THE COMPREHENSIVE
WORD GUIDE

THE
COMPREHENSIVE
WORD GUIDE

By

Norman Lewis

Introduction by

CLARENCE BARNHART

Doubleday & Company, Inc.

GARDEN CITY, NEW YORK

TO

Mary, Margie, and Debra

PREFACE

If you have ever searched in annoyance and frustration for an important word that was seemingly on the very tip of your tongue or pen—a word whose color, feeling, shape, and dimensions would provide you with the special facet of meaning you most needed, but that nevertheless continued to remain tantalizingly elusive—

Or if, less specifically, you have ever wished to verbalize a thought or emotion that you could sense vaguely in your mind but that was either too subtle or too complex to call forth an immediate response from your vocabulary—

Then this book is for you.

For this is a book whose single, simple, and unique purpose is to help you find the words that will quickly, accurately, and effectively express your thoughts, concepts, emotions, and mental imagery.

This is a manual for translating your thinking and ideas into language—

into language that is clear, concise, and forceful—

into language that will communicate to a reader or listener exactly the meaning you wish to convey to him.

Such a translation of your thinking into words can be effected, through this manual, as easily as a problem in addition can be worked out on a calculating machine—and almost as speedily.

As you will see by reading through the instructions ("How to Use This Book," page xvii), THE COMPREHENSIVE WORD GUIDE offers you the following help:

1. It spreads before you, for the purpose of clarifying and refining your thinking, a panorama of the important and useful words that concentrate in a general category of meaning.

2. It unerringly finds for you the exact word that verbalizes a specific thought, idea, concept, fact, condition, action, feeling, object, person, etc.

I do not pretend that this work includes every word in the English language. I have, of course, had to be fairly selective in order to keep the material within publishable bounds. My criterion for inclusion or exclusion of a word has been a simple and, I believe, a logical one: *Is this word one that the general reader is, or is not, likely to look for?* By applying this test I have *excluded* the following types of words:

1. Extremely technical terms in the arts, sciences, crafts, etc., that, if a writer or speaker needs to use them, he is either likely to know without recourse to a reference work; or, if reference is necessary, he will be better served by a tech-

nical dictionary or manual on the subject. However, THE COMPREHENSIVE WORD GUIDE does contain a vast affluence of those technical and semitechnical terms that have begun to come into general use—words from psychoanalysis, psychopathology, and other medical sciences, from law, chemistry, physics, religion, philosophy, logic, music, art, etc., that the educated layman finds indispensable for the communication of complex ideas.

2. Extremely common, everyday, colloquial, and slang words, expressions, and phrases that spring so readily to mind they would only take up valuable space better used for terms that the reader would be likely to search for in these pages.

3. Most, though not all, standard *phrases* as distinguished from individual *words*. From its conception THE COMPREHENSIVE WORD GUIDE was intended to aid in producing freshness and originality of style, in the achievement of which ingenious writers often devise picturesque or unusual combinations of words. To lard one's writing or public speeches with formalized phrases is to run the obvious risk of falling into hackneyed expression and triteness of style—with the inevitably resultant fuzziness of meaning and communication that this book hopes to help a writer or speaker avoid. (The few phrases admitted to these pages are the less common, more picturesque and expressive ones that have not yet deteriorated into clichés.)

4. Archaic, obsolete, and rare words and usages—but I have included occasional archaic terms that I feel have some currency in modern writing. All such are so labeled.

THE COMPREHENSIVE WORD GUIDE is divided into 1144 general categories. Each category has a variable number of sections, depending on the richness or paucity of words and ideas that relate to the category. The order of categories is strictly by meaning, never alphabetically—all interdependent, logically connected, and meaning-associated categories are found in one place.

Thus **STRENGTH** is followed in order by **ENERGY, FORCE, VIOLENCE, POWER,** etc., each category logically deriving from the previous and flowing into the next, so that a browsing reader can rummage through every phase of a concept until he discovers the one that comes closest to his thinking and that he will wish, therefore, to explore thoroughly. **DIFFICULTY** is followed by **EASE; CONVENIENCE** by **INCONVENIENCE; FATE** by **CHANCE, GOOD LUCK, BAD LUCK,** and **MISFORTUNE; PRESENCE** by **EXISTENCE, PREVALENCE, UNIVERSALITY, ABSENCE,** and **LACK.**

The category **BODY** leads into associated categories dealing with various parts, organs, and components, such as **HAND, FINGER, LEG, FOOT, BELLY, BUTTOCKS, BLOOD, VEIN, ARTERY,** etc.

From the category of **NUMBER** as a general concept we proceed through various specific numbers, **ONE, TWO, THREE, FOUR,** etc., and continue logically with **COUNTING, CALCULATION, MATHEMATICS, ANGLES, GEOMETRIC FIGURES,** etc.

MOVEMENT of all kinds forms a long series of categories; **EMOTION** is divided into another extended series; and such other broad generalizations as **WATER, METALS, LANGUAGE, SOUND, ART, SEX, MARRIAGE, TIME, SPACE, LIFE, DEATH,** etc., are covered in still other series.

The Alphabetical Index, which is the mechanism of the book, or, to continue the metaphor used earlier, the brain of the calculating machine with which you will be working, starts on page 697. It is thorough, detailed, and comprehensive, covering 216 pages in triple columns, and attempts to list, within reason, every concept you are likely to search for in it.

Bear in mind that this is an index of ideas, not of words. In looking for a category or entry, explore under the simplest and most common word that expresses your general idea: **belittle** rather than **depreciate; choose** rather than **select; worthy** rather than **meritorious; insult** rather than **affront; go** rather than **proceed; drop, fall,** or **go down** rather than **descend; tease** rather than **badger; annoy** rather than **exasperate; little** rather than **minute; unusual** rather than **extraordinary.**

To find a specific word to translate an idea, decide on the key word of the idea. Hatred of women, for example, is found under **hatred;** prediction by lots or any other means under **prediction;** fear of heights under **fear;** worship of animals under **worship;** inhabitant of Mars under both **inhabitant** and **Mars.** If one key word does not turn up the reference you want, try the other or others. In most cases I have listed references under two or more key words, so that the chances are very good that you will find what you want under almost any key word you decide upon.

In selecting the entries I have included in THE COMPREHENSIVE WORD GUIDE, and in writing the definition of each, I have used as sources a number of major American dictionaries, so that no shade of meaning would be omitted. Dictionaries have varying approaches to word meanings, and it was my intent to offer the reader a kind of amalgam or consensus of lexicographic opinion. Every definition, although in my own words, attempts to fuse the ideas contained in the following dictionaries:

Thorndike-Barnhart Comprehensive Desk Dictionary (Doubleday)
Webster's New World Dictionary (World)
The American College Dictionary (Random House)
Webster's New Collegiate Dictionary (Merriam)
Webster's New International Dictionary (Merriam)
New College Standard Dictionary (Funk and Wagnalls)
The Winston Dictionary (Winston)

For the meanings of medical terms I have relied largely on the *New Gould Medical Dictionary* (Blakiston), and for legal terms on *The College Law Dictionary* (Lawyers Co-operative Publishing Company).

I wish to express my debt and gratitude to these nine reference works, but I hasten to emphasize that, since all definitions are ultimately my own, there is no implication of responsibility to any of these dictionaries for the meanings of the words in THE COMPREHENSIVE WORD GUIDE.

N.L.

INTRODUCTION

by Clarence L. Barnhart

Norman Lewis's COMPREHENSIVE WORD GUIDE is a welcome newcomer among the tools for users of words. All of us, in our variously modest or ambitious activities and aspirations, are word users who can profit from its aid.

What he has produced in THE COMPREHENSIVE WORD GUIDE is a monumental organization of over 120,000 word entries into an ingenious sequence based on the interlockings and overlappings of meaning, and an alphabetical index that leads you readily to the word or word group you want. Its function is complementary to rather than competitive with that of the dictionary; it is much broader in scope than are any of the various books dealing with synonyms.

The arrangement of the semantic categories to make a continuous flow throughout the book is not the least of Mr. Lewis's original contributions, and the numbering system is pursued to a much finer point, so that the Index can carry you either to a section of closely related words or to an individually numbered word entry, as the occasion requires. Mr. Lewis's work also provides brief definitions to give you the means of discriminating between apparently synonymous terms. These definitions play a big part in the indexing of ideas to guide you rapidly to the exact word you are hunting for.

One of the reasons why a writer or speaker or student or any user of words needs the help of a book such as this is that each of us has a vocabulary that consists of two parts—a small, heavily used, smoothly operating *active* vocabulary, the words we use more or less day in and day out in our personal lives and the pursuit of our occupations and the round of our activities, and a large *passive*, or *recognition*, vocabulary made up of words we have heard or read but that aren't part of the stock of words we have ready at hand, available for instant use. We are constantly hearing or reading the utterances and expressions of people whose activities and experiences are different from ours or remote in place, time, or range of content. We hear words and expressions that are natural to another speaker or writer but that we do not assimilate or that we recall with utmost difficulty when we want to make use of them. We are nonetheless entitled to use them when they fit the need and occasion and express what we want to say. They are part of the rich resources of our language, and the writer or speaker who neglects their aid simply because they don't spring to mind is ignoring one of the available and effective ways of making his writing or speaking clear, colorful, and convincing.

In the formation of this passive vocabulary and in the gradual shift of a part of it into our active vocabulary, the dictionary, naturally, plays a big part. An eager and conscientious learner uses the dictionary to hunt down the meanings of new terms as he reads or hears them. Generally speaking, the dictionary does not reverse the process and feed the word back to you. It will, if the word is part of the definition of another word you can think of, or is a synonym of another word you have in mind; but, once you have gone beyond the limits of those possibilities, you need the help of a reference work organized on a different principle.

THE COMPREHENSIVE WORD GUIDE will help you in either of two ways. You can browse among the words belonging to a broad category of meaning, or you can run down a precisely delimited idea in the Index. In the former case you would work as you do with any word list or thesaurus, running through words with some common connection of meaning until you found a word you wanted. In the latter case the detailed Alphabetical Index provides gratifyingly specific references to detailed entries, immediately and directly.

As an easy general example, I looked up the Index entry for **pleasant** and found first a reference to Category 1106, Section 3; that section in the vocabulary turns out to provide half a column of words ranging (alphabetically) from "affable (i.e., pleasant and polite, easy to talk to, etc.)" to "winsome (i.e., wholly delightful, as a child, manner, smile, voice, etc.)." Furthermore the other words involved in the category **TO PLEASE** (which is Category 1106) were immediately at hand in the neighboring sections—verbs, adjectives, abstract nouns, persons who are pleasing, words for special manners of pleasing, and so on. And, if what I really am hunting turns out to be something a little different from **pleasant** or **pleasing,** I can work backward or forward from Category 1106 and find, in one direction, **PLEASURE** (Category 1105) and **MERRIMENT** (Category 1104), in the other, **SATISFACTION** (1107), **TO INDULGE** (1108), and **TO LIKE** (1109).

To try out the more specific and detailed approach through the Alphabetical Index, I went on from the entry **pleasant** and found entries spotting exactly various shadings and accretions of meaning. "Deceptively pleasant" refers us to Section 11 of Category 823 **(DECEPTION),** which provides "bland, oily, oleaginous, slick, smooth, suave, unctious, urbane," and to Category 1106, which provides "plausible" and "specious" in Section 10 **(Pleasing in Appearance or to the Eye or Sight, but Deceptive).** In the same way, I could go on at once to the particular words for "excessively pleasant," "fairly pleasant," "friendly or pleasant," "pleasant in appearance," "pleasant in attitude," "pleasant in movement, action, manner, etc.," "pleasant in sound," "insincerely pleasant," "least pleasant," "made pleasant by maturity," "somewhat pleasant," or—a reverse twist—"unwilling to be pleasant," all of which are covered by Index entries under the main entry **pleasant.**

There is another range of words we can get from THE COMPREHENSIVE WORD GUIDE—words involved in an encyclopedic sort of information that may lie well outside even our passive vocabulary. They are words we may have reason to believe must exist, words connected with certain activities or occupations or places or times or fields of knowledge that are quite outside our experience but that we need to explore the ramifications of an idea or to make a comparison or to give a touch of circumstantial detail or local color or simply, in Pooh-Bah's words, "to give artistic verisimilitude to an otherwise bald and unconvincing narrative."

As an example, I recall a recent conversation in which someone pointed out that we have a word (misogny) for "hatred of women" and a word (misanthropy) for "hatred of mankind," and wondered whether we have a word for women's hatred of men (if and when they do!). There is indeed such a word. It is indexed in this book both under **male** and under **hatred;** the reference is to word entry (3) in Section 17 **(Selected Specific Hatreds or Aversions)** in Category 880 **(HATE),** and the word is "misandry."

For another check I thought of the difficulty of learning and remembering the names of cloud formations. Through the Index I was led easily to Category 1057 **(CLOUDS)** and specifically to Section 4 **(Cloud Forms, Masses, or Layers),** where I found the terms (with explanatory notes)—not only the technical terms from "altocumulus" to "stratus," but also some plainer and vividly descriptive terms such as "cauliflower," "woolpack," and "mare's-tail."

Other examples of the sort of words we may need to locate through a reference book of this kind come easily to mind. You might be hunting for names of articles of clothing of a particular time or place, or the name for some specific phobia, or for a whole range of verbs that mean "to place" in various specific positions or manners, or for adjectives that relate to a certain animal, mineral, etc., or for names of musical instruments, or precious stones, or the branch of knowledge that deals with some specific topic, or terms for groups of certain animals, and so on and so on.

Now I suppose most of us could have long and prosperous careers without having to know that the word for a group of jack rabbits is a **husk,** or that you can express "having a wide jaw" with the word **eurygnathic,** or that the technical name for fear of snakes is **ophidiophobia,** or that abnormal hairiness can be referred to as **hypertrichosis** or **hypertrichiasis,** and I would not in the least suggest that you enliven your style by throwing in without good cause such Greco-Latin startlers as **butyraceous** or **desquamation** or **lamellibranchiate** or **pseudosyllogism,** but it is a comfort to discover that, if we *should* need any of them on a specific occasion, we can find them here when we are hunting for the things they designate.

The vocabulary portion of THE COMPREHENSIVE WORD GUIDE contains more than 120,000 word entries. This makes it about the same size, in that respect, as the "college" dictionaries, those that serve for all general uses and are the largest on the market except for the big unabridged dictionaries containing all of the technical and special words that are on record. From the few examples quoted in the preceding paragraph it is obvious, however, that the vocabulary of this book and that of the college dictionaries do not exactly coincide, for some of Mr. Lewis's terms are more special than would be needed for a college dictionary; this is offset by the fact that some parts of the everyday vocabulary do not need the treatment that this book affords.

A few words now about the arrangement of the entries in the vocabulary section of THE COMPREHENSIVE WORD GUIDE. There have been many other schemes for organizing our stock of words by categories of meaning. Typically, they start from some assumption of a few broad general categories that are refined step by step into more and more distinct groupings; at the end of this process you get numerous small groups of words that may or may not be related to the groups immediately adjacent—the only guaranteed relationship is from a small subdivision back to a larger division and thence to a larger branch and so on back to one of the major categories with which the classification started, just as the twigs on a tree are connected through branches and stems back to the trunk. Continuous numbering in such a system is an aid in indexing, but there is no necessary assurance that the words in one of the numbers will be closely related to those under the preceding or the following number.

The major division of THE COMPREHENSIVE WORD GUIDE vocabulary is into 1144 numbered categories. If you examine the list of these categories, you will note a strikingly continuous flow of interconnected ideas. The continuity is not absolute, of course. Now and again through the list you will see points at which one line of exploration runs out and a main thread is picked up again. For instance, the first nine categories run from **STRENGTH** to **INFLUENCE**; the negative ideas connected with those categories occupy Category 10, **WEAKNESS**, through Category 14, **AWKWARDNESS; UNSKILLFULNESS**; then at Category 15 the main development resumes with **CAUSE**.

I do not know what line of thought led Mr. Lewis to begin his flow of categories with "strength," "energy," "force," and "violence," but I was fascinated to observe that after working through 1144 categories of meanings he wound up with "peace," "comfort," "relief; reduction of severity or intensity," "mildness," and "gentleness." I just hope that isn't a descending order of importance for "violence" and "peace" in this turbulent world! What is wondrous to note is that Mr. Lewis could have begun with the "peace" to "gentleness" categories and ended with "force" and "violence" as contrasting categories; that is, I get the feeling that we have turned through a circle of ideas and are starting back over the track again. Or to say it another way, that Mr. Lewis's organization of his categories is indeed a sequence of interconnected ideas that, like a circle, might be started anywhere; and wherever you might start you would find related ideas in the categories, both behind you and ahead.

The selection and ordering of the 1144 categories is not the final point of the numbering of the entries in THE COMPREHENSIVE WORD GUIDE vocabulary. There are two further divisions. Each category is divided into numbered sections, some of which have no further subdivision, some of which are divided into a few or many numbered word entries. The section organization is partly a matter of connection of meaning, partly a matter of grammatical function (that is, grouping adjectives with adjectives, nouns with nouns, etc.); the details need not concern us here. This detailed numbering system is, naturally, one of the devices that make for thorough and effective indexing so that an index entry can carry us either to a fairly broad or large group in a section or to a surprisingly minute detail covered by a single word entry.

The word entries are covered by definitions. A definition may be general, covering the idea common to all words of a section—for instance, **Sour; Sour in, or to, the Taste,** followed by "acerb, acetose, acetous, acid, acidulent, acidulous, astringent, austere, tart, vinegary"—or a separate one for each word entry. The latter can be exemplified by Category 369 **(HAIR)**, Section 10 **(Resembling Hair or a Hair, adj.)**. In that section each word entry is defined; thus: **1. bristlelike**—resembling a short, thick hair; **2. bristly**—resembling short, thick hairs, or a short, thick hair; **3. capillary**—resembling a hair in slenderness; hairlike; and so on through **downy, fluffy, furry, hairlike, hairy,** and **trichoid.** As you will see, the definitions go immediately to the point and provide enough meaning to distinguish each entry from any other entry with which it is associated and compared.

To carry out the purpose of supplying a word to fit an idea you may have in mind, Mr. Lewis sometimes achieves the curious result of supplying a word to suit an entry that in a dictionary would be the definition. Thus, in Section 3 of Category 369, the only entry is **Growth of Hair in Unusual Places and in Unusual Amounts,** followed by the word this phrase defines; that is, "hirsutism." This, you will see, is one of the ways in which Mr. Lewis provides ideas that can be indexed as keys to a word you may be hunting for. Similarly, in Category 633 **(OPINION)**, I note Section 4, **Figurative Means of Airing, or Giving Publicity to, One's Opinions, or of Presenting One's Opinions to a Public Audience,** followed by the words "rostrum" and "soapbox," and Section 5, **To Be Purposely Ambiguous in the Expression of One's Opinions,** for which the words given are "equivocate" and "pussyfoot (colloq.)."

As a dictionary editor on a busman's holiday, I am startled and entertained by the spectacle of this reversal of the roles of the entry word and the definition: the definition becomes the expression of an idea for which, in this book, the corresponding word is located and supplied. We can cite some more complicated examples than those of the preceding paragraph. Witness Category 1009, Section 37: **To Remove, Destroy, or Eliminate the Glassy Properties of; To Cause (Glass) to Become Opaque, Crystalline, and Hard.** If I may be ponderously playful for a moment, it seems to me that here we have the making of a fine guessing game: What word *does* fit this definition and express this idea? But to resume, in all seriousness, the word that THE COMPREHENSIVE WORD GUIDE will feed to you to meet this specification of meaning is "devitrify."

Do you know what, said of the skin, means **To Come or Peel Off in Scales in the Course of a Disease or a Diseased Condition?** The answer: "desquamate," as you will find at Category 972, Section 15.

The key to locating all of these various words of the vocabulary is the Alphabetical Index. The use of the Index is described in the instructions on the use of the book, and I need here only one comment on a point of especial convenience in the use of the Index. That is, that where a word you consult has different sets of meanings and connotations, especially ones falling in different categories, the Index saves time and encourages precision of thinking by separating and identifying the various references. Under the entry for **spontaneous,** for instance, you get references to categories and sections for the meanings **natural, openly emotional,** and **unplanned.** The entry for **develop** leads you to different sets of words for the sense of **grow** (several sections in Category 731) and for the sense of **happen** (in Category 29). The entry for **unsavory** sorts out the separate references for "flavorless and insipid," "charmless," "disagreeable," and "affronting."

In *The Education of Henry Adams* we read that "no one means all he says, and yet very few say what they mean, for words are slippery and thought is viscous." Words are indeed slippery, and all of us who attempt to use them precisely and effectively need all the help we can get to pin them down; thought is usually, alas, all too viscous and we need all the help we can get to start it flowing. THE COM- PREHENSIVE WORD GUIDE gives you some ideas to loosen up the flow of your thought and helps you put your finger on those elusive words and pin them down!

HOW TO USE THIS BOOK

I

THE COMPREHENSIVE WORD GUIDE consists of two parts:

1. The Vocabulary, pages 1 to 695, containing over 120,000 word entries arranged under 1144 numbered categories of meaning. Each category is divided into numbered sections, and each section contains the relevant word entries, which are also numbered if the section is subdivided.

2. The Alphabetical Index, which begins on page 697.

II

The 1144 numbered categories are listed on pages xix–xxiii. Since these categories follow one another in a sequence of related and partially overlapping ideas, it is possible—if you want to do some leisurely hunting among a large number of words connected with some general topic—to find the number of your category from this list and turn directly to it. However, this is not a typical use of THE COMPREHENSIVE WORD GUIDE. Ordinarily you will want to locate the idea more precisely by starting with the Alphabetical Index.

III

The comprehensive numbering system of the Vocabulary makes it possible to refer instantly to category and section, or to category, section, and word entry.

An Index reference may be of this form:

9.1—which means Category 9, Section 1;

or this:

1106.9,15—which means Category 1106, Sections 9 and 15;

or this:

1073.36(11)—which means Category 1073, Section 36, Word Entry 11;

or this:

564.1(31,39,50)—which means Category 564, Section 1, Word Entries 31, 39, and 50.

Each column of the Vocabulary has a boldface heading showing the numbers of the category or categories and section or sections that appear in that column. This continuous numbering of the columns by category and section numbers enables you to turn speedily to the Vocabulary page where any item located through the Index appears.

IV

Let us suppose, by way of example, that you are hunting a descriptive word that has the general idea of "weak" but means a little more or a little less or has some added connotation.

You look in the Alphabetical Index and find the entry:

weak, adj., 10.1; 830.5.

At this point you can do either of two things:

1. You can turn immediately to Section 1 under Category 10, and to Section 5 under Category 830, and consider all of the words in these sections until you have the one that says just what you want to say.

You will find that Category 830 (taking the shorter) deals with FAULT, and that Section 5 under that category gives you *ten* adjectives sharing a common core of meaning, Containing a Fault or Faults: "blemished, defective, deficient, faulty, flawed, imperfect, marred, unsound, vicious, weak"—and, for good measure, the abstract nouns that are formed from these adjectives.

It is quite possible that that was not the kind of weakness you set out to describe. In that case you will linger longer on the first of the Index references, that is, Section 1 in Category 10 (Index reference 10.1). You will find this a much broader coverage of the idea "weak." Category 10 deals with WEAKNESS generally, and Section 1 under that category lists and defines seventy-five words that are related through the core meaning "Weak; Lacking Power, Force, Energy, etc." You have your pick of "1. adynamic—lacking, or having lost, vital force or power as a result of disease, 2. anile—weak, as it were like an old woman," and so on, down through "73. weak-kneed—not strong in mental determination or decision, 74. weakly—weak, 75. wishy-washy—weak and thin; without strength or force."

Beyond this you may wish to explore suggestions for stating your thought in some manner or form, from Section 2, Weakness, i.e., State of Being Weak; Section 3, A Weakness; Section 4, A Weak Person; Section 5, To Weaken, i.e., Make Weak or Weaker; Section 6, A Weakening, i.e., Making Weak or Weaker; Section 7, State of Being Weakened; and so on, down through Section 13, That Which Reduces the Force of a Blow (the words in this section are "buffer" and "cushion"), and Section 14, A Weakness of Character (with six numbered word entries and definitions from "1. failing" to "6. vice").

Furthermore, if your interest suggests a widening of your search to include a gradual shading away from the idea of "weakness," you may pursue your hunt through Categories 11 (DELICACY), 12 (FATIGUE), and 13 (DISABLEMENT)—or, if you are interested in the opposite ideas of "strength" and its close congeners, you may work backward through the categories that precede Category 10, where we began this exploration.

2. The second of your alternatives is to do more exploring right in the Alphabetical Index before you leave the entry weak. You can pinpoint the entries in the Vocabulary by looking through the subentries of the Index until you find an exact refinement of the idea "weak" that is just what you are hunting. The Index entry for weak begins, as we have observed, with the main entry:

weak, adj., 10.1; 830.5.

Following this are subentries in this style:

become ~, 10.8

This entry, of course, means "become weak"

become ~ with disappointment, 1121.8

(Observe that this picks up a point of contact with another category, DISAPPOINTMENT)

becoming ~, 10.10
delicate and ~, 11.1(5,6,11)

This takes us into the closely related Category 11, DELICACY

~ from disease, 10.1(1,6,36,69)

From this entry you go directly to Category 10, Section 1, Word Entries 1. adynamic; 6. cachexic, cachetic; 36. lassitudinous; and 69. valetudinarian, valetudinary—all with definitions provided.

~ from indulgence in luxuries, 10.1(16)

This takes you immediately to effete ("weak and worn out because of activity, advanced age, or the luxuries of civilization or indulgent living").

And so on through further refinements of the idea "weak," such as "weak from mixture with water," "weak from old age," "helpless and weak," "weak in appearance," "weak in argument," "weak in color," "weak in determination," "weak in excuses," and still others that are set out in the rest of the subentries under the Index entry weak.

You may also, before leaving the Index, consult the main entries immediately following the entry and subentries for weak; these give you the needed references for weaken, weakened, weakening (as adjective and as noun), and weakness.

V

Any time you are hunting for a word you know or feel is in the semantic range of a word you can start from, you can use the Index and the Vocabulary in the way described for weak in the preceding discussion. You can do it with accuse or bubble or cold or full (to the top: brimful; to overflowing: bursting; to the limit: chock-full; with things in disorder: cluttered; so that passage is blocked: congested—and so on for twenty-six more) or merciless or sparkle—or for hundreds of others.

VI

That does not exhaust THE COMPREHENSIVE WORD GUIDE's possibilities. Far from it. It will supply you with thousands of technical and special terms you know *must* exist but that lie outside of your ordinary experience or that you may have heard or seen but don't recall.

What, for instance, is the term for a portion of the circumference of a circle? The Index, under circle, refers you to 508.16, Selected Parts of a Circle, under which you find: "arc—portion of the circumference of a circle."

What is the term for a substance that causes fever? The Index, under fever, takes you to 1063.5, "febrifacient" or "pyrogen."

What are the names of the rays from radioactive materials? The Index, under radioactive and under ray, leads you to 1069.23, "alpha rays" and several others, with brief definitions.

What adjective or adjectives are available to express "like clay"? The Index, under clay, takes you to the answer at 1002.1, "argillaceous, clayey, clayish, claylike."

What are the names of the grasslands of Russia, South Africa, and South America, respectively? The Index, under grassland, locates these terms at 986.16, 17, and 18.

How do we designate silver or gold in bars or ingots? The Index, under silver and under gold, refers you to 1015.2, "bullion."

Fear of being shut in is called "claustrophobia." Is there a correlative term for fear of open spaces? There is. The Index, under fear, will take you to "agoraphobia" at 570.11(2). In the same section (570.11) you will find the terms for an assortment of other abnormal or pathological fears, if you need them.

Is there an adjective to describe a structure that has columns at each end? There is. It is "amphistylar," which you can locate at 1023.6 through the Index, under column.

What is the title of the ruler of Baroda? Under both ruler and Baroda, in the Index, you will be referred to the answer, Gaekwar, at 1073.36(11).

VII

A few abbreviations are employed both in the Vocabulary and in the Index to label parts of speech (adj., n., v., etc.); singular (sing.) and plural (pl.); masculine (masc.) and feminine (fem.); and colloquial (colloq.). Most other qualifying terms are written out in full.

VIII

The Vocabulary contains a fair number of words and phrases from other languages—especially French, German, Italian, and Latin—which, although freely used in English, retain their foreign form and are customarily printed in italics. They are not italicized in this book, but they are labeled according to language of origin. Examples: "bon vivant (French)"; "furor scribendi (Latin)"; "simpático (Spanish)"; etc.

THE CATEGORIES

1. Strength
2. Energy
3. Force
4. Violence
5. Power
6. Privilege; Right
7. Skill; Ability
8. Control
9. Influence
10. Weakness
11. Delicacy
12. Fatigue
13. Disablement
14. Awkwardness;
    Unskillfulness
15. Cause
16. Result
17. Ineffectiveness
18. Attempt
19. Test
20. Competition
21. Struggle
22. Defeat
23. Success
24. Failure
25. Difficulty
26. Ease
27. Convenience
28. Inconvenience
29. Occurrence
30. Likelihood
31. Possibility
32. An Experience
33. Fate
34. Chance
35. Good Luck
36. Bad Luck
37. Misfortune
38. Presence
39. Existence
40. Prevalence
41. Universality
42. Absence
43. Lack
44. State; Condition
45. Purpose
46. Plan
47. Plot; Scheme
48. Preparation
49. Do
50. Manner; Means; Method
51. Do or Act Together
52. Action
53. Treatment
54. Reaction
55. Behavior
56. Principle; Rule
57. Activity
58. Inactivity
59. Lack of Motion
60. Posture
61. Stand

62. Sit
63. Seat
64. Crouch
65. Lie; Recline
66. Rest
67. Sleep
68. Sleeping Quarters
69. Bed; Bedding
70. Hypnotism
71. Dream
72. Awake
73. Not Do
74. Hold Back from Doing
75. Hesitation
76. Avoidance
77. Self-Control; Self-Denial
78. Prevention
79. Motion
80. Playful Motion
81. Motion on All Fours
82. Secret Motion
83. Nervous Motion
84. Confused Motion
85. Motion Requiring Effort
86. Clumsy Motion
87. Unsteadiness
88. Steadiness
89. Sudden Motion
90. Easy Motion
91. Violent Motion
92. Noisy Motion
93. Motion in Waves
94. Rapid Motion
95. Rapidity
96. Run
97. Flight
98. Aircraft
99. Rate
100. Slowness
101. Biological Movement
102. Gesture
103. Bodily Exercise
104. Horse Movements
105. Rhythm
106. Drive
107. Walk
108. Step
109. Dance
110. Jump
111. Shake
112. Flow
113. Float
114. Swimmer
115. Watercraft
116. Sail
117. Row
118. Come
119. Go
120. Pass
121. Cross
122. A Passage
123. Road

124. Travel
125. Visit
126. Greet
127. Farewell
128. Wander
129. Gypsy
130. Go Beyond
131. Accompaniment
132. Approach
133. Entrance
134. Take In
135. Bring In
136. Inside
137. Center
138. Outside
139. Surface
140. Come Out
141. Go Away
142. Desertion
143. Disappearance
144. Cause to Go Away
145. Move, Come, or Go Back
146. Back-and-Forth Motion
147. Sway; Swing
148. Turn
149. Turn Over
150. Turn Round
151. Roll
152. Bend
153. Lean
154. Slant; Slope
155. Curve
156. Twist; Wind
157. Fold
158. Wrinkle
159. Rise
160. A Step (for Rising)
161. Rise and Fall
162. Up and Down Motion
163. Raise
164. Height
165. Top
166. Hill; Mountain
167. Come, Go, or Move Down
168. Fall
169. Lowness
170. Depth
171. Dig
172. Hang
173. Follow
174. Forward Motion
175. Precede
176. Lead
177. Guide
178. Follower
179. Direction
180. Straightness
181. Crookedness
182. Directness
183. Indirectness
184. Bank
185. Front

186. Side
187. Throw
188. Scatter
189. Send
190. Carry
191. Bring Back
192. Vehicle
193. Pull
194. Stretch
195. Spread
196. Attraction
197. Push
198. Press
199. Play
200. Amusement
201. Merrymaking
202. Mischief
203. Work
204. Occupation
205. Worker
206. Labor Relations
207. Non-Professional
208. Busy
209. Lack of Work
210. Business
211. Purchase
212. Sale
213. Money
214. Interest in Money
215. Money Profit
216. Wealth
217. Poverty
218. Debt
219. Payment
220. Bribery
221. Payment in Kind
222. Recompense
223. Charge
224. Spend
225. Waste
226. Economy
227. Stinginess
228. Self
229. Generosity
230. Give
231. Distribution
232. Charity
233. Supply
234. Give Back
235. Give Forth
236. Give Up
237. Offer
238. Suggestion
239. Hint
240. Get
241. Inheritance
242. Legal Will
243. Heredity
244. Trap
245. Acceptance
246. Tolerance
247. Take
248. Plunder
249. Removal
250. Steal
251. Take Back
252. Choice
253. Appointment
254. Voting
255. Possession
256. Belong
257. Hold
258. A Handle
259. Inclusion
260. Contain
261. Container
262. Storage
263. Preservation
264. Loss
265. Desire
266. The Will
267. Hope
268. Expectation
269. Unexpectedness
270. Suddenness
271. Surprise

272. Wait
273. Need
274. Demand
275. Order; Command
276. Beg
277. Urge
278. Advice
279. Use
280. Equipment
281. Rent
282. Use Up
283. Misuse
284. Disuse
285. Waste; Refuse
286. Elimination
287. Bodily Discharge
288. Belch
289. Spit
290. Vomit
291. Sweat
292. Menstruation
293. Defecation
294. Urination
295. Toilet
296. Keep Out
297. Closure
298. Open
299. A Hollow
300. Surround
301. Keep In
302. Attachment
303. Tightness
304. Looseness
305. Sew
306. Thread
307. Weave
308. Network
309. Freedom
310. Slavery
311. Arrangement
312. Classification
313. Rank
314. Social Class
315. Layer
316. Line
317. Type; Model
318. Group
319. Collect; Gather
320. Mixture
321. Put Together
322. A Meeting
323. Place; Put
324. Substitution
325. Separation
326. Parts
327. Detail
328. Completeness
329. Incompleteness
330. Alone
331. Privacy
332. Cut
333. Sting
334. Sharpness
335. A Point
336. Dullness
337. Tear
338. Body
339. Arm
340. Wing
341. Feather
342. Fin
343. Hand
344. Finger; Toe
345. Leg
346. Foot
347. Belly
348. Buttocks
349. Tail
350. Sac
351. Heart
352. Blood
353. Vein; Artery
354. Bone
355. Horn; Scale; Shell
356. Skull
357. Brain

358. Head
359. Neck
360. Breast
361. Eye
362. Ear
363. Nose
364. Throat
365. Face
366. Jaw
367. Mouth
368. Tooth
369. Hair
370. Beard
371. Hair Removal
372. Wig
373. Wool
374. Lung
375. Windpipe
376. Breathe
377. Muscle
378. Nerve
379. Sex Organ
380. Egg
381. Biological Cell
382. Skin
383. Pus
384. Skin Color
385. Flesh
386. Leather
387. Membrane
388. Other Bodily Parts
389. Illness
390. Tumor; Cancer
391. Hernia
392. Inflammation
393. Plague
394. Thyroid and Pituitary Disorders
395. Vitamin Deficiency Disorders
396. Other Diseases
397. Health
398. Cure
399. Drug
400. Medical Treatment
401. Medical Branches
402. Surgery
403. Animal
404. Bat
405. Bird
406. Cat
407. Dog
408. Horse
409. Ass; Donkey
410. Bovine
411. Sheep
412. Goat
413. Deer
414. Camel
415. Giraffe
416. Bear
417. Elephant; Hippopotamus
418. Kangaroo
419. Hog
420. Monkey
421. Rodent
422. Water Animal
423. Marine or Aquatic Mammal
424. Frog
425. Reptile
426. Dinosaur
427. Worm
428. Insect
429. Mankind
430. Race
431. Person
432. The Senses
433. Perception
434. Physical Sensation
435. Lack of Sensation
436. Touch
437. Hit
438. Rub
439. Smoothness
440. Roughness

441. Hardness
442. Stiffness
443. Softness
444. Limpness
445. Smell
446. Taste
447. Juice
448. Sweetness
449. Sugar
450. Candy
451. Honey
452. Sourness
453. Listen
454. Hearing
455. Sound
456. Animal Sound
457. Infant Sound
458. Bell Sound
459. Water Sound
460. Body Sound
461. Air Sound
462. Deep Sound
463. Loud Sound
464. Shout
465. High Sound
466. Harsh Sound
467. Sweet Sound
468. Unhappy Sound
469. Sound of Movement
470. Monotonous Sound
471. Echo
472. Hiss
473. Confused Sound
474. Voice
475. Silence
476. Sing
477. Hymn
478. Melody
479. Music
480. Vision
481. Visual Defects
482. Mental Image
483. Visibility
484. Look
485. Examination
486. Search
487. Find
488. Color
489. Lack of Color
490. Black
491. Dark Color
492. Blue
493. Green
494. Purple
495. Red
496. Pink
497. Brown
498. Gray
499. White
500. Yellow
501. Spot
502. Stripe
503. Mark
504. Appearance
505. Beauty
506. Ugliness
507. Form; Shape
508. Roundness
509. Arch
510. Fatness
511. Width
512. Narrowness
513. Thinness
514. Shortness (of Appearance)
515. Tallness
516. Length (of Appearance)
517. Thickness
518. Swell
519. Flatness
520. Relationship
521. Pertinence
522. Involvement
523. Relations
524. Association
525. Condition; Provision

526. Dependence
527. Responsibility
528. Duty
529. Similarity
530. Comparison
531. Uniformity
532. Imitation
533. Copy
534. Equality
535. Commonness
536. Unusualness
537. Freak of Nature
538. Foreign
539. Change
540. Difference
541. Agreement
542. Disagreement
543. Debate
544. Opposition
545. Challenge
546. Opposite
547. Denial
548. Refusal
549. Disobedience
550. Unruliness
551. Obedience
552. Submission
553. Stubbornness
554. Permission
555. Prohibition
556. Help
557. To Hinder
558. Restraint; Restriction
559. Interference
560. Attack
561. Attack in Words
562. Fight
563. War
564. Soldier
565. Firearm
566. Bow and Arrow
567. Aim
568. Protection
569. Protection against Disease
570. Take Care of
571. Save from Danger
572. Danger
573. Threat
574. Warning
575. Bravery
576. Fear
577. Care
578. Carelessness
579. To Pay Attention
580. Interest
581. Inattentiveness
582. Neglect
583. Uninteresting
584. The Mind
585. Thought
586. Idea
587. Imagination
588. Guess
589. Reasoning
590. Reasonableness
591. Unreasonableness
592. Decision
593. Comprehension
594. Intelligence
595. Cleverness; Shrewdness
596. Wisdom
597. Stupidity
598. Clarity
599. Explanation
600. A Reason
601. Solution
602. Problem
603. Unclearness
604. Mystery
605. Confusion
606. Dizziness
607. Meaning
608. Nonsense
609. Frivolousness
610. Serious

611. Knowledge
612. Know
613. Make Known
614. Publicity
615. Fame
616. Rumor
617. Description
618. Map
619. Experience
620. Inexperienced
621. Instruction
622. Study
623. School
624. Discovery
625. Question
626. Answer
627. Memory
628. Forgetfulness
629. Habit
630. Inclination
631. Fashion
632. Belief
633. Opinion
634. Prejudice
635. Unfairness
636. Lack of Prejudice
637. Fairness
638. Persuasion
639. Disbelief
640. Uncertainty
641. Certainty
642. Religion
643. Religiousness
644. Religious Community
645. Church
646. Clergyman
647. To Preach
648. The Bible; Sacred Writings
649. Prayer
650. Sacred
651. Saint
652. A Cross
653. Christ
654. God
655. Angel
656. To Worship
657. Devotion
658. Loyalty
659. Disloyalty
660. Devil
661. Hell
662. Supernaturalism
663. Magic
664. Language
665. To Express
666. Word
667. Use of Words
668. Syllable
669. Figure of Speech
670. Pronunciation
671. Talk
672. Discussion
673. Reference
674. Say
675. Admission
676. A Saying
677. Handwriting
678. A Letter
679. Written Symbol
680. Punctuation Mark
681. Spelling
682. Writing
683. Secret Writing
684. Manuscript
685. Story
686. Author
687. Book
688. Literature
689. Poetry
690. Printing
691. A Publication
692. Reading
693. Call
694. Name
695. Study of Names

696. Signature
697. Seal
698. Label
699. Title
700. Love
701. Caress
702. Marriage
703. Married Person
704. Engagement
705. Divorce
706. Unmarried Person
707. Male
708. Female
709. Sex
710. Sexual Intercourse
711. Prostitute
712. Sexual Immorality
713. Obscenity
714. Pregnancy
715. Fertility
716. Sterility
717. Give Birth
718. Childbirth
719. Breed
720. Birth
721. Child
722. Relative
723. Ancestry
724. Father
725. Mother
726. Make
727. Build
728. Origin
729. Beginning
730. Introduction
731. Growth
732. Maturity
733. Immaturity
734. Eat
735. Bite
736. Swallow
737. Hunger
738. Feed
739. Nourishment
740. Food
741. Restaurant
742. Soup
743. Meat
744. Milk
745. Fruit
746. Jelly
747. Coffee
748. Drink
749. Alcoholic Liquor
750. Live
751. Life
752. Liveliness
753. Living Quarters
754. Continuation
755. Endlessness
756. Impermanence
757. Remain
758. Age
759. Old
760. Young
761. New
762. Time
763. Geologic Time
764. Same Time
765. Timeliness
766. Early
767. Late
768. Delay
769. Period of Time
770. Season
771. The Present
772. Prediction
773. Sign of the Future
774. Time Measurement
775. Morning
776. Day
777. Evening
778. Night
779. Week
780. Month
781. Year

782. Place
783. Surroundings
784. Nation
785. City
786. Countrified
787. Space
788. Distance
789. Far
790. Near
791. Stop
792. End
793. Boundary
794. Death
795. Suicide
796. Kill
797. Burial
798. Cremation
799. Funeral
800. Poison
801. Destruction
802. Breakage
803. Harm
804. Unharmed
805. Spoilage
806. Decay
807. Reality
808. Thing
809. Unreality
810. Naturalness
811. Unnaturalness
812. Truth
813. Honesty
814. Fact
815. Correctness
816. Perfection
817. Suitability
818. Properness
819. Formality
820. Falseness
821. A Lie
822. Dishonesty
823. Deception
824. A Trick
825. Cheat
826. Pretense
827. Incorrectness
828. Improperness
829. Mistake
830. Fault
831. Excellence
832. Restoration
833. Superiority
834. Best
835. Improvement
836. Advantage
837. Favorableness
838. Unfavorableness
839. Value
840. To Belittle
841. Worthiness
842. Kindness
843. Moral Principles
844. Nobility
845. Moral Purity
846. Dignity
847. Magnificence
848. Importance
849. Unimportance
850. Approval
851. Praise
852. Flattery
853. Applause
854. Support
855. Admiration
856. Respect
857. Honor
858. Politeness
859. Refinement
860. Impoliteness
861. Disrespect
862. Boldness; Forwardness
863. Unrefinement
864. Coarseness
865. Roughness
866. Uncivilized
867. Insult

868. Offense
869. Ridicule
870. Contempt
871. Pride
872. Boast
873. Modesty
874. Annoyance
875. Tease
876. Bad-Tempered
877. Bitterness
878. Anger
879. Hostility
880. Hate
881. Disgust
882. Curse
883. Badness
884. Sin
885. Conscience
886. Corruption; Immorality
887. Meanness
888. Worthlessness
889. Cruelty
890. Harshness
891. Disgrace
892. Accusation
893. Blame
894. Disapproval
895. Scold
896. Punishment
897. Forgiveness
898. An Excuse
899. Cleanness
900. Purification
901. Strainer
902. Neatness
903. Untidiness
904. Dirt
905. Impurity
906. Size
907. Increase
908. Addition
909. Smallness
910. Decrease
911. Shortness
912. Summary
913. Length
914. Amount; Quantity
915. Supply
916. Large Amount
917. Small Amount
918. Drop (of Liquid, etc.)
919. Enough
920. Excess
921. Excessiveness
922. Extremeness
923. Moderation
924. Greatness (in Degree, etc.)
925. Fullness
926. Emptiness
927. A Number
928. Nothing
929. Half
930. One
931. Two
932. Three
933. Four
934. Five
935. Six
936. Seven
937. Eight; Nine
938. Ten
939. Twenty
940. Other Numbers
941. Counting
942. Calculation
943. Mathematics
944. Angle
945. Geometric Figures
946. Measurement
947. Weight
948. Heaviness
949. Lightness
950. Balance
951. Show
952. Conspicuousness

953. Representation
954. Symbolism
955. Symptom
956. Signal
957. Flag
958. Stick Out
959. Ornamentation
960. Simplicity
961. Jewelry
962. Diamonds
963. Pearls
964. Objects of Art
965. Art
966. Carving; Sculpture
967. Photography
968. Motion Pictures
969. Drama; Theater
970. Concealment
971. Secrecy
972. Cover
973. Roof
974. Clothing; Dress
975. Formal Dress
976. Coat
977. Neckwear
978. Gloves
979. Footwear
980. Trousers
981. Underwear
982. A Woman's Dress
983. Hat
984. Undress
985. Plants
986. Grass
987. Grain
988. Tobacco
989. Rubber
990. Branch
991. Stem
992. Root
993. Leaf
994. Flower
995. Seed
996. Tree
997. Wood
998. Farming
999. Soil
1000. Mud
1001. Dust; Powder
1002. Clay
1003. Land
1004. Earth
1005. Earthquake
1006. Rock
1007. Sand
1008. Minerals
1009. Glass
1010. Coal
1011. Salt
1012. Metal
1013. Gold
1014. Platinum
1015. Silver
1016. Copper
1017. Iron
1018. Lead

1019. Zinc
1020. Tin
1021. Mercury
1022. Support; Hold Up
1023. Column
1024. Wall
1025. Floor
1026. Water
1027. Liquid
1028. Bubble; Foam
1029. Body of Water
1030. Island
1031. Water Movement
1032. Ocean Wave
1033. Water Structure
1034. Wetness
1035. Dip
1036. Pour
1037. Rain
1038. Dryness
1039. Snow
1040. Ice
1041. Fog
1042. Wind
1043. To Blow
1044. Thunder; Lightning
1045. Air
1046. The Atmosphere
1047. Weather
1048. Gas
1049. Oxygen
1050. Smoke
1051. Sky; Heaven
1052. Universe
1053. Heavenly Body
1054. The Moon
1055. The Sun
1056. Stars
1057. Clouds
1058. Coldness
1059. Freeze
1060. Heat
1061. Cookery
1062. Bread; Cake; Pie
1063. Fever
1064. Fire
1065. Light
1066. Electricity
1067. Candle
1068. Wax
1069. X-Rays; Radioactivity
1070. Darkness; Lack of Light
1071. Shadow
1072. Dullness; Lack of Shine
1073. Government; Rule
1074. Feudalism
1075. Citizenship
1076. Politics
1077. Official; Officer
1078. Police
1079. Law
1080. Legislation
1081. Court of Law
1082. Court Case
1083. A Judge
1084. Jury

1085. Lawyer
1086. Statement under Oath
1087. Illegality
1088. Crime
1089. The Soul
1090. Spirituality
1091. One's Nature
1092. Emotion
1093. Sensitiveness
1094. Sentimentality
1095. Enthusiasm
1096. Friendliness
1097. Emotional Lack, Coldness, Indifference, etc.
1098. Emotionally Hardened
1099. Emotional Effect
1100. Excitement
1101. Commotion; Disturbance
1102. Happiness
1103. Cheerfulness
1104. Merriment
1105. Pleasure
1106. To Please
1107. Satisfaction
1108. To Indulge
1109. To Like
1110. Thanks
1111. To Laugh
1112. To Smile
1113. Funny; Laughable
1114. Humor
1115. Joking
1116. A Clown
1117. Unpleasantness
1118. Offensiveness
1119. Dissatisfaction
1120. Complaint
1121. Disappointment
1122. Promise
1123. Low Spirits; Depression
1124. Gloom
1125. Sadness
1126. Regret
1127. To Weep
1128. Tears
1129. Pity; Sympathy
1130. Emotional or Mental Suffering
1131. Anxiety; Worry
1132. Disturbance of Mind or Emotion
1133. Nervousness; Emotional Pressure
1134. Restlessness
1135. Emotional or Personality Disorder
1136. Insanity
1137. Pain
1138. Torture
1139. To Calm; To Soothe
1140. Peace
1141. Comfort
1142. Relief; Reduction of Severity or Intensity
1143. Mildness
1144. Gentleness

1. STRENGTH

1. Strong: bouncing, brawny, forceful, forcible, rugged; sinewy, sinewed, or sinewous; stalwart, stanch or staunch, strengthful, substanial, unweakened,adj.; *Also:*

1. **burly**—big and strong
2. **hefty, husky**—big and strong (colloq.)
3. **Herculean**—amazingly strong and powerful, like Hercules, the mythical character famed for his strength
4. **manly, virile**—having, or exhibiting, manly strength
5. **mighty**—powerfully strong; physically strong
6. **rock-ribbed**—very strong, as if ribbed by, or of, rock
7. **Tarzanish**—prodigious in strength, like the character in the E. R. Burroughs novels
8. **titanic**—gigantically or tremendously strong
9. **wiry**—strong and slim
10. **withy**—strong, but bending easily

2. Strength,n. *From Sec. 1:* brawniness, force or forcefulness, forcibleness or forcibility, ruggedness, sinewiness or sinewousness, stalwartness, stanchness or staunchness, substantiality or substantialness; burliness, heftiness, huskiness, manliness or virility, might or mightiness, wiriness

3. Strong Person,n. *From Sec. 1:* stalwart; Hercules, husky, Tarzan, Titan; *Also:*

1. **Atlas**—very strong person, after the deity in Greek mythology who supported the world on his shoulders
2. **Samson**—very strong man, after the Biblical character

4. Someone Who Unexpectedly Proves Too Strong for the One Who Attacks Him: Tartar,n. (usually in the phrase *catch a Tartar*)

5. Strong and Healthy: athletic, robust; robustious (humorous); sound, strapping, vigorous,adj. (robustness, soundness, vigor or vigorousness,n.)

6. Strong in Body or Build: able-bodied, bouncing, burly, muscular, robust; robustious (humorous); stalwart, stocky, stout, sturdy, adj. (burliness, muscularity, robustness, stalwartness, stockiness, stoutness, sturdiness,n. stalwart,n.)

7. Having Strength of Muscles: brawny, muscular,adj. (brawn or brawniness, muscularity,n.)

8. Vigorous: bouncing, rugged, sinewy, sinewed, or sinewous; sound, tough, vibrant, virile (of men),adj.

9. Vigor: birr, pith, ruggedness, sinewiness or sinewousness, soundness, stamina, toughness, vibrancy, vigorousness, vim, virility, vitality, zip,n. (staminal,adj.)

10. Vigorous and Young: blooming, youthful, adj. (bloom, youth or youthfulness,n.)

11. To Be in a State of Vigor and Freshness: bloom,v. (bloom,n.)

12. Vigorous and Full of Life: lusty, vital,adj. (lustiness, vitality or vitalness,n.)

13. Vigor of the Physiological Functions of a Bodily Organ or Organs, or of the Body as a Whole: tone, tonicity, or tonus,n. (tonic, adj.)

14. Vigor as of, or Suggestive of, Freshly Growing Plants: verdure,n.

15. Time of Greatest Vigor: bloom, prime,n.

16. Strong in the Sense of Being Able to Withstand or Endure Fatigue, Injury, Extremes of Temperature, or Similar Hardships: hardy, rugged, stalwart, sturdy, tough, adj.

17. Such Strength to Withstand or Endure: hardiness, ruggedness, stalwartness, stamina, sturdiness, toughness,n. (staminal,adj.)

18. Strong (of Qualities, Abstractions, etc.): intense,adj. (intensity, intenseness,n.)

19. Full of Strength or Vigor (of Language, Style, etc.): forceful, pithy, racy, sinewy, trenchant, vigorous, virile, vivid,adj. (forcefulness or force, pithiness or pith, raciness, sinewiness, trenchancy, vigor or vigorousness, virility, vividness,n.)

20. Strong and Distinct (of Colors): vivid, adj. (vividness,n.)

21. Strong (of Wind, Water Current, etc.): stiff,adj. (stiffness,n.)

22. Strength of Character: backbone,n.

23. Remaining Strong; Not Weakening: unflagging,adj.

24. With No Weak Points for an Opponent to Attack: airtight,adj. (of arguments, etc.)

25. Strong in the Sense of Not Being Diluted: concentrated, condensed, undiluted, adj. (concentrate, condensate,n.)

26. Undiluted (of Alcoholic Drinks): neat, straight,adj.

27. To Be or Prove Stronger: prevail,v.

28. Source of Strength: sinews,n.

29. To Strengthen, i.e., Make Strong, Stronger, or Vigorous; To Give Strength or Vigor to,v.

1. **arm**—strengthen morally
2. **brace**—give strength to
3. **concentrate**—strengthen by removing diluting agents from; make the action of stronger (concentration,n.)
4. **condense**—strengthen by removing water or other nonessentials from (condensation,n.)
5. **confirm**—strengthen, generally in a habit, feeling, etc. (confirmation,n.)
6. **consolidate**—strengthen (consolidation, n.)
7. **fortify**—make strong physically, mentally, morally, or in any other conceivable way (fortification,n.)
8. **heighten**—strengthen, figuratively; intensify
9. **intensify**—make (a quality, color, or other abstraction) stronger (intensification,n.)
10. **invigorate, innerve, vitalize**—give strength or vigor to; make strong or stronger (invigoration, vitalization,n.)
11. **prop up**—strengthen
12. **refresh**—strengthen; give fresh strength or vigor to (refreshment,n.)
13. **reinforce**—strengthen; strengthen by the addition of something or with new materials (reinforcement,n.)
14. **reinvigorate**—make stronger (reinvigoration,n.)
15. **sinew**—make strong; give strength to
16. **stiffen**—strengthen, figuratively
17. **tone up**—make stronger in color, volume, etc.
18. **toughen**—make strong or stronger, vigorous, hardy, etc.

30. To Strengthen, i.e., Become Strong, Stronger, or Vigorous,v. *From Sec. 29:* concentrate, condense, consolidate, intensify, refresh, stiffen, toughen (concentration, condensation, consolidation, intensification, refreshment,n.)

31. Strengthening, i.e., Giving Strength to, adj. *From Sec. 29:* bracing, fortifying, intensifying, etc. *Also:* roborant, tonic, vital; *Also:* 1. **brisk, crisp**—invigorating and sharp, as climate, etc. (briskness, crispness,n.)

32. That Which Gives Strength: tonic,n.

33. Medicine That Gives Strength: roborant, tonic,n.

1

34. Drink That Gives Strength: bracer,n.

35. To Make Strong or Vigorous Again; To Restore Strength to; To Give New Strength to: invigorate, refresh, regenerate, reinvigorate, rejuvenate, rejuvenize, renew, revive,v. (invigoration, refreshment, regeneration, reinvigoration, rejuvenation, renewal, revival, n.)

36. Making Strong or Vigorous Again: analeptic (medical), invigorating, refreshing, regenerating or regenerative, reinvigorating, rejuvenating or rejuvenative, rejuvenizing, renewing, reviving, tonic,adj.

37. To Regain Strength: rally, refresh, rejuvenate, rejuvenesce, revive,v. (rally, refreshment, rejuvenation, rejuvenescence, revival,n. rejuvenescent,adj.)

38. To Call upon One's Strength: brace up,v.

39. Giant in Greek Mythology Who Was Invincible in Wrestling because Every Time He Touched the Ground His Strength Was Renewed: Antaeus,n. (Antaean,adj.)

2. ENERGY

1. Energy: bang, birr, verve, zip,n.

2. Energy of Action or Motion: bang, dash, n.

3. Active Energy: vigor, vim, vitality,n.

4. Active Energy to Start Something New: enterprise, initiative,n.

5. Nervous Energy: sinew,n.

6. Available Energy: motivity,n.

7. Potential Energy (Physics): ergal,n.

8. Energetic: aggressive, demoniac, dynamic or dynamical, lively, sappy, strenuous, vibrant, vigorous, vital; zippy (colloq.),adj. (aggressiveness, liveliness; strenuousness, strenuosity, or strenuity; vibrancy, vigor or vigorousness, vitality,n.)

9. Having the Active Energy to Start Something New: enterprising,adj.

10. Possessing Such Abundancy of Energy as Rarely if Ever to Become Tired: indefatigable,adj. (indefatigableness or indefatigability,n.)

11. Energetic Person: demon. dynamo, Trojan,n.

12. Giving an Impression of Energy: vibrant, adj. (vibrancy,n.)

13. Not Losing Energy: unflagging,adj.

14. To Direct One's Energies to: address oneself to, apply oneself to, buckle down to, devote oneself to,v. (application, devotion,n.)

15. To Expend Energy,v.
  1. energize—put forth energy
  2. exert oneself—put forth energy
  3. spurt—put forth unusually increased energy for a short time
  4. struggle—put forth great bodily energy
  5. toil, labor—exert great energy and effort, usually with fatigue, suffering, or pain
  6. travail—engage in the painful expenditure of energy; toil

16. Expenditure of Energy,n. *From Sec. 15:* exertion, spurt, struggle, toil, labor, travail; *Also:* 1. effort—expenditure of mental or physical energy to produce that which is desired, attain a result, accomplish something, etc.

17. Requiring Great Energy: arduous, laborious, strenuous, toilsome,adj. (arduousness, laboriousness, strenuousness, toilsomeness,n.)

18. To Give Energy to: brace, energize, vitalize,v. (vitalization,n.)

19. To Give New Energy to: invigorate, reinvigorate,v. (invigoration, reinvigoration,n.)

20. To Give Nervous Energy to: innervate, innerve,v. (innervation,n.)

21. Pert. to Energy: dynamic, energic,adj.

22. Pert. to Explanation in Terms of Energy: energic,adj.

23. Machine that Converts Mechanical Energy into Electrical Energy: dynamo,n.

24. Unit of Energy,n.
  1. dinamode—unit of energy equal to the work necessary to raise one ton one meter against the force of gravity
  2. erg, ergon—unit of energy
  3. joule—unit of energy equal to 10^7 ergs
  4. quantum—smallest unit of energy that can exist independently

25. Device to Measure Energy,n.
  1. dynamometer—device to measure energy
  2. ergmeter—device to measure energy in terms of ergs
  3. ergometer—device to measure energy expended (ergometric,adj.)
  4. joulemeter—device to measure energy in terms of joules

26. Place Where Energy Is Exerted: arena,n.

27. Certain Theories of Energy,n.
  1. dynamism—that energy is the final physical reality (dynamist,n. dynamistic, adj.)
  2. energetics—that matter is an arrangement of energy in space; theory of the conditions or laws governing the manifestations of energy (energetistic,adj.)
  3. energism—that mental states and other abstract phenomena are explainable in terms of energy (energist,n.)

28. Science that Treats of the Conditions and Laws of the Manifestations of Energy: energetics,n. (energeticist,n. energetistic,adj.)

29. Path Followed by Energy: ergodic,n.

30. Process by Which the Psychic Energy Is Focused upon an Idea, Object, Person, etc., Thus Giving It a Special Significance (psychoanalysis): cathexis,n. (cathectic,adj.)

3. FORCE

1. Force,n.
  1. agent—active force
  2. birr—force; driving force
  3. brunt—main force of a blow, or of attack or violence; main force in a struggle or conflict
  4. counterbalance—force that serves to neutralize an opposing force.
  5. counterpoise—force of equal power acting as a balance or in opposition
  6. dint—force
  7. energy—force
  8. impetus—driving force; technically, force by which a moving body maintains its speed
  9. might—force
  10. momentum—force of movement that keeps something going
  11. pith—concentrated force
  12. power—force
  13. soul—spiritual force
  14. strain—force that causes tension
  15. stress—physical force; distressing, painful, or opposing force
  16. vehemence—force; great force
  17. vim—force
  18. violence—extreme force

2. Forceful,adj.
  1. dynamic—forceful
  2. elemental—exerting a strong force, though simple or uncomplicated

3. **energetic**—operating with force, strength, and effectiveness; possessing a capacity for exerting force; forcible
4. **forcible**—possessing, or characterized by, force; obtained or accomplished by force (forcibleness, forcibility,n.)
5. **mighty**—forceful (might, mightiness,n.)
6. **pithy**—full of force (pithiness,n.)
7. **potent**—forceful (potency,n.)
8. **powerful**—forceful (power, powerfulness, n.)
9. **puissant**—forceful—poetic term (puissance,n.)
10. **punchy**—forceful (punch,n.)
11. **spasmodic**—forceful and sudden, but lasting only a short time
12. **stringent**—forceful (stringency,n.)
13. **titanic**—having tremendous force
14. **vehement**—full of force; acting with great force (vehemence,n.)
15. **vigorous**—forceful; forceful in mind or body (vigor, vigorousness,n.)
16. **violent**—possessing or acting with great, harmful, or destructive force (violence, n.)

3. To Force; To Use Force; To Use Force against,v.
1. **bludgeon**—force, by threats or otherwise
2. **coerce** (. . . into)—use force to compel obedience, make (someone) do something, or restrain him from doing it
3. **compel**—force; accomplish or get by force; force to yield
4. **constrain**—force (to do something)
5. **counterbalance**—use force in such a way as to neutralize an opposing force
6. **counterpoise**—use a force of equal power to balance or oppose another force
7. **dislodge**—force out of hiding
8. **draft**—force into the armed services
9. **dragoon** (. . . into)—force (to do something) by persecution or oppression
10. **enforce**—compel obedience to
11. **exact**—demand and force to give
12. **extort**—force to give
13. **impress**—force into the naval service
14. **oblige**—force (to do something) by a promise, duty, etc.
15. **press**—force into service or duty against one's will; force into military or naval service
16. **require**—force
17. **subject** (. . . to)—force to undergo (an experience, usually an unpleasant one)
18. **twist**—force out of normal shape
19. **violate**—use force against
20. **wrest**—extort
21. **wring**—force out by twisting or squeezing, literally or figuratively; extort

4. Use of Force,n. *From Sec. 3:* coercion, compulsion, constraint, dislodgment, draft, enforcement, exaction, extortion, impress, impressment, requirement, subjection, violation; *Also:*
1. **coaction**—coercion
2. **duress**—compulsion; coercion
3. **violence**—unlawful use of force

5. Using Force,adj. *From Sec. 3:* coercive, compulsory or compulsive; extortive, extortionary, extortionate; obligatory, violative; *From Sec. 4:* coactive, violent; *Also:* 1. **mandatory**—compulsory by official order

6. State of Being Forced,n. *From Sec. 3:* compulsion, constraint, obligation, subjection; *From Sec. 4:* duress

7. With Great Force: with a vengeance

8. Legally Enforceable: valid,adj. (validity, n.)

9. Pert. to Physical Force or Forces: dynamic,adj.

10. Science of Forces,n.
1. **dynamics**—branch of mechanics dealing with the action of forces in producing or changing the motion of bodies (dynamic, adj.)
2. **kinetics**—science dealing with the changes of motion caused by forces (kinetic,adj.)
3. **mechanics**—science dealing with the action of forces (mechanical,adj.)
4. **physics**—science comprising mechanics, heat, electricity, light, sound, etc. (physicist,n. physical,adj.)
5. **statics**—science of forces in equilibrium (statical,adj.)

11. Process, Means, or Art of Measuring Forces Engaged in Work: dynamometry,n. (dynamometric, dynamometrical,adj.)

12. Device for Measuring Any Kind of Force: dynamometer, ergometer,n. (dynamometric or dynamometrical, ergometric,adj.)

13. Any Theory Viewing the Universe as Constituted of Forces: dynamism,n. (dynamist,n. dynamistic,adj.)

4. VIOLENCE

1. Violent; Acting or Moving with Violence: blustery, blusterous, fierce, furious, mad, rabid, raging, rampageous, rampant, stormy, tempestuous, turbulent, unbridled, wild,adj.

2. Violence; Violence of Action or Movement: fierceness, fury or furiousness, madness, rabidness or rabidity, rage, rampageousness, rampancy, storminess, tempestuousness, turbulence or turbulency, wildness,n.

3. Violent Action, Behavior, or Movement: fury, rage, rampage, storm, violence,n.

4. To Act, Behave, or Move with Violence: bluster, rage, rampage, storm,v.

5. To Be Extremely Violent, or to Use Extreme Violence (of People): out-Herod Herod,v.

6. Violent and Rapid: headlong,adj.

7. Violently and Rapidly: headlong,adv.

8. Marked by Unrestrained Violence, as a Fight, Struggle, etc.: rough-and-tumble,adj.

9. Descr. of Violent Weather, Storms, etc.: rude,adj.

10. Violent and Sudden Effort, Force, Feeling, Expense of Energy, etc., That Lasts for a Short Time Only: spasm,n.

11. Violent and Sudden, but Lasting Only a Short Time: spasmodic, spasmodical,adj.

12. Violent in Feelings: vehement,adj. (vehemence,n.)

13. To Act, Behave, or Talk with Noise and Violence: bluster,v. (blusterer,n. blusterous, blustery,adj.)

14. Violence and Confused Noise or Uproar: bluster, tumult,n.

15. Violent and Full of Confused Noise: blusterous, blustery, tumultuary, tumultuous, adj. (tumultuousness,n.)

16. Violence and Disorder of a Crowd: tumult,n.

17. With Great Violence: hammer and tongs, with a vengeance,adv. phrase

18. Political Violence,n.
1. **anarchism**—violent and terroristic resistance to government (anarchist,n. anarchistic,adj.)
2. **nihilism**—use of violence against government (nihilist,n. nihilistic,adj.)
3. **terrorism**—use of violence in opposition to government; government by violence (terrorist,n. terroristic,adj.)

19. Fierce: ferocious, grim, lupine, savage, tigerish, truculent, wolfish,adj.

20. Fierceness: ferity, ferocity, or ferociousness, fury, grimness; savagery, savageness, or savagism; truculence or truculency, wolfishness,n.

21. Fierce and Cruel: fell, truculent,adj. (fellness, truculence or truculency,n.)

22. Fierce Person: savage, tiger, wolf,n.

23. Fierce and Cruel or Bloodthirsty Person: tiger,n.

24. Fiercely, Desperately, and Courageously, though Often against Superior Odds: tooth and nail,adv. phrase

25. Savage: barbarous, brutal, brute, feral, ferine, ferocious,adj. (barbarousness, brutality, ferity, ferineness, ferocity or ferociousness,n.)

26. Savage, Like a Beast: bestial, brutal, brute, feral, ferine (i.e., like a wild beast), lupine (i.e., like a wolf), wolfish,adj. (bestiality, brutality, ferity, ferineness, wolfishness, n.)

27. Savage and without Mercy: grim,adj. (grimness,n.)

28. Savage Person: brute, savage, wolf,n.

29. Savage Act: brutality, savagery,n.

30. To Treat in a Savage Manner: brutalize, savage,v. (brutalization,n.)

31. To Attack (Someone) in a Savage Manner: savage,v.

5. POWER

1. Power,n.
1. **ability**—power to do; power to do well
2. **almightiness**—all-embracing power
3. **animal magnetism**—hypnotic power
4. **armipotence**—power in battle
5. **effectuality**—adequate power to produce an effect
6. **efficacy, efficaciousness**—power to produce the desired effect or result
7. **faculty**—physical or mental power
8. **force**—active power; power to cause a physical effect; power of effective action; power to convince; power for war; power exercised upon a thing or person
9. **influence**—power to produce a change
10. **might**—power; physical power
11. **omnipotence**—unlimited power
12. **potency**—power; physical power; sexual power; procreative power
13. **prepotency**—unusual power
14. **puissance**—power (poetic)
15. **sinews**—muscular power
16. **thews**—muscular power
17. **vigor**—power; healthy power; sexual power; power of mind or body
18. **vim**—power
19. **virtue**—power to cause results or effects
20. **witchcraft**—supernatural or magical power
21. **wizardry**—magical power

2. Powerful,adj. *From Sec. 1:* able, almighty, armipotent, effectual, efficacious, forceful or forcible, influential, mighty, omnipotent, potent, prepotent, puissant; sinewy, sinewed, or sinewous; thewy, vigorous; *Also:*
1. **Herculean**—amazingly powerful and strong
2. **husky**—powerful, strong, and big
3. **titanic**—possessed of tremendous power

3. Powerful Person,n. *From Sec. 1:* influence, witch, wizard; *From Sec. 2:* Hercules, Titan or titan; *Also:* 1. **leviathan**—one who (or that which) is tremendously powerful

4. Power, in the General Sense of Authority; Authority; Power over,n.
1. **accreditation**—official authority
2. **ascendancy, ascendency, ascendance, ascendence**—dominance

3. **authorization**—power; power established by precedent
4. **autocracy**—independent or self-derived power; uncontrolled power of an absolute monarch or of an individual who need answer to no one
5. **charter**—written or official authority
6. **command**—power; authority
7. **commission**—formal written authority
8. **control**—authority or power over
9. **diadem**—royal power
10. **dominance, dominancy, domination**—power; the most power in a group or class
11. **dominion**—supreme authority; power of governing or controlling; dominance
12. **imperium**—supreme power (usually political)
13. **jurisdiction**—authority to act as judge; legal authority; authority to govern or make laws; control
14. **license**—official authority to do; official authority to practice a profession
15. **paramountcy**—highest power, authority or jurisdiction
16. **plutocracy**—power owing to wealth
17. **predominance, predominancy, predomination**—superiority of authority
18. **preponderance**—superiority of power or authority
19. **prestige**—authority derived from one's known accomplishments, abilities, etc.
20. **regency**—dominion
21. **scepter, sceptre**—authority; sovereignty
22. **sovereignty**—supreme power; supreme political power
23. **supremacy**—highest authority or power
24. **sway**—power
25. **Vatican**—power or authority of the Pope
26. **Vaticanism**—the Pope's supreme power (usually derogatory)
27. **warrant**—authority; authorization

5. Powerful; Authoritative,adj. *From Sec. 4:* ascendant, authorized, autocratic, chartered, commanding, controlling, dominant or dominating, imperial, paramount, plutocratic, predominant; preponderant, preponderate, or preponderating; prestigious, sovereign, supreme; *Also:*
1. **cathedral**—authoritative
2. **ex cathedra**—fully authoritative
3. **magisterial**—authoritative
4. **official**—authoritative
5. **oracular**—authoritative, as if given by a god (of decisions, statements, answers, etc.)
6. **plenipotentiary**—invested with full and unrestricted power or authority
7. **thetic**—set down as authoritative
8. **top**—having the highest or greatest power or authority
9. **upmost, uppermost**—top

6. To Have or Exercise Power or Authority, v. *From Sec. 4:* control, dominate, predominate, preponderate

7. To Give Power or Authority to,v. *From Sec. 4:* accredit, authorize, charter, commission, license, warrant (accreditation, authorization,n.) ; *Also:*
1. **empower**—give authority to (empowerment,n.)
2. **enthrone**—give or invest with supreme political or other power (enthronement, n.)
3. **implement**—provide the necessary power or authority to render (something) effective (implementation,n.)
4. **qualify**—give legal authority to (qualification,n.)
5. **vest**—furnish with power or authority

8. Person with Power or Authority,n. *From Sec. 4:* authority, autocrat, commander, emperor, licensee, licentiate, plutocrat, regent; *From Sec. 5:* official, plenipotentiary; *Also:* 1. **baron**—powerful industrialist

2. **mogul**—powerful and important person
3. **potentate**—person with political power
4. **sachem**—very powerful person in an organization
5. **upstart**—one who has suddenly risen from a lowly position to one of power (upstart,adj.)

9. Pert. to Power or Authority,adj. *From Sec. 4:* imperial, jurisdictional, plutocratic; vaticanal, vaticanic, or vaticanical; Vaticanist

10. One Who Has the Power or Authority to Act for Another or For Others,n.
   1. **agent, agency**—one who (or that which) has the power or authority to act for another (agential,adj.)
   2. **delegate**—one who has authority to act for another (delegation, delegacy, collective,n.)
   3. **deputy, surrogate**—one who has been given the authority to act for another (deputation, collective n.)
   4. **proxy**—one who has the authority or power to act or vote for another
   5. **regent**—one who has the authority or power to act for one, usually a monarch who is too young, incapable for some reason, etc.; one who has delegated or vicarious power

11. Power or Authority to Act for Another, n. *From Sec. 10:* delegacy, proxy, regency; *Also:* 1. **commission**—authority to act for another

12. To Give Power or Authority to Act for Another,v. *From Sec. 10:* delegate, depute or deputize; *From Sec. 11:* commission

13. To Increase the Power of: aggrandize,v. (aggrandizement,n.)

14. Based on Authority or Legal Power: valid,adj. (validity,n.)

15. Means or Source of Power or Authority, n.
   1. **authorization**—that which grants authority or power
   2. **precedent**—act or event that serves as an authorization for similar acts or events
   3. **sinew, sinews**—means or source of power
   4. **warrant**—document granting authority

16. Symbol of Power, Political Power, or Authority: scepter, sceptre,n.

17. One Who Upholds Authority: Ghibelline, n.

18. Descr. of Power Wielded by the Mother: matripotestal,adj.

19. Region or Place of Power,n.
   1. **bailiwick**—one's special region of power
   2. **bourn**—realm
   3. **circle**—realm
   4. **demesne**—domain; realm
   5. **domain**—region in which one is powerful or exercises power, influence, or authority
   6. **dominion**—place subject to one's authority or power
   7. **field**—province
   8. **jurisdiction**—region of authority; territory in which power is or may be exercised
   9. **province**—region of power
   10. **purview**—region of authority or power
   11. **realm**—region of power
   12. **regency**—dominion of a ruler deriving his power from another
   13. **scope**—region of power
   14. **sphere**—region, figurative or literal, over which power is exercised

20. Feeling of Abnormal Power: exaltation,n.

21. Exceeding Legal Power or Authority: ultra vires (Latin)

22. Device to Measure Muscular or Motor Power: dynamometer,n.

6. PRIVILEGE; RIGHT

1. Privilege; Right,n.
   1. **angary**—right of a belligerent nation to take, use, or destroy property of a neutral nation in wartime
   2. **appurtenance**—minor privilege or right
   3. **authority**—right
   4. **authorization**—right
   5. **entitlement**—specially acquired right or privilege
   6. **franchise**—special and generally exclusive privilege or right granted by a government (for example, to operate a bus line, etc.)
   7. **perquisite**—that which is held or claimed as a sole right
   8. **prerogative**—unique privilege or right

2. To Give a Privilege or Right to,v. *From Sec. 1:* authorize, entitle, franchise (authorization, entitlement, franchisement,n.)

3. One Who Holds or Claims a Sole Right: perquisitor,n.

4. Pert. to the Private Rights of a Person: civil,adj.

5. Entitled to Inherit a Throne, Title, Position, etc.: apparent,adj. (following the designation, as *heir-apparent,* etc.)

6. Possessing or Enjoying Royal Privilege or Privileges: palatine,adj.

7. To Take Away the Privilege of Doing, or the Right to Do: disqualify,v. (disqualification,n.)

7. SKILL; ABILITY

1. Skill; Ability,n.
   1. **ableness**—skill; above-average ability; competence
   2. **accomplishment**—skill achieved by training or education; skill in social manners so achieved
   3. **address**—skill; self-assured ability
   4. **adeptness**—ability resulting from a combination of skill and training
   5. **adequacy**—ability that is sufficient but no more than sufficient; competence
   6. **adroitness**—manual skill of a high order; intellectual ability in handling difficult tasks or situations
   7. **ambidexterity, ambidextrousness**—equal skill in both left and right hands
   8. **appetency**—instinctive, rather than learned, ability to perform an action
   9. **aptitude**—natural or native ability rather than that which comes from learning or experience
   10. **aptness**—skill
   11. **architectonics**—structural skill
   12. **artfulness**—ingenious skill, esp. in attaining an objective; adroitness
   13. **artifice**—skill in contriving; ingenuity
   14. **artistry, art**—skill; skill in working or doing; ability or skill that shows talent and inspiration
   15. **attainment**—mental ability; ability
   16. **bent**—aptitude
   17. **brilliance, brilliancy**—great ability
   18. **caliber**—ability; mental capacity
   19. **canniness**—skill
   20. **capability**—potential ability
   21. **capacity**—potential ability (a person's ability is judged by his actual performance; his capacity or capability is inferred from past performance)
   22. **cleverness**—skill
   23. **compass**—capacity
   24. **competence**—ability equal to the requirements of a job
   25. **consummateness**—great skill; finished, or perfect, ability
   26. **craft**—special skill

27. **craftiness, craft**—skill in deception
28. **deftness**—manual or mental skill
29. **delicacy**—skillfulness of touch; tact
30. **dexterity, dextrousness**—skill in the use of the hands or the mind
31. **diplomacy**—skill in dealing with people, managing human relationships, avoiding the arousal of hostile emotions, etc.
32. **diplomatism**—diplomacy
33. **efficiency**—ability of a high order that results in successful production without waste of time, motion, energy, etc.
34. **endowment**—specific ability or capability that is bestowed by nature, as it were, i.e., that one is born with
35. **expertness**—skillful ability that comes from training, knowledge, and experience
36. **facility**—skill that makes a task easy, and that usually results from special talent or experience; ability to do something with skill, ease, smoothness, etc.
37. **faculty**—physical ability; natural aptitude of any kind
38. **finesse**—skill in the execution of a difficult task; skill in handling a difficult or delicate situation
39. **flair**—natural ability in a special field, so that one does something in a uniquely successful way
40. **genius**—unique or extraordinary natural ability
41. **gift**—natural ability of a very high order for some special work
42. **habilitation**—ableness; expertness
43. **handicraft**—skill in the use of the hands
44. **handiness**—skill in using the hands
45. **ingenuity, ingeniousness**—skill in contriving new ways of getting things done, or in devising, creating, or inventing
46. **initiative**—active ability to start something new, begin a course of action, etc.
47. **knack**—natural ability that helps one do something easily
48. **masterliness**—great skill
49. **mastery**—skill in a subject or field
50. **neatness**—skill
51. **nimbleness**—skill and quickness in doing; physical skill
52. **practice, practise**—skill
53. **proficiency**—above-average ability in working or doing
54. **prowess**—unusual ability or skill; superiority of technique
55. **prudence**—skill in management of one's affairs
56. **qualification**—capability; competence
57. **resource, resourcefulness**—skill in handling difficult situations, getting out of difficulties, etc.; ingenuity
58. **savoir-faire**—ability to say and do the right thing at the right time
59. **strategy**—skill in execution or planning
60. **superability**—extraordinary ability
61. **tact, tactfulness**—ability to do or say the proper thing; ability to deal with, or get along with, people
62. **talent**—native, rather than acquired, ability; natural ability of high order; unusual ability and intelligence in a field
63. **technique**—skill or expertness in the procedure, details, or performance of an art, science, etc.
64. **turn**—natural ability
65. **versatility**—capability in many directions; ability to do many different kinds of things with competence or skill
66. **verve**—talent; great aptitude
67. **virtuosity**—consummate skill in musical performance, or, less commonly, in the performance of any fine art; by extension, such skill in the performance of any very difficult task, project, work, etc.
68. **wizardry**—amazing skill; magical skill
69. **woodcraft**—skill in working on wood; skill in hunting, trapping, or other activities connected with the forest or woods
70. **workmanship**—ability, skill, or artistry of a worker in his work

2. Skillful; Skilled,adj. *From Sec. 1:* able, accomplished, adept, adequate, adroit, ambidextrous or ambidexter, apt, artful, artistic, brilliant, canny, capable, clever, competent, consummate, crafty, deft, delicate, dexterous, diplomatic, efficient, endowed, expert, facile, gifted, habile, handy, ingenious, masterly, neat, nimble, proficient, practiced or practised, prudent or prudential, qualified, resourceful, tactful, talented, versatile, workmanlike; *Also:*

1. **au fait**—expert
2. **equal**—sufficiently able
3. **facile**—skillful in the use of language
4. **light-fingered**—skillful in stealing, esp. in picking pockets
5. **many-sided**—versatile
6. **sciential**—capable
7. **top-flight**—highest in ability
8. **trained**—skillful through practice, repetition, or education
9. **versed**—skilled

3. Skillful or Able Person,n. *From Sec. 1:* adept, ambidexter, artificer, artist, craftsman, diplomat or diplomatist, expert, genius, master, strategist, technician, virtuoso, wizard, woodsman; *Also:*

1. **ace**—one who excels in ability or skill
2. **authority**—expert in a subject or field
3. **master workman**—one especially skilled in an art, handicraft, or trade
4. **past master**—one particularly skilled in something
5. **prodigy**—extraordinarily skillful person
6. **shark, whiz**—person extremely skillful in something
7. **tactician**—skillful maneuverer or manager

4. Special Area of Ability: forte,n.

5. To Show Unusual Mental or Other Ability: shine,v.

6. Showing Skill of Actions, etc.; Made or Done with Skill,adj.

1. **cunning**—made with great skill
2. **daedal**—done with clever skill
3. **strategic**—showing skill in execution or planning (of actions)
4. **tactical**—characterized by skillful procedures or actions
5. **tricky**—showing skill (a tricky arrangement, etc.)
6. **well handled**—managed or done skillfully
7. **workmanlike**—showing skill of execution

7. Act Showing Skill,n.

1. **achievement, accomplishment**—act showing great skill
2. **deed, exploit**—act accomplished through skill
3. **feat**—act of skill, ingenuity, or dexterity
4. **stunt**—act requiring great skill and usually done to attract attention

8. Requiring Skill or Ability,adj.

1. **delicate**—requiring the greatest skill (delicacy,n.)
2. **tender**—requiring tact
3. **ticklish**—requiring skillful, careful, or tactful handling (ticklishness,n.)
4. **tricky**—requiring skill, delicacy, or tact in doing, handling, etc. (trickiness,n.)

9. To Be Capable or Competent,v.

1. **qualify**—be capable (qualification,n.)
2. **suffice**—be competent or equal to a task or demand

10. To Become Skillful,v.

1. **master**—become skillful in
2. **train**—become skillful through practice or repetition

11. To Make Skilful or Able,v.
1. **capacitate**—make capable; qualify (capacitation,n.)
2. **empower**—give ability to (empowerment, n.)
3. **enable**—give ability to (enablement,n.)
4. **qualify**—give sufficient ability to (qualification,n.)
5. **train**—make skillful through practice or repetition
6. **verse**—make skillful

12. To Make (Something) Efficient: streamline,v.

8. CONTROL

1. To Control; To Exercise Control over,v.
1. **awe**—control by inspiring with fear
2. **bridle**—control
3. **censor**—control by examining and passing on (written material), deleting that which is considered objectionable
4. **check**—control
5. **command**—have or exercise control over
6. **contain**—control
7. **corner**—get control of
8. **cow**—exercise control over by frightening
9. **curb**—control
10. **determine**—control
11. **direct**—control; exercise control over, or be in control of, the affairs of (an institution, company, group, etc.)
12. **dominate**—exercise control over
13. **govern**—control the actions, conduct, or operation of; restrain
14. **hold sway over**—have control over
15. **hypnotize**—exercise control over the mind or actions of through the power of suggestion
16. **manipulate**—control skillfully; control cleverly but fraudulently; control for one's own purposes
17. **master**—control; get control of; have control over; keep under control
18. **monopolize**—have exclusive control over (a commodity, etc.)
19. **navigate**—control (an airplane or ship)
20. **predominate**—have control or controlling authority or influence over
21. **pull strings, pull wires, wirepull**—exercise secret control
22. **regiment**—keep under strict and uniform control, allowing little or no real freedom
23. **regulate**—control; keep under control
24. **restrain**—keep under control
25. **rule**—exercise control; have control over
26. **subject**—bring under one's control
27. **subjugate**—bring under one's control
28. **subordinate (to)**—bring under the controlling power (of)
29. **sway**—exercise control; have a controlling influence or power over

2. Control,n. *From Sec. 1:* censorship, check, command, containment, corner, curb, direction; domination, dominance, or dominancy; government, manipulation, mastery, monopoly, navigation; predomination, predominance, or predominancy; wirepulling, regimentation, regulation, restraint, rule, subjection, subjugation, subordination, sway; *Also:*
1. **address**—skillful control
2. **ascendancy**—control
3. **autocracy**—undisputed and unqualified control
4. **charge**—control
5. **oligopoly**—almost complete control of an industry by a few giant corporations in secret alliance
6. **rein**—control
7. **strategy**—skillful control
8. **upper hand**—control
9. **whip hand**—control

3. Controller; One Who Controls or Is in Control,n. *From Sec. 1:* censor, commander, director, governor, manipulator, master, monopolist, navigator, wirepuller, ruler; *From Sec. 2:* autocrat

4. A Control; That Which Controls,n. *From Sec. 1:* check, determinant, governor, regulator; *Also:*
1. **bit**—that which, figuratively, curbs or restrains
2. **lever**—device or part, usually in the form of a bar of some kind, that starts and controls the operation of a machine
3. **pedal**—lever worked by the foot
4. **robot**—automatic control that almost seems capable of using human judgment
5. **switch**—device for controlling a machine, etc., by turning electricity on or off, or by changing from one operation or action to another
6. **treadle**—lever worked by foot pressure

5. Controlling; Pert. to, or Descr. of, Control,adj. *From Sec. 1:* awful or awesome, censorial, commanding, curbing, determining or determinant, directorial or directive, dominating or dominant, governing, hypnotic, masterful, monopolistic, predominating or predominant, regulative or regulatory, restraining, ruling; *From Sec. 2:* ascendant, autocratic or autocratical, oligopolistic; *Also:*
1. **top**—having highest control

6. Controlled,adj. *From Sec. 1:* bridled, contained, etc., subject (to), subordinate (to); *Also:*
1. **androcentric**—male-dominated
2. **dependent on**—controlled by
3. **heteronomous**—subject to government or control by an outside agent
4. **tributary**—subject to the controlling power or influence of another

7. Controllable,adj. *From Sec. 1:* censorable, containable, governable, hypnotizable, masterable, navigable, restrainable, subjugable; *Also:*
1. **dirigible**—able to be controlled
2. **docile**—easily controlled (docility,n.)
3. **tractable**—easily controlled

8. To Control Harshly, Cruelly, Arrogantly, Arbitrarily, etc.,v.
1. **browbeat**—domineer
2. **bully**—domineer
3. **despotize over**—exercise absolute and harsh control over; tyrannize over
4. **domineer**—exercise one's control over (someone) in an imperious, arrogant, and/or arbitrary manner
5. **hector**—domineer
6. **lord over**—domineer
7. **oppress**—control with harshness and cruelty
8. **tyrannize over**—control, or exercise controlling power or authority over, in a harsh, unjust, severe, and cruel manner

9. Harsh, etc., Control,n. *From Sec. 8:* despotism, oppression, tyranny

10. One Who Exercises Harsh, etc., Control, n. *From Sec. 8:* browbeater, bully, despot, hector, oppressor, tyrant; *Also:*
1. **autocrat**—domineering person; despot
2. **bruiser**—bully
3. **bucko**—domineering and aggressive person; bully
4. **dictator**—one who arrogantly imposes control over others

11. Descr. of Harsh, etc., Control; Tending to Control Harshly, etc.,adj. *From Sec. 8:* browbeating, bullying, despotic, domineering, hectoring, oppressive; tyrannical, tyrannic, or tyrannous; *From Sec. 10:* autocratic, dictatorial; *Also:*
1. **absolutist, absolutistic**—despotic; tyrannical

2. **arbitrary**—tyrannical
3. **authoritative**—dictatorial
4. **imperious**—arrogantly domineering
5. **magisterial**—dictatorial
6. **masterful**—tending to give orders or domineer
7. **peremptory**—dictatorial
8. **rigorous**—oppressive

12. **Harshness, etc., of Control; Tendency to Control Harshly, etc.,**n. *From Sec. 11:* despotism, domineeringness, oppressiveness, tyranny; autocracy, dictatorialness; arbitrariness, authoritativeness, imperiousness, masterfulness, peremptoriness, rigorousness

13. **Oppressed:** downtrodden,adj.

14. **To Control the Affairs of; To Direct,**v.
   1. **administer, administrate**—control or direct the affairs of
   2. **be in charge of**—direct; administer
   3. **govern**—direct; control or direct the affairs of
   4. **husband**—control or direct wisely and economically so that there is no waste
   5. **manage**—direct
   6. **mismanage**—control or direct poorly
   7. **overlook**—direct
   8. **oversee**—direct
   9. **proctor**—supervise (an examination) in a college, school, etc.
   10. **superintend**—direct
   11. **supervise**—direct; direct the course, workings, or actions of

15. **Control; Direction,**n. *From Sec. 14:* administration, charge, government, husbandry, management, mismanagement, superintendence or superintendency, supervision; *Also:*
   1. **telesis**—intelligent or rational direction of natural and social forces to a desirable goal

16. **Director; One Who Is in Charge,**n. *From Sec. 14:* administrator, governor, manager, overseer, proctor, supervisor; *Also:*
   1. **caretaker**—one who is in charge of a place
   2. **comprador**—native in charge of native workers in a commercial establishment owned by foreign agents
   3. **curator**—person in charge of a museum, library, or other public building; supervisor
   4. **custodian**—one who is in charge of a public building or apartment house
   5. **executive**—person who does administrative work, usually in a business, industry, etc.
   6. **gerent**—one who manages
   7. **impresario**—manager or organizer of an opera or concert company
   8. **matron**—woman who supervises children, growing girls, other women, etc., as in an institution, etc.
   9. **proctor**—one who manages the affairs of another
   10. **steward**—manager; caretaker

17. **Directorial; Directive,**adj. *From Sec. 14:* administrative or administerial, managerial, proctorial, supervisory; *From Sec. 16:* curatorial, custodial, executive, proctorial

18. **System of Management:** regime,n.

19. **One Who Is under the Control of Another,**n.
   1. **serf**—one under the control of another, i.e., in a position of complete servitude (serfdom, serfhood,n.)
   2. **slave**—one completely controlled by, or under the domination of, another (slavery,n.)
   3. **subject**—someone under the control of another (subjection,n.)
   4. **Trilby**—one (usually a woman) under the hypnotic control of another
   5. **vassal**—one subject to control by another (vassalage,n.)

20. **Position of Control:** helm,n.

21. **Means of Controlling:** rein, reins,n.

22. **To Give Control to,**v.
   1. **nationalize**—give control of (an industry) to the central government of a country (nationalization,n.)
   2. **vest (in)**—put under the control (of)

23. **To Bring under One Main Control:** centralize,v. (centralization,n.)

24. **To Remove from Central or Main Control:** decentralize,v. (decentralization,n.)

25. **To Deprive of Controlling Power:** overthrow, overturn,v. (overthrow, overturn,n.)

26. **Loss of Control:** tailspin,n. (from airplane terminology)

27. **Without Control,**adj.
   1. **involuntary**—without conscious control or direction by the mind or body
   2. **reflex, reflexive**—acting or functioning through no conscious control
   3. **subconscious, unconscious**—outside the control of the conscious mind

9. INFLUENCE

1. **To Influence,**v.
   1. **affect**—influence; impress
   2. **bias**—influence (someone) toward forming a strong feeling for or against
   3. **dispose**—influence (someone) toward (action, feeling, attitude, etc.)
   4. **govern**—influence
   5. **impress**—have a deep or strong influence upon the mind or emotions of (someone)
   6. **incline**—influence (someone) toward (an action, attitude, etc.)
   7. **inspire**—influence (someone) strongly (usually toward some good action, achievement, work, etc.)
   8. **move**—impress
   9. **obsess**—influence (someone) to an unusual or unreasonable extent (generally said of a notion, fear, desire, fixed idea, etc.)
   10. **possess**—exert a powerful influence upon (someone)
   11. **predispose**—influence (someone) beforehand
   12. **prejudice**—bias; predispose
   13. **sway**—exert a controlling influence over
   14. **touch**—impress

2. **Influence,**n. *From Sec. 1:* bias, impression, inspiration, obsession, prejudice, sway; *Also:*
   1. **ascendancy, ascendency, ascendance, ascendence**—ruling, dominating, governing, paramount, or controlling influence
   2. **atmosphere**—pervading or surrounding influence
   3. **authority**—influence that engenders confidence and respect
   4. **effect**—influence
   5. **hegemony**—leading influence of one nation in a group
   6. **leaven**—strong and pervading influence toward change
   7. **lever**—influence for accomplishing a purpose
   8. **metapsychosis**—influence of one mind upon another through no physical or explainable means
   9. **miasma**—noxious or foul influence
   10. **pressure**—compelling influence; confining or restraining influence
   11. **prestige**—influence derived from one's known accomplishments, ability, etc.
   12. **stress**—influence upon one's feelings
   13. **weight**—influence
   14. **witchcraft**—magical or supernatural influence
   15. **witchery**—irresistible influence

3. Influential; Exerting an Influence,adj.
From Sec. 1: affecting, impressive, inspiring or inspirational, moving, obsessive, prejudicial, touching; *From Sec. 2:* ascendant, effective, hegemonic or hegemonical, weighty; *Also:*
  1. **moral**—exercising a good influence
  2. **upmost, uppermost**—most influential

4. To Be More Influential,v.
  1. **outweigh**—be more influential than
  2. **predominate**—have superiority of influence (predomination or predominance,n. predominant,adj.)
  3. **preponderate**—be greater in influence (preponderance or preponderancy,n. preponderant, adj.)

5. To Act or Work as an Influence against: militate against,v. (militation,n.)

6. To Serve as an Influence to Neutralize an Opposing Influence: counterbalance,v. (counterbalance,n.)

7. To Exert Secret Influence: pull strings, pull wires, wirepull,v. (wirepuller,n. wirepulling,n.)

8. Sphere of Influence: bailiwick, orbit, province, scope,n.

9. Open to Influence or Able to Be Influenced,adj.
  1. **accessible to**—capable of being influenced by (accessibility,n.)
  2. **amenable to**—open to influence by (amenability,n.)
  3. **impressible**—capable of having one's mind or emotions deeply or strongly influenced (impressibility, impressibleness, n.)
  4. **impressionable**—easily influenced; impressible (impressionability, impressionableness,n.)
  5. **morbid**—unusually impressible by things that are sad or gloomy (morbidness,n.)
  6. **plastic**—easily influenced; impressible (plasticity,n.)
  7. **pliable**—easily influenced (pliability, pliableness,n.)
  8. **pliant**—easily influenced (pliancy, pliantness,n.)
  9. **sensitive**—easily influenced (sensitiveness, sensitivity,n.)
  10. **suggestible**—easily influenced by suggestion (suggestibility, suggestibleness,n.)
  11. **susceptible**—easily influenced or moved in feelings (susceptibility, susceptibleness, n.)
  12. **susceptive**—susceptible (susceptiveness, n.)
  13. **waxen, waxy**—impressible (waxiness, n.)

10. Under the Influence of: subject to,adj.

11. Under the Influence of (Another): subordinate to,adj. (subordination,n.)

12. Group That Attempts to Influence Legislation: lobby,n. (lobby,v. lobbyist,n.)

13. An Attempt to Exert Illegal or Corrupt Influence on a Court or Jury: embracery,n.

14. To Attempt to Exert Illegal or Corrupt Influence on (a Court, Jury, etc.): embrace, v. (embracer, embraceor,n.)

10. WEAKNESS

1. Weak; Lacking Power, Force, Energy, etc.,adj.
  1. **adynamic**—lacking, or having lost, vital force or power as a result of disease
  2. **anile**—weak, as it were like an old woman
  3. **apathetic**—lacking in energy
  4. **asthenic**—lacking, or having lost, bodily strength or vigor (medical)
  5. **atonic**—weak or lacking in vital energy (descr. of a bodily organ, part, or system)

  6. **cachexic, cachectic**—weak and wasted in body owing to some chronic disease (medical)
  7. **characterless**—weak (i.e., without character)
  8. **decrepit**—weak with, or owing to, old age
  9. **delicate**—weak in color; weak in health
  10. **dilute**—weak because mixed with water or similar substance
  11. **doddered**—infirm
  12. **doddering**—senile
  13. **doddery**—infirm; senile
  14. **dotard**—senile
  15. **effeminate**—lacking in manly strength
  16. **effete**—weak and worn out because of activity, advanced age, or the luxuries of civilization or indulgent living
  17. **faint**—weak; weak in color or volume of sound
  18. **feckless**—weak and helpless
  19. **feeble**—weak; lacking in the necessary strength or endurance; lacking in power or authority; weak from advanced age
  20. **flabby**—weak; lacking in force or firmness
  21. **flaccid**—weak in the sense of offering no resistance
  22. **flimsy**—weak in the sense of having little substance (as a flimsy argument, excuse, etc.)
  23. **fragile**—weak
  24. **frail**—weak; weak in health or constitution
  25. **helpless**—weak; destitute of strength
  26. **hyposthenic**—lacking in strength (medical)
  27. **impotent**—weak; lacking in power, ability, authority, etc.; sexually weak (of a man)
  28. **impuissant**—weak; totally lacking in power (poetic term)
  29. **infirm**—weak (often from advanced age)
  30. **insipid**—weak, i.e., lacking in flavor, liveliness, etc.
  31. **insubstantial**—flimsy
  32. **lackadaisical**—weak; bereft of energy; listless
  33. **lame**—weak (applicable to abstractions, as a *lame excuse, lame attempt,* etc.)
  34. **languid**—weak; lacking in energy
  35. **languorous**—lacking in energy or vigor
  36. **lassitudinous**—weak as a result of illness, mental disturbance, etc.; lacking energy
  37. **limp**—as if ready to drop from exhaustion; without strength or firmness (figuratively) ; flaccid
  38. **listless**—lacking the energy to be active
  39. **lymphatic**—temperamentally lacking in energy
  40. **marrowless**—lacking in animal vigor
  41. **moony**—lacking in energy
  42. **namby-pamby, namby-pambical**—insipid
  43. **nerveless**—totally lacking in strength or power
  44. **nugatory**—having no force (of actions, abstractions, etc.)
  45. **papier-mâché**—of no intrinsic strength or permanence
  46. **pithless**—lacking in vigor, force, or strength of life
  47. **powerless**—totally lacking in power
  48. **prostrate**—weak and helpless
  49. **puny**—weak and small; weaker than normal
  50. **quaggy**—flabby
  51. **rickety**—weak in the joints
  52. **sapless**—feeble
  53. **sear, sere**—weak
  54. **senile**—having the mental and physical weakness of advanced old age
  55. **sheepish**—weak
  56. **sinewless**—lacking in strength

57. **slack**—weak (in strictness, force, severity, etc.)
58. **slight**—weak; flimsy; frail
59. **slim**—weak (of abstractions, as a *slim excuse,* etc.)
60. **sluggish**—lacking in energy or vigor
61. **spent**—without energy
62. **spineless**—weak
63. **strengthless**—lacking in strength
64. **subtle**—faint
65. **supine**—lacking in energy; lacking in physical or moral endurance
66. **tender**—not strong or hardy
67. **thin**—weak (of abstractions, as a *thin excuse,* etc.)
68. **torpid**—devoid of energy
69. **valetudinarian, valetudinary**—weak from illness
70. **wan**—weak; weak-looking
71. **washy**—weak; lacking in strength; flabby
72. **watery**—weak; flabby
73. **weak-kneed**—not strong in mental determination or decision
74. **weakly**—weak
75. **wishy-washy**—weak and thin; without strength or force

2. Weakness, i.e., State of Being Weak,n. *From Sec. 1:* adynamia, anility, apathy, asthenia, atony, atonia, cachexia, characterlessness, decrepitude or decrepitness, delicateness or delicacy, dilution, dotardism or dotardy, effeminacy or effeminateness, effeteness, faintness, fecklessness, feebleness, flabbiness, flaccidity or flaccidness, flimsiness, fragility, frailty or frailness, helplessness, hyposthenia, impotence or impotency, impuissance, infirmity, insipidity or insipidness, insubstantiality, lameness, languidness, languor, or languorousness, lassitude, limpness, listlessness, mooniness, namby-pambiness or namby-pambism, nervelessness, powerlessness, prostration, puniness, quagginess, ricketiness, saplessness, senility, sheepishness, slackness, slightness, slimness, sluggishness, spinelessness, strengthlessness, subtlety, supineness, tenderness, thinness; torpor, torpidity, or torpidness; valetudinarianism, wanness, wateriness, wishy-washiness; *Also:*
  1. **dotage**—senility
  2. **inanition**—weakness from lack of food
3. A Weakness,n. *From Sec. 1:* frailty, infirmity
4. A Weak Person,n. *From Sec. 1:* dotard, effeminate, feebling, namby-pamby, valetudinarian, weakling; *Also:* 1. **tenderfoot**—someone who has not become used to the hardships or rigors of nature

5. To Weaken, i.e., Make Weak or Weaker, v.
  1. **abate**—reduce in intensity; moderate
  2. **attemper**—reduce in force by mixture
  3. **attenuate**—weaken; decrease the force of
  4. **confound**—render powerless with confusion
  5. **cripple**—weaken
  6. **cushion**—weaken the sound or impact of
  7. **deaden**—weaken
  8. **debilitate**—weaken by sapping the strength, vitality, or physical vigor of
  9. **devitalize**—rob of strength or vigor, literally or figuratively
  10. **dilute**—reduce the strength of by mixing with water or similar substance; attenuate
  11. **diminish**—lessen in power, authority, strength, etc.
  12. **disable**—deprive of power, function, or capacity
  13. **discourage**—weaken the resolution or determination of
  14. **effeminate, effeminatize, effeminize**—weaken; cause to have, or to develop, womanly weakness; deprive of manly strength

15. **emasculate**—deprive of all vigor, strength, vitality, etc., leaving only an empty shell
16. **enervate**—deprive of energy, strength, or vitality
17. **enfeeble**—make or leave weak and helpless
18. **eviscerate**—weaken; deprive of force or strength by the removal of vital parts
19. **exhaust**—drain of all strength
20. **extenuate**—diminish
21. **fade**—make weak (in color, intensity, brilliance, etc.)
22. **impair**—weaken
23. **incapacitate**—deprive of natural power; rob of mental or physical power; disable
24. **mitigate**—moderate; temper
25. **moderate**—decrease the force or violence of
26. **modify**—moderate; temper
27. **modulate**—temper
28. **palsy**—deprive of energy
29. **prostrate**—render weak and helpless
30. **qualify**—weaken or make less strong (abstractions)
31. **relax**—weaken in strictness, force, severity, etc.
32. **remit**—reduce the force or intensity of
33. **sap**—weaken; weaken gradually or slowly; undermine
34. **slacken, slack**—relax
35. **slake**—weaken; make less intense or less strong
36. **starve**—weaken by depriving of food or some other essential
37. **subdue**—reduce in force
38. **temper**—weaken; reduce the intensity, force, power, or strength of by adding some thing, quality, or ingredient
39. **thin**—dilute
40. **undermine**—weaken; weaken secretly, slyly, insidiously, or unfairly; weaken gradually
41. **vitiate**—weaken; reduce the strength of
42. **waste**—weaken (usually the body or a bodily part)
43. **wilt**—weaken; rob of vigor or freshness
44. **wither**—deprive of strength or force

6. A Weakening, i.e., Making Weak or Weaker,n. *From Sec. 5:* abatement, attenuation, confoundment, debilitation, devitalization, dilution, diminution or diminishment, disablement, discouragement, effemination or effeminization, emasculation, enervation, enfeeblement, evisceration, exhaustion, extenuation, impairment, incapacitation, mitigation, moderation, modification, modulation, prostration, qualification, relaxation, remission, starvation, subdual, vitiation

7. State of Being Weakened,n. *From Sec. 5:* abatement, attenuation, confoundment, debilitation, debility, devitalization, dilution, diminution or diminishment, disability or disablement, discouragement, emasculation, enervation, enfeeblement, evisceration, exhaustion, impairment, incapacity, moderation, palsy, relaxation, remissiveness, slackness, starvation, vitiation, waste, wilt

8. To Weaken, i.e., Become Weak or Weaker,v. *From Sec. 5:* abate, dilute, diminish, effeminate, fade, moderate, palsy, relax, slacken or slack off, slake, starve, waste or waste away, wilt, wither; *Also:*
  1. **decay**—lose power or strength
  2. **decline**—grow weak or weaker; lose mental, moral, or physical strength
  3. **deteriorate**—lose mental, moral, or physical strength
  4. **droop**—become weak; lose strength
  5. **dwindle**—decrease gradually in power
  6. **fail**—become weaker; lose vigor
  7. **flag**—lost strength, force, or power; become weak
  8. **languish**—lose force, power, energy or strength

9. **taper**—become gradually less in force or intensity
10. **wane**—decline in power, authority, strength, influence, intensity, etc.
11. **waver**—begin to lose strength of resolution

9. A Becoming Weak or Weaker,n. *From Sec. 5:* abatement, dilution, diminution or diminishment, effemination, moderation, relaxation, starvation; *From Sec. 8:* decay, decline, deterioration, languishment

10. Becoming Weak or Weaker,adj. *From Sec. 5:* abating, diminishing, fading, moderating, slackening, wilting, withering; *From Sec. 8:* decaying, declining, deteriorating, drooping or droopy, dwindling, failing, flagging, languishing, tapering, waning, wavering; *Also:* 1. **decrescent**—growing less powerful

11. Weak Spot,n.
   1. **Achilles' heel**—figurative spot or place where one is most weak
   2. **foible**—weak point

12. To Be beyond the Power of: beggar (description, etc.,v.)

13. That Which Reduces the Force of a Blow: buffer, cushion,n.

14. A Weakness of Character,n.
   1. **failing**—a slight weakness of character of which one may not be aware
   2. **fault**—a weakness, but not a serious weakness, of character
   3. **foible**—a weakness of character or temperament that is harmless and inoffensive
   4. **frailty**—a weakness of character that makes one a victim of temptation
   5. **shortcoming**—failing; fault
   6. **vice**—any weakness of character

11. DELICACY

1. Delicate,adj.
   1. **dainty**—delicate (daintiness,n.)
   2. **ethereal**—unusually delicate (etherealness,n.)
   3. **exquisite**—delicate; delicate and beautiful (exquisiteness,n.)
   4. **fine**—delicate, small, and thin (fineness, n.)
   5. **fragile**—delicate and weak, i.e., easily broken (fragility,n.)
   6. **frail**—delicate and weak (frailty, frailness,n.)
   7. **mincing**—affectedly delicate
   8. **minikin**—delicate; affectedly delicate
   9. **minion**—delicate
   10. **rose water**—affectedly delicate
   11. **slight**—frail (slightness,n.)
   12. **subtle**—delicate and elusive (subtlety, n.)

12. FATIGUE

1. Fatigued; Tired,adj.
   1. **bedraggled**—tired and soiled
   2. **blasé**—tired of normal or conventional pleasures
   3. **bushed**—completely fatigued (colloq.)
   4. **careworn**—tired; showing fatigue
   5. **dead-beat**—completely exhausted (colloq.)
   6. **dead-tired**—extremely tired; completely fatigued or exhausted
   7. **dog-tired**—completely fatigued
   8. **dog-weary**—completely fatigued
   9. **drooping**—figuratively or literally hanging down from extreme fatigue
   10. **droopy**—drooping
   11. **enervated**—mentally, physically, and/or emotionally tired; unpleasantly tired
   12. **exhausted**—tired to an extreme degree; drained of all strength or energy

13. **fagged, fagged out**—tired; tired out
14. **footsore**—tired, i.e., with one's feet sore or tender, from much walking
15. **foot-weary**—fatigued from walking or traveling
16. **footworn**—foot-weary; tired in the feet
17. **jaded**—tired by hard, tedious, or monotonous tasks; blasé
18. **languid**—drooping; languorous
19. **languorous**—having a feeling of general tiredness, physical, mental, and emotional, so that one has no energy or desire to do anything, no zest, spirit, or enthusiasm
20. **lassitudinous**—tired
21. **life-weary**—tired of living
22. **listless**—tired and bored
23. **outspent**—completely fatigued; exhausted
24. **overfatigued**—overtired
25. **overtired**—excessively or abnormally tired
26. **overwearied**—overtired
27. **prostrated**—completely fatigued; utterly exhausted
28. **sear, sere**—exhausted
29. **spent**—exhausted
30. **tuckered, tuckered out**—completely fatigued
31. **war-weary**—tired of, or from, war
32. **washed out**—completely fatigued
33. **way-weary**—tired from traveling
34. **wayworn**—tired from traveling
35. **wearied**—fatigued; exhausted
36. **weary**—tired
37. **weary-footed**—foot-weary
38. **weary-laden**—burdened with fatigue
39. **weary-winged**—wing-weary
40. **weary-worn**—worn out with fatigue
41. **wing-weary**—tired from traveling
42. **world-weary**—tired of living
43. **worn out**—completely tired out

2. Fatigue; Tiredness,n. *From Sec. 1:* bedragglement, dead-tiredness, dog-tiredness, dog-weariness, droopiness, enervation, exhaustion, footsoreness, foot-weariness, languidness, languor or languorousness, lassitude, listlessness, overfatigue, overtiredness, overweariness, prostration, war-weariness, weariness, world-weariness

3. To Fatigue or Tire, i.e., Cause to Be Fatigued or Tired,v. *From Sec. 1:* bedraggle, bush, enervate, exhaust, fag, jade, overfatigue, overtire, prostrate, tucker or tucker out, weary

4. Fatiguing; Tiring; Causing Fatigue or Tiredness,adj. *From Sec. 1:* enervating, exhausting, fagging, wearying; *Also:* poky, tedious, tiresome, weariful, wearing, wearisome, weary

5. Tiresomeness,n. *From Sec. 4:* pokiness, tedium or tediousness, wearifulness, wearisomeness, weariness

6. To Fatigue or Tire, i.e., Become Fatigued or Tired,v. *From Sec. 1:* droop, weary; *Also:*
   1. **flag**—become tired
   2. **languish**—droop; flag
   3. **succumb**—sink down in complete fatigue

7. Writer's Fatigue: graphospasm,n.

8. Tired-Looking,adj.
   1. **haggard**—looking worn out from fatigue, worry, pain, or similar experiences; looking wild-eyed and fatigued (haggardness, n.)
   2. **languishing**—looking emotionally weary, or assuming such a look in order to evoke sympathy
   3. **toil-worn**—appearing fatigued by hard work
   4. **wan**—tired-looking (wanness,n.)
   5. **weary-looking**—tired-looking

9. Easily Fatigued: fatigable,adj. (fatigability,n.)

10. Not Becoming Tired: indefatigable, tireless, unfailing, unflagging, untiring, unwearied, wearless,adj. (indefatigability or indefatigableness, tirelessness,n.)

13. DISABLEMENT

1. To Disable,v.
1. cripple—disable
2. disarm—make powerless
3. disqualify—make unable to do something
4. hamstring, hock—disable, either literally or figuratively, in allusion to cutting the hamstring, a tendon at the back of the knee; make inefficient
5. incapacitate—disable; deprive of ability or power
6. lame—disable; disable in the leg or legs, foot or feet
7. maim—disable
8. paralyze, palsy—render incapable of action or motion
9. pinion—disable by holding the arms of
10. unfit—disable

2. Disablement,n. From Sec. 1: disqualification, incapacitation, paralysis

3. Disabled,adj. From Sec. 1: crippled, disarmed, etc.; Also:
1. hors de combat (French)—disabled from fighting or struggling
2. powerless, helpless, impotent—completely lacking in ability or power

4. Disability,n. From Sec. 1: incapacity, lameness, paralysis, palsy; From Sec. 3: powerlessness, helplessness, impotence or impotency

14. AWKWARDNESS; UNSKILLFULNESS

1. Awkward; Unskillful; Unskilled; Clumsy, adj.
1. amateur, amateurish—awkward in the sense of doing something poorly or unskillfully, like a beginner
2. ambisinister—clumsy in the use of both hands
3. artless—unskilled
4. awkward—unskillful; manually unskillful; clumsy
5. backhanded—clumsy
6. blunderheaded—blundering and stupid
7. blundering, blunderous—working, doing, acting, etc., in a clumsy, wrong, or stupid fashion; clumsy
8. bobbling—fumbling
9. boggling—blundering; botchy
10. boorish—clumsy
11. botching—doing in a poor and clumsy fashion
12. botchy—doing, or done, in a poor and clumsy fashion
13. bungling—doing or making in an unskillful or clumsy fashion
14. clownish—clumsy and ill-mannered
15. elephantine—ungainly
16. floundering—clumsy; going or moving clumsily
17. footless—clumsy; inept
18. fumbling—feeling or groping about awkwardly or clumsily; awkward in one's attempts to do or find something
19. gauche—socially awkward; awkward in social graces or contacts, in getting along with people, etc.
20. gawkish—gawky
21. gawky—awkward in motions or physical movement; clumsy and stupid; awkward and foolish; clumsy
22. graceless—lacking in grace; hence, awkward or clumsy
23. heavy-handed—clumsy; awkward
24. helpless—incompetent

25. improficient—incompetent
26. imprudent—showing no skill in the management of one's affairs
27. inadept—awkward in the sense of not having the ability that results from skill and training
28. inadequate—incompetent
29. inapt—showing no natural or native ability or capacity
30. inartistic—showing no skill, talent, or inspiration
31. incapable—totally lacking in ability, or in any potential skill or ability
32. incompetent—not possessed of the ability required for the task, work, etc.
33. inefficient—incapable of doing or working without waste of time, motions, effort, energy, etc.
34. inelegant—graceless
35. inept—awkward; lacking skill
36. inexpert—unskilled
37. left-handed—awkward; clumsy
38. limping—awkward and halting
39. loutish—awkward and stupid
40. lubberly—big and clumsy
41. maladroit—mentally or socially awkward; clumsy in accomplishing things; tactless
42. oafish—lubberly
43. ponderous—heavy and clumsy or awkward, literally or figuratively (as a ponderous beast, ponderous style of writing, etc.)
44. rude—unskillful; not expert
45. rustic—awkward; clumsy
46. rusty—out of practice; hence, no longer as skillful as before
47. shiftless—inefficient
48. splay—awkward; ungraceful
49. sternforemost—awkward (literally with the back in front)
50. stiff—awkward
51. tactless—unable to do or say the proper thing; showing no skill in dealing with, or getting along with, people
52. unable—lacking in ability
53. unaccomplished—unskillful; lacking in the skill that comes from training; socially unskillful
54. unadept—lacking in ability
55. unadroit—not skillful
56. unapt—inapt
57. uncouth—awkward; clumsy
58. undexterous, undextrous—lacking in skill; not able to use the hands skillfully
59. undiplomatic—showing no skill in dealing with people; unskillful in human relationships
60. uneasy—awkward; stiffly awkward
61. unendowed—ungifted
62. unfit—incapable; incompetent
63. ungainly—awkward and lacking grace in manner or movement
64. ungifted—possessing no natural ability or talent
65. ungraceful—lacking smoothness in movement or action
66. unhandy—manually awkward
67. unpracticed—unskilled
68. unproficient—incompetent
69. unqualified—incapable; incompetent
70. unresourceful—showing no skill in handling difficult situations, getting rid of difficulties, etc.
71. untactful—tactless
72. untalented—having no special abilities, gifts, or capacities
73. untoward—awkward; ungraceful
74. unworkmanlike—showing no skill or ability (of actions, jobs, etc.)
75. weedy—physically ungraceful
76. wooden—clumsy

2. Awkwardness; Unskillfulness; Clumsiness,n. From Sec. 1: amateurism, amateurishness, artlessness, awkwardness, backhandedness, blunderheadedness, boorishness, botchiness, botchery, clownishness, gaucher, gawkishness, gawkiness, gracelessness, heavyhandedness, helplessness, improficiency, imprudence, inadeptness, inadequacy, inaptitude, inartisticness, incapability or incapacity, incompetence, inefficiency, inelegance, ineptness or ineptitude, inexpertness, left-handedness, loutishness, lubberliness, maladroitness, oafishness, ponderousness or ponderosity, rudeness, rusticity, rustiness, shiftlessness, stiffness, tactlessness, inability, uncouthness, uneasiness, unfitness, ungainliness, ungracefulness, unhandiness, unresourcefulness, untactfulness, untowardness, weediness, woodenness

3. Awkward, Clumsy, or Unskillful Person, n. *From Sec. 1:* amateur, blunderhead, blunderer, boggler, boor, botcher, bungler, clown, fumbler, gawk or gawky, incompetent, lout, lubber, oaf, rustic; *Also:*
1. **blunderbuss**—clumsy and stupid person who always does the wrong thing
2. **cobbler**—botchy worker
3. **dabster**—unskillful worker
4. **duffer**—clumsy, awkward, or unskilled player in a game or participant in a contest
5. **gawk**—person who is awkward owing to his abnormally large size
6. **hobbledehoy**—awkward or clumsy young man
7. **looby**—awkward person
8. **lummox**—clumsy, inept, and stupid person
9. **lumpkin**—gawk
10. **ne'er-do-well**—hopelessly incompetent and incapable person
11. **slouch**—clumsy, inefficient person
12. **tinker**—unskilled, botchy, or clumsy worker or performer

4. To Be Awkward, Clumsy, or Unskillful; To Do Awkwardly, Clumsily, or Unskillfully, v. *From Sec. 1:* blunder, bobble, boggle, botch, bungle, flounder, fumble, gawk, limp; *Also:*
1. **foozle**—do (something) clumsily and unsuccessfully
2. **muddle**—bungle
3. **muff**—handle awkwardly; bungle

5. Clumsy to Handle Because of Its Shape, Large Size, etc.: bulky, cumbersome or cumbrous, unwieldy,adj. (bulkiness, cumbersomeness or cumbrousness, unwieldiness,n.)

15. CAUSE

1. To Cause; To Bring About, v.
1. **anticipate**—cause to happen sooner
2. **beget**—be the cause of
3. **brew**—bring about
4. **conclude**—effect
5. **contribute**—help bring about
6. **contrive**—bring about
7. **effect**—bring about; cause to happen
8. **effectuate**—bring about; cause; cause to happen
9. **engender**—cause; bring about
10. **foment**—cause (usually some unpleasant action, as *foment dissension, rebellion, discontent,* etc.)
11. **generate**—cause
12. **incur**—bring (something unpleasant) upon oneself (by one's acts)
13. **induce**—cause; bring on; bring about
14. **maneuver**—bring about by artful managing, trickery, or clever planning
15. **precipitate**—cause to happen faster, unexpectedly, or before one is ready
16. **produce**—bring about; cause to happen; cause to be
17. **provoke, prompt, inspire, occasion**—cause; bring about

18. **render**—cause to become
19. **stage-manage**—cause to happen by artificial or external direction and control rather than allowing spontaneous occurrence
20. **synchronize**—cause to happen at the same time
21. **trigger**—cause to happen, i.e., do that one thing that, circumstances being proper, adds the necessary factor for causing a process or action to start

2. Causation, n. *From Sec. 1:* anticipation, conclusion, contribution, contrivance, effectuation, engenderment, generation, incurrence, inducement, precipitation, production, provocation or inspiration, synchronization

3. Causative,adj. *From Sec. 1:* anticipatory, contributory, effective or effectual, productive, provocative

4. A Cause,n. *From Sec. 1:* contribution, inducement, provocation or inspiration, trigger; *Also:*
1. **agent**—cause
2. **antecedent**—loosely, that which acts as a cause of (strictly, that which comes or occurs before)
3. **causation**—that which causes
4. **parent**—cause

5. To Consider as Caused by, or as the Cause of: accredit (to), ascribe (to), attribute (to), blame (for), credit,v. (accreditation, ascription, attribution,n. ascriptive, attributive,adj.)

6. Caused by Internal Factors: endogenous, adj.

7. Caused by External Factors: exogenous, adj.

8. Pert. or Relating to Cause, or to Cause and Effect,adj.
1. **causal**—pert. to cause; showing cause; pert. to cause and effect
2. **causative**—pert. to cause, or to cause and effect

9. Relation of Cause and Effect: causality, causation,n.

10. Doctrine That Every Effect Has a Cause: causality, causation,n.

11. Science of Causes: etiology,n.

16. RESULT

1. Result: aftermath, conclusion, consequence, creature, effect, eventuality, fruit, issue, offspring, outcome, outgrowth, product, resultant, sequela, sequence, sequent, spawn (derogatory), upshot,n.; *Also:*
1. **aftereffect**—result that comes later
2. **by-product**—unintended result
3. **conclusion**—final result
4. **corollary**—that which follows naturally as a result
5. **denouement**—result of a complicated situation
6. **engram**—permanent psychological effect left upon a personality by an experience
7. **harvest**—result of one's efforts or actions
8. **offshoot**—that which results from the main part, idea, branch, etc.
9. **repercussion**—indirect or reciprocal effect from a happening, act, or action
10. **sequel**—result of an action

2. Results: fruit, sequelae, spawn (derogatory),n.; *Also:*
1. **backfire**—unfortunate results, contrary to those expected or planned
2. **harvest**—results of one's efforts or actions

3. To Result; To Come or Happen as a Result: ensue, eventualize, eventuate, follow, issue, pan out, turn out,v. (eventuation,n.); *Also:*

1. **accrue**—come as a natural or logical result (accrual, accruement,n.)
2. **attend**—accompany or follow as a result
3. **redound** (on or upon)—come or flow back (to) as a result

4. **Resulting; Coming or Happening as a Result**: consequent, consequential, ensuing, resultant, sequent, sequential,adj. *Also:*
   1. **accruing**—naturally or logically resulting
   2. **aleatory**—resulting from luck
   3. **attendant, attending**—following or accompanying as a result
   4. **corollary**—following naturally as a result

5. **To Involve as a Result**: entail,v. (entailment,n.)

6. **To Have Unfortunate Results, Contrary to Those Expected**: backfire,v.

7. **To Get as the Results of One's Efforts**: harvest, reap,v.

8. **To Produce as a Result**: afford, beget, determine, effect; spawn (derogatory),v.

9. **To Produce a Result**: operate,v.

10. **To Help in Producing (a Result)**: contribute to,v. (contribution,n. contributory, adj.)

11. **Effective; Producing, or Capable of Producing, the Desired Effect**: effectual, efficacious, forceful, fruitful, operative, potent, telling, trenchant, valid,adj.

12. **Effectiveness**: effectuality, efficacy or efficaciousness, forcefulness, fruitfulness, potency, trenchancy, validity,n.

13. **Powerful in Effect**: potent, vigorous,adj. (potency, vigor or vigorousness,n.)

14. **Able to Bring About Desired Results or Effects with a Minimum of Effort or Time (of Persons, Things, or Action)**: efficient,adj. (efficiency,n.)

15. **Producing a Clear and Definite Result**: decisive,adj.

16. **Productive of Noteworthy Results**: eventful,adj. (eventfulness,n.)

17. **Involving Momentous or Decisive Results**: fateful,adj. (fatefulness,n.)

18. **Tending to Bring About the Desired Result**: expedient,adj. (expedience, expediency, n.)

19. **Capable of Becoming Effective**: potential, adj. (potentiality,n.)

20. **Giving Results to One Person though Done by Another**: vicarious,adj.

21. **In Effect though Not in Fact or Name**: moral, practical, virtual,adj.

22. **To Make Effective by Providing Power, Influence, Means, etc.**: implement,v. (implementation,n.)

23. **To Put into Effect or Force**: administer, administrate, execute, perform,v.

24. **A Putting into Effect or Force**: administration, execution, performance, pursuance,n.

25. **To Put into Effect or Force, and Compel Obedience to (Laws, Commands, Demands, etc.)**: enforce, execute,v. (enforcement, execution,n.)

26. **Legally Enforceable**: valid,adj. (validity, n.)

27. **To Figure the Possible Results of**: appraise,v. (appraisal,n.)

28. **Concern with Practical Results Rather than Theoretical Concepts**: pragmatism,n. (pragmatist,n. pragmatic or pragmatical, adj.)

29. **Philosophy or Doctrine that an Idea Is of Value Only in Respect to Its Results**: pragmatism,n. (pragmatist,n. pragmatic or pragmatical,adj.)

17. INEFFECTIVENESS

1. **Ineffective; Incapable of Having an Effect or Producing a Result**,adj.
   1. **anticlimactic**—noticeably or ridiculously dropping in effectiveness from preceding events, statements, etc.
   2. **bathetic**—strained and unsuccessful in an attempt at pathetic effect; anticlimactic
   3. **bootless**—fruitless
   4. **defeasible**—ineffective because capable of being annulled
   5. **feckless**—ineffective; futile
   6. **fruitless**—without result; ineffectual
   7. **futile**—incapable of becoming effective
   8. **impotent**—incapable of producing a result or effect
   9. **indecisive**—producing no clear or definite result
   10. **ineffectual**—not producing the desired, expected, or usual effect; futile
   11. **inefficacious**—incapable of producing the desired results
   12. **inexpedient**—not likely to bring about the desired result or effect
   13. **innocuous**—having no effect
   14. **inoperative**—causing no effect
   15. **invalid**—ineffective
   16. **nugatory**—ineffective
   17. **null**—of no force; of no effect
   18. **outworn**—no longer effective
   19. **sterile**—ineffective; not producing results; futile
   20. **stillborn**—ineffective when produced
   21. **unavailing**—futile
   22. **unfruitful**—not producing results
   23. **vain**—futile
   24. **void**—without legal force
   25. **weak**—ineffective
   26. **withered**—without force or effect

2. **Ineffectiveness**,n. *From Sec. 1:* anticlimax, bathos, bootlessness, defeasibility, fecklessness, fruitlessness, futility, impotence, indecisiveness, ineffectualness or ineffectuality, inefficaciousness or inefficacy, inexpedience or inexpediency, innocuousness, inoperativeness, invalidity, nullity, sterility, unfruitfulness, vainness, weakness

3. **That Which Noticeably or Ridiculously Falls Off in Effectiveness**: anticlimax,n.

4. **To Lose Effectiveness**: wither,v.

5. **To Make Ineffective**,v.
   1. **abolish**—make null and void
   2. **abrogate**—make void or invalid by legislative or authoritative act
   3. **annihilate**—make totally ineffective
   4. **annul**—make void or invalid
   5. **baffle**—frustrate by causing confusion
   6. **balk**—render ineffective by placing obstacles or hindrances in the path of realization or fulfillment; frustrate
   7. **bilk**—make ineffective; frustrate
   8. **blight**—frustrate
   9. **cancel**—make null and void; neutralize
   10. **circumvent**—render ineffective by ingeniously preventing completion or fulfillment
   11. **counterbalance**—neutralize (an opposing influence)
   12. **countermand**—cancel (a contrary or previous order or command)
   13. **countermine**—frustrate by secret measures
   14. **countervail**—frustrate by opposing force
   15. **dash**—frustrate
   16. **defeat**—cause to be without force or effect; frustrate (a plan, purpose, hope, desire, etc.)
   17. **destroy**—make void
   18. **disannul**—annul completely
   19. **discharge**—cancel or set aside (a court order)
   20. **discomfit**—annul the plans of; frustrate

21. **foil**—make (someone's efforts, plans, etc.) ineffective; frustrate
22. **frustrate**—make (someone's efforts, plans, etc.) ineffective; prevent (someone) from achieving fulfillment or realization of efforts, plans, desires, etc.
23. **invalidate**—cause to be no longer operative or effective
24. **negate**—make ineffective
25. **neutralize**—make ineffective or ineffectual by means of an opposing force or substance
26. **nullify**—make null and void
27. **override**—make ineffective
28. **paralyze**—make ineffective
29. **preclude**—make ineffectual
30. **quash**—nullify an action (in law); make void or inoperative
31. **repeal**—cancel (a law, order, etc.)
32. **rescind**—make void or without force or effect; annul
33. **revoke**—annul
34. **ruin**—destroy the effectiveness of
35. **scotch**—make ineffective
36. **spike**—make ineffective
37. **stultify**—make ineffective or futile
38. **stymie**—make ineffective; frustrate
39. **supersede**—cause to be ineffective or of no further force
40. **suspend**—make temporarily inoperative
41. **thwart**—make ineffective by vigorous opposition; frustrate
42. **vacate**—nullify
43. **vitiate**—make ineffective or without force; invalidate
44. **void**—nullify
45. **wither**—cause to lose force

6. A Making Ineffective,n. *From Sec. 5:* abolishment or abolition, abrogation, annihilation, annulment, bafflement, cancellation, circumvention, defeat, destruction, disannulment, discharge, discomfiture, frustration, invalidation, negation, neutralization, nullification, paralysis, preclusion, repeal, rescission, revocation, ruin, stultification, supersedure or supersession, suspension, vacation, vitiation, voidance; *Also:* **1. defeasance**—a rendering null and void (legal)

7. Making, or Serving to Make, Ineffective,adj. *From Sec. 5:* annihilative, circumventive, destructive, rescissory, supersessive, suspensive

8. Philosophy that Everything Is Futile, Esp. Human Efforts or Aspirations: futilitarianism,n. (futilitarian,n. futilitarian,adj.)

18. ATTEMPT

1. To Try; To Attempt,v.
1. **agonize**—try desperately
2. **angle for**—try for; try to get
3. **bid for**—make an attempt to get, win, or attract
4. **buffet**—strive
5. **compete for**—attempt to get in rivalry with others who have the same goal
6. **contend**—strive in opposition, rivalry, or competition
7. **contest**—compete; strive; strive or struggle to gain or hold
8. **dispute**—try to win
9. **endeavor**—try; try hard; try earnestly; try to do something fairly difficult or requiring great effort
10. **essay, assay**—make tentative attempts at something particularly difficult
11. **exert oneself**—put forth energy in an attempt
12. **pursue**—try to get
13. **rival**—try to equal or surpass
14. **seek**—try; try to get
15. **snatch at**—attempt to seize
16. **solicit**—try to get by asking

17. **storm**—attempt to seize by attack
18. **strain**—try as hard as possible
19. **strive**—try hard and persistently against odds or opposition; try hard
20. **struggle**—try hard; make great attempts
21. **tackle**—try to deal with
22. **toil**—exert great energy in an attempt
23. **tout**—try to get customers, business, votes, etc.
24. **travail**—exert energy in a great or painful attempt
25. **vie**—strive for superiority
26. **woo**—try to get, persuade or win; try to get the love of
27. **wrestle**—try earnestly

2. Attempt; Try; an Attempting or Trying, n. *From Sec. 1:* agony, bid, competition, contention, contest or contestation, endeavor or endeavors, essay, exertion, pursuit, rivalry, solicitation, storm, strain, struggle, toil, travail, wrestle; *Also:*
1. **application**—continued attempt or attempts
2. **attentat**—attempt to commit a crime of violence; unsuccessful attempt to commit a crime of violence
3. **captation**—attempt to get by flattery
4. **conation**—a striving toward a conscious or unconscious goal
5. **conatus**—a striving
6. **effort**—attempt
7. **heat**—a single attempt
8. **nisus**—a striving
9. **pains**—careful or laborious attempt
10. **shot**—a try
11. **siege**—long and tenacious attempt to gain possession
12. **stroke**—successful or bold attempt
13. **throes**—anguished attempt (usually in the phrase *in the throes*)
14. **trial**—an attempt
15. **whack**—an attempt
16. **wild-goose chase**—an attempt, apparently doomed to failure from the beginning, to find or accomplish something

3. Attempter,n. *From Sec. 1:* bidder, competitor, contender, contestant or contester, rival, seeker, solicitor, striver, struggler, toiler, wrestler

4. Descr. of Attempting,adj. *From Sec. 1:* competitive, exertive, rival; *From Sec. 2:* conative, conational (from *conation*)

5. Place of Endeavor: vineyard,n.

6. That Which One Strives for: ambition,n.

7. That Which One Has Long Striven to Attain, Long Wished for, etc.: mecca,n.

19. TEST

1. Test; Means of Testing,n.
1. **acid test**—final and most severe or revealing test of a person's or thing's quality, value, character, etc.
2. **bout**—test of strength or superiority
3. **check**—test
4. **criterion**—test; means of testing
5. **crucible**—severe test (after the container in which metals are dissolved)
6. **examination**—test of ability (as in school, for a position, etc.)
7. **experiment**—test or trial to discover something
8. **ordeal**—painful, unpleasant, or severe test; in ancient times, a test of a person's guilt or innocence by forcing him to endanger himself, on the theory that an innocent person would come through unharmed
9. **plummet**—test; means of testing
10. **probation**—test of one's ability, conduct, etc.
11. **quiz**—short examination

12. **shibboleth**—test; means of testing
13. **touchstone**—test of, or means of testing, the quality of something (so called from the black stone that tests the genuineness of gold or silver)
14. **trial**—test; means of subjecting to proof
15. **trial balloon, feeler**—tentative announcement of a plan, project, etc., to test the reaction of the public or of others
16. **yardstick**—criterion by which one measures some intangible thing

2. To Test,v. *From Sec. 1:* check, examine, experiment or experimentalize, quiz, try; *Also:* 1. **validate**—test the soundness of

3. A Testing,n. *From Sec. 1:* examination, experimentation, trial; *From Sec. 2:* validation

4. Tester,n. *From Sec. 1:* checker, examiner, experimenter or experimentator

5. Serving to Test, adj. *From Sec. 1:* experimental or experimentative, probationary, trial; *Also:*
   1. **pilot**—serving as a test of a new process, thing, development, etc.
   2. **probative**—serving to test
   3. **tentative**—done as a trial or experiment

6. One Who Is Tested,n. *From Sec. 1:* probationer

7. State or Condition of Being Tested,n. *From Sec. 1:* probation, trial

8. Based or Dependent on Experiment: empirical,adj.

9. Science, Art, Practice, etc., of Testing,n.
   1. **docimasy**—art or practice of testing, in science, to ascertain quality, characteristics, etc.
   2. **empiricism**—pursuit of knowledge by experiment and observation (empiricist,n. empiric or empirical,adj.)
   3. **experimentalism**—theory or practice of relying on experiment (experimentalist, n.)
   4. **psychometrics**—science of testing intelligence, emotional reactions, etc. (psychometrist,n. psychometric,adj.)

10. Place for Testing,n.
   1. **laboratory**—place where experiments are carried on or experimental work or studies are engaged in
   2. **proving ground**—place for testing or experimenting

11. Treatise on the Art of Testing: docimology,n.

12. Period of Time in Which One's Ability, Conduct, etc., Are Tested: probation,n.

13. Not Tested; Not Yet Tested: untested, untried, virgin or virginal,adj.

20. COMPETITION

1. To Compete,v.
   1. **contend (with)**—strive in competition (with)
   2. **contest**—compete; struggle for superiority in a competition
   3. **cope with**—contend with, usually on equal terms
   4. **duel**—engage in a competition with another, whether with weapons or with words, etc.
   5. **joust (with)**—engage in a competition (with)
   6. **pit oneself against**—compete with; struggle in competition with or against
   7. **race**—engage in a contest of speed
   8. **strive**—struggle in competition
   9. **tilt, tourney**—engage in a competition

2. A Competition, Contest, or Race,n. *From Sec. 1:* contest, duel, joust, race, tourney; *Also:*
   1. **bout**—contest

2. **course**—event in athletic contests, esp. those connected with racing; race
3. **decathlon**—athletic contest of ten events
4. **derby**—horse race run annually near London; any similar race; any race or contest, by extension, of similar prominence to the original derby
5. **gymkhana**—meeting for athletic contests, esp. racing
6. **heat**—single event in an athletic contest or race
7. **marathon**—long contest or race
8. **match**—contest
9. **pentathlon**—athletic contest consisting of five events
10. **regatta**—rowing race; boat race; series of boat races
11. **steeplechase**—horse race over obstacles or across country
12. **sweepstake**—race or other contest, esp. a horse race, in which the stake is given either entirely to the winner or in shares to the several winners
13. **tournament**—athletic contests of various kinds; contest; series of contests in a field; knightly contests
14. **tug of war**—contest between two opposing sides to gain ascendancy or supremacy
15. **walkaway**—contest won without any great effort

3. Competitor,n. *From Sec. 1:* contender, contestant, duelist or dueler, jouster, racer; *Also:*
   1. **also-ran**—horse or contestant that fails to win any place
   2. **corrival**—rival
   3. **dark horse**—little-known competitor or contestant
   4. **entry**—one entered in a contest of any sort
   5. **finalist**—one who survives previous elimination contests and is entered in the last and decisive contest
   6. **protagonist**—main contender in a conflict, struggle, contest, activity, etc.
   7. **rival**—one who competes with another for the same thing, goal, etc.

4. State of Being in Competition with Another: rivalry,n.

5. Having Competitive Claims: corrival, rival,adj.

6. To Place in Competition,v.
   1. **pit (against)**—place in rivalry or competition (with)
   2. **race**—place (animals) in a running contest

7. Place of Competition,n.
   1. **arena**—place in which a contest takes place
   2. **pit**—place where a cockfight takes place; by extension, place of any competition

8. Person Who Comes in Second in a Contest: runner-up,n.

9. Loser in a Contest: underdog,n.

10. A Draw,n.
   1. **dead heat**—reaching of the goal simultaneously by two or more contestants in a race
   2. **standoff**—draw in a game
   3. **stalemate**—draw in a game or contest
   4. **tie**—draw; dead heat

11. Horse Racing: the track, the turf,n.

12. Place Where Horses Race: course, racecourse, race track, track, the turf,n.

13. Pert. to or Characteristic of Horse Racing: turfy,adj.

14. Verbs Indicating Order of Winners in a Horse Race
   1. **place**—come in second
   2. **show**—come in third
   3. **win**—come in first

21. STRUGGLE

1. To Struggle, v.
1. battle—struggle
2. buckle—struggle
3. buffet—struggle; strive
4. contend—struggle in rivalry or competition
5. contest—struggle to get or keep; struggle for superiority; strive
6. cope with—struggle with on equal terms and, usually, successfully
7. grapple (with)—struggle (with)
8. pit oneself against—struggle with in rivalry, competition, or antagonism
9. scrimmage—engage in a rough and confused struggle
10. scuffle—struggle at close quarters and in some confusion
11. skirmish—struggle
12. strive—struggle in opposition, rivalry, or competition
13. toil—struggle hard
14. tussle—struggle; scuffle; wrestle
15. vie—struggle for advantage or superiority
16. wrestle—struggle; struggle bodily with, attempting to pin to the ground

2. Struggle, n. *From Sec. 1:* battle, contention, contest, scrimmage, scuffle, skirmish, toil, tussle, wrestle; *Also:*
1. agony—final struggle before death
2. bout—struggle
3. brush—short, quick struggle
4. throes—anguished struggle (usually in the phrase in the throes)

3. Struggler, n. *From Sec. 1:* battler, contender, contestant or contester, grappler, scrimmager, scuffler, skirmisher, toiler, tussler, wrestler

4. Wrestling School of Ancient Times: palaestra, palestra, n.

22. DEFEAT

1. To Defeat: beat, best; lick (colloq.); overcome, overpower, overthrow, overturn, prevail against, prevail over; trim (colloq.); triumph over; trounce (in a contest); vanquish; whip (colloq.); worst, v.

2. Defeat: beating; licking (colloq.); overthrow, overturn, trimming (colloq.), triumph; trouncing (in a contest); vanquishment; whipping (colloq.), n.; *Also:*
1. reverse, reversal—defeat that is suffered
2. Waterloo—crushing defeat that is suffered

3. To Defeat Thoroughly or Completely: checkmate, crush, discomfit, overpower, overwhelm, put to rout, rout, smash, vanquish, v.

4. Thorough or Complete Defeat: checkmate, discomfiture, rout, vanquishment, n.

5. To Defeat Decisively, or by a Wide Margin, as in a Contest: drub, thrash, whitewash, v.

6. Decisive Defeat, as in a Contest: drubbing, thrashing, whitewash, n.

7. To Defeat (Opponents) in a Contest in Such a Thorough Way that They Make No Score: whitewash, v. (whitewash, n.)

8. To Defeat by Guile, Deception, or a Plot: euchre (colloq.), v.

9. To Defeat Unfairly: trim (colloq.), v. (trimming, n.)

10. One Who Has Defeated (an Opponent, Enemy, etc.): master, victor, winner, n.

11. Having Defeated an Opponent, Enemy, etc.: master, successful, triumphant, victorious, adj. (successfulness, victoriousness, n.)

12. State or Fact of Having Defeated an Opponent, Enemy, etc.: mastery, success, triumph, victory, n.

13. Victory Gained with Excessive Losses or at Too Great a Cost: Pyrrhic victory, n.

14. Easy Victory, as in a Contest, etc.: walkaway, walkover, n.

15. Pert. to, or Marked by, Victory: triumphal, triumphant, victorious, adj.

16. In Celebration or Commemoration of a Victory: triumphal, triumphant, adj.

17. Rejoicing over a Victory: exultant, exulting, triumphant, adj. (exultance, exultancy, or exultation, n.)

18. To Rejoice over a Victory: exult, v. (exultation, n.)

19. Song or Expression of Victory: paean, pean, n.

20. What Is Won in a Contest, Conquest, War, etc.: spoils, n.

21. Capable of Being Defeated: beatable, defeatable, adj.

22. Incapable of Being Defeated: unbeatable, undefeatable, adj.

23. To Overcome: beat (in a contest), conquer, overmaster, overpower, overthrow, overwhelm, prevail against, prevail over, subdue, triumph over, vanquish, v. (conquest, overthrow, subdual, triumph, vanquishment, n.)

24. To Overcome Completely: crush, overmaster, overpower, overwhelm, vanquish, v. (vanquishment, n.)

25. To Overcome the Feelings or Mind of: crush, overmaster, overpower, overwhelm, shock, stun, swamp, v. (shock, n.)

26. To Be Overcome by Difficulties, Hardships, etc.: swamp, v.

27. To Overcome (an Obstacle, Difficulty, etc.): conquer, hurdle, negotiate, prevail over, surmount, triumph over, vanquish, v. (conquest, negotiation, triumph, vanquishment, n. conquerable, surmountable, vanquishable, adj. insurmountable, unconquerable, unvanquishable, neg.adj.)

28. To Overcome the Obstacles, Difficulties, or Problems of: conquer, master, triumph over, vanquish, v. (conquest, mastery, triumph, vanquishment, n. conquerable, masterable, vanquishable, adj. unconquerable, unmasterable, unvanquishable, neg.adj.)

29. To Overcome (Someone) Physically, or by Superior Strength: overpower, subdue, v. (subdual, n. subduer, n. subduable, adj. unsubduable, neg.adj.)

30. Means of Crushing Opposition: steam roller, n. (steam roller, adj.)

31. Capable of Being Overcome: beatable, conquerable, masterable, superable, surmountable, vanquishable, vincible, adj.

32. Incapable of Being Overcome: impregnable (as reasoning, an argument, etc.), indomitable, ineluctable, insuperable, insurmountable, invincible, unbeatable, unconquerable, unmasterable, unvanquishable, adj.

33. Hard to Overcome: formidable, adj. (formidableness, formidability, n.)

34. To Overthrow: defeat, overturn, overwhelm, smash, subvert, topple, upset, v.

35. Overthrow: debacle, defeat, downcome, downthrow, overturn, smash, subversion, upset, n.

36. Tending or Acting to Overthrow or to Cause an Overthrow: subversive, adj. (subversiveness, n. subversive, n.)

37. Sudden Act That Illegally Overthrows the Government: coup d'état (French), n.

38. To Force to Submit: bring to terms

39. To Put Down, as Opposition, Revolt, Disorder, or Anything Not Desired: crush, quash, quell, repress, squash, squelch, subdue, suppress, tame,v. (repression, subdual, suppression,n. subduer, suppressor, tamer,n. repressive, suppressive,adj.)

40. Capable of Being Put Down: domitable, repressible, subduable, suppressible, tamable, adj.

41. Incapable of Being Put Down: indomitable, irrepressible, insuppressible, unrepressible, unsubduable, unsuppressible, untamable, adj.

42. To Put Down or Subdue by Withholding Food or Other Essentials from: starve,v. (starvation,n.)

43. To Conquer; To Conquer and Bring under Domination: master, overcome, overmaster, overpower, subdue, subjugate, vanquish,v.

44. Conquest; Conquest and Domination: mastery, subdual, subjugation, vanquishment, n.

45. State of Being Conquered, or Conquered and Dominated: subdual, subjugation, vanquishment,n.

46. Conqueror: master, subduer, subjugator, vanquisher,n.

47. Leader of the Spanish Conquest of North or South America: conquistador,n.

48. Conquerable: masterable, subduable, subjugable, superable, vanquishable, vincible,adj.

49. Unconquerable: indomitable, insuperable, invincible, unmasterable, unsubduable, unvanquishable,adj.

50. Conquerable by Assault or Attack, as a Place, etc.: pregnable,adj.

51. Unconquerable by Assault or Attack, as a Place, etc.: impregnable, inexpugnable,adj.

23. SUCCESS

1. To Succeed; To Be Successful: batten, bloom, blossom, flourish, prevail, prosper, thrive, triumph,v.

2. Successful: blooming, blossoming, flourishing, fruitful, palmy, prosperous, thrifty, thriving, triumphant,adj.

3. Unusually Successful, as a Crop, etc.: bumper,adj.

4. Success; Successfulness: fruitfulness or fruition, prosperity or prosperousness, thriftiness, triumph,n.

5. Successful over an Enemy in Battle or an Opponent in a Contest, Struggle, etc.; Successful in One's Attempt: triumphant, victorious,adj. (triumph, victory or victoriousness,n. triumph,v.)

6. Brilliant Success: éclat,n.

7. Success Bought at Too High a Cost: Pyrrhic victory,n.

8. Critical, Rather than Commercial, Success, as of a Play, Novel, Other Work of Art, etc.; Such a Play, Novel, etc.: succès d'estime (French),n.

9. To Do Successfully: accomplish,v. (accomplishment,n.)

10. To Succeed in Completing; To Bring to a Successful Completion or Conclusion: accomplish, achieve,v. (accomplishment, achievement,n.)

11. To Succeed Financially: flourish, prosper,v. (flourishing, prosperous,adj. prosperity or prosperousness,n.)

12. To Be Successful against, or in One's Opposition to: prevail against, resist, withstand,v. (resistance,n.)

13. To Come Successfully Through, as Storms, Dangers, Hardships, etc.: weather, v.

14. Successful Person,n.
1. **arrivé (French)**—one who has newly won success; parvenu (contemptuous)
2. **parvenu**—one who, usually by commercial success, has risen to a higher station than the one to which he was born (contemptuous)
3. **upstart**—one who, through commercial success usually, has risen from a humble or lowly position to one of honor, wealth, etc. (upstart,adj.)
4. **victor**—one who is successful in an attempt, or over an enemy, opponent, etc.

15. Indicating or Promising Probable Success: auspicious, promising,adj. (auspiciousness,n.)

24. FAILURE

1. To Fail,v.
1. **abort**—fail of complete development; be totally unsuccessful; fail after having barely started
2. **collapse**—fail completely
3. **crash**—fail in business
4. **fizzle**—fail after a successful start (colloq.)
5. **flop**—fail (slang)
6. **flunk**—fail in, or as if in, a test; fail a subject in school
7. **foozle**—do unsuccessfully and clumsily
8. **founder**—fail
9. **miscarry**—fail to achieve the desired end
10. **misfire**—fail, by turning out differently from what had been planned
11. **overreach oneself**—fail by trying for too much, or by being too clever or too tricky
12. **peter out**—gradually fail

2. Failure,n. *From Sec. 1:* abortion, collapse, crash, fizzle, flop, foozle, miscarriage, misfire; *Also:*
1. **cropper**—failure (esp. in the pattern *come, fall, or get a cropper*)
2. **debacle**—complete and unfortunate failure
3. **dud**—effort that turns out to be completely unsuccessful (colloq.)
4. **fiasco**—complete, unmitigated, and often ridiculous failure
5. **stillbirth**—abortion
6. **unsuccess**—failure; lack of success
7. **washout**—complete failure

3. Not Successful,adj.
1. **abortive**—totally unsuccessful; failing after having barely started; failing of complete development (abortiveness,n.)
2. **barren**—totally unsuccessful (barrenness, n.)
3. **sterile**—barren (sterility,n.)
4. **stillborn**—abortive
5. **unavailing**—unsuccessful
6. **unfruitful**—barren (unfruitfulness,n.)
7. **unprosperous**—lacking in success, often from a financial viewpoint (unprosperousness,n.)
8. **unsuccessful**—lacking in success (unsuccessfulness,n.)
9. **vain**—unsuccessful

4. One Who Fails or Has Failed: dud (colloq.), failure, ne'er-do-well,n.

5. To Give Someone a Failing Mark in a School Subject: fail, flunk,v.

6. Unlikely to Bring Success: disadvantageous,adj. (disadvantageousness,n.)

7. Indicating Probable Failure: inauspicious,adj. (inauspiciousness,n.)

25. DIFFICULTY

1. Difficult,adj.
1. **arduous**—difficult to do

2. **baffling**—too difficult to understand or solve
3. **complex**—difficult in the sense either of lacking simplicity or of having many confusing elements
4. **complicated**—difficult to explain, solve, understand, disentangle, etc.
5. **entangled**—complicated
6. **formidable**—so difficult as to cause dread, fear, or doubt of success
7. **hard**—difficult
8. **intricate**—difficult to understand; containing many confusing difficulties
9. **involved**—complex
10. **knotty**—difficult; intricate
11. **painful**—difficult
12. **problematic, problematical**—difficult; both difficult and uncertain
13. **prohibitive**—so difficult as to prevent or forbid doing
14. **queasy**—full of difficulties
15. **ramified**—full of complex divisions and subdivisions
16. **reticular**—complex; intricate
17. **scabrous**—very difficult to solve
18. **severe**—difficult; difficult in the sense of causing hardships
19. **snaggy**—full of hidden or unexpected difficulties
20. **snarled**—complicated
21. **spiny**—full of difficulties; thorny
22. **tangled**—complicated
23. **thorny**—difficult; hard to settle; full of problems, obstacles, or controversial points
24. **tough**—difficult
25. **tricky**—complicated
26. **troublesome, troublous**—causing difficulty; difficult
27. **uphill**—difficult, as if one were trudging up a steep slope
28. **vicissitudinary, vicissitudinous**—full of the difficulties or hardships of life that are beyond one's control

2. **Difficulty,**n. *From Sec. 1:* arduousness, complexity, complication or complicacy, entanglement, formidability, hardship, intricacy, involvement, knottiness, problem, ramification, reticularity, severity, snag, snarl, tangle, thorniness, trickiness, troublesomeness or trouble, vicissitude; *Also:*
1. **Chinese puzzle**—anything very complex or intricate
2. **inconvenience**—difficulty
3. **pitfall**—difficulty into which one may be trapped or in which one may trap oneself

3. **To Be Too Difficult for (Someone) to Understand or Solve:** baffle,v.

4. **To Cause Difficulties in, or Make Difficult:** complicate, entangle, snag, snarl or snarl up,v.

5. **One Who Causes Difficulties:** stormy petrel, troublemaker,n.

6. **Mischievous Person Who Causes Difficulties:** hellion,n.

7. **One Who Heralds Imminent Difficulties:** stormy petrel,n.

8. **One Who Finds and Eliminates the Causes of Difficulties:** trouble shooter,n. (trouble shooting,n.)

9. **Difficult Situation, Position, Condition, or Circumstance,**n.
1. **dilemma**—situation requiring a decision between alternatives that are equally difficult, unpleasant, unfavorable, etc.
2. **entanglement**—complicated situation or condition
3. **fix**—predicament (colloq.)
4. **imbroglio**—difficult (and often embarrassing) situation
5. **impasse**—difficult situation from which there is no escape, or to which there is no solution

6. **jam**—difficult situation (colloq.)
7. **mire**—difficult or complicated situation
8. **morass**—unpleasant circumstances or conditions from which one finds it difficult to extricate oneself
9. **pickle**—difficult situation or condition; predicament
10. **plight**—difficult situation or condition
11. **predicament**—difficult, unfortunate, and/or unpleasant situation
12. **quagmire**—situation, position, or condition of difficulty or attended by difficulties, or one from which it is difficult to extricate oneself
13. **quandary**—predicament
14. **rattrap**—difficult situation in which one is hopelessly caught
15. **scrape**—difficult situation; predicament
16. **snarl**—complicated situation
17. **straits**—difficult situation
18. **tangle**—complicated situation
19. **vicious circle**—one difficult and undesirable circumstance producing another, which in turn aggravates the first, and so on

26. EASE

1. **Easy,**adj.
1. **effortless**—capable of being done, achieved, or accomplished with no, or practically no, difficulty, effort, or expense of energy (effortlessness,n.)
2. **elementary**—dealing with the simplest parts or things, those that precede the more difficult or complicated ones; simple
3. **simple**—easy; not difficult (simplicity,n.)
4. **simplified**—easy because of having been made less difficult
5. **uncomplicated**—not difficult
2. **To Cause to Be Easy,**v.
1. **expedite**—make (an action, etc.) easy to accomplish
2. **facilitate**—make easy or easier; remove the difficulty from (facilitation,n.)
3. **simplify**—make less difficult (simplification,n.)
3. **Ease,**n.
1. **abandon**—careless ease
2. **facility**—ease; lack of difficulty (in doing); power or ability to do something easily
3. **legerity**—ease, lightness, and nimbleness of touch, movement, or action
4. **Extremely Easy Job or Position, or One Paying Well but Involving Little or No Work or Responsibility:** sinecure,n.
5. **To Do Easily,**v.
1. **take in one's stride**—do easily, without great effort or difficulty
2. **toss off**—do easily and quickly

27. CONVENIENCE

1. **Convenient,** adj.
1. **available**—handy (availability,n.)
2. **central**—convenient to get to from all places (centralness, centrality,n.)
3. **commodious**—convenient and spacious (commodiousness,n.)
4. **handy**—conveniently close or at hand; convenient to use or get to (handiness,n.)
2. **Things That Make Actions More Convenient, Easier, etc.:** facilities,n.

28. INCONVENIENCE

1. **Inconvenient:** awkward, bothersome, incommodious, troublesome, unhandy, untoward, adj.
2. **Inconvenience:** awkwardness, bother, bothersomeness, discommodity, incommodi-

ousness, trouble, troublesomeness, untowardness,n.

3. To Inconvenience: bother, discommode,
disoblige, incommode, trouble,v.

**4. Inconvenient to Handle or Manage,
Owing to Its Awkward Size, Weight, Dimensions, etc.:** awkward, bulky, unhandy, unmanageable, unwieldy,adj. (awkwardness,
bulkiness, unmanageableness, unwieldiness,
n.)

5. Inconvenient to Get to: remote,adj. (remoteness,n.)

29. OCCURRENCE

1. To Happen,v.
  1. **accompany**—happen at the same time;
  happen with (some other event)
  2. **alternate**—happen by turns
  3. **antedate, predate**—happen before (some
  other thing or event)
  4. **arise**—happen
  5. **bechance**—happen
  6. **befall**—happen; happen to
  7. **betide**—befall
  8. **coincide**—happen at the same time
  9. **concur**—happen at the same time
  10. **develop**—happen finally
  11. **ensue**—happen as a result of a previous
  occurrence
  12. **eventualize**—happen as a result, possibility, or accident
  13. **eventuate**—happen finally; happen at the
  end
  14. **intervene**—happen between other occurrences
  15. **materialize**—happen
  16. **occur**—happen
  17. **perseverate**—recur repeatedly in the
  mind without any associative cause (said
  of an idea, image, etc.)
  18. **persist**—happen over and over again
  19. **precede, antecede**—happen before (some
  other thing or event)
  20. **predominate**—happen more often
  21. **recrudesce**—happen again, after a period
  of inactivity (of a disease, symptom, feeling, or other abstraction)
  22. **recur**—happen again; happen over and
  over again
  23. **subvene**—happen by way of help or relief
  24. **supervene**—happen as something added,
  unexpected, or unneeded
  25. **synchronize**—happen at the same time
  26. **take place**—happen
  27. **terminate**—happen at the end of
  28. **transpire**—happen

2. Act, Fact, or Process of Happening,n.
From Sec. 1: accompaniment, alternation, coincidence, concurrence, development, eventuation, intervention, materialization, occurrence, perseveration, persistence, precession,
precedence or antecedence; predominance or
predomination, recrudescence, recurrence,
supervention, synchronization, transpiration;
Also:
  1. **accident**—act or fact of happening by
  chance rather than plan
  2. **conjunction**—act or fact of happening
  together
  3. **relapse**—recurrence

3. Happening,adj.
  1. **accidental**—happening by chance
  2. **acronical, acronycal**—happening at sunset (astronomy)
  3. **adventitious**—accidental (adventitiousness,n.)
  4. **afoot**—happening
  5. **alternate**—happening by turns
  6. **ambulatory**—happening while walking
  7. **ante bellum**—happening at some time
  previous to the, or a, war, or to the Civil
  War

  8. **antecedent**—happening before (antecedence, antecedency,n.)
  9. **anticlimactic**—happening as the last of
  the series of events, and ridiculously less
  important than the one before (anticlimax,n.)
  10. **aperiodic**—happening with no regularity
  (aperiodicity,n.)
  11. **bathetic**—anticlimactic (bathos,n.)
  12. **casual**—accidental; occasional
  13. **chronogeneous**—happening at a given
  time or period
  14. **circumstantial**—incidental (circumstantiality,n.)
  15. **climactic**—happening at the end, or at
  the most important final point
  16. **coincident, coincidental**—happening at
  practically the same time (coincidence,n.)
  17. **concomitant**—happening at the same
  time (concomitance,n.)
  18. **concurrent**—happening together, or at
  the same time (concurrence, concurrency,n.)
  19. **conjunctional, conjunctive**—happening
  together (conjunction,n.)
  20. **conjunctural**—happening together or in
  combination (conjuncture,n.)
  21. **consecutive, successive**—happening one
  after the other (consecutiveness, succes-
  siveness,n.)
  22. **constant**—regularly recurrent (constancy,n.)
  23. **contingent**—happening unexpectedly or
  accidentally (contingency,n.)
  24. **current**—happening commonly or frequently; happening at this time (currency,n.)
  25. **darkling**—happening in the dark
  26. **ensuing**—happening later; happening as
  a result of previous happenings
  27. **ex post facto**—happening after something, but nevertheless applying to, or
  influencing, it
  28. **fortuitous**—happening by pure chance
  (fortuitousness,n.)
  29. **frequent**—happening often (frequency,n.)
  30. **haphazard**—happening irregularly and
  by chance (haphazardness,n.)
  31. **immediate**—happening at once or without delay (immediacy, immediateness,n.)
  32. **incidental**—happening along with something more important; happening by
  chance
  33. **infrequent**—happening only once in a
  while (infrequency,n.)
  34. **instantaneous**—happening for just an
  instant; happening immediately after
  (instantaneousness,n.)
  35. **intermittent**—happening, stopping, then
  happening again, etc.; happening with
  stops or interruptions (intermittence, intermittency,n.)
  36. **isochronal, isochronous**—recurrent at
  regular intervals of time
  37. **minutely**—happening every minute
  38. **miraculous**—happening contrary to the
  laws of nature (miraculousness,n.)
  39. **occasional**—happening once in a while
  or infrequently
  40. **occurrent**—happening
  41. **opportune**—happening at such a time
  that full advantage can be taken; happening at the right or best time (opportuneness,n.)
  42. **passing**—happening at the present time
  43. **periodic**—happening at regular intervals;
  happening every once in a while (periodicity,n.)
  44. **perseverating**—happening repeatedly in
  the mind without any associative cause
  (said of an idea, image, etc.)
  45. **persistent**—happening over and over
  again (persistence, persistency,n.)
  46. **precedent, preceding**—happening before

or previously (precedence, precedency,n.)

47. **predominant**—happening more often (predominance, predominancy,n.)
48. **premature**—happening too soon (prematurity, prematureness,n.)
49. **prevalent**—widespread (prevalence,n.)
50. **prodigious**—happening outside the normal range of occurrences (prodigiousness,n.)
51. **random**—haphazard (randomness,n.)
52. **rare**—infrequent (rarity,n.)
53. **recrudescent**—happening again, esp. after a period of inactivity (of a disease, symptom, feeling, or other abstraction)
54. **recurrent**—happening again or repeatedly
55. **recurring**—recurrent
56. **rife**—happening frequently (rifeness,n.)
57. **seasonable, timely**—happening at the right time (seasonableness, timeliness,n.)
58. **secular**—happening only once in an age or century (secularity,n.)
59. **sparse**—happening in scattered places (sparseness,n.)
60. **spasmodic**—happening irregularly or with irregular frequency
61. **spontaneous**—happening by itself and not through some artificial or external suggestion, cause, help, or motivation (spontaneity, spontaneousness,n.)
62. **sporadic, sporadical**—happening irregularly or after irregular intervals of time; happening in scattered places; happening by itself (sporadicalness,n.)
63. **subvenient, subventive**—happening by way of help or relief (subvenience,n.)
64. **supervenient, superventive**—happening as something added, unexpected, or unneeded (supervenience,n.)
65. **swift**—happening suddenly, immediately, or without warning (swiftness,n.)
66. **synchronous, synchronal**—happening at the same time (synchronousness,n.)
67. **terminal**—happening at the end
68. **unseasonable, untimely**—happening too early, at the wrong time, or in the wrong season (unseasonableness, untimeliness, n.)
69. **widespread**—happening in many different places

4. Never Having Happened Before: unexampled, unprecedented,adj.

5. Depending for Occurrence on Something Uncertain: contingent,adj. (contingency,n.)

6. A Happening; That Which Happens,n.
1. **accident**—an unfortunate, unintended, or unexpected happening; that which happens by chance rather than plan (accidental,adj.)
2. **act of God**—accident that could not have been foreseen or prevented (legal)
3. **antecedent**—a prior happening
4. **anticlimax**—a happening, the last of a series, ridiculously less important than the one before (anticlimactic,adj.)
5. **authority**—precedent
6. **calamity**—disaster (calamitous,adj.)
7. **casualty**—an unfortunate happening
8. **cataclysm**—an unfortunate or tragic happening that causes violent and extreme changes (cataclysmic, cataclysmal, adj.)
9. **catastrophe**—a happening that causes great changes in the order of things; a sudden and disastrous happening (catastrophic, catastrophal,adj.)
10. **circumstance**—a happening (circumstantial,adj.)
11. **climax**—the final and most important happening, usually of a series (climactic, adj.)
12. **coincidence**—that which happens at the same time as something else, but without

any cause-and-effect relationship (coincidental,adj.)
13. **contingency, contingent**—a possible happening; an incidental, accidental, or unexpected happening; a happening that depends on something uncertain
14. **contretemps**—an embarrassing or unfavorable happening, or one that interferes with one's plans
15. **debacle**—disaster
16. **development**—that which happens finally
17. **disaster**—an unexpected and unfortunate happening, often causing great destruction or ruin (disastrous,adj.)
18. **episode**—a happening, in a novel or in real life, that is somewhat distinct and separate from previous or following happenings (episodic,adj.)
19. **event**—a happening; an important happening
20. **eventuality**—a possible happening
21. **happenstance**—a happening caused by chance (colloq.)
22. **incident**—that which has happened; a subordinate or less important happening (incidental,adj.)
23. **interlude**—an unimportant happening that fills the time between more important happenings
24. **milestone**—an important happening in progress
25. **miracle**—a happening contrary to laws of nature (miraculous,adj.)
26. **misadventure**—an unfortunate happening
27. **mischance**—an unlucky or unfortunate happening
28. **mishap**—an unfortunate happening; an unfortunate accident
29. **occasion**—a happening
30. **occurrence**—a happening
31. **phenomenon**—a happening that is observed; a happening that is perceived through the senses; an unusual, rare, or unique happening (phenomena, phenomenons,pl., adj.)
32. **portent**—a happening that forebodes future evil or misfortune
33. **precedent**—a happening that serves as an example or authorization for similar and following happenings
34. **proceeding, proceedings, process**—what happens
35. **prodigy**—an abnormal happening
36. **rarity**—an unusual or infrequent happening
37. **recurrence**—that which happens again
38. **sequel**—a happening that follows
39. **sequela**—that which by necessity happens at the same time
40. **supervention**—that which happens as something added, unexpected, or unneeded
41. **synchronal**—that which happens at the same time (synchronal,adj.)
42. **tragedy**—a sad, unfortunate, or terrible happening (tragic,adj.)
43. **tragicomedy**—a happening containing a combination of tragic and comic elements (tragicomic,adj.)

7. Happenings or Group of Happenings,n.
1. **conjuncture**—combination of happenings (conjunctural,adj.)
2. **consecution**—sequence of happenings
3. **episode**—related group of happenings, in a novel or in real life, that are somewhat distinct and separate from previous or following happenings (episodic,adj.)
4. **farce**—an absurd, or absurdly improbable, set of happenings (farcical,adj.)
5. **rash**—happenings that figuratively break out
6. **sequel**—happenings that follow, either purely in time or as a result

7. **sequelae**—happenings that necessarily occur at the same time
8. **tragedy**—sad, unfortunate, or terrible happenings (tragic,adj.)
9. **tragicomedy**—happenings that have a combination of tragic and comic elements (tragicomic,adj.)
10. **train**—series or succession of happenings
11. **wake**—resulting happenings

8. Pert. to, Descr. of, or Referring to the Happenings of the Day or of the Time: topical,adj.

9. The Sum Total of What Will Happen to One: destiny, fate, fortune,n.

10. What Finally Happens: upshot,n.

11. Full of Important Happenings: eventful, adj. (eventfulness,n.)

12. Without Unusual or Important Happenings: uneventful,adj. (uneventfulness,n.)

13. Range of Happening: incidence,n.

14. Place of Happening: locale, scene, setting, stage, theater,n.

15. Instrument to Examine or Indicate Simultaneous Occurrence of Two Actions: synchroscope,n.

16. About to Happen: imminent, impendent, impending, overhanging, pendent, pending, adj. (imminence or imminency, impendence or impendency, pendency,n.)

17. About to Happen within a Short Time or at Any Moment: momentary,adj. (momentariness,n.)

18. To Be About to Happen: impend, overhang, pend,v.

19. To Prepare to Happen: brew,v. (brewing, adj.)

20. To Be on the Point of Breaking Out or Boiling Up as a Happening: simmer,v. (simmering,adj. simmer,n.)

21. Certain to Happen: ineluctable, inevitable,adj. (ineluctability, inevitability or inevitableness,n.)

22. To Be in Store for: await,v.

23. Likely to Happen: eventual, probable,adj. (eventuality, probability,n.)

24. Likely to Happen Soon: imminent,adj. (imminence or imminency,n.)

25. Likely to Happen (of Unpleasant Events); Threatening to Happen: impendent, impending, looming, threatening,adj. (impendence or impendency, threat,n. impend, loom, threaten,v.)

26. Threatening to Happen Shortly: imminent, impendent, impending,adj. (imminence or imminency, impendence or impendency,n. impend,v.)

27. Likely either to Happen or Not to Happen: contingent,adj. (contingency,n.)

28. Expected to Happen in the Future: prospective,adj. (prospect,n.)

29. What Seems Likely to Happen in the Future: outlook, prospect,n.

30. That Which May Happen: contingency, eventuality, possibility,n.

31. Possibility of Something Happening: chance,n.

30. LIKELIHOOD

1. Likely: probable,adj.

2. Likely to: apt to, liable to (considered by some a misusage), adj.

3. Likelihood: probability,n.

4. To Be Likely to Move or Go in the Direction of: tend to, tend toward,v.

5. Likelihood of Going or Moving in a Certain Direction: tendency, trend,n.

6. Based on Likelihood or Probability: presumptive,adj.

31. POSSIBILITY

1. Possible,adj.
  1. **contingent**—possible
  2. **eventual**—possible, depending on preceding or on uncertain events
  3. **potential**—existing as a possibility, but not as an actuality
  4. **thinkable**—possible

2. Possibility,n. *From Sec. 1:* contingency, eventuality, potentiality; *Also:* 1. **chance**—possibility of something happening

3. To Figure the Possibilities of a Thing, Action, Occurrence, etc.: appraise,v. (appraisal,n.)

32. AN EXPERIENCE

1. An Experience,n.
  1. **adventure**—an exciting experience; an unusual experience
  2. **escapade**—a wild, reckless, or unrestrained adventure
  3. **lark**—a pleasurable adventure
  4. **nightmare**—an experience resembling a frightful dream
  5. **ordeal**—a painful, unpleasant, or severe experience

2. To Experience: suffer, sustain, undergo,v.

3. To Cause to Undergo an Unpleasant Experience: subject,v. (subjection,n.)

4. State of Being Caused to Undergo an Unpleasant Experience: subjection,n.

5. Mystical Experience or the Capacity for It: theopathy,n. (theopathetic, theopathic, adj.)

33. FATE

1. Fate,n.
  1. **destiny**—one's fate; that which happens to one finally despite any efforts to change it
  2. **doom**—fate; unhappy destiny
  3. **foredoom**—destiny
  4. **kismet**—fate; destiny
  5. **lot**—one's fate; that which is fated to happen to one
  6. **portion**—one's fate in life
  7. **predestination**—fate; destiny

2. Fate Personified: Weird Sisters,n.

3. Controlled by Fate: fateful,adj.

4. Pert. to Fate: weird,adj.

5. To Fate, i.e., to Cause to Have as One's Fate,v.
  1. **destine, destinate**—fate; doom; foreordain
  2. **doom**—fix, beyond hope of change, the (often unpleasant or undesirable) fate of
  3. **foredoom**—doom beforehand
  4. **foreordain, foreordinate**—fate; cause to be the fate of beyond any possibility of change
  5. **predestine, predestinate**—fate; doom; foreordain
  6. **preordain**—foreordain

6. Act or Process of Fating,n. *From Sec. 5:* destination, foreordainment, foreordination, predestination, preordination

7. Fated,adj. *From Sec. 5:* destined, doomed, foredoomed, foreordained, predestined, predestinate, preordained

8. Belief in Fate,n.
  1. **fatalism**—belief that events are controlled by fate and are therefore inevitable and unchangeable

2. **predestinarianism**—predestination
3. **predestination,**   **predestinationism**—theory that what happens has been foreordained by fate and cannot be avoided
9. **One Who Believes in Fate,**n. *From Sec. 8:* fatalist, predestinarian, predestinationist
10. **Believing in Fate,**adj. *From Sec. 8:* fatalistic, predestinarian
11. **Pert. to a Belief in Fate,**adj. *From Sec. 8:* predestinarian, predestinational

34. CHANCE

1. **Chance:** accident, fortune, hap, haphazard, hazard, luck, peradventure,n.
2. **Dangerous Chance:** hazard, risk,n.
3. **An Even Chance:** tossup,n.
4. **By Chance; Happening by Chance:** accidental, adventitious, at random, casual, chance, contingent, fortuitous, haphazard, incidental, random,adj. (adventitiousness, casualness, contingency, fortuitousness, haphazardness, randomness,n.)
5. **Happening by Chance and Turning Out Well:** fortunate, happy, lucky,adj. (fortunateness,n.)
6. **Subject to Chance:** chancy (colloq.), hazardous,adj. (hazardousness,n.)
7. **Subject to, or Attended by, Dangerous Chance:** hazardous, risky, venturesome, venturous,adj. (hazardousness, venturesomeness, venturousness,n.)
8. **Full of Chance, but Promising Unusual Financial or Commercial Reward or Profit if Successful:** speculative,adj. (speculativeness,n. speculation,n.)
9. **Something Full of Chance:** gamble, lottery, raffle,n.
10. **Theory That Events Are Controlled Purely by Chance:** casualism,n. (casualist,n.)
11. **To Take a Chance:** chance it, gamble, gamble on it, risk it,v. (gamble,n. gambler,n.)
12. **To Expose to, or Allow to Depend upon, the Workings of Chance:** bet, gamble, hazard, risk, stake, venture, wager,v. (bet, gamble, hazard, risk, stake, venture, wager,n. bettor, gambler, venturer, wagerer,n.)
13. **To Go into a Business or Other Venture That Is Full of Chance but That, if Successful, Promises Unusual Profits:** speculate, wildcat,v. (speculation,n. speculative,adj. speculator, wildcatter,n.)
14. **Gambling Scheme,**n.
    1. **lottery**—gambling scheme in which prizes or rewards are distributed by chance
    2. **numbers,   numbers   game,   numbers pool, policy**—illegal lottery in which bets are made on the possibility of certain numbers appearing, as in racing totals, bank clearings, etc.
    3. **raffle**—gambling scheme in which a number of people pay or share, one of them winning the prize

35. GOOD LUCK

1. **Good Luck,**n.
    1. **fluke**—piece of unexpected good luck
    2. **stroke**—piece of good luck
    3. **windfall**—unexpected good luck
2. **Lucky, i.e., Causing, Indicating, or Resulting from Good Luck,**adj.
    1. **auspicious**—fortunate
    2. **fortuitous**—loosely, fortunate (strictly, occurring by chance)
    3. **fortunate**—bringing, causing, or resulting from good luck

4. **propitious**—indicating good luck; fortunate
5. **providential**—lucky, as if God had intervened
3. **Possessed of Good Luck:** fortunate, lucky, adj.
4. **To Have Good Luck:** prosper,v.
5. **That Which Is Relied on for Good Luck,** n.
    1. **amulet**—ornament worn as a charm against bad luck
    2. **charm**—anything worn for the purpose of averting bad luck
    3. **grigri, greegree**—African amulet
    4. **mascot**—that which is relied on for, or is supposed to bring, good luck
    5. **periapt**—charm worn to protect against misfortune, disease, etc.
    6. **rabbit's-foot,   rabbit-foot**—any good-luck piece (originally the hind foot of a rabbit)
    7. **talisman**—that which is believed to have magic power to bring good luck or to ward off bad luck
6. **Pert. to, or Resulting from, Luck:** aleatory,adj.

36. BAD LUCK

1. **Bad Luck:** adversity (with the implication of previous good luck), ambsace, ill-fortune, ill-luck, misadventure, mischance, misfortune, mishap,n.
2. **A Piece or Stroke of Bad Luck:** adversity, misadventure, mischance, misfortune, mishap, reverse,n.
3. **Unlucky, i.e., Having or Attended by Bad Luck,**adj.
    1. **black**—unlucky (of conditions, times, events, etc.)
    2. **disastrous**—most unlucky (of conditions, events, etc.)
    3. **hapless**—unlucky
    4. **ill-omened**—doomed to bad luck because of a lack of favorable signs or circumstances
    5. **ill-starred**—unlucky because of a start or birth under unlucky stars
    6. **inauspicious**—unlucky because operating under malign signs, auspices, or omens (of time, circumstances, events, undertakings, etc.)
    7. **jinxed**—attended by ill-luck
    8. **luckless**—unlucky
    9. **misadventurous**—unlucky
    10. **sinister**—unlucky or inauspicious (of things, signs, events, conditions, etc.)
    11. **sinistrous**—unlucky; ill-omened
    12. **unfortunate**—unlucky
    13. **unhappy**—unlucky
    14. **unpropitious**—ill-omened
    15. **untoward**—unlucky
4. **One Who Encounters or Incurs Bad Luck:** misadventurer,n.
5. **One Who, or That Which, Causes Bad Luck:** jinx,n.
6. **To Cause Bad Luck to:** jinx,v.

37. MISFORTUNE

1. **Misfortune,**n.
    1. **adversity**—a misfortune; a stroke of misfortune
    2. **blow**—sudden misfortune
    3. **calamity**—great misfortune, often affecting many people and causing keen distress
    4. **casualty**—any misfortune
    5. **cataclysm**—misfortune, often of a type caused by nature, as an earthquake, flood,

etc.; misfortune of the kind that causes violent and extreme changes; calamity
6. **catastrophe**—great misfortune; sudden calamity
7. **debacle**—disaster
8. **disaster**—unexpected misfortune, often causing great destruction or ruin
9. **misadventure**—misfortune
10. **mischance**—misfortune
11. **mishap**—misfortune
12. **reverse**—misfortune
13. **tragedy**—unexpected misfortune

2. Causing, Indicating, Accompanied by, Full of, Descr. of, Pert. to, or Relating to, Misfortune,adj. *From Sec. 1:* adverse, calamitous; cataclysmic, cataclysmal, or cataclysmatic; catastrophic or catastrophal, disastrous, tragic; *Also:*
1. **direful**—full of misfortune; calamitous
2. **foreboding, premonitory**—indicating coming misfortune or disaster
3. **sinister**—causing or indicating misfortune (of things, signs, events, conditions, etc.)

3. Doomed to Misfortune: disastrous, ill-fated, ill-omened, ill-starred, inauspicious, jinxed, sinistrous, unpropitious,adj.

4. One Who Encounters or Incurs Misfortune: misadventurer,n.

5. One Who, or That Which, Causes Misfortune: jinx,n.

6. To Cause Misfortune to: jinx,v.

7. A Feeling of Coming Misfortune: foreboding, misgiving, premonition, presage, presentiment, presurmise,n. (presentimental, adj.)

8. To Have a Feeling of Coming Misfortune: forebode, presage,v.

38. PRESENCE

1. Present,adj.
1. **attendant, attending**—present
2. **latent**—present but inactive (of qualities, etc.)
3. **omnipresent**—present everywhere at the same time
4. **ubiquitous**—omnipresent

2. Presence,n. *From Sec. 1:* attendance, latency, omnipresence, ubiquitousness or ubiquity

3. One Who Is Present,n. *From Sec. 1:* attender, attendant; *Also:* 1. **bystander**—one who is present at, but does not participate in, an activity

4. To Be Present at: attend,v.

39. EXISTENCE

1. To Exist,v.
1. **coexist**—exist together at the same time
2. **obtain**—exist
3. **outlast**—exist longer than
4. **pre-exist**—exist before; exist previously in another condition or state
5. **prevail**—exist in many places; continue to exist
6. **smolder**—exist within but give no outward manifestation; exist though suppressed
7. **subsist**—exist; continue to exist

2. Existing; Existent,adj. *From Sec. 1:* coexistent, pre-existent, prevailing or prevalent, smoldering, subsistent; *Also:*
1. **extant**—in existence; existing
2. **latent**—existing but inactive

3. Existence,n. *From Sec. 1:* coexistence, pre-existence, prevalence, subsistence; *From Sec. 2:* latency

40. PREVALENCE

1. Prevalent: abundant, common, current, diffuse, dominant, epidemic, extensive, general, obtaining, omnipresent, predominant or predominating, prevailing, reigning, rife, superabundant, ubiquitous or ubiquitary, universal, widespread,adj.

2. Prevalence: abundance or abundancy, commonness, currency, diffuseness, dominance or dominancy, extensiveness, generality, omnipresence; predominance, predominancy, or predomination; rifeness, superabundance, ubiquitousness or ubiquity, universality,n.

3. To Be Prevalent: abound, dominate, obtain, predominate, prevail, reign, superabound,v.

41. UNIVERSALITY

1. Universal; General,adj.
1. **catholic**—universal in application (catholicity,n.)
2. **ecumenical, ecumenic**—universal or general in extent, influence, power, effect, etc.
3. **epidemic**—so general as to be like a disease that affects great multitudes at the same time
4. **pandemic**—universal; general

42. ABSENCE

1. Absence,n.
1. **absenteeism**—absence from the place or activity where one's presence is expected or needed; habitual absence of this sort
2. **French leave**—absence without permission
3. **furlough**—official leave of absence
4. **hooky**—absence without permission; truancy
5. **leave**—leave of absence; leave of absence from military duty; leave of absence, for an extended period, of a sailor from his ship
6. **leave of absence**—absence with permission; legal or proper absence
7. **liberty**—leave of absence of a sailor from his ship for a short period
8. **non-attendance**—absence
9. **sabbatical, sabbatical leave**—leave of absence from work, office, or duty for purposes of education, travel, etc. (often with full or partial salary)
10. **truancy, truantry, truantism**—absence from school, work, duty, etc., without permission

2. Absent,adj. *From Sec. 1:* absentee, non-attendant, truant; *Also:*
1. **away**—absent
2. **missing**—absent

3. To Be Absent,v. *From Sec. 1:* absent oneself, take French leave, play hooky, truant

4. Act of Being Absent,n. *From Sec. 3:* absentation, truancy

5. One Who Is Absent,n. *From Sec. 1:* absentee, hooky player, non-attender, truant

6. Pert. to an Absence,adj. *From Sec. 1:* sabbatical

7. While Absent: in absentia (Latin)

43. LACK

1. Lack,n.
1. **dearth**—lack
2. **defect**—lack; lack of something needed for completion or perfection
3. **deficiency**—lack of that which is needed; lack of the required amount

4. **deficit**—lack of a specific amount of money
5. **destitution**—lack
6. **ellipsis**—lack of a part or parts; lack of a word
7. **insufficiency**—lack
8. **paucity**—deficiency
9. **poverty**—lack
10. **privation**—lack of that which is needed to live, or to live with a minimum of comfort; lack of something needed
11. **scantness, scantiness**—lack of enough
12. **shortage**—specific lack of that which is needed
13. **shortcoming**—lack of that which is proper or desirable in conduct, action, function, etc.
14. **want**—lack; lack of that which is needed

2. Lacking or Lacking in,adj. *From Sec. 1:* defective, deficient, destitute (of), elliptic or elliptical, insufficient (in), poor (in), scant, scanty, short, wanting (in); *Also:*
1. **devoid of**—utterly lacking in
2. **shy**—lacking a certain amount (shy ten dollars, etc.)
3. **shy of**—lacking; lacking in
4. **void of**—lacking; lacking in

3. To Lack,v. *From Sec. 1:* want

4. Causing, Characterized by, or Indicating Lack of That Which Is Needed to Live, or Needed to Live in Minimum Comfort: privative,adj.

44. STATE; CONDITION

1. State; Condition,n.
1. **aspect**—state
2. **auspice**—favorable condition (auspicial, adj.)
3. **circumstance**—condition (circumstantial,adj.)
4. **estate**—condition or state of being
5. **phase**—state
6. **plight**—unfortunate state or condition
7. **situation**—state (situational,adj.)
8. **status**—condition; condition of affairs or circumstances; state
9. **status quo**—present condition or state; existing condition
10. **temper**—condition

2. Combination of Conditions: situation,n. (situational,adj.)

45. PURPOSE

1. Purpose,n.
1. **aim**—purpose that one directs one's energy and efforts to attain
2. **arrière-pensée (French)**—hidden purpose
3. **bourn**—goal
4. **calculation**—deliberate purpose
5. **design**—deliberate, carefully calculated, or carefully thought-out purpose; secret purpose; aim; secret aim
6. **destiny**—probable or inevitable end or goal
7. **determination**—deliberate purpose; aim
8. **end**—purpose one hopes or expects to attain
9. **goal**—purpose for which one struggles or is willing to struggle, or which one hopes or plans to reach; final purpose
10. **intention, intent**—deliberate purpose
11. **mecca**—goal of many people
12. **mission**—purpose in life
13. **nonce**—particular purpose, as in *for the nonce*
14. **notion**—intention
15. **object**—purpose one must, or wishes to, attain
16. **objective**—final purpose; purpose one directs one's efforts and energy to attain

17. **resolution, resolve**—deliberate purpose to do or not do something
18. **terminus**—final goal
19. **will**—purpose

2. To Have as One's Purpose: aim, contemplate, determine, intend, propose, purpose, resolve,v. (contemplation, intention, proposal, resolve or resolution,n.)

3. To Determine or Resolve to Sin No More: repent,v. (repenter,n. repentant,adj. repentance,n.)

4. Firmly Fixed or Unwavering in Purpose: assured, bent, bound, decided, determined, firm, intent, purposive, resolute, resolved, stalwart,adj. (assurance, decidedness, determination, firmness, intentness, purposiveness, resoluteness or resolution, resolve, stalwartness,n.)

5. Purposeful: calculated, purposive, teleological, willful,adj. (calculation, purposiveness, teleology, willfulness,n.)

6. Expressive of Serious Purpose: intense, adj. (intensity, intenseness,n.)

7. Having a Conscious Purpose; Tending to Fulfill a Conscious Purpose; Pert. to, Characterized by, of the Nature of, or Adapted to a Purpose: purposive,adj. (purposiveness, n.)

8. Having But One Purpose in Mind: single-minded,adj. (single-mindedness,n.)

9. Tending to a Preconceived Purpose: telic,adj.

10. Having Good Intentions: well-intentioned, well-meaning,adj.

11. Arising from Good or Acceptable Intentions: well-intended, well-meant,adj.

12. Done, Said, etc., on Purpose: aforethought, calculated, conscious, considered, deliberate, designful, intended, intentional, meant, premeditated, studied, voluntary, willful, witting,adj. (deliberateness, intention or intentionality, premeditation or premeditatedness, voluntariness, willfulness,n.)

13. On Purpose: advisedly, calculatedly, consciously, deliberately, designedly, intentionally, purposely, voluntarily, willfully, wittingly,adv.

14. Not Done, Said, etc., on Purpose: accidental, inadvertent, involuntary, uncalculated, unconscious, undeliberate, unintended, unintentional, unmeant, unpremeditated, unthinking, unwilled, unwitting,adj. (accident, inadvertence or inadvertency, involuntariness, undeliberateness, unintentionality or unintentionalness, unpremeditation or unpremeditatedness, unthinkingness, unwittingness,n.)

15. That Which Is Unintentional: accident,n.

16. For a Certain Purpose Only; For This Purpose Only: ad hoc (Latin)

17. Suiting One's Purpose: expedient,adj. (expediency, expedience,n.)

18. That Which Suits a Purpose: expedient, n. (expediential,adj.)

19. Theory or Doctrine of Purpose,n.
1. **predestination, predestinationism, predestinarianism, predetermination**—theory that God has a purpose in respect to all happenings (predestinationist, predestinarian,n. predestinational, predestinarian,adj.)
2. **teleology, teleologism**—doctrine of purposefulness in nature; theory that everything in nature is governed by a purpose or general plan (teleologist,n. teleological, adj.)

20. Without Purpose: aimless, designless, driftless, haphazard, purposeless, random, undirected,adj. (aimlessness, driftlessness, haphazardness, purposelessness, randomness,n.)

21. Figuratively Jumping from One Thing to Another without Aim, Purpose, or System: desultory,adj. (desultoriness,n.)

22. To Move or Go without Aim or Purpose: drift,v. (drifter,n.)

23. Lack of Intellectual Purpose: flânerie (French),n.

24. One Who Lacks Intellectual Purpose: flâneur (French),n.

46. PLAN

1. To Plan: aim (to), arrange, brew, cogitate, contemplate, contrive, design, devise; intend (to); meditate, project, purpose (to),v.; *Also:*
1. **aim for, bargain for, count on, reckon on**—plan on
2. **concert**—plan together
3. **maneuver**—plan artfully
4. **outline**—make a general plan of
5. **plot**—engage in a secret, and generally wicked, mischievous, or illegal plan or plans; plan the outline of (a story or novel)
6. **prearrange, premeditate**—plan beforehand
7. **scheme**—plan; plan mentally; engage in an underhanded plan or plans to gain an advantage
8. **sketch out**—make a rough plan of

2. Planning,n. *From Sec. 1:* arrangement, cogitation, contemplation, contrivance, intention, meditation, projection; prearrangement, premeditation, schemery; *Also:*
1. **prudence**—wise planning
2. **strategy**—skillful planning; skillful planning to achieve a goal
3. **strategy, strategics**—skillful planning and managing of war
4. **telesis**—intelligent or rational planning of natural and social forces toward a desirable objective

3. Plan,n. *From Sec. 1:* aim, arrangement, contrivance, design, device, intention or intent, project; maneuver, outline, plot, prearrangement, scheme, sketch; *From Sec. 2:* strategy; *Also:* conception, counsel, deal, proposal, proposition, system; *Also:*
1. **bubble**—plan that is deceptively sound but soon bursts into nothing
2. **castle in the air, castle in Spain**—visionary and impractical plan
3. **program**—plan of an activity, or of a sequence of activities
4. **scheme**—plan of action, or of a sequence of activities
5. **system**—plan of action

4. Planner,n. *From Sec. 1:* arranger, cogitator, contriver, designer, deviser; maneuverer, plotter, schemer; *From Sec. 2:* strategist; *From Sec. 3:* programmer, schemist

5. Pert. to, or Descr. of, Planning or a Plan,adj. *From Sec. 1:* projective; *From Sec. 2:* strategic; *From Sec. 3:* programmatic, schematic, systematic

6. Tending to Plan Wisely: prudent,adj. (prudence,n.)

7. Planning Wisely for the Future: farseeing,adj.

8. Having High or Grandiose Plans: ambitious, lofty,adj. (ambitiousness or ambition, loftiness,n.)

9. Able to Plan Wisely for the Future: farsighted,adj. (farsightedness,n.)

10. Showing Poor Planning: shortsighted,adj. (shortsightedness,n.)

11. Planned,adj.
1. **advised**—carefully planned

2. **put-up**—planned (generally in a bad sense)
3. **studied**—deliberately planned

12. Unplanned,adj.
1. **casual**—unplanned and unexpected (casualness,n.)
2. **extemporaneous**—unplanned; impromptu (extemporaneousness, extemporaneity,n.)
3. **impetuous**—descr. of unplanned actions that result from sudden, vehement, or rash feelings (impetuousness, impetuosity,n.)
4. **impromptu**—done or spoken without previous planning
5. **improvised**—done, made, said, sung, acted, etc., without previous planning
6. **impulsive**—descr. of actions, etc., that result from sudden feelings rather than from cool planning (impulsiveness, impulsivity,n.)
7. **spontaneous**—arising or resulting from sudden feeling rather than plan; unpremeditated (spontaneity, spontaneousness, n.)
8. **uncalculated**—unplanned
9. **unintended**—unplanned
10. **unintentional**—unplanned (unintentionality, unintentionalness,n.)
11. **unpremeditated**—unplanned; not planned beforehand (unpremeditatedness, unpremeditation,n.)
12. **unstudied**—unplanned

13. Without Plan,adj.
1. **aimless**—without plan (aimlessness,n.)
2. **casual**—without plan (casualness,n.)
3. **desultory**—descr. of actions, etc., that show a jumping from one thing to another without plan or order (desultoriness,n.)
4. **haphazard**—without plan (haphazardness,n.)
5. **planless**—without plan; having no plan (planlessness,n.)
6. **random**—without plan or purpose (randomness,n.)
7. **unstudied**—without plan

47. PLOT; SCHEME

1. To Plot; To Scheme,v.
1. **agitate**—plot (agitation,n.)
2. **brew**—plot
3. **cabal**—plot secretly, with others, to do something evil, illegal, treasonable, etc.; scheme in secret
4. **colleague**—conspire
5. **compass**—plot
6. **complot**—plot together
7. **conspire**—engage, with others, in a plot to do something evil, illegal, treasonable, etc. (conspiracy,n.)
8. **contrive**—plot; scheme (contrivance,n.)
9. **countermine**—plot together; devise a counterscheme; devise a scheme to ward off attack
10. **counterplot**—engage in a plot to oppose another plot
11. **design**—plot; scheme; scheme secretly or underhandedly
12. **devise**—scheme
13. **intrigue**—scheme in a secret or underhanded manner to gain one's purpose (intrigue,n.)
14. **machinate**—scheme to bring harm, injury, or misfortune to others; plot or scheme in an artful, cunning, and evil manner (machination,n.)
15. **project**—scheme (projection,n.)

2. A Plot; Scheme,n. *From Sec. 1:* complot, conspiracy, countermine, counterplot, design, device, intrigue, machination, project; *Also:*
1. **racket**—dishonest or fraudulent scheme
2. **shift**—scheme
3. **stratagem**—scheme intended to deceive

4. subterfuge—scheme; scheme intended to deceive

3. Plotter; Schemer,n. *From Sec. 1:* agitator, complotter, conspirator, contriver, counterplotter, deviser, intriguer or intrigant, machinator; *From Sec. 2:* racketeer; *Also:* **1.** adventurer—one who plots to get money, attain social position, etc. (adventuress,fem.)

4. Plotters or Schemers, Collectively,n. *From Sec. 1:* cabal; *Also:* **1.** junto—number of people combined to engage in political scheming; cabal

5. Plotting; Scheming; Tending to Plot or Scheme,adj. *From Sec. 1:* conspiratorial, designing or designful

48. PREPARATION

1. To Prepare (Something or Someone),v.
1. arm—prepare (someone) against danger or attack
2. arrange—prepare
3. brew—prepare
4. cure—prepare (meats and other foods, leather, etc.) for keeping or use
5. dispense—prepare and give
6. extemporize—prepare on very little notice
7. forearm—prepare (someone) against danger or threat beforehand
8. prime—prepare (someone) in the sense of giving information to him
9. provide—prepare; prepare beforehand
10. ready—prepare
11. rehearse—prepare (someone or something) for a later performance
12. unlimber—prepare for action or use
13. winterize—prepare to withstand the winter

2. To Prepare, i.e., Get or Become Prepared, v. *From Sec. 1:* arm, arrange, forearm, rehearse, unlimber; *Also:* **1.** compose oneself—prepare; get ready

3. Preparation,n. *From Sec. 1 or 2:* arrangement, cure, dispensation, extemporization, provision, rehearsal, winterization

4. A Preparation, i.e., That Which Has Been or Is Prepared,n. *From Sec. 1:* arrangement, brew, provision

5. Prepared,adj. *From Sec. 1:* armed, arranged, etc.; ready; *Also:*
1. available—ready
2. pat—prepared; rehearsed (*a pat answer,* etc.)
3. prompt—ready and eager
4. put-up—rehearsed (in a bad sense)

6. Preparedness,n. *From Sec. 5:* readiness; availability, patness, promptness or promptitude

7. Preparatory; Preparative: preliminary, adj.

8. To Be Ready for: await,v.

9. To Do, etc., without Previous Preparation,v.
1. extemporize—do, make, speak, etc., without devoting time to preparation (extemporization,n.)
2. improvise, improvisate—do, make, say, sing, act, etc., on the spur of the moment without preparation (improvisation,n. improviser,n. improvisatory, improvisatorial,adj.)

10. Done, etc., without Preparation,adj. *From Sec. 9:* extemporal, extemporaneous, extemporary, or extempore; improvised or improviso; *Also:*
1. impromptu—done or spoken without time having been devoted to preparation, or without previous thought or study
2. offhand—done, said, etc., without previous preparation

11. That Which Is Done, Performed, Made, Said, Sung, Acted, etc., on the Spur of the Moment and without Preparation: impromptu, improvisation,n.

12. Prepared Hastily, Suddenly, or on the Spur of the Moment: impromptu,adj.

49. DO

1. To Do,v.
1. accomplish—do successfully
2. achieve—do successfully
3. anticipate—do or take care of beforehand or ahead of time
4. assume—undertake
5. attain—do successfully
6. carry out—do; do completely
7. commit—do (a crime, sin, or other illegal activity)
8. compass—do; do successfully
9. dabble (in)—do, or engage in, in a superficial way
10. discharge—do; do completely (discharge a duty, etc.)
11. dispatch—do (something) quickly, finishing it off without delay
12. dispose of—do (something) and get it out of the way
13. engage in—do as a regular practice; do as a business, profession, etc.
14. execute—carry out
15. expedite—carry out quickly and without delay
16. fulfill—do successfully and completely
17. minister (to)—do what is necessary or helpful (for)
18. officiate—perform the duties of one's office or position
19. overdo—do too much; exceed what is reasonable in doing
20. overwork—overdo
21. perform—do; do completely
22. perpetrate—do (that which is offensive, sinful, or illegal)
23. practice, practise—do; do as a matter of habit or custom; do repeatedly to gain proficiency or skill
24. proceed—continue doing
25. prosecute—carry out
26. pursue—carry out
27. recast—do again in another form
28. reiterate—do again and again
29. render—perform (music, a dramatic part, etc.)
30. repeat—do again
31. requite—do in return
32. resume—do again; start doing again
33. scamp—do (something) in an imperfect, careless, or hasty manner
34. scrimp—do less than one should
35. skimp—do less well than necessary; do poorly
36. supererogate—do more than required by duty; do more than necessary or required
37. take care of—do (that which needs to be done)
38. transact—do (business, etc.)
39. undertake—do; be in the process of doing; expect to do
40. wade into—do (work, tasks, etc.) with vigor and determination
41. wage—do successfully; continue doing
42. work—do; accomplish
43. wreak—do (something) in anger

2. A Doing,n. *From Sec. 1:* accomplishment, achievement, anticipation, assumption, attainment, commission, discharge, dispatch, disposal, disposition, engagement, execution, expedition, fulfillment, ministration, officiation, performance, perpetration, practice or practise, procedure or process, prosecution, pursuance or pursuit, recast, reiteration, repetition, requital, resumption, supererogation, transaction, work; *Also:* **1. facture**—act of doing something (in the fine arts)

3. Doer,n. *From Sec. 1:* accomplisher, achiever, anticipator or anticipant, assumer, attainer, committer, dabbler, executive or executor, expediter, minister, officiator, performer, perpetrator, repeater, transactor, undertaker, wager, worker; *Also:*

1. **dilettante**—one who engages in an activity (usually some fine art, profession, etc.) in a superficial manner rather than to attain skill, success, etc.
2. **practitioner**—person engaged in doing something
3. **star**—leading or prominent performer in an action or activity

4. Doing, Descr. of Doing, or Tending or Acting to Do,adj. *From Sec. 1:* anticipative or anticipatory, expeditious, ministrant, reiterative, repetitive, resumptive, skimpy, supererogatory

5. Capable of Being Done,adj. *From Sec. 1:* accomplishable, achievable, attainable, dischargeable, performable; *Also:*

1. **feasible**—reasonably capable of being done, accomplished, realized, worked out, etc.
2. **practicable**—capable of being done or accomplished

6. That Which One Does; That Which Is or Has Been Done,n.

1. **accomplishment**—that which is done successfully; that which is done with skill
2. **achievement**—feat
3. **adventure**—exciting, different, somewhat dangerous, and therefore brave, undertaking
4. **attainment**—accomplishment
5. **deed**—that which is done
6. **exploit**—brave deed
7. **feat**—that which is done in a remarkable or unusual fashion; that which is done with skill, daring, etc.; that which is done successfully
8. **performance**—that which one does
9. **practice**—that which one does routinely, habitually, or repeatedly
10. **precaution**—that which is done to ward off danger or failure
11. **proceeding, proceedings, process**—that which is done
12. **project**—undertaking
13. **pursuit**—that which one does as a business, profession, etc.
14. **res gestae** (Latin)—heroic deeds
15. **stunt**—remarkable deed (usually to gain attention)
16. **tour de force**—feat of strength; ingenious accomplishment
17. **transaction**—piece of business one does
18. **undertaking**—anything one does, attempts to do, or engages in
19. **venture**—hazardous or daring undertaking
20. **work**—that which one does or has done; that which is done

7. Things, or List of Things, to be Done: agenda,n. (agendum,sing.)

8. Done After Something, but Nevertheless Applying to, or Influencing, It: ex post facto

9. Done: wrought,adj. (the somewhat archaic past participle of the verb *to work*)

50. MANNER; MEANS; METHOD

1. Manner, Means, or Method,n.
1. **agency**—means (agential,adj.)
2. **agent**—means (agential,adj.)
3. **avenue**—manner or means of entering, approaching, or leaving, or of getting something done

4. **beadledom**—unnecessary and stupid official procedure
5. **ceremony**—special procedure suitable to dignified occasions (ceremonial,adj.)
6. **course**—method or manner of procedure; manner of acting
7. **detour**—roundabout or indirect manner or means
8. **facture**—manner of doing something connected with the fine arts
9. **fashion**—manner
10. **form**—manner or method, esp. that established, fixed, or prescribed (formal,adj.)
11. **formula**—fixed or conventional method (formulary, formular, or formulaic,adj.)
12. **instrument**—means by which something is done, accomplished, or effected (instrumental,adj.)
13. **instrumentality**—means
14. **manner**—method by which something is done or in which something occurs; method of doing or acting
15. **means**—that by which, or manner in which, something is effected or done
16. **measure**—means to an end
17. **medium**—means through which something is done (media,pl.)
18. **method**—means or manner of doing something by orderly and logical procedure, arrangement, etc. (methodical, methodic,adj.)
19. **mode**—manner; methods; means
20. **modus operandi** (Latin)—method, manner, or means of acting, functioning, doing, etc.
21. **modus vivendi** (Latin)—method, manner, or means of living
22. **path**—means
23. **procedure, process, proceeding, proceedings**—means by which, or manner in which, something is done (procedural, adj.)
24. **receipt**—method of putting ingredients together in making something, or in cooking, baking, etc.
25. **recipe**—method for compounding medicine; method for preparing, cooking, baking, etc.; means to achieve a result
26. **ritual, ritualism**—rigid manner in, or method by, which something is done (ritual, ritualist, or ritualistic,adj.)
27. **road**—means
28. **rote**—mechanical manner or means of doing, with no understanding of underlying meaning or purpose
29. **route**—manner or means by which one achieves an end or result
30. **routine**—regular method or procedure by which something is done; habitual method or procedure (routine,adj.)
31. **rubric**—prescribed method
32. **rut**—established and fixed method of acting or doing, and from which one does not easily deviate
33. **scheme**—method; system (schematic, adj.)
34. **short cut**—method or manner of doing something more directly and rapidly than by ordinary means
35. **step**—means
36. **steppingstone**—means of advancing
37. **style**—manner
38. **system**—method; body of methods or means (systematic,adj.)
39. **tack**—method of action, often one different or changed from the previous one
40. **tactics**—means; method; methods; procedure; procedure followed to gain an advantage or win success (tactical,adj.)
41. **technics**—technique
42. **technique**—method, manner, or means of getting something done (technical,adj.)
43. **theory**—methods and/or principles (theoretic, theoretical,adj.)
44. **tool**—means

45. **usage**—method or manner of treatment, doing, etc.
46. **vehicle**—means; medium
47. **way**—means; manner
48. **ways and means**—methods for getting something done

2. One Skilled in Methods or Means,n. *From Sec. 1:* tactician, technician

3. Following, or Characterized by, a Regular Method,adj.
1. **businesslike**—methodical
2. **methodical, methodic**—following, or characterized by, regular and orderly method (methodicalness, methodicality, methodism,n.)
3. **routine**—following a regular method (routinism, routine,n.)
4. **systematic, systematical**—following some regular method; regular, orderly, and thorough in method of conduct or performance (systematicness, systematicality,n.)

4. To Give Method or System to: methodize, organize, routinize, schematize, systematize or systemize,v. (methodization, organization, routinization, schematization; systematism, systematization, or systemization,n. organizer, routinizer; systematizer, systemizer, systematist, or systematician,n.)

5. Devotion or Adherence to Method,n.
1. **conventionality, conventionalism**—adherence to social methods, manners, forms, usages, or procedures (conventionalist,n. conventional,adj.)
2. **formalism**—devotion to prescribed or established methods or forms, esp. in religion (formalist,n. formalistic, formalist, adj.)
3. **formality**—devotion to established method (formal,adj.)
4. **formularism**—strict adherence to established methods or formulas (formularistic,adj.)
5. **methodism**—excessive devotion to methods (methodist,n.)
6. **ritualism**—excessive devotion to established or ceremonial methods, esp. in religious worship (ritualist,n. ritualistic, adj.)
7. **routinism**—adherence to doing things by a mechanical, regular, or undeviating method or technique (routinist,n. routinish,adj.)

6. Science of Method: methodics, methodology,n. (methodologist,n. methodological,adj.)
7. Art and Principles of Method: methodics, n.
8. To Provide the Means,v.
1. **enable**—provide (someone) the means to do something (enablement,n.)
2. **implement**—provide the means to render (something) effective (implementation, n.)

51. DO OR ACT TOGETHER

1. To Do or Act Together,v.
1. **coact**—do or act together
2. **cofunction**—act together
3. **collaborate**—act jointly
4. **collude**—act together and/or at the same time; do or act together in secret; co-operate secretly, deceitfully, and, often, illegally; conspire
5. **concert**—do or act together and/or at the same time
6. **concur**—act together or in agreement
7. **connive**—do or act together secretly
8. **conspire**—act together to a common end; act together in harmony; act together toward an illegal or treasonous goal
9. **co-operate**—do or act together in harmony or agreement

10. **co-ordinate**—act together in harmony
11. **partake in**—do with others
12. **participate (in)**—do with others
13. **share (in)**—do with others

2. A Doing or Acting Together,n. *From Sec. 1:* coaction, collaboration, collusion, concert, concurrence or concurrency, connivance, concert, spiracy, co-operation, co-ordination; participation, participance, or participancy; *Also:*
1. **coadjuvancy**—a doing or acting together in harmony
2. **communion**—an acting together with others
3. **complicity**—a taking part with others in illegal, wrong, or sinful action or activity
4. **teamwork**—a harmonious doing or acting together in an attempt or endeavor

3. Doing or Acting Together; Tending to Do or Act Together,adj. *From Sec. 1:* coactive, collaborative, collusive, concerted, concurrent, connivant, conspiratorial, co-operative, participant or participative (coactivity, collusiveness, concurrence or concurrency, connivance, co-operativeness,n.) ; *From Sec. 2:* coadjuvant; *Also:*
1. **en masse (French)**—(acting) all together in a group
2. **in concert**—(acting) all together

4. One Who Does or Acts with Another or Others,n. *From Sec. 1:* collaborator, colluder, conniver, co-operator, partaker, participant or participator, sharer

5. Done Together,adj. *From Sec. 1:* collaborative, concerted, concurrent, co-operative, shared; *Also:*
1. **bilateral**—done, shared in, etc., by both parties
2. **collective**—done, shared in, etc., as a body by all concerned
3. **common**—conjoint
4. **conjoint**—done, carried on, etc., by two or more in co-operation or combination; joint
5. **joint**—done, produced, shared, etc., by two or more acting together
6. **multilateral**—done, shared in, etc., by a number of nations, parties, groups, etc.
7. **mutual**—done, shared in, etc., by two or more at the same time
8. **trilateral**—done, shared in, etc., by three together or in co-operation

6. Leading Participant: principal, protagonist, star,n. (star,v.)

52. ACTION

1. To Act,v.
1. **aggress**—commit an unprovoked act
2. **antic**—commit an absurd act
3. **behave**—act
4. **bluster**—act noisily and stormily
5. **burst**—act in an explosive way
6. **demean oneself**—act
7. **function**—act
8. **interact**—act upon each other
9. **officiate**—act in the capacity of one's office or position
10. **operate**—act
11. **overdo**—go or carry too far in one's action or actions
12. **override**—act despite objections
13. **perk up**—act with animation or briskness
14. **retroact**—act upon one another; act in opposition; act in such a way as to influence preceding events (of deeds, events, etc.)
15. **roister**—act noisily
16. **run riot**—act without control or restraint
17. **star**—take a leading or prominent part in an action or activity
18. **temporize**—act as the time or circumstances dictate
19. **trifle**—act without seriousness

2. Action,n. *From Sec. 1:* aggression, antics, behavior, bluster, burst, demeanor, function, interaction, officiation, operation, retroaction; *Also:*

1. **automatism**—self-action; action without outside control or stimulation
2. **interplay**—interaction
3. **violence**—rough and harmful action

3. Acting; Descr. of Action; Tending to Act, adj. *From Sec. 1:* aggressive, antic, blusterous or blustery, interactive, operative, overriding, retroactive, roistering (aggressiveness, retro-activity,n.); *From Sec. 2:* automatic, violent; *Also:*

1. **impetuous**—acting suddenly, and often without due consideration (impetuous-ness, impetuosity,n.)
2. **impulsive**—acting out of sudden desire or inclination (impulsiveness, impulsivity, n.)
3. **mutual, reciprocal**—acting upon one another (mutuality, reciprocity,n.)
4. **practical**—tending to action rather than thinking (practicality,n.)
5. **reflexive**—acting through no conscious volition or control, as an immediate response to some stimulus; automatic (reflexiveness,n.)

4. Actor, i.e., One Who Acts,n. *From Sec. 1:* aggressor, blusterer, officiator, roisterer, star, temporizer, trifler; *From Sec. 2:* automaton

5. An Act or Action; Acts or Actions,n.

1. **aggression**—unprovoked act
2. **amenity**—act that makes for easy and pleasing social relationships
3. **antic**—absurd act
4. **atrocity**—cruel or savage act
5. **attentions**—public acts in courtship
6. **barbarity**—inhuman or cruel act
7. **beau geste (French)**—graceful act
8. **benefaction**—kind, merciful, or generous act
9. **beneficence**—kind act
10. **benevolence**—act of charity
11. **benignancy**—kind or gracious act
12. **benignity**—kind act
13. **byplay**—action that is not part of the main action
14. **caprice**—unmotivated and apparently irrational action
15. **ceremonial**—formal act or action suitable to an occasion
16. **ceremony**—special acts suitable to dignified occasions
17. **charity**—kind act
18. **contumely**—insulting, scornful, or insolent act or action
19. **coup (French)**—brilliant, often unexpected, and usually successful act or action
20. **coup de grâce (French)**—final or finishing act or action
21. **courtesy**—thoughtful or considerate act
22. **custom**—habitual action; habitual action or actions in a region, among a class of people, etc.
23. **deed**—glorious act
24. **deliration**—irrational action
25. **devilry, deviltry**—reckless act
26. **exploit**—brave act
27. **feat**—remarkable act; act accomplished through skill, daring, etc.
28. **folly**—foolish act
29. **indignity**—act that shows contempt
30. **indiscretion**—act of carelessness
31. **knight-errantry**—chivalrous actions
32. **officialism**—action or actions characteristic of officials
33. **outrage**—act of violence
34. **precaution**—act to ward off danger or failure
35. **proceeding, proceedings, process**—action; act; acts
36. **reflex**—action that occurs through no

conscious volition or control, or as an immediate response to a stimulus

37. **res gestae (Latin)**—heroic acts
38. **ritual**—act or action rigidly and repeatedly followed or engaged in
39. **stunt**—act showing cleverness, skill, boldness, strength, etc., and usually done to attract attention
40. **tour de force (French)**—skillful act
41. **venture**—hazardous or daring act

6. Course of Action,n.

1. **campaign**—methodical course of action designed to accomplish a purpose
2. **current**—course of action
3. **démarche (French)**—course of action involving a change of plan or policy (as in diplomacy)
4. **drift**—trend
5. **practice, practise**—general or customary course of action
6. **tack**—course of action, often changed from the previous course
7. **tendency**—course of action in a certain direction
8. **tenor**—general course of action
9. **track**—course of action
10. **trend**—prevailing or general course of action in a certain direction

7. To Follow a Course of Action,v.

1. **adhere to**—continue following (a course of action)
2. **practice, practise**—follow a course of action
3. **prosecute**—continue on (a course of action)
4. **pursue**—follow (a course of action)
5. **steer**—follow a course of action

8. A Following of a Course of Action,n. *From Sec. 7:* adherence, practice or practise, prosecution, pursuit or pursuance

9. To Excite or Stimulate to Action; To Cause to Act,v.

1. **activate**—make, or cause to become, active
2. **actuate**—put into action; move or influence to act
3. **agitate**—stimulate public discussion or interest with the view of effecting action, change, or reform
4. **arouse**—excite to action
5. **bestir**—rouse
6. **catalyze**—accelerate the action of
7. **develop**—make active
8. **excite**—cause activity in
9. **foment**—arouse
10. **galvanize**—arouse as if by an electric shock
11. **goad**—urge
12. **impel**—provide with a driving power or strong wish to act; activate; urge forward or on
13. **incite**—excite to (often less than praiseworthy) action
14. **induce**—give (someone) a motive for acting by promising advantage, reward, etc.
15. **innervate**—stimulate to action or activity
16. **inspire, prompt**—affect in such a way as to create a desire to act
17. **instigate**—arouse; stir up (action)
18. **jog**—move to action by figuratively pushing or shaking out of inaction
19. **mobilize**—put into effective action
20. **motivate**—create a desire to act
21. **move**—excite to action by emotional appeal or by affecting the emotions
22. **needle**—excite to action by sharp (figurative) prods, remarks, gibes, etc.
23. **pique**—excite to action; stimulate; sting; urge
24. **predetermine**—impel beforehand
25. **prod**—excite to action; urge
26. **propel**—cause to act
27. **provoke**—stimulate

28. **push**—cause to act
29. **quicken**—excite to activity or action
30. **rouse**—stir out of inactivity or passiveness; excite to action; stir up out of hiding
31. **spur**—stimulate into activity, action, or movement
32. **stimulate**—cause to become more active or to increase or speed up one's activity; excite to action or activity
33. **sting**—excite to action as if by piercing or paining
34. **stir, stir up**—arouse
35. **suggest**—motivate; inspire
36. **urge**—move, or attempt to move, to action; serve as a driving force toward action
37. **waken**—move to action

10. **To Become Excited to Action,v.** *From Sec. 9:* bestir, mobilize, quicken, rouse, stir, waken

11. **Excitation or Stimulation to Act,n.** *From Sec. 9 or 10:* activation, actuation, agitation, arousal, catalysis, development, excitation or excitement, galvanization, impulsion, incitement, inducement, innervation, inspiration, instigation, mobilization, motivation, predetermination, propulsion, provocation, stimulation, suggestion

12. **That Which Excites or Stimulates to Action,n.** *From Sec. 9:* activator, catalyst or catalytic agent, excitant or excitator, goad, impulse or impulsion, inducement, inspiration, jog, motive or motivation, needle, prod, provocation, push, spur, stimulant or stimulus, suggestion, urge; *Also:*
    1. **incentive**—external cause of a desire to act or to achieve a goal
    2. **spring, springs**—underlying, often unconscious or unrecognized, motive or motives

13. **One Who Excites or Stimulates to Action,n.** *From Sec. 9:* agitator, arouser, catalyst or catalytic agent, fomenter, inciter, inspiration or inspirer, instigator, mobilizer, mover, needler, provoker; *Also:* 1. **agent provocateur (French)**—one who associates with a group for the purpose of inciting the members to illegal acts so that they may be apprehended and punished; instigator

14. **Exciting, or Serving to Excite, to Action,** adj. *From Sec. 9:* activating, actuating, catalytic, excitative or excitatory, galvanizing, goading, inciting, indecisive, innervating, inspiring or inspirational, instigating or instigative, motivating or motivational, moving, needling, predetermining, prodding, propelling, provocative or provoking, rousing, spurring, stimulating or stimulative, stirring, suggestive, urgent

15. **Relying on, or Taking Advantage of, Human Motivation to Excite to Action:** psychological,adj.

53. TREATMENT

1. **To Treat, i.e., Act toward,v.**
    1. **abuse**—treat badly
    2. **brutalize**—treat cruelly
    3. **consider**—treat thoughtfuly or kindly
    4. **disserve**—treat badly
    5. **handle**—treat
    6. **ill-treat**—treat cruelly
    7. **maltreat**—treat badly, cruelly, or roughly
    8. **manhandle**—treat roughly, i.e., with physical roughness
    9. **maul, mall**—handle roughly; manhandle
    10. **mishandle**—treat or handle badly, roughly, or cruelly
    11. **mistreat**—treat badly or cruelly
    12. **oppress**—treat harshly

13. **trample on or upon**—treat cruelly or harshly
14. **trifle with**—treat without seriousness
15. **violate**—treat roughly and harmfully

2. **Treatment,n.** *From Sec. 1:* abuse, brutalization, consideration, disservice, handling, ill-treatment, maltreatment, manhandling, mauling, mishandling, mistreatment, oppression, trifling, violation or violence

3. **Descr. of Treatment,adj.** *From Sec. 1:* abusive, considerate, oppressive, violent

4. **One Who Treats,n.** *From Sec. 1:* abuser, ill-treater, maltreator, mauler, oppressor, trampler, trifler, violator

5. **Roughly or Harshly Treated:** downtrodden,adj. (downtroddenness,n.)

54. REACTION

1. **Reaction,n.**
    1. **boomerang**—harmful reaction back on the perpetrator
    2. **hydrolysis**—chemical reaction with water (hydrolytic,adj.)
    3. **repercussion**—indirect reaction to a happening, act, or action
    4. **response**—strong or prompt reaction to stimulation
    5. **reverberation**—reaction to something
    6. **revulsion**—sudden and violent reaction
    7. **tone**—normal bodily reaction to stimuli
    8. **tonus, tonicity**—healthy bodily reaction to stimuli (tonic,adj.)
    9. **tropism**—involuntary physical reaction of a plant or animal in response to a stimulus (tropismatic, tropistic,adj.)

2. **To React,v.**
    1. **backfire**—boomerang
    2. **boomerang**—react back on one; react harmfully back on the perpetrator
    3. **respond**—react to stimulation

3. **Reacting,adj.**
    1. **reactive**—reacting (reactiveness, reactivity,n.)
    2. **responsive**—reacting readily or strongly to stimulation (responsiveness,n.)
    3. **sensitive**—reacting strongly or on slight stimulus or provocation (sensitiveness, sensitivity,n.)
    4. **susceptible**—sensitive (susceptibility,n.)

4. **Resulting from, Tending to, or Characterized by, Reaction:** reactive,adj. (reactiveness, reactivity,n.)

5. **Pert. to or Descr. of Reaction:** reactive, reactional,adj.

6. **Power to React:** reactivity,n.

7. **Science of Human Reactions:** reactology, n. (reactological,adj.)

8. **One Who or That Which Reacts:** reactor, reagent, reagency,n.

9. **Action of One Who, or That Which, Reacts:** reagency,n.

10. **Chemical or Other Substance That Takes Part in Chemical Reactions:** reagent, n.

11. **One Who Reacts to a Stimulus in a Psychological Experiment:** reagent,n.

12. **To Speed Up the Reaction of:** catalyze,v. (catalysis,n. catalyst, catalytic agent,n. catalytic,adj.)

55. BEHAVIOR

1. **Behavior; Manner of Behaving:** address, bearing, carriage, comportment, conduct, demeanor, deportment, mien,n.

2. **To Behave:** acquit oneself, comport one-

self, conduct oneself, demean oneself, deport oneself,v.

3. Certain Specific Behavior,n.
1. **antics**—absurd behavior (antic,adj.)
2. **ceremony**—formally polite behavior (ceremonial, ceremonious,adj.)
3. **decency**—behavior that is proper, acceptable, in good taste, etc. (decent,adj.)
4. **decorum**—seemly, dignified, and suitable behavior (decorous,adj.)
5. **derring-do**—daring behavior
6. **devilment, deviltry, devilry**—reckless or devilish behavior
7. **etiquette**—behavior prescribed or required by good breeding, social customs, convention, etc.
8. **folly**—foolish behavior
9. **knight-errantry**—chivalrous behavior
10. **levity**—frivolous and unseemly behavior
11. **misbehavior**—bad or sinful behavior
12. **misdemeanor**—bad behavior
13. **morals**—behavior in questions of right and wrong (moral,adj.)
14. **propriety**—proper behavior
15. **rampage**—violent behavior (rampageous, adj.)
16. **ritual, ritualism**—behavior rigidly, compulsively, and repeatedly followed (ritualistic,adj.)
17. **second nature**—fixed, almost reflexive, behavior

4. To Behave in a Specific Manner,v. *From Sec. 3:* antic, misbehave, misdemean, rampage

5. Science, Study, etc., of Behavior,n.
1. **anthroponomics, anthroponomy**—science of human behavior, actions, etc. (anthroponomist,n. anthroponomic,adj.)
2. **philosophy**—science or study of the facts and principles of human behavior (philosopher,n. philosophic, philosophical, adj.)
3. **psychology**—science of human behavior and motivation (psychologist,n. psychologic, psychological,adj.)
4. **sociology**—science of group behavior (sociologist,n. sociologic, sociological, adj.)
5. **sociometry**—measurement or analysis of human behavior in the social group or within the framework of society (sociometrist,n. sociometric,adj.)

6. Pert. to Behavior: behavioral,adj.

7. Doctrine that Psychology Should Concern Itself Only with Observed Behavior: behaviorism,n. (behaviorist,n. behavioristic,adj.)

56. PRINCIPLE; RULE

1. Principle; Principles; Rule; Rules,n.
1. **ABC**—principles of a subject
2. **axiom**—established principle (axiomatic, adj.)
3. **basis**—fundamental principle or principles (basic,adj.)
4. **canon**—rule; fundamental principle (canonical,adj.)
5. **code**—set of rules
6. **credenda (pl.)**—in religion, those doctrines that are to be believed
7. **dictum**—authoritative rule (dicta,pl.)
8. **doctrine**—principle, or body of principles, taught by a school of religion, philosophy, politics, etc. (doctrinal,adj.)
9. **dogma**—body of authoritative doctrines of an organized church or religion (dogmatic,adj.)
10. **evangel**—that doctrine that is of the utmost importance and is used as a guide
11. **fundamental**—principle or rule that forms the basis of a system (fundamental, adj.)
12. **gospel**—doctrine of the first importance;

any principles or doctrines earnestly and unquestioningly believed
13. **ideology**—fundamental doctrines (ideological,adj.)
14. **keynote**—guiding or fundamental principle
15. **keystone**—essential principle, in that all other parts or principles are dependent on it
16. **law**—principle; body of rules or principles
17. **logos**—in philosophy, the rational principle of the universe
18. **philosophy**—broad principles of a subject or field of knowledge, human activity, etc. (philosophic, philosophical, adj.)
19. **platform**—principles of a political party
20. **polestar, lodestar**—guiding principle
21. **postulate**—essential or fundamental principle
22. **prescript**—rule (prescriptive,adj.)
23. **protocol**—rules of rank, order, or honor due to people or positions of importance, etc.
24. **regimen**—rule (regiminal, regimental, adj.)
25. **regulation**—rule
26. **rudiment**—first principle of a subject, field of knowledge, art, science, etc. (rudimentary,adj.)
27. **system**—aggregate of principles of a philosophy, religion, form of government, school of thinking, etc.
28. **tenet**—principle or doctrine considered true and accepted by members of a group, sect, organization, etc.
29. **theorem**—principle; principle to be proved or that can be proved
30. **theory**—general principles advanced to explain phenomena or occurrences; principles and/or methods of an art or science; general or abstract principles (theoretic, theoretical,adj.)

2. To Lay Down Principles or Rules,v.
1. **postulate**—lay down essential or fundamental principles (postulation,n.)
2. **prescribe**—lay down as a rule of conduct or behavior (prescription,n. prescriptive, adj.)
3. **theorize**—lay down principles to be, or that can be, proved

3. Principles or Rules of Conduct,n.
1. **discipline**—rules for conduct (disciplinary, disciplinarian, disciplinal,adj.)
2. **law**—obligatory rules of conduct
3. **philosophy**—principles of human conduct (philosophic, philosophical,adj.)
4. **precept**—practical rule of conduct given generally as an order, instruction, etc. (preceptual, preceptive,adj.)
5. **prescript, prescription**—rule of conduct or behavior (prescriptive,adj.)
6. **principle**—rule of conduct
7. **proprieties**—rules of conduct
8. **protocol**—rules of conduct in diplomatic or formal relations
9. **punctilio**—precise rule of conduct

4. Careful to Observe Precise Rules of Conduct: punctilious,adj. (punctiliousness, punctilio,n.)

5. Doctrine or Practice of Observing Principles or Rules of Conduct,n.
1. **formalism**—doctrine of strict adherence to rules, conventions, etc. (formalist,n. formalistic,adj.)
2. **legalism**—doctrine of strict conformance to laws (legalist,n. legalistic, legalist, adj.)
3. **nomism**—practice of basing conduct, from a religious or ethical viewpoint, on obedience to moral law (nomistic,adj.)
4. **rationalism**—practice of, or belief in, making one's conduct conform to reason (rationalist,n. rationalistic, rationalist, adj.)

57. ACTIVITY

1. Activity,n.
1. **bluster**—noisy or stormy activity
2. **burst**—sudden and energetic display of activity
3. **bustle**—excited or noisy activity
4. **buzz**—activity
5. **hum**—activity
6. **hustle-bustle**—fast activity
7. **liveliness**—activity
8. **niggling**—unimportant activity
9. **photokinesis**—activity caused by light (photokinetic,adj.)
10. **pother**—bustle
11. **sally**—sudden burst of activity
12. **stir**—activity; restless or excited activity
13. **tinker**—useless or ineffective activity
14. **tonus, tonicity, tone**—healthy physiological activity of an organ, muscle, bodily part, etc. (tonic,adj.)
15. **vortex**—whirl of activity that sucks one in like a whirlpool
16. **whirl**—rapid round of activity; bustle
17. **whirlwind**—rush of activity
18. **white heat**—intense activity

2. Filled with Activity,adj. *From Sec. 1:* blusterous or blustery, bustling, buzzing, humming, lively, whirling

3. To Be Active or Filled with Activity,v. *From Sec. 1:* bluster, bustle, buzz, hum

4. Active,adj.
1. **aggressive**—active
2. **agile**—active in the sense of being able to move one's limbs with skill and ease
3. **alert**—active; brisk
4. **alive**—active; continuing activity
5. **astir**—active; not quiet
6. **brisk**—quick and active
7. **dapper**—small and active
8. **energetic**—physically active as a result of abundant and healthy vigor
9. **light**—nimble
10. **lightsome**—gracefully nimble
11. **lissome**—agile; nimble
12. **lively**—active
13. **militant**—aggressively active
14. **nimble**—skillfully, quickly, and light-footedly active
15. **pragmatic, pragmatical**—active
16. **smart**—active
17. **spry**—agile; nimble
18. **strenuous**—active (as in *a strenuous life*, etc.)
19. **supple**—agile
20. **tripping**—nimble
21. **vibrant**—active; giving an impression of activity
22. **vigorous**—active and strong
23. **volant**—agile
24. **withy**—agile and strong

5. Activity, i.e., State of Being Active,n. *From Sec. 4:* aggressiveness, agility, alertness, briskness, dapperness, energy, lightness, lightsomeness, lissomeness, liveliness, militancy, nimbleness, smartness, spryness, strenuousness, strenuosity, or strenuity; suppleness, vibrancy, vigor or vigorousness; *Also:* 1. **legerity**—nimbleness or agility combined with speed

6. Area of Activity,n.
1. **arena**—region or sphere of activity
2. **focus**—center of activity
3. **hub**—center of activity
4. **orbit**—area in which one is active
5. **province**—sphere, department, or division of activity

7. To Become Active,v.
1. **develop**—become active (development,n.)
2. **quicken**—become more active (quickening,n. quickening,adj.)
3. **recrudesce**—become active again, after a period of inactivity—said usually of unhealthy or dangerous conditions (recrudescence,n. recrudescent,adj.)
4. **resurge**—become, or tend to become, active again (resurgence,n resurgent, adj.)
5. **sally**—show a sudden burst of activity (sally,n.)
6. **stir**—become active (stir,n. stirring,adj.)

8. Disposition toward Activity: ergasia,n.

9. An Activity,n.
1. **project**—activity involving research
2. **pursuit**—activity in which one is engaged

10. Activities Followed to Gain an Advantage or Win Success: tactics,n.

58. INACTIVITY

1. Inactive; Made Inactive,adj.
1. **abeyant**—temporarily inactive; with its activity temporarily suspended
2. **arrested**—with its activity stopped or suspended; made or caused to be inactive
3. **bedridden**—kept to bed and rendered inactive by illness
4. **deadlocked**—reduced to a state of inactivity by the equality of action and resistance; brought to a complete standstill
5. **deedless**—inactive
6. **dormant, dormient**—inactive (i.e., figuratively asleep; thus flower bulbs may remain dormant, i.e., inactive, during the winter; a trait, characteristic, or talent may be dormant, in the sense that it is present in a personality but not active or functioning)
7. **fallow**—not active, in the sense in which land is plowed but left unseeded in order to restore strength
8. **inactivated**—rendered inactive
9. **inert**—tending to be inactive, to do nothing, to remain as before, or to refrain from, or avoid, action
10. **languid**—inactive, or hard to rouse to activity by nature, personality, disposition, or character
11. **languorous**—sluggish
12. **latent**—present but inactive
13. **leaden**—sluggish
14. **lethargic**—unable or unwilling to rouse oneself to action; inactive because of total indifference, a state out of which one is unwilling to be roused; dully or heavily inactive owing to illness, fatigue, emotional shock, etc.
15. **listless**—lacking the energy to be active
16. **passive**—inactive; acted upon but not reacting
17. **phlegmatic**—emotionally inactive
18. **potential**—latent
19. **quiescent**—with its activity temporarily quieted or arrested (implying, however, the possibility of a resumption or flare-up of previous activity)
20. **quiet**—inactive
21. **recumbent**—inactive
22. **sedentary**—inactive
23. **slack**—showing little or no activity
24. **slaked**—less active; made less active
25. **slothful**—inclined to inactivity
26. **sluggish**—inactive; hard to rouse to activity or movement
27. **slumberous**—inactive, the implication being that such a state is temporary
28. **soporific**—lethargic
29. **spiritless**—inactive; languid; sluggish
30. **stagnant**—not active
31. **stalemated**—brought to a point where no action can be taken by either side; deadlocked
32. **static**—inactive
33. **still, stilled**—inactive; with its activity stopped

34. **stuporous**—lethargic
35. **supine**—sunk into inactivity; lazily inactive; sluggish
36. **suspended**—temporarily made inactive
37. **torpid**—inactive by nature; dormant
38. **vegetative**—inert

2. Inactivity,n. *From Sec. 1:* abeyance or abeyancy, arrest, deadlock, dormancy, fallowness, inactivation, inertia or inertness; languidness, languor, or languorousness; latency, leadenness, lethargy, listlessness, passivity or passiveness, potentiality, quiescence, quietness, recumbency, sedentariness, slackness, sloth or slothfulness, sluggishness, slumberousness, spiritlessness; stagnation, stagnance, or stagnancy; stalemate, stupor or stuporousness, supineness, suspension; torpor, torpidness, or torpidity; vegetativeness; *Also:*
  1. **doldrums**—listlessness
  2. **entropy**—inactive condition
  3. **faineance, faineancy**—inactivity
  4. **lassitude**—sluggishness
  5. **oscitancy**—sluggishness; torpor
  6. **somnolentia**—torpor
  7. **standstill**—state of inactivity

3. To Make Inactive; To Cause to Become Inactive,v. *From Sec. 1:* arrest, deadlock, inactivate, quiet, slake, stalemate, still, suspend (arrest, inactivation, suspension,n.)

4. That Which Puts an End to Activity: quietus,n.

5. Causing Reduction in Bodily Activity, adj.
  1. **depressive, depressant**—reducing bodily activity (depressant, depressive,n. depress,v.)
  2. **depressomotor**—curtailing, inhibiting, or reducing motor responses of the body (depressomotor,n.)
  3. **narcotic**—causing a reduction in bodily activity (narcotic,n.)

6. To Become Inactive or Less Active,v.
  1. **languish**—become inactive (languishment,n.)
  2. **lull**—subside (lull,n.)
  3. **quiet**—become inactive
  4. **slack, slacken, slack off**—show less activity than before
  5. **slake**—become less active
  6. **stagnate**—become inactive (stagnation, n.)
  7. **still**—become inactive
  8. **subside**—become less active; calm down after activity; become inactive (subsidence,n.)

7. Becoming Inactive or Less Active,adj. *From Sec. 6:* languishing, quieting, slackening, stagnating, subsident or subsiding; *Also:*
1. **latescent**—becoming inactive though still present (latescence,n.)

8. To Be Inactive,v.
  1. **estivate**—pass the summer in an inactive state, as certain organisms (estivation, n.)
  2. **hibernate**—spend the winter in inactivity; go through any period of inactivity (hibernation,n.)
  3. **slumber**—be inactive; be temporarily inactive
  4. **stagnate**—be inactive (stagnation,n.)
  5. **vegetate**—live a dull, inactive life, doing little beyond eating, sleeping, and growing, like a vegetable or plant (vegetation, n.)

9. Period of Inactivity: interregnum,n.

10. Cessation of Activity: lull, respite,n.

11. A Suspension of Activity: recess,n. (recess,v.)

12. Feeling of Inactivity That Comes with the First Warm Weather: spring fever,n.

59. LACK OF MOTION

1. Not Moving,adj.
  1. **fixed**—immobile
  2. **immobile**—not moving; standing or remaining absolutely still
  3. **immovable**—not moving; standing, or remaining, absolutely still
  4. **motionless**—not moving; standing or remaining absolutely still
  5. **quiescent**—motionless
  6. **quiet**—not moving; moving very little or very slowly
  7. **stable**—not moving; not likely to move
  8. **stagnant**—not moving or progressing; not flowing; standing still
  9. **stalled**—lacking in movement; no longer moving
  10. **standing**—not moving
  11. **static**—not moving or progressing; standing still
  12. **stationary**—not moving or progressing
  13. **steadfast**—not moving
  14. **still**—motionless; quiet

2. State or Condition of Not Moving,n. *From Sec. 1:* immobility, immovability, motionlessness, quiescence; quiet, quietness, or quietude; stability, stagnation or stagnancy, stall, stand or standstill, steadfastness, still or stillness; *Also:* 1. **entropy**—static condition

3. Not to Move,v. *From Sec. 1:* stagnate, stall, stand still

4. To Stop (Something) from Moving,v. *From Sec. 1:* fix, stall, still

5. Unable to Move,adj.
  1. **apoplectic**—figuratively unable to move (from the stress of an emotion)
  2. **immobile**—unable to move
  3. **immobilized**—immobile
  4. **inert**—having no power of movement
  5. **numb**—temporarily without ability to move
  6. **palsied**—paralyzed
  7. **paralyzed**—unable to move
  8. **petrified**—unable to move because of some strong emotion
  9. **sessile**—not free to move about because of being permanently attached (of biological organisms)
  10. **spellbound**—unable to move by reason of strong fascination
  11. **torpid**—lacking in the power to move, as animals in hibernation
  12. **transfixed**—absolutely unable to move, owing usually to some deep emotion or to being pierced by someone's gaze

6. Inability to Move,n. *From Sec. 5:* apoplexy, immobility, immobilization, inertia or inertness, numbness, palsy, paralysis, petrifaction or petrification, sessility; torpor, torpidity, or torpidness; transfixion, transfixture, transfixation; *Also:* 1. **trance**—inability to move or react to the surroundings

7. To Cause to Be Unable to Move,v. *From Sec. 5:* immobilize, numb, palsy, paralyze, petrify, transfix (immobilization, paralysis, petrifaction or petrification, transfixion or transfixation,n. petrifactive,adj.)

8. Unable to Be Moved: immovable,adj. (immovability,n.)

60. POSTURE

1. Posture: air, attitude, bearing, carriage, demeanor, port, pose, stance,n.

2. Pert. to Posture: attitudinal, postural,adj.

3. To Strike or Hold a Posture: pose, posture, posturize,v. (poser, posturer,n.)

4. Posture of a Figure in Painting or Sculpture: attitude,n. (attitudinal,adj.)

5. To Place in a Bodily Position: pose, posturize,v.

6. Position in Which the Body Is Close to the Ground and the Limbs Close to the Body: crouch,n. (crouch,v.)

7. With the Hands on Hips, the Elbows Pointing Outward: akimbo,adj. or adv.

61. STAND

1. To Stand,v.
1. **bestraddle, bestride, straddle, stride**—stand with one leg on each side of
2. **cock**—stand up (of a dog's ears, etc.)
3. **confront**—stand facing (confrontation, n.)
4. **lounge**—stand lazily
5. **poise**—stand balanced or in balance
6. **slouch**—stand in a drooping, stooping, or overrelaxed manner
7. **stoop**—stand with the head and shoulders bent forward
8. **straddle**—stand with the legs spread apart
9. **totter**—stand unsteadily

2. Way of Standing,n. *From Sec. 1:* straddle, stride, lounge, poise, slouch, stoop, straddle, totter; *Also:* pose, posture, stance

3. Stander,n. *From Sec. 1:* lounger, sloucher, stooper, straddler, totterer; *Also:*
1. **bystander**—one who stands around
2. **standee**—one who stands while others sit, as in a theater, train, bus, etc.

4. Standing,adj. *From Sec. 1:* astraddle or straddle-legged, astride, slouchy, tottery; *Also:*
1. **erect, upright, upstanding**—standing up straight
2. **knock-kneed, valgus**—standing with the knees bent in and touching, or almost touching, each other

5. To Stand (Something) on Its End or Top: upend,v.

62. SIT

1. To Sit,v.
1. **baby-sit**—sit with (i.e., take care of) babies when the parents leave for a short period
2. **bestraddle, bestride, straddle, stride**—sit with one leg on each side of
3. **brood**—sit on eggs for the purpose of hatching them
4. **hatch**—sit on (eggs) to give birth to young
5. **incubate**—sit on (eggs) so they will hatch; keep (eggs) warm for hatching, simulating the circumstances of the mother hen sitting on them (incubation, n.)
6. **lounge**—sit lazily
7. **nestle**—sit close and comfortably
8. **perch**—sit on, or as if on, a pole, bar, etc.; sit the way a bird does
9. **roost**—sit on, or as if on, a pole or bar
10. **set**—sit (on eggs)
11. **slouch**—sit in a drooping, overrelaxed manner
12. **squat**—sit on the floor or ground, or on one's heels, with the legs drawn close to the body
13. **straddle**—sit with the legs spread apart

2. Manner of Sitting,n. *From Sec. 1:* straddle, stride, lounge, slouch, squat, straddle; *Also:* 1. **seat**—manner of sitting

3. Sitter,n. *From Sec. 1:* baby-sitter or sitter, straddler, incubator, lounger, nestler, percher, rooster, sloucher, squatter, straddler

4. Sitting,adj. *From Sec. 1:* astraddle or straddle-legged, astride, brood, perched or perching, slouchy, squat, astraddle; *Also:*
1. **insessorial**—perching (usually of birds)
2. **sedentary**—sitting

5. A Sitting: séance, session,n.

6. A Ceremonial Sitting with a Corpse before Its Burial: wake,n.

7. Pert. to, or Adapted for, Sitting on a Perch: insessorial,adj.

8. Pert. to, Characterized by, or Requiring, Sitting: sedentary,adj.

9. Accustomed to Sitting for Long Periods: sedentary,adj.

63. SEAT

1. Seat; Chair,n.
1. **armchair**—chair with arms; upholstered chair with arms
2. **bench**—long seat for two or more people; simple seat without back or arms
3. **cathedra**—bishop's throne; chair of a teacher or any person in authority (cathedral,adj.)
4. **easy chair**—upholstered chair for comfortable sitting or reclining
5. **fauteuil (French)**—armchair
6. **footstool**—low rest for the feet, occasionally used for sitting
7. **form**—long seat; bench
8. **howdah**—passenger's seat, usually covered, on the back of an elephant
9. **Morris chair**—easy chair with adjustable back and removable cushions
10. **musnud**—large draped seat (in India, Persia, etc.)
11. **ottoman**—upholstered backless and armless seat
12. **perch**—elevated seat
13. **pouf**—circular armless seat
14. **rocker**—chair that rocks
15. **roost**—elevated seat; any place to sit
16. **saddle**—seat on a horse
17. **settle**—long wooden bench with arms, high, solid back, and enclosed base
18. **settle bed**—long wooden bench convertible into a bed
19. **squab**—ottoman
20. **stall**—seat, usually in a church
21. **still**—seat; bench
22. **stool**—small seat without back or arms
23. **taboret**—seat without back or arms
24. **throne**—seat on a dais and with a canopy, usually for a sovereign

2. Couch,n.
1. **causeuse (French)**—couch for two (literally place to sit while chatting); tête-à-tête
2. **chaise longue**—a kind of couch with the back support at one end and at a reclining angle
3. **chesterfield**—type of large couch
4. **davenport**—large couch, sometimes convertible for sleeping
5. **day bed**—couch convertible for sleeping
6. **divan**—couchlike article of furniture; strictly a couch without arms or back, but in current use any couch
7. **lounge**—a kind of couch for reclining
8. **love seat**—small couch for two
9. **settee**—couch
10. **sofa**—upholstered couch
11. **squab**—couch
12. **tête-à-tête (French)**—short couch for two people that is so designed that they face each other

3. Footstool,n.
1. **cricket**—low wooden footstool
2. **hassock**—small upholstered footstool
3. **ottoman, squab**—upholstered footstool

4. Structure of Seats,n.
   1. **amphitheater**—circular structure with seats rising in tiers around a central space
   2. **bleachers**—structure of seats for spectators at a game, contest, etc.
   3. **grandstand**—principal section of seats at a race track, sports event, or other outdoor spectacle
   4. **pew**—compartment of seats in a church

64. CROUCH

1. To Crouch,v.
   1. **cower**—stay in a crouching position while trembling and shrinking
   2. **cringe**—crouch in fear or humbleness
   3. **grovel**—crouch in abject humbleness
   4. **squat**—crouch on the heels, low to the ground

2. Crouch,n. *From Sec. 1:* cower, cringe, grovel, squat

3. Crouching,adj. *From Sec. 1:* cowering, cringing, groveling, squat or squatting

65. LIE; RECLINE

1. To Lie; To Recline,v.
   1. **bask**—lie in the warmth of
   2. **border**—lie along the edge or boundary of (a thing or place)
   3. **bundle**—lie (with a member of the opposite sex) in the same bed without undressing—a practice during courtship in colonial days (bundling,n)
   4. **couch**—lie down
   5. **cuddle**—lie close for comfort and warmth (cuddle,n.)
   6. **grovel**—lie face downward in abject humbleness (grovel,n.)
   7. **loll**—recline in a lazy and/or relaxed manner (loll,n.)
   8. **lounge**—lie lazily (lounge,n.)
   9. **nestle**—lie close and comfortably (nestle, n.)
   10. **nuzzle**—lie close and intimate; cuddle; nestle (nuzzle,n.)
   11. **prostrate oneself**—lie down flat (prostration,n.)
   12. **puddle**—lie about in the mud
   13. **repose**—lie down to sleep (repose,n.)
   14. **rest**—lie (rest,n.)
   15. **skirt**—lie along the edge or border of (a place)
   16. **snuggle**—cuddle; nestle (snuggle,n.)
   17. **sprawl**—lie down and move the limbs awkwardly; lie with one's limbs carelessly or awkwardly spread (sprawl,n.)
   18. **squat**—lie close to the ground to escape observation (squat,n.)
   19. **wallow, welter**—lie soaked or drenched (wallow,n.)

2. Recliner,n. *From Sec. 1:* basker, bundler, cuddler, groveler, loller, lounger, nestler, nuzzler, reposer, rester, snuggler, sprawler, wallower; *Also:*
   1. **incubus**—evil spirit that supposedly lies on top of, and ravishes, women in their sleep
   2. **succubus**—demon in female form that supposedly lies under men who are asleep and has sexual intercourse with them (succubine,adj.)

3. Lying; Reclining,adj.
   1. **accumbent**—reclining; lying against something (accumbency,n.)
   2. **couchant**—lying down; in heraldry, lying down with head raised
   3. **couché (French)**—reclining (term in heraldry, said of things usually erect)
   4. **cubatory**—lying down
   5. **decumbent**—lying down (decumbence, decumbency,n.)

   6. **dormient**—lying asleep (dormience,n.)
   7. **incumbent**—lying on; lying on with downward pressure (incumbency,n.)
   8. **overlying**—lying over or on top
   9. **procumbent**—lying face downward (procumbency,n.)
   10. **prone**—lying face downward; loosely, lying flat or on one's back (proneness,n.)
   11. **prostrate**—lying flat; lying either prone or supine (prostration,n.)
   12. **recumbent**—lying down in rest; reclining (recumbency,n.)
   13. **resupine**—supine
   14. **subjacent**—lying under (subjacency,n.)
   15. **superincumbent**—lying over or on top of (superincumbency,n.)
   16. **superjacent**—lying on top of or above
   17. **supine**—lying on one's back (supineness, n.)
   18. **underlying**—lying under or below

66. REST

1. To Rest,v.
   1. **float**—rest on the surface of water or any fluid without sinking
   2. **kneel**—rest on the knees
   3. **lounge**—rest lazily
   4. **repose**—rest
   5. **roost**—rest in a place; come to rest
   6. **settle**—rest; come to rest

2. Place to Rest,n.
   1. **lounge**—place in which to rest
   2. **roost**—place in which to come to rest

3. State of Resting: quietude, recumbency, repose, rest,n. (quiet, recumbent,adj.)

4. State of Resting on the Top or Surface: supernatance,n. (supernatant,adj.)

5. Science of Bodies at Rest: statics,n.

6. Pert. to a Rest from Work: sabbatical,adj.

7. A Rest; Period of Rest,n.
   1. **intermission**—a rest or period of rest in some work, study, activity, etc.
   2. **interval**—a rest or period of rest between activities
   3. **lull**—a rest, i.e., a cessation of activity
   4. **recess**—a rest or period of rest from work, study, or other activity
   5. **respite**—a rest or period of rest from work, trouble, pain, etc.
   6. **siesta**—a midday rest
   7. **spell**—a period of rest from work or duty
   8. **truce**—a rest from distress, suffering, pain, etc.

67. SLEEP

1. To Sleep; To Go to Sleep,v.
   1. **bunk**—sleep; sleep in a crude or makeshift bed; go to sleep
   2. **doze**—be in a light sleep
   3. **drowse**—fall into a light sleep, or into short stretches of light sleep
   4. **nap**—sleep for a short time
   5. **oversleep**—sleep later than intended or expected
   6. **retire**—go to bed in order to sleep
   7. **slumber**—sleep; be in a light sleep
   8. **snooze**—sleep; take a nap

2. Sleep; State of Sleep,n. *From Sec. 1:* doze, drowse, nap, slumber, slumbers, snooze; *Also:*
   1. **cataplexy**—hypnotic sleep
   2. **cat nap**—short sleep
   3. **forty winks**—short sleep
   4. **narcohypnosis**—state of deep sleep induced by hypnosis
   5. **narcosis, narcotism**—state of sleep
   6. **sopor**—deep sleep
   7. **somnipathy**—hypnotic sleep (somnipathist,n.)

3. Asleep; Sleeping,adj. *From Sec. 1:* dozing, napping; slumbering, slumberous, or slumbery; snoozing; *Also:* **1. dormient**—lying asleep

4. State or Condition of Lying Asleep: dormience, repose,n.

5. Sleeplike State: trance,n.

6. Act of Falling Asleep: dormition,n.

7. Descr. of Unbroken Sleep: deep, sound, wakeless,adj.

8. Sleepy: dozy, drowsy, poppied, slumberous, slumbery, somniferous, soporific,adj.

9. Sleepiness: doziness, drowsiness, narcosis, narcotism, oscitancy, slumberousness,n.

10. To Be Sleepy: doze, drowse,v.

11. Unnaturally Sleepy: lethargic, somnolent, soporose,adj.

12. Unnatural Sleepiness: lethargy, narcotism, somnolence, somnolency,n.

13. One Who Is Usually Sleepy, or Who Likes to Sleep a Lot: somnolent,n.

14. Sleep-Drunkenness: somnolentia,n.

15. Morbid Condition, the Victim of Which Falls Involuntarily into Short Fits of Deep Sleep: narcolepsy,n. (narcolept,n. narcoleptic,adj.)

16. Any Disorder in the Functioning of Sleep: somnipathy,n. (somnipathist,n.)

17. Causing Sleep or Sleepiness: dormitive, hypnagogic, hypnogenetic, hypnotic, narcotic, opiate, poppied, sleep-inducing, slumberous, slumbery, somnifacient, somniferous, somnific, somnolent, soporiferous, soporific,adj.

18. Agent, Substance, or Drug That Causes Sleep or Sleepiness: barbiturate, dormitive, hypnotic, narcotic, opiate, sleeping pill, somnifacient, soporific,n.

19. Science of Sleep, Esp. Hypnotic Sleep: hypnology,n. (hypnologist,n. hypnologic, hypnological,adj.)

20. Sleeplike: hypnoid, hypnoidal,adj.

21. Descr. or Characteristic of the Process of Falling Asleep: hypnagogic,adj.

22. God of Sleep: Morpheus,n.

23. Pert. to Sleep: morphetic, soporific,adj.

68. SLEEPING QUARTERS

1. Sleeping Quarters,n.
1. **accommodation, accommodations**—sleeping quarters; sleeping quarters and meals
2. **bunkhouse**—sleeping quarters of a crude sort for laborers
3. **cubicle**—partitioned space in a dormitory
4. **dormitory**—building with many sleeping rooms; single large room with many beds

2. To Provide with Sleeping Quarters,v.
1. **accommodate**—provide with a place to sleep; provide with sleeping quarters and meals (accommodation,n.)
2. **bed**—provide with a place to sleep
3. **camp**—accommodate
4. **lodge**—provide with sleeping quarters, usually for a temporary period (lodgment,n.)

69. BED; BEDDING

1. Bed; Bedding,n.
1. **bunk**—narrow, shelflike bed set against a wall
2. **litter**—bedding for animals
3. **paillasse, palliasse**—straw mattress or bedding
4. **pallet**—small, shabby bed; bed of straw;

anything spread on the floor to serve as a bed
5. **truckle bed, trundle bed**—low bed, on casters or wheels, that can be pushed under a higher bed when not in use

2. Bedspread: counterpane, coverlet,n.

3. Pillow,n.
1. **bolster**—long pillow
2. **cushion**—little pillow
3. **sham**—decorative pillow (or decorative cover for a pillow) removed at night

70. HYPNOTISM

1. Hypnotism: animal magnetism, hypnogenesis, magnetism, mesmerism,n.

2. To Hypnotize: magnetize, mesmerize,v.

3. Hypnotist: magnetizer, mesmerist; Svengali (after the character in a George du Maurier novel),n.

4. Hypnotic: hypnogenetic, magnetic, mesmeric,adj.

5. Pert. to Hypnotism: hypnotic,adj.

6. Resembling Hypnotism: hypnotoid,adj.

7. Resulting from Hypnotism: hypnotoid, adj.

8. One Who Is Susceptible to Hypnotism or Is in a Hypnotic State: hypnotic,n.

9. Hypnotic Power: animal magnetism,n.

10. Hypnotic State: hypnosis, trance,n.

11. Self-Induced Hypnotic State: autohypnosis, self-hypnosis,n.

12. Deep Hypnosis: cataleptic or somnambulistic hypnosis,n.

13. Light Hypnosis: lethargic hypnosis,n.

14. Resembling a Hypnotic State: hypnoid, hypnoidal,adj.

15. Onset of the Hypnotic State: hypnogenesis,n.

16. Study of Hypnosis: hypnotism,n.

71. DREAM

1. Dream: vision,n.

2. Frightful Dream: incubus, nightmare,n.

3. Like a Dream,adj.
1. **dreamlike, dreamy**—like a dream
2. **nightmarish**—like a frightful dream
3. **phantasmagoric, phantasmagorical, phantasmagorial, phantasmagorian**—dreamlike in the way pictures or images shift and change suddenly in size

4. Dreamy (of People): moony, visionary, adj.

5. Dreamy State: trance,n.

6. Daydream: castle in the air, castle in Spain, fantasy, phantasy, reverie, revery,n.

7. Given to Daydreaming: moony,adj

8. Full of Daydreams: visionary,adj

9. One Who Tends to Have Daydreams: phantast, visionary,n.

72. AWAKE

1. To Awake: arise, awaken, get up rise rouse, wake, waken, wake up,v. (rise rouse,n awakener, riser, waker, wakener,n awake wakeful,adj.)

2. To Get Up from Bed after Sleeping arise,v.

3. To Awake in the Morning: rise,v rise,n riser,n.)

4. To Awake Slightly: stir,v. (stir,n.)

5. To Cause to Awake: arouse, awake, awaken; get (someone) up; rouse, wake, waken, wake up,v. (arousal, rouse,n. arouser, awakener, rouser, waker, wakener,n.)

6. To Cause to Awake Slightly: stir,v.

7. Wakefulness,n.
1. **insomnia**—morbid inability to sleep over a protracted period of time (insomniac, n. insomniac,adj.)
2. **sleeplessness**—wakefulness (sleepless, adj.)
3. **vigil**—wakefulness; wakefulness at times when sleep is normal or needed
4. **vigilance**—wakefulness; inability to sleep; a not sleeping (vigilant,adj.)

8. A Staying Awake to Watch or Guard: vigil,n.

9. Keeping Awake: vigilant,adj. (vigilance, n.)

10. Fully Awake: wide-awake,adj. (wide-awakeness,n.)

11. Out of Bed after Sleeping: astir,adj.

12. Descr. of Waking up,adj.
1. **hypnagogic**—descr. of the process of waking up
2. **hypnopompic**—descr. of the state on awakening from sleep

13. Driving Sleep Away: hypnopompic,adj.

73. NOT DO

1. Not Do,v.
1. **abate**—fail to do
2. **abstain from**—not do; not take part in
3. **avoid**—abstain from
4. **default**—fail to do something required
5. **desist**—refrain from doing
6. **forbear (to do)**—refrain (from)
7. **forgo**—voluntarily refrain (from)
8. **neglect**—not do; fail to do
9. **omit**—fail to do
10. **pretermit**—fail to do
11. **refrain**—not do that which one wants to do
12. **resist**—keep oneself from doing
13. **shirk**—not do one's share
14. **skip**—fail to do

2. A Not Doing,n. *From Sec. 1:* abatement, abstention or abstinence, avoidance, default, desistance, forbearance, neglect, omission, pretermission, resistance; *Also:*
1. **defection**—failure to do
2. **non-feasance**—failure to do that which should have been done (legal)

3. Not Doing,adj. *From Sec. 1:* abstinent or abstentious, defaulting, forbearing, neglectful or negligent, omissive, pretermissive, resistant or resistive (abstinence, forbearance; neglectfulness, negligence, or neglect; resistance or resistiveness,n.)

4. One Who Does Not Do,n. *From Sec. 1:* abstainer, avoider, defaulter, forgoer, shirk or shirker; *From Sec. 2:* non-feasor

74. HOLD BACK FROM DOING

1. To Hold (Oneself) Back from Doing,v.
1. **abstain (from)**—hold oneself back (from indulgence of one's appetites, from sexual pleasures, etc.); voluntarily hold back (from doing that which one has an impulse to do)
2. **boggle (at)**—hold back (from doing) owing to fear
3. **eschew**—abstain from activities, companionship, indulgences, etc., that one may find momentarily pleasurable but that are morally wrong or may eventually be harmful
4. **forbear (to do)**—refrain from (doing something)

5. forgo—abstain from

6. hesitate (to do)—hold back (from doing) through unwillingness (the motivation is usually fear, doubt, or some similar emotion)

7. refrain (from)—hold oneself back (from doing or saying what one has an impulse to do or say)

8. resist—keep oneself from (doing)

2. A Holding Back from Doing,n. *From Sec. 1:* abstention or abstinence, eschewal, forbearance; hesitation, hesitance, or hesitancy; resistance

3. Holding Back from Doing,adj. *From Sec. 1:* abstinent or abstentious, forbearing; hesitant, hesitative, or hesitatory; resistant or resistive (abstinence, forbearance, hesitancy, resistance or resistiveness,n.)

75. HESITATION

1. To Hesitate,v.
1. **boggle (at)**—hesitate from fear
2. **demur**—hesitate to do something
3. **falter**—hesitate
4. **shilly-shally**—hesitate
5. **stagger**—hesitate
6. **stickle**—hesitate on moral grounds or because of dictates of conscience
7. **waver**—hesitate

2. Hesitation: demurral, hesitance, hesitancy, indecision, waver,n.

3. Feeling of Hesitation about Doing Something That May or May Not Be Ethical, Right, Wise, etc.: scruple, scruples,n.

4. Hesitant: faltering, halting, hesitative, hesitatory, indecisive, wavering,adj.

5. To Cause to Hesitate: stagger,v.

76. AVOIDANCE

1. To Avoid,v.
1. **abstain from**—voluntarily avoid (indulgence in the fleshly or earthly pleasures)
2. **avert**—avoid (something)
3. **bilk**—evade payment of
4. **blink**—purposely avoid; shirk
5. **by-pass**—avoid
6. **circumvent**—avoid; get around by guile or deception
7. **dodge**—avoid by trickery or deceit
8. **elude**—avoid by cleverness, skill, artfulness, trickery, or some ruse
9. **escape**—avoid
10. **eschew**—avoid (those things, activities that, or people who, are, or might be, harmful or dangerous)
11. **evade**—avoid by artfulness, trickery, etc.
12. **fence**—avoid an issue, as in a dispute or argument
13. **fend off**—avoid, keep off, or ward off (a blow, attack, etc.) by proper defense
14. **fight shy of**—avoid; keep away from
15. **give a wide berth to**—avoid; keep far away from
16. **parry**—avoid or evade (a blow, question, attempt, etc.) by turning it aside or warding it off
17. **quibble**—avoid the point or truth by twisting the meanings of words, by using words of ambiguous meaning, etc.
18. **shirk**—avoid (duty, work, danger, etc.), often by artfulness, deception, trickery, etc.; get out of doing
19. **shun**—avoid; keep away from
20. **shy clear of**—avoid; keep away from
21. **side-step**—avoid; avoid (an issue or point of argument)
22. **skirt**—avoid by passing along the edge or outside of; avoid by going around
23. **stall**—evade

24. **stall off**—keep (something or someone) away by a pretext or trick
25. **stave off**—avoid; keep (something) away or at a distance
26. **straddle**—avoid taking sides in an issue
27. **tergiversate**—practice purposeful and artful or tricky avoidance
28. **ward off**—keep (something) away
29. **welsh, welch**—avoid paying one's gambling debt (slang)

2. Avoidance,n. *From Sec. 1:* abstention or abstinence, circumvention, dodge, elusion, escape, eschewal, evasion, parry, quibble, stall, tergiversation; *Also:*
 1. **escapism**—avoidance of the monotony, drabness, or harshness of reality by illusions, fantasy, etc.
 2. **ichthyophobia**—avoidance of fish because of taboo
 3. **precaution**—avoidance of danger or failure by direct action
 4. **quiddity**—quibble
 5. **whifflery**—the use of evasions or dodges in argument

3. Avoider,n. *From Sec. 1:* abstainer, bilker, blinker, dodger, eluder, eschewer, evader, fencer, parrier, quibbler, shirk or shirker, shunner, side-stepper, staller, straddler, tergiversator, welsher or welcher; *From Sec. 2:* escapist, whiffler; *Also:* 1. **slacker**—one who shirks work, duty, etc.; someone who avoids, or tries to avoid, military duty in wartime

4. Avoiding; Tending to Avoid,adj. *From Sec. 1:* abstinent or abstentious, circumventive, elusive, evasive, tergiversatory (elusiveness, evasiveness,n.); *From Sec. 2:* escapist; precautious, precautionary, or precautional (precautiousness,n.)

5. To Swear to Avoid: abjure,v. (abjuration, n. abjuratory,adj.)

6. To Try to Ward Off by Prayer: deprecate, v. (deprecation,n. deprecative, deprecatory, adj.)

7. Avoidable: avertable, avertible, eludible, evitable,adj.

8. Unavoidable: imperative, ineludible, inescapable, unavertable, unavertible,adj.

9. Unavoidable and Certain to Happen: ineluctable, inevitable,adj. (ineluctability, inevitability, or inevitableness,n.)

10. To Make Unavoidable: necessitate,v. (necessitation,n.)

77. SELF-CONTROL; SELF-DENIAL

1. Self-Control; Self-Denial,n.
 1. **abstemiousness**—self-denial of the gross pleasures of eating and/or drinking
 2. **abstinence, abstention**—state or act of holding oneself back in the indulgence of one's appetites, sexual desires, etc.
 3. **aloofness**—restraint; reserve
 4. **asceticism**—self-denial of the fleshly or gross pleasures; belief that self-denial, especially of the grosser pleasures, will lead to intellectual and spiritual refinement
 5. **astringency**—austerity
 6. **austerity**—condition of leading a severe, simple, and unindulgent existence; severe self-discipline
 7. **celibacy**—self-denial of romantic contacts or involvements with the opposite sex, or of sexual relations of any sort
 8. **composure**—self-control
 9. **constraint**—restraint
 10. **control**—self-control
 11. **discipline**—self-control
 12. **inhibition**—inner control that holds back the gratification of one's feelings, needs, desires, etc.

13. **mortification**—conquest of desires of the flesh through self-denial, or through religious or other disciplines
14. **offishness**—reserve
15. **prudence**—self-discipline through reasoning
16. **repression**—according to psychoanalytic theory, the process by which one not only denies oneself certain desires and feelings that are thought to be socially or morally unacceptable, but actually pushes out of one's conscious mind all awareness of these desires or feelings (repress,v.)
17. **reserve**—quality of holding back one's feelings
18. **restraint**—tendency to hold back feelings
19. **retenue (French)**—self-control; self-restraint
20. **reticence**—restraint in speaking
21. **self-abnegation**—self-denial of life's pleasures
22. **self-begrudgment**—unwillingness to allow oneself indulgence in pleasure
23. **self-discipline**—strict self-control, including the curbing of one's primitive impulses, for the purposes of improving one's mind, character, etc.
24. **self-mortification**—mortification
25. **self-renunciation**—self-denial of one's wishes or needs
26. **self-restraint**—holding oneself back from gratifying one's bodily appetites or other desires, impulses, or needs
27. **self-sacrifice**—sacrifice of one's own interests, needs, desires, etc., out of a greater desire to see a loved one's advancement or gratification
28. **Spartanism**—strict self-discipline
29. **stoicism**—practice of not giving in to one's emotions
30. **sublimation**—rerouting of primitive or carnal desires into socially acceptable activities or channels (sublimate,v.)
31. **suppression**—in psychoanalytic theory, conscious exclusion from one's mind of certain feelings, desires, etc. (suppress, v.)
32. **temperance, temperateness**—self-restraint
33. **undemonstrativeness**—reserve
34. **yoga**—mental self-control by concentration (a Hindu concept)

2. Exercising Self-Control or Self-Denial, adj. *From Sec. 1:* abstemious, abstinent or abstentious, aloof, ascetic, astringent, austere, celibate, constrained, controlled, disciplined, inhibited, offish, prudent, repressed, reserved, restrained, reticent, self-abnegating, self-begrudging, self-disciplined, self-renouncing, self-restrained, self-sacrificing, Spartan, stoic or stoical, suppressed, temperate, undemonstrative

3. One Who Exercises Self-Control or Self-Denial,n. *From Sec. 1:* ascetic, celibate, Spartan, stoic, yogi

4. To Exercise Self-Control or Self-Denial, v. *From Sec. 1:* abstain (from), control oneself, inhibit oneself, mortify oneself or one's flesh, begrudge oneself, discipline oneself, restrain oneself, sublimate

78. PREVENTION

1. To Prevent,v.
 1. **avert**—prevent from happening
 2. **deter**—prevent (someone) from doing something, usually by causing fear, fear of consequences, etc.
 3. **discourage**—deter
 4. **forbid**—prevent as if by effective command; prohibit
 5. **forestall**—prevent (an occurrence, etc.) by prior action or by doing something that makes the occurrence impossible

6. **frustrate**—prevent (some effort, etc.) from achieving fulfillment
7. **preclude**—prevent
8. **prohibit**—prevent because of difficulty, expense, etc.
9. **stave off**—prevent
10. **stay**—prevent from happening or from falling
11. **stop**—prevent
12. **thwart**—frustrate
13. **trammel**—prevent free action, movement, or progress
14. **ward off**—prevent from happening

2. **Prevention,** n. *From Sec. 1:* deterrence or determent, discouragement, forestallment, frustration, preclusion, prohibition, stay

3. **A Preventive,**n. *From Sec. 1:* deterrent or determent, prohibition, trammels

4. **Preventive,**adj. *From Sec. 1:* avertive, deterrent, frustrating, preclusive, prohibitive, thwarting, trammeling

5. **To Try to Prevent by Showing One's Disapproval:** discourage,v. (discouragement,n.)

79. MOTION

1. **To Move About, Around, or from Place to Place,**v.
    1. **ambulate**—move about; move from place to place
    2. **circulate**—move around from place to place; move around regularly
    3. **drift**—move about aimlessly in whatever direction offers the least resistance
    4. **locomote**—move about; move from place to place (colloq.)
    5. **maneuver**—move around, when in a tight spot, as part of a strategy
    6. **maunder**—move about without purpose
    7. **paddle**—move the hands or feet about idly in shallow water
    8. **stir**—move about
    9. **sweep**—move about or around over a wide range

2. **Movement About, Around, or from Place to Place,**n. *From Sec. 1:* ambulation, circulation, drift or driftage, locomotion, sweep; *Also:*
    1. **circuit**—movement around a place
    2. **course**—movement considered in reference to direction or objective
    3. **current**—movement (of air, water, etc.)

3. **Moving About, Around, or from Place to Place,**adj. *From Sec. 1:* ambulant, ambulative, ambulatory, ambulatorial; circulating or circulative, drifting, locomotive, maundering, stirring; *Also:*
    1. **ambient**—moving around
    2. **vagabond**—moving from place to place
    3. **volitant**—moving about

4. **To Move (Something or Someone) About, Around, or from Place to Place,**v. *From Sec. 1:* circulate, drift, maneuver, paddle, stir; *Also:*
    1. **manipulate**—move around with the hands (manipulation,n.)
    2. **shunt**—move out of the way
    3. **transplant**—move from one place to another; move (a population or group of people) from one country or region and settle them in another (transplantation, n.)

5. **To Move, or Cause to Move, Very Slightly:** budge, stir,v.

6. **Very Slight Movement:** budge, stir,n.

7. **To Move Past:** cross, pass,v.

8. **To Move Irregularly:** toss, twist, wind,v.

9. **Irregular Movement:** toss, twist, wind,n.

10. **To Move in Numbers,**v.
    1. **mill (around)**—move in a confused mass

2. **stampede**—move in a general rush (stampede,n.)
3. **swarm**—move in great numbers and packed close together
4. **throng**—move in a crowd
5. **troop**—move together

11. **To Move on the Ground or on the Surface of Water:** taxi,v. (of an airplane)

12. **To Move One Within the Other:** telescope,v.

13. **To Move Weakly:** crawl, creep,v.

14. **To Move Continuously:** stream,v.

15. **Continuously Moving:** restless, streaming,adj. (restlessness,n.)

16. **To Move, or Move Something, on, or as if on, Wheels:** roll, truckle, trundle, wheel,v.

17. **To Move (Something) with Force, or by the Use of Considerable Force:** pry,v.

18. **Military Movements of Troops, Ships, etc.:** maneuver,n.

19. **First Perceptible Movements of a Fetus:** quickening,n.

20. **Regular Movement:** rhythm,n. (rhythmic, rhythmical,adj.)

21. **Repeated Movement:** stroke,n.

22. **Line of Motion:** track,n.

23. **Self-Moving:** automotive, automobile, locomobile,adj.

24. **Dainty and Affected in Motion:** mincing, adj.

25. **Able to Move,**adj.
    1. **locomobile**—having the power to move about (locomobility,n.)
    2. **locomotive**—able to move from place to place (locomotivity, locomotiveness, locomotion, locomotility,n.)
    3. **mobile**—able to move (mobility,n.)
    4. **motile**—capable of self-generated or spontaneous movement or motion (motility,n.)

26. **Able to Be Moved,** adj.
    1. **ambulatory**—movable
    2. **mobile**—easily moved (mobility,n.)
    3. **movable**—capable of being moved (movability,n.)

27. **Pert. or Relating to Movement,**adj.
    1. **circulatory**—pert. to motion from place to place
    2. **dynamic**—pert. to forces that produce motion
    3. **gestic**—pert. to bodily motion
    4. **kinematic**—pert. to the motions of physical bodies
    5. **kinetic, kinesic**—pert. to, or resulting from, motion

28. **Science of Motion,**n.
    1. **dynamics**—science comprising both kinematics and kinetics (dynamic,adj.)
    2. **kinematics**—science of motion (kinematic,adj.)
    3. **kinetics**—science of changes in motions produced by forces (kinetical,adj.)
    4. **physics**—science of motion and matter (physical,adj. physicist,n.)

29. **Instrument for Studying the Motion of a Body, esp. a Rapidly Rotating or Vibrating Body:** stroboscope,n. (stroboscopic, adj.)

80. PLAYFUL MOTION

1. **To Move Playfully, etc.,**v.
    1. **cavort**—move about playfully
    2. **frisk, curvet**—move in a gay and playful manner (frisky,adj.)
    3. **frolic**—move about in a playful manner
    4. **gambol**—frisk about

5. **prance, caper**—move proudly, gaily, or boastfully
6. **romp**—frolic happily (rompish, rompy, adj.)

2. Playful, etc., Movement or Motion,n. *From Sec. 1:* frisk or curvet, frolic, gambol, prance or caper, romp; *Also:* 1. **tittup**—brisk physical movements such as capering, frisking, prancing, etc., indicative of high spirits

81. MOTION ON ALL FOURS

1. To Move on All Fours,v.
1. **crawl**—move on all fours
2. **creep**—move on all fours, and/or with the body prone and close to the ground
3. **grovel**—literally or figuratively crawl in abject humbleness at someone's feet
4. **scrabble, scramble**—crawl and climb simultaneously

2. Movement on All Fours,n. *From Sec. 1:* crawl, creep, grovel, scrabble, scramble; *Also:*
1. **reptation**—a creeping
2. **vermiculation**—a crawling like a worm

3. Moving, or Characterized by Movement, on All Fours,adj. *From Sec. 1:* crawly or crawling, creepy or creeping, groveling; *From Sec. 2:* reptant; repent (of animals or plants); reptatorial, reptatory, vermiculate or vermicular; *Also:* 1. **reptile**—creeping; creeping on the belly or on very short legs; groveling

82. SECRET MOTION

1. To Move Secretly, Stealthily, Sneakily, etc.,v.
1. **crawl**—creep
2. **creep**—move stealthily
3. **lurk**—move sneakily or stealthily
4. **prowl**—move about in a secret, stealthy, or sneaky fashion, often looking for something to steal, eat, take, etc.
5. **pussyfoot**—move warily, secretly, and quietly, like a cat (colloq.)
6. **sidle**—move in a way to attract little or no attention; move in a furtive manner, as if sideways
7. **skulk**—move in a sneaky way
8. **slink**—move in a quiet, secret manner, as if afraid or ashamed, or as if guilty of some wrongdoing
9. **sneak**—move in a stealthy or furtive manner
10. **steal**—move secretly, quietly, inconspicuously, gently, etc.

2. Secret, Stealthy, etc., Movement,n. *From Sec. 1:* crawl, creep; lurk (most often in the phrase *on the lurk*); prowl, sidle, slink, sneak, steal

3. Secret, Stealthy, etc., in Movement,adj. *From Sec. 1:* crawling or crawly, creeping or creepy, lurking, prowling, skulking, slinking or slinky, sneaking or sneaky

4. One Who Moves Secretly, Stealthily, etc., n. *From Sec. 1:* crawler, creeper, lurker, prowler, pussyfooter, skulk or skulker, sneak

83. NERVOUS MOTION

1. To Move Nervously, Fearfully, Restlessly, etc.,v.
1. **buck**—start (often of horses)
2. **crawl, creep**—move fearfully
3. **fidget**—move around restlessly or nervously
4. **jerk**—move suddenly and nervously
5. **jiggle**—move in nervous jerks
6. **shy**—move away from sudden fright; start
7. **start, startle**—make a sudden and involuntary movement from fear

8. **stir**—move restlessly
9. **thrash, thrash about, thrash around, toss, toss about, toss around**—move around fitfully in bed, or while lying down or sleeping
10. **twitch**—move with nervous jerks
11. **vellicate**—twitch; move in nervous spasms

2. Nervous, Fearful, Restless, etc., Movement,n. *From Sec. 1:* buck, crawl, creep, fidget, jerk, jiggle, shy, start, startle, thrash, toss, twitch, vellication; *Also:*
1. **jactitation, jactation**—frequent tossing or jerking of the body (medical)
2. **tic**—twitch

3. Nervous, Fearful, Restless, etc., in Movement,adj. *From Sec. 1:* fidgety, jerky, jiggly, thrashing, tossing, twitchy; twitchety (colloq.); *Also:*
1. **restive**—fidgety
2. **restless**—moving nervously or fitfully
3. **skittish**—likely to start or shy nervously

4. To Move (Something) Nervously, etc.,v. *From Sec. 1:* fidget, jerk, jiggle, thrash, toss, twitch, vellicate

84. CONFUSED MOTION

1. To Move in Confusion,v.
1. **flounce, flounder**—move about in confusion
2. **mill (around)**—move in a confused mass
3. **tumble**—move in a confused and disorderly manner

2. Confused Movement,n. *From Sec. 1:* flounce, flounder, tumble; *Also:* 1. **hurryscurry**—fast and confused motion

85. MOTION REQUIRING EFFORT

1. To Move with Effort, etc.,v.
1. **flounder**—struggle, as if held back by something (flounder,n.)
2. **plow, plough**—move ahead slowly and laboriously
3. **struggle**—move with great effort or difficulty (struggle,n.)
4. **toil**—move with pain, suffering, or difficulty (toil,n.)
5. **trail**—move in, or as if in, fatigue, weariness, or reluctance
6. **work (up, down, through, in, out, etc.)**—move with great effort and/or slowness

86. CLUMSY MOTION

1. To Move Clumsily, Awkwardly, Heavily, Unsteadily, etc.,v.
1. **barge**—move clumsily and slowly
2. **bicker**—move rapidly but unsteadily
3. **blunder**—move clumsily or blindly
4. **crawl, creep**—move awkwardly and slowly on hands and knees
5. **falter**—move in an awkward, unsteady, and/or hesitating manner
6. **flop**—move heavily and clumsily
7. **flounce, flounder**—move about clumsily
8. **jog**—move heavily; move heavily and slowly
9. **limp**—move in an awkward and halting manner
10. **lumber**—move heavily and clumsily
11. **reel, stagger**—move unsteadily or in halting, unsure steps
12. **scramble**—move clumsily on, or as if on, hands and feet
13. **shuffle**—move while scraping or dragging the feet
14. **slither**—move unsteadily and against little or no friction or resistance
15. **slouch**—move in an awkward, drooping, overrelaxed, or stooping manner

16. **sprawl**—move awkwardly
17. **teeter**—move unsteadily
18. **waddle**—move clumsily
19. **wobble, wabble**—move unsteadily or clumsily and with a staggering, side-to-side sway
20. **yaw**—move unsteadily

2. Clumsy, etc., Movement,n. *From Sec. 1:* crawl, creep, falter, flop, flounce, flounder, jog, limp, reel, stagger, scramble, shuffle, slither, slouch, sprawl, teeter, waddle, wobble, wabble, yaw; *Also:*
1. **parakinesia**—clumsy or awkward movements or motion (of a person) owing to a nervous disorder
2. **titubation**—unsteady, staggering movement in walking occurring in some nervous afflictions

3. Clumsy, etc., in Movement,adj. *From Sec. 1:* blundering, crawling, creeping, faltering, floppy or flopping, floundering, jogging, limping, lumbering, reeling, staggering or staggery, shuffling, slithering or slithery, slouching or slouchy, sprawling or sprawly, waddling or waddly; wobbling or wobbly, wabbling or wabbly; yawing; *From Sec. 2:* parakinetic; *Also:*
1. **lame**—moving in an awkward and halting manner
2. **logy**—moving heavily
3. **sluggish, sullen**—heavy and slow in movement

87. UNSTEADINESS

1. Unsteady,adj.
1. **groggy**—unsteady (said of a person who, owing to sleepiness, intoxication, bodily shock, or any similar cause, is unable to maintain his physical steadiness)
2. **joggly**—unsteady (colloq.)
3. **ramshackle**—shaky and loose
4. **rickety**—unsteady; shaky
5. **rocky**—shaky
6. **shaky**—unsteady; so unsteady as to shake easily or be easily shaken
7. **staggering, staggery**—unsteady
8. **ticklish**—unsteady; easily turned over
9. **tippy**—unsteady, i.e., likely to turn over
10. **tipsy**—unsteady, i.e., likely to tip or turn over
11. **top-heavy**—unsteady because the weight of the top overbalances that of the base
12. **tottering, tottery**—unsteady; beginning to fall
13. **unstable**—unsteady
14. **wayward**—unsteady
15. **wavery**—unsteady
16. **wobbly, wabbly**—unsteady; shaky

2. Unsteadiness,n. *From Sec. 1:* grogginess, ricketiness, rockiness, shakiness, tippiness, tipsiness, top-heaviness, instability, waywardness, wobbliness, wabbliness

3. To Be or Become Unsteady,v. *From Sec. 1:* rock, shake, stagger, tip, totter, waver, wobble, wabble

4. To Cause to Be Unsteady,v. *From Sec. 1:* rock, shake, stagger; wobble, wabble (colloq.)

88. STEADINESS

1. Steady; Not Easily Moved, Shaken, Thrown off Balance, etc.; Not Shaking or Swaying: firm, solid, stable, stalwart, stanch, staunch, stiff, stout, sturdy, substantial, tough,adj.

2. Steadiness: firmness, solidity, solidness, stability, stableness, stalwartness, stanchness, staunchness, stiffness, stoutness, sturdiness, substantiality, substantialness, toughness,n.

3. To Cause to Be Steady: ballast (figura-

tively), brace, firm, stabilize, steady, stiffen,v. (stabilization,n. ballast, brace, stabilizer,n.)

4. To Become Steady: firm, steady, stiffen,v.

5. Firmly Built: stocky,adj. (stockiness,n.)

89. SUDDEN MOTION

1. To Move Suddenly and/or Jerkily,v.
1. **arrow**—move suddenly upward
2. **bob**—move in a sudden, jerky fashion
3. **bound**—move with sudden jumps
4. **buck**—start jerkily
5. **charge**—move suddenly, violently, and quickly at or toward
6. **convulse**—move jerkily
7. **dangle**—move jerkily while hanging loosely
8. **dart**—move suddenly and quickly
9. **dartle**—dart over and over
10. **dodge**—move suddenly to one side to, or as if to, avoid contact
11. **flit**—move suddenly and quickly
12. **flounce**—move jerkily, and in such a way as to show impatience, anger, etc.
13. **hitch**—move jerkily
14. **jerk**—move sharply and suddenly
15. **jiggle**—move in quick, nervous jerks
16. **joggle**—move jerkily
17. **jump**—move suddenly into the air
18. **lash**—move suddenly
19. **leap**—move suddenly; jump
20. **lunge**—move suddenly and violently forward
21. **lurch**—move suddenly to one side
22. **shoot**—move suddenly and very swiftly
23. **shy**—move away suddenly from fright; start
24. **skid**—move in a sudden sideways slide
25. **spring**—move suddenly and rapidly
26. **start, startle**—move suddenly; make a sudden, involuntary movement from fear or surprise
27. **twitch**—move with a nervous jerk
28. **vellicate**—move in jerks or spasms; twitch
29. **whip**—move suddenly
30. **wiggle**—move with quick jerks from side to side
31. **zoom**—move suddenly upward

2. Sudden or Jerky Movement,n. *From Sec. 1:* bob, bound, buck, charge, convulsion, dart, dodge, flit, flounce, hitch, jerk, jiggle, joggle, jump, lash, leap, lunge, lurch, shy, skid, spring, start, twitch, vellication, wiggle, zoom; *Also:*
1. **jactitation, jactation**—frequent jerking of the body
2. **spasm**—sudden movement

3. Sudden or Jerky in Movement,adj. *From Sec. 1:* bobbing, bucking, convulsive, darting, dodging, flitting, jerky or jerking, jiggly or jiggling, joggly, lunging, lurching, skidding, springy, twitching, wiggly or wiggling, zooming; *Also:*
1. **skittish**—likely to shy or start nervously
2. **working**—twitching in spasms as an indication of intense emotion (esp. the facial muscles)

4. To Cause to Move Suddenly or Jerkily, v. *From Sec. 1:* convulse, dangle, hitch, jerk, jiggle, lash, shoot, startle, twitch, vellicate, whip, wiggle, zoom

90. EASY MOTION

1. To Move Easily, Smoothly, etc.,v.
1. **brush**—move so lightly as to be scarcely felt or seen; move with agility and speed
2. **coast**—move easily; slide downhill
3. **dance**—move in a lively manner
4. **float**—move easily on the surface of water or any fluid without sinking

5. **flow**—move smoothly and easily
6. **glide**—move flowingly and smoothly
7. **jog**—move in a leisurely manner
8. **lounge**—move lazily
9. **skid**—slide sideways
10. **skim**—move lightly and, often, rapidly over the surface of; move lightly and rapidly (over, along, near, or at the surface); glide along; slide along
11. **skip**—trip
12. **skitter**—glide or trip along the surface; glide lightly or in haste
13. **slide**—move smoothly or easily along a surface; move smoothly with little friction or resistance
14. **slip**—slide; glide
15. **slither**—slide down or along a surface; slide unsteadily
16. **trip**—move lightly in quick steps
17. **waltz**—move with agility, as in the dance of the same name
18. **whisk**—move lightly and quickly

2. Easy, Smooth, etc., Movement,n. *From Sec. 1:* brush, coast, dance, float, flow, glide, jog, lounge, skid, skim, skip, skitter, slide, slip, slither, trip, waltz, whisk; *Also:* **1. flick** —light and very quick movement

3. Easy, Smooth, etc., in Movement, adj. *From Sec. 1:* brushing, dancing, floating, flowing, gliding, jogging, skidding, skipping, skittering, sliding, slithering, slithery, tripping; *Also:*
1. **agile**—nimble (agility,n.)
2. **lambent**—moving lightly on or over a surface; gliding (lambency,n.)
3. **lightsome**—light in movement (lightsomeness,n.)
4. **lissome**—nimble (lissomeness,n.)
5. **mobile**—moving easily (mobility,n.)
6. **nimble**—moving lightly, easily, skillfully, and quickly (nimbleness,n.)
7. **spanking**—moving in a lively fashion

4. Able to Move Lightly, Easily, etc., adj.
1. **agile, nimble**—able to move lightly, easily, and skillfully (agility, nimbleness,n.)
2. **mobile**—able to move easily or freely (mobility,n.)

91. VIOLENT MOTION

1. To Move Forcefully or Violently,v.
1. **charge**—move at, toward, or against violently, suddenly, and/or quickly
2. **dash**—move violently and quickly; move forward forcefully or violently
3. **hurtle**—move violently and rapidly
4. **lunge**—move forward violently and suddenly
5. **plunge**—move violently and quickly (into, or as if into, water)
6. **rampage**—rush about in a wild or excited fashion
7. **run amuck**—rush around, furiously attacking
8. **rush**—move violently and quickly
9. **smash**—move with tremendous or crushing force or violence
10. **stampede**—move in a general rush
11. **storm**—move about violently
12. **surge**—rush
13. **thrash**—move with violence
14. **whip**—thrash about

2. Forceful or Violent Movement,n. *From Sec. 1:* charge, dash, lunge, plunge, rampage, rush, smash, stampede, storm, thrash, whip; *Also:*
1. **commotion**—violent or excited motion
2. **debacle**—violent rush of debris-laden waters
3. **fury**—movement containing great violence
4. **inrush**—a rushing in
5. **onrush**—strong forward rush

6. **precipitation, precipitance, precipitancy** —violent, rapid, and headlong movement
7. **spasm**—violent movement
8. **tidal wave**—any overwhelming movement

3. Forceful or Violent in Movement,adj. *From Sec. 1:* charging, dashing, hurtling, lunging, plunging, rampaging or rampageous, rushing, smashing, stampeding, stormy, surging, thrashing, whipping; *From Sec. 2:* furious, inrushing, onrushing, precipitate or precipitant (precipitance, precipitancy,n.)

92. NOISY MOTION

1. To Move with a Sound,v.
1. **bicker**—move with a noise repeated rapidly
2. **birr**—move with a whirring sound
3. **chug**—move with the sharp, explosive sound of an engine's exhaust
4. **clatter**—move noisily
5. **crash**—move with a sudden and very loud noise
6. **hurtle**—move rapidly and with a clattering noise
7. **rumble**—move with a low, rolling, deep, and continuous sound
8. **skirr**—move rapidly with a whirring sound
9. **smash**—crash
10. **swish**—move with a light, hissing or brushing sound
11. **whir, whirr**—move quickly with a buzzing sound, or with the characteristic sound of bodies rushing through air
12. **whish**—move with a brushing, hissing, or rushing sound
13. **whiz**—move with a humming or hissing sound

93. MOTION IN WAVES

1. To Move in Waves,v.
1. **billow**—surge; undulate
2. **fluctuate**—move in a wave or waves; move irregularly, alternately, up and down, or back and forth in waves
3. **purl**—move in small or gentle waves; undulate
4. **ripple**—move in small waves
5. **surge**—move in strong, large, or high waves
6. **undulate**—move in waves; have a wavy motion

2. Movement in Waves,n. *From Sec. 1:* billow, fluctuation, purl, ripple, surge, undulation; *Also:*
1. **peristalsis**—wavelike movement in a hollow organ by which contents are pushed inward, esp. such movement of the alimentary canal, stomach, or intestines
2. **wafture**—wavelike motion

3. Moving in Waves,adj. *From Sec. 1:* billowy or billowing, fluctuant or fluctuating, purling, ripply or rippling, surging; undulative, undulatory, undular, undulate, or undulating; *From Sec. 2:* peristaltic

94. RAPID MOTION

1. To Move Rapidly,v.
1. **arrow**—shoot upward (like an arrow)
2. **bicker**—move rapidly but unsteadily
3. **bob**—move with quick, short, or jerky motions, often up and down
4. **bolt**—move suddenly and quickly
5. **bound**—move with fast jumps
6. **brush**—move so quickly as to be scarcely seen or felt; move with speed and agility
7. **career**—move rapidly
8. **charge**—rush at or toward suddenly

9. **chase**—hurry
10. **course**—move fast
11. **cruise**—move at a speed of maximum efficiency or comfort
12. **dart**—move quickly and suddenly
13. **dartle**—dart over and over again
14. **dash**—move quickly and violently
15. **flit**—move quickly and suddenly
16. **flitter**—flutter
17. **flounce**—toss about
18. **flutter**—move rapidly but aimlessly
19. **fly**—move at high speed
20. **hasten**—move quickly; move with undue, unthinking, rash, or confused quickness
21. **hurry**—move with quickness or with confused or flustered speed; move with a kind of tense quickness; hasten
22. **hurtle**—move very rapidly; move rapidly and violently; move rapidly and with a clattering noise
23. **hustle**—move rapidly and determinedly; move with confused quickness
24. **jig**—move in a quick, nervous fashion
25. **jiggle**—move in quick, nervous jerks
26. **jump**—leap
27. **leap**—move quickly; move quickly into the air
28. **nod**—make a quick downward or forward motion
29. **plunge**—move quickly and violently (into, or as if into, water)
30. **race**—move as speedily as possible
31. **rampage**—rush about in a wild or excited fashion
32. **run**—move rapidly
33. **run amuck**—rush around furiously attacking
34. **rush**—move quickly and violently; move very quickly
35. **scamper**—move in a quick and hurried manner
36. **scud**—move rapidly
37. **scurry**—move with brisk speed
38. **scutter**—scurry
39. **shoot**—move very swiftly and, often, suddenly
40. **skim**—move rapidly and lightly over the surface of; move rapidly and lightly (over, along, near, or at the surface)
41. **skip**—trip
42. **skirr**—move with speed or haste; move rapidly with a whirring sound
43. **skitter**—move rapidly and smoothly; trip along the surface
44. **smash**—rush
45. **speed**—move rapidly
46. **spring**—move rapidly and suddenly
47. **spurt**—move with a sudden burst of speed
48. **stampede**—move in a general rush
49. **surge**—rush
50. **tear**—move very rapidly
51. **toss**—move with a quick, sometimes scornful, motion
52. **trip**—move lightly in quick steps
53. **twinkle**—move quickly
54. **waltz**—move with rapidity, as in the dance of the same name
55. **whir, whirr**—move quickly with the characteristic sounds of bodies rushing through air
56. **whirl**—move quickly or with haste
57. **whisk**—move quickly and lightly
58. **whiz**—move speedily with a humming or hissing sound

2. Rapid Movement,n. *From Sec. 1:* bob, bolt, bound, brush, charge, chase, dart, dash, flit, flitter, flounce, flutter, jig, jiggle, jump, leap, nod, plunge, race, rampage, run, rush, scamper, scurry, skip, skitter, smash, spring, spurt, stampede, surge, tear, toss, twinkle, waltz, whirl, whisk; *Also:*
1. **flick**—light and very quick movement
2. **hurry-scurry**—fast and disordered or confused motion

3. **lilt**—springy motion or movement
4. **precipitation, precipitance**—very rapid, headlong movement or rush
5. **tantivy**—rapid and impetuous movement

3. Rapid in Movement,adj. *From Sec. 1:* arrowy, bobbing, bounding, charging, coursing, cruising, darting, flitting, fluttering, flying, hasty, hurrying or hurried, hurtling, jiggling or jiggly, jumping, leaping, plunging, racing, rampaging, rampageous, running, rushing, scampering, scurrying, shooting, skipping, skittering, speedy or speeding, springy, stampeding, surging, tripping, twinkling, whirring; *From Sec. 2:* lilting, precipitate or precipitant; *Also:*
1. **agile**—moving, or moving about, quickly and lightly
2. **arrowy**—swift, like an arrow in motion
3. **brisk**—moving rapidly and with animation
4. **fast**—moving rapidly
5. **fleet**—moving rapidly; rapid in motion
6. **lissome**—nimble
7. **lively**—brisk
8. **nimble**—moving quickly, lightly, easily, and skillfully
9. **quick**—moving rapidly
10. **supersonic**—moving faster than the speed of sound
11. **swift**—fast-moving
12. **transsonic**—so fast as to be moving at approximately the speed of sound (which is 738 miles an hour) or at a speed between 600–900 miles per hour
13. **ultrasonic**—supersonic
14. **velocious**—speedy
15. **volant**—nimble

4. Rapidity of Movement,n. *From Sec. 1:* haste, hurry, rampageousness, rush, speed, speediness; *From Sec. 2:* lilt, precipitance or precipitancy; *From Sec. 3:* agility, briskness, fleetness, lissomeness, liveliness, nimbleness, quickness, swiftness, velocity; *Also:* 1. **legerity** —nimbleness

5. To Move (Something) Rapidly; To Cause to Move Rapidly,v. *From Sec. 1:* chase, flutter, hasten, hurry, hustle, jiggle, plunge, race, rush, shoot, skitter, whirl, whisk; *From Sec. 2:* precipitate; *Also:* 1. **wing**—give speed to

6. To Move Faster,v.
1. **accelerate**—move faster; pick up speed (acceleration,n.)
2. **gain upon**—move faster than (as in a race, etc.)
3. **hasten**—move faster; hurry
4. **hurry**—move faster, and with increased urgency or tenseness
5. **outstrip**—move faster than
6. **overhaul**—gain upon
7. **quicken**—move faster

7. To Cause to Move Faster,v. *From Sec. 1:* accelerate (acceleration,n.), hasten, hurry, quicken; *Also:*
1. **bundle off**—hurry (someone) off
2. **cause**—cause to move faster
3. **wing**—give increased speed to the movements of

8. Able to Move Rapidly,adj.
1. **agile**—able to move, or move about, rapidly (agility,n.)
2. **fast**—able to move rapidly
3. **fleet**—able to move rapidly (fleetness,n.)
4. **fleet-footed, fleet-foot**—able to move rapidly by or on foot (fleet-footedness, n.)
5. **lissome**—nimble (lissomeness,n.)
6. **nimble**—able to move rapidly, lightly, and skillfully (nimbleness,n.)
7. **nimble-footed**—able to move rapidly, lightly, and skillfully by or on foot (nimble-footedness,n.)
8. **quick**—able to move rapidly (quickness, n.)

9. **quick-footed**—fleet-footed (quick-footedness,n.)
10. **rapid**—able to move very fast (rapidness, rapidity,n.)
11. **speedy**—rapid (speediness,n.)
12. **swift**—rapid (swiftness,n.)
13. **volant**—nimble
14. **wing-footed**—fleet; fleet-footed (wing-footedness,n.)

9. Speedy and Smart in Appearance: rakish, adj. (of ships)

95. RAPIDITY

1. Rapid; Fast; Quick,adj.
   1. **abrupt**—hasty
   2. **alacritous**—cheerfully fast
   3. **alert**—quick to act
   4. **brash**—hasty and reckless
   5. **cursory**—descr. of that which is done quickly and superficially, and with little attention to detail
   6. **expeditious**—descr. of that which is done quickly and without delay
   7. **hasty**—unduly, unthinkingly, confusedly, or rashly quick; descr. of that which is done with such quickness
   8. **headlong**—rapid and violent; heedlessly hasty
   9. **hurried**—descr. of that which is done quickly or with tense quickness; quick; hasty
   10. **nimble**—quick and skillful
   11. **overhasty**—excessively or unnecessarily hasty
   12. **precipitate, precipitant**—very fast; acting or doing in a recklessly hasty manner
   13. **premature**—excessively or unnecessarily hasty
   14. **quick-fire**—rapidly following one after the other (of actions, questions, etc.)
   15. **rapid-fire**—quick-fire
   16. **rash**—overhasty in action, speech, decision, etc.; precipitant
   17. **slapdash**—hasty and careless
   18. **speedy**—fast
   19. **superficial**—quick and careless (of actions)
   20. **swift**—fast; very fast
   21. **winged**—rapid

2. Rapidity; Quickness,n. *From Sec. 1:* abruptness; (with) alacrity, alertness, brashness, cursoriness, expeditiousness or expedition, haste or hastiness, hurry, nimbleness, overhastiness, precipitance or precipitancy, prematurity, rashness, speed or speediness, superficiality, swiftness; *Also:* celerity, dispatch

3. In Full Speed of Action or Activity: in full career

4. Sudden Burst of Speed: spurt,n.

5. Quickly,adv.
   1. **amain**—in great haste; at full speed
   2. **headlong**—rapidly and violently; with unthinking haste
   3. **like wildfire**—very rapidly and uncontrollably
   4. **pell-mell**—in great and confused haste
   5. **posthaste**—very quickly; by the fastest means
   6. **presto**—quickly

6. To Go, Do, Act, etc., Quickly,v.
   1. **fly**—go at top speed
   2. **hasten**—go, do, act, etc., quickly or with undue, unthinking, confused, or rash quickness
   3. **hurry**—go, do, act, etc., with a kind of tense quickness
   4. **hustle**—go with confused haste
   5. **speed**—go, do, etc., quickly
   6. **spurt**—go, do, etc., with a sudden burst of speed

7. To Do Faster than: outstrip,v.
8. To Cause to Go, Act, Happen, etc., Faster,v.
   1. **accelerate**—make (something) go or develop faster (acceleration,n. accelerative, acceleratory,adj.)
   2. **anticipate**—make happen faster (anticipation,n.)
   3. **bundle off**—hurry (someone) off
   4. **catalyze**—cause (a chemical reaction, or, by extension, any process) to happen or develop faster without itself undergoing any change (catalysis,n. catalytic,adj.)
   5. **expedite**—cause (something, some process, act, etc.) to happen, develop, etc., faster (expedition,n.)
   6. **hasten**—speed
   7. **hurry**—make go, happen, etc., faster
   8. **precipitate**—make happen faster (precipitation,n.)
   9. **speed**—make go, or happen, faster
   10. **wing**—cause to go faster

9. That Which Causes Speed,n. *From Sec. 8:* accelerant or accelerator, catalyst or catalytic agent, precipitator

10. One Who Causes Speed,n. *From Sec. 8:* expediter, precipitator

11. Fast, in Music,adj. or adv. (Italian)
   1. **allegro**—fast, brisk, and lively
   2. **prestissimo**—very fast
   3. **presto**—fast

12. Fast, a Direction in Music,adj. (Italian)
   1. **veloce**—fast and dashing
   2. **volante**—with lightning rapidity

96. RUN

1. To Run,v.
   1. **career**—run
   2. **course**—run over or through; run swiftly
   3. **dart**—run fast after a quick start
   4. **dash**—run quickly
   5. **gallop**—run with a jumping, leaping, or springy gait
   6. **lope**—run with a long, effortless stride or gait
   7. **pad**—run with quiet and steady steps; run quietly and softly
   8. **race**—run swiftly
   9. **scamper**—run hurriedly
   10. **scoot**—run suddenly
   11. **scud**—run
   12. **scurry, scutter**—run briskly
   13. **scuttle**—run swiftly
   14. **sprint**—run at top speed for a short distance
   15. **squint**—run in a slanting direction
   16. **trot**—run without great speed
   17. **whirl**—run a short distance

2. A Run; A Running,n. *From Sec. 1:* career, course, dart, dash, gallop, lope, pad, race, scamper, scoot, scurry, scutter, sprint, trot, whirl; *Also:* 1. decurrence, decurrency—a running downward

3. Running,adj. *From Sec. 1:* careering, coursing, darting, etc.; *From Sec. 2:* decurrent; *Also:*
   1. **cursive**—running; descr. of running and flowing style of handwriting
   2. **procursive**—running forward

4. Adapted to Running: cursorial,adj.

5. To Participate in a Running Contest: race,v.

6. A Running Contest: race,n.

97. FLIGHT

1. To Fly,v.
   1. **airplane**—fly in an airplane
   2. **aviate**—fly aircraft

3. **buzz**—fly low over (a place) in a plane
4. **flit**—fly along; flutter
5. **flush**—fly out or up suddenly from, or as from, cover (of birds)
6. **flutter, flitter**—fly with flapping wings or movements
7. **glide**—fly at a descending angle with engine cut off (of a plane); fly smoothly, as a bird, etc.
8. **hover**—fly back and forth and around in a small area, watchfully (of birds and other flying creatures)
9. **sail**—fly or travel through the air, as planes, birds, objects, etc.
10. **skirr**—fly with speed and haste
11. **soar**—fly up
12. **swarm**—fly in great numbers and packed close together
13. **take wing**—fly away
14. **volplane**—glide in an airplane
15. **whir**—fly quickly with a buzzing sound
16. **wing**—fly
17. **zoom**—fly suddenly upward; fly upward at a sharp angle

2. Flight,n. *From Sec. 1:* aviation, flit, flutter, glide, hover, soar, volplane, zoom; *Also:*
1. **volation, volitation**—flight

3. Flying,adj. *From Sec. 1:* flitting, fluttering, gliding, hovering, skirring, soaring, swarming or aswarm, whirring, zooming; *From Sec. 2:* volant or volitant

4. Disposed to Fly: fugacious,adj. (fugaciousness, fugacity,n.)

5. Able to Fly: volant, volitant,adj.

6. Power of Flight: volation, volitation,n.

7. Pert. or Relating to, or Descr. of, Flying, adj.
1. **aerobatic**—pert. to stunts or feats performed by an airplane
2. **aeronautic, aeronautical**—pert. to flight in a plane or other air vehicle, or to one who rides in such
3. **flight**—pert. to, or descr. of, flying
4. **volar**—pert. to flight or flying; used in flying

8. Science of Flying,n.
1. **aerodonetics**—science of gliding in the air
2. **aeronautics**—science and/or art of operating aircraft
3. **aviation**—art or practice of piloting aircraft
4. **avigation**—science of handling aircraft while in the air

9. Feats, Tricks, or Stunts Performed by Airplane: aerobatics,n.

98. AIRCRAFT

1. Common Aircraft,n.
1. **airplane, aeroplane**—heavier-than-air aircraft
2. **airship**—lighter-than-air and self-propelled aircraft
3. **amphibian**—airplane that can land on, and take off from, both land and water
4. **autogiro, autogyro**—aircraft with horizontal revolving wings
5. **balloon**—bag filled with gas (usually helium) so that it can rise and float in the air, and with an attached compartment for passengers
6. **biplane**—airplane with two wings, one above the other
7. **blimp**—small air balloon, not rigid
8. **craft**—airplane
9. **dirigible**—airship
10. **glider**—airplane without an engine
11. **helicopter**—aircraft with propellers revolving around a vertical axis
12. **hydroplane**—airplane that lands on, and takes off from, water

13. **monoplane**—airplane with only one supporting surface
14. **plane**—airplane
15. **seaplane**—hydroplane
16. **zeppelin**—rigid airship; balloon that can be steered

2. Flier of, or in, Aircraft,n. *From Sec. 1:* airplanist, balloonist, monoplanist; *Also:*
1. **aeronaut**—operator of, or traveler in, a balloon or other aircraft
2. **aviator**—one who flies an aircraft
3. **pilot**—one who flies, or directs the flying of, an aircraft
4. **volplanist**—one who glides in an airplane

3. Pert. to Aircraft: aerial,adj.

4. Airport: aerodrome,n.

5. Shed for Aircraft: hangar,n.

99. RATE

1. Rate,n.
1. **acceleration**—rate of change in the speed of inanimate objects (mechanics)
2. **gradient**—rate of change
3. **pace**—rate of movement or speed
4. **permillage**—rate per thousand
5. **speed**—rate of movement, action, etc.
6. **tempo**—rate of movement, activity, action, etc.
7. **velocity**—rate of movement of inanimate things

2. One Who or That Which Sets a Rate: pacemaker, pacer,n.

3. Instrument to Measure Rate,n.
1. **accelerometer**—instrument for measuring acceleration of a moving vehicle
2. **decelerometer**—instrument that measures change in the rate of a vehicle that is slowing down
3. **speedometer**—instrument to measure the speed of a moving vehicle
4. **tachograph**—device that registers the speed of something
5. **tachometer**—instrument to measure speed, or the RPM of an engine
6. **tachymeter**—instrument for measuring the speed of a moving object
7. **velocimeter**—instrument for measuring the speed of inanimate things (engines, vessels, projectiles, etc.)

4. Measurement of the Speed of a Moving Object: tachometry, tachymetry,n.

5. Record of Rate,n.
1. **log**—record of the rate of a ship's speed or progress
2. **tachograph, tachogram**—record made of speed, or of engine RPM

6. Science of Rate Measurement: tachymetry,n.

7. Pert. to the Speed of Sound,adj.
1. **sonic**—pert. to the speed of sound traveling through air, approx. 738 miles per hour
2. **subsonic**—pert. to speeds slower than that of sound
3. **supersonic, ultrasonic**—pert. to speeds greater than that of sound
4. **transsonic**—pert. to the speed of sound in air, or to speeds between 600 and 900 miles per hour

100. SLOWNESS

1. To Move, Do, Act, Go., etc., Slowly,v.
1. **barge**—move slowly and in a clumsy or heavy manner
2. **crawl**—move slowly; move slowly and awkwardly on hands and knees; move slowly by dragging the body along the ground or floor; creep

3. **creep**—move slowly; move slowly on all fours; move, go, or act with extreme slowness
4. **delay**—move or go slowly
5. **forge**—move ahead slowly but steadily
6. **jog**—move slowly; move slowly and heavily
7. **loiter**—move slowly
8. **plow, plough**—move ahead slowly and laboriously
9. **prowl**—move about in a slow and stealthy, secret, or sneaky fashion, often looking for something to steal, take, eat, etc.
10. **slug**—move at a slow pace
11. **steal**—move slowly
12. **tarry**—move slowly; not move fast
13. **taxi**—move slowly (of a vehicle, or of a plane on the ground or on the surface of the water)
14. **trail**—move or go slowly
15. **work (up, down, through, in, out, etc.)**—move slowly and/or with great effort

2. Slow Movement, Action, etc.,n. *From Sec. 1:* crawl, creep, delay, jog, prowl

3. To Move, Do, Act, Go, etc., More Slowly, v.
1. **brake**—slow down
2. **decelerate**—move more slowly; decrease speed; slow down
3. **lag**—move or do something slower than expected, slower than others, slower than planned, etc.
4. **slack, slacken**—move or go more slowly; decrease speed
5. **slow down, slow up, slow**—move, go, do, act, etc., more slowly
6. **stall**—lose the speed necessary for maintaining itself in the air (of an airplane)
7. **trail**—lag

4. Slower Movement, Action, etc.,n. *From Sec. 3:* deceleration, lag, stall

5. To Cause to Move, etc., More Slowly,v. *From Sec. 3:* brake, decelerate, slack, slacken, slow down, slow up, slow (deceleration,n.); *Also:*
1. **delay**—make move, go, etc., more slowly (delay,n.)
2. **retard, retardate**—cause to go, etc., more slowly; slow down the progress of; slow down by placing hindrances in the path, progress, or advance of (retardation, retardance, retardence, retardment,n. retardant,n. retardative, retardatory, retardant, retardent,adj.)

6. Slow; Slow-Moving; Slower; Slowed,adj.
1. **backward**—not progressing with normal speed
2. **bovine**—slow (in allusion to an ox or cow)
3. **crawling**—slow-moving
4. **creeping, creepy**—characterized by slow motion; extremely slow in motion or action
5. **decelerated**—with the speed decreased; going or moving less quickly
6. **delayed**—slowed
7. **inert**—slow
8. **jogging**—moving slowly, or slowly and heavily
9. **laggard**—slow; slow-moving; not fast enough
10. **lagging**—moving, progressing, etc., more slowly than others, than expected, etc.
11. **leisurely**—not hurried; slow in the sense of taking plenty of time
12. **lentitudinous**—slow; slow-moving
13. **loitering**—moving slowly
14. **poky**—slow; moving with lazy slowness; slow and lazy
15. **retarded**—with its progress slowed down; slow in developing or maturing
16. **slack**—slow; slow-moving
17. **slackened**—slowed

18. **slackening**—decreasing in speed
19. **slow-footed**—moving or act at a very slow rate
20. **slowing**—decreasing in speed
21. **slowish**—somewhat or rather slow
22. **slow-paced**—moving or progressing at a very slow rate
23. **slow-witted**—mentally slow
24. **sluggard**—slow-moving
25. **sluggish**—slow-moving
26. **snail-like**—slow, like a snail
27. **snail-paced**—moving at a very slow rate, like a snail
28. **sullen**—sluggish
29. **tardigrade**—moving slowly; stepping slowly
30. **tardy**—slow; slow-moving
31. **tarrying**—moving slowly
32. **testudineous, testudinous**—slow-moving, like a turtle
33. **tortoise-like**—slow, like a tortoise
34. **trailing**—lagging
35. **turtle-like**—slow, like a turtle

7. Slowness,n. *From Sec. 6:* backwardness, bovinity, creepiness, inertness or inertia, leisureliness, lentitude, pokiness, retardation or retardment, slow-footedness, slow-wittedness, sluggishness, snail's pace, tardiness

8. Slow Person,n. *From Sec. 6:* laggard, loiterer, poke, snail, tarrier, tortoise, turtle; *Also:* 1. slowpoke—annoyingly slow person

9. Vehicle, Ship, etc., That Moves Slowly: slug,n.

10. Slow, in Music,adj. or adv. (Italian)
1. **allegretto**—slow, though faster than andante
2. **andante**—moderately slow, faster than larghetto
3. **andantino**—faster than andante, slower than allegretto
4. **larghetto**—rather slow, though less so than largo
5. **largo**—very slow
6. **lentamente**—slow
7. **lentando**—slowing down
8. **lentissimo**—very slow
9. **lento**—slow

11. Gradual: gradational or gradative (i.e., by regular steps or gradations); imperceptible (so gradual as to defy perception); piecemeal, step-by-step,adj.

12. State of Being Gradual: gradualness or graduality,n.

13. Gradually: bit by bit, by degrees, by slow degrees, drop by drop; gradatim (Latin); gradationally or gradatively (i.e., by regular steps or gradations); imperceptibly (so gradually as to defy perception); inch by inch, little by little, piece by piece, piecemeal, step by step,adv.

14. The Doctrine or Theory that It Is Best to Proceed Gradually toward a Desired Goal or Objective: gradualism,n. (gradualist,n. gradualistic,adj.)

101. BIOLOGICAL MOVEMENT

1. Movement of a Biological Organism,n.
1. **apheliotropism**—movement away from the sun (apheliotropic,adj.)
2. **chemotaxis, chemotaxy**—taxis in which a chemical substance (or substances) is the stimulating agent (chemotactic,adj.)
3. **chemotropism**—tropism in which a chemical substance (or substances) is the stimulating agent (chemotropic,adj.)
4. **geotaxis, geotaxy**—taxis in which gravitational force is the stimulating agent (geotactic,adj.)
5. **geotropism, geotropy**—tropism in which gravitational force is the stimulating agent (geotropic,adj.)

6. **heliotaxis**—taxis in which the light of the sun is the stimulating agent (heliotactic,adj.)
7. **heliotropism**—tropism in which the light of the sun is the stimulating agent (heliotropic, heliotropical,adj.)
8. **hydrotaxis**—taxis in which water is the stimulating agent (hydrotactic,adj.)
9. **hydrotropism**—tropism in which water is the stimulating agent (hydrotropic, adj.)
10. **photokinesis**—physiological motion or activity stimulated, caused, or provoked by light (photokinetic,adj.)
11. **phototaxis, phototaxy**—taxis in which light is the stimulating agent (phototactic,adj.)
12. **phototropism**—tropism in which light is the stimulating agent (phototropic,adj.)
13. **taxis**—movement to or away from a stimulating agent, usually involving a change of place (tactic,adj.)
14. **thermotaxis**—taxis in which heat is the stimulating agent (thermotaxic, thermotactic,adj.)
15. **thermotropism**—tropism in which change in temperature is the stimulating agent (thermotropic,adj.)
16. **tropism**—involuntary movement of a biological organism or any of its parts toward or away from a stimulating agent (tropistic, tropismatic, tropic,adj.)

2. Pert. to Stimulation by Light: photic,adj.

102. GESTURE

1. To Gesture,v.
1. **beck, beckon**—make a summoning gesture
2. **bow**—bend the head or body in gesture
3. **curtsy**—make a physical gesture of politeness or reverence (said of a woman)
4. **genuflect**—bend the knees to, as a mark of respect or worship
5. **gesticulate**—gesture; make gestures
6. **nod**—bend the head as a gesture of assent, summoning, etc., or in indication of drowsiness, inattention, etc.
7. **pantomime**—gesture without words to express something
8. **salaam**—bow very low to show respect or deference, with the palm of the hand placed on the forehead, as in the Orient
9. **salute**—make any of various gestures of honor or respect to
10. **shrug**—raise and contract the shoulders in a gesture to express dislike, doubt, indifference, annoyance, or similar feeling

2. Gesture; Gesturing,n. *From Sec. 1:* beck, beckon, bow, curtsy, genuflection, gesticulation, nod, pantomime or pantomimicry, salaam, salute or salutation, shrug; *Also:*
1. **nutation**—a nod, or a nodding, of the head
2. **obeisance**—gesture or gesturing indicative of deep respect

3. Gesturer,n. *From Sec. 1:* beckoner, genuflector, gesticulator, nodder, pantomimic; *Also:* 1. **pantomimist, pantomimic**—actor in a pantomime play

4. Gestural,adj. *From Sec. 1:* genuflectory; gesticulative, gesticulatory, or gesticular; pantomimic or pantomime, salutatory

5. Making a Gesture,adj. *From Sec. 2:* obeisant; *Also:* 1. **cernuous**—nodding; nodding the head

6. Author or Composer of a Pantomime Play: pantomimist,n.

7. Art of Gesturing with the Hands in Pantomime, Acting, Oratory, etc.: chironomy,n.

8. Art of Expressive Gestures or Bodily Movements, Esp. to Interpret Musical Compositions: eurhythmics, eurythmics,n.

9. Science of Communication by Gesture, Rather than in Words: kinesics,n.

10. To Play a Pantomime Part in a Drama, Sketch, etc.: mime,v. (mime, mimer,n.)

11. Pert. to Bodily Movements: gestic,adj.

103. BODILY EXERCISE

1. Bodily Exercise or Exercises,n.
1. **acrobatics**—gymnastics performed on a trapeze, tightrope, etc.
2. **athletics**—physical exercises
3. **calisthenics**—bodily exercises for improvement of health, posture, etc.
4. **gymnastics**—bodily exercise, especially as performed in a gymnasium
5. **hydrogymnastics**—energetic bodily exercises performed in water
6. **palaestra**—athletics or gymnastics in ancient times

2. Art, Practice, etc., of Bodily Exercise,n. *From Sec. 1:* acrobatics, athletics, calisthenics, gymnastics, hydrogymnastics; *Also:* 1. **agonistics**—art of athletic exercise

3. Pert. to, or Descr. of, Bodily Exercise, adj. *From Sec. 1:* acrobatic, athletic, calisthenic, gymnastic, hydrogymnastic

4. One Who Performs Exercises,n. *From Sec. 1:* acrobat, athlete, gymnast, hydrogymnast; *Also:*
1. **aerialist**—acrobat on a trapeze
2. **contortionist**—acrobat who twists his body or limbs into unnatural positions
3. **tumbler**—one who performs acrobatic tricks, esp. in public (tumble,v.)

5. Instrument to Exercise the Fingers,n.
1. **chirogymnast**—device used by pianists for exercising the fingers
2. **digitorium**—mock piano keyboard, used by pianists to exercise the fingers

104. HORSE MOVEMENTS

1. Horse Movements; Gait of a Horse,n.
1. **amble**—gait in which, in alternation, the legs of each side are moved simultaneously (amble,v.)
2. **canter**—gait with moderate bounds or leaps, slower than, though similar to, a gallop (canter,v.)
3. **capriole**—upward leap (capriole,v.)
4. **caracole**—half turn to either the left or right
5. **gallop**—fast and springing gait, in which all four legs are off the ground in each stride (gallop,v.)
6. **manège**—movement of a trained horse
7. **pace**—gait in which the legs move in alternating lateral pairs, one pair on the ground while the other is in the air
8. **prance**—capering movement from the hind legs (prance,v.)
9. **rack**—gait that is either pace or single-foot
10. **run**—rapid gallop (run,v.)
11. **single-foot**—gait in which each leg hits the ground singly, and the horse is alternately supported by one foot and two feet, the others being raised (single-foot, v.)
12. **stride**—the complete cycle of a horse's gait
13. **trot**—gait in which the legs move in diagonal pairs (trot,v.)
14. **walk**—gait in which there are always two feet on the ground (walk,v.)

105. RHYTHM

1. Rhythm,n.
1. cadence, cadency—rhythm
2. eurhythmy, eurythmy—pleasant rhythm
3. lilt—gay and swinging rhythm
4. measure—rhythm
5. meter, metre—rhythm in poetry
6. tempo—rhythm; characteristic rhythm

2. Rhythmical,adj. *From Sec. 1:* cadent; eurhythmic, eurythmical, eurythmic, or eurythmical; lilting, measured, metrical

3. To Beat; To Beat Rhythmically, etc.,v.
1. flutter—beat weakly and irregularly
2. palpitate—beat rapidly, strongly, steadily, or rhythmically; flutter
3. pant—pulsate; throb
4. pitter-patter—go through a succession of rapid and light beats
5. pulsate—beat rhythmically
6. pulse—beat regularly
7. throb—beat; beat rapidly and strongly; beat rhythmically, steadily, or painfully
8. thump—beat violently or noisily
9. tick—beat regularly and with little sound
10. vibrate—beat regularly

4. Beat or Beating,n. *From Sec. 3:* flutter, palpitation, pant, pitter-patter, pulsation, pulse, throb, thump, tick, vibration; *Also:*
1. cadence, cadency—rhythmical beat
2. stroke—beat; throb
3. tattoo—pulsation like the beating of a drum

5. Beating,adj. *From Sec. 3:* fluttering or fluttery, palpitating or palpitant, panting, pitter-patter or pitapat; pulsating, pulsatile, or pulsative; pulsing, throbbing, thumping, ticking; vibrating, vibrant, or vibratory; *From Sec. 4:* cadent

106. DRIVE

1. To Drive, i.e., Force or Cause to Move,v.
1. corner—drive into a place from which there is no escape
2. dislodge—drive from an occupied position (dislodgment,n.)
3. drift—drive into piles or heaps, as snow, etc. (drift, driftage,n.)
4. flush—drive (birds) out of hiding or cover
5. goad—drive (someone) on
6. impel—drive or drive forward, literally or, more commonly, figuratively (impulsion,n.)
7. lash—drive with, or as if with, a whip
8. propel—drive forward (propulsion,n.)
9. urge—drive; drive forward with effort; drive forward with threats, force, etc.

2. That Which Drives,n. *From Sec. 1:* goad, impellent or impulse, lash; propeller, propellant, propellent, propulsion or propulsor; urge; *Also:* drift, impetus, pressure

3. Driving,adj. *From Sec. 1:* goading; impulsive, impellent, or impelling; propellent, propulsive, propulsory, or propelling

4. Driving Force or Movement: drift,n.

5. To Be Driven Along by, or as if by, Air, Wind, Water, etc.; To Be Driven into Piles or Heaps, as Snow, etc.: drift,v. (drift, driftage,n.)

6. Matter That Has Been So Driven: driftage,n.

7. Bird, or Flock of Birds, Driven out of Cover: flush,n.

107. WALK

1. To Walk,v.
1. amble—walk about aimlessly and slowly or with an easy and purposeless pace
2. ambulate—walk
3. bestraddle—bestride
4. bestride—walk across or over; walk with the legs spread apart
5. canter—walk with moderate bounds or leaps
6. clump—walk clumsily
7. debouch—march out from a narrow or closed-in place into open territory (usually of an army or military unit)
8. defile—walk or march in a line
9. hike—walk some distance
10. hobble—walk in an awkwardly lame or limping manner
11. lag—walk slowly and thus fall behind others
12. limp—walk lamely; walk as if one or both feet were lame or had defects; walk with a halting and awkward gait; walk with difficulty
13. march—walk in a grave or dignified fashion; walk in step with others
14. mince—walk with little and dainty steps
15. pace—walk over with careful steps; walk up and down or back and forth
16. pad—walk with dull or quiet and steady steps; walk quietly or softly
17. paddle—toddle
18. parade—walk in public with others; walk in public with a good deal of ostentation
19. pat—walk with a light sound
20. patter—walk with rapid, light footsteps
21. peacock—strut
22. perambulate—walk about
23. pitter-patter—patter
24. plod—walk heavily, slowly, or laboriously
25. prance—walk proudly, gaily, boastfully, etc.
26. promenade—walk for pleasure or relaxation
27. reel—walk unsteadily, often swaying from side to side
28. saunter—walk about with no destination; walk in an aimless, slow, or leisurely manner
29. scuff—walk without lifting the feet from the ground
30. shamble—walk unsteadily or clumsily
31. shuffle—walk without lifting the feet from the ground
32. skip—trip
33. slog—walk heavily, because the feet meet, or as if the feet were meeting, resistance on the ground
34. slouch—walk in a drooping, overrelaxed, awkward, or stooping manner
35. stagger—reel from dizziness, drunkenness, a heavy burden, etc.
36. stalk—walk in a stiff, proud manner
37. step—walk; walk with slow, graceful, or deliberate movements
38. stoop—walk with the head and shoulders bent forward
39. straddle—walk with the legs spread apart
40. stride—walk in long steps
41. stroll—walk aimlessly or in a leisurely way
42. strut—walk in a conceited, self-important, or haughty manner
43. stumble—walk clumsily or unsteadily
44. swagger—walk in a conceited, bold, impolite, or superior manner
45. sweep—walk in long robes that trail after one; walk in a proud or stately manner
46. tiptoe—walk very quietly or secretly, on, or as if on, the tips of one's toes
47. toddle—walk like an infant just learning, that is, in short, uncertain steps
48. trail—walk in, or as if in, fatigue, weariness, or reluctance
49. traipse—walk without purpose; walk idly (colloq.)
50. tramp—walk heavily
51. trample—walk on heavily and thus bruise, injure, or crush

52. **traverse**—walk in a crosswise direction
53. **tread**—walk on, through, or over (past tense: trod; past participle: trod or trodden)
54. **trek**—walk slowly or with difficulty
55. **trip**—walk with light and rapid steps
56. **troop**—walk; walk with others to the same place; march
57. **trudge**—walk wearily or with great effort
58. **waddle**—walk like a duck, that is, in short steps and with a swaying motion
59. **wade (through)**—walk through (a medium that obstructs free movement, as water, snow, etc.)

2. A Walk; Manner of Walking,n. *From Sec. 1:* amble, canter, clump, hike, hobble, limp, march, pad, paddle, parade, patter, prance, promenade, reel, saunter, scuff, shamble, shuffle, skip, slog, slouch, stagger, stalk, stoop, straddle, stride, stroll, strut, stumble, swagger, sweep, toddle, tramp, trample, tread, trek, trudge, waddle; *Also:*
1. **constitutional**—walk taken as a health measure
2. **gait**—manner of walking
3. **titubation**—unsteady, staggering walk occurring in some nervous afflictions
4. **whirl**—short walk

3. Act of Walking,n. *From Sec. 1:* ambulation, debouchment, perambulation, traversal; *Also:*
1. **noctambulism**—walking by night (may or may not imply sleepwalking)
2. **somnambulism, somnambulation**—sleep-walking

4. Walking; Given to Walking,adj. *From Sec. 1:* ambulant or ambulatory, perambulatory; *From Sec. 3:* noctambulant or noctambulous, somnambulant or somnambulistic; *Also:*
1. **afoot**—walking
2. **biped**—walking upright on two limbs
3. **digitigrade**—walking on the digits or front part of the foot only (descr. of certain animals)
4. **itinerant**—walking from place to place in the conduct of one's business
5. **knock-kneed, valgus**—walking with the knees bent in and touching, or almost touching, each other
6. **on foot**—walking
7. **peripatetic**—walking around from place to place in the conduct of one's business (as a traveling teacher, visiting nurse, etc.)
8. **plantigrade**—walking by placing both the sole and heel of the foot simultaneously on the ground (descr. of certain animals)
9. **quadruped**—walking on four feet
10. **slipshod**—walking without lifting one's feet from the ground
11. **taligrade**—walking with the weight on the ankles

5. One Who Walks or Is Given to Walking, n. *From Sec. 1:* ambler or ambulator, hiker, hobbler, lagger or laggard, limper, marcher, parader, perambulator, plodder, prancer, promenader, saunterer, shuffler, skipper, sloucher, strider, stroller, strutter, swaggerer, toddler, trampler, trooper, trudger, waddler, wader; *From Sec. 3:* noctambulist or noctambule, somnambulist; *From Sec. 4:* biped, quadruped; *Also:*
1. **funambulist**—one who walks a tightrope, as in a circus
2. **passer-by**—one who walks by
3. **pedestrian**—one who walks, walks around, or gets to a destination by walking

6. Adapted to or for Walking,adj.
1. **gradient**—adapted to walking
2. **gressorial**—adapted for walking (said of the feet of certain birds and insects)

7. Able to Walk, i.e., Not Bedridden: ambulatory,adj.
8. Unable to Walk Properly: crippled, lame, adj. (lameness,n. cripple,n.)
9. A Walk, i.e., a Place to Walk or for Walking,n.
1. **alameda**—public walk or promenade (so called in the Southwest)
2. **alley**—walk in a garden or park
3. **ambulatory**—covered walk
4. **boardwalk**—walk of planking; promenade near or at the beach
5. **catwalk**—narrow walk along a bridge
6. **cloister**—covered walk
7. **crossing**—paved walk across a street
8. **crosswalk**—crossing
9. **esplanade**—public open place for walking
10. **gallery**—covered space for walking; roofed promenade
11. **mall**—shaded public walk
12. **parade**—public walk
13. **portico**—covered walk, formed by a roof on columns
14. **promenade**—public place for walking
15. **sidewalk**—walk by the side of a road or street

10. Device to Measure Walking,n.
1. **odograph**—device for measuring and recording the steps taken by a walker
2. **pedograph**—instrument carried while walking to record the topography of one's journey
3. **pedometer**—instrument carried while walking to record the distance traveled

108. STEP

1. To Step,v.
1. **skip**—step lightly
2. **tiptoe**—step softly and lightly
3. **tramp**—step heavily
4. **trip**—step lightly

2. To Step on,v.
1. **scotch**—stamp
2. **stamp (on)**—step on forcibly
3. **tramp (on)**—step on hard and repeatedly
4. **trample (on)**—step on heavily and thus bruise, injure, or crush; stamp on or down
5. **tread**—step on; trample

3. To Step over: bestride,v.

4. A Step,n.
1. **footpace**—step by foot
2. **footstep**—step in walking
3. **pace**—step in walking
4. **skip**—trip
5. **tramp**—heavy step
6. **tread**—footstep
7. **trip**—light, quick step

5. Moving Step by Step: gradient,adj.

109. DANCE

1. Dance, i.e., Type of Dance,n.
1. **ballet**—elaborate stage dance, often telling a story
2. **buck and wing**—American Negro clog dance
3. **cakewalk**—stage dance developed from an American Negro form
4. **cancan**—stage dance of French origin characterized by high kicking
5. **Charleston**—kind of dance in four-four time, characterized by kicking heels, popular in the 1920's
6. **clog dance**—dance in which wooden-soled shoes are used to tap out rhythm on the floor
7. **conga**—kind of Cuban dance
8. **contredanse, contradance**—dance in which the participants are arranged in

two lines, the partners facing each other; earlier form of the quadrille

9. **cotillon**—complicated dance at a formal ball, in which the dancers follow the lead of a single couple
10. **country dance**—British contredanse
11. **fandango**—Spanish or Latin-American dance, performed by a single couple and with castanets
12. **fling**—lively dance with gestures
13. **folk dance**—dance originating among the masses and transmitted from generation to generation
14. **fox trot**—ballroom dance in four-four time
15. **german**—intricate type of dance involving suddenly changing steps
16. **habanera**—voluptuous dance imported from Africa and popular in Cuba
17. **Highland fling**—folk dance popular among inhabitants of the Scottish Highlands, involving three or four dancers, and characterized by high kicking
18. **hornpipe**—lively and animated dance, popular among sailors, usually done by one person to the accompaniment of hornpipes
19. **hula, hula-hula**—native Hawaiian dance, often of lascivious character, performed by women to the accompaniment of drumbeats and chanting
20. **jig**—kind of lively dance
21. **lindy**—jazz version of the fox trot
22. **mambo**—Puerto Rican ritual dance
23. **mazurka**—kind of Polish dance
24. **paso-doble**—dance representing a Spanish bullfight
25. **peabody**—fast fox trot
26. **polka**—lively hopping dance of Bohemian origin
27. **polonaise**—stately Polish dance
28. **promenade**—opening dance of a formal ball
29. **quadrille**—square dance of five figures
30. **reel**—animated dance of circular figures performed with gliding movements; Virginia reel
31. **round dance**—country dance in which the participants form a ring; ballroom dance in which the partners move counterclockwise around the room
32. **rumba**—Cuban Negro dance of violent movements
33. **samba**—Brazilian dance derived from an African dance
34. **saraband**—rude, lively, often somewhat sensual Spanish dance performed with castanets
35. **schottische**—nineteenth-century round dance with hopping and gliding steps, similar to, but slower than, the polka
36. **shimmy**—jazz dance characterized by shaking of the body
37. **square dance**—dance in which the performers are arranged in a square
38. **tango**—Latin-American ballroom dance in four-four time
39. **tap dance**—dance tapped out audibly by the soles of the shoes
40. **tarantella**—lively Neapolitan folk dance
41. **toe dance**—dance performed on the tips of the toes
42. **two-step**—ballroom dance done in march or polka time
43. **Virginia reel**—country dance for any number of participants
44. **waltz**—kind of round dance in three-quarter time in which the partners whirl around
45. **zarabanda**—saraband

2. To Dance,v. *From Sec. 1:* cakewalk, Charleston, conga, cotillon, fox-trot, jig, lindy, polonaise, promenade, quadrille, rumba, samba, schottische, square-dance, tango, tapdance, toe-dance; *Also:*

1. **frisk**—dance around in a playful manner
2. **shuffle**—dance while scraping or dragging the feet

3. **Group of Steps in a Dance:** figure,n.

4. **Dancing,**n.
   1. **choregraphy**—dancing; stage dancing
   2. **choreography**—ballet dancing
   3. **eurhythmics, eurythmics**—kind of dancing that depends on musical patterns, phrasing, etc.
   4. **saltation**—dancing marked by leaping or jumping

5. **A Dance, i.e., the Holding of a Dance,**n.
   1. **ball**—formal dance
   2. **masquerade, masquerade ball**—formal dance in which the participants dress in fancy costumes, wear masks, etc.
   3. **prom**—dance given by a college or high-school class

6. **Dancer,**n.
   1. **artiste**—professional dancer
   2. **ballerina**—professional female ballet dancer
   3. **choreographer**—ballet dancer
   4. **chorine**—female member of a professional dancing group
   5. **clog dancer**—one who taps out the rhythm of a dance with wooden shoes or soles
   6. **coryphee**—female ballet dancer; leader of a ballet
   7. **danseuse**—female ballet dancer
   8. **funambulist**—one who dances on a tightrope
   9. **geisha, geisha girl**—professional Japanese dancing and singing girl
   10. **nautch girl**—professional dancing girl of India
   11. **tap dancer**—one who taps out dances audibly with the toes or heels of the shoes
   12. **taxi dancer**—girl in a public dance hall who, for so much a dance, dances with patrons
   13. **terpsichorean, terpsichore**—dancer
   14. **toe dancer**—one who dances on the tips of the toes

7. **Dancing Group,**n.
   1. **chorus**—organized group of dancers and singers
   2. **corps de ballet (French)**—company of ballet dancers

8. **Frenzied Dance:** corybantic,n.

9. **Dancing:** saltant,adj.

10. **Pert. to Dancing or Dancers,**adj.
    1. **choreographic**—pert. to ballet dancing or to a ballet dancer or dancers
    2. **gestic**—pert. to bodily motions in dancing
    3. **saltatorial**—pert. to, or marked by, dancing
    4. **saltatory**—pert. to dancing
    5. **terpsichorean, terpsichoreal**—pert. to dancing

11. **The Writing or Arranging of Dances for the Ballet:** choreography, choregraphy,n. (choreographer,n.)

12. **Ballet Enthusiast:** balletomane,n.

13. **Medical Affliction Marked by an Uncontrollable Desire to Dance, by Melancholy and by Stupor:** tarantism,n. (tarantist,n.)

14. **Art of Representing Dancing by Symbols:** choregraphy,n.

15. **Muse of Dancing and Choral Song:** Terpsichore,n.

110. JUMP

1. **To Jump,**v.
   1. **boggle**—jump with fright
   2. **bounce**—jump like a ball; jump suddenly

3. **bound**—jump; jump quickly or suddenly
4. **buck**—jump jerkily; jump into the air with the back stiffly curved and land with the legs straight and taut (of horses)
5. **canter**—move in moderate jumps
6. **caper**—jump around lightly or joyously
7. **capriole**—jump in dancing; jump upward (of a horse)
8. **carom**—rebound after striking
9. **cavort**—jump around in high humor
10. **curvet**—jump; bound; jump with the forelegs first, then finally the hind legs, so that all four legs are off the ground at the same time (of a horse)
11. **dance**—jump up and down
12. **frisk**—jump around in a playful manner
13. **gambol**—skip about playfully
14. **hop**—jump in quick and short movements
15. **hurdle**—jump over while running
16. **jounce**—bounce around in riding
17. **leap**—jump
18. **lollop**—jump; bound
19. **plummet**—jump down heavily and suddenly
20. **plunge**—jump (into, or as if into, water)
21. **pounce**—jump upon suddenly
22. **rebound**—jump back to previous position
23. **recoil**—jump back
24. **ricochet**—jump or skip (said of something hitting along a surface, rebounding or jumping away, hitting again, then again rebounding, etc.)
25. **skip**—jump lightly; go jumping or bounding along a surface
26. **somersault, summersault, somerset**—jump in such a way as to turn head over heels
27. **spring**—jump
28. **start**—jump suddenly in, or as if in, surprise or fear
29. **startle**—start
30. **submerge, submerse**—jump into water
31. **take off**—jump from the ground
32. **trip**—skip
33. **upspring**—jump into the air
34. **vault**—jump; jump over with the help of a pole; jump on or over, using the hands

2. A Jump; A Jumping,n. *From Sec. 1:* boggle, bounce, bound, buck, canter, caper, capriole, carom; curvet (of a horse); dance, frisk, gambol, hop, hurdle, jounce, leap, lollop, plummet, plunge, pounce, rebound, recoil, ricochet, skip; somersault, summersault, or somerset; spring, start, startle, submergence or submersion, take-off, upspring, vault; *Also:*
1. **breach**—jump of a whale out of water
2. **saltation**—a jumping forward; a jumping; a jump

3. Tending to Jump,adj.
1. **frisky**—tending to jump around in a playful manner (friskiness,n.)
2. **jumpy, skittish**—tending to jump nervously (jumpiness, skittishness,n.)
3. **transilient**—tending to jump suddenly from one thing to another, figuratively speaking (transilience,n.)

4. Jumping: saltant,adj.

5. Able to Spring Back into Shape or Position: buoyant, elastic, resilient, springy,adj. (buoyancy, elasticity, resilience or resiliency, spring or springiness,n.)

6. Capable of Springing Back to Original Shape when Pressed, etc., Like Rubber: rubbery,adj. (rubberiness,n.)

7. Able to Spring Back into Shape when Squeezed: spongy,adj. (sponginess,n.)

8. Adapted to or for Jumping,adj.
1. **saltatorial, saltatory**—adapted to jumping
2. **saltigrade**—descr. of those animals whose feet or legs are adapted for jumping

9. Of the Nature of, or Characterized by, Jumping: saltatorial, saltatory,adj.

10. To Cause to Jump,v.
1. **bounce**—cause to jump like a ball
2. **jounce**—cause to bounce around while riding
3. **skip**—send jumping along a surface
4. **startle**—cause to jump with fear or surprise

111. SHAKE

1. To Shake; To Tremble,v.
1. **bicker**—shake; tremble
2. **churn**—shake violently
3. **convulse**—shake in irregular spasms
4. **dangle**—shake jerkily while hanging
5. **dodder**—shake or tremble, generally as a result of weakness or old age
6. **flicker**—shake; shake involuntarily; shake back and forth in short, quick movements
7. **flutter**—tremble; vibrate
8. **jiggle**—shake in quick, nervous movements
9. **jog**—shake slightly
10. **joggle**—shake slightly
11. **jolt**—shake up and down while moving
12. **jounce**—be shaken up roughly in riding
13. **librate**—vibrate in balance
14. **oscillate**—vibrate
15. **palpitate**—shake; tremble
16. **pulsate**—shake; tremble; vibrate
17. **quake**—shake; tremble; shudder
18. **quaver**—shake; tremble
19. **quiver**—shake; tremble
20. **ripple**—undulate
21. **rock**—shake violently; totter; vibrate
22. **shimmy**—shake or vibrate abnormally
23. **shiver**—tremble; shake from, or as from, fear, cold, illness, etc.
24. **shudder**—tremble convulsively from fear or horror
25. **thrill**—tremble; vibrate
26. **throb**—vibrate
27. **totter**—shake as if about to fall
28. **twiddle**—tremble
29. **twitter**—tremble with excitement; feel a nervous tremble
30. **undulate**—shake in a wavy motion
31. **vibrate**—shake rapidly back and forth; tremble
32. **wag**—shake
33. **waggle**—shake from side to side
34. **waver**—shake; tremble
35. **wiggle**—shake with quick jerks from side to side
36. **wobble, wabble**—shake; tremble

2. A Shaking; A Trembling; A Shake; A Tremble,n. *From Sec. 1:* bicker, churn, convulsion, dangle, dodder, flicker, flutter, jiggle, jog, joggle, jolt, jounce, libration, oscillation, palpitation, pulsation, quake, quaver, quiver, ripple, rock, shimmy, shiver, shudder, throb, thrill, totter, twiddle, twitter, undulation, vibration, wag, waggle, waver, wiggle, wobble, wabble; *Also:*
1. **ague**—a shaking
2. **concussion**—a shaking; a violent shaking
3. **crispation**—muscular quiver
4. **jactation**—a shaking
5. **tremor**—a tremble; fit of trembling
6. **trepidation**—a trembling; a trembling from fear

3. Shaking; Trembling; Atremble,adj. *From Sec. 1:* bickering, churning, dangling or adangle, flickering or aflicker, fluttering or aflutter, jiggling, jogging, joggling, jouncing, oscillating, palpitating, quaking, quavering, quivering or aquiver, rippling or aripple, rocking, shivering or ashiver, shuddering, throbbing, tottering, twiddling, twittering or atwitter, undulating, vibrating, wagging or awag, waggling, wavering, wiggling or awiggle, wobbling, wabbling; *Also:*

1. **aspen**—trembling
2. **blubbery**—shaking like jelly
3. **lambent**—flickering; flickering lightly
4. **tremulous, tremulant, tremulent**—trembling; trembling with fear (tremulousness,n.)

4. Shaky; Trembly; Characterized by, of the Nature of, or Given to, Shaking or Trembling; Tending to Shake or Tremble, adj. *From Sec. 1:* convulsive, convulsional, or convulsionary; dangly, doddery, flickery, fluttery, jiggly, joggly, jolty, jouncy, oscillatory, palpitant; pulsative, pulsatory, pulsatile, pulsational; quaky, quavery, quivery, ripply, rocky, shivery, shuddery, tottery, twiddly, twittery; undulatory, undulant, undulative, undulate; vibrant or vibratory, waggy, waggly, wavery, wiggly, wobbly, wabbly (pulsatility, vibrancy,n.); *From Sec. 3:* tremulous, tremulant, or tremulent (tremulousness,n.); *Also:*
1. **aspen**—tremulous
2. **blubbery**—shaky, like jelly
3. **lambent**—characterized by flickering (lambency,n.)
4. **ramshackle**—shaky and loose
5. **rickety**—shaky (ricketiness,n.)
6. **unsteady**—shaky (unsteadiness,n.)

5. To Shake (Someone or Something); To Cause to Shake, v. *From Sec. 1:* churn, convulse, dangle, flicker, flutter, jiggle, jog, joggle, jolt, jounce, oscillate, ripple, rock, thrill, twiddle, vibrate, wag, waggle, wiggle (convulsive,adj.); *Also:*
1. **agitate**—shake violently (agitation,n.)
2. **brandish**—shake or wave threateningly (brandish,n. brandisher,n.)
3. **flourish**—brandish (flourish,n. flourisher, n.)
4. **jar**—shake; make shake from an impact, blow, etc. (jar,n. jarring,adj.)
5. **jerk**—give a sudden quick shake to (jerk, n. jerky,adj.)
6. **jolt**—shake suddenly and somewhat forcibly (jolt,n. jolting,adj.)
7. **nod**—shake (the head); shake the head in agreement or assent (nod,n. nodding, adj.)
8. **stagger**—cause to tremble (staggering, adj.)
9. **succuss**—shake forcibly (succussion, succussation,n. successive, successatory, adj.)
10. **wave**—shake in the air
11. **worry**—seize and shake with the teeth

112. FLOW

1. To Flow, v.
1. **deluge**—flow over; flow over the land (of water)
2. **ebb**—flow back
3. **flood**—flow over; flow over onto land (of a body of water not ordinarily in contact with the land)
4. **gurgle**—flow in an irregular and noisy current
5. **gush**—flow suddenly and in great amounts
6. **inundate**—flow over completely; flow over completely, covering with water
7. **lave**—flow along or against (poetic)
8. **ooze**—flow along or against (poetic)
9. **overflow**—flow over
10. **pour**—flow
11. **purl**—flow in swirls and/or with a murmuring sound; flow around obstructions
12. **recede**—flow back
13. **regurgitate**—flow back forcibly; flow out again forcibly
14. **spout**—flow out forcibly
15. **spurt**—flow out suddenly and/or rapidly; gush
16. **stream**—flow steadily
17. **swamp**—deluge

18. **trickle**—flow in drops or in a very thin or slow manner
19. **wash**—flow in a current or stream
20. **well**—flow

2. A Flowing; A Flow, n. *From Sec. 1:* deluge, ebb, flood, gurgle, gush, inundation, ooze, overflow, pour, purl, recession, regurgitation, spout, spurt, stream, trickle, wash; *Also:*
1. **affluence**—a flowing toward or to; inflow
2. **afflux, affluxion**—a flowing (of something) to or toward
3. **alluvion**—flow of water against the shore; flooding; overflow
4. **backflow**—a flowing back; backward flow
5. **breach**—a flowing of water over
6. **confluence, conflux**—a flowing together
7. **current**—a flowing; flow
8. **defluxion**—flow, or a flowing, downward; downflow of fluids in the body
9. **downflow**—a flowing down; downward flow
10. **downpour**—downflow
11. **efflux**—outflow
12. **emanation**—a flowing forth
13. **flux**—a flowing; flow; copious flow; outflow
14. **fluxion**—a flowing; flow; unnatural or unhealthy flow of blood or fluid toward an organ of the body
15. **hydrorrhea**—excessive flow of a watery liquid in the body
16. **inflow**—a flowing in; inward flow
17. **influx**—inflow
18. **inpour**—inflow
19. **outflow**—a flowing out; outward flow
20. **outpour**—outflow
21. **profluence**—onward or forward flow
22. **profluvium**—outflow
23. **refluence**—reflux
24. **reflux**—a flowing back; backward flow
25. **torrent**—flow; rapid or violent flow; strong flow; flood
26. **transflux**—a flowing, or flow, across, beyond, or through

3. Flowing, adj. *From Sec. 1:* ebbing, flooding, gurgling, gushing, inundating or inundant, oozing, overflowing, pouring, purling, receding or recessive, regurgitating; regurgitant (medical); spouting, streaming, trickling; *From Sec. 2:* affluent, backflowing, confluent, defluent or defluous, downflowing, downpouring, effluent, fluent, inflowing or influent, inpouring, outflowing, outpouring, refluent or reflux, torrential or torrent, transfluent (fluency,n.); *Also:*
1. **affluent**—flowing in abundance
2. **circumfluent, circumfluous**—flowing around
3. **decurrent**—flowing downward
4. **excurrent**—flowing outward
5. **mellifluous, mellifluent**—flowing smoothly or sweetly
6. **profluent**—flowing smoothly or abundantly in, or as if in, a stream
7. **superfluent**—flowing above; flowing on the top or from the top
8. **tributary**—flowing into a larger stream or body of water

4. That Which Flows, n. *From Sec. 1:* ooze, overflow, stream, trickle; *From Sec. 2:* backflow, defluent, downflow, downpour, efflux or effluence, emanation, fluxion, inflow, influent, inpour, outflow, outpour; *From Sec. 3:* profluent; *Also:* 1. **effluvium, efflux**—that which flows out as a vapor or odor

5. Capable of Flowing: fluent, fluid,adj. (fluency, fluidity,n.)

6. Overflowed by Water: awash,adj.

7. Flood: alluvion, cataclysm, cataract, deluge, inundation, tide, torrent,n.

8. Flood Caused in a Stream by Heavy Melting Snow or Rain: freshet,n.

9. Pert. to, or Descr. of, a Flood: cataclysmal, cataclysmic, cataractal, cataractine, diluvial, diluvian, tidal, torrential,adj.

10. After the Biblical Flood: post-diluvial, adj.

11. Before the Biblical Flood: ante-diluvian, adj.

113. FLOAT

1. To Float, i.e., Be or Send Floating: drift (as in water or on air) ; waft (esp. on air),v. (drifter, wafter,n.)

2. To Set (a Vessel) Afloat: launch,v. (launcher,n.)

3. Floating; State of Floating: drift, driftage, flotage or floatage, flotation or floatation, waft, waftage,n.

4. Act or Process of Floating: drift, driftage, flotage or floatage, flotation or floatation, natation; waft, waftage, wafture,n.

5. Act of Floating on the Top or Surface: supernatation,n.

6. Act of Sending Floating: flotage or floatage, flotation or floatation; waft, waftage, wafture,n.

7. The Floating of Bonds, Stocks, etc., on the Market: flotation,n. (float,v.)

8. Floating: adrift, afloat; awaft (esp. on air) ; natant,adj.; *Also:*
 1. awash—floating in water
 2. fluctuant—floating on the waves
 3. supernatant—floating on the top or surface

9. Art of Floating: natation,n.

10. Power to Float: flotage or floatage,n.

11. Able to Float: buoyant,adj. (buoyancy,n.)

12. That Which Is Floating,n.
 1. driftage—anything floating, esp. in water
 2. driftwood—wood floating in, and carried by, water; figuratively, anything floating as if on or in water
 3. float—something that floats on the surface
 4. flotage, floatage—something floating; floating things or substances
 5. flotsam—floating wreckage of a vessel and/or cargo; driftage
 6. flotsam and jetsam—wreckage of a vessel and/or cargo found either floating on the water or washed upon the land
 7. supernatant—any substance floating on the surface

13. One Who Floats, Figuratively Speaking, from Place to Place, with No Permanent or Continuous Residence: drifter, floater,n.

14. Persons Figuratively Floating Around with No Permanent Residence, Often Unemployed or Disinclined to Work, etc.: flotsam, flotsam and jetsam,n.

114. SWIMMER

1. Swimmer,n.
 1. mermaid—beautiful girl swimmer
 2. naiad—girl swimmer (in Greek mythology naiads were nymphs who lived in streams and rivers)
 3. natator—swimmer

2. To Swim toward the Bottom: sound,v.

3. Swimming: natant, natatorial,adj.

4. Act or Art of Swimming: natation,n.

5. Pert. to, Descr. of, Adapted for, or Used in, Swimming: natatorial, natatory,adj.

6. Indoor Swimming Pool: natatorium,n.

7. Water Sports (Including Swimming): nautics,n.

115. WATERCRAFT

1. Watercraft (Generic),n.
 1. boat—watercraft; small watercraft; small watercraft attached to, or used by, a larger one
 2. craft—vessel
 3. ship—larger watercraft not propelled by oars
 4. vessel—watercraft that is larger than a rowboat; boat; ship

2. Boats, Ships, and Vessels, Collectively: craft,pl. n.

3. Boats (Selected),n.
 1. ark—clumsy boat
 2. barge—boat; flat-bottomed, roomy boat; pleasure boat; flag officer's personal boat
 3. canoe—small, light boat propelled by paddle
 4. craft—boat
 5. cutter—ship's boat with a broad, square stern
 6. dinghy—small rowboat; small two- or four-oared boat for communication with the shore; small, undecked racing boat
 7. dory—flat-bottomed small boat with a sharp bow
 8. gig—commanding officer's personal boat
 9. kayak—Eskimo canoe
 10. punt—flat-bottomed boat with square ends, used primarily for painting and repairs
 11. rowboat—small open boat propelled by oars
 12. sampan—Chinese boat; skiff, usually propelled by a scull, sometimes by sail, used in the waters of Japan and China and neighboring islands
 13. scull—racing boat for one or two rowers, each pulling two oars
 14. skiff—light rowboat
 15. tender—boat used to communicate between shore and a larger vessel; boat used to bring provisions, etc., to a larger vessel
 16. trawler—fishing boat
 17. umiak—open Eskimo boat
 18. wherry—lightly built boat pulling two or four oars
 19. yawl—ship's small boat

4. To Go by, or Ride in, a Boat: boat,v. (boating,n. boater,n.)

5. To Carry or Transport in or by Boat: boat,v.

6. Skill in Maneuvering, Steering, Using, etc., Boats: boatmanship,n. (boatman,n.)

7. Vessels (Selected),n.
 1. argosy—large merchant vessel
 2. ark—large flush-decked, full-bellied vessel; large flatboat
 3. barge—pleasure vessel
 4. bathysphere—vessel for diving to the depths of a sea for purposes of observation of fish life, etc.
 5. bottom—vessel
 6. cabin cruiser—power vessel so built and appointed (i.e., containing a cabin, etc.) that one or more people may live on it (generally privately owned and used for pleasure)
 7. craft—vessel
 8. cruiser—vessel; vessel that carries "round-trip" passengers exclusively or primarily; pleasure vessel with living accommodations; cabin cruiser
 9. ferry, ferryboat—boat used to carry passengers, vehicles, etc., over a river or other narrow body of water
 10. flatboat—vessel with a flat bottom, used for heavy freight in shallow waters
 11. freighter—vessel used for transporting cargo
 12. galley—large, low vessel used in ancient

times, in the Middle Ages, and in later times

13. **lighter**—large boat used to carry goods to or from a vessel not tied up at a dock (lighterage,n. lighter,v.)
14. **liner**—one of a fleet of commercial vessels, as *ocean liner*, etc.
15. **merchantman**—merchant vessel
16. **packet**—vessel; vessel transporting mail, passengers, etc., and having regular days of departure and arrival
17. **scow**—large flat-bottomed, square-ended vessel for carrying refuse to the point of disposal, or goods to and from another vessel
18. **ship**—vessel
19. **steamboat**—vessel propelled by steam along the coast or inland waterways (steam, steamboat,v. steamboating,n.)
20. **steamer, steamship**—vessel, usually seagoing, propelled by steam (steam,v.)
21. **tug, tugboat**—vessel used to tow larger vessels
22. **warship**—armed vessel used in attack on, or defense against, enemy vessels
23. **yacht**—privately owned pleasure vessel

8. To Go on Board a Vessel: embark, ship, v. (embarkation, embarcation,n.)

9. To Receive, or Put, on Board a Vessel: embark,v. (embarkation, embarcation,n.)

10. Operator of a Ferry: Charon (humorous), ferryman,n. (charonian, charonic,adj.)

11. One Who Works on, Operates, Makes, or Sells Vessels: boatman, waterman,n.

12. Builder of Vessels: shipbuilder,n. (shipbuilding,n.)

13. To Send or Transport by Vessel: ship,v. (shipping,n. shipper,n.)

14. Galley,n.
  1. **bireme**—galley with two banks of oars
  2. **quadrireme**—galley with four banks of oars
  3. **quinquereme**—galley with five banks of oars
  4. **trireme**—galley with three banks of oars

15. Pirate Ship: brigantine (formerly), corsair, rover,n.

16. Naval Vessels; Warships (Selected),n.
  1. **aircraft carrier**—naval vessel that carries aircraft
  2. **battleship**—one of the largest and heaviest kind of armed and armored warship
  3. **corvette**—small sailing warship of earlier times; modern escort or patrolling naval vessel
  4. **cruiser**—warship less heavily armed and armored than a battleship but faster; fast naval vessel, unarmored or thinly armored, with guns of less than ten inches' diameter of bore
  5. **destroyer**—originally a torpedo-boat destroyer; now a small, fast, anti-submarine and patrol vessel, larger than a modern corvette or frigate
  6. **dreadnaught**—kind of battleship
  7. **flagship**—naval vessel on which the commander of a fleet or squadron rides, and which carries his flag
  8. **flattop**—aircraft carrier
  9. **frigate**—warship of the era of sail that carried some of her guns mounted below the upper deck; modern escort or patrolling naval vessel
  10. **gunboat**—light armed naval vessel
  11. **man-of-war**—warship
  12. **submarine**—underwater naval vessel, usually armed with torpedoes, often with deck guns
  13. **U-Boat**—German submarine; by extension, any submarine

17. Private Armed Ship with the Privilege of Sailing against the Commercial Ships or Warships of an Enemy in Times of War: corsair (esp. along the Barbary coast), privateer,n. (privateer,v. privateer, privateersman,n.)

18. Group of Naval Vessels,n.
  1. **armada**—fleet
  2. **division**—small group of naval vessels of similar type; smallest homogeneous group of naval vessels
  3. **fleet**—group of naval vessels; such a group under one commander
  4. **flotilla**—small fleet
  5. **navy**—naval vessels of a country
  6. **squadron**—large group of naval vessels of similar type or function
  7. **task force**—group of naval vessels gathered under one command to perform a specific mission

19. Pert. to Vessels of War: naval,adj.

20. Sailing Vessels (Selected),n.
  1. **bark, barque**—sailing vessel with three masts, the after one of which is fore-and-aft rigged, the others square-rigged
  2. **barkentine, barquentine**—sailing vessel with three or more masts, each of which is fore-and-aft rigged except the forward one, which is square-rigged
  3. **brig**—two-masted square-rigged sailing vessel
  4. **brigantine**—brig, except that the after-mast is fore-and-aft rigged
  5. **catboat**—small sailing craft with only one sail, whose mast has few or no stays
  6. **clipper**—fast sailing vessel
  7. **cutter**—one-masted sailing vessel with more than one headsail (staysail); specifically such a vessel that has not more than twice as much length of deck aft of the mast as forward of the mast
  8. **junk**—seagoing, generally flat-bottomed sailing vessel, usually plying the waters near and around China, with square sails and a high stern
  9. **ketch**—sailing vessel with two masts fore-and-aft rigged, the aftermast of which is shorter than the forward mast and stepped forward of the rudderpost
  10. **lugger**—sailing vessel propelled by lug-sails
  11. **sailboat, sailing boat**—small boat with a sail or sails
  12. **sailer**—sailing vessel
  13. **sailship**—sailing vessel
  14. **schooner**—sailing vessel with two or more masts, all of which are fore-and-aft rigged
  15. **ship**—sailing vessel with three or more masts, all of which are square-rigged
  16. **sloop**—one-masted sailing vessel
  17. **smack**—sailing vessel, usually a cutter or sloop, used mainly in fishing or in traveling along the coast
  18. **three-master, two-master, etc.**—sailing vessel with three masts, two masts, etc.
  19. **yawl**—two-masted fore-and-aft-rigged sailing vessel whose aftermast is smaller than the forward one and is stepped abaft the rudderpost

21. To Manage, Ride in, Steer, etc., a Sailboat (Esp. for Sport) or Other Sailing Vessel: sail,v. (sailing,n.)

22. Group of Vessels,n.
  1. **argosy**—fleet of large merchant vessels
  2. **fleet**—group of vessels engaged in the same business or activity
  3. **flotilla**—group of small boats

23. Pert. to Watercraft: maritime, nautical, adj.

24. Pert. to Seagoing Watercraft: marine, adj.

25. To Manage, Steer, Ride in, or Travel or Go by, Any Type of Watercraft: sail,v. (sailing,n.)

26. To Go or Travel upon, over, or through (a Body of Water): sail,v.

116. SAIL

1. To Sail,v.
1. **circumnavigate**—sail around
2. **cruise**—sail about
3. **navigate**—sail, steer, or direct a ship; sail or travel on water

2. Sailing; Sail,n. *From Sec. 1:* circumnavigation, cruise, navigation; *Also:*
1. **cabotage**—navigation along the coast
2. **sailoring, sailorizing**—act or practice of sailing, esp. as a sailor

3. Sailor; One Who Sails,n. *From Sec. 1:* circumnavigator, cruiser, navigator; *Also:*
1. **deck hand**—sailor
2. **gob**—sailor (colloq.)
3. **mariner**—seaman (restricted to technical uses)
4. **sailorman**—sailor
5. **salt, tar**—old and experienced sailor or seaman (colloq.)
6. **seaman**—sailor, i.e., one who works on a ship

4. Members of a Ship's Company, Exclusive of the Master: crew,n.

5. Personnel of a Ship: ship,n.

6. Commanding Officer of a Ship: captain, master, skipper,n.

7. Pert. to Sailors: maritime, nautical,adj.

8. Like, or Characteristic of, Sailors or a Sailor: maritime, sailorly,adj.

9. Duties, Occupation, or Life of a Sailor: sailoring,n.

10. Work of a Sailor: sailoring, sailorizing,n.

11. Pert. to Sailing, or to Sailing on a Sea or Ocean: marine, maritime, nautical, navigational,adj.

12. Science or Art of Navigation: nautics,n.

13. Sufficiently Deep and Wide for Ships to Sail Through: navigable,adj. (navigability,n.)

117. ROW

1. To Row Easily or Slowly: paddle,v.
2. To Propel a Boat at Its Stern, Using One Oar: scull,v.

3. Oar,n.
1. **paddle**—broad-bladed oar used to propel or steer a canoe or other boat
2. **scull**—oar used to propel a boat at its stern; short oar
3. **sweep**—long oar used to propel or steer a boat or other vessel

4. Rower,n.
1. **oarsman**—rower (oarswoman,fem.)
2. **paddler**—rower, i.e., one who uses a paddle
3. **sculler**—rower, i.e., one who propels a boat at its stern, using one oar
4. **stroke**—rower who sets the timing for other rowers

5. Rowers of a Boat: crew,n.

6. Skill in Rowing: oarsmanship, watermanship,n. (oarsman,n.)

7. Art of Rowing: oarsmanship, watermanship,n.

8. In the Form of, Shaped Like, or Used as, an Oar: oarlike, oary,adj.

118. COME

1. To Come,v.
1. **accede to**—come finally to (a state or condition)
2. **appear**—come; come into sight
3. **arrive**—come; come finally
4. **attain**—come to; come to finally; come to (a state or condition) finally
5. **bring up the rear**—come last
6. **burst**—come with great force or violence
7. **flare**—burst suddenly into existence
8. **gain**—reach
9. **hail from**—come from (a place of origin, birth, or previous residence)
10. **interlope**—come where one is unwelcome
11. **intervene**—come between
12. **intrude**—come where one is neither asked nor welcome
13. **obtrude**—come though uninvited and unwanted
14. **reach**—come to; come to finally
15. **regain**—come to again
16. **run**—come quickly
17. **rush**—come quickly and with forceful haste
18. **slip**—come quietly or inconspicuously
19. **steal**—come slowly, gently, quietly, or secretly
20. **subvene**—come under
21. **supervene**—come as something additional
22. **troop**—come in large numbers
23. **visit**—come to see

2. A Coming,n. *From Sec. 1:* accession (to), appearance, arrival, attainment, flare or flare-up, intervention, intrusion, obtrusion, run, rush, slip, steal, subvention, supervention, visit; *Also:* 1. **advent**—a coming

3. One Who Comes,n. *From Sec. 1:* arrival, interloper, intruder, obtruder, visitant; *Also:* 1. **newcomer**—one who has just, or recently, come

119. GO

1. To Go,v.
1. **adjourn to**—go to (some other place)
2. **advance**—go forward or ahead
3. **betake oneself**—go
4. **burrow**—work one's way indirectly, secretly, under the surface, etc.
5. **burst**—go with great force or violence
6. **butt**—go headfirst
7. **by-pass**—go around
8. **canvass**—go through a region or from door to door, soliciting business, votes, etc. (canvass a town, neighborhood, etc.)
9. **circulate**—go around from place to place or person to person; go and return to a starting place; go in a circle; go around regularly
10. **circumvent**—go around
11. **crash**—go with a loud noise
12. **crisscross**—traverse in opposite directions
13. **cross**—go across; go past
14. **crowd**—force one's way
15. **delay**—go slowly
16. **detour**—go off one's direct course; go around
17. **flare**—burst suddenly into existence
18. **force one's way**—go as a result of effort or expense of energy
19. **hasten**—go fast
20. **head**—go in a certain direction
21. **hie**—go quickly
22. **hurry**—go quickly
23. **hustle**—go quickly and determinedly
24. **interlope**—go where one is unwelcome
25. **intrude**—go where one is neither asked nor welcome
26. **make one's way**—go; go with some effort
27. **migrate**—go from one place to settle in another; go from one area to another according to season
28. **navigate**—make one's way through, sometimes with difficulty
29. **obtrude**—go though uninvited and unwanted

30. **patrol**—go around protecting, guarding, watching, etc.
31. **pioneer**—go into new territory
32. **proceed**—go ahead
33. **repair**—go
34. **resort**—go; go habitually; go often
35. **run**—go quickly
36. **rush**—go quickly and with forceful haste
37. **scamper**—go in a quick and hurried manner
38. **scoot**—go quickly and suddenly
39. **scurry, scutter**—go with brisk speed
40. **scuttle**—go quickly
41. **seek**—go to (*water seeks its level*, etc.)
42. **slip**—go quietly or inconspicuously
43. **squint**—go in a slanting direction
44. **steal**—go slowly, gently, quietly, or secretly
45. **strike out**—go suddenly or quickly
46. **submerge, submerse**—go under water
47. **substitute for**—go in the place of
48. **take oneself**—go
49. **tend**—go in a certain direction
50. **thread**—wind one's way
51. **trace**—make one's way through
52. **trail**—go along slowly
53. **transmigrate**—go from one country or place to another
54. **traverse**—go back and forth over
55. **trend**—go in a certain direction; go in a certain course (as events, a stream, river, etc.)
56. **troop**—go; go in large numbers
57. **unthread**—make one's way through
58. **visit**—go to see
59. **wade through**—go through with difficulty or effort, or despite obstacles
60. **wangle**—proceed with difficulty
61. **weave**—go by winding in and out
62. **wend**—go; make one's way (often in the pattern *wend one's way*)
63. **whir, whirr**—hurry
64. **wind one's way**—go in a winding fashion
65. **work one's way**—go with some effort or difficulty
66. **worm**—go by twisting and wriggling
67. **wreathe**—go in a twisting fashion
68. **wriggle**—go by indirect or devious paths

2. A Going,n. *From Sec. 1:* adjournment, advance or advancement, burst, by-pass, canvass, circulation, circumvention, delay, detour, flare, intrusion, migration, navigation, obtrusion, patrol, repair, run, rush, scamper, scoot, scurry, slip, steal, strike, submergence, submersion, substitution, tendency, transmigration, traversal, trend, visit, wade, weave, wreathe, wriggle

3. One Who Goes,n. *From Sec. 1:* canvasser, hastener, hurrier, interloper, intruder, migrant, obtruder, patrolman, runner, scooter, substitute, transmigrant, traverser, visitor or visitant

4. Descr. of Going,adj. *From Sec. 1:* intrusive, migrant, migratory, obtrusive, substitutive or substitutional, transmigratory, visitant

120. PASS

1. To Pass,v.
1. **circulate**—pass from person to person
2. **elapse**—pass by (generally of a period of time)
3. **skirt**—pass along the edge or border of (a place or thing)
4. **slide**—pass easily from one place to another
5. **transit**—pass
6. **transmigrate**—pass from one condition or body to another; pass at death into another's body (of the soul)

2. Passage,n. *From Sec. 1:* circulation, lapse, slide, transit or transition, transmigration

3. Passing,adj. *From Sec. 1:* transient, transitory, or transitional; transmigratory; *Also:*
1. **current**—passing from person to person
4. That Which, or One Who, Passes,n. *From Sec. 1:* transmigrant or transmigrator

121. CROSS

1. To Cross; To Go or Pass Through or Over,v.
1. **bisect**—cross, as one thing over or through another
2. **bridge**—go over; go across
3. **cleave**—pass through
4. **crisscross**—move across in opposite directions
5. **cut through**—cross
6. **decussate**—cross in the form of an X; pass through
7. **disembogue**—pass through the mouth of a river into open sea
8. **intersect**—pass through
9. **negotiate**—pass over or through; go past
10. **osmose**—pass through a semi-permeable membrane (chemistry); figuratively, penetrate through a separating medium
11. **penetrate**—go through; pass through; pierce
12. **percolate**—permeate
13. **perforate**—pierce through; pierce the surface of
14. **permeate**—pass through the whole of (something); pass through the pores, holes, or spaces of
15. **pierce**—go through with, or as if with, a pointed instrument
16. **plow, plough**—cross through the surface of
17. **scour**—go or pass quickly through or over, looking for something
18. **transpierce**—penetrate; pierce
19. **transude**—pass as or like sweat through the pores or texture
20. **traverse**—cross through or over; move in a crosswise direction
21. **wade**—cross with difficulty or effort

2. A Crossing; A Going or Passing Through or Over,n. *From Sec. 1:* bisection, cleavage, decussation, disembouement, intersection, negotiation, osmosis, penetration, percolation, perforation, permeation, transudation, traversal, wade; *Also:*
1. **dialysis**—a passing through a membrane (chemistry)
2. **transience**—a passing through without stopping

3. Crossing; Going or Passing Through,adj. *From Sec. 1:* osmotic, penetrative or penetrant, permeative; *From Sec. 2:* transient

4. Able to Be Crossed or Passed Through, adj. *From Sec. 1:* penetrable, perforable, permeable, traversible; *Also:* 1. **passable**—able to be crossed

5. Unable to Be Crossed or Passed Through, adj. *From Sec. 4:* impenetrable, imperforable, impermeable, impassable

6. One Who Is Passing Through: transient, n.

7. To Cause to Pass Through a Membrane: dialyze, osmose,v. (dialysis, osmosis,n. dialytic, osmotic,adj.)

8. Lying, Going, or Running Across,adj.
1. **cross**—going or lying across
2. **crosswise**—cross
3. **diagonal**—lying or running across (diagonal,n.)
4. **horizontal**—going across
5. **transversal**—running or lying across (transversal,n.)
6. **transverse**—lying across

9. Across: athwart, crosswise, transverse,adv.

122. A PASSAGE

1. A Passage,n.
1. access—passage by which a place may be approached or reached
2. aisle—narrow passage flanked by structures
3. alley—passage between buildings; passage into a building or house; passage in a garden or park
4. alleyway—narrow passage
5. approach—passage by means of which a place or building may be approached
6. arcade—long, arched passage
7. avenue—passage
8. blind alley—alley closed at one end
9. channel—passage
10. cloister—any covered passage or arcade
11. corridor—passage; hall; entrance hall
12. course—passage
13. cul-de-sac (French)—dead end
14. cut—passage made by digging, or worn by natural action
15. dead end—passage closed at one end
16. driveway—passage along which animals, game, cars, or carriages may be driven
17. gallery—corridorlike passage
18. gap—mountain passage
19. gorge—narrow passage
20. hall—passage in a building or house
21. hallway—hall; entrance hall
22. hoistway—passage through which something may be lifted; elevator shaft
23. impasse—dead end
24. lane—narrow passage
25. lobby—wide passage between rooms; entrance hall
26. overpass—passage over a railroad or other road
27. pass—passage
28. passageway—passage; way or means through which one may pass
29. path—passage; pathway
30. pathway—passage that is much used
31. run—passage used regularly by animals
32. shaft—deep passage in the earth; any long passage
33. subway—underground passage
34. thoroughfare—constantly used passage; passage going all the way through
35. tunnel—underground passage
36. vault—arched passage
37. vestibule—passage between rooms, railroad cars, etc. (vestibule,adj.)
38. way—passage of any kind

123. ROAD

1. Road,n.
1. alley—narrow road between tall structures; public road through the middle of a block giving access to the rear of a building or buildings; narrow street
2. alleyway—alley
3. approach—road by which a place or building may be reached
4. artery—main road
5. avenue—broad street
6. beeline—shortest, most direct route to a place
7. blind alley—alley closed at one end
8. boardwalk—military road of brush and timber over mud
9. boulevard—broad street
10. by-pass—road around a place
11. bypath—private road; indirect or side road
12. byroad—side road
13. bystreet—side street
14. byway—side road
15. causeway—raised road above shallow water or wet ground; paved road; main road
16. course—road; foot road; trail

17. court—short street enclosed by dwellings on all sides
18. crossroad—road that crosses a main road or roads
19. crossway—crossroad
20. cul-de-sac (French)—dead end
21. dead end—road closed at one end
22. detour—roundabout or indirect road
23. driveway—road leading from a street into a garage or up to the entrance of a house
24. footpath—narrow road for pedestrians only
25. gap—mountain road
26. gradient—rising or sloping road
27. highroad—highway
28. highway—main road; public road
29. impasse—road with no exit
30. itinerary—route of a journey
31. lane—narrow road; narrow country road
32. overpass—road over a railroad, other road, etc.
33. parkway—broad main road bordered by trees, lawns, etc.
34. pass—road
35. passage—road; foot road
36. path—road; foot road; route
37. pathway—path
38. place—short street
39. ramp—sloping road, usually leading to or descending from an elevated highway
40. roadway—road; part of the road over which traffic travels; road leading to another road
41. route—road that is followed or traveled over; road or roads by means of which one goes somewhere
42. row—short street, so made by houses (that are connected or close together) on both sides
43. run—regular or habitual route
44. short cut—more direct road than ordinarily followed
45. shun-pike—side road used as a means of avoiding a toll road
46. speedway, freeway, thruway—main road for fast-moving vehicles
47. street—road with sidewalks or footpaths flanking it; public road; main road
48. subway—underground road
49. switchback—very winding or zigzag road in mountainous region
50. terrace—street along or on top of a slope
51. thoroughfare—public road; main road
52. towpath—road or foot road along a canal, used by men or animals towing boats
53. track—road; foot road; trail
54. trail—road or foot road through a wilderness
55. turnpike—road on which a toll must be paid
56. underpass—road under a bridge, railroad track, etc.
57. viaduct—road over a valley, part of a city, gorge, etc.
58. walk—foot road
59. way—road

2. Pert. to a Road,adj.
1. arterial—pert. to, descr. of, etc., a main road
2. viatic—pert. to a road

3. Winding Paths: ambages,n.

4. Path of a Moving Body,n.
1. locus—path of a point or curve (mathematics)
2. orbit—path of a moving body around a stationary object
3. trajectory—curved path of a body moving in space

5. Place Where Roads Cross: crossroads, intersection,n.

6. Edge of a Road: wayside,n.

7. Having Four Roads That Meet at One Point: quadrivial,adj.

8. Descr. of Roads That Lead in Four Directions: quadrivial,adj.

9. By Way of: via

124. TRAVEL

1. To Travel; To Take a Trip,v.
1. **barnstorm**—travel about giving entertainments, lecturing, or making political speeches in small towns or communities over a wide area
2. **caravan**—travel with a group through the desert, through enemy territory, or over dangerous terrain, esp. in Asia or Africa
3. **circuit**—travel around
4. **commute**—travel to and from work
5. **cross**—travel across water or the ocean
6. **cruise**—travel about
7. **jaunt**—take a short pleasure trip
8. **journey**—travel from place to place; go on a trip
9. **junket**—take a trip at public expense (of congressmen and other officials)
10. **migrate**—travel from one place or country to another, esp. with the view of taking up residence
11. **navigate**—travel on water
12. **peregrinate**—travel around from place to place
13. **ply**—travel regularly over
14. **safari**—travel (with others); take a trip, with others, for a special purpose; take part in a hunting trip, esp. in Africa
15. **sally forth**—leave one's home, etc., for a trip
16. **stump**—travel across (a place) in an effort to get votes
17. **tour**—travel through (a place); go traveling
18. **tramp**—travel on foot
19. **transmigrate**—travel through a country not one's own on the way to a foreign country where one intends to take up permanent residence
20. **trek**—travel by wagon; travel by ox wagon; travel in a group and by wagons, cars, train, etc., to a new home; take a slow or difficult trip
21. **voyage**—travel by water; take any long trip

2. A Traveling; Travel; Trip,n. *From Sec. 1:* circuit, commutation, crossing, cruise, jaunt, journey, junket, migration, navigation, peregrination, safari, sally, tour, tramp, transmigration, trek, voyage; *Also:*
1. **excursion**—short trip, usually for pleasure or amusement
2. **expedition**—trip for a special purpose
3. **globe-trotting**—traveling around or to various parts of the world, often for sight-seeing (colloq.)
4. **hadj (Arabic)**—pilgrimage made by a Moslem to Mecca
5. **junket**—pleasure trip
6. **outing**—trip for pleasure; excursion
7. **picnic**—trip to a woods, beach, or other outdoor place for a basket lunch, etc.
8. **pilgrimage**—trip to a place to worship; long, sometimes tedious trip
9. **run**—trip
10. **tour**—trip that returns to the starting place
11. **tourism**—traveling around for pleasure
12. **wayfaring**—traveling, usually on foot

3. Traveler,n. *From Sec. 1:* barnstormer; caravanist, caravanner, or caravaneer; commuter, journeyor, junketer; migrant, migrator, or migratory; navigator, peregrinator, tourist, tramp or tramper, transmigrant or transmigrator, trekker, voyager; *From Sec. 2:* excursionist, expeditionist, globe-trotter, junketer, picnicker, pilgrim, tourist, wayfarer; *Also:*

1. passenger—traveler on a public conveyance

2. viator—traveler

4. Traveling; Engaged in Travel,adj. *From Sec. 1:* migrant, migratory, migrative, or migratorial; transmigrant, transmigratory, or transmigratorial; *From Sec. 2:* expeditionary, globe-trotting: *From Sec. 3:* viatorial; *Also:*
1. **itinerant**—traveling from one place to another in the conduct of business
2. **peripatetic**—traveling from place to place in the conduct of one's business

5. Pert. to, or Descr. of, Traveling,adj. *From Sec. 1:* migratorial, migratory, or migrational; transmigratory or transmigratorial; *From Sec. 2:* expeditionary, pilgrim, tourist; *Also:*
1. **itinerary**—pert. to a trip or to traveling
2. **viatic**—pert. to a trip or to traveling
3. **viatorial**—pert. to traveling

6. Stage of a Journey: trek,n.

7. Line of Travel: track,n.

8. Plan or Route of a Trip or of Traveling: itinerary,n.

9. In the Process of Traveling: en route

10. Year of Traveling before Settling Down: wanderjahr (German), wanderyear,n.

11. Need or Desire to Travel,n.
1. **dromomania**—pathological need to travel
2. **wanderlust**—irresistible need or desire to travel away from home

12. Business of Managing or Directing Pleasure Trips: tourism,n.

125. VISIT

1. To Visit,v.
1. **call on**—visit
2. **frequent**—visit often or habitually (frequentation,n.)
3. **haunt**—visit frequently

2. A Visit,n.
1. **call**—visit
2. **visitation**—official visit of inspection; visit by animals in unusual numbers or in an unusual place; unpleasant visit (visitationary,adj.)

3. Visitor,n.
1. **caller**—visitor
2. **frequenter**—frequent or habitual visitor
3. **habitué (French)**—frequent visitor to a place
4. **haunter**—frequent visitor

4. Place Visited,n.
1. **haunt, haunts**—place or places one habitually visits
2. **mecca**—place visited by many people; place that attracts many visitors; place one has long wished to visit
3. **stamping ground**—place frequently visited

5. Visiting Card: calling card, pasteboard,n.

6. Descr. of Places Unvisited by People,adj.
1. **cloistered**—shut off from the rest of the world, hence rarely if at all visited by people
2. **desolate**—lonely; solitary (desolation, desolateness,n.)
3. **insular**—isolated, as if an island (insularity,n.)
4. **isolated**—cut off from the world, hence not visited by people (isolation,n.)
5. **lonely**—not visited by people (loneliness, n.)
6. **lonesome**—lonely (lonesomeness,n.)
7. **out-of-the-way**—rarely visited by people; isolated
8. **private**—isolated; solitary (privacy,n.)
9. **quiet**—free from crowds; visited by few people (quietness,n.)

10. **remote**—out-of-the-way (remoteness,n.)
11. **retired**—isolated
12. **secluded**—isolated (seclusion,n.)
13. **sequestered**—isolated (sequestration,n.)
14. **solitary**—visited by few or no people (solitude, solitariness,n.)
15. **unfrequented**—unvisited
16. **withdrawn**—isolated

126. GREET

1. To Greet,v.
1. **accost**—greet
2. **hail**—greet in welcome
3. **salaam**—greet with a very low bow
4. **salute**—greet; welcome
5. **welcome**—greet kindly, hospitably, warmly, or joyfully

2. A Greeting,n. *From Sec. 1:* hail, salaam, salute or salutation, welcome; *Also:*
1. **aloha**—Hawaiian greeting
2. **banzai**—Japanese word of greeting, meaning *May you live 10,000 years*
3. **compellation**—act of greeting
4. **ovation**—enthusiastic public greeting

3. Greeter,n. *From Sec. 1:* saluter, welcomer; *Also:* 1. **salutatorian**—in an institution of learning, at graduation exercises, the student (usually second in scholastic achievement) who makes the greeting address to the audience

4. To Express in Greeting: bid,v.

5. Style of Greeting: compellation, salute,n.

6. Pert. to, or Descr. of, Greetings: salutatory,adj.

127. FAREWELL

1. A Farewell; A Good-by,n.
1. **adieu**—farewell
2. **aloha**—Hawaiian farewell
3. **apopemptic**—that which is said or sung to one who is departing (apopemptic,adj.)
4. **bon voyage**—expression of farewell to one going on a sea voyage (bon voyage, adj.)
5. **farewell**—good-by said at parting (farewell,adj.)
6. **vale**—farewell
7. **valediction**—farewell (valedictory,adj.)

2. A Farewell Speech: valediction, valedictory,n.

3. A Saying or Bidding Farewell: valediction,n.

4. Student Who, at Graduation Exercises, Delivers the Farewell Address: valedictorian, n.

5. Good-by, in Various Languages
1. **adios**—in Spanish
2. **aloha**—in Hawaiian
3. **a mañana**—in Spanish
4. **arivederci**—in Italian
5. **auf Wiedersehen**—in German
6. **au revoir**—in French
7. **bon jour**—in French

128. WANDER

1. To Wander,v.
1. **aberrate**—wander off the normal, usual, or proper course (most often in a figurative sense)
2. **cruise**—wander about
3. **digress**—wander off the main theme
4. **divagate**—wander off; wander about; wander from a subject in talk or writing; digress
5. **extravagate**—wander; ramble
6. **gad**—wander about idly, looking for diversion or pleasure

7. **gallivant**—wander about in search of pleasure
8. **jaunt**—wander around for pleasure
9. **meander**—wander without purpose or energy
10. **peregrinate**—wander
11. **prowl**—wander about in a slow and stealthy fashion
12. **ramble**—wander leisurely; wander aimlessly; wander off a topic in talking or writing
13. **range**—wander over or through
14. **roam**—wander; wander over
15. **rove**—wander; wander aimlessly or in a leisurely manner
16. **straggle**—wander off a course; wander away from the rest; wander about
17. **stray**—wander away; wander off the course; wander off limits
18. **stroll**—wander in a leisurely manner
19. **tramp**—wander on foot
20. **vagabond**—wander freely or irresponsibly
21. **vagabondize**—wander idly

2. A Wandering; A Wander,n. *From Sec. 1:* aberration, cruise, digression, divagation, extravagation, jaunt, meander, peregrination, prowl, ramble, range, roam, rove, straggle, stray, stroll, tramp; *Also:*
1. **deliration**—aberration
2. **excursion**—a wandering away from the subject or central point
3. **noctivagation**—a wandering at night

3. Wanderer,n. *From Sec. 1:* aberrator, cruiser, gadabout, gallivanter, meanderer, peregrinator, prowler, rambler, ranger, roamer, rover, straggler, stray, stroller, vagabond, vagabondizer; *Also:*
1. **beachcomber**—wanderer living on what he can salvage on a beach
2. **Bedouin**—nomad
3. **gypsy, gipsy**—wanderer
4. **nomad**—one who wanders from place to place instead of living with any permanency in one place
5. **pilgrim**—wanderer
6. **runabout**—person who wanders from place to place
7. **tramp**—wanderer who begs his sustenance from place to place
8. **vagabond**—person of no fixed living place; tramp
9. **vagrant**—wanderer; tramp

4. Wandering, Tending to Wander, or Given to Wandering,adj. *From Sec. 1:* aberrant, cruising, digressive or digressory, gadabout or gadding, meandrous or meandering, prowling, rambling, ranging, roaming, roving, straggling or straggly, stray or astray, strolling, vagabond; *From Sec. 2:* excursive, noctivagant or noctivagous; *From Sec. 3:* gypsy, gipsy, nomadic, vagabond, vagrant; *Also:*
1. **afield**—wandering off
2. **delirious**—wandering mentally
3. **devious**—wandering off a straight line
4. **discursive**—wandering without system from one subject to another (of speech or writing)
5. **errant**—wandering; straying
6. **erratic, erratical**—wandering off a regular course; wandering
7. **fugitive**—wandering; having no fixed place to live
8. **migratory**—wandering from place to place; nomadic
9. **planetary**—wandering; not fixed
10. **skimble-skamble**—rambling

5. Tendency to Wander,n. *From Sec. 1:* aberrance or aberrancy, digressiveness, vagabondage or vagabondism; *From Sec. 2:* excursiveness; *From Sec. 3:* vagabondage, vagabondism, vagrancy; *From Sec. 4:* deliriousness, deviousness, discursiveness, errantness, erraticalness, fugitiveness or fugitivity

6. Irresistible Desire to Wander from Home: wanderlust,n.

129. GYPSY

1. A Gypsy,n.
1. Romany—gypsy
2. tzigane (Hungarian)—gypsy; Hungarian gypsy
3. zingaro (Italian)—gypsy (zingara,fem.)

2. One Who Associates with Gypsies: Romany rye,n.

3. Pert. to, Descr. of, or Resembling Gypsies,adj.
1. gypsy, gipsy—pert. to, descr. of, or resembling a gypsy or gypsies
2. Romany—pert. to gypsies
3. tzigane (Hungarian)—pert. to, resembling, characteristic of, or descr. of gypsies

130. GO BEYOND

1. To Go Beyond,v.
1. encroach (on or upon)—go beyond one's rights or privileges and thereby enter upon (the rights or privileges of another); go beyond one's rightful territory (into the territory of another); go beyond normal or acceptable limits
2. exceed—go beyond (set bounds)
3. extravagate—go beyond normal bounds
4. impinge (on or upon)—encroach; trespass
5. infringe (on or upon)—go beyond one's legal or other rights
6. invade—go beyond; encroach
7. lap over—extend over and beyond
8. overlap—extend over and beyond; go beyond (what was expected or planned)
9. overrun—go beyond (time set aside for something)
10. overstep—go beyond; go beyond (set bounds or accepted standards)
11. overtop—transcend
12. surpass—go beyond
13. transcend—go beyond; go beyond the powers of; go beyond (normal limits or bounds)
14. transgress—go beyond; go beyond the limits of
15. trench (on or upon)—trespass
16. trespass (on or upon)—go beyond the boundaries of propriety, right, legality, courtesy, etc.
17. violate—infringe; trespass

2. A Going Beyond,n. *From Sec. 1:* encroachment, impingement, infringement, invasion, overlap, transcendence, transgression, trespass, violation; *Also:* 1. inroad—a forcible going beyond what is moderate; encroachment

3. One Who Goes Beyond,n. *From Sec. 1:* encroacher, impinger, infringer, invader, transgressor, trespasser, violator

4. Going Beyond,adj. *From Sec. 1:* invasive, transcendent (transcendence, transcendency, transcendentness,n.), transgressive; *Also:* 1. ultra—going beyond all limits

131. ACCOMPANIMENT

1. To Accompany,v.
1. attend—accompany
2. chaperon—accompany for the sake of convention or propriety
3. conduct—usher
4. convoy—accompany for the purpose of protecting, generally in a military, police, or other official sense

5. escort—accompany for purposes of protection
6. matronize—chaperon
7. retinue—accompany (usually said of a train of attendants or a permanent staff that accompanies an important person)
8. squire—escort (a woman, usually)
9. usher—accompany to a place or seat (usually in a theater, assembly hall, etc.)

2. Accompaniment,n. *From Sec. 1:* attendance, chaperonage, convoy

3. Accompanier,n. *From Sec. 1:* attendant, chaperon (chaperone,fem.), conductor, convoy, escort, squire, usher; *Also:*
1. accompanist—one who accompanies, esp. another musician in performing a piece
2. accompanyist—accompanier
3. beau—escort
4. cavalier—courteous or chivalrous escort for a lady
5. companion—one who accompanies another
6. duenna—elderly woman who is the chaperone of a young girl, guarding her morals, censoring her contacts with the opposite sex, etc. (derived from the custom in Spain and Portugal)
7. gigolo—man who, for a fee, escorts a woman to places of amusement
8. page—uniformed usher in a theater or in Congress
9. yokefellow—constant companion

4. Group That Accompanies,n. *From Sec. 1:* convoy, escort, retinue; *Also:*
1. attendance—retinue
2. company—retinue
3. cortege—group of attendants that accompanies an important person, member of royalty, etc.
4. entourage—those who accompany a person of importance, as family, servants, secretaries, staff, etc.
5. suite—personal staff that accompanies an important person

5. That Which Accompanies,n.
1. accessory—that which accompanies, usually in a subordinate capacity
2. accompaniment—anything that accompanies
3. appanage—natural accompaniment
4. obbligato—accompanying part in music; accompanying sound or noise; accompaniment
5. vade mecum (Latin)—something carried along with one as a kind of companion

6. Accompanying,adj.
1. accessory—accompanying in a subordinate capacity (of things)
2. attendant—accompanying
3. collateral—accompanying, but less important (collaterality,n.)
4. concomitant—accompanying (something else) at the same time (concomitance,n.)

7. To Involve as a Necessary or Required Accompaniment: entail,v. (entailment,n.)

8. Protection or Attendance of a Chaperon: chaperonage,n.

132. APPROACH

1. To Approach,v.
1. accost—approach; approach and speak to
2. draw near—approach
3. make advances—approach personally with suggestions for settling a disagreement or with any other suggestions
4. near—approach
5. stalk—approach secretly

2. Approach,n. *From Sec. 1:* stalk; *Also:* access, accession

3. Approacher,n. *From Sec. 1:* accoster, stalker

4. Means of Approach: access, adit, avenue, n.

5. Approaching: forthcoming (in time), nearing, oncoming,adj.

6. To Cause to Approach: attract,v. (attraction,n. attractive,adj.)

7. Approachable: accessible,adj. (accessibility,n.)

8. Unapproachable,adj.
1. **forbidding**—looking as if approach is unwelcome, or would be dangerous or unpleasant (forbiddingness,n.)
2. **formidable**—repelling approach (formidability, formidableness,n.)
3. **inaccessible, unaccessible**—incapable of being approached (inaccessibility, inaccessibleness, unaccessibility, unaccessibleness,n.)
4. **remote**—hard or impossible to approach (remoteness,n.)

133. ENTRANCE

1. To Enter,v.
1. **barge in, barge into**—enter unexpectedly and impolitely
2. **breach**—break through and enter
3. **burglarize**—enter (a place) forcibly and illegally, then steal what is found inside
4. **encroach (on or upon)**—enter stealthily and gradually into (the rights or privileges of another) ; intrude; trespass
5. **escalade**—enter by climbing a ladder
6. **filter, filter into**—percolate
7. **immigrate**—enter a foreign country or region to live
8. **infiltrate**—enter, singly and secretly, into enemy territory; enter into the pores or interstices of
9. **intrude**—enter without permission or invitation
10. **invade**—enter (a place) for hostile purposes, by force, or as if to take possession
11. **penetrate**—enter in or into; enter and pass through
12. **percolate**—enter into the holes, openings, spaces, etc., of
13. **permeate**—penetrate
14. **pierce**—enter deeply into
15. **pounce into**—enter suddenly
16. **raid**—enter by force; gain entrance, seize booty, and leave
17. **stab**—pierce
18. **straggle in, into**—enter irregularly, one by one, or a few at a time
19. **trench (upon)**—trespass on
20. **trespass (on or upon)**—enter (someone else's property) without right, permission, or invitation
21. **violate**—enter by force or without right

2. Entrance; Entry,n. *From Sec. 1:* breach, burglary, encroachment, escalade, immigration, infiltration, intrusion, invasion, penetration, percolation, raid, stab, trespass, violation; *Also:*
1. **admission**—entry
2. **debut**—entrance into formal society (generally of women)
3. **incursion**—hostile entry in force
4. **influx**—entrance by, or as if by, flowing
5. **ingress, ingression**—entrance
6. **inpour**—influx
7. **inrush**—influx
8. **irruption**—violent and sudden invasion

3. Entrant; One Who Enters,n. *From Sec. 1:* burglar, encroacher, immigrant, infiltrator, intruder, invader, raider, straggler, trespasser, violator; *From Sec. 2:* debutante; *Also:*
1. **entry**—one who enters a contest
2. **incomer**—one who enters; immigrant

4. Entering; Tending to Enter,adj. *From Sec. 1:* burglarious, immigrant, intrusive, invasive, penetrative or penetrant, permeative; *From Sec. 2:* incursive, ingressive, inpouring, inrushing, irruptive; *From Sec. 3:* incoming; *Also:* 1. **inbound**—entering (of trains, ships, passengers, etc.)

5. Pert. to, or Descr. of, Entering: ingressive,adj.

6. To Go on Board,v.
1. **embark**—go on board ship, preparatory to leaving; by extension, go on board a train for the same purpose (embarkation, n.)
2. **emplane**—go on board an airplane
3. **entrain**—go on board a train (entrainment,n.)

7. Way or Means of Entering,n.
1. **access**—means of entering
2. **adit**—access
3. **avenue**—way or means of entering
4. **door**—way, means, or place of entering
5. **doorway**—means of entering
6. **entrance**—place through which to enter
7. **entranceway**—entrance
8. **entree**—access
9. **entry**—means by which entrance is made
10. **gate, gateway**—place for entering
11. **ingress**—place for entering
12. **ingress, ingression**—access
13. **limen**—threshold—psychological term (liminal,adj.)
14. **lobby**—entrance hall
15. **portal**—imposing entrance, door, gate, etc.
16. **portcullis**—massive and strong iron gate or grating sliding up and down in the entrance of ancient castles or forts to permit (or prohibit) entering
17. **sill**—threshold
18. **threshold**—place for, or means of, entering; entering point
19. **toe hold**—place or means of gaining entry
20. **vestibule**—entrance hall (vestibular,adj.)
21. **wicket**—small door or gate

8. Doorkeeper or Gatekeeper: concierge, porter,n.

9. Permission, Right, etc., to Enter,n.
1. **admission**—permission or right to enter
2. **admittance**—permission or right to enter
3. **entree**—freedom or privilege to enter
4. **ingress, ingression**—power or right to enter

10. That Which Gives Admittance or Opens Doors (Figuratively): open-sesame,n.

11. Ease of Entering: access,n.

12. Price Paid to Enter: admission,n.

13. To Permit Entry: admit,v. (admission, admittance,n.)

14. Capable of Being Entered,adj.
1. **accessible**—capable of being entered
2. **penetrable**—capable of being entered, pierced, penetrated, etc. (penetrability,n.)
3. **permeable**—penetrable (permeability,n.)
4. **pervious**—penetrable (perviousness,n.)
5. **porous**—penetrable by water or liquids (porousness,n.)

15. Unable to Be Entered,adj. *From Sec. 14:* inaccessible, impenetrable, impermeable, impervious; *Also:* 1. **adamantine**—impenetrable

134. TAKE IN

1. To Take In,v.
1. **absorb**—take in; take in and cause to lose identity; suck in (absorption,n.)
2. **accept**—take in (acceptance,n.)
3. **admit**—take in (admission, admittance, n.)

4. **assimilate**—take into the general body or group; absorb (assimilation,n.)
5. **devour**—take in through the senses with great eagerness or figurative hunger
6. **imbibe**—take in (learning); take in mentally and retain
7. **receive**—take in (reception, recipience, receipt,n.)
8. **resorb**—take (that which has been eliminated or exuded) back in (resorption,n.)
9. **soak up**—take in
10. **sop up**—take in; take in eagerly; suck in
11. **sponge**—take in
12. **suck (in or up)**—draw in with, or as if with, the mouth (suction,n.)
13. **swallow**—absorb

2. Taking In; Able to Take In,adj. *From Sec. 1:* absorbent or absorptive, admissive, assimilative or assimilatory; receptive, receptible, or recipient; resorbent, spongy; *Also:*
1. **bibulous**—highly absorbent of water or moisture
2. **hygroscopic**—freely absorbing and retaining moisture
3. **porous**—admitting or absorbing water or liquids

3. Tendency or Ability to Take In,n. *From Sec. 2:* absorbency, absorptivity or absorptiveness; receptiveness, receptivity, receptibility, or recipience; resorbence, sponginess, bibulousness, porousness or porosity; *Also:* 1. **capillary attraction,**—ability of a porous substance to absorb liquids by contact

4. Pert. to Taking In That Which Has Been Eliminated: resorptive,adj.

5. Causing to Take In That Which Has Been Eliminated: resorptive,adj.

6. Adapted for Sucking: suctorial,adj.

7. Operating by Suction: vacuum,adj.

8. That Which Absorbs: sponge,n.

9. To Become Absorbed: assimilate,v. (assimilation,n.)

135. BRING IN

1. To Bring In,v.
1. **adhibit**—bring in
2. **import**—bring in from outside the country, region, system, etc. (importation,n.)
3. **superinduce**—bring in as something added or additional (superinduction, superinducement,n.)
4. **track in**—bring in (something or some soil) on one's shoes

2. One Who Brings In from the Outside: importer,n.

3. That Which Is Brought In from the Outside: import, importation,n.

136. INSIDE

1. Inside; Inner,adj.
1. **domestic**—inside or within a state, country, etc.
2. **innermost, inmost**—farthest inside or within
3. **interior**—inside (interiority,n.)
4. **internal**—inner (internality,n.)
5. **intestine**—domestic, with regard to disorders or calamities
6. **intimate**—innermost
7. **intrinsic**—inner (intrinsicality,n.)
8. **inward**—inside; inner
9. **within**—inside

2. The Inside; Insides; Inside Part or Parts,n.
1. **bowels**—inside; inside parts
2. **core**—innermost part of anything
3. **heart**—innermost part of anything

4. **innards**—inside; inside parts (colloq.)
5. **interior**—inside; inside part, parts, or section
6. **inward**—inside; inner part
7. **midst**—inner part or place
8. **penetralia**—innermost parts of a thing or place, esp. of a palace or temple
9. **pith**—soft or spongy inner part of a body

3. Inside Section, Region, Territory, etc., of a Country: inland, inlands, interior, midlands, upcountry,n. (inland, interior, midland, upcountry,adj.)

4. Inhabitant of the Inside Section, etc., of a Country: inlander, midlander,n.

137. CENTER

1. Center,n.
1. **axis**—line, real or theoretical, passing through the center of a body, and around which the body revolves; hence, loosely, center or center line
2. **barycenter**—center of gravity
3. **bull's-eye**—center of a target; hence, loosely, center
4. **center**—middle point or place
5. **centroid**—center of mass of a body or system of bodies; center of the position of stars being discussed in respect to motion; center of an electrical charge
6. **centrosphere**—center part of the earth
7. **centrum**—center
8. **compromise**—some abstraction that is an intermediate between two extremes
9. **core**—center; center portion of a fruit
10. **deep**—middle
11. **focus**—center point; center of activity, action, attention, etc. (foci or focuses, pl. n.)
12. **heart**—center of activity; center part of a tree, fruit, etc.; part nearest the center of anything
13. **hub**—center; center of activity; center portion of a wheel
14. **intermediary**—intermediate
15. **intermediate**—that which is, lies, or occurs in, or near, the middle between extremes or limits
16. **kernel**—center part
17. **mean**—middle point between extremes, numbers, etc.
18. **median**—middle point, number, line, etc., between extremes
19. **medium**—that which lies in, or near, the middle between extremes; middle state, quality, degree, etc.; mean
20. **middle**—point or part equidistant from extremities or exterior points or limits; center part or portion
21. **midst**—middle; center part or place
22. **navel**—center; middle
23. **nucleus**—center portion; center part of something around which other parts collect or to which other parts are added
24. **omphalos**—center; center point; hub
25. **pivot**—center member on which something turns; axis

2. Central; Pert. to, Descr. of, Near, Situated at, etc., the Center,adj. *From Sec. 1:* axial, barycentric, bull's-eye; central, centric, or centrical; centroidal, compromise, focal, intermediate, mean, median, medium, middle, navel, nuclear, pivotal; *Also:*
1. **equidistant**—in the center between two or more limits or points
2. **halfway**—in the middle; middle
3. **medial**—middle; occurring, situated, etc. in the middle or between extremes
4. **mesial**—medial
5. **mid**—denoting the middle or middle part; occupying a middle position; middle
6. **middling**—medium in size, quality, value, etc.

7. **midmost, middlemost**—in the precise middle or center
8. **midway**—halfway between two things, places, etc.
9. **umbilical**—central; pert. to or occupying the center.

3. Centrality,n. *From Sec. 2:* axiality; centrality, centricity, or centricality; intermediateness or intermediacy, equidistance

4. To Bring, etc., to a Center,v.
1. **center**—bring, put, place, collect, etc., at or on a center or central point.
2. **centralize**—bring, draw, gather, collect, etc., at, into, or about a center or central point (centralization, concentralization, n.)
3. **concenter, concentre**—bring, draw, or gather to a common center
4. **concentrate**—bring together to a common center (concentration,n.)
5. **focus**—bring to a central point
6. **medialize**—cause to be in the middle or between extremes (medialization,n.)

5. To Come to a Center,v. *From Sec. 4:* center, centralize, concenter, concentre, concentrate

6. Proceeding or Directed toward the Center: centripetal,adj. (centripetence, centripetency, centripetalism,n.)

7. Converging to a Center: centrolineal,adj. (of lines)

8. Having the Same or a Common Center: concentric, homocentric,adj. (concentricity, homocentricity,n.)

9. To Have a Common Center: concenter, concentre,v.

10. That Which Has a Common Center with Something Else: concentric,n.

11. Having Different Centers: eccentric, eccentrical,adj. (eccentricity,n.)

12. Not Having a Center: acentric,adj. (acentricity,n.)

13. Not Centered: acentric,adj. (acentricity, n.)

14. Proceeding, Fleeing, or Flying Away from the Center: centrifugal,adj.

15. To Cause to Undergo Centrifugal Action: centrifuge, centrifugate, centrifugalize,v. (centrifugation, centrifugalization,n.)

16. Machine That Causes Something to Undergo Centrifugal Action: centrifuge,n.

138. OUTSIDE

1. Outside,adj.
1. **alfresco**—outdoor
2. **eccentric**—directed, occurring, or lying outside the self as a center—term in psychology
3. **ecdemic**—originating from the outside (medical)
4. **exoteric**—from, or pert. to, the outside or outside world; external
5. **exterior**—outside; pert. to or descr. of the outside of something (exteriority,n.)
6. **external**—outside; pert. to or descr. of the outside of a thing or person; turned to the outside; seen from the outside (externality,n.)
7. **extraliminal**—extramarginal
8. **extramarginal**—outside the limits of awareness or consciousness (psychology)
9. **extramundane**—outside the material world; extraterrestrial
10. **extramural**—outside the walls of a fortified city; outside (the walls of) an educational institution
11. **extraneous**—originating from the outside (extraneousness,n.)

12. **extrasolar**—outside (or beyond) the solar system
13. **extraterrestrial**—originating or existing outside the earth or its atmosphere
14. **extraterritorial**—outside the territorial limits of a jurisdiction
15. **extrinsic, extrinsical**—coming from, or originating on, the outside; external (extrinsicalness,n.)
16. **foreign**—outside a country
17. **marginal**—peripheral
18. **objective, objectivist, objectivistic**—treating phenomena or events as external rather than as a reflection of one's own feelings and emotions (objectiveness, objectivity, or objectivism,n. objectivist,n.)
19. **outdoor, outdoors**—happening outside the home, outside any shelter, in the open air, etc.
20. **outer**—outside; external
21. **outermost**—on the extreme outside
22. **outlying**—exterior
23. **outmost**—farthest outside
24. **outward**—turned to, facing toward, or seen on, the outside; external
25. **peripheral**—pert. to or descr. of the outside or the outside surface or part
26. **superficial**—pert. to the outside only; exterior (superficiality, superficialness,n.)
27. **surface**—pert. to the outside of a body or thing

2. The Outside; That Which Is Outside,n. *From Sec. 1:* exterior, external, margin, outdoors, periphery, superficies, surface; *Also:*
1. **bounds, boundary**—outside limits
2. **limit, limits**—outer parts, portions, or sections
3. **outskirts**—outer parts of a place or city
4. **superstratum**—outside layer

3. To Cause to Be Outside or on the Outside,v. *From Sec. 1:* exteriorize, externalize, objectify or objectivate (exteriorization, externalization, objectification, objectivation, n.)

139. SURFACE

1. Surface,n.
1. **area**—flat surface
2. **burr**—rough surface
3. **expanse**—large and/or wide surface
4. **face**—surface; front surface; principal surface; principal flat surface
5. **facet**—one of the small plane surfaces of a crystal, diamond, or other cut gem
6. **obverse**—main surface
7. **periphery**—outer surface (peripheral, adj.)
8. **plane**—flat and level surface
9. **platform**—raised level surface
10. **slick**—smooth and/or slippery surface
11. **stretch**—continuous surface
12. **stubble**—rough surface
13. **superficies**—surface (superficial,adj.)
14. **sward**—grassy surface

2. On the Surface Only: shallow, skin-deep, superficial,adj. (shallowness, superficiality or superficialness,n.)

3. Having a Number of Plane Surfaces,adj.
1. **dodecahedral**—having 12 plane surfaces
2. **hexahedral**—having 6 plane surfaces
3. **multifaceted**—having many facets or plane surfaces
4. **octahedral**—having 8 plane surfaces
5. **pentahedral**—having 5 plane surfaces
6. **polyhedral**—having 7 or more plane surfaces

4. Instrument to Measure Plane Surfaces: planimeter,n. (planimetry,n.)

5. To Come to the Surface: crop up or out, surface,v.

6. To Give a Surface to: surface,v.

7. To Bring (a Submarine, etc.) to the Surface: surface,v.

140. COME OUT

1. To Come Out; To Come Forth,v.
1. **blaze**—burst out
2. **burst (out, forth)**—come out or forth suddenly and violently
3. **debouch**—come out from a confined space (said of armies, troups, etc.); come out into a more open place; issue
4. **discharge**—come forth
5. **disembogue**—come out
6. **effloresce**—burst forth
7. **egress**—come forth (from a place)
8. **emanate**—come out
9. **emerge**—come out; come out from obscurity into full view
10. **erupt**—burst out or forth
11. **escape**—come out (of any enclosure or confinement)
12. **exit**—come out (from a place)
13. **explode**—burst out (literally or figuratively)
14. **gush**—come out or forth in a violent pour
15. **issue**—come out or forth (from a place)
16. **jet**—come out forcefully through a narrow opening (of liquids, gases, etc.)
17. **leak**—escape (of fluids)
18. **ooze**—escape slowly
19. **peep through**—come out from concealment
20. **peer**—come partly out
21. **proceed**—come forth
22. **rampage**—come out wildly, riotously, suddenly, violently, etc.
23. **rush out or forth**—come out or forth with great force or violence
24. **sally**—burst out; rush out or forth
25. **seep**—escape (often slowly) through small openings
26. **spout**—come out in a stream (of liquids)
27. **spring**—burst out or forth
28. **spurt**—gush
29. **squirt**—come out in a forcible stream
30. **wallow**—come out or forth in a pouring and swirling motion

2. A Coming Out,n. *From Sec. 1:* burst; debouchment, debouch, or debouché; discharge, disemboguement, efflorescence, egression, emanation, emergence, eruption, escape, exit, explosion, gush, issue, jet, leak, leakage, ooze, rampage, sally, seepage, spout, spring, spurt, squirt, wallow; *Also:*
1. **outbreak**—a bursting out
2. **outburst**—a bursting out or forth
3. **spate**—a sudden bursting out or forth (usually of words)
4. **wave**—a bursting out (of emotion, feelings, etc.)

3. That Which Comes Out or Forth,n. *From Sec. 1:* burst, discharge, emanation, gush, issue, jet, leakage, ooze, process, seepage, spout, squirt; *Also:*
1. **effluvium, efflux**—emanation that cannot be seen, but may be smelled (effluviums, effluvia,pl. n. effluvial,adj.)
2. **exhalation**—that which comes out as a product of breathing, or as if breathed out

4. Coming Out or Forth,adj. *From Sec. 1:* efflorescent, emergent, eruptive, explosive, rampageous

5. Means or Place of Coming or Going Out,n.
1. **avenue**—way of coming out
2. **egress**—means of coming or going out; exit
3. **exit**—place or door for coming or going out
4. **leak**—hole or opening through which fluid, gas, etc., comes out

5. **outlet**—means of coming or going out
6. **spout**—place from which something comes out
7. **vent**—way or means of coming or going out

6. Privilege or Right to Come or Go Out from a Place: egress,n.

7. To Spring a Leak: bilge,v.

141. GO AWAY

1. To Go Away; To Get Away; To Depart; To Leave; To Escape,v.
1. **abandon**—leave (a place) completely, with no thought of returning
2. **abdicate**—voluntarily leave an office, position of trust, etc.
3. **abscond**—depart secretly; leave secretly and hide away
4. **bolt**—run away
5. **break out**—escape from restraint or confinement
6. **by-pass**—get away from
7. **debark**—disembark
8. **decamp**—leave secretly; escape; run away; break up a camp secretly and steal away; flee
9. **desert**—run away from duty; leave or abandon (a place or person) when needed
10. **detrain**—leave a train
11. **disband**—scatter
12. **disembark**—leave a ship
13. **disperse**—scatter
14. **elude**—get away from by some clever ruse, etc.; leave one's memory, recollection, mind, etc. (*his name eludes me*)
15. **embark**—go on a vessel for purposes of departing
16. **emigrate**—depart from one's country to live permanently in another
17. **evacuate**—depart from (an occupied position—said of military troops); depart (from a city, etc., that is in danger of military attack, bombing, flood, volcanic eruption, etc.); depart (from a premises)
18. **evade**—get away from by artfulness, trickery, etc.
19. **expatriate**—leave one's native country to live in another
20. **flee**—run away; escape, or try to escape, by running away
21. **lapse**—pass away; slip away
22. **maroon**—escape and become a fugitive slave
23. **migrate**—depart permanently from one place or country to another; depart periodically from one place to another
24. **part**—go away; go away from one another
25. **pass away**—go away
26. **quit**—leave (a place)
27. **resign**—leave an office or position
28. **retire**—leave an occupation, place, following, etc.
29. **run away**—go away quickly; try to escape; escape
30. **scatter**—go away in different directions (of groups)
31. **secede**—depart officially from an organization, religious body, group, etc.
32. **skedaddle**—run away (colloq.)
33. **skip**—leave in a hurry
34. **slip away**—go away unnoticed; go away secretly
35. **stampede**—run away in sudden and panicky manner (of groups of animals or people)
36. **steal away**—leave secretly or stealthily
37. **tergiversate, tergiverse**—leave one party, cause, affiliation, faith, etc., and go over to another
38. **troop**—go away (usually of groups)

39. vacate—leave (in the sense of giving up occupancy)

40. withdraw (from)—go away; leave

2. A Going Away, Leaving, Departure, or Escape,n. *From Sec. 1:* abandonment, abdication, bolt, breakout or outbreak, by-pass, decampment, desertion, detrainment, disbandment, disembarkation, dispersal or dispersion, embarkation, emigration, evacuation, evasion, expatriation, flight, lapse, migration, resignation, retirement, secession, stampede, tergiversation, vacation, withdrawal; *Also:*

1. **abstraction**—withdrawal from worldly or earthy interests
2. **demission**—abdication
3. **exodus**—general and widespread departure of many people from a place
4. **farewell**—departure
5. **French leave**—informal or secret departure, esp. without paying one's debts
6. **fugue**—figurative flight from familiar surroundings during a state of amnesia (psychology)
7. **hegira**—flight, in analogy to the flight of Mohammed from Mecca; departure that is similar to a flight
8. **stampede**—exodus
9. **wilding**—escape

3. One Who Goes Away,n. *From Sec. 1:* abandoner, abdicator, absconder, bolter, deserter, emigrant, evacuee, expatriate, maroon, migrant, runaway, tergiversator, vacator; *Also:*

1. **departer**—one who departs
2. **escapee**—one who has escaped
3. **escaper**—one who escapes
4. **fugitive**—one who flees, or has fled, in order to avoid arrest, imprisonment, detection, etc.
5. **refugee**—one who flees for safety
6. **runagate**—fugitive
7. **transient**—one who soon leaves

4. Descr. of Going Away; Tending to Go Away,adj. *From Sec. 1:* abdicant, elusive, emigrant, evasive, migratory or migrant, runaway, secessive; *From Sec. 3:* fugitive, transient; *Also:*

1. **fleeting**—leaving after remaining only a very short time
2. **fugacious**—disposed to fly away quickly
3. **fugitive**—leaving quickly, i.e., not remaining long
4. **passing**—fleeting
5. **transitory**—leaving quickly
6. **volatile**—fleeting

5. Tendency to Go Away,n. *From Sec. 4:* elusiveness, evasiveness; transience; fugaciousness and fugacity, fugitiveness or fugitivity, transitoriness, volatility

6. To Provide Escape,v.

1. **canalize**—provide a means of issue or escape (canalization,n.)
2. **vent**—allow or make a means for an escape of air, gas, etc., from
3. **ventilate**—provide with an opening for the escape of air or gas (ventilation,n.)

7. Means of Escape,n.

1. **leak**—hole or opening through which something can or does escape
2. **loophole**—hole or opening through which escape is possible, either literally or figuratively
3. **vent**—means for the escape of air, gas, etc.

8. Place or Passage without an Exit: blind alley, cul-de-sac (French), dead end,n.

9. Place, Position, Condition, or State of No Escape,n.

1. **(at) bay**—position, condition, or state in which escape or flight is no longer possible and one must turn and face the opponent, pursuer, antagonist, etc.

2. **blind alley, cul-de-sac (French), dead end**—place or position from which there is no escape except by retracing one's actions or steps

142. DESERTION

1. To Desert,v.

1. **abandon**—desert
2. **apostatize**—desert one's religion, party, principles, the cause one has supported, etc.
3. **betray**—desert when most needed
4. **bolt**—desert and refuse to support (a party, cause, etc.)
5. **forsake**—desert (that which, or one whom, one has treasured, protected, loved, believed in, etc.)
6. **leave**—desert
7. **maroon**—desert (someone) in a helpless, difficult, or unfortunate position, or in an isolated place
8. **strand**—desert (someone) in a helpless or unfavorable position, or in a position he cannot leave or from which he cannot extricate himself
9. **tergiversate, tergiverse**—desert (a cause, party, etc.)

2. Desertion,n. *From Sec. 1:* abandonment, apostasy or apostatism, betrayal or betrayment, bolt, tergiversation; *Also:* **1. defection** —desertion of that to which allegiance is owed

3. Deserter,n. *From Sec. 1:* apostate, betrayer, tergiversator or tergiversant; *Also:* **1. renegade, renegado, turncoat**—one who deserts a party, cause, political or religious faith, etc., in favor of another (the latter often opposed or hostile to the former)

4. Pert. to, or Descr. of, Desertion or a Deserter,adj. *From Secs. 1 and 3:* apostate, apostalic, or apostalical; tergiversant, tergiversatory or tergiverse; renegade, turncoat

143. DISAPPEARANCE

1. To Disappear,v.

1. **dematerialize**—lose physical form, hence disappear (dematerialization,n.)
2. **dissipate**—disappear completely; separate into components and disappear (dissipation,n.)
3. **dissolve**—fade (dissolution,n.)
4. **evaporate**—disappear into air; disappear completely, like vapor
5. **fade (away)**—disappear gradually
6. **melt (away)**—disappear by scattering; disappear completely
7. **perish**—disappear
8. **vanish**—disappear completely

2. Tending to Disappear, or to Disappear Gradually: fugitive,adj. (fugitiveness, fugitivity,n.)

3. To Begin to Disappear: evanesce, fade,v. (evanescence,n. evanescent, fading, adj.)

144. CAUSE TO GO AWAY

1. To Cause to Go Away; To Send Away; To Drive Away or Out,v.

1. **banish**—force to leave; condemn to leave and remain out of a (or one's native) country; drive away (banishment,n.)
2. **bounce**—eject
3. **cast out**—banish; expel from home and friends; exorcise
4. **chase**—put to flight; cause to go away by threats, etc.; drive away; expel
5. **deport**—banish from a country (deportation,n.)
6. **detrain**—cause (someone) to leave a train (detrainment,n.)

7. **disband**—disperse (disbandment,n.)
8. **dislodge**—drive out of hiding (dislodgment,n.)
9. **dismiss**—send away (dismissal,n. dismissive,adj.)
10. **dispel**—drive away (generally something unpleasant, as fear, gloom, worry, etc.)
11. **disperse**—drive away by making flee in all directions (dispersal, dispersion,n. dispersive,adj.)
12. **displace**—force out and take the place of (displacement,n.)
13. **dispossess**—force to give up occupancy or possession of land, living quarters, etc. (dispossession,n. dispossessory,adj.)
14. **dissipate**—drive away and make disappear (dissipation,n. dissipative,adj.)
15. **eject**—cause (a person) to leave by forcibly driving him out (ejection, ejectment, n. ejective,adj.)
16. **evict**—put (someone) out from a place he is occupying or living in, usually by legal process (eviction,n. evictive,adj.)
17. **exile**—force or condemn to leave and remain out of one's native country (exile, n.)
18. **exorcise**—drive out (something evil or an evil spirit) by prayer, magic, etc. (exorcism,n.)
19. **expatriate**—make (someone) leave his native country and live in another (expatriation,n.)
20. **expel, expulse**—make (someone) leave; drive or force out (expulsion,n. expulsive, expulsory, or expulsatory,adj.)
21. **force out**—make leave
22. **ostracize**—banish from a country or place (ostracism,n.)
23. **oust**—turn, drive, or force out (someone) who is in, or in possession of, a place, position, etc. (ouster,n.)
24. **rebuff**—figuratively drive away (by one's attitude); drive away (rebuff,n.)
25. **relegate (to)**—send away; banish (relegation,n.)
26. **repel, repulse**—drive away, literally or figuratively (repulse, repulsion,n. repulsive,adj.)
27. **rout**—put (an enemy or opponent) to flight in defeat (rout,n.)
28. **scatter**—disperse
29. **wean (from)**—cause to leave the protection (of)

2. State or Fact of Being Sent or Driven Away, etc.,n. *From Sec. 1:* banishment, deportation, disbandment, dislodgment, dismissal, dispersal or dispersion, displacement, dispossession, ejection, eviction, exile, expatriation, expulsion, ostracism, ouster, rebuff, relegation, repulse or repulsion, rout; *Also:* 1. coventry—ostracism

3. One Who Is Sent or Driven Away, etc.,n. *From Sec. 1:* outcast (from *cast out*), deportee; déporté (French); exile, expatriate (expatriate,adj.)

4. To Dismiss or Remove from a Position, Membership, etc.,v.
1. **bounce**—dismiss from employment
2. **cashier**—dismiss (an employee or member of an organization) under circumstances of disgrace
3. **defrock**—dismiss from the position, office, privileges, etc., of the clergy
4. **demount**—remove from a high position
5. **depone**—depose
6. **depose**—remove from office (deposal, deposition,n.)
7. **dethrone**—remove from office or position (dethronement,n.)
8. **discharge**—dismiss from employment (discharge,n.)
9. **disenthrone**—dethrone (disenthronement,n.)
10. **disfrock**—defrock

11. **disseat**—unseat
12. **disthrone**—dethrone
13. **expel**—dismiss from membership (expulsion,n.)
14. **fire**—dismiss from employment
15. **shelve**—dismiss from service
16. **suspend**—temporarily dismiss from office, membership, etc. (suspension,n.)
17. **unfrock**—defrock
18. **unmiter, unmitre**—dismiss from one's position as bishop
19. **unseat**—remove from position or office

145. MOVE, COME, OR GO BACK

1. To Move, Come, or Go Back,v.
1. **backslide**—relapse into moral wrong, crime, sin, etc., after correction; return to former habits after having cultivated new and better ones
2. **backtrack**—go back over a previously traversed route, course, road, etc.; go back, figuratively, from what one has said, promised, etc.; retreat
3. **cringe, blench**—shrink
4. **draw back**—go back; go back in fear or hesitation
5. **ebb**—go back from a high point
6. **fall back**—go back to a previous position; go back from danger, difficulty, etc.; go back out of fear; go back to a position of safety
7. **flinch**—draw back in fear or pain, or as if in fear or from pain
8. **pull back**—draw back; fall back
9. **quail**—shrink
10. **recede**—move or go back; go back to a previous position
11. **recoil**—go, move, draw, or fall back; return to previous position
12. **recur**—come or go back; go back (to); come back again
13. **regress**—move or go back or in a backward direction; come or go back to a lower, lesser, or less advanced state
14. **regurgitate**—come back with some force; come back in waves
15. **relapse**—go back or slip back into a former state or condition, or into former evil or illness
16. **remigrate**—go or come back
17. **retire**—go back; draw back; fall back
18. **retrace**—go back over
19. **retreat**—move or go back, usually from danger, difficulty, or an enemy; go back to be safe; go back out of fear
20. **retrocede**—move or go back or in a backward direction
21. **retrograde**—go backward; go back to a previously worse condition; retrocede
22. **retrogress**—move or go back, esp. to a worse, less advanced, or inferior position or condition
23. **return**—come back; go back
24. **revert**—go back to a former condition, belief, habit, etc.
25. **shrink**—draw back in fear
26. **slip back**—move, go, or come back inconspicuously, easily, smoothly, secretly, etc.
27. **wince**—draw back suddenly; shrink slightly
28. **withdraw**—go back; draw back; fall back

2. A Moving, Coming, or Going Back,n. *From Sec. 1:* backslide, blench, cringe, ebb, flinch, quail, recession, recoil, recurrence, regression, regurgitation, relapse, remigration, retirement, retracement, retreat, retrocession or retrocedence; retrogradation, retrograde, or retrogression; return, reversion, shrink, wince, withdrawal; *Also:*
1. **atavism**—a going back to a more primitive, less advanced, less civilized, etc., type

2. **recidivism**—a return to former criminal or sinful habits or activities after a period of correction
3. **throwback**—a going back to some earlier biological type or ancestor

3. Moving, Coming, or Going Back,adj. *From Sec. 1:* backsliding, blenching, cringing, ebbing, flinching, quailing, receding or recessive, recoiling, recurring or recurrent, regressing or regressive; regurgitating or regurgitant (medical); relapsing, remigrating, retiring, retreating, retrocessive, retrograde, retrogressing or retrogressive, returning, revertive or reversive, shrinking; *From Sec. 2:* atavistic, recidivous or recidivistic

4. One Who Moves, Comes, or Goes Back, n. *From Sec. 1:* backslider, remigrant, retreater, retrograde, reverter; *From Sec. 2:* atavist, recidivist, throwback; *Also:* **1.** revenant—one who comes back after death, or after a long absence

5. Person Who Is Inclined to Go Back: retrogressionist, retrogressive,n.

6. To Ask or Cause to Come Back: recall,v. (recall,n.)

146. BACK-AND-FORTH MOTION

1. To Move Back and Forth,v.
1. **corkscrew**—twist
2. **flap**—move back and forth while remaining attached to a place
3. **flop**—move back and forth; flap awkwardly
4. **fluctuate**—move lightly back and forth as if on waves
5. **lop**—move back and forth loosely
6. **pivot**—move back and forth on, or as if on, a fixed support
7. **rock**—move back and forth on, or as if on, a pivot
8. **roll**—move back and forth; rock
9. **seesaw**—move back and forth
10. **shuttle**—move back and forth over a short space
11. **sway**—move back and forth
12. **swing**—move back and forth, often with some regularity; move back and forth while hanging
13. **teeter, teeter-totter**—seesaw
14. **twist**—move back and forth in a crooked or irregular fashion
15. **wave**—move back and forth in the air
16. **waver**—move back and forth between points
17. **wigwag**—move back and forth
18. **wind**—twist

2. Back-and-Forth Movement,n. *From Sec. 1:* flap, flop, fluctuation, rock, roll, seesaw, sway, swing, teeter, twist, wave, waver, wigwag, wind

3. To Move (Something or Someone) Back and Forth,v. *From Sec. 1:* flap, pivot, rock, roll, seesaw, shuttle, sway, swing, teeter, twist, wave, wigwag, wind

4. Moving Back and Forth,adj. *From Sec. 1:* corkscrew, corkscrewing, or corkscrewy; flapping, floppy, fluctuating or fluctuant, pivoting, rocking or rocky, rolling, seesawing, swaying or asway; swinging, swingy, or aswing; twisting or twisty, waving, winding

147. SWAY; SWING

1. To Sway; To Swing,v.
1. **careen**—sway or swing from side to side
2. **dangle**—wave jerkily while hanging
3. **flap**—swing up and down or back and forth while remaining attached to a place
4. **flicker**—sway back and forth in short, quick motions

5. **flop**—flap awkwardly
6. **fluctuate**—swing back and forth, often figuratively
7. **flutter**—swing or sway back and forth
8. **lop**—sway loosely
9. **lurch**—sway suddenly to the side
10. **oscillate**—swing back and forth like a pendulum; swing between limits
11. **pivot**—swing on, or as if on, a support
12. **reel**—sway dizzily or unsteadily on one's feet as if abnormally weak or drunk
13. **rock**—sway backward and forward on a support; reel; totter
14. **roll**—sway from side to side
15. **seesaw**—swing up and down or back and forth, like the child's toy
16. **stagger**—sway from one side to another, from dizziness, weakness, drunkenness, a heavy burden, etc.
17. **switch**—swing in a wide arc
18. **swivel**—swing round
19. **teeter, teeter-totter**—swing back and forth; seesaw
20. **thrash**—swing about or back and forth wildly
21. **toss**—sway irregularly; sway from side to side
22. **totter**—sway as if about to fall
23. **undulate**—sway or swing in a wavy motion
24. **vibrate**—swing rapidly back and forth
25. **waddle**—move with the swaying motion of a duck
26. **wag**—sway; swing back and forth or up and down quickly and in short motions
27. **waggle**—swing or sway from side to side
28. **waltz**—whirl
29. **wave**—sway or swing back and forth
30. **waver**—sway in one direction or another; reel; totter
31. **whirl**—swing round and round rapidly
32. **wiggle**—move from side to side in quick jerks; waggle
33. **wobble, wabble**—sway; move with a side-to-side sway

2. Sway; Swing; Swaying or Swinging Motion,n. *From Sec. 1:* careen, dangle, flap, flicker, flop, fluctuation, flutter, lurch, oscillation, reel, rock, roll, seesaw, stagger, switch, teeter, thrash, toss, totter, undulation, vibration, waddle, wag, waggle, wave, waver, whirl, wiggle, wobble, wabble; *Also:* **1.** swaging or swaying motion

3. Swaying; Swinging,adj. *From Sec. 1:* careening, dangling, dangly, or adangle; flapping; flickering, flickery, or aflicker; floppy, fluctuating or fluctuant; fluttering, fluttery, or aflutter; lurching, oscillating or oscillatory, reeling, seesawing, staggering, swiveling, teetering, thrashing, tossing; tottering, tottery, or totterish; undulating, undulatory, undulant, or undulate; vibrating, vibrant, vibratory, or vibratile; waddling or waddly; wagging, waggy, or awag; waggling or waggly, waving or wavy, wavering or wavery; whirling, whirligig, whirly, or awhirl; wiggling, wiggly, or awiggle; wobbling, wabbling, or wobbly, wabbly; *Also:*
1. **billowy**—undulating
2. **pendulous**—swinging

4. To Cause to Sway or Swing,v. *From Sec. 1:* careen (a vehicle, ship, etc.), dangle, flap, flicker, flutter, oscillate, reel, rock, roll, seesaw, stagger, switch, swivel, teeter, thrash, toss, undulate, vibrate, wag, waggle, wave, whirl, wiggle

5. Swinging Body or Object: pendulum,n.

148. TURN

1. To Turn, i.e., Make a Turn, v.
1. **bend**—turn from a straight direction
2. **branch (out or off)**—diverge

3. **caracole**—make a half turn to either the left or right (of a horse)
4. **curve**—turn gradually; turn from a direct path
5. **deflect**—turn aside; turn aside from a position, course, straight line, etc.
6. **detour**—turn off one's direct course or path
7. **deviate (from)**—turn away or aside (from a course, topic, normality, etc.)
8. **digress (from)**—turn away or aside (from the topic being discussed)
9. **dip**—turn; turn downward
10. **divaricate**—diverge into two parts or branches
11. **diverge**—turn away in various directions from a common center or from the same point (either literally, in reference to actual motion, or figuratively, as in a turning away from normal, etc.)
12. **fork**—diverge
13. **incline**—turn away from a line, course, or direction
14. **orient, orientate**—turn toward the east; turn toward any desired or indicated direction
15. **pivot**—turn on a central point or fixed support
16. **radiate**—turn away from the center or central point
17. **retroflex**—turn sharply backward
18. **reverse**—turn in an opposite direction; turn back; turn inside out
19. **revert**—turn back to a former condition, belief, habit, etc.
20. **sheer**—turn aside; turn from the original course
21. **shunt**—turn away or aside; turn off
22. **skew**—turn sharply to one side
23. **swerve**—turn aside
24. **swing**—turn back and forth, often with some regularity
25. **tip**—turn
26. **twist**—turn
27. **veer**—turn sharply
28. **warp**—turn out of shape
29. **whirl**—turn aside quickly and suddenly
30. **wiggle, wriggle**—turn and twist like a worm
31. **wind**—turn gradually or repeatedly in direction (of a road, etc.)
32. **writhe**—turn and twist, often in discomfort or pain
33. **yaw**—turn from a straight or directed course; turn crazily (of ships over which control has been lost)
34. **zigzag**—turn at sharp and short angles

2. A Turn; A Turning,n. *From Sec. 1:* bend, branch, caracole; curve, curvature, or curvation; deflection, deflexure, or deflexion; detour, deviation, digression, dip, divarication, divergence or divergency, fork, incline or inclination, orientation, radiation, reversal, reversion, shunt, skew, swerve, swing, tip, twist, veer, warp, whirl, wind, wiggle, wriggle, writhe, yaw, zigzag; *Also:*
1. **crotch**—fork
2. **dextrogyration**—dextrorotation
3. **dextrorotation**—a turning toward the right side; a turning in a clockwise direction
4. **retroflexion, retroflection**—the turning back of an organ upon itself (medical)
5. **retroversion**—a turning back or backward
6. **quirk**—sudden turn; turn of the pen in writing
7. **sinistrogyration**—a turning toward the left; a turning in a counterclockwise direction
8. **upturn**—a turning up
9. **whirligig**—rapidly turning motion

3. Turning,adj. *From Sec. 1:* bending, branching, caracoling, curving, or curvy, deflected, deviating, digressing or digressive, dipping, divaricating, diverging or divergent, forking; inclining, inclined, or inclinatory; pivoting, radiating or radial, swerving, swinging, twisting or twisty, whirling, winding, wiggling or wiggly, wriggling or wriggly, writhing, yawing, zigzag, zigzagging, or zigzaggy; *From Sec. 2:* dextrogyrate, dextrogyrous, or dextrogyre; dextrorotatory, sinistrogyrate or sinistrogyric; *Also:*
1. **eccentric**—turning away from the center
2. **eely**—wriggling like an eel
3. **intricate**—turning and twisting (of a passage, path, etc.)
4. **sinuous, sinuose**—winding
5. **voluble**—turning easily

4. State or Quality of Turning,n. *From Sec. 3:* curviness, digressiveness, divergence or divergency, fork, swerve, twist, zigzag; eccentricity, intricacy, sinuousness or sinuosity, volubility or volubleness

5. Tending to Turn,adj. *From Sec. 1:* deflective, deviative, digressive, orientative (digressiveness,n.)

6. To Turn, i.e., Cause to Turn,v. *From Sec. 1:* bend, curve, deflect, detour, deviate, diverge, incline, orient, orientate, retroflex, reverse, shunt, swing, tip, twist, warp, wriggle; *Also:*
1. **deflex**—bend or curve downward
2. **divert**—turn away from its proper or expected course, destination, or direction
3. **evaginate**—turn inside out
4. **evert**—turn outward; turn inside out
5. **invert**—turn inside out
6. **obvert**—turn so that a different face, aspect, or surface is seen
7. **parry**—turn aside (a blow, question, attempt, etc.)
8. **pronate**—turn the limbs or other joints in a direction forward and toward the body
9. **reflect**—turn back (sound waves, light rays, etc.)
10. **reflex**—turn back
11. **retrovert**—turn backward
12. **supinate**—turn the limbs or other joints in a direction backward and away from the body
13. **ward off**—turn aside; parry

7. A Causing to Turn,n. *From Sec. 6:* curvation, deflection, deviation, inclination, orientation, retroflexion, reversal; deflexure or deflection, diversion, evagination, eversion, inversion, obversion, parry, pronation, reflection, supination

8. Causing to Turn,adj. *From Sec. 6:* deflective, diversive, eversive, orientative, reflective, reversive

9. State of Being Turned,n. *From Sec. 6:* deflection, deviation, orientation, evagination, inversion, pronation, reflection, retroversion, supination

10. Turned,adj. *From Sec. 6:* bent, curved, deflected, deviate, deviated, inclined, retroflex, reversed, tipped, twisted, warped; evaginated, inverted, pronate, retroverted, supine; *Also:*
1. **askew**—turned to one side
2. **awry**—turned to one side
3. **splay**—turned outward or toward the outside

11. Having Two Turns: biflex,adj.

12. Full of Turns,adj.
1. **anfractuous**—full of turnings and windings (anfractuosity,n.)
2. **sinuous, sinuose**—full of turns and curves (sinuousness, sinuosity,n.)

13. That Which Is Full of Turns: crinkumcrankum,n.

14. That on Which Something Turns: pivot, swivel,n.

15. Traffic Island around Which Cars Turn: rotary,n.

16. **Tendency to Turn toward a Magnetized Pole:** verticity,n.

149. TURN OVER

1. **To Turn (Something) Over,**v.
1. **capsize**—turn bottom end up or turn over (generally a small boat)
2. **invert**—turn upside-down
3. **overturn**—turn upside-down
4. **plow, plough**—turn over (the soil)
5. **reverse**—turn upside-down
6. **roll**—turn over and over
7. **tip**—turn over
8. **upend**—turn (something) over so that it now stands on its other end
9. **upset**—overturn
10. **upturn**—turn over

2. **To Turn Over, i.e., Be Turned Over,**v. *From Sec. 1:* capsize, overturn, reverse, roll, tip, upset, upturn; *Also:* 1. somersault, somerset, summersault, tumble—turn over completely, head over heels (of a person or animal)

3. **A Turning Over,**n. *From Sec. 1:* capsizal or capsize, inversion, overturn, reversal, roll, upset, upturn; *From Sec. 2:* somersault, somerset, or summersault.

4. **Turned Over,**adj. *From Sec. 1:* capsized, inverted, overturned, plowed, ploughed, reversed, upended, upturned; *Also:*
1. **sternforemost**—topsy-turvy
2. **topsy-turvy**—turned upside-down
3. **upside-down**—turned over

150. TURN ROUND

1. **To Turn Round,**v.
1. **birl**—spin; whir
2. **circle**—revolve
3. **circumvolve**—revolve
4. **gyrate**—revolve round a center
5. **pirouette**—spin on the toes or on one foot
6. **pivot**—turn round on a central point
7. **pronate**—rotate in a direction forward or toward the body (of the limbs or joints)
8. **revolve**—turn round in a circle; turn like a wheel
9. **roll**—revolve on an axis; rotate without sliding
10. **rotate**—turn like a wheel; turn in a circle or around a center or axis
11. **spin**—turn round rapidly
12. **supinate**—rotate in a direction backward and away from the body (of the limbs or joints)
13. **swirl**—whirl, twist, and curl simultaneously
14. **swivel**—turn round on a support or hinge
15. **troll**—turn round and round; revolve
16. **trundle**—roll; rotate; twirl
17. **tumble**—whirl round
18. **turn**—revolve
19. **twirl**—turn round and round rapidly or idly
20. **waltz**—whirl
21. **whir, whirr**—turn round and round very rapidly and with the characteristic sound made by a fast-moving body through the air
22. **whirl**—turn round and round rapidly

2. **To Cause (Someone or Something) to Turn Round,**v. *From Sec. 1:* pronate, revolve, roll, rotate, spin, supinate, swirl, swivel, troll, trundle, tumble, turn, twirl, whirl; *Also:*
1. **bowl**—roll or spin (a ball, hoop, etc.)
2. **twiddle**—turn (something) round idly and nervously

3. **A Turning Round,**n. *From Sec. 1:* birl, circumvolution, gyration, pirouette, pronation, revolution, roll, rotation, spin, supina-

tion, swirl, troll, trundle, tumble, turn, twirl, whirl; *From Sec. 2:* twiddle

4. **Turning Round,** adj. *From Sec. 1:* birling, gyrating or gyratory, pirouetting, pivoting, revolving; rotating, rotary, rotative, or rotatory; spinning, swirling, tumbling, turning, twirling, whirring, whirling; *Also:*
1. **vertiginous**—revolving
2. **voluble**—rotating
3. **vortical, vorticular, vorticose, vortiginous**—whirling

5. **Ability or Tendency to Turn Round:** revolvency,n.

6. **That Which Turns Round,**n.
1. **rotator, rotor**—something that revolves
2. **rundle**—anything that turns about an axis

7. **Science of Rotating Bodies:** gyrostatics,n. (gyrostatic,adj.)

8. **Rapidly Spinning Wheel or Disc on an Axis:** gyroscope,n. (gyroscopic,adj.)

151. ROLL

1. **To Roll,**v.
1. **billow**—roll in waves
2. **convolve**—roll together
3. **devolve**—roll on; roll in a downward direction
4. **fluctuate**—roll here and there
5. **lurch**—roll suddenly to one side
6. **revolve**—roll round on an axis
7. **rock**—roll back and forth
8. **toss**—roll nervously
9. **trundle**—roll along
10. **tumble**—roll over, or back and forth
11. **wallow (in)**—roll round (in)
12. **welter**—roll or toss about; roll round in a sinful or depraved condition

2. **A Roll; A Rolling,**n. *From Sec. 1:* billow, fluctuation, lurch, revolution, rock, toss, trundle, tumble, wallow, welter

3. **To Roll (Something) Tightly:** furl,v.

4. **Tending to Roll; Rolling Easily:** voluble, adj. (volubility,n.)

5. **Full of Rolls:** billowy,adj.

152. BEND

1. **To Bend,**v.
1. **bow**—bend; bend the head or upper part of the body
2. **crook**—bend
3. **crouch**—bend down slavishly, humbly, or timidly; bend low
4. **curve**—bend gradually
5. **decline**—bend downward; bend aside
6. **flex**—bend
7. **genuflect**—bend the knee in, or as in, worship
8. **incline**—bend; bow
9. **kneel**—bend the knee
10. **lean**—bend
11. **nod**—bend so that the upper part comes forward
12. **recline**—bend backward
13. **retroflex**—bend sharply back
14. **sag**—bend in the middle
15. **salaam**—bow low as a form of greeting or salutation
16. **stoop**—bend forward and downward
17. **tilt**—bend
18. **twist**—bend
19. **verge**—bend

2. **To Cause (Something) to Bend; To Bend (Something),**v. *From Sec. 1:* bow, crook, curve, flex, incline, lean, nod, recline, tilt, twist

3. **A Bend; A Bending,**n. *From Sec. 1:* bow, crook, crouch; curve, curvature, or curvation;

declination; flexure, flection, or flexion; genuflection, inclination, kneel, lean or leaning, nod, reclination, retroflexion, sag, salaam, stoop, tilt, twist; *Also:*
1. **bight**—bend; bend in a river, coast, coast line, mountain chain, etc.
2. **nutation**—a nodding; involuntary nodding of the head
3. **retroflexion, retroflection**—a bending back of an organ upon itself (medical)
4. **retroversion**—a bending back or backward
5. **sinus**—bend

4. **Bending,adj.** *From Sec. 1:* crouching, curving or curvy, genuflectory, inclining or inclinatory, kneeling, leaning, nodding, reclining, sagging or saggy, stooping, tilting, twisting or twisty; *From Sec. 3:* nutant; *Also:*
1. **sinuous, sinuose**—bending in and out (sinuousness, sinuosity,n.)

5. **Bent,adj.** *From Sec. 1:* bowed, crooked, curved, curvate, or curvated, declinate, flexed, inclined, retroflex, saggy, stooped, tilted, twisted; *Also:*
1. **biflected**—bent twice
2. **biflex**—bent in two directions; having two bends
3. **crumpled**—bent spirally
4. **geniculate**—bent sharply at an angle
5. **genuflexuous**—bent like the knee; bent sharply at an angle
6. **hooked**—bent sharply like a hook
7. **retrorse**—bent downward or backward
8. **uncinate, uncinated**—bent like a hook

6. **State of Being Bent,n.** *From Sec. 5:* crookedness, curvature or curvation, flexure, retroflexion, sagginess; geniculation (flexural,adj.)

7. **Capable of Bending; Bending Easily,adj.**
1. **flexible**—capable of bending or being bent without breaking (flexibility, flexibleness,n.)
2. **limber**—bending easily (limberness,n.)
3. **lissome**—limber (lissomeness,n.)
4. **lithe, lithesome**—bending easily (litheness, lithesomeness,n.)
5. **pliable**—easily bent; flexible (pliability, pliableness,n.)
6. **pliant**—bending easily; flexible (pliancy, n.)
7. **supple**—bending easily (suppleness,n.)
8. **svelte**—lithe
9. **tough**—bending without breaking (toughness,n.)
10. **waxen**—pliable
11. **withy**—flexible but strong (withiness, n.)

153. LEAN

1. **To Lean,v.**
1. **cant**—list
2. **careen**—list
3. **decline**—lean downward
4. **heel**—list
5. **incline**—lean
6. **list**—lean to one side (of ships, vehicles, etc.)
7. **recline**—lean backward
8. **tilt**—lean; lean slightly
9. **tip**—lean slightly

2. **To Cause to Lean,v.** *From Sec. 1:* careen, incline, recline, tilt, tip

3. **A Leaning,n.** *From Sec. 1:* cant, careen, declination, list, reclination, tilt

4. **Leaning,adj.** *From Sec. 1:* canting, careening, declining, heeling, inclining or inclinatory, listing, reclining, tilting; *Also:*
1. **incumbent**—leaning; reclining on and exerting a downward pressure (incumbency,n.)
2. **lopsided**—leaning sharply to one side (lopsidedness,n.)

3. **recumbent**—leaning; reclining (recumbency,n.)

154. SLANT; SLOPE

1. **To Slant or Slope, i.e., Have a Slant or Slope,v.**
1. **ascend**—slope upward
2. **bank**—slope
3. **batter**—slope in a slight and gradual backward decline (usually of a wall)
4. **bevel**—slant; slope
5. **cant**—slant; slope
6. **decline**—slope downward
7. **descend**—slope downward
8. **dip**—slope downward
9. **drop**—slope downward
10. **fall**—slope downward
11. **incline**—slope
12. **lean**—slope
13. **pitch**—slope downward
14. **rake**—slant; slope; slope from the vertical
15. **shelve**—slope gradually
16. **skew**—slant
17. **splay**—slant
18. **tilt**—slant; slope
19. **tip**—slant; slope

2. **To Slant or Slope, i.e., Cause to Slant or Slope,v.** *From Sec. 1:* bank, bevel, dip, incline, splay, tilt, tip

3. **A Slanting or Sloping; A Slant or Slope, n.** *From Sec. 1:* ascent, bank, batter, bevel, cant; declination, decline, or declension; descent, dip, drop, fall, inclination or incline, lean, pitch, rake, shelf, tilt; *Also:*
1. **acclivity**—upward slope (of a hill, road, etc.)
2. **chute**—steep slope; inclined slope for letting things slide down
3. **declivity**—gradual downward slope
4. **downgrade**—downward slope
5. **grade**—slope
6. **gradient**—rising or falling slope
7. **helicline**—slope that gradually curves as it ascends
8. **hill**—slope; fairly steep slope
9. **precipice**—very steep, almost vertical, slope
10. **talus**—slope
11. **upgrade**—upward slope
12. **uprise, uprising**—upward slope
13. **versant**—slope of a mountain range; general slope of a country

4. **Slanting or Sloping,adj.** *From Sec. 1:* ascending, banked, beveled, declining, descending, dipping, dropping, falling, inclining or inclined, rakish, skew; tilting, tilted, or atilt; *From. Sec. 3:* acclivous, declivitous, declivous, or declivate; hilly, uprising; *Also:*
1. **abrupt**—very steeply inclined (abruptness,n.)
2. **declivitous**—sloping sharply downward
3. **oblique**—slanting; neither straight up and down nor right to left (obliquity, obliqueness,n.)
4. **pendent**—sloping sharply down (pendency,n.)
5. **precipitant**—sloping perpendicularly downward (precipitance, precipitancy,n.)
6. **precipitous**—very steeply inclined, like a precipice (precipitousness,n.)
7. **steep**—sloping sharply (steepness,n.)
8. **synclinal**—sloping from opposite directions in such a manner as to meet at a point (synclinality, synclination,n.)
9. **tipsy**—slanting; sloping

5. **Instrument to Measure Slope,n.**
1. **clinometer**—instrument to measure the angles of slope
2. **declinometer**—instrument to measure the degree or angle of downward slopes

6. **In a Slanting Direction:** aslant, aslantwise, aslope, athwart,adv.

155. CURVE

1. To Curve, i.e., Move Curvingly,v.
1. arch—curve in the form of any portion of a circle
2. bow—curve
3. bulge—curve outward
4. concave—curve inward
5. convex—curve outward
6. crook—curve
7. curl—curve; move in curves or spirals
8. gyrate—spiral about an axis or central point
9. hook—curve
10. loop—curve
11. snake—curve like a snake, in a winding fashion
12. spiral—curve in such a way as to go round and round in a widening circle
13. swerve—curve
14. swirl—curl
15. twist—curve; wind
16. wind—move curvingly or in continuous curves
17. wreathe—curl; wind

2. A Curve; A Curving,n. *From Sec. 1:* arch, bow, bulge, concavity, convexity, crook, curl, gyration, hook, loop, spiral, swerve, swirl, twist, wind; *Also:*
1. arc—curve
2. bight—long curve in a coast line
3. contour—curve
4. curvation, curvature—act or instance of curving
5. ellipse—closed curve in the shape of a flattened circle
6. quirk—sudden curve

3. Curving,adj. *From Sec. 1:* bulging, curling, gyrating or gyratory, spiral; swirling, swirly, or aswirl; twisting or atwist, winding

4. Curvy; Curved,adj. *From Sec. 1:* arched, bowed, bulgy or bulged, concave, convex, crooked, curly or curled, gyrate, hooked, loopy or looped, snaky, spiral, twisty or twisted, wreathed or wreathy; *From Sec. 2:* contoured; *Also:*
1. adunc, aduncous—curved inward
2. arciform—curved
3. arcuate—curved like a bow
4. bandy—curved outward
5. biconcave—concave on two sides
6. biconvex—convex on two sides
7. biflected—curved twice
8. compass—curved
9. concavo-concave—concave on both sides
10. concavo-convex—concave on one side, convex on the other
11. convexo-concave—convex on one side, concave on the other
12. convexo-convex—convex on both sides
13. corkscrew, corkscrewy—spiral
14. curvate, curvated—curved
15. sigmate—curved like the Greek sigma, or S
16. sigmoid—curved like the letter S
17. sinuous, sinuose—full of curves and turns
18. tortuous—full of curves and twists
19. uncinate, uncinated—curved like a hook

5. Curviness,n. *From Sec. 4:* bulginess, concavity, convexity, crookedness, curliness, snakiness, twistiness; aduncity, biconcavity, biconvexity, curvation, curvature, sinuousness or sinuosity, tortuousness; *Also:* 1. curvature —state of being abnormally curved (medical)

6. Curved Part,n. *From Sec. 1:* arch, crook, hook, loop

7. Act of Curving,n. *From Sec. 1:* gyration; *Also:* 1. curvature or curvation—act of curving

8. To Curve (Something); To Cause (Something) to Curve,v. *From Sec. 1:* arch, bow,

bulge, concave, convex, crook, curl, hook, loop, twist, wind, wreathe

9. Outline of the Curves of a Figure or Region: contour,n. (contour,adj. contour,v.)

10. Inner Surface of a Curve: concavity,n.

11. Outer Surface of a Curve: convexity,n.

12. Hooked Instrument: crook, hook,n.

13. Instrument That Measures Curvature of a Surface: spherometer,n.

156. TWIST; WIND

1. To Wind or Twist, i.e., Move in a Winding or Twisting Fashion,v.
1. coil—wind spirally or cylindrically
2. convolute—twist around elaborately; writhe
3. corkscrew—wind around or through; wind around in the shape of a spiral
4. crimp—twist into waves
5. crisp—twist into short folds or ringlets
6. crook—wind
7. curl—twist into rings or curves; twist out of shape
8. entangle—twist together or interweave in such a way that separation is difficult
9. entwine—wind together and around; twist together
10. gyrate—wind; wind around as in a spiral
11. interlace—wind or weave together by or as by lacing
12. intertwine—interlace
13. intertwist—twist together
14. interweave—wind in and around; wind together
15. interwind—wind together, or one through the other
16. interwreathe—interweave; wreathe
17. involute—wind inward at the edges; coil
18. kink—twist or curl (said of thread, rope, hair, etc.)
19. knot—twist into knots; become twisted; become twisted together
20. mat—twist thickly together
21. meander—wind intricately or aimlessly (from the Maiandros River in Phrygia, famous for its winding course)
22. skew—twist to one side
23. slither—move in a winding, snakelike manner
24. snake—wind around like a snake
25. spiral—wind around a center
26. squirm—twist around in nervousness, boredom, embarrassment, confusion, etc.; move by twisting and turning
27. swirl—move in a twisting, curling, and whirling manner
28. tangle—twist together into a confused jumble
29. twine—wind around; twist together; wind in an irregular course
30. warp—twist out of shape by drying or shrinking or, figuratively, by going off in a wrong or unhealthy direction
31. weave—wind in and around
32. whip (around, through)—wind (around or through) quickly
33. wrap (around)—wind (around)
34. wreathe—twist; twist into folds or creases; interweave into a circle; entwine
35. wriggle—twist and turn like a worm; squirm
36. writhe—twist and turn; twist and turn in discomfort or pain

2. To Wind or Twist (Something),v. *From Sec. 1:* coil, convolute, crimp, crisp, curl, entangle, entwine, interlace, intertwine, intertwist, interweave, interwind, interwreathe, involute, kink, knot, mat, spiral, swirl, tangle, twine, warp, weave, whip, wrap, wreathe, wriggle, writhe; *Also:*
1. braid—twist, wind, or weave

2. **complect**—wind, weave, or plait together
3. **complicate**—twist together
4. **contort**—twist back upon itself; twist together; twist (something) in such a way as to give it a grotesque or painful appearance
5. **convolve**—twist one part of on another
6. **cue**—braid
7. **deform**—twist in physical form; twist out of shape
8. **distort**—twist out of shape (literally or figuratively)
9. **gnarl**—twist out of shape
10. **intort**—twist inward; twist in and out
11. **plait**—wind together by strands; weave
12. **raddle**—twist together; interlace; interweave
13. **ravel**—twist; tangle
14. **reel**—wind
15. **torture**—twist out of shape
16. **tweak**—simultaneously twist, pinch, and pull
17. **twiddle**—twist slightly with the fingers
18. **twinge**—tweak
19. **wattle**—twist together or weave (branches, twigs, etc.)
20. **wrench**—twist forcibly or violently
21. **wrest**—twist away violently
22. **wring**—twist; twist and squeeze forcibly

3. A Winding or Twisting; A Wind or Twist, n. *From Secs. 1 and 2:* coil, convolution, crimp, crispation or crispature, crook, curl, entanglement, gyration, interlacement, intertwine, intertwist, involution, kink, knot, mat, meander, slither, spiral, squirm, swirl, tangle, twine, warp or warpage, whip, wrap, wriggle, writhe; braid, complication, contortion, convolution, deformation, distortion, intorsion, plait, raddle, ravel, torture, tweak, twiddle, twinge, wattle, wrench, wrest, wring; *Also:*
1. **curlicue**—fancy twist; fancy curl; spiral
2. **ply**—twist
3. **quirk**—sudden twist; twist of the pen in writing
4. **torsion**—act of twisting
5. **vermiculation**—a twisting or writhing like a worm

4. That Which Winds or Twists or Is Full of Winds or Twists,n. *From Sec. 1:* coil, convolution, corkscrew, crimp, curl, kink, knot, mat, spiral, tangle; *From Sec. 2:* braid; cue, or, in reference to hair, queue; plait; *From Sec. 3:* curlicue; *Also:*
1. **kinkum-crankum**—anything full of windings or twistings
2. **helix**—spiral
3. **labyrinth**—maze
4. **whorl**—coil; convolution

5. Winding; Twisting; Twisted; Full of Winds or Twists,adj. *From Sec. 1:* coiled, convolute or convoluted, corkscrew or corkscrewy, crimpy, crisp, crispate, or crispy; crooked; curling, curly, or curled; entangled, entwined, gyrate or gyratory, interlaced, intertwined, intertwisted, interwoven or interwound, interwreathed, involute or involuted, kinky, knotty, matted or matty, meandrous or meandering, askew, snaky, spiral or spiry, squirming or squirmy; swirling, swirly, or aswirl; tangled or tangly, twined or twining, warped, wreathed, wriggling or wriggly, writhing; *From Sec. 2:* braided, complected or complex, complicated; contortive, contorsive, contort, contorted, or contortioned; deformed, distorted, gnarled or gnarly, intorted, plaited, raddled, raveled, tortured or torturous, wattled; *From Sec. 4:* helical or helicoid, labyrinthian or labyrinthine, mazy, whorled; *Also:*
1. **ambagious**—winding
2. **anfractuous**—full of windings and turnings
3. **awry**—askew
4. **circuitous**—winding

5. **cirrose**—curly, like curly hair
6. **crooked**—twisted; twisted out of shape
7. **devious**—winding away from a direct course; twisting; winding (as a path, road, etc.); figuratively winding (as a discussion, reasoning, etc.)
8. **dextrorse, dextrorsal**—twining in a spiral from left to right (botany)
9. **eely**—wriggling, like an eel
10. **flexuous**—full of winding turns
11. **intricate**—twisting and turning (as a passage, path, etc.)
12. **knurly**—gnarled
13. **plexiform**—wound or winding, like a network; complicated
14. **reticular**—intricate, like a net
15. **serpentine**—winding or twisting, like a serpent
16. **sinistrorse, sinistrorsal**—twining in a spiral form from right to left (botany)
17. **sinuous**—winding; weaving in and out; winding in a snakelike manner
18. **tortile**—twisted; coiled
19. **tortuous**—winding in different directions; full of twists and curves (literally or figuratively)
20. **voluminous**—full of twists or windings
21. **volute**—spiral
22. **wry**—twisted to one side; with the features of the face twisted out of normal shape; distorted

6. State of Being Wound or Twisted,n. *From Sec. 5:* convolution, crispation, entanglement, tangle; complicacy, contortion, deformity, distortion or torsion; ambagiousness, anfractuosity, circuity or circuitousness, crookedness, deviousness, flexuousness, intricacy, sinuosity or sinuousness, tortuosity or tortuousness, voluminousness, wryness

7. To Curl Up in Comfort: cuddle, nestle, snuggle,v.

8. To Unwind or Untwist: disentangle, disentwine, ravel, reel out, unbraid, uncoil, unreel, untangle, untwine, unweave, unwrap, unwreathe,v.

157. FOLD

1. To Fold, i.e., Put a Fold or Folds in,v.
1. **cockle**—pucker
2. **complicate**—fold together
3. **corrugate**—form a long, somewhat hollow fold in; form into raised folds
4. **crease**—fold; fold into a line or wrinkle
5. **crimp**—press into small, regular folds
6. **crinkle**—form into many small and irregular folds or beginnings of folds
7. **crisp**—fold into small curls
8. **crumple**—crush into folds
9. **enfold**—infold
10. **furrow**—crease
11. **groove**—form a long, somewhat hollow fold in (something)
12. **infold**—fold over; cover with folds; make a fold in
13. **loop**—fold; fold back (rope, string, or that which is likened to rope or string)
14. **plait**—fold; make or form into folds
15. **pleat**—fold; make or form into folds
16. **pucker**—draw or contract into folds
17. **purse**—pucker
18. **replicate**—fold back; fold over or back upon itself
19. **ridge**—form into raised folds
20. **ruffle**—draw or make into folds
21. **rumple**—squeeze or make into numerous and irregular folds
22. **seam**—groove; ridge
23. **wreathe**—twist into folds

2. To Fold, i.e., Become Folded,v. *From Sec. 1:* cockle, corrugate, crease, crimp, crinkle, crisp, crumple, loop, pucker, purse, ridge, ruffle, rumple, seam

3. A Folding,n. *From Secs. 1 and 2:* complication, corrugation, crispation or crispature, enfoldment, infoldment; *Also:*

1. **circumvolution**—a folding of one thing about another
2. **involution**—process of folding inward
3. **plication**—act of folding

4. A Fold,n. *From Sec. 1:* cockle, complication, corrugation, crease, crimp, crinkle, crumple, furrow, groove, infolding, loop, plait, pleat, pucker, ridge, ruffle, rumple, seam; *From Sec. 3:* circumvolution, plication; *Also:*

1. **convolution, convolute**—fold; twisted fold
2. **flection**—fold
3. **plica**—fold
4. **ply**—fold

5. Folded; Having Folds,adj. *From Sec. 1:* cockled; cockle (of the surface of paper); complicated, corrugated or corrugate, creased, crimped, crinkled or crinkly, crisped or crispy, crumpled, enfolded, furrowed, grooved, infolded, looped or loopy, plaited, pleated, puckered or puckery, pursed or pursy, replicate or replicative, ridged, ruffled or ruffly, rumpled or rumply, seamed or seamy, wreathed; *From Sec. 4:* convoluted; *Also:*

1. **bullate**—puckered
2. **voluminous**—full of folds; full of twisting, winding, or complicated folds

6. Easily Contracting into Folds: puckery, adj.

7. Folded Part: plica,n.

8. Fold of Skin: plica,n.

158. WRINKLE

1. To Wrinkle, i.e., Put a Wrinkle or Wrinkles in,v.

1. **cockle**—wrinkle; pucker
2. **contract**—wrinkle (the forehead)
3. **corrugate**—wrinkle in deep folds
4. **crease**—wrinkle; make wrinkles in by folding or as if by folding
5. **crinkle**—wrinkle; turn or wind into wrinkles
6. **crisp**—wrinkle into small folds or curls
7. **crumple**—crush into wrinkles
8. **furrow**—wrinkle
9. **pucker**—draw or contract into wrinkles
10. **purse**—pucker
11. **ruffle**—draw or make into wrinkles
12. **rumple**—wrinkle; crush into wrinkles; squeeze or make into numerous wrinkles
13. **seam**—wrinkle
14. **shrivel**—wrinkle
15. **wither**—wrinkle
16. **wreathe**—twist into wrinkles

2. To Wrinkle, i.e., Become Wrinkled,v. *From Sec. 1:* cockle, corrugate, crease, crinkle, crisp, crumple, pucker, purse, ruffle, rumple, seam, shrivel, wither

3. A Wrinkling,n. *From Secs. 1 and 2:* contraction, corrugation, crispation or crispature

4. A Wrinkle,n. *From Sec. 1:* cockle, corrugation, crease, crinkle, crumple, furrow, pucker, ruffle, rumple, seam; *Also:*

1. **crow's-foot**—wrinkle at the outer corner of the eye
2. **rugosity**—wrinkle

5. Wrinkled,adj. *From Sec. 1:* cockled, cockle (of the surface of paper), contracted, corrugated or corrugate, creased, crinkled or crinkly, crisped or crispy, crumpled, furrowed, puckered or puckery, pursed or pursy, ruffled or ruffly, rumpled or rumply, seamed or seamy, shriveled, withered, wreathed; *From Sec. 4:* rugose (rugosity,n.); *Also:*

1. **bullate**—puckered
2. **rugged**—wrinkled

6. Wrinkled Place: rugosity,n.

159. RISE

1. To Rise; To Go, Come, or Move Up or Upward,v.

1. **arise**—go up; move upward
2. **arrow**—go up; move swiftly upward
3. **ascend**—go up; go higher; climb
4. **billow**—rise like an ocean wave
5. **bristle**—rise erect (of hair)
6. **clamber**—climb on hands and feet
7. **climb**—go up or go higher by, or as if by, the use of the hands and feet to hold on; go up with difficulty or continuous effort; go up gradually; rise; rear (of horses); mount
8. **crop up, out**—come up to the surface
9. **dominate**—rise high above
10. **emerge**—come up from a lower state into a higher or better one
11. **escalade**—climb by means of ladder or ladders; scale as if by ladder
12. **jump**—move upward suddenly
13. **levitate**—rise into the air and float without support; do this by a magical trick depending on illusion
14. **lift**—come up; rise
15. **mount**—rise; go up; get up on; climb to the top of
16. **overtop**—rise above
17. **rear**—rise up on the hind legs (of animals)
18. **resurge**—rise again; rise again from, or as if from, death, destruction, inactivity, etc.
19. **rocket**—rise suddenly and very fast
20. **scale**—climb, through effort and perseverance, that which is difficult to get to the top of
21. **scramble, scrabble**—climb and crawl simultaneously
22. **shinny up**—climb up (a pole, tree, etc.) by the use of the shins
23. **skyrocket**—rise to amazing heights; rise very fast to great heights
24. **soar**—rise high, or higher than normal; rise in spirits; rise in spirits above worldly things or thoughts
25. **surface**—come up to the top (usually of a body of water)
26. **surge**—rise strongly; rise in or like waves
27. **surmount**—go up and over; rise above
28. **swarm**—climb; shin
29. **swell**—rise above a point or level
30. **take off**—rise from the ground (of birds, planes, etc.)
31. **top**—rise above or higher
32. **tower**—rise high; rise high above the surroundings
33. **transcend**—rise beyond the power to control or grasp
34. **uprear**—rise up
35. **upspring**—rise up
36. **vault**—mount by jumping on
37. **wallow**—rise in swirls; billow; surge
38. **well up**—rise
39. **wreathe**—move upward in rings or circular arrangement
40. **zoom**—move suddenly upward, or upward at a sharp angle

2. Rise or Rising,n. *From Sec. 1:* ascent or ascension, billow, clamber, climb, domination, emergence, jump, levitation, lift, mount, rear, resurgence, scramble, scrabble, soar, surge, swell, take-off, transcendence, upspring, vault, wallow, zoom; *Also:*

1. **aurora**—figurative rise
2. **upheaval**—a rising up of the earth's crust

3. Riser,n. *From Sec. 1:* ascendant, climber, levitator, scaler, vaulter

4. Rising,adj. *From Sec. 1:* ascending, ascendant, or ascensive; billowing or billowy, clambering, climbing, dominating or dominant, emergent, mounting, rearing, resurging or resurgent, soaring, surging, swelling, tow-

ering, transcending or transcendent, wallowing, wreathing, zooming; *Also:*
1. **bluff**—rising with a high, flat front (of hills, natural configurations of land, etc.)
2. **emersed**—rising above the surface of the water
3. **lofty**—rising high, figuratively (lofty desires, etc.)
4. **rampant**—rising up on the hind legs, the forelegs raised
5. **scandent**—climbing (usually of plants)

5. Adapted to Climbing (of Animals or Animal Anatomy): scansorial,adj.

6. Means of Rising (Figuratively): ladder, steppingstone,n.

7. Vehicle for Transporting to Higher Levels: elevator,n.

8. To Go Over the Head of an Official to a Higher Authority: by-pass,v.

9. Climber,n.
1. **Alpinist**—mountain climber, esp. in the Alps
2. **cragsman**—cliff climber
3. **mountaineer**—mountain climber
4. **steeplejack**—person whose occupation it is to climb high places to make repairs, paint, etc.

10. Practice of Mountain Climbing (Esp. in the Alps): Alpinism,n.

11. Staff Used in Mountain Climbing: alpenstock,n.

12. Climbing Irons: crampons,n.

160. A STEP (FOR RISING)

1. A Step; One of a Group of Steps: stair, stairstep,n.

2. Step of a Ladder: bar, rundle, rung, spoke, stave, tread,n.

3. That Part of a Step on Which the Feet Are Placed in Climbing: tread,n.

4. The Vertical Part of a Step: riser,n.

5. Step or Steps for Going over a Fence or Wall: stile,n.

6. Group of Steps That Goes from One Level of a Building to the Next Higher or Lower: flight, flog, stairs; staircase or stairway (with its framework, etc.),n.

7. Such Groups, One after the Other: staircase, stairway,n.

8. Group or Series of Steps at the Entrance to a House: stoop,n.

9. Moving Staircase or Stairway: escalator, n.

10. A Way or Passage Up or Down by Means of Stairs: stairway,n.

11. The Open Shaft or Compartment Containing a Staircase: stair well,n.

12. The Top or Head of a Staircase: stairhead,n.

13. Platform or Section of Floor between Groups or Flights of Stairs in a Building: landing,n.

14. Railing of a Staircase: baluster, balustrade, banister,n.

15. Support in a Staircase Railing: baluster, rail, upright,n.

16. First, or Final, Support of a Staircase Railing: newel, newel post,n.

17. Central Support from Which Winding Stairs Radiate: newel,n.

18. Having Stairs: staired,adj.

19. Arranged or Grouped Like Stairs or Steps: staired, stairstep,adj.

20. The Construction Involved in Making Stairs: stairwork,n.

21. Scored Like the Rungs of a Ladder; Ladderlike: scalariform,adj.

161. RISE AND FALL

1. To Rise and Fall,v.
1. **billow**—rise and fall in waves
2. **dip**—fall and rise
3. **post**—rise and sink in a saddle in synchronization with a horse's movements
4. **surge**—rise and fall
5. **undulate**—rise and fall like ocean waves
6. **welter**—rise and fall stormily

2. A Rising and Falling,n. *From Sec. 1:* billow, dip, post, surge, undulation, welter; *Also:* 1. **tide**—rhythmic rise and fall

3. Rising and Falling,adj. *From Sec. 1:* billowy or billowing, dipping, surging; undulatory, undulating, or undulate; weltering

4. That Which Rises and Falls like the Ocean: tide,n.

162. UP AND DOWN MOTION

1. To Move Up and Down,v.
1. **bob**—move up and down with quick, short, or jerky motions
2. **flap**—move up and down while remaining attached to a place
3. **jog**—move up and down with a shaking motion
4. **pump**—move up and down
5. **seesaw**—move up and down
6. **teeter-totter**—seesaw

2. Up-and-Down Movement,n. *From Sec. 1:* bob, flap, jog, pump, seesaw, teeter-totter

163. RAISE

1. To Raise; To Lift,v.
1. **boost**—lift or raise up from below
2. **bristle**—make (the hair) rise erect
3. **elevate**—raise up high, whether literally or figuratively
4. **emboss**—raise in relief from the surface (of printing, ornamentation, etc.)
5. **exalt**—raise high in honor, rank, etc.
6. **heave**—raise, using considerable energy, force, or exertion
7. **heft**—lift in order to judge or estimate the weight of; heave
8. **heighten**—make higher
9. **hoist**—raise, esp. with a tackle; raise aloft; raise higher
10. **levitate**—cause to rise into the air and float without support; do this by a magic trick depending on illusion
11. **perk (up)**—raise or lift smartly; lift the head
12. **poise**—raise
13. **pry**—raise with force or effort
14. **rear**—raise upright or erect
15. **toss**—lift or raise quickly
16. **upraise**—raise up
17. **uprear**—raise

2. A Raising; A Lifting; A Lift,n. *From Sec. 1:* boost, elevation, embossment, exaltation, heave, hoist, levitation, pry, toss

3. To Bring Up from, or as if from, the Bottom: dredge,v.

4. Machine or Device for Raising or Lifting, n.
1. **capstan**—machine for lifting or pulling
2. **dredge**—device for raising earth, sand, marine specimens, etc., from the bottom of the sea
3. **elevator**—machine or device for lifting or raising

4. **hoist**—apparatus for lifting or raising heavy loads; elevator
5. **lift**—apparatus for lifting or raising
6. **tackle**—apparatus consisting of ropes and blocks for raising and lowering
7. **winch**—machine for raising or hoisting, turned by a crank
8. **windlass**—machine for raising or hoisting

5. Elevator Car: cage,n.

164. HEIGHT

1. High,adj.
1. **abrupt**—steep
2. **alpine**—high, like a mountain
3. **declivitous**—fairly steep
4. **elevated**—high; raised up high, literally or figuratively
5. **exalted**—raised up high in honor, rank, etc.
6. **lofty**—high; having an impressive height; figuratively high
7. **precipitous**—steep
8. **steep**—high; unusually high
9. **sublime**—exalted
10. **supernal**—high in position
11. **tall**—high
12. **towering**—very high
13. **upborne**—raised high
14. **winged**—figuratively high

2. Height,n. *From Sec. 1:* abruptness, elevation, loftiness, precipitousness, steepness, sublimity or sublimeness, tallness; *Also:*
1. **altitude**—height
2. **stature**—height

3. High above the Ground: aloft,adv.

4. Higher: superior, upper,adj. (superiority, n.)

5. Going Higher: upward,adj. or adv.

6. Highest,adj.
1. **maximal**—highest
2. **supreme**—highest in authority, influence, power, or position; highest in degree; highest in quality (supremacy,n.)
3. **tiptop**—highest
4. **top**—highest
5. **top-drawer**—highest in rank, social level, excellence, or importance
6. **top-flight**—highest in rank, ability, eminence, or excellence
7. **topmost**—highest
8. **top-notch**—highest in excellence
9. **upmost, uppermost**—highest
10. **utmost**—highest

7. To Be High or Higher,v.
1. **command**—dominate (command,n.)
2. **dominate**—occupy a high or higher geographical position (domination, dominance, dominancy,n.)
3. **overlook**—be higher than (geographically)
4. **surmount**—be above; be higher than
5. **top**—be higher than
6. **tower (above)**—be very high; be higher than similar or surrounding people or things
7. **transcend**—be higher than (transcendence, transcendency,n. transcendent,adj.)

8. Measurement of Heights, Esp. Heights of Natural Protuberances, Such as Hills, Mountains, etc., in Reference to Sea Level: hypsography, hypsometry,n.

9. Instrument to Measure Height,n.
1. **altimeter**—device for measuring altitude
2. **altometer**—device for measuring elevations
3. **hypsometer**—device to measure the height of lands or mountains in reference to sea level

4. **quadrant**—instrument for measuring heights
5. **tachymeter**—device that measures the height and distance of a remote object

165. TOP

1. Top; High or Highest Point,n.
1. **acme**—topmost point (acmic, acmatic, adj.)
2. **apex**—top, climax, or tip—the implication being that all lines or efforts have converged to this point (apical,adj.)
3. **apogee**—highest point in a movement (In astronomy, the apogee of a comet, planet, etc., is that point in its orbit when it is farthest from the earth. The term need not be applied only to praiseworthy things; we may speak of the *apogee of man's cruelty,* the *apogee of the depression,* etc.)
4. **climax**—highest point of a process (climactic,adj.)
5. **cope**—vertex
6. **crest**—topmost part, as of a hill, mountain, wave, etc.
7. **crown**—top; highest part (coronal,adj.)
8. **culmination**—highest point in a process, development, career, etc. (culminant,adj.)
9. **cusp**—apex; peak
10. **height**—highest point; summit
11. **meridian**—highest point, in analogy to the highest point reached by the sun in a day (meridian,adj.)
12. **ne plus ultra (Latin)**—the final pinnacle of achievement or accomplishment
13. **noon**—highest point
14. **noontide**—highest point; culmination
15. **peak**—pointed top of a hill or mountain (implying a range, so that there may be higher peaks on other hills or mountains within the range); topmost or highest point, though often a temporary one
16. **pinnacle**—highest point of achievement, progress, etc.; possibly insecure and abnormally high point
17. **ridge**—long and narrow top; top of an animal's back; crest
18. **solstice**—highest point (solstitial,adj.)
19. **spire**—pointed top
20. **summit**—top; highest point; highest point or level attainable by human effort; top of a hill or mountain
21. **tip**—very top; highest point
22. **tiptop**—very top; highest point
23. **vertex**—top or highest point (vertical, adj.)
24. **zenith**—highest point of achievement or distinction; summit; in astronomy the point in the heavens directly overhead (zenithal,adj.)

2. To Reach the Top or Highest Point,v.
1. **culminate**—reach the highest point in development, in a process, etc. (culmination,n. culminant,adj.)
2. **mount**—get to the top of
3. **surmount**—get to the top of
4. **top**—reach the top of

3. To Be at or on the Top of: crown, top,v.

166. HILL; MOUNTAIN

1. Hill; Mountain; High Place,n.
1. **alp**—high mountain
2. **bank**—raised piece of ground; raised place under the sea; embankment
3. **bluff**—steep cliff or bank
4. **cliff**—high face of a rock; rocky height
5. **cope**—height
6. **cordillera**—long mountain range
7. **elevation**—height
8. **embankment**—raised structure of earth

to prevent water from flowing onto level land

9. **eminence**—high place; hill
10. **escarp, escarpment**—long cliff
11. **height**—hill; mountain; high place or region
12. **highland**—elevated land; mountainous land
13. **hillock**—small hill
14. **hummock**—small rise of ground; small rounded hill
15. **hurst**—wooded hill
16. **knoll**—little round hill; mound
17. **mesa**—rocky hill with a flat or flattened top
18. **mound**—small hill; man-made bank or hill of earth or stones
19. **mount**—high hill; mountain
20. **precipice**—high cliff
21. **promontory**—high point of land projecting into the sea
22. **ridge**—range of mountains or hills; raised piece of ground; raised strip of anything
23. **rise**—stretch of high ground
24. **scar**—rocky height
25. **scarp**—long cliff
26. **sierra**—irregular mountain range
27. **terrace**—flat, raised strip of land
28. **tumulus**—artificially made small hill or mound, often over a grave
29. **upland**—highland
30. **volcano**—hill or mountain, conical in shape and topped by a crater, from which (if the volcano is active) hot or molten rock and steam may issue; hill or mountain formed by lava

2. Pert. to, or Descr. of, a Hill, etc.,adj. *From Sec. 1:* alpine or alpestrine, highland, tumular, volcanic or vulcanian

3. Hilly, Mountainous, etc.,adj. *From Sec. 1:* highland, hillocky or hillocked, hummocky, knolly, precipitous, tumulose, volcanic

4. Located as to a Mountain or Mountains, adj.

1. **intermontane**—between mountains
2. **piedmont**—lying at the base of a mountain
3. **submontane**—located at or near the foot of a mountain
4. **tramontane**—lying or coming from the other side of the mountain (usually, from the other side of the Alps, viewed from Italy)
5. **transmontane**—tramontane
6. **ultramontane**—beyond the mountains (esp. the Alps in reference to Italy)

5. One Who Comes from, or Lives on, the Other Side of the Mountain,n.

1. **tramontane**—one who comes from the other side of the mountain (usually from the other side of the Alps, as viewed from Italy)
2. **ultramontane**—one who lives on the other side of the mountain (esp. the Alps in reference to Italy)

6. Science of Mountains: orography, orology,n.

7. Science of Volcanic Phenomena: volcanology, vulcanology,n.

8. Action of a Volcano: volcanicity, volcanism, vulcanism,n.

9. Process of Mountain Development: orogeny,n.

167. COME, GO, OR MOVE DOWN

1. To Come, Go, or Move Down, Downward, or Lower; To Fall or Drop,v.

1. **alight**—come down from the air and stop on the ground or on something solid, like a plane or bird

2. **cascade**—fall or drop sharply, like a waterfall
3. **cataract**—fall or drop sharply or steeply, like a waterfall
4. **cave in**—fall down
5. **chute**—cataract
6. **coast**—move easily or smoothly downhill
7. **collapse**—fall down
8. **crash**—drop or fall suddenly, violently, and/or with a loud noise
9. **decline**—move or go down or downward; drop to a less honorable position
10. **descend**—go down; go lower; come down from parent to child (of qualities, titles, etc.)
11. **dip**—go lower; drop
12. **dribble**—fall in drops
13. **drip**—dribble
14. **drizzle**—fall in small drops
15. **droop**—sink down from physical fatigue, lack of food, etc.
16. **duck**—move the head suddenly downward to, or as if to, avoid a blow, contact, etc.
17. **lower**—move to a lower position or in a downward direction; come down
18. **nod**—make a quick motion downward
19. **plop**—fall or drop suddenly
20. **plummet**—fall or drop heavily and straight down
21. **plump**—fall, drop, or sink suddenly and heavily
22. **plunge**—come down suddenly; fall or drop suddenly and forcefully
23. **poach**—sink into mud while walking
24. **pounce on, upon, or at**—come down suddenly and seize
25. **prolapse**—fall down or forward (medical term referring to organs, muscles, etc.)
26. **rain**—fall or drop (said of things that come down); come down in large numbers
27. **sag**—fall or sink under, or as if under, weight or pressure; sink in the middle
28. **settle**—fall, drop, or sink to the bottom
29. **shower**—come down like heavy rain
30. **sink**—go lower; go down; go to the bottom; fall; fall slowly or gradually
31. **slide**—come down or fall gradually
32. **slip**—drop down a little
33. **slough off**—drop off
34. **slump**—fall, drop, or sink suddenly or heavily
35. **spatter**—fall in drops or particles
36. **spray**—shower in forcibly ejected drops
37. **sprinkle**—fall in drops
38. **subside**—fall to the bottom or to a lower level
39. **swamp**—sink after filling with water
40. **swoop, swoop down**—come down rapidly; come down in a sudden attack
41. **toboggan**—go sharply lower
42. **topple**—fall forward; fall or tumble down; fall down because of the unbalanced weight at the top
43. **trickle**—fall in drops or in a very thin or slow stream
44. **tumble**—fall suddenly and with force
45. **weep**—dribble

2. A Fall or Falling; A Drop or Dropping, etc.,n. *From Sec. 1:* cascade, cataract, cave-in, chute, coast, collapse, crash, declination or declension, descent, dip, dribble, drip, drizzle, droop, duck, nod, plop, plummet, plunge, pounce, prolapse, rain, sag, settlement, shower, sinkage, slide, slip, slump, spatter, spray, sprinkle, subsidence, swoop, toboggan, topple, trickle, tumble; *Also:*

1. **anticlimax**—a sudden drop from the important to the unimportant, the sublime to the ridiculous, the serious to the frivolous, etc.
2. **avalanche**—sudden and overwhelming descent of anything
3. **bathos**—anticlimax

4. **nutation**—a nodding; a nod
5. **precipitation**—a falling down from a height
6. **ptosis**—falling or dropping of a part, member, tissue, etc., often specifically referring to the drooping of the upper eyelid (medical)
7. **storm**—a shower of things, articles, words, etc.
8. **tail spin**—any rapid descent, figuratively; downward, nose-first, spinning motion of a plane out of control

3. Falling, Dropping, etc.,adj. *From Sec. 1:* alighting, cascading, cataracting, coasting, declining, descending or descendant, dipping, dribbling, dripping, drizzling, drooping or droopy, ducking, lowering, nodding, plummeting, plunging, prolapsed, sagging, settling, sinking, sliding, slipping, slumping, spattering, subsident, swooping, toppling, trickling, tumbling; *From Sec. 2:* anticlimactic, bathetic, nutant, precipitant or precipitate; *Also:*
  1. **precipitous**—falling rapidly
  2. **sheer**—sharply dropping downward

4. To Cause to, or Let, Fall or Drop,v. *From Sec. 1:* cataract, cave in, collapse, dip, droop, duck, lower, plunge, settle, shower, sink, slough off, spatter, spray, sprinkle, swamp, topple, tumble; *Also:*
  1. **countersink**—sink (something, such as a nail, screw, etc.) below the surface
  2. **depress**—let or cause to come down, fall, etc. (depression,n.)
  3. **dip**—lower and raise quickly; lower into and raise out of water
  4. **knock down**—cause a violent drop in (price, value, etc.)
  5. **plunk**—drop suddenly and forcibly
  6. **scuttle**—make (a ship) sink (scuttlement,n.)
  7. **shed**—let fall; slough off

5. To Begin to Fall: slip, totter,v.

6. Falling Off,adj.
  1. **caducous**—falling off
  2. **deciduous**—falling off or out after a period of maturity (as the leaves of trees, the first teeth, etc.)
  3. **fugacious**—falling off (of the petals of a flower or the leaves of a tree)

7. Likely to Fall Down: ramshackle,adj.

8. Seemingly about to Fall Down: tottery, adj.

9. Ready to Fall Down: tumble-down,adj.

10. To Get Off, or Down Off,v.
  1. **alight (from)**—get down off (something high)
  2. **debark**—disembark (debarkation,n.)
  3. **detrain**—get off a train (detrainment,n.)
  4. **disembark**—get off a ship (disembarkation, disembarkment,n.)
  5. **dismount**—get down off a horse or from a vehicle

168. FALL

1. To Fall, i.e., Lose One's Balance,v.
  1. **blunder**—stumble
  2. **collapse**—fall down
  3. **founder**—stumble and fall; stumble around awkwardly and helplessly, either literally or figuratively
  4. **slide**—lose one's footing, support, balance, etc.; fall as a result of this
  5. **slip**—lose one's balance and fall
  6. **stumble**—fall while walking
  7. **topple**—fall down; fall forward
  8. **trip**—stumble
  9. **tumble**—fall suddenly and with force

2. A Fall,n. *From Sec. 1:* blunder, collapse, founder, slide, slip, stumble, topple, trip, tumble; *Also:* **1. cropper**—heavy fall

3. To Cause to Fall,v. *From Sec. 1:* topple, trip, tumble; *Also:*
  1. **bowl down, bowl over**—cause to fall by hitting against, etc.
  2. **knock down, knock over**—cause to fall by bumping into, hitting against, etc.
  3. **overthrow**—cause to fall
  4. **overturn**—cause to fall

4. To Begin to Fall; To Lose One's Balance and Begin to Fall: slide, slip, totter, trip,v.

169. LOWNESS

1. Low and Broad; Low and Flat: squat, squatty,adj. (squatness, squattiness,n.)

2. Lower,adj.
  1. **inferior**—lower in value or position (inferiority,n.)
  2. **minor**—lower in rank, value, importance, position, etc. (minority,n.)
  3. **nether**—lower; situated lower
  4. **subjacent**—lower in position (subjacency, n.)

3. Lowest,adj.
  1. **bottom**—lowest
  2. **bottommost**—lowest
  3. **nethermost**—lowest
  4. **rock-bottom**—very lowest

4. Lowest Point; Bottom,n.
  1. **abyss**—lowest depths; bottom waters of a sea (abysmal, abyssal,adj.)
  2. **base**—bottom; supporting bottom (basal, adj.)
  3. **basement**—lowest part
  4. **bed**—bottom on which something rests; bottom surface
  5. **bedrock**—bottom
  6. **benthos, benthon**—bottom of the sea or ocean (benthal, benthonic, benthic,adj.)
  7. **bilge**—lowest part of the inside of a ship; bottom of a ship's hull
  8. **Davy Jones's locker**—bottom of the ocean
  9. **depths**—loosely, the lowest point or part
  10. **floor**—bottom, or supporting bottom, of a room, place, etc.
  11. **foundation**—bottom; supporting bottom (fundamental, foundational, foundationary,adj.)
  12. **fundament**—foundation (fundamental, adj.)
  13. **fundus**—bottom of the inside of a hollow organ (medical)
  14. **nadir**—lowest point; lowest point reached

170. DEPTH

1. Deep,adj.
  1. **abysmal**—so deep as to be apparently bottomless; too deep for measurement; profound (abyss,n.)
  2. **abyssal**—deep beyond measurement
  3. **bottomless**—deep beyond measurement (bottomlessness,n.)
  4. **depthless**—so deep as to be beyond measurement
  5. **fathomless**—so deep as to be beyond measurement (fathomlessness,n.)
  6. **inmost**—innermost
  7. **innermost**—deepest inside or within
  8. **intense**—deep in feeling, emotion, etc. (intenseness, intensity,n.)
  9. **profound**—extremely deep; intellectually deep; so deep as to be difficult to understand; very intense (profoundness, profundity,n.)
  10. **sound**—deep—of sleep (soundness,n.)
  11. **unfathomable**—so deep as to be beyond measurement (unfathomability,n.)
  12. **unplumbed**—so deep as never to have been measured

2. Having Constant Depth: isobath, isobathic,adj. (isobath,n.)

3. To Make Deeper,v.
1. **deepen**—make deeper
2. **dredge**—make (channels, river bottoms, etc.) deeper through excavating
3. **intensify**—make deeper, figuratively (intensification,n.)

4. To Become Deeper: deepen,v.

5. To Become Figuratively Deeper: intensify,v. (intensification,n.)

6. To Measure the Depth of: fathom, plumb, sound,v.

7. Unit of Measurement of Water Depth: fathom,n.

8. Device to Measure Depth of Water: fathomer,n.

9. Deep Place, Space, or Part; Depth,n.
1. **abysm**—abyss (abysmal, abyssal,adj.)
2. **abyss**—space of unmeasurable depth or without apparent bottom; bottomless hole (abyssal,adj.)
3. **benthos, benthon**—depth of the ocean (benthal, benthonic, benthic,adj.)
4. **briny deep**—depths of the ocean or other body of salt water
5. **chasm**—yawning abyss; deep opening in the earth
6. **crevasse**—deep opening, as in the earth, etc.
7. **deep**—deep part, place, or space; deep part of a body of water
8. **depth**—deep or deepest part; abyss
9. **depths**—deepest part or parts
10. **gulf**—abyss; chasm
11. **pit**—abyss
12. **valley**—deep place between hills, mountains, or other elevations

10. Valley,n.
1. **canyon, cañon**—deep valley with steep slopes
2. **coomb, combe, comb, coombe, coom**—valley
3. **dale**—valley (poetic)
4. **dell**—small sheltered valley
5. **dingle**—small wooded valley
6. **gap**—mountain ravine
7. **glen**—narrow and sheltered valley; narrow valley between hills or mountains
8. **gorge**—ravine with high and rocky sides
9. **gulch**—ravine
10. **gully**—small valley; ravine in the face of a precipice
11. **notch**—mountain ravine
12. **ravine**—narrow and steep valley; such worn by running water
13. **strath**—wide river valley
14. **vale**—valley (poetic)

11. Not Deep,adj.
1. **depthless**—having no depth; shallow
2. **shallow**—not deep; superficial
3. **shoal**—not deep
4. **superficial**—not deep (i.e., on the surface only)
5. **trifling**—superficial
6. **trivial**—superficial
7. **unsound**—not deep (of sleep)

12. Lack of Depth,n. *From Sec. 11:* shallowness, shoalness or shoaliness, superficiality, triviality or trivialness, unsoundness

13. Place Where the Water Is Not Deep,n. *From Sec. 11:* shallow, shoal; *Also:* 1. **sand bar**—shoal

14. To Become or Make Less Deep,v. *From Sec. 11:* shallow, shoal

15. Full of Shoals: shoaly,adj. (shoaliness,n.)

16. To Dive,v.
1. **duck**—dive (duck,n.)
2. **plunge**—dive, usually into water (plunge, n.)
3. **shoal**—dive
4. **submerge**—dive under water (submergence,n.)

1. To Dig,v.
1. **bail**—scoop out water from a boat
2. **bore**—dig
3. **burrow**—dig; dig a hole in the ground for shelter
4. **delve**—dig with a shovel
5. **disentomb**—dig up out of its burial place
6. **disinhume**—disinter
7. **disinter**—dig up (a corpse) out of its grave
8. **ditch**—dig a ditch; dig a ditch or ditches in
9. **dredge**—dig in order to deepen; dig up from the bottom
10. **drill**—dig a hole or holes into with an instrument or machine made for that purpose
11. **excavate**—dig and remove what is dug; make a hollow by digging; make a hole by digging
12. **exhume**—dig up out of the ground
13. **gouge**—dig out with, or as if with, a scoop
14. **grub**—dig in or under the ground, usually for something hard to get to or get out
15. **grub up**—dig up by the roots
16. **hollow out**—dig a hole or groove into
17. **mine**—dig a mine; dig away the foundation of; dig in, or below, the surface of
18. **quarry**—dig from, or as from, a pit, excavation, etc.
19. **resurrect**—illegally dig (a corpse) up out of its grave in order to sell it to anatomy students
20. **root**—dig down to, or around, the bottom of; dig with the snout
21. **rout**—dig with the snout
22. **sap**—dig under; dig under the foundation of (literally or figuratively)
23. **scoop**—dig out; hollow out
24. **shovel into**—dig into; dig into with an implement
25. **spade**—dig; dig with an implement
26. **trench**—dig a deep ditch or groove into
27. **trowel**—spade
28. **tunnel**—dig one's way underground; dig into or through the ground

2. Digging,n. *From Sec. 1:* disentombment, disinhumation, disinterment, excavation, exhumation, resurrection or resurrectionism

3. A Digger,n. *From Sec. 1:* borer, burrower, delver, driller, excavator, miner, quarrier, resurrectionist, sapper, shoveler, tunneler

4. Digging Instrument,n. *From Sec. 1:* bail or bailer, bore, dredge, drill, gouge, scoop, shovel, spade, trowel; *Also:*
1. **bulldozer**—large machine for digging holes for the foundations of buildings
2. **mattock**—instrument for digging and cutting roots
3. **wimble**—scoop

5. So Constituted as to Be Able to Dig: fossorial, fossorious,adj. (of animal anatomy)

1. To Hang, i.e., Be Hanging,v.
1. **beetle**—overhang and stick out
2. **brood over**—hang close over; hover
3. **dangle**—hang loosely and move jerkily while so hanging
4. **depend**—hang down
5. **droop**—hang down listlessly
6. **hover over**—hang over in a fluttering manner; remain hanging over
7. **jut**—project
8. **loll**—hang loosely or listlessly
9. **lop**—hang loosely down
10. **overhang**—hang over; hang out over
11. **poise**—hang suspended or in balance; hover
12. **project**—hang out over

13. **sag**—hang down unevenly
14. **suspend**—hang down; be hanging; hang down from a support
15. **swing**—hang; hang from a support and wave back and forth
16. **topple**—overhang unsteadily

2. To Hang, i.e., Let or Cause to Hang,v. *From Sec. 1:* dangle, droop, jut, lop, overhang, poise, project, suspend, swing; *Also:*
1. **gibbet**—hang the body of (an executed person, generally in chains) on a gallows as a warning to other malefactors and to expose to disgrace; hang as if from a gallows, i.e., on something with a projecting arm
2. **loll**—let (the tongue) hang out when fatigued and hot (of an animal)

3. A Hanging,n. *From Secs. 1 and 2:* dangle, droop, hover, loll, overhang, poise, projection, sag, suspension, swing, topple

4. Hanging,adj. *From Sec. 1:* beetle or beetling, dangling or adangle, dependent, drooping or droopy, hovering, jutting, lolling, lop or loppy, overhanging, poised, projecting or projective, sagging; suspending, suspended, or suspensory; swinging or aswing; *Also:*
1. **cernuous**—pendulous; drooping
2. **nutant**—drooping
3. **pendant, pendent**—hanging; overhanging
4. **pending**—hanging
5. **pendulous**—hanging loosely
6. **pensile**—hanging

5. Device for Hanging,n.
1. **gallows**—wooden device on which criminals are hanged
2. **gibbet**—kind of gallows
3. **pendant**—that by which something hangs
4. **rack**—place on which things can be hung
5. **scaffold**—structure on which a criminal is hanged
6. **suspenders**—device in the form of two straps from which a man's trousers hang while being worn

6. That Which Hangs: pendant,n.

7. Hanging Ornament: pendant,n.

173. FOLLOW

1. To Follow, i.e., Come After or Next,v.
1. **draggle**—follow slowly
2. **ensue**—follow as a result (said of occurrences)
3. **succeed**—come after; come next; follow in order; follow another in a position, privilege, etc.
4. **supervene**—follow closely
5. **tag (after)**—follow closely (after)
6. **trail**—follow; follow along behind; follow in an irregular line

2. A Coming After or Next,n. *From Sec. 1:* succession, supervention; *Also:*
1. **catenation**—succession in a connected series
2. **concatenation**—succession as in a chain
3. **sequence**—a following of one thing after another

3. One Who Comes After or Next,n. *From Sec. 1:* successor, trailer

4. Coming After; Next; Following,adj.
1. **after**—following (in combinations, as aftereffects, etc.)
2. **attendant**—following as a result
3. **consecutive**—following immediately one after the other (consecutiveness,n.)
4. **consequent**—following as a result
5. **consequential**—following as a result; following logically; following in order (consequentiality,n.)
6. **ensuing**—following; following as a result; next following
7. **later**—following

8. **posterior**—following in time or order (posteriority,n.)
9. **proximate**—next following
10. **quick-fire**—following in rapid succession
11. **sequacious**—following; following logically (sequacity, sequaciousness,n.)
12. **sequent**—sequential (sequence,n.)
13. **sequential**—following in order or as a result (sequentiality,n.)
14. **serial, seriate**—following in order
15. **seriatim**—following in order, one after the other
16. **subsequent**—following in time
17. **succeeding**—following next (succession, n.)
18. **successive**—following one after the others, but with no necessary implication of closeness in time or space
19. **supervenient**—following closely (supervenience,n.)
20. **trailing**—following behind

5. Following: in the wake of,prep. phrase

6. That Which Comes After or Next; That Which Follows,n.
1. **consecution**—sequence of events
2. **consequence**—that which follows as a result
3. **sequel**—that which follows; events that follow; that which follows logically
4. **sequela**—event, condition, etc., that follows (sequelae,pl.)
5. **sequelant**—a thing which follows as a result
6. **sequence**—that which follows after or as a result
7. **sequent**—that which follows as a result, in a series, etc.
8. **series**—things following one after another

7. Order of Following: sequence,n.

8. Logically Following in Meaning or Implication: sequacious,adj. (sequacity, sequaciousness,n.)

9. A Series,n.
1. **array**—imposing or impressive series of things
2. **barrage**—rapid-fire series of questions, remarks, statements, etc.
3. **catena**—connected series (catenary,adj.)
4. **chain**—series of things or ideas connected in some way
5. **concatenation**—series, as if in a chain, each event or thing linked to the preceding and following one
6. **consecution**—series; chain of logical reasoning
7. **continuum**—unbroken series
8. **course**—series of motions or acts arranged in order
9. **cycle**—complete series (cyclic,adj.)
10. **line**—series of objects counted as one (linear,adj.)
11. **litany**—repeated series
12. **nexus**—connected series
13. **range**—series of things in a row
14. **ritual**—series of actions so rigidly followed as to be in effect a ceremony (ritual, ritualistic,adj.)
15. **row**—series of objects or persons arranged in a line
16. **run**—series; succession
17. **sequence**—connected series
18. **set**—series (of books, etc.) related in subject by common authorship, etc.; series of various other things
19. **succession**—continuous or uninterrupted series; connected series
20. **suit**—series of cards of the same device (clubs, diamonds, hearts, or spades)
21. **suite**—series of things; series of rooms
22. **train**—series of happenings; series of connected ideas

10. To Form into a Connected Series: catenate, concatenate,v. (concatenation,n.)

11. Forming, or United in, a Connected Series: catenated, concatenate,adj.

12. To Follow, i.e., Pursue,v.
1. **chase**—follow in order to catch
2. **persecute**—pursue in order to annoy, attack, harass, harm, etc.
3. **shadow**—follow closely and in secret
4. **spoor**—follow the track or trail of (a wild animal, etc.)
5. **stalk**—follow secretly
6. **tag (after)**—follow closely (after)
7. **tail**—follow closely after; follow secretly in order to observe the movements of
8. **trace**—follow by the signs, tracks, or trail left behind; follow the movements or course of
9. **track**—follow by the marks or traces left; follow the footprints, smell, or other indications of
10. **trail**—follow

13. Pursuit,n. *From Sec. 12:* chase, persecution, stalk

14. Pursuer, Follower,n. *From Sec. 12:* persecutor, shadow, shadower, stalker, tail, tracer, tracker

15. Tending to Pursue,adj. *From Sec. 12:* persecuting, persecutive (persecutiveness,n.)

16. Pert. to Pursuit,adj. *From Sec. 12:* persecutional, persecutory

17. Passionate or Eager Pursuit of Something Desired: zeal,n.

174. FORWARD MOTION

1. To Move Ahead, Forward, etc.,v.
1. **advance**—move forward
2. **dash**—move forward forcefully or violently
3. **edge**—move ahead gradually
4. **forge**—move ahead slowly and steadily
5. **lunge**—move forward suddenly and violently
6. **plow, plough**—move ahead slowly and with effort
7. **proceed**—move forward; move forward in an orderly fashion
8. **progress**—move forward
9. **ramp**—move forward with arms raised in attack

2. Forward Movement,n. *From Sec. 1:* advance, dash, lunge, process or procedure, progress or progression, ramp; *Also:*
1. **course**—forward or onward movement
2. **current**—forward or onward movement of a stream or any similarly moving body
3. **saltation**—forward movement made by jumping

3. Moving Forward,adj. *From Sec. 1:* advancing, dashing, etc.; progressive

4. Line of Progress or Advance: course,n.

175. PRECEDE

1. To Go or Come Before,v.
1. **antecede**—come before
2. **antedate**—come before
3. **forerun**—come before as a sign of that which will follow; precede
4. **guide**—go before to show the way
5. **harbinger**—go before to secure lodgings for another or others; come before as a sign of that which, or those who, will follow
6. **head**—go or come in front of
7. **herald**—come before as an announcement of that which will follow
8. **introduce**—usher in
9. **lead**—go before; go before to show the way
10. **pioneer**—go into uncivilized country before anyone else

11. **precede**—go or come before, whether in time or space
12. **precurse**—herald
13. **preface**—prelude
14. **prelude**—precede as an introduction; precede
15. **usher in**—come before as a sign of that which will follow

2. A Going or Coming Before,n. *From Sec. 1:* antecedence, introduction, precedence or precession

3. Going or Coming Before,adj. *From Sec. 1:* antecedent, head, introductory or introductive, leading or lead, pioneer or pioneering, preceding or precedent, precursory or precursive, prefatory or prefatorial; prelusive, prelusory, preludious, or preludial; *Also:*
1. **aforementioned**—coming before in speech or writing
2. **aforesaid**—aforementioned
3. **anterior**—coming before, in time or place
4. **before-mentioned**—aforementioned
5. **early**—coming before the usual, expected, or planned-for time
6. **foregoing**—coming before, esp. in speech or writing
7. **former**—preceding
8. **precursory, precursive**—preliminary; preceding
9. **preliminary**—coming before, in time; coming before the main part
10. **prevenient**—coming before
11. **previous**—coming before, in time
12. **prior**—coming before, in time
13. **prodromal**—preceding; preliminary
14. **proemial**—prefatory

4. State or Quality of Going or Coming Before,n. *From Sec. 1:* antecedence or antecedency, precedence or precedency; *From Sec. 3:* anteriority, earliness, prevenience, previousness, priority

5. One Who or That Which Goes or Comes Before,n. *From Sec. 1:* antecedent or antecessor, forerunner, guide, harbinger, herald, introduction, pioneer, precedent or precess, precursor, prelude, prelusion; *From Sec. 3:* foregoing, former, preliminary, proem; *Also:*
1. **ancestor**—one who or that which comes or has come before
2. **antecessor**—one who has previously held a position or post
3. **avant-courier (French)**—someone who comes before to give notice of the approach of another or others
4. **forebear, forbear**—ancestor
5. **forerunner**—predecessor
6. **precursor**—one who precedes in an office or condition
7. **predecessor**—one who previously held the same position or office; one who came before; that which has come before and is followed by another
8. **progenitor**—ancestor
9. **vaunt-courier (French)**—herald

176. LEAD

1. To Lead,v.
1. **abduct, abduce**—lead away
2. **betray**—lead into danger, error, or sin
3. **concentrate, concenter**—lead to a common center
4. **conduct**—lead (someone somewhere)
5. **convey**—conduct
6. **decoy**—lead into a trap; lead into danger
7. **guide**—conduct
8. **inveigle into**—lead (someone) into (doing something) by trickery, deception, or cajolery
9. **marshal**—lead (someone) ceremoniously (into a place)
10. **pervert**—lead along bad or wrong courses
11. **pilot**—lead

12. **pioneer**—take the lead in some new activity
13. **seduce**—lead astray; lead into error, sin, etc.
14. **shepherd**—conduct

2. A Leading,n. *From Sec. 1:* abduction, betrayal or betrayment, concentration, conduction, conveyance, guidance, inveiglement, perversion, pilotage, seduction or seducement; *Also:*
1. **demagoguery, demagogy, demagogism**—false leading or leadership
2. **hegemony**—political leadership of one nation in a group

3. Leader; One Who Leads,n. *From Sec. 1:* abductor, betrayer, conductor, conveyor, decoy, guide, inveigler, marshal, perverter, pilot, pioneer, seducer, shepherd; *From Sec. 2:* demagogue; *Also:*
1. **bellwether**—male sheep, wearing a bell, that leads a flock; leader of a mob or of thoughtless or foolish people
2. **captain**—leader
3. **caudillo (Spanish)**—military leader of irregular troops
4. **chair**—leader of a discussion group
5. **chairman, chairwoman**—leader of a discussion group
6. **chief**—leader of a tribe, group, army, band, etc.
7. **commander**—leader; chief
8. **commander in chief**—head leader of a group, army, etc.
9. **coryphaeus**—leader of a school of thought, party, sect, etc.
10. **croupier**—assistant chairman at a public dinner
11. **Führer (German)**—leader
12. **gauleiter (German)**—nazi district leader
13. **head**—leader
14. **Judas goat**—goat that leads sheep into a slaughterhouse
15. **protagonist**—leader
16. **ringleader**—leader of an illegal, disorderly, or conspiring group
17. **skipper**—loosely, the captain of any ship; strictly, the captain of a fishing boat or small trading ship
18. **standard bearer**—leader of a movement, cause, party, group, etc.
19. **vanguard, avant-garde**—leaders of a movement

4. That Which Leads,n. *From Sec. 1:* conductor, conveyance or conveyor, decoy; *Also:* 1. **preliminary**—that which leads to something else or something more important

5. Leading; Serving to Lead; Pert. to Leading,adj. *From Sec. 1:* conductive, conveyor, perversive, pioneering or pioneer, seductive; *From Sec. 2:* demagogic, hegemonic; *From Sec. 3:* vanguard; *From Sec. 4:* preliminary

6. Without a Leader: acephalous, leaderless, adj.

177. GUIDE

1. To Guide,v.
1. **beacon**—guide
2. **conduct**—guide (someone to a place)
3. **conn**—steer (a ship)
4. **convey**—conduct
5. **coxswain**—steer (a ship)
6. **direct**—act as a guide; guide through a course
7. **fugle**—act as a guide
8. **helm**—steer; direct
9. **marshal**—guide ceremoniously (to a place)
10. **misdirect**—guide in the wrong direction
11. **navigate**—steer (an airplane or ship)
12. **pervert**—guide in the wrong direction (figurative)

13. **pilot**—guide; steer; steer (a plane or ship)
14. **shepherd**—guide spiritually; conduct
15. **steer**—guide the movement or course of

2. Guidance,n. *From Sec. 1:* conduction, conveyance, direction or misdirection, navigation, perversion, steerage

3. A Guide, i.e., One Who Guides,n. *From Sec. 1:* conductor, conveyor, coxswain, director, fugleman, helmsman, marshal, navigator, perverter, pilot, shepherd, steersman or steerer; *Also:* 1. **cicerone**—guide for sightseers (ciceroni, cicerones,pl.)

4. A Guide, i.e., That Which Guides,n. *From Sec. 1:* conductor, conveyor; *Also:*
1. **Baedeker**—guidebook
2. **beacon**—guiding signal; guiding light; anything that is figuratively or symbolically a guiding light
3. **clue, clew**—that which guides one to the solution of a problem, crime, puzzle, etc.
4. **cynosure**—that which serves to guide or direct
5. **guideboard**—board on a guidepost giving directions
6. **guidebook**—book giving directions, etc.
7. **guidepost**—post on the road, usually at a fork or intersection, containing a guideboard with directions for reaching various places; hence, by extension, anything that guides
8. **lodestar, loadstar**—guiding star; cynosure
9. **polestar**—guide
10. **rudder**—something that guides a person's course, actions, etc.
11. **signpost**—guide; that which guides; guidepost
12. **tiller**—lever for steering a boat; hence, loosely, any steering lever

5. Guiding; Serving to Guide; Pert. to Guidance,adj. *From Sec. 1:* conductive, conveyor; directive, directional, or directorial; navigational or navigative; *Also:* 1. **polar**—guiding

6. Position or Place for Guiding or Steering,n.
1. **conn**—station for steering a ship
2. **conning tower**—tower from which one steers a ship
3. **helm, saddle**—position from which one guides and controls

7. Capable of Being Steered: dirigible, navigable,adj. (dirigibility, navigability,n.)

8. Without Guidance or Light to Show the Way: beaconless,adj.

178. FOLLOWER

1. A Follower,n.
1. **adherent**—follower (of a cause, party, group, etc.)
2. **attendant**—follower, in the sense of one who accompanies an important person
3. **bootlicker**—obsequious or fawning follower
4. **dangler**—hanger-on
5. **devotee**—enthusiastic follower (of an art, hobby, cult, fashion, philosophy, etc.)
6. **disciple**—follower of a school (of learning, belief, philosophy, etc.)
7. **espouser**—follower (of a cause, etc.)
8. **fan**—enthusiastic follower (of a sport, author, motion-picture actor, etc.)
9. **footlicker**—bootlicker; sycophant
10. **hanger-on**—follower, usually an undesirable one
11. **henchman**—close and trusted follower
12. **lackey**—servile, obsequious follower
13. **lickspittle, lickspit**—contemptible follower; contemptible sycophant
14. **minion**—follower

15. **myrmidon**—obedient and unprotesting follower
16. **parasite**—hanger-on
17. **partisan**—follower of a party, cause, principle, etc., often on emotional rather than rational grounds
18. **satellite**—follower of an important person; fawning, obsequious follower or sycophant
19. **sectary**—zealous follower of a sect
20. **servitor**—follower; attendant
21. **sycophant**—follower of the wealthy or influential
22. **toady**—sycophant
23. **tufthunter**—sycophant who seeks the acquaintance of persons with titles
24. **vassal**—follower
25. **votary**—devoted follower (votaress, votress,fem.)
26. **zealot**—extreme devotee

2. To Be a Follower of,v. *From Sec. 1:* bootlick, espouse, toady to

3. Act, Fact, or State of Being a Follower, n. *From Sec. 1:* discipleship, espousal, parasitism, partisanship, sycophancy, vassalage, zealotry

4. Following; Pert. to, or Characteristic of, a Follower,adj. *From Sec. 1:* parasitic, partisan, sycophantic, vassal, votary, zealous

5. Followers,n.
1. **following**—those who are followers of a person, thing, cause, etc.
2. **retinue**—a person's, or an important person's, followers
3. **rout**—retinue
4. **train**—group of followers

6. Inclined to Follow and Be Subservient to a Leader: sequacious,adj. (sequacity, sequaciousness,n.)

179. DIRECTION

1. Direction,n.
1. **aspect**—direction in which something faces or fronts
2. **bearing**—direction of one point in respect to another or in reference to the points of the compass
3. **bent**—particular direction
4. **course**—general direction
5. **current**—general direction
6. **dip**—downward direction
7. **drift**—direction of driving or being driven; general direction; trend
8. **inclination**—trend
9. **lee, leeward**—direction toward which the wind blows
10. **run**—general direction
11. **stream**—general direction
12. **stretch**—direction
13. **tack**—direction of action, often changed from the previous one
14. **tendency**—trend
15. **tenor**—general direction
16. **tide**—general direction
17. **trend**—general direction, as of events, a river, etc.
18. **windward**—direction from which the wind blows

2. To Go or Point in a Direction,v. *From Sec. 1:* bear, bend, course, dip, drift, incline, run, stream, tend, trend; *Also:*
1. **orient, orientate**—face or point to the east or to a specific direction (orientation,n. orientative,adj.)
2. **verge**—tend

3. To Place Facing the East or Other Specific Direction: orient, orientate,v. (orientation,n. orientative,adj.)

4. To Ascertain the Direction of in Respect to the Compass: orient,v.

5. Four Principal Directions of the Compass: cardinal points

6. One of the 32 Directions of the Compass: point,n.

7. Special Stand or Container for a Compass on a Ship: binnacle,n.

8. In a Direction,adj.
1. **bifarious**—pointing in two directions
2. **clockwise**—in the direction in which the hands of a clock turn
3. **counterclockwise, contraclockwise**—in the direction opposite to that in which the hands of a clock turn
4. **horizontal**—parallel to the horizon
5. **leeward**—in the direction in which the wind is blowing
6. **parallel**—going or tending evenly in the same direction (parallelism,n.)
7. **quadrivial**—leading in four directions (of roads)
8. **reverse**—in an opposite direction
9. **single-track**—moving always in the same direction
10. **windward**—in the direction from which the wind is blowing

9. To Make Parallel: collimate,v. (collimation,n.)

10. Northern,adj.
1. **arctic**—northern, i.e., pert. to or situated near or around the North Pole
2. **boreal**—pert. to the north
3. **hyperborean**—northern; northernmost
4. **northerly**—situated, moving, or directed toward the north; blowing from the north (of winds)
5. **northernmost**—farthest north
6. **septentrional**—pert. to the north

11. Inhabitant of the North: Hyperborean, Northerner, northerner,n.

12. Eastern,adj.
1. **easterly**—situated in, moving, or directed toward the east; blowing from the east (of winds)
2. **easternmost**—farthest east
3. **oriental**—pert. to the East (i.e., the Far East)

13. Inhabitant of the East: easterner, Easterner, Eastern, Oriental (of the Far East),n.

14. Easterly Direction: easting,n.

15. Southern,adj.
1. **antarctic**—southern, i.e., pert. to, or situated near or around, the South Pole
2. **austral**—southern
3. **meridional**—pert. to, characteristic of, etc., the south
4. **southerly**—situated, moving, or directed toward the south; blowing from the south (of winds)
5. **southernmost**—farthest south

16. Inhabitant of the South: southerner, Southerner,n.

17. The South: auster,n.

18. Western,adj.
1. **occidental**—pert. to the west, Western world, or Western Hemisphere
2. **westerly**—situated in, moving, or directed toward the west; blowing from the west (of winds)
3. **westernmost**—farthest west

19. Inhabitant of the West: Occidental, westerner, Westerner,n.

20. The West or Western Hemisphere: occident,n.

21. Pert. to, or Relating to, the Right,adj.
1. **dexter**—pert. to or on the right hand or side
2. **dextral**—belonging to, pert. to, or functioning on the right side (dextrality,n.)
3. **starboard**—pert. to or toward the right side, of a ship when facing forward (starboard,n.)

22. Toward the Right: dextrad,adv. (anatomy)

23. Pert. to, or Relating to, the Left,adj.
1. **larboard**—pert. to or toward the left side of a ship, when facing forward, today generally replaced by port (larboard,n.)
2. **port**—larboard (port,n.)
3. **sinister**—left; toward or on the left (sinisterness,n.)
4. **sinistral, sinistrous**—pert. to the left; inclining toward the left (sinistrality, sinistration,n.)

24. Toward the Left: sinistrad,adv. (anatomy)

180. STRAIGHTNESS

1. Straight,adj.
1. **direct**—straight, without turns or detours (directness,n.)
2. **erect**—straight up (erectness,n.)
3. **even**—straight one with another (evenness,n.)
4. **horizontal**—straight with the horizon; at right angles to vertical
5. **perpendicular**—at right angles to the base; upright; vertical (perpendicularity, n.)
6. **plumb**—exactly vertical
7. **precipitous**—sheer (precipitousness,n.)
8. **sheer**—straight up and down (sheerness, n.)
9. **true**—even
10. **unbent**—straight (in the sense of not being bent or crooked)
11. **undeviating**—straight in the sense of being without break or stops
12. **upright**—straight up in posture or position (uprightness,n.)
13. **vertical**—straight up and down

2. Lying in the Same Straight Line: collinear,adj.

3. Moving in, or Forming, a Straight Line: rectilinear, rectilineal,adj.

181. CROOKEDNESS

1. Crooked, i.e., Not Straight,adj.
1. **askew**—off to one side (of that which is expected to be straight, or looks better when straight)
2. **awry**—turned to one side instead of true or straight
3. **bent**—crooked; off true line; not straight
4. **rakish**—not conventionally straight in appearance
5. **tipsy**—not standing straight
6. **wry**—crooked

182. DIRECTNESS

1. Direct, Figuratively,adj.
1. **bald**—direct (baldness,n.)
2. **blunt**—direct and to the point (bluntness,n.)
3. **categorical**—direct
4. **forthright**—direct (forthrightness,n.)
5. **personal**—descr. of that which is done directly or in person
6. **plump**—direct
7. **point-blank**—direct (point-blankness,n.)
8. **straightforward**—direct (straightforwardness,n.)
9. **summary**—direct and prompt (summariness,n.)

183. INDIRECTNESS

1. Indirect, Figuratively or Literally,adj.
1. **ambagious, ambagitory**—indirect in manner, means, proceedings, etc.
2. **backhand, backhanded**—indirect
3. **circuitous**—indirect
4. **circular**—indirect
5. **collateral**—indirect
6. **devious**—indirect; wandering off a straight line; not approaching a question, topic, request, etc., directly or straightforwardly
7. **oblique, obliquitous**—indirect; not direct or straightforward
8. **roundabout**—indirect
9. **sinuous**—indirect
10. **tortuous**—indirect; not straightforward

2. Indirectness,n. From Sec. 1: ambagiousness, ambagiosity, backhandedness, circuitousness or circuity, circularity, deviousness, obliqueness, obliquitousness or obliquity, sinuousness or sinuosity, tortuousness or tortuosity

3. Indirect or Roundabout Means, Manner, etc.: ambages (pl.); circumbendibus (humorous),n.

184. BACK

1. Back or Back Part of a Thing,n.
1. **background**—that part of a picture or scene that is in the back, i.e., farthest away from the observer
2. **behind**—back part
3. **rear**—back portion; back
4. **reverse**—back
5. **stern**—back, or back part, of a ship or, by extension, of anything else
6. **tail**—rear

2. Back,adj. From Sec. 1: background, behind, rear, reverse, stern, tail; Also:
1. **hind**—pert. to or descr. of that part, person, or thing that is in the rear
2. **hinder**—pert. or relating to the part or end that is in the rear
3. **hindmost, hindermost, hindhand**—farthest in the rear
4. **posterior**—situated in or toward the back
5. **postern**—situated at the rear
6. **tail**—coming from the rear (of a wind, etc.)

3. With the Back in Front: backward, rearward, tailfirst,adj. or adv.

4. One in Back of the Other: tandem,adj. or adv.

5. Toward or to the Rear: astern, backward, rearward,adj. or adv.

6. Behind, or toward the Back of, a Ship: astern,adv.

7. Moving toward the Back: backward, rearward,adj.

8. Back or Back Part of a Person or Animal,n.
1. **dorsum**—back of a person or animal (dorsal,adj.)
2. **hind, hindquarter**—back part of the carcass of an animal
3. **posterior**—back or back portion of a person or animal
4. **small**—narrowest part of the back
5. **tergum**—back of a person or animal (tergal,adj.)

9. Highest Part of a Horse's or Other Animal's Back: withers,n.

10. Toward the Back End of the Body: caudad, caudalward,adv.

11. At, near, or in, the Back End of the Body: caudal,adj.

12. To Turn the Back, as in Running Away: tergiversate,v. (tergiversation,n. tergiversator, tergiversant,n. tergiversatory, tergiversant, adj.)

185. FRONT

1. Front; Front Part,n.
1. **anterior**—front of the body
2. **façade**—front of anything, esp. of a building or similar structure; false front, figuratively or literally
3. **face**—front as contrasted to the back; front surface; front of a building, arch, etc.
4. **fore**—front
5. **forefront**—front part or place
6. **foreground**—front part of a picture or natural scene, i.e., the part nearest the observer
7. **frontage**—front of a building or lot
8. **frontal**—façade
9. **obverse**—front; front turned to the observer
10. **van**—front part of an army or of any moving group
11. **vanguard**—front; front part; van

2. Frontal; In, on, toward, etc., the Front, adj. *From Sec. 1:* anterior, facial, fore, foreground, obverse, vanward (anteriority, anteriorness,n.) ; *Also:*
1. **advanced**—ahead of others in thinking, grade, etc.
2. **ahead**—in front; in the front
3. **ventral**—pert. to, or situated on, the front part of the body

3. One Who or That Which Is, or Those Who Are, in the Front,n. *From Sec. 1:* fore, frontage, van, vanguard

4. To or toward the Front: vanward,adv.

5. Toward the Front of the Body: anteriad, adv.

6. Front Position or View: foreground, proscenium,n.

7. Size of the Front of a Building, Lot, etc.: frontage,n.

8. With the Back in Front: sternforemost, adj. or adv.

9. Having Two Fronts: bifacial,adj.

10. Front or Front Part of a Ship: bow, nose, prow, stem,n.

11. Curved End of a Ship's Prow: rostrum,n.

12. Part of the Prow on Ancient Ships Used to Ram an Enemy Ship: beak,n.

186. SIDE

1. Side,n.
1. **aspect**—side that faces in a certain direction
2. **behind**—back side
3. **face**—principal side of anything
4. **facet**—side, figuratively, as of a question, subject, topic, etc.
5. **flank**—side of an animal; side of anything
6. **flitch**—salted and cured side of a hog; side of bacon; side of an animal
7. **obverse**—front side; side turned to the observer; side of a coin or medal that has the main design
8. **pane**—flat side of something
9. **reverse**—side on the back

2. Pert. to Sides, a Side, or the Side: lateral, adj.

3. Situated at the Side: postern,adj.

4. Side-by-Side: abreast, collateral, juxtaposed,adj. (juxtaposition,n. juxtapose,v.)

5. Having Sides,adj.
1. **bilateral**—two-sided (bilateralism, bilateralness,n.)
2. **equilateral**—having equal sides
3. **multifaceted**—having many (figurative) sides

4. **multilateral**—many-sided
5. **polyhedral**—having many sides
6. **quadrilateral**—four-sided
7. **tetrahedral**—four-sided
8. **trilateral**—three-sided
9. **unilateral**—one-sided

6. Involving One Side Only: unilateral,adj.

7. Pert. to, or Affecting, Two or Both Sides, Literally or Figuratively: bilateral,adj. (bilaterality,n.)

8. To Move to the Side,v.
1. **dodge**—move suddenly to one side, to, or as if to, avoid a blow or any other type of contact (dodge,n.)
2. **duck**—move the head quickly and suddenly to the side to, or as if to, avoid a blow, contact, etc. (duck,n.)
3. **lurch**—move suddenly to one side (lurch, n.)
4. **side-skip**—skip to one side (side-skip,n.)
5. **sideslip**—skid of a vehicle (sideslip,n.)
6. **side-step**—step to one side (side-step,n.)
7. **sidle**—move sideways; move, as if sideways, in a furtive manner (sidle,n.)
8. **skew**—swerve
9. **skid**—move sideways in a smooth, easy, or sudden manner (skid,n.)
10. **swerve**—move suddenly to the side; turn aside (swerve,n.)
11. **veer**—turn aside (veer,n.)

9. To Move from Side to Side: sway, swing, v. (sway, swing,n.)

187. THROW

1. To Throw,v.
1. **bandy**—throw back and forth
2. **barrage**—hurl a rapid-fire succession of words, questions, statements, accusations, or missiles at
3. **beam**—emit
4. **belch**—throw out forcibly or in gushes
5. **besprinkle**—scatter over
6. **bestrew**—scatter over; strew over
7. **bombard**—throw shells, shot, bombs, bullets, words, etc., on, at, or into
8. **broadcast**—scatter in all directions
9. **bung**—throw forcibly
10. **cant**—throw with a sudden movement
11. **cast**—throw
12. **catapult**—throw with great force
13. **chuck**—throw; toss, the arm not moving in its full arc
14. **dart**—throw suddenly and quickly
15. **dash**—throw violently
16. **defenestrate**—throw out of the window
17. **discharge**—eject
18. **dump**—throw down
19. **ejaculate**—eject (bodily fluids)
20. **eject**—throw out, usually forcibly
21. **emit**—throw off; throw out
22. **expel**—eject
23. **fling**—throw with force or violence
24. **flip**—throw with a quick, jerking or snapping movement
25. **flirt**—throw unexpectedly or with a jerk
26. **heave**—throw; throw forcefully
27. **hurl**—throw forcefully
28. **inject**—throw in (figuratively)
29. **jerk**—throw with a quick, twisting, and suddenly arrested motion
30. **lapidate**—stone
31. **launch**—throw (some missile)
32. **lob**—throw slowly and heavily
33. **pellet**—throw (small, round things, etc.) at
34. **pelt**—throw at rapidly or heavily
35. **pepper**—shower at; shower (shot, bullets, missiles, questions, accusations, etc.) at
36. **pitch**—throw
37. **plunge**—throw forcibly and violently into; throw oneself violently forward and downward

38. **precipitate**—throw down from a height
39. **project**—throw forward
40. **prostrate oneself**—throw oneself down
41. **reflect**—throw back (sound, images, etc.)
42. **regurgitate**—throw back
43. **scatter**—throw here and there at random
44. **shoot**—throw with force
45. **shower**—throw on or over from, or as if from, a spray
46. **shy**—throw quickly and suddenly in a sidewise manner
47. **slam**—throw with great force and noise
48. **slap**—throw forcibly, carelessly, and/or hastily
49. **sling**—throw with force
50. **spatter**—splash; scatter around
51. **splash**—throw (water, liquid, or mud) on or around
52. **splatter**—splash
53. **spout**—throw out in a stream
54. **spray**—shower in small pieces or drops
55. **sprinkle**—scatter
56. **stone**—throw stones at
57. **strew**—throw here and there or at random
58. **thrash**—throw oneself around violently in bed or while lying down
59. **toss**—throw gently, with the hand palm upwards; throw about, back and forth, continuously; throw upward; throw (a coin) to see on which side it lands; throw oneself around in bed or while lying down
60. **twirl**—throw with a twisting motion; throw (a ball)
61. **volley**—throw or throw out in quick succession; throw back and forth
62. **vomit**—throw out forcibly or in gushes
63. **waft**—throw through the air or over the water

2. A Throwing; A Throw,n. *From Sec. 1:* barrage, belch, bestrewment, bombardment, broadcast, cant, cast, chuck, defenestration, discharge, dumpage, ejaculation, ejection or ejectment, emission, expulsion, fling, flip, flirt, heave, hurl, injection, lapidation, lob, pitch, plunge, precipitation, projection, prostration, reflection, regurgitation, scatter or scatteration, shy, sling, strewage, thrash, toss, twirl, volley, waftage or wafture; *Also:* **1.** jaculation—a throwing, hurling, or tossing

3. Pert. to, or Descr. of, Throwing,adj. *From Sec. 1:* ejaculatory or ejaculative, ejective, emissive; expellant, expellent, expulsive, or expulsory; injective, projective or projectile, reflective

4. That Which Is Thrown,n. *From Sec. 1:* barrage, beam, dart, discharge; ejecta (pl.); pellet, projectile, reflection, shot, shower, volley, vomit or vomitus; *Also:*
 1. **fusillade**—barrage
 2. **missile**—that which is thrown
 3. **storm**—violent or heavy shower of anything, literally or figuratively

5. Place Where Things Are Thrown Down: dump, tip,n.

6. Capable of Being Thrown: missile,adj.

7. Discus Thrower: discobolus,n.

188. SCATTER

1. To Scatter,v.
 1. **besprinkle**—scatter over
 2. **bestrew**—scatter all around or over (bestrewment,n.)
 3. **disperse**—dissipate (dispersal, dispersion, n. dispersive,adj.)
 4. **dissipate**—scatter aimlessly and without system (dissipation,n. dissipative,adj.)
 5. **intersperse**—scatter here and there among other things (interspersion,n. interspersive,adj.)
 6. **shed**—scatter all around

7. **sow**—scatter widespread
8. **spatter**—scatter (particles) over
9. **spray**—scatter in all directions
10. **spread**—scatter (spread,n.)
11. **sprinkle**—scatter around in small quantities
12. **strew**—scatter all around (strewage,n.)

2. The Scattering or Dispersion of the Jews, Esp. after Their Exile from Babylonia; The Body of Jews Thus Scattered; Jewish Christians Living Outside of Palestine in Early Times: Diaspora,n.

189. SEND

1. To Send,v.
 1. **accompany**—send together with (accompaniment,n.)
 2. **broadcast**—send by radio or television (broadcast,n.)
 3. **circulate**—send around from place to place or person to person (circulation,n.)
 4. **consign**—send (consignment,n.)
 5. **detail**—send on a special errand
 6. **direct**—send by showing the way (direction,n.)
 7. **dispatch**—send off; send off on official or business functions (dispatch,n.)
 8. **export**—send out of a country or region (exportation, export,n.)
 9. **issue**—send out, i.e., put into circulation (issuance, issue,n.)
10. **mail**—send by postal service
11. **misdirect**—send to the wrong place (misdirection,n.)
12. **route**—send by means of
13. **ship**—send by ship, train, mail, etc.
14. **summon**—send for (summons,n.)
15. **transmit**—send over; send out by radio (transmission, transmittal,n.)
16. **troll**—send around or circulate (as when a cup is passed around and each in turn drinks from it)

2. One Who, or Group That, Is Sent,n.
 1. **ambassador**—official messenger; official government envoy
 2. **courier**—special messenger
 3. **detachment**—group (of soldiers, police, etc.) sent on a special errand
 4. **detail**—small group sent out on a special errand
 5. **embassy**—ambassador together with his staff; group of envoys from one nation to another
 6. **envoy**—one sent on a mission; one sent as a messenger
 7. **errand boy**—one (often a boy) sent on an errand
 8. **mercury**—messenger (after the Roman god who functioned as such)
 9. **messenger**—one sent to do something, carry news, etc.
10. **page**—young boy (or, less commonly, girl) who works as a messenger, does errands, etc.

3. Sent by Special Messenger or Arrangement: missive,adj.

4. Place to Which Sent: destination,n.

5. That Which One Is Sent to Do: errand, mission,n.

6. Information One Is Sent to Deliver: message,n.

190. CARRY

1. To Carry,v.
 1. **bear**—carry
 2. **bring**—cause to come by carrying, literally or figuratively
 3. **cart**—loosely, carry from one place to another; carry by cart
 4. **convey**—carry from one place to another

5. **dangle**—carry loosely, allowing to swing
6. **deliver**—carry and give to the person or persons for whom intended
7. **dray**—carry, or carry from place to place, by cart; loosely, transport
8. **ferry**—carry over water by boat
9. **haul**—transport; strictly, transport by pulling
10. **lug**—carry with great effort
11. **shoulder**—carry (a burden or as a burden)
12. **taxi**—convey by, or as if by, taxicab
13. **tote**—carry; carry in one's arms or on one's shoulders
14. **transport**—carry from one place to another
15. **truck**—carry by truck
16. **waft**—carry through the air; carry over or on the surface of water
17. **whiff**—carry on a puff of air or wind
18. **whirl**—carry away quickly
19. **whisk**—take and carry away quickly

2. Carriage,n. *From Sec. 1:* cartage, conveyance, delivery, drayage, ferriage, haulage, transportation, truckage, waftage or wafture; *Also:*
1. **portage**—act of carrying; the carrying of boats, goods, etc., overland between navigable waterways
2. **transit**—a carrying

3. Carrier,n. *From Sec. 1:* bearer, bringer, carter, conveyor; deliverer, deliveryman, etc.; drayman, hauler, lugger, toter, transporter, trucker; *Also:*
1. **carrier, common carrier**—person or company in the transportation business
2. **porter**—one who carries people's luggage
3. **teamster**—trucker

4. That Which Carries,n. *From Sec. 1:* cart, conveyance or conveyor, ferry or ferryboat, transport, truck; *Also:*
1. **carriage**—conveyance; wheeled conveyance for passengers
2. **channel**—means, medium, or thing that conveys
3. **conduit**—channel for carrying water, fluids, electric wires, etc., over great distances
4. **duct**—tube, etc., that carries fluids, etc.
5. **litter**—couch supported on rails for carrying passengers; stretcher
6. **stretcher**—device, usually of cloth stretched across two poles, for carrying the sick or wounded
7. **vehicle**—conveyance

5. Able to Be Carried,adj. *From Sec. 1:* cartable, conveyable, haulable, transportable; *Also:* 1. **portable**—able to be carried, usually by hand

6. A Being Carried Across or Through: transit,n.

7. Carrying the Young in a Pouch, Like a Kangaroo, Opossum, etc.: marsupial,adj.

8. Able to Carry: portative,adj.

9. That Which Is Carried,n.
1. **burden**—that which is carried
2. **cargo**—that which is carried, usually on a ship
3. **cumbrance**—encumbrance
4. **encumbrance**—something carried that makes progress, action, or movement difficult, slow, etc.
5. **freight**—that which is transported, whether by land or sea; cargo
6. **lading**—burden; cargo
7. **load**—burden; cargo
8. **pack**—bundle carried, or to be carried, on the back of a person or animal

10. Hard to Carry,adj.
1. **burdensome**—hard to carry, literally or figuratively
2. **carking**—burdensome, figuratively

3. **clumsy**—unwieldy
4. **cumbersome**—unwieldy
5. **cumbrous**—unwieldy
6. **unwieldy**—hard to carry because of awkward size, shape, etc.

11. That Which Is Figuratively Hard to Carry: burden,n.

12. Science of Military Transportation and Supply: logistics,n.

191. BRING BACK

1. To Bring Back,v.
1. **fetch**—bring back after going for
2. **reclaim**—bring back to good condition; bring back into usefulness (reclamation, n.)
3. **repatriate**—bring (someone) back to his own country (repatriation,n.)
4. **restore**—bring back to a previous state (restoration,n. restorative,adj.)
5. **retrieve**—bring back after finding (retrieval, retrievement,n.)

192. VEHICLE

1. Vehicle (General), n.
1. **automobile**—self-propelled vehicle (automobilist,n. automobile,v.)
2. **car**—any closed or partly closed vehicle
3. **caravan**—covered vehicle
4. **carriage**—vehicle with wheels; wheeled vehicle pulled by a horse or horses
5. **cart**—vehicle with wheels
6. **conveyance**—vehicle for carrying people from one place to another
7. **cycle**—vehicle consisting mainly of a wheel or wheels, a seat for the rider, and controls (cyclist,n.)
8. **rattletrap**—old, rattling, rickety, and not particularly trustworthy vehicle
9. **sled**—vehicle with runners for use on snow or ice (sledder,n. sled,v.)
10. **streetcar**—electric vehicle, running on tracks, for transporting people, usually within a city
11. **trundle**—small cart
12. **wagon**—four-wheeled vehicle for transporting goods, merchandise, etc.

2. Vehicles Traveled in by People Going through a Desert or Enemy Territory: caravan,n. (caravanist, caravanner, caravaneer,n. caravan,v.)

3. Vehicle for Moving the Sick or Wounded: ambulance,n.

4. Pert. to a Vehicle or Vehicles: vehicular, adj.

5. Wide Board Towed behind a Motorboat, Ridden for Sport or Pleasure: aquaplane,n. (aquaplanist,n. aquaplane,v.)

6. Automobile; Motor Vehicle,n.
1. **brougham**—automobile with a closed body
2. **bus**—omnibus
3. **cab**—taxi
4. **cabriolet**—convertible coupé
5. **car**—automobile
6. **charabanc**—open omnibus, used in sightseeing
7. **coach**—two-door automobile
8. **convertible coupé**—coupé of which the top comes down
9. **coupé**—two-door automobile
10. **hack**—taxi (slang)
11. **hackney**—taxi
12. **horseless carriage**—original name for the automobile
13. **jalopy**—run-down automobile (colloq.)
14. **landau**—enclosed automobile with a division between the front and rear seats, and a convertible top on the back

15. **limousine**—automobile with the driver's seat technically on the outside though generally under a roof
16. **motorcar**—automobile
17. **omnibus**—public motor vehicle
18. **phaeton**—open automobile with front and back seats
19. **rattletrap**—old and rickety automobile
20. **roadster**—open automobile with front seat and luggage compartment or rumble seat
21. **sedan**—four-door closed automobile
22. **station wagon**—automobile with rear seats that fold down to make room for cargo
23. **suburban**—station wagon
24. **taxi, taxicab**—motor vehicle for hire
25. **touring car**—open automobile with front and back seats, and a canvas top
26. **tractor**—motor vehicle for pulling or hauling
27. **truck**—motor vehicle for transporting goods

7. To Drive, or Ride in, a Motor Vehicle,v. *From Sec. 6:* cab (colloq.), hack, motor, taxi

8. Driver of, or Ride in, a Motor Vehicle,n. *From Sec. 6:* bus driver, cabdriver, charabancer, hacker, motorist, taxi driver, taxicab driver, truckman, trucker, truck driver; *Also:*
1. **autoist, automobilist**—one who drives, or rides in, an automobile
2. **chauffeur**—one who drives an automobile for pay
3. **jehu**—cabdriver (humorous)

9. Man-Drawn Vehicle,n.
1. **cart**—hand-drawn vehicle
2. **jinrikisha, jinricksha**—two-wheeled vehicle, hand-drawn by one or two men, originally used in Japan
3. **palanquin, palankeen**—conveyance used in the Orient for one person, borne by foot. (The seat is supported by poles that rest on the shoulders of the men who carry it around.)
4. **rickshaw**—term used by foreigners for jinrikisha
5. **sedan, sedan chair**—portable, covered vehicle for a single person

10. Streetcar,n.
1. **tram, tramcar**—streetcar (generally British, though occasionally used in U.S.)
2. **trolley, trolly, trolley car**—streetcar (trolley,v.—colloq.)

11. Driver of a Streetcar: motorman,n.

12. Horse-Drawn Carriage,n.
1. **barouche**—four-wheeled carriage, with an outside seat for the driver, and two inside, facing seats
2. **brougham**—light, closed carriage
3. **buggy**—light carriage drawn by one horse
4. **cab**—carriage used for hire
5. **cabriolet**—light carriage with two wheels and a single seat, and pulled by one horse; cab
6. **cart**—open, two-wheeled carriage
7. **chaise**—two- or four-wheeled carriage; light carriage
8. **chariot**—two-wheeled vehicle, pulled by a horse, popular in ancient Rome and other places of antiquity
9. **clarence**—closed carriage for four people
10. **coach**—large, closed carriage with four wheels
11. **coach-and-four**—coach with four horses
12. **diligence**—stagecoach
13. **droshky**—low, open, four-wheeled carriage used in Russia
14. **four-in-hand**—carriage pulled by four horses and driven by one person
15. **gig**—light, two-wheeled carriage, drawn by a single horse
16. **hackney**—carriage for hire
17. **hansom**—light carriage with two wheels,

with the driver's seat elevated at the rear, often used for hire
18. **landau**—four-wheeled enclosed carriage, with a division between the front and rear seats, and a convertible top on back
19. **landaulet**—small landau
20. **phaeton**—light, four-wheeled carriage, with, usually, two seats facing forward
21. **shay**—chaise (colloq.)
22. **stagecoach**—public carriage making regular runs between stations
23. **sulky**—light carriage, with two wheels, for a single rider
24. **surrey**—carriage with four wheels for two riders
25. **tandem**—carriage drawn by horses harnessed one in front of the other
26. **victoria**—low, four-wheeled carriage for two passengers, with a raised driver's seat in front

13. To Drive, or Ride in, a Carriage,v. *From Sec. 12:* gig, tandem or tandemize

14. Driver of, or Rider in, a Carriage,n. *From Sec. 12:* charioteer; diligence (pl.); tandemer or tandemist; *Also:*
1. **coachman, coach driver**—one whose business is driving carriages
2. **jehu**—coachman (humorous)
3. **phaeton**—one who drives a coach or chariot at reckless speed

15. Pert. to Carriages: curricular,adj.

16. Baby Carriage,n.
1. **bassinet**—child's carriage in the form of a basket
2. **gocart**—baby carriage, with adjustable back, and having larger rear wheels than front wheels
3. **perambulator, pram**—small carriage in which an infant is pushed (British)
4. **stroller**—kind of baby carriage; gocart

17. Cycle,n.
1. **bicycle**—two-wheeled cycle; child's three-wheeled cycle
2. **hydrocycle**—cycle used on water
3. **monocycle**—one-wheeled cycle
4. **motorcycle**—cycle propelled by motor
5. **quadricycle**—four-wheeled cycle, esp. for use on railroads
6. **tandem**—bicycle with two seats, one behind the other
7. **tricycle**—three-wheeled cycle
8. **unicycle**—one-wheeled cycle
9. **velocipede**—three-wheeled cycle; early bicycle; child's tricycle
10. **wheel**—bicycle

18. To Cycle,v. *From Sec. 17:* bicycle, motorcycle, tandem or tandemize, tricycle, velocipede

19. Cyclist,n. *From Sec. 17:* bicyclist or bicycler, hydrocyclist, motorcyclist, quadricyclist or quadricycler, tandemer or tandemist, tricyclist or tricycler, unicyclist; velocipedist, velocipeder, velocipedean, or velocipedian

20. Sled,n.
1. **bobsled, bobsleigh, bob**—short sled, usually joined to another; the combined sled so formed
2. **cutter**—sled drawn by a single horse
3. **double-ripper, double-runner**—sled formed by joining one behind the other with a board; bobsled
4. **sledge**—sled
5. **sleigh**—sled
6. **toboggan**—long sled with a flat bottom, capable of holding many riders

21. To Sled,v. *From Sec. 20:* bobsled; sleigh (generally in the present participle, as *to go,* or *come sleighing,* etc.) toboggan

22. Sledder,n. *From Sec. 20:* bobsledder, bobsleigher or sleigher, tobboganer or tobboganist. *Also:* 1. **coaster**—one who rides downhill on a sled

23. Wagon,n.
1. **buggy**—small wagon used for short hauls
2. **caisson**—ammunition wagon
3. **cart**—small vehicle for transporting; light commercial wagon
4. **Conestoga wagon**—covered wagon, having large wheels, for traveling on prairies, etc.
5. **prairie schooner**—long, covered wagon used in early days by people crossing the prairies to settle in the West
6. **truck**—large vehicle for transporting goods
7. **van**—large, covered vehicle for transporting household goods to a new residence, wild animals on exhibition, furniture to a new location, etc.; truck

24. Maker or Repairer of Wagons: wainwright, wagonsmith, wagonwright,n.

25. To Ride Downhill: coast,v. (coast,n.)

26. One Who Drives a Train: engineer,n.

27. Fast Driver of a Vehicle: jehu,n. (humorous)

28. Someone Who Rides in, Rather than Drives, a Vehicle: passenger,n.

29. Pert. to Driving: curricular,adj.

193. PULL

1. To Pull; To Draw,v.
1. **absorb**—draw up
2. **attract**—draw or pull to oneself or itself
3. **drag**—draw heavily; draw slowly; pull by physical force against implied resistance; draw or pull along
4. **dredge**—pull up from the bottom
5. **haul**—pull or drag forcefully
6. **jerk**—pull with a quick, twisting, and suddenly arrested motion
7. **lug**—pull along with great effort
8. **manhandle**—pull and/or push (someone) about roughly
9. **maul**—hit (someone) and pull (him) about roughly
10. **pluck**—pull at
11. **strain**—pull hard
12. **stretch**—pull or draw out longer or to full length
13. **tear**—pull hard
14. **thrum**—pluck a stringed instrument aimlessly or idly
15. **tow**—pull by a rope or chain
16. **trail**—pull or drag behind one
17. **tug**—pull hard
18. **tweak**—simultaneously pull, pinch, and twist
19. **twinge**—tweak
20. **twist**—wrench
21. **twitch**—pull at sharply or suddenly
22. **wrench**—pull or jerk forcibly

2. A Pulling; A Pull,n. *From Sec. 1:* absorption, attraction, drag, haulage, haul, jerk, lug, maul, pluck, strain, stretch, tear, thrum, tow or towage, tug, tweak, twinge, twist, twitch, wrench; *Also:*
1. **stress**—strain
2. **stroke**—a pull on an oar or oars
3. **traction**—a pulling or drawing

3. That Which Pulls or Draws,n. *From Sec. 1:* attraction, attractor, or attrahent; dredge, stretcher; *From Sec. 2:* tractor (thing or vehicle)

4. Descr. of Pulling or Drawing,adj. *From Sec. 1:* absorbent or absorptive, attractive or attrahent (absorbency, absorptiveness, absorptivity, attractiveness, attractivity,n.); *From Sec. 2:* tractive, tractional

5. Condition Caused by Pulling or Drawing,n. *From Sec. 1:* strain, stretch; *From Sec. 2:* stress, traction

6. That Which Is Pulled or Drawn,n.
1. **trailer**—that which, or vehicle that, is pulled or drawn along behind
2. **train**—something drawn or pulled behind one

7. To Be Pulled or Drawn Along Behind: trail,v.

8. To Pull or Draw (Something) In, Back, etc.,v.
1. **absorb**—suck in
2. **reel in**—pull in, on, or as if on, a round disc
3. **resorb**—draw back in that which has been eliminated or exuded
4. **retract**—draw back or inward
5. **sheathe**—draw back (claws)
6. **suck**—draw in; draw into the mouth; draw in with the mouth

9. A Pulling or Drawing In, Back, etc.,n. *From Sec. 8:* absorption, resorption, retraction, suction or suck

10. Descr. of Pulling or Drawing In, Back, etc.,adj. *From Sec. 8:* absorbent or absorptive, resorbent, retractive or retractile, suctorial (absorbency, absorptiveness, absorptivity, resorbence, retractiveness, retractility,n.)

11. Capable of Being Drawn Back or Inward: retractible, retractile,adj. (retractibility, retractility,n.)

12. Device for Drawing In Fluids and Expelling Them in a Stream: syringe,n.

13. To Draw (Things) Together,v.
1. **clench**—draw the parts of tightly together
2. **constrict**—draw together; contract
3. **constringe**—cause a drawing together of
4. **contract**—draw together the parts of
5. **tuck**—draw together

14. A Drawing Together,n. *From Sec. 13:* clench, constriction, contraction

15. That Which Draws Together,n. *From Sec. 13:* constrictor, contractor

16. Descr. of or Capable of, Drawing Together,adj. *From Sec. 13:* constrictive, constringent, contractive or contractile (constringency, contractiveness, contractility,n.)

17. Condition of Being Drawn Together,n. *From Sec. 13:* constriction, contraction

18. To Pull or Draw (Something) Out, Off, Forth, Away, Apart, etc.; To Stretch (something),v.
1. **abstract**—draw off or out
2. **broaden**—extend
3. **catheterize**—draw out fluid from by passing a tube through a bodily opening
4. **crane**—stretch (the neck)
5. **crop**—pluck
6. **dislocate**—pull (a bodily member) out of joint
7. **distill**—draw out through refinement (used figuratively, as to distill an attitude from someone's remarks, etc)
8. **educe**—draw forth or out of a person (that which is potentially or latently present in him); draw forth (information, facts, etc.) from a source
9. **elicit**—draw out (an abstraction or intangible)
10. **elongate**—stretch out (to a greater length)
11. **evaporate**—draw off (liquid) by heat, so that a more solid form remains
12. **evoke**—draw or pull forth or out (some intangible or abstraction)
13. **extend**—draw out in time or space; pull out, in order to make larger; stretch out in time or treatment to cover many things, subjects, aspects, etc.
14. **extract**—draw or pull out

15. **pluck**—pull off; pull the feathers or hair off of
16. **prolong, prolongate**—stretch out in time
17. **pry**—pull away, off, or apart
18. **rack**—stretch; strain
19. **rend**—pull apart violently
20. **siphon, siphon off**—draw off through, or as if through, a tube or pipe
21. **strain**—pull or draw tight; stretch; stretch as hard as possible; stretch too far; stretch beyond reasonable limits
22. **tense**—stretch tight
23. **tweeze**—pull out with a sharp-pointed instrument
24. **unsheathe**—draw (a knife, sword, etc.) from its sheath or holder
25. **whip out**—pull out suddenly
26. **withdraw**—draw out; draw away; draw from
27. **wrest**—pull away violently

19. A Pulling or Drawing Out, etc.; A Stretching; A Stretching,n. *From Sec. 18:* abstraction, catheterization, crane, dislocation, distillation, education, elicitation, elongation, evaporation, evocation, extension, extraction, prolongation, pry, rend or rent, strain, tension, tweeze, withdrawal, wrest; *Also:*
  1. **discerption**—a pulling to pieces
  2. **stress**—strain

20. That Which Pulls or Draws Out, etc.; Stretcher,n. *From Sec. 18:* abstracter, catheter, extender, extractor, rack, siphon, tweezer or tweezers

21. Descr. of Pulling or Drawing Out, Stretching, etc.,adj. *From Sec. 18:* abstractive, eductive, evocative or evocatory, extensive or extensional, extractive, tensive or tensional

22. Condition of Being Pulled or Drawn Out, Stretched, etc.,n. *From Sec. 18:* dislocation, extension, strain, tension; *From Sec. 19:* stress

23. Pert. to Cord Tension: funicular,adj.

24. Capable of Being Pulled Out, Drawn Out, or Stretched,adj.
  1. **ductile**—of metals, capable of being permanently drawn out, or of being drawn out into wire or thread (ductility,n.)
  2. **elastic**—capable of being stretched, and of then springing back to original shape (elasticity,n.)
  3. **extendible**—capable of being pulled out to greater length; capable of being drawn out in time or space (extendibility,n.)
  4. **extensible**—capable of being stretched; extendible (extensibility,n.)
  5. **extensile**—capable of being stretched; extendible (extensility,n.)
  6. **stretchable**—capable of being stretched
  7. **tensile, tensible**—capable of being stretched (tensility, tensileness,n.)
  8. **tractile**—capable of being stretched in length, or to a greater length (tractility, n.)

25. Stretched Tight: taut, tense,adj. (tautness; tensity or tenseness,n.)

194. STRETCH

1. To Stretch, i.e., Become Stretched,v.
  1. **branch out**—stretch out (in the range of one's activities)
  2. **bridge**—stretch out over; span
  3. **extend**—stretch out, whether in space or time
  4. **overlap**—stretch out beyond (what was expected or planned)
  5. **overrun**—stretch out beyond control
  6. **ramble**—stretch out with no regularity
  7. **range**—stretch out in a certain direction
  8. **reach**—stretch out in time, influence, dimensions, etc.

9. **span**—stretch out between two limits or supports; stretch out over
10. **spread**—stretch out
11. **strain**—stretch with effort or difficulty or as hard as possible
12. **subtend**—stretch across
13. **tense**—stretch tight

2. A Stretching or Stretch,n. *From Sec. 1:* extension or extent, overlap, range, reach, span, spread, strain, tension (extensional, tensional,adj.) ; *Also:*
  1. **amplitude**—extent
  2. **breadth**—extent
  3. **compass**—extent; reach
  4. **gamut**—range, from lowest to highest
  5. **purview**—extent of authority, activity, power, influence, ability, or knowledge
  6. **scope**—extent

3. That Which Stretches Out,n. *From Sec. 1:* branch, bridge, extension, span

4. Having a Wide Extent,adj.
  1. **cyclopedic, encyclopedic, encyclopedical**—having a wide extent of knowledge
  2. **extensive**—having a wide extent (extensiveness,n.)

5. Capable of Stretching,adj.
  1. **elastic**—capable of stretching and then springing back to former size or shape (elasticity,n.)
  2. **tensile**—capable of stretching (tensility, tensileness,n.)

195. SPREAD

1. To Spread, i.e., Be, Become, or Lie Spread,v.
  1. **bestrew**—lie spread over
  2. **deploy**—spread out along the front (of military troops)
  3. **diffuse**—spread widely; spread out over a wide area or surface
  4. **extend**—spread out in space, area, influence, etc.
  5. **mantle**—spread over, like a cloak; spread out—first one, then the other, over an outstretched leg (of a bird's wings)
  6. **overrun**—spread beyond control
  7. **overspread**—be spread over
  8. **penetrate**—spread through completely
  9. **permeate**—spread through the whole of
  10. **pervade**—spread throughout
  11. **proliferate**—spread by growing rapidly, developing new parts, etc.
  12. **radiate**—spread in all directions from, or as if from, a center or central point
  13. **ramble**—spread with no regularity
  14. **ramify**—spread out; spread out into branches and subbranches, or into divisions and subdivisions
  15. **scatter**—spread widely or all over
  16. **splay**—spread out
  17. **sprawl**—spread out ungracefully (of the limbs) ; spread irregularly or ungracefully over
  18. **stalk through**—spread through
  19. **straggle**—spread in an irregular manner
  20. **stretch**—spread
  21. **strew**—be spread all over
  22. **suffuse**—spread over
  23. **transfuse**—spread through
  24. **unfold**—be or become spread open or out from a previously closed or folded state
  25. **unfurl**—be or become spread open or out from a previously curled, folded, or closed state
  26. **unroll**—spread forth to be seen

2. To Spread (Something),v. *From Sec. 1:* deploy, diffuse, extend, mantle, overspread, scatter, splay, sprawl, stretch, strew, suffuse, transfuse, unfold, unfurl, unroll; *Also:*
  1. **broadcast**—spread (information, seed, etc.) in all directions
  2. **circumfuse**—spread over or around

3. **daub**—smear
4. **disseminate**—spread in all directions or far and wide (ideas, principles, or similar intangibles)
5. **dissipate**—spread aimlessly and without system (something intangible)
6. **propagate**—spread, or cause to spread, from person to person (ideas, doctrines, etc.); disseminate
7. **sow**—spread (ideas, information, seed, etc.) far and wide
8. **smear**—spread (something thick, soft, or greasy)
9. **sprinkle**—spread in drops or particles

3. To Spread a Place or Person with,v. *From Sec. 1:* bestrew (with); diffuse (with); overrun (with); overspread (with); strew (with); suffuse (with); transfuse (with); *From Sec. 2:* circumfuse (with); smear (with); sprinkle (with); *Also:*
1. **bedaub (with)**—spread (with something soft, sticky, greasy, etc.)
2. **besmear (with)**—bedaub
3. **bespread (with)**—spread thickly over, on, or through
4. **besprinkle (with)**—sprinkle
5. **perfuse (with)**—suffuse or sprinkle; spread all through or over
6. **plaster (with)**—spread all over

4. A Spreading,n. *From Sec. 1:* bestrewment, deployment, diffusion, extension, penetration, permeation, pervasion, proliferation, radiation, ramification, scatter, scatteration, splay, sprawl, stretch, strewage, suffusion, transfusion; *From Sec. 2:* broadcast, circumfusion, dissemination, dissipation; *From Sec. 3:* perfusion

5. Descr. of Spreading; Tending to Spread, adj. *From Sec. 1:* diffusive, overrunning, over-spreading; penetrating, penetrant, or penetrative; permeating, permeant, or permeative; pervading or pervasive, proliferating or proliferative, radiating or radiatory, rambling, ramifying, sprawling or sprawly, straggling or straggly, suffusive; *From Sec. 2:* disseminative, dissipative, propagative or propagatory, smeary; *From Sec. 3:* perfusive; *Also:* 1. **infectious**—spreading from person to person (infectiousness,n.)

6. Spread,adj. *From Sec. 1:* bestrewed, deployed, diffused or diffuse, extensive, overrun, overspread, permeated, ramified, scattered, splay, sprawly, straggly, strewed, suffused, transfused, unfolded, unfurled, unrolled; *From Sec. 2:* broadcast, circumfused, disseminated, propagated, sowed or sown, sprinkled, smeared; *From Sec. 3:* bedaubed, besmeared, bespread, besprinkled, perfused, plastered; *Also:*
1. **far-flung**—widely spread over a great (literal or figurative) range or distance
2. **outspread**—spread out
3. **patulous**—spread open
4. **rotate**—having parts spread out from a center, like the spokes of a wheel
5. **widespread**—spread over a large area

7. Device for Spreading,n.
1. **spatula**—implement for spreading thick substances
2. **spreader**—instrument for spreading butter, jam, and similar foods; machine for spreading seeds, a coating over something, etc.

196. ATTRACTION

1. To Attract,v.
1. **allure**—attract by offering some bait or advantage; fascinate; tempt
2. **appeal (to)**—be attractive (to)
3. **bait**—allure; captivate; entice
4. **beckon**—attract; lure; tempt
5. **beguile**—attract

6. **bewitch**—fascinate
7. **captivate**—attract by charm, delightfulness, or artistry
8. **charm**—attract
9. **decoy**—lure into danger or a trap
10. **enchant**—attract greatly with one's charm or delightfulness
11. **enthrall**—fascinate
12. **entice**—attract, often to or into something considered wicked, immoral, or unpleasant, by arousing or holding out hopes of reward, the satisfaction of desire, special or sensual pleasures, etc.
13. **fascinate**—attract and hold by one's charm
14. **intrigue**—strongly attract the interest or curiosity of
15. **invite**—attract; tempt
16. **lure**—attract, often to something harmful, by promise of pleasure or reward or by arousing desire
17. **magnetize**—attract (almost against or beyond the will of the one attracted)
18. **seduce**—attract into wrongdoing, vice, foolish or unwise actions, etc.; attract away from propriety or rectitude by overcoming qualms, scruples, or better instincts
19. **solicit**—tempt to do wrong or to commit immoral acts
20. **spellbind**—fascinate
21. **tempt**—attract to an action or activity; attract into evil actions; attract into what is wrong by promise of pleasure or reward
22. **troll**—allure; entice
23. **wile**—attract by, or as if by, magic; entice.
24. **witch**—fascinate

2. Attraction,n. *From Sec. 1:* allure or allurement, appeal, beguilement, bewitchment, captivation, charm, enchantment, enthrallment, enticement, fascination, invitation, lure, seduction or seducement, solicitation, temptation, witchery or witchcraft

3. An Attraction, i.e., That Which Attracts, n. *From Sec. 1:* allurement, bait, charm, decoy, enticement, lure, magnet, temptation, wiles; *Also:*
1. **ignis fatuus (Latin)**—will-o'-the-wisp
2. **loadstone, lodestone**—anything which strongly attracts as if by magnetic force
3. **will-o'-the-wisp, wisp**—that which lures one on but is deceptive, misleading, or nonexistent

4. One Who Attracts,n. *From Sec. 1:* beguiler, bewitcher, charmer, decoy, enchanter or, fem., enchantress, fascinator; seducer or, fem., seductress, spellbinder, solicitor, tempter or, fem., temptress, troll, witch; *Also:*
1. **affinity**—person to whom one is naturally attracted
2. **Delilah**—temptress
3. **lorelei**—temptress
4. **siren**—temptress

5. Attractive,adj. *From Sec. 1:* alluring, appealing, beckoning, beguiling, bewitching, captivating, charming, enchanting, enthralling, enticing, fascinating, intriguing, inviting, luring, magnetic, seductive, tempting; *Also:*
1. **adorable**—delightfully and exquisitely attractive
2. **catching**—attractive; fascinating
3. **catchy**—attractive
4. **engaging**—attractive and charming, either in personality or in appearance, but more often the former
5. **fetching**—attractive
6. **glamorous**—possessing or exercising a kind of exciting fascination
7. **idyllic**—naturally simple and attractive (esp. of ways of living)
8. **meretricious**—attractive by false show;

alluring or tempting through false values, benefits, charms, enticements, etc.
9. **orphic**—fascinating, after Orpheus, who could fascinate with the music of his lyre
10. **piquant**—attractive in a lively, stimulating way
11. **rose-colored**—alluring
12. **seductive**—alluring; captivating; fascinating
13. **serpentine**—tempting
14. **siren, sirenic**—tempting
15. **suggestive**—tempting
16. **taking**—captivating
17. **winning**—attractive
18. **winsome**—attractive

6. Attractiveness; Attractive Quality or Qualities,n. *From Sec. 1:* allure, appeal, charm, fascination, lure, magnetism, seductiveness, temptation, wiles, witchery or witchcraft; *From Sec. 5:* adorableness, catchiness, glamour, meretriciousness, piquancy, seductiveness, suggestiveness, winsomeness; *Also:*
1. **spell**—fascination

7. Unattractive,adj. *From Sec. 1:* unalluring, unappealing, charmless, unenchanting, unfascinating, unintriguing, uninviting, untempting; *From Sec. 5:* unglamorous; *Also:* 1. **arid**—totally without appeal

8. Attraction, i.e., State of Being Attracted, n. *From Sec. 1:* bewitchment, enchantment, enthrallment, fascination, seduction; *Also:*
1. **affinity**—natural attraction to someone or something
2. **penchant (for)**—strong attraction (to)

9. Strongly Attracted: smitten,adj.

10. To Be Strongly Attracted to: gravitate toward,v. (gravitation,n.)

11. Center of Attraction,n.
1. **blazing star**—brilliant center of attraction
2. **cynosure**—center of attraction
3. **lodestar, loadstar**—center of attraction

12. Scientific Attraction,n.
1. **adhesion**—attraction that holds molecules attached together
2. **capillary attraction, capillarity**—force that attracts surface liquids
3. **gravity**—natural force that pulls objects toward the center of the earth

13. Device to Measure Intensity of Magnetic Forces: magnetometer,n.

197. PUSH

1. To Push (Something or Someone),v.
1. **boost**—push up from below
2. **buck**—push with lowered head
3. **bump**—push against, but without great force
4. **bunt**—push with the head lowered
5. **butt**—push with the head lowered
6. **crowd**—push; push forward; push (a large number or quantity) into too small a place for comfort; shove
7. **detrude**—push forcibly down, out, or away
8. **displace**—push out and take the place of
9. **drive**—urge
10. **eject**—push out forcibly
11. **expel, expulse**—push out
12. **extrude**—push out
13. **impel**—propel, literally or, more often, figuratively
14. **inject**—push in, figuratively or literally
15. **insinuate**—push in gradually, slowly, indirectly, subtly, etc.
16. **intrude**—push in upon (often what is not welcome or wanted)
17. **jab**—push, or push at, with something sharp or pointed
18. **jerk**—push with a quick, twisting, and then suddenly arrested movement

19. **jog**—push slightly, literally or figuratively
20. **jostle**—push against roughly
21. **lunge**—thrust
22. **manhandle**—push and/or pull (someone) about roughly
23. **maul**—manhandle; beat and manhandle
24. **nudge**—push gently; push (someone) gently with the elbow to call his attention to something
25. **nuzzle**—push, push at, or push around with the nose
26. **obtrude**—push forward (what is unwanted and unwelcome); push out forcibly
27. **oust**—push out (someone who is in, or in possession of, a place, office, etc.)
28. **outthrust**—thrust out
29. **pack**—push (a large number or quantity) into a small space; tamp
30. **plump**—push into suddenly and heavily
31. **plunge**—push into (usually with force and suddenness)
32. **poke**—push, or push at, with one's arm, something pointed, etc.
33. **press**—continue a pushing motion upon, while in contact; push ahead or forward
34. **prod**—push, or push at, with something pointed, etc.; push, figuratively
35. **propel**—push forward
36. **protrude**—push out
37. **ram**—push; push down; force down by pushing
38. **rebuff**—push back or away, figuratively (as by one's attitude, words, actions, etc.)
39. **reel out**—push out by, or as if by, unwinding from a wheel or round disc
40. **relegate**—push aside
41. **repel, repulse**—push back, literally or figuratively; push back by one's attitude
42. **retrude**—thrust back
43. **root**—poke around
44. **sheathe**—push forcibly into flesh
45. **shoulder**—push with, or as if with, the shoulder; push aside
46. **shove**—push by main strength; push carelessly or impolitely
47. **slam**—push with great force and noise
48. **slide**—push along a surface
49. **spread**—push apart
50. **squirt**—push (liquid) out in a forcible stream
51. **stab at**—thrust at with, or as if with, a pointed instrument
52. **strain**—push through a sieve
53. **tamp**—push in or down by gently hitting
54. **thrust**—push forcibly (in some direction)
55. **trundle**—push along
56. **tuck**—push into a small or out-of-the-way place; push (the ends of a garment, sheet, blanket, etc.) into place
57. **urge**—push forward with threats of force, literally or figuratively
58. **wedge**—push in or through a tight place
59. **whiff**—push out in puffs

2. To Push; To Push Oneself or Itself; To Go or Come by Pushing,v. *From Sec. 1:* crowd (of groups), drive, extrude, intrude, lunge, obtrude, pack (of groups); plunge, press, protrude, reel out, squirt, thrust; *Also:*
1. **barge in, into**—thrust oneself in or into unexpectedly and impolitely
2. **project**—push out
3. **slop**—push through snow, slush, soft mud, mire, etc.
4. **squeeze**—push one's way with difficulty or effort
5. **throng**—push into too small a place for comfort (of large groups)

3. A Pushing,n. *From Sec. 1:* detrusion, displacement, drive, ejection, expulsion, extrusion, impulsion or impulse, injection, insinuation, intrusion, lunge, obtrusion, ouster, outthrust, plunge, poke, press or pressure, propulsion or propelment, protrusion, rebuff, relegation, repulsion, retrusion, squirt, thrust; *From Sec. 2:* projection, squeeze

4. A Push,n. *From Sec. 1:* boost, buck, bump, bunt, drive, impulse, jab, jog, jostle, lunge, nudge, nuzzle, plunge, poke, press, prod, rebuff, shove, squirt, tamp, thrust, tuck, whiff; *Also:* **1. upthrust**—upward push

5. Pert. to, or Descr. of, Pushing or a Push, adj. *From Sec. 1:* detrusive, driving, ejective, expellant or expellent; expulsive, expulsatory, or expulsory; extrusive; impellent, impulsive, or impulsory; insinuative or insinuatory, intrusive, obtrusive, propulsive or propellent, protrusive, repulsive or repellent, retrusive, urgent (detrusiveness, ejectivity, impulsiveness or impulsivity, intrusiveness, obtrusiveness, repulsiveness, urgency,n.); *From Sec. 2:* projectile, projectional or projective

6. Pusher,n. *From Sec. 1:* driver, impeller, intruder, jostler, mauler, obtruder, shover

7. That Which Pushes,n. *From Sec. 1:* detrusor, drive, ejector, expeller, expulsor, extruder, impeller or impellent, impulse, injector, obtruder, ouster, plunger, poker, presser, prod; propeller, propellant, propellent; repellent, tamp

8. Capable of Being Pushed,adj. *From Sec. 1:* protrusible or protrusile, retrusible; *Also:* **1. protractile**—capable of being thrust out

9. A Being Pushed Back: retroversion,n.

10. Pushed Out: outthrust,adj.

198. PRESS

1. To Press; To Squeeze,v.
1. **astringe**—compress
2. **bear down**—press
3. **choke**—press or squeeze the windpipe of hard enough to cause or almost to cause, a cessation of breathing
4. **clamp**—press and hold together
5. **compress**—press or squeeze together and thus cause to take less space
6. **corrugate**—press into folds
7. **cram**—press; compress
8. **crumple**—press or squeeze into folds or wrinkles
9. **crunch**—crush noisily
10. **crush**—squeeze hard; squeeze so hard as to break, bruise, or harm
11. **cuddle**—nestle; snuggle
12. **depress**—press down
13. **express**—press or squeeze out
14. **hug**—press close within, or as if within, the arms
15. **jam**—press together tightly or in a tight position
16. **knead**—press and squeeze by hand, as dough in baking, the muscles or flesh in massaging, etc.
17. **mash**—crush into a soft or pulpy mass
18. **nestle**—press close (so that part of the body is in contact with something), often for comfort or security
19. **nuzzle**—press with the nose; nestle
20. **pinch, sandwich**—squeeze between two things
21. **ram**—press tightly or closely together; press together into a limited or compact space
22. **snuggle**—press close for affection, warmth, comfort, etc.
23. **squash**—press or squeeze until flat and soft; crush; crush to a pulp
24. **squelch**—press with enough force to break or bruise; crush
25. **strain**—press through a sieve; press closely; squeeze; hug
26. **strangle**—press so hard on the windpipe of (a person or animal) as to cause death by preventing from breathing

27. **strangulate**—press (a person, organ, etc.) hard enough to stop circulation of blood or breathing
28. **stuff**—jam
29. **throttle**—squeeze the throat of; strangle
30. **trample**—crush by stepping on heavily
31. **tread**—press on with the feet; crush
32. **triturate**—crush into a fine powder
33. **wad**—press into a soft mass; jam; jam with something soft
34. **wedge**—squeeze in, or through, a tight place
35. **wring**—squeeze; squeeze and twist forcibly

2. A Pressing; A Squeezing; Pressure; Squeeze,n. *From Sec. 1:* compression, corrugation, crunch, crush, cuddle, depression, expression, hug, jam, nestle, nuzzle, pinch, snuggle, strangulation, trample, trituration, wring; *Also:*
1. **brunt**—chief pressure in a struggle or conflict
2. **strain**—stress
3. **stress**—pressure upon one's endurance

3. Acting, Serving, or Tending to Press,adj. *From Sec. 1:* compressive, depressive, expressive, strangulative

4. One Who Presses or Squeezes,n. *From Sec. 1:* cuddler, nestler, nuzzler, pincher, snuggler, strangler, stuffer, throttler, trampler

5. That Which Presses or Squeezes,n. *From Sec. 1:* clamp, crusher, masher, wringer; *Also:*
1. **nipper, nippers**—instrument or device for squeezing
2. **vise**—implement with two jaws for squeezing or pressing

6. Device to Measure Pressure,n.
1. **manometer**—device for measuring pressure, as of gases or vapors
2. **piezometer**—device to measure pressure
3. **sphygmomanometer**—device to measure blood pressure

7. Measurement of the Compressibility of Liquids: piezometry,n. (piezometer,n. piezometric, piezometrical,adj.)

8. To Free from Pressure: decompress,v. (decompression,n.)

9. To Pinch,v.
1. **nip**—pinch (nip,n.)
2. **tweak**—simultaneously pinch, pull, and twist (tweak,n.)
3. **twinge**—tweak (twinge,n.)
4. **vellicate**—pinch (vellication,n. vellicative,adj.)

199. PLAY

1. To Play,v.
1. **dabble, dabble in**—play in (water)
2. **dally**—play
3. **dandle**—play with (a child) by bumping it up and down on one's knees or in one's arms
4. **disport**—play
5. **frisk**—frolic
6. **frolic**—play merrily
7. **gambol**—frolic
8. **lark**—play
9. **romp**—play in a rough, rough-and-tumble, or lively fashion
10. **skylark**—play
11. **sport**—play
12. **toy with**—play with
13. **twiddle**—play with

2. One Who Plays,n. *From Sec. 1:* dabbler, dallier, frisker, frolicker, romper, skylarker

3. Play,n. *From Sec. 1:* dalliance, frisk, frolic, gambol, romp, sport; *Also:*

1. **beer and skittles**—drink and play
2. **recreation**—play
4. **Playful**,adj. *From Sec. 1:* frisky, frolicsome, rompish or rompy, sportive or sportful; *Also:*
    1. **arch**—playful
    2. **coltish**—playful, like a colt
    3. **kittenish**—playful, like a kitten
5. **Playful Child or Animal:** wanton,n.
6. **Done in a Spirit of Play:** waggish,adj.
7. **To Spend (Time or a Portion of Time) in Play:** beguile,v.
8. **To Play More Skillfully** than, as in a Game or Contest: outplay,v.
9. **One Who Enjoys, Is Interested in, or Participates in, Outdoor Games:** sportsman, sport,n.
10. **To Play with,** i.e., **Not Be Serious with:** toy with, trifle with,v.
11. **To Play at, Rather than Work at Seriously:** dabble at, dabble in,v. (dabbler,n.)
12. **A Toy**,n.
    1. **bauble**—cheap and showy plaything
    2. **gewgaw**—toy; worthless, cheap, and showy plaything
    3. **kickshaw**—toy
    4. **plaything**—toy; something to play with
13. **A Playing Card:** pasteboard,n.

200. AMUSEMENT

1. **To Amuse**,v.
    1. **beguile**—amuse
    2. **divert**—amuse; entertain lightly
    3. **entertain**—interest and amuse
    4. **regale**—amuse or entertain, usually with something charming or delightful; entertain with choice food or a sumptuous meal
    5. **tickle**—amuse
2. **Amusement,** i.e., **Act of Amusing**,n. *From Sec. 1:* beguilement, diversion, entertainment, regalement
3. **Amusing**,adj. *From Sec. 1:* beguiling, diverting, entertaining, regaling; *Also:*
    1. **droll**—quaint and amusing
    2. **funny**—amusing
    3. **priceless**—amusing
4. **Amusement,** i.e., **State of Being Amused,** n. *From Sec. 1:* beguilement, diversion, entertainment, regalement; *Also:*
    1. **fun**—merry amusement
    2. **mirth**—amusement
    3. **recreation**—amusement; diversion
    4. **sport**—amusement; diversion
5. **An Amusement**,n. *From Sec. 1:* diversion, entertainment, regalement; *From Sec. 4:* recreation, sport; *Also:*
    1. **divertissement**—diversion
    2. **nautch**—an entertainment by dancing girls (in India)
    3. **pastime**—an amusement; a recreation; that which helps one pass time pleasantly, though itself of no further value or purpose
6. **Entertainments**,n.
    1. **repertoire, repertory**—entertainments that a company or person is prepared to give
    2. **revels**—entertainments provided at a celebration, wedding, etc.
7. **To Amuse Oneself**,v.
    1. **disport**—amuse oneself
    2. **play with, toy with**—amuse oneself with
8. **To Spend (Time or a Portion of Time) in Fun, Amusement, or Entertainment:** beguile,v.
9. **Place of Amusement:** resort,n.

10. **A Traveling Group of Entertainers, Shows, Amusement Devices, etc.:** carnival,n.
11. **Hobby:** avocation, pastime,n.
12. **One Who Follows a Hobby**,n.
    1. **amateur**—one who pursues a study, science, calling, etc., as a hobby rather than to make money
    2. **dabbler, dilettante**—one who follows a profession or engages in a fine art as a hobby rather than in a serious manner (dilettanti,pl.)
    3. **hobbyist**—one who habitually pursues hobbies
13. **Quality or State of Following a Hobby,** n. *From Sec. 12:* amateurism, dabbling, dilettantism, hobbyism
14. **Descr. of Following a Hobby**,adj. *From Sec. 12:* amateur, dabbling, dilettante or dilettantish; hobbyhorsical (humorous)

201. MERRYMAKING

1. **Merrymaking:** bacchanal or bacchanalianism (drunken, and often somewhat in the nature of an orgy); carousing, carousal, or carouse (drunken and noisy); celebration (in honor of an event, accomplishment, time, anniversary, etc.); festival, festivity or festivities; orgy (wild, drunken, riotous, lascivious, etc.) or orgies (such in ancient Rome and ancient Greece in the worship of certain gods, esp. Dionysus); racket; revel, revelry, or reveling (usually boisterous or noisy); roistering (noisy or wild); wassailing (marked by much drinking, or by the drinking of toasts),n.
2. **A Merrymaking,** i.e., **a Party, Celebration, Revel, or Similar Occasion**,n. *From Sec. 1:* bacchanal or bacchanalia, carousal or carouse, celebration, festival, festivity, orgy, revel or revels, wassail; *Also:*
    1. **affair**—party; elaborate party
    2. **Bacchanalia, bacchanals**—ancient Roman celebration in honor of the god Bacchus, characterized by rites in the nature of an orgy
    3. **feast**—religious or other celebration
    4. **festival, festivity**—religious or other celebration, esp. one recurring periodically
    5. **frolic**—gay or merry party
    6. **function, social function**—formal social party
    7. **gala**—occasion of merrymaking; celebration; festival
    8. **gathering**—party; social party in someone's home
    9. **house party**—entertainment of guests at someone's home for a period of time, as overnight, for the weekend, etc.; loosely, a party at someone's home, as in the evening.
    10. **housewarming**—party that celebrates someone's moving into a new house, home, apartment, etc.
    11. **Kaffeeklatsch (German)**—informal social party, so called because coffee is served
    12. **masquerade**—social party in which costumes and masks are worn
    13. **reception**—party, i.e., one in which guests are received; formal party; party given in someone's honor, so the guests can meet him
    14. **shower**—party for the presentation of gifts to a prospective bride, an infant, etc.
    15. **social, sociable**—social party; social party given by a church, institution, etc.
    16. **soirée**—evening party
    17. **spree**—lively and gay party
    18. **tea**—afternoon party at which, theoretically but not always in practice, tea is served

3. To Make Merry; To Engage in Merry-making, or in a Party, Celebration, etc.,v. *From Sec. 1:* bacchanalize, carouse, celebrate, racket, revel, roister, wassail (bacchanalization, celebration,n.) ; *From Sec. 2:* frolic

4. Merrymaker,n. *From Sec. 1:* bacchanal, bacchanalian, or bacchant; carouser; celebrator, celebrater, or celebrant; orgiast, reveler, roisterer, wassailer (bacchantic,adj.) ; *From Sec. 2:* bacchanal, bacchanalian, bacchant, or, fem., bacchante; frolicker, masquerader (bacchantic, bacchant, Bacchic,adj.)

5. Women Who Participated in the Ancient Roman Bacchanalia: Bacchae,pl.n.

6. Merrymaking, i.e., Making Merry or Participating in Merrymaking,adj. *From Sec. 1:* bacchanalian or bacchanal, carousing, celebrating, rackety, reveling, roisterous or roistering, wassailing; *From Sec. 2:* frolicking

7. Pert. to Merrymaking or to a Party,adj. *From Sec. 1:* bacchanalian or bacchanal; festival, festal, or festive; orgiac, orgiastic, orgiastical, or orgic; *From Sec. 2:* bacchanalian or bacchanal; festival, festal, or festive; gala

8. Like, of the Nature of, or Suitable for, Merrymaking or Parties,adj. *From Sec. 1:* bacchanalian or bacchanal, celebratory, festal or festive, orgiastic or orgiastical (bacchanalianism, festivity or festiveness,n.) ; *From Sec. 2:* bacchanalian or bacchanal, festal or festive, gala (bacchanalianism, festivity or festiveness,n) ; *Also:* convivial (conviviality, n.)

9. Characterized by Merrymaking,adj. *From Sec. 1:* orgiastic or orgiastical; *From Sec. 2:* gala

10. Intended, or Kept Separate, for Celebrations: celebrative,adj.

11. Fond of, or Given to, Merrymaking: rackety,adj.

12. To Turn (Merrymaking) into Drunken Revelry: bacchanalize,v. (bacchanalization, n.)

13. The Pleasure or Gaiety of Parties or Celebrations: conviviality, festivity,n.

14. The Activities, or What Goes On, at Parties or Celebrations: festivities,pl.n.

15. Rapid Round of Parties: whirl,n.

16. Place Where Guests Are Received, Parties Held, etc.: salon,n.

17. Guests, Collectively: company, party,n.

18. One Who Gives a Party: host or, fem., hostess,n.

19. Unknown or Secret Host: amphitryon,n.

202. MISCHIEF

1. Mischievous,adj.
1. **arch**—mischievous
2. **devilish**—mischievous
3. **elfin**—mischievous, like an elf
4. **hoydenish**—mischievous (of a young girl)
5. **impish**—mischievous, like an imp
6. **naughty**—mischievous (of children)
7. **parlous**—dangerously mischievous
8. **prankish**—mischievous (i.e., tending to play mischievous tricks)
9. **puckish**—mischievous
10. **rascal, rascally**—mischievous
11. **roguish**—playfully or pleasantly mischievous
12. **sly**—playfully mischievous
13. **villainous**—mischievous (humorous)
14. **waggish**—mischievous and merry

2. Mischief; Mischievousness,n. *From Sec. 1:* archness; devilishness, devilry, deviltry, or devilment; impishness, naughtiness, prank-

ishness or pranks, puckishness, rascality, roguishness or roguery, slyness, villainy, waggishness or waggery; *Also:*
1. **knaveries**—mischievous tricks
2. **shenanigan, shenanigans**—mischief (colloq.)

3. Mischievous Person,n. *From Sec. 1:* devil; imp (a child), prankster, puck, rascal, rogue, villain, wag; *Also:*
1. **devilkin**—mischievous child
2. **harlequin**—mischievous person
3. **hellion**—mischievous and troublesome person
4. **hobgoblin**—mischievous spirit
5. **hoyden**—mischievous young girl
6. **minx**—mischievous girl
7. **mischief-maker**—one who does mischievous things
8. **scamp**—mischievous child
9. **tyke, tike**—mischievous child
10. **urchin**—mischievous child or boy
11. **vagabond**—mischievous child

203. WORK

1. To Work,v.
1. **apply oneself**—set to work and continue working
2. **boggle**—work clumsily
3. **boondoggle**—do unnecessary or useless work, merely for the sake of keeping or looking busy (colloq.)
4. **char, chare**—do odd jobs; work by the day; do odd jobs, or work by the day at cleaning, in a home, office building, factory, etc. (of women)
5. **clerk**—work as a salesperson in a store; work on records, accounts, etc., in an office
6. **collaborate**—work together, especially in a literary, scientific, or artistic effort
7. **connive with**—co-operate with secretly
8. **co-operate**—work together and to mutual advantage
9. **dabble (at, in)**—work (at) with no intensity
10. **delve**—work with a shovel
11. **drudge**—engage in hard, tiresome, monotonous, disagreeable, and/or dull work
12. **endeavor**—work earnestly toward a goal
13. **grind**—drudge (colloq.)
14. **grub**—work at menial jobs; drudge; plod
15. **labor**—work; work hard
16. **moil**—work hard; work hard at monotonous or unpleasant tasks
17. **niggle**—work in an ineffective manner
18. **operate**—work
19. **overwork**—work too hard or too long
20. **piddle**—work in a petty, ineffective, trifling, or mean fashion
21. **plod**—work patiently and laboriously, or at a monotonous or unpleasant task
22. **ply**—work away at; continue working, or working at; work busily; work busily at
23. **potter**—work at unimportant or trifling things
24. **pursue**—work at (a career, profession, business, etc.)
25. **slave**—work very hard, often at a monotonous or disagreeable task
26. **specialize (in)**—devote oneself to some limited type of work or restricted field of a profession
27. **strive**—work hard
28. **struggle**—work hard
29. **synergize**—co-operate
30. **tinker**—work in a botchy and unskillful way; work at unimportant tasks
31. **toil**—work hard or with great effort or exertion
32. **tool**—work with tools; do mechanical work by hand
33. **travail**—engage in hard work or painful work

2. To Cause to Work,v. *From Sec. 1:* operate (a machine, etc.), overwork; *Also:* **1. manipulate**—operate with the hands

3. Act or Process of Working,n. *From Sec. 1:* application, collaboration, connivance, co-operation, drudgery, endeavor or endeavors, labor or labors, operation, overwork, pursuit, slavery, specialization or specialism, struggle, synergy, toil, travail; *From Sec. 2:* manipulation; *Also:*
1. **mechanism**—the working together of parts
2. **synergism**—co-operation between different things so that the combined effect is greater than the total of separate effects (term in physiology; for example, codeine and aspirin taken together are more effective than the sum of their individual effects)
3. **teamwork**—co-operation in an endeavor

4. Work; Type of Work,n. *From Sec. 1:* drudgery, grind, labor, moil, overwork, slavery, toil, travail; *Also:*
1. **handicraft**—work requiring manual skill
2. **niggling**—unimportant, trifling, or over-meticulous work
3. **servitude**—forced work (usually as punishment)
4. **trade**—skilled work; work involving the buying and selling of commodities

5. Piece of Work,n. *From Sec. 1:* boondoggle, char, endeavor or endeavors, labor or labors; *Also:*
1. **arrears**—unfinished pieces of work
2. **chore**—small or odd piece of work, often one that is routine or unpleasant
3. **job**—piece of work; piece of work complete in itself; piece of hard work
4. **stint**—assigned task or job
5. **task**—piece of work, usually imposed on one; piece of work complete in itself; piece of hard work

6. Descr. of, Pert. to, or Relating to, Work, adj. *From Sec. 1:* clerical (from *clerk*), collaborative, co-operative, operative, synergetic or synergistic; *From Sec. 2:* manipulative; *From Sec. 3:* mechanical, synergistic; *Also:*
1. **conjoint**—working together
2. **daedal**—working cunningly, skillfully, or cleverly

7. Worker,n. *From Sec. 1:* boondoggler, charwoman, clerk, collaborator, conniver, co-operator, dabbler, delver, drudge or drudger, grind, grub, laborer, niggler, operator, piddler, plodder, potterer, slave, specialist, struggler, tinker or tinkerer, toiler, tooler or toolman; *From Sec. 2:* manipulator; *From Sec. 3:* teamworker; *Also:*
1. **artificer**—skilled worker or mechanic; craftsman
2. **artisan**—worker in a manual art or trade
3. **artist**—skillful worker
4. **beaver**—hard worker
5. **cobbler**—awkward worker
6. **coolie**—common laborer in India or China; laborer of oriental extraction
7. **co-worker**—one who works with another
8. **craftsman**—one who is engaged in some mechanical or manual work, usually exhibiting some skill; specially skilled worker
9. **dabster**—unskilled worker
10. **day laborer**—one who accepts manual work on a day-to-day basis
11. **employee**—one who works for money, salary, etc.
12. **factotum**—someone engaged to do all kinds of work (commonly found in the phrase *general factotum*)
13. **floater**—worker who moves from employment to employment, not remaining in one job for any length of time
14. **foreman**—worker who supervises other workers

15. **grisette**—young woman of the working class in France
16. **hack**—one who will do any kind of (usually literary) work, often without any particular skill; drudge
17. **hand**—worker, esp. a manual worker
18. **handy man**—man who works at odd jobs around a place
19. **hired man**—worker hired to help on a farm, etc.
20. **hireling, pensioner**—one who works purely for money, and not out of belief in a cause or principle, nor out of interest in the work (derogative)
21. **hustler**—one who works with determined purpose or ambition
22. **journeyman**—worker who has finished his training and is now skilled or qualified
23. **laborer**—one who works at jobs requiring no skill but only strength
24. **mate**—one's fellow worker
25. **mechanic**—worker at, on, or with machinery
26. **office worker**—clerk in an office
27. **Okie**—migratory worker, esp. one from Oklahoma
28. **outlier**—one who works away from his living quarters
29. **peon**—in the Southwest, one who works off a debt; hence, also, a poorly paid, almost enslaved worker (peonage, peonism, n.)
30. **practitioner**—person engaged in a profession
31. **proletarian**—one who works for a living; member of the working classes
32. **roustabout**—laborer on a wharf, Mississippi River steamboat, in a mine, oil field, circus, etc.; worker who does odd jobs anywhere; one who wanders around the countryside doing odd jobs when he needs money
33. **wage earner**—one who works for regular pay
34. **white-collar worker**—one who, by working in an office or at a non-manual occupation, can dress in business clothes
35. **workfellow**—one who works with another
36. **working girl, work girl**—girl working in a factory, store, etc.
37. **workingman, workman, workingwoman** —man or woman who works usually at manual or unskilled labor; more generally, one who works for wages

8. Pert. to, or Descr. of, a Worker,adj. *From Sec. 7:* clerical (from *clerk*), hack, journeyman, mechanical, proletarian

9. Workers, Collectively,n.
1. **crew**—group of people engaged in some common work
2. **gang**—group of workers operating under common direction; crew
3. **help**—workers in a store, factory, home, etc.
4. **personnel**—workers in an institution, factory or corporation
5. **proletariat**—those people who work for a living; the working class of people as distinguished from the capitalists, tradesmen, entrepreneurs, professional people, etc. (proletarian,adj.)

10. Lacking the Required Number of Workers: shorthanded,adj.

11. Place of Work,n.
1. **atelier**—studio; workshop
2. **billet**—working quarters to which one is assigned
3. **factory**—place where work, usually that connected with manufacturing, is done
4. **plant**—factory
5. **position**—situation
6. **shop**—place where work is done
7. **situation**—place where one works

8. **studio**—place where an artist of any kind (painter, writer, etc.) works
9. **vineyard**—place of labor
10. **workshop**—place where work is done

12. Period of Work,n.
1. **char, chare**—turn at work
2. **hitch**—period of work
3. **shift**—period of work; turn of work
4. **spell**—period of work
5. **tour**—spell
6. **trick**—spell; sailor's period of work at the wheel or helm (generally two hours)
7. **turn**—period of work alternating with another or others

13. Quality of Work: workmanship,n.

14. Manner in Which Parts Work Together: mechanism,n.

15. Manner, Method, or Means of Working: modus operandi,n. (Latin)

16. Easy to Work with: tractable,adj. (tractability,n.)

17. Amount of Work to Be Done: stint,n.

18. Disposition toward Work: ergasia,n.

19. One Who Is Morbidly Addicted to Working: ergomaniac,n.

20. Hard-Working,adj.
1. **assiduous**—hard-working, in the sense of paying close and constant attention to one's job (assiduity, assiduousness,n.)
2. **diligent**—steady and sincere in one's application to one's job; assiduous (diligence,n.)
3. **industrious**—hard-working and busy (industry, industriousness,n.)
4. **laborious**—hard-working (laboriousness, n.)
5. **operose**—hard-working; industrious (operoseness,n.)
6. **sedulous**—working hard, carefully, and painstakingly toward a goal or objective; industrious (sedulousness,n.)

21. Requiring Work,adj.
1. **arduous**—strenuous (arduousness,n.)
2. **laborious**—requiring hard work (laboriousness,n.)
3. **operose**—requiring or involving work (operoseness,n.)
4. **strenuous**—requiring hard work, in the sense of a great expense of energy (strenuousness, strenuosity, strenuity, n.)
5. **toilful**—full of, involving, or demanding hard work
6. **toilsome**—requiring hard work (toilsomeness,n.)

22. Study of the Effects of Work on the Human Organism: ergology,n.

23. One for Whom Work Is Done,n.
1. **employer, boss**—one for whom another works for pay
2. **taskmaster**—person who imposes duties, work, etc., on another, or who is very strict in his demands on his workers and assistants

204. OCCUPATION

1. Occupation,n.
1. **business**—work in which one is gainfully engaged; work one generally does to earn money; type of work one does for a livelihood
2. **calling**—one's usual work or occupation; one's business, profession, or trade
3. **career**—one's occupation, business, profession, etc.
4. **craft**—occupation, trade, or work requiring skill or training
5. **employment**—occupation; business; trade
6. **field**—specialty

7. **handicraft**—trade requiring manual skill
8. **line**—business
9. **livelihood**—business or profession through which one earns the money to stay alive
10. **métier**—one's occupation, work, or profession; the work or type of work in which one is particularly skilled or with which one is particularly familiar
11. **profession**—work for which one has been specially trained and involving, often, though not necessarily, self-employment; work requiring unusual skill or talent; work in the arts or sciences, etc. (professional,adj.)
12. **pursuit**—one's occupation, business, or profession
13. **specialty**—limited area in which one is engaged as an occupation or profession
14. **trade**—kind of work (usually skilled) that one engages in (in common use, requiring less training than a profession)
15. **vocation**—occupation, business, trade, or profession (vocational,adj.)
16. **work**—occupation

2. Science of Vocational Selection, Stress, and Fatigue: ergology,n.

205. WORKER

1. Worker with Animals,n.
1. **blacksmith, smith, horseshoer, or (British) farrier**—one who makes horseshoes and fits them on horses
2. **broncobuster, bronchobuster**—one who breaks untrained Western horses, as broncos, mustangs, ponies, etc., to the saddle
3. **cameleer**—camel driver
4. **caravaneer**—driver or leader of the camels in a caravan
5. **cowboy, broncobuster or bronchobuster, buckaroo or buckayro, cowpuncher, or, in the Southwest, vaquero (Spanish)**—worker with cows, steers, etc., on a farm or ranch
6. **cowherd, neatherd**—one who tends cows
7. **drover**—dealer in cattle
8. **groom, hostler**—one who takes care of, or is in charge of, horses
9. **hostler**—one who takes care of horses at an inn or stable
10. **mahout**—keeper or driver of an elephant
11. **muleteer**—mule driver
12. **saddler**—one who makes, repairs, or deals in saddles and other equipment for horses
13. **shepherd, sheepherder**—one who herds sheep (shepherdess, fem.n.)

2. Such Work; the Business of Such a Worker,n. *From Sec. 1:* blacksmithing, smithery, or (British) farriery; cowherding, saddlery, sheepherding

3. Shop of Such a Worker,n. *From Sec. 1:* smithy, or (British) farriery; saddlery

4. To Fit Horseshoes on (a Horse): horseshoe, v.

5. Clothing Worker,n.
1. **clothier**—manufacturer or retailer of clothing
2. **cobbler**—one who repairs shoes
3. **corsetier (French)**—maker, seller, or fitter of corsets (corsetière,fem.n.)
4. **costumer, costumier**—one who makes or sells clothing for dances, the theater, etc.; one who makes fancy or elegant clothing for women
5. **dressmaker, couturier (French), modiste**—one who makes or alters women's clothing (couturière,fem.n.)
6. **furrier**—dealer in furs; one who makes or repairs fur garments; one who dresses furs

7. glovemaker, glover—manufacturer of gloves

8. glover—dealer in gloves

9. haberdasher—dealer in articles of clothing for men, as shirts, ties, etc.

10. hatter—manufacturer of, or dealer in, hats

11. hosier—manufacturer of, or dealer in, stockings or similar knit goods

12. outfitter—one who sells clothing

13. sartor—tailor (humorous)

14. seamstress, sempstress, needlewoman—woman who sews clothing or other fabrics

15. shirtmaker—manufacturer of shirts

16. shoemaker—one who makes or repairs shoes

17. tailor—one who makes, alters, or repairs clothing

18. valet—one who cleans and presses clothing for residents in a hotel or apartment house; loosely, one in the business of cleaning and pressing clothes (valet,v.)

6. The Work, Occupation, etc., of a Clothing Worker,n. *From Sec. 5:* cobblery or cobbling, corsetry, costumery, dressmaking or dressmakery, furriery, glovemaking, hosiery; needlework or needle trade (from *seamstress*); shoemaking or shoecraft, tailoring

7. Pert. to a Tailor or to Tailoring: sartorial,adj.

8. Shop of a Dealer in Men's Furnishings: haberdashery,n.

9. Worker with Wood,n.

1. **cabinetmaker**—one who makes fine wood furniture (cabinetmaking,n.)

2. **carpenter**—one who makes or repairs things of wood (carpentry, carpentering, n. carpenter,v.)

3. **joiner**—one who joins pieces of wood together to make articles; one who, by this means, makes the woodwork, doors, windows, stairs, etc., in buildings under construction (joinery,n.)

4. **logger**—one who fells trees, cuts the trunks into proper lengths, and transports the logs to the sawmill (logging,n. log,v.)

5. **lumberjack, lumberman, woodchopper, woodcutter, woodsman**—one who chops, cuts, or otherwise fells trees for their wood (lumbering, woodcutting,n. lumber, v.)

6. **woodcraftsman**—one who is skilled in making or carving things out of wood (woodcraft,n.)

7. **woodworker**—one who makes things out of wood (woodworking,n.)

10. Product of a Worker with Wood,n. *From Sec. 9:* carpentry, joinery, woodwork

11. Waiter in a Restaurant, etc.: garçon (French; used affectedly in English), server, n.

12. Chief Waiter: captain, headwaiter; maître d'hôtel (French),n.

13. Chief Waitress: hostess,n.

14. Servant: menial, minion, retainer, servitor, slavey, vassal,n. (vassalage,n. menial, vassal,adj.); *Also:*

1. **amah**—female servant in the Orient

2. **ayah**—lady's maid in India

3. **butler**—head male servant of a large household; male servant in charge of the pantry and table service (butlership,n.)

4. **chambermaid**—female servant who makes beds, cleans bedrooms, etc.

5. **dayworker, charwoman**—servant who works on a day-to-day basis, or one or more days a week, in a household

6. **domestic**—household servant (domestic, adj.)

7. **flunkey, flunky**—contemptuous term for

a liveried male servant (flunkeyism, flunkyism,n.)

8. **handmaid, handmaiden**—female servant; by extension, one who is a servant to another or others

9. **housekeeper**—woman employed to take charge of a household (housekeeping,n.)

10. **lackey, lacquey, footman**—liveried male servant of various duties—greeting and announcing visitors, opening doors, accompanying people to their automobiles or, formerly, carriages, waiting on table, etc.

11. **lady's maid**—personal servant to a woman

12. **maid, maidservant; bonne** (French); **housemaid, houseworker**—female household servant

13. **major-domo, maître d'hôtel** (French)—man in complete charge of the domestic affairs of a great or rich household

14. **slavey**—submissive servant

15. **steward**—man who supervises the household affairs of a large estate (stewardship,n.)

16. **valet, or, French, valet de chambre**—male servant who attends to a man's personal needs, takes care of his clothing, etc.

15. To Be a Servant to,v. *From Sec. 14:* lackey or lacquey, valet

16. To Act as a Servant,v. *From Sec. 14:* valet

17. Household Employment: service,n.

18. Position as a Worker: appointment, berth, billet, capacity; job (colloq.); place, post,n.; *Also:*

1. **appointment**—position of authority for which one is selected or nominated

2. **office**—elective or appointive position of authority or trust

3. **place**—position in a household

4. **post, office**—position of duty, responsibility, trust, authority, etc.

5. **situation**—subordinate position, as in an office, factory, shop, household, etc.

19. To Give a Position to: appoint, berth, billet, employ, engage, hire, place,v. (appointment, employment, engagement, hire, placement,n.)

20. State or Condition of Being Given a Position: appointment, employment, hire, placement,n.

21. To Give Work to: employ, engage, hire,v. (employment, engagement, hire,n.)

22. To Accept a Position: hire out,v.

206. LABOR RELATIONS

1. Concepts in Labor Relations,n.

1. **checkoff**—collection of union dues by the employer from the worker's wages

2. **closed shop**—plant in which only union members are hired or in which new non-union employees must apply for membership; contrarily, plant in which union members are not hired

3. **labor union**—organization of workers

4. **lockout**—process or act of closing a plant so that the employees cannot enter

5. **non-unionism**—non-support of labor unions; theory that labor unions are not beneficial

6. **non-union shop**—plant that will not hire union members

7. **open shop**—shop or plant in which both union and non-union members are employed

8. **sit-down strike**—strike in which workers remain continuously in the plant, but not working

9. **strike**—refusal on the part of the employees to work (strike,v.)

10. **syndicalism**—plan or method by which control of industry and government will fall to the labor unions
11. **trade union**—labor union
12. **union**—labor union
13. **unionism**—principles of the labor unions; system of labor unions
14. **union shop**—shop or plant that recognizes labor unions
15. **walkout**—strike
16. **wildcat strike**—strike that is unauthorized by union officials

2. One Involved in Labor Relations,n.
1. **fink**—strikebreaker
2. **goon**—terrorizer of workers or strikers, supplied by gangsters or racketeers employed by the management of corporations
3. **picket, picketer**—guard outside a struck plant to keep workers out and induce the public not to patronize (picket,v.)
4. **scab**—someone who accepts a job in a struck factory, business, etc.; employee who works for lower wages than those prescribed by the union (scab,v.)
5. **strikebreaker**—one who goes to work in a business or factory that is on strike
6. **striker**—employee who refuses to work (strike,v.)
7. **unionist**—one who forms, organizes, or joins a labor union (unionize,v.)

207. NON-PROFESSIONAL

1. Non-Professional Person,n.
1. **amateur**—one engaged in work, activity, sport, etc., in other than a professional capacity, i.e., as a hobby
2. **dabbler**—dilettante
3. **dilettante**—one engaged in an art or branch of science as a pastime rather than in a professional capacity (dilettanti,pl.)
4. **layman**—one not belonging to a specific profession or to the clergy

2. State or Quality of Being a Non-Professional Person,n. *From Sec. 1:* amateurism, dilettantism, laymanship

3. Pert. to a Non-Professional Person,adj. *From Sec. 1:* amateur, dilettante; lay, laic, laical, or layman; *Also:* 1. **secular**—pert. to, or descr. of, control or possession by laymen rather than by the church (secularity,n.)

4. People Not Connected with the Church or with a Specific Profession, as Distinguished from Those So Connected: laity,n. (lay, laic, laical,adj.)

5. To Give Over to, Make Available to, or Put Under the Control of, Non-Professional People: laicize, secularize,v. (laicization, secularization,n.)

208. BUSY

1. Busy,adj.
1. **bustling**—noisily and hurriedly busy (of places)
2. **humming**—busy with activity (of places)
3. **industrious**—keeping busy in advantageous pursuits
4. **occupied**—busy
5. **operose**—industrious
6. **pragmatic**—busy
7. **sedulous**—industrious

2. To Be or Keep Busy,v. *From Sec. 1:* bustle, hum; occupy (oneself); *Also:*
1. **busy oneself (in, with)**—keep busy (at)
2. **tinker**—keep busy doing things of no importance
3. **twiddle**—be busy doing unimportant things

3. State or Fact of Being Busy,n. *From Sec. 1:* bustle, hum, industry or industriousness, occupation, operoseness, sedulousness

4. To Cause (Someone) to Be Busy; To Keep (Someone) Busy: occupy,v.

209. LACK OF WORK

1. Lazy; Unwilling to Work,adj.
1. **do-nothing**—lazy
2. **faineant**—lazy
3. **idle**—lazy; not willing to work
4. **indolent**—lazy, in the sense of avoiding or disliking exertion or expenditure of energy, or of being unacceptably fond of ease and passivity
5. **lymphatic**—temperamentally disinclined to exertion
6. **shiftless**—lazy
7. **slothful**—extremely lazy; inclined to inactivity; unwilling to work
8. **slovenly**—generally lazy in habits
9. **sluggard**—lazy; idle
10. **sluggish**—lazy; habitually or temperamentally disinclined to activity or exertion
11. **supine**—lazily inactive

2. Laziness,n. *From Sec. 1:* do-nothingness or do-nothingism, faineance, idleness, indolence, lymphatism, shiftlessness, sloth or slothfulness, slovenliness, sluggishness, supineness; *Also:* 1. acedia—sloth

3. Lazy Person,n. *From Sec. 1:* do-nothing, faineant, idler, indolent, sloth, sloven, sluggard; *From Sec. 2:* acediast; *Also:*
1. **bum**—someone who will not work; vagabond
2. **drone**—one unwilling to work
3. **hooligan**—loafer
4. **lazybones**—lazy person
5. **loafer**—one who indulges his laziness
6. **lounger**—one who moves, sits, rests, or stands lazily
7. **poke**—slow and lazy person
8. **slouch**—lazy, unambitious person
9. **slugabed**—sluggard
10. **vagabond**—lazy, irresponsible person

4. To Be Lazy,v.
1. **idle**—spend time lazily or inactively
2. **laze**—be or act lazy; spend or waste time lazily
3. **loaf**—indulge one's desire to be lazy
4. **lounge**—rest, sit, stand, or move lazily

5. Not to Work,v.
1. **dally**—loaf
2. **gold-brick**—loaf while supposedly working (slang)
3. **idle**—not work; habitually not work; be unemployed
4. **loaf**—not work; spend time not working
5. **malinger**—avoid work by pretending illness
6. **retire**—withdraw from business life; no longer work, usually because of advanced age
7. **soldier**—pretend to work but not actually do so; malinger

6. Not Working,adj. *From Sec. 5:* dallying, idle, retired; *Also:*
1. **emeritus**—retired from the service (usually of a college or university) without loss of one's rank or title
2. **superannuated, superannuate**—retired on a pension because of advanced years
3. **unemployed**—not working at gainful labor

7. To Cause Not to Work,v. *From Sec. 5:* idle, retire (retirement,n.); *From Sec. 6:* superannuate (superannuation,n.)

8. Act, State, or Fact of Not Working,n. *From Sec. 5:* dalliance, gold-bricking, idleness or, poetic, idlesse, loafing, malingering, retirement, soldiering; *From Sec. 6:* superannuation, unemployment

9. One Who Is Not Working,n. *From Sec. 5:* dallier, gold-brick or gold-bricker, idler, loafer, malingerer; *From Sec. 6:* superannuate; *Also:* 1. lazzarone—in Naples, homeless idler living by begging or occasional work (lazzaroni,pl.)

10. Not Working or Operating (of Machinery, etc.): out of commission,adj.

11. Those Who Are Out of Work: the unemployed,n.

12. Freedom from Work,n.
1. **busman's holiday**—leisure time spent doing the same thing as on one's regular job, but without pay
2. **fiesta**—holiday
3. **holiday**—time off from work (holiday,v.)
4. **leisure**—time free from work
5. **spell**—relief given by one person to another by taking over his work, duty, etc. (spell,v.)
6. **vacation**—extended holiday (vacation,v.)

13. Pert. to, Descr. of, or Like, a Holiday, adj.
1. **carnival**—holiday-like; holiday-like and gay
2. **festive, festal**—pert. to, descr. of, or like, a holiday
3. **gala**—pert. to, or suitable for, holidays

14. Christmas,n.
1. **Noel**—Christmas
2. **yule**—Christmas; Christmas time
3. **yuletide**—Christmas time

15. Santa Claus: Kriss Kringle, St. Nicholas, n.

16. Easter: Eastertide, Easter time,n.

17. Pert. to Easter: paschal,adj.

210. BUSINESS

1. Business; Business Dealing,n.
1. **barter**—trade involving the exchange of goods rather than money
2. **commerce**—business; business intercourse or relations
3. **deal**—business arrangement
4. **dealings**—business; traffic
5. **industry**—business; branch of business
6. **merchantry**—commercial business; retail business; trade
7. **negotiation, negotiations**—business dealings
8. **trade**—buying and selling; exchange of goods or things
9. **traffic**—business of buying and selling; trade
10. **transaction**—business deal; piece of business; business matter
11. **transactions**—business; business dealings
12. **truck**—business

2. To Do Business,v. *From Sec. 1:* barter, deal with or in, negotiate, trade; traffic (in); transact, truck

3. Pert. to Business or Business Dealings, adj. *From Sec. 1:* commercial, industrial, negotiative, transactional; *Also:* 1. mercantile—pert. to trade or commerce

4. Businessman; One Who Is Engaged in Business,n. *From Sec. 1:* barterer, dealer, industrialist, merchant; merchantry (collective); negotiator, trader or tradesman, trafficker, transactor; *Also:*
1. **Babbitt**—businessman who conforms to middle-class mediocrity and worship of success—derogative term, from Sinclair Lewis's character (Babbittry,n.)
2. **baron**—industrial executive
3. **capitalist**—person whose money is invested in business

4. **entrepreneur**—one who starts and manages a business or industry, assuming the risks and taking the profits
5. **executive**—one in charge of a business; one in a managerial capacity in a business
6. **tycoon**—important and influential business leader or executive

5. To Make into a Business,v. *From Sec. 1:* commercialize, industrialize (commercialization, industrialization,n.)

6. Practice, Theory, etc., of Business,n.
1. **capitalism**—theory or practice of economic organization in which natural wealth is in private hands and competition is prevalent (capitalist,n. capitalist, capitalistic,adj.)
2. **commercialism, commerciality**—commercial spirit, method, or philosophy (commercialist,n. commercialistic,adj.)
3. **industrialism**—social organization in which industries are dominant (industrialist,adj.)
4. **mercantilism**—spirit, theory, or practice of business pursuits; devotion to commercial endeavors; commercialism (mercantilist,n. mercantilist, mercantilistic, adj.)

7. A Business Organization,n.
1. **cartel**—group of businesses that agree to fix prices, control production, etc.
2. **company**—business organization (company,adj.)
3. **concern**—business organization
4. **corporation**—business organization that is a legal entity or individual (corporate, adj.)
5. **enterprise**—business organization
6. **establishment**—business organization
7. **firm**—business organization
8. **holding company**—business organization that owns the major part or all of the stock of other companies; operating company that does this
9. **house**—business organization (house, adj.)
10. **monopoly**—business organization that has full control over all phases of an industry
11. **organization**—business organization (organizational,adj.)
12. **partnership**—business organization owned by two or more individuals in which each is liable for the debts of the organization
13. **pool**—combination of business firms in an industry formed to control trade by eliminating competition
14. **syndicate**—group of people who combine to carry out an industrial or financial project
15. **trust**—organization that controls the policies of a number of independent firms, thus cutting down competition, controlling prices, etc.

8. Phases of Business Cycles,n.
1. **adjustment**—euphemism for a slight downturn in business activity
2. **boom**—time of great and rapid increase in the value of commodities (boom,adj.)
3. **commercial crisis**—latter part of a depression in which there is much unemployment, contraction of credit, falling prices and profits, etc.
4. **crash**—time when many businesses fail
5. **crisis**—end of a period of business prosperity followed by the onset of depression or recession (critical,adj.)
6. **deflation**—time of increase in the value of money and of decrease in the price or money value of goods (deflationary,adj.)
7. **depression**—period of great reduction or stagnation of trade, profits, earnings, and general business activity

8. **inflation**—abnormal increase in prices owing to causes over which the economists are still arguing; concomitant factors are great increase in money and credit supply, decrease in supply of goods, etc. (inflationary,adj.)

9. **prosperity**—that phase in which there is wide employment, confidence in the future, high prices and wages, abundance of money in circulation, etc. (prosperous, adj.)

10. **recession**—time of a slowing down of business and industrial activity (less severe than a depression)

11. **slump**—period when prices and business activity fall or drop suddenly and markedly

9. To Engage in Reckless Business Practices,v.
1. **speculate**—engage in unsound business practices (speculator,n. speculation,n. speculative,adj.)
2. **wildcat**—use or engage in unsound or reckless business practices (wildcatter,n. wildcat,adj.)

10. Science of Industrial Management; Industrial Arts or Science: technology,n. (technologist,n. technological,adj.)

11. God of Business or Commerce: Mercury, n.

12. Stock Exchange,n.
1. **bourse**—stock exchange in Paris or other European cities
2. **curb**—stock exchange in which securities not listed on the main exchange are traded (now called, in New York, the American Stock Exchange, to distinguish it from the main exchange, called the New York Stock Exchange)

13. Rising or Falling Stock Market,n.
1. **bear market**—market of falling stock prices (bear,n. bearish,adj.)
2. **bull market**—market of rising stock prices (bull,n. bullish,adj.)

211. PURCHASE

1. To Buy,v.
1. **coempt**—buy the entire supply of (a commodity) in order to gain a monopoly
2. **deal in**—buy and sell
3. **engross**—buy up most or all of (some commodity) in order to exercise a monopoly and thereby be able to fix the price
4. **market**—shop, usually for food, etc.
5. **patronize**—buy regularly from; buy from (a retail establishment); be a customer or a regular customer at (a retail establishment, theater, library, or other institution)
6. **pre-empt**—buy (esp. public lands) before anyone else can
7. **purchase**—buy
8. **ransom**—buy the release or freedom of (someone)
9. **redeem**—buy back
10. **shop**—buy in a store
11. **trade in**—buy and sell
12. **traffic in**—buy and sell
13. **truck**—buy and sell

2. A Buying,n. *From Sec. 1:* coemption, engrossment, marketing, patronage, pre-emption, purchase, ransom, redemption, shopping, trade, traffic, truck; *Also:*
1. **custom**—frequent patronage
2. **emptio (Latin)**—buying (legal)
3. **emption**—buying (legal)
4. **mongering, mongery**—buying and selling (contemptuous)

3. Descr. of or Pert. to Buying,adj. *From Sec. 1:* coemptive or coemptional, pre-emptive, redemptive; *From Sec. 2:* emptional

4. Buyer,n. *From Sec. 1:* coemptor, dealer, engrosser, marketer, patron, pre-emptor, purchaser, redeemer, shopper, trader, trafficker; *From Sec. 2:* customer, emptor, monger; *Also:*
1. **client**—one who uses the services of a professional person, businessman, etc.; customer (cliental,adj.)
2. **customer**—one who buys at a place of business, market, etc. (custom,adj.)
3. **vendee**—one to whom something is sold

5. Customers, Collectively,n.
1. **clientele, clientage, clientry**—body of customers or clients
2. **custom**—customers collectively (custom, adj.)
3. **patronage**—body of customers
4. **trade**—customers

6. Without Clients: briefless,adj. (of lawyers)

7. Addiction to Shopping, or to Buying Beyond Realistic Needs: oniomania,n. (oniomaniac,n.)

8. That Which Is Bought,n.
1. **bargain**—something bought at a price below its true value
2. **buy**—that which is bought; bargain
3. **commodity**—anything bought and sold
4. **purchase**—that which is bought
5. **steal**—great bargain (colloq.)

212. SALE

1. To Sell,v.
1. **auction**—sell, in public, to the highest bidder
2. **bootleg**—sell secretly (anything illegal or forbidden)
3. **canvass**—sell from door to door
4. **costermonger**—peddle fruits and vegetables in the street (British)
5. **deal in**—buy and sell
6. **hawk**—sell in the streets, usually by shouting one's wares
7. **higgle**—hawk (provisions)
8. **market**—sell; sell in a market
9. **merchandise**—sell; retail
10. **merchant**—retail
11. **negotiate**—sell (something of value) for money or other valuable thing
12. **peddle**—travel about selling; sell from place to place
13. **regrate**—sell at a profit (commodities bought at a market or fair); retail
14. **resell**—sell again; sell after having bought
15. **retail**—sell to the ultimate consumer
16. **trade in**—buy and sell
17. **traffic in**—buy and sell
18. **truck**—buy and sell
19. **undersell, undercut**—sell at a lower price than
20. **vend**—sell
21. **wholesale**—sell in large quantities to that person who will then sell to the ultimate consumer

2. Sale,n. *From Sec. 1:* auction, negotiation, resale; *Also:* 1. mongering, mongery—a buying and selling (contemptuous)

3. Seller,n. *From Sec. 1:* auctioneer, bootlegger, canvasser, costermonger, dealer, hawker, higgler, marketer, merchant, negotiator, peddler or pedlar, regrater, retailer, trader or tradesman, trafficker, vendor or vender, wholesaler; *From Sec. 2:* monger; *Also:*
1. **bagman**—traveler (British)
2. **butcher**—seller or hawker of wares on trains, in theaters, etc.
3. **chandler**—dealer in groceries, provisions, etc.; seller of candles
4. **chapman**—peddler (British)
5. **colporteur, colporter**—hawker; peddler of religious books and articles

6. **commercial traveler**—traveler
7. **drummer**—one who sells on the road for a wholesaler or middleman; traveling salesman
8. **huckster**—peddler
9. **jobber**—middleman
10. **middleman**—one who buys from the manufacturer and sells to the retailer or consumer
11. **monger**—petty trader in some commodity; trader in some illegal or disreputable commodity
12. **packman**—peddler (i.e., one who carries around a pack)
13. **salesman, salesperson, saleswoman, salesclerk, etc.**—one who sells
14. **solicitor**—one who sells from door to door
15. **traveler**—traveling salesman

4. That Which Is for Sale, Is Sold, etc.,n.
1. **commodity**—anything bought and sold
2. **goods**—merchandise
3. **merchandise**—that which is for sale
4. **vendibles**—articles for sale
5. **wares**—articles for sale

5. To Be Sold for: bring, fetch,v.

6. Salable: marketable, merchantable, negotiable, trafficable, vendible,adj.

7. Place of Selling,n.
1. **bazaar**—fair where goods are sold; store where fancy goods are sold
2. **emporium**—store where things are sold, especially a variety of things; market
3. **fair**—place where things are sold, often for charitable purposes; outdoor meeting, at a specific time or for a specific number of days, at which goods are sold, amusement provided, etc.; place where members of a trade, industry, etc., meet by appointment and at a specific time to display their wares to retailers
4. **market**—place where things are sold
5. **market place**—market
6. **mart**—any store that sells a variety of goods; market
7. **shop**—store
8. **store**—place where things are sold at retail

8. Public Auction Sale: vendue,n.

9. The Selling of Sacred Things; The Crime of Selling Positions or Promotions in the Church: simony,n. (simoniac,n. simoniacal, adj.)

213. MONEY

1. Money (Unqualified),n.
1. **cash**—money
2. **currency**—loosely, money
3. **funds**—money
4. **legal tender**—loosely, money
5. **lucre**—money (contemptuous)
6. **means**—money
7. **medium of exchange**—money
8. **pelf**—money (contemptuous, the implication being that it is debasing)
9. **wampum**—articles used by the American Indians as money (usually beads made of shell) ; hence, colloquially, money

2. Money in Various Forms,n.
1. **bill**—piece of paper money
2. **change**—money in coins
3. **coin**—piece of metal money
4. **coinage**—coin; coins collectively
5. **deuce**—two-dollar bill
6. **greenback**—U.S. bill with a green-printed back, first issued in 1862; loosely, any bill
7. **mill**—1/10 of a cent
8. **mintage**—coin
9. **silver**—money in silver form; silver coins
10. **specie**—money in coin form, usually gold or silver
11. **talent**—ancient unit of money

12. **token**—piece of metal money having a higher nominal than intrinsic value
13. **wad**—roll of paper money (colloq.)

3. Money for Various Purposes or with Other Qualifications,n.
1. **advance**—money lent on collateral, against future earnings, etc.
2. **boodle**—money for a bribe
3. **capital**—money used to carry on business
4. **change**—excess of money returned to one on paying for a purchase with a bill or coins of denomination larger than the cost of the purchase
5. **currency**—that which passes freely as a medium of exchange or as money
6. **dole**—public money paid to the poor
7. **graft**—money obtained dishonestly through one's official influence or power
8. **legal tender**—money authorized by a government for paying all debts, obligations, etc.
9. **proceeds**—money obtained from business, sale of something, etc.
10. **stake**—sum of money risked, gambled, etc.; gambler's capital
11. **sterling**—legal money of Great Britain
12. **swag**—boodle; graft (colloq.)
13. **treasure**—hoarded money
14. **viaticum**—money for a journey
15. **wherewithal**—money to buy something with

4. Money Resources,n.
1. **capital**—money resources of a company or business
2. **exchequer**—money resources; finances
3. **finances**—money resources of a person, company, state, etc.
4. **funds**—money resources

5. Amount of Money,n.
1. **budget**—amount of money available (budgetary,adj.)
2. **principal**—amount of money on which interest is paid
3. **sum**—amount of money
4. **trifle**—small amount of money

6. To Have the Money for: afford,v.

7. To Make Money,v.
1. **earn**—make (money) as salary, wages, etc.; be paid (money) for services, etc.
2. **eke out**—barely make enough (money) to stay alive, and even so by irregular and unremunerative occupations or work

8. Money-Maker,n.
1. **breadwinner**—person who earns money to support a family
2. **earner**—one who earns money at a position
3. **wage earner**—one who earns money as wages or salary

9. Means of Earning Money: livelihood,n.

10. Estimate of Amount of Money to Be Spent: budget,n. (budgetary,adj.)

11. Collection of Money at Religious Services: offertory,n.

12. Pert. to Money, Money Matters, Coins, etc.,adj.
1. **financial**—pert. to money or money matters
2. **fiscal**—pert. to public money, financial control, or money matters
3. **monetary**—pert. to money, coinage, or currency
4. **numismatic**—pert. to, or containing, coins
5. **nummary, nummulary**—pert. to or dealing with coins or money
6. **nummular, nummulary**—pert. to money
7. **pecuniary**—pert. or relating to, or consisting of, money

13. Person in Charge of Money,n.
1. **banker**—one who keeps a business for the deposit and loan of money

2. **bursar**—person to whom money is paid in any organization; treasurer of a college (bursarial,adj.)
3. **cashier**—one in charge of money
4. **chamberlain**—treasurer
5. **comptroller**—controller
6. **controller**—officer in charge of financial expenditures
7. **financier**—one who is active in financial matters, who manages large sums of money, or whose business is the management or investment of large sums of money
8. **paymaster**—one whose function it is to pay salaries, as in the navy, army, a large corporation, etc.
9. **purser**—cashier; paymaster; paymaster of a ship
10. **steward**—officer or agent in charge of finances
11. **teller**—employee of a bank directly engaged in the handling of money
12. **treasurer**—officer (of an association, company, government, etc.) in charge of the money or financial accounts

14. Person Skilled in Rates or Processes of Money Exchange of Various Countries: cambist,n.

15. Place Where Money Is Kept or Dealt with,n.
1. **bank**—institution for the deposit and lending of money; place, box, etc., where money is kept
2. **bursary**—treasury of a college or monastery (bursarial,adj.)
3. **cash register**—device in which to keep (and keep the records of) the money taken in
4. **coffer**—chest for money and other valuables
5. **exchequer**—loosely, treasury; strictly, the public treasury of Great Britain
6. **fisc**—state or royal treasury; exchequer
7. **purse**—treasury
8. **safe**—place for storing money and other valuables
9. **till**—drawer for money in a bank, shop, etc.
10. **treasury**—place of deposit and payment of funds, usually public; place or building where money is kept
11. **vault**—room for the safekeeping of money and other valuables

16. To Manufacture Money,v.
1. **coin**—stamp coins for issue (coinage,n.)
2. **counterfeit**—manufacture money illegally, by copying, etc.
3. **mint**—make money by stamping (mintage,n.)
4. **monetize**—convert or coin into money (monetization,n.)

17. Place Where Money is Coined: mint,n.

18. Counterfeiter: coiner,n.

19. Use of Metal for Money,n.
1. **bimetallism**—use of two metals (usually gold and silver) as the legal standard of money (bimetallic,adj.)
2. **monometallism**—use of only one metal (either gold or silver) as the legal standard of money (monometallic,adj.)

20. Sciences of Money, Coins, etc.,n.
1. **chrysology**—science of the production and value of gold, silver, and other precious metals
2. **economics**—science dealing with the production, distribution, etc., of material wealth (economist,n. economic,adj.)
3. **finance**—science and practice of raising and spending public revenue; science of money management (financier,n. financial,adj.)
4. **numismatics**—science of coins, paper

money, etc. (numismatist,n. numismatic, adj.)
5. **numismatology**—numismatics (numismatologist,n. numismatological,adj.)
6. **political economy**—economics (political economist,n.)

21. Written Descriptions of Coins, Medals, etc.: numismatography,n.

22. Management of Money or Moneys, Esp. on a Large Scale; Management of Public Funds: finance,n. (financier,n.)

23. Money Record,n.
1. **account**—statement of money taken in or paid out
2. **budget**—financial statement of expected revenues and expenditures of a country (budgetary,adj.)

24. The Keeping of Money Records,n.
1. **accounting, accountancy**—art or business of keeping money records (accountant,n.)
2. **bookkeeping**—the keeping of money records (bookkeeper,n.)

25. To Give Value as Money,v.
1. **monetize**—give value as money (monetization,n.)
2. **remonetize**—restore to use as lawful money (remonetization,n.)

26. Capable of Being Given a Money Value or Appraisal: tangible,adj. (tangible,n.)

27. To Take Away Money Value,v.
1. **demonetize**—deprive (some metal, type of currency, etc.) of its value or use as money (demonetization,n.)
2. **devaluate**—lower the official value of currency (devaluation,n.)

---

214. INTEREST IN MONEY

1. Interested in Money or Wealth,adj.
1. **bourgeois**—wrapped up in material interests or possessions (bourgeois,n.)
2. **hireling**—serving purely from motives of monetary gain
3. **mammonish, mammonistic**—concentrating one's interest on increasing one's wealth (mammonist,n. mammonism,n.)
4. **mercenary**—solely motivated by a desire for money or financial gain
5. **pensionary**—hireling
6. **Philistine**—interested only in business, the making of money, etc.
7. **sordid**—mercenary
8. **venal**—mercenary

2. Interest in Money or Wealth,n. *From Sec. 1:* mammonism, mercenariness, Philistinism, sordidness, venality

3. One Who Is Interested in Money or Wealth,n. *From Sec. 1:* bourgeois, hireling, mammonist, pensionary, Philistine; *Also:*
1. **fortune hunter**—one who seeks wealth by marriage
2. **gold-digger**—woman whose relations with men are based on the desire for monetary gain
3. **huckster**—mercenary person
4. **miser**—one who wants money merely for the thrill of possession, and who often lives poorly in order to increase his store of money
5. **moneygrubber**—person who has a mean and exaggerated interest in the accumulation of money

---

215. MONEY PROFIT

1. Profit in Money,n.
1. **gain**—money profit; return
2. **perquisite**—profit made incidentally in one's work and in addition to one's regular pay

3. **return**—profit from work, sales, investments, etc.

2. Profitable in Money,adj.
  1. **gainful**—showing a money profit
  2. **lucrative**—producing money; resulting in money gain or financial profit
  3. **money-making**—financially profitable
  4. **paying**—giving a money return
  5. **prosperous**—making money
  6. **remunerative**—profitable in money
  7. **well-paying**—giving a good return in money

3. To Take Advantage of Public Need to Make Extortionate or Exorbitant Profits: profiteer,v. (profiteer,n.)

216. WEALTH

1. Rich; Wealthy,adj.
  1. **affluent**—possessing rich and perhaps increasing material resources; moneyed
  2. **flush**—affluent; prosperous
  3. **moneyed**—rich; possessing a good amount of money
  4. **opulent**—inordinately wealthy
  5. **pecunious**—rich; possessing a good deal of money
  6. **prosperous**—rich; making a good deal of money
  7. **substantial**—rich in money or property
  8. **well-fixed, well-to-do**—rich; prosperous
  9. **well-off**—fairly rich

2. Richness; Wealth; State of Being Rich or Wealthy,n. *From Sec. 1:* affluence, opulence, prosperity, substantiality; *Also:* 1. luxury—state of self-indulgent wealth

3. Riches; Wealth; That Which Constitutes Wealth,n. *From Sec. 1:* affluence, opulence, substance; *Also:*
  1. **assets**—wealth
  2. **capital**—stock of accumulated wealth
  3. **fortune**—store of wealth
  4. **lucre**—wealth (contemptuous)
  5. **means**—wealth
  6. **pelf**—wealth (contemptuous, the implication being that it is debasing)
  7. **resources**—wealth
  8. **treasure**—stored or saved-up wealth

4. To Make Wealthy or Wealthier: enrich, v. (enrichment,n.)

5. Wealthy Person,n.
  1. **arrivé (French)**—parvenu
  2. **billionaire**—person whose wealth is in the billions
  3. **bourgeois**—capitalist
  4. **capitalist**—person whose wealth is employed in business
  5. **Croesus**—very rich man (so called after the King of Lydia in the sixth century B.C., famed for his tremendous wealth)
  6. **Dives**—rich man (so called after the person of great wealth in the Bible)
  7. **Midas**—rich man; someone whose projects always turn out with financial success (so called after the mythological king whose touch turned everything into gold)
  8. **millionaire**—person whose wealth is in millions of dollars
  9. **multimillionaire**—one even richer than a millionaire, possessing many millions of dollars
  10. **nabob**—person of great wealth, so called from the East Indian title for a provincial governor (nabobess,fem.)
  11. **nawab**—nabob
  12. **nouveau riche (French)**—parvenu; someone who has recently acquired wealth and vulgarly or obnoxiously makes a display of it
  13. **parvenu**—one who, by the acquisition of wealth, has risen to a station above that to which he was born; one who has great

ambitions or pretensions because of his wealth; upstart
  14. **plutocrat**—someone who is powerful or influential owing to his great wealth
  15. **richling**—rich youth
  16. **upstart**—one who has risen suddenly from poverty or humble position to one of wealth and power
  17. **vulgarian**—rich person of low standards or taste; rich person without good breeding or manners

6. Descr. or Characteristic of a Wealthy Person or Persons,adj. *From Sec. 5:* bourgeois, capitalistic, nabobical or nabobish, nouveau riche (French), parvenu, plutocratic, upstart, vulgarian

7. Behavior, Characteristics, etc., of a Wealthy Person or Persons,n. *From Sec. 5:* nabobery or nabobism, parvenuism, vulgarianism

8. Rich People; Wealthy Class,n. *From Sec. 5:* bourgeoisie, nabobery, plutocracy; *Also:*
  1. **society**—people of wealth and fashion
  2. **villadom**—the world of self-satisfied, financially independent, and mediocre people
  3. **zaibatsu**—the wealthy families controlling most of Japanese industry before and during World War II

9. Source or Means of Wealth,n.
  1. **bonanza**—anything yielding an unusually good or large financial return; strictly, a good strike in a gold or silver mine
  2. **Golconda**—source of tremendous wealth
  3. **resources**—means of wealth

10. Science of Wealth,n.
  1. **economics**—science of wealth, its production, distribution, and consumption (economist,n. economic,adj.)
  2. **plutology**—scientific study of wealth (plutologist,n. plutological,adj.)
  3. **plutonomy**—economics; plutology (plutonomist,n. plutonomic,adj.)
  4. **political economy**—economics (political economist,n.)

11. Greek God of Wealth: Plutus,n.

12. Demon of Desire for Material Possessions: Mammon,n.

13. Luxurious: Corinthian, palatial, palatine, adj.

217. POVERTY

1. Poor (in Money),adj.
  1. **bankrupt**—having no further resources; impoverished
  2. **beggared**—impoverished
  3. **beggarly**—very poor; reduced to poverty
  4. **broke**—out of money; bankrupt (colloq.)
  5. **destitute**—in extreme want; lacking even the necessities that money can buy
  6. **distressed**—in painful circumstances owing to lack of money
  7. **down-and-out**—thoroughly incapacitated by lack of money; destitute
  8. **embarrassed**—lacking money (a euphemism, usually in the phrase *embarrassed circumstances*)
  9. **impecunious, impecuniary**—possessing very little or no money; habitually without money
  10. **impoverished**—made poor; reduced to poverty; poor
  11. **indigent**—poor; lacking in money
  12. **insolvent**—lacking in the money to pay one's debts
  13. **miserable**—poor and mean (of places, surroundings, etc.)
  14. **moneyless**—totally lacking in money
  15. **necessitous**—poor; without money; destitute; needy

16. **needful**—needy
17. **needy**—poor; in unfortunate circumstances owing to lack of money; impoverished
18. **pauperized**—totally lacking in money
19. **penniless**—totally without money
20. **pinched**—distressed
21. **poverty-stricken**—without money
22. **reduced**—distressed (often in the phrase *reduced circumstances*)
23. **sordid**—meanly poor (of places, surroundings, etc.)
24. **squalid**—poor, mean, and dirty (of places, surroundings, etc.)
25. **straitened**—restricted or embarrassed because of lack of money
26. **stranded**—alone and without money
27. **strapped**—penniless (colloq.)
28. **unmoneyed**—penniless

2. Poverty,n. *From Sec. 1:* bankruptcy, beggary or beggarliness, destitution, distress, impecuniousness or impecuniosity, impoverishment, indigence, insolvency, misery or miserableness, necessitousness; need, needfulness or neediness; pauperism, pauperization, pauperage, or pauperdom; pennilessness, sordidness, squalor; *Also:*
1. **adversity**—state of being without money, though previously otherwise
2. **penury**—lack of money or material resources; extreme poverty
3. **want**—poverty; penury

3. To Cause to Be Poor; To Reduce to Poverty,v. *From Sec. 1:* bankrupt, beggar; break (colloq.); destitute, distress, impoverish; pauperize, pauper or pauperate; straiten, strand, strap (destitution, impoverishment, pauperization,n.)

4. Poor Person,n. *From Sec. 1:* bankrupt, beggar, indigent, insolvent, pauper, pauperess (fem.); *Also:* 1. **poorling**—poor person

5. Poor People, Collectively,n. *From Sec. 1:* bankrupt, beggary, indigent, insolvent, pauperism or pauperdom

218. DEBT

1. Debt; Debts,n.
1. **arrear, arrears, arrearage**—debt; debts
2. **debit**—debt
3. **dues**—debt
4. **indebtedness, indebtment**—debts, collectively; that which is owed
5. **liabilities**—debts, collectively
6. **liability**—debt; that which one is under obligation to pay
7. **obligation**—debt incurred by accepting a kindness, favor, etc.

2. To Place under a Debt,v.
1. **astrict**—place under legal or moral debt (astriction,n.)
2. **bind**—obligate
3. **indebt**—place under a debt; obligate
4. **obligate**—place under moral or social debt (obligation,n.)

3. Placed under a Debt,adj. *From Sec. 2:* astricted, bound or bounden, indebted, obligated (indebtedness or indebtment, obligation,n.); *Also:* 1. **beholden**—indebted; obligated

4. To Be in Debt: owe,v.

5. Record of a Debt,n.
1. **account**—record of that which is owed
2. **bill**—statement of money owed
3. **check**—ticket, slip, etc., on which amount due is shown
4. **chirograph**—statement of obligation written and signed in one's own hand
5. **chit**—signed admission of a small debt
6. **debenture**—certificate of debt, usually of corporations

7. **debit**—record of debt
8. **invoice**—written account or itemized statement of merchandise shipped, with prices, money that will be due, etc.
9. **I.O.U.**—signed paper acknowledging a debt
10. **manifest**—invoice of a ship's cargo
11. **memorandum, memo**—statement of commodities shipped or delivered for which the receiver is in debt, but that may be returned for full credit
12. **note**—written or printed paper acknowledging indebtedness and promising payment
13. **obligation**—contract or agreement by which one is bound
14. **promissory note**—written and signed agreement to pay a debt on demand or on a specified date
15. **reckoning**—bill, as at a hotel, restaurant, etc. (somewhat archaic, but occasionally found in modern usage)
16. **score**—record of money due
17. **statement**—abstract of an account, showing balance due
18. **tab**—account; account at a hotel, restaurant, etc.
19. **tally**—score kept in duplicate

6. Written Acknowledgment of Payment of a Debt: receipt, voucher,n. (receipt,v.)

7. One Who Is in Debt,n.
1. **debtor**—one who is in debt
2. **mortgagor**—one who owes money for which he has put up a house, property, etc., as collateral

8. One to Whom Is Owed,n.
1. **creditor**—the person to whom something is owed
2. **debtee**—creditor
3. **mortgagee**—one who has lent money with a house or other property as collateral
4. **Shylock**—greedy creditor

9. Moneylender,n.
1. **banker**—one who lends money at interest
2. **money broker**—moneylender
3. **moneymonger**—moneylender
4. **pawnbroker**—one who lends money on things left as security or collateral
5. **Shylock**—usurer (Shylock,adj.)
6. **usurer**—one who lends money at exorbitant or illegal rates of interest (usury,n. usurious,adj.)

10. Pert. to a Pawnbroker: avuncular,adj. (humorous)

11. To Lend Money on Collateral or against Future Earnings: advance,v.

12. Exorbitant or Illegal Rate of Interest Charged for the Loan of Money: usury,n. (usurious,adj.)

13. Capable of Paying Financial Debts: solvent,adj. (solvency,n.)

14. Incapable of Paying Financial Debts: bankrupt, insolvent,adj. (bankruptcy, insolvency,n. bankrupt, insolvent,n.)

15. To Announce as Bankrupt: gazette,v. (gazetted,adj.)

16. Not to Pay Debts,v.
1. **default**—fail to pay (what is owed) when due
2. **dishonor**—refuse to pay (a note or other document of indebtedness)
3. **repudiate**—refuse to honor or pay (one's debts)
4. **welsh, welch**—not pay one's gambling debts (colloq.)

17. A Not Paying of Debts,n. *From Sec. 16:* default, repudiation

18. One Who Does Not Pay Debts,n. *From Sec. 16:* defaulter or defaultant, repudiator, welsher or welcher; *Also:*

1. **dead beat**—person who does not pay his debts, or is known not to pay his debts
2. **delinquent**—one who has not paid a due or overdue debt

19. Not Having Paid Debts when Due: in default, delinquent,adj. (delinquency,n.)

20. Unpaid (of a Debt, Bill, etc.): delinquent, outstanding,adj. (delinquency,n.)

219. PAYMENT

1. To Pay,v.
1. **acquit**—make complete payment of (what is owed)
2. **amortize**—make gradual payments of (total sum owed)
3. **award**—grant money payment, as in a competition or contest to the winner, or in a legal action to the successful litigant, etc.
4. **compensate**—pay for loss, services, etc.
5. **defray**—pay (costs, expenses, etc.)
6. **deposit**—pay (part) as a promise or guarantee of later full payment
7. **disburse**—pay (funds, money, salaries, or other due financial obligations)
8. **discharge**—pay off (a debt) and thus get rid of it
9. **indemnify**—pay for loss, injury, damage, inconvenience, etc.
10. **liquidate**—pay off (a debt, obligation, etc.)
11. **pension**—make payments to (a person) in lieu of salary or wages (as when he retires, suffers incapacitating injuries, etc.)
12. **prepay**—pay the charge on beforehand
13. **ransom**—pay for the delivery or setting free of (someone held captive)
14. **rebate**—return (a payment or part of a payment)
15. **recompense**—pay for (services, losses, damages suffered, etc.)
16. **redeem**—pay off the full amount of (a loan)
17. **refund**—repay (money), as when someone makes a purchase, then returns the merchandise, etc.
18. **reimburse**—pay back to (someone) money he has spent on one's behalf
19. **remit**—pay (money in any form—cash, check, money order, etc.) through the mails or by messenger, telegraph, etc.
20. **remunerate**—pay (someone) for work done or services rendered
21. **render**—pay (that which is due)
22. **repay**—pay back
23. **replace**—repay
24. **requite**—pay in return; make payment for injuries, etc.
25. **return**—pay interest on investments
26. **reward**—pay (someone) for special services
27. **satisfy**—pay (what is due)
28. **settle**—pay off; pay up
29. **square**—settle (debts, accounts, etc.)
30. **subsidize**—pay money to, usually as an aid, as to a college student completing his course, or to business for reasons of benefit to the state, etc.
31. **support**—pay the costs of maintaining
32. **tip**—make a voluntary payment to (someone) for menial services, in addition to the payment agreed upon or charged, as to a messenger, waiter, etc.

2. Payment,i.e., Act of Paying,n. *From Sec. 1:* acquittance or acquittal, amortization, award, compensation, defrayal or defrayment, deposit, disbursement, discharge, indemnification, liquidation, prepayment, ransom, rebate, recompense, redemption, refund, reimbursement, remittance, remuneration, repayment, replacement, requital or requitement, return,

satisfaction, settlement, subsidization or subsidy, support; *Also:*
1. **clearance**—paying off of claims or debts (banking)
2. **quittance**—acquittance; recompense
3. **reckoning**—paying up of one's accounts
4. **restitution**—repayment to the rightful or legal owner of money (or other valuables) that has been stolen, embezzled, illegally confiscated, etc.

3. Payment or Pay, i.e., That Which Is Paid,n. *From Sec. 1:* award, compensation, deposit, indemnity, pension, prepayment, ransom, rebate, recompense, redemption, refund, remittance, remuneration, repayment, return, reward, satisfaction, settlement, subsidy, support, tip; *Also:*
1. **alimony**—sums paid to one's wife or former wife for her subsistence, pending or after divorce
2. **allowance**—fixed sum granted to one's dependent for personal use; sum granted for expenses
3. **amends**—payment or recompense for loss, injury, insult, harm, etc.
4. **annuity**—sum paid yearly or more often, as from investments, insurance policies, etc.
5. **arbitrament**—award by an arbitrator
6. **bonus**—payment additional to that agreed upon
7. **bounty**—payment, usually by a government agency, for specific acts, such as destruction of pests, capture of harmful animals, etc.
8. **brokerage**—fee for doing business as a broker
9. **cartage**—payment made for carting or transporting
10. **commission**—payment, usually at a percentage of the price of sale, for goods sold or for services rendered in buying or selling or in collecting money
11. **consideration**—payment for services; payment in money or otherwise
12. **demurrage**—payment made for retaining any vessel or carrier beyond the time needed for loading and unloading
13. **dividend**—interest payment from stocks, bonds, or other form of investment
14. **dole**—payment of public money to the poor, on the basis of need rather than of services performed
15. **douceur (French)**—bonus; honorarium
16. **drayage**—cartage
17. **dues**—fee; toll; tribute
18. **duty**—payment required or recoverable by law
19. **earnest**—payment of something of value to seal a bargain; installment; token payment
20. **earnings**—salary, wages, fees, profits, etc., paid to a person, institution, or corporation
21. **emolument**—regular periodic payment for one's job, work, etc.
22. **expressage**—payment for transportation
23. **fare**—payment for riding on a common carrier
24. **fee**—payment; payment for professional services
25. **fine**—payment exacted as punishment for error, wrong, infraction of the law, etc.
26. **footing**—payment demanded of a newcomer in a school, trade, or other relationship to establish his standing in the group
27. **freightage**—cartage
28. **grant**—payment by a government agency or private institution for valuable work to be done
29. **honorarium**—strictly, payment for professional or other valuable service for which custom forbids the donor to set a fee; actually, in present use, a fee

30. **income**—payment from work, business, investments, etc.
31. **installment**—part payment on a debt
32. **interest**—percentage paid by a borrower for the use of money
33. **moorage**—payment for anchoring a vessel
34. **perquisite**—payment in addition to salary or wages, usually expected or guaranteed; payment for work
35. **pittance**—pitifully small payment, allowance, wage, etc.
36. **portal-to-portal pay**—pay from the time a worker enters a plant, factory, etc. (i.e., passes through the portals or gates), until he leaves, whether or not he is actually engaged in work
37. **poundage**—payment per pound; payment for the release of impounded animals
38. **premium**—additional or extra payment, offered or promised as an incentive, charged for special quality, etc.
39. **primage**—added payment made to the owner or captain of a freight vessel
40. **prize**—payment in money or other valuable thing to the winner in a contest or competition
41. **quid pro quo (Latin)**—payment on the basis of equal return
42. **receipts**—payment received from sale of goods
43. **relief**—payments on the part of a government to those unable to support themselves, sufficient for food, clothing, shelter, etc.; dole
44. **rent**—payment for use of property
45. **reparation**—payment for injury or harm
46. **revenue**—payment from investments; payment received by government agency
47. **royalty**—payment of a percentage or share of the sale of a product, as to an author on his books, a playwright on performances of his play, an owner of land on oil or metals extracted from it, etc.
48. **salary**—payment for services, usually on a weekly, monthly, or yearly basis
49. **salvage**—payment for rescuing a ship and/or its cargo at sea
50. **solatium**—payment for suffering, loss, injury, etc.
51. **stipend**—payment for services (In America the word may have the implication of a remuneration just barely enough for subsistence; in England it is the common synonym for our word *salary*.)
52. **stipendium**—stipend
53. **subvention**—grant from a government or philanthropic agency
54. **tithe**—payment of a small part of one's income to support a religious organization
55. **token payment**—very small partial payment on a debt as an evidence of good faith and intention
56. **toll**—that which is paid
57. **tonnage**—payment per ton
58. **tontine**—yearly sum paid to a group of people (When one of the group dies, his share is divided among the others, until finally the total annual payment is made to the last survivor.)
59. **towage**—payment for towing
60. **tribute**—money or other consideration paid by one nation to another in order not to be attacked; any payment made unwillingly but without choice; payment as a token of thanks, respect, loyalty, etc.
61. **wage, wages**—payment, at regular intervals, for manual, menial, mechanical, or other labor or work

4. Descr. of, or Pert. to, Payment,adj. *From Sec. 1:* compensatory, pensionary, redemptive, remunerative, subsidiary; *From Sec. 3:* reparative, stipendiary, tontine, tributary

5. **Person Paid,**n. *From Sec. 1:* pensioner or pensionary; *From Sec. 3:* annuitant, stipendiary
6. **To Agree to Pay the Expenses of:** underwrite,v.
7. **Paying Well:** lucrative, profitable, remunerative, well-paying,adj.
8. **A Tip,**n.
   1. **baksheesh**—tip, so called in the Near East
   2. **cumshaw**—tip, from the Chinese phrase of thanks used by beggars
   3. **douceur (French)**—tip
   4. **gratuity**—tip
   5. **perquisite**—tip, esp. one established by custom
   6. **pourboire**—tip (from the French, literally [*money*] *for drinking*)
   7. **primage**—tip paid to the owner or captain of a freight vessel
9. **The Exaction of Tips:** perquisition,n.
10. **One Who Exacts Tips:** perquisitor,n.
11. **Reward, Prize, etc.,**n.
    1. **accolade**—award
    2. **award**—something given as a prize, as in a contest, dispute, etc.; prize for excellence, merit, etc.
    3. **bays**—honorary crown or garland given as a prize for excellence or victory
    4. **booty**—prize
    5. **crown**—reward; wreath or garland to be worn around the head and bestowed as a reward for victory, etc.
    6. **desert**—suitable reward
    7. **garland**—wreath made of branches, precious stones, etc., given as a reward to the victor in ancient games
    8. **guerdon**—reward (poetic)
    9. **laurel**—reward for excellence, superiority, etc., in the form of a crown made of leaves from the laurel tree; such figuratively
    10. **medal**—reward for bravery, excellence, merit, etc., in the form of a flat, circular piece of metal, often silver or gold, with an inscription, design, etc.; such a piece of metal struck in memory of, or to honor, a person, event, etc. (medallic, adj.)
    11. **medallion**—large medal
    12. **meed**—reward (poetic)
    13. **palm**—prize (the palm is a symbol of success, victory, triumph, etc.)
    14. **plume**—reward or prize for skill, prowess, honor, etc.
    15. **purse**—money prize
    16. **stake**—prize
    17. **stakes**—prize or prizes in a contest
    18. **trophy**—reward of victory (as in a contest, tournament, etc.)
    19. **visitation**—reward from heaven (visitationary,adj.)
    20. **wreath**—symbolic reward for a winner or victor
12. **To Reward,**v. *From Sec. 11:* award, crown, garland, laurel or laureate, medal or decorate, plume (decoration, laureation,n.)
13. **One Who Receives a Reward,**n. *From Sec. 11:* laureate, medalist,n. (laureate,adj.)
14. **Description of Medals and Coins:** numismatography,n.
15. **Science of Medals and Coins:** numismatics, numismatology,n. (numismatist, numismatician, or numismatologist,n. numismatic or numismatical,adj.)
16. **One Who Makes, Engraves, or Designs Medals:** medalist,n.
17. **That Which Deserves Reward:** merit,n.
18. **Tax,**n.
    1. **assessment**—tax; amount of tax (assess, v.)

2. **capitation**—tax levied per head or per person
3. **custom**—tax on imports
4. **dues**—tax; tax for a privilege or right
5. **duty**—tax on imports, exports, consumption of goods, etc.
6. **excise, excise tax**—tax on manufacture, sales, etc., within a country (excise, adj.)
7. **gabelle**—tax on salt (once imposed in France and China)
8. **impost**—tax on imports
9. **levy**—that which is taken by the government to satisfy tax warrants (levy,v.)
10. **poll, poll tax**—tax of so much per person, levied usually on males over a certain age
11. **rate**—local tax
12. **tariff**—tax on imports or, less commonly, exports
13. **tithe**—small part of one's income (originally a tenth) to support a religious organization, and levied generally as a tax
14. **toll**—tax for some privilege or right, as going over a bridge

220. BRIBERY

1. To Bribe,v.
1. **buy**—bribe
2. **corrupt**—bribe
3. **embrace**—bribe, or attempt to bribe, for purposes of influencing a decision, a court, jury, etc. (legal)
4. **fix**—bribe (colloq.)
5. **grease (or tickle) the palm of**—bribe
6. **suborn**—cause a person, by bribery, to commit a crime
7. **tamper with**—bribe

2. Bribery,n. *From Sec. 1:* corruption, embracery, subornation

3. Briber,n. *From Sec. 1:* corruptor, embraceor or embracer, fixer, suborner

4. Acting to Bribe,adj. *From Sec. 1:* corruptive, subornative

5. A Bribe,n.
1. **boodle**—money for a bribe
2. **douceur (French)**—bribe
3. **graft**—bribe; money for a bribe
4. **sop**—bribe
5. **swag**—boodle (colloq.)

6. Open to Bribery,adj.
1. **bribable**—open to bribery; capable of being bribed
2. **corruptible**—bribable (corruptibility, corruptibleness,n.)
3. **rotten**—open to bribery (rottenness,n.)
4. **venal**—open to bribery; capable of being bribed; selling for money that which should not be sold (venality,n.)
5. **vendible**—venal (vendibility,n.)

7. To Take a Bribe in Return for Not Prosecuting a Crime: compound a felony

221. PAYMENT IN KIND

1. To Pay, or Pay Back, in Kind,v.
1. **avenge**—pay back by inflicting merited punishment
2. **reciprocate**—pay back to another in the same kind or to the same extent (generally restricted to pleasant, friendly, or at least neutral actions, as distinguished from *retaliate*)
3. **recompense**—pay back in kind; pay in return
4. **repay**—pay back in kind
5. **requite**—pay back in kind; pay in return; retaliate; revenge
6. **retaliate**—pay back evil with evil or

wrong for wrong (i.e., with the same harm or injury visited upon oneself)
7. **retort**—repay
8. **revenge**—pay back, sometimes spitefully, for injury or harm inflicted

2. Payment in Kind,n. *From Sec. 1:* avengement, reciprocation or reciprocity, recompense, repayment, requital or requitement, retaliation, retort, revenge; *Also:*
1. **feud**—bitter quarreling or violence, including bloodshed, between families, groups, etc., in revenge for previous wrongs
2. **reprisal**—retaliation; revenge
3. **retribution**—a paying back for evil or, occasionally, for good
4. **talion**—retaliation; retaliation by the Mosaic code (eye for an eye, etc.)
5. **tit for tat**—retaliation
6. **vendetta**—blood feud (i.e., one in which friends or relatives of the wronged or murdered person take extreme revenge on the one who has caused the wrong or committed the injury)
7. **vengeance**—retribution; unrestrained or passionate revenge or retaliation

3. Tending or Acting to Pay in Kind,adj. *From Sec. 1:* reciprocal, retaliatory, revengeful; *From Sec. 2:* retributive, talionic, vengeful; *Also:*
1. **grudgeful**—vindictive
2. **vindictive**—likely to bear and hold a grudge and to attempt to retaliate maliciously; vengeful

222. RECOMPENSE

1. To Make Up for,v.
1. **atone, atone for**—make up for (an offense, sin, crime, etc.)
2. **compensate for**—make up for (what is lacking); make up for (damage, loss, suffering, etc.)
3. **countervail**—make up for some harm or harmful influence; make up for injury, damage, or suffering caused by a harmful influence
4. **expiate**—make complete satisfaction for; atone for
5. **indemnify**—make up to (someone) for loss or damage
6. **make amends (for)**—make up (for injury or loss)
7. **offset**—make up for; compensate for
8. **overcompensate**—make up for a trait by exaggerating a contrasting or opposite trait
9. **propitiate**—atone (religious term)
10. **recompense**—make up to (someone) for loss or injury
11. **recoup**—make up to oneself for loss or damage
12. **recover**—make up for
13. **redeem**—make up for; atone
14. **redress**—give satisfaction for (wrongs, injustice, moral errors, etc.)
15. **requite**—make up for
16. **retrieve**—make up for; make amends for
17. **satisfy**—make up for (damage, loss, etc.)

2. A Making Up for,n. *From Sec. 1:* atonement, compensation, expiation, indemnification, overcompensation, propitiation, recompense, recoupment, recovery, redemption, redress, requital or requitement, retrieval or retrievement, satisfaction; *Also:*
1. **amende**—reparation
2. **amende honorable**—reparation to such extent as will restore the injured honor of the one wronged
3. **amende profitable**—reparation by means of a sum of money sworn by the plaintiff to be less than necessary for the restoration of his honor

4. **reparation**—act of making amends or giving compensation for a wrong or injury
5. **restitution**—compensation for loss, damage, etc.

3. Descr. of Compensation,adj. *From Sec. 1:* compensatory, compensative or compensational; expiatory, expiative or expiational; indemnificatory, propitiatory or propitiatory, redemptive; *From Sec. 2:* reparative, restitutive or restitutory; *Also:*
1. **piacular**—expiatory
2. **purgatorial**—making up for guilt

4. Capable of Being Made Up for,adj. *From Sec. 1:* atonable, expiable, recoverable, redeemable, retrievable; *From Sec. 2:* reparable

5. Incapable of Being Made Up for,adj. *From Sec. 4:* unatonable, inexpiable, irrecoverable, unredeemable, irretrievable, irreparable

223. CHARGE

1. Charge,n.
1. **amount**—charge
2. **capitation**—charge levied per head or per person
3. **dues**—legal charge; fee; toll
4. **fare**—charge for riding on a public vehicle, train, ship, etc.
5. **fee**—charge for professional or other services
6. **overcharge**—excessive charge (overcharge,v.)
7. **price**—charge (price,v.)
8. **rent**—charge for the use of something
9. **surcharge**—charge on top of other charges; excessive charge (surcharge,v.)
10. **tariff**—charge
11. **toll**—charge for a privilege, right, or service

2. Certain Specific Charges,n.
1. **admission**—charge for entering
2. **brokerage**—charge by a broker for transacting business
3. **cartage**—charge for transporting goods
4. **drayage**—charge for transporting of goods
5. **expressage**—charge for transporting
6. **freightage**—cartage
7. **moorage**—charge for anchoring a vessel
8. **pierage**—wharfage
9. **poundage**—charge per pound; charge for the release of impounded animals
10. **quayage**—wharfage
11. **salvage**—charge for the rescue of a ship at sea, its cargo, passengers, etc.
12. **tonnage**—charge per ton
13. **towage**—charge for towing
14. **wharfage**—charge for using a wharf

3. Table or List of Charges or Prices: tariff, n.

4. Cost of Operation: budget,n. (budgetary, adj.)

5. Cost of Keeping in Operation and Repair: upkeep,n.

6. Appraised or Estimated Price: valuation, n.

7. Amount Added to the Buying Price to Arrive at the Selling Price: markup,n.

8. Price Paid by One Nation to Another in Order Not to Be Attacked: tribute,n. (tributary,n. tributary,adj.)

9. To Discuss Price,v.
1. **bargain**—discuss price; discuss price in a petty or argumentative fashion
2. **chaffer**—discuss price; haggle
3. **dicker**—discuss price; arrive at a mutually agreeable price; haggle
4. **haggle**—discuss price pettily and disputatiously

5. **higgle**—engage in a petty dispute about the price of something
6. **negotiate**—discuss price with a view to coming to an agreement
7. **palter**—haggle

10. Discussion of Price,n. *From Sec. 9:* bargaining, chaffer or chaffering, dickering, haggle or haggling, higgling, negotiation, paltering; *Also:* 1. **huckstery**—bargaining; haggling

11. To Offer a Price,v.
1. **bid**—offer a price
2. **outbid**—offer a higher price than
3. **overbid**—outbid (overbid,n.)
4. **underbid**—offer a lower price than (underbid,n.)

12. Government Price Control of a Commodity: valorization,n. (valorize,v.)

13. Free of Charge or Cost: complimentary, free, gratis, gratuitous,adj.

14. Expensive,adj.
1. **costly**—expensive (costliness,n.)
2. **dear**—expensive (dearness,n.)
3. **excessive**—higher in price than reasonable or normal (excessiveness,n.)
4. **exorbitant**—excessively or unreasonably expensive (exorbitance, exorbitancy,n.)
5. **extortionate**—exorbitant (extortionateness,n.)
6. **extravagant**—excessively or unreasonably expensive (extravagance, extravagancy, n.)
7. **high**—expensive
8. **high-priced**—expensive
9. **immoderate**—unreasonably expensive (immoderateness,n.)
10. **luxurious**—very expensive and also rich, elegant, and beautiful (luxuriousness,n.)
11. **prohibitive**—inordinately expensive; so expensive as to prohibit or prevent buying or doing (prohibitiveness,n.)
12. **sumptuous**—expensive; luxurious (sumptuousness,n.)
13. **unreasonable**—abnormally expensive (unreasonableness,n.)

15. Inexpensive,adj.
1. **catchpenny**—inexpensive and worthless (i.e., made to catch the pennies of the unwary or ignorant)
2. **cheap**—inexpensive (cheapness,n.)
3. **cut-rate**—at reduced prices
4. **dirt-cheap**—extremely inexpensive
5. **low**—inexpensive
6. **low-priced**—inexpensive
7. **moderate**—not expensive (moderateness, n.)
8. **nominal**—low in price; so low as to be no more than token in price
9. **reasonable**—moderately priced; inexpensive (reasonableness,n.)
10. **tin-horn**—inexpensive and flashy

16. That Which Is Inexpensive: catchpenny n.

224. SPEND

1. To Spend,v.
1. **consume**—spend
2. **disburse**—spend; spend (public funds)
3. **dissipate**—spend imprudently or wastefully
4. **economize**—spend money frugally
5. **expend**—spend (money, time, energy, etc.)
6. **lavish**—spend extravagantly; squander
7. **misspend**—spend badly or foolishly
8. **outlay**—spend (money, time, energy, etc.)
9. **splurge**—spend extravagantly
10. **squander**—spend lavishly, prodigally, profusely, foolishly, or wastefully
11. **waste**—spend foolishly, needlessly, and without valuable result

2. A Spending,n. *From Sec. 1:* consumption, disbursement, dissipation, economy, expenditure or expense, outlay, splurge, squander, waste

3. That Which Is Spent,n. *From Sec. 1:* disbursement, expenditure, outlay

4. Cause of Spending: expense,n.

5. Pert. to, or Controlling, Spending: sumptuary,adj.

225. WASTE

1. To Waste; To Be Wasteful with: dissipate, fribble, fribble away, frivol away, fritter, fritter away, lavish, squander, squander away,v. (dissipation, squander,n. dissipator, squanderer,n. dissipative,adj.)

2. Wasteful: extravagant, improvident, lavish; pound-foolish (in the phrase *penny-wise and pound-foolish*); prodigal, profligate, profuse in, profuse of; shiftless (i.e., not showing thrift); spendthrift, wanton,adj. (extravagance, improvidence, lavishness, prodigality, profligacy or profligateness, profuseness, shiftlessness, wantonness,n.)

3. Wasteful in Producing: extravagant, lavish,adj. (extravagance, lavishness,n.)

4. Wasteful Person: dissipator, prodigal, profligate, scattergood, spendthrift, squanderer, wastrel,n.

226. ECONOMY

1. Economical,adj.
  1. **canny**—thrifty
  2. **chary**—cautiously economical or frugal
  3. **frugal**—sparing and careful in using resources or spending money
  4. **parsimonious**—excessively economical or frugal
  5. **penny-wise**—exceedingly economical in expenditure (in the phrase *penny-wise and pound-foolish*)
  6. **penurious**—exceedingly economical in the expenditure of money
  7. **provident**—economical; frugal; thrifty
  8. **prudent, prudential**—using resources carefully and economically
  9. **saving**—economical
  10. **scrimpy**—sparing
  11. **skimpy**—too economical in using
  12. **sparing**—careful or economical in using
  13. **Spartan**—frugal
  14. **stinting**—economical in using
  15. **thrifty**—economical; careful or wise in spending

2. Economy,n. *From Sec. 1:* canniness, chariness, frugality, parsimoniousness or parsimony, penuriousness, providence, prudence, scrimpiness, skimpiness, Spartanism, thrift or thriftiness; *Also:* 1. **husbandry**—thrift

3. To Be Economical,v.
  1. **economize**—be sparing or frugal in money expenditures (economy,n.)
  2. **husband**—economize in using; be frugal in using (husbandry,n.)
  3. **pinch**—be excessively economical
  4. **retrench**—cut down expenses (retrenchment,n.)
  5. **scrimp**—be very frugal or sparing in the use of something
  6. **shepherd**—be thrifty in spending
  7. **skimp**—be very frugal in expenditure or use
  8. **stint**—be economical in using

227. STINGINESS

1. Stingy,adj.
  1. **anal**—stingy in character or personality (psychoanalysis)

  2. **avaricious**—stingy in reference to, and greedy for, money (avariciousness, avarice,n.)
  3. **chary**—stingy (chariness,n.)
  4. **churlish**—meanly stingy (churlishness, n.)
  5. **costive**d—stingy (closefistedness,n.)
  6. **costive**—stingy (costiveness,n.)
  7. **illiberal**—stingy, i.e., not generous (illiberality,n.)
  8. **miserly**—stingy, esp. in reference to money; refusing to part with any part of what one has; avaricious (miserliness,n.)
  9. **niggardly**—meanly stingy (niggardliness, n.)
  10. **parsimonious**—stingy through demands of economy or frugality (parsimoniousness, parsimony,n.)
  11. **penny-pinching**—meanly stingy (colloq.)
  12. **penurious**—stingy, or excessively stingy, in the spending or giving of money (penuriousness,n.)
  13. **petty**—stingy (pettiness,n.)
  14. **scabby**—stingy (scabbiness,n.)
  15. **shabby**—stingy (shabbiness,n.)
  16. **small-minded**—stingy (small-mindedness,n.)
  17. **sordid**—stingy (sordidness,n.)
  18. **tight**—stingy (tightness,n.)
  19. **tightfisted**—excessively stingy (tightfistedness,n.)
  20. **uncharitable**—not generous in giving to the poor (uncharitableness,n.)
  21. **unchristian**—stingy
  22. **ungenerous**—stingy (ungenerousness,n.)

2. To Be Stingy: pinch,v.

3. Stingy Person,n.
  1. **miser**—stingy person who refuses to part with what he has an abundance of or no need for
  2. **niggard**—meanly stingy person; miser
  3. **penny-pincher**—niggard (colloq.)
  4. **Scrooge**—miser (in allusion to the character in Dickens)
  5. **skinflint**—unusually stingy person
  6. **tightwad**—extremely stingy person

4. Selfish,adj.
  1. **base**—selfish (baseness,n.)
  2. **calculating**—selfish (calculation,n.)
  3. **small**—selfish (smallness,n.)
  4. **small-minded**—selfish in attitude (small-mindedness,n.)
  5. **sordid**—meanly selfish (sordidness,n.)

5. Woman Whose Relations with Men Are Based on Selfish Gain: gold-digger,n.

228. SELF

1. Self,n.
  1. **alter ego**—one's other self
  2. **alter idem**—alter ego
  3. **ego**—the self in the sense of one's inner feelings, thoughts, needs, etc. (the Latin pronoun for "I")
  4. **id**—in psychoanalytic terminology, the primitive, uninhibited self
  5. **psyche**—the self
  6. **superego**—in psychoanalytic terminology, the self that acts as the conscience or censor

2. By Itself,adv. phrase
  1. **intrinsically**—by and of itself
  2. **per se (Latin)**—by, in, or of itself; by and of itself

3. Self-Interest,n.
  1. **autism**—absorption in the inner world of fancy with attendant neglect of the world of reality
  2. **egocentricity**—consideration of everything as relating to oneself; interest in people or objects as they affect oneself
  3. **egoism**—excessive and often obnoxious

love of, and interest in, oneself as reflected in selfishness, contempt for the
needs or desires of others, or exaltation
of one's own way of living

4. **egomania**—egoism carried to an abnormal degree
5. **egotism**—concentration on, or interest
in, self, generally evidenced by conceit,
self-praise, conversation devoted to one's
praise, etc.
6. **introspection**—self-examination, analysis, etc.; analysis of one's motives,
actions, etc. (introspect,v.)
7. **introversion**—in psychology, the turning
of the psychic energy inward; in everyday use, greater interest in the inner
world of thought and fancy than in the
outer world of people, objects, and reality
8. **narcissism, narcism**—condition of conscious or unconscious erotic gratification
from, or interest in, one's self, one's
body, one's intellectual and emotional
processes, etc.; fixation at, or regression
to, the infantile level where this is normal
9. **self-absorption**—absorption in oneself,
one's needs, desires, ambitions, etc.
10. **self-centeredness, self-centration, self-
centerment**—egocentricity
11. **self-concern**—extreme self-interest
12. **self-contemplation**—introspection
13. **self-intentness**—intensity of interest in,
and devotion to, oneself; extreme self-interest
14. **selfishness**—interest in one's gratification, advancement, etc., even at the expense of others; egocentricity; egotism
15. **self-reflection**—introspection
16. **self-seeking**—excessive and exclusive interest in one's own advancement, advantage, or pleasure
17. **subjectiveness**—excessive or moody introspection

**4. Pert. to, Descr. of, or Characteristic of,
Self-Interest**,adj. *From Sec. 3:* autistic, egocentric or ego-centered, egoistic, egomaniacal,
egotistic or egotistical, introspective, introverted, narcissistic or narcistic, self-absorbed,
self-centered, self-concerned, self-contempla-
tive, self-intent, selfish, self-reflective, self-
seeking, subjective

5. One Who Is Self-Interested,n. *From Sec.
3:* autist, egocentric, egoist, egomaniac, egotist, introvert, narcissist or narcist, self-
seeker

**6. Based on Self-Interest Rather than
Moral Right:** expedient,adj. (expedience, expediency,n.)

229. GENEROSITY

1. Generous,adj.
1. **altruistic**—having a greater regard for
the welfare and needs of others than for
one's own desires
2. **beneficent**—arising out of generosity (of
acts, motives, etc.)
3. **big**—generous
4. **bighearted**—generous
5. **bounteous**—giving, or given, freely, generously, or in large and unrestricted
quantities
6. **bountiful**—bounteous
7. **charitable**—generous in giving to the
poor; generous in forgiving
8. **extravagant**—overgenerous
9. **free**—generous (of people)
10. **freehanded**—generous in giving or spending (of people)
11. **handsome**—generous
12. **hospitable**—generous and kind to guests
or strangers
13. **lavish**—giving, or given, richly, abundantly, or without restrictions, and with

the added connotation, at times, of generous indulgence
14. **liberal**—giving, or given, generously and
without limit
15. **magnanimous**—generous in forgiving
slights, sins, transgressions, etc.
16. **munificent**—generous to an extreme,
overwhelming, or breath-taking extent
17. **openhanded**—generous
18. **openhearted**—generous
19. **philanthropic**—generous to the poor or
to those in need of charity
20. **princely**—extremely generous
21. **prodigal**—lavish
22. **profuse**—freely giving; bountiful; lavish
23. **selfless**—unselfish
24. **sumptuous**—lavish
25. **uncalculating**—unselfish
26. **ungrudging**—not reluctant to give
27. **unselfish**—generous; altruistic
28. **unsparing**—generous; liberal
29. **unstinting**—liberal

2. Generosity, n. *From Sec. 1:* altruism,
beneficence, bigness, bigheartedness, boun-
teousness or bounty, bountifulness or bounty,
charitableness or charity, extravagance, free-
handedness, handsomeness, hospitableness or
hospitality, lavishness, liberality, magnanimousness or magnanimity, munificence, open-
handedness, openheartedness, philanthropy,
princeliness, prodigality, profuseness or profusion, selflessness, sumptuousness, unselfish-
ness

3. Generous Person,n. *From Sec. 1:* altruist,
philanthropist

4. To Be Generous with,v. *From Sec. 1:*
lavish

5. Act of Generosity: benefaction,n.

230. GIVE

1. To Give,v.
1. **accompany with**—give together with
(something else)
2. **accord**—give (that which is proper or
fit); give or give formally (that which
is requested)
3. **administer**—give; dispense
4. **advance**—give beforehand
5. **afford**—give
6. **assign**—hand over (legal)
7. **award**—give by judicial procedures; give
after careful consideration; grant
8. **bequeath**—give to one who comes, or
those who come, later (child or children,
successor, posterity, etc.); give possession of after one has gone or died; hand
on; hand on through heredity
9. **bestow (on, upon)**—give; make a gift
of; give in marriage; grant
10. **cater (to)**—give whatever is requested or
desired; give means of enjoyment (to)
11. **cede**—grant; hand over
12. **communicate**—give (one's disease, etc.);
impart
13. **concede**—grant (a right or privilege)
14. **condescend**—give a favor with an air of
superiority, as if lowering oneself to another's inferior position or rank
15. **confer**—grant
16. **consign**—hand over
17. **contribute**—give along with others
18. **deal**—give
19. **delegate**—give (power, privilege, authority, duty, etc.), usually with the right to
take back
20. **deliver**—give; hand over; surrender
21. **dispense**—give; prepare and give
22. **distribute**—give (to many)
23. **dole out**—give grudgingly, in small
amounts, etc.
24. **donate**—give, without expectation of
recompense

25. **dower**—endow
26. **endow**—make a gift to (of some quality or faculty)
27. **endue**—endow
28. **grant**—give formally; give in response to a request, prayer, etc.
29. **hand**—give with, or as if with, the hands
30. **hand down, pass on**—give (to one's successor, son, next in line, etc.); transmit
31. **hand on, pass along, pass on**—give with, or as if with, the hands (that which one has received from another)
32. **hand over**—give (to another that which one has or has control over); surrender
33. **impart**—give (a quality); give from one's store of
34. **inflict (on)**—give (something unpleasant, such as pain, punishment, disease, troubles, etc.)
35. **lavish (on, upon)**—give generously or recklessly
36. **leave**—give possession of after one has gone or died
37. **pass**—hand
38. **ply**—keep giving
39. **pool**—contribute to a collection for mutual use or advantage
40. **present**—give; make a gift of; give formally or ceremoniously
41. **relay**—give (to someone else) that which one has received; hand on
42. **render**—give
43. **reward**—give to, in return for services, ability, etc.
44. **shower**—give, or give to, liberally or generously
45. **subsidize**—make gifts of financial aid to
46. **supply**—give (what is needed)
47. **surrender**—give into the power or possession (of another), often on demand
48. **transfer**—hand over
49. **transmit**—hand on; hand on through heredity (to one's descendants); leave (to posterity)
50. **vest (in)**—give into the possession or power (of); endow
51. **vouchsafe**—bestow; grant (a right or privilege); grant with an air of superiority
52. **yield**—give; grant

2. A Giving,n. *From Sec. 1:* accompaniment, accordance, administration, advance, assignment or assignation, bequeathal or bequeathment, bestowal, cession, communication, concession, condescension or condescendence, conferment or conferral, consignment or consignation, contribution, deal, delegation, delivery, dispensation, distribution, donation, endowment, infliction, lavishment, presentation, rendition, subsidization, surrender; transfer, transferrence, or transferral; transmission or transmittal, vouchsafement; *Also:*
1. **almsgiving**—a giving to the poor
2. **charity**—a giving to the poor
3. **largess, largesse**—a very generous giving
4. **philanthropy**—a giving of money for human benefit or to the poor

3. Giver,n. *From Sec. 1:* accorder, administrator or, fem., administratress, assigner or assignor, awarder, bequeather, bestower, caterer, ceder, conferrer, consigner or consignor, contributor, dealer, delegator, deliverer, dispenser or, fem., dispensatrix, distributor; donor, donator, or, fem., donatress; grantor, imparter, passer, relayer, renderer, rewarder, subsidizer, supplier, transferrer or transferror, transmitter; *From Sec. 2:* almsgiver, philanthropist

4. One to Whom Is Given,n. *From Sec. 1:* assign or assignee; cessionary (from *cede*), consignee; donee, transferee

5. Descr. of, or Pert. to, Giving,adj. *From Sec. 1:* concessive or concessional, condescensive; contributive, contributory or contribu-

tional; distributive or distributional, inflictive, lavish, presentational, transferential; transmissive, transmissory, or transmissional; *From Sec. 2:* philanthropic

6. That Which Is Given; A Gift,n. *From Sec. 1:* advance, award, bequest, concession, consignment, contribution, delivery, dispensation, distribution, dole, donation or donative, dower, endowment, grant, infliction, present or presentation, reward, subsidy, vouchsafement; *From Sec. 2:* alms, charity, largess or largesse; *Also:*
1. **amatorio (Italian)**—gift that shows love
2. **benefice**—something good or of value given to a church official, such as living quarters, etc.
3. **boon**—gift
4. **bounty**—that which is given generously
5. **douceur (French)**—gift for service either already rendered or expected to be rendered
6. **gratuity**—gift; that which is given in return for a favor or service; that which is given freely and without expectation of return
7. **handsel**—gift made on some special occasion connected with starting a new venture, moving into new quarters, etc. (Such a gift indicates the donor's hopes for the recipient's good fortune.)
8. **keepsake**—gift that is an indication of friendship, and intended to be kept by the recipient as a reminder of the giver
9. **lagniappe**—gift of little value made to a customer
10. **oblation**—gift to a church
11. **offering**—gift to a church
12. **relief**—public money or assistance given to people without resources
13. **sop**—conciliatory gift
14. **sportula**—gift; generous gift
15. **subvention**—gift or grant from the government or from a philanthropic agency
16. **token**—slight gift to be valued more as a symbol than for its intrinsic value; keepsake
17. **tribute**—gift as a token of thanks, respect, loyalty, etc.
18. **widow's mite**—small contribution that is as much as one can afford but that one gives gladly

7. To Give for Safekeeping,v.
1. **commend**—give over for safekeeping
2. **commit**—give in trust or for safekeeping (commitment,n.)
3. **confide**—give for safekeeping; entrust
4. **consign**—entrust (consignment,n.)
5. **deliver**—commit (delivery,n.)
6. **entrust**—give for protection or safekeeping; give over in trust
7. **intrust**—entrust

8. To Give a Part or Share of,v.
1. **communicate**—give (to another) so he may have a share of (a feeling, disease, attitude, etc.); impart (communication, n.)
2. **impart**—give a part or share of (what one has)
3. **share (with)**—give part of (to another or others)

231. DISTRIBUTION

1. To Distribute; To Give in Shares,v.
1. **allocate**—distribute in shares or parts; apportion
2. **allot**—distribute in shares or parts
3. **allow**—assign
4. **apportion**—distribute by parts; divide and distribute by shares
5. **assign**—give as a share or portion; apportion
6. **award**—give as a share after careful consideration

7. **bootleg**—distribute (illegal or forbidden commodities)
8. **deal**—distribute; give shares
9. **disburse**—distribute (funds, money, salaries, etc.)
10. **dispense**—distribute; give out in portions or shares
11. **divide**—distribute by parts or shares
12. **dole out**—distribute sparingly, in small quantities, or unwillingly
13. **mete out**—distribute by shares
14. **parcel out**—distribute share by share
15. **partition**—take apart and distribute
16. **proportion**—distribute by shares
17. **prorate**—distribute proportionally
18. **ration**—distribute according to each one's share
19. **share (with)**—distribute part or parts (to others)
20. **spread**—distribute

2. Distribution,n. *From Sec. 1:* allocation, allotment, allowance, apportionment, assignment or assignation, deal, disbursement, dispensation, division, partition or partitionment, proration, spread

3. That Which Is Distributed,n. *From Sec. 1:* allocation, allotment, allowance, portion, assignment or assignation, award, disbursement, dispensation, division, dole, ration, share

232. CHARITY

1. To Give in, or to, Charity,v.
1. **dole**—give or distribute in charity
2. **donate**—give (to charity)

2. A Giving in, or to, Charity,n. *From Sec. 1:* dole, donation; *Also:*
1. **almsgiving**—a giving to charity
2. **philanthropy**—a giving to charity (philanthropic,adj.)

3. Giver to Charity,n. *From Sec. 1:* donor or donator; *From Sec. 2:* almsgiver, philanthropist; *Also:*
1. **almoner**—one who has official charge of distributing charity for another
2. **benefactor**—one who donates to charity (benefactress,fem.)

4. Charity; Charitable Gift,n. *From Sec. 1:* dole, donation; *From Sec. 2:* alms, philanthropies; *From Sec. 3:* benefaction; *Also:* 1. **oblation**—gift to charity

5. Pert. or Relating to Charity: eleemosynary,adj.

6. Place Where Charity Is Given,n.
1. **almonry**—place where alms are distributed
2. **almshouse**—place for recipients of charity
3. **beadhouse, bedehouse**—almshouse in which inmates pray for their supporters
4. **poorhouse**—almshouse

7. One Who Receives, or Lives on, Charity, n.
1. **almsman, almswoman**—receiver of charity
2. **mendicant**—one who lives on charity (mendicancy, mendicity,n.)
3. **pauper**—person so poor that he must live on charity (pauperism,n.)

8. Act of Charity: beneficence, benevolence, n.

233. SUPPLY

1. To Supply,v.
1. **accommodate**—supply with sleeping quarters and food; supply room for comfortably and conveniently; supply with what is wanted or wished for

2. **accouter**—supply with clothing, or with military clothing
3. **administer**—supply
4. **afford**—provide
5. **cater**—supply provisions
6. **dower**—supply with a dowry
7. **endow**—supply with an income for support
8. **endue**—supply (with a quality or power)
9. **equip**—supply with what is necessary for use, action, etc.
10. **forage**—supply (horses, cattle, etc.) with food
11. **furnish**—supply
12. **maintain**—sustain
13. **outfit**—equip
14. **ply**—keep supplying
15. **provender**—forage
16. **provide**—supply for use; supply what is needed
17. **provision**—supply with food; victual
18. **purvey**—supply; provide
19. **render**—supply
20. **replenish**—supply again that which has been used up
21. **serve**—supply; supply food, drink, services, commodities, etc., to
22. **skimp**—supply in a lesser amount than needed or wanted
23. **sustain**—supply with food and similar needs
24. **victual**—supply; supply (an army) with food, provisions, etc.

2. A Supplying,n. *From Sec. 1:* accommodation, accouterment, administration, endowment, equipment, maintenance, provision, purveyance, rendition, replenishment, service, sustainment or sustention

3. That Which Is Supplied,n. *From Sec. 1:* accommodations, accouterments, endowment, equipment, maintenance, outfit, provision or provisions, service, sustenance, victuals; *Also:* 1. **manna**—anything unexpectedly provided

4. Supplier,n. *From Sec. 1:* adminstrator, caterer, furnisher, maintainer, provider, provisioner, purveyor or purveyancer, renderer, server, sustainer, victualer; *Also:*
1. **chandler**—one who sells provisions, groceries, etc.
2. **quartermaster**—person who supplies troops with clothing, food, etc.
3. **sutler**—one who follows an army and sells provisions, food, liquor, etc., to the troops
4. **vivandière**—woman who follows an army and sells the troops food, provisions, and liquor (most generally the French Army in previous times in history)

5. Science of Military Supply and Transportation: logistics,n.

234. GIVE BACK

1. To Give Back,v.
1. **rebate**—give back (a payment or part of a payment)
2. **reciprocate**—give back the like of that which is received
3. **render**—give back
4. **restore**—give back
5. **return**—give back

2. A Giving Back,n. *From Sec. 1:* rebate, reciprocation, rendition, restoration, return; *Also:* 1. **restitution**—a giving back to the rightful owner

3. That Which Is Given Back,n. *From Sec. 1:* rebate, return

4. Tending or Acting to Give Back,adj. *From Sec. 1:* reciprocal, restorative (reciprocity,n.); *From Sec. 2:* restitutive or restitutory

5. To Give in Return: reciprocate, render, requite, return,v. (reciprocation, rendition, requital or requitement, return,n.)

235. GIVE FORTH

1. To Give Forth; To Give Off,v.
1. **afford**—give forth
2. **beam**—emit
3. **belch**—give off or forth in gushes or spasms
4. **disgorge**—vomit (contents)
5. **emit**—give off; give forth
6. **exude**—give forth; give forth from the pores or openings
7. **radiate**—emit
8. **secrete**—give off (of cells, glands, or organs of the body)
9. **shed**—give off
10. **spew**—vomit
11. **vomit**—give forth in great quantities
12. **yield**—give forth

2. A Giving Forth or Off,n. *From Sec. 1:* emission, exudation, radiation, secretion

3. That Which Is Given Forth or Off,n. *From Sec. 1:* beam, belch, emission, exudation or exudate, radiation, secretion, vomit, yield

4. Descr. of Giving Forth or Off,adj. *From Sec. 1:* emissive, exudative; radiant, radiative, or radiational; secretive, secretory, or secretionary

236. GIVE UP

1. To Give (Something or Someone) Up,v.
1. **abandon**—give up without intending to reclaim at any future time; give up to the care or charge of someone else; give (oneself) up
2. **abdicate**—give up an office or position of trust, power, or responsibility
3. **abjure**—give up solemnly; solemnly give up claim or right to
4. **abnegate**—give up; renounce
5. **apostatize**—give up one's principles or faith, the cause one has supported, one's religion, political party, etc.
6. **betray**—deliver (someone or something) to the enemy through deceit, fraud, or treachery
7. **cede**—give up (rights or property to another)
8. **deliver**—give up; give up completely
9. **desert**—give up to another's care, mercy, or charge, esp. when one is needed
10. **disgorge**—give up by discharging from the throat or through the mouth; give up unwillingly, through coercion, pressure, violence, etc.
11. **disown**—give up ownership of or claim to
12. **divorce oneself from**—give up official connection with
13. **extradite**—give up (a prisoner) to the legal authority of another state or territorial division
14. **forfeit**—give up (something, some privilege, etc.) as a penalty for one's crime or error
15. **forsake**—give up (what one has treasured or believed in); desert
16. **forswear**—abjure
17. **immolate**—sacrifice; sacrifice to the gods, by killing
18. **quit**—give up; surrender
19. **recant**—give up one's belief or what one has professed or taught
20. **release**—give up
21. **relinquish**—give up all claim to
22. **renegade**—apostatize
23. **renege**—desert; renounce
24. **renounce**—give up; give up (rights, privileges, etc.); abandon

25. **resign**—give up office or position
26. **retire (from)**—give up an occupation, activity, etc.
27. **sacrifice**—give up in the expectation of getting something better or some gain or advantage
28. **submit**—give oneself up to the power or authority of another
29. **surrender**—give up completely
30. **tergiversate**—give up one's party, cause, affiliation, faith, etc., and go over to another or opposing one
31. **vacate**—give up occupancy of
32. **waive**—give up; give up a right to
33. **yield**—give up; give up one's place; surrender

2. A Giving Up,n. *From Sec. 1:* abandonment, abdication, abjuration or abjurement, abnegation, apostasy or apostatism, betrayal or betrayment, cession, delivery, desertion, disownment, divorce, extradition, forfeiture, immolation, recantation, release, relinquishment, renege, renunciation or renouncement, resignation, retirement, sacrifice, submission or submittal, surrender, tergiversation, vacation, waiver; *Also:*
1. **demission**—a giving up; abdication
2. **dereliction**—a giving up or abandoning
3. **hecatomb**—sacrifice of a great number of victims
4. **self-sacrifice**—sacrifice of oneself, one's interests, advantage, etc., for the good of another or as a duty

3. One Who Gives Up,n. *From Sec. 1:* abandoner, abdicator, abjurer, abnegator, apostate, betrayer, ceder, deserter, disgorger, disowner, forsaker, immolator, recanter, relinquisher, renegade, reneger, renouncer or renunciator, submitter, tergiversator or tergiversant, yielder; *From Sec. 2:* self-sacrificer; *Also:*
1. **martyr**—one who sacrifices everything, including even his life, in defense of a (usually unpopular or unacceptable) principle or religious belief
2. **protomartyr**—the first or earliest martyr

4. Descr. of Giving Up,adj. *From Sec. 1:* abjuratory, abnegative; apostate, apostatic, or apostatical; renegade, renunciatory, sacrificial, submissive, tergiversatory or tergiversant; *From Sec. 2:* self-sacrificial

5. One Who or That Which Is or Can Be Given Up,n. *From Sec. 1:* forfeit, immolation, sacrifice; *From Sec. 2:* derelict; *Also:*
1. **gambit**—apparent sacrifice; in chess, sacrifice calculated to gain an advantage
2. **pawn**—unimportant person or factor capable of being sacrificed for an advantage
3. **victim**—one who or that which is sacrificed

6. Given Up,adj. *From Sec. 1:* abandoned, deserted, forfeit or forfeited, forsaken, surrendered, vacant or vacated; *From Sec. 2:* derelict; *Also:*
1. **forlorn**—abandoned; deserted
2. **lorn**—forsaken

7. State of Being Abandoned: dereliction,n.

8. That to Which One Is Sacrificed,n.
1. **juggernaut**—cause or thing to which a person is blindly devoted and to which he is, finally, ruthlessly sacrificed (after the idol of the Hindu god, Krishna; devotees threw themselves under the rolling cart in which Krishna was exhibited and were crushed to death)
2. **moloch**—person or thing that demands the sacrifice of one's life (after a Semitic deity)

9. Worth Sacrificing to the Enemy: expendable,adj.

237. OFFER

1. To Offer,v.
1. **adduce**—offer as proof, instance, or evidence; bring forward as an argument
2. **advance**—bring forward as an offer or proposal
3. **bid**—offer as a price
4. **ply**—keep offering
5. **pose**—offer for discussion
6. **premise**—offer as an explanation
7. **present**—offer
8. **proffer**—offer for acceptance
9. **propose**—offer for consideration; offer marriage
10. **propound**—offer for consideration
11. **render**—offer for approval, consideration, etc.
12. **submit**—offer; offer for the judgment or conclusions of another; tender
13. **suggest**—offer for consideration
14. **tender**—offer formally or officially
15. **volunteer**—make an offer out of one's free choice or will; offer one's services

2. An Offering; An Offer,n. *From Sec. 1:* advancement, bid, presentation, proffer, proposal or proposition, propoundment, rendition, submission or submittal, suggestion, tender; *Also:*
1. **beau geste (French)**—generous offer
2. **oblation**—religious offering
3. **overture**—offer; proposal

3. One Who Offers,n. *From Sec. 1:* bidder, proponent or proposer, submitter, suggester, tenderer, volunteer

4. Too Ready to Offer Services, Advice, etc.: officious,adj. (officiousness,n.)

238. SUGGESTION

1. To Suggest,v.
1. **advance**—suggest
2. **advise**—use statements to make suggestions or recommendations
3. **broach**—suggest; suggest for discussion
4. **commend**—recommend
5. **emend**—suggest changes for correcting errors in (esp. in written material)
6. **exhort**—suggest with great emphasis or earnestness
7. **imply**—suggest
8. **insinuate**—suggest indirectly (often something insulting, derogatory, unpleasant, etc.)
9. **intimate**—suggest indirectly
10. **make advances**—approach personally with suggestions for settling an argument or with any other suggestions
11. **propose**—suggest for consideration
12. **recommend**—suggest as good, praiseworthy, or favorable
13. **signify**—suggest
14. **symbolize**—suggest something else by virtue of conventional association
15. **tout**—recommend with great praise (colloq.)

2. A Suggesting; Suggestion,n. *From Sec. 1:* advancement, advice, commendation, emendation, exhortation, implication, insinuation, intimation, proposal or proposition, recommendation, signification, symbolization or symbol; *Also:*
1. **innuendo**—derogatory suggestion; insinuation
2. **insinuendo**—combination of innuendo and insinuation
3. **overtone**—in language, that which suggests a wealth of associations, implications, or relationships
4. **testimonial**—paper or statement recommending someone or something as qualified, valuable, etc.; recommendation

5. **thesis**—proposition advanced subject to debate or discussion
6. **tip**—suggestion

3. Suggester,n. *From Sec. 1:* adviser or advisor, exhorter, insinuator, intimater, proponent or proposer, recommender, symbolist; *From Sec. 2:* tipster (on race horses, stocks, etc.); *Also:* 1. **snide**—one who slyly suggests but does not directly say (usually something derogatory or unpleasant)

4. Suggestive,adj. *From Sec. 1:* advisory, commendatory, emendatory, exhortatory, implicative, insinuative or insinuatory, recommendatory, significant, symbolic (significance, symbolism,n.); *From Sec. 3:* snide; *Also:*
1. **pregnant**—suggestive—said of language, words, etc. (pregnancy,n.)
2. **redolent (of)**—suggestive (of); suggestive of an odor (redolence, redolency,n.)

5. Suggested,adj. *From Sec. 1:* implied or implicit, proposed, recommended, symbolized; *Also:*
1. **constructive**—implied
2. **tacit**—implied, but not expressed in words

6. Art of Suggesting by Symbols: symbology, symbolism,n. (symbologist,n. symbological,adj.)

7. Self-Suggestion,n.
1. **autosuggestion**—suggestion to and by oneself
2. **Couéism**—therapeutic system of self-suggestion leading, supposedly, to increased health

239. HINT

1. To Hint; To Hint at; To Give a Hint to, v.
1. **cue**—give a hint or hints to (someone) as to the proper words, actions, etc., esp. in a play
2. **imply**—hint; hint at
3. **insinuate**—imply (often something insulting, derogatory, unpleasant, etc.)
4. **intimate**—hint
5. **prompt**—give hints to (someone) as to the proper actions or words to be used
6. **suggest**—hint

2. A Hinting; Hint,n. *From Sec. 1:* cue, implication, insinuation, intimation, prompt, suggestion; *Also:*
1. **inkling**—slight hint
2. **innuendo**—derogatory hint
3. **insinuendo**—combination of innuendo and insinuation
4. **suspicion**—hint; inkling
5. **tag**—cue to the next actor to speak
6. **tip**—useful hint
7. **wrinkle**—useful hint

3. Hinter,n. *From Sec. 1:* insinuator, intimater, prompter, suggester

240. GET

1. To Get; To Receive; To Gain, etc.,v.
1. **accede to**—attain (an office)
2. **accept**—receive willingly; receive with favor
3. **accomplish**—achieve
4. **achieve**—get by effort or by trying for
5. **acquire**—get; gain
6. **attain**—get by effort
7. **bag**—get possession of by stealth or ruse
8. **capture**—get by skill, cleverness, or effort; get possession of
9. **coax**—manage to get by gentle and persuasive words
10. **collect**—get payment of (a debt); get from a number of sources
11. **compel**—get by force

12. **conquer**—get by overcoming obstacles or resistance
13. **contract**—get (a disease)
14. **corral**—get and keep
15. **derive**—obtain from the origin or source; obtain from some source
16. **exact**—get by demanding
17. **fetch**—go for, get, and bring back
18. **harvest**—get as the results of one's efforts
19. **impetrate**—get through entreaty
20. **inherit**—receive from an ancestor, previous holder of an office, etc.; receive by will
21. **obtain**—get; get possession of; get by effort
22. **partake (of)**—get a share or part (of)
23. **procure**—get; gain; obtain
24. **profit**—gain; derive an amount of gain over expenditure
25. **pry**—get (something) only after great effort or difficulty
26. **realize**—get actual possession of; get as the result of trying or planning; gain
27. **reap**—get as the result of effort
28. **recruit**—get (new members) for an organization; get as a new member or as new members for an organization
29. **relay**—receive (from someone) and give (to someone else)
30. **secure**—get; go and get; go out and get
31. **share**—get a portion of
32. **steal**—get by charm; get by trickery, force, dishonesty, etc.
33. **strike**—get by figuring (as in *strike a total*)
34. **wangle**—get by trickery, deception, indirection, persuasion, scheming, etc.
35. **wheedle**—get by soft words, flattery, coaxing, etc.
36. **win**—get; get through effort or against competition
37. **worm**—get by secret and persistent methods, or by slow, indirect, devious, and insidious methods
38. **wring**—get by twisting and squeezing, literally or figuratively; get by force, persuasion, etc.

2. A Getting, Receiving, Gaining, etc.,n. *From Sec. 1:* accession (to), acceptance, accomplishment, achievement, acquirement or acquisition, attainment, capture, collection, conquest, contraction, derivation, exaction, impetration, inheritance, procurement, realization, recruitment, relay; *Also:* 1. receipt, reception, recipience—act of receiving

3. That Which Is Gotten, Received, Gained, etc.,n. *From Sec. 1:* accomplishment, achievement, acquirement or acquisition, attainment, capture, collection, conquest, derivative, harvest, inheritance, profit, share; *From Sec. 2:* receipts; *Also:* 1. windfall—unexpected gain or profit

4. Receiver; Gainer, etc.,n. *From Sec. 1:* acceptor, accomplisher, achiever, acquirer, attainer, captor or capturer, collector, conqueror, harvester, inheritor, obtainer, partaker, procurer, profiter, reaper, recruiter, sharer, winner; *Also:*
1. **beneficiary**—one who is on the receiving end of a good deed; one who receives money or gifts by a will, gets the proceeds of an insurance policy, or is the recipient of a gift, favor, or any other token of generosity
2. **fence**—receiver of stolen goods for purposes of illicit resale
3. **heir**—one who inherits (heiress,fem.)
4. **receptionist**—one who is employed to receive visitors, callers, customers, clients, etc., in a business or professional office
5. **recipient**—one who receives

5. Able to Be Gotten, Received, Gained, etc.,adj. *From Sec. 1:* achievable, acquirable,

attainable, collectible, contractible, inheritable, obtainable, procurable, realizable, securable; *Also:*
1. **accessible**—capable of being obtained
2. **available**—capable of being gotten
3. **receptible**—able to be received

6. Acquired from the Outside, Rather than Being a Natural Part of: adventitious,adj.

7. Acquired by Wickedness, Evil Means, Trickery, etc.: ill-gotten,adj.

8. Obtained by Corrupt Purchase: venal, adj.

9. Manner or Ceremony of Receiving Visitors or Guests: reception,n.

10. That Which Acknowledges Receiving,n.
1. **acquittance**—receipt in full
2. **receipt**—paper acknowledging that something has been received
3. **voucher**—receipt in proof of payment

11. To Try to Get,v.
1. **contest**—try to get (contestation,n. contester, contestant,n.)
2. **court**—try to get; act in such a way as to get; woo
3. **solicit**—try to get (solicitation,n. solicitor,n.)
4. **sue for**—try to get (suit,n. suitor,n.)
5. **woo**—try to get; try to get (someone's favor or love); try to get the love or affection of, often with a view to marriage (wooer,n.)

12. To Get Back: recapture, recoup, recover, recuperate, regain, repossess, retake, retrieve, v. (recapture, recoupment, recovery, recuperation, repossession, retrieval or retrievement, n. recuperative or recuperatory,adj.)

13. To Get Back (Property) by Repaying the Money Borrowed against It: redeem,v. (redemption,n. redemptive,adj.)

14. To Get Back One's Strength, Vigor, Losses, Previous Position, etc.: recuperate,v. (recuperation,n. recuperative, recuperatory, adj.)

241. INHERITANCE

1. Act or Process of Inheriting: inheritance, n.

2. Joint Inheritance: coinheritance, coparcenary, coparceny, parcenary,n.

3. System of Inheritance,n.
1. **matriheritage**—system of inheritance from the mother, property or title descending only in the female line (matriherital,adj.)
2. **primogeniture**—system of inheritance by which the estate goes to the eldest son
3. **ultimogeniture**—system of inheritance by which the estate goes to the youngest son

4. An Inheritance, i.e., That Which Is Inherited,n.
1. **birthright**—property inherited, or to be inherited, by reason of one's first birth in a family
2. **coinheritance**—shared inheritance
3. **estate**—property of a person that is inherited, or is to be inherited, after his death
4. **heirloom**—some personal possession owned for several generations by a family and passed down by successive inheritance
5. **hereditament**—property that may be inherited (legal)
6. **heredity**—physical or mental characteristics that are inherited from the parents or ancestors
7. **heritage, heritance**—that which one in-

herits, either biologically or through a will
8. **legacy**—inheritance; inheritance received through a will; that which is inherited from an ancestor or ancestors, from a predecessor, or from the past or past times, and in the form either of tangible possessions or of qualities, feelings, or other abstractions (legatary,adj.)
9. **patrimony**—property or money inherited, or to be inherited, from one's father

5. Inheritor,n.
1. **beneficiary**—one who receives the proceeds of a life insurance policy on the death of the insured
2. **coheir**—one who shares an inheritance (coheiress,fem.n. coheirship,n.)
3. **coparcener**—coheir
4. **crown prince**—one expected to inherit or gain a position after the death or retirement of the one presently holding it
5. **heir**—one who inherits money, property, etc., from another; one entitled to, or who is going to, receive such inheritance (heiress,fem.n. heirdom, heirship,n.)
6. **legatee**—one who receives an inheritance, whether through a will or otherwise
7. **parcener**—coheir

6. Right of Inheriting: heirship,n.

7. Privileges of an Heir: heirship,n.

8. Pert. to, or Derived from, Inheritance: hereditary,adj.

9. Existing by Hereditary Right or Privilege: legitimate,adj.

10. Capable of Being Inherited, by either Biological or Legal Inheritance: heritable, inheritable,adj.

11. Person or Institution Appointed by a Court to Settle an Estate: administrator (masc.), administratrix (fem.),n.

242. LEGAL WILL

1. Legal Term for a Will Properly Signed, Witnessed, etc.: testament,n. (testamentary, adj.)

2. A Will (or a Clause in a Will) Leaving Real Property: devise,n.

3. An Addition to a Will, Changing Some of Its Provisions: codicil,n. (codiciliary,adj.)

4. To Give by Will,v.
1. **bequeath, bequest**—give by will (usually, money, personal property, etc., rather than real estate)
2. **devise**—give by will (usually real estate)
3. **leave**—give by will
4. **legate**—bequeath

5. A Giving by Will,n. *From Sec. 4:* bequeathal, bequeathment, or bequest; devisal or devise

6. One Who Gives by Will,n. *From Sec. 4:* bequeather, devisor or deviser, legator (legatorial,adj.); *Also:* 1. **testator** or, fem., **testatrix**—one who leaves a will

7. One Who Receives by Will,n. *From Sec. 4:* devisee, legatee

8. That Which Is Left by a Will,n. *From Sec. 4:* bequest, devise, legacy (legatary,adj.)

9. Having Left a Will: testate,adj. (testacy, n.)

10. Not Having Left a Will: intestate,adj. (intestacy,n.)

11. Descr. of a Will Made Orally Rather than in Writing: nuncupative,adj.

12. To Take Legal or Official Steps to File and Prove Genuine the Will of a Person Who Is Deceased: probate,v.

13. Person Legally Appointed by the Signer of a Will to Carry Out the Provision of the Will: executor (masc.), executrix (fem.),n.

14. To Cut Out of One's Will; To Cut Off from Inheriting One's Money or Property: disinherit, disherit,v. (disinheritance,n.)

243. HEREDITY

1. Science or Study of Heredity,n.
1. **dysgenics**—study of the deterioration of the heredity of a race (dysgenic,adj.)
2. **eugenics**—science dealing with the production of human beings with improved heredity (eugenic, adj. eugenist,n.)
3. **genesiology**—science of heredity (genesiologist,n. genesiological,adj.)
4. **genetics**—the science of the transmission of hereditary characteristics from parents to offspring (geneticist,n. genetic, adj.)

2. Theories of Heredity,n.
1. **blastogenesis**—theory that characteristics are transmitted through the germ plasm (blastogenetic,adj.)
2. **Mendelian theory**—Gregor Mendel's theory of heredity (Mendelian,adj.)
3. **predeterminism**—belief that an individual's development is determined by heredity (predeterministic,adj.)

3. Beneficial to Heredity: eugenic,adj.

4. Detrimental to Heredity: dysgenic,adj.

5. Certain Heredity Factors,n.
1. **allelomorph**—either of two contrasting Mendelian characteristics (a dominant or a recessive) in heredity; the gene that transmits this characteristic (allelomorphic,adj.)
2. **chromosome**—special body, found within the cells of a living organism, that contains the genes (chromosomal,adj.)
3. **dominant character, characteristic, or trait**—the one of two contrasting factors (as tallness and shortness, brown eyes and blue eyes, etc.) that predominates over the other in its occurrence in offspring (dominant,adj.)
4. **gene**—theoretical particle of the germ cell that transmits hereditary factors from parent to offspring (genic, genetic, adj.)
5. **recessive character, characteristic, or trait**—hereditary factor in the chromosomes that does not manifest itself in the individual but is nevertheless present and latent—for example, a person with brown eyes may have a blue-eyed recessive characteristic, inherited from an ancestor, which when properly paired off with a blue-eyed characteristic in a mate may appear in a certain proportion of his descendants (recessive,adj.)
6. **x-chromosome**—chromosome that determines femaleness in heredity; if two are present (one from each parent), the egg develops into a female infant
7. **y-chromosome**—chromosome that determines maleness in heredity; a fertilized egg need contain but one such to develop into a male infant

6. Hereditary Quality or Character: strain, n.

244. TRAP

1. To Trap; To Catch,v.
1. **ambuscade**—ambush
2. **ambush**—trap; lie in wait to trap (an enemy) by surprise

3. **circumvent**—catch in, or as if in, a trap
4. **decoy**—trap; lead into a trap
5. **enmesh**—catch, figuratively, as if in a net or mesh
6. **ensnare**—trap; catch in, or as if in, a trap
7. **entangle**—catch in an involved, difficult, confusing, or tangled-up situation; trap into such a situation
8. **entrap**—catch in, or as if in, a trap
9. **hook**—catch by trickery; catch (fish); catch hold of; catch on (an animal's) horns
10. **insnare**—ensnare
11. **lasso**—catch (animals, fleeing criminals, etc.) with a rope
12. **mesh**—catch or entangle in, or as if in, a net
13. **net**—trap or catch (figuratively or literally)
14. **seine**—catch fish in a net; use a net to catch fish
15. **snag**—catch on a projection
16. **snare**—trap; catch in a trap
17. **surprise**—catch unprepared
18. **tangle**—catch and imprison in a snare or net
19. **trammel**—entangle
20. **trick**—trap (into saying or doing that which one does not wish to say or do)
21. **trip up**—catch in an error or untruth

2. A Catching or Trapping,n. *From Sec. 1:* circumvention, ensnarement, entanglement, entrapment, insnarement, tanglement

3. A Trap,n. *From Sec. 1:* ambuscade, ambush, decoy, hook, meshes, net, snare, trick; *Also:*
1. **booby trap**—trap to catch the unsuspecting; that which looks innocent or harmless but turns out to be dangerous or ensnaring
2. **catch**—trap
3. **noose**—trap
4. **pitfall**—trap
5. **quicksand**—trap (i.e., something as treacherous and overwhelming as quicksand)
6. **toils**—trap

4. That Which Catches,n. *From Sec. 1:* hook, lasso, net, seine, snag, trammel

5. Acting or Tending to Trap or Catch,adj. *From Sec. 1:* enmeshing, ensnaring, entangling, entrapping, tangling, tricky; *Also:*
1. **captious**—apt to trap (captiousness,n.)
2. **catchy**—tending to catch (someone) in a trap
3. **cobwebby**—entangling, like a spider's web
4. **insidious**—full of traps for the unwary (insidiousness,n.)

6. One Who Traps Animals as a Business: trapper,n.

7. Situation in Which One Is Caught,n.
1. **morass**—unpleasant circumstance or condition from which it is hard to extricate oneself
2. **quagmire**—situation from which it is hard to extricate oneself
3. **rattrap**—situation in which one is hopelessly caught

8. Hard to Catch,adj.
1. **elusive**—hard to catch or get hold of (elusiveness,n.)
2. **subtile**—subtle (subtileness, subtility,n.)
3. **subtle**—elusive; elusive and delicate (subtlety, subtleness,n.)
4. **tenuous**—elusive; elusive and delicate (tenuousness, tenuity,n.)

9. To Catch Up to or with: gain on, gain upon, overhaul, overtake,v.

245. ACCEPTANCE

1. To Accept,v.
1. **abide**—accept the consequences of
2. **abide by**—accept; accept and follow
3. **accredit**—accept and believe; accept as coming up to a standard
4. **admit**—accept as true or valid
5. **adopt**—accept formally
6. **approve**—accept as satisfactory
7. **assume**—accept as one's own; accept for oneself; suppose
8. **initiate**—accept into a club, society, etc., with ceremony and ritual
9. **lap up**—accept eagerly
10. **receive**—accept
11. **reconcile oneself to**—resign oneself to
12. **resign oneself to**—accept patiently, quietly, or without protest or complaint
13. **shoulder**—accept (a burden or as a burden)
14. **suppose**—accept as true, probable, or possible
15. **swallow**—accept with little investigation or demand for proof
16. **take**—accept
17. **tolerate**—accept (practices, beliefs, customs, behavior, attitudes, etc., that are quite different from, or even opposed to, one's own, and without repugnance or hostility)
18. **welcome**—accept gladly or freely

2. Acceptance,n. *From Sec. 1:* accreditation, admission, adoption, approval, assumption, initiation; reception, recipience, or recipiency; reconcilement or reconciliation, resignation or resignedness, supposition, toleration or tolerance

3. That Which Is Accepted,n. *From Sec. 1:* assumption, supposition; *Also:* 1. **standard**—that which is generally accepted

4. Descr. of Accepting,adj. *From Sec. 1:* admissive, adoptive, assumptive, initiatory, receptive or recipient, tolerant

5. Acceptable,adj. *From Sec. 1:* admissible, adoptable, receptible, tolerable; *Also:*
1. **palatable**—acceptable
2. **standard**—acceptable; acceptable as an authority

6. Generally Accepted: current, popular, standard,adj. (currency, popularity,n.)

7. No Longer Accepted: outmoded, passé, adj.

8. Ready or Willing to Accept,adj.
1. **broad-minded**—tolerant (broad-mindedness,n.)
2. **open-minded**—receptive to new ideas or new arguments (open-mindedness,n.)
3. **receptive, recipient**—ready or willing to accept suggestions, ideas, etc. (receptiveness or receptivity, recipience or recipiency,n.)
4. **susceptive**—receptive (susceptiveness, susceptivity,n.)
5. **tolerant**—willing to accept, without hostility, practices or beliefs different from one's own (tolerance,n.)

9. That Which Is Bitter to Accept: gall,n.

246. TOLERANCE

1. To Bear; To Bear Up under,v.
1. **abide**—bear with patience; tolerate
2. **bide**—bear; bear up under; bear patiently or without anger
3. **brook**—bear, bear up under, or put up with (usually in the negative or interrogative)
4. **endure**—bear without complaint; bear up under; put up with
5. **put up with**—bear without anger, impatience, suffering, or resentment

6. **resist**—withstand
7. **stomach**—bear; bear without showing one's dislike; put up with
8. **suffer**—resign oneself to enduring or tolerating; be forced to endure or tolerate; put up with
9. **support**—endure, usually in silence
10. **sustain**—bear; bear up under; endure
11. **swallow**—put up with
12. **tolerate**—bear; bear up under; bear the effects of (a drug, medication, etc.) without becoming ill or poisoned; endure
13. **undergo**—endure
14. **weather**—bear up under or endure, and come through successful or uninjured
15. **wink at**—endure (something bad)
16. **withstand**—bear up under without injury

2. A Bearing; A Bearing Up,n. *From Sec. 1:* endurance, resistance, sufferance, support, sustainment, toleration or tolerance; *Also:*
1. **forbearance**—a bearing without complaint or impatience
2. **fortitude**—a bearing of hardship, suffering, or pain without complaint or impatience

3. Descr. of Bearing or Bearing Up under, adj. *From Sec. 1:* abiding, enduring, resistant or resistive, suffering, tolerant (resistivity, tolerance, toleration,n.); *From Sec. 2:* forbearing, fortitudinous; *Also:*
1. **longanimous**—tending to bear suffering with patience (longanimity,n.)
2. **long-suffering**—enduring anything unpleasant for a long time with great patience
3. **meek**—enduring without complaint (meekness,n.)
4. **patient**—enduring calmly (patience,n.)

4. Bearable,adj. *From Sec. 1:* endurable, sustainable, tolerable

5. Unbearable,adj. *From Sec. 1:* unendurable, insufferable, insupportable, intolerable; *Also:* 1. **excessive**—unbearable

6. Hard to Bear: burdensome, onerous, tough,adj.

7. That Which Is Hard to Bear: burden,n.

8. Ability to Bear, or Bear Up under,n.
1. **endurance**—ability to bear, endure, withstand, etc.
2. **fortitude**—ability to withstand difficulties, adversity, etc., with coolness and courage
3. **hardiness**—ability to withstand difficulties, injuries, extremes of temperature, etc.
4. **resilience**—ability to withstand difficulties or troubles without loss of composure
5. **resistance, resistivity**—ability to withstand illness, injury, etc.
6. **ruggedness**—hardiness
7. **stalwartness**—hardiness
8. **stamina**—ability to endure strain (staminal,adj.)
9. **sturdiness**—hardiness
10. **tolerance**—ability to bear the effects of a drug
11. **toughness**—hardiness

9. Able to Bear, or Bear Up under,adj. *From Sec. 8:* fortitudinous, hardy, resilient, resistive, rugged, stalwart, sturdy, tough

10. One Who Can Endure Hardships or Unusual Strain: Trojan,n. (colloq.)

11. That Which Bears the Brunt of Force or Conflict: buffer,n.

247. TAKE

1. To Take,v.
1. **accept**—take as is
2. **adopt**—take and use; take for one's own;

take and put into practice; take and bring up as one's own (the child of another); voluntarily take into some relationship
3. **allot**—take for a special purpose
4. **antedate**—take before the proper or correct time
5. **appropriate**—take for one's own use; take for a particular use
6. **arrogate**—take presumptuously and without right
7. **assume**—appropriate; usurp
8. **attach**—take as payment for a debt (legal)
9. **capture**—take by force, skill, or trickery
10. **clutch**—take and hold tightly; take eagerly
11. **commandeer**—take by force
12. **confiscate**—take by authority or official power, without the approval or consent of the owner; take, as a penalty; take, as a penalty, for public use
13. **draft**—take, by lots or other means of selection, men to serve in the armed forces
14. **expropriate**—take (property, possessions, etc.) for public use
15. **extort**—take by force, violence, fraud, deception, threats, or other illegal use of power (a thing or an abstraction from someone)
16. **garnishee**—attach (money or property) through legal processes
17. **hale**—take (someone) by force (to a place to which he is unwilling to go)
18. **impress**—take by force or authority for public service; draft for naval service
19. **intercept**—take (someone or something) on his or its way to a destination
20. **misappropriate**—take for one's own use (that which is entrusted to one, though belonging to another)
21. **occupy**—take possession of
22. **partake (of)**—take a share or part (of)
23. **pre-empt**—take before anyone else does or can
24. **rape**—take by robbery or violence
25. **remove**—take away; take off; take from one position or place and put in another
26. **seize**—take, or take possession of, by force
27. **sequester, sequestrate**—take (property) until a debt or claim is satisfied; confiscate
28. **smuggle**—take somewhere (originally in or out of a country) secretly and/or illegally
29. **snatch**—take suddenly
30. **sneak**—take in a stealthy or furtive manner
31. **steal**—take that which does not belong to one; take secretly or thievishly
32. **usurp**—take (often by force) and keep without right (applied to a place, position, power, authority, privilege, etc.)
33. **whip**—take suddenly
34. **whisk**—take and carry away quickly
35. **wrest**—take by force
36. **wring**—extort as if by twisting

2. A Taking,n. *From Sec. 1:* acceptance, adoption, allotment, appropriation, arrogation, assumption, attachment, capture, confiscation, draft, expropriation, extortion, impressment, interception, misappropriation, occupation or occupancy, pre-emption, rape or rapine, removal, seizure, sequestration, usurpation, wrest, wring

3. Taker,n. *From Sec. 1:* adopter, appropriator, captor, confiscator, expropriator; extortioner, extorter, or extortionist; interceptor, misappropriator, occupier or occupant, partaker, pre-emptor, smuggler, sneak, usurper, wrester

4. Descr. of Taking,adj. *From Sec. 1:* adoptive, appropriative, assumptive, confiscatory;

extortive, extortionary, or extortionate; interceptive, pre-emptive or pre-emptory

**5. That Which Is Taken by Sovereign or
Royal Privilege:** seigniorage,n.

6. To Seize,v.
1. **abduct**—seize (a person) by force, take
him away, and hold him, usually for
ransom
2. **apprehend**—arrest
3. **arrest**—seize and hold legally; capture
4. **bag**—seize; capture
5. **capture**—seize, or seize possession of,
forcibly
6. **clutch**—seize eagerly; seize and hold
tightly
7. **collar**—seize by the collar; capture
8. **commandeer**—seize by force
9. **corral**—capture
10. **grab**—seize with a sudden motion; clutch;
grasp
11. **grapple (with)**—seize and hold fast
12. **grasp**—seize with the hand and hold tight
13. **grip**—seize firmly; grasp
14. **hook**—seize and pull with, or as if with,
a hook; seize secretly or sneakily (slang)
15. **impound**—seize and hold through legal
processes
16. **intercept**—seize (someone or something)
on his or its way to a destination
17. **kidnap**—abduct
18. **pounce on or upon**—come down suddenly
and seize
19. **prey on or upon**—seize (a person or
animal) for purposes of eating, killing,
etc.
20. **rape**—seize and carry off by force
21. **ravish**—rape
22. **sequester**—seize by legal authority; seize
and keep
23. **snatch**—seize hastily or suddenly; seize
as it passes
24. **swoop up, swoop away, swoop off**—seize
in one motion; pounce upon
25. **tackle**—seize, often for the purpose of
subduing
26. **tong**—seize with tongs
27. **twitch**—snatch

7. Seizure,n. *From Sec. 6:* abduction, apprehension, arrest, capture, clutch, grab, grapple,
grasp, grip, impoundage or impoundment, interception, pounce, rape or rapine, ravishment, sequestration, snatch, swoop, tackle,
twitch; *Also:* **1. prehension**—act of seizing or
grasping with the hand or other bodily member (of animals)

8. One Who Seizes,n. *From Sec. 6:* abductor,
apprehender, captor, grabber, grappler, interceptor, kidnaper, pouncer, raper, ravisher,
snatcher, swooper, tackler

9. One Who or That Which Is Seized,n.
From Sec. 6: captive, prey; *Also:*
1. **booty**—prize
2. **prize**—that which, or one who, is taken
captive; enemy ship and cargo captured
in wartime

**10. Tendency to Seize That Which One De-
sires; Habit of Seizing by Force or Violence:**
rapacity, rapaciousness, raven, ravin,n.
(rapacious, ravenous,adj.)

**11. Descr. of a Bodily Member That Is
Adapted for Seizing or Grasping:** prehensile,
prehensive, prehensorial, prehensory,adj.
(prehensility, prehensiveness,n.)

**12. Descr. of a Bird's Beak, Claws, etc., That
Are Adapted for Seizing Prey:** raptorial,adj.

13. Open to Seizure through Attack: pregnable,adj. (pregnability,n. impregnable, im-
pregnability,neg.)

14. To Attempt to Seize,v.
1. **besiege**—surround with armed forces for
the purpose of capturing (siege,n.)
2. **storm**—attempt to seize by attack (a

city, fortified place, etc., or, figuratively,
a person's affections, etc.)

15. Instrument or Device for Seizing,n.
1. **forceps**—instrument for seizing and holding, esp. in surgical operations
2. **grapnel**—device of various hooks or
clamps for grasping; grapple
3. **grapple**—hook by which a ship seizes
onto and holds another
4. **grappling iron, grappling hook**—grapnel; grapple
5. **grip**—device for seizing or grasping
6. **hook**—curved instrument, piece of metal,
etc., for seizing and/or holding
7. **pincers, pinchers**—tool for seizing and
holding, made up of two jaws and handles
8. **pliers**—small pincers
9. **tongs**—instrument of various kinds for
seizing or grasping
10. **tweezers**—small two-pronged instrument
for grasping small things

16. Grasping Human Hands or Fingers:
talons,n.

17. To Take (a Person) Away,v.
1. **abduct**—kidnap (abduction,n. abductor,
n.)
2. **alienate**—estrange (alienation,n. alienator,n.)
3. **estrange**—figuratively take (someone)
away from the one for whom he has
tender or sympathetic feelings (estrangement,n. estranger,n.)
4. **kidnap**—take (a person) away by force
and hold him against his will, usually for
ransom (kidnaping,n. kidnaper,n.)
5. **ravish**—kidnap (a woman) for immoral
purposes (ravishment,n. ravisher,n.)
6. **shanghai**—take (a person) away by
trickery or force; drug or render (a person) unconscious and then take him
away, esp. aboard ship to serve as a sailor
7. **snatch**—kidnap (slang)
8. **wean**—figuratively take (a person) gradually away from the one he loves, from a
habit or the enjoyment of a habit, from
an occupation, etc.

18. To Take (an Abstraction) Away,v.
1. **abridge**—take (rights, privileges, etc.)
away (abridgment,n.)
2. **alienate**—take away (such abstractions
as privileges, friendship, love, etc.) and
give to another or keep for oneself
(alienation,n. alienator,n.)
3. **derogate (from)**—detract (derogation,n.
derogator,n. derogatory, derogative,adj.)
4. **detract (from)**—take away a part (from
reputation, credit, honor, etc.); take away
credit from (detraction,n. detractor,n.
detractive, detractory,adj.)
5. **subtract (from)**—detract (subtraction,n.
subtractive,adj.)

19. Not to Be Taken Away,adj.
1. **imprescriptible**—not to be taken away
by law or legal processes
2. **inalienable**—descr. of those rights, privileges, etc., that are not to be taken away

**20. To Take (an Amount, Part, Quantity,
Number, etc.) Away:** abate, deduct, subtract,v. (abatement, deduction, subtraction,
n.)

21. Amount Taken Away: abatement, deduction, subtrahend,n.

**22. Tending, or Having the Power, to Sub-
tract; Involving Subtraction:** subtractive,
adj.

**23. To Take Something from a Person or
Place,**v.
1. **bereave (. . . of)**—take (joy, hope, etc.)
from (someone); take (something) from
(someone) without hope of return
2. **bleed**—take money, usually in large
amounts, from (someone) by threats, etc.
3. **defrock**—unfrock

4. **deplume**—take away all possessions, wealth, honor, honors, etc., from (someone)

5. **deprive** (. . . **of**)—take (a thing, privilege, right, power, ability, faculty, etc.) from (someone) either by force or contrary to the will or desire of the owner or possessor; take (a quality, characteristic, etc.) from (a place or thing)

6. **disbar**—take away the license to practice (from a lawyer)

7. **disentitle**—deprive of title, claim, or right

8. **disestablish**—deprive (a church) of its support from, or connection with, the state

9. **disfrock**—unfrock

10. **disfurnish**—take furniture, furnishing, or equipment from (a place); strip (a place)

11. **dispossess** (. . . **of**)—deprive (someone) of the possession of (something)

12. **divest** (. . . **of**)—take (a privilege, power, right, title, holding, clothing, arms, equipment, anything carried, etc.) from (someone) by making him give it up; take (anything) from (a place or thing)

13. **fleece**—strip (someone) of valuables

14. **loot**—strip (a place) by stealing, by political corruption, by trickery, or after capture in war

15. **mulct** (. . . **of**)—deprive (someone) of (something) as a penalty, or by trickery, fraud, or deception

16. **plunder**—strip (a place or person) completely of valuables, through force or violence, or after capture in war

17. **prey (on, upon)**—take possessions from (someone) through attacks or violence

18. **ransack**—search through and take everything of value from (a place)

19. **raven, ravin**—prey

20. **rifle**—strip (a place) bare

21. **rob** (. . . **of**)—take from (a person that to which he has a right or which is due him); take (a quality, characteristic, ability, power, or other abstraction) from (a person or place)

22. **sack**—loot; plunder

23. **strip** (. . . **of**)—take the entire contents or covering from (a place); take (a thing, quality, privilege, power, right, etc.) completely from (a person or place)

24. **unfrock**—take away (a clergyman's) privileges, office, right to preach, etc.

24. Taking Something from a Person or Place,n. *From Sec. 23:* bereavement, deplumation; deprivation, deprival, or deprivement; disbarment, disestablishment, disfurnishment, dispossession; divestiture, divesture, or divestment; plunder or plunderage, raven or ravin, robbery, sack

25. One Who Takes Something from a Person or Place,n. *From Sec. 23:* bereaver; bloodsucker (from *bleed*); depriver, dispossessor, looter, plunderer, preyer, ransacker, rifler, robber, sacker

26. That Which Is Taken from a Person or Place,n. *From Sec. 23:* loot, plunder

27. Descr. of Taking from a Person or Place, adj. *From Sec. 23:* deprivative, plunderous

28. One Who Advocates Depriving a Church of Its Support from, or Connection with, the State: disestablishmentarian,n. (disestablishmentarianism,n.)

248. PLUNDER

1. To Plunder (a Place or People); To Commit Plunder,v.
1. **depredate**—plunder; commit plunder
2. **despoil**—plunder; pillage
3. **fleece**—plunder

4. **forage**—plunder; plunder of supplies; commit plunder

5. **foray**—commit pillage

6. **gut**—plunder of contents

7. **loot**—plunder

8. **pillage**—plunder completely of valuables by means of violence or after capture in war; commit plunder

9. **ransack**—pillage

10. **ravage**—plunder; pillage; sack

11. **raven, ravin**—go about plundering

12. **rob**—plunder; plunder completely; commit plunder

13. **sack**—plunder after capture

14. **spoil**—commit plunder

15. **spoliate**—plunder; pillage

16. **strip**—plunder

2. A Plundering; Plunder or Plunderage,n. *From Sec. 1:* depredation, despoliation or despoilment, pillage, ravage, robbery, sack, spoliation; *Also:*
1. **rapine**—plunder; pillage
2. **spoliation**—authorized plunder of a neutral ship at sea

3. Plunderer,n. *From Sec. 1:* depredator or depredationist, despoiler, fleecer, forager, forayer, looter, pillager, ransacker, ravager, robber, sacker, spoiler, spoliator

4. Plunderous,adj. *From Sec. 1:* depredatory, spoliatory or spoliative; *Also:* 1. **predatory**—pert. to or descr. of plundering

5. Plunder, i.e., That Which Is Taken,n. *From Sec. 1:* loot, pillage, spoils; *Also:*
1. **booty**—plunder; things of value taken from the enemy in war
2. **swag**—plunder (colloq.)

6. To Search for Plunder or Prey,v.
1. **filibuster**—go about in search of plunder
2. **forage**—raven
3. **maraud**—go about seeking plunder
4. **prowl**—wander about quietly, secretly, or persistently in search of plunder
5. **raven, ravin**—seek plunder or prey

7. A Search or Searching for Plunder,n. *From Sec. 6:* maraud, prowl

8. One Who Searches for Plunder,n. *From Sec. 6:* filibuster or filibusterer, forager, marauder, prowler; *Also:* 1. **freebooter**—one who goes about in search of plunder

9. Living off Prey or Plunder; Tending to Prey or Plunder,adj.
1. **depredatory**—tending to prey or plunder
2. **predaceous, predacious**—living off prey or by preying (literally or figuratively)
3. **predatory, predative**—living by prey or plundering; living by preying upon other animals; tending to plunder, prey upon, or pillage; tending to prey upon other animals
4. **rapacious**—living on prey; in the habit of preying on others; predatory
5. **raptatorial, raptatory**—predaceous
6. **raptorial**—living on prey (esp. of birds); preying, or tending to prey, upon other animals
7. **ravenous**—rapacious

10. A Living off Prey or Plunder; Tendency to Prey or Plunder,n. *From Sec. 9:* predacity, predaceousness or predaciousness; predatoriness, predatism (of animals), rapacity or rapaciousness; ravin, raven, or ravenousness; *Also:*
1. **brigandage, brigandism**—a living by plunder and robbery
2. **vampirism**—a preying upon others

11. A Preyer,n. *From Sec. 9:* predator; *From Sec. 10:* brigand, vampire; *Also:* 1. **harpy**—one who preys upon others

12. To Prey or Prey Upon: depredate,v. (depredation,n.)

13. Prey: quarry, raven, ravin,n.

249. REMOVAL

1. To Remove, v.
1. **abstract**—remove (abstraction,n.)
2. **brush**—remove from a place by, or as by, a sweeping motion
3. **cart**—remove from one place to another (cartage,n.)
4. **decenter**—remove from the center (decentration,n.)
5. **delocalize**—remove from its location (delocalization,n.)
6. **detach**—loosen and remove (detachment, n.)
7. **dislocate**—displace (dislocation,n.)
8. **dislodge**—remove from its proper place (dislodgment,n.)
9. **displace**—remove from its proper place to make room for something else (displacement,n.)
10. **disroot**—dislodge
11. **relegate**—remove; remove from sight or thinking (relegation,n.)
12. **rend**—remove forcibly
13. **sequester**—remove from public use, contact, or view (sequestration,n.)
14. **strip**—remove
15. **sweep**—remove from the surface
16. **tear**—remove by effort
17. **transplant**—remove from one soil and plant in another; remove (tissue) from one person or part of the body and cause to grow in another (transplantation,n.)
18. **withdraw**—remove from a place or position (withdrawal,n.)

2. To Remove Something from, v.
1. **cream**—remove the best part from
2. **disfurnish**—remove furniture, furnishings, or equipment from
3. **eviscerate**—remove the viscera from
4. **pit**—remove the pit from
5. **ream**—remove the cream from the top of
6. **skim**—remove film or scum from the top of (a liquid); remove cream or other substance from the top of; figuratively, remove something from the top of
7. **stone**—remove the pit from
8. **top**—remove the top from

250. STEAL

1. To Steal, v.
1. **abstract**—steal; take by dishonest removal; purloin
2. **burglarize**—steal from (a place) after entering forcibly and illegally
3. **cabbage**—steal
4. **crib**—steal; pilfer; plagiarize; purloin
5. **defalcate**—commit embezzlement
6. **depredate**—take away illegally and, often, with violence
7. **despoil**—rob
8. **embezzle**—fraudulently appropriate to one's own use (money or property entrusted to one's care)
9. **filch**—steal sneakily or secretly (usually something of small value); pilfer
10. **fleece**—fraudulently take all money or property from
11. **loot**—steal from (a place); corruptly steal from (a place over which one has political control, etc.); commit thievery; burglarize; rob
12. **peculate**—steal (funds entrusted to one's care, esp. public funds); steal public funds or other funds over which one has control; embezzle
13. **pilfer**—steal (something of small value, or in small amounts)
14. **pillage**—engage in open robbery through violence; plunder
15. **pirate**—rob at sea; steal (another's artistic creation, invention, or mental product) and pass it off as one's own

16. **plagiarize**—steal (the literary or other composition of another) and pass it off as one's own original work
17. **plunder**—rob (a place or people) through open force; fraudulently take all money or property from; engage in robbery through open force
18. **purloin**—steal (something) secretly and take it away
19. **rape**—take by robbery
20. **rifle**—steal; go through or search (a place) and then steal what one wants or is looking for
21. **rob**—take personal property from (someone) feloniously and forcibly, by intimidation, or against his will; steal from (a place or person) by force or fraud
22. **rustle**—steal (cattle)
23. **sneak**—steal when no one is looking
24. **spoil**—rob
25. **thieve**—steal, usually when no one is looking

2. Stealing, n. *From Sec. 1:* abstraction, burglary, defalcation, depredation, despoilment or despoliation, embezzlement, filchery, peculation, pilferage, pillage, piracy, plagiarism or plagiary, plunder or plunderage, purloinment, rape or rapine, robbery, spoliation, thievery or theft; *Also:*
1. **banditry**—robbery
2. **bibliokleptomania**—the stealing of books
3. **brigandage, brigandism**—robbery
4. **dacoity, dacoitage**—robbery by murderous thieves in India or Burma, where they operate in organized gangs
5. **grand larceny**—thievery of a sum of money (or of property valued at a sum of money) higher than a certain amount, usually fifty dollars
6. **kleptomania**—morbid and pathologic thievery, usually of the petty variety, and with no thought of economic gain
7. **larceny**—thievery; thievery of personal property
8. **petit larceny**—thievery of a sum of money (or of property valued at a sum of money) under a statutory limit, usually fifty dollars
9. **petty larceny**—petit larceny
10. **plunderage**—embezzlement of goods on a ship at sea
11. **racket**—fraudulent extortion of money under threat of violence
12. **shoplifting**—surreptitious stealing from the open counters of a shop.

3. One Who Steals, n. *From Sec. 1:* burglar, cribber, defalcator, depredator or depredationist, despoiler, embezzler, filcher, looter, peculator, pilferer, pillager, pirate, plagiarist or plagiary, plunderer, purloiner, rapist, rifler, robber, rustler, sneak, spoiler, thief; *From Sec. 2:* bandit, bibliokleptomaniac, brigand, dacoit, kleptomaniac, larcener or larcenist, racketeer, shoplifter; *Also:*
1. **bravo**—robber
2. **cracksman**—burglar or safebreaker (slang)
3. **cutpurse**—pickpocket
4. **footpad**—robber on foot
5. **highwayman**—robber on the highway or public roads (originally, on horse)
6. **hijacker**—one who holds up a truck and steals the cargo, or the truck and cargo
7. **ladrone**—thief
8. **latron**—robber
9. **picklock**—burglar; thief
10. **pickpocket**—one who surreptitiously steals from people's pockets
11. **safebreaker, safecracker**—one who breaks open safes to steal the contents
12. **yegg**—burglar; safebreaker

4. Descr. of Stealing, adj. *From Sec. 1:* abstractive, burglarious, depredatory, piratic or piratical, plagiaristic or plagiary, plunderous, sneaky, spoliative, thievish; *From Sec. 2:* bibliokleptomaniacal, kleptomaniacal, larcenous or larcenish

5. That Which Is Stolen,n. *From Sec. 1:* defalcation, loot, pilferage, pillage, piracy, plagiarism, plunder, spoils; *Also:*
 1. **booty**—that which is stolen
 2. **haul, swag**—booty (colloq.)
 3. **pelf**—stolen property
 4. **plunderage**—goods embezzled aboard a ship at sea

6. Pirate: buccaneer, corsair, filibuster, freebooter, picaroon, rover, sea rover,n.

7. Norseman Pirate Who Plundered the Coast of Europe from the Eighth to Tenth Centuries: Viking,n.

8. To Commit Piracy; To Act or Play the Pirate: pirate,v.

9. Descr. of, or Pert. to, a Pirate or Piracy: piratic, piratical,adj.

10. Resembling a Pirate: piratelike, piraty, adj.

11. Pirate Flag: black flag, blackjack, Jolly Roger, Roger, or roger,n.

251. TAKE BACK

1. To Take Back,v.
 1. **countermand**—take (a contrary order or command) back (countermand,n.)
 2. **palinode**—recant; retract (palinode,n. palinodist,n.)
 3. **recant**—take back one's belief or what one has professed or taught (recantation, n. recanter,n.)
 4. **retract**—take back an offer, promise, charge, statement, accusation, etc. (retraction,n. retractive,adj.)
 5. **revoke**—take back (revocation, revokement,n.)
 6. **withdraw**—take back (withdrawal,adj.)

2. Able to Be Taken Back: revocable,adj. (revocability,n.)

3. Unable to Be Taken Back: irrevocable, adj. (irrevocability,n.)

252. CHOICE

1. To Choose,v.
 1. **co-opt, co-optate**—choose (someone) to be a fellow member in an organization
 2. **cull**—choose carefully (the best of the lot)
 3. **elect**—choose, with the implication of previous deliberation or mature consideration, and the added implication of rejecting alternative courses or possibilities; choose for public office
 4. **excerpt**—select and take out (written material from a larger body of such material)
 5. **extract**—choose from the general body (usually of what is said or written); select and take out
 6. **garble**—make an unfair selection of (those parts or passages of written or spoken material as will serve one's purpose)
 7. **glean**—cull or select out
 8. **pick**—cull; select
 9. **prefer** (. . . to)—choose as better or more desirable (than)
 10. **select**—choose from a wide range or from a large number
 11. **sift out**—separate and choose from the rest (those that are desired)
 12. **single out**—choose from among others
 13. **winnow**—choose (some) from among the rest

2. Choice, i.e., Act of Choosing,n. *From Sec. 1:* co-optation or co-option, election, excerption, extraction, garble, preference, selection; *Also:* 1. **volition**—act of choosing

3. Chooser,n. *From Sec. 1:* elector, electorate (collective), excerptor, picker, selector, winnower

4. Descr. of Choosing,adj. *From Sec. 1:* co-optative or co-optive, electoral or elective, excerptive, preferential, selective; *Also:*
 1. **eclectic**—acting to choose from all systems or sources that which best fits one's needs
 2. **volitional**—acting to make a free choice
 3. **voluntary**—acting freely from one's own choice

5. A Choice,n.
 1. **alternative**—choice between two (or, loosely, more) possibilities, things, courses of action, etc.
 2. **chrestomathy**—selection of literary passages used in learning a foreign language
 3. **cull**—something selected to be removed or eliminated owing to inferiority
 4. **dilemma**—difficult choice between things equally bad or unfavorable
 5. **election**—that which is chosen in preference to other things, courses of action, etc.
 6. **excerpt, excerption**—written material selected and taken out from a larger body of such material
 7. **extract**—selection from written material
 8. **garble**—unfair selection of parts from speech or writing
 9. **Hobson's choice**—nominal choice that is not actually a choice, since there is no alternative
 10. **option**—that which is offered as a choice
 11. **pick**—choice from a wide range
 12. **predilection**—preference
 13. **preference**—choice according to one's desires or judgment
 14. **quandary**—dilemma
 15. **selection**—that which is chosen from a wide range

6. Wide Range from Which a Choice May Be Made: selection,n.

7. State of Choice: volition,n.

8. Having the Power to Elect: constituent, adj.

9. Freedom or Power to Choose,n.
 1. **discretion**—freedom or right to make a choice based on one's judgment
 2. **option**—right to choose; power of making a free choice

10. Specially Chosen,adj.
 1. **choice**—chosen as the best or most desirable
 2. **elect**—specially chosen; taken by choice as the best
 3. **select**—specially chosen; chosen as the best

11. Chosen, but Not Yet Installed in Office: elect,adj. (mayor-elect, etc.)

12. Capable of Being Chosen; Suitable for Choice,adj.
 1. **alternative**—descr. of one of two possibilities, things, or courses of action that may be chosen
 2. **eligible**—suitable for choice
 3. **facultative**—optional
 4. **optional**—left to one's choice (i.e., not obligatory or compulsory)
 5. **preferable**—more suitable for choice

13. Those Who Are Chosen as the Best: elite,n.

14. The Choice Part: elite,n.

15. Choosy,adj.
 1. **dainty**—particular, overparticular, or fastidious in one's tastes or feelings (daintiness,n.)

2. **delicate**—fastidious (delicacy,n.)

3. **discriminating, discriminative, discriminatory**—tending to make careful choice by considering or weighing the differences (discrimination,n.)

4. **eclectic**—tending to choose for one's use that which one considers the best from various sources, systems, philosophies, religions, principles, etc., rather than methodically following or using one source, system, etc. (eclecticism,n. eclectic,n.)

5. **fastidious**—possessing extremely high and rigid standards in one's selection of food, dress, friends, associates, etc. (fastidiousness,n.)

6. **finical**—excessively fastidious in one's likes and dislikes (finicality, finicalness, finicism,n.)

7. **finicky, finikin, finicking**—finical (finickiness, finickingness,n.)

8. **fussy**—excessively fastidious in one's likes and dislikes (fussiness,n.)

9. **overfastidious**—too fastidious (overfastidiousness,n.)

10. **overparticular**—too particular (overparticularity,n.)

11. **particular**—tending to make careful choice or choices based on high standards (particularity,n.)

12. **pernickety**—fastidious; finical (pernicketiness,n.)

13. **picky**—choosy; fastidious (pickiness,n.)

14. **prissy**—excessively fastidious (prissiness, n.)

15. **queasy**—fastidious (queasiness,n.)

16. **select**—careful in choosing

17. **selective**—choosing carefully and discriminatingly (selectiveness,n.)

18. **squeamish**—very fastidious or particular (squeamishness,n.)

16. Having No Choice: willy-nilly,adj. and adv.

17. Allowing No Choice,adj.
1. **compulsory**—allowing no choice
2. **mandatory**—made compulsory by official order
3. **obligatory**—allowing no choice
4. **peremptory**—leaving no choice
5. **prescribed**—allowing no choice
6. **required**—allowing no choice

18. To Allow No Choice,v. *From Sec. 17:* compel, oblige, prescribe, require

19. That Which Allows No Choice,n. *From Sec. 17:* compulsion, mandate, obligation, requirement

253. APPOINTMENT

1. To Appoint,v.
1. **assign**—appoint to a place, post, or duty
2. **commission**—appoint; appoint to a duty, office, etc.
3. **constitute**—appoint to an office or function
4. **delegate**—appoint as a representative or deputy
5. **depute**—appoint as an agent, substitute, etc.
6. **deputize**—appoint to act in one's behalf
7. **designate**—appoint
8. **ordain**—appoint officially to the clergy

2. Appointment,n. *From Sec. 1:* assignment, commission, constitution, delegation or delegacy, deputation, designation, ordination

3. One Who Is Appointed,n. *From Sec. 1:* commissioner, delegate, deputy

4. Those Appointed,n. *From Sec. 1:* commission, delegation or delegacy, deputation

5. Descr. of Appointment,adj. *From Sec. 1:* delegatory, designative

6. **Having the Power to Appoint:** constituent,adj.

7. **Appointed but Not Yet Installed in Office:** designate,adj. (secretary-designate, etc.)

254. VOTING

1. The Right to Vote,n.
1. **ballot**—right to vote
2. **franchise**—right to vote
3. **proxy**—right or power to vote for someone else
4. **referendum**—right of the citizens to vote accepting or rejecting laws passed or proposed by a legislative body
5. **suffrage**—right to vote (suffragial,adj.)

2. To Give the Right to Vote to: enfranchise,v. (enfranchisement,n.)

3. To Take Away (Someone's) Right to Vote: disenfranchise, disfranchise,v. (disenfranchisement, disfranchisement,n.)

4. To Vote,v.
1. **ballot**—vote
2. **blackball**—vote against secretly
3. **plump for**—give all one's votes to (one candidate)
4. **poll**—cast a vote

5. Voting,n.
1. **chirotony**—voting by the showing or raising of hands
2. **plebiscite**—voting of the people of a region as to a choice of government, sovereignty, or the country to rule them
3. **poll**—voting
4. **referendum**—voting by the people accepting or rejecting laws passed or proposed by a legislative body

6. A Vote,n.
1. **aye**—affirmative vote
2. **ballot**—vote
3. **blackball**—secret negative vote, excluding from membership
4. **nay**—negative vote
5. **suffrage**—vote, whether favorable or unfavorable; favorable vote (suffragial,adj.)
6. **yea**—affirmative vote

7. Voter,n.
1. **constituent**—resident or voter of a voting or election district (constituency, collective n.)
2. **elector**—voter (electorate, collective n.)
3. **floater**—one who votes illegally at several polling places

8. Place Where Votes Are Cast: polling place, polls,n.

9. Box into Which Votes Are Dropped: ballot box,n.

10. Paper on Which a Vote Is Indicated: ballot,n.

11. Collection or Number of Votes Cast: poll,n.

12. To Take and Register the Votes of: poll,v.

13. One Who Carefully Examines the Votes Cast: scrutineer, scrutator,n.

14. An Advocate of Extending the Vote,n.
1. **suffragette**—female advocate of extending the vote to women (suffragettism,n.)
2. **suffragist**—advocate of extending the vote to women, or to others not possessing it (suffragism,n. suffragist, suffragistic, adj.)

255. POSSESSION

1. To Possess; To Have,v.
1. **contain**—possess; have; have inside or within

2. **hold**—possess; have in one's possession
3. **occupy**—have possession of (a place)
4. **own**—possess; have
5. **recapture**—have (a feeling, experience, etc.) again

2. Possession,n. *From Sec. 1:* occupancy or occupation, ownership, recapture; *Also:*
1. **community**—common ownership
2. **coparcenary, coparceny**—joint ownership (legal)
3. **copartnership**—joint partnership
4. **partnership**—ownership by two or more
5. **proprietorship**—ownership
6. **tenancy**—occupancy of a place under lease, payment of rent, etc.
7. **tenure**—possession of a thing, office, position, etc.; possession of the real property of a superior in return for services to be given

3. Possessor,n. *From Sec. 1:* container, holder, occupant or occupier, owner; *From Sec. 2:* copartner, partner, proprietor, proprietress (fem.), tenant; *Also:*
1. **bourgeois**—property owner
2. **squire**—landowner

4. Possessors, Collectively,n. *From Sec. 3:* proprietariat, tenantry, bourgeoisie, squirearchy; *Also:* 1. **landed gentry**—landowners, collectively

5. Descr. of Possession or a Possessor,adj. *From Secs. 2 and 3:* proprietary, proprietory, or proprietorial; tenurial; *Also:* 1. **landed**—owning land

6. Period, Conditions, or Right of Possession of an Office, Position, Place, etc.: tenure,n. (tenurial,adj.)

7. Owned by Two or More People in Common: communal,adj.

8. To Give into Common Ownership of Two or More People: communalize,v.

9. Owned Privately or Exclusively: peculiar, adj.

10. A Possession; Possessions,n.
1. **appurtenance**—that which is owned; that which belongs to someone
2. **asset**—a possession of any value
3. **belonging**—possession
4. **capital**—total property owned by a corporation or person
5. **chattel**—piece of personal property; property other than real estate
6. **effects**—possessions, often personal
7. **estate**—sum total of one's property; sum total of property that may be, or is, left to heirs
8. **holdings**—property, esp. stocks, bonds, real estate, etc.
9. **lares and penates**—cherished household or family possessions
10. **paraphernalia**—personal possessions
11. **personal effects**—personal possessions
12. **personalty**—personal property
13. **property**—possessions of value
14. **real estate**—property in the forms of land, buildings, etc.
15. **real property**—real estate
16. **realty**—real estate
17. **substance**—property
18. **traps**—personal possessions, esp. those carried on a trip
19. **white elephant**—possession requiring great expense or trouble to keep, and yielding little profit or enjoyment, yet hard to get rid of; troublesome possession

11. Economic System Based on Private Property: capitalism,n.

12. Pert. to Capitalism: bourgeois, capitalist, capitalistic,adj.

13. Believer in, or Advocate of, Capitalism: capitalist,n.

256. BELONG

1. To Belong,v.
1. **appertain**—belong as a part; belong legally
2. **inhere in**—belong to as an integral part, essential quality, etc.
3. **pertain (to)**—belong (to)
4. **reside in**—belong to as an essential quality

2. Belonging,adj. *From Sec. 1:* appurtenant, inherent, pertinent, resident (appurtenance, inherence, pertinence or pertinency, residence, n.); *Also:*
1. **appropriate**—peculiarly or specially belonging (appropriateness,n.)
2. **endemic, endemical**—belonging (to a particular country, region, or people)
3. **intrinsic, intrinsical**—belonging to the innermost make-up or nature of a thing (intrinsicality, intrinsicalness,n.)
4. **particular**—belonging distinctively to an individual, thing, group, etc. (particularity,n.)
5. **peculiar**—particular (peculiarity,n.)

3. That Which Belongs,n. *From Sec. 2:* appurtenance; particularity, peculiarity; *Also:* 1. **perquisite**—something advantageous that especially belongs (to an office, position, etc.)

4. To Pass into the Possession of: vest in,v.

5. To Consider (a Quality or Other Abstraction) as Belonging to: accredit to, ascribe to, attribute to, credit to, impute to,v. (accreditation, ascription, attribution, imputation,n.)

6. Not Belonging: extraneous, extrinsic, extrinsical,adj. (extraneousness, extrinsicality, extrinsicalness,n.)

257. HOLD

1. To Hold,v.
1. **brace**—hold steady; hold firmly in place
2. **cherish**—hold tenaciously in the mind
3. **clasp**—hold firmly; hold firmly with the hand or arm
4. **clench**—hold tight or firmly; clinch
5. **clinch**—take or maintain a tight hold in fighting or wrestling; hug
6. **clutch**—hold tightly
7. **cradle**—hold as in a cradle
8. **cuddle**—hold close for comfort or warmth
9. **embrace**—hold within the arms
10. **grapple**—hold fast or tight, as in wrestling, fighting, etc.
11. **grasp**—hold tight
12. **grip**—hold fast; hold tight
13. **gripe**—hold tight or fast
14. **hug**—hold within the arms
15. **keep**—hold in one's possession
16. **maintain**—hold and defend; hold and keep
17. **nourish**—cherish
18. **occupy**—hold and have possession of (a place)
19. **possess**—hold; hold as property; hold under control
20. **retain**—hold; keep hold of; hold in one's possession
21. **seize**—lay hold of suddenly and by force
22. **suspend**—hold in place as if hanging
23. **trammel**—hold as if in a net
24. **vise**—hold with, or as if with, an implement with two jaws
25. **wield**—hold and use
26. **wring**—clasp; clasp and twist

2. A Holding; A Hold,n. *From Sec. 1:* clasp, clench, clinch, clutch, cuddle, embrace, grapple, grasp, grip, gripe, hug, maintenance, nourishment, occupation or occupancy, possession, retention, seizure, suspension, wring; *Also:* 1. **purchase**—firm hold when moving or raising something heavy; firm hold in such circumstance to avoid slipping

3. One Who Holds,n. *From Sec. 1:* cherisher, clutcher, cuddler, grasper, keeper, occupant or occupier, possessor, retainer, wielder

4. That Which, or Implement That, Holds, n. *From Sec. 1:* brace, clasp, clench, clutch, cradle, grip, gripe, vise; *Also:* 1. **clamp**—device for holding something tight

5. Acting or Tending to Hold,adj. *From Sec. 1:* possessive, retentive, suspensive (possessiveness, retentiveness,n.) ; *Also:*
1. **hygroscopic**—retaining moisture after freely absorbing it
2. **pertinacious**—holding (an opinion, idea, etc.) stubbornly or strongly in the mind (pertinacity, pertinaciousness,n.)
3. **tenacious**—holding firm (tenacity, tenaciousness,n.)
4. **viselike**—holding tight, as in the jaws of a vise

6. Able to Hold: portative,adj.

7. Capable of Being Held, Often of Literal or Figurative Position: tenable,adj. (tenableness, tenability,n.)

8. To Try to Hold onto: contest,v. (contestation,n.)

9. Unable to Hold onto Something: butterfingered,adj. (butterfingers,n.)

258. A HANDLE

1. A Handle,n.
1. **brace**—handle for a boring bit
2. **butt**—handle end of a tool, pistol, or other weapon, etc.
3. **crop**—handle of a whip
4. **grip**—handle; hilt
5. **haft**—handle of a knife, sword, dagger, etc.
6. **helve**—handle of such tools as hatchets, hammers, axes, etc.
7. **hilt**—handle of a sword or dagger
8. **hold**—handle
9. **lug**—projecting part by which something may be held
10. **shaft**—handle of an implement or weapon
11. **snath**—handle of a scythe
12. **steal, stele**—handle; shaft
13. **stock**—handle of a whip, fishing rod, gun, etc.
14. **withe**—resilient handle for a tool to decrease the effect of the vibration when in use

2. With a Handle or Part That Serves as, or Resembles, a Handle: ansate,adj.

259. INCLUSION

1. To Include,v.
1. **comprehend**—include within the scope
2. **comprise**—include; include (those parts that are essential)
3. **embody**—include (within or as if within the total body)
4. **embrace**—include as part of an entity
5. **encompass**—include by containing
6. **incorporate**—include as one or more of its parts
7. **involve**—include (something) as if it were rolled up with the whole
8. **number** (. . . **among**)—include as one of a collection, group, etc.
9. **reckon** (. . . **among**)—number
10. **subsume**—include within a classification

2. Inclusion,n. *From Sec. 1:* comprehension, comprisal, embodiment, embracement, encompassment, incorporation, involvement, subsumption

3. Including Most or All of Something: allembracing, all-inclusive, broad, comprehensive, embracive, exhaustive, expansive, extensive, full, inclusive, sweeping, vast, wide,adj. (all-inclusiveness, breadth, comprehensiveness, exhaustiveness, expansiveness, fullness, inclusiveness, vastness,n.)

4. All-Inclusive, without Regard for Distinctions or Differences: indiscriminate,adj. (indiscriminateness, indiscrimination,n.)

5. All-Inclusive in Sympathies (of a Person): expansive,adj. (expansiveness,n.)

260. CONTAIN

1. To Contain,v.
1. **accommodate**—contain; have room for (accommodation,n.)
2. **have, hold**—contain
3. **include**—contain (a part of the total, or one factor of the whole) within itself or within a category (inclusion,n.)
4. **receive**—contain
5. **take in**—contain
6. **teem with**—contain great numbers of (moving things or people)

2. That Which Is Contained: contents,n.

3. Amount Contained: content,n.

4. To Be Able to Contain: admit, hold, take in,v.

5. To Be Able to Hold: contain,v.

6. Able to Contain a Large Amount: capacious, roomy,adj. (capaciousness, roominess, n.)

7. Ability to Contain, in Reference to Quantity: capacity, contents,n.

8. Cubic Contents: volume,n.

9. Measurement of Cubic Contents: stereometry,n. (stereometer,n.)

261. CONTAINER

1. Container,n.
1. **bag**—closed container, or container that may be closed, made of flexible material such as cloth, paper, etc.
2. **barrel**—round and bulging container, greater in length than width, usually made of wooden staves
3. **barrelet**—small barrel
4. **basket**—container made of twigs or woven materials; container, usually of wood, for shipping produce
5. **bin**—container for storing
6. **box**—any comparatively rectangular container
7. **bucket**—pail; wooden pail
8. **caisson**—ammunition chest
9. **can**—tin or metal container
10. **canister**—small box or can
11. **cannikin**—small can
12. **carton**—box with cover attached, usually made of cardboard
13. **case**—box
14. **casket**—small chest
15. **censer**—vessel in which incense is burned
16. **chest**—large box with a hinged cover
17. **coffer**—container for valuables, such as jewels, gold, silver, money, etc.
18. **crate**—container for fruits, vegetables, etc., the sides and bottoms having openings as a means of ventilation
19. **crib**—manger
20. **drum**—metal barrel for liquids; cylindrical box
21. **firkin**—small cask made of wood
22. **gallipot**—small container for medicines or drugs (used by druggists)
23. **hamper**—large basket with a cover
24. **holder**—container
25. **holster**—leather container for a pistol
26. **hope chest**—chest or box in which a young girl collects various articles that

will be useful for setting up house after marriage

27. **hopper**—funnel-shaped box with an opening at the lower end
28. **horn**—vessel made of an animal horn for carrying gunpowder in former times
29. **housewife**—container for needles, thread, and other sewing implements
30. **humidor**—container for keeping things moist; container for cigars
31. **hussy, huswif**—housewife
32. **hutch**—box; chest
33. **keg**—small barrel, containing, usually, less than ten gallons
34. **manger**—container from which horses and cattle eat hay and other feed
35. **mortar**—strong vessel in which materials may be beaten or pounded to a powder or paste
36. **pail**—round container, usually of metal, with a flat bottom and open top, often wider at the top than at the bottom
37. **pannier**—large basket, often of wicker
38. **quiver**—container for arrows
39. **receptacle**—container; that which receives and holds something
40. **reliquary**—small box for holding or exhibiting a sacred relic
41. **scabbard**—container for a sword or dagger
42. **sheath**—close-fitting container or scabbard
43. **tabernacle**—that which contains something sacred
44. **tin**—can
45. **tray**—flat container, usually with a low rim, for holding or carrying things
46. **tub**—round wooden container
47. **vessel**—hollow, rounded container

2. Rounded Part of a Barrel: bilge,n.

3. One of the Narrow Strips of Wood or Metal Forming the Sides of a Barrel: stave, n.

4. Maker or Repairer of Barrels: cooper,n. (cooperage, coopery,n. cooper.v.)

5. Tray,n.
1. **hod**—wooden tray with a handle
2. **salver**—tray
3. **waiter**—tray

6. Container for Coal,n.
1. **brazier**—container for hot coals, usually to heat a room
2. **hod**—scuttle
3. **scuttle**—container for carrying coal

7. Container or Vessel for Liquids, etc.,n.
1. **amphora**—a kind of jar or vase with a handle on each side
2. **ampulla**—flask of globular shape
3. **basin**—hollow, usually circular, container, generally for water or other fluids
4. **beaker**—vessel with a pouring lip
5. **bottle**—hollow container, usually of glass or pottery, with a comparatively narrow neck
6. **bowl**—vessel, concave and hollow, for holding liquids
7. **bucket**—container for water or other fluids; pail; wooden pail
8. **canteen**—small container for water or other beverages, to be carried on a hike, journey, etc.
9. **carafe**—glass bottle for holding water or other liquids
10. **carboy**—large bottle enclosed in wickerwork
11. **cask, firkin**—barrel-shaped vessel, usually of wood, for liquids
12. **censer**—vessel for perfumes
13. **chamber, chamber pot**—vessel in which to urinate, kept by the bedside at night
14. **churn**—vessel in which butter is made from milk and cream
15. **cistern**—underground tank for storing water

16. **crock**—earthenware jar
17. **cruet**—glass bottle that holds vinegar, oil, etc., and placed on a dining table
18. **cruse**—earthenware jar
19. **decanter**—container, usually of glass, for storing and serving wines or liquors
20. **demijohn**—large bottle, enclosed by wickerwork, with a narrow neck
21. **ewer**—jug with a wide mouth
22. **flacon (French)**—small bottle; flask
23. **flagon**—container for fluids
24. **flask**—bottle-shaped container for liquids or liquor; thin, flat container for liquor, designed to be carried by a man in his hip pocket
25. **flasket**—small flask
26. **jar**—vessel with a wide mouth
27. **jeroboam**—very large bottle or bowl
28. **jug**—earthenware pitcher; narrow-necked pitcher with a spout and handle
29. **magnum**—two-quart bottle for wine, champagne, whiskey, etc.
30. **pail**—round, usually metal, container with a flat bottom and open top, for liquids, etc.
31. **phial**—vial
32. **pitcher**—vessel with handle and spout for holding and pouring liquids
33. **stoup**—flagon
34. **tank**—large vessel for liquids
35. **Toby**—small jug or pitcher, shaped like a fat man, and used for serving beer or ale
36. **tub**—large vessel for washing or bathing
37. **tun**—large cask
38. **urn**—vase with a pedestal or foot
39. **vase**—vessel or jar, usually of greater depth than width, used for holding flowers or for other ornamental purposes
40. **vat**—large tank
41. **vial**—bottle; small bottle for medicines or other liquids
42. **vinaigrette**—small ornamental bottle

8. Drinking Vessel; Cup; Glass,n.
1. **beaker**—wide drinking cup
2. **bowl**—drinking vessel for wine and other alcoholic beverages
3. **calabash**—gourd
4. **cannikin**—small drinking vessel
5. **chalice**—drinking cup, usually used in religious ceremonies
6. **cruse**—earthenware cup
7. **cup**—comparatively shallow vessel, with a handle, for drinking
8. **demitasse**—very small cup; small cup in which strong black coffee is served
9. **glass**—hollow drinking vessel, usually made of glass
10. **goblet**—drinking glass resting on a stem and base
11. **gourd**—any drinking vessel, after the scooped-out shell of the gourd, a species of fruit, so used
12. **horn**—drinking cup, so called since such cups were originally made from animal horns (Horns used for drinking had, of course, no base, and so the contents had to be drained before the vessel could be set down.)
13. **jeroboam**—very large goblet
14. **mug**—drinking cup
15. **noggin**—small drinking cup
16. **pannikin**—small cup
17. **rummer**—tall drinking glass
18. **stein**—large mug for beer
19. **stoup**—drinking vessel
20. **tankard**—large drinking glass, with a hinged cover and handle, and often ornamented
21. **Toby**—mug, shaped and ornamented to look like a fat man, for beer or ale
22. **tumbler**—large drinking glass (originally made so that it would not stand, i.e., so that it could not be put down until the contents had been drained)

9. Container or Vessel for Eating out of, or for Serving Foods,n.
1. **bowl**—concave, hollow vessel for liquids, such as soup, etc.
2. **buffet**—piece of furniture for holding dishes, serving food, etc.
3. **casserole**—vessel, usually of earthenware, in which food may be cooked and served
4. **crockery**—earthenware dishes, vessels, etc.
5. **dish**—comparatively flat or shallow vessel for serving up food at the table
6. **plate**—shallow, generally circular, container from which food is eaten
7. **platter**—large plate or dish for serving food at the table
8. **porringer**—bowl or dish for porridge
9. **ramekin**—pottery dish in which a single portion of food of certain kinds is baked and served
10. **tureen**—large container for serving soup at the table

10. Container or Vessel for Heating or Cooking,n.
1. **boiler**—container in which something may be boiled
2. **caldron, cauldron**—large boiler; large kettle
3. **crucible**—container or pot in which metals or other things are melted
4. **kettle**—vessel, usually of metal, for boiling liquids
5. **pan**—shallow vessel, often for heating or cooking
6. **pannikin**—small pan
7. **pot**—vessel for cooking food
8. **retort**—vessel in which substances are distilled or decomposed by the use of heat
9. **samovar**—metal urn used for making tea (in Russia)
10. **saucepan**—shallow pan for heating foods
11. **skillet**—pan for frying
12. **spider**—cast-iron pan for frying
13. **urn**—vessel for making and serving coffee or tea

11. Earthenware: bone china, ceramics or ceramic ware, china or chinaware, crockery, Dresden, Limoges or Limoges ware, porcelain or porcelain ware, pottery, Sèvres, Spode, stoneware, terra cotta,n.

12. Manufacture of Earthenware: pottery,n. (potter,n.)

13. Pert. to Earthenware or the Making of Earthenware: ceramic,adj.

14. Art of Making Earthenware: ceramics, pottery,n.

15. Bag,n.
1. **caddie bag**—bag for golf clubs
2. **handbag**—woman's purse
3. **poke**—bag or sack (now archaic, except in the phrase *pig in a poke*)
4. **porte-monnaie**—small purse
5. **pouch**—bag; sack
6. **purse**—bag for carrying money (generally, today, signifying a woman's bag)
7. **reticule**—small bag carried by women
8. **sack**—large cloth bag or other large bag
9. **wallet**—bag for carrying things, usually money, papers, etc., on the person

16. Container for Traveling; Traveling Bag, n.
1. **bag**—traveling bag
2. **Boston bag**—small traveling bag for books, papers, small articles of clothing, etc.
3. **brief case, brief bag**—small flat bag for carrying papers flat, books, etc.
4. **carpetbag**—kind of traveling bag
5. **duffel bag**—cloth bag for carrying supplies
6. **Gladstone**—light leather traveling bag with flexible sides
7. **grip, gripsack**—small traveling bag

8. **handbag**—traveling bag small enough to be carried by hand
9. **haversack**—bag or case, generally made of cloth, in which provisions for a journey are carried by a traveler or soldier
10. **kit**—bag or box in which equipment or implements are carried while traveling
11. **knapsack**—leather or cloth traveling bag containing clothing or necessities and carried on the back
12. **portfolio**—brief case
13. **portmanteau**—large traveling bag
14. **rucksack**—loose flat bag carried on the back when traveling
15. **satchel**—small traveling bag
16. **suitcase**—larger traveling bag
17. **trunk**—big box or chest in which traveling things are packed
18. **valise**—traveling bag
19. **wallet**—knapsack

17. Traveling Bags Collectively: baggage, impedimenta, luggage,n.

262. STORAGE

1. To Store,v.
1. **bank**—save (money) in a bank; put into a storage place
2. **bin**—store in a bin
3. **garner**—store
4. **hoard**—amass and store away, presumably for future use (hoarder,n.)
5. **hutch**—store in a box, bin, chest, etc.; hoard
6. **lay away, lay up**—store away; store up
7. **reserve**—hold or keep for future use (reservation,n.)
8. **salt away**—store away (colloq.)
9. **save**—store (literally or figuratively) for future use (saver,n.)
10. **stock**—store for future use
11. **stockpile**—store for future use when needed
12. **stow away**—put away safely in a convenient place for future use
13. **treasure**—collect and store for future use
14. **victual**—store up supplies

2. Store,n. *From Sec. 1:* bank, garner, hoard, reserve, savings, stock, stockpile, treasure

3. Place of Storage,n.
1. **armory**—storage place for equipment for war, weapons, etc.
2. **arsenal**—place where weapons are kept (or manufactured); armory; storehouse
3. **bank**—storage place
4. **bin**—container for storing
5. **buttery**—storeroom for liquors or other provisions
6. **cistern**—tank for storing water
7. **conservatoire**—conservatory
8. **conservatory**—place for safekeeping
9. **crib**—container for stored grain (usually a building or other structure)
10. **depositary**—depository
11. **depository**—place where commodities or valuables are stored
12. **depot**—place to which military supplies are shipped for storage and later distribution; storehouse
13. **garner**—granary
14. **granary**—storehouse for grain
15. **humidor**—box, case, or container for storing cigars or tobacco in order to prevent drying out
16. **larder**—place where food is stored
17. **lazarette, lazaret, lazaretto**—storage space or compartment on certain ships; storage room between decks on certain merchant ships
18. **magazine**—place for storing ammunition, explosives, etc.; place for storage, as in a gun, camera, stove, etc.; arsenal; storehouse; warehouse

19. **pantry**—room or closet for storing provisions, dishes, pots and pans, etc.
20. **repertory**—storehouse
21. **repository**—depository
22. **reservoir**—place where anything is stored; lake, etc., where water is stored
23. **shed**—one-story building for storage
24. **silo**—structure for storing fodder that will be converted into winter feed for domestic animals
25. **storage**—place where something is stored
26. **storehouse**—place, structure, etc., for storage
27. **storeroom**—room for storage
28. **tank**—receptacle for storing liquids, etc.
29. **thesaurus**—storehouse; treasury
30. **treasure house**—building where valuables are stored
31. **treasury**—storehouse of wealth; storehouse of information
32. **vault**—room or place for storing and safety; place for the storing and safekeeping of valuables; underground storehouse
33. **warehouse**—storehouse for goods or merchandise

263. PRESERVATION

1. Preserve, i.e., Treat to Keep from Spoiling or Decaying,v.
1. **brine**—steep or soak in a strong salt solution to preserve
2. **confect**—preserve; pickle
3. **conserve**—prepare (usually fruits) with sugar in order to preserve
4. **corn**—preserve with seasonings
5. **cure**—prepare (meat, fish, etc.) by salting, drying, etc., in order to preserve
6. **embalm**—preserve against the ravages of time; preserve figuratively; treat (a corpse) with chemicals or other preservatives to retard decay
7. **kipper**—cure (fish, etc.)
8. **marinate, marinade**—brine
9. **mummify**—preserve (a corpse) from decay
10. **pickle**—preserve with a solution of salt, vinegar, spices, etc.
11. **salt**—preserve with salt
12. **smoke**—prepare (meat, fish, etc.) by exposure to smoke in order to preserve
13. **souse**—pickle

2. Preservation,n. *From Sec. 1:* confection, mummification
3. Preservative,n. *From Sec. 1:* brine, marinade, pickle, salt
4. Acting to Preserve: preservative,adj.

264. LOSS

1. To Lose,v.
1. **forfeit**—lose, or lose the right to, by some fault, mistake, etc.
2. **leach**—lose soluble parts or particles through the effects of water running over or through
3. **mislay**—lose by putting in a place and then forgetting where
4. **misplace**—mislay

2. Loss,n. *From Sec. 1:* forfeit or forfeiture, misplacement; *Also:*
1. **bereavement**—loss, as of a person through death, or of some tangible, as property, etc.
2. **decrement**—loss
3. **deprivation**—loss
4. **penalty**—loss attached to some act or condition
5. **perdition**—complete and irrevocable loss; loss of one's soul; loss of the possibility of going to heaven

3. That Which Is Lost,n. *From Secs. 1 and 2:*

forfeit or forfeiture, penalty; *Also:* 1. **toll**—that which is lost

4. Lost,adj. *From Sec. 1:* forfeited or forfeit, leached, mislaid, misplaced; *Also:*
1. **astray**—lost
2. **bewildered**—lost and puzzled
3. **missing**—lost

5. Having Lost,adj.
1. **bereaved of**—having lost (often by death)
2. **bereft of**—having lost (something immaterial, intangible, or abstract)

6. One Who Has, or Those Who Have, Lost a Relative by Death: the bereaved,n.

7. To Be or Become Lost,v.
1. **disappear**—be or become lost (disappearance,n.)
2. **stray**—become lost

8. Lost Person, Thing, or Animal,n.
1. **stray**—lost animal, child, etc.
2. **waif**—lost person, animal, or thing

265. DESIRE

1. To Desire,v.
1. **ache for**—have an insistent and painful desire for
2. **aspire to**—desire earnestly to attain, reach, or get (something great, or some high or honorable position)
3. **begrudge**—covet; envy (someone) for possessing
4. **covet**—desire excessively (that which rightfully belongs to another)
5. **crave (for)**—desire keenly; have abnormal or morbid desires for
6. **desiderate**—look upon (something) as desirable
7. **envy**—feel a strong desire for (the possessions, position, attributes, etc., of someone), while being unhappy that he has it or them
8. **gasp for, gasp after**—desire; desire eagerly; crave
9. **grudge**—covet; envy (someone) for possessing
10. **hanker for, hanker after**—desire eagerly; crave
11. **hunger for, hunger after**—have a compelling and unceasing desire for
12. **itch for, itch after**—desire; desire (to do)
13. **languish for**—have or feel a strong and painful desire for; suffer with desire for
14. **long (for)**—have a strong desire (for); crave
15. **lust for, lust after**—desire strongly, excessively, or sinfully
16. **pant for**—desire eagerly
17. **pine for**—desire painfully, strongly, greatly, keenly, etc.
18. **prefer**—find more desirable
19. **require**—desire
20. **sigh for**—desire keenly, greatly, etc.
21. **starve for**—desire strongly; crave
22. **thirst for, thirst after**—desire keenly or greatly; crave
23. **want**—desire
24. **wish**—desire
25. **yearn for, yearn after**—desire greatly, keenly, etc.

2. Desire,n. *From Sec. 1:* ache, aspiration, craving, desideration, envy, hankering, hunger or hungering, itch, longing, lust, pining, preference, requirement, thirst, want, wish, yearning; *Also:*
1. **accord**—voluntary desire to act or do
2. **ambition**—strong desire
3. **appetency**—strong, unwavering desire; appetite
4. **appetite**—desire or craving for that which fills a bodily, mental or emotional need; desire for food

5. **avarice**—excessive, unseemly, and abnormal desire for gain, wealth, or possession
6. **cacoëthes**—desire so strong or frenzied as to be beyond satisfying; morbidly urgent, excessive, or uncontrollable desire
7. **caprice**—irrational, unexplainable, and apparently unmotivated desire or desires
8. **cathexis**—desire concentrated upon a wished-for object or upon some idea—a concept in psychoanalysis (cathectic, adj.)
9. **conatus**—natural impulse
10. **crotchet**—strange desire
11. **fancy**—caprice
12. **gluttony**—insatiable desire
13. **greed**—unrestrained desire, often for something evil
14. **impulse**—sudden and strong desire, usually to act or do
15. **mania**—excessive or uncontrollable desire
16. **motive, motivation**—desire that stimulates to action
17. **nostalgia**—keen desire for home, past surroundings, or to relive previous pleasant experiences
18. **notion**—whim
19. **nympholepsy**—frenzied desire for something unattainable
20. **obsession**—desire or impulse that haunts or besets the mind
21. **oestrus**—violent desire or impulse
22. **passion (for)**—strong desire (for)
23. **solicitude**—anxious or eager desire
24. **stomach**—desire; appetite (usually used in the negative: *no stomach for such things*)
25. **urge**—strong desire
26. **vagary**—caprice
27. **velleity**—very faint desire
28. **whim**—quaint or strange desire
29. **whoredom**—sinful desire
30. **will**—desire
31. **yen**—intense desire; sharp craving
32. **zeal**—eager desire

3. Desirous,adj. *From Sec. 1:* aspirant or aspiring, covetous, envious, itchy, longing, lustful, thirsty or athirst, wishful, yearning; *From Sec. 2:* ambitious, avaricious, capricious, crotchety, gluttonous, greedy, nostalgic, nympholeptic, solicitous, vagarious, willing, zealous; *Also:*

1. **acquisitive**—desirous of gaining, adding to, and holding possessions and/or power
2. **avid (for)**—keenly desirous (of)
3. **cormorant**—excessively grasping
4. **eager (for)**—keenly desirous (of)
5. **flighty**—full of sudden and strange desires
6. **grasping**—desirous of gaining the possessions of others, often through unethical or illegal means
7. **lickerish, liquorish**—desirous; lustful
8. **miserly**—avaricious; grasping and covetous
9. **rapacious**—excessively grasping
10. **ravenous, ravening**—excessively grasping
11. **wistful**—keenly desirous, usually with little or no expectation of obtaining what one wants
12. **would-be**—wishing to be (*would-be gentlemen*, etc.)

4. Desirousness,n. *From Sec. 1:* covetousness, enviousness or envy, lustfulness or lust, wishfulness; *From Sec. 2:* ambitiousness or ambition, avariciousness or avarice, capriciousness or caprice, crotchetiness, gluttonousness or gluttony, greediness or greed, solicitousness or solicitude, vagarity, willingness, zealousness or zeal; *From Sec. 3:* acquisitiveness, avidness or avidity, eagerness, flightiness, graspingness, lickerishness, liquorishness, miserliness, rapaciousness or rapacity, ravenousness, wistfulness

5. Desirer,n. *From Sec. 1:* aspirant, coveter, craver, envier, grudger, longer, luster, thirster, wisher, yearner; *From Sec. 2:* glutton, nympholept, zealot; *From Sec. 3:* cormorant, miser; *Also:*

1. **buzzard**—grasping person
2. **candidate**—one who desires to attain an office, post, position, etc.

6. With Envy: askance,adv.

7. Something Desired,n.
1. **ambition**—that which one desires strongly, or desires to attain
2. **desideratum, desideration, desiderative** —something desired or considered desirable and/or necessary (desiderata,pl.)
3. **desire**—that which is wished or wished for
4. **passion**—that which one desires to attain
5. **plum**—something esp. desirable
6. **rage, craze, fad**—object of eager and popular desire

8. Arising out of, Based on, etc., Desire,adj.
1. **arbitrary**—based on, or derived from, one's own desires or caprice with no regard for reasonableness, rule, law, etc. (arbitrariness,n.)
2. **capricious**—arbitrary (capriciousness, caprice,n.)
3. **impulsive**—arising out of a sudden desire, usually to act (impulsiveness, impulsivity,n.)
4. **spontaneous**—caused by natural desire (spontaneity, spontaneousness,n.)

9. Expressive of Desire: optative,adj.

10. Pert. to, Descr. of, or Signifying Desire: desiderative,adj.

11. Fulfilling Desires: welcome,adj.

12. To Arouse Desire,v.
1. **fire**—inspire
2. **inspire**—arouse the desire (to do or act)
3. **motivate**—create a desire in (someone) to do or act
4. **obsess**—haunt the mind with a desire or impulse
5. **suggest**—indirectly arouse (a desire) in the mind

13. Arousal of Desire,n. *From Sec. 12:* inspiration, motivation, obsession, suggestion

14. Arousing Desire,adj. *From Sec. 12:* inspiring or inspirational, motivating, obsessive, suggestive; *Also:*
1. **enviable**—causing or exciting desire or envy
2. **savory**—exciting desire

15. That Which Arouses Desire,n. *From Sec. 12:* inspiration, motivation or motive; *Also:*
1. **incentive**—cause of a desire to act or achieve a goal

16. Greedy,adj.
1. **acquisitive**—greedy
2. **avaricious**—greedy for riches or money for, generally, the mere sake of hoarding; greedy and stingy
3. **avid**—greedy
4. **cormorant**—ravenous; voracious
5. **covetous**—greedy, esp. for what belongs to another
6. **esurient**—greedy; voracious
7. **gluttonous**—excessively greedy; greedy for food
8. **grasping**—greedy, in the sense of desiring to get all one possibly can
9. **hoggish**—greedy, like a hog
10. **lickerish, liquorish**—greedy for delicious food
11. **miserly**—greedy; greedy for money; avaricious
12. **openmouthed**—greedy; excessively greedy
13. **piggish**—greedy, like a pig
14. **rapacious**—excessively greedy or grasping

15. **ravening**—voracious; eating, feeding, or devouring greedily
16. **ravenous**—extremely greedy
17. **sordid**—greedy
18. **swinish**—hoggish
19. **voracious**—greedy, as if ready to devour
20. **vulturous**—greedy, unscrupulous, and ruthless
21. **wolfish**—greedy; greedy and cruel

17. Greed; Greediness,n. *From Sec. 16:* acquisitiveness, avarice or avariciousness, avidity or avidness, covetousness, esurience, gluttony or gluttonousness, graspingness, hoggishness, lickerishness, liquorishness, miserliness, piggishness, rapacity or rapaciousness, ravenousness, sordidness, swinishness, voracity or voraciousness, vulturousness, wolfishness; *Also:* 1. **cupidity**—neurotic, almost pathological greed for wealth and material possessions

18. Greedy Person,n. *From Sec. 16:* cormorant, esurient, glutton, hog, miser, pig, swine, vulture, wolf; *Also:*
1. **buzzard**—grasping person
2. **curmudgeon**—avaricious person
3. **harpy**—extremely greedy person
4. **Shylock**—greedy creditor

19. Eager,adj.
1. **ablaze**—eager
2. **ambitious**—eager to get ahead in the world; eager to attain advancement
3. **ardent**—eager
4. **athirst**—eager
5. **avid**—eager
6. **cormorant**—excessively eager
7. **lickerish, liquorish**—eager, esp. to enjoy or taste
8. **prompt**—eager and ready
9. **solicitous**—anxiously eager
10. **thirsty**—eager
11. **vehement**—eager
12. **voracious**—excessively eager
13. **warm-blooded**—eager
14. **whole-souled**—eager and sincere
15. **wild**—intensely eager (colloq.)
16. **zealous**—eager

20. Eagerness,n. *From Sec. 19:* ambitiousness or ambition, ardor or ardency, thirst, avidity or avidness, lickerishness, liquorishness, promptness or promptitude, solicitude or solicitousness, thirst, vehemence, voracity or voraciousness, warm-bloodedness, zeal or zealousness; *Also:* 1. **élan** (French)—warm and spirited eagerness

21. Eager Person,n. *From Sec. 19:* cormorant, zealot

22. To Make Eager: whet (the appetite, curiosity, etc.),v.

23. Willing,adj.
1. **accommodating**—willing to help
2. **alacritous**—cheerfully willing
3. **cheerful**—willing
4. **disposed (to)**—possessed of a willingness (to do)
5. **inclined (to)**—disposed (to do)
6. **minded**—disposed
7. **obliging**—willing; willing to do favors
8. **patient**—willing to wait, suffer, endure, etc., calmly
9. **prone (to)**—having a willingness (to do)
10. **solicitous**—anxiously willing
11. **voluntary, unforced**—willing

24. Willingness,n. *From Sec. 23:* accommodation, alacrity, cheerfulness, disposition, inclination, patience, proneness, solicitude or solicitousness, voluntariness or volition

25. To Make Willing,v. *From Sec. 23:* dispose, incline

26. Unwilling,adj.
1. **averse**—unwilling because something is distasteful or unpleasant
2. **backward**—reluctant

3. **begrudging**—grudging
4. **disinclined (to)**—unwilling (to do or act)
5. **disobliging**—unwilling to oblige, do favors, or be pleasant
6. **grudging**—descr. of that which is given unwillingly
7. **hesitant, hesitative**—unwilling
8. **impatient**—unwilling to accept or stand delay
9. **indisposed (to)**—unwilling (to do or act)
10. **involuntary, forced**—unwilling; given, done, etc., unwillingly or under compulsion
11. **loath, loth**—reluctant
12. **reluctant**—unwilling; preferring not (to do or act)
13. **unaccommodating**—unwilling to help
14. **uncheerful**—unwilling
15. **uninclined (to)**—disinclined
16. **unobliging**—unwilling; unwilling to do favors

27. Unwillingness,n. *From Sec. 26:* aversion or averseness, backwardness, disinclination; hesitation, hesitancy, or hesitance; impatience, indisposition, involuntariness, loathness, reluctance or reluctancy

28. To Be Unwilling,v. *From Sec. 26:* begrudge, grudge, hesitate

266. THE WILL

1. The Will: volition,n. (volitional, volitionary, volitive,adj.)

2. One's Free Will: accord, voluntariness,n. (voluntary,adj.)

3. Act of Willing; Exercise of the Will: volition,n. (volitional, volitionary,adj.)

4. To Will; To Exercise the Will: volitionate,v.

5. Power of Exercising the Will,n.
1. **volitiency**—power to will (volitient,adj.)
2. **volition**—power of willing (volitionary, volitive,adj.)
3. **volitionality**—possession of the power of using the will (volitional,adj.)
4. **voluntariness**—ability to exercise one's free will (voluntary,adj.)

6. Based on One's Own Will, with No Regard for Reasonableness, Rule, Law, etc.: arbitrary, capricious, despotic,adj. (arbitrariness, capriciousness or caprice,n.)

7. Controlled by the Will: voluntary,adj. (voluntariness,n.)

8. Incomplete or Imperfect Volition: velleity,n.

9. Not Controlled by the Will: involuntary, reflex, reflexive, unwilled,adj. (involuntariness, reflexiveness,n.)

10. Lack or Loss of Will Power, Found in Certain Neurotic or Insane Conditions: abulia,n. (abulic,adj.)

11. Doctrine, Philosophy, or Theory of the Will,n.
1. **determinism**—doctrine or philosophy that acts of will are determined by cause (determinist,n. determinist, deterministic, adj.)
2. **indeterminism**—doctrine or philosophy that the will is free (indeterminist,n. indeterminist, indeterministic,adj.)
3. **libertarianism**—doctrine or philosophy that the will is free (libertarian,n.)
4. **necessarianism**—necessitarianism (necessarian,n. necessarian,adj.)
5. **necessitarianism**—doctrine or philosophy that the will is not free (necessitarian,n. necessitarian,adj.)
6. **Pelagianism**—doctrines of Pelagius, British monk who lived in the fourth century,

that man has freedom of will and is not doomed by original sin (Pelagian,adj.)

7. voluntarism—theory that the will is the dominant factor in experience or in the make-up of the world (voluntarist,n. voluntaristic,adj.)

267. HOPE

1. Hopeful,adj.
1. **buoyant**—hopeful
2. **optimistic**—hopeful; feeling or believing that everything will turn out favorably
3. **Pollyanna, Pollyanna-like, Pollyannish** —sickeningly, irrepressibly, or incorrigibly optimistic (from the character in a novel by Eleanor Porter; Pollyanna labeled herself the "glad girl"—nothing ever depressed her, no matter how calamitous or disastrous)
4. **roseate, rose-colored, rosy**—hopeful (of views, attitudes, etc.)
5. **sanguine, sanguineous**—tending to take a hopeful view; cheerfully optimistic
6. **unflagging**—not becoming discouraged; not losing hope

2. Hopefulness, Hope,n. *From Sec. 1:* buoyancy, optimism, Pollyannaism, rosiness, sanguineness or sanguineousness; *Also:* 1. **encouragement**—hope; hopefulness; hope to go on or continue

3. Hopeful Person,n. *From Sec. 1:* optimist, Pollyanna

4. Belief or Philosophy that Everything Will Turn Out Well, Favorably, or for the Best: optimism,n. (optimist,n. optimistic, adj.)

5. To Give Hope to: boost, brace up, buck up, buoy up, encourage, hearten,v. (encouragement,n.)

6. Giving or Holding Out Hope: encouraging, heartening, rosy,adj.

7. Hoped-for: prospective,adj.

8. That Which Is Hoped for: prospect,n.

9. Hopelessness; Feeling of Hopelessness; Lack of Hope,n.
1. **abjectness**—hopelessness
2. **chill**—discouragement
3. **damp**—discouragement
4. **despair**—lack of hope
5. **desperation**—hopelessness
6. **despondency**—hopelessness; feeling that all hope is gone or that everything is hopeless
7. **disconsolateness**—feeling that there is no hope
8. **discouragement, disheartenment, downheartedness**—lack or loss of hope; feeling of hopelessness; feeling that success is beyond hope, grasp, or attainment
9. **dismay**—discouragement caused by what one sees, hears, or learns, or by danger, difficulty, or a problem; utter discouragement or disheartenment at learning something previously unknown and unsuspected
10. **futility**—hopelessness, i.e., absence of hope for effectiveness or success
11. **pessimism, dyspepsia**—tendency to feel hopeless, or to feel that there is no hope
12. **slough, slough of despond**—feeling of complete hopelessness
13. **Weltschmerz** (German)—pessimism about the world, the state of the world, the way things are, etc.

10. Hopeless, i.e., Feeling Hopeless,adj. *From Sec. 9:* abject, chilled, dampened, despairing, desperate, despondent, disconsolate; discouraged, disheartened, or downhearted; dismayed, pessimistic

11. One Who Tends to Feel Hopeless,n. *From Sec. 9:* pessimist

12. To Give Up or Lose Hope,v. *From Sec. 9:* despair, despond

13. Hopeless, i.e., Descr. of That Which Is Hopeless or Offers No Hope,adj. *From Sec. 9:* desperate, futile (desperateness, futility, futileness,n.); *Also:* 1. **forlorn**—hopeless (forlornness,n.)

14. To Give a Feeling of Hopelessness to, or Take Hope from,v. *From Sec. 9:* chill, dampen, discourage, dishearten, dismay; *Also:* daunt, wet-blanket,v.

15. One Who Takes Away Hope,n. *From Sec. 9:* dampener, discourager, disheartener; *From Sec. 14:* daunter, wet blanket

16. Robbing of Hope,adj. *From Sec. 9:* chilly, dampening, discouraging, disheartening

17. Influence, Feeling, or Thing That Robs of Hope: chill, dampener, damper, despair, discouragement,n.

18. Undertaking That Is Hopeless, or Nearly So, i.e., Certain, or Almost Certain, to Fail; A Useless or Futile Hope: forlorn hope,n.

19. Philosophy of Hopelessness,n.
1. **futilitarianism**—belief or philosophy that human hopes are futile, or that it is hopeless to strive or aspire (futilitarian, n. futilitarian,adj.)
2. **pessimism**—belief or philosophy that life is not worth while and that evils predominate; belief or philosophy that the worst will happen, that things will turn out badly, etc. (pessimist,n. pessimistic, adj.)

20. Attack of Hopelessness Occurring in Certain Neurotic States: psycholepsy,n. (psycholeptic,adj.)

21. A Box, the Gift to Pandora from Zeus, That Contained All the Gods' Blessings—When, out of Curiosity, She Opened It, All the Blessings Escaped except Hope; According to an Earlier Version, the Box Contained the Evils That Afflict Mankind—These Escaped under Similar Circumstances; Hence, in Modern Use, Anything Best Left Unopened, Untouched, Undisturbed, etc., Lest It Cause Trouble, Difficulties, Misfortunes, etc.: Pandora's box,n.

268. EXPECTATION

1. To Expect: anticipate; apprehend (with fear or anxiety); await, calculate, contemplate, count on, envision, foresee, look for, look forward to; purpose (to do); reckon on; undertake (to do),v.

2. Expectation; Expectance; Expectancy: anticipation; apprehension (i.e., of misfortune, etc.); calculation, contemplation, view, n.

3. Expecter: anticipant or anticipator,n.

4. Expectant: anticipant, anticipative, or anticipatory; anxious or apprehensive (i.e., with uneasiness or fear); breathless (i.e., figuratively holding one's breath in expectation); eager (i.e., with delight, pleasure, or impatience); impatient (i.e., nervously, anxiously, or restlessly so),adj.

5. Such Expectancy,n. *From Sec. 4:* anticipancy or anticipation; anxiety or anxiousness, apprehensiveness or apprehension; breathlessness, eagerness, impatience

6. Anxious, Eager, or Excited Condition of Expectancy: suspense; tenterhooks (esp. in the phrase *on tenterhooks*),n.

7. Expected: anticipated, awaited, contemplated, counted on, foreseen, prospective, reckoned on,adj.

8. Reasonably Expected or to Be Expected: logical, prospective,adj.

9. That Which Is Expected, or Can Reasonably Be Expected: prospect,n.

10. Figuratively or Literally Holding One's Breath in Expectation: with bated breath, adv. phrase

11. To Be in Such a State of Eager Expectation that the Saliva Literally or Figuratively Runs from the Mouth: drool,v. (drooler,n. drooling,adj.)

12. To Expect and Desire: hope for, hope that,v. (hope,n. hopefulness,n. hoper,n. hopeful,adj.)

13. To Expect to Get: anticipate; bargain for (as in *more than one bargained for,* etc.); reckon on,v.

14. Through an Error of Judgment or Reasoning, to Expect to Happen Something That Does Not Happen: miscalculate,v. (miscalculation,n.)

269. UNEXPECTEDNESS

1. Unexpected,adj.
1. abrupt—unexpected
2. astounding—so unexpected as to shock or stun
3. casual—unexpected
4. contingent—unexpected
5. precipitous, precipitate, precipitant— unexpected; fast and unexpected
6. sudden—coming or happening unexpectedly or with no, or very little, notice
7. unanticipated—unexpected
8. unbargained for—unexpectedly received
9. uncalculated—unexpected
10. uncontemplated—unexpected
11. unforeseen—unexpected
12. unhoped for—unexpected and undesired
13. unlooked for—unexpected

2. Unexpectedness,n. *From Sec. 1:* abruptness, contingency; precipitance, precipitation, or precipitousness; suddenness

3. That Which Is Unexpected,n. *From Sec. 1:* contingency; *Also:* **1. godsend**—that which comes unexpectedly in answer to a great need, as if sent by God

4. To Bring on Unexpectedly: precipitate,v. (precipitation,n.)

270. SUDDENNESS

1. Sudden,adj.
1. abrupt—sudden
2. acute—sudden and sharp
3. impulsive—resulting from sudden feeling or whim
4. precipitous, precipitate, precipitant— unusually sudden
5. spasmodic—sudden and forceful or violent, but lasting only a short time
6. swift—happening suddenly

2. Suddenness,n. *From Sec. 1:* abruptness, acuteness, impulsiveness or impulsivity; precipitousness, precipitateness, precipitance, or precipitancy; swiftness

3. That Which Is Sudden,n. *From Sec. 1:* impulse, spasm; *Also:* **1. thunderclap**—anything very sudden

4. To Bring On Suddenly: precipitate,v. (precipitation,n.)

5. Suddenly and Heavily: plump,adv.

6. Acting, or Likely to Act, out of Sudden Feeling or Desire, and without Proper Care, Thought, or Consideration: impetuous,adj. (impetuousness, impetuosity,n.)

271. SURPRISE

1. Surprising,adj.
1. amazing—so surprising as to cause wonder
2. astonishing—so surprising as to be almost beyond belief
3. astounding—so surprising as to shock or stun
4. awing, awesome—filling with surprise and fear
5. breath-taking—extremely surprising
6. consternating—filling with, or causing, surprise and fear
7. dumfounding, dumbfounding—so surprising and puzzling as to leave one mute
8. fabulous—amazing, in the sense that anything so described occurs in fables rather than real life
9. flabbergasting—so surprising as to leave one silent or unable to react
10. marvelous—astonishing; wonderful
11. shocking—striking with surprise
12. spectacular—exciting surprise
13. staggering—so surprising as almost to make one reel or lose one's balance; astonishing
14. startling—surprising and frightening
15. stunning—overpowering with surprise; stupefying
16. stupefying, stupefactive—surprising to an extreme degree, or to the point where the mind is unable to function
17. stupendous—amazing; astonishing
18. wonderful—exciting surprise because of excellence, strangeness, etc.

2. To Surprise,v. *From Sec. 1:* amaze, astonish, astound, awe, consternate, dumfound or dumbfound, flabbergast, shock, stagger, startle, stun, stupefy

3. Surprise, i.e., State of Surprise,n. *From Sec. 1:* amazement, astonishment, astoundment, awe, consternation, dumfoundment or dumbfoundment, shock, stupefaction, wonder or wonderment

4. Surprised,adj. *From Sec. 1:* amazed, astonished, etc.; *Also:*
1. aghast—amazed
2. taken aback—surprised
3. thunderstruck, thunderstricken— amazed; astounded

5. Gaping in Surprise: openmouthed,adj.

6. Figuratively or Literally Holding One's Breath in Wonder: with bated breath

7. By Surprise: unaware, unawares,adv.

8. To Feel Surprised,v.
1. marvel (at)—feel great wonder or astonishment (at)
2. wonder—feel surprised by something strange or amazing

9. To Show Surprise,v.
1. gape—show surprise or wonder by staring with open mouth (gape,n.)
2. start—give an involuntary twitch or jump from surprise (start,n.)
3. startle—move suddenly owing to surprise (startle,n.)

10. That Which Causes Surprise: bombshell, marvel, surprise, thunderbolt, thunderclap, wonder, wonderment,n.

272. WAIT

1. To Wait,v.
1. abide—wait for; wait for eagerly
2. attend—wait
3. await—wait for
4. bide—wait; wait expectantly
5. bide one's time—wait patiently
6. dangle—wait or be left hanging in suspense

7. **delay**—wait
8. **hover**—wait around or near, usually uncertainly and/or watchfully
9. **lurk**—wait secretly or in concealment
10. **queue, queue up**—wait in line with other people; form a waiting line with other people
11. **tarry**—wait; wait expectantly
12. **waylay**—lie in wait for someone for the purpose of attacking and/or robbing him

2. A Wait; A Waiting,n. *From Sec. 1:* attendance, delay

3. State of Waiting,n. *From Sec. 1:* danglement, delay, tarry

4. Waiter,n. *From Sec. 1:* bider, delayer, lurker, tarrier, waylayer

5. Those Who Wait in Line: queue,n.

6. To Keep (Someone) Waiting: delay, detain,v. (delay, detainment, detention,n.)

7. Patient,adj.
1. **bovine**—patient, in allusion to a cow or ox
2. **forbearing**—patient
3. **fortitudinous**—patiently enduring hardship, pain, suffering, etc.
4. **longanimous**—tending to bear suffering with patience
5. **long-suffering**—enduring pain, suffering, insult, etc., for a long time with unusual patience
6. **meek**—patiently enduring or suffering

8. Patience,n. *From Sec. 7:* bovinity, forbearance, fortitude, longanimity, meekness

9. To Be Patient: forbear,v. (forbearance, n.)

10. Impatient,adj.
1. **chafing**—impatient
2. **choleric**—angrily impatient
3. **hasty**—impatient; done impatiently
4. **quick**—impatient
5. **testy**—impatient

11. Impatience,n. *From Sec. 10:* choler, hastiness or haste, testiness

12. To Be Impatient: chafe,v.

13. To Lose Patience with: tire of, weary of, v.

273. NEED

1. To Need,v.
1. **crave**—need
2. **demand**—need
3. **desiderate**—consider necessary
4. **postulate**—need
5. **require**—need
6. **want**—need; feel the need of

2. Need,n.
1. **compulsion, compulsiveness**—irresistible need to do something
2. **craving**—keen need
3. **demand**—need
4. **extremity**—state or condition of being in the greatest need
5. **necessity**—need
6. **want**—need

3. A Need, i.e., That Which Is Necessary or Needed,n.
1. **competence, competency**—that which is needed to sustain life adequately
2. **demand**—that which is needed
3. **desideratum**—something considered necessary and desirable (desiderata,pl.)
4. **essence**—necessary part of something
5. **godsend**—something sorely needed and coming unexpectedly, as if sent by God
6. **necessity**—that which is necessary, needed, or cannot be done without
7. **postulate**—necessary condition
8. **prerequisite**—that which is needed beforehand

9. **qualification**—that which is needed
10. **requirement**—that which is needed
11. **requisite**—that which is needed; that for which circumstances dictate a need
12. **sine qua non (Latin)**—that which is absolutely necessary
13. **vitals**—necessary parts
14. **want**—a need

4. Fulfilling Needs: welcome,adj.

5. Pert. to, or Affecting, Bodily Needs: material,adj.

6. Necessary; Needed; Made Necessary,adj.
1. **basic**—essential
2. **bounden**—required
3. **compulsory**—required
4. **critical**—absolutely necessary but in short supply—of supplies, materials, etc. (criticalness,n.)
5. **demanded**—required
6. **de rigueur (French)**—needed or required for the sake of etiquette or good form
7. **entailed**—required
8. **essential**—needed; necessary; indispensable (essentiality,n.)
9. **imperative**—absolutely necessary and urgent (imperativeness,n.)
10. **incumbent**—falling upon one as a necessity
11. **indispensable**—descr. of that which one cannot get along without or do without; needed; necessary (indispensability,n.)
12. **integral**—necessary to the complete whole, or to completeness
13. **key**—essential, in that other things cannot function without it
14. **mandatory**—required by an official or authoritative order
15. **necessitated**—made necessary
16. **necessitous**—made necessary
17. **needful**—necessary
18. **obligatory**—required
19. **organic**—needed; necessary; indispensable; vital
20. **postulated**—required
21. **prerequisite**—necessary or required beforehand
22. **required**—needed; necessary; made necessary
23. **requisite**—necessary; needed; made necessary by circumstances
24. **strategic**—most necessary in the carrying out of something, or to being successful in an endeavor; necessary to the prosecution of war (of materials or supplies)
25. **substantive**—needed; necessary; indispensable
26. **vital**—most necessary; indispensable to life or continued living

7. To Be Necessary for; To Be Necessary as a Duty or Obligation: behoove,v.

8. To Make Necessary: compel, demand, entail, necessitate, postulate, require,v. (compulsion, demand, entailment, necessitation, postulation, requirement,n. necessitative,adj.)

9. Necessarily; By Necessity: perforce,adv.

10. Doctrine or Philosophy that Necessity Dictates the Way Things Are: determinism, n. (determinist,n. determinist, deterministic, adj.)

11. Unneeded; Unnecessary,adj.
1. **dispensable**—descr. of that which one does not need or can do without (dispensability,n.)
2. **excess**—unneeded
3. **extrinsic**—inessential
4. **gratuitous, uncalled for**—descr. of that which is said, done, etc., when there is no need for it, when the circumstances do not require it, when there is no rational motivation, etc—generally used with an unpleasant connotation (gratuitousness,n.)

5. **inessential**—not needed; descr. of that which one can get along without
6. **needless**—unnecessary; inessential (needlessness,n.)
7. **non-strategic**—not necessary for the carrying out of something; not vital for the conduct of war (of supplies, materials, etc.)
8. **superfluous**—unnecessary; inessential (superfluousness, superfluity,n.)
9. **uncritical**—not absolutely essential (of materials, supplies, etc.)
10. **undemanded**—unneeded
11. **unessential**—inessential
12. **unincumbent**—not falling upon one as a necessity
13. **unneedful**—unnecessary
14. **unrequired**—unneeded

12. To Make Unnecessary: obviate,v. (obviation,n.)

274. DEMAND

1. To Demand; To Ask; To Ask for,v.
1. **abuse**—make excessive demands upon (abuse one's patience, etc.)
2. **adjure**—ask solemnly or earnestly
3. **appeal for**—request earnestly
4. **apply for**—request
5. **arrogate**—demand presumptuously and without right
6. **badger**—nag without cease
7. **beg**—ask for that which is a favor; ask for persistently or earnestly
8. **besiege**—make insistent and repeated demands upon or requests to
9. **bid**—ask to come; appeal (for)
10. **charge**—ask as a price
11. **claim**—demand; demand that which is due or which is one's right
12. **clamor for**—demand insistently and in loud tones
13. **consult**—ask for instruction or information
14. **counterclaim**—demand in opposition to the demand of another, or to offset such a demand
15. **dun**—constantly and repeatedly demand payment from
16. **entreat**—ask earnestly for; ask for persuasively; ask for in such a way as to overcome someone's resistance, reluctance, or automatically negative reaction
17. **exact**—demand; demand and force to give
18. **impetrate**—entreat
19. **implore**—ask for (something) out of great need, desire, eagerness, or anguish
20. **importune**—ask, demand, or request with annoying persistence
21. **impose upon**—make unfair or unreasonable demands upon
22. **insist on or upon**—continue asking or demanding
23. **invite**—ask to come; ask for
24. **nag**—make annoyingly persistent demands or requests
25. **pester**—make continual and annoying petty requests to
26. **petition**—make a written and signed request to an authority for (some favor, privilege, etc.)
27. **plead for**—ask for earnestly; implore
28. **ply**—keep asking (ply someone with demands, etc.)
29. **poll**—ask for, and register or classify, the opinions of on a specific, and usually public, question or problem
30. **postulate**—demand
31. **recall**—ask to come back
32. **reclaim**—demand the return of
33. **request**—ask; ask as a favor
34. **require**—demand
35. **requisition**—demand; make a formal demand for

36. **seek**—ask for
37. **solicit**—try to get by asking; ask earnestly or eagerly for
38. **SOS**—ask for help
39. **stipulate**—demand as a condition of agreement
40. **sue for**—ask urgently for
41. **supplicate**—ask humbly and seriously
42. **tax**—make great demands on
43. **urge**—demand insistently

2. A Demand; A Demanding,n. *From Sec. 1:* adjuration, appeal, application, arrogation, bid, charge, claim, clamor, consultation, counterclaim, dun, entreaty or entreatment, exaction, impetration, imploration, importunity, imposition, insistence or insistency, invitation, petition, plea, poll, recall, reclaim, request, requirement, requisition, solicitation, SOS, stipulation, suit, supplication, tax; *Also:*
1. **lien**—legal claim on a property by a creditor
2. **recourse**—appeal for aid or protection
3. **round robin**—petition with the signatures in a circle so that no one can tell who signed first
4. **ultimatum**—final demand, demands, or statement of demands

3. Demander,n. *From Sec. 1:* adjurer or adjuror, appellant, applicant, arrogator, beggar, claimant, consultant, exactor, impetrator, implorer, importuner, imposer, nag or nagger, pest, petitioner, pleader, pollster, seeker, solicitor, suitor; suppliant, supplicant or supplicator; *Also:*
1. **scold**—nag
2. **termagant**—nagging woman
3. **virago**—nagging woman

4. Demanding,adj. *From Sec. 1:* appealing, badgering, begging, etc.; adjuratory, appellant, clamorous, importunate, insistent, pestiferous, petitionary; suppliant, supplicant, or supplicatory (clamorousness; importunateness, importunacy, or importunity; insistence or insistency, pestiferousness, supplicancy, n.); *Also:*
1. **ambitious**—making great claims or demands (ambitiousness,n.)
2. **exigent**—making great demands on one; demanding immediate action or attention (exigency,n.)
3. **imperious**—arrogantly demanding (imperiousness,n.)
4. **pressing**—urgent
5. **urgent**—demanding immediate action or attention (urgency,n.)

5. Pert. to an Earnest Request: appellant, appellate,adj.

6. Person Appealed to for Help or Protection: recourse,n.

7. To Argue for,v.
1. **advocate**—argue for (advocacy,n. advocate,n.)
2. **urge**—argue for insistently

275. ORDER; COMMAND

1. To Order; To Command,v.
1. **adjudge**—order by law; decree
2. **adjure**—command under oath or pain of punishment (to do)
3. **bid**—order in a somewhat arbitrary or peremptory manner (to do or act)
4. **charge**—order (to do or complete a task, duty, etc.)
5. **decree**—order or command with authority
6. **dictate (to)**—give peremptory orders or commands (to)
7. **direct**—order (to do)
8. **enjoin**—order or command
9. **lord over**—order about
10. **ordain**—order

11. **prescribe**—order
12. **require**—order (to do)
13. **subpoena**—summon into court by the serving of legal papers upon
14. **summon**—order to come

2. Order or Command; An Ordering or Commanding,n. *From Sec. 1:* adjuration, bid, charge; decree, decretal, or decreement; dictate or dictation, direction or directive, enjoinment, ordinance or ordainment, prescription, requirement, subpoena, summons; *Also:*
  1. **behest**—order; command
  2. **bull**—official order by the Pope
  3. **canon**—decree; decree by the church
  4. **decretal**—authoritative ecclesiastical decree
  5. **directive**—order of the type that explains how a thing is to be done
  6. **edict**—order, command, or decree issued by public authority
  7. **injunction**—order commanding a person to do something, or to refrain from doing something
  8. **mandate**—official or authoritative order
  9. **prescript**—order; that which is ordered or prescribed
  10. **rescript**—official order
  11. **summons**—order demanding a person's appearance in court
  12. **ukase**—official decree, or decree having the force of law (generally derogatory)
  13. **writ**—formal legal or court order directing or restraining

3. One Who Orders,n. *From Sec. 1:* adjurer or adjuror, dictator, director, ordainer, summoner

4. Ordering; Tending to Order; Containing, or Pert. to, an Order,adj. *From Sec. 1:* adjuratory; decretive, decretal, or decretory; dictatorial, directorial or directive, prescriptive; *From Sec. 2:* canonical, decretal, directive, injunctive, mandatory

5. Ordered,adj. *From Sec. 1:* adjured, bidden, charged, etc.; *Also:*
  1. **decretory**—fixed by decree
  2. **mandatory**—required by an official order
  3. **prescript**—set down by authoritative or official order
  4. **subpoenal**—ordered under threat of punishment
  5. **thetic**—ordered

6. Ruled or Governed by Decree: decretory, adj.

7. The Right to Give Orders: authority, command,n.

8. To Order Not to: forbid,v. (forbiddance, n. forbidder,n.)

9. To Issue an Order or Command Revoking a Previous and Contrary Order or Command: countermand,v. (countermand,n.)

10. To Order, i.e., Put in an Order for,v.
  1. **arrange for**—order (something) for which one will pay (arrangement,n.)
  2. **bespeak**—arrange for in advance
  3. **engage**—order the services of (engagement,n.)
  4. **prescribe**—order for treatment (prescription,n.)
  5. **reserve**—order in advance (reservation, n.)
  6. **speak for**—arrange for in advance

276. BEG

1. To Beg,v.
  1. **adjure**—entreat
  2. **advocate**—plead for
  3. **appeal for**—earnestly beg for (aid, sympathy, or other support)
  4. **beseech**—beg earnestly or urgently for
  5. **bum**—beg (colloq.)

6. **cadge**—beg, or live by begging (colloq.)
7. **conjure** (. . . to)—beg earnestly or solemnly (to do)
8. **crave**—bag as a favor
9. **entreat**—beg earnestly
10. **impetrate**—beg earnestly
11. **implore**—beg with great earnestness or extreme urgency
12. **importune**—beg so repeatedly and insistently as to constitute a nuisance
13. **intercede**—plead on someone's behalf
14. **obsecrate**—beg humbly; beg earnestly or urgently for
15. **obtest**—beg; obsecrate
16. **panhandle**—beg in the streets (slang)
17. **petition**—formally plead for (something) from a sovereign, person in high authority, judge, etc.
18. **plead (for)**—beg earnestly; beg with great earnestness or urgency
19. **pray**—beg; entreat; implore
20. **seek**—beg
21. **solicit**—beg; try to get by entreating
22. **sponge on**—live by begging from (colloq.)
23. **sue for**—beg; plead for
24. **supplicate**—beg by praying or by a prayerful attitude, as to a sovereign or someone in high authority
25. **urge**—plead earnestly for
26. **whine (for)**—beg in low nasal tones
27. **woo**—beg; solicit

2. Begging,n. *From Sec. 1:* adjuration, advocacy, appeal, entreaty, impetration, importunity, intercession, obsecration, obtestation, petition, plea, prayer, solicitation, suit, supplication or suppliance

3. One Who Begs; Beggar,n. *From Sec. 1:* adjurer or adjuror, advocate, appellant, beseecher, bum, cadger, impetrator, implorer, interceder, panhandler, petitioner, pleader, solicitor, sponge, suitor; supplicant, suppliant, or supplicator; wooer; *Also:*
  1. **fakir, fakeer**—member of a Mohammedan sect who has taken a vow of poverty and lives by begging
  2. **lazarus**—leprous beggar
  3. **mendicant**—beggar from house to house, person to person, etc., for alms or charity

4. Descr. of Begging,adj. *From Sec. 1:* adjuratory, appellant, beseeching, entreating, imploring, importunate, intercessive, petitionary, pleading; supplicatory, supplicant, or suppliant; *From Sec. 3:* mendicant; *Also:*
  1. **precatory**—expressive of entreaty or supplication
  2. **recreant**—begging and crying for mercy

5. Quality or Practice of Begging,n. *From Sec. 4:* beseechingness; importunateness, importunacy, or importunity; supplicance, mendicance or mendicity, recreance; *Also:* 1. **beggary**—practice of begging or of being a beggar

6. Pert. to Begging,adj. *From Sec. 1:* appellate; *From Sec. 4:* precatory

7. Beggars Collectively: beggary,n.

8. Responsive to Entreaty: exorable,adj. (exorability,n.)

9. Unresponsive to Entreaty: inexorable,adj. (inexorability,n.)

10. What Is Given to a Beggar: handout,n. (slang or colloq.)

11. Like a Beggar: beggarly,adj. (beggarliness, n.)

277. URGE

1. To Urge,v.
  1. **abet**—encourage in wrongdoing
  2. **admonish**—urge strongly
  3. **connive with**—encourage secretly in wrongdoing

4. **countenance**—encourage
5. **encourage**—urge subtly and sympathetically (to go on)
6. **exhort**—strongly or earnestly urge (someone to do something)
7. **goad**—urge on
8. **impel**—urge on
9. **incite**—urge on
10. **invite**—urge courteously (to do something)
11. **ply**—keep urging on (someone)
12. **preach**—urge in words; urge or exhort wearisomely
13. **preachify**—urge moral actions to the point of nausea (colloq.)
14. **precipitate**—urge on with haste or force
15. **press**—urge
16. **prevail on, prevail upon**—urge with arguments or persuasions; urge successfully
17. **prod**—urge; urge on
18. **spur**—urge on
19. **submit**—urge respectfully

2. Act of Urging,n. *From Sec. 1:* admonishment or admonition, connivance, encouragement, exhortation, impulsion, incitation or incitement, invitation, preachment, preachification, precipitation, submission; *Also:* 1. suasion—act of urging

3. Urging; Descr. of Urging,adj. *From Sec. 1:* admonishing or admonitory, encouraging, exhortative or exhortatory, goading; impelling, impellent, impulsive, or impulsory; inciting or incitant, pressing, prodding, spurring; *From Sec. 2:* suasive; *Also:*
1. **hortative, hortatory**—serving to encourage or exhort
2. **vehement**—urging

4. That Which Serves to Urge,n. *From Sec. 1:* admonition, encouragement, exhortation, goad, impellent or impulsion, incitation or incitement, invitation, preachment, prod, spur

278. ADVICE

1. To Advise,v.
1. **admonish**—advise
2. **admonish (not to)**—advise against
3. **caution (not to)**—advise against (an action or procedure)
4. **counsel**—advise actions, procedures, etc.; give advice; give professional advice
5. **exhort**—advise strongly, earnestly, or warmly
6. **preach**—give advice
7. **preachify**—advise moral actions to the point of nausea (colloq.)
8. **recommend**—advise
9. **urge**—advise strongly

2. Act of Advising,n. *From Sec. 1:* admonishment or admonition, exhortation, preachment, preachification, recommendation; *Also:* 1. suasion—act of advising

3. Advice,n. *From Sec. 1:* admonition, caution, counsel, exhortation, preachment, recommendation

4. Advisory,adj. *From Sec. 1:* admonishing or admonitory, cautionary, exhortative or exhortatory; *From Sec. 2:* suasive; *Also:*
1. **consultive, consultative, consultatory, consultary, consulting**—advisory
2. **hortative**—advisory; giving advice
3. **prudential**—advisory

5. Adviser; Advisor,n. *From Sec. 1:* admonisher or admonitor, cautioner, counselor, preacher, recommender; *Also:*
1. **consultant**—one who gives professional advice on a problem or question
2. **councilman**—councilor (councilmanic, adj.)

3. **councilor, councillor**—member of an advisory group or assembly
4. **counsel**—one who gives advice, usually in legal matters
5. **counselor, counsellor**—one who gives professional or legal advice; councilor
6. **mentor**—adviser (after the character in the *Odyssey* to whom Odysseus entrusted the education of his son)
7. **Nestor**—wise old adviser (after the adviser of the Greeks in the Trojan War)

279. USE

1. To Use,v.
1. **adopt**—take and use; take and put into use
2. **anticipate**—use before or ahead of time
3. **apply**—use; put to use; put to practical use; use for a special purpose; use (a word) appropriately
4. **avail oneself of**—use
5. **capitalize on**—use to full advantage
6. **christen**—use for the first time
7. **consume**—use
8. **employ**—use; make use of
9. **exert**—put into active or vigorous use
10. **exploit**—get the inherent use out of; use to one's own advantage or profit without return or advantage to the person or group so used
11. **husband**—use wisely and economically
12. **invest**—use (money, time, etc.) in such a way as to produce a profit
13. **make capital of**—use to one's advantage
14. **mobilize**—put into effective use
15. **overwork**—use too often or too much
16. **ply**—use
17. **practice, practise**—use; put into use
18. **scavenge**—find and use what others have discarded as useless
19. **scrimp on**—use less of than required
20. **skimp on**—use economically or sparingly; use too little of
21. **utilize**—use; turn to profitable or practical use
22. **wield**—hold and use; use with skill

2. Use,n. *From Sec. 1:* adoption, anticipation, application, capitalization (on), consumption, employment, exertion, exploitation, husbandry, investment, mobilization, practice, utilization; *Also:* 1. usage—use; process of being used; habitual or customary use; customary use by many people (of a word, phrase, or language construction)

3. User,n. *From Sec. 1:* adopter, anticipator, applier, consumer, employer, exploiter, husbander, investor, mobilizer, practicer, practiser, scavenger, scrimper, skimper, utilizer, wielder

4. Using; Tending to Use; Pert. to Using, adj. *From Sec. 1:* adoptive; anticipating, anticipative, anticipatory, or anticipant; exploitative

5. Put to Practical Use, i.e., Opposed to "Pure" or "Theoretical": applied,adj.

6. Way of Using: application,n.

7. Legal Right to Use the Products or Benefits of That Which Belongs to Someone Else: usufruct,n. (usufructuary,adj.)

8. Adapted for Use: commodious,adj.

9. Easy to Use: convenient, handy,adj. (convenience, handiness,n.)

10. In Use,adj.
1. **current**—presently or generally in use
2. **employed**—in use
3. **obtaining**—descr. of that which is in general use
4. **popular**—in widespread or common use
5. **prevalent, prevailing**—generally in use

6. **reputable**—in common use among educated people (of words)
7. **vulgar**—in common use

11. State of Being in Use,n. *From Sec. 10:* currency, employment, popularity, prevalence, reputability, vulgarity

12. To Be in Use,v. *From Sec. 10:* obtain, prevail

13. To Cause to Be in Use,v. *From Sec. 10:* popularize, vulgarize

14. Bring Back to Use: restore, resurrect, revive,v. (restoration, resurrection, revival,n.)

15. Person Used by Another for the Latter's Advantage: cat's-paw, creature, pawn, tool, n.

16. That Which Is Used for Someone's Gain or Advantage: pawn,n.

17. Useful; Usable,adj.
 1. **adaptable**—capable of being taken and used or put into use
 2. **advantageous**—useful
 3. **applicable**—usable; able to be put to use or to practical use; usable for a special purpose
 4. **available**—accessible for ready use; useful for a purpose
 5. **commodious**—serviceable
 6. **employable**—usable; able to be made use of
 7. **exploitable**—usable for one's own advantage or profit; descr. of that which one can get the inherent use out of
 8. **functional**—serving a useful purpose
 9. **handy**—capable of being used or put to use
 10. **practicable**—usable; able to be put into use or practice
 11. **practical**—capable of being put into actual practice rather than being merely theoretical
 12. **pragmatic, pragmatical**—practical
 13. **purposive**—useful or serving a useful function, though not so planned
 14. **serviceable**—capable of being put to use
 15. **subsidiary**—useful in assisting or supplementing
 16. **utile**—useful; practical
 17. **utilitarian**—useful rather than decorative or beautiful
 18. **utilizable**—usable; capable of being turned to practical or profitable use
 19. **valuable**—highly useful
 20. **wieldy**—able to be held and used
 21. **workaday**—practical
 22. **worthy**—useful

18. Use, Usefulness, or Usability,n. *From Sec. 17:* advantage or advantageousness, applicability, avail or availability, commodiousness, employability, exploitability, functionality or function, handiness, practicability, practicality, purposiveness, service or serviceability, utility, utilitarianism, value, wieldiness, worth or worthiness

19. To Be of Use; To Be Useful or Usable,v.
 1. **apply**—be useful
 2. **avail**—be of use; answer the need or purpose
 3. **bestead**—be of use
 4. **boot**—be of use
 5. **do**—be useful; be usable
 6. **serve**—be of use; be usable
 7. **subserve**—be useful; be usable

20. To Become More Useful: develop,v. (development,n.)

21. To Make More Useful by Keeping or Storing for a Time: season,v.

22. That Which Is Useful or Used,n.
 1. **agency**—means
 2. **asset**—anything useful
 3. **commodity**—that which is useful
 4. **facilities**—things that are used or useful

5. **expedient**—that which is useful (generally for lack of anything better) to accomplish an end or serve a purpose
6. **instrument**—that which can be used to accomplish a purpose
7. **instrumentality**—means
8. **makeshift**—stopgap
9. **means**—that which is useful for accomplishing a purpose
10. **medium**—means
11. **resource**—that on which one depends or falls back to accomplish a purpose or end
12. **shift**—temporary (and often not entirely honest) expedient
13. **stopgap**—something that can be used temporarily
14. **utility**—any useful factor or thing

23. Concern with Usefulness or Practical Results Rather than with Theoretical Concepts: pragmatism,n. (pragmatist,n. pragmatic, pragmatical,adj.)

24. Belief That What Is Useful Is Good: Benthamism, utilitarianism,n. (Benthamite, utilitarian,n. utilitarian,adj.)

280. EQUIPMENT

1. Equipment,n.
 1. **accouterment, accouterments**—equipment; soldier's equipment other than arms
 2. **apparatus**—necessary or mechanical equipment for some special purpose
 3. **appointments**—equipment; furnishings
 4. **armament**—military equipment
 5. **equipage**—equipment; equipment for a ship so that it can sail; equipment that outfits a ship, soldier, army, etc., for war or for military action; furniture
 6. **fittings**—necessary fixtures
 7. **fixtures**—equipment or apparatus fixed in place in a home, shop, office, etc.
 8. **furnishings**—equipment for a home; apparatus; fixtures; necessary fixtures
 9. **furniture**—equipment; equipment for a home, office, etc.
 10. **gear**—equipment for a boat; household equipment; nautical equipment; rigging
 11. **kit**—implements, tools, etc., forming the equipment of a worker
 12. **layette**—complete equipment for a newborn infant
 13. **machinery**—mechanical equipment
 14. **matériel**—equipment of an institution, army, etc.
 15. **mechanism**—mechanical equipment
 16. **outfit**—equipment
 17. **paraphernalia**—equipment; apparatus; furnishings
 18. **rig**—necessary equipment; equipment for a ship
 19. **rigging**—equipment; that equipment of a ship that works the sails, masts, etc.; gear
 20. **supplies**—equipment; kit
 21. **tackle**—equipment; apparatus; gear; rigging
 22. **trim**—equipment
 23. **trousseau**—equipment, i.e., clothing, linens, etc., for a bride

2. To Equip,v. *From Sec. 1:* accouter, arm, fit out, furnish, mechanize, outfit, rig, supply

3. Equipment, i.e., Act of Equipping,n. *From Sec. 1:* accouterment, mechanization

4. Place to Get Equipment: commissary,n.

5. Having Good Equipment: well-appointed, adj.

6. Piece of Equipment,n.
 1. **accessory**—piece of equipment that adds to the effect or usefulness of some other equipment

2. **apparatus**—complex piece of equipment for some special purpose
3. **appliance**—piece of mechanical equipment, generally powered by electricity
4. **attachment**—piece of equipment that works when attached to a larger piece of equipment
5. **automaton**—piece of self-functioning equipment
6. **contraption**—piece of equipment; piece of mechanical or complex equipment
7. **contrivance**—piece of mechanical equipment
8. **device**—piece of mechanical equipment; apparatus
9. **gadget**—apparatus; contrivance (colloq.)
10. **implement**—piece of useful equipment; piece of equipment necessary for some work
11. **instrument**—implement
12. **machine**—piece of mechanical equipment; apparatus
13. **mechanism**—machine
14. **neolith**—polished stone implement used in the early days of man
15. **robot**—automaton
16. **tool**—implement, often for handwork
17. **utensil**—kitchen implement; any implement
18. **utility**—piece of useful equipment; accessory

7. Pert. to Machines or Machinery: mechanical,adj.

8. One Who Works on Machines or Machinery: mechanic,n.

9. The Use of Automatic Devices to Operate and Control Machinery, as in Industrial Plants, etc.: automation,n.

281. RENT

1. To Rent to or from,v.
1. **charter**—rent; hire
2. **hire**—engage (something) for temporary use; give someone the temporary use of (something) for a fee
3. **lease**—give the temporary use of (often land, buildings, etc.) under contract for a period of time; get the temporary use of similarly
4. **let**—give or get the use of, for a fee
5. **sublease**—get the use of (usually land, buildings, etc.) from someone who is not the owner but has himself obtained such use under a contract; give the use of similarly
6. **sublet**—sublease
7. **underlease**—sublease
8. **underlet**—sublease

2. A Renting,n. *From Sec. 1:* charter, hire, lease, sublease, underlease

3. One Who Rents to Another,n. *From Sec. 1:* leaser, lessor, sublessor, subletter, underletter

4. One Who Rents from Another,n. *From Sec. 1:* lessee, sublessee, underlessee

282. USE UP

1. To Use Up,v.
1. **consume**—use up
2. **deplete**—use up
3. **devour**—use up
4. **exhaust**—use up completely
5. **expend**—use up
6. **sap**—slowly use up; use up completely
7. **spend**—use up wastefully; use up completely
8. **tire**—use up (someone's) patience, attention, interest, or enjoyment

9. **wear out**—use up (by constant use, until no value or service is left)

2. A Using Up,n. *From Sec. 1:* consumption, depletion, exhaustion, expenditure

3. One Who Uses Up,n. *From Sec. 1:* consumer, devourer, expender, spender

4. Using Up,adj. *From Sec. 1:* consumptive, depletory or depletive, devouring, exhaustive

5. Capable of Being Used Up,adj. *From Sec. 1:* consumable, exhaustible (inexhaustible, neg.), expendable

6. Used Too Much,adj.
1. **hackneyed**—used too much, hence no longer novel, fresh, or interesting (of language, phraseology, attitudes, and other abstractions)
2. **moth-eaten**—hackneyed; worn out
3. **overused**—used too much
4. **overworked**—hackneyed
5. **sear, sere**—worn out by age or use
6. **shabby**—considerably worn
7. **stale**—hackneyed
8. **trite**—hackneyed
9. **well-worn**—used too much; hackneyed
10. **worm-eaten**—hackneyed; worn out
11. **worn**—used to the point where the original function is no longer served
12. **worn out**—used until no longer serving any function; hackneyed

283. MISUSE

1. To Misuse,v.
1. **abuse**—put to incorrect or evil use; misuse
2. **maltreat**—abuse
3. **mistreat**—abuse
4. **pervert**—use in a wrong way or for wrong purposes
5. **profane**—put to vile, unworthy, or wrong use
6. **prostitute**—put to a base or unworthy use

2. Misuse; Act of Misusing,n. *From Sec. 1:* abuse, maltreatment, mistreatment, perversion, profanation, prostitution

3. Misuser,n. *From Sec. 1:* abuser, maltreator, perverter, profaner, prostitutor

4. Tending or Acting to Misuse; Misusing, adj. *From Sec. 1:* abusive, perversive or perversionary, profane or profanatory

284. DISUSE

1. To Fall into Disuse: lapse, obsolesce,v. (lapse, obsolescence,n. lapsing, obsolescent, adj.)

2. Tending to Go out of Use: obsolescent, adj. (obsolescence,n.)

3. Not in Use,adj.
1. **fallow**—not used, so that strength can be regained for future use (of land, the mind, etc.)
2. **idle**—not in use
3. **vacant**—not being used (generally of a place, building, land, etc.)

4. Disuse,n. *From Sec. 3:* fallowness, idleness, vacancy; *Also:* 1. **desuetude**—state or condition of disuse

5. To Cause to Be in Disuse,v. *From Sec. 3:* idle

6. To Stop Using: disuse,v. (disuse,n.)

7. Not Yet Used: virgin, virginal,adj. (virginity,n.)

8. No Longer in Use,adj.
1. **antiquated**—obsolete
2. **archaic, archaistic**—obsolete (of a word, phrase, language use, etc.)

3. **dated**—no longer in current use, i.e., reminiscent of past rather than present usage
4. **obsolete**—no longer in use (as words, designs, meanings, customs, theories, etc.)
5. **old-fashioned**—dated; obsolete
6. **out-of-date**—no longer in use
7. **passé**—no longer in current use

9. **State of No Longer Being in Use,**n. *From Sec. 8:* archaism, obsoleteness, obsoletism
10. **To Put out of Use,**v. *From Sec. 8:* antiquate, archaize, date
11. **That Which Is No Longer in Use,**n. *From Sec. 8:* archaism, obsolete or obsoletism (words, meanings, etc.)
12. **Useless; Not Usable,**adj.
   1. **impracticable**—not usable
   2. **impractical**—not useful; not usable
   3. **inapplicable**—not usable; having no practical use; not usable for a special purpose
   4. **inutile**—useless
   5. **paltry**—useless
   6. **rubbishy**—useless
   7. **scrap**—useless; no longer of use
   8. **scrubby**—useless
   9. **trashy**—useless
   10. **unavailable**—not accessible for ready use; not useful for a particular purpose
   11. **unemployable**—not able to be used
   12. **unfunctional**—having no use or uses
   13. **unhandy**—not capable of being put to use
   14. **unserviceable**—not capable of being put to use
   15. **unwieldy**—not capable of being held and used
   16. **waste**—not usable or useful
   17. **worthless**—useless
13. **Uselessness; Incapability of Being Used,** n. *From Sec. 12:* impracticability, impracticality, inapplicability, inutility, paltriness, trashiness, unavailability or unavailableness, unemployability, unhandiness, unserviceability, unwieldiness, worthlessness
14. **To Make Unfit for Use; To Make Useless or Less Useful,**v.
   1. **contaminate**—make unfit for use by adulterating
   2. **destroy**—make useless
   3. **deteriorate**—impair
   4. **impair**—decrease the usefulness of
   5. **negate**—make useless
   6. **nullify**—destroy the usefulness of
   7. **ruin**—destroy the usefulness of
   8. **spoil**—make unfit for use
   9. **void**—make useless
15. **A Making Useless or Less Useful,**n. *From Sec. 14:* contamination, destruction, deterioration, impairment, negation, nullification, ruin, spoilage
16. **Making, or Tending to Make, Useless or Less Useful,**adj. *From Sec. 14:* contaminative, destructive, deteriorative, ruinous
17. **To Declare Unfit for Use:** condemn,v. (condemnation,n. condemnatory,adj.)
18. **To Lose Usefulness:** deteriorate,v. (deterioration,n. deteriorative,adj.)
19. **To Become Unfit for Use:** spoil,v. (spoilage,n.)
20. **Useless Thing or Things,**n.
   1. **chaff**—anything useless
   2. **debris**—rubbish
   3. **dross**—rubbish
   4. **inutility**—useless factor; useless thing
   5. **jetsam**—anything useless
   6. **jettison**—jetsam
   7. **junk**—useless things (colloq.)
   8. **rubbish**—useless thing or things
   9. **rubbishry**—rubbish
   10. **rubble**—rubbish

11. **rummage**—odds and ends of little use
12. **scrap**—useless particle, fragment, or bit; useless bits or things
13. **spoilage**—something no longer fit for use
14. **trash**—useless things
15. **waste**—useless material, bits, fragments, or things
16. **wastements**—useless pieces, fragments, or bits

21. **Impractical,**adj.
   1. **quixotic**—impractical and idealistic (quixotism, quixotry,n.)
   2. **theoretic, theoretical**—impractical
   3. **utopian**—ideal but impractical, in reference to social systems, plans, laws, etc. (utopianism,n utopian,ñ.)
   4. **visionary**—impractical (visionary,n.)

285. WASTE; REFUSE

1. **Waste; Refuse; That Which Is, Has Been, or Is to Be, Discarded, etc.,**n.
   1. **castoff**—that which has been discarded
   2. **debris**—discarded things
   3. **decrement**—waste
   4. **discard**—that which is thrown away
   5. **draft**—refuse; waste matter; brewery refuse
   6. **dregs**—waste part of anything
   7. **dross**—waste matter or refuse; rubbish
   8. **exuviae**—castoff or discarded skins, shells, coverings, or other parts of animals (exuvial,adj.)
   9. **garbage**—refuse (esp. from a kitchen); offal
   10. **jetsam**—that which is thrown overboard from a sinking ship and often washes ashore
   11. **jettison**—jetsam
   12. **junk**—valueless refuse or trash (colloq.)
   13. **offal**—waste parts of an animal that is butchered for food; that which is taken off as unsuitable or useless; any refuse, garbage, or rubbish
   14. **offaling**—offal
   15. **offscouring**—refuse
   16. **offscum**—refuse; dross; scum that has been removed
   17. **outscouring**—scouring
   18. **recrement**—dross
   19. **reject**—that which is discarded as useless
   20. **rejectamenta**—rubbish
   21. **riffraff**—refuse; rubbish
   22. **rubbish**—waste; waste matter; anything useless and therefore thrown out or to be thrown out
   23. **rubbishry**—rubbish
   24. **rubble**—rubbish; trash
   25. **rummage**—that which is to be thrown away
   26. **scoria**—refuse from the melting of metals; dross; slag (scoriac, scoriaceous, adj.)
   27. **scouring**—material removed in the process of cleansing; refuse
   28. **scrap**—that which is discarded as useless
   29. **scum**—film of waste or foul matter on top of a liquid; refuse
   30. **sewage**—refuse carried off by sewers
   31. **shoddy**—refuse
   32. **slag**—waste when metal ore is refined
   33. **slops**—liquid refuse; such refuse fed to hogs or other domestic farm animals
   34. **slough**—castoff skin of an animal that regularly sheds its skin; that which may be cast off or discarded, as a habit, covering, etc.
   35. **sordes**—refuse
   36. **sordor**—refuse; dregs
   37. **spilth**—refuse; refuse in the street
   38. **sullage**—refuse; sewage
   39. **sweepings**—refuse; rubbish
   40. **swill**—partly liquid kitchen refuse, often fed to hogs; garbage

41. **trash**—refuse; worthless and discarded things; rubbish
42. **wastements**—waste pieces or fragments

2. Receptacle for Refuse,n.
1. **cesspool**—receptacle to collect refuse from sinks and bathrooms
2. **cloaca**—sewer (cloacal,adj.)
3. **cloaca maxima**—main sewer (after the one in ancient Rome)
4. **drain**—sewer
5. **septic tank**—tank in which solid part of refuse is stored until decomposed by anaerobic bacteria
6. **sewer**—pipe, or system of pipes, for conducting refuse to some point of ultimate disposal
7. **sump**—cesspool

286. ELIMINATION

1. To Eliminate; To Discard; To Do Away with; To Throw Away, Off, or Out,v.
1. **abolish**—do away with completely (usually a law, custom, institution, etc.)
2. **abrogate**—do away with; abolish by legislative or authoritative act
3. **blot out**—eliminate every trace of by, or as if by, rubbing out
4. **blue-pencil**—eliminate with, or as if with, a blue or editor's pencil (words, expressions, etc.)
5. **bowdlerize**—eliminate parts (of a story, book, play, etc.) that are considered obscene, indelicate, unusually frank, etc.
6. **burke**—get rid of secretly or quietly
7. **cancel**—strike out
8. **cashier**—discard; reject
9. **cast**—throw off
10. **cast away**—reject
11. **cast off**—discard; get rid of
12. **cast out**—discard; throw away
13. **censor**—eliminate (written or printed material considered harmful, dangerous, obscene, immoral, etc.)
14. **cross out**—delete
15. **delete**—eliminate (a word, letter, passage, etc.) from a manuscript or other written or printed matter, usually by marking it out
16. **deracinate**—eliminate by pulling out by the roots
17. **disburden oneself of**—get rid of (that which is burdensome or oppressive)
18. **discharge**—get rid of; dismiss
19. **dismiss**—get rid of (a person) by removing him from office, position, etc.; get rid of (an idea, fear, thought, etc.) by pushing it out of the mind
20. **dispose of**—get rid of; take care of and thereby eliminate as a responsibility; throw away
21. **disroot**—uproot
22. **drop**—get rid of; dismiss
23. **efface**—eliminate; do away with; eliminate by rubbing out or as if by rubbing out; wipe out
24. **eradicate**—eliminate completely, as if plucking out by the roots
25. **erase**—eliminate by, or as if by, rubbing out
26. **excind**—excise
27. **excise**—eliminate by cutting out
28. **expunge**—eliminate completely by, or as if by, blotting or rubbing out
29. **expurgate**—eliminate (objectionable or offensive passages or parts) from literary material, thereby cleansing it
30. **exsect**—excise
31. **exterminate**—eliminate by destroying completely
32. **extirpate**—eliminate by, or as if by, plucking out by the roots
33. **exuviate**—shed a covering or skin (said of animals that go through this process)

34. **jettison**—throw overboard (that which lightens a sinking vessel) ; discard (that which is no longer of any use)
35. **jilt**—discard (a lover)
36. **liquidate**—eliminate politically or as a political force or power
37. **molt**—shed the skin, feathers, fur, etc., preparatory to growing new (said of animals, such as birds, snakes, etc., that undergo this natural process)
38. **obliterate**—eliminate every trace of by, or as if by, rubbing or blotting out
39. **outroot**—eliminate completely
40. **reject**—throw away as useless or inadequate
41. **remove**—get rid of by taking away from a present location, position, office, etc.
42. **rid (. . . of)**—eliminate (something unpleasant) from (a place or person) ; eliminate (an offensive person or his presence) from (a place or person)
43. **root out**—eliminate by, or as if by, pulling out by the roots
44. **rub out**—eliminate by, or as if by, rubbing until gone
45. **scotch**—do away with
46. **scrap**—discard as no longer useful; discard when worn out
47. **scrape away or off**—eliminate by harsh rubbing
48. **screen out**—eliminate by, or as if by, sifting out
49. **scuttle**—eliminate by destroying
50. **shed**—get rid of; cast off (skin, hair, etc.)
51. **shuffle off**—get rid of
52. **shunt, shunt off**—get rid of
53. **slough, slough off**—discard; shed
54. **stamp out**—eliminate as if by stepping on forcibly and thus destroying
55. **strike out**—eliminate by crossing out, marking out, rubbing out, etc.
56. **unload**—get rid of
57. **unroot**—uproot
58. **uproot**—eliminate and destroy by, or as if by, pulling or tearing up violently by the roots
59. **void**—throw out (a clause, phrase, etc.)
60. **weed out**—get rid of (the less desirable parts or members of something)
61. **whittle down or away**—eliminate little by little, as if cutting away piece by piece
62. **wipe out**—eliminate completely; get rid of by, or as if by, wiping away

2. Elimination,n. *From Sec. 1:* abolition or abolishment, abrogation, bowdlerization or bowdlerism, cancellation, censorship, deletion, deracination, disburdenment, discharge, dismissal, disposal, effacement, eradication, erasure, excision, expunction or expungement, expurgation, exsection, extermination, extirpation, exuviation, liquidation, obliteration, rejection, removal, riddance; *Also:*
1. **abreaction**—elimination of a personality complex or suppression by working it through with the analyst (psychoanalysis)
2. **evulsion**—elimination by plucking out, or by pulling out by the roots
3. **rasure**—obliteration

3. A Discard, i.e., That Which Is Eliminated,n. *From Sec. 1:* castoff, deletion, discharge, erasure, exuviae, reject, scrap, slough (skin)

4. Eliminative,adj. *From Sec. 1:* abrogative, deletory, deracinative, eradicative; expurgative, expurgatory, or expurgatorial; exterminative or exterminatory, extirpative or extirpatory, obliterative, rejective

5. Capable of Being Eliminated,adj. *From Sec. 1:* abrogable, cancelable, censorable, dischargeable, disposable, eradicable, erasable, excisable, expungeable, exsectile, exterminable, obliterable

6. Incapable of Being Eliminated,adj. *From Sec. 1:* non-cancelable, indelible (from delete), ineradicable, inerasable, inexpungeable

7. To Direct a Typesetter to Eliminate Words, Letters, etc.: dele,v. (printing)

287. BODILY DISCHARGE

1. To Discharge from, or in, the Body,v.
 1. **belch**—discharge, through the mouth, gas or wind from the stomach in a spasmodic fashion
 2. **break wind**—discharge gas through the anus
 3. **defecate**—discharge waste through the anus
 4. **disgorge**—discharge from the throat or mouth
 5. **egest**—discharge from any of the organs or tissues of the body
 6. **ejaculate**—discharge from the body; discharge semen from the penis
 7. **eliminate**—discharge from the body; excrete
 8. **excrete**—discharge any waste or harmful matter from the body or from any organs of the body
 9. **exude, exudate**—discharge from the pores or openings of the body
 10. **menstruate**—discharge the monthly flow of blood from the vagina
 11. **secern**—secrete
 12. **secrete**—discharge from the cells or glands of the body
 13. **spit**—discharge from the mouth
 14. **sweat**—discharge moisture from the pores of the skin
 15. **urinate**—discharge water from the kidneys or bladder
 16. **vomit**—discharge from the stomach through the mouth

2. Discharge from, or in, the Body,n. *From Sec. 1:* belch, defecation, egestion, ejaculation, elimination, excretion, exudation, menstruation, secernment, secretion, urination; *Also:*
 1. **blennorrhea**—abnormal secretion and discharge of mucus
 2. **eccrisis**—excretion in disease
 3. **flux**—fluid discharge, usually excessive and abnormal, from the bowels or other part of the body
 4. **leucorrhea**—discharge of a whitish, greenish-white, or yellowish viscid mucus from the vagina (familiarly called *the whites*)
 5. **mucorrhea**—excessive discharge of mucus

3. A Bodily Discharge; Discharged Matter,n. *From Sec. 1:* wind (from *break wind*), feces (from *defecate*), egesta, excretion or excreta, exudate, secretion or secreta, spit or spittle, sweat, urine, vomit; *From Sec. 2:* eccrisis, flux; *Also:*
 1. **afterbirth**—matter discharged from the uterus following the birth of a child
 2. **dejecta**—waste matter discharged from the body, such as vomit, excreta, etc.
 3. **lochia**—matter discharged through the vagina following childbirth
 4. **secundines,**pl.—afterbirth
 5. **waste**—that which is excreted by humans or animals

4. Descr. of, or Pert. to, Bodily Discharge,adj. *From Sec. 1:* egestive, eliminative, excretive or excretory, exudative, menstrual, secernent; secretive, secretory, secretional, or secretionary; urinary, vomitive; *From Sec. 2:* blennorrheal, eccritic, leucorrheal

5. Discharging Organ,n.
 1. **emunctory**—organ that functions in elimination
 2. **follicle**—small gland (follicular,adj.)

3. gland—organ that discharges various substances used in, or excreted by, the body (glandular, glandulous,adj.)

6. A Secretion,n.
 1. **autacoid**—internal secretion (autacoidal, adj.)
 2. **chalone**—internal secretion that acts as a depressant
 3. **endocrine**—internal secretion (endocrine, endocrinal, endocritic,adj.)
 4. **hormone**—internal secretion that acts as a stimulant (hormonal,adj.)
 5. **mucus**—viscid secretion from certain membranes (mucous,adj.)

7. Secreting Internally: endocrine,adj.

8. Certain Specific Secretions or Hormones,n.
 1. **adrenalin, adrenaline**—secretion of the glands on the upper part of the kidneys, called the adrenal or suprarenal glands
 2. **bile**—secretion of the liver (bilious,adj.)
 3. **colostrum**—first watery secretion from the breasts of a mother after childbirth
 4. **epinephrine, epinephrin**—secretion of the suprarenal glands
 5. **gall**—bile; ox bile
 6. **gastrin**—hormone that stimulates secretion of the stomach glands
 7. **insulin**—extract from the hormones of the pancreas, used in treating diabetes
 8. **sebum**—fatty matter secreted by certain glands of the skin (sebaceous,adj.)
 9. **secretin**—hormone produced in the duodenum
 10. **thyroxin, thyroxine**—hormone of the thyroid gland

9. Conveying Bile: biliary,adj.

10. Secreting Fatty Matter through the Pores of the Skin: sebaceous,adj.

11. Morbid Increase in the Secretion of Fatty Matter by the Glands of the Skin: seborrhea, seborrhagia, stearrhea,n. (seborrheal, seborrheic,adj.)

12. Certain Sex Hormones,n.
 1. **androgen**—hormone that produces or controls secondary sex characteristics of males
 2. **androsterone**—sex hormone present in the urine of the human male
 3. **estrogen**—loosely, female sex hormone; substance acting like a hormone that produces sexual desire
 4. **estrone**—estrogenic hormone found in the ovaries, urine, etc.
 5. **progesterone**—sex hormone found in the corpus luteum
 6. **testosterone**—male sex hormone secreted in the testes
 7. **theelin**—estrone

13. Mucus,n.
 1. **phlegm**—mucus, esp. an extraordinary amount, in the respiratory passages
 2. **pituite**—mucus; phlegm
 3. **rheum**—watery discharge from the mucous membranes, usually of the eyes or nose
 4. **snivel**—mucus running from the nose
 5. **snot**—mucus from the nose

14. Pert. to, Descr. of, etc., Mucus,adj. *From Sec. 13:* phlegmy, pituitous, rheumy, snotty; *Also:*
 1. **mucous**—pert. to, resembling, secreting, or covered with mucus
 2. **muculent**—full of mucus
 3. **pituitary**—pert. to, or secreting, mucus

15. Science of Excretions and Secretions,n.
 1. **eccrinology**—science of excretions and secretions
 2. **endocrinology**—science of internal secretions (endocrinologist,n. endocrinological,adj.)

288. BELCH

1. To Belch: burp (colloq.), eruct, eructate, v.

2. Belching: eructation,n.

3. A Belch: burp (colloq.), eructation,n.

4. Belching,adj.
  1. burping—belching (colloq.)
  2. carminative—expelling gas from the alimentary canal
  3. eructative—given to belching
  4. flatulent—belching because of the accumulation of gas in the stomach, bowels, or alimentary canal (flatulence, flatulency,n.)

5. Pert. to Belching: eructative,adj.

6. To Cause (an Infant) to Belch after Drinking Milk: bubble, burp,v. (both colloq.)

7. Gas Brought Up by Belching: flatus,n.

289. SPIT

1. To Spit; To Discharge from the Mouth or Throat,v.
  1. disgorge—discharge from the throat or through the mouth
  2. drivel—let spit or saliva flow slowly from the mouth
  3. drool—let saliva run from the mouth, often in anticipation of what one enjoys
  4. expectorate—spit; cough up and spit out
  5. salivate—secrete or produce spit, esp. in abnormal amounts
  6. slaver—let spit run from the mouth; smear spit over
  7. slobber—slaver
  8. splutter—spit while talking
  9. sputter—spit out saliva or bits of food while talking or in excitement

2. A Spitting; A Spit,n. From Sec. 1: drool, expectoration, salivation, splutter, sputter; Also: 1. hemoptysis—spitting of blood

3. Spit,n. From Sec. 1: drivel, drool, saliva, slaver, slobber; Also:
  1. spittle—spit
  2. sputum—spit; matter brought up from the lungs and spat out (sputa,pl.)

4. Pert. to Saliva: salivary, salivous,adj.

5. Pert. to the Saliva Glands: salivary,adj.

6. Producing or Carrying Saliva: salivary, adj.

7. Resembling, or of the Nature of, Saliva: salivous, sialoid,adj.

8. Flow of Saliva,n.
  1. ptyalism—flow of saliva; excessive flow of saliva
  2. salivation—flow, or unusually copious flow, of saliva

9. To Cause a Flow of Saliva,v. From Sec. 8: ptyalize, salivate

10. Agent or Substance Causing One to Expectorate, or Facilitating Expectoration: expectorant,n.

11. Agent or Substance That Promotes the Flow of Saliva: salivant, salivator, sialagogue or sialogogue,n.

12. Promoting or Causing a Flow of Saliva: salivant, salivatory, sialagogic or sialogogic, adj.

13. Vessel for Spitting into: cuspidor, spittoon,n.

290. VOMIT

1. To Vomit: bring up, puke, regurgitate, spew, spit up, throw up; upchuck (colloq.),v.

2. To Vomit or Vomit Up (Something): bring up, puke, regorge, regurgitate, reject, spit up, throw up; upchuck (colloq.),v.

3. Vomiting: regurgitation, rejection,n.

4. Vomiting with the Bringing Up of Very Little Matter: vomiturition,n.

5. Vomit: puke, spew,n.

6. Bloody Vomit or Vomiting Symptomatic of Yellow Fever: black vomit,n.

7. Causing to Vomit: vomitive,adj.

8. To Cause to Vomit: gag,v.

9. A Bringing About of Vomiting with Little Trouble: vomiturition,n.

10. That Which Causes Vomiting: emetic, vomitive, vomitory,n.

11. Dried Root Used as an Emetic: ipecac,n.

12. To Make Feel Like Vomiting: gag, nauseate,v. (nauseation,n.)

13. To the Point of Nausea: ad nauseam (Latin)

14. Causing a Desire to Vomit: brackish (of fluids), disgustful; nauseant (medical); nauseating, nauseous,adj. (brackishness, nauseousness,n.)

15. Substance That Causes a Desire to Vomit: nauseant (medical),n.

16. To Feel Like Vomiting: gag, nauseate,v. (nauseation,n.)

17. Feeling Like Vomiting: nauseated, nauseous, queasy, squeamish, sick,adj. (nausea, queasiness, squeamishness, sickness,n.)

18. Nausea and Dizziness from the Rolling of a Ship at Sea: mal de mer (French), seasickness,n. (seasick,adj.)

19. Easily Nauseated: queasy, squeamish,adj. (queasiness, squeamishness,n.)

20. To Strain or Try to Vomit: heave, keck, retch,v.

21. Unsuccessful Attempts to Vomit: vomiturition,n.

291. SWEAT

1. To Sweat,v.
  1. exude, exudate—sweat; discharge from the pores of the skin
  2. ooze—exude moisture
  3. perspire—sweat
  4. swelter—sweat; sweat a lot
  5. transpire—give off as sweat

2. Act of Sweating,n. From Sec. 1: exudation, perspiration, transpiration; Also: 1. polyhidrosis—excessive secretion of sweat

3. Sweat,n. From Sec. 1: exudation or exudate, ooze, perspiration; Also:
  1. sudor—sweat
  2. suint—dried sweat of sheep that is deposited in the wool
  3. yolk—dried sweat of sheep found as part of the wool fat, or lanolin, in the wool

4. Pert. to Sweating or Sweat,adj. From Sec. 1: exudative, perspiratory, transpiratory; From Sec. 3: sudary, sudoral, or sudoric

5. To Pass or Come through the Pores or Texture Like Sweat: transude,v. (transudation,n. transudative, transudatory,adj.)

6. That Which Passes or Comes through the Pores or Texture Like Sweat: transudate, transudation,n.

7. Artificially Induced Increase in Sweating: diaphoresis,n.

8. Secreting Sweat: sudoriferous, sudoriparous,adj.

9. Pathological Condition in Which Sweat Has a Bad Odor: osmidrosis,n.

10. Characterized or Accompanied by Sweating: sudoral,adj.

11. Derived from Sweat: sudoric,adj.

12. Caused by Sweat: sudoral,adj.

13. Causing Sweating or Sweat: sudatory, sudorific,adj.

14. Causing an Increase in Sweating or Sweat: diaphoretic, sudatory, sudorific,*adj.*

15. Agent or Substance That Causes Sweating or an Increase in Sweating: diaphoretic, sudorific,n.

16. Producing Sweat: sudoriferous, sudoriparous,adj.

17. Cloth for Wiping Sweat from the Face: sudarium,n.

18. Sweating Room in a Bathing Place: sudatorium, sudarium, sudatory,n.

292. MENSTRUATION

1. Menstruation,n.
 1. **catamenia**—menses
 2. **dysmenorrhea**—difficult or painful menstruation
 3. **menorrhagia**—excessive menstrual flow
 4. **menses**—uterine flow of blood in the human female, occurring normally once every month
 5. **monthly**—menstruation, since the phenomenon occurs once a month (colloq.)
 6. **period**—condition, state, or act of menstruating

2. Pert. to, or Descr. of, Menstruation,adj. *From Sec. 1:* catamenial, dysmenorrheal, menorrhagic, periodic; *Also:* **1. menstrual,** menstruous—pert. to or descr. of menstruation

3. To Be in a State of Menstruation: menstruate,v.

4. Menstruating: menstruous, unwell,adj.

5. That Which Causes Menstruation or Starts the Menstrual Flow: emmenagogue,n.

6. Time of the First Menstrual Discharge in a Young Girl: menarche,n.

7. Unhealthy or Pathological Lack of a Menstrual Flow when Due: amenorrhea,n. (amenorrheal,adj.)

8. Time of the Natural Cessation of Menstruation, Occurring Normally between the Ages of 45 and 50: change of life, climacteric or climacterical, critical age, menopause,n. (climacterical, menopausal or menopausic, adj.)

293. DEFECATION

1. To Defecate: eliminate, evacuate, evacuate the bowels, excrete, have a bowel movement, move one's bowels, relieve oneself; soil (of infants),v.

2. Defecation: bowel movement, dejection, elimination, evacuation, excretion, stool,n.

3. Pert. to Defecation: eliminative, evacuative, excretive, excretory,adj.

4. To Defecate Frequently: purge,v. (purgation,n.)

5. Defecation of Loose or Fluid Matter,n.
 1. **bloody flux**—dysentery
 2. **diarrhea**—profuse defecation of watery or fluid matter (diarrheal, diarrheic, adj.)
 3. **dysentery**—disease marked by the defecation of mucus and blood, a constant desire to move the bowels, and griping pains (dysenteric,adj.)
 4. **flux**—defecation, usually excessive, of fluid matter
 5. **lientery, lienteric, lienteria**—diarrhea in

which food is excreted only partly digested (lienteric,adj.)

6. Feces: bowel movement, dejecta, dejection, dregs, egesta, evacuation, excrement, excreta, excretes, excretion, fecal matter, feculence, ordure, rejectamenta, sordes, stool,n.

7. Mass of Hardened Feces: coprolith,n.

8. Fluid Discharge of Feces: flux,n.

9. Animal Feces: droppings, dung, manure, ordure,n.; *Also:*
 1. **chiropterite**—partly decomposed feces of prehistoric bats
 2. **coprolite**—hardened or fossilized animal feces
 3. **guano**—partly decomposed feces of seafowl, bats, fish, and other animals, used as fertilizer
 4. **muck**—moist manure

10. Pert. to, or Descr. of, Feces: dreggy, excremental, excrementary, excrementitial, excrementitious, excretal, fecal, feculent, ordurous, scatologic, scatological,adj.

11. Pert. to, or Characteristic of, Animal Feces: ordurous, stercoraceous, stercorous, adj.

12. Resembling or Containing Feces: dreggy, feculent,adj. (dregginess, feculence, feculency, n.)

13. A Cleansing or Opening of the Bowels: catharsis, depuration, laxation, purgation, purge,n.

14. To Cleanse or Open the Bowels: depurate, purge,v.

15. To Cause Frequent Defecation in (a Person): purge,v.

16. Medicine, Drug, Substance, or Agent That Cleanses or Opens the Bowels, or Causes Defecation,n.
 1. **aperient, aperitive**—substance which acts as a gentle laxative, causes defecation, or relieves constipation
 2. **cathartic**—drug or medicine that cleanses the bowels
 3. **clyster**—enema
 4. **deobstruent**—aperient
 5. **depurative, depurator**—agent or medicine that cleanses the bowels
 6. **eccoprotic**—laxative
 7. **eccritic**—agent that causes defecation
 8. **enema**—injection of liquid into the rectum to aid defecation; the device for such injection
 9. **hydragogue**—purgative that causes copious watery discharges
 10. **laxative**—substance, medicine, or drug that loosens the bowels, causes defecation, or releases from constipation
 11. **lenitive**—mild laxative
 12. **physic**—substance or medicine that induces defecation
 13. **purgative, purge**—medicine or drug that cleanses or empties the bowels

17. Cleansing or Opening the Bowels, or Causing Defecation,adj. *From Sec. 16:* aperient, aperitive, cathartic, deobstruent, depurative, eccoprotic, laxative, lenitive, purgative; *Also:* **1.** excretive—promoting defecation

18. To Undergo a Cleansing of the Bowels: purge,v.

19. Difficulty in Defecating: constipation,n.

20. To Cause (Someone) to Have Difficulty in Defecation: constipate,v.

21. Constipation,n.
 1. **astriction**—constipation
 2. **binding**—constipation
 3. **constriction**—constipation
 4. **costiveness**—state of being constipated
 5. **ileus**—complete constipation resulting from intestinal obstruction
 6. **obstipation**—extreme constipation

22. To Constipate,v. *From Sec. 21:* bind, constrict or constringe; *Also:* 1. glutinate—constipate

23. Constipating,adj. *From Sec. 21:* astrictive or astringent, binding, constrictive or constringent, costive; *From Sec. 22:* glutinative

24. Constipated,adj. *From Sec. 21:* bound, constricted, costive

25. Need, or Apparent Need, to Defecate, but without Success: tenesmus,n.

26. Ability to Control Defecation and/or Urination: continence,n. (continent,adj.)

27. Inability to Control Defecation and/or Urination: incontinence,n. (incontinent,adj.)

28. Abnormal Interest in Feces: coprophilia, coprophilism,n. (coprophiliac,n. coprophilic, adj.)

29. Constant Talking about Feces: coprolalia, n.

30. Living or Growing in Animal Feces: coprophilous, coprozoic, stercoricolous,adj.

31. The Study of Feces: coprology, scatology, n. (scatologist,n. scatological,adj.)

32. Inspection of Feces, as for Diagnosis or Divination: scatoscopy,n. (scatoscopic,adj.)

294. URINATION

1. To Urinate: eliminate, excrete, micturate, make water, piddle (of dogs), relieve oneself, stale (of horses and cattle), void, wet (usually of children and animals),v.

2. To Drop Urine Like a Dog: piddle,v.

3. Urination: elimination, excretion, miction, micturition,n.

4. Urine: excreta, excretes, excretion; piddle (of dogs); stale (of horses and cattle); water,n.

5. Pert. or Related to Urine or Organs Involved in Urination,adj.
1. uretic—pert. to the urine
2. uric—pert. to, or obtained from, urine
3. urinary—pert. to urine or the organs involved in urination
4. urinelike—resembling urine
5. uriniferous—carrying urine
6. urinous—pert. to urine; smelling like urine; resembling urine
7. urogenital, urinogenital, genitourinary—pert. to both the urinary and sexual or reproductive organs
8. urogenous—producing urine; derived from urine

6. Ability to Control Urination and/or Defecation,n. (continent,adj.)

7. Inability to Control Urination,n.
1. bed-wetting—inability to hold urine while asleep (bed wetter,n.)
2. enuresis—morbid condition in which the urine cannot be held back or controlled but flows out beyond the volition of the patient; bed-wetting (enuretic,adj.)
3. incontinence—inability to keep voluntary control over urination and/or defecation (incontinent,adj.)
4. nocturia, nycturia—involuntary urination while asleep

8. Certain Urinary Ailments or Abnormalities,n.
1. albuminuria—presence of albumen in the urine
2. alcoholuria—presence of alcohol in the urine
3. anuria, anuresis—absence of urine; deficient discharge of urine (anuretic,adj.)
4. bacteriuria—presence of bacteria in the urine
5. dextrosuria—glycosuria

6. diabetes—disease characterized by excessive discharge of urine, excessive sugar in the urine, unusual thirst and hunger, and other symptoms (diabetic,adj. diabetic,n.)
7. diuresis—excessive or abnormal discharge of urine
8. dysuria—difficult or painful discharge of urine (dysuretic,adj.)
9. glycosuria—excretion of sugar into the urine (glycosuric,adj.)
10. hematuria—discharge of urine containing blood
11. hyposthenuria—diminution in the secretion of urine or urinary solids
12. micturition—excessive frequency of urination owing to disease
13. nocturia, nycturia—excessive urination at night
14. oliguresis, oliguria—condition of discharging a very small and deficient amount of urine; diminution of the amount of urine discharged (oliguretic, adj.)
15. phosphaturia—abnormal presence of phosphates in the urine
16. polyuria—excessive discharge of urine (polyuretic,adj.)
17. pyuria—presence of pus in the urine (pyuretic,adj.)
18. strangury—painful, drop-by-drop discharge of urine
19. tenesmus—need, or apparent need, to urinate, but without success

9. Causing Increased Urination: diuretic, diuretical, uretic,adj.

10. Medicine That Causes Increased Urination: diuretic,n.

11. Urinary Duct or Canal,n.
1. ureter—duct that serves to carry the urine from the kidneys to the bladder (ureteral, ureteric,adj.)
2. urethra—canal through which urine is discharged from the bladder (urethral, adj.)

12. Analysis of Urine,n.
1. urinalysis—chemical analysis of urine
2. uroscopy—diagnosis of disease by examining the urine (uroscopist,n. uroscopic, adj.)

13. Chemical Present in the Urine of Humans and Other Mammals: urea,n.

14. Vessel in Which to Urinate,n.
1. bedpan—vessel for urinating and defecating (for a bedridden invalid)
2. chamber pot, chamber—bedside vessel for urinating
3. sanitary—urinal
4. urinal, urinary—vessel or device in which to urinate

295. TOILET

1. Toilet,n.
1. bathroom—room containing urinal, sink, bathtub, etc.
2. can—toilet (slang)
3. cloaca—toilet (cloacal,adj.)
4. closet—toilet
5. comfort station—public toilet
6. head—toilet on a boat
7. john—toilet (slang)
8. latrine—toilet, generally in a public place such as a camp, army installation, office building, school, factory, etc.
9. lavatory—loosely, toilet or bathroom
10. outhouse—privy
11. powder room—bathroom
12. privy—toilet; outdoor toilet
13. rest room—comfort station
14. sanitary—toilet; urinal
15. urinal, urinary—closet or building in which to urinate

16. **washroom**—bathroom
17. **water closet**—toilet

296. KEEP OUT

1. To Keep (Someone or Something) Out; To Shut Out,v.
1. **bar**—exclude
2. **blackball**—exclude from membership by secretly voting against
3. **blink**—shut out of sight
4. **debar**—keep out; keep from entering
5. **exclude**—keep or shut out from entering, joining, becoming a member, enjoying privileges, etc.
6. **excommunicate**—shut out or cut off from communion with the church
7. **lock out**—keep out by locking a door or entrance against
8. **occlude**—shut out
9. **ostracize**—exclude from privileges of society or human relationships
10. **preclude**—shut out

2. A Keeping or Shutting Out,n. *From Sec. 1:* debarment, exclusion, excommunication, lockout, occlusion, ostracism, preclusion

3. State of Being Kept or Shut Out,n. *From Sec. 1:* excommunication, occlusion, ostracism; *Also:* 1. **coventry**—state of ostracism

4. One Who Advocates Keeping or Shutting Out,n. *From Sec. 1:* exclusionist

5. One Who Has Been Shut Out,n. *From Sec. 1:* excommunicant

6. That Which Keeps or Shuts Out,n. *From Sec. 1:* bar, occlusion

7. Keeping or Shutting Out,adj. *From Sec. 1:* exclusive, excommunicative, occlusive, preclusive

8. To Shut Off,v.
1. **beleaguer**—blockade with a surrounding force
2. **blockade**—shut off a place with military force so that entrance and exit are impossible
3. **seclude**—shut off by itself; shut off to protect

9. Act of Shutting Off,n. *From Sec. 8:* beleaguerment, blockade, seclusion

10. State of Being Shut Off,n. *From Sec. 8:* beleaguerment, blockade, seclusion

297. CLOSURE

1. To Close (Something),v.
1. **bolt**—close tight; close tight with a sliding bar; latch
2. **fasten**—close so that it cannot be easily opened or will not open by itself
3. **latch**—close with a lever for holding (a door, gate, window, etc.) closed
4. **lock**—close tight; latch
5. **padlock**—close tight with a portable lock
6. **seal**—close tight
7. **secure**—close firmly
8. **shut**—close; close tight
9. **slam**—close noisily; shut forcibly and noisily
10. **wink**—close and open in rapid alternation

2. To Close, i.e., Become Closed,v. *From Sec. 1:* bolt, fasten, latch, lock, seal, secure, shut, slam, wink

3. Closed,adj. *From Sec. 1:* bolted, fastened, latched, locked, sealed, secure or secured, shut

4. That Which Causes Closing,n. *From Sec. 1:* bolt, fastener or fastening, latch, lock, padlock, seal; *Also:* 1. **closure**—that which closes, closes tight, or keeps something closed

5. Act of Closing: closure,n.

6. State or Condition of Being Closed: closure,n.

7. The Closing Down of a Factory or Place of Business: shutdown,n.

8. To Close Up an Opening; To Close Up the Opening of or in,v.
1. **bung**—close (a cask or barrel) with a stopper
2. **calk**—stop or seal the cracks of or in (boats, window frames, walls, wood, etc.), usually with a special compound
3. **cork**—close up (an opening)
4. **occlude**—close up (an opening) of (occlusion,n. occludent, occlusive,adj.)
5. **plug**—close up (an opening)
6. **seal**—close up (an opening) tightly
7. **stopper**—close up (an opening)
8. **stopple**—stopper
9. **stop up**—close up (an opening)

9. That Which Closes Up an Opening,n. *From Sec. 8:* bung, cork, occludent, plug, seal, stopper, stopple; *Also:*
1. **tampon**—medical cotton plug inserted into a cavity to absorb blood; such a plug inserted into the vagina to absorb menstrual flow
2. **tap**—plug

10. Having No Opening: blind,adj.

11. To Wink: bat (of the eyes only), blink, nictate, nictitate, twink, twinkle,v.

12. To Wink (the Eyes): bat, blink,v.

13. A Wink; A Winking: bat (of the eyes only), blink, nictation, nictitation, twink, twinkle,n.

14. Winking: blinking, nictitant, nictitating, twinking, twinkling, twinkly,adj.

15. Unusual or Morbid Frequency of Winking of the Eyes: nictitation,n.

16. Time Required to Wink the Eyes: twinkling,n.

298. OPEN

1. To Open (Something); To Cause to Open; To Make an Opening in,v.
1. **breach**—break an opening into or through
2. **broach**—tap (a cask, or other container) to let out liquid; open by making a hole; open for the first time
3. **burst**—open suddenly; break open
4. **fissure**—open by splitting
5. **gap**—make or break an opening in or into
6. **lacerate**—tear open
7. **lance**—cut open
8. **pop**—burst
9. **puncture**—make an opening in or into
10. **scuttle**—make an opening in (a wall or roof, or the deck or side of a ship)
11. **sever**—break open; cut open
12. **slit**—cut a long and narrow opening in or into
13. **slot**—cut a narrow opening in (in order to insert something)
14. **socket**—make an opening in, so that something may rest inside
15. **split**—break a lengthwise opening in
16. **spread**—open; open up
17. **stave**—break an opening in
18. **tap**—open by taking out the plug or stopper (from a barrel, cask, etc.); open outlets from (pipes, power lines, etc.)
19. **unbolt**—open; unlock
20. **uncork**—open by removing the cork from
21. **unfasten**—open (that which is closed or closed tight)
22. **unlatch**—open; unlock
23. **unlock**—open by removing the lock from or the locking of

146

24. **unplug**—open by removing the plug from
25. **unseal**—open (that which is sealed)
26. **unstop, unstopper**—open; open by taking the stopper out of
27. **unwrap**—open up by removing the wrappings from
28. **vent**—make an opening in for the escape of air or gas
29. **ventilate**—provide with an opening for the escape of gas or air

2. To Open, i.e., Become Open,v. *From Sec. 1:* burst, fissure, pop, sever, split, spread, unbolt, unfasten, unlatch, unlock, unseal; *Also:*
1. **dehisce**—burst open and discharge contents (of abscesses, ripe pods, etc.)
2. **frondesce**—open up its leaves (of plants)
3. **gap**—open by means of the separation of parts normally closed or together
4. **gape**—open wide; open the mouth wide as an indication of sleepiness, forgetfulness, surprise, an intention to devour, a desire to conquer, etc.
5. **unfold**—open (of flowers, leaves, etc.)
6. **yawn**—open wide; open the mouth in a gesture indicating sleepiness
7. **yawp, yaup**—yawn noisily; gape

3. Act or Process of Opening,n. *From Sec. 1:* breach, laceration, puncture, severance, ventilation; *From Sec. 2:* burst, dehiscence, frondescence, gape, yawn; *Also:* 1. **gape**—yawn

4. An Opening,n. *From Sec. 1:* breach, fissure, gap, laceration, puncture, slit, slot, socket, split, spread, vent, ventilation; *From Sec. 2:* gap, yawn; *Also:*
1. **aperture**—opening of any kind
2. **avenue**—opening through which to go
3. **break**—opening; opening that has been broken through
4. **bung, bunghole**—opening in a cask or barrel
5. **cavity**—hollow opening
6. **chink**—narrow opening; opening caused by cracking or splitting
7. **cleft**—opening caused by cracking or splitting
8. **crack**—opening caused by cracking or splitting
9. **cranny**—small opening; narrow opening caused by cracking or splitting
10. **crenel**—opening in a battlement
11. **crevasse**—deep opening, usually in the ice of a glacier
12. **crevice**—narrow opening caused by breaking, cracking, splitting, etc.
13. **cut**—opening made by a sharp instrument
14. **excavation**—large opening made by digging
15. **gape**—open space; opening in parts normally closed or together
16. **hatch, hatchway**—rectangular opening in a floor or roof of a building, or deck of a ship, for the lowering of merchandise, cargo, etc.
17. **hiatus**—opening; opening in parts normally closed or together
18. **hole**—opening; hollow opening
19. **hollow**—hollow opening
20. **interstice**—opening between things closely packed (interstitial,adj.)
21. **leak**—opening through which something can or does escape
22. **loculus**—small cavity (locular,adj.)
23. **loophole**—opening through which escape is possible, either literally or figuratively
24. **louver**—opening in a wall, a ship's side, an automobile hood or body, etc.
25. **orifice**—opening, usually similar in appearance to a mouth; small opening; opening for the escape of gas or air
26. **ostiole**—small opening; orifice (ostiolar, adj.)
27. **perforation**—opening made by piercing
28. **pigeonhole**—one of a row of boxlike openings in a desk or cabinet

29. **pore**—tiny opening in the texture of something, for, or as if for, breathing; tiny opening in a rock
30. **recess**—opening set back from the surface
31. **rent**—opening made by tearing
32. **rift**—opening made by splitting, breaking, or cracking
33. **scupper**—opening in the deck of a ship so water washed overboard may drain off
34. **scuttle**—opening in a wall or roof, with a cover; opening in the side, deck, or bottom of a ship; hatch
35. **spout**—opening through which liquid flows
36. **tear**—opening made by tearing
37. **vein**—fissure
38. **vent**—small opening
39. **vomitory**—opening through which something is discharged or emitted
40. **wicket**—small opening
41. **window**—opening in a wall, roof, etc., to admit light and/or air

5. Open; Opened; Full of, or Containing, Openings, Holes, etc.,adj. *From Sec. 1:* breached, broached, burst, fissured, lacerated, lanced, popped, punctured, scuttled, severed, slit, slotted, socketed, split, spread, staved in, tapped, unbolted, uncorked, unfastened, unlatched, unlocked, unplugged, unsealed, unstopped, unstoppered, unwrapped, vented, ventilated; *From Sec. 2:* dehiscent, frondescent, gaping or gapy, unfolded, yawning; *From Sec. 4:* cleft, cracked, crannied, crenelated, cut, excavated, gaping, holey, hollow, leaky, louvered, perforated, porous, rent, torn, veined, vented, windowed; *Also:*
1. **ajar**—slightly open (of doors)
2. **blind**—having only one opening
3. **cavernous**—full of small openings, holes, cavities, etc.; porous
4. **leachy**—porous
5. **patulous**—open, in the sense of spread open
6. **rimose**—full of small openings, chinks, crevices, etc.
7. **spongy**—of an open and loose texture; porous

6. That Which Serves to Open a Way for One to Proceed (Figuratively): wedge, entering wedge, opening wedge,n.

7. Charge in a Restaurant for Each Bottle of Wine or Liquor Opened and Served, Esp. Those Brought In by the Patron: corkage,n.

8. Anatomical Opening,n.
1. **antrum**—hollow opening in the body or in a bodily organ; sinus
2. **anus**—external opening at the end of the rectum (anal,adj.)
3. **atrium**—cavity
4. **bursa**—saclike cavity (bursal,adj.)
5. **cavity**—hollow opening in the body or in a bodily organ
6. **follicle**—small cavity (follicular, folliculate,adj.)
7. **foramen**—small opening in plant or animal tissue or organs (foramina,pl. foraminous, foraminate,adj.)
8. **nares**—nostrils
9. **nostril**—one of the two external openings of the nose
10. **ostiole**—pore (ostiolar,adj.)
11. **pore**—tiny opening, usually for breathing or absorption in the skin, a membrane, a leaf, etc. (porous,adj.)
12. **pyloris**—opening from the stomach to the intestines (pyloric,adj.)
13. **rictus**—opening of the mouth (rictal,adj.)
14. **sinus**—opening or cavity, usually in the skull bones
15. **stoma**—mouthlike opening in the lower animals (stomata,pl. stomatal, stomatous, adj.)
16. **ventricle**—hollow opening in a bodily organ (ventricular,adj.)

17. vesicle—cavity filled with fluid; membranous cavity (vesicular,adj.)

9. Opening in the Earth,n.
1. **abyss**—opening in the earth of such depth as to appear bottomless (abyssal, abysmal,adj.)
2. **cave**—opening, generally horizontal, into a hill or mountain
3. **chasm**—deep opening in the earth
4. **crater**—opening in the earth caused by an explosion or earthquake (cratered, adj.)
5. **ditch**—long and narrow opening made in the earth by digging
6. **excavation**—large opening dug into the earth
7. **gulf**—abyss
8. **mine**—opening in the earth from which metals, stone, minerals, etc., are dug out
9. **trench**—ditch
10. **tunnel**—opening into the ground, through a hill or mountain, etc.
11. **yawn**—chasm

10. Cave,n.
1. **cavern**—cave; large cave
2. **grotto**—cave; artificial cave for pleasant retreat
3. **subterrane**—cave

11. Full of Large Caves: cavernous,adj.

12. Pert. to Caves: cavernous, spelaean, spelean,adj.

13. Cave Dweller,n.
1. **cave man**—cave dweller; prehistoric human of the Stone Age who lived in caves
2. **troglodyte**—member of a primitive or savage race that lives in caves; cave dweller

14. Living in Caves: spelaean, spelean, trogladytic,adj.

15. Exploration of Caves: spelunking,n.

16. Explorer of Caves: spelunker,n.

17. Science or Scientific Study of Caves: speleology,n. (speleologist,n. speleological, adj.)

18. Formations in Caves,n.
1. **stalactite**—formation hanging from the roof of a cave
2. **stalagmite**—formation pointing up from the floor of a cave

19. To Make a Hole or Holes in,v.
1. **bore**—make a hole by pushing, digging, etc.
2. **drill**—pierce with holes; put a hole or holes into
3. **perforate**—make rows of holes in (perforation,n.)
4. **pit**—make holes in the surface of; make a hole in the ground
5. **punch**—put holes into
6. **puncture**—make a hole in (puncture,n.)
7. **riddle**—pierce with a great number of holes
8. **scuttle**—cut a hole or holes in the side or bottom of (a ship) below the water line

20. A Hole,n. *From Sec. 19:* perforation, pit, puncture; *Also:*
1. **burrow**—hole dug in the ground by an animal to live in
2. **cavity**—hole
3. **crater**—deep hole; hole in the earth caused by an explosion
4. **excavation**—large hole made by digging; large hole dug into the earth
5. **leak**—hole through which something can or does escape
6. **loophole**—hole through which escape is possible, either literally or figuratively
7. **mine**—excavation from which metals, etc., are dug out
8. **pothole**—deep hole, as in a road, etc.; deep pit; deep hole, more or less round

in shape, formed in the rock of the bed of a river or other body of water by the grinding action of gravel and other material in the swirling waters
9. **wallow**—hole in the ground where an animal comes to roll around; figuratively, such a hole (as in *wallow of despair*, etc.)
10. **well**—hole sunk in the ground to obtain any underground resources

21. Instrument for Making Holes,n. *From Sec. 19:* bore, drill, punch; *Also:*
1. **auger**—device for boring holes
2. **awl**—hand instrument for piercing small holes in something
3. **bit**—tool for boring or drilling
4. **broach**—small tool for making a hole in a cask, barrel, etc., so the contents may pour out
5. **gimlet**—small tool for boring holes
6. **reamer**—tool for making a hole the right size and shape
7. **wimble**—instrument for boring holes

22. To Make a Hole Larger or the Proper Size or Shape: ream,v.

23. Special Key That Opens All the Locks in a Place: masterkey, passe partout (French), passkey, skeleton key,n.

24. Private Key: passkey,n.

299. A HOLLOW

1. A Hollow; A Hollow Place or Part,n.
1. **bight**—hollow
2. **bowl**—hollow, round part of anything
3. **cavern**—hollow place
4. **cavity**—hollow place
5. **chamber**—hollow place
6. **channel**—narrow ditch; ditch made by running water
7. **chase**—narrow ditch; ditch made by running water
8. **cleft**—hollow; hollow caused by cracking or splitting
9. **compartment**—hollow place
10. **concavity**—rounded or curved hollow
11. **corrugation**—long and narrow hollow or hollow place
12. **dent**—hollow caused by, or as if by, a blow
13. **depression**—hollow; hollow set back from the surface
14. **ditch**—long and narrow hollow dug into the earth
15. **excavation**—hollow made by digging
16. **furrow**—narrow hollow cut in the ground by a tool or wheel
17. **gouge**—hollow dug or scooped out
18. **groove**—narrow hollow cut in the ground by a tool, wheel, or the passage of people, vehicles, or water; narrow hollow cut in the surface of anything
19. **grotto**—artificial cavelike recess
20. **gulf**—deep hollow; hollow place in the earth
21. **gully**—ditch; furrow made by running water
22. **gutter**—furrow made by running water
23. **hole**—hollow place
24. **indentation, indention**—deep recess
25. **niche**—recess in a wall for a statue, ornament, etc.
26. **notch**—angular hollow on a surface or edge
27. **pit**—small hollow in the surface
28. **rabbet**—narrow hollow cut out of the surface of something, often a board of wood
29. **recess, recession**—hollow set back from the surface
30. **rut**—narrow hollow in the ground worn by wheels or the passage of people or vehicles
31. **sinus**—curved hollow

32. **socket**—hollow place in which something rests, is held, or is received
33. **sulcation**—groove
34. **track**—rut
35. **trench**—ditch; ditch of which the loose soil is banked on top as protection; furrow
36. **trough**—long hollow between ridges
37. **umbilication**—navel-like depression
38. **wallow**—depression in the ground where an animal comes to roll around; figuratively, such a hollow (as in *wallow of despair*, etc.)

2. Hollow,adj. *From Sec. 1:* cavernous, chambered, channeled, chased, cleft, concave, corrugate or corrugated, dented, furrowed, grooved, gullied, indented, notched, pitted, rabbeted, recessed, rutted, socketed, sulcate or sulcated, umbilicate or umbilicated; *Also:*
1. **alveolate**—having compartments like a honeycomb
2. **bisulcate**—having two grooves
3. **concavo-concave**—hollow on both sides
4. **concavo-convex**—hollow on one side, rounded or protuberant on the other
5. **fistulous**—hollow, like a pipe
6. **flatulent**—hollow
7. **variolar, variolous**—having pits or depressions resembling those of smallpox

3. Hollowness,n. *From Sec. 2:* concavity, flatulence

4. To Make Hollow; To Hollow Out,v. *From Sec. 1:* channel, chase, corrugate, dent, excavate, furrow, gouge (out), groove, indent, notch, pit, rabbet, rut, socket

300. SURROUND

1. To Surround,v.
1. **bathe**—surround, figuratively
2. **beleaguer**—surround; besiege
3. **belt**—encircle with, or as if with, a belt
4. **beset**—surround
5. **besiege**—surround with armed forces in an attempt to capture
6. **bound**—circumscribe
7. **box**—enclose
8. **cincture**—surround; encircle; encompass
9. **circle**—surround
10. **circumfuse**—surround
11. **circumscribe**—surround; draw a line around; encircle
12. **circumvallate**—surround with a fortifying wall, rampart, trench, etc.
13. **compass**—surround
14. **corral**—surround
15. **embower**—surround with a floral or leafy shelter
16. **encircle**—surround; surround by forming a circle around
17. **enclose**—surround with, or as if with, a fence or wall
18. **encompass**—surround; enclose
19. **endue**—invest
20. **engulf**—surround completely
21. **enswathe**—envelop
22. **entrench**—surround with trenches
23. **envelop**—surround with a covering or wrapping, literally or figuratively
24. **fence**—surround with, or as if with, a fence
25. **gird**—surround; encircle with, or as if with, a belt or girdle; hem in
26. **girdle**—surround; enclose
27. **girt**—encircle with a belt or girdle
28. **girth**—encircle
29. **hedge in**—surround to prevent escape
30. **hem in, around, or about**—surround on all sides and thus confine or prevent from escaping
31. **immure**—surround by walls; enclose
32. **impound**—enclose in, or as if in, a pen or pound

33. **inclose**—enclose
34. **invest**—surround as if with clothing or cover
35. **mure**—immure
36. **ring**—surround in or with a circle
37. **siege**—surround (an enemy-held fortified place) to compel surrender
38. **swathe**—surround or envelop with, or as if with, bandages
39. **wreathe**—surround; encircle; envelop

2. A Surrounding,n. *From Sec. 1:* beleaguerment, cincture, circumfusion, circumscription, circumvallation, embowerment, encirclement, enclosure, encompassment, engulfment, enswathement, entrenchment, envelopment, immurement, impoundment, inclosure, investment, siege; *Also:*
1. **ambience**—a surrounding
2. **annulation**—a ringing; a surrounding by a ring (botany)
3. **circumambience**—a surrounding; encirclement
4. **circumfluence**—a surrounding, in the sense of, or as if, flowing all around
5. **paling**—a surrounding with a fence

3. Surrounding,adj. *From Sec. 1:* beleaguering, besetting, besieging, circumfusive, circumscribing or circumscriptive, encircling, enclosing, encompassing, engulfing, enveloping, inclosing; *From Sec. 2:* circumambient, circumfluent or circumfluous

4. That Which Surrounds,n. *From Sec. 1:* belt, boundary, cincture, circle, circumfusion, circumvallation, bower (from embower), enclosure, envelope, girdle, inclosure, investment, ring, wreath; *Also:*
1. **aura**—that which comes from something and surrounds it; distinctive atmosphere surrounding a person or thing (aural, adj.)
2. **cordon**—line or circle of people or things surrounding a place

5. Enclosed by Curved Lines or Boundaries: curvilinear,adj.

6. Descr. of, or Pert. to, a Siege: obsidional, adj.

7. Enclosure, i.e., Enclosed Space or Place, n.
1. **compass**—enclosed space
2. **compound**—enclosed space (with buildings, etc.) occupied by foreigners
3. **coop**—small enclosure
4. **corral**—enclosure for animals
5. **cote**—enclosure for small animals
6. **cubbyhole, cubby**—small enclosed space
7. **fold**—enclosure for sheep or, less commonly, other domestic animals
8. **hutch**—pen for rabbits or other small animals
9. **pale**—enclosure
10. **pen**—small enclosure
11. **pound**—enclosure for stray animals; enclosure that provides shelter for animals
12. **stockade**—enclosure made with posts
13. **yard**—enclosed ground

8. Fence,n.
1. **barrier**—any kind of fence; that which serves as a fence
2. **enclosure**—that which serves as a fence by confining or enclosing
3. **pale**—confining barrier
4. **paling**—fence
5. **palisade**—fence used for defense, enclosing, or restricting
6. **railing**—fence of rails

9. Part of a Fence,n.
1. **pale**—post
2. **paling**—posts
3. **palisade**—long, pointed stick set in the ground with other sticks to form a protective, enclosing, or confining fence
4. **panel**—section between two posts
5. **picket**—pointed fence post

6. **post**—strong, upright wooden or metal support of a fence
7. **rail**—wooden or metal bar set horizontally in a fence
8. **stake**—pointed post driven into the ground
9. **upright**—vertical member of a fence

301. KEEP IN

1. To Keep or Shut In; To Confine; To Imprison, v.
1. **box up**—shut in
2. **cage**—encage
3. **closet**—shut up in a private or secret place
4. **commit**—confine (to a prison, etc.)
5. **constrain**—confine; imprison
6. **coop up**—confine in a small or restricted area
7. **cramp**—confine in a small or limited space
8. **detain**—confine
9. **encage, incage**—confine in, or as if in, a cage
10. **fence in**—keep within a restricted area; confine; keep confined
11. **fold**—confine (sheep) in an enclosed place
12. **immure**—put behind the walls of a prison; imprison
13. **impound**—confine or imprison in, or as if in, an enclosure
14. **incarcerate**—imprison; put into prison or some place of confinement
15. **intern**—confine to a place
16. **jail**—imprison for minor infractions of the law
17. **jug**—imprison (colloq.)
18. **lock up**—imprison; jail
19. **mure**—immure
20. **occlude**—shut in
21. **pen**—keep within an enclosure or restricted area
22. **pinfold**—put (animals) into an enclosure; put or keep in a place of confinement
23. **pound**—impound
24. **restrain**—keep in confinement or prison
25. **stockade**—confine within a pen or enclosure
26. **trammel**—confine

2. A Keeping or Shutting In; Confinement; Imprisonment, n. *From Sec. 1:* commitment, constraint, detainment or detention, immurement, impoundage, incarceration, internment, occlusion, restraint

3. Confinement or Imprisonment, i.e., State of Being Kept or Shut In, Confined, or Imprisoned, n. *From Sec. 1:* constraint, detention, restraint; *Also:*
1. **bonds**—imprisonment
2. **captivity**—imprisonment
3. **custody**—confinement; detention in prison
4. **durance**—imprisonment (poetic)
5. **duress**—imprisonment; detention
6. **reclusion**—solitary imprisonment; solitary confinement

4. Place of Confinement; Prison, n. *From Sec. 1:* cage, coop, fold, jail, jug, lockup, pen, pinfold, pound, stockade; *Also:*
1. **barracoon**—enclosure for temporary confinement of prisoners or slaves
2. **bastile**—prison, esp one run in tyrannical fashion
3. **black hole**—dungeon
4. **bridewell**—prison
5. **brig**—prison or place of confinement on a warship; any prison or guardhouse
6. **bullpen**—place for prisoners in times of riot
7. **calaboose**—jail (colloq.)
8. **cell**—small room in a prison

9. **clink**—prison or prison cell (colloq.)
10. **cooler**—prison (colloq.)
11. **coop**—small cage; jail (colloq.)
12. **dungeon**—underground prison; any dark, enclosed prison or cell
13. **gaol**—jail (British official spelling)
14. **guardhouse**—military jail where soldiers are confined for minor offenses or while waiting trial for more serious offenses
15. **hole**—dungeon
16. **oubliette**—dungeon where the only opening or means of access or egress is at the top
17. **penal institution**—prison; penitentiary
18. **penitentiary**—prison; place where prisoners are kept for purposes of detention, punishment, etc.; prison for those who have committed serious crimes
19. **reformatory**—a kind of prison where young criminal offenders are sent for training and rehabilitation
20. **stir**—jail (slang)

5. Prisoner, n. *From Sec. 1:* detenu (from *detain*), intern or internee; *From Sec. 3:* captive; *Also:*
1. **convict**—one sentenced to imprisonment; one serving a term of imprisonment
2. **inmate**—someone confined to an institution, such as a hospital, asylum, prison, etc.; animal so confined, as in a zoo

6. One Who Is Confined by Illness, etc.: shut-in, n.

7. Convicts of a Prison, Collectively: felonry, n.

8. To Send Back to Prison: recommit, remand, v.

9. Period of Imprisonment: stretch, n. (colloq.)

10. Kept in Solitary Confinement: incommunicado, adj.

11. Closely Confined; Shut Up in Close Confinement: pent, adj.

12. Confined Indoors by Bad Weather, Storms, Snow, etc.: snowbound, stormbound, weather-bound, adj.

13. To Make a Prisoner of: capture, v. (capture, n.)

14. State of Being Held a Prisoner: captivity, n.

15. Held as a Prisoner: captive, adj.

16. To Keep under Guard: detain, v. (detainment, detention, n.)

17. Head of a Prison: warden, n.

18. Division of a Prison: ward, n.

19. Science of Prison Management: penology, n. (penologist, n. penological, adj.)

20. Confined in Space (of Places): cramped, two-by-four, adj.

302. ATTACHMENT

1. To Attach; To Fasten; To Attach by Fastening, v.
1. **adhibit**—attach
2. **affix**—attach; fasten
3. **annex**—attach as a result or consequence
4. **append (to)**—attach; attach at the end (of)
5. **belt**—attach with, or as if with, a belt
6. **bind**—fasten with a bond of some sort
7. **bolt**—attach firmly or fasten with some kind of sliding bar
8. **brace**—fasten tightly
9. **buckle**—fasten with a tongue and link device of some sort
10. **button**—fasten with a button or buttons
11. **chain**—fasten securely with, or as strongly as if with, a chain
12. **cinch**—girt tightly

13. **clamp**—fasten with a device that holds things tightly within its jaws
14. **clasp**—fasten together
15. **clinch**—fasten with a kind of clamp (nautical)
16. **clip**—fasten
17. **couple**—attach (one thing to another)
18. **engage**—attach by the gears or teeth of (machinery); interlock
19. **fix**—fasten
20. **gird**—fasten with, or as if with, a belt
21. **girt, girth**—fasten with a band or strap
22. **grapple**—attach fast; fasten; fasten with, or as if with, a grappling iron
23. **hasp**—fasten with a kind of fastener
24. **hitch**—fasten with, or as if with, a hook
25. **hook**—fasten with, or as if with, a hook
26. **interlock**—attach securely into one another; attach closely to one another
27. **interweave**—attach closely into the texture of
28. **join**—attach
29. **latch**—fasten by means of a kind of lock
30. **link**—attach
31. **lock**—attach securely
32. **miter, mitre**—attach at the proper angle so that the parts fit evenly (of wood in construction)
33. **moor**—fasten (a ship) to a dock, wharf, etc.; fasten (anything) as if to a dock or by an anchor
34. **mortise**—fasten securely; attach securely with a mortise and tenon arrangement, the mortise being a square hole into which the tenon, a tongue cut to the same shape, securely fits
35. **nail**—attach; fasten by, or as if by, nails
36. **padlock**—attach securely with a portable lock
37. **pin**—attach by, or as if by, pins
38. **postfix**—annex; suffix
39. **prefix**—attach to the beginning of, or to the beginning of a word
40. **rabbet**—attach the edges (of boards) by interlocking grooves and ridges
41. **rivet**—fasten very strongly
42. **root**—attach deeply or firmly
43. **screw**—attach by screws
44. **seal**—attach securely; fasten tightly
45. **secure**—attach firmly
46. **spike**—fasten with long nails
47. **staple**—fasten with wire
48. **strap**—attach by a belt, strap, etc.
49. **suffix**—attach to the end of; attach to the end of a word
50. **tack**—attach or fasten in a slight or temporary fashion
51. **tie**—attach; attach by rope, cord, etc.; attach figuratively
52. **unite**—attach closely
53. **wedge**—attach or fasten with a wedge or pointed piece of wood
54. **yoke**—attach (an animal, usually a horse or ox) to a vehicle to be pulled; attach as if in this manner
55. **zip**—fasten by closing a slide fastener

2. Attachment; Fastening,n. *From Sec. 1:* adhibition; affixion, affixation, or affixture; annexation, appendage, engagement; junction (from *join*); linkage, moorage, prefixion or prefixture, suffixion or suffixment, union

3. Fastener; Fastening,n. *From Sec. 1:* belt, binder, bolt, brace, buckle, button, chain, clamp, clasp, clinch, clip, coupling, hasp, hook, latch, link, lock; mortise (figurative); nail, padlock, pin, rivet, screw, spike, staple, strap, tack, tie, union, wedge, yoke, zipper or slide fastener; *Also:*
1. **tendril**—threadlike part of a plant that attaches to something for climbing or support; anything that may be figuratively likened to this
2. **tentacle**—any of the various processes of animals used to attach to a surface; tendril

4. To Attach or Fasten, i.e., Become Attached or Fastened,v. *From Sec. 1:* bolt, buckle, button, clamp, clasp, clip, engage, hook, interlock, join, latch, link, lock, moor, nail, pin, rabbet, root, screw, seal, secure, strap, tack, tie, unite; *Also:*
1. **accrete**—become attached by growing together
2. **mesh**—engage with each other (of the teeth or gears of machinery)

5. Act, Process, or State of Being or Becoming Attached or Fastened,n. *From Sec. 4:* engagement, junction (from *join*), linkage, moorage, union, accretion

6. An Attachment, i.e., That Which Is Attached,n. *From Sec. 1:* affix or affixation, appendage, postfix, prefix or prefixture, suffix (appendicular, postfixal or postfixial, prefixal, suffixal,adj.); *Also:*
1. **appendicle**—small appendage (appendicular,adj.)

7. To Unfasten,v. *From Sec. 1:* unbelt, unbind, unbolt, unbuckle, unbutton, unchain, unclamp, unclasp, unclip, uncouple, disengage, unfasten, ungird, unhitch, unhook, unlatch, unlink, unlock, unmoor, unpin, unscrew, unseal, unstrap, untack, untie, unyoke, unzip; *Also:*
1. **detach**—remove the attachment of
2. **unpeg**—unfasten
3. **unsnap**—unfasten

8. Attached: appendant, appendent,adj.

9. Permanently Attached to Some Base and Hence Unable to Move About Freely (of Animal Forms): sessile,adj. (sessility,n.)

10. To Hold (Things) Together,v.
1. **brace**—hold (the parts of) together
2. **clamp**—press and hold tightly together
3. **clench**—hold (the parts of) tightly together (as the fist, teeth, etc.)

11. Implement That Holds Things Together, n. *From Sec. 10:* brace, clamp

12. To Attach by Causing to Stick Together, v.
1. **agglutinate**—cause to stick together with, or as if with, glue or similar substance
2. **bind**—make stick
3. **braze**—solder with any hard alloy or with brass
4. **cement**—cause to stick together with, or as if with, cement
5. **conglutinate**—cause to stick together by glue or some gluey substance
6. **engage**—cause to stick together
7. **glue**—attach or cause to stick with some sticky substance or with glue
8. **glutinate**—attach as with glue
9. **gum**—attach with a gummy or sticky substance
10. **paste**—cause to attach or stick by paste or some sticky substance
11. **plaster**—paste
12. **seal**—paste tightly
13. **solder**—cause to stick or be attached by solder, a form of molten alloy

13. Attachment by Causing to Stick Together,n. *From Sec. 12:* agglutination, conglutination, engagement, glutination

14. That Which Causes Attachment by Sticking,n. *From Sec. 12:* agglutinant, cement, glue, glutinative, gum, paste, plaster, solder; *Also:*
1. **adhesive**—that which causes sticking, or attachment by sticking
2. **mucilage**—watery solution used as an adhesive

15. Causing to Attach by Sticking,adj. *From Sec. 12:* agglutinant or agglutinative, conglutinant or conglutinative, glutinative; *Also:*
1. **cohesive**—causing to stick together

151

16. To Become Attached by Sticking To-gether,v. *From Sec. 12:* conglutinate, engage, glue, paste, seal, solder; *Also:*
  1. **adhere**—stick; stay attached by sticking
  2. **cherish**—cling to (figuratively)
  3. **cleave**—stick closely
  4. **cling**—stick, often by intertwining, literally or figuratively
  5. **cohere**—stick together

17. A Sticking to or Together,n. *From Sec. 16:* conglutination, engagement; adherence or adhesion, cleavage, coherence or cohesion

18. Sticking or Tending to Stick,adj. *From Sec. 12:* agglutinative, conglutinative, gluey, gummy, pasty; *From Sec. 16:* adherent or adhesive, clingy or clinging, coherent or cohesive; *Also:* **1. tenacious**—clinging tightly to; clinging tightly together

19. Tendency to Stick,n. *From Sec. 18:* agglutinativeness, conglutinativeness, glueyness, gumminess, pastiness; adhesiveness, clingingness, cohesiveness; tenacity

20. Stuck Together,adj. *From Sec. 12:* agglutinate, conglutinate (agglutination, conglutination,n.)

21. To Unstick,v. *From Sec. 12:* unbind, disengage, unglue, unpaste, unseal, unsolder

22. One Who Clings Tightly: barnacle, clinger,n.

23. A Sticking Together of Bodily Tissues That Are Normally Separated: adhesion,n.

24. Sticky,adj.
  1. **adhesive**—sticky; sticking easily; smeared with sticky substance
  2. **agglutinative**—sticky; sticking easily
  3. **clammy**—sticky, damp, and cold
  4. **doughy**—sticky, like paste
  5. **gelatinous**—sticky, like glue
  6. **gluey**—sticky
  7. **glutinose, glutinous**—sticky, like glue
  8. **gummous, gummose, gummy**—sticky, like gum
  9. **mucid**—mucous; slimy
  10. **mucilaginous**—moist and sticky
  11. **mucous**—covered with mucus or other sticky and semi-fluid matter
  12. **muculent**—moist and sticky; slimy
  13. **pasty**—sticky, like paste
  14. **pituitous**—mucous
  15. **ropy**—sticky
  16. **slimy**—sticky and semi-fluid
  17. **stringy**—adhesive; gluey
  18. **tacky**—sticky
  19. **tenacious**—sticky, like glue
  20. **viscid**—sticky; gluey
  21. **viscidulous, viscoid, viscoidal**—slightly sticky or gluey
  22. **viscous, viscose**—sticky; gluey
  23. **waxy**—sticky

25. Stickiness,n. *From Sec. 24:* adhesiveness, clamminess, doughiness, gelatinousness, glueyness, glutinosity or glutinousness, mucilaginousness, pastiness, pituitousness, ropiness, sliminess, stringiness, tackiness, tenaciousness, viscidity or viscidness, viscousness or viscosity, waxiness

26. Sticky Substance,n. *From Sec. 24:* adhesive, glue, gum, mucus, paste, slime

27. To Cause to Be Sticky Like Glue: glutinize,v.

28. To Attach or Fasten by Tying; To Tie or Tie Up,v.
  1. **astrict**—tie up
  2. **astringe**—bind fast
  3. **band**—tie with a cord, ligament, etc.
  4. **bandage**—bind (wounds, injured parts, etc.) with a strip of material
  5. **belay**—turn a rope around (something) in order to hold it securely (nautical)
  6. **belt**—tie with a belt

  7. **bind**—tie; tie with a cord, band, rope, etc.; bandage
  8. **bond**—tie firmly together
  9. **brace**—tie; bind
  10. **chain**—tie with a chain or as strongly as with a chain
  11. **cinch**—girt tightly
  12. **colligate**—tie together into a union
  13. **couple**—tie (one thing to another)
  14. **enchain**—tie in chains; chain
  15. **gird**—tie with a flexible band or belt
  16. **girt, girth**—tie with a strap or band
  17. **harness**—tie with, or as if with, a horse's harness
  18. **hitch**—fasten with, or as with, a knot
  19. **interknit**—interlace; knit
  20. **interknot**—knot together
  21. **interlace**—attach or fasten by, or as if by, lacing together
  22. **interlock**—interlace firmly
  23. **intertwine**—interlace
  24. **intertwist**—interlace
  25. **interweave**—interlace
  26. **knit**—tie together; attach by, or as if by, knots
  27. **knot**—tie or attach with, or as if with, a knot
  28. **lace**—tie; attach with, or as if with, laces
  29. **lash**—tie with rope, cord, etc.
  30. **leash**—tie together with, or as with, a leather strap
  31. **ligate**—tie up; bind
  32. **moor**—tie (a vessel) fast to an anchor or other stationary object
  33. **pinion**—bind; bind the arms of
  34. **raddle**—interlace
  35. **rope**—tie with a rope
  36. **sew**—attach by stitches of thread
  37. **sheave**—tie into a bundle after gathering (wheat, grain, etc.)
  38. **splice**—attach (two ropes or similar things) or parts of (a rope, etc.) by interweaving the strands
  39. **strap**—attach by a strap
  40. **string**—tie; attach with string or light cord
  41. **swathe**—bind with wrapping, bands, bandage, etc.
  42. **tether**—tie (an animal or person, usually) with a rope, chain, etc., that allows just so much room for wandering or grazing
  43. **trice up**—pull up and tie with a small rope (nautical)
  44. **truss**—tie the wings and legs of (fowl) before cooking; tie; bind
  45. **wattle**—tie with interwoven twigs or branches

29. Attachment by Tying; A Tying or Tying Up,n. *From Sec. 28:* colligation, enchainment, interlacement, ligation, moorage

30. To Become Tied or Attached by Tying,v. *From Sec. 28:* couple, harness, hitch, interknit, interlace, interlock, intertwine, intertwist, interweave, knit, knot, lace, lash, moor, strap

31. To Untie,v. *From Sec. 28:* unbandage, unbelt, unbind, unchain, uncouple, ungird, unharness, unhitch, unknit, unknot, unlace, unlash, unleash, unmoor, unstrap, unstring, untether, untruss; *Also:*
  1. **loose, loosen, unloose, unloosen**—untie
  2. **unbridle**—untie and remove the bridle from (a horse, etc.)

32. Cord, Rope, or Other Material for Tying,n.
  1. **band**—anything used for tying or that ties
  2. **bandage**—strips of material for tying up a wound, injured part, etc.
  3. **belt**—leather strap
  4. **binder**—that which ties
  5. **binding**—that which ties; bandage

6. **bond**—anything that ties or fastens by tying
7. **brace**—rope that passes through a block (nautical)
8. **cable**—strong wire rope or chain
9. **chain**—metal rope of links
10. **harness**—leather straps that tie a horse to a vehicle
11. **lace**—thin cord used for tying parts of a shoe, corset, etc., together
12. **lariat**—rope used for catching animals; lasso
13. **lashing**—rope, cord, etc., used for tying
14. **lasso**—long rope with a noose at the end used for catching animals
15. **leash**—cord, or leather strap, used to hold a dog
16. **ligament**—that which ties two parts together; bond
17. **ligature**—anything used to tie, tie up, or attach by tying
18. **raffia**—fiber from a kind of palm used in binding
19. **ribbon**—narrow strip of silk, satin, etc., used for tying, or for decorative tying
20. **strand**—rope of twisted cords or threads
21. **strap**—narrow strip of leather or other material used for tying
22. **string**—light cord
23. **tether**—rope or chain by which an animal is tied to a stake or other stationary object
24. **thong**—narrow strip of leather used for tying or lacing
25. **torsade**—twisted cord
26. **twine**—strong cord; strictly, cord made of threads wound together
27. **wire**—long and thin cords of metal that may be used for tying

33. Parts of a Rope,n.
1. **bight**—middle part of a rope; loop (of rope)
2. **halter**—noose put around a victim's neck in hanging
3. **loop**—fold of cord, rope, thread, etc., through which another part of the cord, etc., may be pulled and so tightened
4. **noose**—loop in a rope that tightens when pulled

34. Knot in Rope, Thread, Hair, etc.: kink, n. (kinky,adj.)

35. Full of Knots: knotty,adj.

303. TIGHTNESS

1. To Make Tight,v.
1. **brace**—draw tight (the nerves, a drum, a bow, etc.)
2. **constrict, constringe, astrict, astringe**—make tight by binding or drawing together (constriction,n. constrictive, constringent, astrictive, astringent,adj.)
3. **strain**—draw tight (strain,n.)
4. **tauten**—draw, pull, or stretch tight
5. **tense, tensify**—make, draw, or stretch tight (tension,n. tensive,adj.)
6. **tighten**—make, draw, or stretch tight

2. Tight or Tightened,adj. *From Sec. 1:* braced, constricted, astricted, strained, taut, tense; *Also:*
1. **airtight, hermetic**—too tight for air or gas to enter or escape
2. **snug**—tight in fit; fitting tight
3. **watertight**—too tight for water to enter or escape

3. Tightness,n. *From Sec. 1:* constriction, astriction, strain, tautness; tenseness, tension, or tensity; *From Sec. 2:* snugness

4. That Which Causes Tightness,n. *From Sec. 1:* constrictor, astringent

5. To Become Tight,v. *From Sec. 1:* constrict, tense, tighten

6. Sensation of Tightness,n. *From Sec. 1:* constriction, tension

304. LOOSENESS

1. Loose; Loosened,adj.
1. **baggy**—loose and billowing
2. **flabby**—hanging loose of its own weight, as tissue or flesh
3. **flimsy**—loose in structure or texture
4. **lax**—loose; not tight or taut
5. **loppy**—hanging loose
6. **ramshackle**—loose and shaky (of buildings, structures or anything put together); loose-jointed
7. **relaxed**—loose; loosened
8. **slack**—loose; not taut or tense
9. **slackened**—loose; loosened
10. **ungirt**—loose; not tight, or not tightened, for use

2. Looseness,n. *From Sec. 1:* bagginess, flabbiness, flimsiness, laxity or laxness, relaxation, slack or slackness

3. To Loosen, i.e., Make Loose,v. *From Sec 1:* relax, slack, slacken; *Also:*
1. **detach**—loosen and remove (detachment, n.)
2. **relax**—loosen (one's grip, hold, etc.)
3. **unstring**—loosen; loosen the tension of

4. To Loosen, i.e., Become Loose,v. *From Sec. 1:* bag, lop, relax, slack, slacken

5. Act of Loosening or State of Being Loose: relaxation,n.

6. Causing or Producing Looseness: relaxative,adj.

305. SEW

1. To Sew,v.
1. **baste**—sew with long stitches for temporary holding until a final permanent sewing is made
2. **darn**—mend with a special kind of stitch
3. **hem**—fold back and sew down the edge of
4. **hemstitch**—sew along a line from which threads have been drawn out, stitching the cross threads into groups
5. **mend**—sew in order to repair
6. **seam**—sew pieces together along a line
7. **stitch**—sew
8. **suture**—join surgically by sewing (sutural,adj.)
9. **tack**—sew with long stitches
10. **tuck**—sew a fold

2. A Stitch,n. *From Sec. 1:* baste, hemstitch, seam, suture, tack, tuck

3. Woman Who Sews for a Living: seamstress, sempstress,n.

306. THREAD

1. Thread; Threads,n.
1. **fiber**—slender thread; fine, threadlike piece; very fine threads, collectively
2. **fibril**—very fine or thin thread; hairlike thread on a root
3. **filament**—very fine thread
4. **lint**—tiny bits or fluffs of thread
5. **meshes**—threads that form the open spaces of a net
6. **nap**—soft, woolly threads on the surface of cloth
7. **strand**—threads that constitute, when twisted together, a rope, cord, etc.; thread; thread from the texture of something; fiber; filament
8. **warp**—lengthwise threads in woven material
9. **weft, woof**—threads running from side to side

10. yarn—thread; thin length of twisted threads

2. Pert. to, or Descr. of, Thread or Threads, adj. *From Sec. 1:* fibrous, fibrilar, filamentary or filamentous, linty; *Also:* **1. filar**—pert. to threads

3. Resembling, or in the Form of, Threads, adj. *From Sec. 1:* fibrous, fibriform, or fibroid; fibriliform, filamentous, linty; *Also:* **1. capillaceous**—threadlike

4. Having or Bearing Threads, adj. *From Sec. 1:* fibrous, fibrilose, filamentous; *Also:*
1. **bifilar**—two-threaded
2. **filar**—having threads
3. **threaded**—having threads

5. Fine, Threadlike Structure: filament,n.

6. To Form into Thread: spin,v.

7. Act of Forming into Threads: filature,n.

8. Involving the Use of Two Threads: bifilar,adj.

307. WEAVE

1. To Weave; To Form by Weaving, v.
1. **braid**—weave; interweave (strands of hair)
2. **crochet**—knit with a hooked needle
3. **interknit**—knit together, each with the other
4. **interlace**—weave together
5. **interlock**—weave together firmly
6. **intertwine**—twine together
7. **interweave**—weave together (the various threads, strands, etc.)
8. **knit**—interweave (loops of thread or yarn) by hand or machine; make or form by such interweaving
9. **lace**—interlace
10. **plait**—interweave (strands of hair)
11. **plat**—interweave; interweave (strands of hair)
12. **pleach**—interweave and so unite; interweave (strands of hair)
13. **raddle**—interweave (provincial English)
14. **spin**—make (yarn) by interweaving fibers or threads
15. **texture**—form or make by weaving; make as if by weaving
16. **trellis**—interweave (strips of wood, metal, etc.) to form a lattice
17. **twill**—weave (cloth) in a certain way
18. **twine**—weave; form or make by weaving threads together
19. **wattle**—interweave (usually twigs, etc.); form or make by interweaving twigs; interweave (strands of hair)

2. Woven, adj. *From Sec. 1:* braided, crocheted, interknit, interlaced, interlocked, intertwined, interwoven, knit, laced, plaited, platted, raddled, spun, textured, trellised, twilled, wattled; *Also:*
1. **textile**—woven
2. **vimineous**—woven from twigs

3. That Which Is Woven, n. *From Sec. 1:* braid, lace, plait, plat, texture, trellis, twill, twine; *Also:*
1. **fabric**—woven cloth or material
2. **lattice, latticework**—structure of interwoven wood or metal strips
3. **mesh**—net
4. **net**—system or combination of woven threads or cords
5. **textile**—woven material

4. Act of Weaving Together: contexture, intertexture,n.

5. Characteristic Structure of Woven or Interwoven Threads: contexture, texture,n. (textural,adj.)

6. Manner, Fact, or State of Being Woven Together: contexture, intertexture,n.

7. Weaving Together: contexive,adj.

8. Machine for Weaving: loom, spinning wheel,n.

9. Capable of Being Woven: textile,adj.

10. Formed by Weaving: textile,adj.

11. Pert. to Weaving: textile,adj.

12. Pert. to Woven Materials: textile, textural,adj.

13. Material Suitable for Weaving: textile,n.

308. NETWORK

1. Network; A Net, n.
1. **cobweb**—net or network spun by a spider; network (figuratively) of intrigue or plotting
2. **gossamer**—net or network spun by a spider
3. **mesh**—net; network
4. **meshwork**—network
5. **reticulation**—network; arrangement of network
6. **seine**—large net, usually for catching fish
7. **texture**—network
8. **tissue**—net; network
9. **toils**—net or nets spread for wild game
10. **web**—network; cobweb
11. **webbing**—network
12. **weft**—network

2. Netted; Descr. of, or Resembling, Network, adj. *From Sec. 1:* cobwebby, gossamer, meshed or meshy, reticulate or reticular, textured, webbed or webby

3. Like a Cobweb: arachnoid, cobwebby,adj.

4. To Form into a Network: reticulate,v. (reticulation,n.)

5. Fabric Made of Network: netting,n.

6. Able to Make a Web to Catch Prey: retiary,adj.

7. Possessing, or Armed with, a Net: retiary, adj.

8. Pert. to Nets, or to the Construction of Nets: retiary,adj.

9. Operating Like, or Having the Effects of, a Net: reticular,adj.

10. Open Space of a Net or of Network: mesh,n.

309. FREEDOM

1. To Free or Set Free (Literally), v.
1. **affranchise**—free from slavery
2. **bail**—effect the release of (a prisoner) by payment of security for his reappearance
3. **deliver**—set free; rescue
4. **disengage**—free
5. **emancipate**—free from slavery
6. **enfranchise**—free from slavery or prison
7. **extricate**—free from that which is holding one fast
8. **go bail for**—make the necessary payment to effect the release of (a prisoner)
9. **let loose**—free; set free
10. **liberate**—free; set free
11. **loose, loosen**—free; set free
12. **manumit**—formally free from slavery
13. **parole**—release (a prisoner) before his term has been served
14. **ransom**—effect the freedom or release of (someone held prisoner or captive) by payment, usually of money
15. **redeem**—rescue by paying a ransom
16. **release**—set free
17. **rescue**—free from danger or confinement
18. **set loose**—free; set free
19. **unbind**—set free; set free from that which holds

20. **unbridle**—free
21. **uncage**—set free from, or as if from, a cage
22. **unchain**—set free
23. **uncoop**—set free from, or as if from, a coop or place of confinement
24. **unfetter**—free
25. **unhand**—free; let escape
26. **unhandcuff**—set free from handcuffs
27. **unhobble**—set free from that which hinders foot motions, or from foot shackles
28. **unimprison**—set free from prison
29. **unleash**—set free
30. **unloose, unloosen**—set free
31. **unmanacle**—set free from handcuffs
32. **unmew**—free from prison or confinement
33. **unmuzzle**—set free from a muzzle
34. **unpinion**—set free from that which binds the arms
35. **unshackle**—free; set free; free from bonds or from that which keeps one tied up
36. **untie**—free; set free

2. A Freeing or Setting Free,n. *From Sec. 1:* affranchisement, deliverance or delivery, disengagement, emancipation, enfranchisement, extrication, liberation, manumission, redemption, release, rescue; *Also:* **1. probation**—the release of a young or first-offender from punishment provided he avoids further entanglement with the law (probationary,adj.)

3. Freedom,n. *From Sec. 1:* disengagement, emancipation, enfranchisement, liberation or liberty, redemption; *From Sec. 2:* probation

4. One Who Frees,n. *From Sec. 1:* deliverer, emancipator, enfranchiser, liberator, ransomer, redeemer, rescuer

5. One Who Is, or Has Been, Freed,n. *From Sec. 1:* parolee; *From Sec. 2:* probationer; *Also:* **1. freedman, freeman**—one who has been set free

6. That Which Frees,n. *From Sec. 1:* bail, ransom

7. Freeing; Serving to Free,adj. *From Sec. 1:* emancipative; *From Sec. 2:* probationary

8. Not Imprisoned: uncommitted,adj.

9. Elimination of Negro Slavery in the United States: abolition,n.

10. Advocacy of the Elimination of Negro Slavery in the United States: abolitionism,n. (abolitionist,n.)

11. To Free, i.e., Make Free of,v.
1. **absolve**—free of duty, obligation, responsibility, promise, blame, or guilt
2. **affranchise**—free of obligation or dependence
3. **clear**—free of impurities; free of blame, accusation, or imputation of guilt
4. **decontaminate**—free of contamination or impurities
5. **decontrol**—free of control
6. **delouse**—free of lice
7. **demilitarize**—free of control by the army
8. **deobstruct**—free of obstructions
9. **disabuse**—free of incorrect notions or false beliefs or understanding
10. **disaccustom**—free of a habit
11. **disburden**—free of a burden, load, or oppression; disencumber
12. **discharge**—free of a burden, charge, or oppression
13. **disembarrass**—free of embarrassment, uneasiness, or an entangling situation; free of that which entangles or impedes
14. **disenchant**—free of pleasant illusions; disillusion
15. **disencumber**—free by taking away or lifting off a literal or figurative burden
16. **disengage**—free of an obligation or involvement
17. **disentangle**—free of entanglement

18. **disillusion**—free of one's illusions, or of one's high regard for someone or something
19. **disinfect**—free of infection
20. **disinfest**—free of infestation of rodents, insects, etc.
21. **enfranchise**—free of obligation
22. **excuse**—free of obligation or duty
23. **exempt**—free of that duty, obligation, liability, etc., to which others are subject
24. **exonerate**—free of guilt, charge, obligation, or hardship
25. **extricate**—free of difficulties, of a difficult situation, of an entanglement, or of anything holding one back, literally or figuratively
26. **liberate**—free of duty, requirement, obligation, etc.
27. **release**—free of obligation or duty; free from being held or held back, literally or figuratively
28. **relieve**—free of duty by taking the place of; free of some figurative or literal burden
29. **rid**—free of
30. **spare**—free for other uses
31. **unblock**—free by removing hindrances or obstructions
32. **unbridle**—free of restraint
33. **unclog**—free by removing obstructions
34. **uncork**—free from a stopped-up or pent-up condition
35. **unfetter**—free of restraint
36. **ungag**—free of restraints upon one's speech
37. **unleash**—free of control or restrictions
38. **unmuzzle**—free of restraints upon one's speech
39. **unpinion**—free of restraint
40. **unplug**—free by removing the plug, literally or figuratively
41. **unravel**—free of complication, difficulty, or entanglement
42. **unshackle**—free of restraint
43. **unstick**—free (that which is stuck together)
44. **unstop**—free of obstruction
45. **unstopple**—unplug
46. **untrammel**—free of restrictions or hindrances

12. A Freeing; A Freeing of or from Something,n. *From Sec. 11:* absolution, affranchisement, decontamination, decontrol, demilitarization, deobstruction, disburdenment, discharge, disembarrassment, disenchantment, disencumberment, disengagement, disentanglement, disillusionment, disinfection, disinfestation, enfranchisement, exemption, exoneration, extrication, liberation, release, relief, riddance, unravelment

13. Serving or Acting to Free, or to Free from Something,adj. *From Sec. 11:* decontaminative, deobstructive, disillusive or disillusioning, disinfective, exemptive

14. Freedom; Freedom from Something,n. *From Sec. 11:* absolution, decontamination, decontrol, demilitarization, disenchantment, disengagement, disillusionment, enfranchisement, exemption, liberation or liberty, release, relief; *Also:*
1. **abandon, abandonment**—freedom from ordinary control or restraint; unrestrained freedom in the following of impulses or natural desires
2. **anarchy**—freedom from all government
3. **autarchy, autarky**—economic freedom of a country
4. **autocracy**—freedom from any outside control
5. **autonomy**—freedom from outside government, control, or influence
6. **carte blanche (French)**—freedom to use one's own judgment in actions
7. **dissoluteness**—freedom from convention,

conscience, self-control, or other restrictions upon conduct or behavior

8. **expansiveness**—freedom from inhibitions or inner restraint
9. **impunity**—freedom or exemption from punishment or loss (generally preceded by *with*, as *to break the law with impunity*)
10. **independence**—freedom, in the sense of lack of subjection to outside will, rule, government, or control
11. **latitude**—freedom from narrow bounds or restraints
12. **libertinism**—freedom from control, restraint, or moral restraint; dissoluteness; license
13. **license, licentiousness**—lack of restraint by law or morals
14. **looseness**—freedom from attachment or restraint; freedom from obligation, duty, or constraint; freedom from moral restraint
15. **rampancy**—freedom from restraint
16. **rein**—freedom, i.e., lack of control (in the phrase *give rein to*)
17. **riotousness, riot**—freedom, in the sense of living or acting without restraint
18. **sovereignty**—political independence; autonomy
19. **unattachment**—freedom, in the sense of lack of attachment or figurative bonds (to a person, cause, etc.)
20. **unconstraint**—freedom from force or compulsion of natural feelings
21. **unscrupulousness**—freedom from the restrictions of conscience or morality
22. **volition**—freedom to act according to one's own decisions or choice
23. **wantonness**—excessive freedom from normal inner restraint
24. **wildness**—lack of control, regulation, or restraint

15. Free; Free of, or from, Something,adj. *From Sec. 11:* absolved, affranchised, etc.; clear, exempt, rid, unstuck; *From Sec. 14:* abandoned, anarchic, autarchic or autarkic, autocratic, autonomous, dissolute, expansive, independent, libertine, licentious or licentiate, loose, rampant, riotous, sovereign, unattached, unconstrained, unscrupulous, wanton, wild; *Also:*

1. **absolute**—free from outside control
2. **fancy-free**—free of any commitment to a loved one
3. **foot-loose**—free in the sense of having no figurative attachments
4. **madcap**—uncontrolled
5. **reinless**—unchecked; unrestrained
6. **substantive**—independent
7. **unchecked**—free in the sense that no hindrance or check is imposed
8. **uncircumscribed**—unrestricted
9. **uncommitted**—not bound by previous decision
10. **unconfined**—free in the sense of not held within limits or bounds; unrestrained
11. **unconscionable**—free from control or guidance by the conscience
12. **unconstricted**—free in the sense of not being held in
13. **uncontained**—free in the sense of not being held back; unrestrained
14. **uncontrolled**—unchecked; uncontained
15. **uncramped**—unrestricted
16. **uncurbed**—unrestrained
17. **undammed**—free in the sense of not having its flow restrained or impeded
18. **undominated**—free in the sense of not being subject to the will of another
19. **unencumbered**—free in the sense of not being burdened, or of not being hindered by burdens
20. **ungoverned**—unrestrained
21. **unhampered**—free in action; free of restrictions or impediments

22. **unhindered**—free in the sense of not being held back by obstacles
23. **unimpeded**—unhindered
24. **uninhibited**—free of emotional self-control
25. **unlimited**—free in the sense that there is no imposition of conditions or restrictions
26. **unobstructed**—free in the sense that nothing is in the way
27. **unprincipled**—free of moral principles or of the restraint of morals or conscience
28. **unqualified**—free of all limits or qualifications
29. **unregulated**—free of outside control
30. **unreined**—unchecked; unrestrained
31. **unrepressed**—free in the sense of not being held back
32. **unreserved**—unrestrained; unrestricted
33. **unrestrained**—free in the sense of not being held back, held in, kept down, kept back, or limited in any way
34. **unrestricted**—free in the sense that action is not limited or hindered
35. **unstemmed**—free in the sense that there is no obstacle to a free flow or flowing
36. **unstifled**—free in the sense of not being choked back, kept back, or held back
37. **unsuppressed**—unstifled
38. **wildcat**—unchecked; uncontained; unregulated

16. One Who Is Free of Something,n. *From Sec. 14:* autocrat, libertine, rioter, wanton; *Also:* 1. **maverick**—one who bolts his political party or group and acts independently (from the name given to an unbranded calf)

17. Advocate of Freedom,n. *From Sec. 14:* anarchist, autarchist or autarkist; *Also:* 1. **libertarian**—advocate of freedom of thought and conduct (libertarianism,n.)

18. Abuse of Freedom by Ignoring All Restraints: license,n.

19. Frantic Desire for Freedom: eleutheromania,n. (eleutheromaniac,n. eleutheromaniac,adj.)

20. Movement toward Political Freedom in a Dependent Country: nationalism,n. (nationalist,n. nationalist, nationalistic,adj.)

21. To Be or Become Free,v.
1. **discharge, disburden**—free oneself of (a burden or load)
2. **disentangle**—become free of entanglement (disentanglement,n.)
3. **relax**—free oneself of care, anxiety, worry, etc. (relaxation, laxation,n.)
4. **riot**—live or act in complete freedom from restraint
5. **thaw**—become free or freer in manner
6. **unbend**—relax; thaw

22. Wild: feral, ferine, fierce, savage, undomesticated, untamed,adj.

23. Wildness: ferineness, ferity, fierceness, savagery, savagism,n.

310. SLAVERY

1. **To Enslave,**v.
1. **bind**—enslave; indenture
2. **enthrall**—reduce to a condition of moral or mental slavery (enthrallment,n.)
3. **indenture**—hand over into slavery for a stated period of time under a contract (indenture,n.)
4. **subject**—subjugate (subjection,n.)
5. **subjugate**—cause to be, or live like, a slave (subjugation,n.)
6. **thrall, bethrall**—enslave morally, emotionally, or mentally
7. **yoke**—enslave; hold in slavery or subjection

2. **Slavery:** bondage, chains, enslavement, helotry, helotism, serfdom, serfage, serfism,

serfhood, servitude, subjection, subjugation, vassalage, vassalism, yoke,n.

3. Mental or Moral Slavery: enthrallment, thrall, thralldom,n.

4. Bondage for a Stated Period of Time under a Contract: indenture,n.

5. Slave: bondmaid (fem.), bondsman, bondman, bond servant, bond slave; bondwoman (fem.); bondswoman (fem.); chattel, helot; mameluke (Mohammedan); serf, thrall, vassal,n.

6. Fugitive Slave in the West Indies or Guiana: maroon,n.

7. One Who Is Mentally or Morally Enslaved: thrall,n.

8. Female Slave in a Harem: odalisque,n.

9. Peasant Bound to the Land and His Master: serf,n.

10. Group of Slaves Chained Together: coffle, n.

11. Pert. to, Descr. or Characteristic of, Like, or Acting Like, a Slave: abject, servile, slavish, subservient, supine,adj. (abjectness, servility or servileness, slavishness, subservience or subservientness, supineness,n. subservient,n.)

12. Causing Slavery: slavish,adj.

13. That Which Holds in Slavery or Subjection: bonds, chains, yoke,n.

14. Symbol of Slavery: bonds, chains, yoke,n.

15. Lacking in Freedom from Convention, Conventional Restrictions, etc.: slavish,adj. (slavishness,n.)

311. ARRANGEMENT

1. Arrangement,n.
1. **alignment**—arrangement in a line
2. **alternation**—arrangement by turns (first one, then the other, etc.)
3. **architectonics**—structural design
4. **array, arrayal**—arrangement in order
5. **catalogue**—arrangement in a list
6. **chronology**—arrangement of events in accordance with the time in which they have occurred
7. **codification**—arrangement into a system
8. **collocation**—arrangement in a definite order
9. **composition**—arrangement of parts in an artistic work, etc.
10. **configuration**—arrangement of the parts (of a thing)
11. **cosmos**—orderly arrangement of the world
12. **crisscross**—arrangement of crossing lines
13. **design**—arrangement of details, color, etc., in a picture or painting; arrangement of parts
14. **disposal, disposition**—arrangement
15. **echelon**—arrangement of military troops, planes, etc., in steplike form; arrangement of executives or other officers of an institution, corporation, etc., in figuratively similar form, the lowest in rank in the greatest numbers at the bottom, rank increasing and number decreasing toward the top
16. **file**—orderly arrangement of papers, letters, cards, etc., for easy reference
17. **harmony**—arrangement in which the components are orderly and fit together pleasingly
18. **homotaxis, homotaxy, homotaxia**—similarity in arrangement; similarity in the arrangement of layers or of fossils in strata of different regions (geology)
19. **menology**—calendar arrangement of the lives of saints
20. **method**—arrangement by some orderly or logical means
21. **methodology**—orderly or logical arrangement
22. **network**—arrangement of things crossing, and connected with, each other
23. **order**—formal arrangement; sensible or logical arrangement
24. **ordination**—arrangement
25. **organization**—arrangement of parts into a working or effective combination
26. **patchwork**—checkered or variegated arrangement
27. **pattern**—decorative or orderly arrangement
28. **phalanx**—massed arrangement of people, things, animals, etc. (phalanxes, phalanges,pl.)
29. **prearrangement**—arrangement beforehand
30. **rally**—rearrangement in order
31. **range**—arrangement in some order
32. **rank**—orderly arrangement
33. **realignment**—rearrangement in a line
34. **rearrangement**—new or different arrangement
35. **reticulation**—netlike arrangement; network
36. **scheme**—orderly arrangement
37. **seriation**—arrangement in orderly sequence
38. **series**—arrangement in rows
39. **stichometry**—arrangement of reading material in lines suited to meaning (a method used before the adoption of punctuation)
40. **stratification**—arrangement in layers
41. **structure**—arrangement of parts
42. **symmetry**—arrangement in which there is a balance or correspondence of both sides
43. **system**—orderly arrangement
44. **tabulation**—arrangement in lists or tables
45. **tessellation**—arrangement in checkerboard form
46. **texture**—arrangement of threads in a woven fabric; arrangement of parts in anything
47. **typography**—arrangement of printed matter

2. To Arrange,v. *From Sec. 1:* align, alternate, array, catalogue, chronologize, codify, collocate, compose, design, dispose, file, harmonize, methodize, organize, rally, range, rank, realign, rearrange, reticulate, schematize, seriate; serialize (from *series*); stratify, structure, symmetrize, systematize, tabulate or tabularize, tessellate; *Also:*
1. **list**—arrange in bands or stripes
2. **marshal**—arrange in effective order
3. **pack**—rig
4. **rig**—arrange dishonestly or fraudulently to one's own advantage
5. **stage**—arrange; arrange as in a theater
6. **stage-manage**—arrange for maximum effect on people or the public
7. **stagger**—arrange in alternating order
8. **string**—arrange in a row
9. **tier**—arrange in rows, layers, or ranks, each higher than the preceding one

3. Arrangement, i.e., an Arranging,n. *From Sec. 2:* alignment, alternation, arrayal, codification, collocation, composition, disposal or disposition, organization, realignment, rearrangement, reticulation, schematization, serialization, stratification, systematization, tabulation or tabularization, tessellation, stagemanagement

4. Arranged; Descr. of, or Pert. to, Arrangement,adj. *From Sec. 1:* aligned, alternated, architectonic, arrayed; catalogued, catalogic, or catalogical; chronological, codified, compositional, configurational or configurative, cosmic, crisscrossed, filed, harmonious; homotaxial, homotaxic, homotaxeous, or homotactic; methodic or methodical, methodological, orderly or ordered, patterned, phalangeal, prearranged, ranked, realigned, rearranged, reticular or reticulate, schematic, seriate; serial (from *series*); stichometric, stratified, structural, symmetric or symmetrical, systematic or systematical, tabular or tabulated, tessellate or tessellated, textural, typographical; *From Sec. 2:* marshaled, rigged, staged, stage-managed, staggered, strung, tiered; *Also:*

1. **bibliothetic**—pert. to, or descr. of, the arrangement of books in a bookstore, library, etc.
2. **bicyclic**—arranged in two circles
3. **cathedral**—arranged like the aisles of a big church
4. **cycloid**—arranged in circles
5. **tegular**—arranged like tiles

5. Arranger,n. *From Sec. 2:* cataloguer, cataloguist, catalogist, or cataloger; chronologer or chronologist, codifier, composer, designer, filer or file clerk, organizer, schematizer, systematizer, tabulator; stager, stage-manager

6. Place Where Things Can Be Arranged: rack,n.

7. Place or Container for Papers in Orderly Arrangement: file,n.

8. Design,n.
1. **chevron**—design in the form of bars, inverted *V's*, etc., worn to indicate military or other rank, service, wounds, etc.
2. **crisscross**—design of crossing lines
3. **decalcomania**—design transferred to china, glass, wood, etc.
4. **intaglio**—design cut into or below the surface
5. **kaleidoscope**—variegated and changing design (kaleidoscopic,adj.)
6. **mosaic**—design formed by differently colored pieces of glass, stone, etc.
7. **patchwork**—checkered or variegated design
8. **pattern**—design
9. **pyrography, pyrogravure**—design (or designs) burned into the surface of something (pyrographic,adj.)
10. **tattoo**—design pricked or marked into the skin
11. **tessellation**—checked or checkerboard mosaic
12. **vignette**—decorative design in a book, often on the title page

9. To Prick or Mark a Design into the Skin: tattoo,v.

10. Art or Process of Burning Designs into a Surface: pyrography, pyrogravure,n. (pyrographer,n. pyrographic,adj.)

11. A Row,n.
1. **column**—row of print on a page of a newspaper, magazine, etc.; row of figures
2. **file**—row of people or things one behind the other; one of the vertical rows of squares on a chessboard
3. **line**—row
4. **list**—row of numbers, names, words, etc.
5. **range**—row
6. **rank**—row; one of the horizontal rows of squares on a chessboard; row of soldiers, military vehicles, etc., side by side
7. **series**—row
8. **string**—row (of things)
9. **swath**—row cut by a scythe, mower, etc.
10. **table**—row of figures, facts, etc.
11. **tier**—row; one of a number of rows, each higher than the preceding one
12. **windrow**—row of hay or grain swept together to dry; row of dust, dry leaves, etc., swept together by the wind

12. Arranged in Rows,adj. *From Sec. 11:* columnar or columned, lined up, ranged, ranked, serial or seriate, strung, tabular,

tiered; *Also:* **1. tristichous**—arranged in three rows

13. To Arrange in a Row or Rows,v. *From Sec. 11:* line up, list, range, rank, serialize, string; tabularize or tabulate (from *table*); tier, windrow (serialization, tabularization, tabulation,n.)

14. To Be or Become Arranged in a Row or Rows,v. *From Sec. 11:* line up, range, rank, tier

15. Rows; Things Arranged in a Row: series, n.

16. Figures or Facts Arranged in Rows: table,n.

17. To Move in a Row: file,v.

18. To Go Out in a Row: file out,v.

19. A List,n.
1. **canon**—list; list of works of an author
2. **catalogue**—list (catalogic, catalogical, adj.)
3. **index**—alphabetical list of the contents
4. **register**—list of events, items, etc.; list of names
5. **roll**—list; list of names; list of names for checking attendance
6. **schedule**—list of details; list of recurring events with the times of their expected recurrence
7. **screed**—long written list
8. **table**—systematic list of contents, details, parts, figures, etc. (tabular,adj.)

20. To List,v. *From Sec. 19:* catalogue, index, schedule, tabularize or tabulate (tabularization, tabulation,n.)

21. To Put on, or in, a List,v. *From Sec. 19:* catalogue, register, enroll, schedule (registration, registry, enrollment,n.)

22. One Who Makes, or Puts in, or on, a List,n. *From Sec. 19:* cataloguer, cataloguist, catalogist, or cataloger; indexer, registrar, tabulator

312. CLASSIFICATION

1. Class, Classification, Kind, or Sort,n.
1. **assortment**—kind
2. **bracket**—classification
3. **brand**—kind
4. **breed**—class; kind; sort
5. **brood**—kind; distinct kind; class; sort
6. **cast**—kind; sort
7. **category**—class; classification
8. **character**—kind; sort
9. **color**—distinctive or strong quality
10. **denomination**—class; classification
11. **description**—class; classification
12. **division**—class; classification
13. **feather**—kind; sort
14. **genre**—kind, sort, or type (esp. in literature or the fine arts)
15. **grade**—class or kind of things or people of the same quality, rank, etc.; classification in school
16. **group**—related class or kind
17. **grouping**—classification
18. **ilk**—class, kind, or sort (often used in the phrase *of that ilk,* or in phrases like *the human ilk, the bovine ilk,* etc., occasionally with humorous intent)
19. **kidney**—class; kind; sort
20. **mold**—distinctive kind or sort
21. **nature**—kind; sort
22. **persuasion**—class; kind; sort
23. **quality**—class, kind, or type that something is
24. **quintessence**—purest kind
25. **race**—classification; kind; sort
26. **rank**—class; classification
27. **section**—class; classification; subdivision
28. **sort**—class; classification; kind
29. **species**—kind; distinct kind

30. **stamp**—class; classification; kind; sort
31. **strain**—kind; sort
32. **stripe**—kind; sort
33. **style**—class; kind; sort
34. **subdivision**—class or classification within a larger class or classification
35. **tier**—class; classification
36. **tribe**—classification; kind; sort
37. **type**—kind having similar or common characteristics
38. **variety**—kind

2. To Classify,v. *From Sec. 1:* assort, bracket, categorize, class, divide, group, rank, section, sort, type; *Also:*
1. **codify**—classify into a system
2. **pigeonhole**—classify; put into the proper classification
3. **screen**—sort by, or as if by, sifting
4. **winnow**—sort out

3. Act or Process of Classifying,n. *From Sec. 1:* assortment, categorization, division; *From Sec. 2:* codification

4. Sciences of Classification,n.
1. **nosology**—science of the classification of diseases (nosologist,n. nosological,adj.)
2. **systematics**—science of classification (systematician,n.)
3. **taxonomy**—branch of any science dealing with classification (taxonomist, taxonomen,n. taxonomic, taxonomical,adj.)

5. Pert. to, or Concerned with, Classification,adj.
1. **bibliothetic**—pert. to the classification of books in a bookstore, library, etc.
2. **categorical**—pert. to classification
3. **classificatory**—pert. or relating to, or using, classification
4. **systematic**—pert. to, or concerned with, classification

6. Of No Particular Kind or Type,adj.
1. **amorphous**—of no clear kind or type
2. **mongrel**—of no special or pure kind
3. **nondescript**—not easily classified as to kind; of no particular kind

7. Of the Same Kind: consubstantial, homogeneous, kindred,adj. (consubstantiality, homogeneity, homogeneousness, kindredness, n.)

8. Of the Same Genus or Species: congeneric,adj.

9. Member of the Same Genus or Species: congener,n.

10. Of Several or Different Types or Kinds, adj.
1. **assorted**—of several kinds (assortment, n.)
2. **biform**—having, or combining the characteristics of, two types, as a *mermaid, centaur,* etc.
3. **bigeneric**—of two genera
4. **hybrid**—of two or more species, strains, breeds, kinds, etc.
5. **manifold**—of many kinds
6. **mixed**—assorted (mixture,n.)
7. **mongrel**—hybrid
8. **multifarious**—of many different kinds (multifariousness,n.)
9. **omnifarious**—of all kinds or sorts (omnifariousness,n.)
10. **triform**—of three different kinds
11. **varicolored**—of different kinds (varicolor, n.)
12. **varied**—assorted (variety,n.)
13. **variegated**—assorted (variegation,n.)
14. **various**—of different kinds (variousness, variety,n.)

11. One Who Is of Several Types or Kinds,n. *From Sec. 10:* bigener, hybrid, mongrel

12. To Cause to Be of Several Kinds,v. *From Sec. 10:* assort, mix, variegate, vary (assortment, mixture, variegation, variation,n.)

13. **Having Only One Type:** monotypic,adj.
14. **Having Many Types:** polytypic,adj.

313. RANK

1. Rank,n.
1. **class**—rank; rank in school
2. **classification**—rank
3. **echelon**—rank of command, as in the army, a corporation, etc.
4. **estate**—political rank
5. **grade**—rank; rank in school
6. **level**—figurative rank
7. **position**—rank
8. **sphere**—rank
9. **station**—rank

2. To Rank, i.e., Place in a Rank or Ranks, v. *From Sec. 1:* class, classify, grade (classification,n.)

3. To Rank, i.e., Hold a Rank,v. *From Sec. 1:* class, grade

4. High Rank: estate,n.

5. High in Rank: major,adj. (majority,n.)

6. The Higher Ranks in a Church, College, etc: hierarchy,n. (hierarchic, hierarchical, adj.)

7. Higher in Rank: major, senior,adj. (majority, seniority,n.)

8. To Hold a Higher Rank than: outrank, rank,v.

9. Highest or First in Rank: first-string, paramount, premier, prime, ranking, sovereign, supreme, top-drawer, top-flight,adj. (paramountcy, primacy, sovereignty, supremacy,n.)

10. To Raise in Rank,v.
1. **advance**—raise to a higher rank or grade
2. **promote**—raise in rank, grade, etc.
3. **skip**—raise to a higher class in school by allowing to jump a grade
4. **upgrade**—raise in rank or grade

11. To Rise in Rank,v. *From Sec. 10:* advance, skip

12. A Raising or Raise in Rank,n. *From Sec. 10:* advancement, promotion, upgrading; *Also:* 1. preferment—promotion

13. A Rising or Rise in Rank,n. *From Sec. 10:* advance or advancement, skip; *Also:* 1. ascent —advance in position or rank

14. A Person of High, Higher or Highest Rank,n.
1. **chief, head, leader**—person of highest rank in an organization or group
2. **dignitary**—person of high position or rank
3. **grandee**—person of high rank
4. **magnifico**—person of high position or rank
5. **major**—person of high rank in a group
6. **officer**—person of high or higher rank in an organization
7. **prince**—one who is first in his class, type, profession, etc.
8. **senior**—person of higher rank in an organization
9. **superior**—person of higher rank in an organization

15. Having Too Many Officers or Personnel in the Higher Ranks in Relation to Those in the Lower Ranks: top-heavy,adj.

16. Of Low Class or Rank: rude,adj.

17. Lower in Rank: junior, minor, second-string, subordinate,adj.

18. Person of Lower Rank: junior, subordinate,n.

19. To Reduce in Rank,v.
1. **abase**—reduce in rank or position (abasement,n.)

2. **degrade**—reduce to a lower grade
3. **demote**—reduce in grade or put back to a lower grade or rank (demotion,n.)
4. **disrate**—reduce in rank (in the Navy)
5. **downgrade**—reduce in grade or rank

314. SOCIAL CLASS

1. Social Class, Position, or Rank,n.
1. **caste**—division of social classes, indigenous to India, but applicable also to any other regions where such divisions are practiced
2. **class**—rank of society; high social rank
3. **estate**—social class or rank
4. **sphere**—social position or class
5. **station**—social position or rank
6. **stratum**—social class containing people of approximately the same education, wealth, background, etc. (strata,pl.)

2. People or Class as to Social Rank,n.
1. **aristocracy**—upper social class
2. **beau monde**—upper class of society
3. **bon ton**—high society; upper class society
4. **bourgeoisie**—conservative, property-owning, materialistic middle class
5. **classes**—upper social classes, as contrasted to the masses
6. **commons**—class that is not the aristocracy
7. **elite**—socially select or superior class of society
8. **equites**—privileged social class of ancient Rome
9. **first estate**—the clergy in England and France
10. **gentlefolk, gentlefolks**—people of good social rank
11. **gentry**—upper social classes
12. **lower class**—people of low social position, as manual workers, menials, etc.
13. **masses**—common people
14. **middle class**—class between the upper and lower class
15. **nobility**—upper social class in a country where social titles are used
16. **patricians**—higher social class in ancient Rome or, later, in certain medieval German, Swiss, and Italian free cities
17. **peasantry**—social class, in Europe, of workers on the soil
18. **peerage**—nobility
19. **plebs, plebes**—lower social class in ancient Rome
20. **proletariat**—working class or classes
21. **quality**—high social class or classes
22. **second estate**—aristocracy
23. **society**—higher social class or classes; people of fashion and wealth
24. **third estate**—common people
25. **upper class**—higher social class
26. **upper crust**—highest of the higher social classes

3. Member of a Social Class,n. *From Sec. 2:* aristocrat, bourgeois, commoner, noble, patrician, peasant, peer, pleb, plebs, or plebeian, proletarian; *Also:*
1. **blue blood**—person of upper social class descent
2. **parvenu**—one who has suddenly risen to a higher social position, often through, or by means of, acquired wealth, and who is unfamiliar with the graces or customs of the higher classes (derogative)
3. **patrician**—member of the higher social classes
4. **socialite**—well-known member of high society
5. **underdog**—member of the less privileged social classes
6. **untouchable**—member of one of the lowest castes in India

4. Pert. to, or Descr. of, Social Class,adj.

From Sec. 2: aristocratic, bourgeois, common, equestrian (from *equites*), lower-class, middle-class, noble or nobiliary, patrician, peasant, plebeian, proletarian, upper-class; *From Sec. 3:* patrician

5. One Who Has the Tastes or Atttitudes of the Upper Social Classes: aristocrat,n.

6. Placing of Greater Value on Social Position than on Genuine Worth: snobbishness, snobbism, snobbery,n. (snob,n. snobbish,adj.)

7. A Noble; A Nobleman,n.
1. **archduke**—prince (Austria)
2. **baron**—member of the lowest rank of nobility
3. **chevalier**—member of the lowest rank of former French nobility
4. **count**—European nobleman corresponding in rank to a British earl
5. **duke**—British or other European nobleman of the highest rank after that of a prince; prince
6. **earl**—British nobleman of a rank higher than a viscount but lower than a marquis
7. **grand duke**—person holding the title 'just below that of the king in certain countries; formerly, son of the ruler or Czar of Russia, or direct male descendant of the Czar
8. **grandee**—Spanish or Portuguese nobleman of the highest rank
9. **landgrave**—German count or prince
10. **lord**—British nobleman; baron; any British nobleman from baron to marquis
11. **marchese**—Italian nobleman of a rank below prince
12. **margrave**—marquis
13. **marquis**—nobleman of the rank next below that of a duke
14. **peer**—nobleman; member of the British nobility
15. **prince**—male member of the royal family
16. **viscount**—nobleman higher in rank than a baron but below a count or earl

8. Noblewoman,n. *From Sec. 7:* archduchess, baroness, duchess, grand duchess, landgravine or landgravess, marchesa, margravine, marquise or marchioness, peeress, princess, viscountess; *Also:* 1. countess—wife or widow of an earl; female equivalent of an earl

9. Rank of a Noble,n. *From Sec. 7:* baronage or barony, dukedom, earldom, grand dukedom, lordship, landgraviate, margraviate, marquisate, peerage; princedom, princehood or princeship; viscountcy, viscounty, or viscountship

10. Domain of a Noble,n. *From Sec. 7:* archdukedom or archduchy, barony, dukedom or duchy, earldom, grand dukedom or grand duchy, landgraviate, margraviate, princedom

11. Noble; Pert. to, or Descr. of, a Noble, adj. *From Sec. 7:* archducal, baronial, grandducal, lordly, margravial or margravely, marquisal, princely

12. A Little or Petty Prince: princekin, princelet, princeling,n.

13. Nobles, Collectively,n.
1. **baronage**—nobles collectively; barons collectively
2. **nobility**—nobles as a class or collectively
3. **peerage**—nobles collectively; peers collectively
4. **second estate**—nobles as a class or collectively

14. Pert. to, or Descr. of, the Nobility: noble, nobiliary,adj.

15. Having a Title of Nobility: titled,adj.

16. Person with a Title below That of Nobility,n.
1. **baronet**—person with a title just below that of a baron, but not included in the nobility (baronetcy, baronetage,n.)

2. **cavalier**—knight
3. **esquire**—person with a title below that of a knight (British)
4. **knight**—in Britain, a person with a title below that of a baronet (knighthood,n.)

17. Title Prefixed to the Name of a Baronet or Knight: Sir,n.

18. Baronets Collectively: baronetage,n.

19. Abbreviation of the Title Baronet: Bart. (generally follows the name)

20. To Raise to the Rank of Esquire: esquire, v.

21. To Raise to the Rank of Knight: knight, v.

315. LAYER

1. Layer,n.
1. **bedrock**—lowest layer
2. **cortex**—outer layer of an anatomical organ, tree, etc. (cortical,adj.)
3. **film**—thin or slight layer (filmy,adj.)
4. **lamina, lamination**—thin layer; layer lying over another—of minerals, bones, etc. (laminae,pl. laminar, laminate,adj.)
5. **membrane**—layer of thin animal or vegetable matter; thin layer of animal tissue (membranous,adj.)
6. **ply**—layer
7. **scum**—thin layer that rises to the top of a liquid (scummy,adj.)
8. **stratification**—layer of rock (stratified, adj.)
9. **stratum**—layer of material, esp. one of several such parallel layers; layer of society; layer of rock (strata,pl. stratiform, adj.)
10. **streak**—layer
11. **substratum**—layer under another layer (substrata,pl.)
12. **superstratum**—layer on the top of other layers (superstrata,pl.)
13. **tier**—layer (tiered,adj.)
14. **veneer**—surface layer; thin layer of something fine used for covering (veneered,adj.)

2. Primary Germ Layers of an Embryo,n.
1. **ectoderm**—outermost germ layer of an embryo (ectodermal, ectodermic,adj.)
2. **endoderm, entoderm**—innermost of the three germ layers of the embryo (endodermal,endodermic, entodermal, entodermic,adj.)
3. **mesoderm**—middle layer, between the ectoderm and endoderm (mesodermal, mesodermic,adj.)

3. To Split (Something) into Thin Layers: delaminate, laminate,v. (delamination, lamination,n.)

4. To Form into, Cover with, or Arrange in, a Layer or Layers,v.
1. **laminate**—build layer upon layer; cover with layers; beat or roll (metal) into a layer (lamination,n.)
2. **stratify**—form into rigid professional, business, social, economic, etc., layers, so that members of a lower layer cannot easily rise to a higher one; form into rigid, unchangeable layers; arrange in layers (stratification,n.)
3. **veneer**—cover with a thin layer of finer material

5. To Become Formed or Arranged in Layers: stratify,v. (stratification,n.)

6. To Lie in Layers (of Rock): stratify,v. (stratification,n.)

316. LINE

1. A Line,n.
1. **queue**—waiting line of people

2. **streak**—long line
3. **stripe**—line of color different from its background
4. **train**—line of people, animals, or things moving along together
5. **transversal**—line that crosses two or more lines
6. **underline, underscore**—line drawn under (usually written material)

2. Pert. or Relating to Lines,adj.
1. **bilinear**—pert. to, or having, two lines (bilinearity,n.)
2. **collinear**—lying in one straight line (collinearity,n.)
3. **interlineal, interlinear**—placed between the lines (usually of writing or printing)
4. **lineal, linear**—pert. to, or of the nature of, a line or lines (linearity,n.)
5. **lineate**—marked by or with lines (lineation,n.)
6. **rectilinear**—pert. to, moving in, characterized by, or bounded with, straight lines (rectilinearity,n.)
7. **trilinear**—pert. to, or included among, three lines

3. Number of Lines of Writing or Printing: linage,n.

4. To Make a Line or Lines; To Form a Line,v.
1. **align, aline**—bring or form into line; form a line out of (alignment, alinement, n.)
2. **interlineate**—mark between the lines (interlineation,n.)
3. **lineate**—mark with lines (lineation,n.)
4. **queue up**—form a line, with other people, to wait for something
5. **underline, underscore**—mark a line under, usually under written or printed material (underlineation, underlinement, n.)

317. TYPE; MODEL

1. Type; Model; Example,n.
1. **antetype**—earlier type; prototype
2. **antitype**—opposite type; corresponding type
3. **archetype**—original type or model
4. **beau ideal**—perfect type or model
5. **case**—example that shows or illustrates the existence of what is being discussed
6. **countertype**—opposite type; corresponding type
7. **cross section**—representative specimen
8. **embodiment**—incarnation
9. **examplar**—one who, or that which, is a typical model (of something); ideal or perfect type or model
10. **exemplification**—illustration
11. **exponent**—one who, or that which, serves as a type or example (of something)
12. **fugleman**—model or example (of something)
13. **ideal**—perfect model
14. **illustration**—example that clarifies, explains, or throws light on what is being discussed
15. **incarnation**—one who, or that which, represents the type of typical form (of something)
16. **instance**—illustration
17. **monotype**—only example of its kind
18. **nonesuch**—paragon
19. **paradigm**—type; model
20. **paragon**—model; model of perfection or excellence
21. **pattern**—model; model to be copied
22. **personification**—incarnation
23. **precedent**—act or event that serves as an example for similar acts or events
24. **prefiguration**—prototype
25. **prototype**—primary type (of something); model from which something is copied

26. **quintessence**—perfect, most characteristic, or typical model or example
27. **sample**—specimen
28. **specimen**—one of a kind or group that is an example of the others or that shows what the others are like
29. **standard**—model
30. **stereotype**—conventional model; model showing no originality, creative thinking, etc.
31. **typification**—typical example; typical specimen

2. Typical; Exemplary; Pert. to, or Descr. of, a Type, Model, or Example,adj. *From Sec. 1:* antetypal, antitypal, archetypal, countertypal, illustrative, incarnate, monotypal, paradigmatic; prototypal, prototypic, or prototypical; quintessential, stereotyped

3. To Serve as a Type, Model, or Example of,v. *From Sec. 1:* embody, illustrate, incarnate, personify, prefigure

4. To Make a Model of: model,v.

5. To Give Examples of: exemplify,v. (exemplification,n.)

6. To Give Examples (of) for Purposes of Clarifying: illustrate,v. (illustration,n. illustrative,adj.)

7. For Example: exempli gratia—Latin (commonly abbreviated to *e.g.*), par exemple (French)

318. GROUP

1. A Group,n.
1. **aggregation**—group of human beings, whether organized or not
2. **array**—group of people in proper order
3. **assemblage**—group; group of people
4. **assembly**—group of people gathered together for some serious purpose or for legislative action
5. **assortment**—group of different or various kinds
6. **band**—group
7. **batch**—group of people or things of the same kind; such a group taken at one time
8. **battalion**—organized group of people
9. **battery**—group of personality, psychological, intelligence, etc., tests
10. **bevy**—group of women
11. **bloc**—group formed for some purpose, usually legislative or political
12. **block**—group of persons or things considered as a unit; bloc
13. **board**—administrative group
14. **body**—group of people or things; group fighting as a unit; group of people united by some common interest; force
15. **body politic**—group organized for government
16. **bracket**—group of things or people; things or people considered as a group
17. **brigade**—group of people organized to act in co-operation
18. **bunch**—group of things of the same kind; group of people (colloq.); clique (colloq.)
19. **bundle**—group
20. **cabal**—secret group engaged in plots, or in plotting evil, illegal, or treasonable acts
21. **caboodle**—group of people or things (colloq.)
22. **caravan**—group of travelers, merchants, or pilgrims on a long journey, esp. through a desert, unfriendly territory, etc., often in Asia or Africa
23. **category**—group of people or things of similar character
24. **cell**—communist group, esp. in a government or industry
25. **circle**—group of people related by some common interest

26. **clan**—group of people with related or common interests; group of related families; clique; society
27. **claque**—body of paid applauders at a performance; body of fawning toadies
28. **class**—group of things or persons with some common similarities; group of students
29. **clique**—group of people of common interests, the main characteristic of which is the exclusion from social relations of those not acceptable to the group
30. **cluster, clump**—group of people or things so arranged as if growing on a common vine, like grapes
31. **cohort**—group; group of people
32. **collection**—group of people or things
33. **colony**—group or community of people transplanted from their homeland to a new country or province and still subject to the jurisdiction of the mother country; group of people from a foreign country living together in one area; group of people of the same occupation living together in an area; isolated community of people living under supervision; group of self-supporting inmates of a public institution living outside the parent organization
34. **committee**—group of people formed for a specific action, purpose, etc.
35. **community**—group of people of similar interests or common organization, or living under the same laws and government; group organized for government
36. **company**—group of people
37. **concourse**—assemblage
38. **congregation**—group of people gathered together for religious worship
39. **contingent**—group belonging to a larger group
40. **corps**—group of people formed into a single, well-knit body
41. **cortege**—group of accompanying attendants
42. **coterie**—group of people who meet socially
43. **covey**—group of people; bevy
44. **crew**—group rowing a boat or manning a ship; loosely, any group of people
45. **crowd**—large, usually disordered, group of people, pressed closely together
46. **deputation**—group of people appointed or authorized to act for someone
47. **detachment**—group of soldiers, police, etc., sent on a special errand
48. **detail**—small group sent out on a special errand
49. **directorate, directory**—group of directors of an institution; group of people in control of the affairs of an institution
50. **division**—group of some common characteristics
51. **elite**—the very best, most competent, most honored, etc., group of any category
52. **embassy**—group of envoys from one nation to another
53. **entourage**—accompanying group
54. **estate**—political or social group in a nation having different rights and duties from other groups (esp. formerly in England and France), as the *first estate*, or clergy, *second estate*, or aristocracy, and *third estate*, or commoners
55. **family**—group of people related by blood or marriage and living in one household; group of comets, asteroids, etc.
56. **felonry**—criminals, felons, or convicts of a prison as a group
57. **flock**—large group of people; group of people attending the same church; group of people in relation to the one in charge; group of children in one family
58. **force**—group of people prepared for action, work, etc.

59. **gang**—number moving in, acting as, or forming a group; group acting under common direction or supervision; group of people associated for some evil, criminal, or, at the very least, disreputable purpose
60. **gathering**—assemblage; assembly
61. **genus**—class (genera, genuses,pl.)
62. **harem**—group of women emotionally attached to, or living with, a man
63. **herd**—group of (so-called) common or lower class people (derogative)
64. **huddle**—confused group of people
65. **junta, junto**—group of people who meet for political purposes, or often for political plotting
66. **knot**—group; small, massed group of people; cluster
67. **majority**—group with the greater number of people or votes
68. **minority**—racial, religious, political, national, or other group containing fewer people than, and differing in specific ways from, the larger and dominant group
69. **order**—group of people united by some common obligation or honorary distinction
70. **outfit**—group of people engaged in an activity, such as mining, exploring, railroad building, herding, etc., or in some particular industry or pursuit
71. **pack**—group of people closely associated, usually in some less than respectable endeavor; group of people for whom one expresses contempt; large group of people or things
72. **party**—group united in opinion or sentiment as opposed to the rest of the community; group forming one side of a contest; temporary group of people associated in some endeavor; detachment
73. **persuasion**—group or party adhering to a common creed
74. **platoon**—organized group of police
75. **posse**—armed group; force with legal authority
76. **posse comitatus (Latin)**—force with legal authority
77. **procession**—group moving forward in a formal or orderly manner
78. **push**—clique (colloq.)
79. **race**—class of individuals with common characteristics, interests, habits, appearance, etc.
80. **secretariat**—group of secretaries in an office
81. **sect**—group of people following a religious belief, philosophical or other doctrines, etc.
82. **section**—group formed from a larger group
83. **sept**—social group descended, or believed to be descended, from a common ancestor
84. **set**—group; group associated by custom, opinion, etc; clique
85. **society**—co-operating social group; the group of a community that is distinguished by special aims, standard of living, or behavior; leisure group
86. **sodality**—group with common interests
87. **squad**—small group of people working together
88. **squadron**—organized group of people
89. **string**—group of players or contestants ranked according to skill or competence
90. **subclass**—primary division of a class
91. **subdivision**—group further divided from a larger group
92. **system**—related group
93. **team**—group of persons acting or pulling together, constituting one side in a contest; group of workers that finishes one of a set of tasks or operations
94. **tribe**—group of people of a distinct religion, race, or ancestry; group of per-

sons of common character or occupation (often contemptuous) ; social group made up of a number of clans, families, etc.; group of primitive people under one leader
95. **troop**—group of people
96. **troupe**—group; group of people; traveling group of actors
97. **unit**—single group regarded as an individual member of a larger group
98. **wing**—part of a group in disagreement with the rest

2. Pert. to, or Descr. of, a Group,adj. *From Sec. 1:* cabalistic, categorical or categorial, cliquy or cliquish, collective, colonial, communal or communal, congregational, directorial, divisional, familial, generic or generical, processional, racial, sectarian, sectional, societal, subdivisional, systemic, tribal, unital or unitary

3. Member of a Group,n. *From Sec. 1:* cabalist; caravaneer, caravanist, or caravanner; clansman, colonial, committeeman (or committeewoman), crewman, deputy, director, felon, gangster, posseman, secretary, sectary, tribesman, trouper (actor); *Also:* **1.** **recruit**—new member of a group

4. To Group; i.e., Put Together, Collect, or Cause to Form into a Group,v. *From Sec. 1:* array, assemble, assort, bracket, bunch, bundle, collect, colonize, crowd, divide, gather, group, section, subdivide, team; *From Sec. 3:* recruit

5. To Group, i.e., Be Together, Come Together, Get Together, or Go Together in a Group,v. *From Sec. 1:* assemble, band together, bunch, bundle together, cluster, collect, colonize, congregate, crowd, flock, gang up, gather, huddle, team up

6. Tending to Form into Groups,adj. *From Sec. 1:* cliquy or cliquish (cliquishness, cliquism,n.)

7. Common, Enthusiastic Spirit of Cooperation and Loyalty in a Group; Group Spirit: esprit de corps,n. (French)

8. Biological Category,n.
1. **breed**—race or variety of animals or plants related by descent and similar in most characteristics; group of domestic animals or plants developed through the influence of man, and, in this sense, denoting a wider group than strain; race; stock; strain
2. **class**—comprehensive category of animals or plants next below a phylum and above an order
3. **family**—category of plants or animals ranking higher than a genus and lower than an order (familial,adj.)
4. **genus**—category of animals or plants ranking between a family and a species (genera,pl. generic, generical,adj.)
5. **group**—category of animals or plants conceived of as having certain natural relationships to each other
6. **legion**—category of animals sometimes considered identical to a superfamily, sometimes to a class
7. **order**—category of animals or plants above a family and below a class
8. **phylon**—category of animals or plants related by common ancestry; family
9. **phylum**—large and primary category of plants and animals (phyla,pl. phylar, adj.)
10. **race**—category of organisms having certain similarities but not sufficiently distinct to constitute a species; group of individuals differing from other members of a species; subspecies (racial, adj.)
11. **species**—category of plants or animals of common physical characteristics (specific, adj.)

12. **stock**—category of genetically related individuals in a breed or species
13. **strain**—group of domestic animals of common lineage but not sufficiently distinct to constitute a breed; group of plants within a variety having some distinct difference in physiology
14. **subclass**—category below a class and above an order
15. **subfamily**—category below a family and above a genus
16. **subgenus**—category below a genus and above a species
17. **suborder**—category below an order and above a family; superfamily
18. **subphylum**—primary division of a phylum
19. **subspecies**—division of a species; race; variety
20. **superfamily**—category above a family; category between a suborder and a family; suborder
21. **variety**—division of a species (varietal, adj.)

9. A Crowd,n.
1. **concourse**—crowd
2. **confluence**—crowd
3. **conflux**—crowd
4. **conglomeration**—crowd of different kinds of people
5. **crew**—crowd
6. **crush**—crowd of people
7. **drove**—crowd of people all moving in the same direction
8. **flock**—crowd
9. **gathering**—crowd
10. **herd**—crowd of people (derogative)
11. **horde**—noisy and particularly disorderly crowd
12. **host**—great crowd
13. **huddle**—confused crowd of persons or animals
14. **jam**—mass of people crowded together
15. **mass**—crowd
16. **mob**—crowd that is particularly unruly and disordered, and generally bent on violence or destruction
17. **multitude**—crowd
18. **posse**—crowd; throng
19. **push**—crowd (colloq.)
20. **rabble**—noisy and disorderly crowd of people; mob
21. **ragtag; rag, tag, and bobtail**—rabble
22. **ribble-rabble**—rabble
23. **rout**—rabble
24. **ruck**—crowd of ordinary persons
25. **scum**—mob of low-class or worthless people
26. **swarm**—crowd of people moving about in confusion and/or in close contact
27. **throng**—crowd in motion, with the implication of pushing by the individual members

10. To Crowd, i.e., Be, Collect, or Move in a Crowd,v. *From Sec. 9:* conglomerate, flock, gather, herd, huddle, jam, mass, mob, swarm, throng; *Also:*
1. **besiege**—crowd around (a person or place)
2. **congregate**—collect in a crowd
3. **pack**—crowd together in (a place)—of people
4. **serry**—crowd close together

11. To Crowd, i.e., Bring Together or Collect into a Crowd,v. *From Sec. 9:* conglomerate, gather, herd, huddle, jam, mass, throng; *From Sec. 10:* congregate, pack, serry

12. Crowded,adj. *From Sec. 9:* jammed, massed, mobbed, swarming, thronged; *From Sec. 10:* packed, serried; *Also:*
1. **bristling**—crowded
2. **chockablock**—crowded or jammed close together
3. **congested**—overcrowded (congestion,n.)

4. **conglomerate**—crowded into a mass
5. **crammed**—crowded
6. **overcrowded**—extremely or excessively crowded
7. **slum**—crowded, poor, and dirty (of areas where people live, usually in a large city)
8. **teeming**—crowded
9. **tumid**—crowded (tumidity,n.)

13. To Be Crowded,v. *From Sec. 9:* swarm, throng; *From Sec. 12:* bristle, teem

14. Crowded Place,n.
1. **slum, slums**—crowded, poor, and dirty part of a city (slummy,adj.)
2. **warren**—place or district that is very crowded, like a rabbit's breeding ground

15. Parade,n.
1. **callithump**—noisy parade, with discordant sounds, blowing of horns, etc.
2. **cavalcade**—parade; parade of people on horseback
3. **motorcade**—parade of motorcars
4. **pageant**—elaborate parade
5. **procession**—parade (processional,adj.)

16. A Collection,n.
1. **accumulation**—collection
2. **aggregate**—collection
3. **aggregation**—collection
4. **ana**—collection of items of information about a subject
5. **assemblage, assembly**—collection of people
6. **assortment**—collection of various kinds
7. **body**—collection of individuals
8. **bunch**—collection; cluster of things of the same kind
9. **bundle**—collection
10. **cluster**—collection of things growing together
11. **clutter**—confused collection
12. **collectanea**—collection of writings, passages, specimens, or excerpts
13. **compilation**—collection of several similar things; collection of literary works
14. **concentration**—collection of things or people at a common center, or in one place, body, mass, or force
15. **congeries**—collection of different things in one mass or body
16. **conglobation**—collection in the form of a rounded mass
17. **conglomeration**—collection of different things in the form of a ball or mass
18. **congregation**—collection
19. **convention**—collection of people in a meeting
20. **convocation**—collection of people called together
21. **crop**—collection (as if harvested)
22. **crowd**—large collection of people or things
23. **cumulation**—collection
24. **fardel**—miscellaneous collection
25. **flock**—collection
26. **gathering**—collection
27. **gleanings**—collection of things gathered together patiently, little by little, or with some difficulty
28. **heap**—collection of things laid in a body or so thrown together as to form an elevation
29. **hoard**—large collection stored up or away, or concealed
30. **jumble**—collection lacking any order
31. **knot**—collection of people or things
32. **mass**—collection of things that cohere into a single body, or that together form a single body
33. **miscellanea**—miscellany; literary miscellany
34. **miscellany**—collection of different things
35. **muster**—collection; collection of people
36. **olio**—varied collection
37. **olla-podrida**—varied collection of different kinds of things

38. **omnium-gatherum**—olla-podrida
39. **pack**—large collection of people or things; set of playing cards
40. **parcel**—collection of things
41. **patchwork**—collection of things that do not normally go together; jumble
42. **pile**—collection in the form of a mass or heap; collection of things laid one on top of the other
43. **pool**—collection of things or people to be used as necessary
44. **potpourri**—varied collection of different kinds of things
45. **ragtag; rag, tag, and bobtail**—disreputable and/or disorderly collection of people
46. **repertoire**—collection; collection of dramatic pieces, etc., that a person or group has rehearsed and is ready to perform
47. **repertory**—repertoire
48. **roundup**—collection of previously scattered people or animals
49. **ruck**—collection of ordinary things
50. **rummage**—collection achieved by, or as if by, searching
51. **set**—collection of things that usually go or are used together; assortment
52. **stock pile**—stored collection
53. **store**—large collection
54. **treasure**—collection stored for future use
55. **truss**—collection of things tied together or packed in a receptacle
56. **wilderness**—bewildering or confusing collection

17. That Which Is Collected (Usually Men for the Armed Forces or Money) by Governmental or Other Authority or Power: levy,n.

18. A Heap, Pile, or Bundle,n.
1. **accumulation**—heap
2. **agglomeration**—heap; cluster
3. **bale**—large bundle prepared for transportation or storing; large bundle pressed tight and wrapped with cord or twine; heap or pile (colloq.)
4. **bank**—long pile
5. **bunch**—cluster of things of the same kind
6. **clump**—heap
7. **cluster**—heap of things growing together, or appearing as if growing together, on a common vine, stem, etc.
8. **cock**—pile of hay in the shape of a cone
9. **cumulation**—heap
10. **fascicle**—small bundle; small cluster
11. **mound**—heap
12. **pack**—bundle ready for carrying, or for carrying on the back; bale
13. **package**—bundle prepared for transportation
14. **packet**—small package
15. **parcel**—small package
16. **pinnacle**—tall and slim, pointed pile
17. **roll**—heap of things rolled together
18. **sheaf**—bundle; tied bundle
19. **shock**—bundle, or pile of bundles, of wheat, grain, etc., set up in a field
20. **stack**—orderly pile of anything
21. **stock pile**—stored heap or pile
22. **store**—large heap or pile
23. **truss**—bundle of hay or straw
24. **tuft**—bunch or cluster joined at one end
25. **wad**—compact bundle or roll
26. **wisp**—small bundle; small bunch

19. A Mass,n.
1. **accumulation**—mass
2. **agglomeration**—mass
3. **aggregate**—mass
4. **aggregation**—mass
5. **bank**—long or high mass
6. **billow**—rolling or surging mass
7. **bulk**—mass
8. **cake**—hard mass
9. **clot**—thickened mass
10. **clump**—mass

11. **coalescence**—combined mass
12. **conglobation**—rounded mass (conglobate,adj.)
13. **cumulation**—mass
14. **dab**—small, soft, and usually wet mass
15. **formation**—rock or mineral mass
16. **glomeration**—round mass
17. **grume**—clot, often of blood (grumous, adj.)
18. **heap**—mass
19. **huddle**—confused mass of people
20. **jam**—mass of people or things crowded together
21. **jumble**—mass lacking any order
22. **mound**—mass
23. **pat**—small, shaped mass
24. **pile**—mass of things thrown together; mass of buildings
25. **pinnacle**—tall and slim, pointed mass
26. **pomace**—crushed or soft mass
27. **pulp**—soft mass (pulpy,adj.)
28. **roll**—things rolled together into a mass
29. **shock**—thick mass
30. **wad**—small, soft mass
31. **wilderness**—bewildering or confusing mass

20. To Be Formed into or Become a Mass,v. *From Sec. 19:* accumulate, agglomerate, aggregate, bulk, cake, clot, coalesce, heap up, huddle, jam, jumble, pile up (accumulation, agglomeration, aggregation, coalescence,n.)

21. To Put or Form into a Mass,v. *From Sec. 19:* bank, bulk, clot, heap up, jam, jumble, pat, pile

319. COLLECT; GATHER

1. To Collect or Gather; To Bring or Put Together in a Collection,v.
1. **accumulate**—collect; collect in or into a mass or heap; collect bit by bit
2. **adsorb**—collect (gas, dissolved substance, etc.) and hold on the surface after condensation
3. **agglomerate**—gather into a heap or ball
4. **aggregate**—collect; collect into a mass or body
5. **amass**—collect; collect into a mass or heap; collect for oneself; collect a large quantity of
6. **assemble**—collect in one place
7. **bank**—collect into a long or high pile
8. **bulk**—pile
9. **bunch**—gather into a bunch or group
10. **centralize**—gather together toward the center; collect at the center
11. **cluster**—gather into a bunch or bunches
12. **cock**—pile (hay, etc.) in a conical heap
13. **compile**—collect (several like things) into one list or place; collect (literary works) into one volume
14. **concenter, concentre**—collect at a point or center
15. **concentrate**—collect at, or gather toward, a common center; gather into one place, body, mass, or force
16. **conglobe, conglobate**—collect into a ball or rounded mass
17. **conglomerate**—collect into a ball, bunch, mass, or in large numbers
18. **congregate**—collect, or gather together, into a group or mass
19. **convene**—assemble (people) in a meeting
20. **convoke**—assemble (people) by summons
21. **crowd**—mass
22. **cumulate**—collect; heap
23. **focus**—collect at, or gather toward, a center point
24. **garner**—gather for purposes of storing away
25. **glean**—gather patiently, little by little, gradually, with some difficulty, etc. (in analogy to those who gather stray bits of

grain from a field when the reapers have already finished gathering the harvest)
26. **harvest**—gather (a crop); gather as if a crop; gather the crop from
27. **heap, heap up**—gather together into a pile or mass
28. **hoard**—collect and store away; collect and hide; collect money, goods, valuables, etc.
29. **huddle**—collect into a confused or disorderly heap
30. **hutch**—hoard
31. **jam**—mass
32. **levy**—collect (men for the armed forces, or money)—of governmental or other authority
33. **mass**—collect into a single continuous body
34. **mobilize**—gather together for war or action
35. **muster**—gather together; collect; collect in one place; collect as part of a body, group, force, etc.
36. **pack**—collect (persons, facts, etc.) to suit one's own purposes, with an implication of lack of honesty
37. **pile, pile up**—collect into a heap or mass
38. **pool**—collect for mutual use or advantage
39. **rake**—gather; gather together; collect slowly or laboriously
40. **rally**—collect; collect that which has been, or those who have been, scattered or dispersed; collect or gather (people) for common action
41. **round up**—gather or collect (scattered people or animals) into one place
42. **rummage**—collect by or as if by searching
43. **scrape together**—collect with difficulty; collect by scraping
44. **sheave**—gather and tie into a bundle
45. **shepherd**—gather
46. **shock**—gather (wheat, grain, etc.) together into a bundle or bundles and set up in a field
47. **stack**—gather into a pile
48. **stock-pile**—accumulate and store
49. **sum up**—collect into a total or whole
50. **treasure**—collect and store for future use

2. To Collect or Gather, i.e., Come Together in a Collection or Gathering,v. *From Sec. 1:* accumulate, agglomerate, aggregate, assemble, bunch, cluster, concenter or concentre, concentrate, conglobe or conglobate, conglomerate, congregate, convene, crowd, cumulate, focus, huddle, jam, mass, mobilize, muster, rally or rally round; *Also:*
1. **crowd**—gather in large numbers
2. **flock**—gather in groups, companies, or large numbers
3. **meet**—collect at a point or place
4. **swarm**—collect or gather in a large multitude
5. **throng**—collect in great numbers
6. **troop**—gather into groups

3. Collection, i.e., a Collecting or Gathering,n. *From Secs. 1 and 2:* accumulation, adsorption, agglomeration, aggregation, amassment, assemblage or assembly, centralization, compilation, concentration, conglobation, conglomeration, congregation, convention, convocation, cumulation, levy, mobilization, muster, rally, roundup

4. Collector; Gatherer,n. *From Sec. 1:* accumulator, amasser, assembler, compiler, congregator, convener, convoker, gleaner, harvester, hoarder, mobilizer, rallier, shepherd, stock piler; *From Sec. 2:* assembler, congregator, huddler, meeter, swarmer, thronger

5. Descr. of Collecting or Gathering,adj. *From Sec. 1:* accumulative, adsorptive, agglomerative, aggregative, concentrative, conglobative, conglomerative, congregative, cumulative

6. Collected; Gathered,adj. *From Sec. 1:*

accumulated, adsorbed, etc.; agglomerate, aggregate, conglobate, conglomerate, cumulate; *Also:*
1. **collective**—collected; formed by collection
2. **indiscrete**—not separated into individual parts, but collected in a compact mass

7. To Pack,v.
1. **box**—pack into a box
2. **compact**—pack together firmly; pack close together
3. **cram**—pack tightly
4. **crate**—pack into a crate
5. **stow**—pack closely together (stowage,n.)
6. **stuff**—pack tightly
7. **tamp**—pack down
8. **truss**—pack into a bundle
9. **wad**—pack tightly

8. Packed Closely or Firmly Together: compact,adj. (compactness,n.)

9. Instrument Used for Packing Down: tamp, tamper,n.

320. MIXTURE

1. To Mix or Combine (Things or, Sometimes, People),v.
1. **admix**—mix in
2. **aerate**—mix with air
3. **alloy**—mix (metals); mix (metallic and non-metallic elements)
4. **amalgamate**—mix (those that go together harmoniously); mix (a metal) with mercury; combine
5. **blend**—mix thoroughly and in such a way that the components are indistinguishable
6. **commingle**—mix together; combine into a mass; blend
7. **commix**—mix; blend
8. **compound**—mix together into a unified whole, so that the parts are indistinguishable one from the other
9. **concoct**—combine (various things) to produce something unusual in the way of a mixture
10. **confect**—mix together and produce a final whole or mixture
11. **conflate**—combine (two readings of a text) into a composite whole
12. **conjoin**—combine
13. **dissolve (in)**—mix (something into) some fluid so that it disappears in the solution; merge completely (figuratively)
14. **emulsify**—mix (liquids) so that one is suspended within the other rather than dissolving within it
15. **fuse**—mix in such a way that there can be no separation of elements
16. **immingle**—mix intimately; mix together; blend
17. **incorporate**—combine into a single body or whole
18. **interlard**—mix in (that which is different or extraneous)
19. **intermingle**—mix together
20. **intermix**—mix together
21. **jumble**—mix together in a confused or disordered manner
22. **merge**—mix or combine so that one or more elements disappear or are lost
23. **mingle**—mix; mix together; combine into a mass
24. **muddle**—mix together; mix into a confused mess
25. **scramble**—mix together unevenly or in confusion
26. **shuffle**—mix so as to change the order or arrangement
27. **synthesize**—combine; combine into a whole; combine to form a final product
28. **unite**—combine

2. To Mix, or Combine, i.e., Come Together in Mixture or Combination,v. *From Sec. 1:*

alloy, amalgamate, blend, commingle, commix, conjoin, dissolve, fuse, immingle, intermingle, intermix, merge, mingle, unite; *Also:*
1. **coalesce**—mix or combine because of a natural affinity for each other; combine into one body or mass

3. Mixture or Combination, i.e., a Mixing or Combining,n. *From Sec. 1:* admixture, aeration, amalgamation, commixture or commixtion, concoction, confection, conflation, conjunction, emulsification, fusion, incorporation, intermixture, merger, shuffle, synthesis, synthesization or synthetization, union

4. A Mixture or Combination, i.e., the Result of Mixing or Combining,n. *From Sec. 1:* admixture, alloy, amalgam or amalgamation, blend, commixture, compound, concoction, confection, conflation; solution (from *dissolve*); emulsion (emulsive,adj.), fusion, intermixture, jumble, merger, muddle, scramble, shuffle, synthesis or synthetic, union; *Also:*
1. **brine**—any strong salt solution
2. **coalition**—combination
3. **collectanea**—miscellany
4. **composition**—mixture
5. **farrago**—odd, confused, or incongruous mixture
6. **gallimaufry**—hodgepodge
7. **hash**—mixture; mixture of ground meat and potatoes; confused or disordered mixture
8. **hodgepodge, hotchpotch**—incongruous mixture
9. **medley**—mixture of things not ordinarily mixed together
10. **melange**—mixture; medley
11. **mess**—disagreeable and confused mixture
12. **miscellany, miscellanea**—mixture of different things, yet in which no one thing loses its separateness or identity
13. **mishmash**—confused or disordered mixture; mess
14. **motley**—mixture; incongruous mixture
15. **olio**—heterogeneous or incongruous mixture
16. **olla-podrida**—heterogeneous mixture
17. **pasticcio (Italian)**—medley
18. **patchwork**—mixture made up of incongruous and different things; confused or disordered mixture
19. **phantasmagoria, phantasmagory**—constantly changing mixture or medley (phantasmagorial, phantasmagoric,adj.)
20. **potpourri**—heterogeneous and varied mixture or medley
21. **puddle**—confused mixture
22. **salmagundi**—varied mixture or medley
23. **suspension**—mixture in which particles of a solid remain suspended and undissolved in a fluid
24. **tincture**—solution of a medicine or drug in alcohol

5. In a Disorderly and Heterogeneous Mixture: promiscuous,adj. (promiscuity,n.)

6. Capable of Being Mixed: miscible,adj. (miscibility,n.)

7. Incapable of Being Mixed: immiscible, adj. (immiscibility,n.)

8. Tending or Able to Cause Combination; Pert. to Combination; Characterized by, or Resulting from, Combination: combinative, adj.

9. Combining into One Body or Mass: coalescent,adj. (coalescence,n.)

10. Tending to Mix with People: gregarious, adj. (gregariousness,n.)

11. To Mix or Stir (Something),v.
1. **agitate**—stir violently (agitation,n.)
2. **beat**—stir thoroughly
3. **levigate**—mix (usually semi-fluids) thoroughly, and thereby make smooth (levigation,n.)

4. **muddle**—mix or stir
5. **stir**—mix by moving around with an implement
6. **swizzle**—mix or stir (usually, alcoholic drinks) with a special stick made for this purpose

12. Implement for Mixing,n. *From Sec. 11:* agitator, beater, muddler, stirrer or stirring rod, swizzle stick; *Also:* 1. **spatula**—implement used for mixing drugs

321. PUT TOGETHER

1. To Put Together, Join, Connect, or Unite,v.
1. **affiliate**—bring into close connection; unite as a member or in fellowship
2. **agglutinate**—unite with, or as if with, glue or similar substances
3. **align, aline**—cause to join those on the side of, or against, a cause
4. **ally**—unite by formal agreement or understanding; connect by some relationship
5. **amalgamate**—unite
6. **anastomose**—connect (one anatomical vessel) to an anatomical vessel of a different system; inosculate
7. **annex**—join or unite (something smaller) to something larger
8. **articulate**—unite through, or by means of, joints; fit together in a joint
9. **assemble**—put, join, or fit the parts of together
10. **associate**—join; unite
11. **attach**—connect; join
12. **bind**—tie into firm connection
13. **blend**—unite intimately; merge
14. **bond**—join firmly together
15. **bracket**—unite into a common group; group together
16. **catenate**—connect in a series; link
17. **colligate**—join together into a union
18. **combine**—join; unite; unite harmoniously; link closely together
19. **compose**—put together the parts of; put together the necessary parts of (a literary or other artistic work)
20. **compound**—put together (parts, etc.) to form a whole; unite; combine
21. **concatenate**—connect or unite in a linked series; unite in a chain; link together
22. **concenter, concentre**—concentrate
23. **concentrate**—put or bring together at or toward a common center or point of connection or joining
24. **confederate**—unite into a league, association, or conspiracy
25. **conglutinate**—unite by, or as if by, glue or some gluey substance
26. **conjoin**—join together; unite
27. **consolidate**—unite into a single entity
28. **consort**—join; unite
29. **correlate**—connect by some system or method
30. **counite**—join together; unite
31. **couple**—join (two things or people) together, literally or figuratively
32. **crowd**—put together in large numbers
33. **dovetail**—join or fit together exactly or harmoniously (literally or figuratively); join or fit (pieces of wood) by means of tongue and groove or mortise and tenon
34. **embody**—put together into one body or form
35. **engraft**—graft
36. **fasten**—connect or join by, or as by, nailing, tying, pinning, etc.
37. **fit together**—put together in smooth connection or at the proper joints
38. **focus**—concentrate
39. **fuse**—unite or combine by, or as if by, melting together into one whole

40. **graft**—join (one naturally growing thing) to another (as plant shoots, skin, etc.) so that the two will grow together
41. **group**—put together in, or into, a common class or category
42. **herd**—put together in a crowd
43. **incorporate**—unite into a single body or entity
44. **inosculate**—unite by contact; unite or join in so as to make one
45. **integrate**—unite in a relationship that is complete and forms a whole
46. **interconnect**—join together one to the other
47. **interknit**—knit together
48. **joint**—unite at a place of connection or joining
49. **knit**—unite firmly or closely; join together; unite; consolidate
50. **link**—connect, literally or figuratively, in analogy to the rings of a chain
51. **marry**—unite in a close or permanent union or relationship
52. **merge**—cause to unite or combine, often in such a way that the components lose their identity
53. **paste**—unite by, or as by, glue or other adhesive substance
54. **rejoin**—join again
55. **splice**—join by weaving the strands of together
56. **synthesize, synthetize**—put together to form a whole
57. **tie**—connect; unite; connect or unite by, or as if by, cord, rope, etc.
58. **unify**—unite
59. **weld**—unite (two metals); unite in a very close bond
60. **yoke**—unite; join or unite in a close bond

2. To Come Together, Join, Connect, or Unite,v. *From Sec. 1:* affiliate, agglutinate; align or aline (with); ally (with); amalgamate, anastomose; associate (with); attach, blend, combine, concenter or concentre, concentrate, confederate, conglutinate, conjoin, consolidate, consort, counite, couple, crowd, dovetail, fasten, fit together, focus, fuse, graft, group, herd, inosculate, integrate, interconnect, interknit, joint, knit, link, merge, rejoin, tie, weld; *Also:*
1. **coalesce**—unite or combine into one body or mass
2. **cohere**—connect logically (in speech or writing)
3. **communicate**—join or connect (of rooms, offices, apartments, etc.)
4. **concur**—join together or combine toward a common object or effect; unite in action
5. **converge**—draw together toward a common point
6. **copulate**—unite in sexual intercourse
7. **enlist**—join in a common venture
8. **make common cause with**—join in support of
9. **meet**—come together at a point

3. A Putting or Coming Together, Joining, Connection, or Union,n. *From Secs. 1 and 2:* affiliation, agglutination, alignment or alinement, alliance, amalgamation, anastomosis, annexation, articulation, assemblage or assembly, association, attachment, catenation, colligation, combination, composition, concatenation, concentration, confederation, conglutination; conjunction (from *conjoin*); consolidation, consortion or consortium, correlation; copulation (from *couple*); embodiment, fusion, incorporation, inosculation, integration, interconnection, linkage, marriage, merger or mergence; synthesis, synthesization, or synthetization; unification; *From Sec. 2:* coalescence, coherence, communication, concurrence or concurrency, convergence or convergency, copulation, enlistment, meeting; *Also:*

1. **coalition**—a joining or union into one body or mass
2. **junction, juncture**—a joining

4. Connection or Union, i.e., State of Being Joined, Connected, United, or the Result of Joining, Connecting, or Uniting,n. *From Secs. 1 and 2:* affiliation, agglutination, alignment or alinement, alliance, amalgamation or amalgam, articulation, assemblage or assembly, association, attachment, blend, combination, composition, compound, concatenation, concentration, confederation, conglutination, conjunction, consolidation, consortium, correlation, crowd, embodiment, fusion, group or grouping, herd; corporation (from *incorporate*); integration, interconnection, linkage, marriage, splice, synthesis, unification; *From Sec. 2:* coalescence, coherence, communication, concurrence or concurrency, convergence or convergency; *From Sec. 3:* junction; *Also:*
1. **concert**—union
2. **unity**—state of being united; result of being united

5. Connector or Connective, i.e., That Which Causes or Effects Joining, Connection, or Union,n. *From Sec. 1:* agglutinant, attachment, binding or binder, bond, bracket, coupling, dovetail, fastener or fastening, link, tie, yoke; *Also:*
1. **additive**—word or element that joins or links other words or things
2. **conjunction**—word that joins other words, phrases, or clauses
3. **copula**—that which connects things; link
4. **nexus**—connector; link

6. One Who, or That Which, Is Joined, Connected, or United,n. *From Sec. 1:* affiliate, ally, annex or annexation, associate; confederate (mainly in a conspiracy or other wrongdoing); correlate, fusion, graft, link

7. Place of Joining, Connection, or Union, n. *From Sec. 1:* articulation, conjunction or conjuncture, convergence or convergency, graft, splice, weld; *Also:*
1. **commissure**—joint where two parts unite
2. **connection**—place where things connect or are connected
3. **joint**—place where things join or are joined
4. **junction, juncture**—place where joining occurs
5. **seam**—line or mark where edges join or are joined

8. Joined, Connected, or United,adj. *From Sec. 1:* affiliated, agglutinated, aligned, etc.; affiliate, agglutinate, anastomotic, articulate, concatenate, confederate, conglutinate, conjunct, corporate (from *incorporate*), integral, joint, synthetic; *From Sec. 2:* coalescent, coherent, concurrent, convergent; *Also:*
1. **compact**—closely united
2. **concrete**—united in growth
3. **conjugate**—coupled
4. **glomerate**—joined together in a cluster
5. **syndetic, syndetical**—connected; interconnected

9. Connective; Acting or Serving to Join, Connect, or Unite,adj. *From Sec. 1:* agglutinant or agglutinative, associative, combinative or combinatory, confederative, conglutinant or conglutinative, conjunctive, consolidative, correlative, incorporative, integrative

10. Connectional; Pert. to, or Descr. of, Joining, Connection, or Union,adj. *From Sec. 1:* anastomotic, articular, associational or associative, combinative or combinatory, compositional, conjunctional; corporate or corporative (from *incorporate*); *From Sec. 3:* junctional or junctural

11. One Who Fits Scissors Blades, Pipes, Wires, etc., Together at the Joints: jointer, n.

322. A MEETING

1. A Meeting,n.
1. **assemblage**—a meeting
2. **assembly**—a meeting
3. **assignation**—a meeting for illicit sexual relations
4. **bee**—a community meeting for work, amusement, competition, etc.
5. **caucus**—a meeting of a political party or other group to set up policy or determine candidates
6. **chautauqua**—a meeting for educational purposes, often held outdoors in the summer
7. **conclave**—a secret or private meeting
8. **concourse**—a meeting of large numbers in an open area
9. **concurrence, concurrency**—a meeting at the same point; concourse
10. **conference**—a meeting of people in allied fields of endeavor for purposes of comparing ideas or holding discussions; a meeting for discussion or advice
11. **confluence**—a meeting of two bodies that flow together, such as streams, crowds of people, etc.
12. **congregation**—a meeting for the worship of God or for religious instruction
13. **congress**—a meeting; a meeting of lawmakers, policy makers, etc.
14. **conjunction**—a meeting of two or more celestial bodies in the same degree of the Zodiac
15. **consultation**—a meeting to consider a special case; a meeting for advice
16. **conventicle**—a meeting for secret or unauthorized religious worship
17. **convention**—a formal meeting of delegates, etc., for specific purposes
18. **conversazione (Italian)**—a social meeting for conversation about literature and the arts
19. **convocation**—a meeting of people or officials called together for specific purposes
20. **council**—a meeting for advice or to consider or discuss a special problem, case, etc.
21. **diet**—a formal public meeting; congress; convention
22. **encounter**—a meeting, strictly face to face, between two people or groups; a hostile meeting
23. **gathering**—a meeting; congregation
24. **interview**—a meeting for purposes of discussion; a meeting between the press and a person of importance so the latter may answer questions, give his views, etc.
25. **Kaffeeklatsch**—an informal social meeting, so called since coffee is often served
26. **mass meeting**—large or general meeting of the people to discuss problems or matters of common concern
27. **plenum**—full meeting of all legislative parts or members
28. **rally**—a mass meeting for the purpose of arousing public action, feeling, support, etc.
29. **rencounter**—a casual meeting
30. **rendezvous**—a meeting by appointment; a meeting for illicit sexual relations
31. **riot**—a disorderly meeting that disturbs the peace
32. **séance**—a meeting in which spiritualists or mediums allegedly communicate with the dead
33. **session**—a constructive meeting of the members of a legislature, court, class in school, etc.
34. **sitting**—session
35. **synagogue**—a meeting of Jews for worship or religious instruction
36. **synod**—a formal meeting to formulate church policy; a meeting; convention
37. **tournament, tourney**—a meeting for competition in athletics or sports; encounter
38. **tryst**—a prearranged meeting, usually for romantic purposes
39. **turnout**—a meeting of people, usually for entertainment or for some other specific purpose

2. Pert. to, or Descr. of, a Meeting,adj. *From Sec. 1:* chautauqua or chautauquan, concurrent, confluent, congregational, congressional, conjunctional; consultative, consultatory, consultive, or consultary; conventical or conventicular (from *conventicle*), conventional, convocational, plenary, riotous, sessional or sessionary; synodal, synodic, or synodical

3. To Meet, i.e., to Meet Together,v. *From Sec. 1:* assemble, caucus, confer, congregate, convene, encounter, gather, rally, rendezvous, riot, sit, tourney, tryst, turn out (assemblage or assembly, conferment or conference, congregation, convention, encounter,n.); *Also:*
1. **forgather**—meet as a group; meet together; meet by chance
2. **rejoin**—meet again

4. Meeter; Member or Attender of a Meeting,n. *From Sec. 1:* assembler, chautauquan, conferee or conferree, congressman, congresswoman, consulter or consultant, conventicler, convener or conventioner, convocator, councilor or councillor, rioter, tryster

5. Those Who Meet,n. *From Sec. 1:* assemblage or assembly, congregation, congress, convention, council

6. To Call a Meeting of,v. *From Sec. 1:* assemble, congregate, convene, convoke, rally, rendezvous (assemblage or assembly, congregation, convention, convocation,n. convener or convocator,n.)

7. Agreement to Meet,n. *From Sec. 1:* rendezvous, tryst; *Also:* 1. **appointment, engagement**—agreement to meet

8. Place of Meeting,n. *From Sec. 1:* concourse, confluence, conventicle, rendezvous, synagogue, tryst; *Also:*
1. **consistory**—meeting place, usually of a council
2. **crossroads**—meeting place for people living far from each other
3. **crotch**—place where two things meet in a V
4. **forum**—public meeting place for discussions, debates, etc.
5. **junction, juncture**—place where things meet

9. To Meet (Something or Someone),v.
1. **come upon**—meet
2. **confront**—meet face to face (confrontation, confrontment,n.)
3. **dare**—meet and defy or resist
4. **encounter**—meet; meet unexpectedly (encounter,n.)
5. **find**—meet
6. **overtake**—meet suddenly

10. To Tend to Meet in a Point or Line, or Draw toward a Meeting Point, though Coming from Different Directions: converge,v. (convergence, convergency,n. convergent, adj.)

11. To Cause to Draw toward a Meeting Point: converge,v. (convergence,n.)

323. PLACE; PUT

1. To Place; To Put,v.
1. **adhibit**—put on
2. **apply**—put; put on
3. **appose**—place opposite, facing, or in front of; place side by side, or close by each other; put; put on
4. **bed**—embed

5. **berth**—put in allotted place or position; place (a ship) at anchor or at a wharf or dock
6. **brace**—put firmly in place
7. **bunch**—put into a group
8. **camp**—put into camp
9. **clap**—put in place with force
10. **collocate**—place side by side
11. **compose oneself**—place or put oneself (in a position, etc.)
12. **confront** (. . . with)—place in front of
13. **couch**—place or put down
14. **dab**—put on with soft and light strokes
15. **deposit**—place or put down; put in a safe place
16. **embed, imbed**—place firmly (into surrounding material)
17. **enclose, inclose**—place or put inside
18. **engraft**—graft; insert in such a way as to make part of something
19. **ensconce**—put comfortably (in a place)
20. **entrench**—put firmly in a place as if protected from ouster by trenches
21. **establish**—put in a place or position
22. **fix**—put firmly in place; put in a place or position; put in a certain place
23. **graft**—insert into a stem, branch, or root of another plant; implant (living tissue)
24. **implant**—place or put securely or deeply in; place or put (living tissue) into a living site
25. **impose**—put on, usually by force, force of authority, etc.
26. **impregnate**—infuse a modifying element or principle into
27. **indent**—place in from the margin or edge
28. **infix**—fix by pushing in forcibly; place or put securely or deeply in or into
29. **infuse**—introduce by, or as by, pouring
30. **inject**—insert forcibly; interpolate; interpose
31. **inlay**—place or put into the surface of
32. **insert**—place or put in or within
33. **insinuate**—place or put gently or slowly in or into; insert; instill
34. **install**—put in or into (a place)
35. **instill**—place or put in, little by little or drop by drop, literally or figuratively; inject; insinuate
36. **intercalate**—insert (matter, writing, etc.) at a later time
37. **interject**—insert; interpolate; interpose
38. **interlineate**—put or place (writing) between two lines of writing or printing
39. **interpolate**—insert (words, phrases, etc.) into a book, document, etc.; insert between two other things; insert (a remark) into a discussion or conversation
40. **interpose**—place or put between two things; put in an interruption, objection, or opposing remark, statement, or question
41. **introduce**—put into (a place); insert
42. **juxtapose**—place or put side by side
43. **lay**—place; put; place or put down
44. **locate**—place or put (in a certain area, district, region, etc.)
45. **lodge**—place or put (in a place); put (in a place) for safekeeping
46. **maroon**—put (someone) in a helpless and unfortunate position and leave him there; put (someone) in an isolated place
47. **nestle**—place or put (something in a close and comfortable position)
48. **pack**—place in with others
49. **park**—put and leave somewhere (colloq.)
50. **pigeonhole**—put away in the memory for further reference
51. **plank down**—put down forcibly (colloq.)
52. **plant**—place or put in the ground to grow; place or put firmly in, or as if in, the ground; embed
53. **plop down**—put down forcibly (colloq.)
54. **plump down**—plunk
55. **plunk**—put down suddenly and forcibly

56. **post**—put at a specific place
57. **recess**—place or put back from the surface
58. **reposit**—place or put away or in safekeeping
59. **seat**—put in place; place or put in or on a seat; put in or into (a place); embed
60. **secrete**—put in a secret or concealed place
61. **set**—place; put
62. **settle**—place; establish; locate
63. **situate**—place; locate
64. **slam**—slap
65. **slap**—place or put forcibly, carelessly, and/or hastily
66. **station**—place in (a location, spot, position, etc.); post
67. **stow**—place or put into a compact mass or arrangement
68. **submerge, submerse**—put under water
69. **substitute**—put in place of (something else)
70. **superimpose, superpose**—place on top of or over
71. **thrust**—put forcibly into (some place or condition)
72. **tip**—put on the top or end of
73. **top**—put on the top of
74. **transplant**—put somewhere else after removing; put (tissue that has been removed from one person or one part of the body) into another and cause it to grow
75. **wedge**—put with others into (a small, cramped, or tight place)

2. Placing; Putting,n. *From Sec. 1:* adhibition, application, apposition, collocation, composure, confrontation or confrontment, dab, deposit, enclosure, inclosure, engraftation, entrenchment, establishment, implantation, imposition, impregnation, indentation or indenture, infixion, infusion, injection, insertion, insinuation, installation or installment, instillment or instillation, intercalation, interjection, interlineation, interpolation, interposition, introduction, juxtaposition, location, lodgment, secretion, settlement, situation, stowage, submergence or submersion, substitution, superimposition, superposition, thrust, transplantation

3. That Which Is Placed or Put,n. *From Sec. 1:* dab, deposit, enclosure, inclosure, graft, implant, impregnation, infusion, injection, inlay, insert or insertion, instillation, interjection, interpolation, interposition, plant, stowage, substitute or substitution, transplant; *Also:* 1. **inset**—that which is placed or put in something larger

4. Place Where Something Is Put,n. *From Sec. 1:* bed, berth, bunch, depository, enclosure, inclosure, location, post, recess, repository, seat, situation, station

5. Placing or Putting,adj. *From Sec. 1:* depository, infusive, insertive, insinuative or insinuatory, substitutive

6. Pert. to Placing or Putting,adj. *From Sec. 1:* appositive or appositional, insertive, intercalary, interlinear, substitutional

7. Capable of Being Placed Opposite Something: apposable,adj. (apposability,n.)

8. The Setting Out of a Military Camp: castrametation,n.

9. Insertion of a Unit of Time: embolism, n.

10. Bad Placing: malposition,n. (malposed, adj.)

11. The Act of Placing, or the State of Being Placed, After: postposition,n. (postpositional, postpositive,adj. postpositive,n.)

12. Position Before: preposition,n.

13. Situated Away from the Main Body: outlying,adj. (outlier,n.)

14. To Deposit Fine Earth as a Sediment (of Moving Water): silt,v. (silt,n.)

15. To Put Back,v.
1. **re-establish**—put back into former place or position (re-establishment,n.)
2. **reinsert**—put (that which has been taken out) back in (reinsertion,n.)
3. **reinstall**—put back into place or position (reinstallation, reinstallment,n.)
4. **reinstate**—place again in a former position; put back to former power or condition (reinstatement,n.)
5. **replace**—put back from where taken (replacement,n.)
6. **restore**—put back; put back in former place or position (restoration,n. restorative,adj.)
7. **return**—put back; replace (return,n.)

16. To Put or Set Aside,v.
1. **by-pass**—set aside (rules, laws, etc.) to reach a goal
2. **override**—set aside
3. **pigeonhole**—put aside with the intention of forgetting, neglecting, ignoring, etc.; put away or aside indefinitely
4. **shelve**—put aside; put aside for later consideration
5. **shunt**—put aside
6. **supplant**—set aside (supplantation,n.)
7. **suspend**—temporarily put or set aside (suspension,n. suspensive,adj.)

17. To Put Out of Place: displace, supersede, supplant,v. (displacement, supersedure or supersession, supplantation,n.)

18. To Put Out of Proper Place: dislocate,v. (dislocation,n.)

19. To Put in a Wrong Place: misplace,v. (misplacement,n.)

20. To Put (a Bodily Joint) Out of Place: dislocate, luxate,v. (dislocation, luxation,n.)

21. Out of Place: dislocated, displaced, incongruent, incongruous, misplaced, strange, adj. (dislocation, displacement, incongruence, incongruousness, incongruity, strangeness,n.)

22. To Instill, Figuratively,v.
1. **imbue** (. . . with)—instill (attitudes, principles, beliefs, feelings, etc.) into the mind of (imbuement,n.)
2. **implant**—instill (knowledge, feelings, attitudes, etc.) deeply and permanently (implantation,n.)
3. **impregnate** (. . . with)—imbue (impregnation,n.)
4. **impress** (. . . with)—imbue (impression, n.)
5. **inculcate** (. . . with)—instill (feelings, ideas, attitudes, etc.) into the mind of through repeated effort; instill (feelings, etc.) into the mind of (inculcation,n.)
6. **indoctrinate**—instill with principles or doctrines; instill with a partisan or biased viewpoint (indoctrination,n.)
7. **infect** (. . . with)—instill (harmful beliefs, opinions, feelings, or attitudes) into the mind of (infection,n.)
8. **infix**—instill; inculcate (infixion,n.)
9. **infuse**—instill as if by pouring in; imbue (infusion,n.)
10. **ingrain, engrain**—thoroughly instill into (someone's mind or nature)
11. **inoculate** (. . . with)—instill (feelings, etc.) into the mind of (inoculation,n.)
12. **inspire** (. . . with)—instill an impelling or exalting influence into the mind of (inspiration,n.)
13. **plant**—implant

23. Established; Deep-Seated,adj.
1. **confirmed**—firmly established and growing stronger as time passes
2. **deep-rooted**—firmly established in the sense of having roots deeply planted (deep-rootedness,n.)

3. **fixed**—established
4. **imbued**—ingrained
5. **inbred**—thoroughly deep-seated or deep-rooted as a result of strong breeding from infancy
6. **ingrained**—so firmly established as to have become part, as it were, of the grain or structure; deep-seated
7. **inveterate**—firmly established over a long period of time (inveteracy,n.)
8. **profound**—deep-seated (profoundness, profundity,n.)
9. **rock-ribbed**—firmly established
10. **rooted**—well-established; so well established as to have, figuratively, already become attached at the roots (rootedness, n.)

324. SUBSTITUTION

1. To Substitute, i.e., Put in the Place of,v.
1. **change**—substitute
2. **commute**—substitute; interchange
3. **exchange**—substitute (one thing) for another; put in the place of
4. **interchange**—put (each one) in the place of the other
5. **replace** (. . . with)—put in place of
6. **subrogate**—substitute (one person) for another
7. **supersede** (. . . with)—put in the place of; put (someone) in the position or place of (another)
8. **supplant** (. . . with)—put in the place of; put in the place of through trickery, treachery, or unfair methods
9. **surrogate**—substitute (someone) in place of another
10. **swap**—exchange
11. **switch**—put (one) in place of (the other)

2. To Substitute for, i.e., Take the Place of,v. *From Sec. 1:* change, exchange, interchange, replace, supersede, supplant, switch; *Also:*
1. **displace**—take the place of
2. **represent**—stand in, or take, the place of
3. **succeed**—take the place or position left vacant by
4. **symbolize**—stand for (something else)

3. Substitution,n. *From Sec. 1:* change, commutation, exchange, interchange, replacement, subrogation, supersedure or supersession, supplantation, swap, switch; *From Sec. 2:* displacement, representation, succession (to), symbolism or symbolization

4. A Substitute or Substitution, i.e., One Who, or That Which, Is Substituted,n. *From Sec. 1:* replacement, supplanter, surrogate; *From Sec. 2:* representative or representation, successor or succedaneum, symbol; *Also:*
1. **alternate**—one who will substitute for another if the latter cannot function, attend, etc.
2. **apology**—poor and inadequate substitute
3. **auxiliary**—that which takes the place of (something)
4. **delegate**—representative
5. **deputy**—one who substitutes for another, esp. in an official capacity
6. **envoy**—one sent to represent another
7. **ersatz**—substitute for the real thing
8. **locum tenens**—one who substitutes temporarily for another who is away, esp. in the medical and clerical professions
9. **makeshift**—something used temporarily as a substitute for the right thing
10. **pinch hitter**—one who substitutes for another in an emergency
11. **postiche (French)**—imitation substituted for the genuine thing
12. **proxy**—one who substitutes for another by authority of the latter
13. **ringer**—substitute entered falsely in a contest, race, etc., owing to its similarity

or resemblance to the one supposedly entered (colloq.)

14. **stand-in**—one who functions as a substitute
15. **stopgap**—temporary substitute
16. **understudy**—one who substitutes for another (often an actor) who cannot function
17. **vicar**—substitute; deputy; representative

5. Substitute; Substitutive,adj. *From Sec. 1:* exchange, supersessive, surrogate; *From Sec. 2:* representative, succedaneous, symbolic; *From Sec. 4:* alternate, auxiliary, deputy, ersatz, makeshift, stopgap, vicarial or vicarious

6. Capable of Substitution,adj. *From Sec. 1:* changeable, exchangeable, interchangeable, replaceable, supersedable; *Also:*
 1. **mutual, reciprocal**—interchangeable
 2. **substitute, substitutive**—capable of substitution

7. Pert. to, or Descr. of, Substitution: substitutional, substitutionary,adj.

8. Falsely Substituted for the Genuine: supposititious,adj.

325. SEPARATION

1. To Separate; To Take Apart; To Cause to Come Apart,v.
 1. **abstract**—separate; separate in one's mind (one thing from another)
 2. **analyze**—separate into component parts
 3. **anatomize**—take apart to see or show the relationship of parts; analyze
 4. **assay**—separate into component parts in order to determine the make-up of
 5. **assort**—separate into groups
 6. **bifurcate**—separate into two branches or forks; separate figuratively into two parts
 7. **branch**—separate into divisions or sections
 8. **break down**—separate into component parts
 9. **burst**—cause to fly or break apart suddenly and forcibly
 10. **class**—separate into different qualities, grades, groups, etc.
 11. **classify**—separate into groups according to some method or plan
 12. **cleave**—separate by a blow; separate figuratively as if with a knife or blow; separate along natural lines of division
 13. **collapse**—break apart
 14. **decompose**—break up into component parts
 15. **demarcate**—separate
 16. **demobilize**—disband (troops)
 17. **detach**—separate; disunite; unfasten
 18. **dichotomize**—separate into two parts
 19. **disaffiliate**—separate from its affiliation or association with
 20. **disarticulate**—separate at the joints, or separate joint from joint
 21. **disassemble**—take apart, usually in an orderly fashion (parts that have been put together)
 22. **disassociate**—put a stop to an association
 23. **disband**—break up into separate units
 24. **discerp**—dismember
 25. **disconnect**—separate the connection of, or at the connecting points
 26. **disengage**—separate (those parts that are connected or engaged); separate at the points of junction
 27. **disentangle**—separate (parts that are tangled or twined together)
 28. **disentwine**—disentangle
 29. **disintegrate**—separate into pieces; destroy the unity of; decompose
 30. **disject**—separate forcibly
 31. **disjoin**—separate; separate at the points of joining; dissolve (that which is joined)
 32. **disjoint**—break up into parts; separate joints from; separate at the joints
 33. **dismantle**—take apart (generally that which has been put together by human hands, as a machine, building, etc.)
 34. **dismember**—separate the members of, one from another, or from the main body, literally or figuratively
 35. **dismount**—separate the parts of (a machine)
 36. **dissect**—cut into separate parts (an animal, corpse, plant, etc.) for examination; analyze (an idea, principle, or other intangible) by critically studying it part by part; anatomize
 37. **dissever**—separate completely (used almost exclusively for intangibles, as one's connection with an organization, one's relationship to a group, etc.)
 38. **dissociate**—separate; break up the union or association of; separate from connection or association with an organization, group, or other intangible
 39. **dissolve**—separate back into its individual parts (often some association or other intangible, such as a political organization, business empire, federation of nations, etc.)
 40. **distinguish**—separate (in the mind) into kinds or categories
 41. **disunite**—separate; break or end the union, association, etc., of; disjoin
 42. **divide**—separate; separate into parts
 43. **divorce**—separate (usually two people, things, ideas, etc.) so that any former relationship is ended and each goes a separate path or is to be considered separately
 44. **explode**—burst with great noise and violence
 45. **fraction, fractionize**—separate into parts or pieces
 46. **fractionate**—separate (a mixture) into its components, or into parts of different character, as by distillation or crystallization
 47. **itemize**—separate figuratively into its specific parts
 48. **part**—separate one from the other; separate into parts
 49. **partition**—separate into parts or shares; take apart and distribute
 50. **ravel**—unravel
 51. **resolve**—separate into component parts
 52. **rift**—rive
 53. **rive**—tear apart; cleave; split
 54. **rupture**—break or burst apart
 55. **secern**—separate
 56. **section**—cut into separate or component parts; separate from the main body
 57. **segment**—separate into natural parts or divisions
 58. **sever**—separate from an attachment; separate from association or connection; part
 59. **sift**—separate into component pieces or particles, large particles from small, etc.
 60. **sort**—separate into groups
 61. **splinter**—break into long, thin pieces
 62. **split**—separate into parts or into different or dissenting groups
 63. **spread**—separate one from the other
 64. **sunder**—separate by force; split
 65. **tear**—pull apart forcibly
 66. **trichotomize**—separate into three branches, parts, groups, ranks, classes, etc.
 67. **unassemble**—disassemble
 68. **unbind**—separate from its attachment or fastening
 69. **unchain**—separate from its chains
 70. **unclasp**—separate the fastenings of
 71. **uncouple**—separate (two things that are joined together)
 72. **unfasten**—separate the fastenings of, or from its fastenings

73. **unknit**—disunite
74. **unlink**—disconnect
75. **unmoor**—separate from its anchorage
76. **unmount**—take apart
77. **unpack**—separate and remove the contents of
78. **unravel**—separate the woven threads of; pull apart
79. **unsolder**—separate; tear apart; sunder
80. **untangle**—disentangle
81. **untie**—separate from bonds or from that which ties together
82. **untwine**—disentangle
83. **unweave**—take apart
84. **wedge**—separate by, or as if by, pushing a tapered piece of wood between, literally or figuratively
85. **winnow**—separate

2. To Separate, i.e., Come Apart,v. *From Sec. 1:* bifurcate, branch or branch out, break down, burst, cleave, collapse, decompose, demobilize, detach, dichotomize, disarticulate, disband, disconnect, disengage, disentangle, disentwine, disintegrate, disjoin, disjoint, dissociate or dissociate oneself, dissolve, disunite, divide, explode, fractionize, part, resolve, rift, rive, rupture, segment, sever, splinter, split, spread, tear, trichotomize, unfasten, unknit, unravel, untie, untwine; *Also:*
1. **divaricate**—separate into two branches or parts
2. **fork**—separate into two or more branches, as a road, stem, tree trunk, etc.
3. **fragment**—separate into pieces
4. **furcate**—fork; branch like a fork

3. Separation,n. *From Secs. 1 and 2:* abstraction, analysis, assay, assortment, bifurcation, breakdown, classification, cleavage, collapse, decomposition, demarcation, demobilization, detachment, dichotomization, disaffiliation, disarticulation, disassembly, disassociation, disbandment, discerption, disconnection, disengagement, disentanglement, disintegration, disjection; disjunction (from *disjoin*); dismantlement, dismemberment, dissection, disseverance or disseverment, dissociation, dissolution (from *dissolve*); disunion (from *disunite*); division, divorce or divorcement, explosion, fractionization; fractionation (from *fractionate*); itemization, partition; resolution (from *resolve*); rupture, secernment, segmentation, severance, split, sunderance, trichotomy; *From Sec. 2:* divarication, fragmentation, furcation; *Also:*
1. **abruption**—sudden or unexpected breaking off or away
2. **avulsion**—forcible separation
3. **concision**—separation by cutting
4. **divulsion**—separation by tearing apart
5. **fission**—a splitting into parts
6. **schism**—separation; a split into unfriendly groups; division owing to difference of opinion in a party, religious group, organization, etc.
7. **scission**—division
8. **separatism**—separation of a group (as in a party, church, organization, etc.) from the larger body
9. **trichotomy**—division of man into body, soul, and spirit
10. **vertebration**—segmentation or division like that of the backbone

4. One Who, or That Which, Separates,n. *From Sec. 1:* analyst, anatomist, assayer, assorter, classifier, dichotomist, dissector, sifter, wedge; *From Sec. 3:* separatist (separatist, adj.)

5. Separative; Separatory; Causing, Producing, or Inclined to Separation,adj. *From Sec. 1:* abstractive, analytic or analytical, classificatory, dichotomous; disjunctive (from *disjoin*); dissective, divisive, divorcive, explosive or explosible, partitive, splintery; *From Sec. 3:* schismatic, separatistic; *Also:*

1. **ramshackle**—tending or likely to fall apart or come apart

6. One Who or That Which Is Separate or Has Been Separated,n. *From Sec. 1:* bifurcation, branch, discerption; *From Sec. 2:* divarication, furcation; *From Sec. 3:* avulsion; *Also:*
1. **entity, individual**—that which has, or which is considered as having, a separate and distinct existence

7. A Separation,n. *From Sec. 1:* division, rift, rupture, split, spread, tear; *Also:*
1. **gulf**—wide separation
2. **valley**—separation between the female breasts

8. Separate; Separated,adj. *From Sec. 1:* bifurcated, branched, classified, etc.; bifurcate, burst; cleft or cloven (from *cleave*); dichotomous, disarticulate; disjunct (from *disjoin*); riven; asunder (from *sunder*); trichotomous or trichotomic; *From Sec. 2:* divaricate, furcate; *Also:*
1. **apart**—separate; separated
2. **discrete**—separate; composed of individually separate or distinct parts (discreteness, n.)
3. **distinct**—separate, in the sense of being unconnected with others of the same type (distinctness, n.)
4. **individual**—separate; existing as a separate entity (individuality, n.)
5. **multifid**—cut into many parts or divisions
6. **particular**—separate; separate from others; considered separately (particularity, n.)
7. **remote**—separate (remoteness, n.)
8. **segregate**—separate; separated from others of the same kind (segregation, n.)
9. **singular**—separate (singularity, n.)

9. Separable,adj. *From Sec. 1:* classifiable, collapsible, detachable, discerptible or discerptible, disengageable, dismountable, dissoluble, divisible, divorceable or divorcible, explodable or explosible, partible, resoluble, sectionable, sortable; *From Sec. 3:* fissionable

10. Inseparable,adj. *From Sec. 9:* unclassifiable, undetachable, indissoluble, indivisible, impartible, irresoluble, unfissionable; *Also:*
1. **infrangible**—not capable of being broken or separated into its parts
2. **tenacious**—not easily pulled apart
3. **ultimate**—incapable of further division

11. Pert. to Separation,adj. *From Sec. 1:* analytic or analytical, classificatory, dichotomous or dichotomic, dissectional, explosive, fractional, sectional, trichotomic; *From Sec. 2:* fragmental; *From Sec. 3:* schismatic, trichotomic; *Also:* 1. **splinter**—pert. to small groups that separate from a larger organization owing to differences in opinion

12. To Set Apart,v.
1. **appropriate**—set apart for a particular use (appropriation, n.)
2. **consign**—set apart (consignment, n.)
3. **dedicate**—set apart for special use (dedication, n. dedicative, dedicatory, adj.)
4. **designate**—set apart for a purpose (designation, n.)
5. **destine**—set apart for special purpose or use
6. **distinguish**—set apart from others by special qualities or differences, as a *rocky soil distinguishes the region*
7. **earmark**—set apart for a particular purpose
8. **isolate**—set apart; cut off from communication or contacts with others (isolation, n. isolate, n. isolate, adj.)
9. **quarantine**—isolate (someone with infectious or contagious disease) so that others will not catch it; isolate (someone) for any other reason (quarantine, n.)

10. **reserve**—set apart for later use, special purpose, or a particular person (reservation,n.)
11. **sanctify**—set apart for sacred use, observance, etc. (sanctification,n.)
12. **secern**—distinguish (secernment,n.)
13. **segregate**—set apart; set apart by itself from the rest; isolate (segregation,n. segregative, segregational,adj. segregate, adj.)
14. **sequester**—set apart (sequestration,n.)
15. **taboo, tabu**—set apart as sacred or, contrarily, as profane (taboo, tabu,n.)

13. Set Apart as Sacred: sacrosanct (sometimes ironic), sanctified, taboo or tabu,adj. (sacrosanctness or sacrosanctity,n.)

14. To Show the Separateness of, through Special Differences, from the General Class: distinguish,v.

15. To Make into a Separate and Distinct Entity: individualize, individuate,v. (individualization, individuation,n.)

16. To Make into, or Regard as, a Separate and Distinct Substance: hypostasize, hypostatize,v. (hypostasization, hypostatization,n.)

17. Segregation of Negroes in the U.S., esp. Southern U.S.: Jim Crow,n. (jim-crow, Jim-Crow, adj.)

18. Racial Segregation in South Africa: apartheid,n.

326. PARTS

1. A Part (General or Miscellaneous),n.
1. **accessory**—less important part
2. **appurtenance**—part that belongs
3. **articulation**—segment
4. **aspect**—part facing a particular direction
5. **branch**—part; part that extends
6. **bulk**—larger part
7. **butt**—part at the bottom
8. **cantlet**—incomplete part
9. **core**—innermost part
10. **detail**—unimportant part
11. **division**—part; part complete in itself though ultimately part of a larger body; segment
12. **dregs**—worst, most debased, most corrupt, least attractive, or bitterest part of anything
13. **epitome**—part that represents, or is typical of, the whole
14. **factor**—part that serves to help something function
15. **feature**—single part of the face; conspicuous or prominent part of anything
16. **fragment**—incomplete part
17. **installment**—one part of a succession or series, as of a debt, of a story or novel published in newspaper- or magazine-form, etc.
18. **item**—separate part specified or particularized in a list, accounting, etc.
19. **joint**—part where two things join; movable part of the body where two bones or other parts join; segment
20. **limb**—extended part
21. **moiety**—part; one of two equal parts
22. **particular**—individual part
23. **partition**—part
24. **piece**—part; portion
25. **plica**—folded part
26. **portion**—part; part that is someone's share
27. **prime**—best or first part
28. **ramus**—projecting part
29. **rudiment**—part to be learned first in a subject or field
30. **section**—part
31. **segment**—part; part that is easily and cleanly broken off from the whole or into which the whole easily breaks or naturally separates; marked-off part

32. **shard**—fragment; fragment of earthenware
33. **share**—part belonging to, owed to, or contributed by, a person or group
34. **slice**—thin part cut from the whole
35. **strip**—long and narrow part
36. **stub**—short, blunt part of anything after the rest has been removed, broken off, or used up; short, thick, projecting part; stump
37. **stump**—bottom part after the rest has been removed; stub
38. **subdivision**—part made by still further dividing
39. **tatter**—torn and hanging part
40. **tentacle**—projecting part used to feel, touch, hold, move, etc.; figuratively, growing part of anything that goes into new places, esp. for evil purposes

2. Descr. of, or Pert. to, a Part,adj. *From Sec. 1:* divisional, epitomic or epitomical, factorial, featural, fragmental or fragmentary, particular, partitional, portional, rudimentary, sectional, segmentary or segmental, subdivisional, tentacular

3. To Separate (Something) into Parts,v. *From Sec. 1:* articulate, divide, epitomize, factor, itemize, particularize, partition, portion or apportion, section, segment, slice, strip, subdivide

4. Parts Forming a Related Group: system, n. (systemic,adj.)

5. The Parts of Something: composition,n. (compositional,adj.)

6. Part in the Sense of Division or Section, n.
1. **branch**—division
2. **compartment**—division or section of some closed space
3. **cut**—division
4. **detachment**—division or section of troops, a fleet, or police sent on a special mission
5. **detail**—detachment
6. **group**—section
7. **limb**—division
8. **member**—division of a party, organization, group, etc.
9. **partition**—division
10. **segment**—division
11. **subdivision**—section made by still further division
12. **unit**—division
13. **wing**—part of an organization; part of a group not in agreement with the rest

7. Divisional; Sectional,adj. *From Sec. 6:* compartmental, partitional, segmental or segmentary, subdivisional, unitary or unital

8. To Divide or Section; To Separate (Something) into Divisions or Sections,v. *From Sec. 6:* compartmentalize, partition, segment, subdivide

9. Part That Makes Up the Whole,n.
1. **base**—chief constituent (basal,adj.)
2. **basis**—chief constituent or ingredient (basic,adj.)
3. **component**—part necessary to make up the whole; part that has an individual wholeness or entity, of which something, tangible or intangible, is made (component,adj.)
4. **constituent**—tangible or intangible part essential to make up the whole, or that influences the character of the whole (constituent,adj.)
5. **element**—one of the very simple or simplest parts of which a thing or quality is made (elemental,adj.)
6. **factor**—constituent; element that helps produce a result (factorial,adj.)
7. **ingredient**—part that goes into a mixture; figurative part that, with others, makes up a quality or other intangible

8. **integrant**—part that is necessary in the make-up of the whole (integrant, integral,adj.)
9. **leaven**—element that tempers or modifies the whole
10. **staple**—chief part necessary to make up the whole (staple,adj.)
11. **unit**—distinct part of the whole (unitary, unital,adj.)

10. Broken, Torn, or Cut-Off Part or Piece, n.
1. **bit**—piece broken or bitten off
2. **cantlet**—fragment
3. **chip**—small, broken or chopped-off piece
4. **clipping**—piece or part cut or clipped off
5. **collop**—small slice
6. **cross section**—part cut transversely out of something; transverse slice
7. **crumb**—small piece (of food or bread) broken or rubbed off; small fragment
8. **cut**—part or portion cut off
9. **cutting**—part cut, cut off, or cut out
10. **division**—distinct segment or section
11. **fraction**—part broken off, or as if broken off, from a larger piece
12. **fragment**—part broken or cut off from the whole, generally a small or incomplete part
13. **oddment**—fragment
14. **morsel**—fragment
15. **paring**—surface part cut or shaved off
16. **partition**—section
17. **potsherd**—fragment of earthenware
18. **rasher**—thin slice (of meat) cut for cooking, broiling, or frying, or already cooked, broiled, or fried
19. **scrap**—small piece cut or torn off; fragment
20. **section**—part cut off
21. **segment**—broken-off part
22. **shard**—fragment; fragment of earthenware
23. **shaving**—part shaved off from the surface
24. **shiver**—small splinter
25. **shred**—long, narrow piece cut or torn off
26. **sippet**—broken piece; small broken piece
27. **slab**—thick slice
28. **slice**—flat piece cut off and across something; cross section
29. **sliver**—long, thin piece broken off or cut off from a larger piece
30. **snatch**—fragment (usually of something heard)
31. **snip, snippet**—small piece cut off; fragment
32. **splint, splinter**—long, thin piece, usually that has split off or been split off
33. **tatter**—part torn off

11. Descr. of a Broken, Torn, or Cut-Off Part or Piece,adj. *From Sec. 10:* crumby, divisional, fractional, fragmental or fragmentary, partitional, segmental or segmentary, splintery

12. To Break, Cut, or Tear (Something) into Parts or Pieces; To Break, Cut, or Tear a Part or Piece Off,v. *From Sec. 10:* cross-section, divide, fraction or fractionize, partition, section, segment, shiver, shred, slice

13. To Become Broken, Cut, or Torn into Pieces,v. *From Sec. 10:* chip, divide, fragment, section, segment, shiver, shred, slice, splinter, tatter

14. Broken or Cut-Off Parts or Pieces,n.
1. **debris**—scattered and broken parts
2. **disjecta membra** (Latin)—broken or broken-off and scattered parts
3. **flinders**—long, thin, broken, split, or split-off pieces
4. **rubble**—mass, mixture, or collection of broken pieces or parts
5. **smithereens**—small broken pieces

15. A Piece: cantlet, shred, slice, stitch,n.; *Also:*
1. **lump**—piece of irregular shape
2. **nugget**—lump (of some substance, esp. gold, etc.)
3. **slab**—thick, flat piece of stone, wood, or other thing or substance
4. **slat**—strip of wood, metal, etc., used as a support for a mattress or spring in a bed, or as one of the horizontal pieces in a venetian blind
5. **strip**—long, narrow piece

16. To Divide (Something) into Pieces,v. *From Sec. 15:* shred, slice; slab, strip

17. Small Piece: bit, crumb, morsel, particle, patch, scrap, shiver, shred, snippet, stitch; wisp (figurative),n. (crumby, patchy, wispy or wispish,adj.)

18. Small Hanging Piece: tag, tatter,n.

19. To Divide or Break (Something) into Small Pieces: crumb, crumble, morsel, shred, v.

20. To Become Broken into Small Pieces or Particles: crumble, molder,v.

21. Something That Is Breaking, or Has Broken, into Small Pieces: crumble,n.

22. Large Piece: dollop; hunk (slang),n.

23. Small Part: bit, cantlet, crumb, detail, fraction, fragment, moiety, morsel, particle, patch, shred, slice, snippet, tithe,n. (fractional, fragmental or fragmentary,adj.)

24. Small Part That Is Left: remnant, stub, stump,n.

25. Minute Part of Matter: particle,n.

26. Any Least or Very Small Part: stitch,n. (colloq.)

27. Small Part or Bit (of Something Heard): snatch,n.

28. To Divide (Something) into Small Parts: fraction, fractionize, morsel, shred, slice,v.

29. Main, Important, or Essential Part: backbone, base, basis, bedrock, body, core, crux, essence, kernel, keynote, marrow, mass, meat, nucleus, pith, principle, substance, trunk,n.

30. Part on Which Other Parts Depend: keystone,n.

31. Main or Most Important Part, Happening, Thing, etc., in a Series or Collection: pièce de résistance,n. (French)

32. Necessary Parts: vitals,n.

33. Central Part: core, heart, kernel, middle, midst, nucleus,n.

34. Central Part of a Tree, Fruit, etc.: heart, n.

35. Central Portion of a Wheel: hub,n.

36. A Share: portion, proportion,n.

37. That Share of the Total Amount That Is Due from or to Each Person, Group, etc.: quota,n.

38. One's Share of the Total, Esp. When There Is a Scarcity of Supply: ration,n.

39. By Share: proportionally, proportionately, adv.

40. According to Equal Shares: pro rata

41. To Be a Part of,v.
1. **appertain to**—belong as a part of
2. **compose**—be one of the parts of
3. **constitute**—be, with others, a part of (constitution,n.)
4. **epitomize**—be that part that typically represents the whole of (epitomization, n.)
5. **inhere in**—be a permanent and inseparable part of (inherence, inherency,n.)

6. **make up**—be a part or the parts of
7. **reside in**—exist as a part or element of (residence,n.)

42. Being a Part of,adj. *From Sec. 41:* appertaining or appurtenant, component, constituent, inherent, resident (appurtenance, inherence or inherency, residence,n.)

43. That Which Is a Permanent and Inseparable Part or Element: inherency,n.

44. Being a Necessary Part or Element in the Make-Up of the Whole: constitutive, essential, intrinsic or intrinsical, material, adj. (constitutiveness, essentiality or essentialness, intrinsicality, materiality or materialness,n.)

45. Something That Is Such a Necessary Part or Element: essentiality, materiality,n.

46. To Cause to Become Part of the Body of: embody, incorporate,v. (embodiment, incorporation,n.)

47. Made Up of Parts,adj.
 1. **anisometric**—made up of parts that do not correspond
 2. **articulate, articulated**—made up of separate and distinct parts
 3. **biform**—made up of the parts or characteristics of two forms, kinds, or forms of life
 4. **combined of**—made up of (parts put together)
 5. **compact of**—composed of
 6. **complex**—made up of very different parts
 7. **complicated**—made up of many different parts
 8. **composed of**—made up of (various parts put together)
 9. **composite**—made up of distinct parts or elements; compound
 10. **compound**—made up of two or more parts put together
 11. **comprised of**—made up of (various parts put together or combined)
 12. **consisting of**—made up of (parts that form the whole)
 13. **constituted of**—made up of (parts)
 14. **constructed of**—made up of (parts that form the whole)
 15. **containing**—made up of (parts held within, literally or figuratively)
 16. **cosmopolitan**—made up of parts from all over the world
 17. **dual**—made up of two parts
 18. **fabricated**—made up (of parts united into a whole)
 19. **formed of**—made up of (parts)
 20. **mixed**—made up (of parts combined together into a smooth whole)
 21. **organized from**—made up of (interdependent parts, each having its special purpose or function)
 22. **segmentate, segmented**—articulate
 23. **structured of**—made up of (parts, organs, etc., arranged into one substance or body); constructed of
 24. **synthesized, synthetic**—made up (of parts put together into a whole)
 25. **textured of**—made up of (parts that are, literally or figuratively, woven together)
 26. **triform**—made up of three parts
 27. **triple, triplex**—made up of three parts

48. State of Being Made Up of Parts,n. *From Sec. 47:* anisometry, articulateness or articulation, biformity, complexity, complication, compositeness, constitution, construction, cosmopolitanism, duality, formation, organization, segmentation, triformity, triplicity or triplexity

49. Make-Up; Manner of Make-Up,n. *From Sec. 47:* combination, composition, consistency, constitution, construction, content or contents, fabric, formation, mixture, organization, structure, texture

50. That Which Is Made Up of Parts,n. *From Sec. 47:* articulation, combination, complex or complexity, complication, composition, composite, compound, construction, fabric or fabrication, formation, mixture, organization or organism, structure, texture, triplex; *Also:*
 1. **network**—fabric or structure of wires, cords, threads, or similar things crossing each other and interconnecting; complex organization; system; system of lines or channels intercrossing and interconnecting
 2. **system**—that which is made up of parts arranged into a unified whole

51. To Be Made Up of (Parts),v. *From Sec. 47:* comprise, consist of, contain (comprisal, n.)

52. To Make Up (Something) from Parts,v. *From Sec. 47:* compose, compound, constitute, construct, fabricate, form, mix, organize, structure, synthesize, texture (composition, constitution, construction, fabrication, formation, mixture, organization, synthesis,n.)

53. Having, or Divided into, Parts,adj.
 1. **bipartite**—having two corresponding parts (bipartition,n.)
 2. **multipartite**—having, or divided into, a number of parts
 3. **tripartite**—having three corresponding parts; divided into three parts (tripartition,n.)

54. Not a Part of: adventitious, extrinsic, extrinsical,adj. (adventitiousness, extrinsicality,n.)

327. DETAIL

1. Detail,n.
 1. **accessory**—subordinate detail
 2. **circumstance**—detail
 3. **fact**—true detail
 4. **item**—specific detail
 5. **particular**—specific detail
 6. **punctilio**—precise detail of convention or form
 7. **specification**—particular detail
 8. **technicality**—detail of a very specialized nature

2. Small, Minor, or Unimportant Details: minutiae, trivia,n.

3. List of Details: schedule,n.

4. To Give Details,v.
 1. **amplify**—give more details to; add details to
 2. **circumstantiate**—show or support with details; give full and accurate details about
 3. **elaborate (on or upon)**—add details (to an idea, subject, theme, etc.)
 4. **embellish**—add interesting and usually fanciful or false details to (a story, account, report, etc.)
 5. **individualize**—particularize
 6. **itemize**—give the specific details of
 7. **particularize**—give details about
 8. **recite**—tell about in detail
 9. **recount**—tell in detail; tell the specific details of; specify one by one
 10. **rehearse**—tell in detail
 11. **specialize**—give the details or particulars of
 12. **specify**—give particular details about; mention, describe, or name in detail

5. A Giving of Details,n. *From Sec. 4:* amplification, circumstantiation; elaboration (of, on, or upon); embellishment, individualization, itemization, particularization, recital or recitation, recountal, rehearsal, specialization, specification

6. In Detail; Detailed,adj. *From Sec. 4:* amplified, circumstantial or circumstantiated, elaborate or elaborated, embellished, individualized, itemized, particularized or particular, specified or specific (circumstantiality, elaborateness, particularity, specificity,n.)

328. COMPLETENESS

1. Complete; Whole,adj.
1. **absolute**—complete; complete in itself; whole
2. **aggregate**—complete; entire
3. **all-embracing**—complete in the sense of covering everything, or every part, aspect, etc.
4. **all-inclusive**—complete in the sense of including everything
5. **arrant**—complete or thoroughgoing, in a bad sense
6. **blank**—complete; absolute (as a *blank refusal*, etc.)
7. **circumstantial**—complete, in the sense that full and accurate particulars and details are given
8. **consummate**—complete; finished
9. **downright**—absolute (often derogative)
10. **entire**—complete in all parts; whole; undiminished; undivided
11. **exhaustive**—thorough, in the sense of leaving out nothing important
12. **finished**—complete, in the sense that everything leading toward completeness has been done
13. **full**—complete; entire
14. **full-fledged**—complete
15. **gross**—complete; whole; entire (as a *gross sum, weight*, etc.)
16. **imperforate**—whole, i.e., not pierced
17. **indiscrete**—not separated into individual parts, but in a compact whole
18. **intact**—complete, with no parts missing
19. **integral**—complete; whole; with nothing missing
20. **integrated**—complete, in the sense that all the parts needed for completeness are present
21. **intensive**—thorough and deep
22. **organic**—organized into a co-ordinated whole
23. **out-and-out**—complete; thorough (often derogative, as an *out-and-out coward*, etc.)
24. **outright**—complete (often derogative)
25. **plenary**—complete, absolute, or entire (of power, authority, privileges, etc.)
26. **radical**—complete; thoroughgoing
27. **sheer**—complete; absolute (as *sheer madness, effrontery, delight*, etc.)
28. **sound**—complete; thorough
29. **sweeping**—complete or nearly complete; covering the whole range; all-embracing
30. **systematic**—thorough and regular in conduct or performance
31. **thorough**—complete; doing everything necessary
32. **thoroughgoing**—complete in every way
33. **total**—complete; entire
34. **unabridged**—complete; not shortened; with nothing taken out or removed
35. **unbroken**—complete or whole, in the sense of not being broken, interrupted, etc.
36. **unconditional**—absolute
37. **uncut**—whole, in the sense of not being cut; unabridged
38. **undiminished**—whole or complete, in the sense of not having lost any parts
39. **undivided**—whole, in the sense of not having been divided into parts
40. **unexpurgated**—complete in the sense that no (usually objectionable) parts or passages have been removed (of books, written material, etc.)
41. **unitary**—whole; not divided
42. **unmitigated**—absolute
43. **unqualified**—absolute

44. **unreduced**—undiminished
45. **unsevered**—whole, in the sense that no part has been cut or cut off
46. **utter**—complete; absolute

2. Completeness; Wholeness,n. *From Sec. 1:* absoluteness, all-inclusiveness, circumstantiality, consummateness, downrightness, entirety or entireness, exhaustiveness, fullness, intactness, integrity, intensiveness, outrightness, soundness, systematicness, thoroughness, thoroughgoingness, totality or totalness, unbrokenness, undividedness, utterness.

3. To Complete; To Make Complete,v.
1. **accomplish**—complete
2. **clinch**—complete successfully
3. **complement**—complete (something that would otherwise be incomplete); fill in the lacks or deficiencies of (another person); serve to make complete
4. **conclude**—complete
5. **consummate**—bring to completion
6. **crown**—make complete
7. **finish**—complete
8. **integrate**—make complete by bringing together the parts that form a whole
9. **top off**—complete

4. Completion,n. *From Sec. 3:* accomplishment, conclusion, consummation, integration

5. Completive,adj. *From Sec. 3:* complemental or complementary, conclusive, integrative

6. That Which, or One Who, Completes,n.
1. **complement**—that which completes or, by adding to something else, makes up the full amount; word or words serving to complete a grammatical construction; one of two things or persons serving to fill in the other's lacks or deficiencies
2. **copestone**—finishing touch
3. **counterpart**—person or thing that is the complement of another person or thing
4. **obverse**—complement

7. Necessary to Completeness: integral,adj.

8. That Which; A Whole,n.
1. **aggregate**—sum of parts or particulars
2. **aggregation**—combined whole; aggregate
3. **body**—collective whole
4. **complex**—whole made up of different parts
5. **entirety**—whole
6. **sum**—whole; whole amount
7. **total, totality**—whole; aggregate
8. **unity**—systematic whole; whole made up of related parts

329. INCOMPLETENESS

1. Incomplete,adj.
1. **abridged**—incomplete, in the sense that parts have been removed (of written material)
2. **expurgated**—incomplete, in the sense that (usually objectionable) parts or passages have been removed of books, written material, etc.)
3. **fragmentary**—incomplete; made up, or as if made up, of disconnected fragments
4. **inchoate**—incomplete
5. **partial**—not complete
6. **rude, crude, rough**—in an incomplete state
7. **rudimentary**—incomplete
8. **sketchy**—incomplete; roughly outlined but not complete
9. **unconsummated**—not yet brought to completion
10. **unfinished, unpolished, incondite**—incomplete

2. Incompleteness,n. *From Sec. 1:* fragmentariness, inchoateness, rudeness, crudeness or crudity, roughness, rudimentariness, sketchiness

330. ALONE

1. Alone; Left Alone; Living Alone, etc., adj.
1. **abandoned**—left alone
2. **beached**—stranded
3. **bereaved (of)**—left desolate through loss or death (of someone)
4. **cloistered**—shut off from the world
5. **companionless**—alone, in the sense of having no friends
6. **derelict**—abandoned; given up by owner or guardian
7. **deserted**—left alone
8. **desolate**—alone; left alone; without others; without friends or companions; lonesome
9. **forlorn**—left alone; lonely
10. **forsaken**—left alone
11. **friendless**—alone, i.e., without friends
12. **incommunicado**—held alone or apart so that one cannot be in communication with others; kept in solitary confinement
13. **insular**—isolated
14. **isolated, isolate**—alone; kept or shut off alone; by itself or oneself; lonely
15. **lone**—alone; by itself or oneself; without others
16. **lonely**—alone; not with others; unhappy at being alone
17. **lonesome**—feeling alone; unhappy at being alone; longing for company
18. **lorn**—forlorn
19. **marooned**—left alone on a desolate island or shore; placed in helpless isolation
20. **quarantined**—kept alone or shut off from others or in order to prevent the spread of an infectious disease
21. **retired**—living a secluded life
22. **secluded**—shut off by itself; having few or no contacts with other people; isolated
23. **segregated**—put off alone; isolated; secluded
24. **sequestered**—segregated
25. **single**—alone
26. **singlehanded**—doing, working, or accomplishing alone or without help
27. **sole**—alone; without help
28. **solitary**—alone; without others; done alone; lonely
29. **solitudinous**—marked by loneliness, isolation, or solitariness
30. **stranded**—alone and without money
31. **stray**—by itself or oneself
32. **unaccompanied**—alone, in the sense of being without others
33. **unaided**—alone, in the sense of having no help from others
34. **unassisted**—unaided
35. **unattended**—unaccompanied
36. **withdrawn**—secluded

2. Aloneness,n. *From Sec. 1:* abandonment, bereavement, dereliction, desolation, forlornness, forsakenness, friendlessness, insularity, isolation, loneness, loneliness, lonesomeness, quarantine, retirement, secludedness or seclusion, segregation, sequestration, singleness, solitariness or solitude

3. To Leave, or Cause to Be, Alone,v. *From Sec. 1:* abandon, beach, bereave (of), cloister, desert, forsake, isolate, maroon, quarantine, seclude, segregate, sequester, strand

4. Act, Fact, or Process of Leaving, or Causing to Be, Alone,n. *From Sec. 1:* abandonment, bereavement, dereliction, desertion, forsakement, isolation, quarantine, seclusion, segregation, sequestration

5. One Who Is Alone; One Who Is Left, or Has Been Left, Alone,n. *From Sec. 1:* derelict, isolate, maroon, solitudinarian

6. Preferring to Be Alone,adj.
1. **non-gregarious**—preferring solitude to the company of others

2. **retiring**—tending to withdraw from contacts with others
3. **shy**—retiring
4. **unsociable**—preferring not to have contacts with others; preferring to be alone
5. **withdrawn**—tending to stay alone; preferring aloneness to contacts with others

7. One Who Lives Alone or in Seclusion,n.
1. **anchoress**—female anchorite
2. **anchoret**—anchorite
3. **anchorite**—one who, for religious reasons, lives in seclusion
4. **anchoritess**—female anchorite
5. **ascetic**—one who lives a solitary and contemplative life and is much given to self-discipline
6. **castaway**—shipwrecked person
7. **eremite**—one who lives in solitude for religious reasons; hermit
8. **hermit**—one who retires from society and lives in seclusion, often, though not necessarily, for religious reasons
9. **Hieronymite, Hieronymian**—member of any of the hermit orders named after St. Jerome
10. **Marabout**—Mohammedan hermit
11. **monk**—one who is a member of a religious order that requires solitary living
12. **pillarist**—stylite
13. **recluse**—one who shuts himself off from the world and lives a solitary existence
14. **santon**—hermit, esp. in Mohammedan cultures
15. **solitaire, solitary**—hermit; recluse
16. **solitudinarian**—recluse
17. **stylite**—one who lives an ascetic and secluded life on the top of a pillar, chiefly in Syria
18. **troglodyte**—person living a hermitlike existence; hermit

8. State or Condition of Living Alone or in Seclusion,n. *From Sec. 7:* anchoritism, asceticism, eremitism, monkery (derogatory), monkhood, or monasticism, reclusion

9. Descr. of, Pert. to, or Characteristic of, One Who Lives Alone or in Seclusion,adj. *From Sec. 7:* anchoritic or anchoritish, ascetic; eremitic, eremitical, or eremitish; hermit, Hieronymite; monkish (often derogatory) or monastic; reclusive, troglodytic

10. Place of Living Alone or in Seclusion,n. *From Sec. 7:* hermitage, monastery (from monk); *Also:* 1. **ribat**—Algerian monastery

331. PRIVACY

1. Private,adj.
1. **cloistered**—private, i.e., protected from interference (of places)
2. **closet**—private
3. **confidential**—private (of material, information, etc.)
4. **covert**—private
5. **isolated**—secluded
6. **out-of-the-way**—secluded
7. **personal**—private
8. **quiet**—secluded
9. **remote**—secluded
10. **secluded**—shut off by itself, hence private (of places)
11. **singular**—private

2. Privacy,n. *From Sec. 1:* isolation, quietness, remoteness, seclusion; *Also:* 1. **penetralia(**pl.**)**—privacy

3. Private Place,n.
1. **adytum**—sanctum
2. **retreat**—place of privacy or seclusion
3. **sanctum**—private place to which one can retire; place where one is free from intrusion
4. **sanctum sanctorum**—most private place
5. **seclusion**—private place of retirement

4. Privately,adv.
1. **in camera (Latin)**—privately; in private; behind shut doors
2. **sotto voce (Italian)**—privately (of something said, etc.)
3. **tête-à-tête (French)**—for two people in private; two together in private

332. CUT

1. To Cut; To Cut Off; To Cut Out, etc.,v.
1. **amputate**—cut off; cut parts from
2. **bisect**—cut in half; cut through the center of; cut into two equal parts
3. **bob**—cut short (hair, a tail, etc.)
4. **carve**—cut; cut artistically; cut into slices
5. **chine**—cut through the backbone
6. **chip**—cut off in small, thin pieces; cut, chop, or break off a piece or part of; cut or chop with, or as if with, a chisel, ax, etc.
7. **chisel**—cut with a chisel or other cutting tool
8. **chop**—cut by repeatedly hitting with a sharp instrument; cut and separate by a stroke of an ax or similar instrument
9. **cleave, rive**—cut along a natural line of division; cut apart with a single blow; sever by, or as if by, splitting
10. **clip**—cut; cut short; trim
11. **crop**—cut or clip the tops or tips of; cut off short
12. **decollate**—sever at the neck
13. **decussate**—cut in the form of an X
14. **dice**—cut into small cubes
15. **dichotomize**—cut into two parts
16. **dirk**—cut with a dagger
17. **disembowel**—cut out the viscera or bowels of, as in cleaning a chicken, or as in killing someone
18. **dissect**—cut apart or into its various parts
19. **dock**—cut off the end of (most commonly in reference to the tails of animals, or to wages or salary)
20. **excide, excind, excise, exscind, exsect**—cut out
21. **gash**—cut; cut deeply; make a deep and long cut in
22. **guillotine**—cut; cut short
23. **hack**—cut roughly or unevenly
24. **hackle**—cut roughly
25. **hew**—cut into shape with a sharp instrument
26. **incise**—cut into; cut into with a sharp instrument
27. **intersect**—cut across
28. **knife**—cut or stab with a knife, dagger, or other cutting instrument
29. **lance**—cut open
30. **lop**—cut or trim off (that which is in excess), literally or figuratively
31. **mangle**—cut violently and with continuous blows
32. **mince**—chop into fine pieces
33. **mow**—cut down (as grass, or as if what is being cut is grass)
34. **mutilate**—cut off a limb or a bodily or other essential part of
35. **nip off**—snip off
36. **notch**—make a V-shaped cut in
37. **pare**—cut or shave off the surface, skin, or outside of
38. **pierce**—cut through with, or as if with, a pointed instrument; stab
39. **plow, plough**—cut through the surface of
40. **poll, pollard**—cut off; cut short or clip the hair, horns, wool, etc., of; cut short or off the foliage and branches of (a plant or tree)
41. **prune**—cut off (what is in excess, unnecessary, or superfluous); trim
42. **rabbet**—cut a groove in the surface of

43. **raze**—shave off
44. **rend**—split
45. **retrench**—cut away; cut down; cut off
46. **rough-hew**—hew roughly, as wood, rock, etc., without finishing or smoothing
47. **saw**—cut with, or as if with, a saw or other toothed implement
48. **scarify**—make slight cuts in (the skin)
49. **scotch**—cut; cut the surface of; gash
50. **sculpt**—cut or carve out of stone, metal, wood, etc.
51. **section**—cut; cut into parts or portions
52. **sever**—cut off; cut open
53. **shave**—cut into very thin slices; cut hair from with a razor
54. **shear**—cut; cut with scissors; cut the wool or fleece of; cut close; cut off
55. **shred**—cut into strips or pieces
56. **skive**—cut (leather) into layers; cut off (leather or rubber) in thin layers; shave off in thin layers
57. **slash**—cut with long, sweeping strokes
58. **slice**—cut up into shares, portions, or flat pieces
59. **slip**—cut a branch or branches from (a plant) to grow new plants
60. **slit**—cut down the length of; cut with a long incision; make a straight cut in
61. **slot**—cut a narrow opening in
62. **snip**—cut suddenly; cut with small, quick strokes of a scissors
63. **split**—cleave lengthwise
64. **stab**—cut through or into with a pointed weapon
65. **transect**—cut across
66. **trench**—make a deep cut in
67. **trim**—cut away unneeded parts from
68. **trisect**—cut into three equal parts
69. **truncate**—cut off; cut short
70. **whittle**—cut shavings or small pieces from (wood, etc.) to shape into something; carve

2. Act or Process of Cutting,n. *From Sec. 1:* amputation, bisection, cleavage, decollation, decussation, dichotomy, disembowelment, dissection; dockage (of wages); excision, exsection, guillotinade, incision, intersection, mutilation, retrenchment, scarification, sculpture, section, severance, shave, transection, trisection, truncation; *Also:*
1. **abscission**—act of cutting off
2. **fission**—a splitting of the nucleus of the atom; a splitting or cutting into parts
3. **scission**—act of cutting or splitting

3. A Cut,n. *From Sec. 1:* bob, chip, chop, clip, dichotomy, gash, hack, incision, intersection, nip, notch, pierce, rent, scarification, slash, slit, slot, snip, split, stab, trench, trim, whittle

4. State of Being Cut,n. *From Sec. 1:* cleavage, dichotomy; *From Sec. 2:* abscission, scission

5. Cutter, i.e, One Who Cuts,n. *From Sec. 1:* carver, chopper, dissector, sculptor, shaver, skiver, whittler

6. Cutting,adj. *From Sec. 1:* dichotomous, dissective, incisive, intersectant

7. Cut,adj. *From Sec. 1:* amputated, bisected, bobbed, etc.; cleft or cloven (from *cleave*); riven, decussate, dichotomous, hewn, mown, rent, rough-hewn, sawn, sectional, shaven; *Also:*
1. **bifid, bifidate**—cut into two equal lobes or parts
2. **décolleté**—cut low in the neck (of a dress, etc.)
3. **multifid**—cut into many parts or divisions

8. A Cutting, i.e., That Which Is Cut or Cut Off,n. *From Sec. 1:* carving, chip, chop, clipping, paring, section, shaving, shred, slice, slip, trimming, whittling; *Also:* 1. **splinter**—piece cut, chopped, or chiseled off

9. Cutter, i.e., **Cutting Instrument,**n. *From Sec. 1:* carver, chisel, chopper, cleaver, clipper or clippers, dicer, knife, mower, nippers, paring knife; plow or plough (agricultural); pruning shears, razor, saw, shears, shredder, skiver, slicer, whittling knife; *Also:*
1. **ax, axe**—cutting or chopping instrument with a bladed head on a handle
2. **bolo**—large Philippine knife
3. **bowie knife**—long hunting knife
4. **coping saw**—saw used to cut curves
5. **dagger**—short, pointed instrument for thrusting and stabbing
6. **file**—metal tool with small teeth on the surface, for cutting, shaping, etc.
7. **hack saw**—saw used for cutting metal
8. **machete**—large, heavy knife used in tropical climates to cut sugar cane, cut away underbrush, etc.
9. **rasp**—coarse file
10. **scissors**—cutting tool of two interacting blades
11. **scythe**—instrument for cutting grass or grain by hand
12. **shears**—scissors
13. **sickle**—short implement with a curved blade used to cut grass, weeds, etc.
14. **snickersnee**—knife used as a weapon
15. **spear**—long instrument with a sharp, pointed head or end used for throwing or thrusting
16. **sword**—cutting weapon of various kinds, with a sharp, long blade and a short handle
17. **yataghan, yatagan**—Mohammedan long knife

10. Edged Cutting Instruments or Implements, Esp. Those Used in Eating: cutlery,n.

11. Cutting Part of an Instrument or Weapon: blade,n.

12. Person Who Makes, Sells, and Repairs Knives, Scissors, and Other Cutting Instruments: cutler,n.

13. Ax,n.
1. **adz, adze**—kind of ax
2. **battle-ax, battle-axe**—ax used as a weapon of war
3. **hatchet**—small ax for use by one hand
4. **mattock**—instrument shaped like a pick, with one broad end, for loosening the soil in digging
5. **pick**—curved hand ax, pointed at one or both ends, for loosening the soil in digging
6. **pickax, pickaxe**—pick
7. **tomahawk**—light ax used by American Indians

14. Dagger,n.
1. **bayonet**—dagger fitting at the end of a rifle
2. **couteau (French)**—two-edged dagger
3. **creese**—Malayan dagger with a curvy blade
4. **dirk**—dagger
5. **poniard**—kind of dagger
6. **stiletto**—kind of dagger with a thin blade

15. Spear,n.
1. **assagai, assegai**—slender spear, made of hard wood and with an iron tip, used by tribes in South Africa either to throw or stab; light javelin
2. **dart**—short spear; sharp-pointed missile of any sort
3. **javelin**—light spear for hurling at game or adversaries
4. **lance**—long spear
5. **pike**—wooden spear with a metal head
6. **shaft**—spear
7. **trident**—three-pronged spear

16. Stem of a Spear: shaft,n.

17. Sword,n.
1. **blade**—sword

2. **broadsword**—flat, broad, and straight sword
3. **cutlass**—short, heavy, curving sword
4. **épée**—sword with a point but a dull edge, used in dueling or fencing
5. **Excalibur**—King Arthur's magic sword
6. **foil**—long, narrow sword with an unsharpened point used in fencing
7. **rapier**—two-edged sword
8. **saber, sabre**—sword with a curved blade
9. **scimitar, scimiter**—saber used by Turks, Mohammedans, etc.
10. **yataghan, yatagan**—Mohammedan short saber

18. Weaker Part of a Sword Blade: foible,n.

19. Capable of Being Cut,adj.
1. **fissile**—capable of being cut in the direction of the grain (of wood), or along natural lines of splitting (of crystals)
2. **scissile**—lending itself to smooth cutting or easy splitting
3. **sectile**—capable of being smoothly cut

20. Adapted for Cutting: incisive, incisory, adj. (of teeth, etc.)

21. Appearing as if Neatly Cut by a Chisel: chiseled,adj.

22. To Pierce,v.
1. **bayonet**—pierce with a bayonet
2. **cleave**—pierce
3. **dirk**—stab with a dagger
4. **impale**—pierce with anything pointed
5. **knife**—pierce
6. **lance**—pierce
7. **lancinate**—pierce sharply
8. **penetrate**—pierce; pierce and go through
9. **percolate**—penetrate
10. **perforate**—pierce through, or through the surface of
11. **permeate**—penetrate
12. **pink**—pierce the surface of with, or as if with, a pointed instrument
13. **prick**—pierce slightly
14. **prong**—pierce or stab with something pointed
15. **puncture**—pierce with, or as if with, a point or pointed instrument
16. **spear**—pierce with, or as if with, a spear
17. **spike**—pierce with something containing a long, sharp point, or with a long, pointed nail
18. **spit**—pierce with a long rod; impale
19. **stab**—pierce; pierce with a pointed instrument; pierce suddenly and sharply
20. **stick**—pierce with a pointed instrument
21. **sting**—pierce slightly; pierce slightly with a point
22. **thrust**—pierce; stab
23. **transfix**—pierce; pierce through
24. **transpierce**—pierce; pierce through; pierce and go through

23. A Piercing,n. *From Sec. 22:* cleavage, impalement, lancination, penetration, percolation, perforation, permeation, pink, prick, puncture, stab, sting, thrust, transfixion or transfixation; *Also:* 1. **acupuncture**—a piercing of bodily tissue

24. State of Being Pierced,n. *From Sec. 22:* impalement, penetration, perforation, permeation, puncture, transfixion or transfixation

25. Piercing,adj. *From Sec. 22:* penetrative, permeant or permeative (penetrativeness, permeance,n.) ; *Also:*
1. **cutting**—piercing
2. **pervious**—penetrating
3. **pointed**—penetrating, figuratively—of language, etc. (pointedness,n.)
4. **pungent**—sharply piercing, figuratively—of flavors, smells, and other abstractions (pungency,n.)
5. **searching**—figuratively piercing or penetrating (of a glance, examination, etc.)
6. **shrill**—high-pitched and piercing, or so

high-pitched as to pierce figuratively the eardrums—of sound (shrillness,n.)

26. Capable of Being Pierced,adj. *From Sec. 22:* penetrable, permeable, puncturable; *Also:*
1. **pervious**—capable of being pierced or penetrated

27. Incapable of Being Pierced,adj. *From Sec. 26:* impenetrable, impermeable, punctureproof, impervious; *Also:* 1. **adamantine**—impenetrable

28. Pierced: cleft, cloven, perforate,adj.

29. Not Pierced: imperforate,adj.

30. To Scratch,v.
1. **claw**—scratch, or scratch at, with the nails
2. **scarify**—scratch (the skin) on the surface (scarification,n.)
3. **scrabble**—scratch about with the hands or feet, often searching for something (scrabble,n.)

31. A Scratch: claw mark, scarification,n.

32. Habituated to Scratching the Ground for Food: rasorial,adj. (of animals)

333. STING

1. To Sting (Someone),v.
1. **bite**—sting
2. **prick**—sting; sting sharply
3. **prickle**—sting sharply
4. **smart**—sting
5. **urticate**—sting with, or as if with, a nettle or nettles (urtication,n.)

2. To Sting, i.e., Feel a Stinging Sensation, v. *From Sec. 1:* prickle, smart

3. A Sting; A Sensation of Stinging,n. *From Sec. 1:* bite, prick; prickle, prickling, or prickliness; smart or smarting, urtication

4. Stinging,adj. *From Sec. 1:* biting, pricking, prickly or prickling, smarting, urticant; *Also:*
1. **acanthaceous**—prickly (of a plant)
2. **acid**—stinging (acidity, acidness,n.)
3. **aculeate**—stinging
4. **bitter**—of language, stinging (bitterness, n.)
5. **peppery**—of words or language, stinging (pepperiness,n.)
6. **pungent**—of language, stinging (pungency,n.)
7. **sharp**—stinging (sharpness,n.)

5. Substance That Stings: urticant,n.

6. Adapted for Stinging: urticant,adj. (of insects, etc.)

334. SHARPNESS

1. Sharp,adj.
1. **acid**—sharp; sharp in language or temper (acidity, acidness,n.)
2. **acuate**—sharp; having a sharp point
3. **aculeate**—full of sharp prickles
4. **acuminate**—ending in a point (biology)
5. **acute**—sharp; sharp and sudden; sharp and severe (acuteness, acuity,n.)
6. **barbed**—full of sharp points or prickles; sharp in language
7. **biting**—sharp (of language, the wind, etc.)
8. **corrosive**—sharp, literally or figuratively (corrosiveness,n.)
9. **cultrate**—sharp-edged
10. **cutting**—sharp
11. **echinated**—set with sharp prickles, as on a hedgehog
12. **edged**—having a sharp edge
13. **excruciating**—so sharp as to be intensely painful or torturous
14. **incisive**—sharp; trenchant (incisiveness, incision,n.)
15. **keen**—sharp, literally or figuratively (keenness,n.)
16. **mucronate**—ending in a sharp point
17. **muricate**—possessing sharp points
18. **prickly**—sharp and stinging; having sharp points (prickliness,n.)
19. **shrill**—sharp in sound (shrillness,n.)
20. **splintery**—full of sharp edges (splinteriness,n.)
21. **trenchant**—figuratively sharp—of reasoning, thinking, etc. (trenchancy,n.)
22. **vitriolic**—sharp (of language)

2. To Sharpen,v.
1. **acuminate**—make sharp or keen
2. **hone**—sharpen on a whetstone
3. **strop**—sharpen (a razor) on a strap
4. **whet**—sharpen, literally or figuratively

3. Implement for Sharpening,n.
1. **hone**—whetstone for sharpening razors
2. **strop**—strap for sharpening razors
3. **whetstone**—stone for sharpening knives and other tools

335. A POINT

1. Point; Pointed End; Pointed Part,n.
1. **apex**—point; pointed end; highest point
2. **barb**—point, or pointed part, projecting back from a main point; thorn
3. **cusp**—pointed end
4. **fang**—pointed part
5. **jag**—sharp point
6. **neb**—pointed end; point of a pen
7. **nib**—pointed part; pointed end; point of a pen
8. **peak**—apex
9. **pen point**—point of a pen
10. **pike**—point; spike
11. **pricket**—sharp metal point on which to stick a candle
12. **prickle**—sharp point; sharp-pointed process on a plant
13. **prong**—pointed, projecting part; pointed end; point of a fork
14. **quill**—stiff, sharp spine, as on a porcupine
15. **spike**—sharp-pointed end, part, or piece; sharp-pointed piece of metal
16. **spine**—pointed projection on something; pointy process or projection on a plant or on an animal's body; thorn
17. **spire**—sharp pointed end
18. **taper**—spire
19. **thorn**—sharp point; pointed growth on a plant
20. **tine**—sharp, projecting point; pointed, projecting part of an antler; point of a fork
21. **tip**—pointed end
22. **vertex**—point opposite the base of a pyramid or triangle; apex (vertices,pl.n. vertical,adj.)
23. **wedge**—something that tapers to a point

2. Pointed; Pointy,adj. *From Sec. 1:* apical, barbed, cuspate or cuspidate, jagged or jaggy, peaked, prickly, pronged, spiny, spired, tapered or tapering, thorny, tined, tipped; *Also:*
1. **acanthoid**—resembling a prickle or spine
2. **acerate, acerose**—having a sharp point, as on a needle
3. **acuate**—pointed
4. **aculeate**—full of sharp points or prickles
5. **acuminate**—pointed; tapering to a point (biology)
6. **acute**—having a sharp point
7. **bicuspid**—having, or ending, in two points
8. **echinated**—set with sharp prickles, as on a hedgehog
9. **hispid**—covered with small spines
10. **mucronate**—with, or ending in, a sharp point
11. **multifid**—having many points or prongs

12. **muricate**—having sharp points
13. **tricuspidate**—three-pointed
14. **trident, tridentate**—three-pointed
15. **trifid**—three-pointed;   having   three prongs

3. To Come to a Point: taper,v.

4. Becoming Spiny or Thorny: spinescent, spinulescent,adj.

5. Pert. to a Mathematical Point: punctual, adj.

336. DULLNESS

1. Dull or Dulled, i.e., Not Sharp,adj.
1. **blunt, blunted**—having a dull edge; with its edge dulled; not sharp (all literally or figurative)
2. **deadened**—dull or dulled (often figurative)
3. **obtuse**—not sharp or acute; not sharp, i.e., greater than 90° but less than 180° (of angles) ; with its sharpness reduced, esp. figuratively, as of the mind or senses; blunt

2. To Dull,v. *From Sec. 1:* blunt, deaden, obtund

3. Causing to Be Dull,adj. *From Sec. 1:* obtundent

4. That Which Dulls,n. *From Sec. 1:* obtundent

337. TEAR

1. To Tear (Something),v.
1. **dilacerate**—tear to pieces
2. **discerp**—tear in pieces from the whole
3. **disembowel**—tear out the viscera or bowels of
4. **disject**—tear apart violently
5. **divulse**—tear apart; tear apart violently
6. **fray**—tear
7. **frazzle**—tear
8. **lacerate**—tear; tear open
9. **mangle**—tear violently and with repeated blows
10. **peel**—tear off the outer covering of
11. **rend**—tear apart violently
12. **rip**—tear forcibly
13. **rive**—tear apart
14. **shred**—tear into strips or pieces
15. **sunder**—tear apart
16. **tatter**—tear into pieces or shreds
17. **unsolder**—tear apart
18. **wrest**—tear away violently

2. To Tear, i.e., Become Torn,v. *From Sec. 1:* fray, frazzle, rip, shred, tatter

3. A Tearing,n. *From Sec. 1:* dilaceration, disembowelment, disjection, divulsion, laceration, sunderance; *Also:* **1. avulsion**—a forcible tearing off

4. A Tear,n. *From Sec. 1:* fray, frazzle, rent, rip, tatter

5. Part Torn Off,n. *From Sec. 1:* shred, tatter; *From Sec. 3:* avulsion

6. Tearing,adj. *From Sec. 1:* disjective, divulsive, lacerative

7. With Torn Edges or Surface: ragged,adj. (raggedness,n.)

8. Looking Torn or Tattered: shabby,adj. (shabbiness,n.)

9. Able to Be Torn Apart: discerpible, discerptible,adj.

338. BODY

1. The Body,n.
1. **person**—the body of a human being
2. **system**—the body in its entirety, from a physiological point of view

3. **tabernacle**—the body conceived as the temporary abode of the soul

2. Human Body, Exclusive of Head and Limbs: torso, trunk,n.

3. Small Area of the Body around Something: areola, areole,n. (areolar,adj.)

4. Figure of the Human Body, Used by Tailors, etc.: manikin, mannequin,n.

5. Main Body of Something: corpus,n.

6. A Legal Body: corporation,n. (corporate, corporative,adj.)

7. Pert. to, Descr. of, etc., the Body,adj.
1. **bodily**—pert. to, or descr. of, the body
2. **corporal**—affecting, descr. of, or pert. to, the body
3. **corporeal**—physical
4. **personal**—pert. to the body of a human being
5. **physical**—pert. to, or descr. of, the body (rather than the emotions, mind, etc.)
6. **psychosomatic**—pert. to both body and mind
7. **somatic**—pert. to, arising from, or affecting the body
8. **systemic**—pert. to the body from its physiological aspects

8. Pert. to, or Descr. of, the Appetites or Passions of the Body: carnal, fleshly, sensual, adj.

9. Bodily Structure, Shape, etc.,n.
1. **anatomy**—bodily structure of a person or animal (anatomical,adj.)
2. **constitution**—bodily organization (constitutional,adj.)
3. **figure**—bodily shape (more commonly applied to women)
4. **physique**—structure and appearance of the body (popularly in reference to a man)

10. Anatomy,n.
1. **anthropotomy, androtomy**—anatomy of the human body
2. **herpetotomy**—anatomy of reptiles
3. **hippotomy**—anatomy of the horse
4. **ichthyotomy**—anatomy of fishes
5. **ornithotomy**—anatomy of birds
6. **topology**—anatomy of a bodily region
7. **zootomy**—anatomy of animals

11. Descr. of Body Types,adj.
1. **asthenic**—descr. of a body type that is slight, slim, and slender in build, with little muscular development
2. **athletic**—descr. of a body type characterized by long arms and legs, strong muscles, and well-developed chest
3. **ectomorphic**—descr. of a frail, delicate, unmuscular body type
4. **endomorphic**—descr. of a body type characterized by well-developed visceral structures
5. **mesomorphic**—descr. of a body type characterized by hard, firm muscles, thick skin, and well-developed structures
6. **pituitary**—descr. of a body type characterized by long legs and arms, and generally large bones—believed caused by excessive secretion of the pituitary gland
7. **pyknic**—descr. of a round and fat body type

12. Person As to Body Type,n. *From Sec. 11:* asthenic, ectomorph, endomorph, mesomorph, pyknic

13. Having, or Having the Form of, a Body, adj.
1. **bodied**—having a body
2. **bodily**—having a body; having the form of a body
3. **corporeal**—consisting of, or having, a physical body (corporeality, corporealness, corporeity, corporality,n.)
4. **embodied**—having, or being represented

in, the form of a body—said of abstract qualities, as *embodied virtue, courage*, etc. (embodiment,n.)

5. **incarnate, incarnated**—in, or taking on, the form of the human or other body (incarnation,n.)
6. **material**—having a bodily form (materiality,n.)
7. **personified**—embodied
8. **physical**—material

14. That Which Is in the Form of a Body,n. *From Sec. 13:* embodiment, incarnation, personification; *Also:*
1. avatar—incarnation; embodiment
2. soul—embodiment

15. To Give Bodily Form to, or to Represent in Bodily Form,v. *From Sec. 13:* embody, incarnate, personify (embodiment, incarnation, personification,n.)

16. Lacking in a Body or in Bodily Form, adj.
1. **asomatous**—immaterial
2. **bodiless**—having no body (bodilessness, n.)
3. **discarnate**—immaterial
4. **disembodied**—lacking in a physical body (disembodiment,n.)
5. **immaterial**—having no physical body (immateriality,n.)
6. **incorporate**—incorporeal
7. **incorporeal**—having no physical body (incorporeality, incorporeity,n.)
8. **trunkless**—lacking the main part of the body

17. To Deprive of a Body or Bodily Existence: discarnate, disembody,v. (discarnation, disembodiment,n.)

18. Science of the Body,n.
1. **anatomy**—science of the physical structure of the body (anatomist,n. anatomic, anatomical,adj.)
2. **anthropology**—science of human development, physical and otherwise (anthropologist,n. anthropological,adj.)
3. **anthropometry**—science of bodily measurements of a human being (anthropometric, anthropometrical,adj.)
4. **anthroposomatology**—science that treats of the development, structure, and functions of the human body (anthroposomatologist,n. anthroposomatological,adj.)
5. **physiology**—science of the functions of the body (physiologist,n. physiological, adj.)
6. **somatology**—branch of anthropology that investigates comparative development, etc., of the human body (somatologist,n. somatological,adj.)

339. ARM

1. Arm: limb, member,n.
2. Pert. to the Arm: brachial,adj.
3. Pert. to the Armpit: axillary,adj.
4. Part of the Arm between the Elbow and the Wrist: forearm,n.
5. Pert. to the Inside of the Forearm: ulnar, adj.
6. Pert. to the Shoulder: humeral, scapular, adj.
7. Shoulder Blade: scapular, scapulary,n. (scapular, scapulary,adj.)
8. The Elbow: ancon,n.

340. WING

1. Wing: pennon, penna, pinion,n.
2. Pert. to a Wing or Wings: alar, alary,adj.
3. Resembling a Wing: aliform,adj.

4. Having Wings; Winged,adj.
1. **alar**—winged
2. **alate, alated**—winged; having wings or winglike appendages
3. **dipterous**—having two wings or winglike parts
4. **micropterous**—having small or rudimentary wings (micropterism,n.)
5. **pennate**—having wings
6. **tetrapterous**—having four wings

5. Having the Shape of a Wing: pennate, adj.

6. Wingless: apterous,adj.

341. FEATHER

1. Feather,n.
1. **penna**—feather
2. **pinfeather**—young feather; feather just piercing the skin
3. **pinion**—feather; flight feather of a bird
4. **pinna**—feather
5. **plume**—feather; large, long, and ornamental feather; feather worn as a decoration
6. **plumelet**—small plume
7. **plumule**—down feather
8. **quill**—large, stiff feather
9. **vibrissa**—long feather growing along the side of the mouth of certain birds (vibrissae,pl.)

2. Feathers; Group of Feathers,n.
1. **crest**—tuft of feathers on the head of a bird; plume on a helmet
2. **down**—covering of soft feathers
3. **fluff**—plumage between the thighs and on the abdomen of domestic birds
4. **hackles**—long, narrow neck feathers of certain birds and domestic fowls
5. **panache**—tuft of feathers worn as a decoration, usually on a helmet
6. **plumage**—bird's coat of feathers; any coat of feathers
7. **plume**—tuft of feathers worn as a decoration
8. **plumelet**—small plume
9. **ruff**—fringe of feathers on the neck of some birds
10. **topknot**—crown of feathers at the top of the head
11. **tuft**—bunch of feathers joined at one end

3. Feathered,adj. *From Sec. 2:* crested, downy, plumed, ruffed, tufted; *Also:*
1. **fledged**—feathered; having the feathers needed for flight
2. **fledgy**—feathered; covered with feathers or down
3. **full-fledged**—feathered with the complete plumage
4. **pennate**—feathered
5. **plumose**—feathered

4. Feathery; Resembling Feathers or a Feather: downy, featherlike, fledgy, fluffy, pennate, penniform, pinnate, plumate, plumelike, plumose,adj.

5. To Be or Become Feathery: feather,v.

6. Certain Parts of a Feather,n.
1. **barb**—side branch of a feather
2. **barbicel**—side branch of a barbule
3. **barbule**—side branch of a barb
4. **barrel**—quill
5. **calamus**—quill
6. **filament**—side branch of a down feather
7. **fluff**—downy part of a feather near or at the base
8. **pinnula**—barb
9. **quill**—that part of the stem of a feather that is nearer to the body; hollow stem of a large, stiff feather
10. **rachis**—that part of the stem of a feather farther from the body

11. shaft—stem of a feather
12. vane—flat, soft part of a feather
7. **Part or Organ Resembling the Barb of a Feather:** pinnule, pinnula,n. (pinnular,adj.)
8. **To Grow Feathers Needed for Flying:** fledge,v.
9. **To Grow Feathers:** feather,v.
10. **To Put Feathers on (Something),**v.
   1. feather—clothe, cover, or provide with feathers
   2. fledge—put feathers on; put feathers on (an arrow)
   3. fletch—put feathers or a feather on (an arrow)
   4. plume—ornament, cover, or furnish with feathers
11. **To Smooth or Trim (the Feathers) with the Beak:** plume, preen,v.
12. **To Remove the Feathers from,**v.
   1. deplume—strip the feathers from (deplumation,n.)
   2. dress—pull feathers from (poultry) as a preparation for marketing or cooking
   3. pinion—cut off the flight feathers (from a bird's wing)
13. **To Shed the Feathers Preparatory to Growing New Ones:** molt, moult,v.
14. **Not Yet Having Developed Feathers:** callow, featherless, squab, unfledged,adj.

342. FIN

1. **Fin:** pinna,n.
2. **Small, Finlike Appendage of Certain Fishes:** finlet, pinnule, pinnula,n. (pinnular, adj.)
3. **Part or Organ Resembling a Fin:** pinnule, pinnula,n. (pinnular,adj.)
4. **Having Pinnules:** pinnulate, pinnulated, adj.

343. HAND

1. **Hand, i.e., the End of a Limb:** extremity, n.
2. **The Clenched Hand:** fist,n.
3. **Pert. to the Hand:** chiral, manual,adj.
4. **Pert. to the Right Hand:** dexter,adj.
5. **Inside of the Hand:** palm, thenar,n.
6. **Pert. to the Palm of the Hand:** palmar, thenar, volar,adj.
7. **Having Hands,**adj.
   1. bimanous—two-handed
   2. Briarean—many-handed
   3. quadrumanous—four-handed
8. **Right-Handed:** dexterical, dexterous, dextral, dextromanual, dextrous,adj.
9. **Right-Handedness:** dextrality,n.
10. **Preference for Using the Right Hand:** dextrality,n.
11. **Left-Handed:** sinistral, sinistromanual, sinistrous,adj.
12. **Left-Handedness:** mancinism, sinistrality, n.
13. **Left-Handed Person,**n.
   1. dextrosinistral—one who is naturally left-handed but has been trained to use the right hand in writing (dextrosinistral, adj.)
   2. southpaw—one who is left-handed, esp. in a sport in which the arm is used to throw, hit, etc. (colloq.)
14. **Preferring to Use the Left Hand:** sinistrodextral,adj.
15. **Able to Use Both Hands Equally Well:** ambidextrous,adj. (ambidexterity,n.)

16. **Capable of Distinguishing the Right Hand from the Left Hand:** chirognostic,adj.
17. **Done with, or Requiring, Two Hands:** bimanual,adj.
18. **Care of the Hands and Fingernails:** manicure,n. (manicure,v. manicurist,n.)
19. **Study of the Hand:** chirology,n. (chirologist,n. chirological,adj.)
20. **Increase in Hand Size:** chiromegaly,n. (medical)
21. **The Wrist:** carpus,n. (carpal,adj.)
22. **Organ of Touch of an Insect or Other Creature:** antenna (antennae,pl.), feeler, tentacle,n. (tentacular,adj.)

344. FINGER; TOE

1. **A Finger or Toe:** digit,n.
2. **Child's Toes:** pettitoes,n.
3. **The Thumb:** pollex,n.
4. **Elevation at the Base of the Thumb:** thenar,n.
5. **In Reference to Fingers or Toes,**adj.
   1. dactylate—pert. to the fingers
   2. dactyloid—resembling a finger
   3. digital—pert. to the fingers or toes; done by the fingers
   4. digitate—resembling fingers
6. **Fingered; Toed,**adj.
   1. artiodactyl,   artiodactylous—having either two or four toes, as the pig, deer, etc.
   2. digitate—having fingers
   3. isodactylous—having all fingers or toes of equal length
   4. macrodactylous—having   abnormally large fingers or toes
   5. microdactylous—having   abnormally small fingers or toes
   6. monodactylous—having only one finger or toe on each hand or foot
   7. pigeon-toed—with the toes turned inward
   8. polydactyl, polydactyle, polydactylous —having more than the normal number of fingers or toes
   9. prestidigital—fast- or light-fingered
   10. syndactyle—having two or more fingers or toes completely or partially fused
   11. totipalmate—having all four toes webbed, as certain birds
7. **Condition of Fingers or Toes,**n. *From Sec. 6:* artiodactylism, isodactylism, macrodactylia or macrodactylism, microdactylia or microdactylism, monodactylism, polydactylism, syndactylism, totipalmation; *Also:* 1. dactylion—syndactylism
8. **Reflexive Extension of the Great Toe Combined with Fanning of the Other Toes when the Sole of the Foot is Excited, Tickled, etc.:** Babinski reflex,n.
9. **Fingerprint:** dactylogram, dactylograph, whorl,n.
10. **Fingerprint Science, Classification, etc.,** n.
   1. dactylography—science of identification by means of fingerprints
   2. dactyloscopy—classification of fingerprints for purposes of identification; identification through fingerprints (dactyloscopic,adj.)
11. **Claw; Nail,**n.
   1. chela—claw of spiders, scorpions, crabs, lobsters, etc.
   2. pounce—claw of a bird of prey
   3. talon—claw of a bird of prey; claw of an animal

4. unguis—claw or nail on a mammal's finger or toe
5. ungula—claw; nail
12. Having Claws,adj.
   1. chelate—having claws
   2. cheliferous—having a claw or claws (of spiders, scorpions, crabs, lobsters, etc.)
   3. clawed—having claws
   4. ungual—having a claw or claws
13. Pert. to, or Resembling, a Claw: ungual, adj.

345. LEG

1. Leg: limb, shank,n.
2. Wooden Leg: stump,n.
3. Person's Legs: underpinnings,n.
4. Selected Leg Parts,n.
   1. calf—back of the human leg below the knee
   2. shank—part of the leg between the knee and ankle; lower leg; any leglike part
   3. shin—front of the leg below the knee
   4. thigh—part of the leg above the knee
5. Pert. to the Leg: crural,adj.
6. Pert. to the Calf of the Leg: sural,adj.
7. Legged,adj.
   1. bandy-legged—having crooked legs; bowlegged
   2. biped—having two legs (biped,n.)
   3. bowlegged—with the legs curved outward
   4. knock-kneed—with the legs curved inward
   5. leggy—having long or conspicuous legs
   6. spindle-legged, spindle-shanked—having long, slim legs
   7. tripodal, tripodic—three-legged
   8. valgus—bowlegged; knock-kneed
   9. varus—bowlegged
8. Condition of Legs,n. From Sec. 7: bandyleg, bowleg, knock-knee, valgus
9. Bowlegged or Knock-Kneed Person: valgus,n.
10. With One Leg on Each Side; With the Legs Far Apart: astraddle, astride, straddle, straddle-fashion, straddle-legged, straddleways, straddlewise,adv.
11. With the Legs Crossed: cross-legged,adj. or adv.
12. Appendage; Limb,n.
   1. appendicle—small appendage (appendicular,adj.)
   2. appendix—appendage (appendicular,adj.)
   3. extremity—limb, or end of a limb, of the body
   4. process—appendage
   5. tentacle—slim, flexible appendage of an animal, esp. an invertebrate (tentacular, adj.)
13. Having Two Long, Slender Appendages: biflagellate,adj.
14. Pert. to the Thigh: crural, femoral,adj.
15. Hip: coxa, haunch,n.
16. Hip Joint: coxa,n.
17. Part around the Hip: haunch,n.
18. Pert. to the Hip or the Region of the Hip; in the Hip Region: sciatic,adj.
19. Back and Side Parts, or Region between the Hipbone and the So-Called False Ribs, in a Human Being or Four-Footed Animal: loins,n.
20. Pert. to the Loins: lumbar,adj.
21. Neuralgia, or Any Other Affliction, of the Hip or Hip Region: sciatica,n.
22. Pert. to the Knee: genual,adj.
23. Kneecap: patella,n. (patellar,adj.)

24. Ankle: talus, tarsus,n. (talaric, tarsal, adj.)
25. Anklebone: astragal, talus,n. (talaric, adj.)

346. FOOT

1. Foot,n.
   1. extremity—foot, i.e., end of the leg
   2. forefoot—front foot of an animal
   3. pad—foot of certain animals, as the fox, hare, otter, wolf, etc.
   4. hind foot—back foot of an animal
   5. hoof—foot, or the horny covering on the foot, of certain animals, as horses, donkeys, cattle, deer, hogs, etc.
   6. paw—foot of an animal; such a foot with claws
   7. trotter—foot of an animal, esp. that of a pig or sheep when used as food
2. To Beat, Strike, or Scrape (a Place) with Its Foot or Feet; To Beat, Strike, or Scrape the Ground with Its Foot or Feet—of an Animal: paw,v.
3. Footlike Process of Single-Cell Animals Such as the Amoeba, Used for Locomotion: pseudopod, pseudopodium,n. (pseudopodia, pl.n. pseudopodal,adj.)
4. Hoof: unguis, ungula,n. (ungual, ungular, adj.)
5. Resembling a Hoof: ungual, ungular,adj.
6. Having a Hoof or Hoofs: hoofed, ungual, ungulate,adj.
7. Child's Feet: pettitoes,n.
8. Bottom of the Foot: sole,n.
9. Pert. to the Foot: pedal, podal,adj.
10. Pert. to the Sole of the Foot: plantar, volar,adj.
11. Having Feet; Descr. of the Condition of the Foot or Feet,adj.
   1. biped—two-footed
   2. chiropodous—having feet that function as hands in grasping (of certain animals)
   3. cloven-footed, bisulcate, cloven-hoofed —having split or divided feet or hoofs
   4. clubfooted, taliped—having a congenital deformity in which the forefoot is inverted and turned
   5. flat-footed, splayfooted—having the arch of the foot flattened
   6. lame, crippled, halt—disabled in the foot (or leg) so that walking is difficult, awkward, or impossible
   7. megapod—having large feet
   8. micropod, micropodous—having unusually small feet
   9. multiped—having many feet
   10. pedate—having a foot or feet
   11. pedigerous—having feet
   12. pigeon-toed—having the feet (or toes) turned inward
   13. quadruped—four-footed
   14. spavined—lame (of horses)
   15. splayfooted—having broad, flat feet turned somewhat outward
   16. tripedal, tripodal, tripodic—three-footed
12. Condition of the Foot or Feet,n. From Sec. 11: clubfoot or talipes; flatfoot, flatfootedness, flat feet, or splayfoot; lameness splayfoot; Also:
   1. stringhalt—lameness in horses, resulting from muscular spasms in the back legs
   2. valgus—clubfoot; extreme flat-footedness, splayfoot
13. Creature or Person as to Feet,n. From Sec. 11: biped, cripple, multiped, quadruped
14. To Cause a Condition of the Feet,v From Sec. 11: cripple, lame
15. To Walk in a Lame Fashion: limp,v.

16. Without Feet: apodal,adj.

17. Care of the Feet, Esp. Trimming, Polishing, etc., the Toenails: pedicure,n.

18. To Give Such Care to (the Feet, Toenails, etc.): pedicure,v. (pedicurist,n.)

347. BELLY

1. Belly, Stomach, etc.,n.
1. abdomen—belly
2. craw—animal's stomach
3. crop—digestive organ in certain animals
4. maw—stomach
5. paunch—belly; stomach
6. pelvis—lower belly
7. potbelly, paunch—protuberant belly
8. venter—belly; stomach

2. Pert. to, or Descr. of, the Belly or Stomach,adj. *From Sec. 1:* abdominal, pelvic, potbellied, ventral; *Also:*
1. alvine—pert. to the belly
2. cardiac—pert. to the stomach, esp. that part into which the esophagus opens
3. gastric—pert. to the stomach
4. stomachic, stomachical—pert. to the stomach

3. Upon, or on Top of, the Stomach: epigastric,adj.

4. Pert. to the Cavity of the Abdomen: coeliac, celiac,adj.

5. Point on the Stomach Wall, below the Breastbone, Where a Blow Will Affect the Network of Nerves in the Upper Abdomen: solar plexus,n.

6. Tube Connecting the Mouth with the Stomach: esophagus, gullet,n. (esophageal, adj.)

7. Baglike Enlargement of the Gullet of Certain Birds, in Which Food Is Held and Partly Digested: craw, crop,n.

8. Similar Part of Certain Insects: craw,n.

9. Intestine; Intestines; Part of the Intestines,n.
1. anus—opening of the lower end of the rectum
2. appendix, vermiform appendix—narrow tube, with a blind end, extending from the caecum
3. bowels—intestines
4. caecum, cecum—first part of the large intestine into which the small intestine opens
5. colon—part of the large intestine from the caecum to the sigmoid flexure
6. duodenum—first part of the small intestine leading from the stomach
7. entrails—intestines; internal organs of the abdominal cavity; any internal organs
8. gut—intestine
9. guts—intestines; entrails
10. ileum—last part of the small intestine, following the jejunum
11. inwards, innards—entrails
12. jejunum—middle part of the small intestine
13. large intestine—lower part of the intestines
14. pylorus—opening from the stomach into the small intestine
15. rectum—final section of the large intestine
16. sigmoid flexure, sigmoid—S-shaped bend at the lower end of the colon just before the rectum
17. small intestine—upper part of the intestine
18. viscera—internal organs of the abdominal cavity

10. Intestinal, etc.,adj. *From Sec. 9:* anal, appendicial, appendiceal, caecal, colonic or colic, duodenal, ileac, jejunal, pyloric, rectal, sigmoid or sigmoidal, visceral; *Also:*
1. alvine—pert. to the intestines
2. enteric—pert. to the intestine
3. splanchnic—visceral

11. Tubal Passage from the Mouth to the Anus: alimentary canal, enteron,n. (enteric, adj.)

12. Inflammations or Disorders of a Visceral Organ or Part,n.
1. appendicitis—inflammation of the appendix
2. colitis—inflammation of the colon
3. enteritis—inflammation of the intestinal tract
4. gastritis—inflammation of the stomach or of its mucous lining
5. gastroenteritis—inflammation of the stomach and intestine
6. hemorrhoids—painful dilatation of the vein or veins at the anus (hemorrhoidal, adj.)
7. peritonitis—inflammation of the peritoneum, the membrane that surrounds the viscera
8. splenitis—inflammation of the spleen

13. Belly Button: navel, omphalos, umbilicus, n. (omphalic, umbilical or umbilicar,adj.)

14. Resembling a Belly Button: omphaloid, adj.

348. BUTTOCKS

1. The Buttocks: backside, behind, bottom, breech; bum (vulgar); can (slang); crupper; derrière (elegant); fanny (slang); fundament, posteriors; prat (slang); rear, rear end, rump, seat; tail (colloq.),n.

2. Horse's Buttocks: croup, crupper,n.

3. Buttocks of a Four-Footed Animal: croup,n.

4. Pert. to, or in the Region of, the Buttocks: gluteal, pygal,adj.

5. One of the Two Buttocks: cheek,n.

6. Having Beautiful Buttocks: callipygian, adj.

7. Having Excessively Fat Buttocks (Esp. of Females), as among the Hottentots: steatopygic, steatopygous,adj. (steatopygia, n.)

8. Region of the Body Including the Buttock, Hip, and Upper, or Fleshy, Part of the Thigh: haunch,n.

349. TAIL

1. Tail; Appendage Like a Tail: cauda,n.

2. Pert. to the Tail,adj.
1. caudal—pert. to a tail or tails; near or at the tail
2. cephalocaudal—pert. to head and tail

3. Having a Tail,adj.
1. caudate—having a tail or some appendage resembling a tail
2. crinite—having a hairy tail
3. longicaudal—having a long tail

4. Without a Tail: acaudal, anurous, excaudate, tailless,adj.

5. Toward the Tail or Tail End: caudad, caudalward,adv.

6. Fleshy Part of the Tail as Distinguished from the Hair or Fur: dock,n.

7. Part of the Tail Left after Cutting: dock, n.

8. End of the Tail in Certain Animals, esp. the Cow or Ox: switch,n.

350. SAC

1. Baglike Part of the Body,n.
1. **bladder**—membranous sac for fluids
2. **bursa**—sac; small sac between two movable parts of the body (bursate,adj.)
3. **cyst**—bladder; sac with a wall and containing fluid or other matter (cystic,adj.)
4. **follicle**—small sac (follicular, folliculate, adj.)
5. **marsupium**—external baglike part of an animal, such as a kangaroo or opossum, for carrying its young (marsupial,adj.)
6. **pouch**—marsupium
7. **sac**—baglike part of the body
8. **saccule**—little sac
9. **vesica**—bladder; urinary bladder (vesical, adj.)
10. **vesicle**—bladder; sac filled with fluid (vesicular,adj.)

2. Inflammation of the Bursa: bursitis,n.

3. Bladderlike: ampullaceous, utriculate,adj.

4. Pert. to the Gall Bladder: biliary, cystic, adj.

5. Selected Disorders of the Bladder,n.
1. **cystitis**—inflammation of the bladder
2. **cystocele**—hernia of the urinary bladder
3. **cystolithiasis**—a stone in the bladder

351. HEART

1. Heart Activity,n.
1. **diastole**—dilation of the heart (diastolic, adj.)
2. **palpitation**—abnormally rapid beating of the heart (palpitate,v.)
3. **systole**—contraction of the heart (systolic,adj.)
4. **tachycardia**—very rapid heartbeat (tachycardial,adj.)

2. Chamber of the Heart: auricle, ventricle, n.

3. Pert. to the Heart: cardiac,adj.

4. Located within the Heart: endocardial, intracardiac,adj.

5. Instrument for Heart Measurement,n.
1. **cardiograph**—instrument used to trace the motion and beat of the heart (cardiogram,n.)
2. **electrocardiograph**—cardiograph (electrocardiogram,n.)
3. **myocardiograph**—instrument for making tracings of heart action (myocardiogram, n.)

6. Selected Heart Disorders,n.
1. **angina pectoris**—heart disease causing severe pains and feelings of suffocation in the chest
2. **cardiac thrombosis**—formation of a blood clot in the heart
3. **carditis**—inflammation of the muscles of the heart wall
4. **coronary occlusion**—a stopping up of the branch of the arterial system that supplies blood to the heart muscle
5. **coronary thrombosis**—a clot of blood in the coronary arteries of the heart
6. **endocarditis**—inflammation of the membrane lining the heart cavities
7. **myocarditis**—carditis
8. **pericarditis**—inflammation of the membrane enclosing the heart

7. One Who Suffers from a Heart Disorder: cardiac,n.

8. The Pulse: sphygmus,n. (sphygmic,adj.)

9. Resembling the Pulse: sphygmoid,adj.

10. Instrument to Measure Pulse,n.
1. **sphygmograph**—instrument that records characteristics of the arterial pulse
2. **sphygmometer**—instrument for measuring strength of the pulse

352. BLOOD

1. Blood,n.
1. **clot**—soft mass of blood
2. **cruor**—clotted part of blood
3. **gore**—blood; clotted blood
4. **plasma**—fluid part of the blood

2. Certain Blood Organs, Parts, Elements, etc.,n.
1. **arteriole**—small artery (arteriolar,adj.)
2. **artery**—tube that carries the blood away from the heart (arterial,adj.)
3. **blood vessel**—any vessel or part (as an artery, vein, or capillary) by means of which blood circulates
4. **capillary**—very tiny blood vessel connecting arteries and veins (capillary,adj.)
5. **corpuscle**—blood cell, of which there are two types, red and white (corpuscular, adj.)
6. **erythrocyte**—red blood corpuscle (erythrocytic,adj.)
7. **hemoglobin**—important component of the red corpuscles
8. **leucocyte**—white blood corpuscle (leucocytic,adj.)
9. **metarteriole**—blood vessel intermediate in position and structure between an arteriole and a capillary
10. **phagocyte**—white blood corpuscle that destroys harmful substances in the blood (phagocytic,adj.)
11. **plexus**—network of blood vessels
12. **thrombin**—element in the blood that causes clotting
13. **vein**—tube that carries blood to the heart (venous,adj.)

3. Pert. to, Descr. of, or Having to Do with, Blood,n.
1. **bloody**—pert. to, containing, of the nature of, or stained by, blood (bloodiness, n.)
2. **hemal**—pert. to blood
3. **hematal**—pert. to the blood
4. **hematic**—pert. to the blood; of the color of blood; containing blood
5. **hematogenous**—producing blood; produced by the blood
6. **hematoid**—similar to blood
7. **hematose**—full of blood
8. **hemic**—pert. to the blood
9. **hemoid**—hematoid
10. **Rh positive, Rh negative**—descr. of blood that possesses a special factor (85 per cent of people are Rh positive; the remainder, Rh negative, will react adversely to a second transfusion of Rh-positive blood)
11. **sanguicolous**—living in the blood
12. **sanguiferous**—carrying or transmitting blood
13. **sanguine**—possessing an active circulation of blood
14. **sanguineous**—pert. to or containing blood
15. **sanguinolent**—containing blood
16. **sanguinous**—containing blood
17. **sanguivorous**—subsisting on blood
18. **thromboplastic**—pert. to blood-clotting; causing blood to clot faster
19. **venous**—descr. of the dark red blood found in veins (venosity,n.)

4. Bloody; Bloodied,adj.
1. **crimson**—bloody; sanguinary
2. **ensanguined**—bloodied (ensanguine,v.)
3. **gory**—covered with blood
4. **hematose**—bloody
5. **imbrued**—stained with blood (imbrue,v.)
6. **sanguinary**—bloody, i.e., pert. to, or attended by, the shedding of blood
7. **sanguine**—sanguinary
8. **sanguinolent**—tinged with blood

5. To Be, or Become, Suffused with Blood: mantle,v.

6. Action of the Blood,n.
1. **circulation**—movement of blood within the body, to and from the heart, through the veins and arteries, etc. (circulate,v. circulatory,adj.)
2. **clotting**—formation of a thickened mass of blood, either within the body or on exposure to air at an opening (clot,v.)
3. **coagulation**—changing of blood from its normal fluidity to a thickened mass on exposure to air at a small opening (coagulate,v.)
4. **hematosis**—formation of blood
5. **phagocytosis**—action or process by which the white blood corpuscles destroy harmful substances in the blood

7. To Draw or Let Blood,v.
1. **bleed**—draw or let blood, often for healing purposes
2. **cup**—draw blood to, or from, the surface of the body by suction
3. **leech**—draw or let blood by suction
4. **phlebotomize**—let blood flow by cutting into a vein

8. The Drawing or Letting of Blood,n. *From Sec. 7:* bleeding, cupping, phlebotomy; *Also:*
1. **venesection**—phlebotomy

9. Bloodletter,n. *From Sec. 7:* cupper, leech, phlebotomist

10. Bloodsucker,n.
1. **leech**—bloodsucking worm
2. **vampire**—bloodsucking bat; figuratively, bloodsucker; supernatural being that supposedly sucks the blood of sleeping people (vampirism,n.)

11. Bloodsucking, Like a Leech: sanguisugous,adj.

12. Transfer of Blood from the Veins or Arteries of One Person to Those of Another: transfusion,n. (transfuse,v.)

13. To Stop the Bleeding of: stanch,v.

14. Stopping the Flow of Blood,adj.
1. **hemostatic**—checking the flow or loss of blood by compressing the blood vessels
2. **styptic**—checking bleeding by contracting the blood vessels (stypsis,n.)

15. Agent That Checks Bleeding,n.
1. **hemostat**—device that checks bleeding by compressing a blood vessel
2. **styptic**—agent that checks bleeding, usually by causing contraction of the blood vessels
3. **tourniquet**—agent that checks bleeding by forcibly compressing a blood vessel, as a bandage twisted tightly, a pad pressed down by a screw, etc.

16. To Cut Off the Blood Supply from, by Pressing: strangulate,v. (strangulation,n. strangulative, strangulatory,adj.)

17. Warm-Blooded: hemathermal,adj.

18. Bloodless,adj.
1. **anemic**—deficient in hemoglobin and red blood cells (anemia,n.)
2. **exsanguine**—bloodless; anemic (exsanguinity,n.)
3. **pale**—bloodless, i.e., lacking in healthy color (pallor, paleness,n.)

19. Without Bloodshed: bloodless,adj.

20. Medical Instrument for Measuring the Blood Pressure in an Artery: sphygmomanometer,n.

21. Pert. to, Descr. of, or Relating to, Blood Vessels,adj.
1. **cirsoid**—varicose
2. **hemal, hematal**—pert. to blood vessels
3. **varicose**—descr. of blood vessels that are swollen, dilated, knotted, etc. (varicosity, n.)
4. **vascular**—pert. to, containing, etc., blood vessels or the blood-vessel system (vascularity,adj.)

5. **vasoconstrictor**—causing contraction of blood vessels (vasoconstrictor,n.)
6. **vasodilator**—causing dilation of blood vessels (vasodilator,n.)
7. **vasomotor**—regulating the size, tension, etc., of blood vessels

22. Blood-Vessel System of the Body: circulatory system,n.

23. Selected Disorders of the Blood,n.
1. **anemia**—condition in which there is a deficiency of the red corpuscles of the blood
2. **anoxemia**—deficient oxygenation of the blood
3. **chlorosis**—disease of young women, characterized by a pronounced reduction of hemoglobin in the blood, greenish or yellowish-gray color of the skin, menstrual disorders, poor digestion, general weakness, palpitations, etc.
4. **embolism**—solid or foreign substance or particle in the blood
5. **embolus**—embolism
6. **greensickness**—chlorosis
7. **hemotopathy**—any blood disease
8. **hemophilia**—inheritable disease, occurring usually only in males, marked by abnormal bleeding and slow coagulation from any wound, however small
9. **hemorrhage**—escape of blood from blood vessels, because of rupture of the vessels or some other injury
10. **hyperemia**—excess or congestion of blood in a part, organ, or member
11. **leucocythemia**—leukemia
12. **leukemia**—disease characterized by an excess of white blood corpuscles
13. **oligocythemia**—form of anemia
14. **plethora**—pathological condition of an excess of blood in the body
15. **pyemia**—blood poisoning in combination with the development of abscesses
16. **septicemia**—blood poisoning caused by the absorption of both bacteria and their toxins into the system
17. **sleeping sickness**—popular name for a group of tropical diseases caused by the presence of trypanosomes in the blood, transmitted through the African tsetse fly
18. **spanemia**—anemia
19. **thrombosis**—blood clot in a blood vessel or in the heart
20. **toxemia**—blood poisoning caused by the absorption of poisonous substances into the system
21. **uremia**—accumulation in the blood of poisonous or harmful waste products that are normally voided in the urine

24. Pert. to, Descr. of, or Suffering from, a Blood Disorder,adj. *From Sec. 23:* anemic, anoxemic, chlorotic, embolic, greensick, hematopathic, hemophiliac, hemorrhagic, hyperemic, leucocythemic, oligocythemic, plethoric, pyemic, septicemic, spanemic, toxemic, uremic

25. Sufferer from a Blood Disorder,n. *From Sec. 23:* anemic, hemophiliac

26. Selected Disorders of Blood Pressure,n.
1. **hyperpiesia, hyperpiesis**—abnormally high blood pressure (hyperpietic,adj.)
2. **hypertension**—abnormally high blood pressure (hypertensive,adj.)
3. **hypopiesia, hypopiesis**—abnormally low arterial blood pressure
4. **hypotension**—abnormally low blood pressure (hypotensive,adj.)

353. VEIN; ARTERY

1. Vein,n.
1. **veinlet, veinule**—small vein

2. **vena**—vein (medical)
3. **venule**—small vein

2. System or Arrangement of the Veins of a Leaf or an Insect's Wing; These Veins, Collectively: nervation, neuration, venation, n.

3. Vein of a Leaf or Insect's Wing: nerve, nervure,n.

4. Pert. to, Descr. of, or Relating to, a Vein or Veins,adj.
1. **cirsoid**—varicose
2. **phleboid, phleboidal**—having the qualities of veins; characterized by veins
3. **varicose**—descr. of veins that are swollen, knotty, etc.
4. **veiny**—full of veins
5. **venous**—pert. to a vein or veins

5. Into, or Inside, a Vein: intravenous,adj.

6. Penetration or Puncture of a Vein, Usually by a Hypodermic Needle: venepuncture, n.

7. Selected Disorder of Vein or Artery,n.
1. **arteriosclerosis**—abnormal thickening and hardening of the artery walls (arteriosclerotic,adj.)
2. **arteritis**—inflammation of the arteries (arteritic,adj.)
3. **phlebitis**—inflammation of a vein
4. **varicosis**—development of enlarged veins or arteries (varicose,adj.)
5. **varix**—enlarged vein or artery (varices, pl.)

354. BONE

1. Bone,n.
1. **cementum, cement**—layer of bone at the root of the tooth
2. **clavicle**—collarbone
3. **fibula**—thin outer bone of the lower leg
4. **mastoid**—process of the temporal bone behind the ear
5. **os (Latin)**—bone (ossa,pl.)
6. **ossicle**—small bone or bonelike part
7. **radius**—bone of the forearm on the thumb side
8. **shinbone**—tibia
9. **sternum**—breastbone; chestbone
10. **tibia**—inner bone of the lower leg
11. **ulna**—bone of the forearm, on the side away from the thumb

2. Pert. to, Descr. of, or Resembling, Bone or a Bone,adj. *From Sec. 1:* clavicular, fibular, mastoid, ossal, radial, sternal, tibial, ulnar; *Also:*
1. **bony**—pert. to, descr. of, containing, resembling, or full of bone or bones
2. **osseous**—containing, made up of, or resembling bone
3. **osteal**—pert. to or resembling bone
4. **osteoid**—resembling bone

3. To Make Bony or Bonelike: ossify,v. (ossification,n.)

4. To Change, or Become Changed, into Bone: ossify,v. (ossification,n.)

5. Bone Formation: ossification, osteogenesis, osteogeny,n.

6. Producing or Generating Bone: ossific, osteoplastic,adj.

7. Bony Structure,n.
1. **osteology**—bony structure of an organism (osteological,adj.)
2. **skeleton**—bony structure of the body (skeletal,adj.)

8. Backbone,n.
1. **coccyx**—lower end of the backbone
2. **spinal column**—backbone
3. **spine**—backbone
4. **vertebra**—one of the bones or segments of the backbone (vertebrae,pl.)
5. **vertebral column**—backbone

9. **Pert. to the Backbone,**adj. *From Sec. 8:* coccygeal, spinal, vertebral; *Also:* 1. sacral—pert. to the lower spine

10. **Pert. to the Spinal Cord or to Bone Marrow:** myeloid,adj.

11. **Having a Backbone:** vertebrate,adj.

12. **Lacking a Backbone:** invertebrate,adj.

13. **Rib:** costa,n. (costal,adj.)

14. **Between the Ribs:** intercostal,adj.

15. **The Wishbone:** furculum, merrythought, n.

16. **Selected Bone Disorders,**n.
1. **mastoiditis**—inflammation of the process of the temporal bone behind the ear
2. **osteitis**—bone inflammation
3. **osteomyelitis**—pussy inflammation of the marrow of the bone
4. **pigeon breast**—physical deformity in which the sternum comes to a sharp point or projects conspicuously (pigeon-breasted,adj.)
5. **rachitis**—rickets (rachitic,adj.)
6. **rheumatism**—general term for diseases of the bones (rheumatic,adj.)
7. **rickets**—childhood disease that affects the structure of the bones (rickety,adj.)

17. **Selected Disorders of the Backbone or Spinal Cord,**n.
1. **curvature of the spine**—abnormal bending of the vertebral column
2. **encephalomyelitis**—inflammation of the brain and spinal cord
3. **humpback, hump**—roundly protuberant back caused by an angular curvature of the spine
4. **hunchback**—humpback
5. **infantile paralysis**—poliomyelitis
6. **kyphosis**—angular curvature of the spine, popularly called *humpback* or *hunchback*
7. **lordosis**—forward curvature of the spine
8. **meningitis**—inflammation of the meninges, or membranous lining of the brain and spinal cord
9. **poliomyelitis**—inflammation of the gray matter of the spinal cord (popularly called *infantile paralysis* or *polio*)
10. **spondylitis**—inflammation of the backbone
11. **sway-back**—abnormal concave curvature of the spine, found esp. in horses

18. **Having, or Pert. to, a Disorder of the Backbone,**adj. *From Sec. 17:* humpbacked, hunchbacked, kyphotic, spondylitic, swaybacked; *Also:* 1. gibbous—humpbacked (gibbosity,n.)

19. **One Who Is Humpbacked:** humpback, hunchback,n.

355. HORN; SCALE; SHELL

1. Horn,n.
1. **antler**—deer's horn; branch of a deer's horn
2. **attire**—antlers of a buck or stag
3. **beam**—main stem of an antler

2. Having Horns,adj.
1. **antlered**—horned (of a deer)
2. **beamy**—antlered
3. **bicorn, bicornuate, bicornuous**—two-horned
4. **horned**—having horns
5. **tricorn**—having three horns

3. Horny; Scaly,adj.
1. **chitinous**—horny, as the shells of certain insects, or of shrimps, crabs, etc.
2. **corneous**—horny
3. **keratoid**—horny; like horny tissue
4. **leprose**—scaly
5. **sclerodermatous**—scaly or horny—of skin (scleroderma,n.)

6. **scutate**—covered with large scales or horny plates (of certain animal forms)
7. **scutellate**—covered with small scales or horny plates (of certain animal forms)
8. **squamate, squamose, squamous**—covered with scales; scaly; scalelike

4. Arrangement of Scales on an Animal's Skin: squamation,n.

5. Scaly Material: scurf,n.

6. Covered by Scaly Material or Substance: leprose, scurfy, scurvy,adj.

7. Scaly Crust That Forms over a Skin Lesion: eschar, scab,n. (scabby, scabious,adj.)

8. Scales of the Hairy Skin of an Animal: dander,n.

9. Causing a Scaly Crust to Form: escharotic,adj. (of certain medications)

10. Shell of an Animal,n.
1. **carapace**—protective shell that covers creatures like lobsters, crabs, turtles, armadillos, etc.
2. **chitin**—horny shell
3. **conch**—spiral sea shell
4. **crust**—hard outer shell of an animal
5. **lorica**—hard protective shell of an animal
6. **test**—hard shell, or shell-like covering, of certain lower creatures; lorica

11. Pert. to, or Resembling, a Shell or Shells, adj.
1. **crustaceous**—of the nature of, or pert. to, a shell; shell-like
2. **crustal**—pert. to the hard outer shell of an animal
3. **testacious**—pert. to shells
4. **testudinal, testudinarious**—pert. to, or resembling, a turtle shell
5. **testudinate**—resembling a turtle's shell

12. Having a Shell,adj.
1. **conchiferous**—having a shell
2. **testacious**—having a hard shell, as lobsters, etc.

13. Discarded Shells of Marine Forms: exuviae,n. (exuvial,adj.)

14. Science of Marine Shells: conchology,n. (conchologist,n. conchological,adj.)

356. SKULL

1. The Skull: cranium, poll,n. (cranial,adj.)

2. Skull Part,n.
1. **brainpan**—cranium
2. **corona**—upper part or crown of the skull (coronal,adj.)
3. **cranium**—part of the skull enveloping the brain (cranial,adj.)
4. **occiput**—back part of the skull (occipital,adj.)
5. **sinciput**—upper half of the skull (sincipital,adj.)
6. **vertex**—highest point of the skull

3. Pert. to the Base of the Skull: basilar, adj.

4. Having a Skull: craniate,adj.

5. Selected Skull Conditions,n.
1. **acrocephaly**—unusual pointiness of the skull (acrocephalic, acrocephalous,adj. acrocephalic,n.)
2. **macrencephaly**—unusually large size or length of the skull (macrencephalic, macrencephalous,adj.)
3. **oxycephaly, oxycephalism**—unusual height of the skull (oxycephalic, oxycephalous,adj.)

6. Opening or Space in the Skull of a Newborn Infant: fontanel, fontanelle,n.

7. Science or Study of the Skull,n.
1. **craniography**—descriptive craniology (craniographer,n. craniographical,adj.)
2. **craniology**—science of the physical proportions of the cranium, particularly in the various races of man (craniologist,n. craniological,adj.)
3. **craniometry**—science of skull measurement for determining race, sex, etc. (craniometrist,n. craniometric, craniometrical,adj.)
4. **phrenology**—study of the shape or contours of the skull to determine mental abilities, faculties, or natural characteristics (phrenologist,n. phrenological,adj.)

8. Instrument for Measuring the Skull,n.
1. **craniometer**—instrument for making skull measurements
2. **encephalometer**—instrument for measuring the cranium to locate regions of the brain

357. BRAIN

1. The Brain: encephalon,n.

2. Unusually Small Brain: micrencephalon, n.

3. Having an Unusually Small Brain: micrencephalic, micrencephalous,adj. (micrencephaly,n.)

4. Pert. to the Brain: cerebral,adj.

5. Selected Brain Parts or Components,n.
1. **alba**—white matter of the brain
2. **cerebellum**—one of the divisions of the brain, lying below the cerebrum and above the pons and medulla (cerebellar, adj.)
3. **cerebral cortex**—gray matter
4. **cerebrum**—main part of the brain, occupying the upper part of the cranium (cerebral,adj.)
5. **convolutions**—raised ridges of the gray matter of the brain
6. **cortex**—external gray layer of the brain; gray matter (cortical,adj.)
7. **fissures**—grooves or clefts in the brain matter, i.e., the valleys between the convolutions
8. **ganglion**—mass of gray matter in the brain (ganglionic,adj.)
9. **gray matter**—nerve cells of the brain
10. **gyri**—convolutions (gyrus,sing.)
11. **medulla oblongata**—a portion of the brain, the upper enlarged part of the spinal cord
12. **pons**—white eminence at the base of the brain
13. **sulci**—furrows, grooves, or valleys in the brain matter (sulcus,sing.)
14. **white matter**—nerve fibers arising from the nerve cells of the brain

6. Resembling the Brain in Form or Structure: cerebriform, encephaloid,adj.

7. Brain Activity: cerebration,n. (cerebrate, v.)

8. X-Ray Photograph of the Brain: encephalogram, encephalograph,n. (encephalography,n.)

9. Instrument for Tracing Brain Waves: electroencephalograph,n. (electroencephalography,n. electroencephalographic,adj. electroencephalogram,n.)

10. Selected Brain Disorders,n.
1. **cephalitis**—encephalitis
2. **cephalocele**—hernia of the brain
3. **cerebral edema**—excessive accumulation of fluids in the brain
4. **cerebritis**—encephalitis
5. **encephalatrophy**—atrophy of the brain
6. **encephalitis**—inflammation of the brain
7. **encephalitis lethargica**—brain inflammation of such symptoms as often to be termed sleeping sickness
8. **encephalocele**—brain hernia

9. **encephalomyelitis**—inflammation of the brain and spinal cord
10. **encephalopathy**—disease of the brain
11. **encephalosclerosis**—hardening of the brain tissue
12. **encephalosepsis**—gangrene of the brain
13. **encephalosis**—degenerative brain disease
14. **hydrocephalus, hydrocephaly**—condition of excessive pressure of the spinal fluid in the skull cavity
15. **meningitis**—inflammation of the meninges, or membranous lining of the brain and spinal cord
16. **phrenitis**—brain fever
17. **polioencephalitis**—inflammation of the gray matter of the brain
18. **sleeping sickness**—popular name for *encephalitis lethargica*

358. HEAD

1. **The Head:** costard (contemptuous or humorous); nob (slang); noddle (humorous); noggin (colloq.); noodle (slang); pate, poll,n.
2. **Pert. to the Head:** cephalic,adj .
3. **Pert. to the Head and Tail; Lying between the Head and Tail:** cephalocaudal,adj.
4. **Part of the Head,n.**
   1. forehead—front of the head
   2. occiput—back part of the head (occipital,adj.)
   3. pate—top of the head
   4. poll—back of the head
   5. sinciput—front of the head (sincipital, adj.)
   6. vertex—top of the head
5. **Forehead:** brow, frons, sinciput,n.
6. **Pert. to the Forehead:** frontal, metopic, sincipital,adj.
7. **Flattened Surface on Each Side of the Forehead:** temple,n. (temporal,adj.)
8. **Pert. to the Side of the Head:** malar,adj.
9. **Any Part That Resembles a Small Head in Shape or Appearance:** capitellum, capitulum,n. (anatomy)
10. **Resembling a Head in Appearance:** cephaloid, headlike,adj.
11. **Figured by the Head, i.e., by the Person or Individual:** capitatim, per capita
12. **Having a Head:** cephalate, cephalophorous, cephalous,adj.
13. **Having Two Heads:** bicephalic, bicephalous, dicephalous, two-headed,adj. (dicephalism,n.)
14. **Monster with Two Heads:** craniodidymus, dicephalus,n.
15. **Having Three Heads:** tricephalous, three-headed,adj.
16. **Monster with Three Heads:** cephalotridymus, tricephalus,n.
17. **Having a Broad or Short Head:** brachycephalic, brachycephalous,adj. (brachycephalism, brachycephaly,n.)
18. **Person with a Broad or Short Head:** brachycephal,n. (brachycephali, brachycephales,pl.)
19. **Having an Abnormally Large Head:** macrocephalic, macrocephalous,adj. (macrocephaly, macrocephalia,n.)
20. **Person with an Abnormally Large Head:** macrocephalus,n.
21. **Having an Abnormally Small Head:** microcephalic, microcephalous,adj. (microcephaly, microcephalism, microcephalia,n.)
22. **Person with an Abnormally Small Head:** microcephalus,n.

23. **Without a Head:** acephalous, headless, adj.
24. **Instrument for Measuring the Head:** cephalometer,n.
25. **Science of the Head:** cephalology,n.

359. NECK

1. **Neck:** cervix,n.
2. **Necklike Part or Organ:** cervix,n.
3. **Back of the Neck:** nape, nucha, nuque, poll, scruff,n.
4. **Pert. to the Neck:** cervical, jugular,adj.
5. **Thick-Necked:** bull-necked,adj.
6. **Ailment That Causes a Twisting of the Neck and Therefore an Unnatural Position of the Head:** torticollis, wryneck,n.
7. **Sufferer from a Twisted Neck:** wryneck,n.

360. BREAST

1. **Breast; Breasts,n.**
   1. bosom—breast; breasts
   2. bust—breast; woman's breasts
   3. dug—breast of a female suckling mammal
   4. mamma—breast (mammae,pl.)
   5. mammary gland—individual female breast, so called from its milk-giving capacity
   6. udder—breasts or milk glands of certain mammals, strictly when baggy and possessing more than one nipple
2. **Pert. to the Breast or Breasts:** mammary, pectoral,adj.
3. **Resembling a Breast:** mastoid,adj.
4. **Breast-Shaped:** mammillary,adj.
5. **Having Breasts or a Breast:** (*The following terms are self-explanatory*) bare-bosomed, big-bosomed, big-breasted, black-breasted, broad-bosomed, broad-breasted, chicken-breasted, dark-bosomed, darkbreasted, deep-bosomed, double-breasted, flat-breasted, flat-chested, full-bosomed, full-breasted, high-bosomed, high-breasted, large-bosomed, large-breasted, long-bosomed, low-bosomed, low-breasted, narrow-bosomed, narrow-breasted, pigeon-breasted, round-bosomed, round-breasted, small-bosomed, small-breasted, swan-bosomed, white-breasted, white-breasted, wide-bosomed, wide-breasted, adj.; *Also:*
   1. bathycolpian, bathycolpic, bathukolpian—deep-bosomed
   2. bimastic—having two breasts (bimastism,n.)
   3. bosomy—having a prominent bosom (colloq.)
   4. callimastian—having beautiful breasts
   5. mammiferous—having breasts
6. **Excessive Development of Breasts in the Male:** gynecomastia, gynecomastism,n.
7. **Overgrowth of the Breasts:** hypermastia, n.
8. **Presence of More than Two Breasts:** hypermastia,n.
9. **Abnormal Smallness of the Breasts:** hypomastia, hypomazia,n.
10. **Inflammation of the Breast or Mammary Gland:** mastitis,n.
11. **To Feed (an Infant) at the Breast:** give suck to, lactate, nurse, suckle,v. (lactation,n. lactational,adj.)
12. **To Feed (a Child Belonging to Another) at One's Breast:** wet-nurse,v. (wet nurse, or, in the Orient, amah,n.)
13. **To Drink from the Breast:** nurse, suck, suckle,v.

14. To Take (a Child) off the Breast and Feed Other than Mother's Milk to: ablactate, wean,v. (ablactation,n.)

15. Nipple,n.
1. **dug**—nipple, commonly of suckling mammals
2. **mammilla**—nipple (mammillae,pl. mammillary,adj.)
3. **pacifier**—rubber nipple upon which an infant sucks
4. **pap**—anything in the shape of a nipple
5. **papilla**—nipple; nipplelike projection (papillary,adj.)
6. **teat**—nipple
7. **tit**—nipple

16. Having Nipples: mammillate,adj.

17. Nipplelike: mastoid,adj.

18. Inflammation of the Nipple: thelitis,n.

361. EYE

1. The Eye: optic; orb (poetic),n.

2. Pert to the Eye: ocular, ophthalmic, optic, optical,adj.

3. In the Region of the Eye: ophthalmic,adj.

4. Selected Parts of the Eye,n.
1. **conjunctiva**—mucous membrane that lines the inner surface of the eyelid and reflects over the front of the eyeball (conjunctival,adj.)
2. **cornea**—transparent coating of the ball of the eye (corneal,adj.)
3. **eyeball**—ball of the eye
4. **iris**—colored part surrounding the pupil of the eye
5. **lens**—part of the eye that focuses rays of light upon the retina
6. **lid, eyelid**—skin that covers the eye when the eye is closed
7. **pupil**—expanding and contracting circular opening in the eye (pupillary,adj.)
8. **retina**—membrane of the eye sensitive to light (retinal,adj.)

5. Descr. of a Person, Vision, etc., in Reference to the Eyes,n.
1. **binocular**—using both eyes
2. **blear-eyed, bleary-eyed, bleary**—having the eyes dimmed by tears, or red and sore as from sleeplessness or fatigue
3. **brunet, brunette**—having dark eyes
4. **cross-eyed**—with the eyes converging instead of focusing simultaneously on the same point
5. **dextrocular**—using the right eye more, or more effectively, than the left eye
6. **exophthalmic**—with the eyeballs protruding abnormally
7. **gimlet-eyed**—having sharp and piercing eyes
8. **goggle-eyed**—having bulging, staring, or rolling eyes
9. **megalophthalmic**—having unusually large eyes
10. **monocular, monoculate**—one-eyed; using only one eye
11. **monoptic, monoptical**—one-eyed
12. **moon-eyed**—round-eyed from some emotion
13. **mydriatic**—with the pupils of the eyes excessively or abnormally dilated
14. **myotic**—with the pupils of the eyes abnormally contracted
15. **nystagmic**—with the eyeballs moving rapidly and involuntarily
16. **popeyed**—with the eyes bulging, or, less frequently, staring
17. **round-eyed**—with the eyes unusually round
18. **sinistrocular**—habitually using, or more effectively using, the left eye
19. **sloe-eyed**—having eyes shaped like sloes, a kind of plum

20. **squint-eyed**—cross-eyed
21. **starry-eyed**—with the eyes shining or twinkling like stars
22. **strabismic**—cross-eyed; walleyed
23. **walleyed**—with the eyes diverging instead of focusing simultaneously on the same point; having eyes that glare or look fierce

6. Condition or Disorder of the Eyes,n.
From Sec. 5: binocularity, bleariness, crosseye or cross-eyes, dextrocularity, exophthalmos or exophthalmus, megalophthalmus, monocularity, mydriasis, myosis, nystagmus, popeye, squint-eye or squint, strabismus, walleye; *Also:*
1. **cast**—slight squint of the eye
2. **cataract**—opacity of the lens of the eye
3. **conjunctivitis**—inflammation of the conjunctiva of the eye
4. **glaucoma**—pathological hardness of the eyeball, often resulting in poor vision or blindness (glaucomatous,adj.)
5. **hippus**—eye disorder marked by spasmodic variation in pupil size
6. **hyalitis**—inflammation of the vitreous body of the eye
7. **iritis**—inflammation of the iris of the eye
8. **leucoma**—disease of the eye in which the cornea becomes white and opaque
9. **ophthalmia, ophthalmitis**—inflammation or infection of the membrane around the eye
10. **pinkeye**—highly contagious form of conjunctivitis
11. **synizesis**—closure or obliteration of the pupil of the eye

7. To Cause (the Eyes) to Become Sore, Watery, Inflamed, etc.: blear,v.

8. With the Eyes Looking Crookedly off to the Side: asquint,adv.

9. Deep-Set (of the Eyes): cavernous,adj.

10. Adapted for the Use of One Eye Only: monocular,adj.

11. Adapted for the Use of Two Eyes: binocular,adj.

12. Intersection of the Optic Nerves: chiasma, optic chiasma,n. (chiasmic, chiasmal, adj.)

13. Pert. to the Eyebrow: superciliary,adj.

14. Having Thick and Overhanging Eyebrows: beetle-browed,adj.

15. Eyelashes: cilia,n. (ciliary,adj.)

16. Pert. to the Eyelids: blepharal, palpebral, adj.

17. Selected Disorders of the Eyelids,n.
1. **blepharism**—spasm of the eyelids; rapid, involuntary, or spasmodic winking of the eyelids
2. **blepharitis**—inflammation of the eyelids
3. **trachoma**—granulation or inflammation of the eyelids (trachomatous,adj.)

362. EAR

1. Medical Term for the Ear: auris,n.

2. Projecting External Parts of the Ear: auricle, pinna,n.

3. Pert. or Relating to the Ear,adj.
1. **aural**—pert. to the ear
2. **auricular**—pert. to the ear
3. **binaural**—requiring or involving the use of two ears
4. **binotic**—pert. to the two ears
5. **dichotic**—having a different effect on each ear; bringing simultaneously a different sound to each ear
6. **entotic**—pert. to the ear's interior
7. **otic**—pert. to, or found in the region of, the ear
8. **otogenic**—originating in the ear
9. **parotic**—near the ear

10. **periotic**—around or surrounding the ear or internal ear

4. **Having Ears,adj.**
   1. **aurated**—having ears
   2. **auriculate**—having ears, or appendages shaped like ears
   3. **binaural**—having two ears
   4. **lop-eared**—having loosely hanging or drooping ears

5. **The Eardrum:** tympanic membrane,n.

6. **The Middle Ear:** tympanum,n. (tympanic, adj.)

7. **Inflammation of the Ear:** otitis,n.

8. **Inflammation of the Eardrum:** tympanitis,n.

363. NOSE

1. **Human Nose:** beak (contemptuous); bill (contemptuous); proboscis (humorous); snoot (slang),n.

2. **Noselike, Bony Formation of Birds:** beak, bill, neb,n.

3. **Nose of an Animal:** neb,n.

4. **Projecting Nose, Mouth, and Jaws of Those Animals Whose Heads Are So Built:** proboscis, snout,n.

5. **Long Nasal Appendage of the Elephant:** proboscis, trunk,n.

6. **Bony Part of the Nose:** bridge,n.

7. **The Two External Openings of the Nose:** nares, nostrils,n.

8. **Glandular Tissue behind the Nose:** adenoids,n.

9. **Descr. of the Nose,adj.**
   1. **aquiline**—having the hooked appearance of an eagle's beak
   2. **beaked**—turned down, like a bird's beak
   3. **hooked, hook**—bent, usually downward, like a hook
   4. **pug**—short and turning up at the end
   5. **retroussé**—turned up; pug
   6. **Roman**—having a prominent bridge; somewhat beaked
   7. **snub**—short and turned up
   8. **uptilted, upturned**—turned up

10. **Having a Broad, Short Nose:** platyrrhinian,adj. (platyrrhinism, platyrrhiny,n.)

11. **Person with a Broad, Short Nose:** platyrrhinian,n.

12. **Pert. to the Nose:** nasal, rhinal,adj.

13. **Uttered through, or Coming from, the Nose:** nasal,adj.

14. **To Sneeze:** sternutate,v.

15. **A Sneeze; Fact or Act of Sneezing; Noise of a Sneeze:** sternutation,n.

16. **Sneezing; Pert. to Sneezing or the Sound of Sneezing:** errhine (medical), sternutative, sternutatory,adj.

17. **A Cold:** rheum, rhinitis, roup,n.

18. **A Head Cold:** coryza,n.

19. **A Slight Head Cold:** the sniffles,n.

20. **Inflammation, Irritation, or Affection of the Mucous Membranes of the Nose,n.**
   1. **catarrh**—inflammation of the mucous membranes, esp. of the nose and air passages (catarrhal, catarrhous,adj.)
   2. **coryza**—acute inflammation of the mucous membranes of the nasal cavities
   3. **hay fever, allergic rhinitis, pollenosis, pollinosis**—irritation or affection of the mucous membranes of the nose, eyes, and air passages, caused by certain pollens
   4. **rhinitis**—inflammation of the mucous membranes of the nose

364. THROAT

1. **The Throat:** craw, gorge, gullet, maw, throttle, weasand,n.

2. **Pert. to the Throat:** guttural, jugular,adj.

3. **The Organ Situated between the Windpipe and the Base of the Tongue, and Serving as the Organ of Voice:** larynx,n. (laryngeal,adj.)

4. **Produced in the Larynx:** laryngal,adj.

5. **Tonsil:** amygdala,n.

6. **Small, Fleshy Process Hanging Down from the Middle of the Soft Palate above the Back of the Tongue:** uvula,n. (uvular, adj.)

7. **A Cough,n.**
   1. **bark**—hoarse cough
   2. **hack**—short, dry cough
   3. **hawk**—voluntary cough to clear the throat of phlegm
   4. **tussis**—cough (medical)

8. **To Cough,v.** From Sec. 7: bark, hack, hawk; Also: 1. **expectorate**—cough up and spit out (expectoration,n.)

9. **Pert. to, or Evidenced by, a Cough:** tussal,adj.

10. **Pert. to, or Caused by, a Cough:** tussive, adj.

11. **Spasm, or Gasping Sound, after a Cough:** whoop,n. (whoop,v.)

12. **Selected Disorders, Marked by Coughing, n.**
   1. **croup**—disorder of the windpipe or larynx (usually in children) marked by a harsh, hoarse cough and labored breathing (croupous, croupy,adj.)
   2. **pertussis**—whooping cough (pertussal, adj.)
   3. **whooping cough**—infectious childhood disease marked by fits of severe coughing

13. **Inflammation of the Throat or Related Parts,n.**
   1. **laryngitis**—inflammation of the larynx
   2. **pharyngitis**—inflammation of the pharynx
   3. **quinsy**—inflammation of the throat; a kind of tonsillitis
   4. **tonsillitis**—inflammation of the tonsils

365. FACE

1. **Face; Facial Features or Appearance,n.**
   1. **aspect**—face
   2. **countenance**—face
   3. **dead pan, poker face**—expressionless face (colloq.)
   4. **features**—components of the face, eyes, nose, etc.; loosely, general facial appearance
   5. **lineament**—outline of the face; features or parts of the face
   6. **mask**—likeness of a face, made by molding wax, plastic, etc., to one's features
   7. **physiognomy**—face; kind of facial features
   8. **profile**—face, or outline of the face, seen from a side view
   9. **visage**—face

2. **Facial Expression or Gesture,n.**
   1. **aspect**—expression of the face
   2. **countenance**—expression on the face
   3. **fleer**—wry facial expression indicative of contempt; coarse grimace (fleer,v.)
   4. **frown**—facial expression of displeasure, disapproval, annoyance, or similar emotion made by contracting or lowering the eyebrows (frown,v.)
   5. **grimace**—wry facial expression or gesture indicative of pain, displeasure, annoyance, disgust, etc. (grimace,v.)

6. **lower, lour**—frown; scowl (lower, lour,v.)

7. **mien**—facial expression

8. **moue** (French)—grimace indicative of discontent, annoyance, petulance, etc.; pout

9. **pout**—facial expression, characterized by lips thrust forward or out, indicative of sullenness, displeasure, discontent, etc. (pout,v.)

10. **scowl**—facial expression, made often by lowering the eyebrows, of anger, threat, gloom, annoyance, etc. (scowl,v.)

11. **smile**—facial expression of pleasure, amusement, etc. (smile,v.)

12. **sneer**—facial expression indicative of contempt or scorn (sneer,v.)

13. **snoot**—facial expression of contempt or scorn (snoot,v.)

3. Expressionless as to Face: dead pan or poker-faced (colloq.), stony, stony-faced,adj.)

4. Art of Deducing Character or Nature from a Study of Facial Features or Bodily Shape: physiognomy,n. (physiognomist,n. physiognomical,adj.)

5. Having Two Faces: bifacial, Janus-faced, adj. (bifaciality,n.)

6. To Face: confront, front,v. (confrontation, n.)

7. Face-to-Face: vis-à-vis,adv.

366. JAW

1. Jaw,n.
1. **jowl**—jaw, lower jaw, or part just under the jaw, esp. when hanging loosely and conspicuously
2. **mandible**—jaw; jaw of an insect or bird; lower jaw
3. **maxilla**—jaw; upper jaw
4. **submaxilla**—lower jaw
5. **underjaw**—lower jaw

2. Pert. to the Jaw,adj. *From Sec. 1:* mandibular, maxillary, submaxillary; *Also:* 1. gnathic—pert. to the jaw

3. Situated under the Lower Jaw: submaxillary,adj.

4. Jaws,n.
1. **chops**—jaws, usually of an animal
2. **maw**—jaws
3. **muzzle**—mouth and jaws of an animal
4. **snout**—projecting jaws, nose, and mouth of those animals whose heads are so built

5. Pert. to Both Jaws: bimaxillary,adj.

6. Upper Jawbone: maxilla,n. (maxillary, adj.)

7. Lower Jawbone: mandible, mandibular, submaxilla,n. (mandibular, submaxillary,adj.)

8. Situated under the Lower Jawbone: submaxillary,adj.

9. Having, or Descr. of, a Jaw or Jaws of a Particular Kind,adj.
1. **eurygnathic**—having a wide jaw (eurygnathism,n.)
2. **lantern-jawed**—having a long, thin lower jaw that sticks out, usually with hollow cheeks
3. **macrognathic**—having long jaws; having protruding jaws (macrognathism,n.)
4. **mandibulate**—having a lower jaw adapted for chewing, as in certain types of insects; having a lower jaw
5. **mesognathous**—having moderate-sized, slightly projecting jaws (mesognathism, mesognathy,n.)
6. **opisthognathous**—having receding jaws (opisthognathism,n.)
7. **orthognathous, orthognathic**—having straight, unprojecting jaws (orthognathism, orthognathy,n.)

8. **overshot**—having, or descr. of, the upper jaw protruding beyond the lower

9. **prognathous, prognathic**—having protruding jaws (prognathism, prognathy,n.)

10. **underhung**—having, or descr. of, a lower jaw that sticks out considerably farther than the upper jaw

11. **underjawed**—having a prominent underjaw

12. **undershot**—having, or descr. of, a lower jaw that sticks out

10. Unusual Smallness of the Jaws; Unusual Smallness of the Lower Jaw: micrognathia, n.

11. Without Jaws: agnathic, agnathous,adj.

12. Lack of, or Deficient Development of, the Jaws: agnathia,n.

13. The Cheek; Low-Hanging Cheek: jowl,n.

14. Having Large or Low-Hanging Cheeks: jowly,adj.

15. Pert. to to the Cheek or Cheeks: buccal, malar,adj.

16. Hanging Part of a Double Chin: jowl,n.

17. Pert. to the Chin: mental,n.

367. MOUTH

1. Mouth,n.
1. **maw**—mouth
2. **muzzle**—mouth; mouth and jaws of an animal
3. **neb**—person's mouth
4. **snout**—projecting mouth, nose, and jaws of those animals whose heads are so built
5. **stoma**—mouthlike opening in the lower animals (stomata,pl.)

2. Area or Region around the Mouth: peristome, peristoma,n.

3. Roof of the Mouth: palate,n. (palatal, adj.)

4. Soft Palate: velum,n. (velar,adj.)

5. Pert. or Relating to the Mouth or a Mouth,adj.
1. **buccal**—pert. to the mouth cavity, mouth, or sides of the mouth
2. **oral**—pert. to, emanating from, or in the region of the mouth
3. **oscular**—pert. to the mouth
4. **preoral**—in front of the mouth
5. **stomatal**—pert. to a mouthlike opening
6. **stomatic**—pert. to the mouth
7. **stomatous**—pert. to or resembling a mouthlike opening

6. Having a Mouth,adj.
1. **cyclostomate, cyclostomatous**—having a circular mouth (biology)
2. **microstomatous, microstomous**—having a very small mouth
3. **monostomous**—having one mouth

7. Mouth of a River: embouchure,n.

8. Mouthpiece of a Musical Instrument: embouchure,n.

9. Selected Mouth Ailments,n.
1. **stomatitis**—inflammation of the soft tissues of the mouth
2. **thrush**—mouth disease in infants, caused by a yeast
3. **trench mouth**—form of stomatitis

10. Shapely Line of the Lips: cupid's bow,n.

11. Pert. to the Lips: labial,adj.

12. Having Two Lips: bilabial,adj.

13. Pert. to the Tongue: glossal, lingual,adj.

14. Using the Tongue: lingual,adj.

15. Characteristic of the Tongue: lingual, adj.

368. TOOTH

1. Tooth,n.
1. **bicuspid**—premolar, so called because it has two cusps or pointed tops
2. **bucktooth**—tooth that projects beyond the line of the rest of the teeth
3. **cheek tooth**—molar
4. **canine**—one of the four pointed teeth next after the incisors and just before the first premolars, so called from its similarity in appearance to the prominent teeth of dogs
5. **cuspid**—canine
6. **denticle**—small tooth
7. **eyetooth**—upper canine
8. **fang**—snake's tooth through which poison is injected; dog's tooth; tooth like that of a dog
9. **impacted tooth**—tooth that is prevented from erupting, usually because it is lodged between the jawbone and another tooth
10. **incisor**—one of the eight front teeth, four upper and four lower, so called from its function of cutting
11. **molar**—one of the three back teeth, in each quarter of the mouth, just behind the two premolars
12. **premolar**—one of the two teeth, in each quarter of the mouth, coming just after the canine and before, as the name implies, the molar
13. **snaggletooth**—rough, irregular, or broken tooth
14. **stomach tooth**—lower canine
15. **tricuspid**—tooth with three points
16. **tusk**—long, projecting tooth, as in an elephant, walrus, etc.
17. **wisdom tooth**—the third, or last, molar

2. Teeth,n.
1. **buckteeth**—teeth that project beyond the lips when the mouth is open
2. **deciduous teeth**—the first, or temporary, teeth, twenty in number (eight incisors, four canines, and eight molars)
3. **milk teeth**—deciduous teeth
4. **permanent teeth**—second set of teeth (eight incisors, four canines, eight premolars, twelve molars)

3. Tooth, Other than Human or Animal,n.
1. **cog**—tooth in a wheel for interlocking with teeth of another wheel; tooth of a gear
2. **prong**—tine
3. **serration**—one of the teeth of a saw
4. **tine**—tooth of a fork

4. Pert. or Relating to a Tooth or Teeth, adj.
1. **deciduous**—pert. to, or descr. of, the first, or temporary, teeth
2. **dental**—pert. to a tooth or teeth
3. **interdental**—between the teeth
4. **periodontal, peridental**—surrounding a tooth or the teeth
5. **succedaneous**—pert. to, or descr. of, those teeth that come in after the early teeth fall out

5. Resembling a Tooth: odontoid, toothlike, adj.

6. Selected Parts of a Tooth,n.
1. **corona**—upper part, or crown, of a tooth
2. **crown**—the portion of the tooth above the gum, covered by enamel; loosely, the top of the tooth (coronary,adj.)
3. **cusp**—point on the crown of a tooth (cuspal,adj.)
4. **dentine**—bonelike major portion of the tooth
5. **enamel**—thin external covering of the tooth, the hardest substance in the body
6. **fang**—root of the tooth
7. **neck**—line joining the crown and root of a tooth

8. **pulp**—soft, vital tissue that fills the center and root canals of the teeth
9. **root**—bottom of the tooth, imbedded in the jaw
10. **root canal**—channel between the top of the tooth and the pulp chamber

7. Having Teeth,adj.
1. **bidentate**—having two teeth
2. **macrodont**—having large teeth (macrodontism,n.)
3. **microdont**—having very small teeth (microdontism,n.)
4. **oligodontous**—having very few teeth
5. **saber-toothed**—having long, sharp, canine teeth
6. **serrate**—toothed like a saw
7. **serrulate**—having fine, sawlike teeth
8. **snaggle-toothed**—having rough, irregular, or broken teeth
9. **toothed**—having teeth
10. **trident, tridentate**—three-toothed
11. **trifid**—three-toothed

8. Occurrence of an Abnormal Number of Teeth: polydontia,n.

9. Without Teeth: toothless,adj.

10. Tooth Arrangement,n.
1. **dentition**—arrangement of teeth
2. **serration**—arrangement like the teeth of a saw
3. **serrulation**—arrangement of fine, sawlike teeth

11. Tooth Contact,n.
1. **articulation**—loosely, occlusion
2. **bite**—occlusion
3. **malocclusion**—irregular, abnormal, or incorrect contact between upper and lower teeth
4. **occlusion**—the contact, at rest, of the upper and lower teeth

12. Tooth Production or Eruption,n.
1. **dentition**—eruption of teeth; teething
2. **odontogeny**—production of teeth
3. **primary dentition**—eruption of the 20 deciduous teeth
4. **secondary dentition**—eruption of the 32 permanent teeth
5. **teething**—growing or cutting of teeth (teethe,v.)

13. Replacement of a Tooth, Teeth, or Part of a Tooth, by Artificial Means: prosthesis or prothesis,n. (prosthetic,adj.)

14. Device for Attaching a False Tooth to a Real Tooth: bridge,n.

15. Dental Bridge or Bridges: bridgework,n.

16. Artificial Replacement for the Natural Top of the Tooth: crown,n.

17. Set of False Teeth: denture, plate,n.

18. Substance Used to Fill a Tooth Cavity: filling,n.

19. Finished Filling Inserted into a Tooth Cavity and Held by Cement: inlay,n.

20. Decay of the Teeth: caries,n. (carious, adj.)

21. Pussy Inflammation of the Sockets of the Teeth: pyorrhea, Rigg's disease,n. (pyorrheal,adj.)

22. The Gum; The Gums: gingiva,n. (gingival,adj.)

23. Inflammation of the Gums: gingivitis,n.

369. HAIR

1. Hair; Hairy Growth; A Hair,n.
1. **axillary hair**—hair in the armpit
2. **bangs**—hair cut straight and even over the forehead
3. **beard**—hair on the face or side of the face, generally of a man

4. **braid**—lock of hair entwined with other locks
5. **bristle**—a short, stiff hair or hairlike growth
6. **bun**—coil of hair, usually at the top or back of the head
7. **chignon**—knob of hair worn at the back or top of the head
8. **coat**—hairy or furry covering, usually of an animal
9. **cowlick**—tuft turned up over the forehead
10. **crew cut**—hair clipped very short
11. **crop**—clipped hair; hair cut short
12. **curl**—portion of hair or number of hairs in a curving, spiral, circular, etc., form
13. **daglock**—clotted or dirty mass or cluster of hair on an animal
14. **down**—short, silky hairs; soft and slight growth of hair
15. **fluff**—down
16. **frizzle, friz, frizz**—curl
17. **fur**—thick, hairy growth on the hide of certain animals
18. **fuzz**—down
19. **hackles**—erectile hairs on the neck and back of a dog
20. **hirsuties**—covering of hair
21. **lanugo**—down
22. **lock**—portion of hair; number of hairs together in one cluster
23. **locks**—hair on the head
24. **mane**—hair that is thick, long, and heavy; long and heavy hair growing about the neck of certain animals
25. **mop**—mass of thick hair
26. **patch**—small, separate area of hair
27. **pelage**—hair coat of a mammal; fur
28. **pigtail**—hair, tightly braided, hanging down the back
29. **pile**—soft hair
30. **plait**—braid
31. **pubes, pubescence, pubic hair**—hair on the genital region
32. **queue**—pigtail, esp. that of a Chinese
33. **quill**—a stiff, sharp, and pointed hair, as on a porcupine
34. **ringlet**—small curl of hair
35. **ruff**—fringe of hair on the neck of some animals
36. **shag**—rough, matted hair; mass of rough, matted hair
37. **shock**—thick, bushy hair or head of hair
38. **strand**—lock
39. **thatch**—head of thick, usually unkempt, hair
40. **topknot**—crown of hair at the top of the head
41. **tousle**—mop
42. **tress**—lock, usually a girl's, child's, or woman's
43. **tresses**—woman's long, unbound hair
44. **tuft**—small cluster of long hairs
45. **vibrissa**—one of the short, stiff hairs around the nose or mouth of certain animals (vibrissae,pl.)
46. **whiskers, whisker**—hair on the side of a man's face and chin; long, protruding hair or hairs around the mouth or nose of an animal
47. **widow's peak**—hair coming to a point on the forehead
48. **wig**—false hair worn to cover baldness, or for ornamental purposes
49. **wool**—thick, hairy growth on certain animals, as sheep, etc.

2. Depression or Cavity from Which a Hair Grows: hair follicle,n.

3. Growth of Hair in Unusual Places and in Unusual Amounts: hirsutism,n.

4. Excessive or Abnormal Growth of Hair: hirsuties, hypertrichosis, hypertrichiasis,n.

5. Pert. to, or Characteristic of, Hair: hirsute,adj.

6. Hairy; Having, or Covered with, Hair,adj.
1. **barbigerous**—hairy
2. **bristly, bristled**—full of, or covered with, short, thick hairs
3. **comate**—hairy
4. **cottony**—covered with down or fine hairs
5. **crinite**—hairy; having hairy growths
6. **downy**—covered with down
7. **fluffy**—downy
8. **furry**—covered with fur
9. **fuzzy**—having, or covered with, fuzz or down
10. **hirsute**—unusually hairy; covered with rough, long, and somewhat stiff hair
11. **hispid**—covered with rough, stiff hairs
12. **lanate**—covered with fine hair
13. **lanuginous, lanuginose**—covered with down
14. **pileous, pilous, pilose**—hairy; covered with soft hair
15. **pubescent**—covered with down or soft hair; hairy
16. **setaceous, setose**—bristly (biology)
17. **shaggy**—covered with thick hair
18. **tomentose**—covered with thick and matty hair
19. **tufted**—having a small cluster of long hairs
20. **velutinous**—covered with fine and silky hairs
21. **villous**—covered with silky hairs
22. **woolly**—covered with wool

7. Hairiness, etc.,n. *From Sec. 6:* bristliness, downiness, fluffiness, furriness, fuzziness, hirsuteness or hirsuties, hispidity, pubescence, shagginess, vollosity, woolliness; *Also:*
1. **hirsutism**—excessive hairiness
2. **hypertrichosis, hypertrichiasis**—abnormal hairiness

8. To Make Hairy: shag,v.

9. Development of Pubic Hair: pubescence, n. (pubescent,adj.)

10. Resembling Hair or a Hair,adj.
1. **bristlelike**—resembling a short, thick hair
2. **bristly**—resembling short, thick hairs, or a short, thick hair (bristliness,n.)
3. **capillary**—resembling a hair in slenderness; hairlike
4. **downy**—resembling down (downiness,n.)
5. **fluffy**—downy (fluffiness,n.)
6. **furry**—resembling fur (furriness,n.)
7. **fuzzy**—resembling fuzz (fuzziness,n.)
8. **hairlike**—resembling hair or a hair
9. **hairy**—resembling hair or a hair
10. **trichoid**—resembling hair

11. Having Hair of a Certain Kind,adj.
1. **bristly**—having short, thick hairs
2. **curly-headed, curly-haired**—having curly hair
3. **fuzzy-headed, fuzzy-haired**—having hair like down; having curly hair (fuzzy-wuzzy,n.)
4. **long-haired**—having long hair
5. **short-haired**—having short hair
6. **ulotrichous**—having woolly hair
7. **wire-haired**—having coarse, curly, short hair like wire
8. **woolly, woolly-headed**—having thick and curly hair

12. Having a Certain Color of Hair,adj.
1. **albino**—having hair without pigment; white-haired
2. **auburn-haired**—having reddish-brown or yellowish-brown hair
3. **auricomous**—golden-haired
4. **blond, blonde**—having light- or yellowish-colored hair
5. **brunet, brunette**—having dark or brown hair
6. **carroty**—having red hair
7. **fair-haired**—having light hair
8. **grizzled**—gray-haired

9. **melanocomous**—having dark hair
10. **melanous**—black-haired and dark-skinned
11. **sandy, sandy-haired**—having hair of a yellowish-red color
12. **towheaded, towhaired**—having whitish hair
13. **xanthochroid**—belonging to the ethnic group with light or yellowish hair and fair complexion
13. **Descr. of Hair Color**,adj. *From Sec. 12:* albino, auburn, blond or blonde, brunet or brunette, carroty, sandy
14. **Condition of Having Hair of a Certain Color**,n. *From Sec. 12:* albinism, blondness or blondeness, melanism
15. **Person of a Certain Color of Hair**,n. *From Sec. 12:* albino; blond (masc. and fem.); blonde (fem.); brunet (masc.); brunette (fem.); carrottop, towhead, xanthochroid; *Also:* 1. **brownette**—woman or girl with brown hair
16. **With the Hair Combed:** coifed,adj.
17. **Hair Style**,n.
    1. **bob**—style of short hair worn by women or, less often, children
    2. **coiffure**—manner of combing or wearing the hair, generally by women
    3. **croquignole**—a type of permanent wave
    4. **marcel**—style in which a deep wave is produced in the hair by a special curling iron
    5. **permanent wave**—style in which a long-lasting wave is produced in the hair by a special technique
    6. **pompadour**—style of wearing the hair high over the forehead
    7. **updo, upsweep**—style of wearing the hair in which it is piled on top of the head
18. **Descr. of Hair Style, Appearance, etc.**, adj. *From Sec. 17:* bobbed, marcelled; permanented (colloq.); upswept; *Also:*
    1. **braided**—worn in braids
    2. **curled**—having a curl produced artificially
    3. **curly**—having curls; not straight
    4. **lank**—straight, devoid of curl or wave
    5. **plaited**—worn in braids
    6. **tressed**—worn in braids
    7. **waved**—having an artificially produced wave
    8. **wavy**—having waves
19. **Hairdresser**,n.
    1. **barber**—one who cuts, trims, or dresses hair
    2. **coiffeur (French)**—male hairdresser
    3. **coiffeuse (French)**—female hairdresser
20. **Pert. to a Barber:** tonsorial,adj.
21. **Substance Used on the Hair**,n.
    1. **brilliantine**—oily dressing or tonic for the hair
    2. **pomade, pomatum**—hair oil, dressing, etc. (pomade,v.)
22. **Morbid Anxiety about the Condition or Health of the Hair:** trichopathophobia,n.
23. **Bristling of the Hair on Head or Body:** horripilation,n.
24. **Hair Disease:** trichopathy, trichosis,n.
25. **Scalp Disease That Causes Specks of White in the Hair:** dander, dandruff, furfur, scurf,n. (furfuraceous, scurfy,adj.)

370. BEARD

1. **Beard, Whiskers, etc.**,n.
    1. **burnsides**—sideburns (colloq.)
    2. **goatee**—small, pointed chin beard
    3. **handle-bar mustache**—long, curving mustache remindful of the handle bars of a bicycle

4. **imperial**—pointed tuft of hair on a man's chin or below his underlip
5. **mustache, moustache, mustachio**—hair on the upper lip
6. **mutton chops**—patch of whiskers on each side of the face (muttonchop,adj.)
7. **sideburns**—whiskers on the side of the face, starting, usually, at the hairline and coming to below the ears, with the chin clean-shaven
8. **stubble**—rough, short growth of beard
9. **Vandyke**—small, pointed beard
10. **vibrissae**—whiskers of a cat and certain other animals
11. **walrus, walrus mustache**—mustache with ends that curve or hang down
2. **Bearded; Whiskered**,adj. *From Sec. 1:* goateed; mustached, moustached, or mustachioed; stubbled; *Also:* barbate, barbigerous, bewhiskered
3. **Not Having or Wearing a Beard:** clean-shaven, shaven, unbearded, unwhiskered,adj.
4. **Beardlike; Relating to a Beard:** pogonic, adj.
5. **The Growing or Cultivation of a Beard or Beards:** pogonotrophy,n.
6. **The Study of Beards; A Treatise on Beards:** pogonology,n. (pogonologist,n. pogonological,adj.)
7. **State of Having an Unusually Full Beard; Excessive Growth of a Man's Beard; Occurrence of a Beard in a Woman:** pogoniasis,n. (medical)
8. **The Cutting or Trimming of the Beard:** pogonotomy,n. (humorous)

371. HAIR REMOVAL

1. **To Remove Hair**,v.
    1. **barber**—cut or trim the hair of
    2. **depilate**—remove the hair from
    3. **shave**—cut or scrape off (hair) with a razor; cut hair from with a razor
    4. **tonsure**—shave the head of; cut the hair of; shave the head or part of the head of, as a religious practice, before entry into the priesthood, etc.
2. **Hair Removal**,n. *From Sec. 1:* depilation, shave, tonsure; *Also:*
    1. **coupage**—process of taking the hair off skins
    2. **electrolysis**—removal of hair by electrical processes or equipment
3. **State of Having One's Hair Shaved Off:** tonsure,n.
4. **Shaven Part of a Monk's or Cleric's Head:** tonsure,n.
5. **Substance That Removes Hair:** depilatory,n.
6. **Removing, or Serving to Remove, Hair:** depilatory,adj.
7. **Pert. to a Haircutting:** tonsorial,adj.
8. **Pathological Desire to Break Off the Hair on One's Head:** trichoclasmania,n.
9. **Morbid Compulsion to Pull Out One's Hair:** trichotillomania,n.
10. **The Tearing Out of One's Hair:** trichologia,n.
11. **Hairless**,adj.
    1. **bald, bald-headed**—without hair
    2. **glabrous, glabrate**—smooth and hairless (zoology)
12. **Baldness; Loss of Hair**,n.
    1. **alopecia, defluvium**—baldness; loss of hair (medical)
    2. **trichorrhea**—rapid and abnormal loss of hair (medical)
13. **Bald Person:** baldhead, baldpate,n.

14. Skin Disease Characterized by Loss of Hair, etc.: mange, the mange,n. (mangy,adj.)

372. WIG

1. Wig,n.
　1. **periwig**—wig, esp. of the white or powdered variety, worn in the eighteenth century
　2. **peruke**—wig; periwig
　3. **switch**—false hair worn by women in addition to their own hair
　4. **toupee**—small wig covering a bald area
　5. **transformation**—wig worn by women; wig added to natural hair by women
　6. **wiggery**—wig

2. Wigs, Collectively: wiggery,n.

3. The Use of Wigs: wiggery,n.

4. Wearing a Wig: bewigged, wigged,adj.

5. Wig Maker: perruquier (French),n.

373. WOOL

1. Wool,n.
　1. **fleece**—wool covering of any wool-bearing animal
　2. **pelage**—wool coat of an animal
　3. **shag**—rough, matted wool; mass of rough, matted wool
　4. **yarn**—spun wool

2. Woolly,adj.
　1. **fleecy**—woolly (fleeciness,n.)
　2. **floccose**—woolly
　3. **flocculent**—woolly; consisting of soft and woolly masses (flocculence, flocculency, n.)
　4. **flocky**—flocculent
　5. **lanate, lanose**—woolly (lanosity,n.)
　6. **villous**—woolly (villosity,n.)

3. Pert. to, Consisting of, or Made of, Silk: sericeous, silken, silky,adj.

4. Silky; Resembling Silk: sericeous, silken, adj.

5. Production of Silk by Keeping and Raising Silkworms: sericulture,n. (sericulturist, n. sericultural,adj.)

374. LUNG

1. Pert. to, or Affecting, the Lungs: pneumonic, pulmonary, pulmonic,adj.

2. Pert. to the Air Cells of the Lungs: alveolar, vesicular,adj.

3. Possessing Lungs or Organs Similar to Lungs: pulmonate,adj.

4. Inflammation of the Lung or Lungs: pneumonia,n. (pneumonic, pulmonic,adj.)

5. Suffering from Pneumonia: pneumonic, adj.

6. Inflammation of the Membrane of the Lung: pleurisy,n. (pleuritic,adj.)

7. Suffering from Pleurisy: pleuritic,adj.

8. Tuberculosis of the Lungs: consumption, phthisic, phthisis, pulmonary tuberculosis, white plague,n.

9. Pert. or Referring to Tuberculosis of the Lungs: consumptive, phthisical, tubercular, tuberculous,adj.

10. Suffering from Tuberculosis of the Lungs: consumptive, phthisical, phthisicky, tubercular, tuberculous,adj.

11. Sufferer from Tuberculosis of the Lungs: consumptive, tubercular,n.

12. Showing the Wasting Signs of Tuberculosis: hectic,adj.

13. Sufferer from a Disease of the Lungs: pulmonic,n.

14. Pathological Condition in Which There Is Gas or Air in the Pleural Cavity: pneumothorax,n.

375. WINDPIPE

1. Windpipe: throttle, trachea, weasand,n. (tracheal,adj.)

2. The Two Major Subdivisions of the Windpipe: bronchi,pl.n. (bronchus,sing.n. bronchial,adj.)

3. Subdivisions of the Bronchi: bronchia, pl.n. (bronchial,adj.)

4. Inflammation of the Windpipe: tracheitis,n.

5. Inflammation of the Mucous Membrane of the Windpipe and Bronchial Tubes: bronchitis,n. (bronchitic,adj.)

376. BREATHE

1. To Breathe,v.
　1. **aspire**—breathe
　2. **blow**—breathe out; emit the breath
　3. **exhale**—breathe out
　4. **expire**—breathe out air from the lungs
　5. **gasp**—catch the breath sharply and audibly
　6. **gulp**—catch the breath sharply
　7. **huff**—emit the breath
　8. **inhale**—breathe in
　9. **inspire**—breathe in
　10. **insufflate**—breathe (something) in
　11. **pant**—emit quick and sharp breaths
　12. **puff**—emit the breath with some difficulty
　13. **respire**—breathe
　14. **sigh**—let out a long, deep breath, as in the expression of some emotion
　15. **sniff**—draw air audibly up the nose
　16. **sniffle**—breathe with difficulty through a partly clogged nose; draw air up through such a nose
　17. **snivel**—audibly draw or breathe mucus up the nose; sniffle
　18. **snore**—breathe noisily while asleep
　19. **snort**—expel the breath noisily through the nose
　20. **snuff**—breathe or draw in forcibly through the nose; breathe in powdered tobacco through the nose
　21. **snuffle**—breathe or breathe in audibly and continuously through the nose; do such when the nose passage is partly obstructed; breathe in mucus through the nostrils
　22. **suspire**—sigh, or take a long breath (poetic)
　23. **wheeze**—breathe with audible chest sounds, as in asthma
　24. **whiff**—exhale breath or smoke in puffs

2. Breathing,n. *From Sec. 1:* aspiration, exhalation, expiration, inhalation, inspiration, insufflation, respiration; *Also:*
　1. **dyspnea**—faulty, labored, painful, or abnormal breathing
　2. **eupnea**—good, normal, unlabored breathing
　3. **hyperpnea**—unusually rapid breathing
　4. **stertor**—act or fact of snoring
　5. **tachypnea**—abnormally rapid breathing

3. A Breath,n. *From Sec. 1:* aspiration, gasp, gulp, huff, pant, puff, sigh, sniff, sniffle, snivel, snore, snort, snuff, snuffle, wheeze, whiff; *Also:* 1. **suspiration**—a long or prolonged sigh

4. Pert. to, or Descr. of, Breathing,adj. *From Sec. 1:* aspiratory, expiratory, inspiratory, respiratory, wheezy; *From Sec. 2:* dyspneal, dyspneic, or dyspnoic

5. Breathing,adj. *From Sec. 1:* aspiring, blowing, exhaling or exhalant, etc.; *Also:* 1. **stertorous**—snoring deeply

6. Sound of Breathing,n. *From Sec. 1:* gasp, gulp, pant, sigh, sniff, sniffle, snivel, snore, snort, snuffle, wheeze; *From Sec. 2:* stertor; *Also:*
1. **murmur**—abnormal sound in the lungs or heart (murmurous,adj.)
2. **râle (French)**—abnormal sound accompanying breathing
3. **rhonchus**—snoring or whistling sound heard in the chest; râle (rhonchal, rhonchial,adj.)
4. **sough**—sighing sound (sough,v.)
5. **stridor**—harsh and shrill sound during breathing caused by some obstruction in the larynx, windpipe, bronchi, etc.
6. **whoop**—deep, gasping sound after a cough (whoop,v.)

7. Breathing Abnormally or with Difficulty, adj.
1. **adenoidal**—breathing as if the nose passages were stopped up by enlarged tissues
2. **asthmatic**—breathing with difficulty or in a labored fashion, with a feeling of tightness, etc. (asthma,n. asthmatic,n.)
3. **pursy**—short-winded owing to stoutness (pursiness,n.)
4. **short-winded**—getting out of breath from exertion in less time than normal; breathing with difficulty; short of breath; susceptible to difficulty in breathing
5. **stertorous**—breathing hoarsely (stertorousness,n.)
6. **winded**—having lost one's breath, or the power to breathe normally, as a result of physical effort

8. Inflammation of the Mucous Membranes of the Respiratory Tract: catarrh,n. (catarrhal,adj.)

9. The Breath: halitus,n.

10. Offensive or Foul Breath: halitosis, ozostomia,n.

11. Something Breathed Out: exhalation,n.

12. Breathing Apparatus, Medication, Device, or Organ,n.
1. **branchiae, branchia**—gills (branchial, adj.)
2. **gill**—anatomical process for breathing under water, occurring in fish, tadpoles, etc.
3. **inhalant**—medication that is breathed in, usually a substance to clear the air passages; apparatus used for breathing in (inhalant,adj.)
4. **inhalation**—medication to be breathed in
5. **inhaler**—apparatus used in breathing in medication, anesthetics, etc.; respirator
6. **lung**—organ of breathing in man and certain higher animals
7. **Pulmotor**—device for pumping air into the lungs of victims of drowning, suffocation, etc.
8. **respirator**—device for artificial breathing; device worn over the nose and/or mouth to prevent the inhalation of noxious gases, substances, etc.

13. Possessing Gills: branchiate,adj.

14. Below the Gills: hypobranchial,adj.

15. Scientific Study of the Respiratory Organs: pneumology,n. (pneumological,adj.)

16. To Stop or Impair the Breathing of,v.
1. **asphyxiate**—send into a coma by depriving of oxygen, thus causing an excess of carbon dioxide in the blood; smother; stifle
2. **choke**—stop from breathing by compressing the throat
3. **garrote, garote, garotte, garrotte**—throttle, generally in order to rob
4. **smother**—deprive of air so that breathing is impossible
5. **stifle**—stop from breathing

6. **strangle, strangulate**—choke; choke to death; stifle (strangulative, strangulatory,adj.)
7. **suffocate**—obstruct the breathing of; smother; stifle
8. **throttle**—cut off breathing by pressure on the throat

17. To Stop Breathing; To Be Unable to Breathe,v. *From Sec. 16:* asphyxiate, choke, smother, stifle, strangle, suffocate, throttle

18. A Stoppage or Impairment of Breathing, n. *From Sec. 16:* asphyxiation; garrote, garote, garotte, or garrotte; strangulation, suffocation

19. Condition of Stopped Breathing,n. *From Sec. 16:* asphyxia or asphyxiation

20. That Which Causes Stoppage or Impairment of Breathing,n. *From Sec. 16:* asphyxiant, suffocant

377. MUSCLE

1. Selected Muscles,n.
1. **biceps**—muscle with two heads or origins, as the one on the front of the upper arm, or the one on the back of the thigh (bicipital,adj.)
2. **depressor**—muscle that lowers a part or organ
3. **extensor**—muscle that extends or straightens a part
4. **flexor**—muscle that bends a limb or part
5. **gluteus**—muscle in the buttocks (gluteal, adj.)
6. **levator**—muscle that raises a limb or part
7. **masseter**—large jaw muscle used in chewing
8. **quadriceps**—great muscle of the thigh
9. **sphincter**—muscle organ surrounding an opening (sphincteral,adj.)
10. **tensor**—muscle that stretches or tightens
11. **thew**—muscle (usually in pl.)
12. **triceps**—muscle with three heads or origins; muscle at the back of the upper arm (tricipital,adj.)

2. Muscles, Muscle Arrangement, or Muscle System of a Body: musculature,n.

3. Pert. to, or Descr. of, Muscle: muscular, sarcous,adj.

4. Into Muscular Tissue: intramuscular,adj.

5. Band That Connects a Muscle to Bone or Other Part: sinew, tendon,n. (sinewy, tendinous,adj.)

6. Muscular, i.e., Having Well-Developed Muscles,adj.
1. **brawny**—muscular
2. **sinewy, sinewed, sinewous**—muscular; muscular and thin
3. **stringy**—muscular; muscular and thin
4. **tendinous**—muscular
5. **thewed**—muscular
6. **thewy**—muscular; muscular and strong
7. **torose**—muscular; bulging with well-developed muscles
8. **wiry**—muscular and thin

7. Muscularity,n. *From Sec. 6:* brawn or brawniness, sinewiness or sinewousness, stringiness, toroseness or torosity, wiriness

8. Muscular Power: sinews, thews,n.

9. Action, Condition, State, or Disorder of, or Involving, Muscles, Joints, Tendons, etc. (Selected),n.
1. **ankylosis**—stiffness or fixation of a joint (ankylose,v.)
2. **apraxia**—loss or impairment of ability to make co-ordinated bodily or muscular movements
3. **arthritis**—inflammation of a joint or of the joints; gout
4. **ataxia**—lack of ability to co-ordinate muscular movements

5. **catalepsy, catalepsis**—pathological muscular rigidity; a fit involving this and accompanied by unconsciousness
6. **cataplexy**—loss of muscle tone caused by sudden emotional shock
7. **charley horse**—strained muscle; stiffness from a strained muscle
8. **clonus**—alternating contractions and partial relaxations of a muscle
9. **contracture**—permanent contraction of a muscle
10. **convulsion**—violent muscular spasm
11. **cramp**—painful spasm
12. **eclampsia**—convulsions, esp. during pregnancy or while giving birth
13. **gout**—painful inflammation of the joints, esp. in the great toe, or also in the hands or feet
14. **holotonia**—general muscular spasms; tetanus
15. **hyperkinesia, hyperkinesis**—abnormal increase in muscular movement
16. **hypertonicity, hypertonia, hypertonus**—greater than normal muscular tone
17. **hypotonicity, hypotonia, hypotonus**—lower than normal muscular tone
18. **kinesthesia**—muscular movement or response
19. **lockjaw**—tetanus; tetanus of the lower jaw
20. **locomotor ataxia**—pathological condition, of syphilitic origin, causing lack of control over walking and other muscular movements
21. **myalgia**—muscular rheumatism
22. **myositis**—inflammation of a muscle or of muscles
23. **parakinesia**—jerky, spasmodic, and uncontrollable muscular movements of the body resulting from nervous disorder
24. **rheumatism**—general name indicating a disease of the muscles, tendons, or joints
25. **rigor mortis (Latin)**—stiffness of muscles after death
26. **sarcitis**—inflammation of the muscles or fleshy tissue
27. **spasm**—sudden, unusual, and involuntary muscular contraction
28. **spasticity**—complete or partial loss of voluntary muscular control, combined with a state of sustained contraction or tension of a muscle
29. **tenonitis**—inflammation of a tendon
30. **tetanus**—frequently fatal disease characterized by violent spasms and muscle stiffness; state of a muscle undergoing continuous contraction
31. **tetany**—state of continuous contraction of muscles, mainly in the extremities
32. **tic**—involuntary, usually nervous, muscular movement or jerk, esp. of the face
33. **tone**—tonicity
34. **tonicity**—healthy tension or partial contraction of muscle fibers at rest
35. **tonus**—slight degree of contraction of muscles at rest; continuous spasm
36. **trismus**—tetanus of the lower jaw

10. Descr. of, Pert. to, Suffering from, etc., Such Action, Condition, State, or Disorder, adj. *From Sec. 9:* ankylotic, apraxic, arthritic, ataxic, cataleptic, cataplectic, clonic, convulsive, eclamptic, holotonic, hyperkinetic, hypertonic, hypotonic, kinesthetic, myalgic, myositic, parakinetic, rheumatic or rheumatoid; spasmic, spasmodic, or spastic; tetanic, tonal or tonic, trismic

11. Sufferer from Such a Condition or Disorder,n. *From Sec. 9:* arthritic, cataleptic, eclamptic, rheumatic, spastic

12. Resembling Rheumatism: rheumatoid, adj.

13. Pert. to Muscular Reaction Governed by Mental Processes: psychomotor,adj.

14. To Contract the Muscles Involuntarily: cringe,v.

15. Paralysis,n.
1. **apoplexy**—sudden loss or decrease of sensation, movement, or consciousness caused by the rupture of a blood vessel in the brain or by the cutting off of the blood supply to the brain; figurative paralysis by the stress of some emotion
2. **cerebral palsy**—paralysis caused by brain injury
3. **hemiplegia**—paralysis of one side of the body
4. **laloplegia**—paralysis of the speech muscles (except those of the tongue) resulting in an inability to talk
5. **monoplegia**—paralysis of one member, part, or limb of the body
6. **palsy**—paralysis
7. **paraplegia**—complete paralysis of the lower portion of the body
8. **paresis**—partial paralysis of muscular power
9. **petrifaction**—paralysis, often figurative, from fear, surprise, or other strong emotion
10. **stroke**—apoplexy
11. **stupefaction**—paralysis of the mind

16. Paralytic, i.e., Paralyzed,adj. *From Sec. 15:* apoplectic, hemiplegic, monoplegic, palsied, paraplegic, paretic, petrified, stupefied

17. A Paralytic,n. *From Sec. 15:* apoplectic, hemiplegic, paraplegic, paretic

18. To Paralyze,v. *From Sec. 15:* palsy, petrify, stupefy

19. Paralytic, i.e., Paralyzing,adj. *From Sec. 15:* petrifactive, stupefactive

378. NERVE

1. Nerve Center: ganglion,n. (ganglia,pl.n. ganglionic,adj.)

2. Nerve Tissue in a Mass: ganglion,n. (ganglia,pl.n. ganglionic,adj.)

3. Network of Nerves: plexus,n.

4. Network of Nerves in the Upper Abdomen: solar plexus,n.

5. System of Nerves: nervous system,n.

6. Nerve Cell: neuron,n. (neuronic,adj.)

7. Point Where a Nerve Impulse Goes from One Nerve Cell to Another: synapse,n. (synaptic,adj.)

8. Pert. to, Affecting, or Relating to, the Nerves or Nervous System,adj.
1. **nervine**—reacting on the nerves
2. **nervous**—pert. to, associated with, arising from, etc., the nerves
3. **neural, nerval**—pert. to the nerves or nervous system

9. Any Activity of the Nervous System: neurosis,n. (neurotic,adj.)

10. Substance or Agent Harmful to the Nervous System: neurotic,n.

11. Selected Nervous Disorders,n.
1. **chorea**—disease of the nerves marked by spasmodic twitching
2. **epilepsy**—chronic nervous disease marked by convulsions, dizziness, unconsciousness, etc.
3. **grand mal (French)**—complete or pronounced epilepsy
4. **neuritis**—inflammation of the nerve or nerves, or condition caused by this
5. **neuropathy**—ailment of a nerve or of the nervous system
6. **petit mal (French)**—mild epilepsy
7. **St. Vitus's dance**—chorea
8. **tarantism**—nervous ailment, the symptoms of which are morbid dejection, stupor, and a compulsive need to dance

12. Pert. to, Descr. of, or Suffering from a Nervous Disorder,adj. *From Sec. 11:* choreic, epileptic, neuropathic

13. Sufferer from a Nervous Disorder,n. *From Sec. 11:* epileptic or epileptoid, neuropath, tarantist

14. Resembling Epilepsy: epileptoid, epileptiform,adj.

379. SEX ORGAN

1. Sex or Reproductive Organ or Organs, Gland, Part, etc.,n.
1. **clitoris**—female erectile organ, homologous to the penis (clitoral,adj.)
2. **epididymus**—organ in which the sperm ripens (epididymal,adj.)
3. **genitals, genitalia**—external sex or reproduction organs (genital,adj.)
4. **glans, glans penis**—conical end of the penis
5. **gonad**—sex gland, such as the ovary or testis (gonadal,adj.)
6. **hymen, maidenhead**—membrane at the opening of the vagina (hymeneal,adj.)
7. **labia majora (Latin)**—two outer folds of skin at the opening of the female genitals
8. **labia minora (Latin), nympha**—two inner membranous folds of skin at the opening of the female genitals
9. **milt**—reproductive glands of male fishes
10. **mons Veneris (Latin)**—external rounded eminence of the female genitals
11. **muliebria, pudenda, pudendum, vulva** —female genitals (pudendal or pudic, vulval,adj.)
12. **ovary, ovarium**—organ in the female where the unfertilized eggs are formed (ovarian,adj.)
13. **oviduct**—tube that carries eggs from the ovary
14. **ovipositor**—egg-laying organ of certain insects
15. **penis, phallus, priapus, male member, virile member**—male erectile sex organ (penal, phallic, priapal,adj.)
16. **placenta**—organ in wall of the uterus through which the embryo or fetus receives nourishment from the mother (placental,adj.)
17. **prepuce, foreskin**—fold of skin covering the head of the penis
18. **prostate, prostate gland**—gland that surrounds the male urethra (prostatic, adj.)
19. **pubic region, pubes**—region of the male or female genitals
20. **scrotum**—sac containing the testicles (scrotal,adj.)
21. **testicle, testis, spermary**—male reproductive gland in which the sperm originates (testes,pl.n. testicular, orchic,adj.)
22. **urethra**—tube, in the male, that carries semen (urethral,adj.)
23. **uterus, womb, matrix**—female organ that receives and holds the fertilized egg during pregnancy (uterine, matricular, adj.)
24. **vagina**—tube, in females, from the uterus to the exterior (vaginal,adj.)
25. **virilia (Latin)**—male sexual organs

2. Pert. to Both the Sexual or Reproductive Organs and the Urinary Organs: genitourinary, urogenital, urinogenital,adj.

3. Part of the Body That Responds to Sexual Excitation: erogenous zone,n.

4. Symbol or Representation of the Penis: phallus,n. (phallic,adj.)

5. Possession of Unusually Small Genital Organs: microgenitalism,n.

6. Reproductive Cell,n.
1. **gamete, generative cell**—one of the two germ cells that unite in reproduction; mature reproductive cell (gametic,adj.)
2. **germ cell**—sexual reproductive cell (germinal,adj.)
3. **milt**—sperm of male fishes
4. **oöcyte**—female germ cell in the stage of maturation
5. **oösphere**—female gamete
6. **ovum**—female germ cell; cell that, when fertilized, develops into the embryo (ova,pl.)
7. **seed, sperm, spermatozoon**—male reproductive cell (seed, sperm, spermatozoa, pl.n. spermatic, spermatozoal,adj.)
8. **zygote**—cell resulting from the union of gametes

7. Male Impregnating Fluid Containing Germ Cells: seed, semen, sperm,n. (seminal, spermatic,adj.)

8. Producing Semen: seminiferous,adj.

9. Selected Diseases or Disorders of the Sex or Reproductive Organs,n.
1. **blennorrhea**—gonorrhea (blennorrheal, adj.)
2. **chancre**—venereal or syphilitic ulcer (chancrous,adj.)
3. **clap**—gonorrhea
4. **cryptorchidism**—condition in which the testicles have not descended, or fail to descend, normally
5. **gonorrhea**—contagious venereal disease that causes inflammation of the genitourinary tract (gonorrheal,adj.)
6. **lues**—syphilis (luetic,adj.)
7. **metritis**—inflammation of the uterus
8. **orchitis**—inflammation of the testicles (orchitic,adj.)
9. **ovaritis**—inflammation of the ovaries
10. **priapism**—pathological and more or less continuous erection of the penis without sexual desire
11. **prostatitis**—inflammation of the prostate
12. **social disease**—venereal disease, esp. syphilis or gonorrhea
13. **syphilis**—venereal infection caused by a spirochete (syphilitic,adj.)
14. **urethritis**—inflammation of the urethra
15. **vaginismus**—painful contraction of the vagina
16. **vaginitis**—inflammation of the vagina
17. **venereal disease**—infection contracted through sexual intercourse; disease of the sexual organs (venereal,adj.)
18. **vulvitis**—inflammation of the vulva

10. One Who Has Syphilis: luetic, syphilitic, n.

380. EGG

1. Egg,n.
1. **embryo**—fertilized egg in its earliest development (embryonic,adj.)
2. **germ**—embryo in its earliest stages
3. **nit**—egg of a louse; egg of a parasitic insect
4. **oösperm**—fertilized egg
5. **oösphere**—unfertilized egg
6. **ovule**—egg in early stages; small egg (ovular,adj.)
7. **ovum**—female egg; egg that, when fertilized, develops into a new individual (ova,pl.)

2. Eggs,n.
1. **caviar**—sturgeon eggs
2. **clutch**—eggs in a nest
3. **roe**—fish eggs
4. **spawn**—eggs of fishes and other marine forms

3. White of an Egg: albumen, glair,n. (albuminous,adj.)

4. Yellow of an Egg: yolk,n.

5. Pert. to, or Resembling, the Yolk of an Egg: vitelline,adj.

6. Egg-Shaped: oval,adj.

7. Like an Egg: ovoid,adj.

8. Carrying or Serving to Carry or Bear Eggs: oviferous,adj.

9. Process of Producing an Egg, or of Discharging an Egg from the Ovary: ovulation, n. (ovulate,v.)

10. Science of Bird's Eggs: oölogy,n.

11. To Examine Eggs, by Holding Them Up to a Light, for Imperfections: candle,v. (candler,n.)

381. BIOLOGICAL CELL

1. Small Cell: cellule,n.

2. Reproductive Cell: germ cell,n.

3. Selected Cell Components,n.
1. **chromosome**—one of the small bodies in certain cells (chromosomal,adj.)
2. **cytoplasm, cytoplast**—protoplasm of a cell, not including the nucleus (cytoplasmic,adj.)
3. **nucleolus**—rounded body found in the nucleus (nucleolar,adj.)
4. **nucleus**—central specialized portion of the protoplasm (nuclear,adj.)
5. **protoplasm**—living substance of all cells (protoplasmic,adj.)

4. Cell Division,n.
1. **amitosis**—direct method of cell division (amitotic,adj.)
2. **cleavage**—cell division
3. **meiosis**—process of maturation of germ cells involving two divisions (meiotic, adj.)
4. **mitosis**—indirect method of cell division (mitotic,adj.)

5. Cell Structure, Function, Organic Processes, etc.: cytology,n. (cytological,adj.)

6. Cell Disintegration: cytolysis,n.

7. The Devouring of Cells of an Organism by Other Cells in the Organism: cytophagy, n. (cytophagous,adj.)

8. Having a Single Cell: unicellular,adj.

9. Having Two Cells: bicellular,adj.

10. Divided into Two Cells: bilocular, biloculate,adj.

11. Pert. to, or Containing, Cells: cellular, adj.

12. Science of Cell Structure, Functions, etc.: cytology,n. (cytologist,n. cytological, adj.)

382. SKIN

1. Skin; Part of the Skin,n.
1. **agnail**—hangnail
2. **callus**—hardened or thickened part of the skin
3. **corium**—deep vascular layer of skin under the epidermis; derma
4. **cuticle**—dead skin around the edges of the fingernails and toenails; epidermis
5. **cutis**—corium
6. **derma**—layer of skin between the epidermis and the tissue under the skin
7. **dermis**—skin
8. **epidermis**—protective outer layer of skin
9. **hangnail**—strip of skin lying loose at the root of the fingernail
10. **hide**—skin of an animal
11. **integument**—skin
12. **parchment**—skin of an animal prepared for writing

13. **peel**—skin of a fruit, etc.
14. **pellicle**—thin skin
15. **pelt**—skin of any fur-bearing animal
16. **peltry**—animal skin with fur on it
17. **rind**—outer skin of fruit, cheese, etc.
18. **scalp**—skin of the upper part of the head, usually including the tissues underneath
19. **slough**—shed skin of a snake or other reptile; layer of dead skin that drops off a healing wound
20. **vellum**—skin of a lamb, calf, or kid prepared for bookbinding or as parchment

2. Pert. to, Descr. of, or Affecting, the Skin,adj. *From Sec. 1:* cuticular, dermal, epidermal, vellum; *Also:* 1. **cutaneous**—pert. to, affecting, or on the skin

3. Skins of Animals,n.
1. **exuviae**—skins or other coverings cast off by snakes, animals, etc. (exuvial,adj.)
2. **peltry**—skins of fur-bearing animals

4. Fold of Skin: plica,n.

5. Scales of Dead Skin: scurf,n. (scurfy, adj.)

6. Resembling Skin: dermatoid,adj.

7. Between the Layers of Skin: intradermal, adj.

8. Under the Skin: subcutaneous,adj.

9. Pert. to the Region beneath the Skin: hypodermic,adj.

10. The Art of Stuffing the Skins of Dead Animals: taxidermy,n. (taxidermist,n. taxidermal, taxidermic,adj.)

11. Selected Skin Disorders, Conditions, or Diseases in Which Symptoms Show on the Skin,n.
1. **acne**—common disease of the skin, esp. among adolescents, in which pimples break out on face, back, and chest
2. **blotch**—broken-out area on the skin
3. **breakout**—bumps, spots, pimples, sores, etc., on the skin
4. **callosity**—callus; condition of the skin in which calluses are present
5. **callus**—thickened or hardened area, part, or place on the skin
6. **chicken pox**—contagious childhood disease marked by skin eruptions
7. **corn**—horny callus, esp. on the toes or feet
8. **cowpox**—skin disease of cows that, when communicated to humans, immunizes against smallpox
9. **dermatitis**—inflammation of the skin
10. **dermatopathy, dermatopathia**—any skin disease
11. **dermatosis**—any skin disease
12. **eczema**—itching, non-contagious, inflammatory disease of the skin
13. **elephantiasis**—disease marked by great thickening, roughness, hardening, and cracking of the skin together with tremendous enlargement of the part or parts affected
14. **eruption**—rash
15. **erysipelas**—infectious disease marked by fever, inflamed skin, etc.
16. **frambesia**—contagious skin disease of tropical climates marked by raspberry-like eruptions
17. **German measles**—rubella
18. **hives**—eruptive skin disease
19. **ichthyosis**—disease in which the skin is thick, rough, and scaly
20. **impetigo**—infectious skin disease characterized by pussy pimples
21. **induration**—hardened area of tissue under the skin
22. **(the) itch**—contagious disease caused by a mite that burrows into the skin
23. **lepra**—leprosy
24. **leprosy**—infectious disease characterized by ulceration, thickening of the skin, de-

velopment of red areas on the skin, deformities, etc.
25. lupus—tuberculous skin disease
26. (the) mange—skin disease affecting domestic animals and, less commonly, human beings
27. measles—contagious disease marked by red spots on the skin
28. morbilli—measles
29. myxedema—dryness and swelling of the skin caused by defective thyroid functioning
30. pachyderma, pachydermia—abnormal or pathological thickness of skin; elephantiasis
31. pimple—small bump, swelling, or elevation on the skin, usually inflamed
32. pityriasis—branlike skin disease or rash
33. pox—disease that covers the skin with spots, pimples, sores, etc.
34. prurigo—skin disorder marked by itching pimples, etc.
35. pruritus—itching of the skin
36. psoriasis—inflammatory skin disease
37. rash—a breaking out on the skin of bumps, spots, pimples, sores, etc.
38. ringworm—contagious skin disease caused by a fungus
39. roseola—rose-colored rash
40. rubella—infectious disease similar to measles, but milder
41. rubeola—measles; rubella
42. scabies—the itch; the mange
43. scarlatina—scarlet fever; mild form of scarlet fever
44. scarlet fever—contagious disease marked by fever and a scarlet rash, and caused by a streptococcus
45. scleroderma—hard, scaly, or thorny condition of the skin
46. shingles—acute inflammatory skin disease of nervous origin
47. smallpox—contagious eruptive skin disease, characterized by fever, and leaving permanent scars
48. sore—broken or bruised area or place on the skin
49. tinea—any fungus disease of the skin; ringworm
50. uredo—hives
51. urticaria—hives
52. vaccinia—cowpox
53. varicella—chicken pox
54. variola—smallpox
55. varioloid—mild form of smallpox
56. xeroderma—skin disease in which there are pathological dryness, roughness, and flakiness
57. yaws—frambesia

12. Pert. to a Skin Condition or Disorder, or to a Person Affected with a Skin Disorder, adj. *From Sec. 11:* blotchy, callous or calloused, dermatopathic, eczemous, erupted, erysipelatous, ichthyotic, impetiginous, indurated, lepric, leprous or leprosied, lupous, mangy, myxedemic or myxedematous, pachydermal or pachydermatous, pimpled or pimply, pityriasic, pruritic, psoriatic, roseolar or roseolous, rubeolar, scabious, sclerodermatous, urticarial, variolar or variolous, varioloid; xerodermic, xerodermatic, or xerodermatous

13. Sufferer from a Skin Disorder or Disease, n. *From Sec 11:* leper or lazar, psoriatic

14. Resembling a Skin Disorder or Disease, adj. *From Sec. 11:* acneform or acneiform, leproid, rubeoloid, varicelloid; varioloid (from *variola*)

15. Hospital for Lepers: lazaret, lazarette, or lazaretto, leprosarium, leprosery,n.

16. A Boil,n.
1. anthrax—malignant carbuncle, an indication of anthrax, an infectious and often fatal disease of cattle, sheep, and certain

other animals that is transmissible to humans
2. carbuncle—large boil, caused by inflammation of the tissue under the skin (carbuncular, carbuncled,adj.)
3. excrescence—disfiguring boil
4. furuncle—boil (furuncular, furunculous, adj.)
5. sore—boil

17. Small, Black-Tipped, Fatty Mass on the Skin of the Face: blackhead, comedo,n.

18. A Pimple,n.
1. fester—pustule
2. papule, papula—small, usually pointed pimple that is inflamed but not pussy
3. phlyctena—small pustule
4. phlyctenule, phlyctenula—small phlyctena
5. pustule, pustulation—pimple; pussy pimple; inflamed pimplelike elevation
6. whelk—papule; pustule

19. Pert. or Referring to a Pimple,adj. *From Sec. 18:* phlyctenar, phlyctenular, pustular or pustulous

20. Pimpled; Pimply,adj. *From Sec. 18:* papular, papulate, papulated, papuliferous, papulose, or papulous; phlyctenous; pustulate, pustulated, pustulous, pustuled, or pustulatous

21. To Pimple,v. *From Sec. 18:* pustulate

22. Eruption or Formation of Pimples,n. *From Sec. 18:* papulation, pustulation; *Also:* 1. empyesis—eruption of pustules

23. Causing or Producing Pimples,adj. *From Sec. 18:* pustulant

24. A Blister: bleb, bulla, vesication, vesicle, vesicula, vesicule,n.

25. Having, or Marked by, Blisters: blebby, blistered, blisterous, blistery, bullate, bullated, vesicular,adj.

26. To Blister: vesicate, vesiculate,v. (vesication, vesiculation,n.)

27. Causing Blisters: vesicant, vesicatory,adj. (vesicant, vesicatory,n.)

383. PUS

1. Pus: matter, purulence, suppuration,n.

2. Pus Sore; A Collection or Accumulation of Pus,n.
1. abscess—collection or accumulation of pus somewhere in or on the body, often from bacterial action
2. canker—corroding or gangrenous ulcer
3. chancre—venereal or syphilitic ulcer
4. empyema—collection or accumulation of pus in a region of the body, esp. the pleural cavity
5. fester—small ulcer
6. phagedena—ulcer that spreads rapidly
7. ulcer, ulceration—open pus sore, usually at the surface

3. Pussy,adj. *From Sec. 2:* abscessed, cankerous or cankered, chancrous, empyemic, festered; phagedenic, phagedenical, or phagedenous; ulcerous, ulcerated, or ulcerative; *Also:*
1. purulent—pussy
2. pyic—pussy

4. To Become Pussy; To Generate Pus,v. *From Sec. 2:* canker, fester, ulcer or ulcerate; *Also:* 1. matter, maturate, suppurate—generate pus

5. Generation of Pus,n. *From Sec. 4:* ulceration; maturation, suppuration; *Also:* 1. purulence, purulency, pyosis—generation of pus

6. Generating Pus,adj. *From Sec. 4:* maturative, suppurative; *From Sec. 5:* purulent

7. To Cause to Become Pussy,v. *From Sec. 4:* canker, fester, ulcer or ulcerate (ulceration, n. ulcerative,adj.)

8. Pussiness,n. *From Sec. 3:* ulcerousness, purulence or purulency; *Also:* **1. suppuration** —pussy condition

9. To Discharge Pus: fester, matter, maturate, suppurate,v.

10. Discharge of Pus: maturation, pyorrhea, pyosis, suppuration,n.

11. Discharging Pus: festering, maturating or maturative, pyorrheal, suppurating or suppurative,adj.

12. Resembling Pus: puriform, puruloid, pyoid,adj.

384. SKIN COLOR

1. General Color and Appearance of the Skin: complexion,n. (complexioned,adj.)

2. Abnormal Blueness of Skin, Resulting from a Deficiency of Oxygen in the Blood: cyanosis,n. (cyanotic,adj.)

3. Dark-Skinned,adj.
1. **black**—belonging to the ethnic group of people having dark-pigmented skin
2. **brunet, brunette**—having dark skin
3. **dusky**—dark and dull, but not black, of skin
4. **melanic, melanistic, melanous, melanian**—belonging to the ethnic group having dark skin, hair, and eyes
5. **melanochroous, melanochroic**—dark-skinned
6. **melanodermic**—having black skin as an abnormal condition
7. **Negro**—belonging to an ethnic group having dark, black, or brownish-black skin
8. **Negroid**—somewhat, or resembling, Negro
9. **swarthy, swart**—dark-skinned

4. Condition of Dark Skin,n. *From Sec. 3:* blackness, duskiness; melanism, melanoderma, or melanodermia; swarthiness, swartness

5. Person with Dark Skin,n. *From Sec. 3:* black or Black, brunet or, fem., brunette, Negro or, fem., Negress, Negroid

6. Black Pigment: melanin,n.

7. Light-Skinned,adj.
1. **blond, blonde, blondine**—light-skinned and light-haired
2. **fair, fair-skinned**—light-skinned
3. **leucochroic**—white or fairly white in complexion
4. **leucodermic, leucodermatous**—having spots of abnormally white skin
5. **Melanochroid**—belonging to the ethnic group characterized by light skin and dark hair
6. **xanthochroid**—belonging to the ethnic group having light skin and light or yellowish hair

8. Condition of Light Skin,n. *From Sec. 7:* blondness or blondeness, fairness, leucoderma

9. Person with Light Skin,n. *From Sec. 7:* blond or blonde (fem.), blondine, xanthochroid

10. Ethnic Group with Light Skin,n. *From Sec. 7:* Melanochroi, Xanthochroi

11. Pale in Complexion,adj.
1. **ashen**—deathly pale
2. **ashy**—pale as ashes; deathly pale
3. **blanched**—pale, esp. from fear, illness, etc.
4. **bleached**—pale
5. **blenched**—pale; blanched
6. **cadaverous**—pale and thin, looking, as it were, like a corpse
7. **doughy**—pale and flabby; pasty
8. **ghastly**—pale as a ghost

9. **palish**—somewhat pale
10. **pallid**—pale; lacking in color; wan
11. **pasty**—pale, like paste
12. **wan**—pale; having an unnatural or sickly paleness
13. **waxen**—pale
14. **wheyfaced**—with a face very pale from some emotion
15. **white**—pale

12. Paleness,n. *From Sec. 11:* cadaverousness, ghastliness, pallor, pastiness, wanness, whiteness

13. Pale Person,n. *From Sec. 11:* wheyface

14. To Become, or Cause to Become, Pale,v. *From Sec. 11:* blanch, bleach, blench, pale, wan (poetic), whiten

15. Having a Sickly Yellow Complexion: sallow,adj. (sallowness,n.)

16. To Cause to Have a Sickly Yellow Complexion: sallow,v.

17. Red in Complexion,adj.
1. **blooming**—having a healthy rosy or pinkish color of cheeks
2. **blowzy, blowzed**—having a red complexion; having a healthy red complexion; coarse-looking and red-faced; fat, red-faced, and untidy
3. **erythematous**—having an abnormal redness of the skin caused by capillary congestion
4. **florid**—red; having a healthy red complexion
5. **flush, flushed**—having a healthy red complexion, or cheeks of this complexion
6. **glowing**—blooming; rosy
7. **inflamed**—red, hot, and swollen (of skin, tissues, etc.)
8. **rosy**—having a fresh and healthy redness of complexion
9. **rubicund**—tending to redness; ruddy
10. **ruddy**—having a healthy red color of complexion
11. **sanguine**—ruddy, owing to an active circulation of blood

18. Redness of Complexion,n. *From Sec. 17:* bloom, erythema, floridness or floridity, flush, glow, inflammation, rosiness, rubicundity, ruddiness (erythemic, erythematic,adj.)

19. To Redden (the Skin),v. *From Sec. 17:* flush, inflame (inflammation,n.)

20. Causing Redness of the Skin: inflammatory or inflammative, rubefacient, rubific, adj. (inflammatory or inflammative, rubefacient,n. rubefaction,n.)

21. To Turn or Become Red of Complexion, v.
1. **bloom**—develop a healthy pink cheek color; flush (bloom,n.)
2. **blush**—turn red from embarrassment, modesty, shame, etc. (blush,n.)
3. **crimson**—turn deep red; blush
4. **flush**—turn red in complexion; blush (flush,n.)
5. **glow**—develop a healthy pink color in the cheeks or face (glow,n.)
6. **mantle**—blush; flush
7. **redden**—become red; blush

22. To Cause to Turn Red,v. *From Sec. 20:* blush, crimson, flush, redden

23. Being, Becoming, or Growing Red,adj. *From Sec. 20:* blooming, blushing, etc.; blushful or ablush, crimson, flush or aflush, red; *Also:*
1. **erubescent**—turning red; blushing (erubescence,n.)
2. **rosy**—blushing (rosiness,n.)
3. **rubescent**—growing, turning, or becoming red; blushing (rubescence,n.)

24. Sunburned: adust, bronzed, browned or brown, burned, tanned or tan, toasted,adj.

25. To Sunburn, i.e., Become, or Cause to Become, Sunburned: bronze, brown, burn, tan, toast,v.

26. Small, Brownish Yellow Spot on the Skin: freckle, lentigo,n. (freckled, freckly, lentiginous,adj. freckle,v.)

385. FLESH

1. Flesh; Fleshy Growth,n.
  1. caruncle—fleshy growth on the head of certain birds; comb (caruncular, carunculous, caruncinate, caruncinated,adj.)
  2. comb—fleshy growth on the head of fowl
  3. crest—fleshy growth on an animal's head; comb (crested,adj.)
  4. dewlap—loose fold of flesh on the throat of a person, or hanging under the throat of cattle, dogs, etc. (dewlapped,adj.)
  5. jowl—fleshy part under the lower jaw; dewlap of cattle; wattle
  6. quick—sensitive part of the flesh under the fingernails
  7. wattle—one of the two red, fleshy processes hanging down from the throat of poultry, certain birds, etc. (wattled,adj.)

2. Pert. to Flesh: sarcous,adj.

3. Fleshy,adj.
  1. brawny—fleshy, of people (brawn, brawniness,n.)
  2. pulpy, pulpous—fleshy (of fruit, vegetables, etc.)

4. Flesh-Colored: incarnadine, incarnate, adj. (incarnadine,n. incarnadine,v.)

5. To Invest with Flesh, Figuratively: incarnate,v. (incarnation,n.)

6. In the Flesh (Figuratively): incarnate, adj.

7. To Turn into, or Be Turned into, Flesh; To Make, or Become, Fleshlike: carnify,v.

386. LEATHER

1. Leather Made from the Skin of the Indicated Animal: alligator; buckskin (originally from a deer or buck, now usually from a sheep); buff (from a buffalo or an ox); calfskin; capeskin (from a Cape goat, and chiefly used in gloves); chamois (from a kind of antelope; also from a goat or sheep); cowhide, crocodile, deerskin; doeskin (from a female deer); goatskin, horsehide; kid or kidskin (from a young goat); lizard; morocco or morocco leather (from a goat, and tanned with sumac); pigskin; pin seal (from a young seal); seal, sheepskin, snakeskin,n.

2. A Kind of Fine Leather Originally Made at Cordova, Spain: cordovan,n.

3. Calfskin or, Formerly, Kidskin, Buffed on the Flesh Side into a Nap: suede or suède, n.

4. Thin Sheepskin Used in Bookbinding: skiver,n.

5. Thin and Cheap Leather: skiver,n.

6. Strip of Leather Used for Fastening or Tying: belt or strap (with a buckle), thong,n.

7. Strap Used to Hold a Slipper or Low Shoe on the Foot: sandal,n.

8. Resembling Leather: coriaceous, leather, leatherlike, leathern, leathery,adj. (leatheriness,n.)

9. Made of Leather: coriaceous, leather, leathern,adj.

10. Place Where Hides Are Made into Leather: tannery,n.

11. To Make Hides into Leather: tan,v. (tanning,n. tanner,n.)

12. To Prepare Tanned Leather for Use: curry,v. (currier,n.)

13. To Cover with Leather; To Put Leather On; To Bind with Leather: leather,v.

14. Imitation Leather, Generally Cloth, Paper, or Plastic: leatherette or leatheret,n.

15. Hide of Animals, Esp. Cattle, That Is Untanned or Only Partially Tanned: rawhide,n.

16. A Rope or Whip Made of Such Hide: rawhide,n.

17. To Beat or Hit with Such a Whip: rawhide,v.

18. Soap for Cleaning and Softening Leather: saddle soap,n.

387. MEMBRANE

1. Membrane,n.
  1. arachnoid—serous membrane, between the dura and pia mater, around the brain and spinal cord (arachnoid,adj.)
  2. caul—membrane that may still cover the head of a newborn infant
  3. dura, dura mater—fibrous membrane covering the brain and spinal cord (dural, adj.)
  4. endocardium—membrane lining the cavities of the heart (endocardial,adj.)
  5. endometrium—mucous membrane lining the uterus (endometrial,adj.)
  6. frenum—connecting fold of membrane that restricts or supports a part
  7. meninges (pl.)—membranous lining of the brain and spinal cord; the three membranes, arachnoid, dura, and pia mater (meningeal,adj.)
  8. mucosa—mucous membrane (mucosal, adj.)
  9. mucous membrane—membrane covering certain body openings and passages
  10. pellicle—thin membrane
  11. pericardium—membrane enclosing the heart (pericardial, pericardiac,adj.)
  12. peritoneum—membrane that lines the cavity of the abdomen in mammals (peritoneal,adj.)
  13. pia mater—vascular membrane around the brain and spinal cord
  14. pleura—membrane around the lung (pleural,adj.)

2. Consisting of, Pert. to, or Resembling, a Membrane or Membranes: membranous, membranaceous,adj.

3. Of the Nature of a Membrane: membranate,adj.

388. OTHER BODILY PARTS

1. Bodily Part,n.
  1. middle—waist
  2. midriff—diaphragm
  3. milt—spleen
  4. thorax—chest; chest cavity (thoracic, adj.)
  5. tomalley—lobster's liver, green when cooked
  6. vestige—bodily part now only in its rudimentary or undeveloped state, but having once, in earlier stages of growth or in earlier generations, been fully developed, like the appendix (vestigeal,adj.)

2. Referring to a Bodily Part,adj.
  1. adrenal—situated near, or close to, the kidneys
  2. diaphragmatic—pert. to the diaphragm
  3. hepatic—pert. to, or affecting, the liver
  4. inguinal—pert. to the region of the groin
  5. nephric, nephritic—pert. to the kidney or kidneys

6. **organic**—pert. to an organ, often internal
7. **pancreatic**—pert. to the pancreas
8. **pectoral**—pert. to the chest
9. **phrenic**—pert. to the diaphragm
10. **renal**—pert. to the kidney or kidneys
11. **splenic**—pert. to the spleen
12. **suprarenal**—located above or in front of the kidneys

3. Selected Kidney Disorders,n.
1. **Bright's disease**—a kidney disease
2. **nephrism**—chronic disease of the kidney, or condition resulting from this
3. **nephritis**—inflammation of the kidney or kidneys (nephritic,adj.)
4. **nephrosis**—non-inflammatory degenerative condition of the kidneys
5. **pyelitis**—inflammation of the kidney pelvis

4. Selected Liver Disorders,n.
1. **biliousness**—any liver disorder, or the resulting condition from such a disorder (bilious, biliary,adj.)
2. **cirrhosis**—disease characterized by certain changes in the structure of the liver (cirrhotic,adj.)
3. **hepatitis**—inflammation of the liver

5. Selected Lymph Disorders,n.
1. **bubo**—inflammation and swelling of a lymph gland, usually in the groin or armpit
2. **bubonic plague**—devastating contagious and epidemic disease, usually carried by rat fleas, and characterized by buboes, chills, fever, prostration, etc.
3. **lymphangitis**—inflammation of a lymph vessel
4. **scrofula**—tuberculosis of the lymph glands

6. Pert. to, or Suffering from, a Lymph Disorder,adj. *From Sec. 5:* bubonic, scrofulous; *Also:* 1. **strumatic**—scrofulous

389. ILLNESS

1. Illness; Disease,n.
1. **affection**—abnormal or morbid bodily state or condition
2. **affliction**—any (usually serious) illness, esp. one causing pain, distress, etc.
3. **ailment**—illness, usually not major; any sick or unhealthy condition
4. **autoinfection**—self-infection, rather than from external sources
5. **blight**—disease that causes a plant to wither
6. **cachexia**—general illness
7. **complaint**—ailment
8. **complication**—secondary condition resulting from, or modifying, a disease
9. **contagion**—disease communicated by contact, whether direct or indirect
10. **disorder**—illness
11. **endemic**—disease peculiar to a geographical place, region, or people
12. **epidemic**—disease that infects a large part of the people (or animals) of a community, region, etc.
13. **idiopathy**—any disease that is primary, i.e., not preceded by or caused by any other disease
14. **ill-health**—illness; condition of being ill or in poor health
15. **indisposition**—slight illness
16. **infection**—disease caused by germs
17. **infirmity**—illness, usually characterized by weakness
18. **invalidism**—illness or ill-health, usually to the extent that a normal or active life cannot be led
19. **malady**—any illness, disease, ailment, etc.
20. **malaise**—general feeling of physical discomfort or illness
21. **morbidity**—disease; unhealthy or unwholesome condition, literally or figuratively
22. **pathology**—disease
23. **pathosis**—any diseased condition
24. **pest**—deadly epidemic disease
25. **pestilence**—devastating contagious disease
26. **plague**—deadly, highly contagious, and rapidly spreading disease
27. **sequela**—unhealthy state or condition resulting from a disease (sequelae,pl.)
28. **shock**—disturbance of the body
29. **sickliness**—state of being ill
30. **sickness**—illness; disease
31. **trauma, traumatism**—physical condition resulting from physical or emotional shock, injury, etc.
32. **unhealthiness**—state of being ill
33. **unsoundness**—unhealthiness
34. **unwholesomeness**—unhealthiness
35. **upset**—physical disorder, usually of the stomach

2. Ill; Diseased,adj. *From Sec. 1:* affected, afflicted, ailing, cachectic or cachexic; complaining (of); disordered, indisposed, infected, infirm, invalid, morbid, pathological, sickly, sick, traumatized, unhealthy, unsound, unwholesome, upset; *Also:*
1. **peaked**—sickly and thin
2. **pestiferous**—infected with a contagious disease
3. **smitten**—deeply afflicted
4. **stricken**—seriously ill
5. **unwell**—sick
6. **valetudinary**—sick

3. Referring to Illness or Disease,adj. *From Sec. 1:* afflictive, cachectic or cachexic, contagious, endemic, epidemic, idiopathic, infective or infectious, morbid, pathological, pestilential, traumatic; *Also:*
1. **critical**—capable of causing, or resulting in, death
2. **cryptogenic**—of puzzling or unknown origin
3. **epizootic**—affecting many animals of a species simultaneously
4. **exopathic**—produced by external causes
5. **fatal**—causing, or able to cause, death (fatality,n.)
6. **insidious**—having a greater effect than is shown by the symptoms (insidiousness, n.)
7. **malignant**—fatal; likely to be fatal (malignancy,n.)
8. **pandemic**—affecting most of the people in a region, country, the world, etc.
9. **toxicopathic**—caused by poison
10. **virulent**—progressing rapidly and dangerously (virulence, virulency,n.)
11. **zymotic**—contagious; infectious

4. To Make Ill; To Cause Illness or Disease in,v. *From Sec 1:* affect, afflict, blight, indispose, infect, invalid, shock, sicken, traumatize, upset

5. To Be, Become, or Grow Ill,v.
1. **ail**—be ill
2. **catch**—get (a contagious disease)
3. **complain of**—have as an illness
4. **contract**—get (a disease); catch
5. **pine (away)**—grow sick from grief, longing, pain, hunger, etc.
6. **sicken**—become ill
7. **waste away**—lose health

6. Ill Person,n.
1. **invalid**—someone ill enough not to be able to lead a normal or active life
2. **outpatient**—patient who does not live in a hospital, but visits it, or is visited by its staff, for treatment
3. **patient**—ill person under a doctor's care

4. shut-in—person confined to his room or house because of illness
5. valetudinarian—ill person

7. Pert. to What Can Be Observed about a Disease: clinical,adj.

8. Simulation of the Symptoms of a Disease, an Occurrence in Certain Neurotic and/or Psychotic States: pathomimesis,n. (pathomimetic,adj.)

9. Specific Unhealthy Physical Reaction to Some Special Factor, Food, Drug, Plant, Substance, etc.: allergy,n.

10. That Which Causes Such a Reaction,n. *From Sec. 9:* allergen (allergenic,adj.)

11. Susceptible to Such a Reaction,adj. *From Sec. 9:* allergic

12. Pert. to the Functions or Activities of a Sickroom: clinical,adj.

13. Liability to Disease,n.
  1. **diathesis**—predisposition to a disease or class of diseases
  2. **predisposition**—state of having a special susceptibility to a specific disease or type of disease (predisposed,adj.)
  3. **susceptibility**—a characteristic that renders someone likely to contract a disease if exposed to the cause (susceptible,adj.)
  4. **tendency**—predisposition

14. Pert. to, or Dependent on, a Predisposition to a Disease: diathetic,adj.

15. Easily Falling Ill: delicate, sickly,adj.

16. Looking Ill: bilious, peaked, sickly, wan, adj. (biliousness,n.)

17. Cause of Disease,n.
  1. **carrier**—person who has disease germs, and, though himself immune to them, can transmit them to another person; any person who has disease germs in his body and is therefore a source of infection
  2. **contagium**—matter that can spread disease germs
  3. **germ**—disease-producing bacterium, microorganism, etc.
  4. **microbe**—disease-causing bacterium (microbial, microbic,adj.)
  5. **pathogen**—disease-producing organism (pathogenic, adj.)
  6. **vector**—organism or insect that transmits disease germs (vectorial,adj.)
  7. **virus**—submicroscopic organism that causes disease (viral,adj.)

18. Not Healthful; Causing Illness or Disease,adj.
  1. **insalubrious**—not healthful
  2. **insanitary**—unsanitary
  3. **morbific**—causing or producing a disease (less commonly used than *pathogenic*)
  4. **nocuous, noxious**—not healthful (nocuousness, noxiousness,n.)
  5. **pathogenic**—capable of causing or producing a disease
  6. **peccant**—causing or inducing disease (peccancy,n.)
  7. **pestiferous**—causing or carrying disease or infection
  8. **pestilential**—causing or carrying, or likely to cause, a devastating contagious disease
  9. **unhealthful**—not healthful (unhealthfulness,n.)
  10. **unhealthy**—not promotive of, or conducive to, health (unhealthiness,n.)
  11. **unhygienic**—not promoting health
  12. **unsanitary**—not healthful; promoting or encouraging disease
  13. **unwholesome**—not healthful (unwholesomeness,n.)
  14. **zymotic**—causing a contagious or infectious disease

19. Caused by Disease: pathological,adj.

20. Onset or Origin of Disease: pathogenesis, pathogeny,n. (pathogenetic, pathogenic,adj.)

21. Catching (of Diseases),adj.
  1. **communicable**—capable of being imparted from one person to another (communicability,n.)
  2. **contagious**—communicable by contact (contagiousness,n.)
  3. **infectious**—communicable through the medium of germs or germ carriers (infectiousness,n.)

22. The Spreading of Disease, etc.,n. *From Sec. 21:* communication, contagion, infection; *Also:*
  1. **autoinoculation**—spread of infection from one part to the rest of the body
  2. **vection**—transmission of disease germs from a sick to an uninfected person

23. The Period of Time between the Contraction of an Infectious Disease and the Appearance or Manifestation of Symptoms: incubation,n.

24. Place Where Epidemic Disease is Rampant or Likely to Occur: pesthole,n.

25. Change or Turning Point in a Disease, toward either Recovery or Death: crisis,n. (critical,adj.)

26. Gradual Cessation or Termination of a Disease without an Abrupt Crisis: lysis,n. (lyterian,adj.)

390. TUMOR; CANCER

1. Selected Tumors,n.
  1. **adenoma**—benign tumor of glandular organ
  2. **angioma**—tumor of dilated blood or lymph vessels
  3. **cancer**—malignant tumor; spreading tumor; tumor likely to cause death
  4. **chondroma**—tumor of cartilage
  5. **encephaloma**—brain tumor
  6. **excrescence**—disfiguring wart
  7. **fibroma**—non-cancerous tumor of fibrous tissues
  8. **growth**—tumor
  9. **hematoma**—blood-containing tumor
  10. **lipoma**—tumor of fatty tissue
  11. **malignancy**—any tumorous growth
  12. **melanoma**—dark-pigmented tumor
  13. **myoma**—tumor of muscular tissue
  14. **neoplasm**—tumor
  15. **nevus**—vascular tumor
  16. **osteoma**—benign tumor of the bone; bony tumor
  17. **papilloma**—epithelial tumor
  18. **polyp**—mucous tumor
  19. **tumefaction**—tumor
  20. **verruca**—wart
  21. **wart**—small, hard skin tumor
  22. **wen**—benignant skin tumor

2. Tumorous,adj. *From Sec. 1:* cancerous, neoplastic, verrucose, warty

3. Selected Cancers or Cancerous Conditions,n.
  1. **carcinoma**—cancer originating in epithelial tissue (carcinomata,pl. carcinomatous,adj.)
  2. **encephaloma**—brain cancer
  3. **epithelioma**—cancer of the epithelium
  4. **leukemia, leucemia**—cancerous condition of the blood, characterized by excessive production of white blood cells
  5. **malignancy**—cancerous growth
  6. **sarcoma**—cancer of connective tissue
  7. **scirrhus**—hard cancer; hard and cancerous tumor

4. Affected with Cancer: cancerous,adj.

5. Resembling Cancer: cancerous, cancroid, adj.

6. Condition Characterized by the Development of Many Epithelial Cancers: carcinomatosis,n. (carcinomatous,adj.)

7. Origin or Production of a Cancer: carcinogenesis,n. (carcinogenetic,adj.)

8. Causing Cancer: carcinogenic,adj. (carcinogenicity,n.)

9. Substance or Agent That Causes Cancer: carcinogen,n.

10. The Spreading (of a Cancer) from One Part of the Body to Another: metastasis,n. (metastatic,adj. metastasize,v.)

391. HERNIA

1. Hernia: breach, herniation, rupture,n.

2. Having a Hernia: herniated, ruptured,adj.

3. Pert. to, or Descr. of, a Hernia: hernial, adj.

4. To Come Through as a Hernia: herniate, rupture,v. (herniation, rupture,n.)

392. INFLAMMATION

1. Inflammation,n.
1. **blain**—inflammatory sore
2. **chilblain**—inflammation on the hands and feet produced by undue exposure to cold and dampness
3. **phlogosis**—inflammation of an external part or member of the body, or of bodily tissue

2. Pert. to Inflammation,adj.
1. **inflammatory**—pert. to, or associated with, inflammation
2. **phlogistic**—pert. to inflammations and fevers; inflammatory
3. **phlogotic**—pert. to an inflammation of an external tissue, or of an external part of the body

3. To Cause Inflammation of or in: inflame, v. (inflammation,n.)

4. Causing Inflammation: inflammative, inflammatory, phlogistic,adj.

5. Counteracting Inflammation: antiphlogistic,adj. (antiphlogistic,n.)

6. To Develop an Inflammation: inflame,v. (inflammation,n.)

393. PLAGUE

1. The Plague,n.
1. **black death**—violent and often fatal plague that ravished Europe and Asia in the 14th century
2. **bubonic plague**—contagious, pestilential, and often fatal disease, marked by fever, chills, inflammation of the lymph glands of the groin, etc.
3. **murrain**—plague affecting domestic animals
4. **pest**—the plague
5. **pestilence**—bubonic or other plague

394. THYROID AND PITUITARY DISORDERS

1. Selected Thyroid Disorders,n.
1. **exophthalmic goiter**—type of goiter so called because protrusion of the eyeballs is a characteristic symptom
2. **goiter**—morbid enlargement of the thyroid gland
3. **Graves' disease**—exophthalmic goiter
4. **hyperthyroidism**—abnormal activity of the thryroid gland, or the resultant mental or physical state (hyperthyroid,adj.)

5. **hypothyroidism**—deficient activity of the thyroid gland or the resultant mental or physical state (hypothyroid,adj.)
6. **myxedema**—defective thyroid functioning resulting in dryness and swelling of the skin (myxedematic, myxedematous,adj.)
7. **thyroiditis**—inflammation of the thyroid gland
8. **thyrotoxicosis**—morbid condition resulting from overactive or abnormally acting thyroid gland
9. **struma**—goiter (strumous, strumose, strumatic,adj.)

2. Selected Pituitary Disorders,n.
1. **hyperpituitarism**—excessive activity of the pituitary gland, causing abnormal increase in size of members of the body
2. **hypopituitarism**—deficient activity of the pituitary gland or the resultant condition, generally marked stoutness, weak sexual activity, etc.

395. VITAMIN DEFICIENCY DISORDERS

1. Selected Vitamin Deficiency Disorders,n.
1. **avitaminosis**—pathological condition resulting from a deficiency of vitamins
2. **beriberi**—disease prevalent in the Orient and resulting from a lack or insufficiency of Vitamin B
3. **pellagra**—disease prevalent in parts of Italy, Southeastern U.S., and other places, and believed to be the result of vitamin deficiency, esp. niacin (pellagrous,adj.)
4. **rachitis**—rickets (rachitic,adj.)
5. **rickets**—childhood disease marked by soft bones, caused by lack of Vitamin D or other nutritional elements (rickety,adj.)
6. **scurvy**—disease caused by lack of Vitamin C and resulting in tendency to hemorrhage, poor healing of wounds, etc. (scurvied, scorbutic,adj.)

396. OTHER DISEASES

1. Certain Diseases or Disorders,n.
1. **ague**—ailment characterized by chills, shaking, and fever
2. **ancylostomiasis**—hookworm disease
3. **anthrax**—infectious disease of cattle and sheep, usually fatal
4. **black vomit**—yellow fever
5. **breakbone fever**—dengue
6. **brucellosis**—undulant fever
7. **caisson disease**—disease caused by too abrupt a change in pressure when rising from the sea depths
8. **dengue**—epidemic and infectious fever of warm climates, causing severe pains in muscles and joints
9. **dropsy**—disease characterized by abnormal accumulation of water in the tissues (dropsical, dropsied,adj.)
10. **edema**—dropsy (edematous, edematose, adj.)
11. **endocrinopathy**—disease resulting from the improper functioning of an endocrine gland (endocrinopathic,adj.)
12. **enteric fever, enteric**—typhoid fever
13. **erethism**—medical condition of excessive irritability of tissue (erethismic, erethistic, erethitic,adj.)
14. **farcy**—contagious disease of horses
15. **glanders**—contagious disease of horses, mules, and certain other animals, characterized by hardening of the glands of the lower jaw
16. **hookworm disease**—disease, characterized by anemia and weakness, that is caused by the hookworm
17. **hydrophobia**—rabies (hydrophobic,adj.)
18. **icterus**—jaundice (icteric,adj.)

19. **jaundice**—disease that causes yellowness of skin, eyes, and urine (jaundice,v.)
20. **malaria**—disease marked by fever, chills, and sweating, and caused by protozoans transmitted to humans by the anopheles mosquito (malarial, malarious, malarian, adj.)
21. **mycosis**—disease caused by infestation of fungi
22. **paludism**—malaria; malarial disease (paludal,adj.)
23. **parrot fever**—psittacosis
24. **psittacosis**—contagious disease of parrots and allied species communicable to humans
25. **rabbit fever**—tularemia
26. **rabies**—infectious disease often afflicting dogs and other animals and transmissible to humans (rabid,adj.)
27. **taeniasis, teniasis**—pathological condition of having tapeworms
28. **trichinosis, trichiniasis**—disease contracted by eating diseased and undercooked pork; the ailment is caused by trichinae, organisms that infect the flesh of unhealthy pigs and are killed by sufficient cooking
29. **tularemia**—disease of rabbits, squirrels, etc., communicable to humans
30. **typhoid fever**—infectious disease, often fatal, contracted through food and water
31. **typhus**—infectious disease caused by microorganisms transmitted to humans by lice and fleas (typhous,adj.)
32. **uncinariasis**—hookworm disease (uncinariatic,adj.)
33. **undulant fever**—ailment caused by a microorganism found in the raw milk of diseased cows and goats
34. **virosis**—any disease caused by a virus
35. **yellow fever**—disease, often fatal, caused by a virus transmitted to humans by the stegomyia mosquito, and usually found in warm climates
36. **yellow jack**—yellow fever

2. Resembling Typhoid Fever: entericoid, paratyphoid,adj.

3. Infected with the Trichina Parasite: trichinous,adj. (of pork)

4. Curing, or Serving to Cure, Jaundice: icteric,adj. (icteric,n.)

397. HEALTH

1. Healthy,adj.
1. **able-bodied**—healthy and strong; physically fit
2. **athletic**—healthy and strong
3. **blooming**—in a state of great health; possessing the glow of health
4. **bouncing**—healthy
5. **eudaemonic**—possessed of health and happiness, resulting from a life lived according to the precepts of reason—an Aristotelian concept
6. **euphoric**—possessed of a sense of physical and/or emotional well-being
7. **fit**—in good health; in good physical condition
8. **hale**—healthy; free from illness (often applied to those old people still in good mental and physical condition)
9. **hearty**—healthy and strong; vigorous
10. **robust**—healthy and strong
11. **robustious**—robust (humorous)
12. **sane**—mentally healthy
13. **sound**—healthy
14. **strapping**—healthy and strong; big and healthy
15. **tonic**—in a healthy condition (of the body or a bodily part)
16. **trig**—in healthy physical condition
17. **trim**—in good physical condition

18. **vigorous**—healthy; possessed of the power that results from good health
19. **whole**—healthy; again healthy after illness
20. **wholesome**—healthy

2. Good Health; Health,n. *From Sec. 1:* bloom, eudaemonia, euphoria, fitness, haleness, heartiness, robustness, sanity, soundness, tone, tonicity or tonus, trim or trimness, vigor or vigorousness, wholeness, wholesomeness; *Also:*
1. **pink**—most healthy state, as *in the pink*
2. **prime**—healthiest or most vigorous state
3. **verdure**—healthy condition
4. **well-being**—health and happiness

3. Healthy-Looking: wholesome,adj. (wholesomeness,n.)

4. Time of Greatest Health or Vigor: prime, n.

5. Pert. to Health,adj.
1. **hygienic**—pert. to health
2. **sanitarian**—pert. to health or to the laws of health
3. **sanitary**—pert. to health, to staying healthy, or to restoring health

6. Healthful; Promoting Health,adj.
1. **beneficial**—productive of physical well-being (beneficialness,n.)
2. **hygienic**—promoting health
3. **nutritious**—healthful, or promoting health, growth, vigor, etc.—of food (nutritiousness,n.)
4. **salubrious**—healthful (salubriousness, salubrity,n.)
5. **salutary**—healthful (salutariness,n.)
6. **sanatory**—promoting health
7. **sanitary**—favorable to health; healthful in the sense of being free of germs, dirt, etc.
8. **wholesome**—healthful; promoting health or well-being (wholesomeness,n.)

7. Health Science,n.
1. **hygiene, hygienics**—science of health preservation (hygienist, hygeist, hygieist, n. hygienic,adj.)
2. **sanitation**—science of conditions that are conducive to health, as cleanliness, lack of germs, etc. (sanitarian,n. sanitary, sanitarian,adj.)

8. Application of Measures Conducive to Health: sanitation,n. (sanitarian,n. sanitary, sanitarian,adj.)

9. Health Resort: sanatorium, sanitarium,n.

10. Concerned about One's Health,adj.
1. **atrabilious, atrabiliar**—hypochondriac
2. **hypochondriac, hypochondriacal**—morbidly concerned about one's health; suffering from delusions of ill-health though there is no organic disease (hypochondria,n. hypochondriac,n.)
3. **valetudinary**—unduly or almost morbidly and constantly concerned about one's health; hypochondriac (valetudinarianism,n. valetudinarian,n.)

11. Greek Goddess of Health: Hygeia,n.

12. Prevention of Disease: prophylaxis,n. (prophylactic,adj. prophylactic,n.)

13. Pert. to, or Descr. of, Precautions against Disease: sanitary,adj.

14. Use of Precautions against Disease: sanitation,n.

398. CURE

1. To Cure; To Heal,v.
1. **cicatrize**—cause (a wound, etc.) to heal by inducing the formation of scar tissue
2. **glutinate**—heal (a wound)
3. **medicate**—cure; heal

4. **physic**—cure; heal; relieve the medical symptoms of
5. **remedy**—cure

2. **Cure; Curing,**n. *From Sec. 1:* cicatrization, glutination, medication

3. **Curing; Curative; Healing,**adj. *From Sec. 1:* glutinative, remedial; *Also:*
   1. **Aesculapian**—medicinal
   2. **medicative, medicatory**—curative; healing
   3. **medicinal**—curative; healing
   4. **sanative, sanatory**—curative; healing
   5. **therapeutic**—curative
   6. **vulnerary**—used or useful in healing wounds

4. **A Cure or Curative, i.e., That Which Cures or Heals,**n. *From Sec. 1:* glutinative, physic, remedy; *From Sec. 3:* medication, medicine, sanative, therapeutic, vulnerary; *Also:*
   1. **balm**—any healing substance
   2. **capsule**—small gelatinous pill containing medicine to be swallowed
   3. **demulcent**—medication used to soothe an irritated mucous membrane or other bodily part
   4. **drug**—chemical substance employed to cure or heal, to prevent disease, restore health, etc.
   5. **lotion**—preparation for healing the skin
   6. **lozenge**—little, flavored candy containing a drug, medicine, etc., and intended to be sucked
   7. **medicament**—any preparation used as a healing or curative agent
   8. **nostrum**—remedy or cure for social problems (derogatory); quack medicine (derogatory)
   9. **officinal**—standard or recognized drug or medication
   10. **ointment**—substance used to heal the skin
   11. **pellet**—small ball of medicine
   12. **pill**—small ball of medicine, to be swallowed whole
   13. **placebo**—medication of no value other than to please the kind of patient who wants a medicine for his ailment
   14. **poultice, cataplasm**—that which is applied as medication to a sore or inflamed part of the body (poultice,v.)
   15. **proprietary**—medicine of which the formula is kept secret
   16. **restorative**—agent, drug, substance, etc., that is used to restore an unconscious person to consciousness; that which restores health
   17. **salve**—healing agent
   18. **serum**—fluid, obtained from an animal that has been rendered immune to a disease, used as a curative for, or preventive of, that disease
   19. **slippery elm**—prepared inner bark of the slippery elm tree used as a demulcent
   20. **specific**—particular drug, substance, or method for curing an individual ailment or disease
   21. **synergist**—remedy used in conjunction with another remedy to which it is similar and the effect of which it enhances
   22. **tablet**—medication in the form of a small, flat cake intended to be sucked or swallowed
   23. **troche**—pill, lozenge, or tablet designed for sucking, usually to soothe the throat
   24. **unguent**—ointment; salve applied to sores
   25. **vaccine**—preparation from the killed or immobilized virus of certain diseases used as an inoculation to immunize against that disease

5. **Referring to a Curative or Healing Agent,**adj. *From Sec. 4:* capsular, medicamentary, officinal, proprietary, restorative, serous,

synergistic or synergistical, unguentary, vaccinal; *Also:*
   1. **medicinal**—pert. to any medicine, medication, or remedy
   2. **pharmacal**—pert. to drugs or medications

6. **Certain Specific Remedies or Drugs,**n.
   1. **antacid**—remedy for acidity (antacid, adj.)
   2. **antirachitic**—medicine that prevents, checks, or cures rickets (antirachitic, adj.)
   3. **antiscorbutic**—medicine that prevents, checks, or cures scurvy (antiscorbutic, adj.)
   4. **chaulmoogra oil**—oil used in treating leprosy, now superseded by more modern remedies
   5. **digitalis**—medication made from the dried leaves of the foxglove and used as a heart stimulant and diuretic
   6. **diuretic**—medicine or agent used to increase the flow of urine (diuretic,adj.)
   7. **ergot**—medication used to stop a hemorrhage
   8. **hemostatic**—medication or agent used to stop a hemorrhage
   9. **mydriatic**—drug that causes pupil dilation (mydriatic, adj.)
   10. **myotic**—drug that causes pupil contraction (myotic,adj.)
   11. **parturifacient**—medicine or drug that induces childbirth or delivery (parturifacient,adj.)
   12. **vaccine**—serum used in immunizing against smallpox (vaccinal,adj.)
   13. **vitamer**—substance that relieves a vitamin deficiency (vitameric,adj.)

7. **Morbid Craving for Medication; Compulsive and Pathological Urge to Self-Medication:** pharmacomania,n.

8. **Substance or Agent That Destroys Bacteria, Microbes, Fungi, etc., or Destroys or Expels Worms,**n.
   1. **anthelmintic**—agent or medicine that destroys or expels intestinal worms (anthelmintic,adj.)
   2. **anti-bacterial**—substance or medication that destroys or counteracts bacteria (anti-bacterial,adj.)
   3. **antibiotic**—substance, produced by fungi, molds, etc., that acts as a destroying agent of certain bacteria; the drugs made from this, such as penicillin, aureomycin, streptomycin, terramycin, etc. (antibiotic, adj.)
   4. **antibody**—substance in the blood that destroys, weakens, or counteracts bacteria, poisons, etc.
   5. **bactericide**—substance or agent that destroys bacteria (bactericidal,adj.)
   6. **bacteriophage**—agent or substance that destroys bacteria, and normally present in the blood, urine, etc., of those recovering from a bacterial disease (bacteriophagic,adj.)
   7. **disinfectant**—agent that destroys disease germs (disinfection,n. disinfect,v.)
   8. **fungicide**—agent that destroys fungi (fungicidal,adj.)
   9. **germicide**—agent that destroys disease germs (germicidal,adj.)
   10. **microbicide**—agent that destroys disease-producing bacteria or other microorganisms (microbicidal,adj.)
   11. **parasiticide**—agent that destroys parasites (parasiticide, adj.)
   12. **sulfa drugs**—group of drugs used as antibacterials
   13. **taeniacide, teniacide**—substance or agent that destroys tapeworms (taeniacidal, teniacidal,adj.)
   14. **taeniafuge, teniafuge**—substance that expels tapeworms
   15. **vermicide**—substance or drug that de-

stroys parasitic intestinal worms (vermicidal,adj.)

16. vermifuge—substance or agent that destroys or expels intestinal worms (vermifugal,adj.)

9. Substance That Causes the System to Produce Antibodies: antigen,n.

10. Checking Bacterial Growth without Destroying the Bacteria: bacteriostatic,adj.

11. Universal Remedy; Cure for All Ills: catholicon, cure-all, elixir, panacea,n. (panacean,adj.)

12. Believer in Universal Remedies: panaceist,n.

13. Any Substance or Matter Used in Medicines, Medications, Remedies, etc.: materia medica

14. Pert. to Curing or Healing,adj.
1. **Aesculapian**—medical
2. **medical**—pert. to healing or the healing arts
3. **medicinal**—pert. to medical healing; therapeutic
4. **orthogenic**—pert. to, descr. of, or designating, such medical, psychological, or surgical techniques that are designed to correct emotional, mental, or nervous ailments of children
5. **sanatory**—pert. to healing
6. **therapeutic**—pert. to the art of healing or to the treatment and cure of disease

15. Curative Power or Quality: therapy,n.

16. Curable: medicable, remediable,adj.

17. Incurable: immedicable, irremediable,adj.

18. Capable of Being Healed: medicable,adj. (immedicable,neg.)

19. To Become Healed by the Formation of Scar Tissue: cicatrize,v. (cicatrization,n.)

20. Scar Tissue That Forms over a Healed Wound: cicatrix, cicatrice,n. (cicatricial, cicatricose,adj.)

21. To Get Well: convalesce, heal, mend, rally, recover, recuperate, revalesce,v. (convalescence, rally, recovery, recuperation, revalescence,n. convalescent, revalescent,n. convalescent, recuperative, revalescent,adj.)

399. DRUG

1. Drug Science or Art,n.
1. **pharmaceutics**—art of compounding drugs, medications, etc.
2. **pharmacodynamics**—science of the action of drugs
3. **pharmacognosy**—science of crude drugs
4. **pharmacography**—pharmacognosy
5. **pharmacology**—science of the actions, nature, and properties of drugs
6. **pharmacy**—art of compounding drugs, medications, etc.

2. Pert. to, or Descr. of, Drug Science, etc., adj. *From Sec. 1:* pharmaceutical, pharmacodynamic, pharmacographic or pharmacographical, pharmacological, pharmacal

3. Student or Practitioner of a Drug Science, etc., n. *From Sec. 1:* pharmaceutist, pharmacologist, pharmacist; *Also:*
1. **apothecary**—druggist
2. **druggist**—one who compounds and dispenses drugs, medications, etc.
3. **gallipot**—druggist (colloq.)

4. Kept in Stock by a Druggist: officinal,adj.

5. Place Where Drugs or Medications Are Prepared, etc.,n.
1. **dispensary, dispensatory**—place where medications are prepared and distributed or sold
2. **pharmacy, drugstore**—a store or place

where drugs and medications are kept, compounded, or dispensed

6. Book of Drugs, Medications, etc.,n.
1. **dispensatory**—book that explains how medicines are to be prepared, and containing a list of the drugs used in medicine
2. **pharmacopoeia**—book describing official list of drugs, medications, etc., and their components (pharmacopoeial,adj.)

7. Narcotic,n.
1. **barbiturate**—one of a general class of drugs, derived from barbituric acid, and used to induce sleep, or as a hypnotic or sedative (Affects the higher centers of the brain, and does not normally injure the heart or kidneys. Common examples are phenobarbital, nembutal, etc.)
2. **cocaine**—alkaloid, derived from coca leaves, that acts first as a stimulant, then as a narcotic
3. **codeine**—alkaloid derived from opium
4. **dope**—preparation of opium used for smoking, or, loosely, any narcotic (colloq.)
5. **drug**—narcotic
6. **hashish**—narcotic derived from the oriental hemp plant
7. **heroin**—habit-forming derivative of morphine used as a sedative or narcotic
8. **hypnotic**—drug used to induce sleep or as a sedative
9. **laudanum**—tincture of opium
10. **marijuana**—narcotic made from the dried leaves or flowers of the hemp, usually smoked in cigarettes
11. **morphia**—morphine
12. **morphine**—derivative of opium (morphinic,adj.)
13. **opiate**—narcotic; a derivative of opium; anything that has a narcotic effect
14. **opium**—narcotic derived from the opium poppy
15. **paregoric**—camphorated tincture of opium, a very mild narcotic often used with infants
16. **phenobarbital**—chemical substance used as a hypnotic
17. **sedative**—drug used to calm, soothe, or reduce pain, irritability, excitement, or functional activity
18. **soporific**—drug that causes sleep

8. Narcotic,adj. *From Sec. 7:* hypnotic, opiate, sedative, soporific

9. To Put under the Influence of a Narcotic,v. *From Sec. 7:* drug, morphinize, sedate (morphinization, sedation,n.); *Also:* 1. narcotize—put under the influence of a narcotic (narcotization,n.)

10. Narcotic State,n. *From Sec. 9:* sedation, narcosis or narcotism

11. Under the Influence of a Narcotic,adj. *From Sec. 9:* drugged, morphinized, sedated, narcotized; *Also:* 1. **poppied**—drugged

12. Addiction to Narcotics,n.
1. **cocainism, cocainomania**—to cocaine
2. **morphinism**—to morphine
3. **narcotism, narcoticism**—to narcotics
4. **opiumism**—to opium

13. Narcotics Addict,n. *From Sec. 12:* cocainist or cocainomaniac, morphinist, narcotic; *Also:* 1. **dope fiend, drug fiend**—narcotics addict (colloq.)

14. Action or Influence of a Narcotic or of Narcotics: narcotism,n.

15. Illness from Drugs or Narcotics,n.
1. **cocainism**—illness produced by the habitual and excessive use of cocaine
2. **cocainomania**—insanity resulting from the cocaine habit
3. **digitalism**—morbid condition resulting from excessive use of digitalis

4. **jag**—intoxication from narcotics (colloq.)
5. **morphinism**—morbid condition produced by habitual use of morphine
6. **narcoma**—stupor from the use of narcotics (narcomatous,adj.)
7. **narcosis**—stupor or unconsciousness produced by narcotics (narcose, narcous, adj.)
8. **nicotinism**—pathological condition caused by excessive use of tobacco
9. **opiumism**—unhealthy condition resulting from habituation to opium

16. **Morbid Desire for Narcotics:** narcomania, n. (narcomaniac,adj.)

400. MEDICAL TREATMENT

1. **To Treat Medically,**v.
1. **doctor**—treat medically; medicate
2. **medicament**—treat with medicines or medication
3. **medicate**—treat with medicine for purposes of healing or curing
4. **physic**—treat with medicine, esp. a laxative, purgative, or cathartic

2. **Medical Treatment,**n. *From Sec. 1:* medicamentation, medication; *Also:* 1. **therapy**—treatment of disease or of emotional difficulties or disturbances (therapist,n.)

3. **Referring or Pert. to the Treatment of Disease:** clinical, therapeutic,adj.

4. **To Receive Medical Treatment:** doctor,v.

5. **Place of Treatment,**n.
1. **asylum**—place of treatment for special afflictions, esp. insanity
2. **clinic**—part of a hospital or medical school where non-resident patients receive treatment, sometimes at low cost or as charity
3. **hospital**—institution for the treatment of sick or injured people
4. **infirmary**—place where the sick or injured come for treatment
5. **pesthouse**—hospital for those infected with virulent or contagious diseases
6. **polyclinic**—hospital or clinic for treating many kinds of diseases
7. **sanatorium, sanitarium**—place for mental or physical rehabilitation, or for treatment of disease

6. **Special or Specialized Treatment; Method of Treatment; Therapy,**n.
1. **aerotherapy, aerotherapeutics**—treatment of ailments with air or other gases
2. **allopathy**—system of medical treatment that combats diseases with substances that produce effects opposite to those caused by the diseases (allopathic,adj.)
3. **analysis**—psychoanalysis (analytic, analytical,adj.)
4. **balneotherapy**—treatment of disease by baths
5. **bibliotherapy**—treatment of emotional disorders by inspiring the patient to read certain kinds of books
6. **chemotherapy**—treatment of internal ailments by chemical agents
7. **chiropractic**—treatment of physical ailments by manipulating the articulations of the body, esp. those connected to the spinal column
8. **Christian Science**—system and religion of healing based on the concept that the cause and effect of disease are mental
9. **collapse therapy**—method of decreasing volume of the lung in the treatment of pulmonary tuberculosis
10. **Couéism**—therapy by self-suggestion
11. **crymotherapy**—therapy by the application of cold
12. **cult**—unorthodox or spurious system of treatment based on the theory that all

disease has the same underlying cause (derogative)
13. **electrotherapy, electroshock therapy**—method of passing up to 110 volts of electricity through the brain for $\frac{1}{10}$ to $\frac{1}{5}$ of a second in the treatment of certain mental ailments
14. **endocrinotherapy**—treatment of disease with endocrines
15. **fever therapy**—method of artificially inducing high temperatures in the body as a treatment for certain diseases
16. **group therapy**—psychotherapy administered to a small, usually unchanging group of patients who learn to relate to each other and to the therapist as they discuss their problems
17. **heliotherapy**—treatment of ailments by sun baths
18. **homeopathy**—therapy following the theory originated by Dr. Samuel Hahnemann in 1796 that "disease can be cured by drugs that are capable of producing in a healthy individual symptoms similar to those of the disease to be treated" (homeopathic,adj.)
19. **hydropathy**—the use of water, both by drinking and bathing, for the treatment of disease (hydropathic,adj.)
20. **hydrotherapy**—treatment of disease with water, baths, etc.
21. **hypnoanalysis**—psychoanalysis of a patient who is under hypnosis or the influence of a sedating drug
22. **hypnotherapy**—treatment of mental or physical disease through, or while the patient is under, hypnosis
23. **insulin therapy**—method of causing shock by the injection of large doses of insulin, in the treatment of mental disorders
24. **kinesiatrics**—therapy involving proper muscular movements (kinesiatric,adj.)
25. **malariotherapy**—treatment of the early stages of syphilis by infecting with malaria, the fever thus produced often killing the spirochetes
26. **massotherapy**—treatment of ailments by massage
27. **medication**—treatment by the use of drugs, medicine, etc.
28. **metrazol shock therapy**—method of causing convulsions and brain-wave changes by intravenous injections of metrazol, in the treatment of mental disorders
29. **narcosynthesis**—treatment of neurosis in which narcotics are used; while under the influence of these the patient is induced to recall incidents or experiences from his past
30. **naturopathy**—treatment (non-medical in concept) by assisting nature (naturopathic,adj.)
31. **occupational therapy**—method of getting the patient interested in certain kinds of hobbies or manual occupations as a treatment for certain disorders or during convalescence
32. **pharmacotherapy**—treatment with drugs
33. **phototherapy, phototherapeutics**—treatment of diseases, usually skin ailments, with light
34. **physical therapy, physiotherapy**—treatment of disease by light, heat, massage, electricity, and other physical means
35. **pneumothorax, artificial pneumothorax**—treatment of pulmonary tuberculosis by collapsing the lung
36. **prosthesis**—addition of an artificial part or member to the human body, as a denture, artificial limb, etc. (prosthetic,adj.)
37. **psychiatry**—treatment of mental or emotional disorders (psychiatric,adj.)
38. **psychoanalysis**—treatment of mental or

emotional disorders or maladjustment by the use of Dr. Sigmund Freud's technique of discovering and exploring the unconscious (psychoanalytic, psychoanalytical, adj.)

39. **psychotherapy**—any kind of treatment of emotional disorders (psychotherapeutic, adj.)
40. **pyretotherapy**—treatment of certain diseases by inducing fever
41. **radiotherapy**—treatment of disease with X-rays or other radioactive substances
42. **radium therapy**—the use of radium to destroy malignant tissue, usually in the treatment of cancer
43. **roentgenotherapy**—treatment with X-rays
44. **therapeutics**—therapy
45. **X-ray therapy**—treatment of disease or morbid growths by X-rays

7. Therapist; Practitioner of a Therapy,n. *From Sec. 6:* allopath, analyst, chiropractor, Christian Scientist, homeopath, naturopath or naturopathist, physical therapist or physiotherapist, prosthetist, psychoanalyst, psychotherapist, therapeutist; *Also:* 1. **healer**—practitioner of Christian Science (term not accepted by the Christian Scientists)

401. MEDICAL BRANCHES

1. Selected Medical or Related Branches, Sciences, or Studies,n.
1. **alienism**—study or science of mental illness and its treatment (The term is today relatively unused, psychiatry having taken its place.)
2. **analysis**—psychoanalysis
3. **andriatrics, andriatry**—medical specialty dealing with the diseases peculiar to men, esp. diseases of the male sexual organs
4. **anesthesiology**—specialty concerned with the study and use of anesthesia and anesthetics
5. **anesthetics**—science of anesthesia and anesthetics
6. **balneology**—science of healing with baths of natural mineral water
7. **cardiology**—medical science relating to the heart
8. **chiropody**—science of treatment of foot ailments; podiatry
9. **cystology**—medical science of the bladder
10. **dentistry**—branch dealing with the care and repair of the teeth
11. **dermatology**—science of the skin, its diseases, treatment, etc.
12. **diagnostics, diagnostic**—science or art of recognition of diseases and symptoms
13. **dosology, dosiology**—science of doses (of medication, etc.)
14. **encephalology**—scientific study of the brain
15. **endemiology**—science of those diseases that are peculiar to a locality, region, etc.
16. **endocrinology**—specialty relating to the treatment of disorders of the endocrine glands
17. **enterology**—former term for gastroenterology
18. **epidemiology**—medical science relating to epidemics, plagues, etc.
19. **etiology**—science of the causes of disease
20. **exodontia**—branch of dentistry specializing in extraction of teeth
21. **forensic medicine**—science of the relationship of medical facts to law
22. **gastroenterology**—branch that deals with the stomach and intestines, diseases peculiar to them, etc.
23. **gastrology**—medical science of the stomach, its functions, processes, diseases, etc.

24. **geriatrics**—specialty concerned with the medical care of the aged
25. **glossology**—medical study of the tongue
26. **gynecology**—medical science of diseases peculiar to women, especially ailments of the genitourinary tract, reproductive organs, etc.
27. **gyniatrics**—branch dealing with the treatment of diseases peculiar to women
28. **hematology**—science of the blood
29. **hemopathology**—science of blood diseases
30. **herniology**—science of ruptures
31. **histology**—science relating to the minute structure of animal and plant tissue
32. **immunology**—science of immunity to disease
33. **internal medicine**—specialty concerned with the diagnosis and treatment of diseases of the interior of the body
34. **kinesiology**—science of movements as a therapeutic agency
35. **laryngology**—specialty concerned with diseases of the larynx
36. **lay analysis**—the practice of psychoanalysis by a non-medical therapist
37. **legal medicine**—forensic medicine
38. **leprology**—science of leprosy and its treatment
39. **maieutics**—obstetrics
40. **malariology**—medical study of malaria
41. **materia medica**—medical science dealing with those substances used in curing disease, or in medicines, medications, or remedies
42. **medical jurisprudence**—forensic medicine
43. **medicine**—science or art of curing without surgery
44. **mental hygiene**—science of the promotion of mental health and prevention of mental disease
45. **midwifery**—practice (by someone other than a medical doctor) of assisting in the delivery of a child
46. **myology**—medical science dealing with muscles
47. **nasology**—medical science dealing with the nose
48. **nephrology**—medical science of the kidneys, their diseases, treatment, etc.
49. **neurology**—specialty dealing with the organic diseases of the nervous system, esp. of the brain, spinal cord, and peripheral nerves
50. **neuropathology**—study of the diseases of the nerves
51. **neuropsychiatry**—specialty dealing with the diagnosis and treatment of nervous and mental diseases
52. **nosology**—science of disease or disease classification
53. **obstetrics**—specialty concerned with the treatment of women during pregnancy and childbirth, and with the delivery of the infant
54. **odontology**—science of the structure, development, and diseases of the teeth
55. **oncology**—medical study or science of tumors
56. **ophthalmology**—medical specialty dealing with the structure, diseases, treatment, etc., of the eye
57. **optometry**—science of correction of visual defects through the fitting of glasses
58. **organology**—science of organic structure; splanchnology
59. **orthodontia, orthodontics**—division of dentistry that corrects irregularity of the position of the teeth
60. **orthopedics**—specialty concerned with the treatment, often by surgery, of injuries, deformities, and diseases of the bones, joints, muscles, tendons, ligaments, and peripheral nerves

61. **orthopedic surgery**—orthopedics
62. **orthopsychiatry**—preventive psychiatry
63. **orthoptics**—science or practice of correcting vision through mechanical means other than the use of glasses
64. **osteology**—science of the anatomy and structure of the bones
65. **osteopathy**—science and practice deriving from the medical theory that diseases arise from displacement of bones with resultant pressure on blood vessels, and that treatment and cure are found in the manipulation of affected parts
66. **otolaryngology**—specialty concerned with the treatment of the throat and ear
67. **otology**—medical science dealing with the ear, its ailments, etc.
68. **otorhinolaryngology**—medical branch dealing with the diseases of the ear, nose, and throat
69. **pathology**—medical specialty dealing with the causes, symptoms, nature, etc., of disease; medical practice devoted to post-mortem examinations to determine cause or causes of death, or to the examination of tissues removed by operation
70. **pediatrics**—medical branch specializing in the care and treatment of children
71. **pedodontia**—branch of dentistry specializing in the care and treatment of children's teeth
72. **periodontia**—branch of dentistry dealing with diseases of the gums and other tissue surrounding the teeth
73. **pharyngology**—medical science of the diseases of the pharynx
74. **physic**—profession of healing; practice of medicine (archaic)
75. **physiology**—science of the functions of living organs or organisms
76. **podiatry**—study and treatment of ailments of the foot
77. **podology**—science treating of the structure, etc., of the foot
78. **posology**—dosology
79. **proctology**—medical science of the diseases of the rectum and anus
80. **prosthetics**—branch of surgery or dentistry supplying artificial members, parts, teeth, etc., for the human body
81. **prosthodontia**—branch of dentistry specializing in the replacement of teeth, fitting of false teeth, etc.
82. **psychiatry**—specialty devoted to the care of the mentally ill, the restoration of sanity, and the alleviation of emotional disturbances
83. **psychoanalysis**—the science of treating emotional disturbances by helping patients to probe their unconscious, mainly through techniques devised by Dr. Sigmund Freud of Vienna
84. **psychopathology**—science of mental and emotional disorders
85. **psychotherapeutics**—science of the treatment of mental or emotional disorders
86. **psychotherapy**—art or science of treating emotional disorders
87. **pyretology**—medical science relating to fever
88. **radiology**—science of radioactive substances and X-rays in the diagnosis and treatment of disease
89. **rhinology**—science of the diseases of the nose
90. **roentgenology**—science of X-rays and their use in medicine and dentistry
91. **semeiology**—science of the symptoms of disease
92. **serology**—science of serums, their preparation, use, etc.
93. **somatology, somatics**—science of the comparative structure, function, etc., of the human body

94. **specialty, specialism**—the concentration of practice upon certain diseases, organs, parts of the body, etc.
95. **splanchnology**—medical science of the viscera and visceral diseases
96. **stomatology**—medical science of the mouth and its diseases
97. **surgery**—science or practice of the correction of medical defects through operation
98. **symptomatology**—science of the symptoms of disease
99. **syphilology**—medical science dealing with syphilis and other venereal diseases
100. **teratology**—science dealing with anatomical freaks and monstrosities
101. **therapeutics**—science dealing with remedies for disease
102. **theriatrics**—veterinary medicine as a science
103. **tocology**—obstetrics
104. **toxicology**—science of poisons and their antidotes
105. **trichology**—science treating of hair and its diseases
106. **urology**—specialty dealing with the treatment of diseases of the genitourinary system, including the kidneys, bladder, and male genital organs
107. **venereology**—medical specialty dealing with venereal disease
108. **veterinary medicine**—specialty dealing with the treatment of sick or injured horses or other animals
109. **virology**—medical science of viruses and virus diseases

2. Doctor; Practitioner or Student of a Medical or Related Branch,n. *From Sec. 1:* anesthesiologist, cardiologist, etc.; alienist, analyst, chiropodist, dentist, diagnostician, exodontist, geriatrician, internist, lay analyst, midwife, neuropsychiatrist, obstetrician, optometrist, orthodontist, orthopedist, orthopedic surgeon, orthopsychiatrist, osteopath or osteopathic physician, pediatrician, pedodontist, periodontist, podiatrist, prosthetist, prosthodontist, psychiatrist, psychoanalyst, psychotherapeutist, psychotherapist, specialist surgeon, therapeutist, veterinarian or veterinary; *Also:*

1. **accoucheur**—obstetrician
2. **accoucheuse**—female obstetrician; midwife
3. **Aesculapian**—medical doctor
4. **alienist**—psychiatrist who specializes in legal aspects of insanity
5. **allergist**—doctor who specializes in the discovery and treatment of abnormal sensitivity to various substances, such as strawberries, dust, feathers, paint, hair of animals, pollen, etc.
6. **anesthetist**—one who administers anesthetics
7. **aurist**—specialist in ear diseases
8. **clinician**—doctor concerned with the treatment of disease or the observation of the symptoms or progress of a disease
9. **farrier**—horse doctor
10. **general practitioner**—one who practices general medicine rather than specializing in any limited field
11. **healer**—one who heals or cures
12. **intern, interne**—resident doctor in a hospital who is preparing for private practice
13. **leech**—former name, and now contemptuous term, for a physician, in allusion to the ancient custom of bleeding patients
14. **medic**—medical doctor
15. **medical doctor**—licensed practitioner of the art and science of curing disease
16. **medicine man**—person who, among certain primitive peoples and North American Indians, cures, or claims to cure,

disease by various herbs, drugs, magical charms, and incantations, etc.
17. **medico**—medical doctor; medical student
18. **neuropathist**—neurologist
19. **oculist**—ophthalmologist
20. **physician**—medical doctor, strictly one who heals with medicines or drugs rather than through surgery
21. **quack**—unskillful doctor (contemptuous)
22. **quacksalver**—quack
23. **shaman**—healer by magic (shamanic, shamanistic,adj.)
24. **witch doctor**—medicine man among African peoples

3. Pert. to, or Descr. of, a Medical or Related Branch,adj. *From Sec. 1:* anesthesiological, cardiological, etc.; analytic, diagnostic, exodontic, geriatric, neuropsychiatric, obstetrical, optometric, orthodontic, orthopedic, orthopsychiatric, orthoptic, osteopathic, pediatric, pedodontic, periodontic, podiatric, prosthetic, prosthodontic, psychiatric, psychoanalytic, psychotherapeutic, surgical, veterinarian or veterinary

4. To Practice, Be Engaged in, or Do the Work of, a Medical or Related Branch,v. *From Sec. 1:* analyze, diagnose, psychoanalyze, specialize; *From Sec. 2:* intern

5. Pert. to the Art of the Physician: Aesculapian,adj.

6. Prescribed by a Medical Doctor: magistral,adj.

7. Symbol of the Medical Doctor—a Serpent-Wreathed Staff: caduceus,n.

8. God of Medicine or Medical Arts: Asclepius (Greek) ; Aesculapius (Roman) ,n.

9. Oath Taken by a Doctor in Reference to His Ethical Duties to Patients, etc.: Hippocratic oath,n.

10. Commonly Known Medical Tests,n.
1. **Aschheim-Zondek test**—test for pregnancy
2. **Dick test**—test to determine susceptibility to scarlet fever
3. **ink-blot test**—Rorschach test
4. **rabbit test**—Aschheim-Zondek test
5. **Rorschach test**—test in which a subject's emotional attitudes can be analyzed by his reactions to ten standard ink blots
6. **Schick test**—test of immunity to diphtheria
7. **Wassermann test**—test for syphilis made with a sample of a person's blood

402. SURGERY

1. Surgery, General; Surgical Removal or Cutting,n.
1. **ablation**—surgical removal
2. **anaplasty**—plastic surgery
3. **anatomy**—dissection of animals or plants
4. **autoplasty**—surgical repair of wounds or lesions with tissue taken from the same body
5. **autopsy**—dissection of a corpse to determine the cause of death
6. **biopsy**—surgical removal of tissue from a living organism for microscopic examinations and diagnosis
7. **dissection**—cutting of an animal or organism apart or into its component parts for purposes of study of its structure, functions, etc.
8. **excision**—surgical removal
9. **exsection**—excision
10. **incision**—a surgical cutting into; cut made by surgery
11. **microtomy**—cutting of sections of tissue for microscopic examination
12. **necrotomy**—dissection of corpses

13. **neoplasty**—surgical restoration of a missing part or tissue; autoplasty
14. **neurosurgery**—surgery of the brain and nervous system
15. **operation**—surgical cutting, repair, removal, etc.
16. **plastic surgery**—surgery intended to improve the appearance of the body or members of the body
17. **prosection**—dissection of bodies for anatomical instruction
18. **psychosurgery**—surgery on the brain in order to correct emotional or mental disorders
19. **resection**—a surgical cutting away, or cutting away of a part
20. **scarification**—surface scratches or incisions made in the skin or a wound
21. **section**—a surgical cutting or division
22. **vivisection**—surgery performed on a live animal for research or scientific purposes

2. To Cut Surgically or Perform Surgery (on),v. *From Sec. 1:* dissect; excise, excide, or exscind; exsect, incise, operate, prosect, resect, scarify, section, vivisect

3. Surgeon,n. *From Sec. 1:* anatomist, microtomist, necrotomist, neurosurgeon, operator, plastic surgeon, prosector, vivisector or vivisectionist

4. Surgical,adj. *From Sec. 1:* anaplastic, autoplastic, biopsic, dissective or dissectional, microtomic or microtomical, necrotomic, neoplastic, neurosurgical, operative, vivisectional

5. Selected Specific Surgeries,n.
1. **amputation**—surgical removal of a limb or part of a limb
2. **apicoectomy**—surgical removal of the root of a tooth
3. **appendectomy**—surgical removal of the appendix
4. **Caesarean section, Caesarean**—delivery of a child by cutting through the abdomen and uterus of the mother
5. **cephalotomy**—cutting or opening the head of the fetus to facilitate delivery during birth
6. **chiroplasty**—plastic surgery of the hand
7. **circumcision**—surgical removal of the prepuce of the penis as a religious rite or health measure
8. **cirsotomy**—surgical incision of a swollen vein
9. **colostomy**—surgical formation of an artificial anal opening, or opening for elimination, in the colon
10. **costectomy**—surgical removal of a rib
11. **costotomy**—surgical incision into a rib
12. **craniectomy**—surgical removal of parts of the skull bones
13. **cranioclasis, cranioclasty**—crushing of the fetal head during delivery
14. **cranioplasty**—surgical correction of skull deficiencies
15. **craniotomy**—cutting or breaking of the fetal head during delivery; surgical removal of part of the skull
16. **cystectomy**—surgical removal of the gall bladder
17. **cystolithotomy**—surgical removal of a stone from the bladder
18. **cystotomy**—surgical incision into the bladder
19. **dermatotomy**—surgical incision of the skin
20. **encephalotomy**—dissection of the brain; destruction of the brain of the fetus to make delivery possible
21. **episiotomy**—surgical enlarging of the vulvar opening during childbirth
22. **exodontia, extraction**—surgical removal of a tooth
23. **frontal lobotomy, prefrontal lobotomy**

—brain surgery to correct certain emotional disorders

24. **glossectomy**—surgical removal of the tongue
25. **herniotomy**—surgical removal of a rupture
26. **hysterectomy**—surgical removal of the womb
27. **leucotomy, leukotomy, prefrontal leucotomy**—frontal lobotomy
28. **lobotomy**—cutting of brain tissue; frontal lobotomy
29. **mastectomy**—surgical removal of the breast
30. **mastostomy, mastotomy**—surgical incision in, of, or into the breast
31. **necrotomy**—surgical removal of dead bone
32. **nephrotomy**—surgical cutting into a kidney
33. **ostectomy**—surgical excision of bone
34. **osteoplasty**—surgical operation to correct bone ailment or loss
35. **osteotomy**—surgical operation in which bone is cut into, or in which a piece of bone is cut out
36. **otoplasty**—plastic surgery to restore the external ear
37. **ototomy**—cutting of any ear tissue; surgical operation of or in the ear
38. **ovariectomy, ovariotomy**—surgical excision of an ovary
39. **phlebotomy**—surgical cutting into a vein or veins
40. **pneumectomy**—surgical removal of part of a lung
41. **psychosurgery**—frontal lobotomy
42. **rhinoplasty**—plastic surgery of the nose
43. **scarification**—the making of slight incisions in the skin
44. **thyroidectomy**—surgical removal of thyroid tissue
45. **tonsillectomy**—removal of the tonsils by surgery
46. **varicotomy**—surgical incision of a varicose or swollen vein
47. **venesection**—phlebotomy

6. To Perform Surgery (upon),v. *From Sec. 5:* amputate, circumcise, extract, nephrotomize, phlebotomize, scarify; *Also:* 1. trepan, trephine—cut or bore through the skull with a special surgical instrument

7. Surgeon,n. *From Sec. 5:* exodontist, necrotomist, phlebotomist

8. Surgical,adj. *From Sec. 5:* Caesarean, chiroplastic, exodontic, necrotomic, rhinoplastic

9. One Who Has Had a Limb or Limbs Removed in Surgery: amputee,n.

10. Capable of Being Operated Upon: operable,adj. (inoperable,neg.)

11. One Who Is Opposed to Surgery on Live Animals: anti-vivisectionist,n. (anti-vivisection,n.)

12. One Who Favors Surgery on Live Animals: vivisectionist,n.

13. Selected Surgical Instruments,n.
1. **auriscalp**—device for scraping the interior of the ear
2. **dermatome**—instrument for cutting skin
3. **lancet**—sharp surgical knife
4. **microtome**—instrument for cutting sections of tissue for microscopic examination
5. **scalpel**—surgical knife with a thin blade
6. **scarificator**—instrument for making surface incisions or scratches in the skin or a wound
7. **trepan, trephine**—instrument for cutting or boring through the skull
8. **xyster**—instrument for scraping bone

403. ANIMAL

1. Animal Life,n.
1. **aborigines**—original animal life of a region (aboriginal,adj.)
2. **animality**—animal life
3. **avifauna**—bird life of a region (avifaunal, adj.)
4. **benthos**—animal life on the bottom of a sea or of a body of fresh water (benthonic,adj.)
5. **biota**—animal and plant life of a region
6. **fauna**—animal life of a region or period (faunal,adj.)
7. **ichthyofauna**—fish life of a region
8. **microbiota**—microscopic animal and plant life of a region (microbiotic,adj.)
9. **ornis**—bird life of a particular place or region
10. **piscifauna**—fish life of a region
11. **plankton**—animal life used as food by larger marine life in a body of water (planktonic,adj.)
12. **vermin**—troublesome, harmful, or disgusting animal life, such as roaches, lice, bedbugs, mice, fleas, etc. (verminous,adj.)

2. Treatise on the Animal Life of a Region or Time: fauna,n. (faunal,adj.)

3. The Animal World: animality,n.

4. Animals,n.
1. **cattle**—live animals raised for food, milk, etc., generally of the bovine species; any domesticated four-footed animals
2. **game**—wild animals hunted for food or sport
3. **livestock**—domestic animals kept on a farm or ranch
4. **stud**—animals kept for breeding purposes

5. Group of Animals,n.
1. **apiary**—of bees kept for their honey
2. **ascension**—of larks
3. **bale**—of turtles
4. **band**—of jays
5. **barren**—of mules
6. **bevy**—of larks, partridge, quail, or roes
7. **brood**—of newborn chicks, grouse, or other birds of the same kind
8. **cete**—of badgers
9. **charm**—of goldfinches
10. **clowder**—of wildcats
11. **clutch**—brood
12. **colony**—of ants, bees, or wasps
13. **community**—of animals living in a common home or having common interests
14. **congregation**—of plover
15. **covey**—of partridge, quail, or other birds
16. **crash**—of rhinoceroses
17. **down**—of hares
18. **dray**—of squirrels
19. **drift**—of hogs
20. **drove**—of cattle, swine, or other animals that are driven in a flock
21. **dule**—of turtledoves
22. **exaltation**—of larks
23. **eye**—of pheasants
24. **fall**—of woodcocks
25. **farrow**—of pigs, or of pigs in a litter
26. **fesymes**—of ferrets
27. **flight**—of swallows, or, occasionally, of other birds
28. **flock**—of animals that feed together, such as sheep, goats, geese, or other birds, etc.
29. **fold**—of sheep, or of sheep in an enclosure
30. **gaggle**—of geese on the water
31. **gam**—of whales (New England idiom)
32. **gang**—of elk
33. **hatch**—brood
34. **herd**—of cattle, elephants, whales, or other animals
35. **hive**—of bees
36. **host**—of locusts
37. **hover**—of trout
38. **husk**—of jack rabbits

39. **insectarium**—of live insects
40. **kennel**—of dogs or other animals
41. **kindle**—of kittens
42. **labor**—of moles
43. **lepe**—of leopards
44. **litter**—of newborn animals
45. **murmuration**—of starlings
46. **muster**—of peacocks
47. **mustering**—of storks
48. **nest**—of cottontails
49. **nide**—of pheasants in a nest (British)
50. **pace**—of asses
51. **pack**—of dogs, hounds, wolves, or certain other animals
52. **pod**—of seals, whales, or certain other animals or birds
53. **pride**—of lions
54. **raft**—of game birds afloat in water
55. **rafter**—of turkeys
56. **rag**—of colts
57. **rich**—of martens
58. **rout**—of wolves
59. **school**—of fish or other water animals swimming together
60. **sedge**—of herons
61. **shoal**—of porpoises; school
62. **shrewdness**—of apes
63. **singular**—of boars
64. **skein**—of wild ducks, wild geese, or other wild fowl, esp. in flight
65. **skulk**—of foxes
66. **sloth**—of bears
67. **smack**—of jellyfish
68. **sord**—of mallards
69. **sounder**—of wild swine
70. **spring**—of teals
71. **stud**—of mares
72. **swarm**—of bees or other insects, esp. in motion
73. **team**—of horses, oxen, etc., harnessed to a vehicle
74. **tribe**—of goats or sparrows
75. **trip**—of seals
76. **troop**—of various animals
77. **vespiary**—of social wasps in a nest
78. **walk**—of snipe
79. **watch**—of nightingales
80. **wisp**—of snipe or other birds

6. Of Animals as to General Category,adj.
1. **arthropod, arthropodal, arthropodan, arthropodous**—of the category of animals containing the crustaceans (lobsters, shrimps, crabs, etc.), the insects, and the spiders and scorpions
2. **articulate**—of invertebrate animals that have bodies composed of ringlike segments
3. **bestial, beastly**—of four-footed animals
4. **biped, bipedal**—of two-footed creatures, such as man
5. **brindle**—of animals of gray or tan color, with darker streaks or spots
6. **brute, brutish**—of dumb animals
7. **carnivorous**—of meat-eating animals
8. **creatural**—of animals; of any living beings other than plants
9. **crossbred**—of animals bred from different species, genera, breeds, etc.
10. **gregarious**—of animals that move, feed, and live in flocks
11. **herbivorous**—of grass- or grain-eating animals
12. **hybrid**—of animals whose parents are of different breeds, species, genera, etc.
13. **insectivorous**—of insect-eating animals
14. **invertebrate**—of animals that lack a backbone
15. **mammalian**—of animals that suckle their young
16. **metazoal, metazoan, metazoic**—of animals that are higher in development than the one-celled forms
17. **microorganic**—of microscopic forms of animal life
18. **mongrel**—hybrid

19. **monopode**—of one-footed animal forms
20. **omnivorous**—of animals that eat both flesh and vegetation
21. **organic**—of any living organisms
22. **polyped**—of animal forms possessing many feet
23. **protozoan**—of one-celled animal forms
24. **quadrupedal**—of four-footed animals
25. **unguiculate**—of animals that have claws or nails rather than hoofs
26. **vertebrate**—of animals with backbones
27. **zoic**—of animals or animal life
28. **zoological**—of animals

7. The Animal,n. *From Sec. 6:* arthropod, beast, biped, brindle, brute, carnivore, creature, crossbreed or crossbred, herbivore, hybrid, insectivore, invertebrate, mammal or mammalian, metazoan or metazoon, microorganism, mongrel, monopode, omnivore, polyped, protozoan or protozoon, quadruped, unguiculate, vertebrate; *Also:*
1. **albino**—animal deficient in pigmentation
2. **anthropoglot**—animal possessing a tongue similar to that of man
3. **behemoth**—very large and strong animal
4. **cosset**—pet
5. **fatling**—young domestic animal fattened for slaughter
6. **hominoid**—animal that resembles a human being
7. **monster**—horrible or grotesque animal, fabulous or actual; very large animal; animal that is a freak of nature
8. **monstrosity**—monster
9. **organism**—any living being
10. **pet**—domestic animal kept for pleasure, company, or amusement
11. **pollard**—animal without horns, esp. a sheep, goat, stag, ox, etc.
12. **rogue**—animal that, because of its nontypical savage nature, lives, or is forced to live, apart from the herd
13. **sport**—animal that deviates from its parents or parent form to an unusual degree
14. **stud**—animal kept for breeding purposes
15. **whiffet**—small and unimportant animal
16. **wildling**—wild animal
17. **yearling**—year-old animal, or one in its second year
18. **zoophyte**—lower-order animal resembling, or living like, a plant

8. Animal-Like: bestial, beastly, brute, brutish, theroid, zooid,adj.

9. Having the Form of an Animal: theriomorphic,adj.

10. Of Animals as to Habitat,adj.
1. **amphibious, amphibian**—living both on land and in water
2. **aquatic**—living in water or growing in or on the margins of bodies of water
3. **arboreal**—living in trees
4. **gregarious**—living in flocks
5. **marine**—living in the sea or ocean
6. **rupicolous, rupicoline, rupestrine**—living among rocks
7. **terrestrial**—living on land

11. Of Selected Specific Animals or Animal Categories, Not Later Classified,adj.
1. **amphibian**—of the frogs, toads, newts, salamanders, and related forms
2. **bovid**—of the group comprised of sheep, goats, oxen, and true antelopes
3. **bradypodoid**—of the sloths
4. **edentate**—of the group comprised of the aardvarks, anteaters, armadillos, and pangolins
5. **herpestine**—of mongooses
6. **hippotigrine**—of zebras
7. **lutrine**—of the otters, except sea otters
8. **meline**—of the badgers
9. **mephitine**—of the American skunks
10. **musteline, mustelid, mustelinous**—of the group composed of badgers, skunks,

otters, martens, weasels, minks, ferrets, ermines, polecats, etc.
11. **procyonine**—of raccoons
12. **ruminant**—of the category of even-toed hoofed mammals, comprised of the antelopes, camels, chevrotains, deer, giraffes, goats, oxen, and sheep
13. **solidungular, solidungulous, solidungulate**—of those animals that have a single hoof on each foot, as horses, asses, zebras, etc.
14. **soliped**—solidungular
15. **soricine, soricid**—of the shrews
16. **ungulate**—of horses, rhinoceroses, elephants, and other hoofed animals
17. **viverrine**—of civets
18. **zebrine**—of zebras

12. Resembling a Specific Animal or Animals,adj. *From Sec. 11:* hippotigrine, soricine, viverrine or viverriform, zebrine or zebroid

13. The Animal,n. *From Sec. 11:* amphibian, bovid, bradypod or bradypode, edentate, herpestine, meline, mephitine, musteline or mustelid, ruminant, solidungulate, soliped, soricid, ungulate, viverrine; *Also:*
1. **ichneumon**—the mongoose
2. **stoat**—the ermine when it has its brown summer fur

14. Prematurely Born Animal: slink,n.

15. Young of a Beast of Prey: whelp,n.

16. The Young of an Animal Brought Forth at One Birth: litter,n.

17. Member of the Same Litter: sib,n.

18. Infested with Animals,adj.
1. **crawling**—infested with creatures that crawl
2. **lousy**—infested with lice
3. **pediculous, pedicular**—lousy
4. **swarming**—infested with insects
5. **vermiculate, vermicular**—full of worms
6. **vermigerous**—infested with intestinal worms
7. **verminous**—infested with roaches, lice, bedbugs, fleas, or other disgusting animal life; infested with worms; infested with parasites

19. Infestation with Animals,n. *From Sec. 18:* lousiness, pediculosis, vermiculation, verminousness or vermination

20. To Be Infested with Animals,v. *From Sec. 18:* crawl, swarm, vermiculate, verminate; *Also:* 1. **formicate**—be infested with ants

21. Selected Organisms, Microorganisms, or Bacteria,n.
1. **aerobe**—microorganism that can survive only when in contact with oxygen (aerobic,adj.)
2. **amoeba**—simplest kind of one-celled organism that moves by extruding part of itself (amoebic,adj.)
3. **anaerobe**—microorganism that can live where there is no air (anaerobic,adj.)
4. **animalcule, animalculum**—very tiny animal organism, either invisible to the naked eye or nearly so (animalcula, animalculae,pl.)
5. **bacillus**—rod-shaped bacterium (bacilli, pl. bacillary,adj.)
6. **germ**—microorganism, esp. a disease-causing microorganism
7. **gonococcus**—bacterium that produces gonorrhea (gonococci,pl. gonococcal, gonococcic,adj.)
8. **infusorian**—most highly developed of the one-celled organisms (infusorial,adj.)
9. **microbe**—very minute organism, too small to be seen by the naked eye, and esp. one that causes disease (microbic, microbial,adj.)

10. **micrococcus**—a kind of bacterium (micrococci,pl. micrococcal,adj.)
11. **microzoan, microzoon**—microscopic, usually one-celled, organism (microzoa, pl. microzoan, microzoic,adj.)
12. **monad**—one-celled organism
13. **paramecium**—a type of infusorian, known also, from its shape, as the slipper animalcule (paramecia,pl.)
14. **pneumobacillus**—bacillus that causes pneumonia (pneumobacilli,pl.)
15. **pneumococcus**—bacterium that causes lobar pneumonia (pneumococci,pl. pneumococcal, pneumococcic, pneumococcous, adj.)
16. **protozoan, protozoon**—organism consisting of a single cell (protozoa,pl. protozoan, protozoal,adj.)
17. **pseudopod**—type of one-celled organism that protrudes part of itself for purposes of locomotion, as if on false feet (pseudopodal,adj.)
18. **spirochete**—a bacterial microorganism (one variety of which, the *Spirochaeta pallida*, causes syphilis)
19. **staphylococcus**—a kind of disease-producing bacterium (staphylococci, pl. staphylococcal, staphylococcic,adj.)
20. **streptococcus**—a kind of disease-producing bacterium (streptococci,pl. streptococcal, streptococcic,adj.)
21. **tubercle bacillus**—microorganism that causes tuberculosis

22. Quarters Where Animals (Other than Birds) Live, Are Kept, Breed, etc.,n.
1. **alveary, alvearium**—beehive
2. **apiary**—place where bees are kept
3. **aquarium**—place where fish and other aquatic forms are kept for exhibition
4. **barn**—stable
5. **beehive**—place where bees live or are kept
6. **burrow**—opening in the ground in which a rabbit, fox, or other small animal lives
7. **byre**—place where cows are kept
8. **coop**—wired house for chickens or other fowl
9. **corral**—enclosure for animals
10. **cot, cote**—shed for small animals, esp. sheep
11. **cowshed, cowhouse, etc.**—barn for cows
12. **den**—place where a wild beast lives
13. **fishery**—place where fish are caught
14. **fold**—enclosure for sheep or other animals
15. **form**—lair of a hare or other animal
16. **formicary**—ant's nest
17. **hatchery**—place where the eggs of fowl or fish are hatched
18. **haunt**—den or lair of an animal
19. **hive**—beehive
20. **hole**—burrow
21. **hutch**—pen for rabbits or other small animals
22. **insectarium**—place where live insects are kept
23. **kennel**—place where dogs sleep, or are kept or bred
24. **lair**—place where a wild animal lives, rests, or lies down
25. **lodge**—living quarters of beavers or other animals
26. **menagerie**—place where animals are kept
27. **nest**—place where various egg-laying animals, as insects, birds, etc., deposit their eggs and where the young are hatched and reared
28. **nidus**—breeding place for germs; nest of certain insects
29. **pen**—small enclosure for animals
30. **piggery**—place for pigs
31. **pigpen, pigsty**—enclosure for pigs
32. **pinfold**—enclosure for animals
33. **piscary**—place where fish are kept
34. **pound**—enclosure for stray animals or

for animals seized by public authority; sheltering enclosure for animals

35. **ranarium**—place where frogs are raised and/or kept
36. **rookery**—breeding place of seals
37. **sealery**—place where seals are hunted
38. **snakery**—house for snakes
39. **stable**—building that houses domestic animals
40. **sty**—enclosure for pigs
41. **terrarium**—vivarium containing no water, or for animals that live solely on land
42. **vespiary**—nest of social wasps
43. **vivarium**—enclosed place for raising animals indoors
44. **warren**—place where rabbits live, breed, are bred, or are found in large quantities
45. **zoo, zoological gardens**—place where wild animals are kept on exhibition

23. To Keep or Confine Animals in a Place, v. *From Sec. 22:* coop up, corral, kennel, lair, pen, pinfold, stable

24. One Who Maintains Quarters for Animals,n. *From Sec. 22:* apiarist or apiculturist, warrener

25. To Live in Animal Quarters,v. *From Sec. 22:* den, haunt, lair

26. Science, or Scientific Study, of Animals,n.
   1. **amphibiology**—science of those animals that can live on both land and water, as frogs, salamanders, newts, etc.
   2. **anthropobiology**—scientific study of anthropoid apes
   3. **arachnology**—science of spiders, scorpions, and related forms
   4. **bacteriology**—science relating to bacteria
   5. **biochemistry**—chemistry of plants and animals
   6. **biodynamics**—science of vital and active phenomena of plants and animals
   7. **biology**—science of plants and animals
   8. **bionomics, bionomy**—science of the relationship of animals to their environment
   9. **biostatics**—science of structure of plants and animals in relation to function
   10. **carcinology**—science of crustaceans, i.e., crabs, lobsters, shrimps, etc.
   11. **conchology**—science of mollusks, i.e., clams, oysters, etc.
   12. **crustaceology**—carcinology
   13. **dipterology**—science of flies, mosquitoes, gnats, and related two-winged insects
   14. **ecology**—science dealing with the mutual relations between organisms and environment
   15. **entomology**—science of, or scientific study of, insects
   16. **helminthology**—study, science, or natural history of parasitic worms
   17. **hemipterology**—science of such forms as the bedbug, squash bug, chinch bug, and related organisms
   18. **herpetology**—science of reptiles
   19. **hippology**—science or study of horses
   20. **ichthyology**—science of fishes
   21. **ichthyopaleontology**—science of the fishes of past geological periods
   22. **lepidopterology**—science of butterflies and moths
   23. **malacology**—science of mollusks, i.e., oysters, clams, snails, slugs, and related shellfish
   24. **mammalogy, mammalology**—science of mammals
   25. **mastology**—mammalogy
   26. **morphology**—science dealing with the form and structure of animal or plant organisms
   27. **myrmecology**—science of ants
   28. **nematology**—science of roundworms

   29. **ophiology**—science of snakes and serpents
   30. **ornithology**—science of birds
   31. **orthopterology**—science dealing with locusts, grasshoppers, crickets, cockroaches, and related insects
   32. **paleontology**—science of animal and plant life of past geological periods
   33. **paleoornithology**—science of fossil birds
   34. **paleozoology**—science of the animals of past geological periods
   35. **parasitology**—science of animal parasites
   36. **promorphology**—morphology from a geometrical point of view
   37. **protozoology**—scientific study of one-celled organisms
   38. **taxonomy**—science of the classification of animals and plants
   39. **zoogeography**—study of the geographical distribution of the animals of the world
   40. **zoography**—descriptive zoology
   41. **zoology**—branch of biology dealing with animals
   42. **zoometry**—science of animal measurement
   43. **zoopaleontology**—paleozoology
   44. **zootomy**—science dealing with animal anatomy

27. Student of an Animal Science,n. *From Sec. 26:* amphibiologist, anthropobiologist, etc.; biochemist, bionomist, dipterist or dipterologist, hemipterist or hemipterologist, lepidopterist or lepidopterologist, orthopterist or orthopterologist, taxonomer or taxonomist, zoogeographer, zoometrician, zootomist; *Also:*
   1. **herterocerist**—student of moths
   2. **naturalist**—student of animal and plant life
   3. **rhopalocerist**—student of butterflies

28. Pert. to, or Descr. of, an Animal Science, adj. *From Sec. 26:* amphibiological, anthropobiological, etc.; biochemical, biodynamic, bionomic, biostatic, taxonomic, zoogeographic, zoographic, zoometric, zootomic

29. Scientific Description of Animals and Their Habits: zoography,n. (zoographic,adj.)

30. Business Connected with Animals,n.
   1. **animal husbandry**—breeding, production, etc., of farm animals (animal husbandman,n.)
   2. **apiculture**—beekeeping as a business (apiculturist, apiarist,n. apicultural,adj.)
   3. **aviculture**—scientific rearing of, and care for, birds (aviculturist,n.)
   4. **hiruniniculture**—the breeding of leeches, or bloodsucking worms
   5. **pisciculture**—scientific breeding and cultivation of fish (pisciculturist,n. piscicultural,adj.)
   6. **sericulture**—raising of silkworms for their raw silk (sericulturist,n. sericultural,adj.)
   7. **taxidermy**—art of stuffing the skins of animals (taxidermist,n. taxidermic,adj.)

31. Deserted by the Mother and Brought Up as a Pet by a Human: cade,adj. (of animals)

404. BAT

1. Bat,n.
   1. **chiropteran**—a bat (chiropteran, chiropterous,adj.)
   2. **flying fox**—fruit bat
   3. **megachiropteran**—fruit bat (megachiropteran, megachiropterous,adj.)
   4. **microchiropteran**—bat other than the fruit bat (microchiropteran, microchiropterous,adj.)
   5. **vespertilionid**—common bat of the temperate region (vespertilionine, vespertilionid,adj.)

2. Resembling a Bat in Habits, Activities, Appearance, etc.: vespertilian,adj.

405. BIRD

1. Bird,n.
1. **bantam**—small or dwarf domestic bird of various breeds
2. **biddy**—chicken
3. **cageling**—bird kept in a cage
4. **culver**—dove; pigeon
5. **fowl**—large, usually domesticated, edible bird
6. **gallinacean**—domestic bird
7. **passerine**—member of the category of perching birds that sing
8. **roc**—fabled bird of tremendous size
9. **sitter**—bird sitting on eggs
10. **songbird, songster**—singing bird
11. **trochilus**—hummingbird
12. **visitant**—migratory bird
13. **warbler**—singing bird

2. Male Bird,n.
1. **capon**—castrated male chicken
2. **chanticleer**—cock
3. **cob**—male swan
4. **cock**—male chicken or other bird
5. **drake**—male duck
6. **gander**—male goose
7. **rooster**—male chicken

3. Female Bird,n.
1. **biddy**—hen
2. **duck**—female duck, as distinguished from the drake
3. **fowl**—mature hen
4. **goose**—female goose, as distinguished from the gander
5. **hen**—female chicken or other bird
6. **pen**—female swan

4. Young Bird,n.
1. **birdling**—young bird
2. **chick**—young bird, chicken, etc.
3. **cockerel**—young domesticated male bird or fowl
4. **cygnet**—young swan
5. **duckling**—young duck
6. **eaglet**—young eagle
7. **fledgling**—young bird just developing flight feathers
8. **gosling**—young goose
9. **nestling**—young bird still in the nest
10. **owlet**—young owl
11. **poulard**—pullet fattened for slaughter
12. **poult**—young turkey or pheasant; young domestic bird
13. **pullet**—young hen less than a year old; young chicken
14. **ravenling**—young raven
15. **squab**—young pigeon

5. Young Birds, Collectively,n.
1. **aerie, aery, eyrie, eyry**—young eagles; young birds of prey
2. **brood**—the young of birds newly hatched from eggs
3. **clutch**—brood of chicks

6. Domesticated and Edible Birds, Such as Chickens, Ducks, Turkeys, etc.: fowl, poultry,n.

7. Pert. to, Descr. of, or Referring to, Birds, adj.: avicular, avian, ornithic,adj.

8. Of Birds as to Habits, Activities, Condition, etc.,adj.
1. **acciptrine**—of birds of prey
2. **gallinaceous, gallinacean**—of domestic fowl
3. **gregarious**—of such birds, as ducks, that move, feed, and live in flocks
4. **insessorial**—of perching birds
5. **migratory**—of birds that go periodically from one location or region to another
6. **oscine, oscinine**—of various kinds of songbirds
7. **passerine**—of perching songbirds
8. **pensile**—of birds that live in, or build, hanging nests
9. **precocial**—of those newly hatched birds

that are covered with down and can run about
10. **raptorial**—of birds that live on prey, as hawks, eagles, etc.
11. **rasorial**—of birds that scratch the ground in search of food; of domestic fowl
12. **sedentary**—of birds that do not migrate but are permanently settled in one place or area

9. Of Specific Birds, adj.
1. **accipitral**—of hawks
2. **anserine**—of geese
3. **aquiline**—of eagles
4. **columbaceous**—of pigeons
5. **columbine**—of doves
6. **corvine**—of crows
7. **hirundine**—of swallows
8. **hirundinous**—of swallows and martins
9. **odontophorine**—of partridge and quail
10. **trochiline, trochilidine**—of hummingbirds

10. Resembling a Specific Bird or Birds,adj.
From Sec. 9: accipitral or accipitrine, anserine, aquiline, columbine, corvine, hirundine, *Also:*
1. **gallinaceous**—resembling pheasants
2. **parroty**—resembling a parrot or parrots

11. Quarters for Birds,n.
1. **aerie, aery, eyrie, eyry**—high nest of an eagle or other bird of prey
2. **aviary**—place for keeping or rearing birds
3. **birdhouse**—house for birds
4. **columbary**—pigeon house; dovecote
5. **cot, cote**—shed or other enclosure for doves or other birds
6. **dovecote**—shelter for doves
7. **nest**—place where birds breed or are bred
8. **ravenry**—place where ravens are bred and kept
9. **rookery**—breeding place of birds that live in flocks
10. **roost**—house or place for birds or fowl to roost in or on
11. **swannery**—place for keeping or breeding swans
12. **volery**—aviary

12. One Who Keeps Birds: aviarist,n.

406. CAT

1. Domestic Cat,n.
1. **feline**—cat
2. **grimalkin**—cat; she-cat
3. **mouser**—cat that catches mice
4. **puss, pussy**—cat (usually affectionate)
5. **ratter**—rat-catching cat
6. **tabby**—cat
7. **tiger cat**—domestic cat with markings like those of a tiger
8. **tom, tomcat**—male cat

2. Young Cat: catling, kitten,n.

3. Member of the Cat Family (Generic): felid, feline,n.

4. Member of the Cat Family (Specific): American lion, bobcat, cheetah, catamount, catamountain, cougar, jaguar, leopard, lion, lynx, mountain lion, mountain panther, ocelot, panther, puma; sabertooth (extinct); serval, tiger, wildcat,n.

5. Baby Lion, Tiger, etc.: cub,n.

6. Nickname for a Lion: Leo,n.

7. Small or Young Lion: lionet,n.

8. Cross between a Lion and a Tiger: liger, tiglon,n.

9. Small or Young Tiger: tigerkin, tigerling,n.

10. Female Member of the Cat Family: lioness, pantheress, tigress,n.

11. Pert. to, Descr. of, or Referring to, a Cat or Cats, or a Member or Members of the Cat Family: feline,adj.

12. Resembling, or Characteristic of, a Cat or Cats, etc.: feliform, feline, feloid,adj. (felinity, felineness,n.)

13. Pert. to, Descr. of, or Referring to, a Specific Member or Members of the Cat Family: leonine (lion); lyncean or lyncine (lynx); pantherine, tigerish or tigrine,adj.

14. Resembling or Characteristic of, a Specific Member or Members of the Cat Family: leonine (lion), pantherine; tigerish, tigrine, or tigroid,adj.

407. DOG

1. Dog: canine, hound,n.

2. Female Dog: bitch, slut,n.

3. Dog of Mixed or Unknown Ancestry: cur, mongrel; mutt (colloq.),n.

4. Young or Baby Dog: pup, puppy, whelp,n.

5. Rat-Catching Dog: ratter,n.

6. Hunting Dog: hound, pointer,n.

7. Pert. to, Descr. of, Resembling, or Characteristic of, a Dog or Dogs: canine,adj.

8. Kindness to Dogs: caninity,n.

9. Any Member of the Dog Family: canid, canine,n.

10. Pert. to, Descr. of, or Resembling, any Member or Members of the Dog Family: canine,adj.

11. Certain Members of the Dog Family: coyote, dingo, fennec, fox, jackal, wolf,n.

12. Female Fox: vixen,n.

13. Pert. to, or Descr. of, a Fox: vulpecular, vulpine,adj.

14. Pert. to, or Descr. of, a Young Fox: vulpecular,adj.

15. Resembling a Fox, Esp. in Cunning or Other Characteristics: foxy, vulpine,adj.

16. Pert. to, Descr. of, or Resembling, a Wolf: lupine, wolfish,adj.

17. Young Fox, Wolf, etc.: cub,n.

408. HORSE

1. Horse (Generic): Dobbin, equine; nag (derogatory); steed,n.

2. Male Horse,n.
1. colt—male horse under four years of age
2. gelding—castrated male horse
3. sire—male parent of a horse
4. stallion—male horse over four years of age
5. stud, studhorse—stallion kept for breeding purposes

3. Female Horse,n.
1. brood mare—mare kept for breeding purposes
2. dam—female parent of a horse
3. filly—female horse under four years of age
4. mare—female horse over four years of age

4. Young or Baby Horse,n.
1. colt—baby horse
2. filly—female baby horse; female newborn horse
3. foal—newborn horse
4. yearling—year-old horse, or one in its second year

5. Horse as to Breed, etc.,n.
1. Arab—one of a breed of horses native to Arabia

2. Belgian—draft horse noted for its strength and weight, bred in Belgium, generally of roan or chestnut color
3. bronco, broncho—somewhat wild small horse or pony, found in the West
4. cayuse—small horse, found in the West, and descended from stock introduced by the Spaniards
5. cow pony—horse with lineage going back to Spanish horses imported from Mexico at the time of the Spanish invasion of that country
6. Indian pony—smaller, and usually stockier, relative of the cow pony
7. jennet—small Spanish horse
8. Morgan—one of a breed of light horses that originated in Vermont
9. mustang—half-wild horse of the Southwest
10. palomino—horse of Arabian ancestry of cream or tan color
11. Percheron, Percheron Norman—one of a breed of draft horse that originated in Le Perche, France
12. pony—one of a special small breed of horse
13. Shetland pony—one of a small and hardy breed of ponies that originated in the Shetland Islands
14. Shire—one of a breed of draft horse from England
15. thoroughbred—horse with lineage going back to Arabian stallions bred to European mares; specially bred horse
16. Waler—Australian horse

6. Horse as to Use, Activity, Quality, etc.,n.
1. ambler—horse that goes at an easy pace
2. carriage horse—horse of smart appearance used for drawing carriages
3. charger—war horse; officer's horse; horse trained to attack
4. clipper—fast horse
5. cob—stocky and short-legged horse
6. courser—fast horse; war horse (poetic)
7. crock—old or broken-down horse
8. Dobbin—name or term for a farm horse
9. draft horse, dray horse—horse for pulling heavy loads
10. gigster—horse suitable for pulling a gig, a type of light carriage
11. maiden—race horse that has not won a race; show horse that has not won a blue ribbon
12. mount—horse on which one rides
13. pacer, pacemaker—horse used to set the pace for another horse in racing
14. pad—horse with an easy pace
15. padnag—ambling or slowly moving horse
16. palfrey—saddle horse, generally a small and gentle one for ladies to ride
17. pony—loosely, any small horse
18. race horse—horse trained for racing
19. remount—another and fresh horse to take the place of one fatigued, disabled, etc.
20. roadster—horse used for light work or driving
21. Rosinante—worn-out, useless horse, so called from the horse in *Don Quixote*
22. saddle horse—horse suitable for riding, owing to its strong back and other attributes
23. steed—spirited horse
24. stepper—high-spirited horse
25. sumpter—pack horse
26. tit—small and poor horse
27. trotter—horse trained for trotting races

7. Horse as to Color,n.
1. bay—horse of a reddish-brown color (bay,adj.)
2. bayard—reddish-brown, or chestnut-colored horse
3. chestnut—brownish-colored horse (chestnut,adj.)

4. **dapple**—horse with a coat marked by small, gray spots (dappled,adj.)
5. **palomino**—cream-colored or tan horse of Arabian ancestry
6. **piebald**—horse whose coat has spots and patches of black and white (piebald,adj.)
7. **pinto**—spotted horse
8. **roan**—horse of any solid color with white hairs mixed through its coat (roan,adj.)
9. **skewbald**—horse whose coat is a mixture of brown and white or bay and white (skewbald,adj.)
10. **sorrel**—horse of a light reddish-brown color (sorrel,adj.)

8. The Color of a Horse,n. *From Sec. 7:* bay, chestnut, roan, sorrel; *Also:* 1. **blossom**—color of a horse whose bay or sorrel hair contains an admixture of white hairs

9. Horses, Collectively,n.
1. **bloodstock**—thoroughbred horses kept for racing
2. **stable**—race horses kept and trained in one place, owned by one person, etc.
3. **stud**—horses kept for breeding purposes
4. **tandem**—two horses harnessed one behind the other
5. **team**—two or more horses harnessed together to pull a carriage, plow, vehicle, etc.; such horses together with the vehicle

10. Draft Horse Together with the Vehicle Pulled: team,n.
11. Alexander the Great's War Horse: Bucephalus,n.
12. Flying Horse of Greek Fable: Pegasus,n.
13. Fabled Horselike Animal with One Horn: unicorn,n. (unicorn,adj.)
14. Like or Resembling a Unicorn: unicorn, unicornic,adj.
15. First-Known and Primitive Type of Prehistoric Four-Toed Horse: eohippus,n.
16. Pert. to, Descr. of, or Referring to, a Horse or Horses: cabaline, equine,adj.
17. Resembling or Characteristic of a Horse or Horses: cabaline, equine, equoid,adj.
18. Cross between a Horse and a Zebra,n.
1. **zebrinny**—cross between a male horse and a female zebra
2. **zebroid, zebrula**—cross between a female horse and a male zebra

19. Horse Rider: horseman, equestrian; equestrienne (fem.),n.
20. Rider of Race Horses: jockey,n.
21. Pert. to Horse Riding: equestrian,adj.
22. Skill in Riding Horses: horsemanship, equitation,n.
23. Person Skilled in Riding or Managing Horses: horseman,n.
24. Art of Riding Horses: manège,n.
25. On a Horse: à cheval (French), mounted
26. On a Horse but without a Saddle: bareback,adj. and adv.
27. Riding Academy: manège,n.

409. ASS; DONKEY

1. Ass; Donkey,n.
1. **burro**—small donkey
2. **chigetai**—wild ass of Mongolia
3. **dickey**—donkey
4. **hinny**—hybrid between a stallion and a she-ass
5. **jackass, jack**—male ass; donkey
6. **jennet, jenny, jenny ass**—female ass
7. **kiang**—wild ass of Tibet
8. **mule**—offspring of a male ass and a mare
9. **onager**—wild ass of Asia
10. **she-ass**—female ass

11. **sumpter**—pack mule
2. Pert. to, Descr. of, Resembling, or Characteristic of, an Ass: asinine,adj. (asininity, n.)

410. BOVINE

1. Bovine,n.
1. **bovoid**—bovine
2. **bull**—male bovine
3. **bullock**—castrated male bovine not previously used in reproduction; steer
4. **cow**—female bovine
5. **kine**—cow (archaic)
6. **ox**—bovine; adult castrated male bovine (oxen,pl.)
7. **ruminant**—cud-chewing animal
8. **runt**—small cow or ox
9. **steer**—castrated male bovine
10. **taurine**—bull
11. **zebu**—bovine domesticated in India, East Africa, etc.

2. Young Bovine,n.
1. **calf**—young bovine
2. **heifer**—young cow
3. **maverick**—motherless calf
4. **slink**—prematurely born calf
5. **stirk**—young cow or bull between one and two years old

3. Bovines, Collectively,n.
1. **cattle**—bovine domesticated animals
2. **kine**—cattle (archaic)
3. **neat**—cattle
4. **oxen**—bovines

4. Of Cows, Bulls, Cattle, etc.,adj.
1. **bovine**—of a cow or cows, or other wild and domestic cattle (bovinity,n.)
2. **ruminant**—of cud-chewing animals
3. **taurian**—of bulls
4. **taurine**—of bulls; of cattle
5. **vaccine**—of cows
6. **vituline**—of a calf or calves

5. Resembling, or Characteristic of, a Cow, Calf, or Cattle,adj. *From Sec. 4:* bovine or bovoid, vituline (bovinity,n.)

6. Derived from Cows: vaccine,adj.

7. Kinds of Wild Oxen or Buffalo: aurochs, bison, carabao, cattalo, gaur, water buffalo, yak,n.

8. Kinds of Antelopes: addax, chamois, eland, gazelle, gnu, hartebeest, kudu, nilgai, oryx, pronghorn, serow, springbok or springbuck, steinbok, takin,n.

411. SHEEP

1. Kinds of Sheep: argali, mouflon or mouflon, urial,n.

2. Male Sheep,n.
1. **bellwether**—male sheep that leads the flock, with a bell on its neck
2. **ram**—male sheep
3. **tup**—male sheep
4. **wether**—castrated male sheep

3. Female Sheep: ewe,n.
4. Hornless Sheep: pollard,n.
5. Young or Baby Sheep,n.
1. **cosset**—pet lamb
2. **lamb, lambkin**—young or baby sheep
3. **yeanling**—young sheep

6. Sheep in its Second Year: tag, teg,n.
7. Pert. to, Descr. of, or Resembling, Sheep or a Sheep: ovine,adj.

412. GOAT

1. Kinds of Wild Goat: ibex, markhor,n.
2. Male Goat: billy goat,n.

3. Female Goat: nanny goat, she-goat,n.

4. Hornless Goat: pollard,n.

5. Young Goat: kid, yeanling,n.

6. Mythical Creature, Half Goat and Half Stag: hircocervus,n.

7. Pert. to, Descr. of, Smelling Like, or Resembling, a Goat or Goats: hircine,adj.

413. DEER

1. Male Deer: buck, hart, roebuck, stag,n.

2. Female Deer: doe, hind, roe,n.

3. Small Deer: roe,n.

4. Young Deer,n.
 1. fawn—young deer
 2. yearling—year-old deer; deer in its second year

5. Kinds of Deer: caribou, chevrotain, elk, kanchil, moose, moose deer, musk deer, napu, red deer, reindeer, sambar, wapiti,n.

6. Pert. to, Descr. of, or Resembling, a Deer or Deer: cervine,adj.

414. CAMEL

1. Camel,n.
 1. Bactrian camel—two-humped camel
 2. dromedary—one-humped camel
 3. llama—kind of South American ruminant allied to the camel

415. GIRAFFE

1. Giraffe: camelopard,n.

2. Giraffe-Like Mammal of the Belgian Congo: okapi,n.

416. BEAR

1. Bear: bruin,n.

2. Young or Baby Bear: cub, whelp,n.

3. Pert. to, Descr. of, or Resembling, a Bear or Bears: ursine,adj.

4. Kinds of Bears: black bear, brown bear, cinnamon bear, grizzly bear, ice bear, polar bear, sloth bear, Syrian bear; Teddy bear (toy),n.

417. ELEPHANT; HIPPOPOTAMUS

1. Elephant,n.
 1. mammoth—extinct elephant that abounded at some prehistoric period (though scientifically describing a number of genera, the word usually refers in everyday use to the form that had curved tusks and a woolly hide)
 2. mastodon—kind of large prehistoric elephant-like mammal
 3. pachyderm—elephant
 4. proboscidian—member of the elephant order
 5. tusker—elephant with large tusks

2. Male Elephant: bull,n.

3. Young or Baby Elephant: calf,n.

4. Resembling an Elephant: elephantic, elephantine, elephantoid,adj.

5. Belonging to the Elephant Order: proboscidean, proboscidian,adj.

6. Pert. to, Descr. of, or Resembling, Elephants or Rhinoceroses, or, Sometimes, Hippopotamuses and Other Thick-Skinned Animals: pachydermal, pachydermatoid, pachydermatous, pachydermic, pachydermoid, pachydermous,adj.

7. Pert. to, Descr. of, or Resembling, a Hippopotamus or Hippopotamuses: hippopotamian, hippopotamic, hippopotamine, hippopotamoid,adj.

418. KANGAROO

1. Kangaroo: marsupial (since the young are kept in a pouch),n.

2. Kinds of Kangaroos: bettong, jerboa kangaroo, wallaby, wallaroo,n.

3. Pert. to, or Descr. of, Kangaroos, Opossums, Wombats, Bandicoots, and Related Mammals That Carry the Young in a Pouch: marsupial,adj.

419. HOG

1. Hog: pig, porker, swine,n.

2. Male Hog,n.
 1. barrow—castrated male hog
 2. boar—uncastrated male hog

3. Female Hog: sow,n.

4. Young or Small Hog: pig, piggie, piggy, piglet, pigling, shoat,n.

5. Hogs, Collectively: hoggery, piggery, porkery, swine,n.

6. Litter of Pigs: farrow,n.

7. Kinds of Hogs: babirusa; boar (wild); peccary, razorback; tusker (wild); wart hog (wild),n.

8. Pert. to, or Descr. of, the Hog Family: porcine,adj.

9. Resembling, or Characteristic of, a Hog or Hogs: hoggish, piggish, porcine, swinish, adj.

420. MONKEY

1. Any Monkey or Related Animal: primate, primatal,n.

2. Pert. to, or Descr. of, Monkeys and Related Animals: primate, primatal,adj.

3. Any Monkey or Ape: anthropoid, simian, n.

4. Pert. to, Descr. of, or Resembling, Monkeys and Apes: anthropoid, anthropoidal, anthropoidean, apish, simiad, simial, simian, simious,adj. (simianity,n.)

5. Familiar Name for a Monkey: Jocko,n.

6. Kinds of Monkeys or Related Animals: anthropoid ape, ape, aye-aye, baboon, chacma, chimpanzee, drill, gibbon, gorilla, lemur, lemurid, lemuroid, macaco, macaque, mandrill, marmoset, orang-utan, rhesus, tarsier, troglodyte,n.

7. Pert. to, Descr. of, or Resembling, a Kind of Monkey: apish, lemurian, lemuriform, lemurine, lemuroid, troglodytal, troglodyte, adj.

421. RODENT

1. Any Rodent: rodentian,n.

2. Rabbit: bunny, cottontail, hare, jack rabbit, leporid,n.

3. Young Hare in Its First Year: leveret,n.

4. Pert. to, or Descr. of, Rabbits and Hares: leporid,adj.

5. Pert. to, Descr. of, or Resembling, a Hare or Hares: leporine,adj.

6. Certain Other Rodents: beaver, chinchilla, chipmunk, coypu or nutria, gopher, ground hog, guinea pig, hamster, hedgehog, jerboa, marmot, mouse, muskrat, porcupine, prairie dog, rat, squirrel, white rat, woodchuck,n.

7. Pert. to, or Descr. of, Rodents: glirine, rodent,adj.

8. Any Squirrel, Marmot, or Related Rodent: sciurid, sciurine,n.

9. Pert. to, or Descr. of, a Squirrel, Marmot, or Related Rodent: sciurid, sciurine, adj.

10. Resembling a Squirrel, Marmot, or Related Rodent: sciurine, sciuroid,adj.

422. WATER ANIMAL

1. Of Certain Categories of Water Animals or Forms,adj.
1. **actinozoal, actinozoan**—anthozoan
2. **anthozoan, anthozoic**—of corals, sea anemones, and related sea animals
3. **aquarian**—of fish kept on exhibition
4. **asteroid, asteroidean, asteroidal**—of the starfishes
5. **bivalve, bivalvular, bivalved**—of oysters, clams, mussels, and other two-shelled organisms
6. **brachiopod, brachiopodous**—bivalve
7. **brachyuran, brachyural, brachyurous**—of the common crabs
8. **bryozoan**—of masslike marine animals
9. **cephalopod**—of squids, cuttlefish, octopuses, nautiluses, and related forms
10. **clupeid, clupeoid**—of herrings, or of that family of fishes containing the herrings, sardines, shads, and menhaden
11. **coelenterate, coelenteric**—of corals, polyps, sea anemones, jellyfish, and related forms
12. **crinoid, crinoidean**—of the sea lilies, stone lilies, feather stars, and related forms
13. **crustacean**—of lobsters, shrimps, crabs, barnacles, and related forms
14. **ctenophoral, ctenophoran, ctenophoric, ctenophorous**—of marine animals of the jellyfish type
15. **cyclostome, cyclostomate, cyclostomatous**—of lampreys and hagfishes
16. **echinoderm, echinodermic, echinodermatous**—of starfish, sea urchins, and related marine animals
17. **echinoid**—of sea urchins
18. **elasmobranch**—of sharks and rays
19. **finny**—of fish
20. **gastropod, gastropodous**—of slugs, snails, whelks, and related one-shelled forms
21. **holothurian**—of the sea cucumbers
22. **hydroid**—of polyps; hydrozoal
23. **hydrozoal, hydrozoan**—of a kind of polyp or jellyfish
24. **ichthyic**—of fish
25. **lamellibranch, lamellibranchiate**—of clams, oysters, mussels and related forms
26. **medusal, medusan**—of the typical jellyfish
27. **molluscan, molluscous**—of oysters, clams, snails, slugs, whelks, limpets, cuttlefishes, conchs, scallops, and related shellfish other than the crustaceans
28. **octopod, octopodan, octopodous**—of octopuses, argonauts, and other eight-armed forms
29. **piscatorial, piscatorian, piscatory, piscine, piscian**—of fishes
30. **polypean**—of polyps
31. **poriferal, poriferan, poriferous**—of the sponges
32. **spongian**—of sponges
33. **univalve, univalved**—gastropod

34. **xiphosuran, xiphosurous**—of the king crabs

2. Resembling a Water Animal, Animals, or Forms,adj. *From Sec. 1:* asteroid, clupeoid or clupeiform, echinoid, hydroid; icthyoid, ichthyic, ichthyomorphic, or ichthyomorphous; medusal or medusoid, piscoid, poriferous, spongoid or spongy; *Also:*
1. **cancroid**—resembling a crab
2. **eely**—resembling an eel or eels
3. **fishy**—resembling fish

3. The Water Animal or Form,n. *From Sec. 1:* actinozoan, anthozoan, asteroid or asteroidean, bivalve or bivalvian, brachiopod, brachyuran or brachyure, bryozoan, cephalopod, clupeid, coelenterate, crinoid or crinoidean, crustacean, ctenophore or ctenophoran, cyclostome, echinoderm, echinoid, elasmobranch, gastropod, holothurian, hydrozoan, lamellibranch or lamellibranchiate, medusa or medusan, mollusk or molluscan, octopod or octopodan, polypean, poriferan, univalve, xiphosuran or xiphosure; *Also:*
1. **blue point**—oyster from a bed near Blue Point, Long Island, usually eaten raw; any similar oyster
2. **fingerling**—very small fish, about the size of a finger
3. **milter**—male fish during the breeding season
4. **quahog, quahaug**—a kind of clam
5. **samlet**—small salmon
6. **smolt**—two-year-old salmon

4. Young or Baby Water Animal,n.
1. **alevin**—young trout
2. **codling**—young codfish
3. **cub**—young shark
4. **grilse**—young salmon after its first trip to the sea
5. **parr**—young salmon
6. **samlet**—young salmon
7. **set**—young oyster
8. **spat**—young oyster

5. Crop of Young Oysters in a Locality: set,n.

6. The Newly Expelled Eggs of Fish, Oysters, and Other Marine Life: spawn,n.

7. Containing an Abundance of Fish: finny, fishy,adj.

423. MARINE OR AQUATIC MAMMAL

1. Any Marine or Aquatic Mammal: cetacean,n.

2. Pert. to, or Descr. of, Marine or Aquatic Mammals: cetacean, cetaceous,adj.

3. Kind of Whale: balaenid, baleen whale, bottlehead, bottlenose, blackfish, blue whale, cachalot, finback, grampus, humpback, mysticete, odontocete, porpoise whale, right whale, rorqual, sperm whale, sulphur-bottom, whalebone whale; zeuglodon or zeuglodont (now extinct),n. (mysticetous, odontocete or odontocetous, zeuglodont or zeuglodontoid, adj.)

4. Young or Baby Whale: calf, cub,n.

5. Other Marine or Aquatic Mammals: beluga, bottlenose, bottle-nosed dolphin, bottle-nosed porpoise, dolphin, dugong, killer or killer whale, manatee, narwhal, porpoise, seal, sea lion, sea otter, walrus, white whale,n. (narwhalian,adj.)

6. Pert. to, or Descr. of, Porpoises: phocaenine,adj.

7. A Seal: phoca, phocid,n.

8. Pert. to, or Descr. of, Seals: phocacean, phocaceous, phocal, phocid, phocine,adj.

9. Resembling a Seal: phociform, phocoid, adj.

10. Young or Baby Seal: calf, pup,n.

424. FROG

1. Frog,n.
1. amphibian—loosely, a frog or toad, though there are other creatures in this category
2. anuran—frog; toad
3. batrachian—frog; toad
4. bullfrog—large frog, so called from its heavy build and bellowing voice
5. croaker—frog
6. salient batrachian, salient amphibian —frog; toad
7. salientian—frog; toad
8. toad—animal very much like a frog, but spending most of its time on land; loosely, a frog; any amphibian without a tail

2. Early or Immature Developmental Form of a Frog or Toad: polliwog, tadpole,n.

3. Pert. to, or Descr. of, Frogs and Toads or the Category to Which They Belong: amphibian, amphibious, anuran, batrachian, batrachiate, salientian,adj.

4. Resembling Frogs and Toads: batrachoid, adj.

425. REPTILE

1. A Reptile: reptilian,n.

2. Pert. to, or Descr. of, Any Reptile, Including Snakes, Lizards, Alligators, Crocodiles, etc.: reptile, reptilian, reptiliary,adj.

3. Resembling, or Characteristic of, a Reptile: reptile, reptilian, reptiliary, reptiloid, adj.

4. Habits, Character, Behavior, etc., of Reptiles: reptilism, reptility,n.

5. In the Form of a Reptile: reptiliform,adj.

6. Scientific Description of Reptiles: herpetography,n.

7. Snake: ophidian, reptilian, reptile, serpent; viper (venomous),n.

8. Kind of Snake: adder, anaconda, asp, belltail, boa, boa constrictor, cobra, colubrid, copperhead, garden snake, garter snake, moccasin, pit viper, python, rattler, rattlesnake, viper, viperid, viperine, water moccasin, water snake,n.

9. Pert. to, or Descr. or, a Snake, Snakes, or a Category of Snakes: anguine, colubrid, colubrine, ophidian, pythonic, serpentile, serpentine, viperid, viperine,adj.

10. Resembling, or Characteristic of, Snakes or a Snake: anguineous, colubriform, colubrine, colubroid, serpentine, sinuous, viperiform, viperine, viperoid, viperous, viperoid, vipery,adj.

11. Suggestive of Snakes: anguine,adj.

12. A Lizard, Generically: saurian,n.

13. Kind of Lizard: basilisk, chameleon, dragon, eft, gecko, Gila monster, horned toad, iguana, iguanid, newt, skink,n. (chameleonic, iguanian, iguanid,adj.)

14. Pert. to, or Descr. of, Lizards as a Category: saurian,adj.

15. Turtle: chelonian, testudinate, tortoise,n.

16. A Kind of North American Turtle: terrapin,n.

17. Pert. to, or Descr. of, the Turtle or Tortoise Family: chelonian, testudinal, testudinarious, testudinate,adj.

18. Resembling a Tortoise: testudinal, testudinarious, testudineal,adj.

19. Resembling a Tortoise Shell: testudinal, testudinarious, testudinate, testudineal,adj.

20. Pert. to, Descr. of, or Resembling, Crocodiles or a Crocodile: crocodilian, crocodiline, crocodiloid,adj.

426. DINOSAUR

1. A Dinosaur, Generically: dinosaurian,n.

2. Kind of Dinosaur: Atlantosaurus, brachiosaur, brontosaurus, ceratopsian, Ceratosaurus, diplodocus, megalosaur or megalosaurian, morosaurian, ornithopod, sauropod, stegosaur or stegosaurian, theropod, titanosaur, triceratops, tyrannosaur,n. (ceratopsian, megalosaurian, morosaurian, sauropod or sauropodous, stegosaurian, theropod or theropodous,adj.)

3. Pert. to, or Descr. of, Dinosaurs as a Category: dinosaurian,adj.

427. WORM

1. Common Worm: angleworm, earthworm, n.

2. Pert. to, or Descr. of, Earthworms: lumbricine,adj.

3. Resembling an Earthworm: lumbriciform, lumbricoid,adj.

4. Segmented Worm: annelid, annelidan, annelidian, annulate,n.

5. Pert. to, or Descr. of, Segmented Worms: annelid, annelidan, annelidian, annelidous, adj.

6. Resembling a Segmented Worm: anneloid,adj.

7. Intestinal Worm: helminth, taenia, tapeworm,n. (helminthic,adj.)

8. Bloodsucking Worm: hirudinean, leech,n.

9. Of Leeches or Bloodsucking Worms: hirudinean, hirudine,adj.

10. Resembling a Leech: hirudinoid,adj.

11. Roundworm: hookworm (parasitic), nema, nemathelminth, nematode, nematoid, nematoidean,n. (nemathelminthic, nematoid, nematoidean,adj.)

12. Flatworm: nemertean, nemertian, nemertine, nemertinean, nemertoid, platyhelminth, n. (nemertean, nemertian, nemertine, nemertinean, nemertoid, platyhelminthic,adj.)

13. Of the Category Including Both Roundworms and Flatworms: helminthic,adj. (helminth,n.)

14. Of Worms, Generally: vermian,adj.

15. Wormlike, As in Form, Shape, Motion, etc.: lumbriciform, vermian, vermicular, vermiculate, vermiculated, vermiform, wormy, adj.

16. Creeping Like a Worm: vermigrade,adj.

17. Worm-Eaten: vermiculate, vermiculated, adj. (vermiculation,n.)

428. INSECT

1. Of Insects, Bugs, Spiders, etc.,adj.
1. acarine—of mites, ticks, etc.
2. apian, apiarian—of bees
3. arachnid, arachnidan—of spiders, scorpions, mites, etc.
4. arthrogastran—of scorpions
5. diplopterous—of wasps
6. dipteran, dipterous, dipteral—of flies,

mosquitoes, gnats, and related two-winged insects

7. **formic, formicarian, formicid, formicine, formicate**—of ants
8. **hemipteral, hemipteran, hemipterous**—of bedbugs, squash bugs, chinch bugs, and other related bugs
9. **herterocerous**—of moths
10. **hexapod, hexapodal, hexapodan, hexapodous**—of six-legged insects
11. **homopteran, homopterous**—of cicadas, aphids, scale insects, and related forms
12. **hydrophilid**—of a kind of aquatic and scavenging beetle
13. **insectile, insectival**—of insects
14. **isopterous**—of termites
15. **lepidopteral, lepidopteran, lepidopterous**—of the order of insects that includes the butterflies and moths
16. **orthopteran, orthopterous**—of locusts, grasshoppers, crickets, cockroaches, and related insects
17. **papilionine, papilionid**—of butterflies
18. **pedicular**—of lice
19. **pieridine, pierine, pierid**—of a kind of butterfly
20. **rhopalocerous**—of butterflies
21. **tinean, tineid, tineine**—of a certain kind of moth
22. **tortricid, tortricine**—of a certain kind of moth
23. **trachearian**—of mites, ticks, and allied forms
24. **vespine, vespid**—of wasps, esp. social wasps
25. **xylotomous**—of those insects that are able to cut or bore into wood

2. Resembling an Insect, Bug, Spider, etc., adj. *From Sec. 1:* acaroid, formicine, hydrophiloid, insectile or insectival, papilionaceous or papilionid, tineoid, tortricoid; *Also:* 1. scorpioid—resembling a scorpion

3. The Insect, Bug, Spider, etc., n. *From Sec. 1:* acarid, arachnid or arachnidan, arthrogastran, dipteran, formicid, hemipter or hemipteran, hexapod, homopteran, hydrophilid; lepidopteran, lepidopteron, or lepidopterid; orthopteran or orthopteron, papilionid, pierid or pierine, tinean or tineid, tortricid or tortricine, trachearian, vespid; *Also:*

1. **blight**—insect that causes a plant to wither and decay
2. **centipede**—insect with many legs
3. **millipede**—insect with many legs
4. **pest**—destructive insect
5. **pismire**—ant
6. **stegomyia**—mosquito that transmits yellow fever
7. **weevil**—kind of beetle

4. Young of Insects, n.
1. **aurelia**—pupa, esp. of butterflies (aurelian,adj.)
2. **brood**—eggs and young of bees
3. **chrysalis, chrysalid**—pupa, esp. of butterflies (chrysalid, chrysalidal, chrysalidian,adj.)
4. **grub**—thick, wormlike larva, esp. of the beetle
5. **larva**—immature, wingless, and wormlike form in which certain insects hatch from the egg (larvae,pl. larval,adj.)
6. **maggot**—wormlike larva of certain insects, esp. when living on decaying matter or flesh
7. **nit**—newborn parasitic insect
8. **nymph, nympha**—premature or preadult form of certain insects (nymphal,adj.)
9. **pupa**—young insect in the stage between the larva and the mature adult (pupae, pl. pupal,adj. pupate,v.)

5. Agent for Dispersing or Repelling Insects: insectifuge,n.

6. Repellant of Mosquitoes or Other Insects: citronella,n.

429. MANKIND

1. Mankind: anthropos; Hominidae (biology); homo, Homo (biology); Homo sapiens, human beings, humanity, humankind, human race, humans, human species, man, mortality, n. (Hominian, human, mortal,adj.)

2. Category of Animals to Which Mankind (and Also Monkeys, Apes, Lemurs, etc.) Belongs: Primates,n. (primate, primatal,adj.)

3. A Human Being, n.
1. **anthropos**—human being
2. **automaton**—human who seems to act mechanically, like a machine, without full power to reason, etc. (automata,pl.)
3. **beast**—human who is animal-like
4. **biped**—human being, i.e., a two-footed animal (bipedal,adj.)
5. **creature**—human being (creatural,adj.)
6. **earthling**—human being, i.e., a dweller of the earth
7. **Hominian, hominid**—human animal (biology)
8. **human**—human being (human,adj.)
9. **man**—human being
10. **mortal**—human being, i.e., someone who is not eternal and will eventually die (mortal,adj.)
11. **person**—human being (personal,adj.)
12. **primate, primatal**—member of the biological category to which human beings, monkeys, apes, lemurs, etc., belong (primate, primatal,adj.)
13. **robot**—human being who acts, moves, or works in a dull, mechanical, unthinking way, as if he were more a machine than a human being
14. **soul**—human being
15. **wight**—human being (archaic or humorous)
16. **worldling**—earthling

4. Mechanical Man: automaton (automata, pl.), robot,n.

5. Automaton in Human Form: android,n. (androidal,adj.)

6. Early Man, n.
1. **anthropolith**—any petrified prehistoric man (anthropolithic,adj.)
2. **cave man**—man living in the Stone Age
3. **Cro-Magnon man**—member of a group of prehistoric men, tall and erect, believed to be the same species as modern man
4. **Java man**—Pithecanthropus
5. **Neanderthal man**—early man in paleolithic Europe
6. **neolithic man**—man of the new Stone Age
7. **paleolithic man**—man of the old Stone Age
8. **Peking man**—species of early man known to have existed from remains found in China
9. **Piltdown man**—early prehistoric man with retreating chin and apelike appearance (recently proved spurious)
10. **Pithecanthropus, Pithecanthropus erectus**—very early type of prehistoric man of apelike appearance (pithecanthropi, pl.)

7. Resembling a Human Being, As in Form, Appearance, Characteristics, etc.: andromorphous, anthropoid, anthropomorphous, hominiform, hominoid, humanoid,adj. (hominoid, humanoid,n.)

8. Both Human and Divine: theanthropic, theanthropical,adj. (theanthropism,n.)

9. Beyond What Is Human; above or beyond Normal Human Power: preterhuman, superhuman,adj.

10. To Make Human, v.
1. **anthropomorphose**—transform into human form (anthropomorphosis,n.)

2. **hominify**—to turn into a human being (hominification,n.)
3. **humanize**—make human (humanization, n.)
4. **personalize**—personify (personalization, n.)
5. **personate**—personify in art or poetry (personation,n.)
6. **personify**—represent as a human being; give human characteristics to (personification,n.)
7. **virify**—make into a man (virification,n.)

11. **To Become Human:** humanize,v. (humanization,n.)

12. **Ascription of Human Characteristics to Something Non-Human,n.**
   1. **animatism**—ascription of consciousness, personality, will, etc., to inanimate objects (animatistic,adj.)
   2. **animism**—belief that nature and inanimate objects have consciousness, or that inanimate objects have souls (animist,n. animist, animistic,adj.)
   3. **anthropomorphism**—ascription to non-human creatures or forces of the mental processes or attributes of a human being (anthropomorphist,n. anthropomorphic, anthropomorphist,adj. anthropomorphize, v.)
   4. **anthropomorphology**—application to God or to a god of terms descr. of a human (anthropomorphological,adj.)
   5. **anthropopathy**—anthropomorphism; anthropophuism (anthropopathic,adj.)
   6. **anthropophuism**—anthropomorphism in reference to a deity (anthropomorphotheist,n. anthropophuistic,adj.)
   7. **anthropopsychism**—ascription of a human type of soul to nature or natural forces (anthropopsychic,adj.)
   8. **personification**—ascription of human characteristics to non-humans or inanimate objects (personify,v.)
   9. **theanthropism, theanthropology**—anthropomorphism; anthropophuism (theanthropist,n.)

13. **To Deprive of Human Characteristics,v.**
   1. **brutalize, brutify**—make inhuman, i.e., more like an animal (brutalization,n.)
   2. **dehumanize**—take human attributes from (dehumanization,n.)
   3. **imbrute, embrute**—cause to sink to the level of an animal (imbrutement, embrutement,n.)

14. **To Sink to the Level of an Animal:** brutalize, brutify, imbrute, embrute,v. (brutalization, imbrutement, embrutement,n.)

15. **The Animal Nature of a Human:** animality, beast, brute, flesh,n.

16. **Philosophy that Humans Have No Spiritual Superiority over Animals:** animalism,n. (animalist,n. animalistic,adj.)

17. **Philosophy or Theory that Man Is the Center of the Universe and/or the Final Purpose of Creation:** anthropocentrism,n. (anthropocentrist,n. anthropocentric,adj.)

18. **Active Interest in the Welfare of Humanity or Desire for the Betterment of Mankind:** humanitarianism, philanthropy, philanthropism,n. (humanitarian, philanthropist or philanthrope,n. humanitarian; philanthropic, philanthropical, philanthropian, adj.)

19. **Hatred of All Mankind:** misanthropy,n. (misanthrope, misanthropist,n. misanthropic, adj.)

20. **Theory of Human Origin,n.**
   1. **monogenesis, monogenesy, monogenism, monogeny**—theory that all humanity originated from a single created pair of people, or from one ancestral type (monogenesist, monogenist,n. monogenetic, monogenistic, monogenic,adj.)
   2. **polygenesis**—theory that several branches of the human race originated and developed independently (polygenesist,n. polygenesic, polygenetic,adj.)
   3. **polygenism, polygeny**—theory that all human races derived from two or more distinct ancestral types (polygenist,n. polygenistic,adj.)
   4. **polyphylesis, polyphyly**—polygenesis (polyphyletic,adj.)

21. **Origin of Man,n.**
   1. **ethnogeny**—origin of human races (ethnogenic,adj.)
   2. **monogenesis**—origin of man from a single ancestral type (monogenetic,adj.)
   3. **polygenesis**—polyphylesis (polygenetic, adj.)
   4. **polyphylesis, polyphyly**—origin of man from more than one ancestral type or race (polyphyletic,adj.)

22. **Science or Study of Man or of Race,n.**
   1. **anthropobiology**—biological study of man (anthropobiological,adj.)
   2. **anthropogenesis, anthropogeny**—science that treats of the origin and development of the human race (anthropogenetic,adj.)
   3. **anthropogeography**—science that explores and studies the geographic distribution of the human race (anthropogeographical,adj.)
   4. **anthropography**—science that treats of the distribution of the divisions of the human race (anthropographic,adj.)
   5. **anthropology**—science that treats of the development of the human race (anthropological,adj.)
   6. **anthroponomy, anthroponomics**—science of human actions, behavior, etc. (anthroponomic,adj.)
   7. **anthroposociology**—study of the reciprocal action of race and environment (anthroposociological,adj.)
   8. **cacogenics**—science or study of the degeneration of a race (cacogenic,adj.)
   9. **ethnogeny**—science of the origin of human races; ethnology (ethnogenic,adj.)
   10. **ethnography**—descriptive ethnology (ethnographic,adj.)
   11. **ethnology**—science that treats of the races of mankind (ethnological,adj.)
   12. **eugenics**—science of race improvement through selective breeding (eugenic,adj.)
   13. **genetics**—science of human heredity (genetic,adj.)
   14. **paleoanthropology**—science of primitive man (paleoanthropological,adj.)
   15. **paleoethnography**—descriptive ethnology of early prehistoric or paleolithic man (paleoethnographic,adj.)
   16. **paleoethnology**—science of the races of prehistoric man (paleoethnological,adj.)
   17. **philosophy**—science or study of the facts or principles of human behavior (philosophic, philosophical,adj.)
   18. **psychology**—science of human behavior, actions, motives, etc. (psychological,adj.)
   19. **sociology**—science of how humans live together (sociological,adj.)

23. **Student of a Science of Man or of Race, n. From Sec. 22:** anthropobiologist, anthropogeographer, anthropologist, anthroponomist, anthroposociologist, ethnologist, eugenist, geneticist, paleoanthropologist, philosopher, psychologist, sociologist

430. RACE

1. **Race:** breed, lineage; phylon (biology); stock, strain,n.
2. **Of the Races of Man:** Caucasian

("white") ; Mongoloid ("yellow") ; Negroid ("black") ,adj. (Caucasian, Mongoloid, Negroid or Negro,n.)

3. Racial: ethnic, phyletic,adj.

4. Race Degeneration: cacogenics,n. (cacogenic,adj.)

5. Race History of Animal or Plant Types: phylogeny,n. (phylogenetic,adj.)

6. Person of Mixed Race or Blood,n.
   1. albino—term for octoroon in Mexico
   2. cafuso (Portuguese)—zambo
   3. creole—person part Negro and part French or Spanish
   4. Eurasian—person of mixed European and Asiatic blood
   5. fustee—offspring of a white person and a mustee
   6. griffado—offspring of a white and a quadroon
   7. griffe—child of a mulatto mother and a Negro father; person of mixed Negro and American Indian blood; mulatto
   8. half-blood—half-breed
   9. half-breed—person of mixed race; person of mixed American Indian and white blood
   10. half-caste—person born of a European parent and a Mohammedan or Hindu parent; half-breed
   11. hybrid—person of mixed race (hybridism, hybridity,n.)
   12. Ladino—one not of pure Spanish blood or birth but who still speaks Spanish or a Spanish dialect with fluency; person of mixed Spanish and Indian blood (term used in Latin America or the Spanish colonies)
   13. marabou—person of five-eighths Negro blood; child of a mulatto and a griffe (term used in Louisiana)
   14. mestizo—offspring of parents of different races, esp. one of mixed Spanish and Indian blood, of mixed Chinese and Negro blood in the Philippines, or of mixed European and Oriental blood; any person of mixed racial extraction
   15. métis—person of mixed blood; octoroon, in the U.S.; half-breed, in Canada (métisse,fem.)
   16. miscegine, miscegenate—child born of parents of different races
   17. mulatto—person of mixed white and Negro blood; strictly, the offspring of a pure white and a pure Negro
   18. mustee, mestee—person of mixed racial origin (term used in the West Indies or in India)
   19. octoroon—person with seven-eighths white blood, one-eighth Negro blood
   20. quadroon—person of three-fourths white blood, one-fourth Negro blood
   21. quintoon—offspring of a quadroon and a white person
   22. sacatra—person of approximately seven-eighths Negro blood and one-eighth white blood
   23. sambo—person of mixed Indian and Negro blood (term used in the Honduras) ; person of mixed Negro and Indian, or mixed Negro and mulatto blood
   24. zambo—person of mixed Indian and Negro blood, esp. of a Negro father and Indian mother; sambo

7. Negro,n.
   1. Afro-American, Aframerican—American Negro (Afro-American, Aframerican,adj.)
   2. blackamoor—Negro
   3. colored person—Negro (colored,adj.)
   4. Negroid, Negrillo—member of a diminutive Negro people in Africa

8. Resembling a Negro; Characteristic of Negroes: Negroid,adj.

9. White Person,n.
   1. Caucasian—member of the white race (Caucasian,adj.)
   2. Creole—white person descended from the French settlers of Louisiana (Creole, adj.)
   3. griffin, griff—white person newly arrived in the Orient (griffinage,n.)
   4. paleface—white person, so called by the American Indians
   5. xanthochroid—person with fair complexion and light or yellowish hair (xanthochroid,adj.)

10. White People,n.
   1. albiculi—white people (derogatory)
   2. Xanthochroi—division of the Caucasian races made up largely of fair-haired Northern Europeans and their descendants (Xanthochroic,adj.)

11. Indian,n.
   1. Amerind—American Indian
   2. red man, redskin—American Indian
   3. squaw—female of the American Indian

12. A Japanese or Part Japanese,n.
   1. Issei—Japanese immigrant to the U.S.
   2. Nipponese—Japanese (Nipponese,adj.)
   3. Nisei—native-born American of immigrant Japanese parents
   4. Oriental—Japanese (Oriental,adj.)
   5. Sansei—child born of Nisei parents

13. The Japanese People: Nipponese,n.

14. A Chinese,n.
   1. Celestial—native of China (Celestial,adj.)
   2. Oriental—Chinese (Oriental,adj.)

15. Pert. to Races with Yellow Skin: xanthous,adj.

16. Knowledge of Chinese or Far Eastern Languages, Customs, Culture, etc.: Orientalism,n. (Orientalist,n. Orientalist,adj.)

17. Science of the Chinese, Their Culture, Customs, etc.: Sinology,n. (Sinologist,n. Sinological,adj.)

18. To Make or Become Oriental; To Cause to Conform to Oriental Culture: orientalize, v. (orientalization,n.)

19. Any Oriental Trait, Characteristic, Custom, etc.: orientalism,n.

431. PERSON

1. A Person,n.
   1. cog—person functioning somewhat anonymously or routinely in an organization
   2. homunculus—little person
   3. individual—person
   4. manikin—little person
   5. personage—person
   6. soul—person
   7. specimen—person (colloq. and often derogatory)

2. Person by Person: per capita

3. People; The People,n.
   1. body politic—people as a group organized for government; organized society
   2. commonalty—people as a group
   3. commonwealth—people constituting a political division; body politic
   4. community—people living together in one region and having common interests, etc.; public
   5. crowd—people in general
   6. demos—the people
   7. folk, folks—people
   8. gens—people
   9. parish—people of the district or region served by a church
   10. personnel—people working in, or attached to, an organization, public or private
   11. plebs—the people

12. **populace**—people of a place
13. **population**—people who live in a place
14. **public**—the people
15. **quick**—living people, usually in the phrase *the quick and the dead*
16. **rank and file**—people constituting the body of a society, nation, party, etc., as distinguished from the leaders
17. **society**—people of a place or time; all people
18. **Tom, Dick, and Harry**—any people at all, without discrimination (derogatory)
19. **world**—all people; people in general

4. Referring to People or the People,adj. *From Sec. 3:* community, demotic, folk, popular, public, societal or social; *Also:*
1. **communal**—pert. or belonging to all the people
2. **pandemic**—pert. to or affecting all people
3. **vulgar**—pert. to the people in general; popular; public

5. Containing Many People: populous,adj. (populousness,n.)

6. The Common People (Neutral Term): commonalty, commonality, commonage, commons, crowd, demos, hoi polloi, masses, multitude, peasantry, plebs, populace, ruck; Third Estate (formerly, in France and England); vulgus,n. (common, demotic, mass, peasant, plebeian, vulgar,adj.)

7. One of the Common People (Neutral Term): commoner, peasant, plebeian,n.

8. Common or Low-Class People (Derogatory or Contemptuous Term): canaille, cattle, crowd, dregs, herd, horde, mob, peasantry, rabble, raff, ragtag; rag, tag, and bobtail; ribble-rabble, riffraff, rout, ruck, scum, varletry,n.

9. One of the Common or Low-Class People (Derogatory or Contemptuous Term): peasant, plebeian, scum, varlet,n.

10. The Mob as a Ruling Class: mobocracy,n. (mobocratic, mobocratical,adj.)

11. The People Who Work for a Living: proletariat,n. (proletarian, proletary; prolétaire (French),n. proletarian,adj.)

12. Doctrine or Philosophy that the Person is Superior to, and More Important than, Society or the Community: individualism,n. (individualist,n. individualist, individualistic, adj.)

13. Population Science,n.
1. **demography**—science of statistics of births, deaths, marriages, diseases, and other social or vital statistics of population (demographic, demographical,adj.)
2. **demotics**—sociology
3. **larithmics**—science or scientific study of population size (larithmic,adj.)
4. **sociology**—science that investigates how people live together in a society (sociological,adj.)

14. Student of Population,n. *From Sec. 13:* demographer or demographist, sociologist

15. Facts about the People in a Country or Region, Such as Number, Sex, Age, Business, etc.: vital statistics,n.

432. THE SENSES

1. Process of Using One of the Five Senses: sensation,n.

2. Pert. or Referring to the Senses (General): sensational, sensorial, sensory, sensual, sensuous,adj.

3. Sense of Hearing: audition,n.

4. Sense of Taste: gustation, palate,n.

5. Sense of Smell: olfaction, scent,n.

6. Sense of Seeing: sight, vision,n.

7. Sense of Touch: feel, tactility,n.

8. Pert. to the Sense of Hearing: acoustic, audile, auditive, auditory, aural, auricular, adj.

9. Pert. to the Sense of Taste: gustatory, palatal,adj.

10. Pert. to the Sense of Smell: olfactory,adj.

11. Pert. to the Sense of Seeing: visual,adj.

12. Pert. to the Sense of Touch: tactile, tactual,adj.

13. Pert. to the Senses of both Hearing and Seeing: audiovisual,adj.

14. The Entire Sensory Apparatus: sensorium,n.

15. Operation or Functioning of the Senses: sensation,n. (sensational,adj.)

16. Capable of Having Sensations: conscious, esthetic, passible, sensible, sensitive, sentient, adj.

17. Capability of Having Sensations: consciousness, esthesia, passibility, sensibility, sensitiveness, sentience,n.

433. PERCEPTION

1. Perception through the Senses,n.
1. **apperception**—clear or conscious perception through any of the senses
2. **feeling**—perception by touch
3. **perceptiveness**—power or faculty of perceiving
4. **percipience, percipiency**—perception; act of perceiving; physical or mental ability to perceive; quick or sharp perception
5. **sensation**—perception through the senses; faculty of perceiving stimuli

2. Perceiving; Able to Perceive,adj. *From Sec. 1:* apperceptive, perceptive, percipient, sensitive

3. Pert. to, or Descr. of, Perception,adj. *From Sec. 1:* apperceptive, perceptive, sensational; *Also:*
1. **perceptional**—pert. to, or descr. of, perception
2. **perceptual**—pert. to, descr. of, or involving, perception
3. **sensory, sensorial, sensual**—pert. to perception through the senses

4. To Perceive,v. *From Sec. 1:* apperceive, feel, sense

5. Perceiver,n. *From Sec. 1:* percipient

6. Organs or Powers of Perception: perceptives,pl. n.

7. That Which Is Perceived; Product of Perceiving; Object of Perception: percept,n.

8. Capable of Being Perceived,adj.
1. **palpable**—easily perceived by any of the senses
2. **perceptible, perceivable**—capable of being perceived, or of being grasped by the senses
3. **phenomenal**—perceptible through the senses, rather than thought or imagined
4. **sensible**—capable of being perceived by one of the senses
5. **tangible**—possessing substance, hence capable of being perceived
6. **tenuous**—barely capable of being perceived

9. Ability to Be Perceived,n. *From Sec. 8:* palpability, perceptibility, perceivability, sensibility, tangibility, tenuousness, tenuity

10. Not Able to Be Perceived,adj. *From Sec. 8:* impalpable, imperceptible, unperceivable, insensible, intangible; *Also:*

1. **extrasensory**—beyond perception by the five senses
2. **supersensible, supersensory**—beyond what is perceptible by the senses
3. **supersensual**—beyond the range of the normal senses

11. Inability to Be Perceived,n. *From Sec. 10:* impalpability, imperceptibility, insensibility, intangibility

12. Abnormal Perception,n.
   1. **clairvoyance**—perception, through sight, of things or actions that are beyond the range of vision
   2. **extrasensory perception**—perception by some means other than one of the five senses
   3. **sixth sense**—psychic, supernatural, or intuitive perception; perception without or beyond the normal senses
   4. **telepathy**—communication of minds by other than normal means
   5. **telesthesia**—sensation, perception, or impression received from a distance and beyond the normal power of the sensory organs

13. Having Abnormal Perception,adj. *From Sec. 12:* clairvoyant, telepathic; *Also:* **1. psychic**—especially susceptible to, or capable of, extrasensory perception

14. Person with Abnormal Perception,n. *From Sec. 12:* clairvoyant, telepathist or telepath; *From Sec. 13:* psychic

15. Pert. to, Descr. of, or Related to, Abnormal Perception,adj. *From Sec. 12:* extrasensory, telepathic; *From Sec. 13:* psychic, psychical

16. One Who Is a Student of, or Believer in, Abnormal Perception,n. *From Sec. 12:* telepathist

17. Study That Investigates Extrasensory Phenomena Such as Clairvoyance, Telepathy, etc.: parapsychology,n.

18. Sensitivity, Sensitiveness,n.
   1. **algesia**—sensitivity to pain
   2. **allergy**—abnormal physical or bodily sensitiveness to a drug, substance, pollen, food, etc., followed by strong reactions on exposure
   3. **anaphylaxis**—increased sensitivity to a foreign protein, drug, serum, antibiotic, etc., resulting from previous exposure to, or treatment with, it
   4. **hyperalgesia**—excessive sensitivity to pain
   5. **hyperesthesia**—morbid acuteness of the senses
   6. **hypersensitivity**—abnormal, or abnormally acute, sensitivity
   7. **idiosyncrasy**—individual and non-typical sensitivity to a drug
   8. **impressibility**—sensitiveness
   9. **irritation**—abnormal or pathologic sensitivity of a bodily part or organ, etc.
   10. **photosensitivity**—sensitivity to light
   11. **phototonus**—sensitivity to light (of a plant or organism)
   12. **soreness**—sensitivity to pain (of a bodily part or organ)

19. Sensitive,adj. *From Sec. 18:* allergic, anaphylactic, hyperalgesic, hyperesthetic, hypersensitive, impressible, irritated, photosensitive, phototonic, sore

20. To Cause to Be Sensitive: sensitize,v. (sensitization,n.)

21. To Cause (a Bodily Part or Member) to Be Abnormally Sensitive: irritate,v. (irritation,n.)

22. To Eliminate or Reduce the Natural Sensitivity of (a Person, Animal, Organ, Tissue, Bodily Part, etc.): desensitize,v. (desensitization,n.)

434. PHYSICAL SENSATION

1. Physical Sensation,n.
   1. **crawliness**—sensation as if creatures were crawling on one's skin
   2. **creepiness**—sensation that insects are moving along one's skin
   3. **feel**—physical sensation, esp. of something touched or touching
   4. **formication**—imaginary sensation of ants crawling on the skin
   5. **impression**—sensation
   6. **itch, itching, itchiness**—peculiar sensation on the skin that causes one to scratch or want to scratch
   7. **paresthesia**—sensations of prickliness, tingling, etc., of the skin from no apparent cause
   8. **prickle, prickliness**—stinging or sharply painful sensation
   9. **pruritus**—itching of the skin though there is no visible rash or eruption
   10. **pseudesthesia**—false or imaginary sensation, as in a limb that has been amputated
   11. **synesthesia**—sensation felt in one part of the body though the stimulus has been applied to a different part; secondary or subjective sensation (for example, a sensation of sound or color aroused by an actual sensation of taste or touch, etc.)
   12. **tickle**—sensation that causes a desire to laugh; sensation of being lightly touched, as by a feather, the fingers, etc.
   13. **tingle**—stinging sensation, either of touch or hearing
   14. **trichoesthesia**—sensation when the hair is touched
   15. **urtication**—stinging or itching feeling in or on the skin

2. Descr. of, or Having, a Physical Sensation,adj. *From Sec. 1:* crawly, creepy, formicative, itchy or itching, paresthetic, prickly, pruritic, synesthetic, tingly

3. To Feel a Sensation,v. *From Sec. 1:* crawl, creep, itch, prickle, tickle, tingle

4. Causing a Sensation,adj. *From Sec. 1:* prickling, pruritic, tickling, tingling, urticant

435. LACK OF SENSATION

1. Dullness, Lack, or Loss of Sensation; Insensitivity; Unconsciousness,n.
   1. **analgesia**—insensitivity to pain
   2. **anesthesia**—loss of feeling or sensation
   3. **apathism**—insensitivity
   4. **bemusement**—numbness and confusion
   5. **besottedness**—dullness; stupefaction; torpor
   6. **black-out**—unconsciousness
   7. **bloodlessness**—torpor
   8. **coma**—deep unconsciousness caused by some morbid physiological state
   9. **daze**—numbness combined with confusion; stupefaction
   10. **deadness**—complete lack of sensation; numbness
   11. **faint**—temporary loss of consciousness; state of unconsciousness
   12. **hebetude**—dullness of senses
   13. **hypesthesia**—imperfect power of sensation; dullness of the senses
   14. **impassivity, impassiveness**—lack of ability to feel sensation; unconsciousness
   15. **insensateness**—lack of the power of sensation
   16. **insensibility**—lack of sensation; unconsciousness
   17. **insentience**—lack of the sensations of animate creatures
   18. **numbness**—temporary lack of sensation or the ability to feel

19. **petrifaction, petrification**—numbness caused by some strong emotion
20. **senselessness**—unconsciousness
21. **stupefaction**—dullness of sensation; loss of consciousness; torpor
22. **stupor**—loss or lack of capacity for sensation; near unconsciousness; numbness
23. **swoon**—faint
24. **syncope**—unconsciousness caused by cerebral anemia
25. **torpor, torpidity, torpidness**—lack of the power of sensation, as in a hibernating animal
26. **trance**—unconsciousness or insensibility somewhat like sleep; partly unconscious condition; stupor
27. **twilight sleep**—partial anesthesia, effected by injection of morphine and scopolamine

2. To Cause Lack or Reduction of Sensation or Consciousness,v. *From Sec. 1:* anesthetize, bemuse, besot, daze, deaden, hebetate, numb, petrify, stupefy, torpify (anesthetization, bemusement, hebetation, petrifaction or petrification, stupefaction,n.); *Also:*
1. **benumb**—make numb; deprive of sensation; stupefy
2. **chloroform**—anesthetize with chloroform
3. **etherize**—anesthetize with ether (etherization,n.)
4. **knock out**—render unconscious (colloq. or slang)
5. **stun**—knock unconscious

3. Lacking in Sensation; Insensitive; Unconscious,adj. *From Sec. 1:* apathic, bloodless; comate, comatose, or comose; dead, hebetudinous, hypesthesic, impassive, insensate, insensible, insentient, numb, senseless, stuporous or stupid, torpid; *From Sec. 2:* anesthetized, bemused, besotted or besot, dazed, deadened, hebetate or hebetated, numbed, petrified, stupefied; benumbed, chloroformed, etherized, knocked out, stunned; *Also:* 1. narcose, narcous—in a state of stupor

4. Causing Lack of Sensation or Unconsciousness,adj. *From Sec. 1:* analgesic, anesthetic, hebetative, petrifactive, stupefactive or stupefacient, torporific; *Also:* 1. narcotic—causing a reduction in sensation

5. Agent or Substance That Reduces or Removes Sensation,n. *From Sec. 1:* analgesic, anesthetic or anesthetizer, stupefacient or stupefier; *From Sec. 2:* chloroform, ether; *From Sec. 4:* narcotic

6. To Lose Sensation or Consciousness,v. *From Sec. 1:* black out, faint, hebetate, swoon (hebetation,n.)

7. To Soothe to Unconsciousness, Figuratively: narcotize,v. (narcotization,n.)

8. To Bring Back (Someone) to Consciousness: resuscitate, revive,v. (resuscitation, revival,n. resuscitative,adj.)

9. To Return to Consciousness: resuscitate, revive,v. (resuscitation, revival,n.)

436. TOUCH

1. To Touch; To Come into Contact (with), v.
1. **abut**—touch upon geographically
2. **adjoin**—touch in the geographical or spatial sense
3. **beat against**—lap against
4. **brush**—touch very lightly in passing
5. **caress**—touch, pat, stroke, etc., lovingly or affectionately
6. **carom**—strike and then rebound, as in billiards
7. **chuck**—touch or stroke lightly, usually under the chin

8. **clank (against)**—hit or strike (against) with a metallic sound
9. **collide (with or against)**—come into violent contact (of moving objects or vehicles)
10. **contact**—move into touch with; be in touch with; touch
11. **crash (into)**—collide (with) with a very loud noise
12. **dab**—touch lightly; stroke softly and lightly or with something soft and wet
13. **feel**—touch in order to examine or get a sensation from
14. **graze**—touch very lightly while passing
15. **grope**—feel about with the hands, owing to inability to see, as through blindness, darkness, etc.
16. **handle**—touch with the hands; feel with the hands
17. **hit**—come into contact (with); collide
18. **impinge (on, upon, or against)**—come into contact (with); collide
19. **kiss**—touch for the fraction of a second; barely touch
20. **lap, lap against, lap at**—touch repeatedly and gently against
21. **lick**—touch or pass over with, or as if with, a tongue; draw the tongue over
22. **manipulate**—handle
23. **osculate**—come into close physical contact
24. **palpate**—touch in order to examine; examine by touch (medical)
25. **pat**—stroke lightly
26. **patter against, patter on**—touch repeatedly with a succession of slight sounds
27. **percuss**—touch against forcibly; tap (a part of the body) sharply to listen to the sounds produced and thus form an opinion or diagnosis of an ailment (medical)
28. **ram**—make forcible contact with
29. **shave**—just barely touch; touch lightly while passing
30. **strike**—come into forcible contact with
31. **stroke**—pass the hand over gently and lightly
32. **suck**—lick
33. **tag**—touch with the hand, as in the child's game
34. **tap**—touch lightly; touch lightly and repeatedly and with enough force to make a slight sound
35. **tickle**—touch gently; touch with the fingers, a feather, etc., in such a way as to cause to laugh
36. **tip**—tap
37. **twiddle**—touch slightly or lightly

2. A Touching; A Touch,n. *From Sec. 1:* abuttal or abutment, brush, caress, carom, chuck, collision, contact, crash, dab, feel, graze, grope, hit, impingement, kiss, lap, lick, manipulation, osculation, palpation, pat, patter, percussion, ram, shave, stroke, suck, tap, tickle, twiddle; *Also:*
1. **impact**—strong contact or collision
2. **palpation**—act of touching; act of touching to examine or get a sensation from
3. **shock**—sudden or violent impact
4. **smashup**—bad collision
5. **taction**—touch; contact

3. Touching; Descr. of Touch,adj. *From Sec. 1:* caressive, impingent, manipulative, osculatory, palpatory, percussive (impingence, n.); *Also:*
1. **approximal**—touching (medical)
2. **contiguous**—touching geographically or spatially (contiguity, contiguousness,n.)
3. **contingent**—touching (contingence,n.)
4. **tangent, tangential**—touching; touching at one point only (tangency, tangentiality,n.)

4. Shock Caused by Bodies Colliding: concussion,n. (concussional,adj.)

5. Sense of Touch: feel, tactility,n.

6. Pert. to Touch, Sense of Touch, Contact, etc.,adj.
   1. contactual—pert. to contact
   2. tactile—pert. to touch or to the sense of touch
   3. tactual—pert. to touch, or to the sense or organs of touch

7. Quality of Something Perceived by Touching: feel,n.

8. Caused by Touching: tactual,adj.

9. Causing the Sensation of Touching: tactual,adj.

10. Capable of Touching Each of the Other Fingers (as of the Thumb): apposable,adj. (apposability,n.)

11. Perceivable by Touch,adj.
   1. palpable—capable of being felt or touched (palpability,n.)
   2. tactile—perceivable by touch (tactility,n.)
   3. tangible—having substance and therefore capable of being touched or felt (tangibility,n.)

12. Not Perceivable by Touch,adj. *From Sec. 11:* impalpable, intangible (impalpability, intangibility,n.)

13. Untouched by That Which Might Harm or Injure: intact,adj. (intactness,n.)

437. HIT

1. To Hit, Strike, Beat, Whip, etc.,v.
   1. bang—beat or strike with a loud noise
   2. bash—hit with a smashing blow
   3. baste—hit; beat; whip
   4. bastinado, bastinade—beat with a stick
   5. bat—hit or strike with a stick or club
   6. batter—beat with repeated blows; beat so as to wound or destroy
   7. belabor—beat with strong and repeated blows; beat with words
   8. belt—beat with a belt; hit
   9. birch—whip
   10. blackjack—strike or beat with a short, usually leather-covered, club
   11. bludgeon—hit or beat with a club
   12. bob—rap
   13. bounce—bang; bump
   14. box—hit with the open palm, often on the ear
   15. brain—hit so hard on the head as to, or almost as to, dash out the brains of
   16. buck—hit with lowered head
   17. buffet—hit; strike; hit repeatedly; knock about; slap
   18. bump—hit against (something), but without great force
   19. bunt—hit with the head lowered, as does a goat
   20. bust—hit (slang or colloq.)
   21. butt—hit with the head lowered
   22. cane—hit or beat with a stick or cane
   23. chastise—beat, whip, or spank, literally or figuratively
   24. clang—hit or strike together with a metallic, bell-like sound
   25. clap—hit, or hit together, with a resounding noise
   26. clip—deliver a sharp blow upon (someone) with the fist (colloq.)
   27. clobber—hit, or hit forcefully (slang)
   28. clout—hit; strike
   29. club—beat with a stick
   30. cowhide—whip with a leather strap
   31. cudgel—beat with a club
   32. cuff—hit with the flat of the hand
   33. dash—strike violently, often in order to break
   34. drub—hit repeatedly with, or as with, a stick
   35. drum—beat on with rhythmical motions; beat a drum

36. fell—knock down with, or as if with, a blow
37. ferule—strike on the hand (usually children) with a rod or ruler
38. flagellate—whip; flog
39. flagellate oneself—beat or whip oneself fanatically or frenziedly, for religious purification or discipline (flagellant,n.)
40. flail—beat; strike; whip
41. flog—beat hard with a stick, whip, etc.
42. fustigate—beat; cudgel (fustigatory,adj.)
43. glance—beat or strike obliquely, then swerve off at an angle
44. hammer—beat with, or as if with, a hammer; strike blows on or upon with, or as if with, a hammer
45. horsewhip—beat or whip with a horsewhip
46. knock—hit; strike; beat
47. knock about—hit repeatedly and thereby cause to move or jump from place to place
48. knock down—hit (someone or something) so as to make him or it fall
49. knock out—hit (an opponent in a prize fight) so hard that he falls and cannot rise before the count of ten
50. knout—whip as a form of punishment
51. lambaste—beat soundly (slang)
52. larrup—beat soundly; whip (colloq.)
53. lash—beat or strike forcibly, with, or as with, a whip
54. lick—beat; whip (colloq.)
55. lob—hit (a tennis ball) too high
56. loft—hit (a golf ball) so it will have a good rise
57. mash—beat into a soft or pulpy mass
58. maul—beat and pull about
59. paddle—beat; whip
60. paddywhack—spank (colloq.)
61. paste—hit with a sharp blow on the face or body (slang)
62. pat—hit lightly; tap
63. pellet—hit with a small ball or balls
64. pelt—beat heavily upon; hit with successive blows
65. percuss—strike against; strike so as to shake or jar; strike against the ear—of sounds (percussive,adj.)
66. pestle—pound into a powder
67. pistol-whip—whip with a pistol
68. pommel, pummel—beat or hit thoroughly or repeatedly
69. pound—beat or strike repeatedly and heavily
70. punch—strike with the fist; deliver a quick, smart blow with the fist
71. quirt—hit with a riding whip; whip
72. rap—hit with a light but sharp blow
73. scourge—whip
74. sideswipe—hit with a glancing blow along the side of
75. slam—hit or strike with great force or noise
76. slap—strike with the open hand
77. slash—strike violently; strike with a knife, sword, or other sharp implement; whip
78. slate—whip
79. slog—hit heavily, but with little or no aim
80. slug—hit heavily, generally with the fist (colloq.)
81. smack—hit sharply
82. smash—hit with a strong or violent impact
83. smite—hit; strike; strike with the hand or with some weapon held in the hand; hit with great force; strike down (smote, past tense); smitten, past participle)
84. sock—strike violently (colloq.)
85. spank—hit with the open hand, esp. on the buttocks, and usually as punishment
86. stamp—hit forcibly; hit forcibly with the sole of the foot

87. **strap**—hit, beat, or whip with a strap, usually as punishment
88. **stub**—hit (one's foot, toe, finger, etc.) against something
89. **swat**—hit hard; strike a crushing blow against
90. **swinge**—beat; whip
91. **swipe**—hit with a sweeping blow
92. **switch**—beat; whip
93. **tag**—tap with the hand, as in the child's game
94. **tamp**—hit gently to pack down
95. **tan**—whip (colloq.)
96. **tap**—hit with a light blow; hit with a light, audible blow
97. **thrash**—beat; whip
98. **thresh**—beat (wheat, etc.) to separate grain or seeds
99. **thrum**—drum or tap the fingers idly upon
100. **thump**—hit with something thick and heavy, making a dull sound; hit heavily, making a dull sound; pound
101. **thwack**—hit hard with something flat, or with a stick
102. **tip**—hit with a light blow
103. **trounce**—beat or whip severely
104. **truncheon**—beat with a club
105. **uppercut**—hit with a swinging blow started low and directed upward (term in boxing)
106. **urticate**—whip (a numb or paralyzed limb) with nettles in order to bring back sensation or stimulate blood circulation
107. **wallop**—beat, hit, or strike with great force (colloq.)
108. **whack**—beat; hit; strike; hit with a smart and loud blow (colloq.)
109. **whale**—beat; hit; hit forcibly; whip (colloq.)
110. **whisk**—beat lightly (as eggs, etc.)

2. A Blow, Hit, or Strike; A Hitting, Striking, Beating, or Whipping,n. *From Sec. 1:* bang, bash, baste, bastinado or bastinade, bat, belaboring, belt or belting, birching, box, buffet or buffeting, bump, bunt, bust, butt, caning, chastisement, clap, clip, clout, clubbing, cowhiding, cudgeling, cuff, drub or drubbing, drum, flagellation or self-flagellation, flailing, flogging, fustigation, glance, hammering, horsewhipping, lambasting, larruping, lash or lashing, licking, lob, mauling, paddling, paddywhacking, paste, pat, pelting, percussion, pistol-whipping, pommeling or pummeling, pounding, punch, quirting, rap, sideswipe, slam, slap, slash, slugging, smack, smash, smite, sock, spank or spanking, stamp, strapping, swat, swingeing, swipe, switch or switching, tamp, tanning, tap, thrashing, thrum, thump, thwack, trouncing, uppercut, urtication, wallop or walloping, whack or whacking, whaling; *Also:*
1. **coup de grâce (French)**—merciful deathblow that ends suffering
2. **deathblow**—final and fatal blow, literally or figuratively
3. **fisticuff**—blow by the fist
4. **flick**—light and very quick blow
5. **impact**—a striking or hitting together; a striking or hitting of one thing upon another, literally or figuratively
6. **quietus**—finishing blow
7. **shock**—sudden and violent blow; sudden or violent impact
8. **spat**—light blow or slap
9. **stroke**—blow
10. **thud**—blow

3. Blow for Blow: tit for tat

4. That Which One Tries to Hit: target,n.

5. A Whip; A Club; A Stick Used for Beating or Hitting, or as a Weapon,n.
1. **bastinado, bastinade**—stick for beating someone
2. **bat**—strong stick or club

3. **billy, night stick**—policeman's club
4. **birch**—rod or twig of a birch tree used as a whip
5. **blackjack**—short, usually leather-covered, club
6. **bludgeon**—club that is thicker at the striking end
7. **cat-o'-nine-tails**—whip for flogging
8. **crop**—riding whip
9. **cudgel**—short and heavy club
10. **ferule**—cane, rod, or stick for punishing children by striking them on their palms
11. **flail**—stick used to thresh grain
12. **horsewhip**—whip for horses
13. **knout**—kind of whip once used in Russia for beating criminals
14. **lash**—anything used as a whip
15. **pestle**—instrument for pounding something into a powder
16. **pike**—pole with a small metal tip, once used as a weapon
17. **quarterstaff**—weapon in the form of a six- to eight-foot heavy pole, with an iron tip, once used in England
18. **quirt**—short-handled riding whip
19. **scourge**—whip
20. **shillelagh**—short club used for hitting or as a weapon
21. **stave**—short and heavy club
22. **switch**—light stick used to beat or whip with
23. **truncheon**—policeman's club

6. Part of a Whip below the Handle: lash, thong, whiplash,n.

7. Other Stick,n.
1. **baton**—rod or staff as symbol of office; orchestra leader's stick
2. **cane**—walking stick
3. **crook**—shepherd's staff
4. **crosier, crozier**—bishop's or abbot's staff
5. **pikestaff**—staff with a pointed end of metal, used by foot travelers
6. **pole**—long, comparatively slender stick, often round
7. **rod**—shaped stick of any kind or material
8. **spit**—slender rod
9. **staff**—fairly long and heavy stick
10. **stake**—pointed stick, to be driven into the ground
11. **stave**—stick
12. **wand**—slender rod

8. Stick, Rod, Pin, etc., for Holding Meat while Broiling, Roasting, etc.: broach, brochette, skewer, spit,n.

9. Hammer,n.
1. **cock**—hammer of a firearm
2. **gavel**—small wooden hammer used by a judge, presiding officer, etc., to call for attention, etc.
3. **mallet**—wooden hammer
4. **maul, mall**—heavy hammer
5. **sledge, sledge hammer**—large and heavy hammer, generally for use with both hands

438. RUB

1. To Rub,v.
1. **abrade**—rub off or away
2. **anoint**—rub with oil, often as a religious ceremony
3. **bark**—rub the skin off
4. **bray**—rub fine
5. **brush**—wipe
6. **buff**—rub until smooth; polish
7. **burnish**—polish (a surface)
8. **chafe**—rub; rub in such a way as to wear away or irritate (the skin)
9. **excoriate**—chafe (the skin)
10. **furbish**—rub (a weapon, armor, etc.) until clean and bright; polish

11. **grate**—rub against a rough surface for the purpose of reducing to small particles; rub (things) together, or be rubbed one against the other, and produce a harsh or unpleasant sound
12. **massage**—rub (the body or parts of the body) usually for therapeutic purposes
13. **mop**—rub with, or as if with, a mop
14. **pat**—stroke
15. **plaster**—rub; smear
16. **polish**—rub until smooth and bright
17. **pumice**—polish with, or as if with, pumice
18. **rasp**—rub harshly; rub with, or as if with, a rough instrument or file; grate
19. **raze**—rub off harshly or roughly
20. **scour**—rub clean
21. **scrape**—rub harshly or roughly; roughly rub the top layer or surface of or from; rub against (something) with a harsh noise
22. **scrub**—rub hard; rub hard in cleaning or washing
23. **scuff**—rub harshly, or scrape, with the foot or feet
24. **shine**—polish
25. **sleek**—rub until smooth and shiny
26. **smear**—rub something thick or greasy on
27. **sponge**—wipe; wipe with, or as if with, a sponge
28. **stroke**—rub gently or smoothly in one direction
29. **swab**—wipe
30. **towel**—rub with a towel
31. **triturate**—rub into a fine powder
32. **wax**—rub or polish with wax
33. **wipe**—rub dry or clean

2. A Rubbing; A Rub,n. *From Sec. 1:* abrasion, anointment, excoriation, massage, pat, polish, scour, scrape, scrub, scuff, shine, smear, sponge, stroke, swab, trituration, wipe; *Also:*
1. **attrition**—a rubbing away, together, or off
2. **chirapsia**—massage by hand
3. **friction**—rubbing of one object against another (frictional,adj.)
4. **rubdown**—massage
5. **traction**—friction of the kind that permits a body, such as a wheel, to stick to a surface (tractional,adj.)
6. **unction**—anointment

3. A Rubbed Place,n. *From Sec. 1:* abrasion, chafe, excoriation, scrape, scuff

4. Substance or Thing Used for, or in, Rubbing,n. *From Sec. 1:* abrasive, brush, buffer, grate or grater, mop, polish or polisher, pumice, rasp, razor, sponge, swab, towel, triturator, wax or waxer, wiper

5. One Who Rubs,n. *From Sec. 1:* burnisher, furbisher, masseur (masc.) or masseuse (fem.), polisher, wiper

6. Causing a Rubbed State or Place,adj. *From Sec. 1:* abrasive; *From Sec. 2:* attritive

7. To Make Sore by Rubbing or Friction: gall,v.

8. To Grind,v.
1. **bray**—grind fine
2. **bruise**—pulverize (drugs, food, etc.)
3. **comminute**—grind into a fine powder; pulverize
4. **crunch**—grind noisily
5. **levigate**—grind to a powder
6. **pulverize**—grind to powder or dust
7. **triturate**—grind into a fine powder

9. A Grinding; A Grind,n. *From Sec. 8:* comminution, crunch, levigation, pulverization, trituration; *Also:* 1. **attrition**—a grinding down by friction

10. To Become Powdery: effloresce,v. (efflorescence,n. efflorescent,adj.)

439. SMOOTHNESS

1. Smooth,adj.
1. **alabaster**—smooth and white, or near white, like marble
2. **bland**—smooth
3. **creamy**—smooth and soft in consistency (creaminess,n.)
4. **glabrous**—smooth and hairless; smooth, i.e., without bumps
5. **glacé (French)**—smooth and glossy
6. **glassy**—smooth, like glass (glassiness,n.)
7. **glossy**—smooth and shiny (gloss, glossiness,n.)
8. **lubricous**—smooth and slippery; smooth of surface; having an oily smoothness (lubricity,n.)
9. **polished**—naturally glossy
10. **silken, silky**—pleasantly smooth (silkiness,n.)
11. **sleek**—glossy (sleekness,n.)
12. **slick**—glossy (slickness,n.)
13. **slippery**—extremely smooth and shiny, as if able to cause one to slip if walked on (slipperiness,n.)
14. **unwrinkled**—smooth in the sense of having no folds or wrinkles
15. **velutinous**—velvety (generally of plants)
16. **velvety**—smooth; smooth and soft to the touch or in appearance (velvetiness,n.)
17. **waxen**—smooth and shining
18. **waxy**—resembling wax in smoothness and shine (waxiness,n.)

2. To Smooth; To Make Smooth,v.
1. **buff**—make smooth by rubbing
2. **file**—make smooth with, or as if with, a file
3. **iron**—smooth with a heated iron or similar device
4. **levigate**—make smooth by thoroughly mixing (levigation,n.)
5. **lubricate**—make smooth and/or slippery by, or as if by, coating with oil or similar substance (lubrication,n. lubricatory, adj.)
6. **mangle**—iron with an electrical machine designed for that purpose
7. **oil**—lubricate
8. **pat**—smooth by lightly stroking
9. **plane**—smooth the surface of
10. **planish**—make smooth; make smooth, tough, and shiny by lightly hammering
11. **polish**—make smooth and/or shiny by rubbing
12. **preen**—smooth the feathers (of birds)
13. **pumice**—smooth with, or as with, pumice
14. **sleek**—make smooth and shiny by brushing
15. **sleeken**—make smooth and gentle
16. **slick, slick up**—make smooth or smooth and bright; polish
17. **unwrinkle**—smooth by removing the wrinkles from
18. **wax**—make smooth

3. Smooth Place: slick,n.

4. An Iron,n.
1. **flatiron, sadiron**—iron with a flat bottom
2. **mangle**—electrical ironing machine that works by roller pressure

5. Slippery,adj.
1. **lubricous**—slippery and smooth (lubricity,n.)
2. **saponacious**—slippery
3. **slick**—slippery (slickness,n.)

6. A Slippery Place: slick,n.

440. ROUGHNESS

1. Rough, Literally, i.e., Not Smooth,adj.
1. **brambly**—rough in texture
2. **chapped**—rough or roughened by exposure to cold, etc. (of the skin)

3. **choppy**—rough (of the sea)
4. **coarse**—rough; not smooth
5. **craggy**—of roughhewn, rocklike appearance or features
6. **crisp, crispy**—roughened into small curls or folds
7. **crude**—rough
8. **harsh**—rough to any of the senses, esp. touch and hearing
9. **ragged**—with rough edges or surface
10. **rude**—rough; roughly made
11. **ruffled**—rough; rugged
12. **rugged**—rough or harsh in surface, outline, or shape
13. **rustic**—rough in construction, as furniture, etc.
14. **scabrous**—rough to the touch because of small bumps or projections
15. **scraggly**—ragged
16. **scraggy**—rough; rugged
17. **shaggy**—long, thick, and rough
18. **splintery**—rough in surface
19. **uneven**—rough; rugged
20. **unpolished**—still rough because not rubbed smooth
21. **wrinkled**—rough because full of wrinkles

2. Roughness,n. *From Sec. 1:* brambliness, choppiness, coarseness, cragginess, crispness, crudeness or crudity, harshness, raggedness, rudeness, ruggedness, rusticity, scabrousness, scragginess, shagginess, splinteriness, unevenness

3. To Roughen, i.e., Make or Become Rough,v. *From Sec. 1:* chap, coarsen, crisp, ruffle, shag, splinter, wrinkle

4. Rough Spot or Place on the Skin Caused by Exposure to Cold, etc.: chap,n.

441. HARDNESS

1. Hard; Hardened,adj.
1. **adamantine**—hard, like a diamond
2. **callous**—hardened (usually of skin)
3. **congealed**—hard or hardened from, or as from, cold or freezing
4. **coriaceous**—tough, like leather
5. **crisp, crispy**—hard and thin; hard but easily broken
6. **crusty**—hard, like crust
7. **firm**—hard in the sense of being unyielding to pressure
8. **flinty**—hard as flint; terrifically hard
9. **impermeable**—so hard as to resist piercing
10. **indurate, indurated**—hardened
11. **leathern**—leathery
12. **leathery**—tough, like leather
13. **ossified**—hard, or hardened, like bone
14. **petrified**—hard, like stone
15. **petrous, petrosal**—hard, like stone
16. **planished**—made tough, shiny, and smooth by light hammering
17. **sclerous**—hard, hardened (of body tissue)
18. **stale**—hard and dry (of bread, etc.)
19. **steely**—hard, like steel
20. **stony**—hard, like stone
21. **tough**—hard; hard to cut, chew, tear, etc.
22. **weather-beaten**—hardened by weather

2. Hardness,n. *From Sec. 1:* callosity, crispness, crustiness, firmness, flintiness, impermeability, leatheriness, staleness, steeliness, stoniness, toughness

3. To Harden, i.e., Make Hard,v. *From Sec. 1:* callous, congeal, crisp, firm, indurate, ossify, petrify, planish, stale, toughen

4. To Harden, i.e., Become Hard,v. *From Sec. 1:* callous, congeal, crisp, firm, indurate, ossify, petrify, stale, toughen

5. A Making or Becoming Hard,n. *From Sec. 1:* congealment or congelation, induration, ossification, petrifaction or petrification

6. **Anything Terrifically Hard:** flint,n.

7. **Device That Measures the Relative Hardness of Substances, Usually Minerals:** sclerometer,n.

442. STIFFNESS

1. Stiff: firm, inflexible, rigid, tense, tough, unbending, unyielding,adj.

2. Stiffness: firmness, inflexibility, rigidness or rigidity; tenseness, tensity, or tension; toughness,n.

3. To Make or Cause to Be Stiff: brace, firm, petrify, stiffen, tense, toughen,v. (petrifaction or petrification,n. petrifactive,adj.)

4. To Become Stiff: firm, petrify, stiffen, tense, toughen,v. (petrifaction or petrifaction,n.)

5. That Which Makes or Holds Rigid: brace, n.

6. Degree of Firmness or Stiffness: consistency,n.

443. SOFTNESS

1. Soft,adj.
1. **cottony**—soft, like cotton
2. **creamy**—soft and smooth in consistency
3. **delicate**—soft
4. **flabby**—soft in the sense of lacking firmness
5. **fleecy**—soft and white, like a sheep's wool
6. **flexible**—soft in the sense of lacking stiffness
7. **flocculent**—soft and woolly
8. **limp**—lacking stiffness, firmness, rigidity, etc.
9. **mellow**—soft (of fruit)
10. **pulpy**—soft, like the inner part of a fruit
11. **quaggy**—yielding; not rigid; flabby
12. **silken, silky**—soft and shiny
13. **slack**—soft; not firm
14. **sleek**—soft and shiny
15. **sodden**—soggy
16. **soggy**—soft and heavy with moisture
17. **squashy**—soft
18. **supple**—soft in feel
19. **tender**—soft
20. **velutinous**—velvety (generally of plants)
21. **velvety**—soft and smooth to the touch or in appearance

2. Softness,n. *From Sec. 1:* creaminess, delicacy, flabbiness, fleeciness, flexibility, flocculence, limpness, mellowness, pulpiness, silkiness, slackness, sleekness, soddenness, sogginess, squashiness, suppleness, tenderness, velvetiness; *Also:*
1. **mollities**—softness
2. **patina**—softness of appearance caused by the passage of time

3. To Soften,v.
1. **intenerate**—make soft or softer (inteneration,n.)
2. **macerate**—make or become soft by soaking in water or other liquid; make (food) soft by using a solvent (maceration,n.)
3. **sodden**—make or become soft and heavy with moisture

4. Tending to Soften: mollescent,adj. (mollescence,n.)

5. That Which is So Soft as to Be Easily Crushed: squash,n.

6. Soft Inner Part of Something: pulp,n.

7. Causing a Part, Tissue, etc., to Become Soft (of Drugs, Medications, Applications, etc.): lenitive,adj. (lenitive,n.)

444. LIMPNESS

1. Limp, i.e., Not Firm or Rigid, adj.
1. **drooping, droopy**—limp or hanging down from lack of strength, fatigue, loss of vital fluids (as plants), etc.
2. **flabby**—soft and limp and drooping loosely from its own weight
3. **flaccid**—limp in the sense of having lost its stiffness, shape, ability to resist pressure, etc.
4. **sagging**—drooping
5. **slack**—limp, i.e., not firm, taut, or rigid
6. **sodden**—limp and heavy with moisture; flaccid
7. **soggy**—limp with moisture
8. **wilted**—flaccid from heat, lack of water, etc. (of plants)

2. Limpness, n. *From Sec. 1:* droop or droopiness, flabbiness, flaccidity or flaccidness, slackness or slack, soddenness, sogginess

3. To Become Limp, v. *From Sec. 1:* droop, sag, slack or slacken, sodden, wilt (droop, wilt,n.)

4. To Cause to Be or Become Limp, v. *From Sec. 1:* sag, slack or slacken, sodden, wilt

445. SMELL

1. To Smell, i.e., Engage in Smelling, v.
1. **scent**—smell
2. **sniff**—smell by deliberately drawing (an odor) up the nose (sniff,n.)
3. **snuff**—smell; sniff (snuff,n.)

2. Act of Smelling: olfaction, osmesis,n. (osmetic,adj.)

3. Sense of Smell: olfaction, scent,n.

4. Pert. to the Sense of Smell: olfactory,adj.

5. Having a Well-Developed Sense of Smell: macrosmatic,adj.

6. Descr. of Animals or Organisms That Have Organs of Smell: osmatic,adj. (osmatism,n.)

7. Pathologic Condition in Which the Sense of Smell Is Absent, Lacking, or Has Been Lost: anosmia,n. (anosmic, anosmatic, adj.)

8. Science Treating of Odors and the Sense of Smell: osmology,n.

9. An Odor; A Smell, n.
1. **aroma**—agreeable and characteristic odor, usually strong and pervasive
2. **aura**—subtle scent
3. **bouquet**—characteristic aroma of wine
4. **effluvium, efflux**—odor characteristic of some invisible thing
5. **emanation**—odor coming out of something
6. **essence**—perfume
7. **exhalation**—odor of something breathed out
8. **fragrance**—pleasant or sweet odor, usually emanating from flowers or plants
9. **fumet**—odor of meat that has been kept too long; odor of meat cooking
10. **incense**—pleasant or sweet odor; perfume from something burning, usually spices, gums, resins, etc.
11. **malodor**—evil or offensive odor
12. **mephitis**—foul odor emanating from the earth; any foul odor
13. **musk**—odor from the secretion of an animal, esp. the male musk deer; any odor similar to this
14. **must**—evil odor, as from age, mold, or lack of air
15. **perfume**—pleasant or sweet odor
16. **pungency, pungence**—sharp, penetrating, but not unpleasant odor, as of spices; sharp and bitter odor

17. **reek**—conspicuous and unpleasant odor
18. **savor**—characteristic and distinctive odor and/or taste, usually pleasant
19. **scent**—characteristic odor, usually pleasant; odor left along one's track, as by animals
20. **sniff**—perceived odor
21. **snuff**—odor
22. **spice**—strong and pleasing aroma
23. **stench**—disgustingly offensive odor
24. **stink**—stench
25. **tang**—strong or distinctive odor
26. **tincture**—tinge
27. **tinge**—trace of some characteristic odor
28. **trail**—scent left by animal or person
29. **whiff**—slight, faint, or temporary odor

10. Odorous; Having an Odor or Smell, adj. *From Sec. 9:* aromatic, effluvious, fragrant, malodorous, mephitic, musky, musty, perfumed, pungent, reeking, savory, scented or scentful, spicy, stenching or stenchy, stinking or stinky, tangy (fragrance, malodorousness, mustiness, pungency, savoriness, spiciness, n.); *Also:*
1. **acrid**—sharp and bitter in odor (acridness, acridity,n.)
2. **alliaceous**—smelling of garlic or onions
3. **balmy**—aromatic; fragrant (balminess, n.)
4. **dank**—damp or musty in odor (dankness, n.)
5. **delicious**—pleasant to the sense of smell (deliciousness,n.)
6. **evil-smelling**—having an evil or offensive odor
7. **fetid**—offensive or disgusting in odor (fetidness, fetidity,n.)
8. **flavorous, flavorsome**—pleasant in, or to the sense of, smell
9. **foul**—noisome (foulness,n.)
10. **frowzy, frowsy, frouzy**—having an unpleasant or musty odor (frowziness,n.)
11. **fusty**—evil-smelling, as from lack of cleanliness or air (fustiness,n.)
12. **hircine**—smelling like a goat
13. **ill-smelling**—having a bad odor
14. **moldy**—stale and musty in odor (moldiness,n.)
15. **noisome**—disgusting, offensive, unwholesome, or poisonous in odor (noisomeness, n.)
16. **odoriferous**—giving off an odor, usually sweet or pleasant, though not necessarily (odoriferousness,n.)
17. **putrid**—evil-smelling, as from decaying animal matter (putridness, putridity,n.)
18. **rancid**—having an unpleasant, stale, or decayed odor (rancidness, rancidity,n.)
19. **rank**—strong and offensive in odor; rancid (rankness,n.)
20. **redolent (of)**—smelling (of); having a sweet or pleasant odor (redolence, redolency,n.)
21. **rotten**—smelling of decay (rottenness,n.)
22. **smelly**—having a bad odor; having an odor
23. **stagnant**—foul- or ill-smelling from lack of motion (stagnancy,n.)
24. **unsavory**—unpleasant in smell (unsavoriness,n.)

11. To Have an Odor or Smell; To Smell, v. *From Sec. 9:* reek (of); savor (of); stink (of or from)

12. To Give an Odor to, v. *From Sec. 9:* aromatize, odorize, perfume, savor, scent, tincture, tinge; *Also:*
1. **cense**—perfume with scent from burning incense
2. **fumigate**—perfume

13. Liquid That Lends a Pleasant or Sweet Odor: perfume,n.

14. Material That, When Burned, Emits a Pleasant Odor: incense,n.

15. Perfume, etc.: balm, cologne, eau de cologne, essence, patchouli, scent, toilet water,n.

16. Perfumed Powder, or a Small Bag Containing This: sachet,n.

17. Substance Used in Making Perfume or Incense,n.
1. ambergris—secretion of the sperm whale used in making perfume
2. attar—aromatic oil from roses, used in making perfume
3. civet—substance with a musky odor obtained from civet cats, used in making perfume
4. frankincense—fragrant resin used in the manufacture of incense
5. musk—secretion from the musk deer or other animal, used in the manufacture of perfume
6. myrrh—aromatic resinous substance from certain plants, used in making incense, perfume, etc.

18. Place Where Perfumes Are Kept, Made, Sold, etc.: perfumery,n.

19. One Who Makes and/or Sells Perfume: perfumer,n.

20. Measurement of the Effect of Odors on the Sense of Smell: odorimetry,n.

21. Unit in the Measurement of the Stimulus of Odors on the Sense of Smell: olfacty, n.

22. Instrument That Measures the Ability to Detect Odors: olfactometer, osmometer,n.

23. Inability to Tolerate Certain Odors: osmodysphoria,n.

24. Lacking in Odor: deodorized, odorless, scentless, unaromatic, unperfumed, unscented, adj.

25. To Remove an Odor (Usually Unpleasant) from: deodorize,v. (deodorization,n. deodorant,n. deodorant,adj.)

446. TASTE

1. Sense of Taste: gustation, palate,n.

2. Pert. to the Sense of Taste: gustatory, adj.

3. Part of the Mouth Incorrectly Believed to be the Seat of Taste: palate,n.

4. Perverted Sense of Taste: parageusia,n.

5. Perceivable by the Organs of Taste: sapid,adj. (sapidity,n.)

6. To Taste: savor, sip,v.

7. Act of Tasting: gustation,n.

8. A Taste: sip, snack, soupçon,n.

9. Foretaste: antepast, prelibation,n.

10. Taste; Flavor,n.
1. aroma—flavor
2. relish—characteristic or pleasing flavor; taste or flavor
3. sapor—flavor; the property of something to which the sense of taste reacts; savor
4. savor—characteristic and distinctive taste and/or odor, usually pleasant
5. smack—taste; flavor
6. stingo—zest (slang)
7. tang—strong or distinctive flavor or taste
8. tincture—tinge
9. tinge—trace of some characteristic flavor
10. zest—exciting or stimulating flavor

11. To Have Taste or Flavor: relish,v.

12. To Have the Taste or Flavor of: savor of, smack of,v.

13. Descr. of Taste or Flavor,adj.
1. acid—sharp to the taste (acidity, acidness,n.)

2. acrid—sharp and bitter to the taste (acridity, acridness,n.)

3. appetizing—exciting, or appealing to, the taste

4. aromatic—having a strong, pervasive, and characteristic flavor

5. dainty—delicious

6. delicious—highly pleasing to the taste (deliciousness,n.)

7. flavorful—full of flavor

8. flavorsome, flavorous, flavory—pleasant in flavor; full of flavor; pleasant to the taste

9. full-flavored—having a strong flavor

10. gingery—sharp and spicy, like ginger (gingeriness,n.)

11. mellow—ripe-flavored—of fruit (mellowness,n.)

12. palatable—agreeable to the sense of taste; savory (palatability, palatableness, n.)

13. piquant—pleasantly sharp to the taste (piquancy,n.)

14. pungent—sharp to the sense of taste (pungency,n.)

15. racy—having a strong and fresh flavor; having an unusual but pleasant taste (raciness,n.)

16. rancid—having an unpleasant, stale, or decayed taste (rancidness, rancidity,n.)

17. rank—strong and offensive in taste (rankness,n.)

18. sapid—having flavor, or a distinctive and pleasant taste (sapidity,n.)

19. saporous—sapid

20. savory, savorous—having flavor; pleasant in flavor or taste; appetizing (savoriness, n.)

21. sharp—biting in flavor or taste (sharpness,n.)

22. sour—having the taste of vinegar, lemon, acid, etc. (sourness,n.)

23. spicy—full of flavor (spiciness,n.)

24. tangy—full of flavor (tanginess,n.)

25. tart—sharp in taste (tartness,n.)

26. tasty—agreeable in taste or flavor (tastiness,n.)

27. toothsome—pleasing to the taste

28. velvety—mild or smooth in taste (velvetiness,n.)

29. vinegary—sour or sharp in taste (vinegariness,n.)

30. unsavory—unpleasant in taste (unsavoriness,n.)

31. zestful—having an exciting or stimulating taste or flavor (zestfulness,n.)

14. To Give or Add Flavor to: flavor, season, spice, tincture, tinge, zest,v.

15. To Improve the Flavor of: season,v.

16. Giving or Adding a Flavor or Taste: saporific,adj.

17. Substance That Adds or Improves Flavor or Taste: condiment, flavor, flavoring, pepper, salt, seasoning, spice, vanilla; vanillin (synthetic) ; zest,n.

18. Lacking, or Dull, in Flavor or Taste: flat, flavorless, insipid, jejune, namby-pamby, sapidless, savorless, tasteless, unflavored, unsavory, vapid, zestless,adj.

19. Lack, or Dullness, of Flavor or Taste: flatness, insipidity or insipidness, tastelessness, unsavoriness, vapidity or vapidness,n.

20. Tasteless because No Longer Fresh: stale,adj. (staleness,n.)

21. To Make Tasteless or Flavorless: stale,v.

447. JUICE

1. Juicy: pulpy, succulent,adj. (succulence, n.)

2. Juicy and Sweet: luscious; mellow (of fruit),adj. (lusciousness, mellowness,n.)

3. Sour Juice of Certain Unripe Fruits: verjuice,n.

4. Juices and Fat That Drip from Roasting or Cooking Meat: gravy,n.

5. Served in Gravy or Its Own Natural Juices (of Meat, etc.): au jus (French)

448. SWEETNESS

1. Sweet,adj.
1. candied—sweet; honeyed
2. honeyed—sweet as honey, literally or figuratively
3. luscious—sweet and juicy (lusciousness, n.)
4. mellifluous, mellifluent—sweet, like honey; sweetened with, or as with, honey (mellifluousness, mellifluence,n.)
5. mellow—sweet and juicy—of fruit (mellowness,n.)
6. saccharine—sweet; sickeningly sweet; sugary (saccharinity,n.)
7. sugared—honeyed
8. sugary—sweet; excessively sweet, either literally or figuratively (sugariness,n.)
9. syrupy—excessively sweet, figuratively (syrupiness,n.)

449. SUGAR

1. Sugar,n.
1. beet sugar—sugar made from beets
2. cane—sugar cane
3. caramel—burnt sugar
4. corn sugar—dextrose derived from corn
5. dextroglucose—dextrose
6. dextrose—crystalline sugar, occurring naturally in certain plant and animal organism
7. fondant—thick sugar paste used in candymaking
8. fructose—fruit sugar
9. galactose—white crystalline sugar
10. glucose—a kind of sugar
11. grape sugar—natural sugar found in ripe grapes
12. invert sugar—mixture of levulose and dextrose, occurring naturally in fruits; dextrose obtained from starch
13. lactose—sugar occurring in milk
14. levulose—kind of sugar found in honey and sweet fruits
15. maltose—crystalline reducing sugar used in brewing and distilling
16. malt sugar—maltose
17. milk sugar—lactose
18. molasses—brownish by-product in the manufacture of sugar
19. saccharose—cane or beet sugar
20. simple syrup—syrup with no added flavoring
21. sorghum—syrup obtained from a sorgo, a kind of tropical grass
22. sucrose—cane or beet sugar
23. syrup—concentrated mixture of sugar and water
24. theriaca, theriac—molasses (theriacal, adj.)
25. treacle—molasses (British, though occasionally used in U.S.)

2. Coal-Tar Product Used as a Sugar Substitute: saccharine,n.

3. Preserved or Coated with Sugar,adj.
1. candied—preserved or coated with sugar (candy,v.)
2. glacé (French)—coated with a sugar icing or frosting—of foods, esp. desserts (glacé,v.)

4. Producing, Yielding, or Containing Sugar: sacchariferous, saccharine,adj.

5. To Convert into, or Fill with, Sugar: saccharify, saccharize,v. (saccharification, saccharization,n.)

6. Instrument to Measure the Amount of Sugar in a Solution: saccharimeter, saccharometer,n.

7. Capable of Converting, or Pert. to the Conversion of, Sugar into Starch: diastatic, adj.

450. CANDY

1. Candy; A Piece of Candy,n.
1. bonbon—piece of candy; fruit, nut, etc., dipped in chocolate
2. butterscotch—a kind of taffy made with butter
3. caramel—a kind of candy in small, hard blocks
4. chocolate—a candy made or coated with cocoa
5. confection—a candy (confections, confectionary,pl.)
6. confiture—a candy; a dried root, seed, or fruit preserved with sugar
7. cream—a candy with a soft center and coated with chocolate
8. fondant—thick, creamy, sugar paste used as the center of many candies; a candy with such a center
9. fudge—a kind of candy made of sugar, butter, milk, and chocolate, often prepared in the home
10. kiss—a candy of various small shapes
11. licorice—sweet-tasting dried root, used as candy
12. lollipop—a candy, hard candy, piece of taffy, etc., on the end of a stick, for sucking
13. mint—a candy flavored with peppermint
14. nougat—a pastelike candy, containing nuts, etc.
15. peppermint—candy flavored with peppermint
16. sugarplum—bonbon
17. sweet—a candy
18. sweetmeat—any candy (usually in the plural)
19. taffy—candy of boiled-down sugar or molasses
20. toffee—taffy

2. One Who Manufactures or Sells Candy: confectioner,n.

3. Place Where Candy Is Made or Sold: confectionery,n.

4. Business of Making or Selling Candy: confectionery,n.

451. HONEY

1. Honey: mel,n. (pharmacy)

2. Honey Diluted with Water: hydromel,n.

3. Fermented Honey and Water: mead, metheglin,n.

4. Producing Honey: melliferous,adj.

5. Resembling Honey in the Way It Flows, Its Sweetness or Smoothness, etc.: mellifluent, mellifluous,adj. (mellifluence, mellifluousness,n.)

452. SOURNESS

1. Sour; Sour in, or to the, Taste: acerb, acetose, acetous, acid, acidulent, acidulous, astringent, austere, tart, vinegary,adj.

2. Sourness: acerbity, acidity, acidness, astringency, austereness, tartness, verjuice, vinegariness,n.

3. To Make, Turn, or Cause to Be Sour: acerbate, acidify, acidulate, sour,v. (acerbation, acidification, acidulation,n.)

4. To Cause to Turn Sour and Thick: curdle,v.

5. To Become Sour: acidify, sour,v. (acidification,n.)

6. To Become Sour and Thick: clabber, curdle,v.

7. To Make, Become, or Turn Sour, Figuratively: curdle, sour,v.

8. Vinegar: acetum,n. (pharmacy)

9. Referring to Vinegar,adj.
1. acetic—pert. to, producing, or derived from, vinegar
2. acetous, acetose—pert. to, or producing, vinegar
3. vinegary—pert. to, resembling, or tasting like, vinegar (vinegariness,n.)

10. To Turn or Convert, or Become Converted, into Vinegar: acetify,v. (acetification,n.)

11. Bitter,adj.
1. absinthial,   absinthian—bitter,   like wormwood
2. acrid—sharp and bitter to the taste (acridity, acridness,n.)

12. Anything Very Bitter, Figuratively: gall, wormwood,in.

13. Bitterness (Figurative): wormwood,n.

453. LISTEN

1. To Listen,v.
1. attend—listen to
2. audit—sit in on a course of instruction as a mere listener, i.e., without taking active part or receiving scholastic or other credit
3. audition—listen to (an actor, singer, etc.) to determine his qualifications for a role, position, etc.
4. auscultate, auscult—listen, with a stethoscope or other instrument, to the sounds inside of (the chest, abdomen, back, etc.) in order to detect symptoms of disease, pregnancy, etc.
5. eavesdrop—listen secretly
6. give ear—listen
7. hark—listen (chiefly in the imperative)
8. harken, hearken—listen
9. lend an ear—listen
10. monitor—listen to (radio broadcasts) to check on legality, adherence to code, or, in the case of programs of foreign origin, political significance
11. stethoscope—listen with a special medical device to the sounds within (the chest or other parts of the body)

2. Listening,n. From Sec. 1: attention, audition, auscultation, stethoscopy; Also: 1. auscultation—act of listening

3. Descr. of, or Pert. to, Listening,adj. From Sec. 1: attentive, auscultative or auscultatory, stethoscopic or stethoscopical; Also: 1. audient—listening

4. Listener,n. From Sec. 1: auditor, auscultator, eavesdropper, monitor, stethoscopist; Also: 1. auditor—listener

5. Group of People Who Listen: audience,n.

6. Place Where People Listen to Music, Plays, Lectures, etc.: auditorium,n.

7. To Force to Listen to What One Has to Say: buttonhole,v.

454. HEARING

1. Act, Sense, or Power of Hearing: audition,n.

2. Pert. to, or Descr. of, Hearing or the Sense of Hearing: acoustic, audile, auditive, auditory, aural, auricular,adj.

3. Pert. or Appealing to Both Hearing and Sight: audiovisual,adj.

4. Aiding Hearing: acoustical,adj. (acoustic, n.)

5. To Hear Incorrectly: mishear,v.

6. To Hear That Which Was Not Intended for the Listener's Ears: overhear,v.

7. Hearing: audient,adj.

8. One Who Hears: auditor,n.

9. Those Who Hear; Group That Hears: audience,n.

10. Chance to Be Heard: audience, hearing,n.

11. Heard,adj.
1. audible—heard
2. auricular—heard privately; actually and directly heard
3. distinct—clearly heard
4. hearsay—heard from another

12. That Which Is Heard,n.
1. audition—that which is heard
2. hearsay—that which is heard from another rather than seen or experienced by oneself

13. Able to Be Heard,adj.
1. audible—able to be heard; loud enough to be heard (audibility,n.)
2. distinct—clearly audible (distinctness,n.)

14. Unable to Be Heard,adj. From Sec. 13: inaudible, indistinct (inaudibility, indistinctness,n.)

15. To Make (a Sound or Sounds) Inaudible: deafen, drown, drown out,v.

16. Easy to Hear; Easily Heard: clear, distinct, plain,adj. (clearness or clarity, distinctness, plainness,n.)

17. Hard to Hear: faint, indistinct, unclear, adj. (faintness, indistinctness, unclearness,n.)

18. One Who Is Hearing-Minded, i.e., Can Best Understand or Remember from Hearing, Rather than from Seeing or Doing: audile,n.

19. Science of Hearing: audiology,n.

20. Hearing or Listening Instrument,n.
1. audiometer—device for measuring one's power of hearing
2. auscultator—stethoscope
3. Dictograph—telephonic instrument, of a highly sensitive character, for listening, sometimes secretly, to conversations in another room, making a record of them, etc.
4. hydrophone—device for detecting sounds in, or transmitted through, water
5. sonometer—audiometer
6. stethoscope—medical device for listening to sounds in the chest and other parts of the body

21. Hearing Aid,n.
1. audiphone—hearing aid that is placed against the teeth and conveys sound waves to the auditory nerve
2. auriphone—a kind of ear trumpet
3. dentiphone—audiphone
4. ear trumpet—device, held to the ear by the hard of hearing, for magnifying sounds
5. osteophone—hearing aid that attaches to skull bones and transmits sound waves to the inner ear

22. Hearing Defect,n.
1. deaf-mutism, deaf-muteness—inability to hear or speak
2. deafness—inability to hear; unwillingness to listen or hear
3. otosis—defective hearing; mishearing of sounds

4. **pseudacusis**—false hearing; hearing of sounds that do not exist
5. **stone-deafness**—complete deafness
6. **tinnitus**—hearing of sounds or noises that actually do not exist

23. Having a Hearing Defect,adj. *From Sec. 22:* deaf, deaf-mute or deaf and dumb, stone-deaf; *Also:* 1. **hard of hearing**—somewhat or slightly deaf; having difficulty with one's hearing

24. Deaf-and-Dumb Person: deaf-mute,n.

25. To Cause to Be Deaf: deafen,v. (deafening,adj.)

455. SOUND

1. Sound,n.
1. **cadence, cadency**—rhythmical sound (cadent,adj.)
2. **noise**—sound (noisy,adj.)
3. **note**—musical sound
4. **peep**—any sound (peep,v.)
5. **siren**—warning sound
6. **sonance**—a sound
7. **static**—loosely, interfering sound (or sounds), esp. in radio reception
8. **tone**—any sound thought of with reference to its physical characteristics (tonal,adj.)
9. **undulation**—wave of sound

2. The Striking of Sounds against the Ear: percussion,n. (percussive,adj. percuss,v.)

3. A Succession of Rapid, Light Sounds: pitter-patter,n.

4. A Multiplicity of Sounds: polyphony,n. (polyphonic,adj.)

5. Pert. to, Descr. of, or Relating to, Sound or Sounds,adj.
1. **acoustic**—pert. to sound
2. **audiogenic**—produced by sound
3. **isacoustic**—pert. to equal strength or intensity of sound
4. **multisonous, multisonant**—having or making many sounds
5. **phonic**—pert. to sound or sounds
6. **polyphonic**—pert. to, or consisting of, a multiplicity of sounds
7. **sonant**—pert. to sound
8. **sonic**—pert. to, or using, sound waves
9. **stereophonic**—descr. of sound that gives the effect of coming simultaneously from two or more directions
10. **supersonic**—having to do with sounds of greater frequencies than those audible to the human ear
11. **ultrasonic**—supersonic

6. Nature, Character, or Quality of Sound or Sounds,n.
1. **cadence, cadency**—rhythmic rise and fall of sound
2. **harmony**—any pleasing quality of sound; simultaneous combination of sounds
3. **inflection**—variety in the pitch of the voice
4. **intensity**—volume
5. **intonation**—rise and fall in the pitch of the voice
6. **melody**—succession of single musical sounds
7. **modulation**—pleasing change in the tone of the voice or other sound
8. **monotony**—unvarying pitch or quality
9. **pitch**—frequency of vibration of a sound or sound wave
10. **quality**—character or nature of a sound, without considering its pitch or volume
11. **resonance**—reverberation or echoing quality of sound
12. **rhythm**—regular beat or accent of sound
13. **sonority, sonorousness**—fullness of sound; resonance; rich resonance

14. **tone**—quality
15. **volume**—amount or fullness of sound

7. Similarity of Sound or Sounds,n.
1. **accord**—harmony
2. **assonance**—similarity in sound between syllables or words (assonant,adj.)
3. **consonance, consonancy**—any (often pleasing) similarity of sounds (consonant,adj.)
4. **harmony**—similarity of sounds (harmonious,adj.)
5. **homophony**—similarity or identity of sound (homophonic, homophonous,adj.)
6. **unison**—identity of pitch of sound or identity in tuning of sounds, as when several people speak or sing at the same time (unisonous, unisonal, unisonant, adj.)

8. Standing for the Same Sound (of Letters, Symbols, etc.): homophonous,adj.

9. Sound Instrument or Device,n.
1. **Dictaphone**—instrument that records a message or dictation for later transcription
2. **Ediphone**—variety of Dictaphone, manufactured by another company
3. **electrophone**—instrument for producing sounds by means of electrical impulses
4. **Gramophone**—trade name for a certain type of phonograph
5. **Graphophone**—trade name for a type of sound recorder
6. **megaphone**—device for making sound louder
7. **microphone**—instrument that makes comparatively soft sounds louder or audible, through electrical connections, over large distances
8. **optophone**—instrument for transforming light energy into sound energy
9. **phonograph**—instrument for recording and reproducing sounds (including music, singing, talking, etc.)
10. **phonometer**—device that measures characteristics of sound or sounds (phonometry,n.)
11. **radio**—device for receiving sound transmitted over air waves
12. **siren**—device for making a warning sound
13. **telegraph**—apparatus for transmitting messages through electrical impulses over wires or through radio waves (telegraphy, n. telegrapher, telegraphist,n. telegram, n. telegraphic, telegraphical,adj. telegraph,v.)
14. **telephone**—instrument for transmitting the spoken word through electrical impulses over wires (telephoner,n. telephony,n. telephonic,adj. telephone,v.)
15. **topophone**—device for estimating the direction from which sounds are coming
16. **Victrola**—trade name for a certain make of phonograph

10. Unit of Sound Volume: decibel,n.

11. Making, or Able to Make, a Sound or Sounds,adj.
1. **sonant**—making a sound or sounds (sonance,n.)
2. **soniferous**—producing sound
3. **sonorescent**—able to give forth sound as a reaction to light—a term in physics (sonorescence,n.)
4. **sonoriferous**—soniferous
5. **sonorous**—capable of emitting sound when struck (sonorousness, sonority,n.)

12. Science of Sound or Sounds,n.
1. **acoustics**—science of production, transmission, and effects of sound (acoustician, n. acoustic, acoustical,adj.)
2. **catacoustics**—science of reflected sounds
3. **harmonics**—science of musical sounds
4. **phonics**—science of sound or sounds

5. **supersonics**—science of sounds of greater frequency than those audible to the human ear

456. ANIMAL SOUND

1. Animal Sound or Sounds,n.
1. **bark**—noise or sound made by a dog
2. **bay**—bark; prolonged bark
3. **bell**—sound of a stag or buck, or of a deer in heat; bellow; roar
4. **bellow**—roar of a bull
5. **blat**—cry of a calf or lamb
6. **bleat**—sound or cry of a goat, calf, sheep, etc.
7. **boom**—hollow cry of a bittern, a kind of heron; resonant hum of a beetle
8. **bray**—sound of a donkey or ass
9. **buzz**—low, humming sound of bees
10. **cackle**—sound or sounds made by a hen or goose
11. **caterwaul**—sounds of a cat in heat
12. **caw**—sound made by a crow or raven
13. **chatter**—sound or sounds of monkeys or magpies
14. **cheep**—faint, high-pitched cry of a young bird or mouse
15. **chirp, chip**—short, sharp sound or sounds of a bird or cricket
16. **chirr**—trilled sound of grasshoppers, cicadas, and certain birds
17. **chirrup**—chirp; repeated and lively chirping
18. **chitter**—chirp; twitter
19. **chuck**—chirrup; cluck
20. **chuckle**—cackle; cluck
21. **churr**—whirring or vibrating sound made by the cockchafer or other insects, or the nightjar, partridge, or certain other birds
22. **clang**—cry of a crane or goose
23. **cluck**—sound made by a hen calling to her chicks
24. **cock**—sound made in the morning by a rooster or certain other male fowl
25. **cock-a-doodle-doo,   cock-a-doodle**—sound of a rooster or certain other male fowl
26. **cockcrowing**—sound of a cock or rooster
27. **coo**—sound characteristic of doves
28. **creak**—sharp and grating sound of crickets
29. **crick**—slight and sudden sound of a grasshopper
30. **croak**—sound of a frog, crow, or raven
31. **cronk**—hoarse sound of a raven; sound of a wild goose
32. **crow**—sound of a rooster
33. **cry**—sound or call of an animal
34. **cuckoo**—two-syllable whistle of the cuckoo
35. **drone**—sound or sounds of a bee or beetle
36. **gabble**—sounds of fowl or geese
37. **gobble**—throaty sound of the male turkey
38. **growl**—deep and threatening sound made by a dog, lion, etc.
39. **grunt**—throaty sound of a hog
40. **hiss**—sound of an angry goose or snake
41. **honk**—cry of the wild goose
42. **hoot**—characteristic cry of an owl
43. **howl**—long, low mournful sound of a dog or wolf; cry of a wild beast
44. **hum**—sound of a bee in flight; sound of a beetle, mosquito, gnat, or certain other insects
45. **latration**—a barking
46. **low**—sound characteristic of a cow
47. **mew**—sound made by a cat
48. **miaou, miaow**—sound made by a cat
49. **miaul**—cry or sound of a cat; caterwaul
50. **moo**—characteristic sound made by a cow
51. **neigh**—characteristic sound of a horse
52. **peep**—weak and shrill sound of a newly hatched bird

53. **pipe**—call or note of a bird or insect; whistle
54. **purr, pur**—low, rhythmic sound of a contented cat
55. **quack**—sound made by a duck
56. **rattle**—sound made by the tail of a rattlesnake
57. **roar**—deep, loud sound of a bull, lion, or certain other wild animals
58. **scape**—cry of a snipe suddenly roused to flight
59. **scream**—shrill, loud sound of an eagle or certain other wild beasts or birds
60. **screech**—harsh and shrill cry of an owl or certain other birds
61. **snarl**—deep, threatening, and angry sound, accompanied by a gnashing or snapping of its teeth, of a dog, lion, or certain other animals
62. **snort**—sound of air blown explosively through the nose by a high-spirited horse
63. **squall**—harsh scream of a bird or animal
64. **squawk**—harsh scream of a fowl, bird, or certain other animals
65. **squeak**—sharp, shrill, and short, but not very loud, sound of a mouse or certain other animals
66. **squeal**—shrill sound of a pig
67. **stridulation**—creaking, high-pitched, musical sound of a katydid, grasshopper, cicada, cricket, or certain other insects
68. **troat**—cry of a buck or certain other animals in heat
69. **trumpet**—sound made by an elephant; sound of a mosquito or gnat
70. **tu-whit, tu-whoo**—sound of an owl
71. **tweet**—sound made by a young bird
72. **twitter**—tremulous sound or sounds of a bird
73. **ululation**—hooting of an owl; howling; wailing of a jackal
74. **ululu**—wail
75. **wail**—low, mournful cry of a jackal or certain other animals
76. **whicker**—neigh; whinny
77. **whinny**—gentle neigh
78. **whistle**—shrill note or notes of a blackbird or certain other birds
79. **whoop**—cry of an owl or crane
80. **yap**—high-pitched bark
81. **yarr**—growl; snarl
82. **yelp**—sharp cry of a dog, fox, or female wild turkey
83. **yip**—yelp; high-pitched yelp
84. **yowl**—long and loud, mournful cry of a cat, dog, or certain other animals

2. To Make a Sound (of an Animal); To Make an Animal Sound or Sounds,v. *From Sec. 1:* bark, bay, bell, bellow, blat, bleat, boom, bray, buzz, cackle, caterwaul, caw, chatter, cheep, chirp or chip, chirr, chirrup, chitter, chuck, chuckle, churr, clang, cluck, cock-a-doodle, coo, creak, crick, croak, cronk, crow, cry, cuckoo, drone, gabble, gobble, growl, grunt, hiss, honk, hoot, howl, hum, low, mew, miaou or miaow, miaul, moo, neigh, peep, pipe, purr or pur, quack, rattle, roar, scream, screech, snarl, snort, squall, squawk, squeak, squeal, stridulate, troat, trumpet, tu-whit, tu-whoo, tweet, twitter, ululate, wail, whicker, whinny, whistle, whoop, yap, yarr, yelp, yip, yowl; *Also:*
1. **blow**—make a hissing sound (of a snake)
2. **curr**—make a low, murmuring sound (of a dove) ; make the sound of a dove; purr
3. **gaggle**—make the sound of a goose or pheasant; cackle; gabble
4. **plunk**—make a harsh sound (of a raven)

3. Making an Animal Sound,adj. *From Sec. 1:* barking, baying, etc.; stridulous, stridulent, or stridulatory; ululant or ululatory; *Also:* 1. **mugient**—bellowing; lowing (mugience, mugiency,n.)

457. INFANT SOUND

1. Infant Sound or Sounds,n.
  1. **babble**—vocal sounds of an infant
  2. **crow**—happy sound of an infant
  3. **gurgle, gurgulation**—liquid sound or sounds of an infant

2. To Make an Infant Sound,v. *From Sec. 1:* babble, crow, gurgle; *Also:* 1. **guggle**—gurgle

458. BELL SOUND

1. Sound of Bells; Ringing Sound,n.
  1. **carillon**—sound made by a group of stationary bells
  2. **chime**—musical sound of bells
  3. **clang**—characteristic sound of bells
  4. **clangor**—harsh, loud, and often sharp ringing sound
  5. **clank**—metallic ringing sound, but less shrill than a clang
  6. **ding**—sound of a ringing bell
  7. **dingdong**—sound of a bell struck repeatedly
  8. **jingle**—sound made by small bells
  9. **knell**—sound of a bell rung slowly and mournfully, as at a funeral
  10. **peal**—loud sound made by a bell or bells
  11. **ring**—sound made by a bell
  12. **stroke**—sound of a bell or gong
  13. **ting**—clear and ringing sound of a bell
  14. **ting-a-ling**—sound of a small bell
  15. **tinkle**—sound of small bells
  16. **tintinnabulation**—sound or sounds of bells; bell-like sound or sounds
  17. **toll**—sound, often solemn, made by the slow, regular, and repeated striking of a bell or gong
  18. **treble**—highest-pitched peal

2. To Sound (of a Bell); To Make a Bell-Like or Ringing Sound,v. *From Sec. 1:* chime, clang, clangor, clank, ding, jingle, knell, peal, ring, strike, ting, tinkle, tintinnabulate, toll

3. To Cause a Bell to Sound,v. *From Sec. 1:* chime, clang, clank, ding, jingle, ring, strike, ting, tinkle, tintinnabulate, toll

4. The Ringing of a Bell or Bells,n. *From Sec. 1:* chime, clang, knell, peal, ring, tinkle, tintinnabulation, toll

5. Pert. to, or Descr. of, a Bell-Like Sound, adj. *From Sec. 1:* clangorous, jingly, tinkly; tintinnabulant, tintinnabulary, tintinnabular, tintinnabulous, or tintinnabulatory

6. Bell; Bells,n.
  1. **Big Ben**—bell in the Parliament clock tower in London
  2. **carillon**—group of stationary bells sounded by striking with a hammer or similar device
  3. **chime, chimes**—set of metal plates that, when struck, sound like bells; carillon
  4. **curfew**—bell that rings a signal to clear the streets and go indoors
  5. **cymbals**—pair of brass plates that, struck together, give off a clear, ringing sound (cymbalist, cymbaleer, cymbaler, n.)
  6. **gong**—flat bell, shaped like a saucer; loosely, any bell
  7. **peal**—set of bells or chimes
  8. **tocsin**—alarm bell
  9. **vesper**—evening bell

7. Pert. to Bells or the Ringing of Bells: tintinnabulant, tintinnabular, tintinnabulary, tintinnabulous, tintinnabulatory,adj.

8. That Part by Which a Bell Is Hung: cannon,n.

9. Tongue of a Bell: clapper,n.

10. Bell Tower,n.
  1. **belfry**—bell tower

2. campanile—bell tower, usually built separately from the church to which it belongs

11. Science of Bells; Art of Bell Ringing: campanology,n. (campanologer, campanologist,n.)

459. WATER SOUND

1. Water Sounds,n.
  1. **burble**—bubbling sound
  2. **gurgle, gurgulation**—sound of water flowing irregularly, as over or around rocks, etc.
  3. **purl**—low, murmuring sound, as of gently flowing water
  4. **ripple**—sound of, or like, small waves breaking
  5. **splash**—sound of some heavy object falling into water
  6. **swash**—sound as of water hitting an object

2. To Make a Sound or Sounds (of Water); To Make a Sound Like That of Water,v. *From Sec. 1:* burble, gurgle, purl, ripple, splash, swash; *Also:* 1. **guggle**—make a sound like that of liquid pouring from a bottle; gurgle

3. Having the Sound of Ocean Waves, or Sounds Resembling Those of Ocean Breakers: fluctisonous, adj.

460. BODY SOUND

1. Certain Body Sounds,n.
  1. **croak**—throaty, low, and harsh sound
  2. **death rattle**—rattle noticed in a dying person just before the final moment
  3. **grunt**—short, deep, and throaty sound
  4. **hawk**—harsh, unpleasant sound of clearing the throat
  5. **murmur**—abnormal sound in the heart or lungs
  6. **rattle**—sound in the throat produced by air passing through mucus
  7. **rumble**—deep sound in, or by, the stomach
  8. **smack**—sharp noise of, or as of, the lips being compressed and then opened suddenly and forcibly
  9. **splutter**—spitting sound
  10. **sputter**—spitting sound or sounds
  11. **twang**—sharp nasal tone of voice

2. To Make a Body Sound,v. *From Sec. 1:* croak, grunt, hawk, rattle, rumble, smack, splutter, sputter, twang

3. Descr. of Body Sounds,adj. *From Sec. 1:* croaky, spluttery, sputtery, twangy; *Also:*
  1. **guttural**—descr. of throatlike sounds or sounds made in the throat (gutturalness, n.)
  2. **husky**—sounding dry-throated (huskiness,n.)
  3. **nasal**—uttered through, or sounding as if uttered through, the nose (nasality,n.)
  4. **nasalized**—nasal
  5. **throaty**—descr. of, or similar to, sounds made in the throat (throatiness,n.)

4. Hoarse,adj.
  1. **gruff**—deep, hoarse, and harsh in sound —generally applicable to the human voice (gruffness,n.)
  2. **husky**—hoarse (huskiness,n.)
  3. **raucous**—hoarse (raucousness,n.)
  4. **roupy**—hoarse (roup,n.)
  5. **stertorous**—breathing hoarsely (stertorousness,n.)
  6. **throaty**—hoarse and deep (throatiness, n.)

461. AIR SOUND

1. Sound of a Wind Instrument,n.
1. **blare**—loud and harsh sound of, or like that of, a trumpet
2. **blast**—sound of, or like that of, a wind instrument
3. **clang**—loud, ringing sound of, or like that of, a trumpet
4. **fanfare, flourish**—short air, tune, or call of trumpets or similar instruments
5. **pipe**—shrill sound of reed instruments
6. **tantara**—blare or flourish of a trumpet, horn, etc.
7. **toot**—short blast on a horn, whistle, or any other wind instrument
8. **tootle**—continuous or repeated toot, gentle or melodious in sound

2. To Make the Sound or Sounds of Wind Instruments,v. *From Sec. 1:* blare, blast, clang, pipe, toot, tootle

3. Having the Sound of a Reed Instrument: reedy,adj. (reediness,n.)

4. Other Air Sounds,n.
1. **bang**—loud and sudden sound of an explosion
2. **blast**—sound of, or like that of, a steam whistle
3. **chug**—sharp, explosive sound of an engine exhaust
4. **explosion**—sound of the violent expansion of air
5. **pop**—sound as of a light explosion
6. **whistle**—sound that is sharp and shrill and produced by expulsion of air against or through an obstruction or obstructing device

5. To Make a Sound of Air,v. *From Sec. 4:* bang, blast, chug, explode, pop, whistle

6. Having the Sound of Violent Expansion of Air: explosive,adj. (explosiveness,n.)

462. DEEP SOUND

1. Deep or Low Sound,n.
1. **boom**—deep and hollow sound
2. **buzz**—low, vibrating sound, as of bees
3. **croak**—low, harsh, throaty sound, resembling that of a crow or frog
4. **drone**—low sound, often in a monotone; hum; murmur
5. **growl**—deep, low sound
6. **grunt**—short and deep, throaty sound
7. **gurgulation**—rumbling
8. **hum**—continuous low buzz or murmur
9. **muffle**—deadened or muted sound
10. **mumble**—low, confused sound
11. **murmur**—soft, low, and indistinct sound
12. **purl**—low, murmuring sound, as of gently flowing water
13. **purr, pur**—low, rhythmic sound of a contented cat
14. **roll**—deep or booming and continuous sound
15. **rumble**—low, rolling, deep, and continuing sound
16. **undertone**—low tone or sound, as of speech
17. **whisper**—low, hissing sound

2. To Make a Deep or Low Sound,v. *From Sec. 1:* boom, buzz, croak, drone, growl, grunt, hum, mumble, murmur, purl, purr, pur, roll, rumble, whisper

3. Low or Deep in Sound; Descr. of a Deep or Low Sound,adj. *From Sec. 1:* booming, buzzing, croaking, etc.; growly, muffled, mumbly, murmurous, purry, whisperous or whispery; *Also:*
1. **bass**—low or deep in tone or sound
2. **faint**—very low; so low as to be hard to hear (faintness,n.)

3. **gruff**—deep, hoarse and harsh (gruffness, n.)
4. **guttural**—deep and harsh, like sounds made in the throat (gutturalness,n.)
5. **hoarse**—deep, harsh, and grating—of the human or animal voice (hoarseness,n.)
6. **inaudible**—so low as not to be heard (inaudibility,n.)
7. **pianissimo**—very soft, in music
8. **piano**—soft, in music
9. **sepulchral**—unnaturally deep and low
10. **soft**—low in sound (softness,n.)
11. **throaty**—deep and hoarse; low-pitched (throatiness,n.)
12. **velvety**—soft in sound (velvetiness,n.)

4. Having a Soft and Gentle Voice: soft-spoken,adj.

5. In a Low Tone Not Intended to Be Overheard; In an Undertone: sotto voce (Italian)

6. Murmur; Murmuring Sound or Sounds, n.
1. **babble**—murmur; murmuring sounds
2. **buzz**—murmur
3. **drone**—low, murmuring sound, usually in a monotone; hum
4. **hum**—continuous, low, murmuring sound
5. **purl**—low, murmuring sound, as of gently flowing water
6. **purr, pur**—low, murmuring sound of, or as of, a contented cat
7. **simmer**—murmuring sound of something gently boiling
8. **sough**—murmuring sound, as of leaves or the wind
9. **susurration**—murmur
10. **susurrus**—murmuring sound
11. **whiz**—humming sound

7. To Make a Murmuring Sound,v. *From Sec. 6:* babble, buzz, drone, hum, purl, purr, pur, simmer, sough, susurrate; *Also:* 1. **curr**—make the murmuring sound of a dove or of a contented cat

8. Murmurous; Descr. of, or Making, a Murmuring Sound,adj. *From Sec. 6:* babbling, buzzing, droning, etc.; susurrant or susurrous

9. Whisper; Whispering Sound,n.
1. **buzz**—whisper
2. **susurration**—whisper
3. **susurrus**—whispering sound; sound of whispering

10. To Whisper,v. *From Sec. 9:* buzz, susurrate; *Also:* 1. **breathe**—whisper

11. Whisperous; Whispery,adj. *From Sec. 9:* buzzing, susurrant or susurrous

12. In a Whispered Voice: sotto voce (Italian)

13. Dull Sound,n.
1. **drone**—dull, low, continuous sound
2. **hum**—drone
3. **pad**—dull sound made by light contact
4. **thud**—dull, muted sound
5. **thump**—dull and heavy sound

14. To Make a Dull Sound,v. *From Sec. 13:* drone, hum, thud, thump

15. To Make Lower in Sound,v.
1. **cushion**—soften (the sound of)
2. **deaden**—reduce the intensity of (sound)
3. **depress**—lower the pitch of (voice or sound)
4. **modulate**—soften; tone down (modulatory,adj.)
5. **muffle**—deaden or dull the sound of
6. **mute**—muffle (a musical instrument, sound, etc.)
7. **soften**—make (sound, voice, etc.) lower, less strong, less harsh, etc.
8. **subdue**—reduce the volume of (sound)
9. **tone down**—make lower or softer in volume; soften

16. To Become Lower in Sound,v. *From Sec. 15:* modulate, soften, tone down; *Also:* 1.

taper, taper off—grow gradually less in force or volume

17. A Making or Becoming Lower in Sound, n. *From Secs. 15 and 16:* depression, modulation, subdual; *Also:*
1. **decrescendo**—gradual decrease of the volume or force of sound (music)
2. **diminuendo**—gradual decrease of the loudness or force of sound (music)

18. Becoming Lower in Sound,adj. *From Sec. 17:* decrescendo, diminuendo

19. To Keep Sound out of: deaden, soundproof,v. (soundproof,adj.)

463. LOUD SOUND

1. Loud or Sharp Sound; Noise,n.
1. **bang**—sudden loud noise, as of an explosion
2. **bark**—loud and harsh sound
3. **bedlam**—confused and loud noise or noises; noise and confusion
4. **bellow**—roar
5. **blare**—loud and harsh sound
6. **bluster**—noise of activity or action
7. **brawl**—loud and confused noise; noise like that of a fight or quarrel
8. **bray**—loud and harsh sound, like that of a donkey
9. **chirm**—noise; noise of many sounds
10. **clamor**—continuous loud noise
11. **clang**—loud, ringing sound, like that of a trumpet or of metals striking together
12. **clangor**—loud, harsh, and often sharp sound, of the nature of ringing
13. **clap**—loud sound, as of the impact of bodies
14. **clarion**—loud and clear sound
15. **clash**—loud, sharp sound, as of impact, collision, etc.
16. **crackle**—sharp, repeated, sudden, but not prolonged sound or sounds
17. **crash**—sudden and very loud noise, as of the impact of heavy bodies
18. **crepitation**—crackle
19. **cry**—loud sound
20. **din**—loud noise
21. **disquiet, disquietude**—lack of quietness; noise; noisiness
22. **hubbub**—tumultuous noise or uproar of, or as of, many voices shouting
23. **hullabaloo**—confused noise or uproar
24. **hurly-burly, hurly**—noise; uproar
25. **outcry**—great noise
26. **peal**—loud and long sound or sounds, as of bells or thunder
27. **racket**—loud noise
28. **report**—loud, sudden sound, as of a shot or explosion
29. **riot**—loud and confused noise
30. **roar**—loud, full, and deep sound or noise
31. **roll**—loud or heavy, rising and falling sound
32. **rumpus**—noise; uproar
33. **salvo**—noise of the simultaneous firing of many guns
34. **screak**—screech
35. **scream**—loud, shrill sound
36. **screech**—loud, shrill sound
37. **shout**—loud-voiced sound or sounds
38. **shriek**—loud, sharp, and high-pitched sound
39. **slam**—great noise
40. **squall**—loud or violent scream
41. **squawk**—loud, harsh sound
42. **thunder**—loud sound or noise, like that of thunder
43. **thunderclap**—any very loud sound
44. **tumult**—noise; confused, loud noise
45. **uproar**—loud and/or confused noise or noises
46. **yawp**—harsh, loud noise
47. **zing**—sharp, humming or singing sound
48. **zoom**—loud and humming sound

2. To Make a Loud Sound or Noise,v. *From Sec. 1:* bang, bark, bellow, blare, bluster, brawl, bray, clamor, clang, clangor, clap, clash, crackle, crash, crepitate, cry, din, peal, racket, roar, roll, screak, scream, screech, shout, shriek, slam, squall, squawk, thunder, yawp, zing, zoom; *Also:*
1. **deafen**—shock or stun (someone) with noise; make such a loud sound as to cause (another sound) to be inaudible
2. **drown (out)**—be so noisy or loud as to push (other sounds) out of audibility
3. **noise**—to make a noise or clamor
4. **resound**—sound loudly; be filled with sound
5. **roister**—be noisy
6. **ruffle**—grow noisy; become rough and noisy
7. **skirl**—shriek

3. Loud; Noisy; Making a Loud or Sharp Sound,adj. *From Sec. 1:* banging, barking, etc.; bedlam, blusterous or blustery, brawly, clamorous, clangorous, clarion, crepitant, hurly-burly, rackety, riotous, screechy, squally, squawky, thunderous, tumultuous or tumultuary, uproarious; *Also:*
1. **blatant**—loud and offensive; noisy; clamorous
2. **boisterous**—noisy; rough and noisy
3. **brazen**—loud and harsh in sound
4. **canorous**—pleasantly loud and rich in sound
5. **disorderly**—noisy
6. **efferverscent**—boisterous or noisy with lively and high spirits
7. **forte**—loud (music)
8. **fortissimo**—very loud (music)
9. **obstreperous**—noisy beyond control
10. **rambunctious**—noisy
11. **reedy**—sharp and thin in sound, like that of a reed instrument
12. **rip-roaring**—very noisy
13. **rowdy**—noisy and rough
14. **sonorous**—loud in sound or tone
15. **stentorian**—unusually loud in sound (of voice)
16. **strepent**—noisy; loud
17. **strepitous, strepitant**—noisy; making a great clamor or uproar; boisterous
18. **vociferous**—loud; noisy

4. Loudness; Noisiness,n. *From Sec. 3:* blusterousness or blusteriness, clamorousness, riotousness, thunderousness, tumultuousness or tumultuariness, uproariousness; blatancy, boisterousness, brazenness, canorousness, disorderliness, effervescence, obstreperousness, rambunctiousness, reediness, rowdiness, sonority or sonorousness, vociferousness

5. In a Loud Voice,adv.
1. **aloud**—in or with a loud voice
2. **viva voce**—aloud and all together

6. One Who Has a Loud Voice: stentor,n.

7. Noisy Woman: scold,n.

8. Noisy and Unmanageable Person or Child: terror,n.

9. To Make or Cause to Be Louder: amplify, boost, increase, raise,v. (amplification, boost, increase,n.)

10. To Become Louder: increase, rise, swell, uprise,v. (increase, rise, swell, uprise,n.)

11. Gradual Increase in the Volume or Force of Sound: crescendo,n. (crescendo,adj. or adv.)

12. Tendency to Increase in Sound: resonance (physics),n. (resonant,adj.)

464. SHOUT

1. A Shout; Shouting,n.
1. **bark**—harsh and hostile shout
2. **bawl**—shout; public shout

3. **bellow**—shout
4. **cheer**—shout of encouragement, praise, approval, etc.
5. **clamor**—loud shout or shouting; shouting by many people
6. **cry**—shout; scream
7. **hue**—shout or public shouting, in a chase (used only in the phrase *hue and cry*)
8. **outcry**—great shout; great public shout; scream
9. **oyez, oyes**—shout used in courts to obtain silence when court opens, the judge enters, a proclamation is to be read, etc.
10. **roar**—shout
11. **salvo**—burst of shouting from an audience or crowd
12. **screak**—screech
13. **scream**—loud, shrill shout
14. **screech**—loud, very shrill shout
15. **shriek**—loud, sharp, and high-pitched shout
16. **squall**—loud or violent shout
17. **squawk**—loud, harsh, and shrill shout
18. **tallyho!**—hunter's shout when the fox comes into view
19. **tumult**—confused shouting of many people
20. **view halloo**—shout made by hunters in catching sight of a fox
21. **vociferation**—shouting
22. **whoop**—shout; shout of joy; loud shout
23. **yammer**—shout; yell
24. **yap**—bark
25. **yawp**—harsh, loud shout; noisy scream
26. **yell**—strong and loud shout; shout of pain, fear, etc.; patterned or traditional shout or cheer used by a college or other institution
27. **yoicks**—shout used to encourage hounds in fox hunting

2. To Shout,v. *From Sec. 1:* bark, bawl, bellow, cheer, clamor, cry, roar, screak, scream, screech, shriek, squall, squawk, vociferate, whoop, yammer, yap, yawp, yell

3. Shouting; Descr. of Shouting,adj. *From Sec. 1:* clamorous, screechy, squally, squawky, tumultuous or tumultuary, vociferant or vociferous

465. HIGH SOUND

1. High-Pitched Sound,n.
1. **cheep**—faint, high-pitched cry, like that of a young bird
2. **chirr**—high-pitched, creaking sound
3. **clarion**—clear, high-pitched sound
4. **cry**—scream
5. **peep**—weak and high-pitched sound, like that of a newly hatched bird
6. **scream**—high-pitched and piercing sound or cry
7. **screech**—loud, high-pitched, and piercing sound or cry
8. **shriek**—loud, high-pitched, and piercing sound or cry
9. **shrill**—high-pitched, piercing sound
10. **skirl**—high-pitched sound characteristic of Scottish bagpipes; any high-pitched sound
11. **squall**—loud or violent scream
12. **squawk**—harsh scream
13. **squeak**—short, high-pitched, and sharp sound
14. **squeal**—high-pitched, sharp sound, like that of a pig
15. **stridor**—high-pitched and harsh sound
16. **stridulation**—high-pitched and creaking sound
17. **ting**—high-pitched, clear, and ringing sound
18. **treble**—high-pitched, sharp sound
19. **whine**—high-pitched, piercing, and moaning sound, as of the wind, machinery, etc.

20. **whistle**—high-pitched, sharp sound
21. **yap**—high-pitched, barking sound of a dog
22. **yawp**—noisy scream
23. **yelp**—high-pitched sound, like the cry of a fox or dog
24. **yip**—yelp; very high-pitched yelp
25. **zing**—high-pitched, humming sound

2. To Make a High-Pitched Sound,v. *From Sec. 1:* cheep, chirr, cry, peep, scream, screech, shriek, shrill, skirl, squall, squawk, squeak, squeal, stridulate, ting, whine, whistle, yap, yawp, yelp, yip, zing; *Also:* 1. **pipe**—make a high-pitched sound

3. High-Pitched,adj. *From Sec. 1:* cheeping, chirring, etc.; clarion, screechy, shrill, squally, squawky, squeaky; strident, stridulous, stridulant, or stridulatory; treble (screechiness, shrillness, squeakiness, stridence or stridency,n.) ; *Also:* 1. **reedy**—having a high-pitched, thin sound, like that of an oboe or certain other reed instruments (reediness,n.)

466. HARSH SOUND

1. Harsh or Unpleasant Sound or Sounds, n.
1. **bark**—harsh, loud sound
2. **blare**—harsh and loud sound
3. **bray**—harsh and loud sound, resembling that of an ass or donkey
4. **cacophony**—harsh, unpleasant sound or sounds
5. **caterwaul**—harsh and wailing sound; harsh and wailing sounds of a cat in heat
6. **chirr, churr**—high-pitched creak
7. **clangor**—harsh, loud, and often sharp sound, of the nature of ringing
8. **clash**—harsh sound of colliding hard surfaces
9. **creak**—extended, grating sound, as of things rubbing against each other
10. **crepitation**—creak; creaking sound or sounds
11. **croak**—low, harsh sound made deep in the throat, resembling that of a frog or crow
12. **discord**—harsh combination of musical sounds; harsh sound; sounds of conflict, fighting, quarreling, etc.
13. **discordance**—harsh or jarring combination of sounds
14. **disharmony**—discordance
15. **dissonance, dissonancy**—harsh sound; discord
16. **hawk**—harsh, unpleasant sound made by noisily clearing the throat
17. **jangle**—harsh and discordant sound
18. **noise**—unpleasant and loud sound
19. **quack**—harsh cry or sound
20. **rasp**—harsh and grating sound; harsh or grating effect of sound on the ears
21. **screak**—noisy creak
22. **skirr**—grating sound
23. **squawk**—harsh scream; loud, harsh sound
24. **stridor**—disagreeably harsh and shrill sound; creak
25. **yawp**—harsh, loud noise or cry

2. To Make a Harsh or Unpleasant Sound, v. *From Sec. 1:* bark, blare, bray, caterwaul, chirr, churr, clangor, clash, creak, crepitate, croak, hawk, jangle, quack, rasp, screak, squawk, yawp; *Also:*
1. **grate**—make a harsh and unpleasant sound, as of things rubbing against each other; have a harsh or unpleasant effect on the ear
2. **jar**—sound harshly or unpleasantly; have a harsh or unpleasant effect on the ear

3. Harsh-   or   Unpleasant-Sounding,adj. *From Sec. 1:* blaring, cacophonous, clangorous, clashing, creaking or creaky, crepitant, croaky, discordant, disharmonious, dissonant, jangling, noisy, rasping or raspy, screaky, squawky, strident (cacophony, creakiness, discordance or discordancy, disharmony, dissonance or dissonancy, noisiness, raspingness, screakiness, stridence or stridency,n.) ; *From Sec. 2*: grating, jarring; *Also:*

1. **barbarous**—harsh-sounding (barbarousness,n.)
2. **brazen**—loud and harsh in sound (brazenness,n.)
3. **gruff**—deep and harsh; hoarse (gruffness, n.)
4. **guttural**—deep and harsh, like a sound made in the throat (gutturalness,n.)
5. **hoarse**—harsh, deep, and grating in sound—particularly descr. of the sound of the human or, less often, the animal voice (hoarseness,n.)
6. **husky**—harsh in tone (huskiness,n.)
7. **inharmonious**—discordant
8. **raucous**—harsh-sounding (raucousness, n.)
9. **rude**—harsh or discordant in sound (rudeness,n.)
10. **rugged**—harsh in sound
11. **scrannel**—harsh in sound
12. **uneuphonious**—not pleasant in sound (uneuphoniousness,n.)
13. **unharmonious**—discordant
14. **unmelodious**—unmusical (unmelodiousness,n.)
15. **unmusical**—harsh or discordant in sound

4. To Cause to Make a Harsh or Unpleasant Sound: jangle,v.

467. SWEET SOUND

1. Sweet, Pleasant, or Musical Sound,n.
1. **chime**—musical sound of bells
2. **coo**—sound of love, so called from the characteristic sounds of the dove
3. **euphony**—pleasant sound
4. **harmony**—pleasant, musical, or sweet sound or combination of sounds
5. **melody**—sweet, pleasant, or agreeable sound or succession of sounds
6. **musicality, musicalness**—sweet and pleasant sound
7. **pizzicato**—musical sound made by plucking a string
8. **purr**—sound of contentment, like that of a happy cat
9. **symphony**—harmony of sounds made by musical instruments
10. **tone**—musical sound
11. **tune**—melody

2. To Make a Sweet, Pleasant, or Musical Sound,v. *From Sec. 1*: chime, coo, purr

3. Sweet-, Pleasant-, or Musical-Sounding, adj. *From Sec. 1:* euphonious or euphonic, harmonious or harmonic, melodious or melodic, musical, symphonic, tuneful (euphoniousness or euphony, harmoniousness or harmony, melodiousness or melody, tunefulness,n.) ; *Also:*

1. **canorous**—pleasantly full in tone; melodious (canorousness,n.)
2. **cantabile**—smoothly musical; melodious
3. **dulcet**—sweet, agreeable, and/or soothing in sound
4. **mellifluous, mellifluent**—descr. of sounds that flow smoothly or sweetly (mellifluousness, mellifluence,n.)
5. **mellow**—full, rich, and soft in sound (mellowness,n.)
6. **orotund**—strong, rich, full, and clear—of voice sounds (orotundity,n.)
7. **rotund**—having full, rich, or glowing sounds or tones (rotundity,n.)
8. **silvery**—like silver in sound
9. **sonorous**—full or rich in sound or tone (sonorousness, sonority,n.)

4. System of Musical Sounds: tonality,n. (tonal,adj.)

468. UNHAPPY SOUND

1. Unhappy, etc., Sound,n.
1. **bay**—prolonged howl
2. **bleat**—complaining sound or cry
3. **catcall**—sound or cry of disapproval
4. **caterwaul**—harsh wail
5. **cry**—wail
6. **groan**—deep sound expressive of suffering, pain, or some similar emotion or feeling
7. **growl**—deep and throaty sound of anger, hostility, complaint, etc.
8. **grumble**—sound or sounds, often somewhat indistinct, of complaint, discontentment, ill-humor, etc.
9. **howl**—long, low, and plaintive, anguished, pained, or unhappy cry
10. **knell**—mournful sound, as of a bell rung slowly at a funeral; warning sound of approaching death, misfortune, etc.
11. **moan**—sound of pain or grief
12. **outcry**—loud cry, usually of distress, alarm, or fear
13. **snarl**—sharp or angry growl
14. **sough**—hollow, moaning sound; moan
15. **ululation**—howl similar to that of a dog or wolf; wail
16. **wail**—prolonged cry of grief or distress
17. **whimper**—low, unhappy, and broken sound
18. **whine**—complaining, fretful, peevish, or distressed sound or cry
19. **yarr**—growl; snarl

2. To Make an Unhappy, etc., Sound,v. *From Sec. 1:* bay, bleat, catcall, caterwaul, cry, groan, growl, grumble, howl, knell, moan, snarl, sough, ululate, wail, whimper, whine, yarr; *Also:* 1. pule—whimper; whine

3. Unhappy, etc., in Sound,adj. *From Sec. 1:* baying, bleating, etc.; growly, grumbly, ululant or ululatory, wailful or wailsome, whiny; *Also:*
1. **blatant**—bleating
2. **sullen**—mournful in tone

469. SOUND OF MOVEMENT

1. Sound of Movement, Vibration, or Trembling,n.
1. **birr**—whirr
2. **buzz**—low, vibrating sound
3. **churr**—vibrating sound; whirr
4. **crackle**—short, sharp sound, as when stiff paper is crushed
5. **crepitation**—crackle
6. **crinkle**—crackle
7. **crunch**—grinding or crushing sound
8. **flop**—sound of a fall or drop; thud
9. **gurgle**—bubbling sound
10. **gurgulation**—bubbling sound
11. **hum**—buzz
12. **purl**—low sound of, or as of, gently flowing water
13. **quaver**—trembling sound, esp. of the voice or of a musical instrument
14. **quiver**—quaver
15. **roll**—trill; trill of certain birds
16. **rustle**—small sound like that of tree leaves moved by the wind, silk swishing, paper being moved, etc.
17. **skirr**—whirr
18. **sough**—rustling sound, as of leaves in the wind
19. **susurration**—rustle
20. **susurrus**—rustling sound
21. **swirring**—whirring sound
22. **swish**—brushing sound
23. **thud**—sound of some heavy object falling
24. **tremble**—quaver (of the voice)

25. **tremolo**—vibrating or trembling sound, tone, or note, esp. of the voice or of a musical instrument
26. **tremor**—trembling sound or note
27. **trill**—trembling or vibrating sound
28. **twang**—sharp sound made by vibration, as of a taut metal wire
29. **twitter**—series of tremulous sounds like those of a bird
30. **vibrato**—vibrating sound in singing or in a bowed musical instrument
31. **whirr**—characteristic sound made by a body moving very rapidly through the air
32. **whish**—rushing sound
33. **whiz**—vibrating or hissing sound of an object moving rapidly through the air
34. **zing**—high-pitched hum
35. **zoom**—continuous hum

2. To Make a Sound of Movement, Vibration, or Trembling,v. *From Sec. 1:* birr, buzz, churr, crackle, crepitate, crinkle, gurgle, hum, purl, quaver, quiver, rustle, roll, sough, susurrate, swish, thud, tremble, trill, twang, twitter, whirr, whish, whiz, zing, zoom; *Also:* 1. **guggle**—make a sound like that of liquid pouring from a bottle; gurgle

3. Descr. of a Sound of Movement, Vibration, or Trembling,adj. *From Sec. 1:* birring, buzzing, etc.; crackly, crepitant, crinkly, gurgly, quavery, quivery, susurrant or susurrous, swishy, trembly, tremoloso (Italian), tremulous or tremulant (from tremor or tremble), twangy

4. Shaking or Oscillating Motion of a String or Other Sounding Body That Produces a Musical Sound: vibration,n.

5. Sound of Walking, etc.,n.
1. **clump**—sound of heavy footfalls
2. **patter**—sound of light footsteps
3. **scuff**—sound as if someone were walking without lifting the feet from the ground
4. **tramp**—sound of heavy footsteps
5. **trample**—sound of heavy stepping
6. **tread**—sound of someone's footsteps

6. To Make a Sound of Walking, etc.,v. *From Sec. 5:* clump, patter, scuff, tramp

7. Contact Sound; Metallic Sound or Sounds,n.
1. **beat**—sound of striking or of a blow
2. **chatter**—sound of things hitting together rapidly and repeatedly
3. **chink**—short, sharp, metallic sound, as of coins or glasses striking each other
4. **clack**—short click; chatter
5. **clang**—loud sound of metals striking together
6. **clank**—metallic sound, less ringing or shrill than a clang, similar to that of the impact between things that resound when struck
7. **clap**—loud sound, as of the impact of bodies or heavy objects
8. **clash**—harsh sound of colliding hard surfaces
9. **clatter**—rattle
10. **click**—slight, sharp, somewhat metallic sound
11. **clink**—slight but sharp sound, as of metals making contact
12. **clip-clop**—sound of a horse's hoofs striking on hard ground, pavement, etc.; sound of chopping
13. **crash**—sudden, loud sound caused by the impact or collision of heavy bodies or objects
14. **creak**—sound of hard surfaces rubbing against each other
15. **crepitation**—creak; rattle
16. **drumbeat**—sound of a drum being beaten
17. **jingle**—sound of small pieces of metal striking lightly against each other
18. **pad**—dull or muted sound made by the light impact of two objects

19. **pat**—sound made by light strokes
20. **patter**—sound of light, rapid strokes
21. **ping**—sharp, somewhat metallic sound; sound of a bullet striking
22. **plunk**—metallic and hollow sound
23. **rap**—sound of a quick blow or knock
24. **rasp**—harsh sound of surfaces rubbing together
25. **rataplan**—repeated sound of something being beaten, as a drum; rub-a-dub
26. **rattle**—short, sharp sound or sounds, as of things repeatedly striking each other
27. **roll**—continuous sound of a drum being beaten rapidly
28. **rote**—sound of waves beating against the shore
29. **rub-a-dub, rubadub**—sound of a drum being beaten
30. **ruffle**—low and continuous sound of a drum being beaten
31. **screak**—noisy creak
32. **scuff**—sound of two things being harshly rubbed against each other
33. **slam**—sound made by forcible closing, contact, or impact
34. **squeak**—high-pitched creak
35. **stroke**—sound made by striking
36. **tap**—sound made by a light blow
37. **tattoo**—series of continuous raps, taps, etc.
38. **tick**—barely audible sound, as of the regular beat of something
39. **tom-tom**—monotonous and rhythmic drumbeat or any sound like it

8. To Make a Sound of Contact or of Metal,v. *From Sec. 7:* beat, chatter, chink, clack, clang, clank, clap, clash, clatter, click, clink, clip-clop, crash, creak, crepitate, jingle, patter, ping, plunk, rap, rasp, rattle, roll, screak, slam, squeak, strike, tap, tick; *Also:* 1. **grate**—make the unpleasant sound of things rubbing against each other

9. To Cause to Make a Sound of Contact or of Metal,v. *From Sec. 7:* beat, clack, clank, clap, clash, clatter, click, clink, crash, creak, jingle, rap, rataplan, rattle, roll, ruffle, slam, squeak, strike, tap; *From Sec. 8:* grate

10. Descr. of a Sound of Contact or of Metal, adj. *From Sec. 7:* beating, chattering, etc.; clattery, clip-clop, creaky, crepitant, jingly, raspy, rattly, screaky, squeaky; *Also:* 1. **tinny** —descr. of a sound like that of tin being struck; resembling tin in sound

470. MONOTONOUS SOUND

1. Monotonous Sound,n.
1. **chant**—monotonous tone of voice
2. **drone**—monotonous, dull, continuous sound
3. **hum**—drone
4. **monotone**—sound that does not vary in pitch or tone
5. **singsong**—tone of voice that rises and falls monotonously
6. **thrum**—monotonous sound, as of someone idly plucking a stringed instrument
7. **tom-tom**—monotonous and rhythmic drumbeat or sound resembling this

2. To Make a Monotonous Sound,v. *From Sec. 1:* chant, drone, hum

3. Monotonous in Sound,adj.
1. **singsong**—descr. of a tone of voice which rises and falls monotonously
2. **toneless**—monotonous in sound; devoid of expression or change of the voice

471. ECHO

1. Echo; Echoing Sound,n.
1. **rebound**—echo
2. **re-echo**—echo of an echo

3. **repercussion**—re-echo
4. **replication**—echo
5. **reverberation**—re-echo; series of continuing echoes

2. To Echo, i.e., Come Back as an Echo, v. *From Sec. 1:* rebound, re-echo, reverberate or reverb; *Also:*
　1. **redound**—resound
　2. **resound**—echo; re-echo; reverberate
　3. **vibrate**—echo; re-echo; reverberate

3. To Echo, i.e., Send Back as an Echo, v. *From Sec. 2:* rebound, re-echo, reverberate or reverb, resound

4. An Echoing, or a Sending of an Echo, n. *From Sec. 1:* rebound, re-echo, repercussion, replication, reverberation; *From Sec. 2:* redound, vibration

5. Echoing; Descr. of Echoing, adj. *From Sec. 1:* rebounding, re-echoing, etc.; repercussive, replicative; reverberant, reverberative, or reverberatory; *From Sec. 2:* vibrant, vibrative, or vibratory; *Also:*
　1. **plangent**—reverberating deeply and loudly, like the clang of bells or the breaking of waves upon the shore (plangency,n.)
　2. **reboant**—loudly resounding
　3. **resonant**—echoing; re-echoing; reverberating (resonance,n.)

472. HISS

1. Hissing Sound or Sounds; Hiss, n.
　1. **fizz**—hissing sound
　2. **sibilance, sibilation**—hissing or *"S"* sounds
　3. **sibilant**—hissing sound; an *"S"* sound
　4. **sizzle**—hissing sound, as of something frying in hot grease
　5. **swish**—light, hissing sound
　6. **whisper**—low, hissing sound
　7. **whiz**—hissing sound
　8. **zip**—sudden hissing sound

2. To Hiss; To Make a Hissing Sound, v. *From Sec. 1:* fizz, sibilate, sizzle, swish, whisper, whiz, zip

3. Hissing, adj. *From Sec. 1:* sibilant, whisperous or whispery

473. CONFUSED SOUND

1. Confused Sound or Sounds, n.
　1. **babel**—confusion of sounds, noises, cries, etc.
　2. **bedlam**—confused and loud noise
　3. **brawl**—confused and loud sound or sounds
　4. **clatter**—confused noise
　5. **clutter**—confused noise
　6. **din**—confusion of loud noises; confused and loud noise
　7. **hubbub**—confusion of loud sounds or noises; confusion of many voices
　8. **hullabaloo**—confused noise; uproar
　9. **mumble**—low, confused sound
　10. **pandemonium**—any great confused noise; tumult
　11. **racket**—confused noise
　12. **riot**—loud and confused noise
　13. **tumult**—confused noise, as of many people shouting
　14. **uproar**—confused and loud noise or noises

2. To Make a Confused Sound or Sounds, v. *From Sec. 1:* brawl, clatter, clutter, din, mumble, racket, riot

3. Descr. of a Confused Sound or Sounds, adj. *From Sec. 1:* bedlam, clattery, rackety, riotous, tumultuous or tumultuary, uproarious

4. Place of Noise and Confusion: babel, bedlam,n.

474. VOICE

1. Voice, n.
　1. **monotone**—voice of an unvarying pitch or tone
　2. **undertone**—low voice
　3. **vox populi (Latin)**—voice of the people

2. Pert. to the Voice, adj.
　1. **phonetic**—pert. to the voice or the sound of the voice
　2. **vocal**—pert. to the voice

3. Sound or Sounds of the Voice, n.
　1. **accents**—tone of voice
　2. **chatter**—rapid but unintelligible vocal sounds
　3. **clack**—chatter
　4. **tone**—sound of the human voice

4. To Make Sounds with the Voice, v. *From Sec. 3:* chatter, clack; *Also:*
　1. **intonate, intone**—utter (sounds) in a particular voice or in a special tone (intonation,n.)
　2. **phonate**—make sounds with the voice (phonation,n.)
　3. **vocalize**—use the voice; make sounds with the voice (vocalization,n.)
　4. **voice**—say, express, etc., with the voice

5. Use of the Voice: vocalism,n.

6. Pronounced or Said with the Voice: laryngal, sonant, vocal, voiced,adj.

7. Very Thin in Quality (of the Voice): tinny,adj. (tinniness,n.)

8. Art of Throwing One's Voice: ventriloquism, ventriloquy,n. (ventriloquist,n. ventriloquial, ventriloquistic, ventriloqual,adj. ventriloquize,v.)

9. Organ of Voice: larynx,n. (laryngeal,adj.)

10. Organ of Voice in Birds: syrinx,n. (syringeal,adj.)

475. SILENCE

1. Silent, adj.
　1. **dumb**—silent; speechless
　2. **glum**—silent and gloomy
　3. **hushed**—silent, usually following noise or clamor
　4. **inarticulate**—silent through inability to speak or to express one's thoughts
　5. **mousy**—quiet, like a mouse
　6. **mum**—silent; not uttering any sound
　7. **mute**—silent; uttering no sound
　8. **noiseless**—silent; making no sound or noise
　9. **quiet**—free from, or making no, noise or sound
　10. **saturnine**—gloomily silent
　11. **soundless**—making no sound
　12. **speechless**—silent; struck silent
　13. **sphinxian**—silent, like a sphinx
　14. **still**—silent; making no sound
　15. **stilly**—making no noise or sound
　16. **sulky**—angrily silent owing to resentment or offense
　17. **sullen**—silent and in bad humor; disagreeably silent
　18. **tacit**—silent or unspoken (of an agreement, feeling, approval, or similar abstractions)
　19. **tongue-tied**—silent or speechless through the force of some feeling, such as fear, shyness, embarrassment, etc.
　20. **unspoken**—silent in the sense of not being said or spoken, though often expressed in some other fashion (of feeling, agreement, approval, disapproval, or similar abstractions)
　21. **voiceless**—silent; mute
　22. **wordless**—silent; mute

2. Silence, n. *From Sec. 1:* dumbness, glumness, hush, inarticulateness, mousiness, muteness, noiselessness, quietness or quietude, saturninity or saturnineness, soundlessness, speechlessness, stillness, sulkiness or sulk, sullenness, voicelessness, wordlessness

3. Silent Person,n. *From Sec. 1:* dummy, sphinx, sulk or sulker

4. Tending to Be Silent: reticent, taciturn, uncommunicative,adj. (reticence or reticency, taciturnity, uncommunicativeness,n.)

5. To Silence; To Stop from Talking,v.
1. gag—stop the mouth of and prevent talking; prevent from exercising freedom of speech
2. hush—make silent
3. muzzle—stop from speaking, or from speaking freely
4. quiet, quieten—silence
5. squelch—silence (a person, group, etc.)
6. still—silence
7. tongue-tie—silence

6. To Be or Become Silent,v.
1. dummy up—become silent
2. hold one's tongue—remain silent
3. hush—become silent
4. quiet, quiet down—become silent
5. sulk—be angrily silent

7. Not Permitted to Express Opinions: voiceless,adj.

8. Not Said: unbreathed, unmentioned, unsaid, unspoken, untold,adj.

9. Beyond That Which Is Directly Said: ulterior,adj.

10. Pronounced without the Use of the Vocal Cords: surd, voiceless,adj.

476. SING

1. To Sing,v.
1. accompany—sing with (some featured soloist)
2. cantillate—chant or recite against a musical background, generally in religious ceremonies
3. carol—sing; sing a joyous hymn
4. chant—sing; sing in a musical monotone
5. croon—sing in a low, affectionate voice, showing emotion or sentimentality
6. harmonize—sing together in harmony (colloq.)
7. hum—sing without opening the lips
8. intonate—chant
9. intone—say in a singing voice; chant
10. serenade—sing a love song; sing to (a woman one loves)
11. solo—sing by oneself; sing as the featured singer, with musical accompaniment
12. trill—sing in trembling or quavering sounds
13. troll—sing loudly; sing in a full voice; sing in a roundelay
14. vocalize—sing
15. warble—sing; sing with trills, quavers, etc.
16. yodel, yodle—sing; sing with sudden and repeated changes from normal to falsetto or shrill tones

2. Singing,n. *From Sec. 1:* accompaniment, cantillation, chant, croon, hum, intonation, serenade, trill, vocalization or vocalism, warble, yodel or yodle; *Also:*
1. antiphony—singing by groups in turn, as if answering each other, esp. in worship (antiphonal,adj.)
2. calypso—form of improvised, jazz-like singing of the natives of the British West Indies (calypso,adj.)
3. minstrelsy—singing; singing by a medieval musician who accompanied himself on an instrument
4. psalmody—practice or act of singing psalms or hymns during worship

3. Singer,n. *From Sec. 1:* accompanist, caroler, chanter, crooner, hummer, intoner, serenader, soloist, vocalizer or vocalist, warbler, yodeler or yodler; *From Sec. 2:* calypso singer, minstrel; *Also:*
1. artist, artiste—professional singer
2. buffo—male singer of comic-opera roles
3. cantatrice—woman who sings professionally
4. cantor—leader of a church choir; loosely, any singer, usually in religious ceremonies
5. chanteuse (French)—woman who sings professionally
6. choralist—singer in a chorus
7. chorine—girl who sings in a chorus in a theater, etc. (colloq.)
8. chorister—singer in a choir
9. chorus girl—chorine
10. diva—female operatic star; prima donna
11. prima donna—chief female singer in an opera, concert, etc.
12. songster—one who sings; accomplished singer

4. Song or Part of a Song,n. *From Sec. 1:* carol, chant, croon, serenade, solo, trill, troll, vocal (colloq.), warble, yodel or yodle; *From Sec. 2:* antiphon or antiphony; *Also:*
1. air—aria
2. anthem—patriotic, praising, devotional, glorifying, or sacred song
3. apopemptic—song of farewell
4. aria—song to be sung by a single voice
5. arietta—short aria
6. ballad, ballade—romantic song
7. berceuse (French)—soothing song; lullaby
8. burden—chorus of a song; repeated verse in a song
9. callithump, callithumpian—charivari; farcical serenade
10. canon—song sung by two or more kinds of voices in the same or in a different pitch
11. cantata—dramatic composition for singing, usually to be accompanied by organ, piano, or full orchestra
12. canticle—hymn
13. canzonet—light, graceful, and short song
14. chanson—song
15. chantey, chanty—song sung by sailors at work; song sung by any workers in rhythm with their movements
16. charivari—discordant song to a newly married couple
17. chorale, choral—sacred song; hymn
18. chorus—part of a song that others join in singing with the principal singer
19. dirge—song of grief over someone's death
20. ditty—short and simple song
21. duet, duo—song for two people
22. encore—another song, or a repetition of one previously sung, in response to a demand from the audience
23. epithalamium, epithalamion, epithalamy—song in honor of a newly married couple
24. folk song—simple song handed down from generation to generation, or one that imitates it
25. glee—song for three or more solo voices
26. hymeneal, hymen—marriage or wedding song
27. hymn—song of praise or adoration to a deity
28. lilt—gay and lively song
29. lullaby—song to put someone, often a child, to sleep
30. melody—song; poem that is sung
31. monody—funeral song; song of grief; song in which one voice carries the melody
32. noel—Christmas carol
33. number—song, in theatrical parlance

34. **oratorio**—elaborate dramatic song, often religious in theme, for single voices, chorus, and orchestra
35. **paean, pean**—song of praise, triumph, or happiness
36. **palinode**—song retracting what one has sung in a previous song
37. **prothalamion, prothalamium**—song that celebrates a marriage
38. **psalm**—sacred or religious song (psalmody, collective)
39. **recitative**—passage of music in which the words are rendered more as speech than singing
40. **refrain**—phrase or verse occurring repeatedly in a song; chorus
41. **Requiem, requiem**—song, chant, dirge, or hymn in honor of, or for the repose of the souls of, the dead; song or chant that asks rest or peace for the living
42. **round**—short canon that several voices sing at regular intervals
43. **roundelay**—song in which a phrase or line is constantly repeated
44. **spiritual**—religious folk song originated by the American Negro
45. **strephonade**—love song; sentimental song
46. **threnody, threnode**—song for the dead; song of lamentation
47. **tune**—song
48. **verse, stanza**—separate part or portion of a song
49. **vesper**—hymn

5. Pert. to, Descr. of, or in the Manner of, a Song,adj. *From Sec. 4:* antiphonal; arioso (from *aria*); callithumpian; choral or choric (from *chorus*); epithalamic or epithalamial, hymnal or hymnic, palinodal; psalmic, psalmodic or psalmodial; threnodial, threnodian, threnodic, or threnodical; stanzaic or stanzaical

6. Writer of a Song,n. *From Sec. 4:* ballader, epithalamiast, hymnist, palinodist, psalmist or psalmodist, threnodist

7. To Write a Song in Honor of a Newly Married Couple: epithalamize,v.

8. The Writing of Sacred or Religious Songs: psalmography,n.

9. Collection of Songs or of Folk Songs: minstrelsy,n.

10. Book of Antiphons: antiphonal, antiphonary,n.

11. Art or Technique of Singing: vocalism,n.

12. Art of a Minstrel: minstrelsy,n.

13. Pert. to, Suitable for, or Adapted to, Singing: cantabile, lyric, melic, vocal,adj.

14. Adapted for Singing by a Chorus or Choir: choral,adj.

15. Intended for Singing: vocal,adj.

16. Songlike: cantabile,adj.

17. Sung: vocal,adj.

18. Sung by a Chorus or Choir: choral,adj.

19. Singing Group,n.
1. **choir**—group of singers at a church service or generally functioning at church services (choral,adj.)
2. **chorus**—organized group of singers, or of singers and dancers (choral, choric,adj.)
3. **duo, duet**—group of two singers
4. **ensemble**—small group of singers
5. **glee club**—club or company for singing glees; today, generally, any chorus or company for singing ballads, roundelays, or other songs, esp. in a school or college
6. **octet, octette**—group of eight singers
7. **quartet, quartette**—group of four singers
8. **quintet, quintette**—group of five singers
9. **septet, septette, septuor**—group of seven singers
10. **sextet, sextette, sestet**—group of six singers
11. **trio**—group of three singers

20. Leader of a Singing Group,n.
1. **choragus**—leader of a singing group in ancient Greece (choragic,adj.)
2. **chorister**—leader of a choir
3. **coryphaeus**—leader of a choir or chorus; leader of the chorus in a Greek drama of ancient times
4. **precentor**—one who directs the singing of a congregation or choir (precent,v. precentorial,adj. precentorship,n.)

21. Singing Voice,n.
1. **alto**—female voice of lowest range
2. **baritone**—male singing voice between bass and tenor
3. **bass**—lowest male voice
4. **basso profundo**—unusually deep and heavy, low male voice
5. **coloratura**—high, clear soprano
6. **coloratura soprano**—soprano voice singing, or capable of singing, vocal music highly ornamented with trills and runs
7. **contrabass**—voice lower in range than normal bass
8. **contralto**—lowest female voice
9. **countertenor**—male alto
10. **falsetto**—voice singing high-pitched notes above the natural range; unnaturally high-pitched male voice
11. **mezzo-soprano**—female voice between soprano and contralto
12. **soprano**—highest singing voice, usually in women or young boys
13. **tenor**—highest male voice (except falsetto)

22. Possessor of a Singing Voice,n. *From Sec. 21:* alto, baritone, bass or basso, basso profundo, coloratura, coloratura soprano, contrabass, contralto, falsetto, mezzo-soprano, soprano, tenor

23. Descr. of a Singing Voice,adj. *From Sec. 21:* alto, baritone, bass, contralto, falsetto, soprano, tenor

477. HYMN

1. Pert. to, or Descr. of, Hymns: hymnal, hymnic,adj.

2. Using Hymns: hymnal,adj.

3. Resembling a Hymn: hymnic,adj.

4. A Composition That Resembles a Hymn: hymnic,n.

5. A Book of Hymns: hymnal, hymnbook,n.

6. The Writing of Hymns: hymnography, hymnody, hymnology,n. (hymnographer, hymnodist, hymnologist,n. hymnodical, hymnologic, hymnological,adj.)

7. Writing about Hymns: hymnography,n. (hymnographer,n.)

8. The Science or Study of Hymns: hymnology,n. (hymnologist,n. hymnologic, hymnological, adj.)

9. To Praise, Worship, or Celebrate in Hymns, or by Singing Hymns: hymn,v. (hymner,n.)

10. The Singing of, or Art of Singing, Hymns: hymnody,n. (hymnodist,n. hymnodical,adj.)

11. A Compiler of Hymns: hymnologist,n.

12. Hymns Collectively: hymnody, hymnology,n.

13. Tune of, or for, a Hymn: choral, chorale,n.

14. Composer of Hymn Tunes: choralist,n.

478. MELODY

1. Melody,n.
1. air—melody
2. aria—melody (arioso,adj.)
3. arietta—short melody
4. cadenza—flourish
5. cavatina—simple melody
6. counterpoint—melody that combines with another melody; plural melody (contrapuntal,adj.)
7. descant—subordinate melody
8. flourish—ostentatious musical passage
9. lilt—gay and lively melody
10. strain—melody; passage or sounds of music
11. theme—principal melody in a musical composition (thematic,adj.)
12. triad—musical chord of three tones
13. tune—melody

2. Pert. or Relating to Melody: melodic,adj.

3. Containing or Characterized by, Melody: melodic, melodious, tuneful,adj. (melodiousness, tunefulness,n.)

4. Theory of Melody: melodics,n.

5. Art of Adding a Related but Independent Melody or Melodies to a Basic Melody: counterpoint,n. (contrapuntist,n.)

6. Composer of Melodies; Singer of Melodies: melodist,n.

7. To Compose Melodies; To Set to Melody: melodize,v.

479. MUSIC

1. Music; Form of Music; Selected Musical Compositions; Division of Music,n.
1. accompaniment—instrumental accompanying part of music that gives the main part a richer effect
2. aubade (French)—musical composition to be performed in the morning; music suggestive of morning
3. berceuse (French)—soothing musical composition
4. cavatina—simple musical composition
5. concerto—long musical composition (usually in symphonic form) for a principal instrument or instruments to be accompanied by an orchestra (concertos, concerti,pl.)
6. dirge—mourning music; music to express sorrow over someone's death, often played at a funeral, etc.
7. fugue—polyphonic musical composition of one or more themes (fugue,v. fuguist, n.)
8. impromptu, improvisation—extemporaneous or improvised musical piece; a piece composed in this style
9. intermezzo—short musical composition between larger parts of a work (intermezzi, intermezzos,pl.)
10. movement—main division of a symphony or other long composition
11. obbligato, obligato—accompaniment of special character and importance (obbligato, obligato,adj.)
12. oratorio—long dramatic musical composition (usually of religious nature) performed without scenery, costumes, etc.
13. overture—opening or introductory music to an opera, musical play, etc.
14. piece—musical composition, generally short
15. postlude—concluding musical composition; concluding movement; organ voluntary at the end of a church service
16. prelude—short, somewhat improvised, musical composition; movement or short composition preceding a more important

movement; overture to an opera; opening music at a church service
17. Requiem, requiem—musical church service for the dead
18. rhapsody—musical composition of irregular form
19. serenade—piece of music to a woman by her lover (serenader,n. serenade,v.)
20. sonata—long instrumental musical composition, usually of three or four movements, with contrasting moods and related tonalities
21. sonatina—short or simple sonata
22. symphony—long instrumental composition for full orchestra, usually in three or four movements (symphonist,n. symphonic,adj.)
23. theme—principal subject in a musical composition (thematic,adj.)
24. toccata—free and lively virtuosic composition for the piano, organ, or other keyboard instrument in the form of an improvisation
25. tone poem, symphonic poem—elaborate composition for full orchestra, usually in one movement
26. voluntary—improvised or spontaneous musical composition; piece of organ music played in church

2. Musical Composition as to Number of Instruments, Players, or Singers,n.
1. duet, duo—musical composition for two players, instruments, or voices
2. octet, octette—musical composition for eight players, instruments, or voices
3. quartet, quartette—musical composition for four players, instruments, or voices
4. quintet, quintette—musical composition for five players, instruments, or voices
5. septet, septette, septuor—musical composition for seven players, instruments, or voices
6. sextet, sextette, sestet—musical composition for six players, instruments, or voices
7. solo—musical composition for one instrument, player, or voice
8. trio—musical composition for three players, instruments, or voices

3. To Play a Musical Instrument (General),v.
1. accompany—play music with (some featured soloist)
2. bow—play (a stringed instrument) with a bow
3. perform—play a musical instrument, usually in public
4. saw—bow
5. strum—play (a stringed instrument) idly, unskillfully, noisily, or aimlessly
6. thrum—play (a stringed instrument) by plucking the strings
7. trill—play (a musical instrument) in quavering sounds

4. The Playing of an Instrument,n. *From Sec. 3:* accompaniment, performance, strum, thrum, trill; *Also:*
1. aubade—morning musical concert
2. concert—musical performance
3. debut—one's first performance of music in public
4. ensemble—performance by all the instruments of an orchestra or by all the singers of a chorus
5. obbligato, obligato—musical accompaniment, often played by a single instrument
6. recital—musical performance, usually by one person (often with an accompanist)
7. solo—musical performance by one person

5. Player of a Musical Instrument,n. *From Sec. 3:* accompanist, performer, strummer, thrummer; *From Sec. 4:* recitalist, soloist; *Also:*

1. **artist, artiste**—professional, and usually skilled, musician
2. **harmonist**—musician
3. **instrumentalist**—one who performs on a musical instrument
4. **musician**—one who plays a musical instrument, usually professionally
5. **symphonist**—one who plays a musical instrument in a symphony orchestra
6. **virtuoso**—extremely gifted musician (virtuosos, virtuosi,pl.)

6. To Give, Perform in, or Manage Concerts or Recitals: concertize,v. (concertizer, n.)

7. Skill in Music: musicianship, virtuosity, n.

8. Selected Musical Instruments,n.
1. **alto**—viola
2. **barrel organ**—mechanical musical instrument played by turning a crank
3. **bass drum**—largest member of the drum family
4. **bass viol**—deep-toned, large, violin-like instrument; viola da gamba
5. **celesta**—keyboard instrument like a piano, the hammers striking steel plates
6. **cello**—violoncello
7. **cithara**—ancient Greek instrument similar to a lyre, and with a wooden case
8. **clavichord**—stringed instrument, with keyboard, from which the piano developed
9. **clavier**—stringed instrument with a keyboard
10. **concertina**—small accordion-like musical instrument
11. **contrabass**—largest instrument of the viol type
12. **fiddle**—violin (colloq.)
13. **glockenspiel**—a kind of xylophone-like instrument
14. **hand organ**—large music box, played by turning a crank; barrel organ; hurdy-gurdy
15. **harpsichord**—keyboard instrument in which the strings are plucked, and, like the clavichord, one of the forerunners of the piano
16. **hurdy-gurdy**—street organ, played by turning a crank
17. **lyre**—stringed instrument, similar to a harp, used by the ancient Greeks
18. **lyrichord**—a kind of harpsichord
19. **marimba**—a kind of xylophone-like instrument
20. **orchestrina, orchestrion**—large mechanical music box that gives the effect of an orchestra
21. **pianoforte**—former name for the piano, so called from its ability to play both soft (piano) and loud (forte)
22. **recorder**—early form of the flute, once again popular
23. **reed**—rustic musical instrument; wind instrument with a narrowed opening in the mouthpiece
24. **sousaphone**—brass wind instrument similar to a tuba
25. **Stradivarius**—violin made by Antonio Stradivari of Italy; loosely, a violin
26. **tabor**—small, one-headed drum
27. **taboret, taborine, tabret**—small tabor
28. **tambour**—drum
29. **tambourine**—small drum; small hand drum with one head, containing jingling disks on the sides
30. **timpani, tympani**—set of kettledrums
31. **tom-tom, tam-tam**—native drum, usually of primitive or savage peoples
32. **tympan**—kettledrum (tympani,pl. tympanic,adj.)
33. **vibraphone**—a sort of marimba with electrically operated valves
34. **viol**—any stringed instrument resembling

the violin; a kind of medieval instrument of this type
35. **viola**—instrument resembling a violin, but considerably larger; tenor or alto violin
36. **viola da gamba**—forerunner of the violoncello
37. **violoncello**—bass instrument resembling a violin
38. **violone**—contrabass

9. Player of a Specific Musical Instrument, n. *From Sec. 8:* cellist, citharist, clavichordist, clavierist, concertinist, contrabassist, fiddler; organ grinder (from *hand organ*); harpsichordist, hurdy-gurdist, hurdy-gurdyist or hurdy-gurdy man, lyrist, taborer, tambour, tambourine, timpanist or tympanist, violist, violoncellist; *Also:*
1. **accordionist**—accordion player
2. **banjoist**—banjo player
3. **bassoonist**—bassoon player
4. **bugler**—bugle player
5. **clarinetist, clarinettist**—clarinet player
6. **cornetist, cornettist**—cornet player
7. **cymbalist, cymbaler, cymbaleer**—player of cymbals
8. **drummer**—drum player
9. **fifer**—fife player
10. **flautist, flutist**—flute player
11. **guitarist**—guitar player
12. **harpist, harper**—harp player
13. **hornist**—horn player
14. **kettledrummer**—kettledrum player
15. **lutanist, lutist, luter**—lute player
16. **mandolinist**—mandolin player
17. **oboist**—oboe player
18. **organist, organer**—organ player
19. **pianist**—piano player, esp. one of skill
20. **piccoloist**—piccolo player
21. **piper**—bagpipe player; player on any pipe
22. **saxophonist**—saxophone player
23. **trombonist**—trombone player
24. **trumpeter**—trumpet player
25. **violinist**—violin player
26. **xylophonist**—xylophone player
27. **zitherist**—zither player

10. To Play a Specific Instrument,v. *From Sec. 8:* fiddle, lyre, tom-tom; *From Sec. 9:* bugle, drum, fife, flute, pipe, trumpet

11. Musical Instruments as to Group,n.
1. **brass, brasses, brass winds**—instruments containing coiled metal tubes and played by blowing into a mouthpiece (brass wind, adj.)
2. **percussion instruments**—instruments played by beating or striking, as drums, xylophones, pianos, etc.
3. **reeds**—wind instruments with cane, bamboo, etc., reeds on the mouthpieces
4. **strings**—stringed instruments, esp. those played with a bow
5. **winds**—instruments played by blowing air into a mouthpiece (wind,adj.)
6. **wood winds**—wind instruments that are, or originally were, made of wood, esp. today the bassoon, clarinet, English horn, flute, and oboe

12. Keyboard of an Organ or Piano; Dummy Keyboard for Practice: clavier,n.

13. Maker of Lutes: lutist,n.

14. Small Piece of Ivory, Metal, etc., Used to Pluck the Strings of Musical Instruments Such as the Zither, Mandolin, etc.: plectrum,n.

15. Pert. to a Lyre or Harp: lyric,adj.

16. Shaped Like a Lyre: lyriform,adj.

17. Group of Musicians,n.
1. **band**—group of musicians playing together, esp. on percussion and wind instruments

2. **duet, duo**—group of two musicians
3. **ensemble**—small group of musicians
4. **octet, octette**—group of eight musicians
5. **orchestra**—group or company of musicians (orchestral,adj.)
6. **quartet, quartette**—group of four musicians
7. **quintet, quintette**—group of five musicians
8. **septet, septette, septuor**—group of seven musicians
9. **sextet, sextette, sestet**—group of six musicians
10. **strings**—group in an orchestra that plays the stringed instruments
11. **trio**—group of three musicians

18. Florid Style of Music: bravura,n.

19. Arrangement or Composition of Music, n.
1. **instrumentation**—arrangement or composition of music for instruments; orchestration
2. **orchestration**—arrangement or composition of music for playing by an orchestra (orchestrate,v.)

20. District Where Musicians, Singers, Song Composers, etc., Congregate or Work: tinpan alley,n.

21. Admirer of, or Anyone Connected with the Performance of, the Works of Gilbert and Sullivan: Savoyard,n. (Savoyard,adj.)

22. Music As a Science or Field of Investigation, Rather than As a Performing Art: musicology,n. (musicologist,n. musicological, adj.)

23. To Write Music: compose,v. (composer,n. composition,n.)

480. VISION

1. To See,v.
1. **behold**—see
2. **descry**—catch sight of (something that is some distance away and has either just come into view or is difficult to see clearly)
3. **discern, decern**—see; see clearly; see (something that stands out clearly from the background)
4. **discover**—see (something not previously seen)
5. **espy**—catch sight of
6. **glimpse**—see for just a moment
7. **note**—see
8. **notice**—see
9. **observe**—see
10. **penetrate**—see into
11. **perceive**—see
12. **pierce**—see through, literally or figuratively
13. **preview, prevue**—see before the general public does
14. **remark**—see
15. **sight**—see
16. **spy**—catch sight of
17. **view**—see
18. **witness**—see (something happen)

2. Seeing,n. *From Sec. 1:* descrial, discernment, decernment, discovery, espial, glimpse, notice, observation, penetration, perception, preview, prevue, view

3. One Who Sees,n. *From Sec. 1:* beholder, discoverer, observer, perceiver, viewer, witness; *Also:*
1. **eyewitness**—one who sees an occurrence with his own eyes
2. **visionary**—one who sees visions

4. Sense of Seeing: sight, vision,n.

5. Power of Seeing: view, vision,n.

6. Pert. or Relating to Sight or Vision: ocular, optic, optical, visional, visual,adj.

7. Obtained through Sight: ocular,adj.

8. Pert. or Appealing to Both Sight and Hearing: audiovisual,adj.

9. Sensation of Seeing Something after It Has Disappeared or Passed: afterimage,n.

10. Capable of Seeing,adj.
1. **binocular**—having good vision in both eyes (binocularity,n.)
2. **clairvoyant**—able to see things ordinarily not visible to normal senses (clairvoyance,n. clairvoyant,n.)
3. **farseeing**—able to see a great distance
4. **farsighted**—able to see distant objects more clearly than those nearby; farseeing (farsightedness,n.)
5. **lynx-eyed, lyncean**—possessing sharp vision, like that of a lynx
6. **observant**—quick or skillful in seeing or noticing (observation, observance,n.)
7. **perceptive**—capable of, or quick or skillful in, perceiving through the eyes (perception, perceptiveness, perceptivity,n.)
8. **percipient**—capable of perceiving quickly and actively through the eyes (percipience,n.)
9. **periscopic**—able to see on all sides or all around
10. **photopic**—able to see in bright light, artificial or natural (photopia,n.)
11. **sharp-sighted**—having keen eyesight (sharp-sightedness,n.)
12. **sighted**—able to see, i.e., not blind
13. **stereoptic**—possessing vision in depth; able to see in three dimensions (stereopsis,n.)
14. **stereoscopic**—capable of seeing in depth (stereoscopy,n.)
15. **telescopic**—able to see things at a great distance

11. View,n.
1. **aspect**—view
2. **bird's-eye view**—view from a considerable distance above
3. **diorama**—view through, or as if through, a small opening, of something in, or seemingly in, miniature (dioramic,adj.)
4. **glimpse**—quick view
5. **ken**—range of sight
6. **outlook**—view from a place
7. **panorama**—wide and unobstructed view of the surroundings (panoramic,adj.)
8. **prospect**—broad view; outlook
9. **retrospect**—view of past things, experiences, etc.
10. **vista**—view; long view through a narrow passage; mental view extending over a whole series of events

12. Point of View, Literal or Figurative,n.
1. **angle**—point of view, literal or figurative
2. **aspect**—point of view, literal or figurative
3. **facet**—figurative point of view, as of a question, subject, topic, etc.
4. **outlook**—point of view, literal or figurative
5. **perspective**—point of view toward events of the past or future; point of view of things or events in proper or logical relationship
6. **retrospect**—point of view on the past
7. **standpoint**—point of view, literal or figurative
8. **viewpoint**—point of view, literal or figurative

13. Place for Seeing,n.
1. **conning tower**—observation tower on a submarine
2. **crow's-nest**—high position used for observation
3. **observatory**—place where observations of natural or celestial phenomena may be

made; place from which a wide view of the surroundings can be had
4. **outlook**—place from which to get a view

14. Offering a View,adj.
1. **dioramic**—offering a view through, or as if through, a small opening
2. **panoramic**—offering a wide and unobstructed view of the surroundings
3. **pantoscopic**—offering, or having, a wide and unobstructed view

15. Science of Vision,n.
1. **ophthalmology**—medical science of vision, the eyes, etc. (ophthalmologist,n. ophthalmological,adj.)
2. **optics**—science of vision and light (optical,adj.)
3. **optometry**—science dealing with measurement of vision (optometrist,n. optometric,adj.)
4. **stereoscopy**—science dealing with vision in depth (stereoscopic,adj.)

16. Eyeglasses,n.
1. **bifocals**—eyeglasses containing lenses of two parts or kinds—one for close vision, the other for distant vision
2. **cheaters**—eyeglasses (colloq.)
3. **eyeglass**—monocle
4. **glasses**—eyeglasses
5. **goggles**—large eyeglasses; large eyeglasses with side guards to protect against wind, dust, etc.
6. **lens**—piece of glass or other transparent substance made so as to correct specific visual defects
7. **lorgnette**—eyeglasses on a long handle
8. **lorgnon (French)**—pince-nez
9. **monocle**—glass for one eye
10. **pince-nez**—eyeglasses that clip onto the nose
11. **spectacles**—eyeglasses
12. **trifocals**—eyeglasses that contain three types of lenses—for near, intermediate, and far vision
13. **winkers**—eyeglasses

17. Other Instrument or Device to Aid Vision,n.
1. **binoculars**—portable telescope for two eyes
2. **field glass**—portable telescope
3. **field glasses**—portable telescope for two eyes
4. **hydroscope**—device for viewing below the surface of water (hydroscopic,adj.)
5. **periscope**—instrument enabling an observer in a submarine or trench to view the surface (periscopic,adj.)
6. **spyglass**—small telescope
7. **stereoscope, stereopticon**—instrument that, by fusing two images, permits the viewer to see pictures in, or with the illusion of, depth (stereoscopic,adj.)
8. **tachistoscope**—instrument used to speed up visual perception (tachistoscopic,adj.)
9. **telescope**—instrument for seeing things at a great distance (telescopic,adj.)

18. Instrument to Measure Vision: optometer,n.

19. Instrument to Measure Refraction of the Eye: dioptometer,n.

20. One Who Manufactures or Sells Optical Goods, Grinds Lenses, etc.: optician,n.

481. VISUAL DEFECTS

1. Selected Visual Defects,n.
1. **ablepsia**—lack of sight; blindness
2. **amaurosis**—loss of sight without structural or organic change
3. **amblyopia**—beginning of fading eyesight; dimness of vision
4. **aniseikonia**—visual defect in which each eye gets a somewhat different image

5. **anopsia**—blindness
6. **astigmatism**—indistinctness or inaccuracy of vision occurring from specific irregularities in the curvature of one or more of the refractive surfaces of the eye
7. **blindness**—inability to see
8. **cross-eye**—converging strabismus
9. **Daltonism**—inability to distinguish red and green—a congenital defect
10. **darkness**—blindness
11. **dichromatism**—ability to see only two basic colors
12. **diplopia**—double vision, i.e., seeing something in a double image
13. **esophoria**—tendency of the visual axes of the eyes to deviate inward from parallelism when the eyes are at rest
14. **exophoria**—condition like esophoria, except that the deviation is outward
15. **farsightedness**—ability to see objects at a distance more clearly than those closer to one's eyes
16. **hemeralopia**—visual defect by which one can see, see clearly, or see without pain, only in faint light or at night
17. **heterophoria**—tendency of the eyes to deviate from the position that is correct for binocular vision
18. **hypermetropia**—farsightedness
19. **hyperopia**—farsightedness
20. **hyperphoria**—condition in which the visual axis of one eye tends to deviate above that of the other
21. **hypophoria**—condition in which the visual axis of one eye tends to deviate below that of the other
22. **macropsia, macropsy**—abnormality of vision in which objects seem larger than in reality
23. **megalopia, megalopsia**—macropsia
24. **micropsia**—abnormality of vision in which objects seem smaller than in reality
25. **myopia**—nearsightedness
26. **nearsightedness**—ability to see clearly only at close distances
27. **nyctalopia**—visual condition that permits clear sight only in daylight or strong artificial light
28. **presbyopia**—defect of vision, usually occurring in old age, in which objects near at hand cannot be clearly seen
29. **purblindness**—partial blindness
30. **shortsightedness**—nearsightedness
31. **strabismus**—defect of vision in which the two eyes are not simultaneously focused on the same point (There are two forms—cross-eye, in which the eyes converge; wall-eye, in which they diverge.)
32. **typhlosis**—blindness
33. **wall-eye**—divergent strabismus

2. Having, or Descr. of, a Visual Defect,adj. *From Sec. 1:* ableptical, amaurotic, amblyopic, aniseikonic, astigmatic or astigmic, blind, cross-eyed, diplopic, esophoric, exophoric, farsighted, hemeralopic, hypermetropic, hyperopic, hyperphoric, myopic, nearsighted, nyctalopic, presbyopic, purblind, shortsighted, strabismic, typhlotic, wall-eyed; *Also:*
1. **sand-blind**—weak-sighted; nearly blind
2. **sightless**—blind
3. **stone-blind**—totally blind
4. **unsighted**—blind

3. One Who Has a Visual Defect,n. *From Sec. 1:* amblyope, hemeralope, myope, nyctalope

4. Science of Blindness: typhlology,n.

5. To Blind: darken, seel,v.

6. To Make Nearly or Partly Blind: purblind,v.

7. To Become Blind: darken,v.

8. To Shut the Eyes of: seel,v.

9. Lacking in Figurative Vision,adj.
1. **blind**—lacking in figurative vision (blindness,n.)
2. **dark**—spiritually or morally blind
3. **imperceptive**—not skillful in seeing, esp. in seeing what lies beneath the surface, figuratively speaking (imperceptiveness, imperceptivity,n.)
4. **impercipient**—imperceptive (impercipience,n. impercipient,n.)
5. **myopic**—able to see, figuratively, only that which is close by, with no vision or understanding of less conspicuous things; shortsighted (myopia,n.)
6. **nearsighted**—shortsighted (nearsightedness,n.)
7. **purblind**—lacking in figurative vision (purblindness,n. purblind,v.)
8. **shortsighted**—lacking in figurative vision; lacking foresight (shortsightedness,n.)
9. **undiscerning**—imperceptive

482. MENTAL IMAGE

1. Mental Images, Collectively: imagery,n.

2. To Form a Mental Image or Images: envisage, envision, image, imagine, picture, vision, visualize,v.

3. Formation of Mental Images: envisagement, imagination, visualization,n.

4. Power of Forming Mental Images: imagination, phantasy, vision,n.

5. To Form a Mental Image of Beforehand: anticipate, foresee,v.

6. Formation of Mental Images Beforehand: anticipation, foresight, prevision, providence,n.

7. Power of Forming Mental Images Beforehand: foresight,n.

8. Pert. to Mental Images: visual,adj.

9. Science of Mental Imagery: eidology,n.

10. One Who Has Unusually Vivid and Often Persistent Mental Images: eidetic,n.

483. VISIBILITY

1. Visible,adj.
1. **apparent**—plain or easy to see (apparency, apparentness,n.)
2. **clear**—easy to see (clearness, clarity,n.)
3. **clinical**—visible as a symptom
4. **conspicuous**—easy to see (conspicuousness, conspicuity,n.)
5. **discernible**—perceptible (discernibleness, n.)
6. **discoverable**—perceptible (discoverability,n.)
7. **distinct**—clearly visible (distinctness,n.)
8. **eidetic**—clearly perceptible (psychology)
9. **evident**—easily seen; clear to the eye; easy to see (evidence,n.)
10. **limpid**—clear to the sight (limpidness, limpidity,n.)
11. **macroscopic**—capable of being seen by the naked eye
12. **manifest**—plain to the sight (manifestness,n.)
13. **marked**—very noticeable (markedness,n.)
14. **noticeable**—capable of being seen (noticeability,n.)
15. **observable**—capable of being seen or noticed (observability,n.)
16. **obvious**—inescapable to the sight (obviousness,n.)
17. **pellucid**—limpid, esp. of water (pellucidness, pellucidity,n.)
18. **perceptible, perceivable**—able to be caught by the sense of sight (percepti-

bility, perceptibleness, perceivability, perceivableness,n.)
19. **plain**—easy to see (plainness,n.)
20. **pointed**—noticeable (pointedness,n.)
21. **predominant**—most noticeable (predominance,n.)
22. **prominent**—easy to see (prominence,n.)
23. **pronounced**—extremely conspicuous
24. **salient**—noticeable (salience,n.)
25. **striking**—noticeable
26. **transparent**—obvious—of abstractions, subterfuges, etc. (transparence, transparency, transparentness,n.)
27. **visual**—visible
28. **vivid**—clearly perceptible (vividness,n.)

2. To Make Visible: visualize,v. (visualization,n.)

3. To Be Visible or Seen; To Appear,v.
1. **crop up, crop out**—appear suddenly or unexpectedly; come into view
2. **darkle**—loom in the dark
3. **dawn**—appear
4. **emerge**—come from obscurity into full view
5. **loom**—appear indistinctly and, often, at a distance; appear in distorted or menacing shape, literally or figuratively
6. **materialize**—appear in bodily form
7. **occur**—appear
8. **reappear**—appear again
9. **recur**—appear again; appear repeatedly
10. **twinkle**—appear and vanish in a rapid motion
11. **visualize**—become visible

4. Appearance, i.e., Act of Appearing,n. *From Sec. 3:* dawn, emergence, materialization, occurrence, reappearance, recurrence, twinkle, visualization; *Also:*
1. **apparition**—appearance; sudden and unexpected appearance
2. **encore**—repetition of an appearance of a public entertainer in response to audience demand

5. Appearing,adj. *From Sec. 3:* emergent, occurrent, recurrent

6. Appearing at a Given Time or Period: chronogeneous,adj.

7. At First View; On First Appearance: prima facie,adj.

8. That Which Is Seen,n.
1. **afterimage**—image that persists in the mind for a time even though the actual thing, object, etc., is no longer in view
2. **apparition**—appearance; unreal or ghostly appearance; sudden and unexpected appearance (apparitional,adj.)
3. **appearance**—anything seen; something seen that is unreal, ghostly, or unexpected
4. **bird's-eye view**—that which is seen from a considerable distance above
5. **concept**—image formed by mental activity (conceptual,adj.)
6. **diorama**—miniature scene in three dimensions (dioramic,adj.)
7. **eidolon**—insubstantial image; phantom
8. **hallucination**—false or deceptive sight (hallucinatory,adj.)
9. **illusion**—false and misleading image or sight (illusional, illusionary,adj.)
10. **image**—visual impression of something seen through a mirror, lens, etc.; visual impression
11. **mirage**—optical phenomenon or illusion resulting from the reflection of light rays, so that one seems to see what is not really there; something falsely seen though actually nonexistent in the place where it is observed
12. **outlook**—that which one sees on looking out or ahead, literally or figuratively
13. **perspective**—things as they appear to the sight

14. **phantasm**—deceptive or delusional sight (phantasmal, phantasmic,adj.)
15. **phantasmagoria, phantasmagory**—thing or things, either real or imagined, seen as if on a screen, and suddenly and violently increasing or decreasing in size (phantasmagorial, phantasmagoric, phantasmagorical,adj.)
16. **phantasy**—image
17. **phantom**—ghostly appearance; vague or shadowy appearance; mental image (phantom,adj.)
18. **photogene**—afterimage
19. **prospect**—that which is seen when one looks around
20. **reflection**—that which is seen through a mirror, etc. (reflectional,adj.)
21. **scene**—that which is seen; spectacle
22. **scintilla**—something barely perceptible
23. **sight**—that which is seen; unusual or spectacular thing or person seen
24. **spectacle**—something to look at or worth seeing
25. **tableau**—striking scene
26. **view**—that which is seen; mental image
27. **vision**—something seen; something seen in the mind or imagination; sight; beautiful sight (visional,adj.)

9. A Mirror,n.
1. **looking glass**—mirror
2. **reflector**—that which acts as a mirror, i.e., reflects an image
3. **speculum**—metal mirror

10. Transparent,adj.
1. **crystalline**—transparent and clear
2. **gauzy**—transparent and thin (gauziness, n.)
3. **hyaloid**—transparent (of an anatomical structure or of body tissue)
4. **limpid**—clear and transparent, often of water, air, etc. (limpidness, limpidity,n.)
5. **lucid**—transparent (lucidness, lucidity, n.)
6. **luculent**—transparent
7. **pellucid**—transparent (pellucidness, pellucidity,n.)
8. **sheer**—transparent, or almost transparent, owing to thinness (sheerness,n.)
9. **transpicuous**—transparent (transpicuity, n.)

11. Not Transparent: opaque,adj. (opaqueness, opacity,n.)

12. Hard or Impossible to See,adj.
1. **faint**—hard to see (faintness,n.)
2. **imperceptible**—not able to be perceived by the eye (imperceptibility,n.)
3. **inconspicuous**—not easy to see; not striking to the eye (inconspicuousness, inconspicuity,n.)
4. **indistinct**—not clear to the sight (indistinctness,n.)
5. **indistinguishable**—not easy to see (indistinguishability,n.)
6. **invisible**—impossible to see (invisibility, n.)
7. **microscopic**—so small as to be visible only through a microscope
8. **obliterated**—imperceptible because erased or blotted out
9. **perdu**—lost to view
10. **subclinical**—not visible as a symptom
11. **submicroscopic**—so small as to be invisible, even under a microscope
12. **tenuous**—scarcely visible (tenuousness, tenuity,n.)
13. **ulterior**—beyond that which can be directly seen
14. **undiscernible**—imperceptible
15. **unevident**—not clear to the sight
16. **unnoticeable**—inconspicuous
17. **unobvious**—not immediately striking to the sight
18. **unperceivable**—imperceptible
19. **unpronounced**—inconspicuous

484. LOOK

1. To Look; To Look at,v.
1. **admire**—look at with wonder, appreciation, delight, pleasure, or approval
2. **behold**—look at
3. **blink**—look while winking
4. **contemplate**—look at for a long time; gaze at
5. **examine**—look at closely and critically for purposes of gaining information, etc.
6. **eye**—look at; look at narrowly, fixedly, or carefully
7. **gape**—stare in openmouthed wonder or surprise
8. **gawk**—stare stupidly (colloq.)
9. **gaze**—look fixedly, steadily, or attentively
10. **glare**—stare with anger, fierceness, hostility, etc.
11. **gloat (over)**—stare (at) in great satisfaction
12. **glower**—stare in anger
13. **goggle**—stare while rolling the eyes in surprise or admiration
14. **inspect**—look at
15. **leer**—look lustfully, one's expression intimating indecent proposals
16. **lower**—give a sullen and angry look
17. **moon**—gaze listlessly
18. **muse on or upon**—gaze thoughtfully or wonderingly at
19. **note**—observe
20. **notice**—observe; regard
21. **observe**—look, or look at, carefully
22. **ogle**—look at with desirous eyes; stare at amorously or flirtatiously; look at in such a way as to invite amorous advances
23. **overlook**—look at from above
24. **oversee**—survey; watch
25. **peek**—look slyly or quickly; peep; spy
26. **peep**—look secretly or cautiously
27. **peer**—look closely in order to see better
28. **pore over**—look or gaze at long and steadily, studying and pondering
29. **pry**—look where one has no business or right; look inquisitively; peep
30. **regard**—look at or upon, often closely
31. **remark**—observe
32. **retrospect**—look back mentally
33. **review**—look at again
34. **scan**—look at carefully or closely; contrarily, look over quickly and carelessly
35. **scout**—observe (a region) to gain information
36. **scowl**—look with a threatening expression
37. **sight**—look at
38. **skew**—squint
39. **snoop**—try to look secretly at that which one is not supposed to see
40. **spy (upon)**—look (at) secretly
41. **squint**—look with the eyes partly closed; look sideways; look indirectly; look crosseyed; partly close the eyes in looking, as in a strong light; look with envy; distrust, or similar emotion
42. **stare**—look directly and fixedly for some time
43. **supervise**—watch and manage (work, functions, operations, etc.)
44. **survey**—look over or around; look at in detail; look at the whole of
45. **trace**—observe
46. **view**—look at
47. **watch**—look, or look at, with care, attention, expectation, etc.
48. **yawp**—gape

2. A Looking; A Look,n. *From Sec. 1:* admiration, blink, contemplation, examination, gape, gaze, glare, gloat, glower, goggle, inspection, leer, note, notice, observation, ogle, peek, peep, pry, regard, retrospect or retrospection, review, scan or scansion, scowl, snoop, squint, stare, supervision, survey, view, watch, yawp; *Also:*

1. **auspice**—observation of signs or omens
2. **retroversion**—a looking back
3. **surveillance**—close watch kept over a person, often one suspected of crimes or criminal intent
4. **vigil**—alert watching

3. Looker,n. *From Sec. 1:* admirer, beholder, contemplator, examiner, eyer, gaper, gazer, gloater, inspector, muser, observer, ogler, overseer, peeker, peeper, pry, reviewer, scout, scowler, snoop or snooper, spy, supervisor, surveyor, viewer, watcher; *Also:*
1. **bystander**—onlooker
2. **looker-on**—one who watches; spectator
3. **onlooker**—one who looks on; observer
4. **Peeping Tom, voyeur**—one who peeps secretly at women undressing, sexual encounters, etc. (voyeurism,n.)
5. **spectator**—one who looks or watches but does not take part

4. Descr. of Looking,adj. *From Sec. 1:* contemplative, inspective or inspectional, moony, observant, retrospective, scansive, snoopy, squinty or squint-eyed, supervisory, watchful; *Also:*
1. **beetle-browed**—scowling
2. **openmouthed**—gaping in surprise
3. **vigilant**—watchful; wide-awake and watchful
4. **wall-eyed**—staring blankly; having a blank stare

5. Spectators of a Tennis Match: dedans (French),n.

6. Spying,n.
1. **counterintelligence**—system of spying designed to block the enemy's sources of information
2. **espial**—act or incident of spying
3. **espionage**—act or practice of spying

7. Use of Spies: espionage,n.

8. Sexual Pleasure Derived from Looking at the Sex Organs of Others, or One's Own Sex Organs, or from Having One's Sex Organs Looked At by Another: scopophilia, scoptophilia,n.

485. EXAMINATION

1. To Examine,v.
1. **analyze**—examine the parts of carefully and critically; examine carefully and in detail
2. **assay**—examine
3. **audit**—examine officially and check the accounts of (a business, etc.)
4. **canvass**—examine; examine carefully; examine to determine the opinion or sentiment of
5. **check**—examine; examine closely
6. **extrospect**—examine that which is outside oneself
7. **inspect**—examine closely
8. **introspect**—examine one's own thoughts, feelings, motions, attitudes, etc.
9. **observe**—examine at length
10. **overhaul**—examine carefully for needed repairs
11. **overlook**—inspect
12. **palpate**—examine by touching
13. **prospect**—examine to find something
14. **reconnoiter**—make a preliminary examination to gain information, often for military purposes
15. **review**—examine again
16. **scrutinize, scrutinate**—examine with close attention to details
17. **search**—examine carefully to find something, or something hidden
18. **sift**—examine closely
19. **spy**—examine closely or carefully
20. **study**—examine carefully

21. **survey**—examine; examine carefully or in detail; examine officially or formally; examine the whole of (a field, etc.)
22. **test**—examine; examine by questioning
23. **test for**—examine for the presence of
24. **view**—examine

2. Examination,n. *From Sec. 1:* analysis, assay, audit, canvass, check or checkup, extrospection, inspection, introspection, observation, overhaul, palpation, reconnoiter, review, scrutiny or scrutinization, search, study, survey, test; *Also:*
1. **aperçu (French)**—survey
2. **coup d'oeil**—brief survey
3. **panorama**—comprehensive survey of a subject or field of knowledge
4. **reconnaissance**—examination or survey to gain information, usually for military purposes

3. Examiner,n. *From Sec. 1:* analyst or analyzer, assayer, auditor, canvasser, checker, inspector, observer, prospector, reviewer, scrutinizer, scrutineer, or scrutator; searcher, student, surveyor, tester; *Also:* 1. **commentator**—one who analyzes news events or other phenomena and reports his findings via radio or television

4. Examining,adj. *From Sec. 1:* analytic or analytical, extrospective, inspective, introspective, palpatory, scrutinous, studious

5. Selected Medical Examinations,n.
1. **auscultation**—examination by listening, either directly or through a stethoscope, to the sounds in the chest, abdomen, back, etc.
2. **autopsy**—examination, usually by dissection, of a corpse to determine cause of death, extent of disease or lesions, etc.
3. **bacterioscopy**—examination of bacteria under the microscope
4. **biopsy**—examination of tissue removed from a living body, esp. under the microscope, for purposes of diagnosis
5. **bioscopy**—examination of a body to discover whether it is still alive
6. **bronchoscopy**—visual examination, by instrument, of the bronchi, or subdivisions of the windpipe
7. **cystoscopy**—visual examination, by instrument, of the bladder, kidneys, and ureter
8. **encephaloscopy**—instrument examination of the cavities in brain matter
9. **fluoroscopy**—visual examination of the body through an apparatus employing X-rays
10. **gastroscopy**—visual examination, by instrument, of the inside of the stomach
11. **laryngoscopy**—examination, by instrument, of the inside of the larynx
12. **micrography**—examination through the microscope
13. **microscopy**—examination under the microscope, esp. of or for microorganisms
14. **necropsy, necroscopy**—autopsy
15. **otoscopy**—examination, by instrument, of the interior of the ear
16. **palpation**—examination of the body or a bodily part by gently touching
17. **pharyngoscopy**—examination, by instrument, of the pharynx
18. **post-mortem**—examination of a corpse, often to determine the cause of death
19. **rhinoscopy**—examination, by instrument, of the nasal cavity
20. **tracheoscopy**—examination, by instrument, of the inside of the windpipe

6. Descr. of, or Pert. to, a Medical Examination,adj. *From Sec. 5:* auscultative or auscultatory, autopsic or autopsical, bacterioscopic, biopsic, bioscopic, bronchoscopic, cystoscopic, fluoroscopic, gastroscopic, laryngoscopic or laryngoscopical, micrographic, microscopic, necroscopic, otoscopic, palpatory, pharyngoscopic, rhinoscopic, tracheoscopic

7. Instrument Used in a Medical Examination,n. *From Sec. 5:* auscultator, bronchoscope, cystoscope, encephaloscope, fluoroscope, gastroscope, laryngoscope, microscope, otoscope, pharyngoscope, rhinoscope; *Also:*
1. **auriscope**—instrument for looking into the ear
2. **endoscope**—medical instrument for viewing or examining the interior of an organ
3. **stethoscope**—instrument used to listen to sounds within the body

8. One Who Examines Medically,n. *From Sec. 5:* auscultator, bacterioscopist, bronchoscopist, cystoscopist, gastroscopist, laryngoscopist, micrographer, microscopist, tracheoscopist

9. To Examine Medically,v. *From Sec. 5:* auscultate or auscult, autopsy, palpate

486. SEARCH

1. To Search, Seek, or Look for,v.
1. **adventure**—search for excitement or danger
2. **burrow**—search
3. **cast about**—search
4. **chase after**—hunt
5. **comb**—search thoroughly
6. **court**—look for (court danger, defeat, etc.)
7. **delve**—search hard for information
8. **dowse**—use a divining rod in a search for water, ores, etc.
9. **explore**—search into for the purpose of discovery
10. **ferret**—search out with crafty questioning; search or hunt as a ferret does a rabbit
11. **forage**—go about looking for food, or for anything else needed
12. **gun for**—seek
13. **hunt, hunt for**—look for; go about in search of
14. **inquire**—seek out, often by questioning
15. **introspect**—search within oneself for the sources, causes, and meanings of one's feelings, attitudes, etc.
16. **investigate**—search or seek out by patient and methodical examination, observation, asking of questions, etc.
17. **maraud**—go about in search of plunder
18. **mouse**—search around or hunt, the way a cat does for a mouse
19. **philosophize**—search into the reasons for natural or universal phenomena
20. **prospect (for)**—look for; explore
21. **pry (into)**—attempt to get information, esp. information that is not one's concern
22. **pursue**—look for
23. **puzzle over**—try to find the answer to
24. **quest**—search; look for; go about in search of; hunt
25. **rake**—search through thoroughly
26. **ransack**—search thoroughly; search every part of
27. **research**—search for facts, truth, etc.; investigate; investigate studiously and thoroughly
28. **rifle**—go through or search (a place), looking between (in it), often stealing what one has found
29. **root**—search
30. **rout**—search with the snout
31. **rummage**—search thoroughly, in every corner, by moving things around or turning them over; search in a confused or disorderly manner
32. **scour**—go or pass quickly through or over, looking for something
33. **scout (for)**—hunt around (for)
34. **scrimmage**—look for busily

35. **shop around**—search around, making comparisons, before deciding what to buy, which to choose, etc.
36. **sleuth**—search around, like a detective; play the detective; act like a detective
37. **snoop**—go about looking for things, often in violations of rules, laws, orders, etc., in a sneaky, prying way
38. **trace**—try to find, or find out about, by following clues, indications left behind, etc.
39. **track**—seek by following indications left behind; trail
40. **trail**—search for by following the track, smell, footprints, or other indications of

2. Search,n. *From Sec. 1:* chase, exploration, hunt, inquiry, introspection, investigation, pursuit, quest, research, rummage; *Also:*
1. **inquest**—official investigation
2. **perquisition**—thorough search, usually of a house, by authority of a search warrant
3. **réclame (French)**—the seeking of publicity
4. **wild-goose chase**—chase or hunt for something that cannot be found or caught
5. **witch hunt**—a pretended seeking out of wrongdoers, though actually an attempt to persecute or defame political opponents

3. Descr. of Searching or Seeking,adj. *From Sec. 1:* exploratory, inquisitive, introspective, investigative or investigatory, philosophical, snoopy (inquisitiveness, introspectiveness,n.) ; *Also:*
1. **curious**—seeking learning or knowledge (curiosity,n.)
2. **nosy**—inquisitive (nosiness,n.)
3. **rogatory**—looking for information

4. Searcher; Seeker,n. *From Sec. 1:* adventurer, burrower, delver, dowser, explorer, ferret, forager, hunter or fem., huntress, investigator, marauder, mouser, philosopher, prospector, pry, pursuer, quester, ransacker, researcher, rifler, scouter, scrimmager, sleuth, snoop or snooper, tracer, tracker; *From Sec. 2:* perquisitor; *Also:*
1. **detective**—one who seeks out solutions to crimes, those who committed the crimes, etc.
2. **hydroscopist**—dowser
3. **quidnunc**—inquisitive person (from the Latin for *"What now?"*)
4. **sleuth**—detective

5. Forked Rod Used to Search for Underground Water or Metals: dipping rod, divining rod, divining stick, dowser, dowsing rod,n.

6. Motivating (Someone) to Investigate Further: heuristic,adj.

7. That Which Is Sought,n.
1. **big game**—anything sought that is very important; large animals that hunters seek
2. **chase**—hunted animal or thing; that which is sought
3. **quarry**—animal sought in hunting; that which is chased, hunted, pursued, or looked for
4. **quest**—that which is hunted or searched for

8. Without Further Investigation: prima facie,adj.

9. To Hunt Animals,v.
1. **chase**—hunt as a sport
2. **course**—hunt or chase after game
3. **gun**—hunt with a firearm
4. **poach**—hunt on another's property
5. **scent**—hunt (animals) by pursuing their odor
6. **wolf**—hunt wolves

10. Hunting,n.
1. **chase**—hunting as a sport or art
2. **gunning**—hunting with a firearm

3. **sealery**—hunting of seals
4. **venery**—hunting; art of hunting

11. Hunter,n.
1. **chasseur**—hunter
2. **Diana**—huntress, after the Roman goddess of the woods
3. **gunner**—hunter with a firearm
4. **huntress**—female hunter
5. **huntsman**—hunter
6. **Nimrod**—hunter, after the character so described in the Bible
7. **poacher**—one who hunts on another's property
8. **sealer**—one who, or ship that, hunts seals
9. **wolver**—wolf hunter
10. **woodman**—hunter of forest animals
11. **woodsman**—one skilled in hunting

12. Pert. to, or Used in, Hunting; Fond of Hunting; Existing by Hunting: venatic,adj.

13. To Fish,v.
1. **angle**—fish
2. **chum**—throw fish, pieces of fish, or other edibles from a boat to attract fish
3. **poach**—fish on another's property
4. **seine**—trawl
5. **trawl**—fish by dragging a net across the bottom of the water
6. **troll**—fish with a line kept moving through the water

14. Fisher; Fisherman,n. *From Sec. 13:* angler, poacher, trawler, troller; *Also:* 1. piscator—fisherman

15. Gear Used in Fishing: tackle,n.

16. Line, Hook, Lure, etc., Used in Trolling: troll,n.

17. Fishing Place: piscary,n.

18. Legal Right to Fish in Waters Owned by Another: piscary,n.

19. Science of Fishing: piscatology,n.

20. Pert. to Fishing: piscatorial, piscatory, adj.

487. FIND

1. To Find,v.
1. **alight upon**—find by chance
2. **chance on or upon**—come upon
3. **come upon**—find; find unexpectedly
4. **descry**—find by observing or investigating
5. **detect**—find the presence or existence of
6. **develop**—find the possibilities of
7. **discover**—find
8. **encounter**—find; come upon
9. **locate**—find; find the place where someone or something is
10. **meet**—come upon
11. **overtake**—find suddenly; come upon
12. **pin-point**—find or locate exactly
13. **retrieve**—find and bring back
14. **scavenge**—find and use what others have discarded as useless
15. **scent**—find by, or as if by, the sense of smell
16. **sight**—find in the range of vision
17. **sniff**—detect
18. **snuff**—detect by smelling
19. **spot**—find; find by seeing; detect
20. **strike**—find, as if by hitting against suddenly
21. **stumble upon or across**—find by accident
22. **surprise**—find unexpectedly
23. **trace**—find signs of; find by searching
24. **track**—find by searching
25. **turn up**—find
26. **uncover**—find by figuratively removing the covering or concealment of
27. **unearth**—find (something hidden, figuratively buried, lost sight of, forgotten, etc.)
28. **upturn**—find in, or as if in, digging

2. Finding,n. *From Sec. 1:* detection, development, discovery, encounter, location, retrieval or retrievement, strike; *Also:* 1. water witching—the finding of a source of underground water by means of a wand

3. Finder,n. *From Sec. 1:* descrier, detector or detective, developer, discoverer, locator, overtaker, retriever, scavenger, spotter, tracer, tracker

4. Able to Be Found,adj. *From Sec. 1:* detectable or detectible, discoverable, retrievable, traceable

5. Unable to Be Found; Hard to Find,adj. *From Sec. 4:* undetectable or undetectible, undiscoverable, irretrievable, untraceable; *Also:*
1. **elusive**—hard to find (elusiveness,n.)
2. **inscrutable**—incapable of being discovered (inscrutability,n.)
3. **obscure**—hard to find; not easily found (obscurity,n.)
4. **scarce**—hard to find (scarcity, scarceness, n.)
5. **subtile**—elusive and delicate (subtileness, subtility, subtilty,n.)
6. **subtle**—elusive and delicate (subtlety, subtleness,n.)
7. **tenuous**—elusive and delicate (tenuousness, tenuity,n.)

6. That Which Is Found: discovery, find,n.

7. Valuable Find: treasure, treasure-trove,n.

8. Money, etc., the Ownership of Which Is Unknown, That Is Found Hidden or Buried: treasure-trove,n.

488. COLOR

1. General Color or Coloring,n.
1. **cast**—slight amount of color
2. **coloration**—combination or pattern of coloring; distinctive color
3. **dye**—color produced by dyeing
4. **hue**—color
5. **pastel**—pale color
6. **pigment**—color
7. **pigmentation**—coloring
8. **shade**—variety or variation of color, esp. toward dark
9. **tincture**—tinge
10. **tinge**—slight trace of color
11. **tint**—pale or delicate color; slight color; trace of a color; shade
12. **tone**—shade
13. **undertone**—subdued color; color changed by the one under it

2. Color Quality,n.
1. **blare**—brightness of color
2. **brilliance, brilliancy**—degree of resemblance to white or remoteness from black
3. **chroma**—quality that combines both hue and saturation; intensity; saturation
4. **hue**—variation or modification of color
5. **intensity**—sharpness, strength, or purity of color
6. **nuance**—shade of difference in color
7. **purity**—saturation
8. **saturation**—purity of color; degree of remoteness from gray; degree of freedom from mixture with white
9. **shade**—degree of color; degree of darkness of a color; intensity
10. **tint**—shade
11. **tone**—shade

3. Softening or Mellowing of Color Caused by the Passage of Time: patina,n.

4. Play of Colors: chatoyancy,n.

5. The Colors Placed or Mixed on an Artist's Mixing Board: palette,n.

6. Band of Colors Formed When a Beam of Light Is Passed through a Prism: spectrum,n.

7. Effect of Color, Light, and Shade in a Picture: tone,n.

8. Colored; Having Color,adj.
1. **bicolored, bicolor**—having two colors
2. **blazing**—showing bright colors
3. **chatoyant**—having a play of colors (chatoyancy,n.)
4. **colorful**—full of color; having lots of color; having many or bright colors (colorfulness,n.)
5. **columbine**—having the color of a dove
6. **dichroic, dichroitic**—showing varying colors in different directions according to how it is viewed, or showing varying colors in two different directions owing to transmitted light—of crystals (dichroism, dichromaticism,n.)
7. **dichromatic, dichromic, dichroic**—showing or having only two colors; having two color phases or periods—of certain birds and insects (dichromatism, dichroism,n.)
8. **duotone**—in two colors or two tones of the same color
9. **heterochromatic**—possessing a variety or complexity of colors
10. **heterochromous**—possessing a variety of different colors
11. **homochromatic, homochrome**—possessing one color (homochromatism,n.)
12. **homochromous**—of the same or uniform color
13. **hued**—colored
14. **incarnadine**—flesh-colored
15. **iridescent**—possessing a variety of colors, or varying colors, like a rainbow (iridescence,n.)
16. **isochromatic**—having the same color or tint
17. **isochrous**—of the same color or tint throughout
18. **many-colored**—having a variety of colors
19. **mellow**—full, rich and soft in color (mellowness,n.)
20. **monochromatic, monochroic**—containing only one color
21. **motley**—varicolored
22. **multicolored**—having many, or a variety of, colors
23. **pale**—not bright in color (paleness,n.)
24. **parti-colored, party-colored**—colored in different tints
25. **pastel**—pale in color
26. **piebald**—varicolored
27. **pied**—containing colors in blotches; varicolored
28. **pigmented**—colored
29. **polychromatic, polychrome, polychromic**—having, showing, or decorated in, a variety of colors (polychromy,n.)
30. **prismatic**—highly or brilliantly colored
31. **stellular**—colored in starlike spots
32. **trichroic**—showing colors in three different directions—of crystals (trichroism,n.)
33. **trichromatic**—consisting of, or using, three colors (trichromatism,n.)
34. **varicolored**—having different colors
35. **varied**—marked by a number of different colors (variegation,n.)
36. **variegated**—marked in different colors (variegation,n.)
37. **versicolor**—changeable in color; having a rainbowlike range of colors; varicolored

9. Painting or Drawing That Has Only One Color: monochrome,n. (monochromist,n. monochromic, monochromical,adj.)

10. State of Having Color: coloration, pigmentation,n.

11. Art of Combining Colors: coloration, polychromy,n.

12. Of No Decided or Particular Color: neutral,adj.

13. Pert. to Color,adj.
1. **chromatic**—pert. to color or colors
2. **heterochromatic**—pert. to a variety or complexity of color
3. **homochromatic**—pert. to one color
4. **pigmentary**—pert. to color or coloring
5. **tinctorial**—pert. or relating to color
6. **trichromatic**—pert. to three colors

14. Colors as to Category,n.
1. **achromatic colors**—black, white, and shades of gray
2. **chromatic colors**—brown, green, red, purple, etc.
3. **fundamental or physiological primaries**—red, green, and blue
4. **primary colors**—red, blue, and yellow (in painting)
5. **psychological primaries**—red, yellow, blue, green, black, and white
6. **secondary colors**—colors derived from mixing other colors

15. To Color; To Change or Vary the Color of,v.
1. **discolor**—change the color of; change to a different color
2. **dye**—give a color to; change the color of
3. **shade**—change to a darker or different degree of color
4. **stain**—color in a desired way; give color to; discolor
5. **tarnish**—discolor
6. **tincture**—stain; tinge
7. **tinge**—give a slight color to
8. **tint**—color slightly
9. **tone**—change the color of
10. **tone down**—make (a color) less sharp; make less sharp in color
11. **variegate**—mark with different colors

16. To Color, i.e., Become Colored, Take On Color, or Become Changed in Color,v. *From Sec. 15:* discolor, dye, shade, stain, tarnish; *Also:*
1. **blend**—shade into each other (of colors)
2. **tone**—take on a color or color quality; agree in color; blend

17. A Coloring; A Changing in, or of, Color, n. *From Sec. 15:* discoloration or discolorment, variegation; *Also:* 1. **coloration**—act of coloring

18. Change of Color: metachromatism,n.

19. Pert. or Relating to Staining or Dyeing: tinctorial,adj.

20. Discoloration,n.
1. **bruise**—discoloration of the skin caused by a blow, etc. (bruise,v.)
2. **speck**—small discoloration
3. **tarnish**—discoloration (tarnish,v.)

21. Discolored,adj.
1. **livid**—discolored—of the skin (lividness, lividity,n.)
2. **tarnished**—discolored (tarnish,n.)
3. **ustulate**—discolored as if by fire or burning

22. Coloring Matter,n.
1. **color**—coloring matter
2. **dye**—coloring matter used to change color
3. **dyestuff**—matter used to dye or change color
4. **lipstick**—stick of red or other colored matter used on the lips
5. **mascara**—coloring matter used on eyelashes to make them attractive, conspicuous, etc.
6. **pigment**—coloring matter
7. **rouge**—red powder used as coloring matter; coloring matter used to add a red tinge to the cheeks, lips, etc.

23. To Show Bright Colors: blaze,v.

24. Science of Color,n.
1. **chromatics**—science of hue and saturation of color (chromatist,n.)

2. chromatology—science of color (chromatologist,n.)

25. A Treatise or Essay on Colors: chromatography, chromatology,n.

26. Device for Dealing with Color,n.
1. chromatometer—device to test one's color perception
2. colorimeter—device for measuring intensity of color, determining colors, etc. (colorimetry,n. colorimetric, colorimetrical,adj.)
3. prism—device that separates light into its component colors (prismatic,adj.)

489. LACK OF COLOR

1. Lacking Color,adj.
1. achromatic, achromatous—without color; deficient in color
2. achromic—without color; free from color
3. colorless—without color
4. faded—without color; having lost its color
5. pale—lacking in color
6. pallid—lacking in color
7. washed-out—colorless; faded

2. Lack of Color,n. From Sec. 1: achromatism, colorlessness, fadedness, paleness, pallor

3. To Lose Color,v. From Sec. 1: fade, pale

4. To Remove Color from,v. From Sec. 1: achromatize, fade, pale; Also: 1. decolor, decolorize—remove color from

5. That Which Removes Color: decolorant, n.

6. Person, Animal, or Plant Deficient in Pigmentation: albino,n. (albinism,n. albinic, albinistic,adj.)

490. BLACK

1. Black; Blackish,adj.
1. coal-black, coaly—resembling coal in blackness; as black as coal
2. ebony—black, like the wood of the ebony tree
3. ink-black, inky-black, inky—black; as black as ink
4. jet, jet-black, jetty—shiny black, like the mineral from which the word is derived
5. melanoid—blackish
6. nigrescent—somewhat black
7. nigricant—black
8. nigrine—black
9. nigritudinous—black
10. nigrous—black
11. obsidian—very black, like the material from a volcano
12. pitch-black, pitchy—black, like pitch; as black as pitch
13. raven, raven-black—glossy and black
14. sable—black, like the color of the animal's fur
15. sloe, sloe-black, sloe-colored—purplish-black or bluish-black, like the color of a kind of plum
16. sooty—blackish; brownish black in color; blackened

2. Blackness,n. From Sec. 1: inky-blackness, jet-blackness, nigrescence, nigritude, pitch-blackness, sootiness

3. The Color Black,n. From Sec. 1: ebony, jet, raven, sable

4. To Make or Cause to Be Black: black, blacken, denigrate,v. (denigration,n.)

5. To Become Black: black, blacken,v.

6. Something Black: nigritude,n.

7. Black and Blue: livid,adj. (lividness, lividity,n.)

491. DARK COLOR

1. Dark or Darkish in Color,adj.
1. darksome—dark; darkish
2. dusky—dark and dull, but not quite black (duskiness,n.)
3. nigricant—dark
4. nigritudinous—extremely dark (nigritude,n.)
5. sable—very dark, like the color of the animal's fur
6. sooty—dark-colored (sootiness,n.)
7. swarthy, swart—dark (swarthiness, swartness,n.)

2. To Make or Become Dark or Darker: darken,v.

492. BLUE

1. Greenish or Green Blues: aquamarine, baby blue, beryl or beryl blue, cobalt blue, eggshell blue, glaucous blue, Italian blue, jouvence blue, marine or marine blue, Nile blue, peacock blue, robin's-egg blue, sea blue, turquoise or turquoise blue,n. (aquamarine, baby-blue, beryl-blue or berylline, cobalt-blue, glaucous, peacock-blue, robin's-egg-blue, turquoise,adj.)

2. Peacock-Blue: pavonian, pavonine,adj.

3. Reddish Blues: cadet blue, damson, French blue, hyacinth blue, indigo, indigo blue, madder blue, midnight blue, periwinkle, periwinkle blue, mulberry, wisteria blue,n. (hyacinthine, indigo, indigotic, indigo-blue, adj.)

4. Sky Blues: azure, azure blue, azury, cerulean, lapis lazuli, sky color,n.

5. Sky-Blue: azure-blue, azurean, azurine, azurous, azury, cerulean, ceruleous, sky-color, adj.

6. Deep or Dark Blues: French blue, marine, marine blue, navy, navy blue, royal blue, sapphire, ultramarine,n.

7. Deep or Dark Blue: navy, navy-blue, perse, sapphire, ultramarine,adj.

8. A Light and Kind of Dusty Blue: powder blue,n.

9. Light Blue: cerulescent,adj.

10. Violet or Purplish Blues: indigo, indigo blue, sloe blue,n. (indigo, indigotic, indigo-blue, sloe-blue,adj.)

11. Certain Other Blues: Berlin blue, bronze blue, Brunswick blue, Dresden blue, Hortense blue, milori blue, Paris blue, Prussian blue, slate blue, steel blue, Swiss blue,n. (slate-blue, steel-blue,adj.)

12. Having a Blue Tinge: cyanic,adj. (of flowers)

13. To Make, Cause to Be, Turn, or Become Blue: blue,v.

493. GREEN

1. Yellow or Yellowish Greens: apple green, bladder green, boa, chartreuse, emerald, fir or fir green, glaucous green, jade or jade green, mignonette or mignonette green, Montpelier green, moss or moss green, mousse, Nile green, olive, olive drab, Paris green, pea green, peacock green, reseda, sap green, sea green, shamrock or shamrock green, Spanish green, verdet, verdigris or verdigris green, viridian, viridine green, willow green,n. (apple-green, chartreuse, emerald, glaucous, jade-green, moss-green, olive or olivaceous, olive-drab, pea-green, peacock-green, reseda, sea-green, viridian,adj.)

2. Blue or Bluish Greens: aquamarine, bird's-egg green, eggshell green, glaucous

green, jade or jade green, myrtle or myrtle green, Nile green, sea green, turquoise or turquoise green,n. (aquamarine, glaucous, jade-green, sea-green, turquoise,adj.)

3. Dull Green: olive,n. (olive, olivaceous, adj.)

4. Somewhat or Slightly Green; Greenish: viridescent,adj.

5. Green with Grass or Growing Plants: verdant,adj. (verdancy,n.)

6. Becoming or Growing Green: virescent, adj. (virescence,n.)

7. Greenness: viridity,n.

8. Greenness of Fresh, Growing Plants: greenery, verdure,n.

9. Greenish Tinge on Copper Caused by the Passage of Time: patina,n.

10. To Become, or Cause to Be, Green: green, v.

494. PURPLE

1. Purple,n.
 1. **amethyst**—purple; bluish purple
 2. **lavender**—pale purple
 3. **lilac**—pale and reddish purple
 4. **magenta**—reddish purple
 5. **mauve**—pale or delicate purple
 6. **mulberry**—dull, dark, and reddish purple
 7. **orchid**—light purple
 8. **plum**—deep bluish or reddish purple
 9. **royal purple**—deep and somewhat bluish purple
 10. **Tyrian purple**—kind of purple
 11. **violet**—bluish purple

2. Purple,adj. *From Sec. 1:* amethyst or amethystine, lavender, lilac or lilaceous, mauve, orchid, plum-colored, Tyrian, violet, adj.; *Also:*
 1. **perse**—very deep purple
 2. **violaceous**—violet

3. Purplish: livid, purplescent, violescent, adj. (lividness, lividity,n.)

4. Growing or Becoming Purple: purplescent,adj.

5. To Color Purple or with a Shade of Purple: empurple, purple,v.

6. To Become Purple: purple,v.

495. RED

1. Red,n.
 1. **blood red**—red, like the color of blood
 2. **cardinal**—bright red; deep and rich red
 3. **carmine**—rich red; deep red
 4. **cerise**—red, like the color of cherries
 5. **cherry**—bright red
 6. **crimson**—deep red
 7. **incarnadine**—red; blood red
 8. **maroon**—brownish red
 9. **minium**—vermilion
 10. **murrey**—dark red
 11. **orange**—yellowish red
 12. **pink**—pale or light red
 13. **puce**—a kind of red
 14. **ruby, ruby red**—deep, glowing red
 15. **scarlet**—very bright red
 16. **terra cotta**—dull, brownish red
 17. **vermilion**—bright red
 18. **wine**—dark red

2. Red,adj. *From Sec. 1:* blood-red, carmine or incarmined, cerise, cherry, crimson, incarnadine, maroon, orange, pink, puce, ruby, scarlet, terra-cotta, vermilion, wine-colored; *Also:*
 1. **erubescent**—red
 2. **ferruginous**—of the color of rusty iron
 3. **hematic**—of the color of blood
 4. **rubescent**—red

5. **rubiginous, rubiginose**—brownish-red; ferruginous
6. **rubineous**—of a deep and glowing red color, like that of the ruby
7. **rufous**—brownish red
8. **rust-colored**—of the color of rusty iron
9. **sanguine**—blood-red

3. Redness: erubescence, rubedity, rubescence, rubricity,n.

4. To Become Red: crimson, redden,v.

5. Growing or Becoming Red: erubescent, rubescent,adj. (erubescence, rubescence,n.)

6. To Make or Cause to Be Red,v.
 1. **carmine**—color a rich or deep red
 2. **crimson**—color a deep red
 3. **incarnadine**—make or dye red, blood-red, or deep red
 4. **redden**—make or color red
 5. **rubric**—ornament with red; redden
 6. **rubricate**—mark or color with red (rubrication,n.)
 7. **ruby**—redden
 8. **ruddle**—color red with red ochre; redden
 9. **vermilion**—make or color deep red

7. Act of Causing Redness, as on the Skin or Elsewhere: rubefaction, rubification,n.

8. Causing Redness: rubefacient, rubific, rubificative, rubrific,adj.

9. Marked with Red: rubricate,adj.

10. Colored, Marked, or Printed in Red: rubric, rubrical,adj. (rubricality,n.)

11. To Mark the Chapters, Titles, or Headings of a Book, etc., in Red: rubricate, rubricize,v. (rubrication,n.)

12. Red Marking, as in a Book, Manuscript, etc.: rubric,n.

13. Reddish Color,n.
 1. **carnelian**—reddish color, resembling that of flesh
 2. **copper**—reddish color, resembling that of the metal
 3. **puce**—reddish color

14. Reddish: carnelian, carroty, copper, coppery, erubescent, puce, rubedinous, rubescent, rubicund, rubricose, ruddy, rufescent, rufous, adj.

15. Reddishness: erubescence, rubedity, rubescence, rubicundity, ruddiness, rufescence, n.

16. Tinged with Red: rufescent, rufous,adj. (rufescence,n.)

17. Blue, Bluish, Purple, or Purplish Reds: burgundy, carmine, carnation, claret, crimson, dahlia, dahlia carmine, dahlia purple, fuchsia, gridelin, heliotrope, hellebore red, hyacinth, lilac, magenta, mallow, mauve, solferino,n. (carmine, claret, crimson, fuchsia, hyacinthine, lilac or lilaceous, magenta, mauve,adj.)

18. Yellow or Yellowish Reds: blood red, blossom, orange, rust, tangerine, tea rose, terra cotta, titian, Venetian pink,n.

19. Yellow- or Yellowish-Red: blood-red, carroty, orange, rufous, rust-colored, sandy, tea-rose, terra-cotta,adj.

496. PINK

1. Pink,n.
 1. **apricot**—yellowish pink
 2. **coral**—deep pink
 3. **flesh, flesh color**—whitish or yellowish pink, the color of the skin of a white person
 4. **fuchsia**—deep and purplish pink
 5. **incarnadine**—flesh
 6. **peach**—yellowish pink
 7. **rose**—pink; deep pink

8. **salmon**—yellowish pink
9. **tea rose**—yellowish pink

2. Pink,adj. *From Sec. 1:* apricot, coral or coralline, flesh-color or flesh-colored, fuchsia, incarnadine, peach; rose, roseate, rose-colored, or rosy; salmon or salmon-colored, tea-rose

3. To Cause to Become Flesh Pink in Color: incarnadine,v.

4. Tinged with a Deep Pink Color: roseate, adj.

5. Pinkish, or Deep Pink, Tinge: blush,n.

6. To Turn Pinkish: blush,v. (of flowers, the sky, etc.)

497. BROWN

1. Brown,n.
1. **amber**—yellowish brown
2. **auburn**—reddish brown; golden brown
3. **bay**—reddish brown
4. **beige**—pale brown; tan; the natural color of unbleached cotton
5. **biscuit**—very light tan
6. **bister, bistre**—dark brown
7. **brindle**—tan, with darker streaks or spots (of animals)
8. **bronze**—yellowish or reddish brown
9. **burnt almond**—reddish or yellowish brown
10. **burnt umber**—reddish brown
11. **café-au-lait**—light chocolate brown, similar to the color of a beverage of half coffee and half milk
12. **chestnut**—reddish brown
13. **chocolate**—dark brown
14. **cinnamon**—light reddish brown
15. **cocoa**—brown; yellowish or reddish brown
16. **coffee**—dark brown
17. **copper**—reddish, metallic brown, like that of the metal
18. **dun**—dull brown; grayish brown
19. **ecru**—light tan, like the color of unbleached cloth
20. **fawn**—light brown
21. **hazel**—light reddish brown, the color of hazelnuts
22. **henna**—reddish brown
23. **hyacinth red**—reddish brown
24. **khaki**—yellowish brown; tan
25. **mahogany**—reddish brown, like the color of the wood
26. **puce**—dark brown; purplish brown
27. **russet**—yellowish or reddish brown
28. **rust**—reddish brown
29. **sepia**—dark brown
30. **sorrel**—light reddish brown
31. **tan**—yellowish brown
32. **tawny**—dull and yellowish brown
33. **titian**—golden or yellowish brown
34. **topaz**—yellowish brown
35. **umber**—brown; reddish brown

2. Brown,adj. *From Sec. 1:* amber, auburn, bay, beige, brindle or brindled, bronze, café-au-lait, chestnut, chocolate, cinnamon, cocoa, coppery, dun or dun-colored, ecru, fawn, hazel, henna, hyacinthine, khaki, mahogany, puce, russet, rust-colored, sepia, tawny, titian, umber; *Also:*
1. **castaneous**—chestnut
2. **ferruginous**—of the color of iron rust
3. **fulvous**—dull brown
4. **rubiginous, rubiginose**—rust-colored
5. **spadiceous**—bright, clear brown

3. To Make or Become Brown: brown, tan,v.

498. GRAY

1. Gray,n.
1. **ash color**—ash gray

2. **ash gray**—pale gray, like the color of ashes
3. **brindle**—gray, with darker streaks or spots (of animals)
4. **dove color**—warm gray with a slight tint of pink or purple
5. **dove gray**—dove color
6. **drab**—dull yellowish or brownish gray
7. **oyster white**—very light gray with a somewhat yellow or green tinge
8. **pearl gray**—soft, neutral, bluish gray
9. **slate gray**—gray with a reddish or yellowish tone
10. **taupe**—dark, brownish gray

2. Gray,adj. *From Sec. 1:* ash-colored, ash-gray, brindle or brindled, dove-colored, dove-gray, drab, oyster-white, pearl-gray, slate-gray, taupe; *Also:*
1. **ashen**—ash-gray
2. **cinereal, cinereous**—ash-gray
3. **columbine**—dove-colored
4. **dapple-gray, dappled-gray**—gray with spots of a different color (often of animals)
5. **fulvous**—dull and yellowish gray in color
6. **grizzled**—streaked with gray
7. **hoar**—light gray; gray with advanced age
8. **hoary**—gray; gray with advanced age

3. To Make, Cause to Be or Appear Gray; To Become Gray: gray,v.

499. WHITE

1. White or Whitish,adj.
1. **alabaster**—white, or near-white, and smooth, like marble
2. **albescent**—somewhat white; whitish
3. **argent**—white; silvery white
4. **cream, creamy, cream-color, cream-colored**—yellowish-white in color
5. **fleecy**—white and soft, like a sheep's wool
6. **flesh-color, flesh-colored**—pinkish-white, like the color of a white person's skin
7. **hoar, hoary**—white; whitish; white or whitish as a result of advanced age
8. **ivory**—yellowish white, or whitish, like ivory
9. **leucochroic**—white; fairly white
10. **leucous**—white
11. **marmoreal, marmorean**—white and cold, like marble
12. **milk-white, milky**—white, or somewhat bluish-white, like milk
13. **off-white**—not quite white; not stark white; white with a touch of gray
14. **piebald**—mottled white and black
15. **snowy**—white, like snow
16. **wintry, wintery**—white

2. White,n. *From Sec. 1:* cream or cream color, flesh or flesh color, ivory, off-white

3. Whiteness,n. *From Sec. 1:* albescence, creaminess, fleeciness, hoariness or hoar, milkiness, snowiness, wintriness, winteriness; *Also:* 1. **albedo**—whiteness

4. Becoming or Growing White: albescent, albicant, canescent,adj. (albescence, albication, canescence,n.)

5. To Make White,v.
1. **blanch**—make white or whiter
2. **bleach**—blanch
3. **blench**—blanch
4. **etiolate**—blanch (plants) by excluding sunlight
5. **whiten**—make white or whiter

6. A Making White,n. *From Sec. 5:* etiolation; *Also:* 1. **albification**—process or act of making white

7. To Become or Turn White,v. *From Sec. 5:* blanch, bleach, blench, whiten

8. Whitening Agent: bleach,n.

9. Able to Cause Whitening: albificative,adj.

500. YELLOW

1. Yellow,n.
1. amber—brownish yellow; yellow
2. apricot—pale orange yellow, like the color of the fruit
3. bisque—reddish yellow
4. blond—light yellow; reddish yellow
5. brimstone, brimstone yellow—sulphur
6. buff—dull yellow
7. canary, canary yellow—light yellow
8. carbuncle—brownish or reddish yellow
9. chrome, chrome yellow—deep yellow; light yellow; reddish yellow
10. citrine—reddish yellow
11. citron, citron yellow—reddish yellow
12. citrus—sulphur
13. cream—yellowish color, like that of cream
14. crocus—saffron
15. flesh color, flesh—pinkish yellow
16. gold—yellow, like the metal
17. lemon, lemon yellow—yellow, the color of the ripe fruit
18. ochre—brownish yellow
19. olive—greenish yellow
20. orange—reddish yellow
21. peach—reddish or pinkish yellow
22. primrose—pale yellow
23. rust—reddish yellow
24. saffron—orange yellow
25. sulphur, sulphur yellow—very bright yellow
26. tawny—brownish yellow
27. tea rose—reddish yellow
28. titian—reddish yellow
29. topaz—yellow, like the color of the gem

2. Yellow; Yellowish,adj. *From Sec. 1:* amber, apricot, blond, buff; canary, canary-colored, or canary-yellow; citrine or citrean, citreous (from *citron*) ; cream, creamy, cream-color, or cream-colored; flesh-color or flesh-colored, gold or golden, lemon-colored or lemon-yellow; ocherous, ochery, ochreous, or ochry; olive or olive-colored, orange, peach or peach-colored, primrose, rust-colored, saffron, tawny, tea-rose, titian, topazine; *Also:*
1. aureate—golden
2. aurulent—gold in color (aurulence,n.)
3. citrine—lemon
4. flavescent—yellowish
5. flaxen—pale yellow or blond, like the color of flax or straw
6. fulvescent—tending toward dull yellow in color
7. fulvous—dull yellow
8. glaucous—yellowish
9. leucous—blond
10. lurid—reddish yellow
11. luteolous—yellowish or somewhat yellow (of plants and animals)
12. luteous—yellow
13. lutescent—yellowish (lutescence,n.)
14. meline—canary-yellow
15. rufous—reddish-yellow
16. stramineous—straw-colored
17. straw-colored—light yellow, like straw
18. vitelline—yellowish, like the yolk of an egg
19. xanthic—yellowish
20. xanthous—yellow

3. Becoming or Turning Yellow: flavescent, adj.

4. Pert. to Yellow: xanthic,adj.

5. Yellow Pigment,n.
1. xanthin—yellow coloring matter extracted from yellow flowers
2. xanthophyll—natural yellow pigment

6. To Make, Cause to Be, Turn, or Become Yellow: yellow,v.

7. To Make Yellow as if with Jaundice: jaundice,v.

501. SPOT

1. Spotted,adj.
1. blotchy, blotched—irregularly spotted
2. brindle, brindled—spotted (of animals)
3. dappled, dapple—spotted; marked with small, usually gray, spots (of animals)
4. dotted—with small spots
5. flecked—marked with tiny spots
6. flyspecked—marked with small spots
7. freckled—marked by small, brownish skin spots
8. lentiginous—freckled (medical)
9. maculate—blotchy; splotched
10. mottled—marked with varicolored spots
11. patchy—spotted; irregularly spotted
12. pocked, pock-marked—marked by spots; of the skin, marked by the pitted spots left by certain diseases, as smallpox, chicken pox, etc.
13. punctate—dotted with small spots
14. specked—marked with small spots
15. speckled—spotted; specked
16. splotched, splotchy—spotted; marked with large and irregular spots
17. spotty—containing spots
18. sprinkled—dotted
19. stippled—dotted

2. To Spot,v. *From Sec. 1:* blotch, dapple, dot, fleck, flyspeck, freckle, macule or maculate, mottle, pock, pockmark, speck, speckle, splotch, sprinkle, stipple; *Also:* 1. stigmatize —produce spots on; produce spots on an animal (stigmatization,n.)

3. A Spot,n. *From Sec. 1:* blotch, dot, fleck, flyspeck, freckle, lentigo; macula, macule, or mackle; mottle, patch, pock, pockmark, speck, speckle, splotch; *Also:*
1. albugo—white spot on the cornea of the eye
2. blaze—white spot on an animal's face
3. mole—skin spot, usually brown, present from birth
4. mote—speck of dust
5. pip—distinguishing spot on a playing card
6. stigma—abnormal spot on the skin; small spot on an animal or organ (stigmata, pl. stigmatic,adj.)

4. Condition of Abnormal Spots on the Skin: stigmatism,n.

5. Spotted Appearance or State: dapple,n.

6. Arrangement of Spots on an Animal: maculation,n.

502. STRIPE

1. Stripe; Streak,n.
1. band—long, narrow stripe, different in some way, usually in color, from adjacent stripes or parts, and generally going around or over something
2. belt—encircling stripe
3. cincture—belt
4. cingulum—band, usually on an animal
5. girdle—encircling stripe or band
6. list—stripe of color
7. ring—circular band
8. striation—stripe; streak
9. vein—streak or wave, as in wood
10. wale—streak left on the skin by a blow or whipping
11. wave—curvy streak
12. weal—wale
13. welt—wale
14. wheal—wale

2. Striped, Streaked,adj. *From Sec. 1:* banded, belted, cinctured, cingulate, girdled, striated or striate, veined; *Also:*

1. **brindle, brindled**—streaked
2. **gyrose**—marked with wavy lines
3. **To Stripe; To Streak,**v. *From Sec. 1:* band, belt, girdle, striate, vein

503. MARK

1. **Mark; Marking; Marks,**n.
   1. **badge**—characteristic mark
   2. **birthmark, nevus**—mark on the skin present at birth
   3. **blaze**—mark on a tree made by chipping off pieces from the bark; white mark on an animal's face
   4. **brand**—mark burned or otherwise placed on animals or criminals; mark burned on the skin; figurative mark of disgrace; stigma
   5. **earmark**—identifying or distinguishing mark; such a mark placed on the ear of a domestic animal to show possession
   6. **lineation**—line markings
   7. **ring**—circular mark
   8. **scar**—mark left on the skin by a healed wound or lesion
   9. **score, scoring**—line markings
   10. **scuff**—mark left on the surface by continued use
   11. **sear**—brand; stigma
   12. **stigma**—mark of disgrace, literally or figuratively; characteristic mark of a disease, deterioration, etc.; small mark on an animal or organ; abnormal mark on the skin (stigmata,pl. stigmatic,adj.)
   13. **streak**—long mark
   14. **stroke**—mark made by something
   15. **trace**—mark left by someone or something
   16. **track**—mark left by the wheels of a moving vehicle, a passing person or animal, etc.
   17. **vermiculation**—marks in the form of wormlike designs or tracks
   18. **vestige**—trace (vestigial,adj.)
   19. **wake**—mark left by a moving ship or object

2. **To Mark; To Make or Leave a Mark on,** v. *From Sec. 1:* blaze, brand, earmark, lineate, scar, score, scuff, sear, stigmatize, streak, vermiculate (stigmatization, vermiculation, n.)

3. **Marked,**adj. *From Sec. 2:* blazed, branded, etc.; lineate, streaky, vermiculate or vermicular

504. APPEARANCE

1. **Appearance:** aspect, cast, complexion, guise, look; mien (of a person); person (of a person); phase, species, visage,n.

2. **External, Outward, or Surface Appearance:** guise, semblance, superficies, veneer,n.

3. **Exact Appearance:** vraisemblance,n. (French)

4. **Netlike Appearance:** reticulation,n.

5. **Complete or Radical Change in Appearance:** metamorphosis or metamorphism, transformation,n. (metamorphic or metamorphous, transformational,adj.)

6. **To Effect a Complete or Radical Change in the Appearance of:** metamorphose, transform,v. (metamorphosis, transformation,n.)

7. **Misleading, Deceptive, or False Appearance,**n.
   1. **disguise**—misleading appearance
   2. **gloss**—false, superficial appearance of goodness or quality hiding inferiority underneath
   3. **guise**—outward appearance, with the implication that the inner fact or reality may be very different

4. **illusion**—misleading or deceptive appearance (illusional,adj.)
5. **semblance**—assumed or false appearance
6. **varnish**—deceptive appearance

8. **Having the Appearance,**adj.
   1. **apparent**—having the appearance of; seeming (apparentness,n.)
   2. **ostensible**—apparent but not necessarily actual
   3. **quasi**—apparent but not actual (used as a prefix, as quasi-intelligence, etc.)
   4. **seeming**—having the appearance of; to all outward appearances; appearing to be but not actually so
   5. **token**—having the superficial appearance of, but not genuinely so

9. **Appear to Be:** look, look as if, seem, seem to be,v.

10. **To Have the Appearance of, but Not Really Be:** purport to be,v.

11. **Way of Carrying Oneself:** address, air, bearing, carriage, demeanor, mien, poise,n.

505. BEAUTY

1. **Beautiful, etc.,**adj.
   1. **adorable**—extremely beautiful (colloq.)
   2. **aesthetic, esthetic**—beautiful in the sense of pleasing one's sense of form or beauty
   3. **angelic**—lovely
   4. **attractive**—beautiful, i.e., appealing to the sense of sight
   5. **beauteous**—beautiful; sensually beautiful
   6. **becoming**—attractive
   7. **bonny**—pleasant to look at; pretty
   8. **comely**—pleasing to the eye
   9. **cunning**—quaintly appealing to the sight —of something little, or of a child (colog.)
   10. **cute**—pleasing to look at
   11. **dainty**—delicately beautiful; pretty and fresh
   12. **ethereal**—descr. of the type of beauty that seems not of this earth, but airy, spiritual, unusually delicate, etc.
   13. **exquisite**—delicately and breath-takingly beautiful
   14. **fair**—pretty (applied to girls or women)
   15. **good-looking**—appealing to the sense of sight
   16. **gorgeous**—exceedingly and excitingly beautiful
   17. **handsome**—pleasing to the eye; having a fine appearance
   18. **lovely**—exceedingly or exquisitely beautiful; of a beauty that appeals to both the eye and the emotions; spiritually beautiful
   19. **personable**—pleasing in appearance; attractive
   20. **pretty**—having pleasing physical characteristics short of actual beauty (of women, girls, and children)
   21. **pulchritudinous**—beautiful
   22. **ravishing**—enchantingly beautiful
   23. **sculpturesque**—statuesque
   24. **sightly**—pleasing in appearance; attractive
   25. **statuesque**—beautiful, tall, graceful, and shapely, like a statue
   26. **stunning**—so beautiful as to stun, shock, take away the breath, etc. (colloq.)
   27. **well-favored**—having a pleasing or attractive appearance

2. **Beauty, etc.,**n. *From Sec. 1:* adorableness or adorability, attractiveness, beauteousness, bonniness, comeliness, cunningness, cuteness, daintiness, etherealness, exquisiteness, fairness, gorgeousness, handsomeness, loveliness, personability, prettiness, pulchritude, sculpturesqueness, statuesqueness; *Also:*
   1. **beau ideal**—ideal beauty

2. **beaux yeux** (French)—facial beauty or attractiveness

3. **Glow of Beauty and Health:** bloom,n.

4. **Beautiful Woman or Girl,**n.
   1. **belle**—a beautiful woman who is also the object of wide admiration
   2. **dryad**—attractive country girl
   3. **nymph**—beautiful young woman
   4. **Venus**—woman of extraordinary beauty
   5. **vision**—beautiful woman

5. **Handsome Man,**n.
   1. **Adonis**—young man who is strikingly handsome in face and physique—so called after the youth in Greek mythology with whom the goddess Aphrodite fell in love
   2. **Apollo**—young man who is handsome and graceful in both face and figure—so called from the Greek god of manly beauty (Apollonian, Apollonic,adj.)

6. **Pert. to Beauty:** aesthetic, cosmetic, esthetic,adj.

7. **Pert. to Beauty of the Complexion:** cosmetic,adj.

8. **Reacting Emotionally or Sensitively to Beauty; Sensitive to Beauty:** aesthetic, esthetic,adj.

9. **One Who Is Particularly Sensitive to Beauty; One Who So Pretends:** aesthete, esthete,n.

10. **To Cause to Be Beautiful,**v.
    1. **adorn**—add beauty to (adornment,n.)
    2. **beautify**—make beautiful (beautification, n.)
    3. **deck**—decorate
    4. **decorate**—make beautiful with ornaments (decoration,n.)
    5. **prettify**—make pretty in a petty or superficial manner (prettification,n.)

11. **Any Agent or Substance That Makes Beautiful, or That Hides or Changes That Which Would Detract from One's Appearance:** cosmetic,n.

12. **Designed to Beautify the Skin, Hair, Nails, etc.; Beautifying or Intended to Beautify:** cosmetic,adj.

13. **Art of Giving Beautifying Treatments:** cosmetology,n. (cosmetologist,n.)

14. **Professional Operator of, or Worker in, a "Beauty Parlor":** beautician, cosmetician,n.

15. **Excessive Obsession with Beauty and Grace:** callomania,n.

16. **Study of Beauty; Philosophy of Beauty; Science of Beauty:** aesthetics, esthetics,n. (aesthetician, esthetician,n.)

17. **Love of Anything Beautiful:** philocaly,n.

18. **Acceptance of Artistic Beauty and Taste as More Important than Ethical or Other Standards:** aestheticism, estheticism,n.

19. **Goddess of Beauty and Love:** Aphrodite (Greek) ; Venus (Roman),n.

20. **Greek God of Manly Beauty:** Apollo,n.

506. UGLINESS

1. **Ugly; Not Beautiful; Not Appealing to the Sight,**adj.
   1. **deformed**—ugly (deformity,n.)
   2. **hideous**—revoltingly or repulsively ugly (hideousness,n.)
   3. **homely**—not handsome or beautiful, though not quite ugly—of facial appearance (homeliness,n.)
   4. **ill-favored**—ugly, in the sense that nature has failed to show favor
   5. **ogrish, ogreish**—ugly (ogrishness, ogreishness,n.)
   6. **plain**—homely (plainness,n.)

7. **repulsive**—so ugly as to push one away (repulsiveness,n.)
8. **unaesthetic, unesthetic**—not pleasing to one's sense of form or beauty
9. **unattractive**—not appealing to the sense of sight (unattractiveness,n.)
10. **unbecoming**—unattractive
11. **unfair**—not pretty
12. **unfavorable**—ugly; repulsively ugly
13. **unhandsome**—not pleasing to the eye
14. **unlovely**—lacking in any beauty (unloveliness,n.)
15. **unpersonable**—unattractive
16. **unpretty**—not pretty
17. **unsightly**—ugly; unpleasant to look at (unsightliness,n.)

2. **Ugly Woman,**n.
   1. **gorgon**—unusually ugly woman
   2. **hag, harridan**—ugly old woman, often of evil character
   3. **ogress**—ugly and cruel woman

3. **Ugly and Cruel Man:** ogre,n.

507. FORM; SHAPE

1. **Form; Shape,**n.
   1. **angulation**—angular shape
   2. **cast**—form
   3. **conformation**—external form
   4. **embodiment**—definite, concrete form
   5. **figuration**—form; shape
   6. **malformation**—irregular shape
   7. **metamorphosis, metamorphism**—new and changed form (metamorphic,adj.)
   8. **mold**—form; shape
   9. **quintessence**—purest form (quintessential,adj.)
   10. **recast**—new form
   11. **reticulation**—netlike form (reticular, adj.)
   12. **ripple**—shape resembling a small ocean wave
   13. **roughcast**—rough or crude form
   14. **simulacrum**—vague, shadowy form
   15. **species**—form; shape
   16. **structure**—form (structural,adj.)
   17. **symmetry**—shape

2. **To Form; To Shape; To Give a Form or Shape to,**v.
   1. **canalize**—give a fixed form to (canalization,n.)
   2. **crystallize**—cause to come finally into a definite form or shape (crystallization, n.)
   3. **embody**—give to (something abstract) a definite form (embodiment,n.)
   4. **mold**—give form or shape to
   5. **pat**—shape by lightly stroking
   6. **roughcast, roughhew**—give a rough or crude form to; shape into a rough or crude form
   7. **streamline**—so shape as to offer the least possible resistance to wind, air, or water
   8. **symmetrize**—give balance and correspondence of shape to
   9. **whittle**—shape by cutting small pieces from

3. **To Come Finally into a Definite Form or Shape:** crystallize,v. (crystallization,n.)

4. **To Give a New Form or Shape to:** recast, reform,v. (recast, reformation,n.)

5. **To Take on a New Form or Shape:** reform,v. (reformation,n.)

6. **Evenness, Balance, or Correspondence of Shape of Both or All Sides:** symmetry,n. (symmetric, symmetrical,adj.)

7. **A Plastic Mold of the Form or Shape of Something, Often Made to Preserve or Present Evidence in Criminal Investigations·** moulage,n. (French)

8. Shaping of the Mouth in Blowing a Wind Instrument: embouchure,n.

9. Referring or Pert. to Shaping: plastic, adj.

10. Capable of Being Shaped,adj.
 1. **malleable**—capable of being shaped by hammer blows (malleability,n.)
 2. **plastic**—capable of being shaped (plasticity,n.)
 3. **viscous**—capable of changing its shape under pressure (viscousness, viscosity,n.)

11. Hammered or Beaten into Shape: wrought,adj.

12. Having Many Forms or Shapes,adj.
 1. **biform, biformed**—having, or combining, the characteristics of two forms—as a mermaid, centaur, satyr, etc. (biformity, n.)
 2. **dimorphic, dimorphous**—occurring in two different forms
 3. **multiform**—of many forms (multiformity,n. multiform,n.)
 4. **polymorphic, polymorphous**—in many varied forms, shapes, etc. (polymorphism, n.)
 5. **triform**—in three forms or shapes (triformity,n.)

13. Shapely,adj.
 1. **chiseled**—even or regular in shape
 2. **curvaceous**—shapely; having shapely curves—said of a woman's figure (curvaceousness,n.)
 3. **graceful**—having a pleasant or beautiful shape (grace, gracefulness,n.)
 4. **petite**—small and shapely—of a child, girl, or woman (petiteness,n.)
 5. **sculpturesque**—statuesque (sculpturesqueness,n.)
 6. **spheral**—symmetrical (spherality,n.)
 7. **statuesque**—shapely, tall, beautiful, and graceful, like a statue (statuesqueness,n.)
 8. **sylphlike**—shapely and slim—of a woman
 9. **symmetrical, symmetric**—having balance and correspondence of shape on both sides (symmetry,n.)

14. Irregular or Unpleasant in Shape or Form,adj.
 1. **anisometric**—having parts that are not symmetrical or do not correspond
 2. **asymmetrical**—not symmetrical in shape (asymmetry,n.)
 3. **baroque**—irregular in shape
 4. **bastard**—of irregular, questionable, or non-standard form
 5. **deformed**—misshapen (deformity,n. deform,v.)
 6. **erose**—shaped irregularly, as if eaten away; irregular in shape or form
 7. **malformed**—of irregular shape or form; misshapen (malformation,n.)
 8. **misshapen**—distorted in shape or appearance (misshapenness,n. misshape,v.)
 9. **roughhewn, roughcast**—roughly or crudely shaped or formed
 10. **shapeless**—of unpleasant or ill-defined shape (shapelessness,n.)
 11. **skew**—not symmetrical (skew,v.)
 12. **ungraceful**—unpleasant in shape or form (ungracefulness,n.)
 13. **unshaped, unshapen**—misshapen

15. Physical Deformity: vice,n.

16. Shapeless; Formless: amorphous, unshaped, unshapen,adj. (amorphousness,n.)

17. Descr. of Specific Form or Shape,adj.
 1. **acanthoid**—shaped like a prickle or spine, as in a plant, animal's foot, etc.
 2. **acerate, aciform**—needle-shaped
 3. **aciniform**—shaped like a grape cluster
 4. **alary, aliform**—wing-shaped
 5. **alveolate**—shaped like a honeycomb
 6. **ampullaceous**—bladder-shaped; flask-shaped

 7. **amygdaloid**—almond-shaped
 8. **arciform**—arch-shaped
 9. **bacillary, bacilliform, baculiform**—rod-shaped
 10. **bicorn**—crescent-shaped
 11. **botyroid**—in the form of a bunch of grapes
 12. **bursiform**—purse-shaped; sac-shaped
 13. **campanulate**—bell-shaped
 14. **capsular**—capsule-shaped (capsularity,n.)
 15. **cheliform**—claw-shaped
 16. **clavate, claviform**—club-shaped
 17. **clupeiform**—herring-shaped
 18. **clypeate, clypeiform**—shield-shaped (biology)
 19. **cochleate**—shaped like the shell of a snail
 20. **colubriform**—shaped like a snake
 21. **cordate, cordiform**—heart-shaped
 22. **crenate**—having the edges shaped in round scallops (crenation, crenature,n.)
 23. **crescent**—shaped like the first-quarter moon
 24. **crinoid**—lily-shaped
 25. **crosswise**—in the form of a cross
 26. **cruciate, crucial, cruciform**—shaped like, or in the form of, a cross
 27. **cucumiform**—cucumber-shaped
 28. **cuneate, cuneatic**—wedge-shaped
 29. **cystoid**—bladder-shaped
 30. **dactylose**—finger-shaped
 31. **deltoid**—triangle-shaped
 32. **dentiform**—tooth-shaped
 33. **digitiform**—finger-shaped
 34. **domical**—dome-shaped
 35. **ensiform**—sword-shaped
 36. **feliform**—catlike in form
 37. **galeate, galeiform**—helmet-shaped
 38. **gliriform**—rodentlike in form
 39. **granular, granulose**—having a form as if made up of grains
 40. **helical**—spiral-shaped
 41. **helicoid**—spiral-shaped; shaped like a snail's shell
 42. **herbaceous**—of the form of a leaf
 43. **ichthyomorphic**—fish-shaped
 44. **infundibular**—funnel-shaped
 45. **linguiform, lingulate**—tongue-shaped
 46. **lunate**—crescent-shaped
 47. **luniform**—moon-shaped
 48. **mammillary**—breast-shaped
 49. **napiform**—turnip-shaped
 50. **navicular**—boat-shaped
 51. **nuciform**—nut-shaped
 52. **nummiform, nummulary**—coin-shaped
 53. **olivary**—olive-shaped
 54. **oval, ovate, oviform, ovoid, ovular**—egg-shaped
 55. **palmate**—shaped like a hand
 56. **pediform**—shaped like a foot
 57. **peltate**—shield-shaped
 58. **petiolate**—stalk-shaped; stem-shaped
 59. **piliform**—hair-shaped
 60. **pisciform**—fish-shaped
 61. **pyramidoid**—pyramid-shaped
 62. **pyriform**—pear-shaped
 63. **quadrate**—square; roughly square in shape
 64. **reticular, reticulate**—netlike in form (reticularity, reticulation,n.)
 65. **rhombic**—diamond-shaped
 66. **rotate**—wheel-shaped
 67. **sagittal**—shaped like an arrow or arrow-head
 68. **sagittate, sagittiform**—shaped like an arrowhead
 69. **scaphoid**—boat-shaped
 70. **scutiform**—shield-shaped
 71. **semilunar**—shaped like a half-moon
 72. **setiform**—bristle-shaped
 73. **sinuous**—snakelike in form (sinuousness, sinuosity,n.)
 74. **spatulate**—spoon-shaped
 75. **sphenoid**—wedge-shaped
 76. **stellate, stelliform**—star-shaped

77. **tabular, tabulate**—table-shaped
78. **theriomorphic**—animal-like in form
79. **trapeziform**—trapezium-shaped
80. **triagonal**—triangle-shaped
81. **trochal**—wheel-shaped (zoology)
82. **umbilicate, umbilicated, umbiliform**—navel-shaped
83. **unciniform**—hook-shaped
84. **undulant, undulating, undulatory**—wavy in form or shape
85. **ungulate**—hoof-shaped
86. **urceolate**—urn-shaped
87. **vermicular, vermiform**—wormlike in shape
88. **villiform**—resembling in form the pile of velvet
89. **viperiform**—snakelike in form
90. **virgate**—wand-shaped; rod-shaped
91. **virgulate**—rod-shaped
92. **viverriform**—civetlike in form
93. **wavy**—in the shape of waves (waviness, n.)
94. **xiphoid**—sword-shaped (medical)

18. That Which Is Horn-Shaped: cornet,n.

19. Line That Indicates the Outer Shape of Something: outline,n.

20. Outline,n.
1. **circumscription**—outline
2. **conformation**—external outline
3. **contour**—outline of the curves of a figure or region
4. **diagram**—outline (diagrammatic,adj.)
5. **figuration**—outline
6. **lineation**—outline
7. **lines**—outline; contour
8. **profile**—outline; outline of a person's face
9. **shadow**—outline of a person, animal, or object on a surface, caused by the sun or light
10. **silhouette**—outline, blacked in, of a person, figure, or shape

21. To Outline,v. *From Sec. 20:* circumscribe, contour, diagram, profile, silhouette (circumscription,n.); *Also:* 1. **roughhew**—give a rough or crude outline to

508. ROUNDNESS

1. Round; Rounded,adj.
1. **beady**—round, small, and shiny (beadiness,n.)
2. **circular**—round (circularity,n.)
3. **cylindrical, cylindric**—round and long, with flat ends (cylindricality, cylindricalness,n.)
4. **lobate**—rounded and projecting
5. **orbiculate**—round; rounded
6. **rotund**—round; rounded (rotundity,n.)
7. **spherical, spheric**—round, like a ball, globe, or sphere; perfectly round (sphericity,n.)

2. Almost, but Not Completely, Round: spheroid, spheroidal,adj. (spheroidicity,n.)

3. Circular: compass, cycloid, orbicular, orbiculate,adj. (orbicularity, orbicularness,n.)

4. Circular and Flat: discoid,adj.

5. Semicircular: compass,adj.

6. Almost Circular in Form: orbiculate,adj.

7. Spherical: ampullaceous, global, globate, globated, globoid, globose, globous, globular, orbicular, rotund, spheriform,adj. (globoseness, globosity, globousness, globularness, orbicularity, orbicularness, rotundity,n.)

8. Ball: globe, orb, sphere,n.

9. Other Round Objects or Formations,n.
1. **cylinder**—long, round object with flat ends (cylindrical, cylindric,adj.)
2. **globule**—sphere-shaped particle (globular,adj.)

3. **lobation**—rounded and projecting formation
4. **lobe**—rounded part, usually projecting (lobar,adj.)
5. **spheroid**—body shaped like a sphere, but not truly spherical (spheroidicity,n. spheroid, spheroidal,adj.)

10. Flattened Circle: ellipse,n.

11. Having the Shape of an Ellipse: elliptical, elliptoid, oval, ovoid,adj.

12. Circle; Ring,n.
1. **annulation**—part or formation in the shape of a ring
2. **annulet**—little ring
3. **annulus**—ring; part, band, or space in the shape of a ring (annular,adj.)
4. **circlet**—small circle; ring
5. **equator**—any circle or circular band dividing the surface of a body into two equal and symmetrical parts; imaginary great circle on the earth's surface doing this to the earth (equatorial,adj.)
6. **gyre**—circle or ring (poetic)
7. **ringlet**—small circle; small ring
8. **wreath**—ring; part or formation in the shape of a ring or circle; circle of leaves and/or flowers twisted together

13. In the Form of a Ring: annular,adj. (annularity,n.)

14. Having Rings or Circles, or Bands in the Form of Rings: annulate, annulose, armillary,adj.

15. Formation into Rings: annulation,n.

16. Selected Parts of a Circle,n.
1. **arc**—portion of the circumference of a circle
2. **circumference**—external border of a circle (circumferential,adj.)
3. **diameter**—line through the center of a circle (diametric,adj.)
4. **octant**—eighth of a circle
5. **quadrant**—fourth of a circle
6. **radius**—line from the center of a circle to the circumference (radial,adj.)
7. **semicircle**—half a circle (semicircular, adj.)
8. **sextant**—sixth of a circle

17. Pert. to a Circle: circular,adj.

18. Device for Measuring the Arcs of Circles: cyclometer,n.

19. To Move in Circles or a Circular Path or Fashion: circle, circulate, gyrate, mill around, purl, revolve, ring, roll, rotate,v. (circulation, gyration, revolution, rotation,n. circulative, circulatory, gyratory, revolutionary, rotative, rotatory,adj.)

20. Lobed,adj.
1. **bifid**—divided into two equal lobes
2. **bilobate, bilobated, bilobed**—divided into two lobes
3. **lobate**—lobed; in the form of a lobe (lobation,n.)
4. **trilobate, trilobated, trilobal**—three-lobed (trilobation,n. trilobe,n. trilobe,v.)

21. Rayed,adj.
1. **actiniform**—having rays or radial members
2. **actinoid**—having rays, as a starfish
3. **radial**—arranged in rays
4. **radiate, radiated**—having rays
5. **spoked**—rayed
6. **starry**—arranged in rays
7. **triradiate**—having three rays, radiating branches, or spokes

22. Raylike: actinoid,adj.

509. ARCH

1. Arched Structure, Often Serving As a Roof, Ceiling, etc.: dome, vault,n. (domical, adj.)

2. Series of Arches: arcade, vault,n.

3. Pointed Arch: ogive,n. (ogival,adj.)

4. Arched Space: vault,n.

5. To Make in the Form of an Arch; To Cover with an Arch: arcade, arch, dome, vault,v.

6. To Become Formed, Rise, or Swell Out, into an Arch: arch, dome,v.

7. Arched: arch-shaped, arciform, domed, dome-shaped, domical, testudinate, vaulted, adj.

510. FATNESS

1. Fat; Stout,adj.

1. **adipose**—fat; obese (medical)
2. **beefy**—fat, in the sense of having an excess of flesh
3. **blowzy, blowzed**—fat, red-faced, and untidy
4. **blubbery**—fat; fat, as of a whale, i.e., having a lot of blubber
5. **bouncing**—stout; plump
6. **burly**—heavily built; stout-bodied
7. **buxom**—plump, but pleasing and attractive (applied to women)
8. **chubby**—fat, esp. in reference to children or unusually short people; plump
9. **chunky**—somewhat stout and short; thickly built and short
10. **corpulent**—possessed of bodily fleshiness, bulk, etc.; stout
11. **dumpy**—stout and short
12. **Falstaffian**—fat and jolly
13. **fattish**—somewhat fat
14. **fleshy, fleshly**—fat, in the sense of having an abundance of flesh
15. **heavy**—carrying more than usual, average, or normal weight
16. **obese**—very fat, far beyond normal, with a strong connotation of a diseased condition
17. **overweight**—fat, in the sense of more than is healthy; heavy
18. **paunchy**—fat, with most of the excess weight in the belly
19. **plump**—fat, in the sense of being well rounded or filled out
20. **podgy**—stout and short
21. **portly**—stout, and yet somehow imposing and dignified
22. **pudgy**—fat and short; thickset
23. **pursy**—fat
24. **roly-poly**—fat and short
25. **rotund**—fat, with the implication of roundness, squatness, or shortness
26. **squat, squatty**—fat and short
27. **stocky**—thickset
28. **stubby**—thickset
29. **thickset**—stout and short; thick in body
30. **tubby**—fat and short, like a tub
31. **well-fed**—fat; looking fat or plump from good eating

2. Fatness; Stoutness,n. *From Sec. 1:* adiposis or adiposity, beefiness, burliness, buxomness, chubbiness, chunkiness, corpulence, dumpiness, fleshiness, fleshliness, heaviness, obeseness or obesity, overweight, paunchiness, plumpness, podginess, portliness, pudginess, pursiness, roly-poliness, rotundity, squatness, stockiness, stubbiness, tubbiness; *Also:*

1. **avoirdupois**—weight, i.e., conspicuous weight or overweight (colloq.)
2. **embonpoint (French)**—plumpness
3. **polysarcia**—obesity (medical)

3. Having a Chubby and Innocent Face: cherubic,adj.

4. Fat Person,n.

1. **cherub**—one who has a chubby and innocent face (cherubic,adj.)
2. **fatty**—fat person (colloq.)

3. **punchinello**—fat, short, and odd-looking person
4. **roly-poly**—fat and short person
5. **tub**—fat person (colloq.)

5. To Grow, Become, or Cause to Be Fat: batten, fatten,v.

6. Big-Bellied; Having a Protuberant Belly: abdominous, paunchy, potbellied, ventricose, ventricous,adj. (paunchiness, potbelly, ventricoseness, ventricosity,n.)

7. A Big, Protuberant, or Prominent Belly: paunch,n.

8. Fat,n.

1. **blubber**—fat from the whale or other marine mammal
2. **butter**—fat of milk separated and processed for use
3. **butterfat**—fat of milk
4. **cream**—fatty part of milk that rises to the top
5. **grease**—melted animal fat, esp. when soft; any fatty matter; lubricant
6. **lanolin**—wool fat
7. **lard**—pig fat
8. **lubricant**—fat used to make something work smoothly
9. **margarine, oleomargarine**—vegetable or animal fat, or a combination, highly purified, and used as a butter substitute
10. **sebum**—fatty substance secreted by the sebacious glands
11. **shortening**—butter or other type of fat used in cooking or baking
12. **suet**—hard fat around the kidneys and loins of cattle and sheep
13. **tallow**—fat of animals of the ox or sheep family used in making candles, soap, certain kinds of margarine, etc.

9. Fatty; Fatlike; Referring to Fat,adj.

1. **adipose**—fatty or fatlike (adiposity, adiposeness,n.)
2. **blubbery**—like, or rich in, blubber
3. **buttery**—like, containing, or spread with, butter
4. **butyraceous**—like, or containing, butter
5. **creamy**—like, or containing, cream
6. **greasy**—like grease in feel or appearance; made up of, containing, smeared with, or soiled with, grease (greasiness,n.)
7. **liparoid, lipoid**—fatty; fatlike
8. **pinguid**—fatty
9. **sebacious**—fatty; pert. to fat; greasy
10. **slick**—greasy
11. **unctuous**—fatty; greasy (unctuousness, n.)

10. Causing or Promoting the Use or Consumption of Fat: lipotropic,adj.

11. Secreting a Fatty Substance, as Certain Glands of the Body: sebacious,adj.

12. To Put Fat on; To Cover or Smear with Fat: grease, lubricate, tallow,v. (lubrication, n. lubricator,n. lubricative,adj.)

13. Oil,n.

1. **lubricant**—oil or oil product used to make something work smoothly
2. **petrolatum**—mineral oil
3. **petroleum**—oil as taken from the ground
4. **unction**—oil used in anointing

14. Oily; Referring to Oil,adj.

1. **greasy**—oily (greasiness,n.)
2. **oleaginous**—oily; like, or producing, oil
3. **oleic**—pert. to, coming from, or deposited in, oil
4. **pinguid**—oily
5. **unctuous**—like an oil (unctuousness,n.)

15. Oil-Covered Place or Area, as on the Ocean, a Highway, etc.: slick,n.

16. To Oil,v.

1. **anoint**—pour or rub oil on; do so as a religious ceremony

2. **grease**—put grease on; smear with grease; lubricate

3. **lubricate**—apply oil or grease to in order to make work smoothly and without friction (lubricator,n. lubricative,adj.)

17. Act of Oiling,n. *From Sec. 16:* anointment, lubrication; *Also:* 1. **unction**—anointment

18. Place Where Cars Are Oiled, Greased, etc.: lubritorium,n. (colloq.)

19. To Drill for Oil in Unproven Areas: wildcat,v. (wildcatter,n.)

511. WIDTH

1. Wide,adj.
  1. **broad**—wide
  2. **splay**—wide and flat
  3. **squat, squatty**—wide and low

2. Width,n. *From Sec. 1:* broadness or breadth, squatness; *Also:* 1. **amplitude**—width

3. To Make or Cause to Be Wide or Wider; To Become or Grow Wide or Wider: broaden, dilate, expand, stretch, widen,v. (dilation or dilatation, expansion,n.)

4. To Make an Opening or Hole Wider: ream,v.

5. State of Being Widened: dilation, dilatation,n.

6. Widening: dilatant,adj. (dilatancy,n.)

7. Serving, Causing, or Tending to Widen: dilative, dilatative,adj.

8. Widened Part or Organ: dilatation,n.

512. NARROWNESS

1. Narrow: hairbreadth, necessitous, slender, adj. (slenderness,n.)

2. A Narrowing; A Morbid Narrowing of Some Tube or Organ of the Body: stricture, n.

513. THINNESS

1. Thin; Slender; Slim; Not Fat,adj.
  1. **angular**—thin and with the bones prominent through the skin
  2. **bony**—thin and with the bones prominent or sticking out through the skin
  3. **cadaverous**—thin and pale, like a corpse
  4. **consumptive**—wasted
  5. **elongate, elongated**—slender and long
  6. **emaciated**—abnormally, perhaps even morbidly, thin, as if one has wasted away from lack of food
  7. **gangling**—slender and tall, but awkwardly and loosely built
  8. **gaunt**—thin, bony, and haggard, as from suffering, illness, or starvation
  9. **gracile**—gracefully slender
  10. **lanky, lank**—ungracefully thin and tall, with the added implication of being loose-jointed
  11. **lean**—having little fleshy fat
  12. **macerated**—wasted
  13. **peaked**—thin and sickly
  14. **rangy**—slim, with long limbs
  15. **rawboned**—thin in the sense of having little flesh on the bones
  16. **reedy**—slender and long
  17. **scraggy**—thin and bony; lean and tough
  18. **scrawny**—thin and bony; very thin
  19. **skeleton-like**—so thin as to be almost all bones and no flesh
  20. **skinny**—very thin
  21. **slab-sided**—thin and tall
  22. **slight**—slender
  23. **spare**—thin; lean

  24. **spindly, spindling**—unusually or excessively thin and long or thin and tall
  25. **stringy**—thin and long; thin and tall
  26. **svelte**—slender; slender and graceful of figure (often of women)
  27. **sylphlike**—slim and shapely (of women)
  28. **waspish, wasp-waisted**—having an unusually slender waist, like that of a wasp
  29. **wasted**—having lost flesh to an abnormal or morbid degree
  30. **willowy**—slender; slim and graceful
  31. **wiry**—slim, strong, and tough
  32. **wispy**—slender
  33. **withy**—wiry and agile
  34. **wraithlike**—thin to the point of looking like a ghost

2. Thinness; Slenderness; Slimness,n. *From Sec. 1:* angularity, boniness, cadaverousness, consumptiveness, emaciation, gauntness, gracility, lankiness, lankness, leanness, peakedness, ranginess, reediness, scragginess, scrawniness, skinniness, slightness, spareness, waspishness, wasp-waistedness, willowiness, wiriness, wispiness

3. Thin, Slender, or Slim Person,n. *From Sec. 1:* cadaver, scrag, skeleton, spindling, sylph, wisp, wraith; *Also:* 1. **slip**—slim, young person, usually a female

4. To Make Thin, Slender, or Slim,v. *From Sec. 1:* emaciate, macerate, skeletonize, waste (emaciation, maceration,n.) ; *Also:*
  1. **slenderize**—make slender
  2. **slim, slim down**—make slim
  3. **thin**—make thin

5. To Become or Grow Thin, Slender, or Slim,v. *From Sec. 4:* macerate, waste away; slenderize, slim or slim down, thin

6. Thin, i.e., Not Thick,adj.
  1. **attenuate, attenuated**—thin; fine
  2. **capillary**—very thin, i.e., as thin as a hair
  3. **cobwebby**—so thin as to resemble a spider's web
  4. **diaphanous**—so thin as to be translucent or transparent
  5. **filmy**—as thin as a mere film
  6. **fine**—thin, small, and delicate; very thin
  7. **fine-drawn**—fine-spun
  8. **fine-spun**—amazingly thin, as if, or because of having been, drawn out to a fine thread
  9. **gauzy**—thin and transparent
  10. **gossamer**—incredibly thin and filmy, like a spider's web
  11. **laminated**—beaten or rolled into a thin plate (of metal)
  12. **papery**—thin, like paper
  13. **sheer**—very thin; so thin as to be transparent or almost transparent
  14. **wispy**—filmy

7. Thinness,n. *From Sec. 6:* attenuation, capillarity, diaphanousness or diaphaneity, filminess, fineness, gauziness, sheerness

8. That Which Is Thin,n. *From Sec. 6:* cobweb, film, gauze, gossamer, wisp

9. To Make Thin,v. *From Sec. 6:* attenuate, laminate (attenuation, lamination,n. attenuant,adj.).

10. To Become Thin,v. *From Sec. 6:* attenuate (attenuation,n.)

11. Capable of Being Hammered Thin (of Metals): ductile, tensile,adj. (ductility, tensility,n.)

12. Thin or Thinned; Insubstantial; Not Dense,adj.
  1. **aerial**—thin, insubstantial, and light as air
  2. **airy**—insubstantial
  3. **attenuate, attenuated**—thin; thinned; made less dense; slender
  4. **cobwebby**—insubstantial, like a spider's web

5. **dilute, diluted**—thin, because mixed with water or other thinning agent; thin and weak
6. **extenuate**—attenuate
7. **fine-spun**—highly or excessively rarefied
8. **flimsy**—thin, in the sense of being without substance
9. **frothy**—insubstantial, like foam
10. **meager**—thin; having little flesh or substance
11. **rare**—thin, in the sense of not being dense
12. **rarefied**—thin; not dense; thinned; made less dense
13. **serous**—thin and watery
14. **sleazy**—flimsy
15. **slender**—without, or with very little, substance
16. **slight**—slender
17. **subtile**—so thin or so nearly insubstantial as almost to escape detection or perception; subtle
18. **subtle**—thin; insubstantial; not dense; rarefied (of liquids)
19. **tenuous**—thin; not dense (of air or fluid); without substance; so nearly insubstantial as to be hard to grasp or perceive
20. **unsubstantial**—insubstantial
21. **vaporous**—insubstantial
22. **watery, waterish**—thin; thin and transparent (of liquids)
23. **wishy-washy**—thin and pale; thin and weak; having no substance
24. **wispy**—insubstantial
25. **wraithlike**—insubstantial

13. **Thinness; Insubstantiality,n.** *From Sec. 12:* airiness, attenuation, diluteness or dilution, flimsiness, frothiness, meagerness, rarity; rarefaction (from *rarefied*); serousness or serosity, sleaziness, slenderness, slightness; subtileness, subtilety or subtilty; subtleness or subtlety, tenuousness or tenuity, vaporousness or vaporosity, wateriness

14. **That Which Thins,n.** *From Sec. 12:* attenuant, diluent, extenuative

15. **That Which Is Thin,n.** *From Sec. 12:* cobweb, froth, vapor, wisp, wraith

16. **To Make Thin or Thinner,v.** *From Sec. 12:* attenuate, dilute, extenuate, subtilize (attenuation, dilution, extenuation, subtilization,n.)

17. **Making, or Causing to Be, Thin or Thinner,adj.** *From Sec. 12:* attenuant, diluent, extenuative or extenuatory, rarefactive

18. **To Become Thin,v.** *From Sec. 12:* attenuate, extenuate,v. (attenuation, extenuation,n.)

514. SHORTNESS
(OF APPEARANCE)

1. **Short,adj.**
1. **chunky**—short and thickly built; short and somewhat stout or stocky (chunkiness,n.)
2. **dumpy**—short and stout (dumpiness,n.)
3. **podgy**—short and stout (podginess,n.)
4. **pudgy**—short and fat; short and thick or thickset (pudginess,n.)
5. **roly-poly**—short and fat (roly-poliness, n.)
6. **rotund**—fat, with the implication of shortness (rotundity,n.)
7. **squat, squatty**—short and fat; short and thickset (squatness,n.)
8. **stocky**—short and thickset (stockiness,n.)
9. **stubby**—short and thickset (stubbiness, n.)
10. **stumpy**—short and thick
11. **thickset**—short and stout
12. **tubby**—short and fat, like a tub (tubbiness,n.)

2. **Short and Fat Person:** roly-poly; tub (colloq.),n.

515. TALLNESS

1. **Tall,adj.**
1. **Amazonian**—unusually tall, or unusually tall and strong (of women)
2. **gangling**—tall and slender, but awkwardly and loosely built; awkwardly lanky
3. **high**—tall (of buildings, structures, mountains, etc.)
4. **Junoesque**—tall and stately (of women)
5. **lanky, lank**—ungracefully tall and thin, with the added implication of being loose-jointed (lankiness, lankness,n.)
6. **rangy**—long-limbed and slim (ranginess, n.)
7. **sculpturesque**—statuesque (sculpturesqueness,n.)
8. **slab-sided**—tall and thin
9. **slender**—tall and slim (slenderness,n.)
10. **spindly, spindling**—unusually or excessively tall and thin
11. **statuesque**—tall, beautiful, graceful, and shapely, like a statue—usually of women (statuesqueness,n.)
12. **stringy**—tall and thin
13. **towering**—very tall; taller than the surroundings
14. **willowy**—tall and graceful (willowiness, n.)

2. **Tall Person,n.** *From Sec. 1:* Amazon, Juno, spindling

3. **Degree of Tallness:** height, stature,n.

4. **To Be Taller than:** tower over,v.

516. LENGTH
(OF APPEARANCE)

1. **Long,adj.**
1. **elongate, elongated**—long and thin in shape or appearance
2. **oblong**—elongate
3. **reedy**—long and slender (reediness,n.)
4. **spindly, spindling**—unusually or excessively long and thin (spindliness,n.)
5. **stringy**—long and thin

2. **Degree of Longness:** length,n.

3. **Longer than Wide:** oblong,adj.

4. **To Make Longer:** draw out, elongate, extend, lengthen, prolong, prolongate, stretch,v. (elongation, extension, prolongment, prolongation,n. elongative,adj.)

5. **To Become Longer:** elongate, extend, lengthen, stretch,v. (elongation, extension,n.)

517. THICKNESS

1. **To Thicken, i.e., Make Thick,v.**
1. **clabber**—curdle
2. **clot**—thicken; form into a thick mass; coagulate
3. **coagulate**—change from a fluid state to one of thickness, or of syrupy thickness
4. **congeal**—thicken; thicken through cold or freezing
5. **curd**—thicken; coagulate; curdle
6. **curdle**—thicken; make thick and sour; coagulate
7. **inspissate**—thicken; thicken by evaporation

2. **To Become Thick,v.** *From Sec. 1:* clabber, clot, coagulate, congeal, curd, curdle, inspissate

3. **A Making or Becoming Thick,n.** *From Sec. 1:* coagulation, congealment or congelation, inspissation

4. Thick or Thickened,adj. *From Sec. 1:* clabbered, clotted, etc.; clotty; *Also:*
1. **grumous**—thick; clotted (grumousness, n.)
2. **ropy**—viscid (ropiness,n.)
3. **turbid**—thick with sediment or mud (turbidness, turbidity,n.)
4. **viscid, viscous**—thick and syrupy; thick and sticky, like syrup or glue (viscidness, viscidity, viscousness, viscosity,n.)

5. Thickening Agent,n. *From Sec. 1:* coagulant, inspissator; *Also:* 1. **rennet**—substance used to thicken milk

6. Thickened Mass: clot,n.

7. Thick in Body or Arrangement,adj.
1. **chunky**—thickset and short (chunkiness, n.)
2. **dense**—thick in the sense of the individual parts closely packed together (denseness, density,n.)
3. **pudgy**—thickset and short (pudginess,n.)
4. **squat, squatty**—thick and short, or thickset and short—of the body, persons, animals, etc. (squatness,n.)
5. **stocky**—thick for one's, or its, height; thickset and short (stockiness,n.)
6. **stubby**—stocky (stubbiness,n.)
7. **stumpy**—thick and short
8. **thickset**—thick in arrangement; of thick build or body; dense

8. To Make or Become Thick or Dense: densen, densify,v. (densification,n. densifier, n.)

9. Instrument to Measure Density: densimeter, densitometer,n. (densimetry,n. densimetric,adj.)

10. Instrument to Measure Photographic Density: densitometer,n.

11. A Thickness: ply,n.

518. SWELL

1. To Swell; To Become Swollen,v.
1. **balloon**—swell out; distend
2. **belly**—swell out
3. **bilge**—swell out
4. **billow**—swell
5. **blister**—swell; turn into a watery swelling
6. **bloat**—swell; swell up; swell out
7. **bulge**—swell
8. **bulk, bulk up**—swell
9. **distend**—swell from inward pressure
10. **erect**—fill with blood and swell (of the penis)
11. **expand**—swell
12. **fester**—become gradually red, hot, and swollen
13. **inflame**—become red, hot, and swollen
14. **inflate**—swell up by being filled with air, gas, etc.
15. **intumesce**—swell up
16. **protuberate**—swell out
17. **puff up**—swell; inflate
18. **surge**—swell and rise
19. **tumefy**—swell; become swollen
20. **wallow**—swell; surge

2. To Swell, i.e., Cause to Swell or Become Swollen,v. *From Sec. 1:* balloon, belly, bilge, blister, bloat, bulge, bulk out, distend, expand, fester, inflame, inflate, puff up, tumefy; *Also:* 1. **blubber**—swell (the face)

3. Act, Fact, or Process of Swelling, Becoming Swollen, or Causing to Swell,n. *From Secs. 1 and 2:* distention or distension, erection, expansion, inflammation, inflation, intumescence, protuberance or protuberancy, surge, tumefaction, wallow; *Also:* 1. **swell**—act of swelling

4. Swollen, Swelled,adj. *From Sec. 1:* ballooned, bellied, etc.; billowy, bulgy, distent,

erect, intumescent, protuberant, puffy, surgy; *Also:*
1. **angry**—painfully inflamed
2. **blubber, blubbery**—swollen
3. **bumpy**—swollen; knobby
4. **dropsical**—swollen
5. **edematous, edematose**—swollen and filled with serous fluid (of the tissues, abdomen, etc.)
6. **emphysematous**—swollen
7. **flatulent**—swollen with air or gas, esp. as applied to a distensible organ such as the stomach
8. **knobby, knobbed**—having, or full of, rounded swellings
9. **knurled**—knobby
10. **lumpy**—having, or full of, small swellings
11. **nodous, nodose**—full of swellings
12. **nodular**—having small swellings
13. **nodulous, nodulose**—full of small swellings
14. **patulous**—swollen
15. **plethoric**—swollen
16. **torose, torous**—swollen; bulging with well-developed muscles; knobby
17. **tuberous**—covered with swellings or rounded knobs or protuberances
18. **tumescent**—slightly swollen
19. **tumid**—swollen; so swollen as to be bursting or ready to burst
20. **tumorous**—swollen; having swollen parts
21. **turgid**—swollen, often from some internal pressure or force
22. **utriculate**—swollen like a bladder
23. **varicose**—irregularly swollen (medical)
24. **ventricose**—swollen; swollen out on one side (zoology and botany)
25. **ventricular**—swollen

5. Swollenness; State or Condition of Being Swollen,n. *From Sec. 1:* bloatedness, expansion, inflammation, inflatedness or inflation, tumefaction; *From Sec. 4:* billowiness, bulginess, distention or distension, erectness or erection, intumescence, protuberance or protuberancy, puffiness; angriness, bumpiness, flatulence, lumpiness, nodosity, patulousness, torosity, tuberousness, tumescence, tumidness or tumidity, turgidness or turgidity, varicosity, ventricoseness or ventricosity; *Also:*
1. **dropsy**—edema (dropsical,adj.)
2. **edema**—swollen condition of tissues, or distention of the abdomen, caused by the abnormal accumulation of serous fluids in various cavities and spaces of the body (edematous, edematose, edemic,adj.)
3. **emphysema**—swollen state caused by gas or air in the body tissues (emphysematous, adj.)
4. **meteorism**—state in which the abdomen is swollen with air or gas
5. **swell**—state or condition of being swollen
6. **turgor**—state of normal swollenness in living cells (physiology)
7. **tympanism, tympanites, tympanosis, tympany**—meteorism (tympanitic,adj.)
8. **tympany**—distention

6. A Swelling,n. *From Sec. 1:* belly, billow, blister, bulge, fester, inflammation, intumescence, protuberance or protuberancy, puff, tumefaction; *From Sec. 4:* bump, knob, knurl, lump, node, nodule, tuberosity, tumor, varicosity (nodal, nodular,adj.); *Also:*
1. **blain**—inflammatory swelling
2. **bunion**—inflamed swelling on the first joint of the big toe
3. **chilblain**—inflammatory swelling on the hands or feet from exposure to cold
4. **mouse**—dark swelling caused by a blow (slang)
5. **tuber**—swelling (anatomy)
6. **wheal**—small swelling on the skin that burns or itches

7. Causing Swelling,adj. *From Sec. 1:* distensive, inflammative or inflammatory, tumefacient

8. Swelling; Becoming Swollen: surgent, turgescent, ventricular,adj. (turgescence, turgescency, or turgor,n.)

9. Capable of Being Distended: distensible, distensive,adj. (distensibility,n.)

10. Swollen Part: swell,n.

519. FLATNESS

1. Flat,adj.
1. discoid—flat and circular
2. level—flat, i.e., with no part higher or lower than any other (levelness,n.)
3. oblate—flat or flattened at the ends
4. plane—flat; level
5. spatulate—flat; flattened
6. splay—flat and wide
7. squat, squatty—flat and close to the ground; flat and low (squatness,n.)
8. tabular, tabulate—flat

2. A Flat Surface: level, plane,n.

3. To Become Flat: flatten, flatten out, level, level off, level out,v.

4. To Flatten, i.e., Make Flat,v.
1. crush—flatten by great pressure
2. level, level off, level out—make flat or level
3. pat—flatten by stroking lightly
4. plane—make flat or level by cutting or shaving
5. squash—flatten by striking

5. A Plate,n.
1. discus—heavy plate to be thrown in a contest of skill
1. disk, disc—flat, circular plate
3. spangle—plate of shiny metal

520. RELATIONSHIP

1. Relationship,n.
1. affiliation—relationship
2. affinity—relationship; relationship through marriage; spiritual relationship between two people of opposite sex
3. alliance—relationship of qualities; relationship of people or groups having some common interest, purpose, or goal
4. association—relationship; relationship in thought
5. cognation—relationship by birth, origin, descent, nature, or quality
6. communion—intimate relationship, esp. spiritual
7. concern—relationship
8. congeneracy—relationship in origin, nature, or action
9. connection—relationship
10. consanguinity—close relationship; relationship by blood
11. consociation—relationship
12. contact—mental relationship
13. contingency—close relationship
14. correlation—mutual relationship
15. dependence, dependency—relationship in which one is influenced by another
16. equation—equal relationship
17. integration—complete relationship
18. interconnection—mutual relationship
19. interdependence, interdependency—mutual dependence
20. interrelation, interrelationship—mutual relationship
21. intimacy—close relationship; close, friendly relationship
22. kindredship, kindredness—relationship by birth or blood; close relationship; kinship

23. kinship—relationship; blood relationship; loosely, relationship through marriage; relationship in quality, character, or kind; close relationship
24. liaison—relationship between parts of the army, a corporation, etc., that is intended to insure co-operation, knowledge of what each is doing, etc.
25. linkage, link—relationship of thought, ideas, etc.
26. mutuality—interdependence; reciprocity
27. pertinence, pertinency—relationship to the matter under discussion
28. proportion—relationship between parts
29. ratio—proportion
30. reciprocity—relationship of feeling; relationship in which each influences the other
31. sympathy—relationship in which one is affected by, or responds to, what affects another or elicits a response from another
32. terms—personal relationship
33. theorem—mathematical relationship expressed as a formula or equation
34. ubiety—relationship in place
35. union—relationship in which the parts or people are joined
36. unity—union

2. To Relate, i.e., Have a Relationship or Be Related,v. *From Sec. 1:* ally, connect, consociate, correlate, depend, integrate, interconnect, interdepend, interrelate, link, pertain, unite

3. To Relate, i.e., Bring into Relationship or Consider as Being Related,v. *From Sec. 1:* ally, associate, connect, consociate, correlate, equate, interconnect, interrelate, link; *Also:*
1. bracket—form a relationship in the mind or in one's speaking between (things); think, or speak of, as related or associated

4. Related,adj. *From Sec. 1:* affiliated, allied, etc.; cognate, congeneric or congenerous, consanguineous, consociate, contingent, correlative, dependent, interconnective, interdependent, intimate, kindred, kin, pertinent, proportional or proportionate, reciprocal, sympathetic; *Also:*
1. connatural—allied
2. equiparent—having the same relationship to each other (term in logic)

5. One Who, or That Which, Is in a Relationship,n. *From Sec. 1:* cognate (cognatal, adj.), congener, consociate, correlate, dependent, reciprocal; *Also:* 1. cousin—that which is related to another

6. Network of Interrelating Parts: plexus, n.

7. Tending to Have a Close Relationship with the Members of One's Family: clannish,adj. (clannishness,n.)

8. Presenting Events to Show Interrelationship: pragmatic,adj.

9. To Bring into Proper Relationship,v.
1. adjust—bring into proper relationship (adjustment,n. adjustive,adj.)
2. correlate—bring into proper relationship, one with the other (correlation,n. correlative,adj.)
3. orient, orientate—bring into correct relationship with the surroundings (orientation,n. orientative,adj.)

10. In Proportion: commensurate, proportional, proportionate,adj. (commensurateness, proportionality, proportionateness, proportion,n.)

11. Not in Proportion: disproportional, disproportionate, incommensurate,adj. (disproportionality, disproportionateness, disproportion, incommensurateness,n.)

521. PERTINENCE

1. Pertinent: applicable, apposite, appurtenant, apropos, apt, connected, germane, material, pat, relevant, to the point,adj.

2. Pertinence: applicability, application, appositeness, appurtenance, aptness, bearing, connection, germaneness, materiality, patness, pertinency, relevance, relevancy,n.

3. To Pertain: appertain, apply, bear upon, connect,v.

4. Legally Pertinent: appurtenant,adj. (appurtenance,n.)

5. Pertinent in Time: opportune,adj. (opportuneness,n.)

6. Not Pertinent: extraneous, immaterial, impertinent, inapplicable, inapposite, inappurtenant, inapropos, inconsequential, irrelevant, non-germane, pointless, remote, unapt, unconnected,adj.

7. Lack of Pertinence: extraneousness, immateriality, impertinence, impertinency, inapplicability, inappositeness, inappurtenance, inconsequentiality, irrelevance, irrelevancy, non-germaneness, pointlessness, remoteness, unaptness, unconnectedness,n.

8. That Which Is Not Pertinent: irrelevancy,n.

9. Not Pertinent in Time: inopportune,adj. (inopportuneness,n.)

522. INVOLVEMENT

1. To Involve,v.
1. **entail**—involve (an act, action, circumstance, happening, etc.) as a necessary or required accompaniment or result of another act, action, etc. (entailment,n.)
2. **entangle**—involve in a difficult, confused, or tangled-up situation (entanglement,n.)
3. **implicate**—involve in something, usually something illegal, wrong, or sinful (implication,n.)
4. **incriminate**—involve in a crime, sin, or other wrongdoing (incrimination,n.)
5. **inculpate**—involve in a guilty action (inculpation,n.)
6. **mire**—involve in a difficult or complicated situation
7. **tangle**—involve in something that hinders, embarrasses, or obstructs (tanglement,n.)

2. Involved As an Essential Part: implicit, adj.

3. Involvement in Wrongdoing: complicity, n.

523. RELATIONS

1. Relations,n.
1. **commerce**—social relations or intercourse
2. **conversation**—social intercourse
3. **dealings**—business or friendly relations
4. **intercourse**—intimate relations among people, groups, or nations
5. **terms**—personal relations
6. **traffic**—relations; commercial relations; intercourse
7. **truck**—relations (usually derogatory)

2. To Have Relations,v. *From Sec. 1:* deal, traffic, truck; *Also:*
1. **fraternize**—have relations (fraternization,n. fraternizer,n.)
2. **socialize**—have social or friendly relations (socialization,n.)

3. Science of Human Relations,n.
1. **social science**—science, or one of the sciences, dealing with human relations in any of their aspects (social scientist,n.)

2. **sociology**—science of human relations in society or in groups (sociologist,n. sociologic, sociological,adj.)

4. Management of Relations between Nations: diplomacy,n. (diplomat,n. diplomatic,adj.)

5. Art of the Management of Relations between Nations: diplomatics,n. (diplomatist,n. diplomatic,adj.)

6. A Diplomat,n.
1. **ambassador**—highest diplomatic representative (ambassadorial,adj.)
2. **attaché**—member of a diplomatic staff
3. **chargé d'affaires**—diplomatic representative of lower rank
4. **consul**—diplomatic representative who lives in the foreign country to which he is accredited in order to protect the business and other interests of the citizens of his own country (consular,adj.)
5. **envoy**—diplomatic agent lower in rank than an ambassador, higher than a minister
6. **internuncio**—diplomatic representative of the Pope, lower in rank than a nuncio (internuncial, internunciary,adj.)
7. **legate**—ambassador; envoy (legatine, adj.)
8. **minister**—diplomatic representative of a nation or government (ministerial,adj.)
9. **nuncio**—permanent representative of the Pope to a foreign government
10. **plenipotentiary**—diplomat of any rank with full power to negotiate for his government (plenipotentiary,adj.)

7. Ambassador and His Staff: embassy, legation,n.

8. Envoys As a Group: embassy,n.

9. Office or Residence of a Diplomat or Diplomats: consulate, embassy, legation,n.

524. ASSOCIATION

1. To Associate; To Come into Association or Form an Association with,v.
1. **affiliate**—associate in action, endeavor, or interests
2. **ally**—come into voluntary association because of similar interests or goals (of people, groups, countries, etc.)
3. **colleague**—ally
4. **confederate**—ally
5. **consociate**—associate
6. **consort**—associate
7. **conspire**—associate in an illegal act or plot
8. **federate**—ally
9. **fraternize**—associate; associate in a friendly or brotherly fashion; associate in an intimate or friendly fashion with the citizens of a conquered or enemy country
10. **hobnob**—associate on friendly or intimate terms
11. **league**—form an association for some definite purpose (of people, groups, or nations)
12. **mingle**—associate
13. **syndicate**—form an association to engage in some joint business, industrial, or financial endeavor
14. **unite**—associate in an endeavor or toward an end

2. To Bring into Association,v. *From Sec. 1:* affiliate, ally, confederate, consociate, federate, fraternize, syndicate, unite

3. Association; A Coming or Bringing into Association,n. *From Secs. 1 and 2:* affiliation, alliance, consociation, consortion, conspiracy, federation, fraternization, syndication, union; *Also:*

1. **comether**—friendly association
2. **copartnership**—equal partnership
3. **partnership**—association between two or more people in a mutual endeavor

4. An Association,n. *From Sec. 1:* alliance, confederacy or confederation, federation, league, syndicate, union; *Also:*
1. **coalition**—temporary association of statesmen or countries for some specific purpose
2. **federation**—association, often of political divisions, in which the components retain certain local powers
3. **phalanx, phalanstery**—association of people organized under principles of community ownership advanced by François Fourier

5. An Associate; One Who Associates; Member of an Association,n. *From Sec. 1:* affiliate, ally, colleague, consociate, consort or consorter, conspirator, fraternizer; *From Sec. 3:* copartner, partner; *From Sec. 4:* coalitioner or coalitionist; *Also:*
1. **accomplice**—associate in wrongdoing or crime
2. **adjunct**—associate; subordinate associate
3. **colleague**—associate in a profession
4. **confederate**—associate in an illegal, unethical, or unacceptable act
5. **confrère**—associate in an occupation, profession, endeavor, etc.
6. **particeps criminis (Latin)**—criminal accomplice (legal)

6. Associate or Associated,adj. *From Sec. 1:* affiliated, allied, etc.; affiliate, confederate, consociate, federate

7. Associational or Associative; Pert. or Referring to Association,adj. *From Sec. 1:* consociational or consociative, conspiratorial, federal or federative; *From Sec. 4:* coalitional

8. Tending to Associate Only with Members of One's Group: clannish, cliquish, cliquy,adj. (clannishness, cliquishness,n.)

9. An Association, Club, or Society,n.
1. **academy**—society of scholars for the advancement of an art, subject, profession, etc. (academician,n.)
2. **athenaeum**—literary or scientific society
3. **Black Hand**—criminal society, originating in Italy, practicing murder and blackmail in the U.S.
4. **brotherhood**—association of people in the same profession, occupation, etc., or with a common purpose or similar interests (brother,n.)
5. **confraternity**—association of men for some purpose; brotherhood (confrère,n. confraternal,adj.)
6. **consortium**—club; society (consortial, adj.)
7. **fellowship**—association of people of similar tastes and interests
8. **fraternity**—association of boys or men in a school or college; a club of "brothers" ("frater,"n.)
9. **league**—association of people with common purpose, interests, etc.
10. **order**—society united by common obligation or honorary distinction; fraternity; monastic fraternity
11. **organization**—association or club of people united in a common purpose (organizational,adj.)
12. **sisterhood**—association of women with a common purpose (sister,n.)
13. **sodality**—association; club
14. **sorority**—club of girls, or "sisters," in a school or college
15. **sorosis**—woman's club; sisterhood
16. **tong**—secret Chinese association either in China or America

17. **Turnverein (German)**—club for athletic or gymnastic exercises (turner,n.)

525. CONDITION; PROVISION

1. Condition; Provision,n.
1. **codicil**—added or explanatory provision
2. **contingency, contingent**—condition dependent on something uncertain or unknown
3. **postulate**—necessary condition
4. **proviso**—condition; sentence or clause in an agreement that states a condition
5. **qualification**—condition that must be met beforehand
6. **stipulation**—condition in an agreement, bargain, contract, etc.

2. Conditional; Provisional,adj. *From Sec. 1:* codicillary, contingent, stipulative; *Also:*
1. **dependent**—conditional
2. **provisory**—provisional
3. **subject (to)**—conditional (on or upon)
4. **tentative**—done provisionally and subject to change; conditional

3. To Condition; To Provide,v. *From Sec. 1:* postulate, stipulate (postulation, stipulation,n.)

526. DEPENDENCE

1. To Depend on or upon: bank on, hinge on or upon, reckon on, rely on or upon,v. (reliance,n.)

2. To Depend Mutually: interdepend,v. (interdependence, interdependency,n.)

3. To Depend on for Support, Literally or Figuratively: lean on,v.

4. A Dependent Person: client, dependent, pensioner,n.

5. One Who Is Dependent on the Will of Another: puppet,n.

6. Able to Be Depended upon: dependable, reliable, responsible, stable, steady, trustworthy, trusty, unfailing,adj. (dependability, reliability, responsibleness or responsibility, stableness or stability, steadiness, trustworthiness, trustiness,n.)

7. Person or Thing That Can Be Depended upon when Needed: stand-by,n.

8. That on Which One Relies for Lack of Anything Else: recourse, refuge, resort, resource,n.

527. RESPONSIBILITY

1. Responsibility: blame, burden, onus,n.

2. To Place the Responsibility on: blame,v.

3. To Be Responsible for: answer for, sponsor, vouch for,v. (sponsor,n. sponsorship,n.)

4. To Give an Unbearable Responsibility to: burden,v.

5. To Shift Responsibility to Someone Else: pass the buck,v. (colloq.)

6. Irresponsible: fly-by-night,adj.

528. DUTY

1. Duty: liability, obligation, onus, province, responsibility,n.

2. Required by Duty or As a Duty: duteous, dutiful, obligatory,adj.

3. Resting on (One) As a Duty: incumbent on,adj.

4. Arising or Proceeding from a Sense of Duty: duteous, dutiful,adj.

5. Doing What Is Required by Duty: duteous, dutiful,adj.

6. Failure in, or Neglect of, Duty: default, defection, delinquency, dereliction, misprision, n. (defaultant or defaulter, delinquent,n. defaultant, delinquent, derelict, adj. default, v.)

7. Neglect of Official or Legal Duty: nonfeasance,n. (non-feasor,n.)

8. Failure to Meet Financial Duties: default, delinquency,n. (defaultant or defaulter, delinquent,n. defaultant, delinquent,adj. default,v.)

9. Science or Theory of Duty,n.
  1. deontology—science or theory of duty or moral obligation (deontologist,n. deontological,adj.)
  2. ethics—science of moral duty (ethical, adj.)
  3. eudaemonism—theory of ethics that enforces duty according to its relation to happiness or well-being (eudaemonist,n. eudaemonistic, eudaemonistical,adj.)

529. SIMILARITY

1. Similar; Same,adj.
  1. akin—of the same kind; allied by natural qualities
  2. alike—similar; without difference
  3. allied—similar in kind, structure, function, descent, etc.
  4. analogous—similar in some respect (of things, ideas, or abstractions that are essentially different)
  5. approximate—somewhat similar
  6. coinciding, coincident, coincidental—corresponding exactly
  7. collateral—similar; corresponding
  8. commensurate—corresponding
  9. companion—corresponding; matching
  10. congeneric, congenerous—of the same genus or species
  11. congruent—exactly the same or alike in spatial shape
  12. consubstantial—similar in kind or nature
  13. corresponding, correspondent—similar; similar in shape, size, color, or other attributes
  14. homogeneous—similar; of the same kind; having a similarity owing to common origin
  15. homologous, homological, homologic—similar in position, proportion, structure or value
  16. homotaxic, homotaxial, homotaxeous, homotactic—similar in arrangement, esp. in reference to fossils or other geological deposits
  17. identical—exactly the same; exactly alike
  18. kindred, kin—similar; similar or alike in kind or type
  19. matching—similar in size, color, shape, etc.
  20. parallel—similar; corresponding
  21. proportional, proportionate—corresponding; symmetrical
  22. reciprocal—corresponding one to the other
  23. regular—symmetrical
  24. self-same—the very same in every way
  25. symmetrical—similar and balanced in size and shape on both sides
  26. twin—exactly the same as another

2. Similarity, Sameness, or Likeness,n. *From Sec. 1:* analogy, approximation, coincidence or coincidency, commensurateness, congruence or congruity, consubstantiality, correspondence, homogeneity or homogeneousness, homology; homotaxis, homotaxy, or homotaxia; identity, kinship, parallelism;

proportion, proportionality, or proportionateness; reciprocity, regularity, self-sameness, symmetry; *Also:*
  1. affinity—similarity
  2. community—similarity; likeness; identity
  3. conformity, conformance—similarity in form or character
  4. resemblance—similarity
  5. semblance—similarity; likeness
  6. similitude—similarity

3. One Who, or That Which, Is Similar or the Same,n. *From Sec. 1:* analogue, companion, congener, correspondent, homologue or homolog, kin, match, parallel, reciprocal, twin; *From Sec. 2:* semblance, similitude; *Also:*
  1. copy—one who, or that which, is the same as another
  2. counterpart—person or thing that bears a close resemblance to another; corresponding person or thing
  3. double—one who, or that which, is exactly the same as another
  4. Doppelgänger (German), doubleganger—fictional, unreal, or ghostly counterpart or double of an actual person
  5. duplicate—something exactly the same as something else
  6. image—counterpart; reflection
  7. likeness—one who, or that which, is strikingly similar to another person or thing, to an original, etc.
  8. mate—one of a pair that are the same
  9. mirror image—double
  10. obverse—counterpart
  11. opposite number—one who holds a similar or corresponding rank, position, etc., in another institution or organization
  12. reflection—that which is the same as another
  13. simulacre—likeness; reflection (simulacral,adj.)
  14. simulacrum—shadowy, unreal, faint, or insubstantial likeness

4. To Be or Become Similar or the Same,v. *From Sec. 1:* approximate, coincide, correspond, identify, match, parallel, reciprocate (approximation, coincidence, correspondence, identification, reciprocation,n.); *From Sec. 2:* conform, resemble (conformance, resemblance, n.); *From Sec. 3:* duplicate (duplication,n.); *Also:*
  1. agree—be the same; correspond exactly (agreement,n.)
  2. assimilate—become similar to the rest (assimilation,n.)
  3. border on—be similar to
  4. compare—be similar

5. To Make Similar or the Same,v. *From Sec. 1:* homologize, identify, reciprocalize, symmetrize (identification, symmetrization, n.); *From Sec. 2:* conform; *From Sec. 4:* assimilate (assimilation,n.); *Also:*
  1. reconcile—make the same; adjust the differences to make the same (reconcilement,n.)
  2. standardize—make (all) similar to, or the same as, an agreed-upon model (standardization,n.)

6. Made Up of People or Things That Are Similar: homogeneous,adj. (homogeneousness, homogeneity,n.)

7. Similarity of Interests: solidarity,n.

8. Resemblance to Truth or Real Life: verisimilitude; vraisemblance (French),n. (verisimilar,adj.)

9. Superficial Resemblance of an Animal to Surroundings As a Means of Protection: mimesis, mimicry, protective coloration,n.

10. Matching Set of Furniture: suite,n.

11. Two Things, People, etc., Absolutely Alike: tweedledum and tweedledee,n.

12. To Find or Show Points of Similarity: collate, compare, liken,v. (collation, comparison,n. comparative,adj.)

530. COMPARISON

1. Comparison of Differences: contrast,n. (contrast,v.)

2. Capable of Being Compared: commensurable, commensurate, comparable,adj. (commensurability, commensurateness, commensuration, comparableness, comparability, n.)

3. Incapable of Being Compared: disparate, incommensurable, incommensurate, incomparable,adj. (disparateness, incommensurableness, incommensurability, incommensurateness, incomparableness, incomparability,n.)

4. Basis of Comparison: criterion, norm, standard, yardstick,n. (criteria,pl. normal, standard,adj.)

5. To Compare with a Standard: standardize,v. (standardization,n.)

531. UNIFORMITY

1. Unchanging: changeless, consistent, constant, even, fixed, immutable, invariable, rigid, stable, static, steady, unchangeable, undeviating, uniform, unvarying, unwavering,adj. (changelessness, consistency, constancy, evenness, fixity, immutability, invariability, rigidity, stability or stableness, staticness, steadiness, unchangeability or unchangeableness, uniformity or uniformness,n. stabilize, steady,v.)

2. Uniform: consistent, constant, even, homogeneous, invariable; isochronal, isochrone, isochronic, isochronical, or isochronous (in time); level; monolithic (of cultures, political or social states, conditions, structures, etc.), regular, stable, steady, undiversified,adj. (consistency, constancy, evenness, homogeneousness or homogeneity, invariability, isochronism, levelness, regularity, stability or stableness, steadiness,n. isochronize, stabilize, steady,v.)

3. Boringly, Tediously, or Wearisomely Unchanging: colorless, drab, humdrum, monotonous, tiresome; toneless (in sound); treadmill (in the routine of living or working); unrelieved,adj. (colorlessness, drabness, humdrumness, monotony or monotonousness, tiresomeness, tonelessness, treadmill,n.)

4. Occurring Uniformly: isochronal, isochrone, isochronic, isochronical, or isochronous (in time), periodic, regular, seasonal,adj. (isochronism, periodicity, regularity,n. isochronize,v.)

5. Unchanging in Purpose, Support, etc.: resolute, stalwart, stanch or staunch, steadfast or stedfast, steady, undeviating, unwavering,adj. (resoluteness or resolution, stalwartness, steadfastness or stedfastness, steadiness,n.)

6. Unchanging when Heated: thermostable, adj. (thermostability,n.)

7. Unchanging in Arrangement: unshifting, adj.

8. Incapable of Being Changed: fated, fateful, immutable, inflexible, invariable, irreversible, unalterable, unchangeable, unmodifiable,adj.

9. Beyond Change to Something Better (of People): incorrigible,adj.

10. That Which Doesn't Change or Vary: continuum,n.

532. IMITATION

1. To Imitate,v.
 1. ape—imitate; imitate in a servile way; mimic
 2. burlesque—imitate a serious subject, or something serious or solemn, in a ludicrous and frivolous manner or for purposes of ridiculing
 3. caricature—imitate by humorously or satirically exaggerating the distinctive characteristics of (a person or group of people)
 4. copy—imitate
 5. counterfeit—imitate for purposes of deception or fraud
 6. emulate—imitate for the purpose of equaling or excelling in accomplishments or actions
 7. feign—imitate for purposes of deception
 8. forge—imitate (the signature of another) for purposes of fraud
 9. mimic, mime—imitate faithfully or closely; imitate for purposes of ridiculing
 10. mock—imitate (the real or genuine); imitate in joke or play; mimic
 11. parody—imitate (an author or actor, or his style, characteristics, etc.), usually for purposes of satire, humor, or ridicule
 12. parrot—imitate without understanding, like a parrot
 13. pattern (oneself or something) after—imitate; emulate
 14. sham—counterfeit
 15. simulate—imitate
 16. travesty—imitate (something serious or a serious literary work) in such a way as to make it seem absurd or ridiculous

2. Imitation; An Imitation,n. *From Sec. 1:* apery, burlesque, caricature, copy, counterfeit, emulation, forgery, mimicry, mockery or mock, parody, parrotism or parrotry, sham, simulation, travesty; *Also:*
 1. mimesis—imitation of the words of another (rhetoric)
 2. mockery—bad or frivolous imitation
 3. pastiche—writing or painting that imitates other writing or painting for purposes, usually, of ridicule
 4. postiche (French)—imitation substituted for the genuine thing

3. Imitator,n. *From Sec. 1:* ape or aper, caricaturist, copyist or copycat, counterfeiter, emulator, feigner, forger, mimic or mimicker, mime, mocker, parodist, parrot, shammer, simulator

4. Imitative,adj. *From Sec. 1:* apish, burlesque, caricatural or caricature, counterfeit, emulous, mimic or mimetic, mock, parodic or parody, parrot, sham; simulant, simulative, or simulatory; *Also:*
 1. artful—imitative
 2. rivalrous—emulous

5. Imitativeness: apishness, apery, artfulness,n.

6. Capable of Being Imitated: imitable,adj.

7. Incapable of Being Imitated: inimitable,adj. (inimitability, inimitableness,n.)

8. Art of Imitation: mimicry,n.

9. That Which Is Worth Imitating: example, model, pattern,n. (exemplary, model, adj.)

533. COPY

1. To Copy, i.e., Make a Copy of,v.
 1. duplicate—make a copy of
 2. engross—copy in large or formalized handwriting, as a document, statute, etc.
 3. manifold—make several copies of
 4. reproduce—make a copy of

5. **trace**—copy by following the lines or outlines of
6. **transcribe**—make a written or typed copy of (some paper, document, page, shorthand notes, recording, etc.)

2. A Copy,n. *From Sec. 1:* duplicate, engrossment, manifold, reproduction, tracery, transcription; *Also:*
1. **autotype**—facsimile (autotypic,adj.)
2. **carbon**—exact copy
3. **ectype**—copy of an original; copy of an artist's original
4. **facsimile**—exact copy
5. **likeness**—copy
6. **miniature**—copy reduced in scale
7. **replica**—close copy, often of an original artistic production
8. **similitude**—copy; exact copy

3. Act or Process of Copying,n. *From Sec. 1:* duplication, engrossment, reproduction, transcription (duplicative, reproductive, transcriptive,adj.) ; *From Sec. 2:* autotypy,n.

4. One Who or That Which Copies,n. *From Sec. 1:* duplicator, engrosser, reproducer, tracer, transcriber; *Also:*
1. **amanuensis**—one who copies at another's dictation
2. **copyist**—one who copies

5. That Which Is Copied: model, original, pattern,n.

6. Copied Word for Word: verbatim,adj. or adv.

534. EQUALITY

1. Equal,adj.
1. **abreast**—in an equally advanced position
2. **coequal**—equal
3. **commensurate, commeasurable**—equal in measure or extent
4. **comparable**—equal
5. **co-ordinate**—of equal rank, importance, value, etc.
6. **equidistant**—equal in distance from a place or point
7. **equipollent**—equal in force, power, or meaning
8. **equiponderant, equiponderous**—equal in weight
9. **equipotential**—equal in power, ability, capacity, or potentiality
10. **equivalent**—equal in value, force, meaning, extent, etc.
11. **homologous, homologic**—of equal value
12. **isochronal, isochrone, isochronic, isochronical, isochronous**—of equal time; equal in time
13. **isonomic, isonomous**—equal in law or rights
14. **isopolitical**—equal in political rights
15. **matching**—equal; equal in ability, force, power, etc.
16. **parallel**—equal in all essential details
17. **tantamount**—equal in effect, meaning, value, etc.
18. **worth**—equal in value to

2. Equality,n. *From Sec. 1:* coequality, commensurateness or commensuration, comparability, co-ordination, equidistance, equipollence, equiponderance or equiponderancy, equipotentiality, equivalence or equivalency, homology, isochronism, isonomy, isopolity, parallelism; *Also:*
1. **equipoise**—equality of weight
2. **par**—equality
3. **parity**—equality

3. An Equal; One Who, or That Which, Is Equal,n. *From Sec. 1:* coequal, co-ordinate, equipollent, equivalent, homologue or homolog, isopolite, match, parallel; *Also:*
1. **compeer**—one's equal
2. **peer**—an equal

3. **rival**—an equal
4. **tit for tat**—an equivalent

4. To Equal,v. *From Sec. 1:* commeasure, compare, equiponderate, match, parallel; *From Sec. 2:* equipoise

5. To Make Equal,v. *From Sec. 1:* co-ordinate, equiponderate, isochronize, match (co-ordination, equiponderation,n.) ; *From Sec. 2:* equipoise; *Also:*
1. **equalize**—make equal (equalization,n.)
2. **equate**—make equal; treat as equal; represent as equal (equation,n.)

6. To Try to Equal in Accomplishments, Actions, etc.: emulate, rival,v. (emulation, rivalry, rivalism,n. emulator, rival,n. emulous, rivalrous,adj.)

7. Statement of Equality between Numerical or Mathematical Quantities: equation,n.

8. At an Equal Pace; To an Equal Extent or Degree: pari passu (Latin)

9. Having Equal Angles: equiangular, isogonal,adj. (equiangularity, isogonality,n. isogonic,adj.)

10. Having Equal Sides: equilateral,adj. (equilateral,n.)

11. Having Equal Distances Around: isoperimetric, isoperimetrical,adj.

12. The Doctrine or Philosophy That Asserts That All Men Are Socially and Politically Equal: egalitarianism, equalitarianism, n. (egalitarian, equalitarian,n. egalitarian, equalitarian,adj.)

13. Without Equal: incomparable, matchless, nonpareil, peerless, unequaled, unexampled, unique, unparalleled, unrivaled,adj.

14. Never Having Been Equaled: unequaled, adj.

15. Person or Thing without Equal: nonesuch, nonpareil,n.

16. Unequal: disparate, incommensurate, unequivalent,adj.

17. Inequality: disparateness, disparity, imparity, incommensurateness, unequality, unequivalence,n.

18. Having an Unequal Relationship to Each Other (Term in Logic): disquiparant,adj. (disquiparancy, disquiparation,n.)

535. COMMONNESS

1. Common, i.e., Usual: accustomed, average, bread-and-butter, commonplace, customary, everyday, familiar, frequent, garden variety, general, habitual, normal, ordinary, popular, prevailing, prevalent, regular, stock, typical, unexceptional, vulgar, wonted, workaday,adj.

2. Descr. of That Which One Commonly or Usually Does, Has, Wears, Says, Is, etc.: accustomed, customary, familiar, general, habitual, natural, regular, typical, wonted, adj.

3. One Who, or That Which, Is Common: commonplace,n.

4. To Be Common or Usual: prevail,v. (prevalence,n.)

5. Common in the Sense of Lacking Originality, Imagination, or Freshness: banal; bathetic (writing or speech) ; bromidic, commonplace, conventional, drab, hackneyed, humdrum, moth-eaten, musty, obvious; pedestrian (writing, acting, the fine arts, etc.) ; platitudinous, plebeian, prosaic, slavish, stale, stereotyped, stodgy, threadbare, trite, unexciting, unimaginative, unoriginal, well-worn,adj. (banality, bathos, commonplaceness, conventionality, drabness, mustiness, obviousness, pedestrianism, platitude, prosaicness or prosaism, slavishness, staleness, stereotypy, stodginess, threadbareness, triteness, unimaginativeness, unoriginality,n.)

6. Common, Unoriginal, etc., Phrase, Expression, Action, etc.: banality, bromide, cliché, commonplace, platitude, stereotype,n.

7. Common, Unoriginal, etc., Person: bromide, humdrum, plebeian, stereotype,n.

8. To Say or Speak in Unoriginal, Trite, etc., Sentiments: platitudinize,v.

9. To Do, Act, Go, etc., in a Common, Unoriginal Manner: humdrum,v.

10. Common in the Sense of Lacking Distinction: baseborn, bourgeois, characterless, cheap, colorless, commonplace, drab, humdrum, mediocre, middling, nondescript, obvious, ordinary, passable, philistine, plain, plebeian, prosaic, prosy, raffish, stodgy, tolerable, undistinctive, undistinguished, vulgar, adj. (characterlessness, cheapness, colorlessness, commonplaceness, drabness, mediocrity, nondescriptness, obviousness, ordinariness, plainness, prosaicness or prosaism, prosiness, raffishness, stodginess, vulgarism or vulgarity, n.)

11. Common, Undistinguished Thing, Act, Event, Attitude, etc.: commonplace, mediocrity, nondescript,n.

12. Common, Undistinguished Person: mediocrity, nondescript, plebeian, vulgarian,n.

13. To Cause to Be Common: cheapen, vulgarize,v. (vulgarization,n.)

536. UNUSUALNESS

1. Unusual in the Sense of Odd, Peculiar, or Strange,adj.
1. alien—strange
2. baroque—odd and ornate, and, often, in bad taste; bizarre; fantastic
3. bizarre—unusual in the sense of possessing wild and strange contrasts or unexpected combinations (bizarreness,n.)
4. curious—mildly strange and unusual, and therefore attracting attention (curiousness, curiosity,n.)
5. droll—odd and at the same time amusing; quaint
6. eccentric—odd; peculiar; strange (eccentricity,n.)
7. eerie, eery—strange and fearful because associated, or as if associated, with ghosts or spirits (eeriness,n.)
8. erratic—odd; peculiar
9. exceptional—unusual; out of the ordinary (exceptionalness, exceptionality,n.)
10. exotic—strikingly unusual in appearance (exoticness, exoticism,n.)
11. extraordinary—unusual (extraordinariness,n.)
12. fantastic—wildly strange or odd
13. fresh—unusual and original (freshness, n.)
14. grotesque—bizarre; absurdly incongruous (grotesqueness, grotesquery, grotesquerie, n.)
15. incongruous—odd in the sense of being out of place or unexpected (incongruity, incongruousness,n.)
16. marvelous—unusual (marvelousness,n.)
17. novel—unusual and new (novelty,n.)
18. outlandish—peculiar or strange in appearance; odd; bizarre; queer (outlandishness,n.)
19. out-of-the-ordinary—unusual
20. out-of-the-way—unusual; infrequently met
21. outré (French)—unusual; out of the ordinary run of things; bizarre
22. outstanding—so unusual as to be conspicuous or draw attention

23. peregrine—strange
24. phenomenal—unusual (phenomenality, n.)
25. portentous—prodigious (portentousness, n.)
26. prodigious—unusual; extraordinarily or marvelously unusual (prodigiousness,n.)
27. quaint—odd, peculiar, or strange in an interesting, pleasing, or amusing way; strange because reminiscent of past generations, customs, etc., and therefore also interesting or pleasing (quaintness,n.)
28. queer—peculiar; odd; strange (queerness, n.)
29. quizzical—queer
30. rare—unusual; seldom found, seen, or occurring (rarity, rareness,n.)
31. remarkable—unusual; sufficiently unusual or uncommon to be noticed (remarkableness,n.)
32. scarce—unusual (scarcity, scarceness,n.)
33. singular—unusual; strange; peculiar; being the only one of its kind (singularity, n.)
34. sui generis (Latin)—in a class by itself; being the only one of its kind; unique
35. supernatural—eerie (supernaturalness, supernaturalism,n.)
36. thundering—unusual
37. transcendental—fantastic (transcendentalism,n.)
38. unaccustomed—unusual
39. uncanny—eerie (uncanniness,n.)
40. uncommon—unusual (uncommonness,n.)
41. uncouth—strange in an unpleasant way (uncouthness,n.)
42. uncustomary—unusual
43. unearthly—strange; eerie (unearthliness, n.)
44. unfamiliar—unusual; strange (unfamiliarity,n.)
45. unheard-of—so unusual as never to have been heard of or encountered before
46. unique—unusual in the sense of being the only one of its kind (uniqueness,n.)
47. unprecedented—unusual in the sense that no similar thing, occurrence, etc., has ever happened before
48. unwonted—unusual
49. weird—strange; supernaturally strange; fantastic
50. whimsical—odd; quaint (whimsicality, whimsicalness,n.)

2. An Oddity or Peculiarity; Unusual, Odd, Peculiar, or Strange Person, Thing, Act, Occurrence, etc.,n. *From Sec. 1:* curiosity, drollery, eccentricity (act), eccentric (person), grotesque or grotesquerie, incongruity, marvel, novelty; phenomenon (phenomena, pl.); portent, prodigy, rarity, singularity, whimsey or whimsy; *Also:*
1. crank—odd act
2. customer—strange or unusual person
3. foible—a kind of general eccentricity
4. kickshaw—any fantastic thing
5. kink—mental or emotional peculiarity
6. punchinello—odd-looking and squat person
7. quip—anything odd or queer
8. quirk—individual peculiarity or eccentricity
9. rara avis (Latin)—anyone or anything unique, extraordinary, or extremely uncommon
10. treasure—something rare
11. vagary—strange, unexpected, unexplainable, or odd action, turn, movement, etc.

3. The Only One of Its Kind, Group, Species, etc.: monotype,n.

4. Unusual in the Sense of Lying or Occurring outside Normal or Natural Bounds: aberrant, abnormal, anomalous, atypic or atypical, eccentric, exceptional, freakish or freaky, heteroclite, inordinate, irregular, miraculous, monstrous, phenomenal, preternatural, prodigious, supernatural, uncommon, unconventional, unnatural, untypical, adj. (aberrancy or aberration, abnormality or abnormity, anomalousness or anomaly, atypicality, eccentricity, exceptionalness or exceptionality, freakishness or freakiness, inordinateness, irregularity, miraculousness, monstrousness or monstrosity, phenomenality, preternaturalness or preternaturalism, prodigiousness, supernaturalness or supernaturalism, uncommonness, unconventionality, unnaturalness,n.)

5. Person, Act, Action, Happening, or Thing That Is Unusual in the Sense of Lying or Occurring outside Normal or Natural Bounds: aberration, abnormality or abnormity, anomaly or anomalism, eccentric (person); eccentricity (act, etc.); exception, freak, heteroclite, irregularity, miracle, monster or monstrosity; phenomenon (phenomena,pl.); preternaturalism, prodigy,n.

6. Noticeable Irregularity That Indicates or Accompanies Disease: symptom,n.

7. Person, Often an Artist, Writer, Actor, etc., Who Lives an Unconventional, Free-and-Easy Life: Bohemian,n. (Bohemianism, n. Bohemian,adj.)

8. Less or Lower than Normal: subnormal, substandard,adj. (subnormality,n. subnormal, n.)

9. Beyond, Higher, or Better than Normal: supernormal, supranormal,adj.

537. FREAK OF NATURE

1. Freak of Nature (General): abnormity, lusus naturae (Latin), monster, monstrosity, sport, teratism,n. (monstrous, teratical,adj.)

2. Freak Plant: rogue,n.

3. Freaks Collectively: freakery,n.

4. Of the Nature of a Freak: freakish, freaky, monstrous,adj. (freakishness, freakiness, monstrousness or monstrosity,n.)

5. Full of Freaks: freakful, freakish, freaky, adj

6. State of Being a Freak: teratism,n. (teratical,adj.)

7. Resembling a Freak: teratoid,adj.

8. Giving Rise or Birth to Freaks: teratogenic,adj. (teratogeny,n.)

9. Medical Science of Human Freaks: teratology,n. (teratologist,n. teratological,adj.)

10. Selected Human Freaks or Monsters,n.
1. **cephalodiprosopus**—anatomical monstrosity in which a second, incomplete parasitical head is attached to the head
2. **cephalomelus**—anatomical monstrosity possessing an extra limb attached to the head
3. **cephalopagus**—twins born with joined heads (cephalopagy,n.)
4. **cephalotridymus**—monster with three heads
5. **craniodidymus**—two-headed monster
6. **dicephalus**—two-headed monster
7. **tricephalus**—three-headed monster

538. FOREIGN

1. Foreign,adj.
1. **alien**—foreign; belonging or owing allegiance to another country
2. **exotic**—foreign; from a foreign country (exoticness, exoticism,n.)
3. **heterochthonous**—not native; from a different land
4. **outland**—foreign; from a foreign land

5. **peregrine**—foreign
6. **remote**—foreign
7. **strange**—foreign

2. Having Come from a Different Country but Now a Citizen: naturalized,adj.

3. Foreign Thing, Plant, or Word: exotic,n.

4. A Foreigner,n.
1. **alien**—citizen of one country living in another (alienage, alienism,n.)
2. **baboo, babu**—native of a foreign land who has some education in English—contemptuous term (babooism, babuism,n.)
3. **immigrant**—one who comes into a foreign country or region to live (immigration,n. immigrant,adj. immigrate,v.)
4. **issei**—Japanese immigrant to the U.S.
5. **outlander**—foreigner
6. **stranger**—foreigner
7. **tramontane**—foreigner

539. CHANGE

1. To Change, i.e., Cause to Change, Make or Cause a Change in, or Make or Cause to Be Different,v.
1. **accommodate**—adapt; adjust; make necessary adjustments in
2. **adapt**—change for or to a different or new use, environment, etc., or so as to be able to conform to, or be comfortable in, a new environment, etc.; adjust
3. **adjust**—make changes in so as to bring into conformity with what is desired or desirable
4. **alter**—change; cause to be different
5. **alternate**—arrange, use, etc., by turns, first one, then the other, and so on
6. **amend**—change for the better; change the wording of
7. **arrange**—adapt (music) to instruments or voices for which it was not written
8. **bacterize**—modify by bacterial action
9. **bedevil**—change and thus spoil
10. **blue-pencil**—change (written material) with, or as if with, a blue or editor's pencil
11. **bowdlerize**—change parts of (a story, book, play, etc.) that are considered obscene, indelicate, unusually frank, etc.
12. **censor**—change (written or printed material considered harmful, dangerous, obscene, immoral, etc.)
13. **convert**—change into something else
14. **counterchange**—cause to change places; shift; vary
15. **deflect**—change the direction of (something) by blocking the direction in which it was going
16. **deviate**—cause to change in course or direction, or from a standard, the norm, a topic, etc
17. **disguise**—change the appearance of
18. **dissimilate**—change; make different
19. **diversify**—give variety to
20. **edit**—make necessary changes in (material) so that it will be suitable for publication
21. **emend**—change by correcting the faults or errors of (esp. written material)
22. **exchange**—change (one thing) for another
23. **fluctuate**—cause to change constantly from point to point
24. **forge**—alter (a legal document) for purposes of fraud
25. **garble**—so change (a story, a written account, etc.) as to mislead purposely and confuse
26. **gradate**—change by gradual steps or stages
27. **inflect**—change the pitch of (the voice)
28. **innovate**—make a change (to something new)

29. **interchange**—change (each thing) from its own position to that of the other; alternate
30. **metamorphose, metamorphize**—change completely, noticeably, or strikingly the form, structure, appearance, or character of
31. **modify**—change somewhat; make moderate changes in the form or appearance of
32. **modulate**—alter (the tone of voice) to give pleasing expression to; adjust
33. **mutate**—change; alter
34. **permutate**—change; change in order or arrangement; interchange
35. **permute**—alter; permutate
36. **pervert**—cause to change to something abnormal or unnatural
37. **qualify**—change to some extent
38. **quantify**—change the quantity of
39. **recondition**—change the emotional attitude of
40. **redact**—edit; revise
41. **reform**—cause to change to something better; cause (a person) to change by giving up bad habits or behavior for good; change the shape or form of; change (anything evil or vicious) by eliminating bad qualities
42. **relieve**—give variety or change to
43. **resolve**—change by disintegration into some other form or constituency; convert
44. **revamp**—change by putting into a new form
45. **reverse**—change to the opposite thing or direction
46. **revise**—change by correcting or improving
47. **revolutionize**—cause a complete and radical change in
48. **rotate**—alternate
49. **shift**—change; change from one place or person to another; change the arrangement of; change gears in an automobile
50. **socialize**—adapt (someone or something) to community or social needs
51. **specialize**—adapt (a biological organism or some part of it) to special or particular uses or functions
52. **switch**—change from one to another
53. **tailor**—change or adapt to what is required or requested
54. **tamper with, doctor**—change so as to damage; make changes in that rob of genuineness or authenticity
55. **tinge**—change slightly
56. **transfer**—change from one person or place to another
57. **transfigure**—cause a complete change in the form or appearance of; change so as to make glorified or exalted
58. **transform**—cause a change in appearance, character, nature, kind, etc.; effect a complete change in
59. **translate**—change (words, etc.) from one language to another; change into different words; change from one place, position, condition, etc., to another
60. **transliterate**—change into the letters or characters of a different kind of alphabet or that of another language
61. **transmogrify**—cause a complete and ridiculous change in; transform
62. **transmute**—change from one substance, form, or nature to another; change (base metal) into gold
63. **transpose**—change the order of; change the position of; change from one side to another; change the usual order of (the letters of a word); interchange
64. **transship, tranship**—change from one ship, or from one means of conveyance, to another for continued transportation
65. **transubstantiate**—change into another substance

66. **trim**—cause a change in to suit the circumstances
67. **turn the tide**—cause a change to the opposite
68. **variegate**—give variety to; diversify; diversify in appearance
69. **vary**—change; make changes in; make different; alter in form, substance, appearance, etc.; diversify; modify
70. **warp**—pervert

2. To Change, i.e., Undergo Change, or Be or Become Changed or Different, v. *From Sec. 1:* accommodate, adapt, adjust, alter, alternate, convert, deviate, dissimilate, fluctuate, gradate, interchange, modify, modulate, reform, reverse, rotate, shift, specialize, switch, transfer, transform, vary; *Also:*
1. **digress**—change from one topic to another in speaking or writing
2. **diverge**—vary or deviate from normal, typical, or standard
3. **go off on a tangent**—change suddenly from one course of action or thinking to another
4. **mutate**—undergo change; change in form, quality, or structure; undergo, in biology, a sudden change from parental forms
5. **oscillate**—fluctuate between fixed points; fluctuate between opposing beliefs, doctrines, etc.
6. **range**—undergo changes; change within the stated limits
7. **repent**—change one's mind or opinion, owing to dissatisfaction or regret
8. **shift**—change in direction
9. **switch**—change from one direction, place, opinion, etc., to another
10. **tergiversate**—change in one's attitude or opinion on a subject or in respect to a cause
11. **trail off**—change little by little to something else
12. **vacillate**—change one's mind or feeling back and forth; fluctuate
13. **veer**—change in direction or course
14. **waver**—change in intensity; vacillate
15. **whiffle**—change in course; keep changing one's course of action, plans, opinions, etc.

3. A Changing or Change, n. *From Secs. 1 and 2:* accommodation, adaptation, adjustment, alteration, alternation, amendment, arrangement, bacterization, bedevilment, bowdlerization or bowdlerism, censorship, conversion, deflection, deviation, disguise, dissimilation, diversification, emendation, exchange, fluctuation, forgery, gradation, inflection, innovation, interchange, metamorphosis or metamorphism, modification, modulation, mutation, permutation, perversion, qualification, quantification, redaction, reform or reformation, relief, resolution, reversal, revision or revisal, revolution, rotation, shift, socialization, specialization, switch; transfer, transference, or transferral; transfiguration or transfigurement, transformation, translation, transliteration, transmogrification, transmutation, transposition or transposal, transshipment or transhipment, transubstantiation; variegation, variation or variance; *From Sec. 2:* digression, divergence or divergency, mutation, oscillation, range, repentance, shift, switch, tergiversation, vacillation, veer, waver, whiffery; *Also:*
1. **about-face**—turnabout
2. **fluxion, flux**—continuous change
3. **freak**—impulsive change of mind
4. **metastasis**—transformation
5. **metathesis**—transposition of sounds, syllables, or letters in a word
6. **permutation**—transformation
7. **phantasmagoria, phantasmagory**—sudden and violent change in size, or unex-

pected shift in appearance or surroundings—often applied to scenes in dreams, fever, delirium, etc.
8. **reverse**—change to bad luck or misfortune
9. **revulsion**—sudden and violent change
10. **saltation**—sudden change
11. **symptom**—noticeable change that indicates or accompanies disease
12. **tolerance**—permitted small variation from the exact standard of measurement, weight, etc.
13. **transit**—change
14. **transition**—change from one activity, place, condition, state, idea, thought, stage, period, etc., to another or to the next one
15. **turnabout**—complete or reversing change
16. **vicissitude**—change in fortunes, conditions, circumstances, etc.; irregular change
17. **volte-face (French)**—change of policy; turnabout

4. One Who Causes or Makes Changes,n. *From Sec. 1:* adapter, arranger, bowdlerizer, censor, editor, forger, innovator, perverter, redactor, reformer, reviser, translator

5. One Who, or That Which, Changes, Undergoes Change, or Is Changed,n. *From Sec. 1:* deviate or deviator, variant; *From Sec. 2:* digressor, mutation or mutant, oscillator, repenter, tergiversator, vacillator, whiffler; *Also:* **1. turncoat**—one who changes in his principles or beliefs

6. Causing to Change,adj. *From Sec. 1:* accommodative, alterative, amendatory, deflective, deviative, dissimilative, emendatory, perversive, reformative, revisory or revisionary, transliterative, transmutative, transubstantiative; *From Sec. 3:* revulsive

7. Changing; Tending to Change,adj. *From Sec. 2:* accommodative, adaptive, adjustive, deviative, fluctuant, reformative, rotative; digressive, mutative, oscillative or oscillatory, repentant, tergiversative, vacillatory; *From Sec. 3:* phantasmagorial, phantasmagoric, or phantasmagorical; revulsive, transitive, vicissitudinous

8. Descr. of, Pert. or Relating to, Change, adj. *From Sec. 1:* adaptational, conversional, deviatory, dissimilative or dissimilatory, inflectional; metamorphic, metamorphosic, metamorphosian, or metamorphotic; mutational, permutational, revolutionary, transferential, transformational, transmutational, transpositional, variational; *From Sec. 3:* phantasmagorial, phantasmagoric, or phantasmagorical; revulsionary, transitional, vicissitudinary

9. Changeable, i.e., Capable of Being Changed,adj. *From Sec. 1:* adaptable, adjustable, alterable, amendable, convertible, diversifiable, emendable, interchangeable, modifiable, mutable, permutable, pervertible, reformable, resolvable, reversible, transferable, translatable, transmutable, transposable or transposible, variable; *Also:* **1. corrigible**—capable of being changed for the better
2. reciprocal—interchangeable

10. That Which Transforms: alembic,n.

11. With the Necessary Changes: mutatis mutandis (Latin)

12. To Exchange,v.
1. **bandy**—exchange in a rapid give and take
2. **barter**—exchange (one kind of goods for another)
3. **commute**—exchange; exchange (one for the other)
4. **convert**—exchange

5. **interchange**—exchange (one for the other)
6. **reciprocate**—exchange (one for the other)
7. **substitute**—exchange
8. **swap**—exchange; barter
9. **trade**—barter
10. **truck**—exchange; barter

13. Exchange,n. *From Sec. 12:* barter, commutation, conversion, interchange, reciprocation, substitution, swap, trade

14. Exchange of Witty Remarks: repartee,n.

15. Action, etc., That Represents a Change, n.
1. **caprice**—action, course, desire, feeling, attitude, etc., that is a sudden and unexpected change from the former action, course, etc. (capriciousness,n capricious, adj.)
2. **démarche (French)**—course of action involving a change of policy or principle, esp. in diplomacy
3. **whim**—caprice (whimsicality, whimsicalness,n. whimsical,adj.)
4. **whimsey, whimsy**—caprice

16. Time or Point of Change,n.
1. **apex**—crisis (apical,adj.)
2. **conjuncture**—crisis produced by a combination of happenings or circumstances (conjunctural,adj.)
3. **crisis**—point at which circumstances change sharply for the better or worse; turning point (critical,adj.)
4. **transition**—period of change; period of change to the next stage (transitional, adj.)
5. **turning point**—point at which there is an important change
6. **zero hour**—crisis

17. A Pervasive Influence toward Change: leaven,n.

18. Favoring Extremes in Change or Reform: radical,adj. (radical,n. radicalism, radicality, n.)

19. To Become, or Cause to Become, Radical, Esp. in Politics: radicalize,v. (radicalization,n.)

20. Radicals, Collectively: radicality,n.

21. Changeable in the Sense of Not Remaining Constant, i.e., Changing Suddenly, Unexpectedly, etc.,adj.
1. **abrupt**—with sudden changes from one thing to another—of style of writing (abruptness,n.)
2. **adaptable**—flexible (adaptability,n.)
3. **amphibolic**—changing (medical)
4. **arbitrary**—capricious (arbitrariness,n.)
5. **capricious**—changing suddenly, unexpectedly, and from no apparent or logical motivation, with the added implication of impulsiveness, inconstancy, and lack of consideration for others (capriciousness, caprice,n.)
6. **chameleonic**, **chameleon-like**—highly changeable; constantly changing, in allusion to the lizard whose skin color changes in adaptation to the surroundings
7. **changeful**—full of change (changefulness,n.)
8. **checkered**—marked with frequent changes
9. **erratic**—changing capriciously and unexpectedly in course, actions, attitude, etc. (erraticness,n.)
10. **fickle**—capriciously changeable, esp. in one's affections or allegiance (fickleness, n.)
11. **flexible**—capable of changing or willing to change according to changing circumstances (flexibility, flexibleness,n.)

12. **freakish, freaky**—changing suddenly and unexpectedly (freakishness, freakiness,n.)
13. **inconstant**—changeable; fickle (inconstancy,n.)
14. **irresolute**—vacillating (irresoluteness, irresolution,n.)
15. **kaleidoscopic**—continuously changing in pattern, shape, etc., like things viewed in a kaleidoscope
16. **mercurial**—changeable; constantly changing; volatile
17. **moody**—of frequently changeable mood (moodiness,n.)
18. **moonish**—capricious
19. **mutable**—changeable; fickle (mutability, mutableness,n.)
20. **opportunistic**—changing in action, course, opinions, etc., according to the advantage to be secured (opportunism,n.)
21. **protean**—very changeable; readily assuming changing form, shape, type, appearance, etc., after Proteus, in Greek legend, a sea god who had this power
22. **skittish**—changeable; capricious (skittishness,n.)
23. **streaky**—changeable or variable in character, personality, or mood (streakiness, n.)
24. **supple**—readily changing to fit the environment; adaptable to changing requirements (suppleness,n.)
25. **tangential**—going off on a tangent; erratic (tangentiality,n.)
26. **temperamental**—changeable in mood; moody (temperamentalness, temperament, n.)
27. **timeserving**—changing according to the tenor of the times or the wishes of those in power
28. **transient**—changeable in form or appearance (transience,n.)
29. **transilient**—marked by abrupt changes or variations (transilience,n.)
30. **unreliable**—changeable; likely to change (unreliability,n.)
31. **unstable**—changeable (instability,n.)
32. **unsteady**—changeable (unsteadiness,n.)
33. **vacillating**—constantly changing one's opinions, mind, intentions, etc. (vacillation,n.)
34. **variable**—constantly changing; fickle (variability, variableness,n.)
35. **various**—changeable
36. **volatile**—changing easily, rapidly, and usually unexpectedly from one mood or condition to another; fickle (volatility,n.)
37. **whimsical**—capricious (whimsicality, whimsicalness,n.)

22. **Changeable Person,n.** *From Sec. 21:* chameleon, opportunist, timeserver; *Also:* 1. **prima donna**—woman (or, in irony, man) who acts in a maddeningly capricious manner

23. **Changeable, i.e., Irregular or without Uniformity,**adj.
1. **aperiodic**—occurring with no regularity (aperiodicity,n.)
2. **casual**—irregular (casualness,n.)
3. **convulsive**—irregular in the sense of moving jerkily and without rhythm—of that which usually moves rhythmically (convulsiveness,n.)
4. **erratic**—following no regular course or time schedule (erraticness,n.)
5. **fitful**—irregular in the sense of stopping and starting with no particular rhythm (fitfulness,n.)
6. **haphazard**—irregular (haphazardness,n.)
7. **inconsistent**—not uniform (inconsistency, n.)
8. **intermittent**—happening, stopping, happening again, etc., at irregular intervals (intermittence, intermittency,n.)
9. **occasional**—happening at irregular intervals

10. **spasmodic**—irregular; happening with irregular frequency (spasmodicness,n.)
11. **sporadic**—irregular; happening irregularly or in scattered places (sporadicness, n.)
12. **spotty**—irregular; not uniform (spottiness,n.)
13. **unreliable**—so irregular as not to be relied upon (unreliability,n.)
14. **unstable**—irregular (instability,n.)
15. **ununiform**—irregular (ununiformity,n.)
16. **vagabond**—following an irregular course
17. **vagrant**—following no definite course (vagrancy,n.)
18. **wayward**—irregular (waywardness,n.)
19. **wild**—irregular; erratic (wildness,n.)
24. **Subject to Change or Variation:** fluid, mutable, provisional, temporary, tentative, adj. (fluidity or fluidness, tentativeness,n.)

540. DIFFERENCE

1. **Different,**adj.
1. **alien**—entirely different in character
2. **antithetic**—contrasting; contrasting in ideas, such contrast being emphasized by the position of the words
3. **asymmetrical**—not the same on both sides
4. **atypic, atypical**—not similar to the type
5. **colorful**—full of contrasts
6. **contradistinct, contradistinctive**—different by contrast
7. **contrary**—completely different
8. **contrasting**—strikingly different when compared
9. **discrepant**—different
10. **disparate**—not alike in type or character; fundamentally different
11. **dissimilar**—different
12. **distinct**—clearly different
13. **distinctive**—so different as to stand out clearly from the group, surroundings, etc.
14. **divergent**—different; different from the typical, normal, or standard
15. **divers**—different and unrelated
16. **diverse**—different; clearly different
17. **diversiform**—different in form
18. **incommensurable**—having no common basis of comparison
19. **incomparable**—so different that no basis of comparison exists
20. **individual**—different in personality, character, make-up, quality, nature, design, etc., from the rest; distinctive
21. **manifold**—many and different
22. **mismatched**—not the same; mismated
23. **mismated**—not forming a homogeneous, similar, or suitable pair
24. **motley**—inharmoniously different
25. **novel**—new and different
26. **original**—different in the sense of showing new, distinctive, and unusual characteristics, trends, techniques, etc.
27. **particular**—different from others, from others of its kind, or from the ordinary
28. **remote**—entirely different
29. **special**—different from others of its kind
30. **sundry**—different; different and unrelated
31. **unlike**—different
32. **unrelated**—different from its group
33. **unwonted**—different from that which is habitual
34. **variant**—different; different from the standard, normal, average, typical, etc.
35. **varied**—different, i.e., lacking in monotonous sameness
36. **variform, variformed**—different in form
37. **various**—different

2. **Difference,n.** *From Sec. 1:* antithesis, asymmetry, atypicality or atypicalness, colorfulness, contradistinction (mostly in the phrase *in contradistinction to*), contrariety,

contrast, discrepancy, disparateness or disparity, dissimilarity or dissimilitude; distinctness, distinctiveness, or distinction; divergence or divergency, diversity or diverseness, incommensurability, incomparability, individuality or individualism, novelty, originality, particularity, remoteness, specialness, unlikeness, unrelatedness, variance; variation or variety (from *varied*); variformity; *Also:*

1. **chasm**—wide difference in feeling or interests
2. **dash**—distinctiveness of action, acting, motion, etc.
3. **differential**—difference in time, rate, amount, etc.
4. **dissemblance**—difference; lack of resemblance
5. **gulf**—chasm
6. **nicety**—minute or subtle distinction
7. **quiddity**—fine or subtle difference
8. **subtlety**—fine or delicate distinction
9. **tone**—distinctiveness

3. To Differ; To Be Different,v. *From Sec. 1:* contrast, diverge, vary (contrast, divergence, divergency, variation,n.)

4. One Who or That Which Is Different,n. *From Sec. 1:* contrast, individual, novelty, variant or variation; *Also:*

1. **deviate**—one who is considerably different from the average or normal in any respect
2. **individualist**—one who thinks or acts differently from the rest (individualistic, adj.)
3. **varietist**—one who differs from the average, norm, or standard (varietism,n.)
4. **wilding**—something or someone quite different from the type or average

5. Different or Unlike People or Things: dissimilars,n.

6. Various, Different, or Miscellaneous Small Articles, Items, etc.: sundries,n.

7. Person or Thing That, by Contrast, Enhances the Appearance or Value of Someone or Something Else: foil,n.

8. To Pair Things or People Who Are Not the Same or Do Not Go Well Together: mismatch, mismate,v. (mismatch,n.)

9. Of, Containing, or Having Different Kinds or Forms,adj.

1. **assorted**—of various kinds (assortment, n. assort,v.)
2. **biform**—of two different kinds or forms (biformity,n.)
3. **diversified**—variegated (diversification,n. diversify,v.)
4. **diversiform**—having different forms
5. **heterogeneous**—of different kinds; made up of differing types, classes, etc. (heterogeneity, heterogeneousness,n.)
6. **manifold**—of many different kinds
7. **miscellaneous**—of different kinds; consisting of unrelated things, kinds, forms, etc. (miscellaneousness, miscellany,n.)
8. **multifarious**—of many different kinds (multifariousness,n.)
9. **omnifarious**—of all different kinds or sorts (omnifariousness,n.)
10. **sundry**—of different kinds
11. **triform**—of three different kinds (triformity,n.)
12. **varicolored**—of different kinds (varicolor, n.)
13. **varied**—containing different kinds (variety,n. vary,v.)
14. **variegated**—marked by, or made up of, different shapes, sizes, kinds, etc. (variegation,n. variegate,v.)
15. **variform, variformed**—having different forms (variformity,n.)

10. Different Form of Something: variety,n. (varietal,adj.)

11. Pert. to, Relating to, Indicating, Producing, Constituting, Resulting from, Involved with, etc., Differences: differential,adj.

12. Degree or Extent of Difference: disparity, range,n.

13. Very Slight Degree of Difference: nuance, shade,n.

14. To Find, or Make Note of, Differences; To Make Distinctions,v.

1. **contradistinguish**—distinguish by contrasting opposite qualities
2. **differentiate**—see or note the differences in; distinguish between (differentiation, n.)
3. **discern**—see and understand differences (discernment,n.)
4. **discriminate**—find or make distinctions (discrimination,n.)
5. **distinguish**—tell one thing, quality, or abstraction from another through recognizing special differences despite a general or possible similarity—followed by *between* or *from*, depending on the construction (distinction,n.)
6. **split hairs**—make excessively fine and perhaps unnecessary distinctions

15. Making or Finding, Capable of Making or Finding, or Tending to Make or Find, Differences or Distinctions,adj. *From Sec. 14:* discerning; discriminating, discriminative, or discriminatory (discernment, discrimination,n.); *Also:*

1. **nice**—capable of making subtle distinctions (nicety,n.)
2. **perceptive**—capable of making keen, subtle, or fine distinctions (perceptiveness, perceptivity,n.)
3. **schizotrichiatic**—tending to split hairs, i.e., make fine distinctions
4. **subtile**—subtle (subtileness, subtility, subtilty,n.)
5. **subtle**—capable of making keen or fine distinctions (subtlety, subtleness,n.)

16. To Use or Introduce Fine Distinctions in the Discussion of: subtilize,v. (subtilization, n.)

17. To Examine or Arrange for the Purpose of Noting Differences: contrast,v.

18. Not Finding or Making, or Unable to Find or Make, Distinctions,adj.

1. **imperceptive**—incapable of making keen, subtle, or fine distinctions (imperceptiveness,n.)
2. **indiscriminate**—showing no perception of distinctions or differences; not taking differences or distinctions into account (indiscriminateness, indiscrimination,n.)
3. **promiscuous**—not discriminating in the bestowal of one's favors; showing no discrimination; making no distinctions (promiscuousness, promiscuity,n.)
4. **undiscriminating**—unable to make important distinctions

19. To Be Unable to See Differences or Tell Apart: confuse, mix up,v. (confusion,n.)

20. To Set (a Person, Thing, Place, etc.) Apart by Special or Visible Differences: characterize, demarcate, differentiate, distinguish, individualize, individuate, mark,v. (characterization, demarcation, differentiation, individualization, individuation,n.)

21. That Which Sets a Person, Thing, or Place Apart as Different from the Rest: differentia (term in logic), differential, distinction, mark, marking, markings,n.

22. To Arrange for the Purpose of Showing Differences: contrast,v.

23. To Express a Contrast of Ideas by the Emphatic Position of Words: antithesize,v. (antithesis, antithesism,n.)

24. To Give Special Differences to: individualize, individuate, specialize,v. (individualization, individuation, specialization,n.)

25. Special: ad hoc (Latin), especial, express, individual, particular, singular, specialized, specific,adj. (individuality, particularity, singularity, specificity,n.)

26. To Make Special: specialize,v. (specialization,n.)

27. Applied to This Special Case Only: ad hoc (Latin)

28. Special Detail, Aspect, Fact, etc., of a Subject, Art, Science, Business, Profession, etc.: technicality,n. (technical,adj.)

541. AGREEMENT

1. To Agree, i.e., Give or Show Agreement,v.
1. accede (to)—agree (to)
2. accept—agree to
3. accord (with)—agree (with)
4. acquiesce (in)—agree (to) ; assent tacitly (to)
5. assent—agree; admit one's agreement
6. concur (in)—agree with an opinion, finding, conclusion, etc.
7. consent (to)—agree (to)
8. nod—bow and raise the head quickly as a sign of agreement
9. subscribe to—agree with or to
10. sustain—agree with
11. uphold—agree with

2. Agreement, i.e., Giving or Showing Agreement,n. From Sec. 1: accession (to), acceptance, accord, acquiescence, assent, concurrence or concurrency, consent or consentment, nod, subscription; sustainment, sustention, or sustentation; Also:
1. adherence—assent
2. assentation—ready assent, esp. insincere or obsequious; practice of giving insincere or obsequious assent

3. One Who Gives or Shows Agreement,n. From Sec. 1: acquiescer; assentor, assenter, or assentient; consenter, subscriber, sustainer; Also: 1. yes man—person who, sincerely or otherwise, agrees with everything his superior says

4. Agreeing; Agreeable; Giving or Showing Agreement,adj. From Sec. 1: accordant, acquiescent, assentive or assentient, concurrent, consentant or consentive, sustentive or sustentative (accordance, accordancy, or accord, assentiveness, concurrence or concurrency,n.) ; Also:
1. affirmative—agreeing; giving or showing agreement (affirmativeness,n.)
2. consentaneous—agreeing in opinion; unanimous (consentaneousness, consentaneity,n.)
3. consentful—consenting fully
4. consentient—agreeing; unanimous (consentience,n.)
5. unanimous—giving or showing agreement by all concerned (unanimousness, unanimity,n.)

5. Ready or Willing to Agree: assentaneous, assentatious,adj.

6. Agreement of Opinion or Views among a Number of People: consensus,n.

7. Done by Complete Agreement: consentaneous, unanimous,adj. (consentaneousness or consentaneity, unanimousness or unanimity,n.)

8. Existing by Mere Consent: consensual, adj. (legal)

9. To Feel Agreement (with): sympathize (with),v. (sympathy, sympathies,n. sympathizer,n. sympathetic,adj.)

10. To Agree, i.e., Make, or Come to, an Agreement,v.
1. accord—come to an agreement
2. bargain—come to terms of agreement; stipulate
3. collude—make a secret agreement in defiance of law
4. come to terms—agree
5. compact—agree; make an agreement
6. compromise—come to an agreement by making mutual concessions
7. conspire—agree with another or with others to commit an illegal or evil act or action
8. contract—agree; agree formally in writing, or by means of a legally enforceable document
9. covenant—make a solemn or legal agreement (of people, or of groups of people)
10. settle—come to an agreement, often by composing or adjusting differences
11. stipulate—agree definitely to do or not to do

11. Agreement, i.e., a Making of, or Coming to, an Agreement,n. From Sec. 10: arrangement, collusion, compaction, compromise, conspiracy, contraction, settlement, stipulation; Also: 1. accord—agreement

12. One Who Agrees, i.e., Makes or Comes to an Agreement,n. From Sec. 10: bargainer, colluder, compacter or compactor, compromiser; conspirator, conspirer, or conspirant; contractor, covenanter or covenantor, stipulator

13. An Agreement,n. From Sec. 10: arrangement, bargain, collusion, compact or compaction, compromise, conspiracy, contract, covenant, settlement, stipulation; From Sec. 11: accord; Also:
1. accord—informal agreement between sovereign states
2. bond—binding agreement
3. concord, concordance—formal agreement
4. concordat—formal agreement between the Pope and a secular government; any formal or solemn agreement
5. convention—agreement; general agreement as to customs, actions, thoughts, social usages, etc.
6. entente—agreement between governments, groups, or official bodies
7. indenture—written agreement
8. pact—agreement
9. pool—agreement between companies to control prices and thereby eliminate competition
10. treaty—agreement between independent nations
11. understanding—agreement

14. Agreeing, i.e., Making, or Coming to, an Agreement,adj. From Sec. 10: bargaining, colluding, etc.; accordant, collusive, conspirant or conspirative (collusiveness,n.)

15. Descr. of, Pert. to, or of the Nature of, Agreement or an Agreement,adj. From Sec. 10: collusive, conspiratorial, contractual, stipulative; From Sec. 13: conventional

16. To Attempt to Come to an Agreement: bargain,v. (bargainer,n.)

17. To Agree, i.e., Do, Be, Act, Go Together, etc., in Harmony,v.
1. accord—be in agreement
2. blend—go well together; harmonize
3. chime—agree; be in agreement or harmony
4. coincide—agree exactly (of spatial relationships) ; agree exactly in nature, time, character, etc.
5. concert—act in harmony
6. concur—be in agreement
7. conform—act in agreement or harmony with another or others, or with customs, etc. (conformer, conformist,n.)

8. **conspire**—act in harmony
9. **co-ordinate**—function or act together in agreement or harmony
10. **correspond**—agree; agree in details; be in harmony
11. **harmonize**—be or act in agreement in feelings, sound, proportions, etc.
12. **jibe**—be in agreement
13. **match**—go well together; agree in color, size, shape, etc.
14. **tally**—agree; correspond
15. **tone in**—blend or harmonize in color

18. Agreement; A Doing, Being, etc., in Harmony,n. *From Sec. 17:* coincidence, concurrence or concurrency; conformance, conformation or conformity; conspiracy, co-ordination, correspondence, harmonization

19. Agreeing; Agreeable; Doing, Being, etc., in Agreement or Harmony,adj. *From Sec. 17:* blending, chiming, etc.; accordant, coincident or coincidental, concurrent, conformant or conformable, conspirant or conspirative, co-ordinate, correspondent, harmonious; *Also:*
1. **attune, atune, attuned**—in harmony
2. **coherent**—consistent
3. **compatible**—living, existing, or getting along together in agreement or harmony, i.e., without conflict or discord
4. **concordant**—harmonious; without clashing, discord, or conflict
5. **congenial**—agreeing in tastes, likes, attitudes, etc.
6. **congruent**—agreeing throughout in spatial shape
7. **congruous**—in harmonious agreement with the surroundings
8. **consistent**—in agreement in logical or broad principles; in logical agreement
9. **consonant**—in agreement; lacking in clash or discord; conformant; correspondent
10. **cosmic**—harmonious
11. **en rapport (French)**—in harmonious agreement
12. **in tune with**—in agreement or harmony with
13. **legitimate**—in agreement with recognized principles or standards
14. **orthodox**—in agreement with accepted, standard, or commonly held beliefs, as in religion, politics, etc.; in agreement with established custom, true religion, etc.
15. **pursuant**—acting according to; in accordance with; conforming
16. **unisonous**—in agreement or harmony

20. Agreement; Agreeableness; State or Condition of Being, Doing, etc., in Agreement or Harmony,n. *From Sec. 17:* accord, accordance, or accordancy; coincidence, concert, concurrence or concurrency; conformance, conformity, conformableness, or conformability; co-ordination, correspondence or correspondency, harmoniousness or harmony, match, tally; *From Sec. 19:* coherence or coherency, compatibleness or compatibility, concord or concordance, congeniality, congruence, congruousness or congruity, consistency, consonance, cosmos, rapport (from *en rapport*), legitimateness or legitimacy, orthodoxy, unison; *Also:*
1. **accord**—harmony of sounds
2. **concert**—musical harmoniousness; agreement in design or plan
3. **concinnity**—internal harmony (said of style)
4. **unity**—agreement; harmony

21. To Cause to Agree or Come to an Agreement; To Settle,v.
1. **adjudge**—settle by law
2. **adjudicate**—settle (adjudication,n. adjudicatory or adjudicative,adj.)
3. **adjust**—so arrange that all interested parties are in agreement (adjustment,n. adjustive,adj.)

4. **bring to terms**—cause to agree
5. **clinch**—settle conclusively
6. **compose**—settle or reconcile (a quarrel, disagreement, differences, etc.)
7. **compromise**—settle (a disagreement) by means of a yielding by both parties (compromise,n.)
8. **concert**—settle by conference or agreement
9. **conciliate**—make agree (conciliation,n. conciliatory, conciliative,adj.)
10. **decide**—settle (decision,n. decisive,adj.)
11. **negotiate**—arrange, or arrange for, an agreement (negotiation,n. negotiatory, negotiative,adj.)
12. **patch (up)**—settle (a quarrel, argument, differences, etc.)
13. **preconcert**—settle by previous agreement
14. **reconcile**—bring into agreement; remove grounds of opposition or disagreement; settle (reconciliation or reconcilement,n. reconciliatory,adj.)

22. State of Having Been Brought into Agreement,n. *From Sec. 21:* adjustment, compromise, reconciliation or reconcilement

23. One Who Causes Agreement; One Who Settles,n. *From Sec. 21:* adjudicator, adjuster, compromiser, conciliator, decider, negotiator or negotiant

24. Able to Be Settled or Brought into Agreement,adj. *From Sec. 21:* adjudicable, adjustable, negotiable, reconcilable; *Also:* 1. **mediable**—able to be settled by agreement

25. Arranged by Agreement: concerted,adj.

26. To Act or Attempt to Settle an Argument; To Attempt to Cause Agreement,v.
1. **intercede**—act between disputants to settle, or attempt to settle, an argument (intercession,n. intercessive,adj.)
2. **intervene**—come or act between disputants to settle an argument (intervention,n. interventive,adj.)
3. **mediate**—act in an argument or controversy in order to bring about agreement (mediation,n. mediatory, mediative, adj.)
4. **negotiate**—act with others to effect an agreement or settlement (negotiation,n. negotiatory, negotiative,adj.)

27. One Who Acts or Attempts to Settle an Argument or to Cause Agreement,n. *From Sec. 26:* interceder, intervener, mediator, mediatress or, fem., mediatrix, negotiator or negotiant

28. To Make Agreeable or Harmonious; To Bring into Agreement,v.
1. **accommodate**—bring into agreement; make harmonious (accommodation,n. accommodative,adj.)
2. **adjust**—get rid of differences or discrepancies; make conform (adjustment,n. adjustive,adj.)
3. **attemper**—put in tune
4. **attune**—bring into agreement or harmony (attunement,n.)
5. **conciliate**—make harmonious; make compatible (conciliation,n. conciliatory, conciliative,adj.)
6. **consort**—bring into agreement
7. **harmonize**—bring into agreement (harmonization,n.)
8. **match**—cause to correspond or agree
9. **normalize**—make conform to a standard (normalization,n.)
10. **reconcile**—bring into agreement; make consistent (reconciliation, reconcilement, n. reconciliatory,adj.)
11. **standardize**—make in accord with recognized or accepted measurements, specifications, etc. (standardization,n.)
12. **stylize**—make conform to convention, or to conventional form (stylization,n.)

13. tally—make agree or correspond
14. tune—make agree
29. State of Having Been Made Agreeable or Harmonious,n. *From Sec. 28:* accommodation, adjustment, harmonization, reconciliation or reconcilement
30. One Who Makes Agreeable or Harmonious,n. *From Sec. 28:* accommodator, adjuster, conciliator, harmonizer, tuner
31. Able to Be Made Agreeable or Harmonious,adj. *From Sec. 28:* adjustable, reconcilable

542. DISAGREEMENT

1. Disagreement, i.e., State of Disagreement or Lack of Harmony,n.
1. clash—discord
2. **conflict**—disagreement of interests, desires, needs, etc.
3. **disaccord, disaccordance**—disagreement; lack of harmony or harmonious relationship
4. **discongruity**—incongruity
5. **discord, discordance, discordancy**—lack of agreement (when the word refers to relations among people, there is the added implication of quarreling or other symptoms of disharmony)
6. **discrepancy**—lack of agreement or consistency
7. **disharmony, disharmonism**—discord
8. **dissension, dissentience**—strong disagreement in feeling or opinion, often resulting in disputes, quarrels, ill-will, etc.
9. **dissidence**—strong disagreement, often with the rest of the group
10. **dissonance**—lack of agreement or harmony
11. **divergence, divergency**—disagreement, with the implication of former or original agreement
12. **embroilment**—condition or state of confused discord
13. **faction, factionalism**—conflict or strife among members of a group; dissension (factional,adj.)
14. **friction**—disagreement caused by opposing motivations or by a clash of desires or goals (frictional,adj.)
15. **incompatibility, incompatibleness**—state or condition of not getting along well or harmoniously together
16. **incongruity, incongruousness**—state or condition of being inconsistent or in disharmony, esp. with the surroundings
17. **inconsistency**—lack of logical agreement or harmony
18. **rift**—disagreement that causes a split or break in a group or organization
19. **strife**—quarrelsome lack of harmony
20. **variance**—disagreement in opinion
21. **war**—strong disagreement or conflict
22. **warfare**—conflict

2. Disagreeing; In Disagreement; Not in Harmony,adj. *From Sec. 1:* clashing, conflicting or conflictive, disaccordant, discordant, discrepant; disharmonious, unharmonious, or inharmonious; dissenting or dissentient, dissident, dissonant, divergent, embroiled, factious or factional, incompatible, incongruous, inconsistent, warring; *Also:*
1. **absonant**—not harmonious
2. **ajar**—in disagreement
3. **alien**—not harmonious; not in agreement
4. **at loggerheads**—in total disagreement
5. **jarring**—out of harmony with surrounding things

3. To Be in, or Show, Disagreement, or Be Lacking in Harmony,v. *From Sec. 1:* conflict, disaccord, discord, disharmonize, dissent, diverge, war; *From Sec. 2:* jar

4. One Who Is in, or Shows, Disagreement, n. *From Sec. 1:* dissenter, dissident, factionist, incompatible

5. Unable to Be Brought into Agreement (of People or Things): incompatible, irreconcilable,adj. (incompatibility or incompatibleness, irreconcilability,n.)

6. Things, Drugs, Ideas, etc., That Do Not Go Together Harmoniously: incompatibles, n.

7. People Who, or Things That, Cannot Be Brought into Agreement or Harmony: irreconcilables,n.

8. One Who Refuses to Agree: irreconcilable,n.

9. Caused by Disagreement within the Group: factious,adj.

10. Disagreement; Dispute; Argument; Quarrel,n.
1. **action**—suit in which one demands or enforces one's rights
2. **affray**—noisy quarrel; public argument
3. **altercation**—angry argument or dispute, generally in words, perhaps becoming violent or, rarely, even leading to blows
4. **bicker**—petulant quarreling or disagreement; wrangle
5. **bout**—argument; dispute
6. **brabble**—wrangle
7. **brawl**—noisy quarrel
8. **breach**—quarrel; end of friendly or peaceful agreement or relations
9. **break**—breach
10. **broil**—noisy quarrel
11. **cause célèbre (French)**—famous dispute, often legal
12. **clash**—disagreement; dispute; argument
13. **conflict**—dispute; argument
14. **contention**—argument
15. **contest, contestation**—dispute; legal dispute; argument
16. **controversy**—dispute; occasionally, a quarrel (controversial,adj.)
17. **debate**—public argument in which each side to a controversy presents its contentions
18. **difference**—argument; quarrel
19. **disception**—disagreement; dispute
20. **disputation**—dispute
21. **embroilment**—dispute; quarrel
22. **feud**—quarrel between families, in which members of one attempt to retaliate for the acts of members of the other; any such continued quarrel between individuals or groups
23. **fracas**—noisy quarrel
24. **fray**—noisy quarrel
25. **haggle**—argument about price
26. **higgle**—petty argument over price
27. **litigation**—legal dispute; suit
28. **logomachy**—dispute or quarrel in words only; dispute about words, their meaning, use, etc. (logomachic, logomachical, adj.)
29. **melee**—noisy quarrel
30. **misunderstanding**—disagreement; quarrel
31. **polemic, polemical**—dispute or argument involving aggressive attack on one another's opinions, doctrines, etc. (polemic, polemical,adj.)
32. **quibble**—argument over trifles in order to avoid the main point at issue
33. **rift**—disagreement or dispute that causes a split or break in an organization
34. **row**—disagreement; quarrel; noisy quarrel
35. **ruckus**—dispute; quarrel (slang)
36. **rumpus**—noisy quarrel
37. **rupture**—end of agreement; breach
38. **set-to**—dispute; quarrel
39. **skirmish**—disagreement; argument

40. spat—quarrel over trivial or petty matters

41. split—breach; breach in a political party

42. squabble—noisy or angry quarrel

43. suit, lawsuit—dispute brought into a law court

44. tiff—quarrel over unimportant matters

45. tussle—rough argument, dispute, or quarrel

46. variance—dispute; quarrel

47. velitation—dispute; disagreement; argument

48. vendetta—feud for blood revenge

49. war—serious argument, dispute, or quarrel

50. wrangle—angry and ill-tempered quarrel or argument

11. To Disagree; To Dispute; To Argue; To Quarrel,v. *From Sec. 10:* altercate, bicker, brawl, clash, contend, contest, controvert or controversialize, debate, differ, discept, feud, haggle, higgle, litigate, logomachize, quibble, row, skirmish, spat, squabble, sue, wrangle; *Also:*
1. **caterwaul**—quarrel like cats
2. **palter**—argue about price
3. **spar**—argue
4. **stickle**—argue on trifling or insufficient grounds

12. Disputer, Disputator, or Disputant; Arguer; Quarreler,n. *From Sec. 10:* bickerer, brawler, contestant or contester; controverter, controvertist, or controversialist; debater, feuder or feudist, haggler, higgler, litigant; logomachist, logomacher, or logomach; polemic, polemicist, polemist, or polemician; quibbler, rower, skirmisher, squabbler, vendettist, wrangler; *From Sec. 11:* caterwauler, palterer, stickler

13. Open to Disagreement, Dispute, etc.; Disputable; Arguable,adj. *From Sec. 10:* actionable, contestable, controversial or controvertible, debatable; *Also:*
1. **moot**—subject to debate or argument
2. **questionable**—open to argument

14. Indisputable; Unarguable,adj. *From Sec. 13:* incontestable, uncontroversial or incontrovertible, undebatable, unquestionable

15. Engaged in a Quarrel or Dispute: at odds, embattled, embroiled,adj.

16. Complicated or Embarrassing Situation Characterized by Quarreling, Friction, etc.: imbroglio,n.

17. Disposed to Disagree, Argue, or Dispute; Quarrelsome,adj.
1. **argumentative**—disposed to argue, dispute, or disagree (argumentativeness,n.)
2. **bellicose**—quarrelsome in temperament or attitude (bellicosity, bellicoseness,n.)
3. **belligerent**—quarrelsome in temper (belligerency, belligerence,n.)
4. **bickering**—tending to quarrel in a peevish or ill-humored manner or over trifles
5. **cantankerous**—argumentative (cantankerousness,n.)
6. **combative**—tending to look for a quarrel (combativeness,n.)
7. **contentious**—tending to provoke and persistently maintain a dispute or quarrel (contentiousness,n.)
8. **disputatious, disputative**—inclined to provoke and take part in disputes, arguments, controversies, etc. (disputatiousness,n.)
9. **dissentious**—quarrelsome; tending to ally oneself with one party in a dispute against another (dissentiousness,n.)
10. **eristic**—inclined to argument or dispute
11. **factious**—enjoying, or tending to provoke, disagreement or dispute within a group (factiousness,n.)
12. **litigious**—tending, or eager, to bring disputes into a court of law, or to take frequent legal action under slight pretexts (litigiousness,n.)
13. **polemical**—disputatious
14. **pugnacious**—disposed or eager to quarrel, pick a quarrel, engage in quarreling, etc. (pugnacity, pugnaciousness,n.)
15. **rowdy, rowdyish**—noisily quarrelsome (rowdiness, rowdyishness, rowdyism,n.)
16. **ugly**—quarrelsome (ugliness,n.)
17. **warlike**—bellicose (warlikeness,n.)

18. Quarrelsome Person: rowdy,n.

19. Quarrelsome Woman: brimstone, harridan, shrew, termagant, virago, vixen,n. (shrewish, viraginian, vixenish,adj.)

20. To Involve (Someone) in a Dispute: embroil,v. (embroilment,n.)

21. Causing, or Tending to Cause, Dispute or Disagreement: disruptive, divisive,adj. (disruptiveness, divisiveness,n.)

22. One Who Causes People to Quarrel: firebrand, mischief-maker, trouble-maker,n.

23. Suitable for Disputation: eristic,adj.

24. Expression Used When a Telling Point Has Been Made in an Argument: touché (French)

543. DEBATE

1. To Debate: agitate, argue, controvert, discept, dispute,v.

2. Debate; Debating: agitation, argument, argumentation, controversy, disceptation, disputation,n.

3. Debater: arguer, disceptator, disputant or disputer,n.

4. Clever Debater; Person Who Uses His Wits Skillfully in Debating: picador,n.

5. To Debate Noisily: wrangle,v. (wrangle, n. wrangler,n.)

6. Relating to Public Debate: forensic,adj.

7. Debate or Argumentation According to the Laws of Logic: dialectic,n.

8. The Practice of Debating According to the Principles of Logic: dialecticism,n.

9. Art of Debate,n.
1. **dialectic, dialectics**—art of debate or argument—a branch of logic (dialectic, dialectical,adj.)
2. **polemics**—art of debate, esp. in public (polemic, polemical,adj.)

10. One Versed in the Art of Debate,n. *From Sec. 9:* dialectician; polemic, polemicist, polemist, or polemician

544. OPPOSITION

1. To Oppose; To Be or Act in Opposition; To Show Opposition,v.
1. **affront**—confront defiantly
2. **antagonize**—oppose; act in opposition to
3. **balk**—oppose by hindering or placing obstacles, and thus make ineffective
4. **bar**—oppose; show opposition to by words
5. **buck**—oppose; act or fight in stubborn opposition to
6. **challenge**—object to (a juror, vote, etc.) as illegal
7. **compete against, compete with**—be or strive in opposition with
8. **confront**—oppose; face boldly in opposition
9. **contradict**—be in opposition to; say that which is in opposition to
10. **contravene**—act in opposition to
11. **controvert**—oppose with argument
12. **counter**—oppose; say or do in opposition to

13. **counteract**—act in opposition to; neutralize a contrary action
14. **counterbalance**—oppose with equal power or weight
15. **countermine**—oppose by secret measures
16. **counterpoise**—counterbalance
17. **counterweigh**—counterbalance
18. **counterwork**—work in opposition
19. **dare**—defy; meet and defy
20. **defy**—resist openly and stubbornly
21. **demur**—object
22. **disaffirm**—contradict
23. **disagree (with)**—show by one's statement that one is in opposition (to what another has said); be in opposition (to)
24. **dispute**—oppose by argument
25. **gainsay**—speak against; contradict
26. **neutralize**—oppose the action of, and thus destroy the effectiveness or result of
27. **object (to), take exception (to)**—oppose; show opposition in words
28. **offset**—neutralize the influence of
29. **oppugn, oppugnate**—be in opposition to; controvert
30. **protest**—object; object to
31. **rebel (against)**—show opposition or defiance (to authority)
32. **rebut**—contradict by argument
33. **recalcitrate**—show obstinate opposition to, or defiance of, authority or orders; object strongly
34. **remonstrate**—give strong reasons against; object
35. **repel, repulse**—oppose successfully
36. **resist**—oppose; act or fight against
37. **stickle**—make trifling objections
38. **violate**—act in opposition to
39. **withstand**—successfully oppose

2. Opposition, i.e., Act or Fact of Opposing, or State of Being Opposed or in Opposition, n. *From Sec. 1:* affront, antagonism, challenge, competition or competitiveness, confrontation or confrontment; contradiction, contradictoriness, or contradictiveness; contravention, controversion, counteraction, counterbalance, counterpoise, counterweight, defiance, demurral, disaffirmance or disaffirmation, disagreement, disputation or dispute, neutralization, objection or exception, oppugnance or oppugnancy, protest or protestation, rebellion or rebelliousness, rebuttal; recalcitration, recalcitrance, or recalcitrancy; remonstration or remonstrance, repulsion, resistance or resistiveness, violation; *Also:*
1. **adverseness**—opposition
2. **antinomy**—opposition of one law or rule to another
3. **antithesis**—opposition
4. **aversion**—opposition
5. **bravado**—boastful opposition masking a reluctance for actual fight
6. **civil disobedience**—passive opposition to laws
7. **contrariness, contrariety**—tendency to oppose authority, commands, demands, etc.
8. **enmity**—active opposition of a person to something or someone
9. **frowardness**—contrariness
10. **hostility**—enmity
11. **iconoclasm**—opposition to the worship of religious images; opposition to tradition
12. **inimicalness, inimicality**—opposition in tendency, influence, or effects; enmity
13. **negativism**—quality of doing the opposite of what is demanded, of opposing the wishes of others, of being contrary, of saying no to suggestions, etc.
14. **pacifism**—opposition to war or armed conflict
15. **perversity, perverseness**—contrariness
16. **renitence**—state of strong opposition or resistance, esp. to pressure; stubborn resistance to authority
17. **repugnance, repugnancy**—opposition in nature or character
18. **terrorism**—opposition to government or rule by creating great fear
19. **unfavorableness**—opposition
20. **unfriendliness**—enmity
21. **waywardness**—contrariness

3. Opposed; In Opposition; Opposing,adj. *From Sec. 1:* antagonistic, balky, competitive, contradictory or contradictive, counter, counteractant or counteractive, defiant, disaffirmatory, oppugnant, protestant, rebellious, recalcitrant, remonstrant, repellent or repulsive, resistant or resistive, violative; *From Sec. 2:* adverse, antinomous, antithetic, averse, contrary or contrariant, froward, hostile, iconoclastic, inimical, negative or negativistic, pacifistic, perverse, renitent, repugnant, unfavorable, unfriendly, wayward; *Also:*
1. **against**—opposed to
2. **alien**—opposed
3. **die-hard**—opposed to the very end
4. **unbowed**—not submissive
5. **underground**—secretly resistive to a government or tyranny
6. **versus**—opposed to (often abbreviated vs.)

4. Opposer; Opponent,n. *From Sec. 1:* antagonist, challenger, competitor or competer, contradicter, contravener, controverter, defier, disputant or disputer; objector, objectioner, or objectionist; oppugner, protester or protestant, rebel, rebutter, remonstrator, repeller, resister, stickler, violator; *From Sec. 2:* adversary, enemy, iconoclast, pacifist, terrorist; *From Sec. 3:* die-hard; *Also:*
1. **archenemy**—chief enemy
2. **foe**—opponent; one who is opposed to a person, thing, institution, etc.
3. **Guelph, Guelf**—one who opposes authority—after a member of the political party that opposed the authority of the German emperors in Italy from the twelfth to the fifteenth centuries (Guelphic, Guelfic,adj.)

5. That Which Opposes, Serves to Oppose, or Is in Opposition,n. *From Sec. 1:* bar, counter, counteractant or counteractive, counterbalance, counterpoise, counterweight, counterwork, demurral, neutralizer, objection or exception, protest, rebutter or rebuttal, remonstration, resister; *Also:*
1. **antagonism**—opposing agent or principle
2. **antidote**—that which counteracts an evil or harmful effect
3. **counteragent**—that which acts in opposition

6. Opposable,adj. *From Sec. 1:* contradictable, controvertible, defiable, disputable, objectionable or exceptionable, rebuttable, resistible (disputability, disputableness; objectionableness, objectionability, or exceptionableness; resistibility or resistibleness,n.)

7. Unopposable,adj. *From Sec. 1:* uncontradictable; incontrovertible, uncontrovertible, or uncontrovertable; indisputable or undisputable, unobjectionable or unexceptionable, unrebuttable, irresistible or unresistible (uncontradictableness; incontrovertibility, incontrovertibleness, uncontrovertibility, incontrovertibleness, uncontrovertibleness, or uncontrovertableness; indisputability, indisputableness, or undisputableness; unobjectionableness or unexceptionableness, unrebuttableness, irresistibility or irresistibleness,n.); *Also:* 1. **ineluctable**—irresistible (ineluctability,n.)

8. Opposed to Change or Progress,adj.
1. **bourgeois**—conservative; stubbornly and stupidly conservative

2. **conservative**—indisposed to change; preferring things the way they are
3. **die-hard**—strongly and stubbornly opposed to all change
4. **hidebound**—stubbornly and stupidly conservative
5. **old-line**—conservative
6. **Philistine**—opposed to education, culture, progress, or progressive theories; opposed to artists, people of artistic temperament, artistic ideas, etc.
7. **reactionary**—favoring a return to former, less progressive, states; hence, loosely, opposed to change or progress
8. **square-toed**—conservative
9. **standpat**—opposing change; wanting to keep things as they are

9. **Opposition to Change or Progress,**n. *From Sec. 8:* conservatism, Philistinism, reaction, standpattism; *Also:* 1. Bourbonism—stubborn conservatism

10. **Opponent of Change or Progress,**n. *From Sec. 8:* conservative, die-hard, Philistine, reactionary, standpatter; *From Sec. 9:* Bourbon or Bourbonist

545. CHALLENGE

1. **To Challenge,**v.
   1. **contest**—challenge the legality or validity of (contestation,n.)
   2. **dare**—challenge
   3. **defy**—challenge (to do something considered impossible); challenge to combat (defiance,n.)
   4. **impugn**—challenge as false (impugnment, n.)
   5. **question**—challenge

2. **A Challenge:** dare; defi (colloq.); defial, defiance; defy (colloq.); the gage, the gauntlet, the glove,n.

3. **A Written Challenge to a Duel:** cartel,n.

546. OPPOSITE

1. **Opposite; Contrary,**adj.
   1. **absonant**—contrary
   2. **antilogical**—contradictory in terms or ideas
   3. **antipodal, antipodean, antipodic**—diametrically opposite
   4. **antithetic**—directly opposite; contrary
   5. **antonymous**—opposite in meaning (of words or phrases)
   6. **contradictory, contradictive**—opposite; directly opposite; contrary
   7. **contrary, contrariant**—opposite in nature, character, condition, etc.
   8. **converse**—opposite; contrary
   9. **counter (to)**—opposite (to)
   10. **crosswise**—opposite to what is wanted
   11. **diametric**—completely opposite
   12. **inverse**—opposite in position, direction, meaning, value, etc.
   13. **paradoxical, paradoxal, paradoxial, paradoxic**—contradictory, yet existent or true (of a condition, fact, or situation); self-contradictory, but true (of a statement)
   14. **perverse**—contrary; contrary to what is right, acceptable, or correct
   15. **polar**—completely opposite in character or quality
   16. **repugnant**—contradictory
   17. **reverse**—opposite
   18. **violative of**—contrary to
   19. **vis-à-vis**—opposite
   20. **wayward**—contrary; contrary to expectations

2. **Oppositeness; Contrariness, Contrariety,** n. *From Sec. 1:* antilogy, antithesis, antonymy; contradiction, contradictoriness, or contradictiveness; paradox, paradoxicality, or paradoxicalness; perversity or perverseness, polarity, repugnance or repugnancy, waywardness

3. **An Opposite; A Contrary,**n. *From Sec. 1:* antilogy, antipode, antithesis, antonym, contradiction, converse, inverse, paradox, reverse

4. **To Be Opposite or Contrary,**v. *From Sec. 1:* contradict, violate

5. **Opposite:** vis-à-vis,adv.

6. **On the Contrary:** au contraire (French), per contra

547. DENIAL

1. **To Deny,**v.
   1. **abnegate**—deny and reject
   2. **controvert**—deny
   3. **disaffirm**—deny
   4. **disavow**—deny knowledge about, responsibility for, or approval of
   5. **disclaim**—deny ownership of, connection with, or responsibility for
   6. **dispute**—deny the truth of
   7. **gainsay**—deny
   8. **negate**—deny; claim or prove to be non-existent
   9. **negative**—deny
   10. **protest**—deny
   11. **renege**—deny
   12. **repulse**—deny

2. **Denial,**n. *From Sec. 1:* abnegation, controversion, disaffirmance or disaffirmation, disavowal, disclamation or disclaimer, disputation, negation, protestation, renege, repulsion; *Also:* 1. denegation—denial

3. **Denying,**adj. *From Sec. 1:* abnegative, disaffirmative or disaffirmatory, disputative, negatory, negative, protestant

548. REFUSAL

1. **To Refuse,**v.
   1. **abnegate**—deny and reject; repudiate
   2. **balk**—refuse to continue
   3. **bolt**—refuse to support (a party, cause, etc.) after leaving it or breaking with it
   4. **brush away, brush aside**—refuse to consider
   5. **decline**—refuse politely, esp. that which is offered in a friendly spirit; refuse politely (to do)
   6. **deny**—refuse
   7. **disallow**—refuse to allow
   8. **disavow**—refuse to acknowledge or accept responsibility for
   9. **disclaim**—refuse to accept or acknowledge any responsibility for or connection with
   10. **discountenance**—refuse to approve, or to look upon with approval
   11. **disdain**—refuse to accept because unworthy of one's dignity, status, etc.
   12. **disown**—refuse to admit ownership or authorship of, or responsibility for
   13. **negative**—refuse assent to; veto
   14. **rebuff**—make a sudden and discourteous refusal to a request, offer, advance, etc., or to the person making this request, etc.
   15. **reject**—refuse to accept, believe, use, acknowledge, etc.
   16. **renounce**—disown; repudiate
   17. **repel, repulse**—refuse to accept
   18. **reprobate**—refuse to accept
   19. **repudiate**—refuse to accept, acknowledge, or pay
   20. **scorn**—refuse as unworthy
   21. **scout**—refuse to accept; refuse to believe or believe in; reject with scorn or contempt

22. **spurn**—refuse scornfully
23. **veto**—refuse to admit or approve; refuse assent or consent to

2. Refusal,n. *From Sec. 1:* abnegation, bolt, declension or declination, denial, disallowance, disavowal, disclamation or disclaimer, rebuff, rejection, renouncement, repulsion or repulse (from *repel*), reprobation, repudiation, veto; *Also:* 1. **non-acceptance**—refusal to accept

3. Refuser,n. *From Sec. 1:* abnegator, disavower, disclaimer, disowner, rejector, reprobater, repudiator, scorner, spurner, vetoer

4. Refusing; Tending to Refuse,adj. *From Sec. 1:* abnegating, balking, etc.; balky, disclamatory, disdainful, negative, rejective; repulsive (from *repel*); reprobative or reprobatory

5. Sign of Rejection: thumbs down

6. Power of an Executive to Reject Laws Passed by a Legislature: veto,n.

549. DISOBEDIENCE

1. Disobedient; Rebellious,adj.
1. **balky**—tending to disobey
2. **contrary**—temperamentally unwilling to accept authority, orders, dictation, etc.
3. **contumacious**—stubbornly disobedient, esp. to constituted authority
4. **disorderly**—disobedient
5. **fractious**—disobedient
6. **froward**—so strongly inclined to disobedience that no compliance is made even with reasonable requests or orders
7. **insubordinate**—disobedient; rebellious against authority
8. **insurgent**—rising or rebelling against authority
9. **insurrectionary**—rebellious against civil or political authority
10. **malcontent**—rebellious
11. **mutinous**—refusing to obey those in authority; rebellious against constituted authority, esp. naval or military authority
12. **naughty**—disobediently bad (of a child, pet, etc.)
13. **non-compliant**—disobedient
14. **non-conformist**—failing and/or unwilling to conform to accepted patterns of behavior
15. **perverse**—stubbornly unwilling to obey; contrary
16. **recalcitrant**—disobedient; rebellious to authority, influence, or control; stubbornly defiant of authority or orders
17. **restive**—stubbornly resistive to control
18. **revolutionary**—tending to overthrow a government, system, etc.
19. **uncompliant**—non-compliant
20. **unruly**—disobedient
21. **wayward**—willfully or contrarily disobedient

2. Disobedience; Rebelliousness; Rebellion, n. *From Sec. 1:* contrariness, contumacy or contumaciousness, disorderliness, fractiousness, frowardness, insubordination, insurgence or insurgency, insurrection, mutinousness or mutiny, naughtiness, non-compliance, non-conformity or non-conformance, perversity or perverseness; recalcitrance, recalcitrancy, or recalcitration; restiveness, revolution, unruliness, waywardness; *Also:*
1. **civil disobedience**—refusal to obey the orders, commands, or authority of the government
2. **unrest**—agitation or disturbance coming close to complete rebellion against authority

3. To Disobey; To Rebel,v. *From Sec. 1:* insurrect, rebel, recalcitrate, revolutionize or revolution; *Also:*

1. **arise**—rebel
2. **revolt**—rebel against authority or government

4. An Act of Disobedience or Rebellion; A Rebellion,n. *From Sec. 1:* insurrection, mutiny, revolution; *From Sec. 3:* revolt; *Also:*
1. **commotion**—rebellion; insurrection
2. **outbreak**—rebellion
3. **Putsch (German)**—rebellion; petty rebellion; insurrection
4. **rising**—rebellion; insurrection
5. **uprisal, uprise, uprising**—rebellion; insurrection

5. One Who Disobeys or Rebels; A Rebel,n. *From Sec. 1:* insurgent, insurrectionist, malcontent, mutineer, non-conformist, recalcitrant; revolutionary, revolutionist or revolutioner; *From Sec. 3:* revolter; *From Sec. 4:* putschist, upriser; *Also:* 1. **maverick**—a rebel against one's political party or group

6. Pert. or Relating to, or Descr. of, Rebellion: insurrectionary, rebel, revolutional, revolutionary,adj.

7. Advocacy of Revolutionary Principles: revolutionism,n. (revolutionist,n.)

8. One Who Favored the American Revolution: Revolutionist, Whig,n.

9. Spirit of Rebellion, Often against Social or Artistic Tradition or Conventions: Titanism,n.

10. Incitement of the People to Discontentment with, and/or Rebellion against, the Government or Legal Authority; An Act or Speech of This Nature: sedition,n. (seditionary, seditionist,n. seditionary, seditious,adj.)

550. UNRULINESS

1. Unruly; Disorderly; Uncontrollable; Unmanageable,adj.
1. **fractious**—unruly; difficult to manage or control (fractiousness,n.)
2. **froward**—unmanageable (frowardness,n.)
3. **headstrong**—not easily held back (headstrongness,n.)
4. **incorrigible**—unruly or unmanageable, with the implication that the behavior cannot be changed (incorrigibility,n.)
5. **intractable**—stubbornly hard to manage or control (intractability,n.)
6. **irrepressible**—uncontrollable; unable to be held back (irrepressibility,n.)
7. **obstreperous**—unruly; unmanageable (obstreperousness,n.)
8. **rambunctious**—uncontrollably or noisily unruly (rambunctiousness,n.)
9. **refractory**—uncontrollable; unmanageable; resistive (refractoriness,n.)
10. **resistive**—tending to resist control (resistiveness,n.)
11. **restive**—stubbornly resisting control, guidance, or management (restiveness,n.)
12. **riotous**—disorderly and noisy in behavior (riotousness,n.)
13. **rowdy, rowdyish**—disorderly (rowdiness, rowdyishness,n.)
14. **stormy**—unruly; disorderly (storminess, n.)
15. **temperamental**—governed by sudden emotion and therefore hard to control; willful
16. **tempestuous**—unruly; disorderly (tempestuousness,n.)
17. **tough**—hard to influence or gain power over; disorderly (toughness,n.)
18. **troublesome**—unruly; difficult to manage (troublesomeness,n.)
19. **tumultuous**—characterized by disorder, noisy disorder, noisy commotion, etc. (tumultuousness,n.)
20. **turbulent**—unruly; disorderly (turbulence, turbulency,n.)

21. **ungovernable**—uncontrollable (ungovernableness,n.)
22. **untoward**—hard to manage (untowardness,n.)
23. **uproarious**—disorderly and noisy (uproariousness,n.)
24. **wild**—unruly; disorderly; impatient of control or restraint (wildness,n.)
25. **willful**—uncontrollable, in the sense of not listening to reason (willfulness,n.)

2. Unruly, etc., Act, Acts, Behavior, etc.,n. *From Sec. 1:* riot, tumult, turbulence, uproar

3. Unruly, etc., Person,n. *From Sec. 1:* rowdy, tough; *Also:* 1. terror—noisy and unmanageable person or child

4. Disorderly Public Demonstration: riot,n. (rioter,n. riotous,adj. riot,v.)

5. Likely to Become Unruly or Disorderly: ugly,adj. (ugliness,n.)

6. Uncontrollably and Very Fast: like wildfire

7. Not Reacting Readily to Treatment: refractory,adj.

551. OBEDIENCE

1. Obedient,adj.
1. **biddable**—obedient; manageable
2. **compliant, compliable**—obedient to a request, command, suggestion, etc.
3. **conformable**—obedient
4. **docile**—obedient; manageable
5. **dutiful, duteous**—obedient, esp. in the performance of duties
6. **law-abiding**—obedient to the law
7. **manageable**—capable of being controlled, directed, etc., and reacting to such control or direction obediently
8. **meek**—quietly obedient; submissive
9. **observant of**—obedient to (rules, laws, principles, etc.)
10. **orderly**—obedient; acting obediently
11. **quiet**—orderly
12. **servile**—meanly or slavishly submissive
13. **submissive**—obedient; doing what one is told
14. **subservient**—submissively obedient or compliant; slavishly obedient
15. **tame**—once wild, now able to live with humans and be obedient to their call or demands
16. **well-behaved**—obedient; acting obediently

2. Obedience,n. *From Sec. 1:* compliance, compliancy, or compliableness; conformability, conformity, or conformance; docility, dutifulness, duteousness, manageability, meekness, observance, orderliness, quietness, servility, submissiveness, subservience, tameness; *Also:*
1. **accordance**—conformance
2. **dharma**—obedience to religious law (a term of Hinduism or Buddhism)
3. **subordination**—obedience; willingness to obey

3. To Be Obedient,v. *From Sec. 1:* comply (with), conform, observe, submit; behave (from *well-behaved*)

4. Entitled to Obedience: authoritative,adj. (authoritativeness,n.)

5. One Who Demands, Believes in, or Advocates Obedience,n.
1. **authoritarian**—one who demands or advocates blind obedience to authority (authoritarianism,n. authoritarian,adj.)
2. **disciplinarian**—person who believes in or demands strict obedience
3. **martinet**—one who insists on the strictest, and often most unreasonable and blind, obedience and discipline,

whether in military or civil life (martinetism,n.)
4. **precisian**—one who insists on the strictest obedience to religious practice or, occasionally, other rules or principles

6. To Force Obedience: compel,v. (compulsion,n.)

7. To Force Obedience to (a Law, Command, etc.): enforce,v. (enforcement,n. enforcer,n.)

8. Sternly Enforced: strict,adj. (strictness, n.)

9. Demanding Obedience: strict,adj. (strictness,n.)

10. To Give the Power (to a Law, etc.) to Compel Obedience: put teeth in,v.

11. To Teach Obedience to; To Make Obedient: discipline, tame, train,v. (discipline, training,n. disciplinarian or discipliner, tamer, trainer,n. disciplinary, disciplinative, disciplinatory, disciplinal,adj.)

12. Means Taken by Nations to Force Another to Obey International Law: sanction, n.

13. Obedient Person,n.
1. **minion**—one willing to do whatever he is told to do
2. **myrmidon**—obedient and unprotesting follower; obedient and unprotesting executor of commands
3. **servant**—one who does without question what he is told to do

552. SUBMISSION

1. To Submit; To Yield or Give In,v.
1. **abide**—submit to; submit to without shrinking
2. **acknowledge**—admit or accept the authority of
3. **acquiesce**—yield passively to
4. **appease**—give in to (someone's) of strong demands or requests for the purpose of calming or quieting him
5. **bow**—submit; yield
6. **capitulate**—give in; surrender under agreed conditions
7. **comply**—yield
8. **concede**—give in to another's wishes or demands; yield; surrender
9. **cry quits**—give in
10. **defer (to)**—yield politely (to another or to another's opinion or wishes)
11. **humor**—yield to the whims, moods, caprices, etc., of
12. **indulge**—yield weakly or with weak fondness to the desires of, no matter how unreasonable such desires are
13. **knuckle under**—submit; yield
14. **reconcile oneself to**—bring oneself to submit to
15. **relent**—give way or yield from one's determined or planned action or course, often out of pity
16. **resign oneself to**—submit patiently, quietly, or without protest or complaint to
17. **stoop**—submit; yield
18. **succumb**—yield
19. **surrender**—yield to another's power
20. **truckle (to)**—give in servilely or submissively (to); defer excessively or obsequiously (to)

2. Submission; Submittal; A Submitting, Yielding, or Giving In,n. *From Sec. 1:* acknowledgment, acquiescence, appeasement, capitulation, compliance or compliancy, concession, deference, indulgence, reconcilement, resignation, surrender

3. Submissive; Submitting, Yielding, or Giving In,adj. *From Sec. 1:* acquiescing, appeasing, etc.; acquiescent, compliant or compliable, concessive, deferential, indulgent, reconciled, resigned; *Also:*

1. **amenable**—yielding, or willing to yield, to persuasion
2. **complaisant**—yielding graciously; not stubborn
3. **conformable**—submissive
4. **docile**—yielding; submitting to authority without resistance or reluctance; doing quietly and willingly what one is told
5. **flexible**—inclined to yield to pressure or persuasion; not stubborn
6. **malleable**—amenable; pliable
7. **meek**—timidly submissive
8. **non-resistant**—submissive
9. **obeisant**—politely yielding to another's wishes or opinions
10. **passive**—submissive
11. **pliable, pliant**—yielding; yielding easily; amenable
12. **recreant**—submitting out of fear and cowardice
13. **resistless**—incapable of resisting
14. **sequacious**—tending to suit one's opinion passively to that of another person; inclined to follow and be submissive to a leader
15. **servile**—unnaturally or excessively submissive
16. **slavish**—weakly submissive
17. **spellbound**—unable to resist by reason of fascination
18. **subject to**—submissive to the influence of
19. **subordinate**—submissive to authority
20. **subservient**—submissive
21. **supine**—slavishly submissive
22. **supple**—yielding; servile
23. **tractable**—submitting willingly to control; docile
24. **unresistant, unresisting**—submissive
25. **waxy**—pliable
26. **weak-kneed**—yielding readily to opposition, intimidation, etc.

4. Submissiveness, etc.,n. *From Sec. 1:* acquiescence; compliance, compliancy, or compliableness; deference, indulgence, resignation or resignedness; *From Sec. 3:* amenability or amenableness, complaisance, conformability or conformableness, docility, flexibility or flexibleness, malleability, meekness, non-resistance, obeisance; passivity, passivism, or passiveness; pliability, pliancy, recreancy, resistlessness, sequacity or sequaciousness, servility, slavishness, subjection, subordination, subservience, supineness, suppleness, tractability, waxiness

5. Submitter; Yielder,n. *From Sec. 1:* abider, appeaser, capitulator, truckler; *From Sec. 3:* recreant, slave, subject; *Also:*

1. **milquetoast**—meek and fearful person (colloq.)
2. **puppet**—one who submits to the will of another, or who does what he is told without thinking for himself
3. **quitter**—one who gives up easily
4. **stooge**—one who plays a submissive and/or subordinate role to someone else (slang)

6. Attitude or Philosophy of a Person Who Wishes to Give Up a Struggle, Contest, Attempt, etc., Believing Further Effort Futile or Ill-Advised: defeatism,n. (defeatist,n. defeatist,adj.)

7. Gesture (Curtsy, Bow, Bending of the Knees, etc.) of Submission: obeisance,n.

8. To Force to Yield: compel,v. (compulsion, n.)

9. To Make Subservient: subordinate,v. (subordination,n.)

10. Unable to Resist (a Disease): predisposed (to), subject (to), susceptible (to),adj. (predisposition, susceptibility,n. predispose,v.)

553. STUBBORNNESS

1. Stubborn; Obstinate; Unyielding,adj.

1. **adamant, adamantine**—stubborn; unyielding; immovable
2. **balky**—stubbornly refusing to proceed, move, etc.
3. **bulldogged**—dogged
4. **bullheaded**—stubborn
5. **cussed**—stubborn; obstinate; perverse (colloq.)
6. **dogged**—obstinate; sullenly obstinate
7. **firm**—obstinate; not easily moved or changed
8. **froward**—stubborn; obstinate
9. **headstrong**—stubborn; obstinate; obstinately determined to have one's own way, regardless of consequences
10. **immovable**—stubborn; defying all efforts to make one give in, change, yield, etc.
11. **inexorable**—stubbornly unyielding to, or unmoved by, prayers or entreaty
12. **inflexible**—stubbornly unyielding
13. **intractable**—stubborn and hard to manage or control
14. **intransigeant (French), intransigent**—stubbornly unyielding; stubbornly unwilling to accept any compromise
15. **irreconcilable**—stubbornly unwilling to compromise
16. **mulish**—stubborn; sullenly or silently stubborn
17. **obdurate**—stubborn; stubbornly unyielding in feelings; stubbornly unwilling to repent
18. **opinionated, opinionative**—stubborn; obstinate; stubbornly attached to one's opinions, no matter how illogical these are shown to be
19. **persevering**—stubborn or obstinate despite any counterinfluences, opposition, hardships, etc.
20. **persistent**—stubborn; obstinate
21. **pertinacious**—extremely stubborn, obstinate, or unyielding
22. **perverse**—obstinate; obstinately holding to what is wrong or unacceptable
23. **pervicacious**—very stubborn or obstinate
24. **pigheaded**—stubborn; obstinate
25. **Procrustean, procrustean**—stubborn in making, or stubbornly determined to make, someone or something fit into a system, classification, etc.
26. **refractory**—stubborn
27. **relentless**—stubbornly unyielding
28. **rigid**—stubbornly unwilling to change or compromise
29. **self-willed**—stubborn; obstinate
30. **stern**—unyielding; firm
31. **stiff**—rigid
32. **stiff-necked**—stubborn; extremely obstinate
33. **stony**—unyielding
34. **stout**—stubborn; unyielding
35. **strong-willed**—obstinate
36. **sturdy**—unyielding
37. **tenacious**—stubborn; obstinate
38. **tough**—stubborn
39. **unbending**—unyielding
40. **uncompromising**—unyielding
41. **unmovable**—immovable
42. **unreconstructed**—stubbornly holding to old-fashioned or outmoded political or other beliefs
43. **unrelenting**—stubbornly unyielding
44. **untoward**—stubborn; obstinate
45. **wayward**—stubborn; obstinate
46. **willful**—stubborn; obstinate
47. **wrongheaded**—stubborn when, or even though, wrong
48. **wry**—wrongheaded

2. Stubbornness; Obstinacy or Obstinance, n. *From Sec. 1:* bulldoggedness, bullheadedness; cussedness (colloq.); doggedness, firm-

ness, frowardness, headstrongness, immovability, inexorability, inflexibility, intractability; intransigeance (French), intransigence,
or intransigency; irreconcilability, mulishness,
obduracy, opinionatedness, opinionativeness,
perseverance, persistence or persistency, pertinacity or pertinaciousness, perversity or
perverseness, pigheadedness, refractoriness,
relentlessness, rigidity, self-will, sternness,
stiffness, stoniness, stoutness, sturdiness,
tenacity or tenaciousness, toughness, waywardness, willfulness, wrongheadedness, wryness

**3. Stubborn, Obstinate, or Unyielding Per-
son,n.** From Sec. 1: bullhead, intransigeant
(French) or intransigent, intransigente,
mule, pighead; Also: 1. bitter-ender—one
who will not give in or compromise

**4. To Continue Stubbornly despite Ob-
stacles:** persevere, persist,v. (perseverance,
persistence,n.)

554. PERMISSION

**1. To Allow; To Permit; To Consent; To
Say Yes to,v.**
1. abet—allow to do wrong
2. accede to—consent to; say yes to
3. accept—consent to
4. acquiesce (in)—passively permit
5. agree to—say yes to
6. assent to—say yes to; consent to
7. authorize—permit
8. blink at—condone
9. canonize—permit by churchly authority
10. condone—strictly, treat (an offense) as if
   it had not been committed; hence, by extension, permit (an offense) by not punishing the commission of it
11. empower—permit
12. indulge—permit actions to out of fondness; tolerate
13. let—allow
14. license—officially permit; give official permission to for carrying on a business or
   engaging in an activity that without such
   permission is illegal
15. sanctify, sanction—give permission for;
   give official permission for
16. subscribe to—give one's official permission to; consent to
17. suffer—allow in the sense of putting up
   with or not objecting to; allow, in Biblical
   language
18. tolerate—allow in a passive sense, that
   is, by not stopping or opposing
19. warrant—permit
20. wink at—condone

2. Allowance; Permission; Consent,n. From
Sec. 1: accession, acceptance, acquiescence,
agreement, assent, authorization, canonization, condonation or condonance, empowerment, indulgence, license, sanctification, sanction, subscription, sufferance, toleration or
tolerance, warrant; Also:
1. carte blanche—permission to use one's
   own judgment in actions, or to act as one
   sees fit or wishes
2. dispensation—official permission to disregard or violate a rule
3. imprimatur—official permission to publish; such permission where there is no
   freedom of press; such permission from
   the Roman Catholic Church
4. leave—permission; permission to a sailor
   to go ashore or off duty for a period
   longer than that covered by liberty; permission to be away, go off duty, etc.
5. liberty—permission for a sailor to go
   ashore for a time, usually a number of
   hours

**3. Permitting; Permissive; Consentant;
Consentive,adj.** From Sec. 1: accepting, ac-

quiescing, etc.; acquiescent, agreeable, assentive or assentient, indulgent, tolerant (acquiescence, agreeableness, assentiveness, indulgence, tolerance,n.); Also: 1. susceptible
of—permitting (susceptible of proof, etc.)

4. Saying "Yes" to a Question: affirmative,
adj.

**5. Word or Phrase That Means or Says
"Yes":** affirmative,n.

6. Saying Neither "Yes" nor "No": noncommittal,adj.

7. To Allow to Enter, Pass, etc.: admit, pass,
transmit,v. (admission or admittance, transmission,n.)

**8. Document, etc., Granting Permission,
n.**
1. authorization—document giving official
   permission
2. license—document giving official permission to do certain things or engage in
   certain activities
3. pass—document giving permission to go
   or pass through
4. permit—written permission or license to
   do something
5. warrant—document giving official permission

**9. One Who Has Been Given a License or
Permit:** licensee, licentiate, permittee,n.

10. Gladly and Freely Permitted: welcome,
adj.

**11. Permitted for Consideration; Permitted
in Court as Evidence:** admissible,adj. (ad-
missibility,n.)

12. With or Without Permission: willy-nilly,
adv.

555. PROHIBITION

1. To Forbid; To Prohibit,v.
1. ban—prohibit
2. bar—forbid
3. deprive—prohibit from having; not permit to have or enjoy
4. embargo—prohibit
5. enjoin from—forbid, in the sense of
   ordering not to
6. excommunicate—prohibit from taking
   part in any church services or from enjoying privileges of church membership
7. forfend—forbid (archaic)
8. interdict—prohibit
9. outlaw—prohibit
10. proscribe—forbid as dangerous, harmful,
   or bad
11. suppress—prohibit from publication
12. taboo, tabu—forbid; place a ban upon,
   often as something sacred or, contrarily,
   profane
13. veto—prohibit

**2. Forbiddance, Forbiddal, or Prohibition,
n.** From Sec. 1: ban, bar, deprivation or deprival, embargo, enjoinder, excommunication,
interdiction, outlawry, proscription, suppression, taboo, tabu, veto; Also: 1. injunction
(against)—an order prohibiting a person
from doing something

3. Forbidding, Prohibitive, Prohibitory,adj.
From Sec. 1: banning, barring, etc.; excommunicative or excommunicatory, proscriptive,
suppressive; From Sec. 2: injunctive

4. Forbidden, Prohibited,adj. From Sec. 1:
banned, barred, etc.; taboo, tabu; Also:
1. contraband—prohibited as to trading,
   importation, or export (contraband,n.)
2. verboten (German)—prohibited by authority or law

5. To Prohibit from Entering: bar, debar,
forbid,v.

6. A Government Decree Prohibiting the Entrance and Departure of Ships at a Port: embargo,n. (embargo,v.)

556. HELP

1. To Help; To Aid,v.
1. abet—help in wrongdoing
2. accommodate—help
3. advantage—help
4. assist—help
5. avail—help
6. befriend—come to the aid of
7. benefit—help
8. bestead—help
9. connive with—give secret aid (in wrongdoing or to wrongdoers); help secretly
10. foster—help grow or develop
11. minister (to)—be of help (to) ; do what is helpful (for)
12. oblige—help
13. promote—help to organize
14. rally—come to the aid of a person, group, party, or cause
15. relieve—give help to
16. subserve—promote; be an instrument for promoting; be of use in promoting
17. subsidize—give financial aid to, usually in the form of a gift
18. subvene—happen in the way of help
19. succor—give help to (one in trouble, distress, or difficulty)
20. tide over—help temporarily

2. Help; Aid,n. *From Sec. 1:* accommodation, advantage, assistance or assist, avail, benefit, connivance, promotion, rally, relief, subsidization or subsidy, succor; *Also:*
1. accessory—that which helps in a subordinate capacity
2. adminicle—auxiliary
3. auxiliary—that which helps or furnishes help
4. bounty—financial aid given to encourage some activity
5. crutch—an artificial aid
6. subsidiary—that which furnishes help
7. subvention—subsidy from a government, foundation, etc.
8. yeoman service—loyal help

3. Helper; Aider,n. *From Sec. 1:* abettor, accommodator, assistant or assister, befriender, conniver, fosterer, minister, subsidizer, succor or succorer; *Also:*
1. accessory—one who helps someone commit a legal offense though not present at the actual commission (He may help in the planning, in which case he is an accessory before the fact; or he may provide aid, shelter, or protection afterward, in which case he is an accessory after the fact.)
2. accomplice—one who helps another in wrongdoing
3. acolyte—helper; boy who helps the priest in a Roman Catholic Mass
4. adjutant—assistant; army officer who assists a superior officer (adjutancy,n.)
5. adjutory—helper
6. adjuvant—assistant
7. aide—military or naval assistant
8. aide-de-camp, aid-de-camp—officer assistant to a general
9. ally—helper
10. apprentice—one who is learning (a job, etc.) while helping (apprenticeship,n.)
11. coadjutor—assistant; bishop appointed to help another bishop (coadjutress, coadjutrix, fem.)
12. humanitarian—one who is helpful to humanity
13. Samaritan—one who helps, or is ready to help, people in trouble or distress
14. second—helper
15. subsidiary—one who furnishes help

4. Helping; Aiding; Helpful,adj. *From Sec. 1:* abetting, accommodating, etc.; accommodative, advantageous, assistant, beneficial, ministrant, promotive; *From Sec. 2:* accessory, auxiliary, subsidiary, subventionary; *From Sec. 3:* adjutory or adjutorious, adjuvant, apprentice, humanitarian; *Also:*
1. ancillary—auxiliary
2. constructive—helpful
3. useful—helpful

5. Willing to Help: accommodating, obliging,adj.

6. That to Which, or Person to Whom, One Turns for Help: recourse, resort, resource, stand-by,n.

7. To Turn for Help (to): resort (to),v.

8. A Turning for Help: recourse, resort,n.

9. To Make an Urgent Call for Help: SOS, v. (SOS,n.)

10. To Fail to Help when Help Is Most Needed: betray,v. (betrayal,n.)

11. Needing Help from Others: dependent, adj. (dependence, dependency,n.)

12. Not Needing or Seeking Help from Others: independent,adj. (independence,n.)

13. Having the Attitude that One Needs No Help from Others: independent,adj. (independence,n.)

14. Helpless and Weak: impotent, prostrate, prostrated,adj. (impotence or impotency, prostration,n.)

15. To Render Helpless: prostrate, swamp,v. (prostration,n.)

16. To Become Helpless: swamp,v.

557. TO HINDER

1. To Hinder,v.
1. astrict—restrict
2. baffle—hinder
3. balk—hinder
4. bar—hinder; obstruct
5. barricade, barricado—hinder with a barrier or obstruction
6. block—hinder; obstruct
7. blockade—hinder by throwing up obstructions or barriers in the way of
8. bridle—restrict
9. circumscribe—restrict
10. clog—hinder; obstruct
11. constrict—restrict
12. cramp—restrict
13. cumber—hinder by putting a burden or figurative weight upon
14. encumber—hinder, or hinder from free action, by placing burdens upon, these usually being figurative or intangible
15. fetter—hinder with, or as if with, foot shackles, literally or figuratively
16. frustrate—hinder
17. hamper—hinder from free action
18. hamstring—cause (someone) difficulty in doing something
19. hobble, hopple—hinder so that progress can be made only slowly or awkwardly
20. impede—hinder; get in the way of; stop the progress of
21. interfere with—hinder
22. obstruct—hinder; get in the way of; hinder the progress of
23. pinion—impede; shackle
24. restrict—hinder the free action of
25. retard, retardate—hinder the progress of
26. shackle—hinder the free action of, literally or figuratively; fetter
27. snag—hinder through hidden or unexpected impediments, obstacles, etc., literally or figuratively
28. spike—hinder
29. strait-jacket—hinder the movements of

with, or as if with, a tight jacket, literally
or figuratively

30. **stymie**—hinder
31. **thwart**—hinder
32. **trammel**—hinder the free action, movement, or progress of

2. Hindrance; A Hindering,n. *From Sec. 1:*
astriction, bafflement or baffle, barricade,
blockage, blockade, circumscription, constriction, encumbrance, frustration, interference,
obstruction, restriction; retardation, retardment, or retardance; *Also:* 1. obscurantism—
act of impeding progress or the progress of
knowledge

3. A Hindrance, i.e., That Which Hinders,
n. *From Sec. 1:* bar, barricade, barricado,
block or blockage, blockade, bridle, clog, constriction, cumber or cumbrance, encumbrance,
fetter or fetters, hobble, impediment (impedimenta,pl.), interference, obstruction, restriction, retardant, shackle or shackles,
snag, strait jacket, trammel or trammels;
Also:

1. **baffle**—artificial obstruction to deflect
gases, sounds, etc.
2. **barrier**—hindrance; anything standing in
the way of movement or progress; that
which hinders approach or attack; some
obstacle thrown up to hinder or stop the
enemy
3. **bottleneck**—place, condition, stage, etc.,
that slows down or hinders progress
4. **hitch**—hindrance
5. **hobble**—hindrance that slows the progress of a horse
6. **hopple**—hindrance that slows the progress of a horse or grazing animal
7. **hurdle**—hindrance or barrier to be sur-
mounted
8. **muzzle**—restrictive device placed over
the mouths of animals, usually dogs
9. **obstacle**—hindrance; that which stands
in the way, literally or figuratively
10. **obstruent**—obstruction (medical)
11. **rampart**—protective barrier
12. **strangle hold**—that which hinders free
movement, growth, development, etc.
13. **stumbling block**—that which hinders;
that which hinders progress; obstacle

**4. Hindering; Serving or Tending to
Hinder,** adj. *From Sec. 1:* astricting, baffling,
etc.; astrictive, circumscriptive, constrictive,
cumbrous or cumbersome; impeditive, im-
pedimental, or impedimentary; obstructive,
restrictive; retardative, retardant, or retardatory; *From Sec. 2:* obscurantist or obscurant;
Also:

1. **diriment**—impeding (legal)
2. **obstruent**—obstructing (medical)

5. Full of Obstacles: thorny,adj. (thorniness,n.)

**6. The Hindering of Progress; The Hinder-
ing of Legislation by Delaying Tactics:** ob-
tructionism,n.   (obstructionist,n.   obstructionist,adj.)

**7. Aim or Attempt to Impede Progress or
the Progress of Knowledge:** obscurantism,n.
obscurantist,n. obscurantist, obscurant,adj.)

558. RESTRAINT; RESTRICTION

**1. To Restrain; To Restrict; To Hold or
Keep In or Back,**v.
1. **astrict**—restrict
2. **bar**—obstruct
3. **block**—obstruct
4. **blockade**—hold back by throwing up obstructions or barriers
5. **bound**—confine; limit
6. **bridle**—restrain; restrict
7. **burke**—suppress

8. **chain**—restrain with, or as if with,
chains, figuratively or literally
9. **check**—restrain
10. **checkmate**—restrain completely or to an
extreme degree
11. **choke**—restrain the growth, action, or
progress of
12. **choke back**—hold back; keep back
13. **circumscribe**—restrict; hold within narrow limits
14. **clog**—hold back; choke with obstructions;
obstruct
15. **confine**—hold within limits or bounds
16. **constrain**—restrain; hold back forcibly
17. **constrict**—restrict; limit
18. **contain**—restrain; hold back
19. **control**—restrain; hold back
20. **cork**—restrain
21. **cramp**—restrict; limit
22. **curb**—restrain
23. **daggle**—clog with mud
24. **dam**—restrain or obstruct the flow of
25. **delimit, delimitate**—place limits, bounds,
or boundaries to
26. **demarcate**—delimit
27. **detain**—hold back; keep from going or
leaving
28. **deter**—hold back from doing by fear of
results
29. **determine**—limit
30. **fetter**—restrain with, or as if with, fetters or foot shackles, literally or figuratively
31. **hinder**—hold back the free action of
32. **inhibit**—restrain (that which one in-
stinctively or spontaneously wishes to do
or feel) ; restrain the instinctive or spontaneous wishes, feelings, or actions of
33. **leash**—hold in check, literally or figuratively
34. **limit**—set a point or condition beyond
which one may not go
35. **localize**—limit to a certain place
36. **manacle**—place any physical restraint
upon
37. **obstruct**—hold back by making passage
difficult, or by getting in the way of
38. **occlude**—obstruct
39. **overawe**—restrain by frightening
40. **pinion**—restrain by holding the arms of;
shackle
41. **plug, plug up**—obstruct by, or as if by,
a plug or stopper
42. **qualify**—limit
43. **quench**—suppress
44. **repress**—hold back forcibly
45. **reserve**—hold back for future use
46. **shackle**—restrict the free action of, literally or figuratively; fetter
47. **smother**—keep back; hold back
48. **snag**—hold back through hidden or unexpected impediments, obstacles, etc.
49. **stay**—restrain
50. **stem**—dam
51. **stifle**—hold or keep back
52. **stop up**—obstruct
53. **strait-jacket**—hold back with, or as if
with, a tight jacket that restrains movements, literally or figuratively
54. **strangle**—hold or keep back
55. **stymie**—obstruct completely (figurative)
56. **suppress**—hold back; keep back
57. **taboo, tabu**—restrict as either sacred or
profane
58. **throttle**—hold or keep back
59. **thwart**—obstruct
60. **trammel**—restrain the free action, movement, or progress of
61. **withhold**—hold or keep back

**2. Restraint; Restriction; A Holding or
Keeping In or Back,**n. *From Sec. 1:* astriction, blockage, blockade, check, checkmate,
circumscription, confinement, constraint, constriction, containment, control, delimitation,
demarcation, detainment or detention, de-

terment, determination, hindrance, inhibition, limitation, localization, obstruction, occlusion, qualification, repression, reservation, suppression

3. Restraint, Restrainer, or Restriction, i.e., **That Which Holds or Keeps In or Back, or Serves to Hold or Keep In or Back,**n. *From Sec. 1:* bar, block or blockage, blockade, bounds, bridle, chain or chains, check, clog, confines, constriction, control or controls, cork, cramp, curb, dam, deterrent, determinant, fetter or fetters, hindrance, inhibition or inhibitor, leash, limit or limitation, manacle or manacles, obstruction, occlusion, plug, qualification, shackle or shackles, snag, stay, strait jacket, taboo, tabu, trammel or trammels; *Also:*
1. **bilboes**—long iron bar with sliding shackles used as a fetter
2. **bonds**—chains; shackles
3. **fetters**—foot shackles
4. **gyves**—leg shackles
5. **handcuffs**—restraining device used on the wrists
6. **manacles**—handcuffs
7. **obstruent**—obstruction (medical)
8. **pale**—confining barrier

4. Restraining, Restrictive; Holding or Keeping Back,adj. *From Sec. 1:* astricting, barring, etc.; astrictive, circumscriptive, constrictive, delimitative, detentive, determinative, inhibitive or inhibitory, obstructive, occlusive, repressive, suppressive; *Also:* 1. **obstruent**—obstructive (medical)

5. Restrained, Restricted; Held or Kept In or Back,adj. *From Sec. 1:* astricted, blocked, etc.; taboo, tabu; *Also:*
1. **parochial**—restricted (parochialism,n.)
2. **straitened**—restricted by a lack of that which is needed (often money)
3. **temporal**—limited in time

6. Restricted Place,n.
1. **ghetto**—place in a European city to which, at one time, Jews were restricted in their residence; hence, any area to which any group is restricted
2. **pale**—restricted area
3. **precinct**—limited area

559. INTERFERENCE

1. To Interfere,v.
1. **butt in**—interfere; meddle
2. **intermeddle**—meddle; meddle officiously
3. **meddle**—interfere where one is not wanted; interfere in the affairs of others
4. **tamper with**—interfere with in such a way as to cause unfortunate or unwholesome change or changes in; meddle with

2. Interfering: meddlesome, officious, pragmatic,adj.

3. Interferer: busybody, intermeddler, meddler, tamperer,n.

4. Person Who Interferes Officiously and Thus Ruins, Spoils, or Annuls a Plan, Plot, or Purpose: marplot,n.

5. Interference by One Nation in the Internal Affairs of Another: intervention,n. (interventional,adj.)

6. One Who Advocates Such Interference: interventionist,n. (interventionist,adj.)

560. ATTACK

1. To Attack,v.
1. **aggress**—attack; make an attack upon
2. **ambush**—make a surprise attack upon from a hidden place
3. **assail**—attack repeatedly by blows
4. **assault**—attack with violence

5. **bait**—attack and worry (of dogs); persecute maliciously; set dogs on to attack, for sport
6. **beset**—attack from all directions
7. **besiege**—siege
8. **bombard**—attack strongly or persistently; attack with artillery
9. **charge**—attack
10. **counterattack**—attack in answer to the attack of an opponent or enemy
11. **descend (on or upon)**—make a sudden attack (on or upon)
12. **devour**—prey upon
13. **feint**—make a pretended attack in one direction in order to lure protection away from that part or region where a genuine attack is planned
14. **foray**—make an attack or a sudden attack; make an attack or sudden attack upon the enemy for the purpose of plundering or ravaging
15. **hook**—attack with the horns (of an animal)
16. **maraud**—attack or raid for the purpose of plundering
17. **mug**—attack bodily for purposes of robbery (colloq.)
18. **persecute**—attack in an annoying way, or in order to annoy
19. **pounce upon**—make a sudden attack upon
20. **prey on, prey upon**—make repeated attacks on for the purpose of plundering
21. **raid**—attack; attack suddenly
22. **run amuck**—rush around, attacking in a frenzy; make attacks recklessly and indiscriminately
23. **sally**—make a sudden attack from a defensive position
24. **sick, sic**—attack (of a dog); set (a dog or dogs) to attack (colloq.)
25. **siege**—make a persistent attack upon in an attempt to gain possession of (a place)
26. **storm**—attack; attack and attempt to seize (a city or fortified place)
27. **strike**—make an attack
28. **surprise**—attack unexpectedly
29. **tilt at**—attack
30. **tilt at windmills**—attack an opponent that exists only in the imagination
31. **torpedo**—attack with explosives, bombs, etc.
32. **wade into**—attack, or press an attack on, with vigor and determination
33. **waylay**—attack (someone) as he moves on his way, usually for the purpose of robbing him

2. Attacking; Attack,n. *From Sec. 1:* aggression, assailment, assault, bombardment, charge, counterattack, descent, feint, foray, maraud, persecution, raid, sally, siege, strike; *Also:*
1. **blitzkrieg**—violent and irresistible attack
2. **counteroffensive**—attack made by a person or group that has previously been under attack
3. **dragonnade**—rapid, devastating incursion
4. **incursion**—sudden attack
5. **inroad**—attack; raid
6. **irruption**—violent and/or sudden attack
7. **offense, offensive**—attack
8. **onslaught**—violent or furious attack
9. **razzia**—foray; raid
10. **sortie**—sudden attack made by troops from a defensive position
11. **thrust**—attack

3. Attacker,n. *From Sec. 1:* aggressor, ambusher, assailant or assailer, assaulter, besieger, counterattacker, forayer, marauder, mugger, persecutor, preyer, raider, waylayer

4. Attacking,adj. *From Sec. 1:* besetting, besieging, etc.; aggressive, assailant, assaultive,

persecutive or persecutory; *From Sec. 2:*
blitzkrieg, counteroffensive, incursive, irruptive, offensive; *Also:*
  1. **besetting**—constantly attacking (of danger, sin, temptation, etc.)
  2. **obsidional**—besetting

5. To Advance Suddenly in an Attack upon:
buck, charge, rush at,v. (buck, charge,n. charger,n.)

6. To Advance with Forelegs (if an Animal) or Arms (if a Person) Raised in Attack:
ramp,v. (ramp,n.)

7. To Come Down in a Sudden Attack on:
swoop down on, swoop down upon,v.

8. To Enter (a Place) for the Purpose of Attacking: invade,v. (invasion,n. invader,n. invasive,adj.)

9. A Sudden Invasion: incursion, irruption, n. (incursive, irruptive,adj.)

10. To Threaten or Attempt a Bodily Attack upon (Legal): assault,v. (assault,n. assaulter,n.)

11. Pert. to, or Used in, Attack: offensive,adj.

12. Prepared to Attack: offensive,adj.

13. Means of Attack: ammunition (figurative); weapon (literal or figurative),n.

14. Object of Attack: target,n.

15. One against Whom a Legal Attack Is Made in Court: defendant,n.

16. Position for Attack,n.
  1. **beachhead**—position established by an invading army in hostile territory or on a shore; vantage point for attack of any kind
  2. **bridgehead**—position in hostile territory from which attacks may be made
  3. **offensive**—position for attack

17. Time Set for the Beginning of an Attack: zero hour,n.

18. To Give Means of Attack to: arm,v.

19. Pert. to a Siege: obsidional,adj.

20. Open to Attack: pregnable, vulnerable, adj. (pregnability, vulnerability,n.)

21. Spot or Figurative Place Where One Is Most Open to Attack: Achilles' heel,n.

22. To Attack (of a Disease): affect, afflict,v. (affection, affliction,n. afflictive,adj.)

23. To Attack Suddenly and Violently (of a Disease): fulminate, fulmine,v. (fulmination,n. fulminant, fulminatory,adj.)

24. An Attack, i.e., a Fit,n.
  1. **access**—attack (of a disease or strong emotion)
  2. **affection**—attack of a disease
  3. **bout**—fit; spell
  4. **conniption, conniption fit**—fit of anger or temper (colloq.)
  5. **convulsion**—spasm (convulsionary, convulsive,adj.)
  6. **epitasis**—paroxysm (medical)
  7. **grip**—spasm of pain
  8. **gripe, gripes**—spasm of intestinal pain
  9. **huff**—fit of anger or resentment
  10. **ictus**—sudden attack or fit of some medical condition
  11. **invasion**—attack of a disease or anything harmful
  12. **irruption**—sudden invasion
  13. **onset**—attack, or the beginning of an attack (of a disease, etc.)
  14. **pang**—sharp attack of feeling or pain
  15. **paroxysm**—severe and sudden attack— of an ailment, feeling, emotion, etc. (paroxysmal,adj.)
  16. **pet**—attack or fit of annoyance, anger, or ill-humor
  17. **pique**—fit of anger or resentment

  18. **qualm**—sudden and soon-passing attack of nausea, faintness, illness, or pain
  19. **seizure**—attack; fit
  20. **siege**—long-continued attack (of illness, etc.)
  21. **spasm**—violent and sudden attack or fit that lasts only a short time (spasmodic, adj.)
  22. **spell**—attack (of illness, grief, etc.)
  23. **storm**—attack or fit of anger
  24. **stroke**—sudden attack of disease or paralysis
  25. **throe**—sharp attack of pain

25. Attack of Epilepsy or Apoplexy: fit,n.

561. ATTACK IN WORDS

1. To Attack with Words,v.
  1. **abuse**—attack in harsh and censorious language
  2. **assail**—attack repeatedly in words
  3. **assault**—attack violently in words
  4. **barrage**—attack with a rapid fire of questions, words, abuse, etc.
  5. **baste**—attack in speech
  6. **belabor**—attack with words
  7. **besiege**—make persistent attacks on with questions, demands, attentions, etc.
  8. **blackguard**—attack with abusive language
  9. **blaspheme**—abuse
  10. **blister**—attack with scorching words
  11. **bombard**—attack strongly or persistently with words, questions, insults, etc.
  12. **denounce**—attack with the strongest of censure
  13. **excoriate**—make a violent verbal attack upon
  14. **inveigh against**—make a violent verbal attack upon
  15. **lampoon**—make a malicious verbal attack upon by means of ridicule, and usually in writing
  16. **lash, lash out at**—attack violently in words
  17. **rail at, rail against**—abuse
  18. **rally**—attack with light ridicule, mocking remarks, etc.
  19. **revile**—make a strong and abusive verbal attack on
  20. **satirize**—use language that attacks by ridicule; attack through ridicule; use sarcasm or irony to attack
  21. **smear**—make a malicious verbal attack upon, such attack being calculated to ruin a person's reputation
  22. **snipe at**—underhandedly attack in words
  23. **squib**—make a witty or satirical attack upon in a brief speech or written passage
  24. **vituperate**—attack abusively in language
  25. **whip**—attack in sharp words

2. An Attacking, or Attack, in Words,n.
From Sec. 1: abuse, assailment, assault, barrage, blasphemy, bombardment, denouncement or denunciation, excoriation, invective, lampoon, revilement, satirization or satire, smear, snipe, squib, vituperation; *Also:*
  1. **broadside**—volley or barrage of abuse
  2. **diatribe**—abusive speech leveled against someone or something
  3. **harangue**—noisy, attacking public speech
  4. **iconoclasm**—cynical attack or attacks on cherished or traditional beliefs as frauds or shams; quality or condition of making such attacks
  5. **mudslinging**—verbal attack marked by abusive language, vile accusations, etc.
  6. **philippic**—sharp verbal attack, so called from the denunciatory attacks on Philip of Macedon by Demosthenes
  7. **screed**—long speech of attack or abuse
  8. **tirade**—extended speech of denunciation characterized by its abusive or intemperate language

3. Attacker in Words,n. *From Sec. 1:* abuser, assailant or assailer, assaulter, besieger, blasphemer, denouncer, excoriator, inveigher, lampooner or lampoonist, reviler, satirizer or satirist, sniper, vituperator; *From Sec. 2:* haranguer, iconoclast, mudslinger

4. Attacking in Words,adj. *From Sec. 1:* abusing, assailing, etc.; abusive, assailant, assaultive, blasphemous, denunciatory or denunciative, invective, satiric or satirical, vituperative; *From Sec. 2:* iconoclastic; *Also:*
  1. **catty**—abusive (of women who verbally attack other women)
  2. **vitriolic**—sharply abusive

5. To Expose to Abuse: pillory,v.

6. Object of Abuse: butt, target,n.

7. State of Being Abused: obloquy,n.

8. Abusive Language: abuse, billingsgate, blasphemy, invective, obloquy, scurrility, vituperation,n.

9. Abusive in Language: blasphemous, scurrile, scurrilous, vituperative,adj.

10. Abusive Word: epithet; invective (usually pl.),n.

11. Language That Attacks through Ridicule: satire,n. (satiric, satirical,adj.)

562. FIGHT

1. A Fight; A Battle,n.
  1. **affaire d'honneur (French)**—a duel
  2. **affray**—a public fight
  3. **angelomachy**—a battle between angels
  4. **Armageddon**—a great and final conflict, so called from the Biblical place where such a conflict occurred between the forces of good and evil
  5. **battle royal**—a fight among a number of people; melee
  6. **bout**—a fight; conflict
  7. **brawl**—a noisy fight
  8. **broil**—brawl
  9. **brush**—a short, brisk fight or battle; skirmish
  10. **clash**—conflict
  11. **combat**—a fight; a battle
  12. **conflict**—a fight or battle of opposing sides, elements, etc.
  13. **contest, contention**—a fight in rivalry or competition
  14. **dispute**—a verbal fight
  15. **dogfight**—a fight between dogs; melee
  16. **Donnybrook, Donnybrook Fair**—a riotous or uproarious fight among great numbers
  17. **duel**—battle between two opponents; such a battle with swords or other deadly weapons, under certain conventional rules
  18. **encounter**—a fight; a battle
  19. **engagement**—a fight; a battle; formerly, a duel
  20. **exchange of blows**—a fight
  21. **fracas**—a noisy fight
  22. **fray**—a fight
  23. **free fight, free-for-all**—a riotous, noisy fight
  24. **gladiatorism**—a gladiatorial contest, i.e., a contest in which captives, slaves, criminals, etc., fought in public combat for the amusement of the populace in ancient Rome
  25. **joust**—a fight, figuratively or verbally, i.e., in the manner of knights on horseback; a fight on horseback between knights in the Middle Ages
  26. **match**—a fight between boxers in the ring
  27. **melee**—a fight attended by confusion; a hand-to-hand fight or battle
  28. **monomachy**—a duel

29. naumachia, naumachy—a mock sea fight in ancient Rome

30. naval engagement—a battle between ships of enemy nations

31. prize fight—a professional boxing match

32. scramble—a fight to have; a fight with others for something, often something on the ground

33. scrap—a fight (slang)

34. scrimmage—a rough or confused fight

35. scuffle—a fight at close quarters attended by some confusion

36. set-to—a fight

37. skirmish—a fight between small or isolated groups of soldiers; a small fight

38. struggle—a fight

39. theomachy—a battle between gods

40. tilt—a fight with lances

41. tournament, tourney—a battle; a battle between knights in the Middle Ages

42. tussle—a scuffle

43. velitation—a skirmish

2. To Fight; To Battle,v. *From Sec. 1:* brawl, clash, combat, conflict, contest, contend, dispute, duel, exchange blows, joust, scramble, scrap, scrimmage, scuffle, skirmish, struggle, tilt, tourney, tussle; *Also:*
  1. **box**—fight, or fight scientifically, with the fists in, or as in, the prize ring
  2. **buffet**—fight
  3. **fence**—fight in the manner of swordsmen; fight with swords
  4. **militate against**—fight against, figuratively
  5. **ruffle**—fight
  6. **shadowbox**—box with an imaginary opponent, as in training; fight with an imaginary opponent
  7. **spar**—box scientifically; make motions of attack and defense in boxing
  8. **tilt at**—fight
  9. **tilt at windmills**—fight an imaginary foe or foes
  10. **war, warfare**—engage in armed fighting (of groups, nations, etc.)

3. Fighting; Battling,n. *From Sec. 1:* angelomachy, encounter, engagement, theomachy, tournament, tourney; *From Sec. 2:* brawling, clashing, etc.; combat, conflict, contestation or contention, dispute, struggle; militation, war, warfare; *Also:*
  1. **engagement**—first crossing of the swords in a duel
  2. **fisticuffs**—fighting with the fists (fistic, adj.)
  3. **lists**—tournament
  4. **pugilism**—fist-fighting, esp. in the boxing ring (pugilistic,adj.)
  5. **sciamachy**—fighting with a nonexistent foe; fighting with, or as if with, a shadow; futile fighting with a nonexistent foe
  6. **shadow-fighting**—sciamachy
  7. **strife**—fighting

4. Fighter; Battler,n. *From Sec. 1:* brawler, combatant or combater, contender; disputant, disputer or disputator; dueler or duelist, gladiator, jouster, monomachist, prize fighter, scrapper, scrimmager, scuffler, skirmisher, struggler, tilter, tussler; *From Sec. 2:* boxer, fencer, shadowboxer, warrior or warfarer; *From Sec. 3:* pugilist; *Also:*
  1. **bruiser**—professional boxer
  2. **swashbuckler**—boastful swordsman
  3. **swordsman**—one skilled in fighting with the sword
  4. **wildcat**—person who fights fiercely

5. Fighting; Battling; Engaged in Fighting or Battle,adj. *From Sec. 1:* brawling, clashing, etc.; combatant; *Also:*
  1. **embattled**—engaged in battle
  2. **embroiled**—involved in battle
  3. **militant**—fighting; engaged in fighting or battle

6. Code of Rules Regarding Duels: duello,n.

7. To Take a Fighting Attitude: bristle,v.

8. Scene of Fighting,n.
1. aceldama—scene of bloodshed, so-called from the place where Judas committed suicide
2. arena—scene of a combat; area where gladiatorial contests were held in ancient Rome
3. Armageddon—scene of any great or decisive fighting; according to the Bible, scene of the great and final conflict between the forces of good and evil
4. battlefield, battleground—scene of fighting
5. lists—arena or place of fighting; area where tournaments were held in the Middle Ages

9. Instruments of Fighting: armor, arms, weapons,n.

10. Bearing Weapons: armiferous,adj.

11. Inclined to Fight,adj.
1. aggressive—tending to provoke a fight (aggressiveness,n.)
2. bellicose—tending to look for or stir up a fight (bellicoseness, bellicosity,n.)
3. belligerent—aggressive in temper (belligerence, belligerency,n.)
4. combatant—ready to fight
5. combative—eager to fight; fond of fighting; disposed to fight or pick a fight (combativeness,n.)
6. contentious—disputatious (contentiousness,n.)
7. disputatious, disputative—inclined to engage in verbal fights (disputatiousness, n.)
8. martial—fond of fighting
9. militant—aggressive; bellicose (militancy,n.)
10. pugnacious—disposed or eager to fight, pick a fight or engage in fighting (pugnaciousness, pugnacity,n.)
11. scrappy—inclined to fight; aggressive (colloq.)
12. warlike—bellicose (warlikeness,n.)

12. Small but Pugnacious Person: bantam,n.

13. One Who Does Not Fight, or Is Not Engaged in Fighting, Esp. in Wartime; One Connected with the Armed Forces in Other than a Fighting Capacity; Civilian in Wartime: noncombatant,n.

14. One Who Refuses to Fight in Wartime Owing to Ethical, Moral, or Religious Scruples: conscientious objector,n.

15. Bullfighter,n.
1. matador—person who kills the bull in a bullfight
2. picador—horseman who excites or annoys the bull, but does not kill him
3. tauromachian—bullfighter
4. toreador—bullfighter; mounted bullfighter
5. torero (Spanish)—unmounted bullfighter

16. Bullfighting: tauromachy,n.

17. A Bullfight,n.
1. taurokathapsia—bullfight as depicted in pre-Hellenic art
2. tauromachy—bullfight, esp. as portrayed in art

18. Pert. to, or Favoring, Bullfights: tauromachian,n.

563. WAR

1. War; Warfare,n.
1. blitzkrieg—warfare of a very violent and forceful kind
2. civil war—war between sections of, or groups within, a nation

3. gigantomachy, gigantomachia—war between the giants; war between the Olympians and the giants in Greek mythology
4. rupture—war between nations
5. Titanomachy—war between the Titans and the Olympian gods in Thessaly
6. warfaring—warfare

2. To Engage in War: war, warfare,v.

3. One Engaged in War: soldier, warfarer, warrior,n.

4. Nation Engaged in, or Waging, War: belligerent,n. (belligerent,adj. belligerency,n.)

5. Fond of War: martial, militant, warlike, adj. (militancy, warlikeness,n.)

6. Advocacy of an Aggressive and Bellicose Foreign Policy: jingoism,n. (jingo, jingoist, n. jingo, jingoistic,adj.)

7. Policy of Aggressive Preparation for War: militarism,n. (militarist,n. militaristic, adj.)

8. Active Militarism with a View to Conquest and Control of Other Countries: Prussianism,n.

9. Act or Policy of Stirring Up, or Attempts to Stir Up, War: warmongering,n. (warmonger,n. warmongering,adj.)

10. State of Readiness for War: war footing, n.

11. Able to Fight or Conduct War on Both Land and Sea: amphibian, amphibious,adj.

12. Able to Fight or Conduct War on Land and Sea and in the Air: triphibian, triphibious,adj.

13. Descr. of Raw Materials Essential to the Prosecution of a War but Obtainable, at Least in Part, Only from Other Countries: strategic,adj.

14. Cause of, or Justification for, War: casus belli,n. (Latin)

15. Threatening War: warlike,adj. (warlikeness,n.)

16. Threat of War: war cloud,n.

17. Relating to Warfare: martial, military, warlike,adj.

18. Pert. to the Pomp, Ceremony, or Excitement of War: martial,adj.

19. Before the War: ante-bellum,adj.

20. After the War: post-bellum,adj.

21. God of War: Ares (Greek); Mars (Roman); Odin or Othin (Norse); Tyr (Norse); Woden or Wodan (Norse),n.

22. Goddess of War: Bellona (Roman), Juno Curitis or Juno Quiritis (Roman),n.

23. Maiden Who Flies over a Battlefield, Choosing the Warriors Who Are to Die, and Then Escorting Their Souls to the Warrior's Heaven, According to Norse Mythology: Valkyrie,n.

24. Deeds or Activities of War: arms,n.

564. SOLDIER

1. Soldier; Warrior,n.
1. adventurer—soldier who joins an army that will pay him the greatest salary
2. Amazon—female warrior
3. artillerist—artilleryman; cannoneer
4. artilleryman—soldier attached to a section of the army employing mounted guns
5. Aussie—Australian soldier
6. Beefeater—Yeoman of the Guard
7. Boche—German soldier
8. brave—American Indian warrior
9. campaigner, old campaigner—veteran

10. **cannoneer**—soldier who serves the cannon
11. **carabineer, carbineer**—cavalry soldier armed with a light rifle
12. **cavalryman, cavalier**—horse-mounted soldier
13. **chasseur**—soldier of a body of French light troops, either infantry or cavalry
14. **condottiere (Italian)**—soldier of fortune
15. **Cossack**—Russian cavalryman; member of an armed force used by reactionaries against liberals, etc. (derogatory)
16. **cuirassier**—mounted soldier in the French and other continental armies
17. **doughboy**—U.S. infantryman (colloq.)
18. **dragoon**—cavalry soldier, esp. British
19. **enlisted man**—any soldier in the U.S. Army lower in rank than a commissioned officer or warrant officer
20. **foot soldier**—soldier who serves on foot
21. **franc-tireur**—French partisan soldier; member of a detachment engaged in raids, etc.
22. **free lance**—condottiere
23. **G.I.**—U.S. soldier
24. **grenadier**—soldier who carries and throws grenades; member of a special regiment or corps
25. **guerrilla**—member of an irregular military group; one who engages in predatory forays staged by such a group
26. **gunner**—cannoneer
27. **Hessian**—mercenary
28. **Hun**—German soldier (term used in World War I)
29. **hussar**—cavalryman, originally of Hungary and Croatia, now of many European armies
30. **infantryman**—foot soldier
31. **janizary, janissary**—Turkish soldier
32. **Jerry**—German soldier
33. **legionary**—member of a military force
34. **mameluke**—soldier recruited from slaves converted to Islamism
35. **marine**—soldier trained somewhat like those on land but associated with the naval service and used as a member of a landing force
36. **mercenary**—soldier who serves in an army other than that of his country, with the implication that this is done purely for the pay and not from any principles or ideals
37. **militaster**—military man of little ability (contemptuous)
38. **musketeer**—foot soldier with a light firearm
39. **nizam**—Turkish soldier
40. **officer**—soldier with a commission
41. **poilu**—French soldier
42. **private**—U.S. soldier with the lowest military rank
43. **recruit**—newly inducted soldier
44. **Redcoat**—British soldier, so called since the uniform was originally red in color
45. **rifleman**—soldier armed with a rifle
46. **rookie**—recruit (slang)
47. **sapper**—member of a certain division of the engineer corps of the army engaged in fortification work
48. **sepoy**—Indian native serving as a soldier in the British Army
49. **serviceman**—member of the armed forces
50. **spahi, spahee**—member, originally, of a corps of irregular Turkish cavalry; now, member of Algerian native cavalry in the French Army
51. **swashbuckler**—boasting soldier
52. **Tommy, Tommy Atkins**—British soldier
53. **trooper**—cavalryman
54. **veteran**—honorably discharged soldier, sailor, etc., of the U.S. forces; old and experienced soldier
55. **warfarer**—warrior
56. **yeoman of the guard**—member of the military force acting as a bodyguard to a British sovereign
57. **Zouave**—French soldier stationed in North Africa; soldier in an oriental type of uniform

2. Descr. of, Pert. to, or Characteristic of, a Soldier or Soldiers: military, soldierly, warrior,adj.

3. Soldiers, Collectively: army, array, battalions, forces, the military, ranks, soldiery, troops,n.

4. Soldiers of an Army as Distinguished from the Officers: rank and file, ranks,n.

5. Unit or Group of Soldiers or of Men Engaged in Warfare,n.
   1. **armament**—military or naval forces engaged in an operation
   2. **army**—military organization of a nation for land warfare; independent military unit
   3. **array**—military force
   4. **artillery**—section of an army that handles the mounted guns
   5. **battalion**—unit of an army
   6. **battery**—smallest unit of field artillery
   7. **brigade**—military division
   8. **cavalry**—military force that is horse-mounted
   9. **cohort**—band of warriors
   10. **company**—body of soldiers, esp. infantry
   11. **corps**—large unit of an army
   12. **detachment**—portion of the troops sent on a special mission
   13. **division**—unit of an army or navy (divisional,adj.)
   14. **formation**—body of troops in some military arrangement
   15. **fusiliers, fusileers**—certain British regiments
   16. **garrison**—body of soldiers stationed in a fort
   17. **infantry**—foot soldiers collectively
   18. **legion**—military force; army
   19. **maniple**—small body of soldiers; company
   20. **marine corps**—men and officers associated with a naval service and used as a landing force
   21. **mass**—formation in which the various subdivisions of troops are separated by less than the usual distance
   22. **militia**—body of citizens enrolled as a military force for periodic training
   23. **National Guard**—militia, in the U.S.
   24. **navy**—division of fighting forces engaged in sea warfare
   25. **outfit**—branch or section of an army (colloq.)
   26. **party**—small body of troops sent on a special mission
   27. **phalanx**—body of armed infantry of ancient Greece, massed close and deep (phalangeal,adj.)
   28. **platoon**—military division
   29. **regiment**—military unit of ground forces (regimental,adj.)
   30. **squad**—small group of soldiers
   31. **squadron**—group of soldiers
   32. **troop**—unit of cavalry soldiers
   33. **unit**—military force
   34. **vanguard**—part of an army that moves ahead of the rest
   35. **Wehrmacht**—German Army
   36. **wing**—right or left division of an army or navy

6. Pert. to, or Descr. of, the Army: martial, military,adj.

7. Position or Rank of an Officer in the Army or Navy: commission,n.

8. U. S. Army Ranks: corporal, sergeant, warrant officer, second or first lieutenant, captain, major, lieutenant colonel, colonel, brigadier general, major general, lieutenant general, general, general of the army,n. (corporalship, sergeantcy, lieutenancy, captaincy, majority, colonelcy, generalship,n.)

9. **Military Officer:** brass hat,n. (colloq.)

10. **Military Officers, Collectively:** the brass, n. (colloq.)

11. **Military Officer of High Rank in Various Countries Other than the U.S.:** marshal, n. (marshalcy, marshalship,n.)

12. **Commanding Officer:** commandant,n.

13. **Highest Officer of the Armed Forces:** commander in chief,n.

14. **Military Commission of a Rank Higher than That for Which an Officer Is Paid:** brevet,n. (brevet,v.)

15. **Skeleton Unit of Military Officers and Non-Commissioned Officers:** cadre,n.

16. **To Enroll (a Man or Men) in Military Service:** conscript, draft, induct,v. (conscription, draft, induction,n.)

17. **One Enrolled in Military Service:** conscript, draftee, inductee,n.

18. **Military Service; Military Science:** arms, war, warfare,n.

19. **To Force into Naval Service:** impress,v. (impressment,n.)

20. **Pert. to, or Descr. of, the Navy:** naval, adj.

21. **U. S. Navy Ranks:** petty officer, ensign, lieutenant j.g., lieutenant, lieutenant commander, commander, captain, commodore, rear admiral, vice-admiral, admiral, admiral of the fleet,n. (ensignship or ensigncy, lieutenancy, commandership, captaincy, admiralty,n.)

565. FIREARM

1. **Firearm,n.**
1. **automatic**—automatic firearm; firearm that ejects and loads the cartridge automatically
2. **Big Bertha**—any of the large German mounted guns of long range used in World War I
3. **blunderbuss**—obsolete firearm of short range and inexact aim
4. **bombard**—earliest kind of cannon that threw stones, etc.
5. **breechloader**—gun which is loaded at the breech, or back part
6. **cannon**—mounted gun
7. **carbine**—light rifle
8. **carronade**—kind of short, light cannon no longer in use
9. **culverin**—originally, a primitive kind of musket; later (sixteenth to nineteenth centuries) a long cannon
10. **derringer**—short-barreled pistol
11. **fowling piece**—light gun for shooting birds and small animals
12. **Garand**—semi-automatic rifle
13. **gun**—any portable firearm other than a pistol or revolver; cannon; rifle; rifled cannon
14. **harquebus**—ancient portable gun
15. **howitzer**—kind of cannon delivering curved fire
16. **machine gun**—automatic gun for rapid firing
17. **mortar**—kind of cannon
18. **musket**—hand firearm; firearm carried by a foot soldier
19. **muzzle-loader**—obsolete type of gun loaded at the muzzle
20. **pistol**—short hand firearm
21. **revolver**—pistol with a revolving chamber
22. **rifle**—firearm shot from the shoulder
23. **shotgun**—gun for firing at short range

24. **sidearm**—firearm carried upon the person
25. **torpedo**—tube-launched, self-propelled machine or engine for blowing up enemy ships
26. **weapon**—instrument of attack or defense, including firearms

2. **Firearms, Collectively,n.**
1. **armament**—various weapons of a ship, fortification, etc.
2. **arms**—weapons, including firearms
3. **artillery**—mounted cannons
4. **battery**—two or more pieces of artillery under one command; guns of a warship
5. **broadside**—all the guns that can be fired from one side of a ship
6. **cannon, cannonry**—mounted guns
7. **gunnery**—guns collectively
8. **ordnance**—cannon and other mounted arms and guns collectively
9. **small arms**—portable firearms

3. **To Shoot,v.**
1. **barrage**—fire artillery at; cut off (a road, place, etc.) by laying down a barrier of artillery fire
2. **bomb**—drop bombs on; bombard
3. **bombard**—throw shells, bombs, etc., at or upon
4. **cannonade**—shoot cannon or heavy artillery at
5. **catapult**—shoot as if from the massive crossbow used by the ancient Greeks and Romans
6. **discharge**—shoot
7. **fire**—shoot
8. **gun**—shoot with a gun
9. **machine gun**—shoot with a machine gun
10. **pellet**—shoot bullets at
11. **pistol**—shoot with a pistol
12. **rake**—shoot at rapidly along the whole length of
13. **shell**—bombard
14. **shrapnel**—bombard with a projectile that discharges bullets over a wide area
15. **snipe (at)**—shoot (at) from a hidden place
16. **strafe**—bombard heavily or fiercely; machine-gun from low-flying planes
17. **twang**—shoot (an arrow) from a bow

4. **Shooting,n.** *From Sec. 3:* bombing, bombarding, etc.; barrage, bombardment, discharge, gunfire or gunnery, machine gunnery; *Also:*
1. **broadside**—simultaneous discharge of a number of guns, esp. all those on one side of a vessel
2. **fusillade**—simultaneous discharge of many guns, cannon, etc.
3. **salvo**—simultaneous discharge of several guns
4. **sharpshooting**—skilled shooting
5. **skeet**—shooting at moving clay targets
6. **volley**—simultaneous, or almost simultaneous, discharge of a number of guns

5. **A Shot or Shots,n.** *From Sec. 3:* barrage, bombardment, cannonade, fire, snipe; *From Sec. 4:* broadside, fusillade, salvo, volley; *Also:* 1. musketry—shots from muskets

6. **Shooter,n.** *From Sec. 3:* bomber, bombardier, firer, gunner, machine gunner, sniper, strafer; *From Sec. 4:* sharpshooter

7. **Science of the Use of Guns and the Flight of Bullets or Other Projectiles:** artillery, gunnery,n.

8. **Art or Practice of Shooting Guns:** gunnery, gunning, musketry,n.

9. **To Pull Back the Hammer of (a Gun) Preparatory to Firing It:** cock,v.

10. **Bullet; Projectile,n.**
1. **ball**—solid, spherical or elongated projectile for a cannon, rifle, etc.

2. **bomb**—projectile containing a high explosive and thrown by a mortar or dropped from an airplane

3. **cannon ball**—projectile shot, or to be shot, from a cannon

4. **dumdum**—expanding bullet capable of stopping a man in motion

5. **grenade**—missile containing an explosive, and designed to be thrown

6. **missile**—bullet; anything thrown, shot, etc.

7. **pellet**—small bullet; that which is used as a bullet

8. **petard**—kind of bomb, once used to break down gates, barricades, etc.

9. **shell**—hollow projectile to be fired from a cannon and containing a charge that explodes during flight or on hitting or penetrating

10. **shot**—that which is shot; projectile discharged or designed to be discharged from a firearm, cannon, etc.; bullet or ball of lead, a number of which constitute the charge in a hunter's gun

11. **shrapnel**—projectile that carries a number of bullets to a distance removed from the weapon, discharging them with great force over a wide area

12. **torpedo**—cigar-shaped projectile, self-propelled, and launched from a submarine, etc.

13. **trajectile**—that which is impelled through space, including bullets, shot, shells, etc.

11. Projectiles Collectively: ammunition, shot,n.

12. Pert. to Hurling Missiles: ballistic,adj.

13. Amount of Explosives Set Off at One Time: charge,n.

14. Charge Used in a Cannon to Send a Projectile to Its Target: propellant,n.

15. Container of Bullets and/or Explosives, n.

1. **cartridge**—that which contains the explosive charge and projectile to be fired

2. **petard**—case containing explosives, once used to break down gates, barricades, etc.

3. **shell**—case that holds the charge of explosive and the bullet

4. **torpedo**—case containing dynamite, gunpowder, etc.

16. Science of the Motion, etc., of Bullets, Shells, Bombs, etc.: ballistics,n. (ballistician, n. ballistic,adj.)

17. Other Explosive Device,n.

1. **mine**—explosive device, planted on land or in water, designed to go off on contact (mine,v.)

2. **torpedo**—explosive device for destroying enemy vessels

18. Military Engine That Propelled a Missile without the Use of Gunpowder,n.

1. **ballista, ballist**—ancient Roman engine, usually in the form of a crossbow, for hurling missiles at an angle

2. **catapult**—engine that was used by ancient Greeks and Romans to hurl arrows, stones, etc., and that resembled a tremendous crossbow (catapultic,adj. catapult,v.)

3. **martinet**—old-time war engine that threw large stones

4. **trebuchet, trebucket**—medieval military engine for hurling stones, etc.

19. Missile Hurled by a Ballista: ballista,n.

20. Forked Stick with an Elastic Band for Hurling Small Stones, etc.: catapult, sling, slingshot,n. (slinger, slingsman,n. catapultic, adj. catapult, sling,v.)

21. Missile Hurled from a Slingshot: slingstone,n.

566. BOW AND ARROW

1. Bow,n.

1. **arbalest, arbalester, arbalestre**—crossbow used to throw arrows, darts, and other missiles

2. **backed bow**—bow formed of two or more pieces of wood, the belly of one piece, the back of another

3. **carriage bow**—bow that may be taken apart for traveling convenience or portability

4. **crossbow**—bow set crosswise on a stock for hurling stones, etc. and used in medieval times

5. **longbow**—wooden bow, usually 5½ to 6 feet long; great bow used in medieval England that often was as long as 6 feet 7 inches, and weighed 100 pounds

6. **self-bow**—bow made from a single piece of wood

7. **union bow**—backed bow

2. Side of the Bow Facing the String: belly, n.

3. Side of the Bow Away from the String: back,n.

4. Distance a Bow Throws the Arrow: cast, n.

5. Missile Hurled from a Crossbow: arbalester, arbalestre,n.

6. Arrow,n.

1. **bolt**—arrow; short, blunt-headed, stout arrow; arrow intended to be shot from a crossbow or catapult

2. **dart**—any sharp-pointed weapon used as a missile, including an arrow

3. **quarrel**—square-headed arrow used in a crossbow

4. **shaft**—arrow

5. **vire**—arrow so feathered that it has a rotary motion, and used with a crossbow

7. Arrows in Their Case: quiver,n.

8. Stem of an Arrow: shaft, stele,n.

9. Pointed Part of an Arrow: head,n.

10. Pert. to an Arrow or Arrowhead: sagittal,adj.

11. Resembling an Arrow in Shape, Effect, etc.: arrowy, sagittal,adj.

12. Resembling an Arrowhead: sagittal,adj.

13. Arrow Maker: fletcher,n.

14. To Shoot an Arrow or Arrows: arrow,v.

15. One Who Uses a Bow and Arrow: archer, bowman,n.

16. Use of a Bow and Arrow: archery,n.

17. One Who Uses a Crossbow: arbalester, crossbowman,n.

18. Art of the Bow and Arrow: archery,n. (archer,n.)

19. Study of, Enthusiasm for, and the Practice of Using a Bow and Arrow: toxophily,n. (toxopholite,n. toxopholitic,adj.)

20. Those, Collectively, Who Use, or Are Skilled in Using, the Bow and Arrow: archery,n.

21. Bows and Arrows, Collectively: archery, n.

567. AIM

1. To Aim: beam, direct, level, point, point at, slant, train,v.

2. Aiming: direction,n.

3. To Aim Specifically: direct, slant,v. (direction,n.)

4. To Aim at Exactly: pin-point,v. (pin-point,adj.)

5. To Aim (One's Speech or Writing) to: address,v.

6. That Which Is Aimed at: target,n.

7. Aimed Straight at the Target: point-blank,adj.

8. Descr. of Something Said or Written That Is Specifically Aimed in a Direction: direct, pointed,adj. (directness, pointedness, n.)

568. PROTECTION

1. To Protect; To Make or Keep Safe,v.
1. assure—protect or make safe against change or risk
2. bulwark—protect
3. champion—protect
4. conserve—keep safe; safeguard
5. cradle—protect while very young
6. cushion—protect from sudden shocks, jars, etc.
7. defend—protect by warding off danger or attack
8. guard—protect against danger
9. insulate—protect from contact with what might harm or injure—followed by *from* or *against*
10. panoply—afford complete protection or protective covering, often in a figurative sense; afford a glorious covering and protection, again often in a figurative sense
11. preserve—keep safe; keep from harm or injury
12. safeguard—protect against danger or risk
13. save—make safe; safeguard
14. screen—put up protection or a protective element between (somebody or something and danger)—followed by *from*
15. seclude—protect by shutting off
16. secure—protect against attack, loss, etc.; make safe
17. sentinel—protect against danger or sudden attack
18. shade—protect from light or from the sun
19. sheathe—protect, as if by a hard covering
20. shelter—protect; cover to protect, literally or figuratively
21. shepherd—protect; keep safe; guard
22. shield—protect; protect from danger or damage
23. shutter—protect by keeping away from sight or contact
24. treasure—keep safe
25. veil—protect by covering
26. watch, watch over—guard; keep guard over

2. Protection, i.e., Act of Protecting or Making or Keeping Safe,n. *From Sec. 1:* assurance, championship, conservation, defense, insulation, preservation, seclusion; *Also:*
1. conservation—safeguarding of natural resources against waste, exploitation, etc.
2. custody—a guarding
3. guardianship—protection of a dependent or someone under one's care
4. safekeeping—a keeping safe
5. salvation—protection from evil, destruction, failure, danger or difficulty
6. tutelage—guardianship

3. Protection; State of Being Protected or Safe,n. *From Sec. 1:* assurance, defense, guard, insulation, panoply, safety (from *save*), seclusion, security, shelter; *From Sec. 2:* custody, guardianship, safekeeping, tutelage; *Also:*
1. asylum—protection; safety
2. wardship—protection and care under a guardian

4. Protection or Protector; Means of Protection; Protective Device,n. *From Sec. 1:*

assurance, bulwark, cushion, defense, guard, safeguard, screen, shade, sheath, shelter, shield, shutter, veil; *From Sec. 2:* salvation; *Also:*
1. ammunition—means of defense, figuratively speaking
2. anchorage—means of protection or safety
3. armor—figurative protection
4. bastion—defense
5. buckler—figurative protection or defense
6. buffer—fender
7. cordon—line or circle of things acting as a protection or guard
8. covert, coverture—defense; shelter
9. fender—any device that protects
10. palladium—source of safety; safeguard
11. tower—protection; defense
12. umbrage—shade
13. weapon—instrument or means of defense

5. Protector; Protectors; Protecting Person or Persons,n. *From Sec. 1:* champion, conserver or conservator, defender; guard (sing. or pl.) or guardian; safeguarder, savior, sentinel, shepherd, shield; watch (pl.); *Also:*
1. Argus—watchful guardian
2. bodyguard—one who accompanies, or those who accompany, someone to protect him from assault, attack, etc.
3. Cerberus—surly and alert guard (after the three-headed dog guarding the entrance to Hades)
4. convoy—those who go along as a protection, often in a military, naval, police, or official sense
5. convoyer—one who goes along as a protection, often in a military, naval, police, or official sense
6. cordon—line or circle of people acting as a protection or guard
7. escort—one who accompanies, or those who accompany, to protect
8. garrison—body of troops stationed to protect a place
9. guardian angel—one who protects against harm, danger, etc.
10. lifeguard—one who protects swimmers against the perils of the sea, etc.
11. Messiah—savior
12. paladin—protector; knightly, courtly or chivalrous protector
13. picket—detached body of soldiers serving to guard the army from enemy surprise
14. recourse—person turned to for protection
15. sentry—sentinel
16. vedette—mounted sentinel who watches an enemy and gives notice of danger
17. warden—guard; watchman
18. warder—watchman
19. watchman—one who keeps watch over a building at night, to protect it against thieves, fire, etc.

6. Protective; Pert. to, or Descr. of, Protection, a Protector, etc.,adj. *From Sec. 1:* conservative or conservational, defensive, guardian, preservative, seclusive; *From Sec. 2:* conservational, custodial, tutelary or tutelar; *From Sec. 5:* Cerberean, Messianic; *Also:* 1. benevolent—generously protective (benevolence,n.)

7. Protected,adj. *From Sec. 1:* assured, bulwarked, etc.; safe (from *save*), secure; *From Sec. 4:* armored, bastioned; *From Sec. 5:* convoyed, escorted, garrisoned; *Also:*
1. impregnable—protected or safe against attack
2. inviolable—safe against harm or injury
3. invulnerable—protected or safe against attack, harm, danger, or injury
4. presidial, presidiary—protected by a garrison
5. snug—protected; sheltered
6. unassailable—safe against attack
7. under the wing of—protected by

8. To Accompany for the Purpose of Protecting: convoy (esp. in a military, police, or official sense), escort,v. (convoy, escort,n.)

9. To Go Around Guarding, Protecting, etc.: patrol,v. (patrol,n. patrol, patrolman, patroller,n.)

10. To Take under One's Protection and Care: godfather,v. (godfather,n.)

11. To Give Refuge to: harbor,v.

12. Capable of Being Protected or Defended: defensible, tenable,adj. (indefensible, untenable,neg.)

13. Japanese Art of Self-Defense: judo, jujitsu,n.

14. State of Being a Guardian: guardianship, wardship,n.

15. Pert. to a Guardian: tutelar, tutelary,adj.

16. Pert. to a Garrison: presidial, presidiary, adj.

17. To Give Means of Defense to: arm, armor, v.

18. A Turning for Protection: recourse,n.

19. One Who Is Protected,n.
1. **client**—one who is under the protection of another
2. **protégé**—one who is under the protection of another (protégée,fem.)
3. **ward**—child or person under protection or guardianship; one who is under the protection of the court by reason of youth, incompetence, etc.

20. Protection, Support, and Encouragement Given to a Cause, Artist, Artistic Endeavor, etc.: aegis or egis, auspices, patronage,n. (patron, patroness,n. auspicial,adj. patronize,v.)

21. Patron of the Arts or Literature: Maecenas,n.

22. Protective Covering against Attack,n.
1. **armature**—armor for the body
2. **armor**—protective covering against attack, as on the body, a ship, etc.
3. **breastplate**—plate of metal used as armor to cover the breast of a soldier
4. **buckler**—a kind of shield
5. **shield**—broad piece of armor, metal plate, etc., carried on the arm by soldiers or fighters in former times

23. Protective Device against Light, Sun, Rain, etc.: canopy, parasol, screen, shade, sunshade, umbrella,n.

24. To Guard the Side of (Military Troops): flank,v.

25. Rapid Artillery Fire Laid Down as a Protective Screen: barrage,n.

26. Protected, Safe, or Fortified Place; Place of Protection,n.
1. **alcazar**—fortress
2. **ark**—place of refuge, in analogy to Noah's ark
3. **asylum**—place of protection, refuge, or retreat; inviolable sanctuary once given to criminals and debtors, now to refugees from political tyranny; place of refuge, shelter, and protection for the insane, orphans, the blind, and other helpless or afflicted persons
4. **burrow**—place of retreat or shelter
5. **castle, château**—large, fortified building
6. **citadel**—fortified place; safe place; place of refuge; fortress; stronghold
7. **corral**—enclosure for defense or protection
8. **covert, coverture**—covering and protective place; shelter
9. **depository**—repository
10. **fastness**—safe and protected place
11. **fort**—strong, protected, or fortified place; such a place occupied by troops and surrounded by various defensive devices and barriers
12. **fortification**—fortified place
13. **fortress**—large, permanent, fortified place; stronghold
14. **garrison**—fortified place manned by troops
15. **harbor**—refuge
16. **haven**—place of safety, literally or figuratively
17. **lee**—place or side that affords protection against the wind
18. **oasis**—refuge in an otherwise barren region
19. **preserve**—place where game, fish, etc., are kept by certain restrictions against their being hunted, killed, etc.
20. **presidio**—any place protected by a garrison
21. **redoubt**—small fort
22. **refuge**—place of protection, safety, or shelter
23. **repository**—place for safekeeping
24. **retreat**—place of safety
25. **sanctuary**—place of protection or safety; place of refuge or protection from the law
26. **shelter**—place of protection or refuge
27. **stockade**—protected position made by thick posts set in the ground
28. **stronghold**—fortified place; safe and protected place
29. **tower**—high structure used as a fortress or stronghold

27. Head of a Castle or Fort: castellan, chatelain,n. (chatelaine,fem.)

28. To Protect a Place or Military Installation,v.
1. **barricade**—fortify with a hastily constructed defensive obstruction
2. **bulwark**—fortify with a wall-like structure; rampart
3. **fortify**—make safe against attack; make safe with defensive and protective devices, forts, etc.
4. **fortress**—fortify
5. **garrison**—make safe against attack by fortresses occupied by troops; place troops in to protect; (of troops) protect against danger
6. **rampart**—protect with a barrier or embankment
7. **stockade**—protect with, strictly, thick posts set in the ground

29. Protection of a Place,n. *From Sec. 28:* fortification

30. That Which Affords Protection to a Place,n. *From Sec. 28:* barricade or barricado, bulwark, fortification, rampart, stockade; *Also:*
1. **barrier**—that which hinders attack
2. **bastion**—fortification
3. **battlement**—parapet with open spaces for shooting through
4. **breastwork**—fortification thrown up hastily
5. **earthwork**—fortification made of earth
6. **machicolation**—projecting parapet with openings through which molten lead, missiles, etc., were thrown upon the enemy below
7. **moat**—deep, water-filled, protective trench around a fortified place
8. **outwork**—part of the fortifications outside the main fortifications
9. **palisade**—fence used for protection
10. **parapet**—protective wall, elevation, or defense for soldiers; fortification
11. **ravelin**—triangular outside fortification beyond the main trench
12. **redoubt**—inner fortification; temporary fortification on hilltops, passes, etc.
13. **trench**—protective ditch
14. **vallation**—rampart

15. work—any structure designed as a fortification

31. Protected or Fortified,adj. *From Sec. 28:* barricaded, bulwarked, etc.; *From Sec. 30:* bastioned, battlemented; *Also:* 1. walled—fortified

32. To Furnish (a Structure) with Battlements or Open-Spaced Parapets: crenel, crenelate, crenellate,v. (crenelation, crenellation,n. crenelate, crenellate, crenelated, crenellated,adj.)

33. Open Space in a Battlement: crenel,n.

34. Solid Part between the Open Spaces of a Battlement: merlon,n.

35. Opening in the Floor between the Corbels, or Supports, of a Projecting Parapet: machicolation,n. (machicolated,adj. machicolate,v.)

569. PROTECTION AGAINST DISEASE

1. To Protect against Disease, Poison, etc., v.
1. **immunize**—protect against disease, poison, or similar harmful agent
2. **inoculate**—protect against (a disease) by introducing germs or viruses that will cause a mild attack of, and eventual immunity to, the disease
3. **vaccinate**—inoculate with the virus of cowpox and thus render immune to smallpox; loosely, inoculate with the modified virus of various other diseases
4. **variolate**—inoculate with the unmodified virus of smallpox, usually taken directly from a human afflicted with the disease—a practice forbidden in most countries

2. Protection against Disease, etc.,n. *From Sec. 1:* immunization, inoculation, vaccination, variolation; *Also:* 1. **tachyphylaxis**—rapid immunization

3. One Who Protects against Disease,n. *From Sec. 1:* inoculator, vaccinator

4. Substance Used in Protection against Disease,n. *From Sec. 1:* inoculant or inoculum, vaccine; *Also:* 1. **toxin-antitoxin**—mixture of a poisonous substance and its antidote used to immunize a person against the substance

5. Pert. to, Descr. of, etc., Protection against Disease,adj. *From Sec. 1:* inoculative, vaccine or vaccinal

6. The Scar Resulting from Inoculation against Smallpox: vaccination,n.

7. Instrument Used in Vaccinating: vaccinator,n.

8. Advocate of Vaccination: vaccinationist, n.

9. Protection Built Up against Disease, Poison, etc.: immunity,n. (immune,adj.)

10. Immunity against Poison, Built Up Gradually by Taking at First Minute Then Increasing Quantities: mithridatism,n.

11. Reduction or Loss of Acquired Immunity: anergy,n.

12. Medical Science Dealing with Immunity and Its Production: immunology,n. (immunologist,n. immunological,adj.)

13. Art of Guarding against, or Preventing, Disease: prophylaxis,n.

570. TAKE CARE OF

1. To Take Care of; To Care for,v.
1. **attend to**—take thoughtful care of
2. **cherish**—care for with great tenderness
3. **foster**—cherish

4. **mind**—take care of; care for protectively
5. **nurse**—take care of; care for tenderly or solicitously
6. **nurture**—take care of; care for; cherish
7. **shepherd**—take good care of
8. **tend**—take care of; care for and watch over
9. **treasure**—take particularly good care of
10. **watch, watch over**—take alert care of; mind
11. **wet-nurse**—take overindulgent care of, doing (for someone) many of the things he should do, or is capable of doing, for himself

2. One Who Cares for,n. *From Sec. 1:* attendant, cherisher, nurse, shepherd, tender, wet nurse; *Also:* 1. **handmaid, handmaiden**—female attendant; by extension, anyone who takes thoughtful care of (another)

3. One Who Takes Care of a Place: caretaker, curator, custodian,n. (curatorial, custodial,adj.)

4. Care: charge, custody,n. (custodial,adj.)

5. Patronage and Care: aegis or egis, auspices,n. (auspicial,adj.)

6. Care and Protection of a Guardian: guardianship, tutelage, wardship,n. (tutelar, tutelary,adj.)

7. Showing Care for: solicitous,adj. (solicitude, solicitousness,n.)

8. One Who Is Cared for: charge, protégé,n. (protégée,fem.)

10. A Nurse: amah (Orient); ayah (India); bonne (French); governess, nursemaid,n.

571. SAVE FROM DANGER

1. To Save from Danger, etc.,v.
1. **deliver**—rescue
2. **rescue**—save from danger, capture, etc.
3. **salvage, salve**—save (a ship at sea) from shipwreck, capture, ruin, fire, or other calamity; save what one can in any disaster

2. Act or Process of Saving,n. *From Sec. 1:* deliverance or delivery, rescue, salvage; *Also:*
1. **redemption**—salvation (religion)
2. **salvation**—saving; saving of the soul from spiritual destruction, sin, evil, etc.

3. One Who Saves,n. *From Sec. 1:* deliverer, rescuer, salvager or salvor; *From Sec. 2:* redeemer; *Also:*
1. **lifesaver**—one who saves someone's life or who comes to his rescue
2. **Messiah**—savior; expected savior of the Hebrews (Messianic,adj. Messiahship,n.)
3. **savior**—one who saves, rescues, or delivers

4. State of Being Saved; State of Having One's Soul Saved from Spiritual Destruction, Sin, etc.: salvation,n.

572. DANGER

1. Dangerous,adj.
1. **adventurous, adventuresome**—dangerous; risky
2. **chancy**—risky
3. **critical**—dangerous; dangerously capable of following an unfortunate course
4. **hazardous**—dangerous, i.e., full of possibilities of harm, evil, or mischance
5. **insecure**—dangerous; not properly protected
6. **jeopardous**—dangerous, i.e., full of risk of danger, death, injury, etc. ·
7. **parlous**—mischievously dangerous
8. **perilous**—full of immediate danger, or of a threatened immediacy of danger
9. **precarious**—dangerous in the sense of

being unsafe for a footing or as a support; dangerous in the sense of being dependent on circumstances beyond one's control

10. **queasy**—dangerous
11. **risky**—dangerous, i.e., likely to result in harm, with the implication that the possible harm is known beforehand
12. **serpentine**—treacherous and tricky
13. **speculative**—involving possible loss, danger, damage, etc. (of business ventures)
14. **ticklish**—risky
15. **touch-and-go**—risky and uncertain
16. **treacherous**—falsely seeming safe or secure, but actually dangerous
17. **ugly**—dangerous
18. **unsafe**—dangerous
19. **venturesome**—dangerous; involving risks
20. **venturous**—dangerous; risky
21. **viperous**—dangerous and hateful; treacherous

2. Dangerousness,n. *From Sec. 1:* adventurousness, criticalness, hazardousness, insecurity, perilousness, precariousness, queasiness, riskiness, speculativeness, ticklishness, touch and go, treacherousness or treachery, unsafeness or unsafety, venturesomeness, venturousness

3. Danger; A Danger,n. *From Sec. 1:* chance, hazard, insecurity, jeopardy, peril, risk; *Also:* 1. **pitfall**—danger in which one may be trapped

4. To Endanger; To Expose to Danger,v. *From Sec. 1:* hazard, jeopardize, peril or imperil, risk, speculate with, venture; *Also:* 1. **compromise**—endanger

5. To Accept Danger; To Accept the Danger of,v. *From Sec. 1:* hazard, risk, speculate, venture

6. Time of Danger: crisis,n. (critical,adj.)

7. Dangerous-Looking: forbidding,adj.

8. Business Undertaking Involving Possible Loss, Danger, etc.: speculation,n. (speculator, n. speculative,v.)

9. Dangerous Act or Undertaking: hazard,n.

10. Dangerous Person,n.
1. **femme fatale (French)**—woman whose beauty and allure cause men to commit foolhardy, desperate, and self-destructive actions
2. **serpent**—dangerous, untrustworthy, backbiting person
3. **viper**—dangerous and hateful person

11. That Which Is Risked: stake, venture,n.

573. THREAT

1. Threatening; Sounding or Looking Threatening,adj.
1. **barking**—speaking or shouting threateningly
2. **black**—threatening
3. **comminatory**—threatening
4. **dire**—threatening evil
5. **fateful**—ominous (fatefulness,n.)
6. **fulminant, fulminating, fulminatory**—uttering threats
7. **gnarling**—growling
8. **gnarring**—growling with a snapping or gnashing of the teeth (of dogs)
9. **growling**—making deep, threatening sounds
10. **impending, impendent**—hanging over threateningly—of those events that are likely to occur, or likely to occur shortly (impendence, impendency,n.)
11. **looming**—appearing as a threat
12. **lowering**—looking threatening and dark
13. **menacing**—threatening danger and thereby, perhaps, causing, or attempting

to cause, fear; threatening evil, harm, etc.

14. **minacious, minatorial, minatory**—threatening; menacing (minaciousness, minacity,n.)
15. **ominous**—of such a character as to threaten danger, evil, harm, etc., and thereby causing, or capable of causing, fear or fright (ominousness,n.)
16. **overhanging**—impending
17. **portentous, portending**—threatening (to happen); giving a threatening sign or token (portentousness, portentosity,n.)
18. **rampant**—threatening in attitude, manner, bearing, or action (rampancy,n.)
19. **scowling**—looking threatening
20. **sinister**—containing, or indicating the possibilities of, a threat of harm or evil (sinisterness,n.)
21. **snarling**—growling with a snapping or gnashing of the teeth (of animals)
22. **thundering**—uttering terrible threats
23. **ugly**—threatening
24. **yarring**—growling; snarling (of animals)

2. To Threaten; To Make Threatening Sounds; To Look Threatening,v. *From Sec. 1:* bark, comminate, fulminate or fulmine, gnarl, gnar or gnarr, growl, impend, loom, lower or lour, menace, overhang, portend, scowl, snarl, thunder, yarr (commination, fulmination, impendence,n.); *Also:*
1. **assault**—threaten to commit bodily attack upon (legal)
2. **blackmail**—make unlawful threats to expose (someone's) folly, weakness, crimes, etc., in order to extort money from him
3. **bluff**—make threats that cannot be carried out
4. **ramp**—stand, maintain a posture, or move forward with the forelegs (if an animal) or the arms (if a person) raised in a threatening manner

3. Threatener,n. *From Sec. 1:* barker, fulminator, growler, menacer, scowler, snarler, thunderer; *From Sec. 2:* assaulter, blackmailer, bluffer

4. Threat; Threats; Threatening Action, Appearance, Sound, Sign, etc.,n. *From Sec. 1:* bark, commination, fulmination, gnarl, growl, lower or lour, menace, omen, portent, scowl, snarl, thunder, yarr; *From Sec. 2:* assault, blackmail, bluff, ramp

5. Supposed Threat to the White Race of Domination by the Yellow Race: yellow menace, yellow peril,n.

574. WARNING

1. To Warn,v.
1. **admonish**—warn; say in a warning manner (admonishment, admonition,n.)
2. **alert**—warn of approaching danger
3. **caution**—warn of threat or danger; warn to exercise care or be careful
4. **exhort**—warn strongly or earnestly (exhortation,n.)
5. **forewarn**—warn beforehand
6. **growl**—make a deep, low sound of angry warning
7. **monitor**—admonish
8. **portend**—warn of; give a warning sign or token of
9. **premonish**—warn beforehand
10. **threaten**—warn of danger, harm, or something bad
11. **tip off**—warn (colloq.)

2. A Warning,n. *From Sec. 1:* admonition or admonishment, caution, exhortation, forewarning, growl, portent, premonition, threat; *Also:*
1. **caveat**—a warning
2. **monition**—a warning

3. Warner, One Who Warns,n. *From Sec. 1:* admonisher or admonitor, cautioner, exhorter, forewarner, growler, premonitor, threatener; *Also:*
1. **Cassandra**—woman who warns of disaster, but is not believed
2. **lookout**—one who watches in order to warn of danger
3. **monitor**—one who warns about behavior

4. That Which Gives Warning,n. *From Sec. 1:* forewarner, premonitor, portent; *Also:*
1. **alarm**—device for making sounds of warning
2. **monitor**—that which gives warning
3. **Mother Carey's chicken**—stormy petrel
4. **siren**—device for sounding warning
5. **stormy petrel**—that which warns of trouble or difficulties ahead

5. Warning; Serving to Warn,adj. *From Sec. 1:* admonitory, cautionary, exhortatory, portentous, premonitory or premonitive; *Also:*
1. **dire**—warning of evil
2. **exemplary**—serving as a warning
3. **monitory, monitorial**—warning
4. **precursory**—warning, or serving to warn, beforehand

6. A Warning Signal or Sound,n.
1. **alarm**—sound that warns of danger
2. **alarum**—alarm (archaic)
3. **alert**—alarm that warns of the approach of danger, attack, enemy aircraft, etc.
4. **beacon**—warning signal
5. **knell**—warning sound of imminent death, failure, misfortune, etc.
6. **portent**—sign that warns of future evil or misfortune
7. **siren**—warning sound
8. **tocsin**—warning signal; alarm; alarm sounded on a bell

575. BRAVERY

1. Brave; Bold,adj.
1. **adventuresome**—bold; daring
2. **adventurous**—ready to take risks; daring
3. **assured**—bold
4. **audacious**—contemptuous of danger or risk; daring
5. **aweless**—free from fear
6. **brash**—rash; reckless
7. **courageous**—willing and able to face up to danger without shrinking
8. **daredevil**—bold; contemptuous of danger
9. **daring**—lacking fear in circumstances of danger, or in situations that might frighten others
10. **dauntless**—lacking in fear; not subject to fright or intimidation
11. **desperate**—frantically rash or reckless, since there is no, or almost no, hope anyway
12. **devilish**—daring
13. **doughty**—brave; bold; undismayed by danger; daring; heroic (The term is now somewhat archaic, unless used humorously.)
14. **enterprising**—showing courage, venturesomeness, boldness, imagination, and energy in starting new projects
15. **fearless**—free from fear
16. **foolhardy**—foolishly bold or daring; rash
17. **gallant**—brave in spirit and noble in bearing
18. **game**—plucky
19. **hardy**—brave; bold; daring
20. **harum-scarum**—rash; reckless
21. **headlong**—heedless of risk (of actions)
22. **heroic**—exceptionally brave, esp. against greater odds or extreme danger
23. **impavid**—free from fear
24. **impetuous**—acting rashly and suddenly
25. **intrepid**—not subject to fear, anxiety, or trembling; lacking fear, even when in frightening circumstances
26. **lionhearted**—brave, like a lion
27. **madcap**—reckless; reckless and wild
28. **manful**—brave
29. **manly**—brave, i.e., the way a man should be
30. **martial**—brave
31. **nervy**—bold; undaunted by fear or risk
32. **plucky**—full of spirited courage
33. **pot-valiant**—brave when, or if, drunk
34. **rash**—acting without thought of danger or possible consequences (The term is not complimentary and implies undue haste or thoughtlessness of action.)
35. **reckless**—unduly indifferent to danger; rash
36. **red-blooded**—courageous
37. **resolute**—bold; daring
38. **soldierly**—brave, like a soldier
39. **Spartan**—not easily frightened
40. **spunky**—full of spirited courage
41. **stalwart**—brave; brave and strong
42. **stout**—brave; bold
43. **stouthearted**—brave; courageous
44. **temerarious**—abnormally contemptuous of risk or danger; senselessly rash or reckless
45. **Trojan**—courageous; plucky
46. **two-fisted**—brave
47. **unafraid**—possessing no fear
48. **unalarmed**—not frightened
49. **unapprehensive**—not frightened; without fear
50. **undaunted**—still courageous despite obstacles or fearful circumstances
51. **unfaltering**—not hesitating through fear
52. **unflinching**—brave; not drawing back in the face of danger
53. **unfrightened**—not frightened
54. **unscared**—not frightened
55. **unshrinking**—unflinching
56. **unterrified**—not frightened
57. **valiant**—undismayed by danger; heroic; stouthearted
58. **valorous**—possessing the kind of bravery that enables one to meet danger without worry or weakness
59. **venturesome**—inclined to take risks; daring
60. **venturous**—bold; running risks; exposing oneself to danger; ready or eager to face danger or take risks; daring
61. **wildcat**—reckless
62. **yeomanly**—brave

2. Bravery; Boldness,n. *From Sec. 1:* adventuresomeness, adventurousness, assurance, audacity or audaciousness, awelessness, brashness, courageousness or courage, daring, devilishness, doughtiness, enterprise, fearlessness, foolhardiness, gallantry, gameness, hardihood, heroism, impetuousness or impetuosity, intrepidity, lionheartedness, manfulness, manliness, nerve or nerviness, pluck, pot-valiance, rashness, recklessness, redbloodedness, resolution or resoluteness, Spartanism, spunk, stalwartness, stoutheartedness, temerity, two-fistedness, unapprehensiveness, valiancy, valiance or valiantness, valor or valorousness, venturesomeness, venturousness; *Also:*
1. **fortitude**—bravery in face of danger, pain, suffering, hardship, etc.
2. **grit**—courage and perseverance in the face of hardship or difficulties
3. **guts**—courage to endure adversity, hardship or danger (colloq.)
4. **manhood**—manly courage
5. **mettle**—courage
6. **prowess**—heroic bravery; daring
7. **soul**—courage
8. **spirit**—courage

3. Brave Person,n. *From Sec. 1:* adventurer, daredevil, gallant, hero or, fem., heroine, harum-scarum, lion, madcap, Spartan, stalwart, Trojan, yeoman; *Also:*

1. **Bayard**—man of great honor and indomitable courage
2. **blade**—sharp-witted and reckless man
3. **scapegrace**—reckless and worthless person

4. To Be Brave or Show Bravery,v. *From Sec. 1:* adventure, dare, venture

5. Show of Pretended Bravery: bravado,n.

6. Action or Utterance Pretending Bravery: bravado,n.

7. Brave or Bold Act, Action, or Undertaking,n.

1. **deed**—glorious exploit
2. **exploit**—brave or heroic act
3. **feat**—act or deed accomplished through daring
4. **stunt**—bold act, usually performed to attract attention
5. **venture**—daring act or undertaking

8. Bold Actions; Daring Behavior: derringdo,n.

9. Heroic Deeds: res gestae,n. (Latin)

10. To Make Brave or Bold; To Give Courage to: assure, embolden, encourage, reassure,v. (assurance, encouragement, reassurance,n.)

11. To Call Upon One's Courage: brace up,v.

576. FEAR

1. Afraid; Frightened; Fearful,adj.

1. **aghast**—filled with great fear, horror, or terror
2. **alarmed**—suddenly or unexpectedly frightened by danger or threat of danger
3. **anxious**—fearful; apprehensive
4. **appalled**—overwhelmed with fear
5. **apprehensive**—possessing fear, usually on realistic or rational grounds; fearful of the future
6. **awed**—inspired with fear; inspired with fear and wonder or worship
7. **base**—cowardly
8. **breathless**—figuratively holding one's breath in fear
9. **browbeaten**—frightened into doing something by stern or threatening words or looks
10. **bulldozed**—frightened by threats or violence (colloq.)
11. **chickenhearted**—fearful; cowardly; timid
12. **cowardly**—meanly fearful; totally lacking in courage
13. **cowed**—dominated by fear
14. **cowering**—showing abject fear in the face of danger, the presence of enemies, etc.; crouching or shrinking in fear
15. **craven**—full of petty, base, or ignoble fears; totally lacking in the merest iota of courage
16. **creepy**—nervously fearful
17. **cringing**—shrinking back in fear; crouching in fear
18. **crouching**—assuming a position with the body close to the ground and the limbs close to the body, indicating fear
19. **dastardly**—cowardly in a mean and sneaky way
20. **daunted**—frightened
21. **dismayed**—frightened; rendered impotent or unable to continue, owing to alarm or terror
22. **faint**—lacking in courage
23. **fainthearted**—cowardly
24. **flinching**—fearfully drawing back in the face of danger
25. **horrified**—filled with a combination of fear, dread, disgust, and intense hatred, usually most painful and unnerving
26. **horror-struck, horror-stricken**—horrified

27. **intimidated**—inspired with fear by threats; prevented from doing something by fear, threats of reprisal, etc.
28. **jumpy**—nervously fearful
29. **lily-livered**—cowardly
30. **nerveless**—totally lacking in courage
31. **nervous**—timid
32. **overawed**—overcome with fear; frightened and thus restrained
33. **panic-stricken, panicky**—overpowered by fright (sometimes groundless), and therefore prone to irrational or unthinking actions or reactions
34. **phobic**—full of morbid and irrational fear (of some specific thing, activity, group, etc.)
35. **pigeonhearted**—fearful; cowardly; timid
36. **planet-stricken, planet-struck**—panicstricken
37. **pusillanimous**—fearful, or lacking in courage, in a petty and contemptible manner
38. **pussyfooting**—timid about revealing one's opinion or taking a stand (considered slang by some authorities)
39. **quaking**—shuddering
40. **qualmish**—having a sudden fear that one is doing, or is contemplating doing, the wrong thing
41. **quivery, quivering**—trembling
42. **recreant**—submitting out of fear and shameful cowardice; cowardly; craven
43. **scared**—struck suddenly with fear or alarm
44. **scary**—generally or easily frightened (colloq.)
45. **sheepish**—timid
46. **shivering, shivery**—shaking from fear
47. **shocked**—caused to feel great terror or horror
48. **shrinking**—drawing back in fear
49. **shuddering, shuddery**—trembling in a convulsive manner, figuratively or literally, from fear or horror
50. **shy**—easily frightened or frightened away; timid
51. **skittish**—easily frightened
52. **sneaky**—cowardly; acting in a cowardly fashion
53. **solicitous**—fearful; anxious
54. **spineless**—lacking in courage
55. **startled**—simultaneously alarmed and surprised; jumping out of sudden alarm
56. **superstitious**—full of irrational fears of the unknown or mysterious, esp. in religion
57. **terrified**—overwhelmed by fear; shocked with overwhelming fear
58. **terror-stricken, terrorized**—overcome by extremely intense fear or overwhelming dread, or a combination of the two emotions
59. **timid**—fearful, esp. in contact with new situations or unfamiliar surroundings or circumstances
60. **timorous**—full of fears, esp. in circumstances that require aggressiveness, independence, self-assurance, etc.
61. **trembling**—feeling fear; shaking involuntarily from fear
62. **tremulous**—timid; trembling
63. **unmanned**—having had one's courage taken away
64. **unstrung**—fearful
65. **white-livered**—cowardly
66. **wilted**—frightened; having lost one's courage
67. **yellow**—cowardly

2. Fear; Fright; Fearfulness,n. *From Sec. 1:* alarm, anxiety or anxiousness, apprehension or apprehensiveness, awe, baseness, chickenheartedness, cowardice or cowardliness, cravenness, creepiness, dastardliness, dismay, faintness, faintheartedness, horror, jumpiness, nervelessness, nervousness, panic, phobia, pigeonheartedness, pusillanimity, quake, qualm or qualms, recreancy or recreance, scare, sheepishness, shivers, shock, shyness, skittishness, sneakiness, solicitousness or solicitude, spinelessness, startle, superstition, terror or terrorism, timidity or timidness, timorousness, trembles, tremulousness, yellowness; *Also:*

1. **consternation**—amazed fear that paralyzes or confounds
2. **dread**—intense fear, often of imminent evil, combined with total loss of courage
3. **misdoubt**—fear
4. **misgiving**—feeling of fear
5. **poltroonery**—thoroughgoing, out-and-out cowardice
6. **stage fright**—fear over, or when, appearing before an audience
7. **trepidation**—fear; state of fear or alarm; nervousness or trembling from fear or alarm
8. **turn**—fright; scare
9. **white feather**—cowardice
10. **yellow streak**—cowardice; streak of cowardice

3. To Fear; To Be or Become Afraid, Frightened, or Fearful; To Show Fear or Signs of Fear,v. *From Sec. 1:* apprehend, cower, cringe, crouch, flinch, pussyfoot, quake, quiver, scare, shiver, shock, shrink, shudder, startle, tremble, wilt; *From Sec. 2:* dread, misdoubt; *Also:*

1. **falter**—lose courage in what one is doing
2. **quail**—become fearful; lose all courage at the threat of danger; shrink back in fear
3. **show the white feather**—show cowardice or timidity
4. **shy**—jump with fear
5. **start**—jump in sudden fear

4. An Act, Movement, or Sign of Fear,n. *From Sec. 1:* cringe, crouch, flinch, quake, quiver, shiver, shrink, shudder, startle, tremble; *From Sec. 3:* falter, shy, start; *Also:*

1. **crispation**—shudder
2. **funk**—a shrinking back with fear

5. One Who Fears; One Who Is Afraid, Frightened, or Fearful,n. *From Sec. 1:* coward, craven, cringer, dastard, flincher, pussyfooter, recreant, sneak; *From Sec. 2:* poltroon, white feather; *Also:*

1. **milksop**—coward
2. **milquetoast**—fearful and meek person
3. **quitter**—coward
4. **Scaramouch**—cowardly fool

6. To Cause Fear to; To Frighten; To Make Afraid or Fearful,v. *From Sec. 1:* alarm, appall, awe, browbeat, bulldoze, cow, daunt, dismay, horrify, intimidate, overawe, panic, scare, shock, startle, terrify or terror, terrorize, unman, unstring, wilt (horrification, intimidation, terrorization or terrorism,n.); *From Sec. 2:* consternate; *Also:*

1. **bully**—intimidate by threats, or by an overbearing manner
2. **hector**—bully
3. **tame**—deprive of courage

7. Frightful or Fearful, i.e., Frightening or Causing Fear,adj. *From Sec. 1:* alarming, appalling; awesome, awful, or awe-inspiring; browbeating, bulldozing, creepy; horrifying, horrific, or horrible; scary, shocking, shuddersome, startling; terrifying, terrorful, terrorific, or terrible; *From Sec. 2:* consternating, dread or dreadful; *Also:*

1. **bloodcurdling**—horrifying; terrifying
2. **chimerical**—frightening but imaginary
3. **dire**—causing great fear
4. **eerie, eery**—frightening, unnatural, and strange, as if associated with ghosts or spirits (eeriness,n.)
5. **fierce**—capable of inspiring great fear (fierceness,n.)

6. **formidable**—tending to excite fear (formidableness, formidability,n.)
7. **ghastly**—horrifying (ghastliness,n.)
8. **ghoulish**—horrifying (ghoulishness,n.)
9. **grisly**—causing dread or shuddering; horrifying (grisliness,n.)
10. **gruesome, grewsome**—repulsively horrifying (gruesomeness, grewsomeness,n.)
11. **horrendous**—causing intense fear; exciting horror
12. **macabre**—horrifying (literally, suggestive of the dance of death)
13. **monstrous**—exciting horror owing to its incredible shape, form, or general appearance (monstrousness, monstrosity,n.)
14. **morbid**—frightful (morbidness, morbidity,n.)
15. **redoubtable, redoubted**—exciting fear or dread
16. **tremendous**—terrifying, usually owing to its extraordinarily large size
17. **uncanny**—eerie (uncanniness,n.)
18. **unearthly**—frightful; eerie (unearthliness,n.)

8. Frightener; One Who Causes Fear or Frightens,n. *From Sec. 1:* browbeater, bulldozer, scarer, intimidator, terrorizer or terror; *From Sec. 6:* bully, hector; *Also:*

1. **alarmist**—one who attempts to make others needlessly frightened or fearful (alarmism,n. alarmist,adj.)
2. **scaremonger**—one who needlessly causes alarm
3. **terrorist**—scaremonger

9. Symbol of Cowardice: white feather, white flag,n.

10. Object of Fear,n.

1. **bête noire**—whoever or whatever is particularly feared
2. **bogy, bogey, bogie**—anything that is superstitiously feared; bugbear
3. **bugaboo**—some nonexistent thing that is feared
4. **bugbear**—any object of fear; some imaginary monster used by adults to excite fear in a child
5. **chimera, chimaera**—object of fear that exists only in the imagination
6. **hobgoblin**—bogy
7. **monstrosity**—something of fearful and incredible shape, form, or appearance
8. **thunderbolt**—sudden act, thing, happening, etc., that causes fear

11. Selected Abnormal or Pathological Fears,n.

1. **acrophobia**—of high places, riding in elevators, climbing ladders, etc.
2. **agoraphobia**—of open spaces, or of the necessity of leaving the sheltering protection of home, parents, friends, etc.
3. **ailurophobia**—of cats
4. **algophobia**—of pain
5. **amaxophobia**—of being in vehicles
6. **androphobia**—of males
7. **anemophobia**—of winds
8. **Anglophobia**—of British customs, people, etc.
9. **anthropophobia**—of people
10. **apiphobia**—of bees, or of being stung by bees
11. **astraphobia**—of lightning, or of thunderstorms
12. **astrophobia**—of the stars
13. **aurophobia**—of gold
14. **autophobia**—of being alone
15. **bacteriophobia**—of bacteria, or of germs
16. **bathophobia**—of depths
17. **batrachophobia**—of frogs and toads
18. **bibliophobia**—of books
19. **brontophobia**—of thunder
20. **cardiophobia**—of heart disease
21. **chromatophobia, chromophobia**—of certain colors

22. **claustrophobia**—of being shut in, or of confining places
23. **coitophobia**—of sexual intercourse
24. **coprophobia**—of feces, or of defecation
25. **cynophobia**—of dogs
26. **cypridophobia**—of venereal disease
27. **demonophobia**—of demons, or of devils
28. **dipsophobia**—of drinking
29. **dromophobia**—of wandering
30. **erotophobia**—of sexual love
31. **erythrophobia**—of the color red
32. **feminophobia**—of women
33. **Francophobia**—of France, French customs, influence, etc.
34. **gamophobia**—of marriage
35. **genophobia**—of sex
36. **Germanophobia**—of Germany, Germans, German ideas, etc.
37. **geumaphobia**—of taste
38. **graphophobia**—of writing
39. **Grecophobia**—of Greeks, Greek customs, etc.
40. **gymnophobia**—of nakedness
41. **gynephobia**—of the female sex
42. **hadephobia**—of hell
43. **Hellenophobia**—of Greek people, customs, etc.
44. **hematophobia, hemophobia**—of the sight of blood
45. **hodophobia**—of traveling
46. **hydrophobia**—of water
47. **hylophobia**—of the forest
48. **ichthyophobia**—of fish
49. **kleptophobia**—of robbers, or of robbery
50. **lyssophobia**—of insanity, or of becoming insane; of rabies
51. **monophobia**—of being alone
52. **mysophobia**—of dirt, or of contamination
53. **mythophobia**—of telling untruths
54. **necrophobia**—of corpses, or of death
55. **negrophobia**—of Negroes
56. **neophobia**—of newness, or of novelty
57. **nosophobia**—of disease
58. **nyctophobia**—of darkness, or of night
59. **ochlophobia**—of crowds
60. **onomatophobia**—of hearing certain words
61. **ophidiophobia**—of snakes
62. **ophthalmophobia**—of being stared at
63. **ornithophobia**—of birds
64. **osmophobia**—of odors
65. **paralipophobia**—of neglecting one's duty
66. **pedophobia**—of infants
67. **pharmacophobia**—of medicine
68. **phobophobia**—of fearing, or of fear
69. **phonophobia**—of noise
70. **photophobia**—of light
71. **pyrophobia**—of fire
72. **rhabdophobia**—of being beaten
73. **Russophobia**—of Russia, Russian people, customs, etc.
74. **scopophobia**—of being looked at, or of being seen
75. **siderodromophobia**—of railroad travel
76. **sitophobia**—of food, or of eating
77. **Slavophobia**—of Slavic peoples, customs, etc.
78. **taphephobia**—of being buried alive
79. **teratophobia**—of deformity, of giving birth to monsters, or of deformed people
80. **thanatophobia**—of death
81. **tocophobia**—of giving birth
82. **toxicophobia, toxiphobia**—of being poisoned
83. **trichophobia**—of hair
84. **trikaidekaphobia**—of the number 13
85. **vermiphobia**—of worms
86. **xenophobia**—of strangers
87. **zoophobia**—of animals

12. Having, or Descr. of, a Specific Abnormal or Pathological Fear or Dread,adj. *From Sec. 11:* acrophobic, agoraphobic, etc.

13. One Who Is the Victim of a Specific Ab-

normal or Pathological Fear or Dread,n. *From Sec. 11:* acrophobe, agoraphobe, etc.

577. CARE

1. Careful,adj.
1. **assiduous**—attentively careful
2. **cagey**—wary (colloq.)
3. **calculating**—careful
4. **canny**—cautious; wary
5. **cautious**—very careful; tending to avoid risk or danger
6. **chary**—excessively cautious in one's actions
7. **circumspect**—careful in the sense of looking around before taking action, or of considering all the possible consequences of an action or decision
8. **closemouthed**—cautious in speaking
9. **conscientious**—careful to do what is right; exercising conscience-dictated care
10. **diligent**—careful and painstaking
11. **discreet**—avoiding unnecessary recklessness or imprudence; sensibly cautious
12. **Fabian**—cautious—so called from the Roman general, Quintus Fabius Maximus, who avoided decisive battles when Rome was under attack by Hannibal
13. **gingerly**—most cautious, as if in expectation of danger or threat
14. **guarded**—careful; cautious
15. **heedful (of)**—careful (of)
16. **meticulous**—extremely careful, esp. in attention to even the slightest of details
17. **mindful (of)**—careful (of)
18. **painstaking**—most careful (in the doing of something)
19. **particular**—most careful (to do, or get, things right)
20. **precautious**—taking care, or being careful, beforehand
21. **provident**—careful to take possible future needs into account
22. **prudent**—careful or cautious in actions, conduct of affairs, management, etc.
23. **punctilious**—excessively careful to observe the exact principles of law, etiquette, morality, convention, etc.; meticulous
24. **regardful (of)**—careful (of)
25. **religious**—conscientiously careful
26. **reserved**—cautious in the way one acts or speaks
27. **scrupulous**—careful to a great degree, esp. as to exactness and propriety, with the implication that such care is caused by one's principles or conscience
28. **shy**—wary
29. **solicitous (of)**—showing care (about)
30. **strict**—most careful in observance of rule or form
31. **studious**—careful and thoughtful
32. **thorough**—careful about details
33. **vigilant**—cautious; circumspect; wary
34. **wary**—careful in the sense of expecting danger, of being suspicious of attack, etc.
35. **watchful**—cautious; circumspect; wary

2. Care; Carefulness,n. *From Sec. 1:* assiduity or assiduousness, cageyness, canniness, caution or cautiousness, chariness, circumspection or circumspectness, conscientiousness, diligence, discretion or discreetness, gingerliness, guardedness, heed or heedfulness, meticulousness or meticulosity, mindfulness, pains, particularity, precaution, providence, prudence, punctiliousness or punctilio, regard or regardfulness, religiousness, reserve, scrupulosity or scrupulousness, shyness, solicitude or solicitousness, strictness, studiousness, thoroughness, vigilance, wariness, watchfulness; *Also:*
1. **attention**—observant care
2. **oversight**—watchful care
3. **retenue**—caution in doing things

3. A Careful Taking into Account of Probable Future Events or Contingencies: foresight, precaution,n. (foresighted, precautional, precautionary,adj.)

4. Careful to Be on Time, as for Meetings, Appointments, etc.: punctual,adj. (punctuality, punctualness,n.)

5. Done with Care: assiduous, cautious, conscientious, diligent, meticulous, painstaking, punctilious, scrupulous, strict, studious, thorough,adj.

6. Done Only after Careful Thinking or Planning: considered,adj.

7. Done with Great and Studied Care and Fine Attention to Detail: elaborate,adj. (elaborateness,n.)

8. To Give Care and Thought (to): attend, heed,v.

9. To Be Careful of: beware, beware of, heed, watch out for,v.

10. To Advise or Urge Care: caution,v.

11. Advising or Urging Care: cautionary, precautional, precautionary,adj.

12. Requiring Care: pernickety, tender, ticklish,adj.

578. CARELESSNESS

1. Careless (of a Person, Attitude, etc.), adj.
1. casual—careless
2. cursory—careless; doing in a rapid, superficial, and careless manner that which should receive careful or exhaustive treatment; hasty
3. harebrained—reckless
4. harum-scarum—rash; reckless
5. hasty—careless and rapid
6. heedless—careless
7. impetuous—acting without due thought, care, etc.; rash
8. improvident—giving no care or thought to the future; making no careful provision for the future
9. imprudent—lacking in caution or discretion
10. inadvertent—careless, i.e., not paying proper attention
11. incautious—not showing any caution
12. indiscreet—not careful or cautious
13. lax—careless
14. madcap—wild and reckless
15. napping—off one's guard; lacking in caution
16. neglectful, negligent—careless; not showing proper or required care
17. perfunctory—careless; not showing careful attention to details; superficial
18. pococurante—careless
19. pound-foolish—careless in spending large sums of money (usually in the phrase *penny-wise and pound-foolish*)
20. precipitate—rash
21. rash—acting without thought of possible consequences and with undue haste or carelessness
22. reckless—not exercising normal caution; rash
23. regardless (of)—careless (of); showing no concern, attention, or heed (to)
24. remiss—careless
25. riotous—acting or living without caution
26. slack—careless; not exercising due care or caution
27. slipshod—careless; careless in dress, speech, etc.; careless by nature or habit
28. sloppy—careless; careless and untidy
29. slovenly—generally careless in appearance, habits, performance, etc.
30. superficial—careless; not thorough; hasty
31. thoughtless—showing no care

32. unmindful (of)—careless (of)
33. unthinking—careless; thoughtless
34. untidy—careless in habits, dress, etc.
35. unwary—not cautious or careful; not alert to danger; not on guard against danger

2. Careless (of Acts); Done Carelessly,adj. *From Sec. 1:* casual, cursory, harebrained, hasty, heedless, impetuous, imprudent, inadvertent, incautious, indiscreet, madcap, perfunctory, precipitate, rash, reckless, slipshod, sloppy, slovenly, superficial, thoughtless, unthinking; *Also:*
1. slapdash—careless and hasty
2. unadvised—careless; rash

3. Carelessness,n. *From Secs. 1 and 2:* casualness, cursoriness, haste or hastiness, heedlessness, impetuousness or impetuosity, improvidence, imprudence, inadvertence, incaution or incautiousness, indiscretion or indiscreetness, laxity or laxness; neglect, neglectfulness, or negligence; perfunctoriness, prococurantism, precipitateness, rashness, recklessness, remissness, riotousness, slackness, slipshodness, sloppiness, slovenliness, superficiality, thoughtlessness, unthinkingness, untidiness, unwariness

4. To Be Careless or Act Carelessly,v. *From Sec. 1:* nap, neglect (something), riot away or riot out (time); *Also:*
1. palter—act carelessly
2. plunge (into)—act hastily, recklessly, without thought
3. slur over—pass over without due care

5. Careless Act or Action: indiscretion,n.

6. Careless Person: pococurante,n.

7. Not Careful to Be on Time: unpunctual, adj. (unpunctuality,n.)

579. TO PAY ATTENTION

1. To Pay Attention,v.
1. address oneself to—apply oneself to
2. advert to—turn the attention to
3. apply oneself to—pay close attention to (application,n.)
4. attend—pay attention to (attention,n.)
5. concentrate on—turn the mind to without distraction or wandering; pay close attention to (concentration,n.)
6. heed—pay careful attention to; take notice of
7. mind—pay close attention to
8. note—pay attention to
9. notice—turn one's attention to
10. observe—pay close attention to (observation,n.)
11. remark—note; notice
12. scout—observe (a region) to gain information

2. Attention,n. *From Sec. 1:* application, concentration, heed, mind, notice, observation; *Also:* 1. micrology—attention to small and unimportant things or differences

3. Attentions Paid in Courtship: addresses, n.

4. Attentive,adj.
1. absorbed (in)—with one's attention so firmly fixed or captured that there is no room for distraction
2. advertent—attentive; mindful
3. alert (to)—closely or carefully attentive; vigilant
4. Argus-eyed—carefully observant; watchful
5. assiduous—carefully attentive
6. awake (to)—alert (to)
7. bemused (by)—absorbed (in)
8. engrossed (in)—with one's attentions fully taken up
9. enrapt—rapt

10. **enthralled (by)**—with one's attention captured and held, as if by magic
11. **fascinated (by)**—enthralled
12. **heedful (of)**—attentive; carefully attentive
13. **immersed (in)**—completely absorbed (in)
14. **intent (on)**—with one's attention firmly fixed (on)
15. **mindful (of)**—carefully attentive (to)
16. **observant**—attentive; paying careful attention; watchful
17. **on the qui vive**—alert; watchful
18. **open-eyed**—watchful
19. **particular**—attentive to details
20. **preoccupied (in or with)**—engrossed (in)
21. **punctilious**—attentive to precise details of conduct, form, etiquette, ceremony, etc.
22. **rapt**—intensely absorbed
23. **regardful**—attentive; mindful
24. **solicitous**—particular
25. **spellbound**—enthralled
26. **vigilant**—attentive to possibilities of harm or danger; carefully attentive
27. **wakeful**—watchful
28. **watchful**—closely or carefully attentive
29. **wide-awake**—alert
30. **wrapped up (in)**—absorbed (in)

5. **Attentiveness or Attention,n.** *From Sec. 4:* absorption, advertence or advertency, alertness, assiduity or assiduousness, engrossment, enthrallment, fascination, heed or heedfulness, immersion, intentness, mindfulness, observation, particularity, preoccupation, punctiliousness, raptness, regardfulness or regard, solicitude or solicitousness, vigilance, wakefulness, watchfulness, wide-awakeness; *Also:* 1. **trance**—totally absorbed state

6. **To Occupy the Attention of,v.** *From Sec. 1:* absorb, engross, enthrall, fascinate, preoccupy

7. **To Be Attentive to (a Person),v.**
1. **court**—be attentive to, in order to please or gain favor from
2. **curry favor with**—seek favor or friendliness from by insincere flattery or by constant attentions
3. **fawn on, fawn upon**—be attentive to in a servile and exaggeratedly deferential manner

8. **Attentive to a Person or His Needs,adj.**
1. **considerate**—attentive or alert to the feelings of others
2. **gallant**—attentive and polite to women
3. **obsequious**—servilely and, usually, insincerely attentive
4. **thoughtful**—unselfishly attentive to the needs or desires of others

9. **Attentiveness to a Person or His Needs,** n. *From Sec. 8:* considerateness or consideration, gallantry, obsequiousness, thoughtfulness; *Also:* 1. **prévenance (French)**—attentiveness to the needs of others

10. **One Who Is Courteously Attentive to Women:** chevalier, gallant,n.

11. **An Action or Speech That Indicates One's Courteous Attentiveness to a Woman:** gallantry,n.

12. **Attentiveness Intended to Win Illicit Sexual Favors from a Woman:** gallantry,n.

13. **Done with Fine Attention to Detail:** elaborate,adj. (elaborateness,n.)

14. **Indicating Careful Attention to Details:** minute,adj. (minuteness,n.)

15. **One Who Devotes His Complete Attention, Time, and Energy to One All-Consuming Interest:** monomaniac,n. (monomania,n. monomaniacal,adj.)

16. **One Whose Attention Is Occupied with Himself, His Thoughts, and His Fantasies, Rather than with the Outside World:** introvert,n. (introversion,n. introverted,adj.)

17. **One Whose Attention Is Turned toward the Outside World, Rather than Back in on Himself:** extravert, extrovert,n. (extraversion, extroversion,n. extraverted, extroverted, adj.)

18. **Unusually Engrossed with One's Own Thoughts and Feelings:** introspective,adj. (introspectiveness,n.)

19. **Able to Give Attention to Only One Thing at a Time (of the Mind, Personality, etc.):** single-track,adj.

20. **To Call Attention to,v.**
1. **advertise**—call attention to (advertisement,n.)
2. **alert**—call the attention of (someone)
3. **obtrude upon**—push oneself or itself upon the attention of (obtrusion,n.)
4. **show off**—constantly call attention to oneself, one's virtues, possessions, etc.
5. **urge**—call one's attention to insistently

21. **Calling, or Tending to Call, Attention, adj.** *From Sec. 20:* obtrusive, urgent (obtrusiveness, urgency,n.) ; *Also:*
1. **blatant**—offensively obtrusive
2. **exhibitionistic**—tending to call attention either to that which normal modesty usually requires the concealment of (as one's sexual organs), or, by extension, to one's qualities, vices, suffering, deformities, etc. (exhibitionism,n.)
3. **ostentatious**—tending to call attention to oneself by excessive display (ostentatiousness, ostentation,n.)
4. **protrusive**—calling attention to oneself by conspicuous manner, speech, behavior, etc.

22. **One Who Calls Attention to Himself,n.** *From Sec. 20:* show-off; *From Sec. 21:* exhibitionist

23. **Done to Attract Attention:** ostentatious, adj.

24. **Attracting Attention:** striking,adj.

25. **Demanding or Compelling Attention; Demanding or Requiring Immediate Attention,adj.**
1. **crying**—demanding attention
2. **exigent**—requiring immediate attention, decision, action, remedy, etc. (exigency, n.)
3. **insistent**—compelling attention (insistence, insistency,n.)
4. **pressing**—urgent
5. **striking**—compelling attention
6. **urgent**—demanding or requiring immediate attention (urgency,n.)

26. **That Which Requires Immediate Attention,n.**
1. **emergency**—that which arises suddenly or unexpectedly and requires immediate attention, action, etc.
2. **exigency**—situation or condition that requires immediate attention, decision, action, remedy, etc.

27. **Hindu System of Deep Concentration and Meditation:** Yoga or yoga,n.

28. **Practitioner of Yoga:** yogi,n.

29. **Practice or Belief of Yogis:** yogi,n.

30. **Center of Attention:** focus,n.

31. **Conspicuous Center of Public Attention, Interest, or Notice:** limelight, spotlight,n.

32. **One Who, or That Which, Is a Brilliant Center of Attention:** blazing star, cynosure, n.

580. INTEREST

1. **To Interest; To Be Interesting to,v.**
1. **absorb**—interest; capture and hold the interest of

2. **appeal to**—be interesting to
3. **concern**—interest
4. **entertain**—interest and amuse (entertainment,n.)
5. **enthrall, inthrall**—capture and hold, as if by magic, the interest of (enthrallment, inthrallment,n.)
6. **fascinate**—enthrall (fascination,n.)
7. **pique**—arouse the interest of

2. Interesting,adj. *From Sec. 1:* absorbing, appealing, entertaining, enthralling, inthralling, fascinating, piquant; *Also:*
1. **breezy**—interesting and light
2. **colorful**—interesting
3. **dateless**—of lasting interest
4. **engrossing**—absorbing; so interesting as to completely absorb one's attention
5. **glamorous**—such as to attract great interest; full of interest and charm; fascinating
6. **picturesque**—interesting
7. **racy**—spicy
8. **salty**—spicy
9. **spicy**—lively and interesting
10. **succulent**—interesting
11. **zestful**—full of interest and charm

3. Interest, i.e., Quality of Being Interesting,n. *From Sec. 1:* appeal, fascination, piquancy; *From Sec. 2:* breeziness, color or colorfulness, glamour or glamorousness, picturesqueness, raciness, salt or saltiness; spice, spiciness, or spicery; succulence, zest

4. To Make Interesting,v. *From Sec. 2:* glamorize, salt, spice; *Also:*
1. **flavor**—give an interesting flavor or atmosphere to
2. **romanticize**—invest with an atmosphere of romantic or attractive interest
3. **savor**—flavor
4. **season**—flavor

5. Ability to Arouse Interest: salt, savor, spice,n.

6. To Reawaken an Interest in: revive,v. (revival,n.)

7. A Reawakening of Interest in Religion: revival, revival of religion,n. (revivalism,n. revivalist,n.)

8. To Become Interested: perk up,v.

9. Keen and Happy Interest: élan,n. (French)

10. Figuratively Holding One's Breath in Interest: breathless,adj.

11. Object of Deep Interest: passion,n.

12. One's Subordinate Interest: avocation,n.

13. Sphere of Interest: scope,n.

581. INATTENTIVENESS

1. Inattentive; Not Paying Attention,adj.
1. **absent**—inattentive (*absent look,* etc.)
2. **absent-minded**—inattentive to one's environment or to what is happening around one
3. **abstracted**—inattentive; with one's thoughts diverted elsewhere; absent-minded
4. **bemused**—lost in thought
5. **deaf**—inattentive
6. **disregardful**—heedless
7. **distracted**—with the mind or attention drawn away
8. **distrait**—inattentive, often owing to worry, care, or anxiety; absent-minded
9. **giddy**—heedless
10. **harebrained**—heedless
11. **heedless (of)**—carelessly inattentive (to)
12. **neglectful, negligent**—not showing proper or required attention
13. **oblivious (of or to)**—inattentive (to); paying no attention (to)

14. **preoccupied**—inattentive because lost in thought
15. **scatterbrained**—inattentive; unable to concentrate
16. **thoughtless (of)**—carelessly inattentive; heedless (of)
17. **unaware (of)**—heedless (of)
18. **unconscious (of)**—inattentive (to)
19. **unmindful (of)**—heedless (of)
20. **woolgathering**—lost in daydreams, fancying, or idle thought; absent-minded

2. Inattentiveness; Inattention,n. *From Sec. 1:* absentness, absent-mindedness, abstractedness or abstraction, bemusement, deafness, disregardfulness, distractedness or distraction, heedlessness, obliviousness or oblivion, preoccupation, thoughtlessness, unawareness, unconsciousness, unmindfulness; *Also:* 1. inadvertence—inattentiveness

3. Inattentive Person,n. *From Sec. 1:* scatterbrain, woolgatherer

4. To Make or Become Carelessly Inattentive: giddy,v.

5. Done through Inattentiveness: inadvertent,adj.

6. To Pay No Attention to; To Ignore,v.
1. **blink at**—ignore
2. **by-pass**—ignore; ignore (rules, laws, etc.) to reach a goal
3. **cushion**—ignore (a complaint, etc.)
4. **cut**—snub
5. **disregard**—pay no attention to; take no notice of; ignore (disregard, disregardance,n. disregardant,adj.)
6. **miss**—fail to see
7. **neglect**—pay no attention to (neglect,n.)
8. **ostracize**—totally ignore (a person), as if he did not exist, thus cutting him off from all human relationships—said when a group so acts (ostracism, ostracization, n.)
9. **overlook**—pay no attention to; miss
10. **override**—disregard the feelings or wishes of (overriding,adj.)
11. **pretermit**—let pass without paying attention to; overlook (pretermission,n.)
12. **ride roughshod over**—disregard the feelings or wishes of in a harsh or domineering manner
13. **shrug off**—pay no attention to; ignore as unimportant
14. **skip**—neglect; fail to see, notice, or do
15. **slight**—pay little or no attention to; ignore
16. **slur over**—pass over without due attention or regard
17. **snub**—discourteously ignore (a person or his friendly overtures)
18. **wink at**—ignore; overlook

7. One Who Pays No Attention, or Who Ignores,n. *From Sec. 6:* disregarder, neglecter or neglector, overlooker, pretermitter, snubber

8. Inattention; Instance of Inattention,n. *From Sec. 6:* cut, disregard, neglect, ostracism, slight, slur, snub

9. State of Being Ignored,n. *From Sec. 6:* ostracism; *Also:* 1. coventry—ostracism

10. Someone Ostracized by Society: castaway, outcast, pariah,n.

11. To Publicize Someone's Name as Unworthy of Employment, or of Acceptance into a Group: blacklist,v.

12. Organized Movement to Refuse to Have Business Dealings or Social Relations with: boycott,n. (boycott,v.)

13. Capable of Being Disregarded: negligible, adj. (negligibility,n.)

14. To Act, or Continue to Act, in Total Disregard of, or of the Feelings or Wishes of:

override, ride roughshod over,v. (overriding, adj.)

15. To Draw (Someone's) Attention Away: abstract, distract,v. (distraction,n.)

16. That Which Draws Someone's Attention Away: distraction,n.

17. Device to Draw Attention Away from an Issue: red herring,n.

582. NEGLECT

1. To Neglect,v.
1. **by-pass**—neglect (rules, laws, etc.) to reach a goal
2. **default**—neglect to do something required; neglect to make a required payment
3. **disregard**—neglect to notice, consider, or pay attention to
4. **omit**—neglect (to do)
5. **overlook**—neglect, as if by not seeing
6. **pretermit**—neglect; overlook
7. **slight**—neglect
8. **violate**—neglect to do or perform (what is required or has been promised)

2. Neglect; Act of Neglecting,n. *From Sec. 1:* default, disregard or disregardance, omission, pretermission, violation; *Also:*
1. **breach**—neglect
2. **defection**—neglect of duty
3. **dereliction**—neglect of duty
4. **misprision**—neglect of duty
5. **non-feasance**—neglect to do what should have been done, or omission of duties that should have been performed (said chiefly of public or other officials)
6. **oversight**—neglect to notice or think of something

3. Neglectful; Neglecting,adj. *From Sec. 1:* defaultant, disregardful or disregardant, omissive, violative; *From Sec. 2:* derelict; *Also:*
1. **delinquent**—neglectful of duty; neglectful in one's payments
2. **lax**—neglectful
3. **negligent**—neglectful
4. **remiss**—neglectful; neglectful in one's duty

4. Neglectfulness; Neglect,n. *From Sec. 3:* disregardfulness; delinquency, laxness or laxity, negligence, remissness

5. Neglector; One Who Neglects or Is Neglectful,n. *From Sec. 1:* defaulter or defaultant, disregarder, overlooker, pretermitter, violator; *From Sec. 2:* derelict, non-feasor; *From Sec. 3:* delinquent

6. State or Condition of Neglect,n.
1. **dilapidation**—state of such complete neglect that decay or a falling apart has set in (of places, buildings, things, etc.)
2. **limbo**—condition of complete neglect

7. Neglected: dilapidated, unkempt,adj.

8. Capable of Being Neglected: negligible, adj. (negligibility,n.)

583. UNINTERESTING

1. Uninteresting; Dull; Boring,adj.
1. **arid**—totally without interest (aridity,n.)
2. **boresome**—boring
3. **bromidic**—totally lacking in interest; dull
4. **characterless**—uninteresting (characterlessness,n.)
5. **cloying**—boring, owing to excess, even though originally pleasurable
6. **colorless**—uninteresting; dull (colorlessness,n.)
7. **commonplace**—lacking in interest (commonplaceness,n.)

8. **drab**—dull; monotonous (drabness,n.)
9. **dry**—totally without interest (dryness,n.)
10. **flat**—uninteresting, often because of lack of change or variety (flatness,n.)
11. **hackneyed**—stale
12. **humdrum**—totally lacking in interest
13. **insipid**—uninteresting or dull, as if without flavor (insipidity, insipidness,n.)
14. **interminable**—uninteresting and seemingly without end (interminability, interminableness,n.)
15. **lifeless**—lacking in any qualities or aspects that might interest (lifelessness,n.)
16. **monotonous**—boringly unchanging or lacking in variety (monotony, monotonousness,n.)
17. **moth-eaten**—trite
18. **musty**—stale (mustiness,n.)
19. **platitudinous**—dull, flat, and insipid in language; dull; insipid (platitude,n.)
20. **plebeian**—commonplace
21. **poky**—dull; boring
22. **prosaic**—totally or tediously lacking in interest (prosaism, prosaicness,n.)
23. **prosy**—dull; boring; unexciting (prosiness,n.)
24. **spiritless**—dull
25. **stale**—uninteresting because old or old-fashioned; lacking in interest (staleness, n.)
26. **stereotyped**—stale; trite
27. **stodgy**—uninteresting; lacking in interest; dull (stodginess,n.)
28. **stuffy**—devoid of interest or sparkle; dull (stuffiness,n.)
29. **tame**—dull (tameness,n.)
30. **tedious**—boring (tedium, tediousness,n.)
31. **threadbare**—stale; trite (threadbareness, n.)
32. **tiresome**—boring (tiresomeness,n.)
33. **trite**—no longer interesting (triteness,n.)
34. **unexciting**—uninteresting; lacking in any spark of interest
35. **vapid**—dull (vapidity, vapidness,n.)
36. **wearisome, wearying**—boring (wearisomeness,n.)
37. **well-worn**—stale; trite
38. **wooden**—dull (woodenness,n.)

2. Bore; That Which Is Uninteresting or Dull,n. *From Sec. 1:* bromide, commonplace, platitude, stereotype

3. Dull, Uninteresting, or Boring Person: bore, bromide,n.

4. Bores, Collectively: boredom,n.

5. Boring Routine of Living or Working: treadmill,n.

6. To Make Uninteresting, Owing to the Passage of Time: stale,v.

7. To Bore,v.
1. **cloy (on)**—bore by an excess of a good thing or of a pleasure
2. **pall (on)**—become boring (to) owing to excessiveness
3. **tire, weary**—bore completely

8. Bored; Uninterested,adj.
1. **apathetic**—lacking in interest; totally uninterested
2. **blasé**—bored with conventional or normal pleasures, owing to overindulgence
3. **detached**—uninterested
4. **ennuyé (French)**—suffering from a feeling of general boredom, dissatisfaction, and lack of interest
5. **incurious**—lacking normal human interest or curiosity
6. **indifferent**—uninterested
7. **jaded**—completely bored by monotony, or by the monotony of good things
8. **languid**—uninterested; totally without interest
9. **languorous**—languid
10. **lassitudinous**—languid
11. **lethargic**—apathetic

12. **listless**—uninterested, bored and tired; lacking in interest owing to fatigue
13. **lukewarm**—showing no great interest
14. **perfunctory**—uninterested
15. **pococurante**—uninterested
16. **tired of**—completely bored with
17. **unconcerned**—uninterested
18. **weary of**—tired of
19. **world-weary**—bored with material or worldly pleasure, or because of overindulgence in these

9. **Boredom; State of Being Uninterested,**n. *From Sec. 8:* apathy, detachment, ennui, incuriosity, indifference, jadedness, languidness, languor or languorousness, lassitude, lethargy, listlessness, lukewarmness, perfunctoriness, pococurantism, unconcern, weariness, world-weariness; *Also:*
  1. **doldrums**—ennui; listlessness
  2. **taedium vitae (Latin)**—weariness of living
  3. **tedium**—complete boredom

10. **To Be Bored with,**v. *From Sec. 8:* tire of, weary of

11. **One Who Is Indifferent:** pococurante,n.

12. **Done as a Matter of Form Rather than Out of Real Interest:** mechanical, perfunctory,adj. (perfunctoriness,n.)

584. THE MIND

1. **The Mind; The Mental Faculties:** intellect, intelligence, mentality, psyche, wits,n.

2. **Of the Mind or Mental Faculties:** intellective, intellectual, mental, phrenic, psychic, psychical, psychologic, psychological,adj.

3. **Native or Inborn Mental Faculties:** mother wit,n.

4. **The Mind before It Has Received Any Impressions:** tabula rasa,n. (Latin)

5. **Pert. to, or Involving, Both Mind and Body:** psychosomatic,adj.

6. **Treatment of Physical Disease through an Understanding of the Relationship between Mind and Body and by the Application of Certain Psychological, Psychiatric, or Psychoanalytic Principles That Show the Influence of the Mind over the Body:** psychosomatic medicine, psychosomatics,n.

7. **Descr. of Such Mental Processes or Activities of Which One Is Aware:** conscious,adj. (consciousness,n.)

8. **Descr. of Such Mental Processes or Activities of Which One Is Unaware:** subconscious, subliminal, unconscious,adj. (subconsciousness, unconsciousness,n.)

9. **That Part of the Mind Containing Mental Experiences That Are Not at the Moment Conscious but That May Be Recalled to Consciousness:** the subconscious, the unconscious,n. (subconscious, unconscious,adj.)

10. **Mental Power:** intellectuality, intelligence, n.

11. **Power of Using the Mind:** intellect, mentality, wits,n.

12. **The Mental Life:** psyche,n.

13. **Originating in the Mind:** psychogenic, psychogenetic,adj.

14. **Happening in the Mind Rather than Being External:** subjective,adj. (subjectivity, subjectiveness,n.)

15. **Descr. of Mental Processes Influenced by, or Involved with, the Emotions:** subjective,adj. (subjectivity, subjectiveness,n.)

16. **Descr. of Mental Processes Not Influenced by Emotional Factors:** objective,adj. (objectivity, objectiveness,n.)

17. **Origin and Development of the Mind:** psychogenesis,n. (psychogenetic,adj.)

18. **To Invest with an Intellectual, Rather than Emotional, Attitude:** intellectualize,v. (intellectualization,n.)

19. **To Come into the Mind of:** occur to, strike,v.

20. **To Bring or Call to the Mind:** suggest,v. (suggestion,n. suggestive,adj.)

21. **Science of the Mind,**n.
  1. **nomology**—science of the laws of the mind (nomologist,n. nomological,adj.)
  2. **psychiatry**—medical science of the mind, its diseases, etc. (psychiatrist,n. psychiatric,adj.)
  3. **psychoanalysis**—science, based on Sigmund Freud's principles, that explores patterns of emotional thinking and the influence of the unconscious, etc., on actions, feelings, behavior, etc. (psychoanalyst,n. psychoanalytic,adj.)
  4. **psychobiology**—science of the relationship between mental and biological processes (psychobiologist,n. psychobiological, adj.)
  5. **psychogenetics**—science of the development of the mind or of mental traits
  6. **psychology**—science of the mind and mental processes (psychologist,n. psychological,adj.)

22. **Study of the Mind and Emotions:** psychognosis,n. (psychognostic,adj.)

23. **Description or Analysis of a Person's Mental Traits, Their Development, Functioning, etc.:** psychography,n. (psychographer,n. psychographic,adj.)

24. **Mental Testing; Measurement of the Speed and Accuracy of the Mental Processes:** psychometrics, psychometry,n. (psychometrist,n. psychometric, psychometrical, adj.)

25. **The Opinion That Introspection into the Conscious Processes of the Mind Is the Proper Province of, or Field of Investigation for, Psychology; Philosophical Doctrine That the Mind Is the Ultimate or Basic Reality; Any Philosophical Doctrine That Claims a Distinction between the Processes of the Mind and the Activity of the Brain That Accompanies Such Processes:** mentalism,n. (mentalist,n. mentalistic,adj.)

26. **One Who Claims the Power of Reading the Mind or Thoughts of Others:** mentalist, mind reader,n. (mind reading,n.)

27. **Art or Process of Curing Bodily Ailments through Hypnotism, or through Influencing the Mind of the One Afflicted:** mental healing, mind healing,n. (mental healer, mind healer,n.)

585. THOUGHT

1. **To Think; To Engage in Mental Activity,** v.
  1. **advert to**—turn the mind to
  2. **analyze**—separate the parts or factors of in the mind
  3. **anticipate**—give thought to beforehand, or before the proper time
  4. **attend**—give thought and care to
  5. **bethink oneself (of or that)**—think (of or that); give thought (to)
  6. **brood (on or about)**—dwell (on) in thought, often moodily or unhappily, and for a long period of time; think continuously of one's misfortunes, unhappiness, or troubles
  7. **cerebrate, cerebrize**—think; engage in thinking
  8. **cogitate (on or upon)**—think; think

over; turn over in the mind; give thought (to)

9. **conceive**—form, work out, or devise in the mind; think; suppose
10. **conclude**—have a mental reaction as a result of thinking, analyzing, reasoning, etc.
11. **consider**—think; give thought to; turn over in one's mind; suppose
12. **contemplate**—give extended thought to; dwell on in the mind; study
13. **cudgel one's brains (over)**—expend effort in thinking (about); think hard (about)
14. **debate**—consider, or turn over in one's mind, the pros and cons of, before coming to a decision or conclusion
15. **decide**—come to a conclusion as a result of thinking
16. **deduce, deduct**—arrive at a conclusion through reasoning
17. **deem**—think
18. **deliberate**—consider in the mind; think out or over with care
19. **entertain**—receive, consider, and/or keep in the mind, as *entertain a hope, notion, fear, grudge,* etc.
20. **excogitate**—think out
21. **introspect**—think about one's own inner mental processes
22. **mark**—consider, as *mark my words,* etc.
23. **meditate (about, on, or over)**—give deep thought (to); engage in deep thinking
24. **mull (over)**—think about; turn over in the mind; ponder
25. **muse (on, about, or over)**—think (about); meditate; think (about) dreamily
26. **ponder, ponder about, ponder on, ponder over**—consider the pros and cons of; meditate
27. **pore on**—think about deeply
28. **premeditate**—consider or turn over in the mind beforehand
29. **puzzle over**—think hard about
30. **ratiocinate**—think exactly
31. **reason**—use various mental processes or types of thinking to reach a conclusion or decision
32. **reckon**—think; consider
33. **reflect**—think; think carefully
34. **retrospect**—think back; think about the past
35. **revolve**—turn over in the mind (some problem, question, etc.)
36. **ruminate**—think; think carefully; engage in deep thought; turn over in the mind
37. **speculate (about or on)**—engage in thought not necessarily based on facts; think (about something in all its aspects)
38. **study**—think carefully about; give close or deep thought or thinking to; apply oneself mentally for the purpose of learning
39. **suppose**—think probable; think reasonable, or in accord with truth, reality, or facts
40. **take account of**—consider
41. **theorize**—speculate
42. **view**—give thought to
43. **weigh**—think about; give thought to before deciding; turn over carefully in the mind the possibilities of
44. **wonder about**—think about

2. Thought; Act or Process of Thinking,n. *From Sec. 1:* analysis, anticipation, attention, cerebration, cogitation; conception (from *conceive*); conclusion, consideration, contemplation, debate, decision, deduction, deliberation, entertainment, excogitation, introspection, meditation, premeditation, ratiocination, reflection, retrospection, rumination, speculation, study, supposition, theorization or theorism

3. A Thought; Result of Thinking,n. *From Sec. 1:* concept (from *conceive*), conclusion,

decision, deduction, reflection, rumination, speculation, supposition, theory; *Also:*

1. **afterthought**—thought that comes too late to be used; later thought
2. **idea**—thought
3. **sentiment**—emotional thought

4. Thoughtful; Engaged in Thought; Given to Thinking, etc.,adj. *From Sec. 1:* analytic or analytical, attentive, brooding, cogitative, contemplative, introspective, meditative, musing, reasoning, reflective, restrospective, ruminative or ruminant, studious, sentimental (attentiveness, cogitativeness, contemplativeness, introspectiveness, meditativeness, reflectiveness, studiousness; *From Sec. 3:* sentimentality,n.); *Also:*

1. **bemused**—lost in dreamy thought or thinking
2. **pensive**—seriously and/or sadly thoughtful; dreamily or musingly thoughtful (pensiveness,n.)
3. **preoccupied**—lost in thought (preoccupation,n.)
4. **wistful**—pensive (wistfulness,n.)

5. Pert. to, or Descr. of, Thinking or Thought,adj. *From Sec. 1:* analytic or analytical, anticipatory or anticipant; cerebrational, cerebrative, or cerebral; cogitative; conceptive, conceptual or conceptional; deductive, deliberative, introspective, premeditative, ratiocinative, reflective, restrospective, ruminative, speculative, theoretic or theoretical; *From Sec. 3:* ideational, sentimental; *Also:*

1. **intellectual**—pert. to, or descr. of, thinking or reasoning
2. **objective**—descr. of thinking or reasoning uninfluenced by emotional factors
3. **subjective**—pert. to, or descr. of, the thoughts or of thinking; descr. of thinking or reasoning colored by emotional involvement

6. Capable of Thinking: cogitative, reasoning,adj.

7. Incapable of Thinking: unreasoning,adj.

8. Able to Think Quickly in Difficult Circumstances: resourceful,adj. (resourcefulness,n.)

9. Able to Think of Only One Thing at a Time: single-track,adj.

10. Inability to Think or Act: trance,n.

11. Area of Thinking in Which One Is Unable to Exercise Judgment: blind spot,n.

12. State of Absorption in Thought: brown study,n.

13. Spontaneous and Uncontrolled Association of Loosely Linked Thoughts or Ideas: free association,n.

14. Meditation While Contemplating the Navel (a Practice of Certain Mystics): omphaloskepsis,n.

15. Dreamy Thinking; State of Dreamy Thinking: reverie, revery,n.

16. Combination of Thinking and Feeling: sentiment,n.

17. Verbalized, or Partially Verbalized, Thinking: stream of consciousness,n.

18. Thinking as Opposed to Doing: theory,n.

19. Pathologically Rapid Mental Activity: tachyphrenia,n. (tachyphrenic,adj.)

20. A Pondering about Death: thanatopsis,n.

21. Under Careful Consideration: under advisement

22. Way of Thinking about Things: view,n.

23. More Given to Thinking or Other Mental Activities than to Physical Activities: intellectual,adj. (intellectual,n. intellectualism, n.)

24. To Arouse Thought (in): suggest (to),v.

25. Carefully Considered or Thought about: advised,adj.

26. Thought of, but Not Yet in Actual Existence: theoretic, theoretical,adj.

27. Commonly Thought: putative,adj.

28. Able to Be Grasped by the Mind: tangible,adj. (tangibility,n. intangible, intangibility,neg.)

29. Able to Be Pictured in the Mind: conceivable,adj. (inconceivable,neg.)

30. To Stop Thinking about: dismiss,v. (from the mind, thoughts, etc.)

586. IDEA

1. An Idea,n.
1. **abstraction**—abstract, theoretical, or visionary idea
2. **archetype**—original idea
3. **brain storm**—sudden and ingenious or inspired idea
4. **bubble**—deceptively sound idea that eventually bursts into nothing
5. **caprice, capriccio**—foolish idea that arises from no rational or apparent motivation
6. **castle in the air, castle in Spain**—visionary and impractical idea
7. **chimera, chimaera**—frightening but totally unrealistic idea or fancy; absurd or wildly foolish idea
8. **conceit**—quaint, affected, or artificial idea; foolish idea
9. **concept, conception**—idea
10. **construct**—complicated idea or image put together in the mind
11. **crank, crinkum-crankum**—odd and foolish idea
12. **crotchet**—odd and foolish idea; quaint or strange idea
13. **fallacy**—false idea; misleading and foolish idea
14. **fancy**—pictured idea; idea; foolish idea; idea with no foundation in fact
15. **fantasy**—product of the imagination; misleading idea
16. **idée fixe (French)**—fixed idea; obsession
17. **image**—idea; pictured idea
18. **impression**—vague or indistinct idea
19. **inspiration**—sudden idea that is so good one feels it has come from heaven, divine influence, etc.
20. **maggot**—queer, foolish, quaint, or strange idea
21. **megrim**—odd and foolish idea
22. **notion**—idea; foolish idea
23. **obsession**—idea that constantly besets or haunts the mind or attention, and from which there seems no escape
24. **old wives' tale**—superstitious idea
25. **phantasm**—pictured idea; sensuous but vague idea
26. **phantasy**—pictured idea; fantasy
27. **preconception**—idea formed beforehand
28. **prenotion**—idea formed without actual experience; idea formed beforehand
29. **reverie, revery**—dreamy or impractical idea
30. **sally**—idea that expresses a flight of imagination
31. **stereotype**—idea showing no originality, creative thinking, etc.
32. **surmise**—idea based on little or insufficient evidence
33. **theory**—idea as opposed to a fact
34. **vacuity**—inane or foolish idea
35. **vagary, vagrancy**—irrational and illogical idea
36. **vapor**—empty idea
37. **view**—idea

38. **vision**—pictured idea
39. **whim, whimsey, whimsy**—quaint or strange idea
40. **wrinkle**—idea; foolish idea; clever new idea; useful idea

2. Descr. of, Pert. to, Containing, or Expressing, an Idea or Ideas,adj. *From Sec. 1:* archetypal, chimerical, conceptual, fallacious, fanciful, fantastic or fantastical, impressional, notional, obsessional, phantasmal, phantasmic or phantasmatic, prenotional, stereotyped, theoretic or theoretical, vagrant (from *vagary*), vaporous, visionary, whimsical (fallaciousness or fallacy, fancifulness or fancy, vagrancy, vaporousness, whimsicality, whimsey, or whimsy,n.); *Also:* **1. pregnant**—full of ideas; expressing significant ideas (pregnancy,n.)

3. Possessing an Idea or Ideas, or Full of Ideas (of People),adj. *From Sec. 1:* crotchety, fanciful, inspired, maggoty, notional, obsessed, visionary, whimsical (crotchetiness, fancifulness,n.); *Also:* **1. resourceful**—full of ideas for getting things done (resourcefulness, n.)

4. Expressing a Complexity of Ideas in a Single Word: holophrastic,adj.

5. Expressing Abstract Ideas: notional,adj.

6. Picture Ideas Formed in the Mind: imagery,n.

7. Series of Connected Ideas: train,n.

8. Group of Ideas and Unconscious Memories That, in Disguised Form, Have an Influence on the Personality: complex,n.

9. The Expression of Loosely Connected, or of Seemingly Unconnected, Ideas as They Occur to the Mind (during Psychoanalysis): free association,n. (free-associate,v.)

10. Existing Only in Ideas or As an Idea: notional, theoretic, theoretical,adj.

11. The Main Idea: burden, core, essence, gist, kernel, keynote, nub, purport, substance, sum, sum and substance,n.

12. To Form an Idea of: conceive of,v. (conception,n.)

13. To Form an Idea of Beforehand: preconceive,v. (preconception,n.)

14. To Form or Have Ideas: ideate,v. (ideation,n. ideational,adj.)

15. To Form in Idea: ideate,v. (ideation,n. ideational,adj.)

16. External Object of Which an Idea is Formed: ideate,n. (philosophy)

17. Ability of the Mind to Have Ideas: ideation,n. (ideational,adj.)

18. Power or Function of Receiving and Reproducing Sensuous Ideas: phantasy,n.

587. IMAGINATION

1. To Imagine: conceive, depicture, envisage, envision, fancy, fantasy, phantasy, picture, surmise, vision, visualize,v. (conception, visualization,n.)

2. To Imagine Beforehand: prefigure,v. (prefiguration,n. prefigurative,adj.)

3. Product of the Imagination: conceit, concept, conception, fancy, fantasy, phantasy, surmise, vision,n.

4. Derived from the Imagination: romantic,adj.

5. To Make Perceptible to the Imagination: visualize,v. (visualization,n.)

6. Imaginative; Possessing, Using, or Showing Imagination,adj.

1. **chimerical**—wildly imaginative (of ideas, thoughts, etc.)
2. **enterprising**—boldly imaginative (of people)
3. **fanciful**—imaginative (of people or things, ideas, etc.)
4. **forgetive**—imaginative (of people)
5. **poetical**—imaginative (of writing or writers)
6. **romantic**—imaginative (of people, ideas, writing, etc.)
7. **visionary**—imaginative, i.e., given to using the imagination

7. **Imaginativeness; Imagination,n.** *From Sec. 6:* enterprise, fancy or fancifulness, romanticism; *Also:*
   1. **sally**—clever imaginativeness
   2. **verve**—creative imaginativeness such as is found in an artist, poet, composer, etc.; clever imaginativeness

8. **Power of Imagining or of Seeing in the Imagination: vision,n.**

9. **Appealing to, or Stimulating, the Imagination: romantic,adj.** (romanticism,n.)

588. GUESS

1. **A Guess,n.**
   1. **conjecture**—a guess arrived at from flimsy evidence
   2. **hypothesis**—a guess rather than a known fact
   3. **speculation**—a guess made from insufficient or little evidence
   4. **surmise**—a guess arrived at on slight evidence and derived from intuition, imagination, etc.
   5. **suspicion**—a guess

2. **To Guess,v.** *From Sec. 1:* conjecture, hypothesize, speculate, surmise, suspect

3. **Pert. to, or Descr. of, a Guess or of Guessing,adj.** *From Sec. 1:* conjectural, hypothetical, speculative

4. **Act of Guessing; Something Arrived at by Guessing,n.** *From Sec. 1:* conjecture, speculation, surmise, suspicion; *Also:* guess, guesswork

589. REASONING

1. **To Reason; To Derive by Reasoning,v.**
   1. **analogize**—reason by similarities or comparisons
   2. **conclude**—derive or determine by reasoning; deduce
   3. **decide**—conclude; come to a conclusion
   4. **deduce, deduct**—reason out a specific application of a general principle
   5. **induce**—reason out a general principle from particular examples, facts, etc.
   6. **infer**—derive by reasoning; draw a conclusion from reasoning
   7. **paralogize**—reason falsely; draw conclusions not justified by the premises
   8. **philosophize**—reason like a philosopher
   9. **ratiocinate**—reason exactly
   10. **syllogize**—reason by drawing or applying a specific application from a general principle; reason by drawing a conclusion from a major and minor premise; reason subtly, speciously, or craftily

2. **Reasoning; Act or Process of Reasoning, n.** *From Sec. 1:* analogism, conclusion, decision, deduction, induction, inference, paralogism or paralogy, ratiocination, syllogization or syllogism; *Also:*
   1. **analysis**—reasoning
   2. **apriority**—reasoning from a general principle to a specific instance
   3. **argument, argumentation**—act or process of reasoning

4. **dianoetic**—discursive reasoning
5. **illation**—act of inferring

3. **Result or Instance of Reasoning,n.** *From Sec. 1:* analogism, conclusion, decision, deduction, inference, ratiocination; *From Sec. 2:* analysis, argument, illation; *Also:* 1. corollary —that which can be deduced or inferred from what has already been proved

4. **Descr. of, or Pert. to, Reasoning,** *adj.* *From Sec. 1:* deductive, inductive, inferential, paralogistic, ratiocinative, syllogistic; *From Sec. 2:* analytic or analytical, a priori, dianoetic, illative; *From Sec. 3:* corollary; *Also:* 1. rational—descr. of, or pert. to, reasoning

5. **Reasoner,n.** *From Sec. 1:* analogist, paralogist, ratiocinator, syllogist; *Also:*
   1. **dialectician**—reasoner
   2. **logician**—reasoner

6. **Pert. to Those Who Reason by Similarities or Comparisons: analogistic,adj.**

7. **Chain of Logical Reasoning: consecution, n.**

8. **Underlying or Basic Reasoning behind Something: rationale,n.**

9. **Explanation of the Supernatural, or That Which Appears to Be Supernatural, by Means of Reasoning: rationalism,n.** (rationalistic,adj.)

10. **Form of Logical Reasoning Consisting of Two Statements with a Conclusion Drawn from Them: syllogism,n.** (syllogistic, adj.)

11. **Proposition on Which Reasoning Is Based, or from Which a Conclusion Is Drawn: premise, premiss,n.**

12. **Based on Sound or Correct Reasoning: valid,adj.** (validity,n.)

13. **To Find the Reasoning behind: rationalize,v.** (rationalization,n.)

14. **To Cause to Conform to, or Be in Agreement with, Reasoning or Reason: rationalize,v.** (rationalization,n. rationalizer,n.)

15. **Science or Art of Reasoning,n.**
   1. **argumentation**—art of reasoning
   2. **dialectic, dialectics**—art of reasoning about opinions or theories; art of distinguishing truth from error through reasoning; logic (dialectician,n. dialectic, dialectical,adj.)
   3. **logic**—science of reasoning (logician,n. logical,adj.)
   4. **syllogistics**—branch of logic dealing with syllogisms; art of reasoning by means of syllogisms (syllogist,n. syllogistic,adj.)

16. **False Reasoning,n.**
   1. **casuistry**—reasoning that is false, though superficially logical or reasonable, in regard to morals, ethics, law, principles of behavior, etc.
   2. **fallacy**—reasoning that does not follow valid or formal principles
   3. **paralogism, paralogy**—reasoning that is contrary to the rules of logic
   4. **philosophism**—spurious reasoning
   5. **pseudosyllogism**—paralogism
   6. **sophism**—formal reasoning intended to deceive; reasoning containing a fallacy, whether deliberate or unconscious; apparently true but actually false reasoning; clever but misleading reasoning
   7. **sophistry, sophistic**—false, though seemingly true, reasoning

17. **False Reasoner,n.** *From Sec. 16:* casuist, paralogist, philosophist, sophist or sophister

18. **Descr. of, or Pert. to, False Reasoning,** adj. *From Sec. 16:* casuistic or casuistical, fallacious, paralogistic, philosophistic or philosophistical; sophistic, sophistical, or vermiculate

19. Instance of False Reasoning,n. *From Sec. 16:* fallacy, paralogism or paralogy, philosophism, pseudosyllogism, sophism, sophistry

20. False Premise on Which Reasoning Is Built: fallacy,n.

21. Error in Reasoning of Considering that What Follows in Time Is a Result or Effect: post hoc propter hoc fallacy,n. (logic)

590. REASONABLENESS

1. Reasonable: justifiable, legitimate, logical, moderate, philosophical, rational, sane, sensible, sound, temperate, valid,adj. (justifiability, legitimacy; logic, logicality or logicalness; moderateness, rationality, sanity, sensibleness, soundness, temperateness, validity,n.)

2. Seemingly Reasonable: plausible,adj. (plausibility, plausibleness,n.)

3. That Which Is Seemingly Reasonable: plausibility,n.

4. To Make Reasonable: moderate, temper, v. (moderation,n.)

5. Logically Connected: coherent,adj. (coherence, coherency,n.)

591. UNREASONABLENESS

1. Unreasonable: absonant, excessive, exorbitant, extravagant, illegitimate, illogical, immoderate, inordinate, intemperate, invalid, irrational, nonsensical, senseless, unconscionable, unjustifiable, unsound,adj. (excessiveness, exorbitance or exorbitancy, extravagance, illegitimacy; illogic, illogicality, or illogicalness; immoderateness, inordinateness, intemperateness, invalidity, irrationality, nonsensicality, senselessness, unjustifiability, unsoundness,n.)

2. Not Sounding or Seeming Reasonable: implausible,adj. (implausibility, implausibleness,n.)

3. That Which Does Not Sound or Seem Reasonable: implausibility,n.

4. That Which Is Devoid of Reason: nonsense,n.

5. Statement or Conclusion That Does Not Follow Logically; Conclusion That Does Not Reasonably Result from the Premise: non sequitur,n. (Latin)

6. Not Logically Following: farfetched, illogical, inconsequential,adj.

7. Not Logically Connected: disconnected, disjointed, incoherent, irrational, skimbleskamble,adj. (disconnectedness, disjointedness, incoherence or incoherency, irrationality,n.)

592. DECISION

1. To Decide,v.
  1. adjudge—decide by law
  2. adjudicate—decide by law; render a judicial decision on (adjudicative,adj.)
  3. conclude—decide
  4. determine—decide firmly
  5. judge—decide by hearing the facts, various sides or opinions, etc.
  6. overrule—decide against
  7. prearrange—decide beforehand
  8. predetermine—decide beforehand
  9. resolve—decide; decide firmly
  10. rule—decide officially
  11. settle—decide
  12. will—use the power of the mind to make decisions

2. Decision; Act of Deciding,n. *From Sec. 1:* adjudication or adjudicature, conclusion, determination, judgment, prearrangement, predetermination, resolution or resolve, settlement

3. A Decision,n. *From Sec. 1:* adjudication, conclusion, judgment, resolve or resolution, ruling; *Also:*
  1. oracle—wise or divine decision (oracular, adj.)
  2. verdict—decision; decision by judge or jury

4. One Who Decides or Makes or Gives a Decision,n. *From Sec. 1:* adjudicator, judge; *From Sec. 3:* oracle (oracular,adj.)

5. Decided Beforehand: destined, prearranged, predetermined,adj.

6. To Take a Decisive Step, or Make a Decision, That Is Irrevocable or Unalterable: cross the Rubicon,v.

7. Able to Decide, or Come to a Decision, Quickly and without Doubt or Hesitation: crisp, decisive, resolute,adj. (decisiveness or decision, resoluteness or resolution,n.)

8. Capable of Deciding, i.e., Bringing on a Definite Decision, in a Contest, Dispute, Area of Doubt, etc.: conclusive, decisive, peremptory,adj. (conclusiveness, decisiveness, peremptoriness,n.)

9. Power of the Mind to Make Decisions: will,n.

10. Firm and Unyielding in Decision: resolute, unbending,adj. (resoluteness,n.)

11. State of Decision: volition,n. (volitional, adj.)

12. Decided by a Judge or Authority: arbitrary,adj.

593. COMPREHENSION

1. To Understand,v.
  1. apperceive—understand fully; assimilate new ideas with those already held
  2. apprehend—understand the meaning or significance of
  3. assimilate—understand and then absorb
  4. comprehend—understand mentally or intellectually only, rather than emotionally or intuitively
  5. conceive of—understand; understand through mental activity
  6. conclude—come to an understanding through reasoning or the use of various mental processes
  7. construe—understand a meaning from; arrive at an understanding of the meaning of
  8. decipher—arrive at an understanding of the meaning of (illegible, obscure, or secret writing)
  9. digest—understand and then absorb
  10. discern—understand as if seeing through the mind's eye; understand fully; understand as a result of seeing or thinking about; understand distinctions
  11. divine—understand through intuition, feeling, or some means other than intellectual or logical reasoning
  12. fathom—understand by figuratively digging into, penetrating to the depths of, etc.
  13. grasp—understand as if seizing with the mind
  14. infer—understand by reasoning
  15. interpret—arrive at an understanding of the meaning of
  16. intuit—understand not from reasoning but from some mysterious emotional power; apprehend directly
  17. judge—arrive at an understanding of

18. **penetrate**—understand as if seeing into the deepest meanings of
19. **perceive**—understand; gain understanding through the mind, or through seeing, hearing, or any of the senses
20. **realize**—understand fully or vividly
21. **seize**—understand; grasp with the mind

2. Understanding,n. *From Sec. 1:* apperception, apprehension, assimilation, comprehension, conception, conclusion, construction, decipherment, discernment, divination, grasp, inference, interpretation, intuition, judgment, penetration, perception or percipience, realization; *Also:*
1. **acumen**—keen understanding combined with penetrating judgment
2. **grip**—understanding; mental grasp or hold
3. **illation**—inference
4. **impression**—understanding
5. **inkling**—very vague or slight understanding
6. **insight**—understanding into the deepest meanings of something; understanding through some mysterious emotional power
7. **noesis**—exclusively intellectual understanding (philosophy)
8. **notion**—understanding
9. **prehension**—understanding
10. **subreption**—understanding drawn from a deliberate falsification or misrepresentation
11. **sympathy**—mutual understanding arising from similar attitudes, interests, experiences, etc.
12. **theosophy**—special insight (or claim to special insight) into the nature of God
13. **wit**—understanding

3. Understanding,adj. *From Sec. 1:* apperceptive, apprehensive, comprehensive, discerning, intuitive, penetrating or penetrative, perceptive or percipient (apprehensiveness, comprehensiveness, intuitiveness or intuitivism; perceptiveness, percipience or percipiency) ; *From Sec. 2:* acute, sympathetic; *Also:* 1. **perspicacious**—having a keen understanding; discerning (perspicacity, perspicaciousness,n.)

4. Pert. to, or Descr. of, Understanding,adj. *From Sec. 1:* apperceptive; conceptive, conceptual, or conceptional; constructive or constructional, inferential; interpretive, interpretative, or interpretational; intuitive or intutional; perceptive, perceptual, or perceptional; *From Sec. 2:* illative, theosophic or theosophical

5. One Who Understands,n. *From Sec. 1:* apprehender, comprehender, construer, diviner, interpreter, judge, percipient (from *perceive*)

6. That Which Is Understood,n. *From Sec. 1:* concept (from *conceive*), inference, percept; *From Sec. 2:* illation

7. Belief in Spiritual Insight: mysticism,n. (mystic,n. mystic, mystical,adj.)

8. Belief in Special Insight into the Nature of God: theosophism,n. (theosophist,n.)

9. Range of Understanding: ken,n.

10. Great Breadth or Wide Range of Understanding: catholicity, catholicism,n. (catholic,adj.)

11. Quick to Understand: quick on the uptake (colloq.)

12. Slow to Understand: slow on the uptake (colloq.)

13. Generally Understood: accepted,adj. (of a meaning of a word or phrase)

14. To Misunderstand: misapprehend, miscomprehend, misconceive, misinterpret, misjudge,v.

15. Misunderstanding: misapprehension, miscomprehension, misconception, misintelligence, misinterpretation, misjudgment,n.

16. Capable of Being Misunderstood: ambiguous, misintelligible, misintrepretable,adj. (ambiguity or ambiguousness,n.)

17. To Understand a Wrong Meaning from: misconstrue, misinterpret,v. (misconstruction, misinterpretation,n. misconstructive,adj. misconstruable, misinterpretable,adj.)

594. INTELLIGENCE

1. Intelligent; Quick to Understand; Having a Keen or Quick Mind: acute, agile, alert, apt, astucious, astute, brainy, bright, brilliant, clever, discerning, incisive, intellectual, keen, keen-minded, knowledgeable, luminous, nimble, penetrating, penetrative, perceptive, percipient, perspicacious, quick-witted, rational, sagacious, sensible, sharp, sharp-minded, sharp-witted, shrewd, smart, subtle, trenchant, wide-awake,adj.

2. Intelligent, i.e., Showing Intelligence (of Attitudes, Actions, Mental Products, Writing, Reasoning, etc.): acute, astucious, astute, bright, brilliant, incisive, intellectual, keen, luminous, penetrating, penetrative, rational, sensible, sharp, shrewd, smart, subtle, thoughtful, trenchant,adj.

3. Intelligence, i.e., Quality of Possessing or Showing Intelligence: acuity, acumen, acuteness, agility, alertness, aptitude, aptness, astuteness, braininess, brightness, brilliance, brilliancy, cleverness, discernment, incisiveness, intellectuality, intellectualness, luminosity, luminousness, nimbleness, penetration, perception, perceptiveness, percipience, percipiency, perspicaciousness, perspicacity, quick-wittedness, rationality, sagaciousness, sagacity, sense, sensibleness, sharpness, sharp-wittedness, shrewdness, smartness, subtleness, subtlety, trenchancy, wit,n.

4. Quick in Learning: apt, quick,adj. (aptitude, aptness, quickness,n.)

5. Showing Unusual or Abnormal Intelligence for One So Young: precocious,adj. (precocity, precociousness,n.)

6. Extraordinarily Precocious Person: child prodigy, prodigy,n.

7. Mental Ability Achieved by Training or Education: accomplishment,n. (accomplished, adj.)

8. Sudden Display of Intellectual Brilliancy: coruscation,n.

9. Intelligent Person: intellectual,n.

10. Intellectuals as a Class: intelligentsia,n. (often derogatory)

11. Person of Delicate Wit and Graceful Mind: bel-esprit,n. (French)

12. Extraordinarily Intelligent Person: prodigy,n.

13. Certain Intelligence Tests,n.
1. **alpha test**—form of intelligence test
2. **beta test**—form of intelligence test not relying on use of language
3. **Binet test, Binet-Simon test**—intelligence test, originally devised for children, and used to determine intelligence quotient
4. **Stanford-Binet test**—adaptation of the original Binet test, used as an individual test on the pre-adult level

14. One's Intelligence Score, Determined by Standardized Tests, Expressed in Relation to One's Chronological Age: intelligence quotient, I.Q.,n.

595. CLEVERNESS; SHREWDNESS

1. Clever; Shrewd (of People),adj.
1. **artful**—clever; shrewd; cunning
2. **brainy**—clever
3. **bright**—clever
4. **cagey**—shrewd
5. **calculating**—shrewd
6. **canny**—shrewd about worldly things; skillfully clever
7. **crafty**—shrewd; cunning
8. **cunning**—shrewd; shrewd at deception or concealment
9. **cute**—clever; shrewd
10. **designing**—clever; shrewd; cunning
11. **diabolic**—fiendishly clever and evil
12. **discerning**—shrewd
13. **disingenuous**—meanly clever, shrewd, or cunning, though pretending simplicity or frankness
14. **foxy**—shrewd and sly, like a fox
15. **habile**—clever
16. **hardheaded**—shrewd and practical
17. **ingenious**—clever
18. **parlous**—dangerously clever or shrewd
19. **politic**—shrewd in doing or saying that which advances one's interests
20. **resourceful**—clever at devising new ways of doing things
21. **retiary**—clever at entangling or confusing
22. **sagacious**—shrewd
23. **slick**—clever; cunning
24. **sly**—trickily or deceptively clever; cunning
25. **smart**—clever
26. **subtile**—shrewd; cunning
27. **subtle**—shrewd; cunning; sly
28. **vulpine**—shrewd, like a fox
29. **wise**—shrewd; cunning

2. Clever or Shrewd, i.e., Showing Cleverness or Shrewdness on the Part of the Doer, Maker, or Performer,adj. *From. Sec. 1:* artful, cagey, canny, crafty, cunning, cute, diabolic, foxy, hardheaded, ingenious, politic, slick, sly, smart, subtile, subtle, vulpine, wise; *Also:*
1. **daedal**—formed or done cleverly
2. **deep-laid**—made with cleverness or cunning
3. **tricky**—showing cleverness

3. Cleverness; Shrewdness,n. *From Sec. 1:* artfulness, braininess, brightness, cageyness, calculation, canniness, craft or craftiness, cunning, cuteness, discernment, disingenuousness or disingenuity, foxiness, hardheadedness, ingenuity or ingeniousness, parlousness, resourcefulness, sagacity or sagaciousness, slickness, slyness, smartness; subtility, subtilty, or subtileness; subtlety or subtleness; *From Sec. 2:* trickiness; *Also:* 1. **wizardy**—great cleverness

4. Clever or Shrewd Person,n. *From Sec. 1:* fox; *From Sec. 3:* wizard

5. To Use Cleverness to Get Something, Achieve One's Ends, etc.: angle for,v. (angler, n.)

6. To Be Cleverer or Shrewder than: outsmart, outwit,v.

7. Lacking in Shrewdness or Cunning: artless, ingenuous, simple, simple-minded,adj. (ingenuousness,n.)

596. WISDOM

1. Wise (of People); Having or Showing Good Judgment (of People),adj.
1. **astute**—having sharp judgment
2. **deep**—wise
3. **discerning**—showing good judgment
4. **discreet**—showing good and cautious judgment
5. **discriminating**—showing the ability to make wise choices as between things of small though significant differences; showing the ability to make wise distinctions
6. **farsighted**—having good judgment
7. **judicious**—wise; possessing sound judgment
8. **levelheaded, coolheaded**—possessing good judgment
9. **omniscient**—infinitely wise
10. **pansophic, pansophical**—having all-inclusive wisdom
11. **perceptive**—having good intuitive judgment
12. **philosophical**—wise
13. **practical**—having good sense or judgment
14. **prudent**—wise or sensible in actions, conduct, etc.
15. **sagacious**—wise in a practical way; having keen and sensible judgment
16. **sage**—outstanding and profoundly wise; having wisdom that results from experience and meditation; having or showing good judgment
17. **sapient**—wise (sometimes used ironically)
18. **sensible**—wise; having or showing good judgment
19. **shrewd**—able to judge wisely in practical matters
20. **Solomonic**—very wise, like King Solomon of ancient Israel
21. **sophisticated**—worldly-wise
22. **subtle**—able to make keen or fine distinctions; keenly discerning
23. **well-balanced**—sensible
24. **worldly, worldly-wise**—wise in the ways of the world

2. Wise; Showing Wisdom or Good Judgment (of Actions, Attitudes, Mental Products, etc.),adj. *From Sec. 1:* astute, deep, discerning, discreet, discriminating, farsighted, judicious, levelheaded, coolheaded, philosophical, practical, prudent, sage, sensible, shrewd, Solomonic, sophisticated, subtle, worldly, worldly-wise; *Also:*
1. **advisable**—wise; sensible; prudent
2. **expedient**—dictated by practical wisdom, or by a feeling of the demands of a situation (often implying material or selfish motivation)
3. **oracular**—wise, as if given by a god (of statements, decisions, answers, etc.)
4. **politic**—expedient
5. **rational**—showing good judgment
6. **sound**—showing good judgment

3. Wisdom; Good Judgment,n. *From Secs. 1 and 2:* astuteness, depth, discernment, discretion or discreetness, discrimination, farsightedness, judiciousness, levelheadedness, coolheadedness, omniscience, pansophy, perceptiveness, prudence, sagacity or sagaciousness, sageness, sapience or sapiency, sense or sensibleness, shrewdness, sophistication, subtlety or subtleness, worldliness, worldly wisdom; advisability, expedience or expediency, oracularity, rationality, soundness; *Also:*
1. **acumen**—penetrating judgment combined with keen understanding
2. **common sense**—good judgment; judgment free from emotional prejudice; judgment not relying on intellectual cleverness or special or technical knowledge
3. **horse sense**—instinctive common sense; practical common sense (colloq.)
4. **judgment**—ability to make wise decisions or distinctions

4. Wise Person,n. *From Sec. 1:* philosopher, sage, Solomon, sophisticate, worldling; *Also:*
1. **Minerva**—woman of great wisdom
2. **solon**—wise man

5. Unwise,adj. *From Sec. 1:* undiscerning, indiscreet, undiscriminating; shortsighted (from *farsighted*); injudicious, imperceptive, impractical, imprudent, unsagacious; insipient (from *sapient*); senseless, unsophisticated, unworldly; *From Sec. 2:* inadvisable, inexpedient, impolitic, irrational, unsound; *Also:*

1. **foolish**—unwise
2. **ill-advised**—unwise; done, or acting, without sufficient thought or consideration
3. **misguided**—guided into unwise actions; showing unwise guidance
4. **obliquitous**—deviating from sound thinking
5. **unintelligent**—unwise

6. Unwisdom,n. *From Sec. 5:* indiscreetness or indiscretion, shortsightedness, injudiciousness, imperceptiveness, impracticality, imprudence, insipience, senselessness, unsophistication, unworldliness; inadvisability, inexpedience or inexpediency, irrationality, unsoundness; foolishness or folly, misguidedness, obliquity, unintelligence

7. Unwise Act: folly, indiscretion,n.

8. Unwise Person: fool,n.

9. Act, Action, etc., Dictated by Practical Wisdom: expedient,n. (expediential,adj.)

10. One Who Makes Use of, or Advocates the Use of, Expedients: expedientist,n.

11. Pretension or Claim to All-Inclusive Wisdom: pansophism,n. (pansophist,n.)

12. Pert. to Wisdom: Palladian,adj.

13. Goddess of Wisdom: Athena, Athene, Pallas, or Pallas Athena (Greek); Minerva (Roman),n.

597. STUPIDITY

1. Stupid: addlebrained, addleheaded, addlepated, anserine or anserous (like a goose), asinine (like an ass), beef-witted, beetleheaded, besotted, birdbrained, blockheaded, blockish, blunt, boneheaded, bovine (like a cow or ox), brainless, brutish, chuckleheaded, cloddish, clodpated, dense, dim, dim-witted, doltish, dull, dullard, dull-witted, dumb, duncelike, duncical, duncish, dunderheaded, empty-headed, empty-minded, empty-pated, empty-skulled, fatuitous, fatuous, featherbrained, feeble-minded, feeble-witted, half-witted, idiot, idiotic, imbecile, imbecilic, inane, incapacious, insipient, loggerheaded, lumpish, lunkheaded; mentally defective, deficient or retarded; moronic, muddleheaded, numskulled (colloq.), obtuse, opaque, purblind, rattlebrained, rattleheaded, rattlepated, rattleskulled, sapheaded, senseless, silly, simple, simple-headed, simple-minded, simple-witted, sotted, sottish, thick, thickbrained, thick-headed, thick-pated, thick-witted, thoughtless, unintelligent, vacant, vacuous, vapid, witless, wooden,adj.

2. Stupidity: addleheadedness, addlepatedness, asininity, beef-wittedness, bêtise (French), blockheadedness, blockheadism, blockishness, bluntness, boneheadedness, brainlessness, brutishness, chuckleheadedness, cloddishness, denseness, density, dimness, dim-wittedness, doltishness, dullardism, dullardness, dullness, dumbness, duncery, duncishness, dunderheadedness, empty-headedness, fatuity, fatuousness, feeble-mindedness, feeble-wittedness, half-wittedness, idiocy, idiotism, imbecility, incapacity, insipience, loggerheadedness, lumpishness, lunkheadedness, mental defectiveness or deficiency, misintelligence, moroncy, moronism, moronity, muddleheadedness; numskulledness, numskullery, numskullism (colloq.); obtuseness, opacity, opaqueness, purblindness, senselessness, silliness, simple-mindedness, simpleness, simplicity, sottishness, thickness, thickheaded-

ness, thick-wittedness, unintelligence, vacancy, vacuity, vacuousness, vapidity, vapidness, witlessness, woodenness,n.

3. Stupid Person: addlebrain, addlehead, addlepate, ass, beetlehead, block, blockhead, bonehead, boob, booby, chucklehead, clod, clodpate, dimwit, dolt, dullard, dumbbell, dummy, dunce, dunderhead, featherbrain, gaby, goose, half-wit, idiot, imbecile, jackass, loggerhead, loon, lunkhead, mental defective, moron, muddlehead; nitwit (colloq.); noddy, noodle, numskull or numbskull, rattlebrain, rattlehead, rattlepate, rattleskull, saphead; sap (slang); silly (colloq.); simpleton, swine, thickhead, thickskull, thickwit,n.

4. Stupid Act; Instance of Stupidity: asininity; bêtise (French); fatuity, idiocy, idiotism, imbecility, inanity, vapidity,n.

5. Anything Offensively Stupid: tripe,n. (slang)

6. Dull, or Lacking, in Understanding: blunt, dim, dim-witted, imperceptive, obtuse, opaque, purblind, witless,adj. (bluntness, dimness, dim-wittedness, imperceptiveness, obtuseness, opaqueness, opacity, purblindness, witlessness,n.)

7. Possessing, or Indicative of, a Mind That Does Not or Cannot Penetrate beneath the Surface, or That Has No Intellectual Depth: shallow,adj. (shallowness,n.)

8. Not Possessed of the Ability to Think Deeply: asinine, unthinking,adj. (asininity,n.)

9. Showing No Thinking or Intelligence: thoughtless,adj. (thoughtlessness,n.)

10. Indicative of a Lack of Intelligence (of a Stare, Look, Appearance, etc.): empty, vacant, vacuous, vapid, wooden,adj. (emptiness, vacancy, vacuity, vacuousness, woodenness,n.)

11. Stupid, but in a Complacent Manner, i.e., without Realization of One's Stupidity: fatuitous, fatuous,adj. (fatuity, fatuousness, n.)

12. Not Capable of Human Thinking or Reasoning: brute, brutish, unreasoning,adj.

13. Unintelligent and Coarse: crass,adj. (crassness,n.)

14. Stupid and Clumsy: gawky, loutish,adj. (gawkiness, loutishness,n.)

15. Stupid and Clumsy Person: blunderbuss, gawk, lout, lummox,n.

16. Person So Unintelligent that He Seems Like One Revived from Death: zombie,n. (colloq.)

17. Feeble-Minded Person, or One below Average in Mentality, from a Psychological or Medical Viewpoint,n.
1. **cretin**—person with deficient intelligence caused by absence or insufficiency of thyroid secretion—symptoms usually appear at the sixth month of life, and include apathy, protrusion of the tongue, thickening of features, prominence of abdomen, labored breathing, etc.
2. **defective**—person of subnormal intelligence
3. **high-grade moron**—moron of fairly close to normal intelligence, though by no means normal
4. **idiot**—one who is afflicted with so pronounced a degree of mental deficiency as to be unable to guard himself against physical danger; his intelligence is that of a two-year-old, his I.Q. under 25.
5. **idiot-savant, idiotic prodigy**—person of deficient intelligence who has, paradoxically, one or more special and unusually

developed faculties, perhaps for music, calculation, memory of certain categories, etc.

6. **imbecile**—person somewhat higher in the scale than an idiot, with an I.Q. between 25 and 50, and the intelligence of a five-year-old

7. **mental defective**—one who lacks normal intelligence

8. **Mongoloid, Mongoloid idiot, Mongolian** —mental defective of a special physical type, possessing facial similarities to individuals of the Mongolian race, though there is no scientific relationship (Mongolism is a congenital condition, probably caused by some unknown glandular disturbance. The Mongoloid child has typically slanting eyes, large tongue, and a broad, short skull. His life expectancy is short, few Mongoloids reaching adulthood.)

9. **moron**—person who is the most intelligent of the feeble-minded, with an I.Q. between 50 and 74 and the intelligence of a child of eight to twelve

10. **subnormal**—one of subnormal intelligence

18. **Feeble-Mindedness; Lack of Normal Intelligence,**n. *From Sec. 17:* cretinism, defectiveness, idiocy or idiotism, imbecility, mental defectiveness or deficiency, Mongolism or Mongolianism, moronism, moronity, or moroncy, subnormality; *Also:*
   1. **amentia**—term that encompasses idiocy, imbecility, moronity, and all other states in which deficient intelligence is prevalent from birth or the early months of existence
   2. **hebetude**—dullness of intellect
   3. **morosis**—moronity

19. **Feeble-Minded; Lacking in Normal Intelligence,**adj. *From Sec. 17:* cretinous, defective, idiot or idiotic, imbecile or imbecilic, mentally defective or deficient, Mongolian or Mongoloid, moronic, subnormal; *Also:* 1. **mentally retarded, retarded**—of subnormal intelligence

20. **To Make Stupid, i.e., Numb the Mental Faculties of,**v.
   1. **benumb**—stupefy
   2. **besot**—make stupid; stupefy with drink
   3. **blunt**—make slow of understanding; make stupid
   4. **daze**—stupefy with shock, surprise, a blow, etc.
   5. **dull**—make stupid
   6. **hebetate**—blunt (hebetation,n.)
   7. **sodden**—make stupid; dull mentally by dissipation, drinking, sexual excesses, etc.
   8. **stultify**—make stupid (stultification,n.)
   9. **stun**—cause to be unable to think
   10. **stupefy**—make stupid; daze; stun (stupefaction,n.)
   11. **torpify**—numb mentally; make mentally sluggish; stupefy

21. **In a Stupid or Stupefied Condition,**adj. *From Sec. 20:* benumbed, besotted, dazed, etc.; blunt, dull, sodden, torpid; *Also:*
   1. **groggy**—dazed
   2. **silly**—dazed (*knocked silly*, etc.)
   3. **sottish**—stupefied, as by alcoholic indulgence
   4. **supine**—in mental lethargy

22. **Stupid or Stupefied Condition,**n. *From Sec. 20:* bluntness, daze, dullness, soddenness, stultification, stupefaction or stupor; *From Sec. 21:* grogginess, sottishness, supineness

23. **Causing a Stupid or Dazed Condition:** stupefactive,adj.

24. **To Cause to Appear or Look Stupid:** stultify,v. (stultification,n.)

25. **Stupid-Looking:** sodden,adj. (soddenness,n.)

26. **Mentally Weak Owing to Advanced Age:** senile,adj.

27. **Mental Weakness of Old Age:** dotage, senility,n.

28. **One Who Is Mentally Weak from Old Age:** dotard,n.

598. CLARITY

1. **Clear in the Sense of Not Being Cloudy, Muddy, etc.:** cloudless, crystalline, limpid (often of water, air, crystal, etc.), lucent, lucid, pellucid, transparent,adj. (limpidity or limpidness, lucency or lucence, lucidity or lucidness, pellucidity or pellucidness, transparency or transparence,n.)

2. **Clear and Sharp, Usually of Weather, the Atmosphere, etc.:** crisp, crispy,adj. (crispness,n.)

3. **Clear and Bright; Clear and Calm:** serene,adj. (serenity,n.)

4. **Clear to the Senses:** palpable,adj. (palpability,n.)

5. **Clear to the Sight or Hearing,**adj.
   1. **articulate**—distinct
   2. **clarion**—clear and high-pitched in sound
   3. **clear-cut**—with clearly defined outlines; distinctly defined
   4. **conspicuous**—clear to the sight
   5. **decided**—clear-cut; definite
   6. **definite**—not vague; clearly defined
   7. **distinct**—clear to the eye or ear; clearly seen; clearly visible; clearly heard; clearly audible
   8. **evident**—clear to the eye
   9. **inescapable**—so clear to the sight that one cannot possibly miss it
   10. **lucent**—clear
   11. **manifest**—clear to the eye
   12. **obvious**—inescapably clear to the sight
   13. **plain**—clear to the sight or hearing
   14. **shrill**—clear and high-pitched in sound
   15. **unmistakable**—obvious
   16. **vivid**—clearly perceptible to the sight; clear and sharp

6. **Clearness or Clarity of Appearance or Sound,**n. *From Sec. 5:* articulateness, conspicuousness or conspicuity, decidedness, definiteness, distinctness, inescapableness, lucency or lucence, obviousness, plainness, shrillness, unmistakableness, vividness

7. **To Make or Become Clear:** clarify, clear, clear up,v. (clarification,n.)

8. **Clear to the Mind or Understanding; Clear in Meaning,**adj.
   1. **categorical**—explicit
   2. **clear-cut**—with no fuzziness or confusion, hence sharply clear to the mind
   3. **decided**—not vague; clear-cut
   4. **definite**—not vague
   5. **distinct**—clear to the mind
   6. **evident**—clear to the mind
   7. **explicit**—clear, distinct, and definite as to meaning, with no possibilities of confusion
   8. **graphic**—clear to the mind because presenting, or making one able to visualize, pictures, imagery, action, etc.; clear in detail
   9. **inescapable**—so clear to the mind that one cannot possibly miss it
   10. **limpid**—free from obscurity
   11. **lucid, lucent, luculent**—clear to the understanding; not confused
   12. **luminous**—clear to the understanding
   13. **manifest**—clear to the understanding
   14. **obvious**—inescapably clear to the understanding
   15. **palpable**—obvious

16. **pellucid**—extremely clear to the understanding
17. **perspicuous**—clear to the understanding
18. **plain**—clear to the understanding
19. **precise**—lacking any hint of vagueness or indefiniteness, hence sharply clear to the understanding
20. **simple**—clear to the understanding
21. **specific**—not vague
22. **tangible**—not vague
23. **transparent**—perfectly clear to the understanding
24. **trenchant**—sharply clear to the understanding; clear-cut; showing clear thinking on the part of the person who presents an argument, analysis, piece of writing, etc.
25. **unambiguous**—clear in meaning; lacking in any possibility of being misunderstood
26. **understandable**—clear to the understanding
27. **unequivocal**—clear in meaning
28. **unmistakable**—clear; obvious
29. **vivid**—sharp and clear, so that a strong impress is made on the mind

9. Clearness or Clarity,n. *From Sec. 8:* decidedness, definiteness, distinctness, explicitness, inescapableness, limpidity or limpidness, lucidity or lucidness, lucency or lucidness, luculence, luminosity or luminousness, obviousness, palpability, pellucidity or pellucidness, perspicuity or perspicuousness, plainness, precision or preciseness, simplicity, specificity, tangibility or tangibleness, transparency or transparence, trenchancy, unambiguity or unambiguousness, understandability, unequivocalness, unmistakableness, vividness

10. To Make Clear or Clearer; To Eliminate or Reduce the Confusion or Obscurity of,v.
1. **clarify**—make clear or clearer (clarification,n.)
2. **clear up**—clarify
3. **elucidate**—make clear by explaining; make clear by giving examples, illustrations, etc. (elucidation,n.)
4. **expound**—clarify the meaning of
5. **illuminate, illumine**—make clear by figuratively throwing more light upon (illumination,n.)
6. **illustrate**—clarify by giving examples (illustration,n.)
7. **ravel, ravel out**—make clear, as if by removing the tanglement of meaning
8. **resolve**—clear up (problems, confusions, mysteries, etc.) ; make (mysteries, riddles, etc.) clear (resolution,n.)
9. **solve**—clear up (solution,n.)
10. **uncloud**—clear from vagueness or obscurity
11. **unravel**—clear up (a mystery, puzzle, problem, confusion, etc.) as if by unwinding the parts (unravelment,n.)
12. **untangle**—clear up (a mystery, etc.) by straightening out the confusion or tanglement
13. **vivify**—make sharp and clear to the mind, or make capable of producing a clear and strong impression on the mind or imagination (vivification,n.)

11. To Become Clear or Clearer to the Mind, etc.,v. *From Sec. 10:* clarify, clear or clear up, resolve, uncloud, unravel (clarification, resolution, unravelment,n.) ; *Also:* 1. **dawn on**—become clear to

12. Clarifying: elucidative, illuminating, illuminative, illustrative, luciferous, vivifying, adj.

13. Evident: apparent, clear, manifest, obvious, palpable, patent, plain, transparent, unmistakable,adj. (apparentness, obviousness, palpability, patency, transparency, unmistakableness,n.)

14. **Evident without Proof:** axiomatic, axiomatical, self-evident,adj. (self-evidence,n.)
15. **Relating to, Descr. of, or Concerned Only with, What Is Obvious or Apparent:** superficial,adj. (superficiality,n.)
16. **Understandable; Easy to Understand; Easily Understood:** apprehensible, clear, comprehensible, conceivable, fathomable, intelligible, lucent, lucid, luculent, luminous, obvious, pellucid, perspicuous, plain, rational, simple,adj. (apprehensibility, clarity or clearness, comprehensibility, conceivability or conceivableness, intelligibility, lucency or lucence, lucidity or lucidness, luculence, luminosity or luminousness, obviousness, pellucidity or pellucidness, perspicuity or perspicuousness, plainness, rationality, simplicity,n.)
17. **Capable of Being Understood, though Some of the Letters or Words May Be Hard to Make Out (of Writing):** decipherable,adj.
18. **Understandable by the General Public, That Is, by Those Who Have No Special Information, Training, etc.:** exoteric,adj. (exotericism,n.)
19. **Understandable without Further Explanation:** self-explanatory,adj.
20. **Easy to Understand, though an Effort Is Made at Concealment or Disguise (of Motives, Attitudes, etc.):** transparent,adj. (transparency,n.)
21. **Not Capable of Being Misunderstood:** unmistakable,adj. (unmistakableness,n.)
22. **So Made That There Is No Chance of Misunderstanding:** watertight,adj.
23. **To Become Understandable to:** dawn on, v.

599. EXPLANATION

1. To Explain,v.
1. **account for**—explain
2. **annotate**—provide (a book, manuscript, etc.) with explanatory notes
3. **construe**—explain; explain the meaning of
4. **define**—explain the meaning of
5. **diagram**—explain with an outline, plan, chart, etc.
6. **elucidate**—explain by examples, illustrations, and other means of clarifying
7. **enucleate**—explain, in the sense of peeling off the covering and getting out the nucleus or core of meaning
8. **explicate**—explain
9. **expound**—explain; explain the meaning of
10. **gloss**—explain by comments or notes; make explanations, by written comments or notes, in a book, manuscript, etc.
11. **interpret**—explain the meaning of
12. **justify**—explain the reasons for
13. **outline**—explain the general plan of
14. **rationalize**—explain according to reason; explain the reasons for or the reasoning behind
15. **resolve**—explain (a problem, dilemma, etc.)
16. **riddle**—explain
17. **solve**—explain
18. **spell out**—explain in clear detail
19. **translate**—explain the meaning of

2. Explanation,n. *From Sec. 1:* annotation, construction, definition, elucidation, enucleation, explication, glossography, interpretation, justification, rationalization, resolution, solution, translation; *Also:*
1. **commentary**—explanation
2. **epexegesis**—the addition of a word or words to explain a preceding word or sentence

3. **exegesis**—critical explanation; critical explanation or interpretation of the Bible
4. **exposition**—explanation
5. **theodicy**—explanation of why God permits the existence of evil

3. An Explanation,n. *From Sec. 1:* account or accounting, annotation, definition, diagram, elucidation, explication, gloss, interpretation, justification, outline, rationalization, resolution, solution, translation; *From Sec. 2:* commentary, epexegesis, exegesis, exposition; *Also:*
1. **afterthought**—later explanation
2. **apostil, postil**—note of explanation in the margin of a page
3. **codicil**—explanation of previous points or provisions
4. **comment**—explanatory remark
5. **commentary**—explanatory notes, remarks, or writings
6. **epexegesis**—added explanation or explanatory matter beyond the exegesis
7. **exegesis**—explanatory note
8. **exposition**—speech or writing of the nature to explain something rather than tell a story, etc.
9. **glossary**—collection of explanations of the words and passages in a volume, work, or author
10. **scholium**—marginal comment in a book (scholia,pl.)
11. **theory**—explanation; explanation of the principles of something worked out in the mind; explanation worked out through observing and forming conclusions; general principle advanced to explain phenomena or occurrences

4. Explainer,n. *From Sec. 1:* annotator, elucidator, enucleator, expounder; glossographer, glossograph, glossarian, or glossarist; interpreter, translator; *From Sec. 2:* commentator, exegete, expositor; *From Sec. 3:* commentator, glossarian or glossarist, scholiast, theoretician; *Also:*
1. **commentator**—one who explains news events or other things on radio or television
2. **exponent**—one who explains or interprets (some art, cause, movement, etc.)
3. **hierophant**—explainer of sacred mysteries
4. **mystagogue**—explainer of mysteries

5. Explanatory; Explanative,adj. *From Sec. 1:* annotative or annotatory, diagrammatic, explicative or explicatory, glossographical, interpretive or interpretative, justificative or justificatory; *From Sec. 2:* epexegetic or epexegetical, exegetic or exegetical, expository, theodicean; *From Sec. 3:* codiciliary, theoretic or theoretical; hierophantic

6. Explainable,adj. *From Sec. 1:* accountable, construable, definable, explicable, justifiable, resolvable, solvable, translatable (accountability or accountableness, construability, definability, explicability, justifiability, resolvability or resolvableness, solvability or solvableness, translatability or translatableness,n.)

7. Unexplainable; Inexplainable,adj. *From Sec. 6:* unaccountable, inconstruable or unconstruable, indefinable or undefinable, inexplicable, unjustifiable, unresolvable, unsolvable, untranslatable (unaccountability, indefinability or undefinability, inexplicability or inexplicableness, unjustifiability, untranslatability or untranslatableness,n.); *Also:*
1. **ambiguous**—incapable of explanation (ambiguity, ambiguousness,n.)
2. **mysterious**—impossible to explain (mysteriousness, mystery,n.)
3. **preternatural**—incapable of rational explanation because outside the realm of

the natural (preternaturalism, preternaturalness,n.)
4. **supernatural**—preternatural (supernaturalism, supernaturalness,n.)

8. That Which Is Unexplainable: ambiguity, mystery,n.

9. Hard to Explain: complex, complicated, adj. (complexity, complicacy, complication,n.)

10. That Which Is Hard to Explain: complexity, complicacy, complication, crux,n.

11. Requiring Explanation (Term in Logic): exponible,adj. (exponible,n.)

12. To Ask (Someone) for an Explanation (of His Actions, etc.): call to account,v.

13. Science of Explanation: exegetics, hermeneutics,n.

14. Science of Explanation of Scripture: exegetics,n.

15. Pert. to Explanations: exegetic,adj.

16. To Explain Incorrectly: misconstrue, misinterpret, mistranslate,v. (misconstruction, misinterpretation, mistranslation,n. misconstruer, misinterpreter,n. misconstructive,adj. misconstruable, misinterpretable,adj.)

600. A REASON

1. A Reason,n.
1. **account**—reason
2. **cause**—reason
3. **excuse**—reason for being excused
4. **ground, grounds**—good and sufficient reason
5. **justification**—reason; satisfactory reason
6. **raison d'être (French)**—reason for being in existence
7. **rationale**—underlying or basic reason behind something
8. **warrant**—satisfactory reason

2. Statement of Reasons: account, accounting,n.

3. To Give or Afford Reason or Reasons for: account for, excuse, justify, warrant,v. (excuse, justification,n.)

4. To Give as a Reason: adduce, allege,v. (allegation,n.)

5. To Find the Reasons for: rationalize,v. (rationalization,n.)

6. Without Good Reason: groundless, inexcusable, unjustified, unwarranted,adj.

601. SOLUTION

1. To Solve: disentangle, puzzle out, ravel, ravel out, resolve, riddle, unravel, unriddle, unscramble, unsnarl, untangle, unweave,v. (resolution, unravelment,n.)

2. Act of Solving: solution,n.

3. To Solve a Vexing or Complicated Problem: cut the Gordian knot,v.

4. Result of Solving: answer, solution,n.

5. Able to Be Solved: resoluble, resolvable, soluble, solvable, unravelable,adj.

6. Unable to Be Solved: insoluble, irresoluble, irresolvable, unresolvable, unsoluble, unsolvable,adj.

7. To Solve (Secret Writing): decipher, decode,v. (decipherment,n. decipherer,n. decipherable,adj. indecipherable or undecipherable, neg.)

8. The Key to Secret Writing: cipher,n.

9. Piece of Black Basalt That Furnished the Key to Egyptian Hieroglyphics: Rosetta stone,n.

10. The Solution of a Complicated Situation: denouement,n.

11. That Which Guides or Points the Way to a Solution: clew, clue, key,n.

12. That Which Makes Solution Possible: key,n.

13. Some Artificial and Unconvincing Character or Circumstance Dragged into a Story, Play, etc., Solely to Solve a Problem and Thereby Extricate the Author from His Difficulties: deus ex machina (Latin),n.

602. PROBLEM

1. A Problem,n.
1. conundrum—puzzling or mysterious problem; problem to which the answer involves a play on words
2. dilemma—problem requiring a decision between alternatives that are equally unpleasant, unfavorable, etc.
3. Gordian knot—vexing and complicated problem
4. logogriph—kind of riddle in which a particular word must be discovered
5. puzzle, puzzler—problem that is hard to solve; problem contrived to test the solver's ingenuity
6. quandary—dilemma
7. question—problem under discussion, for discussion, to be solved, etc.
8. rebus—puzzle or riddle in which words are represented by pictures
9. riddle—puzzling problem; problem or puzzle offered for guessing; conundrum

2. Of the Nature of a Problem: problematic or problematical,adj.

3. To Offer Riddles or Conundrums for Guessing or Solution: riddle,v.

603. UNCLEARNESS

1. Unclear to the Mind or Senses; Unclear in Form, Sound, Meaning, etc.,adj.
1. ambiguous—unclear in meaning
2. aoristic—indefinite
3. blurred, blurry—unclear in form or outline; indistinct or faint to the vision
4. casual—indefinite; vague
5. cloudy, clouded—not clear, as a liquid; obscure; indistinct; vague
6. confused—indistinct
7. dark—obscure
8. dim—not clear to the sight; vague
9. equivocal—purposely unclear in meaning
10. faint—not clear to the sight; not clear in sound, color, etc.
11. foggy—dim; obscure; indistinct or vague, as if blurred by fog
12. fuzzy—blurred; indistinct
13. hazy—not clear or distinct in form; vague
14. impalpable—indefinite or vague, as if it could not be clearly felt or touched
15. imprecise—not sharply or exactly defined or definite; vague
16. inarticulate—not clear or distinct in sound
17. inconspicuous—not immediately clear or striking to the sight
18. indefinite—not clearly defined; not clear in meaning, nature, or purpose
19. indeterminate—indefinite; indistinct
20. indistinct—not clear; not clear to the eye or ear
21. inexplicit—not absolutely clear in meaning
22. intangible—indefinite
23. misty—indistinct or vague, as if blurred by a mist
24. muddy—not clear, because, or as if, clouded with mud
25. murky, mirky—obscure
26. nebulated—not clearly marked; cloudy
27. nebulous, nebulose—cloudy; indefinite; vague
28. nubilous—indefinite; indistinct; vague
29. obscure—not at all, or not immediately, clear to the sight or understanding; not clear in meaning, expression, or form; indefinite; vague
30. roily—not clear; cloudy; cloudy owing to violent movement, as water
31. shadowy—indistinct
32. sketchy—not clearly presented; lacking in clearness (of writing, mental products, ideas, etc.)
33. subtle—faint
34. tenuous—faint
35. transcendental—indefinite; indistinct; vague
36. turbid—not clear; cloudy
37. undecided—indefinite
38. unevident—not evident
39. unobvious—not immediately clear to the sight or understanding
40. vague—not absolutely clear in character, form, meaning, thought, understanding, etc.; not absolutely clear to the sight or other senses

2. Unclearness,n. From Sec. 1: ambiguity or ambiguousness, cloudiness, confusion or confusedness, dark or darkness, dimness, equivocalness, faintness, fogginess, fuzziness, haziness, impalpability, imprecision, inarticulateness, inconspicuousness, indeterminateness or indeterminacy, indistinctness, inexplicitness, intangibility or intangibleness, mistiness, muddiness, murkiness, mirkiness, nebulation, nebulosity or nebulousness, obscurity or obscureness, shadowiness, sketchiness, subtlety or subtleness, tenuity or tenuousness, transcendentalism, turbidity or turbidness, undecidedness, unobviousness, vagueness

3. To Become Unclear,v. From Sec. 1: cloud, darken, dim, fog, mist

4. To Make or Cause to Be Unclear,v. From Sec. 1: befog, blurr, cloud, confuse, darken, dim, fog, mist, muddy, obscure, roil, shadow (confusion, obscuration,n.) ; Also:
1. becloud—make unclear with, or as if with, clouds
2. befog—make foggy; obscure
3. blot out—obscure
4. enshroud—obscure and hide, as if with a veil

5. State of Being Obscured: obscuration,n.

6. One Who Obscures or Causes Obscurity: obscurant, obscurantist,n. (obscurantism,n. obscurant, obscurantist,adj.)

7. That Which, or One Who, Is Obscure: obscurity,n.

8. Obscurity or Vagueness of Mind: haze,n.

9. To Use Purposely Unclear or Ambiguous Language: equivocate,v. (equivocation,n. equivocator,n. equivocalness,n. equivocal,adj.)

604. MYSTERY

1. Hard or Impossible to Understand; Mysterious,adj.
1. abstract—hard to understand
2. abstruse—hard to understand
3. arcane—deeply mysterious
4. baffling—defying understanding; confusing
5. bewildering—hard to understand owing to confusing elements; defying understanding
6. cabalistic—mysterious; mystical
7. carking—perplexing
8. complex—having many confusing elements and therefore hard to understand
9. complicated—hard to understand
10. confounding—perplexing

11. confusing—hard to understand owing to the variety and complexity of elements
12. cryptic—having a hidden or secret meaning; mysterious; perplexing
13. dark—hard to understand
14. deep—hard to understand owing to obscurity, complexity, etc.
15. Delphic—oracular
16. difficult—hard to understand
17. elusive—hard to understand; mysterious
18. enigmatic—presenting a baffling or puzzling mystery; mysterious
19. fathomless—incapable of being understood, i.e., defying all attempts to get to the bottom or depths
20. impalpable—difficult or almost impossible to understand
21. incomprehensible—impossible to understand
22. inconceivable—impossible to understand
23. indecipherable—impossible to understand (of writing)
24. inscrutable—so mysterious or obscure as to defy understanding
25. intangible—difficult to understand, in the sense of not being the sort of thing the mind can touch or grasp; defying understanding
26. intricate—hard to understand; complex
27. involved—complex
28. knotty—complex
29. labyrinthine, labyrinthic, labyrinthian, labyrinthal—complex
30. mazy—complex
31. metaphysical—very hard to understand, i.e., delving into the rarefied depths of metaphysics, the branch of philosophy that attempts to explain reality
32. mystical, mystic—having a secret meaning; defying human understanding
33. mystifying—bewildering; perplexing
34. obscure—not clear in meaning; not expressing meaning in a quickly and easily understandable manner
35. occult—mysterious
36. opaque—hard to understand
37. oracular—containing an obscure or hidden meaning
38. perplexing—hard to understand in the sense of containing or presenting many confusing and complex elements, difficulties, problems, etc.
39. preternatural—mysterious
40. problematic, problematical—perplexing
41. profound—so deep as to be difficult to understand
42. puzzling—bewildering; perplexing
43. recondite—hard to understand; obscure
44. reticular—full of intricacies and complexities, like a net
45. runic—mysterious
46. scabrous—complex
47. sphinxian—enigmatic; inscrutable
48. subtle—mysterious
49. transcendental—defying, i.e., going beyond understanding; mysterious
50. tricky—complicated
51. turbid—not easy to understand, i.e., not clear or lucid
52. uncanny—mysterious
53. unfathomable—beyond understanding; fathomless
54. unintelligible—incapable of being understood
55. weird—supernaturally mysterious

2. State or Condition of Being Hard or Impossible to Understand; Mysteriousness,n. From Sec. 1: abstractness or abstraction, abstruseness, cabalism, complexity, complicacy or complication, depth, difficulty, elusiveness, impalpability, incomprehensibility, indecipherability, inscrutability or inscrutableness, intangibility or intangibleness, intricacy, involvement, knottiness, labyrinth, mysticalness, obscurity, opacity or opaqueness, pre-

ternaturalism, profundity, reticularity, scabrousness, subtlety or subtleness, transcendentalism, trickiness, turbidity or turbidness, uncanniness, unfathomability, unintelligibility, weirdness

3. That Which, or a Factor or Part That, Is Hard or Impossible to Understand; A Mystery,n. From Sec. 1: abstraction, arcana (pl.), cabala, complexity, complication or complicacy, difficulty, enigma, intangible, intricacy, involvement, labyrinth, maze, obscurity, occult, oracle, perplexity, problem; puzzle, puzzlement, or puzzler; rune, subtlety; Also:
1. Chinese puzzle—anything full of complexities
2. conundrum—anything puzzling
3. crux—anything puzzling or mysterious
4. cryptogram, cryptograph—symbol or representation that has a mysterious or hidden meaning
5. riddle—mystery; anything hard to guess or understand; anything mysterious
6. snarl—complication

4. One Who Is a Mystery or Hard to Understand,n. From Sec. 1: enigma, obscurity, problem, puzzle; From Sec. 3: riddle

5. To Cause to Be Hard or Impossible to Understand,v. From Sec. 1: complicate, confuse, darken, involve, obscure (complication, confusion, obscuration,n.) ; From Sec. 3: snarl

6. Study of, Belief in, or Doctrines Relating to, Mysteries: cabalism, mysticism, occultism,n. (cabalist, mystic, occultist,n. cabalistic, mystic, occultist,adj.)

7. Understood Only by the Select Few: esoteric, esoterical,adj.

8. Expounder of Sacred Mysteries: hierophant,n.

9. One Who Initiates Someone into, or Explains, Mysteries: mystagogue,n.

10. Mysterious, Unknowable, Puzzling, and Silent Person: sphinx,n.

605. CONFUSION

1. To Confuse (a Person),v.
1. abash—cause confusion and embarrassment to
2. addle—make confused
3. baffle—confuse
4. bamboozle—perplex (colloq.)
5. bedevil—confuse completely
6. befog—confuse; bewilder; perplex
7. befuddle—confuse by weakening the mental faculties of, as with drugs, liquor, shock, etc.
8. bemuddle—confuse; muddle
9. bemuse—confuse; bewilder
10. beset—perplex
11. bewilder—confuse by external complexities, or by presenting such a variety of problems or considerations as to defy understanding; make lose one's sense of location or direction; perplex
12. confound—confuse; throw into complete confusion; perplex
13. daze—confuse; bewilder
14. dazzle—confuse by a display of literal or figurative brilliance
15. demoralize—throw into confusion
16. disconcert—throw into confusion
17. discountenance—disconcert
18. disorient, disorientate—confuse as to one's relation to one's environment or to reality; confuse as to where compass directions are
19. distract—confuse (someone) by drawing his mind from idea to idea, etc.
20. flurry—fluster
21. fluster—cause temporary or momentary

confusion to; confuse (someone) by doing that which momentarily robs him of the ability to think clearly

22. **flutter**—throw into confusion; make confused
23. **fog**—confuse; perplex
24. **fuddle**—befuddle; muddle
25. **mix up**—cause to be confused
26. **muddle**—make confused; make stupidly or drunkenly confused; bewilder; perplex
27. **mystify**—bewilder; perplex
28. **non-plus**—confuse, bewilder, or perplex completely; reduce (a person) to a state in which he does not know what to do or say
29. **perplex**—confuse by complexity, difficulty, or mystery; bewilder
30. **puzzle**—bewilder; perplex
31. **rattle**—cause confusion of mind in
32. **stagger**—cause confusion of mind in
33. **stump**—bewilder; perplex
34. **stun**—bewilder

2. Confusion, i.e., Act of Confusing,n. *From Sec. 1:* bafflement, bamboozlement, bedevilment, befuddlement, bemuddlement, bemusement, bewilderment, demoralization, disconcertion or disconcertment, disorientation, distraction, mystification

3. Confusion, i.e., State of Being Confused, n. *From Sec. 1:* bafflement, bedevilment, befuddlement, bemusement, bewilderment, daze, dazzle or dazzlement, demoralization, disconcertion or disconcertment, disorientation, distraction, flurry, fluster, flutter, fog, mix-up, muddle, mystification, perplexity, puzzlement or puzzle; *Also:*
1. **haze**—mental confusion
2. **maze**—state of bewildered confusion
3. **quandary**—state of confusion or perplexity, usually as to what course to take, what action to follow, what decision to make, etc.
4. **whirl**—state of confusion

4. Confusing; Causing One to Be Confused, adj. *From Sec. 1:* baffling, bedeviling, etc.; *Also:* 1. **carking**—perplexing

5. Confused,adj. *From Sec. 1:* abashed, addled, etc.; *From Sec. 3:* hazy, whirling; *Also:*
1. **addle**—confused (of one's brains)
2. **addlebrained, addleheaded, addlepated** —confused or mixed up (addlebrain, addlehead, addlepate,n.)
3. **dizzy**—confused
4. **groggy**—mentally confused
5. **muzzy**—confused; drunkenly or stupidly confused; bewildered

6. That Which Causes One to Be Confused, n. *From Sec. 1:* distraction, perplexity; puzzle, puzzlement, or puzzler

7. To Become Confused: addle,v.

8. To Act in a Confused and Purposeless Fashion: maunder,v.

9. To Feel Confused and Dizzy: reel, whirl, v.

10. To Confuse, i.e., Not Be Able to Tell Apart: confound, mix up,v.

11. To Reduce (a Place or Things) to Confusion; To Make (Something) Confused,v.
1. **becloud**—make (something) confused, as an issue, argument, problem, thinking, or similar abstraction
2. **bedlamize**—throw (a place) into noisy confusion
3. **befog**—becloud
4. **clutter**—cause a confused disorder or disarray of things in (a place)
5. **derange**—disorder
6. **disarrange**—disorder
7. **disarray**—disorder
8. **discreate**—cause (things) to be in the wildest confusion

9. **disorder**—reduce (things) to confusion by disturbing their proper order, arrangement, etc.
10. **disorganize**—throw into confusion; remove all systematic order or organization from (things or a place)
11. **embrangle**—tangle (things) up in confusion
12. **embroil**—throw (things) into confusion
13. **entangle**—confuse (things) in, or as if in, a tangle
14. **fog**—becloud
15. **jumble**—mix (things) together into a confused mass; put or throw (things) together in confusion
16. **litter**—scatter things about (a place) in confused disorder
17. **mess, mess up**—throw (things or a place) into confused disorder
18. **mix up**—put (things) into a confused mixture
19. **muddle**—jumble
20. **muss, muss up**—disorder (colloq.)
21. **obfuscate**—deliberately confuse (an issue, problem, question or similar abstraction) by eliminating clearness, or by making it unnecessarily devious or complicated
22. **rumple, rumple up**—disorder (usually hair, clothing, etc.)
23. **snarl**—involve (something) in tangled confusion
24. **tangle**—cause (things) to be wound or twisted together in confusion, literally or figuratively
25. **tousle**—disorder (usually hair, clothing, etc.)
26. **tumble**—throw (things) into disorder or confusion

12. Confusion, i.e., a Reducing to Confusion, or Making Confused,n. *From Sec. 11:* derangement, disarrangement, discreation, disorganization, embranglement, embroilment, entanglement, obfuscation

13. Confusion, i.e., State of Being Confused or in Confusion,n. *From Sec. 11:* bedlam, clutter, derangement, disarrangement, disarray, disorder or disorderedness, disorganization, embranglement, embroilment, entanglement, jumble, litter, mess, mix-up or mix, muddle, muss, snarl, tangle; *Also:*
1. **anarchy**—complete confusion, in the sense of lack of order, rule, etc.
2. **babel**—confusion of sounds, cries, voices, or languages
3. **chaos**—complete, totally confused disorder; confused state of things before an orderly process was evolved on the earth
4. **din**—confusion of loud noises
5. **hubbub**—noisy confusion, often with shouting, uproar, etc.
6. **hurly-burly**—confusion; noisy confusion
7. **hurry-scurry**—disordered confusion
8. **intricacy**—state of perplexing or confusing complexity
9. **maelstrom**—wild confusion
10. **moil**—state of confusion
11. **pandemonium**—noisy confusion
12. **perplexity**—bewildering confusion
13. **pother**—confusion
14. **rabblement**—noisy confusion
15. **racket**—noisy confusion
16. **riot**—wild confusion
17. **rummage**—confusion
18. **tophet**—chaos
19. **topsy-turviness, topsy-turvydom**—confusion; disorder
20. **tumult**—confusion
21. **turbidity**—confusion
22. **turbulence**—disorder; violent confusion
23. **turmoil**—great confusion of sounds, movements, thinking, etc.
24. **uproar**—noisy confusion
25. **welter**—great confusion
26. **whirl**—confusion

14. Confused,adj. *From Sec. 11:* beclouded, befogged, etc.; *From Sec. 13:* anarchic, chaotic, intricate, rackety, riotous, topsy-turvy, tumultuous, turbid, turbulent, uproarious; *Also:*
  1. **addle**—confused (of talk)
  2. **bedlam**—confused and noisy
  3. **macaronic**—mixed up and confused, like macaroni
  4. **upside-down**—all confused
15. To Be in a Great Confusion or Turmoil: welter,v.

16. Scene or Place of Confusion,n.
  1. **babel**—place of noise and confusion
  2. **bedlam**—place or scene of wild confusion and noise
  3. **madhouse**—place or scene of wild confusion
  4. **maelstrom**—scene of confusion and wild turmoil
  5. **shambles**—place or scene of great confusion; place of confusion and killing

17. Place Full of Confusing Passageways, Confusingly Winding Roads or Paths, etc.: labyrinth, maze,n. (labyrinthine, labyrinthic, labyrinthian, labyrinthal, mazy,adj.)

18. Confusing or Bewildering State of Things: bewilderment, labyrinth, maze, perplexity,n.

19. Confusing Mass or Collection of Things: wilderness,n.

20. Time of Confusion between Governments, or between Changes of Government: interregnum,n.

21. In Confusion,adv.
  1. **helter-skelter**—in hurried confusion
  2. **pell-mell**—in disordered confusion

606. DIZZINESS

1. Dizzy, Literally or Figuratively: flighty (figuratively only), giddy; harebrained (figuratively only); lightheaded, reeling, swimming; vertiginous (literally only); whirling, adj. (flightiness, giddiness, lightheadedness, vertigo, whirl,n.)

2. Causing Dizziness: dizzy, dizzying, giddy, heady, vertiginous,adj. (headiness,n.)

3. To Be Dizzy: reel, swim,v.

4. To Become Dizzy: giddy, reel,v.

5. To Feel Dizzy and Confused: reel, whirl, v.

6. To Make Dizzy: dizzy, giddy,v.

7. Flighty Woman: flibbertigibbet,n.

607. MEANING

1. To Mean,v.
  1. **connote**—have as an added or suggested meaning above and beyond the literal meaning (of a word or phrase)
  2. **denote**—have as the literal or actual meaning (of a word or phrase)
  3. **imply**—mean, though not express directly or distinctly
  4. **import**—mean; signify
  5. **intend**—mean
  6. **omen**—portend
  7. **portend**—have a threatening meaning; have a meaning that indicates future events
  8. **purport**—mean; have as its meaning
  9. **signify**—mean; have a deep meaning; have a meaning that may not be immediately apparent; have a meaning conveyed by language
  10. **spell**—mean (*this spells victory*, etc.)
  11. **suggest**—have as a hidden or indirect meaning; imply

2. Meaning,n. *From Sec. 1:* connotation, denotation, implication, import, intent, omen, portent, purport, significance or signification, suggestion; *Also:*
  1. **acceptation**—usual, general, or generally accepted meaning (of a word or phrase)
  2. **anagoge, anagogy**—spiritual or mystical meaning of words (anagogic, anagogical, adj.)
  3. **arrière-pensée (French)**—hidden meaning
  4. **definition**—meaning (usually of a word, phrase, term, etc.)
  5. **idea**—meaning
  6. **point**—final meaning
  7. **sense**—meaning
  8. **substance**—real meaning
  9. **tenor**—general meaning

3. Central Meaning: content, core, essence, gist, idea, kernel, nub, pith, point, substance, sum,n.

4. Shade of Difference in Meaning: nuance, n.

5. Equal in Meaning: equipollent,adj. (equipollence,n.)

6. Meant, but Not Directly Expressed: implicit, implied,adj. (implicitness,adj.)

7. Having No Disgused Meaning: explicit, adj. (explicitness,n.)

8. To Seem Meaningful; To Become Meaningful: bulk,v.

9. Having Meaning or a Meaning; Full of Meaning,adj.
  1. **cabalistic**—having a mystical meaning (cabalism,n.)
  2. **concise**—having much meaning in few words (conciseness, concision,n.)
  3. **cryptic**—having a hidden or secret meaning
  4. **meaningful**—full of meaning; significant (meaningfulness,n.)
  5. **meaty**—full of important meaning (meatiness,n.)
  6. **mystical**—having a spiritual or secret meaning (mysticalness,n.)
  7. **ominous**—portentous (ominousness,n.)
  8. **oracular**—containing an obscure or hidden meaning (oracularity,n.)
  9. **pithy**—full of meaning; full of clear meaning (pithiness,n.)
  10. **pointed**—full of meaning; full of clear meaning (pointedness,n.)
  11. **portentous**—full of threatening meaning; full of meaning that indicates future events (portentousness,n.)
  12. **pregnant**—full of important meaning; suggestive (pregnancy,n.)
  13. **sappy**—meaty; pithy
  14. **sententious**—packed with meaning (sententiousness,n.)
  15. **significant, significative**—full of deep meaning; having a meaning; having a special or concealed meaning; suggestive (significance, significancy,n.)
  16. **succinct**—containing much meaning, though expressed in few words
  17. **suggestive**—having an indirect meaning (suggestiveness,n.)

10. Descr. of, or Pert. to, Meaning,adj.
  1. **connotative**—descr. of, or pert. to, the added or suggested meaning above and beyond the literal meaning
  2. **denotative**—descr. of, or pert. to, the literal or actual meaning
  3. **figurative**—descr. of the non-literal, or extended, meaning of a word or phrase; metaphorical
  4. **literal**—descr. of the strict, primary, and unextended meaning of a word or phrase (The literal meaning of *sweep* is the use of a broom to push dirt, etc., while the figurative meaning of this word is found

in phrases like *a clean sweep in the elections, a sweeping statement,* etc.)

5. **metaphorical**—descr. of significance gained by using a word with one meaning to describe something of different meaning, in order to show figurative similarity

6. **semantic**—pert. to, or descr. of, meaning, meaning of language, or meaning of language forms

7. **significative**—pert. to meaning

11. **Having Several Meanings,**adj.
1. **ambiguous**—capable of being interpreted in two or more different ways; having two or more different meanings (ambiguity, ambiguousness,n.)
2. **amphibolic, amphibolous, amphibological**—ambiguous; equivocal (amphibology, n.)
3. **equivocal**—purposely admitting of two or more meanings or interpretations (equivocalness,n.)
4. **ironic, ironical**—having a meaning directly opposite to that expressed (irony, n.)
5. **oracular**—capable of many interpretations; ambiguous (oracularity,n.)
6. **sarcastic**—having a meaning contrary to that literally expressed by the words, and generally showing contempt, ridicule, mockery, or hostility (sarcasm,n.)

12. **Word, Phrase, Term, etc., That Has Several Meanings,**n. *From Sec. 11:* ambiguity, amphibologism or amphibology; *Also:*
1. **double-entendre (French)**—expression, pun, or other statement of ambiguous meaning, one seemingly innocent and likely to be so understood by the naïve, the other obscene or sexy
2. **equivoque, equivoke**—term or expression with a double or ambiguous meaning
3. **paronomasia**—pun
4. **pun**—word or phrase capable of more than one meaning, and used with humorous intent

13. **Using Words, Phrases, etc., in Such a Way that Several Meanings May Be Understood,**adj. *From Sec. 11:* ambiguous, equivocal, ironic or ironical, oracular, sarcastic,adj.

14. **The Use of Words, etc., in This Manner,** n. *From Sec. 11:* ambiguity or ambiguousness, equivocalness or equivocation, irony, sarcasm (equivocate,v.); *From Sec. 12:* paronomasia, punning (pun,v.)

15. **Pert. to, or Descr. of, Punning or a Pun:** paronomastic, paronomastical,adj.

16. **Acceptance or Understanding of, or Inclination to Accept or Understand, Words in Their Strict, Primary, and Unextended Meanings Only:** literalism, literal-mindedness, verbalism,n. (literalist, verbalist,n. literal, literal-minded,adj.)

17. **To Give, Explain, etc., the Meaning of,**v.
1. **construe**—translate; translate orally; interpret (construction,n.)
2. **define**—give and/or explain the meaning of (definition,n.)
3. **explain**—make clear the meaning of (explanation,n.)
4. **explicate**—unfold the meaning of (explication,n.)
5. **expound**—explain the meaning of
6. **interpret**—show, explain, or tell the meaning of (interpretation,n.)
7. **maximize**—give the broadest possible interpretation to
8. **metaphrase**—translate from one language into another
9. **paraphrase**—restate in other words, but with essentially the same meaning; translate freely or loosely
10. **render**—translate
11. **translate**—explain the meaning of; re-

state with the same meaning, but in another language (translation,n.)

18. **That Which Gives, Explains, etc., Meaning,**n. *From Sec. 17:* construction, definition, explanation, explication, interpretation, metaphrase, paraphrase, rendering, translation; *Also:*
1. **crib**—translation of a literary work used by a student as an aid in learning a foreign language
2. **trot, pony**—translation of a work in a foreign language, generally word for word, used by students as an aid in their classwork (colloq.)
3. **version**—translation

19. **Giving, Explaining, etc., Meaning,**adj. *From Sec. 17:* constructive, explanatory or explanative, explicative or explicatory, interpretive or interpretative, paraphrastic; *Also:*
1. **hermeneutic**—unfolding meaning; interpretative

20. **Giver, Explainer, etc., of Meaning,**n. *From Sec. 17:* construer, definer, explainer, explicator, expounder, interpreter, paraphraser or paraphrast, translator; *Also:*
1. **dragoman**—interpreter, in the Far East
2. **oneirocritic**—interpreter of dreams

21. **To Give a Wrong Meaning,**v.
1. **distort**—twist the meaning of (distortion,n.)
2. **do violence to**—alter, without justification, the meaning or wording of
3. **gloss, gloss over**—give a false, though seemingly true or plausible, interpretation of (gloss,n.)
4. **misconstrue**—misinterpret (misconstruction,n.)
5. **misinterpret**—give the wrong meaning of, or a wrong meaning to (misinterpretation,n.)
6. **mistranslate**—give a wrong meaning to, or the wrong meaning of (mistranslation, n.)
7. **pervert**—give a wrong meaning to (perversion,n.)
8. **torture**—twist the meaning of (torture, n.)
9. **twist**—give a wrong meaning to
10. **wrench**—twist out of the original meaning
11. **wrest**—turn or twist violently from the proper meaning

22. **Science of Meaning,**n.
1. **hermeneutics**—science of interpretation and explanation
2. **semantics**—science of the meanings of words, esp. their emotional effects and connotations (semanticist,n. semantic, adj.)
3. **semantology**—semantics (semantological, adj.)
4. **semasiology**—science of the meanings of words (semasiologist,n. semasiological, adj.)
5. **sematology**—semantics
6. **significs**—semantics

23. **Meaningless:** empty, inane, nonsensical, pointless, senseless, skimble-skamble, vacuous,adj. (emptiness, inanity, nonsensicality or nonsensicalness, pointlessness, senselessness, vacuity or vacuousness,n.)

24. **That Which Has No Meaning; Words or Language without Meaning:** nonsense,n.

25. **To Make Nonsense of:** nonsensify,v. (nonsensification,n.)

26. **Meaningless or Nonsensical Talk:** abracadabra, babble, balderdash, bilge, blather, bosh, buncombe, bunk, bunkum, cackle, drivel; flapdoodle (colloq.); flummery, gabble, galimatias, gibber, gibberish, jabber, jargon, poppycock, prate, prattle, raving, ravings, rigmarole, slaver, slush, twaddle, twattle,n.

27. To Talk Meaninglessly or Nonsensically: babble, blat, blather, bleat, burble, cackle, drivel, gabble, gibber, jabber, jargon, prate, prattle, rattle on, rave, slaver, twaddle, twattle,v.

28. Nonsensical Talk Designed to Distract the Mind While Deception Is Practiced: hocus-pocus,n.

29. Meaningless or Nonsensical Words or Sounds Supposed or Pretended to Have Meaning: mumbo-jumbo,n.

30. Nonsensical Talk That Is an Insult to One's Intelligence: pap,n.

31. Succession of Meaningless Statements: rigmarole,n. (rigmarole,adj.)

32. Given to Foolish or Nonsensical Talk: vaporous, vapory,adj. (vaporousness, vaporosity,n.)

608. NONSENSE

1. Nonsense: balderdash; bavardage (French); bilge, bosh, buncombe, bunk, bunkum; flapdoodle (colloq.); pap, poppycock, slaver, tomfoolery, tommyrot, trumpery,n.

2. Nonsense Designed to Distract the Mind While Deception Is Practiced: hocus-pocus,n.

3. Nonsense That Is an Insult to One's Intelligence: pap,n.

4. Anything Offensively Foolish: tripe,n. (colloq.)

5. Nonsensical; Foolish: absurd, apish, asinine, balmy, barmy, barmybrained; besotted (of a person); brainless, childish, crazy, daft; dizzy (colloq.); empty, fantastic, fantastical, farcical, fatuitous, fatuous, idiotic, inane, irrational, ludicrous, lunatic, mad, meaningless, pointless, preposterous, priceless, puerile, ridiculous, senseless, silly; simple (of a person); simple-minded (of a person); stupid, unearthly, unreasonable, unwise, vacuous, vapid, witless, zany, zanyish, adj.

6. Nonsensicality; Foolishness: absurdity, apishness, asininity, balminess; bêtise (French); brainlessness, childishness, craziness, daftness; dizziness (colloq.); emptiness, fantasticality, fantasticalness, farcicality, fatuity, fatuousness, folly, idiocy, inanity, irrationality, ludicrousness, lunacy, madness, meaninglessness, pointlessness, preposterousness, pricelessness, puerility, ridiculousness, senselessness, silliness, simplicity, simple-mindedness, stupidity, unearthliness, unreason, unreasonableness, unwisdom, vacuity, vacuousness, vapidity, vapidness, witlessness, zaniness,n.

7. Absurd or Preposterous in Actions or Appearance: antic,adj.

8. Exceedingly Foolish in Talk: blithering, adj.

9. Instance of Nonsensicality or Foolishness: absurdity, asininity; bêtise (French); fatuity, folly, idiocy, inanity, lunacy, puerility, stupidity, vacuity, vapidity,n.

10. Nonsensical or Foolish Act or Action: antic, apery, folly, stupidity, zanyism,n.

11. To Act or Behave Foolishly: antic, drivel, v.

12. Ridiculous Show: farce,n. (farcial, farcical,adj.)

13. Absurdly Improbable Situation: farce,n. (farcical,adj.)

14. Reduction to Absurdity: reductio ad absurdum (Latin)

15. Treatment That Makes Something Serious Seem Absurd or Ridiculous: travesty,n. (travesty,v.)

16. Fool; Foolish or Silly Person: ape, ass, boob, chump, clown, half-wit, idiot, lunatic, nincompoop, ninny, nitwit, noddy, noodle; silly (colloq.); simpleton, zany,n.

17. Foolish Young Man: pup, puppy,n.

18. Cowardly Fool: scaramouch,n.

19. Someone Who Pretends to Understanding but Is in Actuality a Fool: witling,n.

20. Silly, Conceited, and Talkative Person: popinjay,n.

21. Silly, Flirtatious Woman: fizgig,n.

22. Foolish People as a Class: booboisie,n. (term coined by H. L. Mencken from *boob*, in analogy to *bourgeoisie*)

23. Given to Foolish Ideas: vaporous, vapory, adj. (vaporousness, vaporosity,n.)

24. To Make, or Cause to Be, Foolish: besot, v.

25. To Treat as a Fool: befool,v.

609. FRIVOLOUSNESS

1. Frivolous: barmy, barmybrained, facetious, flighty; flip (colloq.); flippant, fribble, giddy, harebrained, idle, lightheaded, playful, rattlebrained, rattleheaded, rattlepated, skittish, sportive, tongue-in-cheek, trifling, volatile, whimsical, yeasty,adj.

2. Frivolousness: facetiousness, flightiness, flippancy or flippantness, fribble, frivolity, giddiness, levity, lightheadedness, playfulness, skittishness, sportiveness, trifling, volatility, whiffiery, whimsicality, whimsey, whimsy, yeastiness,n.

3. Frivolous Person: flip (colloq.), fribble, lighthead, rattlebrain, rattlehead, rattlepate, trifler, whiffler,n.

4. Frivolous Young Woman: soubrette,n.

5. Frivolous and Chattering Woman: flibbertigibbet,n.

6. To Act the Frivolous and Chattering Woman: flibbertigibbet,v.

7. To Act Frivolously: fribble, frivol, trifle,v. (fribbler, frivoler, trifler,n.)

8. Frivolous Act: frivolity,n.

9. To Talk Frivolously: trifle,v. (trifler,n.)

10. To Talk to, Act toward, or Treat, without Seriousness: play with, toy with, trifle with,v.

610. SERIOUS

1. Serious: astringent, austere, demure, earnest, funereal, grave; grievous (of things); pontifical, saturnine, sedate; severe (of things); sober, solemn, somber, sore (of things); staid (of people); weighty (of things),adj. (astringency, austerity, demureness, earnestness, funerealness, gravity, grievousness, sedateness, severity, sobriety or soberness, solemnity or solemnness, somberness, soreness, staidness, weightiness,n.)

2. Serious in Appearance or Looks: demure, solemn, somber,adj. (demureness, solemnity or solemnness, somberness,n.)

3. Quiet and Serious: sedate, staid,adj. (sedateness, staidness,n.)

4. Combining Seriousness and Humor: seriocomic,adj.

5. To Make Serious; To Treat Seriously: solemnify, solemnize,v. (solemnization,n.)

6. To Make More Serious: aggravate,v. (aggravation,n.)

611. KNOWLEDGE

1. Having Knowledge, adj.

1. **abreast**—informed of the latest developments or events
2. **acquainted with**—knowing about; having knowledge or personal knowledge of; having knowledge of (something) gained through experience or education (acquaintance, acquaintanceship, n.)
3. **appreciative of**—having knowledge of; aware of (appreciativeness, appreciation, n.)
4. **au fait (French)**—familiar with the material or facts (of something)
5. **aware**—having conscious knowledge (awareness, n.)
6. **cognizant (of)**—aware (of) by knowledge or by direct experience (cognizance, n.)
7. **conscious**—aware (consciousness, n.)
8. **conversant with**—having knowledge of, or familiarity with (conversance, n.)
9. **erudite**—learned (erudition, eruditeness, n.)
10. **familiar with**—having knowledge about (familiarity, n.)
11. **informed (in or about)**—having knowledge (of or about)
12. **knowledgeable**—full of knowledge; possessing knowledge
13. **learned**—having knowledge gained through study or education (learnedness, n.)
14. **omniscient**—having knowledge of everything (omniscience, n.)
15. **pansophic, pansophical**—having all-inclusive knowledge
16. **prescient**—having knowledge of things before they happen; having knowledge of the future (prescience, n.)
17. **privy to**—having private or secret knowledge of (privity, n.)
18. **sciential**—having efficient knowledge
19. **sensible to**—aware of (sensibility, n.)
20. **sophisticated**—having knowledge of the ways of the world (sophistication, n.)
21. **versed in**—acquainted with; familiar with
22. **well-informed**—having a good deal of knowledge about a certain thing, or about many things
23. **wise**—having knowledge (wisdom, n.)
24. **worldly, worldly-wise**—sophisticated (worldly wisdom, n.)

2. Knowledge, n. *From Sec. 1:* cognizance, erudition, information, learning, omniscience, pansophy, prescience, sophistication, wisdom, worldly wisdom; *Also:*

1. **afflatus**—knowledge derived from a divine or supernatural source
2. **anthroposophy**—knowledge of man's nature (anthroposophical, adj. anthroposophist, n.)
3. **cabala, cabalism**—esoteric knowledge (cabalistic, cabalic, adj. cabalist, n.)
4. **daylight**—full knowledge of what before had been puzzling or obscure
5. **foreknowledge**—knowledge of an event before it happens; knowledge of the future
6. **intuition**—knowledge derived not from reasoning but from instinct or some emotional source or power (intuitive, intuitional, adj.)
7. **lore**—knowledge; body of knowledge about a particular subject, or possessed by a group and handed down from previous generations
8. **prevision**—foreknowledge (previsional, adj.)
9. **realization**—knowledge gained through seeing, hearing, perception of any sort, learning, etc.
10. **science**—knowledge gained from practice, study, and experience; systematized body of knowledge (scientist, n. scientific, adj.)

11. **sciolism**—superficial knowledge (sciolist, n. sciolistic, adj.)
12. **smattering, smatter**—slight and superficial knowledge
13. **theory**—abstract knowledge

3. Not Having Knowledge; Ignorant, adj. *From Sec. 1:* unacquainted with, unappreciative of, unaware, incognizant or uncognizant, unconscious, unconversant, inerudite, unfamiliar with, uninformed, unlearned, insensible, unsophisticated, unversed in, unwise (unacquaintance, unappreciativeness, unawareness, incognizance, unconsciousness, inerudition, unfamiliarity, unintuitiveness, unlearnedness, insensibility, unsophistication, unwisdom, n.); *Also:*

1. **artless**—ignorant (artlessness, n.)
2. **benighted**—ignorant of, or showing ignorance of, morality (benightedness, n.)
3. **dark**—ignorant (darkness, dark, n.)
4. **naïve; naïf (French)**—lacking in worldly knowledge (naïveté, n.)
5. **nescient**—ignorant (nescience, n.)
6. **sophomoric**—ignorant but pretending to great wisdom
7. **troglodytic**—knowing nothing of what has been happening in the world (troglodyte, n.)
8. **unwitting**—not aware or conscious; not knowing or realizing (unwittingness, n.)

4. Person without Knowledge: ignoramus, n.

5. Pretended Ignorance Displayed by Asking Subtle Questions That on the Surface Are for the Purpose of Gaining Information but in Reality Are Intended to Show the One Questioned the Errors in His Thinking: Socratic irony, n.

6. Doctrine of the Condition, Necessity, and Extent of Human Ignorance: agnoiology, n. (metaphysics)

7. Pert. to Knowledge: sciential, adj.

8. Object of Knowledge: cognitum, n.

9. Theory that All Knowledge Is Gained through Experience: empiricism, n. (empiricist, n. empiricist, adj.)

10. Pretension to All-Inclusive Knowledge: pansophism, n. (pansophist, n.)

11. Summary of Knowledge in a Field; Summary or Digest of General Knowledge: cyclopedia, encyclopedia, n. (cyclopedist, encyclopedist, n. cyclopedic, encyclopedic, adj.)

12. Range of Knowledge: ken, n.

13. Department or Division of Knowledge: province, n.

14. Methodical View of Knowledge in General, of General Knowledge, or of All Knowledge: pantology, n. (pantologist, n. pantologic, pantological, adj.)

15. To Spread (Knowledge) for Instructive Purposes; To Sow Seeds of (Knowledge): disseminate, v. (dissemination, semination, n.)

16. Science, Study, or Philosophy of General Knowledge, Its Origins, Limits, Validity, etc.: epistemology, n. (epistemologist, n. epistemological, adj.)

17. Means for Gaining Knowledge: organon, n.

18. Able to Apply Knowledge or Theory: practical, adj. (practicality, n.)

612. KNOW

1. To Know; To Have Knowledge of: appreciate, cognize, realize, v. (appreciation, cognition, realization, n.)

2. To Gain Knowledge through the Mind or Senses: perceive, v. (perception, n.)

3. To Know Beforehand: foreknow, v.

4. To Know on Seeing Again: recognize,v. (recognition,n. recognizable,adj.)

5. Process of Knowing: cognition,n. (cognitive,adj.)

6. Product of the Process of Knowing: cognition,n.

7. Knowable: cognizable, cognoscible,adj. (cognizability, cognoscibility,n. cognoscible, n.)

8. One Who Is in the Know, or Who Has Knowledge: cognoscente,n. (cognoscenti,pl.)

9. One Who Has Knowledge of the Ways of the World: sophisticate, worldling,n.

10. To Become Known (of Facts, etc.): transpire,v. (transpiration,n.)

11. Generally or Widely Known: common, exoteric, familiar, proverbial,adj. (commonness, exotericism, familiarity,n.)

12. Known to the Mind: conscious,adj. (consciousness,n.)

13. Above the Threshold of Consciousness: supraliminal,adj.

14. Known Only to a Few; Not Well Known: esoteric, little-known, obscure, orphic, recondite, secret, unfamiliar,adj. (obscurity, reconditeness, secrecy, unfamiliarity,n.)

15. One Who Has Knowledge of Those Things, Doctrines, or Practices Known Only to a Few: esoteric,n.

16. Unknowable: incalculable, incognizable, incognoscible, inscrutable,adj. (incalculability, incognoscibility, inscrutability,n.)

17. Outside the Possible Bounds of Human Knowledge: occult,adj.

18. Beyond the Possibility of Knowledge from Actual Experience: metempiric, metempirical,adj.

19. An Unknowable Fact, Factor, or Possibility: imponderable,n. (imponderables or imponderabilia,pl.)

20. Concern with, or Doctrine That Stresses, Facts, Material, etc., That Are beyond the Possibility of Knowledge through Actual Experience: metempiricism,n. (metempiricist, n.)

21. Science or Study of Those Relations and Concepts That Are Beyond the Possibility of Knowledge through Actual Experience: metempirics,n. (metempiric, metempirical,adj.)

22. Doctrine that All Knowledge Is Relative and Uncertain: agnosticism,n. (agnostic,n. agnostic,adj.)

23. Unknown: strange, unascertained, undeduced, undetermined, undiagnosed, undiscovered, unexplored, unfamiliar, unfathomed, unlearned, unplumbed,adj.

24. Descr. of That Which Remains Unknown because of Lack of Facts or Conditions to Permit Successful or Useful Pondering upon, Consideration of, or Thinking about: imponderable,adj. (imponderability,n.)

25. Still Unknown or Unexplored Area in Any Subject or Field of Knowledge: terra incognita,n.

26. That Part of a Science Not Yet Conclusively Known and So Subject to Theorizing, Speculating, or Conjecturing: theoretics,n.

613. MAKE KNOWN

1. To Make (Something, or Some Information) Known,v.
1. advertise—make known
2. air—make known; make public disclosure of

3. announce—make known to the public; make the arrival or presence of known; make known to the senses or to the mind

4. babble—make known in loose talk (that which should have been kept secret)

5. betray—disclose (what one has promised to keep secret); make known without intending to

6. blab—make (secrets) known; disclose thoughtlessly

7. blaze—make known to all the public

8. blazon—make known publicly

9. blurt out—divulge without meaning to

10. communicate—make known; give knowledge of

11. convey—make known

12. declare—make known

13. develop—make known

14. disclose—make known (often that which was once secret or unknown)

15. disembosom oneself of—disclose

16. disseminate—spread (information) for purposes of instruction

17. divulge—make known publicly (that which was formerly kept secret)

18. expose—make known (what has heretofore been kept secret or remained unknown); make (something discreditable) known

19. herald—make known

20. impart—make known; disclose

21. noise (it) around—make known generally

22. proclaim—make known

23. promulgate, promulge—make known

24. publicize—make known to the general public; make known to many

25. publish—make generally or commonly known; make known by printing and distributing

26. report—make one's whereabouts or presence known; make known (the misconduct, etc., of someone, usually to his superior, the authorities, etc.)

27. resound—make known loudly

28. reveal—make known; disclose (that which had been hidden, secret, or concealed)

29. signify—make known by words or signs

30. squeal—make a secret known (colloq.)

31. tattle—make another's secret or secrets known; make known (the secrets of another)

32. tell—make known by words or signs

33. unbosom oneself of—disclose (one's secret or secrets)

34. unburden oneself of—make known (that which, kept secret, remains a weight or burden on one's mind or conscience)

35. unmask—expose

36. vend—publish for all to see

37. ventilate—make known to all; air

38. voice—make known (a feeling, etc.) through words or actions

2. A Making Something or Information Known,n. *From Sec. 1:* announcement, betrayal, blazonment, communication, conveyance, declaration, development, disclosure, dissemination or semination; divulgement, divulgence, or divulgation; exposure, exposal, or exposé; impartation or impartance, proclamation; publication (from *publish*); revelation or revealment, signification, unburdenment, ventilation; *Also:* 1. showdown—a forced or frank revealing of facts

3. That Which Is Made Known,n. *From Sec. 1:* disclosure, communication, revelation

4. Means of Making Known; That Which Makes Known,n. *From Sec. 1:* advertisement, announcement, babble, blab, communication, conveyance, declaration, exposure or exposé, proclamation, publicity, publication, report, tattle

5. One Who Makes Known,n. *From Sec. 1:* advertiser, announcer or annunciator, babbler, betrayer; blab, blabber or blabbermouth; blazoner, blurter, communicator, conveyor, disseminator; divulger, divulgater, or divulgator; exposer, herald, imparter, proclaimer or proclamator, promulgator or promulger, publicizer, publisher; revealer, revelator, or revelationer; squealer, tattler, tattletale, or taleteller, teller, unbosomer, vendor

6. Making, or Serving to Make, Known,adj. *From Sec. 1:* annunciative or annunciatory (from *announce*), declarative or declaratory, divulgatory, impartive, proclamatory, revelative or revelatory, significant or significative; *Also:* **1. telltale**—revealing that which was intended to be hidden

7. Pert. to Making Known,adj. *From Sec. 1:* annunciative or annunciatory, communicative or communicatory, proclamatory, revelatory or revelational

8. To Make Known the Faults, Crimes, or Other Shameful Things about (a Person): expose; report (esp. to a superior, the authorities, etc.), unmask,v. (exposure,n.)

9. To Give Away the Secrets of (Someone): betray,v. (betrayal,n. betrayer,n.)

10. To Give Incriminating Information about a Person: bear or carry tales; inform (on); peach (slang); snitch (slang); squeak (slang); squeal (colloq.); tattle,v.

11. One Who Informs on Another or Others: betrayer, blab, blabber, informer; snitcher (slang); squeaker (slang); squealer (colloq.); stool pigeon (slang); talebearer, taleteller, tattletale, telltale,n.

12. To Announce,v.
1. **annunciate**—announce
2. **blazon**—announce publicly
3. **enunciate**—announce; announce publicly
4. **herald**—announce publicly
5. **proclaim**—announce publicly
6. **promulgate, promulge**—announce officially or formally
7. **publish**—announce publicly, officially, or formally
8. **resound**—proclaim loudly
9. **toll**—announce by striking a bell
10. **trumpet**—announce publicly on, or as if on, a trumpet

13. Announcement, i.e., Act of Announcing, n. *From Sec. 12:* blazonment, enunciation, proclamation, promulgation, publication

14. An Announcement,n. *From Sec. 12:* proclamation; *Also:*
1. **bill**—written or printed public announcement
2. **bull**—official announcement by the Pope
3. **manifesto**—public announcement of principles or policy by a group, government, etc.
4. **notice**—announcement
5. **placard**—publicly posted announcement
6. **poster**—placard
7. **pronouncement**—formal announcement
8. **pronunciamento**—formal or public announcement
9. **trial balloon**—announcement made to test public reaction or opinion

15. Announcer,n. *From Sec. 12:* annunciator, blazoner, enunciator, herald, proclaimer or proclamator, promulgator or promulger; *Also:* 1. **crier**—one who announces orders in a court

16. Announcing,adj. *From Sec. 12:* annunciative or annunciatory, enunciative or enunciatory, proclamatory

17. To Tell,v.
1. **communicate**—tell
2. **confide**—tell, knowing or believing that what is told will be kept secret

3. **dictate**—tell (something) to another, who writes it down
4. **disclose**—tell
5. **narrate**—tell (a story)
6. **recite**—tell in detail
7. **recount**—tell in detail
8. **rehearse**—tell in detail
9. **relate**—tell
10. **report**—tell
11. **reveal**—tell
12. **signify**—tell; tell by words or signs
13. **summarize**—tell the main points of
14. **transmit**—tell (information, news, etc.)

18. A Telling,n. *From Sec. 17:* communication, dictation, disclosure, narration or narrative, recital or recitation, recountal, rehearsal, relation, revealment or revelation, signification, summarization, transmission, transmittal, or transmittance

19. Teller,n. *From Sec. 17:* communicator, confider, dictator, discloser, narrator, reciter, recounter, rehearser, relater or relator, reporter, revealer, summarizer, transmitter

20. That Which Is Told,n. *From Sec. 17:* communication, confidence, dictation, narrative or narration, recital or recitation, relation, report, revelation; *Also:*
1. **account**—that which is told in words, whether oral or written
2. **cahier** (French)—report
3. **canard**—false report designedly propagated to mislead people, and usually defamatory
4. **compte rendu** (French)—report of happenings
5. **story**—account
6. **tale**—that which is told; report intended to injure the reputation
7. **version**—account from one point of view
8. **white paper, white book**—official government report

21. Serving to Tell; Descr. of Telling,adj. *From Sec. 17:* communicative or communicatory, narrative, revelative or revelatory, significant or significative

22. Pert. to a Reporter or His Duties: reportorial,adj.

23. To Tell about,v.
1. **describe**—tell about; give an account of
2. **detail**—tell completely about; tell all about; tell about item by item
3. **herald**—tell news of
4. **narrate**—tell about in story form; give an account of
5. **outline**—tell the general plan of
6. **recite**—report on a prepared lesson to a teacher; tell about in detail
7. **recount**—tell about in detail
8. **rehearse**—recount
9. **relate**—tell the story of
10. **report**—give an account of; tell about officially
11. **testify, testify to**—tell about under oath in court; witness
12. **witness**—tell under oath in court, about what one has seen, heard, or knows from actual experience

24. A Telling about,n. *From Sec. 23:* description, narration or narrative, recitation or recital, recountal, rehearsal, relation, report

25. That Which Tells about,n. *From Sec. 23:* description, narrative or narration, outline, recitation or recital, relation, report, testimony

26. One Who Tells about,n. *From Sec. 23:* describer, detailer, herald, narrator, reciter, recounter, rehearser, relater or relator, reporter, testifier, witness

27. Telling about,adj. *From Sec. 23:* descriptive, narrative

28. To Tell or Inform (Someone); To Let (Someone) Know,v.
  1. **acquaint** (. . . with)—let know; inform; tell (usually that which is the beginning of one's knowledge of something)
  2. **advertise** (. . . of)—inform; give notice to
  3. **advise** (. . . of or that)—give information or notice to
  4. **apprize, apprise** (. . . of)—tell (something of interest or importance) to, often by means of a message; inform; notify
  5. **circularize**—send a notice or advertisement to
  6. **communicate with**—give or send information to
  7. **confide in**—tell one's troubles to
  8. **enlighten**—inform (with truth)
  9. **familiarize** (. . . with)—acquaint
  10. **misinform**—give misleading or false information to
  11. **notify** (. . . of or that)—tell by calling one's notice (often to things that require attention); give notice to; inform; let know; tell
  12. **orient, orientate**—acquaint with the existing situation; familiarize
  13. **tip off**—give secret information to
  14. **warn** (. . . of or that)—inform (of possible or approaching danger or risk)

29. Act of Telling or Informing Someone,n. *From Sec. 28:* circularization, communication, enlightenment, notification, orientation; *Also:*
  1. **intercourse**—communication of ideas, feelings, etc., between people, groups, etc.
  2. **telecommunication**—communication at a distance by any of various means (radio, telegraph, etc.)
  3. **telepathy**—communication of thought by extranormal or psychical means; thought transference (telepathist,n. telepathic, adj.)

30. Information,n. *From Sec. 28:* advertisement, advice or advisory, circular, communication, confidence, misinformation, notification, tip or tip-off, warning; *Also:*
  1. **aviso**—information; notification
  2. **communiqué**—official information told or given out by a nation, army, headquarters of an organization, etc.
  3. **dossier**—collection of data, documents, or detailed information about a person or thing
  4. **intelligence**—information; news
  5. **message**—information or communication in speech or writing delivered by a third person
  6. **missive**—written message
  7. **news**—information on happenings
  8. **notice**—information
  9. **propaganda**—information spread by an interested group
  10. **scoop**—piece of news published by one newspaper before others publish it
  11. **side light**—incidental information
  12. **tidings**—information; news

31. Informant,n. *From Sec. 28:* adviser or advisor, communicator, enlightener, misinformant or misinformer, notifier, warner; *From Sec. 30:* messenger, propagandist; *Also:*
  1. **herald**—messenger
  2. **tipster**—one who gives or tells special or secret information to be used in gambling

32. Informative,adj. *From Sec. 28:* advisory, orientative, warning; *Also:* 1. **newsy**—full of news, usually trivial

33. Inclined to Give Information: communicative,adj. (communicativeness,n.)

34. To Give Tips on a Horserace in Return for a Share of the Winnings: tout,v.

35. One Who Gives Such Tips: tout,n.

36. Place or Person from Which or Whom Information Is Obtained: source,n.

37. Someone in Whom One Confides, or to Whom One Tells One's Secrets: confidant,n. (confidante,fem.n.)

38. Descr. of Information Suitable for the General Public: exoteric,adj. (exotericism,n.)

39. State of Being Informed: enlightenment, illumination,n. (enlightened,adj.)

40. State of Being Spiritually Informed: illumination,n.

41. Claim to Special Spiritual or Intellectual Information Not Accessible to Most People: illuminism,n. (illuministic,adj.)

42. One Who Claims Special Information or Enlightenment: illuminato (illuminati,pl.), illuminee,n.

614. PUBLICITY

1. Publicity,n.
  1. **ballyhoo**—noisy or blatant publicity
  2. **notoriety**—publicity about one's wickedness, errors, sins, etc.
  3. **puffery**—exaggerated publicity; exaggeratedly laudatory publicity
  4. **réclame (French)**—publicity

2. To Give Publicity to,v. *From Sec. 1:* ballyhoo, puff; *Also:*
  1. **advertise**—give wide publicity to
  2. **publicize**—give publicity to

3. The Seeking of Publicity: réclame,n. (French)

4. The Business of Publicity: press-agentry, public relations,n.

5. Someone in the Business of Publicity: huckster (derogatory), press agent or publicity agent, publicist, public relations counselor,n.

615. FAME

1. Famous; Well-Known,adj.
  1. **celebrated**—famous; well-known
  2. **classic, classical**—famous in literature
  3. **crying**—notorious
  4. **distinguished**—famous or well-known for excellence, superiority, etc.
  5. **eminent**—well-known for one's distinguished accomplishments or high position in a group
  6. **famed**—famous
  7. **familiar**—well-known
  8. **illustrious**—famous; known far and wide for one's achievements
  9. **immortal**—forever famous
  10. **laureate**—distinguished, esp. for poetic achievement
  11. **notable**—distinguished
  12. **noted**—famous; well-known; known by reputation
  13. **notorious**—well and widely known for bad, immoral, wicked, or unpleasant things, acts, or behavior
  14. **outstanding**—well-known
  15. **prominent**—famous; well-known
  16. **proverbial**—well-known (of things, qualities, etc.)
  17. **redoubted**—renowned
  18. **renowned**—gloriously famous
  19. **splendent**—famous; illustrious
  20. **storied**—celebrated in history or stories
  21. **supereminent**—eminent to a great degree
  22. **top-flight**—most highly eminent
  23. **upmost, uppermost**—most well-known

2. Fame; State of Being Well-Known,n. *From Sec. 1:* distinction, eminence, familiarity, illustriousness, immortality, laureateship, notoriety or notoriousness, prominence, renown, supereminence; *Also:*

1. **kudos**—fame
2. **prestige**—fame; renown
3. **repute**—fame
4. **rumor**—notoriety; public fame

3. Famous or Well-Known Person,n. *From Sec. 1:* celebrity, immortal, laureate, notable; *Also:*

1. **luminary**—famous person
2. **personage**—famous person

4. To Make Famous or Well-Known,v. *From Sec. 1:* celebrate, familiarize, immortalize (celebration, familiarization, immortalization, n.); *Also:*

1. **emblazon**—make famous, perhaps by literally inscribing the name conspicuously and publicly, or in some way giving bright and conspicuous publicity to (emblazonment, emblazonry,n.)
2. **eternize**—make famous for all time
3. **publicize**—make well-known by giving publicity to

5. Book, Story, Poem, Author, etc., That Is Famous in Literature: classic,n.

6. To Bring from a State of Obscurity into Public Notice or View: disinter,v. (disinterment,n.)

616. RUMOR

1. Rumor: buzz, comment, hearsay, report, repute; scuttlebutt (navy term),n.

2. A Rumor: report,n.

3. Idle or Malicious Rumor: gossip, scandal, tales, tattle, tittle-tattle,n.

4. A Malicious Rumor: canard, tale,n.

5. To Spread Rumor or a Rumor: buzz, gossip; noise (it) about, abroad, around, etc., tattle, tittle-tattle,v.

6. To Spread a Rumor about (Someone or Something); To Spread by Rumor: noise about, abroad, around, etc., rumor,v.

7. Rumored: bruited, bruited about, buzzed, gossiped, noised around, reported, reputed, adj.

8. Spreading, or Tending to Spread, Rumors: gossipy,adj.

9. Pert. to a Rumor; Of the Character of a Rumor; Filled with Rumor: rumorous,adj.

10. One Who Spreads Rumor, a Rumor, or Rumors: gossip, newsmonger, quidnunc, rumorer, rumormonger, talebearer, taleteller, tattler, telltale, tittle-tattle,n.

617. DESCRIPTION

1. To Describe,v.

1. **characterize**—describe; describe the special features of
2. **delineate**—describe
3. **depict, depicture**—describe; portray
4. **explicate**—give a thorough and detailed description of
5. **geographize**—describe the earth, or a part of the earth, in reference to air, land, sea, inhabitants, natural features, etc.
6. **limn**—describe or picture in words
7. **picture**—describe graphically, vividly, or clearly; describe in words
8. **portray**—describe in words that give a picture; describe vividly or very clearly
9. **specify, specificate**—describe definitely or in detail

2. Description,n. *From Sec. 1:* characterization, delineation, depiction, depicture, explication, geography or geographics; portrayal, portrait, or portraiture; specification; *Also:*
1. **chorography**—description of a region

2. **topography**—exact description, in minute details, of the physical features of a region, usually by means of maps or charts
3. **version**—description from one point of view
4. **vignette**—short description

3. One Who Describes,n. *From Sec. 1:* delineator, depicter or depictor, geographer, portrayer or portrayist; *From Sec. 2:* chorographer, topographer or topographist

4. Descriptive,adj. *From Sec. 1:* delineative, depictive, explicative or explicatory; specific, specifical or specificative; *From Sec. 2:* topographic or topographical

5. Pert. to, or Characteristic of, Description,adj. *From Sec. 1:* delineatory, explicatory; *From Sec. 2:* chorographic or chorographical, topographic or topographical

6. Hard to Describe: indescribable, ineffable, nondescript, subtle,adj. (indescribability, ineffability or ineffableness, subtlety or subtleness,n.)

618. MAP

1. A Map,n.
1. **cartogram**—a kind of map
2. **chart**—map
3. **chorography**—map of a region
4. **plat**—map of the site where a town is to be built

2. Book of Maps: atlas,n.

3. Art or Practice of Making or Drawing Maps,n.
1. **cartography**—art or practice of drawing maps (cartographer,n. cartographic, cartographical,adj.)
2. **chorography**—art or practice of making a map of a region (chorographer,n. chorograph, chorographical,adj.)
3. **topography**—art or practice of making maps showing the exact description, in minute detail, of the physical features of a place (topographer, topographist,n. topographic, topographical,adj.)

4. Sphere Containing a Map of the Earth or Heavens: globe,n.

619. EXPERIENCE

1. Experienced,adj.
1. **accustomed to**—experienced in
2. **bookish**—experienced in books or academic learning, but not in practical affairs (bookishness,n.)
3. **cosmopolitan**—experienced in worldly things or in the world's ways (cosmopolitanism,n.)
4. **practical**—experienced in actual work or practice (practicality,n.)
5. **practiced, practised**—experienced
6. **seasoned**—experienced
7. **sophisticated**—experienced in the world's ways (sophistication,n.)
8. **trained**—experienced, in the sense of having undergone instruction combined with practice and experience in some work or profession
9. **versed (in)**—experienced (in)
10. **veteran**—experienced; long experienced in an activity, profession, etc.
11. **worldly, worldly-wise**—experienced in the ways of the world (worldliness, worldly wisdom,n.)

2. Experience,n. *From Sec. 1:* practice, practise, seasoning, training

3. To Become Experienced,v. *From Sec. 1:* practice, practise, train (in or for)

4. To Make Experienced,v. *From Sec. 1:* season, train

5. Experienced Person,n. *From Sec. 1:* cosmopolite, sophisticate, veteran, worldling

6. One's Complete Experience, Training, etc.: background,n.

7. Reliance on Methods or Techniques Based on Experience, Observation, Experiment, etc.; Undue Reliance on Such Methods or Techniques, without Proper Regard for Theoretical Knowledge: empiricism,n. (empiric, empiricist,n. empirical, empiric, empiricist,adj.)

8. Relating or Pert. to, or Based on, Experience,adj.
1. **empirical, empiric**—guided by, or dependent, founded, or resting upon, practical experience rather than upon theory; founded or dependent solely upon empirical knowledge without regard for theory or theoretical knowledge, esp. in medicine
2. **experiential**—based on, or relating to, experience
3. **practical**—relating or pert. to experience or practice

620. INEXPERIENCED

1. Inexperienced,adj.
1. **bookish**—experienced in books or academic learning, but not in practical affairs (bookishness,n.)
2. **callow**—inexperienced or unsophisticated because of immaturity or youth (callowness,n.)
3. **green**—inexperienced (greenness,n.)
4. **innocent**—sexually inexperienced; unsophisticated (innocence,n.)
5. **naïve; naïf (French)**—lacking in worldly experience (naïveté,n.)
6. **raw**—inexperienced (rawness,n.)
7. **sophomoric**—inexperienced, but pretending to great wisdom, knowledge, or experience
8. **strange at or in**—inexperienced at or in
9. **unaccustomed to**—inexperienced in
10. **unpracticed, unpractised**—inexperienced
11. **unseasoned**—inexperienced
12. **unsophisticated**—inexperienced in the world's ways; sexually inexperienced (unsophication,n.)
13. **untrained**—inexperienced, in the sense of not having had instruction combined with practice
14. **unworldly**—inexperienced in the ways of the world (unworldliness,n.)
15. **verdant**—inexperienced; unsophisticated (verdancy,n.)
16. **virgin to**—inexperienced in

2. Inexperienced Person,n.
1. **babe**—inexperienced, innocent and naïve person
2. **colt**—inexperienced person
3. **greenhorn**—someone totally inexperienced in something
4. **virgin**—one who is sexually inexperienced

3. Time of Youthful Inexperience: salad days,n.

621. INSTRUCTION

1. To Teach (Someone); To Train (Someone),v.
1. **catechize**—teach by asking questions to be answered
2. **coach**—train; help to prepare for a test
3. **cradle**—train while very young
4. **cultivate**—train; improve or develop by teaching or training
5. **discipline**—train; train the mind or character of
6. **domesticate**—train (animals) to live with people, to live in a human habitation, etc.

7. **edify**—teach for purposes of moral improvement
8. **educate**—teach; train
9. **enlighten**—instruct; shed upon (someone) the figurative light of truth, knowledge, or true information; free (someone) from the figurative darkness of ignorance, misunderstanding, or error
10. **ground (. . . in)**—give elementary or basic training (in)
11. **illuminate, illumine**—enlighten
12. **implant (. . . with)**—figuratively plant (learning or knowledge) in
13. **inculcate (. . . with)**—teach by frequent example
14. **indoctrinate, indoctrine (. . . with)**—teach the rudiments or principles of (a field, belief, etc.) to
15. **initiate (. . . in)**—teach the principles of (a subject) to
16. **instruct**—teach, often under formal circumstances
17. **nurture**—teach; train
18. **recondition**—re-educate
19. **re-educate**—educate over again; teach or train again; teach new things, ideas, or principles to, to take the place of old or discarded ones
20. **school**—teach; train
21. **tutor**—teach; give individual instruction to; train; discipline

2. To Teach (Something),v. *From Sec. 1:* implant, inculcate, indoctrinate

3. Teaching; Training,n. *From Sec. 1:* catechism, cultivation, discipline, domestication, edification, education, enlightenment, illumination, implantation, inculcation, indoctrination, initiation, instruction, nurture, re-education; *Also:*
1. **cabala, cabalism**—secret teaching
2. **catechesis**—instruction given orally in doctrines of the church
3. **clinic**—instruction through direct attack on specific problems; medical instruction by this means
4. **coeducation**—education of students of both sexes at the same institution
5. **propaedeutics**—preliminary instruction or introductory teaching in any field; preparatory instruction in an art or science, etc.
6. **propaganda**—instruction spread by an interested group
7. **tuition**—instruction; teaching
8. **tutelage**—instruction

4. One's Education; State of Being Taught or Trained,n. *From Sec. 1:* cultivation, edification, enlightenment, grounding, illumination, indoctrination, initiation, nurture, schooling; *Also:*
1. **background**—one's complete training, education, experience, etc.
2. **breeding**—training in the ways of polite society
3. **culture**—development by training or teaching
4. **literacy**—education

5. Serving to Teach or Train,adj. *From Sec. 1:* catechistic, disciplinary or disciplinarian, edifying, educational or educative, enlightening, inculcative or inculcatory, initiative or initiatory, instructive or instructional, re-educative; *From Sec. 3:* catachetic, propaedeutic, propagandistic; *From Sec. 4:* cultural; *Also:*
1. **didactic**—intended for purposes of teaching; serving to teach; serving to teach a moral lesson
2. **preceptive, preceptory**—serving to teach

6. Descr. of, or Pert. to, Teaching,adj. *From Sec. 1:* catechistic, disciplinal, educational, inculcatory, initiative or initiatory, instructional, re-educational, tutorial; *From Sec. 3:*

cabalic or cabalistic, clinical or clinic, coeducational, tuitional or tuitionary; *From Sec. 4:* cultural; *Also:*

1. **academic**—pert. to higher education; classical
2. **classical**—descr. of, or pert. to, the teaching of general subjects, general sciences, humanities, etc.
3. **deductive**—descr. of a type of teaching in which principles are first explained, then examples drawn
4. **homiletic**—pert. to, or descr. of, moral teaching through sermons
5. **inductive**—descr. of a method of teaching whereby principles are derived from a study of examples
6. **pedagogic, pedagogical**—pert. to teaching or education
7. **scholastic**—pert. to education

7. Teacher; Trainer,n. *From Sec. 1:* coach, cultivator, disciplinarian, edifier, educator, enlightener, implanter, inculcator, indoctrinator; initiator or, fem., initiatress or initiatrix; instructor or, fem., instructress, nurturer, tutor or, fem., tutoress; *Also:*

1. **abecedarian, abecedary**—teacher of the rudiments or beginning principles of a subject; teacher of the alphabet
2. **docent**—teacher or lecturer (shortened form of *Privatdocent*)
3. **dominie**—schoolmaster (Scottish)
4. **don**—tutor at Oxford or Cambridge
5. **lecturer**—one who teaches by addressing a large group
6. **mentor**—teacher
7. **pedagogue**—teacher of children; any teacher (often derogatory); pedantic teacher
8. **preceptor**—teacher in a school (preceptress,fem.)
9. **Privatdocent (German)**—teacher in a German college whose fees are paid by his students
10. **professor**—person holding the highest rank in the faculty of a college (sometimes called *full professor*; below the professor, in descending rank, are the *associate professor, assistant professor, instructor, tutor, fellow,* etc.)
11. **pundit**—learned teacher (often faintly derogatory)
12. **schoolman**—teacher in a school
13. **schoolmarm**, **schoolma'am**—female teacher in a school
14. **schoolmaster**—teacher (schoolmistress, fem.)
15. **schoolteacher**—teacher in a school

8. Teachers Collectively,n. *From Sec. 7:* tutoriate or tutorhood; professorate or professoriate; *Also:* **1. faculty, staff**—body of teachers in an institution

9. State or Rank of Teacher,n. *From Sec. 7:* instructorship, tutorship; preceptorate, professorship, professorate or professoriate; *Also:* **1. teacherhood, teachership**—state of being a teacher

10. Teacherlike; Teacherish; Pert. to, Descr. of, Characteristic of, or Resembling a Teacher,adj. *From Sec. 7:* tutorial; donnish; pedagogic, pedagogical or pedagoguish; preceptoral or preceptorial, professorial, schoolmarmish; schoolmasterly, schoolmasterish, or schoolmastery; schoolmistressy; schoolteacherish, schoolteacherly, or schoolteachery (donnishness, pedagogism or pedagoguery, schoolmasterishness,n.) ; *Also:* **1. didactic**—inclined to act too much like a teacher (didacticism,n.)

11. Taught; Trained,adj. *From Sec. 1:* cultivated, disciplined, etc.; *From Sec. 4:* well-bred, cultured, literate; *Also:* **1. lettered**—taught; educated

12. Untaught; Untrained,adj. *From Sec. 1:* uncultivated, undisciplined, etc.; *From Sec. 4:* unbred or ill-bred, uncultured, illiterate; *From Sec. 11:* unlettered; *Also:*

1. **ignorant**—uninstructed (ignorance,n.)
2. **Philistine**—unenlightened; uncultured
3. **raw**—untrained (rawness,n.)
4. **unlearned**—uneducated
5. **virgin to**—untrained to

13. Untaught or Untrained Person,n. *From Sec. 4:* illiterate; *From Sec. 12:* ignoramus, Philistine (Philistinism,n.) ; *Also:* **1. empiric**—one who is untrained, i.e., who relies exclusively on practical experience in the type of work for which theoretical training is required

14. The Well-Educated Class: clerisy,n.

15. System of Spiritual Self-Improvement and Education: biosophy,n. (biosophical, adj.)

16. Branch of Instruction: discipline,n.

17. Outdoor Meeting, Usually of Adults, for Educational Purposes: chautauqua,n. (chautauquan,n. chautauqua, chautauquan,adj.)

18. Science, Art, Rules, etc., of Teaching,n.
1. **didactics**—art of teaching; principles of teaching; pedagogy
2. **pedagogics**—science or art of teaching; pedagogy
3. **pedagogy**—methods, principles, or rules of teaching (pedagogic, pedagogical,adj.)

19. Books for Instruction,n.
1. **catechism**—book of questions and proper answers used for religious instruction
2. **manual**—book of instruction
3. **text, textbook**—book used in instruction

20. Fees Paid for Instruction in a School or Other Institution of Learning: tuition,n.

622. STUDY

1. To Study,v.
1. **brush up on**—study to refresh one's knowledge of
2. **coach in or with**—receive instruction in or from; study with (someone), acting as the teacher
3. **lucubrate**—study late at night; study hard or with great effort
4. **major in**—study as one's main field in school or college
5. **minor in**—study as one's secondary field in school or college
6. **review**—study again
7. **specialize (in)**—study some special branch of knowledge
8. **train in**—get practical education in (some work or profession)
9. **tutor in or with**—take individual instruction in (some subject) or with (someone acting as the teacher)

2. Study, i.e., Act or Process of Studying,n. *From Sec. 1:* coaching, lucubration, review, specialization or specialism, training, tutoring

3. A Study; That Which Is Studied; Course of Study,n. *From Sec. 1:* major, minor, specialty; *Also:*
1. **class**—subject, or course of study, pursued in a school
2. **content**—matter included or dealt with in a field of study
3. **course**—one of a systematic series of studies; subject
4. **curriculum**—course of study in an institution of learning
5. **lesson**—that which is, or is to be, studied
6. **moral**—practical lesson taught in a story, fable, etc.
7. **seminar**—course of study pursued by graduate or other students engaged in original research

8. **subject**—study pursued in a school, college, etc.
9. **syllabus**—course of study in a field

4. Pert. to, or Descr. of, Studying, Study, or Studies,adj. *From Sec. 1:* lucubratory, major, minor; *From Sec. 3:* curricular; *Also:*
1. **academic**—pert. to, or descr. of, studies or studying in school or college
2. **chautauquan, chautauqua**—pert. to, or descr. of, studies or studying by adults, originally in outdoor assemblies, now in any courses specifically for adults
3. **classical**—pert. to, or descr. of, courses of general culture
4. **collegiate**—pert. to, or descr. of, studies or courses in college
5. **extension**—descr. of courses given by a college for students, often adults, not working for a degree
6. **liberal**—descr. of courses for general, rather than vocational, technical, or professional, education; classical
7. **postgraduate**—pert. to, or descr. of, courses or studying subsequent to graduation
8. **scholarly**—pert. to, or descr. of, studies or studying
9. **scholastic**—pert. to, or descr. of, studies or studying in school or college
10. **studious**—pert. to, characterized by, or concerned with, study or studying
11. **undergraduate**—pert. to, or descr. of, courses taken before graduation

5. Student; Learner,n. *From Sec. 1:* lucubrator, major, specialist, trainee; *Also:*
1. **abecedarian, abecedary**—someone who is learning the very beginnings of a subject
2. **academic**—university or college student
3. **apprentice**—one who is learning, by practical experience, some job or calling
4. **autodidact**—self-learner (autodidactic, adj.)
5. **cadet**—boy in military school
6. **Cantabrigian**—student at the University of Cambridge
7. **catechumen**—one who is learning the beginning principles, esp. of church doctrines
8. **classmate**—fellow student in a group
9. **coed**—girl in an institution of learning attended by both sexes
10. **collegian**—student at a college
11. **condisciple**—fellow learner or student
12. **disciple**—one who receives instruction from another
13. **neophyte**—learner in any field, esp. in religious instruction
14. **novice**—learner in a field
15. **Oxonian**—student at Oxford University
16. **postgraduate**—student who pursues courses after graduation (postgraduate, adj.)
17. **pupil**—student of a teacher or class
18. **scholar**—student at a school or of a teacher (scholastic,adj.)
19. **schoolmate**—fellow student at a school
20. **seminarian, seminarist**—student in a school for those entering the clergy (seminarianism,n. seminaristic,adj.)
21. **seminarist**—student of a seminar, or class engaged in original research (seminaristic,adj.)
22. **tyro**—new learner in a field
23. **undergraduate**—student in a college who has not yet received his degree (undergraduate,adj.)
24. **votary, votarist**—devoted student of something (votaress, votress,fem.n. votary,adj.)

6. Student According to Years of Attendance,n.
1. **freshman**—first-year student in college or high school (freshman,adj.)
2. **junior**—student in the third year of a

secondary school or college (junior,adj.)
3. **lowerclassman**—freshman or sophomore (lowerclass,adj.)
4. **senior**—student in the fourth or final year of a secondary school or college (senior,adj.)
5. **sophomore**—student in the second year of a secondary school or college (sophomore,adj.)
6. **upperclassman**—junior or senior (upperclass,adj.)

7. Students Collectively, Usually in a Schoolroom: class,n.

8. Class of Graduate or Other Students Pursuing Original Research: seminar,n.

9. Fond of, or Given to, Studying: bookish, scholarly, studious,adj. (bookishness, scholarliness, studiousness,n.)

10. Quick to Learn: apt,adj. (aptitude, aptness,n.)

11. Eager to Learn: curious,adj. (curiosity,n.)

12. To Create a Desire in (a Pupil) to Learn: motivate,v. (motivation,n.)

13. Learning,n.
1. **culture**—learning
2. **education**—learning; learning derived from school
3. **erudition**—learning; learning that comes from books rather than from practical experience
4. **lore**—learning; body of learning about a particular subject, or possessed by a group and handed down from previous generations
5. **scholarship**—learning

14. Learned,adj. *From Sec. 13:* cultured, educated, erudite, scholarly (of people or their mental products) or schooled; *Also:*
1. **abstruse**—learned (of writing, mental products, etc.)
2. **literate**—learned; educated

15. Learnedness,n. *From Sec. 14:* culture, erudition or eruditeness, scholarliness; abstruseness, literacy

16. Pert. to, Descr. of, or Indicating, Learning,adj. *From Sec. 13:* cultural, erudite, scholarly; *From Sec. 14:* abstruse, literate; *Also:*
1. **Chaldean**—pert. to occult learning
2. **Palladian**—pert. to learning

17. A Learned Person,n.
1. **bookman**—scholar
2. **Brahman**—person of the highest culture; an intellectual; a supercilious intellectual (the term is derogatory or satirical)
3. **intellectual**—one whose interests are in learning, or who has attained a high degree of learning (now sometimes faintly derogatory)
4. **literatus**—one who is above average in learning
5. **Minerva**—woman of great learning
6. **polyhistor**—person with incredibly vast learning
7. **pundit**—learned teacher; any learned man (often faintly derogatory)
8. **savant**—person of great learning
9. **scholar**—person of great learning

18. Learned People; Learned People as a Class: clerisy, literati,n.

19. Person Versed in the Learning of Ancient Babylonia: Chaldean,n.

20. Unnecessary or Excessive Display of Learning, Often by an Insistence on Correctness and Distinctions: bookishness, pedantism, pedantry,n. (pedant,n. bookish, pedantic, pedantical,adj.)

21. To Act Like a Pedant: pedantize,v.

22. A Pedantic Expression, Idea, Action, Trait, etc.: pedanticism, pedantism, pedantry, n.

623. SCHOOL

1. A School or Other Institution of Learning,n.
1. **academy**—place or institution of learning; secondary school; institution of higher learning; college or university (academic,adj.)
2. **alma mater**—school or college one attends, or from which one has graduated
3. **college**—institution of higher learning (collegiate,adj.)
4. **conservatory, conservatoire, conservatorium, conservatorio**—institution of learning, usually of music or the fine arts
5. **elementary school**—school going through the first six or eight grades
6. **finishing school**—private school for girls in which the curriculum is intended to prepare the students for cultural and social pursuits
7. **grammar school**—elementary school
8. **high school**—school going through four years beyond elementary school or, in some places, three years beyond junior high school
9. **institute**—institution devoted to technical subjects or to specialized teaching of advanced professional subjects
10. **junior college**—college going through two years (often for women)
11. **junior high school**—in some localities, school going through the seventh, eighth, and ninth grades, providing a transition to the last three years of high school
12. **lyceum**—place for instruction by means of lectures
13. **manège**—school for teaching the art of horse riding
14. **normal school**—school for training future teachers
15. **pension**—boarding school, usually in Europe
16. **preparatory school**—private school that prepares a student for college
17. **primary school**—elementary school
18. **public school**—elementary school; any non-private elementary or high school
19. **secondary school**—high school
20. **seminary**—institution of learning; private school; school for the ministry or priesthood; institution of learning for young women (seminarial,adj.)
21. **university**—institution of higher learning that includes a college of liberal arts, etc., and also various professional, technical, and postgraduate schools

2. Pert. or Relating to School: academic, scholastic,adj.

3. Conforming to the Rules or Traditions of School or of a School: academic,adj.

4. Descr. of, Relating to, or Pert. to, Activities in a School outside of the Regular Course of Study: extracurricular,adj.

5. Descr. of Extracurricular Activities Restricted to the Grounds or Student Body of a College or High School: intramural,adj.

6. Descr. of Such Activities Engaged in on the Grounds of, or with the Student Body of, Other Colleges or Schools: extramural, adj.

7. Head of a School,n.
1. **dean**—administrative head of a division of a university or college
2. **preceptor**—principal   (preceptress,fem. preceptoral, preceptorial,adj.)
3. **president**—administrative head of a college or university (presidential,adj.)

4. **principal**—head of an elementary or secondary school

8. Office or Rank of the Head of a School, n. From Sec. 7: deanery, preceptorate, presidency, principalship

9. To Enroll in a College: matriculate,v. (matriculation,n. matriculant, matriculator, n. matriculatory,adj.)

10. To Accept into the Student Body of a College: matriculate,v.   (matriculation,n. matriculatory,adj.)

11. Student Who Has Enrolled in and Been Accepted by a College: matriculate,n. (matriculate, matriculated,adj.)

12. Graduate of a School,n.
1. **alumna**—female graduate of an institution of learning (alumnae,pl.)
2. **alumnus**—male graduate of an institution of learning (alumni,pl.)
3. **bachelor**—graduate of a college
4. **Cantabrigian**—graduate of the University of Cambridge
5. **collegian**—graduate of a college
6. **diplomate**—one who has received a diploma or advanced degree, and (in medicine) who has been accepted into membership of a society of specialists
7. **doctor**—graduate of an advanced course of university study (doctoral, doctorial, adj.)
8. **master**—holder of a degree, conferred for advanced study in a college, between that of a bachelor and that of a doctor
9. **Oxonian**—graduate of Oxford University

13. The Degree or Title Conferred on a Graduate,n. From Sec. 12: baccalaureate (from bachelor), doctorate, masterate, master, or master's (baccalaureate, doctoral, doctorial,adj.)

14. Certificate Granted on Graduation: diploma,n.

15. Graduation Exercises at a School: commencement,n.

16. The Liberal Arts in the Middle Ages,n.
1. **quadrivium**—the four liberal arts of the Middle Ages—arithmetic, music, geometry, and astronomy
2. **trivium**—the lower group of the liberal arts of the Middle Ages—grammar, logic, and rhetoric

624. DISCOVERY

1. To Find Out,v.
1. **analyze**—determine the elements or parts of
2. **ascertain**—find out for sure through one's own experience or senses
3. **authenticate**—find out the truth of
4. **certify**—find out the truth of
5. **deduce**—find out by logically tracing the movement or course of; discover by drawing a conclusion from what is known or accepted
6. **descry**—determine by observing or investigating
7. **detect**—find out (whether something exists); find out (something that is concealed)
8. **determine**—find out; find out the truth or facts of (a matter)
9. **diagnose, diagnosticate**—find out the type or cause of (disease) or the cause and classification of (any difficulty or problem) by examining scientifically the symptoms, indications, etc.
10. **discern**—find out by seeing or by understanding
11. **discover**—find out (something not previously known)
12. **divine**—find out; find out by intuition,

feeling, guessing, or some means other than logical deduction

13. **fathom**—find out by digging into, figuratively penetrating the depth of, etc.
14. **ferret out**—discover (that which is hidden or intended to be kept hidden) often by ingenious questions or similar strategy
15. **get to the bottom of**—find out the truth, causes, or basis of
16. **learn**—find out without any great search or effort
17. **perceive**—find out through one of the five senses or through the use of the mind
18. **pin-point**—determine exactly
19. **plumb**—discover all the secrets, complexities, depths, or ramifications of; get to the bottom of, figuratively
20. **tell**—find out; determine; learn
21. **trace**—find out by searching
22. **track down**—find out by searching or following clues to
23. **uncover**—find out by figuratively removing the covering of or by nullifying efforts to conceal
24. **unearth**—find out (something hidden, figuratively buried, lost sight of, forgotten, etc.)
25. **unravel**—find out by solving the mystery of, or by simplifying the complications of
26. **verify**—find out or ascertain the truth, truthfulness, or accuracy of

2. A Finding Out,n. *From Sec. 1:* analysis, ascertainment, authentication, certification, deduction, detection, determination, diagnosis, diagnostication, discernment, discovery, divination, perception, unravelment, verification

3. Finding Out; Tending or Serving to Find Out,adj. *From Sec. 1:* analytic or analytical, deductive, detective, determinative, diagnostic, perceptive; *Also:* 1. **diacritic**—diagnostic (medical)

4. One Who Finds Out,n. *From Sec. 1:* analyst, deducer, detective or detector, discerner, discoverer, diviner, ferret or ferreter, tracer, tracker, unraveler, verifier

5. Capable of Being Found Out,adj. *From Sec. 1:* analyzable, ascertainable, etc.

6. Easily Detected: transparent,adj. (transparency,n.)

7. To Gain Information by Observing an Area: scout,v. (scout,n.)

8. To Seek or Attempt to Find Out or Gain Information,v.
1. **examine**—look at carefully to find out about; subject (a patient) to various tests or procedures in order to make a diagnosis or determine the state of health; investigate
2. **inquire into, enquire into**—seek to find out by asking questions about; investigate
3. **inquisite, inquisit**—inquire into; investigate
4. **investigate**—seek to find out about; seek answers to questions about
5. **pry into**—seek impudently to find out about (matters, circumstances, conditions, etc., that are not one's concern)
6. **research into**—make a studious and thorough attempt to find out about
7. **study**—examine carefully to learn about

9. A Seeking, Attempting, or Attempt to Find Out,n. *From Sec. 8:* examination, inquiry, enquiry, investigation, research, study; *Also:*
1. **disquisition**—formal and/or elaborate inquiry into a matter
2. **inquest**—inquiry or investigation, usually official
3. **inquirendo**—inquiry; investigation

10. One Who Seeks to Find Out,n. *From Sec.*

8: examiner or examinant, inquirer, enquirer, inquisitor, investigator, pry, researcher, student; *From Sec. 9:* disquisitor

11. Given to Seeking Information,adj. *From Sec. 8:* inquiring or inquisitive, investigative, prying, studious

12. Pert. or Relating to Seeking Information or to an Attempt to Find Out,adj. *From Sec. 8:* examinational, examinative, examinatory, or examinatorial; inquisitional or inquisitorial; investigative, investigatory, or investigational; research, studious; *From Sec. 9:* disquisitive, disquisitional, disquisitory, or disquisitorial

13. Pert. to an Inquisitor: inquisitorial,adj.

14. Making Offensive or Searching Inquiry: inquisitorial, inquisitional,adj.

15. Eager to Find Out,adj.
1. **curious**—eager to find out, gain information, knowledge, etc. (curiosity,n.)
2. **inquisitive**—curious; eager to find out what is not one's concern (inquisitiveness, n.)
3. **inquisiturient**—eager to inquire

625. QUESTION

1. To Question, i.e., Ask Questions,v.
1. **catechize**—ask a formal set of questions of; question formally
2. **challenge**—call on for an answer or explanation
3. **cross-examine**—question very closely; question (a witness) in lawsuits—said of the opposing side to that which the witness is on
4. **cross-question**—question closely
5. **examine**—question in order to test (someone's) knowledge, ability, qualifications, etc.
6. **grill**—question persistently
7. **inquire of, enquire of**—question for the purpose of discovering facts, information, truth, etc.
8. **inquisition, inquisite, inquisit**—subject to a thorough and searching series of questions, sometimes for the purpose of persecuting or embarrassing; make a judicial or official inquiry of before a jury
9. **interrogate**—question; question formally or thoroughly; ask questions of (a witness, etc.)
10. **interview**—ask questions of (someone) in order to gain information, get material for an article, biography, or other written report, etc.
11. **ply with questions**—keep asking questions of
12. **pry (into)**—ask searching and impudent questions (about circumstances, matters, conditions, etc., that are not one's concern)
13. **pump**—question in order to get information from
14. **query**—question
15. **quiz**—ask a series of questions of; question in order to test
16. **sound**—ask questions about the feelings, attitudes, motives, etc., of
17. **test**—ask questions of (someone) in order to determine his knowledge

2. A Questioning,n. *From Sec. 1:* catechism or catechization, challenge, cross-examination, examination, inquiry or enquiry, inquisition, interrogation, interview

3. A Question,n. *From Sec. 1:* inquiry or enquiry, interrogation or interrogatory, query; *Also:*
1. **conundrum**—question to which the answer is a play on words
2. **crux**—puzzling question

3. **rhetorical question**—question asked only for effect, not because an answer is desired
4. **riddle**—conundrum

4. Set, Series, Group, etc., of Questions,n. *From Sec. 1:* catechism, cross-examination, examination, grilling; inquiry, enquiry or inquisition; interrogation, interview, quiz, test; *Also:*
1. **barrage**—rapid fire of questions
2. **inquest**—inquiry, usually of an official nature
3. **questionnaire, questionary**—written list of questions to be answered

5. Questioner,n. *From Sec. 1:* catechist or catechizer, challenger, cross-examiner, cross-questioner, examiner, inquirer or enquirer, inquisitor or inquisitionist, interrogator, interviewer, pry, quizzer, tester

6. One Who Is Questioned,n. *From Sec. 1:* examinee or examinate, interrogatee, interviewee

7. Descr. of, or Pert. to, Questioning; Serving to Question,adj. *From Sec. 1:* catechistic, challenging; examinative, examinatory, examinatorial or examinational; inquisitional or inquisitorial, interrogative or interrogatory, prying, quizzical

8. A Formal Set of Questions and Answers on a Subject: catechism,n.

9. The Use of a Series of Questions Leading Someone to Think, Discover the Errors in His Thinking, Learn, etc.: Socratic method, n.

10. To Ask a Question: demand, inquire or enquire, query,v.

11. Inclined or Eager to Ask Questions,adj.
1. **curious**—inclined to ask questions in order to learn, know, or find out (curiosity,n.)
2. **inquisitive**—curious; disposed to ask questions about things that are not one's concern (inquisitiveness,n.)
3. **nosy**—inquisitive—colloq. or slang (nosiness,n.)
4. **personal**—inclined to ask intimate and hence offensive questions
5. **prying**—disposed to ask questions about matters that are not one's concern

12. Inquisitive Person: bluenose, busybody, inquisitive, nosybody, pry, quidnunc,n.

13. A Seeking of Answers to Questions: investigation,n. (investigator,n. investigative, investigatory,adj. investigate,v.)

14. The Use of Torture, Usually by the Police, to Force a Suspect to Answer Questions or Confess a Crime: third degree,n. (third-degree,v.—colloq.)

15. Authorized to Question Witnesses in Order to Gain Information: rogatory,adj.

626. ANSWER

1. An Answer,n.
1. **echo**—answer that indicates a sympathetic feeling; answer thrown back by the reflection of sound waves
2. **nay, no**—negative answer
3. **oracle**—answer, of divine origin, usually capable of many interpretations; wise or authoritative answer
4. **rejoinder**—answer
5. **repartee**—clever or witty answer
6. **reply**—answer in words or action
7. **response**—answer in words or actions
8. **retort**—answer given sharply or angrily; answer combined with a counterargument, counteraccusation, etc.; answer made in a way that pays back in kind what has been said to one

9. **return**—answer
10. **riposte**—quick and/or clever answer; quick retort
11. **squelcher**—retort that leaves someone speechless (colloq.)
12. **yea, yes**—affirmative answer

2. To Answer,v. *From Sec. 1:* echo, rejoin, reply, respond, retort, return

3. Answer, i.e., an Answering or Act of Answering,n. *From Sec. 1:* rejoinder, repartee, reply, response or respondence, retort, return

4. Answerer,n. *From Sec. 1:* oracle, replier; responder, respondent, or responser; retorter

5. Answering; Making an Answer,adj. *From Sec. 1:* echoing; respondent, responsive, or responsorial (respondence, responsiveness or responsivity,n.)

6. Descr. of, or Pert. to, an Answer or Answering,adj. *From Sec. 1:* oracular, responsorial

7. Means by Which a Divine and Usually Ambiguous Answer Is Given: oracle,n. (oracular,adj.)

8. Sharp in Answer: snippy,adj.

9. Answering Aloud and All Together: viva voce,adv. phrase

627. MEMORY

1. To Remember,v.
1. **bethink oneself of**—remember
2. **recall**—bring back to one's memory
3. **recapture**—bring back to one's memory
4. **recognize**—remember on seeing or hearing again
5. **recollect**—remember; bring back to one's memory
6. **reminisce**—recall past experiences
7. **reproduce**—remember; bring back through memory to one's mind
8. **retain**—keep in one's memory
9. **retrospect**—remember past experiences

2. Remembrance, i.e., Act of Remembering, n. *From Sec. 1:* recall, recapture, recognition, recollection, reminiscence, reproduction, retention, retrospection; *Also:*
1. **anamnesis**—recollection
2. **memory**—act or process of remembering

3. Able to Remember,adj. *From Sec. 1:* recollective, retentive

4. Ability to Remember,n. *From Sec. 1:* recall, recognition, recollection or recollectiveness, reminiscence; retention, retentiveness, or retentivity; *From Sec. 2:* memory; *Also:*
1. **hypermnesia, hypermnesis**—increased efficiency or retentiveness of memory
2. **remembrance**—ability to remember

5. Descr. of, or Pert. to, Remembering or Memory,adj. *From Sec. 1:* recognitional, recognitive, recognition, or recognitory; recollective; reminiscent, reminiscential, or reminiscitory; reproductive, retrospective; *Also:*
1. **eidetic**—pert. to extremely clear recollection of mental imagery
2. **memorial**—pert. to memory; contained in memory
3. **mnemonic**—pert. to memory
4. **mnesic**—pert. or relating to memory
5. **mnestic**—pert. to memory

6. That Which Is Remembered,n. *From Sec. 1:* recollection, reminiscence; *From Sec. 2:* memory; *Also:*
1. **complex**—group of unconscious memories and ideas which, in disguise, influence the personality
2. **mneme**—a persistent memory of past experiences which affects behavior (mnemic, adj.)

3. **remembrance**—that which is remembered; remembered image, experience, or fact

7. **To Remember Incorrectly:** misremember, v. (misremembrance,n.)

8. **Period of Time through Which One's Memory Reaches:** remembrance,n.

9. **Person Who Can Vividly Recall His Mental Images:** eidetic,n.

10. **To Go Back to the Past in Memory:** retrospect,v. (retrospection,n. retrospective, adj.)

11. **To Spend Time Indulging in Memories of Past Experiences:** reminisce,v. (reminiscence,n.)

12. **Given to, or in the Habit of, Indulging in Memories of Past Experiences:** reminiscent,adj.

13. **To Commit to Memory:** memorize,v. (memorization,n. memorizer,n.)

14. **Aiding, or Serving to Aid, the Memory:** memorial, mnemonic,adj.

15. **Trick or Device That Aids, or Serves to Aid, the Memory:** mnemonic, mnemonicon,n.

16. **Type of Memorizing without Understanding:** rote,n.

17. **From or by Memory:** by heart; memoriter (Latin),adv.

18. **Full of Memories:** memoried,adj.

19. **Easy to Remember; Hard to Forget,adj.**
 1. **catchy**—easy to remember (catchiness, n.)
 2. **indelible**—descr. of that which can never be washed from the memory (indelibility, n.)
 3. **memorable**—not easily forgotten (memorability,n.)
 4. **rememberable**—memorable (rememberability,n.)

20. **Worth Remembering,adj.**
 1. **memorable**—worth remembering
 2. **red-letter**—esp. worth remembering as having been productive of joy, triumph, or similar emotion
 3. **rememberable**—memorable

21. **Remarkable Things Worth Remembering:** memorabilia,n.

22. **A Record of Remarkable Things Worth Remembering:** memorabilia,n.

23. **Art of Improving the Memory:** mnemonics, mnemotechny,n.

24. **Act or Process of Improving the Memory:** mnemonism,n.

25. **Illusion of Remembering Having Undergone an Experience Before, though in Actuality Undergoing It for the First Time:** paramnesia,n.

26. **Descr. of the Illusion that One Remembers Having Previously Experienced the Same Circumstances, Situation, etc., that One Is Now Experiencing:** déjà vu,adj. (French)

27. **Account of One's Remembered Experiences,n.**
 1. **memoirs**—written account of one's remembered personal experiences
 2. **memorials**—memoirs
 3. **reminiscences**—written or oral account of one's remembered experiences

28. **Writer or Teller of Remembered Experiences,n.** From Sec. 27: memoirist, memorialist, reminiscent

29. **The Writing of Remembered Experiences,** n. From Sec. 27: memoirism

30. **To Cause (Someone) to Remember; To Make (Someone or Something) Remembered,v.**

1. **admonish**—remind
2. **commemorate**—call to one's memory; preserve the memory of (a person, thing, or event)
3. **din into**—make remember by means of frequent repetitions
4. **jog**—stir or stimulate (the or someone's memory) by a reminder or hint
5. **memorialize**—commemorate
6. **perpetuate**—keep the memory of (someone or something) alive
7. **prod**—jog sharply; remind sharply
8. **prompt**—jog the memory of; jog (someone's memory)
9. **recall to**—awaken (someone's) memory of
10. **remind**—bring back to the mind or memory of; cause (someone) to remember
11. **suggest**—recall to the mind or memory
12. **twit, twitter**—remind (someone) of previous words, plans, mistakes, etc., for the purpose of ridiculing him

31. **A Causing to Remember; A Making Remembered,n.** From Sec. 30: admonition or admonishment, commemoration, memorialization, perpetuation or perpetuance, prompt, recall, reminder, suggestion, twit

32. **Serving to Cause Remembrance,adj.** From Sec. 30: admonitory, commemorative, memorial, remindful, suggestive; Also:
 1. **mnemonic**—aiding the memory
 2. **redolent (of)**—suggestive of the memory (of something); suggestive (of), or recalling the memory (of), by odor, atmosphere, etc. (redolence,n.)
 3. **reminiscent**—suggestive of something remembered; remindful

33. **One Who Causes Someone to Remember, or Who Keeps the Memory of Someone or Something Alive,n.** From Sec. 30: admonisher or admonitor, commemorator, jogger, memorializer, perpetuator, prodder, prompter, recaller, reminder, suggester, twitter; Also:
 1. **prompter**—one who, in the theater, jogs the memory of actors who forget their lines, by supplying cues, etc.
 2. **remembrancer**—one who reminds, or who is engaged to remind, someone of something

34. **That Which Causes, or Serves to Cause, Remembrance,n.** From Sec. 30: admonition or admonishment, commemoration, jog, memorial, prod, prompt, reminder, suggestion, twit; From Sec. 32: mnemonic or mnemonicon; Also:
 1. **aide-mémoire (French)**—memorandum of agreement, discussion, etc.
 2. **cairn**—memorial made of a heap of stones
 3. **commemoration**—celebration or function in honor of someone's memory, or to recall some noteworthy event to memory
 4. **jubilee**—joyful commemoration, usually of the twenty-fifth or fiftieth anniversary of an event
 5. **keepsake**—gift made, or that which is taken, as a reminder of friendship, a pleasant experience, etc.; souvenir
 6. **memento**—token to awaken or recall a memory
 7. **memento mori (Latin)**—reminder of death, or of impending death
 8. **memoir**—memorandum; memorial to a person
 9. **memorandum, memo**—note to jog one's memory (memoranda,pl.)
 10. **monument**—memorial; building, sculpture, etc., that serves as a memorial; written memorial
 11. **note**—something set down to help the memory
 12. **phylactery**—reminder
 13. **relic**—souvenir or remembrance of the past

14. **remembrance**—token of something worth remembering
15. **remembrancer**—memento; souvenir
16. **souvenir**—token to help one remember past experiences, things in the past, etc.
17. **testimonial**—something done for, or established to, the memory of someone (testimonial,adj.)
18. **token**—reminder; souvenir
19. **trophy**—memorial of victory, as in a tournament, contest, etc.
35. **Greek Goddess of Memory:** Mnemosyne,n.
36. **Extending Back beyond the Range of Human Memory:** immemorial,adj.

628. FORGETFULNESS

1. **Forgetfulness; Loss of Memory,**n.
   1. **absent-mindedness**—such preoccupation with one's thoughts that one tends to be forgetful of other things
   2. **amnesia**—complete loss of memory from pathological or morbid causes; loosely, any lapse of memory (amnesic, amnestic, adj.)
   3. **amnesty**—forgetfulness, esp. of someone's offenses, sins, etc.
   4. **fugue**—prolonged state of amnesia in which the victim may tend to flee from familiar surroundings (medical)
   5. **Lethe**—loss of memory; forgetfulness (Lethean,adj.)
   6. **nirvana**—oblivion to pain, anxiety, and other mortal woes; oblivion to external reality (nirvanic,adj.)
   7. **oblivion, obliviousness**—forgetfulness
   8. **unmindfulness**—forgetfulness
2. **Forgetful,**adj. *From Sec. 1:* absent-minded, amnesic or amnestic, oblivious, un-mindful
3. **Causing Forgetfulness:** Lethean, oblivial, oblivious,adj.
4. **That Which Causes One to Forget,**n.
   1. **Lethe**—a drink that, supposedly, causes one to forget the past
   2. **nepenthe**—anything that causes forgetfulness, esp. of pain or sorrow
5. **Act of Forgetting:** oblivion,n.
6. **Able to Be Forgotten:** obliviscible,adj.
7. **State or Condition of Being Completely Forgotten:** limbo, oblivion,n.
8. **Process of Becoming Forgotten or Falling into Oblivion:** obliviscence,n. (obliviscent,adj.)
9. **Place Where Someone or Something Is Completely Forgotten:** limbo,n.
10. **Memory Disorder,**n.
    1. **hypomnesia**—weakened memory
    2. **paramnesia**—any memory disorder; memory disorder causing an inability to remember the proper meanings of words
11. **Relating to Impairment of Memory:** amnemonic,adj.

629. HABIT

1. **Habit or Habits; Custom or Customs,**n.
   1. **amenities**—conventions that make for easy and pleasing social relations
   2. **consuetude**—habit; social custom; social usage; usage that has the force of law
   3. **convention**—fixed social custom; practices that are based on social custom (conventional,adj.)
   4. **etiquette**—social convention
   5. **fashion**—habit of the time; prevailing habit or habits, esp. as to dress, manners, ways of doing things, etc.
   6. **fixation**—strong habit

7. **mores** (Latin)—traditional customs; social or ethical customs
8. **observance**—custom; practice
9. **orthodoxy**—conventional practice
10. **perversion**—unnatural or abnormal habit
11. **practice**—habit; habitual action or procedure
12. **proprieties**—conventions
13. **routine**—habit of doing something in the same way; habitual method or procedure
14. **second nature**—fixed, almost reflexive habits
15. **stereotype**—convention
16. **tradition**—customs or practices handed down from the past (traditional,adj.)
17. **usage**—habit; habitual use, action, or procedure
18. **vice**—undesirable habit
19. **vulgarism**—coarse habit
20. **wont**—habit; habitual action or procedure

2. **Habitual; Customary,**adj. *From Sec. 1:* consuetudinary or consuetudinal, conventional, fashionable, orthodox, practiced or practised, routine, second-nature, stereotyped, traditional or traditionary, wonted (conventionality, fashionableness, orthodoxy, traditionality, wontedness,n.); *Also:*
   1. **academic**—conventional
   2. **accustomed**—habitual
   3. **ingrained**—habitual in pattern
   4. **inveterate**—habitual over a long period of time (inveteracy,n.)

3. **Not Habitual; Contrary to, or Not Following, Habit, Custom, or Convention,** adj. *From Sec. 1:* unconventional, uncustomary, unfashionable, unorthodox, unstereotyped, untraditional, unwonted (unconventionality, unfashionableness, unorthodoxy, unwontedness,n.); *From Sec. 2:* unacademic, unaccustomed; *Also:* 1. **strange**—contrary to, or not following, habit or the usual habit (strangeness,n.)

4. **Habitual Attitude of Mind:** habitude,n.

5. **Adhering or Conforming to Habit, Custom, or Convention,**adj.
   1. **academic**—conforming to scholastic traditions; conventional
   2. **addicted to**—adhering or given up to (a strong habit or a drug habit)
   3. **confirmed**—adhering strongly to a habit or habits
   4. **conventional**—adhering or conforming to fixed social customs or to practices based on social custom
   5. **decorous**—adhering to or observing the conventional rules of behavior
   6. **fashionable**—conforming to the habits or customs of the time, or to prevailing custom in dress
   7. **formal, formalist, formalistic**—conventional; conventional in matters of religious practice
   8. **orthodox**—conforming to established custom or convention; conforming to established religious practice
   9. **prim**—stiffly conventional (of people)
   10. **punctilious**—adhering or conforming strictly to precise details of convention
   11. **traditional**—conforming or adhering to the customs or conventions handed down from the past

6. **Adherence or Conformity to Habit, Custom, or Convention,**n. *From Sec. 5:* academicism or academism, addiction or addictedness, conventionalism or conventionality, decorum or decorousness, fashionableness, formalism, orthodoxy, primness, punctiliousness or punctilio, traditionalism or traditionality; *Also:*
   1. **academicism**—conventionalism or traditionalism in literature, art, etc.

2. routinism—adherence to a customary course of action or way of doing things

7. One Who Adheres or Conforms, or Believes in Adhering or Conforming, to Habit, Custom, or Convention,n. *From Sec. 5:* addict, conventionalist, formalist, orthodox, traditionalist or traditionary; *From Sec. 6:* routinist

8. To Cause to Conform to Convention; To Make Conventional,v. *From Sec. 5:* academize, conventionalize, formalize, traditionalize (academization, conventionalization, formalization,n.)

9. Precise Detail of Convention: punctilio,n.

10. Violating Conventions: indelicate,adj. (indelicacy,n.)

11. Custom or Customs of a Specific Country or Place,n.
   1. Americanism—custom peculiar to the United States
   2. Frenchism, frenchism—French custom
   3. Hibernicism—Irish custom
   4. monkery—customs, practices, etc., of monks (disparaging)
   5. Occidentalism—customs of Western peoples
   6. Orientalism—customs of Oriental peoples
   7. Sinicism—custom peculiar to the Chinese
   8. Slavicism—Slavic customs

12. To Be Customary: obtain, prevail,v. (prevalence,n.)

13. Strengthened by Habit: confirmed,adj. (*confirmed alcoholism,* etc.)

14. Strengthened in One's Habits by Constant Repetition: confirmed,adj. (*confirmed alcoholic,* etc.)

15. Strengthened in One's Habits over a Long Period of Time: inveterate,adj. (inveteracy,n.)

16. Of Good Habits: steady,adj. (steadiness, n.)

17. Of Bad or Corrupt Habits: vicious,adj. (viciousness,n.)

18. To Be in the Habit of Doing: practice, practise,v.

19. To Become Accustomed to: adjust to, get used to,v. (adjustment,n.)

20. To Become Accustomed to a New Climate or Environment, or, Loosely, New Conditions or Circumstances: acclimate, acclimatize,v. (acclimation, acclimatization, n. acclimatable, acclimatizable,adj.)

21. To Become Set in a Conventional or Customary Pattern: ossify,v. (ossification,n.)

22. A Falling Back, Relapse, or Return to Previous Criminal Habits after Punishment; A Relapse into any Former Habits, Usually Bad, after Correction: recidivism,n. (recidivist,n. recidivous, recidivistic,adj.)

23. To Accustom; To Make Accustomed,v.
   1. acclimate—accustom to a new climate or environment, or, loosely, new conditions or circumstances (acclimation,n.)
   2. acclimatize—accustom to a new climate or environment (acclimatization,n.)
   3. habituate—accustom; make accustomed (habituation,n.)
   4. inure—accustom; accustom (to burdens, difficulties, painful circumstances, etc.); accustom to something painful or difficult (inurement,n.)
   5. season—accustom (to something) through wide experience
   6. wean from—accustom to do without or be without; accustom to being away from

24. Accustomed,adj. *From Sec. 23:* acclimated, acclimatized, etc.; *Also:*
   1. adjusted to—accustomed to
   2. used to—accustomed to; in the habit of

25. Unaccustomed,adj. *From Sec. 23:* unacclimated, unacclimatized, etc.; *From Sec. 24:* unadjusted, unused to; *Also:* **1. strange to**—unaccustomed to

26. To Devote Oneself Habitually to; To Give Oneself Over to (a Habit): addict oneself to,v. (addictedness, addiction,n. addict,n. addicted,adj.)

27. State of Being a Slave to a Drug or Narcotics Habit: addiction,n. (addict,n. addicted,adj.)

630. INCLINATION

1. Inclination; Tendency,n.
   1. addiction—strong inclination
   2. aptitude—inclination; habitual inclination; disposition
   3. bent—inclination
   4. bias—inclination or tendency, esp. one that does not permit unprejudiced considerations
   5. conatus—natural inclination or tendency
   6. disposition—mental or physical inclination or tendency
   7. impulse—sudden tendency to act
   8. leaning—inclination; tendency
   9. mind—inclination
   10. partiality—bias
   11. penchant—strong inclination
   12. predisposition—previous inclination, tendency, or disposition
   13. proclivity—mental or emotional inclination
   14. proneness—inclination; tendency
   15. propensity—natural inclination or tendency
   16. slant—mental inclination; tendency; bias
   17. temper—inclination of mind
   18. trend—inclination; tendency

2. Inclined,adj. *From Sec. 1:* apt (to), biased, disposed, minded, partial, predisposed, prone

3. To Incline or Tend; To Be Inclined,v. *From Sec. 1:* bend, lean, trend; *Also:* **1. verge**—incline or tend

4. To Incline, i.e., Cause to Incline or Tend, v. *From Sec. 1:* bend, dispose; impel (from *impulse*) ; predispose

631. FASHION

1. Fashion,n.
   1. bon ton—high fashion; sophisticated fashion
   2. craze—sudden and very popular fashion or fad, usually of short duration
   3. cult, cultus—intellectual or social fashion of devotion to, or worship of, a person, principle, or idea
   4. dernier cri (French)—newest fashion
   5. fad—fashion of dress, use, speech, or any other action that is enthusiastically followed for a short time
   6. mode—fashion
   7. style—fashion; fashion of dress
   8. vogue—fashion; accepted fashion

2. The Following of, or Addiction to, Fashion or Fashions,n. *From Sec. 1:* cultism, faddism

3. One Who Follows, or Is Addicted to, a Fashion or Fashions,n. *From Sec. 1:* cultist (cult, collective), faddist

4. Given to, or Following, a Fad: faddish, faddist,adj.

5. Like a Fad: faddish,adj. (faddishness,n.)

6. Fashionable: chic, current, modish; newfangled (usually derogative); popular, smart, stylish,adj. (chic, currency, modishness, popularity, smartness, stylishness,n.)

7. Fashionable in Dress or Appearance: chic, dapper, dashing, dashy, jaunty, modish, natty; nifty (colloq.); rakish, saucy, smart, smug, sporty, spruce, stylish; swank (colloq.); swanky (colloq.); trim, trig,adj. (chic, dapperness, dash, jauntiness, modishness, nattiness, niftiness, rakishness, sauciness, smartness, smugness, sportiness, spruceness, stylishness, swank, swankiness, trimness,n.)

8. Fashionable and Neat in Appearance or Dress: natty, smart, smug, spruce, trim, trig, adj. (nattiness, smartness, smugness, spruceness, trimness,n.)

9. Stylish, Smart, Neat, and Speedy in Appearance (of Ships, Cars, etc.): rakish,adj. (rakishness,n.)

10. According to the Latest Fashion: à la mode,adv.

11. People or World of Fashion: beau monde, bon ton, fashionable society; haut monde (usually ironic); society,n.

12. Old-Fashioned; Out-of-Date: anachronistic, anachronous, antediluvian, antiquated, antique, archaic, dated, moss-grown, motheaten, obsolete, old-fangled, outdated, outmoded, passé, stale, superannuated, timeworn, worm-eaten,adj. (antiquity, datedness, obsoleteness or obsoletism, staleness,n.)

13. To Make Old-Fashioned or Out-of-Date: antiquate, archaize, date, obsolete, outdate, outmode, stale,v.

14. To Become Old-Fashioned or Out-of-Date: date, obsolesce, stale,v.

15. Going out of Fashion; Becoming Out-of-Date: obsolescent,adj. (obsolescence,n.)

16. Old-Fashioned or Out-of-Date Thing, Attitude, Action, Word, or Phrase: anachronism (thing, action, or attitude); antique (thing); archaism (thing, word, or phrase); obsoletism (thing, word, or phrase),n.

17. Old-Fashioned (of People Only): fogyish, fusty, old-fogyish, square-toed,adj. (fogyism, fustiness,n.)

18. Old-Fashioned or Out-of-Date Person: anachronism, antediluvian, fogey, fogy, fossil, old fogey, old fogy, square-toes,n.

632. BELIEF

1. To Believe,v.
1. accept—believe (acceptance,n.)
2. account—believe to be
3. accredit—believe (accreditation,n.)
4. assume—suppose; take for granted
5. consider—believe or suppose (that); believe to be (consideration,n.)
6. credit—believe (something), often because of the reputation for honesty of the person offering what is to be believed; believe (that)
7. deem—believe to be; suppose
8. posit—assume as a fact
9. postulate—take for granted (postulation, n.)
10. premise—presuppose
11. presume—take for granted; suppose (presumption,n.)
12. presuppose—take for granted; accept the truth of; suppose beforehand (presupposition,n.)
13. reckon—believe to be; suppose
14. suppose—believe on little evidence; tend to believe
15. suspect—believe (that something is true, likely, etc.) on little or no evidence (suspicion,n.)
16. swallow—believe with little investigation or demand for proof
17. take for granted—believe to be true
18. think—believe; believe to be

2. To Believe in; To Have Faith or Belief in,v.
1. accredit—trust (accreditation,n.)
2. confide in—have faith in (confidence,n.)
3. depend on—trust (dependence,n.)
4. rely on—have faith, or full faith, in (reliance,n.)
5. trust—believe in; have faith or belief in (trust,n.)

3. To Have a False Belief or Beliefs: misbelieve,v. (misbelief,n. misbeliever,n.)

4. To Believe in a False Religion: misbelieve, v. (misbelief,n. misbeliever,n.)

5. To Change in One's Beliefs: convert,v. (conversion,n. convert,n.)

6. Belief, i.e., State of Believing,n.
1. acceptance—belief
2. affiance—faith
3. assumption—belief
4. confidence—faith; full faith
5. conviction—strong belief
6. credence—belief
7. credit—belief; faith; faith in a person's ability and intention to pay his debts
8. faith—belief out of feeling rather than through logic or evidence; belief in God
9. heresy—belief sharply in opposition to accepted or commonly held belief—in religion, science, etc.
10. heterodoxy—belief contrary to, or not in accordance with, accepted belief or teaching
11. illusion—belief in something that seems true or real, but is in actuality untrue or nonexistent
12. misbelief—false or incorrect belief; heresy
13. orthodoxy—approved, or officially accepted or approved, belief
14. reliance—faith
15. superstition—belief based on an acceptance of magic, the powers of the supernatural, etc.; unfounded belief
16. trust—faith
17. unorthodoxy—unapproved, or officially unaccepted or unapproved, belief

7. A Belief, i.e., That Which One Believes or Believes in; That Which Is Believed,n. From Sec. 6: assumption, conviction, credit, heresy, heterodoxy, illusion, misbelief, superstition; Also:
1. creed, credo, persuasion—one's religious faith or belief; one's belief in any other field
2. delusion, misconception, misimpression —false or mistaken belief
3. gospel—that which is earnestly and unquestioningly believed
4. notion, impression—belief; vague belief
5. old wives' tale—foolish belief; superstition
6. persuasion—one's belief; one's induced belief
7. presupposition—belief that one takes for granted
8. shibboleth—something superstitiously or blindly believed in by members of a group
9. supposition, suspicion—belief one forms on little evidence
10. tenet, doctrine, dogma—belief considered true by members of a sect, organization, etc.
11. theory, hypothesis, postulate—belief based on insufficient evidence, but accepted subject to further proof or investigation

8. Beliefs; Body or Summary of Beliefs,n. From Sec. 6: heresy, heterodoxy, orthodoxy, unorthodoxy; From Sec. 7: creed, credo, persuasion, doctrine, dogma; Also:
1. credenda (pl.)—those religious doctrines or tenets that are to be believed, or that are to be accepted on belief alone

2. credo—one's expressed beliefs as to ethical behavior or the philosophy of living

3. ideology—fundamental tenets

4. propaganda—beliefs or doctrines of a group that are systematically spread throughout a place, country, the world, etc.

5. tradition—beliefs handed down from the past

9. Descr. of, or Pert. or Relating to, Belief, a Belief, or Beliefs,adj. *From Sec. 6:* assumptive, convictional, heretic or heretical, heterodox; illusional, illusionary, illusory, or illusive; orthodox, superstitious, unorthodox; *From Sec. 7:* delusional, delusive, or delusory, notional, suppositional, doctrinal, dogmatic, theoretic or theoretical, hypothetic or hypothetical; *From Sec. 8:* ideological, propagandist, traditional or traditionary; *Also:* **1. opinionative**—pert. to, concerned with, or consisting of, beliefs

10. Holder of a Belief or Beliefs,n. *From Sec. 6:* accepter or acceptor, heretic, misbeliever, orthodox; *From Sec. 8:* traditionalist

11. Leader of Heretics or of a Heretic Movement: heresiarch,n.

12. Reconciliation or Adjustment of Beliefs, Often Religious, into a Single Movement: syncretism,n. (syncretize,v.)

13. Based on Belief or Theory, Not on Actual Experience, Evidence, or Observation: a priori,adj. (apriority,n.)

14. Based on Faith, Trust, or Confidence: fiduciary,adj.

15. Giving Grounds for a Strong Belief; Based on Belief: a priori, presumptive,adj. (apriority,n.)

16. Tending to Cause Beliefs Not Founded on Fact or Truth: prejudicial,adj.

17. To Spread Systematically One's, or a Group's, Beliefs: propagandize,v. (propagandism,n. propagandist,n. propagandist, propagandistic,adj.)

18. Believing; Tending to Believe,adj.
1. confident—full of faith or belief; full of faith in oneself (confidence,n.)
2. credent—believing
3. credulous—tending to believe; not prone to skepticism; likely to believe on flimsy evidence (credulity, credulousness,n.)
4. gullible—easily led to believe what is patently false (gullibility,n.)
5. heterodox—holding beliefs contrary to those considered generally acceptable, or contrary to those officially approved (heterodoxy,n.)
6. intransigent, intransigeant—uncompromising (intransigence, intransigeance,n.)
7. naïve; naïf (French)—believing almost anything, owing to one's lack of sophistication or experience (naïveté)
8. orthodox—holding approved, or officially accepted or approved, beliefs (orthodoxy, n.)
9. superstitious—believing in magic, in the supernatural, or in other things for which there is no objective evidence (superstitiousness,n.)
10. trusting, trustful—believing; believing what one is told (trustfulness, trust,n.)
11. uncompromising—firm and unyielding in one's beliefs
12. unorthodox—holding beliefs not generally approved or officially sanctioned (unorthodoxy,n.)

19. One Who Is Firm and Unyielding in One's Beliefs: intransigent, intransigeant,n.

20. One Who Believes Obvious Falsehoods: dupe,n.

21. Believable: authentic, credible,adj. (authenticity, credibility,n.)

22. Believable because of the Honesty, Reputation, etc., of the Source: creditable,adj. (creditability,n.)

23. Believable because Reasonable or Making Sense: plausible,adj. (plausibility,n.)

24. Entitled to Belief: authoritative,adj. (authoritativeness,n.)

25. Worthy of Belief, Confidence, Faith, or Trust: authentic, dependable, reliable, tried, trustworthy, trusty,adj. (authenticity, dependability or dependableness, reliability or reliableness, trustworthiness, trustiness,n.)

26. Entitling to Confidence or Belief: credential,adj.

27. That Which Entitles One to Confidence or Belief: credential,n.

28. Documents That Entitle One to Confidence or Belief: credentials,n.

29. Commonly or Generally Believed: accepted, putative, reputed,adj.

633. OPINION

1. To Form or Have an Opinion; To Have as an Opinion; To Express an Opinion,v.
1. account—judge
2. adjudge—judge
3. approve—have or express a good opinion of (approval,n.)
4. conclude—form an opinion through considering all pertinent factors (conclusion, n.)
5. consider—judge (consideration,n.)
6. deem—judge
7. estimate—judge (estimation,n.)
8. hold—judge
9. judge—have or give an opinion of; arrive at as an opinion after investigation or analysis (judgment,n.)
10. misjudge—judge incorrectly (misjudgment,n.)
11. opine—have or express an opinion
12. preconceive—form an opinion of beforehand, without knowing the facts (preconception,n.)
13. prejudge—judge before knowing all the facts (prejudgment,n.)
14. pronounce—give an opinion of (pronouncement,n.)
15. reckon—conclude
16. speculate—conclude from little or insufficient evidence (speculation,n.)
17. suppose—have or form an opinion; hold as opinion (supposition,n.)
18. think—suppose

2. Expression of Opinion from a Group: resolution,n.

3. Overwhelming Display of Popular or Group Opinion: tidal wave,n.

4. Figurative Means of Airing, or Giving Publicity to, One's Opinions, or of Presenting One's Opinions to a Public Audience: rostrum, soapbox,n.

5. To Be Purposely Ambiguous in the Expression of One's Opinions: equivocate; pussyfoot (colloq.),v. (equivocation,n. equivocal,adj. equivocator, pussyfooter,n.)

6. Tending to Have the Opinions Required of One: sequacious,adj. (sequacity, sequaciousness,n.)

7. Not Expressing an Opinion: noncommittal,adj.

8. An Opinion,n.
1. apprehension—opinion
2. concept—opinion (conceptional, conceptual,adj.)

3. **conclusion**—opinion arrived at after considering all pertinent factors
4. **consideration**—opinion arrived at after mature reflection
5. **deliverance**—formally expressed opinion or judgment
6. **dogma**—that which is held as an established opinion (dogmatic,adj.)
7. **estimate, estimation**—opinion; judgment
8. **judgment**—opinion; opinion arrived at after investigation or analysis
9. **misjudgment**—incorrect judgment
10. **notion**—opinion (notional,adj.)
11. **parti pris (French)**—preconceived opinion
12. **persuasion**—one's induced opinion
13. **preconception**—opinion formed before all the facts are known (preconceptional, adj.)
14. **prejudgment**—preconception
15. **prejudice**—opinion formed for or against without considering the pros and cons; favorable or unfavorable opinion formed beforehand or without logical reason
16. **pronouncement**—expressed opinion
17. **pulse**—personal opinion of people on a question or subject
18. **sense**—general opinion of a group
19. **sentiment**—personal opinion
20. **slant**—personal and characteristic opinion
21. **thesis**—opinion advanced subject to discussion or debate, or to be defended against objections
22. **view**—opinion

9. One's Opinions Expressed in Writing and Sent to Some Authority: address,n.

10. Collection of Opinions on a Subject: symposium (symposia,pl.), symposiac, symposition,n.

11. One Who Contributes to a Symposium: symposiast,n.

12. Pert. to, or Concerned with, Opinions: opinionative,adj.

13. Based on Opinion, Not on Actual Experience or Evidence: a priori,adj. (apriority,n.)

14. Based on, or Derived from, One's Own Opinion, with No Regard for Reasonableness, Rule, Law, etc.: arbitrary, high-handed,adj. (arbitrariness, highhandedness, n.)

15. Admitting of Opinion or Opinions: opinionable,adj.

16. Full of Opinions,adj.
1. **opinionated**—full of firmly held opinions (opinionatedness,n.)
2. **opinioned**—full of opinions

17. Firm in Opinion or Opinions; Expressing Opinion or Opinions Firmly, Positively, or as if Fact,adj.
1. **assertive**—overconfident or overcertain in one's expression of opinion (assertiveness,n.)
2. **dogmatic**—extremely positive in asserting one's opinion; asserting one's opinions in such a way as to brook no dissent or qualification, and/or as if one were the highest authority (dogmatism, dogmaticness,n.)
3. **intransigent, intransigeant**—uncompromising (intransigence, intransigeance,n.)
4. **opinionated, opinionative**—expressing one's opinions in a dogmatic way, closing the door on all arguments; expressing opinions as if they were facts; firmly or perversely adhering to one's opinions (opinionatedness, opinionativeness,n.)
5. **oracular**—expressing one's opinions with pompous dogmatism or authority, as if they were divinely inspired (oracularity, n.)

6. **peremptory**—most positive in the expression of one's opinion (peremptoriness,n.)
7. **positive**—overcertain or overconfident in one's opinions (positiveness,n.)
8. **pragmatic, pragmatical**—dogmatic; opinionated (pragmatism,n. pragmatical-ity,n. pragmatic, pragmatist,n.)
9. **uncompromising**—firm in opinions; stubbornly unwilling to change in opinions

18. An Adjustment of Opinion: compromise, understanding,n. (compromise,v.)

634. PREJUDICE

1. Prejudice; State of Being Prejudiced,n.
1. **anti-Semitism**—prejudice against the Jews
2. **bias**—prejudice (for or against)
3. **bigotry**—intolerant and blind prejudice (against)
4. **discrimination**—prejudice for or against in particular cases
5. **favoritism**—prejudice toward or in favor of a person, institution, etc.
6. **illiberality, illiberalness**—bigotry
7. **inclination**—prejudice (toward)
8. **intolerance**—tendency not to accept opinions, attitudes, races, religions, political feelings, etc., that are different from, or opposed to, one's own
9. **jaundice**—feeling of prejudice, or state of feeling prejudiced, owing to jealousy, envy, bitterness, etc., with the result that one's judgment is colored, unreasonable, etc.
10. **Jim Crowism, Jim Crow**—prejudice against Negroes, usually evidenced by segregation or attempts at segregation
11. **narrow-mindedness**—prejudice; bigotry
12. **nativism**—bias toward the natives of a country, and against foreigners or immigrants
13. **Papism, papism**—partisanship toward the Pope (derogatory)
14. **partiality**—prejudice (toward)
15. **parti pris (French)**—prejudice; partiality
16. **partisanship**—favorable and usually unreasonable prejudice caused by one's emotional leanings
17. **preconception**—prejudice
18. **predilection**—prejudice in favor of something
19. **predisposition**—prejudice (toward)
20. **prepossession**—prejudice
21. **propensity**—prejudice (toward)
22. **race prejudice**—racialism; racism
23. **racialism**—prejudice, either toward or against, but usually against, a race or races
24. **racism**—belief in the superiority of a race or of races, with consequent prejudice against other races
25. **sectarianism**—narrow prejudice in favor of a group, denomination, religious sect, etc.; bigotry
26. **sectionalism**—bias toward one's own section of the state or country
27. **slant**—bias
28. **subjectivity, subjectiveness**—state of being prejudiced or biased owing to one's personal or individual emotional reactions
29. **unfairness**—bias
30. **zealotry, zealotism**—fanatical partisanship

2. Prejudiced; Showing Prejudice,adj. *From Sec. 1:* anti-Semitic, biased, bigoted, discriminatory, favorable, illiberal, inclined, intolerant, jaundiced, Jim-Crow or jim-crow, narrow-minded, nativistic, Papist or papist, partial, partisan, predisposed, prepossessed, racialist, racist, sectarian, sectional, slanted, subjective, unfair, zealot or zealotic; *Also:*

1. **colored**—prejudiced (of feeling, statements, expressions of ideas, etc.)
2. **squint-eyed**—biased
3. **Person Who Is Prejudiced or Who Shows Prejudice,n.** *From Sec. 1:* anti-Semite, bigot, nativist, Papist or papist, partisan, racialist, racist, sectarian, sectionalist, zealot or zealotist
4. **To Prejudice; To Cause Prejudice in (Someone),v.** *From Sec. 1:* bias, incline, jaundice, predispose, prepossess, sectarianize (predisposition, prepossession,n.) ; *Also:*
   1. **indoctrinate**—instill with a partisan or biased viewpoint (indoctrination,n.)
   2. **predetermine**—bias or prejudice for or against (predetermination,n. predeterminative,adj.)
5. **To Show or Feel Prejudice,v.** *From Sec. 1:* discriminate, favor, incline; slant (writing, statements, etc.) ; *From Sec. 2:* color; *Also:* 1. **angle**—distort in presenting or writing about, so as to favor the author's prejudice or point of view
6. **Directed to One's Prejudices Rather than to One's Intellect or Sense of Logic:** ad hominem (of reasoning, arguing, argument, etc.—logic)
7. **Narrow-Mindedness, Generally or Specifically,n.**
   1. **illiberality, illiberalness**—narrow-mindedness; lack of a broad point of view
   2. **insularity**—narrow-mindedness from restricted experiences
   3. **localism**—tendency to consider, or habit of considering, local affairs more important than national or international affairs; hence loosely, narrowness
   4. **narrowness**—lack of comprehensiveness of sympathy or point of view
   5. **parochialism**—state of being narrow, limited, or restricted in opinions or interests
   6. **pettiness**—narrow-mindedness
   7. **provincialism, provinciality**—narrowness of interests, knowledge, or understanding
   8. **sectarianism**—narrowness of interests or character; restriction of interest to one's own group, denomination, religious sect, etc.
   9. **sectionalism**—restriction of one's interests to one's own section of the state or country
   10. **Victorianism**—narrow-mindedness in respect to behavior, morals, or conduct
8. **Narrow-Minded; Indicating Narrow-Mindedness,adj.** *From Sec. 7:* illiberal, insular; local, localist, or localistic; narrow, parochial, petty, provincial, sectarian, sectional, Victorian; *Also:*
   1. **bourgeois**—hidebound
   2. **hidebound**—stubbornly and stupidly narrow-minded
9. **Narrow-Minded Person; One Who Shows General or Specific Narrow-Mindedness,n.** *From Sec. 7:* localist, parochialist, provincialist or provincial, sectarian, sectionalist, Victorian
10. **To Cause to Be Narrow-Minded,v.** *From Sec. 7:* provincialize, sectarianize (provincialization,n.)

635. UNFAIRNESS

1. **Unfair:** discriminatory, excessive, inequitable, iniquitous, shabby, underhand, underhanded, unjust, unreasonable, unrighteous, unsporting, unsportsmanlike, unsportsmanly, wrongful,adj.
2. **Unfairness:** discrimination, excessiveness, favoritism, inequity, iniquitousness, iniquity, injustice, shabbiness, underhandedness, unjustness, unreasonability, unreasonableness, unrighteousness, wrongfulness,n.
3. **To Be Unfair to; To Treat Unfairly:** discriminate against, wrong,v. (discrimination, n.)
4. **Unfair Action:** inequity, iniquity, injustice, wrong,n.
5. **To Represent Unfairly:** distort, skew, twist,v. (distortion,n.)
6. **Unfair in the Exercise of Power or Authority:** arbitrary, despotic, tyrannic, tyrannical, tyrannous,adj. (arbitrariness, despotism, tyrannicalness, tyranny,n. despot, tyrant, tyrannizer,n. tyrannize, tyrannize over,v.)
7. **Playing Games or Competing in Sports Unfairly:** unsportsmanlike, unsportsmanly, adj.

636. LACK OF PREJUDICE

1. **Unprejudiced,adj.**
   1. **broad-minded**—free from prejudice or bigotry; tolerant of liberal, radical, or unconventional opinions or acts
   2. **candid**—impartial; free from bias
   3. **catholic**—broad-minded
   4. **detached**—not influenced by what is going on around one or by one's feelings; objective
   5. **disinterested**—impartial or objective, because one's own personal interests are not involved
   6. **dispassionate, dispassioned**—lacking in any bias that might be caused by the influence of emotion or strong feelings; unprejudiced by one's emotional reactions; impartial
   7. **fair, fair-minded**—unprejudiced; unbiased
   8. **impartial**—showing no prejudice for or against; showing no favoritism
   9. **impersonal**—objective
   10. **liberal**—free from prejudice; tolerant
   11. **neutral**—sympathetic to neither one side nor another in a dispute, etc.
   12. **non-partisan**—unprejudiced by emotional leanings or bias
   13. **objective**—unprejudiced by one's own thinking, feelings, or personal interests
   14. **tolerant**—unprejudiced against attitudes, opinions, races, religions, political feelings, etc., that are different from, or opposed to, one's own
   15. **unbiased**—unprejudiced
   16. **unbigoted**—lacking in blind prejudice
   17. **uncolored**—lacking in any expression of prejudice (of writing, language, etc.)
   18. **unslanted**—uncolored
2. **Lack of Prejudice,n.** *From Sec. 1:* broad-mindedness, candor or candidness, catholicity or catholicism, detachment, disinterest, dispassionateness, fairness, fair-mindedness, impartiality, impersonality, liberality or liberalness, neutrality, non-partisanship; objectiveness, objectivity, or objectivism; tolerance
3. **Person without Prejudice,n.** *From Sec. 1:* neutral, non-partisan
4. **Broadness of Sympathies, Attitudes, Point of View, etc.,n.**
   1. **breadth, breadth of mind**—liberality
   2. **catholicity, catholicism**—broadness or comprehensiveness of sympathies, tastes, likes, interests, attitudes, etc.
   3. **cosmopolitanism**—broad, world-wide, outlook or point of view
   4. **liberality, liberalness**—lack of narrowness of mind, point of view, etc.
5. **Broad in Sympathies, etc.,adj.** *From Sec. 4:* catholic, cosmopolitan, liberal

6. One Who Has a Broad, World-Wide Outlook or Point of View: cosmopolitan, cosmopolite,n.

7. To Make or Become Liberal: liberalize,v. (liberalization,n.)

637. FAIRNESS

1. Fair: candid, equitable, evenhanded, fairminded, impartial, just, reasonable, sporting, sportsmanlike, sportsmanly, square, unbiased, unprejudiced,adj.

2. Fairness: candidness, candor, equitableness, equity, evenhandedness, fair-mindedness, impartiality, justice, justness, reasonability, reasonableness, sportsmanship, squareness,n.

3. Person Who Is Fair: sportsman, squareshooter,n.

4. Playing Games or Competing in Sports with Fairness: sportsmanlike, sportsmanly, adj. (sportsmanship,n. sportsman,n.)

638. PERSUASION

1. To Persuade,v.
1. **align (with or against)**—persuade to join or support (a cause for or against)
2. **argue (into)**—persuade by reason, reasoning, or reasons (to)
3. **blandish**—cajole; coax
4. **blarney**—use smooth coaxing upon; wheedle
5. **cajole (into)**—persuade (to) by making deceitful or artful promises, or by ingenious flattery
6. **coax (to, into)**—persuade (to) by gentle words
7. **convert**—persuade to change beliefs; turn from one belief to another; turn from one religious belief to another
8. **convince**—persuade by logic, argument, or proof; satisfy by proof; cause to believe in the truth (of)
9. **disarm**—make lose suspicion, or the desire to be suspicious
10. **dissuade (from)**—persuade not to (do)
11. **enlist**—persuade to join or support (an undertaking, project, etc.)
12. **induce**—persuade by any of various means (to do something) by influencing reason or judgment
13. **inveigle (into)**—cajole (into), often by deception or trickery
14. **prevail on, prevail upon**—persuade successfully
15. **proselytize, proselyte**—convert, by persuasion or teaching, to a religion, sect, opinion, belief, political party, etc.
16. **seduce (into)**—persuade (into wrongdoing, foolish actions, etc.)
17. **suborn**—secretly persuade to do something wrong or illegal, or to give deliberately false testimony
18. **sway**—persuade by causing the mind or feelings to turn in a certain direction
19. **wheedle (into)**—persuade by soft words, flattery, offers of rewards, etc.; coax
20. **win over**—persuade to one's way of thinking

2. Persuasion; A Persuading,n. *From Sec. 1:* alignment, conversion, convincement or conviction, dissuasion, enlistment, inveiglement, proselytization or proselytism, seduction or seducement, subornation; *Also:* 1. suasion—persuasion

3. Persuasion, i.e., State of Being Persuaded,n. *From Sec. 1:* alignment, conversion, conviction, dissuasion, proselytism, seduction or seducement

4. Persuasion, i.e., That Which Persuades; Persuasive Talk, Thing, etc.,n. *From Sec. 1:* argument, blandishment, blarney, cajolery, dissuasion or dissuasiveness, inducement, seduction; *Also:* 1. taffy—cajolery

5. One Who Persuades,n. *From Sec. 1:* cajoler, coaxer, dissuader, inducer, inveigler; proselytizer, proselyter, or proselytist; seducer, suborner, wheedler; *From Sec. 2:* suasionist

6. One Who Has Been Persuaded,n. *From Sec. 1:* convert or convertite, proselyte, seducee

7. Persuasive,adj. *From Sec. 1:* cajoling, coaxing, etc.; coaxy, convictive, dissuasive, seductive, subornative; *From Sec. 2:* suasive; *Also:*
1. **cogent**—persuasive or convincing because of logic, force, clearness, etc.
2. **conclusive**—convincing
3. **stringent**—penetratingly persuasive; convincing
4. **unctuous**—persuasive and soothing, esp. in speech or language (of people, manner, writing, etc.)

8. Persuasiveness,n. *From Sec. 7:* convictiveness, dissuasiveness, seductiveness; suasiveness; cogency, conclusiveness, stringency, unctuousness or unctuosity

9. Persuadable; Persuasible,adj. *From Sec. 1:* convertible, convincible, seducible or seduceable; *From Sec. 2:* suasible

10. To Attempt to Persuade,v.
1. **propagandize**—systematically attempt to persuade to one's beliefs, or the beliefs of a group (propaganda,n. propagandism, n. propagandist,n. propagandist, propagandistic, propagandic,adj.)
2. **urge**—attempt to persuade by advancing reasons, by entreaty, etc.
3. **woo**—attempt to persuade (wooer,n.)

11. Person Sent to a Foreign, or, Most Usually, Unchristian, Land to Convert Natives to Christianity; One Sent Out to Convert Anyone to Any Belief: missionary,n. (missionary,adj.)

12. Art of Persuading a God or Supernatural Being to Do, or to Refrain from Doing: theurgy,n. (theurgic,adj.)

13. Not Able to Be Persuaded: impersuadable, impersuasible, inconvincible, uncoaxable, unconvincible, unswayable,adj. (unpersuadableness, impersuasibility, impersuasibleness, unconvincibility,n.)

14. One Who Cannot Be Convinced: inconvincible,n.

15. Not Capable of Persuading: flimsy, lame, or thin (as a *flimsy excuse, explanation, story,* etc.); inconclusive, unconvincing, unpersuasive,adj. (flimsiness, lameness, thinness; inconclusiveness, unconvincingness, unpersuasiveness,n.)

639. DISBELIEF

1. To Disbelieve,v.
1. **discount**—believe only part of, owing to the incredibility or tendency to exaggeration of the source of the information
2. **discredit**—refuse to believe true
3. **distrust**—have no belief, faith, or trust in
4. **doubt**—disbelieve; tend to disbelieve; hesitate to believe
5. **misdoubt**—have doubts or suspicions about
6. **mistrust**—distrust
7. **query**—doubt
8. **question**—doubt
9. **reject**—refuse to believe

10. **scoff (at)**—show or express one's disbelief (in)
11. **scout**—refuse to believe or believe in
12. **suspect**—not believe in; have doubts about; distrust
13. **wonder (at)**—feel doubt, often mixed with curiosity (about); question or doubt in one's mind

2. Disbelief, i.e., Refusal to Believe,n. *From Sec. 1:* distrust, doubt, misdoubt or misdoubts, mistrust, rejection, suspicion, wonderment.

3. Disbelieving; Lacking in Belief,adj.
1. **agnostic**—maintaining that nothing can be implicitly believed, since all knowledge is relative and absolute certainty is unattainable by man
2. **apprehensive**—distrustful of the future
3. **cynical**—skeptical of human virtue, honesty, or nobility, and believing that all human actions reflect self-interest
4. **diffident**—having no faith in oneself; distrustful of one's ability, worth, or powers
5. **disenchanted**—freed from pleasant illusions or beliefs
6. **disillusioned**—disenchanted
7. **distrustful (of)**—having no belief, faith, or trust (in)
8. **doubtful**—disbelieving; tending to disbelieve; hesitant to believe
9. **dubious**—hesitant to believe
10. **heterodox**—rejecting standard, accepted, or orthodox doctrine or beliefs
11. **incredulous**—refusing to believe; tending to disbelieve
12. **mistrustful (of)**—distrustful (of)
13. **nihilistic**—rejecting all accepted beliefs
14. **nullifidian**—disbelieving; having no faith at all; believing in nothing; skeptical
15. **Pyrrhonic**—extremely skeptical (so called after the Greek philosopher Pyrrho, who taught that the evidence of the senses is unreliable)
16. **questioning**—doubtful (of a look, attitude, etc.)
17. **quizzical**—skeptical
18. **rejective**—refusing to believe; tending to refuse belief
19. **scoffing**—showing or expressing disbelief
20. **skeptical, skeptic**—disbelieving; lacking belief; maintaining a disbelieving or highly suspicious attitude; disbelieving, or showing disbelief of, the doctrines of religion
21. **suspicious (of)**—not believing (in); having doubts (about)
22. **umbrageous**—suspicious
23. **unbelieving**—disbelieving; disbelieving as to matters of religion; distrustful; incredulous
24. **unconfident**—lacking in belief or faith; lacking in belief or faith in oneself
25. **unorthodox**—not believing in orthodox or accepted doctrines, tenets, etc.
26. **wary (of)**—suspicious (of)

4. Disbelief; Lack of Belief,n. *From Sec. 3:* agnosticism, apprehension or apprehensiveness, cynicism, diffidence, disenchantment, disillusion or disillusionment, distrust or distrustfulness, doubt or doubtfulness; dubiousness, dubiety, dubitation, or dubiosity; heterodoxy, incredulity or incredulousness, mistrust or mistrustfulness, nihilism, pyrrhonism, quizzicality, skepticalness or skepticism, suspicion or suspiciousness, umbrageousness, unbelievingness, unbelieving, or unbelief; unorthodoxy, wariness; *Also:*
1. **misgiving**—feeling of distrust
2. **non-belief**—disbelief; lack of belief
3. **query**—doubt

5. Disbeliever,n. *From Sec. 3:* agnostic, cynic, distruster, doubter, mistruster, nihilist, nullifidian, Pyrrhonian, questioner, rejecter or rejector, scoffer, unbeliever, unorthodox; *From Sec. 4:* non-believer; *Also:*

1. **doubting Thomas**—one who is generally skeptical
2. **infidel**—disbeliever, esp. in that which is considered the true religion

6. To Cause (Someone) to Lose Belief,v. *From Sec. 3:* disenchant; disillusion, disillusionize, or disillude (disenchantment, disillusionment,n. disenchanter, disillusionist, disillusioner, or disillusionizer,n. disenchanting, disillusioning or disillusive,adj.)

7. Showing, or Having, No Disbelief,adj. *From Sec. 3:* unapprehensive, uncynical, unquestioning, unskeptical, unsuspicious, unwary; *Also:* 1. **implicit**—expressing or showing no doubt (as *implicit faith, confidence, obedience,* etc.)

8. Expressing or Indicating Doubt: dubitative,adj.

9. With Disbelief, Suspicion, Distrust, Skepticism, etc.: askance; cum grano salis (Latin); with a grain of salt

10. Unbelievable; Hard to Believe; Open to Doubt,adj.
1. **doubtful**—open to doubt
2. **dubious**—hard to believe
3. **farfetched**—not naturally following, hence hard to believe
4. **fishy**—not believable (colloq.)
5. **implausible**—not believable owing to its unreasonableness, illogical nature, improbability, etc.
6. **incredible**—unbelievable; impossible to believe
7. **questionable**—open to doubt
8. **suspect**—open to doubt or disbelief
9. **suspicious**—such as to arouse disbelief or doubt; open to doubt

11. Unbelievability, etc.,n. *From Sec. 9:* doubtfulness, dubiousness or dubiety, fishiness, implausibility or implausibleness, incredibility or incredibleness, questionableness, suspiciousness

12. Not Worthy of Belief, Trust, or Confidence: fly-by-night; shifty (of a person); slippery (of a person); treacherous (of a person); unauthentic, undependable, unreliable, untrustworthy,adj. (shiftiness, slipperiness, treacherousness, unauthenticity, undependability, undependableness, unreliability, unreliableness, untrustworthiness,n.)

13. To Show or Express Disbelief about or Doubt in,v.
1. **challenge**—call into doubt or question (challenge,n.)
2. **impeach**—call into doubt or question (impeachment,n.)
3. **impugn**—call into doubt or question; cast doubts upon (impugnation, impugnment, n.)
4. **oppugn**—show one's doubts about; call into question
5. **query**—question the truth of
6. **question**—call into question; express doubts about; query

14. To Destroy Belief in,v.
1. **discredit**—destroy belief or confidence in; cause people to disbelieve (a story, statement, or other abstraction); cause (a story, etc.) to be less believable
2. **explode**—destroy belief in by showing the falsity of (explosion,n.)

15. To Put under Suspicion: compromise,v. (compromising,adj.)

640. UNCERTAINTY

1. Uncertain, i.e., Descr. of That Which One Cannot Be Certain about,adj.
1. **ambiguous**—uncertain, because obscure, faint, or confusing
2. **amphibolic**—uncertain (medical)

3. **borderline**—uncertain, because in between
4. **chancy**—uncertain, because dependent on chance (colloq.)
5. **changeful**—uncertain, because constantly changing
6. **contestable**—controvertible
7. **contingent**—uncertain, because subject to conditions that cannot be foreseen
8. **controversial**—uncertain, because open to argument
9. **controvertible**—uncertain, because open to doubt, argument, disproof, etc.
10. **disputable**—uncertain, i.e., open to dispute
11. **doubtful**—uncertain, because open to doubt
12. **dubious**—doubtful
13. **dubitable**—doubtful
14. **imponderable**—uncertain, because not of the sort that one can think about, ponder on, know about, etc.
15. **incalculable**—uncertain, because not of the sort that one can calculate, rely on, count on, etc.
16. **indecisive**—uncertain; producing no definite decision; doubtful
17. **indefinite**—not certain
18. **indeterminable**—uncertain, because not of the sort that can be decided or settled
19. **indeterminate**—uncertain
20. **moot**—uncertain, i.e., open to argument or discussion
21. **pending, pendent**—still undecided, therefore not yet certain
22. **precarious**—uncertain, often in the sense of depending on the will or pleasure of another
23. **problematic, problematical**—uncertain; doubtful
24. **questionable**—uncertain; doubtful
25. **rocky**—unpleasantly doubtful or uncertain
26. **suspenseful**—full of uncertainty
27. **touch-and-go**—uncertain
28. **unassured**—uncertain
29. **undecided**—uncertain, because still not decided
30. **undependable**—uncertain, i.e., not able to be depended on
31. **unreliable**—uncertain, i.e., not able to be relied on
32. **unsure**—uncertain; unreliable

2. Uncertainty (of Things, Events, etc.),n. *From Sec. 1:* ambiguity or ambiguousness, changefulness, contestability, contingency, controvertibility, disputability, doubtfulness or doubt, dubiousness, dubitability, imponderability, incalculability or incalculableness, indecisiveness, indefiniteness, indeterminableness, indeterminateness or indeterminacy, pendency, precariousness, questionability or questionableness, suspense, touch-and-go, undecidedness, undependability, unreliability or unreliableness, unsureness

3. Uncertain Quality or Thing,n. *From Sec. 1:* imponderable, indeterminable

4. To Remain Undecided: pend,v. (of things, results, etc.)

5. Uncertain, i.e., Feeling Uncertain, or Indicating a Feeling of Uncertainty,adj.
1. **diffident**—uncertain of oneself, one's ability, powers, worth, etc., or showing such uncertainty
2. **doubtful**—uncertain, i.e., full of doubts
3. **dubious**—doubtful
4. **halting**—uncertain; showing uncertainty
5. **indecisive**—unable to make up one's mind; arriving at no definite decision
6. **indefinite**—uncertain
7. **insecure**—uncertain
8. **irresolute**—unable to come to a firm decision; vacillating

9. **shilly-shally, shilly-shallying**—irresolute
10. **unassured**—unconfident
11. **unconfident**—uncertain; not free from doubt
12. **undecided**—uncertain, because not having made up one's mind
13. **unpoised**—not sure of oneself
14. **unpositive**—uncertain; not sure
15. **unself-assured**—not sure of oneself
16. **unself-confident**—not confident of oneself
17. **unsure**—uncertain
18. **vacillating, vacillatory**—uncertain, i.e., swinging back and forth between decisions; unable to make up one's mind; showing indecision
19. **willy-nilly**—vacillating
20. **wobbly, wabbly**—uncertain; undecided; vacillating

6. Uncertainty, i.e., a Feeling or Feelings of Uncertainty,n. *From Sec. 5:* diffidence, doubt or doubtfulness, dubiousness or dubiety, indecisiveness or indecision, indefiniteness, insecurity, irresoluteness or irresolution, shilly-shally, unassurance, unconfidence, undecidedness or indecision, unpositiveness, unself-assurance, unself-confidence, unsureness, vacillation, wobbliness, wabbliness; *Also:*
1. **misgiving**—feeling of doubt
2. **qualm**—scruple
3. **scruple**—feeling of doubt about whether a contemplated act or course is right or wrong, fair or unfair, etc.
4. **suspense**—anxious uncertainty as to an outcome

7. To Be or Feel Uncertain or Show Uncertainty,v. *From Sec. 5:* doubt, shilly-shally, vacillate, wobble, wabble (vacillation,n.); *From Sec. 6:* scruple; *Also:*
1. **oscillate**—swing back and forth between two opposing beliefs, decisions, etc (oscillation,n.)
2. **sway**—vacillate (sway,n.)
3. **waver**—be undecided; be unsure of one's opinion (waver,n.)

8. To Cause (Someone) to Lose Self-Confidence or Poise: abash, embarrass,v. (embarrassment,n.)

9. To Deprive (a Male) of His Self-Confidence (Term in Psychoanalysis): castrate. v. (castration,n.)

10. Situation or Condition of Uncertainty, n.
1. **dilemma**—situation or condition in which there is a good deal of uncertainty, since the alternatives are equally unpleasant
2. **quandary**—state or condition of uncertainty or doubt, usually as to which course to take, what action to follow, or what decision to make; dilemma

641. CERTAINTY

1. Certain, i.e., Descr. of That Which One Is or Can Be Certain about,adj.
1. **absolute**—certain; completely certain
2. **assured**—certain
3. **decided**—unambiguous; unmistakable, unquestionable
4. **decisive**—certain in the sense of putting an end to all dispute or doubt
5. **definite**—certain in the sense of not being a bit vague or doubtful
6. **guaranteed**—certain
7. **incontestable**—certain beyond any question; so certain as to allow no argument or disagreement
8. **incontrovertible**—incontestable
9. **indisputable**—certain beyond any dispute or question
10. **indubitable**—certain beyond any doubt
11. **inevitable**—certain to happen

12. **irrefutable**—undeniable
13. **positive**—certain
14. **secure**—certain
15. **sure**—certain
16. **unambiguous**—certain in the sense of leaving no confusion or doubt in the mind
17. **undeniable**—certain in the sense of not being susceptible to denial or refutation
18. **undoubted**—certain; without doubt
19. **unfailing**—certain; certain to happen
20. **unmistakable**—certain in the sense that one cannot make a mistake about it
21. **unquestionable**—certain beyond doubt or question

2. **Certainty (of Things, Events, Circumstances, etc.),n.** *From Sec. 1:* absoluteness, decidedness, decisiveness, definiteness, incontestability or incontestableness, incontrovertibility or incontrovertibleness, indisputability or indisputableness, indubitableness, inevitability or inevitableness, irrefutability or irrefutableness, positiveness, security, surety or sureness, unambiguity or unambiguousness, undeniableness, unmistakableness, unquestionableness; *Also:* 1. certitude—certainty

3. **A Certainty,n.** *From Sec. 1:* inevitability, surety

4. **To Make (Something) Certain or Sure,v.**
1. **assure**—make (a thing or occurrence) sure (assurance,n.)
2. **certify**—make certain; assure (certification,n.)
3. **corroborate**—make more certain (corroboration,n. corroborator,n. corroborative, corroboratory, corroborant,adj.)
4. **ensure, insure**—make sure or certain—usually, that something will happen (ensurance, insurance,n.)
5. **guarantee, guaranty**—make sure or certain (guarantor, guarantee, guaranty,n.)
6. **secure**—make certain; ensure
7. **warrant**—guarantee (warranty,n. warranter,n.)

5. **Fact, Thing, or Statement That Makes Certain or Sure,n.** *From Sec. 4:* assurance, corroboration, guarantee or guaranty, insurance, security, warrant or warranty

6. **Certain, i.e., Feeling Certain, or Indicating a Feeling of Certainty,adj.**
1. **absolute**—certain; completely certain
2. **assured**—certain; confident
3. **cocksure**—absolutely or offensively sure or positive
4. **confident**—certain; free from doubt; self-assured
5. **decided**—free from doubt
6. **decisive**—characterized by a complete lack of doubt or uncertainty
7. **definite**—certain; without doubt or any feeling of vagueness
8. **overweening**—excessively and intolerably self-confident
9. **poised**—self-confident
10. **positive**—certain
11. **presumptuous**—overconfident
12. **secure**—certain; confident; free from doubt
13. **self-assured**—sure of oneself
14. **self-confident**—sure of oneself
15. **sure**—certain

7. **Certainty, i.e., Feeling or Feelings of Certainty,n.** *From Sec. 6:* absoluteness, assurance or assuredness, cocksureness, confidence, decidedness or decision, decisiveness or decision, definiteness, poise, positiveness, presumptuousness or presumption, security, self-assurance, self-confidence, sureness or surety; *Also:*
1. **aplomb**—self-assurance
2. **brass**—bold self-assurance
3. **certitude**—certainty
4. **sufficiency**—self-confidence

8. **To Be Certain or Sure of:** bank on, depend on, rely on, trust,v.

9. **To Cause (Someone) to Feel Certain, Sure, or Confident:** assure, encourage, reassure, warrant,v. (assurance, encouragement, reassurance, warranty,n.)

642. RELIGION

1. **Religion, Generally,n.**
1. **creed**—one's religion or religious belief or beliefs
2. **cult**—false or unorthodox religion (cultism,n. cultist,n.)
3. **faith**—one's religion
4. **orthodoxy**—that religion or form of religion that is considered the true and genuine (orthodox,n. orthodox,adj.)

2. **Pert. to Religion:** religious, solemn,adj.

3. **Certain Specific Religions or Types of Religion,n.**
1. **Brahmanism**—religion of the orthodox Hindus
2. **Buddhism**—Asian religion, based on the teachings of Buddha
3. **Catholicism**—religion of the Roman Catholic Church
4. **Christianity**—religion of the Christians
5. **Confucianism**—philosophical and ethical system of Confucius that forms the basis of one of the religions of China
6. **gospel**—Christian faith
7. **heathenism**—paganism
8. **Hinduism, Hindooism**—native religion of India
9. **Islam, Islamism**—religion of the Mohammedans
10. **Jainism**—heterodox religion founded as a revolt against Hinduism
11. **Judaism**—religion of the Jews
12. **Mohammedanism**—religion of the Mohammedans, or Moslems
13. **Moslemism**—Mohammedanism
14. **Mussulmanism**—Mohammedanism
15. **paganism**—religion other than Christianity, Judaism, or Mohammedanism; religion of the early Greeks and Romans
16. **Protestantism**—religion of the Protestants
17. **Shinto, Shintoism**—religion of the Japanese, a form of ancestor worship
18. **Sikhism**—religion founded in India by a Hindu reformer—originally a Hindu sect, now an independent religion
19. **Taoism**—one of the three main religions (the other two are Buddhism and Confucianism) of China
20. **therianthropism**—religion in which the deities are part man, part animal
21. **Zoroastrianism, Zoroastrism**—religion founded in ancient Persia; religion of the Persians before their conversion to Mohammedanism

4. **Descr. of, or Pert. to, a Religion or Member of a Religion,adj.** *From Sec. 3:* Brahman, Brahmanic, Brahmanist, or Brahmanistic; Buddhist or Buddhistic, Catholic, Christian, Confucian or Confucianist, heathen, Hindu; Islam, Islamic, Islamistic, or Islamitic; Jaina; Judaic, Judaistic, Judean, Jewish, Hebrew, Israelite, or Israelitish; Mohammedan; Moslem, Moslemic, or Moslemite; Mussulmanic; pagan, paganist, or paganistic; Protestant, Shintoist or Shintoistic, Sikh, Taoist or Taoistic, therianthropic, Zoroastrian; *Also:* 1. gentile—Christian rather than Jewish; pert. to any people who are not Jewish; pagan

5. **Member of, or Believer in, a Religion,n.** *From Sec. 3:* Buddhist, Catholic, Christian, Confucian or Confucianist, heathen, Hindu, Islamist or Islamite; Jain, Jaina, or Jainist;

Judaist, Judean, Judaean, Jew, Hebrew, or Israelite; Mohammedan, Moslem or Moslemite, Mussulman, pagan or paganist, Protestant, Shintoist, Sikh, Taoist, Zoroastrian; *From Sec. 4:* gentile; *Also:*

1. **coreligionist**—member of the same religion
2. **giaour**—Christian, so called by Mohammedans
3. **infidel**—member of a different religious faith
4. **Nazarene**—Christian; early Christian
5. **paynim**—Mohammedan, so called by Christians

6. Like, Resembling, or Characteristic of a Religion,adj. *From Sec. 3:* Brahmanistic, Buddhistic, heathenish, Islamistic, Judaistic, paganish or paganistic, Shintoistic

7. Members Collectively of a Religion,n. *From Sec. 3:* Christendom, heathendom, Jewry, pagandom; *Also:*

1. **paynim**—Mohammedans collectively, so called by Christians
2. **Zion**—Jews collectively

8. To Convert (Someone) to a Religion,v. *From Sec. 3:* Catholicize, Christianize, heathenize, Islamize, Judaize, Mohammedanize, paganize, Protestantize (Christianization, Islamization, Judaization, Mohammedanization, paganization,n. Catholicizer, Christianizer, etc.,n.) ; *Also:*

1. **evangelize**—convert to Christianity (evangelization,n. evangelizer, evangelist, or evangel,n. evangelistic,adj.)
2. **proselytize, proselyte**—convert to a religion (proselytization, proselytism,n. proselytizer, proselyter, proselytist,n. proselytical, proselytistic,adj.)
3. **Romanize**—convert to Roman Catholicism (Romanization,n. Romanizer,n.)

9. To Convert, i.e., Be Converted to a Religion,v. *From Sec. 3:* Catholicize, Christianize, heathenize, Islamize, Judaize, paganize (Christianization, Islamization, Judaization, paganization,n.)

10. A Convert to a Religion,n.

1. **neophyte**—new convert; new convert to Christianity (neophytic,adj. neophytism, n.)
2. **novice, novitiate, noviciate**—new convert to Christianity
3. **proselyte**—convert to Christianity, Judaism, or certain other religions (proselytization, proselytism,n.)

11. Roman Catholic,adj.

1. **papist, Papist, papistic, papistical**—pert. to, or characteristic of, the Roman Catholic religion, its forms, ceremonies, government, etc. (derogatory)
2. **popish**—Roman Catholic (derogatory)
3. **Roman**—pert. to the Roman Catholic religion, ritual, church, etc.
4. **Romanist, Romanistic**—pert. to the Roman Catholic religion (derogatory)
5. **Romish**—descr. of the Roman Catholic Church or religion (derogatory)

12. Roman Catholicism,n. *From Sec. 11:* papistry, popishness or popery, Romanism, Romishness

13. A Roman Catholic,n. *From Sec. 11:* papist or Papist, Roman, Romanist

14. To Conform to, or Be Prejudiced toward, Roman Catholic Beliefs: Romanize,v. (Romanization,n. Romanizer,n.)

15. Christian Revelation: gospel,n.

16. Movement to Colonize the Jews in Palestine: Zionism,n. (Zionist,n. Zionist,adj.)

17. Group Forming Part of a Larger Religion: denomination, sect,n. (denominational, sectarial or sectarian,adj. sectarian or sectary,n. sectarianism,n.)

18. Group Dissenting from the Established Religion or Church: cult, sect,n. (cultist, sectarian,n.)

19. System of Religion or Religious Beliefs: theology,n. (theological,adj.)

20. Science or Study of Religion or of Religious Practices: divinity, theology,n. (theologian,n. theological,adj.)

21. Scientific Study of Comparative Religion: hierology,n. (hierologist,n. hierologic, hierological,adj.)

643. RELIGIOUSNESS

1. Religious,adj.

1. **devoted**—sincerely religious
2. **devout**—sincerely devoted to, and conscientiously practicing, religious principles
3. **God-fearing**—devoutly religious; feeling reverence for God
4. **godly**—religious; devout; pious
5. **holy**—religious; devout; pious
6. **pietistic, pietistical**—deeply religious in feeling or emotion rather than from intellectual decision or cool reasoning; exaggeratedly religious
7. **pious**—zealous in the practice of religion or religious worship; showing reverence to God
8. **religionistic**—strictly or zealously devoted to religion

2. Religiousness,n. *From Sec. 1:* devotion, devoutness, godliness, holiness, pietism, piousness or piety, religionism; *Also:* 1. **religiosity** —religiousness; intense or excessive religiousness

3. Religious Person,n.

1. **devotee**—one devoted to religious practices or ceremonies; religious fanatic
2. **religionist**—one who is strictly or zealously devoted to a religion

4. To Be Strictly or Zealously Devoted to Religion; To Practice Religion Strictly or Zealously: religionize,v.

5. Strong Religious Emotion or Ecstasy, or the Capacity for It, Caused by Thinking about God: theopathy,n. (theopathetic, theopathic,adj.)

6. One Who Has Fits of Religious Mania: convulsionary,n. (convulsionary,adj.)

7. Arising out of Religious Motives: pious, adj. (piety, piousness,n.)

8. The Advocacy of Strict Observance of Sunday as a Religious Day: Sabbatarianism, n. (Sabbatarian, Sabbatist,n. Sabbatarian, adj.)

9. Strict Religious Observance of the Seventh Day, Sunday, or the Sabbath: sabbatism,n.

10. Hypocritical, Insincere, or Affected Religiousness: pharisaism, phariseeism, pietism, piety, piousness, religionism, religiosity, sanctimoniousness, sanctimony, self-righteousness,n. (pharisaic or pharisaical, pietistic or pietistical, pious, religionist or religionistic, sanctimonious, self-righteous,adj. pharisee, religionist,n.)

11. Arising out of a Pretense of Religious Motives: pious,adj. (piety, piousness,n.)

12. Not Religious; Having No Religion; Not Believing in or Not Revering God,adj.

1. **atheistic, atheistical**—not believing in God or in the existence of a supreme being (atheism,n.)
2. **godless**—acknowledging no god (godlessness,n.)
3. **heathen**—professing no belief in the God

of Revelation; irreligious (heathenism, heathenry, heathendom,n.)
4. **impious**—not religious; having no reverence for God (impiety, impiousness,n.)
5. **infidel**—having no religious faith; not having a particular faith (applied by Mohammedans to those who are not Mohammedan and by Christians to those who are not Christian); heathen (infidelity,n.)
6. **irreligious**—not religious; against religion or contrary to religion (irreligion, irreligiousness,n.)
7. **pagan**—having no religion; neither Christian, Jewish, nor Mohammedan; heathen (paganism,n.)
8. **unchristian**—heathen; pagan (unchristianity, unchristianness,n.)
9. **uncircumcised**—irreligious (generally, of Jews)
10. **ungodly**—godless; irreligious (ungodliness,n.)
11. **unholy**—impious (unholiness,n.)

13. One Who Is Not Religious, etc.,n. *From Sec. 12:* atheist, heathen, infidel, pagan or paganist, unchristian; *Also:* 1. **paynim**—infidel; pagan

14. Resembling, or Characteristic of, One Who Is Not Religious, etc.,adj. *From Sec. 13:* atheistic or atheistical, heathenish, paganish, paganistic, or paganic

15. To Make Irreligious, etc.,v. *From Sec. 12:* heathenize, paganize, unchristianize (paganization,n.)

16. To Become Irreligious, etc.,v. *From Sec. 12:* heathenize, paganize (paganization,n.)

17. Not Related to Religion or Religious Activities: secular, temporal,adj. (secularity, temporality,n.)

18. Political or Social Rejection of All Forms of Religious Faith or Worship: secularism,n. (secularist,n. secularistic,adj.)

19. Attitude that Civil, Political, or Educational Matters Should Not Contain Any Religious Element: secularism,n. (secularist, n. secularistic,adj.)

644. RELIGIOUS COMMUNITY

1. Religious Community,n.
1. **abbey**—convent; monastery (abbatial, adj.)
2. **cloister**—convent or monastery the members of which are comparatively withdrawn from worldly living (cloistral,adj.)
3. **convent**—secluded religious community for females or nuns (conventual,adj.)
4. **lamasery**—monastery in parts of the Orient
5. **monastery**—place of religious retreat where monks live in seclusion (monastic or, derogatory, monkish,adj.)
6. **nunnery**—convent
7. **priory, priorate**—religious house dependent on an abbey

2. Head of a Religious Community,n. *From Sec. 1:* abbot or, fem., abbess, prior or, fem., prioress (abbatial,adj.) ; *Also:*
1. **archimandrite**—head of a large monastery of an Eastern church
2. **hegumen**—head of a small monastery of an Eastern church

3. Office, Jurisdiction, or Tenure of a Head of a Religious Community,n. *From Sec. 2:* abbacy, priorate,n.

4. Life in a Monastery: monasticism,n.

5. Inhabitant of a Religious Community,n.
1. **canoness**—woman in a convent who has not taken perpetual vows
2. **cenobite**—member of a monastery or convent (cenobitism,n. cenobitic,adj.)

3. **cloistress**—female who lives in a cloister; nun
4. **conventual**—member of a convent
5. **dervish**—Mohammedan monk
6. **fra**—Italian monk or friar
7. **friar**—member of a religious order of "brothers"
8. **monk, monastic**—inhabitant of a monastery; someone living in religious seclusion in a monastery (monasticism, n. monastic, monachal, or, derogatory, monkish,adj.)
9. **nun**—woman in a convent who has taken religious vows
10. **religieuse (French)**—nun
11. **religieux (French)**—monk
12. **sister**—nun
13. **vestal virgin**—nun

6. To Make Monklike: cowl,v.

7. Person Bound by Religious Vows to a Way of Life: devotee, votarist, votary,n. (votaress, votress, fem.n. votary,adj.)

8. Women United in a Religious Faith or Organization: sisterhood,n. (sister,n.)

9. Candidate for Membership in a Religious Order: postulant,n.

10. One Newly Accepted into a Religious Order: novice, novitiate, or noviciate,n.

11. Period or State of Probation in a Religious Order: novitiate or noviciate,n.

12. Not Belonging to a Religious Order: lay, secular,adj. (of clergymen)

645. CHURCH

1. Church; Place of Worship,n.
1. **abbey**—church of a monastery
2. **bethel**—church for sailors
3. **cathedral**—large or important church; originally, the bishop's church
4. **Catholicity**—the Roman Catholic Church
5. **chapel**—small place or room for godly worship
6. **conventicle**—place of meeting for secret or unauthorized religious worship (conventicler,n.)
7. **fold**—the church; a particular church
8. **minster**—large church; church attached to, or once attached to, a monastery
9. **oratory**—place for praying
10. **parish**—local or district church
11. **shrine**—place of worship
12. **synagogue**—meeting place for Jewish worship or religious instruction
13. **tabernacle**—place of worship for many people; synagogue
14. **temple**—building for the worship of God or of a god; synagogue
15. **Zion**—church of God

2. Pert. to, or Descr. of, a Church,adj. *From Sec. 1:* abbatial, cathedral, Catholic, parochial (from *parish*), synagogical or synagogal, tabernacular; *Also:*
1. **apostolic**—papal
2. **ecclesiastic**—pert. to the church
3. **papal**—pert. to the Roman Catholic Church
4. **spiritual**—of the church

3. One Who Attends, etc., a Church: churchgoer, parishioner, worshiper,n. (worship,v.)

4. Those Who Attend, or Worship in, a Church: congregation, flock,n. (congregational,adj.)

5. One Newly Received into a Church: novice, novitiate, or noviciate,n.

6. Period or State of Probation as a New Member of a Church: novitiate or noviciate, n.

7. Devotion to the Interests or Principles of the Church: ecclesiasticism,n.

8. Science of Church Art, Architecture, Ornamentation, and Antiquities: ecclesiology,n. (ecclesiologist,n. ecclesiologic, ecclesiological,adj.)

9. Spirit, Principles, or Practices, of a Church: ecclesiasticism,n.

10. Doctrines, Principles, Tenets, Beliefs, Practices, etc., of the Roman Catholic Church: Catholicity or, derogatory, Romanism,n. (Romanist,n. Romanist, Romanistic, adj.)

11. Not Controlled by, Related to, etc., the Church: lay, secular, temporal,adj. (secularity, temporality,n.)

12. Opposed to the Church, esp. to Its Influence in Secular Matters: anti-clerical,adj. (anti-clericalism,n. anti-clerical,n.)

13. Refusal to Conform to the Principles of a Church: dissent,n. (dissenter,n. dissent,v.)

14. Refusal, in Early Times in England, to Attend the Anglican, or Established, Church: recusance, recusancy,n. (recusant,n. recusant,adj.)

646. CLERGYMAN

1. Clergyman or Other Church Officer,n.
1. archbishop—chief bishop
2. archdeacon—chief deacon
3. bishop—clergyman of the higher or highest rank
4. canon—clergyman of a cathedral or large church
5. cardinal—high official of the Roman Catholic Church
6. cassock—clergyman, so called from the characteristic dress
7. chaplain—clergyman officially appointed to duty in the armed forces or in an institution
8. cleric—clergyman
9. curate—assistant pastor, rector, or vicar
10. curé—parish priest
11. deacon—clergyman next below a priest in rank; assistant clergyman who does not preach
12. dean—high official of the church
13. divine—clergyman
14. ecclesiastic—clergyman
15. father—priest
16. lama—Tibetan priest
17. metropolitan—archbishop with limited authority over the bishops of an ecclesiastical province; clergyman below a patriarch in the Russian Orthodox Church
18. minister—member of the clergy
19. monsignor—title of honor of certain prelates
20. padre—priest, esp. so called in Italy, Spain, Portugal, and Latin America; chaplain, in military parlance
21. parson—clergyman; clergyman at the head of a parish
22. pastor—clergyman of a church or parish; spiritual adviser or overseer
23. patriarch—bishop in the Russian Orthodox Church
24. pontiff—Pope; high or chief priest; bishop; bishop of Rome
25. Pope, Holy Father, His Holiness—head of the Roman Catholic Church; Bishop of Rome
26. preacher—clergyman, i.e., one who preaches
27. prelate—clergyman of high rank
28. presbyter—priest
29. priest—member of the clergy; clergyman ranking next below a bishop
30. primate—highest bishop of a region
31. pulpiteer—preacher (contemptuous, in allusion to the pulpit from which he speaks)
32. rabbi—clergyman of the Jewish religion
33. rector—clergyman officiating in a church or parish
34. reverend—clergyman (loose or colloq.)
35. shaveling—priest (contemptuous, in allusion to his shaven head)
36. shepherd—pastor
37. suffragan—bishop who assists another bishop, an archbishop, or a metropolitan
38. vicar—clergyman of a special kind, depending on the denomination

2. The Office, Rank, etc., of a Clergyman,n. *From Sec. 1:* archbishopric or archiepiscopate; archdeaconry, archdeaconship, archdeaconate, or archidiaconate; bishopric; canonicate, canonry, or canonship; cardinalate, cassock, curacy; deaconship, deaconate, or diaconate; deanery, deanship, or decanate; ministership; pastorate, pastorage, or pastorship; patriarchate, popedom or papacy; prelacy, prelature, or prelatism; presbyterate, priesthood, primacy, rabbinate, rectorate or rectorship; vicarate, vicariate, or vicarage; *Also:*
1. episcopacy—rank of bishop
2. Holy See—office of the Pope

3. Descr. of, or Pert. to, Clergymen, a Clergyman, or the Office or Rank of a Clergyman,adj. *From Sec. 1:* archiepiscopal (from *archbishop*); archidiaconal (from *archdeacon*); canonical or canonic, clerical, deaconal or diaconal; decanal (from *dean*); ecclesiastical, metropolitan, ministerial, monsignorial, pastoral, patriarchal, pontifical; papal or apostolic (from *Pope*); prelatic, prelatical, or prelatial; priestly, rabbinical or rabbinic, rectorial or rectoral, suffragan, vicarial; *Also:*
1. episcopal—pert. to bishops
2. sacerdotal—pert. to, or descr. of, a priest or his office

4. The Clergy; Clergymen as a Group or Body; Group or Body of Clergymen,n. *From Sec. 1:* canonicate or canonry, cardinalate, deaconry or diaconate, ministry, pastorate, the pulpit, prelacy, presbyterate, priesthood, rabbinate; *Also:*
1. (the) cloth—the clergy
2. conclave—group of cardinals
3. episcopacy, episcopate, episcopature—bishops, collectively
4. (the) First Estate—the clergy, in England, esp. formerly
5. (the) Lords Spiritual—the First Estate
6. (the) Spiritualty—the clergy

5. Territory or Jurisdiction of a Clergyman, *n.* From Sec. 1: archbishopric or archiepiscopate, archdeaconry or archdiocese, bishopric, deanery or decanate, patriarchate, popedom or papacy (archdiocesan,adj.); *Also:*
1. diocese—district over which a bishop has authority (diocesan,adj.)
2. episcopate—diocese
3. Holy See—jurisdiction of the Pope; Diocese of Rome
4. parish—part of a diocese under a priest, minister, pastor, etc. (parochial,adj.)
5. see—diocese

6. Residence of a Clergyman,n. *From Sec. 1:* archdeaconry, deanery or decanate, parsonage, pastorage or pastorate, patriarchate, presbytery, rectory; *Also:*
1. manse—house of a church official
2. rectory—parsonage
3. Vatican—residence of the Pope

7. Part of the Church for the Use of the Clergy: presbytery,n.

8. Profession, Functions, etc., of a Clergyman: the clergy, the ministry,n.

9. Believing in the Divinity of the Priestly Office: sacerdotal,adj. (sacerdotalism,n.)

10. To Officiate as a Bishop or Pope: pontificate,v.

11. An Adherent of the Pope: papist,n. (papistry,n. papist, papistic, papistical,adj.)

12. Favoring the Supremacy of the Pope: ultramontane,adj.

13. Opposed to the Clergy, Esp. to Its Influence in Non-Religious Affairs: anti-clerical,adj. (anti-clericalism,n. anti-clerical,n.)

14. Other Church Officers,n.
1. **beadle**—subordinate church officer
2. **elder**—governing officer of a Protestant church
3. **sexton**—minor officer of the church who takes care of church property
4. **verger**—custodian of the interior of a church building
5. **vestryman**—member of the committee that manages the business affairs of a church or parish (vestry, collective)

15. Office or Rank of a Governing Official of a Protestant Church: presbyterate,n.

647. TO PREACH

1. To Preach,v.
1. **evangelize**—preach the gospel; preach the gospel to (someone)
2. **preachify**—preach unskillfully or tiresomely
3. **pulpit**—preach from a pulpit
4. **pulpiteer**—preach
5. **sermonize**—preach

2. Preaching,n. *From Sec. 1:* evangelization or evangelism, preachification, pulpit, pulpiteering, sermonizing

3. A Preaching, i.e., That Which Is Preached,n. *From Sec. 1:* preachification, sermon; *Also:*
1. **homily**—sermon; sermon for moral instruction; sermon on a Biblical topic
2. **preachment**—sermon; tiresome sermon

4. Preacher,n. *From Sec. 1:* evangelist, evangelizer, or evangel; preachifier, pulpiter; pulpiteer (often contemptuous); sermonizer; *From Sec. 3:* homilist; *Also:* 1. predicant, predicator, pulpitarian—preacher

5. Descr. of, or Pert. to, Preaching, a Preaching, or a Preacher,adj. *From Sec. 1:* evangelistic, pulpital or pulpitarian; *From Sec. 3:* homiletic; *Also:* 1. predicatory—descr. of, or pert. to, preaching

6. Preaching: preachifying, predicant, predicative, predicatory, pulpiteering, sermonizing, adj.

7. Addicted to Preaching: predicant,adj.

8. The Art of Preaching: homiletics,n.

9. A Characteristic Habit, Idea, etc., of Preaching or of Preachers: pulpitism,n.

10. To Talk Like a Preacher: preacherize,v.

11. Preachingly: preachily,adv.

12. To Supply with Preaching or a Pulpit: pulpit,v.

13. Without a Pulpit: pulpitless,adj.

648. THE BIBLE; SACRED WRITINGS

1. The Bible; Selected Books of the Bible; Sacred Writings,n.
1. **Apocalypse**—last book of the New Testament, also called Revelation, Revelations, or, in full, The Revelation of St. John the Divine (apocalyptic,adj.)
2. **Apocrypha**—fourteen books of the Bible, not considered canonical, but included in the Septuagint and the Vulgate as an appendix to the Old Testament; religious writings of uncertain authorship, considered by some to be inspired (Apocryphal, apocryphal,adj.)
3. **codex**—manuscript volume of the Scriptures
4. **Evangel**—one of the four Gospels
5. **Genesis**—first book of the Old Testament, describing the creation of the world and of man (Genesiac, Genesitic,adj.)
6. **Good Book**—the Bible
7. **Gospels**—first four books of the New Testament
8. **Heptateuch**—first seven books of the Old Testament
9. **Hexateuch**—first six books of the Old Testament
10. **Holy Writ**—the Bible
11. **Koran, Alcoran**—Mohammedan sacred writings
12. **New Testament**—books in the Bible produced by the early Christian church and added to the Old Testament
13. **Old Testament**—collection of books forming the first of the two main divisions of the Bible
14. **oracles**—Scripture
15. **Pentateuch**—first five books of the Old Testament
16. **Scripture, The Scriptures, Holy Scripture**—the Bible; the sacred writings of the Old and/or New Testament (Scriptural,adj.)
17. **Septuagint**—Greek version of the Old Testament
18. **Talmud**—books of Jewish law (Talmudic, adj.)
19. **Upanishad**—theological documents of ancient Hinduism
20. **Veda**—collection of sacred writings of the Hindus (Vedaic,adj.)
21. **Vulgate**—edition of the Bible used in Roman Catholic churches (Vulgate,adj.)

2. The Ten Commandments: Decalogue,n.

3. Alphabetical Index of the Important Words of the Bible: concordance,n.

4. Writings Falsely Ascribed to Biblical Characters: pseudepigrapha,n. (pseudepigraphic, pseudepigraphous,adj.)

5. Bible Scholar, etc.,n.
1. **Biblicist**—expert on the Bible
2. **Biblist**—Bible scholar
3. **Talmudist**—student of the book of Jewish laws

6. One Who Accepts Only the Bible as a Guide to Religious Faith: Biblist,n.

7. Literal or Strict Adherence to the Bible: Biblicism, textualism,n. (Biblicist, textualist, n. Biblicistic,adj.)

649. PRAYER

1. Prayer,n.
1. **Ave Maria, Ave Mary**—salutation and prayer to the Virgin Mary
2. **benedicite**—grace said at table
3. **confiteor**—prayer in which one confesses one's sins
4. **devotions**—form of prayer (devotional, adj.)
5. **grace**—short prayer preceding or following a meal
6. **Hail Mary**—Ave Maria
7. **invocation**—prayer for help or protection (invocational,adj.)
8. **litany**—kind of formal prayer in which both the minister and congregation speak
9. **orison**—prayer
10. **Pater Noster**—the Lord's Prayer
11. **requiescat (Latin)**—prayer for the peace of a dead soul

12. vesper—evening prayer

2. Prayers,n.
1. devotions—prayers (devotional,adj.)
2. Mass—series of prayers and rites in the Roman Catholic Church
3. Requiem—Mass for the dead
4. Rosary—series of prayers

3. Special Time for Prayers: canonical hour, n.

4. Night of Prayer: vigil,n.

5. To Call Upon by Prayer: invoke,v. (invocation,n.)

6. Person Who Prays, or Who Is Paid to Pray, for Someone: beadsman, bedesman,n.

650. SACRED

1. Sacred,adj.
1. anointed—consecrated by the process of pouring oil
2. blessed—sacred (blessedness,n.)
3. consecrated—sacred; made or declared sacred
4. enshrined—treated as sacred
5. hallowed—sacred; observed or honored as sacred; consecrated (hallowedness,n.)
6. hieratic—consecrated to sacred usage
7. holy—sacred (holiness,n.)
8. inviolable—sacred, i.e., not to be profaned, violated, etc. (inviolability,n.)
9. pious—sacred rather than secular (piousness,n.)
10. sacrosanct—most sacred; set apart as sacred—sometimes ironic (sacrosanctity, sacrosanctness,n.)
11. sainted—sacred; consecrated (saintedness,n.)
12. sanctified—sacred; made sacred; set apart for sacred use, observance, etc. (sanctity,n.)
13. solemn—sacred (solemnity,n.)
14. spiritual—sacred (spiritualness, spirituality, spiritualism,n.)
15. taboo, tabu—set apart as sacred among the Polynesians and other South Pacific races
16. venerable—sacred by religious or other associations (venerability, venerableness, n.)

2. To Make, Declare, Observe as, or Set Aside as, Sacred,v. *From Sec. 1:* anoint, bless, consecrate, enshrine, hallow, sanctify (anointment, consecration, enshrinement, sanctification,n. consecratory,adj.)

3. To Give the Appearance of Sacredness to: sanctify,v. (sanctification,n.)

4. Making a Show or Pretense of Sacredness: sanctimonious,adj. (sanctimony, sanctimoniousness,n.)

5. History of Sacred Writings: hagiology,n. (hagiologist,n. hagiologic, hagiological,adj.)

6. Body of Knowledge of Sacred Things: hierology,n. (hierologist,n. hierologic, hierological,adj.)

7. Writings on Sacred Subjects: hierography,n.

8. Sacred Place: bethel, sanctuary, sanctum, sanctum sanctorum, shrine,n.

9. To Violate the Sacredness of (a Sacred Thing or Person): commit sacrilege, desecrate, dishallow, pollute, profane, unconsecrate, unhallow, violate,v. (sacrilege, desecration, pollution, profanation,n. desecrater, profaner,n. sacrilegious, desecrative, profanatory or profane,adj.)

10. To Make the Previous Consecration Null: disanoint, unbless, unconsecrate, unsanctify,v. (unsanctification,n.)

11. Not Sacred: profane, secular, unanointed,

unblessed, unblest, unconsecrated, unhallowed, unholy, unsanctified,adj. (unblessedness, unconsecratedness, unhallowedness, unholiness, unsanctifiedness,n.)

651. SAINT

1. Like or Befitting a Saint: angelic, angelical, sainted, saintly,adj. (saintliness, sanctity,n.)

2. State of Being a Saint; Character of a Saint: sainthood,n.

3. Saints, Collectively: sainthood,n.

4. Pretense of Saintliness: sanctimoniousness, sanctimony,n. (sanctimonious,adj.)

5. To Declare (a Dead Person) a Saint; To Include in the Catalogue of Saints: canonize, saint,v. (canonization,n.)

6. Descr. of the Three Degrees of Recognized Sainthood in the Roman Catholic Church (in order): venerable, beatified, canonized,adj. (beatification, canonization,n. beatify, canonize,v.)

7. Catalogue of Saints: canon (Roman Catholic), hagiology, hierology, sanctilogy,n.

8. Writings about, or Stories of, the Lives of Saints: hagiography, hagiology; menology (in calendar form),n. (hagiographer or hagiographist, hagiologist,n. hagiographic or hagiographical, hagiologic or hagiological,adj.)

9. Calendar of Saints, with a Brief Life of Each: menology,n.

10. Pert. to St. Peter, His Teachings, etc.: Petrine,adj.

11. Not Befitting a Saint: unsaintly,adj.

12. To Remove from Status as a Saint: discanonize, unsaint,v. (discanonization,n.)

652. A CROSS

1. The Christian Cross: crucifix, rood,n.

2. Cross; Cross in Heraldry: crux,n. (crucial, adj.)

3. To Nail or Bind to a Cross, Literally or Figuratively: crucify,v. (crucifixion,n.)

4. One Who Carries a Cross in Religious Parades or Processions: crucifer,n.

653. CHRIST

1. Christ: Jesus, Jesus Christ, the Lord, the Messiah, the Nazarene, the Saviour,n. (Messianic,adj.)

2. The Infant Christ as Represented in Art: the Bambino,n. (Italian)

3. Image of Christ on the Cross: crucifix, rood,n.

4. Pert. to Christ as the Lord: dominical, adj.

5. False Christ; Enemy of Christ; One Who Denies Christ: antichrist,n.

6. Doctrine Taught by Christ and His Disciples: gospel,n.

7. Happy News about Salvation Announced by Christ: gospel,n.

8. Happy News about the Redemption of the World through Christ: evangel,n.

9. Story of Christ's Life and Teachings: gospel,n.

10. Selected Beliefs or Doctrines about Christ,n.
1. Adventism—belief or doctrine that the second coming of Christ and the end of the world are imminent (adventist,adj. adventist,n.)

2. **chiliasm**—belief that Christ will return to earth at the millennium (chiliastic,adj. chiliast,n.)
3. **millenarianism, milleniarism, millenialism**—chiliasm (millenarian, millenary, millenial,adj. millenarian, millenarist, millenialist, millenian,n.)
4. **psilanthropy**—doctrine or belief that Christ had no divinity, but existed only as a human being (psilanthropic, psilanthropist,adj. psilanthropist,n.)

11. **The Virgin Mary**: the Holy Virgin, the Madonna; Mater Dolorosa,n.

654. GOD

1. **God; The Supreme Deity**: the Absolute Being, the All Holy, the All Knowing, the All Merciful, the Almighty, the All Powerful, the All Wise; Ancient of Days (Biblical); Brahma (Hindu); the Creator, the Deity, the Divinity, the Eternal, the Eternal Being, Father, the Godhead, the Holy Spirit, the Infinite, the Infinite Being; Jehovah (Old Testament); the King of Kings, the Lord, the Lord of Lords, the Maker, the Master Workman, monad, the Omnipotent, the Omnipotent Being, the Omniscient, the Omniscient Being, the Preserver, Providence, the Spirit, the Supreme Being, the Supreme Soul; Varuna (Hindu); the World Spirit; Yahweh, Yahwe, Yahveh, Jahveh, Jave, or Jehovah (Hebrew text of the Old Testament),n.

2. **A God or Goddess**,n.
1. **Baal**—false god
2. **celestial**—heavenly being
3. **daemon, daimon**—protective deity of ancient Greek mythology; deity of the ancient Greek religion that was thought of as a power rather than a person (daemonic, daimonic,adj.)
4. **deity**—god; goddess
5. **demigod, demigoddess**—minor god; god whose ancestry is partly human
6. **Demiurge**—god, subordinate to the Supreme Deity, who created the world, according to some Gnostic systems; god who was the originator of evil (demiurgic, demiurgical, demiurgeous,adj. demiurgism,n.)
7. **divinity**—god; goddess
8. **godling**—local or lower god
9. **Jupiter, Jove**—head of the Roman gods of ancient mythology (Jovial,adj.)
10. **muse**—goddess who inspires poets or other artists
11. **numen**—divine spirit in the ancient Roman religion
12. **nymph**—lower female deity in Greek and Roman mythology
13. **satyr**—deity of the woods, in Greek mythology, depicted either as part human and part goat, or of human form with the tail and ears of a horse, notorious for lasciviousness and riotousness (satyric, satyrical,adj.)
14. **siren**—minor female deity associated with death, in the ancient Greek religion (siren, sirenic, sirenical,adj.)
15. **Titan**—earliest deity of Greek mythology (Titanic,adj.)
16. **Zeus**—head of all the Greek gods of ancient mythology

3. **Gods**,n.
1. **lares (Latin)**—Roman household gods
2. **pantheon**—collection of gods that a people worships
3. **penates (Latin)**—protective gods of the household and state in ancient Rome, worshiped in conjunction with the lares

4. **Divine; Descr. of, Relating to, or Pert. to, God, Gods, or a God**,adj.

1. **ambrosial, ambrosian**—divine; worthy of gods; belonging to gods
2. **celestial**—divine
3. **godlike**—befitting God or a god
4. **godly**—divine
5. **Olympian**—divine
6. **providential**—proceeding from divine power or intervention
7. **theanthropic**—both divine and human

5. **Divinity**,n. *From Sec. 4:* godlikeness, godliness, theanthropism; *Also:* 1. **godhead, godhood, godship**—character, rank, or status of a god

6. **Like or Resembling God or a God**,adj.
1. **daemonic, daimonic, daimonistic**—like one of the ancient Greek protective deities
2. **deiform**—godlike (deiformity,n.)
3. **divine**—godlike (divinity,n.)
4. **godlike**—like or resembling a god (godlikeness,n.)
5. **Olympian**—like a Greek god
6. **theomorphic**—having the appearance of God (theomorphism,n.)

7. **To Create in the Image or Appearance of God**: theomorphize,v.

8. **Union of the Father, the Son, and the Holy Ghost into One God**: Trinity,n. (Trinitarian,adj.)

9. **Manifestation, Incarnation, or Appearance of God or a God on Earth**: avatar (Hindu mythology or religion), theophany,n. (theophanic, theophanous,adj. theophanism, n.)

10. **Action of God or of a God**: theurgy,n. (theurgic, theurgical,adj.)

11. **To Make into, or Treat Like, a God**,v.
1. **apotheosize**—exalt or glorify (a human being) to the heights of a god (apotheosis,n.)
2. **deify**—make into, or treat like, a god (deification,n. deific,adj.)
3. **god**—treat like a god
4. **theologize**—give a godlike character to (theologization,n. theologizer,n.)

12. **Selected Beliefs in, or Beliefs or Doctrines about, God, a God, or Gods**,n.
1. **agnosticism**—belief that the existence of the Deity is neither known nor capable of being known; suspended judgment about the existence of God (agnostic,n. agnostic,adj.)
2. **anthropolatry**—belief in a god of human form (anthropolater,n. anthropolatrous, adj.)
3. **anthropomorphism**—conception of a deity with human attributes (anthropomorphist,n. anthropomorphic,adj.)
4. **anthropotheism**—primitive religious theory that the gods were originally human beings (anthropotheist,n. anthropotheistic,adj.)
5. **atheism**—belief that there is no supreme deity, i.e., denial of the existence of God (atheist,n. atheistic, atheistical,adj.)
6. **bitheism**—belief in the existence of two gods, one good, the other evil (bitheist,n. bitheistic,adj.)
7. **deism**—belief that the existence and nature of God can be proved rationally, without recourse to supernatural revelation (deist,n. deistic,adj.)
8. **ditheism**—belief in the existence of two gods (ditheist,n. ditheistic,adj.)
9. **freethinking**—beliefs about God that are not influenced by the church or by formal doctrine; agnosticism (freethinker,n.)
10. **godlessness**—refusal to acknowledge a god (godless,adj.)
11. **heathenism**—lack of belief in the God of the Bible (heathen,n. heathen, heathenish,adj.)
12. **henotheism**—belief in one principal god,

but with the acceptance of the existence of others (henotheist,n. henotheistic,adj.)

13. **mechanomorphism**—belief in, or concept of, the Deity as energy or force working by natural laws (mechanomorphist,n. mechanomorphic,adj.)

14. **monotheism**—belief in only one God—Christianity, Judaism, and Islam are the three great religions based on this faith (monotheist,n. monotheistic,adj.)

15. **pantheism**—belief that God is the entire universe, that "God is all, and all is God"—Brahmanism is a typical religion based on this faith (pantheist,n. pantheistic,adj.)

16. **polytheism**—belief in many gods, as among the ancient Greeks and Romans (polytheist,n. polytheistic,adj.)

17. **theanthropism**—belief in gods who are both divine and human (theanthropist, n. theanthropic,adj.)

18. **theism**—belief in a personal God, the creator and ruler of the universe (theist, n. theistic,adj.)

19. **theocentricism, theocentrism**—theory of the universe that assumes God as the center (theocentric,adj.)

20. **theopantism**—doctrine that God is the only reality

21. **tritheism**—doctrine or opinion that the Father, the Son, and the Holy Ghost are three separate Gods (tritheist,n. tritheistic,adj.)

13. **Science or Study of God:** divinity, theology,n. (theologian,n. theologic, theological, adj.)

14. **Knowledge of God:** theology,n. (theologic, theological,adj.)

15. **Science of Divine Things:** divinity,n.

16. **To Speculate or Theorize about God or Related Subjects:** theologize,v. (theologization,n. theologizer,n.)

17. **Muse,n.**
   1. **Calliope**—Muse of eloquence and heroic poetry
   2. **Clio**—Muse of history
   3. **Erato**—Muse of love poetry
   4. **Euterpe**—Muse of lyric poetry and music
   5. **Melpomene**—Muse of tragedy
   6. **Polyhymnia**—Muse of sacred song
   7. **Terpsichore**—Muse of dancing and choral song (terpsichorean,adj.)
   8. **Thalia**—Muse of comedy and bucolic poetry
   9. **Urania**—Muse of astronomy

18. **Pert. to the Muses, Worship of the Muses, or Inspiration by the Muses:** Pierian, adj.

19. **Nymph,n.**
   1. **dryad**—tree nymph
   2. **hamadryad**—dryad
   3. **hyad**—nymph of the heavens (hyads, hyades,pl.)
   4. **naiad**—water nymph; one of the nymphs of Greek mythology who guarded streams, ponds, rivers, etc. (naiads, naiades,pl.)
   5. **Nereid**—sea nymph
   6. **oceanid**—ocean nymph
   7. **oread**—mountain nymph

655. ANGEL

1. **An Angel:** spirit,n.

2. **Chief Angel:** archangel,n.

3. **Member of the Highest Order of Angels:** seraph,n. (seraphs, seraphim,pl. seraphic, seraphical,adj.)

4. **Member of the Second Order of Angels:** cherub,n. (cherubs, cherubim,pl. cherubic, adj.)

5. **Pert. to, or Descr. of, Angels:** angelic, angelical, incorporeal,adj.

6. **Like or Befitting an Angel:** angelic, angelical,adj.

656. TO WORSHIP

1. **To Worship,v**
   1. **adore**—worship; worship as, or as if, a deity
   2. **Baalize**—worship idols or false gods
   3. **deify**—worship as, or as if, a god
   4. **genuflect**—bend the knee in worship
   5. **glorify**—worship; adore
   6. **hymn**—worship by singing hymns
   7. **idolatrize**—worship; worship idols; idolize
   8. **idolize**—worship as an idol; regard with blind worship
   9. **misworship**—worship foolishly
   10. **revere**—worship
   11. **venerate**—worship
   12. **whore**—worship falsely; worship false gods; worship in a false religion; worship idols

2. **Worship,n.** *From Sec. 1:* adoration, Baalism, deification, genuflection, glorification, idolatry or idolism, idolization or idolism, misworship, reverence, veneration, whoredom; *Also:*
   1. **awe**—fear and worship
   2. **chapel**—service of worship conducted in a small room or place set aside for that purpose
   3. **cult**—system of religious worship; almost religious worship of a person or thing
   4. **devotions**—religious worship
   5. **dulia**—worship accorded to saints, since these are the servants and friends of God—in the Roman Catholic religion
   6. **hyperdulia**—worship accorded to the Virgin Mary—in the Roman Catholic religion
   7. **latria**—supreme worship, accorded only to God—in the Roman Catholic religion
   8. **liturgy**—public worship
   9. **Rite, rite**—public worship
   10. **ritual**—prescribed form of worship
   11. **ritualism**—practice of following the prescribed form of worship
   12. **service, services**—public religious worship according to prescribed form; prescribed form of public worship

3. **Worshipful,adj.** *From Sec. 1:* adoring, deifying, etc.; deific, idolatrous, reverent or reverential

4. **Worshiper,n.** *From Sec. 1:* adorer, Baalist or Baalite, deifier, genuflector, glorifier, hymner, idolater or, fem., idolatress, idolatrizer or idolist, idolizer or idolist, misworshiper, reverer, venerator; *Also:* 1. liturgist—one who leads in public worship

5. **Pert. to, or Descr. of, Worship or a Worshiper,adj.** *From Sec. 1:* Baalitical, genuflectory, idolatorous, idolistic, reverential; *From Sec. 2:* devotional, liturgic or liturgical; ritual, ritualist or ritualistic

6. **Worthy of Worship,adj.** *From Sec. 1:* reverend, venerable; *From Sec. 2:* awful

7. **Glorification or Aggrandizement into an Object of Worship:** avatar,n.

8. **One Who, or That Which, Is Worshiped, n.**
   1. **Baal**—idol
   2. **cult**—object of such intense worship and devotion as to be almost religious in character
   3. **idol**—person or object passionately worshiped; religious image or representation that is the object of worship
   4. **relic**—that which belonged to a saint or holy person and is therefore worshiped

9. Ceremony or Rule of Worship,n.
1. cult—rites and ceremonies of a religion
2. liturgy—prescribed rites and ceremonies of religious worship (liturgic, liturgical, adj.)
3. rite—ceremony, prescribed form, etc., of religious worship
4. ritual—prescribed ceremony of worship (ritual, ritualistic, adj.)
5. rubric—rule for the conduct of public worship (rubrical,adj.)

10. Adherence to Ceremonies or Forms of Public Worship: liturgism, ritualism,n. (ritualist,n. ritualist, ritualistic,adj.)

11. Compiler of Ceremonies of Worship: liturgist,n.

12. Science of Ceremonies of Worship: liturgiology,n. (liturgiologist,n. liturgiological, adj.)

13. Science of Worship: liturgics,n. (liturgician,n.)

14. Song or Expression of Worship: hymn,n.

15. Worship of Certain Specific Things or People,n.
1. anthropolatry—of a human being as if he were a god
2. bibliolatry—of the Bible, or of any book or books
3. cosmolatry—of the natural world
4. dendrolatry—of trees
5. ecclesiolatry—of the church
6. geniolatry—of genii or spirits
7. gyneolatry—of women
8. hagiolatry—of saints
9. heliolatry—of the sun
10. ichthyolatry—of fish, or of fish-shaped icons
11. iconolatry—of images
12. litholatry—of stones
13. lordolatry—of a person of high rank
14. mariolatry—of the Virgin Mary (contemptuous)
15. monolatry—of one god only, though more than one may be recognized
16. necrolatry—of dead people, or of death
17. onolatry—of asses
18. ophiolatry—of serpents
19. pantheism—of all gods, of whatever religion (pantheistic,adj.)
20. phallicism, phallism—of the penis, or of the principle of generation, propagation, etc.
21. physiolatry—of nature
22. pyrolatry—of fire
23. Sabaism—of the stars
24. staurolatry—of the crucifix (derogatory)
25. symbololatry—of symbols
26. thaumatolatry—of magic
27. theocrasy, theokrasia—of different types of gods (theocrasical,adj.)
28. zoolatry—of animals

16. Worshiper,n. From Sec. 15: anthropolater, bibliolater, etc.; pantheist, phallicist or phallist, Sabaist

17. Worshipful,adj. From Sec. 15: anthropolatrous, bibliolatrous, etc.

657. DEVOTION

1. Devotion,n.
1. adherence—devotion
2. allegiance—devotion to a country or ruler; devotion and loyalty
3. consecration—devotion to a purpose or to a sacred purpose; devotion to the service of God
4. consignment—devotion
5. cult—intense devotion to a person, principle, or idea; such devotion considered a fad or temporary intellectual or social fashion
6. dedication—devotion to the services of the Deity or of that which is considered sacred or worthy of worship
7. devotedness—devotion
8. devotement—devotion
9. devoutness—sincere devotion to principles, religious or otherwise
10. fetishism, fetichism—intense, unreasonable, almost irrational devotion
11. idolatry—blind devotion and worship
12. idolism—extreme devotion
13. idolization—blind devotion
14. religionism, religiosity—strict, intense, or affected devotion to religion
15. ritualism—excessive devotion to ritual (derogatory)
16. sectarianism—devotion to one's religious or other sect
17. worship—devotion to God

2. To Devote,v. From Sec. 1: consecrate, consign, dedicate

3. To Be Devoted to,v. From Sec. 1: adhere (to), fetish, fetich, idolatrize, idolize, religionize, worship

4. One Who Is Devoted, or Who Shows Devotion,n. From Sec. 1: adherent, cultist, fetishist or fetichist, idolater (idolatress, fem.) or idolatrizer, idolist, idolizer, religionist, ritualist, sectarian, worshiper; Also:
1. devotee—one enthusiastically devoted to anything; one zealously and ardently devoted to religion or to a religion
2. fiend—one excessively devoted to a habit, hobby, activity, etc.
3. votary, votarist—one who is worshipfully devoted to something; devoted admirer or follower (votaress, votress,fem.)

5. Descr. of, or Pert. to, Devotion or One Who Is Devoted,adj. From Sec. 1: consecratory, dedicative or dedicatory, fetishistic, fetichistic, idolatrous, idolistic, religionist or religionistic, ritualist or ritualistic, sectarian; From Sec. 4: votary

6. Devoted,adj. From Sec. 1: adherent, consecrated, dedicated, devout, fetishistic or fetichistic, idolatrous, idolistic, religionistic, ritualistic, sectarian, worshipful; Also:
1. religious—extremely devoted
2. wrapped up in—devoted to

7. Object of Devotion,n. From Sec. 1: fetish or fetich, idol

8. Given in Devotion: votive,adj. (votiveness,n.)

658. LOYALTY

1. Loyal,adj.
1. adherent—loyal or faithful (to a party, cause, group, etc.)
2. attached—loyal
3. constant—faithful
4. devoted—loyal
5. faithful—strongly loyal over a long period of time to one to whom, or that to which, one is bound by duty, promise, or obligation; loyal to one's word, promise, vow, etc.
6. liege—loyal
7. loyalist—loyal to the constituted government in times of revolution
8. religious—extremely faithful
9. stanch, staunch—loyal
10. steadfast—loyal; not wavering in loyalty
11. tried—loyal; faithful
12. true—loyal
13. unfailing—loyal

2. Loyalty,n. From Sec. 1: adherence or adhesion, attachment, constancy, devotion; faithfulness, faith, or fidelity; loyalism, religiousness, stanchness, staunchness, steadfastness, trueness; Also:

1. **allegiance**—loyalty to country or sovereign; loyalty and devotion
2. **esprit de corps (French)**—common spirit of loyalty to the group shown by all members
3. **fealty**—loyalty to a person, institution, or thing to whom or to which loyalty is owed
4. **troth**—loyalty; faithfulness

3. Loyal Person,n. *From Sec. 1:* adherent, devotee, loyalist; *Also:*
1. **fidus Achates (Latin)**—loyal friend
2. **votary, votarist**—devoted adherent of something; loyal admirer or follower (votaress, votress,fem. votary,adj.)

4. Bound by Loyalty: liege,adj.

5. To Stay Loyal to: abide by,v.

659. DISLOYALTY

1. Disloyal,adj.
1. **faithless**—disloyal; having severed one's loyalty
2. **false**—disloyal; treacherous
3. **perfidious**—disloyal to one's trust, vow, or promise
4. **punic**—disloyal; treacherous
5. **recreant**—disloyal; traitorous
6. **snaky**—treacherous, like a snake
7. **traitorous**—disloyal to one's country, one's ideals, etc.; disloyal to one who, or that which, has a claim on one's allegiance; treasonous
8. **treacherous**—disloyal to that to which one owes allegiance; perfidious; traitorous
9. **treasonable**—treasonous
10. **treasonous**—disloyal to the government, country, or ruler by giving comfort to the enemy in times of war, or by attempting to overthrow the government, etc. (of acts)
11. **unfaithful**—disloyal; not true to one's faith, promise, obligation, marriage vows, etc.
12. **untrue**—disloyal; unfaithful

2. Disloyalty,n. *From Sec. 1:* faithlessness, falsity or falseness, perfidy or perfidiousness, recreancy, traitorousness, treachery or treacherousness, treasonableness, treason, unfaithfulness, untrueness; *Also:*
1. **defection**—loss of loyalty
2. **disaffection**—disloyalty
3. **high treason**—treason
4. **infidelity**—disloyalty to faith, duty, marriage vows, etc.
5. **lese majesty**—treason
6. **whoredom**—falseness to God

3. To Be Disloyal (to),v. *From Sec. 1:* treason, treason against (treason,n.) ; *Also:* 1. **betray**—be disloyal or traitorous to (betrayal, betrayment,n.)

4. Disloyal Person,n. *From Sec. 1:* recreant, snake, traitor (traitress, fem.), treasonist; *From Sec. 3:* treasonist; betrayer; *Also:*
1. **quisling**—traitor to one's country, cause, race, etc.; one who treacherously helps an enemy to occupy his country or who becomes the agent of the occupying power—after Vidkun Quisling of Norway, who accepted ruling power of his country when the nazis invaded it in 1940
2. **renegade, renegado**—disloyal or traitorous person
3. **serpent**—subtly treacherous and malicious person
4. **turncoat**—renegade
5. **viper**—serpent

5. Stimulation of the Populace to Disloyalty to the Government by Speeches, Writing, etc.; Behavior Just Short of Treason, since No Overt Act Is Committed: sedition,n.

(seditious, seditionary,adj. seditiousness,n. seditionist, seditionary,n.)

660. DEVIL

1. The Devil; A Devil; God or Inhabitant of the Lower World,n.
1. **archenemy**—the Devil; Satan
2. **archfiend**—the Devil; Satan
3. **Beelzebub**—the Devil
4. **Belial**—the Devil; Satan
5. **cacodemon, cacodaemon**—devil
6. **Davy Jones**—sea devil
7. **demogorgon**—evil god of the underworld
8. **demon, daemon, daimon**—devil; fiend
9. **devilkin**—little devil
10. **Diabolus**—the Devil; (not cap.) a devil
11. **fiend**—devil; evil spirit; Satan
12. **Hades**—Pluto
13. **imp**—little devil
14. **Lucifer**—the Devil; Satan
15. **Mephistopheles**—one of the seven chief devils
16. **Old Nick**—the Devil
17. **Pluto**—god of Hell; god of the lower world
18. **Satan**—the Devil; chief of the evil spirits
19. **spirit**—demon

2. Devilish; Pert. to, Resembling, or Descr. of, a Devil or the Devil,adj. *From Sec. 1:* cacodemonic, cacodemoniac, cacodemonial, cacodaemonic, cacodaemoniac, or cacodaemonial; demoniac, demonic, demonian, daemonic, daimonic, or daimonistic; fiendish, Hadean, impish, Mephistophelian, Plutonian or Plutonic, satanic or satanical; *Also:*
1. **chthonian**—pert. to, relating to, or designating, the gods of the underworld
2. **cloven-footed, cloven-hoofed**—devilish; pert. to the Devil
3. **diabolic, diabolical, infernal, serpentine**—pert. to, or characteristic of, the Devil or a devil

3. Devilishness; Devilish Actions, Nature, etc.,n. *From Sec. 1:* fiendishness, impishness, Satanism; *From Sec. 2:* diabolicalness or diabolism; *Also:*
1. **deviltry, devilry**—devilish art or magic
2. **diablerie, diablery**—actions or powers within the province of the Devil; magic or art of devils

4. Sign or Indication of the Devil or Devilishness, or, by Extension, of Temptation to Evil (Figurative): cloven foot, cloven hoof,n.

5. Spirits and Gods of the Lower World, According to the Ancient Roman Religion: manes,n.

6. Intercourse with the Devil or with Evil Spirits: diabolism, witchcraft,n. (diabolize,v.)

7. One Who Has Intercourse or Dealings with a Demon, the Devil, or Evil Spirits: demonist, diabolist, witch,n.

8. Knowledge about, Belief in, Study of, etc., Demons or Devils,n.
1. **demonianism**—belief in possession by demons
2. **demonism**—knowledge about demons; description of belief in demons; description of demons; demonology (demonist,n.)
3. **demonology**—belief in demons; description or study of belief in demons; theory or doctrine of demons (demonologist,n.)
4. **deviltry, devilry**—demonology
5. **diablerie, diablery**—lore about demons; demonology
6. **diabolism**—belief in devils; doctrine about devils (diabolist,n.)
7. **diabolology, diabology**—study of the Devil; study of beliefs in devils; doctrine of, or knowledge about, devils (diabological,adj.)

9. Realm or Province of Demons: diablerie, diablery,n.

10. Worship of Demons, Devils, or the Devil: demonism, demonolatry, diabolatry, diabolism, Satanism,n.

11. Worshiper of Demons, Devils, or the Devil: demonist, demonolater, diabolater, Satanist, Satanophil,n.

12. Worshipful of Demons, Devils, or the Devil: demonolatrous, diabolatrous,adj.

13. To Turn (Someone) into a Devil: demonize, diabolify, diabolize,v. (diabolification, diabolization,n.)

14. Possessed by a Demon: demoniac,adj.

15. Inspired as if by a Demon: demonic,adj.

16. To Possess (Someone) by a Demon or by the Devil: demonize, Satanize,v.

17. One Possessed by an Evil Spirit: cacodemon or cacodaemon, demoniac,n.

18. The Victim of an Evil Spirit: energumen, n.

19. Possession by Demons: demonianism,n.

20. To Subject to the Influence of Demons or the Devil: demonize, diabolize,v. (diabolization,n.)

21. To Represent as Devilish or as a Devil: diabolify, diabolize,v. (diabolification, diabolization,n.)

661. HELL

1. Hell: the abyss, Acheron, Avernus; Gehenna (New Testament) ; Hades, the inferno, the lower regions, the lower world; pandemonium (from John Milton's term for Satan's palace) ; the pit; Tartarus (Greek mythology) ; Tophet, the underworld,n.

2. Descr. of, Pert. to, Characteristic of, or Resembling, Hell: Avernal, Hadean, infernal, Plutonian or Plutonic; Stygian (from the river Styx of the lower world) ; sulfurous, sulphurous; Tartarean (Greek mythology), adj.

3. Gloomy Realm under the Earth Where Pluto Rules over the Spirits of the Dead: Hades,n.

4. Any Part of Hell: pit,n.

5. Any Place Like Hell: inferno, tophet,n.

662. SUPERNATURALISM

1. Supernatural,adj.
  1. **eerie, eery**—weird
  2. **ethereal**—not earthy or of this earth
  3. **ghostly**—supernatural, i.e., of the nature of ghosts
  4. **miraculous**—supernatural; happening outside the laws of nature
  5. **occult**—supernatural
  6. **otherwordly**—transcendent; ultramundane
  7. **preternatural**—beyond the natural or ordinary course of nature
  8. **psychic, psychical**—supernatural
  9. **superlunary**—not earthly; not part of this world
  10. **theurgic, theurgical**—miraculous, as if performed by God or a god
  11. **transcendent, transcendental**—supernatural; existing apart from the world or universe as we know it
  12. **transmundane**—ultramundane
  13. **ultramundane**—lying or being outside the limits of this world
  14. **uncanny**—supernatural
  15. **unearthly**—supernatural
  16. **unworldly**—not of this world, hence supernatural

  17. **weird**—supernatural; pert. to the supernatural; supernaturally mysterious
  18. **wondrous**—miraculous

2. Supernaturalism; Supernatural Quality or State,n. From Sec. 1: eeriness, ethereality or etherealness, ghostliness, miraculousness, otherworldliness, preternaturalism; transcendence, transcendency, or transcendentalism; uncanniness, unearthliness, unworldliness, weirdness, wondrousness

3. Supernatural Happening or Thing,n. From Sec. 1: miracle, occult, theurgy, wonder, wonderment, or wonderwork

4. Supernatural Power, Powers, or Practice, n.
  1. **occultism**—the practice or powers of supernatural agencies
  2. **sorcery**—use of power gained from evil spirits; power to control evil spirits
  3. **spiritism**—action of spirits or of a supernatural agency
  4. **spiritualism, spiritism**—communication with the dead
  5. **telekinesis**—supposed ability of a medium to produce motion or activity in things without physical or understandable contact or influence
  6. **thaumaturgy**—performance of miracles
  7. **theurgy**—performance of miracles
  8. **witchcraft**—supernatural power or influence; sorcery
  9. **wizardry**—sorcery

5. One Who Has, or Claims to Have, Supernatural Power or Powers,n. From Sec. 4: occultist, sorcerer or, fem., sorceress, spiritist, spiritualist or spiritist, theurgist or theurgic, thaumaturgist or thaumaturge, witch, wizard; Also:
  1. **medium**—person supposedly possessed of supernatural power, esp. to summon the spirits of the dead
  2. **psychic**—medium

6. Descr. of, or Pert. to, Supernatural Power or Powers,adj. From Sec. 4: occultist, spiritistic, spiritualistic, telekinetic, theurgic or theurgical, thaumaturgic or thaumaturgical; From Sec. 5: mediumistic, psychic or psychical

7. Spirit; Selected Supernatural or Imaginary Beings,n.
  1. **apparition**—specter
  2. **barghest**—goblin whose appearance presages misfortune
  3. **bogle**—goblin
  4. **brownie**—good-natured and helpful fairy who performs kind deeds while people sleep
  5. **cacodemon, cacodaemon**—evil or malevolent spirit
  6. **daemon, daimon, demon**—protective spirit of the ancient Greek religion
  7. **Davy Jones**—spirit of the sea
  8. **demon**—evil spirit
  9. **devil**—evil spirit
  10. **dibbuk**—evil spirit who has gained possession of a person, according to Jewish folklore
  11. **dwarf**—supernatural being of folklore and mythology, of very small size and human appearance, and known for knowledge of and skill in fashioning minerals and metals
  12. **elf, elfin**—supernatural being, of diminutive size, possessing certain powers of magic and generally conceived of as interfering mischievously in human affairs; fairy; mischievous fairy; sprite (elves,pl.)
  13. **eudaemon, eudemon**—good spirit
  14. **fairy**—supernatural being, of diminutive human form, possessed of magic power
  15. **fay**—elf; fairy
  16. **genie**—genius; jinni
  17. **genius**—attendant spirit guiding the

destiny of a place or person; nature demon or spirit of Arabian and Mohammedan folklore; jinni (genii,pl.)

18. **giant**—imaginary being of supernatural strength and superhuman size; one of a race of such beings in Greek mythology who were finally conquered by the Olympian gods (giantess,fem.)
19. **gnome**—imaginary diminutive being living deep in the earth and guarding the earth's treasures, and generally pictured as a shriveled old man
20. **goblin**—grotesque or ugly and usually evil, though sometimes only mischievous, sprite
21. **gremlin**—sportive elf said to be responsible for mischief or unexplainable trouble
22. **hobgoblin**—mischievous elf or sprite
23. **imp**—evil spirit
24. **incorporeal**—spirit, i.e., a being without a body
25. **incubus**—evil spirit supposed to visit women at night and violate them sexually (incubi,pl.)
26. **jinni, jinnee**—supernatural being with magic power, in Mohammedan mythology; demon of the wilderness, in ancient Arabian mythology (jinni,pl.)
27. **lamia**—female demon; vampire
28. **leprechaun**—in Irish folklore, fairy or sprite represented as a mischievous old man who, when caught, shows where a treasure is hidden
29. **Mammon**—demon of desire for material things
30. **nightmare**—incubus believed at one time to oppress sleepers
31. **nix**—water fairy, in Teutonic mythology (nixie, nixe,fem. nixes, nixen,pl.)
32. **ouphe**—elf; goblin
33. **pixy, pixie**—fairy; fairy who delights in leading humans astray; sprite
34. **poltergeist**—spirit responsible for otherwise unexplainable noises, sounds, tappings, rappings, etc.
35. **puck**—evil spirit; mischievous fairy
36. **sandman**—imaginary creature who makes children sleepy
37. **specter, spectre**—visible spirit, esp. one of a terrifying appearance or nature
38. **spirit**—supernatural being or force; elf; specter; sprite
39. **sprite**—imaginary being, of the class of fairies, elves, etc., generally pleasing in appearance and nimble in motion, usually friendly, though sometimes mischievous or hostile; fairy; elf
40. **succubus**—evil spirit of female form supposed to lie under men while they are asleep, in order to have sexual relations with them (succubi,pl.)
41. **sylph**—light and dainty imaginary being who lives in the air
42. **sylphid**—little sylph; young sylph; female sylph
43. **troll**—supernatural being, of ugly and grotesque appearance, either a dwarf or giant, who inhabits caves, other underground places, hills, etc.—in Scandinavian folklore
44. **undine**—female water spirit who can become human by marrying a human being
45. **vampire**—bloodsucking supernatural being
46. **vision**—supernatural being, without material or bodily form, yet able to be seen
47. **wraith**—specter

8. Pert. to, Descr. of, or Resembling, a Spirit or Supernatural or Imaginary Being, adj. *From Sec. 7:* apparitional, cacodemoniac, cacodemonic, cacodemonial, cacodaemoniac, cacodaemonic, cacodaemonial; demonic or demoniac, daemonic, daimonic, daimonistic; devilish, dwarf or dwarfish; elfin, elfish, elvish, or elflike; fairy, fairylike; giant, gigan-

tic, gigantean, or gigantesque; gnomelike, goblin, impish, incorporeal, mammonish, pixyish, puckish, spectral, succubine; sylphy, sylphish, or sylphlike; vampiric or vampirish, wraithy or wraithlike (devilishness, dwarfishness, giantism or gigantism, impishness, puckishness, spectralness or spectrality,n.) ; *Also:* 1. **fey**—elfin

9. Belief in Spirits or Supernatural Beings, n. *From Sec. 7:* demonism or demonology, fairyism, vampirism (demonist, demonologist, n.)

10. Spirits, etc., Collectively,n.
1. **fairy, fairyhood**—fairies collectively
2. **giantry, giantkind**—race of giants
3. **manes**—in the ancient Roman religion, any ancestral spirits considered gods and so worshiped
4. **rakshasa**—class of goblins or evil spirits in Hindu mythology

11. Nature of a Fairy or Fairies: fairyhood, fairyism,n.

12. Where Fairies Live: fairyland,n.

13. Story about Fairies: fairy tale,n.

14. Led Astray by Pixies: pixy-led,adj.

15. Peculiarity or Custom of Giants: giantism,n.

16. Stories about Giants: giantry,n.

17. Befitting a Giant: gigantesque,adj.

18. The Spirit World; Place Where Supernatural Beings Live: other world,n.

19. Ghost,n.
1. **apparition**—ghost; specter
2. **banshee**—ghost who wails as a warning of approaching death in a family
3. **bogle**—specter
4. **eidolon**—ghost
5. **lamia**—vampire
6. **phantasm, phantasma, fantasm**—ghost; specter (phantasmata,pl.)
7. **phantom**—ghost
8. **poltergeist**—noisy ghost; ghost responsible for otherwise unexplainable noises, sounds, rappings, tappings, etc.
9. **revenant**—ghost, i.e., one who returns after death
10. **shade**—ghost; spirit of a dead person
11. **specter, spectre**—visible ghost, esp. one of terrifying appearance or nature
12. **spirit**—ghost; specter
13. **spook**—ghost
14. **sprite**—ghost; shade
15. **vampire**—bloodsucking ghost
16. **wraith**—ghost; ghost of a person seen just before or after his death; specter

20. A Ghostly Appearance,n. *From Sec. 19:* apparition; phantasm, phantasma, or fantasma; specter or spectre, sprite, wraith

21. Ghostly; Ghostlike,adj. *From Sec. 19:* apparitional, eidolic, phantasmal or phantasmic, phantom, spectral, spooky, vampiric or vampirish, wraithy or wraithlike (spectrality or spectralness, spookiness,n.) ; *Also:*
1. **eerie, eery**—ghostly, and therefore causing fear (eeriness,n.)
2. **ghastly**—like a ghost in appearance (ghastliness,n.)
3. **shadowy**—pert. to the spirits of the dead; spectral
4. **uncanny**—ghostly (uncanniness,n.)

22. Belief in Ghosts,n. *From Sec. 19:* eidolism, vampirism

23. Visited, or Lived in, by Ghosts: haunted, adj. (haunt,v.)

24. Certain Mythical Animals,n.
1. **Chimera, Chimaera**—mythical she-monster, represented as vomiting flames, and combining variously the parts of a lion, goat, and serpent; (not cap.) imaginary monster of this type (chimeric,adj.)

2. **griffin, griffon, gryphon**—creature in Greek mythology, half lion and half eagle
3. **hippogriff, hippogryph**—mythical animal with the wings, head, and claws of a griffin and the body and legs of a horse
4. **monster, monstrosity**—mythical animal, often horrible or grotesque in appearance, or combining various animal, or animal and human, forms (monstrous, adj.)
5. **thunderbird**—mythical bird causing thunder and lightning; supernatural eagle considered the spirit of thunder (concept of the American Indians)

25. Certain Mythical Serpents or Reptiles,n.
1. **basilisk**—mythical serpent, lizard, or dragon whose hissing drove away all other reptiles, and whose glance and breath were fatal
2. **cockatrice**—mythical serpent with a fatal glance, supposedly hatched by a reptile from a cock's egg
3. **dipsas**—mythical serpent whose bite caused agonizing thirst
4. **dragon**—mythical monster in the form of a huge winged and scaly serpent with a crested head and enormous claws, and generally pictured as breathing out fire and smoke (draconic,adj.)
5. **Python**—monstrous serpent of Greek mythology, finally slain by Apollo
6. **salamander**—mythical lizard, or lizard-like animal or serpent, supposedly able to live in fire without being harmed (salamandrine,adj.)

26. Certain Mythical Creatures, Part Human, Part Animal,n.
1. **bucentaur**—mythical creature, half man, half ox
2. **centaur**—mythical creature, half man, half horse (centaurial, centaurian, centauric,adj.)
3. **Harpy**—mythical creature, with the lower body of a bird and the head and upper body of a woman, that seized the souls of the dead—pictured as a filthy and greedy monster
4. **lamia**—mythical creature with the body of a serpent and the head and breast of a woman
5. **Lorelei, Lurlei**—siren of German legend
6. **mermaid**—mythical sea creature, the upper half woman, the lower half fish
7. **merman**—masculine counterpart of a mermaid
8. **Minotaur**—mythical creature, half man, half bull
9. **Pan**—Greek deity of flocks, wild life of forests, etc., human in form except for the legs and often the horns and ears of a goat (Pandean, Panic,adj.)
10. **satyr**—Greek deity of the woods, depicted either as part human and part goat, or of human form with the tail and ears of a horse, notorious for lasciviousness and riotousness (satyric, satyrical,adj.)
11. **siren**—one of a class of minor deities of the ancient Greek religion in the form of a bird but with the head, and sometimes the arms and breast, of a woman; mermaid (siren, sirenic, sirenical,adj.)
12. **sphinx**—monster of Greek mythology with the body of a lion, the head and breast of a woman, and wings (sphinxian, adj.)
13. **Triton**—demigod of the sea in Greek mythology, with a fishlike lower body (Tritoness,fem. Tritonic,adj.)

27. Sphinxes of Egyptian Archaeology,n.
1. **androsphinx**—sphinx in the form of a recumbent lion with a man's head
2. **criosphinx**—sphinx in the form of a recumbent lion with a ram's head
3. **hieracosphinx**—sphinx in the form of a recumbent lion with a hawk's head

28. Both Human and Animal in Form,adj.
1. **androcephalous**—having the head of a human on the body of a beast, like the Sphinx
2. **androtauric**—combining the physical appearance of man and bull
3. **biform, biformed**—having, or combining, the characteristics of two forms of life, as a mermaid, satyr, etc.
4. **therianthropic**—both human and animal in form

29. Certain Other Mythical Beings,n.
1. **Charon**—mythical character in Greek mythology who ferried souls of the dead across the river Styx (Charonian, Charonic,adj.)
2. **Cyclops**—one of the race of one-eyed giants of Greek mythology (Cyclopes,pl. Cyclopean, Cyclopic,adj.)
3. **giant**—mythical monster of human form, of tremendous size and strength (giant, gigantic, gigantean,adj.)
4. **Gorgon**—one of the three snake-haired sisters of Greek mythology (Euryale, Medusa, and Stheno) whose horrible appearance turned to stone anyone who looked at them
5. **lycanthrope**—werewolf
6. **ogre**—mythical monster in human form, or a revoltingly ugly giant, who eats human beings; fearful giant (ogress,fem. ogrish, orgrish,adj.)
7. **werewolf**—person supposed to be able to assume a wolf's form; person who has been changed into a wolf

30. Change, by a Human, into a Wolf: lycanthropy,n. (lycanthropic, lycanthropous, adj. lycanthropize,v.)

663. MAGIC

1. Magic,n.
1. **black art**—magic
2. **black magic**—evil magic; sorcery
3. **conjury, conjuration, conjurement**—practice of magic
4. **devilry, deviltry**—devilish magic
5. **diablerie, diablery, diabolism**—evil magic; sorcery
6. **enchantment**—sorcery
7. **hoodoo**—voodoo
8. **necromancy**—magic
9. **rune**—magic
10. **sorcery**—magic practiced with the aid of evil spirits
11. **sortilege**—sorcery
12. **thaumaturgy**—magic; performance of magic
13. **voodoo**—magic and religious rites, of African origin, practiced or believed in by some Negroes of the West Indies and the Southern states of the U.S.; sorcery
14. **voodooism**—magic; magic peculiar to Negro peoples; voodoo
15. **witchcraft, witchery**—black or evil magic; sorcery
16. **wizardry**—magic; sorcery

2. Magician; Performer of Magic,n. *From Sec. 1:* conjurer or conjuror, diabolist, enchanter or, fem., enchantress, necromancer, sorcerer or, fem., sorceress, thaumaturgist or thaumaturge, voodoo, witch, wizard; *Also:*
1. **archimage, archimagus**—great magician or sorcerer
2. **jinni, jinnee**—in Mohammedan mythology a supernatural being with magic powers (jinn,pl.)
3. **magus**—magician
4. **medicine man**—magician among North American Indians and certain primitive peoples
5. **Merlin**—magician, so called in reference to the magician associated with King Arthur

6. **shaman**—tribal magician; medicine man (shamaness,fem.)
7. **witch doctor**—practitioner of sorcery or magic; medicine man among African peoples
3. **A Magic Trick or Feat,n.** *From Sec. 1:* conjuration or conjurement; *Also:* **1. levitation**—magic trick, depending on illusion, whereby someone or something seems to rise in the air and float without support
4. **Magic; Magical; Pert. to, or Descr. of, Magic or Magicians,adj.** *From Sec. 1:* necromantic, runic, thaumaturgic or thaumaturgical, voodoo; *From Sec. 2:* shaman, shamanic or shamanistic, levitational or levitative; *Also:*
   1. hermetic—magic
   2. occult—dealing with, or showing knowledge of, magic
   3. weird—pert. to, or descr. of, magic or witchcraft; suggesting, or caused by, the influence of magic
5. **To Practice or Perform Magic,v.** *From Sec. 1:* conjure, voodoo; *From Sec. 2:* levitate (something or someone)
6. **Act of Performing Magic,n.** *From Sec. 5:* conjuration, conjurement, or conjure, levitation
7. **Belief in Magic,n.** *From Sec. 1:* voodooism (voodooist,n.)
8. **To Summon, Get, or Produce by Magic Arts:** conjure, invoke,v. (conjuration or conjurement, invocation,n.)
9. **To Send Away by Magic Arts:** conjure away, conjure out,v.
10. **Magic Expression,n.**
    1. abracadabra—magic word believed to prevent or cure disease
    2. conjuration—expression used in performing magic
    3. hocus-pocus—expression used in performing magic tricks or sleight of hand
    4. incantation—words uttered to cast a magic spell
    5. invocation—formula for the purpose of calling forth devils or evil spirits by magic
    6. mumbo-jumbo—meaningless sounds supposed to have magic power
    7. rune—verse, sentence, or group of words with a magic meaning
    8. spell—phrase, word, or incantation having magic power
11. **Ornament or Thing Believed to Have Magic Power,n.**
    1. amulet—that which is worn as a magic charm against evil, trouble, witchcraft, etc.
    2. charm—small ornament supposed to have magic power
    3. fetish, fetich—article or object believed to possess magic powers
    4. phylactery—amulet; charm
    5. talisman—something believed to have magic power
12. **To Cast a Magic Spell,v.**
    1. becharm—put under a magic charm
    2. bedevil—cast a magic spell over (bedevilment,n.)
    3. bewitch—put under a magic spell (bewitchment,n.)
    4. charm—affect by magic or magical influence; bewitch
    5. enchant—place under a magic spell (enchantment,n.)
    6. ensorcell—bewitch
    7. enthrall—put and keep under a magic spell (enthrallment,n.)
    8. hex—practice witchcraft upon; bewitch
    9. spellbind—hold by a magic spell; charm
    10. wile—attract by a magic spell
    11. witch—work a magic and evil spell upon; bewitch (witchery,n.)

13. **One Who Casts a Magic Spell,n.** *From Sec. 12:* becharmer, bedeviler, bewitcher, charmer, enchanter (enchantress,fem.), spellbinder, witch; *Also:*
    1. Circe—enchantress (Circean,adj.)
    2. wizard—man who can cast a magic and/or evil spell
14. **Casting a Magic Spell,adj.** *From Sec. 12:* bedeviling, bewitching, etc.; *Also:* **1. siren, sirenic, sirenical**—bewitching
15. **State of Being under a Magic Spell,n.** *From Sec. 12:* bedevilment, bewitchment, enchantment, enthrallment
16. **A Magic Spell,n.** *From Sec. 12:* charm, enchantment, hex, witchery; *Also:* **1. incantation**—magic spell caused by the utterance of magic words or expressions
17. **Like Someone under a Magic Spell:** fey, adj.
18. **Sleight of Hand:** conjuration, conjurement, conjury, hocus-pocus, jugglery, legerdemain, prestidigitation,n. (conjure, juggle, prestidigitate,v. conjurer or conjuror, juggler, prestidigitator or prestidigitateur,n. prestidigitorial,adj.)

664. LANGUAGE

1. **Language,n.**
   1. argot—slang or special language of a group, or of thieves or tramps
   2. billingsgate—coarse, vulgar, foul language—so called from the London fish market notorious for such language
   3. cant—special language of an occupation, trade, profession, etc.; secret language of thieves and members of the underworld; language that hews to convention but is otherwise meaningless and insincere; language that makes a great, but specious, pretense of goodness or holiness
   4. commercialism—language forms used in business
   5. cryptology—secret language
   6. dialect—special form of the parent language prevalent in a geographical area or among special groups of people
   7. gobbledygook—inflated, pretentious, and verbose official language, in which the size or multitude of words gets in the way of the meaning (colloq.)
   8. idiom—language peculiar to a place, people, class, group, etc.
   9. jargon—language restricted to a trade, profession, etc.; formalized and simplified form of a language that can be understood by foreigners
   10. journalese—newspaper language
   11. lingo—special type of language; dialect; jargon
   12. lingua franca—common language used in a large area, generally for commercial purposes, by people of different native tongues
   13. mother tongue—one's native language
   14. parlance—language
   15. patois—illiterate spoken language; dialect; jargon
   16. patter—specialized language of any profession or calling; cant
   17. poetry—language in verse or rhyme; language with poetic feeling, cadence, etc.
   18. prose—ordinary, everyday language; language that is not in verse
   19. rhetoric—elegant or affected language
   20. sillabub—flowery language
   21. slang—language not accepted as formal or in good repute; specialized language of a class, group, occupation, etc.
   22. speech—spoken language
   23. technology—language of the arts or sciences

24. **telegraphese**—language typical of that used in telegrams
25. **tongue**—language; spoken language
26. **Ursprache (German)**—original or parent language
27. **vernacular**—native language; everyday or informal, rather than literary, language; language or form of language of a particular place; special language or language form of a profession, trade, etc.
28. **vulgate**—language that is below acceptable standards; colloquial or unrefined language

2. Descr. of, or Pert. to, Language,adj. *From Sec. 1:* dialectal, dialectic, or dialectical; idiomatic, poetic, prosaic, rhetorical, slang or slangy, technological, vernacular, vulgar; *Also:*
   1. **glottic**—pert. to, or based on, language
   2. **linguistic**—pert. to, or descr. of, language or languages
   3. **semeiotic**—pert. to the language of signs or symbols

3. Confusion of Language or Languages: babel, polyglot,n. (polyglot,adj.)

4. Certain Specific Languages or Language Forms, Omitting Those Commonly Known, n.
   1. **Afrikaans**—South African dialect of the Dutch language
   2. **Attic**—standard Greek; dialect of Athens (Attic,adj.)
   3. **Castilian**—standard Spanish (Castilian, adj.)
   4. **Cockney**—dialect of the East End of London (Cockney,adj.)
   5. **Creole**—French language spoken in Louisiana (Creole,adj.)
   6. **Cymric**—Welsh language (Cymric,adj.)
   7. **Hebraic**—Hebrew language (Hebraic,adj.)
   8. **Hindi**—chief vernacular language of Northern India
   9. **Hindustani**—chief dialect of western Hindi
   10. **Husky**—Eskimo language (Husky,adj.)
   11. **lingua franca**—language composed of Italian combined with French, Spanish, Greek, and Arabic, and used in Mediterranean ports
   12. **Neo-Hebraic**—modern Hebrew language (Neo-Hebraic,adj.)
   13. **Osmanli**—dominant language of Turkey
   14. **pidgin, pidgin English**—jargon, used in dealing with natives of the Far East or South Seas, made up of a combination of English words or corruptions and Chinese grammar (pidgin,adj.)
   15. **Romaic**—modern Greek language (Romaic,adj.)
   16. **Romance language**—any language derived from Latin, as French, Rumanian, Spanish, Portuguese, Italian, etc. (Romance or Romanic,adj.)
   17. **Romany**—language of gypsies
   18. **Urdu**—Hindustani (Urdu,adj.)
   19. **Wallonian, Walloon**—language of southern Belgium (Wallonian,adj.)
   20. **Welsh**—language of Wales (Welsh,adj.)

5. Descr. of Languages Using Various Tones in Speech, as Chinese: tonic,adj.

6. To Make Conform to the Style or Form of the English Language: Anglicize, Anglify, v. (Anglicization, Anglification,n.)

7. Certain Artificial or Man-Made Languages,n.
   1. **Esperanto**—artificial, man-made language, invented by Dr. L. Zamenhof (Esperantist,n. Esperantist,adj.)
   2. **Ido**—artificial language, a simplified version of Esperanto (Idoist,n. Idoistic, adj.)
   3. **pasigraphy**—artificial written language, intended to be universally understood, in which the symbols usually stand for ideas rather than words (pasigraphic or pasigraphical,adj.)
   4. **Volapük**—artificial language invented by Johann Schleyer about 1879 (Volapükist, n.)

8. Speaking, or Capable of Speaking, More than One Language,n.
   1. **bilingual**—speaking, or able to speak, two languages (bilingualism,n.)
   2. **diglot**—capable of speaking two languages equally well
   3. **multilingual**—speaking, or capable of speaking, many languages
   4. **polyglot, polyglottal, polyglottous, polyglotted**—speaking many languages (polyglotry, polyglottery, polyglottism,n.)
   5. **polylingual**—multilingual
   6. **quadrilingual**—speaking, or capable of speaking, four languages
   7. **trilingual**—speaking, or capable of speaking, three languages

9. Expressed in, or Containing, More than One Language,adj. *From Sec. 8:* bilingual, diglot, multilingual, polyglot, polylingual, quadrilingual, trilingual

10. Person Speaking, or Capable of Speaking, More than One Language,n. *From Sec. 8:* bilinguist or bilingual, diglottist, polyglot, polyglottist, polyglotter; *Also:* 1. **linguist**—person capable of speaking many languages; person versed in, or able to speak, various foreign languages

11. Science or Study of Language, Words, etc.,n.
   1. **accidence**—branch of grammar that treats of inflections of words, word order, etc.
   2. **Anglistics**—study of the English language
   3. **dactylology**—science of communicating by use of the fingers, as between deaf-mutes (dactylogical,adj.)
   4. **etymology**—science of the derivation or origin of words (etymological,adj.)
   5. **glossology, glottology**—science or study of language (glossological, glottological, adj.)
   6. **grammar**—science of the relations and functions of the words of a language (grammatical,adj.)
   7. **lexicology**—science of the meanings and derivation of words (lexicological,adj.)
   8. **linguistics**—science or study of language and human speech (linguistic,adj.)
   9. **morphology**—branch of linguistics dealing with the history and function of word inflections, derivation, and structure (morphological,adj.)
   10. **philology**—science of language (philological,adj.)
   11. **syntax**—branch of grammar dealing with relationship or arrangement of words in a sentence (syntactic, syntactical,adj.)

12. Student of Language,n. *From Sec. 11:* Anglist or Anglicist, dactylologist, glossologist, glottologist, etymologist, grammarian, lexicologist, linguist or linguistician, morphologist, philologist, syntactician

13. One Who Is Meticulous about Correctness and Observance of Rule in the Use of Language (derogatory): purist,n. (purism,n. puristic,adj.)

665. TO EXPRESS

1. To Express in Language or Words,v.
   1. **communicate**—express in language
   2. **convey**—express in language
   3. **couch**—express in words
   4. **delineate**—convey clearly

5. **indite**—put into words
6. **phrase**—express (ideas or thoughts) in words
7. **picture**—represent or describe in words, words that draw clear pictures, etc.
8. **reword**—put (the same idea) into different words
9. **sentimentalize**—express one's tender feelings; express one's feelings in an effusive manner
10. **sum up**—express briefly
11. **utter**—express
12. **vent**—express; give expression to; express fully or without restrictions; obtain emotional relief from the expression of
13. **ventilate**—express (one's feelings) fully and without inhibitions or restrictions
14. **verbalize**—put into words; express in carefully chosen words; express (one's feelings) in words
15. **vocalize**—give voiced or spoken expression to
16. **voice**—express
17. **word**—express in words

2. Expression in Language or Words, n. *From Sec. 1:* conveyance or conveyal, delineation, inditement, phraseology, sentimentalization, summation, utterance, vent, ventilation, verbalization or verbalism, vocalization, wording; *Also:* 1. **resolution**—expression in words of one's determination to do or not do

3. Expressive, adj.
  1. **articulate**—vocal; skillfully vocal (articulateness,n.)
  2. **Ciceronian**—eloquent, like Cicero, the Roman orator of ancient times
  3. **eloquent**—expressive of one's thoughts or feelings in moving and emotional language (eloquence, eloquentness,n.)
  4. **facile**—showing ease or effortless skill in the use of language; fluent (facility,n.)
  5. **fluent**—vocal, with the added idea of a copious flow of words (fluency,n.)
  6. **glib**—expressing, or able to express, oneself smoothly, easily, almost too readily (glibness,n.)
  7. **holophrastic**—expressive of a complexity of ideas in one word
  8. **notional**—expressive of ideas, or of abstract ideas
  9. **oratorical**—eloquent (oratory,n.)
  10. **poetic**—expressive of deep feeling, flights of imagination, etc., in suitably noble language (poetry,n.)
  11. **sentimental**—expressive of tender or affectionate feeling; expressive of effusive emotionality (sentimentality,n.)
  12. **silver-tongued**—eloquent
  13. **soulful**—expressive of deep feelings (soulfulness,n.)
  14. **vocal**—able without difficulty to express one's ideas or feelings in words
  15. **voluble**—fluent and smooth (volubility, volubleness,n.)

4. That Which Expresses One's Feelings or Emotions: sentiment,n.

5. Art of Expression in Language or Words, n.
  1. **composition**—art of expressing ideas in writing according to the rules of grammar
  2. **elocution**—oratory (elocutionist, elocutioner,n. elocutionary,adj.)
  3. **oratory**—art of skillful linguistic expression in public (orator,n. oratorical,adj.)
  4. **rhetoric**—art of expression in words (rhetorician, rhetor,n. rhetorical,adj.)

6. Able to Be Expressed: expressible,adj. (expressibility,n.)

7. Not Expressible, adj.
  1. **indefinable**—incapable of being described accurately

2. **indescribable**—beyond description; defying description
3. **ineffable**—defying description or expression in words
4. **inenarrable**—indescribable; defying telling or narration
5. **inexpressible, unexpressible**—defying expression in words
6. **unmentionable**—not to be spoken of
7. **unspeakable**—not expressible in words
8. **unutterable**—not capable of being said or pronounced; descr. of that which one does not dare say

8. Manner of Expression in Speech or Writing (General), n.
  1. **accent, accents**—manner of speaking
  2. **address**—manner of speaking
  3. **delivery**—manner of speaking, esp. in public
  4. **diction**—manner of speaking
  5. **locution**—style of expression
  6. **parlance**—manner of speaking
  7. **phrase, phrasing**—manner of speech
  8. **phraseology**—manner of using words to express ideas; style
  9. **pronunciation**—manner of saying a word or words
  10. **style**—manner of speaking or writing
  11. **terms**—way of speaking
  12. **tone**—manner of speaking
  13. **tongue**—manner of speaking
  14. **vein**—manner of speech or expression

9. Manner or Use of Expression in Speech or Writing (Specific), n.
  1. **barbarism**—use of words or phrases considered substandard
  2. **bathos**—commonplaceness of style in speech or writing
  3. **blatancy**—loud, conspicuous, and offensive speech, with no thought to good taste
  4. **bluffness**—manner of speech that is frank, sincere, good-natured, and unceremonious
  5. **bluntness**—manner of speech that is to the point even at the expense of courtesy or of another's feelings
  6. **bombast**—use of inflated and pretentious language, or of language that is clothed in grandiosity of form and, often, comparative poverty of meaning
  7. **bookishness**—use of stiff, formal, or literary language
  8. **brevity**—economy of language
  9. **bromide**—platitude
  10. **candor, candidness**—frankness
  11. **circumlocution, circumbendibus, circumvolution**—indirect, wordy, or roundabout manner of speaking or expression
  12. **cogency**—manner of expression that is persuasive, or that appeals strongly to the intellect or reason
  13. **coherence**—quality of speech or writing in which the parts are logically connected
  14. **colloquialism**—easy, familiar, or conversational manner of speech or expression
  15. **compactness**—brevity
  16. **conciseness, concision**—manner of expression that is to the point, with no superfluous words
  17. **equivocation**—use of language that can be understood with a variety of meanings, and the purpose of which is to mislead or confuse
  18. **euphuism**—use of affected, pretentiously elegant, flowery, and artificial language
  19. **felicitousness**—use of language or phrasing that is particularly appropriate or suitable
  20. **floridity, floridness**—flowery and pretentious manner of expression
  21. **floweriness**—use of high-sounding language containing many fanciful expressions or figurative allusions

22. **formality**—use of language that strictly follows rule, convention, etc.
23. **frankness**—use of language that expresses freely what one feels or what is in one's mind
24. **fustian**—use of pompous, banal, and absurd language
25. **grandiloquence**—style of expression that is excessively grandiose, lofty, rhetorical, etc.
26. **gruffness**—manner of expression that is uncivil, curt, and often guttural in sound
27. **gush, gushiness**—slush
28. **imagery**—use of language that helps the mind to form pictures
29. **incoherence**—quality of speech or writing in which the parts are not logically connected
30. **irony**—light sarcasm
31. **levity**—frivolous and unseemly manner of speech
32. **macrology**—redundancy
33. **magniloquence**—lofty or grandiose style of expression
34. **obscurity**—manner of expressing ideas in such a way that the meaning is not clear, or defies understanding
35. **oratory**—grandiose use of language
36. **ornateness**—flowery and highly figurative manner of expression
37. **orotundity**—pompous, grandiose, or bombastic manner of expression
38. **periphrasis, periphrase**—roundabout and indirect manner or means of expression
39. **pithiness**—manner of expression that is full of point, meaning, or substance, yet economical of words
40. **platitude**—obvious, flat, and insipid manner of expression
41. **pleonasm**—use of unnecessary words to express meaning
42. **preciosity**—overelegance of expression
43. **provincialism**—manner of speaking peculiar to a narrow area or locality rather than common to the country as a whole
44. **redundancy, redundance**—manner of expression that uses an excessive number of words to convey an idea
45. **rhapsody**—exaggeratedly enthusiastic, overemotional, or wildly ecstatic manner of expression
46. **rhetoric**—artistic use of spoken words
47. **sarcasm**—use of language, statement, or remark, etc., that in form is the opposite of its obvious and clearly intended meaning, the purpose being to express contempt, bitterness, anger, disrespect, etc.
48. **sententiousness**—style of speaking or writing that is full of maxims, sayings, etc.; conciseness and power of expression
49. **slush, slushiness**—use of silly and effusively sentimental or overemotional language
50. **sonorousness**—use of high-sounding, or impressive language
51. **succinctness**—manner of using language that in few words offers much meaning
52. **tautology**—use of language containing needless repetitions
53. **terseness**—manner of expression that is most economical in the use of words
54. **tumidity**—style of language that is full of big words, swollen with pretentious phrases, etc.
55. **turgidity**—style of language that is full of big words, ostentatious or pretentious phraseology, pompousness, etc.
56. **tympany**—bombast
57. **unctuousness**—use of bland, smoothly agreeable, persuasive, or soothing language that may or may not be sincere
58. **vaporing**—inflated, empty, boastful or extravagant manner of expression
59. **volubility**—manner of speaking that is smooth, fluent, and, often, rapid

60. **voluminousness**—style of speaking or writing at great length, as if enough to fill volumes
61. **windiness**—vain and pretentious manner of language

10. **Descr. of Manner or Use of Expression in Speech or Writing**,adj. *From Sec. 9:* bathetic, blatant, bluff, blunt, bombastic, bookish, brief, bromidic; circumlocutory, circumlocutional, or circumlocutionary; cogent, coherent, colloquial, compact, concise, equivocal, euphuistic, felicitous, florid, flowery, formal, frank, fustian, grandiloquent, gruff, gushy, incoherent, ironical or ironic, magniloquent, obscure, oratorical, ornate, orotund, periphrastic, pithy, platitudinous, pleonastic, precious, provincial, redundant, rhapsodic, rhetorical, sarcastic, sententious, slushy, sonorous, succinct, tautological, terse, tumid, turgid, unctuous, vaporous, voluble, voluminous, windy; *Also:*
   1. **dithyrambic**—descr. of a manner of expression that evidences unrestrained emotion in poetic or almost poetic form
   2. **high-flown**—bombastic; turgid
   3. **magnific**—grandiloquent
   4. **orphic**—abstruse or esoteric in language
   5. **plethoric**—swollen, ostentatious, or overelegant in the use of language

666. WORD

1. **Word** (**Non-Descriptive**): expression, locution, term, vocable,n.

2. **Phrase** (**Non-Descriptive**): expression, locution, term,n.

3. **Word or Phrase** (**Descriptive or Qualified**),n.
   1. **abstraction**—abstract word or phrase
   2. **acronym**—word formed by the first letters of the words of a phrase, as *WAC* from *Women's Army Corps*, or from parts of other words, as *motel* from *motor* and *hotel* (acronymic, acronymous,adj. acronymize,v.)
   3. **additive**—word that joins or links
   4. **anagram**—word or phrase formed by rearranging the letters of some other word or phrase (anagrammatic, anagrammatical,adj. anagrammatize,v.)
   5. **archaism**—word no longer in use (archaic,adj.)
   6. **atonic**—word without an accent (atonic, adj.)
   7. **barb**—sharp, prickly, or sarcastic word or phrase
   8. **barbarism**—word or phrase considered substandard or unacceptable in educated usage
   9. **blend**—word formed by combining two or more other words, as *chortle,* from *chuckle* and *snort*
   10. **byword**—pet or favorite word or phrase
   11. **catchword**—word or phrase used over and over by a party, cause, group, etc.
   12. **clipped word**—shortened form of a word, with syllables dropped, as *phone* for *telephone*
   13. **colloquialism**—word or phrase heard especially in everyday conversation rather than in literary speech (colloquial,adj.)
   14. **conceit**—fanciful or affected word or phrase
   15. **contraction**—shortened word made by the omission of letters or by combining two words, as *I'll, can't,* etc.
   16. **countersign**—password
   17. **counterword**—word used more and more frequently with increasing loss of exact meaning, so that finally it loses, or has lost, all but its emotional flavor, as *swell, nice, lousy,* etc.
   18. **element**—word that is found recurrent

in a language with fairly constant meaning

19. **enclitic**—word that is connected in expression or meaning so intimately with the preceding word as to have no accent of its own (enclitic,adj.)

20. **epithet**—uncomplimentary or abusive word or phrase; word applied to a person or thing that expresses a quality or attribute, as Richard the *Lion-Hearted* (epithetic, epithetical,adj. epithet,v. epithetician,n.)

21. **euphemism**—word or phrase substituted for another that might offend decency or delicacy, as *pass away* for *die,* etc. (euphemistic,adj. euphemize,v.)

22. **exclamation**—interjection (exclamational, exclamatory, exclamative,adj.)

23. **expletive**—interjection, often profane, obscene, etc. (expletive, expletory,adj.)

24. **idiom**—word or phrase peculiar to a language (idiomatic,adj.)

25. **interjection**—word that has little or no meaning of its own but that expresses emotion of some sort, as *oh! ah! bah!* etc. (interjectional, interjectory,adj.)

26. **localism**—word or phrase peculiar to a locality

27. **morpheme**—word that shows grammatical relationship (morphemic,adj.)

28. **mot juste (French)**—word that exactly expresses one's meaning; exactly right or applicable word

29. **neologism, neology**—new word or phrase (neologistic, neological,adj.)

30. **nonce word**—word formed for the occasion and not achieving general use; word found only once in all existing writing

31. **obscenity**—obscene, disgusting, foul, or sexy word or phrase

32. **palindrome**—word, phrase, sentence, etc. that reads the same backward as forward (palindromic, palindromical,adj. palindromist,n.)

33. **parenthesis**—word, phrase, or sentence inserted to qualify, comment, or explain (parenthetic, parenthetical,adj. parenthesize,v.)

34. **password**—secret word that permits a person to pass through a guarded place

35. **pejorative**—depreciatory word

36. **pleonasm**—word or phrase used unnecessarily; added word or phrase that does not affect the meaning (pleonastic,adj.)

37. **portmanteau word**—blend

38. **provincialism**—word or phrase peculiar to a narrow area or locality rather than common to the country as a whole (provincial,adj.)

39. **redundancy**—excessive or superfluous word (redundant,adj.)

40. **semanteme**—word that gives an idea or image

41. **sesquipedalian**—long word—contemptuous (sesquipedalian,adj.)

42. **shibboleth**—byword; watchword

43. **slogan**—word or phrase used as a motto, or in advertising

44. **spoonerism**—phrase formed by the transposition of the initial sounds of the words of a phrase, as *blushing crow* for *crushing blow*

45. **term**—word or phrase as used technically, in some profession, occupation, field of knowledge, etc.

46. **tetragram**—four-letter word (tetragrammatic,adj.)

47. **toast**—word or phrase used in drinking to someone's health or honor

48. **usage**—word or phrase commonly used in a language

49. **vernacularism**—word or phrase peculiar to a region, place, country, etc.; word or phrase of the native, everyday, or non-literary language (vernacular,adj.)

50. **vocable**—word from the point of view of sound rather than meaning

51. **vulgarism**—word or phrase used only by ignorant speakers

52. **watchword**—secret word needed to pass a guarded place

4. One Who Coins or Uses a New Word or Words: neologist,n.

5. One Who Makes Up Palindromes: palindromist,n.

6. One Who Coins or Uses Slogans: sloganeer,n.

7. Word or Phrase as to Country,n.
1. **Anglicism**—British word, expression, or idiom
2. **Atticism**—expression peculiar to Athens or to Greece
3. **Briticism**—Anglicism
4. **Cockneyism**—word or phrase of the Cockney dialect of London
5. **Gallicism**—French word or idiom, borrowed by another language
6. **Grecism**—Greek idiom or expression
7. **Hibernicism, Hibernianism**—idiom of Irish English

8. Word as to Its Syllables,n.
1. **decasyllable**—word of ten syllables (decasyllabic,adj.)
2. **dissyllable**—word of two syllables (dissyllabic,adj.)
3. **monosyllable**—word of one syllable (monosyllabic,adj.)
4. **octosyllable**—word of eight syllables (octosyllabic,adj.)
5. **pentasyllable**—word of five syllables (pentasyllabic,adj.)
6. **quadrisyllable**—word of four syllables (quadrisyllabic,adj.)
7. **tetrasyllable**—word of four syllables (tetrasyllabic,adj.)
8. **trisyllable**—word of three syllables (trisyllabic,adj.)

9. Words Collectively,n.
1. **lexicon**—vocabulary, as the *lexicon of youth,* etc.
2. **libretto**—words or text of an opera or musical comedy
3. **lyrics**—words of a song, as distinguished from the music or tune
4. **phrase**—group or combination of related words
5. **phraseology**—words, or combination of words, used in a statement or piece of writing
6. **spate**—rush of words
7. **terminology**—special words or phrases of a subject, field, art, science, etc.; words used to express or describe
8. **text**—exact or actual words of a writer; words on a page, as distinguished from illustrations, etc.
9. **vocabulary**—list or aggregate of words, as in a language, writing, person's knowledge, etc.
10. **wordage**—words collectively; number of words

10. Pert. to, or Descr. of, Words Collectively, adj. *From Sec. 9:* phrasal, phraseological, terminological, textual; *Also:*
1. **lexical**—pert. to words; pert. to the words of a language
2. **verbal**—pert. to words
3. **vocabular**—pert. to words or phraseology
4. **wordy**—pert. to words

11. Writer of the Words of an Opera or Musical Comedy: librettist,n.

12. Words as to Interrelationships,n.
1. **antonyms**—words of opposite meanings (antonym,n. antonymy,n. antonymous, adj.)
2. **cognates**—words of different languages

derived from a common parent word or root (cognate,n. cognate,adj.)

3. **context**—words before or after a word or phrase that help explain the meaning of the word or phrase (contextual,adj.)

4. **doublets**—two words with the same derivation, but, through a differing process of growth, now having somewhat different appearance and meaning, as *guard* and *ward* (doublet,n.)

5. **heteronyms**—words of identical spelling but different pronunciation and meaning, as *row* a boat and have a *row*, i.e., argument (heteronym,n. heteronymous,adj.)

6. **homographs**—words identical in spelling but differing in derivation and meaning (homograph,n. homographic,adj.)

7. **homonyms**—words of similar sound but different meaning and spelling, as *break-brake*, *bear-bare*, etc. (homonym,n. homonymy,n. homonymous,adj.)

8. **homophones**—words pronounced identically, whether or not spelled the same, as *bread* and *bred*, *all* and *awl*, etc. (homophone, homophony,n. homophonous,adj.)

9. **paronyms**—words of the same derivation, as *deduce*, *reduce*, *seduce*, etc. (paronym, n. paronymous,adj.)

10. **synonyms**—words of similar meanings (synonym,n. synonymy,n. synonymous, adj.)

13. **Relationship or Arrangement of Words** in a Sentence: syntax,n. (syntactical,adj.)

14. **To Analyze Word Relationships,**v.
 1. **diagram**—analyze the grammatical relationship of the words of (a sentence) by means of a linear or pictorial arrangement
 2. **parse**—analyze the grammatical relationship of (a word or words in a sentence)

15. **Word Parts,**n.
 1. **affix**—any syllable or part added to a word, either as a prefix or suffix (affixal, adj.)
 2. **element**—part of a word that recurs in a language with fairly constant meaning
 3. **etymon**—stem from which, or on which, a word is formed
 4. **postfix**—suffix (postfixal, postfixial,adj.)
 5. **prefix**—syllable or part at the beginning of a word (prefixal,adj.)
 6. **root**—stem
 7. **stem**—main part of a word, as contrasted to the prefix or suffix
 8. **suffix**—ending of a word (suffixal,adj.)

16. **Placed after or at the End of a Word:** postpositive,adj. (postpositive,n.)

17. **Consisting of, or Expressed in, Words,**adj.
 1. **binomial**—consisting of two words
 2. **literal**—following or translating the exact words
 3. **monomial**—consisting of but one word
 4. **trinomial**—consisting of three words
 5. **verbal**—consisting of words; expressed in words, usually spoken; word-for-word
 6. **verbatim**—word-for-word
 7. **viva-voce**—expressed by spoken words (viva voce,adv.)

18. **Word Games,**n.
 1. **anagrams**—game played by building words by means of adding or transposing letters
 2. **charades**—game in which words, phrases, or syllables of words are acted out
 3. **logomachy**—game in which words are formed from cards, each of which has one letter on it

19. **Word Book,**n.
 1. **dictionary**—volume containing the words of a language in alphabetical arrangement
 2. **lexicon**—dictionary, esp. one of Hebrew, Greek, or Latin

3. **thesaurus**—dictionary as a storehouse of words

20. **Process or Art of Editing or Compiling Dictionaries:** lexicography,n. (lexicographer, n. lexicographic, lexicographical,adj.)

21. **Excessive Attention to Words Rather than Content or Meaning:** verbalism,n. (verbalist,n. verbalistic,adj.)

22. **Omission or Loss of Parts of a Word,**n.
 1. **abbreviation**—omission of letters in a word
 2. **aphaeresis**—dropping of a syllable or letter from the beginning of a word
 3. **aphesis**—gradual loss of the initial vowel of a word when this is short and unaccented
 4. **apocope, apocopation**—dropping of the final syllable or sound of a word
 5. **syncopation**—omission of sounds or letters in the pronunciation of a word
 6. **syncope**—loss of one or more middle sounds of a word, as *e'en* for *even*, etc.

23. **To Omit Parts of (a Word),**v. *From Sec. 22:* abbreviate, apocopate, syncopate

24. **Pert. to, or Descr. of, Loss of Word Parts,** adj. *From Sec. 22:* aphaeretic, aphetic; *Also:*
 1. **catalectic**—having the final syllable missing

25. **The Omission of a Word or Words from a Sentence:** ellipsis,n. (elliptic, elliptical,adj.)

26. **The Splitting of a Compound Word by Inserting One or More Words between the Parts:** tmesis,n. (*what person soever* for *whatsoever person*)

27. **War of, or about, Words:** logomachy,n. (logomachize,v. logomach, logomacher, logomachist,n. logomachic, logomachical,adj.)

28. **Parts of Speech:** adjective, adverb, conjunction, interjection, noun, preposition, pronoun, verb,n. (adjective or adjectival, adverbial, conjunctional, interjectional, nominal, prepositional, pronominal, verbal,adj.)

29. **Descr. of a Verb Whose Action is Directed to an Object:** transitive,adj. (transitiveness,n. intransitiveness,neg.n. intransitive,neg.adj.)

667. USE OF WORDS

1. **Use of Words,**n.
 1. **ambiguity, ambiguousness**—such use of words as to leave the meaning vague or doubtful; such use of words that two or more meanings may be reasonably deduced (ambiguous,adj.)
 2. **amphibology, amphiboly**—ambiguous grammatical construction (amphibolic, adj.)
 3. **anagoge, anagogy**—spiritual or mystical use of words (anagogic, anagogical,adj.)
 4. **diction**—choice of words in talking
 5. **equivocation**—deliberate use of ambiguous words (equivocal,adj. equivocate,v.)
 6. **neologism, neology**—new use of an old word or expression (neologistic,adj.)
 7. **sesquipedalianism**—use of very long words—contemptuous (sesquipedalian, adj.)
 8. **verbalism**—use of words with little or no meaning; use of empty words; skilled use of words

2. **One Who Uses Words,**n. *From Sec. 1:* equivocator, neologist, sesquipedalian, verbalist

3. **Misuse of Words,**n.
 1. **bull**—ridiculous misuse of words
 2. **catachresis**—misuse of an incorrect word for the correct one (catachrestic,adj.)
 3. **malapropism**—ridiculous misuse, or habit of ridiculously misusing, words

4. **misusage**—incorrect use of words
5. **solecism**—illiterate misuse of words (solecistic or solecistical,adj.)
6. **syllepsis**—incorrect use of one word in two grammatical functions (sylleptic, adj.)

4. A Misused Word,n. *From Sec. 2:* bull, malapropism, misusage, solecism; *Also:* 1. **impropriety**—word used in a meaning contrary to correct usage

5. To Use Words or a Word in an Illiterate or Ungrammatical Manner: solecize,v. (solecist, solecizer,n.)

6. Using Too Many Words,adj.
1. **copious**—verbose (of language, etc.)
2. **diffuse, diffusive**—using, or tending to use, more words than necessary in speech or writing, and consequently losing effectiveness, pointedness, and strength
3. **long-winded**—tediously long in speech or writing
4. **pleonastic**—using words that are not essential to the meaning
5. **prolix**—using too many words; long-winded; verbose
6. **redundant**—using too many words to express an idea; using a superfluity of words
7. **verbose**—using far more words than necessary; expressing simple ideas in complicated and unnecessarily superfluous terms
8. **wordy**—verbose

7. Use of Too Many Words; Quality of Using Too Many Words,n. *From Sec. 6:* copiousness; diffuseness, diffusiveness, or diffusion; long-windedness, pleonasm, prolixity, redundance or redundancy, verbosity or verboseness, wordiness; *Also:*
1. **circumlocution, circumbendibus**—use of more words than necessary to express an idea (circumlocutory,adj.)
2. **macrology**—prolixity
3. **periphrasis, periphrase**—circumlocution (periphrastic,adj.)
4. **verbalism**—verbosity
5. **verbiage**—use of more than the necessary number of words; use of unnecessary words; verbosity

8. One Who Uses Too Many Words; Wordy Person: verbalist,n.

9. Overabundance of Unnecessary Words: surplusage, verbiage,n.

10. A Play on Words: equivoke, equivoque, paronomasia, pun,n. (pun,v. punster,n. paronomastic, paronomastical, paronomasial, paronomasian, paronomasiastic,adj.)

11. Making Puns: paronomasia, punning,n. (paronomastic, etc.,adj.)

12. Descr. of Types of Sentences,adj.
1. **balanced**—descr. of a sentence having its component clauses in corresponding order
2. **loose**—not periodic
3. **periodic**—descr. of sentences whose meaning is clear only with the final words

13. Sentence Parts,n.
1. **apodosis**—in a conditional sentence, the clause that expresses the result or conclusion
2. **predicate**—that part of a sentence which asserts something about the subject
3. **protasis**—the clause in a conditional sentence that expresses the condition
4. **subject**—that part of a sentence about which something is asserted

668. SYLLABLE

1. Syllable,n.
1. **antepenult**—syllable of a word that is

two removed from the final syllable (antepenultimate,adj.)
2. **atonic**—syllable without an accent
3. **penult**—next to the last syllable of a word (penultimate,adj.)
4. **tonic**—accented syllable
5. **ultima**—final syllable of a word (ultimate,adj.)

2. To Divide or Form into Syllables: syllabicate, syllabify, syllabize,v. (syllabication, syllabification,n.)

3. Pert. to, or Descr. of, a Syllable: syllabic, syllabical,adj.

4. Sound That Forms a Syllable by Itself: syllabic,n.

5. Shortening of a Long Syllable for Metrical Convenience: systole n. (systolic,adj.)

6. Lengthening of a Short Syllable: diastole, ectasis,n. (diastolic, ectatic,adj.)

7. To Transpose Syllables in a Word: metathesize,v. (metathesis,n.)

8. The Addition of a Syllable to the End of a Word: epithesis, paragoge,n. (paragogic, paragogical,adj.)

669. FIGURE OF SPEECH

1. Figure of Speech, Esp. Irony, Metaphor, Metonymy, and Synecdoche: trope,n. (tropal,adj.)

2. The Use of Figures of Speech: imagery, trope, tropology,n. (tropist,n. tropal, tropological,adj.)

3. Certain Specific Figures of Speech or Other Rhetorical or Grammatical Devices or Effects,n.
1. **allegory**—extended metaphor (allegoric, allegorical,adj.)
2. **alliteration**—repetition of the same sound or sounds in successive words (alliterative, alliteral,adj.)
3. **anaphora**—repetition of the same word at the beginning of successive clauses, sentences, etc.
4. **anastrophe**—inversion of normal word order
5. **anticlimax**—sentence or passage in which the ideas drop off suddenly in force, importance, or dignity toward or at the end (anticlimactic,adj.)
6. **antistrophe**—repetition of previous words in opposite order (antistrophal, antistrophic,adj.)
7. **antithesis**—contrast of ideas emphasized by the position of the contrasting words (antithetic, antithetical,adj.)
8. **apophasis**—mention of something by saying one will not mention it (apophastic, adj.)
9. **aposiopesis**—sudden breaking off of a sentence because of an unwillingness to express one's feelings or thoughts (aposiopetic,adj.)
10. **asyndeton**—deliberate omission of conjunctions in constructions where these are ordinarily used (asyndetic,adj.)
11. **bathos**—anticlimax (bathetic,adj.)
12. **climax**—thoughts expressed in ascending order of importance or effectiveness (climactic,adj.)
13. **echoism**—onomatopoeia (echoic,adj.)
14. **ellipsis**—omission of an understood word or words (elliptic,adj.)
15. **euphemism**—substitution of an inoffensive expression for one that may offend, without changing the meaning or allusion (euphemistic,adj.)
16. **hyperbole**—exaggeration for effect (hyperbolic,adj.)
17. **inversion**—placing of the predicate before

the subject for purposes of emphasis (inverted,adj.)

18. **irony**—use of words that are intended to be understood with a meaning opposite to that expressed (ironical, ironic,adj.)
19. **litotes**—use of understatement to increase effectiveness
20. **metaphor**—implied comparison between unlike things, one of the things being called the other (metaphoric, metaphorical,adj.)
21. **metonymy**—use of another word for the word actually meant, the one being closely allied to and suggestive of the other (metonymical, metonymic, metonymous,adj.)
22. **onomatopoeia, onomatopoesis**—use of words that sound like what they mean, like *bang, crash, whirr,* etc. (onomatopoetic, onomatopoeic, onomatopoeical, onomatopoeial, onomatopoeian,adj.)
23. **oxymoron**—combination of words of contradictory meaning for special effect
24. **paraleipsis, paralepsis, paralipsis**—very brief mention to effect a heightening of the importance or significance of what is omitted
25. **pathetic fallacy**—attribution of human emotions to inanimate objects
26. **personification**—attribution of animate or human characteristics to inanimate or non-human things or creatures (personified,adj.)
27. **polysyndeton**—use of a number of grammatical conjunctions in close succession (polysyndetic,adj.)
28. **simile**—comparison between unlike things, usually with the words *like* or *as*
29. **syncrisis**—comparison of opposites
30. **synecdoche**—use of the part for the whole, or of the whole for the part (synechdochic, synechdochical,adj.)
31. **zeugma**—use of a word to modify two or more other words, though strictly it can modify only one of them (zeugmatic, adj.)

4. To Employ a Specific Figure of Speech, etc.,v. *From Sec. 3:* allegorize, alliterate, antithesize, echoize, euphemize, hyperbolize, invert, personify, similize

5. Employment of a Specific Figure of Speech, etc.,n. *From Sec. 3:* allegorism or allegorization, antithesism, hyperbolism, irony, synecdochism

6. One Who Employs a Specific Figure of Speech, etc.,n. *From Sec. 3:* allegorist or allegorizer, alliterator, echoist, metaphorist

7. Word or Phrase Employed as a Figure of Speech, etc.,n. *From Sec. 3:* antithesism, euphemism, metaphor, metonym; onomatoplasm, or onomatopoeian; simile, synecdochism

8. Allegorizing; Using Allegory; Interpreting as Allegory: allegoristic,adj.

670. PRONUNCIATION

1. Pronunciation; Manner of Pronunciation: accent, articulation, diction, enunciation,n. (accentual, articulative or articulatory,adj.)

2. To Pronounce: accent, articulate, enunciate,v.

3. Correct Pronunciation: orthoëpy,n. (orthoëpic, orthoëpical,adj.)

4. Specific Pronunciation or Manner of Pronunciation,n.
1. **accent, accentuation**—emphasis of the voice on a syllable (accentual,adj.)
2. **articulation**—enunciation (articulative, articulatory,adj.)

3. **aspiration**—pronunciation with an *H* sound
4. **brogue**—Irish accent; any accent peculiar to a region
5. **diaeresis, dieresis**—separation of the vowels of a syllable so that they are pronounced separately, as in *co-operate* (diaeretic, dieretic,adj.)
6. **drawl**—slow manner of pronunciation, with vowel sounds lengthened and various syllables protracted, characteristic of the speech of southern U.S.
7. **elision**—omission, glossing over, or slurring of a syllable or sound in pronunciation
8. **enunciation**—clear or distinct pronunciation
9. **hiatus**—pause between two vowels, each vowel pronounced independently, as in *preempt*
10. **lallation**—infantile pronunciation
11. **nasalization, nasality**—pronunciation through the nose
12. **roll**—trill
13. **sibilance, sibilancy**—pronunciation of an *S* sound (sibilant,adj.)
14. **sibilation**—pronunciation with an initial *S* sound
15. **slurring**—indistinct pronunciation caused by running sounds together
16. **stress**—accent
17. **synaeresis, syneresis**—pronunciation of two vowels as one syllable, though these two vowels are usually pronounced separately
18. **synaloepha, synalepha, synalephe**—the blending into a single syllable of the vowels of consecutive syllables
19. **trill**—pronunciation (usually of the letter *R*) in trembling or vibrating sounds

5. To Pronounce,v. *From Sec. 4:* accent, accentuate, articulate, aspirate, drawl, elide, enunciate, nasalize, roll, sibilate, slur, stress, trill

6. Incorrect Pronunciation: misenunciation, mispronunciation,n. (misenunciate, mispronounce,v.)

7. Certain Incorrect Pronunciations,n.
1. **gammacism**—incorrect pronunciation of the letters *G* and *K,* usually substituting *D* and *T,* respectively
2. **lallation**—incorrect pronunciation of the letter *R* so that it sounds like *L,* as by some Chinese speaking English
3. **lambdacism**—defective pronunciation of *L;* incorrect pronunciation of the letter *R,* substituting *L* in its place
4. **lisp**—incorrect pronunciation of *S* or *Z* like *TH* (lisp,v.)

8. Identical in Pronunciation: homophonous,adj. (homophony,n.)

9. Branch of Grammar Dealing with Pronunciation; Art of Correct Pronunciation: orthoëpy,n. (orthoëpic, orthoëpical,adj. orthoëpist,n. orthoëpistic,adj.)

10. Any Speech Sound: phone, phoneme,n. (phonal or phonic, phonemic,adj.)

11. One of a Group of Related Speech Sounds: phoneme,n. (phonemic,adj.)

12. Consisting of Speech Sounds; Pert. to the Sound or Sounds of Words or Speech: phonetic,adj.

13. The Sounds of a Language: phonology,n. (phonological,adj.)

14. Certain Specific Speech Sounds,n.
1. **aspirate, aspiration**—sound of the letter *H;* any breathed sound (aspirate, aspirated,adj.)
2. **bilabial**—consonant or consonant sound, such as *M, P, B,* etc., formed by the two lips (bilabial,adj.)

3. **consonant**—speech sound caused by some blocking of the breath, such as *P* or *N* in *pan* (consonant, consonantal,adj.)
4. **dental**—consonant, or consonant sound, pronounced by the tip of the tongue against the upper teeth, as *T, D, N, L,* etc. (dental,adj.)
5. **diphthong**—single vowel sound in two parts, produced by a quick succession of differing vowel sounds, as *oi* in *boil,* in which the sounds *aw* and *ee* are fused (diphthongal, dipthongic,adj.)
6. **fricative**—consonant or consonant sound *F, V, S,* or *Z,* pronounced by friction of the breath (fricative,adj.)
7. **labial**—bilabial (labial,adj.)
8. **labiodental**—consonant, or consonant sound, formed both by the lip or lips and the teeth (labiodental,adj.)
9. **schwa**—unaccented vowel sound, such as the *a* in *sofa*
10. **sibilant**—speech sound represented in English by *S, Z, SH, ZH, CH,* and *J* (sibilant,adj.)
11. **tonic**—voiced sound as contrasted to one that is breathed (tonic,adj.)
12. **triphthong**—three vowel sounds forming one syllable (triphthongal,adj.)
13. **velar**—speech sound represented by *K,* hard *G,* the *NG* of *sing,* and certain vowel combinations (velar,adj.)
14. **vowel**—open, unimpeded speech sound (vowel, vocalic,adj.)

15. To Pronounce a Speech Sound,v. *From Sec. 14:* aspirate, dentalize, diphthongize or diphthong, labialize (aspiration, dentalization, diphthongization, diphthongation, labialization,n.)

16. To Change into a Vowel; To Use as a Vowel: vocalize,v. (vocalization,n.)

17. Containing Vowel Sounds: vocalic,adj.

18. Variation of the Vowel of a Root in Related Words: ablaut,n.

19. Variation in a Vowel Resulting from Partial Assimilation to a Following Sound, Esp. in Germanic Languages: umlaut,n.

20. A Vowel So Varied: umlaut,n. (umlaut, v.)

21. Certain Symbols or Letters Representing Speech Sounds,n.
1. **digraph**—two consecutive letters pronounced as one sound, as *ea* in *meat,* *ou* in *four,* *th* in *bath,* etc. (digraphic,adj.)
2. **homophone**—any letter or symbol having the same sound as some other letter or symbol
3. **phonogram**—symbol that represents a single speech sound (phonogrammic, phonogramic,adj.)
4. **thorn**—Anglo-Saxon symbol for either of the two sounds for which, in modern English, we use TH
5. **trigraph**—three consecutive letters pronounced as one sound, as *eau,* pronounced, "O" (trigraphic,adj.)

22. Representing Speech Sounds: phonetic, adj.

23. Description of Speech Sounds, Esp. with Reference to Their Representation: phonography,n. (phonographer, phonographist,n. phonographic,adj.)

24. Transposition of Sounds in a Word: metathesis,n. (metathesize,v.)

25. Science of Speech Sounds,n.
1. **orthoëpy**—phonology (orthoëpist,n.)
2. **phonemics**—science of related speech sounds (phonemic,adj.)
3. **phonetics**—science of the sounds of words as distinguished from their use or meanings (phonetician, phonetist,n. phonetic,adj.)

4. **phonology**—science of speech sounds (phonologist,n. phonological,adj.)

671. TALK

1. To Talk,v.
1. **ad lib**—talk spontaneously or without previous preparation (on the radio, stage, lecture platform, etc.) instead of reading or saying prepared or memorized words (colloq.)
2. **babble**—talk meaninglessly or incoherently; talk foolishly or idly; chatter
3. **banter**—chaff
4. **bark**—talk harshly, angrily, hostilely, etc.
5. **blab**—talk too much; chatter without care as to what one is saying
6. **blarney**—use smooth, coaxing talk
7. **blat**—talk loudly or foolishly
8. **blather, blether**—talk foolishly
9. **bleat**—talk complainingly; talk foolishly
10. **bluster**—talk in a noisy, violent, and often angry way
11. **burble**—talk with a bubbling sound; jabber
12. **cackle**—jabber
13. **chaff**—engage in witty or jesting talk
14. **chaffer**—talk idly about trivialities; chatter
15. **chat**—talk informally
16. **chatter**—talk casually or rapidly about trivialities
17. **chitchat**—engage in trifling and usually familiar conversation
18. **clack**—chatter
19. **clatter**—talk noisily
20. **collogue**—talk together in secret
21. **commune**—talk intimately; engage in friendly conversation
22. **confabulate, confab**—talk familiarly or intimately; chat
23. **converse**—engage in informal talk
24. **coze**—talk or chat intimately
25. **declaim**—talk with rhetorical formality, as if delivering a public address; talk for effect; make a formal public speech
26. **descant**—talk formally and lengthily
27. **discourse**—talk in a formal or extended way
28. **dissertate**—discourse
29. **drawl**—talk slowly, pronouncing words with vowel sounds lengthened and various syllables protracted
30. **drone**—talk monotonously and wearisomely
31. **drool**—talk foolishly (slang)
32. **equivocate**—talk in deliberately vague or ambiguous terms
33. **expatiate**—talk freely and extensively
34. **extemporize**—talk without previous preparation
35. **falter**—talk in a hesitating, stammering fashion
36. **gab**—chatter
37. **gabble**—talk rapidly and with little meaning; engage in silly talk
38. **gibber**—talk foolishly or meaninglessly and with some rapidity or fluency
39. **gossip**—engage in idle, usually malicious chatter
40. **growl**—grumble
41. **grumble**—talk in low and somewhat indistinct fashion, often in complaint or discontent
42. **gush**—talk with annoyingly effusive excitement or enthusiasm
43. **harangue**—make a noisy, passionate, vehement, or wild speech
44. **hedge**—talk in such a way as to escape commitments or definite statements
45. **improvise**—ad lib; extemporize
46. **intone**—talk or recite in a chanting or singing voice

47. **jabber**—talk rapidly, unintelligibly, or indistinctly
48. **jargon**—talk unintelligibly
49. **jaw**—talk; gossip (slang)
50. **jeer**—talk mockingly, sarcastically, or in a way to ridicule
51. **lecture**—deliver a speech or discourse, usually for instructional purposes
52. **lisp**—talk falteringly, or in a childlike manner
53. **maunder**—talk aimlessly, foolishly, or indistinctly; mutter
54. **moralize**—talk in such a way as to be judgmental of the right or wrong of something
55. **mumble**—talk in a low, indistinct manner, with the lips partly closed
56. **murmur**—talk softly, indistinctly, and under the breath
57. **mutter**—talk in a low, indistinct voice, usually in complaint or anger
58. **nasalize**—talk in a nasal manner
59. **not mince matters, words, etc.**—talk frankly
60. **orate**—talk in a grand or pompous fashion
61. **palaver**—talk; talk flatteringly or beguilingly; engage in idle talk
62. **palter**—talk insincerely or deceitfully
63. **parley**—take part in informal talk
64. **patter**—talk quickly, mechanically, and indistinctly; talk rapidly and glibly
65. **peep**—talk in a thin, weak, or small voice
66. **perorate**—deliver a lengthy speech; harangue at length
67. **platitudinize**—talk in flat and commonplace sentiments
68. **pontificate**—talk with the solemnity or authority of the Pope; talk with pompous authority and excessively solemn dignity
69. **prate**—talk a lot but say nothing
70. **prattle**—talk foolishly; babble; chatter
71. **preach**—talk in public on a religious topic or about God
72. **prelect**—talk publicly; lecture
73. **prevaricate**—talk evasively
74. **racket**—engage in loud or noisy talk
75. **rally**—banter; engage in banter
76. **rant**—talk extravagantly, wildly, or violently
77. **rattle on**—talk quickly and, often, tediously or with little meaning
78. **rave**—talk wildly, excitedly, or with little sense; talk with immoderate enthusiasm; talk in raging anger
79. **recite**—deliver a memorized speech, poem, etc., to an audience
80. **rhapsodize**—talk in exaggeratedly enthusiastic, overemotional, or wildly ecstatic language
81. **sermonize**—deliver a religious lecture; talk, or talk tiresomely, about morals, behavior, duty, etc.
82. **shout**—talk in very loud tones, and, often, unrestrained manner
83. **slobber**—talk in a gushy, silly, overeffusive, or sickeningly sentimental manner
84. **snuffle**—talk through, or as if through, the nose; talk in a hypocritical, self-righteous, and insincerely pious manner
85. **soliloquize**—talk aloud to oneself
86. **somniloquize**—talk in one's sleep
87. **speak**—talk
88. **speechify**—make a speech (contemptuous or humorous)
89. **spellbind**—talk in such a way as to capture an audience as if by a magic spell; talk with the purpose of appealing to the emotions of the audience, usually successfully
90. **spout**—talk insincerely
91. **splutter**—talk in a confused, somewhat incoherent manner
92. **sputter**—talk rapidly, nervously, incoherently, or confusedly

93. **squeak**—talk in a high-pitched and thin voice
94. **stage whisper**—so whisper as to be heard by the audience or by others than the one addressed (of an actor in a play)
95. **stammer**—talk hesitantly; talk by involuntarily repeating sounds or by being unable to say a complete word; stumble in one's speech, owing to some emotional difficulty or conflict
96. **stumble**—talk hesitantly or clumsily
97. **stutter**—talk with difficulty in getting sounds out, especially the initial sounds of words; involuntarily repeat sounds or syllables in an effort to say words—usually a constitutional defect
98. **susurrate**—whisper
99. **tattle**—talk foolishly or idly
100. **tittle-tattle**—chatter idly
101. **trifle**—talk without seriousness, or in jest or mockery; talk in a misleading manner
102. **twaddle, twattle**—engage in weak, silly, or meaningless talk
103. **vapor**—talk in inflated, boastful, empty, or extravagant language or manner
104. **ventriloquize**—talk in such a way that one's voice appears to be coming from somewhere else
105. **vociferate**—talk very loudly and, often, insistently
106. **whiffle**—talk idly
107. **whisper**—talk very softly; talk using only the breath and lips, not the vocal cords
108. **yammer**—chatter
109. **yap, yawp, yaup**—talk noisily, foolishly, or angrily (colloq. or slang)

2. Talk; Talking, n. *From Sec. 1:* babble or babblement, banter, blab, blarney, blather, bluster, cackle, chaff, chaffer, chat, chatter, chitchat, clack, clatter, commune, confabulation, conversation or converse, coze, declamation, descant, discourse, drawl, drool, equivocation, expatiation, extemporization, gab, gabble, gibber or gibberish, gossip, growl, grumble, gush, harangue, improvisation, intonation, jabber, jargon, lecture, moralization, mumble, murmur, mutter, nasalization, oration, palaver, parley, patter, peroration, pontification, prate, prattle, preachment, prelection, prevarication, racket, rant, recitation, rhapsody, sermon, slobber, snuffle, soliloquy; somniloquism, somniloquy, or somniloquence; speech, splutter, sputter, stagewhisper, stammer, stutter, susurration, tattle, tittle-tattle, twaddle, twattle, ventriloquism, vociferation, whifflery, whisper, yammer, yap, yawp, yaup; *Also:*
1. **abracadabra**—nonsensical talk; gibberish
2. **address**—formal speech
3. **allocution**—authoritative speech; speech designed to urge or move to action
4. **badinage**—playful, somewhat subtle, or delicate banter; light, teasing talk
5. **blague (French)**—claptrap; raillery
6. **buncombe, bunkum, bunk**—talk of little or no significance
7. **causerie**—casual or informal conversation
8. **claptrap**—insincere talk, often for purposes of gaining approval or applause
9. **colloquy**—conversation
10. **deliration**—irrational talking
11. **dialogue**—formal or literary conversation between two or more people; conversation, esp. in a play, novel, etc.
12. **disquisition**—formal, elaborate, and/or long speech on a subject
13. **dithyramb**—speech delivered in a vehement or passionate fashion
14. **drivel**—foolish, meaningless talk
15. **duologue**—technical term for a dialogue between two, and only two, people
16. **epilogue**—speech addressed to the audience at the end of a play
17. **flapdoodle**—nonsensical talk (colloq.)

18. **flummery**—empty, silly, or nonsensical talk
19. **galimatias**—confused and meaningless talk
20. **gnomology**—talk full of aphorisms
21. **homily**—talk with a moral point or exhortation
22. **interlocution**—conversation; speech between people
23. **monologue**—long speech by one person
24. **oration**—formal public speech
25. **oratory**—fine or effective speaking
26. **parlance**—talk; conversation
27. **persiflage**—slightly teasing or mildly ridiculing talk
28. **pleasantry**—small, unimportant talk; agreeably playful talk; good-humored banter
29. **poppycock**—silly talk
30. **preachment**—long and tedious speech
31. **raillery**—talk that ridicules, but in a good-humored or unmalicious manner
32. **repartee**—talk consisting of clever answers or a rapid flow of witty remarks
33. **rhinolalia**—nasality in speaking; talking through one's nose
34. **ribble-rabble**—ribald chatter; rambling or meaningless chatter
35. **rigmarole**—incoherent or rambling talk
36. **rumor**—general, loose talk; talk that may or may not be true
37. **screed**—long speech, sometimes one of attack or criticism
38. **slush**—silly and effusively sentimental or overemotional talk
39. **small talk**—light, unimportant conversation
40. **tête-à-tête**—private conversation between two people
41. **whimsey, whimsy**—strange or quaint speech

3. Talker,n. *From Sec. 1:* ad-libber, babbler, etc.; blabbermouth, confabulator, conversationalist, dissertator, equivocator, expatiator, gossip, improvisator, moralist, orator, perorator, prelector, prevaricator, rhapsodist, soliloquist, somniloquist, speechifier, ventriloquist, vociferant; *From Sec. 2:* colloquist, homilist, interlocutor, monologist or monologuist, orator, rumorer or rumormonger; *Also:*

1. **prolocutor**—one who speaks for another
2. **rhetor**—orator
3. **spokesman**—one who speaks for another

4. Talking; Pert. to, or Descr. of, Talking, Talk, or a Talker,adj. *From Sec. 1:* babbling, bantering, etc.; conversational, declamatory, equivocal, expatiatory, extemporaneous or extempore, gossipy, gushy; improvisatory, improvisatorial, or improvisational; moralistic, murmurous, oratorical, perorational or peroratorical, pontifical, prevaricatory, rackety, recitative, rhapsodic, somniloquent, sputtery, tittle-tattle, twaddly, vaporous, ventriloquistic or ventriloquial, vociferous or vociferant; *From Sec. 2:* colloquial, dithyrambic, homiletic, interlocutory, monologic, oratorical, slushy; *From Sec. 3:* prolocutory; *Also:*

1. **blithering**—talking irrationally or with exceeding foolishness
2. **demegoric**—pert. to, or descr. of, harangue
3. **mealymouthed**—talking insincerely, though smoothly
4. **mincing**—talking in an affectedly polite, dainty, or elegant manner
5. **outspoken**—speaking, or spoken, freely and without fear
6. **soft-spoken**—talking in a gentle or low voice

5. To Talk about,v.
1. **allude to**—mention quietly, secretly, guardedly, or slightly (allusion,n. allusive,adj.)

2. **belittle**—talk slightingly of (belittler,n.)
3. **broach**—open as a topic of conversation; speak about
4. **chant**—talk about monotonously (chant, n. chanter,n.)
5. **comment on**—talk about (comment,n. commenter,n.)
6. **describe**—talk about the appearance of (description,n. descriptive,adj.)
7. **discuss**—talk over, considering various points of view, often with the aim of arriving at a conclusion (discussion,n. discusser, discussant,n.)
8. **give voice to**—talk about
9. **harp on**—talk about continually and tediously
10. **mention**—talk about (mention,n. mentioner,n.)
11. **noise of**—talk a lot about; talk publicly of
12. **premise**—mention beforehand

6. Commonly or Frequently Talked about or Mentioned: proverbial,adj.

7. To Mention in Detail, Individually, Specifically, etc.: cite, enumerate, itemize, recite, recount, rehearse, relate, specify,v. (citation, enumeration, itemization, recital, recitation, recountal, rehearsal, relation, specification,n.)

8. To Talk to,v.
1. **accost**—talk to first; approach and talk to (accost,n.)
2. **address**—talk to (address,n.)
3. **apostrophize**—directly address (an absent or dead person, or a thing); engage in such address (apostrophe,n. apostrophic,adj.)
4. **banter**—talk to in a teasing or ridiculing, but not malicious, manner
5. **barrage**—hurl a rapid delivery of words, questions, statements, etc., at (barrage, n.)
6. **buttonhole**—talk to (someone) while holding him or forcing him to listen
7. **harangue**—make a noisy, ranting public speech to (harangue,n. haranguer,n.)
8. **rally**—banter
9. **tutoyer**—talk to in familiar tones or manner

9. To Speak against: gainsay,v.

10. Given to Talking in One's Sleep: somniloquous,adj.

11. The Habit of Talking in a Judgmental Manner: moralism,n.

12. Tending to Address the Public in Wild or Ranting Speeches: harangueful,adj.

13. Descr. of a Public Speech That Is Ranting, Vehement, Passionate, etc.: harangueful,adj.

14. Manner of Speaking in Public: delivery, elocution,n.

15. Artificial Manner of Speaking in Public: elocution,n. (elocutionary,n. elocutionist,n.)

16. The Art or Study of Speaking in Public: elocution, public speaking,n.

17. Talkative,adj.
1. **chattering**—talking incessantly
2. **chatty**—talkative
3. **gabby**—loquacious (colloq.)
4. **garrulous**—given to excessive, rambling, meaningless, and therefore tedious talk
5. **loquacious**—given to talking a great deal
6. **mouthy**—emptily or meaninglessly talkative
7. **voluble**—talking a lot; garrulous

18. Talkativeness,n. *From Sec. 17:* chattiness, garrulity or garrulousness, loquacity or loquaciousness, mouthiness, volubility or volubleness; *Also:* 1. **logorrhea**—excessive talkativeness, often including incoherence (medical)

19. Talkative Person,n.
1. **blatherskite**—noisily talkative person
2. **chatterbox**—one who never stops chattering
3. **chatterer**—one who talks incessantly
4. **flibbertigibbet**—chattering, giddy, and flighty woman
5. **jay**—chatterer
6. **magpie**—chatterer
7. **popinjay**—talkative, silly, and conceited person
8. **windbag**—someone who does a lot of talking but never says anything of any consequence (colloq.)

20. Talking Little,adj.
1. **closemouthed**—not saying much
2. **laconic**—so economical in the use of words as to seem almost curt or abrupt; saying no more than is absolutely necessary; making few words convey a wealth of meaning (laconism,n.)
3. **mute**—refraining from talk; silent (muteness,n.)
4. **reticent**—tending to say little (reticence, n.)
5. **silent**—disposed not to talk; disinclined to conversation
6. **taciturn**—disinclined to conversation; preferring to avoid speech (taciturnity,n.)
7. **tight-lipped**—unwilling to give information or to speak
8. **uncommunicative**—not disposed to speak much (uncommunicativeness,n.)
9. **unvocal**—not accustomed to express one's feelings in words

21. Inability to Talk; Selected Speech Ailments or Difficulties,n.
1. **anarthria**—loss of power to say words as a result of a brain injury
2. **aphasia**—loss or great impairment of the ability to use or understand language, resulting from brain injury or severe emotional disturbance (aphasiac, aphasic, adj.)
3. **aphonia**—loss of the voice caused by paralysis of the vocal organs or cords (aphonic,adj.)
4. **baryphony**—difficulty of speech (baryphonic,adj.)
5. **deaf-mutism**—inability to speak or hear, usually a congenital condition
6. **dumbness**—inability to utter sound or to speak (dumb,adj.)
7. **dysphasia**—pathological condition, caused by a brain injury, in which the victim loses the power to use and/or to understand language (dysphasiac, dysphasic, adj.)
8. **dysphonia**—difficulty in making speech sounds (dysphonic,adj.)
9. **impediment, speech impediment**—speech defect of any sort
10. **inarticulateness**—inability to speak intelligibly; inability to speak in words or language (inarticulate,adj.)
11. **laloplegia**—inability to talk, resulting from paralysis of the speech muscles, other than those of the tongue (laloplegic,adj.)
12. **muteness**—inability to talk (mute,adj.)
13. **mutism**—inability to utter language sounds
14. **paralalia**—any speech defect, esp. that of substituting one letter or sound for another
15. **speechlessness**—inability to speak (speechless,adj.)
16. **stammering**—speech that involuntarily repeats sounds, or that is characterized by an inability to say a complete word (possibly a temporary condition)
17. **stuttering**—difficulty in getting speech sounds out, esp. the initial sounds of words; involuntary repetition of sounds

or syllables in an effort to speak (generally a constitutional defect)
18. **tongue-tiedness**—speechlessness through some strong emotion (tongue-tied,adj.)
19. **wordlessness**—speechlessness (wordless, adj.)

22. One Who Is Unable to Talk, or Who Has Difficulty in Talking,n. *From Sec. 21:* aphasiac, aphonic, deaf-mute, dummy, dysphasiac, laloplegic, mute, stammerer, stutterer

23. Pathologically Rapid Speech: tachylogia, tachyphasia, tachyphrasia,n.

24. Descr. of Speech That Is Not Logically Coherent: disconnected, disjointed, incoherent,adj. (disconnectedness, disjointedness, incoherence,n.)

25. To Be Incoherent in Speech or Thinking: wander,v.

26. Subject,n.
1. **motif**—central or dominant theme of a book, play, speech, etc.
2. **text**—subject; topic (textual,adj.)
3. **theme**—subject spoken or written on (thematic, adj.)
4. **thesis**—subject for writing
5. **topic**—subject about which one writes or speaks (topical,adj.)

672. DISCUSSION

1. To Discuss,v.
1. **advise with**—discuss with
2. **argue**—discuss (something)
3. **canvass**—discuss (something)
4. **confer (with)**—discuss (with)
5. **consult with**—discuss with
6. **deliberate**—confer formally (deliberative, adj.)
7. **mention**—discuss (something) casually
8. **negotiate**—discuss or confer, with a view to arriving at an agreement
9. **palaver**—discuss; have a long discussion with African natives
10. **parley**—engage in an informal discussion; engage in an informal discussion with the enemy
11. **thrash out, thresh out**—discuss thoroughly and settle (something)
12. **ventilate**—discuss (something) openly

2. Discussion; A Discussion,n. *From Sec. 1:* argument, conference, consultation, deliberation, negotiation, palaver, parley, ventilation; *Also:*
1. **disquisition**—formal, elaborate and long discussion on a subject
2. **Kaffeeklatsch (German)**—informal discussion, so called because coffee is often served
3. **pourparler (French)**—casual or informal discussion
4. **symposium**—a meeting for discussion (symposia,pl. symposiac,adj.)

3. Discusser,n. *From Sec. 1:* conferee, consultant, deliberator, negotiator (negotiatress or negotiatrix,fem.) or negotiant; *Also:* **1. discussant**—one who engages in a discussion; member of a body devoting itself to discussion

4. Pert. to Discussion: discussional,adj.

5. One Who Presides at a Discussion: symposiarch,n.

6. Group of Discussers: panel, round table, n.

7. Place Where a Group Meets to Discuss: round table,n.

8. Art of Logical Discussion: argumentation, dialectic,n.

9. Subject to Discussion: moot,adj.

10. To Bring (a Point, Topic, etc.) Forward for Discussion: moot,v.

11. Capable of Being Discussed: discussible, adj.

673. REFERENCE

1. To Refer to,v.
  1. **advert to**—refer or allude to (advertence, n.)
  2. **allude to**—refer to by indirection or suggestion (allusion,n. allusive,adj.)
  3. **harp on**—refer to continually and tediously
  4. **mention**—refer to casually or briefly (mention,n.)

2. An Indirect Reference: allusion,n.

3. Derogatory or Insulting Allusion, Usually to a Person: innuendo,n.

4. A Hint by Indirect or Remote Reference: insinuation,n.

674. SAY

1. To Say (Non-Descriptive): deliver oneself of, enounce, express, say, speak, state, utter, vocalize, voice,v. (delivery, expression, statement, utterance, vocalization or vocalism,n.)

2. To Say in Detail: state,v. (statement,n.)

3. Said (Archaic): quoth,v.

4. Descr. of That Which Is Said: expressed, oral, parol, parole, phonic, spoken, stated, uttered, verbal, vocal, vocalized, voiced,adj.

5. Descr. of That Which Is Said in a Certain Way,adj.
  1. **articulate**—said clearly and intelligibly (articulateness,n.)
  2. **distinct**—articulate (distinctness,n.)
  3. **express**—directly and clearly said
  4. **orinasal**—said through the mouth and nose simultaneously (orinasality,n.)

6. Previously Said or Stated: aforementioned, aforesaid,adj.

7. Not to Say What One Wants to Say: refrain,v.

8. To Say or State (Descriptive or Qualified),v.
  1. **add**—say further
  2. **admit**—say, as if reluctantly, and in a way to show acceptance of the truth or validity of another's statement
  3. **affirm**—say with great conviction, because one is sure of the truth of one's statement
  4. **agree**—say in a way that shows one has the same opinion as that of the previous speaker
  5. **allege**—state with assurance but without proof
  6. **announce**—state either publicly or for many listeners
  7. **argue (that . . .)**—maintain
  8. **articulate**—say distinctly
  9. **assert**—state with great positiveness or sureness
  10. **asseverate**—say with great sincerity, sureness, and earnestness
  11. **assure**—say to (someone) with certainty
  12. **aver**—say with great confidence and certainty
  13. **avouch**—affirm; assert
  14. **avow**—say frankly and without concealment
  15. **bawl**—say loudly and as if in pain
  16. **bellow**—say in a voice resembling, or seeming to resemble, the loud and hollow roar of a bull
  17. **blare**—say publicly and loudly; say harshly and loudly

  18. **blat**—say loudly or foolishly
  19. **blubber**—say while crying
  20. **blunder out**—say carelessly or unintentionally
  21. **blurt, blurt out**—say suddenly and recklessly, unintentionally, unwisely, or thoughtlessly
  22. **chant**—say monotonously
  23. **chime**—say in rhythm or singing
  24. **chime in**—add one's statement to what others are saying
  25. **claim**—state as a fact; say strongly
  26. **comment**—make a remark or statement; make an explanatory or critical remark
  27. **complain**—say in protest
  28. **conclude**—make a final statement; say finally
  29. **concur**—make a statement or statements that show one's agreement with what another has said
  30. **confess**—say in a way to show acceptance of one's error, sin, wrongdoing, etc.
  31. **contend (that . . .)**—assert in argument or in answer to expressed or expected opposition
  32. **continue**—go on with what one is saying
  33. **contradict**—say the opposite of
  34. **corroborate**—make a statement that strengthens the truth of another's opinion, testimony, statement, etc.
  35. **counter**—say in opposition
  36. **cry**—say loudly or vehemently
  37. **declaim**—say in a rhetorical style, as if delivering a formal public address; say in public
  38. **declare**—say publicly, or for all to hear; say positively; say openly or strongly; say to be
  39. **deny**—declare to be untrue
  40. **depose, depone**—say under oath
  41. **ejaculate**—say suddenly or as an exclamation, as if the words were thrown out involuntarily
  42. **enounce**—state in public or in formal language
  43. **enunciate**—state definitely or without reservations; declare
  44. **exclaim**—say with surprise or emotion; say suddenly or protestingly
  45. **expound**—state in detail
  46. **gainsay**—contradict
  47. **grant**—say in a way to show one's acceptance of another's statement or opinion
  48. **growl**—say in a low and threatening or angry voice; grumble
  49. **grumble**—say in low or indistinct voice, and in a way to show one's dissatisfaction
  50. **gurgle**—say in liquid tones
  51. **howl**—say in a voice resembling the loud, unhappy cries of dogs, wolves, or other wild beasts
  52. **imply**—state indirectly
  53. **inject**—say by, or as if, throwing (a remark) into a conversation
  54. **insinuate (that . . .)**—say indirectly, subtly, and usually derogatively
  55. **insist (that . . .)**—say in a way to show that one is holding firmly to one's claim, opinion, position, etc.
  56. **interject**—say by throwing (usually an idea, remark, statement, question, etc.) into the midst of a conversation or discussion
  57. **interpolate**—insert (a remark) into a discussion or conversation
  58. **interpose**—insert (an interruption, objection, or opposing remark, statement, or question) into a conversation or discussion
  59. **intonate**—say with a particular tone or expression of voice
  60. **intone**—say in a chanting or singing voice, or in a particular tone
  61. **maintain (that . . .)**—assert as true;

hold to one's previous statements or opinions; state with great conviction
62. **mention (that . . .)**—say incidentally
63. **misstate**—state or say incorrectly
64. **mumble**—say in a very low voice and almost unintelligibly
65. **murmur**—say in a low and somewhat indistinct voice
66. **mutter**—say in a low and fairly indistinct manner, and usually in a way that indicates anger, annoyance, or complaint
67. **object (that . . .)**—say in a way to show one's opposition or disapproval
68. **observe (that . . .)**—say casually
69. **opine (that . . .)**—state as one's thinking or opinion
70. **overstate**—state too strongly
71. **patter**—say quickly, mechanically, and indistinctly
72. **pipe up (that . . .)**—say unexpectedly, or when one is expected to be silent (colloq.)
73. **plead**—say in defense or extenuation of one's actions (legal)
74. **posit**—state as a fact (philosophy)
75. **proclaim**—say publicly; say publicly and officially; say aggressively
76. **profess**—declare openly
77. **pronounce**—say; say to be; declare formally
78. **protest (that . . .)**—say in a way to show one's strong disagreement with another's statement; state solemnly or seriously
79. **quibble**—use statements to avoid the truth or the point under discussion
80. **quip**—make a sharp, biting, or clever remark
81. **rap**—say sharply
82. **rasp**—say with a harsh sound, in a harsh voice, or in such a way as to show one's annoyance or irritation
83. **rattle**—say in an animated manner; say with a noisy clatter
84. **recite**—say as if one's words had been memorized or studied
85. **reel off**—say rapidly and fluently, one after the other
86. **remark (that . . .)**—say casually
87. **remonstrate (that . . .)**—state in a way to show one's opposition or objections; say in protest
88. **repeat**—say again
89. **roar**—say in a very loud, deep, and perhaps confused manner
90. **rumble**—say in a deep, rolling voice
91. **sally**—make a witty or humorous remark
92. **scream**—say in a loud and shrill voice
93. **screech**—scream
94. **shout**—say in a loud voice
95. **shriek**—say in sharp, shrill tones
96. **snap**—say in a hostile, abrupt, irritable, biting, etc., manner
97. **snarl**—say in angry and hostile language or manner
98. **sneer**—say in contempt or scorn
99. **snort**—say while, or as if while, expelling the breath noisily through the nose, and, often, in expression of contempt, anger, etc.
100. **spew**—say as if vomiting out
101. **spout**—say in a loud, affected, insincere, or oratorical manner
102. **squeak**—say in a high-pitched but small voice
103. **squeal**—say in a high-pitched and sharp voice
104. **submit (that . . .)**—say respectfully; say in a way to leave conclusions or judgment to one's listener or listeners; make a statement of perhaps controversial nature in such a way as to ask for agreement from listener or listeners
105. **testify**—say solemnly; say under oath in court

106. **thunder**—say in a loud, deep voice
107. **trumpet**—say in a loud voice so that all can hear
108. **twitter**—say in tremulous tones
109. **understate**—state less strongly than proper
110. **urge (that . . .)**—say with great earnestness
111. **vend**—say publicly
112. **vent**—say from inner compulsion
113. **venture (that . . .)**—dare to say at the risk of criticism, blame, etc.
114. **volunteer**—say without urging, of one's own free will, etc.
115. **vote**—declare by general opinion
116. **vouchsafe**—say in a way to show one's condescension in granting or conceding a point
117. **vow**—say with great seriousness or earnestness
118. **wail**—say in prolonged, mournful tones
119. **warrant (that . . .)**—say in a positive manner or without fear of contradiction (colloq.)
120. **whimper**—say in a nasal tone of complaint or distress, the voice breaking intermittently
121. **whine**—say in begging or complaining tones
122. **whisper**—say very softly, or using only the breath, not the vocal cords
123. **yell**—say loudly and stridently, or in high-pitched tones
124. **yield (that . . .)**—say in a way to show one has finally been convinced by another's reasoning, argument, urging, etc.

9. Statement; A Statement or Statements, n. *From Sec. 8:* admission, affirmation, agreement, allegation, announcement, argument, articulation, assertion, asseveration, assurance, averment, avouchment, avowal, blat, blurt, chant, claim, comment, complaint, conclusion, concurrence, confession, contention, continuation, contradiction, corroboration, cry, declamation, declaration, denial, deposition, ejaculation, exclamation, grumble, implication, injection, insinuation, insistence, interjection, interpolation, interposition, intonation, mention, misstatement, mumble, murmur, mutter, objection, observation, opinion, overstatement, patter, plea, proclamation, profession, pronouncement, protest or protestation, quibble, quip, recitation, remark, remonstrance or remonstration, repetition, sally, scream, screech, shout, shriek, sneer, testimony (from *testify*), understatement, vow, whisper, yell; *Also:*
1. **account**—statement of reasons, causes, etc.
2. **aside**—something said by an actor supposedly not to be heard by the other actors in a play
3. **banality**—statement utterly lacking in originality
4. **barb**—sharp, prickly, or sarcastic statement or remark
5. **bromide**—statement that is flat, dull, commonplace, and totally without freshness
6. **circumlocution, circumbendibus, circumvolution**—statement in an indirect or roundabout manner
7. **cliché**—hackneyed, trite, stereotyped, or timeworn statement
8. **commonplace**—ordinary, trite remark
9. **dictum**—authoritative statement (dicta, pl.)
10. **flummery**—remarks that are grandiose in form but insincere or baseless
11. **inanity**—senseless, stupid, unimaginative statement or remark
12. **jeer**—mocking or sarcastic statement; statement made to ridicule
13. **manifesto**—public declaration of prin-

ciples or policy by a group, government, etc.

14. **mot**—clever or witty remark
15. **Parthian shot**—sharp remark on leaving —after the Parthians, who shot arrows at the enemy after turning their horses around as if to retreat
16. **personalities**—depreciating or offensive remarks about an individual
17. **plank**—statement of the platform of a political party
18. **platitude**—obvious, flat, insipid, or unimaginative remark; dull truism
19. **premise, premiss**—statement leading to a conclusion or to be proved (logic)
20. **pronunciamento**—formal declaration
21. **prospectus**—written or printed statement explaining or describing a new venture
22. **quirk**—clever remark; quip
23. **rigmarole**—series or succession of nonsensical statements
24. **rumor**—statement that has not been proved and may or may not be true
25. **shot**—remark intended to have a sharp effect
26. **theorem**—statement to be proved or that can be proved; such a statement in mathematics
27. **thesis**—statement that is advanced and is subject to discussion or debate, and will be defended against objections
28. **truism**—statement so obviously true that it is banal or trifling to mention it
29. **utterance**—statement; that which is said
30. **vacuity**—inane or foolish statement
31. **weasel words**—statement purposely so worded as to be ambiguous
32. **window dressing**—statements that give a falsely favorable impression, with no sincerity behind them

10. Descr. of, or Pert. to, **Saying, Stating, or Statement**,adj. *From Sec. 8:* admissive, affirmative, assertory, asseverative or asseveratory, contradictory or contradictive, corroborative or corroboratory, declamatory, declarative or declaratory, ejaculatory, enunciatory, exclamatory or exclamative, implicational, insinuative or insinuatory, murmurous, proclamatory, recitative, remonstrant, repetitive, snappish or snappy, whisperous or whispery; *From Sec. 9:* barbed, bromidic, circumlocutory, inane, platitudinous, rigmarole, rumorous, vacuous, weaselworded

11. Disposed to Make Statements with Great Positiveness or Assurance: assertive, dogmatic, positive,adj. (assertiveness, dogmatism, positiveness,n.)

12. Offensively Self-Assertive: aggressive, bumptious,adj. (aggressiveness, bumptiousness,n.)

13. To Say Again; To Repeat,v.
1. **alliterate**—repeat the same sound or sounds in successive words
2. **chant**—repeat monotonously
3. **din into**—impress in the mind with frequent repetitions
4. **echo**—repeat the words or ideas of (another person); repeat a sound
5. **ingeminate**—say again; repeat
6. **iterate**—say again
7. **parrot**—repeat without understanding, like a parrot
8. **practice, practise**—repeat many times in order to become proficient or perfect
9. **quote**—repeat (someone's words) exactly as he said or wrote them
10. **recapitulate**—state again briefly or in summary; restate the main points of
11. **recite**—repeat; repeat from memory, usually to an audience
12. **redouble**—repeat; re-echo
13. **re-echo**—repeat, like an echo; echo back

14. **rehearse**—repeat; by repeating, practice for a later performance
15. **reiterate**—repeat; say again and again
16. **report**—repeat (what one has heard or what has been told to one)
17. **restate**—state again; state (the same idea) in different language
18. **tautologize**—make needless repetition in words or of an idea

14. Repetition,n. *From Sec. 13:* alliteration, chant, echo, ingemination; iteration, iterance, or iterancy; practice, quotation or, colloq., quote, recapitulation, recitation, re-echo, rehearsal, reiteration, report, restatement, tautology or tautologism; *Also:*
1. **nimiety**—unnecessary repetition
2. **rote**—repetition without understanding

15. Repetitive,adj. *From Sec. 13:* chanting, echoing, etc.; alliterative, echoic, iterant or iterative, recapitulatory, reiterative, tautological

16. Repeater,n. *From Sec. 13:* chanter, echoer, etc.; echo, parrot, tautologist

17. Full, or Tiresomely Full, of Repetition or Repetitions: repetitious, repetitive,adj. (repetitiousness, repetitiveness,n.)

18. Morbid Psychological Condition in Which Someone Repeats, Like an Echo, What Others Say: echolalia,n. (echolalic, adj.)

19. Immediate Repetition of a Word for Purposes of Emphasis: palilogy, paliloguia, palilogia,n. (palilogetic,adj.)

20. To Quote, Passage by Passage; To Quote as Proof or Authority: cite,v. (citation,n.)

21. To Quote Incorrectly: misquote,v. (misquotation,n.)

22. Brief Literary Quotation; Brief Quoted Passage: snippet,n.

23. Quotations That Are not Logically Connected: disjecta membra,n. (Latin)

24. To Close or End a Quotation: unquote,v.

25. Repeated Series: litany,n.

26. Repeated Phrase, Line, Sound, etc.,n.
1. **refrain**—phrase, line, or verse regularly repeated in a poem or song
2. **repetend**—repeated tone, sound, phrase, verse, etc.
3. **reprise**—musical phrase, etc., that is repeated

27. Repetition of a Song, Performance, etc., in Response to Audience Demand: encore,n.

28. Direction, in Music, to Repeat a Phrase, etc.: bis,adv.

29. Again: afresh, anew,adv.

675. ADMISSION

1. To Admit,v.
1. **accept**—admit and agree to
2. **acknowledge**—admit as a fact; admit ownership of; admit authorship of; admit as belonging to one; admit the claims of; admit the authority of; admit receiving; admit as true or genuine; confess
3. **agree (that . . .)**—admit (that . . .)
4. **allow**—admit; admit as a fact
5. **assent (to)**—admit that something is true
6. **avouch**—acknowledge
7. **concede**—admit the truth of (another's claims or statements)
8. **confess**—admit one's guilt; admit having done, etc. (that which is wrong, illegal, sinful, in error, etc.)
9. **disbosom oneself of**—confess (that which has been on one's conscience)

10. **grant**—admit; admit for the sake of argument
11. **own**—admit (something) about oneself
12. **profess**—admit openly
13. **write off**—admit as lost

2. Admission,n. *From Sec. 1:* acceptance, acknowledgment, allowance, assent, concession, confession, grant, profession; *Also:*
  1. **peccavis (pl.)**—confession of guilt or of having sinned
  2. **testimony**—open profession of one's faith or belief

3. Admissive; Admissory,adj. *From Sec. 1:* acceptant, concessive, confessional or confessory, professive

4. Implying an Admission: admissive,adj.

5. One Who Confesses: confessant, confesser, confessor,n.

6. One Who Confesses to a Priest: confessant,n.

676. A SAYING

1. A Saying,n.
  1. **adage**—saying that has persevered for a long time and is generally believed
  2. **aphorism**—short saying, full of meaning, that states a generally accepted truth
  3. **apothegm**—short, pointed saying of instructive content
  4. **axiom**—maxim that is generally accepted
  5. **byword**—proverb
  6. **device**—maxim
  7. **dictum**—saying that is current at a certain time
  8. **epigram**—clever or witty saying
  9. **epigraph**—suitable motto at the beginning of a chapter, book, etc.
  10. **gnome**—short, pithy saying containing a universal truth
  11. **maxim**—saying that expresses a general truth or principle of behavior
  12. **moral**—maxim
  13. **moralism**—maxim containing an ethical truth, or a truth about the right way to live or act
  14. **mot**—clever or witty saying
  15. **motto**—appropriate saying inscribed on something; maxim; maxim used as one's guiding principle
  16. **posy**—saying; maxim; sentiment
  17. **precept**—saying intended as a rule of behavior
  18. **proverb**—short and meaningful saying that is popularly used
  19. **quip**—witty saying
  20. **quirk**—witty saying
  21. **saw**—saying; maxim; proverb
  22. **sentiment**—saying, maxim, or toast full of feeling
  23. **shibboleth**—favorite saying of a group, sect, political party, etc.
  24. **slogan**—saying used as a motto, or in advertising; distinctive saying of a group, class, etc.
  25. **toast**—saying when drinking liquor
  26. **war cry**—slogan
  27. **watchword**—motto; slogan
  28. **wheeze**—trite saying

2. Sayings; Sayings Collectively,n. *From Sec. 1:* dicta, gnomology; *Also:* 1. **facetiae**—humorous sayings

3. Descr. of, Pert. to, or Containing, Sayings,adj. *From Sec. 1:* aphoristic, aphorismic, or aphorismatic; apothegmatic, axiomatic, epigrammatic, gnomic or gnomical, preceptive, proverbial; *Also:* 1. **sententious**—full of sayings, maxims, etc. (sometimes derogatory); of the nature of maxims (sententiousness,n.)

4. Given to Using, Speaking in, or Writing Sayings,adj. *From Sec. 1:* aphoristic; *From Sec. 3:* sententious (sententiousness,n.)

5. To Speak in or Write Sayings,v. *From Sec. 1:* aphorize, epigrammatize, moralize

6. One Who Speaks in, or Writes, Sayings,n. *From Sec. 1:* aphorist or aphorizer, epigrammatist or epigrammatizer, gnomist, moralist or moralizer, sloganeer

7. The Use of Clever or Witty Sayings: epigrammatism,n.

677. HANDWRITING

1. Handwriting,n.
  1. **autograph**—one's own handwriting
  2. **cacography**—incorrect or bad handwriting
  3. **calligraphy**—handwriting; beautiful or decorative handwriting
  4. **chirography**—handwriting
  5. **hand**—style of handwriting
  6. **griffonage**—careless or illegible handwriting
  7. **hieroglyphics**—illegible or indecipherable handwriting—so called in allusion to the ancient Egyptian, and once indecipherable, system of writing
  8. **longhand**—handwriting of the usual kind, as against printing, script, etc.
  9. **macrography**—handwriting of great or inordinate size—often considered a symptom of a personality disorder
  10. **manuscription**—writing done by hand
  11. **micrography**—very small handwriting
  12. **penmanship**—style of writing by hand
  13. **printing**—writing by hand, but in block capital letters similar to those found in printed material
  14. **scrabble**—scrawl
  15. **scrawl**—careless or almost illegible handwriting; hasty and careless handwriting
  16. **scribble**—hasty and somewhat illegible handwriting
  17. **script**—form of handwriting similar to lower-case printing
  18. **Spencerian**—form of handwriting once in vogue
  19. **text hand**—large handwriting

2. Descr. of, or Pert. to, Handwriting,adj. *From Sec. 1:* autographic, cacographic, calligraphic, chirographic, hieroglyphic or hieroglyphical, longhand, macrographic, micrographic, scrabbly, scrawly, scribbly, Spencerian; *Also:*
  1. **cramped**—hard to read; small and difficult to make out
  2. **cursive**—flowing; running together
  3. **illegible**—so badly written as to defy reading or deciphering (illegibility,n.)
  4. **indecipherable**—illegible (indecipherability,n.)
  5. **legible**—easy to read or make out (legibility,n.)
  6. **sprawling, sprawly**—spreading unaesthetically across the page (sprawl,v.)

3. To Write by Hand,v. *From Sec. 1:* autograph, scrabble, scrawl, scribble; *Also:* 1. **engross**—write in large or formalized hand, as a document, statute, etc. (engrossment,n.)

4. One Who Writes by Hand,n. *From Sec. 1:* autographer, cacographer, calligrapher or calligraphist, chirographer, macrographer, micrographer, penman, scrawler, scribbler; *From Sec. 3:* engrosser

5. Art of Handwriting,n.
  1. **chirography**—art of writing by hand (chirographer,n. chirographic,adj.)
  2. **micrography**—art of very small handwriting (micrographer,n. micrographic, adj.)
  3. **penmanship**—art of writing by hand (penman,n.)

6. Process of Writing in Very Small Letters: micrography,n.

7. Rapid Writing by Hand: tachygraphy,n. (tachygrapher,n. tachygraphic,adj.)

8. Imitation of Another's Handwriting: forgery, isography,n. (forger, isographer,n. isographic,adj.)

9. Method of Taking Down a Speech in Longhand: logography,n. (logographer,n. logographic,adj.)

10. Curved Shape of a Letter in Handwriting: curl,n.

11. A Fancy Twist, Curl, Spiral, or Other Decoration in Handwriting: curlicue, flourish, quirk,n.

12. Science of the Analysis of Handwriting to Determine Genuineness of Documents, etc.: bibliotics,n. (bibliotist,n. bibliotic,adj.)

13. Study of Handwriting; Analysis of a Person's Character from His Handwriting: graphology,n. (graphologist,n. graphological, adj.)

14. Certain Writing Instruments,n.
1. **cymograph**—instrument that makes tracings of contours, outlines, etc.
2. **micrograph**—instrument for executing extremely tiny writing
3. **polygraph**—instrument for making duplicate copies of writing
4. **psychograph**—instrument for recording communications from the spirit world
5. **stationery**—any materials for writing, as paper, pens, pencil, ink, etc.
6. **stylograph**—fountain pen
7. **stylus**—writing instrument, usually leaving impressions in wax, stencils, etc., but containing no ink, lead, etc.

15. One Who Sells Writing Materials: stationer,n.

16. Table or Desk for Writing: escritoire,n.

17. Place Where the Scribes or Copyists of a Monastery Do Their Writing: scriptorium,n.

678. A LETTER

1. A Letter; A Written Communication,n.
1. **billet-doux**—love letter
2. **communication**—letter
3. **encyclical**—letter from the Pope to Catholic bishops throughout the world
4. **epistle**—communication (epistolary, epistolatory,adj.)
5. **message**—written communication delivered by a third person
6. **missive**—letter
7. **post card, postal card**—written communication on a card suitable for mailing

2. Letters Written, Received, etc.: correspondence, mail,n.

3. To Write Letters: correspond,v. (correspondence,n.)

4. To Write a Letter or Letters to: correspond with, epistolize,v. (correspondence, epistolization,n.)

5. The Writing of Letters: correspondence, epistolography,n.

6. The Practice or Habit of Writing Letters: epistolography,n.

7. In the Habit of, or Occupied in, Writing Letters: epistolarian,adj.

8. Letter Writer: correspondent, epistler, epistolarian, epistoler, epistolist, epistolizer, epistolographer, epistolographist,n.

9. Contained in Letters: epistolary, epistolatory,adj.

10. Carried On by the Writing of Letters: epistolary, epistolatory,adj.

11. Art of Letter Writing: epistolography,n. (epistolographer, epistolographist,n.)

12. To Be Held at the Post Office Until Called For: general delivery, poste restante, adj.

13. Stamp Collecting: philately,n. (philatelist, n. philatelic,adj.)

14. Study of Postage Stamps: philately, timbrology,n. (philatelist, timbrologist,n. philatelic,adj.)

679. WRITTEN SYMBOL

1. Letter; Written Symbol,n.
1. **ampersand**—name of the character &
2. **capital, capital letter**—large letter of the kind used as the first letter of a sentence or proper name (capital,adj.)
3. **character**—letter; written symbol
4. **consonant**—letter of the alphabet other than one of the vowels (consonant, consonantal,adj.)
5. **cryptogram, cryptograph**—secret written symbol or character (cryptogrammic, cryptographic,adj.)
6. **cursive**—letter in flowing handwriting (cursive,adj.)
7. **hieroglyphic, hieroglyph**—symbol of the ancient Egyptian writing system; written symbol with a hidden meaning (hieroglyphic, hieroglyphical,adj.)
8. **ideogram, ideograph, ideographic**—pictorial or written symbol that represents an idea rather than a sound or word (ideogrammic, ideographic, ideographical, adj.)
9. **initial**—first letter of a word, name, etc.
10. **italic**—letter printed on a slant, usually for purposes of emphasis (italic,adj.)
11. **izzard**—the letter Z (dialectal)
12. **logogram, logograph**—written symbol that stands for a word (logogrammatic, adj.)
13. **lower-case letter**—small letter of the alphabet (lower-case,adj.)
14. **majuscule**—large or capital letter (majuscule, majuscular,adj.)
15. **minuscule**—small or lower-case letter (minuscular,adj.)
16. **phonogram**—symbol that represents a single speech sound, word, or syllable (phonogrammic, phonogramic,adj.)
17. **pictogram, pictogram**—pictorial symbol that represents an idea rather than a speech sound (pictographic,adj.)
18. **pothook**—written character resembling a pothook, esp. in shorthand
19. **rune**—alphabet character of ancient Teutonic writing (runic,adj.)
20. **upper-case letter**—capital (upper-case, adj.)
21. **vowel**—one of the five letters, A, E, I, O, U, and, according to its use, Y, of the English language (vocalic,adj.)
22. **zed**—name in British English for the letter Z

2. To Print in Certain Letters,v. *From Sec. 1:* italicize, lower-case, upper-case

3. Representation by Symbols,n. *From Sec. 1:* ideography, pictography; *Also:* 1. notation —representation by symbols

4. Letters; System of Letters or Symbols,n.
1. **alphabet**—letters of a language in their correct order; system of letters or other symbols for representing ideas or sounds
2. **cipher**—system of substitute letters for secret writing
3. **code**—system, often secret, of symbols used to represent words
4. **cryptography**—secret written symbols or letters, collectively
5. **cuneiform**—wedge-shaped letters of the ancient inscriptions of Assyria, Persia, etc. (cuneiform,adj.)
6. **vocalism**—vowel system of a language

5. Pert. to Letters or Written Symbols: literal,adj.

6. Art of Writing in, or of Deciphering or Translating, Cuneiform: sphenography,n. (sphenographer, sphenographist,n. sphenographic,adj.)

7. A Cuneiform Character: sphenogram,n.

8. The Use of a Letter as a Vowel; Transformation into a Vowel: vocalization,n. (vocalize,v.)

9. To Put in Alphabet Order: alphabetize,v. (alphabetization,n. alphabetizer,n.)

10. Alphabetic: abecedarian,adj.

11. Expressed by an Alphabet: alphabetic, alphabetical,adj.

12. To Express by an Alphabet: alphabetize,v. (alphabetization,n.)

13. Descr. of, Pert. to, or Designating the Slavic Alphabet of Russian, Bulgarian, and Similar Languages: Cyrillic,adj.

14. Descr. of, Pert. to, or Designating, the Alphabet Used in English, French, Spanish, and Similar Languages: Roman,adj.

15. Stone, Discovered in 1790, That Gave the Clues That Helped in the Deciphering of Egyptian Hieroglyphics: Rosetta stone,n.

16. Consisting of Letters,adj.
  1. biliteral—consisting of two letters
  2. monoliteral—consisting of one letter
  3. quadriliteral—consisting of four letters
  4. triliteral—consisting of three letters

17. Transposition of Letters in a Word: metathesis,n. (metathesize,v.)

18. A Change into the Letters or Characters of a Different Kind of Alphabet, or That of Another Language: transliteration,n. (transliterative,adj. transliterate,v.)

19. Written in Capital Letters: uncial,adj.

20. One of the Fine Lines, or Fine Cross Strokes at the Top or Bottom, of a Letter in Printing: serif,n.

680. PUNCTUATION MARK

1. Punctuation or Similar Mark,n.
  1. accent, accent mark—mark (′) used to indicate stress in pronunciation
  2. apostrophe—mark (') used to denote a missing letter, show possession, etc. (apostrophic,adj.)
  3. asterisk—star-shaped symbol (*) that refers the reader to a footnote
  4. braces—punctuation sign ({ }) for enclosing parenthetical matter
  5. bracket—punctuation sign ([ ]) used to enclose words, figures, etc.
  6. breve—mark (‿) used to indicate a short syllable
  7. caret—symbol (∧) used to indicate the place in a manuscript where material is to be inserted
  8. cedilla—the symbol (و) under the letter C to denote the sound of S
  9. colon—two dots (:)
  10. comma—the mark (,)
  11. dagger—obelisk (†)
  12. dash—the mark (—)
  13. diacritical mark—any symbol influencing a single letter, as an accent mark, cedilla, etc.
  14. diaeresis, dieresis—mark (··) placed over the second of two vowels to show separate pronunciation, as in coöperate
  15. ditto, ditto mark—device (") used in writing to indicate the exact repetition of the line above
  16. exclamation point or mark—symbol (!) used in place of a period at the end of a sentence to give emphasis

  17. hyphen—dash (-)
  18. interrogation mark or point—question mark (?)
  19. macron—dash placed over vowels to show long quality
  20. obelisk—symbol (†) in the form of a dagger to show reference to a footnote (obeliscal,adj.)
  21. parenthesis—one of the two curved marks ( ) used to enclose parenthetical matter (parenthetic, parenthetical,adj.)
  22. period—point used at the end of a sentence (.)
  23. question mark—punctuation mark (?) at the end of, or to indicate, a question
  24. semicolon—the mark (;)
  25. suspension periods or points—three or, at the end of a sentence, four dots to indicate an interruption, material left out, etc.
  26. tittle—any small mark over a letter, as the dot over a small *j*
  27. umlaut—symbol (··) placed over a vowel in German to indicate partial assimilation to a following sound
  28. virgule—short slanting line (/) between two words, indicating that either may be used or understood

2. To Use a Punctuation Mark on,v. *From Sec. 1:* accent, apostrophize, asterisk, bracket, hyphenate, parenthesize, umlaut

3. Directions or Footnotes to the Reader,n.
  1. *ibid*—footnote referring the reader to the same source as the previous footnote or footnotes—abbreviation for the Latin word *ibidem* (in the same place)
  2. *cf.*—abbreviation directing the reader to compare other material—from the Latin *confer*
  3. *N.B.*, *n.b.*—calling the reader's attention to something important—abbreviation for the Latin phrase *nota bene* (note well)
  4. *q.v.*—abbreviation referring the reader to a previous statement, or to a previous use of a word—from the Latin *quod vide* (which see)
  5. *sic*—word placed in parentheses following a misspelling, misuse, incorrect grammatical form, or other error in quoted material to explain that this is the exact form of the original, that the error so appeared in the original, and that the present quoter is aware of the incorrectness—from Latin *sic* (thus or so)
  6. *v.*—direction calling a reader's attention to some point of reference—abbreviation of the Latin *vide* (see)

681. SPELLING

1. Spelling,n.
  1. heterography—spelling that deviates from accepted usage; the kind of spelling system, of which English is an example, in which the same letter can represent a diversity of sounds (heterographic,adj.)
  2. orthography—spelling; correct spelling (orthographic,adj.)
  3. phonetics—system or kind of spelling in which each symbol always represents the same speech sound, or in which words are spelled exactly the way they are pronounced (phonetic,adj.)
  4. phonography—representation, as by spelling, of words as they are pronounced (phonographic,adj.)

2. Art of Writing with Correct Spelling: orthography,n.

3. Incorrect Spelling: misspelling, pseudography,n.

4. To Spell Incorrectly: misspell,v.

682. WRITING

1. To Write,v.
1. **collaborate (on)**—write, together with another or with others (a story, book, or other effort)
2. **compose**—make up and write
3. **correspond (with)**—write letters (to)
4. **describe**—write about the appearance of
5. **draft**—put into written form
6. **endorse, indorse**—write on the back of (a document, etc.)
7. **enroll**—write down (someone's name) in a list, record, register, etc.
8. **expatiate (on, upon)**—write fully and at length (about)
9. **frame**—compose
10. **indite**—put into writing; compose
11. **inscribe**—write; write on the surface of, in such a way that the writing will endure or be conspicuous; enroll
12. **jot down**—write down in very brief form, and usually quickly
13. **moralize (on, upon, about)**—write in judgment of the right or wrong (of)
14. **note**—put down in writing
15. **record**—put down in writing
16. **redact**—put into writing
17. **register**—enroll
18. **subscribe**—write (one's name) under; write underneath or at the end of
19. **superscribe**—write above, on, on the top of, or on the outside surface of
20. **transcribe**—write in another form (some material or communication, as stenographic notes into English, etc.)

2. Writing; Act or Process of Writing,n. *From Sec. 1:* collaboration, composition, correspondence, description, endorsement, indorsement, enrollment, expatiation, inscription, moralization, redaction, subscription, superscription, transcription; *Also:*
1. **graphorrhea**—ceaseless and incoherent writing as a symptom of abnormal excitation
2. **pseudography**—incorrect writing or printing of words
3. **tachygraphy**—rapid writing

3. Writing or Writings, i.e., That Which Is Written,n. *From Sec. 1:* collaboration, composition, correspondence, description, draft, endorsement, indorsement, inscription, jotting, moralization, note, record, subscript or subscription, superscript or superscription, transcript or transcription; *Also:*
1. **adscript**—something written later or after
2. **amphigory, amphigouri**—nonsense writing
3. **autograph**—something written in one's own handwriting, often an author's signature
4. **circumscription**—inscription around the border of a coin or medal
5. **dedication**—inscription in a book or other literary work in the form of a complimentary statement, usually by the author to someone admired
6. **envoy; envoi (French)**—postscript to a poem or other literary work, often serving as a dedication
7. **epigraph**—permanent inscription on a monument, building, etc.
8. **epigraphy**—epigraphs collectively
9. **epitaph**—inscription on a tomb or gravestone
10. **legend**—inscription on a coin, medal, badge, picture, etc.
11. **manuscript**—literary composition executed in longhand or by typewriter
12. **marginalia**—marginal notes
13. **paleography**—ancient writings collectively
14. **postscript**—something written after;

added thought written after the main body of a letter
15. **pseudograph**—piece of spurious writing
16. **pseudographia**—writing that is false or consists of meaningless marks
17. **psychogram**—written message allegedly sent by a spirit
18. **psychography**—automatic writing used in spiritualism
19. **sketch**—rough draft

4. Written,adj. *From Sec. 1:* subscript, superscript; *From Sec. 3:* adscript, postscript; *Also:*
1. **scriptural**—written

5. Writer,n. *From Sec. 1:* collaborator, composer, correspondent, drafter, endorser or endorsor, indorser or indorsor, expatiator, framer, inditer, inscriber, moralizer or moralist, recorder, redactor, registrar, subscriber, transcriber; *From Sec. 2:* tachygrapher; *From Sec. 3:* autographer, epitapher or epitaphist; *Also:*
1. **amanuensis**—someone who writes what another dictates; someone who copies, for purposes of record, what someone else has written; clerk
2. **clerk**—one whose job it is to keep records, take care of correspondence, etc., as in an office, organization, etc.
3. **copyist**—transcriber
4. **scribe**—clerk
5. **scrivener**—amanuensis; clerk
6. **secretary**—clerk

6. Descr. of, or Pert. to, Writing, Writings, or Writers,adj. *From Sec. 1:* collaborative, compositional, descriptive, expatiatory, inscriptional or inscriptive, moralistic, redactional or redactorial, subscriptive; transcriptional, transcriptural, or transcriptive; *From Sec. 2:* tachygraphic; *From Sec. 3:* autographic; dedicatory, dedicatorial, or dedicative; epigraphic, epitaphic, paleographic; *From Sec. 5:* clerical, secretarial; *Also:* 1. **scriptural**—descr. of, or pert. to, writing

7. Ancient Fashion of Writing: paleography, n. (paleographic,adj.)

8. Habit of Writing in Judgment of the Right or Wrong of Things: moralism,n. (moralist,n.)

9. To Put Writing in a Form Suitable for Publication: edit, redact,v. (redaction,n. editor, redactor,n. editorial, redactorial, redactional,adj.)

10. To Wander from the Subject in Writing: divagate,v. (divagation,n.)

11. To Write or Print Incorrectly: pseudographize,v.

12. Selected Writing Systems,n.
1. **hieroglyphics**—picture-writing system of the ancient Egyptians (hieroglyphic,adj.)
2. **ideography**—system in which written or pictorial symbols stand for ideas (ideographic,adj.)
3. **lexigraphy**—system of writing in which each symbol stands for a complete word, as in Chinese (lexigraphic,adj.)
4. **phonography**—writing according to sound of words or syllables (phonographer, phonographist,n. phonographic, adj.)
5. **shorthand**—phonography; stenography
6. **stenography**—system of using abbreviations or symbols in place of words as a form of writing rapidly (stenographer,n. stenographic,adj.)
7. **stenotypy**—a kind of stenography using ordinary letters rather than special symbols (stenotypist,n. stenotypic,adj.)
8. **tachygraphy**—stenography (tachygrapher,n. tachygraphic,adj.)

13. Something Written in a Special System, n. *From Sec. 12:* stenograph, tachygraph

14. Science, Art, or Study of Writing or Writings,n.
1. **diplomatics**—branch of paleography dealing with ancient documents
2. **diplomatology**—science of ancient documents
3. **epigraphy**—science or study of inscriptions; science or study of ancient inscriptions, or art of deciphering these (epigrapher, epigraphist,n. epigraphic, adj.)
4. **hierology**—science of ancient Egyptian writings or inscriptions (hierologist,n. hierologic, hierological,adj.)
5. **paleography**—study of ancient writing, writings, or modes of writing; science or art of deciphering ancient writings (paleographer, paleographist, paleograph,n. paleographic,adj.)
6. **symboleography**—art of writing or drawing up legal documents

15. Writing, Description, or Treatise on Certain Specific Subjects,n.
1. **dietary**—on diets
2. **glyptography**—on engraved gems
3. **hagiography**—on the lives of saints
4. **heliography**—on the sun
5. **heresiography**—on heresy
6. **hierography**—on religion, or on sacred subjects
7. **hierology**—on ancient Egyptian writings or inscriptions
8. **histography**—on organic tissue
9. **hydrography**—on bodies of water
10. **hyetography**—on the geographic distribution of rainfall
11. **hymnography**—on hymns
12. **ichthyography**—on fish
13. **nosography**—on diseases
14. **odontography**—on the structure of teeth
15. **paleontography**—on fossils
16. **phycography**—on seaweeds
17. **physiography**—on natural phenomena
18. **pneumography**—on the lungs
19. **poetics**—on poetry
20. **pterography**—on feathers
21. **seismography**—on earthquakes
22. **silva, sylva**—on the trees of an area
23. **sitology**—on eating, foods, diet, etc.
24. **stratography**—on matters pertaining to an army
25. **uranography**—on the heavens

16. A Piece of Writing; Literary Writing or Writings,n.
1. **allonym**—work by someone writing under the name of another (allonymous,adj.)
2. **anonym**—work by an unknown author (anonymous,adj.)
3. **article**—piece of writing on a specific topic appearing in a magazine, newspaper, etc.
4. **autobiography**—self-written story of one's life (autobiographic, autobiographical,adj.)
5. **autonym**—work published under one's true name
6. **biography**—written account of a person's life (biographic, biographical,adj.)
7. **causerie**—short, familiar-style article on a subject
8. **composition**—essay written as a school assignment; piece of writing on a subject
9. **disquisition**—dissertation; formal treatise
10. **dissertation**—extended treatment of a subject in writing
11. **epic**—literary composition dealing with heroes, heroic exploits or achievements, etc. (epic, epical,adj.)
12. **erotica**—literary writings on or about sexual love
13. **esoterica**—literary writings of a rare or obscure kind
14. **essay**—literary piece that treats of a sub-

ject—shorter and less elaborate than a treatise
15. **exposition**—explanatory piece of writing (expository,adj.)
16. **foreword**—preface
17. **homily**—piece of writing with a moral point or exhortation (homiletic,adj.)
18. **juvenilia**—youthful or immature literary work or works
19. **lucubration**—literary or learned piece of writing that shows hard work; labored or artificially awkward piece of writing
20. **manuscript**—handwritten or typed piece of writing
21. **monograph**—treatise on one particular subject (monographic,adj.)
22. **monologue**—piece of writing indicative of one person speaking (monologic,adj.)
23. **narrative**—piece of writing that tells a story (narrative,adj.)
24. **pornography**—obscene, lewd, lecherous, etc., writing or piece of writing; books, stories, plays, drawings, pictures, etc., that depict lewd or lascivious scenes (pornographic,adj.)
25. **potboiler**—piece of writing, art, etc., produced quickly for no reason other than the need for the money that will be paid for it
26. **preface**—introductory piece of writing in a book, etc., which explains the purpose, scope, etc., of the material (prefatory, adj.)
27. **prolusion**—an introductory essay (prolusory,adj.)
28. **review**—piece of writing that gives one's opinion of a book, play, etc.
29. **rhyparography**—literary writing that describes mean or sordid scenes, characters, subjects, etc. (rhyparographic,adj.)
30. **script**—piece of writing
31. **scripture**—any piece of sacred writing (scriptural,adj.)
32. **sketch**—light essay on a subject
33. **story**—true or fictitious account of happenings
34. **theme**—piece of expository writing; composition; essay
35. **thesis**—piece of writing that shows the conclusions of original research, often presented to fulfill the requirements of a higher degree in a college or for a diploma; composition; essay
36. **tract, tractate**—treatise
37. **treatise**—methodical and extended piece of writing on a subject
38. **typescript**—manuscript in typed form
39. **vignette**—literary sketch
40. **vita**—brief sketch of one's life
41. **work**—piece of writing, usually somewhat ambitious in scope

17. To Write a Piece, etc.,v. *From Sec. 16:* compose, dissertate, narrate, review

18. Writer of a Piece, etc.,n. *From Sec. 16:* autobiographer, biographer, dissertator, essayist, homilist, pornographer or pornographist, reviewer, rhyparographer or rhyparographist, storyteller, tractator

19. Collection of Writings,n.
1. **analects, analecta**—collection or anthology of various literary passages
2. **anecdotage**—collection of anecdotes
3. **anthology**—collection of writings or poems of different authors, sometimes on a single subject, often with some unifying theme (anthologist,n. anthological,adj. anthologize,v.)
4. **collectanea**—collected writings
5. **corpus**—all the writings on a subject; general collection of writings
6. **facetiae**—collection of humorous writings
7. **legendry, legendary**—collection of legends

8. miscellany, miscellanea—collection of different writings or types of writing

9. mythology—collection of myths

10. omnibus—collection of all the writings of an author, or of all the works on a particular subject

11. pasticcio (Italian)—very varied collection of literary efforts or things

12. pseudepigrapha (pl.)—collection of false writings claimed spuriously to have come from Biblical characters

20. Passage of Writing,n.

1. **chrestomathy**—selection of literary passages used in learning a foreign language
2. **excerpt**—extract
3. **extract**—passage taken from written material
4. **text**—short passage from the Bible

21. Desire to Write,n.

1. **cacoëthes scribendi (Latin)**—itch to write; creative urge for literary composition
2. **graphomania**—morbid or pathological desire to write

22. Able to Write and Read: literate,adj. (literacy,n.)

23. Unable to Write and Read, Owing to Lack of Education: illiterate, unlettered,adj. (illiteracy,n. illiterate,n.)

24. Loss of Ability to Write Caused by a Nervous Disorder: agraphia,n.

683. SECRET WRITING

1. System of Secret Writing in Which Certain Symbols Are Uniformly Substituted for the Letters of Words: cipher, cryptography, steganography,n. (cryptographic, cryptographical, or cryptographal; steganographical,adj.)

2. System of Secret Words: code,n.

3. Secret Characters or Symbols: cryptography, steganography,n.

4. Something Written in Secret Symbols: cryptogram, cryptograph, steganogram,n. (cryptogrammic, cryptogrammatic, cryptogrammatical,adj.)

5. To Express, Translate, or Put into Secret Writing, Symbols, etc.: cipher, code,v.

6. Act or Art of Writing in Secret Symbols: cryptography, steganography,n. (cryptographer or cryptographist, steganographist,n. cryptographic, cryptographical, or cryptographal, steganographical,adj.)

7. To Translate the Secret Symbols or Words of into Understandable English: decipher, decode,v.

8. The Translation of Something Written in Secret Symbols: cryptanalysis, decipherment,n.

9. Translator of Secret Symbols: cryptanalyst, cryptogrammatist, decipherer,n.

10. A Translation of Secret Symbols: decipher,n.

684. MANUSCRIPT

1. Manuscript,n.

1. **autograph**—manuscript written by oneself (autographic,adj.)
2. **holograph**—manuscript in the author's own writing; original typescript, with the author's corrections and additions, of a book (holographic, holographical, holograph,adj.)
3. **opisthograph**—manuscript written on both sides of the paper (opisthographic, opisthographical,adj.)

4. **paleograph**—ancient manuscript (paleographic,adj.)
5. **palimpsest**—manuscript that has been written on two or more times, the previous writings having been erased
6. **parchment**—manuscript; manuscript written on the prepared skin of a goat, sheep, etc.
7. **script**—manuscript
8. **tachygraph**—manuscript in shorthand (tachygraphic,adj.)
9. **typescript**—manuscript written on a typewriter
10. **vellum**—manuscript written on a very fine paper or on specially prepared animal skin, usually that of a lamb, kid, or calf (vellum,adj.)

2. The Writing of Manuscripts Using Both Sides of the Paper: opisthography,n.

3. Ancient Manuscripts Collectively: paleography,n.

4. Document,n.

1. **holograph**—document, such as a will, deed, etc., entirely in the handwriting of the person whose act it claims to be (holograph, holographic,adj.)
2. **paleograph**—ancient document (paleographic,adj.)
3. **parchment**—document; document in the form of the prepared skin of a goat, sheep, etc.

5. Record; Records,n.

1. **annals**—yearly records
2. **archives**—public or official records (archival,adj.)
3. **diary**—daily record of happenings
4. **memorabilia**—records of things worth remembering
5. **minutes**—written records of the happenings at a meeting
6. **note**—record made to help the memory; record of what has happened, what one has learned, etc.
7. **script**—written record

6. One Who Writes or Keeps Records,n. *From Sec. 5:* annalist, archivist, diarist, scribe

7. Place Where Public or Official Records Are Kept: archives,n.

8. Court or Office of Public Records: chancery,n.

9. To Make a Recording of (a Radio Broadcast): transcribe,v. (transcription,n.)

10. Paper,n.

1. **confetti**—strips of paper thrown at festivals, celebrations, etc.
2. **pad**—number of sheets of paper fastened or glued together at one edge
3. **papyrus**—material of the papyrus plant used as writing paper by ancient Greeks, Egyptians, and Romans
4. **parchment**—skin of an animal prepared for writing; any fine writing paper resembling this
5. **quire**—24 or 25 sheets of the same paper
6. **ream**—unit of 500 sheets of paper
7. **scroll**—roll of paper or parchment containing writing
8. **stationery**—paper for writing, or for writing letters
9. **tablet**—pad of writing paper
10. **tissue, tissue paper**—very thin, almost gauzy, paper, or sheet of such paper
11. **vellum**—kind of writing paper that resembles parchment

11. Resembling Paper: chartaceous, papery, adj.

12. Printed Sheet of Paper, Folded to Form One of the Sections of a Bound Book: signature,n.

13. Page of Paper, Both Sides Considered Together, whether Printed or Blank: leaf, sheet,n.

14. Inner Part of a Page of a Checkbook, Account Book, etc., for Recording Information about the Part Torn Off: counterfoil, stub,n.

15. To Give Numbers to Pages in a Volume: page, paginate,v. (pagination,n.)

16. To Put Up or Bind in Pages: paginate,v. (pagination,n.)

17. Number of Pages in a Book (Indicated in Catalogues, etc.): pagination,n.

18. Figures by Which Pages Are Numbered: pagination,n.

19. Pert. to, or Consisting of, Pages: paginal, adj.

20. Page-by-Page: paginal,adj.

21. Phonograph Record: disc, platter, recording, transcription,n.

22. Book of, or for, Such: album,n.

685. STORY

1. Story,n.
 1. account—narrative
 2. allegory—story with a lesson or moral (allegorical,adj.)
 3. anecdote—brief story or narrative of an amusing kind (anecdotal, anecdotic,adj.)
 4. apologue—story intended to teach a lesson
 5. bestiary—allegory on animals
 6. comedy—story, narrative, novel, etc., with a happy ending or written with light or humorous treatment
 7. conte—short story
 8. drama, play—story told in dialogue, and usually presented on the stage
 9. fable—any story or narrative, but often one with a moral or in which animals speak in human language
10. fiction—story invented by the imagination or mind (fictional, fictive, fictitious, adj.)
11. folk tale, folk story—story or legend handed down from generation to generation of the common people
12. kickshaw—fantastic story
13. legend—story handed down from previous generations as historical, but beyond verification and probably not historical; story of the life of a saint (legendary, adj.)
14. memoirs—account as told from memory of one's life and experiences
15. myth—legend designed to explain natural phenomena (mythical,adj.)
16. narrative—story, whether real or fictional, of events, etc. (narrative,adj.)
17. nouvelle (French)—short story; novelette
18. novel—prose tale of fiction, of book length (novelistic,adj.)
19. novelette—short prose tale, less than book length but considerably longer than a short story
20. novella (Italian)—narrative with a compact plot and definite point
21. old wives' tale—foolish story
22. parable—story intended to teach a moral (parabolic,adj.)
23. reminiscence—story of one's memorable experiences
24. roman à clef—novel in which the characters are real people in disguise
25. romance—adventurous, full-of-action story or novel; love story (romantic,adj.)
26. saga—story of heroic actions
27. scenario—story outline of a play, opera, motion picture, etc.

28. sequel—story, play, novel, etc., continuing the narrative of the previous story, etc.
29. serial—story published in parts (serial, adj.)
30. stream of consciousness novel—novel in which the continuous thinking of one or more characters is faithfully recorded
31. succès d'estime (French)—play, novel, etc., that receives critical applause but is unsuccessful commercially
32. tale—story
33. tragedy—story or play with a sad ending
34. tragicomedy—story or play that has a combination of tragic and comic elements
35. yarn—story of someone's adventure; doubtful or somewhat incredible story

2. Stories Collectively,n. *From Sec. 1:* anecdotage, drama, fiction, folklore, legendry or legendary, mythology (fictional, fictive, folkloric, mythological,adj.)

3. To Write or Tell a Story,v. *From Sec. 1:* allegorize, narrate, yarn or spin a yarn

4. To Put in the Form of a Story,v. *From Sec. 1:* allegorize, dramatize, fictionize, novelize, parabolize, serialize

5. One Who Writes or Tells a Story; Storyteller,n. *From Sec. 1:* allegorist, anecdotist, dramatist or playwright; fabulist (from *fable*); fictionist, folklorist, memoirist or memorialist, narrator, novelist, parabolist, romancer, scenarist, serialist, taleteller, yarner (fictionistic, folkloristic,adj.) ; *Also:* 1. raconteur—skillful storyteller

6. Descr. of a Type of Novel in Which the Central Character Wanders Around Having Adventures: picaresque,adj.

7. Science or Study of Myths, Legends, etc., n.
 1. mythology—science of myths (mythologist,n. mythological,adj.)
 2. storiology—study of folk tales, popular legends, etc.; study of the origin and development of these (storiologist,n. storiological,adj.)

8. Interpretation of Myths According to the Doctrine that the Gods Were Deified Humans: euhemerism,n. (euhemerist,n. euhemeristic,adj. euhemerize,v.)

9. To Turn into, or Surround or Envelop with, Myth or Myths: mythicize,v. (mythicism,n.)

686. AUTHOR

1. Author,n.
 1. anonym—author of a work who is or remains unknown
 2. classic—author of acknowledged excellence
 3. coauthor—one who, with another or others, is an author of a work
 4. collaborator—coauthor
 5. composer—author of music, or of a musical composition
 6. hack—author who turns out solely for pay, and generally low pay, material that is not characteristic of his feelings or ability or indicative of originality or creativeness
 7. penman—author
 8. scrivener—professional author (somewhat contemptuous)
 9. writer—author

2. To Be the Author of,v. *From Sec. 1:* coauthor, collaborate on, pen, write; *Also:* author, father

3. Pert. to, or Descr. of, an Author: auctorial, authorial,adj.

4. Line at the Head of a Work Showing Authorship: by-line,n.

5. Line at the End of a Story or Article, etc., Showing Authorship: tag line,n.

6. To Attribute to as Author: ascribe, credit,v. (ascription,n.)

7. Ascription of False Authorship to Writing: pseudepigraphy,n. (pseudepigraphous, adj.)

8. Descr. of Writing in Reference to Author,adj.
  1. **Byronic**—descr. of writing showing pride, cynical contempt, remorse, and irony, like that of the English poet Byron
  2. **Dantesque, Dantean**—descr. of writing having the vividness, intensity, and allegorical quality of Dante's *Inferno*
  3. **Dickensian**—descr. of writing containing humor and pathos in characterization of the lower classes, like that of Charles Dickens
  4. **Homeric, Homerical, Homerian**—descr. of writing, usually of epic style, suggestive of the Greek poet Homer
  5. **Shavian**—descr. of writing similar to that of G. B. Shaw

9. Descr. of, or Pert. to, the Writings or Theories of G. B. Shaw: Shavian,adj.

10. An Admirer of G. B. Shaw or His Writings: Shavian,n.

11. Authors of Ancient Greece or Rome: classics,n.

687. BOOK

1. Book,n.
  1. **album**—blank book for inscribing names, filling with pictures, etc.
  2. **allonym**—book by someone writing under the name of another (allonymous,adj.)
  3. **anonym**—book by an unknown author (anonymous,adj.)
  4. **autonym**—book published under one's true name
  5. **Baedeker**—guidebook, esp. to a foreign country
  6. **booklet**—book of comparatively few pages; small book
  7. **breviary**—book of daily prayers
  8. **brochure**—booklet, today often used for advertising or selling purposes, containing descriptive accounts of some particular thing, etc.
  9. **codex**—book of manuscripts, usually of the Scriptures, of an ancient classic, etc.
  10. **diglot**—edition in two languages
  11. **edition**—one of a number of books printed at the same time; book as to the format in which it appears
  12. **enchiridion**—handbook; manual
  13. **guidebook**—book containing information intended to be useful to travelers
  14. **handbook**—small book intended to help in an occupation, study, or other work; guidebook
  15. **libretto**—book containing the words or text of an opera or musical comedy
  16. **manual**—book intended to instruct
  17. **pamphlet**—thin book with a soft or paper cover
  18. **primer**—book of instruction in the rudiments of a subject
  19. **speller**—book that teaches spelling
  20. **textbook, text**—book for study by members of a school, class, etc.
  21. **tome**—large book and, usually, one dealing with a weighty subject
  22. **tract**—small book or pamphlet on a religious subject; any small book or pamphlet, often published as propaganda
  23. **vade mecum**—book carried around with one as a companion; handbook; manual
  24. **variorum**—book containing the works of an author with notes by different editors;

book containing different versions of an author's text (variorum,adj.)
  25. **volume**—book; one of a group of books dealing in some organized fashion with a subject
  26. **work**—book

2. Writer of a Book,n. *From Sec. 1:* librettist, pamphleteer, tractator

3. To Write Pamphlets: pamphleteer,v.

4. Books; Series of Books,n.
  1. **incunabula (pl.)**—books printed before 1500
  2. **tetralogy**—series of four books, usually by the same author and dealing with the same subject or related subjects, or with the same characters or their offspring, etc. (tetralogic,adj.)
  3. **trilogy**—series of three books, otherwise having the characteristics of a tetralogy (trilogic, trilogical,adj.)

5. Writer of a Trilogy: trilogist,n.

6. Books as to Binding,n.
  1. **duodecimo**—book bound of paper folded into twelve leaves
  2. **folio**—book bound of paper folded into two leaves
  3. **octavo**—book bound of paper folded into eight leaves
  4. **octodecimo**—book bound of paper folded into eighteen leaves
  5. **quarto**—book bound of paper folded into four leaves
  6. **sextodecimo**—book bound of paper folded into sixteen leaves

7. Art of Bookbinding: bibliopegy,n. (bibliopegic,adj.)

8. Bookbinder: bibliopegist,n. (bibliopegistic, bibliopegistical,adj.)

9. Certain Parts of a Book,n.
  1. **addendum**—appendix
  2. **appendix**—additional matter at the end of a book
  3. **chapter**—subdivision of a book
  4. **colophon**—special emblem, device, inscription, etc., to distinguish the publisher of a book; inscription at the end of a book
  5. **concordance**—index of the important words in a book, such as the Bible, or of an author, together with their use and/or special meanings, and references to the passages in which they occur
  6. **contents**—list of what is to be found in a book, chapter titles, etc.
  7. **frontispiece**—illustration opposite the title page of a book
  8. **index**—alphabetical listing of the contents of a book, generally placed at the end

10. Strong Desire for the Acquisition or Accumulation of Books: bibliomania, bibliomanianism, bibliomanism,n. (bibliomaniac, bibliomaniacal, bibliomanian,adj. bibliomane, bibliomaniac, bibliomanian, bibliomanist,n.)

11. One Versed in Books,n.
  1. **bibliognost**—one versed in books, their production, various editions, etc. (bibliognostic,adj.)
  2. **bibliologist**—one versed in knowledge about books (bibliology,n. bibliological, adj.)

12. List of Books or Other Writings on a Particular Subject or of a Particular Author: bibliography, bibliology,n. (bibliographic or bibliographical, bibliological,adj.)

13. One Versed in Bibliography: bibliognost, bibliographer, bibliologist,n. (bibliognostic, adj.)

14. To Make a List of Books on a Subject or of an Author: bibliographize,v.

15. Place Where Books, Magazines, News-papers, etc., Are Kept for Reference and Use: athenaeum, bibliothec, bibliotheca, library,n. (bibliothecal,adj.)

16. Person in Charge of a Library: bibliothec, bibliothecary, librarian,n. (bibliothecarian, bibliothecary,adj.)

17. Book Production: bibliogenesis, bibliogony,n.

18. Bookseller,n.
   1. **bibliopole, bibliopolist**—bookseller; seller of rare or precious books
   2. **colporteur**—seller or peddler of religious books or pamphlets

19. Selling of Books,n. *From Sec. 18:* bibliopoly, bibliopolery, or bibliopolism, colportage

20. Pert. to, or Descr. of, Bookselling or a Bookseller; Engaged in Bookselling: bibliopolar, bibliopolic, bibliopolistic,adj.

21. Irresistible Desire to Steal Books, but without the Motive of Economic Gain: bibliokleptomania,n. (bibliokleptomaniac, biblioklept,n.)

22. Story about Books: bibliology,n. (bibliologist,n. bibliological,adj.)

23. Instrument to Measure Lines in a Book: stichometer,n. (stichometry,n. stichometric, stichometrical,adj.)

24. Book Destruction; Destruction of the Bible: biblioclasm,n.

25. One Who Destroys, Damages, Mutilates, etc., Books: biblioclast,n.

688. LITERATURE

1. Literature,n.
   1. **belles-lettres**—esthetic literature; poetry, literary essays, fiction, etc. (belletristic, adj.)
   2. **classics**—literature of acknowledged excellence; literature of ancient Greece or Rome (classical,adj.)

2. Literary: bookish,adj. (bookishness,n.)

3. Literary Person,n.
   1. **bluestocking**—literary woman
   2. **littérateur**—literary person

4. Highest Era of a National Literature: Augustan Age,n.

689. POETRY

1. Poetry: poesy; rhyme, rhymes, rime; verse,n.; *Also:*
   1. **balladry**—narrative poetry
   2. **blank verse**—unrhymed but metrical poetry
   3. **dithyramb**—ancient Greek poetry in honor of Bacchus
   4. **doggerel**—loose, undignified poetry
   5. **free verse, vers libre**—poetry that has rhythm but no rhyme or meter

2. Poem: poesy, rhyme, rime, verse,n.; *Also:*
   1. **amphigory, amphigouri**—nonsense poem (amphigoric,adj.)
   2. **ballad**—narrative poem; narrative poem set to music (balladic,adj.)
   3. **ballade**—poem, usually of three stanzas, and of a fixed form
   4. **bucolic**—poem about shepherds, country life, etc.
   5. **canzone (Italian)**—Italian song poem
   6. **dithyramb, dithyrambic**—poem written in a wild, vehement, or unrestrained manner and irregular in form (dithyrambic,adj.)
   7. **ditty, lay**—poem that is sung
   8. **elegy**—poem of lamentation or sorrow, especially over someone's death; mourn-

ful or melancholy poem (elegiac, elegiacal,adj.)
   9. **epic**—narrative poem of heroes, heroic achievements, etc. (epic, epical,adj.)
   10. **epithalamium, epithalamion**—poem in honor of a newly married couple (epithalamic, epithalamial,adj.)
   11. **erotic**—poem about sexual love
   12. **hymn**—ode in praise of God, one's country, etc. (hymnic, hymnal,adj.)
   13. **jingle**—short poem with a catchy rhyme (jingly,adj.)
   14. **lyric**—short musical poem expressing emotion (lyricalness, lyricism,n. lyrical, lyric,adj.)
   15. **madrigal**—lyric, generally about love and set to a musical background (madrigalian,adj.)
   16. **madrigaletto**—short madrigal
   17. **ode**—poem that can be sung or set to music (odic,adj.)
   18. **palinode**—poem in which a retraction is made of what was said in a previous poem
   19. **psalm**—sacred or religious poem; poem in worship of God (psalmic, psalmodic, psalmodial,adj.)
   20. **telestich**—poem in which the last letters of the lines, when taken consecutively, form a name

3. To Compose a Poem or Poetry,v. *From Sec. 2:* rhyme or rime, versify; epithalamize (versification,n.) ; *Also:* **2. poetize**—compose poetry (poetization,n.)

4. To Turn or Put into Poetry,v. *From Sec. 2:* rhyme, rime, berhyme or berime; versify (versification,n.) ; *Also:* **1. metrify**—put into meter

5. Poet; Composer of a Poem, Poems, or Poetry,n. *From Sec. 2:* ballader (from *ballad*), dithyrambic, elegist, epithalamiast, hymnist, lyrist, madrigalist or madrigaler, palinodist, psalmodist; *From Sec. 3:* poetizer; *From Sec. 4:* metrifier; *Also:* bard, lutanist, metrist, minstrel, rhymer or rimer, versifier; *Also:*
   1. **metrist**—poet skillful in handling meter
   2. **troubadour**—lyric poet; one of the lyric poets who flourished in parts of Western Europe in the 11th to 13th centuries
   3. **versifier**—one who converts prose into verse
   4. **vers librist, vers libriste**—writer of free verse

6. Italian Poet of the Stated Century: trecentist (14th) ; quatrocentist (15th); cinquecentist (16th),n.

7. Inferior Kind of Poet; One Who Writes Inferior Poetry, or Who Writes Verses Rather than True Poetry: poetaster, rhymer or rimer, rhymester or rimester, versifiaster, versifier,n. (poetastric, poetastrical,adj.)

8. The Writing of Such Poetry or Verses: poetastering, poetasterism, poetastery, or poetastry,n.

9. Art of, or Addiction to, Making Rhymes: rhymery, rimery,n. (derogatory)

10. Poetic Inspiration: Pegasus,n.

11. Pert. to, Descr. of, or Characteristic of, Poetry or Poets: poetic, poetical,adj. (poeticalness, poeticism,n.)

12. Division or Part of a Poem,n.
   1. **antistrophe**—the second of two metrical patterns of a lyric poem; part of an ode, esp. a classical Greek ode, that alternates with the strophe (antistrophal, antistrophic,adj.)
   2. **canto**—primary division of a long poem
   3. **envoy; envoi (French)**—short stanza at the end of a poem in certain early poetry
   4. **octet**—first eight lines of a sonnet
   5. **sestet**—last six lines of a sonnet of the Italian type

6. **sestiad**—one of the six divisions of certain types of poems

7. **stanza, verse**—separate group of lines of a poem in the same meter as previous groups (stanzaic,adj.)

8. **stave**—stanza; stanza set to music or intended for singing

9. **strophe**—separate section of a poem not necessarily repeating the metrical patterns of previous sections; the first of two metrical patterns or metrically corresponding divisions of a lyric poem or classical Greek ode; stanza (strophic, strophical,adj.)

10. **tercet**—group of three successive lines of a poem, either rhyming together or connected by rhyme with previous and following groups

13. **Stanza or Poem of the Stated Number of Lines:** monostich (one), couplet or distich (two), tristich (three), quatrain or tetrastich (four), pentastich (five), rondelet (five); sestet, hexastich, or hexastichon (six); heptastich (seven), rhyme royal (seven), octastich or ochtastichon (eight), roundel (nine), decastich (ten), rondeau or roundel (ten or thirteen), rondel or roundel (fourteen),n. (tristichic, tetrastichic, tetrastichal, hexastichic, adj.) ; *Also*: 1. **sonnet**—type of poem containing fourteen lines, and rhyming according to one of certain fixed patterns, as the Italian, Petrarchan, or regular; the English, Elizabethan, or Shakespearean; or the Spenserian (sonnetary,adj.)

14. **Poet Who Writes in Couplets:** coupleteer, n.

15. **Poet Who Writes Sonnets:** sonneteer,n.

16. **To Write a Sonnet or Sonnets:** sonnet, sonneteer, sonnetize,v.

17. **Line of Poetry:** stich, verse,n. (stichic, adj.)

18. **Two Successive Lines, Rhyming Together, of the Same Meter, Length, etc.:** couplet,n.

19. **Repeated Initial Sound of the Words in a Line of Poetry:** stave,n.

20. **Made Up of Lines of the Same Meter:** stichic,adj.

21. **Specific Type of Metrical Line of Poetry:** verse,n.

22. **Half a Poetic Line:** hemistich,n.

23. **Incomplete, or Shorter than Normal, Poetic Line:** hemistich,n.

24. **Group of Syllables Forming a Metrical Unit in Poetry:** foot,n.

25. **Accent or Stress in a Poetic Foot:** beat, ictus,n.

26. **Rhythmical Arrangement of Words in Poetry:** measure, meter,n. (metrical, metric, adj.)

27. **Having Such a Rhythmical Arrangement:** metrical, metric,adj.

28. **To Mark Off Lines of Poetry by Metrical Feet:** scan,v. (scansion,n.)

29. **To Be Able to Be Marked Off by Metrical Feet:** scan,v. (scannable,adj.)

30. **Particular Style or Form of Metrical Composition:** prosody, verse, versification,n.

31. **Metrical Structure:** versification,n.

32. **Science, Art, or Study of Meter or Poetry,** n.
  1. **metrics**—science of meter; art of composing poetry in meter (metrist, metrician,n.)
  2. **poetics**—metrical structure when studied as a subject
  3. **prosody**—science or study of meter or

metrical structure (prosodist, prosodian, n. prosodic, prosodical, prosodiac, prosodiacal, prosodial,adj.)

33. **Rules or Customs of Composing Poetry:** versification,n.

34. **A Theory of Poetry:** poetics,n.

35. **Literary Criticism Having to Do with the Laws, Rules, and Nature of Poetry:** poetics,n.

36. **Chief Types of Metrical Feet:** amphibrach, anapest or anapaest, dactyl; iamb, iambic, or iambus; spondee, trochee or trochaic, n. (anapestic, dactylic, iambic, spondaic or spondaical, trochaic,adj.)

37. **Unit of Metrical Time Equal to That of a Short Syllable:** mora,n. (morae or moras, pl.n.)

38. **Metrical Foot or Syllable as to Morae:** triseme (three), tetraseme (four),n. (triseme or trisemic, tetraseme or tetrasemic,adj.)

39. **Poetic Line as to Number of Metrical Feet:** monometer (one), dimeter (two), trimeter (three), tetrameter (four), pentameter (five), hexameter (six), heptameter (seven), octameter (eight), decameter (ten),n. (monometric or monometrical, dimetric; trimeter, trimetric, or trimetrical; tetrameter, pentameter; hexameter, hexametral, hexametric, or hexametrical; octameter,adj.)

40. **Poetic Line of Six Iambic Feet:** Alexandrine,n. (Alexandrine,adj.)

41. **Unaccented Metrical Syllable at the Beginning of a Poetic Line:** anacrusis,n.

42. **Descr. of a Poetic Line of Which Part of the Last Foot Is Missing:** catalectic,adj. (catalexis,n.)

43. **Group or Line of the Stated Number of Metrical Feet:** dipody (two), tripody (three), tetrapody (four), pentapody (five), hexapody (six), heptapody (seven), octapody (eight),n. (dipodic, tetrapodic, heptapodic, octapodic, adj.)

44. **The Main Pause within a Poetic Line:** caesura,n. (caesural, caesuric,adj.)

45. **Poetic Line in Which the Meaning Pauses at the End:** end-stop,n. (end-stopped, adj.)

46. **Poetic Line in Which the Meaning Runs Over to a Succeeding Line or Lines:** run-on, n. (run-on,adj.)

690. PRINTING

1. **Printing, as a Process,** n.
  1. **gravure**—printing from engraved copper plates or wood blocks
  2. **lithography**—printing from stone or metal plates (lithographic,adj.)
  3. **offset**—form of printing in which the material is not transferred directly to paper (offset,v.)
  4. **photogravure**—printing from plates made by photography
  5. **rotogravure**—a form of photogravure
  6. **thermography**—printing with the aid of heat (thermographic,adj.)
  7. **typography**—printing; printing by type (typographic, typographical,adj.)

2. **Printer,** n. *From Sec. 1:* lithographer, photogravurist, typographer; *Also:*
  1. **compositor**—typesetter
  2. **pressman**—printer, i.e., one who runs a printing press
  3. **typesetter**—one who sets type in a printing press

3. **Printers; Master Printers:** typothetae,n. (used in names or titles of organizations)

4. Art of Printing by Type: typography,n. (typographer,n. typographic, typographical, adj.)

5. Form of Printing Similar to Handwriting: script,n.

6. Printing System of Raised Dots, for the Blind: Braille or braille,n.

7. Appearance of Printed Matter: typography,n. (typographic, typographical,adj.)

691. A PUBLICATION

1. A Publication; A Magazine, Newspaper, etc.,n.
  1. **annual**—publication appearing once a year
  2. **bimonthly**—publication appearing every two months
  3. **biweekly**—publication appearing every two weeks
  4. **daily**—newspaper issued each day
  5. **digest**—magazine containing condensations of material, or of material published elsewhere in fuller form
  6. **journal**—newspaper, esp. a daily newspaper; magazine, often a trade or professional magazine
  7. **monthly**—publication appearing once a month
  8. **periodical**—publication, such as a newspaper, magazine, etc., that is issued at regular intervals
  9. **review**—publication containing articles on current events, literary or artistic matters, etc.
  10. **quarterly**—publication appearing four times a year, or every three months
  11. **semimonthly**—publication appearing twice a month
  12. **semiweekly**—publication appearing twice a week
  13. **sheet**—newspaper
  14. **tabloid**—newspaper of shorter sheet size than ordinarily, usually containing many pictures
  15. **trimonthly**—publication appearing every three months
  16. **triweekly**—publication appearing every three weeks

2. Periodicals Collectively: the press,n.

3. Newspapers Collectively: journalism, the press,n.

4. Person Connected with Publication,n.
  1. **cub**—young and inexperienced reporter
  2. **editor**—person in charge of a magazine or newspaper, or subdivision of either; person who supervises publishing activities relating directly to manuscripts in a book-publishing business (editorial,adj.)
  3. **journalist**—anyone in the business of writing for, or editing, a newspaper or other publication (journalistic,adj.)
  4. **publisher**—one engaged in publishing books, periodicals, etc.; business head of a newspaper, magazine, or publishing firm
  5. **reporter**—one who gathers and writes up news for a newspaper (reportorial,adj.)

5. Journalists, Collectively: the Fourth Estate, the press,n.

6. Occupation or Business of Writing for, Editing, etc., a Publication: journalism,n. (journalistic,adj.)

7. To Engage in Journalism: journalize,v.

8. Number of Copies of a Publication Sold Regularly: circulation,n.

9. Organization That Sells Material to Newspapers, etc., for Simultaneous Publication: syndicate,n. (syndicate,v.)

10. To Publish: issue,v.

11. To Be Published: appear,v. (appearance, n.)

12. Act or Process of Publishing: publication, publishment,n.

692. READING

1. To Read,v.
  1. **browse**—read a little here and there in a book, magazine, bookstore, library, etc.
  2. **censor**—read and accept; read, and change or delete material considered harmful, dangerous, immoral, obscene, etc. (censorship,n.)
  3. **peruse**—read; read carefully and critically (perusal,n.)
  4. **pore over**—read with deep involvement or close attention
  5. **scan**—read by glancing at; read hastily with much skimming and skipping
  6. **skim**—read quickly and superficially; pass over quickly and superficially in reading; read for main ideas only
  7. **spell out**—read with such lack of skill as almost to examine the spelling of every word before recognizing it
  8. **thumb, thumb through, leaf through**—turn the pages of (a book, manuscript, etc.) rapidly, scanning, skimming, or reading only parts

2. Reader,n. *From Sec. 1:* browser, censor, peruser, skimmer; *Also:* 1. **bookworm**—one who reads a lot

3. To Read Incorrectly: misread,v.

4. A Reading Aloud from Someone's Writings: recital,n.

5. Main Body of Reading Material of a Book or Other Writing, as Distinguished from Pictorial or Other Matter: text,n. (textual,adj.)

6. Easy to Read; Capable of Being Read, adj.
  1. **decipherable**—easy to read in the sense that the handwriting is clear and understandable (decipherability,n.)
  2. **legible**—capable of being read, or easy to read, in the sense that the writing can be understood (legibility,n.)
  3. **readable**—capable of being read; easy to read, owing to the style, use of language, etc. (readability,n.)

7. Incapable of Being Read, or Hard to Read,adj. *From Sec. 6:* indecipherable, illegible, unreadable

8. Able to Read and Write: literate,adj. (literacy,n.)

9. Fond of Reading: bookish,adj. (bookishness,n.)

10. Having Read a Lot; Familiar with Good Books: well-read,adj.

11. Not Familiar with Reading, Good Books, etc.: unread,adj.

12. Unable to Read or Write, Owing to Lack of Education: illiterate, unlettered,adj. (illiteracy,n. illiterate,n.)

13. Certain Reading Difficulties,n.
  1. **alexia**—loss of ability to read; word blindness
  2. **paralexia**—misreading of language, substituting one word for another, or meaningless words for actual ones
  3. **strephosymbolia**—reading disability believed to result from non-subordination of one cerebral hemisphere to the other
  4. **word blindness**—morbid condition, usually owing to brain injury, causing an inability to recognize written or printed words (word-blind,adj.)

14. Eye Movements in Reading,n.
1. **fixation**—during reading, the momentary period of rest when the eyes are fixed upon a portion of print
2. **interfixation**—movement of the eyes between fixations
3. **saccadic movements**—eye movements during reading, a combination of fixations and interfixations

15. Use of Phonetics to Teach Beginners to Read by Independently Pronouncing the Various Syllables of Words: phonics,n.

16. Stand on Which Reading Material Is Placed: lectern,n.

693. CALL

1. To Call,v.
1. **appeal to**—call upon (an authority) for judgment or decision
2. **assemble**—call together in one place
3. **beckon**—call, or call to come, with a signal or gesture
4. **cite**—summon to appear in court
5. **conjure up**—call forth by, or as if by, magic
6. **convene**—call before a tribunal; convoke
7. **convoke**—call together; call to a meeting for a specific purpose
8. **evoke**—call forth
9. **hail**—call loudly after (someone)
10. **invoke**—call upon by prayer; call forth by magic
11. **muster**—call (troops) together for some reason; summon
12. **rally**—call together in meeting for common action
13. **recall**—call back
14. **subpoena**—call for (a person's presence) in court on pain of punishment
15. **summon, summons**—call; call to come; call forth; call by authority to a duty
16. **toll**—call, or call to come, by striking a bell

2. A Calling; A Call,n. *From Sec. 1:* appeal, assembly or assemblage, beck or beckon, citation, conjuration or conjurement, convention, convocation, evocation, hail, invocation, muster, rally, recall, subpoena, summons, toll

3. Descr. of, or Pert. to, Calling or a Call, adj. *From Sec. 1:* appellant or appellate, convocational or convocative, evocative or evocatory, invocative or invocatory; *Also:*
1. **avocatory**—calling back
2. **vocative**—pert. to calling

4. Caller,n. *From Sec. 1:* appellant, beckoner, convener; convoker, convocant, or convocator; evoker or evocator; invoker, invocant, or invocator; summoner

5. One Who Summons Spirits: evocator,n.

694. NAME

1. Name,n.
1. **address**—at the head of a letter, the name of the person to whom the letter is written, the place to which the letter is sent, and the salutation
2. **agnomen**—nickname (agnominal,adj.)
3. **alias**—false name assumed for purposes of deception, usually by a criminal
4. **allonym**—name of someone else assumed by an author (allonymous,adj.)
5. **anonym**—pseudonym
6. **appellation**—name (appellatory,adj.)
7. **appellative**—name; descriptive name
8. **autograph**—signature (autographic,adj.)
9. **autonym**—one's own true name; name given to a tribe by itself as distinguished from that given it by a foreign tribe

10. **byname**—nickname; second name; surname
11. **byword**—nickname
12. **Christian name**—given name
13. **cognomen, cognomination**—family name; last name; loosely, any name or nickname
14. **compellation**—name
15. **denomination**—general name; name of units (denominational,adj.)
16. **designation**—name
17. **diminutive**—affectionate name, usually applied to young children, often ending in *-ie* or *-kins* (diminutive,adj.)
18. **epithet**—name that has meaning or application to the person bearing it (epithetic, epithetical,adj.)
19. **family name**—name derived from one's family, as *Brown* in *John Brown*
20. **first name**—given name
21. **given name**—name given to one on birth, as *John* in *John Brown*
22. **handle**—name (slang)
23. **last name**—family name
24. **matronymic, metronymic**—name derived from the mother (matronymic, metronymic,adj.)
25. **metronymic**—name derived from a female ancestor (metronymic,adj.)
26. **misnomer**—wrong name
27. **moniker**—name or nickname (slang)
28. **nickname**—intimate or substitute name
29. **nom de guerre (French)**—literally, name assumed for concealment during wartime; hence, any fictitious name
30. **nom de plume**—pen name; name assumed by an author for concealment of his identity
31. **nom de théâtre (French)**—stage name
32. **nomen (Latin)**—name, esp. scientific name (nominal,adj.)
33. **paedonymic**—name derived from one's child (paedonymic,adj.)
34. **patronymic, patronym**—name derived from one's father, as *Johnson*, son of John, *Ivanovich*, son of Ivan, etc. (patronymic,adj.)
35. **pen name**—fictitious name used by a writer
36. **praenomen**—in ancient Rome, the first of a person's three names (praenominal, adj.)
37. **proper name**—name of a person, place, etc., usually capitalized
38. **pseudonym**—false or fictitious name adopted for purposes of concealing one's true identity; pen name (pseudonymic, pseudonymal,adj.)
39. **second name**—family name
40. **signature**—one's name signed in one's own handwriting
41. **sobriquet**—nickname
42. **stage name**—fictitious name used professionally by an actor or actress
43. **style**—trade name of a business; descriptive name
44. **surname**—family name
45. **tag**—name
46. **term**—name
47. **title**—name; descriptive name (titular, adj.)
48. **toponym**—place name; scientific name for a region or area that indicates where or how such region or area originated; scientific name for a part of the body (toponymic,adj.)

2. Pert. to, or Consisting of, a Name or Names: onomastic,adj.

3. Place Names of an Area; Place Names in a Language: toponymy,n. (toponymic,adj.)

4. Use of a Man's Name as a Pen Name by a Woman Author: pseudandry,n.

5. To Write One's Name, as on a Document, etc.: sign,v. (signature,n.)

6. To Name, Give a Name to, or Call by Name,v.

1. **acclaim**—name by loud shouting (*acclaimed him king*, etc.)
2. **address**—call, speak to, or write to, by name
3. **baptize**—give a name to; give a name to in a religious ceremony
4. **bound**—name the boundaries of
5. **call**—speak to by name; get the attention of by using the name of; say the name or names of
6. **christen**—name; baptize
7. **cognominate**—give a family name or, loosely, any name to
8. **declare**—acclaim
9. **denominate**—give a name to
10. **designate**—name
11. **dignify**—give a pretentious or high-sounding name to
12. **dub**—give a new name to (somewhat poetic or archaic)
13. **enumerate**—name one by one, in, or as if in, a list
14. **godfather**—give a name to
15. **label**—give a name to
16. **mention**—name; name incidentally
17. **nickname**—give an affectionate or informal name to
18. **nomenclature**—name; designate
19. **nominate**—name as a candidate
20. **specify**—name definitely or individually
21. **style**—give a descriptive or trade name to
22. **tag**—give a name to
23. **term**—name
24. **title**—give a descriptive name to

7. Act or Process of Naming, etc.,n. *From Sec. 6:* acclamation, baptism, christening, declaration, denomination, designation, enumeration, mention, nomination, specification; *Also:* 1. **appellation**—the act of naming, or of calling by name

8. Descr. of, or Pert. to, Naming, etc.,adj. *From Sec. 6:* acclamatory, denominative, designative, enumerative, nomenclative, nominative, appellative or appellatory; *Also:* 1. **onomastic**—descr. of, or pert. to, naming

9. Named,adj. *From Sec. 6:* acclaimed, addressed, etc.; designate; *Also:* 1. **y-clept**—named (archaic, now used only humorously)

10. Self-Named, i.e., So Named or Called by One's Own Claim: self-called, self-christened, self-styled; soi-disant (French),adj.

11. Person Named,n.

1. **cognominal**—namesake
2. **designate**—one named to a post or position
3. **namesake**—one named after another
4. **nominee**—one named as a candidate

12. In Name Only, but Not in Fact: nominal, titular,adj.

13. Having a Name: denominate, nominative, adj.

14. Having a Person's Name: nominative,adj.

15. Source of a Name,n.

1. **denominator**—source from which a name springs
2. **eponym**—person from whose name the name of a city, family, nation, etc., is derived

16. Custom of Deriving a Name from the Female Ancestral Line: metronymy,n.

17. One Who Announces the Names of Guests: nomenclator,n.

18. Without a Name: anonymous, innominate, nameless,adj. (anonymity or anonymousness, innomination, namelessness,n.)

19. Person Whose Name Is Unknown: anonym,n.

20. Written, Composed, Done, or Created by an Unnamed or Unknown Person: anonymous,adj. (anonymity, anonymousness,n.)

21. Containing or Showing the Writer's Name, as Distinguished from Anonymous: onomatous,adj.

22. Having, Using, or Assuming a Fictitious Name,adj.

1. **allonymous**—assuming the name of someone else—said of an author
2. **incognito**—with one's true identity concealed by a fictitious name, as to avoid publicity, undue attention, etc.
3. **pseudonymous**—using or having a fictitious name, assumed for the purpose of concealing one's identity; using or having a pen name

23. State of Having, etc., a Fictitious Name, n. *From Sec. 22:* incognito, pseudonymity or pseudonymousness

24. One Who Has, Uses, or Assumes a Fictitious Name: incognito,n.

25. Under an Assumed Name: incognito,adv.

26. To Call by a Wrong Name or Give a Wrong Name to: miscall, misname, misnomer, misterm,v.

27. Design Composed of the Initials of a Person's Name: monogram,n. (monogrammatic, monogrammatical, monogrammic,adj.)

28. Namely: to wit, viz. (abbreviation of *videlicet*—Latin)

29. Nicknames of States of the United States,n.
1. **Alabama**—Cotton State; Yellowhammer State
2. **Arizona**—Grand Canyon State
3. **Arkansas**—Wonder State; Bear State
4. **California**—Golden State
5. **Colorado**—Centennial State
6. **Connecticut**—Nutmeg State
7. **Delaware**—Diamond State
8. **Florida**—Sunshine State; Peninsula State
9. **Georgia**—Cracker State
10. **Idaho**—Gem State
11. **Illinois**—Prairie State
12. **Indiana**—Hoosier State
13. **Iowa**—Hawkeye State
14. **Kansas**—Sunflower State
15. **Kentucky**—Blue Grass State
16. **Louisiana**—Pelican State; Creole State
17. **Maine**—Pine Tree State
18. **Maryland**—Free State; Old Line State
19. **Massachusetts**—Bay State; Old Colony
20. **Michigan**—Wolverine State
21. **Minnesota**—Gopher State; North Star State
22. **Mississippi**—Magnolia State
23. **Missouri**—Show-Me State
24. **Montana**—Treasure State
25. **Nebraska**—Cornhusker State
26. **Nevada**—Sagebrush State; Silver State
27. **New Hampshire**—Granite State
28. **New Jersey**—Garden State
29. **New Mexico**—Sunshine State
30. **New York**—Empire State
31. **North Carolina**—Tar Heel State
32. **North Dakota**—Flickertail State
33. **Ohio**—Buckeye State
34. **Oklahoma**—Sooner State
35. **Oregon**—Beaver State
36. **Pennsylvania**—Keystone State
37. **Rhode Island**—Little Rhody
38. **South Carolina**—Palmetto State
39. **South Dakota**—Sunshine State; Coyote State
40. **Tennessee**—Volunteer State
41. **Texas**—Lone Star State
42. **Utah**—Beehive State
43. **Vermont**—Green Mountain State
44. **Virginia**—Cavalier State; Old Dominion
45. **Washington**—Evergreen State; Chinook State
46. **West Virginia**—Mountain State

47. **Wisconsin**—Badger State
48. **Wyoming**—Equality State

695. STUDY OF NAMES

1. Study of Names,n.
1. **onomatology**—terminology
2. **patronomatology**—study of names derived from the father
3. **terminology**—study of names of things, or of terms to describe them (terminological,adj.)
4. **toponymics, toponymy**—study, or study of the derivation, of place names, or of names of people or families derived from places (toponymic,adj.)

2. Student of Names,n. *From Sec. 1:* onomatologist, terminologist

3. Science of Names: onomatology,n. (onomatologist,n.)

4. System of Names,n.
1. **glossology**—nomenclature; terminology (glossological,adj.)
2. **nomenclature**—system of names used in classification (nomenclatural, nomenclatorial,adj.)
3. **orismology**—terminology of a science (orismologic, orismological,adj.)
4. **synonymy**—system of scientific names
5. **technology**—terminology used in arts, sciences, etc. (technological,adj.)
6. **terminology**—system of names or terms in a business, art, science, etc. (terminological,adj.)
7. **toponymy**—system of scientific names for parts of the body (toponymic,adj.)

5. List of Names,n.
1. **nomenclature**—list of names (nomenclatural, nomenclatorial, nomenclatory, adj.)
2. **onomasticon**—list of proper names, esp. of people, arranged in some systematic fashion
3. **register**—list or record of names
4. **roll**—roster
5. **roster**—list of names
6. **rota**—roster
7. **synonymy**—list of scientific names

6. To Write the Name of (a Person) in a List: enroll, enter, inscribe, record, register, sign up,v. (enrollment, entrance, inscription, registration,n.)

7. One Who Writes a Person's Name in a List: enroller, recorder, registerer, registrar, n.

8. To Write One's Own Name, or Have One's Name Entered or Written, in a List: enroll, register, sign up,v. (enrollment, registration,n. enroller, registrant or registerer,n.)

9. To Put One's Name Down as a Formal Agreement or Promise to Give Money, etc., or to Buy or Receive a Periodical, Stock, etc.: subscribe,v. (subscription,n. subscriber, n. subscriptive,adj.)

696. SIGNATURE

1. To Sign,v.
1. **attest**—sign as a witness (attestation,n.)
2. **autograph**—sign one's own name to—esp. said of a famous person, author, composer, etc., signing a copy of his work, a blank page in an album, etc. (autography, n.)
3. **cosign**—sign (a document) as a joint signer (cosignature,n.)
4. **countersign**—sign (that which has already been signed by another) as further confirmation (countersignature,n.)
5. **endorse, indorse**—sign one's name on the

back of (a check, etc.) as an acknowledgment of receiving payment (endorsement, indorsement,n.)
6. **forge**—sign (another's name) for purposes of fraud; copy (another's signature) for purposes of fraud (forgery,n.)
7. **subscribe**—sign with one's own handwriting (subscription,n.)
8. **undersign**—sign one's name at the end of (undersignature,n.)
9. **witness**—sign (a document) as evidence of observing someone else sign it

2. A Signature,n. *From Sec. 1:* autograph, cosignature, countersignature, endorsement, indorsement, forgery, subscription, undersignature; *Also:*
1. **sign manual**—signature by one's own hand, esp. of a ruler or official on a document, etc.
2. **visa, vise**—official signature on a passport or other legal document showing that it has been examined and approved

3. Signer,n. *From Sec. 1:* attester, attestor, attestant, or attester; autographer, cosigner or cosignatory, countersigner, endorser, indorser, forger, subscriber, undersigner, witness; *Also:* 1. **signatory**—one who joins in the signing of a document

4. Signing; Pert. to, or Descr. of, Signing, adj. *From Sec. 1:* attestant, attestive, or attestative; autographic, cosignatory, subscriptive; *From Sec. 3:* signatory; *Also:* 1. **onomastic**—pert. to or designating someone's signature to a document written by another

697. SEAL

1. A Seal,n.
1. **bulla, bull**—seal placed on an official document, papal announcement, etc.
2. **cachet**—seal on a letter
3. **sigil**—seal
4. **signet**—seal of authority, or the impression made by such a seal

2. To Put or Impress a Seal On: seal, signet, v.

3. Science of Seals: sphragistics,n. (sphragistic,adj.)

698. LABEL

1. To Label,v.
1. **docket**—mark with a ticket or label
2. **tag**—give a label to
3. **tally**—label
4. **ticket**—label; put a label on

2. A Label: docket, tag, ticket,n.

699. TITLE

1. To Title; To Give a Title to,v.
1. **address**—use the proper title to, in speaking or writing to a person or dignitary
2. **denominate**—give a title to (denomination,n.)
3. **dignify**—give a pretentious or high-sounding title to (dignification,n.)
4. **dub**—give a new title to (poetic or archaic)
5. **entitle**—give a title to (entitlement,n.)
6. **style**—title
7. **subtitle**—give a secondary or subordinate title to
8. **term**—title

2. Title; Style of Title,n. *From Sec. 1:* address, denomination, style, subtitle, term; *Also:*
1. **appellative**—title
2. **compellation**—style of address

3. **designation**—title
4. **heading**—title of a chapter, page, etc.
5. **honorific**—title of honor, as *Your Excellency*, etc.
6. **rubric**—title of a law, chapter, page, etc.
7. **salutation**—address, or style of address, of a letter, as *Dear Sir, Your Excellency,* etc.
8. **titulus**—title (legal)

3. Pert. to, or Descr. of, Titling or a Title, adj. *From Sec. 1:* denominative; *From Sec. 2:* honorific, salutatory; *Also:* 1. **titular**—pert. to a title or titles

4. The Use of a Title Instead of the Proper Name of a Person: antonomasia,n. (antonomastic,adj.)

5. Having a Title: titular,adj.

6. Titled by One's Own Claim: self-styled; soi-disant (French),adj.

7. In Title Only, Not in Actuality: titular, titulary,adj.

8. Miss, as a Title,n.
　1. **Fräulein**—Miss, in German
　2. **Mademoiselle**—Miss, in French
　3. **Senhora, Senhorita**—Miss, in Portuguese
　4. **Señorita**—Miss, in Spanish
　5. **Signorina**—Miss, in Italian

9. Mrs., as a Title,n.
　1. **Doña**—Mrs., in Spanish
　2. **Dona**—Mrs., in Portuguese
　3. **Donna**—Mrs., in Italian
　4. **Frau**—Mrs., in German
　5. **Madame, Mme.**—Mrs., in French
　6. **Mem-sahib**—Mrs., in Hindustani
　7. **Sahibah**—Mrs., in the language of India
　8. **Senhora**—Mrs., in Portuguese
　9. **Señora**—Mrs., in Spanish
　10. **Signora**—Mrs., in Italian
　11. **Vrouw**—Mrs., in Dutch

10. Mr., as a Title,n.
　1. **Herr**—Mr., in German
　2. **Master**—Mr., usually applied to young boys
　3. **Messieurs, Messrs., MM.**—Mr. (plural)
　4. **Monsieur, M'sieu**—Mr., in French
　5. **Senhor**—Mr., in Portuguese
　6. **Señor**—Mr., in Spanish
　7. **Signor**—Mr., in Italian

11. Heading,n.
　1. **banner**—line of large type forming a headline
　2. **caption**—heading of a page, chapter, etc.
　3. **head**—heading
　4. **headline**—line of type forming a heading in a newspaper
　5. **rubric**—heading of a statute, law, chapter, page, etc.
　6. **streamer**—banner
　7. **trope**—heading of a topic

700. LOVE

1. Love; Feeling of Love,n.
　1. **adoration**—love that reaches an extreme, or that amounts almost to worship
　2. **affection, affections, affectionateness**—love; friendly love
　3. **amor**—love
　4. **amorousness**—feeling of love or affection
　5. **amour-propre (French)**—self-love
　6. **attachment**—affection
　7. **autophilia**—self-love (psychiatric)
　8. **brotherliness**—affection of the kind felt by a brother
　9. **calf love**—temporary affection between a young boy and girl
　10. **charity**—love for one's fellows
　11. **devotion**—deep and loyal affection
　12. **fatherliness**—tender and protective affection, like that of a father to a child
　13. **fondness**—affection

14. **idolatry**—love that reaches an excessive degree; love that amounts to worship
15. **infatuation**—foolish and extravagant love or sexual love
16. **maritality**—foolish, extravagant, or excessive fondness for one's husband
17. **motherliness**—tender and protective affection, like that of a mother to a child
18. **narcissism, narcism**—the fixation upon oneself, one's body, or one's personality of that love which is normally directed to another person or a member of the opposite sex (psychoanalysis); loosely, self-love
19. **passion**—sexual love; warm affection
20. **platonic love**—love between man and woman without, or transcending, the sexual element
21. **puppy love**—calf love
22. **reverence**—combination of love, deep respect, and awe
23. **self-love**—love of self
24. **sisterliness**—affection of the kind felt by a sister
25. **tenderness**—affection
26. **uxoriousness**—foolish and fond adoration of one's wife
27. **venery**—sexual love
28. **warmheartedness**—affection
29. **worship**—great or extreme love and admiration
30. **yearning**—affection; tender feelings

2. Loving,adj. *From Sec. 1:* adoring, affectionate, amorous, attached, brotherly, charitable, devoted, fatherly, fond, idolatrous, infatuated, motherly, narcissistic or narcistic, passionate, reverent or reverential, sisterly, tender, uxorious, warmhearted, worshipful, yearning; *Also:*
　1. **doting**—unusually fond; fond and indulgent
　2. **enamored (of)**—in love (with)
　3. **smitten (with)**—enamored (of)

3. To Love; To Feel Love for,v. *From Sec. 1:* adore, idolize, revere or reverence, worship (adoration, idolization or idolism, worship, n.); *From Sec. 2:* dote on, dote upon; *Also:* 1. **yearn**—feel tender affection

4. To Treat Affectionately; To Hold Dear: cherish, enshrine, prize, treasure,v.

5. Loved: adored, beloved, cherished, darling, dear, doted on, doted upon, idolized, pet, precious, prized, revered, treasured, worshiped,adj.

6. One Who Is Loved; Object of Love: beloved, darling, dear, idol, passion, pet, precious, sweetheart, treasure,n.

7. To Make Love,v.
　1. **court**—make love to, often with a view to marrying (courtship,n.)
　2. **gallant**—make love; act as a (male) lover (gallantry,n.)
　3. **spark**—court (a woman)
　4. **spoon**—make love
　5. **woo**—make love; make love to; make love to with a view to marrying

8. To Try to Get the Love of: woo,v. (wooer, n.)

9. To Go About with the Opposite Sex, Esp. in a Frivolous Search for Pleasure: gallivant, galavant, galivant,v. (gallivanter, n.)

10. To Meet to Make Love; To Meet for Romantic Purposes: tryst,v. (tryst,n. tryster, n.)

11. To Make or Offer Love Insincerely, or without Genuine Feeling,v.
　1. **coquet, coquette**—play at love; flirt (coquetry,n.)
　2. **dally (with)**—make love lightly, triflingly, or insincerely (to); play amorously (dalliance,n.)

3. **flirt (with)**—make love (to) purely for amusement; act as if making offers of love, with no serious intention of fulfilling the offers (flirtation,n.)
4. **gallivant**—play at the part of a (male) lover
5. **philander**—make love insincerely—said of a man
6. **trifle (with)**—dally (with)
7. **vampirize**—make love, or flirt, in order to debase one's lover or use him for financial advantage until his money is gone —said of a woman (vampirism,n.)
8. **wanton**—dally

12. One Who Makes or Offers Love Insincerely,n. *From Sec. 11:* coquette (fem.), dallier, flirt, gallivanter, philanderer or philander, trifler, vampire or, slang, vamp, wanton or wantoner; *Also:*
1. **fizgig**—flirtatious and silly woman
2. **gold-digger**—woman who flirts with men for financial gain
3. **soubrette**—flirtatious young woman

13. Making or Offering Love Insincerely,adj. *From Sec. 11:* coquetting, dallying, etc., coquettish or coquet, flirtatious (coquettishness, flirtatiousness,n.)

14. To Excite with Love,v.
1. **enamor**—excite with love
2. **inamorate**—enamor
3. **infatuate**—excite with a foolish and intemperate love or passion (infatuation,n.)

15. One Who Is Excited with a Foolish Love or Passion: infatuate,n.

16. Interested in, or Inclined toward, Love or Love-Making: amative, amorous; romantic (colloq.),adj. (amativeness, amorousness,n.)

17. To Cause to Appeal to One's Affections: endear,v. (endearment,n.)

18. State of Appealing to Someone's Affections: endearment,n.

19. Affectionate Term; Word, Action, etc., Showing Affection or Love: endearment,n.

20. Love Affair,n.
1. **amour**—love affair, usually illicit
2. **flirtation**—frivolous love affair
3. **intrigue**—secret and illicit love affair
4. **romance**—love affair

21. Tending to Show or Express One's Love: demonstrative,adj. (demonstrativeness,n.)

22. Expressive of Love or Fondness: amatorial, amatory, endearing, pet,adj.

23. Lover,n.
1. **admirer**—man who loves a woman
2. **adorer**—one who loves to an extreme degree
3. **amorist**—love-maker; gallant (amoristic,adj.)
4. **beau**—male lover
5. **Casanova**—lover of many women (Casanovanic,adj.)
6. **cavalier**—lover of a married woman; man who is chivalrously attentive to a married woman
7. **cicisbeo (Italian)**—lover of a married woman
8. **Corydon**—rustic gallant
9. **courter**—wooer
10. **dallier**—one who makes love insincerely
11. **enamorato**—male lover
12. **gallant**—male lover; male who engages in illicit love
13. **idolizer**—one who loves to the point of worship
14. **inamorata**—female lover; woman with whom one is in love
15. **inamorato**—male lover
16. **Lothario**—insincere lover of many women
17. **paramour**—lover; one who engages in illicit love; wooer

18. **philanderer**—man who makes love insincerely
19. **Romeo**—male lover
20. **spark**—male lover
21. **spooner**—one who makes love
22. **squire**—male lover
23. **Strephon**—male lover, so called after the shepherd lover in Sir Philip Sydney's *Arcadia*
24. **suitor**—one who asks or desires a woman's hand in marriage
25. **swain**—lover
26. **sweetheart**—lover
27. **valentine**—one's sweetheart; sweetheart chosen on St. Valentine's Day
28. **wooer**—one, usually a man, who makes love to a member of the opposite sex with a view to marriage

24. Love Potion: philter, philtre,n.

25. Pert. to Love or Sexual Love: amatorial, amatorian, amatorious, amatory, amorous, erotic; Paphian (esp. illicit) ; romantic, venereal,adj.

26. One Interested in Sexual Love: erotic,n.

27. God or Goddess of Love,n.
1. **Cupid**—Roman god of love
2. **Eros**—Greek god of sexual love
3. **Venus**—Roman goddess of love and beauty

28. To Cast Aside (a Lover) in an Unfeeling or Inconsiderate Manner: jilt,v. (jilter,n.)

29. Woman Who Casts Aside a Lover: jilt,n.

30. One Who Is Fond of Certain Specific Places, Things, or People,n.
1. **Anglomaniac, Anglophile**—of British customs, people, etc.
2. **bibliophile, bibliophilist**—of books
3. **coprophiliac**—of obscenity, esp. in reading matter, pictures, etc.
4. **demophile**—of the populace
5. **dendrophile**—of trees
6. **Francophile, Gallophile**—of France, French customs, etc.
7. **Germanomaniac, Germanophile**—of Germany, German customs, etc.
8. **Grecomaniac**—of Greece, Greek customs, etc.
9. **hippophile**—of horses
10. **Indophile**—of India, Indian people, customs, etc.
11. **Judaeophile**—of Jews, Jewish customs, etc.
12. **necrophile**—of the dead
13. **Negrophile**—of Negroes
14. **ophiophilist**—of snakes
15. **philalethist**—of truth
16. **philharmonic**—of music
17. **philhellene**—of Greece or the Greeks
18. **philocalist**—of beauty or beautiful things
19. **philodox, philodoxer**—of opinion, or of one's own opinions
20. **philogynist**—of women
21. **philopornist**—of prostitutes
22. **philotheist**—of God
23. **philotherian**—of animals
24. **Russomaniac, Russophile**—of Russia, Russian people, customs, etc.
25. **Slavophile**—of Slavic peoples, customs, etc.
26. **timbrophilist, timbromaniac**—of postage stamps
27. **Turkophile**—of Turkey, Turkish people or customs, etc.
28. **zoophilist**—of animals

31. Fondness for Certain Places, Things, or People,n. *From Sec. 30:* Anglomania, bibliophilism, coprophilia or coprophilism, demophilism, Francophilism, Gallophilism, Germanomania, Grecomania, Indophilism, Judaeophilism, necrophilia, Negrophilism, ophiophilism, philocaly, philogyny, philotheism, philotherianism, Russomania, Russophilism,

Slavophilism, timbrophilism or timbrophily, timbromania, Turkophilism or Turkomania; zoophilia, zoophilism, or zoophily; *Also:*
1. **gerontophilia**—for old people
2. **pedophilia**—for a child or children, esp. one's own
3. **philomathy**—for learning
4. **philoprogenitiveness**—for one's own children
5. **xenomania**—for foreign customs, things, etc.

32. Fond of Certain Places, Things, or People; Descr. of Such Fondness,adj. *From Sec. 30:* Anglophile, bibliophilic, coprophilic, Francophile, Germanophile, necrophilic, philharmonic, philocalic, philodoxical, philogynous, philotheistic, philotherian, timbrophilic, zoophilic; *From Sec. 31:* pedophilic, philomathical, philoprogenitive; *Also:*
1. **Hispanophile**—of Spain, Spanish customs, etc.
2. **philhippic**—of horses
3. **philodemic**—of the populace

701. CARESS

1. To Caress,v.
1. **bill**—caress fondly (as in *bill and coo*), like birds joining bills
2. **chuck**—caress by patting lightly under the chin
3. **cocker**—fondle
4. **cosher**—pet
5. **cosset**—fondle; pet
6. **cuddle**—fondle in the manner of a mother with an infant; hug or hold close and tenderly
7. **dandle**—fondle; pet
8. **embrace**—hug
9. **fondle**—caress or stroke tenderly and lovingly
10. **hug**—put one's arms around as a caress
11. **nuzzle**—cuddle
12. **pat**—caress by tenderly stroking
13. **pet**—caress lovingly or tenderly, or with light strokes to soothe or comfort; caress in an amorous or erotic manner
14. **snuggle**—press closely in love or as an expression of love; cuddle
15. **squeeze**—hug
16. **stroke**—caress lightly with the hands

2. A Caress,n. *From Sec. 1:* chuck, cuddle, embrace, hug, pat, snuggle, squeeze, stroke; *Also:* 1. **endearment**—caress that shows warm affection

3. Caressible,adj. *From Sec. 1:* cuddly or cuddlesome, embraceable, huggable

4. Pert. to, or Characteristic of, a Caress: caressive,adj.

5. Tending to Caress, Cuddle, etc., to Show Love: affectionate,adj.

6. To Kiss,v.
1. **buss**—kiss (archaic or old-fashioned)
2. **osculate**—kiss—the actual touching of the lips or mouth is stressed (osculation, n.)
3. **smack**—kiss loudly

7. A Kiss,n. *From Sec. 6:* buss, osculation, smack; *Also:* 1. **peck**—a quick kiss

8. Pert. to a Kiss: oscular,adj.

9. Pert. to Kissing: osculatory,adj.

10. Kissing: osculatory,adj.

11. The Study of Kissing: philematology,n.

702. MARRIAGE

1. To Marry, or Take in Marriage,v.
1. **elope**—marry secretly; run away to marry secretly (elopement,n. eloper,n.)

2. **espouse**—take in marriage
3. **intermarry**—marry someone of the same family, group, tribe, etc. (intermarriage, n.)
4. **lead to the altar**—marry
5. **mate**—marry
6. **miscegenate**—marry a person of another race (miscegenation,n. miscegenator, miscegenist,n.)
7. **mismate**—marry poorly, unsuccessfully, or unsuitably
8. **remarry**—marry again; take again in marriage (remarriage,n.)
9. **rewed**—remarry
10. **wed**—marry; take in marriage
11. **wive**—marry (a woman); take a wife

2. To Marry, or Unite (Two People) in Marriage,v.
1. **couple**—marry
2. **join**—unite in marriage
3. **mate**—unite as mates in marriage
4. **mismatch**—unite in an unsuitable marriage
5. **mismate**—mismatch
6. **remarry**—unite again in marriage (remarriage,n.)
7. **rewed**—remarry
8. **splice**—unite in marriage (colloq.)
9. **unite**—unite in marriage (union,n.)
10. **wed**—unite in marriage

3. To Become United through Marriage, as Two Families, Tribes, etc.: intermarry,v. (intermarriage,n.)

4. To Unite (Two Families, etc.) through Marriage: ally,v. (alliance,n.)

5. Relationship (of Families, etc.) through Marriage: affinity, alliance, kinship,n.

6. United in Marriage (of Two People): conjugate, coupled, joined, married, matched, mated, united, wed,adj. (conjugacy,n.)

7. Badly or Poorly Married: mismatched, mismated,adj.

8. Marriage,n.
1. **alliance**—marriage
2. **civil marriage**—marriage solemnized by a judge, mayor, etc., rather than by a clergyman
3. **common-law marriage**—marriage entered into by agreement between man and woman, without religious or civil ceremony
4. **companionate marriage**—trial marriage based on legalized birth control and divorce by agreement
5. **consortium**—marriage; marriage relationship (legal)
6. **elopement**—secret marriage
7. **Gretna Green marriage**—marriage contracted by people who have run away—so called from the village in Scotland where runaway couples were married
8. **hymen**—marriage
9. **intermarriage**—marriage between members of a family, clan, tribe, blood group, etc.; marriage between members of different races or religions
10. **mariage de convenance (French), marriage of convenience**—marriage based on convenience or other factors, rather than on love, mutual attraction, etc.
11. **match**—marriage
12. **matrimony**—marriage
13. **mésalliance (French)**—marriage to a person of inferior social rank
14. **misalliance**—unfortunate marriage
15. **miscegenation**—marriage between individuals of different races, as Negro and Caucasian
16. **mismarriage**—poor or unsuitable marriage
17. **mismatch**—mismarriage
18. **mixed marriage**—marriage between people of different religions, races, etc.

19. **monandry**—marriage to but one male at a time
20. **monogamy**—marriage to but one person at a time; marriage to one person only throughout one's life
21. **monogyny**—marriage to but one female at a time
22. **morganatic marriage**—marriage of a man of high social rank to a woman of lower rank, with the understanding that neither she nor her children shall have any claim to his rank or property—contracted by male members of royal families or the nobility in Europe
23. **nuptials**—marriage
24. **union**—marriage
25. **wedding**—marriage
26. **wedlock**—marriage

9. **One Who Practices a Form of Marriage,** n. *From Sec. 8:* eloper, miscegenator or miscegenist, monogamist, monogynist

10. **Pert. to, or Descr. of, Marriage or a Form of Marriage,**adj. *From Sec. 8:* hymeneal, matrimonial, miscegenetic, monandrous or monandric; monogamous, monogamic, monogamistic, or monogamian; monogynous, morganatic, nuptial, wedded; *Also:* 1. **left-handed** —morganatic, so called because the groom, during the ceremony, gives his left hand, instead of his right, to the bride

11. **Practicing a Form of Marriage,**adj. *From Sec. 8:* monogamous, monogamic, monogamian, monogynous

12. **Upholding or Favoring Monogamy:** monogamian, monogamistic, monogamous, adj.

13. **One Who Upholds or Favors Monogamy:** monagamist,n. (monogamistic,adj.)

14. **One Who Favors Mixed Marriages as a Solution to Race Problems:** miscegenationist, n.

15. **Plural Marriage,**n.
    1. **bigamy**—illegal second or subsequent marriages without the legal dissolution of the former marriage or marriages (bigamist,n. bigamous,adj.)
    2. **deuterogamy**—marriage after the death or divorce of one's first spouse (deuterogamist,n.)
    3. **digamy**—deuterogamy (digamous,adj.)
    4. **polyandry, polyandria**—marriage to a plurality of husbands (polyandrist,n. polyandrous, polyandric, polyandrian, adj.)
    5. **polygamy**—marriage to a plurality of wives, or, less commonly, of husbands (polygamist,n. polygamous, polygamic, polygamical,adj.)
    6. **polygyny**—marriage to a plurality of wives (polygynist,n. polygynous,adj.)
    7. **remarriage**—second or subsequent marriage
    8. **trigamy**—marriage for the third time; illegal marriage to three husbands or wives without legal dissolution of previous marriages (trigamist,n. trigamous,adj.)

16. **To Practice Polygamy:** polygamize,v.

17. **Bond of Marriage:** vinculum matrimonii, n. (Latin)

18. **Married Life:** wedlock,n.

19. **State of Being Married:** matrimony, wedlock,n. (matrimonial,adj.)

20. **State of Living Together as, or as if, Husband and Wife:** cohabitation,n. (cohabit,v.)

21. **State of a Woman under Marriage, since She Is under the Cover, Protection, and Authority of Her Husband:** coverture,n.

22. **State of Living Together as Husband and Wife, though Not Legally Married:** concubinage, hetaerism, hetairism,n. (concubi-

nary or concubinarian, hetaeristic, hetairistic,adj.)

23. **Woman Who Lives with a Man though Not Legally Married to Him:** concubine, concubinary, or concubinarian, or, esp. in ancient Greece, hetaera or hetaira,n.

24. **State of Being a Concubine:** concubinage, n.

25. **Marriage Requirement,**n.
    1. **endogamy**—requirement that marriage be contracted within the tribe, caste, or social group—practiced in primitive societies and occasionally by present-day religious groups (endogamic, endogamous, adj.)
    2. **exogamy**—requirement that marriage be contracted only outside the tribe, clan, village, or family group, in order to avoid inbreeding (exogamic, exogamous,adj.)
    3. **levirate**—ancient Hebrew custom requiring an unmarried man to marry his brother's widow if she had no children

26. **Marriage Celebration or Ceremony,**n.
    1. **bridal**—wedding (bridal,adj.)
    2. **espousals, espousal**—marriage ceremony; wedding
    3. **matrimony**—rite or ceremony of marriage (matrimonial,adj.)
    4. **nuptials**—marriage ceremony (nuptial, adj.)
    5. **spousals**—nuptials (spousal,adj.)
    6. **wedding**—marriage ceremony, festival, or celebration

27. **Pert., Relating, or Referring to Marriage,** adj.
    1. **conjugal**—pert. to marriage and its privileges
    2. **connubial**—pert. to marriage or the married state; conjugal
    3. **extramarital**—outside of marriage
    4. **hymeneal**—pert. to marriage (poetic or literary)
    5. **marital**—pert. to marriage or the married state
    6. **matrimonial**—pert. to marriage
    7. **nuptial**—pert. to marriage
    8. **postmarital**—after marriage
    9. **premarital**—before marriage
    10. **spousal**—pert. to marriage

28. **God or Goddess of Marriage,**n.
    1. **Frigg, Frigga**—goddess of Norse mythology who presided over marriage and domestic life
    2. **Hera**—Greek goddess of the married state, so worshiped under the name of Teleia
    3. **Hymen**—Greek god of marriage
    4. **Juno Pronuba**—Roman goddess of marriage

703. MARRIED PERSON

1. **Married Person; Husband; Wife,**n.
    1. **benedict, benedick**—newly married man who had for a long time been a bachelor; any married man
    2. **better half**—one's wife (humorous)
    3. **bride**—newly married woman, or one about to be married (bridal,adj.)
    4. **bridegroom, groom**—newly married man, or one about to be married
    5. **consort**—wife or husband
    6. **feme covert**—married woman (legal)
    7. **helpmate, helpmeet**—wife
    8. **mate, yokemate**—one's husband or wife
    9. **matron**—married woman, usually no longer young (matronly,adj.)
    10. **mulier**—wife (mulierine,adj.)
    11. **newlywed**—one just or recently married
    12. **partner**—one's wife or husband
    13. **prince consort**—husband of the ruling queen
    14. **spouse**—one's wife or husband

15. **squaw**—wife (American Indian)
16. **squaw man**—white man married to a female American Indian, and often living with his wife's tribe

2. Married People,n.
  1. **couple**—two people married to each other
  2. **Darby and Joan**—happily married couple, esp. if elderly

3. Elderly Married Couple of Greek and Roman Mythology: Baucis (the wife) and Philemon

4. Pert. or Relating to a Husband: husbandly, marital,adj.

5. Pert. or Relating to a Wife: wifely,adj.

6. Pert. to the Relations between, or the Relationship of, Husband and Wife: conjugal,adj. (conjugality,n.)

7. To Provide a Wife for: wive,v.

704. ENGAGEMENT

1. Promise of Marriage,n.
  1. **affiance**—marriage contract; engagement
  2. **betrothal**—mutual agreement to marry; engagement
  3. **engagement**—promise of marriage or to marry
  4. **sponsalia**—contract not to marry another (Roman Catholic religion)
  5. **troth**—one's promise to marry

2. To Promise (Someone) in Marriage: affiance, betroth, engage, troth,v. (betrothal or betrothment, engagement,n.)

3. To Promise to Marry: plight one's troth

4. Promised in Marriage: affianced, betrothed, engaged,adj.

5. One Promised in Marriage, or Who Has Promised to Marry: (one's) betrothed, fiancé (masc.), fiancée (fem.), or intended,n.

6. Public Notice, Given in Church, that a Couple will Marry: banns,n.

7. Engagement Ceremony: espousals,n.

8. Suitable for Marriage,adj.
  1. **eligible**—suitable for marriage, whether because of age, financial conditions, attractiveness, or any other qualities
  2. **marriageable**—fit for marrying or getting married
  3. **nubile**—of females, at the age or stage of physical development when marriage can be consummated; hence, marriageable

9. Suitability for Marriage,n. *From Sec. 8:* eligibility, marriageability, nubility; *Also:* 1. concubitancy—marriageability

10. Person Considered Eligible or Suitable for Marriage: match,n.

11. State of Those Who, by Tribal Custom, Are Eligible to Marry Each Other or Are Predestined Mates: concubitancy,n. (concubitant,n. concubitous,adj.)

12. One Who Arranges a Marriage between Two People: matchmaker,n.

13. Professional Arranger of Marriages: marriage broker, matrimonial agent,n.

14. To Make an Offer of Marriage (to): propose (to),v. (proposal,n.)

15. Breaking of One's Promise to Marry (Legal): breach of promise,n.

16. To Refuse to Marry (Someone) after Having Promised to Do So: jilt,v. (jilter,n.)

705. DIVORCE

1. Termination of Marriage,n.
  1. **annulment**—legal or ecclesiastical declaration that a marriage is not, and has never been, in force

2. divorce—legal termination of a marriage
3. divorce a mensa et thoro—type of divorce that prevents husband and wife from living together, but that leaves all other marital obligations and duties in force and permits reconciliation (legal)
4. divorce a vinculo matrimonii—complete and absolute divorce (legal)
5. legal separation—legal separation of husband and wife, though the marriage is still in force

2. To Declare (a Marriage) Not in Force, and Never to Have Been in Force: annul,v. (annulment,n.)

3. To Legally Terminate a Marriage to: divorce,v. (divorce, divorcement,n.)

4. One Who Is Divorced: divorcé (masc.); divorcee (masc. or fem.); divorcée (fem.),n.

5. Woman in the Process of Divorcing Her Husband: divorceuse,n. (French)

6. Causing Divorce: divorcive,adj.

7. Divorce Decree,n.
  1. **Enoch Arden decree**—decree granting divorce on the grounds of unexplained absence of husband or wife for a specified number of years, usually seven (so called from the hero of a Tennyson poem, who, shipwrecked for a number of years, returns finally to his home to find his wife happily remarried; he hides his identity and eventually dies of a broken heart)
  2. **decree nisi**—divorce decree granted on petition, and made final at a later time, usually six months, unless reason for not granting the divorce is shown
  3. **final decree**—absolute divorce decree
  4. **interlocutory decree**—decree granting temporary divorce until there is a final hearing or disposition

8. One Who Is Named in a Divorce Action as the Person with Whom the Spouse Has Committed Adultery: corespondent,n. (corespondency,n.)

706. UNMARRIED PERSON

1. Unmarried Person,n.
  1. **bachelor**—unmarried man
  2. **bachelor girl**—unmarried girl or woman
  3. **celibate, celibatory, celibatarian; célibataire** (French)—one who is unmarried, or, more commonly, one who is forced, has vowed, or has chosen, to remain unmarried; confirmed bachelor or spinster
  4. **feme sole**—unmarried woman (legal)
  5. **maid, maiden**—young, still-unmarried woman
  6. **miss**—young, unmarried woman
  7. **old maid**—spinster
  8. **spinster, spinstress**—unmarried woman beyond the likely age for getting married
  9. **virgin**—young, unmarried woman; unmarried woman

2. Unmarried,adj. *From Sec. 1:* celibate, maiden, virginal or virgin; *Also:*
  1. **husbandless**—unmarried, i.e., without a husband
  2. **single**—unmarried
  3. **spouseless**—unmarried, i.e., without a spouse
  4. **unwed, unwedded**—unmarried
  5. **wifeless**—unmarried, i.e., without a wife

3. State of Being Unmarried,n. *From Sec. 1:* bachelorhood or bachelorship, celibacy, maidenhood, old-maidism, spinsterhood, virginity; *From Sec. 2:* singleness

4. Pert. to an Unmarried Person,n. *From Sec. 1:* celibatic, maidenly, virginal

5. Characteristic of, Descr. of, or Resembling, an Unmarried Person,adj. *From Sec. 1:* bachelorly or bachelorlike, celibatarian, maidenly, old-maidish or old-maidenish; spinsterous, spinsterish, spinsterlike, spinsterly, or spinsterial

6. Advocating or Favoring the Unmarried Life or State: celibatarian,adj.

7. One Who Advocates or Favors the Unmarried Life or State: celibatarian, celibatist, n.

8. Woman Whose Husband Has Died and Who Has Not Yet Remarried: widow,n. (widowhood,n. widowed,adj.)

9. Man Whose Wife Has Died and Who Has Not Yet Remarried: widower,n. (widowerhood, widowership,n. widowered,adj.)

707. MALE

1. Male,n.
   1. **buck**—male of certain animals, including antelopes, deer, goats, rabbits, hares, sheep, etc.
   2. **bull**—male of bovine and certain other animals
   3. **tom**—male of certain animals, including cats, turkeys, etc.

2. Man,n.
   1. **betty**—cotquean (contemptuous)
   2. **cave man**—man who is rough and direct with women
   3. **cotquean**—man who is concerned with feminine affairs or who engages in what is considered feminine pursuits (contemptuous)
   4. **gentleman**—man of good breeding, manners, etc.
   5. **homunculus**—little man
   6. **manikin**—little man

3. Male; Pert. to, Descr. of, Resembling, or Relating or Referring to, a Male or Man,adj.
   1. **androcentric**—revolving around the male rather than the female
   2. **android**—similar to, or resembling, a male or man
   3. **bull**—male
   4. **andromorphous**—having masculine form or physical characteristics—said of females
   5. **manful**—like a man; showing maleness (commendatory)
   6. **manlike, manly**—possessing the admirable traits of a man
   7. **mannish**—like a man—used to describe a woman or anything pert. to a woman
   8. **masculine**—pert. to, or descr. of, a male
   9. **two-fisted**—manly
   10. **virile**—manful; manly

4. Maleness, etc.,n. *From Sec. 3:* andromorphism, manfulness, manliness, mannishness, masculinity, two-fistedness, virility; *Also:*
   1. **manhood**—quality or state of being a man
   2. **prime**—early manhood

5. Development of Maleness,n.
   1. **virilescence**—development of male characteristics in old women (virilescent,adj.)
   2. **virilism**—development of male traits, appearance, or characteristics in a female

6. To Make Manly: virify,v. (virification,n.)

7. Place Where Only Men Were Permitted (in Ancient Greece): andron,n.

8. Having or Exhibiting Womanish Qualities or Characteristics, though a Man: effeminate,adj. (effeminacy, effeminateness, n.)

9. Effeminate: girlish, muliebrous, niminy-piminy, panty-waist, prissy, sissified, sissy, sissyish, unmanly, womanish,adj.

10. Effeminacy: androgyny, girlishness, muliebrity, prissiness, sissiness, sissyishness, unmanliness, womanishness,n.

11. Effeminate Man or Boy: androgyne, effeminate, milksop, mollycoddle, panty-waist, sissy, woman-man,n.

12. To Make, or Cause to Be, Effeminate: effeminate, effeminatize, effeminize, sissify, womanize,v. (effemination, effeminization, sissification, womanization,n.)

13. To Become Effeminate: effeminate, womanize,v. (womanization,n.)

14. The Development by a Man of Feminine Mental Qualities, Attitudes, etc. (psychology): effemination,n.

15. Presence, Medically, of Female Characteristics in a Male: feminism,n.

708. FEMALE

1. Female: gentlewoman, girl, lady, mulier, petticoat, wench, woman,n.

2. Females or Women, Collectively or Generally: distaff, fair sex, female sex, femality, feminality, femininity, feminity, gentle sex, gentler sex, girlery, girlhood, weaker sex, womanhood, womankind; womenfolk (colloq.), n.

3. Women, Collectively, in an Oriental Household: harem,n.

4. Group of Females Attached to, or Associating with, a Single Male of Certain Animal Species: harem,n.

5. Pert. or Relating to, or Descr. of, Females or Women: distaff, female, feminine, girlish, girly, gynecic or gynaecic, muliebrile, petticoat, womanish, womanlike, womanly, adj.

6. Femaleness: femality, feminacy, feminality, femineity, femininity, feminism, feminity, girlhood, girlishness, muliebrity, womanhood, womanishness, womanity, womanliness, womanness,n.

7. State of Possessing Full Womanly Powers: muliebrity,n.

8. Like a Female or Woman in Form or Physical Characteristics: gynecomorphous, adj.

9. To Deprive of Femaleness; To Make Unfeminine: unsex,v.

10. Belief that Women Should Have Equal Political, Social, and Economic Rights with Men: feminism,n. (feminist,n. feminist,adj.)

11. Concern about, and Devotion to, the Interests, Rights, etc., of Women: womanism,n. (womanist,n.)

12. Women's Quarters in Ancient Greece and Rome: gynaeceum, gynaecium,n.

13. Screen used in India to Conceal Women from Public Gaze or View: purdah,n.

14. Certain Specific Types of Females or Women,n.
   1. **adventuress**—woman who seeks a social position or money through dubious, not entirely ethical, or not entirely honest means
   2. **amazon**—tall, powerful, masculine, or aggressive woman; virago (amazonian,adj.)
   3. **androgyne**—masculine woman
   4. **baggage**—pert and lively young woman; worthless woman
   5. **bitch**—low or coarse woman
   6. **dame**—woman of station or authority
   7. **Delilah**—woman who entices a man for her own special benefit, rather than out of sincere emotion—so called after Samson's mistress in the Bible
   8. **grisette**—young woman of the lower classes who works for a living and who is lively and free in manner, etc.
   9. **harridan**—bad-tempered woman; shrew

10. **hussy**—worthless woman; bad-mannered, impertinent woman
11. **jade**—disreputable, contemptible woman
12. **Lorelei**—siren
13. **quean**—bold or brazen woman; hussy
14. **scold**—irritable, abusive, or noisy woman
15. **shrew**—bad-tempered, quarrelsome woman with an acid tongue and a nagging disposition; vexatious, perverse, and turbulent woman (shrewish,adj.)
16. **siren**—alluring, enticing woman
17. **spitfire**—hot-tempered female
18. **termagant**—quarrelsome, scolding woman
19. **virago**—loudmouthed, turbulent woman (viraginian,adj.)
20. **vixen**—quarrelsome and bad-tempered woman—a somewhat affectionate term (vixenish,adj.)
21. **wench**—woman for whom one feels a mild contempt
22. **witch**—woman who attracts men as if by magic power; fascinating, charming, or alluring woman
23. **Xanthippe**—complaining, scolding woman —after Socrates' wife

709. SEX

1. **Pert. or Referring to Sex,adj.**
   1. **bisexual**—pert. to both sexes
   2. **epicene**—common to both sexes
   3. **heterosexual**—pert. to both sexes
   4. **intersexual**—between the sexes
   5. **sexual**—pert. to sex
   6. **unisexual**—pert. to one sex only

2. **Grammatical Sex: gender,n.**

3. **Descr. of Gender:** common (as *person, author,* etc.); feminine (as *girl, woman,* etc.); masculine (as *boy, man,* etc.); neuter (as *book, pencil,* etc.),adj.

4. **Pert. to Sex, i.e., Sexual Activities or Appetites, etc.:** animal, animalistic, bestial, brutish, carnal, erotic, fleshly, gross, Lesbian, sensual, sexual, venereal, voluptuous,adj.

5. **Sexual Character or Nature:** eroticism, sexuality,n.

6. **Sex Life**
   1. **erotism, eroticism**—sex life of a person (psychoanalysis)
   2. **sexuality**—sex life

7. **Sexual Desire, Excitement, or Interest,n.**
   1. **amorousness**—inclination to sexual enjoyment
   2. **andromania**—nymphomania
   3. **animalism, animality**—sensuality (animal, animalistic,adj.)
   4. **aphrodisia**—violent sexual passion
   5. **aphrodisiomania**—exaggerated sexual interest or excitement
   6. **boarishness**—lust
   7. **bestiality**—excessive or degraded sensuality
   8. **brutishness**—sensuality
   9. **carnality**—lust (carnal,adj.)
   10. **concupiscence**—lust
   11. **desire**—sexual desire or appetite
   12. **eroticism, erotism**—sexual desire, excitement, or interest (erotic, erotical,adj.)
   13. **erotomania, eroticomania**—excessive or pathological sexual desire
   14. **goatishness**—lust
   15. **grossness**—sensuality
   16. **gynecomania**—satyriasis
   17. **heat**—sexual desire or excitement in the female mammal (often in the expression *in heat*)
   18. **heterosexuality**—normal attraction to, interest in, or desire for, the opposite sex (heterosexual,adj.)
   19. **incontinence**—lack of control over, or restraint in, sexual desires
   20. **lasciviousness**—lust

21. **lechery, lecherousness**—lust
22. **lewdness**—lust
23. **libertinism**—lack of restraint in sexual appetites
24. **libidinousness**—lust
25. **libido**—sexual desire; lust (libidinal, libidinous,adj.)
26. **licentiousness**—lust
27. **lickerishness**—lust
28. **looseness**—lack of sexual restraint
29. **lubricity**—lust
30. **lust, lustfulness**—sexual desire; sinful, illicit, unbridled, or unrestrained sexual desire, desires, or appetites; strong desire for prohibited sexual pleasures
31. **must**—frenzy from sexual excitement— of the male elephant
32. **narcissism, narcism**—erotic feeling aroused by one's own body (narcissistic, narcistic,adj.)
33. **nymphomania**—morbid and apparently insatiable desire for sexual intercourse— of the female (nymphomaniacal,adj.)
34. **oestrus, estrus**—heat (oestrous, oestrual, estrous, estrual,adj.)
35. **passion, passions**—sexual desire; lust
36. **priapism**—satyriasis, in psychiatric terminology (priapistic,adj.)
37. **prurience**—strong, often unseemly, sexual interest, desire, cravings, thoughts, curiosity, etc.
38. **rammishness**—lust
39. **rut**—sexual heat in certain mammals
40. **ruttishness, ruttiness**—lust
41. **salaciousness, salacity**—tendency to pursue sexual pleasure; lust
42. **satyriasis**—morbid and excessive sexual desire in the male
43. **satyrism**—unrestrained or beastlike lust
44. **sensuality, sensualism**—devotion to sexual pleasures (sensualistic,adj.)
45. **sexuality**—abnormal interest in, or preoccupation with, sex
46. **stimulation**—sexual excitement
47. **sultriness**—sexual passion or excitement
48. **swinishness**—sensuality

8. **Sexually Desirous or Excited; Interested in, or Pursuing, Sex or Sexual Pleasures,adj.** *From Sec. 7:* amorous, animal, boarish, bestial, brutish, concupiscent, erotic or erotical, goatish, gross, heterosexual, hot, incontinent, lascivious, lecherous, lewd, libertine, libidinous, licentious, lickerish or liquorish, loose, lubricous, lustful, must, narcissistic, narcistic, nymphomaniacal, passionate, prurient, rammish, ruttish, rutty, salacious, sensual, stimulated, sultry, swinish; *Also:*
   1. **Cyprian**—lustful
   2. **hircine**—lustful, in allusion to the reputed quality of goats
   3. **hot**—sexually excited

9. **One Who Is Sexually Desirous or Excited, or Who Is Interested in, or Pursues, Sex or Sexual Pleasure,n.** *From Sec. 7:* erotic, erotomaniac, heterosexual, incontinent, lecher, libertine, must (an elephant), narcissist, narcist, nymphomaniac, satyr or satyromaniac, sensualist, swine

10. **Energy, Desire, or Striving Derived from the Sex Instinct (Term in Psychoanalysis):** libido,n. (libidinal, libidinous,adj.)

11. **Arising from Sensual Gratification:** voluptuous,adj.

12. **Sexual Pleasure: volupty,n.**

13. **Period of Sexual Desire in Female Mammals:** estrum, estrus, heat, oestrum, oestrus, rut,n. (estrous, estrual, oestrous, oestrual, adj.)

14. **To Have Sexual Desires, or Sexual Desires toward,v.**
   1. **desire**—wish to have sexual intercourse with

402

2. **lust (for, after)**—have strong sexual desires (for)
3. **oestruate, estruate**—be in heat; rut—of animals (oestruation, estruation,n.)
4. **rut**—have strong sexual impulses during the reproductive period—of cattle, deer, and certain other mammals
5. **want**—desire

15. **To Approach Personally with Sexual Proposals:** make advances to,v.
16. **The Pursuit of Sexual Pleasures:** sensualism, venery,n. (sensualist,n. sensualistic, adj.)
17. **That Which Causes Sexual Desire or Excitement,n.**
   1. **aphrodisiac**—agent that stimulates the sexual appetites
   2. **blister beetle**—beetle that, when dried and powdered, is administered internally, supposedly as an aphrodisiac, though actually serving only to stimulate the genitourinary mucous membranes—called by pharmacists *Spanish fly* or *cantharis*
   3. **cantharis**—blister beetle (cantharides,pl.)
   4. **fetish, fetich**—object or part of the body that abnormally arouses sexual passion
   5. **philter, philtre**—love potion
   6. **Spanish fly**—blister beetle
   7. **stimulant**—substance, agent, etc., that arouses sexual desire

18. **Causing Sexual Desire or Excitement,adj.**
   1. **aphrodisiac**—causing sexual excitement
   2. **erogenous**—stimulating the sexual appetites
   3. **erotic**—causing or arousing sexual desire
   4. **estrogenic**—capable of producing an increase in physiological sex capacity or activity, esp. in females
   5. **stimulating**—arousing sexual interest or desire
   6. **venereal**—aphrodisiac

19. **To Cause Sexual Desire in:** excite, inflame, stimulate,v.
20. **Emphasis on Sex:** sexualism,n.
21. **To Invest with Sexual Atmosphere, Characteristics, Energy, etc.:** eroticize, erotize, libidinize (all psychiatric), sexualize, v. (erotization, libidinization, sexualization, n.)
22. **Psychological Opinion that All Human Activity, Behavior, Interest, Desire, Stimuli, etc., Stem from the Sex Instinct (Not Accepted by Any School of Psychiatry Today):** pansexualism,n. (pansexualist,n. pansexual, pansexualist,adj.)
23. **To Examine, Interpret, or Understand (Human Activity, etc.) According to This Viewpoint:** pansexualize,v.
24. **An Overspreading, Investment, or Imbuement of All Behavior and Experiences with Sexual Feeling:** pansexualism, pansexuality,n. (pansexual,adj.)
25. **Male Sexual Power or Ability:** potency, vigor, virility,n. (potent, vigorous, virile,adj.)
26. **Man Who Annoys Strange Women, Esp. in a Theater, Park, or Other Public Place, with Sexual or Other Advances or Intimacies:** masher,n. (slang)
27. **Period or State in Which Sexual Ability Develops:** puberty,n.
28. **Pert. to Puberty:** hebetic, puberal, pubertal, pubertic, pubescent,adj.
29. **Arriving at, or Having Arrived at, Puberty:** pubescent,adj. (pubescence,n.)
30. **Young Person Who Has Arrived at Puberty:** pubescent,n.
31. **Science of Sex:** sexology,n. (sexologist,n. sexological,adj.)

32. **Literature Devoted to Sexual Themes:** erotica,n.
33. **Books Dealing with Sexual Themes, Esp. in an Obscene or Stimulating Manner—So Called by Book Dealers and Collectors:** curiosa,n.

710. SEXUAL INTERCOURSE

1. **Sexual Intercourse:** aphrodisia, carnality, cohabitation, coition, coitus, commerce, comcubitus, congress, conjugation, connection, conversation, copulation, intercourse; knowledge or carnal knowledge (archaic) ; relations, sexual act, sexual connection, sexual relations, sexual union, union, venery,n. (coital, copulatory, venereal,adj.) ; *Also:*
   1. **adultery**—sexual intercourse between a married person and someone other than the legal spouse (adulterine, adulterous, adj.)
   2. **affair, affaire**—sexual intercourse between two people not married to each other
   3. **consummation**—completion (of a marriage) by sexual intercourse
   4. **criminal conversation**—sexual intercourse with a married woman not one's wife; adultery
   5. **debauchery**—participation in illicit and excessive sexual relations, indulgence, or pleasures
   6. **extramarital relations**—sexual intercourse on the part of a married person with someone other than the legal husband or wife
   7. **fornication**—sexual intercourse between unmarried adults
   8. **fraternization**—illicit sexual intercourse between the women, or a woman, of an occupied country and the enemy soldiers, or soldier
   9. **incest**—sexual intercourse between close blood relatives (incestuous,adj.)
   10. **infidelity, unfaithfulness**—breach of marriage vows, i.e., sexual intercourse with someone other than one's legal spouse
   11. **intimacy**—illicit sexual intercourse
   12. **intrigue**—secret or illicit sexual intercourse
   13. **liaison**—illicit sexual intercourse
   14. **mating**—sexual intercourse or pairing between animals
   15. **polygyny**—mating of a male animal and several female animals
   16. **possession**—sexual intercourse, generally from the viewpoint of the male who, figuratively, possesses, or possesses himself of, the female
   17. **premarital relations**—sexual intercourse before marriage
   18. **prostitution**—sexual intercourse on the part of a woman for money or other valuable considerations, but not out of genuine desire or feelings
   19. **whoredom**—unlawful sexual intercourse
   20. **whoremastery**—sexual intercourse with prostitutes

2. **To Have Sexual Intercourse,v.** *From Sec. 1:* cohabit, conjugate, copulate; consummate (a marriage), debauch, fornicate, fraternize, be intimate, intrigue, mate, prostitute; *Also:*
   1. **bed**—have sexual intercourse with
   2. **couple**—have sexual intercourse
   3. **cover, serve**—copulate with (a female)—of domestic animals
   4. **cuckold**—be unfaithful to (one's husband) by having intercourse with another man or men
   5. **go to bed with, go to sleep with**—have intercourse with
   6. **know**—have sexual intercourse with, i.e., have carnal knowledge of (archaic)

7. **possess**—have sexual intercourse with (a woman)

8. **sleep together**—have sexual intercourse

9. **sleep with**—have sexual intercourse with

10. **wench**—engage in sexual intercourse with loose women

11. **whore**—go around having unlawful intercourse; have intercourse with prostitutes; have intercourse with a man for money

3. One Who Has Sexual Intercourse,n. *From Sec. 1:* cohabitant or cohabiter, adulterer, or, fem., adultress, debauchee, fornicator, or, fem., fornicatress, fraternizer, mate, prostitute, whoremaster or whoremonger; *From Sec. 2:* wencher

4. Engaging in Sexual Intercourse,adj. *From Sec. 1:* adulterous, incestuous, unfaithful, intimate (with), whorish

5. Man Whose Wife Has Intercourse with Other Men: cuckold,n. (cuckoldry,n.)

6. To Make a Cuckold of (a Husband) by Having Intercourse with His Wife: cuckold, v.

7. Referring to Sexual Indulgence: Paphian, Sapphic,adj.

8. A Living Together in Sexual Relationship, though Not Legally Married: cohabitation, concubinage,n. (cohabitant, cohabiter, n. concubinal, concubinarian, concubinary, adj.)

9. Woman Who Lives in a Sexual Relation with a Man, though Not Legally Married to Him: concubine, concubinary,n. (concubinage,n.)

10. Symbol of Adultery: scarlet letter,n.

11. A Meeting for Illicit Sexual Relations: assignation, rendezvous,n. (rendezvous,v.)

12. A Meeting Place for Illicit Sexual Relations: rendezvous,n.

13. To Force Sexual Intercourse upon (a Female): abuse, assault; defile (archaic); outrage, rape, ravish, ruin, violate,v. (abuser, assaulter, defiler, rapist, ravisher, ruiner, violater,n.)

14. Rape: abuse, assault; defilement (archaic); ravishment, stupration, violation,n.

15. To Entice into Sexual Intercourse,v.
  1. **betray**—seduce (a female) by promises, as of marriage, etc., that were not intended to be kept, then desert her (betrayal, betrayment,n. betrayer,n.)
  2. **debauch**—seduce (debauchment,n. debaucher,n.)
  3. **seduce**—entice (a woman, or, perhaps, a young boy or man) into unlawful sexual intercourse (seduction,n. seducer,n. seductress,fem.n.)

16. To Deprive or Rob (a Female) of Virginity through Sexual Intercourse: deflower, v. (defloration,n.)

17. To Debase or Corrupt by Lascivious Sexual Intercourse: whore,v.

18. Certain Other Terms for Men Engaging in Illicit Sexual Activity,n.
  1. **Casanova**—rake (Casanovanic,adj.)
  2. **Don Juan**—irresistible seducer of women
  3. **gallant**—paramour
  4. **gigolo**—man who, for pay, caters to a wealthy woman sexually
  5. **Lothario**—unconscionable seducer of women
  6. **lover**—man with whom a woman has illicit intercourse
  7. **paramour**—man engaged in an illicit sexual relationship; lover
  8. **rake**—man who promiscuously indulges in sexual relationships (rakish,adj.)
  9. **roué**—man who indulges in dissipation,

often including sexual intemperance; man who spends much of his life indulging in sexual vices or excesses; rake

19. Woman Who Has Entered into a Protracted Illicit Sexual Relationship with a Man: concubine; doxy (slang); fancy woman, kept woman, mistress, paramour,n.

20. Mistress of the Better Class, Often of High Intellectual Attainment, of Ancient Greece: hetaera, hetaira,n. (hetaerae, hetairai,pl.n. hetaerism, hetairism,n. hetaeristic, hetairistic,adj.)

21. Well-Known Hetaerae: Lais, Phryne,n.

22. Harem: seraglio, serai, serail, or, in India and Persia, zenana,n.

23. Concubine in a Harem: odalisque,n.

24. Final Physiological Point of Sexual Activity or Intercourse: climax, orgasm,n. (climactic, orgasmic or orgastic,adj.)

25. Withdrawal of the Penis before Orgasm: coitus interruptus, onanism, withdrawal,n. (onanist,n. onanistic,adj.)

26. To Attain Orgasm by Self-Manipulation: masturbate,v. (masturbation,n.)

27. Masturbation: autoeroticism, autoerotism, onanism, self-abuse, self-pollution,n.

28. Masturbator: onanist,n.

29. Pert. or Referring to, or Descr. of, Masturbation: autoerotic, masturbatic, masturbational, masturbatory, onanistic,adj.

30. Inability to Reach Orgasm during Sexual Intercourse: anorgasmy,n.

31. Sexual Aberration; Abnormal or Unnatural Sexual Instinct, Desire, etc.: erotopathy, perversion, sexual deviation, sexual perversion,n. (erotopathic, perverted,adj.)

32. One Possessing a Sexual Aberration, etc.: erotopath, deviate or sexual deviate, pervert or sexual pervert,n.

33. Certain Specific Sexual Aberrations, Perversions, Abnormal Practices, etc.,n.
  1. **algolagnia**—sexual perversion in which the giving or receiving of pain leads to gratification without intercourse
  2. **autofellatio**—fellatio practiced on himself by the male
  3. **bestiality**—sexual relations between humans and animals
  4. **bisexualism, bisexuality**—sexual attraction to both males and females (bisexual, adj.)
  5. **buggery**—sodomy
  6. **coprolagnia**—sexual perversion in which gratification is obtained from thinking of, handling, or seeing fecal matter
  7. **cunnilingus**—abnormal sexual practice in which orgasm is produced in the female by the use of the tongue; practice of using the tongue on the vulva to cause sexual excitement in the female
  8. **eonism**—adoption, by a male, of feminine mannerisms, clothing, habits, etc. (eonistic,adj.)
  9. **erotic zoophilism**—impulse to stroke animals for sexual pleasure
  10. **exhibitionism**—sexual perversion in which pleasure is derived from exhibiting the genital organs to the opposite sex (exhibitionistic,adj.)
  11. **fellatio, fellatorism**—sexual practice in which an orgasm is produced in the male by the use of the tongue or mouth (fellatic,adj.)
  12. **fetishism, fetichism**—fixation of erotic interest on a part of the body or an article of clothing, rather than on a person of the opposite sex (fetishistic, fetichistic, adj.)

13. **fixation**—arresting of sexual development by a strong childhood attachment
14. **flagellation**—practice of whipping to stimulate sexual desire
15. **frottage**—sexual perversion in which orgasm is achieved by rubbing against someone, as in a crowd
16. **gerontophilia**—sexual attraction toward aged people
17. **homoerotism**—sublimated sexual attraction to one's own sex, usually expressed in socially acceptable patterns (homoerotic,adj.)
18. **homogenitality**—perversion marked by genital relations between members of the same sex (homogenital,adj.)
19. **homosexuality, homosexualism**—manifestation of sexual interest in members of the same sex (homosexual,adj.)
20. **iconolagny**—abnormal sexual stimulation or excitement from looking at pictures or statues
21. **irrumation**—fellatio
22. **Lesbianism, Lesbian love**—sexual attraction or relations between women (Lesbian, adj.)
23. **masochism**—sexual perversion in which one of the partners derives intensified gratification and pleasure through the pain, cruelty, or humiliation inflicted by the other (masochistic,adj.)
24. **necrophilism, necrophilia, necrophily**—sexual perversion in which the victim derives pleasure from violating dead bodies (necrophilic, necrophile,adj.)
25. **pederasty**—sexual relations through the anus, practiced by men on young boys (pederastic,adj.)
26. **pedophilia**—pathological sexual desire on the part of an adult for a child (pedophilic,adj.)
27. **sadism**—perversion in which passion is aroused by inflicting cruelty or injury on one's sexual partner (sadistic,adj.)
28. **Sapphism**—Lesbianism
29. **scoptophilia, scopophilia**—sexual pleasure derived from looking or observing; voyeurism (scopophilic,adj.)
30. **self-irrumation**—autofellatio
31. **sexo-aesthetic inversion**—eonism
32. **sexual inversion**—homosexuality
33. **sodomy**—sexual relations through the anus, between males; sexual intercourse with an animal
34. **transvestism, transvestitism**—abnormal desire to dress in the clothing of the opposite sex
35. **tribadism, tribady**—playing of the role of the male by a woman in homosexual practices
36. **voyeurism**—practice of obtaining sexual pleasure from watching, secretly or otherwise, other people having intercourse, or nude people of the opposite sex (voyeuristic,adj.)
37. **zooerasty, zooerastia**—sexual intercourse with animals
38. **zoolagnia**—sexual attraction toward animals
39. **zoophilia, zoophilia erotica**—sexual excitement from petting or stroking animals

34. Possessor or Practicer of a Specific Sexual Aberration, etc.,n. *From Sec. 33:* algolagnist, autofellator, bisexual, bugger, cunnilinguist, eonist, exhibitionist, fellator; fellatrice (fem.); fetishist, fetichist, flagellator, frotteur, homosexual, homosexualist, Lesbian, masochist, necrophile, pederast, sadist, Sapphist, scopophiliac, sexual invert, sodomist or sodomite, transvestite, tribade, voyeur; *Also:*
1. **écouteur**—one who derives abnormal sexual gratification from listening to stories of sexual encounters, etc.
2. **Peeping Tom**—voyeur

---

35. **Homosexuals as a Class, Group, etc.:** third sex,n.
36. **Combination of Male and Female Characteristics, Organs, etc.,n.**
   1. **androgyny, androgynism, androgyneity**—state or condition of having characteristics of both sexes, or of being both male and female; hermaphroditism (androgynous,adj.)
   2. **gynandry, gynandrism, gynandria**—condition of a woman having a masculine physique; hermaphroditism (gynandrous, gynandroid,adj.)
   3. **hermaphroditism**—condition of possessing both ovarian and testicular tissue; condition of possessing the reproductive organs of both sexes, one set, however, being in rudimentary form; possession or exhibition of the physical characteristics or attributes of both sexes (hermaphrodite, hermaphroditic, hermaphroditical, adj.)
37. **One Possessing Male and Female Characteristics, Organs, etc.,n.** *From Sec. 36:* androgyne, gynandroid, hermaphrodite
38. **To Deprive of Sexual Power, Ability, etc., v.**
   1. **alter**—castrate (esp. cats)
   2. **asexualize**—make incapable of sexual reproduction, as by castration or other means
   3. **caponize**—castrate (a rooster or cock), in order to make his meat more tender
   4. **castrate**—deprive a male of sexual power or ability by excising the testicles
   5. **emasculate**—take male sexual power or ability from, by a surgical operation or by some other means
   6. **geld**—castrate (esp. horses)
   7. **mutilate**—castrate
   8. **spay**—remove the ovaries of (a female animal) so that she cannot conceive
   9. **sterilize**—make incapable of reproduction, usually by a surgical operation
   10. **unman**—emasculate
   11. **unsex**—deprive of sex
39. **Deprivation of Sexual Power or Ability, n.** *From Sec. 38:* alteration, asexualization, caponization, castration, emasculation, mutilation, sterilization
40. **Castrated Human Male:** androgyne, eunuch,n.
41. **Resembling a Eunuch:** eunuchoid,adj.
42. **Human Male Castrated in Youth so that He May Retain His Soprano Voice for Singing:** castrato,n. (Italian)
43. **Lack of Sexual Power or Interest,n.**
   1. **anaphrodisia**—lack or impairment of sexual desire
   2. **frigidity**—indifference to, or lack of pleasure from, sexual intercourse; absence of sexual desire in a woman (frigid, adj.)
   3. **impotence, impotency**—inability, on the part of the male, to take part in sexual intercourse (impotent,adj.)
44. **Substance, Agent, etc., that Impairs or Reduces Sexual Desire:** anaphrodisiac,n.
45. **Capable of Impairing or Reducing, or Serving to Impair or Reduce, Sexual Desire:** anaphrodisiac,adj.
46. **To Detour One's Sexual Energy into Non-Sexual and Socially Acceptable Paths:** sublimate,v. (sublimation,n.)
47. **Lack, etc., of Sexual Relations,n.**
   1. **abstention, abstinence**—voluntary forbearance from sexual relations (abstinent,adj.)
   2. **celibacy**—state of refraining from sexual relations (celibate,adj.)

3. **chastity**—non-indulgence in sexual relations (chaste,adj.)
4. **continence**—self-restraint in respect to sexual passions; non-indulgence in sexual relations (continent,adj.)
5. **maidenhead, maidenhood, maidhood**—virginity—of a female (maiden,adj.)
6. **purity**—virginity (pure,adj.)
7. **virginity**—state of not having had sexual intercourse, esp. of a female (virgin, virginal,adj.)
8. **virtue**—chastity (virtuous,adj.)

48. One Who Avoids, Has Not Had, or Does Not Have, Sexual Relations,n. *From Sec. 47:* abstainer, celibate, maiden; virgin, vestal, or vestal virgin

49. To Forbear Voluntarily from Sexual Relations: abstain, maid it, virgin it,v.

50. Part Symbolic of Virginity in a Female: hymen, maidenhead,n.

51. Sexless; Not Related to Sex,adj.
1. **asexual**—not involved with sex; having no reference to sex; having no sex or sexual action
2. **epicene**—sexless
3. **neuter**—without sex; having no relevance to sex; neither male nor female

711. PROSTITUTE

1. Prostitute: cocotte, courtesan or courtezan, Cyprian, Delilah; doxy (slang); drab, fallen woman, fancy woman; fille de joie (French); fille de nuit (French); harlot, meretrix, painted woman, Paphian, quean, scarlet woman, slut, stew, strumpet; tart (slang); trollop, trull, whore,n. (meretricious, sluttish, whorish,adj.)

2. Worn-Out Prostitute: harridan,n.

3. Prostitute Who Solicits Business Publicly: streetwalker,n.

4. Woman Forced Unwillingly into Prostitution: white slave,n.

5. Prostitution: harlotry, white slavery, whoredom,n.

6. To Associate with Prostitutes: drab, wench, whore,v.

7. To Make a Prostitute of: whore,v.

8. One Who Seduces Women into Prostitution: white-slaver,n.

9. House of Prostitution: bagne (Italian); bagnio, bawdyhouse, bordel, bordello, brothel, disorderly house, house of assignation, house of ill-fame, house of ill-repute; panel den or house (where there are secret panels so that accomplices may enter to steal the possessions of the frequenters); seraglio (loose usage); stews, whorehouse,n.

10. Woman Who Keeps a House of Prostitution: bawd, madam,n.

11. Region of Houses of Prostitution: red-light district,n.

12. Japanese District Where Prostitutes Live —So Called by Foreigners after the District in Tokyo: yashiwara,n.

13. District in a City Where Vice and Immorality Abound: tenderloin,n.

14. Descr. of a Place Where the Laws against Prostitution and Other Vice or Sexual Immorality Are Poorly if at all Enforced: wide-open,adj.

15. To Procure Customers for a Prostitute: pander, pimp, procure,v.

16. One Who Procures Customers for a Prostitute: bawd (fem.); madam (fem.); pander, panderer, pimp, procurer; procuress (fem.),n.

17. To Invite Men to Have Sexual Intercourse—said of a Prostitute: solicit,v.

18. Description or Portrayal of, or Writing about, Prostitutes or Prostitution: pornography,n. (pornographer, pornographist,n. pornographic,adj.)

19. Place of Refuge or Rehabilitation for Prostitutes: magdalen,n.

712. SEXUAL IMMORALITY

1. Sexually Loose or Immoral: abandoned, boarish, corrupt, Cyprian, debauched, depraved, dissolute; fast (colloq.); goatish, hircine; Jezebelian or Jazebelish (of the female); lascivious, lecherous, lewd, libertine, libidinous, licentious, lickerish, liquorish, lubricous, pornerastic, profligate, promiscuous; rakehell, rakehellish, rakehelly, rakish (the last four usually of the male); salacious, shameful, shameless; sluttish (of the female); unchaste, vicious, wanton, whorish,adj.

2. Sexual Looseness or Immorality: boarishness, corruption, corruptness, debauchery, depravity, dissoluteness, goatishness, lasciviousness, lecherousness, lechery, lewdness, libertinism, libidinousness, licentiousness, lickerishness, lubricity, profligacy, promiscuity, promiscuousness, salaciousness, salacity, shamefulness, shamelessness, sluttishness, unchasteness, vice, viciousnes, wantonness, whorishness,n.

3. Sexually Loose, Depraved, or Immoral Man: debauchee, Don Juan, lecher, libertine, profligate, rake, roué, swine, wanton, whoremaster,n.

4. Sexually Loose, Depraved, or Immoral Woman: debauchee, cocotte, courtesan, Cyprian, Delilah, demimondaine; doxy (slang); drab, harlot, jade, Jezebel, libertine, meretrix, Messalina, profligate, slut, strumpet; tart (slang); trollop, trull, wanton; wench (somewhat archaic),n.

5. To Indulge in Sexual Looseness, Depravity, or Immorality: debauch, wanton, whore,v. (debauchery,n.)

6. To Lead into Sexual Looseness, etc.: corrupt, debauch, deprave, seduce,v. (corruption, debauchment, depravation, seduction,n. corrupter, debaucher, depraver, seducer, or, fem., seductress,n.)

713. OBSCENITY

1. Obscene,adj.
1. **bawdy**—obscene
2. **breezy**—somewhat risqué or suggestive
3. **broad**—indelicate—often of humor
4. **coarse**—indelicate—often of language or humor
5. **dirty**—obscene
6. **Fescennine**—obscene or scurrilous—after a form of scurrilous poetry that originated in Fescennia, a city of Etruria
7. **filthy**—vulgarly or disgustingly obscene or sexy
8. **foul**—filthy
9. **gross**—obscene, low, or vulgar—often of language or humor
10. **immodest**—obscene—*immodest proposals, offers,* etc.
11. **immoral**—contrary, or flagrantly in opposition, to sexual morality
12. **improper**—obscene; contrary to propriety or decency; immoral
13. **indecent**—obscene; offensive to decency
14. **indecorous**—improper
15. **indelicate**—too grossly or frankly indicative of sexuality, and hence violating pruderies or conventions
16. **ithyphallic**—obscene—in reference to the phallus carried in the festivals of Bacchus

17. **lascivious**—obscene; unduly or vulgarly stimulating sexual desire, response, etc.; offensive to decency, modesty, chastity, or propriety; exposing or emphasizing what decency or modesty forbids exposing or emphasizing

18. **lewd**—obscene; lascivious

19. **licentious**—obscene; lascivious

20. **low**—obscene; fit for only coarse or depraved company or conversation—of language, words, expressions, etc.

21. **lubricous**—lascivious

22. **lurid**—marked by frankness and coarseness in dealing with sexual episodes—of writing

23. **nasty**—filthy

24. **off-color**—risqué

25. **pornographic**—descr. of such writing, painting, or other artistic representation that is intended solely to excite sexual passion and that otherwise has little or no artistic value or integrity

26. **purple**—lurid or risqué—of writing

27. **Rabelaisian**—characterized by a bold, lusty, and humorous approach to sexual matters, with little disguise or delicacy, as in the writing of the French author Rabelais

28. **racy**—risqué

29. **raw**—lewdly obscene

30. **ribald**—descr. of language that is obscene or coarse but nevertheless jesting or humorous in flavor

31. **risqué**—bordering on the obscene—of language, writing, a story, etc.

32. **salacious**—obscene; lascivious

33. **scabrous**—obscene; risqué

34. **scurrilous, scurrile**—humorously obscene —of language

35. **sexy**—emphasizing sex in a frank and purposefully stimulating manner (slang)

36. **shameless, shameful**—obscene

37. **smutty**—disgustingly obscene

38. **spicy**—risqué

39. **suggestive**—tending to suggest or imply indecency or obscenity

40. **unclean**—obscene; filthy

41. **vile**—filthy

42. **vulgar**—obscene

2. Obscenity,n. *From Sec. 1:* bawdiness or bawdry, breeziness, broadness, coarseness, dirt or dirtiness, Fescenninity, filth or filthiness, foulness, grossness, immodesty, immorality, impropriety, indecency, indecorum or indecorousness, indelicacy, lasciviousness, lewdness, licentiousness, lowness, lubricity, luridness, nastiness, pornography, purpleness, raciness, rawness, ribaldry, salaciousness or salacity, scabrousness, scurrility or scurrilousness, sexiness, shamelessness, shamefulness, smut or smuttiness, spice or spiciness, suggestiveness, uncleanness, vileness, vulgarity or vulgarness.

3. Obscene Expression, Language, etc.,n. *From Sec. 1:* bawdry, dirt, filth, impropriety, ribaldry, scurrility, smut, spice, vulgarity; *Also:*

1. **coprophemia**—obscene language

2. **obscenity**—obscene language; an obscene term or expression

4. Obscene Literature or Art; Literature or Art Intended to Be Sexually Stimulating: pornography,n. (pornographer, pornographist, n. pornographic,adj.)

5. Study of, or Interest in, Obscene or Pornographic Literature: scatology, skatology,n. (scatologic, scatological,adj.)

714. PREGNANCY

1. Pregnant: anticipating (slang); big, big with child, childing; enceinte (French); expectant, expecting, full, gravid, great, great with child, heavy, heavy with child, laden, adj.

2. Pregnancy: fetation, foetation, gestation, gravity, gravidness,n. (gestational, gestative, adj.)

3. To Become Pregnant: conceive,v. (conception,n.)

4. To Conceive Again when Already Pregnant: superfetate,v. (superfetation,n. superfetate,adj.)

5. To Carry in the Womb during Pregnancy: gestate,v. (gestation,n. gestational, gestative,adj.)

6. To Make Pregnant: fecundate (biology); fecundify (biology); fertilize (biology); impregnate, inseminate,v. (fecundation, fertilization, impregnation, insemination,n. fecundator, impregnator,n. fecundatory, impregnatory,adj.)

7. Serving to Make Pregnant: fecundative, adj.

8. The Fertilization of Another Ovum, though the Female is Already Pregnant, by a Closely Subsequent Act of Sexual Intercourse: superfecundation, superimpregnation,n.

9. Introduction of Semen into the Vagina by means of an Instrument to Produce Pregnancy: artificial insemination,n.

10. Certain Periods or Events in Pregnancy, n.

1. **conception**—time of becoming pregnant

2. **gestation**—period of pregnancy (gestational, gestative,adj.)

3. **labor**—period when the pains preceding childbirth begin and continue

4. **lightening**—the dropping of the head of the fetus into the pelvic inlet and the accompanying descent of the uterus before labor; sense of decreased abdominal tension felt by the pregnant woman at this point

5. **quickening**—movements of the fetus as first felt by the pregnant woman

6. **term**—period ending pregnancy, when labor starts and the baby is ready to be born

11. To Reach the Period of Pregnancy when Fetal Movements Can Be Felt: quicken,v.

12. Certain Types of Pregnancy,n.

1. **ectopic pregnancy, extrauterine pregnancy**—development of the fertilized ovum outside the uterus

2. **multiple pregnancy, plural pregnancy**—development of two or more fertilized ova within the uterus

3. **pseudocyesis**—false pregnancy

4. **superfetation**—development of a second fetus after one has already started to develop

5. **tubal pregnancy**—development of the fetus within the oviduct

13. Woman in Her First Pregnancy: primigravida, primipara, unigravida,n.

14. Pregnant Woman Who Has Already Had One or More Children: multipara,n.

15. Woman in Any Pregnancy beyond Her Second: multigravida,n.

16. Prevention of Pregnancy during Sexual Intercourse: contraception,n. (contraceptive, n. contraceptive,adj.)

17. Control of Pregnancy or Number of Pregnancies: birth control, planned parenthood,n.

18. Expulsion, Removal, or Destruction of the Fetus before the End of Pregnancy,n.

1. **aborticide**—destruction of the fetus within the uterus

2. **abortion**—expulsion or removal of a non-viable fetus, strictly when less than three or four months in development
3. **criminal abortion**—illegal operation to remove a fetus from a pregnant woman
4. **curettage, dilatation and curettage**—medical abortion of a fetus by scraping the womb
5. **feticide**—aborticide (feticidal,adj.)
6. **immature delivery**—miscarriage
7. **miscarriage**—self-expulsion of a non-viable fetus before the end of the period of pregnancy, or more strictly after the first three months of development

19. Drug or Agent that Causes Abortion: aborticide, abortifacient,n.

20. Causing Abortion: abortifacient,adj.

21. To Cause the Abortion of: abort,v.

22. To Undergo Abortion: abort, miscarry,v.

23. One Who Performs an Illegal Abortion: abortionist,n.

715. FERTILITY

1. Fertile (of the Female): breedy, fecund, fruitful, prolific, uberous,adj. (fecundity, fruitfulness, prolificness, prolificacy, prolification, prolificity, uberty, uberousness,n.)

2. Capable of Reproducing: generative, procreative, reproductive,adj. (generativeness, procreativeness, reproductiveness,adj.)

3. Capable of Reproducing (of the Male): potent, procreative, virile,adj. (potency, procreativeness, virility,n.)

4. Period at Which the Ability to Reproduce is Developed, or the Condition of Developing Such Ability: puberty,n.

5. Pert. to, or Characteristic of, Puberty: hebetic, puberal, pubertal, pubertic, pubescent,adj.

6. Reaching, or Having Reached, Puberty: pubescent,adj. (pubescence, pubescency,n.)

7. Fertile (of Soil, etc.): fecund, fruitful, loamy, luxuriant, mellow, pinguid, productive, rich, vegetative,adj. (fecundity, fruitfulness, loaminess, luxuriance, luxuriancy, pinguidity, productiveness, richness, vegetativeness,n.)

8. Producing Coarse Vegetation with Excessive Fertility: rank,adj. (rankness,n.)

9. Fertile in Other or Figurative Senses,adj.
1. **banner**—most productive
2. **creative**—fertile; able to create easily (creativeness, creativity,n.)
3. **fecund**—producing or able to produce things in abundance, whether inventions, ideas, or anything creative (fecundity,n.)
4. **feracious**—fertile (feracity,n.)
5. **fruitful**—fertile (fruitfulness,n.)
6. **plenteous, plentiful**—yielding or producing in abundance (plenteousness, plentifulness,n.)
7. **procreant**—productive
8. **productive**—yielding or producing richly (productiveness, productivity,n.)
9. **prolific**—fertile; producing freely and abundantly; creating much and easily (prolificacy, prolificness, prolification, prolificity,n.)
10. **pullulating**—very fertile, or producing richly, generally in the figurative sense only
11. **rich**—fertile; producing abundantly (richness,n.)
12. **teeming**—fertile; prolific
13. **uberous**—fertile (uberty, uberousness,n.)

10. To Be Fertile,v.
1. **abound in**—be rich in
2. **pullulate**—be very fertile, or produce abundantly or richly, generally in the figurative sense only (pullulation,n.)
3. **teem with**—be fertile or prolific in

11. To Make Fertile: fecundate, fertilize, fructify,v. (fecundation, fertilization, fructification,n.)

716. STERILITY

1. Sterile; Unproductive,adj.
1. **barren**—unable to produce offspring (of the female); unproductive of children (of a couple); unproductive (barrenness, n.)
2. **childless**—not productive of children (childlessness,n.)
3. **fruitless**—unproductive; unproductive of offspring, results, profit, value, etc. (fruitlessness,n.)
4. **impotent**—unable to father a child; sterile (impotence,n.)
5. **infecund**—not fertile; barren (infecundity,n.)
6. **infertile**—not fertile; sterile; barren (infertility,n.)
7. **issueless**—not productive of offspring
8. **jejune**—sterile or unproductive, literally or figuratively
9. **otiose**—unproductive (otiosity, otioseness,n.)
10. **unfertile**—not fertile; barren (unfertileness, unfertility,n.)
11. **unfruitful**—bearing nothing; unproductive (unfruitfulness,n.)
12. **unprolific**—not fertile

2. Producing Little: lean,adj. (leanness,n.)

3. Not Sufficiently Productive to Repay the Costs of Working, Cultivating, Bringing into Operation, etc.—of Land, Mines, etc.: submarginal,adj.

4. To Render Sterile, i.e., Unable to Produce Offspring: sterilize,v. (sterilization,n.)

5. End or Ending of the Fertile Period in the Female, Signalized by the Cessation of Menstruation: climacteric, climacterical, menopause,n. (climacterical, menopausal, menopausic,adj.)

6. Decrease in Reproductive Power or Activity in the Older Man: climacteric, climacterical, male climacteric,n. (climacterical, adj.)

717. GIVE BIRTH

1. To Give Birth to (of the Female): bear, breed, bring forth, deliver, produce,v. (delivery, production,n.)

2. To Give Birth to Young: teem,v.

3. To Bring Forth Young (of the Human Female): cub,v. (contemptuous)

4. To Give Birth to Twins: twin,v.

5. To Give Birth to, Esp. in Large Numbers, either Children (Disparaging), or Unpleasant Things or Conditions: spawn,v.

6. To Produce (Offspring) by Sexual Union with the Female: beget, breed, engender, father, generate, procreate, produce, sire,v. (engenderment, generation, procreation, production,n. begetter, breeder, father, procreator, procreant, producer,n.)

7. To Have or Produce Young (of the Male and Female Together): breed, multiply, procreate, propagate, pullulate, reproduce,v. (multiplication, procreation, propagation, pullulation, reproduction,n.)

8. Pert. or Relating to Production of Offspring: generative, genesial, genesic, genital, procreative, propagative, reproductive,adj.

9. Pert. to the Organs Used in Reproduction: generative, genesic, genital, reproductive,adj.

10. Symbolic Seat of Procreation: loins,n. (of the male)

11. Male Procreative Power Personified and Worshiped as a God in the Ancient Greek and Roman Religions: Priapus,n. (Priapean, adj.)

12. Certain Other Specific Forms of Reproduction,n.
1. **amphimixis**—reproduction through a sexual union of germ cells
2. **apomixis**—reproduction without sexual union, as in plants
3. **bastardy**—procreation of a child out of wedlock
4. **fission**—reproduction of some primitive biological organisms by simple splitting into two new organisms
5. **schizogenesis**—reproduction by fission (schizogenic, schizogenetic,adj.)
6. **syngenesis**—reproduction resulting from the sexual union of male and female (syngenetic,adj.)
7. **vermination**—multiplication, through breeding, of worms, vermin, or parasites

13. Reputed or Imagined Production of an Offspring Totally Unlike the Parent Form: xenogenesis,n. (xenogenic, xenogenetic,adj.)

14. To Give Birth to Young (Specifically of Animals),v.
1. **brood**—hatch
2. **calve**—bring forth young—of cows, other bovines, elephants, hippopotamuses, rhinoceroses, moose, whales, and certain other large mammals
3. **cast**—give birth to (young), esp. prematurely
4. **cub**—give birth
5. **drop**—give birth to
6. **farrow**—give birth—of swine
7. **fawn**—give birth—of deer
8. **fission**—reproduce by a simple splitting into two new organisms—of certain primitive biological forms
9. **foal**—give birth—of horses
10. **freshen**—give birth—of cows
11. **hatch**—give birth to (young) from eggs (hatch,n.)
12. **incubate**—hatch (incubation,n.)
13. **kid**—give birth to young—of goats
14. **lamb**—give birth—of sheep or goats
15. **pup**—give birth—of dogs or beasts of prey
16. **slink, sling**—give birth prematurely
17. **spawn**—drop the sex cells directly into the water—of certain aquatic forms
18. **throw**—give birth to
19. **whelp**—give birth to; give birth—of dogs and certain beasts of prey
20. **yean**—give birth—of goats and sheep

15. To Produce (a Foal) by Sexual Union with the Female—of the Stallion: sire,v.

16. Procreative Instinct of Birds in the Spring: nisus,n.

17. Giving Birth,adj.
1. **biparous**—giving birth to two young at a time
2. **catadromous**—spawning in salt water, though spending the rest of its life in fresh water—of certain aquatic life
3. **confined**—giving birth—of the human female
4. **fissiparous**—producing new organisms by a simple splitting—of certain primitive forms
5. **multiparous**—producing more than one offspring at a single birth
6. **oviparous**—giving birth through externally deposited eggs, as fish, fowl, etc.
7. **ovoviparous**—giving birth to live young

by hatching the egg or eggs within the body
8. **parturient**—giving birth to young
9. **semioviparous**—giving birth to live, but not fully developed, offspring, as kangaroos and other marsupials
10. **uniparous, uniparient**—producing only one egg or child at a time
11. **viviparous**—giving birth to live young, as mammals

718. CHILDBIRTH

1. Childbirth: accouchement, childbearing, childbed, confinement, delivery, labor, lying-in, parturition, travail,n.

2. To Be in the Process of Childbirth: labor, travail,v.

3. Period of Giving Birth: accouchement, childbirth, labor, travail,n.

4. Period between Childbirth and the Time When the Uterus of the Mother Returns to Normal Size: puerperium,n.

5. To Assist (the Mother) in Expelling the Newborn Infant: deliver,v. (delivery,n.)

6. Certain Types of Delivery,n.
1. **breech delivery**—delivery of a breech presentation, the medical term used when the fetus presents itself in the cervix of the vagina with the buttocks or feet showing, instead of the normal position, in which the head presents itself—in such a situation, the obstetrician must turn the infant before delivery
2. **Caesarean operation, Caesarean section** —delivery of an infant by cutting through the abdominal and uterine walls, when normal birth through the vagina is dangerous or impossible—so called after Julius Caesar, supposed to have been delivered by this means

7. About to Give Birth to Young; About to Give Birth to an Idea, Discovery, etc.: parturient,adj. (parturiency,n.)

8. Condition of the Female Relative to Childbirth,n.
1. **childbed**—condition of a woman giving birth
2. **lying-in**—state of a woman at, or as a result of, childbirth
3. **parity**—condition of having given birth
4. **parturiency**—condition of being in labor (parturient,adj.)
5. **pregnancy**—condition of the female from the time of conception to the time of childbirth (pregnant,adj.)
6. **puerperium**—condition of a woman in labor, or directly following the birth of a child

9. Woman in Labor: puerpera,n.

10. Woman Who Has Just Given Birth: puerpera, puerperant,n.

11. Woman Giving Birth to Her First Child: primipara,n. (primiparity,n. primiparous, adj.)

12. Woman Who Has Borne Only One Child: primipara, unipara,n. (primiparity,n. primiparous, uniparous,adj.)

13. Woman Giving Birth a Second or Subsequent Time, or Who Has Borne Two or More Children: multipara,n (multiparity,n. multiparous,adj.)

14. Woman Who Has Not Yet Borne Children: nullipara,n. (nulliparity,n. nulliparous, nonparous,adj.)

15. Pert. to Childbirth: maternity, puerperal, adj.

16. Before Childbirth: prenatal,adj.

17. After Childbirth: postnatal, postpartum, adj.

18. Infection Occurring during Childbirth: childbed fever, puerperal fever,n.

19. Roman Goddess Who Helped Women in Childbirth: Diana,n.

20. Primitive Custom in Which the Father Takes to Bed at the Birth of a Child, Often Fasting to Become Purified: couvade,n.

719. BREED

1. To Breed, i.e., Cause to Produce Offspring,v.
1. **cross**—cause (members of different species, etc.) to produce offspring
2. **cross-fertilize, cross-pollinate**—cause the fertilization of one plant or flower by the pollen from another, or from another kind or variety, usually to produce a different strain, etc.
3. **crossbreed**—breed (two varieties of the same species); hybridize
4. **hybridize**—cause to produce a mixed strain by breeding different species to each other; cross
5. **inbreed**—breed (closely related individuals, strains, etc.) to each other
6. **interbreed, intercross**—breed by crossing different species, etc., of animals or plants
7. **mate**—pair (animals, one to the other) for breeding, i.e., lead (animals) to have sexual intercourse for breeding purposes
8. **outbreed**—breed by crossing unrelated stocks, species, etc.
9. **propagate**—breed; cause to multiply or have offspring

2. To Breed, i.e., Undergo the Production of Offspring,v. *From Sec. 1:* crossbreed, interbreed, intercross, mate, propagate; *Also:* **1. miscegenate**—breed children—said of members of white races interbreeding with members of non-white races, or, esp. in the U.S., with Negroes, or vice versa

3. Breeding,n. *From Sec. 1:* crossing, crossbreeding, etc.; cross-fertilization, cross-pollination, hybridization or hybridism, intercross, propagation (propagative,adj.); *From Sec. 2:* miscegenation (miscegenetic,adj.); *Also:*
1. **amphimixis**—interbreeding
2. **animal culture**—breeding of animals
3. **animal husbandry**—breeding of farm animals
4. **stirpiculture**—breeding of special strains or stocks (stirpicultural,adj.)
5. **stockbreeding**—breeding of livestock for sale, show, racing, etc.
6. **xenogamy**—cross-fertilization (xenogamous,adj.)

4. Breeder,n. *From Sec. 1:* propagator; *From Sec. 2:* miscegenator or miscegenist; *From Sec. 3:* animal husbandman, stirpiculturist, stockbreeder

5. Result of Breeding,n. *From Sec. 1:* cross, crossbreed, hybrid, intercross; *From Sec. 2:* miscegenate or miscegine; *Also:*
1. **mongrel**—result of a mixture of breeds
2. **purebred, pureblood**—animal of recognized or registered breed, not contaminated by crossing with other breeds
3. **thoroughbred**—animal or horse of unmixed breed

6. Bred,adj. *From Sec. 1:* crossed, crossbred, etc.; hybrid (hybridity, hybridism,n.); *From Sec. 5:* mongrel, purebred, pureblood, thoroughbred; *Also:* **1. blooded**—thoroughbred

7. Breed: race,n.

8. Domestic Animals of a Common Ancestry but Not Sufficiently Distinct in Characteristics to Constitute a Breed: stock, strain,n.

9. Kept for Breeding Purposes: brood (of the female), stud (of the male),adj.

10. Science of Breeding Domesticated Animals or Cultivated Plants: thremmatology,n.

720. BIRTH

1. Birth: creation, nascency, natality, nativity,n.

2. New Birth: palingenesis, renaissance,n. (palingenetic, palingenetical, palingenesian, adj.)

3. Birth of Christ: Nativity,n.

4. Birth of a Dead Fetus: stillbirth,n.

5. Pert. or Relating to Birth,adj.
1. **congenital, connate**—acquired during development in the uterus; present or happening at, or dating from, birth
2. **natal**—pert. to birth
3. **native**—pert. to, or descr. of, the place where someone or something is born
4. **neonatal**—pert. to a new birth
5. **postnatal**—after birth
6. **prenatal**—before birth

6. Pert. to Birthdays; Pert. to the Position and Influence of the Stars on One's Birthday: genethliac, genethlic,adj.

7. To Be Born,v.
1. **drop**—be born—of animals
2. **hatch**—be born from an egg
3. **incubate**—hatch (incubation,n.)
4. **pullulate**—be produced as offspring (pullulation,n.)

8. Being Born: nascent,adj. (nascency, nascence,n.)

9. Born,adj.
1. **abortive**—born too soon (abortiveness,n.)
2. **baseborn**—born of humble parentage
3. **congenital**—born or born so, as *a congenital liar*, etc.
4. **connate**—born together—of qualities or characteristics (connateness, connation, n.)
5. **ignoble**—of low birth (ignobility, ignobleness,n.)
6. **legitimate**—born to parents who are legally married (legitimacy,n.)
7. **misbegotten**—unfortunately born, given birth, begotten, etc.
8. **née**—born—word that precedes the maiden name of a married woman, as *Jane Doe née Roe*
9. **newborn**—just born
10. **noble**—of high or royal birth (nobility, n.)
11. **premature**—born before the end of the normal term of pregnancy (prematurity, n.)
12. **stillborn**—born, or brought into the world, dead (stillbirth,n.)
13. **terrigenous**—born on or of the earth
14. **viable**—born alive and so formed or developed that it can remain alive—of newborn infants (viability,n.)
15. **well-born**—born in a socially or economically higher family
16. **yeanling**—newborn—of animals

10. Born to Unmarried Parents: baseborn, bastard, illegitimate, natural, unfathered,adj. (bastardy, bastardism, illegitimacy,n.)

11. One Born to Unmarried Parents: bantling, bastard, by-blow, illegitimate child, daughter, son, etc.; love-child (colloq.),n.

12. To Declare or Prove (Someone) to Be a Bastard: bastardize,v. (bastardization,n.)

13. People in General Born at about the Same Time: generation,n.

14. Not Yet Born: unborn,adj.

15. Birth Rate: natality,n.

16. Representation of the Stable in Which the Infant Jesus Was Born: crèche,n.

17. Inborn: connate, indigenous, ingenerate, innate, native, natural,adj. (connateness, connation, indigenousness, indigenity, innateness, nativeness, naturalness,n.)

18. Native,adj.
1. **aboriginal**—native from earliest times
2. **autochthonous**—native; aboriginal; indigenous (autochthony,n.)
3. **endemic, endemical**—native to a particular region, country, or people
4. **indigenous**—native to a country or region —esp. of flora, fauna, natural products, attitudes, cultural abstractions, etc. (indigenousness, indigenity,n.)
5. **natal**—native
6. **natural**—native; found, or existing, in its native state
7. **terrigenous**—native to a land or region
8. **vernacular**—native to the place where used—of words, language, etc.; native to a region, country, or people—of a disease, etc.

19. A Native,n. *From Sec. 18:* aborigine, autochthon, indigene

20. Rebirth: palingenesis, recreation, regeneration; renaissance, renascence (generally figurative only); revival,n. (palingenetic, palingenetical, palingenesian, regenerative, adj.)

21. To Be Reborn: regenerate, revive,v.

22. To Give Rebirth to: recreate, regenerate, v. (recreation, regeneration,n. regenerative, adj.)

23. Reborn: recreated, regenerated, renascent, revived,adj.

721. CHILD

1. Child (General): baby; bairn (Scottish); bambino, bantling; bud (affectionate); chick, chit, infant, moppet, nestling; proles (legal—Latin); shaver, sprat, tad, tot, tyke or tike, whelp, youngster,n. (baby, infantile or infantine,adj.)

2. Childhood (General): babyhood, infancy, n.

3. Child (Descriptive),n.
1. **brat**—child (derogatory); impudent or ill-behaved child (bratty,adj.)
2. **cadet**—younger son
3. **changeling**—infant secretly changed for another
4. **cherub**—beautiful, rosy, happy-looking, or good child
5. **daughter**—one's female child
6. **daughter-in-law**—daughter by virtue of her marriage to one's son
7. **descendant**—one's child or offspring, whether directly or indirectly
8. **elf**—small, attractive, and mischievous child—term of affection
9. **enfant terrible** (French)—child whose indiscreet behavior or remarks cause embarrassment to older people
10. **female**—girl child
11. **foster child, fosterling, foster son, foster daughter**—child, son, or daughter brought up by other than the natural parents (fosterage,n.)
12. **foundling**—infant, of unknown parentage, found deserted
13. **heir**—one's child or son, i.e., the one who will inherit one's estate
14. **male**—boy child
15. **minor**—any person under twenty-one years of age; a legal "infant," i.e., one not recognized in law as an adult (minority,n. minor,adj.)
16. **miscegine, miscegenate**—child born of parents of different races

17. **neonate, neonatus**—newborn child (medical)
18. **nursling**—child still suckling at the breast, or, in modern times, the bottle
19. **oaf**—deformed or foolish child
20. **offspring**—child, in reference to its parents
21. **orphan**—child who has lost one or both, usually both, parents by death
22. **papoose**—young American Indian child
23. **pickaninny**—small Negro child
24. **premature infant**—baby born before the full term of pregnancy
25. **ragamuffin**—ragged, ill-dressed child (ragamuffin,adj.)
26. **sibling**—one of two or more children in a family—denotes brother or sister relationship, and is useful in that it does not indicate the sex of the child
27. **son**—one's male child
28. **son-in-law**—son by virtue of his marriage to one's daughter
29. **stepchild, stepson, stepdaughter**—child, son, or daughter whose male or female parent in fact is not the natural parent
30. **stillbirth**—child born dead
31. **suckling**—child who has not yet been weaned from bottle or breast
32. **tyke, tike**—lively child
33. **ugly duckling**—child of little promise or poor appearance who becomes, in adulthood, quite the reverse
34. **urchin**—child in ragged clothing and obviously from poor environment
35. **waif**—homeless and uncared-for child; lost child
36. **ward**—child under the protection of a guardian
37. **weanling**—child who has just been weaned from breast or bottle

4. Mischievous Child: devil, devilkin, elf, imp, rascal, rogue, scamp, tyke or tike, urchin, villain,n.

5. Child as One of a Multiple Birth,n.
1. **fraternal twin**—one of twins not born from same egg
2. **identical twin**—twin born from the same egg
3. **quadruplet**—one of four children from a single pregnancy
4. **quintuplet**—one of five children from a single pregnancy
5. **septuplet**—one of seven children from a single pregnancy
6. **sextuplet**—one of six children from a single pregnancy
7. **Siamese twin**—one of two children born joined together at some point
8. **triplet**—one of three children from a single pregnancy
9. **twin**—one of two children from a single pregnancy

6. Developed from a Single Fertilized Egg, as Identical Twins: monozygotic,adj.

7. Developed from Two Fertilized Eggs, as Fraternal Twins: dizygotic,adj.

8. Child Still Unborn, or in the Womb,n.
1. **embryo**—unborn child from the moment of conception through the earlier stages of growth within the womb, or through the third month of pregnancy (embryonic,adj.)
2. **fetus, foetus**—unborn child from the end of the third month of pregnancy to birth (fetal, foetal,adj.)
3. **homunculus**—fetus
4. **macrocephalus**—fetus with an abnormally developed head
5. **microcephalus**—fetus with an abnormally small head

9. Children, Collectively,n.
1. **brood**—human infants from the same mother

2. flock—children in one family
3. generation—all the children of a parent or parents considered as a step in descent
4. issue—one's children, or the children of a marriage (legal)
5. offspring—children of parents
6. procreation—children of parents
7. progeny—children of parents
8. proles (Latin)—children; legitimate children (legal)
9. seed—one's, strictly a father's, children
10. sibs—children of parents
11. small fry—children
12. spawn—children in large numbers, esp. in reference to their parents (contemptuous)
13. young—children; children of parents

10. Like or Characteristic of a Child: babyish, babylike; childish (often in reference to unpleasant qualities); childlike (in reference to pleasant qualities); immature, infantile, infantine, juvenile; panty-waist (colloq.); puerile,adj. (babiness, childishness, childlikeness, immaturity, infantilism or infantility, juvenility, puerility or puerilism,n.)

11. Retaining the Physical or Anatomical Characteristics of a Child, though an Adult: pedomorphic,adj. (pedomorphism,n.)

12. Childish Behavior in an Adult, as a Symptom or Result of a Mental or Emotional Disorder: puerilism,n.

13. Acting in the Way a Son or Daughter Should; Characteristic of a Son or Daughter: filial,adj. (filialness,n. unfilial,neg.adj.)

14. Attitude of a Child to a Parent: filiality, n.

15. Place for Children,n.
   1. **crèche**—day nursery; hospital for foundlings
   2. **incubator**—device in which premature infants are placed and which simulates, as far as possible, the conditions within the mother's body
   3. **nursery**—place where young children are taken care of; room for a young infant
   4. **orphanage, orphan asylum**—institution for the care of children who have lost one or both parents

16. To Bring Up (a Child or Children): breed, foster, nurture, raise, rear, suckle, uprear,v.

17. Upbringing: breeding, nurture, rearing, uprearing,n.

18. Affected by Upbringing: cultural,adj.

19. To Take Care of (a Child): nurse,v. (nurse,n.)

20. Science of Child Rearing: pedology,n.

21. Art of Successful Child Rearing: pedotrophy,n.

22. Specialty of Training Children: puericulture,n.

23. Woman Employed by the Parents to Live with Their Children in order to Train and Instruct Them: governess,n.

722. RELATIVE

1. Relative; One Related by Blood, Family, etc.,n.
   1. **agnate**—person whose family relationship is through male members or on the father's side (agnatic, agnate,adj.)
   2. **cater-cousin**—first cousin
   3. **clansman**—member of a group of related families
   4. **cognate**—one related by blood; one related by blood on the mother's side (cognate,adj.)
   5. **collateral**—relative of the same ancestry but not in a direct line of descent, as a brother, sister, uncle, nephew, etc. (collateral,adj.)
   6. **consanguinean**—blood relative (consanguineous, consanguine,adj.)
   7. **cousin-german**—first cousin
   8. **first cousin, full cousin, own cousin**—son or daughter of one's aunt or uncle
   9. **kinsman, kinswoman**—person of the same family
   10. **nepote**—nephew (nepotal,adj.)
   11. **sib**—blood relative

2. Related by Blood or Family,adj. *From Sec. 1:* agnate or agnatic, cognate, collateral, consanguineous or consanguine, kindred; *Also:*
   1. **affinal**—related by marriage
   2. **bilateral**—related, or tracing descent, through both maternal and paternal ancestors
   3. **lineal**—related by a direct line of descent, as father and child
   4. **unilateral**—related, or tracing descent, through either maternal or paternal ancestors, but not both

3. Blood or Family Relationship,n. *From Sec. 1:* agnation, cognation, collaterality, consanguinity; kinship, kindred, or kindredship; *From Sec. 2:* lineality; *Also:*
   1. **avunculate**—in primitive or tribal societies, relationship between nephew and maternal uncle
   2. **filiation, affiliation**—family relationship of a child to parents, esp. of a child or son to the father

4. Related People; Related Families,n.
   1. **blood group**—group of people related by blood
   2. **clan**—group of related families
   3. **family**—relatives by blood; close relatives in the same household
   4. **gens**—clan or family connection in ancient Rome, containing the families in the same stock of the male line; clan (gentes,pl.)
   5. **kin, kith**—one's blood relatives, collectively
   6. **kindred**—group of people interrelated by blood; family; family to which one belongs; relatives by blood or, loosely, by marriage; clan
   7. **kinfolk, kinfolks, kinsfolk**—relatives; family
   8. **phratry**—group of related families in ancient Greece
   9. **race**—families descendent from a common ancestor; tribe
   10. **sept**—social group in which the members are believed to be descended from a common ancestor (anthropology)
   11. **sib**—group of people or families descended in a single line from a real or supposed common ancestor; relatives collectively
   12. **tribe**—social group made up of a series of families, clans, generations, etc., considered, in anthropology, to be related by blood; group of people, esp. those in a primitive or nomadic state, from the same stock; group of people having a distinct racial origin or common ancestry

5. Pertaining to Related People,adj. *From Sec. 4:* familial, kindred; phratral, phratriac, phratric, or phratrial; racial, tribal; *Also:*
   1. **gentile**—pert. to a tribe or clan
   2. **gentilic, gentilitian**—pert. to a tribe
   3. **gentilitious**—pert. to a family
   4. **phyletic**—pert. to a race

6. Member of a Group of Related Families in Ancient Greece: phrator,n.

7. Pert. or Relating to a Specific Member of a Family Relationship,adj.
   1. **ancestral**—pert. to an ancestor
   2. **avuncular**—pert. to an uncle

3. **brotherly**—pert. to, characteristic of, or like a brother (brotherliness,n.)
4. **fatherly**—pert. to, characteristic of, or like, a father (fatherliness,n.)
5. **filial**—pert. to, characteristic of, or like, a son or daughter
6. **fraternal**—pert. to brothers, or to a brother
7. **maternal**—pert. to a mother
8. **motherly**—pert. to, characteristic of, or like, a mother (motherliness,n.)
9. **nepotal**—pert. to a nephew
10. **novercal**—pert. to, characteristic of, or fit for, a stepmother
11. **parental**—pert. to a mother or father
12. **paternal**—pert. to a father
13. **sisterly**—pert. to, characteristic of, or like, a sister (sisterliness,n.)
14. **sororal**—pert. to sisters, or to a sister

8. State of Being a Paternal Uncle: patruity,n.

9. Disposal of Political Favors to One's Nephews or Other Relatives; Preferment to One's Relatives in Business, Government, etc., without Distinction as to Merit or Ability: nepotism,n. (nepotic, nepotistic,adj.)

10. One Who Practices Such Favoritism: nepotist,n.

11. Brother; Sister,n.
1. **blood brother**—brother by birth
2. **brother-german**—brother of the same father and mother
3. **brother-in-law**—brother of one's husband or wife
4. **cadet**—younger brother
5. **half brother, half sister**—brother, or sister, sharing one, but not both, parents
6. **sib**—sibling (genetics)
7. **sibling**—generic term including brother and sister
8. **sister-german**—sister of the same father and mother
9. **sister-in-law**—sister of one's husband or wife
10. **stepbrother, stepsister**—brother, or sister, because the child of one's stepparent by a previous marriage
11. **twin**—one's brother or sister born from the same pregnancy
12. Brothers Collectively: brethren,n.
13. Brotherhood: fraternity,n.

723. ANCESTRY

1. Ancestry; Line of Descent: antecedence, bloodline, blood strain, breed, derivation, descent, extraction, family, genealogy; heredity (loose usage) ; line, lineage, origin, parentage, pedigree, stirps, stock, strain,n.

2. Pert. to Ancestry or Line of Descent: ancestral, antecedent, familial, genealogical or genealogic, hereditary, lineal, parental, phyletic,adj.

3. Distinguished Ancestry: pedigree,n.

4. Indirect Branch of Descent: offset, offshoot,n.

5. Line of Family Descent: branch,n.

6. Branch of a Family: stem,n.

7. Sequence of Ancestry of Animals, Considered as Transmitting Traits, etc.: bloodline,n.

8. Ancestor,n.
1. **antecedent**—ancestor
2. **atavus**—ancestor; remote ancestor whose biological characteristics are inherited by an individual, though these did not appear in intervening generations
3. **forebear, forbear**—ancestor or forefather —usually in the plural
4. **forefather**—ancestor; remote ancestor

5. **parent**—ancestor (civil law)
6. **predecessor**—ancestor
7. **primogenitor**—ancestor; one's earliest ancestor
8. **progenitor**—ancestor; ancestor in direct line of descent (progenitress, progenitrix, fem.)
9. **prototype**—biological ancestral form
10. **sire**—male ancestor of an animal, esp. a horse
11. **stirps**—person from whom a family is descended (legal)
12. **stock**—original progenitor; progenitor of a family and his direct descendants

9. Ancestral,adj. From Sec. 8: antecedent, forefatherly, parental, progenitorial, prototypal; Also: 1. atavic—pert. to remote ancestors

10. Reappearance in an Individual of Biological Characteristics of a Remote Ancestor, though These Have Been Absent in Preceding Generations: atavism,n. (atavistic, atavic,adj.)

11. Individual in Whom Such Characteristics Appear: atavist, throwback,n.

12. Study of a Person's Family Origin, Family Tree, Line of Ancestors, etc.: genealogy, n. (genealogist,n. genealogical, genealogic, adj.)

13. To Make Investigations into, or Give an Account of, Ancestry and Descent: genealogize,v.

14. To Trace, or Make a Chart of, the Ancestry and Descent of: genealogize,v.

15. A Descendant: scion; sprig (humorous), n.

16. Indirect or Collateral Descendant: filiation, offset, offshoot,n.

17. Descendants,n.
1. **posterity**—descendants to the farthest time
2. **seed**—descendants
3. **stock**—direct descendants of some ancestor of a family, including the ancestor himself

724. FATHER

1. Father,n.
1. **father-in-law**—father of one's wife or husband
2. **foster father**—one's adoptive father
3. **godfather, godparent**—male who assumes fatherly responsibility for a child at baptism
4. **parent**—father
5. **pater**—father (colloq. term, common in certain classes in England)
6. **paterfamilias**—father head of a household
7. **patriarch**—elderly father
8. **progenitor**—father
9. **sire**—father of an animal, esp. a horse
10. **sponsor**—godfather
11. **stepfather**—person who marries one's mother and steps into the father's role

2. Pert. to, Descr. of, Like, or Characteristic of, a Father,adj. From Sec. 1: godfatherly, patriarchal, progenitorial, stepfatherly; Also: 1. fatherly—pert. to, descr. of, like, or characteristic of, a father (fatherliness,n.)
2. paternal—fatherly (paternalness,n.)

3. To Assume Fatherly Responsibility for (a Child) at Baptism: godfather, sponsor,v.

4. Fatherhood: paternity,n. (paternal,adj.)

5. Psychological Situation Involving Father and Daughter,n.
1. **electra complex**—intricate psychological situation in which (this is oversimplified)

the young daughter feels great fondness or love for the father, with corresponding fear of, or hatred for, the mother

2. Oedipus complex—electra complex; the term is commonly used in reference to either the father or mother (oedipal, edipal,adj.)

6. Having No Father: fatherless,adj.

7. Relationship between Governor and Governed, Employer and Employee, etc., Similar to That Between a Father and Dependent Child: paternalism,n. (paternalist, paternalistic,adj.)

8. One Who, as Governor, Ruler, Employer, etc., Assumes This Relationship; One Who Advocates Such a Relationship: paternalist, n.

9. To Treat (a Subject, Employee, etc.) in this Manner: paternalize,v.

10. Grandfather: atavus,n.

725. MOTHER

1. Mother,n.
1. **dam**—female parent; mother of four-footed animals
2. **foster mother**—adoptive mother
3. **godmother, godparent**—female who assumes motherly responsibility for a child at baptism
4. **mater**—mother (colloq. term in England)
5. **materfamilias**—mother of a household
6. **matriarch**—ruling mother
7. **matron**—woman who is, or has been, a mother
8. **mother-in-law**—mother of one's wife or husband
9. **mulier**—mother
10. **Niobe**—proud mother; in Greek mythology, mother who was excessively proud of her children
11. **progenitress, progenitrix**—mother, i.e., female parent
12. **sponsor**—godmother
13. **stepmother**—woman who marries one's father and steps into the mother's role

2. Pert. to, Descr. of, Characteristic of, or Like, a Mother,adj. *From Sec. 1:* godmotherly, matriarchal, matronly, mulierine, stepmotherly; *Also:*
1. **maternal**—motherly (maternalness, maternality,n.)
2. **motherly**—pert. to, descr. of, characteristic of, or like, a mother (motherliness, n.)

3. To Assume Motherly Responsibility for (a Child) at Baptism: godmother, sponsor,v.

4. Motherhood: maternity,n. (maternal, adj.)

5. To Act in a Motherly Fashion; To Treat (Someone) in a Motherly Fashion: maternalize, mother,v.

6. Intricate Psychological Situation in Which the Young Son Feels Great Fondness or Love for the Mother, with Corresponding Fear of, or Hatred for, the Father (Oversimplified): Oedipus complex,n. (oedipal, edipal,adj.)

7. Having the Same Mother,adj.
1. **uterine**—having the same mother but a different father
2. **whole**—having the same mother and father

8. Having No Mother: motherless,adj.

9. Scientific Study of Motherhood: maternology,n.

10. Grandmother: beldame, grandam; granny (colloq.),n.

1. To Make,v.
1. **blend**—make by mixing various kinds together
2. **bootleg**—make illegally (slang or colloq.)
3. **brew**—make or prepare through fermentation; concoct
4. **build**—make by putting parts or elements together
5. **compound**—make by mixing things together into a unified whole
6. **concoct**—make by mixing various parts or ingredients together, as a spaghetti sauce, etc., with the implication, generally, that something unusual or special results, either because the combination of parts is out of the ordinary or the manner of mixing or combining them is new or ingenious (concoction,n.)
7. **confect**—make; make by mixing; construct (confection,n.)
8. **construct**—make; make by putting the necessary parts of together (construction, n. constructive, constructional,adj.)
9. **contrive**—make as a work of art or as the result of ingenious thinking or planning (contrivance,n.)
10. **create**—make (something new, or something that has not existed previously); make as a work of art or imagination (creation,n. creational,adj.)
11. **decoct**—prepare through a process of boiling or soaking in hot water (decoction,n.)
12. **design**—make as a work of art
13. **devise**—contrive
14. **execute**—make by means of art in accordance with a plan, as a statue, painting, etc. (execution,n.)
15. **fabricate**—make; manufacture (fabrication,n.)
16. **fashion**—contrive
17. **forge**—make or build (something intangible, as a plan, system, philosophy, etc.) in allusion to the way metals are heated in a forge and then hammered into shape
18. **form**—fashion (formation,n. formative, adj.)
19. **manufacture**—make by machinery, or, less commonly, by hand (manufacture,n.)
20. **prepare**—make by some special process; compound (preparation,n.)
21. **produce**—make (production,n. productive,adj.)
22. **synthesize, synthetize**—make by putting or combining parts into a whole (synthesis,n. synthetic,adj.)

2. Maker,n. *From Sec. 1:* blender, bootlegger, brewer, builder, compounder, concocter, constructor, contriver, creator, designer, deviser, fabricator, fashioner, forger, manufacturer, producer; *Also:*
1. **artificer**—one who contrives
2. **wright**—maker of, usually in compounds like *wheelwright, playwright,* etc.

3. That Which Is Made or Results from Making,n. *From Sec. 1:* blend, brew, building, compound, concoction, confection, construction, contrivance, creation, decoction, device, fabrication, formation, manufacture, preparation; product, produce, or production; synthesis or synthetic; *Also:*
1. **artifact**—that which is made by primitive human workmanship; any product of human workmanship or skill; any artificial or synthetic product (artifactitious, adj.)
2. **chef-d'oeuvre**—masterpiece
3. **masterpiece**—the best, chief, or most skillful thing one has made
4. **work**—that which is made or produced by labor

4. Made,adj. *From Sec. 1:* blended, brewed, etc.; *Also:*

1. **artificial**—made by human workmanship or art rather than growing or existing naturally; synthetic (artificiality, artificialness,n.)
2. **compact of**—made of
3. **synthetic**—made through putting things together
4. **wrought (of)**—made, fashioned, or manufactured (of)
5. **Place Where Things Are Manufactured:** factory, manufactory, plant,n.
6. **Place Where Something Is Figuratively Made or Shaped:** forge,n. (in allusion to the metal forge where iron is heated and shaped)
7. **Russian Efficiency System of Industrial Output:** Stakhanovism,n.
8. **To Produce,v.**
   1. **afford**—produce, as fruit, results, profit, etc.
   2. **bear**—produce, as fruit, profit, etc.
   3. **beget**—produce, as results, conditions, etc.
   4. **breed**—produce, as conditions, etc.; engender
   5. **create**—produce, as conditions, etc.
   6. **engender**—produce in the sense of causing to develop, as conditions, results, feelings, etc.
   7. **generate**—produce, as steam, electricity, etc.; beget
   8. **give birth to, give rise to**—produce, as conditions, feelings, etc.
   9. **originate**—produce (something) as new
   10. **provide**—produce, as fruit, results, profit, what is needed, etc.
   11. **pullulate**—produce richly, in the figurative sense
   12. **yield**—produce, as fruit, natural products, results, etc.; produce as a profit, as investments, work, etc.
9. **Production,n.** *From Sec. 8:* creation, engenderment, generation, origination, provision, pullulation (generative,adj.)
10. **Producer,n.** *From Sec. 8:* begetter, breeder, creator, generator, originator, provider
11. **That Which Is Produced,n.** *From Sec. 8:* provision, yield; *Also:*
    1. **by-product**—that which is produced secondarily when something else is produced or made
    2. **outturn**—yield, as from farming, etc.
    3. **produce**—that which is produced, esp. in agriculture
    4. **product, production**—that which is produced
12. **Having the Power or Capacity to Produce, esp. Abundantly:** productive,adj. (productiveness, productivity,n.)
13. **The Total Produced:** output, outturn,n.
14. **A Producing or Generating by Itself, Without Outside Help:** autogeny,n.
15. **Self-Produced; Self-Generated:** autogenetic, autogenous,adj.
16. **Produced by Living Matter:** biogenous, adj.
17. **To Make Up; To Create,v.**
    1. **bring into being, bring into existence**—create
    2. **coin**—make up, as words, etc.; invent
    3. **compose**—make up, as literature, music, etc.
    4. **conceive**—create or invent in the mind
    5. **concoct**—make up, as a story, excuse, etc.
    6. **contrive**—devise; invent
    7. **devise**—think up (something new); invent
    8. **fabricate**—make up, as a lie, legend, etc.
    9. **hatch**—think up (something new, original, etc.)
    10. **improvise**—make up on the spur of the moment and with little, if any, preparation or planning

11. **invent**—create, make up, or think up (something new)
12. **manufacture**—invent, figuratively, as a lie, story, account, etc.
13. **originate**—make up (something new); invent
14. **premeditate**—make up beforehand
15. **produce**—create
16. **think up**—make up out of one's mind
18. **Creation,n.** *From Sec. 17:* coinage, composition, conception, concoction, contrivance, fabrication, improvisation, invention, manufacture, origination, premeditation, production (conceptive, conceptual, or conceptional; improvisatorial, improvisatory, or improvisational; inventive,adj.)
19. **Creator,n.** *From Sec. 17:* coiner, composer, conceiver, concocter, contriver, deviser, fabricator, hatcher, improviser or improvisator, inventor, manufacturer, originator, producer; *Also:*
    1. **architect**—creator or deviser, as of a plan, program, philosophy, etc.
    2. **artificer**—inventor
    3. **demiurge**—power or person who creates a real or imaginary world (demiurgic, demiurgical, demiurgeous,adj.)
20. **Creation, i.e., That Which Is Created,n.** *From Sec. 17:* coinage, composition, conception, concoction, contrivance, fabrication, improvisation, invention, manufacture, origination or original; product, produce, or production; *Also:* 1. **creature**—creation; that which is created, made up, thought up, devised, etc.
21. **An Artistic (Including Musical, Literary, etc.) Creation,n.**
    1. **chef-d'oeuvre**—masterpiece
    2. **composition**—artistic creation
    3. **creation**—artistic creation
    4. **magnum opus**—one's greatest or most ambitious artistic creation
    5. **masterpiece**—one's best, chief, or most skillful artistic creation
    6. **monument**—artistic creation that will, or should, endure
    7. **opus**—artistic creation
    8. **opuscule**—petty or unimportant artistic creation
    9. **work**—artistic creation
22. **Pert. to Creation:** creational, creationary, creative,adj.
23. **Creation of the Universe by God:** the Creation,n.
24. **Doctrine that God Created the Universe out of Nothing:** creationism,n. (creationist, n. creationistic,adj.)
25. **One Who Believes that Different Species of Animals and Plants Were Separately Created:** creationist,n. (creationistic,adj.)
26. **Having the Power or Capacity to Create:** creative,adj. (creativeness, creativity,n.)
27. **Creative,adj.**
    1. **adroit**—inventive (adroitness,n.)
    2. **all-creative, all-creating**—creative of all things, as God
    3. **demiurgic, demiurgical, demiurgeous**—creative
    4. **forgetive**—inventive (forgetiveness,n.)
    5. **ingenious**—skillful at inventing (ingenuity, ingeniousness,n.)
    6. **inventive**—creative; clever at inventing new things or ideas (inventiveness,n.)
    7. **omnific**—all-creative
    8. **original**—able to create something new or different; inventive (originality,n.)
    9. **originative**—creative; inventive
    10. **productive**—creative (productiveness, productivity,n.)
    11. **Promethean**—creative; tending to create daring and original things
28. **Poorly Constructed, esp. in Reference to Literary Creations:** incondite,adj.

727. BUILD

1. To Build,v.
1. **construct**—build by putting the necessary parts or together
2. **engineer**—build
3. **erect**—build (a building or structure) in the sense of causing it to rise from the ground
4. **fabricate**—build by putting together standard parts or sections
5. **jerry-build**—build cheaply, poorly, and quickly
6. **nidificate, nidify**—build a nest
7. **put up**—build (a structure, etc.)
8. **remodel**—build over
9. **superstruct**—build (something) on top of, or over, some building or structure, or on a foundation

2. Building,n. *From Sec. 1:* construction, engineering, erection, fabrication, nidification; *Also:*
1. **architecture**—construction
2. **structure**—construction

3. Builder,n. *From Sec. 1:* engineer, erecter or erector, fabricator, jerry-builder; *Also:*
1. **architect**—one who designs and supervises the construction of buildings (architectonic,adj.)
2. **civil engineer**—one who plans and supervises the construction of bridges, roads, etc.

4. That Which Is Built or Results from Building,n. *From Sec. 1:* construction, erection, fabrication, superstructure; *From Sec. 2:* architecture, structure

5. Pert. to Building: architectonic, architectural, constructional, constructive, structural, tectonic,adj.

6. Manner or Design of Building: architectonic, architectonics, architecture, construction, structure,n. (architectonic, architectural, constructional, structural,adj.)

7. Resembling Architecture, as in Design, Structure, etc.: architectonic,adj.

8. Structural Skill: architectonic, architectonics,n.

9. Given to Building, Constructing, etc.: constructive,adj. (constructiveness,n.)

10. Science of Building,n.
1. **architecture, architectonics, architectonic**—science of the construction of houses, buildings, bridges, etc. (architect, n. architectural, architectonic,adj.)
2. **civil engineering**—science of the construction of bridges, roads, etc. (civil engineer,n.)
3. **engineering**—science of the use of inorganic substances, sources of power, physical forces, etc., in building, heating, lighting, etc. (engineer,n.)
4. **tectonics**—science or art of constructing buildings, ships, implements, etc.

11. Descr. of Certain Common Styles of Architecture,adj.
1. **baroque**—of the style of the 1500's to 1800's, characterized by elaborately curved and contorted forms
2. **Byzantine**—of an elaborate style resembling that of Byzantium, an ancient city in Turkey
3. **classical**—of the style of Greek and Roman antiquity or of any architecture based on this; of the style popular from 1770 to 1840 intended to revive the architecture of Greek and Roman antiquity
4. **colonial**—of the style prevalent in the early colonies of America
5. **Georgian**—of the style popular in Britain during the reigns of the first four Kings George

6. **Gothic**—of the French style of the 1100's to 1500's, characterized by buttresses, pointed arches, vaulting, etc.
7. **Renaissance**—of the style that arose in Italy in the 15th century, based on Roman classical design
8. **rococo**—of the style that arose in France about 1720, characterized by curving lines, elegant and elaborate ornamentation, use of different materials for a total effect, etc. (rococo,n.)
9. **Romanesque**—of the style developed in Italy and characterized by rounded arches, columns, elaborate ornamentation, etc.

12. A Building,n.
1. **alcazar**—palace
2. **arcade**—long, arched building
3. **capitol**—building in which a legislature sits
4. **casino**—building for dancing, card playing, gambling, or other amusements
5. **castle, château**—large, fortified building
6. **edifice**—large, imposing building, usually of a public or semi-public character (edificial,adj.)
7. **hall**—large building used for public or semi-public purposes, as meetings, etc.
8. **lean-to**—shed with a slanting roof
9. **mausoleum**—large and gloomy building
10. **palace**—public building, esp. one very imposing, expensive, etc.; building for residence of a monarch (palatial, palatine,adj.)
11. **pantheon**—building where the tombs or memorials of the illustrious dead of a nation are kept
12. **pile**—large building
13. **rotunda**—circular, usually domed, building
14. **shed**—one-story building for storage, protection against the weather, etc.
15. **skyscraper**—very tall building
16. **structure**—building; anything that is built (structural,adj.)

13. Additional Building to That or Those in Use or Existence: annex,n.

14. Built Like a Castle: castellated,adj.

15. Part of a Building,n.
1. **annex**—wing
2. **extension**—wing
3. **lean-to**—wing with an inclining roof
4. **rotunda**—circular, usually domed, part of a building
5. **superstructure**—part of a building above the cellar or basement; vertical extension of a building (superstructural,adj.)
6. **wing**—part of a building jutting out from the main part

16. Buildings Surrounding a Square or Rectangular Space: quadrangle,n.

17. Certain Other Structures,n.
1. **aerie, aery, eyrie, eyry**—structure built on a very high place
2. **cupola**—small structure built on the roof of a building, today purely for design, though historically serving as a lookout
3. **dome**—large cupola (domical,adj.)
4. **monument**—structure erected to commemorate someone or something
5. **reticulum**—structure in the form of a network
6. **superstructure**—structure built on top of, or over, some other structure (superstructural,adj.)
7. **tower**—high structure, often on top of some building

18. Tower,n.
1. **beacon**—tall tower containing a warning or guiding signal
2. **belfry**—tower; bell tower
3. **donjon**—massive main tower in ancient castles

4. steeple—church tower
5. turret—small tower, usually ornamental

19. Having a Tower or Towers: towered,adj.

20. Having a Small Tower, or Small Towers, Usually as Ornamentation: turreted,adj.

21. Porch, etc.,n.
1. gallery—veranda, so called in the South
2. loggia—covered, outside porch, forming an architectural entity with a house or building
3. patio—open porch
4. piazza—porch
5. porte-cochere—large open porch of a house, under which vehicles drive so that occupants can alight in stormy weather without getting wet
6. portico—roof on columns, forming a kind of porch
7. stoop—porch at the entrance to a home
8. terrace—open porch on a level with the ground
9. veranda—open, but roofed, porch

728. ORIGIN

1. Origin: ancestry, authorship, birth, derivation, descent, genesis, nascency, origination, parentage, primordium, provenance, provenience, source,n. (ancestral, derivational, original, parental,adj.)

2. National Origin: extraction,n.

3. Family Origin: ancestry, descent, extraction, lineage, parentage,n. (ancestral, lineal, parental,adj.)

4. Origin or Source, i.e., That Which Is an Origin, Place of Origin, or Source,n.
1. ancestor—that from which, or one from whom, origin can be traced
2. cradle—place where something begins, or begins to grow
3. cunabula—cradle (cunabular,adj.)
4. font—origin or source in the sense of the figurative spring or fountain from which something comes
5. fount—origin; source
6. fountain, fount—source of water; by extension, any source
7. fountainhead—basic or original source
8. golconda—rich source
9. headspring—source; fountain
10. matrix—that in which something originates and develops (matrical,adj. matrices,pl.n.)
11. mine—rich source
12. original—form or type from which others, or varieties, are derived or descended
13. parent—origin; source
14. principle—origin; source
15. resource—source of supply, help, relief, support, etc.
16. root—deepest origin or source
17. spring—origin; source
18. springhead—origin; source
19. stem—origin; source
20. stock—the original (usually a person, language, or race) from which others have descended or are derived
21. store—source of supply
22. well—source of supply
23. wellhead—origin; source
24. wellspring—source; source of supply; inexhaustible source of supply

5. Acting as Origin or Source: primary,adj.

6. Origin or Origination of the World: cosmogony,n. (cosmogonal, cosmogonic, cosmogonical,adj.)

7. Origin and Descent of Gods: theogony,n. (theogonic,adj.)

8. Origin of a Mental or Personality Trait: psychogenesis,n. (psychogenic,adj.)

9. The Original from Which Others Are Copied: antetype, archetype, model, paradigm, pattern, prototype,n. (archetypal, archetypic, or archetypical, paradigmatic or paradigmatical, prototypal or prototypic,adj.)

10. Original: aboriginal, first, genuine, primal, primary, prime, primigenial, pristine,adj.

11. In Its Original Form or State: primordial,adj.

12. Original in the Growth of an Individual or Organism: primordial,adj.

13. Originating in or from a Source or Place,adj.
1. autogenous—endogenous
2. endogenous—inside or within, or from internal causes
3. exogenous—outside, or from external causes
4. extrinsic—from the outside
5. heterogenous—outside the body
6. monogenetic—from a single cell
7. monophyletic—from a single parent form
8. psychogenic—in or from the emotions
9. xenogenous—from a cause outside the body or organism, or from a foreign body (medical)

14. Of Irregular, Questionable, or Non-Standard Origin: bastard,adj. (bastard,n.)

15. Of Many or Mixed Origin,adj.
1. mongrel—of mixed origin (mongrel,n.)
2. polygenetic—having many different origins; having origins at different times and/or places
3. polyphyletic—having origins in more than one race, family, or ancestral type

16. Of Common or Identical Origin: congenetic, isogenous, monogenic,adj.

17. Certain Theories or Doctrines of Origin, n.
1. abiogenesis, abiogeny—theory, now abandoned, that living matter can originate from inorganic or inanimate matter (abiogenist,n. abiogenetic, abiogenetical, adj.)
2. autogenesis—abiogenesis (autogenetic, adj.)
3. biogenesis, biogeny—doctrine that living matter can originate only from other living matter, not from inorganic or inanimate matter (biogenesist,n. biogenetic,adj.)
4. cosmogony—theory of the origin of the world (cosmogonal, cosmogonic, cosmogonical,adj.)
5. Darwinism—Charles Darwin's theory of the origin and survival of species, including natural selection, survival of the fittest, etc. (Darwinian, Darwinist, Darwinite,n. Darwinian, Darwinist, Darwinistic, adj.)
6. monogenesis—theory that all life originated in and developed from a single cell; monogenism
7. monogenism, monogenesy, monogeny—theory that all humanity has its origins in a single pair or in a single ancestral type (monogenist, monogenesist,n. monogenistic,adj.)
8. polygenesis—theory of plural origins of the human race, i.e., that two or more branches evolved independently of one another (polygenesist,n. polygenesic, polygenic,adj.)
9. polygenism, polygeny—theory that humanity originated in and developed from two or more ancestral types (polygenist, n. polygenic, polygenistic,adj.)
10. spontaneous generation—abiogenesis

18. To Be the Origin of, or Give Origin to: breed, create, give birth to, give rise to, father, generate, hatch (esp. secretly), originate,v. (creation, generation, origination,n.

creator, father, generator, hatcher, originator,n.)

729. BEGINNING

1. To Begin or Start (Something),v.
1. **commence**—begin
2. **constitute**—establish
3. **embark on, embark upon**—start on (some venture, project, etc.)
4. **enter on, enter upon**—make a beginning in (a new project, work, etc.)
5. **establish**—give a beginning to (something new); begin
6. **found**—establish on a strong foundation or base, as a movement, institution, etc.
7. **hatch**—give a beginning to, esp. secretly, as plans, schemes, etc. (hatcher,n.)
8. **inaugurate**—begin; make a formal or ceremonious beginning of; set in motion formally (inaugural,adj.)
9. **initiate**—begin (something new)
10. **innovate**—give a beginning to something new; give a beginning to (something new) for the first time
11. **institute**—begin; establish
12. **introduce**—begin; give a beginning to, as fashions, methods, etc.
13. **launch**—start, in the sense of set going, as a business, a man in his career, an idea, etc.
14. **organize**—start (something) going
15. **originate**—give a beginning to (something new)
16. **preface**—begin, as a speech, remarks, etc.
17. **prime**—start (something) working
18. **set forth on**—begin on (something)
19. **set in motion**—get (something) started
20. **set up**—establish

2. Act or Process of Beginning, or Giving a Beginning to (Something),n. *From Sec. 1:* commencement, constitution, embarkation, entrance, establishment, foundation, inauguration, initiation, innovation, institution, introduction, organization, origination (inaugural, initiative, innovative or innovational, introductory, organizational,adj.)

3. One Who Begins, or Gives a Beginning to (Something),n. *From Sec. 1:* founder, inaugurator, initiator, innovator or innovationist, institutor, introducer, launcher, organizer, originator

4. To Begin (Doing): commence, embark on, embark upon, enter on, enter upon, set about, set forth on, start, undertake,v. (commencement, embarkation,n.)

5. To Begin (Doing) Again, after Having Stopped: resume,v. (resumption,n.)

6. To Begin Doing (Something) and Continue Doing It: apply oneself to, buckle down to,v.

7. To Begin, i.e., Have a Beginning or Origin,v.
1. **arise**—begin; come into being; originate
2. **breed**—originate
3. **brew**—begin to form
4. **commence**—begin
5. **dawn**—begin, as the day
6. **derive (from)**—originate (from)
7. **germinate**—begin to grow or develop
8. **originate**—begin; get a start; have an origin or beginning
9. **resume**—begin again, after having stopped
10. **spring**—come into being at some place of origin
11. **sprout**—begin to grow
12. **start**—begin
13. **stem (from)**—originate (from)
14. **upspring**—come into existence

8. Act, Process, or State of Beginning or Having a Beginning or Origin,n. *From Sec.*

7: rise (from *arise*), commencement, dawn, derivation, germination, origination, resumption, start, upspring (derivative, germinative, adj.)

9. Beginning to Grow or Develop: germinant,adj. (germinance, germinancy,n.)

10. In the Earliest Stages of Growth or Development: germinal,adj.

11. A Beginning,n.
1. **alpha**—beginning, so called from the name of the first letter in the Greek alphabet—often in the phrase *the alpha and the omega,* the beginning and the end
2. **aurora**—beginning (auroral, aurorean, adj.)
3. **birth**—beginning
4. **commencement**—beginning
5. **conception**—earliest beginning as imagined or first given life
6. **creation**—beginning
7. **dawn**—beginning, as of a day, life, career, etc.
8. **debut**—start upon a career or profession
9. **first**—beginning, chiefly in phrases like *from the first, at first,* etc.
10. **genesis**—beginning of an idea, a plan, or any other abstraction
11. **inception**—beginning, as of a work, plan, project, etc.
12. **incunabula**—beginning, in the sense of being the period of infancy, first stages, etc. (incunabular,adj.)
13. **introduction**—beginning, as of a play, artistic work, etc.
14. **nascency**—beginning, i.e., period of being born
15. **nucleus**—beginning to which other things, ideas, etc., will be added, or around which others will collect
16. **onset**—beginning
17. **opening**—beginning, as of a play, book, etc.
18. **origin**—beginning
19. **outset**—beginning
20. **outstart**—beginning
21. **preface**—introduction
22. **prime**—beginning
23. **primordium**—beginning; beginning of a biological organ
24. **rise**—beginning
25. **start**—beginning

12. Starting Point: basis, creation, point of departure, threshold,n.

13. Beginning Principles of a Subject: ABC, elements, rudiments,n.

14. Manner of Beginning: origin,n.

15. Beginning; Dealing with the Beginning; In the Beginning or Earliest Stages,adj.
1. **abecedarian**—elementary
2. **basic**—beginning; elementary
3. **elementary**—dealing with first things, those with which one must begin before proceeding to later or more complicated things or phases
4. **embryonic**—just starting to grow or develop
5. **first**—beginning; coming at the beginning
6. **inceptive**—beginning
7. **inchoate**—in the first or earliest stages; just starting; incipient (inchoateness, inchoation,n.)
8. **incipient**—beginning; beginning to exist or manifest itself (incipience, incipiency, n.)
9. **initial**—beginning
10. **introductory**—beginning
11. **nascent**—beginning to exist, develop, or grow (nascency, nascence,n.)
12. **opening**—beginning
13. **primordial**—existent at the very beginning; first created

14. rudimentary—just starting; elementary (rudimentariness,n.)

16. Recently or Just Begun: inchoate,adj. (inchoateness, inchoation,n.)

17. A Beginner, i.e., One Who Is Just Beginning,n.
1. **abecedarian, alphabetarian**—beginner in a subject or field
2. **apprentice**—beginner, i.e., one who is in the process of learning
3. **initiate**—beginner, in the sense of one who is to be, or has just been, instructed in the first principles
4. **neophyte**—beginner in a field, esp. in religious instruction
5. **novice, novitiate, noviciate**—beginner in a field; tyro
6. **rookie**—inexperienced beginner (colloq.)
7. **tyro, tiro**—beginner in any field; one who, having just begun, is not yet experienced, skilled, or trained

18. State or Period of Being a Beginner,n. *From Sec. 17:* apprenticeship, novitiate, noviciate

19. From the Beginning: ab initio (legal and medical—Latin) ; ab origine (legal and technical—Latin) ; ab ovo (Latin)

20. Willingness to Start Something New, Take the Risks Attendant on New Ventures, etc.: gumption, enterprise, initiative,n. (enterprising,adj.)

730. INTRODUCTION

1. To Introduce,v.
1. **inaugurate**—introduce formally into office, as someone newly elected or appointed
2. **induct (into)**—introduce formally (into office), as someone newly elected or appointed
3. **initiate (into)**—introduce (someone) to principles of learning or art, mysteries, secret knowledge, etc.
4. **innovate**—introduce new things, methods, etc.; introduce changes in (things, methods, etc.)
5. **preface**—act as an introduction to; introduce; make introductory remarks to; be introductory to
6. **prelude**—introduce; be an introduction to
7. **present**—introduce (to someone) ; introduce formally (to a superior or to the world)
8. **usher (in)**—introduce, i.e., come at the beginning of

2. Introduction, i.e., an Introducing,n. *From Sec. 1:* inauguration, induction, initiation, innovation, presentation (inaugural, inductive, initiatory or initiative, innovative, presentational,adj.)

3. Introducer,n. *From Sec. 1:* inaugurator, inductor, initiator, innovator, preluder, presenter

4. An Introduction,n.
1. **exordium**—introductory part of a speech, of written material, etc.
2. **foreword**—preface
3. **overture**—orchestral introduction to an opera, musical comedy, etc.; introduction, as to a poem, etc.
4. **preamble**—introductory material to a speech, document, book, etc.; introduction, i.e., fact, circumstance or happening that indicates or introduces what is coming next
5. **preface**—introduction; introductory matter to a book, poem, or other writing or speaking
6. **preliminary**—introduction
7. **prelude**—introductory act, performance,

etc.; that which introduces, or is introductory to, some following act, circumstance, condition, etc.
8. **prelusion**—introduction; prelude
9. **proem**—preface; prelude
10. **program, programma**—prolegomenon
11. **prolegomenon**—preface; preliminary or introductory remark (generally in the plural, *prolegomena*)
12. **prologue**—introduction; introductory occurrence; introduction to a poem, novel, play, etc.
13. **prolusion**—introductory essay, esp. to a larger work
14. **protasis**—introductory section of a play
15. **ritornel, ritornelle, ritornello**—short instrumental prelude in music

5. Introductory, Introductive,adj. *From Sec. 4:* prefatory, preliminary; prelusive, prelusory, or preludial; proemial; prolegomenary or prolegomenous; prolusory; *Also:* inductive, initiative or initiatory, precursory, preparatory

6. To Compose or Deliver an Introduction, as to a Poem, Novel, Play, etc.: prologize, prologuize,v. (prologizer, prologuizer,n.)

7. Characterized by Tediously and Needlessly Long Introductory Remarks: prolegomenous,adj.

8. Writer of Prefaces: prolegomenist, prologizer, prologuizer,n.

9. One Who Introduces Speakers, as at a Banquet, Meeting, etc.: chairman, toastmaster,n.

731. GROWTH

1. To Begin to Grow,v.
1. **bud**—begin to grow or develop
2. **burgeon**—bud; sprout
3. **germinate**—begin to grow or develop (germination,n. germinative,adj.)
4. **pullulate**—bud; germinate; give forth shoots (pullulation,n.)
5. **sprout**—begin to grow; put out shoots

2. Beginning to Grow: budding, burgeoning, embryonic, germinant, germinating, pullulant, pullulating, sprouting,adj. (germinance, germinancy,n.)

3. To Grow, i.e., Go through Growth,v.
1. **accrete**—grow together
2. **accumulate**—grow into a mass or heap; grow in number
3. **batten**—grow fat, literally or figuratively; thrive
4. **bloom**—grow vigorously
5. **blossom**—flourish; prosper; thrive
6. **boom**—grow rapidly in population, industry, etc.—said of cities, towns, etc.
7. **burgeon**—grow forth; sprout
8. **cluster**—grow in groups
9. **coalesce**—grow together into one body or mass
10. **concresce**—grow together; grow into one body or mass, or into a solid mass
11. **concrete**—grow into a solid mass
12. **develop**—grow; grow to a more advanced or mature stage
13. **evolve**—grow or develop gradually
14. **flourish**—grow abundantly, prosperously, or successfully
15. **flower**—thrive
16. **form**—grow
17. **knit**—grow tightly together
18. **luxuriate**—grow richly and abundantly
19. **maturate**—grow toward maturity; grow ripe
20. **mature**—grow toward full development
21. **outgrow**—grow faster than; grow beyond
22. **overgrow**—grow over or beyond; outgrow
23. **proliferate**—grow rapidly by forming or developing new parts, offshoots, etc. (biology)

24. **prosper**—grow well or richly; thrive
25. **ramble**—grow with no regularity
26. **regenerate**—grow again, after a cessation of growth
27. **ripen**—grow ripe
28. **run riot**—grow without control
29. **shoot, shoot up**—grow suddenly or rapidly
30. **spring**—grow
31. **sprout**—grow or develop rapidly
32. **thrive**—grow successfully, vigorously, or abundantly; grow strong
33. **trail**—grow so long as to fall or creep up on the ground
34. **vegetate**—grow morbidly or with abnormal luxuriance (medical); grow (of plants); grow in the manner of plants
35. **wax**—grow, figuratively, as *wax rich, fat,* etc.

4. Growth,n. *From Sec. 3:* accumulation, coalescence, concretion, development, evolution, formation, luxuriation, maturation, outgrowth, overgrowth, proliferation, regeneration, vegetation (accumulative, concretionary, developmental, evolutional or evolutionary, formative, regenerative, vegetational,adj.); *Also:*

1. **accrescence**—continuous growth
2. **accretion**—growth; growth organically; growth by adding external parts; a growing together of parts that usually stay separate (accretive,adj.)
3. **anabolism**—growth through constructive physiological processes (anabolic,adj.)
4. **catabolism**—growth through destructive physiological processes (catabolic,adj.)
5. **concrescence**—a growing together of parts that are usually separate (biology)
6. **ectogenesis**—development outside the body
7. **evolution**—scientific development of a race (evolutional, evolutionary,adj.)
8. **excrescence, excrescency**—superfluous or abnormal growth
9. **gigantism**—growth to abnormally large size (medical)
10. **hypertrophy**—abnormal and excessive physical growth or development of a member or part of the body, often resulting from unusually great use (hypertrophic,adj.)
11. **individuation**—act of growing, or process by which someone grows, into a distinct individual
12. **metabolism**—combination of anabolism and catabolism in physiological growth (metabolic,adj.)
13. **stature**—figurative growth or development
14. **upgrowth**—process of growing up; development

5. Growing; Developing,adj. *From Sec. 3:* accumulating, battening, blooming, etc.; accumulative, coalescent, luxuriant, proliferous, prosperous, thrifty (usually of plants), vegetant or vegetative (coalescence, luxuriance or luxuriancy, prosperity or prosperousness, thrift or thriftiness, vegetativeness,n.); *From Sec. 4:* accrescent, accretive, excrescent (excrescence, excrescency,n.); *Also:*

1. **acervate**—growing in heaps or clusters
2. **adolescent**—growing or becoming mature (adolescence,n.)
3. **adventive**—growing without cultivation but not native to a place (of plants); growing in a place after being brought in (of animals)
4. **arboricoline**—growing on trees
5. **binate**—growing in pairs or doubles
6. **bushy**—growing thickly (bushiness,n.)
7. **cancerous**—growing wild, like a cancer
8. **clustery**—growing in clusters; growing like grapes on a common vine
9. **crescive**—growing and increasing

10. **florescent**—growing vigorously, abundantly, or successfully, in a figurative sense (florescence,n.)
11. **geogenous**—developing in or on the ground
12. **increscent**—growing (increscence,n.)
13. **lush**—growing richly and thickly—often said of plants (lushness,n.)
14. **neoplastic**—growing abnormally (medical)
15. **palmy**—growing abundantly, richly, or healthily
16. **rambling**—growing irregularly
17. **rampant**—growing unchecked or unrestrained (rampancy,n.)
18. **rank**—growing vigorously and abundantly; growing to excessive heights or limits—usually said of vegetation (rankness,n.)
19. **spontaneous**—growing or developing naturally or without outside help (spontaneity, spontaneousness,n.)
20. **supercrescent**—growing on something (supercrescence,n.)
21. **terrestrial**—growing in the ground

6. The Gland Regulating Bodily Growth: pituitary,n.

7. Period in or of Growth (Non-Descriptive): age, stage,n.

8. Temporary Period in or of Growth or Development: phase,n. (phaseal, phasic,adj.)

9. Specific or Descriptive Period or Point in or of Growth,n.

1. **adolescence**—period of growth between childhood and maturity (adolescent,n. adolescent,adj.)
2. **adulthood**—maturity (adult,n. adult,adj)
3. **apex**—point of final growth (apical,adj.)
4. **autumn, fall**—time of maturity; time of maturity and decline (autumn, autumnal, adj.)
5. **bloom**—time of greatest development
6. **blossom**—period of growth or development analogous to the unfolding of the flower or flowers of a plant
7. **childhood**—period of early growth (child, n. childhood,adj.)
8. **climax**—final and highest point of growth or development (climactic,adj.)
9. **culmination**—highest point in growth or development
10. **florescence**—figurative period of abundant or successful growth (florescent, adj.)
11. **infancy**—period of very early growth (infant,n. infant,adj.)
12. **maturity**—period of full growth (mature, adj.)
13. **middle age**—middle period of growth (middle-aged,adj.)
14. **spring**—first stage of growth; period or stage of growth and progress (vernal,adj.)
15. **summer**—early middle age; period of maturing powers (summer,adj.)
16. **winter**—period of old age or decay (winter, wintry,adj.)

10. To Reach the Highest Point of Growth or Development; To Reach Full Growth or Development: culminate (in),v. (culmination,n. culminant,adj.)

11. Pert. to the Earliest Stage of Growth or Development: embryonic, germinal,adj.

12. Complete Action of Growth That Repeats Itself: cycle,n. (cyclic,adj.)

13. Repetition, in the Development of an Individual, of the Developmental History of the Race or Species: palingenesis,n. (palingenetic, palingenetical,adj.)

14. Lack of Repetition, in the Developmental History of an Individual, of the Development of the Race: cenogenesis,n. (cenogenetic,adj.)

15. Normal Area in Which an Animal or Plant Lives and Grows: habitat,n.

16. History of Development,n.
1. ontogeny, ontogenesis—history of the development of the individual (ontogenetic, ontogenetical, ontogenic,adj.)
2. phylogeny, phylogenesis—history of the development of the race or species (phylogenetic, phylogenetical, phylogenic,adj.)

17. Student of the History of Development, n. *From Sec. 16:* ontogenist, phylogenist

18. Period or State in Phylogeny,n.
1. acme—period of greatest development in numbers and forms in the phylogeny of a group of organisms (acmic, acmatic,adj.)
2. epacme—state of incomplete development in the phylogeny of a group of organisms, before complete development is reached (epacmaic,adj.)
3. paracme—state of decadence or decline in the phylogeny of a group of organisms

19. Capable of Growth or Development: formative (biology); germinative, potential; vegetative (botany); viable (botany),adj. (formativeness, potentiality, vegetativeness, viability,n.)

20. Containing or Showing the Possibility of Future or Further Development: seminal, adj.

21. A Growth, i.e., That Which Grows or Has Grown,n.
1. bud—new or young growth, as on a plant, tree, etc.
2. burr—rounded growth on a tree
3. callus, callosity—hard and thick growth of skin (callous, calloused,adj. callous,v.)
4. cancer—malignant tissue growth (cancerous,adj.)
5. concretion—stone
6. crop—new growth of anything in a season
7. culture—growth of germs carefully prepared for a purpose
8. cyst—abnormal, sac-like growth in the body (cystic,adj.)
9. excrescence—disfiguring external growth, such as a wart, boil, etc.; abnormal growth or outgrowth; also, contradictorily, a natural outgrowth, such as hair, fingernails, etc. (excrescent,adj.)
10. formation—growth
11. malignancy—cancerous growth; growth likely to cause death (malignant,adj.)
12. neoplasm—abnormal bodily growth (neoplastic,adj.)
13. outgrowth—that which grows outside or on the outside
14. overgrowth—that which has grown over something
15. shoot, sprout—new or young growth that emerges suddenly or rapidly on a plant
16. stone—hard, inorganic mass formed in a body cavity or organ
17. stubble—rough growth
18. tumor—abnormal tissue growth (tumorous,adj.)
19. upgrowth—that which has matured or developed
20. vegetation—pathological bodily outgrowth (vegetational,adj.)

22. To Grow, i.e., Cause to Grow,v.
1. cultivate—grow (crops)
2. culture—grow (microbes, etc.) in a special medium
3. develop—cause to grow
4. generate—grow, as a limb or part; cause to grow
5. raise—grow (crops, flowers, etc.)
6. regenerate—grow (new tissues or members) after the loss or death of these
7. sprout—cause to grow

23. Growth, i.e., a Causing to Grow,n. *From Sec. 22:* cultivation, culture, development,

generation, regeneration (developmental, generative, regenerative,adj.) ; *Also:* 1. culture—the growing of a specific crop, product, animal, etc.

24. Causing Growth and Strength: vegetant, adj.

25. Capable of Causing the Growth of Plant Life, as Soil, etc.: vegetative,adj. (vegetativeness,n.)

26. Principal Thing Grown or Produced in an Area: staple,n. (staple,adj.)

27. To Further or Encourage the Growth of: develop, foster, promote,v. (development, fosterage, promotion,n. developmental, promotive,adj.)

28. To Stop or Slow the Growth of: arrest (medical), check, choke, dwarf, retard, stunt, v. (arrest, retardation, retardment,n. retardative, retardatory,adj. arrested, checked, choked, dwarfed, retarded, stunted,adj.)

29. Apparently Held Back in Growth by Poor Environment; Stunted: pauperitic,adj.

30. Arrested or Retarded Development,n.
1. abortion—arrested development of an organ
2. hypoplasia, hypoplasty—arrested physical development of an organ or member of the body (hypoplastic,adj.)
3. infantilism—retarded emotional, physical, and mental development to that of a young child
4. retardation—retarded development

732. MATURITY

1. Mature: adult, full-blown, full-fledged, full-grown, fully grown, full-ripe, grown, grown-up, matured, mellow, mellowed, ripe, seasoned, well-developed,adj.

2. Maturity: adulthood, matureness, mellowness, ripeness,n.

3. To Become Mature: autumn, develop, grow up, maturate, mature, mellow, ripen,v. (development, maturation,n.)

4. Becoming Mature: maturescent, maturing, mellowing, ripening,adj. (maturescence, n.)

5. To Make or Cause to Become Mature: autumn, maturate, mature, mellow, ripen, season,v. (maturation,n.)

6. Causing or Promoting Maturity: maturative, maturing, mellowing, ripening, seasoning,adj.

7. Made Gentle, Sweet, Reasonable, Pleasant, etc., by Maturity or Maturing Experiences: mellow, mellowed,adj. (mellowness,n. mellow,v.)

8. Grown Faster or Bigger than Normal or Pleasing: overgrown,adj.

9. Excessively Developed: overdeveloped,adj.

733. IMMATURITY

1. Immature: bread-and-butter, callow, childish, crude, green, infantile, infantine, juvenile, puerile, raw; sophomoric (esp. intellectually) ; unbaked, undeveloped, unfledged, ungrown, unlicked, unripe, unseasoned; verdant (colloq.) ; young,adj.

2. Immaturity: callowness, childishness, chrysalis, crudeness, crudity, greenness, infantilism, infantility, juvenility, nonage, puerility, rawness, unripeness; verdancy (colloq.) ; youth,n.

3. Lacking, or Showing a Lack of, Mature Wisdom, Judgment, or Experience: half-baked,adj.

4. Immature Person or Thing: bud,n.

5. Animal in an Immature Form, in Analogy to That of the Insect: larva,n. (larval,adj.)

6. Period of a Person's Immaturity: salad days,n.

7. Biologically Undeveloped, or Poorly or Imperfectly Developed—of Organs, Parts, etc.: abortive, embryonal, embryonic; latent (of buds on a plant, etc.); primitive, protomorphic, rudimentary,adj. (abortiveness, primitiveness, rudimentariness,n.)

8. Part or Organ Now Imperfectly Developed though Once Better Developed in an Earlier Stage of the Growth of an Individual, Species, etc.: vestige, vestigium,n. (vestigial,adj.)

9. Still in the Earliest Stages of Biological or, Loosely, Other Development: embryonic, adj.

10. Not Fully or Properly Developed: underdeveloped,adj.

11. Not, or Not Yet, Grown to Full or Normal Size or Height: undergrown,adj.

734. EAT

1. To Eat or Feed, i.e., Take Food,v.
1. **banquet**—eat an elaborate meal
2. **batten**—feed greedily
3. **board (with, at)**—eat and live (with, at)
4. **bolt**—eat (one's food) very rapidly and with little or no chewing
5. **break bread (with)**—eat (with someone)
6. **breakfast**—eat one's morning meal
7. **break one's fast**—eat after a period of abstinence
8. **consume**—eat up
9. **cram**—eat too much; eat greedily
10. **debauch**—indulge in an excess or orgy of eating and drinking
11. **devour**—eat (food) ravenously or eagerly
12. **diet**—feed; eat sparingly; eat special foods for purposes of losing weight or other reasons of health, religion, conscience, etc.
13. **dine**—eat; have one's evening meal
14. **fare**—partake of food
15. **feast**—eat hungrily, sumptuously, or greedily
16. **gluttonize**—stuff oneself with food; eat to excess; eat (food) greedily and to excess
17. **gobble**—eat (food) quickly and greedily
18. **gorge**—eat voraciously, stuffing oneself to satiety
19. **gormandize**—eat greedily; stuff oneself with food
20. **guttle**—eat with greed and coarse enjoyment
21. **ingest**—eat, i.e., take (food, etc.) into the stomach for digestion
22. **lunch**—eat a light midday meal
23. **luxuriate**—feed richly
24. **manducate**—eat
25. **nibble**—eat with small and dainty or quick bites
26. **overeat**—eat too much
27. **partake (of)**—eat (some of)
28. **picnic**—eat outdoors
29. **raven, ravin**—eat or feed greedily; devour
30. **regale**—feast
31. **snack**—eat lightly, often between regular meals
32. **sup**—eat the evening or late evening meal
33. **tiffin**—lunch (British)
34. **tooth**—eat (food) by chewing
35. **victual**—feed (colloq.)
36. **wolf**—eat (food) greedily or ravenously; bolt

2. Eating; Act of Eating,n. *From Sec. 1:* banqueting, battening, etc.; consumption, debauch, gluttony, gormandize, ingestion, luxuriation, picnic, regalement (ingestive,adj.); *Also:*
1. **commensalism**—eating with another or others at the same table
2. **polyphagia**—eating to excess (medical)
3. **repast**—eating of food
4. **surfeit**—excessive eating or indulgence in eating
5. **tachyphagia**—rapid eating (medical)

3. Eater,n. *From Sec. 1:* banqueter, boarder, breakfaster, consumer, devourer, dieter, diner, feaster, glutton, gorger, gormandizer, guttler, luncher, nibbler, partaker, picnicker; *From Sec. 2:* commensal; *Also:* 1. **trencherman**—eater; one who eats heartily or greedily; one who comes frequently for dinner

4. To Eat, or Feed on, Grass, etc. (of Animals): browse, depasture, feed, graze, pasture,v.

5. Feeding Grounds of an Animal: haunt,n.

6. To Be Entertained with Food and Drink: fare,v.

7. Time of Feasting and Celebration: festival, festivity,n. (festival, festive,adj.)

8. Greedy in Eating: cormorant, edacious, gluttonous, ravening, ravenous, voracious,adj. (cormorant, glutton,n. edacity, gluttony, gluttonousness, ravenousness, voracity, voraciousness,n.)

9. Eating Everything; Figuratively Devouring Everything: omnivorous,adj. (omnivorousness,n.)

10. Immoderate or Excessive in Eating: crapulent, crapulous,adj. (crapulence,n.)

11. Illness Resulting from Excessive Eating and Drinking: surfeit,n.

12. Eating with Another or with Others at the Same Table: commensal,adj. (commensality,n.)

13. One Who Enjoys Eating, the Pleasures of Food, etc.,n.
1. **bon vivant (French)**—one who enjoys the pleasures of good eating, esp. in the company of others
2. **convivialist**—one who enjoys the pleasures of eating and drinking in social friendship
3. **epicure, epicurean**—one who enjoys eating as a pleasure, but is choice and critical of food quality and preparation; gourmet
4. **gastronome, gastronomer, gastronomist**—one versed in the art of good eating; epicure; gourmet
5. **gourmand, gormand**—one who is fond of good eating and possessed of a healthy appetite
6. **gourmet**—one who is an expert in the selection of good foods, wines, liquors, etc., or who is choice and finicky about the quality and combinations of what he eats; epicure
7. **visceratonic**—one whose personality make-up predisposes him to the enjoyment of eating and drinking, and of relating to people over a table (psychiatric coinage)

14. Fond of Eating, etc.,adj. *From Sec. 13:* convivial, epicurean, gourmand, visceratonic

15. Fondness for, or Enjoyment of, Eating,n. *From Sec. 13:* conviviality, epicurism, epicureanism; gourmandism, gormandism, or gourmanderie

16. Pert. to, or Characteristic of, Eating and Drinking in Social Friendship: convivial,adj. (conviviality,n.)

17. Fit to Be Eaten: comestible, eatable, edible, esculent,adj. (edibleness, edibility,n.)

18. Unfit to Be Eaten: inedible, uneatable,adj.
(inedibility,n.)

19. Science, Art, or Principles of Eating,n.
1. **dietetics**—science of nutrition (dietitian,
dietician,n. dietetic,adj.)
2. **gastronomy**—art or science of good or
pleasurable eating (gastronomist,n. gas-
tronomic, gastronomical,adj.)
3. **nutrition**—body of principles or knowledge relating to the absorption and utilization of food by the body (nutritionist,n.
nutritional,adj.)
4. **sitology**—science of food; dietetics

**20. One Who, in a Large Institution, Applies
the Laws of Nutrition in Regard to the
Food Served the Members:** dietitian, dietician,n.

21. To Avoid, or Refrain from, Eating: fast,
v. (fast, fasting,n. faster,n.)

**22. Fasting at the Door of Someone in a De-
mand for Justice (in India):** dharna,
dhurna,n.

**23. To Eat Sparingly, or to Eat Only Cer-
tain Foods, Esp. in Religious Observance:**
fast,v. (fast, fasting,n. faster,n.)

24. Eating Sparingly: abstemious,adj. (abstemiousness,n.)

25. Voluntary Avoidance of Certain Foods:
abstemiousness, abstinence,n. (abstemious,
abstinent,adj.)

**26. The Eating of, or Feeding on, Certain
Specific Foods,**n.
1. **anthropophagy**—human flesh, esp. by
humans (anthropophagic, anthropo-
phagical,adj.)
2. **cannibalism**—human flesh by humans,
or one's own kind or species
3. **coprophagy, coprophagia**—dung or feces,
as among birds or insects or, as a form of
insanity, man
4. **geophagy, geophagia, geophagism**—
earth, esp. clay, as among primitive peoples
5. **hippophagy, hippophagism**—horseflesh
6. **ichthyophagy**—fish
7. **omophagy, omophagia**—raw flesh, as a
rite in some primitive religions
8. **phytophagy**—plants, or vegetation
9. **scatophagy**—filth, feces, or dung, as a religious rite or as a morbid obsession
10. **theophagy**—a god, in primitive cultures,
in the symbolized form of a man or animal representing the god
11. **trichophagy, trichophagia**—hair (medical)
12. **vegetarianism**—plant life exclusively, although animal products such as eggs may
be included (vegetarian,adj.)

27. Eating or Feeding on a Specific Food,adj.
From Sec. 26: anthrophagous, cannibal or
cannibalistic, coprophagous, geophagous,
hippophagous, ichthyophagous or ichthi-
ophagian, omophagous or omophagic, phy-
tophagous or phytophagic, scatophagous,
theophagous; *Also:*
1. **androphagous**—human flesh
2. **apivorous**—bees, as among certain birds
3. **baccivorous**—berries
4. **batrachophagous**—frogs
5. **bibliophagic**—books
6. **carcinophagous**—crabs
7. **carnivorous**—flesh only, as by lions,
tigers, wolves, and similar animals
8. **carpophagous**—fruits
9. **carrion**—dead or decaying animal flesh
10. **equivorous**—horseflesh
11. **fructivorous, frugivorous**—fruit
12. **graminivorous**—grasses
13. **granivorous**—grains and seeds
14. **herbivorous**—grains and other plants
only, as by certain animals

15. **hominivorous**—human flesh
16. **hylophagous**—wood (zoology)
17. **insectivorous**—insects, as certain animals
18. **lignivorous**—wood
19. **myrmecophagous**—ants
20. **necrophagous**—dead or decaying animal
flesh
21. **nucivorous**—nuts
22. **omnivorous**—both flesh and vegetation,
as certain animals
23. **ophiophagous**—serpents
24. **panivorous**—bread
25. **phytivorous**—plants or vegetation
26. **piscivorous**—fish
27. **polyphagous**—many kinds of food
28. **rhizophagous**—roots
29. **sanguinivorous**—blood
30. **saprophagous**—decaying matter
31. **saurophagous**—lizards
32. **seminivorous**—seeds
33. **vermivorous**—worms
34. **xylophagous**—wood, as certain crustaceans, insect larvae, etc.

28. Eater of, or Feeder on, a Specific Food,
n. *From Sec. 26:* anthropophagite, cannibal,
coprophagist, geophagist, hippophagist, ich-
thiophagian or ichthiophagan, omophagist,
theophagite; vegetarian (person); *From Sec.
27:* bibliophagist, carnivore, herbivore, insectivore, omnivore, saprophagan, xylophage;
Also: 1. **lactovegetarian**—person who will eat
only plant life and milk products, or, in some
instances, eggs

29. Eaters, Collectively, of a Specific Food,n
From Sec. 26: anthropophagi, hippophagi,
ichthiophagi

30. Animal That Will Eat a Human Being:
man-eater,n. (man-eating,adj.)

**31. Animal or Organism That Feeds on Dead
Organic Matter:** scavenger,n. (scavenge,v.)

735. BITE

1. To Bite,v.
1. **browse**—nibble at twigs, leaves, etc. (of
animals)
2. **champ**—bite and chew loudly or impatiently
3. **crop**—bite off (of grazing animals)
4. **gnaw**—bite upon; bite or bite upon persistently
5. **nibble**—bite gently
6. **nip**—bite sharply and suddenly; bite off
7. **snap at**—make a sudden bite at
8. **tooth**—bite

2. A Bite,n. *From Sec. 1:* champ, crop, nibble,
nip

3. Biting,adj. *From Sec. 1:* browsing,
champing, etc.; *Also:* mordacious, rodent
(mordacity,n.)

4. Gnawing: rodent,adj.

5. Gnawing Animal: rodent,n.

**6. To Wear Away or Eliminate by Con-
tinuous Biting:** gnaw,v.

7. Given to, or in the Habit of, Biting:
mordacious,adj. (mordacity,n.)

**8. To Attempt to Bite; To Jump Forward
to Bite:** snap at,v. (snap,n.)

**9. To Seize with the Teeth and Shake or
Bruise, as One Animal Does to Another; To
Annoy by Continuous Biting or Snapping:**
worry,v. (worry,n.)

10. Bitten Off: premorse,adj.

11. Contact of the Teeth,n.
1. **bruxism**—grinding of the teeth during
sleep
2. **bruxomania**—grinding of the teeth while
asleep or awake, generally a manifestation of neurosis

3. **clamping**—forceful closure of the jaws with isolated upper and lower teeth in contact (clamp,v.)
4. **clenching**—forceful closure of the jaws with the lower teeth in contact with the upper teeth (clench,v.)
5. **gnashing**—grinding (of the teeth), as in pain, anger, etc. (gnash,v. gnash,n.)
6. **grinding**—continuous movement of the lower against the upper teeth (grind,v.)

12. To Chew,v.
1. **champ**—bite and chew loudly or impatiently
2. **crunch, craunch, crump**—chew noisily; crush noisily with the teeth
3. **gnaw**—chew upon
4. **gum**—chew with the gums, since the teeth are missing, in preparation for swallowing (colloq.)
5. **manducate**—chew
6. **masticate**—chew in preparation for swallowing (masticator,n.)
7. **mumble**—chew gently, scarcely using the teeth or with the lips closed
8. **munch**—chew noisily; chew vigorously (muncher, n.)
9. **ruminate**—chew the cud (of cattle, etc.); chew again
10. **scrunch**—crunch

13. Chew, Chewing, i.e., Act of Chewing,n. *From Sec. 12:* champ, crunch, mastication, rumination, scrunch (masticatory, ruminant or ruminative,adj.)

14. Animal That Chews the Cud: ruminant, n.

736. SWALLOW

1. To Swallow,v.
1. **bolt**—swallow (food) very rapidly and without chewing it
2. **devour**—swallow up; swallow greedily and hungrily—both meanings either literal or figurative
3. **englut**—swallow down in gulps
4. **engulf**—figuratively swallow up
5. **glut**—swallow; swallow greedily
6. **gobble, gobble up**—swallow greedily
7. **gorge**—swallow greedily
8. **gulp, gulp down**—swallow food, liquid, etc., eagerly, greedily, and rapidly, or with long swallows
9. **ingurgitate**—swallow greedily or in great amounts
10. **pouch**—swallow
11. **resorb**—swallow (food, etc.) back or again
12. **suck (in, up)**—swallow (up)
13. **swig**—gulp (usually liquids)
14. **swill**—swallow greedily
15. **wolf**—swallow (food) greedily and without chewing it

2. A Swallowing,n. *From Sec. 1:* gulp, ingurgitation, resorption; *Also:* 1. **deglutition**—process or act of swallowing food

3. A Swallow,n. *From Sec. 1:* gulp

4. Swallowing Stones or Gravel: lithophagous,adj. (zoology)

5. Difficulty in Swallowing (Medical): dysphagia, pica,n. (dysphagic,adj.)

737. HUNGER

1. Hungry,adj.
1. **adephagous**—voracious (medical)
2. **bulimic, bulimiac**—having a diseased, excessive, and insatiable desire for food, as a result either of certain forms of insanity or of certain diseases, as diabetes (medical)
3. **empty**—hungry (colloq.)

4. **esurient**—hungry; interested in eating or inclined to eat
5. **famished**—extremely hungry, almost to the point of starvation
6. **gluttonous**—voracious
7. **hollow**—hungry
8. **ravening**—extremely hungry, and implying a fierceness in attempting to find food
9. **ravenous**—extremely hungry or eager for food
10. **starving, starveling**—extremely hungry; suffering from lack of food
11. **voracious**—desiring food in large quantities

2. Hunger; Desire for Food,n. *From Sec. 1:* bulimia, emptiness, esurience or esuriency, famishment, gluttony or gluttonousness, hollowness, ravenousness, starvation, voracity or voraciousness; *Also:*
1. **appetite, appetency**—desire for food
2. **cynorexia**—bulimia (medical)
3. **edacity**—good appetite (humorous)
4. **pica**—abnormal craving for strange foods (medical)
5. **polyphagia**—bulimia (medical)
6. **sitomania**—morbid or pathological craving for food (medical)

3. To Hunger, i.e., Be Hungry,v. *From Sec. 1:* famish, raven or ravin, starve

4. To Cause to Be Hungry,v. *From Sec. 1:* famish, starve (starvation, n.); *Also:* 1. **hunger**—cause to be hungry; starve

5. Starving Person, Animal, or Plant: starveling,n.

6. To Die of Hunger: famish, starve,v. (famishment, starvation,n.)

7. To Cause to Die of Hunger; To Cause to Be Greatly Weakened by Hunger: famish, starve,v. (starvation,n.)

8. Exciting or Tempting the Appetite: appetizing,adj. (appetizer,n.)

9. Lack of Desire for Food,n.
1. **anorexia**—lack of hunger—medical (anorectic, anorectous,adj.)
2. **anorexia nervosa**—morbid or neurotic aversion to food or eating (medical)
3. **inappetence, inappetency**—lack of a desire to eat (inappetent,adj.)

10. Such Complete Lack of Food as to Cause or Threaten Starvation or Death: famine,n.

738. FEED

1. To Feed, i.e., Give Food to,v.
1. **aliment**—give food or nourishment to (alimentation,n.)
2. **breakfast**—provide breakfast for
3. **dine**—serve dinner to as one's guest
4. **dry-nurse**—feed (a child) by hand and attend to his other needs (dry-nurse,n.)
5. **feast**—feed an elaborate meal to
6. **lunch**—provide lunch for
7. **nourish**—feed (nourishment,n.)
8. **nurture**—feed (children or young) during the period of growth
9. **sup**—provide supper for
10. **tiffin**—serve lunch to (British)

2. To Entertain or Delight with Choice Food or an Elaborate Meal: feast, regale,v. (regalement,n.)

3. To Feed Too Much to: overfeed,v.

4. To Feed (Someone) Less than Necessary for Maintaining Good Health and Growth: underfeed, undernourish,v. (undernourishment,n. underfed, undernourished,adj.)

5. Forced Feeding through a Stomach Tube: gavage,n. (medical)

6. To Provide (Domestic Animals) with Growing Grass for Food: depasture, graze, pasture,v.

739. NOURISHMENT

1. Nourishment: alimentation, nutrition,n.

2. Pert. to Nourishment: alimental, alimentary, nutritional, nutritive, trophic,adj.

3. Healthy Nourishment: eutrophy,n. (eutrophic,adj.)

4. Poor or Insufficient Nourishment: dystrophy or dystrophia,n. (dystrophic,adj.)

5. Nourishing: alible, alimentary, alimentative, nutrient, nutritious, nutritive,adj. (alibility, nutritiousness, nutritiveness,n.)

6. Nourishment, i.e., That Which Is Nourishing: aliment, nutrient, nutriment, nutrition, pabulum, subsistence, sustenance,n.

7. Spiritual Nourishment Supplied by God: manna,n.

8. Descr. of Plants or Other Organisms in Reference to Means of Obtaining Nourishment,adj.

  1. allotrophic—dependent on other organisms for nourishment

  2. autophytic—of plants, not dependent on organized food materials for nourishment

  3. autotrophic—getting nourishment from chemical elements in inorganic combinations

  4. heterophytic—of plants, dependent on other plants or on animal organisms for nourishment

  5. heterotrophic—able to obtain nourishment from outside sources (heterotrophy, n.)

  6. parasitic, parasitical—obtaining nourishment from other organisms (parasitism, n.)

  7. saprophytic—of plants, obtaining nourishment from dead or decaying organisms (saprophytism,n.)

9. Plant or Other Organism in Reference to Nourishment,n. *From Sec. 8:* autophyte, heterophyte, heterotroph, parasite, saprophyte

10. Process or Power of Breaking Down Food so that It Can Be Absorbed and Used by the Body: digestion,n. (digest,v.)

11. Pert. to, or Connected with, Digestion: digestive, peptic,adj.

12. Pert. to Digestive Juices: peptic,adj.

13. Promoting or Helpful to Digestion: digestant, digestive, peptic,adj.

14. That Which Promotes or Helps Digestion: digestant, digestive, pepsin, peptic,n.

15. Capable of Being Digested: digestible,adj. (digestibility,n.)

16. Incapable of Being Digested: indigestible, adj. (indigestibility, indigestibleness,n.)

17. Good Digestion: eupepsia,n. (eupeptic, adj.)

18. Having Good Digestion: eupeptic,adj.

19. Poor Digestion: dyspepsia, indigestion,n. (dyspeptic, indigestive,adj.)

20. Having Poor Digestion: dyspeptic,adj.

21. Person with Poor Digestion: dyspeptic,n.

22. Passage of Digested Food into the Blood or Lymph: absorption,n. (absorptive,adj.)

23. Incorporation of Digested Food into the Bodily Substance: assimilation,n. (assimilative, assimilitory,adj. assimilate,v.)

740. FOOD

1. Food (General): aliment; chow (slang); comestible, comestibles, commons, eatables, edible, edibles, esculent, fare; grub (slang); nourishment, nutrient, nutriment, nutrition, pabulum; provender (humorous); provisions, rations, subsistence, sustenance, viand, viands; victuals (colloq.),n.

2. Food (Descriptive),n.

  1. bill of fare—menu

  2. board—one's food and lodging; loosely, one's food, as in the phrase *board and keep*

  3. chyme—semi-digested food passing from the stomach into the intestines (chymal, chymous,adj.)

  4. delicatessen—cold, cooked meats and other foods that are eaten with them, as pickles, potato salad, etc.

  5. diet—food in respect to its qualities or effects; one's regular food; special foods to which one is restricted for reasons of health, weight reduction or gain, etc. (dietary, dietetic,adj.)

  6. dietary—fixed allotment of food

  7. ingesta—food taken into the stomach for digestion

  8. manna—food unexpectedly and miraculously supplied to the Israelites during the Exodus; hence, any needed food

  9. meal—food eaten at one sitting or time

  10. menu—food that is served at a meal, banquet, etc.

  11. pap—soft food for infants

  12. potluck—whatever food happens to be in the house to make a meal of

  13. purée—cooked food passed through a strainer

  14. ration—fixed allowance of food

  15. refection—food that relieves hunger or fatigue; refreshment

  16. refreshment, refreshments—light food

  17. roughage—coarse food; food containing abundant cellulose, such as certain vegetables and fruits, which stimulates stomach action or elimination; coarser parts or kinds of food

  18. snack—refreshment

  19. sop—food soaked in some fluid

  20. tack—poor food (contemptuous)

  21. viands—choice and delicate food or foods

3. Stock, Store, or Supply of Food: provender (humorous), provisions, rations,n.

4. Food for Domestic Animals: bait, feed, fodder, forage, provender,n.

5. Semiliquid Food Made of Garbage, etc., for Pigs: swill,n.

6. Twigs, Leaves, etc., Fit for Food for Grazing Animals: browse,n.

7. Food Brought Back into the Mouth from the First Stomach for Further Chewing by a Cow or Other Ruminant: cud, quid,n.

8. List of Food Served in a Restaurant, at a Formal or Public Dinner, Banquet, etc.: bill of fare, carte, menu,n.

9. Permitting Choice of Dishes from the Entire Menu: à la carte,adj.

10. List of Foods to Which One Is Restricted for Reasons of Health, etc.: diet,n. (dietary, dietetic,adj.)

11. System, Course, or Rule of Diet: dietary, n.

12. Manner of Living in Reference to the Food One Eats: diet,n.

13. Method, Plan, or System of Eating, Exercising, Sleeping, etc., to Improve Health: regimen,n.

14. To Regulate the Food of, Usually for Health Reasons: diet,v.

15. Portion of Food,n.

  1. appetizer; antipasto (Italian); hors d'oeuvre—small portion of food served before or as the first course of a meal

  2. canapé (French)—toasted morsel of bread or cracker topped with some delicacy

3. **confection**—fancy dessert
4. **course**—one of the dishes of a meal
5. **delicacy, dainty, tidbit, titbit**—delicious morsel of food
6. **dessert**—portion of sweets, fruit, etc., served after the main courses of a meal
7. **dish, plate**—portion of food
8. **frappé**—frozen or chilled dessert
9. **morsel, snack, bite**—small portion of food
10. **mouthful**—portion of food that fits into the mouth at one time
11. **pellet**—small ball of food
12. **pièce de résistance (French)**—main dish of a meal
13. **quid**—portion of food suitable for chewing

16. A Meal,n.
1. **bacchanalia**—drunken feast
2. **banquet**—elaborate feast
3. **Barmecide feast**—meal where there is the illusion or pretense of abundance, but where, in reality, there is little or nothing to eat
4. **breakfast**—morning meal
5. **brunch**—combination of breakfast and lunch eaten, usually, by those who have risen late in the morning (colloq.)
6. **buffet meal**—meal served by means of an arrangement of filled dishes from which diners help themselves
7. **collation**—light meal; light meal that takes the place of lunch or supper on religious fast days
8. **dinner**—one's evening or large meal; occasionally one's midday meal if large, esp. on Sundays
9. **feast, festival**—sumptuous meal
10. **feed**—meal (slang)
11. **lunch, luncheon**—light midday meal
12. **mess**—meal served to a group, as in an institution, etc.
13. **picnic**—meal eaten outdoors
14. **potluck**—casual or informal meal
15. **refection**—meal; lunch
16. **refreshment, refreshments**—very light, or incomplete, meal
17. **repast**—meal; sumptuous meal
18. **shore dinner**—meal of seafood, i.e., lobster, shrimp, clams, etc.
19. **snack**—refreshment
20. **supper**—late evening meal
21. **table d'hôte**—meal in a restaurant at a specific price
21. **tiffin**—lunch (British)

17. Meals and Sleeping Quarters: accommodation, accommodations, board, board and keep,n.

18. To Provide Meals and Sleeping Quarters to: accommodate, board, camp,v. (accommodation,n.)

19. Time for a Meal: breakfast time, dinnertime, lunchtime, mealtime, repast, suppertime,n.

20. Pert. or Relating to, or Descr. of, a Meal, adj.
1. **after-dinner**—pert. to time or events after the evening meal or a large meal
2. **bacchanalian**—pert. to a drunken feast
3. **festal, festive**—pert. to, befitting, etc., a feast
4. **Lucullan**—descr. of feasts, banquets, meals, etc., that are sumptuous beyond belief, so called after Lucullus, the Roman consul famous for such feasts
5. **postprandial**—after-dinner
6. **prandial**—pert. to dinner, or to a meal (humorous)
7. **pre-prandial**—before dinner

21. Certain Food Elements: amino acids, carbohydrates, fats, minerals, proteins, starch, sugar, vitamins,n. (starchy, vitaminic, adj.)

22. Unit Used in Expressing the Heat- or Energy-Producing Value of Foods: calorie or calory,n. (caloric,adj.)

741. RESTAURANT

1. Restaurant,n.
1. **automat**—restaurant in which diners serve themselves from machines in which coins are dropped
2. **bistro (French)**—small restaurant
3. **cabaret**—restaurant that provides entertainment as well as food
4. **café**—restaurant
5. **cafeteria**—self-service restaurant
6. **chophouse**—restaurant specializing in steaks, chops, etc.
7. **coffeepot**—small, inexpensive restaurant
8. **coffee shop**—small restaurant, often attached to an institution, where, usually, full-course dinners are not served
9. **diner**—dining car of a train; small restaurant in the shape of a dining car
10. **grill**—restaurant, esp. one where chops, steaks, etc., are fried or broiled to order
11. **inn**—hotel serving meals; loosely, elegant restaurant
12. **lunch wagon**—small restaurant, often in the form of a wagon (colloq.)
13. **night club**—cabaret
14. **rathskeller**—German-style restaurant, often in a cellar or below street level
15. **rotisserie**—restaurant where meats are grilled in full view of the diner
16. **tavern**—restaurant where liquor is served

2. Owner or Manager of a Restaurant: innkeeper, restaurateur, tavern keeper,n.

3. Place Where People Eat, or Are Served Food,n.
1. **canteen**—place where refreshments are served, originally strictly on a military post
2. **commons**—place where food is served to a large number of people at common tables
3. **dining hall**—place where large numbers of people eat
4. **dining room**—place where people eat
5. **grill**—dining hall or dining room of a club, hotel, etc.
6. **lunchroom**—room for dining or lunching
7. **mess hall**—dining hall
8. **refectory**—place for dining in a monastery or convent
9. **restaurant**—public dining place

4. Place Where Food Is Secured or Bought: commissary,n.

5. Place Where French Pastry Is Sold: patisserie,n.

742. SOUP

1. Soup,n.
1. **bisque**—rich purée, usually made from seafood
2. **bouillabaisse**—kind of fish chowder made with vegetables
3. **bouillon**—clear soup, often made from beef
4. **broth**—thin soup
5. **chowder**—thick soup made from fish or seafood
6. **cockaleekie**—soup of boiled fowl and the vegetable leek
7. **consommé**—clear soup, made often from chicken or beef
8. **gumbo**—soup thickened with okra
9. **julienne**—clear soup containing strips of vegetables
10. **minestrone (Italian)**—thick and rich vegetable soup, Italian style
11. **mulligatawny**—curry soup, of East Indian origin

12. **potage (French)**—thick soup containing pieces of meat, vegetables, potato, etc.
13. **pottage**—thick vegetable soup
14. **purée**—soup made from meat, fish, vegetables, etc., the solid substance thoroughly cooked and strained into the broth
15. **vichyssoise**—soup made of potato, cream, leek, etc.

2. Concentrated Liquid, Usually Derived from Boiling Meat, etc., and Often Added to Soups in place of Water: stock,n.

743. MEAT

1. Meat as to the Animal of Origin,n.
1. **bacon**—pig, hog, etc.
2. **beef**—cow, steer, etc.
3. **game**—wild animals hunted for food
4. **ham**—pig, hog, etc.
5. **lamb**—young sheep
6. **mutton**—grown sheep
7. **pork**—pig, hog, etc.
8. **poultry**—domesticated birds
9. **squab**—pigeon
10. **veal**—calf (vituline,adj.)
11. **venison**—deer

2. Sausage: bologna; boloney (colloq.); Bratwurst (German); frankfurter, frankfurt, or frankfort; hot dog (slang), knockwurst, liverwurst, pepperoni, salami; wiener (colloq.),n.

3. Slice of Meat: chop, collop, cut, cutlet, fillet; rasher (of bacon or ham); steak,n.

4. Certain Other Meats or Meat Dishes,n.
1. **bully, bully beef**—canned or pickled beef
2. **chitterlings**—fried or boiled small intestines of the pig
3. **delicatessen**—cold, usually smoked meats
4. **fricassee**—dish made of poultry, veal, or other meats cut into pieces and stewed
5. **goulash**—meat stew with various spices, esp. paprika
6. **hamburg, hamburger**—ground meat, usually in fried or broiled patties
7. **hash**—mixture of cooked ground meat and potatoes
8. **jambalaya**—meat and rice cooked together
9. **pastrami**—highly seasoned and smoked beef, often from the shoulder
10. **scrapple**—scraps of meat, usually pork, boiled with herbs, flour, etc.
11. **stew**—meat, usually in small pieces, cooked by slow boiling, and combined with vegetables, etc.
12. **sweetbread**—the pancreas or thymus of a calf or other animal used as food
13. **tripe**—part of the stomach of a ruminant animal used as food

5. Pert. to, or Caused by, Food Derived from Animal Flesh: creatic,adj.

744. MILK

1. Certain Parts of Milk,n.
1. **butterfat**—fat constituent of milk
2. **cream**—fatty part of the milk that separates out and rises to the top
3. **curd**—thick or solid part of milk that separates from the watery part
4. **whey**—watery part of milk that separates out from the curd when milk sours

2. Curdled Milk: clabber,n.

3. Sourish Liquid Left when Butter Has Been Separated from Milk or Cream: buttermilk,n.

4. Descr. of, or Pert. or Relating to, Milk, adj.
1. **au lait**—with milk—of coffee
2. **galactic**—pert. to, or derived from, milk
3. **homogenized**—descr. of milk in which the cream has been mixed by a special process with the rest of the milk and therefore does not separate out (homogenization,n. homogenize,v.)
4. **lactary, lacteal**—pert. to, having to do with, or resembling, milk
5. **lacteous**—like milk; milky
6. **lactescent**—having a milky appearance; having to do with the secretion of milk; milky; becoming milky (lactescence, lactescency,n.)
7. **lactic**—pert. to milk; derived from sour milk
8. **lactiferous**—secreting milk
9. **milch**—giving milk—of domestic animals, such as cows or goats
10. **milky**—pert. to, descr. of, having the color of, etc., milk (milkiness,n.)
11. **skim**—descr. of milk from which the cream has been removed

5. Place Where Milk Is Prepared, Sold, etc., n.
1. **creamery**—place where milk is prepared for market, and/or where milk products are made
2. **dairy**—place or farm where milk is produced, processed, or made into butter and cheese; store or company that sells these products

6. Business of Producing Milk or Milk Products: dairy,n. (dairyman,n.)

7. Cheesy: caseous,adj.

8. To Make or Become Cheesy: casefy,v. (caseation,n.)

745. FRUIT

1. Certain Fruits,n.
1. **acinus**—grape; berry
2. **comfit, confiture**—fruit, seed, root, etc., preserved with sugar and dried
3. **copra**—dried coconut meat
4. **currant**—seedless raisin
5. **drupe**—a fruit of a certain kind, such as the peach, cherry, plum, etc.
6. **nectarine**—peach with smooth skin
7. **pome**—a fruit of the apple family
8. **pomelo**—grapefruit
9. **tangelo**—cross between the tangerine and grapefruit
10. **tangerine**—small orange-type fruit with loose peel

2. Crop of Grapes of the Year: vintage,n.

3. Juice of Apples, Used for Drinking: cider,n.

4. Crushed Substance of Apples, Used in Cider Making: pomace,n.

5. Dish of Stewed Fruits: compote,n.

6. A Flavor or Concoction of Various Fruits: tutti-frutti,n.

7. Having the Appearance or Form of Fruit: fructiform,adj.

8. Resembling Fruit, Esp. in Flavor, Odor, Taste, etc.: fruity,adj. (fruitiness,n.)

9. Bearing Fruit, or Bearing Fruit Abundantly: feracious, fructiferous, fructuous, fruitful,adj. (feracity, fructuosity, fructuousness, fruitfulness,n.)

10. Having the Capacity to Bear Fruit: fructificative,adj.

11. To Bear Fruit: fructify, fruit,v. (fructification, fruition,n.)

12. To Make Able to Bear Fruit: fructify, fruit,v. (fructification,n.)

13. Bearing Fruit of, or Resembling, the Apple Family: pomiferous,adj.

14. Bearing Berries: baccate, bacciferous,adj.

15. Bearing Nuts: nuciferous, nutty,adj.

16. Full of Nuts; of the Flavor of Nuts: nutty,adj. (nuttiness,n.)

17. Not Producing Fruit: acarpous,adj.

18. Fruit Pit: putamen, stone,n.

19. An Edible Vegetable: esculent, legume,n.

20. Vegetable Such as Peas, Beans, etc.: legume,n.

21. Agricultural Products, Including Fruits and Vegetables: produce,n.

22. Pert. to, Descr. of, Resembling, or Relating to, Certain Fruits or Vegetables,adj.
1. **ammiaceous**—belonging to the carrot family
2. **baccate**—resembling a berry or berries
3. **bromeliaceous**—belonging to the pineapple family
4. **citrus**—descr. of a type of fruit of which the orange, grapefruit, lemon, and lime are representative
5. **drupaceous**—pert. to, resembling, or consisting of peaches, cherries, plums, and similar fruits
6. **leguminous**—pert. to, or characteristic of, peas, beans, etc.
7. **maraschino**—descr. of cherries cooked in a colored and flavored syrup
8. **moracious**—belonging to the mulberry family
9. **musaceous**—belonging to the banana family
10. **oleaceous**—belonging to the olive family
11. **olivaceous**—resembling an olive
12. **vaccinaceous**—belonging to the huckleberry family
13. **vinaceous**—pert. to, or resembling, grapes

23. Seller of Fruits and Vegetables: fruiterer, greengrocer,n.

24. Science of the Fruits and Seeds: carpology,n. (carpologist,n.)

25. The Growing of Fruits or Vegetables,n.
1. **citriculture**—growing of citrus fruits—oranges, grapefruit, lemons, etc. (citriculturist,n.)
2. **fructiculture**—growing of fruit (fructicultural,adj.)
3. **horticulture**—art of growing fruits, vegetables, etc. (horticulturist,n. horticultural,adj.)
4. **olericulture**—growing of vegetables for food (olericulturist,n. olericultural,adj.)
5. **pomiculture**—growing of fruit (pomiculturist,n.)
6. **pomology**—growing of fruit as a science or process (pomologist,n. pomological, adj.)
7. **viniculture**—growing of wine grapes (viniculturist,n. vinicultural,adj.)
8. **viticulture**—growing of grapes (viticulturist, viticulturer,n. viticultural,adj.)

746. JELLY

1. Fruit Jelly: conserve or conserves (with large pieces of fruit), jam; jelly (smooth in consistency); marmalade (often of orange or orange peel); preserves (with large pieces of fruit),n.

2. Base for Fruit Jelly: pectin,n.

3. Like Jelly: gelatinous,adj.

4. Animal Jelly: gelatin,n.

5. Pert. to, or Containing, Gelatin: gelatinous,adj.

6. Like Gelatin: gelatinoid,adj. (gelatinoid, n.)

7. To Become Jelly or Jellylike: gelatinate, gelatinize, jell, jellify, jelly,v. (gelatination, gelatinization, jellification,n.)

8. To Cause to Become Jelly or Jellylike: gelatinate, gelatinize, jellify, jelly,v. (gelatination, gelatinization, jellification,n.)

747. COFFEE

1. Coffee: café; café au lait (with half milk); café noir (black),n. (all French)

2. Small Cup of Strong Black Coffee: demitasse,n.

3. Flavoring of Combined Coffee and Chocolate: mocha,n.

4. Chemical Alkaloid Found in Coffee and Tea: caffeine,n.

5. Very Weak Tea, Mostly Milk and Sugar: cambric tea,n.

6. Belonging to the Tea Family: theaceous, adj.

748. DRINK

1. To Drink,v.
1. **bib**—drink; sip
2. **consume**—drink up
3. **gulp, gulp down**—drink down in big swallows
4. **guzzle**—drink greedily and noisily; drink excessively or continuously
5. **imbibe**—drink or drink in
6. **ingurgitate**—drink greedily, noisily, or in large quantities
7. **lap**—take up in drinking with the tongue, in the manner of certain animals
8. **partake (of)**—drink some of
9. **quaff**—drink; drink deeply; drink with great swallows; drink repeatedly; drink freely (of)
10. **sip**—drink a little at a time; drink, or drink from, little by little
11. **swig**—drink in long draughts
12. **swill**—drink greedily or excessively
13. **toast**—drink to (someone's health or honor)
14. **toss off, toss down**—drink at one swallow

2. Drinking,n. *From Sec. 1:* consumption, ingurgitation, toast; *Also:*
1. **compotation**—drinking together (compotatory,adj.)
2. **draught**—drinking
3. **libation**—drinking (humorous)
4. **potation**—drinking

3. Drinker,n. *From Sec. 1:* consumer, gulper, guzzler, imbiber, partaker, quaffer, sipper, swigger; *From Sec. 2:* compotator

4. A Drink,n. *From Sec. 1:* gulp, quaff, sip, swig, swill; *From Sec. 2:* draught, potation

5. A Drink, i.e., That Which Is Drunk,n.
1. **beverage**—that which is drunk; liquid for drinking
2. **bracer**—stimulating drink
3. **chaser**—drink, usually non-alcoholic, taken after liquor drunk neat
4. **nectar**—drink of the gods; delicious beverage
5. **nightcap**—drink taken at bedtime to produce sleepiness
6. **potion**—drink of medicine, poison, or of any liquid supposed to have magical effect or power
7. **refreshment, refection**—drink that relieves thirst or fatigue
8. **rickey**—drink made of lime juice and carbonated water, with or without the addition of spirits
9. **sherbet**—cold fruit drink

6. Beverages: potables,n.

7. Drinkable: potable,adj.

8. Drinking Fountain: bubbler,n.

9. Thirsty: athirst, dry,adj. (dryness,n.)

10. Excessive Thirst Caused by Disease: dipsosis,n. (medical)

11. To Feel or Be Thirsty: thirst,v.

12. To Drink Alcoholic Beverages or Liquor, v.

1. **bib**—drink heavily; tipple
2. **booze**—drink heavily (colloq.)
3. **bouse**—drink liquor; drink liquor to excess; carouse
4. **carouse**—take part in a drinking party; drink freely or deeply
5. **debauch**—engage in excessive drinking
6. **fuddle**—tipple
7. **guzzle**—drink liquor frequently or to excess
8. **imbibe**—drink liquor
9. **nip**—take liquor in sips; tipple
10. **soak**—drink liquor heavily
11. **souse**—drink to the point of intoxication (slang)
12. **swill**—drink liquor greedily
13. **swizzle**—drink liquor in excess
14. **tipple**—drink liquor; indulge habitually or heavily in the drinking of liquor
15. **toast**—drink liquor to (someone's health or honor)
16. **tope**—drink alcoholic beverages heavily or excessively
17. **tun**—swizzle
18. **wassail**—engage in a drinking bout; drink to the health or success of

13. Drinking of Liquor,n. *From Sec. 12:* bibbing, boozing, etc.; bibation or bibacity, carousal, debauch, swill, toast, wassail (bibitory,adj.) ; *Also:*

1. **compotation**—drinking, or drinking heavily, together (compotatory,adj.)
2. **libation**—drinking (humorous)
3. **potation**—drinking

14. Drinker of Liquor,n. *From Sec. 12:* bibber (chiefly in compounds, as winebibber, etc.), boozer, bouser, carouser, debauchee, guzzler, imbiber, soak, souse, tippler, toper, wassailer; *From Sec. 13:* compotator; *Also:* **1. bacchanal, bacchanalian, bacchant**—devotee of alcoholic revelry, i.e., of Bacchus, the Roman god of wine; carouser (bacchant, bacchantic,adj.)

15. A Drink of Liquor,n. *From Sec. 12:* nip; *From Sec. 13:* libation, potation

16. Drink and Play: beer and skittles,n.

17. Drinking Party or Bout: bouse, carousal, carouse; drunk (colloq.) ; jag (colloq.) ; spree, wassail,n. (carouser, wassailer,n.)

18. Immoderation in Drinking: bibacity, bibulousness, crapulence, inebriacy, insobriety, intemperance, intemperateness, surfeit; winebibbing or winebibbery (of wine),n. (winebibber,n. bibacious, bibulous, crapulent or crapulous, intemperate, winebibbing,adj.)

19. Disposition to Drink with Friends in Sociable Fellowship: conviviality,n. (convivialist,n. convivial,adj.)

20. Descr. of, Pert. to, or Characteristic of, Sociable Drinking: convivial,adj.

21. Toasts Made in Drinking: prosit (Latin), skoal; wassail (ancient times),n.

749. ALCOHOLIC LIQUOR

1. Alcoholic Liquor (General): alcohol, aqua vitae, the bottle; booze (colloq.) ; bouse, drink, firewater, grog; hooch (slang) ; inebriants, intoxicants, John Barleycorn, liquor, pot, potables, pottle; rotgut (of poor quality and unaged—slang) ; rum, schnapps or schnaps, spirit, spirits, spiritus frumenti, stimulants, usquebaugh (Scottish or Irish term), toxicants, whiskey or whisky,n.

2. Liquor Drunk Greedily or to Excess: swill,n.

3. An Alcoholic Drink (General): bracer, drink, inebriant, intoxicant; libation (humor-ous) ; potation, shot, stimulant, toxicant, whiskey, whisky,n.

4. Certain Specific Alcoholic Drinks,n.
1. **appetizer, apéritif (French)**—drink served before a meal, designed to sharpen the appetite
2. **cocktail**—mixed alcoholic drink made of a variety of liquors
3. **fizz, fiz**—alcoholic drink so prepared as to effervesce
4. **highball**—tall glass of liquor mixed with carbonated water, ginger ale, etc., and served with ice
5. **Mickey Finn, mickey finn**—drugged alcoholic drink
6. **nightcap**—alcoholic drink taken at bedtime to produce sleepiness
7. **nog, eggnog**—mixed alcoholic drink, containing an egg or eggs
8. **pousse-café**—alcoholic drink served after coffee, generally made of layers of different kinds and colors of liquors or liqueurs
9. **rickey**—drink made of liquor, lime juice, and carbonated water
10. **sling**—iced alcoholic drink, containing water, sugar, lemon or lime juice, and, usually, gin
11. **swizzle**—mixed alcoholic drink made of crushed ice, sugar, lemon or lime, bitters, and rum or other liquor
12. **toddy, hot toddy**—alcoholic drink of liquor mixed with sweetened hot water and, often, containing a cinnamon stick

5. Certain Popular Cocktails or other Mixed Drinks: alexander, bacardi, bronx, daiquiri, gibson, manhattan, martini, mint julep, old-fashioned, orange blossom, pink lady, scotch mist, side car, tom and jerry, tom collins, whiskey sour, zombie,n.

6. Certain Types of Liquor,n.
1. **applejack**—brandy distilled from cider
2. **aqua vitae**—brandy
3. **blend**—mixture of aged whiskey and grain neutral spirits
4. **bourbon**—whiskey made from corn
5. **brandy**—liquor distilled from wine or from the fermented juice of other fruits
6. **cognac**—brandy from the Cognac region of France; French brandy; loosely, any good brandy
7. **cordial**—liqueur
8. **distilled liquor**—liquor made in a still or distillery by a process of evaporation and condensation
9. **eau de vie (French)**—brandy
10. **fermented liquor**—wine, beer, ale, champagne, etc., prepared through the chemical changes produced by living organisms
11. **gin**—liquor distilled from grain and flavored with juniper berry
12. **grog**—rum or other liquor mixed with water
13. **hard cider**—fermented juice of apples, containing 2%–8% alcohol
14. **home-brew**—liquor manufactured or prepared at home during the prohibition era
15. **liqueur**—syrupy, aromatic, and, usually, sweet liquor
16. **perry**—liquor fermented from pears
17. **rum**—liquor made from fermented sugar cane or molasses
18. **rye**—liquor distilled from rye
19. **scotch**—liquor distilled in Scotland from grains
20. **whiskey, whisky**—liquor distilled from grain
21. **wine**—alcoholic beverage, of low proof, made from the juice of fermented grapes or other fruits

7. Malt Liquor,n.
1. **ale**—fast-fermented liquor from malt and hops

2. **beer**—slow-fermented liquor from malt and hops
3. **bock**—a kind of spring beer
4. **brew, brewage**—any malt liquor or brewed beverage
5. **lager, lager beer**—beer stored for some months before use
6. **near-beer**—beer with a very low alcoholic content
7. **porter**—dark brown, heavy British beer
8. **sake**—Japanese beer, made from rice
9. **stout**—malt liquor; strong ale, beer, or porter
10. **wassail**—beverage of ale flavored with spices, sugar, etc.

8. Descr. of Beverages Containing Alcohol: ardent, hard, spirituous, strong,adj.

9. Alcohol: spirit, spirits,n.

10. Kinds of Alcohol: butanol or butyl alcohol, ethyl alcohol; grain alcohol or grain neutral spirits (used in liquor); isopropyl alcohol, methyl alcohol, wood alcohol,n.

11. Any Preparation Made with Alcohol: alcoholate,n.

12. Alcoholic Strength or Quality: alcoholicity,n.

13. Unit of Strength of the Alcohol in Beverages: proof,n.

14. Device to Measure the Alcohol in, or the Alcoholic Strength of, a Liquid: alcoholometer,n. (alcoholometry,n.)

15. Pert. to, Derived from, or Caused by, Alcohol: alcoholic, vinic,adj.

16. To Treat or Saturate with Alcohol: alcoholize,v. (alcoholization,n.)

17. Wine,n.
1. **champagne**—effervescent white wine from the Champagne region of France; by extension, similar wine from any other place
2. **vin du pays (French)**—wine of a place or country
3. **vin ordinaire (French)**—cheap, everyday table wine
4. **vintage**—wine of a specific crop of grapes, or of a particular type or region in a specific year
5. **vintage wine**—fine wine from a particularly good crop of grapes

18. Act or Time of Making Wine: vintage,n.

19. Relating to, or Descr. of, Wine,adj.
1. **brut (French)**—dry, as applied to wine, esp. champagne
2. **dry**—not sweet, as applied to wine
3. **vinaceous**—pert. to wine; of the color of wine; resembling wine
4. **vinic**—pert. to, or derived from, wine
5. **vinous**—pert. to wine; like wine; produced or caused by wine (vinosity,n.)
6. **winy**—like wine; having a winelike taste

20. Study, Science, etc., of Wines,n.
1. **oenology**—study of wines; knowledge about wines (oenologist,n. oenological, adj.)
2. **viniculture**—science or study of wine making (viniculturist,n. vinicultural,adj.)

21. God of Wine: Bacchus (Roman); Dionysus or Dionysos (Greek),n. (Bacchic or bacchanal, Dionysiac or Dionysian,adj.)

22. Priest or Votary of Bacchus: bacchant, masc. and fem.; bacchante,fem.n. (bacchants or bacchantes,pl.n.; Bacchae,fem.pl.n.; bacchantic,adj.)

23. Female Attendants of Bacchus: Bacchae, pl.n.

24. Follower of Bacchus: bacchanal,n.

25. Roman Festival to Bacchus: Bacchanalia, pl.n. (bacchanalian, bacchanal,adj.)

26. Place Where Liquor Is Made,n.
1. **brewery**—place where malt liquors such as beer or ale are made
2. **distillery**—place where liquor is distilled
3. **winery**—place where wine is made

27. Apparatus for Liquor Manufacture,n.
1. **still**—vessel or apparatus used in distilling liquor
2. **wine press**—machine for pressing out, or vat for treading out, the juice of grapes for wine making

28. To Make Liquor,v.
1. **brew**—make (beer, ale, etc.); make fermented liquor (brewing,n. brewer,n.)
2. **distill**—extract the alcoholic essence from (fruit, grains, etc.) in the making of liquor (distillation,n. distiller,n.)
3. **ferment**—make (beer, wine, etc.) through initiating, etc., certain natural chemical changes (fermentation,n.)

29. To Become Distilled: distill,v. (distillation,n.)

30. Product of Distillation: distillate, distillation,n.

31. To Become Fermented: ferment,v. (fermentation,n.)

32. Fermentation: zymosis,n.

33. Fermenting: barmy,adj.

34. Relating to Fermentation,adj.
1. **fermentative**—pert. to, of the character of, or tending to cause or undergo, fermentation
2. **zymogenic**—producing fermentation
3. **zymotic**—pert. to, causing, or caused by, fermentation

35. Device That Measures Fermentation: zymometer,n.

36. Fermentation Science,n.
1. **zymology**—science of fermentation (zymologist,n. zymologic,adj.)
2. **zymurgy**—chemistry dealing with fermentation, as in brewing, wine making, etc.

37. Place to Obtain Liquor,n.
1. **alehouse**—place where beer, ale, etc., is sold
2. **bar**—room or place where liquor is served
3. **barrel house**—low dive where liquor is served
4. **barroom**—place containing counter where liquor is served
5. **beer parlor, beer house, beer garden**—place where beer is served
6. **bistro (French)**—wineshop
7. **blind pig, blind tiger**—speak-easy
8. **cabaret**—place where food and liquor are served and entertainment is provided
9. **café**—place where alcoholic beverages are served and, usually, entertainment or music provided
10. **cantina**—saloon
11. **dramshop**—saloon
12. **gin mill**—low dive where liquor is served
13. **grogshop, groggery**—saloon
14. **liquor shop, liquor store**—place where liquor is sold
15. **mughouse**—alehouse; pothouse
16. **night club**—cabaret
17. **package store**—store, under state license, that sells liquor packaged to be taken home rather than consumed on the premises
18. **pothouse**—place where beer or ale is sold (British); disreputable tavern
19. **public house, pub**—tavern (British)
20. **rathskeller**—German-style saloon, often in a cellar or below street level
21. **saloon**—place where liquor is served, now usually called a bar
22. **speak-easy**—place where liquor was illegally sold or served during the prohibition era

23. **taphouse**—tavern
24. **taproom**—barroom
25. **tavern**—place where liquor is served
26. **wineshop**—shop where wine is sold

38. Counter for the Mixing or Serving of Alcoholic Drinks: bar,n.

39. Bar for Home Use: cellaret,n.

40. Person Connected with the Sale or Serving of Liquor,n.
1. **alewife**—woman who owns, manages, etc., an alehouse
2. **barkeeper, barkeep**—one who mixes and sells alcoholic drinks
3. **barmaid**—waitress at a bar; girl who serves liquor or mixes drinks at a bar
4. **bartender**—person who serves liquor or mixes drinks at a bar
5. **bootlegger**—seller of illicitly manufactured liquor during the era of prohibition in the U.S.
6. **liquor dealer**—one who owns a liquor store
7. **publican**—keeper of a British tavern
8. **tapster (masc.); tapstress (fem.)**—man or woman who serves drinks at a bar
9. **vintner**—wine merchant

41. Addiction to Liquor: alcoholism, alcoholomania, bibacity, bibulousness; booziness (colloq.); dipsomania; dipsorrhexia (medical),n.

42. Addicted to Liquor: alcoholic, bibacious, bibulous; boozy (colloq.); bousy, dipsomaniacal,adj.

43. One Addicted to Liquor: alcoholic, alcoholist; boozer (colloq.); bouser, dipsomaniac, n.

44. Addiction to Wine: oenomania, oinomania, vinosity,n. (vinous,adj.)

45. Addiction to Drunken Orgies: bacchanalianism,n.

46. Drunk: alcoholized, besotted; boiled (slang); boozy (colloq.); bousy; canned (slang); drunken; half-seas over (colloq.); high (colloq.); inebriate, inebriated, inebrious, in one's cups, intoxicated; lit (slang); loaded (slang); lush (slang); pie-eyed (slang); potted (slang); reeling (slang); sodden, sotted, sottish; soused (slang); three sheets in the wind (colloq.); tight (colloq.); tipsy, under the influence,adj.

47. Drunkenness: acute alcoholism; booziness (colloq.), inebriacy, inebriation, inebriety, insobriety, intoxication, sottishness, tipsiness, n.

48. One Who Is Drunk: drunk (colloq.); inebriate,n.

49. One Who Is Habitually Drunk: bloat (slang); drunkard, inebriate; lush (slang); rummy; soak (slang); sot; souse (slang); toper, tosspot,n.

50. Affected Specifically by Liquor,adj.
1. **bacchic, Bacchic**—merry with liquor
2. **beery**—drunk from, or as from, beer (beeriness,n.)
3. **besotted, sotted**—stupefied with liquor
4. **blind-drunk**—exceedingly drunk
5. **dead-drunk**—exceedingly drunk
6. **groggy**—unsteady or shaky from liquor (grogginess,n.)
7. **high**—somewhat stimulated, dizzy, or foolish from liquor (colloq.)
8. **maudlin**—drunk to the point of tears or silly sentimentality
9. **reeling**—so drunk as not to be able to walk steadily
10. **stimulated**—in a state of heady mellowness from liquor (stimulation,n.)
11. **tipsy**—somewhat, but not completely, drunk; unsteady, or foolish, from liquor (tipsiness,n.)
12. **vinous**—affected by wine (vinosity,n.)

51. To Make Drunk: alcoholize, besot, inebriate, intoxicate,v. (alcoholization, inebriation, intoxication,n. inebriant, inebriative, intoxicant, intoxicative,adj.)

52. To Excite with Liquor: stimulate,v. (stimulation,n. stimulative,adj.)

53. Illness from Excessive Drinking,n.
1. **absinthism**—diseased condition from overindulgence in absinthe
2. **crapulence**—feeling or feelings of distress from excessive drinking (crapulent, crapulous,adj.)
3. **delirium tremens**—violent delirium caused by chronic excessive drinking
4. **hangover**—feeling of prolonged distress from overindulgence in liquor, usually after sobering up, and occurring proverbially the next morning (hung-over, adj.)
5. **surfeit**—illness or discomfort from excessive drinking

54. One Who Frequents Bars, Places Where Liquor Is Served, etc.: barfly,n. (colloq.)

55. Avoidance of Liquor,n.
1. **abstinence, total abstinence**—avoidance of liquor
2. **asceticism**—avoidance of worldly or fleshly pleasures, including alcoholic drinks
3. **nephalism**—teetotalism
4. **Rechabitism**—teetotalism—after Rechab's son, a personage in Jewish history who issued an injunction against drinking alcoholic beverages, planting the vine, and living in houses
5. **teetotalism**—total avoidance of liquor
6. **temperance**—avoidance of liquor

56. Avoiding Liquor,adj. *From Sec. 55:* abstinent, ascetic; *Also:* 1. **on the water wagon**—abstaining completely from liquor though previously having indulged (colloq.)

57. One Who Avoids Liquor,n. *From Sec. 55:* abstainer or total abstainer, ascetic, nephalist, Rechabite, teetotaler or teetotalist

58. Member of a Historical Sect That Condemned Liquor, Sexual Intercourse, Clericalism, and the Use of Animals for Food: Encratite,n. (Encratism,n.)

59. Indulging Only Moderately or Occasionally in Liquor: moderate, sober, temperate, adj. (moderation, soberness or sobriety, temperateness or temperance,n.)

60. Sparing in the Use of Liquor: abstemious, adj. (abstemiousness,n.)

61. Not Drunk: sober, uninebriate, uninebriated, uninebrious, unintoxicated,adj. (soberness or sobriety, uninebriation, unintoxication,n.)

62. Opposed to the Sale of Liquor: antisaloon,adj.

63. Descr. of Places, Cities, etc., Where Liquor May Not Be Legally Sold: dry,adj.

64. Person Who Is Opposed to the Drinking and Sale of Liquor: dry,n.

65. Society Opposed to the Use, Sale, etc., of Liquor: Women's Christian Temperance Union (W.C.T.U.),n.

66. U.S. Temperance Leader: Carry (or, erroneously, Carrie) Amelia Nation (1846–1911)

67. Law Against Liquor,n.
1. **prohibition**—United States law that, by constitutional amendment, prohibited manufacture, sale, or transportation of alcoholic liquor (repealed in 1933)
2. **temperance act**—any law against the sale, etc. of liquor
3. **Volstead Act**—congressional act giving force to the Prohibition Amendment, passed in 1919, repealed in 1933—official title is *The Prohibition Enforcement Act*

68. One Who Advocates Laws against Liquor: dry, prohibitionist,n.

69. Group of Former Alcoholics Banded Together to Help Other Alcoholics Free Themselves of Addiction to Liquor: Alcoholics Anonymous (A.A.),n.

750. LIVE

1. To Live; To Be or Remain Alive,v.
1. abide—live; live temporarily
2. board (at, with)—live (at) and take one's meals (with)
3. breathe—live, i.e., be or remain alive
4. coexist—exist at the same time; exist together
5. cohabit—live together as man and wife, with or without marriage
6. dwell (in)—live (in a place) as home, either a structure or a geographical location
7. exist—live; be alive
8. indwell—live within; live temporarily within; inhabit
9. inhabit—live in (a place)—of people or animals, or, sometimes, conditions or abstractions
10. last—remain alive
11. linger—remain alive, though dying
12. lodge (at, with)—live, usually temporarily (in someone else's home); live, usually temporarily (in a place, house, etc.)
13. luxuriate—live richly or in luxury
14. occupy—live in (a place, home, etc.)
15. outlast, outlive—live longer than
16. outride—remain alive despite (hardships, misfortune, storms, etc.)
17. populate, people—live in (a place)—said of groups or numbers of people
18. postexist—live on after the death of the body—said of the soul
19. pre-exist—live before; live previously in another condition or state
20. reside (at, in)—live in (a place) as one's home
21. settle—live permanently
22. sojourn—live temporarily (in a place) where one is a stranger
23. stay—live for a time (at or in a place)
24. subsist—live; continue to live; live as a result of having food, clothing, and shelter
25. survive—remain, or continue to remain, alive; remain alive after (some condition or event), or after the death of (someone); live longer than
26. tenant—live on (land) or in (a house owned by another)
27. unlive—live down
28. vegetate—live a dull, passive life
29. visit—live with for a short time
30. wallow (in)—live in contentment in (some condition or circumstance), as in luxury, filth, sin, sensuality, etc. (usually derogatory)

2. Living; A Being Alive,n. From Sec. 1: coexistence or coexistency, cohabitation, existence or existency; inhabitancy, inhabitation, or habitation; luxuriation, occupation or occupancy, population, postexistence or postexistency, pre-existence, residence or residency, settlement, sojourn, stay, subsistence, survival or survivance, tenancy or tenantry, vegetation, visit, wallow; Also:
1. being—existence; existence as a mortal
2. entity—existence

3. Living; Alive,adj. From Sec. 1: abiding, boarding, etc.; coexistent, existent, postexistent, pre-existent, resident, subsistent; Also:
1. animate—alive
2. commorant—ordinarily inhabiting; living (in a place)
3. extant—alive

4. gregarious—living in herds, groups, flocks, etc.—of animals (gregariousness, n.)
5. longevous—having a long life (longevity, n.)
6. long-lived, long-living—living a long time
7. quick—alive; living (archaic—used today only in the phrase the quick and the dead)
8. short-lived—living only a short time
9. social—living, or tending to live, with others of the same kind in an organized community
10. urban—living in the city or in cities
11. zoetic—living (biology)

4. One Who or That Which Lives, or Is Alive,n. From Sec. 1: boarder, coexistent, cohabitant or cohabiter, dweller, indweller; inhabitant, inhabiter, or habitant; lodger, occupant or occupier, resident, settler, sojourner; survivor, surviver, or survival; tenant, visitor or visitant, wallower; From Sec. 2: being; From Sec. 3: commorant, urbanite; Also:
1. aborigine—earliest known inhabitant or native of a region (aboriginal,adj.)
2. addressee—one who lives at a certain address
3. cottager—one who lives in a cottage
4. denizen—inhabitant
5. earthling—earth dweller
6. entity—that which has a real and separate existence, whether in actuality or in the mind
7. inmate—one who lives in an institution, hospital, prison, etc.
8. native—original inhabitant of a place or country, as distinguished from one who is a foreigner, or who comes in later, etc. (native,adj.)
9. neighbor—one who lives nearby
10. organism—any living entity
11. roomer—one who lives in a room, or rooms, of another's house
12. tellurian, terrestrial—earth dweller
13. transient—one who lives in a place but a short time, as in a hotel, etc. (transient,adj.)
14. troglodyte—one who lives in primitive or degraded circumstances (troglodytic,adj.)

5. People Who Live in a Place: population, n.

6. Inhabitants of a Region Having Common Interests: community,n. (communal, communital,adj.)

7. Lived in: inhabited, occupied, populated, settled, tenanted,adj.; Also:
1. polyglot—lived in by people who speak different languages
2. populous—inhabited thickly; having an abundance of inhabitants (populousness, n.)

8. Fit to Be Lived in; Suitable for Living in: abidable, habitable, inhabitable, livable, lodgeable, occupiable, tenantable,adj. (habitability, habitableness, inhabitability, livableness, tenantableness,n.)

9. Unfit to Be Lived in; Unsuitable for Living in: unhabitable, uninhabitable, unlivable, untenantable,adj. (unhabitableness, uninhabitableness, unlivableness, untenantableness,n.)

10. To Make (Someone) Fit for Living with Others: socialize,v. (socialization,n.)

11. Enjoying Living with Others: gregarious, social,adj. (gregariousness, socialness,n.)

12. Capable of Remaining Alive,adj.
1. facultative—capable of remaining alive in widely different environments (biology)
2. viable—capable of remaining alive—said of a newborn infant (viability,n.)

13. Power to Live: vitality,n.

14. Pert. to Living Conditions: social,adj.

15. To Settle,v.
1. pre-empt—settle on (land or public land) so that one has a priority in purchasing it (pre-emption,n. pre-emptor,n. pre-emptive, pre-emptory,adj.)
2. squat—settle on land, new land, or public land without permission or right; settle on public land in order to gain title to it (squatter,n.)

16. To Get Along,v.
1. fare—get along
2. fend for oneself—get along without help, or through one's own efforts
3. manage—get along
4. scrape along—get along with difficulty
5. shift—get along

17. Person, Animal, or Plant That Lives Off Another or Others,n.
1. drone—person who lives by the work of others
2. leech—person who lives parasitically upon another, drawing upon the host's wealth or substance for his own benefit, taking and never returning; person who demands and takes from another beyond all reason, as it were, sustaining himself at another's expense
3. lickspittle, lickspit—contemptible parasite (person)
4. parasite—person, animal, or plant that lives off another or others
5. sponge, sponger—parasite (person)
6. sycophant—parasite (person)
7. symbiont, symbion—organism that lives in close association with another, dissimilar organism, each living, as it were, off the other, though occasionally the relationship is profitable only to one (symbiontic,adj.)
8. trencherman—parasite (person)

18. A Living, or State or Quality of Living, Off Another or Others,n. *From Sec. 17:* dronishness, parasitism, sycophancy, symbiosis; *Also:*
1. consortism—symbiosis
2. mutualism—symbiosis beneficial to both symbionts
3. supercrescence—parasitism (biology)

19. Living, or Descr. of Living, Off Another or Others,adj. *From Sec. 17:* dronish, parasitic or parasitical, sycophantic, symbiotic; *From Sec. 18:* supercrescent

20. To Live Off Another or Others,v. *From Sec. 17:* drone; leech (on); sponge (on)

21. Person on Whom, or Animal or Plant on Which, a Parasite Lives: host,n.

22. Living on, or Inside of, Another Plant or Animal, but Not Parasitic on It: commensal, adj. (commensalism, commensality,n.)

23. Plant or Animal That So Lives: commensal,n.

24. Having No Inhabitants: abandoned, bleak, depeopled, depopulated, deserted, desolate, dispeopled, empty, forsaken, undwelt in, unhabited, uninhabited, unlived in, unoccupied, unpeopled, unpopulated, unsettled, untenanted, vacant, waste,adj. (bleakness, desolation or desolateness, emptiness, unoccupiedness, vacancy,n.)

25. Place That Is without Inhabitants: desert, waste, wasteland, wilderness,n.

26. To Cause to Be without Inhabitants; To Deprive of Inhabitants: depeople, depopulate, desolate, dispeople,v. (depopulation, desolation,n.)

27. That Which Deprives a Place of Inhabitants: depopulator,n.

---

1. Life,n.
1. afterlife, hereafter, future life—life after death of the body
2. beer and skittles—pleasant, easygoing life; life without troubles or problems
3. eternity, immortality—everlasting life
4. pilgrimage—life conceived as a journeying
5. spirit—life

2. Course of Life,n.
1. career—course of one's life in a particular field
2. orbit—course of life

3. Length or Duration of Life: longevity,n.

4. Life Force, Energy, Principle, etc.: élan vital (French), soul, spirit; vital force, energy, impulse, or principle,n.

5. Pert. to Life,adj.
1. temporal—pert. to this life, rather than to the hereafter
2. vital—pert. to life
3. zoetic—pert. to life (biology)

6. Similar to Real Life: likelike,adj. (likeness,n.)

7. Representing, in Literature or Art, Human Life with the Exact Fidelity of a Camera or Photograph: photographic,adj.

8. Characteristic of a Simple or Somewhat Primitive Social Life: communal,adj.

9. Two Contrasting Theories of Life,n.
1. mechanism—theory that life is wholly explainable in terms of physics and chemistry (mechanist,n. mechanistic, adj.)
2. vitalism—theory that life cannot be wholly explained by physics and chemistry, but includes some inexplicable special force (vitalist,n. vitalist, vitalistic,adj.)

10. Personal Philosophy That Explains the Purpose of Life: Weltanschauung,n. (German)

11. Substance Reputed, in Ancient Times, to Prolong One's Life Indefinitely: elixir,n.

12. Living Substance of All Cells; Living Substance; Physical Substance of Living Things: protoplasm,n. (protoplasmic,adj.)

13. Certain Sciences of Life,n.
1. biology—science of all living forms, both plant and animal (biologist,n. biological, biologic,adj.)
2. biometry, biometrics—science of biological statistics (biometrician,n. biometric, biometrical,adj.)
3. bionomics—ecology (bionomist,n. bionomic, bionomical,adj.)
4. demotics—sociology (demotic,adj.)
5. ecology—science of the relation between living forms and their environment (ecologist,n. ecological, ecologic,adj.)
6. embryology—science of life in its earliest stages (embryologist,n. embryological, embryologic,adj.)
7. sociology—science of how people live together (sociologist,n. sociological, sociologic,adj.)

14. Doctrine Founded on Biological Reasoning or Manner of Explanation: biologism,n. (biologistic,adj.)

15. Calculation of the Probable Duration of Human Life: biometrics, biometry,n. (biometrician,n. biometric, biometrical,adj.)

16. To Give Life to, i.e., Make Come Alive: animate, enliven, exhilarate, inspirit, invigorate, quicken, vitalize, vivify,v. (animation, exhilaration, invigoration, vitalization, vivification,n. invigorant,n. exhilarative, invigorative,adj.)

17. To Give New Life to: reanimate, re-create, regenerate, reinvigorate, rejuvenate, rejuvenesce, rejuvenize, renew, resurrect; revitalize (figurative only) ; revivify,v. (reanimation, re-creation, regeneration, reinvigoration, rejuvenation, rejuvenescence, renewal, resurrection, revitalization, revivification,n. regenerative, rejuvenative,adj. resurrectional or resurrectionary,adj.)

18. To Bring Back to Life: quicken, rally, resurrect, resuscitate, revive, revivify,v. (rally, resurrection, resuscitation, revival, revivification, reviviscence, or reviviscency,n. resuscitative, reviviscent,adj. resurrectional or resurrectionary,adj. reviviscent,n.)

19. To Come to Life, or Come Alive: quicken, v.

20. To Get New Life: rejuvenate, rejuvenesce, v. (rejuvenation, rejuvenescence,n. rejuvenescent,adj.)

21. To Come Back to Life: rally, resuscitate, revive, revivify,v. (rally, resuscitation, revival; revivification, reviviscence, reviviscency,n. reviviscent,n. reviviscent,adj.)

22. Living Again; Revived: redivivus,adj.

23. The Rising of Jesus from Death: The Resurrection,n.

24. The Rising of All Human Beings from Death before the Last Judgment: resurrection,n. (resurrectional, resurrectionary,adj.)

752. LIVELINESS

1. Lively: active, alacritous, animate, animated, breezy, bright, brisk, coltish, crisp, crispy, dashing, ebullient, effervescent, exhilarated, frisky, mettlesome; peppy (slang) ; perky, racy; snappy (colloq.) ; spanking (esp. of wind) ; sparkling, spirited, sprightly, succulent, tittuppy or tittuppy, vital, vivacious, vivid, volatile; zippy (colloq.) ,adj.

2. Liveliness: activeness, activity, alacrity, animal spirits, animation, bounce, breeziness, brightness, briskness, coltishness, crispness, crispiness, dash, ebullience, ebullition, effervescence, exhilaration, friskiness; peppiness (slang) ; raciness; snap (colloq.) ; sparkle, spirit, spiritedness, sprightliness, succulence, tittup, verve, vitality, vivaciousness, vivacity, vividness, volatility,n.

3. To Be Lively; To Show Liveliness: effervesce, perk up, sparkle, tittup,v.

4. To Cause to Be Lively: animate, enliven, exhilarate; pep up (slang) ; perk up (colloq.), v. (animation, exhilaration,n. exhilarative, adj.)

5. Lively and Cheerful: chipper,adj. (colloq.)

6. Excessively or Nervously Lively: skittish, adj. (skittishness,n.)

753. LIVING QUARTERS

1. Living Quarters,n.
  1. **abode**—place where a person, animal, or, by extension, a thing, quality, or abstraction lives or stays; living quarters
  2. **address**—one's house as identified by road, number, etc.
  3. **apartment, flat**—suite of rooms in a multiple dwelling house
  4. **barracks**—buildings where soldiers live; plain, unrelieved building where many people live; row of identical, attached houses
  5. **berth, billet**—living quarters to which one is assigned
  6. **biosphere**—sphere of all forms of living organisms

  7. **bower**—rustic cottage; summer house
  8. **bungalow**—one-story private residence
  9. **cabaña (Spanish); cabana**—small house; house for undressing before taking a swim; cabin
  10. **cabin**—small, crude house
  11. **chalet**—Swiss-style cottage
  12. **château**—large country house
  13. **cot**—small house
  14. **cottage**—small house
  15. **cunabula**—earliest abode
  16. **diggings**—one's home or house (slang)
  17. **domicile**—home; place where one lives
  18. **dunghill**—vile place to live
  19. **duplex**—two-family house; two-story house or apartment
  20. **dwelling**—structure in which one lives as home
  21. **habitat**—normal area in which an animal or plant naturally lives and grows
  22. **habitation**—place where one lives
  23. **hacienda**—country house, often of Spanish style
  24. **harem**—living quarters of the wives, concubines, and other female relatives of a Mohammedan
  25. **haunt**—abode
  26. **hermitage**—place where a hermit lives
  27. **home**—one's dwelling place; house where one lives
  28. **homestead**—home and its grounds or enclosure
  29. **hotel**—house or building providing lodgings for transients
  30. **house**—building in which one lives as home
  31. **hovel**—small house, not much more than a shelter, unpleasant to live in, inferior in every way, etc.
  32. **hut, hutch**—small, rude, or crude house
  33. **igloo**—Eskimo hut, made of blocks of ice, usually dome-shaped; any similar structure
  34. **lodge**—kind of house, often used as a base for hunting or fishing; temporary home
  35. **lodging, lodgings**—place, house, etc., where one lives; place, rooms, etc., that one rents
  36. **mansion**—substantial, elegant, or wealthy-looking house
  37. **palace**—very elegant and impressive residence, esp. of a king, ruler, member of royalty, etc.
  38. **penthouse**—living quarters or apartment on the roof of a building
  39. **pied-à-terre**—temporary lodgings
  40. **quarters**—place where one lives or stays
  41. **residence**—one's house or living quarters; address
  42. **roost**—place to live
  43. **seat**—abode; residence
  44. **shack**—hut
  45. **shanty**—shabby and small house
  46. **shelter**—one's house or home
  47. **tabernacle**—temporary living place
  48. **tenement**—house or building in which people live; part of a building occupied by a family, i.e., an apartment; usually an apartment in a poor section of a city
  49. **villa**—elegant country or suburban residence
  50. **wickiup, wikiup**—temporary hut

2. To Give Living Quarters to,v. *From Sec. 1:* barrack, berth, billet, domicile or domiciliate, house, lodge, quarter; *Also: 1.* canton-quarter; quarter (soldiers)

3. Pert. to Living Quarters,adj. *From Sec. 1:* biospheric, cunabular, domiciliar or domiciliary; palatine or palatial (from *palace*); residential; *Also:*
  1. **domal**—pert. to a house
  2. **domestic**—pert. to the home
  3. **household**—pert. to the home

4. Devoted to, or Interested in, the Home, Duties around the Home, etc.: domestic,adj. (domesticity,n.)

5. At Home, and Surrounded by the Family: en famille (French)

6. One Who Occupies a House, Generally with His Family: householder,n.

7. Those Who Live as One Family in a House: household, ménage,n.

8. Management of a Home: domestic arts, home economics, homemaking, household arts, housekeeping, ménage,n. (homemaker, housekeeper,n.)

9. Without a Home: homeless, houseless, roofless,adj.

10. Person Expelled from Home, etc.: outcast,n.

11. Homeless and Friendless Person: waif,n.

12. A Longing for Home: Heimweh (German); homesickness; mal du pays (French); nostalgia,n. (homesick, nostalgic,adj.)

13. Mental Disturbance on Returning Home after a Protracted Absence: nostopathy,n. (term coined by Dr. Richard Karpe, Connecticut psychoanalyst)

14. Hotel,n.
1. **boardinghouse**—house or hotel at which one lives and takes one's meals
2. **caravansary, caravanserai**—in the East, place where caravans stop for the night; large hotel (caravanserial,adj.)
3. **hospice**—hotel for travelers or pilgrims, esp. one run by a religious order
4. **hostel**—place of lodging for young people hiking, on bicycle trips, etc.; inn
5. **inn**—place of lodging for tourists, visitors, etc., often of homelike comfort or furnishings
6. **lodge**—hotel
7. **lodginghouse**—house in which rooms are rented out
8. **motel**—lodgings for automobile tourists (combination of the words *motor* and *hotel*)
9. **pension**—boardinghouse in Europe
10. **resort**—summer or vacation hotel
11. **rooming house**—house or hotel where rooms are rented to transient or permanent guests
12. **tavern**—hotel or inn, esp. so called in New England

15. Hotelkeeper: boniface, hosteler, hotelier, innkeeper, tavern keeper, victualer,n.

16. Tent,n.
1. **canvas**—tent
2. **pavilion**—tent; large tent with a rounded or peaked top
3. **tabernacle**—tent
4. **tepee**—American Indian tent
5. **wigwam**—American Indian tent

17. Group of Tents: camp, canvas,n. (camper, n. camp,v.)

18. Group of Any Temporary Shelters: camp, n. (camper,n. camp,v.)

19. The Setting Out of a Camp: castrametation,n.

---

754. CONTINUATION

1. To Continue, i.e., Go On, Keep On, etc., v.
1. **abide**—continue; continue in a certain condition
2. **endure**—continue; keep on
3. **last**—continue; continue in force, existence, etc.
4. **linger**—continue or persist although beginning to stop, vanish, etc., as an illness, custom, etc.

5. **outlast**—continue longer than
6. **persevere**—continue despite obstacles, opposition, etc.
7. **persist**—continue; continue despite obstacles, warning, opposition, etc.; continue existing
8. **proceed (with)**—continue, after stopping; continue an activity; continue (with what one was doing); continue in what one was saying
9. **remain**—continue without change
10. **stand**—continue unchanged; last
11. **stay**—continue as before
12. **survive**—continue longer than

2. Continuation; Continuance,n. *From Sec. 1:* endurance, perseverance, persistence or persistency, survival; *Also:* 1. **duration**—continuation in time

3. Continuing (of Things, Conditions, Actions, etc.),adj. *From Sec. 1:* abiding, enduring, etc.; perseverant, persistent (perseverance, persistence or persistency,n.) ; *Also:*
1. **chronic**—continuing for an indefinite, or an indefinitely long, time; firmly established and persisting despite all efforts at change or cure
2. **constant**—continuing persistently; continual
3. **continual**—continuing over and over, with, or despite, possible regular breaks or interruptions
4. **continuous**—continuing without interruption, whether in time or space (continuousness, continuity,n.)
5. **endless**—continuous, as a belt, ribbon, etc.
6. **intermittent**—continuing with stops or interruptions (intermittence, intermittency,n.)
7. **minutely**—continual
8. **obstinate**—continuing or persisting despite efforts to change or remedy (obstinacy, obstinateness,n.)
9. **perpetual**—continuing without break or interruption
10. **stable**—lasting or enduring without change (stability,n.)
11. **steady**—constant (steadiness,n.)
12. **stubborn**—obstinate (stubbornness,n.)
13. **unbroken**—continuous (unbrokenness,n.)
14. **uninterrupted**—continuous
15. **unremitting**—persevering (unremittingness,n.)

4. Continuous Action: process,n.

5. Continuous or Continued Activity: perseveration,n.

6. That Which Continues, Is Continued, or Is Continuous: continuance, continuant, continuation, continuity,n.

7. That Which Is Continuous and Unchanging: continuum,n.

8. Serving, Acting, Tending, or Causing to Continue: continuative,adj. (continuativeness,n.)

9. To Cause to Continue: prolong, sustain,v. (prolongation or prolongment,n.)

10. Time during Which Something Continues or Lasts: duration, standing, term,n.

11. Continuing or Lasting for a Long, or Very Long, Time: durable, enduring, lasting, long-continued, long-continuing, long-enduring, long-lasting, long-standing, perdurable, perennial, permanent,adj. (durability or durableness, enduringness, lastingness, perdurability or perdurableness, permanence or permanency,n.)

12. Having Continued or Lasted a Long Time: long-standing,adj.

13. Continuing or Lasting for a Stated Time: agelong, daylong, hourlong, monthlong, nightlong, weeklong, yearlong, etc.,adj.

14. Continuing or Lasting through the Centuries: secular,adj.

15. Continuing or Lasting Forever: aeonian, ageless, agelong, dateless, endless, eternal, everlasting, immortal, perdurable, permanent, perpetual, sempiternal, timeless,adj. (agelessness, endlessness, eternalness or eternity, everlastingness, immortality, perdurability or perdurableness, permanence or permanency; perpetuity, perpetuance, perpetualness, or perpetuality; sempiternity, timelessness,n.)

16. That Which Continues or Lasts Forever: eternal, perpetuity,n.

17. To Cause to Continue or Last Forever: eternalize, eternize, perpetuate,v. (eternalization, eternization, perpetuation or perpetuance,n.)

18. Equally Eternal; Eternal Together: co-eternal,adj. (coeternity,n.)

19. To Continue with; To Continue (Doing): carry on, carry on with, go on with, keep going, keep on with, maintain, prolong, prosecute, pursue, stay with, stick with or to, sustain, wage,v. (maintenance, prolongation or prolongment, prosecution, pursuit,n.)

20. Continuing, or Tending to Continue, as in an Activity, Attitude, etc.—of People: assiduous, constant, diligent, dogged, obstinate, perseverant, persevering, persistent, pertinacious, relentless, stick-to-itive, stubborn, tenacious, unfailing, unflagging, unrelenting, unremitting,adj. (assiduity or assiduousness, constancy, diligence, doggedness, obstinacy or obstinateness, perseverance, persistence or persistency, pertinacity or pertinaciousness, relentlessness, stick-to-itiveness, stubbornness, tenacity or tenaciousness, unflaggingness, unrelentingness or unrelentance, unremittingness,n.)

21. To Continue Firmly (in One's Position, Demand, Belief, etc.): insist on, insist that, v. (insistence,n. insistent,adj.)

22. Ability or Capacity to Continue or Endure,n.
  1. **endurance**—ability to continue despite difficulties, hardships, physical demands, etc.
  2. **guts**—stamina (slang)
  3. **stamina**—capacity to continue or endure
  4. **vitality**—power to continue or last

755. ENDLESSNESS

1. Endless, i.e., without Having or Coming to an End: ceaseless, eternal, incessant, infinite, interminable, interminate, perpetual, timeless, unceasing, undying, unended, unending,adj. (ceaselessness, eternalness, incessancy, infiniteness or infinity, interminability or interminableness, perpetualness, timelessness, unceasingness, unendingness,n.)

2. Endless, i.e., Not Stopping: ceaseless, eternal, incessant, perpetual, unceasing, unending, unremitting,adj. (ceaselessness, eternalness, incessancy, perpetualness, unceasingness, unendingness, unremittingness,n.)

3. Endless, i.e., without Bounds or Limits: boundless, illimitable, immeasurable, immense, infinite, interminable, interminant, interminate, limitless, measureless, unbounded, unlimitable, unlimited,adj. (boundlessness, illimitability or illimitableness, immeasurability or immeasurableness, immensity or immenseness, infiniteness or infinity, interminability or interminableness, limitlessness, measurelessness, unlimitableness, unlimitedness,n.)

4. Without Limit; Endlessly: ad infinitum, without stint

5. That Which Is without Bounds or Limits; Space, Time, Quantity, Number, Extent, etc., without Bounds or Limits: immensity, infinity,n.

6. With No Clear or Easily Definable Bounds or Limits: indefinite, indeterminate, adj. (indefiniteness, indeterminateness or indeterminacy,n.)

7. Never Dying: deathless, eternal, immortal, imperishable, perdurable, undying,adj.

8. State or Quality of Never Dying: athanasia, athanasy, deathlessness, eternity, eternalness, immortality, imperishability, imperishableness, perdurability, perdurableness, undyingness,n.

9. One Who Never Dies: immortal,n.

10. Symbol of Immortality: phoenix,n. (so called from the mythical bird said to live 500 years then rise reborn from its funeral pyre)

11. To Make Immortal: eternalize, eternize, immortalize,v. (eternalization, eternization, immortalization,n.)

12. To Keep from Dying Out, as the Species, a Language, Custom, etc.: perpetuate,v. (perpetuation or perpetuance,n. perpetuator, n.)

756. IMPERMANENCE

1. Temporary; Lasting Only a Short Time, adj.
  1. **ad interim**—temporary; for the time being only
  2. **caducous**—transitory (caducity,n.)
  3. **ephemeral**—lasting a very short time (ephemerality, ephemeralness,n.)
  4. **evanescent**—remaining or lasting only a very short time; passing quickly (evanescence,n.)
  5. **fleet**—not lasting; impermanent
  6. **fleeting, fleetful**—lasting but a short time; passing quickly (fleetingness,n.)
  7. **fugacious**—highly temporary, being disposed, as it were, to fly quickly away (fugacity, fugaciousness,n.)
  8. **fugitive**—lasting a very short time (fugitivity, fugitiveness,n.)
  9. **impermanent**—temporary; not permanent; not lasting very long (impermanence, impermanency,n.)
  10. **instantaneous**—lasting for just an instant (instantaneousness,n.)
  11. **momentary**—lasting only a tiny fraction of time (momentariness,n.)
  12. **papier-mâché**—of no intrinsic permanence
  13. **passing**—temporary; fleeting
  14. **pro tempore**—for the time being only—often abbreviated *pro tem.*
  15. **provisional, provisionary**—temporary; of the nature of a temporary arrangement
  16. **shadowy**—transitory (shadowiness,n.)
  17. **short-lived**—not lasting very long
  18. **sometime**—temporary
  19. **spasmodic**—lasting only a short time, but sudden and violent
  20. **temporal**—temporary or fleeting, rather than eternal (temporality,n.)
  21. **transient**—not lasting; soon passing or leaving; not remaining for any length of time; not remaining in a place any great length of time, as a guest in a hotel, etc. (transience, transiency, transientness,n.)
  22. **transitory**—continuing or lasting, by its nature, for a very short time only; passing quickly (transitoriness,n.)
  23. **volatile**—fleeting; transient (volatility, volatileness,n.)

2. That Which Is Temporary or Lasts Only a Short Time,n. *From Sec. 1:* ephemeron (ephemera,pl.), spasm, transient; *Also:* **1.**

vapor—something that is fleeting or transitory

3. Used Temporarily in Place of the Right or Better Thing, Arrangement,etc.: makeshift, stopgap,adj. (makeshift, stopgap,n.)

4. Dealing with Topics of Temporary Interest: fugitive,adj.

757. REMAIN

1. To Stay; To Remain,v.
1. abide—stay
2. bivouac—stay for a short time outdoors, camping without tents or special shelter (bivouac,n. bivouacker,n.)
3. cling to—stay near
4. hover—stay nearby or around, often watchfully or uncertainly (hover,n. hoverer,n.)
5. linger—stay in a place as if, or because, unwilling to leave
6. lodge—stay (in a place) after stopping there, as a bullet in the heart, etc. (lodgment,n.)
7. loiter—stay idly around a place (loiterer, n.)
8. roost—stay; stay for the night
9. sojourn—stay for a short time (sojourn,n. sojourner,n.)
10. survive—remain in existence; remain in existence after (a condition, event, etc.); remain in existence longer than (survival, survivance,n. survivor, surviver, survival, n.)
11. tarry—stay; remain; linger (tarry,n. tarrier,n.)
12. visit—stay with for a short time (visit,n. visitor,n.)

2. Word Used in Manuscripts, Galley Proofs, etc., to Indicate that Something Should Remain though Questioned, or Previously Marked, for Omission: stet (literally, *let it stand*)

3. To So Mark (Something): stet,v.

4. That Which Remains or Is Left,n.
1. ashes—last remaining traces
2. carry-over—that which remains or is left
3. detritus—that which is left after a process of wearing away
4. dregs—worst, most debased, most corrupt, least attractive, or bitterest remains of something
5. fossil—hardened trace or remains, usually found preserved in rocks or the earth, of past animals, people, plants, etc.
6. leavings—that which is left
7. oddment—something left over
8. odds and ends—things left over; remnants
9. rack—vestige
10. relic—that which remains from the past
11. reliquiae—remains; fossil remains
12. remainder—that which, or part which, remains or is left
13. remains—that which, or part which, remains or is left; parts or substances remaining or left in the earth from plant or animal life; remnant
14. remnant—that which, or small part which, remains or is left; remaining or surviving trace
15. residue, residuum—that which remains after some is removed, taken, etc.
16. stump—short, thick part of anything remaining or left
17. surplus—that which remains after all that is needed is used or taken
18. survival—that which is left over from the past
19. trace—anything left as an indication of former presence, existence, or action; vestige
20. vestige, vestigium—visible remains, indi-

cation, mark, etc., of anything no longer present or in existence
21. waste—that which is left over and not usable or needed
22. wreck, wreckage—that which is left of something partially or wholly destroyed

5. Remaining,adj. *From Sec. 4:* fossil, remnant, residual or residuary, surplus, vestigial or vestigiary, waste

6. Mark or Indication Left by One Who, or That Which, Passes,n.
1. spoor—track or trail of a wild animal
2. track, trace—mark, indication, etc., left by the passage of a person, animal, or thing
3. trail—mark, indication, scent, etc., of a person's or animal's passage, and found or looked for by a person or animal following or hunting
4. wake—track left in the water by a moving ship or object; track left behind anywhere by any moving object

7. Footprint Left by a Person or Animal: trace,n.

8. Footprints: track,n.

9. Fossil Footprint: ichnite, ichnolite,n. (ichnolitic,adj.)

10. Scientific Study of Fossil Footprints: ichnolithology, ichnology,n. (ichnological, adj.)

11. Matter That Settles to or at the Bottom, n.
1. dregs (pl.)—solid material that settles at the bottom
2. lees (pl.)—matter that settles to the bottom, as of wine or liquor in a cask, etc.
3. sediment—matter from a liquid that settles to the bottom, as of a container, etc.; dregs; lees (sedimentation,n. sedimentary, sedimental,adj.)
4. silt—fine sand, earth, etc., deposited as sediment by moving water (silty,adj.)

12. To Become Choked or Clogged, or to Choke or Clog, with Silt: silt,v.

758. AGE

1. Person's Age,n.
1. chronological age—actual time a person has lived, as distinguished from his mental, physiological, etc., age
2. majority—age of a person over 21
3. minority—age of a person under 21

2. Person as to Age,n.
1. centenarian—person 100 years old, or older (centenarian,adj.)
2. minor—person under 21 (minor,adj.)
3. nonagenarian—person 90 years old, or between 90 and 100 (nonagenarian,adj.)
4. octogenarian—person 80 years old, or between 80 and 90 (octogenarianism,n. octogenarian, octogenary,adj.)
5. quinquagenarian—person 50 years old, or between 50 and 60 (quinquagenarian, quinquagenary,adj.)
6. septuagenarian—person 70 years old, or between 70 and 80 (septuagenarianism,n. septuagenarian, septuagenary,adj.)
7. sexagenarian—person 60 years old, or between 60 and 70 (sexagenarianism,n. sexagenarian, sexagenary,adj.)

3. Of the Same Age: coetaneous, coeval, contemporary,adj. (coetaneity or coetaneousness, coevality, contemporariness,n.)

4. One Who Is the Same Age as Another or Others: coeval, contemporary,n.

759. OLD

1. Old,adj.
1. aged—old; very old

2. **ancient**—very old; belonging to times of the distant past
3. **antediluvian, antediluvial**—very old or antiquated, as if belonging to the period before the Biblical Flood
4. **antiquated**—old; so old as to belong, in effect, to previous eras
5. **antique**—very old; belonging to times in the remote past
6. **archaic**—of an older time; antiquated
7. **dateless**—so old or ancient that no date can be assigned to it
8. **elderly**—nearly old; beyond middle age
9. **fossil**—antiquated
10. **hoary**—ancient
11. **middle-aged**—in the middle period of one's life, perhaps from 45 to 55 or 60
12. **Noachian, Noachic, Noahic, Noaic**—figuratively so old or antiquated as to date back, as it were, to Noah of the Biblical Flood
13. **olden**—old (poetic)
14. **preadamite, preadamitic, preadamic**—so old as to have been, as it were, in existence before Adam
15. **senectuous**—aged; very old
16. **senile**—very old and possessing the weaknesses and failings of advanced age
17. **superannuated**—antiquated
18. **timeless**—dateless
19. **wintry, wintery**—old

2. Old Age; Oldness,n. *From Sec. 1:* agedness, ancientness or anciently, antiquity, datelessness, elderliness, hoariness, middle age, senectitude or senectude, senility, superannuation, timelessness, wintriness; *Also:*
   1. **anecdotage**—that advanced age in which a person becomes addicted to telling anecdotes
   2. **autumn, fall**—declining years (autumn, autumnal,adj.)
   3. **caducity**—senility
   4. **declining years**—old age
   5. **dotage**—childishness of old age; senility —usually in the phrase *in one's dotage*
   6. **summer**—early middle age (summer,adj.)

3. Old or Aged Person,n. *From Sec. 1:* ancient, antediluvian, elder; *From Sec. 2:* dotard; *Also:* 1. **oldster**—old person

4. That Which Is Old,n. *From Sec. 1:* antique or antiquity, archaism

5. Antiques Collectively: virtu,n.

6. Collector or Admirer of Antiques: antiquarian, antiquary, virtuoso,n.

7. Object That Is Interesting because of Its Age, or because of Its Associations with the Distant Past: relic,n.

8. One Who Lived before Adam: preadamite, n.

9. One Who Lived before the Biblical Flood: antediluvian,n.

10. To Grow Old: age,v.

11. Growing Old: aging, senescent,adj. (senescence,n.)

12. Not Showing, in One's Appearance, the Physical Signs of Old Age: well-preserved, adj.

13. Too Old for a Specific Purpose: overage, adj.

14. Pert. to Old Age: elderly, geratic; gerontal or gerontic (biol.) ; senile,adj.

15. Caused by Extreme Old Age: senile,adj.

16. To Be Older than, in Date or Time: antedate, predate,v.

17. Old Man,n.
   1. **codger**—old man; irritable old man
   2. **dotard**—childish, weak-minded, or foolish old man
   3. **gaffer**—old man (contemptuous)
   4. **geezer**—eccentric old man (colloq.)

5. **grandfather**—old man who is, or is old enough to be, a grandfather
6. **graybeard**—old man whose beard has already turned gray
7. **Methuselah**—very old man, after the character in the Bible who lived almost 1000 years
8. **Nestor**—wise old man who gives good advice
9. **patriarch**—revered old man; old man who is a leader in the community (patriarchal,adj.)

18. Old Woman,n.
   1. **beldam, beldame**—ugly and disgusting old woman; grandmother
   2. **biddy**—older woman (colloq.)
   3. **crone**—old woman, usually withered and shrunk in appearance
   4. **dame**—elderly woman; matron
   5. **dowager**—dignified elderly woman, usually of the upper social classes
   6. **grandmother, grandam, granny**—old woman who is, or is old enough to be, a grandmother
   7. **grimalkin**—old woman (contemptuous, from the term for a she-cat)
   8. **hag**—ugly old woman, often of evil character
   9. **matriarch**—old woman ruling a family, clan, group, tribe, etc. (matriarchal, matriarchic,adj.)
   10. **matron**—woman beyond the first blush of youth, usually married; dignified or motherly old woman
   11. **witch**—ugly old woman

19. Like an Old Woman: anile, old-womanish, adj. (anility,n.)

20. Older (of People): elder, first-born (of children), senior,adj. (seniority,n. elder, senior,n.)

21. State of Appearing Considerably Older than in Actuality: geromorphism,n. (medical)

22. Oldest (of Children in a Family): eldest, first-born,adj.

23. State or Condition of Being the Eldest Born of the Children of a Family: primogeniture,n. (primogenital, primogenitary,adj.)

24. Oldest or Older Member of a Group, Body, Profession, etc.: dean, doyen,n. (doyenness,fem.n.)

25. Science or Study of Old Age,n.
   1. **geriatrics**—medical branch dealing with the diseases of old age (geriatrician,n. geriatric,adj.)
   2. **gerocomy, gerocomia**—medical science dealing with old people (gerocomical,adj.)
   3. **gerontology**—science of aging; study of the phenomena of old age
   4. **nostology**—biological study of the senile or declining stages of an organism (nostologic,adj.)

26. Science or Study of Old Things,n.
   1. **antiquarianism**—study of ancient times through the remains of the past; study of antiques (antiquarian,adj.)
   2. **archaeology, archeology**—science of the relics of ancient times (archaeologic, archaeological, archeological, archeologic, adj.)
   3. **Assyriology**—science or study of ancient Syria, its language, relics, etc. (Assyriological,adj.)
   4. **Egyptology**—science or study of the antiquities of ancient Egypt (Egyptological, Egyptologic,adj.)
   5. **paleobiology**—science that deals with fossils as organisms—a branch of paleontology
   6. **paleology**—study of antiquities, esp. prehistoric antiquities (paleological,adj.)
   7. **paleontology**—science of life of past geo-

logical periods as evidenced by fossils (paleontological, paleontologic,adj.)

27. **Student of Old Things,n.** *From Sec. 26:* antiquary or antiquarian, archaeologist, archeologist, Assyriologist or Assyriologue, Egyptologist or Egyptologer, paleobiologist, paleologist, paleontologist; *Also:*
1. **archaist**—antiquary
2. **medievalist**—one who is versed in the history, etc., of the Middle Ages

28. **Not, or No Longer, New or Fresh,adj.**
1. **banal**—trite (banality,n.)
2. **fusty**—without freshness; moldy (fustiness,n.)
3. **hackneyed**—trite
4. **mildewed**—so lacking in freshness or newness as to be, literally or figuratively, full of mildew
5. **moldy**—so lacking in freshness or newness as to be, literally or figuratively, affected with mold (moldiness,n.)
6. **moss-grown**—so lacking in newness or freshness as already, figuratively, to have begun to sprout moss
7. **moth-eaten**—so lacking in newness or freshness as already, figuratively, to have fallen prey to moths
8. **musty**—stale (mustiness,n.)
9. **outworn**—so lacking in newness or freshness as already to have been cast aside
10. **rancid**—stale, literally (rancidity,n.)
11. **rusty**—so lacking in newness or freshness as to have succumbed, figuratively, to rust (rustiness,n.)
12. **seedy**—not, or no longer, fresh or new (seediness,n.)
13. **stale**—not or no longer fresh (staleness, n.)
14. **stock**—utterly lacking in freshness or newness—of abstractions, as ideas, phrases, attitudes, etc.
15. **threadbare**—so lacking in newness or freshness as, figuratively, to have already been worn down to the threads (threadbareness,n.)
16. **timeworn**—so lacking in newness or freshness as to have already succumbed, figuratively, to the ravages of time
17. **trite**—utterly lacking in freshness or newness, owing to constant and undiscriminating use—of abstractions such as phrases, attitudes, ideas, etc. (triteness, n.)
18. **withered**—lacking in freshness; not, or no longer, fresh
19. **worm-eaten**—so lacking in freshness or newness as to have already, figuratively, been eaten by worms

29. **To Become, or Cause to Be or Become, No Longer New or Fresh,v.** *From Sec. 28:* mildew, mold, rust, stale, wither

30. **Phrase, Attitude, Idea, or Other Abstraction That, Owing to Its Constant and Indiscriminate Use, Is Utterly Lacking in Newness or Freshness:** banality, cliché,n.

760. YOUNG

1. **Young,adj.**
1. **adolescent**—no longer a child but not yet grown up; generally and loosely descr. of the ages between 14 and 21
2. **boyish**—like or characteristic of a boy, i.e., the young male between, loosely, 6 and 20
3. **bread-and-butter**—juvenile
4. **coltish**—like or characteristic of a young and inexperienced person
5. **girlish**—like or characteristic of the female in the early years of life
6. **juvenile**—young in age; characteristic of youth

7. **preadolescent**—pert. to, like, or characteristic of the age before adolescence
8. **tender**—young
9. **vernal**—youthful with springlike vigor or freshness
10. **youngling**—young; youthful
11. **youthful,** **youthlike**—young; acting young; characteristic of young people; characteristic of the ages between childhood and maturity

2. **State or Quality of Being Young,n.** *From Sec. 1:* adolescence, boyishness, coltishness, girlishness, juvenility, tenderness; youthfulness, youth, or youthhood; youthlikeness; *Also:* 1. **prime**—youth; early manhood or womanhood

3. **Young Person,n.** *From Sec. 1:* adolescent, boy, colt, girl, juvenile, preadolescent, youngling, youth; *Also:*
1. **fledgling**—immature young person, likened to a bird that has not yet grown the feathers necessary for flying
2. **minor**—young person under 21 years of age
3. **sapling**—young person
4. **sprig**—youth
5. **teen-ager**—young person in the teens, i.e., from thirteen to nineteen
6. **ward**—young person under the protection of a guardian
7. **youngster**—young person

4. **Symbol of Youth; That Which Is Suggestive of Youth:** dew,n. (dewiness,n. dewy, adj.)

5. **Boy; Young Human Male,n.**
1. **gamin**—young boy who wanders around the streets
2. **gossoon**—boy
3. **hobbledehoy**—male older than a boy but not quite a man; awkward or clumsy male of this age
4. **lad**—boy
5. **shaveling, shaver**—young boy
6. **street Arab, guttersnipe**—homeless boy; gamin
7. **stripling**—young man
8. **urchin**—mischievous boy
9. **whelp**—young male (contemptuous)
10. **youth**—young male

6. **Girl; Young Human Female,n.**
1. **bobby-soxer**—young adolescent girl, usually in her early teens
2. **bud**—debutante
3. **chit**—saucy girl
4. **colleen**—young girl
5. **damsel, demoiselle, damosel, damozel**—girl; young woman; maiden
6. **debutante**—young woman making her entrance into social life
7. **demoiselle**—young woman
8. **filly**—gay or high-spirited young girl (slang)
9. **flapper**—bold, forward, unconventional young girl (colloq.)
10. **giglet**—giddy girl
11. **houri**—young girl of the Mohammedan paradise, eternally beautiful and never aging
12. **hoyden**—boisterous, tomboyish, mischievous and/or pert young girl (hoydenish, adj.)
13. **ingénue**—simple, innocent young woman
14. **jeune fille (French)**—young girl
15. **lass, lassie**—girl; young woman
16. **maid, maiden**—young unmarried woman; virgin (maidenly,adj.)
17. **midinette**—Parisian shopgirl, so called from the French word *midi* (noon), when these girls appeared for lunch
18. **minx**—pert, playful, and mischievous girl
19. **miss**—young woman, still unmarried
20. **petticoat**—girl
21. **romp**—boisterous girl

22. **slip**—girl or woman who is young and slim
23. **street Arab, guttersnipe**—homeless girl
24. **tomboy**—girl who plays in boys' games or prefers the diversions common to boys; wild, noisy girl (tomboyish,adj.)
25. **virgin**—young girl, still unmarried, or who has not yet had sexual intercourse (virgin, virginal,adj.)
26. **wench**—girl; young woman
27. **witch**—fascinating or charming girl or young woman

7. Younger,adj.
1. **junior**—younger in age or time of service (juniority,n. junior,n.)
2. **minor**—younger than 21 years of age (minority,n. minor,n.)
3. **puisne**—junior (legal)

8. Not Old Enough for a Specific Purpose: underage,adj.

9. Condition of Being Underage: nonage,n.

10. Never Growing Old: ageless,adj. (agelessness,n.)

11. Becoming Young, Younger, or Youthful or Again Young or Youthful: juvenescent, rejuvenescent, revirescent,adj. (juvenescence, rejuvenescence,n.)

12. To Become Young, Younger, or Youthful, or Again Young or Youthful: rejuvenate, rejuvenesce,v. (rejuvenation, rejuvenescence,n.)

13. To Make Young, Younger, or Youthful, or Again Young or Youthful: rejuvenate, rejuvenize,v. (rejuvenation,n. rejuvenator,n. rejuvenative,adj.)

14. To Restore the Sexual Vigor of Youth to (Usually a Man): rejuvenate,v. (rejuvenation,n. rejuvenator,n. rejuvenative,adj.)

15. Persistence of Youthful Characteristics in the Adult: juvenilism,n. (medical)

761. NEW

1. New,adj.
1. **brand-new, bran-new, span-new, spick-and-span**—very, entirely, or absolutely new
2. **fresh**—newly made or produced; novel
3. **neoteric**—new and modern
4. **newborn**—new in the sense of having just come into existence
5. **newfangled**—full of novelty or novelties (derogatory)
6. **new-fashioned**—made in a new fashion or form
7. **new-fledged**—new, as if having just sprouted feathers
8. **new-made**—new in the sense of having just been created
9. **novel**—new and different; new and unusual
10. **original**—new; new in the sense of being no copy or imitation of something else; new in the sense of bearing no resemblance to other things; novel
11. **Promethean**—daringly new or original, after Prometheus, who, according to Greek legend, stole fire from heaven and brought it to mankind
12. **recent**—having just been made; having just appeared, etc.
13. **rehashed**—with old ideas restated in a new form or with old material used in a new way (derogatory)
14. **renewed**—made new again
15. **renovated**—made to look new again by repairing, remodeling, etc.
16. **unprecedented**—new or novel in the sense that no similar thing, occurrence, etc., has ever happened before
17. **virgin, virginal**—new, in the sense of not yet having been touched, tried, used, explored, cultivated, etc.

2. Newness,n. *From Sec. 1:* freshness, newfangledness, novelty, originality, recency

3. New Thing, etc.,n. *From Sec. 1:* neoteric or neoterism, novelty, original, rehash; *Also:* 1. **wrinkle**—novelty

4. To Make New,v. *From Sec. 1:* rehash, renew, renovate (renewal, renovation,n.)

5. New Practice or Way of Doing Something: innovation,n. (innovator,n. innovative, adj. innovate,v.)

6. Disposed to New Theories: newfangled, adj. (derogatory)

7. In a New Way: anew,adv.

8. Fresh,adj.
1. **crisp, crispy**—fresh and firm
2. **recent**—freshly made or produced
3. **refreshed**—restored to freshness
4. **renewed**—restored to freshness
5. **succulent**—full of freshness and vitality
6. **unbeaten**—fresh, in the sense of never having been gone through, as, figuratively, paths, roads, etc.
7. **untouched**—fresh in the sense of not having been touched
8. **untried**—fresh in the sense of not having been tried before
9. **untrod, untrodden**—fresh in the sense of not yet having been stepped on, as, literally or figuratively, snow, paths, roads, fields, etc.
10. **vernal**—fresh like the spring of the year
11. **virgin, virginal**—fresh in the sense of not having yet been used, tried, explored, etc.
12. **youthful**—fresh and vigorous

9. Freshness,n. *From Sec. 8:* crispness or crispiness, recency, succulence or succulency, youthfulness; *Also:* 1. **viridity**—freshness

10. To Freshen,v. *From Sec. 8:* refresh, renew (refreshment, renewal,n.)

11. Becoming Fresh Again: revirescent,adj. (revirescence,n.)

12. Symbol of Freshness; That Which Is Suggestive of Freshness: dew,n. (dewiness,n. dewy,adj.)

13. Modern,adj.
1. **futurist, futuristic**—pert. to, or characteristic of, the movement in art or literature that abandons all past and traditional forms and techniques (futurism, n. futurist,n.)
2. **moderne**—ultramodern, esp. in reference to furniture or furnishings (commercial cant)
3. **modernist**—pert. to, or characteristic of, modern taste, quality, style, tendencies, thinking, etc.
4. **modernistic**—modern; extremely or spectacularly modern; modernist
5. **neoteric**—modern and new
6. **new-fashioned**—modern
7. **streamlined**—modern; up-to-date (streamline,v.)
8. **ultramodern, ultramodernistic**—to the extremes in modernity (ultramodernism, n. ultramodern, ultramodernist,n.)
9. **up-to-date, up-to-the-minute**—modern; keeping up with new or present fashions

14. Something Modern: modernism, modernity, neoteric, neoterism,n.

15. Modern Writer, Philosopher, Artist, Thinker, etc.: modern, neoteric,n.

16. One Who Is Modern: modern,n.

17. State or Quality of Being Modern: modernity,n.

18. Modern Character, Thinking, Practices, Tendencies, etc.: modernism,n. (modernist, n.)

762. TIME

1. Time,n.
1. **bloom**—time of blossoming or flowering
2. **eternity**—time after death
3. **future**—later time
4. **geologic time**—time from the earliest days of the earth, esp. before the advent of man
5. **leeway**—time allowing action
6. **past**—earlier time or times
7. **present**—time as of now
8. **season**—proper or suitable time
9. **tempo**—musical time
10. **tempus**—musical or poetical time
11. **tense**—grammatical time
12. **term**—appointed or set time
13. **tide**—time when something has reached its best or highest point

2. Pert. to Time: chronological, temporal, adj.

3. Time without End; Infinite Time: abyss, eternity, infinity, perpetuity,n.

4. Point of Time: date, juncture, moment, point, stage,n. (junctural,adj.)

5. Point of Time of an Event or Events,n.
1. **date**—point of time when an event occurs
2. **juncture**—point of time when important events occur simultaneously (junctural, adj.)

6. Time Flies, a Latin Proverb: tempus fugit

7. For the Time Being; For the Particular Time: for the nonce

8. Characteristic Spirit, Thought, Feeling, or Intellectual or Moral Climate of a Time: zeitgeist,n. (German)

9. Existing in Both Space and Time: spatiotemporal,adj.

10. Order in Time: chronology,n. (chronological,adj.)

11. To Arrange in Order of Time: chronologize,v.

12. To Go On for (a Time): continue, continue for, last, last for, occupy, span, take,v.

13. To Spend (Time) on: devote (time) to,v.

14. To Spend or Pass Time with (Friends, etc.): associate with, consort with, keep company with,v.

15. To Spend or Pass (Time) Easily, Pleasantly, or Enjoyably: while away, wile away,v.

16. To Spend Time on Unimportant Things or Matters: diddle (colloq.), niggle, potter, putter, tinker,v. (putter,n. diddler, niggler, potterer, tinkerer,n.)

17. To Spend Time Lazily or in Idleness: dally, dawdle, dillydally, idle, laze, loaf, loiter, trifle,v. (dalliance,n. dallier, dawdler, idler, loafer, loiterer, trifler,n.)

18. To Spend (Time) Lazily or in Idleness: dally away, dawdle away, idle away, loiter away, slug away, trifle away, while away, wile away (time),v.

19. To Waste Time: dally, dawdle; diddle (colloq.); dillydally, laze, loiter, potter, putter, trifle,v. (dalliance, putter,n. dallier, dawdler, diddler, loiterer, potterer, trifler,n.)

20. To Waste (Time): dally away, dawdle away, loiter away, trifle away (time),v.

763. GEOLOGIC TIME

1. Divisions of Geologic Time: aeon or eon (two or more eras), era; period (subdivision of an era); epoch (subdivision of a period),n.

2. Geologic Eras: Archeozoic, Proterozoic, Paleozoic, Mesozoic, Cenozoic,n. and adj.

3. Pert. to Geologic Time Before There Was Life on the Earth: azoic,adj.

4. Pert. to the Period of Geologic Time When Much of the Earth Was Covered by Glaciers: glacial,adj.

5. Pert. to Recent Geologic Time: postglacial,adj.

764. SAME TIME

1. Existing at the Same Time or for the Same Period of Time: coetaneous, coeval, coexistent, contemporaneous, contemporary, cotemporary,adj. (coetaneousness, coetaneity, coevality, coexistence, coexistency, contemporaneous, contemporaneity, contemporariness,n.)

2. To Exist at the Same Time or for the Same Period of Time: coexist, contemporize, v.

3. One Who Exists or Existed at the Same Time: coeval, contemporary,n.

4. Happening at the Same Time: coeval, coincident, coincidental, concomitant, concurrent, contemporaneous, contemporary, cotemporary, simultaneous, synchronous, synchronal, synchronic, synchronical,adj. (coevality, coincidence, coincidency, concomitance, concurrence, concurrency, contemporaneousness, contemporaneity, simultaneousness, simultaneity, synchronousness, synchronism,n.)

5. That Which Happens at the Same Time As Something Else: coincidence,n.

6. To Happen at the Same Time: coincide, concur, contemporize, synchronize,v. (concurrence, synchronization,n.)

7. To Cause to Happen at the Same Time: contemporize, synchronize,v. (synchronization,n.)

8. Happening at the Same Instant: coinstantaneous,adj. (coinstantaneousness, coinstantaneity,n.)

765. TIMELINESS

1. Timely: auspicious, opportune, pat, propitious, providential, seasonable, towardly, well-timed,adj.

2. Timeliness: auspiciousness, opportuneness, patness, propitiousness, seasonableness, towardliness,n.

3. Just in Time: in the nick of time,adv. phrase; providential,adj.

4. Untimely: inauspicious, inopportune, premature, unpropitious, unseasonable, ill-timed, adj.

5. Untimeliness: inauspiciousness, inopportuneness, prematurity, prematureness, unpropitiousness, unseasonableness,n.

6. Badly Timed: ill-timed, mistimed,adj. (mistime,v.)

7. Happening, Done, Existing, etc., Too Soon, Too Early, or before the Proper Time; Doing, Coming, Speaking, Judging, etc., Too Soon, Too Early, or Too Quickly: premature; previous (colloq.); untimely,adj. (prematurity or prematureness, previousness, untimeliness,n.)

766. EARLY

1. Early,adj.
1. **matutinal**—early (literally, in the morning)
2. **precocious**—extraordinarily early in development (precocity, precociousness,n.)

3. primitive—very early in the history of a movement, art, science, etc. (primitiveness,n.)

4. seasonable—early (seasonableness,n.)

2. Early: betimes,adv.

3. To Make the Time of Earlier: advance,v. (advancement,n.)

4. To Exist Earlier than, Before, or Previous to: antedate, predate, pre-exist,v. (pre-existence,n. pre-existent,adj.)

5. To Exist Earlier, Before, or Previously: pre-exist,v. (pre-existence,n. pre-existent, adj.)

6. Earliest; Pert. or Belonging to Earliest Times,adj.
1. **antediluvian**—primitive (literally, before the Flood)
2. **original**—primitive
3. **prehistoric, prehistorical**—pert. or belonging to the times before recorded history
4. **premier**—earliest
5. **primal, primary**—primitive
6. **primeval**—belonging to the earliest times or ages
7. **primitive**—earliest; pert. or belonging to the earliest ages, periods, or times (primitiveness, primitivity,n.)
8. **primoprimitive**—earliest of the primitive
9. **primordial**—earliest in creation, origin, or existence (primordiality,n.)
10. **pristine**—pert. to the earliest period, state, ages, times, etc.
11. **proleptical**—earliest in time, i.e., before creation, recorded time, or recorded history

7. First, whether in Time or Order,adj.
1. **aboriginal**—very first
2. **initial**—first
3. **maiden**—first—of efforts or creations
4. **original**—first in existence; first in order
5. **premier**—first
6. **primal**—first
7. **primary**—first in time or order
8. **prime**—first in order, rank, importance, value, etc. (primacy,n.)
9. **primigenial**—first formed or generated
10. **primitive**—first
11. **primoprime**—very first
12. **primordial**—first in order (primordiality, n.)
13. **pristine**—original
14. **virgin**—first, as a voyage, effort, etc.

8. One Who Is First in His Class, Type, Profession, etc.: prince,n.

9. Those Who Are the First to Take Up a Cause, Movement, etc.: vanguard,n.

10. On Time: prompt, punctual,adj. (promptitude or promptness, punctuality or punctualness,n.)

11. Soon: anon, betimes, ere long, presently, proximately, shortly,adv.

12. Coming Soon: approaching, oncoming,adj.

13. Very Close in Time: proximate,adj.

14. Immediate: instant, instantaneous, prompt, ready,adj.

15. State of Being Immediate or of Happening, Being Done, etc., Immediately: immediacy, immediateness, instantaneity, instantaneousness, promptitude, promptness, readiness,n.

16. Immediately: at once, directly, instantaneously, instanter, instantly, presto, promptly, right away, straightway, thereon, thereupon,adv.

17. Descr. of That Which Is Done, Happens, etc., without Delay: instant, prompt, summary,adj. (promptitude, promptness, summariness,n. instantly, promptly, summarily, adv.)

767. LATE

1. Late,adj.
1. **behind, behindhand, behind time**—late
2. **belated**—occurring, coming, or being late, too late, or later than proper or expected (belatedness,n.)
3. **dilatory**—tardy (dilatoriness,n.)
4. **overdue**—late beyond the expected time
5. **straggly**—coming in late
6. **tardy**—late; habitually late (tardiness,n.)
7. **unpunctual**—tending to be, or generally or habitually, late for appointments, etc.; not on time (unpunctuality, unpunctualness,n.)

2. Later in Time: subsequent, posterior, ulterior,adj. (posteriority,n.)

3. To Be Late: tarry,v.

4. To Come in Late or Later, Rather than with Others of the Same Kind: straggle, straggle in,v. (straggler,n.)

5. Farthest Removed in Time: ultimate,adj.

768. DELAY

1. To Delay; To Use Delaying Tactics,v.
1. **dally, dilly-dally**—delay by wasting time while in the progress of completing an act, such delay usually occurring through paying attention to nonessentials
2. **dawdle**—delay by wasting time in a pretense of work or activity; dally
3. **demur**—delay
4. **filibuster**—engage in delaying actions in a legislature or similar body by using tactics, such as lengthy and irrelevant speechmaking, that make it impossible to bring a motion to vote
5. **lag, linger, loiter**—dawdle while in progress, often while walking
6. **procrastinate**—delay; tend to delay in doing something, generally out of laziness, unwillingness to face responsibilities, or for other blameworthy reasons
7. **stall**—delay; use a pretext to cause or find delay
8. **tarry**—delay
9. **temporize**—play for time in order to delay facing an issue; put off immediate decision or action in order to gain time or avoid conflict

2. Delaying; Delay,n. *From Sec. 1:* dalliance, demur or demurral, filibuster, lag, procrastination, stall; *Also:*
1. **cunctation**—procrastination
2. **wait**—delay

3. Delayer,n. *From Sec. 1:* dallier, dawdler, demurrer, filibusterer, lagger or laggard, lingerer, loiterer, procrastinator, staller, temporizer; *From Sec. 2:* cunctator

4. Given to Procrastination or Delay; Tending to Procrastinate or Delay: dilatory, tardy,adj. (dilatoriness, tardiness,n.)

5. Period of Delay; Period during Which One May Legally Delay Meeting a Financial Obligation: moratorium,n. (moratoria, moratoriums,pl.n.)

6. Designating a Law Granting a Moratorium: moratory,adj.

7. Pert. to Delay: moratory,adj.

8. To Delay, i.e., Cause a Delay in, or to Be Delayed,v.
1. **adjourn**—put off to a later time
2. **defer**—put off to a future time, usually for good or logical reasons
3. **detain**—delay (someone)
4. **hold up**—delay
5. **pigeonhole**—lay aside; hence, delay indefinitely the consideration of
6. **postpone**—put off to a later time

7. **prorogue, prorogate**—defer the meeting of (a legislative body)
8. **put off**—delay (something or doing something) to a later time
9. **reprieve**—delay; delay the punishment of; postpone (anything evil or unpleasant)
10. **reserve**—put over to a future time
11. **respite**—delay; postpone
12. **retard**—delay the progress of
13. **shelve**—pigeonhole
14. **stall off**—delay
15. **stay**—delay
16. **table**—delay discussing
17. **wait**—delay (a meal) till someone is ready—followed by *for*, as in *wait dinner for someone* (colloq.)
18. **waive**—put off considering to a later time; defer

9. **Delaying; Delay**,n. *From Sec. 8:* adjournment, deferment, detainment or detention, postponement, prorogation, reprieve, respite, retardation or retardment, stay

10. **Having the Purpose or Quality of Causing Delay:** dilatory, Fabian,adj. (dilatoriness, n.)

11. **Delayed beyond the Usual or Expected Time:** belated,adj. (belatedness,n.)

12. **Delayed by Bad Weather:** weather-bound, adj.

13. **Adjourning without Deciding on a Day or Time for Meeting Again**—of Legislative Bodies or Other Groups: sine die

769. PERIOD OF TIME

1. **Period of Time:** age, bout, epoch, extent, era, length, period, season, space, span, spell, stage, stretch, term,n. (epochal, periodic, seasonal,adj.)

2. **Short or Limited Period of Time:** bout, span, spell, term,n.

3. **Extremely Short Period of Time:** flash, instant; jiffy (colloq.); minute, moment, second, trice, twinkle, twinkling,n.

4. **Long Period of Time:** aeon or eon, age, cycle, generation,n.

5. **Endless, or Seemingly Endless, Period of Time:** eternity, infinity,n. (eternal, infinite, adj.)

6. **Period of Time between Events, Things, etc.:** interim, interlude, intermission, interval, parenthesis, space,n.

7. **Period of Time that Something Lasts:** date, duration, term,n.

8. **Certain Other Periods of Time,**n.
   1. **age**—period of time with a predominant feature or a dominant figure
   2. **cycle**—period of time in which there is a completion of a regular round of occurrences or phenomena (cyclic,adj.)
   3. **date**—period of time to which something belongs
   4. **epact**—period of time added so that the lunar and solar calendars agree
   5. **epoch**—period of time in which notable events occurred (epochal,adj.)
   6. **era**—period of time from a given date
   7. **eve**—period of time just preceding an event
   8. **generation**—period of time, commonly accepted as about 33 years, in which a parent is succeeded by a child
   9. **incumbency**—period of holding an office
   10. **intermission**—intervening period of time between parts of an activity or occurrence, such as acts of a play, session of work, study, class, etc.
   11. **interval, interlude**—period of time for pause or rest between activities
   12. **nooning**—midday intermission

13. **phase**—transitory period of time between changes (phaseal, phasic,adj.)
14. **season**—one of the four periods of the year—spring, summer, autumn, winter (seasonal,adj.)
15. **stage**—period of progress in a process, or in the process of growth or development
16. **tenure**—period of time during which anything, such as a position, office, privilege, etc., is held and/or enjoyed (tenurial,adj.)
17. **term**—appointed or set period of time

9. **Certain Ages or Periods of Man,**n.
   1. **ancient times**—earliest times of recorded history, from the first known civilization, as Egypt and Chaldea, and extending to the fall of Rome, A.D. 476 (ancient,adj.)
   2. **antiquity**—time of ancient Greece or Rome; ancient times, esp. before the Middle Ages
   3. **Bronze Age**—age in man's cultural development following the Stone Age, marked by the use of bronze tools
   4. **Dark Ages**—Middle Ages; early part of the Middle Ages, characterized by intellectual stagnation
   5. **eolithic period**—period in the Stone Age when man first used crude stone implements (eolithic,adj.)
   6. **Iron Age**—epoch in the early times of man when he was expert in the use of bronze and iron, domesticated animals, and fashioned pottery, about 1000 B.C. to A.D. 100; in classical mythology, the final and most depraved age of the world
   7. **Middle Ages; moyen âge (French)**—period from about A.D. 400 to about A.D. 1400, or from the fall of Rome to the revival of learning; period between ancient and modern times (medieval,adj.)
   8. **modern times**—period from the end of the Middle Ages, about A.D. 1400, to the present
   9. **neolithic period**—period of the Stone Age when man used polished stone implements and began to domesticate animals (neolithic,adj.)
   10. **paleolithic period**—period of the Stone Age when man used rough or chipped stone implements (paleolithic,adj.)
   11. **prehistoric period**—period before written or recorded history (prehistoric, prehistorical,adj.)
   12. **protolithic period**—earliest part of the Stone Age (protolithic,adj.)
   13. **Renaissance, Renascence**—transitional period between the Middle Ages and modern times, from the 14th to 16th centuries, marked by a revival of classical influences (Renaissance,adj.)
   14. **Stone Age**—prehistoric period in which man used stone implements

770. SEASON

1. **The Four Seasons:** spring, springtime, germinal, prime; summer, summertime, summertide; autumn, fall; winter, wintertide, wintertime,n.

2. **Middle of a Season:** midautumn, midsummer, widwinter,n.

3. **Pert. or Relating to Spring:** spring, springtime, vernal,adj.

4. **Like Spring:** springlike,adj.

5. **Pert. or Relating to Summer:** aestival, estival, midsummer, midsummery, summer, adj.

6. **Like Summer:** midsummery, summerlike, summery,adj.

7. **Pert. to Autumn:** autumn, autumnal, fall, adj.

8. **Like Autumn:** autumnlike,adj.

9. Pert. to Winter: brumal, hiemal, midwinter, winter,adj.

10. Like Winter: brumal, hibernal, midwinterly, midwintry, winterlike, wintery, wintry, adj.

11. To Spend the Season,v.
 1. estivate, aestivate—spend the summer in torpor, as certain organisms (estivation, aestivation,n.)
 2. hibernate—spend the winter; spend the winter in decreased activity, as certain animals (hibernation,n.)
 3. summer—spend the summer
 4. winter—spend the winter

12. In Keeping with the Normal Effects or Weather of a Season: seasonable,adj. (seasonableness,n.)

13. Pert. to, or Depending on, a Season or Seasons: seasonal,adj.

14. Adapted to the Climatic Changes of Seasons—of Plants, etc.: tropophil, tropophilous,adj.

771. THE PRESENT

1. The Present: now, nowadays,n.

2. Now: at present, nowadays, presently,adv.

3. Of the Present,adj.
 1. contemporary—happening or living at the present time, i.e., at the same time as that in which the speaker or writer lives (contemporariness,n.)
 2. current—belonging to, or happening in, the present time (currency,n.)
 3. latter-day—of the present time
 4. modern—of the present time (modernity, n. modern,n.)
 5. up-to-date—extending to the present time (up-to-dateness,n.)

4. The Recent Past: yesterday; yesteryear (poetic),n.

5. The Distant Past: long ago, yore,n.

6. Time So Far Back in the Past as to Defy Reckoning: time immemorial,n.

7. Past Events Collectively: history,n. (historic, historical,adj.)

8. Past: ago (follows the noun), bygone, former; gone by (follows the noun),adj.

9. In the Past: ago,adv.

10. Of Nearby Past Time: latter, latter-day, recent,adj. (recency,n.)

11. Of the Far Past: long-ago,adj.

12. Former: erstwhile, late, previous, quondam, sometime, whilom,adj.

13. Before, in Time: ere,prep.

14. Up to This Time: hereto, heretofore, hereunto, hitherto,adv.

15. Up to That Time: theretofore, thitherto, adv.

16. History,n.
 1. annals—historical records
 2. chronicle—account of historical events in order of time
 3. prehistory—history of what went before
 4. topology—history of a region as indicated by its surface features (topological,adj.)

17. Historian,n. *From Sec. 16:* annalist, chronicler; *Also:* 1. historiographer—historian; one who writes, or is appointed to write, a history or histories

18. The Writing, or Art of Writing, Histories: historiography,n. (historiographic, historiographical,adj.)

19. A Work by a Writer of History: historiography, history,n.

20. Pert. or Related to, or Famous in, History: historic, historical,adj. (historicity,n.)

21. The Future; Future Time: aftertime, futurity, offing, posterity,n.

22. Future Generations; People of the Future: posterity,n.

23. Future State or Quality: futurity,n.

24. Future Event: futurity,n.

25. Pert. to the Future: futural,adj.

26. Future: unborn,adj.

27. Without a Future; Without a Promising or Worth-while Future: futureless,adj.

772. PREDICTION

1. To Predict (Future Events, etc.): anticipate, augur, croak, divine, envision, forebode, forecast, foresee, forespeak, foretell, presage, prognosticate, prophesy, vaticinate,v.

2. To Predict the Future; To Engage in Predictions: augur, divine, forebode, forecast, foretell, hariolate, presage, prophesy, pythonize, soothsay,v.

3. Prediction, i.e., a Predicting: anticipation, augury, divination, forecast, forecasting, fortunetelling, hariolation, mantic, manticism, prognosis, prognostication, prophecy, pythonism, soothsaying, vaticination,n.

4. Art of Prediction: augury, mantic, pythonism, soothsaying,n.

5. A Prediction, i.e., That Which Is Predicted: augury, auspice, divination, foreboding, forecast, presage, prognosis, prognostic, prognostication, prophecy,n.

6. Predictor, i.e., One Who Predicts: augur, Chaldean, diviner, divinator, foreboder, forecaster, foreseer, foreteller, fortuneteller, presager, prognosticator, prophesier, prophet or, fem., prophetess; pythoness (fem.); pythonist; seer or, fem., seeress; sibyl (fem.); soothsayer, sortileger,n.

7. Pert. to a Prophet or Prophets: prophetic, prophetical; pythonic (to a *pythoness*); sibylic, sibyllic, sibylline (to a *sibyl*); vatic, vatical, adj.

8. Predictive: divinatory, fatidic, fortunetelling, mantic, mantistic, prognostic, prophetic, prophetical, sibylic, sibyllic, sibylline, vatic, vatical, vaticinal,adj.

9. Gifted with the Power of Predicting: fatidical, mantic, mantistic,adj.

10. Claiming the Power of Predicting: pythonic,adj.

11. To Predict from Signs or Symptoms: augur, prognosticate,v. (augury, prognostication, prognosis,n. augur, prognosticator,n. prognostic,adj.)

12. Prediction of the Future Course of a Disease: prognosis,n. (prognostic,adj.)

13. To Foresee with Fear, Dread, or Anxiety: apprehend,v. (apprehension,n. apprehensive, adj.)

14. Weather Prediction: aeromancy,n.

15. Official Predictor of Weather: forecaster, n.

16. Divination to Determine Propitious Times for Actions, Practiced in China: chronomancy,n. (chronomantic,adj.)

17. Woman Who Predicts Evil or Misfortune but Is Not Believed: Cassandra,n.

18. To Predict Evil or Misfortune: croak,v.

19. Soothsayer in Ancient Rome: augur, auspex, haruspex,n. (haruspical,adj.)

20. Divination by Specific Methods, or from Specific Things, Actions, Objects, etc.,n.

1. **aeromancy**—from the state of the air or from substances in the atmosphere (aeromancer,n. aeromantic,adj.)
2. **alectryomancy, alectoromancy**—by the following method: a cock is surrounded by grains of corn placed on the letters of the alphabet, and the prediction is made from the order of the grains eaten, that is, the letters spelled out by the order of choice
3. **aleuromancy**—by flour
4. **anthropomancy**—from an examination of human entrails (anthropomantist,n. anthropomantic,adj.)
5. **astrology**—from the position of the stars (astrologer,n. astrologic, astrological,adj.)
6. **astromancy, sideromancy**—by the stars (astromancer,n. astromantic,adj.)
7. **auspice**—by observation of signs, esp. in the flight of birds (auspicial,adj.)
8. **austromancy**—by the south wind
9. **axinomancy**—from the movement of an ax placed on a post
10. **belomancy**—by arrows
11. **bibliomancy**—through books, or by the Bible
12. **botanomancy**—from plants
13. **capnomancy**—from smoke when victims are sacrificed by fire
14. **cephalomancy**—by signs and symbols discovered in a head (cephalomant,n.)
15. **ceromancy**—from the figures formed when melted wax is dropped in water
16. **cleromancy**—by casting lots
17. **coscinomancy**—from the motions of a suspended or balanced sieve
18. **crithomancy**—from the dough of cakes used in ancient sacrifices and the crumbs spread over the victims
19. **crystal gazing, crystallomancy, gastromancy**—by means of a crystal ball (crystal gazer,n.)
20. **dactyliomancy**—from finger rings
21. **gastromancy**—through ventriloquism
22. **genethlialogy**—from the position of the stars at someone's birth (genethlialogic, genethlialogical,adj.)
23. **geomancy**—from lines or figures (geomancer,n. geomantic, geomantical,adj.)
24. **gyromancy**—by the following method: a person continues walking in a circle until he falls from dizziness; the place of his fall indicates the prediction
25. **halomancy**—by salt
26. **haruspication, haruspicy, extispicy**—by examination of the entrails of sacrificial victims, in the religion of ancient Rome (haruspex, haruspice, extispex,n. haruspical, haruspice, extispicious,adj.)
27. **hieromancy, hieroscopy**—from observing objects used in sacrifices
28. **horoscopy**—from a diagram of the stars, planets, etc. (horoscoper, horoscopist,n.)
29. **hydromancy**—by sea tides, water, or other liquids (hydromancer,n. hydromantic, hydromantical,adj.)
30. **ichnomancy**—from footprints
31. **ichthyomancy**—from fish (ichthyomantic,adj.)
32. **keraunoscopia**—from thunder
33. **lithomancy**—by stones or stone charms
34. **molybdomancy**—from lead
35. **myomancy**—by the movements of mice (myomantic,adj.)
36. **necromancy, necromancing, sciomancy**—by communication with the dead (necromancer,n. necromantic, necromancing, sciomantic,adj.)
37. **nomancy**—by letters (of the alphabet)
38. **oenomancy**—from the properties or peculiarities of wine, esp. color
39. **oneiromancy**—from dreams (oneiromancer,n.)

40. **onomancy**—by letters of a name, or other letters
41. **onychomancy**—from nails or claws
42. **ophiomancy**—from serpents
43. **ornithomancy, orniscopy**—by observing the flight or other characteristics of birds (ornithomantist, orniscopist,n. ornithomantic, orniscopic,adj.)
44. **palmistry, chiromancy, chiromance, chirognomy, chirosophy**—from a person's hand, or from the lines or marks in his palm (palmist, chiromancer, chiromancist, chiromant, chirognomist, chirosophist,n. chiromantic, chiromantical, chirognomic, chirosophical,adj.)
45. **pedomancy**—from the soles of the feet
46. **pegomancy**—from fountains
47. **psephomancy**—by pebbles
48. **pyromancy**—by fire or flames (pyromancer,n. pyromantic,adj.)
49. **rhabdomancy**—by wands or rods (rhabdomancer, rhabdomantist,n. rhabdomantic,adj.)
50. **scapulimancy, omoplatoscopy**—by inspecting a shoulder blade, esp. as blotched, cracked, etc., by fire
51. **scatomancy**—by observation of feces
52. **sideromancy**—by observation of straws burning on a hot iron
53. **sorcery, sorcering**—through the aid of evil spirits, or by communication with the dead (sorcerer, sorceress,n. sorcerous,adj. sorcer,v.)
54. **sortilege; sortes (French)**—by the drawing of lots (sortilegic, sortilegious,adj.)
55. **stichomancy**—by the lines or passages in a book
56. **theomancy**—by the answers of divinely inspired oracles (theomantic,adj.)
57. **theriomancy**—by observation of wild animals

21. Diagram of the Stars, Planets, etc., by Which, Supposedly, One's Fortune, Future, etc., Can Be Predicted: horoscope,n. (horoscopic, horoscopical,adj. horoscope,v.)

773. SIGN OF THE FUTURE

1. To Give, or Be, a Sign or Indication of (the Future, Future Event or Events, etc.): adumbrate, augur, bespeak, betoken, bode, forebode, forecast, foreshadow, foreshow, foretell, foretoken, harbinger, herald, omen; portend (often something unpleasant); prefigure, preindicate, presage, preshow, presignify, prognosticate, prophesy,v. (adumbration, bodement, prefigurement, prefiguration, preindication, prognostication,n.)

2. Sign or Indication of the Future or of a Future Event or Events: augury; auspice (usually favorable); foreboding (esp. of misfortune or evil); forerunner, foreshadower, foretoken, harbinger, herald, omen; portent (esp. of misfortune or evil); precursor, preindication, presage, prodigy, prognostic, prognostication,n. (auspicial,adj.)

3. Sign or Indication of Future or Coming Misfortune or Evil: foreboding, omen, portent, premonition, presage,n.

4. Indicative of the Future or Future Events: adumbrative, ominous, portentous, precursory, prefigurative, presageful, prognostic, prognosticative, prophetic, prophetical,adj. (ominousness, portentousness,n.)

5. Indicative of Future or Coming Misfortune or Evil: ominous, portentous, premonitory,adj. (ominousness, portentousness, n.)

6. That Which Is Considered a Revelation of the Future: apocalypse,n. (apocalyptic, apocalyptical,adj.)

774. TIME MEASUREMENT

1. Time Measurement,n.

1. **chronography**—measurement of time intervals by graphic methods (chronographic,adj.)
2. **chronology**—science of time measurement, and of assigning proper dates to occurrences (chronologist, chronologer, chronographer,n. chronological, chronologic,adj.)
3. **chronometry**—measurement of time by periods; art of measuring time (chronometric, chronometrical,adj.)
4. **chronoscopy**—measurement of minute intervals of time (chronoscopic,adj.)
5. **dendrochronology**—figuring of early time periods by studying the rings of ancient trees
6. **horology**—science of time measurement (horologer, horologist,n. horologic, horological,adj.)
7. **horometry**—art of time measurement; measurement of time; method of time measurement (horometrical,adj.)

2. Device to Measure or Indicate Time,n.

1. **chronodeik**—astronomical instrument for calculating approximate time from observation of the stars
2. **chronograph**—instrument for measuring and recording time; watch with an independent second hand (chronographic, adj.)
3. **chronometer**—instrument for measuring time (chronometric, chronometrical,adj.)
4. **chronopher**—device that flashes, by electricity, the correct time to distant places
5. **chronoscope**—instrument for measuring minute time intervals; clock that shows the time by figures visible in holes in the dial
6. **clepsydra**—water clock
7. **clock**—device of various sorts to indicate time
8. **dial**—loosely, any timepiece; originally an instrument for showing the time of day by means of shadows; sundial
9. **ghurry**—instrument that shows or measures time; water clock
10. **gnomon**—object that by the length or position of its shadow indicates time (gnomonic, gnomonical,adj.)
11. **horologe, horologium**—instrument that shows time; clock; dial; watch (horologic, horological,adj.)
12. **hourglass**—instrument for measuring time intervals, esp. hours, consisting of two compartments, joined by a narrow neck, with sand, water, or mercury passing from the top to the bottom compartment
13. **isochronon**—clock designed to keep extremely accurate time
14. **metronome, chronometer**—device used to mark accurate musical time (metronomic, metronomical,adj.)
15. **micronometer**—instrument to measure infinitesimal periods of time
16. **photochronograph**—instrument used by physicists to record extremely minute period of time
17. **sandglass**—hourglass using sand
18. **stem-winder**—watch wound at the stem; loosely, any watch (colloq.)
19. **sundial**—device to show the time of day by a shadow cast by the sun
20. **timepiece, timekeeper**—instrument that shows or measures time
21. **timer**—instrument that measures intervals of time
22. **watch**—small portable timepiece

3. Art of Making Devices That Record Time in Hours: horography,n. (horographer,n.)

4. Principles or Science of Making Time- pieces: horology,n. (horologer, horologist,n. horologic, horological,adj.)

5. Maker of Timepieces: horographer, horologer, horologist, watchmaker,n.

6. Seller of Timepieces: horologer, horologist,n.

7. Time Record,n.

1. **almanac**—book, chart, table, etc., containing a chronology of days, weeks, and months plus other data
2. **annals**—relation or record of events in chronological order, by years
3. **calendar**—system of dividing time into years, months, weeks, and days; table, chart, pad, etc. of such divisions
4. **chronicle**—record of events in the order of their occurrence
5. **chronogram**—record made by a chronograph, a device for measuring and recording time (chronogrammatic,adj.)
6. **chronology**—arrangement or list of events in the order of their occurrence
7. **diary, journal**—daily record of events, or the book in which this is kept (diarist, journalist,n. journalize,v.)
8. **menology**—calendar of months
9. **timetable, schedule**—list of events, arrivals of trains, etc., and the time of each

8. Inserted in the Calendar, as February 29 in Leap Years: intercalary,adj.

9. To Insert in the Calendar: intercalate,v. (intercalation,n.)

10. One Who Investigates the Dates of Occurrences: chronologist,n.

11. About, or Approximately, in Designation of Dates: circa,prep.,adv.

12. Error in Chronology,n.

1. **anachronism**—error in chronology, so that happenings are dated usually before, sometimes after, the actual occurrence (anachronistic, anachronistical, anachronic, anachronismatical,adj.)
2. **metachronism**—error in chronology whereby an event is placed after its actual date
3. **parachronism**—error in chronology, esp. one in which a date is set later than that of the actual occurrence (parachronistic, adj.)
4. **prochronism**—error in chronology by which an event is placed before its actual date
5. **prolepsis**—error in chronology by which an event is dated before its actual occurrence (proleptic, proleptical,adj.)

13. Thing, Act, or Attitude That Is Out of Time, Belonging to either the Past or the Future, or That, in Short, Is Incongruous with the Time in Which It Occurs: anachronism,n.

14. Out of Time with Surrounding Events, etc.: anachronous, anachronistic,adj.

15. To Give an Incorrect Date or Time to,v.

1. **anachronize**—make an error in assigning a time to, i.e., either too early or too late in respect to surrounding events, etc. (anachronist,n.)
2. **antedate, predate**—assign a date to that is earlier than the actual time of occurrence or execution
3. **misdate**—assign an incorrect date to
4. **mistime**—reckon the time of incorrectly
5. **postdate**—assign a date to that is later than the actual time of occurrence or execution

775. MORNING

1. Morning (Poetic): morn, morningtide,n.

2. Sunrise: aurora, dawn, daybreak, daylight, dayspring, sunup,n. (auroral,adj.)

3. Period Just Before Sunrise: crepuscle, crepuscule, crepusculum, dusk, twilight,n. (crepuscular, crepusculine, crepusculous, twilight,adj.)

4. Early Morning, i.e., When the Cock Crows: cockcrow, cockcrowing,n.

5. Part of the Morning before Noon: ante meridiem (abbreviated A.M. or a.m.), foreday, forenoon,n. (antemeridian,adj.)

6. Pert. to Morning: matin, matinal, matutinal,adj.

7. Middle of the Morning: midmorning,n. (midmorning,adj.)

8. Noon: midday, midnoon, noonday, noontide,n.

9. Time after Noon: afternoon, post meridiem,n. (abbreviated P.M. or p.m.)

10. Pert. to the Time after Noon: afternoon, postmeridian,n.

11. Middle of the Afternoon: midafternoon,n. (midafternoon,adj.)

776. DAY

1. Day in the Middle of the Week: weekday,n. (weekday,adj.)

2. Days at the End of a Week: weekend,n. (weekend,adj.)

3. Middle of the Day: midday, noontide,n.

4. Pert. to the Middle of the Day: meridian, midday, noontide,adj.

5. End of the Day: nightfall,n.

6. In Reference to a Day or Days,adj.
  1. **daily**—done, happening, etc., by the day, every day, or every weekday; pert. to each day or weekday
  2. **diurnal**—happening every day (poetic or astronomical)
  3. **hebdomadal**—occurring at seven-day intervals
  4. **per diem**—by the day
  5. **quintan**—occurring every fifth day
  6. **quotidian**—occurring or recurring daily or every day
  7. **semidiurnal**—occurring in half a day or twice a day

7. Having, or Naming, the Extra Day in a Leap Year: bissextile,adj.

8. Comprising a Sequence of Day and Night: noctidiurnal,adj.

9. Sunday as a Day of Religious Observance: Sabbath,n. (Sabbatic, Sabbatical,adj.)

10. Pert. to Sunday as the Lord's Day: dominical, adj.

11. Period of Forty Days: quarantine,n.

777. EVENING

1. Evening: even or eventide (poetic); vesper,n. (vesper, vespertine, vespertinal,adj.)

2. Evening before an Event: eve,n.

3. Middle of the Evening: midevening,n.

4. Twilight: crepuscle, crepuscule, crepusculum, dusk; gloam (poetic); gloaming, nightfall,n. (crepuscular, crepusculine, crepusculous,adj.)

5. Active, etc., in the Evening or Twilight, adj.
  1. **crepuscular**—active in the twilight
  2. **vespertine, vespertinal**—flourishing, active, flying, or blossoming in the evening or twilight

6. Time When the Sun Disappears below the Horizon: sundown, sunset,n.

778. NIGHT

1. Period of the Night: nighttide, nighttime,n.

2. Middle of the Night; Twelve O'Clock at Night: midnight, noontide,n. (midnight,adj.)

3. In Reference to the Night,adj.
  1. **night**—pert. to, happening at, etc., night
  2. **nightly**—pert. to, characteristic of, resembling, or happening at or every, night
  3. **nocturnal**—pert. to, or happening at, night

4. Lasting All Night: all-night, nightlong, overnight,adj.

5. Active, etc., at Night,adj.
  1. **noctambulant, noctambulous**—walking, given to walking, or pert. to walking, at night
  2. **noctiflorous**—flowering at night
  3. **noctilucous**—shining at night
  4. **noctipotent**—powerful at night
  5. **noctivagant, noctivagous**—going about or wandering at night (noctivagation,n.)
  6. **nocturnal**—moving about during the night

6. One Who Stays Up Late at Night: night owl,n. (colloq.)

7. Overtaken by Night: benighted,adj.

8. The Coming of Night: nightfall,n.

779. WEEK

1. A Week: hebdomad,n.

2. Consisting of a Week or Seven Days: hebdomadal, hebdomadary, septenary,adj.

3. Period of Two Weeks: fortnight,n. (fortnightly,adj.)

4. Occurring, Appearing, etc., by the Week, Weeks, or Portion of a Week, adj.
  1. **biweekly**—occurring, appearing, etc., every two weeks
  2. **fortnightly**—occurring, etc., every two weeks
  3. **hebdomadal, hebdomadary, septenary**—occurring, etc., every week, i.e., every seven days
  4. **semiweekly**—occurring, etc., once every half week, or twice a week
  5. **triweekly**—appearing, occurring, done, etc., once every three weeks
  6. **weekly**—occurring, etc., every week

780. MONTH

1. Month,n.
  1. **lunar month**—month of 28 days
  2. **lunation**—month, being the time between successive new moons, approximately 29½ days
  3. **moon**—month (poetic)

2. Period of Two, Three, or Six Months,n.
  1. **bimester**—period of two months (bimestral, bimestrial,adj.)
  2. **semester**—period of six months—now generally refers to the academic half year, about five months in duration, from the middle of September to the end of January and from early February to late May or sometime in June (semestral, semestrial,adj.)
  3. **trimester**—period of three months (trimestral, trimestrial,adj.)

3. Occurring, Appearing, Done, Lasting, etc., by the Month or Months,adj.
  1. **bimensal**—occurring or done once every two months
  2. **bimestrial**—lasting two months; happening or done once in two months
  3. **bimonthly**—occurring every two months

4. **menstrual**—recurring once every month
5. **monthly, mensal**—occurring, appearing, etc., every month or once a month
6. **quadrimestrial**—occurring, etc., every fourth month
7. **quarterly**—occurring, etc., every third month, i.e., four times a year
8. **semestral, semestrial**—occurring, etc., once in six months or every six months
9. **semimonthly**—occurring, etc., every half month, or twice a month
10. **tricenary**—lasting a month, i.e., 30 days
11. **trimestral, trimestrial**—occurring, etc., once in three months or every three months
12. **trimonthly**—occurring or done, etc., once in three months

4. **By the Month:** per mensem (Latin)

5. **Of or in the Next Month:** proximo,adv.

6. **In the Preceding Month to This One:** ultimo,adv. (generally in the abbreviation *ult.*)

7. **Pert. to July and/or August, Considered the Months of the Dog Days:** canicular,adj.

781. YEAR

1. **Leap Year:** bissextile,n.

2. **Middle of the Year:** midyear,n. (midyear,adj.)

3. **Period of Years,n.**
   1. **biennium**—period of two years
   2. **century, centenary**—period of a hundred years
   3. **decade, decennary, decennium**—period of ten years
   4. **millenary, millennium, chiliad**—period of a thousand years
   5. **quadrennium**—period of four years
   6. **quinquennium, quinquenniad, lustrum, pentad**—period of five years
   7. **septenary, septennate, septennium**—period of seven years
   8. **sexcentenary**—period of six hundred years
   9. **sexennium**—period of six years

4. **Pert. to a Period of Years,** adj. *From Sec. 3:* centurial, centenary, centenarian, or centennial; millenarian, millenary, or millennial; sexcentenary; *Also:*
   1. **quindecennial**—pert. to fifteen years
   2. **sesquicentennial**—pert. to one hundred fifty years
   3. **tercentenary, tercentennial, tricentennial**—pert. to three hundred years

5. **In the Year of Our Lord:** anno Domini (usually in the abbreviation A.D.)

6. **In the Year of the World:** anno mundi (Latin)—in calculating dates from the supposed time of creation

7. **By the Year; Each Year:** per annum

8. **Occurring, etc., Once a Year or Once Every Year:** annual, yearly,adj.

9. **Lasting All Year or a Whole Year:** perennial, yearlong,adj.

10. **Lasting for Years; Continuing from Year to Year:** perennial,adj.

11. **Occurring, etc., Twice a Year:** biannual, biyearly, semiannual,adj.

12. **Occurring Every, Consisting of, or Lasting for a, Specified Number of Years,adj.**
   1. **bicentennial**—occurring every two hundred years
   2. **biennial**—occurring every, or lasting for, two years
   3. **centennial, centenary, centenarian**—occurring every, or lasting for, a hundred years

4. **decennial, decennary**—occurring every ten years
5. **millenary**—consisting of a thousand years
6. **octennial**—occurring every, or lasting for, eight years
7. **quadrennial**—occurring every, lasting for, or consisting of, four years
8. **quadricentennial**—recurring every, or lasting for, four hundred years
9. **quinquennial**—occurring every five years, once in five years, or at the end of five years; lasting five years
10. **semicentennial**—occurring at the end of fifty years
11. **septennial, septennary**—recurring every, or lasting for, seven years
12. **sexennial**—occurring every, or lasting for, six years
13. **triennial**—occurring every, or lasting for, three years
14. **vicennial**—occurring every, lasting for, or consisting of, twenty years

13. **Anniversary, or the Celebration of an Anniversary,n.**
   1. **bicentennial, bicentenary**—200th
   2. **biennial**—2nd
   3. **birthday**—one's birth
   4. **centennial, centenary**—100th
   5. **decennial**—10th
   6. **jubilee**—50th, or, occasionally, 25th
   7. **millennial**—1000th
   8. **octennial**—8th
   9. **quadrennial**—4th
   10. **quadricentennial**—400th
   11. **quindecennial**—15th
   12. **semi-centennial**—50th
   13. **septennial**—7th
   14. **sesquicentennial**—150th
   15. **sexcentenary**—600th
   16. **sexennial**—6th
   17. **tercentenary, tricentennial**—300th
   18. **triennial**—3rd

782. PLACE

1. **Place:** area, berth; clime (poetic); compass, demesne, district, locality, location, parts, position, province, quarter, realm, region, seat, section, situation, sphere, spot, station, territory,n. (areal, locational, positional, provincial, regional, sectional, situational, territorial,adj.); *Also:*
   1. **arena**—place where a public contest or competition takes place
   2. **brush, brushwood**—thinly settled region
   3. **confines, suburbs**—region around a boundary
   4. **corner, nook**—out-of-the-way, sheltered, or cozy place
   5. **depository, repository**—place where something is put, esp. for safekeeping
   6. **depot**—railroad station
   7. **district, section**—portion of territory; definite part of some country, state, city, etc. (sectional,adj.)
   8. **frontier**—advance, or not completely explored, region of thinking, knowledge, etc. (figurative)
   9. **locale**—place of some special or characteristic feature, events, or circumstance
   10. **locality**—geographical place
   11. **location**—place for something
   12. **neighborhood**—district, esp. in reference to its inhabitants
   13. **niche**—place, or suitable place, for something or someone
   14. **outremer (French)**—region beyond the sea; foreign regions
   15. **outskirts**—outer districts of a city, town, region, etc.
   16. **pale**—region with certain bounds
   17. **parish**—region served by a church; local ecclesiastical district with its own church and clergyman (parochial,adj.)

18. **point**—place having position but not extending into space; place considered only in reference to its position; particular place

19. **post**—place where a soldier is, or soldiers are, stationed; place to which someone is assigned or appointed

20. **precinct**—limited region or area

21. **presidio**—military post (presidial, presidiary,adj.)

22. **province**—country region; district (provincial,adj.)

23. **range**—open, or thinly populated, region over which domestic animals, livestock, etc., roam, as for feeding

24. **realm**—place where something is found in abundance

25. **recess**—indented or set-back place in a wall; inner place; quiet or secluded place

26. **resort**—place where people meet, gather, relax, or seek amusement

27. **sphere**—place of existence

28. **spot**—particular place or area

29. **standpoint**—fixed point or station

30. **station**—place or spot where a person or thing stands or habitually stands; assigned place; place or region of duty

31. **terrain**—region of land under observation

32. **theater**—region or place of operation or functioning

33. **tract**—region without definite bounds

34. **ward**—district of a city

35. **wilderness**—place in which one cannot find one's way

36. **wonderland**—place that causes wonder and/or admiration

37. **zone**—specially marked off region or area (zonal,adj.)

2. Place of Action or Activity: arena, demesne, domain, field, orbit, province, scene, sphere, stage, theater,n. (domanial, orbital, adj.)

3. Place Where Someone or Something Is, or Is Located: berth, location, position, seat, site, situation, situs, sphere, station, whereabouts,n. (locational, positional, situational, adj.)

4. Natural Position or Place of Something (Scientific): situs,n.

5. Region Where a Plant or Animal Naturally Lives: habitat, range,n.

6. Place or Region of Rule, Administration, Authority, etc.: bourn or bourne (considered erroneous), circle, demesne, department, domain, dominion, jurisdiction, precinct, province, realm, sphere,n. (domanial, jurisdictional, provincial,adj.)

7. Place of Occurrence: locality, scene, stage, theater,n.

8. Place Where a Story, Play, etc., Occurs: locale, scene, setting,n.

9. Sphere of Knowledge, Study, Thought, etc.: demesne, department, domain, dominion, field, province, realm, sphere,n.

10. Region of Influence: bourn or bourne (considered erroneous), circle, demesne, domain, orbit, province, realm, sphere,n.

11. Place Frequently Visited: haunt, purlieu, resort; stamping ground (colloq.),n.

12. Region over Which Repeated Trips Are Made: ambit, circuit,n.

13. Place to Which People Go: haunt, resort, n.

14. Place to Which One Is Going or Traveling: bourn or bourne, destination,n.

15. Pert. or Relating to, Characteristic of, etc., a Particular Place: local, regional, sectional, topical, vernacular,adj.

16. Designed to Be Applied to a Certain Limited Area of the Body: topical,adj.

17. From or to This Place: hither,adv.

18. From or to That Place: thither,adv.

19. In Place (of): in lieu (of); in (one's or its) stead

20. Position: berth, situation, station, ubiety, n.

21. Bad Position: malposition,n.

22. Position After: postposition,n. (postpositional,adj.)

23. Position from Which Things or Ideas Are Looked at and Judged: standpoint,n.

24. Position of Affairs: status,n.

25. Quality of Being in an Abstract Position: ubiety,n.

783. SURROUNDINGS

1. Surroundings;   Surrounding   Places, Parts, Circumstances, Influences, etc.,n.

1. **atmosphere**—surrounding mood or tone (atmospheric,adj.)

2. **aura**—distinctive atmosphere around a person (aural,adj.)

3. **circumambiency**—environment

4. **circumjacencies**—surrounding parts

5. **entourage**—surroundings; environment

6. **environment**—surroundings; surrounding places or parts; surrounding circumstances, influences, etc., that affect a biological organism, a person or a person's behavior, society, etc. (environmental, environal, environic,adj.)

7. **environs, suburbs**—surrounding districts or regions of a place

8. **milieu**—surroundings; environment; setting

9. **mise en scène (French)**—physical surroundings in which something is seen

10. **neighborhood, purlieus, vicinity, vicinage**—surrounding region

11. **precincts**—immediate surroundings

12. **setting**—physical surroundings

13. **terrain**—surroundings;   surrounding places or parts

2. Science or Study of Environment,n.

1. **anthroposociology**—study of the reciprocal action between environment and race (anthroposociologist,n.)

2. **ecology, bionomics**—science of the biological relationship between organisms and their environment (ecologist, bionomist,n. ecological, ecologic, bionomical, bionomic,adj.)

3. **euthenics**—science that deals with and/or attempts to improve human environment or living conditions in order to produce a better race (euthenist,n.)

3. Scenery of a Stage Play: décor (French); mise en scène (French), scene, scenes, setting, n.

4. Scene,n.

1. **arena**—scene of action or public contest

2. **kaleidoscope**—constantly changing and different scene (kaleidoscopic,adj.)

3. **panorama**—continually changing scene (panoramic,adj.)

4. **phantasmagoria, phantasmagory**—suddenly and constantly changing scene (phantasmagorial,   phantasmagoric, phantasmagorical,adj.)

5. **sphere**—scene of action or existence

6. **stage**—scene of action

7. **theater**—scene of important events

5. Corner: angle, bight, coin, nook,n.; *Also:*

1. **inglenook**—chimney corner; corner by the fire

2. **nook**—cozy or sheltered corner

6. Having Corners: angled, angular, cornered,adj. (angularness, angularity,n.)

7. Having Three Corners: tricorn,adj.

784. NATION

1. Nation; Country,n.
1. **buffer state**—country situated between two rival countries
2. **fatherland**—one's native country
3. **motherland**—one's native country; country of one's origin
4. **republic**—nation in which the government ultimately resides in the people (**republican,**adj.)
5. **state**—nation

2. Pert. to a Nation: national,adj.

3. Native or Inhabitant of a Nation or Country: citizen, countryman, national,n.

4. Certain Countries as a Group,n.
1. **Levant**—countries bordering the Eastern Mediterranean Sea (**Levantine,**adj.)
2. **Occident**—countries of Europe or the West, as distinguished from those of Asia or the Far East (**Occidental,**adj.)
3. **Orient**—Japan, China, India, and other countries of Asia or, strictly, of the East or Far East (**Oriental,**adj.)
4. **Scandinavia**—Norway, Sweden, Denmark, and sometimes including Iceland and the Faeroe Islands (**Scandinavian,**adj.)

5. Between Nations; Pert. to Affairs between Nations: international,adj.

6. Within a Nation: intranational,adj.

7. Person from the Same, or from One's Own, Country or Nation: compatriot, countryman,n.

8. Love, etc., of Country,n.
1. **chauvinism, jingoism, nationalism**—exaggerated and often offensive patriotism; excessive boasting about the superiority of one's native land (**chauvinist, jingoist, jingo, nationalist,**n. **chauvinist, chauvinistic, jingoist, jingoistic, jingo, jingoish, nationalist, nationalistic,**adj.)
2. **flag waving**—exaggerated, conspicuous, and offensive patriotism (**flag waver,**n. **flag-waving,**adj.)
3. **patriotism, nationalism**—zealous loyalty to, love of, and solicitousness for, one's country (**patriot, nationalist,**n. **patriotic, nationalist, nationalistic,**adj.)
4. **public spirit**—active interest in the welfare of one's country, community, etc. (**public-spirited,**adj.)
5. **spread-eagleism**—exaggerated patriotism, esp. in reference to the U.S. (**spread-eagleist,**n. **spread-eagle,**adj.)
6. **ultranationalism**—extreme patriotism or nationalism (**ultranationalist,**n. **ultranational, ultranationalist, ultranationalistic,**adj.)

9. Common Substitute Names for Certain Specific Countries or Places,n.
1. **America**—United States (**American,**adj.)
2. **Auld Sod**—Scotland
3. **Cambria**—Wales (poetic or medieval)
4. **Cathay**—old name for China
5. **Celestial Empire**—former Chinese Empire
6. **Columbia**—United States
7. **Dark Continent**—Africa
8. **Eire**—official name of Ireland
9. **Emerald Isle**—Ireland
10. **Helvetia**—Switzerland (poetic)
11. **Hibernia**—Ireland (**Hibernian,**adj.)
12. **Land of the Midnight Sun**—Norway
13. **Land of the Rising Sun, Land of the Cherry Blossoms**—Japan
14. **Land of the Shamrock**—Ireland
15. **Land of the Thousand Lakes**—Finland
16. **Land of the White Elephant**—Siam (Thailand)
17. **Muscovy**—ancient name for Russia (**Muscovite, Muscovitic,**adj.)

18. **Nippon**—Japan, so called by the Japanese (**Nipponese,**adj.)
19. **Seward's Folly**—Alaska
20. **Thailand**—official name of Siam from 1939–45 (**Thai, Tai,**adj.)
21. **Tight Little Island**—Great Britain
22. **Vaterland**—Germany

10. To Make Conform to the Customs or Culture of Certain Countries or Regions,v.
1. **Americanize**—of the United States (**Americanization,**n.)
2. **Anglicize**—of England (**Anglicization,**n.)
3. **Gallicize, Frenchify**—of France (**Gallicization, Frenchification,**n.)
4. **Europeanize**—of Europe (**Europeanization,**n.)
5. **Hellenize, Grecize, Graecize**—of Greece (**Hellenization,**n.)
6. **Occidentalize**—of Western or European countries (**Occidentalization,**n.)
7. **Orientalize**—of Eastern, Far Eastern, or Asian countries (**Orientalization,**n.)
8. **Sinify**—of China (**Sinification,**n.)

11. To Give Greek Form or Characteristics to: Hellenize, Grecize, or Graecize,v. (**Hellenization,**n.)

12. To Change by Chinese Influence: Sinify, v. (**Sinification,**n.)

13. To Become Oriental: Orientalize,v. (**Orientalization,**n.)

14. Expert or Authority on Greek Culture, Customs, Language, etc.: Hellenist,n.

15. Inhabitant or Native of a Specific Country or Other Place,n. (Obvious terms, such as American, Mexican, Italian, etc., are omitted.)
1. **Achaean**—of Greece or ancient Greece
2. **Afrikander**—white inhabitant of South Africa of Dutch or French descent
3. **Argive**—of Greece
4. **Athenian, Attic**—of Athens
5. **Badger**—of Wisconsin
6. **Boche, boche**—of Germany (slang)
7. **Breton**—of Brittany
8. **Cantabrigian**—of Cambridge, England
9. **Canuck**—of French Canada (slang)
10. **Carthaginian**—of ancient Carthage
11. **Celt**—of Ireland, Scotland, Wales, and Brittany
12. **Chinese, Celestial**—of China
13. **citizen**—of a country, state, or city
14. **Cockney**—of the East End of London
15. **Creole**—French or Spanish person born in some non-European colonial region
16. **Dane**—of Denmark
17. **Dutchman, mynheer**—of Holland
18. **Englishman, Britisher, Briton**—of England
19. **Eskimo, Amerind, Husky, Hyperborean**—of the arctic coast of America
20. **Filipino**—of the Philippine Islands
21. **Frenchman**—of France
22. **Gael**—of Scotland, Ireland, or the Isle of Man; Highlander
23. **German, Teuton**—of Germany
24. **Greek, Hellene**—of Greece
25. **Hawaiian, Kanaka**—of Hawaii
26. **Hierosolymitan**—of the city of Jerusalem
27. **Highlander, highlander, Tartan**—of the high regions of Scotland
28. **Hindu**—of India
29. **Hoosier**—of Indiana
30. **Hun**—of Germany (derogatory)
31. **Hyperborean**—of arctic regions
32. **Iberian**—of Spain or Portugal
33. **Irishman, Hibernian**—of Ireland
34. **Israeli**—of modern Israel
35. **Japanese, Nipponese**—of Japan
36. **Levantine**—of a country bordering the Eastern Mediterranean Sea
37. **limey**—of England (slang)
38. **Manxman**—of the Isle of Man

39. **Meridional**—of the south, esp. the south of Europe or of France
40. **Muscovite**—of Russia or, occasionally, of Moscow
41. **Nordic, Scandinavian**—of a Scandinavian country, i.e., Norway, Sweden, or Denmark
42. **Norseman**—of ancient Scandinavia
43. **Norwegian**—of Norway
44. **Occidental**—of the Western world, i.e., not Asia or the Far East
45. **Oriental**—of the East (Asia) or Far East, including China, Japan, India, etc.
46. **Ottoman, Osmanli**—of Turkey, or of Western Turkey
47. **Oxonian**—of the city of Oxford, England
48. **paddy**—of Ireland (colloq.)
49. **Pekingese, Pekinese**—of Peking, or Peiping
50. **Peruvian**—of Peru
51. **Portuguese**—of Portugal
52. **Scotsman, Scot, Scotchman**—of Scotland
53. **Siamese, Thailander**—of Siam
54. **Singhalese, Sinhalese**—of Ceylon
55. **Spaniard**—of Spain
56. **squarehead**—of Germany or Scandinavia (slang and derogatory)
57. **Swede**—of Sweden
58. **Swiss, Helvetian**—of Switzerland
59. **Tangerine**—of Tangier
60. **Tarheel**—of North Carolina
61. **Venetian**—of Venice
62. **Walloon**—of southern Belgium
63. **Welshman, Cambrian**—of Wales
64. **White Russian, Byelorussian**—of the western part of Russia
65. **Wolverine**—of Michigan

16. Pert. or Referring to the Native or Inhabitant of a Country or Place, or to the Country or Place Itself,adj. *From Sec. 15:* Achaean, Athenian or Attic, Breton, Cantabrigian, Carthaginian or Punic, Celtic; Chinese, Celestial, Sinaean, Sinaic, Sinic, or Sinitic; Cockney, Creole, Danish, Dutch, English or British, Eskimo or hyperborean, Filipino; French, Gallic, or Gallican; Gaelic, German or Teutonic, Greek or Hellenic, Hawaiian, Hierosolymitan, Highland or Tartan, Hindu, Hoosier, hyperborean, Iberian, Irish or Hibernian, Israeli, Japanese or Nipponese, Levantine, Manx, meridional, Muscovite or Muscovitic, Nordic or Scandinavian, Norse, Norwegian, Occidental, Oriental, Ottoman or Osmanli, Oxonian, Pekingese or Pekinese, Peruvian, Portuguese; Scots, Scottish, or Scotch; Siamese, Thai, or Tai; Singhalese or Sinhalese, Spanish, Swedish; Swiss, Helvetian, or Helvetic; Tangerine, Venetian, Walloon or Wallonian, Welsh or Cambrian, Byelorussian; *Also:*

1. **antique**—pert. to ancient Greece or Rome
2. **classic, classical**—pert. to ancient Greece or Rome, esp. the life, art, or literature
3. **Hellenic**—pert. to the later period of classical Greek culture
4. **Romaic**—pert. to modern Greece
5. **Trinacrian**—pert. to Sicily

17. Inhabitants or Natives of a Place, Collectively,n.
1. **amphiscians, amphiscii**—of tropical regions
2. **citizenry**—of a nation, state, city, etc.
3. **countryside**—of the country, as distinguished from the city
4. **Manx, Manxmen**—of the Isle of Man
5. **Pekingese, Pekinese**—of Peking or Peiping
6. **Swiss**—of Switzerland
7. **Welsh, Cymry, Kymry**—of Wales (Cymric, Kymric,adj.)

18. According to the Style of the French: à la française (French)

19. According to the Style of the English: à l'anglaise (French)
20. A State in the United States: commonwealth,n.

785. CITY

1. City or Other Political or Geographical Subdivision,n.
1. **borough**—in certain states (notably Connecticut, Pennsylvania, Minnesota, and New Jersey) a municipal corporation corresponding to an incorporated town or village of other states; part of a city, as in New York City
2. **burg**—city or town (colloq.)
3. **capital**—head city of a state or nation
4. **cosmopolis**—city with a very diverse population
5. **hamlet**—small village, no more, usually, than a group of houses
6. **megalopolis**—extremely large city
7. **metropolis**—chief, capital, most important, or most populous city of a region; city that is an important center of something
8. **municipality**—city; self-governing city or locality
9. **suburb, suburbs**—outlying section of a city; section close to a city; small city, village, or town just outside a large city
10. **town, township**—population and business center of a region, incorporated or unincorporated depending on which state it is located in
11. **village**—geographical or political division of a state smaller than a city or town, larger than a hamlet

2. Dweller in a City, etc.,n. *From Sec. 1:* megalopolitan, metropolitan, suburbanite, villager; *Also:*
1. **citizen**—inhabitant of a city, town, state, etc.
2. **city dweller, urbanite**—one who lives in a city
3. **town dweller, townsman, oppidan**—one who lives in a town

3. Pert. or Relating to a City, etc.,adj. *From Sec. 1:* borough, capital, megalopolitan, metropolitan, municipal, suburban, village; *Also:*
1. **civic, urban**—pert. or relating to a city or cities
2. **oppidan**—pert. or relating to a town

4. Those Who Live in the Suburbs, Collectively: suburbia,n.

5. Resembling a City: citified, urban,adj.

6. To Make into, or Similar to, a City: citify, metropolitanize, urbanize,v. (citification, urbanization,n.)

7. Pert. or Relating to the Government of a City: municipal,adj.

8. Characteristic of a Large City: megalopolitan, metropolitan,adj. (megalopolitanism, metropolitanism,n.)

9. Between Cities: interurban,adj.

10. Within a City: intraurban,adj.

786. COUNTRIFIED

1. Countrified; Like or Characteristic of the Country or Country Existence, as Distinguished from the City or City Existence: agrestic, Arcadian, bucolic, bucolical, countrified, countrylike, geoponic, georgic, pastoral, provincial, rural, rustic, rustical, villatic,adj.

2. State or Quality of Being Countrified: countrifiedness, pastoralism, pastorality, peasantry, provincialism, provinciality, rural-

ism, rurality, ruralness, rusticalness, rusticity, rusticness,n.

3. To Become or Make Countrified: rural-
ize, rusticate,v. (ruralization, rustication,n.
rusticator,n.)

**4. To Go into, or Live, Stay, or Spend Time
in, the Country, or Go to the Country as
Punishment:** rusticate,v. (rustication,n. rusticator,n.)

**5. To Banish to the Country, Esp. as Pun-
ishment:** rusticate,v. (rustication,n.)

6. Country Person; Country Dweller: boor;
bucolic (humorous); chuff, churl, clodhopper,
countryman, peasant; rube (slang); rural,
ruralist, ruralite, rustic, rustical,n. (boorish,
chuffy, churlish,adj.); *Also:*

  1. **boor**—clownish country person (boorish,
     adj.)
  2. **bumpkin**—clumsy country person
  3. **rube**—rude and unsophisticated country
     person (slang)
  4. **swain**—young man who lives in the coun-
     try
  5. **yokel**—simple or unsophisticated country
     person (contemptuous)

**7. Peasants Collectively; State or Condition
of Being a Peasant:** peasantry,n.

**8. Artistic Composition on, or Describing,
Country Life,n.**

  1. **bucolic**—poem of country life (bucolic,
     adj.)
  2. **eclogue**—poem of country life or the life
     of shepherds
  3. **idyl, idyll**—poetic, prose, or musical com-
     position on simple, peaceful, or charming
     country life (idylic, idyllic,adj.)
  4. **pastoral, pastorale**—poetic, prose, or
     musical composition on country life, the
     life of shepherds, etc. (pastoral,adj.)

9. Writer of Such a Composition,n. *From
Sec. 8:* bucolic or bucoliast, pastoralist

**10. Combining Elements of Both Country
and City Living:** suburban,adj.

787. SPACE

1. Space,n.

  1. **ambit**—space surrounding a house or
     other building
  2. **area**—total space on the surface; space
     within; extent (areal,adj.)
  3. **berth**—sufficient space to swing at anchor
     or to maneuver under way (nautical)
  4. **circuit**—enclosed space
  5. **clearing**—cleared space
  6. **compartment**—partitioned-off space
  7. **compass**—area
  8. **expanse**—large and/or wide space
  9. **extent**—space that a thing goes or
     stretches to
  10. **field**—open expanse
  11. **headroom, headway**—cleared space
      under a bridge, etc., to allow passage
  12. **immensity**—extremely large expanse of
      space; expanse or extent without bounds
  13. **plenum**—space that is full
  14. **quadrangle**—square or rectangular space
      surrounded by buildings (quadrangular,
      adj.)
  15. **range**—space or extent covered or in-
      cluded
  16. **reach**—continuous expanse or extent
  17. **room**—space or extent of space available
      for use or occupancy; enclosed space
      within a building
  18. **sept**—enclosed space
  19. **spread**—expanse; extent
  20. **stretch**—continuous large or wide space
  21. **sweep**—continuous space, expanse, or ex-
      tent
  22. **territory**—space (territorial,adj.)

  23. **tract**—space without definite bounds;
      expanse
  24. **vastitude or, poetic, vast**—tremendously
      large space or expanse of space
  25. **vault**—arched space
  26. **volume**—cubic space
  27. **wing**—space at the side of a stage

2. Space for Action, Movement, etc.: area,
compass, elbowroom, leeway, range, room,
scope, swing,n.

3. Space of Action, Power, Effect, etc.: extent, field, province, range, reach, sphere,n.

4. Space Between,n.

  1. **gap, breach, chasm**—open space in any-
     thing made by breaking, tearing, or com-
     ing apart
  2. **hiatus**—space between; space that indi-
     cates a part missing
  3. **interstice**—small space between things
     closely packed (interstices,pl.n. inter-
     stitial,adj.)
  4. **lacuna**—blank space in a manuscript or
     other material; any blank space between
     things or parts; space between cells in
     animal or plant tissue (lacunas or lacu-
     nae,pl.n. lacunal, lacunar, lacunary,adj.)
  5. **mesh**—open space in a net, sieve,
     strainer, or screen
  6. **spread**—intervening space

5. Pert. to Space: spatial,adj.

6. Existing in Both Space and Time: spatiotemporal,adj.

7. A Room,n.

  1. **alcove**—small room opening into a larger
     one
  2. **antechamber, anteroom**—small room off
     a larger one, used for waiting
  3. **apartment**—single room
  4. **attic, garret**—room or rooms just below
     the roof, and above the other rooms of
     the house
  5. **bathroom**—room for washing, bathing,
     etc.
  6. **bedroom, chamber, bedchamber**—room
     for sleeping
  7. **booth**—covered compartment; temporary
     compartment, as for voting, at a fair, etc.
  8. **boudoir**—small private dressing room for
     a woman
  9. **cabin**—private room in a ship
  10. **calefactory**—heated apartment, esp. in a
      monastery
  11. **carrell**—small booth for individual study
  12. **casino**—room for dancing, card playing,
      gambling, or other amusements
  13. **cellar, basement**—room or rooms below
      the level of the ground
  14. **chamber**—room; reception room of an
      important person; large room for a legis-
      lative, etc., body
  15. **closet**—small, private room; small room
      for storing things, hanging clothing, etc.;
      monarch's private chamber
  16. **compartment**—separate room, esp. one
      partitioned off from a larger space, as in
      a train, etc.
  17. **cubicle**—small partitioned room for read-
      ing, working, studying, etc.
  18. **cuddy**—small room; closet
  19. **den**—private room
  20. **dining room**—room for eating
  21. **galley**—kitchen of a ship
  22. **hall**—large room for public meetings
  23. **kitchen**—room for cooking
  24. **library**—room for reading, etc.
  25. **living room**—room where the family
      gathers, where guests are entertained,
      etc.
  26. **loft**—upper room, or attic, of a place
  27. **nursery**—room where a child sleeps
  28. **pantry**—room or closet where provisions,
      china, glassware, pots and pans, etc., are
      kept

29. **refectory**—room for dining, esp. in a monastery, school, or other institution
30. **rotunda**—large, circular room
31. **saloon**—large room used for some specific purpose
32. **sanctum**—private room
33. **scullery**—small room off the kitchen where cooking utensils are kept and the rough kitchen work is done
34. **solarium**—room exposed to sunlight
35. **stall**—booth; booth for horses or cattle
36. **stateroom**—bedroom on a ship
37. **studio**—room for working, i.e., writing, painting, sculpturing, etc.
38. **study**—room for work, study, reading, etc.; den
39. **subterrane**—underground room
40. **sun porch**—room, often off the living room, with a wide expanse of windows
41. **vault**—underground room; cellar
42. **vestry**—room in a church for non-religious activities or for the storage of church garments

8. Living Room: drawing room, front room, parlor, sitting room,n.

9. Recessed Portion of a Room: alcove,n.

10. Connecting Series of Rooms for the Use of One Family, Person, etc.: apartment, suite,n.

11. Roomy: ample, broad; capacious (i.e., for containing) ; cavernous (like a cavern) ; commodious, expansive, extensive, immense, spacious, vast; vasty (poetic) ; voluminous (i.e., for containing) ; wide,adj.

12. Roominess: ampleness, amplitude, breadth; capaciousness or capacity (i.e., for containing) ; commodiousness, expansiveness or expansivity, extensiveness, immenseness or immensity, spaciousness, vastness, vastitude, voluminousness, width,n.

13. To Have Room for: accommodate, admit, contain,v.

14. To Furnish Room for: accommodate, stow,v. (accommodation, stowage,n.)

788. DISTANCE

1. Distance,n.
1. **circuit**—distance around a region or space
2. **circumference**—distance around a circle; distance around any area (circumferential,adj.)
3. **diameter**—distance through the center of a circle, object, or place (diametric, adj.)
4. **equidistance**—equal distance from a place or point (equidistant,adj.)
5. **extent, length, compass, reach**—distance from one end to another
6. **light-year**—distance traveled by light in one year, namely about 6,000,000,000,000 miles—used in astronomy to describe the distances of stars, etc., from the earth
7. **offing**—distant part of the sea visible from the shore; remote distance
8. **radius**—distance from a center to the limit, boundary, or circumference of a circle or circular space; distance from the center in any direction (radial,adj.)
9. **range**—distance of distribution
10. **reach**—distance of limited extent
11. **span**—distance between the tip of the thumb and the tip of the little finger; distance between two limits or supports
12. **stretch**—continuous distance or length
13. **stride**—distance traveled in a walking step or in the complete cycle of a horse's use of all four legs

2. To Be a Distance,v. *From Sec. 1:* extend, range, reach, span, stretch

3. Certain Instruments for Measuring Distance,n.
1. **cyclometer**—for measuring the revolutions of a wheel to determine the distance traveled
2. **micrometer**—for measuring minute distances (micrometry,n.)
3. **odograph**—for recording the distance and course of a vehicle, or the speed or number of steps taken in walking
4. **odometer, odograph**—for measuring the distance traversed by a vehicle (odometry, n.)
5. **pedometer**—for measuring the distance traveled on foot (pedometric, pedometrical,adj. pedometrist,n.)
6. **tachymeter**—for measuring the distance and height of a remote object in surveying (tachymetry,n. tachymetric,adj.)
7. **taximeter**—for measuring the distance traveled in a taxi and the cost of trip
8. **telemeter**—for measuring the distance of something from an observer (telemetry, n. telemetric,adj.)

789. FAR

1. Far: distant, faraway, far-off, remote, removed,adj. (remoteness,n.) ; *Also:*
1. **antipodal, antipodean**—situated at the opposite end of the world; hence, very far
2. **distal**—remote from the point of attachment (medical—of an organ, etc.)
3. **outlying, out-of-the-way**—far from the center, or from the main point

2. Beyond or on the Farther Side; More Distant: ulterior,adj.

3. Farthest: farthermost, furthermost, furthest, ultimate,adj.

4. Farthest Away of Things or People in a Series, Line, etc.: endmost,adj.

5. Farthest Point: solstice,n.

6. Farthest in a Specified Direction: easternmost, northernmost, southernmost, westernmost,adj.

7. In, or Pert. to, the Far North: arctic (i.e., North Pole), Hyperborean,adj.

8. In, or Pert. to, the Far South: antarctic, adj. (i.e., South Pole)

9. Far Region or Regions,n.
1. **hinterland**—region far removed from cities, towns, or important cultural or other centers
2. **outskirts**—regions far from the center
3. **provinces**—regions of a country far from the capital city or from a large, or the largest, city (provincial,adj.)
4. **purlieu**—remote region
5. **suburb, suburbs**—outlying part of a city (suburban,adj.)

790. NEAR

1. Near: adjacent, at hand or near at hand, bordering, close, close by or closeby, contiguous, immediate, nearby or near by, neighbor, neighboring, nigh, proximate, vicinal,adj.

2. Lying or Situated Near or Close Together: adjacent, approximate, bordering, contiguous, neighbor or neighboring,adj.

3. Conveniently Close or Nearby: at hand or near at hand, available, convenient, handy, ready,adj. (availability or availableness, convenience, handiness,n.)

4. Nearness: adjacency, closeness, contiguity or contiguousness, immediacy or immediateness, neighborhood, propinquity, proximity, vicinity,n.

5. Living Nearby: neighboring,adj.

6. One Who Lives, or One Who or That Which Is, Nearby: neighbor,n.

7. People Who Live Nearby: neighborhood,n.

8. Nearby Region or Regions: environs, neighborhood, precincts, purlieu, purlieus, vicinage, vicinity,n.

9. To Be, or Be Situated, Near or Close to: border on, border upon, neighbor,v.

10. To Come Near or Close to: approach, approximate, approximate to, border on, border upon, near, shave, trench on, trench upon, verge on, verge upon,v. (approach, approximation,n.)

11. To Bring or Cause to Come Near: approximate, neighbor,v. (approximation,n.)

12. To Draw Near to Each Other: approach, converge,v. (convergence or convergency,n. approaching, converging or convergent,adj.)

13. To Cause to Draw Near Each Other: converge,v.

14. Nearest: immediate, proximal, proximate, adj.

15. Nearest to a Body, Center of Motion, Point of Attachment, or Point of Origin: proximal,adj.

16. Descr. of That End of a Limb or Other Organ That Is Nearest to the Point of Attachment to the Body: proximal,adj.

17. Next; Lying or Situated Next or Touching: abutting, adjacent, adjoining; approximal (anatomy); bordering, conterminal, conterminous, contiguous, immediate, juxtaposed, neighboring, vicinal,adj. (abuttal, adjacency, contiguity, contiguousness, immediacy, immediateness, juxtaposition,n.)

18. That Which Lies Next or Touching: adjacency,n.

19. Series of Things Lying Next to Each Other or Touching: contiguity,n.

20. To Lie or Be Situated Next to, or Touching: abut against, abut on, abut upon, adjoin, border, border on, border upon, neighbor, verge on, verge upon,v. (abutment,n.)

21. To Lie or Be Situated Next to Each Other: abut, adjoin,v. (abutment,n.)

22. To Live Next to: neighbor,v. (neighbor,n. neighbor, neighboring,adj.)

23. Side by Side: juxtaposed,adj.

24. To Place Side by Side: juxtapose,v. (juxtaposition,n.)

---

791. STOP

1. To Stop, i.e., Cause to Stop or End, or Bring to a Stop: arrest, cease, check, choke off, end, halt, stay, stem, terminate,v.; *Also:*

1. **abort**—stop the development or course of, as a disease (medical)
2. **adjourn**—end (a meeting), planning to resume at some other time or place
3. **arrest**—stop the course of, as a disease (medical)
4. **brake**—stop the motion of, as a wheel, machinery, etc.
5. **break off**—put a sudden stop to
6. **cease**—stop (doing)
7. **check**—suddenly and forcibly stop the motion of
8. **choke**—stop the breath, breathing, action, movement, growth, or progress of
9. **cut off**—bring to a sudden end
10. **deter**—stop from doing, continuing, etc., usually by inspiring with fear or doubt
11. **discontinue**—put a stop to (that which was to have continued)
12. **frustrate, thwart**—stop (a person) from doing or accomplishing

13. **intercept, cut off**—stop (a person or thing on his or its way)
14. **interrupt**—stop the continuity of
15. **nip in the bud**—stop at the outset before development, etc.
16. **prevent, prohibit**—stop from doing, happening, etc.
17. **quiet**—stop the motion or activity of
18. **repress, suppress**—stop the normal activity, occurrence, or expression of
19. **stall**—stop the motion of, or bring to a stop, unintentionally
20. **stay**—stop the progress of; stop temporarily by legal or executive order
21. **suspend, pretermit**—stop temporarily or for a time
22. **tie up**—put a stop to (activity, traffic, business, etc.)
23. **waylay**—stop (a person) on his way

2. To Stop, i.e., Come to a Stop,v. *From Sec. 1:* cease, end, halt, terminate, adjourn, break off, cease, discontinue, quiet or quiet down, stall, stay, suspend; *Also:*

1. **balk**—stop and stand still or refuse to go on or continue (balky,adj.)
2. **desist**—stop; stop doing that which one has been doing
3. **pause**—stop temporarily or before continuing
4. **quit**—stop; stop working
5. **stagnate**—stop moving or flowing and remain still (stagnancy, stagnance, stagnation,n. stagnant,adj.)
6. **strike**—stop working in order to get higher wages or better working conditions

3. A Stoppage, Stopping, or Stop,n. *From Sec. 1:* arrest, arrestment, or arrestation, cessation, check, end, halt, stay, termination; adjournment, arrestment, cessation, check, determent, discontinuation or discontinuance, frustration, interception, interruption, prevention, prohibition, repression, suppression, stay, suspension; *From Sec. 2:* desistance, pause, stagnation, strike; *Also:*

1. **armistice, truce**—temporary cessation of hostilities or conflict
2. **breather**—pause for rest
3. **caesura**—pause in the rhythm of poetry or music (caesural,adj.)
4. **hiatus**—pause in continuity, with a part missing
5. **intermission**—stop or pause for a period of time
6. **interval**—pause between activities
7. **lull**—temporary stop or pause in noise, a storm, confusion, etc.
8. **standstill**—stop; pause; complete stoppage of motion or progress
9. **surcease**—cessation (archaic)

4. That Which Serves to Cause Stoppage or a Stopping,n. *From Sec. 1:* check, stay; brake, check, choke, deterrent, interruption, preventive or preventative, prohibition, stay; *Also:*
1. **strangle hold**—that which stops free movement, growth, development, etc.

5. Causing a Stoppage or Stopping,adj. *From Sec. 1:* terminative; abortive, deterrent, interceptive, interruptive or interruptory, preventive, prohibitive or prohibitory, repressive, suppressive, suspensive (deterrence, repressiveness, suppressiveness, suspensiveness,n.)

6. To Stop the Flow of: choke, stanch, staunch, stem, throttle,v.

7. To Interrupt: break in on, cut off, pretermit, punctuate,v. (pretermission, punctuation,n.)

8. To Interrupt with (a Remark, etc.): interject, interpolate, or interpose (a remark, etc.),v. (interjection, interpolation, interposition,n.)

9. Interrupting: interpellant, interruptive, interruptory,adj.

10. To Put an End to: choke off, destroy, dissolve, do away with, end, extinguish, quell, quench, snuff out, spike, squash, stamp out, suppress; surcease (archaic); terminate, wipe out,v.

11. Act of Putting an End to: abscission, destruction, dissolution, extinguishment or extinction, suppression, termination,n. (destructive, extinctive, suppressive, terminative, adj.)

12. Method of Putting an End to Debate or Discussion, and Bringing a Measure to Immediate Vote, in Parliamentary Practice: closure, cloture,n. (closure, cloture,v.)

792. END

1. To End, i.e., Bring to Its End or Its Natural End: close, crown, complete, conclude, finish, terminate, top off, wind up,v. (closure, completion, conclusion, termination, n.)

2. To End, i.e., Come to an End: cease, close, conclude, expire, finish, terminate,v.

3. A Coming to an End: completion, conclusion, dissolution, expiration, expiry, termination,n.

4. To Come to the End of a Stated Period: expire, lapse,v. (expiration, lapse,n.)

5. To Draw to an End: wane,v. (wane,n.)

6. The End or Ending: close, closure, completion, conclusion, expiration, finis, finish, last; omega (often in the phrase *the alpha and the omega*—the beginning and the end); terminal, termination, terminus, upshot, windup,n.; *Also:*
1. **catastrophe**—end or conclusion that is attended by misfortune, usually of great proportions; disastrous end or conclusion (catastrophic,adj.)
2. **denouement**—end or outcome of a story, in which the problem or mystery is solved
3. **dissolution**—end (of an association, business partnership, friendship, enterprise, or some similar intangible); end of a meeting or assembly
4. **outcome, denouement**—resulting end

7. Part That Forms the End: terminal,n.

8. The Opposite Ends of the Earth: antipodes,n. (antipodal, antipodean,adj.)

9. Either End of a Railroad, Trolley, Bus, etc., Line: terminal, terminus,n.

10. Physical or Concrete End of Something, n.
1. **butt**—thicker or broader end of something
2. **extremity**—end part of something
3. **stub**—blunt and short end of something
4. **stump**—short, thick end of something
5. **tag**—loose or torn end of something
6. **tip, edge**—end of a thing or place

11. Pointed End: cusp, neb, nib, prong, spire, tip,n.

12. Ended: complete,adj.

13. Able to Be Ended: terminable,adj. (terminability, terminableness,n.)

14. Having a Determinable End: finite,adj. (finiteness,n.)

15. Final: closing, concluding, conclusive, definitive, dernier, eventual, finishing, last, lattermost; supreme (in reference to one's life, as *the supreme hour*, etc.); terminal, terminating, ultimate,adj. (conclusiveness, definitiveness,n.)

16. The Last Possible: ultimate,adj.

17. Of Two Things, Words, Statements, etc., the Last Mentioned: latter,adj.

18. In Its Fixed and Final Form: definitive, adj. (definitiveness,n.)

19. Coming or Occurring at the End: terminal, ultimate,adj.

20. A Finishing Stroke: coup de grâce,n. (French)

21. Next to the Last in a Series: penultimate, adj. (penult, penultimate,n.)

22. Just Preceding the Next to the Last in a Series: antepenultimate,adj. (antepenultimate,n.)

23. Certain Final or Concluding Things, Parts, etc.,n.
1. **epilogue, epilog**—concluding part of a novel or poem that functions to tie the loose ends together; speech, often in verse, at the conclusion of a play, spoken by one of the actors
2. **finale**—final or concluding number or section of musical or other entertainment, a piece of music, a play, etc.
3. **last, omega**—that which is last
4. **peroration**—last part, or summing up, of a speech or argument (perorate,v.)
5. **summation, summing up**—concluding part, speech, etc., in which the main parts or arguments are reviewed, as in a courtroom, etc. (summational,adj. sum up,v.)
6. **swan song**—person's final artistic work, business, or political accomplishment, etc. —so called from the belief that a swan, otherwise voiceless, sings just on the point of death
7. **tag**—concluding part, as of a speech, action, proceedings, etc.; final lines of a speech in a play, or of a song
8. **tail, tail end, tag end**—final part of anything
9. **ultimate**—last or final thing; last thing possible
10. **upshot**—final point
11. **windup**—final part of an activity

24. Writer of an Epilogue: epilogist,n.

25. Speaker of an Epilogue: epilogist, epilogue,n.

26. Theological Doctrine of Final Things or States, Including Death, Immortality, etc.: eschatology,n. (eschatologist,n. eschatological, adj.)

793. BOUNDARY

1. Boundary or Boundaries of a Place: abuttals, ambit, border, bound or bounds, confines, list, mere, mete, precinct, purlieus, suburbs, terminus,n.; *Also:*
1. **circumference, periphery**—external boundary (circumferential, peripheral, adj.)
2. **compass**—enclosing boundary or bounds
3. **edge**—sharply ending boundary
4. **limit**—farthest boundary
5. **pale**—confining boundary

2. That Boundary of a Country That Is Adjacent to Another Country: border, confines, frontier,n. (frontier,adj.)

3. Boundary of a Country Adjacent to Unsettled Regions: frontier,n. (frontier,adj.)

4. One Who Lives on the Frontier: frontiersman,n.

5. Boundary or Bounds of a Body, Space, or Figure,n.
1. **circumference, periphery**—bounds around a circular or fairly circular space or object (circumferential, peripheral, adj.)
2. **circumscription**—outer boundary of a body
3. **perimeter**—outer bounds of a geometric figure (perimetric, perimetrical,adj.)

6. Boundary Line: borderline, boundary, edge,n.

7. Stone Post or Other Marker Showing a Boundary: terminus,n.

8. To Be or Lie on the Boundary of: border, bound,v.

9. Pert. to a Boundary; Marked as, or Placed at, a Boundary: terminal,adj.

10. Sharing a Common Boundary: conterminal, conterminous, coterminous,adj.

11. Bound by Curved Lines: curvilinear,adj.

12. Outside or Beyond the Territorial Boundaries: extraterritorial,adj.

13. Limit; Limits: barrier, border, borderland, bound or bounds, boundary, compass, confines, solstice, termination, terminus,n.

14. Limiting Line or Thing: bound or bounds, boundary, determinant, limit, limitation,n. (limitary,adj.)

15. To Set or Mark Out the Boundary, Bounds, or Limits of: bound, circumscribe, confine, define, delimit, delimitate, demarcate, determine, limit, terminate,v. (circumscription, confinement, delimitation, demarcation, determination, limitation, termination,n.)

16. Limiting; Serving to Limit, or to Mark Out or Set Limits or Bounds: circumscribing, circumscriptive, confining, delimitative, delimiting, determinative, determining, limitary,adj.

17. Limited; Subject to, or Having Limits: bound, circumscribed, confined, definite, delimitated, delimited, determinate, finite, limitary,adj.

18. Having the Same Limits: conterminal, conterminous, coterminous,adj.

19. At or Near the Lowest Possible Limits: marginal,adj. (as lands, operations, producers, etc.)

20. Edge; Border: brim, brink, fringe, margin, rim, verge,n. (marginal,adj.); *Also:*
1. **brim**—top edge of a cup or dish; projecting edge of a hat
2. **brink**—edge at the top of something steep
3. **burr**—rough edge
4. **fringe**—decorative border or edge; edge of something, but not quite inside
5. **selvage**—edge of a woven fabric so made that the threads will not ravel
6. **wayside**—edge of a road

21. Having an Edge or Border: bordered, fringed, marginate, marginated, rimmed,adj.

22. That Which Serves as an Edge or Border: edging,n.

23. To Form an Edge or Border of: border, edge, rim,v.

24. To Provide with an Edge or Border: border, edge; list (cloth); marginate, rim,v. (margination,n.)

25. To Be on the Edge of, Figuratively: border on, border upon, verge on, verge upon; be on the border, borderline, brim, brink, fringe, or verge of,v.

794. DEATH

1. Death: decease, demise, departure, dissolution; dormition (figurative); eternal rest, happy hunting grounds, last breath, last sleep, night, quietus, rest, tomb,n.

2. Death from Accident: casualty,n.

3. Death of an Intangible: dissolution,n.

4. Death of All Members of a Group, Family, Race, Species, etc.: extinction,n.

5. Death of Large Numbers of People, as from Disease, War, etc.; Death in Relation to Population Figures: mortality,n.

6. Death by Hanging: halter,n.

7. Death of Bodily Tissue or Part of the Body, or of a Bodily Organ: gangrene, mortification, necrosis, phagedena,n.

8. To Be or Become Affected by, or to Affect with, Death of Bodily Tissue, etc.: gangrene, mortify, necrose,v. (mortification, n.)

9. Affected by Death of Bodily Tissue: cankered, cankerous, gangrened, gangrenous, mortified, necrosed, necrotic, phagedenous, adj.

10. Pert. or Relating to Death of Bodily Tissue: gangrenous, necrotic, phagedenic, phagedenical,adj.

11. Causing Death of Bodily Tissue: necrotic, adj.

12. Relating or Referring to Death,adj.
1. **ante-mortem**—before death
2. **lethal**—pert. to death
3. **macabre, macaber**—pert. to or suggestive of the allegorical dance in which Death leads skeletons to the grave
4. **mortal**—pert. or relating to death, or the occasion of death
5. **mortuary**—pert. to, or connected with, death
6. **necrotic**—pert. to death
7. **posthumous**—occurring or awarded at some time after the death of the father, author, creator, artist, etc.—said of the publication of literary efforts, birth of children, exhibition of works of art, etc.
8. **post-mortem**—occurring or done after death
9. **post-obit**—effective or to take effect after death

13. After Death—a Latin Phrase: postobitum

14. Resembling, or Like, Death: deadly, deathful, deathlike, deathly, ghastly, mortal, adj. (deadliness, ghastliness,n.)

15. Death Rate: mortality,n.

16. Published Notice of a Person's Death: necrology, obituary,n. (necrological, obituary or obituarian,adj.)

17. Writer of Death Notices: necrologist, obituarian, obituarist,n.

18. Death Instinct: thanatos,n. (Freudian term, contrasted to *eros*, the life instinct)

19. Morbid Desire for Death: necromania,n. (medical)

20. State after Death: eternity,n.

21. The World beyond Death: other world,n.

22. Punishable by Death—of Crimes, etc.: capital,adj.

23. Punishment by Death: capital punishment,n.

24. Apparent Death, i.e., Temporary Cessation of Vital Functions: suspended animation,n.

25. Suspended Animation Caused by a Deficiency of Oxygen and an Excess of Carbon Dioxide in the Blood: asphyxia,n. (asphyxiation,n. asphyxiator,n. asphyxiant,adj. asphyxial,adj. asphyxiate,v.)

26. Agent That Causes Asphyxia: asphyxiant,n.

27. To Die: breathe one's last; croak (slang); decease, depart, expire; fall, drop, sink, etc., dead; give up the ghost; go to the happy hunting grounds, join one's ancestors; kick the bucket (slang); lose one's life, pass away, pass on, perish, succumb,v.

28. To Die before (Someone Else): predecease,v. (predecease,n.)

29. To Die from Lack of Air: drown (in water, etc.), smother, stifle, strangle, suffocate, throttle,v. (smotheration, strangulation, suffocation,n.)

30. To Die from Lack of Food: starve,v. (starvation,n.)

31. Eventually Dying: mortal,adj. (mortal,n. mortality,n.)

32. Dying Together: commorient,adj. (commorient,n.)

33. Dying—of Customs, Institutions, Cultures, and Other Abstractions: moribund, adj.

34. Dead Body; Dead Person: ashes, cadaver, corpse; corpus (humorous); corse (poetic); the deceased; decedent (legal); the defunct, the departed; relics (poetic); remains,n.; *Also:*
1. carcass, carcase—body of a dead animal; slaughtered and dressed body of an edible animal
2. casualty—person who has died in an accident
3. corpse—anything that has died
4. corpus delicti—actual body of a murdered person (legal)
5. mummy—dead body preserved from decay by the ancient Egyptians
6. victim—one who has been killed, as by disease, accident, murder, etc.
7. zombie—dead person reanimated by magic or supernatural powers

35. Pert. to the Dead: defunctive,adj.

36. Like a Corpse: cadaverous,adj. (cadaverousness,n.)

37. Dwelling Place of the Dead: Elysium or Elysian Fields (Greek mythology), Hades, other world,n.

38. Place Where Corpses Are Kept,n.
1. morgue—place where unidentified corpses are kept until claimed
2. mortuary, undertaking parlor—place where corpses are kept before burial

39. List of People Who Have Died: necrology, n. (necrological,adj.)

40. Morbid Attraction to Corpses: necromania,n.

41. Doctrine or Belief that the Spirits of the Dead Can Communicate with the Living: spiritism, spiritualism,n. (spiritist, spiritualist,n. spiritistic, spiritualistic,adj.)

42. Dead: deceased, defunct, departed, inanimate, late, lifeless,adj. (defunctness, inanimateness, lifelessness,n.)

43. Gone to One's Ancestors, i.e., Dead—a Latin Phrase: ad patres

44. Figuratively Dead—of a Business Firm, Periodical, etc.: defunct,adj. (defunctness,n.)

45. Dead; No Longer Alive—of a Species, Race, etc.: extinct,adj.

46. Dead when Delivered—of a Fetus: stillborn,adj. (stillbirth,n.)

47. Not Possessing Life: brute, exanimate, inanimate, inorganic, lifeless,adj. (inanimateness, lifelessness,n.)

48. Lifeless, Figuratively: arid, dead, exanimate, inanimate, inert, languid, languorous, listless, sluggish, spiritless, stodgy, torpid, vapid, washed-out, wooden, zestless,adj. (aridity or aridness, deadness, inanimateness, inertness, languidness, languor, listlessness, sluggishness, stodginess; torpidity, torpidness, or torpor; vapidity or vapidness, woodenness, n.)

49. Dull and Lifeless, as a Look, Stare, etc.: glassy, glazed, glazy, wooden,adj. (glassiness, woodenness,n.)

795. SUICIDE

1. Suicide: self-destruction, self-killing, self-murder; *Also:*
1. hara-kiri, hari-kari—suicide by disembowelment, practiced as the national and honorable method of self-destruction in Japan
2. self-immolation—literal or figurative self-destruction as a sacrifice to a cause (self-immolating,adj.)
3. seppuku—Japanese term for what we call hara-kiri
4. sutteeism—practice, now outlawed and relatively uncommon, by the Hindu widow of committing suicide by throwing herself onto the burning funeral pyre of her dead husband

2. To Commit Suicide: destroy oneself, kill oneself, murder oneself; suicide (colloq.),v.

3. One Who Commits Suicide: felo-de-se (legal), self-destroyer, self-killer, self-murderer, suicide,n. (felones-de-se or felos-de-se, pl.n.); *Also:* 1. suttee—Hindu widow who commits suicide by throwing herself on the burning funeral pyre of her dead husband

4. One Who Attempts to Commit Suicide: suicide,n.

5. Characterized by Attempts at, or Impulses toward, Suicide: suicidal,adj.

6. Relating, Referring, or Pert. to Suicide: self-destroying, self-destructive, self-killing, suicidal,adj.

7. Sacrifice of One's Life: supreme sacrifice, n.

796. KILL

1. To Kill: butcher, destroy, dispatch, do away with; liquidate (slang); murder, put an end to, put an end to the suffering of, put to death, slaughter, slay, smite, strike dead, strike down, take the life of,v.; *Also:*
1. assassinate—kill by surprise or treacherous attack
2. burke—kill in some manner so that revealing marks of murder are not left on the body
3. butcher, slaughter—kill ruthlessly or in great numbers; kill (a domestic animal) for eating or the market
4. crucify—kill, or put to death, by nailing or tying the hands and feet to a cross
5. decimate—kill a large proportion of; kill every tenth person of, after selection by lots
6. drown—kill by keeping the head of under water or other liquid
7. electrocute—execute by means of electricity; kill by an electric shock
8. execute—put to death in accordance with legal order
9. exterminate—kill off completely (a group, species, race, etc.)
10. hang, gibbet—kill or execute by hanging
11. immolate—kill as a sacrifice, or as a sacrifice to the gods
12. liquidate—do away with by killing secretly
13. lynch—kill by hanging, without due process of law
14. massacre—kill (helpless people) in a wanton and unbridled manner
15. murder—kill illegally and with premeditation, malice aforethought, etc. (legal)
16. pith—kill (an animal) by cutting the spinal cord
17. poison—kill by means of poison
18. stone, lapidate—kill by hurling stones at

2. Killing; A Killing,n. *From Sec. 1:* butchery, destruction, dispatch, liquidation, murder, slaughter, slaying; assassination, butchery or slaughter, crucifixion, decimation, drowning, electrocution, execution, extermination, hanging, immolation, liquidation, lynching, massacre, murder, lapidation; *Also:*

1. **auto-da-fé**—execution, usually by burning, of a heretic
2. **battue**—cruel and ruthless slaughter of great numbers
3. **bloodshed**—killing
4. **carnage**—great slaughter of human life, as in war
5. **euthanasia, mercy killing**—act or practice of painlessly putting to death those with an incurable and agonizing disease
6. **hecatomb**—slaughter of a great number of victims
7. **holocaust**—killing of a large number of people by fire
8. **homicide**—killing of any human being, whether lawfully or unlawfully; in law there are various types: murder, manslaughter, justifiable homicide, excusable homicide, felonious homicide, etc. (homicidal,adj.)
9. **manslaughter**—unlawful killing of another, but without premeditation or malice aforethought—may be accidental or involuntary
10. **noyade**—slaughter of many people by drowning, as during the Reign of Terror in Nantes, France
11. **pogrom**—organized slaughter of helpless people, usually those of a minority religion or race, usually with the knowledge or connivance of government officials; specifically, former slaughter of Jews in Russia and other Slavic countries
12. **suicide**—self-killing (suicidal,adj.)
13. **thuggee, thuggery, thuggism, thuggeeism**—assassination, usually by strangling, by a now supposedly disbanded religious group of fanatics in India who made a profession and crusade of murder and robbery
14. **thuggery**—murder
15. **trucidation**—slaughter

3. Killer,n. *From Sec. 1:* butcher, destroyer, murderer, slaughterer, slayer; assassin or assassinator, burker or burkite, butcher, slaughterer, decimator, electrocutioner, executioner, exterminator, hangman, immolator, lyncher, murderer, poisoner; *From Sec. 2:* bloodshedder, homicide, suicide, thug; *Also:*

1. **assassin, bravo**—one hired or selected to commit murder
2. **Bluebeard**—man who murders one wife after another
3. **Cain, cutthroat**—murderer
4. **highbinder**—member of a Chinese band of criminals in the U.S. who hired himself out for killing or other illegal activities; hence, a ruffian or rowdy, or, loosely, a clever cheat, swindler, or thief

4. Killing; Tending to Kill; Causing, or Tending to Cause, Death,adj. *From Sec. 1:* destructive, murderous, slaughterous (destructiveness, murderousness,n.) ; exterminative or exterminatory, murderous, poisonous (murderousness, poisonousness,n.) ; *From Sec. 2:* homicidal, suicidal; *From Sec. 3:* cutthroat; *Also:* baneful, breakneck, deadly, deathful, deathly, fatal, fell, feral, lethal, lethiferous, malign, malignant, mortal, pestilent, tragic, virulent, vital (banefulness, deadliness, fellness, lethality, malignancy, virulence,n.)

5. Descr. of That Which Is Used to Kill, as a Weapon, etc.: deadly, lethal,adj.

6. Having a Deadly or Malignant Influence: baleful,adj. (balefulness,n.)

7. Characterized by, Involving, or Capable of, Murder; Intending to Murder: murderous,adj. (murderousness,n.)

8. Guilty of Murder: bloodguilty, murder-

ous,adj. (bloodguilt or bloodguiltiness, murderousness,n.)

9. Characterized by Great Slaughter; Descr. of Killing in Which Both or All Sides or Participants Sustain Heavy Losses, or Completely, or Almost Completely, Destroy One Another: internecine,adj.

10. That Which Kills, Causes Death, or Ends Life: bane, killer, lethal, quietus,n.

11. To Kill by Stopping from Breathing: asphyxiate, burke, choke; drown (in water, etc.) ; garrote, garotte, or garrotte; smother, stifle, strangle, strangulate, suffocate, throttle,v. (asphyxiation, smotheration, strangulation, suffocation,n. asphyxiant, strangulative or strangulatory, suffocative, adj.)

12. To Kill by Strangling with the String of a Bow: bowstring,v.

13. One Who Kills by Preventing His Victim from Breathing: burker or burkite, garroter or garrotter, smotherer, strangler, throttler, n.

14. Iron Collar, or Collarlike Device, for Strangling a Victim, as Formerly Used, or Like That Formerly Used, in Spain: garrote, garotte, or garrotte,n.

15. To Sever the Head of; To Kill by Severing the Head of: behead, decapitate, decollate; guillotine (with a machine containing a descending blade),v. (beheading, decapitation, decollation, guillotinade,n. decapitator, decollator,n.)

16. Device with a Descending Blade for Beheading: guillotine,n.

17. To Kill the Disease Germs in, or on: disinfect,v. (disinfection,n. disinfector, disinfectant,n.)

18. To Take the Life out of, Figuratively: devitalize,v. (devitalization,n.)

19. Place of Killing,n.
1. **Aceldama, aceldama**—scene of bloodshed, so called from the place where Judas killed himself
2. **gallows, gibbet, scaffold**—wooden device on which criminals are hanged
3. **shambles**—place or scene of killing or slaughter
4. **slaughterhouse, abattoir, butchery, shamble**—place where domestic animals are killed for the market

20. Insanity Marked by a Desire to Kill: andronophonomania, homicidal mania,n. (homicidal maniac,n.)

21. The Killing of a Specific Person,n.
1. **deicide**—of a divine being, esp. Jesus Christ (deicidal,adj.)
2. **filicide**—of one's own son or daughter (filicidal,adj.)
3. **fratricide**—of one's own brother or sister (fratricidal,adj.)
4. **infanticide**—of one's own newborn infant (infanticidal,adj.)
5. **mariticide**—of one's own husband
6. **matricide**—of one's own mother (matricidal,adj.)
7. **parricide**—of one's own parent of either sex, of any superior member of one's close family, or of one's ruler (parricidal,adj.)
8. **patricide**—of one's own father (patricidal,adj.)
9. **regicide, regicidism**—killing of a, or of one's own, king, ruler, governing head, etc. (regicidal,adj.)
10. **sororicide**—of one's own sister (sororicidal,adj.)
11. **tyrannicide**—of a despot or tyrant (tyrannicidal,adj.)
12. **uxoricide**—of one's own wife (uxoricidal, adj.)
13. **vaticide**—of a prophet

22. Killer of a Specific Person,n. *From Sec. 21:* deicide, filicide, fratricide, infanticide, mariticide, matricide, parricide, patricide, regicide, sororicide, tyrannicide, uxoricide, vaticide

23. The Deliberate Killing, or Measures for the Deliberate Killing, of an Entire Racial, Cultural, Religious, etc., Group, as the Extermination of the Jews by Hitler: genocide, n. (genocidal,adj.)

24. The Killing of a Wolf: lupicide,n.

25. The Killing of a Fox, except While Legally Hunting (British): vulpicide,n. (vulpicidal,adj.)

26. One Who Kills a Fox, except While Legally Hunting (British): vulpicide,n.

27. Agent, Substance, etc., for Killing Certain Creatures,n.
1. **insecticide**—insects, bugs, etc. (insecticide, insecticidal,adj.)
2. **pesticide**—destructive insects, rodents, and other pests
3. **raticide**—rats (raticidal,adj.)
4. **rodenticide**—rodents

28. Not to Kill: spare, spare the life of,v.

797. BURIAL

1. To Bury (a Corpse): ensepulcher or ensepulchre, entomb, inhume, inter, sepulcher or sepulchre, tomb,v.

2. Burial of a Corpse: entombment, inhumation, interment, sepulture,n.

3. Pert. to Burial: charnel, funerary, sepulchral,adj.

4. Act or Practice of Burying Alive: vivisepulture,n.

5. To Wrap a Corpse for Burial: cere, enshroud,v.

6. Cemetery: burial ground or grounds; campo santo (Italian); charnel, golgotha, necropolis,n. (necropolitan,adj.)

7. Underground Cemetery, with Galleries and Wall Recesses for Tombs: catacombs,n.

8. Public Burial Ground for Paupers, Criminals, Vagrants, Unknown People, etc.: potter's field,n.

9. Pert. to, Like, or Suggestive of, a Cemetery: charnel, sepulchral,adj.

10. Grave or Other Place or Structure for Corpses,n.
1. **charnel house, charnel**—structure, vault, etc., in which corpses or bones are piled up
2. **crypt**—underground burial vault
3. **dolmen**—prehistoric tomb, an enclosed space made up of an arrangement of huge stones
4. **golgotha**—place of burial
5. **mausoleum**—magnificent tomb for the dead
6. **ossuary**—place where the bones of the dead are deposited
7. **pantheon**—building where the tombs of the illustrious dead of a nation are kept
8. **sepulcher, sepulchre, sepulture**—burial vault; tomb
9. **shrine**—tomb of a saint or other sacred personage
10. **tomb**—grave, whether in earth or stone; any structure, often magnificent, in which a corpse is laid to rest
11. **urn**—the grave (figurative)
12. **vault**—burial room or structure

11. To Serve as a Tomb for: entomb,v. (entombment,n.)

12. Like, or Suggestive of, a Grave or Burial Place: charnel, gravelike, sepulchral, tomblike,adj.

13. Marker, etc., for a Grave,n.
1. **barrow**—mound of earth or stones over an ancient grave
2. **cairn**—heap of stones erected over a grave (cairned,adj.)
3. **headstone, footstone**—stone at the head, or foot, of a grave
4. **tombstone, stone, monument**—stone, usually with inscriptions, etc., placed over a grave or to mark a burial place

14. Monument to a Celebrated Person Whose Remains Lie Buried Elsewhere: cenotaph,n. (cenotaphic,adj.)

15. Gravedigger; One in Charge of Burials in Early Church Days: fossor,n.

16. Box or Container for a Corpse: casket, coffin, pall,n.

17. Coffin of Stone, Usually of Elaborate Design: sarcophagus,n. (sarcophagi, sarcophaguses,pl.n.)

18. Coffin and Stand: bier,n.

19. Frame for a Coffin: bier, catafalque,n.

20. Cloth, etc., for Wrapping a Corpse for Burial: cerecloth, cerements, shroud, winding sheet,n.

21. Cloth Thrown over a Coffin: pall,n.

22. To Bring or Dig Up from Burial: disentomb, disinhume, disinter, exhume,v. (disentombment, disinterment, exhumation,n.)

23. Grave Robber: body snatcher, ghoul, resurrectionist,n. (resurrectionism,n. resurrectionary,adj.)

24. Like, or Characteristic of, a Grave Robber: ghoulish,adj. (ghoulishness,n.)

25. Evil Demon of Oriental Mythology That Robbed Graves and Fed on Corpses: ghoul, n. (ghoulishness,n. ghoulish,adj.)

798. CREMATION

1. To Burn (a Corpse) to Ashes, Instead of Burying It: cremate,v. (cremation,n. cremator,n. crematory,adj.)

2. Advocate of Cremation: cremationist,n.

3. Furnace for Cremating Corpses: cinerator, cremator, crematorium, crematory,n. (crematoria, crematoriums,pl.n.)

4. Establishment or Place Where Corpses Are Cremated: crematorium, crematory,n.

5. Place Where the Ashes of the Dead Are Kept: cinerarium, columbarium,n.

6. Niches for Crematory Urns in a Columbarium: columbaria,pl.n.

7. Vase Used to Hold the Ashes of the Dead: urn,n.

8. Pile of Wood for the Burning of a Corpse, Usually with Funeral Rites: pyre, funeral pyre,n.

799. FUNERAL

1. Funeral; Funeral Rites: exequies, obsequies,n.

2. Vehicle That Transports the Corpse to the Grave: hearse,n.

3. One Who Prepares a Corpse for Burial and Manages a Funeral: mortician, undertaker,n.

4. One Who Walks with the Coffin at a Funeral: pallbearer,n.

5. Pert. or Relating to a Funeral: defunctive, feral, funeral, funerary, funereal,adj.

6. One Who Attends a Funeral: mourner,n.

7. Traditional Exhibition of Sorrow for the Dead: mourning,n. (mourner,n. mourning,adj. mourn,v.)

800. POISON

1. Poison; Poisonous Substance, etc.,n.
   1. **autotoxin**—poisonous substance secreted within one's own body
   2. **bane**—deadly poison
   3. **endotoxin**—poisonous substance found in bacteria and remaining within the bacterial cell until the cell has disintegrated (endotoxic,adj.)
   4. **exotoxin**—poisonous substance excreted by a microorganism (exotoxic,adj.)
   5. **miasma**—poisonous substances or germs in the atmosphere (miasmal, miasmic, miasmatic,adj.)
   6. **ratsbane**—rat poison
   7. **toxalbumin**—poisonous protein
   8. **toxicant**—poisonous drug, substance, or agent
   9. **toxicodendrol**—poisonous oil from poison ivy
   10. **toxin**—poison secreted by an animal or vegetable organism (toxic, toxical,adj.)
   11. **toxitabella**—tablet of poison with skull and crossbones imprinted upon it
   12. **toxoid**—toxin so treated as to render it harmless yet still capable of causing the blood to produce antibodies to it
   13. **venin**—poisonous substance in snake venom
   14. **venom, virus**—poison secreted by snakes, scorpions, bees, etc.

2. Certain Common Poisons: arsenic, atropine, belladonna, bichloride or bichloride of mercury, carbolic acid or phenol, corrosive sublimate, cyanic acid, cyanide, cyanide of potassium, hemlock; hydrocyanic acid or prussic acid (having the odor of bitter almonds); potassium cyanide, strychnine, tartar emetic,n. (arsenic, arsenical, arsenious, or arsenous; strychnic,adj.)

3. Certain Common Poisonous Plants: banewort, belladonna, black nightshade, deadly nightshade, death camass, hemlock, henbane, Jimson weed, nightshade, nux vomica, poison hemlock, poison ivy, poison oak, poison sumac,n.

4. Moral or Intellectual Poison: virus,n.

5. Pert. or Relating to, or Caused by, Poison: toxic,adj.

6. Having a Gland for the Secretion of Poisonous Substances, as Certain Snakes, Bees, etc.; Able to Inflict a Poisonous Bite, Wound, Sting, etc.: venomous,adj. (venomousness,n.)

7. Poison Fang of a Centipede: toxicognath, n.

8. Resembling Poison: toxicoid,adj.

9. Poisonous: baneful, mephitic, pestilent, toxic, toxical, toxicant, venenous, venomous; viperous (as snakes, etc.); virulent,adj. (banefulness, toxicity, venomousness, virulence,n.)

10. Producing Poison or Poisonous Substances: toxicogenic, toxiferous, toxigenous, adj.

11. To Make Poisonous; To Poison: envenom, taint, venom,v.

12. Any Disease Caused by Poison: toxicopathy,n. (toxicopathic,adj.)

13. Illness Produced by the Excessive Use of Strychnine: strychninism,n.

14. State of Being Poisoned: toxicosis,n.

15. Poisoned State Resulting from Absorption into the Blood Stream of Disease-Pro-

ducing Bacteria: sepsis,n. (septic,n. septic, adj.)

16. Poisoned State Caused by the Accumulation in the Blood of Substances Normally Voided in the Urine: uremia,n. (uremic,adj.)

17. Poisoning: toxication,n.

18. Certain Specific Poisonings,n.
   1. **arsenism, arseniasis**—chronic poisoning from arsenic
   2. **autointoxication, autotoxemia, autotoxicosis, autotoxis**—self-poisoning, i.e., poisoning from the production of toxic materials by one's own body or system
   3. **blood poisoning**—poisoned condition of the blood caused by toxic substances or disease-producing microorganisms
   4. **botulism**—poisoning caused by a bacillus in preserved or canned food
   5. **copremia**—poisoning from absorption by the blood of fecal products
   6. **plumbism**—lead poisoning
   7. **ptomaine poisoning**—poisoning caused by substances formed by the action of putrefactive bacteria
   8. **pyemia**—form of blood poisoning in combination with the development of abscesses (pyemic,adj.)
   9. **sapremia**—form of blood poisoning caused by the toxins from certain putrefactive bacteria (sapremic,adj.)
   10. **septicemia**—blood poisoning caused by bacteria (septicemic,adj.)
   11. **toxemia**—blood poisoning caused by the absorption of poisonous products into the system (toxemic,adj.)

19. Afflicted by Lead Poisoning: saturnine, adj.

20. To Become Gradually More Poisoned—of Tissue, Wounds, etc.: fester,v.

21. Morbid Desire to Consume Poison: toxicomania,n. (toxicomaniac,adj.)

22. Habit of Eating Poison: toxicophagy,n. (toxicophagous,adj.)

23. To Free of Poison: detoxicate,v. (detoxication,n.)

24. That Which Counteracts, etc., the Effects of Poison,n.
   1. **antidote, counterpoison, mithridate**—remedy that neutralizes the effects of a poison (antidotal,adj.)
   2. **antitoxin**—antibody formed in the body that counteracts the effect of a poison or poisonous substance introduced into the body (antitoxic,adj.)
   3. **antivenin**—antitoxin to snake poison; serum containing this
   4. **theriaca**—in ancient medicine, an antidote (theriacal,adj.)
   5. **toxicide**—agent that destroys poisonous substances

25. Counteracting the Effects of Poison: antidotal, antitoxic,adj.

26. Science of Poisons, Their Effects, Antidotes, etc.: toxicology,n. (toxicologist,n. toxicological,adj.)

801. DESTRUCTION

1. To Destroy: blast, blight, break down, consume, demolish, dissolve, obliterate, overthrow, ravage, ruin, ruinate, smash, spoil, unmake, wreck,v.; Also:
   1. **decimate**—destroy a great part of
   2. **dilapidate**—bring (a structure, etc.) to ruin, as by neglect
   3. **disintegrate**—destroy the unity of
   4. **gut**—destroy the interior or contents of
   5. **mutilate**—destroy an essential part of
   6. **pulverize**—destroy as by crushing, smashing, etc.

7. **raze, demolish**—destroy (a structure, etc.) by leveling to the ground
8. **sabotage**—destroy (an employer's property or means of production); destroy (property or means useful in the conduct of war) for the purposes of traitorously aiding the enemy
9. **shipwreck**—destroy (a ship at sea) by any of various means
10. **torpedo**—destroy by blowing up
11. **unmake**—destroy the nature, qualities, or form of
12. **vandalize**—maliciously destroy (works of art, monuments, the property of others, etc.); commit malicious destruction upon such property (vandal, vandalistic, vandalic, vandalish,adj.)
13. **wreck**—destroy by violence

2. Destruction,n. *From Sec. 1:* blight, consumption, demolishment or demolition, dissolution, obliteration, overthrow; ravagement, ravage, or ravages; ruin or ruination, spoilage, wreck or wreckage; decimation, dilapidation, disintegration, mutilation, pulverization, sabotage, shipwreck, vandalism, wreck or wreckage; *Also:* desolation, rack and ruin, smash or smashup, undoing, wrack; *Also:*
1. **biblioclasm**—destruction of books
2. **havoc, ravage**—general and extreme destruction
3. **lysis**—cell destruction (lytic,adj.)
4. **phagocytosis**—destruction of harmful substances by certain white blood corpuscles

3. Destructive,adj. *From Sec. 1:* blasting, blighting, etc.; consumptive, obliterative, ruinous, disintegrative, mutilative; vandalistic, vandal, vandalic, or vandalish (consumptiveness,n.); *Also:* baneful, cutthroat, fell, lethiferous, pernicious, slaughterous (banefulness, fellness, perniciousness,n.)

4. Destroyer,n. *From Sec. 1:* blast, blight, consumer, demolisher, obliterator, spoiler, wrecker; decimator, disintegrator, gutter, mutilator, pulverizer, demolitionist, saboteur, vandal, wrecker; *From Sec. 2:* biblioclast, phagocyte (phagocytal, phagocytic,adj.); *Also:*
1. **bane**—that which destroys
2. **pest**—destructive insect; that which resembles a plague in destructiveness
3. **plague**—source of great destruction
4. **thunderbolt**—that which causes great and sudden destruction

5. Secret Sympathizers with the Enemy in Times of War Who Sabotage, Spy, etc.: fifth column,n. (fifth columnist,n.)

6. Device, Idea, Principle, etc., of Placing Agents within a Foreign Country for Purposes of Sabotage, Subversion, etc.: Trojan horse,n.

7. Policy of Destruction, under Official Orders in Wartime, of All Things of Possible Use to an Invading Enemy: scorched earth,n.

8. Destructive to Crops, etc. (of Insects, Animals, or Pests): predatory,adj.

9. Showing a Desire to Destroy: sinistrous, adj.

10. Philosophy or Doctrine that Destruction Is Good for Its Own Sake, Conditions of Life Being Incorrigibly Bad: nihilism,n. (nihilist,n. nihilistic,adj.)

11. To Destroy, i.e., Lay Waste (a Place): desolate, devastate, ravage, waste,v. (desolation, devastation, ravagement, waste,n.)

12. To Destroy Figuratively: annul, blast, blight, damn, dash, demolish, extinguish, invalidate, nullify, obliterate, overthrow; pulverize (as an argument, etc.); quell, quench, ruin, scuttle, shatter, shipwreck, smash, spoil,

torpedo, undermine, undo, unmake, void, wreck,v.; *Also:*
1. **assassinate**—destroy treacherously, as a person's name, character, reputation, etc.
2. **neutralize**—destroy the intrinsic or individual qualities or properties of
3. **wreck**—destroy the financial status or condition of

13. Figurative Destruction,n. *From Sec. 12:* annulment, damnation, demolishment or demolition, extinguishment or extinction, invalidation, nullification, obliteration, overthrow, pulverization, ruin or ruination, shatterment, shipwreck, smash or smashup, undoing, wreck or wreckage; assassination, neutralization; *Also:*
1. **liberticide**—destruction of freedom (liberticide,n. liberticide, liberticidal,adj.)
2. **suicide**—destruction of one's own best interests or welfare (suicidal,adj.)

14. To Destroy Gradually or Little by Little: corrode, erode, sap, undermine, waste, waste away, whittle, whittle down,v. (corrosion, waste,n. corrosive,adj.)

15. To Destroy or Ruin Completely; To Reduce to Nothing: annihilate, annul, demolish, devour, disannul, discreate, exterminate, extirpate, smash, subvert, undo, void, wreck,v.

16. Complete Destruction or Ruin: annihilation, annulment, demolishment or demolition, disannulment, discreation, extermination, extirpation, perdition, subversion or subversal, undoing, wreck or wreckage,n. (annihilative, exterminative or exterminatory, extirpative, subversive,adj.)

17. To Put Out, as a Fire, Flame, or Analogous Abstraction: extinguish, quench, slake, smother, stifle, snuff out,v. (extinguishment or extinction,n.)

18. To Put Out (a Light): douse (colloq.); extinguish, turn off, turn out,v. (extinguishment,n.)

19. To Go Out, as a Fire, etc., or an Analogous Abstraction: quench,v.

20. To Eat Away,v.
1. **canker**—eat away, as if by ulcers or gangrene
2. **corrode**—eat away by, or as if by, acid or chemical action; eat away by, or as if by, gnawing; eat away gradually (corrosion, n.)
3. **erode**—eat away, usually by mechanical action (erosion,n.)
4. **gnaw**—eat away, literally or figuratively

21. To Become Eaten Away,v. *From Sec. 20:* corrode, erode (corrosion, erosion,n.)

22. Eating, or Capable of Eating, Away,adj. *From Sec. 20:* cankerous, corrosive, erosive (corrosiveness, corrosivity,n.); *Also:* 1. caustic —capable of eating away by chemical action (causticity,n.)

23. Agent or Substance That Eats Away,n. *From Sec. 20:* canker, corrosive; erodent (medical); *From Sec. 22:* caustic

24. Able to Be Eaten Away,adj. *From Sec. 20:* corrodible or corrosible, erodible or erosible (corrodibility, corrosibility, or corrosibleness, n.)

25. To Wear (Something) Away,v.
1. **abrade**—wear away by rubbing or friction
2. **batter**—wear away, or wear away, by hard use
3. **corrode**—wear away gradually
4. **erode**—wear away gradually; wear away (land) by the action of water, etc.
5. **excoriate**—wear away the skin from, as by scratching, rubbing, chafing, etc.
6. **rust**—wear away figuratively, as by time, inaction, etc.
7. **sap, undermine**—wear away the foundation of, literally or figuratively

26. To Wear Away, i.e., Become Worn Away, v. *From Sec. 25:* abrade, corrode, erode, rust (abrasion, corrosion, erosion,n.)

27. A Wearing (Something) Away,n. *From Sec. 25:* abrasion, corrosion, erosion, excoriation; *Also:*
1. **attrition**—a wearing away by friction; gradual process of wearing away or down
2. **detrition**—a wearing away or off

28. Wearing (Something), or Tending to Wear (Something), Away,adj. *From Sec. 25:* abradant or abrasive, corrosive, erosive (corrosiveness,n.) ; *From Sec. 27:* attritive

29. Worn Away,adj. *From Sec. 25:* abraded, battered, corroded, eroded or erose, excoriated or excoriate, rusted or rusty, sapped, undermined; *From Sec. 27:* attrited, detrited

30. A Spot or Place That Is Worn Away,n. *From Sec. 25:* abrasion, excoriation

31. Substance Used for Wearing Away,n. *From Sec. 25:* abradant or abrasive, corrosive; erodent (medical)

32. Able to Be Worn Away,adj. *From Sec. 25:* corrodible or corrosible, erodible or erosible (corrodibility, corrosibility, or corrosibleness, n.)

33. To Be or Become Destroyed or Ruined: blast, blight, break down, perish, ruin, wreck, v. (blight, ruin, wreck or wreckage,n.) ; *Also:*
1. **dilapidate**—fall into partial ruin, as, esp., a structure (dilapidation,n.)
2. **shipwreck**—be destroyed, literally of a ship, or figuratively of hopes, plans, etc. (shipwreck,n.)
3. **waste, waste away**—be gradually destroyed—of body tissue, strength, etc. (waste,n.)

34. Destroyed or Ruined,adj. *From Sec. 33:* blasted, blighted, ruinate or ruinous, dilapidated, wasted or wasted away

35. Able to Be Destroyed or Ruined: destructible, perishable,adj. (destructibility, perishability or perishableness,n.)

36. That Which Can Be Destroyed: perishable,n.

37. Not Able to Be Destroyed: imperishable, indestructible,adj. (imperishability or imperishableness, indestructibility or indestructibleness,n.)

38. That Which Is Left after Destruction: ashes, relics, remains, ruins, wreck, wreckage, n.

39. Person Who Has Been Destroyed: victim, n.

802. BREAKAGE

1. To Break, i.e., Become Broken, Undergo Breakage, etc.,v.
1. **burst**—break apart or into pieces from internal pressure or from strong impact
2. **chip**—break off in thin or small pieces, as china, crockery, bone, etc.
3. **crack**—break with a sharp sound
4. **crash**—break with a sudden and very loud noise
5. **crumble**—break into very small pieces
6. **crush**—break into very fine pieces as a result of being ground, pressed, pounded, etc.
7. **fracture**—break; of a bone, cartilage, etc., become broken or suffer breakage
8. **fragment**—break into small pieces
9. **pulverize**—break into very small particles
10. **rupture**—become broken (of a blood vessel, soft tissue, etc.) ; break apart
11. **sever**—break open; break apart
12. **shatter**—break, or break suddenly, into pieces

13. shiver, splinter—break into many small or thin pieces
14. smash—break suddenly and/or violently into many fragments
15. split—break lengthwise or in or into layers
16. stave—break; become broken; have a hole broken into it, as a ship; have its sides broken or broken in, as a barrel, etc. (stove, past tense and past participle)

2. To Break, i.e., Subject to Breakage or Cause to Break,v. *From Sec. 1:* burst, chip, crack, crash, crumble, crush, fracture, pulverize, rupture, sever, shatter, shiver, splinter, smash, split, stave or stave in; *Also:*
1. **breach**—cause a break in; break an opening in; break an opening in or through (a wall, dike, fortification, etc.)
2. **crackle**—break with rapidly repeated sharp sounds
3. **nick**—cause a small broken place in, as in china, glass, etc.; chip

3. Breakage; A Breaking; A Break,n. *From Sec. 1:* burst, chip, crack, crash, crush, fracture, fragmentation, pulverization, rupture, severance, shatterment, smash or smashage, split; *From Sec. 2:* breach, crackle, nick

4. Breakable; Easily Breaking or Broken, adj. *From Sec. 1:* fracturable, rupturable, severable, shattery, shivery, splintery; *Also:* brittle, crisp, crispy, delicate, fragile, frail, frangible (brittleness, crispness, delicacy, fragility or fragileness, frailness, frangibility, n.)

5. Breaking Easily, Like Glass: vitreous,adj. (vitreosity, vitreousness,n.)

6. Hard, but Breaking Easily: crackly, crisp, crispy,adj. (crispness,n.)

7. Crumbling Easily: crumbly, friable, powdery,adj. (crumbliness, friability or friableness,n.)

8. Broken Place: breach, break, chip, crack, fracture, nick, split,n.

9. To Burst: blow out, blow up, detonate, explode, pop, rend, rift, rive, rupture, shatter, split, split asunder,v.; *Also:*
1. **erupt**—burst forth, as volcanic matter, etc.; burst, throwing matter, as a volcano, geyser, etc.
2. **fulminate**—explode with suddenness and great violence
3. **implode, irrupt**—burst inward

10. To Burst, i.e., Cause to Burst,v. *From Sec. 9:* blow out, blow up, detonate, explode, pop, rift, rupture, shatter, split, split asunder; fulminate; *Also:*
1. **blast**—burst or shatter with an explosive, as dynamite, etc.
2. **bomb**—explode a bomb in, at, or against; hurl or drop a bomb or bombs upon
3. **dynamite**—blow up with dynamite
4. **torpedo**—blow up (a ship) with a torpedo, i.e., a self-powered explosive

11. A Burst; A Bursting,n. *From Sec. 9:* blowout, blowup, detonation, explosion, rupture, shatterment, split; eruption, fulmination, implosion, irruption (detonative, explosive; eruptive, fulminant, irruptive,adj.) ; *From Sec. 10:* blast

12. An Explosive,n. *From Sec. 10:* bomb, dynamite, torpedo (dynamitic,adj.) ; *Also:*
1. **detonator**—substance that explodes; explosive substance that causes another to explode
2. **nitroglycerin, nitroglycerine**—highly explosive liquid
3. **petard**—explosive device used in earlier times to blow in a gate, door, wall, etc.
4. **T.N.T., TNT**—high explosive (abbreviations of *trinitrotoluene* or *trinitrotoluol*)

13. Device, as a Percussion Cap, etc., That Causes a Substance to Explode: detonator, n.

14. One, Esp. a Revolutionary, Who Uses Dynamite: dynamiter, dynamitist,n.

15. To Crack, i.e., Become Cracked,v.
1. chap—of the skin, become cracked, rough, and red, as from cold, etc.; of the earth or of wood, become cracked, or open in cracks
2. fracture—crack

16. To Crack, i.e., Cause a Crack or Cracks in,v. *From Sec. 15:* chap, fracture; *Also:*
1. crackle—crack with rapidly repeated, sharp sounds
2. craze—make tiny cracks on the glaze or surface of (pottery)

17. A Crack,n. *From Sec. 15:* chap, fracture; *From Sec. 16:* craze

18. Network of Tiny Cracks Deliberately Made in the Glaze of Some Porcelain; Cracked Surface of Such Porcelain: crackle, n.

19. Having Cracks in the Surface or Glaze (of Pottery): crackled, crazed,adj.

20. Pottery with Fine Cracks on the Surface or Glaze: crackle, crackleware,n.

21. To Break or Fall Apart: break up, collapse, crash; crumble (colloq.); crumple (colloq.); disintegrate, disrupt, pulverize,v. (breakup, collapse, crash, disintegration, disruption, pulverization,n. disrupt,adj.)

22. Breaking Up of Ice on a River: debacle,n.

23. To Cause to Break or Fall Apart: break up, collapse, disintegrate, disrupt, pulverize,v. (breakup, collapse, disintegration, disruption, pulverization,n. disintegrative, disruptive, adj.)

24. To Break, Pull, or Throw Down (a Structure): demolish, raze, wreck,v. (demolition or demolishment, wreckage,n. demolitionist or demolisher,n.)

25. To Break Up, or Cause to Break Up, into Component Parts: disband (a group), disintegrate, dissolve, pulverize, resolve,v. (disbandment, disintegration, dissolution, pulverization, resolution,n. disintegrative, dissolutive,adj.)

26. To Break Down, or Cause to Break Down, into Partial Ruin, as from Neglect, etc.: dilapidate,v. (dilapidation,n.)

27. Broken-Down (of Structures, etc.): dilapidated, ruinous, tumble-down,adj.

28. To Have a Mental, Moral, or Physical Breakdown: crack up,v. (crack-up,n.)

29. To Break (a Law, Rule, Promise, etc.): breach, contravene, infract, infringe, transgress, violate,v. (breach, contravention, infraction, infringement, transgression, violation,n. contravener, infractor, infringer, transgressor, violator,n. transgressive, violative,adj.)

30. A Gross Violation of Law or Decency: outrage,n.

31. To Commit a Transgression of Law: offend, trespass,v. (offense, trespass,n. offender, trespasser,n.)

32. Violation of the Public Peace: breach of the peace

33. A Breach of Peaceful Relations: rupture, n.

803. HARM

1. To Harm: blemish, bruise, damage; disserve (figuratively); hurt, injure, mar, outrage; prejudice (figuratively or legally);
ravage, scotch, shatter, spoil; trample on (figuratively); wound, wrong,v.; *Also:*
1. bruise, contuse—injure (the skin) but without penetration
2. maim, mutilate—injure by removing a bodily member or limb, or an essential part
3. mangle—bruise or injure badly, or with repeated blows; injure (something) while it is being made
4. prejudice—harm by one's action; harm figuratively, as one's right, cause, etc.
5. raze—wound slightly
6. ruin—damage beyond repair
7. sabotage—damage (property, etc.) maliciously, as by workmen during a strike or by enemy agents during wartime, etc. (saboteur,n.)
8. scathe—injure by fire
9. scuff—injure the surface of by continued use or scraping
10. shock, traumatize—cause physical or emotional injury or wounds to; injure while operating on (medical)
11. sprain, wrench—injure (a bodily part, muscle, joint, etc.) by a sudden twist, etc.
12. stab—wound with a pointed instrument
13. vandalize—damage (works of art, monuments, the property of others, etc.) maliciously; commit malicious damage upon works of art, monuments, the property of others, etc. (vandal,n. vandal, vandalistic, vandalic, vandalish,adj.)
14. wing—wound in the arm or wing; wound, as with a bullet, without killing
15. wound—injure by cutting, stabbing, shooting, etc., i.e., by piercing the skin of

2. Harm; A Harming,n. *From Sec. 1:* bruise, damage, disservice, hurt, injury, mar, prejudice, ravage or ravages, spoilage, wound, wrong; bruise, contusion, mutilation, ruin or ruination, sabotage, scuff, sprain, wrench, shock, trauma (traumata,pl.) or traumatism; stab, vandalism, wound; *Also:*
1. battery—unlawful bodily injury
2. casualty—injury from accident, battle, etc.
3. concussion—injury to the brain, spinal cord, etc., caused by a blow or fall (concussive, concussional,adj.)
4. detriment—harm; injury; damage
5. grievance—wrong or injury considered as grounds for complaint
6. lesion—injury; hurt; wound
7. mayhem, maihem—unlawful and violent bodily injury or mutilation that deprives a person of the use of his limbs or members for self-defense
8. mischief—harm; injury
9. violence—harm; injury; harmful and rough treatment or action
10. wear and tear—normal injury, etc., from use

3. Harmful,adj. *From Sec. 1:* damaging, hurtful, injurious, prejudicial, ravaging; prejudicial, ruinous, traumatic; vandal, vandalistic, vandalic, or vandalish (hurtfulness, injuriousness, ruinousness,n.); *From Sec. 2:* detrimental, mischievous (mischievousness, n.); *Also:* baneful, deleterious, evil, malefic, maleficent, malign, malignant, mephitic, nasty, nocuous, noisome, noxious, outrageous, pernicious, pestilent, scatheful, sinistrous, wicked (banefulness, deleteriousness, evilness, maleficence; malignance, malignancy, or malignity; nastiness, nocuousness, noisomeness, noxiousness, outrageousness, perniciousness, wickedness,n.); *Also:*
1. anti-social—harmful to the welfare of the community
2. baleful, sinistrous—harmful in influence (balefulness,n.)
3. deleterious—harmful to the organism when breathed in, eaten, drunk, etc.

4. dysgenic—harmful to heredity, or to the heredity of a race, stock, etc.

5. nocuous, noisome, noxious, vicious, virulent—harmful to the mind or body (nocuousness, noisomeness, noxiousness, viciousness, virulence or virulency,n.)

6. pestiferous, pestilent—harmful to society, morals, peace, etc.

7. pestilential—morally harmful

8. predatory—harmful to crops, etc.—of insects, rodents, pests, etc.

9. unhealthy, unhealthsome, unwholesome, demoralizing—harmful to morals (unhealthiness, unwholesomeness,n.)

4. Spreading Harmful Notions, Practices, etc.: pestiferous,adj.

5. Known to Be Harmful as a Remedy or Medication: contraindicated,adj.

6. Remedy or Medication That Would Be Harmful in a Specific Circumstance or Case: contraindicant,n.

7. To Show Signs of the Harmfulness of a Remedy or Medication: contraindicate,v. (contraindication,n.)

8. Indicative of the Possibility of Harm: menacing, sinister, threatening,adj. (sinisterness,n.)

9. To Offer or Promise Harm to: menace, threaten,v. (menace, threat,n.)

10. Disposed to Harm: malignant,adj. (malignance, malignancy, malignity,n.)

11. Expression of a Wish that God Bring Harm to Someone: curse, malediction,n. (curse,v. maledictory,adj.)

12. Wishing Harm (to Someone): evilminded, malevolent, malicious, malign,adj. (evil-mindedness, malevolence, malice or maliciousness; malignance, malignancy, or malignity,n.)

13. Cause of Harm: curse, evil; evil eye (i.e., eye that, by a glance, can cause harm or injury),n. (evil-eyed,adj.)

14. Any Harmful Thing That Tends to, or Does, Spread: cancer,n. (cancerous,adj.)

15. Mark of Injury: blemish, scar,n.

16. Surface Injury to, or Mark of Injury on, the Skin or Flesh, as by a Blow, etc.: bruise, contusion, mouse, wale, weal, welt, wheal,n.

17. Wearing Away of the Skin by Friction; The Spot of Such Wearing Away: abrasion,n.

18. Injury That Penetrates the Skin, as by Cutting, etc.: wound,n.

19. To Show the Effects or Marks of Injury: bruise,v.

20. Mark or Effect of an Injury to the Feelings, Reputation, etc.: bruise, scar, wound, n.

21. Injured in One's Rights: aggrieved,adj.

22. To Sustain Harm, Injury, Damage, Loss, Disadvantage, etc.; To Sustain (Such): suffer,v.

23. Easily Hurt, Injured, or Damaged: delicate,adj. (delicacy,n.)

24. Capable of Being Harmed, Injured, or Wounded: vulnerable,adj. (vulnerability or vulnerableness,n.)

25. One Who Is Harmed or Injured: casualty (by accident, battle, etc.), victim,n.

804. UNHARMED

1. Unharmed: intact, scatheless, scot-free, sound, spared, unblemished, unbruised, undamaged, unhurt, uninjured, unmarred; un-

prejudiced (as a case, cause, etc.); unscarred, unscathed, unspoiled, unwounded, whole,adj.

2. Not to Harm: spare,v.

3. Unable to Be Injured or Wounded: inviolable, invulnerable, uninjurable,adj. (inviolability or inviolableness, invulnerability or invulnerableness,n.)

4. To Reduce the Harmfulness of (a Germ, etc.): attenuate,v. (attenuation,n.)

5. Harmless: hurtless, innocent, innocuous, inoffensive, offenseless,adj. (innocence, innocuousness, inoffensiveness,n.)

6. Causing No Harm; Not Harmful: harmless, innocuous, inoffensive, offenseless, undamaging, undetrimental, unhurtful, uninjurious, unpernicious; unprejudicial (to a case, cause, etc.),adj.

805. SPOILAGE

1. To Spoil (Something): blemish, blot, botch, butcher, impair, mar, scar, vitiate,v. (botchery, butchery, impairment, vitiation,n. botcher, butcher, impairer, vitiator,n.); *Also:*

1. adulterate, deacon, doctor—spoil by mixing in something inferior, or in some way rendering impure (adulteration,n. adulterator,n. adulterant,n. adulterant, adj.)

2. batter—impair by hard use

3. botch, butcher—spoil by inferior work or performance (botchery, butchery,n. botcher, butcher,n.)

4. impair—spoil the value or excellence of (impairment,n. impairer,n.)

5. mangle—spoil in making, doing, or performing (mangler,n.)

6. mutilate—spoil by removing, or damaging beyond repair, essential parts or part of (mutilation,n. mutilator,n. mutilative, adj.)

2. To Spoil the Appearance of: blemish, blot, deface, deform, disfeature, disfigure, mar, scar,v. (defacement, deformation, disfeaturement, disfigurement or disfiguration,n. deformative or deformational,adj.); *Also:*

1. deform—mar in form or bodily shape (deformation,n. deformative or deformational,adj.)

2. disfeature—mar the beauty of shape or outline of (disfeaturement,n.)

3. vandalize—deface (artistic works, monuments, the property of others, etc.); commit such defacement (vandalism,n. vandal,n. vandal, vandalistic, vandalic, vandalish,adj.)

3. To Become Marred in Form or Bodily Shape: deform,v. (deformation,n. deformity, n.)

4. To Mar the Appearance of by, or as by, Twisting out of Shape: contort, deform, distort, gnarl, warp,v. (contortion, deformation, distortion, warpage,n. contortive, deformative, distortive or distortional,adj. gnarly, adj.)

5. Mark, Injury, etc., That Spoils the Appearance: blemish, blot, blotch, defacement, deformity, disfigurement, macula, maculation, macule, mar, scar, spot,n.

6. Mark or Blemish Left by a Healed Wound, Burn, etc.: cicatrix, scar,n. (cicatricial,adj. scar,v.)

7. Act of Spoiling: spoilage,n.

8. That Which Is Spoiled: spoilage,n.

9. Unspoiled: inviolate, unadulterated, unblemished, unimpared, unmarred, unscarred, adj. (inviolacy or inviolateness,n.)

806. DECAY

1. To Decay, i.e., **Become Decayed**: blast, blight, consume, crumble, decline, disintegrate, dissolve, fester; molder, moulder, molder away, or moulder away; rot, shrivel, waste away, wither,v.; *Also:*
1. **addle**—become rotten (of eggs)
2. **atrophy**—waste away from lack of nourishment, use, exercise, etc.
3. **decompose**—decay by breaking down or by undergoing disintegrating chemical changes
4. **dilapidate**—fall into decay, as a structure, etc.
5. **perish**—decay and disappear
6. **pine, pine away**—waste away, as from grief, longing, pain, hunger, etc.
7. **putrefy, putresce**—decay, with the attendant offensiveness of odor and appearance (of animal tissue or matter, or organic materials)
8. **spoil**—decay, usually to a limited extent (of food)
9. **wither**—decay from lack of moisture, as flowers, plants, leaves, etc.

2. To Decay, i.e., **Cause to Decay**,v. *From Sec. 1:* blast, blight, disintegrate, fester, molder or moulder, rot, shrivel, waste, wither; addle, atrophy, decompose, dilapidate, putrefy, spoil, wither

3. Decay; Act, Process, or State of Decay or Decaying, or of Causing to Decay,n. *From Sec. 1:* blast, blight, consumption, decline, disintegration, dissolution, rot, waste; atrophy, decomposition, dilapidation, putrefaction, spoilage (atrophic,adj.); *Also:*
1. **breakdown**—chemical decomposition
2. **caries, cariosity**—decay of animal tissue or bone, generally; tooth decay, specifically
3. **contabescence**—a wasting away; atrophy; marasmus
4. **decadence, decadency**—moral, spiritual, social, etc., decay
5. **marasmus**—gradual wasting away of the bodily tissues from poor or insufficient food supply, esp. in infants; wasting away from old age, malnutrition, etc., rather than from disease (marasmic, marasmous, marantic,adj.)

4. Decayed,adj. *From Sec. 1:* blasted, blighted, crumbled, disintegrated, dissolved, festered, rotted or rotten, shriveled, wasted, withered (rottenness,n.); addle, atrophied, decomposed, dilapidated; putrefied, putrefacted, or putrid; spoiled, withered (putridity or putridness,n.); *From Sec. 3:* carious, contabescent, decadent, marismic or marasmous (cariousness or cariosity,n.)

5. In the Process of Becoming Decayed or Putrefied: putrescent,adj. (putrescence, putrescency,n. putresce,v.)

6. Person Who Is Morally, Spiritually, Socially, etc., Decayed: decadent,n.

7. Tending to Decay: putrid,adj. (putridity, putridness,n.)

8. Subject to Decay: perishable (of foods), putrescible, putrefactible,adj. (perishability or perishableness, putrescibility,n.)

9. A Food Subject to Decay: perishable,n.

10. Causing or Producing Decay: putrefacient, putrefactive; pythogenic or pythogenetic (as certain diseases, etc.); saprogenic or saprogenous (as certain bacteria); septic, adj. (pythogenesis,n.)

11. Agent or Substance That Causes or Produces Decay: putrefacient, putrefactive, septic,n.

12. Pert. to Decay: putrefactive, putrescent, putrid, saprogenic, saprogenous, septic,adj.

13. Arising, Resulting, or Deriving from Decay: putrid; pythogenic or pythogenetic (as certain diseases, etc.); saprogenic, saprogenous, septic,adj. (putridity or putridness, pythogenesis,n.)

14. Indicating, or Smelling Like, Decay: putrid,adj. (putridity, putridness,n.)

15. Changes Caused by Decay in Dead Tissues: gangrene,n. (gangrenous,adj.)

16. Decaying Flesh of a Dead Animal: carrion, offal,n.

17. Like the Decaying Flesh of a Dead Animal: carrion,adj.

18. Withering but Not Falling Off—of Leaves, etc.: marcescent,adj. (marcescence, n.)

19. Plant with Such Withered Parts: marcescent,n.

20. Plant Disease That Causes Withering: blight,n.

21. Organism, Insect, or Thing That Causes Decay or Withering: blast, blight,n.

22. Biological Study of the Decaying Stages of Groups, Esp. Those Almost Extinct: geratology,n. (geratologic,adj.)

807. REALITY

1. Real: actual, authentic or authentical; concrete (i.e., not abstract or theoretical); factual, genuine, simon-pure, veritable,adj. (actuality, authenticity, concreteness; fact, factuality, or factualness; genuineness, veritableness or verity,n.)

2. A Reality, i.e., **That Which Is Real**: actuality, fact, verity,n.

3. Real, i.e., **Not Pretended**: candid, frank, genuine, simplehearted, sincere, single, true, unaffected, unashamed, undissembled, undissimulated, unfaked, unfeigned, unpretended, adj. (candidness or candor, frankness, genuineness, simpleheartedness, sincerity or sincereness, singleness, truth or trueness, unaffectedness, undissembledness,n.)

4. Having Real or Actual Existence: actual, concrete, corporeal, material; objective (philosophical term); palpable (i.e., perceivable to the senses); phenomenal (i.e., known through the senses or experience); physical, real; sensible (i.e., perceivable through the senses); substantial, substantive, tangible,adj. (actuality, concreteness; corporeality, corporeity, or corporealness; materiality, objectivity or objectiveness, palpability, phenomenality, physicality, reality, sensibleness, substantiality or substantialness, substantiveness, tangibility or tangibleness,n.)

5. That Which Has a Real or Actual Existence: actuality, concrete, entity, fact, materiality, matter, object, phenomenal; phenomenon (phenomena,pl.); reality, substance, substantial, substantive, verity,n.

6. To Cause to Turn into Reality or Actuality: actualize, corporealize, materialize,v. (actualization, corporealization, materialization,n.)

7. To Turn into or Become Reality: materialize,v. (materialization,n.)

8. In Reality; In Actuality: de facto (Latin)

9. To Assume as a Reality: hypostatize, hypostasize,v. (hypostatization, hypostasization,n.)

10. Concerned with, or Interested in, What Is Real, Rather than with the Theoretical or Ideal: down-to-earth, realistic,adj. (realism,n. realist,n.)

11. Treatment of Subjects, in Literature and Art, with a Fidelity to Reality, Real Life, Nature, etc.: naturalism, realism,n. (naturalist, realist,n. naturalistic, realistic,adj.)

12. Treatment of Subjects, in Literature and Art, with a Free Rein to the Imagination, Rather than with a Fidelity to Reality: idealism, romanticism,n. (idealist, romanticist,n. idealistic, romantic,adj.)

13. Certain Sciences of Reality,n.
   1. metaphysics—branch of philosophy dealing with reality, or with the philosophical basis of reality (metaphysician,n. metaphysical,adj.)
   2. ontology—science that investigates the nature and property of reality; science of reality (ontologist,n. ontological, ontologic,adj.)
   3. philosophy—science that investigates the facts and principles of reality and of human nature, behavior, etc. (philosopher, n. philosophical, philosophic,adj.)

14. Pert. to the Philosophy of Aristotle's Disciples: peripatetic,adj.

15. Pert. to Plato or His Philosophy: Platonic,adj.

16. Philosophy Based on the Principle that Reality Can Be Discovered through Spiritual Intuition, or by Investigating the Processes of Thinking, Rather than through the Objects Perceived by the Senses: transcendentalism,n. (transcendentalist,n. transcendentalist,adj.)

17. Certain Philosophical Theories or Doctrines of Reality,n.
   1. conceptualism—that concepts make it possible for the mind to perceive external or objective reality (conceptualist,n. conceptualistic,adj.)
   2. dualism—that reality is twofold, or explainable in terms of two principles, as mind and matter (dualist,n. dualistic, adj.)
   3. idealism—that mind is the ultimate reality; that reality is of the nature of thought; that reality as one perceives it consists only of ideas (idealist,n. idealistic,adj.)
   4. illusionism—that reality or the material world is an illusion (illusionist,n.)
   5. immaterialism—that there is no reality or material world; that only immaterial things or spiritual beings have existence (immaterialist,n.)
   6. materialism—that matter is the ultimate reality; that the facts of the universe are satisfactorily explained by the nature and property of matter (materialist,n. materialist, materialistic,adj.)
   7. monism—that reality is an organic whole, without independent elements; that there is only one ultimate reality, whether mind, matter, or a third principle or substance on which both mind and matter are based (monist,n. monistic, monistical,adj.)
   8. nominalism—that universals can have names without any corresponding objective reality or existence (nominalist,n. nominalist, nominalistic,adj.)
   9. pluralism—that a number of principles or substances, rather than one (monism) or two (dualism), constitute the ultimate reality (pluralist,n. pluralist, pluralistic, adj.)
   10. realism—that reality exists independently of sense perception; that universals have objective existence (realist,n. realistic, adj.)
   11. substantialism—that unchanging realities are behind phenomena; that matter is a real thing, rather than a composite of centers of force (substantialist,n.)

808. THING

1. A Thing,n.
   1. article—thing of a particular kind; useful thing
   2. commodity—useful thing; thing of value
   3. item—separate thing or article
   4. novelty—new thing; small manufactured article, often more for show than use
   5. object—visible or tangible thing
   6. substance—thing of independent existence

2. Small Articles That Are Useful: notions, n.

3. To Make into, or Cause to Take on the Character of, an Object: objectify,v. (objectification,n.)

4. To Make (an Abstraction or Idea) into, or Treat or Regard (an Abstraction or Idea) as, a Material Object or Concrete Thing: reify,v. (reification,n.)

5. Solid: concrete, substantial,adj. (concreteness, substantiality,n.)

6. To Make, or Become, Solid: concrete, solidify,v. (concretion, solidification,n.)

7. Substance: essence, material, matter, pith, stuff,n.

8. Essence of a Thing; Essential Nature of a Thing: distillation, quiddity,n.

9. Highly Concentrated Form of the Essence of a Thing: distillation, quintessence, n. (quintessential,adj.)

10. Unchanging Essence of a Thing: substance,n.

11. Pert. to Matter: material, physical, substantial,adj.

12. Certain Sciences of Matter,n.
   1. chemistry—science of the composition of matter or of elementary forms of matter (chemist,n. chemical, chemic,adj.)
   2. chemurgy—branch of chemistry devoted to the use of organic raw materials (chemurgic,adj.)
   3. physics—science of matter and motion; science of inanimate matter that does not undergo chemical change (physicist,n. physical,adj.)
   4. somatology, somatics—science of the general properties of substances (somatologist,n. somatological, somatologic, adj.)

13. That Which Is Produced by, or Used in, a Chemical Process: chemical,n.

14. Chemical Action: chemism,n.

15. Chemical Properties, etc.: chemistry,n.

16. Caused by the Operation or Forces of Physics: physical,adj.

809. UNREALITY

1. Unreal,adj.
   1. aerial—imaginary
   2. aeriform—unreal
   3. chimerical—unreal; existing only in the imagination, yet often causing fear; imaginary; wildly fanciful
   4. delusive, delusory—unreal
   5. fabled—not real; fictitious; occurring only in a fable
   6. fabricated, invented—not real, but made up out of the imagination
   7. fanciful—unreal; based on fancy rather than on fact or reality; imaginary
   8. fantastic, fantastical—not real, in the sense of proceeding from or existing solely in the imagination
   9. fictional—not real but only imagined; existing only in fiction, not in real life

10. **fictitious, fictive, figmental**—not real, but made up or imagined
11. **hallucinatory**—not actually present in reality, but believed to be seen or heard
12. **illusional**—imagined or conceived by the senses, but unreal, nonexistent, etc.
13. **illusive, illusory**—unreal
14. **imaginary**—not real, but only imagined
15. **legendary**—not real, i.e., not having existed in historical fact, but only in legend or myth; having no real existence aside from that in fiction, story, or imagination
16. **mythical, mythic**—invented, rather than real; produced by the imagination, but not existing in fact
17. **mythological**—legendary; mythical
18. **nonexistent**—unreal, i.e., having no existence
19. **notional**—not real, but existing only in ideas or as an idea
20. **phantasmagoric, phantasmagorical, phantasmagorial**—produced by, or resembling the figures in, a shifting or changing scene, as in the imagination, dreams, delirium, etc., in which the size of the objects increase or decrease suddenly and violently
21. **phantasmal, phantasmic**—imagined; produced by the imagination or by a disturbed mental condition
22. **phantom**—unreal
23. **quasi**—not real (used as a prefix)
24. **romantic**—not real, i.e., proceeding from the imagination
25. **shadowy**—having no reality or substance
26. **unsubstantial**—having no substantial reality
27. **visionary**—unreal; imaginary

2. Unreality, i.e., Quality, Condition, or State of Being Unreal,n. *From Sec. 1:* delusiveness, fancifulness, fantasticality or fantasticalness, fictitiousness, illusiveness, illusoriness, nonexistence, shadowiness, unsubstantiality

3. An Unreality, i.e., That Which Is Unreal,n. *From Sec. 1:* chimera, delusion, fable, fabrication, invention, fancy, fantasy, fiction, figment, hallucination, illusion, legend, myth, phantasmagoria or phastasmagory, phantasm or phantasma, phantom, shadow; *Also:*
1. **apparition**—something that seems to be there but is not real or of the natural world, such as a ghost, specter, etc. (apparitional,adj.)
2. **mare's nest**—that which was believed to be marvelous, or an unusual discovery, but which turned out to be purely imaginary and nonexistent
3. **mirage**—something falsely seen, though actually nonexistent in the place observed; something imaginary; illusion
4. **nonentity**—that which does not exist, or exists only in the imagination
5. **will-o'-the-wisp, wisp**—nonexistent thing that nevertheless entices, lures, or attracts

4. Imaginary Land or Place Full of Wonders: fairyland, wonderland,n.

810. NATURALNESS

1. Natural, i.e., Not Artificial, Affected, Forced, etc.: artless, inartificial, ingenuous, innocent, naïve, rustic, simple, simplehearted, spontaneous, unaffected, unartful, unartificial, unconstrained, uncontrived, unforced, unlabored, unsophisticate, unsophisticated, unstudied,adj. (artlessness, inartificiality or inartificialness, ingenuousness, innocence or innocency, naïveté, rusticity, simpleness or simplicity, simpleheartedness, spontaneity or spontaneousness, unaffectedness, unartfulness, unartificiality, unconstrainedness or un-

constraint, unforcedness, unsophisticatedness or unsophistication,n.)
2. **Unsophisticated Person:** unsophisticate,n.
3. **Natural, i.e., in Its Natural State, or as Produced by Nature:** crude, raw, unrefined, adj. (crudeness or crudity, rawness,n.)
4. **That Which Is Still in Its Natural State:** crudity,n.
5. **Natural, i.e., Descr. of Qualities, etc., Quite Natural to One, Part of One's Nature,** etc.: inborn, inbred, ingenerate, inherent, innate, native,adj. (inherence or inherency, innateness, nativeness,n.)
6. **Natural, i.e., Pert. to Nature or Natural Laws:** physical,adj.
7. **Natural, i.e., No Longer Contrary to Nature:** unperverted,adj.
8. **To Free from That Which Is Contrary to Nature:** unpervert,v.
9. **State, Condition, or Quality of Being Natural:** naturalness,n.
10. **Adherence to That Which Is Natural:** naturalism,n. (naturalist,n.)
11. **Action That Comes from Natural Instincts and Desires:** naturalism,n.
12. **Imitating Nature:** naturalistic,adj.
13. **To Bring into Accord with Nature:** naturalize,v. (naturalization,n.)
14. **Below What Is Natural:** subternatural, adj.

811. UNNATURALNESS

1. **Unnatural (of Manner, Conduct, Actions, Effect, etc.):** affected, airy, apish, artful, artificial, constrained, contrived, factitious, forced, histrionic, labored, mannered, mincing, minikin; postiche (French); precious, sophisticated, stagy or stagey, studied, theatrical or theatric,adj. (affectedness or affectation, airiness, apishness or apery, artfulness, artificiality or artificialness, constrainedness or constraint, contrivance, factitiousness, laboredness, mincingness, preciosity, sophisticatedness or sophistication, staginess or stageyness, studiedness, theatricality or theatricalism,n.)
2. **One Who Is Unnatural or Affected in Manner, Conduct, etc.:** sophisticate,n.
3. **To Cause to Be Unnatural or Affected in Manner, Conduct, etc.:** sophisticate,v. (sophistication,n.)
4. **Unnatural, i.e., Made by Man Rather than by Nature:** artificial, factitious, synthetic,adj. (artificiality or artificialness, factitiousness,n.)
5. **Deriving from, or Adapted to, an Artificial Standard; Caused or Produced Artificially Rather than Arising Spontaneously:** factitious,adj. (factitiousness,n.)
6. **Unnatural in Shape, Appearance, Kind, etc.:** grotesque, monstrous,adj. (grotesquery or grotesquerie, monstrosity or monstrousness,n.)
7. **That Which Is Unnatural in Shape, Appearance, Kind, etc.:** grotesque, grotesquerie, grotesquery, monster, monstrosity,n.
8. **Grotesque Figure Similar to, or Suggestive of, the Rainspouts Formerly Used on Buildings:** gargoyle,n.
9. **Unnatural, i.e., Contrary to Nature:** aberrant, abnormal, perverted,adj. (aberrance, aberrancy, or aberration, abnormality, pervertedness or perversion,n.)

10. That Which Is Unnatural, i.e., Contrary to Nature: aberration, abnormality, perversion,n.

11. Unnatural, i.e., Beyond or Contrary to Natural Law: eerie or eery, miraculous, preternatural, supernatural, uncanny, unearthly, weird,adj. (eeriness, miraculousness, preternaturalness, supernaturalness or supernaturalism, uncanniness, unearthliness, weirdness,n. miracle,n.)

812. TRUTH

1. True: accurate, authentic or authentical, bona fide, genuine, simon-pure, truthful, valid, veracious, veridical, veritable,adj. (accuracy or accurateness, authenticity, genuineness, truthfulness, validity, veracity or veraciousness, veridicality, veritableness or verity,n.)

2. Obviously True; Self-Evidently True: axiomatic,adj.

3. True beyond Question: unimpeachable, unquestionable,adj. (unimpeachability or unimpeachableness, unquestionability or unquestionableness,n.)

4. True in the Sense of Showing Good Faith; Lacking in Any Manner or Motive of Deceitfulness: bona fide,adj.

5. A Truth: verity,n.

6. Self-Evident Truth: axiom, truism,n.

7. General or Fundamental Truth: principle,n.

8. The Absolute and Undeniable Truth: gospel,n.

9. A Truth So Obvious or Unimportant as to Bar Mentioning, but Mentioned Nevertheless: truism,n.

10. Appearance of Truth: verisimilitude; vraisemblance (French),n. (verisimilar,adj.)

11. Statement, etc., That Has the Appearance of Truth: verisimilitude,n.

12. To Declare or Claim to Be True, Accurate, Genuine, etc.: affirm, attest, authenticate, aver, avouch, certify, confirm, corroborate, maintain, postulate, predicate, substantiate, swear to, validate, verify; vindicate (against denial, etc.); vouch for, warrant,v. (affirmation, attestation, authentication, averment, avouchment, certification, confirmation, corroboration, maintenance, postulation, predication, substantiation, validation, verification, vindication, warranty,n. affirmer; attester, attestor, or attestant; authenticator, certifier, corroborator, maintainer, postulator, swearer, verifier, vindicator, warranter,n. affirmative or affirmatory, attestant, confirmatory or confirmative, corroborative or corroboratory, predicative, substantiative, verificative, vindicative or vindicatory,adj.)

13. Solemn Declaration of the Truth of That Which One Is Saying, by Inference Calling upon God as a Witness or Proof: oath,n.

14. That Which Is Assumed as True Temporarily, as a Basis for Further Argument, Discussion, or Investigation: hypothesis, postulate,n. (postulation,n. hypothetical,adj. hypothesize, postulate,v.)

15. To Show to Be True or Accurate; To Establish the Truth, etc., of; To Prove: argue, attest, authenticate; circumstantiate (by giving details); confirm, corroborate, demonstrate, establish, substantiate, validate, verify, vouch for,v. (attestation, authentication, circumstantiation, confirmation, corroboration, demonstration, establishment, substantiation, validation, verification,n.)

16. Proof, i.e., That Which Proves or Serves as Proof: circumstantiation, confirmation, corroboration, evidence, substantiation,n.

17. That Which Serves as Proof of Authority, Right, Identity, etc.: credentials, documents, papers, token,n. (documentary, documental, adj.)

18. To Give or Present Proof of, in the Form of Papers, Records, Statistics, etc.; To Support by Such Proof: document,v. (documentation,n.)

19. To Prove the Genuineness of: authenticate,v. (authentication,n.)

20. Serving to Prove or as Proof: confirmatory or confirmative; corroborative, corroboratory, or corroborant; demonstrative, evincive, probative or probatory, substantiative, verificative,adj.

21. Capable of Proof: attestable, confirmable, demonstrable, establishable, verifiable,adj. (unconfirmable, undemonstrable, unverifiable, neg.adj.)

22. Pert. to Proof: probatory,adj.

23. Proved: Q.E.D. (abbreviation standing for the Latin *quod erat demonstrandum,* and meaning *what had to be proved*—said or written after a proof is completed)

24. Truly: really, simply, verily,adv.

813. HONESTY

1. Honest: aboveboard, straightforward, truthful, upright, veracious, veridical,adj.

2. Honesty: integrity, probity, rectitude, straightforwardness, truthfulness, uprightness, veracity or veraciousness, veridicality,n.

3. Morally Honest: upright, upstanding,adj. (uprightness,n.)

4. Honest and Fair, or Honest and Frank, Person: square shooter,n. (colloq.)

5. Theory that in Art, Literature, etc., Ugly, Repugnant, Seamy, or Vulgar Things, Incidents, Circumstances, etc., Have a Right to Portrayal Owing to Their Truthfulness: verism,n. (verist,n. verist, veristic,adj.)

6. Frank: aboveboard, candid, direct, forthright, guileless, heart-to-heart, honest, open, openhearted, outspoken, point-blank, square, straightforward, transparent, undeceitful, unguileful, unreserved,adj. (candidness or candor, directness, forthrightness, guilelessness, honesty, openness, openheartedness, outspokenness, straightforwardness, transparency or transparentness, unguilefulness, unreserve or unreservedness,n.); *Also:*

  1. **bluff**—frank in a rough but good-natured way (bluffness,n.)

  2. **blunt, outspoken, point-blank, plump**—frank to the point of being discourteous or wounding someone's feelings; tactlessly or excessively frank (bluntness, outspokenness,n.)

  3. **childlike**—as frank as a child (childlikeness,n.)

  4. **ingenuous**—openly and artlessly frank; frank even where concealment might be advantageous; unable to be anything but frank (ingenuousness,n.)

7. Sincere: aboveboard, artless, bona fide, candid, cordial, devout, earnest, frank, genuine, guileless, heartfelt, heart-to-heart, hearty, simple, simplehearted, singlehearted, single-minded, unaffected, unartful, undeceitful, undesigning, unequivocal, unguileful, wholehearted, whole-souled,adj.

8. Sincerity: artlessness; bona fides (Latin); candor or candidness, cordiality, devoutness, earnestness, frankness, genuineness, good faith, guilelessness, heartiness, simplicity or simpleness, simpleheartedness, sincereness, single-mindedness, unaffectedness, unartfulness, unequivocalness, unguilefulness, wholeheartedness,n.

9. Sincerely,adv. *From Sec. 7:* artlessly, candidly, etc.; *Also:* in good faith,adv.

814. FACT

1. Fact,n.
  1. datum—known, established, or accepted fact (chiefly used in the plural *data*)
  2. fait accompli (French)—accomplished fact, i.e., something already done or finished, with the implication that opposition to it is therefore futile
  3. statistic—fact expressed or clarified in a numerical arrangement (statistical or statistic,adj.)

2. Dealing, or in Accord, with Fact or Facts: de facto (Latin), factual, phenomenal, true, valid, veritable,adj. (fact, factuality, or factualness; phenomenality, truth or trueness, validity, veritableness or verity,n.)

3. In Fact (Whether or Not in Name): de facto (Latin)

4. Science of the Collection and Classification of Facts on a Numerical Basis: statistics,n. (statistician, statist,n. statistical, statistic,adj.)

815. CORRECTNESS

1. Correct: accurate, exact, inerrant, nice, precise, proper, right, rigorous, scrupulous, strict,adj.; *Also:*
  1. Augustan—showing or having correctness, as in taste, judgment, etc.
  2. immaculate—free from errors (of written or printed matter)
  3. punctilious, scrupulous—carefully or minutely correct or exact in observing details or forms of behavior or action
  4. solemn—legally correct in form

2. Correctness,n. *From Sec. 1:* accuracy or accurateness, exactness or exactitude, inerrancy, nicety or niceness, precision or preciseness, properness, rightness, rigorousness, scrupulousness or scrupulosity, strictness; immaculacy or immaculateness, punctiliousness or punctilio, scrupulousness or scrupulosity, solemnity; *Also:*
  1. correctitude—correctness; correctness of behavior; correctness of manners
  2. rectitude—correctness; correctness of decision or action

3. Stated, Defined, Explained, etc., Exactly: precise,adj. (preciseness, precision,n.)

4. Conforming Exactly to Rule: precise,adj. (preciseness, precision,n.)

5. So Made, Fashioned, Performed, etc., that No Part Can Be Criticized as Incorrect: watertight,adj.

6. Nearly Correct or Accurate: approximate, adj.

7. To Correct, i.e., Make Correct: adjust, amend, cure, mend, rectify, redress, remedy, repair, right, revise,v.; *Also:*
  1. disabuse, undeceive—correct the false notions, ideas, or errors of (someone)
  2. emend, emendate—correct the errors or faults in (esp. written material)
  3. repair—correct the actual damage of, or the figurative injury or damage to

8. Correction; A Correction,n. *From Sec. 7:* adjustment, amendment, cure, rectification, redress or redressal, remedy, repair; revision, revisal, or revise; emendation, repair or reparation

9. Corrective; Correctional,adj. *From Sec. 7:* adjustive, amendatory, curative, remedial, reparative; revisory, revisional, or revisionary; emendatory, reparative

10. That Which Serves to Correct: corrective, n.

11. Correctible: adjustable, amendable, correctable, corrigible, curable, emendable, mendable, rectifiable, redressable or redressible, remediable, repairable, reparable, revisable,adj.

12. Uncorrectible: incorrigible, incurable, irremediable, irrepairable, irreparable, remedyless, unadjustable, unamendable, uncorrectable, uncorrigible, unmendable, unrectifiable, unredressable,adj.

13. Adapted or Devised for Extreme Accuracy in Measurement or Operation: precision,adj.

14. One Carefully Correct, or Who Demands Such Correctness, in Observance of Forms, Rules, etc.: formalist; precisian, precisianist, precisionist, or precisioner,n. (formalism, precisianism,n. formalist, formalistic,adj.); *Also:*
  1. pedant—one carefully correct, or who demands such correctness, in scholarship, teaching, etc. (pedantry, pedantism,n. pedantic,adj.)
  2. prig—one whose careful correctness in observance of forms, rules, principles, duty, behavior, manners, speech, etc., is excessive, offensively self-righteous, annoying, etc. (priggery, priggishness, priggism,n. priggish,adj.)
  3. purist—one carefully correct, or who demands such correctness, in the use of language (purism,n. puristic, puristical,adj.)

15. Requiring or Showing Great Accuracy, or Observance of Strictly Correct Form, as a Task, Work, etc.: pernickety, pernicketty, persnickity (all colloq.),adj. (pernicketiness, n.)

16. Incapable of Making an Error: inerrable, infallible, unerring,adj. (inerrability, inerrableness, or inerrancy; infallibility or infallibleness, unerringness,n.)

17. Making No Error: inerrable, unerring,adj. (inerrancy, unerringness,n.)

816. PERFECTION

1. Perfect: absolute, consummate, ideal, sublime, utopian,adj. (absoluteness, consummation, sublimity or sublimeness,n.)

2. Thing That, or Person Who, Is Perfect in Some Category; Model, Instance, or Embodiment of Perfection: paragon, quintessence,n. (quintessential,adj.)

3. Perfect, i.e., Devoid of Fault, Defect, etc.: faultless, flawless, immaculate, impeccable, indefectible, pure, sound, unblemished, unflawed, unmarred,adj. (faultlessness, flawlessness, immaculacy or immaculateness, impeccability, indefectibility, pureness or purity, soundness,n.)

4. One Who Is without Fault or Flaw: impeccable,n.

5. One Who Is Dissatisfied with Anything Short of Perfection: perfectionist,n. (perfectionism,n. perfectionist, perfectionistic,adj.)

6. Capable of Being Made, or of Becoming, Perfect: perfectible,adj. (perfectibility,n.)

7. To Cause to Be, or to Make, Perfect: crown, perfect,v.

8. Impractical Belief in the Possibility of, or Schemes to Achieve, Human Perfection: utopianism,n. (utopian,n. utopian,adj.)

9. Imaginary Place Where There Is Perfect Happiness or Beauty, Nothing Ever Goes Wrong, etc.: Elysian fields, Elysium (after the place in Greek mythology); Erewhon (after Samuel Butler's novel); paradise; Shangri-La (after James Hilton's novel); Utopia,n. (Elysian, Erewhonian, paradisiac or paradisiacal, Utopian,adj.)

10. To Raise, Usually in One's Mind, to Ideal Perfection: idealize,v. (idealization,n.)

817. SUITABILITY

1. Suitable: applicable, appropriate, apropos, apt, becoming, befitting, congruous, consentaneous, decent, decorous; expedient (to the purpose); felicitous or happy (esp. of language or phrasing); fit, fitting, idoneous, likely, meet, pat, proper, right, seemly, suited,adj. (applicability, applicableness, or application; appropriateness, aptness or aptitude, becomingness, congruousness or congruity, consentaneousness or consentaneity, decency or decentness, decorousness or decorum, expedience or expediency, felicity or felicitousness, happiness, fitness, fittingness, patness, propriety or properness, rightness, seemliness, n.)

2. Suitable to a Person, Place, Time, or Occasion: decorous,adj. (decorousness, decorum,n.)

3. Suitable in Time: seasonable, timely,adj. (seasonableness, timeliness,n.)

4. Suitable for Inspection, View, or Presentation: presentable,adj. (presentableness, presentability,n.)

5. To Be Suitable: apply, beseem, fit, suit,v. (application,n.)

6. To Be Suitable to: become, befit, behoove, beseem, fit, suit,v.

7. To Make Suitable: accommodate, adapt, adjust, tailor,v. (accommodation, adaptation, adjustment,n.)

818. PROPERNESS

1. Proper: appropriate, correct, legitimate, right, seemly,adj.

2. Properness: appropriateness, correctness, legitimacy or legitimateness, propriety, rightness, seemliness,n.

3. Morally Proper: decent, equitable, ethical, just, moral, respectable, right, righteous, rightful,adj. (decency, equitableness, ethicalness or ethicality, justness or justice, morality, respectability or respectableness, rightness, righteousness, rightfulness,n.)

4. Pert. to What Is Proper and Improper in Conduct: ethical or ethic, moral,adj.

5. Rules, Customs, or Requirements of Proper Conduct: convention, conventionalities, ethics, morality, morals, proprieties,n.

6. To Cause to Be Ethical; To Consider or Treat as Ethical: ethicize,v.

7. Behaving or Acting Properly: conventional, decent, decorous, demure, moral, proper, staid,adj.

8. Proper Conduct or Behavior: conventionality, correctitude, decency, decorousness, decorum, demureness, etiquette, morality, politesse, propriety, rectitude, staidness,n.

9. Sense of What Is Proper in Conduct or Behavior: shame,n.

10. Stiffly or Excessively Proper in Conduct or Behavior: demure, prim; prissy (colloq.); prudish, puritanic or puritanical, rigid, square-toed, strait-laced,adj. (demureness,

primness, prudishness or prudery, puritanicalness or puritanism, rigidness or rigidity,n.)

11. Stiffly or Excessively Proper Person: bluenose, prude, puritan,n.

12. Demand for the Strictest Propriety in Conduct or Behavior: Grundyism,n. (Grundyist, Grundyite,n.)

13. That Part of the Community That Demands the Strictest Propriety in Conduct or Behavior: Mrs. Grundy,n.

14. To Be Proper for: befit, behoove, beseem,v.

15. Having No Concept of Proper and Improper, Right and Wrong, etc.; Not Concerned with, or Involving, Propriety or Impropriety, etc.: amoral, non-moral, unmoral, adj. (amorality, unmorality,n.)

16. Expressing One's Judgment of Right or Wrong: judgmatic,adj.

17. The Actual Right or Wrong of Something, Irrespective of Technicalities: merits, n.

819. FORMALITY

1. Formal: academic, ceremonial, ceremonious, conventional, ritual, ritualistic, solemn, stereotyped, stereotypic, stereotypical,adj.

2. Stiffly Formal: angular, bookish, sententious, stilted,adj. (angularness or angularity, bookishness, sententiousness,n.)

3. Formality: ceremoniousness, ceremony, conventionality, etiquette, rituality, solemnity, solemnness,n.

4. Meaningless Formality: ceremony,n.

5. Useless, Empty, Ridiculous, Pretentious, or Hypocritical Formality: mummery,n.

6. To Make Formal, Full of Formalities, etc.: ceremonialize, conventionalize, formalize, ritualize,v.

7. To Observe with Formality or Ceremony: solemnize,v. (solemnization,n.)

8. To Act or Be Formal: formalize, stand on ceremony,v.

9. Careful Adherence to, or Observance of, Formality or Form: ceremonial, ceremonialism, ceremoniousness, ceremony, conventionalism, formalism, punctilio, punctiliousness, ritualism,n. (ceremonialist, conventionalist or conventional, formalist, ritualist,n. ceremonialist, ceremonious, conventional, formalistic, punctilious, ritualistic,adj.); *Also:*
1. academism, academicism—adherence to conventional form in art or literature
2. formalism—adherence to the external forms of religion (formalist,n. formalistic, adj.)
3. officialism—careful adherence to the formalities or prescribed routines of office
4. ritualism—excessive adherence to the external forms of religion (ritualist,n. ritualistic,adj.)

10. A Formality,n.
1. ceremonial, ceremony—a formality; a formality of etiquette
2. convention, conventionality, conventionalism—a formality based on custom or usage
3. punctilio—a precise formality of behavior, conduct, or action
4. rite, ritual—a formality in religion or religious worship, or for other solemn occasions; a formality so rigidly followed as to seem almost compulsive in origin

11. System of Formalities,n. *From Sec. 10:* ceremonial, ceremony, convention, ritual

12. Prescribed Form of Religious Worship: rite, ritual,n.

13. Prescribed Form or Formalities of Procedure; Book Containing Such Prescribed Forms or Formalities: ritual,n.

14. Book Describing Rites in the Roman Catholic Religion: ceremonial,n.

15. Set or Rigid Form: rubric, stereotype,n.

16. Informal: casual, easygoing, offhand, unacademic, unceremonial, unceremonious, unconventional, unstereotyped,adj. (casualness, unceremoniousness, unconventionality,n.)

17. Done without Formality: summary,adj. (summariness,n.)

820. FALSENESS

1. False, i.e., Not Genuine or True: adulterate, adulterine, bastard, bogus, counterfeit, delusive, delusory, erroneous; fake or phony (colloq.); fictional, fictitious, illegitimate, inaccurate, mistaken, shoddy, spurious, supposititious, unauthentic, unfathered, untrue, adj. (bogusness, delusiveness, erroneousness, fictitiousness, illegitimacy or illegitimateness, inaccuracy or inaccurateness, shoddiness, spuriousness, supposititiousness, unauthenticity, untrueness or untruth,n. fake or phony, n.)

2. False though Appearing Deceptively True: colorable, plausible, specious,adj. (colorability or colorableness, plausibility or plausibleness, speciousness or speciosity,n.)

3. That Which Is False though Appearing Deceptively True: speciosity,n.

4. False, but in Imitation of the Genuine, Usually for Purposes of Deception: counterfeit, forged, fraudulent, mock; phony (colloq.); postiche (French); sham, shoddy,adj. (fraudulence or fraudulency, shoddiness,n. counterfeit, forgery, fraud, phony, postiche, sham, shoddy,n.)

5. False, i.e., Not from an Authentic Source —Generally of Stories, Accounts, etc.: apocryphal, unauthentic,adj. (unauthenticity,n.)

6. Works or Writings of Questionable Authenticity: apocrypha,n.

7. Obviously False or Untrue: absurd,adj. (absurdity,n.)

8. False, i.e., Not Based on Fact: fallacious, sophistic, sophistical, unsound,adj. (fallaciousness or fallacy, sophisticalness, unsoundness,n.)

9. False—a Prefix Used to Indicate Falsity Despite Pretended Genuineness: pseudo,adj.

10. Giving a False Impression: falsidical,adj.

11. Not Necessarily True: disputable, doubtful, questionable,adj. (disputability, doubtfulness, questionableness,n.)

12. False Character or Nature: fallacy, falsity, vanity,n.

13. False Idea, Notion, Belief, Thinking, etc.: delusion, fallacy, idolism, illusion, misbelief, misconception, misimpression,n. (delusional, fallacious, illusional,adj.)

14. Something False, i.e., Not Genuine or True: bastard, counterfeit; fake (colloq.); fiction, forgery, fraud; postiche (French); sham, simulacrum, untruth,n.

15. Forged or False Document: pseudograph, n. (pseudographer,n.)

16. To Make in False Imitation of the Genuine: counterfeit, fabricate; fake (colloq.); forge, sham,v (fabrication, fakery, forgery,n fabricator, counterfeiter, faker, forger,n.)

17. To Make False; To Give a False Appearance to: deacon, disguise, doctor, falsify, gloss, gloss over, varnish,v. (disguise, falsifi-

cation,n. disguiser, falsifier or falsificator, glosser, varnisher,n.)

18. To Make or Represent Falsely: belie, disguise, falsify, miscolor, misrepresent, trump up,v. (disguise, falsification, misrepresentation,n. disguiser, falsifier or falsificator, misrepresenter,n. misrepresentative,adj.)

19. To Prove to Be False or Untrue: belie, confute, disprove, explode, falsify, give the lie to, rebut, refute,v. (confutation, disproof or disproval, explosion, falsification, rebuttal, refutation or refutal,n. belier, confuter, exploder, rebutter, refuter,n.)

20. That Which Proves Something to Be False or Untrue: confutation, disproof, rebutter, refutation,n.

21. Descr. of Statements, Ideas, etc., That Refute Previous Arguments (in Logic): elenctic,adj.

22. To Attempt to Prove False: controvert, rebut,v. (controversion, rebuttal,n.)

23. To Challenge as False: impugn,v. (impugnation, impugnment,n. impugner,n.)

24. To Declare Untrue: controvert, deny, disaffirm, dispute, gainsay, negate, negative,v. (controversion, denial, disaffirmance or disaffirmation, negation or denegation,n. disaffirmative or disaffirmatory, negatory,adj.)

25. Unable to Be Proved False or Untrue: irrefutable, unanswerable, unconfutable, undisprovable, unrefutable,adj.

26. Unable to Be Declared Untrue: incontrovertible or uncontrovertible, indisputable or undisputable, undeniable,adj.

821. A LIE

1. A Lie: distortion of truth, equivocation, evasion of truth, fable, fabrication, falsehood, falsification, falsification of truth, fiction, figment, flam, invention, misrepresentation of truth, perversion of truth, prevarication, romance, story, tale, untruth,n.; *Also:*
1. fib—trivial lie
2. roorback—defamatory lie published or circulated about a candidate for political office
3. white lie—lie to save another's feelings and devoid of malice; lie about a trivial thing
4. whopper, bouncer—tremendous lie (colloq.)

2. To Lie; To Tell a Lie,v. *From Sec. 1:* distort the truth, equivocate, evade the truth, fable, fabricate, falsify, invent, misrepresent, misrepresent the truth, pervert the truth, prevaricate; fib; *Also:*
1. belie—lie about
2. deceive—lie to; be dishonest with or to
3. lie in one's teeth or throat—lie outrageously
4. palter—tell lies
5. perjure oneself, commit perjury, forswear, forswear oneself—lie willfully while under legal oath to tell the truth
6. trump up—fabricate (a story, charge, etc.) for purposes of deception

3. Lying,n. *From Sec. 1:* distortion of truth, equivocation, evasion of truth, fabrication, falsehood, falsification, invention, misrepresentation, misrepresentation of truth, perversion of truth, prevarication, untruth; *From Sec. 2:* deception, perjury: *Also:*
1. pseudology—lying
2. subreption—deliberate misrepresentation, suppression, or concealment of truth or facts (subreptious,adj.)

4. Liar,n. *From Sec. 1:* distorter of truth, equivocator, evader of truth, fabler or fabu-

list, fabricator, falsifier, inventor, misrepresenter, misrepresenter of truth, perverter of
truth, prevaricator, romancer; fibber; *From
Sec. 2:* deceiver, palterer, perjurer or forswearer; *From Sec. 3:* pseudologist (humorous); *Also:*
1. **Ananias**—liar, after the Biblical character struck dead for his falsehoods
2. **bluffer, bouncer**—liar (colloq.)
3. **mythomaniac, pseudologue**—one who
lies out of pathological or morbid compulsion

5. **Lying; In the Habit of Lying:** dishonest,
mendacious, untruthful,adj. (dishonesty,
mendacity or mendaciousness, untruthfulness,
n.)

6. **Wandering from Truth or Fact:** aberrant,adj. (aberrance, aberrancy,n. aberration,
n.)

7. **Pathological Disposition or Compulsion
to Tell Lies, Invent Fantasies, etc.:** mytho-
mania, pseudologia fantastica, pseudologia
phantastica,n. (mythomaniac,adj.)

8. **Guilty of Deliberately Lying under Oath
in Court:** perjured,adj.

9. **Involving, or Characterized by, Deliberate Lying under Oath in Court:** perjured,
adj.

10. **Amazingly or Fantastically Lied about:**
pseudological,adj.

11. **Descr. of Certain Types of Liars,adj.**
1. **chronic**—of one who lies constantly, at
all times, persistently, etc.
2. **congenital**—of one who has, as it were,
lied from the moment of his birth, who
developed the vice during birth, etc.—an
exaggeration for effect
3. **consummate**—of one who is skillful, finished, or perfect in his ability to lie con-
vincingly
4. **egregious**—of one who tells lies of an outstandingly vicious and harmful kind, or
of lies of this kind
5. **glib**—of one who lies smoothly, fluently,
or without hesitation or embarrassment
6. **incorrigible**—of one who continues lying
despite punishment, correction, or detection
7. **inveterate**—of one who lies from ingrained habit
8. **notorious**—of one who is well known for
lying
9. **pathological, psychopathic**—of one who
cannot differentiate between fact and
falsehood, and for whom lying may be a
symptom of a deep personality disorder
10. **unconscionable**—of one who lies without
regret, compunctions, or twinges of conscience
12. **To Accuse of Lying:** give the lie to,v.

822. DISHONESTY

1. **Dishonest:** crooked, deceitful, devious,
fraudulent, indirect, knavish, scoundrelly,
sinister, thievish, tortuous,adj.

2. **Dishonesty:** crookedness, deceit, deceitfulness, deviousness, fraudulence, fraudulency,
indirection, indirectness, knavery, knavishness, sinisterness, skulduggery, thievery,
thievishness, tortuousness,n.

3. **Dishonest Person:** crook, knave, scoundrel, thief,n.

4. **Dishonest Method of Operation:** racket,
n. (racketeer,n.)

5. **Dishonest and Tricky:** knavish, rascal,
rascally, roguish,adj. (knavishness or knavery, rascality, roguishness or roguery,n.)

6. **Dishonest and Tricky Person:** knave, rascal, rogue,n.

7. **Dishonest and Tricky Act or Practice:**
knavery, rascality, roguery,n.

8. **Of Questionable Honesty:** shady,adj.
(shadiness,n.)

823. DECEPTION

1. **To Deceive (Someone):** bamboozle, befool,
beguile, bilk, blear; bluff (by a bold front);
cheat, chicane, cozen, delude, dupe, flam,
fleece; flimflam (colloq.); fob, fool, gull, hoax,
hocus, hocus-pocus, hoodwink; hornswoggle
(slang); humbug, impose on, impose upon,
jape, mislead, put something over on, sham;
spoof (slang); trick, victimize,v. (bamboozlement, beguilement, delusion, dupery, imposition or imposure, victimization,n.)

2. **To Deceive, i.e., Use or Practice Deception:** bamboozle; bluff (by a bold front);
boggle, cheat, chicane, flam, humbug, pettifog, sham; spoof (slang); stall (slang),v.

3. **To Deceive (Someone) by Giving (Something Fake or Inferior):** fob, foist, impose,
palm or pass off (something) on,v.

4. **To Use Deception to Lead (Someone)
into (an Act, etc.):** inveigle into,v. (inveiglement,n.)

5. **To Give a Deceptive Appearance to:** disguise, gloss, gloss over, varnish,v. (disguiser,
glosser, varnisher,n.)

6. **Deceptive Appearance:** disguise, gloss,
varnish,n.

7. **Deceptive; Deceitful:** ambidexter, ambidextrous, artful, astucious, astute, beguileful,
beguiling, catchy, colorable, crafty, cunning,
delusive, delusory, designing, dishonest, disingenuous, double-dealing, fallacious, feline,
foxy, fraudulent, illusive, illusory, impostrous,
imposturous, indirect, insidious, Janus-faced,
knavish, Machiavellian or Machiavelian,
Mephistophelian, misleading, oblique, obliquitous, rascal, rascally, roguish, scheming, serpentine, shifty, slick, slippery, sly, snaky,
sneaky; snide (colloq.); sophisticated, subtile,
subtle, treacherous, trickish, tricksy, tricky,
two-faced, underhand, underhanded, vulpine,
wily,adj. (ambidexterity, ambidextrousness,
artfulness, astuteness, colorability or colorableness, craftiness or craft, cunningness or
cunning, delusiveness, dishonesty, disingenuousness, fallaciousness or fallacy, foxiness,
fraudulence or fraudulency, illusiveness, illusoriness, insidiousness, knavishness or knavery, Machiavellianism or Machiavellism,
obliqueness, obliquity, roguishness or roguery,
shiftiness, slickness, slipperiness, slyness,
sneakiness; subtileness, subtility, or subtilty;
subtleness or subtlety, treacherousness or
treachery, trickishness, trickiness, two-facedness, underhandedness, wiliness,n.)

8. **Deceptively Simple:** disingenuous,adj.
(disingenuousness,n.)

9. **Deceptive in Appearance:** colorable, illusive, illusory, plausible, specious, varnished,
adj. (colorability or colorableness, illusiveness, illusoriness, plausibility or plausibleness,
speciousness or speciosity,n.)

10. **Deceptively Safe, Easy, etc.:** treacherous,
tricky,adj. (treacherousness, trickiness,n.)

11. **Deceptively Pleasant, Polite, Smooth,
etc.:** bland, oily, oleaginous, slick, smooth,
suave, unctious, urbane,adj. (blandness, oleaginousness, oiliness, slickness, smoothness,
suavity or suaveness, urbanity or urbaneness,
unctuousness, unctuosity, or unction,n.)

12. **Deceitful by Siding with Both of Two
Opposing Parties:** ambidexter, ambidextrous,

double-dealing, Janus-faced, two-faced,adj. (ambidexterity, ambidextrousness, double-dealing, two-facedness,n. ambidexter, double-dealer, Janus-face,n.)

13. Deception; A Deception; Deceptive or Deceitful Practice or Practices: artifice, beguilement, bilk; bluff (by a bold front) ; cheat, cheating, chicane, chicanery, cozenage, cunning, deceit, device, disguise, dodge, double-dealing, dupery, duplicity, feint, flam; flimflam (colloq.); fraud, guile, hoax, hocus-pocus, humbug, humbuggery, illusion, imposition, imposture, indirection, japery, knavery, legerdemain, pettifoggery, pettifogging, pretext, rascality, roguery, ruse, shift; shenanigan or shenanigans (colloq.); skulduggery; spoof (slang); stall (slang); stratagem, subterfuge, swindle, trick, trickery, wile or wiles, wrinkle,n.; *Also:*
1. **disguise**—deceptive condition, manner, covering, etc.
2. **façade, front**—deception in the sense of a false front that is intended to deceive, or that does deceive, the imperceptive
3. **gimmick**—tricky device, strictly one unseen by the audience, used by magicians in their tricks
4. **stratagem**—deception or trick calculated to deceive the enemy
5. **trap, catch**—deception or trick for deceiving and catching the unwary

14. Purposeful Deception to Induce Someone to Part with Property or Surrender Legal Rights: fraud,n.

15. Something That Is Deceiving or Misleading: ignis fatuus (Latin), illusion, mirage, will-o'-the-wisp, wisp,n.

16. Something Believed Marvelous or Unusual but That Turns Out to Be a Deception, Hoax, or Trick: mare's nest,n.

17. Any Thing, Idea, Force, etc., That Lures One On, but Is Deceptive, Misleading, or Nonexistent: will-o'-the-wisp, wisp,n.

18. Some Deceptive Thing That Is Likely to Prove Ruinous: Trojan horse, wooden horse, n. (in reference to the wooden horse of Greek mythology)

19. Pad Placed in a Woman's Brassiere to Give the Illusion of a Fuller Bust: gay deceiver,n.

20. Deceiver; Deceitful Person: ambidexter, bamboozler, beguiler, bilk, bilker, bluff, bluffer, boggler, cheat, cheater, chicaner, cozener, deluder, double-dealer, duper, fleecer; flimflammer (colloq.); fox, fraud, hoaxer, hoodwinker, humbug, humbugger, impostor, Janus-face, japer, knave, misleader, pettifogger, picaro, picaroon, rascal, rogue, scamp, schemer, serpent, shammer; slicker (colloq.); snake, sneak; snide (colloq.); tricker, trickster, victimizer, weasel,n.

21. Boastful Deceiver: mountebank,n.

22. Someone Who Sells Quack Remedies to the Public, Deceiving His Customers with Jokes, Tricks, etc.: mountebank,n.

23. Easily Deceived: dupable, fleeceable, gullible, unsuspecting,adj. (dupability, gullibility, n.)

24. Someone Who Is Easy to Deceive: dupe, gull; sucker (slang),n. (dupery,n.)

25. One Who Is, or Has Been, Deceived: dupe, fool, gull; sucker (slang); victim,n. (dupery, n.)

824. A TRICK

1. A Trick (in a Sense Other than Pure Deception): caper, capriccio, dido,n.

2. Absurd or Fantastic Trick: antic, dido,n.

3. Mischievous Trick: caper, frolic, gambol, joke, lark, practical joke, prank,n. (frolicsome, larksome; prankish, pranksome, or pranky,adj. frolicsomeness, prankishness,n.)

4. To Play Mischievous Tricks: frolic, lark, prank,v.

5. One Who Plays Mischievous Tricks: frolicker, larker, practical joker or jokester, prankster,n.

6. To Perform Tricks: hocus-pocus,v.

825. CHEAT

1. To Cheat (Someone): bamboozle, beguile (of), beguile (out of); bilk; bunco or bunko (colloq.); con (slang); cozen, defraud, fainaigue, finagle, flam, fleece; flimflam (colloq.); gouge (colloq.); gull, hocus; hornswoggle (slang); mulct, overreach, rook, swindle, trick; trim (colloq.); victimize,v. (bamboozlement, beguilement, victimization,n.)

2. To Cheat, i.e., Engage in Cheating: cozen, fainaigue, finagle, flam, overreach,v.

3. To Cheat by Giving Less than the Correct Amount of Change when a Purchase is Made, or by Giving Less than Pretended or than Is Expected or Understood: short-change,v. (short-changer, short-change artist, n.)

4. To Cheat by Not Paying One's Gambling Debts: welch, welsh, welch on, welsh on (all slang),v. (welsher,n.)

5. To Entice or Lure (Someone) to a Place and There Cheat or Swindle Him, as at Cards, Some Other Game, or by Any Other Means: bunco or bunko (colloq.),v. (bunco, bunko, bunco game, or bunko game,n. bunco artist or bunko artist,n.)

6. To Cheat in a Petty Way: cozen,v. (cozenage,n. cozener,n.)

7. Cheating: cozenage; bunco or bunko (colloq.); flam; flimflam (colloq.); fraud, gouge, imposition, imposture, roguery, swindle, trickery,n.

8. Method or Means of Cheating a Victim by First Gaining His Confidence and by Appealing, Usually, to His Desire for Illegal or Unethical Gain: confidence game,n. (confidence man or confidence artist, or, slang, con man,n.)

9. A Cheat; A Cheater: bamboozler, beguiler, bilk, bilker, blackleg; bunco or bunko artist (colloq.); cozener, defrauder, fainaiguer, finagler, fleecer; flimflammer (colloq.); gouger (colloq.); rook, sharper, swindler, tricker or trickster, victimizer,n.

10. Cheating Gambler: blackleg,n.

11. Professional Card Cheat: cardsharp, rook, sharper,n.

12. Professional Cheat at Dice or Other Gambling Games: rook,n.

13. One Easily Cheated: dupe, easy mark, gull,n. (dupery,n.)

14. One Who Has Been Cheated: dupe, gull, victim,n. (dupery,n.)

826. PRETENSE

1. To Pretend to (a Feeling, Quality, Character, Characteristic, Condition, etc.): affect, assume, counterfeit, dissemble, dissimulate, fake, feign, profess, purport, sham, simulate,v. (affectation, dissimulation, fakery, simulation,n. counterfeiter, dissembler, dissimulator, faker, feigner, shammer, simulator,n. dissimulative, simulative or simulatory, adj.)

2. To Pretend to Be: act, act the part, etc., of, assume the character, part, role, etc., of, impersonate, masquerade as, pass oneself off as, personate, pose as, purport to be, represent oneself as,v. (impersonation, masquerade, personation,n. actor, impersonator, masquerader, personator,n. personative,adj.)

3. Pretending to Be: would-be,adj.

4. To Pretend to Have (a Quality, etc.): affect, assume, fake, feign, profess, sham, simulate,v. (affectation, simulation,n. faker, feigner, shammer, simulator,n. simulative, simulatory,adj.)

5. To Pretend, i.e., Make a Pretense or Pretenses: boggle, counterfeit, dissemble, dissimulate, fake, feign, fool, make believe, masquerade; play-act (colloq.); sham,v. (boggle, dissimulation, fakery, play-acting,n. boggler, dissembler, dissimulator, fake or faker, feigner, masquerader, shammer,n. dissimulative,adj.); *Also:*
  1. **bluff**—pretend ability, confidence, strength, etc., that does not exist (bluff, n. bluffer, bluff,n.)
  2. **malinger**—pretend illness or disability in order to avoid work, duty, etc. (malingerer,n.)

6. To Pretend Not to See: blink at, ignore, wink at,v.

7. To Pretend to, or Assume, an Attitude, Air, etc., to Impress Others: attitudinize, peacock, pose, posture, posturize, strike an attitude, pose, etc.,v. (pose, posture,n. attitudinizer or attitudinarian; poser, poseur, or, fem., poseuse; posturer or posturist,n. attitudinarianism,n.)

8. To Pretend Professional or Medical Skill, Ability, or Knowledge That Is Nonexistent: quack,v.

9. To Pretend Not to Have (a Feeling, Quality, Condition, etc.) by Assuming a Contrary or Different Appearance, Show, etc.: cloak, diguise, dissemble, dissimulate, mask, veil,v. (dissimulation,n. disguiser, dissembler, dissimulator,n. cloak, disguise, mask, veil,n. dissimulative,adj.)

10. Pretense: act, affectation, bluff, boggle, disguise, dissimulation, fakery, false show, feint, guise, histrionics, humbuggery, make-believe, mask, masquerade, outward show; play-acting (colloq.); pose; postiche (French); posture, pretension, pretext, role, sham, simulacrum, simulation; stall (slang); veil,n. (dissimulative, simulacral, simulative or simulatory,adj.); *Also:*
  1. **bravado**—pretense of bravery
  2. **charlatanism, charlatanry, quackery**—pretense of nonexistent (usually professional) ability, skill, or knowledge
  3. **hypocrisy, pharisaism, phariseeism**—pretense of nonexistent feelings, virtues, qualities, goodness, righteousness, piety, etc.
  4. **imposture**—pretense of being someone else for purposes of deception or fraud
  5. **quackery**—pretense of nonexistent medical knowledge or skill
  6. **shoddy**—pretense of excellence or superiority, esp. in manufacture, art, etc.

11. Pretended; Characterized by, or Full of, Pretense,adj. *From Sec. 10:* affected, dissimulated or dissimulative, fake or faked, histrionic or histrionical, make-believe; postiche (French); pretentious, sham; simulated, simulate, simulative, or simulatory; charlatan or charlatanic, quack or quackish, hypocritical, pharisaic or pharisaical, impostrous or impostrous, quack or quackish, shoddy; *Also:* artificial, bogus, colorable, counterfeit or counterfeited, factitious, false, feigned, insincere, mock, ostensible, professed; pseudo

(as a prefix); purported, shoddy; soi-disant (French); theatrical, token (affectedness, pretentiousness, shoddiness; artificiality or artificialness, colorability or colorableness, factitiousness, falsity or falseness, insincerity, shoddiness, theatricality or theatricalism,n.)

12. Pretender; One Who Pretends, Is Full of Pretense, etc.,n. *From Sec. 10:* actor, bluff or bluffer, boggler, dissimulator, fake or faker, humbug, hypocrite, make-believe, masquerader, pharisee, playactor, poseur (poseuse, fem.), posturer or posturist, shammer, simulator; charlatan, quack, hypocrite, pharisee, impostor (impostress or impostrix, fem.), quack or quacksalver; *Also:* dissembler, feigner; fraud (colloq.); *Also:*
  1. **mountebank**—bragging and unprincipled pretender
  2. **shoddy**—one who, or that which, though inferior, pretends to excellence or superiority
  3. **tinhorn**—one who pretends wealth, power, influence, etc. (tinhorn,adj.)
  4. **whited sepulcher**—one who, though actually wicked or corrupt, pretends to the greatest goodness, virtue, etc.

13. Pretenses, Collectively: pretension,n.

14. Characterized by a Bland, Suave, or Sentimental Pretense of Spirituality in Manner or Speech: unctuous,adj. (unctuousness, unctuosity, unction,n.)

15. Charlatan: empiric, mountebank, quack, quacksalver,n.

16. To Play the Charlatan: mountebank, quack,v.

17. Descr. of a Remedy Pretending to Cure, but Incapable of Doing So: quack,adj.

18. To Treat with Such Remedies: quack,v.

19. Seller of Such Remedies in Public: mountebank,n.

20. Hypocrite: pharisee, tartufe or tartuffe, whited sepulcher,n.

21. Hypocritical: insincere, Pecksniffian, pharisaic or pharisaical,adj. (insincerity; Pecksniffery, Pecksniffism, or Pecksniffianism; pharisaism or phariseeism,n.)

22. To Speak as if through the Nose, Like a Hypocrite: snuffle,v. (snuffler,n.)

23. Insincere: backhanded, dishonest, disingenuous, empty, hollow, hypocritical, Pecksniffian,adj. (backhandedness, dishonesty, disingenuousness, emptiness, hollowness, hypocrisy, Pecksniffery, Pecksniffism, or Pecksniffianism,n.)

24. Smooth and Soft-Spoken, but Insincere: mealymouthed,adj.

25. To Act Insincerely: palter,v. (palterer,n.)

26. To Be Insincere with: dally with, play with, play fast and loose with, toy with, trifle with,v.

27. Offensive Owing to the Insincerity of Motives: fulsome,adj. (fulsomeness,n.)

827. INCORRECTNESS

1. Incorrect: erroneous, imprecise, improper, inaccurate, inexact, mistaken, unaccurate, unexact, unprecise, wrong,adj. (erroneousness or error, impreciseness or imprecision, improperness or impropriety, inaccuracy or inaccurateness, inexactness or inexactitude, unaccuracy or unaccurateness, unexactness, unpreciseness, wrongness,n.)

2. That Which Is Incorrect: error, mistake, impropriety, inaccuracy,n.

3. To Be Incorrect: err,v.

4. Deviating from What Is Correct: errant, perverse,adj. (perverseness, perversity,n.)

5. Incorrectly Done, Understood, Conceived, etc.: mistaken,adj.

6. To Understand (Something or Someone) Incorrectly: mistake,v.

7. To Be Wrong (of Circumstances, Conditions, etc.): be amiss,v.

8. To Go Wrong (of Circumstances, etc.): go amiss, miscarry, misfire,v. (miscarriage, n.)

9. To Do or Act Wrong: offend,v. (offense,n. offender,n.)

10. To Go Astray: miscarry, stray,v.

11. Full of Wrong; Characterized by Wrong: wrongful,adj. (wrongfulness,n.)

12. Wrong in Judgment or Opinion: wrongheaded,adj. (wrongheadedness,n.)

828. IMPROPERNESS

1. Improper: illegitimate, illicit, inappropriate, incorrect, solecistic, unseemly, wrong, adj.

2. Improperness: illegitimacy, illegitimateness, illicitness, impropriety, inappropriateness, incorrectness, unseemliness, wrongness, n.

3. An Improper Act, Usage, etc.: impropriety,n.

4. Improper and Unnecessary: gratuitous, uncalled-for,adj. (gratuitousness,n.)

5. Deviating from What Is Proper: aberrant, perverse,adj. (aberrance, aberrancy, or aberration; perverseness or perversity,n.)

6. Deviated from the Proper Course: perverted,adj.

7. To Cause to Deviate from the Proper Course: pervert,v. (perversion,n. perverter,n. perversive,adj. pervertible,adj.)

8. Off the Proper Course: astray,adv.

9. Going beyond Set Limits of Propriety: exorbitant, immoderate,adj. (exorbitance or exorbitancy; immoderateness, immoderacy, or immoderation,n.)

10. To Be Improper: be amiss,v.

11. Morally Improper: immoral, indecent, inequitable, inethical, unequitable, unethic, unethical, unjust, unrighteous, unrightful, wrong, wrongful,adj. (immorality, indecency, inequitableness or inequity, unequitableness, unethicalness, unjustness or injustice, unrighteousness, unrightfulness, wrongness, wrongfulness,n.)

12. Behaving or Acting Improperly: immoral, improper, indecent, indecorous, unconventional,adj. (immorality, improperness or impropriety, indecency, indecorum or indecorousness, unconventionality,n.)

13. Unsuitable: ill-befitting, ill-beseeming, ill-suiting, impertinent, improper, inapplicable, inappropriate, inapropos, inapt, incongruous, indecent, indecorous; inexpedient (to the purpose); infelicitous, unfelicitous, or unhappy (of language or phrasing); malapropos, misbecoming, unapt, unbecoming, unbefitting, unbeseeming, uncomely, undue, unfitting, unhandsome, unmeet, unseemly, unsuited; unworthy (of); wrong,adj. (impertinence or impertinency, improperness or impropriety; inapplicability, inapplicableness, or inapplication; inappropriateness, inaptness or inaptitude, incongruity or incongruousness, indecency, indecorum or indecorousness, inexpedience or inexpediency; infelicitousness, in-

felicity, unfelicitousness, or unhappiness; misbecomingness, unaptness, unbecomingness, unbefittingness, unbeseemingness, uncomeliness, unfittingness, unhandsomeness, unmeetness, unseemliness, unworthiness, wrongness,n.)

14. Unsuitable in Time: undue, unseasonable, untimely,adj. (unseasonableness, untimeliness,n.)

15. Unsuitable for Inspection, View, or Presentation: unpresentable,adj. (unpresentableness, unpresentability,n.) ·

16. To Be Unsuitable to: misbecome, unbecome, unbefit, unbeseem,v.

17. To Consider Unsuitable: disdain, scorn,v.

18. To Make Unsuitable: unfit, unsuit,v.

829. MISTAKE

1. A Mistake,n.
  1. blooper—mistake (slang)
  2. blunder—mistake caused by ignorance, stupidity, awkwardness, etc.
  3. boner—absurd or stupid mistake
  4. corrigendum—mistake in a manuscript or printed work that is to be corrected (corrigenda,pl.)
  5. erratum—mistake in writing or printing (errata,pl.)
  6. error, inaccuracy, solecism—mistake
  7. fallacy—mistake in reasoning; mistaken premise upon which reasoning is built
  8. faux pas, gaffe (both French)—social error; mistake in social behavior or convention
  9. fluff—mistake in speaking lines, as on the stage, radio, etc.
  10. gaffe (French)—embarrassing error
  11. howler—especially laughable or ludicrous mistake
  12. lapse—slight mistake; slight mistake in speech or writing
  13. misapprehension—mistake due to misunderstanding (misapprehend,v.)
  14. miscalculation—mistake in calculating (miscalculate,v.)
  15. misconception—mistaken belief or understanding (misconceive,v.)
  16. misconstruction, misinterpretation—mistake in interpreting (misconstrue,v.)
  17. misjudgment—mistake in judgment (misjudge,v.)
  18. misprint—mistake in printing (misprint, v.)
  19. misstep—error in behavior
  20. misunderstanding—mistake in understanding (misunderstand,v.)
  21. oversight—mistake owing to carelessness, inattention, etc.
  22. pitfall—error in which one may be trapped or in which one may trap oneself
  23. slip, slip-up—trivial mistake, or mistake of no great consequence, usually caused by accident or carelessness
  24. slip of the tongue; lapsus linguae (Latin)—inadvertent error in speaking
  25. slip of the pen—inadvertent error in writing
  26. solecism—error of etiquette or conduct
  27. typo—error in print (publisher's slang)

2. To Make a Mistake,v. *From Sec. 1:* blunder, err, fluff, slip, slip up; *Also:* mistake, stumble, trip

3. List of Errors in Published Material, with the Proper Corrections: corrigenda, errata,pl.n.

4. Containing a Mistake or Mistakes: erroneous, faulty, inaccurate, incorrect, solecistic, solecistical,adj. (erroneousness, faultiness, inaccuracy or inaccurateness, incorrectness,n.)

5. Having Made a Mistake; Being in Error: mistaken,adj.

6. By Mistake, to Think One Is Another: confuse, mistake,v. (in patterns such as *confuse one with another, mistake one for another*, etc.)

7. Act of So Mistaking (One for Another): confusion,n.

8. Descr. of That Which May Be Mistaken: mistakable,adj. (unmistakable,neg.adj.)

9. To Cause (Someone) to Make a Mistake: trip, trip up,v.

830. FAULT

1. A Fault: blemish, defect, delinquency, demerit, flaw, imperfection, mar, weakness,n.

2. Slight Fault: peccadillo,n.

3. Moral Fault: vice,n.

4. Physical Defect: vice,n.

5. Containing a Fault or Faults: blemished, defective, deficient, faulty, flawed, imperfect, marred, unsound, vicious, weak,adj. (defectiveness, deficiency, faultiness, imperfectness, unsoundness, viciousness, weakness,n.)

6. To Be Faulty: be amiss,v.

7. Mark Indicating a Fault in Conduct, Placed on One's Record, as in School, etc.: demerit, demerit mark,n.

8. Full of Flaws or Cracks: crazy,adj.

831. EXCELLENCE

1. Excellent: ace, admirable; bully (colloq.); capital, choice, crack, de luxe, exceptional, fine, first-class; first-rate (colloq.); marvelous; par excellence (follows the noun); prime; recherché (sometimes humorous); select, spanking, splendid, sterling, stupendous, superb, supereminent, wonderful, worthy,adj.

2. Excellence: admirableness, dignity, excellency, fineness, marvelousness, merit, prerogative, splendidness, stupendousness, superbness, supereminence, value, virtue, worth, worthiness,n.

3. Model of Excellence: paragon,n.

4. Excellence of Character: quality,n.

5. Person of Excellent Character or Qualities: brick,n. (colloq.)

6. Acceptable in Excellence or Quality: standard,adj.

7. In Good or Excellent Condition: first-rate (colloq.), shipshape, sound; tiptop (colloq.); trim, well-kept,adj.

8. Good or Excellent Condition: pink, prime, soundness, trim, trimness,n.

9. Good Condition of Existence: weal (archaic), welfare, well-being,n.

10. General Welfare; Public Welfare: commonweal,n.

11. Good for One; Bringing, or Productive of, Good: advantageous, benefic, beneficent, beneficial, benignant, fruitful, salutary, serviceable, useful, wholesome,adj. (advantageousness; beneficence, beneficialness or benefit; benignancy, fruitfulness, salutariness, serviceability or serviceableness, usefulness or use, wholesomeness,n.)

12. Good for the Mind: wholesome,adj. (wholesomeness,n.)

13. That Which Is Good for One: advantage, avail, benefit, boon,n.

14. To Be Good for: advantage, avail, benefit, serve,v.

15. Something Especially Good: boon, nugget, plum, treasure; whale (as in *whale of a dividend*, etc.),n.

16. The Highest Good: summum bonum,n. (Latin)

17. To Be Good Enough for the Requirements: avail, do, serve, suffice, suit,v.

18. To Be Good Enough for the Requirements of: satisfy, serve, suit,v.

19. Good Enough for the Requirements: satisfactory, sufficient, suitable,adj.

20. Moderately Good; Good Enough: decent, fair, mediocre, middling, moderate, passable, respectable, tolerable,adj.

21. Neither Good nor Bad: indifferent, mediocre,adj.

22. Belief about What Is Good,n.

　　1. Benthamism—utilitarianism as taught by Jeremy Bentham (Benthamite,n. Benthamic,adj.)

　　2. meliorism—belief or philosophy that the world can be made better, and in fact is getting better (meliorist,n. meliorist, melioristic,adj.)

　　3. utilitarianism—belief that the purpose of behavior is to effect the greatest good for the greatest number of people; belief that what is useful is good (utilitarian,n. utilitarian,adj.)

832. RESTORATION

1. To Bring Back to Good or Healthy Condition: freshen, furbish, mend, recondition, refresh, refurbish, rehabilitate, renew, renovate; repair (what has been damaged, has broken down, etc.); retrieve, revive,v. (refreshment, rehabilitation, renewal, renovation, repair or reparation, retrieval, revival, n.)

2. Restoration after Some Degree of Destruction: instauration,n.

3. Capable of Restoring (Something) to a Normal Condition: corrective,adj. (corrective,n.)

4. Serving to Restore; Capable of Restoring; Pert. to Restoring: restorative,adj. (restorative,n.)

5. To Restore to Brightness, Cleanness, etc.: furbish,v. (furbisher,n.)

6. To Restore (Wasteland, etc.) to Cultivable or Other Useful Condition: reclaim, recover, retrieve,v. (reclamation, recovery, retrieval,n. reclaimable, recoverable, retrievable,adj. irreclaimable, irrecoverable, irretrievable,neg.adj.)

7. To Restore to Popularity, or to Popular Use or Condition: resurrect, resuscitate, revive,v. (resurrection, resuscitation, revival,n. resurrectionary, resuscitative,adj.)

8. To Restore to Citizenship: repatriate,v. (repatriation,n. repatriate,n. repatriable,adj.)

9. To Repair (Something): mend, rebuild, recondition, remodel, renovate,v. (renovation, n.)

10. To Repair Completely; Do All Repairs Necessary on: overhaul,v.

11. To Repair Coarsely or Hastily: cobble, patch, patch up,v. (cobbler, patcher,n.)

12. To Repair in a Botchy and Unskillful Way: tinker,v. (tinkerer,n.)

13. To Repair That Which Is Frayed, Torn, Worn, Broken, etc.; To Repair by Sewing: mend,v. (mender,n.)

14. To Repair Shoes: cobble,v.

15. Repairer of Shoes: cobbler, shoemaker,n. (cobblery or cobbling, shoemaking,n.)

16. To Repair Pots: tinker,v. (tinker,n.)

17. Repairing; Tending to, or Serving for, Repair: reparative,adj.

18. Capable of Being Repaired: mendable, repairable, reparable,adj. (repairableness, reparability,n.)

19. Incapable of Being Repaired: irreparable, irreparable, unmendable,adj. (irreparability or irreparableness, unmendableness,n.)

833. SUPERIORITY

1. Better; Superior: ascendant, banner, choice, exceptional, palmary, pre-eminent, premier, select, singular, supereminent, surpassing, transcendent, transcendental,adj.

2. Superiority: ascendance, ascendancy, distinction, meliority, pre-eminence, prerogative, singularity, supereminence, transcendence, transcendency,n.

3. Superior in Influence, Importance, Power, etc.: dominant, dominating, paramount, predominant, predominating, preponderant, preponderate, preponderating, prevailing, sovereign,adj. (dominance or dominancy, paramountcy, predominance or predominancy, preponderance, prevailingness, sovereignty,n. sovereign,n.)

4. Superior in Position, Order, or Rank: paramount, predominant, predominating, sovereign,adj. (paramountcy, predominance or predominancy, sovereignty,n. sovereign,n.)

5. Superior in Numbers: predominant, predominating, preponderant, preponderate, preponderating,adj. (predominance or predominancy, preponderance,n.)

6. Superior, or Superiority of, Position, Condition, Circumstance, etc., or the Result of This: advantage, vantage,n. (advantageousness,n. advantageous,adj.)

7. To Give an Advantage to: advantage,v.

8. One Who Is Superior (to Someone): superior,n.

9. Those Who Are Superior (to Someone): betters, superiors,n.

10. Belief in German Superiority: Teutonism, n. (Teutonist,n.)

11. To Do Better than: beat, best, better, cap, eclipse, excel, outdistance, outdo, outmatch, outshine, outstrip, overmatch, overtop, put to shame, surpass, top, transcend, trump,v. (eclipse, transcendence,n.)

12. To Try to Do Better than: emulate,v. (emulation,n.   emulousness,n.   emulator,n. emulous,adj.)

13. To Match with Something Better: cap,v.

14. To Get More Points than, in a Contest: outpoint,v.

15. To Be Superior to, or Better than: cap, dominate, dominate over, eclipse, excel, outclass, outshine, overshadow, overtop, predominate over, rise above, surpass, top, tower over, transcend, trump,v. (domination, predomination, transcendence,n.)

16. To Be Superior, as in Power, Authority, Influence, Numbers, etc.: predominate, preponderate, prevail,v.

17. To Get the Better of, or Gain an Advantage over, as by Superior Strategy, Cleverness, etc.: best, circumvent; euchre or euchre out (colloq.); outgeneral, outmaneuver, outwit, overreach, worst,v. (circumvention, outgeneralship,n. circumventive,adj.)

18. To Represent as Better than in Actuality, as in Speaking or Writing about, Por-

traying, etc.: flatter,v. (flattery,n. flatterer, n.)

834. BEST

1. Best: capital, champion, choice, choicest, optimum, prime, superlative, supreme, tiptop, top, top-drawer, top-flight, top-notch, unequaled, unexcelled, unsurpassed,adj. (championship, superlativeness, supremacy,n.)

2. Chosen as the Best: choice, select,adj.

3. One Who Is the Best in a Category: champion, nonpareil,n.

4. The Best in a Category of Sports: champion, titleholder,n. (championship,n.)

5. Those Who Are the Best in a Group or Type: cream; crème de la crème (French); elite, the select,n.

6. Best Part of Something, or of a Group or Category: cream, crème de la crème,n.

835. IMPROVEMENT

1. To Improve, i.e., Become Improved or Better: advance, ameliorate, meliorate, mend, progress, upswing,v.; *Also:*
1. enhance—improve, though already good; improve in value, worth, desirability, etc.
2. reform—become better by changing one's evil or unfortunate habits or tendencies
3. regenerate—improve morally or spiritually

2. To Improve, i.e., Make Improved or Better,v. *From Sec. 1:* advance, ameliorate, meliorate, mend; enhance, reform, regenerate; *Also:*
1. better—improve
2. chasten, correct—improve by discipline, punishment, etc., or by removing faults in
3. cultivate, develop—improve by training, teaching, or practice
4. lard—improve by giving variety to, or by adding new things or qualities to
5. refine—improve by freeing of impurities, coarseness, etc., or by cultivating or practicing, as abilities, skills, etc.
6. refine upon—improve upon (something) by adding better things or qualities, removing faults, etc.
7. revise—improve by making necessary changes in
8. uplift—improve emotionally, spiritually, socially, or morally

3. Improvement,n. *From Sec. 1:* advance or advancement, amelioration, melioration, progress, upswing or upturn; enhancement, reformation or reform, regeneration or regeneracy (ameliorative, meliorative, progressive, progressional; enhancive, reformative, regenerative,adj.); *From Sec. 2:* advancement, amelioration, melioration; enhancement, reformation or reform, regeneration; betterment, correction, cultivation, development, refinement, revision or revisal, uplift or upliftment (ameliorative, meliorative; enhancive, reformative or reformatory, regenerative; correctional, corrective; revisory, revisional, or revisionary; uplift,adj.)

4. Improvable,adj. *From Sec. 2:* ameliorable, meliorable, mendable, reformable, regenerable; correctable or correctible, cultivable, developable, refinable, revisable

5. Improver,n. *From Sec. 2:* ameliorator or ameliorant, meliorator or meliorant, mender; enhancer, reformer, regenerator; corrector, cultivator, developer, refiner, reviser, uplifter

6. To Wage, with Fervor or Religious Zeal, a Campaign to Improve Conditions, Remedy Evil, etc.: crusade,v. (crusade,n. crusader,n.)

836. ADVANTAGE

1. Advantage: avail, behoof, benefit, vantage, n.

2. Advantageous: beneficial, expedient, favorable, serviceable, useful,adj. (beneficialness or benefit, expedience or expediency, favorableness, serviceability or serviceableness, usefulness or use,n.)

3. To Be of Advantage to: advantage, avail, benefit; boot (used with an impersonal subject) ; favor, serve,v.

4. To Come by Way of Advantage: accrue,v. (accrual, accruement,n.)

5. That Which Comes by Way of Advantage: accrual,n.

6. Conducive to Advantage, though Perhaps Unjust: expedient,adj. (expedience, expediency,n.)

7. Position or Condition That Gives One the Advantage over Someone: upper hand, vantage; vantage ground, point, etc.; whip hand,n.

8. An Advantage Gained from Such a Position, etc.: upper hand, vantage, whip hand,n.

9. To Take Advantage of: avail oneself of, capitalize on, make capital of, trade on, turn to one's advantage,v. (capitalization,n.)

10. To Take Advantage of Speedily and Eagerly: snatch at,v.

11. To Take Unfair Advantage, as of Someone's Kindness, Patience, Good Nature, etc.: impose (on or upon) ; presume (on or upon),v. (imposition, presumption,n.)

12. A Regard for Advantage; Practice of Taking Advantage,n.
1. expedience, expediency—regard for the advantage rather than for propriety or justice (expediential,adj.)
2. opportunism—policy or practice of taking advantage of circumstances and opportunities with no regard to principles or conscience (opportunist,n. opportunistic,adj.)

13. Opportunistic Action or Procedure: opportunism,n.

14. Looking for Advantage: expediential,adj.

15. Northerner Who Went to the South after the Civil War to Take Advantage of Unsettled Conditions: carpetbagger,n.

16. Disadvantage,n.
1. detriment, drawback—disadvantage
2. handicap—disadvantage that makes success or accomplishment difficult
3. penalty—disadvantage attached to some act, condition, etc.
4. prejudice—disadvantage that results from another's action or judgment

17. To Subject to a Disadvantage: detriment, disadvantage, handicap, penalize, prejudice,v. (penalization,n.)

18. One Who Is at a Disadvantage: underdog, n.

19. Disadvantageous: detrimental, prejudicial, unfavorable,adj. (detrimentality or detrimentalness, unfavorableness,n.)

837. FAVORABLENESS

1. Favorable: auspicious, advantageous, benign; favonian (i.e., like the west wind) ; fortunate, opportune, propitious,adj. (auspiciousness, advantageousness, benignity, fortunateness, opportuneness, propitiousness,n.)

2. Favorably Disposed or Inclined: benign, inclinable; in favor (of) ; propitious; well-disposed (toward),adj. (benignity, propitiousness,n.)

3. Providing Favorable Results: fortunate, adj. (fortunateness,n.)

838. UNFAVORABLENESS

1. Unfavorable: adverse, contrary, disadvantageous, inauspicious, inopportune, ominous, prejudicial, unfortunate, unpropitious, untoward,adj. (adverseness, contrariness, disadvantageousness, inauspiciousness, inopportuneness, ominousness, unfortunateness, unpropitiousness, untowardness,n.)

2. Unfavorable Opinion, Judgment, or Feeling Formed Beforehand: prejudice,n.

3. Unfavorably Inclined: ill-disposed, unpropitious,adj.

4. Providing Unfavorable Results: unfortunate,adj.

839. VALUE

1. Value; Worth: account, advantage, benefit, caliber, dignity, merit, prerogative,n.

2. Valuable: costly, precious, sterling, worthy,adj. (costliness, preciousness, worthiness,n.)

3. Extremely or Incalculably Valuable: invaluable, priceless,adj. (invaluableness, pricelessness,n.)

4. Of Enough Value or Worth for the Time or Effort: worth-while,adj. (worth-whileness, n.)

5. Something of Value or Worth: asset, commodity, nugget, plum, treasure,n.

6. To Be More Valuable than: outweigh,v.

7. Person of Worth: worthy,n. (often used in irony)

8. Valuable Things Stored or Saved Up: treasure,n.

9. Concern with Practical Values Rather than Theoretical Concepts: pragmatism,n. (pragmatist,n. pragmatic, pragmatical,adj.)

10. To Recognize the Value or Worth of: appreciate,v. (appreciation,n.)

11. To Rise in Value: appreciate, boom, enhance,v. (appreciation, boom, enhancement, n.)

12. To Cause to Rise in Value: enhance,v. (enhancement,n. enhancive,adj.)

13. According to Value: ad valorem

14. To Judge the Value of; To Give a Value to,v.
1. appraise, apprize, rate—figure the money value of; figure or judge the value or worth of (appraisal,n. appraiser,n.)
2. assay—give a critical appraisal of the value of (assayer,n.)
3. assess, rate—set a value upon; set a value upon for tax purposes (assessment,n. assessor,n. assessable,adj.)
4. esteem—set a value upon; consider as having a certain value
5. estimate—set an approximate value upon (estimation,n. estimator,n. estimable, adj.)
6. evaluate—set a value upon; determine the value of (evaluation,n.)
7. transvalue—value on a different, unusual, or unconventional basis (transvaluation, n.)
8. value—set a value on; judge the value of (valuation,n.)

15. To Set a High Value upon: esteem, prize, treasure, value,v.

16. To Set Too High a Value upon: overappraise, overassess, overestimate, overrate, overvalue,v. (overappraisal, overassessment, overestimation, overvaluation,n.)

17. To Lose, or Become Decreased in, Value: cheapen, decline, depreciate, drop, fall, impair,v. (decline, depreciation, drop, fall, impairment,n.)

18. To Become Sharply Lower in Value: toboggan,v.

19. To Lower the Value of: cheapen, debase, depreciate, depress, devaluate, devalue, impair,v. (debasement, depreciation, depression, devaluation, impairment,n. cheapener, debaser, depreciator, impairer,n. depressibility, n. depreciable, depressible,adj.)

20. To Reduce (a Metal) in Value by Mixing in a Less Precious Metal: alloy,v.

21. To Reduce the Value of by Mixing in Something Inferior: adulterate, alloy,v. (adulteration,n. adulterator,n. adulterant,adj. adulterate,adj.)

22. Element That Reduces the Value of Something when Mixed in: adulterant, alloy,n.

23. To Reduce the Purchasing Value of (Money): cheapen, depreciate,v. (depreciation,n. cheapness,n. cheap, depreciated,adj.)

24. To Lower the Value of (Currency) by Official Edict, Process, etc.: decry, devaluate, devalue,v. (decrial, devaluation,n.)

25. To Give a Lower than Actual Value to; To Estimate the Value of Too Low, or Lower than in Actuality: disprize, minimize, underappraise, underassess, underestimate, underrate, undervalue,v. (minimization, underappraisal, underassessment, underestimation, underratement, undervaluation,n. underestimate,n. minimizer, undervaluer,n.)

26. To Estimate the Value of at the Lowest Possible Point: minimize,v. (minimization,n. minimizer,n.)

840. TO BELITTLE

1. To Belittle; To Express a Low Opinion of the Value or Worth of: cheapen, cry down, decry; deprecate (loose usage, considered incorrect); depreciate, derogate from, detract from, disesteem, disparage, dispraise, minimize, vilipend,v. (decrial, depreciation, depreciation, derogation, detraction, disparagement, dispraise, minimization,n. cheapener, decrier, deprecator, depreciator, detractor, disparager, dispraiser, minimizer,n.)

2. Belittling; Expressing a Low Opinion of the Value or Worth of: deprecative or deprecatory (loose usage, considered incorrect), depreciative or depreciatory, derogative or derogatory, detractive or detractory, disparaging, perjorative,adj.

3. Low Opinion of the Value or Worth of (Someone): disesteem,n.

4. Word or Term That Expresses Depreciation or Disparagement: pejorative,n.

5. To Laugh at in Disparagement: ridicule, v. (ridicule,n.)

6. To Treat as of Little Value or Importance: disregard, make light of, slight, vilipend,v.

841. WORTHINESS

1. To Be Worthy of: deserve, merit, rate,v.

2. Worthy: deserving, meritorious,adj. (deservingness, meritoriousness,n.)

3. Worthy of Help: deserving,adj. (deservingness,n.)

4. Worthiness of either Good or Bad: desert, deserts, merit, merits,n.

5. Worthiness of Punishment: desert, deserts,n.

6. Worthiness of Reward: desert, deserts, merit,n.

7. That Which Is Deserved: desert, deserts; meed (poetic) ; merit,n.

8. Deserved: merited, righteous,adj.

9. According to What Is Deserved: deservedly,adv.

10. Not Deserved: undeserved, unmerited,adj.

11. In a Manner Not Deserved: undeservedly, adv.

12. Not Deserving: undeserving (of) ; unworthy (of) ,adj. (unworthiness,n.)

13. To Consider Unworthy: disdain, scorn,v.

14. To Consider Unworthy or Undeserving of One's Notice: disdain, disregard, ignore, scorn, slight,v.

842. KINDNESS

1. Kind; Kindly: affable, amiable, beneficent, benevolent, benign, benignant, bighearted, boon, brotherly, goodhearted, good-natured, gracious, humane, philanthropic or philanthropical,adj.; *Also:*

  1. benignant—kindly toward those socially or economically inferior or dependent

  2. charitable—kind in judging people or their behavior

  3. clement, indulgent, lenient, merciful—disposed to be kind by not punishing severely, as a judge, etc.

  4. gracious—kind and courteous; kind to those dependent on one; condescendingly kind to inferiors

  5. hospitable—kind and generous to guests or strangers

  6. merciful—kind in the sense of refraining from punishing one who deserves punishment; kind beyond expectation, or beyond the demands of justice

2. Kindness; Kindliness,n. *From Sec. 1:* affability or affableness, amiability or amiableness, beneficence, benevolence, benignity, benignancy, bigheartedness, brotherliness, goodheartedness, good nature or good-naturedness; graciousness, grace, or graciosity; humaneness or humanity; benignancy, charitableness or charity, clemency, indulgence or indulgency; lenience, leniency, or lenity; mercifulness or mercy; graciousness, grace, or graciosity; hospitality or hospitableness, mercifulness or mercy; *Also:*

  1. bonhomie, bonhommie—pleasant or affable kindness or good-naturedness

  2. grace—kindness from God

3. To Show Mercy to: spare,v.

4. To Show Kindness to: favor,v.

5. Expressive of Kindness, etc., as Words: tender,adj. (tenderness,n.)

6. Act of Kindness: benefaction, beneficence, benevolence, benignity, charity, favor, kindness, kindliness, lenity,n. (benefactor,n. benefactress,fem.n.)

7. A Favor: accommodation, benignity; boon (archaic) ; courtesy,n.

8. A Favor That Has Been Granted: indulgence,n.

9. To Do a Favor for: accommodate, favor, oblige,v.

10. Willing to Do Favors: accommodating, obliging,adj. (obligingness,n.)

11. A Blessing: benediction, benison, boon, mercy,n.

843. MORAL PRINCIPLES

1. Rules or Principles of Moral Conduct: ethics, moral code, morality, morals,n. (ethic or ethical, moral,adj.)

2. Feudal Japanese Moral Code: Bushido,n.

3. The Practice of Moral Conduct as Distinguished from Religion: moralism,n.

4. Science of Moral Duty, Character, or Conduct: ethics,n. (ethic, ethical,adj.)

5. The Basing of Conduct, or of Religious Conduct, on Moral Law: nomism,n. (nomistic,adj.)

6. Treatise on Moral Conduct: ethics,n.

7. Expressing or Containing Truths about Moral Conduct: moral,adj.

8. To Express One's Thinking or Advice on Moral Conduct or Duty: deliver a sermon, lecture, moralize, preach, sermonize,v. (moralization, preachment,n. lecturer, moralizer, preacher, sermonizer,n. preachy,adj.)

9. To Moralize Tediously or Annoyingly: preach,v. (preachment,n. preacher,n. preachy, adj.)

10. The Habit of Moralizing: moralism,n.

11. To Urge One's Moral Thinking or Attitudes on: lecture, sermonize,v.

12. To Advocate (Moral Conduct): preach,v.

13. Reflections or Advice on Moral Conduct: lecture, preaching, preachment, sermon,n.

14. Tedious Advice on Moral Conduct: preachment,n.

15. Advice on Moral Conduct in a Fable, Story, or Account, or to Be Gained from an Experience: lesson, moral,n.

16. A Saying about Moral Conduct: moralism,n.

17. Observant of Principles of Moral Conduct; Good, in a Moral Sense: conscientious, ethical, honest, honorable, incorrupt, incorruptible, moral, righteous; sainted or saintly (i.e., like a saint); scrupulous, uncorrupt, uncorruptible, upright, virtuous,adj.

18. Observance of, or Quality of Observing, Principles of Moral Conduct; Goodness in a Moral Sense: conscientiousness; dharma (concept of Buddhism and Hinduism); ethicalness or ethicality, honesty, honorableness or honor, incorruptness or incorruption, incorruptibleness or incorruptibility, morality, rectitude, righteousness, saintliness, scrupulousness or scrupulosity, uncorruptness or uncorruption, uncorruptibleness or uncorruptibility, uprightness, virtuousness or virtue,n.

19. The Cardinal Virtues: fortitude, justice, prudence, temperance, and also, sometimes, charity, faith, and hope,n.

20. To Be Good: behave,v.

21. Excessively Strict in Moral Conduct: prudish, puritanical or puritanic, strait-laced, adj. (prudishness or prudery, puritanicalness or puritanism,n. prude, puritan,n.)

22. Extremely Moral in One's Own Self-Opinion and Reproving of Others Considered Less Moral: pharisaic or pharisaical, self-righteous,adj. (pharisaism or phariseeism, self-righteousness,n. pharisee,n.)

23. Good for One's Morals; Promoting Moral Goodness: wholesome,adj. (wholesomeness, n.)

24. Ignorant of Morals: amoral, benighted, non-moral,adj. (amorality, benightedness,n.)

25. Resulting from Moral Ignorance: benighted,adj.

26. Having No Relationship or Reference to Morals: amoral, non-moral,adj. (amorality, n.)

844. NOBILITY

1. Noble: august, dignified, exalted, great, greathearted, great-minded, high-minded, honorable, lofty, magnanimous, majestic, princely, sublime, superb, whole-souled,adj.

2. Nobility; Nobleness: dignity, exaltedness or exaltation, greatness, greatheartedness, great-mindedness, high-mindedness, honorableness, loftiness, magnanimity or magnanimousness, majesty, princeliness, sublimity or sublimeness, superbness,n.

3. Noble Person: greatheart, prince, sublimity,n.

4. That Which Is Noble: sublime, sublimity, n.

5. Noble in Ideas, Thoughts, Sentiments, Language, etc.: dignified, elevated, empyreal, empyrean, exalted, lofty, magnificent, majestic, sublime, winged,adj. (dignity, elevation, exaltedness or exaltation, loftiness, magnificence, majesty, sublimity or sublimeness,n.)

6. To Make Noble: dignify, elevate, ennoble, exalt, glorify, sublimate, sublime,v. (elevation, ennoblement, exaltation, glorification, sublimation,n.)

845. MORAL PURITY

1. Morally Pure: angelic, angelical, seraphic, or seraphical (i.e., like an angel); chaste, clean, immaculate, innocent, intemerate, pure; sainted or saintly (i.e., like a saint); virtuous, white,adj. (angelicalness or seraphicalness, chastity or chasteness, cleanness; immaculateness, immaculacy, or immaculance; innocence, innocency, or innocentness; intemerateness, purity or pureness, saintliness, virtue or virtuousness, whiteness,n.)

2. Pure because Not Made Morally Unclean or Impure: clean, immaculate, intemerate, pure, uncontaminated, uncorrupted, undefiled, uninfected, unpolluted, unseduced, untainted, adj. (cleanness; immaculateness, immaculacy, or immaculance; intemerateness, purity or pureness, uncorruptedness or uncorruption, undefiledness, uninfectedness, untaintedness, n. uncorruptibleness or uncorruptibility,n. uncontaminable, uncorruptible, undefilable, uninfectable, unpollutable, unseducible, untaintable,adj.)

3. Ceremonially Pure; Free of Ceremonial Uncleanness or Impurity; Not Made Ceremonially Unclean or Impure: clean, immaculate, intemerate, inviolate, pure, uncontaminated, undefiled, unpolluted, unprofaned, untainted, unviolated,adj. (immaculateness, immaculacy, or immaculance; intemerateness, inviolacy or inviolateness, purity or pureness, undefiledness, untaintedness,n.)

4. Not to Be, or Not Capable of Being, Made Ceremonially Unclean or Impure: inviolable, uncontaminable, undefilable, unpollutable, unprofanable, untaintable, unviolable,adj. (inviolability or inviolableness, n.)

5. To Render Ceremonially Clean or Pure: cleanse or clean, immaculate, lustrate, purge, purify,v. (cleansing, lustration, purgation or purge, purification,n. purgative, purificatory, adj.)

6. Free of, or without, Blame, Guilt, or Sin: blameless, cleanhanded, guilt-free, guiltless, immaculate, impeccable, impeccant, incorrupt, inculpable, innocent, irreprehensible, irreproachable, reproachless, sin-free, sinless, uncensurable, uncorrupt, unexceptionable, unimpeachable, unreproachable, unreproved,adj. (blamelessness, cleanhandedness, guiltlessness; immaculateness, immaculacy, or immaculance; impeccability, impeccancy, incorruptness or incorruption, inculpableness or inculpability; innocence, innocency, or innocentness; irreprehensibleness, irreproachability or irreproachableness, sinlessness, uncorruptness or uncorruption, unexceptionableness, unreproachableness, unreprovedness,n.)

7. Irreproachable Person: Caesar's wife, impeccable,n.

8. Not Liable to Sin: impeccable,adj. (impeccability,n.)

9. Not Sinning: impeccant,adj. (impeccancy, n.)

10. Unstained, Esp. Morally; Without Moral Stain (of People, Characters, Reputations, etc.): chaste, clean, immaculate, impeccable, pure, spotless, stainless, unattainted or unattaint, unbesmeared, unbesmirched, unblackened, unblemished, unblotted, unblurred, unclouded, undarkened, undefiled, unfouled, unscarred, unsmeared, unsmirched, unsmutched, unsmutted, unsoiled, unspattered, unspotted, unstained, unstigmatized, unsullied, untainted, untarnished, white,adj. (chastity or chasteness, cleanness, immaculacy, immaculateness, or immaculance; impeccability, purity or pureness, spotlessness, stainlessness, unblemishedness, uncloudedness, undefiledness, unsoiledness, unspottedness, unstainedness, unsulliedness, untaintedness, whiteness,n.)

11. Not Guilty of Illicit Sexual Activity: chaste, moral, pure, virtuous,adj. (chastity or chasteness, morality, purity or pureness, virtue or virtuousness,n.)

12. Symbol of Chastity: white,n.

13. Not Open to Bribery: incorrupt, incorruptible, unbribable, unbuyable, uncorrupt, uncorruptible,adj. (incorruptness or incorruption, incorruptibility or incorruptibleness, unbribableness, unbuyableness, uncorruptness or uncorruption, uncorruptibility or uncorruptibleness,n.)

14. Not Guilty of Taking Bribes: cleanhanded,adj. (cleanhandedness, clean hands, n.)

15. To Remove Moral Stain, Guilt, or Sin from: chasten, clean, cleanse, immaculate, lustrate, purge, purify, sanctify,v. (cleansing, lustration, purgation or purge, purification, sanctification,n. lustral; purgatorial, purgatorian, or purgative; purificatory,adj.)

16. To Purify by Propitiatory Offering or Other Ceremony, as in Ancient Rome: lustrate,v. (lustration,n. lustral,adj.)

17. To Sprinkle with, or Immerse into, Holy Water to Wash Away the Sins of: baptize,v. (baptism,n. baptismal,adj.)

18. To Subject to an Experience That Purifies or Cleanses the Character: baptize,v. (baptism,n.)

19. To Do That Which Cleanses Away One's Guilt or Sin: purge oneself,v.

20. To Make Amends for (Guilt, Sin, a Crime, etc.): atone, atone for, expiate,v. (atonement, expiation,n. atoner, expiator,n. expiatory,adj.)

21. Descr. of Such Guilt, etc., for Which Amends Can Be Made: atonable, expiable, adj.

22. To Make Amends for Guilt, Sin, Crime, Offense, etc.: atone,v. (atonement,n. atoner, n.)

23. Of the Nature of Atonement or Expiation: expiatory, piacular, purgatorial, purgatorian,adj.

24. Temporary State after Death for the Purpose of Expiating Venial Sins, etc. (Theological Concept): purgatory,n. (purgatorial, purgatorian,adj.)

25. Condition, State, or Place of Expiation: purgatory,n. (purgatorial,adj.)

846. DIGNITY

1. Dignified: grand, grave, majestic or majestical; pontifical (i.e., like a Pope); portly, stately, togated,adj.

2. Dignity: grandeur, grandness, graveness, gravity, majesty, portliness, stateliness,n.

3. Characterized by Ostentatious Dignity: pompous,adj. (pomp, pompousness, pomposity,n.)

4. Large or Massive, and Dignified, Like a Statue: sculpturesque, statuesque,adj. (sculpturesqueness, statuesqueness,n.)

5. To Give Dignity to: dignify, exalt, grace, v. (exaltation,n.)

6. Falling Off, Usually Ludicrously, in Dignity: anticlimactic, bathetic,adj. (anticlimax, bathos,n.)

847. MAGNIFICENCE

1. Grand; Magnificent: august, brilliant, glorious, grandiose, lustrous, majestic or majestical, noble, Olympian, palatial, pompous, regal, resplendent, royal, sculpturesque; splendid, splendorous, or splendrous; stately, sumptuous, superb,adj.

2. Grandness; Magnificence: augustness, brilliance or brilliancy, gloriousness or glory, grandeur, grandiosity; luster, lustre, or lustrousness; majesty, nobility or nobleness, pomp, resplendence or resplendency, royalty, sculpturesqueness, splendor or splendidness, stateliness, sumptuousness, superbness,n.

3. Ostentatiously Grand or Splendid: grandiose,adj. (grandiosity,n.)

4. Of Such Qualities of Grandness or Magnificence as to Make a Strong Impression on the Mind: arresting, august, commanding, grand, imperial, imposing, impressive; lofty or towering (in height); majestic or majestical, noble, Olympian, stately, striking, sublime,adj. (augustness, grandness or grandeur, imperialness, imposingness, impressiveness, loftiness, majesty, nobility or nobleness, stateliness, sublimity or sublimeness,n.)

5. Grand, Magnificent, etc., Quality or Thing: sublime, sublimity,n.

6. Glory Surrounding Some Idealized Thing: halo,n. (halo,v.)

7. To Invest with Glory; To Make Glorious: exalt, glorify, halo, transfigure,v. (exaltation, glorification, transfiguration or transfigurement,n.)

848. IMPORTANCE

1. Important: eventful, grave, key, material, momentous; notable (of people); outstanding, prominent, serious, significant, substantial, weighty,adj.

2. Importance: concern, concernment, consequence, eventfulness, gravity or graveness, import, materiality or materialness, moment, momentousness; notableness or notability (of people); prominence, seriousness, significance, substantialness or substantiality, weight, weightiness,n.

3. Importance of Social or Other Rank: consequence,n.

4. Important at This Very Instant: imperative, pressing, urgent,adj. (imperativeness, pressingness, urgency,n.)

5. Of First, Leading, or Main Importance; Most Important: arch, banner, capital, cardinal, central, chief, foremost, key, leading, main, master, palmary, paramount, premier, preponderant, preponderating, primal, primary, prime, principal, sovereign, stellar, top, top-drawer,adj. (paramountcy, preponderance or preponderancy,n.)

6. Most Important Thing, Crop, etc., Produced, as in a Region, Country, etc.: staple, n. (staple,adj.)

7. To Be Most Important: preponderate,v. (preponderation,n.)

8. Of Decisive Importance: acute, climacteric, critical, crucial, decisive, fateful, key, momentous, pivotal,adj. (acuteness, criticalness, decisiveness, fatefulness, momentousness,n.)

9. That Which Is of Decisive Importance: crux, pivot,n.

10. Point of Decisive Importance: crux,n.

11. Time of Decisive Importance: apex, climacteric, crisis, turning point,n.

12. Important Point in Progress: milestone, n.

13. So Important as to Be Indispensable: basal, basic, cardinal, essential, fundamental, indispensable, key, material, pivotal, primary, radical, substantial, vital,adj. (essentialness or essentiality, indispensableness or indispensability, materiality or materialness, substantialness or substantiality,n.)

14. That Which Is So Important as to Be Indispensable: core, cornerstone, essential, fundamental, heart, indispensable, pivot,n.

15. Person So Important as to Be Indispensable: indispensable, key man, pivot,n.

16. Important to the Carrying Out of Something, to Being Successful in an Endeavor, or to the Conduct of War: strategic,adj.

17. Equally Important: co-ordinate,adj. (co-ordinateness,n. co-ordinate,n.)

18. Of Greater Importance: major, overshadowing,adj.

19. To Be of Greater Importance than: outweigh, overshadow,v.

20. Priority of Importance: precedence,n.

21. To Have Priority of Importance over: precede,v.

22. Important Person: bigwig (colloq. or humorous), grandee; high-muck-a-muck (slang); magnifico, mogul, notable, notability, personage; worthy (humorous),n.; *Also:*
  1. kingpin—main, or most important, person in a group or undertaking
  2. magnate, tycoon—important person in business or industry
  3. principal—person who occupies the main, chief, or leading position
  4. protagonist—leading person or character in a struggle, conflict, activity, etc.; main character in a play, story, or novel

23. To Seem or Become Important: bulk,v.

24. Having the Air, Manner, or Appearance of an Important Person; Having an Air or Manner of Distinction: distingué, distinguished,adj.

25. To Treat (a Person) as Very Important, as a Celebrity, Person of Social Consequence, etc.: lionize,v. (lionization,n.)

26. A Person So Treated: lion,n.

27. Practice or Custom of So Treating a Person or Persons: lionism,n.

28. State of Being So Treated: lionism,n.

29. To Visit, or Exhibit, the Important Points of Interest in (a Place); To Engage in Such Visits: lionize,v. (lionization,n.)

30. To Place Importance on, or Show that One Considers Important, as by Verbal Expression, Action, etc.: accent, accentuate, emphasize, lay or place emphasis or stress on or upon, point up, punctuate, stress, underline, underscore,v. (accentuation, emphasis, punctuation, stress, underlinement,n. emphatic,adj.)

31. Feeling or Acting Important: consequential, pompous, pretentious, self-important, toplofty,adj. (consequentialness or consequentiality, pompousness or pomposity; pretentiousness, pretension, or pretensions; toploftiness,n.)

32. Action, Speech, or Bearing That Characterizes a Self-Important Person: pomposity, n.

33. Abnormal Feeling of Importance: exaltation,n.

34. Self-Important Person,n.
  1. cockalorum—self-important, and usually undersized, man
  2. whippersnapper—self-important, generally young, person who is in actuality totally unimportant

35. Less Important: accessory or accessorial, minor, secondary, subaltern, subordinate, subsidiary,adj.

36. That Which Is Less Important: accessory, subordinate, subsidiary,n.

37. One Who Holds a Less Important Position or Rank: subaltern, subordinate,n.

38. Accompanying, but of Lesser Importance: accessory, collateral,adj. (accessory, collateral,n.)

39. Falling Off, Usually Ludicrously, in Importance: anticlimactic, bathetic,adj. (anticlimax, bathos,n.)

40. To Treat as Less Important: subordinate, v. (subordination,n.)

41. To Become Less Important: wane,v.

849. UNIMPORTANCE

1. Unimportant: fribble, frivolous, frothy, immaterial, inconsequential, insignificant, lowly, minute, niggling, nonessential, null, paltry, peddling, pettifogging, petty, picayune, picayunish, piddling, puny, scrubby, slight, trifling, trivial, trumpery, unessential, unmomentous, unnotable, vain, yeasty,adj. (fribble, frivolousness or frivolity, frothiness, immateriality or immaterialness, inconsequentiality or inconsequence, insignificance or insignificancy, lowliness, minuteness, nullity, paltriness, pettiness, picayunishness, puniness, scrubbiness, slightness; triviality, trivialness, or trivialism; unessentiality, vainness, yeastiness,n.)

2. Unimportant to the Carrying Out of Actions, Processes, etc.; Unimportant to the Conduct of War: non-critical, non-strategic, adj.

3. Unimportant, i.e., Producing No Important Results, etc.: inconclusive, indecisive, uneventful, unfateful, unmomentous,adj. (inconclusiveness, indecisiveness, uneventfulness, unfatefulness,n.)

4. Unimportant Thing: bagatelle, fico, fribble, frivolity, froth, immateriality, insignificancy, insignificant, nihility, nonentity, nonessential, nullity, picayune, trifle, trivialism, triviality,n.

5. Unimportant Things or Items; Trifles: minutiae, trivia,n.

6. Unimportant Person: cipher, insignificancy, nobody, nonentity, nullity, picayune, snip, squirt, whiffet,n.

7. Unimportant Person, Generally Young, Who Considers Himself Important: whippersnapper,n.

8. To Treat as, or Consider, Unimportant: ignore, pooh-pooh, slight, sneeze at, trifle with,v.

850. APPROVAL

1. To Approve; To Approve of: accept, admire, applaud, approbate, confirm, countenance, endorse, indorse, ratify, sanction, smile on, uphold,v.

2. Approval: acceptance, admiration, applause, approbation, confirmation, countenance, endorsement, indorsement, plaudit, ratification, sanction,n.

3. Approving; Showing, or Descr. of, Approval: applausive, approbative, approbatory, confirmatory, plausive,adj.

4. Approver: accepter, admirer, applauder, endorser, indorser, ratifier, upholder,n.

5. To Shout, or Otherwise Loudly Show, Approval of (Usually by a Crowd, etc.): acclaim, applaud, cheer, cheer for; root for (colloq.),v. (acclaim, acclamation, applause, cheers,n. acclaimer, applauder, rooter,n. acclamatory, applausive,adj.)

6. To Mention, or Speak of, with Approval: commend,v. (commendation,n. commendatory,adj.)

7. Warm Expression of Approval: plaudit,n.

8. To Approve of and Agree with: sympathize with,v. (sympathy,n. sympathizer,n. sympathetic,adj.)

9. To Give Approval (to): consent (to),v. (consent,n.)

10. To Aid by Approval: uphold,v. (upholder, n.)

11. Self-Approval: amour-propre,n. (French)

12. Official Approval (as by the Church, etc.) to Print or Publish: imprimatur,n.

13. Paper or Statement Certifying as to the Quality, Value, Good Character, etc., of Someone or Something: testimonial,n. (testimonial,adj.)

14. Sign of Approval: thumbs up,n.

15. Generally Approved: orthodox (esp. of religious or political beliefs), popular,adj. (orthodoxy, popularity,n.)

16. To Cause to Be Generally Approved: popularize,v. (popularization,n.)

17. Approved in Speech or Language: standard,adj.

18. To Subject (the Actions, Writings, etc., of Others) to Approval or Disapproval: censor, pass on, review,v. (censorship,n. censor,n.)

19. Worthy of Approval: acceptable, admirable, approvable, commendable,adj.

851. PRAISE

1. To Praise: acclaim, applaud, belaud, bepraise; boost (colloq.); celebrate, commend, glorify, laud,v.; *Also:*

1. celebrate—praise in a poem, song, speech, etc.

2. cite—praise, by mentioning publicly, as for heroic action or bravery in war, scholarship, etc.

3. compliment—express light praise for or of

4. eulogize, panegyrize—deliver a speech of high praise of; speak or write of in terms of high praise

5. exalt, extol—praise highly, or in glowing terms

6. flatter—praise insincerely and/or exaggeratedly

7. hymn—sing the praises of

8. overpraise—praise too highly

9. paean, pean—praise in song

10. puff—give exaggerated praise to, esp. in a magazine, book, etc.

11. resound—praise highly and in glowing terms (poetic)

12. tout—praise highly, in glowing terms, insistently, etc. (colloq.)

2. Praise,n. From Sec. 1: acclaim or acclamation, applause, bepraisement, boost, celebration, commendation, glorification, laudation; celebration, citation, compliment, eulogy, panegyric, exaltation, extolment, flattery, hymn, overpraise, paean or pean, puff, puffery; *Also:*

1. accolade—public and ceremonial praise of a high degree

2. éclat—praise or acclaim for a brilliant achievement or success

3. encomium—warm and enthusiastic praise, usually expressed elaborately or formally

4. kudos—great praise from the populace (colloq.)

5. plaudit—praise

6. trade-last—compliment heard about someone and told to that person in exchange for a similar compliment about the teller (colloq.)

7. tribute—high praise

3. Praiser,n. From Sec. 1: acclaimer, applauder, belauder, bepraiser, booster, celebrator, commender, glorifier, lauder; celebrator, eulogizer, panegyrist or panegyrizer, exalter, extoller, flatterer, hymner; *From Sec. 2:* encomiast

4. Praising; Showing, Expressive of, or Descr. of, Praise,adj. From Sec. 1: acclamatory, applausive, commendatory, laudatory or laudative, complimentary, eulogistic, panegyric or panegyrical, flattering; *From Sec. 2:* encomiastic, plausive

5. Advertisement or Opinion Containing Extravagant Praise, Esp. about, or on the Jacket of, a Book: blurb,n. (colloq.)

6. Song of Praise: hymn, laud, paean,n.

7. Composer of a Hymn: hymnist,n.

8. Worthy of, or Deserving, Praise: commendable, creditable, glorious, honorable, laudable, meritorious, praiseworthy,adj. (commendableness, creditability or creditableness, gloriousness, honorableness, laudableness or laudability, meritoriousness, praiseworthiness,n.)

9. One Who, or That Which, Elicits Praise: credit,n.

10. That Which Deserves Praise: merit,n.

11. Claim to Praise: merit,n.

852. FLATTERY

1. To Flatter: beslaver, blandish, blarney, bootlick, butter, butter up, cajole, compliment, salve; sawder (colloq.); soft-soap (colloq.); wheedle,v.; *Also:*

1. **adulate**—overwhelm (often a public or well-publicized figure) with flattery; flatter excessively or servilely
2. **bedaub**—use an excess of flattery upon
3. **blandish**—treat with gentle flattery
4. **jolly**—flatter (a person) to put him in a good humor
5. **puff**—give exaggerated flattery to, esp. in a book or magazine

2. Flattery,n. *From Sec. 1:* blandishment or blandishments; cajolery, cajolement, or cajolements; compliment or compliments, salve; adulation, blandishment, puff or puffery; *Also:*
  1. **courtliness**—flattery, esp. toward a woman or a superior
  2. **flummery**—empty compliment or compliments
  3. **sycophancy**—flattery from a self-seeker
  4. **taffy**—flattery

3. Flattering,adj. *From Sec. 1:* blandishing, bootlicking, cajoling, complimentary, wheedling; adulatory; *From Sec. 2:* courtly, sycophantic; *Also:* assentatory, candied, honeyed

4. Flatterer,n. *From Sec. 1:* blandisher, bootlicker, cajoler, wheedler; adulator; *From Sec. 2:* sycophant; *Also:* assentator, soother,n.

5. To Engage in Flattery: blandish, blarney, bootlick, cajole, flatter, wheedle,v.

6. To Engage in Offensively Obvious Flattery: slaver, slobber,v.

7. To Deceive with Artful Flattery: cajole, v. (cajolement, cajolery,n. cajoler,n.)

8. To Flatter Servilely or Obsequiously in Order to Gain Favor, Friendliness, etc.: bootlick, curry favor with; fawn (on or upon); ingratiate oneself with, toady to,v. (ingratiation or self-ingratiation,n.)

9. One Who Flatters Servilely or Obsequiously in Order to Gain Favor or Friendliness: bootlicker, fawner, flunky or flunkey, lickspittle, sycophant, toady,n.

10. Descr. of One Who Engages in Self-Seeking Flattery, or of His Actions, Attitudes, Speech, etc.: fawning, ingratiating, ingratiatory, obsequious, servile, silken, sycophantic, toadying,adj. (obsequiousness, servility, sycophancy,n.)

853. APPLAUSE

1. To Applaud: clap,v.

2. To Applaud (Someone): acclaim,v.

3. To Applaud a Side or Person in a Contest: cheer for; root for (colloq.),v. (rooter, n.)

4. Applause: acclaim, acclamation, cheers, clapping, plaudit or plaudits,n.

5. Enthusiastic Applause, Esp. for an Entertainer, Speaker, Public Figure, etc., by a Large Group of People: ovation,n.

6. Round of Applause: plaudit,n.

7. Burst or Round of Cheers or Applause from a Crowd or Audience: salvo,n.

8. Group of Paid Applauders at a Play or Other Public Performance; Group of Obsequious Applauders: claque,n.

9. Applauding: acclamatory, applausive, cheering, clapping, plausive,adj.

854. SUPPORT

1. To Support; To Favor: adhere to, advocate, ally oneself with, back, champion, countenance, endorse, espouse, hold a brief for, indorse, make common cause with, rally to, range oneself with, second, side with, subscribe to, take the part of, uphold,v.

2. To Support (an Artist, Artistic Endeavor, etc.): patronize,v. (patronage,n. patron, patroness,n.)

3. Support: adherence, advocacy, backing, championship, countenance, endorsement, espousal, indorsement; subscription (to) ,n.

4. Loyal and Unwavering Support: yeoman service, yeoman's service,n.

5. Supporter; Favorer: adherent, advocate, ally, backer, champion, endorser, espouser, exponent, indorser, proponent, second or seconder, subscriber, upholder,n.

6. Supporter of the Pope: papist,n. (derogatory)

7. Supporter (of an Institution): pillar,n.

8. Loyal Supporter of a Cause, Political Party, etc.: stalwart,n.

9. To Support the Candidacy of: plump for, v.

10. To Seem to Support Both Sides of an Issue Simultaneously, while Actually Taking Neither: straddle,v. (straddler,n.)

11. Movement to Which People Give Their Support: cause,n.

12. To Speak in Favor of: advocate, recommend,v. (advocacy, recommendation,n. advocate, recommender,n.)

13. To Speak Favorably of: boost (colloq.),v. (booster,n.)

14. To Regard Favorably: esteem,v. (esteem, n.)

15. To Defend, i.e., Come to the Defense of: champion, hold a brief for, take up the cudgels for,v. (champion,n.)

16. Defense, in Speech or Writing, of a Cause, Principle, Party, etc.: apologia, apology,n. (apologist, apologizer,n. apologetic, apologetical,adj. apologize,v.)

17. Systematic Defense in Argument, Esp. of the Divine Origin of Christianity: apologetics,n. (apologist,n.)

18. Branch of Theology Dealing with the Defense of Christianity: apologetics,n.

19. One Who Defends the Less Tenable Cause without Any Sincerity, but Merely for the Sake of Starting a Discussion: devil's advocate,n.

20. To Get the Support of: enlist,v. (enlistment,n.)

855. ADMIRATION

1. To Admire Greatly: adore, esteem, idolatrize, idolize, venerate, worship,v.

2. Great Admiration: adoration, esteem, estimation, idolatry, idolism, idolization, veneration, worship,n.

3. Admirer: adorer, idolater or, fem., idolatress, idolizer, venerator, worshiper,n.

4. Admiring: adoring, idolatrous, wondering, worshipful,adj.

5. Affected with Admiration: wonderstricken, wonder-struck,adj.

6. Self-Admiration: narcism, narcissism,n. (narcist, narcissist,n. narcistic, narcissistic, adj.)

7. One Who Is Greatly Admired: idol,n.

8. Worthy of Admiration: admirable, brilliant, estimable, splendid, venerable,adj. (admirableness, brilliance or brilliancy, estimableness, splendor or splendidness, venerableness,n.)

9. That Which Is Given to Indicate Admiration or Respect: testimonial, tribute,n. (testimonial,adj.)

10. To Excite Admiration in (a Person) by a Display of Literal or Figurative Brilliance: dazzle,v.

11. Exciting Admiration: august, dazzling, spectacular,adj. (augustness,n.)

856. RESPECT

1. To Respect: adore, esteem, honor, regard, revere, reverence, venerate, worship,v.

2. Respect: adoration, deference, esteem, homage, honor, obeisance, regard, reverence, veneration, worship,n.

3. Degree of Respect: dignity,n.

4. Popular Respect: repute,n.

5. To Show Abject or Servile Respect to: kotow to, kowtow to,v. (kotower, kowtower,n.)

6. Respectful: deferent, deferential, obeisant, regardful, reverent, reverential,adj.

7. Exhibition of Enthusiastic Respect by the Public: ovation,n.

8. Respectful Act or Action: devoirs,n.

9. Gesture of Respect,n.
  1. bow—a bending from the waist as a gesture of respect
  2. curtsy, curtsey—female gesture of respect in which the body is lowered and the knees bent
  3. genuflection—a bending of the knees in respect, esp. to God
  4. kotow, kowtow—gesture of respect in which a person kneels and bows his head to the ground or hits his head against the ground
  5. obeisance—gesture of deep respect
  6. salaam—very low bow of respect, common in the East, in which the palm of the hand is placed on the forehead
  7. scrape—a drawing back of the foot in making a bow
  8. toast, health, pledge—gesture of respect or wish for a person's continuing good health when drinking, in which the glass is raised toward the person honored

10. To Make a Gesture of Respect,v. *From Sec. 9:* bow, curtsy or curtsey, genuflect, kotow or kowtow, salaam, scrape, toast (genuflector, kotower or kowtower, toaster,n.)

11. To Drink a Toast to: pledge, toast,v.

12. Person to Whom One Drinks a Toast: toast,n.

13. Respected: esteemed, honored, redoubted, reputable, respectable, revered, reverenced, reverend, venerated, well-thought-of,adj. (reputability, respectability or respectableness,n.)

14. Respected or Honored Owing to Age, or to Usage over a Long Period of Time: timehonored,adj.

15. Worthy of Respect: august, decent, estimable, redoubtable, redoubted, respectable, reverend; venerable (often by reason of age, high rank, etc.),adj. (augustness, decency, estimableness, redoubtableness, respectability or respectableness, venerability or venerableness,n.)

16. Respectable People, Collectively: respectability,n.

17. Those Things Generally Considered Respectable: respectabilities,n.

18. Arousing or Commanding Respect: august, redoubtable, sublime,adj. (augustness, redoubtableness, sublimity or sublimeness,n.)

19. Arousing Respect by Age or Dignity of Appearance: venerable,adj. (venerability, venerableness,n.)

20. Advancement in Respect or Esteem: ascent,n.

857. HONOR

1. To Honor: celebrate, crown, grace, dignify,v. (celebration,n.)

2. To Honor (a Holiday): celebrate, observe, v. (celebration, observance,n.)

3. To Honor in Song: chant, troll,v.

4. To Honor by, or as if by, Crowning with Laurel: laureate,v. (laureation,n. laureate, adj.)

5. To Honor with an Entertainment, etc.: fete,v.

6. To Give a Medal, Ribbon, etc., to as an Honor, or in Honor of Some Deed: decorate, v. (decoration,n.)

7. To Mention as Worthy of Honor for Some Military Exploit, Academic Accomplishment, etc.: cite,v. (citation,n.)

8. Honor: credit, distinction,n.

9. Symbol of Honor: crown or garland (worn on the head), distinction, laurel, medal, palm, ribbon,n.

10. Given As, or Indicating, a Symbol of Honor: honorary,adj.

11. Certificate Conferring Scholastic Honors, Privileges, Rights, etc.: diploma,n.

12. One Who Has Received a Diploma: diplomate,n.

13. Descr. of Graduation with Honors in an Institution of Learning (in Ascending Order): cum laude, magna cum laude, summa cum laude (Latin)

14. One Holding a Position of Honor or Dignity, Esp. in a Church: dignitary, dignity, n. (dignitary,adj.)

15. Those Holding Positions of Honor or Dignity, Collectively: dignity,n.

16. One Who Has Been Honored with a Medal: medalist,n.

17. Holding a Position, Rank, or Title Purely As an Honor, without the Usual Monetary Rewards, Duties, Privileges, etc.; Descr. of Such a Position, Rank, or Title: honorary, adj.

18. Worthy of, or Bringing, Honor: creditable, honorable, palmary,adj. (creditability or creditableness, honorableness,n.)

19. One Who, or That Which, Brings Honor: credit,n.

20. To Increase the Honor of: adorn, aggrandize,v. (adornment, aggrandizement,n.)

21. Not Honored: uncelebrated, uncrowned, unhonored, unsung,adj.

858. POLITENESS

1. Polite: attentive, civil, civilized, complaisant, courteous, courtly; debonair, debonaire, or debonaire; genteel; gentlemanly (of the male); gracious; ladylike (of the female); mannerly, refined, well-behaved, well-bred, well-mannered,adj.

2. Politeness: attentiveness or attention, bon ton, breeding, civility, complaisance, comity, courtesy or courteousness, courtliness, debonairness, genteelness; gentlemanliness (of the male); good breeding, good manners, graciousness; ladylikeness (of the female); mannerliness, politesse, refinement,n.

3. Courteous and Kind, Esp. to Those of a Lower Social Position: gracious,adj. (graciousness, graciosity,n.)

4. Polite, Friendly, and Pleasant: affable, adj. (affability, affableness,n.)

5. Polite to Women (of the Male): chivalric, chivalrous, gallant, knightly,adj. (chivalry or chivalrousness, gallantry or gallantness, knightliness or knight-errantry,n.)

6. Chivalrous Man: cavalier, chevalier, gallant,n.

7. Chivalrous Acts, Esp. in Courtship: attentions,n.

8. Japanese Code of Chivalry in Feudal Times: Bushido,n.

9. Extravagantly Chivalrous: quixotic, quixotical,adj. (quixotism,n.)

10. Extravagantly Chivalrous Act: quixotism, n.

11. Extravagantly Chivalrous Actions: knight-errantry,n.

12. Stiffly or Formally Polite: ceremonious, adj.

13. Formal Politeness: ceremoniousness, ceremony, politesse,n.

14. Polite in Speech: well-spoken,adj.

15. Smoothly Polite: suave, urbane,adj. (suavity or suaveness, urbanity or urbaneness, n.)

16. Slavishly Polite: obsequious, servile, subservient,adj. (obsequiousness, servility, subservience or subserviency,n.)

17. Knowledge of, or Training in, the Ways of Polite Society: breeding,n.

18. Polite Formalities of Good Breeding: etiquette,n.

19. Act of Politeness: courtesy,n.

20. Due or Expected Acts of Politeness: devoirs,n.

21. Acts of Politeness That Make for Pleasant Social Living: amenities, civilities, suavities, urbanities,n.

22. Polite Person: gentleman (masc.), lady or gentlewoman (fem.), thoroughbred,n.

23. Spanish Gentleman: caballero,n.

859. REFINEMENT

1. Refined (Figuratively): civilized, cultivated, cultured, genteel, polished, rarefied, suave, urbane,adj.

2. Refined—of Literary or Artistic Style: Attic,adj.

3. Refinement (Figurative): civilization, cultivation, culture, genteelness, gentility, polish, rarefaction, suavity or suaveness, urbanity or urbaneness,n.

4. To Refine (Figuratively): civilize, cultivate, culture, polish, rarefy,v. (civilization, cultivation, rarefaction,n.)

5. A Refinement of Living: nicety,n.

6. Affectedly Refined: niminy-piminy, precious,adj. (preciousness, preciosity,n.)

7. Too Refined: overrefined,adj. (overrefinement,n.)

8. Smooth of Manner, Speech, etc.: bland, polished, silken, sleek, slick, smooth, suave, urbane,adj. (blandness, polish, sleekness, slickness, smoothness, suavity or suaveness, urbanity or urbaneness,n.)

9. Hypocritically Smooth of Manner, Speech, etc.: sleek,adj. (sleekness,n.)

10. Excessively or Sickeningly Smooth of Manner, Speech, etc.: oily, oleaginous, unctuous,adj. (oiliness, oleaginousness; unctuousness, unctuosity, or unction,n.)

860. IMPOLITENESS

1. Impolite: bad-mannered, boorish; caddish (of the male); cavalier, churlish, discourteous, ill-behaved, ill-bred, illiberal, ill-mannered, impertinent, impudent, insolent, inurbane, mannerless, offhand, rude, rustic; snippy (colloq.); unbred, uncivil, uncivilized, uncomplaisant, uncourteous, uncourtly, uncouth, ungenteel; ungentlemanly or ungentlemanlike (of the male); ungracious, unhandsome; unladylike (of the female); unmannered, unmannerly, unpolite, unrefined,adj.

2. Impoliteness: bad or poor manners; boorishness; caddishness (of the male); churlishness, discourtesy or discourteousness, ill breeding, illiberality or illiberalness, impertinence or impertinency; impudence, impudency, or impudentness; incivility, insolence, inurbanity, rudeness, rusticity; snippiness (colloq.); uncivility or uncivilness, uncourtliness, uncouthness, ungenteelness; ungentlemanliness (of the male); ungraciousness, unhandsomeness, unmannerliness, unpoliteness, unrefinement or unrefinedness,n.

3. Scornfully or Contemptuously Impolite, Rude, or Insolent: contumelious,adj. (contumely,n.)

4. Impolite Person: boor; bounder (colloq.); cad (masc.), churl, clown, insolent,n.

5. Bad-Mannered Girl or Woman: hussy,n.

6. Impolite Act, Behavior, Language, or Treatment: discourtesy, impertinence or impertinency, impudence, incivility, insolence,n.

7. Impolite and Unfriendly: inaffable,adj. (inaffability,n.)

8. Violating Good Manners: indelicate, uncalled-for,adj. (indelicacy,n.)

9. Something That Violates Good Manners: indelicacy,n.

10. Impolite to Women (of the Male): caddish, unchivalric, unchivalrous, ungallant,adj. (caddishness, unchivalrousness or unchivalry, ungallantness,n.)

11. Man Who Shows No Courtesy or Chivalry to Women: cad,n.

12. Impolite to Those of a Lower Social Position: ungracious,adj. (ungraciousness, n.)

13. Devoid of Politeness or Ceremoniousness in Manner and/or Speech: abrupt; bluff (implying good nature or lack of malice); blunt or crude (implying a disregard of others' feelings), brief; brusque (implying a certain roughness or sharpness); churlish (implying ill-humor); crusty (implying a possibly kind heart hidden behind sharpness of manner); curt (implying especially disconcerting shortness of speech, answers, commands, etc.); gruff or gruffy (implying a degree of grumpiness or anger with, perhaps—to be literal—a certain hoarseness or throatiness of voice); offhand; outspoken (implying a lack of delicacy of phrasing even at the expense of causing wounded feelings); short, short-spoken; snippy (colloq.); surly (implying ill-temper or ill-humor), unceremonious, adj. (abruptness, bluffness, bluntness, crudeness or crudity, briefness, brusqueness or (French) brusquerie, churlishness, crustiness, curtness, gruffness or gruffiness, outspokenness, shortness, snippiness, surliness, unceremoniousness,n.)

14. To Make Rude, Unkind, or Scoffing Remarks: jeer,v. (jeer,n. jeerer,n. jeering,adj.)

15. To Make Fun of Rudely: jeer, jeer at, laugh at,v.

**16. Impolite to Elders, Those in High Position, or Others Worthy of Respect or

Courtesy: disrespectful,adj. (disrespect, disrespectfulness,n. disrespect,v.)

861. DISRESPECT

1. Disrespectful: awless or aweless; flip (colloq.); flippant; fresh (colloq.); impertinent, impudent, insolent, irreverent, saucy; snippy (colloq.),adj.

2. Disrespect; Disrespectfulness: disesteem, disregard, flippancy or flippantness; freshness (colloq.); impertinence or impertinency; impudence, impudency, or impudentness; insolence, irreverence, sauciness; snippiness (colloq.),n.

3. Disrespectful Person: flip (colloq.), insolent,n.

4. Disrespectful Conduct, Act, Language, Statement, Thing, etc.: impertinence or impertinency, impudence, insolence, irreverence, n.

5. To Feel Disrespect for: disesteem, disrespect,v.

6. To Show Disrespect for: affront, dishonor, disrespect,v. (affront,n.)

7. Disrespectful to Parents: impious, unfilial,adj. (impiousness or impiety,n.)

8. Disrespectful to the Sacred or to That Considered Sacred: blasphemous, impious, irreverent, profane, sacrilegious,adj. (blasphemousness or blasphemy, impiousness or impiety, irreverence, profaneness or profanity, sacrilegiousness or sacrilege,n.)

9. Act, Actions, or Conduct Disrespectful to the Sacred or to That Considered Sacred: blasphemy, impiety, irreverence, profanity, sacrilege,n.

10. Disrespectful Language,n.
1. **blasphemy**—language disrespectful to God or to anything sacred
2. **cursing**—blasphemous language, often used to ask God to bring evil or misfortune to someone or something
3. **profanity**—disrespectful language about holy or sacred people or things
4. **swearing**—blasphemous, and often strictly meaningless, language

11. To Use Disrespectful Language to or about,v. *From Sec. 10:* blaspheme, curse (blasphemer,n.)

12. To Indulge in Disrespectful Language,v. *From Sec. 10:* blaspheme, curse, swear (blasphemer,n.)

13. Term, Word, or Expression That Uses the Name of God or of a Sacred Thing Disrespectfully as a Means of Expressing Anger, Emphasis, etc.: curse, oath, swearword,n.

14. To Treat (Something Sacred) with Disrespect: commit sacrilege upon, desecrate, profane, violate,v. (sacrilege, desecration, profanation, violation,n. desecrater or desecrator, profaner, violator,n. profanatory, violative,adj.)

862. BOLDNESS; FORWARDNESS

1. Bold; Forward; Taking Undue Liberties, etc.: assuming, assumptive, assured, audacious, bantam, barefaced, brash, brashy; brassy (colloq.); brazen, brazenfaced; cheeky (colloq.); cool, defiant; flip (colloq.); flippant; fresh (colloq.); immodest, impertinent, impudent, insolent, malapert; nervy (colloq.); pert (generally of a child or young woman); presumptuous, procacious; saucy (generally of a child or young woman); shameless; snippy (colloq.),adj.

2. Boldness; Forwardness: assumption, assuredness, audacity or audaciousness, barefacedness, brashiness; brass or brassiness (colloq.); brazenness; cheek or cheekiness (colloq.); coolness, defiantness, effrontery, flippancy or flippantness; freshness (colloq.); gall (colloq.); hardihood, immodesty, impertinence or impertinency; impudence, impudency, or impudentness; insolence, malapertness; nerve (colloq.); pertness (generally of a child or young woman); presumption or presumptuousness, procacity; sauciness (generally of a child or young woman); shamelessness; snippiness (colloq.),n.

3. Scornfully or Contemptuously Insolent: contumelious,adj. (contumely,n.)

4. Bold or Forward Person: brazenface; flip (colloq.); insolent, malapert,n.

5. Bold or Impudent Young Person: squirt, n. (colloq.)

6. Bold or Impudent Girl: chit,n.

7. Bold or Impudent Woman: hussy,n.

8. Bold or Forward Act, Action, or Speech: impertinence, impudence, insolence, procacity,n.

9. To Act with Boldness or Forwardness, or in a Way to Take Undue Liberties: presume,v. (presumption,n. presumer,n.)

10. To Be So Bold (as to): dare (to),v.

11. To Face with Boldness, Impudence, etc.: brazen out, brazen through,v.

12. To Make Bold or Impudent: brazen,v.

863. UNREFINEMENT

1. Unrefined (Figuratively): artless, backwood, backwoods, barbarian, barbaric, barbarous, bearish, boorish, clodhopping, coarse, common, crass, crude, gross, illiberal, inurbane, lowbred; lowbrow (colloq.); Philistine, primitive, provincial, raffish, raw, rough, rude, rugged, rustic, savage, uncivilized, uncouth, uncultivated, uncultured, unpolished, vulgar,adj.

2. Unrefinement: artlessness, barbarianism, barbarism, barbarity, barbarousness, boorishness, coarseness, commonness, crassness, crudity or crudeness, grossness, illiberality or illiberalness, inurbanity, Philistinism, primitiveness, provincialism or provinciality, raffishness, rawness, roughness, rudeness, ruggedness, rusticity; savageness, savagery, or savagism; uncouthness; vulgarity, vulgarism, or vulgarness,n.

3. Unrefined Person: barbarian, bear, boor; bounder (colloq.); clodhopper; lowbrow (colloq.); Philistine, provincial, savage, vulgarian,n.

4. Person Contemptuous of Refinement, Culture, Art, Literature, etc. (Derogatory): barbarian, Philistine,n. (barbarianism, Philistinism,n. Philistine,adj.)

5. To Become Unrefined: barbarize, coarsen, v. (barbarization,n.)

6. To Make, or Cause to Become, Unrefined: barbarize, coarsen, rusticate, vulgarize,v. (barbarization, rustication, vulgarization,n.)

7. Unrefined Act or Action: barbarism, savagery or savagism, vulgarism or vulgarity,n.

8. Unrefined Word, Phrase, Term, or Expression: vulgarism, vulgarity,n.

864. COARSENESS

1. Coarse (Figuratively): blatant; broad (of language, humor, etc.); brutal, brute, brutish, common, crass, crude, earthy, gross, indelicate, low, lowbred, vulgar,adj.

2. Coarseness (Figurative): blatancy; broadness (of language, humor, etc); brutality, brutishness, commonness, crassitude, crassness, crudity or crudeness, grossness, indelicacy; vulgarity, vulgarism, or vulgarness,n.

3. Coarse Act or Action: brutality, indelicacy, vulgarism, vulgarity,n.

4. Coarse Person: bounder (colloq.), brute, pig, swine, vulgarian,n.

5. To Become Coarse: coarsen,v.

6. To Make, or Cause to Become, Coarse: coarsen, vulgarize,v. (vulgarization,n.)

7. Coarse-Looking, Red-Faced, and Fat: blowzed, blowzy,adj.

8. Coarsely Human, Rather than Ethereal or Spiritual: earthy,adj.

9. Offensively Coarse: rank,adj. (rankness, n.)

865. ROUGHNESS

1. Rough in Actions, Manner, Behavior, etc.,adj.
1. **bearish, bearlike**—rough in actions or behavior, like a bear
2. **boisterous**—rough and noisy
3. **gruff, gruffy**—rough and cross in manner, attitude, or speech
4. **hooligan**—ruffian (colloq.)
5. **robust**—rough; boisterous
6. **robustious**—rough; boisterous (humorous)
7. **rough-and-ready**—having or showing a rough attitude or vigor, rather than being delicate and refined
8. **rowdy, rowdyish**—rough and ill-behaved or disorderly
9. **rude**—rough in manners or conduct
10. **ruffian, ruffianly**—rough and cruel; rough and lawless
11. **thuggish**—ruffian
12. **tough**—rowdy; ruffian
13. **violent**—rough and strong; rough and harmful in action

2. Roughness,n. *From Sec. 1:* boisterousness, gruffness, gruffiness, robustness, rowdiness, rowdyishness, rudeness, ruffianism, toughness, violence, n.

3. Rough Person,n. *From Sec. 1:* bear, hooligan, rowdy, ruffian, thug, tough; *Also:*
1. **bruiser**—rowdy; ruffian (colloq.)
2. **hoodlum**—ruffian
3. **roughneck**—rough and unrefined person (colloq.)

4. Rough Behavior or Action,n. *From Sec. 1:* hooliganism, rowdyism, ruffianism, thuggery, violence; *From Sec. 3:* hoodlumism; *Also:* 1. **roughhouse**—rowdy behavior (colloq.)

5. To Become Rough, or Rough and Noisy: ruffle,v. (ruffler,n.)

6. Of the Character of Rough Falling, Tumbling, Fighting, Struggling, etc.; Descr. of Such Falling, Fighting, etc.: rough-and-tumble,adj.

7. A Fight, Struggle, etc., of This Nature: rough-and-tumble,n.

8. To Engage in Rough but Kindly Play, esp. Indoors: roughhouse (colloq.),v. (roughhouse,n.)

9. To Push Around, Fight with, etc., Roughly, and in a Spirit of Play: roughhouse,v. (colloq.)

866. UNCIVILIZED

1. Uncivilized: barbarian, barbaric, barbarous, primitive, rude, savage, unchristian,

wild,adj. (barbarianism, barbarism, barbarousness, primitiveness, rudeness; savageness, savagery, or savagism; wildness,n.)

2. Uncivilized Person: barbarian, savage,n.

3. Savage People, Collectively: savagery,n.

4. Savage Act, Behavior, or Character: savagery,n.

5. Study of the Comparative Customs and Mores of Primitive Peoples, Groups, etc.: agriology,n. (agriologist,n. agriological,adj.)

6. Belief or Theory that Primitive Culture or Life is Superior to, or Has Advantages over, Civilization: primitivism,n. (primitivist, n.)

7. Primitive Forces, Instincts, or Desires That Reside in the Unconscious (Psychoanalysis): id,n.

8. Reversion to a More Primitive Type or State, esp. Biologically: atavism,n. (atavist, n. atavistic, atavic,adj.)

9. Reversion of Biological Cells or Tissue to a More Primitive Stage: cataplasia,n.

867. INSULT

1. To Insult,v.
1. **affront**—insult (someone) intentionally, directly, and to his face, whether by words, action, or attitude; insult by lack of respect; insult the dignity or self-respect of
2. **dishonor**—insult
3. **disoblige**—affront
4. **flout**—insult
5. **offend**—insult, usually unintentionally
6. **outrage**—insult; insult to an incredible degree
7. **slight**—insult by treating as if unimportant or not worth bothering with
8. **slur**—insult; make insulting remarks about
9. **snub**—insult by treating with cold indifference or contempt, or by ignoring discourteously
10. **violate**—insult (one's feelings, attitudes, etc.)

2. Insult,n. *From Sec. 1:* affront, dishonor, flout, offense, outrage, slight, slur, snub, violation; *Also:*
1. **brickbat**—insult figuratively thrown at someone
2. **contumely**—insult; insulting language or treatment
3. **despite**—insulting act
4. **indignity**—insult; insult to one's dignity; humiliating insult
5. **insolence**—insulting attitude, behavior, or speech
6. **slap**—insult
7. **taunt**—insulting remark

3. Insulting,adj. *From Sec. 1:* disobliging, offensive, outrageous, violative (disobligingness, offensiveness, outrageousness,n.) ; *From Sec. 2:* contumelious, despiteful, insolent (contumeliousness, despitefulness, insolence,n.)

4. Insulting Word or Term: affront, epithet, slur,n.

5. Insulting Reference: innuendo,n.

6. Below One's Dignity: infra dignitatem (in colloquial usage, abbreviated to *infra dig.*)

868. OFFENSE

1. To Offend (Someone); To Hurt the Feelings of: cut, disoblige, huff, injure, sting, tread on the toes of, wound,v.; *Also:*
1. **affront**—offend in such a way as to cause a loss of self-respect or dignity combined with deep resentment

2. **insult**—offend purposely and maliciously
3. **outrage**—offend deeply; offend to an incredible and unbearable extent
4. **pique**—hurt the feelings, pride, or vanity of; offend by ignoring discourteously

2. Offense,n. *From Sec. 1:* injury, sting, wound; affront, insult, outrage; *Also:*
1. **indignity**—offense, or humiliating offense, to one's dignity or pride
2. **sarcasm**—the use of cutting remarks, usually by irony or by saying the opposite of what one means, though the intent is perfectly clear; such remarks or language

3. Offensive, i.e., Causing Offense or Injury to the Feelings,adj. *From Sec. 1:* cutting, disobliging, stinging, wounding (disobligingness, n.); insulting, outrageous (outrageousness, n.); *From Sec. 2:* sarcastic

4. To Hurt (the Feelings): bruise, injure, lacerate, scarify, wound,v. (bruise, injury, laceration, scarification, wound,n.)

5. Feeling of Being Offended: displeasure, offense, pique, resentment, umbrage,n.; *Also:*
1. **dudgeon, high dudgeon**—feeling of offense and anger at refusal, denial, opposition, etc.
2. **huff**—feeling of offense and annoyance combined with a refusal to continue relations with the offender (*left in a huff,* etc.)
3. **pique**—feeling of hurt pride at someone's offensive or insulting actions

6. Feeling Offended,adj. *From Sec. 5:* displeased, offended, piqued, resentful, umbrageous (resentfulness, umbrageousness,n.)

7. To Feel Hurt or Offended: huff,v.

8. To Feel or Be Hurt or Offended by: resent, take amiss, take exception to,v. (resentment,n.)

9. Easily Hurt or Offended: huffy, sensitive, testy, techy or tetchy, thin-skinned, ticklish, touchy,adj. (huffiness, sensitiveness or sensitivity, testiness, techiness or tetchiness, ticklishness, touchiness,n.)

10. To Cause (Someone) to Feel a Painful Lowering of His Self-Respect, Pride, or Dignity: abash; chagrin (esp. by disappointment or failure); confuse, dash, degrade, discountenance or put out of countenance, disgrace, embarrass, humiliate, mortify, shame or put to shame; wither (as by a look or glance of scorn, contempt, etc.),v. (confusion, degradation, embarrassment, humiliation,n.)

11. Such Feeling or Feelings: abashment, chagrin, confusion, degradation, discomfiture, disgrace, embarrassment, humiliation, ignominy, mortification, pudency, shame, shamefacedness,n.

12. Feeling So; Characterized by, or Exhibiting, Such a Feeling: abashed, ashamed, chagrined, chapfallen or chopfallen, confused, degraded, disgraced, embarrassed, hangdog, humiliated, mortified, put out of countenance, shamed, shamefaced,adj.

13. To Feel Shame about: blush at, blush for, v.

14. Causing Such Feelings; Humiliating: abject, chagrining, degrading, disgraceful, embarrassing, humiliatory, ignominious, mortifying, shameful; withering (as a glance of contempt, etc.),adj. (abjectness, disgracefulness, ignominiousness, shamefulness,n.)

15. A Cause or Source of Such Feelings: disgrace, embarrassment, humiliation, mortification, shame,n.

16. Extreme, Often Public, Shame That Holds One Up to Contempt; Act or Behavior of Such Character: ignominy,n.

17. Humiliating Treatment, Language, Insult, or Action: contumely,n.

18. Characterized by Such: contumelious,adj. (contumeliousness,n.)

19. To Embarrass (Someone); To Make (Someone) Feel Embarrassed: abash, confuse, discomfit, disconcert, discountenance or put out of countenance,v.

20. Embarrassed: abashed, confused, discomfited, disconcerted, ill-at-ease, self-conscious, uncomfortable,adj.

21. Embarrassed, or Awkwardly Embarrassed, in Manner: sheepish,adj. (sheepishness,n.)

22. Exhibiting Shame and Embarrassment: shamefaced,adj. (shamefacedness,n.)

23. Embarrassment: abashment, confusion, discomfiture, discomfort, discomposure, disconcertion, disconcertment, pudency, self-consciousness,n.

24. Embarrassing: discomfiting, disconcerting, adj.

25. Embarrassing or Embarrassed, as a Moment, Pause, etc.: awkward, uncomfortable,adj. (awkwardness, uncomfortableness, n.)

26. A Cause or Source of Embarrassment: embarrassment,n.

27. To Lower in Estimation, Dignity, etc.: abase, bemean, debase, degrade, demean, humble, vilify,v. (abasement, debasement, degradation, vilification,n.)

28. To Lower Oneself in Estimation, Dignity, etc.: abase oneself, bemean oneself, debase oneself, degrade oneself, demean oneself, descend, humble oneself, stoop,v. (self-abasement, self-debasement, self-degradation, self-humiliation,n.)

869. RIDICULE

1. To Ridicule; To Make Fun of: deride; fleer (dialectal); gibe, gibe at, jibe, jibe at; guy (colloq.), jeer or jeer at; josh (colloq.); mock, poke fun at, scoff at, taunt,v.; *Also:*
1. **burlesque**—make fun of by imitation
2. **caricature**—ridicule by grotesque exaggeration or distortion, as in a picture, cartoon, description, etc.
3. **hoot at**—shout one's ridicule or derision of
4. **lampoon**—ridicule (a person) maliciously, in writing
5. **parody**—ridicule (someone) by imitating his style of writing, speaking, etc.
6. **pasquinade**—ridicule or satirize by means of a publicly posted lampoon
7. **satirize**—ridicule by sarcasm or irony
8. **squib**—ridicule in a short satirical or sarcastic statement, remark, speech, or piece of writing
9. **travesty**—ridicule (a serious work) by imitating it mockingly; ridicule (a serious subject) by treating it with unwarranted frivolousness
10. **twit, twitter**—make fun of (someone) by reminding him of previous words, faults, promises, etc.

2. To Engage in Ridicule,v. *From Sec. 1:* gibe or jibe, jeer, mock, poke fun, scoff; burlesque, hoot, squib

3. Ridicule; Word or Words, Language, Treatment, etc., That Ridicules,n. *From Sec. 1:* derision, gibe or jibe, jeer, mockery, scoff, taunt; burlesque, caricature, hoot, lampoon, parody, pasquinade, satire, squib, travesty, twit; *Also:*
1. **asteism**—polite irony, or clever and polite derision (rhetoric)

2. **iconoclasm**—ridicule or mockery of the cherished beliefs of others or of the traditions that most people accept and cherish
3. **irony**—light sarcasm for purposes of ridicule, the literal meaning of which is deliberately the opposite of the one intended and to be understood
4. **pasquil**—pasquinade
5. **pastiche**—writing or painting that caricatures by imitation of style
6. **raillery**—language or remarks containing some satire or sarcasm
7. **sarcasm**—mockery; mocking and often biting remark or remarks; mocking remarks, the literal meaning of which is deliberately the opposite of that intended to be understood
8. **scorn**—ridicule; mockery; derision
9. **sport**—derision; mockery

4. Ridiculer; One Who Pokes Fun,n. *From Sec. 1:* derider, giber or jiber, jeerer, mocker, scoffer, taunter; burlesquer, caricaturist, lampooner or lampoonist, parodist, pasquinader, satirist or satirizer, twitter; *From Sec. 3:* iconoclast

5. Ridiculing; Poking Fun,adj. *From Sec. 1:* gibing, jeering, etc.; derisive or derisory; burlesque, satiric or satirical; *From Sec. 3:* iconoclastic, ironic or ironical, sarcastic; *Also:*
1. **backhanded**—sarcastic (backhandedness,n.)
2. **Hudibrastic**—burlesque or satirical in a sophisticated and playful manner—after Samuel Butler's *Hudibras* (of writing, poetry, etc.)
3. **mordant**—sarcastic (mordancy,n.)
4. **sardonic, sardonical**—sneeringly mocking, ridiculing, or sarcastic; bitterly ironic; contemptuously or bitterly derisive (sardonicism,n.)

6. Art, or Practice, of Writing Malicious Satires against a Person: lampoonery,n. (lampoonist,n.)

7. To Expose to Public Ridicule: pillory,v. (pillory,n.)

8. Wooden Framework, Erected on a Post, with Holes for the Hands and Head, in Which an Offender Was Formerly Exposed to Public Ridicule: pillory,n.

9. To Make Fun of, or Poke Fun at, in a Good-Natured or Non-Malicious Manner: banter, chaff, jolly, josh; kid (slang); rally; rib (colloq.),v.

10. To Engage in Such Good-Natured Ridicule: banter, chaff, josh; kid (slang),v.

11. Good-Natured Ridicule: badinage, banter, chaff, persiflage, raillery,n.

12. Bantering, Chaffing, etc.: quizzical,adj.

13. Object of Ridicule: butt, derision, game, jestingstock, laughingstock, mockery, scoff, scorn, sport, target, victim,n.

14. Greek God of Ridicule and Censure; Ridicule Personified As a God by the Ancient Greeks: Momus,n.

870. CONTEMPT

1. To Feel or Express Contempt (for); To Treat with Contempt,v.
1. **belittle**—express a contemptuous and low opinion of
2. **bridle**—make a characteristic gesture of scorn; become scornful
3. **contemn**—look upon or treat with contempt
4. **deride**—laugh at contemptuously
5. **despise**—be contemptuous of
6. **disdain**—feel scorn for; treat with scorn
7. **disesteem**—look upon with contempt

8. **disregard**—treat as unworthy of one's notice or attention
9. **fleer**—gibe; mock; sneer (dialectal)
10. **flout**—treat with contempt or scorn—as *flout the rules, the law, the orders of someone in authority*, etc.
11. **gibe (at), jibe (at)**—show in one's remarks a sneering, contemptuous attitude (toward)
12. **hoot (at)**—express one's contempt (for); shout one's contempt or scorn (for)
13. **huff**—treat with contempt
14. **jeer (at)**—make contemptuous remarks (about)
15. **misprize**—despise
16. **mock**—act contemptuously to; treat with contempt or scorn
17. **pooh-pooh**—express one's scorn or contempt of
18. **rail at, rail against**—show mocking contempt for
19. **ridicule**—express contempt for
20. **scoff (at)**—show contempt (for) by mocking words or acts
21. **scorn**—have an attitude of extreme contempt for; refuse with contempt
22. **scout**—treat or reject with contempt; show contempt for; flout
23. **sneer (at)**—show contempt or scorn (for) by one's facial expression, or by one's laugh or smile; say in contempt or scorn
24. **sneeze at**—treat with contempt
25. **sniff**—show or express contempt or disdain, as if drawing air through the nose for that purpose
26. **snort**—express contempt by, or as if by, expelling the breath noisily through the nose
27. **snub**—treat with contempt
28. **spurn**—treat contemptuously; show contempt for; refuse with contempt
29. **vilipend**—treat or look upon with contempt

2. Contempt; Contemptuous Remark, Act, etc.,n. *From Sec. 1:* derision, disdain, disesteem, disregard, flout, gibe or jibe, hoot, jeer, mockery, ridicule, scoff, scorn, sneer, sniff, snort, snub, spurn; *Also:*
1. **contumely**—language, action, or treatment that shows contempt
2. **indignity**—act that shows contempt for another
3. **snoot**—facial expression of contempt

3. Contemptuous,adj. *From Sec. 1:* belittling, bridling, etc.; derisive or derisory, disdainful, scornful, sniffy (derisiveness, disdainfulness, scornfulness,n.); *From Sec. 2:* contumelious, snooty (contumeliousness, snootiness,n.) *Also:*
1. **audacious**—contemptuous of restrictions imposed by law, convention, dignity, or religion; contemptuous of danger or risk (audacity, audaciousness,n.)
2. **cavalier**—disdainful; scornful; supercilious
3. **impudent**—showing contempt by one's rudeness or forwardness of speech (impudence, impudency, impudentness,n.)
4. **insolent**—showing contempt or scorn by one's rudeness or disrespect (insolence,n.)
5. **offhand**—cavalier
6. **opprobrious**—expressive of scorn (opprobriousness,n.)
7. **sardonic**—bitterly scornful or derisive (sardonicism,n.)
8. **snippy**—supercilious—colloq. (snippiness, n.)
9. **snobbish**—scornful of those one considers inferior; unwilling to have anything to do with such (snobbishness, snobbism, snobbery,n. snob,n.)
10. **supercilious**—haughtily contemptuous (superciliousness,n.)

11. temperamental—showing, by one's attitude, actions, behavior, etc., contempt for rules, control, etc. (temperamentalness, temperament,n.)

12. toplofty—contemptuous; scornful (toploftiness,n.)

4. One Who Acts in a Maddeningly Temperamental Manner: prima donna,n.

5. With Contempt: askance, askant,adv.

6. To Bring into, or Cause to Come into, Contempt: abase, cheapen, degrade,v. (abasement, degradation,n.)

7. To Expose to Public Contempt or Scorn: pillory,v. (pillory,n.)

8. Worthy of Contempt: abject, beggarly; caitiff (archaic); cheap, contemptible, currish, despicable, ignominious, insignificant, low, mean; measly (slang); miserable, pitiable, pitiful; scabby (colloq.), scummy, scurvy, shabby, sneaky, sorry, swinish, unworthy, wretched, vile,adj. (abjectness or abjection, beggarliness, cheapness, contemptibleness or contemptibility, currishness, despicableness or despicability, ignominiousness, insignificance or insignificancy, lowness, meanness, miserableness, pitiableness, pitifulness, scabbiness, scurviness, shabbiness, sneakiness, sorriness, swinishness, unworthiness, wretchedness, vileness,n.)

9. Worthy of Contemptuous Laughter: derisible,adj.

10. To Act in a Contemptible Manner: sneak,v.

11. Contemptible Person: bugger; buzzard (colloq.); caitiff (archaic), cur, insignificancy, scum, sneak, swine, wretch,n.

12. Person or Thing for Whom or for Which Contempt Is Felt or Shown: byword, scorn,n.

13. Contemptible, Disreputable Woman: jade,n.

14. Woman for Whom One Feels a Certain Contempt: wench,n.

15. Contemptible People: scum, swine,n.

16. Object of Contempt: byword, insignificancy, scorn, target,n.

871. PRIDE

1. Proud,adj.

1. aristocratic, aristocratical—snobbish

2. arrogant—showing, or behaving with, overbearing and insufferable pride; scornfully or excessively proud

3. assuming, assumptive—arrogant

4. bloated—vain

5. bumptious—offensively conceited

6. cavalier—haughty

7. chesty—conceited (slang)

8. cocky, cockish—conceited (colloq.)

9. conceited, self-conceited—having an excessively high opinion of oneself, one's accomplishments, etc.

10. condescending, patronizing—acting out of a feeling of superiority and as if to one's inferior; taking on, or disposed to take on, airs of superiority

11. contumelious—showing one's scornful arrogance in insolent language, action, or treatment

12. coxcombical—conceited

13. dictatorial—imperious; overbearing

14. egotistic, egotistical, egoistic, egoistical—excessively and, often, wearisomely proud of, or conceited about, oneself, one's accomplishments, abilities, etc., such an attitude usually manifested in constant boasting about one's accomplishments, abilities, etc.; conceited and boastful

15. exalted—filled with pride

16. haughty—scornfully or excessively proud

17. high-minded—proud; arrogant

18. immodest—proud; lacking in the reserve or restraint characteristic of humbleness

19. imperious—haughty and domineering

20. inflated—swollen with pride

21. insolent—showing one's arrogance by rude or disrespectful behavior, speech, or attitude

22. lofty—proud; arrogant

23. lordly—proud, like a lord; proudly exercising or displaying one's power or authority

24. magisterial—imperious

25. overbearing—intolerably proud or arrogant

26. overproud—excessively or abnormally proud

27. overweening—conceited; conceitedly proud or arrogant

28. peacockish, peacocky—vain; vainglorious in walk, speech, dress, etc.

29. peremptory—arrogant

30. perk, perky—proud in bearing; cocky

31. pragmatic—conceited

32. presumptuous—offensively or excessively proud

33. prideful—haughty

34. puffed up, swollen—filled, or figuratively distended, with pride

35. purse-proud—proud because of wealth

36. pursy—having, or showing, the scornful pride of wealth

37. self-important—exaggeratedly conceited about one's assumed importance

38. snippy—supercilious (colloq.)

39. snobbish—conscious of, or offensively showing one's consciousness of, one's social or other superiority, and therefore repelling the friendly overtures of one's so-called inferiors

40. snooty—haughty; snobbish (colloq.)

41. stuck-up—conceited; snobbish; supercilious (colloq.)

42. supercilious—filled with pride; arrogant

43. superior—showing, or having, a feeling of being better than others

44. toplofty—haughty

45. uppish, uppity—conceited; haughty

46. vain, self-conceited—conceited; conceited about one's accomplishments or one's pleasing appearance

47. vainglorious—exceedingly proud or conceited about one's accomplishments, as shown by boasting, expressions of elation, etc.

48. vaulting—overweening

49. vaunting—talking with conceit; conceitedly displaying one's worth, accomplishments, etc.

2. Pride,n. From Sec. 1: aristocraticalness, arrogance or arrogancy, assumption, bumptiousness, chestiness, cockiness or cockishness; conceit, conceitedness, or self-conceit; condescension or condescendence, patronage, contumely or contumeliousness, coxcombry, dictatorialness, egotism or egoism, exaltation, haughtiness or hauteur, high-mindedness, immodesty, imperiousness, inflatedness, insolence, loftiness, lordliness, overbearingness, peacockishness or peacockery, peremptoriness, perkiness, pragmatism, presumption or presumptuousness, pridefulness, purse-pride, self-importance, snippiness; snobbishness, snobbery, or snobbism; snootiness, stuck-upness, superciliousness, superiority, toploftiness, uppishness or uppitiness; vanity, vainness, or self-conceit; vainglory or vaingloriousness, vaunt; Also:

1. airs—exhibition of pride, haughtiness, or vanity, as in put on airs, take on airs, etc.

2. amour-propre (French)—self-pride

3. ego—self-pride

4. huff—sudden access of arrogance

5. **pique**—wounded pride
6. **self-pride**—pride in oneself
7. **swagger**—insufferable pride; overbearing show of assumed superiority
8. **swelled head**—pride (slang)
9. **tympany**—conceit

3. To Be Proud; To Show Pride,v. *From Sec. 1:* cavalier, condescend, overween, peacock or peacock oneself, presume, puff up, swell, vaunt (condescension or condescendence,n.) ; *Also:*

1. **bridle**—make a characteristic gesture of pride, i.e., by lifting the head smartly and pulling in the chin
2. **crow**—make sounds showing a combined feeling of happiness and pride
3. **deign**—act as if lowering oneself, while giving the impression of reluctance or unwillingness, and simultaneously evincing a certain superciliousness of attitude; condescend
4. **pride oneself, plume oneself, pique oneself, preen oneself**—feel or show pride or vanity
5. **stoop**—condescend; deign
6. **strut**—walk in a vain or prideful and affected gait (strut,n.)
7. **swagger**—strut defiantly or impudently (swagger,n.)

4. To Cause to Be or Feel Proud,v. *From Sec. 1:* bloat, exalt, inflate, puff up, swell (exaltation, inflation,n.)

5. Proud Person; One Who Feels or Shows Pride,n. *From Sec. 1:* condescender or condescendent, coxcomb, egotist or egoist, peacock, snob, vaunter; *From Sec. 2:* swellhead; *From Sec. 3:* bridler, strutter, swaggerer,n.; *Also:*

1. **popinjay**—conceited, silly, and talkative person
2. **prima donna**—conceited or vain person, or, esp., woman (colloq.)
3. **puppy, pup**—conceited young man

6. Snobs Collectively: snobbery,n.

7. To Treat with Pride or Arrogance: huff, overbear,v.

8. To Treat with Condescension: patronize, v. (patronization,n.)

9. To Talk Conceitedly about; To Make a Conceited Exhibition of: vaunt,v. (vaunt,n. vaunter,n.)

10. To Be Proud of: pique oneself on or upon, plume oneself on or upon, pride oneself on or upon,v.

872. BOAST

1. To Boast: blow, brag, crow; gas (slang) ; rodomontade, roister; spread oneself (colloq.) ; vapor, vaunt,v.

2. To Boast about: brag, vaunt,v.

3. To Boast Noisily: bluster, gasconade, roister, strut, swagger, swank, swash, swashbuckle,v.

4. To Boast Wildly or Extravagantly: gasconade, swash, swashbuckle,v.

5. To Act the Boastful Daredevil, Soldier, Swordsman, or Ruffian: swash, swashbuckle, v. (swashbucklery, swashbuckling,n.)

6. To Place, Put, or Push Forward Boastfully: vaunt,v. (vaunter,n.)

7. Boasting: blow, bounce, brag, braggadocio, braggartism, braggarty, bragging, crowing, fanfaronade, fanfaronading, jactance, jactancy, jactation, jactitation, rodomontade, roistering, vaporing, vaunt, vauntage, vaunting,n.

8. Boasting about Oneself, One's Accomplishments, etc.: vainglory,n.

9. Noisy Boasting: bluster, bounce, fanfaronade, gasconade, rodomontade, roistering, strutting, swagger, swaggering, swank, swashbucklery, swashbuckling, swashing,n.

10. Wild or Extravagant Boasting: gasconade, swashbucklery, swashbuckling, swashing,n.

11. Empty Boasting: braggadocio, fanfaronade, rodomontade,n.

12. Arrogant, or Insufferably Proud, Boasting: vauntage, vauntiness,n.

13. False Boasting (Legal): jactitation,n.

14. Boastful Defiance Masking a Reluctance for Actual Fight: bravado, fanfaronade,n.

15. A Boast: blow, bounce, brag, vaporing, vaunt,n.

16. Boaster: blow, blowhard, or blowoff (slang) ; bouncer (colloq.) ; brag, braggadocio, braggart, bragger, egotist, fanfaron; gasbag (slang) ; gascon, roisterer, vaporer, vaunter; windbag (slang) ,n.

17. Noisy Boaster: blatherskite, blusterer, braggadocio, roisterer, strutter, swaggerer, swashbuckler, swasher,n.

18. Wild or Extravagant Boaster: swashbuckler, swasher,n.

19. Boastful Daredevil, Soldier, Swordsman, or Ruffian: swashbuckler, swasher,n.

20. Empty Boaster: braggadocio, fanfaron,n.

21. A Boaster and Bully: hector,n.

22. Boastful Pretender or Deceiver: mountebank,n.

23. Boastful; Boasting: braggart, braggartly, bragging, crowing, egotistic, egotistical, fanfaron, fanfaronading; gassy (colloq.) ; rodomontade, roistering, thrasonical, vainglorious, vaporous, vaunting, windy,adj. (egotism, vaingloriousness or vainglory, vaporousness or vaporosity,n.)

24. Noisily Boastful; Boasting Noisily: blusterous, blustery, huffish, roistering, strutting, swaggering, swashbuckling,adj. (huffishness,n.)

25. Thing or Person Boasted about: brag,n.

26. Descr. of That Which Is, or Has Been, Boasted about: boasted, bragged-about, vaunted,adj.

873. MODESTY

1. Modest, i.e., Free from Pride, Boastfulness, etc.: humble, meek, sheepish, unassuming,adj. (humbleness or humility, meekness, sheepishness,n.)

2. Contemptibly, Meanly, or Excessively Humble: groveling, wormy,adj. (grovel,v.)

3. To Be Humble, or Act Humbly: humble oneself,v.

4. To Cause to Feel Humble: abase, debase, humble, humiliate,v. (abasement, debasement, humiliation,n.)

5. Modest, i.e., Not Pretentious, etc.: chaste, homely, humble, lowly, mean, plain, quiet, simple, unassuming, unobtrusive, unostentatious, unpretentious,adj. (chasteness, homeliness, humbleness, lowliness, meanness, plainness, quietness, simpleness or simplicity, unobtrusiveness, unostentatiousness, unpretentiousness,n.)

6. Modest, i.e., Having Regard for Decency: chaste, decent, maidenly, proper, pudent, pudibund, adj.

7. Modesty of This Kind: chasteness, decency or decentness, maidenliness, properness or propriety, pudency, pudibundity, pudicitia, pudicity,n.

8. Modesty as Made into a Goddess by the Ancient Romans: Pudicitia,n.

9. To Turn Red of Complexion from Modesty, Embarrassment, etc.: blush, color, crimson, flush, mantle, redden,v.

10. Excessively or Unnaturally Modest,adj.
1. **bashful**—excessively or extremely modest; indicative of excessive or extreme modesty
2. **demure**—unnaturally, exaggeratedly, or affectedly modest
3. **overmodest**—excessively or abnormally modest
4. **prim**—demure
5. **prudish**—excessively, affectedly, or tiresomely modest, esp. in behavior, speech, or dress, or in reference to sex
6. **squeamish, queasy**—overly modest; easily shocked by what is immodest; prudish
7. **strait-laced**—prudish
8. **Victorian**—prudish, esp. in respect to behavior or conduct (prudery, among other qualities, is attributed to the British middle class under Queen Victoria)

11. Excessive or Unnatural Modesty,n. *From Sec. 10:* bashfulness, demureness, overmodesty, primness, prudishness or prudery, squeamishness, queasiness, Victorianism; *Also:*
1. **Grundyism**—conventional prudery
2. **pudency**—intense or extreme prudery
3. **pudibundity**—prudery

12. Excessively or Unnaturally Modest Person,n. *From Sec. 10:* prude, Victorian; *From Sec. 11:* Grundyist or Grundyite

13. To Take On an Expression of Unnatural or Exaggerated Modesty, by Drawing Up the Mouth, Pursing the Lips, etc.; To Draw Up (the Mouth), Purse (the Lips), etc., for this Purpose: prim,v.

14. Bashful; Shy,adj.
1. **backward**—bashful; shy (backwardness, n.)
2. **chary**—shy (chariness,n.)
3. **demure**—affectedly shy (demureness,n.)
4. **diffident**—unduly shy or self-effacing owing to a lack of faith in one's ability, worth, importance, etc. (diffidence,n.)
5. **mousy**—shy (mousiness,n.)
6. **pudent, pudibund**—bashful (pudency, pudibundity,n.)
7. **recessive, reserved**—descr. of a personality that tends to be unaggressive, to shrink from new personal or social contacts, to withdraw into itself, etc. (recessiveness, reserve,n.)
8. **retiring**—shy; tending to withdraw from notice, attention, etc.; avoiding conspicuous show; avoiding contacts with people
9. **self-conscious**—shy; extremely conscious of one's actions, or one's effect on others; embarrassed by the thought of other people looking at one (self-consciousness, n.)
10. **shamefaced**—bashful; shy (shamefacedness,n.)
11. **sheepish**—awkwardly bashful (sheepishness,n.)
12. **shrinking**—excessively shy, hence tending to shrink back from social contacts
13. **timid**—shy and lacking in self-confidence (timidity, timidness,n.)
14. **timorous**—shrinking; timid (timorousness,n.)
15. **verecund**—bashful (verecundity,n.)

15. Bashful or Shy Person: mouse, shrinking violet,n.

16. Pretending Shyness, though Possibly Wishing, in This Manner, to Invite Even

Greater Familiarity, Intimacy, etc.: coy, skittish,adj. (coyness, skittishness,n.)

17. Immodest; Shameless: barefaced; bold (esp. of females); brassy (colloq.); brazen, brazenfaced, impudent, indecent, indelicate, obscene, shameful, unblushing, unseemly,adj.

18. Immodesty; Shamelessness: barefacedness; boldness (esp. of females); brassiness or brass (colloq.); brazenness; impudence, impudency, or impudentness; impudicity, indecency, indelicacy, obscenity, shamefulness, unseemliness,n.

19. Shameless Person: brazenface,n.

874. ANNOYANCE

1. To Annoy (Someone): acerbate; aggravate (colloq.); chafe; devil (colloq.); displease, exacerbate, exasperate, fret, gall, grate, irritate, offend; peeve (colloq.); provoke; rile (colloq.); roil, tread on the toes of, vex,v.; *Also:*
1. **badger**—annoy without end
2. **bait**—annoy in petty ways or with persistent verbal attacks; set dogs on to annoy; harass
3. **bedevil**—torment beyond endurance
4. **bother, pother, disturb, trouble**—annoy; annoy by interfering with the comfort, calmness of mind, or peacefulness of
5. **grate (on, upon), rasp (on, upon)**—have an annoying or irritating effect on (the feelings or ears), or on the feelings or hearing of (someone)
6. **hagride**—annoy or harass (someone) the way a witch does or might
7. **harass, beset, gall**—annoy by repeated attacks or constant irritations
8. **heckle**—annoy (a speaker) with embarrassing or pointless questions, gibes, or contemptuous remarks
9. **hector**—torment with words
10. **importune**—annoy by persistent demands, requests, etc.
11. **infest**—annoy or cause trouble to in great numbers, as rats, vermin, etc.
12. **irk**—annoy by pestering, wearying, or boring
13. **molest**—annoy by disturbing, interfering with, or making unwarranted and undesired physical contact with
14. **nag**—annoy by persistent complaints, requests, faultfinding, scoldings, demands, etc.
15. **needle**—annoy by sharp remarks, gibes, etc.
16. **nettle, pique**—annoy as if by stinging, or by being prickly or aggressive, etc.
17. **persecute**—annoy in petty ways
18. **pester**—annoy; annoy intolerably; harass with petty requests or annoyances
19. **plague**—annoy beyond human endurance; be a source of great annoyance or trouble to; infest
20. **prey (on, upon)**—be a constant source of irritation (to)
21. **ruffle**—annoy by causing (someone) to lose composure or placidity
22. **spite**—do something only to annoy (someone), generally out of malice or hatred
23. **tease**—annoy by jests or jesting requests
24. **torment, devil, macerate**—annoy extremely
25. **worry**—annoy; annoy with unceasing attacks; annoy with unceasing biting or snapping (of dogs, or other animals); bother; plague; torment

2. Annoyance, i.e., State, Act, or Process of Annoying,n. *From Sec. 1:* aggravation, exacerbation, exasperation, irritation, provocation, vexation; bedevilment; botheration (colloq.); disturbance, harassment, besetment, importunity, infestation, molestation, persecution

3. Annoyance, i.e., State of Being Annoyed, n. *From Sec. 1:* aggravation, chafe, displeasure, exacerbation, exasperation, fret, irritation, vexation; bedevilment; botheration (colloq.), disturbance, molestation, ruffle, worry; *Also:*

1. **pet**—fit or attack of annoyance or irritation
2. **petulance**—state of cranky annoyance

4. Annoying, adj. *From Sec. 1:* acerbating, aggravating, etc.; provocative, vexatious; bothersome, troublesome or troublous, importunate, irksome, nettlesome, persecutive or persecutory; pestiferous or pesty (colloq.); plaguy, spiteful, worrisome; *Also:*

1. **acrid**—irritating; irritating to the feelings
2. **carking**—annoying (archaic or poetic)
3. **corrosive**—annoying; vexing; irritating
4. **maddening**—exceedingly annoying, vexing, or irritating
5. **nerve-racking**—extremely annoying, trying, or troublesome; difficult on the nerves
6. **offensive**—annoying; irritating
7. **officious**—annoying in one's illogically strict attitude toward performing one's office or duties
8. **pesky**—annoying
9. **pestilent**—annoying; troublesome
10. **thorny**—annoying or troublesome, i.e., like a thorn
11. **trying**—annoying

5. An Annoyance, i.e., One Who or That Which Annoys or Is a Source of Annoyance, n. *From Sec. 1:* aggravator, exasperater, etc.; aggravation, irritation, peeve, provocation, vexation; bother; botheration (colloq.); trouble, nag, nettle, pest, plague, tease, worry; *From Sec. 4:* thorn; *Also:*

1. **gadfly**—annoying person, in analogy to the insect that bites horses and cattle
2. **nuisance**—one who, or that which, is annoying
3. **pill**—annoying person (slang)
4. **terror**—annoying person

6. Annoyed, adj. *From Sec. 1:* acerbated, aggravated, etc.; *Also:* riley, roily, tempery

7. To Continue to Annoy: pursue, v.

8. To Continue to Be Sharply or Painfully Annoying or Irritating in the Mind, As Unpleasant Experiences, Feelings, etc.: fester, rankle, v.

9. Annoying and Persistent Demands, Requests, etc.: importunities, n.

10. Easily Annoyed: brittle, choleric, cranky, edgy, fretful, huffish, irritable, nettlesome, peevish, perverse, pettish, petulant, raspy; riley (colloq.); techy or tetchy, temperamental, testy, vapory, waspish, adj. (brittleness, choler, crankiness, edginess, fretfulness, huffishness, irritability or irritableness, peevishness, perversity or perverseness, petulance or petulancy, techiness or tetchiness, testiness, waspishness, n.)

11. Person Who Is Easily Annoyed; Irritable Person: crank, n. (colloq.)

12. To Be or Become Annoyed or Irritated: chafe, fret, ruffle, smart, v. (chafe, fret, ruffle, n.)

13. To Show One's Annoyance: fume, v.

14. To Show Annoyance by Contracting the Brows: frown, scowl, v. (frown, scowl, n.)

875. TEASE

1. To Tease (Someone): bait; devil (colloq.); rag (colloq.); rib (colloq.), v.; *Also:*

1. **badger**—tease continuously

2. **banter, badinage, chaff; guy (colloq.); josh (colloq.);** rally—tease in a light, humorous, joking, playful, good-humored, etc., manner
3. **bullyrag, ballyrag**—tease unmercifully
4. **hector**—tease by words
5. **tantalize**—tease; specifically, tease either by offering or promising something desirable only to withdraw the offer or refuse to fulfill the promise, or by awakening hope or expectation for the sole purpose of frustrating it (tantalization, n.)
6. **twit**—tease, esp. by reminding of past faults, promises, etc.

2. Teaser, n. *From Sec. 1:* baiter; badgerer; banterer, chaffer, or josher; hector, tantalizer, twitter; *Also:* 1. tease—one who teases, esp. habitually

3. Light, Playful, Good-Humored, or Humorous Teasing: badinage, banter, chaff, joshing or josh, persiflage, raillery, n.

4. To Engage in Such: banter, chaff, josh, v.

5. Descr. of Such: bantering, bantery, chaffing, joshing, quizzical, adj.

6. Object of Teasing, i.e., One Who Is Teased: butt, n.

876. BAD-TEMPERED

1. Bad-Tempered; Sharp or Sour in Temper: acid, acrid, acrimonious, bilious, cantankerous, choleric, crabbed, crabby, cranky, cross, cross-tempered, curmudgeonly, disagreeable, dyspeptic, fractious; grouchy (colloq.); gruff, grumpish, grumpy, huffish, huffy, ill-humored, ill-natured, ill-tempered, iracund, irascible, irritable, liverish, mean, moody, morose, nasty, out of humor, out of sorts, peevish, peppery, perverse, pettish, petulant, querulous, rugged, sharp, sharp-tempered, short, short-tempered; shrewish (of women), snappish, snappy; snippy (colloq.); sour, sour-tempered; spleenful, spleenish, spleeny, splenetic, splenetical, or splenitive; techy or tetchy, testy, ugly, vapory, vinegary, waspish, adj.; *Also:*

1. **disgruntled**—ill-humored owing to dissatisfaction
2. **dour**—sour-tempered or sullen in appearance, manner, or bearing
3. **glum**—ill-humored and silent
4. **moody, temperamental**—given to fits of bad temper or ill-humor
5. **sore**—disgruntled (colloq.)
6. **sulky**—ill-humored and angrily silent
7. **sullen, morose**—ill-humored and silent or gloomy
8. **surly, churlish**—ill-humored and impolite or unfriendly; disagreeably bad-tempered
9. **tempery, tempersome**—showing ill-temper, irritation, etc.

2. Bad Temper; Sharpness or Sourness of Temper, n. *From Sec. 1:* acidity, acridness, acrimony or acrimoniousness, bile or biliousness, cantankerousness, choler, crabbedness, crabbiness, crankiness, crossness, disagreeableness, dyspepsia, fractiousness, grouchiness, gruffness, grumpiness, huffishness, huffiness, ill humor, ill nature or ill-naturedness, ill temper or ill-temperedness, iracundity, irascibility or irascibleness, irritability or irritableness, meanness, moodiness or moods, moroseness, nastiness, peevishness, pepperiness, perversity or perverseness, petulance or petulancy, querulousness, ruggedness, sharpness, shortness, short temper, shrewishness, snappishness, snappiness, snippiness, sourness, sour temper, spleen, techiness or tetchiness, testiness, ugliness, waspishness; disgruntlement, dourness, glumness, moodiness, soreness, sulkiness, sullenness, moroseness, surliness, churlishness; *Also:*

1. asperity—sharpness of temper or feelings
2. distemper—bad temper; ill-humor
3. verjuice—sourness of feelings or nature

3. Bad-Tempered or Sharp-Tempered Person,n. *From Sec. 1:* crab or crabstick; crank (colloq.); crosspatch, curmudgeon, grouch, grumpy, splenetic, wasp (curmudgeonly,adj.); sorehead, sulk, churl (churlish,adj.); *Also:*

1. brimstone, spitfire—bad- or hot-tempered person, esp. a female (spitfire,adj.)
2. devil—terribly bad-tempered person
3. pill—cranky person (slang)
4. tartar—person with a violent temper

4. Bad-Tempered or Sharp-Tempered Girl or Woman: brimstone, harridan, scold, shrew, spitfire, termagant, virago, vixen; Xanthippe or Xantippe (after the wife of Socrates),n. (shrewish, spitfire, vixenish or vixenly,adj.)

5. Sharp-Tempered and Scolding Wife: Xanthippe or Xantippe,n.

6. Fit of Bad Temper: conniption or conniption fit (colloq.); grouch (colloq.); huff, pet,n.

7. Fit of Violent Bad Temper: tantrum,n.

8. Display, or Violent Display, of Bad Temper: tantrum,n.

9. Fit of Angry and Silent Bad Temper: sulk,n.

10. Temper, i.e., Bad Temper: dander,n. (colloq.)

11. To Make Bad-Tempered: distemper, irritate; peeve (colloq.); roil, sour,v. (irritation, n.)

12. To Make Bad-Tempered by Failing to Satisfy or Please: disgruntle,v.

13. To Make Sullen: cloud,v.

14. To Be Ill-Tempered: crab, fuss; grouch (colloq.),v.

15. To Become Ill-Tempered: fly into a temper, lose one's temper, sour,v.

16. To Be In a State of Silent and Aloof Ill Temper: sulk,v.

17. To Look Sulky or Sullen: lower or lour, pout,v. (lower or lour, pout,n.)

18. To Speak Sharply, in a Bad-Tempered Manner, etc.: bark, snap, snarl,v. (snarl,n. snarler,n.)

19. Snarling: currish,adj.

20. Having a Hot, or Easily Excited, Temper: fiery, hotheaded, hot-tempered, peppery, quick-tempered, short-tempered, tempersome, tempery,adj. (fieriness, hotheadedness, pepperiness,n.)

21. Hot-Tempered Person: brimstone (esp. a female), hothead; spitfire (esp. a female); tinderbox,n.

22. Sharp in Language: acerb, acid, acidulent, acidulous, acrimonious, barbed, biting, bitter, caustic, corrosive, cutting, mordacious, mordant; peppery (of words); pungent, sarcastic, snappish, snappy; snippy (colloq.); stinging, tart, vitriolic,adj. (acerbity, acidity, acidulence, acidulousness, acrimony or acrimoniousness, bitterness, causticity, corrosiveness, mordacity, mordancy, pepperiness, pungency, sarcasm, snappishness, snappiness, snippiness, tartness, vitriol,n.)

23. Sharp and Stinging Word, Statement, etc.: barb,n.

877. BITTERNESS

1. Bitter (Figuratively); Bitter in Feelings: acerbate or acerbated, aerid, embittered, envenomed, exacerbated,adj.; *Also:*

1. acrimonious—bitter and sharp, as in speech, manner, or temper; bitter and angry
2. jaundiced—bitter, or having a bitter attitude, because of an emotional temperament that is characterized by envy, cynicism, hate, etc., and that causes warped judgment, prejudiced reactions, etc.
3. sardonic—scornfully bitter

2. Bitterness (Figurative),n. *From Sec. 1:* acridity or acridness, embitterment, exacerbation; acrimony or acrimoniousness, sardonicism; *Also:*

1. acerbity—bitterness of temper
2. gall—bitterness of feeling or spirit

3. To Cause to Be or Feel Bitter,v. *From Sec. 1:* acerbate, embitter or bitter, envenom or venom, exacerbate; jaundice (embitterment, exacerbation,n.)

4. Bitter Remark: taunt,n.

5. Figurative Bitterness (of Something): wormwood,n.

6. Bitter in Language: acerb, vitriolic,adj. (acerbity, vitriol,n.)

7. Something Bitter to Accept or Endure: gall, wormwood,n.

878. ANGER

1. To Anger, i.e., Make Angry: acerbate, arouse, chafe, gall, huff, incense, inflame, irritate, offend, pique, provoke; rile (colloq.); vex,v. (incensement, inflammation, irritation, provocation, vexation,n.); *Also:*

1. enrage, madden—fill with anger so violent that there is, or may be, loss of control over the feelings or passions; fill with fierce anger
2. infuriate—make fiercely angry (infuriation,n.)
3. pique—anger by being unjust to, hurting the feelings of, etc.
4. tempt—arouse (anger or to anger) as *tempt the fates,* etc.

2. Angered,adj. *From Sec. 1:* acerbated, aroused, chafed, galled, incensed, inflamed, irritated, offended, piqued, provoked, riled or riley, vexed; enraged, maddened, infuriate or infuriated, piqued

3. Angering, i.e., Causing Anger,adj. *From Sec. 1:* chafing, galling, etc.; inflammatory, vexatious; *Also:* 1. corrosive—causing irritation or anger

4. To Cause to Turn Red with Anger: inflame,v. (inflammation,n.)

5. To Cause (Someone's Anger) to Become Sharper or More Bitter: exacerbate,v. (exacerbation,n.)

6. To Anger, i.e., Be or Become Angry; To Show Anger,v.

1. bark—speak, or say, in angry tones
2. blaze—burst into anger; burst out in anger
3. boil—be in a hot rage; be furious; be agitated by anger or angry feelings
4. bridle—hold the head up, chin drawn back, in anger
5. chafe—become angry
6. flare up—become suddenly angry; lose one's temper in sudden anger; burst into anger
7. flounce (away, off, out)—show anger by a rapid and sudden motion of the body
8. frown—contract the brows in anger
9. fume—be extremely angry; show one's anger
10. glower—stare in anger; scowl
11. grouch—be sulkily angry (colloq.)

12. **growl**—make a deep and throaty sound of anger; speak or say in tones of anger
13. **lower, lour**—frown; scowl
14. **madden**—rage
15. **pout**—look sullen or sulky, sometimes by thrusting out the underlip
16. **rage**—act in, feel, or show violent anger
17. **resent**—feel keenly angry and hurt over (an insult, injurious act, etc.)
18. **scowl**—look angry by lowering the eyebrows
19. **snap (at)**—answer, or talk (to), in anger
20. **snarl**—growl and snap or show the teeth in anger, as an animal; speak or say in angry tones
21. **snort**—express anger by noisy expulsion of breath through the nose; say in this manner
22. **storm**—be very angry; say with angry passion or vehemence; rage
23. **sulk**—be angrily silent
24. **take amiss**—be angry over; resent (something)

7. Angry Look,n. *From Sec. 6:* frown, glower, lower or lour, pout, scowl

8. Show or Display of Anger,n. *From Sec. 6:* boil, bridle, flare-up, flounce, rage, snort, sulk

9. Verbal Expression of Anger,n. *From Sec. 6:* growl, snarl, snort

10. Angry; Showing Anger,adj. *From Sec. 6:* blazing, boiling, etc.; grouchy, resentful, snappish or snappy, sulky; *Also:* choleric; heated (as a person, argument, words, etc.); irate, ireful; mad (colloq.); sore (colloq.); spleenful, spleenish, spleeny, splenetic, or splenetical; sulfurous or sulphurous (as words, language, argument, etc.); *Also:*
1. **acrimonious**—bitterly angry; angry and bitter
2. **dour**—sullen, esp. in appearance, manner, or bearing
3. **furious, wild**—extremely or violently angry; so angry as to border on temporary insanity; so angry as to feel an urge to blind destruction
4. **indignant**—angry because of a feeling of injustice, or of having been slighted or hurt
5. **sullen**—silent from anger; showing anger, as in *a sullen look*
6. **sultry**—hot with anger
7. **wrathful, wroth**—extremely angry or indignant, and often wishing to inflict well-deserved punishment on the cause of one's anger
8. **wrathy**—wrathful (colloq.)

11. Anger,n. *From Sec. 6:* boil, chafe, grouchiness, resentment or resentfulness, snappishness or snappiness, sulkiness; *From Sec. 10:* choler, heat or heatedness, ire, irefulness, soreness, spleen; acrimony or acrimoniousness, dourness, fury or furiousness, indignation, sullenness, sultriness, wrath or wrathfulness, wrathiness; *Also:* incensement, inflammation, irritancy, irritation, offense, pique, vexation; *Also:*
1. **animosity, animus**—resentment disposing to hostile acts
2. **dander**—anger (colloq.)
3. **displeasure**—slight or weak anger
4. **dudgeon, high dudgeon**—anger arising from resentment, pique, or hurt, and usually manifested in a desire to end friendly relations with the offender
5. **grudge**—long-standing resentment combined with ill-will
6. **pique**—resentment; resentful anger
7. **rage**—extreme anger; violent anger
8. **spunk**—anger (colloq.)
9. **umbrage**—resentment

12. Fit or Mood of Anger: bluster; conniption or conniption fit (colloq.), fume,n.

13. **Fit of Silent Anger:** grouch (colloq.), sulk,n.
14. **Fit of Violent Anger:** fury, rage, tantrum, n.
15. **Fit of Resentment:** pique,n.
16. **Person Who Shows His Anger in Ill-Tempered Silence:** grouch (colloq.), sulk,n.
17. **Person Easily Angered:** brimstone (esp. a female); crank (colloq.); hothead; spitfire (esp. a female); splenetic, tinderbox, wasp,n.
18. **Easily Angered; Prone or Disposed to Anger:** brittle, choleric, combustible, cranky, edgy, fiery, fretful; grouchy (colloq.); hot-blooded, hotheaded, hot-tempered, inflammable, iracund, irascible, irritable, liverish, passionate, peppery, raspy, quick-tempered; riley (colloq.); short-tempered, snappish, snappy; spleenful, spleenish, spleeny, splenetic, splenetical, or splenitive; techy or tetchy; temperamental, testy, vascular, waspish,adj. (brittleness, choler, combustibleness or combustibility, crankiness, edginess, fieriness, fretfulness, grouchiness, hot-bloodedness, hotheadedness, inflammableness or inflammability, iracundity, irascibleness or irascibility, irritableness or irritability, pepperiness, snappishness, snappiness, techiness or tetchiness, temper, testiness, vascularity, waspishness,n.)
19. **Becoming Angry:** irascent,adj.
20. **To Reduce or Banish the Anger, Hostility, Resentment, etc., of:** appease, calm, conciliate, disarm, mollify, pacify or pacificate, placate, propitiate, reconcile, soothe,v. (appeasement, conciliation, mollification, pacification, placation, propitiation, reconciliation,n. conciliatory, pacificatory, placatory, propitiatory or propitiative, reconciliatory, adj.)

879. HOSTILITY

1. Hostile; Showing, Feeling, or Characterized by, Hostility or Ill Will: adverse, alien, antagonistic, bellicose, deadly, despiteful; dispiteous (poetic); inimical, malevolent, malicious, malign, malignant; nasty (colloq.); oppugnant, poisonous, rancorous, repugnant, snaky, spiteful; spleenful, spleenish, spleeny, splenetical, or splenitive; squint-eyed, venomous; vicious (colloq.); viperous, vipery, virulent, warlike,adj.; *Also:*
1. **aggressive**—acting with hostility; committing unprovoked acts of hostility
2. **cattish**—malicious or spiteful in a sly or underhanded way
3. **wanton**—deliberately malicious or spiteful

2. Hostility; Ill Will,n. *From Sec. 1:* adverseness, antagonism, bellicosity, deadliness, despitefulness or despite, inimicality, malevolence, malice or maliciousness; malignance, malignancy, or malignity; nastiness, oppugnancy, poisonousness, rancor or rancorousness, repugnance or repugnancy, spite or spitefulness, spleen, squint-eyedness, venom or venomousness, viperousness, virulence or virulency, warlikeness; aggressiveness, cattiness or cattishness, wantonness; *Also:*
1. **animosity, animus**—hostility; hostility or ill will manifesting itself in acts, behavior, or conduct
2. **animus**—hostility; hostile spirit; ill will
3. **bad will, bad blood, ill blood**—ill will
4. **disaffection**—state of feeling hostile, alienated, or estranged
5. **enmity**—hostility; ill will
6. **estrangement**—state of now feeling hostile, though previously affectionate or friendly
7. **grudge**—ill will; ill will of long standing,

esp. over a real or fancied insult, injury, etc.

8. **heartburn, heartburning**—secret hostility

9. **war, warfare**—hostility

10. **warpath**—hostility of mind or attitude

3. Hostility between Nations: rupture,n.

4. Hostile Person; One Who Is Hostile,n.

1. **archenemy**—chief enemy

2. **dastard**—malicious and sneaky person (dastardliness,n. dastardly,adj.)

3. **enemy**—one who is hostile to another or to a thing, quality, institution, etc.

4. **foe**—enemy; enemy in war

5. **splenetic**—spitefully hostile person

6. **viper**—malicious or spiteful person

5. Hostile Act or Action: despite,n. (despitefulness,n. despiteful,adj.)

6. Unprovoked Hostile Act: aggression,n.

7. Hostile Course of Action: warpath,n.

8. To Be or Act Hostile; To Feel or Show Hostility or Ill Will,v.

1. **aggress**—act in a hostile fashion; commit an unprovoked act of hostility (aggression,n. aggressor,n.)

2. **begrudge, grudge**—bear ill will toward (someone) because of (something, often something envied)

3. **bristle**—assume a hostile attitude

4. **growl**—say or speak in hostility; make a deep and throaty sound of hostility (growl,n.)

5. **spite**—show ill will toward (a person) by one's actions; do something only to show ill will toward (a person)

9. To Become Spiteful: canker,v.

10. To Cause to Be Hostile or Unfriendly,v.

1. **alienate**—cause to be hostile or unfriendly (alienation,n. alienated,adj.)

2. **antagonize**—arouse the hostility of (antagonization,n. antagonizer,n. antagonized,adj.)

3. **disaffect**—alienate; estrange (disaffection,n. disaffected or ill-affected,adj.)

4. **estrange**—cause to feel hostile or unfriendly, though previously affectionate or friendly (estrangement,n. estranger, n. estranged,adj.)

11. Tending to Arouse Hostility or Ill Will: invidious,adj. (invidiousness,n.)

12. Warlike: bellicose, belligerent,adj. (bellicosity, belligerence or belligerency,n.)

13. Unfriendly: chill or chilly (as an attitude, etc.), ill-affected, ill-disposed, inaffable, inimical, unamiable; unamicable (of relations, actions, etc.); uncompanionable, uncordial; unneighborly (i.e., to a neighbor); unsociable, unsocial, asocial, dissociable or dissocial (i.e., not enjoying, or not inclined to, the society of friends),adj.; *Also:*

1. **aloof, standoff, standoffish**—not welcoming friendliness or approach

2. **anti-social, asocial**—opposed to friendly or social contacts or relationships

3. **gruff**—unfriendly and discourteous

4. **hostile**—actively unfriendly

5. **surly**—unfriendly and ill-tempered (of an animal)

14. Unfriendliness,n. *From Sec. 13:* chill, chillness, or chilliness; ill-affectedness, ill-disposedness, inaffability, inimicality, unamiableness or unamiability, uncordiality, unneighborliness, unsociableness or unsociability, unsocialness; aloofness, standoffishness, or standoff, gruffness, hostility, surliness; *Also:* 1. **aphilanthropy**—aversion to friendly relationship, contact, or intercourse with people

15. To Discourage (Friendly Overtures): stand off,v. (colloq.)

880. HATE

1. To Hate,v.

1. **abhor**—hate to such an extreme degree as to have a feeling close to horror about; feel a combination of hatred, fear, and disgust for; shrink back from in intense hatred (abhorrence,n. abhorrer,n.)

2. **abominate**—feel intense hatred, or hatred and disgust, for, esp. if the object of hatred is shameful, disgraceful, etc. (abominator,n.)

3. **begrudge, grudge**—dislike (someone) because of (something, often something envied)

4. **despise**—feel a mixture of hatred and contempt for (despiser,n.)

5. **detest**—feel intense hatred for (detester, n.)

6. **dislike, disesteem, disfavor, disrelish, distaste, mislike, object to**—have a feeling of not liking, somewhat weaker than hatred, for (disliker, misliker,n.)

7. **execrate**—feel the most intense hatred for; abhor; abominate (execration,n. execrator,n. execrative, execratory,adj.)

8. **loathe**—feel a combination of hatred and disgust for; abhor (loather,n.)

9. **shudder (at)**—feel extreme hatred, fear, and disgust (for); shake or tremble with this feeling

2. Hate; Hatred; Feeling of Hatred or Dislike,n. *From Sec. 1:* abhorrence, abomination, detestation; dislike, disliking, disesteem, disfavor, disrelish, distaste, mislike, misliking, or objection; loathing, shudder or shudders; *Also:*

1. **animosity, animus**—extreme or violent hatred

2. **antipathy**—strong or fixed dislike; repugnance

3. **aversion, averseness**—dislike, strictly combined with a wish to turn away; strong or fixed dislike

4. **disgust**—intense and/or sickening dislike; intense dislike of that which nauseates, offends the senses, etc.

5. **enmity**—hatred

6. **grudge**—dislike of long standing, usually over a real or fancied insult, injury, etc.

7. **horror**—intense dislike or hatred, often combined with fear and/or disgust

8. **rancor, rancorousness**—intense hatred

9. **repugnance, repugnancy**—feeling of deep dislike or distaste, often for something alien or hostile to one's thinking, feeling, instincts, etc.

10. **repulsion**—feeling of acute dislike; repugnance

3. Feeling, Manifesting, or Characterized by, Hate or Hatred,adj. *From Sec. 1:* abhorring, abominating, etc.; abhorrent (of), grudgeful, shuddery; *From Sec. 2:* antipathetic or antipathetical (to); averse (to); disgusted; grudgeful; horrified, horror-stricken, or horror-struck; rancorous, repulsed or repelled; *Also:* 1. **aghast**—filled with horror

4. Hateful; Hatable; Worthy of, or Exciting, Hate or Dislike,adj. *From Sec. 1:* abhorrent, abominable, despicable, detestable; dislikable, distasteful, objectionable, or exceptionable; execrable, loathsome or loathful, shuddersome or shuddery (abominableness, despicableness or despicability, detestableness or detestability; distastefulness, objectionableness, objectionability, or exceptionableness; loathsomeness,n.); *From Sec. 2:* antipathetic or antipathetical, disgusting or disgustful, horrible, repugnant, repulsive or repellent (disgustingness or disgustfulness, horribleness; repulsiveness, repellence, or repellency,n.); *Also:* accursed, blasted, confounded, cursed, curst, damnable, damned; darn or darned (colloq.); foul, heinous, infamous, invidious, obnoxious, odious, offensive, revolting, villainous (accursedness, cursedness, damnableness, foulness, heinousness, infamousness or infamy, invidiousness, obnoxiousness, odiousness, offensiveness, villainousness,n.) ; *Also:*

1. **displeasing**—causing dislike; not likable (displeasingness,n.)
2. **unlikable, unlikeable**—not likable (unlikableness, unlikeableness,n.)
3. **unpopular**—exciting dislike or general dislike (unpopularity or unpopularness, n.)

5. Object of Hatred or Dislike,n. *From Sec. 1:* abhorrence, abomination, detestation, dislike or objection, execration; *From Sec. 2:* antipathy, aversion; *Also:*

1. **anathema**—object of intense hatred (generally followed by *to*)
2. **bête noire (French)**—object of hatred and fear, as a person, thing, or task
3. **hate**—object of hatred
4. **persona non grata (Latin)**—person who is unacceptable, disliked, or unpopular
5. **rotter**—objectionable or repugnant person

6. Horrible Person or Thing: monster, monstrosity,n.

7. Cause of Horror: horror,n.

8. Horrible; Arousing Horror or a Feeling of Horror: ghastly, grim, grisly, gruesome or grewsome, hideous, horrendous, horrid, horrific, horrifying; lurid (in color or hue) ; macabre or macaber (like death) ; monstrous, morbid,adj. (ghastliness, grimness, grisliness, gruesomeness or grewsomeness, hideousness, horridness, luridness, monstrousness or monstrosity, morbidness or morbidity,n.)

9. Enjoying the Horrible and Revolting: ghoulish, morbid,adj. (ghoulishness, morbidness or morbidity,n. ghoul,n.)

10. Not Liked: disesteemed, disfavored, disliked, disrelished, distasteful; in the bad graces (of) ; misliked, out of favor, unesteemed, unfavored, unliked, unpopular, unrelished,adj.

11. State of Being Disliked: disesteem, disfavor, disregard, unpopularity,n.

12. To Dislike the Taste of (Food or Drink): disrelish, distaste,v. (disrelish, distaste,n.)

13. State of Being Hated: odium,n.

14. Act or Action of Hatred: despite,n. (despitefulness,n. despiteful,adj.)

15. Disgrace Attendant on That Which Is Hateful: odium,n.

16. To Arouse Hatred or Dislike in,v.

1. **antagonize**—arouse dislike in (antagonization,n. antagonizer,n. antagonizing, adj.)
2. **disgust**—arouse intense and/or sickening dislike in; arouse dislike and nausea in, as by offending the senses of (disgusting, disgustful,adj.)
3. **displease**—cause dislike to; arouse dislike in (displeasing,adj.)
4. **envenom, venom**—fill with hatred, or with bitter hatred
5. **horrify, shock**—cause intense dislike or hatred in; cause a combination of such a feeling with fear and/or disgust (horrification,n. horrifying,adj.)
6. **offend**—cause dislike; cause dislike in (offense,n. offensiveness,n. offender,n. offensive,adj.)
7. **repel**—arouse the most intense dislike (in), enough, literally or figuratively, to push away (repulsiveness,n. repellent, repulsive,adj.)
8. **scandalize**—horrify by something immoral, an immoral or improper action or activity, etc. (scandalization,n, scandalous, scandalizing,adj.)

17. Selected Specific Hatreds (or Aversions), n.

1. **adypsia**—of drinking
2. **anti-Semitism**—of Jews
3. **misandry**—of the male sex by women
4. **misanthropy, misanthropism**—of all mankind
5. **misogamy**—of marriage
6. **misogyny, misogynism**—of women
7. **misology**—of argument, discussion, or the enlightenment of knowledge
8. **misoneism**—of new or changed things, of change itself, or of any innovations
9. **misopedia, misopedism**—of children, or of one's own children
10. **misosophy**—of wisdom
11. **misotyranny**—of tyranny
12. **misoxeny**—of strangers
13. **taedium vitae (Latin)**—of life

18. Hater of a Specific Thing or Group,n. *From Sec. 17:* anti-Semite, misanthrope or misanthropist, misogamist, misogynist, misologist, misoneist, misopedist, misosopher or misosophist, misoxene; *Also:*

1. **cynic**—of people
2. **misocapnist**—of tobacco smoke
3. **misohellene**—of Greeks
4. **misomath**—of mathematics
5. **misopaterist**—of priests, or of church fathers
6. **oenophobist**—of wine

19. Hating Specific Things or Groups,adj. *From Sec. 17:* anti-Semitic, misanthropic or misanthropical; misogamist, misogamic, or misogamous; misogynous, misogynistic, misogynistical, misogynic, or misogynical; misoneistic; *From Sec. 18:* cynical, misocapnic; *Also:*

1. **misogallic**—the French
2. **misopolemical**—war

20. To Hate, or Cause to Hate, Mankind: misanthropize,v.

881. DISGUST

1. To Disgust,v.

1. **cloy on**—surfeit
2. **nauseate**—disgust; disgust in such a way as to make (one) feel like vomiting (nauseation,n.)
3. **repel**—cause disgust in; cause to be disgusted
4. **revolt**—disgust; nauseate
5. **satiate**—fill (a person) to the point of disgust (satiation,n.)
6. **scandalize**—shock by something immoral; shock (one's) moral sense (scandalization,n.)
7. **shock**—fill with intense disgust
8. **sicken**—disgust; make sick with disgust
9. **surfeit**—disgust by an excess; satiate

2. Disgusting,adj. *From Sec. 1:* cloying, nauseating or nauseous, repellent, revolting, satiating, scandalous or scandalizing, shocking, sickening, surfeiting (nauseousness,n.) ; *Also:* abominable; beastly (colloq.) ; disgustful, foul, frightful, loathful or loathsome, odious, offensive, repulsive, vile (abominableness, beastliness, foulness, frightfulness, loathsomeness, odiousness, offensiveness, repulsiveness, vileness,n.) ; *Also:*

1. **fulsome**—disgusting; disgusting because of, or in its, insincerity (fulsomeness,n.)
2. **gruesome or grewsome, macabre or macaber**—disgusting or repulsive and horrible (gruesomeness or grewsomeness, n.)
3. **hideous**—revolting to one's moral sense or feelings (hideousness,n.)
4. **noisome**—disgusting; disgusting in smell (noisomeness,n.)

3. To the Point of Disgust: ad nauseam (Latin)

4. To Feel Disgust,v. *From Sec. 1:* nauseate, sicken (nauseation,n.)

5. To Be Disgusted by; To Feel Disgust at, v. *From Sec. 1:* nauseate, revolt against, revolt at, sicken at; *Also:*
1. abominate—feel disgust for
2. loathe—feel disgust for; feel physical disgust for (food, drink, etc.)

6. Disgusted,adj. *From Sec. 1:* nauseous or nauseated, repelled, revolted, satiated or satiate, shocked, sick or sickened, surfeited

7. Disgust; Feeling of Disgust; Disgustedness,n. *From Secs. 1 and 6:* nausea, nauseousness, or nauseation; repulsion, revolt, satiety or satiation, sickness, surfeit; *From Sec. 5:* abomination, loathing; *Also:* 1. revulsion—disgust (popular but unsanctioned usage, perhaps from a combination of *revolt* and *repulsion*)

8. Disgusting Thing, etc.,n. *From Sec. 1:* shock; *From Sec. 5:* abomination

9. Disgusting Animal Life, or, by Extension, People: vermin,n. (verminousness,n. verminous,adj.)

10. Sight That Arouses Disgust: object,n. (as in *make an object of oneself*, etc.)

11. Easily Disgusted: fastidious, queasy, squeamish,adj. (fastidiousness, queasiness, squeamishness,n.)

12. Shocking: frightful, ghastly, hideous, horrible, horrid, horrific, horrifying, monstrous, outrageous, scandalous,adj. (frightfulness, ghastliness, hideousness, horribleness, horridness, monstrousness, outrageousness,n.)

882. CURSE

1. A Curse: anathema, ban, curse word, damn, damnation, darn, execration, expletive, imprecation, malediction; malison, oath(often meaningless); swearword,n.

2. Language, or the Use of Language, Containing Curses, or Showing Irreverence to God, Sacred People or Things, etc.: blasphemy, cursing, profanity, swearing,n.

3. An Utterance Containing Curses, etc.: profanity,n.

4. Cursing; Taking the Name of God in Vain; Showing Contempt for God, etc., in Language: blasphemous, impious, profane, swearing,adj. (blasphemousness or blasphemy, impiousness or impiety, profanity,n.)

5. To Curse (Someone or Something): anathematize, ban, damn; darn (colloq.); execrate, imprecate, swear at,v. (execrator, imprecator,n. execrative or execratory, imprecatory,adj. anathematization, execration, imprecation,n.)

6. To Curse, i.e., Indulge in Cursing or in Using Curse Words: anathematize, blaspheme, damn, execrate, imprecate, swear,v. (anathematization, execration, imprecation,n. execrator, imprecator, swearer,n. execrative or execratory, imprecatory,adj.)

7. Prone to Curse: execrative,adj.

8. Cursed: accursed, anathematized, banned, blasted, confounded, curst; damn (colloq.); damned; darn or darned (colloq.); execrated, adj.

9. Worthy of Being Cursed: accursed, cursed, damnable, execrable,adj. (cursedness, n.)

883. BADNESS

1. Bad, i.e., of Bad or Poor Quality: base; bum (colloq.); coarse, common, inferior, low,

meager or meagre, mediocre, poor, scrub; scrubby (of animals); second-rate, third-rate, etc.; shoddy, substandard, wretched,adj. (baseness, coarseness, commonness, inferiority, lowness, meagerness or meagreness, poorness, scrubbiness, shoddiness, wretchedness, n.)

2. Inferior to Gold, Silver, or Other Precious Metals (of Metal): base,adj.

3. Of Poor Quality and Flimsy or Insubstantial in Texture (Generally of Cloth, Material, etc.): sleazy,adj. (sleaziness,n.)

4. Inferior Articles or Things; Inferior Person or Thing Claiming to Be Good, Superior, etc.; Inferior Cloth Made of Reclaimed Wool: shoddy,n.

5. To Condemn (Something, Often a Piece of Literature, Work of Art, etc.) As Inferior: damn,v. (damnation,n. damnatory,adj.)

6. Probably, or Likely to Be, of Poor Quality; of Questionable Quality: dubious,adj. (dubiousness,n.)

7. Very, or Exceedingly, Bad: abominable, atrocious, awful, dreadful, execrable, horrible; incorrigible (beyond correction or reform—of people); lousy (slang); outrageous, putrid; rotten (slang); terrible; tragic (as an error, folly, etc.); worthless,adj. (abominableness, atrociousness, awfulness, dreadfulness, horribleness, incorrigibleness or incorrigibility, putridness, worthlessness,n.); *Also* (esp. of weather, a cold, cough, headache, etc., or other unpleasant condition): beastly, frightful, horrid, nasty, ungodly, unholy, vicious, vile, villainous, wicked, wretched,adj.

8. Outstandingly or Conspicuously Bad: egregious, flagrant, glaring, gross, monstrous, outrageous, rank,adj. (egregiousness, flagrancy or flagrance, glaringness, grossness, monstrousness or monstrosity, outrageousness, rankness,n.)

9. So Bad that One Almost Dare Not Speak of It: unmentionable, unspeakable, unutterable,adj.

10. In Bad Condition: unsound,adj. (unsoundness,n.)

11. To Become Worse; To Lose Excellence, Value, Quality, etc.,v.
1. corrode—deteriorate (corrosion,n.)
2. corrupt—lose excellence, quality, or vigor (corruption,n.)
3. decay—drop from a state of excellence or vigor to one of lower or less robust quality, usually gradually (decay,n.)
4. decline—drop toward a worse or inferior state or condition; lose excellence, value, quality, vigor, etc. (decline, declension, n.)
5. degenerate—drop from previous excellence, vigor, etc., from that of one's forebears or predecessors, or, biologically, from that normal to the type, species, etc. (degeneration,n.)
6. derogate—drop in character; degenerate (derogation,n.)
7. deteriorate—become worse; become gradually worse; lose quality, excellence, value, or character; degenerate (deterioration,n.)
8. impair—become worse; lose excellence, value, etc. (impairment,n.)
9. retrograde—fall back or down to a worse condition, esp. biologically (retrogradation,n.)
10. retrogress—drop back to a previously bad or worse condition; degenerate (retrogression,n.)
11. worsen—become worse

12. State or Condition of Becoming, or of Having Become, Worse, etc.,n. *From Sec. 11:* corrosion, corruption or corruptness, decay, decline or declension; degeneration, degeneracy, or degenerateness; deterioration, impairment, retrogradation; *Also:*

1. **abasement**—degradation
2. **adulteration**—state of being reduced in quality or excellence by the admixture of something inferior
3. **debasement**—state of being reduced in quality or excellence; adulteration
4. **decadence, decadency**—social, aesthetic, intellectual, etc., decay
5. **degradation**—state of being deprived of, or reduced in, quality, excellence, physical excellence, etc. (degradational,adj.)
6. **disrepair**—condition of deterioration that requires repair; condition of needing repairs (of tangible things)

13. Becoming Worse, etc.,adj. *From Sec. 11:* corrupting, decaying, declining, etc.; degenerative, deteriorative, retrogressive; *From Sec. 12:* decadent, degradative; *Also:* 1. **pejorative** —becoming, or tending to become, worse

14. Having Become Worse, etc.,adj. *From Sec. 11:* corroded, corrupt or corrupted, decayed, degenerate or degenerated, deteriorated, impaired, retrograde, worse; *From Sec. 12:* abased, adulterated or adulterate, debased, degraded

15. One Who Is Undergoing, or Has Undergone, Social, Aesthetic, or Intellectual Decay: decadent,n.

16. To Make Worse; To Reduce the Excellence, Value, Quality, etc., of,v. *From Sec. 11:* corrode, corrupt, decay, degenerate, deteriorate, impair, worsen (corrosion, corruption, deterioration, impairment,n.); *From Sec. 12:* abase, adulterate, debase, degrade (abasement, adulteration, debasement, degradation, n.); *Also:*
1. **aggravate**—make worse (aggravation,n.)
2. **alloy**—debase or impair (a quality or thing) by mixing in some inferior or less worthy quality or thing
3. **pervert**—bring to a less good or fine condition (perversion,n.)
4. **vitiate**—pervert (vitiation,n.)

17. Making Worse, etc.,adj. *From Sec. 11:* corrosive, corruptive, deteriorative or deteriorating, impairing; *From Sec. 12:* abasing, adulterating or adulterant, debasing, degrading; *From Sec. 16:* aggravating, perversive, vitiating; *Also:* 1. **pejorative**—making, or tending to make, worse

18. That Which Reduces the Quality or Excellence of Something when Mixed in with It: adulterant,n.

19. Belief in World-Wide Deterioration: deteriorism,n.

20. Worst: seamy (as conditions, environment, etc.),adj. (seaminess,n.)

21. To Make or Serve to Make (a Fault, Offense, Crime, or Anything Bad) Less Bad or Less Serious than It Seems, or to Represent or Treat It As Such: extenuate,v. (extenuation,n. extenuating or extenuative,adj.)

22. Bad, i.e., Wicked or Evil: accursed or cursed (usually of acts), blackhearted; caitiff (somewhat archaic or poetic); corrupt, evil-minded, felon, felonious; foul (of acts, etc.); immoral, iniquitous, malefic, maleficent; malign or malignant (esp. in influence); miscreant, nefarious, placular, sinful, unclean, ungodly, unholy, unregenerate, unrighteous, vicious, vile, villainous,adj.; *Also:*
1. **abandoned**—wicked; wicked beyond reclaim; given over to wickedness; shamelessly wicked
2. **atrocious**—horribly or incredibly wicked (often of acts)
3. **baleful**—evil (esp. of a look, glance, etc.)
4. **demoniac or demoniacal, devilish, dia-**

bolic or diabolical, fiendish, fiendlike, Mephistophelian or Mephistophelean, satanic—evil or wicked, or craftily evil or wicked, like the devil
5. **flagitious**—scandalously or shamefully wicked
6. **heinous**—exceedingly or odiously wicked
7. **infamous**—extremely, shamefully, or disgracefully wicked
8. **monstrous**—incredibly, amazingly, or hideously evil or wicked
9. **obdurate**—willfully, stubbornly, or obstinately wicked
10. **pernicious**—evil or wicked in deed, purpose, or intent
11. **perverted**—obstinately wicked
12. **sinister**—evil (as a look, influence, etc.)
13. **unnatural**—wicked beyond the normal or natural

23. Badness, i.e., Wickedness or Evilness,n. *From Sec. 22:* corruptness or corruption, evil-mindedness, feloniousness, foulness, immorality, iniquity or iniquitousness, maleficence; malignance, malignancy, or malignity; miscreancy, nefariousness, sinfulness, uncleanness, ungodliness, unholiness, unregeneracy, unrighteousness, vice or viciousness, vileness, villainousness; atrociousness or atrocity, balefulness or, poetic, bale; devilishness, devilment, devilry, deviltry, diabolicalness, or fiendishness; flagitiousness, heinousness, infamy or infamousness, monstrousness or monstrosity, obduracy or obdurateness, perniciousness, sinisterness, unnaturalness; *Also:*
1. **enormity**—exceedingly wicked character or quality
2. **evil**—evilness; wickedness

24. Bad, i.e., Wicked or Evil, Act or Deed,n. *From Sec. 22:* immorality, iniquity, malefaction or maleficence, sin, villainy; atrocity, infamy; *From Sec. 23:* enormity; *Also:* 1. **misdeed**, misdemeanor—wicked act

25. Bad, i.e., Wicked or Evil, Person,n. *From Sec. 22:* caitiff, miscreant, sinner, villain; demon, devil, fiend, or Mephistopheles; monster; *Also:* 1. **villain**—evil or wicked character, or main character, in a story, novel, play, etc.

26. Evil or Wicked Acts: malignities,n.

27. Evil or Wicked Action: devilment, maleficence, wrong,n.

28. A Doing of Evil; Commission of Wicked Acts: devilment, evildoing, malefaction, misdoing, outrage, wrongdoing,n.

29. One Who Commits Evil or Wicked Acts: evildoer, malefactor or, fem., malefactress, misdoer, sinner, wrongdoer,n.

30. To Behave Badly or Wrongly: misbehave, misbehave oneself, misconduct oneself, misdemean, misdemean oneself, sin,v. (misbehavior, misconduct, misdemeanor,n. misdemeanant, sinner,n.)

31. Behaving Badly: ill-behaved or, usually of a child, naughty,adj. (naughtiness,n.)

32. Evil or Wicked Thing; An Evil,n.
1. **atrocity**—horribly or incredibly evil or wicked thing
2. **cancer**—evil or wicked thing that has a tendency to spread, or that does spread
3. **curse**—evil; evil that comes as a punishment, or as if in answer to prayer
4. **hydra**—evil of many sources and kinds—in analogy to the nine-headed monster of mythology, slain by Hercules; when one head was cut off, two grew in its place
5. **monster, monstrosity**—incredibly, amazingly, or hideously evil or wicked thing
6. **plague, pestilence**—evil that afflicts one
7. **wrong**—an evil

33. To Afflict with an Evil: plague,v.

34. Reputation of, or for, Evil: infamy,n. (infamous,adj.)

35. Cause of Evil: curse, mischief,n.

36. Area of a City Where Vice and Lawlessness Flourish with the Connivance of the Police: tenderloin,n.

37. Place Where Wickedness, Evil, etc., Is Practiced, or Where the Practitioners of Such Live or Frequently Come to: den or nest (of wickedness, evil, vice, thieves, etc.),n.

38. Place Favorable to the Rapid Growth of Vice, Crime, Evil, Wickedness, or Other Unacceptable Activities; Place Where Such Flourishes, or Where the Practitioners of Such Abound; Less Commonly, Place Favorable to the Rapid Growth or Activity of Anything: hotbed (of vice, crime, thieves, etc.),n.

39. Having an Evil Mind, Character, or Nature; Having Evil Plans, Purposes, or Intentions: evil-minded,adj. (evil-mindedness,n.)

40. Interpreting Innocent Things, Actions, or Words in an Evil or Sexual Light: evil-minded,adj. (evil-mindedness,n.)

884. SIN

1. To Sin; To Do Wrong: err, fall from grace, offend; transgress (against); trespass,v.

2. A Sin: offense, transgression, trespass, wrong,n.

3. Slight or Petty Sin: peccadillo,n.

4. Seven Deadly Sins: anger, covetousness, envy, gluttony, lust, pride, sloth,n.

5. Sin That Lays One Open to, or That Merits, Eternal Punishment: damnation,n.

6. Sinner: offender, transgressor, trespasser, wrongdoer,n.

7. Sinning: erring or errant, offending, peccant, transgressive or transgressing, trespassing,adj. (peccancy,n.)

8. Liable or Likely to Sin; Likely to Succumb to the Temptation to Sin: peccable, adj. (peccability,n.)

9. Guilty of Sin: peccant,adj. (peccancy,n.)

10. Sinful: placular, unregenerate, unrighteous, vile, wrong,adj. (unregeneracy, unrighteousness, vileness, wrongness,n.)

11. Of God, to Reject (a Person) from Salvation Because of Sin: reprobate,v. (reprobation,n.)

12. Having an Uneasy, Sharp, etc., Feeling of Guilt or Sin,adj.
  1. **ashamed**—having a painful feeling of guilt
  2. **compunctious**—having an uneasy and sharp feeling of guilt
  3. **contrite**—thoroughly unhappy because of one's sense of guilt or sin; penitent; thoroughly, humbly, or sincerely penitent
  4. **penitent**—unhappy over one's sin or sins and willing to make atonement; contrite; repentant
  5. **remorseful**—full of deep or sharp regret over sin or wrongdoing; feeling mental pain because of a sense of guilt
  6. **repentant**—regretful or sorry over guilt or sin; having such a feeling combined with a determination to be good in the future

13. Uneasy Feeling of Guilt or Sin,n. *From Sec. 12:* shame, compunction, contriteness or contrition, penitence, remorse or remorsefulness, repentance

14. One Who Has an Uneasy Feeling of Guilt or Sin,n. *From Sec. 12:* penitent or penitential, repenter

15. Lacking in Such a Feeling of Guilt or Sin,adj. *From Sec. 12:* unashamed, uncontrite, impenitent or unpenitent, unremorseful or remorseless, unrepentant or unrepented (impenitence, impenitentness, or unpenitentness; remorselessness, unrepentantness,n. impenitent,n.)

16. Showing, or Indicative of, a Feeling of Guilt: shamefaced,adj. (shamefacedness,n.)

17. To Be Regretful over Guilt or Sin, and Be Willing to Make Atonement or Be Determined to Sin No More: repent (of), rue, v. (repentance,n. repenter, ruer,n.)

18. Arising from Sorrow or Uneasiness over a Sense of Guilt or Sin: compunctious, contrite, penitential, remorseful, repentant,adj.

19. Pert. to, Indicative of, or Expressing, Such Sorrow or Uneasiness: penitential, repentant,adj.

20. Of the Nature of Such Sorrow or Uneasiness: compunctious, remorseful,adj.

21. Caused by, or Causing, Such Sorrow or Uneasiness: compunctious,adj.

22. Utterly without Such Sorrow or Uneasiness: remorseless,adj. (remorselessness,n.)

23. To Admit One's Guilt or Sins: confess,v. (confession,n. confessor, confesser, confessionist, confessant,n.)

24. An Admission of Guilt or Sin: confession, peccavis,n. (confessional,adj.)

25. Having Admitted One's Guilt or Sin: confessed,adj. (as a *confessed murderer*, etc.)

26. To Admit One's Guilt or Sin to a Priest: confess,v. (confession,n. confessor, confesser, confessionist, confessant,n. confessional, confessionary,adj.)

27. One Who Confesses Guilt or Sin to a Priest and Undergoes Penance: penitent,n. (Roman Catholic religion)

28. Priest Who Hears Confessions: confessor,n.

29. Place Where a Priest Hears Confessions: confessional, confessionary,n.

30. Characterized by, Indicative or Expressive of, or Involved in, Guilt: guilty,adj.

31. To Believe Guilty on Little or No Evidence: suspect,v. (suspicion,n. suspecter,n.)

32. Believed Guilty: suspect, suspected,adj.

33. Open to Suspicion: suspect,adj.

34. One Believed Guilty, as of a Crime, etc.: suspect,n.

35. To Prove Guilty: attaint, condemn, convict,v. (attainder or attainture, conviction,n.)

36. To Find Guilty: condemn, convict,v. (condemnation, conviction,n.)

37. One Found Guilty, and under Sentence of Punishment, for a Crime: convict,n.

38. Person Guilty of a Fault, Offense, or Crime: culprit,n.

39. To Call or Declare Guilty: condemn,v. (condemnation,n. condemnatory,adj.)

885. CONSCIENCE

1. Psychoanalytical Term for What Amounts to the Conscience or Moral Censor: superego,n.

2. Determined, Influenced, or Controlled by, Conscience: conscientious, moral,adj. (conscientiousness,n.)

3. In Conformity with Conscience: conscientious, conscionable,adj.

4. Conscience Pain: compunction, pang of conscience or conscience pang, prick of conscience or conscience prick; qualm, qualm of conscience, or conscience qualm; scruple, sting of conscience, twinge or twitch of conscience,n. (compunctious,adj.)

5. Uneasiness of Conscience: compunction, misgiving of conscience, remorse, remorse of conscience,n. (compunctious,adj.)

6. To Hesitate or Be Unwilling, because of Conscience: scruple (followed by an infinitive),v. (scruple,n.)

7. Stung, or Made Uneasy, by Conscience: conscience-smitten, conscience-stricken,adj.

8. Following Dictates of Conscience in Matters of Honesty, Morality, etc.: scrupulous,adj. (scrupulousness, scrupulosity,n.)

9. Not Restricted or Guided by Conscience; Showing No Conscience: conscienceless, unconscionable, unscrupulous,adj. (unconscionableness, unscrupulousness or unscrupulosity, n.)

10. Without Conscience: conscienceless,adj.

886. CORRUPTION; IMMORALITY

1. Corrupt; Immoral; Characterized by, or Indicative of, Low Morals or Lack of Moral Restraint: abandoned, Augean, base, debauched, degenerate, degraded, demoralized, depraved, dishonorable, dissipated, dissolute, evil, graceless, loose, low, miscreant, perverted, profligate, putrid; rakehelly (archaic); rakish, reprobate, rotten, saturnalian, unethical or unethic, unprincipled, unscrupulous, unwholesome, vicious, vile, villainous, wicked,adj.

2. Corruptness; Corruption; Immorality, etc.,n. *From Sec. 1:* baseness, debauchery; degenerateness, degeneration, or degeneracy; degradedness or degradation, demoralization, depravity, dishonorableness, dissipatedness or dissipation, dissoluteness, evilness or evil, gracelessness, looseness, lowness, miscreancy, perversion, profligacy or profligateness, putridness or putridity, rakishness, rottenness, unethicalness, unprincipledness, unscrupulousness or unscrupulosity, unwholesomeness, viciousness or vice, vileness, villainousness or villainy, wickedness,n.; *Also:*
 1. **slough**—condition of moral debasement or degradation
 2. **turpitude, moral turpitude**—innate corruptness or depravity

3. Corrupt, Immoral, etc., Act,n. *From Sec. 1:* depravity, villainy; *From Sec. 2:* turpitude

4. Corrupt, Immoral, or Base Person, or One Lacking in, or of Low, Moral Restraint: debauchee, degenerate, miscreant, pervert, profligate, rakehell, rake or roué, reprobate; rotter (slang); wretch,n.; *Also:* 1. yahoo—degraded, vicious, and filthy person

5. Scoundrel: bezonian, blackguard, knave, rapscallion, rascal, rascalion or rascallion, reprobate, rogue, scamp, scapegrace, varlet, villain,n.

6. Scoundrelly: blackguard or blackguardly, knavish, rascal or rascally, roguish, scoundrel, villainous,adj. (blackguardism, knavishness or knavery, rascality, roguishness or roguery, villainousness or villainy,n.)

7. Scoundrelly Act: knavery, rascality, roguery, villainy,n.

8. Immoral Habit, Custom, or Practice: abomination, depravity, immoralism, immorality, vice,n. (immoralist,n.)

9. Violating, or in Violation of, the Moral Principles of a Business or Profession: unethical,adj. (unethicalness,n.)

10. Without, or Not Hampered by, Moral Scruples: conscienceless, unconscionable, unprincipled, unscrupulous,adj. (unconscionableness, unprincipledness, unscrupulousness or unscrupulosity,n.)

11. Corrupt Place: cesspit, cesspool,n.

12. Corrupting Influence: canker, smutch, ulcer, virus,n.

13. Injurious to Morals: noxious, pestiferous, pestilent, pestilential, unhealthsome, unhealthy, unwholesome,adj. (noxiousness, unhealthsomeness, unhealthiness, unwholesomeness,n.)

14. Something That Defiles Morally: ordure, n.

15. Advocacy of Immorality: immoralism,n. (immoralist,n.)

16. Time of General Immorality: saturnalia, n.

17. To Go Morally Astray: fall (of women), wander,v.

18. Straying from Morality: aberrant, errant or erring, obliquitous, sinuous, wandering, wayward,adj. (aberrance, aberrancy, or aberration; obliquity, sinuousness, waywardness,n.)

19. Having Strayed from Morality (of Women): fallen,adj.

20. In a Moral Lethargy: supine,adj. (supineness,n.)

21. To Indulge in Corrupt, Immoral, or Morally Unrestrained Pleasure or Pleasures: debauch, dissipate,v. (debauchery, dissipation, n. debauchee, dissipater or dissipator,n.)

22. To Become Corrupt: canker, corrupt, taint,v. (corruption,n.)

23. Decaying Morally: decadent,adj. (decadence, decadency,n. decadent,n.)

24. To Corrupt; To Cause to Sink in Morals: canker, debauch, degrade, demoralize, deprave, pervert, seduce, soil, stain, subvert, taint, vilify,v. (debauchment, degradation, demoralization, perversion, seduction, subversion, vilification,n. perversive, seductive, subversive,adj.)

25. Morally Unclean or Impure: contaminated, corrupt, defiled, dirty, filthy, impure, infected, maculate, polluted, seduced, tainted, unchaste, unclean, unvirtuous,adj. (contamination, corruptness, defilement, dirtiness or dirt, filthiness or filth, impureness or impurity, infectedness or infection, pollutedness or pollution, seduction, unchasteness or unchastity, uncleanness, unvirtuousness or unvirtue,n.)

26. To Cause to Be Morally Unclean or Impure: contaminate, corrupt, defile, dirty, filthify, infect, maculate, pollute, seduce, taint,v. (corruption, defilement, infection, pollution, seduction or seducement,n. corruptibleness or corruptibility,n. contaminative, corruptive, seductive,adj. contaminable, corruptible, seducible, taintable,adj.)

27. Place of Moral Uncleanness: cloaca,n. (cloacal,adj.)

28. That Which Makes (Someone or Something) Morally Unclean: ordure,n. (ordurous,adj.)

29. Ceremonially Unclean or Impure: contaminated, defiled, desecrated or desecrate, impure, maculate, polluted, profaned, tainted, unclean, violated,adj. (contamination, defilement, impureness or impurity, pollutedness or pollution, uncleanness, violation,n.)

30. To Make, or Cause to Be, Ceremonially Unclean or Impure: contaminate, defile, desecrate, maculate, pollute, profane, taint, violate,v. (contamination, defilement, desecration, pollution, profanation, violation,n. profanableness, violableness or violability,n. contaminative, profanatory, violative,adj. contaminable, profanable, taintable, violable, adj.)

887. MEANNESS

1. Mean, as in Quality, Character, Temperament, etc.: base, baseborn, beggarly, currish, dirty; hangdog (esp. in appearance); ignoble, low, miserable, nasty; ornery (colloq.); petty, picayune or picayunish, piggish, pusillanimous, raffish, rascal; scabby (colloq.); scoundrel or scoundrelly, scummy, scurvy, shabby, small-minded, sneaky, sordid, soulless, ungenerous, unhandsome, vile; whoreson (archaic); wretched,adj. (baseness, beggarliness, dirtiness, ignobleness or ignobility, lowness, miserableness, nastiness, pettiness, picayunishness, pusillanimity, raffishness, scabbiness, scurviness, shabbiness, small-mindedness, sneakiness, sordidness, unhandsomeness, vileness, wretchedness,n.)

2. Mean, i.e., of Little Value or Importance: beggarly, lowly; measly (slang); menial, miserable, petty, picayune or picayunish, piddling, pitiable, pitiful, poky, scummy, scurvy, shabby, sordid, sorry, unworthy, vile, wretched,adj. (beggarliness, lowliness, miserableness, pettiness, picayunishness, pitiableness, pitifulness, sordidness, sorriness, unworthiness, vileness, wretchedness,n.)

3. Mean, i.e., of Low or Humble Rank: abject, base, baseborn, beggarly, humble, ignoble, menial, shabby, slavish,adj. (baseness, beggarliness, humbleness, ignobleness or ignobility, slavishness,n.)

4. Mean and Wicked: caitiff,adj. (archaic or poetic)

5. Mean, Poor, and/or Dirty, As Surroundings, Conditions, etc.: sordid, squalid,adj. (sordidness, squalidness or squalor,n.)

6. Mean Person: bugger, cur, sneak; whoreson (archaic); worm, wretch,n.

7. Mean or Low People: dregs, raff, scum,n.

8. Mean and Mercenary Person: huckster,n.

9. Not Sordid or Mean: unworldly,adj. (unworldliness,n.)

888. WORTHLESSNESS

1. Worthless: cheap, feckless, good-for-nothing, nugatory, paltry, picayune or picayunish; rascally (humorous); rubbishy, scummy, trashy, vagabond, vain, valueless; verminous (of people only); vile, waste, worm-eaten, wretched,adj. (cheapness, fecklessness, paltriness, picayunishness, trashiness, vainness or vanity, vileness, wretchedness,n.)

2. Showy but Worthless: catchpenny, tinsel, trumpery,adj.

3. Of Little Worth or Value: base; hollow (as a triumph, victory, etc.); paltry, petty, trifling,adj. (baseness, hollowness, paltriness, pettiness,n.)

4. Theoretical Only, and Having No Practical Value: academic,adj.

5. Worthless Person: good-for-nothing, ne'er-do-well, offscouring, scalawag, scapegrace, scamp, snake, vagabond, vermin; *Also:*
  1. **black sheep**—worthless member of a good family, respectable group, etc.
  2. **bum**—idle and worthless person (colloq.)
  3. **cur**—worthless, evil-tempered person

6. Worthless Woman: baggage, hussy,n.

7. Worthless People: dregs, raff, scum, trash, vermin,n.

8. Worthless Thing: picayune, rush,n.

9. Worthless Things: chaff, rubbish, trash, tripe, truck, trumpery, waste,n.

10. Showy but Worthless Thing: bauble, gewgaw, tinsel, trumpery,n.

11. Thing of Little Value: trifle, trinket,n.

889. CRUELTY

1. Cruel: bitter, bloodthirsty, boarish, brutal, brute, cold-blooded, cruel-hearted, fell, felon, flinthearted, grim, hardhearted, heartless, inhuman, inhumane, ironhearted, merciless, ogreish or ogrish, pitiless, ruthless, sanguinary, savage, stonyhearted, unfeeling, unkind, unmerciful, unrelenting,adj.; *Also:*
  1. **atrocious**—horribly or incredibly cruel
  2. **barbarous**—cruel, like savages or uncivilized people
  3. **cannibalistic**—savagely and murderously cruel
  4. **demoniac or demoniacal, devilish, diabolic or diabolical, fiendish, fiendlike, satanic**—cruel, like the devil
  5. **ferocious, tigerish or tigrish, truculent, wolfish**—fiercely cruel
  6. **inclement**—cruel (of temperament, actions, etc.)
  7. **ruffian, ruffianly**—cruel and rough; cruel and lawless
  8. **sadistic**—obtaining joy or psychological gratification from being cruel, or from inflicting pain or humility; cruel from inner and generally pathological compulsion
  9. **tyrannical, tyrannic, tyrannous, oppressive**—cruel in exercising one's power or authority
  10. **unnatural**—cruel to an abnormal or inhuman extent
  11. **vulturous, wolfish**—cruel and greedy; cruel in preying upon others

2. Cruelty,n. *From Sec. 1:* bitterness, bloodthirstiness, boarishness, brutality, coldbloodedness, cruel-heartedness, fellness, grimness, hardheartedness, heartlessness, inhumanity or inhumanness, ironheartedness, mercilessness, pitilessness, ruthlessness, sanguinariness; savageness, savagery, savagism; stonyheartedness, unfeelingness, unkindness, unmercifulness, unrelentingness; atrociousness or atrocity, barbarousness or barbarity, cannibalism; devilishness, diabolicalness, or fiendishness; ferociousness or ferocity, truculence or truculency, wolfishness; inclemency, ruffianism, sadism; tyrannicalness, tyranny, or oppressiveness; unnaturalness, wolfishness

3. Cruel Person,n. *From Sec. 1:* brute, ogre or, fem., ogress, savage; cannibal; demon, devil, or fiend; tiger or wolf; ruffian, sadist; tyrant or oppressor; vulture or wolf

4. Cruel Act: atrocity, barbarity, brutality, rigor, savagery,n.

5. To Make Cruel: barbarize, brutalize,v. (barbarization, brutalization,n.)

6. To Treat Cruelly; To Be Cruel to: brutalize, crucify, ill-treat, maltreat, mistreat, oppress, savage, trample on, trample upon,v. (brutalization, crucifixion, ill-treatment, maltreatment, mistreatment, oppression,n. oppressor,n. oppressive,adj.)

7. To Be Cruel to (a Person or Group) in the Exercise of One's Power or Authority: oppress, tyrannize, tyrannize over,v. (oppression, tyranny,n. oppressiveness, tyrannicalness,n. oppressor, tyrant,n. oppressive; tyrannical, tyrannic, or tyrannous, adj.)

8. Treated Cruelly, Esp. in the Exercise of Power or Authority: downtrodden, oppressed, adj.

9. Eager to Shed Blood: bloodthirsty, sanguinary, tigerish or tigrish,adj. (bloodthirstiness, sanguinariness,n.)

10. Feeling or Showing No Pity or Mercy: bowelless (the bowels were formerly considered the seat of pity and kindness), callous, coldhearted; cutthroat (as competition, etc.); dispiteous, flinthearted, grim, hardhearted, heartless, implacable, inclement, inexorable, inhumane, ironhearted, merciless, obdurate, pitiless, relentless, remorseless, rocky, ruthless, stony, stonyhearted, uncompassionate, unfeeling, unmerciful, unpitying, unrelenting, unsparing, unsympathetic, unsympathizing,adj. (callousness or callosity, coldheartedness, grimness, hardheartedness, heartlessness, implacability or implacableness, inclemency, inexorability or inexorableness, inhumanity, ironheartedness, mercilessness, obduracy or obdurateness, pitilessness, relentlessness, remorselessness, rockiness, ruthlessness, stoniness, stonyheartedness, unmercifulness, unrelentingness,n.)

11. Merciless in Attack, Whether Physically or in Words: slashing,adj.

12. Merciless, Pitiless, or Harsh in Putting to Death or in Inflicting the Death Penalty: sanguinary,adj. (sanguinariness,n.)

13. To Make Unsympathetic to Suffering: callous, harden, sear,v.

14. To Become Unsympathetic to Suffering: callous, harden,v.

15. Very Little Mercy: short shrift,n.

890. HARSHNESS

1. Harsh, as in Manner, Attitude, or Feeling: acerb or acerbic, astringent, austere, bitter; Draconian, Draconic, or Draconical; drastic, hard, iron, obdurate, relentless, rigorous, rugged, severe, stern, uncharitable, unkind,adj.

2. Harshness, as of Manner, Attitude, or Feeling: acerbity, asperity, astringency, austerity or austereness, bitterness, Draconianism, hardness, obduracy or obdurateness, relentlessness, rigorousness or rigor, ruggedness, severity or severeness, sternness, uncharitableness, unkindness,n.

3. Harsh and Repelling Approach: austere, forbidding, grim, stern,adj. (austerity or austereness, forbiddingness, grimness, sternness, n.)

4. Harsh in the Exercise of Power or Authority: absolutist or absolutistic, arbitrary, despotic or despotical; Draconian, Draconic, or Draconical; grinding, hard, hardhanded, ironhanded, oppressive; tyrannical, tyrannous, or tyrannic,adj. (arbitrariness, despotism, Draconianism, hardness, hardhandedness, ironhandedness, oppressiveness, tyranny or tyrannicalness,n. despot, oppressor, tyrant,n. oppress, tyrannize (over),v.)

5. To Treat Harshly: punish (colloq.), trample on, trample upon,v. (punishment,n.)

6. Strict, as People, Attitudes, Laws, Discipline, Enforcement, etc.: astringent, austere; Draconian, Draconic, or Draconical; grim, harsh; ironclad (colloq.); ironhanded, relentless, rigid, rigorous, severe, Spartan; stark (of people only); stern, stiff, stringent, unrelenting,adj. (astringency, austerity or austereness, Draconianism, grimness, harshness, ironhandedness, relentlessness, rigidity or rigidness; rigorousness, rigor, or rigorism; severity or severeness, Spartanism, starkness, sternness, stiffness, stringency,n.)

7. To Treat with Strictness or Sternness: tutor,v.

8. Practice of Strictness: austerities, rigorism,n. (rigorist,n. rigoristic,adj.)

9. Strict in Demands or Requirements: exacting, exactive, stringent,adj. (exactingness, exactiveness, stringency,n.)

10. Strict, Severe, or Stern in Judging Others: censorious, critical, uncharitable, adj. (censoriousness, criticalness, uncharitableness,n.)

11. Illogically Strict in the Performance of One's Office, Official Duties, Functions, or Powers, etc., to the Annoyance of Others: officious,adj. (officiousness,n.)

12. Not Strict: easy, easygoing, informal, lax, lenient, permissive (i.e., allowing deviations from discipline, parental rules, etc.), relaxed, unexacting,adj. (easiness, easygoingness, informality, laxity or laxness, lenience or leniency, permissiveness, relaxedness,n.)

13. To Become Less Strict or Severe: relax,v. (relaxation,n.)

14. To Make (Discipline, Rules, etc.) Less Strict or Severe: relax,v. (relaxation,n.)

15. Lenient in Judging Others: charitable, adj. (charitableness, charity,n.)

16. Severe (of Conditions, Pain, Punishments, and Other Abstractions): acute, austere, crucial, drastic, grievous, hard, harsh, inclement, mortal; nasty (as a cough, cold, etc.); rigid, rigorous, rugged, sharp, smart, sore; stark (of weather); tough; vicious or wicked (as a cold, cough, weather, etc.),adj. (acuteness, austerity, grievousness, hardness, harshness, inclemency, nastiness, rigidness or rigidity, rigorousness or rigor, ruggedness, sharpness, starkness, toughness, viciousness, wickedness,n.)

17. To Make (Conditions, etc.) More Severe: aggravate, intensify,v. (aggravation, intensification,n.)

18. Becoming Gradually More Severe (Medical): ingravescent,adj.

891. DISGRACE

1. To Disgrace; To Bring Disgrace upon: attaint, blot, defile, dishonor, shame,v. (attainder, defilement,n.)

2. To Expose to Disgrace: gibbet,v.

3. To Mark with Disgrace: blot, brand, scar, stigmatize,v. (stigmatization,n.)

4. Mark of Disgrace: blot, brand, scar, stigma,n. (stigmata,pl.n.)

5. Disgrace: attaint, attainture, dishonor, shame,n.; *Also:*

1. **ignominy**—disgrace; disgrace that holds one up to contempt
2. **infamy**—well-publicized or well-known disgrace; public disgrace
3. **obloquy**—disgrace resulting from abuse or accusation by the public or by large numbers of people
4. **odium**—disgrace attached to someone or something widely hated, or, sometimes, that holds one up to general hatred
5. **opprobrium**—disgrace that lays one open to scolding, censure, condemnation, etc.
6. **reproach**—disgrace that one has brought upon oneself
7. **scandal**—disgrace; disgrace of such a kind as to reflect upon, or be borne by, others, esp. those closely related, as by family, friendship, etc.

6. Disgraceful; Causing or Bringing Disgrace,adj. *From Sec. 5:* dishonorable, shameful; ignominious, infamous, opprobrious, scandalous (dishonorableness, shamefulness; ignominiousness, infamousness, opprobriousness,n.) ; *Also:* ignoble, inglorious (ignobleness or ignobility, ingloriousness,n.)

7. That Which Causes Disgrace: disgrace, dishonor, ignominy, opprobrium, reproach, scandal,n.

8. One Who Brings Disgrace upon Another or Others: disgrace, dishonor, reproach, scandal,n.

9. Disgraceful Act, Action, or Happening: disgrace, scandal,n.

10. Given, or Addicted, to Scandal: scandalous,adj.

11. To Injure the Reputation of: disconsider, discredit, disgrace, dishonor, reflect on, reflect upon, reproach,v.

12. Bad Reputation; Loss, or Lack, of Good Reputation: discredit, disesteem, disgrace, dishonor, disrepute; ill fame, ill repute, etc.; infamy, notoriety, obloquy,n.

13. Of Bad Reputation: discreditable, disgraceful, dishonorable, disreputable, disrespectable, doubtful, infamous, notorious, questionable, raffish, shady,adj. (disgracefulness, dishonorableness, disreputability or disreputableness, disrespectability, doubtfulness, infamousness, notoriousness or notoriety, questionableness, raffishness, shadiness, n.)

14. Injurious to the Reputation: discreditable, disgraceful, dishonorable, disreputable, scandalous,adj.

15. Injury to Reputation: discredit, disgrace, dishonor, reproach, scandal,n.

16. One Who Is Injurious to the Reputation of the Group, etc.: discredit, disgrace, dishonor, reproach, scandal,n.

17. To Injure or Attempt to Injure the Character, Reputation, or Good Name of, Esp. in Words,v.
1. **asperse**—spread false rumors about (someone) ; make false and/or damaging statements or insinuations about, or accusations against; blacken the character, name, or reputation of (aspersion,n. asperser,n.)
2. **backbite**—secretly attack the character or reputation of; attack the character or reputation of (one who is not present) ; engage in such attacks (backbiting,n. backbiter,n.)
3. **blacken, besmirch, smirch**—make malicious accusations against (a person, his character, reputation, etc.) in order to detract from his good name
4. **blackguard**—use vile or scurrilous language against; attack (a person, his character, etc.) in such language
5. **blaspheme**—speak evil of; revile (blasphemer,n.)
6. **calumniate**—make false and spiteful accusations against or statements about (calumniation,n. calumniator,n.)
7. **defame, denigrate**—attack the character, reputation, or good name of by saying or writing spiteful things about or by making malicious accusations against (defamation, denigration,n. defamer, denigrator,n.)
8. **discredit**—speak of in such a way as to injure the reputation of
9. **libel**—publish or circulate an accusation calculated to defame or damage the character or reputation of (libeler,n.)
10. **malign**—speak evil of; accuse of evil; make false and spiteful accusations against (maligner,n.)
11. **revile**—use vile or abusive language against; attack in such language (revilement,n. reviler,n.)
12. **slander**—make false and malicious accusations against or statements about, esp.

in speech rather than writing; engage in such accusations or utterances (slanderer, n.)
13. **slur**—cast aspersions upon (a person, his character, reputation, etc.) ; calumniate
14. **smear**—make malicious, and often secret, charges against (a person, his character, reputation, etc.) for purposes of sullying such
15. **spatter, bespatter**—injure the character, reputation, or good name of; defame
16. **traduce**—make derogatory, malicious, and/or false accusations against (a person, his reputation, etc.); speak evilly of; make such derogatory, malicious, and/or false statements about (a person) as are calculated to ruin his reputation (traducement,n. traducer,n.)
17. **vilify, vilipend**—defame; malign (vilification,n. vilifier,n.)
18. **vituperate**—revile (vituperation,n. vituperator,n.)

18. Utterance or Utterances, Word, Accusation, or Accusations, etc., of This Nature or Intent,n. *From Sec. 17:* aspersion, calumny or calumniation, defamation, denigration, libel, revilement, slander, slur, smear or smear word, vilification, vituperation; *Also:*
1. **innuendo**—indirect statement, reference, or gesture of a nature derogatory to character or reputation
2. **insinuation**—sly hint or suggestion of a nature derogatory to character or reputation
3. **insinuendo**—combination of innuendo and insinuation (humorous)
4. **obloquy**—defamatory language; calumny
5. **reflection**—statement that casts discredit or disgrace (upon someone, his motives, character, reputation, etc.)
6. **scandal**—defamatory language or talk

19. Descr. of Language, Statements, Remarks, Accusations, etc., That Are, or Are Intended to Be, Injurious to the Reputation, etc.,adj. *From Sec. 17:* aspersive, backbiting, calumnious or calumniatory, defamatory, libelous, maligning, reviling, slanderous, slurring, traducing, vilifying, vituperative (slanderousness,n.); *From Sec. 18:* insinuative, scandalous

20. The Defamation or Persecution of Political Opponents or Those Connected with Them, Ostensibly for the Purpose of Seeking Out Criminals, Wrongdoers, etc., but Actually for Political Advantage or Profit: witch hunt,n.

21. To Take Away (from Someone's Reputation); To Decrease or Lessen Someone's Reputation, Esp. by Defamation, Slander, etc.: detract,v. (detraction,n. detractor or, fem., detractress,n. detractive, detractory, adj.)

22. To Put a Stain, Esp. a Moral Stain, on, or on the Character, Reputation or Name of: attaint, befoul, besmear, besmirch, bespatter, blacken, blemish, blot, blur, brand, cloud, darken, defile, denigrate, foul, maculate, scar, smear, smirch, smooch, smut, smutch, soil, spatter, spot, stain, stigmatize, sully, taint, tarnish,v. (attainder, defilement, denigration, stigmatization,n.)

23. Stain, Esp. a Moral Stain, on a Person, His Character, Reputation, or Name: attaint, blemish, blot, blur, brand, cloud, maculation, scar, slur, smear, smirch, smutch, spot, stain, stigma, taint, tarnish,n. (stigmata,pl. n.)

24. Stained, Esp. Morally,adj. *From Sec. 22:* befouled, besmeared, etc.; cloudy, maculate; *Also:* scrofulous, unclean

25. To Become Stained, Esp. Morally: sully, taint, tarnish,v.

892. ACCUSATION

1. To Accuse: arraign, blame, charge, denounce or denunciate, impeach, incriminate, inculpate, indict; tax (with),v.

2. Accusation, i.e., Act or Process of Accusing: accusal, arraignment, denouncement or denunciation, impeachment, incrimination, inculpation, indictment,n.

3. Accuser: accusant, arraigner, denouncer or denunciator, impeacher, incriminator, indicter or indictor,n.

4. Pert. to an Accuser: accusatorial,adj.

5. An Accusation: arraignment or arraign, charge, denunciation, indictment,n.

6. Accusatory; Accusing: denunciatory, incriminatory, inculpative, inculpatory,adj.

7. To Make a Formal Accusation, as in Court, etc.: complain,v. (complaint,n. complainant,n.)

8. To Accuse, by Legal Processes, of Wrongdoing, Crime, etc.: indict,v. (indictment,n. indicter,n. indictable,adj.)

9. An Accusation, by Legal Processes, of Wrongdoing, Crime, etc.: indictment,n.

10. Bill of Indictment Endorsed by a Grand Jury: true bill,n.

11. To Accuse (an Officeholder) of Official Wrongdoing or Misconduct: impeach,v. (impeachment,n. impeachability,n. impeacher,n. impeachable,adj.)

12. State of Being Accused of Official Wrongdoing: impeachment,n.

13. To Issue, or Thunder Forth with, Accusations: fulminate,v. (fulmination,n. fulminator,n. fulminant,adj.)

14. To Accuse Rebukingly or Reproachfully: upbraid,v. (upbraider,n. upbraiding,n.)

15. To Make an Accusation against (One's Accuser): countercharge,v.

16. To Make an Accusation or Accusations against One's Accuser; To Charge to One's Accusers the Very Faults or Guilt of Which One Is Accused: recriminate,v. (recrimination,n. recriminative, recriminatory,adj.)

17. An Accusation against One's Accuser: counteraccusation, countercharge, recrimination,n.

18. To Involve in An Accusation: criminate, implicate, incriminate, inculpate,v. (crimination, implication, incrimination, inculpation, n. criminative or criminatory, implicative, incriminatory, inculpative or inculpatory, adj.)

19. To Accuse of a Crime: charge, criminate, impeach, incriminate, inculpate, indict,v. (crimination, incrimination, inculpation, indictment,n. impeachability,n. incriminator, indicter or indictor,n. criminative or criminatory, incriminatory, inculpative or inculpatory,adj. impeachable, indictable,adj.)

20. An Accusation of Crime: indictment,n.

21. Person Accused in Court of a Crime or Offense: the accused, defendant,n.

22. To Charge (a Fault, Discreditable Act, Quality, etc.) to (a Person): blame, impute to,v. (blame, imputation,n. blamableness, imputability or imputableness,n. imputer,n. imputative,adj. blamable, imputable,adj.)

23. To Charge Some Fault, Defect, or Discreditable Quality to: impeach,v. (impeachment,n. impeachability,n. impeachable,adj.)

893. BLAME

1. To Blame: accuse, censure, hold responsible, inculpate, reprehend, reproach,v. (ac-

cusation or accusal, censure, inculpation, reprehension,n. accuser, reproacher,n.)

2. Blame: accusation, censure, discommendation, odium, reprehension, responsibility, reproach,n.

3. Blame Attached to One by the Public, or by Large Numbers of People: obloquy,n.

4. Deserving Blame: blamable, blameful, blameworthy, censurable, discommendable, culpable, guilty, reprehensible, reproachable, responsible,adj. (blamableness, blamefulness, blameworthiness, censurableness or censurability, discommendableness, culpability or culpableness, guilt or guiltiness, reprehensibility or reprehensibleness, reproachableness, responsibility or responsibleness,n.)

5. Deserving Blame and Punishment; Deserving Severe Blame, as for a Crime, Grave Offense, Sin, etc.: guilty,adj. (guilt, guiltiness,n.)

6. One Who Is Blamed for the Sins, Crimes, or Errors of Others: fall guy (slang), scapegoat, whipping boy,n.

7. To Hold or Consider as Responsible for, as Being the Author, Originator, or Possessor of, or as the Cause, Source or Origin of: accredit with, ascribe to, assign to, attribute to, credit with, impute to, refer to,v. (ascription, assignment, attribution, imputation,n. ascribable, assignable, attributable, imputable, referable or referrible,adj. imputative,adj.)

8. To Attribute to (Someone Else) Unwarrantably, Unreasonably, Unduly, or without Justification: arrogate to,v. (arrogation,n.)

894. DISAPPROVAL

1. To Disapprove of; To Have, or Express, an Unfavorable Opinion of; To Find Fault with,v.

1. **animadvert on, animadvert upon**—express disapproval or censure of (a thing, act, etc.), in a way to show hostility, prejudice, and an inclination to pick fault with trifles
2. **blame**—find fault with; censure
3. **castigate**—criticize sharply
4. **censure, call to task, take to task**—find fault with; criticize harshly or hostilely; express one's disapproval of; condemn as wrong, wicked, or sinful
5. **chide**—express disapproval of; find fault with
6. **condemn**—disapprove of; call wrong; make a final and adverse critical judgment of a very harsh, almost merciless, nature upon
7. **criminate**—censure severely
8. **criticize**—find fault with; disapprove of
9. **cry down**—condemn; decry
10. **damn**—denounce angrily, often using abusive language; condemn; condemn as a failure; utter a negative judgment upon
11. **decry**—utter loud and negative judgments upon; censure
12. **denounce, denunciate**—condemn in strong language
13. **deprecate**—express one's strong or critical disapproval of
14. **discommend**—disapprove of; bring into, or expose to, an unfavorable light or censure
15. **discountenance**—refuse to approve, or to look upon with approval; look upon with disfavor
16. **disfavor**—disapprove; consider with disapproval
17. **dispraise**—express one's disapproval of
18. **excoriate**—denounce in the strongest language; flay
19. **exprobrate**—find fault with; criticize harshly; condemn as wrong

20. **flay**—criticize unmercifully, figuratively taking the skin off (the object of one's censure)
21. **frown upon**—look upon with disapproval; disapprove of; show disapproval of
22. **fulminate (against)**—denounce violently; thunder forth with denunciations against
23. **hiss**—show one's disapproval of (someone's public performance) by making a sibilant sound
24. **objurgate**—denounce in strong terms
25. **pan**—criticize adversely (slang)
26. **rebuke**—express stern disapproval of, usually for something considered wrong
27. **reflect on, reflect upon**—show disapproval, usually indirectly, for; serve to bring disapproval or reproach on, as actions, etc.
28. **reprehend**—censure
29. **reprimand (for)**—express stern and usually formal disapproval of, as for actions, wrongdoing, etc.
30. **reproach**—find fault with (someone); censure
31. **reprobate**—disapprove of; censure; denounce as bad or unworthy
32. **reprove**—express disapproval of; find fault with; censure
33. **scathe**—criticize (someone) harshly; denounce (someone) in terms calculated to do serious injury
34. **scold**—find fault with
35. **scorch**—criticize so severely and stingingly that it seems the intent is figuratively to burn or wither; criticize in burning language
36. **slam**—criticize severely (colloq.)
37. **slash**—censure or criticize recklessly and/or harshly, or without mercy
38. **slate**—criticize without mercy; rebuke severely
39. **taunt (with)**—reproach insultingly or mockingly (for)
40. **tax (with)**—censure or criticize (for)
41. **twit (with)**—reproach (for previous faults or promises)
42. **twitter**—taunt; twit
43. **upbraid (for, with)**—reproach (for faults, errors, wrongdoing, etc.)
44. **vituperate**—censure in abusive terms

2. To Express Disapproval; To Engage in Faultfinding or Criticism,v. *From Sec. 1:* animadvert, chide, criticize, fulminate, hiss, scold, upbraid, vituperate; *Also:*
1. **carp**—criticize in an ill-natured manner; pick flaws in a petty way; find fault over trivial causes
2. **cavil**—find fault over trivial matters; be petty in one's criticism; criticize flippantly
3. **object, take exception**—express or feel disapproval
4. **thunder**—utter sharp condemnations

3. Disapproval; Expression of Disapproval; Disapproving Language,n. *From Sec. 1:* animadversion, blame, castigation, censure, condemnation, crimination, criticism, damnation, decrial, denouncement, denunciation, deprecation, discommendation, disfavor, dispraise, excoriation, exprobration, frown, fulmination, hiss, objurgation; panning (slang); rebuke, reflection, reprehension, reprimand, reproach, reprobation, reproval or reproof, scolding; scorcher (colloq.); slam, taunt, twit, upbraiding, vituperation; *From Sec. 2:* cavil, objection or exception; *Also:*
1. **commination**—denunciation
2. **disapprobation**—disapproval
3. **obloquy**—harshly or hostilely critical speech or language; public censure or reproach
4. **odium**—censure or reproach attached to

one who, or to that which, is hated, disgraceful, or shameful
5. **opprobrium**—reproach resulting from wicked or shameful acts
6. **stricture**—censure; criticism; a critical remark or comment
7. **vitriol**—sharp criticism

4. Disapproving; Descr. of Disapproval,adj. *From Sec. 1:* blameful or blaming, castigating, chiding, condemnatory, criminative or criminatory, critical, damnatory, denunciatory, deprecatory or deprecative, flaying, frowning, fulminating or fulminant, hissing, objurgatory, rebuking, reprehensive, reproachful, reprobative, reproving, scathing, scolding, scorching, slashing, taunting, upbraiding, vituperative or vituperatory (criticalness, deprecativeness, reproachfulness,n.); *From Sec. 2:* carping, caviling; *From Sec. 3:* comminatory, disapprobative or disapprobatory, opprobrious, vitriolic (opprobriousness,n.); *Also:*
1. **captious, exceptive**—disposed to find fault, or to criticize in a petty way (captiousness,n.)
2. **censorious**—faultfinding; finding fault in a petty and ill-natured fashion; sharply critical (censoriousness,n.)
3. **cynical**—faultfinding; finding fault with trifles (cynicism, cynicalness,n.)
4. **hypercritical**—excessively critical; critical beyond sense or reason
5. **pharisaic, pharisaical**—self-righteously critical of the behavior or morals of others (pharisaism, pharisaicalness,n.)
6. **overcritical**—too critical
7. **querulous**—faultfinding; tending to find fault (querulousness,n.)
8. **ultracritical**—extremely or excessively critical

5. One Who Disapproves, or Expresses or Shows Disapproval,n. *From Sec. 1:* animadverter, castigator, chider, condemner, critic or criticizer, decrier, denouncer or denunciator, deprecator, discommender, dispraiser, flayer, fulminator, hisser, objurgator, rebuker, reproacher, reprover, scolder, or esp. a woman, scold; slater, taunter, twitter, upbraider, vituperator; *From Sec. 2:* carper, caviler, objector, thunderer; *From Sec. 4:* cynic, hypercritic, pharisee; *Also:*
1. **censor**—faultfinder; critic
2. **Momus**—petty and carping critic or faultfinder

6. State of Being Disapproved of,n. *From Sec. 1:* disfavor, excoriation; *From Sec. 3:* obloquy, odium, opprobrium

7. Worthy of, or Deserving, Disapproval, adj. *From Sec. 1:* censurable, condemnable, criticizable, damnable, discommendable, reprehensible, reproachable, reprovable (censurableness or censurability, damnableness, discommendableness, reprehensibleness or reprehensibility, reproachableness,n.); *From Sec. 2:* objectionable or exceptionable (objectionableness, objectionability, or exceptionableness,n.); *From Sec. 3:* odious, opprobrious (odiousness, opprobriousness,n.); *Also:* 1. culpable—deserving censure

8. Not Deserving Disapproval,adj. *From Sec. 1:* blameless, uncensurable, irreprehensible; irreproachable, unreproachable, or reproachless; unreproved (blamelessness, irreprehensibleness, irreproachability or irreproachableness,n.); *From Sec. 2:* unobjectionable or unexceptionable (unobjectionableness, unexceptionability, or unexceptionableness,n.); *From Sec. 7:* inculpable (inculpableness or inculpability,n.)

9. To Wound Deeply with Harsh Criticism: lacerate, scarify,v. (laceration, scarification, n. scarifier,n. lacerative, scarifying,adj.)

10. To Attack with the Harshest Kind of Criticism: lash, scathe,v. (lashing,n. lashing, scathing,adj.)

11. Sign of Disapproval: thumbs down

12. No Longer Approved: outmoded,adj.

13. To Incur the Disapproval of: displease,v.

895. SCOLD

1. To Scold,v.
1. admonish—scold gently
2. berate—scold vehemently
3. bring to book—reprimand
4. call to account—scold; reprove
5. castigate—scold harshly
6. censure—scold as wrong
7. chide—scold; scold mildly
8. exprobrate—upbraid
9. flay—scold unmercifully, figuratively taking the skin off the object of one's scolding
10. lecture—scold; subject to a formal or public scolding
11. objurgate—scold vehemently or violently
12. rag—scold (colloq.)
13. rail at, rail against—scold in harsh language
14. rant at—scold violently
15. rebuke—scold sharply
16. reprehend—scold (someone for a fault)
17. reprimand—scold severely or formally
18. reproach—scold (someone) gently to show one's displeasure or dissatisfaction with his actions, words, attitude, etc.
19. reprove—scold for a fault or error; scold as unworthy; scold (someone) in a kindly manner in order to persuade to mend his ways
20. revile—scold in harsh, abusive, or vile language
21. slate—scold harshly
22. tax (with)—scold (because of)
23. tongue-lash—give a severe scolding to
24. twit (with)—scold by reminding (of previous promises, faults, etc.)
25. whip—scold in sharp words
26. upbraid—scold for a wrong; scold for good reasons

2. To Scold, i.e., Engage in Scolding,v. *From Sec. 1:* chide, lecture, rail, rant, revile, upbraid

3. Scolding; A Scolding,n. *From Sec. 1:* admonishment or admonition, castigation, censure, chiding, exprobration, lecture, objurgation, ragging or rag, rebuke, reprehension, reprimand, reproach, reproval or reproof, revilement, tongue-lashing, twit, whipping, upbraiding; *Also:*
1. comeuppance—scolding that is deserved (colloq.)
2. curtain lecture—scolding of a husband by his wife after they have gone to bed (colloq.)
3. dressing-down—scolding
4. jobation—long and wearisome scolding (colloq.)
5. lashing—severe scolding
6. speaking-to, talking-to—scolding

4. Scolder,n. *From Sec. 1:* admonisher or admonitor, castigator, chider, flayer, objurgator, rebuker, reproacher, reprover, reviler, slater, twitter, upbraider

5. Scolding,adj. *From Sec. 1:* admonishing, berating, etc.; admonitory, objurgatory, reprehensive, reproachful (reproachfulness,n.)

6. Having a Disposition to Scold—of Women: shrewish, termagant, vixenish, vixenly,adj. (shrewishness, termagancy,n.)

7. A Scolding Woman: harridan, scold, shrew, termagant, virago, Xanthippe or Xantippe,n.

8. Scolding Wife: Xanthippe or Xantippe,n. (after the wife of Socrates)

896. PUNISHMENT

1. To Punish,v.
1. amerce—punish; punish by levying a fine against in the amount decided arbitrarily by the court; fine (amercement,n.)
2. avenge—punish someone for (a wrong he has committed) or on behalf of (the one wronged)
3. bastinado, bastinade—punish (an offender) by beating the soles of his feet with a cudgel
4. castigate—punish severely (castigation, n.)
5. chasten—punish to make morally better—esp. used in a religious sense; chastise
6. chastise—punish by flogging or whipping; administer corporal punishment to (chastisement,n.)
7. correct—punish in order to reform; chastise (correction,n.)
8. crucify—torture (crucifixion,n.)
9. discipline—punish; punish for infraction or wrongdoing; chastise
10. draw and quarter—punish by tying each arm and leg of (an offender) to one of four horses, then driving the horses in four different directions until the victim is dismembered and dies—a practice in the Middle Ages
11. ferule—punish (children) by striking them, usually on the hand, with a rod or ruler
12. fine—punish (an offender) by exacting money for an error, misdeed, slight crime, etc.
13. flog—punish by hitting or beating severely
14. impale—punish by thrusting upon a pointed stake (impalement,n.)
15. keelhaul—haul (an offender) under a ship's keel as a punishment; punish drastically and painfully
16. mulct—fine (mulctation,n.)
17. penalize—impose a specific punishment upon for crime, sin, error, transgression, etc. (penalization,n.)
18. persecute—punish in petty ways for one's religion, religious beliefs, racial origin, nationality, etc. (persecution,n.)
19. pillory, stock—subject to a form of punishment used in former times, in which the offender's hands and head were placed in the openings of a wooden frame in a public place
20. require—avenge (requital,n.)
21. revenge—inflict punishment upon someone for (a wrong one considers malicious, harmful, etc.), or on behalf of (the person so wronged); the distinction between *revenge* and *avenge* is that the latter implies merited punishment upon the offender, while the former may be of petty or malicious motivation
22. scourge—punish severely; punish by whipping or lashing
23. slate—punish
24. smite—punish; strike with punishment
25. strappado—punish (an offender) by pulling him up high by a rope (tied, often, to his wrists), and then letting him plunge the full length of the rope—a practice in former times
26. torture—punish by inflicting great pain upon (torture,n.)
27. trounce—punish with great severity
28. whip—punish by hitting or beating

2. Punishment,n. *From Sec. 1:* amercement; vengeance (from *avenge*), bastinado or bastinade, castigation, chastisement or chastising, correction, crucifixion, discipline, ferule, fine, flogging, impalement, mulct, penalty, persecution, requital, revenge, scourge, strappado or estrapade, torture, trouncing, whipping; *Also:*

1. **amende**—penalty; fine
2. **corporal punishment**—punishment in which the victim is hit, flogged, whipped, etc.
3. **desert, deserts**—suitable, deserved, or due punishment
4. **forfeit**—fine; penalty
5. **gantlet, gauntlet**—form of punishment in which the victim runs between two lines of men who beat him with sticks, whips, etc. (esp. in the phrase *run the gantlet*)
6. **nemesis**—just punishment
7. **penal servitude**—punishment by imprisonment at hard labor
8. **penance**—punishment accepted to pay for a sin, or to atone for a bad action
9. **retribution**—punishment visited upon a wrongdoer; deserved punishment in the hereafter
10. **short shrift**—very little relaxation of punishment; punishment without mercy or delay
11. **visitation**—punishment from heaven
12. **wrath**—deserved punishment; punishment (by God)

3. Punisher,n. *From Sec. 1:* amercer, avenger, castigator, chastener, chastiser, corrector, crucifier, discipliner or disciplinarian, flogger, impaler, persecutor, requiter, revenger, scourger, smiter, torturer, whipper; *Also:* 1. **nemesis**—imposer of just punishment; anyone or anything that makes one pay for one's errors, crimes, neglect, etc.

4. Punishing,adj. *From Sec. 1:* avenging, castigating, etc.; vengeful (from *avenge*), disciplinary or disciplinarian, mulctuary, persecutive or persecutory, revengeful, torturous; *Also:*

1. **grueling**—punishing almost beyond endurance or to the point of exhaustion
2. **nemesic**—avenging
3. **punitive**—inflicting, or intending to inflict, punishment
4. **vindicatory, vindicative**—punishing; avenging

5. Desiring, or Full of a Desire, to Punish, adj. *From Sec. 1:* vengeful (from *avenge*), revengeful (vengefulness, revengefulness,n.); *From Sec. 2:* wrathful (wrathfulness,n.); *Also:* 1. **vindictive**—revengeful (vindictiveness,n.)

6. Descr. of, Pert. to, Involving, etc., Punishment,adj. *From Sec. 1:* vengeful (from *avenge*), disciplinal or disciplinary; mulctatory, mulctative, or mulctary; penal, persecutory or persecutional, revengeful, torturous; *From Sec. 2:* penitential (from *penance*), retributive or retributory, visitational; *Also:* 1. **punitive**—descr. of, or concerned or involved with, punishment

7. Punishable,adj. *From Sec. 1:* amerceable, disciplinable, mulctable or mulctuary, torturable

8. Means or Device Used to Punish,n. *From Sec. 1:* ferule (the rod or ruler); pillory or stocks (the device); scourge; strappado (the device or machine); *Also:*

1. **cucking stool**—a chair once used as a punishment for scolds, dishonest merchants, etc.; the victim was hit with stones, ducked in water, etc.
2. **cutty stool**—seat in Scottish churches where unchaste people sat for public rebuke
3. **ducking stool**—stool in which disorderly women were once tied and then ducked into water
4. **rack**—instrument of punishment

5. **scourge**—means of any kind of punishment

9. Unpunished,adj. *From Sec. 1:* unavenged, uncastigated, unchastened, unchastised, uncorrected, uncrucified, undisciplined, unfined, unflogged, unmulcted, unpenalized, unpersecuted, unpilloried, unrequited, unrevenged, unscourged, unsmitten, untortured, untrounced, unwhipped; *Also:* 1. **scot-free**—unpunished

10. Unpunishable,adj. *From Sec. 1:* unavengeable, unchastisable; incorrigible (from *correct*), undisciplinable, unfloggable, unrequitable,adj. (incorrigibleness, incorrigibility, n.)

11. To Pronounce (a Punishment) upon: adjudge (to), condemn (to), sentence (to),v. (condemnation,n. sentence,n. sentencer,n.)

12. To Give or Bring (to Someone) as Punishment: inflict (on, upon); visit (on, upon), v. (infliction, visitation,n. inflicter or inflictor, n. inflictive,adj.)

13. To Come (to One) as Punishment: visit, v. (visitation,n.)

14. To Impose (Punishment) on: inflict (punishment) on or upon; visit (punishment) on or upon,v. (infliction, visitation,n. inflicter or inflictor,n.)

15. To Impose (a Fine) upon: assess,v. (assessment,n.)

16. To Doom to Eternal Punishment (Religion): damn,v. (damnation,n.)

17. Eternal Punishment (Religion): damnation,n.

18. State of Being Eternally Punished (Religion): damnation, perdition,n.

19. Place or State of Temporary Punishment: purgatory,n. (purgatorial, purgatorian,adj.)

20. State, Condition, or Place in Which Souls of the Dead Are Purified of Sin by Punishment (Roman Catholic Religion): purgatory,n. (purgatorial, purgatorian,adj.)

21. Book of Rules for Imposing Punishments to Expiate a Sin (Religion): penitential,n.

22. One Who Advocates Punishment for Offenses: disciplinarian,n.

23. One Who Advocates or Uses Severe Punishment in a Prison, etc.: correctionalist,n.

24. Deserving of Punishment: disciplinable, punishable,adj. (of offenses, etc.)

25. State or Condition of Deserving Punishment: desert or deserts, punishability,n.

26. Descr. of Severe Punishment That Is Merited by the Extent of the Transgression: condign,adj.

27. To Promise to Punish: threaten,v. (threat,n.)

28. Change of a Stronger to a Lighter Punishment by an Executive Officer, Such as a State Governor, the President, etc.: commutation,n. (commute,v.)

29. Theory or Principle that a Man Who Avenges His Honor by Killing the Seducer of His Wife or Daughter Should Be Unpunished or Only Very Lightly Punished: unwritten law,n.

30. To Restrain or Improve by Punishing: castigate,v. (castigation,n. castigator,n.)

31. Avenging Spirits, in the Ancient Greek Religion, That Inflicted Punishment for Violation of the Laws of Piety or Hospitality, or for Perjury or Homicide: Erinys, Eumenides, Furies, Semnae,pl.n. (Erinys,sing. n.)

32. Greek Goddess of Vengeance or Retributive Justice: Nemesis,n. (nemesic,adj.)

33. To Give Up, Not Have, or No Longer Have, a Desire to Punish (an Offender, Offense, Fault, Crime, etc.): forgive,v. (forgiveness,n. forgivingness,n. forgiver,n. forgiving,adj.)

897. FORGIVENESS

1. To Forgive (a Person for a Slight Fault, Error, etc.): excuse, pardon,v.

2. Forgiveness: pardon,n.

3. One Who Forgives: forgiver,n.

4. Forgiving: placable,adj.   (placability, placableness,n.)

5. Generous in Forgiving: magnanimous,adj. (magnanimity, magnanimousness,n.)

6. To Forgive or Excuse (a Fault, Offense, Guilt, etc.): condone, excuse, extenuate, forgive, justify, overlook, palliate, pardon, remit, vindicate, warrant,v. (condonation, excusal, extenuation, forgiveness, justification, palliation, remission or remittal, vindication, n. extenuator, justifier, palliator, vindicator,n. extenuative or extenuatory, justificative or justificatory, palliative or palliatory, vindicative or vindicatory,adj.)

7. Forgiveness of, or for, a Fault, etc.,n. *From Sec. 6:* pardon, remission; *Also:*
1. **dispensation**—special remission or forgiveness of a fault, etc. (dispensational, adj.)
2. **remission,** remission of sin or sins—forgiveness of sin or sins, esp., in the Roman Catholic religion, through penance, etc.

8. Giving, or Serving to Give, Special Remission or Forgiveness of a Fault, Sin, etc.: dispensative, dispensatory,adj.

9. Able to Be Forgiven or Excused (of a Fault, Offense, Sin, etc.): defensible, excusable, forgivable, justifiable, pardonable, remissible, venial, vindicable, warrantable, adj. (defensibleness or defensibility, excusableness or excusability, forgivableness, justifiableness or justifiability, pardonableness, remissibility, venialness, vindicableness or vindicability, warrantableness,n.)

10. Not Forgivable or Excusable (of a Fault, Offense, Sin, etc.): indefensible, inexcusable, irremissible, unexcusable, unforgivable, unjustifiable, unpardonable, unwarrantable,adj. (indefensibleness or indefensibility, inexcusableness or inexcusability, irremissibleness or irremissibility, unexcusableness, unforgivableness, unjustifiableness, unpardonableness, unwarrantableness,n.)

11. To Ignore Indulgently, or Not Be Troubled by (a Fault, Offense, etc.): blink at, condone, excuse, forgive, overlook, pardon, wink at,v. (condonation, excusal, forgiveness,n. condoner, forgiver,n.)

12. To Forgive, i.e., Free from Punishment or Penalties, or from the Consequences of These: absolve (from), amnesty, excuse, pardon,v. (absolution, excusal,n.); *Also:*
1. **amnesty**—give immunity to punishment for past offenses against the government, or against the laws of war; give (a witness) immunity to punishment in order to make him testify to facts that may incriminate him
2. **indulgence**—attach to (an offense) an exemption for the offender from temporal or purgatorial punishment due for sin after the guilt has been forgiven (Roman Catholic religion)

13. Forgiveness of, or Freedom from, Punishment,n. *From Sec. 12:* absolution, amnesty, pardon; amnesty, indulgence; *Also:*
1. **grace**—pardon; pardon or forgiveness from God
2. **immunity**—freedom from punishment (loose usage)
3. **impunity**—freedom from punishment (esp. in the phrase *with impunity*)
4. **indemnity**—exemption from legal penalties that have been incurred by one's acts; exemption from legal penalties, specially granted to public officials and other persons, for illegal or unconstitutional acts; amnesty

14. Forgiving, or Serving to Forgive, i.e., Freeing from Punishment or Penalties: absolutory, absolvatory, absolvent,adj.

15. Person Who So Forgives, or That Which Serves to Cause Such Forgiveness: absolvent or absolver; pardoner (person only),n.

16. Capable of Being So Forgiven: absolvable, pardonable,adj.

17. Certificate Granting Such Forgiveness: pardon,n.

18. Temporary Immunity from a Penalty: grace,n. (as *period of grace,* etc.)

19. To Delay the Punishment, Esp. the Death Penalty, of (a Person): reprieve, respite,v.

20. Such Delay in Punishment: reprieve, respite,n.

21. Certificate Granting Such Delay: reprieve,n.

22. State of Having Had One's Punishment Delayed: reprieve,n.

23. To Wipe Out (an Offense, Accusation of Guilt, etc.) Legally, by Atonement or Other Suitable Action: purge,v. (purgation,n. purger,n. purgative,adj.)

24. To Free from Blame, Guilt, or Sin: absolve, acquit (of), clear; discharge (legal); disculpate, exculpate, excuse, exonerate, justify, vindicate,v. (absolution, acquittal, discharge, disculpation, exculpation, excusal, exoneration, justification, vindication,n. absolver or absolvent, acquitter, exonerator, justifier, vindicator,n.)

25. Freeing, or Serving to Free, from Blame, Guilt, or Sin: absolutory, absolvatory or absolvent; disculpatory, exculpatory, exonerative, justificative or justificatory, vindicative or vindicatory,adj.

26. Capable of Being So Freed: absolvable, exculpable, excusable, justifiable, vindicable, adj.

27. State of Being So Freed: absolution, acquittal, exoneration, vindication,n.

28. To Free (Someone) from Blame, Fault, or Guilt after Conducting a Perfunctory Official Investigation, or One That Had No Real Intention of Discovering Crimes, Official Misconduct, etc.: whitewash,v. (whitewash,n. whitewasher,n.)

29. To Free from a Charge or Accusation of Guilt, Wrong, Fault, etc.: acquit, clear; discharge (legal); disculpate, exculpate, exonerate, purge,v. (acquittal, discharge, disculpation, exculpation, exoneration, purgation,n. acquitter, exonerator, purger,n. disculpatory, exculpatory, exonerative, purgative,adj. exculpable,adj.)

30. Acquittal of a Person, in Common-Law Trials, if a Certain Number of Friends, etc., Swore to His Innocence—in Effect in Great Britain up to the Early 19th Century: compurgation,n.

31. Person Who So Swore to Another's Innocence: compurgator,n.

32. To Declare or Pronounce Not Guilty: acquit, clear, justify,v. (acquittal, justification,n. acquitter, justifier,n.)

33. To Prove (a Person) Not Guilty: clear,v.

34. Not Inspired or Actuated by a Desire to Punish, a Wish for Revenge, etc.: unrevengeful, unvindictive,adj. (unrevengefulness, unvindictiveness,n.)

35. Not Punishing Severely: clement, lenient, adj. (clemency; leniency, lenience, or lenity, n.)

36. A Lenient Act: lenity,n.

37. To Refrain from Punishing: show mercy to, spare,v. (mercifulness,n. merciful, sparing, adj.)

38. Power to Decide on Punishment or Pardon, or on the Extent of Punishment: mercy,n. (esp. in the phrase *throw oneself on the mercy of*)

39. Merciful: clement (esp. of a judge), compassionate, lenient, sparing,adj.

40. Mercy: clemency (esp. of a judge), compassion or compassionateness, grace; leniency, lenience, or lenity; pity,n.

41. Divine Mercy: grace,n.

42. Mercy Shown to a Defeated Enemy, Opponent, etc.: quarter,n.

43. Disposed to Be Merciful: clement,adj. (clemency,n.)

44. Act of Mercy: clemency, lenity,n.

45. Not Forgiving: merciless, unforgiving, unmerciful, unsparing,adj.

898. AN EXCUSE

1. An Excuse: alibi (colloq.), justification, plea, warrant,n.; *Also:*
1. alibi—plea or fact that a person accused of a crime was at some other place at the time the crime was committed
2. extenuation—partial excuse
3. pretext—excuse that conceals the real reason, motive, or purpose
4. rationalization—justification for one's action, behavior, or thinking by a claim of worthy or creditable motives, though unconscious motives of a different, probably less creditable nature, may inspire such action, behavior, or thinking—concept in psychoanalysis or psychology
5. stall—pretext to cause delay (colloq.)
6. subterfuge—excuse intended to deceive

2. To Make Excuses, or An Excuse, for,v. *From Sec. 1:* alibi (colloq.), excuse, justify; extenuate, rationalize

3. To Make or Offer Excuses,v. *From Sec. 1:* alibi (colloq.); rationalize,v. (rationalization, n.)

4. Speech or Argument Used to Excuse or Vindicate: defense,n.

5. To Urge or Offer as an Excuse: allege, plead,v. (allegation,n.)

6. Statement Offered as an Excuse: allegation,n.

7. Note Explaining or Certifying Illness as an Excuse (for Absence, Not Doing Something, etc.): aeger,n. (Latin)

8. To Tender Excuses or Regrets for That Which One Has Done, as for an Offense, Insult, Harmful or Inconveniencing Act, etc.: apologize,v. (apology,n. apologizer,n.)

9. Formal and Humble or Humiliating Apology for an Offense: amende, amende honorable,n.

10. Full or Complete Apology: amende,n.

11. Apologetic: apologetical, deprecatory, excusatory,adj.

899. CLEANNESS

1. To Clean,v.
1. absterge—clean; clean by wiping; wipe clean
2. brush—clean by rubbing or passing a brush over
3. cleanse—clean
4. debride—clean, in surgery, by removing lacerated or infected tissue from
5. deterge—clean; clean away; wipe clean; clean (a wound, etc.) by removing filth or diseased matter from
6. dry-clean, dry-cleanse—clean, as clothing, rugs, upholstery, etc., with gasoline, benzine, some other chemical, etc., rather than with water
7. dust—clean of dust by wiping
8. mop—clean with, or as if with, a mop; clean by wiping; wipe clean
9. pumice—clean with or as if with pumice, a form of powdered volcanic glass used as an abrasive
10. purge—clean by washing away all dirt or impurities from; clean by eliminating undesirable things, members, or opponents from
11. scavenge—clean of filth, esp. places, streets, etc.
12. scour—rub clean; clean by rubbing
13. scrub—clean by rubbing hard; rub clean
14. sponge—clean with, or as if with, a wet sponge; wipe clean
15. swab—clean by wiping away dirt or other impurities from; clean with a mop (as the deck of a ship), a sponge, piece of cloth, etc.
16. sweep—clean by brushing (as a floor, street, etc.) with a broom
17. vacuum—clean (a rug, floor, etc.) with a vacuum sweeper
18. wash—clean with water, soap and water, etc.
19. wipe—rub clean; clean by rubbing

2. A Cleaning; Act of Cleaning,n. *From Sec. 1:* abstersion, brushing, cleansing, debridement; detersion (medical); dry-cleaning, dusting, mopping; purge, purgation, or purging; scour or scouring, scrub or scrubbing, sponging, swabbing, sweeping, vacuuming, wash or washing, wipe or wiping; *Also:*
1. ablution—a cleansing, as a religious ceremony or rite of purification, though often used humorously in a general sense (ablutionary,adj.)
2. catharsis—a cleansing of the emotions, often through art or artistic experience (cathartic, cathartical,adj.)
3. lavation—a cleansing (lavational,adj.)

3. Serving or Acting to Clean or Make Clean,adj. *From Sec. 1:* abstergent or abstersive, cleansing, detergent or, medical, detersive, purgative (abstersiveness, detersiveness,n.); *From Sec. 2:* cathartic or cathartical; *Also:* 1. abluent—cleansing

4. One Who Cleans,n. *From Sec. 1:* drycleaner, duster, mopper, purger, scavenger; scourer, scrubber, sponger, swabber, sweeper; washer, washerman, or washerwoman; wiper

5. Cleaner, i.e., That Which (as a Substance, Material, Thing, Machine, etc.) Cleans or Is Used in Cleaning,n. *From Sec. 1:* abstergent or abstersive, cleanser, detergent or, medical, detersive, dry-cleaner, duster, mop, pumice or pumice soap; scourer, scour, scouring powder, etc.; scrubber, sponge, swab; vacuum (colloq.), vacuum cleaner, or vacuum sweeper, etc.; washer, wiper; *From Sec. 3:* abluent; *Also:*

1. **ablution**—liquid used in cleansing or washing in a religious ceremony or purification rite
2. **aurilave**—device for cleaning or washing out the ear
3. **dentifrice, toothpaste, tooth powder**—cleansing agent for the teeth
4. **dishwasher**—machine for washing dishes
5. **lotion**—preparation for cleansing the skin
6. **soap**—substance used in cleaning or washing
7. **washing machine, washer**—machine for washing clothes

6. Power or Quality of Cleaning: detergency or detergence,n.

7. Pert. to, of the Nature of, etc., Pumice: pumiceous,adj.

8. Place That Has Been Scoured: scour,n.

9. To Become Clean of All Dirt, Impurities, etc.: purge,v. (purgation,n.)

10. To Make Clean in the Sense of Destroying the Germs or Microorganisms in,v.
  1. **antisepticize**—destroy the germs or microorganisms in (antisepsis,n. antiseptic, adj.)
  2. **disinfect**—destroy the germs or microorganisms in (a place, object, thing, etc.) as by a chemical, etc. (disinfection,n. disinfector,n.)
  3. **fumigate**—disinfect by means of smoke or vapor (fumigation,n. fumigator,n.)
  4. **sterilize**—render absolutely clean, i.e., completely free of disease germs, by raising to a very high temperature, as by boiling in water, using steam or dry heat upon or with a chemical, etc. (sterilization,n.)

11. Clean, in This Sense,adj. *From Sec. 10:* antiseptic, disinfected, fumigated, sterile or sterilized; *Also:*
  1. **aseptic**—free of disease germs, microorganisms, etc.
  2. **hygienic**—clean in the sense of being free of such germs or other conditions as would adversely affect the body or health
  3. **sanitary**—clean in the sense of being free from germs or disease-producing organisms, or dirt that might harbor these
  4. **uncontaminated, uninfected**—not tainted with disease germs

12. Cleanness, in This Sense,n. *From Sec. 11:* sterility; asepsis, sanitariness

13. To Make So Clean,v. *From Sec. 11:* sanitize (sanitation,n.)

14. Cleansing in This Sense, or Having Such Cleansing Properties,adj. *From Sec. 10:* antiseptic, disinfectant or disinfective, sterilizing

15. Agent, Substance, or Thing That So Cleanses,n. *From Sec. 10:* antiseptic, disinfectant or disinfector, fumigant, sterilizer

16. Place Where Plants Are Fumigated to Destroy Insects, etc.: fumigator,n.

17. To Clean (Writing, Books, Publications, etc.) in the Sense of Removing Objectionable, Obscene, Indelicate, or Overly Frank, Material: bowdlerize, censor, expurgate,v. (bowdlerization, censorship, expurgation,n. expurgatorial,adj.)

18. One Who Cleans Up Writing, etc., in This Manner: censor, expurgator,n. (censorship,n. censorial, expurgatorial,adj.)

19. Descr. of Writing, etc., So Cleaned Up: bowdlerized, censored, expurgated or expurgate,adj.

20. Tendency, Practice, etc., to So Clean Up Writing: bowdlerism,n.

21. Index or List of Books the Reading of Which Is Prohibited by the Catholic Church, Unless Expurgated; Any Similar Index or List of Books: Expurgatory Index, Index Expurgatorius, Index of Prohibited Books, or Prohibitory Index,n.

22. Descr. of Writing Not So Cleaned Up: unbowdlerized, uncensored, unexpurgated,adj.

23. Absolutely or Spotlessly Clean: immaculate, snowy, spotless,adj. (immaculateness, immaculacy, or immaculature; snowiness, spotlessness,n.)

24. Clean and Tidy: neat (of people, things, places, etc.); spick-and-span (of places or things),adj. (neatness,n.)

25. Careful to Keep Oneself or One's Surroundings Clean; Clean as a Matter of Habit or Personality: clean, cleanly,adj. (cleanness, cleanliness,n.)

26. Clean; Kept Clean: cleanly,adj. (cleanliness,n.)

27. Quality of Being Clean: cleanness, cleanliness,n.

28. Able to Be Cleaned: cleanable, cleansable, adj.

29. Unstained: clean, spotless, stainless, unblemished, unblotched, unblotted, unblurred, immaculate, unsmeared, unsmudged, unsmutched, unsplotched, unspotted, unsullied, untarnished,adj. (cleanness; immaculateness, immaculacy, or immaculature,n.)

30. Street Cleaner: scavenger, street sweeper, whitewing,n.

31. Department of Street Cleaning: Department of Sanitation

32. To Sweep (Dust, Crumbs, Particles, etc.) from a Surface: brush, whisk,v.

33. Broom; Twigs Tied Together as a Broom: besom,n.

34. Small Broom for Brushing Clothes, etc.: clothesbrush, whisk, whisk broom, wisp,n.

35. To Wash,v.
  1. **bathe**—wash oneself while covered with water; wash (someone or something) similarly
  2. **douche**—wash (some bodily cavity, or, in popular use, the vagina) with a jet or current of water; give oneself such a washing
  3. **gargle**—wash (the throat) with liquid; give one's throat such a washing
  4. **launder**—wash (usually clothes) and including the process of drying, ironing or folding, etc.
  5. **lave**—wash (poetic)
  6. **rinse**—wash (something) lightly in water
  7. **shampoo**—wash (hair, rugs, etc.) with soap and water; give one's hair such a washing
  8. **swill**—wash by pouring water over
  9. **tub**—wash (clothes, etc.)

36. A Wash or Washing,n. *From Sec. 35:* bath, douche, gargle, laundering, rinse or rinsing, shampoo; *Also:*
  1. **ablution**—a washing for the purpose of cleansing, as a religious ceremony or purifying rite, though sometimes used humorously for any washing (ablutionary,adj.)
  2. **lavage**—a washing; the washing out of an organ of the body (medical)
  3. **lavation**—a washing (lavational,adj.)

37. Agent, Substance, Thing, Device, etc., Used for or in Washing,n. *From Sec. 35:* bathtub, douche, gargle; laver (poetic); rinse, shampoo, tub or washtub; *Also:*
  1. **lavabo**—washbasin
  2. **lavatory**—place or equipment for washing oneself
  3. **sink**—basin, receptacle, etc., for washing, with faucets, drain, etc.

4. **washbasin, washbowl**—receptacle for washing

38. Place to Wash Clothes: laundry, laundry room,n.

39. Person Who Washes Clothes: launderer, laundress (fem.), washerman, washerwoman, n.

40. To Rub Soap on, Cover with Soap, etc.: soap, suds,v.

41. Full of, Like, of the Nature of, etc., Soap: saponacious, soaplike, soapy, sudsy,adj. (soapiness,n.)

42. Containing, Covered with, or Pert. to, Soap: soapy,adj.

43. To Convert (a Fat) into Soap; To Become Soap: saponify,v. (saponification,n. saponifier,n. saponifiable,adj.)

44. Foam Produced by An Agitation of Soap in Water: lather, suds,n. (sudsy,adj.)

45. Soapy Water: suds,n. (sudsy,adj.)

46. To Form Foam or Suds—of Soap: lather, suds,v.

47. To Cover with Soapy Foam, or Put Soapy Foam on: lather, suds,v.

48. To Bathe, i.e., Take a Bath,v.
  1. **lave**—bathe
  2. **shower**—take a bath with water raining down on one from a height
  3. **sponge-bathe**—bathe in a small amount of water, using a sponge, washcloth, etc., for cleansing oneself
  4. **tub**—bathe (esp. British)

49. A Bath,n. *From Sec. 48:* shower or shower bath, sponge or sponge bath; *Also:*
  1. **pediluvium**—foot bath (medical)
  2. **sitz bath**—bath taken by sitting in a tub, usually of very hot water
  3. **Turkish bath**—bath in a very hot room, so that one perspires freely; usually followed by a brisk rubdown, etc.

50. Apparatus, etc., for Bathing,n. *From Sec. 48:* shower or shower bath, tub; *From Sec. 49:* sitz bath; *Also:* 1. bathtub, tub—receptacle for bathing

51. Place for Bathing: balneary,n.

52. Act of Bathing: balneation,n.

53. Place Where Sweat Baths Are Taken; Sweating Room in a Bathing Establishment: sudatorium,n.

54. Room Where Warm Baths Are Taken: tepidarium,n.

55. Place Where Sun Baths Are Taken: solarium,n.

56. Pert. to a Bath: balneal, balneatory,adj.

57. Writing about, or Descriptions of, Baths, Bathing, Using Baths for Curing Disease, etc.: balneography,n. (balneographer,n.)

58. Use of Baths to Cure Illness, Treat Patients, etc.: balneotherapy,n.

59. Science of Using Natural Mineral Water as Baths for Healing Purposes; Science of Bathing: balneology,n. (balneologist,n. balneologic, balneological,adj.)

900. PURIFICATION

1. To Purify, i.e., Make Pure: clarify, cleanse, depurate, distill, rarefy, refine,v. (clarification, depuration; distillation, distillment, or distilment; rarefaction, refinement, n. clarifier, cleanser, depurator or depurative, refiner,n. depurative, rarefactive,adj.)

2. That Which, or One Who, Figuratively Purifies: alembic,n.

3. To Purify by Melting, as Fats, etc.: render,v.

4. To Purify with Fresh Air: ventilate,v. (ventilation,n. ventilator,n. ventilative,adj.)

5. To Purify of Harmful or Incorrect Things or Qualities: expurgate,v. (expurgation,n. expurgatory or expurgatorial,adj.)

6. To Free from Contamination, or from Poison Gas or Harmful Radioactivity: decontaminate,v. (decontamination,n.)

7. Place or Plant Where Metal, Oil, Sugar, etc., Is Purified: refinery,n.

8. A Purification of the Emotions, Often through Art or Artistic Experience: catharsis,n. (cathartic, cathartical,adj.)

9. To Purify, i.e., Become Pure: clarify, depurate, rarefy, refine,v. (clarification, depuration, rarefaction, refinement,n.)

10. Pure: clean, immaculate, intemerate, pristine; sheer (of qualities, as *sheer nerve,* etc.); single, snowy, taintless, unadulterated, unalloyed, uncontaminated, undebased, undefiled, unpolluted, untainted, unvitiated,adj. (cleanness; immaculateness, immaculacy, or immaculance; snowiness,n.)

11. Purified: clarified, cleansed, depurated, distilled, rarefied, refined,adj.

12. Highly or Excessively Refined: fine-spun, adj.

13. Still Pure; of Original Purity: pristine, adj.

14. Pure in Literary or Artistic Style: Attic, adj.

15. Pure in Style: chaste,adj. (chasteness, chastity,n.)

16. To Make Pure in Style: chasten,v.

17. Relative Purity, Esp. of Metals: alloy,n.

901. STRAINER

1. A Strainer,n.
  1. **colander, cullender**—vessel-shaped strainer, generally used for draining off liquids in cooking
  2. **riddle**—coarse strainer, as for sifting sand
  3. **sieve**—a kind of strainer with fine holes.
  4. **sifter**—strainer for flour, sand, or other similar substances

2. To Strain,v. *From Sec. 1:* riddle, sieve, sift

902. NEATNESS

1. Neat,adj.
  1. **dapper, natty**—neat and stylish in appearance or dress
  2. **prim**—stiffly neat
  3. **sleek, groomed, well-groomed**—neatly dressed, combed, smoothed, brushed, etc.
  4. **smug**—spruce; trim
  5. **spick-and-span**—neat and clean
  6. **spruce**—neat; neat and stylish in dress or appearance
  7. **taut**—neat; tidy
  8. **tidy**—neat; neat in appearance, habit, or arrangement
  9. **trig**—neat; spruce
  10. **trim**—pleasantly neat in appearance
  11. **well-kept**—neat (of things, houses, places, etc.)

2. Neatness,n. *From Sec. 1:* dapperness, nattiness, primness, sleekness, smugness, spruceness, tautness, tidiness, trimness

3. To Neaten; To Make Neat,v. *From Sec. 1:* prim; sleek, sleeken, or sleek up; groom, spruce or spruce up, tauten, tidy or tidy up; trig, trig up, or trig out; *Also:*
  1. **slick up**—sleek (colloq.)
  2. **smarten**—spruce

3. **titivate, tittivate**—make neat and smart or stylish in dress or appearance (titivation,n.)

4. **trim**—make neat by cutting superfluous or straggly parts away, as from a tree, bush, lawn, or other thing

4. To Make Oneself Neat,v. *From Sec. 1:* spruce up, tidy up; *From Sec. 3:* titivate or tittivate (titivation,n. titivator,n.)

5. To Become Neat or Tidy: tauten,v.

6. In Good Order; Orderly: neat, shipshape, taut, tidy, trim, uncluttered, unlittered,adj. (neatness, tautness, tidiness, trimness,n.)

7. Having Orderly Habits: methodical, neat, orderly, systematic, tidy,adj. (methodicalness, neatness, orderliness, systematicness, tidiness, n.)

8. Excessively or Compulsively Orderly: anal,adj. (psychoanalysis)

9. To Bring Back to Order, Often from a Confused State: unscramble,v. (colloq.)

903. UNTIDINESS

1. Untidy; In Disorder,adj.
1. **bedraggled**—untidy; disheveled
2. **blowzy, blowzed**—untidy and dirty; disheveled; slovenly; fat, red-faced, and untidy
3. **cluttered**—with things lying, or thrown, around in disorderly piles—of places
4. **disarranged**—in a disordered state
5. **disarrayed**—in a disordered state, esp. as to dress
6. **disheveled**—untidy; hanging loosely in an untidy condition, as dress, hair, etc.; so dressed; with the hair so hanging
7. **disorderly, disordered, unorderly, un-ordered**—untidy; lacking any kind of order or orderliness
8. **dowdy, dowdyish**—dressed in an untidy or slovenly manner—esp. of women
9. **draggly, draggletailed, drabbletailed**—untidy; slatternly; sluttish
10. **frowzy, frowsy, frouzy**—untidy and dirty; slovenly
11. **frumpy, frumpish**—dowdy; dowdy and ill-tempered
12. **grubby**—slovenly
13. **jumbled**—thrown together in disorder—of things
14. **littered, littery**—untidy with things thrown around in confused disorder—of places, rooms, etc.
15. **messy**—untidy
16. **poky, pokey**—dowdy
17. **rumpled**—disheveled
18. **slatternly**—untidy and slovenly—of females
19. **slipshod**—untidy; slovenly
20. **sloppy**—untidy in dress; slovenly (colloq.)
21. **slovenly**—untidy; generally untidy and/or unclean in appearance, habits, way of working or doing things, etc.
22. **sluttish**—untidy and unclean—of women
23. **tacky**—dowdy
24. **tousled, tously**—disheveled
25. **unkempt**—untidy; disheveled

2. Untidiness; Untidy State or Condition; Disorder,n. *From Sec. 1:* bedragglement, clutter or clutterment, disarrangement, disarray, dishevelment, disorderliness, dowdiness, draggletailedness, frowziness, frumpiness or frumpishness, grubbiness, jumble, litter, mess or messiness, slipshodness, sloppiness, slovenliness, sluttishness, tousle, unkemptness

3. To Make, or Cause to Be, Untidy,v. *From Sec. 1:* bedraggle, clutter, disarrange, disarray, dishevel, jumble, litter, mess or mess up, rumple, tousle

4. Untidy Person,n. *From Sec. 1:* dowd or dowdy (woman); drabbletail or draggletail (esp. a woman), frump (woman); slattern (woman); sloven, slut (woman); *Also:*
1. **drab**—untidy and unclean or slovenly woman (drabbish,adj.)
2. **draggletail, drabbletail**—untidy and slovenly woman who lets her dress trail in the dirt, mud, etc.
3. **slob**—slovenly and unclean person
4. **trollop**—untidy and slovenly woman

5. To Throw (Things) Around in Disorder: litter,v.

6. Without Orderly Habits or Methods: disorderly, unmethodical, unorderly, unsystematic,adj. (disorderliness, unmethodicalness, n.)

7. Untidy because Superfluous or Straggly Parts Have Not Been Cut Away (of Trees, Bushes, Lawns, or Other Things): untrimmed,adj.

8. Shabby: mangy, poky or pokey; ratty (colloq.); seedy; tacky (colloq.); threadbare, adj. (manginess, seediness, threadbareness, n.)

9. Shabby and Dirty: mangy,adj. (manginess,n.)

10. Wearing Shabby Clothes: seedy, threadbare,adj. (seediness, threadbareness,n.)

11. Person in Shabby Clothes: scarecrow,n.

12. Person in Torn and Ragged Clothes: tatterdemalion,n.

13. Uncombed (of Hair, or of a Person in Respect to His Hair): bedraggled, blowzy or blowzed, disheveled, rumpled, tousled, unkempt,adj.

904. DIRT

1. Dirty,adj.
1. **Augean**—incredibly dirty—so called after the stables of King Augeas, cleaned by Hercules
2. **bedraggled, draggled, draggly, drabbled**—soiled and wet, or soiled and limp, as if dragged through mud, water, dust, dirt, etc.
3. **dingy**—dirty in appearance, rather than fresh or clean, and appearing as if in need of painting, cleaning, or brightening up, etc.—of things or places only
4. **feculent, dreggy**—filthy with foul matter, feces, or impurities
5. **filthy**—disgustingly dirty
6. **foul**—dirty or filthy—esp. of places, clothing, containers, etc.
7. **frowzy, frowsy, frouzy**—dirty and untidy
8. **grimy, collied**—dirty; soiled with rubbed-in dirt, soot, smut, etc.
9. **grubby**—dirty; filthy; dirty or filthy as if infested with insect larvae
10. **mangy**—dirty and shabby
11. **messy**—dirty
12. **mucky**—dirty; disgustingly dirty
13. **nasty**—disgustingly dirty; physically filthy
14. **ordurous**—filthy
15. **piggish**—filthy—esp. of people
16. **polluted**—dirty; foul
17. **slimy**—covered or smeared with thick and sticky filth
18. **sloppy**—soiled with spilled or splashed liquid
19. **slovenly**—dirty and untidy
20. **slum, slummy**—dirty, poor, and crowded—of areas where people live, usually in a large city
21. **sluttish**—dirty and untidy—of women
22. **smeared, smeary**—soiled with something oily or sticky

23. smudged, smudgy—soiled with a dirty mark or with something oily or sticky
24. smutched, smutchy—dirty; smudged; soiled
25. smutty—dirty; dirty with grime or soot; grimy
26. soiled—dirty or smudged, esp. on the surface
27. sooty—soiled with soot or other black substance
28. sordid—dirty; filthy
29. squalid—dirty; filthy; dirty or filthy from lack of care or attention, as places, surroundings, etc.
30. stained—marked or smeared with dirt, oil, grease, etc.
31. unclean, uncleanly—dirty; filthy

2. Dirtiness; Quality or State of Being Dirty,n. *From Sec. 1:* bedragglement, dinginess, feculence or dregginess, filthiness or filth, foulness, frowziness, griminess, grubbiness, manginess, messiness or mess, nastiness, piggishness, pollutedness or pollution, sliminess, sloppiness, slovenliness, sluttishness, smeariness, smudginess, smuttiness, soilage, sootiness, sordidness, squalor or squalidness, uncleanness or uncleanliness; *Also:* 1. sullage—filthiness

3. Dirt,n. *From Sec. 1:* feculence or dregs, filth, grime, mess, muck, ordure, pollution, slime, smut, soil, soot, squalor; *Also:* 1. sullage, sully—filth

4. Dirty Mark, Streak, etc.,n. *From Sec. 1:* smear, smudge, smut, smutch, stain

5. To Dirty, i.e., Make Dirty or Leave a Mark of Dirt upon,v. *From Sec. 1:* bedraggle, draggle, drabble, or bedrabble; filthify, foul or befoul, grime or begrime, mess or mess up, pollute, slime, slop or slop up, smear or besmear, smudge or besmudge, smutch or besmutch, smut or besmut, soil or besoil, soot, stain (soilage,n.); *Also:*
1. bemire, mire—soil with wet mud or filth; throw wet mud over
2. besmirch, smirch—soil with some dirty substance, or with dirt, dust, soot, etc.
3. bespatter, spatter—soil with mud, dirt, slush, etc.
4. blur—smudge
5. defile—make dirty, filthy, or foul (defilement,n.)
6. splash, splatter, plash—soil by throwing mud, water, or other liquids on (splash, splatter, plash,n.)
7. sully—make dirty; soil

6. Not Dirty; Clean because Not Dirty,adj. *From Sec. 1:* unbedraggled, unfoul, unsmutty, unsoiled, unsooty, unstained

7. Not Dirtied; Clean because Not Dirtied, adj. *From Sec. 5:* unbedraggled, unfouled, ungrimed or unbegrimed, unpolluted, unslopped, unsmeared or unbesmeared, unsmudged, unsmutched, unsmutted or unbesmutted, unsoiled, unstained; unbesmirched or unsmirched, unspattered, unblurred, undefiled; unsplashed, unsplattered, or unplashed; unsullied

8. To Dirty, i.e., Become Dirty,v. *From Sec. 1:* draggle or drabble, foul, smudge, soil, stain; *From Sec. 5:* sully

9. Causing, or Caused by, Filth, as Certain Diseases: pythogenic or pythogenetic,adj. (pythogenesis,n.)

10. Dirty in the Sense of Not Being Free of Germs, esp. Disease-Producing Germs: contaminated, infected, insanitary or unsanitary; septic or septical (having putrefactive germs, bacteria, etc.); unhygienic, unsterile or unsterilized,adj. (contamination, infectedness or infection; insanitariness, unsanitariness, insanitation or unsanitation; septicity,n.)

11. To Make Dirty in This Sense: contaminate, infect,v. (contamination, infection,n. contaminant,n. contaminative, infectant,adj.)
12. Tending to Dirty or Soil: smeary,adj.
13. Having Dirty Habits: uncleanly,adj. (uncleanliness,n.)
14. Filthy Place: cesspit, cesspool, pigsty, sty, n.
15. Dirty, Poor, and Crowded Area of a City: slum, slums,n.
16. Dirty Language: filth, foulness, ordure,n. (filthy, foul, ordurous,adj.)
17. To Stain, i.e., Cause or Leave a Stain on: blot, blotch, blur, discolor, maculate, splotch, spot, sully, tarnish,v.
18. A Stain: blemish, blot, blotch, blur, discoloration; maculation, macula, or macule; smear (esp. an oily, greasy, etc., stain); smudge, smutch, speck, speckle, splotch, spot, sully, tarnish,n.
19. Stained; Having Stains: blemished, blotted, blotched or blotchy, blurred, discolored, maculate, smeared or smeary, smudged or smudgy, smutched, specked, speckled, splotched or splotchy, spotted or spotty, sullied, tarnished,adj.
20. To Become Stained: stain, sully, tarnish, v.
21. Able to Be Stained or Become Stained: stainable, tarnishable,adj.
22. Not Becoming Stained: stainless, unstainable, untarnishable,adj.
23. Stain of Ink on Paper, Cloth, etc.: blot, blotch,n.
24. To Stain with Blood: imbrue or imbue,v. (imbruement or imbuement,n.)

905. IMPURITY

1. To Make Impure by Mixing in an Inferior or Less Pure Substance: adulterate, alloy, contaminate, debase, pollute,v. (adulteration, contamination, debasement,n. adulterant, contaminative,adj.)
2. That Which Acts to Make Impure by Admixture: adulterant, alloy, contaminant,n.
3. Impure through Admixture: adulterated, alloyed, contaminated, debased, polluted,adj. (adulteration, contamination, debasement, pollutedness or pollution,n.)
4. Pert. to, or Resulting from, Adulteration: adulterine,adj.
5. To Make (a Precious Metal) Impure by Mixing in a Base Metal: alloy,v. (alloy,n.)
6. To Make (Drinking Water) Impure and Hence Not Fit for Drinking: contaminate, pollute,v. (contamination, pollution,n. contaminant,n. contaminative,adj.)
7. To Make Impure by Contact: contaminate, corrupt, defile, maculate, pollute, taint, vitiate,v. (contamination, corruption, defilement, pollution, vitiation,n. contaminant,n. contaminative, corruptive,adj. contaminable, taintable, vitiable,adj.)
8. Impure as a Result of Contact: contaminated, corrupt or corrupted, defiled, maculate, polluted, tainted, unclean, vitiated,adj.
9. Impurity as a Result of Contact: contamination, corruptness or corruption, defilement, pollutedness or pollution, sullage, uncleanness, vitiation,n.
10. To Destroy the Purity of: tarnish,v.
11. Trace of Impurity: taint,n.
12. To Become Impure: taint,v.

13. That Which Is, or Causes Something to Be, Impure: impurity,n.

14. Filthy with Impurities: feculent,adj. (feculence,n.)

15. To Contaminate with Disease-Producing Germs, Microorganisms, etc.: infect,v. (infection,n. infectant,adj.)

906. SIZE

1. Size: admeasurement, bulk, dimensions, extent, magnitude, mass, measure,n. (dimensional,adj.)

2. Size That Takes Up Space: amplitude, area, bulk, expanse, extent, volume,n. (areal, voluminous,adj.)

3. Big: ample, beamy, bouncing, bulky, bull, decuman, great, gross; king-size (colloq.); large, magnitudinous, massive, monumental, sizable, substantial; thumping (colloq.); thundering (usually of abstractions); voluminous; whacking; whopping or whapping (colloq.),adj. (ampleness or amplitude, bulkiness, greatness, grossness, largeness, magnitude, massiveness or mass, sizableness, substantiality or substantialness, voluminousness or voluminosity,n.); Also:
  1. lubberly—big and clumsy or stupid—of people (lubberliness,n.)
  2. massive, gross, ponderous—big and heavy; big and solid (massiveness, grossness, ponderousness or ponderosity,n.)
  3. monumental—large and enduring, like a monument
  4. strapping—big and healthy
  5. voluminous—of large size—of clothing, drapes, etc. (voluminousness, voluminosity,n.)

4. Large, or Unusually Large—of the Facial Features, Head, or Forehead: massive,adj. (massiveness,n.)

5. Of Such Large Size as to Be Difficult to Handle or Manage: bulky, gross, massive, ponderous, unwieldy,adj. (bulkiness, grossness, massiveness, ponderousness or ponderosity, unwieldiness,n.)

6. Of Such Large Size and, Often, Dignified Appearance as to Make a Strong Impression on the Mind: imposing, impressive, massive, monumental, stately,adj. (imposingness, impressiveness, massiveness, stateliness,n.)

7. Having the Imposing Size and Dignity of a Statue: sculpturesque, statuesque,adj. (sculpturesqueness, statuesqueness,n.)

8. Big and Strong: burly; hefty (colloq.); husky (colloq.),adj. (burliness, huskiness,n.)

9. Unusually Large—of Crops, Yields, Returns, etc.: bumper,adj.

10. Larger than Normal, Usual, Conventional, or Standard: outsize or outsized, oversize or oversized,adj. (outsize, oversize,n.)

11. Having Grown to an Excessive Size: overgrown,adj.

12. Very, Extremely, or Amazingly Big or Large: astronomic or astronomical (in analogy to the figures used in astronomy); Brobdingnagian (from Brobdingnag, the place described in *Gulliver's Travels*, in which everything and everyone was enormous); colossal, cosmic; Cyclopean or Cyclopic (after the mythical race of one-eyed giants); elephantine, enormous; Gargantuan (after the giant in Rabelais's *Gargantua* and *Pantagruel*); giant, gigantean, gigantic, goliath; herculean (after Hercules); huge, immense; jumbo (colloq.); mammoth (after the prehistoric kind of elephant); monster, monstrous, monumental; mountainous (like a mountain); prodigious, stupendous, Titan or titan, Titanic or

titanic; thumping (colloq.); tremendous, vast; whopping or whapping (colloq.),adj. (enormousness, giganticness, hugeness, immensity or immenseness, monstrousness or monstrosity, mountainousness, prodigiousness, stupendousness, tremendousness, vastness,n.)

13. Very, Extremely, or Amazingly Large for Its Kind: thumping, whopping, or whapping (all colloq.),adj.

14. Extremely Large, or Gigantic, and Rough: Cyclopean, Cyclopic,adj.

15. Extremely Large in a Clumsy or Ungainly Way: elephantine,adj.

16. Large Enough for the Requirements: ample, substantial,adj.

17. So Large in Extent as to Be, or Seem to Be, without Bounds or End: boundless, illimitable, immeasurable, immense, infinite, limitless, measureless, unbounded, unlimitable, unlimited, vast,adj. (boundlessness, illimitableness or illimitability, immeasurableness or immeasurability, immenseness or immensity; infiniteness, infinity or infinitude; limitlessness, measurelessness, unlimitableness, unlimitedness, vastness,n.)

18. Very, Extremely, or Amazingly Large Thing, Person, Animal, etc.,n.
  1. behemoth—anything very large; very large and, often, powerful person or animal
  2. Brobdingnagian—enormous thing, animal, or person
  3. colossus—anything or anyone so large as to be almost beyond belief, or as to dominate all similar things in size (colossi, colossuses,pl.n.)
  4. Cyclops—mythical giant possessing but one eye, in the middle of his forehead (Cyclopes,pl.n. Cyclopean, Cyclopic,adj.)
  5. Gargantua—good-humored giant, noted for his tremendous capacity for food and drink, of Rabelais's story
  6. giant—person or thing of enormous size and/or strength (giant, gigantic, gigantean, gigantesque,adj.)
  7. goliath—extremely big person,.thing, institution, etc.—after the giant slain by David
  8. jumbo—extremely big, and sometimes clumsy, animal, thing, or person
  9. leviathan—anything enormous in size, esp. for its kind; very large ship; very large marine animal, as a whale, etc.; extremely large and powerful person or thing
  10. lubber—big and clumsy, or sometimes stupid, person (lubberly,adj.)
  11. monster—thing or animal of extremely large size
  12. oversize—something larger than normal, customary, etc.
  13. Pantagruel—giant, the son of Gargantua, generally drunk and usually manifesting a coarse good humor with a seriously satirical purpose (Pantagruelism,n. Pantagruelist,n. Pantagruelian, Pantagruelic, Pantagrueline, Pantagruelistic,adj. Pantagruelize,v.)
  14. Titan, titan—anyone or anything of tremendous size and/or strength—after the giants of Greek mythology (Titanic, titanic,adj.)
  15. whopper, whapper—something unusually large for its kind (colloq.)

19. To Make Seem Larger than in Actuality: aggrandize, amplify, exaggerate, magnify, overstate,v. (aggrandizement, amplification, exaggeration, magnification, overstatement,n. exaggerative or exaggeratory,adj.)

20. Exaggerated: aggrandized, amplified, bouncing, magnified, overstated, vaulting,adj.

21. To Draw, Describe, etc., in Distorted Exaggeration: caricature,v. (caricature,n. caricaturist,n. caricatural,adj.)

22. To Make Seem Larger through a Microscope, Lens, etc.: magnify,v. (magnification, n.)

23. To Make Abnormally or Unnaturally Large: exaggerate,v. (exaggeration,n.)

24. To Seem Large: bulk,v.

907. INCREASE

1. To Increase, i.e., Make or Cause to Be Larger: aggrandize, amplify, augment, boost, bulk, develop, dilate, enlarge, expand, magnify, swell,v.; *Also:*

1. **aggrandize**—increase in power, rank, honor, wealth, etc.; increase in force, intensity, etc.
2. **boost**—increase the force or intensity of
3. **distend**—increase the size of by stretching or causing to swell, often through internal pressure
4. **enhance**—increase (something good or favorable), as advantage, value, position, beauty, etc.
5. **enlarge**—increase the capacity of
6. **expand, extend**—increase the scope, power, etc., of
7. **heighten**—increase in certain figurative senses, as enjoyment, beauty, appeal, etc.
8. **inflate**—increase (prices, money supply, etc.) abnormally or excessively; increase (someone's ego, self-pride, etc.)
9. **maximize**—increase to the highest or greatest possible
10. **multiply**—increase quantitatively, numerically, or by reproduction
11. **pad**—increase (talk, written material, etc.) with unnecessary words, phrases, details, etc.
12. **propagate**—cause to increase in number; cause to increase by reproduction
13. **raise, lift, step up**—increase in height, force, intensity, volume, amount, value, price, etc.
14. **redouble**—increase greatly
15. **step up**—increase by degrees, as in force, intensity, etc.
16. **swell**—increase in force, degree, intensity, volume, etc., esp. from internal pressure
17. **up**—increase, as in value, number, price, force, etc. (colloq.)

2. To Increase, i.e., Become Larger or Increased,v. *From Sec. 1:* augment, bulk, develop, dilate, enlarge, expand, swell; distend, enhance, enlarge, expand or extend, heighten, inflate, multiply, propagate; rise, lift, or step up; redouble, step up, swell; *Also:*

1. **accumulate, cumulate**—increase in number or amount
2. **grow**—increase; become larger
3. **overgrow**—grow to excessive size
4. **surge**—increase suddenly and greatly
5. **swell, surge**—increase suddenly within one (of an emotion)
6. **wax**—increase in size, quantity, extent, power, etc.

3. Increase; An Increasing; A Being or Becoming Increased,n. *From Secs. 1 and 2:* aggrandizement, amplification, augmentation, boost, development, dilation or dilatation, enlargement, expansion, magnification, swell; aggrandizement, boost, distention or distension, enhancement, enlargement, expansion or extension, inflation, maximization, multiplication, propagation, raise (or rise), step-up, swell; *From Sec. 2:* accumulation or cumulation, growth, overgrowth, surge, swell or surge; *Also:*

1. **access, accession**—increase by addition
2. **accretion**—increase by addition from the outside; growth

3. crescendo—gradual increase in the volume, force, or loudness of sound, esp. of musical sound
4. diastole—normal rhythmical dilatation of the heart
5. dilatation—enlargement, or morbid enlargement, of a bodily organ or cavity; abnormal enlargement, made for surgical purposes, of a cavity, canal, or duct (medical)
6. excrescence—abnormal increase
7. increment—increase; regular or periodic increase

4. Increasing; Becoming Larger,adj. *From Sec. 2:* augmenting, developing, etc.; dilatant (dilatancy,n.); *From Sec. 3:* accretive, crescendo; *Also:* addititious, crescent, crescive, increscent (increscence,n.); *Also:*

1. **accumulative, cumulative**—increasing in force, quantity, etc., by successive additions or growths (accumulativeness, cumulativeness,n.)
2. **towering**—becoming greater and greater, stronger and stronger, etc., as anger, etc.

5. Tending to, Characterized by, of the Nature of, or Pert. to, Increase,adj. *From Sec. 1:* amplificatory, augmentative, developmental, dilatant or dilative; expansile, expansive, propagative; *From Sec. 2:* accumulative or cumulative; *From Sec. 3:* accretive or accretionary, diastolic, incremental

6. Increasable,adj. *From Sec. 1:* augmentable, developable, dilatable, enlargeable, expansible; distensible, enlargeable

7. Capable of Expanding: expansile, expansive,adj. (expansiveness,n.)

8. Policy of Expanding the Territory of a Nation or State, the Supply of Money in Circulation, etc.: expansionism,n. (expansionist,n.)

9. To Increase (Something) the Stated Amount,v.

1. **centuple, centuplicate**—a hundredfold (centuplication,n. centuple, centuplicate, adj.)
2. **decuple**—tenfold (decuple,adj.)
3. **double, duplicate, redouble**—twofold (duplication,n. double, doubled, duple, duplex, redoubled,adj.)
4. **octuple, octuplicate**—eightfold (octuplication,n. octuple, octuplicate,adj.)
5. **quadruple, quadruplicate**—fourfold (quadruplication, quadruplicature,n.)
6. **quintuple, quintuplicate**—fivefold (quintuplication,n.)
7. **septuple, septuplicate**—sevenfold (septuplication,n. septuple, septuplicate,adj.)
8. **sextuple, sextuplicate**—sixfold (sextuple, sextuplicate,adj.)
9. **treble, triple, triplicate**—threefold (triplication, triplicature,n. treble, triple, or triplicate,adj. triplicative,adj.)

10. To Become Increased the Stated Amount,v. *From Sec. 9:* double or redouble, octuple, quadruple, quintuple, sextuple, treble or triple (quadruplication, quintuplication,n.)

11. To Multiply (Something) by the Stated Number,v. *From Sec. 9:* centuple or centuplicate, decuple, double, octuple or octuplicate, quadruple or quadruplicate, quintuple or quintuplicate, septuple or septuplicate, sextuple, sextuplicate, or sextiply; treble, triple, or triplicate

12. To Increase the Material, Details, Illustrations, etc., of (a Subject) in Speaking or Writing: amplify, develop, dilate on or upon; elaborate (on or upon); enlarge on or upon, extend,v. (amplification, development, dilation, elaboration, enlargement, expansion, expatiation, extension,n.)

13. Abnormal Bodily Enlargement,n.

1. **acromegaly**—disease characterized by abnormal and permanent enlargement of the head, hands, feet, chest, etc.—caused by abnormal activity of the pituitary gland (acromegalic,adj.)

2. **elephantiasis**—disease characterized by enormous, often grotesque, enlargement of certain parts of the body, esp. the legs and genital organs

3. **giantism, gigantism**—enlargement, to an abnormal extent, of the entire body or of certain parts—caused, generally, by abnormal activity of the pituitary gland

14. Sufferer from Such Enlargement,n. *From Sec. 13:* acromegalic, giant,n.

15. To Come (as a Person) as an Increase: accrue,v. (accruement or accrual,n.)

16. That Which Comes to a Person as an Increase: accrual,n.

908. ADDITION

1. To Add (Something): admix; annex (esp. to something more important, bigger, etc.); append (as something subordinate, or to something more important, bigger, etc.); appose (to something else); attach, superadd,v.

2. Addition, i.e., Act or Process of Adding (Something),n. *From Sec. 1:* admixture, annexation, apposition, attachment, superaddition,n.

3. An Addition, i.e., Something Added: accession; accessory (as an adornment or convenience); accretion (later or extraneously); addendum (addenda,pl.n.); additament, additive, additory, additum, adjunct; apanage, appanage, appurtenance, or appurtenant (though not an essential part); admixture, affix; annex, annexation, or annexment (to something more important or bigger); appendage, appendant, or appendent (as subordinate, or to something more important, bigger, etc.); attachment, enlargement, increment, supplement,n. (accessional, accessorial, adjunctive, incremental, supplemental or supplementary, adj.)

4. That Which Comes as an Addition, or Is Added by Natural Growth or Increase: accrual,n.

5. Disfiguring Addition of Any Kind, Such as to a Building, to the Body (as a Wart, Boil, or External Tumor), etc.: excrescence, n.

6. Added Part, Stretching Out from the Main Part or Body: extension, limb, prolongation,n.

7. To Add at the Beginning; To Add as a First Syllable or Part (to a Word); To Add a First Part to (a Word): prefix,v. (prefixion, prefixture,n.)

8. Something Added at the Beginning, Esp. a Part or Syllable to a Word: prefix, prefixture,n. (prefixal,adj.)

9. To Add in Addition, or over and above Other Additions; To Add (Something Unnecessary, Extraordinary, etc.): superadd,v. (superaddition,n. superadditional,adj.)

10. To Add to What Has Already Been Said; To Say in Addition: superadd,v. (superaddition,n. superadditional,adj.)

11. To Add the Finishing Touches to: cap, crown, top,v.

12. To Add to (Something) in Order to Make It Enough or Sufficient for the Needs: eke out, supplement,v. (supplementation,n.)

13. Added to Make Enough or Sufficient for the Needs: adscititious, auxiliary, subsidiary, supplemental, supplementary, suppletory,adj.

14. That Which Is Added to Make Enough or Sufficient for the Needs: subsidiary, supplement, supplementer,n.

15. To Add at the End: affix, annex, append, attach, postfix; subjoin (esp. of something spoken or written); suffix,v. (affixation, affixion, or affixture; annexation, attachment, subjunction, suffixion or suffixment,n.)

16. That Which Is Added at the End: affix; annex, annexation, or annexment; postfix, postscript, or subjunction (esp. of something spoken or written),n.

17. To Add (a Part or Syllable) to the End of (a Word); To Add as an Ending (to a Word): postfix, suffix,v. (suffixation, suffixion, or suffixment,n.)

18. Part or Syllable Added at the End of a Word: postfix, suffix,n. (postfixal or postfixial, suffixal,adj.)

19. To Add (a Part or Syllable) either to the End or to the Beginning of a Word: affix,v. (affixation, affixture,n.)

20. Part or Syllable Added either at the Beginning or at the End of a Word: affix,n. (affixal,adj.)

21. Part Added to a Document, Treaty, etc.: annex, supplement,n.

22. An Addition to, or Additional Matter at the End of, a Book: addendum, appendix, n. (addenda, appendices or appendixes,pl.n. appendical,adj.)

23. Additional Part to a Book or Document to Correct Mistakes, Provide Needed Material, etc.: supplement,n.

24. Additional and Special Section of a Newspaper or Magazine: supplement,n.

25. An Addition to a Will, Explaining or Changing Provisions; Similar Addition to Any Other Document: codicil,n. (codiciliary, adj.)

26. An Addition to Property (Legal): accession,n. (accessional,adj.)

27. An Addition to Knowledge, or by Way of Scientific Discovery: additum,n.

28. To Add (New Territory)—of a Country, State, etc.: annex,v. (annexation,n.)

29. New Territory Added: annexation,n.

30. One Who Favors Adding New Territory: annexationist, annexionist,n.

31. Favoring the Addition of New Territory: annexational,adj.

32. To Add by Mixing In: admix,v. (admixture,n.)

33. That Which Is Added In by Mixing: admixture,n.

34. Small Amount Added to a Mixture: dash, drop, pinch, splash, splatter,n.

35. To Add Up (Numbers or Amounts): sum or sum up, tot or tot up, total or total up,v. (summation,n.)

36. To Add Up to—of Numbers or Amounts: aggregate, total, total to,v.

37. The Amount to Which Numbers Add Up: aggregate, sum, summation, total,n.

38. Number Added, or to Be Added, to Another or to Others: addend, summand,n.

39. Numbers to Be Added Together: sum,n.

40. Additional: added, adjunct, adjunctive, adscititious, auxiliary, collateral, subsidiary, superadditional, supplemental, supplementary, suppletory,adj.

41. Added from the Outside, or Extrinsically: adscititious, adventitious,adj. (adventitiousness,n.)

42. To Be Added; Resulting from, or Allowing, Addition; of the Nature of Addition: additive,adj. (additivity,n.)

43. Tending or Serving to Add: additory,adj.

44. Capable of Being Added: addible,adj.

45. To Come as An Addition or as Something Additional: accrue; supervene (on or upon),v. (accrual or accruement, supervenience or supervention,n.)

46. Coming as Additional or as Something Additional: accruing, supervenient,adj. (supervenience,n.)

909. SMALLNESS

1. Small,adj.
1. **baby**—very small of its type
2. **bantam**—small
3. **dapper**—small and active (dapperness,n.)
4. **diminutive**—unusually small in physical size (diminutiveness,n.)
5. **dwarf, dwarfish**—smaller than normal (dwarfishness, dwarfism, or nanism,n.)
6. **fine**—small, thin, and delicate (fineness, n.)
7. **infinitesimal**—immeasurably small in size
8. **insignificant**—too small to be of any consequence or importance (insignificance, insignificancy,n.)
9. **Lilliputian**—diminutive in stature, or smaller than normal or natural—in analogy to the inhabitants of Lilliput, the imaginary land in Swift's *Gulliver's Travels*, who were six inches in height
10. **little**—small (littleness,n.)
11. **microscopic**—minutely small; so small as to be seen only through a microscope
12. **miniature**—tiny; small or reduced in scale or size
13. **minikin**—very tiny
14. **minimal, minim**—very small
15. **minuscule**—very small
16. **minute**—very small (minuteness,n.)
17. **petite**—small; tiny; of a child, girl, or woman, small and shapely (petiteness,n.)
18. **pint-size, pint-sized**—small; smaller than normal (colloq.)
19. **poky, pokey**—small and cramped—of places (colloq.)
20. **puny**—small and weak; smaller than normal
21. **pygmy**—unusually small
22. **runty**—smaller than normal; stunted (runtiness,n.)
23. **scrub, scrubby**—smaller than normal; stunted (scrubbiness,n.)
24. **slight**—small (slightness,n.)
25. **smallish**—somewhat small; undersized
26. **snug**—small but compact; small but sufficient; small but comfortable—all generally of places, living quarters, etc. (snugness,n.)
27. **stunted**—small because of some stoppage of growth so that normal size was not attained
28. **submicroscopic**—so small as not to be seen even through a microscope
29. **tiny, teeny**—very, very small (tininess,n.)
30. **toy**—small for its breed, but so bred—of dogs
31. **undergrown**—of small size
32. **undersized**—smaller than normal
33. **vest pocket**—very small in size, i.e., figuratively small enough to fit into a vest pocket
34. **wee**—small; very small

2. Smallest: minim, minimal, minimum,adj.

3. Small Person,n.
1. **bantam**—person small in size but pugnacious in character
2. **dwarf**—abnormally small person, esp. one

stunted in growth, and with a large head and malformed body (dwarfism, nanism, n.)
3. **gnome**—mythical dwarf who lives within the earth and guards the treasures of mines, quarries, etc. (gnomish, gnome-like,adj.)
4. **homunculus**—man of small size; dwarf
5. **insignificancy**—person too small to be of any importance
6. **Lilliputian**—person of small size; diminutive being; inhabitant of Swift's imaginary land, Lilliput
7. **manikin**—little man; dwarf; pygmy
8. **midge**—very small person
9. **peewee**—very small person but without malformation
10. **peewee**—very tiny person
11. **Pygmy, Pigmy**—member of a Negroid race of short height
12. **pygmy**—any very little or short person; dwarf
13. **runt**—unusually small or stunted person
14. **shrimp**—small and somewhat insignificant or contemptible person
15. **snip**—small person; small and insignificant person (colloq.)
16. **Tom Thumb**—very small man; dwarf; midget; midget of folk stories
17. **tot**—small child

4. Small Animal or Creature,n.
1. **dwarf**—stunted animal (dwarfism, nanism,n.)
2. **midget**—animal small for its kind
3. **mite**—extremely small creature
4. **pygmy**—animal small for its kind
5. **runt**—unusually small or stunted animal
6. **shrimp**—animal small for its kind
7. **stunt**—creature or animal prevented from reaching full growth
8. **toy**—dog of a particular species bred to be of small size

5. Small Thing,n.
1. **ambsace, amesace**—smallest, least, and/or most worthless thing possible
2. **insignificancy**—thing too small to be of any importance
3. **midget**—small thing for its kind
4. **miniature**—something in very small or reduced form representative of something larger; small painting, esp. a portrait
5. **minim**—anything very tiny
6. **mite**—extremely small thing
7. **peewee**—anything very tiny
8. **pygmy**—something small for its kind
9. **scrub**—something smaller than normal
10. **shrimp**—anything both unusually small and somewhat insignificant or contemptible
11. **snippet**—small thing
12. **tot**—small thing
13. **toy**—small thing; small thing of no actual value but considered valuable by the possessor

6. To Cause to Be Small,v.
1. **dwarf**—make into a small or stunted creature or person; cause to be like a dwarf; prevent from attaining full or proper size or growth
2. **micrify**—make small; make insignificantly small; make small and insignificant
3. **minify**—make small
4. **stunt**—prevent from attaining full or proper size or growth; dwarf (stunt,n.)

7. To Become Small; To Become Stunted: dwarf,v.

8. To Make Seem Smaller: diminish, minify, v. (diminution,n.)

9. To Make Seem Small by Contrast: dwarf, v.

10. Art of Executing Very Small Paintings, Esp. Portraits: miniature,n. (miniaturist,n.)

11. Slight, i.e., Lacking in Substantial Qualities or Solidness: flimsy, footless, insubstantial, slender, slim, tenuous, unsubstantial,adj. (filmsiness, insubstantiality, slenderness, slimness, tenuousness or tenuity, unsubstantiality or unsubstantialness,n.)

12. Slight, as a Chance, Possibility, Hope, etc.: bare, flimsy, frail, insignificant, lean, little, meager, rare, remote, scant, slender, slim, small, tiny, weak, wee,adj.

910. DECREASE

1. To Decrease, i.e., Make Smaller or Less, v.

1. **abate, bate**—decrease in amount, force, strength, intensity, etc.; diminish; lessen
2. **abridge**—diminish; lessen; reduce to a smaller scale; rework or reconstruct on a smaller scale; reduce (esp. power, rights, etc.)
3. **alleviate**—lessen, as pain, painful or unpleasant conditions, etc.
4. **astringe**—compress; constrict
5. **attemper**—decrease or moderate by mixture (with something less strong, etc.); decrease or reduce (some harsh quality, attribute, attitude, etc.)
6. **compress**—make smaller by squeezing into a less voluminous shape
7. **condense**—make smaller or less by eliminating nonessentials, reducing to a denser or more compact form, etc.
8. **constrict**—make smaller by tightening up the parts of, or the spaces between the parts of
9. **constringe**—compress; constrict
10. **contract**—make smaller, or decrease the bulk of, by drawing together the parts of
11. **curtail**—diminish; reduce
12. **cut, cut down**—lessen; reduce
13. **deflate**—make smaller by allowing air or gas to escape; reduce (prices, money in circulation, someone's ego, self-pride, etc.)
14. **deplete**—reduce by using up; decrease the amount or fullness of
15. **depress**—decrease the value, rate, activity, price, cost, etc., of; decrease in amount
16. **diminish**—lessen in quantity, size, number, dignity, authority, etc.; make smaller
17. **dwindle**—make gradually smaller and smaller, or less and less, in size, quantity, power, effect, value, etc.
18. **extenuate**—reduce in power, strength, authority, etc.
19. **halve, dimidiate**—decrease to half
20. **impair**—reduce in value, goodness, etc.
21. **lessen**—make less
22. **lower**—reduce in force, degree, amount, price, value, etc.
23. **minify**—make less or smaller
24. **minimize**—decrease to the least, or to the smallest possible, amount, degree, or extent
25. **mitigate**—decrease the force, strength, or intensity of (pain, painful conditions, anger, or similar emotions, harshness, severity, etc.)
26. **moderate**—decrease in force, violence, intensity, severity, excessiveness, etc.
27. **modify**—decrease in degree or extent; moderate
28. **pare, pare down**—decrease by, or as if by, cutting; decrease gradually, or little by little
29. **reduce**—make less or smaller, as in quantity, number, size, degree, extent, intensity, etc.
30. **remit**—decrease the intensity, extremity, or force of
31. **retrench**—diminish; reduce; reduce (expenses)

32. **sag**—lessen (prices, values, etc.)
33. **shade, shave**—lessen (price, cost, etc.) a little
34. **shrink**—make smaller than originally, esp. by cold, heat, water, etc.; make less in value, price, extent, degree, scope, etc.
35. **sink**—reduce (prices, values, etc.)
36. **slacken, slack**—reduce in intensity, strength, force, activity, etc.
37. **slash**—decrease radically or sharply in price, number, size, etc.
38. **subdue, soften, tone down**—reduce in force, volume, intensity, sharpness, etc. (sound, color, light, etc.)
39. **taper, taper off**—decrease gradually; make gradually smaller toward one end; make gradually less in force, activity, or intensity
40. **whittle down**—reduce, esp. gradually, in amount; reduce (expenses), esp. gradually

2. To Decrease, i.e., Become Smaller or Less,v. *From Sec. 1:* abate, condense, contract, diminish, dwindle, impair, lessen, lower, moderate, reduce, remit, sag, shrink, sink, slacken or slack off, taper or taper off; *Also:*

1. **come down, go down, decline, descend, drop, fall**—decrease (of prices, values, etc.)
2. **decline**—become less, as in power, force, influence, value, etc.
3. **peter out**—decrease gradually and finally stop or disappear (colloq.)
4. **subside**—decrease in activity, intensity, force, strength, noise, violence, etc.
5. **toboggan**—decrease sharply and suddenly (of price, value, etc.)
6. **wane**—decrease gradually, as in power, force, strength, importance, wealth, value, etc.; become gradually smaller or less

3. Decrease,n. *From Sec. 1 or 2:* abatement, abridgment, alleviation, compression, condensation, constriction or striction, contraction, curtailment, deflation, depletion, depression, dimidiation, diminution, extenuation, impairment, minimization, mitigation, moderation, modification, reduction, remission, retrenchment, sag, shrinkage or shrink, sinkage, slack, slash, subdual, taper; *From Sec. 2:* decline or declension, descent, drop, fall, subsidence, wane; *Also:*

1. **cutback**—reduction in number, rate, etc.
2. **decrement**—decrease; gradual decrease
3. **decrescence**—a lessening; a growing smaller in size, number, amount, etc.
4. **decrescendo, diminuendo**—gradual decrease in the volume or force of sound in music, or, loosely, of any sound
5. **stricture**—unhealthy contraction of a canal, duct, etc., of the body
6. **systole**—rhythmical contraction of the heart that causes blood circulation (systolic,adj.)

4. Decreasing,adj. *From Sec. 2:* abating, contracting, diminishing, dwindling, lessening, moderating, sagging, shrinking, sinking, slackening or slacking, tapering; declining, descending, dropping, falling, subsiding or subsident, tobogganing, waning; *From Sec. 3:* decrescent, decrescendo or diminuendo (decrescence,n.); *Also:*

1. **remittent**—temporarily decreasing in strength or intensity, as, esp., a fever (remittence, remittency,n.)
2. **systaltic**—contracting rhythmically (of organs of the body)

5. Causing, or Tending to Cause, Decrease, etc.,adj. *From Sec. 1:* abating, abridging, etc.; alleviative or alleviatory; astringent (medical); compressive, constrictive, constringent, contractive, deflationary, depletory or depletive, depressive, extenuative or extenuatory; mitigative, mitigatory, or mitigant; modificatory or modificative, reductive, remissive (astringency, constringency, contractiveness, remissiveness,n.) ; *Also:* **1. styptic, styptical**—causing contraction of bodily or organic tissues (stypticity,n.)

6. Able to Be Decreased,adj. *From Sec. 1:* abatable, abridgeable, compressible, condensable or condensible, contractible or contractile, deflatable, depressible, diminishable, mitigable, modifiable, reducible, shrinkable (compressibility, condensability; contractibility, contractibleness, or contractility; reducibility,n.)

7. Capable of Causing Contraction: contractile,adj. (contractility,n.)

8. One Who Decreases, i.e., Causes Decrease,n. *From Sec. 1:* abridger, alleviator, compressor, condenser, constrictor, contractor, curtailer, deflator, depressor, extenuator, impairer, minimizer, mitigator, moderator, modifier, reducer

9. That Which Decreases, i.e., Causes Decrease,n. *From Sec. 1:* alleviation, alleviative, or alleviator; compressor, condenser, constriction or constrictor, contractor, deflator, depressor or, medical, depressant, mitigator, moderator, modifier, reducer

10. Advocating, or Pursuing, Policies That Reduce Prices, Money in Circulation, etc.: deflationist,adj. (deflationist,n.)

11. To Make One's Expenses Smaller or Less: economize, retrench,v. (economy, retrenchment,n. economical,adj.)

12. Causing the Tissues of the Body to Contract, and Forcing Blood from Them: astringent,adj. (astringency,n.)

13. Substance, Agent, etc., That Contracts the Cavities, Tissues, etc., of the Body: astringent, styptic,n.

14. The Use of Such Substances or Agents: stypsis,n.

15. Having Alternate Contraction and Dilatation (i.e., Systole and Diastole), as the Heart: systaltic,adj.

16. To Contract and Expand in Rhythmical Fashion, as the Heart or Something Likened to It in Such Action: pulsate, pulse, throb, v. (pulsation, pulse, throb,n. pulsator, throbber,n. pulsatile, pulsative, pulsatory, or pulsating; pulsing, throbbing,adj.)

17. Lesser: minor,adj.

18. Less than Natural: subternatural,adj.

19. Less by Subtraction: minus,adj.

911. SHORTNESS

1. Short or Shortened in Length,adj.
1. **abbreviated**—short or shortened, as an account, performance, dress, etc.; shortened by the omission of letters, as words
2. **abridged**—shortened; shortened through the elimination of nonessential words or points, but with the main idea intact; rewritten in shorter form
3. **bobbed**—cut short; shortened
4. **bobtail, bobtailed**—shortened; abbreviated; curtailed
5. **brief**—short; concise—of language, writing, etc. (brevity, briefness,n.)
6. **clipped**—shortened
7. **compact**—condensed; terse (compactness, n.)
8. **compendious**—short, but without loss of any of the essentials of a subject; concise (compendiousness,n.)
9. **concise**—short and to the point, with no superfluous words (conciseness, concision, n.)
10. **condensed**—shortened by the elimination

of nonessentials, as a story, account, book, etc.
11. **curtailed**—shortened by being cut off suddenly or by having the end cut off or eliminated
12. **cut**—cut short; shortened by having parts cut out, as *a cut version,* etc.
13. **detruncated, truncate, truncated**—shortened because parts have been cut or lopped off
14. **succinct**—short and to the point (succinctness,n.)
15. **summary**—short and to the point; short, but without the omission of any essentials —of accounts, etc. (summariness,n.)
16. **syncopated**—shortened or contracted in pronunciation or sound by the omission of letters or syllables from the middle—of a word
17. **tabloid**—short; shortened; condensed—all of accounts, versions, stories, etc.
18. **telescoped**—shortened or condensed, in analogy to the way the parts of a telescope slide one into the other
19. **terse**—short and to the point in language (terseness,n.)

2. To Shorten, i.e., Make or Cut (Something) Short,v. *From Sec. 1:* abbreviate, abridge, bob, bobtail, clip, compact, condense, curtail, cut, detruncate or truncate, syncopate, telescope (abbreviation, abridgment, condensation, curtailment, detruncation or truncation, syncopation or syncope,n. abbreviator, abridger, condenser, curtailer,n.) ; *Also:*
1. **abstract**—make a condensation, summary, or abridgment of (information, written material, etc.) ; abridge (abstracter,n.)
2. **contract**—shorten (a word, or two consecutive words) by omitting parts (contraction,n.)
3. **digest**—shorten (a story, speech, information, or any other language material) by leaving out nonessentials, rearranging in systematic form, summarizing, etc. (digester,n.)
4. **dock**—shorten by cutting the end off (dockage,n.)
5. **epitomize**—shorten or condense (material) by summarizing, stating the main points or ideas, etc. (epitomization,n. epitomizer, epitomist,n.)
6. **summarize**—say, state, or express the main points of, leaving out all superfluous material (summarization,n. summarizer, n.)

3. Shortened Form, Version, etc.,n. *From Sec. 1:* abbreviation, abridgment, brief, condensation; *From Sec. 2:* abstract, contraction, digest, epitome, summary; *Also:* **1. conspectus** —digest

4. To Be a Condensed Symbol, Representation, etc., of (a Quality, Group, etc.): epitomize,v. (epitomization,n.)

5. Such a Condensed Symbol or Representation: epitome,n.

6. To Become Shorter: shorten,v.

7. Short in Time; Lasting Only a Short Time: brief,adj. (brevity, briefness,n.)

8. To Cut Short the Tail of (Esp. a Dog or Horse): bobtail, dock,v.

9. To Cut Short, or Cut the End Off (a Tail): bob, dock,v.

10. Part of the Tail Left after the End Has Been Cut Off: dock,n.

11. Tail That Has Been Cut Short; Animal with Such a Tail, Esp. a Dog or Horse: bobtail,n.

12. With the Tail Cut Short: bobtail, bobtailed,adj.

13. To Cut (Hair) Short: bob,v. (bob,n.)

14. Style of Hair Cut Short: bob,n.

15. In Poetry, the Shortening of a Syllable That Is Normally Long: systole,n. (systolic, adj.)

16. In Poetry, the Lengthening of a Syllable That Is Normally Short: diastole,n. (diastolic,adj.)

912. SUMMARY

1. A Summary,n.
1. **abstract**—summary of a statement, idea, information, book, article, court record, etc. (abstractive,adj.)
2. **abstract of title, brief of title**—summary of the previous ownership of land, real estate, property, etc.
3. **aperçu (French)**—summary; outline; quick or brief sketch of the broad outlines (of a subject, work, etc.) but without details
4. **brief**—summary; summary of facts or conditions; summary or outline of information, arguments, etc., as in a debate, controversy, law case, etc.
5. **compendium, compend**—short summary of the substance of a work or subject
6. **conspectus**—summary, digest, synopsis, or outline of a subject
7. **digest**—summary of a story, article, account, speech, or other literary, scientific, historical, legal, etc., material, usually in systematic form and condensed in length
8. **epitome**—summary, esp. of a literary work or other literary material
9. **outline**—short summary of a longer thing, work, speech, etc.
10. **précis**—short summary embracing all essential points
11. **recapitulation**—brief summary of main points, as at the end of a speech, chapter, etc.
12. **résumé**—summary
13. **sum**—summary
14. **synopsis**—summary; summary of a story or book; summary giving a general outline of a subject; summary of a subject containing short captions, paragraphs, etc. (synoptic, synoptical,adj.)

2. To Summarize; To Give or Make a Summary of,v. *From Sec. 1:* abstract, digest, epitomize, outline, précis, recapitulate, résumé, sum or sum up, synopsize,v. (recapitulative or recapitulatory,adj.)

3. Summarizer,n. *From Sec. 2:* abstracter, digester, epitomizer or epitomist,n.

4. Summarization,n. *From Sec. 2:* epitomization, outline, recapitulation, résumé, summation or summing up

5. To Be a Summary of: summarize,v.

6. A Final Summarizing of Arguments in a Court of Law before a Case Goes to the Jury: summation,n.

913. LENGTH

1. To Make Longer in Duration or Time: continue, draw out, extend, lengthen, prolong, protract, stretch or stretch out,v. (continuation, extension, prolongation or prolongment, protraction,n. protractive,adj.)

2. To Make Longer by Continuing (Something) beyond the Time Expected, Desired, or Provided: prolong,v. (prolongation, prolongment,n.)

3. To Make Tediously or Unnecessarily Long in Time: protract,v. (protraction,n. protractive,adj.)

4. To Make a Speech or Written Material Unnecessarily Long, by Adding Superfluous Material, etc., Generally to Consume Time: pad,v. (padding,n.)

5. To Become Longer in Time: lengthen,v.

6. To Go On in Time: continue, stretch,v. (continuation or continuance,n.)

7. State of Being Made Longer in Time: continuance, continuation, extension, prolongation or prolongment, protraction,n.

8. Long, or Lengthened, in Time: drawn out, extended, lengthy, prolonged, protracted, adj. (lengthiness, protractedness,n.)

9. Tediously Long: interminable, lengthy, long-drawn-out, prolix, protracted,adj. (interminableness or interminability, lengthiness, prolixity or prolixness, protractedness, n.)

914. AMOUNT; QUANTITY

1. Amount, Quantity, or Number: deal (as in *good deal, great deal,* etc.), measure, sum, volume,n.; *Also:*
1. **backlog, reserve, stock, store, supply**—amount or quantity kept for future use (reserve,adj.)
2. **batch**—amount produced at one time
3. **bulk, mass**—greater amount (of something)
4. **complement**—full amount or quantity; amount or quantity that makes something complete (complemental, complementary, adj.)
5. **continuum**—continuous quantity
6. **decrement**—amount of decrease, waste, or loss
7. **extent**—amount that a thing stretches to or is stretched to
8. **figure**—amount expressed in numerical terms
9. **increment**—amount added, gained, etc., or by which something is increased (incremental,adj.)
10. **majority, plurality**—amount, quantity, or number more than half of the total (major,adj.)
11. **minority**—amount, quantity, or number less than half of the total (minor,adj.)
12. **overbalance**—amount that causes a loss of balance
13. **quorum**—the number of members of a legislative or other group necessary for decisions to be legal or binding
14. **series**—number of things following one after another or arranged in rows
15. **supply**—amount or quantity available, provided, etc.
16. **variety**—number (of things) of different kinds; such a number of things

2. Pert. to, Expressing, Denoting, etc., Number: numeral, numeric, numerical,adj.

3. Pert. to Quantity or Amount; Able to Be Estimated in Terms of Quantity or Amount; Pert. to the Description or Measurement of Quantity or Amount: quantitative,adj. (quantitativeness,n.)

4. Total Amount: aggregate, entirety, sum, total, whole,n.

5. Total: aggregate, complete, entire, gross, whole,adj.

6. At a Certain Amount Per Head, Person, or Unit: capitatim,adj.

7. To Amount to: number,v. (as *their members number several hundred,* etc.)

915. SUPPLY

1. Large or Full Supply: abundance or abundancy, affluence, luxuriance, opulence, plenitude, plenty, profusion, reservoir, shower, wealth,n.

2. **Unusually Large or Full Supply:** abundance or abundancy, plethora, superabundance, wealth,n.

3. **Undiminishing Supply of Good Things:** cornucopia,n.

4. **In Great or Full Supply:** abounding, abundant, affluent, ample; aplenty (used after the noun); copious, exuberant, lavish, luxuriant, opulent, overflowing, plenteous, plentiful, profuse, rife, superabundant, torrential,adj. (abundance or abundancy, affluence, ampleness or amplitude, copiousness, exuberance or exuberancy, lavishness, luxuriance or luxuriancy, opulence or opulency, plenteousness, plentifulness, profuseness or profusion, superabundance,n.)

5. **To Be in Large, Full, or Unusually Large or Full, Supply:** abound, exuberate, superabound,v.

6. **To Have a Large, Full, or Unusually Large or Full, Supply of:** abound in or with, flow with, overflow with, superabound in or with,v.

7. **Well, Fully, or Abundantly Supplied:** replete (with), wealthy (in),adj. (repleteness, wealth or wealthiness,n.)

8. **Too Great, or Excessive, Supply:** excess, glut, overabundance, overflow, overstock, oversupply, plethora, surfeit, superabundance, n.

9. **Too Great in Supply:** excessive, overabundant, overflowing, superabundant,adj. (excessiveness, overabundance, superabundance,n.)

10. **To Be in Too Great Supply:** overabound, superabound,v.

11. **To Give a Very Great, or Too Great a Supply to:** deluge, flood, glut, load, overflow, overstock, oversupply, satiate, saturate, surfeit, swamp,v. (glut, satiation, saturation,n.)

12. **Possessed of Too Great a Supply:** deluged, flooded, glutted, loaded, overflowing (with), overstocked, oversupplied, saturated, surfeited, swamped,adj.

13. **Supply Kept for Future Use:** backlog, hoard, reserve, stock, stockpile or stock pile, store,n.

14. **Available Supply:** resources,n.

15. **Adequate Supply:** adequacy, sufficiency,n.

16. **Supplies:** provisions, subsistence,n.

17. **Supplies or Money for a Journey:** viaticum,n.

18. **Military Supplies:** munitions, ordnance,n.

916. LARGE AMOUNT

1. **Large Amount or Quantity:** abundance or abundancy, affluence, dollop; flood, deluge, shower, or torrent (as if pouring out or over); immensity, luxuriance, mass, mint; oodles (colloq.); opulence; peck (colloq.); pile, plenitude, plenty, profusion; raft (colloq.); rain (of something falling); ream (of something written or spoken, as words, etc.); shower; slew or slue (colloq.); superabundance, wealth,n.

2. **An Amount or Quantity So Large as to Be Infinite, or beyond Measuring:** infinitude, infinity,n.

3. **Too Large an Amount or Quantity:** spate, superabundance,n.

4. **A Large Number (of Things, People, etc.):** army, crowd, host, legion, loads, lots, multiplicity, multitude, myriad, plurality; raft (colloq.); sea or ocean (spread out over a wide area); slew or slue (colloq.); swarm (esp. moving); throng,n.

5. **A Great or Overwhelming Number (of Words), as if Coming Out in a Flood:** spate, n.

6. **An Indefinitely Large Number (of Things, People, etc.), or So Large a Number as to Defy Counting:** infinitude, infinity, myriad,n.

7. **The Greater Number (of Things, People, etc.), Strictly More than Half:** majority, plurality,n. (major,adj.)

8. **The Greatest Amount, Quantity, or Number Possible:** maximum,n. (maxima,pl.n. maximum or maximal,adj.)

9. **Many:** considerable or great (usually in the predicate), multitudinous, numerous, rife,adj. (multitudinousness or multitude, numerousness,n.)

10. **Many and Different:** divers, manifold, multiple, multiplex, multiplicate, sundry, various,adj. (multiplicity,n.)

11. **Not Quite Many, but More than One or Two:** several,adj.

12. **Large in Amount, Quantity, or Number; Large (of an Amount, Quantity, or Number):** abundant, ample, astronomical or astronomic, considerable, copious, exuberant, great; legion (in the predicate); multitudinous, numerous, overwhelming, plenteous, plentiful, profuse, rife, substantial, superabundant; tidy (colloq.); vast,adj. (abundance or abundancy, ampleness or amplitude, copiousness, exuberance or exuberancy, multitudinousness or multitude, plenteousness, plentifulness, profuseness or profusion, substantialness, superabundance, vastness,n.)

13. **Large Enough in Amount, Quantity, or Number:** adequate, ample, sufficient,adj. (adequacy or adequateness, ampleness, sufficiency,n. suffice,v.)

14. **Unusually Large in Amount, Quantity, or Number:** torrential,adj.

15. **So Large in Number or Quantity as to Defy Counting:** countless, incalculable, infinite, innumerable, innumerous, myriad, numberless, uncountable, uncounted, unnumberable, unnumbered, untold,adj.

16. **In Great Quantities:** galore,adv. (follows the noun)

17. **To Exist in Large Amounts, Quantities, or Numbers:** abound, exuberate, pullulate, superabound, swarm, teem,v. (pullulation,n.)

18. **To Spring Up in Abundance or Great Numbers:** pullulate,v. (pullulation,n.)

19. **To Have Great Numbers or Quantities of:** abound in or with, be crowded or swarming with, superabound in or with, swarm with, teem with,v.

20. **Possessed of Great Numbers or Quantities of:** abounding in or with, crowded with, rife with, superabounding in or with, swarming with, teeming with,adj.

21. **Swarming with Birds:** winged,adj.

22. **To Have Great Numbers or Quantities of (Insects, Vermin, Rodents, Undesirable People or Things, etc.):** be crawling with, be infested or overrun with or by, crawl with,v.

23. **Possessed of Great Numbers or Quantities of (Insects, Vermin, Rodents, Undesirable People or Things, etc.):** crawling with, infested with or by, overrun with or by,adj.

24. **To Be in Existence, Action, or Movement in (a Place) in Very Large Numbers, as, Esp., Insects, Vermin, Rodents, or Undesirable People or Things Likened to These:**

infest, overrun, swarm over,v. (infestation, .n.)

25. To Be Too Large in Numbers or Quantity: overabound, superabound,v.

26. Too Large a Number, Quantity, or Amount: excess, glut, overabundance, superabundance,n.

27. To Be in, Appear in, Come to, etc., (a Place) in Extremely Large, or Too Large, Numbers or Quantity: crowd, deluge, flood, overcrowd, swamp,v.

917. SMALL AMOUNT

1. Small or Slight Amount or Quantity: atom, bit, crumb, dab, dash, dribble, driblet or dribblet, drop, gram, infinitesimal, iota, jot, little, minim; mite (colloq.); modicum, morsel, particle, patch, pinch, pittance; rap (esp. in the phrase *give a rap*, etc.); scantling, scintilla, scrap, shade, snip, snippet; snuff (strictly equal to that which can be held between two fingers); soupçon, speck, tittle, tot, trace; trickle (esp. of moving objects or persons); trifle, vestige; whit (usually in negative constructions),n.

2. Choice or Pleasing Bit (of Something): morsel, tidbit, titbit,n.

3. Small, Scattered Amount, Quantity, or Number: scattering, sprinkle, sprinkling,n.

4. A Little Bit Cut Off, or as if Cut Off: snip, snippet,n.

5. A Small, Disconnected Bit, as of a Story, Conversation, Song, or Anything Heard: snatch,n.

6. A Small Amount, as of Material, Road, or Something Similar: patch,n.

7. A Slight Amount Added, as to a Mixture: dash, drop, pinch, splash, splatter,n.

8. Small Quantity of Drink: tot,n.

9. Small Sum of Money: mite,n.

10. Very Small Amount of Contribution, as of Money, etc., but All that One Can Manage: mite,n.

11. Coin of Small Value: mite,n.

12. The Smaller of Two Quantities or Amounts: minority,n.

13. Smallest Bit: atom,n.

14. Smallest, or Least Possible, Amount or Quantity: ambace or amesace, minimum,n. (minimal,adj.)

15. Small, Minute, or Tiny Particle: ambace or amesace, atom, bit, corpuscle or corpuscule, fleck, grain, granule, molecule; mote (esp. of dust); scintilla, speck,n.

16. A Trace (of a Thing or Quality): bit, drop, element, iota, jot; mite (colloq.); modicum, patch, rack, shade, show, smack, soupçon, spice, strain, streak, suggestion, suspicion, tang, tincture, tinge, vein, vestige, whisper, wisp,n.

17. A Trace (of Some Intangible or Abstraction): atom; beam, flicker, gleam, ray or spark (as of hope, etc.); bit; breath (as of scandal, etc.); drop, element, grain, inkling, iota, jot; mite (colloq.); modicum, molecule, particle, patch, scintilla, shade, shadow, show, shred, speck, suggestion, vestige, wisp,n.

18. Noticeable Trace: savor,n.

19. Small in Amount, Quantity, or Number; Small (of Amount, Quantity, or Number): exiguous, few, inconsequential, inconsiderable, infinitesimal, insignificant, lean, meager or meagre, minute, paltry, petty, piddling, scant, scanty, short, skimpy, slender, slight,

slim, spare, sparse, stingy, trifling, trivial, woeful or woful,adj.

20. Smallness of, or in, Amount, Quantity, or Number: exiguousness or exiguity, fewness, insignificance, leanness, meagerness, paltriness, paucity, pettiness, poverty; scantness, scantity, or scantiness; shortness, skimpiness, slenderness, slightness, slimness, spareness, sparsity or sparseness, stinginess, woefulness or wofulness,n.

21. So Small in Amount as to Defy, or Practically to Defy, Perception; Descr. of Such Smallness (of Amount): imperceptible,adj.

22. So Small or Slight in Amount as Not to Be Worth Considering: inconsiderable, adj.

23. Immeasurably Small in Amount or Quantity; So Small as to Approach Zero: infinitesimal,adj.

24. Meanly Small in Amount or Quantity: niggardly, stingy,adj. (niggardliness, stinginess,n.)

25. Smallest in Amount or Quantity: least, minimal, minimum,adj.

26. Smaller (of Two Quantities): less, lesser, adj.

27. Not Abundant: infrequent, rare, scant, scanty, scarce, sparse, unabundant,adj. (infrequency or infrequence, rareness or rarity; scantness, scantity, or scantiness; scarceness or scarcity, sparseness or sparsity, unabundance,n.)

28. Scarcity: dearth, paucity, poverty,n.

29. Very Great Scarcity: dearth, famine,n.

30. Not in Full or Great Supply; Limited in Supply: infrequent, unabundant, uncopious, unexuberant, unlavish, unluxuriant, unopulent, unplenteous, unplentiful, unprofuse,adj. (infrequency or infrequence, unabundance, unopulence, unplentifulness, unprofuseness,n.)

918. DROP (OF LIQUID, ETC.)

1. A Drop (of Liquid, etc.): bead, blob, dribble, minim,n.

2. A Falling Drop: driblet or dribblet,n.

3. A Drop, or Drops, Thrown, Splashed, etc., on Someone or Something: plash, splash, splatter,n.

4. Drops of Water or Other Liquid in, or Falling or Blowing in, the Air: spray,n.

5. Liquid That Falls in Drops: drip, drizzle, trickle,n.

6. That Which Falls, Flows, Runs, Comes, etc., in Drops: trickle,n.

7. Small Amount or Quantity Coming Down in Drops, or in Scattered Drops: sprinkle, sprinkling,n.

8. Fine Drops of Rain: drizzle,n. (drizzly, adj.)

9. To Come Down or Out, Fall, Flow, etc., in Drops: dribble; drip (usually uniformly or continuously); drizzle, drop, rain, plash; shower (in heavy drops); spatter, splash, splatter; spray (forcibly ejected); sprinkle, trickle, weep,v. (drip, rain, plash, spatter, splash, splatter, spray, sprinkle, trickle,n. plashy, splashy,adj.)

10. To Let Come Down or Out, or Let Fall or Flow, etc., in Drops: dribble; drip (usually uniformly or continuously); drizzle, drop, rain, plash, shower, spatter, splash, splatter; spray (forcibly ejected); sprinkle, trickle, weep,v.

11. Sound of Drops Coming Down and Hitting Something: spatter, splash, splatter,n.

12. **To Rain in Small or Fine Drops:** drizzle, sprinkle,v.

919. ENOUGH

1. **Enough:** adequate, ample; competent (for the purpose) or enow (archaic, now used only poetically); plenty, sufficient,adj. (adequacy or adequateness, ampleness, competence or competency, plenty, sufficiency,n.)

2. **An Amount or Quantity That Is Enough:** adequacy, competence or competency, enough, plenitude, plenty, sufficiency,n.

3. **Fully Enough:** abundant, ample, copious, plenteous, plentiful, plenty,adj. (abundance or abundancy, ampleness, copiousness, plenteousness, plentifulness, plenty,n.)

4. **Enough to Be Perceived, Measured, or Estimated:** appreciable,adj.

5. **Barely Enough:** scant, scanty, skimpy, adj. (scantness or scantity, scantiness, skimpiness,n.)

6. **More than Enough:** excess, overabundant, plethoric, superabundant,adj. (excess, overabundance, plethora, superabundance or overplus,n.)

7. **To Be Enough:** avail, do, serve, suffice,v.

8. **To Be Enough for (a Person) for a Time:** tide (a person) over,v.

9. **Almost:** nearly, nigh, practically, virtually, well-nigh,adv.

10. **Not Enough:** deficient, inadequate, incommensurate (to); incompetent (as in strength, ability, qualifications, etc., for the purpose or requirements); insufficient, lacking, scant, scanty; short or shy (a certain amount); skimpy, unample,adj.

11. **Quality of Not Being Enough:** deficiency, inadequacy or inadequateness, incommensurateness; incompetence or incompetency (of strength, ability, qualifications, etc., for the purpose or requirements); insufficiency, paucity, poverty; scantness, scantiness, or scantity; shortage, skimpiness,n.

12. **Quantity or Amount That Is Not Enough:** deficiency, insufficiency, paucity, poverty,n.

13. **To Have Not Enough (by a Certain Amount):** be lacking, short, or shy (a certain amount), lack (a certain amount),v.

14. **Not Having Enough (by a Certain Amount):** lacking, short, shy,adj.

15. **The Amount Lacked:** deficiency; deficit (money); shortage,n.

920. EXCESS

1. **In Excess of Needs, Requirements, Desires, etc.:** de trop (French), excess, excrescent, extra, overabundant, plethoric, recrementitious, redundant, spare, superabundant, supererogatory, superfluous, supernumerary, surplus,adj.

2. **State, Condition, Character, or Quality of Being in Excess of Needs, etc.:** excess, glut, nimiety, overabundance, overflow, overplus, plethora, redundancy or redundance, superabundance, supererogation, superfluousness or superfluity, surfeit, surplus or surplusage,n.

3. **That Which Is in Excess of Needs, etc.:** extra, redundancy or redundance, spare, superfluity, supernumerary,n.

4. **Things That Are in Excess of Needs, etc.:** excess, extras, overflow, overplus, redundancies, spares, superfluities, supernumeraries, surfeit, surplus or surplusage,n.

5. **Excess Matter Separated Out from What Is Needed or Useful:** recrement,n. (recremental,adj.)

6. **Amount That Is in Excess of Needs, etc.:** excess, overabundance, overplus, plethora, superabundance, surfeit, surplus or surplusage,n.

7. **Person Who Is in Excess of Needs, etc.:** superfluity, supernumerary,n.

8. **Employee, Official, etc., in Excess of the Number Required:** supernumerary,n.

9. **To Be in Excess:** overabound, superabound,v.

10. **To Do, Go, etc., in Excess of:** exceed,v.

11. **More than:** upwards of

12. **More than Half:** major,adj.

13. **More than Expected:** with a vengeance, adv. phrase

14. **More than Demanded or Required by Duty:** supererogatory,adj.

15. **To Do More than Is Demanded or Required by Duty:** supererogate,v. (supererogation,n.)

16. **To Do More than:** better, exceed, improve upon, surpass, top,v.

17. **To Be More than:** better, exceed, outnumber, surpass, top,v.

18. **The Most Possible:** extreme, limit, maximum, utmost, uttermost,n.

19. **Too Much, or Too Many; Hence, by Extension, Undesirable, in the Way, etc.:** de trop (French)

20. **Too Much of a Good Thing:** embarrassment of riches or, French, embarras de, or des, richesses; toujours perdrix—French (literally, *always partridge*)

21. **Too Much to Choose from, i.e., So Many Good Things as to Make Choice Difficult or Impossible:** embarras de, or du, choix (French), embarrassment of riches, or, French, embarras de, or des, richesses

921. EXCESSIVENESS

1. Excessive,adj.
 1. exceeding—excessive
 2. exorbitant, extortionate—excessive; going beyond the bounds of the normal, reasonable, or fair, esp. in amount, quantity, price, extent, degree, etc.
 3. extravagant—going beyond the bounds of reason, good sense, etc., as actions, feelings, opinions, requests, etc.; going beyond the bounds of wisdom in spending; exorbitant
 4. extreme—going beyond the bounds of moderation
 5. immoderate—excessive; going beyond reasonable, sensible, just, etc., limits; characterized by excessiveness, i.e., going too far, being too much, etc.
 6. inordinate—excessive; beyond reasonable, normal, expected, or justifiable bounds or limits
 7. intemperate—excessive in indulgence of appetites, bodily pleasures, passions, etc.; excessive in indulgence in alcohol; immoderate
 8. outrageous—going beyond the bounds of reasonableness, decency, etc.
 9. prohibitive—so excessive in cost, expense, difficulty, etc., as to prohibit purchase, use, doing, etc.
10. ultra—excessive
11. unconscionable—excessive to an unreasonable degree
12. undue—excessive

13. unreasonable—going beyond the bounds of reason or good sense; exorbitant; immoderate

2. Excessiveness,n. *From Sec. 1:* exorbitance or exorbitancy, extravagance or extravagancy; extremeness, extremism, or extremity; immoderateness, immoderacy, or immoderation; inordinacy or inordinateness, intemperateness or intemperance, outrageousness, prohibitiveness, unconscionableness, unreasonableness; *Also:* 1. excess—excessiveness; going beyond sensible, reasonable, proper, etc., bounds or limits; immoderateness or intemperance in drinking or eating

3. Unexcessive,adj. *From Sec. 1:* unexorbitant, unextravagant, unextreme, unprohibitive; *Also:* moderate

4. Action, Opinion, Feeling, etc., That Goes beyond the Bounds of Reason: extravagance, extravagancy,n.

5. Excessive Degree or Amount: excess, extreme,n.

6. To Go beyond the Bounds of Reasonableness, Propriety, etc.: extravagate,v.

7. To Indulge Excessively in Anything: surfeit,v.

8. Excessively: exceedingly; exorbitantly (as to amount, price, etc.); extravagantly, extremely, immoderately, inordinately, outrageously, overly, overmuch; parlous or parlously (somewhat archaic); prohibitively (as to price, difficulty, etc.); terribly (colloq.); unduly, unreasonably,adv.

922. EXTREMENESS

1. Extreme: dire, drastic, exceeding, immoderate; mortal (as *mortal fear, insult,* etc.); radical; rank (as *rank obscenity,* etc.); ultra, utter, violent,adj.

2. Extreme in Influence, Effect, Result, Intention, etc.: drastic,adj. (as *drastic measures, steps,* etc.)

3. Going to Extremes, as in Opinions, Actions, Practices, etc.: rabid, radical, violent, adj. (rabidness or rabidity, radicalness,n. radical,n. radicalism,n.)

4. Going to Extremes in Matters of Reform: radical,adj. (radicalness or radicalism, n. radical,n.)

5. Extreme in Opinions on Questions of Religion or Morality, or in One's Religious Zeal: fanatic, fanatical,adj. (fanaticism,n. fanatic,n. unfanatical,neg.adj.)

6. To Show, or Act with, Extreme Religious, Moral, or Other Zeal: fanaticize,v.

7. To Cause to Show, or Act with, Such: fanaticize,v.

8. Extreme in Intensity, Violence, Degree, etc.: towering,adj. (as rage, etc.)

9. Extreme Degree, Extent, etc.: excess, extremity, nth degree, utmost, uttermost,n.

10. Extreme Limit: utmost, uttermost,n. (utmost, uttermost,adj.)

11. Situated at an Extreme Point: extremital, utmost, uttermost,adj.

12. To the Extreme: to the nth degree

13. An Extreme; The Extreme: an ultimate, the ultimate,n.

14. The Greatest Extremity; The Last Extremity; The Bitter End: outrance,n. (French)

15. Extreme Measures, Actions, Steps, etc.: extremities,n.

16. Extreme Point, Part, Boundary, Limit, etc.: extremity,n.

17. Condition or State of Extreme Need, Suffering, Misfortune, etc.: extremity or extremities,n.

18. In Such a Condition or State of Need, Suffering, Misfortune, etc.; Hence, Near, or at the Point of, Death: in extremis (Latin)

19. Tendency or Disposition to Go to Extremes: extremism, radicalism or radicality, ultraism,n. (extremist or extremistic, radical, ultraist or ultraistic,adj.)

20. One Who Holds, Follows, or Advocates Extreme Principles, Measures, etc.: extremist, radical, ultraist,n.

21. One Who Goes to Extremes: extremist, radical, ultra, ultraist,n.

22. Radicals as a Group: radicality,n.

23. To Become, or Cause to Become, Politically Radical: radicalize,v. (radicalization, n.)

24. Advocacy of Extremes, Extreme Measures to Attain a Goal, Extreme Principles, etc.: extremism, radicalism, ultraism,n. (extremist, radical, ultraist,n. extremist or extremistic, radical, ultraist or ultraistic,adj.)

25. Principles or Practices of Those Who Hold Extreme Views or Opinions, or Advocate Extreme Steps, Measures, etc.: radicalism, ultraism,n.

26. An Extreme Opinion, View, Act, etc.: ultraism,n.

27. Extremely: drastically, exceedingly, immoderately, mortally; parlous or parlously (somewhat archaic); radically, utterly, violently, with a vengeance,adv.

28. Not Extreme: moderate, unextreme, unradical,adj.

923. MODERATION

1. Moderate, i.e., Not Excessive or Extreme, adj.
1. abstemious—moderate in eating or drinking; avoiding overindulgence in food or drink for religious, health, or economic reasons
2. conservative, middle-of-the-road—moderate; not radical or extreme, esp. in politics
3. medium—moderate; to neither one extreme nor the other
4. reasonable—moderate; not excessive; moderate in price
5. temperate—moderate; not going to extremes; moderate in appetites, passions, etc.; moderate in alcoholic indulgence; moderate in degree or extent

2. Quality or Condition of Being Moderate, n. *From Sec. 1:* abstemiousness, conservativeness, reasonableness, temperateness or, esp. as to appetites, liquor, etc., temperance; *Also:* moderateness, moderation, or moderantism

3. Not Moderate: immoderate, intemperate, unconservative, unreasonable,adj. (immoderateness, immoderacy, or immoderation; intemperateness or intemperance, unreasonableness,n.)

4. One Who Advocates Moderation: moderationist,n.

5. One Who Holds Moderate Opinions or Views: conservative, moderate, moderatist,n.

6. Moderation in Principles, Action, Opinions, or Views: golden mean, moderatism,n.

7. Moderating Factor: moderant, moderator, temperer,n.

8. To Cause to Be Moderate: moderate, temper,v. (moderation,n.)

924. GREATNESS (IN DEGREE, ETC.)

1. Very Great (in Degree, Extent, etc.): exceptional, extraordinary, extreme; grievous or severe (as pain, sorrow, or other unpleasant conditions or circumstances); intense, mighty; mortal (as fear, insult, error, etc.); profound, stupendous, surpassing; towering (as anger, etc.); transcendent, violent,adj. (exceptionalness, extraordinariness, extremeness; grievousness, severity, or severeness; intensity or intenseness, mightiness, profoundness, stupendousness, surpassingness, transcendence or transcendency, violence,n.)

2. Greatest Possible (in Degree, Extent, etc.): maximal, maximum, sovereign, supreme, top, utmost, uttermost,adj.

3. Greatest Possible Degree, Extent, etc.: maximum, utmost, uttermost,n.

4. Brought to the Greatest Possible Degree or Extent: consummate,adj.

5. To Raise or Bring to the Greatest Possible Degree: consummate,v. (consummation, n.)

6. Greater in Number, Position, Value, etc.: superior,adj. (superiority,n.)

7. To Make, or Become, Greater or Very Great in Degree: intensify,v. (intensification, n.)

8. To Be Greater than in Degree, Quality, Excellence, etc.: exceed, surpass, transcend, v.

925. FULLNESS

1. Full, Filled, or Filled Up, Literally, as with Things, Matter, etc.,adj.
1. **brimful, brimming**—full to the top
2. **bursting**—very full; full to overflowing
3. **charged**—filled with the amount capable of being held or intended to be held; filled with other matter, as in diffusion or solution—of the atmosphere, water, etc.; filled with carbon dioxide—of water
4. **chock-full, choke-full, chuck-full**—full to the capacity, limit, extreme, top, etc.
5. **choked or choked up, clogged or clogged up, gorged**—filled up; full, or filled up,'to the point where no passage is possible (of roads, places, openings, canals, ducts, etc.)
6. **cluttered**—filled with things in disorder, in confused or untidy arrangement, etc. (of places, etc.)
7. **complete**—full; filled up
8. **congested**—excessively full; filled to excess; so overfull that passage is blocked or stopped up, as lungs, traffic, streets, etc.
9. **crammed, cram-full**—filled by force to absolute capacity; filled with more than can be conveniently held; filled with an excess; stuffed
10. **crowded**—filled to capacity or excess; filled with crowds of people
11. **glutted**—filled to the point of excess, as the market with supplies, etc.
12. **imbued**—filled with liquid, moisture, or color; saturated
13. **impregnated, impregnate**—having the spaces filled (with something); saturated
14. **loaded, laden**—filled with as much as can be carried; filled abundantly
15. **overcrowded**—filled to excess; filled with an excess of people
16. **overflowing**—so full that the contents flow over the sides
17. **overfull, overfilled**—so excessively full that the contents spill, flow, or run over
18. **packed**—filled with a neat arrangement of things; crammed; crowded
19. **padded**—filled with soft material, stuffing, etc.
20. **plethoric**—overfull
21. **replete (with)**—full; well filled (with); filled to the point where no more can be held; crowded
22. **saturated**—filled to capacity, or to the point where no more can be absorbed, used, tolerated, etc., as the market; filled with moisture or liquid to the point where no more can be held or absorbed; filled with other matter to the point where no more can be accommodated, as the atmosphere, etc.
23. **stuffed**—filled, filled to capacity, or filled to the limit—of a container, opening, passage, cavity, etc.; filled with bread, seasoning, etc.—of fowl, meat, etc.; filled out with material and looking lifelike—of the skins of dead animals, birds, etc.; padded
24. **suffused**—filled, as with liquid or color—eyes with tears, cheeks with a blush, etc.; the connotation is a filling by means of spreading over
25. **teeming (with)**—full (of); full to overflowing; crowded
26. **topfull, topful**—full to the top

2. To Fill; To Make Full,v. *From Sec. 1:* brim or brimfill, charge, choke or choke up, clog or clog up, clutter, congest, cram, crowd, glut, imbue, impregnate, load or lade, overcrowd, overflow, overfill, pack, pad, saturate, stuff, suffuse; *Also:*
1. **bulk out**—pad
2. **lade**—load (a ship)
3. **lumber**—fill with rubbish or useless articles
4. **ram**—cram; stuff
5. **refill**—fill again
6. **replenish**—fill again; bring back to a former state of fullness, as by supplying what has been used up, etc.
7. **swamp**—fill (a ship, etc.) with water and so sink it
8. **tamp**—pack (a hole) with dirt, etc. (in blasting), after the charge has been deposited in it

3. Act of Filling,n. *From Sec. 2:* congestion, glut, imbuement, impregnation, saturation, suffusion; replenishment; *Also:* **1. impletion** —act of filling

4. Fullness; State or Condition of Being Full or Filled,n. *From Sec. 1:* brimfulness, clutterment, completeness, congestion, crowdedness, glut, impregnation, overcrowdedness, overflow, overfullness, plethora, repletion, saturation, suffusion; *From Sec. 2:* replenishment; *From Sec. 3:* impletion; *Also:*
1. **plenum**—state or condition of being full or filled, esp. with things of a similar kind
2. **plenitude**—fullness; state or condition of being full or filled; fullness of amount, quantity, or degree

5. That Which Fills,n. *From Sec. 1:* load, padding or pad, stuffing, suffusion; *Also:* fill, filler, filling, impletion

6. Filling; Causing to Be Full or Filled, adj. *From Sec. 1:* choking, clogging, congesting or congestive, glutting, imbuing, impregnating, repletive, saturating or saturant, suffusive or suffusing

7. To Be Filled or Full,v. *From Sec. 1:* brim, burst, choke, overflow, teem; *Also:* **1. abound** in or with—be filled with

8. To Fill, i.e., Become Filled,v. *From Sec. 1:* choke or choke up, clog or clog up, congest, overfill; *From Sec. 2:* refill, swamp

9. Fillable,adj. *From Sec. 1:* congestible, saturable (saturability,n.); *From Sec. 2:* refillable

10. A Whole Space That Is Full of Matter: plenum,n.

11. A Cup, Bowl, Glass, etc., That Is Full to the Top: brimmer,n.

12. Point of Such Fullness that No More Can Be Absorbed: saturation point,n.

13. At the Time When Fullness Is Reached, i.e., at the Proper or Appointed Time: in the fullness of time

14. Laborer Who Loads and Unloads Ships: longshoreman, stevedore,n. (the latter decides on the manner, the former merely does the carrying)

15. Full, i.e., without Qualification, as Power, Authority, Right, etc.: absolute, complete, plenary,adj. (absoluteness, completeness,n.)

16. Very Full—of Clothing, Drapes, etc.: voluminous,adj. (voluminousness, voluminosity,n.)

17. Filled, Figuratively, as with an Emotion, Quality, etc.: brimful or brimming, bursting, charged; chock-full, choke-full, or chuck-full; choked up or choked; crowded (as the mind with thoughts, etc.); fraught (as with danger, sadness, delight, etc.); imbued (with feelings, ideas, teaching, etc., as the mind or a person); impregnated or impregnate; instinct (with some quality, often an intrinsic quality); loaded or laden (as the mind with care, worry, etc., or some burdensome thing, quality, or emotion); overcrowded (as the mind with thoughts); overflowing, packed; redolent (with a quality or feeling, as a tone of voice, a period of time, etc.); rife (with figurative things or qualities, as errors, danger, etc.); saturated (thoroughly or completely, as with a quality, doctrine, etc.); steeped in (a quality, knowledge, teaching, doctrines, etc.); suffused (with an emotion, etc., as if overspread by it); teeming or pullulating (as with ideas, emotions, etc.); tinctured (with an alien quality); transfused (as with some strong emotion, etc., that was, as it were, poured in),adj.

18. To So Fill, Figuratively, v. *From Sec. 17:* charge, crowd, imbue, impregnate, load, overcrowd, pack, saturate, steep, suffuse, tincture, transfuse (imbuement, impregnation, saturation,n.)

19. To Be, or Become, So Filled or Full,v. *From Sec. 17:* brim, choke up, overflow, teem or pullulate (pullulation,n.)

20. Full, Filled, or Filled Up—of a Person, as with Food, Drink, or Too Much Food, Drink, etc.: bursting; chock-full, choke-full, or chuck-full; crammed; full up (colloq.); gorged; glutted (to the point of disgust or weariness, as with food, pleasure, etc.); loaded (colloq.); overfull; packed (colloq.); replete (to the point of disgust, lack of interest, etc., as with food); sated, satiated, or satiate (to the point of disgust, lack of interest or desire, etc., as with food, pleasure, etc.); stuffed; surfeited (to the point of disgust, nausea, or lack of interest or desire),adj.

21. Such Fullness,n. *From Sec. 20:* glut, overfullness, repletion; satiation or satiety, surfeit

22. To So Fill (a Person),v. *From Sec. 20:* cram, glut, overfill; pack (colloq.); sate or satiate, stuff, surfeit (satiation,n.) *Also:* 1. stodge—fill with food to the point of capacity; surfeit

23. To Become So Filled,v. *From Sec. 20:* cram oneself, gorge oneself, stuff or stuff oneself

24. Able to Be Filled with Food, etc., to the Point of Complete Satisfaction: satiable, adj. (satiableness or satiability,n.)

25. Unable to Be Filled with Food, etc., to the Point of Complete Satisfaction: insatiable, insatiate,adj. (insatiableness or insatiability,n.)

26. Full of Thoughts or Words, as Style, Manner of Speaking or Writing, etc.: copious,adj. (copiousness,n.)

27. Sufficiently or Pleasingly Full of Thoughts or Words, as Style, etc.: ample, adj. (ampleness, amplitude,n.)

28. To Decrease the Fullness of: deplete,v. (depletion,n. depletive, depletory,adj.)

926. EMPTINESS

1. Empty: bare, barren; blank (as a space, paper, etc.); inane; vacant (i.e., without contents, or blank, as a space, etc.); vacuous (i.e., without contents), void,adj. (bareness, barrenness, blankness, inanity or inanition, vacancy, vacuousness or vacuity, void,n.)

2. Empty of: destitute of, devoid of, lacking, void of, wanting,adj. (destituteness or destitution, lack, void, want,n. lack, want,v.)

3. Figurative Emptiness in the Sense of Nothing Happening, etc.: vacuum, void,n.

4. Nearly Empty: bare,adj. (bareness,n.)

5. Empty in Speech; Figuratively Empty, though Having the Appearance of Fullness or Substance: flatulent,adj. (flatulence, flatulency,n.)

6. Empty, i.e., without Occupant or Occupants, as a Place, House, Chair, etc.: unoccupied, untenanted, vacant,adj. (vacancy, n.)

7. Empty, i.e., without an Incumbent, as an Office or Position: open, void,adj.

8. Containing Only Empty Space, or Air, Rather than Being Solid, as a Wall, Tree, etc.: hollow,adj. (hollowness,n.)

9. Figuratively Empty: bare, barren, hollow, inane,adj. (bareness, barrenness, hollowness, inanity,n.)

10. Empty, as a Stare, Look, Expression of the Face, etc.: blank, inane, stupid, vacant, vacuous,adj. (blankness, inanity, stupidity or stupidness, vacancy, vacuousness or vacuity, n.)

11. Empty, i.e., Devoid of Expression, Intelligence, etc., as a Face or the Features, etc.: blank, stupid, vacant,adj. (blankness, stupidity or stupidness, vacancy,n.)

12. Empty of Ideas, Thinking, Intelligence, Mentality, etc.: inane, stupid, vacant, vacuous,adj. (inanity, stupidity or stupidness, vacancy, vacuousness or vacuity,n.)

13. Empty Space: blank, gap; hiatus (where something should be, or has been omitted, as in a manuscript, etc.); hollow (within some enclosure, etc.); interstice (between things or parts); lacuna (where something has been omitted or has come out, as in a manuscript, etc.); vacancy, vacuity, vacuum, void,n. (interstitial; lacunal, lacunar, or lacunary,adj. lacunae,pl.n.)

14. Something Empty: inane, vacancy,n.

15. Infinite Empty Space: infinite, infinity, void,n.

16. The Emptiness of Infinite Space: inane,n.

17. In Empty Space; In Emptiness: in vacuo, adv. phrase (Latin)

18. Into Empty Space: in vacuo,adv. phrase (Latin)

19. Space Left Empty by the Departure or Death of the Usual Occupant; Emptiness Left by the Departure or Death of Someone Usually Present: void,n.

20. Empty Office or Position; Empty Place, as a Room, Apartment, etc.: vacancy,n.

21. To Empty (Something); To Cause (Someone or Something) to Be or Become Empty,v.
1. clear—empty (a place) of people, contents, furniture, etc. (clearance,n.)
2. deplete—empty partially or completely; exhaust, strength, financial or other resources, etc.; exhaust to a point of danger, or to a point where survival is difficult; empty (the bodily vessels or organs) by letting blood, purging, etc. (depletion,n. depletive, depletory,adj.)
3. discharge—empty of a load; unload (a ship, etc.); empty (its load), as a truck, etc.; empty (its passengers), as a bus, train, etc.; empty (its contents, esp. fluid contents), as a pipe, bodily organ, river, etc. (discharge,n.)
4. disembogue—empty (its waters) at the mouth—of a river, etc. (disemboguement, n.)
5. drain—empty gradually of fluid; empty completely of fluid; empty gradually or completely of energy, strength, possessions, contents, etc. (drain, drainage,n.)
6. evacuate—empty; empty (a place, etc.) of inhabitants; leave empty by withdrawing from (a town, etc.); empty (one's bowels, etc.); empty of contents (evacuation,n.)
7. exhaust—empty of contents; leave completely empty by drawing off air, etc.; leave empty of energy, strength, financial resources, patience, etc.; empty completely, so that none of the former contents is left, as a mine, source, etc. (exhaustion,n. exhaustive,adj.)
8. strip—empty of contents, as a house, tree, orchard, etc.
9. unload, unlade—empty of cargo, load, etc.
10. unship, unlade—empty (a ship) of cargo, load, etc.
11. vacate—leave empty; cause (a place) to be empty by removing the occupants from it; cause (a place, house, apartment, room, etc.) to be empty by leaving it, or by removing one's residence from it (vacation,n.)
12. void—empty the contents of (as the bladder, etc.); empty out (voidance,n.)

22. Emptied,adj. *From Sec. 21:* cleared, depleted, discharged, drained, evacuated, exhausted, stripped, unloaded or unladen, unshipped or unladen, vacated, voided

23. State of Being Emptied,n. *From Sec. 1:* depletion, drain or drainage, evacuation, exhaustion

24. Able to Be Emptied,adj. *From Sec. 1:* clearable, drainable, exhaustible, vacatable (exhaustibility,n.)

25. Unable to Be Emptied or Reduced to Emptiness, i.e., in a Sense Always Remaining Full or Still Possessing Contents No Matter How Much Is Removed: exhaustless, inexhaustible, infinite, unfailing,adj. (exhaustlessness, inexhaustibleness or inexhaustibility, infiniteness,n.)

26. State of Exhaustion from Loss of Blood: depletion,n.

27. One Who Is Evacuated, as from a City, Country, etc.: evacuee,n.

28. With Empty Hands, i.e., Bringing or Taking Nothing: empty-handed,adj.

29. To Empty, i.e., Become Empty or Emptied; To Become Empty or Emptied by Discharging Its Contents; To Empty Out,v.
1. discharge—empty, or empty out, as the fluid or water of a bodily organ, river, etc. (discharge,n.)

2. disembogue—empty by discharging or pouring forth its contents, as a river, etc.
3. drain—become gradually empty by the flowing off or discharge of fluid, water, etc. (drain, drainage,n.)
4. peter out—become gradually exhausted, as of energy or strength (colloq.)
5. unload, unlade—become empty by discharging its cargo, contents, etc., as a ship, truck, etc.

927. A NUMBER

1. A Number: figure, numeral,n.; *Also:*
1. addend, summand—number added, or to be added, to another or others
2. Arabic number, cipher—number used in ordinary notation, as 1, 2, 3, 4, etc.
3. augend—number to which another is added or is to be added
4. cardinal, cardinal number, cardinal numeral—number such as 1, 2, 3, etc., as distinguished from an ordinal number (cardinal,adj.)
5. decimal, decimal fraction—number less than 1, written in the form .5, .06, etc. (decimal,adj.)
6. decuple—number ten times greater (than another)
7. denominator—divisor, i.e., bottom number, in a fraction
8. digit, figure—single number, i.e., 0 through 9; 5874 is a numer of four digits or figures
9. dividend—number being divided, or that is to be divided, by another
10. divisor—number that divides, or is to divide, another
11. factor—number which, when multiplied by another, produces a certain product; even divisor, as 3 is a factor of 12 (factorial,adj.)
12. fraction—number less than 1 expressed as a division or decimal, as ½ or .5 (fractional,adj.)
13. googol—any extremely large number (strictly, one followed by 100 zeros)
14. infinity—indefinitely great or large number
15. integer, whole number—number that is not a fraction; one of the numbers 1, 2, 3, 4, etc. (integral, whole,adj.)
16. minuend—number from which another is, or is to be, subtracted
17. multiple—number that is exactly a certain times another, as 12 is a multiple of 4
18. multiplicand, faciend—number that is, or is to be, multiplied by another
19. multiplier—number that multiplies, or is to multiply, another
20. numerator—number to be divided, i.e., top number, in a fraction
21. ordinal, ordinal number, ordinal numeral—number indicating succession, as first, second, third, etc. (ordinal,adj.)
22. prime—number that can be divided equally only by itself and one, as 5, 11, 19, etc. (prime,adj.)
23. product—number that results from multiplication
24. quotient—number resulting from division
25. remainder—number resulting from subtraction; number remaining after division
26. Roman number, Roman numeral—number used by the ancient Romans, or in their notation, as I, II, III, etc.
27. subtrahend—number that is, or is to be, subtracted from another
28. sum—number resulting from addition

2. Word Denoting a Number: numeral,n.

3. Pert. to a Number or to Numbers: numeral, numerary, numeric, numerical,adj.

4. Consisting of, Denoting, Expressing, Ex-

pressed by, etc., a Number or Numbers: numeral, numeric, numerical,adj.

5. Descr. of Part of a Number That Does Not Divide Evenly into It: aliquant,adj. (as 4 is an aliquant part of 11)

6. Descr. of Part of a Number That Divides Evenly into It: aliquot,adj. (as 4 is an aliquot part of 12)

7. Study of Numbers as Influences upon One's Life, Future, etc.; Study of Secret Meanings of Numbers; Prophecy by Numbers; Science of Numbers: numerology,n. (numerological,adj.)

8. Art or System of Reading or Naming Numbers: numeration,n. (numerative,adj.)

9. System of Numbers; Process of Naming by Numbers: notation,n. (notational,adj.)

10. Arabic System of Notation: algorism, cipher,n. (algorismic,adj.)

11. Specialized System of Notation for Special Relationships: algebra,n.

12. To Read or Say (a Number, or Numerical Expression) According to Some System: numerate,v. (numeration,n.)

13. To Give a Number or Numbers to: number,v.

14. Numbered; Having Numbers: numerate, adj.

15. Having No Number; Without a Number or Numbers: numberless, unnumbered,adj.

16. Descr. of Grammatical Number: common (either singular or plural); plural (more than one); singular (one only),adj.

17. Morbid and Compulsive Interest in, or Constant Thinking about, Numbers: arithmomania,n.

928. NOTHING

1. Nothing: nil; naught or nought (archaic or literary), zero,n.

2. Nothingness: nihility, nullity,n.

3. Amounting to Nothing: null,adj.

4. Zero: aught, cipher, naught, nought, ought,n.

929. HALF

1. A Half; Roughly a Half: moiety,n.

2. To Divide into Halves: bisect, dimidiate, halve,v. (bisection, dimidiation,n.)

3. Divided into Halves: bisected, dimidiate, halved,adj.

930. ONE

1. The Number One: unit, unity,n.

2. One Thing, Person, Group, etc.: entity, individual, individuality, single; singleton (different from others in the group); unit,n. (individual, unitary,adj.)

3. Single: alone (used in the predicate), exclusive, individual, particular, sole,adj. (individuality, particularity,n.)

4. Pert. to, or Descr. of, One (Person, Thing, etc.) Only: exclusive, individual, particular, single,adj.

5. One Only: single,adj.

6. One and Only: single, singular, sole, unique,adj. (singleness, singularity, uniqueness,n.)

7. A Unique Thing: singularity,n.

8. Individual: exclusive, particular, peculiar, personal, respective, single, singular, sole,

special, specific, unique,adj. (particularity, peculiarity, singleness, singularity, speciality, specificity, uniqueness,n.)

9. Pert. Individually to Each: respective, adj.

10. To Give an Individual Character to; To Make Individual: individualize, individuate, particularize, singularize, specify,v. (individualization, individuation, particularization, specification,n.)

11. State of Being Made Individual: individualization, individuation,n.

12. To Consider or Treat Individually: individualize,v. (individualization,n.)

13. Individual Character: individualism, individuality, particularity, personality,n.

14. Existence as an Individual: individuality, individuation,n.

15. One at a Time; One by One: individually, respectively, separately, severally, singly,adv.

16. Only: exclusive, single, sole, unique,adj.

17. Only: alone, exclusively, solely,adv.

18. To Make into One: unify, unite,v. (unification, union,n. unific, unitive,adj.)

19. Made One: unified, united,adj.

20. Capable of Being Made One: unitable, unifiable,adj. (unitability,n.)

21. To Become One: unite,v.

22. State of Being One: individuality, oneness, singleness, unity,n.

23. State of Being Made, or of Having Become, One: unification, union, unitedness, unity,n.

24. Single Playing Card, the Only One of its Suit Held in a Hand: singleton,n.

931. TWO

1. Two; Group of Two: brace, couple; mates (as shoes, gloves, etc.); pair; span (of horses or other animals harnessed and driven together); twain (archaic or poetic); twins (similar, related, or identical); twosome,n. (twain, twin,adj.)

2. Relating to Two; Pert. to Two: dual,adj.

3. Of, or Having, Two Different, Contrasting, or Opposing Natures or Characters: dual, dualistic,adj. (duality, dualism,n.)

4. State of Being Two: dualism, duality, twoness,n.

5. For, or of, Two People, Implying a Degree of Privacy or Intimacy: à deux (French), tête-à-tête,adv. (tête-à-tête,adj.)

6. Two at a Time: à deux (French),adv.

7. Consisting of, or Divided into, Two Parts, Branches, etc.: bifid, biforked, bifurcate or bifurcated, binary, bipartite, dichotomous or dichotomic, diploid, double, dual, dualistic, duple, duplex, duplicate, forked; twin (separate and equal, or similar and connected, joined, or related); twofold,adj. (bifidity, bifurcation, bipartition, dichotomy, doubleness, duality or dualism, duplexity or duplicity, forkedness,n.)

8. To Divide, or Cause to Divide, into Two Parts, etc.: bifurcate, dichotomize, fork,v. (bifurcation, dichotomization,n.)

9. Divided into Two Lobes: bifid, bilobate, bilobated, bilobed,adj. (bifidity,n.)

10. Coming, Combined, or Occurring in Groups of Two: coupled, double, dual, geminate, paired, twin,adj.

11. To Become, Form, Combine, or Make into a Group of Two: couple, geminate, pair, twin,v. (gemination,n.)

12. To Make Twice As Great or Twofold: double, duplicate, duplify, redouble,v. (duplication,n.)

13. To Become Twice As Great or Twofold: double, redouble,v.

14. Twice As Great: double, doubled, duple, redoubled,adj.

15. Twofold: bifold, binal, binary, double, dual, duple, duplex, twin,adj. (doubleness, duality, duplexity or duplicity,n.)

16. Involving, or Participated in by, Two People, Parties, Groups, or Nations: bilateral, bipartite,adj.

17. Involving, Representing, or Having Members from Two (Esp. Political) Parties: bipartisan,adj. (bipartisanship,n.)

18. Shared, Felt, Experienced, Manifested, or Performed by, or Pert. to, Two or More in Relationship to One Another: common; dual (two only) ; mutual, reciprocal,adj. (commonness, duality, mutuality, reciprocity,n.)

19. Involving, Comprised of, or Manifesting Two (Things, Elements, etc.): binary, dual, adj. (duality or dualism,n.)

20. One Whole Composed of Two Parts, Elements, etc.: binary,n.

21. Belonging or Pert. to the Second in Order, Rank, etc.: secondary,adj.

22. The Second Power (Mathematics): square,n.

23. To Raise to the Second Power: square,v.

24. The Act of Squaring: quadrature,n.

25. Involving the Second Power or Degree (Algebra): quadratic,adj.

26. Two Times: twice,adv. or adj.

27. Playing Card, or the Side of One of a Pair of Dice, Having Two Pips: deuce,n.

932. THREE

1. Group of Three: leash, ternary, ternion, threesome, triad, trine, trinity, trio, triple, triplet, triplicity, triumvirate, triune,n. (triadic,adj.)

2. Group of Three People (Two Men and a Woman, or Two Women and a Man), Involved in a Love Situation: triangle,n.

3. Three of a Kind: triplets,n.

4. One of Three of a Kind: triplet,n.

5. Group of Three People in Power or Office: triumvirate,n.

6. One of Such a Group: triumvir,n. (triumviral,adj.)

7. Group of Three (Hounds, Greyhounds, Hares, etc.): leash,n.

8. Set, Group, Arrangement, or Object Made Up of Three Related Units: trefoil,n. (trefoil,adj.)

9. Chord of Three Tones: triad,n. (triadic,adj.)

10. Three, in Reference to Cards, Dice, or Dominoes: trey,n.

11. Playing Card, Side of a Die, or a Domino with Three Pips: trey,n.

12. Threefold: ternary, treble, trinal, trinary, trine, triple, triplex, triplicate,adj. (tripleness, triplicity,n.)

13. Based on the Number Three: ternary,adj.

14. Moving, Counting, Going, or Coming, by Threes: trinary,adj.

15. Involving or Comprising Three; Made Up of Three: ternary, ternate, triangular, triple,adj.

16. Arranged in Groups of Three: ternate, adj.

17. Of the Third Order, Rank, etc.: ternate, tertiary,adj.

18. Third: tertiary,adj.

19. Made Up of, or Divided into, Three Parts: threefold, trichotomous or trichotomic, trifid, triform or triformed, trifurcate or trifurcated, triparted, tripartite, triple, triplex, triplicate,adj. (trichotomy, triformity, trifurcation, tripartition, tripleness, triplicity, n.)

20. To Divide into Three Parts, etc.: trichotomize, trifurcate,v. (trifurcation,n.)

21. Divided or Cleft into, or Having, Three Lobes: trifid, trilobate, trilobed,adj.

22. Thing, Figure, or Object with Three Branches: tribrach,n. (tribrachial,adj.)

23. Division of Man's Nature into the Three Elements or Parts of Body, Soul, and Spirit: trichotomy,n. (trichotomous or trichotomic, adj. trichotomize,v.)

24. Involving, or Participated in by, Three People, Parties, Groups, or Nations: triangular, tripartite,adj.

25. State of Being Three: triadism, threeness, trinity, tripleness, triplicity, triunity,n.

26. Combination of Three in One: trinity, triunity,n.

27. Three in One: triune,adj. (triunity,n.)

28. Three Times; In a Threefold Manner: threefold, thrice, trebly, triply,adv.

29. To Make Three Times As Great; To Multiply by Three: treble, triple, triplicate,v. (triplication or triplicature,n. triplicative, adj.)

30. To Become Three Times As Great: treble, triple,v.

31. Something Made Three Times As Great: triplex, triplication,n.

32. Something, as a Number or Amount, Three Times As Great As Another: triple,n.

33. One of Three Things: triplicate,n.

34. Made in or into, or Forming, Three Identical Copies: in triplicate, triplicate,adj.

35. To Make Three Identical Copies of: triplicate,v. (triplication,n.)

36. Recurring Every Third Day—of Medical Conditions, Diseases, Fevers, Ague, etc.: tertian,adj.

37. The Third Power (Mathematics): cube,n. (cubic,adj.)

38. To Raise to the Third Power (Mathematics): cube,v.

933. FOUR

1. The Number Four: quaternary, tetrad,n.

2. Group of Four: foursome; quadruplet (usually of the same kind) ; quartet or quartette, quaternary, quaternion, tetrad,n.

3. Set of Four Parts: quaternion,n.

4. Fourfold: quadrigeminal, quadrigeminous, quadruple, quadruplex, quadruplicate,adj.

5. Having a Fourfold Character, Nature, or Shape: quadriform,adj.

6. Consisting of, or Divided into, Four Parts: fourfold, quadrifid, quadrifurcated, quadruple, quadruplex, quadripartite, quaternary, tetramerous,adj. (quadrifurcation, quadripartition,n. quadrifurcate,v.)

7. Arranged, etc., in Groups of Four: quadruple, quaternary, quaternate,adj.

8. To Divide into Four Equal Parts, Sections, etc.: quadrisect, quarter,v. (quadrisection, quarter,n.)

9. Consisting of Four: quaternary,adj.

10. To Make Four Times As Great; To Multiply by Four: quadruple, quadruplicate, v. (quadruplication or quadruplicature,n.)

11. To Become Four Times As Great: quadruple,v. (quadruplication,n.)

12. One of Four Things: quadruplicate,n.

13. Involving, or Participated in by, Four People, Groups, Parties, Nations, etc.: quadripartite,adj.

14. Card, Die, Domino, etc., with Four Pips: quatre,n.

15. To Make Four Identical Copies of: quadruplicate,v. (quadruplication,n.)

16. One Such Copy: quadruplicate,n.

17. Occurring Every Fourth Day, Esp. of a Fever; Pert. or Relating to the Fourth (of Something): quartan,adj.

934. FIVE

1. The Number Five: pentad,n.

2. The Five in Cards or Dice: cinque,n.

3. Group of Five: cinquain, pentad, quintet or quintette, quintuplet,n. (pentadicity,n.)

4. To Divide into Five Equal, or Approximately Equal, Parts: quinquesect,v. (quinquesection,n.)

5. Consisting of, or Divided into, Five Parts: fivefold, pentamerous, quinary, quinquefid, quinquepartite, quintuple,adj.

6. Fifth, i.e., Occurring after the First Four; Occurring Every Fifth Day: quintan, adj.

7. Put in Arrangements of Five; Made Up of Five: quinary, quinquenary,adj.

8. Something with Five Units, Members, or Parts: quinary,n.

9. Fivefold: quintuple,adj.

10. To Make Five Times As Great; To Multiply by Five: quintuple, quintuplicate,v. (quintuplication,n.)

11. To Become Five Times As Great: quintuple,v. (quintuplication,n.)

12. A Number or Amount Five Times As Great As Another: quintuple,n.

935. SIX

1. The Number Six: hexad,n.

2. Pert. to the Number Six: senary,adj.

3. Group of Six: hexad, sextet or sextette, sextuplet,n. (hexadic,adj.)

4. Sixfold: senary, sextuple, sextuplicate,adj.

5. Consisting of, or Divided into, Six Parts: hexamerous, sexpartite, sextipartite, sextuple, sixfold,adj. (sextipartition,n.)

6. To Make Six Times As Great; To Multiply by Six: sextiply, sextuple, sextuplicate, v.

7. To Become Six Times As Great: sextuple, v.

8. Six Times As Great: sextuple,adj.

936. SEVEN

1. The Number Seven: hebdomad, heptad,n.

2. Pert. to the Number Seven: septenary, adj.

3. Seven Things as a Total: hebdomad,n.

4. Group of Seven: heptad, septenary, septet or septette,n.

5. Making Up a Group of Seven: septenary, adj.

6. Consisting of, or Divided into, Seven Parts: heptamerous, sevenfold,adj.

7. Sevenfold: septuple, septuplicate,adj.

8. To Make Seven Times As Great; To Multiply by Seven: septuple, septuplicate, v. (septuplication,n.)

9. Seven Times As Great: septuple, septuplicate,adj.

10. Occurring at Intervening Periods of Seven Days: hebdomadal, hebdomadary, septenary, weekly,adj.

937. EIGHT; NINE

1. The Number Eight: ogdoad,n.

2. Pert. to the Number Eight: octonal, octonary,adj.

3. Group of Eight: octad, octave, octet or octette, octonary, ogdoad,n. (octadic, octaval, adj.)

4. Made Up, or Consisting, of Eight: octonal, octonary,adj.

5. In Groups or Sets of Eight: octonal, octonary,adj.

6. Occurring or Recurring Every Eighth Day (of Medical Conditions, Fevers, Ague, etc.): octan,adj.

7. Consisting of, or Divided into, Eight Parts: eightfold, octamerous, octofid,adj.

8. Having Eight Operating Elements or Units: octuple,adj.

9. Eightfold: octuple, octuplicate,adj.

10. To Make Eight Times As Great; To Multiply by Eight: octuple, octuplicate,v. (octuplication,n.)

11. To Become Eight Times As Great: octuple,v.

12. Eight Times As Great: octuple,adj.

13. Made Up of Nine: nonary, nonuple,adj.

14. Ninefold: nonary, nonuple,adj.

15. Considered in Sets of Nine: nonary, nonuple,adj.

938. TEN

1. Pert. to the Number Ten; Pert. to Tenths: decimal, denary,adj.

2. Group of Ten: decade,n.

3. Consisting of, or Divided into, Ten Parts: decamerous, tenfold,adj.

4. System Based on Tens: decimal system,n.

5. To Make into a Decimal System: decimalize,v. (decimalization,n.)

6. Being, or Pert. to, Every Tenth in a Series: decuman,adj.

7. Tenfold: decuple, denary,adj.

8. A Tenfold Quantity, Amount, or Multiple: decuple,n.

9. To Make Ten Times Greater; To Multiply by Ten: decuple,v.

10. Ten Times As Great: decuple,adj.

11. Containing Ten: denary,adj.

12. Moving, Coming, or Going, by Tens: decimal, denary,adj.

13. Based on Tens: denary,adj.

14. A One-Tenth Part, Esp. in Reference to Something or to Some Tax Contributed Voluntarily: tithe,n. (tithe,adj.)

939. TWENTY

1. Group, Set, Amount, or Quantity of Twenty: score,n.

2. Pert. to, or Consisting of, Twenty: vicenary, vigesimal,adj.

3. Consisting of, or Divided into, Twenty Parts: twentyfold, vigesimal,adj.

4. Counting Twenty by Twenty: vigesimal, adj.

5. Twentieth: vigesimal,adj.

940. OTHER NUMBERS

1. Twelve: dozen,n.

2. Relating to Twelve; Relating to Twelfths: duodecimal,adj.

3. Counting, or Being Counted, by Twelves: duodecimal,adj. (duodecimality,n.)

4. Part That Is a Twelfth of a Whole: duodecimal,n.

5. Made Up of Twelves; Twelvefold: duodecuple,adj.

6. Thirteen: baker's dozen,n.

7. Comprised of Thirty; To the Number of Thirty: tricenary,adj.

8. Forty; Group, Quantity, or Amount of Forty: twoscore,n. and adj.

9. Consisting of Forty; Continuing Forty Days, as the Lenten Fast: quadragesimal,adj.

10. Fifty: twoscore and ten,n. and adj.

11. Lasting, or Consisting of, Fifty Days: quinquagesimal,adj.

12. Sixty; Group, Quantity, or Amount of Sixty: threescore,n. and adj.

13. Pert. to the Number Sixty: sexagenary, sexagesimal,adj.

14. Based on the Number Sixty: sexagesimal, adj.

15. Consisting of, Counting by, or Proceeding by, Sixties: sexagenary,adj.

16. Seventy: threescore and ten,n. and adj.

17. Composed, Consisting, or Made Up, of Seventy: septuagenarian, septuagenary,adj.

18. Eighty: fourscore,n. and adj.

19. Ninety: fourscore and ten,n. and adj.

20. Ninetieth: nonagesimal,adj.

21. Hundred: fivescore,n. and adj.

22. Hundredth; Pert. to Hundredths or Division into Hundredths: centesimal,adj.

23. Hundredfold: centuple, centuplicate,adj.

24. Number, Amount, or Quantity Made a Hundred Times Greater: centuplicate,n.

25. To Make a Hundred Times Greater; To Multiply by One Hundred: centuple, centuplicate,v. (centuplication,n.)

26. One Hundred Forty-Four as a Quantity, i.e., Twelve Dozen: gross,n.

27. Having, Made Up of, or Consisting of, Four Hundred: quadrigenarious,adj.

28. Pert. to Six Hundred: sexcentenary,adj.

29. A Thousand: chiliad, millenary,n.

30. A Thousand Dollars: grand,n. (slang)

31. Total of a Thousand: millenary,n.

32. Pert. to a Thousand: millenarian, millenary,adj.

33. Consisting, or Composed, of a Thousand: millenary,adj.

34. Thousandth: millesimal,adj.

35. Thousandth Part: millesimal,n.

36. Consisting of Parts in the Thousandths: millesimal,adj.

37. Pert. to a Thousandth or to Thousandth Parts: millesimal,adj.

38. By the Thousand: per mill or per mil

39. One Thousand Seven Hundred Twenty-Eight, as a Quantity, i.e., Twelve Gross: great gross,n.

40. Ten Thousand: myriad,n. and adj.

41. Numbers beyond a Thousand (According to the United States System),n. and adj. Beyond a thousand, names for numbers are as follows, each one representing one thousand times the previous one (the first is one thousand times a thousand): million; billion, or less commonly, milliard; trillion; quadrillion; quintillion; sextillion; septillion; octillion; nonillion; decillion; undecillion; duodecillion; tredecillion; quattuordecillion; quindecillion; sexdecillion; septendecillion; octodecillion; novemdecillion; vigintillion; *Also:*

1. centillion—the number 1 followed by three hundred zeros
2. googol—the number 1 followed by one hundred zeros—this term and the next were coined by the American mathematician Edward Kasner
3. googolplex—the number 1 followed by a googol of zeros, i.e., ten to the exponent ten, which itself is raised to the hundredth power
4. zillion—the number 1 followed by some tremendous and indeterminate number of zeros—a colloquial, humorous, and non-mathematical term

941. COUNTING

1. To Count: enumerate, numerate, reckon, tally,v. (enumeration, numeration, reckoning, tally,n. enumerator, tallier, reckoner,n. enumerative, adj.)

2. To Count One by One: tell, tell down, tell off, tell out,v.

3. Counting; Descr. of That Which Is Used in Counting: numerant,adj.

4. Official Count of the People of a Place, Country, etc.: census, enumeration, numeration,n.

5. Art of Counting by Means of One's Fingers: dactylonomy,n.

6. Decimal System of Counting: algorism,n.

7. Able to Be Counted: countable, numberable,adj. (countableness, numerableness,n.)

8. Unable to Be Counted: countless, innumerable, innumerous, uncountable,adj. (innumerableness or innumerability, uncountableness,n.)

9. Number of Things Counted and Written Down: count, tally,n.

10. Morbid Compulsion to Count Things: arithmomania,n.

942. CALCULATION

1. To Calculate,v.
1. cipher—do, or figure out, by arithmetic; do arithmetic addition
2. compute—figure out mathematically (usually simpler problems, etc.)
3. estimate—calculate approximately, rather than exactly

4. **figure**—calculate; compute; do computations
5. **gauge, gage**—estimate; estimate the size, contents, quantity, force, etc., of
6. **miscalculate**—calculate incorrectly; make an error in calculation
7. **reckon**—compute; compute mentally
8. **sum**—calculate by adding; calculate the total of
9. **tally**—compute; calculate (a score)

2. Calculation,n. *From Sec. 1:* ciphering, computation, gauge or gage, estimation or estimate, figuring, miscalculation, reckoning, sum, tally

3. Calculator,n. *From Sec. 1:* cipherer, computer, estimator, figurer, gauger, miscalculator, reckoner, tallier; *Also:* **1. abacist**—calculator

4. Calculable,adj. *From Sec. 1:* cipherable, computable, estimable, figurable, gaugeable or gageable, reckonable, talliable

5. Incalculable,adj. *From Sec. 1:* uncomputable or incomputable, inestimable or unestimable, unfigurable, unreckonable

6. Pert. to Calculation: calculative,adj.

7. Based on, or Pert. to, Approximate Calculation; Capable of Making an Approximate Calculation: estimative,adj.

8. One Who Calculates Insurance Risks: actuary,n. (actuarial,adj.)

9. Number of Things Serving as a Unit of Calculating: tally,n.

10. Art of Calculating with Arabic Numbers, or with Some Other Form of Notation: algorism or algorithm,n. (algorismic, algorithmic,adj.)

11. Special Method or Process of Calculation: algorithm, calculus,n. (algorithmic,adj.)

12. Method of Calculation Using a Special Algebraic Notation: calculus,n.

13. Calculating Device or Machine,n.
   1. **abacus**—device for calculating on which beads are slid across wires
   2. **adding machine, calculating machine**—machine that automatically prints and adds, subtracts, multiplies, and/or divides numbers
   3. **calculator**—book of tables for calculating; adding machine
   4. **Comptometer**—high-speed calculating machine (a trade-marked name)
   5. **reckoner**—book, pamphlet, or collection of mathematical tables or charts, or other tables or charts of information, statistics, figures, etc., useful in calculation
   6. **slide rule**—device for fast calculation consisting of a rule with a sliding rule within it, both containing logarithmic scales

14. One Who Uses an Abacus: abacist,n.

943. MATHEMATICS

1. Selected Branches of Mathematics,n.
   1. **algebra**—branch dealing with quantitative relationship and properties considered through letters and other symbols
   2. **arithmetic, algorism, algorithm**—branch dealing with numbers and calculation
   3. **geodesy, geodetics**—branch dealing with the calculation of points, areas, shapes, dimensions, etc., of the earth's surface or of large tracts of land
   4. **geometry**—branch dealing with the measurements, properties, etc., of solids, lines, angles, etc.
   5. **mensuration**—branch dealing with the calculation of length, area, and volume
   6. **metageometry**—geometry not based exclusively on Euclidean principles or axioms
   7. **quadratics**—branch of algebra dealing with quadratic equations
   8. **topology**—branch dealing with geometric shapes and surfaces that persist even under drastic deformation, as squeezing, crushing, etc.
   9. **trigonometry**—branch dealing with the measurement of, and relationship between, the sides and angles of a triangle

2. Mathematician,n. *From Sec. 1:* algebraist, arithmetician, geodesist, geometrician, metageometer, trigonometer or trigonometrician

3. Mathematical; Mathematic,adj. *From Sec. 1:* algebraic or algebraical; arithmetic, arithmetical, algorismic or algorithmic; geodetic or geodetical, geometric or geometrical, metageometrical, topologic or topological, trigonometric or trigonometrical

4. Algebraic Expression of the Stated Number of Terms: monomial (one), binomial (two), trinomial (three), quadrinomial (four), n. (monomial, binomial, trinomial, quadrinomial,adj.)

944. ANGLE

1. An Angle: bight, corner,n.

2. Outside Angle of a Building or Wall: quoin,n.

3. Having Angles: angular,adj. (angularity, n.)

4. Having a Number of Angles: polygonal, adj.

5. Having the Stated Number of Angles, adj.
   1. **biangular**—two
   2. **decagonal**—ten
   3. **dodecagonal**—twelve
   4. **heptagonal**—seven
   5. **hexagonal, hexangular**—six
   6. **octagonal, octangular, octangle**—eight
   7. **pentagonal**—five
   8. **quadrangular, tetragonal**—four
   9. **triangular, triangulate, triagonal, trigonal, trigonous, triquetral, triquetrous**—three (triangularity,n.)

6. Having Equal Angles: equiangular, isogonal, isogonic,adj.

7. Descr. of a 90° Angle: right,adj.

8. Having Right Angles: orthogonal, rectangular, right-angled, square,adj. (rectangularity, squareness,n.)

9. Having Four Right Angles: rectangular, adj.

10. Meeting at Right Angles: perpendicular, square,adj. (perpendicularity, squareness,n.)

11. Pert. to, or Involving, Right Angles, or Lines That Meet at Right Angles: orthogonal,adj.

12. Descr. of an Angle That Is Not a Right Angle: oblique,adj.

13. Descr. of an Angle That Is Less than 90°: acute,adj.

14. Descr. of an Angle That Is More Than 90° but Less Than 180°: obtuse,adj.

15. Descr. of 180° Angle: straight,adj.

16. Descr. of an Angle That Is More than 180°: reflex,adj.

17. Not Forming an Angle: agonic,adj.

18. Measurement of Angles, Esp. Solid Angles: goniometry,n. (goniometric, goniometrical,adj.)

19. Measurement of the Angles of the Head: goniocraniometry,n.

20. Selected Devices or Instruments for Measuring Angles,n.

1. **goniocraniometer**—device for measuring the angles of the head
2. **goniometer, graphometer**—instrument for measuring angles, esp. solid angles, as of crystals, or in surveying, skull measurements, etc. (goniometric or goniometrical, graphometric or graphometrical, adj.)
3. **protractor**—device, in the form of a semicircle, for measuring or drawing angles on paper
4. **transit, theodolite**—instrument for measuring vertical or horizontal angles in surveying (theodolitic,adj.)

945. GEOMETRIC FIGURES

1. **Closed Geometric Plane Figure of a Number of Sides and Angles:** polygon,n. (polygonal,adj.)
2. **Polygon of the Stated Number of Sides and Angles,n.**
   1. **decagon**—ten (decagonal,adj.)
   2. **dodecagon**—twelve (dodecagonal,adj.)
   3. **heptagon**—seven (heptagonal,adj.)
   4. **hexagon**—six (hexagonal,adj.)
   5. **nonagon**—nine
   6. **octagon, octangle**—eight (octagonal, octangular,adj.)
   7. **pentagon**—five (pentagonal,adj.)
   8. **quadrilateral, quadrangle, tetragon**—four (quadrilateral, quadrangular, tetragonal,adj.)
   9. **quindecagon**—fifteen
   10. **triangle, trigon**—three (triangularity,n. triangular, trigonal, deltoid,adj.)
   11. **undecagon**—eleven
3. **Descr. of a Triangle with Two Equal Sides:** isosceles,adj.
4. **Figure, Ornament, Decoration, etc., in the Shape of a Triangle:** triquetra,n. (triquetral, triquetrous,adj.)
5. **Descr. of a Geometric Figure with Equal Sides:** equilateral,adj.
6. **Figure Formed by Six Intersecting Lines; Six-Pointed, Star-Shaped Figure So Formed:** hexagram,n.
7. **Selected Four-Sided Geometric Figures, or Quadrilaterals,n.**
   1. **diamond, lozenge, rhombus**—equilateral parallelogram without right angles (rhombic, rhombical,adj.)
   2. **oblong**—rectangle (oblong,adj.)
   3. **parallelogram**—quadrilateral whose opposite sides are parallel
   4. **rectangle**—quadrilateral with right angles and opposite sides that are equal (rectangular,adj.)
   5. **rhomboid**—parallelogram without right angles and with two pairs of equal sides (rhomboid, rhomboidal,adj.)
   6. **square, quadrate**—rectangle with four equal sides (square,adj.)
   7. **trapezium**—quadrilateral no two sides of which are parallel
   8. **trapezoid**—quadrilateral only two of whose sides are parallel (trapezoid, trapezoidal,adj.)
8. **Square:** quadrate, quadratic, quadriform, adj.
9. **Something in the Form or Shape of a Square or Rectangle:** quadrate,n. (quadrate,adj.)
10. **In the Form or Shape of a Rectangle:** quadrate, rectangular,adj.
11. **Selected Geometrical Solids with the Stated Number of Faces:** trihedron (three), tetrahedron (four), pentahedron (five), hexahedron (six), heptahedron (seven), octa-

hedron (eight), decahedron (ten), dodecahedron (twelve), icosahedron (twenty), tetrahexahedron (twenty-four equal triangular), trisoctahedron (twenty-four equal),n. (trihedral, tetrahedral, pentahedral, hexahedral, heptahedral, octahedral, decahedral, dodecahedral, icosahedral, tetrahexahedral, trisoctahedral,adj.)

12. **Geometrical Solid of Many Faces:** polyhedron,n. (polyhedral,adj.)
13. **Geometrical Solid of Six Identical Faces or Square Sides; i.e., a Regular Hexahedron:** cube,n. (cubic,adj.)
14. **Shaped Like a Cube:** cube-shaped, cubic, cubical,adj. (cubicalness,n.)
15. **Roughly or Approximately Shaped Like a Cube:** cuboid,adj.
16. **Geometrical Solid with Ends That Are Parallel Polygons of Equal Size and Identical Shape:** prism,n. (prismatic, prismatical, adj.)
17. **Prism with Six Sides and Faces in the Shape of Parallograms:** parallelepiped, parallelopiped, parallelepipedon,n. (parallelepipedal, parallelepipedic,adj.)

946. MEASUREMENT

1. **To Measure (Something),v.**
   1. **admeasure**—measure; measure off; measure out
   2. **gauge, gage**—measure the quantity, contents, size, force, etc., of; measure accurately, as with a special device or gauge
   3. **meter**—measure, as with a special recording device or meter
   4. **pace off**—measure (distance, or the distance of a place, room, etc.) by taking regular steps over it
   5. **plumb, plumb line, fathom, sound**—measure (depth) or the depth of (water in the sea, ocean, etc.), by dropping a weighted line to the bottom
   6. **quantify, quantitate**—measure the quantity of
   7. **span**—measure, esp. by, or as if by, means of the outstretched hand
   8. **survey**—determine the measurements, boundaries, extent, etc., of (land)
2. **Measurement; Act or Process of Measuring,n.** *From Sec. 1:* admeasurement or admensuration, meterage, quantification, survey or surveying; *Also:* measure, mensuration,n.
3. **Device for Measuring,n.** *From Sec. 1:* gauge, meter, plumb line; *Also:* measure,n.
4. **Measurable,adj.** *From Sec. 1:* gaugeable or gageable, plumbable or fathomable; quantifiable, quantitative, or quantitive; surveyable (quantitativeness,n.); *Also:*
   1. **commensurable, commeasurable, commensurate**—of two or more things, qualities, etc., measurable by the same unit, measure, standard, number, quantity, etc. (commensurability or commensurableness, commensurateness or commensuration,n.)
   2. **mensurable**—measurable (mensurability, n.)
5. **Not Measurable,adj.** *From Sec. 1:* fathomless or unfathomable, unquantitative, unsurveyable (unfathomableness or unfathomability, n.); *From Sec. 4:* incommensurable, incommensurate, uncommensurable, or uncommensurate; immensurable or unmensurable (incommensurability, incommensurableness, incommensurateness, uncommensurability, or uncommensurableness,n.); *Also:*
   1. **abyssal**—so deep as to be beyond fathoming or measuring—esp. of waters of the ocean, etc.

2. **immeasurable, unmeasurable**—not measurable (immeasurability, immeasurableness, unmeasurableness,n.)
3. **measureless**—not measurable (measurelessness,n.)

6. Figuratively Immeasurable: abyssal, fathomless, immeasurable, infinite, measureless, unfathomable,adj. (immeasurability or immeasurableness, infiniteness, measurelessness, unfathomableness or unfathomability, n.)

7. Figuratively Unmeasured: unfathomed, unplumbed, unsounded,adj.

8. So Large, Great, Extensive, etc., as to Be beyond Measuring: immeasurable, immense, infinite, measureless,adj. (immeasurability or immeasurableness, immensity or immenseness; infiniteness, infinity, or infinitude; measurelessness,n.)

9. Pert. or Relating to Measure or Measurement: mensural, mensurative, mensurational; quantitative or quantitive (of quantity),adj. (quantitativeness,n.)

10. Adapted for Making, or for Being Used in Making, Measurements: mensurative,adj.

11. Art of Measurement: mensuration; stereometry (size and volume of solids); surveying (land),n. (mensurational, stereometric or stereometrical,adj.)

12. Occupation of Determining the Measurements, Boundaries, Extent, etc., of Land: surveying,n. (surveyor,n.)

13. To Determine, Mark, or Correct the Gradations of (a Measuring Instrument): calibrate,v. (calibration,n. calibrator,n.)

14. To Be of a Certain Measure; To Allow of Measurement: measure,v.

15. To Be Equal in Measure to: commeasure, commensurate,v. (commensuration,n.)

16. To Make Equal in Measure: commensurate,v. (commensuration,n.)

17. Equal in Measure: commeasurable, commensurate, isometric, isometrical,adj.

18. Equality of Measure: commensurateness, commensuration, isometry,n. (isometric, isometrical,adj.)

19. Standard of Measurement: criterion, gauge; mark (as *below the mark,* etc.); measure, norm, standard, touchstone, yardstick,n. (criterional,adj.)

20. System of Measurements Used in Preparing and Dispensing Liquid Drugs: apothecaries' measure,n.

21. Decimal System of Measurements: metric system,n.

22. System of Measurements and Weights: metrology,n. (metrological,adj.)

23. Science of Measurements and Weights: metrology,n. (metrologist,n. metrological, adj.)

24. Essay or Treatise on Measurements and Weights: metrology,n.

25. Standardized Unit of Measurement: module,n. (modular,adj.)

26. Selected Units of Measurement of Length or Distance: inch; foot (12 inches); yard (3 feet); rod (16½ feet); mile or statute mile (5280 feet),n.; *Also:*
1. **agate**—1/14 inch (used in printing)
2. **bolt**—40 yards (in measuring cloth)
3. **cable**—about 600 feet (for measuring cable lengths)
4. **chain**—66 feet (used in surveying)
5. **cubit**—about 18–22 inches (ancient unit of length)
6. **ell, English ell**—1¼ yards (in measuring cloth)
7. **fathom**—6 feet (for water depths and cables)
8. **furlong**—⅛ mile
9. **hand**—4 inches (for measuring the height of a horse from the withers)
10. **league**—about 3 miles
11. **light-year**—5,880,000,000,000 miles, the distance traveled by light in one year (used in astronomy)
12. **link**—1/100 of a chain, 7.92 inches (used in surveying)
13. **mil**—.001 inch (for measuring wire size)
14. **nautical, geographical, or sea mile**—6080.2 feet
15. **pace**—distance covered in a step in walking, usually 2 to 3 feet
16. **parsec**—about 3.26 light-years (used in astronomy)
17. **pica**—⅙ inch (used in printing)
18. **point**—about 1/72 inch (used in printing)
19. **rood**—5½ to 8 rods, depending on locality
20. **span**—9 inches

27. Unit of Measurement of Length in the Metric System, Equal to 39.37 Inches: meter, n. (metric, metrical,adj.)

28. Metric Units of Length or Distance: millimeter (.001 meter); centimeter (.01 meter); decimeter (.1 meter); dekameter or decameter (10 meters); hectometer (100 meters); kilometer (1000 meters),n. (kilometric or kilometrical,adj.); *Also:*
1. **angstrom**—.0001 micron (in measuring length of light waves)
2. **micron**—.001 millimeter (in scientific measurements)
3. **millimicron**—.001 micron

29. Measurement Around (Something), Usually at Its Widest Point: girth,n.

30. Measurement Around (a Circle or Circular Area): circumference,n. (circumferential, adj.)

31. Length of a Line Passing through the Center of a Circle or Other Object and Going from One Side to the Other: diameter,n. (diametric, diametrical,adj.)

32. Length of a Line from the Center of a Circle or Circular Object to the Circumference: radius,n. (radial,adj.)

33. Measurement Around the Outer Boundaries (of an Object or Figure of Two Dimensions, a Place, etc.): perimeter,n. (perimetric, perimetrical,adj.)

34. Measurement in One Direction, as Length, Width, Breadth, etc.: dimension,n. (dimensional,adj.)

35. Having Two Dimensions: bidimensional, adj.

36. Having Three Dimensions: cubic, tridimensional,adj. (tridimensionality,n.)

37. Unit of Square Measurement, Equal to about One Square Rod: rood,n.

38. Unit of Land Measure Equal to 43,560 Square Feet: acre,n.

39. Size or Area in Acres; Acres Collectively: acreage,n.

40. Unit of Land Measure Equal to ¼ Acre, or 40 Square Rods: rood,n.

41. Unit of Land Measure in the Metric System, Equal to 2.471 Acres: hectare or hektare,n.

42. Square Feet within a Plane Surface: area,n. (areal,adj.)

43. Special Terms for Surface Area in the Metric System (Other than Square Meters, Square Millimeters, etc.): centare or centiare (square meter); are (100 square meters); hectare or hektare (10,000 square meters),n.

44. Circular Measure: second; minute (60 seconds); degree (60 minutes),n.

45. Ratio of the Circumference of a Circle to the Diameter, Roughly 3.1416: pi,n.

46. Selected Fluid Units of Measurement: ounce, gill (4 ounces), pint (16 ounces), quart (32 ounces), gallon (4 quarts),n.; *Also:*
  1. barrel—31½ gallons
  2. dram—60 minims or ⅛ ounce
  3. firkin—¼ barrel
  4. flagon—2 quarts
  5. hogshead—2 barrels
  6. jigger—1½ to 2 ounces (esp. in measuring whiskey)
  7. minim—smallest unit of fluid measure, about a drop
  8. pipe—2 hogsheads (esp. in measuring wines)
  9. tun—252 gallons or more (esp. in measuring wines)

47. Two-Quart Bottle (for Wine): magnum, n.

48. Metric System Unit of Capacity, Equal to 1.0567 Quarts Fluid or .9081 Quart Dry: liter,n.

49. Metric Units of Capacity: milliliter (.001 liter); centiliter (.01 liter); deciliter (.1 liter); dekaliter (10 liters); hectoliter (100 liters); kiloliter (1000 liters),n.

50. Measurement, Amount, Contents, or Size (of Something) in Three Dimensions: cubic measure, volume,n. (cubic, cubical,adj.)

51. Measurement by Volume: volumetry,n. (volumetric, volumetrical,adj.)

52. Device to Measure Volume: volumeter,n.

53. To Measure the Cubic Volume of: cube,v.

54. Units of Dry Measure: pint; quart (2 pints); peck (16 pints); bushel (64 pints),n.

55. Descr. of Measures and Weights According to the British System: imperial,adj. (as *imperial quart*, etc.)

947. WEIGHT

1. Weight: avoirdupois (colloq.), gravity, heft (colloq.),n.

2. A Person's Weight: avoirdupois (colloq.), n.

3. Too Much, or Extra, Weight; Greater Weight: overweight,n.

4. Weighing Too Much; Weighing More than Normal or Necessary: overweight,adj.

5. To Be More than in Weight; To Weigh More than: outweigh, overbalance, overweigh,v.

6. Weight That Causes Someone or Something to Fall, Lose Balance, etc.: overbalance,n.

7. Equality or Equivalence of Weight: balance, equipoise; equiponderance, equiponderancy, or equiponderation,n.

8. To Be of Equal Weight: balance, equiponderate,v.

9. To Make Equal in Weight: equiponderate, v.

10. Equal in Weight: balanced, equiponderant,adj.

11. Equal Distribution of Weight: balance, equipoise,n.

12. A Weight Equal to, or That Balances, Another: counterweight,n.

13. A Weight That Serves to Balance Out an Opposing Weight; An Equal Weight Functioning in Opposition: counterbalance, counterpoise, counterweight, equipoise,n.

14. To Act as Such a Weight to: counterbalance, counterpoise, counterweigh or counterweight, equipoise,v.

15. Certain Other Specific Weights,n.
  1. ballast—heavy weight on a vessel or aircraft to furnish stability
  2. bob—hanging weight
  3. pendulum—swinging weight, as in a clock
  4. plumb, plumb bob, plummet—small weight of lead, attached to a line, to determine depth of water, verticality of walls, etc.

16. To Put a Heavy Weight on (a Vessel, Aircraft, etc.) to Furnish Stability: ballast, v.

17. Line and Lead Weight Combined, for Determining Water Depths, Verticality of Walls, etc.: plumb line, plummet,n.

18. To Test the Weight of by Lifting: heft,v.

19. To Weigh (Something) in, or as if in, a Device for This Purpose: balance, scale,v.

20. To Have a Weight of: scale,v.

21. Having Weight; Able to Be Weighed: ponderable,adj. (ponderability,n.)

22. Lacking in Measurable Weight; Incapable of Being Weighed: imponderable,adj. (imponderability, imponderableness,n.)

23. Ratio of Weight or Mass of a Certain Volume of a Substance to That of the Same Volume of Water, if the Substance is a Liquid or Solid; or of Air or Hydrogen, if the Substance is a Gas: specific gravity,n.

24. Determination of the Specific Gravity of a Liquid: hydrometry,n. (hydrometric, hydrometrical,adj.)

25. Device for Determining Specific Gravity: gravimeter or hydrometer (of liquids); oleometer (of oils),n.

26. Measurement of Weight or Density: gravimetry,n. (gravimetric, gravimetrical, adj.)

27. Device for Determining Weight: balance; scale or scales,n.

28. Either Pan or Dish of a Balance: scale,n.

29. The Weight of the Container, Wrapping, Vessel, etc., as Distinguished from Gross Weight; Weight of a Vehicle, Bus, Truck, etc., without Its Passengers or Cargo; Weight of Container, Vehicle, etc., Deducted from Gross Weight to Determine the Weight of the Contents or Cargo; The Deduction so Made: tare,n.

30. To Determine, Mark, or Allow for the Weight of (the Container, Vehicle, etc.): tare,v.

31. System of Weights,n.
  1. apothecaries' weight—system used in mixing and dispensing drugs
  2. avoirdupois, avoirdupois weight—system used for substances other than drugs, gems, or precious metals
  3. metric system—system used in science, and for general purposes in many countries (metric,adj.)
  4. troy, troy weight—system used for gems and precious metals (troy,adj.)

32. Smallest Unit in Apothecaries', Avoirdupois, and Troy Weight: grain,n.

33. Units in Apothecaries' Weight: scruple (20 grains); dram (60 grains or 3 scruples); ounce (480 grains or 8 drams); pound (12 ounces),n.

34. Units in Troy Weight: pennyweight (24 grains), ounce (20 pennyweights), pound (12 ounces),n.

35. Units in Avoirdupois Weight: dram (27.3438 grains), ounce (16 drams), pound (16 ounces), hundredweight or quintal (100 pounds), ton (2000 pounds),n.

36. British Term for Fourteen Pounds Avoirdupois: stone,n.

37. British Hundredweight, 112 Pounds: long hundredweight,n.

38. British Ton, 2240 Pounds: long ton,n.

39. Weight in Terms of Tons; Capacity of a Ship in Terms of Tons; Duty or Tax on Ships Based on Tons Carried; Charge Per Ton on Cargo or Freight: tonnage or tunnage,n.

40. Weight of a Ship's Cargo: burden,n.

41. Standard Unit of Weight in the Metric System, Equal to Approximately ⅛ Ounce Avoirdupois: gram,n.

42. Units of the Metric System of Weights, in Terms of Grams: milligram (.001 gram); centigram (.01 gram); decigram (.1 gram); dekagram (10 grams); hectogram (100 grams); kilogram (1000 grams); quintal (100 kilograms or 100,000 grams); metric ton (1000 kilograms or 1,000,000 grams) ,n.

43. Unit of Weight in Gems, Equal to 200 milligrams, or Approximately 3 Grains Troy: carat,n.

44. One Hundredth of a Carat: point,n.

45. Unit of Weight for Pearls, Equal to ¼ Carat: pearl grain,n.

46. An Ancient Unit of Weight: talent,n.

47. A Boxer, Prize Fighter, Wrestler, etc., in Respect to Weight: flyweight (not over 112 pounds); bantamweight (113–118); featherweight (119–126); lightweight (127–135); welterweight (136–147); middleweight (148–160); light heavyweight (161–175); heavyweight (over 175) ,n.

948. HEAVINESS

1. Heavy,adj.
1. **burdensome**—heavy; extremely or oppressively heavy
2. **cumbersome, cumbrous**—so heavy and big as to be difficult to manage, use, carry, move, etc.; heavy and unwieldy
3. **hefty**—heavy; heavy in appearance; heavy in feel when held or lifted (colloq.)
4. **leaden**—heavy, like lead; as heavy as lead; inertly heavy like, or possessed of the inert heaviness of, lead, and therefore hard to lift, move, etc.
5. **massive**—big and heavy; clumsy and heavy; of great weight
6. **ponderous**—heavy because of size or bulk; clumsy and heavy; of great weight
7. **sodden, soggy**—heavy and moist; heavy because of poor baking or cooking (of bread, cake, food, etc.)
8. **thumping**—heavy (colloq.)
9. **top-heavy**—too heavy at the top; so heavy at the top as to be likely to fall
10. **weighty**—heavy; having great weight

2. Heaviness,n. From Sec. 1: burdensomeness, cumbersomeness, cumbrousness; heft (colloq.); leadenness, massiveness, ponderousness or ponderosity, soddenness, sogginess, topheaviness, weightiness; Also: 1. gravity-heaviness

3. Amount of Heaviness: weight,n.

4. To Become, or Make, Heavy and Moist, or Heavy because of Poor Baking or Cooking: sodden,v.

5. Heavily and Suddenly: plump,adv.

6. One over the Average in Weight: heavyweight,n.

7. To Be Too Heavy for: outweigh, overbalance, overweigh,v.

8. To Be, or Put, a Literal or Figurative Burden, Heavy Burden, or Heavy Weight
Upon: burden, charge, cumber; encumber or incumber (chiefly figurative); lade (chiefly in the past participle laden), load or load down; oppress (figurative); overweigh or overweight (figurative); prey on or upon (i.e., be burdensome upon, esp. fear, anxiety, responsibility, etc.); task (figurative); tax (figurative); weigh down; weigh on or upon (figurative); weight,v. (oppression,n. oppressor,n.)

9. To Burden with Cruel or Unfair Demands, Restrictions, Exercise of Power or Authority, etc.: oppress,v. (oppression,n. oppressor,n.)

10. To Burden with Debt or Legal Obligations: encumber or incumber,v.

11. To Put Too Heavy a Literal or Figurative Burden Upon: overburden; overlade (chiefly in the past participle overladen); overload,v.

12. To Be Too Heavy a Literal or Figurative Burden Upon; To Be Too Burdensome for: outweigh, overbalance, overburden; overlade (figurative, chiefly in the past participle overladen); overload, overweigh, overweight,v.

13. Burdensome,adj.
1. **carking**—burdensome, figuratively (somewhat archaic or poetic)
2. **cumbersome, cumbrous**—burdensome (cumbersomeness, cumbrousness,n.)
3. **heavy**—burdensome (heaviness,n.)
4. **leaden**—oppressive, as the air or atmosphere (leadenness,n.)
5. **onerous**—burdensome and distasteful or unpleasant (onerousness,n.)
6. **oppressive**—burdensome; burdensome and uncomfortable, as heat, etc. (oppressiveness,n.)
7. **overburdensome**—excessively burdensome
8. **weighty**—burdensome (weightiness, weight,n.)

14. A Literal or Figurative Burden,n.
1. **charge**—burden
2. **cumber**—burden (chiefly figurative)
3. **cumbrance, encumbrance, incumbrance**—burden, chiefly figurative; burden of debt or legal obligation
4. **incubus**—burden that seems figuratively to oppress one, or lie on top of one, like a nightmare
5. **load**—burden
6. **millstone**—heavy burden (figurative)
7. **onus**—burden (figurative)
8. **oppression**—burden (figurative); that which figuratively weighs down upon one
9. **overburden**—excessive burden (chiefly figurative)
10. **overload**—excessive burden (chiefly figurative)
11. **plummet**—figurative burden, i.e., something that weighs heavily upon one
12. **responsibility**—burden of obligation or duty
13. **surcharge**—excessive or additional burden, as of cost, load, etc.
14. **tax**—figurative burden, in the nature of duty, obligation, requirement, demand, etc.
15. **weight**—burden (figurative)

15. One Who Carries a Heavy (Chiefly Figurative) Burden, So Called after the God in Greek Mythology Who Supported the World on His Shoulder: Atlas,n.

16. State or Feeling of Being Burdened in Mind, Spirit, or Bodily Powers; State of Being Burdened with Cruel and Unfair Exercise of Power, Authority, etc.: oppression,n.

17. Literally or Figuratively Burdened; Carrying a Heavy Literal or Figurative Burden: cumbered; encumbered or incumbered (chiefly figurative); heavy-laden, laden, loaded, loaded down; oppressed (figurative); overweighed or overweighted (figurative); taxed (figurative); weighed down,adj.

18. Overburdened: overladen, overloaded, overweighed, overweighted,adj.

19. To Free of a Burden: disburden, disencumber, disload, lighten, relieve, unload,v. (disburdenment, disencumberment, relief,n.)

20. To Get Rid of One's or Its Burden: disburden, disload, unload,v.

21. To Make Less Burdensome: lighten,v.

949. LIGHTNESS

1. Light (in Weight, Appearance, etc.),adj.
1. aerial—light as air
2. airy—light as air; light and insubstantial; light in appearance
3. bantam—light in weight
4. ethereal, aethereal—airy; airy and delicate
5. featherweight—light; light and unimportant
6. feathery—light and insubstantial
7. frothy, yeasty—lacking in (figurative) weight, i.e., light as froth or foam
8. lightsome—light in appearance, form, etc.
9. lightweight—light in weight

2. Lightness,n. *From Sec. 1:* airiness, etherealness or ethereality, featheriness, frothiness, yeastiness, lightsomeness; *Also:* 1. levity—lightness of weight

3. One Who Is Lighter than Average in Weight: featherweight, lightweight,n.

4. Less than Normal, Usual, Average, or Required Weight: underweight,adj. (underweight,n.)

5. One Who Is of Average Weight: middleweight,n.

6. Possessed of a Light and Graceful Beauty: aerial, ethereal,adj. (etherealness, ethereality,n.)

7. Light in Movement; Moving Lightly,adj.
1. agile, lightsome, nimble—light and quick in movement
2. airy, lightsome—light, or light and graceful, in movement
3. lambent—moving lightly on or over a surface
4. light-footed, nimble-footed—stepping or walking lightly, or lightly and quickly
5. lively—light and quick in movement, as a step, dance, etc.
6. nimble-stepping—stepping lightly and quickly
7. tripping—moving or proceeding with lightness and ease, lightness and rhythm, etc., as music, dance, step, measure, etc.; light and quick, as a step, movement, dance, etc.
8. volant—light and quick (chiefly poetic)

8. Lightness of, or in, Movement,n. *From Sec. 7:* agility, lightsomeness, or nimbleness; airiness or lightsomeness, lambency, lightfootedness, liveliness; *Also:* 1. legerity—lightness, or lightness and quickness, of movement

9. That Which Moves Lightly on or over a Surface: lambency,n.

10. Having Fingers That Move Lightly and Quickly, or Lightly, Quickly, and Skillfully: light-fingered, nimble-fingered,adj. (light-fingeredness,n.)

11. Having a Light and Delicate or Skillful Touch: light-fingered, light-handed, nimble-fingered,adj. (light-fingeredness, light-handedness,n.)

12. Having or Showing a Light, Graceful, and Brilliant (Figurative) Touch, as Irony, Style of Writing, Humor, etc.; Playing

Gracefully and Lightly over a Subject, as Humor, Wit, etc.: lambent,adj. (lambency,n.)

13. That Which Is Lambent in This Sense: lambency,n.

14. To Make Lighter in Weight: lighten,v.

950. BALANCE

1. Balance; State of Balance: counterbalance, counterpoise, equilibrium, equipoise, equiponderance or equiponderancy, libration, poise,n. (equilibrial,adj.)

2. Balance and Correspondence in Size, Shape, and Relationship of Both Sides: symmetricalness, symmetry,n. (symmetrical, symmetric,adj.)

3. To Make Symmetrical: symmetrize,v. (symmetrization,n.)

4. To Bring into, or Keep in, Balance: balance, counterbalance, counterpoise, equilibrate, equipoise, equiponderate, poise,v. (equilibration, equiponderation,n.)

5. Acting to Bring into, or Keep in, Balance: equilibrative, equilibratory,adj.

6. Balanced; In Balance: counterbalanced, counterpoised, equilibristic, equipoised, equiponderant, poised,adj.

7. To Be in Balance: balance, counterbalance, equilibrate, librate, poise,v. (equilibration, libration,n.)

8. To Be in Balance with: equilibrate,v. (equilibration,n.)

9. To Vibrate Like a Balance before Stopping: librate,v. (libration,n.)

10. Moving to a State of Balance; Moving or Vibrating Like a Balance toward Equilibrium: libratory,adj.

11. One Who Can Balance Himself in Unnatural or Dangerous Poses, Esp. on a Tightrope: equilibrist,n. (equilibristic,adj.)

12. To Act as a Balance against (Some Other Thing, etc.): balance, counterbalance, counterweigh, counterweight; equiponderate (in force, power, weight, importance, etc.); offset, redeem (as *redeeming virtues*, etc.),v.

13. That Which Acts as Such a Balance: balance, counterbalance, counterweight, offset,n.

14. To Balance (One Thing, etc., against Another): balance, counterbalance, offset,v.

15. Science Dealing with Forces in Balance —a Branch of Mechanics: statics,n.

16. Lack of Balance: imbalance, unbalance,n. (imbalanced, unbalanced,adj.)

17. To Cause a Loss of Balance to; To Make Unbalanced: unbalance,v.

18. Not Balanced and Corresponding in Size, Shape, and Relationship of Both Sides: asymmetric, asymmetrical, disproportional, disproportionate, dissymmetric, dissymmetrical, imbalanced, unbalanced, unsymmetric, unsymmetrical,adj. (asymmetry, disproportion, disproportionateness, dissymmetry, imbalance, unbalance, unsymmetricalness, unsymmetry,n.)

951. SHOW

1. To Show (Something, Some Quality, etc.),v.
1. adumbrate—indicate, esp. in advance; indicate in some vague, obscure, or incomplete manner
2. advertise—show in such a way as to attract attention to
3. argue—show or indicate, or show or give evidence or indication of (a quality, attri-

bute, etc., as *an attitude that argues fear,*
gift that argues generosity, etc.)

4. **attest, attest to**—show plainly or clearly,
or give indication or evidence of (a quality, attribute, emotion, etc.)

5. **augur, augur of**—indicate as a probable
result or outcome; be a sign or indication
of

6. **bare, lay bare**—show (that which has
been secret or covered, or kept secret or
covered, whether an actual thing or a
quality, feeling, attribute, etc.)

7. **betoken, bespeak, token**—show, indicate,
or give signs or indications of (a quality,
etc.)

8. **betray**—show or reveal without meaning
to, as a secret, etc.; show or reveal (that
which was not at first evident, as a quality, feeling, etc.)

9. **blaze, blazon**—show conspicuously, brilliantly, or vividly

10. **demonstrate**—show openly or plainly
(esp. a feeling or attribute, etc.); show
in public; show the workings of (a device,
etc.)

11. **denote**—be an indication of (attributes,
qualities, etc.)

12. **designate**—show; indicate; point out

13. **develop**—disclose or reveal, usually gradually

14. **disclose**—show; make known by showing
or revealing; expose to the sight

15. **display**—show; show publicly or to the
public; show or betray (a feeling, quality,
attribute, etc.); show in such a way as
to attract attention to; show off

16. **emblazon, emblaze**—show or display
brilliantly

17. **evidence**—show plainly or clearly (a
quality, emotion, attribute, etc.)

18. **evince**—show plainly or clearly (a quality,
emotion, attribute, etc.); show the possession of (such a quality, etc.)

19. **exemplify**—show by example

20. **exhibit**—show publicly; show by outward
signs (as a quality, emotion, attribute,
etc.); show to view; put (art, etc.) on
show

21. **expose**—show or reveal (that which has
been kept secret or what someone has
kept or wishes to be kept secret); show
(what has been covered or is usually
covered); show to view; show publicly;
show the faults of; bare

22. **feature**—give special space, display, or
prominence to, as in a newspaper, magazine, store, etc.

23. **flaunt**—show boastfully, arrogantly,
offensively, or in order to gain notice or
attention

24. **flourish**—show (something) conspicuously by waving it; show boastfully,
ostentatiously, etc., as one's possessions,
wealth, honors, etc.

25. **indicate**—show; show in general; point
out; show, usually by symptoms, the presence of (a disease); show (a remedy,
medicine, etc.) to be proper for treatment; be a sign of

26. **lay open**—expose

27. **manifest**—show plainly or clearly (a
quality, emotion, attribute, etc.) to the
eye or understanding; be a clear indication or evidence of

28. **mark**—show a person to be; indicate by,
or as if by, marks

29. **mirror, image, reflect**—show an image or
likeness of

30. **open to view**—show to the sight; show
publicly

31. **parade**—show ostentatiously, conceitedly,
or pompously (one's possessions, qualities,
attributes, emotions, etc.)

32. **picture**—show to the sight in, or as if
in, a picture

33. **point out**—show; show in such a way as
to call attention to

34. **present**—show; show publicly or to the
public; show (oneself) to another, or at
a certain place or time

35. **preview**—show (to someone) before showing to the general public, as a stage performance, motion picture, etc.

36. **reflect**—show (the ideas, opinions, etc.)
of another

37. **represent**—show to the mind; show an
image or likeness of, as a picture, drawing, etc.; be a sign of; denote

38. **reveal**—show or show publicly (that
which previously had been covered, secret,
concealed, etc.); show by, or as if by,
drawing the cover from; expose to view;
display

39. **show off**—show conceitedly or ostentatiously

40. **show up**—show to the sight; expose (a
fault); expose the faults of

41. **sign**—show by gesture or other visible
indication

42. **signal**—show by gesture or other visible
indication; be an indication of

43. **signalize**—show or indicate especially;
show in such a way as to call attention
to; show conspicuously; indicate by signal
or signals

44. **signify**—show by a sign; be a sign of

45. **spread**—display fully; lay out (merchandise, etc.) in display

46. **stage**—show publicly in, or as if in, a
theater

47. **suggest**—show indirectly, faintly, or
slightly

48. **symbolize**—serve as, or be, a sign, token,
or indication of

49. **symptomatize**—be an indication of; be
indicative of

50. **testify, testify to**—be or give a sign of;
indicate (a quality, attribute, feeling,
etc.)

51. **uncloak**—show (that which had been
hidden or kept secret); show the true
character of

52. **uncover, uncurtain, unshroud, unthatch**
—show or reveal (that which had been
hidden or kept secret); bare

53. **unfold, unfurl**—show; reveal; show gradually, detail by detail or step by step, as
a plan or idea, etc.

54. **unmask**—reveal (that which had been
hidden, disguised, kept secret, etc.); expose the true character of

55. **unroll**—show; display; spread forth so
that people may see

56. **unveil**—show to view; reveal; disclose

2. Show, i.e., a Showing or Act of Showing,
n. *From Sec. 1:* adumbration, advertisement,
attestation, betrayal, blazonment, demonstration, denotation, designation, development,
disclosure, display, emblazonment, exemplification, exhibition or exhibit, exposure or exposal, flaunt, indication, manifestation, presentation, reflection, representation, revealment or revelation, show-off, signification,
suggestion, symbolization, unveilment

**3. Show; Display; A Show; That Which Is
Shown,** n. *From Sec. 1:* blazonry, demonstration, disclosure, display, emblazonry or emblazonment, exhibit or exhibition, flourish,
image or reflection, parade, presentation, preview or, esp. in reference to motion pictures,
prevue, reflection, representation, revelation,
spread; *Also:*

1. **array, arrayal**—impressive display of
people or things, often in some formal
grouping

2. **blaze**—bright or violent display (of a
quality)

3. **bravura**—display of brilliance or daring

4. **circus**—public traveling exhibition of

trained animal acts, acrobatics, etc.; any public exhibition; display of rowdy or riotous entertainment, sport, frivolity, etc.
5. **dumb show**—display or demonstration with gestures only, i.e., without words (dumb-show,adj.)
6. **exposition**—public exhibition, as of a country's, state's, city's, etc., artistic, commercial, manufacturing, etc., products
7. **fair**—public display or exhibition of agricultural products, animals that have been bred, etc., usually competitive; exhibition (and sale) of other goods and products, often to raise money for charitable purposes
8. **fanfare**—noisy display
9. **farce**—empty show; ludicrous show (farcial, farcical,adj.)
10. **flash**—sudden display (of emotion, as delight etc., humor, or other attribute), not lasting very long
11. **frippery**—empty show
12. **gesture**—indication or demonstration, as by words or action, intended to show a feeling, attitude, or purpose, or such an indication or demonstration made for effect, as *a gesture of devotion, friendship*, etc.
13. **gloss, varnish**—outside or external show; mere show
14. **mummery, puppetry**—empty or pretentious display, as in ceremony, performance, etc.
15. **pageant**—empty or specious display; mere show; elaborate or spectacular exhibition (pageantry, collective n.)
16. **pageantry**—spectacular, gorgeous, or splendid display; empty or specious display
17. **panorama**—comprehensive presentation of a subject or field of knowledge (panoramic,adj.)
18. **pomp**—brilliant, impressive, magnificent, or splendid display; vain or empty display
19. **pyrotechnics, fireworks**—fiery or dazzling display, figuratively, as of emotion, passion, eloquence, wit, etc.
20. **riot**—brilliant or vivid display, as of color, etc.
21. **scene**—display of excited or violent feelings in public or in front of others
22. **spectacle**—public display; public show on a grand scale (spectacular,adj.)
23. **vainglory**—empty show (vainglorious, adj.)
24. **veneer**—pleasing but not genuine show

4. That Which Shows; A Sign, Indicator or Indication, etc.,n. *From Sec. 1:* attestation, augury, betokener or token, betrayer, demonstrator, denotation, designator, discloser, evidence, exemplification or exemplifier; indication, indicant, or indicator; manifestation, marker or mark, mirror or reflector, revealer, sign, signal, signifier, suggestion, symbol, symptom, testimony (from *testify*); *From Sec. 3:* gesture; *Also:*
1. **auspice**—sign; sign (esp. favorable sign) as to the future or outcome (auspicial, adj.)
2. **badge**—external sign; sign or device of office, achievement, membership, etc.; emblem (badge,v.)
3. **banner**—something indicating or displayed to indicate belief in principles, as *banner of courage*, etc.
4. **bar sinister**—sign of bastard birth or lineage (popular but erroneous usage)
5. **baton, bend sinister, bar sinister**—heraldic sign of bastard birth or lineage
6. **brassard**—badge or emblem worn on the upper arm
7. **coronet**—insigne worn on the head by members of the nobility

8. **earmark**—sign; identifying sign (earmark,v.)
9. **earnest**—something that indicates what is to follow
10. **emblem**—sign; visible sign of a thing, class of people, idea, class of ideas, etc.; badge (emblematic, emblematical,adj.)
11. **ensign**—sign or token; badge or emblem of office, rank, or authority; emblem
12. **hallmark**—special mark or indication of worth, quality, value, genuineness, etc.
13. **index**—sign, indication, or token (of an attribute, quality, etc.); something used to point out or indicate
14. **indicium**—sign; characteristic sign or indication (indicia,pl.n., more commonly used than the singular)
15. **insigne**—distinguishing sign, badge, or emblem of one's state, condition, profession, military, naval, or other rank, etc. (insignia,pl.n.—this plural erroneously, but popularly, used for the singular)
16. **label, ticket**—indication, as a slip of paper, etc., to show contents, size, group, etc., or as a word to show class of people, political party, or other group (label, ticket,v.)
17. **mark**—sign; identifying sign; indication; token; visible or other sign taken on oneself, accruing to one, or imposed on one, as *the marks of an educated man, mark of infamy,* etc.; sign (usually a cross) made by an illiterate person who cannot write his name; sign that indicates position, as a *page mark* (mark,v.)
18. **omen**—sign; sign of good or bad luck to follow; sign of what is to follow
19. **pledge**—something accepted as a sign or token of some other thing
20. **preamble**—happening, fact, or circumstance that indicates what is to follow, or what will probably follow, as *preamble to war,* etc.
21. **prognostic**—sign; indication
22. **shingle**—sign, often in the form of a plaque, placed outside the office of a professional man, as a doctor, lawyer, architect, etc.
23. **symbol**—sign; token; emblem (symbolic, symbolical,adj.)
24. **symptom**—sign or indication (of something); sign or indication of the presence of disease (symptomatic, symptomatical, adj.)
25. **telltale**—sign; indication; sign or indication of something kept secret; indicating device
26. **token**—visible sign (of a quality, emotion, attribute, etc.); sign of friendship; characteristic sign or indication
27. **trace, vestige**—sign, indication, or remaining evidence of former presence, existence, or action of something, or of some quality, attribute, etc. (vestigial, adj.)

5. Showing; Indicating; Tending, Serving, or Acting to Show or Indicate,adj. *From Sec. 1:* adumbrating, advertising, etc.; adumbrative, augural, token, demonstrative, denotative, designative, evidential or evidentiary, evincive, exemplificative, exhibitive or exhibitory, flaunty, indicative, indicant, or indicatory; manifestative, reflective, representative, revelative or revelatory, significant or significative, suggestive; *Also:*
1. **apocalyptic, apocalyptical**—conveying or giving a revelation
2. **auspicious, auspicial**—containing or affording indications or signs of probable success (auspiciousness,n.)
3. **inauspicious**—containing or affording indications or signs of probable failure
4. **ostensive**—showing; exhibiting; revealing
5. **symptomatic, symptomatical (of)**—indicative (of)

6. telltale—showing or revealing what was intended to be, or to be kept, secret, as *a telltale blush, stammer, slip of the tongue*, etc.

6. Capable of Being Shown,adj. *From Sec. 1:* demonstrable, displayable, evincible, exhibitable, picturable, presentable, representable, revealable

7. As a Sign, Indication, or Evidence of: in token of

8. Something That Is a Token of Victory, Triumph, Skill, Bravery, etc.: trophy,n.

9. Distinguishing Signs, Badges, Emblems, etc., of Royalty, or of Any Office, Association, Rank, etc.: regalia,n.

10. One Who Designs or Produces Emblems: emblematist,n.

11. Study of Emblems; Description of Emblems: emblematology,n.

12. Pert. to Signs; Pert. to the Language or Meaning of Signs: semiotic, semiotical, semeiotic, or semeiotical,adj.

13. Science of Signs; Art of Signs; Art of Using Signs, as in Signaling, Expressing Ideas, etc.; **Sign Language:** semiology or semeiology,n. (semiologist or semeiologist,n. semiologic, semiological, semeiologic, or semeiological,adj.)

14. Description or Analysis, from a Scientific Viewpoint, of Signs: semigraphy or semeiography,n.

15. Art of Expressing Thought by Signs Made with the Fingers: dactylology,n.

16. An Item in a Public Exhibition: exhibit, n.

17. To Make a Public Show of Feelings or Sentiments, as by Meetings, Parades, Concerted Action to Gain Attention, etc.: demonstrate,v. (demonstrator, demonstrationist, demonstrant,n. demonstrational,adj. demonstration,n.)

18. To Make a Public Show of Military Might, Equipment, etc., **as a Nation,** etc.: demonstrate,v. (demonstration,n. demonstrational,adj.)

19. To Make a Public Demonstration for Political Effect or Purposes: manifest,v. (manifestation,n. manifestant,n.)

20. An Exposure or Revealment of Some Secret, Sinister, Wicked, Criminal or Otherwise Discreditable Act, Circumstance, Plan, etc., **of Another or Others:** exposé,n.

21. To Expose Corruption in Public, Political, or Business Life or Affairs, Esp. by Writing or Publishing Accounts to This End: muckrake,v. (muckraking,n. muckraker, n.)

22. To Show or Indicate Suppressed Feeling, Esp. One of Righteous Anger or Indignation, as the Eyes, etc.: smolder, smoulder,v.

23. To Make a Sudden Display, as of Anger, Joy, Humor, etc., **as the Eyes:** flash,v. (colloq.)

24. To Show Itself Suddenly or Unexpectedly: crop out, crop up,v.

25. To Show One's True Character, Intentions, Plans, Purposes, etc., **Usually by Accident:** betray oneself,v. (self-betrayal,n. self-betrayed,adj. self-betraying,adj.)

26. To Be Shown, Disclosed, or Revealed: develop; unfold (as a plot, plan, etc.); unroll (as a plot, story, etc.),v.

27. Indicated in Some Way Other than by Words or Verbal Expression, as Agreement, Approval, etc.: tacit,adj. (tacitness,n.)

28. Place for Showing, or Where a Show, etc., **Is Given,**n.

1. botanical gardens—place where plants, flowers, etc., are exhibited

2. circus—place for the exhibition of trained-animal acts, acrobatics, etc.

3. fairground, fairgrounds—place where an exhibition of farm products or other products sold for charitable or other purposes is held and occasionally including various amusements, entertainments, etc.

4. menagerie—place where wild or strange animals are exhibited

5. museum—place where things of interest are exhibited, esp. works of art, scientific specimens, etc.

6. salon—place where works of art are exhibited

7. theater—place for the presentation of plays, motion pictures, lectures, etc.

8. waxworks—place where wax figures of famous or notorious people, or other wax figures or ornaments, are exhibited

9. zoo, zoological gardens—place where wild animals are kept on exhibition

29. Famous Paris Museum of Art: Louvre,n.

30. Famous London Waxworks: Madame Tussaud's,n.

31. Pathological Tendency to Show One's Intimate Bodily Members or Organs in Public; Excessive Tendency to Show Off One's Skill, Ability, Accomplishments, Intimate Affairs, etc.—**In Either Case for the Purpose, Conscious or Unconscious, of Gaining Attention:** exhibitionism,n. (exhibitionist,n. exhibitionistic,adj.)

32. To Make a Conceited or Ostentatious Show of One's Abilities, Skill, Accomplishments, Possessions, etc.: flaunt, prank, show off; splurge (colloq.); spread oneself (colloq.); swagger, swank, swash,v. (show-off,n. flaunter, show-off, splurger, swaggerer,n.)

33. To Walk Up and Down in a Public Place to Show Off, or to Show Oneself: parade,v. (parader,n.)

34. Showy: dashing, dashy, flamboyant, flashy, flatulent, flaunty, gay, glittery, grandiose, jaunty; loud (colloq.); ostentatious, pretentious; splashy (colloq.); sporty (as clothes, etc.); swank or swanky (colloq.); theatrical or stagy, tinsel,adj.; *Also:*
1. **brummagen, trumpery**—showy but valueless or of little or inferior quality
2. **fussy**—showy, i.e., full of showy details or adornments
3. **garish**—showy in an excessively and unpleasantly bright or harshly glaring fashion; excessively or crudely showy
4. **gewgaw, gimcrack**—showy and worthless
5. **spectacular**—making a bright show or eye-catching display

35. Showiness,n. *From Sec. 34:* dash, flamboyance or flamboyancy, flashiness, flatulence or flatulency, flauntiness; gayness, gaiety, or gayety; glitter, grandiosity, jauntiness, loudness, ostentatiousness or ostentation; pretentiousness, pretension, or pretense; sportiness, swankiness or swank; theatricality, theatricalism, or staginess; tinsel, fussiness, garishness

36. Anything That Is, or Things That Are, Showy,n. *From Sec. 34:* tinsel; brummagem, trumpery, gewgaw, gimcrack; *Also:*
1. **catchpenny**—something for sale that is cheap and showy but of no intrinsic value
2. **gaudery**—showy things
3. **peddlery**—anything that is, or things that are, showy but worthless or of inferior quality

37. To Be Showy and Colorful: glitter,v.

38. Characteristic or Descr. of a Showiness That Results from Someone's Exaggerated Self-Importance or Fondness for Ceremony,

Excessive Formality, etc.; **Characteristic or Descr. of Such a Person:** grandiose; highfalutin, hifalutin, or highfaluting (colloq.); pompous, pretentious, stilted, toplofty (colloq.), vainglorious,adj. (grandiosity, pompousness or pomposity; pretentiousness, pretension, or pretense; toploftiness, vaingloriousness or vainglory,n.)

39. Pretentious Person of Low Standards or Tastes: vulgarian,n.

40. Showy or Ostentatious Display; Display Intended to Impress Others: dash, display, fanfare, flash, flaunt, frippery, gaudery; mummery (esp. in ceremony or performance); ostentation, pageant, pageantry, parade, pomp, pretension or pretense, show, splash, splurge, swagger, swank, swash, tinsel, vainglory,n.

41. Cheaply or Vulgarly Showy: catchpenny, flashy, gaudy, meretricious, raffish; sporty (colloq.); tawdry; tinhorn (colloq. or slang); tinsel,adj.

42. Cheap or Vulgar Showiness: flashiness, gaudiness, meretriciousness, raffishness; sportiness (colloq.); tawdriness, tinsel, tinselry,n.

43. Cheaply or Vulgarly Showy Person: tinhorn,n. (colloq. or slang)

44. To Make Showy, Esp. in a Glittering Way: gloss, tinsel, varnish,v.

45. Ostentatiously Stylish: swank or swanky (colloq.),adj. (swank, swankiness,n.)

46. Showy Ornaments: finery, frippery, gaudery, regalia,n.

47. Making a Fine Show: brave,adj.

48. Showy—of Language, Expression, Style of Writing or Discourse, i.e., Full of Excessive Figures of Speech or Other Blatant or Conspicuous Ornamentation: bombastic or bombastical, Corinthian, embellished, flamboyant, florid, flowery, grandiose, inflated, luxuriant, ornamented, ornate, orotund, plethoric, purple, rhetorical, stilted, turgid, adj. (bombast, embellishment, flamboyance or flamboyancy, floridity or floridness, floweriness, grandiosity, luxuriance or luxuriancy, inflatedness, ornateness, orotundity, purpleness, turgidity or turgidness,n.)

49. Ostentatiously Lofty or Dignified—of Language, Style, etc.; Descr. of Language, Style, etc., Characterized by Showy Loftiness or Grandeur: bombastic, grandiose; highfalutin, hifalutin, or highfaluting (colloq.); high-flown, high-sounding, inflated, pompous, pretentious, stilted, swollen; toplofty (colloq.); turgid,adj. (bombast, grandiosity, inflatedness, pomposity or pompousness, pretentiousness or pretension, toploftiness, turgidity or turgidness,n.)

50. Someone or Something That Is Hardly More than Mere Show: idol, phantom,n. (phantom,adj.)

952. CONSPICUOUSNESS

1. Conspicuous: apparent, arresting, bold, clear, evident, eye-catching; glaring (esp. of something bad, wrong, unpleasant, etc.); manifest, marked, noticeable, observable, obtrusive, obvious, outstanding, pointed, prominent, pronounced, protrusive, remarkable, salient, signal, striking, visible,adj.; *Also:*
 1. blatant—conspicuous to the point of being offensive
 2. in relief, in bold relief, etc.—conspicuous or prominent because of contrast

2. Conspicuousness; Conspicuity,n. *From Sec. 1:* apparentness, boldness, clearness, evidentness, glaringness, manifestness, marked-

ness, noticeability, observableness or observability, obtrusiveness, obviousness, outstandingness, pointedness, prominence, protrusiveness, remarkability or remarkableness, salience or saliency, visibility or visibleness; blatancy, relief

3. To Make Conspicuous: advertise, blaze, feature, mark, point up, show up, signalize,v.

4. To Be Conspicuous: call attention to oneself or itself, obtrude, show up, stand out, strike the eye,v.

5. Calling for Notice or Attention: crying, adj.

6. Attracting Attention because Mildly Strange or Unusual: curious,adj. (curiousness, curiosity,n.)

7. That Which So Attracts Attention: curiosity,n.

8. Most Conspicuous: predominant, preeminent,adj. (predominance or predominancy, pre-eminence,n.)

9. Not Conspicuous: inapparent, inconspicuous, inevident, inobservable, inobtrusive, inobvious, obscure, unapparent, unarresting, unclear, unevident, unmarked, unnoticeable, unobservable, unobtrusive, unobvious, unpointed, unpronounced, unprotrusive, unremarkable, unstriking,adj. (inconspicuousness, inevidence, inobtrusiveness, obscurity or obscureness, unapparentness, unclearness, unnoticeableness, unobtrusiveness,n.)

10. Position of Little Notice: background,n.

953. REPRESENTATION

1. To Represent,v.
 1. delineate—represent by picture or pictures; represent accurately (delineation, n. delineator,n. delineative,adj.)
 2. depict, depicture, feature—represent by painting, picture, or words, usually with great vividness of detail (depiction, depicture,n. depicter, depictor,n. depictive, adj.)
 3. feature—represent the features of by picture or pictures
 4. limn—represent by means of, or in, painting, drawing, or other art
 5. picture, depicture—represent visually
 6. portray—represent by drawing, painting, or other form of art, or in words (portrayal or portraiture,n. portrayer,n.)
 7. present—represent on the stage (presentation,n. presenter,n. presentational,adj.)
 8. stage—represent in, or as if in, a theater
 9. symbolize—represent by a symbol or symbols, type, model, etc. (symbolization, n.)
 10. typify—represent by a symbol, type, model, etc. (typification,n. typifier,n.)

2. To Represent by an Emblem: emblematize,v.

3. To Represent Beforehand by a Figure, Type, Symbol, Model, etc.: prefigure, pretypify, typify,v. (prefiguration or prefigurement, typification,n. prefigurativeness,n. prefigurative,adj.)

4. To Represent Unfairly or Inaccurately: contort, distort, misrepresent, pervert, skew, twist,v. (contortion, distortion, misrepresentation, perversion, twist,n. contortionist, distorter or distortionist, misrepresenter, perverter, twister,n. contortive or contorsive, distortive, misrepresentative, perversive,adj. contortional, contortionist, or contortionistic; distortional,adj.)

5. To Give a Vague Representation of: adumbrate,v. (adumbration,n. adumbrative, adj.)

6. A Representation of Words or Syllables by Pictures: rebus,n.

7. Representation by People Posing in Costume: tableau; tableau vivant (French),n.

8. A Representation (of Someone or Something) Made by Drawing, Photography, Painting, etc.: picture,n.

9. A Physical Representation (of an Abstract Idea, Quality, etc.): phantom,n.

10. Symbolic Representation: iconology, symbolism,n.

954. SYMBOLISM

1. Symbol,n.
1. badge—symbol; identifying symbol
2. calathus—symbol of productivity or fertility, after the basket filled with fruits and usually carried on the head in ancient Greece
3. cryptogram, cryptograph—symbolic figure with a secret, mysterious, or hidden meaning (cryptogrammic,adj.)
4. denotation—symbol
5. emblem—symbol; identifying symbol; visible symbol of an idea, class of ideas, class of people or things, etc. (emblematic, emblematical,adj.)
6. exponent—that which or one who is a symbol (of something)
7. image—symbol; emblem
8. mark—written or printed symbol; indicating or identifying symbol; symbol used to rate, as in school, etc.
9. scepter, sceptre—baton or other rod carried by a ruler as a symbol of his power, rule, authority, etc.
10. sign—conventional or generally accepted symbol
11. swastika—symbol of the Nazi party and Third Reich in Germany before and during World War II
12. token—symbol; identifying or indicating symbol; symbol of friendship, etc.
13. totem—anything regarded by primitive cultures or the American Indians as emblematic of the family, group, clan, etc. (totemic,adj.)
14. zoomorph—symbol of a god or supernatural being in animal form (zoomorphic,adj.)

2. To Symbolize, i.e., Be a Symbol of: betoken, denote, emblematize, image, represent, stand for, symbol, token, typify,v. (denotation, representation, typification,n.)

3. Symbolic; Symbolical: denotative, emblematic or emblematical, representative, symbolistic, typical or typic,adj.

4. Symbolicalness: emblematicalness, symbolism, typicalness,n.

5. Spiritually Symbolic: mystic, mystical, adj. (mysticity, mysticalness,n.)

6. To Treat as, or Consider, Symbolic: symbolize,v. (symbolization,n.)

7. To Use Symbols: symbolize,v. (symbolizaiton or symbolism,n. symbolist,n. symbolistic, adj.)

8. To Show by Symbol or Symbols: emblematize, represent, symbolize,v. (representation, symbolization or symbolism,n. symbolistic,adj.)

9. Practice of Showing by Symbols: symbolism,n. (symbolist,n. symbolistic,adj.)

10. System of Symbols; Group of Symbols: symbolism,n. (symbolistic,adj.)

11. The Use of Symbols: iconology, representation, symbolism, symbology,n. (symbolist, symbologist,n. symbolistic, symbological,adj.)

12. Study of Symbols; Interpretation of Symbols; Art of Using Symbols to Express Ideas: symbology,n. (symbologist,n. symbological,adj.)

13. Symbolic Meaning: symbolism,n. (symbolistic,adj.)

14. Writer or Artist Whose Work Is Symbolic in Character: symbolist,n. (symbolistic,adj.)

15. Group of Such Writers or Artists: symbolism,n.

16. Principles, Theories, or Practices of Such Writers or Artists: symbolism,n.

17. Excessive Use of Symbolism; Worship of Symbols or Symbolism: symbolatry,n.

18. Symbolic Writing: symbolography,n. (symbolographist,n.)

19. Use of Totems; Belief in Totems; Fact of Having Totems: totemism,n. (totemist,n. totemistic or totemic,adj.)

20. The Act or Process of Developing or Adopting Totems: totemization,n.

21. Post, Column, etc., Carved and Painted with Symbols or Representations of Totems: totem pole, totem post,n.

22. Symbolism by Means of Animal Forms: zoomorphism, zoomorphy,n.

23. To Symbolize (a God or Supernatural Being) as an Animal or in Animal Form: zoomorphize,v. (zoomorphism, zoomorphy,n.)

955. SYMPTOM

1. Medical Symptom That Is a Warning of an Imminent Condition or Disease: prodrome,n. (prodromal,adj.)

2. Combination of Related Medical Symptoms Characteristic of a Disease: syndrome, n. (syndromic,adj.)

3. Combination of Related Symptoms (Chiefly Deafness, Dizziness, Nausea, Vomiting, Oscillation of Eyeballs, and Imaginary Hissing or Ringing in the Ears) Characteristic of a Disease of the Middle or Internal Ear: Ménière's syndrome,n.

4. The Medical Symptoms, Collectively, of a Disease: symptomatology,n. (symptomatological,adj.)

5. Scientific Description of the Medical Symptoms of Disease: semiography or semeiography,n.

6. To Act as a Symptom of; To Be a Medical Symptom of: symptomatize,v.

7. Pert. to the Period of a Disease before the Appearance of Recognized Symptoms Permitting Diagnosis: preclinical,adj.

8. Having Medical Symptoms That Periodically Increase and Decrease in Severity: stormy,adj.

9. Pert. to Medical Symptoms: semiotic, semiotical, semeiotic, or semeiotical; symptomatic or symptomatical,adj.

10. Of the Nature of, Attended by, Being, According to, etc., a Medical Symptom or Symptoms: symptomatic, symptomatical, adj.

11. Pert. to the Symptoms and Course of a Disease as Observed by a Doctor: clinical, adj.

12. Branch of Medicine Dealing with Symptoms: semiology or semeiology, semiotics or semeiotics, symptomatics, symptomatology,n. (semiologist or semeiologist,n. semiologic, semiological, semeiologic, or semeiological; symptomatological,adj.)

956. SIGNAL

1. Signal,n.

1. **alarm**—warning signal; sound or shout that signals approaching peril; signal to rouse from sleep; signal to gain attention
2. **beacon**—signal; signal fire or light; warning or guiding signal
3. **beckon, beck**—summoning signal or gesture
4. **countersign**—secret signal or password to be given in order to pass a sentry or on challenge by a guard
5. **curfew**—signal of some kind for children to come off the streets and go home; signal that people are to leave the streets and stay indoors after a certain hour
6. **foghorn**—warning signal, made on a horn, in foggy weather (on ships, etc.)
7. **gesture, high sign**—signal made with the hands, arms, head, etc.
8. **heliogram**—signal, or message, sent by a device that flashes beams of light by means of a movable mirror
9. **reveille**—signal to waken, made by a drum or bugle, etc., in the army, camp, etc.
10. **sign**—signal made by gesturing
11. **taps**—signal on drum or bugle for lights-out in military or naval quarters, camps, schools, etc.
12. **tattoo**—signal on drums, fife, bugle, etc., calling soldiers to their quarters
13. **tocsin**—warning signal sounded on a bell or bells
14. **toll**—signal made by striking a bell; such a signal to summon or dismiss
15. **wave**—signal made by shaking something in the air, as the hand, a flag, etc.
16. **wigwag**—signal; signal made by waving one's arms, a flag, a light, etc., in accordance with a code
17. **wink**—signal made by winking the eye

2. To Signal (a Message, etc.),v. *From Sec. 1:* gesture or gesticulate, heliograph, toll, wave, wigwag, wink; *Also:*

1. **flag**—signal with, or as if with, a flag
2. **semaphore**—signal with flags or some special device
3. **signalize**—indicate, announce, etc., by signal or signals

3. To Signal, i.e., Signal to,v. *From Sec. 1:* alarm, beacon, beckon or beck, gesture or gesticulate to or at, sign to, toll, wave at, wigwag at, wink at; *From Sec. 2:* flag, semaphore, signalize; *Also:* **1. whistle at or to**—signal to by blowing breath audibly through the pursed lips or by using some acoustical device

4. To Signal, i.e., Engage in Signaling; To Make Signals,v. *From Sec. 1:* beacon, beckon or beck, gesture or gesticulate, heliograph, sign, toll, wave, wigwag, wink; *From Sec. 2:* semaphore; *From Sec. 3:* whistle

5. Signalment, i.e., Act of Signaling,n. *From Sec. 1:* beckon, gesture or gesticulation, toll, wave, wigwag, wink (gesticulatory or gesticulative,adj.)

6. Signaler, i.e., Signaling Device,n. *From Sec. 1:* alarm, beacon, foghorn, heliograph, tocsin (heliographic,adj.); *From Sec. 2:* flag, semaphore (semaphoric or semaphorical, adj.); *From Sec. 3:* whistle; *Also:*

1. **Angelus, angelus**—bell rung to signal the time for the Angelus, a prayer to observe the Annunciation (Roman Catholic religion)
2. **blinker**—device for flashing light signals
3. **signal smoke**—smoke from a fire used to signal
4. **signal tower**—tower from which signals are displayed

5. **siren**—device used to give sound signals, often of warning

7. Signaler, Signalman, or Signalist, i.e., One Who Signals,n. *From Sec. 1:* beckoner, gesturer or gesticulator, heliographer, waver, wigwagger, winker; *From Sec. 2:* flagger, semaphorist; *From Sec. 3:* whistler

8. System of Signals: code,n.

9. System of Signaling by Flags: semaphore, n.

10. System, Occupation, Practice, or Art of Signaling with a Heliograph: heliography,n. (heliographer,n. heliographic, heliographical, adj.)

11. System of Dots, Dashes, etc., Used in Signaling, Telegraphy, etc.: Morse code or Morse alphabet,n. (Morse,adj.)

12. System of Marine Signaling by Flags, Used by All Leading Nations: International Code,n.

957. FLAG

1. Flag,n.

1. **banderole, banderol, bannerol**—small flag or streamer, generally tied on a lance, flown from a masthead, etc.; square banner carried at the funeral of a famous person and placed over his tomb
2. **banner**—nation's flag; flag of an army or other group; flag bearing some inscription, etc., and carried in parades; piece of cloth on a staff, etc., used formerly as the personal flag of a ruler, knight, lord, etc.
3. **banneret, bannerette**—small banner
4. **blue peter**—blue nautical flag containing a white square in the center, and used as a signal
5. **burgee**—flag or pennant of swallow-tailed shape, used on ships
6. **colors**—flag, as of a country, military group, ship, etc.
7. **ensign**—flag, esp. of a nation; banner; military or naval banner
8. **gonfalon**—flag or banner hanging from a crosspiece or crossbar, sometimes having a number of tails or streamers; flag of the Italian republics in medieval times
9. **guidon**—identification flag of a United States military group; small military flag used for guiding, identification, or signaling
10. **jack**—small flag used by a ship as a signal
11. **oriflamme**—standard; ensign; battle standard; red military ensign of the early kings of France
12. **pennant**—long, narrow, usually triangular flag, used on ships, esp. for signaling; school or college banner, esp. one symbolizing victory or hope of victory, in an athletic contest
13. **pennon**—flag; banner; pennant; flag once flown on the lance of a knight or used by a regiment of lancers
14. **standard**—flag; personal flag of the ruler of a nation; flag that is an emblem of a nation, group, etc.; flag raised on a pole, etc., to indicate a rallying point, as for soldiers, etc.
15. **streamer**—narrow and long flag or pennant
16. **union jack**—flag containing as a device only an emblem of union

2. One Who Carries the Flag,n. *From Sec. 1:* gonfalonier, guidon or guidon bearer, standard bearer

3. U. S. Flag: Old Glory; the Red, White, and Blue; the Star-Spangled Banner; the Stars and Stripes,n.

4. Flag of the Confederate States of America: the Stars and Bars,n.

5. The British Flag: Union Jack,n.

6. The French Flag: tricolor,n.

7. Flags Collectively; Flags of a Ship: bunting,n.

8. Cloth Used for Flags; Flag Material Used to Decorate Buildings, as on Holidays, etc.: bunting,n.

9. To Decorate with Flags or Bunting; To Put a Flag on: flag,v.

10. To Trap (Game, etc.) by Waving a Flag: flag,v.

11. White Cloth, etc., Used to Signal a Desire to Surrender to, or for a Discussion with, the Enemy: flag of truce, white flag,n.

12. To Lower the Flag: strike the flag

13. Position of a Flag Halfway Down its Pole as a Token of Mourning or Trouble: half-mast,n.

14. To Place (a Flag) Thus: half-mast,v.

15. The Flag Flown in Reverse, a Signal of Trouble at Sea: union down

16. Pole on Which a Flag is Hung or Flown: flagpole, flagstaff,n.

17. Device on a Flag, a Symbol of Unity: union,n.

18. Descr. of Flags or Other Things Ending in Deeply Forked Points: swallow-tailed,adj.

958. STICK OUT

1. To Stick Out: beetle, bulge, extrude, jut or jut out, project, protrude, protuberate, push out, stand out, stretch out, thrust out,v. (extrusion, projection, protrusion,n.)

2. To Stick Out Over: beetle, overhang,v. (beetle or beetling, overhanging,adj.)

3. To Cause (Something) to Stick Out: bulge, emboss, extrude, jut, outstretch, outthrust, project; protract (anatomy); protrude, push out, stretch out, thrust out,v. (embossment, extrusion, projection, protraction, protrusion,n. extrusive, projective, protractive, protrusive,adj.)

4. Able to Be Stuck Out: projectile (of anatomical members or parts in animals), projective, protractile; protrudable, protrusible, or protrusile,adj.

5. Sticking Out: beetle or beetling; bulging, bulgy, or bulbous; extrusive, jutting or jutting out, outstanding, outstretched, outthrust, projecting or projective, prominent; protruding, protrudent, or protrusive; protuberant, adj. (jut, outthrust, prominence or prominency, protrusiveness, protuberance or protuberancy,n.)

6. Sticking Out Sharply, Irregularly, or Roughly: snaggy,adj.

7. That Which, or Part Which, Sticks Out: bulge, bump, embossment, jut, lump, node, nub, outstanding, overhang, projection, prominence, protrusion, protuberance, spur, tooth,n.; *Also:*
  1. **barb**—sharp projection
  2. **blob**—small lump
  3. **brow**—projecting upper part of something high
  4. **denticle, denticulation, dentation**—small, toothlike projection
  5. **hump, bulge, knob, node, nub**—rounded projection or protuberance (nodal,adj.)
  6. **knot, node**—small projection on a plant (nodal,adj.)
  7. **lobe, lobation**—rounded projection or protuberance; rounded projecting part of something divided; projecting and rounded formation
  8. **nodule**—small node, knot, knob, lump, protuberance, etc. (nodular,adj.)
  9. **nubble, nubbin**—small knot, knob, lump, protuberance, etc.
  10. **pommel, pummel**—rounded knob, as on a saddle, handle of a sword, etc.
  11. **ramus**—part that sticks out like a branch (biology)
  12. **snag**—rough projection
  13. **stud**—protuberance sticking out from a surface or part, esp. as an ornament
  14. **torus**—smooth and round, or rounded, prominence in, on, or of the body (anatomical term)

8. Having, or Full of, Projections, etc.,adj. *From Sec. 7:* bumpy, lumpy, spurred, toothed; barbed; denticulate, denticulated, or dentate; humped, knobbed or knobby, nodose or nodous; lobed, lobate, or lobated; nodular, nodulous, or nodulose; nubbly, snaggy (bumpiness, lumpiness; denticulation or dentation, nodosity,n.)

9. To Stick Up Conspicuously or Prominently: cock,v.

10. To Cause (the Head, Ears, etc.) to Stick Up or Out, Often in a Meaningful, Listening, etc., Manner; To Cause (the Hat, etc.) to Stick Out to One Side in a Jaunty, etc., Manner: cock,v. (cock,n.)

11. The Position of the Head, Ears, Hat, etc., So Stuck Up, Out, or to One Side: cock,n.

12. To Rise in a Rounded Projection or Protuberance; To Raise (the Back) in Such a Projection or Protuberance: hump,v. (hump,n.)

959. ORNAMENTATION

1. To Ornament: adorn, apparel, array, bedeck, blazon, deck, decorate; doll up (colloq.); dress, embellish, emblaze, emblazon, garnish, grace, prank, trim, varnish,v.; *Also:*
  1. **bedaub**—ornament in a flashy or gaudy manner; ornament excessively
  2. **bedizen**—adorn with cheap or gaudy finery
  3. **beset**—set with ornaments
  4. **bespangle, spangle**—decorate with shiny metal, ornaments, pieces, bits, objects, etc.
  5. **diadem**—decorate the head of with a crown or headband
  6. **elaborate**—adorn or embellish with painstaking labor and minute attention to details
  7. **emblazon, emblaze**—ornament (with heraldic coats of arms, etc.)
  8. **emboss**—ornament; ornament with a design raised from the surface; embellish
  9. **enchase, chase**—ornament with cuts, engravings, gems, jewels, etc.
  10. **engrave**—cut or carve ornamentation, designs, letters, etc., upon (esp. a hard surface, metal, etc.)
  11. **festoon**—decorate or ornament with, or as if with garlands, wreaths, drapes, etc., hung in curving shapes
  12. **flounce**—decorate (esp. the bottom of a woman's skirt) with a wide strip of gathered material
  13. **flourish**—ornament with color, designs, etc.; ornament (handwriting) with artistic and sweeping lines, curves, etc.
  14. **foliate**—decorate with leaves or foliage
  15. **frill**—ornament or trim with cloth or lace strips or edging
  16. **fringe**—ornament with a decorative border of projecting lengths of thread, cord, etc.

17. **furbelow**—ornament or decorate with a showy trimming, or with plaited or gathered material
18. **garland**—ornament with floral or other wreaths
19. **garnish**—ornament (food, prepared dishes, etc.) with decorations, trimmings, scallops, etc.
20. **mosaic**—decorate (something) by inlaying pieces of glass, stone, etc., of different colors in its surface, thus forming a design, pattern, picture, etc.
21. **overdecorate, overdeck**—ornament excessively or in an extravagant fashion
22. **overhang**—ornament (a place, room, window, etc.) with hangings, drapes, curtains, etc.
23. **pink**—decorate (cloth, paper, etc.) at the edge with ornamental curves, perforations, etc.
24. **plume**—decorate with feathers
25. **prank**—ornament in a showy manner
26. **scallop, scollop, escalop, escallop**—decorate the edge or border of (cloth, paper, etc.) with ornamental curves or projections
27. **stud**—decorate with projecting and scattered ornaments or other objects
28. **tattoo**—prick an ornamental design into (the skin) or into the skin of; prick (an ornamental design) in the skin
29. **tessellate**—decorate with a checked or checkerboard design
30. **tinsel**—ornament with shiny metallic thread or yarn
31. **tool**—ornament by working designs into with a tool or implement

2. Ornamentation i.e., Act or Process of Ornamenting,n. *From Sec. 1:* adornment, arrayal, blazonment or blazonry, decoration, embellishment, emblazonment, garnishment; elaboration, emblazonry, embossment, foliation, garnishment, overdecoration, tattoo, tessellation

3. Ornament; Ornamentation,n. *From Sec. 1:* adornment, apparel, decking, decoration, embellishment; garnish, garnishment, or garniture; trimming; spangle (from *bespangle*); diadem, engraving, festoon, festoonery); flounce, flouncing, flourish (in handwriting), foliation, frill or frilling, fringe, furbelow, garland, garnish, mosaic, overdecoration, plume; scallop, scollop, escalop, or escallop; stud, tattoo, tessellation; tinsel, tinselry, or clinquant; tooling; *Also:*
1. **aiguillette**—ornament in the form of a loop, cord, tag, etc., on a military or naval uniform
2. **arabesque**—complicated ornament or ornamentation in which various objects (as fruits, flowers, leaves, figures, etc.) are intertwined in design (arabesque, adj.)
3. **centerpiece**—silver, glass, cloth, etc., ornament for the center of a table
4. **circlet**—circular ornament, esp. for the head
5. **crest**—ornament, esp. a plume, for the top of a helmet
6. **décor** (French)—decoration; ornamentation; a decoration; interior decoration of a home or room
7. **epaulet, epaulette**—shoulder ornament, esp. on military or naval uniforms
8. **epergne**—centerpiece for holding flowers, fruits, etc.
9. **floriation**—ornament or ornamentation of, or resembling, flowers
10. **frill**—something unimportant added for show or decoration, and having no function or other value
11. **gaud**—ornament; showy ornament
12. **medallion**—ornament or decoration in somewhat the shape of a medal, and containing a design, figure, portrait, etc.—often woven into carpets, lace, etc.; plaque identifying an automobile, taxis in New York City, etc.
13. **ornamental**—something ornamental; something used as an ornament; ornamental plant
14. **pendant**—hanging ornament; hanging ornament worn by women
15. **plaque**—ornament in the form of a plate or flat disc; flat ornament worn as an emblem of an honorary organization
16. **postiche** (French)—ornament added superfluously or inappropriately
17. **ruffle**—gathered material used as a trimming on a dress, garment, etc.
18. **scroll, scrollwork**—ornament, or ornamentation, in spiral, coiled, etc., forms or shapes
19. **spray**—ornament similar to a plant branch, including leaves, blossoms, fruit, etc.
20. **sunburst**—ornament, decoration, piece of jewelry, etc., in the form of the sun and its rays
21. **tracery**—ornamentation by delicate, interlacing lines, as in engraving, embroidery, etc.
22. **trinket**—small ornament

4. Ornaments, Collectively,n. *From Sec. 1:* festoonery, tinselry; *Also:*
1. **bric-a-brac**—various ornamental articles placed about a room, etc.
2. **regalia**—special decorations of office, rank, membership in an association, etc.
3. **trappings**—ornaments; surface decorations
4. **waxwork**—ornaments made of wax

5. Cheap, Worthless, and Showy Ornament: bauble, gaud, gewgaw, gimcrack, knickknack, nicknack, trinket,n. (gewgaw, gimcrack,adj.)

6. Showy Ornaments: finery, frippery, gaudery, regalia,n.

7. Cheap, Vulgar, or Showy Ornamentation: tinsel, tinselry,n.

8. Ornamented,adj. *From Sec. 1:* adorned, appareled, arrayed, etc.; bedaubed, bedizened, beset, bespangled, etc.; elaborate, frilly, fringy, mosaic, tessellate, tinselly; *From Sec. 3:* aiguilletted, arabesque, crested, epauleted or epauletted; floriated, floreated, or floriate; frilly, gaudy, ruffled, traceried; *Also:*
1. **baroque**—ornate but tasteless; showily or vulgarly ornate; descr. of a style of architecture characterized by great ornamentation and curved lines
2. **clinquant**—decorated with tinsel; decorated with gaudy embellishments or ornaments
3. **Corinthian**—ornate in a graceful way
4. **fancy**—ornamented; decorated; not plain
5. **flamboyant**—conspicuously and ornately decorated; overornamented; overdecorated; ornate; excessively ornate (flamboyance, flamboyancy,n.)
6. **floreted**—ornamented with small flowers
7. **florid**—highly ornamented or decorated; ornate (floridity, floridness,n.)
8. **luxuriant**—marked by rich, extravagant, or highly decorated ornamentation (luxuriance, luxuriancy,n.)
9. **ornate**—heavily or intricately ornamented (ornateness,n.)
10. **rococo**—excessively ornamented; tastelessly and awkwardly or excessively ornamented; descr. of a style of architecture of profuse and intricate ornamentation
11. **wrought**—ornamented

9. Plain; Unornamented,adj. *From Sec. 1:* unadorned, unappareled, unarrayed, unbedecked, undecked, undecorated, undressed, unembellished, unemblazoned, ungarnished, unpranked, untrimmed, unvarnished; unbedaubed, unbedizened; unspangled (from *be-spangled*); undiademed; unelaborated, un-elaborate, inelaborated, or inelaborate; un-emblazoned, unembossed, unengraved or un-engraven, unfestooned, unflounced, unflour-ished, unfoliated, unfrilled, unfringed, un-furbelowed, ungarlanded, ungarnished, un-plumed, unpranked, unscalloped or unescal-loped, unstudded, untattooed, untessellated, untinseled, untooled; *From Sec. 3:* uncrested, unepauleted, unfrilled, ungaudy, unruffled; *From Sec. 8:* unfancy, unflamboyant, un-florid, unornate; *Also:* bald, bare, severe, simple, stark; *Also:*

1. **austere**—severely simple; totally un-adorned; without any ornamentation, as writing, style, way of living, etc.
2. **chaste**—plain or unadorned in style or manner
3. **classical, classic, Attic, Augustan**—un-adorned, or severely simple, in literary or artistic style, like that of ancient Greece or ancient Rome
4. **homely**—plain and simple, as surround-ings, food, pleasures, tastes, etc.
5. **rustic**—plain in a rough, unfinished, countrylike, or primitive way
6. **Spartan**—harshly plain, i.e., suggestive of the ancient Spartans

10. **Plainness; Lack of Ornamentation or Adornment,**n. *From Sec. 9:* unadornment or unadornedness, untrimmedness; baldness, bareness, severity or severeness, simplicity or simpleness, starkness; austerity or austere-ness, chastity or chasteness, classicality, homeliness, rusticity, Spartanism

11. **Descr. of Facts, Truth or Truths, State-ments, etc., That Are Unadorned:** bald, bare, blunt, crude, dry, matter-of-fact, naked, plain, simple, stark, unembellished, unvar-nished,adj. (baldness, bareness, bluntness, crudity or crudeness, nakedness, plainness, simpleness, starkness,n.)

12. **Art of Heraldic Ornamentation:** blazon-ry, emblazonry,n.

13. **Descr. of Ornamentation Added Super-fluously, Inappropriately, Unnecessarily, etc.:** postiche,adj. (French)

14. **To Use Ornamentation in the Letters of One's Handwriting:** flourish,v.

15. **Practice of Pricking Ornamental Designs into the Skin:** tattoo, tattooing,n. (tattooer, n.)

16. **Pert. to Ornament:** ornamental,adj.

17. **Used for, or of the Nature of, Ornament; Serving to Ornament:** decorative, fancy, ornamental,adj. (decorativeness, ornamental-ity,n.)

18. **To Make Ornamental:** ornamentalize,v.

19. **Professional Ornamenter:** ornamentalist, ornamentist,n.

20. **The Use of Ornament:** ornamentation,n.

21. **Habitual Use of Ornament; Addiction to Ornament:** ornamentalism,n.

22. **Not Ornamental:** undecorative, unfancy, unornamental,adj. (unornamentalness,n.)

23. **Not Capable of Being Ornamented:** un-adornable,adj.

960. SIMPLICITY

1. **Simple, i.e., Not Elaborate:** artless, in-elaborate or unelaborate, plain, primitive, unsophisticated,adj.; *Also:*
   1. **austere**—severely simple
   2. **chaste**—simple in style
   3. **homely**—simple and plain, as surround-ings, phrases, pleasures, tastes, food, etc.
   4. **idyllic**—naturally simple and charming—

esp. of ways of living; simple, charming, and poetic
   5. **rustic**—simple in a rough, unfinished, primitive, or countrified way
   6. **Spartan**—severely simple in manner of living, tastes, or desires
   7. **unpretentious**—simple and tasteful

2. **Simplicity; Simpleness,**n. *From Sec. 1:* artlessness, plainness, primitiveness or prim-itivity, unsophisticatedness or unsophistica-tion; austerity or austereness, chastity or chasteness, homeliness, rusticity, Spartanism

3. **Simple and Fine in Literary or Artistic Style, Like That of Ancient Greece or Rome:** Attic, Augustan, classic, classical,adj. (classicality,n.)

4. **Simple, i.e., Not Complex or Compound:** elemental, elementary, simplex, uncomplex, uncomplicated, uncompounded,adj. (elemen-tariness, simplexity, uncompoundedness,n.)

5. **Simple but Powerful; Simple but Having Great Force:** elemental,adj.

6. **To Make or Cause to Be Simple or Simpler:** simplicize, simplify,v. (simplifica-tion,n. simplifier or simplificator,n. simplifica-tive,adj. simplified,adj.)

7. **Pretense of Simplicity:** simplism,n. (sim-plicist,n.)

8. **One Who Advocates the Simple Life:** simplicitarian,n.

9. **One Who Advocates, or Believes in, Sim-plification:** simplist,n.

961. JEWELRY

1. **Piece of Jewelry; Ornament Worn on the Person, or as Jewelry,**n.
   1. **anklet**—circular ornament, or piece of jewelry, for the ankle
   2. **armlet**—circular ornament, or piece of jewelry, for the arm
   3. **bangle**—bracelet; anklet
   4. **bead**—small ball of glass, precious stone, pearl, etc.
   5. **beads**—necklace; rosary
   6. **bijou**—jewel
   7. **bracelet, wristlet**—circular ornament, or piece of jewelry, for the wrist or arm
   8. **brooch**—ornamental piece of jewelry, with a pin on its back, for fastening to a dress, etc.
   9. **chain**—ornamental piece of jewelry made up of links of gold, silver, or other metal
   10. **chatelaine**—ornament, or piece of jewel-ry, that pins to a woman's lapel
   11. **choker**—necklace that tightly hugs the neck
   12. **circlet**—bracelet; ring
   13. **earring**—ornament, or piece of jewelry, worn on the ear
   14. **gem, gem stone**—stone, mineral, or other petrified substance used in jewelry
   15. **intaglio**—piece of jewelry with a cut or sunken design (intaglios, intagli,pl.n.)
   16. **jewel**—ornament set with gems; gem, precious stone, etc., in a mounting
   17. **lavaliere, lavalier**—ornament, often jeweled, hanging from a chain around the neck, worn by women
   18. **locket**—small case, usually of precious metal, for miniature pictures, locks of hair, etc., worn suspended from a chain around the neck
   19. **necklace, necklet**—ornament, jeweled ornament, string of beads, pearls, dia-monds, or other stones, etc., worn around the neck
   20. **pendant**—hanging ornament or piece of jewelry, esp. a necklace, earring, etc.
   21. **pin**—ornament, or piece of jewelry, that pins to the clothing

22. **ring**—ornamental or jeweled band for the finger
23. **rosary**—string of beads used in keeping count while saying a series of certain prayers
24. **torque**—twisted narrow band of gold, silver, or other precious metal, worn as a necklace or similar ornament, esp. by the Gauls and Britons of antiquity
25. **trinket, bauble**—small piece or bit of jewelry, usually not very valuable or costly

2. Jeweled Ornament or Band Worn on the Head: coronet, crown; tiara (by women),n.

3. To Place Such on the Head of, or Adorn the Head of with Such: crown,v.

4. To Adorn, Ornament, etc., with, or as with, Jewels, Jewelry or Gems: bejewel, enchase, encrust or incrust, gem, jewel, set,v. (encrustation or incrustation,n. bejeweled, encrusted or incrusted, gemmed, jeweled,adj.)

5. To Set with Jewels or Gems: enchase, gem, jewel,v.

6. Manufacturer or Seller of, or Dealer in, Jewels or Jewelry: jeweler,n.

7. Magnifying Glass That Jewelers Use, Generally Held in the Eye: loupe,n.

8. Like a Jewel: gemlike, jewel-like,adj.

9. Jewelry: bijouterie,n.

10. Cut or Polished Stone Used in Jewelry: gem, jewel, stone,n.

11. Such a Stone of Exceptional Beauty and Rarity: precious stone,n.

12. Stone, Gem, Mineral, etc., Used in Jewelry: agate, alexandrite, amethyst, aquamarine, beryl, bloodstone or heliotrope, carbuncle, carnelian or cornelian, cat's-eye, chalcedony, chrysoberyl, chrysolite or olivine, chrysoprase, citrine, coral, corundum, demantoid, diamond, emerald, garnet; girasol, girasole, or girosol; hyacinth or jacinth; hydrophane, jade, jargon, jasper, kunzite, lapis lazuli, morganite, moonstone, onyx, opal, pearl, peridot, plasma, rose quartz, ruby, sapphire, sard, sardonyx; scarab (cut in the form of a beetle); spinel, topaz, tourmaline, turquoise, zircon,n. (amethystine, beryline, carbuncular, diamond, hyacinthine, hydrophanous, opaline, pearl or pearly, sapphirine, topazine,adj.)

13. Gem or Stone Engraved in Relief in Such a Way that the Background is of One Color, the Design of Another; Such an Engraving: cameo,n. (cameo,v.)

14. Gem or Stone So Engraved that the Design Is Cut or Sunk below the Surface; Such an Engraving; The Art or Process of So Engraving: intaglio,n. (intaglios, intagli, pl.n.; intaglio,v.)

15. Stone or Gem Selected for Wear by People Born in a Certain Month, and Supposedly Having Special Power: birthstone,n.

16. Birthstone for the Stated Month: garnet (January); amethyst (February); aquamarine, jasper, or bloodstone (March); diamond (April); emerald (May); pearl, agate, or alexandrite (June); ruby (July); peridot or carnelian (August); sapphire (September); opal or tourmaline (October); topaz (November); turquoise or zircon (December),n.

17. Gem with Numerous Facets: brilliant,n.

18. Gem with Less than Perfect Brilliancy: loupe,n.

19. Gem Cut in a Long, Rectangular Shape; Such a Shape of a Gem: baguette,n.

20. Artificial Gem Made of Glass, Paste, etc., Sometimes Cut Like a Diamond: rhinestone, n.

21. Mythical Gem of Such Hardness as to Be Impenetrable: adamant,n. (adamantean, adamantine,adj.)

22. Science or Study of Gems: gemology,n. (gemologist,n. gemological,adj.)

23. Having, or Producing, Gems: gemmiferous,adj.

24. One Who Is Versed in Gems and Precious Stones and Skillful in Cutting Them: lapidarist,n.

25. One Who Cuts and Polishes Gems and Precious Stones: lapidary,n.

26. Pert. to the Cutting of Gems and Precious Stones: lapidary,adj.

27. Pert. to, or Descr. of, the Carving or Engraving of Gems or Precious Stones: glyptic,adj.

28. Art or Process of Carving or Engraving Gems or Precious Stones: glyptics, glyptography,n. (glyptographer,n.) glyptographic, adj.)

29. Study of Engraved Gems or Precious Stones: glyptography, glyptology,n. (glyptographer, glyptologist,n. glyptographical, glyptological,adj.)

30. Description of Engraved Gems or Precious Stones: glyptography,n.

962. DIAMONDS

1. Diamond,n.
1. **baguette**—diamond cut in a long, rectangular shape
2. **brilliant**—diamond with numerous facets
3. **briolette**—oval diamond with triangular facets
4. **fisheye**—diamond cut so that it is too shallow, and lacking, therefore, in proper brilliancy
5. **Hope diamond**—famous blue diamond, over 44 carats in weight
6. **industrial diamond**—diamond used as an abrasive in grinding lenses, in dentists' drills, etc.
7. **Jonker diamond**—726-carat diamond discovered in South Africa in 1934
8. **Jubilee diamond**—famous 634-carat diamond discovered in South Africa
9. **paragon**—perfect diamond weighing at least 100 carats
10. **solitaire**—single large diamond, or, occasionally, other precious stone, set in a ring

2. Former Name for a Diamond: adamant, n. (adamantean, adamantine,adj.)

3. Certain Qualities of a Diamond,n.
1. **brilliance, brilliancy**—effect produced by refraction and interior reflection, i.e., the amount of light from the internal and external facets
2. **hardness**—resistance to being scratched
3. **luster**—appearance of the surface in reflected light

4. Descr. of a Diamond, or Other Precious Stone, as to Cut,adj.
1. **brilliant-cut**—so cut that it has numerous facets, usually 58 (33 on top, 25 on bottom)
2. **emerald-cut**—step-cut in such a way that the color is enhanced, or the lack of color emphasized, usually in 58 facets of rectangular shape
3. **full-cut**—so cut that it has 58 facets, regardless of size
4. **marquise-cut**—brilliant-cut with double-pointed, boat-shaped outline and 58 facets
5. **single-cut**—so cut that it has 17 or 18 facets
6. **square-cut**—step-cut, with 30 facets and a table

7. step-cut—so cut that all facets are four-sided and in steps or rows

5. The Cut of a Diamond or Other Precious Stone,n. *From Sec. 4:* brilliant cut, emerald cut, full cut, marquise cut, single cut, square cut, step cut; *Also:* 1. **baguette**—a style of step cut with 25 facets

6. Parts of a Diamond,n.
1. **bezel**—sloping surface of the crown between the table and the girdle
2. **crown**—part of a faceted diamond above the girdle
3. **culet**—small facet polished on what would be the point of the pavilion
4. **facet**—one of the small plane surfaces of a cut diamond
5. **girdle**—outer edge of a fashioned diamond, i.e., the portion grasped by the setting or mounting
6. **pavilion**—portion of the cut diamond below the girdle
7. **table**—horizontal flat facet in the crown of the diamond

7. Any Foreign Body Enclosed by Nature within a Diamond That Is Not Flawless: inclusion,n.

8. Having the Hardness or Luster of a Diamond: adamantine,adj.

9. Made of Diamonds: diamond,adj.

10. To Ornament or Set with Diamonds: diamond,v.

11. Containing or Bearing Diamonds: diamantiferous,adj.

12. Diamond-Bearing Rock of South Africa: kimberlite,n.

963. PEARLS

1. Types of Pearls,n.
1. **baroque pearl**—pearl of irregular shape
2. **conch pearl**—pearl naturally grown in a conch, but not considered by jewelers to be a true pearl
3. **cultured pearl**—natural pearl artificially propagated in a captive oyster (Usually, a tiny core of mother-of-pearl is deposited in the oyster, which then coats the core with concentric layers of nacre.)
4. **cyst pearl**—true pearl that occurs within a sac or pouch in the tissues of a mollusk
5. **fine pearl**—natural pearl possessing the qualities of a gem stone
6. **fresh-water pearl, unio pearl**—pearl from the unio, a fresh-water mussel
7. **one-year pearl**—inferior cultured pearl with relatively few layers of nacre
8. **oriental pearl**—true pearl occurring naturally (i.e., not cultured), and not coming from a fresh-water mollusk, abalone, or mussel
9. **pearlet**—small pearl
10. **seed pearl**—very small pearl, often irregular in shape
11. **true pearl**—naturally grown pearl not attached to the shell of the mollusk and formed from layers of nacre

2. The Play of Color in and Just below the Surface of a Pearl: orient,n.

3. Surface Appearance of a Pearl in Reflected Light: luster or pearl luster,n.

4. The Substance of True Pearls, Formed in Thin Concentric Layers around a Nucleus: nacre,n.

5. Pearly Substance Attached to the Shell of a Mollusk: blister pearl,n.

6. Pearly Internal Layers of Certain Marine Shells: mother-of-pearl, nacre, pearl,n. (mother-of-pearl,adj.)

7. Pert. to, Resembling, Consisting of, or Yielding, Nacre: nacreous, nacrous, nacry, or nacred,adj.

8. Lined or Covered with Nacre: nacred,adj.

9. The Principal Mineral Constituent of the Nacre of a Pearl: aragonite,n.

10. To Become, or Cause to Be or Become, Like a Pearl or Pearls in Shape, Color, Appearance, etc.: pearl,v.

11. To Dive, Fish, or Look for Pearls: pearl,v.

12. One Who Dives for Pearls: pearl diver, pearler,n.

13. One Who Hires Pearl Divers: pearler,n.

14. Boat Used in Fishing for Pearls: pearler, n.

15. Pert. to, Like, of the Color of, etc., a Pearl, Pearls, or Mother-of-Pearl: pearl, pearly,adj. (pearliness,n.)

16. Ornamented with, or Abounding in, Pearls: pearl, pearly,adj.

17. To Ornament with Pearls: pearl,v.

964. OBJECTS OF ART

1. Object of Art: bibelot (French), curio; objet d'art (French),n.

2. Objects of Art, Collectively: bijouterie, bric-a-brac, virtu,n.

3. Taste for, Interest in, or Knowledge about, Objects of Art: virtu or vertu, virtuosity,n.

4. Excellence or Quality of an Object of Art: virtu,n.

5. Collector, Admirer, Student, or Connoisseur of Objects of Art: virtuoso,n.

965. ART

1. Picture; Pictorial Representation,n.
1. **abstraction**—picture, painting, or other artistic work that does not depict realities or concrete things, that does not contain objects present in nature, etc.
2. **aquarelle**—transparent water-color painting
3. **aquatint**—etching made in imitation of an ink or water-color drawing
4. **bust**—picture of the head, shoulders, and chest of a person
5. **canvas**—oil painting on a piece of heavy cloth made for this purpose
6. **caricature**—picture, drawing, etc., exaggerating, in an amusing, ludicrous, or sometimes ridiculing manner, the characteristics, peculiarities, or faults of a person
7. **cartoon**—amusing drawing, esp. in a magazine or newspaper; drawing, picture, or caricature, commenting on the current scene, esp. in a magazine or newspaper; drawing that is to be transferred or copied
8. **chiaroscuro, chiaro-oscuro**—picture, sketch, painting, etc., made only in light and shade, thereby achieving an illusion of third dimension
9. **cyclorama**—large, circular picture or pictorial representation on the walls of a circular room, surrounding the spectators and often containing real objects
10. **daub**—unskillfully painted picture; unskillful painting
11. **decalcomania, decal**—picture or design transferred, or to be transferred, to china, glass, wood, etc.
12. **delineation**—drawing; portrait; sketch; rough sketch

13. **depiction**—drawing, painting, or other art form representing or portraying something

14. **design**—drawing or sketch made as a pattern from which to work; finished painting or other artistic work

15. **diorama**—picture, scene, or representation set up in miniature, usually either in third dimension or simulating third dimension, and often viewed through an opening, with special lighting effects

16. **distemper, tempera**—painting, usually a mural or scene, made by using a special medium that is essentially an emulsion prepared in a number of ways and containing, often, thickened oil, egg and water, resin, etc.

17. **draft**—first or preliminary drawing or sketch, either of work to be done or to be finished or filled in later

18. **drawing**—picture, representation, etc., esp. one made with a pen, crayon, or pencil

19. **eidolon**—picture of a small, winged figure painted on early Greek vases

20. **emblazonment**—picture, representation, design, etc., on a heraldic shield

21. **etching**—drawing made on metal by means of acid or other corrosive agent, and transferred later to some other medium

22. **figure**—picture, or pictorial representation, of something, or of the human body

23. **fresco**—painting on fresh, and still wet, plaster

24. **gouache (French)**—painting made with opaque water pigments mixed with gum

25. **icon, ikon, eikon**—picture; image; in the Orthodox Church, sacred image, or picture of Jesus

26. **idol**—image of a deity used as an object of worship

27. **illustration**—picture, drawing, etc., that goes along with, explains, or decorates the text

28. **image**—picture drawn, painted, etc., of something or someone; picture of something or someone reflected, as in a mirror, etc.

29. **landscape**—picture of some natural inland or coastal scenery

30. **likeness**—picture of someone or something

31. **lithograph**—picture produced by a process of putting an impression in stone or other material with a greasy substance, then printing

32. **master, old master**—painting, etc., done by a skilled artist of the past, esp. of a period considerably earlier than the present

33. **miniature**—very small painting, or other pictorial representation, esp. a portrait, and often on metal or other special material

34. **mosaic**—picture (or other decoration) made by inlaying pieces of stone, glass, etc., of various colors on a surface

35. **mural**—painting hung or done on a wall

36. **nude**—picture, painting, or other work of art of the unclothed human figure, generally female

37. **painting**—picture done with color or pigment

38. **panorama**—picture or pictorial representation of a wide extent of scenery; scene pictured on a wide canvas, often shown part by part as it passes in front of viewers

39. **pastel**—drawing made with crayons of soft paste

40. **pastiche; pasticcio (Italian)**—artistic work, as a painting, picture, or literary or musical work, imitating and ridiculing the style of another artist, writer, musician, etc.

41. **photograph**—picture taken by a camera

42. **portrait, portraiture**—picture of a person, or of a person's face, esp. when painted, drawn, etc., from life

43. **portraiture, portrayal**—picture; pictorial representation

44. **potboiler**—picture or other artistic work produced merely to gain enough money to live, not out of inspiration, etc. (colloq.)

45. **primitive**—painting or other work of art by an artist in his early period or by an artist before the Renaissance

46. **production**—work of art, in any sense

47. **representation**—picture; figure; image; likeness

48. **scene**—picture; picture of a place, action, incident, etc.

49. **seascape**—picture representing a view at, or over, the sea

50. **sketch**—drawing or picture in rough outline, omitting the details, etc.

51. **stereochrome**—picture or painting, esp. a mural, made by using water glass mixed with the pigments as a fixative or preservative, or by fixing or preserving with water glass

52. **stereogram**—picture with the illusion of depth

53. **stereograph, stereogram**—single or double picture designed for use in a stereoscope, an optical instrument that gives a realistic illusion of depth to objects viewed in it

54. **still life**—picture, painting, etc., of lifeless objects, as fruit, bottles, flowers, etc.

55. **tableau**—picture, esp. of a scene

56. **tracing**—drawing; drawing of the general outlines of a thing, figure, etc.; drawing of the lines of something, or of some picture made by copying through a transparent sheet of paper, etc.; sketch

57. **view**—picture of a scene, place, action, incident, etc.

58. **water color**—painting made with pigments using water, rather than oil, as a base

59. **zoomorph**—picture or image of a god or supernatural being in animal form

2. To Picture; To Make, etc. (a Picture); To Represent Pictorially,v. *From Sec. 1:* aquatint, caricature, cartoon, daub, delineate, depict or depicture, design, distemper, draft, draw, emblazon or emblaze, etch, fresco; illustrate (text, story, book, etc.); lithograph, miniature, mosaic, paint, photograph, portray, represent, sketch, trace, zoomorphize; *Also:*

1. **limn**—draw; paint; represent by, or in, drawing or painting

2. **pictorialize**—represent by, or in, a picture or pictures

3. **picture**—execute a picture of; represent or show pictorially

4. **picturize**—execute a picture or pictures of

3. To Engage in Making a Picture or Pictures, or in Pictorial Representation,v. *From Sec. 1:* aquatint, daub, design, draw, etch, paint, photograph, sketch, trace

4. Pictorial Representation; a Making, etc., of a Picture or Pictures,n. *From Sec. 1:* caricaturing, cartooning, etc.; daubery, daubry, or daub; delineation, depiction, emblazonment or emblazonry, iconography, illustration, portrayal, representation, zoomorphism or zoomorphy; *From Sec. 2:* pictorialization, picturization; *Also:* 1. scenography—the painting of scenes, as in ancient Greece

5. Process, Method, or Style in, or of, Making Pictures, Artistic Works, Pictorial Representations, etc.,n. *From Sec. 1:* abstractionism, aquatint, caricature, chiaroscuro or chiaro-oscuro; decalcomania (of transferring); distemper or tempera, fresco; gouache (French); lithography, mosaic, photography, stereochromy, water color; *Also:* 1. wash—process of painting in water color by applying a thin and even layer by continuous brush strokes

6. **Art of Making Pictures, Pictorial Representations, etc.,**n. *From Sec. 1:* caricature; decalcomania (of transferring); delineation, design, drafting, drawing, emblazonry, etching, fresco, iconography, landscape, lithography, miniature, painting, pastel, photography; portraiture (from *portrait*); stereography (from *stereogram*); water color; *Also:*
1. calcography—art of drawing with chalk, or with crayons of soft paste
2. fine arts; beaux-arts (French)—arts of aesthetic expression, esp. drawing, painting, sculpture, architecture, engraving, ceramics, etc.—sometimes, also, music, dancing, dramatics, and literature
3. graphic arts—those arts, such as painting, drawing, engraving, etching, photography, etc., that deal with visual presentation or the use of lines, strokes, etc., to make such a presentation
4. graphics—art of drawing in conformity with the rules of mathematics, as in architecture, engineering, etc.
5. perspective, scenography—art of showing things, figures, etc., on a plane surface with a simulation of depth or distance

7. **Artist; One Who Makes, Draws, Paints, etc.,** a Picture or Pictures,n. *From Sec. 1:* abstractionist, aquarellist, caricaturist, cartoonist, chiaroscurist, dauber, delineator, depicter or depictor, designer; drafter, draftsman, or draughtsman; drawer, emblazoner, etcher, frescoer, illustrator, landscapist, lithographer, master or old master, miniaturist, mosaicist, muralist, painter, pastelist, photographer; portraitist (from *portrait*) ; primitive, seascapist, sketcher, tracer, water-colorist; *From Sec. 2:* limner, picturer; *From Sec. 6:* calcographer, scenographer or scenograph; *Also:*
1. colorist—artist who uses color in his work; artist who specializes in unusual color effects
2. master—extremely skillful artist
3. primitive—artist or painter belonging to the earliest part of the development of a style

8. **Pictorial; Pictural; Pert. to, or Descr. of,** a Picture, Pictorial Process, Art, etc., adj. *From Sec. 1:* abstractionist, abstract, nonobjective, or nonrepresentational; caricatural, cycloramic, delineative, depictive, dioramic; iconic, iconical, iconographic, or iconographical; illustrative, lithographic or lithographical, mosaic, mural, panoramic, photographic or photographical, representational, scenic, sketchy, stereochromic; stereographic or stereographical (from *stereogram*); still life, water color or water-colored, zoomorphic; *From Sec. 6:* calcographic or calcographical; graphic or graphical (from *graphic arts*) ; perspective, scenographic, or scenographical

9. **Pictures Collectively or Generally,**n. *From Sec. 1:* iconology, imagery; portraiture (from *portrait*); *Also:*
1. gallery—collection of pictures or other art works in exhibition
2. picture gallery—group, collection, etc., of pictures
3. rogues' gallery—collection of pictures of criminals

10. **Place Where Pictures, etc., Are Exhibited,** n. *From Sec. 1:* diorama; *From Sec. 9:* gallery, picture gallery; *Also:* 1. museum, salon—place where works of art are exhibited

11. **Serving or Tending to Picture,**adj. *From Sec. 1:* delineative, depictive, illustrative

12. **Picturable; Capable of Being Drawn, Painted, etc.,**adj. *From Sec. 1:* caricaturable, paintable, portrayable, sketchable

13. **Work or Skill of Someone Engaged in Drafting:** draftsmanship or draughtsmanship,n.

14. **To Go Along with, Explain, or Decorate the Text—of Pictures, Drawings, etc.:** illustrate,v. (illustration,n. illustrative,adj.)

15. **The Category of Pictures of Natural Inland or Coastal Scenery:** landscape,n.

16. **Drawn Only in Rough Outline:** sketchy, adj. (sketchiness,n.)

17. **Book in Which to Make Drawings in Rough Outline:** sketchbook,n.

18. **The Study, Description, Interpretation, Analysis, etc., of Pictures, Images, or Icons:** iconography, iconology,n. (iconologist,n. iconographic or iconographical, iconological,adj.)

19. **The Study of the Portraits of a Particular Person:** iconography,n. (iconographic, iconographical,adj.)

20. **In Accord with the Standards of Art:** artistic, artistical,adj.

21. **Skill, Effect, or Quality in Art:** artistry,n.

22. **The Following or Practice of Art or Arts:** artistry,n.

23. **Pert. to, Resembling, or Suitable for, an Artist:** artistic, artistical,adj.

24. **Suitable for a Picture, for Picturing, Painting, Drawing, etc.:** picturable,adj. (picturability, picturableness,n.)

25. **Like, or Suggestive of, a Picture:** colorful, pictorial, picturesque, pictury; scenic (i.e., like natural scenery),adj. (colorfulness, picturesqueness,n.)

26. **Descr. of Literary Style That Presents Clear Pictures or Imagery to the Mind:** graphic, pictorial, picturesque, vivid,adj. (picturesqueness, vividness,n.)

27. **Constituents or Elements of an Art:** technique,n. (technical,adj.)

28. **Method, or Skill, in Executing, or (in Music), Rendering or Interpreting, an Artistic Work:** technique or technic,n. (technician,n.)

29. **Pert. to Industrial or Mechanical Arts:** technical,adj.

30. **Object Represented on a Plane Surface with the Illusion of Depth or Distance:** scenogram,n.

31. **Extremely Varied Collection of Artistic Efforts, as in Painting, Literature, Music, etc.; A Painting, or other Artistic, Literary, or Musical Work Made Up of Bits and Patches from Varied Sources, or of Themes or Ideas Borrowed from Other Artists, esp. the Masters:** pasticcio,n. (Italian)

32. **Word Used with an Artist's Name on His Picture or Painting:** delineavit, pinxit (Latin)

33. **An Italian Artist (or Writer, etc.) of the Stated Century:** trecentest (14th); quattrocentist (15th); cinquecentist (16th),n.

34. **The Stated Century in Reference to Italian Art or Literature:** trecento (14th); quattrocento (15th); cinquecento (16th),n. (quattrocentism, cinquecentism,n. trecento, quattrocento, cinquecento,adj.)

35. **Work of Art Produced in Italy in the 16th Century:** cinquecento,n.

36. **The Effect Achieved by an Artist by His Treatment of Light and Shade, or His Dis-**

tribution of Light and Shade in a Picture: chiaroscuro, chiaro-oscuro,n.

37. To Draw or Trace a Line Around (Something): circumscribe,v. (circumscription,n. circumscriptive,adj.)

38. Series of Drawings in Panels Appearing in a Newspaper or Magazine and Narrating Funny Incidents, Adventures, etc.: cartoon, comic strip,n. (cartoonist,n.)

39. Selected Special Broad Principles, Theories, Styles, or Methods of Artistic Expression; Selected Schools or Movements in Art, n.

1. **abstractionism**—principles, methods, etc., of an art that does not depict realities or actual objects, that uses geometric rather than representational design, etc. (abstractionist,n. abstractionist, abstract, nonobjective, or nonrepresentational,adj.)
2. **classicism**—principles, methods, etc., of an art that follows the models of Greek and Roman antiquity; belief in, or adherence to, these principles or methods (classicist, classicalist,n. classical, classic,adj.)
3. **cubism**—principles, methods, etc., of expressing the emotion of the painter by the arrangement of various geometrical forms (cubist,n. cubist, cubistic,adj.)
4. **Dadaism**, Dada, dadaism, dada—movement, cult, etc., in art, painting, sculpture, and literature popular during and after World War I that was characterized by formlessness, fantastic subconscious symbolism, incongruous arrangements or combinations, etc. (dadaist,n.)
5. **expressionism**—theory or method of art based on the free expression of the artist's emotion, rather than on faithful representation (expressionist,n. expressionist, expressionistic,adj.)
6. **Fauvism**—school of art that, among other things, used color for its symbolic properties, violated natural forms, etc. (Fauve,n. Fauvist,adj.)
7. **futurism**—principles, methods, school, or movement in art and literature calling for a rejection of traditional forms and the expression of life in terms of the mechanistic, dynamic, revolutionary, etc., present and future (futurist,n. futurist, futuristic,adj.)
8. **idealism**—method or principles of treating subjects in art and literature according to the artist's or author's ideal of perfection, or according to high ethical concepts (idealist,n. idealist, idealistic,adj.)
9. **impressionism**—method, school, theory, etc., of art and literature expressing the artist's immediate over-all impression of the subject without too much attention to detail (impressionist,n. impressionist, impressionistic,adj.)
10. **modernism**—school, method, etc., of art that rejects traditional devices, forms, etc.—sometimes derogatory (modernist,n. modernist, modernistic,adj.)
11. **naturalism**—theory, principle, practice, etc., in painting and literature of having artistic expression maintain a close fidelity to nature, natural forms and objects, etc. (naturalist,n. naturalist, naturalistic,adj.)
12. **neoclassicism**—style, method, etc., in painting, architecture, literature, etc., that is a revival of classical forms (neoclassicist,n. neoclassical, neoclassic,adj.)
13. **neoimpressionism**—theory, style, practice, etc., in painting that attempted to make impressionism strictly scientific, esp. by the use of the pointillist technique (neoimpressionist,n. neoimpressionist, adj.)
14. **pointillism**—style, method, etc., of painting in which a canvas is covered by dots

or points of pure color that blend together when viewed from a distance (pointillist, n. pointillist,adj.)
15. **postimpressionism**—theory, doctrine, school, movement, etc., of painting that rejected certain tenets of impressionism, esp. its casual effects and naturalistic tendencies, and emphasized the subjective viewpoint of the artist (postimpressionist,n. postimpressionist, postimpressionistic,adj.)
16. **realism**—theory, method, style, etc., in art and literature based on representing things, people, life, etc., with fidelity to reality (realist,n. realist, realistic,adj.)
17. **romanticism**, romantic movement—movement, style, tendency, etc., in art and literature characterized by greater freedom of subject, form, and treatment, more rein to the imagination, emphasis on feeling, etc.—a revolt against neoclassicism (romanticist, romantic,n. romantic, adj.)
18. **surrealism**—movement in art and literature based on the expression of the content of the unconscious and of dreams (surrealist,n. surrealist, surrealistic,adj.)
19. **symbolism**—principles, theory, practice, etc., in art and literature based on the suggestion of ideas, emotions, etc., by the objects pictured or the color used, or, in literature, by words, sounds, etc. (symbolist,n. symbolistic,adj.)
20. **vorticism**—theory in art that pictures and forms should portray modern industrial civilization (vorticist,n.)

40. One Who Is Strongly Interested in Any or a Number of the Fine Arts and Possesses Discriminating Taste in Artistic Works: virtuoso,n.

41. Such People Collectively: virtuosity,n.

42. Such Interest and Taste; Such Interest and Taste on the Part of an Amateur: virtuosity,n.

966. CARVING; SCULPTURE

1. To Carve or Cut (Designs, Figures, etc.), v.

1. **cameo**—carve (a gem, stone, etc.) in relief so that the design or figure stands out in a different color from its background
2. **chase**, enchase—carve or engrave (designs); carve or engrave designs, etc., in or on
3. **emboss**—carve (a design or figure) in relief or above a surface; carve such a design or figure in or on (embossment,n.)
4. **engrave**, grave—carve (designs, letters, figures, etc.) on a hard surface, as metal, stone, etc.; carve such designs, etc., in or on (engravement,n.)
5. **etch**—carve or engrave (designs, pictures, etc.) on metal by means of acid or other corrosive agent; engrave such designs, etc., on (metal)
6. **intaglio**—carve or cut (designs, etc.) into and below the surface of stone, metal, or other hard substance; carve or cut designs, etc., into and below the surface of (stone, metal, etc.)
7. **mezzotint**—engrave (designs, etc.) on steel or copper by a special process of burnishing or scraping away a previously roughened surface
8. **model**—carve or fashion (a figure, object, etc.) in some plastic or comparatively soft material, as clay, wax, etc.
9. **sculpt**—sculpture (colloq.)
10. **sculpture**—carve, fashion, or mold (figures, statues, objects, etc.) in hard or soft materials (sculptural,adj.)
11. **whittle**—carve or cut (a stick or other piece of wood) to form a figure or object;

carve or cut (such a figure or object) from a piece of wood

2. To Engage in Such Carving, etc.,v. *From Sec. 1:* etch, model, sculpture, sculpt, whittle

3. Carving; The Process or Art of Carving, etc.,n. *From Sec. 1:* cameo, chasing, embossing, engraving, etching, intaglio, mezzotint, modeling, sculpture, whittling; *Also:*

1. **chalcography**—art or process of engraving on brass or copper, generally for reproduction in printing (chalcographic, chalcographical,adj.)
2. **iconography**—process of carving representational figures (iconographic, iconographical,adj.)
3. **petroglyphy**—art or process of carving designs, figures, writing, etc., on rock (petroglyphic,adj.)
4. **pyrography, pyrogravure**—art or process of burning designs, etc., into the surface of something, usually leather, wood, etc. (pyrographic,adj.)
5. **wood engraving, xylography**—art or process of engraving designs, pictures, patterns, etc., on wood (xylographic, xylographical,adj.)

4. Carver; One Who Carves Designs, Figures, etc.,n. *From Sec. 1:* chaser, embosser, engraver, etcher, mezzotinter, modeler, sculptor or sculptress, whittler; *From Sec. 3:* chalcographer or chalcographist, iconographer, pyrographer, wood engraver or xylographer

5. A Carving; Carved Design, Figure, Object, etc.,n. *From Sec. 1:* cameo, embossment or embossing, engraving or engravement, etching, intaglio, mezzotint; model (often to be reproduced in a harder or more durable substance); sculpture; *From Sec. 3:* chalcograph; petroglyph (esp. from prehistoric times); pyrograph or pyrogravure; wood engraving, woodcut, woodprint, or wood block; *Also:*

1. **glyph, glyphic**—carved figure, letter, etc., of ancient times (glyphic,adj.)
2. **mold**—some figure, object, etc., shaped or fashioned in a hollow form
3. **relief**—piece of carving, sculpture, etc., raised or projected from its background
4. **statue**—figure sculptured in the round (statuary,adj.)

6. Carved,adj. *From Sec. 1:* cameoed, chased, embossed, engraved or graven, etched, intagliated, intaglioed, modeled, sculptured, whittled (intagliation,n.); *Also:* 1. **glyphic, sculptile**—engraved; sculptured

7. Pert. to Any Type of Carving or Engraving: glyphic,adj.

8. The Projection of Carved Work, Sculpture, etc., from Its Background: relief, relievo, or Italian, rilievo,n.

9. Types of Relief in Sculpture,n.

1. **alto-relievo; alto-rilievo (Italian); high relief**—projection of the figures by half, or, usually, more than half, of their depth from the background
2. **bas-relief; basso-rilievo (Italian); low relief**—projection of the figures only a little from the background
3. **mezzo-relievo; mezzo-rilievo (Italian); half relief**—projection of the figures about halfway from the background

10. So Carved, Sculptured, etc., as to Project from the Background: in relief

11. Map So Shaded, Colored, or Drawn as to Show the Relief, or Projection, etc., of Land Forms, as Hills, Mountains, Valleys, etc.: relief map,n.

12. Word after the Artist's Name on His Engraving, Carving, Sculpture, etc.: sculpsit (Latin)

13. Suggestive of, Resembling, etc., a Piece of Sculpture: sculptitory, sculpturesque,adj. (sculpturesqueness,n.)

14. To Decorate with Sculptural Works: sculpture,v.

15. Sculptural Works Generally or Collectively; sculpture,n. (sculptural,adj.)

16. Branch of Sculpture Dealing with Figures in the Round: statuary,n. (statuary, adj.)

17. Sculptor of Statues: statuary,n.

18. Statue,n.

1. **abstraction**—statue that is unrelated to reality, not representational, etc. (abstract, nonobjective, nonrepresentational, adj.)
2. **acrolith**—statue with a trunk of wood, but hands, feet, and head of stone or marble (acrolithic, acrolithan,adj.)
3. **bust**—statue of the head, shoulders, and chest of a person
4. **Colossus, colossus**—ancient bronze statue of Apollo at Rhodes; any tremendously large statue (colossal,adj.)
5. **effigy**—statue, portrait, or other likeness of a person; such a statue, etc., of one who is the object of general hatred or contempt
6. **figure**—statue or other sculptural representation of a person, animal, or thing
7. **figurine**—small ornamental figure; small statue
8. **icon, ikon, eikon**—statue; large statue of a person (iconic, iconical,adj.)
9. **idol**—statue of a deity; statue worshiped as a deity
10. **image**—statue; statue or sculptured figure worshiped as a deity or idol
11. **manikin, mannikin, manakin**—figure of the human body used for teaching anatomy, demonstrating surgical operations, etc.
12. **mannequin, manikin, dummy, model**—figure of a person, or of the human body, on which clothing is exhibited, as in a store, store window, etc.; such a figure used by tailors, artists, etc.
13. **monument**—statue in memory of a person or event (monumental,adj.)
14. **sculpture**—statue (sculptural,adj.)
15. **statuette**—small statue
16. **torso**—statue of a human body from which the head and limbs have been broken off; statue of the nude trunk of the human figure
17. **waxwork**—statue made of wax

19. Statuary, i.e., Statues Collectively, or Collection of Statues,n. *From Sec. 18:* imagery, sculpture, waxwork

20. Suggestive of, or Resembling, a Statue: sculptural, sculpturesque, statuesque,adj. (sculpturesqueness, statuesqueness,n.)

21. Descr. of Statues or Busts That Are of Conventional, Traditional, or Fixed Style: iconic, iconical,adj.

22. To Hang or Burn the Statue, Portrait, or Other Likeness of (a Person, Usually One Held in General Hatred): hang or burn (a person) in effigy

967. PHOTOGRAPHY

1. Photograph,n.

1. **daguerreotype**—early type of photograph
2. **ferrotype, tintype**—photograph on a sensitized sheet of tin, enameled iron, etc.
3. **microphotograph, photomicrograph**—very small photograph that must be enlarged before the details are visible; very small photograph of bulky material, large books, newspapers, manuscripts, etc., made to conserve space, as in libraries

4. microprint—printed microphotograph of a book, manuscript, etc., read with the aid of a magnifying glass

5. nephogram—photograph of clouds or of a cloud

6. photochrome—photograph taken in colors; photograph in color

7. photochronograph, chronophotograph—photograph—one of a series taken in rapid succession—that records motion

8. photoengraving, heliograph—print made from a process of reproducing photographs on printing plates

9. photogram—photograph; photograph of a scene; photograph of a region used in making maps or in surveying

10. photogravure—print made from a process of reproducing photographs on intaglio printing plates

11. photolithograph—picture produced by photoengraving

12. photomicrograph, microphotograph—photograph taken through a microscope

13. photomural—extremely large photograph covering all or most of a wall

14. photostat—photographic reproduction, made directly on sensitized paper, of documents, book pages, etc.

15. phototelegraph, telephotograph—photograph transmitted over communication wires, by radio, etc.

16. phototype—print made from a block or plate on which a photograph is reproduced

17. picture—photograph

18. portrait—photograph of a person, esp. of his face

19. print, positive—photograph printed from a negative

20. sculptograph—photograph in which the objects or figures seem to stand out in relief

21. shot—photograph; small photograph

22. snapshot, snap—small photograph

23. telephotograph—photograph of distant objects

24. tintype—loosely, any photograph

2. To Photograph; To Make a Photograph of,v. *From Sec. 1:* daguerreotype, microphotograph, photoengrave, photolithograph, photostat, print, snap, shoot

3. Photographer; One Who Makes a Photograph,n. *From Sec. 1:* daguerreotyper or daguerrotypist, photoengraver, photogravurist, photomicographer, portraitist, printer

4. Process in Photography,n. *From Sec. 1:* daguerreotype or daguerreotypy, ferrotype, microphotography or photomicrography, photochromy, photochronography or chronophotography, photoengraving or heliogravure, photogrammetry, photogravure, photolithography, photomicography or microphotography, phototelegraphy or telephotography, phototypy or phototype, portraiture, printing, sculptography, telephotography

5. Camera, etc., Used in Photography,n. *From Sec. 1:* nephograph, photochronograph; photogrammeter or phototheodolite (in surveying or map making); photostat

6. Photographic,adj. *From Sec. 1:* daguerreotypic or daguerrean, microphotographic or photomicrographic, photochromic or photochromatic, photochronographic or photochronographical, photoengraved; photogrammetric or photogrammetrical (of the camera used in surveying or map making); photolithographic, photomicrographic or microphotographic, photostatic, phototelegraphic or telephotographic, phototypic, telephotographic

7. A Combination or Grouping of a Number of Photographs Mounted for Special Effect: photomontage,n.

8. Suitable for Photographing Owing to Attractiveness or Other Qualities; Able to Turn Out Attractively when Photographed: photogenic,adj.

9. Descr. of a Photograph That Is Unposed: candid,adj.

968. MOTION PICTURES

1. Motion Picture: cinema, cinemelodrama, film; flicker (colloq.); motion picture show; movie (colloq.); moving picture, photodrama, photoplay, picture; picture show (colloq.); screen play; show (colloq.),n. (cinematic or cinematograph, photodramatic,adj.)

2. The Motion-Picture Industry, etc.: filmland (colloq.); films, motion pictures; moviedom or movieland (colloq.); the movies (colloq.); moving pictures; pictures (colloq.); the screen, the silver screen, Hollywood,n.

3. Art or Science of Motion Pictures, of Taking or Producing Motion Pictures, etc.: cinematography,n. (cinematographic,adj.)

4. To Photograph (a Scene, Story, etc.) with a Motion-Picture Camera: film; cinematize (British); cinematograph, shoot,v. (cinematographer or cameraman,n.)

5. Motion-Picture Camera: cinematograph, n. (cinematographic, cinematographical,adj.)

6. Motion-Picture Projector: bioscope, cinematograph,n. (cinematographic, cinematographical,adj.)

7. To Make (a Story, etc.) into a Motion Picture: film, picturize,v. (picturization,n.)

8. One Who Writes a Story, etc., for Motion Pictures: photodramatist, photoplaywright, scenarist, screen writer,n.

9. Motion-Picture Theater: cinema or cinematograph (largely British); movie theater or house (colloq.); nickelodeon (in earlier days —admission 5¢); picture theater (colloq.),n.

10. Motion Picture Taken of a Person, Scene, etc., at Close Range and Therefore in Comparatively Large Size: close-up,n.

11. Single Photograph of a Person or Scene, esp. in Motion Pictures, and Displayed outside a Theater: still,n.

12. Motion Picture or Illustrated Lecture Describing Foreign or Unusual Places: travelogue,n.

13. Motion Picture with Animated Drawings for Characters, Usually Comic or Farcical in Nature: cartoon,n.

969. DRAMA; THEATER

1. Drama; Dramatic or Theatrical Performance or Presentation,n.

1. aquacade—performance of swimming, water dancing, and other entertaining pursuits on or in water—so called at the New York World's Fair of 1939

2. burlesque—dramatic composition that treats lofty subjects in a vulgar or ludicrous manner; dramatic performance or entertainment involving vulgar situations, the degree of female nudity permitted by the authorities, etc.

3. comedy—play, etc., of light or humorous nature, or in which there is a happy ending

4. comedy of manners—comedy of social life or of people in the higher strata of social life

5. curtain raiser, curtain lifter—short dramatic sketch or play given before a longer or more serious work

6. dialogue, duologue—performance, sketch,

etc., in which two actors engage in conversation

7. **dramalogue**—performance in which a play is read, often by one person, rather than acted out by a company

8. **drawing-room comedy, drama, etc.**—comedy, drama, etc., acted out in the setting of a drawing room

9. **duodrama**—drama for two actors, usually with accompanying music

10. **entr'acte**—performance of any kind, as music, dancing, etc., between the acts of a play or other dramatic presentation

11. **extravaganza**—musical or dramatic composition of irregular form and elaborate or spectacular settings, costumes, etc.

12. **farce**—light play, satirical and/or humorous in type, containing improbable plot, events, characters, etc.

13. **harlequinade**—pantomime, or other play, in which the principal part is acted by a clown or other ludicrous character dressed in colorful tights, carrying a wooden sword, etc.

14. **impersonation, impression**—performance by an actor who imitates the appearance, characteristics, voice, etc., of a well-known person

15. **legitimate drama, legitimate play**—drama or play presented on the stage, as opposed to a motion picture

16. **light comedy**—comedy written with cleverness, delicacy, grace, wit, etc.

17. **low comedy**—comedy close to farce in character; comedy that depicts the seamy side of life

18. **mask, masque**—dramatic performance or composition, popular in the 16th and 17th centuries, consisting of dancing and pantomime, in which the actors wore masks

19. **melodrama**—sensational drama that shows no particular fidelity to real life in the working out of cause and effect, and in which sentiment and passions are exaggerated

20. **mime**—farce of ancient Greek and Roman times characterized by ludicrous gestures and actions

21. **monodrama, monodram, monodrame**—drama acted out by a single character; drama explaining what goes on in a person's mind

22. **monologue**—drama, play, sketch, etc., for a single actor or speaker

23. **morality play, morality**—allegorical play, popular in the 14th to 16th centuries, in which the actors took the parts of conventional virtues and vices, and the purpose of which was to extol morality

24. **mummery**—performance in mask or disguise, esp. on holidays

25. **musical comedy, musical**—play with music, singing, and dancing, and a light or, often, vague plot

26. **one-act play, one-acter, one-act**—play in one act

27. **opera**—musical drama; drama in which the music and singing are an integral part

28. **opéra bouffe (French)**—comic or farcical opera

29. **opéra comique (Italian)**—comic opera

30. **operetta**—short opera, usually of light character and pleasant plot

31. **pageant**—elaborate, costumed performance, often of a historical nature or setting

32. **pantomime**—drama, or dramatic performance, without words, i.e., in gesture or actions only

33. **play**—drama; dramatic composition or performance

34. **playlet**—short play

35. **première (French)**—first performance

(of a drama, motion picture, musical composition, etc.)

36. **presentation**—performance in a theater, as of a drama, etc.

37. **production**—drama, play, or any other work of art for the theater, or produced or performed in the theater

38. **revue, review**—musical show of various loosely combined, or, at times, totally unrelated, songs, dances, skits, etc.

39. **show**—performance of any kind in the theater

40. **sketch**—short play; slight dramatic performance, as in a revue, musical comedy, vaudeville, etc.

41. **skit**—short play, usually of comic character; comic sketch

42. **slapstick comedy**—comedy in which there is a good deal of rough or rowdy action, etc.

43. **solo**—performance by an actor, singer, musician, etc., unaided by others, or with background acompaniment

44. **spectacle**—public performance using a very large company of actors, elaborate scenery or settings, etc.

45. **stage show**—performance on the stage, as distinguished from a motion picture

46. **tragedy, tragic drama**—drama of serious or solemn character, with an unhappy ending

47. **tragicomedy, comitragedy**—tragedy with comic elements

48. **variety show, vaudeville show**—performance, by various individuals or groups, of acts, sketches, skits, music, dancing, singing, tumbling, acrobatics, etc.

49. **vehicle**—play conceived as a means of displaying the talents or virtuosity of a particular actor or company, or as a means of communicating a special theme, idea, etc.

2. Drama, or Dramatic or Theatrical Performance or Presentation, as a Category,n. *From Sec. 1:* burlesque, comedy, farce, legitimate drama or theatrical stage, light comedy, low comedy, one-act play, opera, opéra bouffe, opéra comique, operetta, pantomime, slapstick; tragedy, tragic drama, or buskin; tragicomedy or comitragedy, variety, vaudeville

3. Actor: artist, artiste, entertainer; mummer (humorous); performer, player; Thespian (often humorous or pretentious); trouper,n.; *From Sec. 1:* comedian, dialogist; farceur (French); Harlequin, impersonator, low comedian, mime; monologist, monologuist, or monologian; mummer; pantomimist, pantomimic, pantomime, mime, or mimer; player, soloist, tragedian or Thespian, variety artist, vaudevillian or vaudevillist; *Also:*

1. **comedian, comic, comique, mime**—comic actor

2. **diseur (French)**—professional entertainer who talks, gives monologues, recitations, etc.

3. **extra**—motion-picture actor engaged, usually by the day, to play a member of a crowd, mob, etc.

4. **hero**—person taking the main male part in a play

5. **impersonator, personator**—one who takes the part of a character in a play

6. **lead**—one who takes the main part in a play

7. **star**—leading or most prominent performer in a theatrical production

8. **straight man, or, colloq., stooge**—person who acts as a comic's assistant, asking questions to which funny answers are given

9. **supernumerary**—actor hired to play a member of a crowd, etc.

10. **trouper**—member of a traveling company of actors; experienced actor

11. **understudy**—actor who is prepared to take over another's role if the latter cannot play
12. **villain**—actor taking the part of the evil, wicked, malicious, etc., character in a drama or melodrama

4. Actress,n. *From Sec. 1:* comedienne, tragedienne; *From Sec. 3:* comedienne; diseuse (French); heroine, villainess; *Also:*
1. **ingénue**—actress who takes the part of a young girl, often a naïve or innocent young girl
2. **première (French)**—leading actress in a play
3. **show girl**—female member of the cast of a musical comedy, revue, etc., who does not sing, dance, or speak any lines, but serves chiefly as a costumed decoration
4. **soubrette**—actress taking the part of a flirtatious or frivolous young woman
5. **starlet**—young actress, esp. in motion pictures

5. To Act, i.e., Engage in Acting,v. *From Sec. 1:* mime, mum, pantomime, play, solo, tragedize (tragedization,n.); *From Sec. 3:* entertain, perform; star, stooge; *Also:*
1. **audition**—act for someone who watches in order to make a decision as to the usefulness, skill, etc., of the actor
2. **tread the boards**—act, or take parts, in a play, sketch, etc.

6. To Act or Act Out, Take the Part of, etc., v. *From Sec. 1:* impersonate, mime, pantomime, play (impersonation,n.); *From Sec. 3:* perform; impersonate or personate, understudy (impersonation or personation,n.); *From Sec. 5:* audition; *Also:*
1. **enact**—act out; act or take the part of (enactment,n.)
2. **present**—act or take the part of (presentation,n.)

7. To Dramatize; To Put or Represent in the Form of (a Drama, etc.),v. *From Sec. 1:* burlesque, farcialize, melodramatize, present, produce, show, tragedize (presentation, production, tragedization,n.); *Also:* 1. **stage**—put (a play) on the stage

8. Dramatist; Dramatizer; Writer of Drama, etc.,n. *From Sec. 1:* comedian, dialogist; farceur (French); melodramatist, mimographer, monodramatist, pantomimist, playwright or stagewright; producer, tragedian; *Also:* 1. dramaturgist, dramaturge—dramatist

9. Dramatic; Pert. to, or Descr. of, Drama, Acting, an Actor, etc.,adj. *From Sec. 1:* burlesque, comic or comical, farcical or farcial, legitimate, light, low, melodramatic or melodramatical, monodramatic, one-act, operatic; pantomime, pantomimic, or pantomimical; première, slapstick, solo, spectacular; tragic, tragical, or buskined; tragicomic or tragicomical, variety, vaudevillian or vaudeville; *From Sec. 3:* artistic, extra, leading, straight; *Also:*
1. **Grand Guignol**—descr. of plays dealing with horror—after the name of the theater in Paris that specialized in these (Grand-Guignolism,n.)
2. **histrionic, histrionical**—pert. to, or descr. of, acting, the stage, the theater, actors, etc (histrionism,n.)
3. **stellar**—pert. to, or descr. of, a stage or film star, or to the role played by such a star
4. **theatrical, theatric**—pert. to, descr. of, or suggestive of the stage, acting, dramatic performance or presentation, etc.
5. **Thespian**—pert to drama or tragedy

10. Part in a Play or Dramatic Performance, n

1. **ingénue**—part of a young girl, or of a naïve and innocent young girl
2. **lead**—main part in a play
3. **role, character**—part in a play
4. **walk-on**—minor part containing no spoken lines

11. The Fact or Instance of an Actor Playing Two Parts or Characters in a Play: dual role,n.

12. Having a Strong Desire to Become an Actor or Actress, to Play in the Theater, etc.: stage-struck,adj.

13. Interval between Two Acts of a Play, etc.: entr'acte,n.

14. Words of a Play, or of an Actor's Part in a Play: lines,n.

15. Group of Actors in, or Putting On, a Play: cast, company, dramatis personae; show (colloq.); troupe,n.; *Also:*
1. **buskin**—actors in an ancient Greek or ancient Roman tragic drama
2. **repertory company, stock company**—group of actors that puts on various plays alternating one with the other or successively
3. **summer stock company**—repertory company playing in a summer resort or traveling to various summer resorts
4. **troupe**—company of traveling actors

16. Plays a Company Can or Does Put On, n. *From Sec. 15:* repertory or repertoire, stock, summer stock

17. To Travel as a Company of Actors, Putting on Plays, etc., Esp. in Small Country Towns: barnstorm, troupe,v.

18. Actor in Such a Traveling Company: barnstormer, trouper,n.

19. Science or Art of Writing Dramas: drama, dramaturgy,n. (dramaturgist,n. dramaturgic, dramaturgical,adj.)

20. Art of Producing or Presenting Dramas, Theatrical Productions, etc.: drama, dramatics, dramaturgy, showmanship, theatrics, n. (dramaturgist, showman,n. dramaturgic or dramaturgical,adj.)

21. Acting: dramatics, histrionicism, histrionics,n.

22. Descr. of Extravagantly Exaggerated Acting: histrionic, theatrical,adj. (histrionics or histrionism, theatricality or theatricalism,n.)

23. Art of Acting: dramatics, histrionics, theater,n.

24. Profession of Acting: footlights; show business (colloq.); the stage, the theater,n.

25. The Dramatic Works of an Author, Nation, Time, etc.: drama, theater,n.

26. Dramatic Productions by Amateurs: dramatics, theatricals,pl.n.

27. The Stage, in Theatrical Parlance: the boards, the footlights,n.

28. Stage for Addressing an Audience: rostrum,n.

29. Front of the Stage, i.e., Part of the Stage in Front of the Curtain, and Often Including the Curtain and its Framework; The Arch Separating the Stage from the Seats in the Theater or Auditorium: proscenium,n.

30. Spaces on the Left and Right Sides of the Stage: wings,pl.n.

31. A Theater: amphitheater (with tiers of seats around a central open area); auditorium (for dramatic performances, speeches, concerts, etc.); bowl (for athletic contests, etc.); coliseum or colosseum (for sports events, public meetings, various entertainments, etc.); hippodrome (for athletic contests, games, spectacles, etc.); odeum; opera house

or opera (for operatic performances); play-
house or house (for plays, musicals, etc.);
stadium (for outdoor meetings, games, etc.),
n. (amphitheatric, amphitheatrical, or amphi-
theatral,adj.)

32. Pert. to a Theater: theatral,adj.

33. Section of Seats in a Theater,n.
   1. **balcony**—section of seats above the main
      floor, or orchestra, and projecting partly
      over it
   2. **box**—small compartment of seats on each
      side of a theater, on various levels
   3. **dress circle**—section of seats behind and
      usually above the orchestra
   4. **gallery**—balcony; highest balcony; the
      least expensive seats
   5. **mezzanine**—first balcony; front rows of
      the first balcony, separated from the
      other rows by a railing
   6. **orchestra, parquet**—main floor of seats
   7. **orchestra circle, parquet circle, parterre**
      —section of seats on the main floor be-
      hind the orchestra seats and under the
      overhanging balcony
   8. **pit**—main floor of seats, esp. those at the
      rear (British); small section of seats, usu-
      ally somewhat sunken, for the musicians
      of the theater orchestra

34. Parts of a Drama,n.
   1. **act**—one of the main sections into which
      a play or opera is divided
   2. **catastasis**—part before the catastrophe,
      when the action is most intense
   3. **catastrophe**—culminating event or un-
      raveling of the plot, esp. of a tragedy
      (catastrophic, catastrophal,adj.)
   4. **climax**—turning point of the plot (cli-
      mactic, climactical,adj.)
   5. **crisis**—point (in a drama, story, etc.)
      when the conflict between opposing forces,
      characters, etc., is strongest
   6. **denouement**—part (in a drama, story,
      etc.) in which there is the final clarifica-
      tion or unraveling of the plot
   7. **epitasis**—part in which the main action is
      developed and in which the events lead to
      the catastrophe (esp. in ancient drama)
   8. **prologue**—introductory lines, often in
      verse, spoken by one of the leading actors
      in the cast before the play starts, pre-
      paring the audience for the theme, etc.;
      introductory act of a dramatic perform-
      ance
   9. **protasis**—introductory part (esp. in an-
      cient drama)
   10. **scene**—section of an act of a play, or of
       the play itself; section of a play occurring
       in one place

35. Actor Who Delivers the Prologue: prologue, prologuizer,n.

36. To Deliver a Prologue: prologuize or prologize,v.

37. Form of Psychological Therapy in Which
the Patient Acts Out, Improvising as He
Goes Along, the Situations That Relate to
His Problems, Usually with the Aid of
Other Patients Who Enact the Roles of
Various Members of His Family, etc.: psy-
chodrama,n.

38. One Who Attends the Theater: playgoer,
theatergoer,n.

39. One Who Regularly Attends the Openings of Plays, Operas, etc.: first-nighter,n.

40. Dolls Used in Dramatic Performances:
marionette (moved by strings or by hand);
puppet (with jointed limbs, and moved by
wires, etc.),n.

41. Puppets or Puppet Shows Collectively:
puppetry,n.

42. Performance of Marionettes or Puppets: marionette show, puppet show,n.

43. Art of Putting on a Marionette or Puppet Show, Making Marionettes or Puppets
Perform, etc.: puppetry,n.

44. Manipulator of Puppets: puppeteer,n.

45. Famous Puppet Show: Punch-and-Judy
show,n.

46. Show in Which Action Is Seen through
an Opening, Magnifying Glass, etc.: peep
show,n.

47. To Choose (Actors) for a Play or Other
Dramatic Performance; To Make Such a
Selection of Actors; To Give the Parts of (a
Play) to Various Actors: cast,v.

48. The Actors So Chosen, or to Whom Parts
Are Given: cast,n.

49. Theater District of New York City:
Broadway, the Rialto,n.

970. CONCEALMENT

1. To Conceal or Hide (Something): blot
out; burrow (in, or as in, a hole dug in the
ground); cache, cloak, cover or cover up, curtain; cushion (by, or as if by, a cushion);
enshroud, mantle, mask, obliterate, obscure,
occult, pall, screen, secrete, shade, shroud,
stow, veil, visor or vizor, wrap,v.

2. Concealment, i.e., Act of Concealing or
Hiding (Something): obliteration, obscuration, occultation,n. (obliterative,adj.)

3. That Which Conceals or Hides, or
Serves to Conceal or Hide; Means of Concealing or Hiding: cloak, concealment,
cover, covering, covert, coverture; cover-up
(colloq.); curtain, mantle, mask, pall, screen,
shade, shroud, veil, visor or vizor, vizard or
visard, wraps,n.

4. To Conceal or Hide (Something) in a
Secret Place: cache, harbor, secrete,v. (secretor,n.)

5. To Conceal or Hide (a Person) in a
Place Where He Will Not Be Found: harbor, secrete,v.

6. To Conceal or Hide the Face of: muffle,v.
(muffler,n.)

7. To Conceal or Hide (That Which Is
Illegal, Unethical, Shameful, etc.): cloak,v.
(cloak,n.)

8. To Wrap (Something) for Purposes of
Concealment: muffle,v.

9. To Conceal or Hide (Something) in One's
Hand: palm,v.

10. To Conceal (Information, etc.) in the
Sense of Keeping It from Public Knowledge,
Preventing Its Disclosure, etc.: suppress,v.
(suppression,n.   suppressor,n.   suppressive,
adj.)

11. To Conceal or Cover Up the Faults,
Crimes, Bad Conduct, Mistakes, etc., of:
whitewash,v. (whitewasher,n.)

12. That Which Conceals or Covers Up
Such: whitewash,n.

13. To Conceal or Hide (Something, or a
Quality, etc.) by Giving a False Appearance to It: camouflage, cloak, disguise, mask,
masquerade, veil,v.

14. Such Concealment: camouflage, cloak,
coverture, disguise, mask, masquerade, veil,n.

15. That Which So Conceals: blind (action,
intention, etc.), camouflage, cloak, coverture;
cover-up (colloq.); disguise, mask, veil, visor
or vizor, vizard or visard,n.

16. Military Art of Such Concealment of
Troops, Installations, Cannon, etc.: camouflage,n.

17. To Disguise Oneself: mask, masquerade, v. (masquerader,n.)

18. To Conceal the True Character or Nature of: dissemble, dissimulate,v. (dissimulation,n. dissembler, dissimulator,n. dissimulative,adj.)

19. To Conceal One's Real Feelings or Motives by Pretending to Other or Contrary Feelings or Motives: dissemble, dissimulate, v. (dissimulation,n. dissembler, dissimulator, n. dissimulative,adj.)

20. That Which Is Designed to Hide from Others One's Real Purpose, Motive, Aim, Objective, etc.: smoke screen,n.

21. Action, Behavior, Way of Acting or Behaving, Belief, etc., Produced or Prompted by Unconscious Processes, That Conceals from Oneself and/or from Others One's Unacceptable, Uncomfortable, or Painful Feelings, Impulses, Tendencies, Memories, etc.: defense mechanism,n.

22. Tendency or Ability to Conceal or Hide Mental Disorder by Appearing Normal—a Quality in Paranoia: dissimulation,n. (psychiatric term)

23. Face Mask: false face, visor or vizor, vizard or visard,n.

24. To Put a Face Mask on (Someone): mask, visor or vizor,v.

25. To Don or Wear a Face Mask: mask,v.

26. One Who Wears a Face Mask: masker, masquer,n.

27. Dance, Party, etc., Where Masks, Costumes, etc., Are Worn: masked ball, masquerade,n.

28. Costume, etc., for Such a Dance or Party: masquerade,n.

29. To Attend Such a Dance or Party: masquerade,v. (masquerader,n.)

30. To Hide, or Become Hidden, from View: occult,v. (occultation,n.)

31. To Hide, i.e., Be or Stay Hidden: burrow, conceal oneself, couch, keep or stay out of sight; lie low (colloq.) ; secrete oneself,v. (concealment,n. burrower, coucher,n.)

32. To Lie in Hiding; To Lie in Hiding, or Stay Hidden, for Some Evil Purpose: couch, lurk, skulk,v. (skulk,n. coucher, lurker, skulk or skulker,n.)

33. To Lie in Hiding, Waiting to Attack by Surprise: ambuscade, ambush, lurk,v. (ambush or ambushment,n. ambuscader, ambusher, lurker,n.)

34. Those Who Thus Hide; Arrangement of Soldiers Who Thus Hide: ambuscade, ambush,n.

35. To Hide in a Sneaky or Cowardly Fashion: skulk,v. (skulk,n. skulk, skulker,n.)

36. In Hiding: snug,adj.

37. To Hide Aboard a Ship, Plane, etc., So as to Ride Free, or So as to Get Passage though Otherwise Barred: stow away,v.

38. One Who So Hides: stowaway,n.

39. To Drive out of Hiding: dislodge,v. (dislodgment,n.)

40. To Drive (Birds) out of Hiding: flush,v.

41. Hiding Place,n.
1. ambush, ambuscade—hiding place where soldiers or others wait in order to launch a surprise attack
2. blind—place where hunters conceal themselves
3. cache—secret hiding place for food, supplies, or other valuables
4. concealment—place of hiding

5. den—place where thieves or criminals hide; place of concealment
6. covert—hiding place; hiding place for game, i.e., hunted animals, etc.
7. hideaway—place in which to hide, or, loosely, retire in seclusion
8. hideout—place to hide; place for a criminal to hide

42. Concealed; Hidden: arcane or arcanal (i.e., from general knowledge), blind, blotted out, cached, cloaked, covered, covered up, covert, cushioned, cryptic or cryptical, dark, enshrouded, masked, obliterated, obscure or obscured, perdu or perdue, recondite, screened; secret (i.e, from others) ; secreted, shrouded, snug, subterranean or subterraneous, under cover or undercover, underground, under wraps, unseen, veiled,adj.

43. State of Being Concealed or Hidden: concealment, cover, covertness, darkness, obliteration; obscuration, obscurity, or obscureness; occultation, reconditeness; secrecy (from others) ; snugness,n.

44. To Keep (Something) Concealed or Hidden: secrete,v.

45. Concealed or Hidden, i.e., Not Showing or Manifesting Itself, but Nonetheless Present, as a Quality, Condition, etc.: latent, adj. (latency,n.)

46. Becoming Latent: latescent,adj. (latescency,n.)

47. Purposely Kept Concealed or Hidden, as Motives, Plans, Purposes, etc.: ulterior, adj.

48. Hidden or Secret in the Sense of Not Being Shown: undisclosed, undisplayed, unexposed, unmanifested or unmanifest, unrevealed, unshown, etc.,adj. (See also Sec. 951.1.)

49. Hidden or Secret in the Sense of Not Being Told, Made Known, etc.: hushed-up, occult, smothered, suppressed, unadvertised, unaired, unannounced, unbetrayed, uncommunicated, unconveyed, undeclared, undisclosed, undivulged, unheralded, unimparted, unproclaimed, unpromulgated, unpublicized, unpublished, unreported, unrevealed, untold, unvoiced, etc.,adj. (See also Sec. 613.1.)

50. To Keep (Information, etc.) Hidden in the Sense of Preventing the Telling of It: hush up, keep quiet, smother, suppress,v. (suppression,n.)

51. Hidden in the Sense of Having a False Appearance, as a Thing, Quality, etc.: camouflaged, cloaked, covert, disguised, masked, veiled,adj.

52. Something, as Food, Supplies, or Other Valuables, Hidden in a Secret Place: cache, n.

53. A Barely Perceptible, Almost Hidden, Feeling, Tenor, Tendency, Attitude, Opinion, etc., Contrary to or Different from That Openly Shown, Expressed, Seen, etc.: undercurrent,n.

54. An Atmosphere, Condition, Attitude, etc., That Lies beneath the Surface, That Is Not Openly Revealed, etc.: undertone,n.

55. Not Concealed or Hidden: aboveboard, bald, bare, exposed, open, overt, uncloaked, unconcealed, uncovered, unhidden, unmasked, unobliterated, unobscured, unscreened, unsecreted, unshrouded, unveiled, visible,adj. (baldness, bareness, openness, overtness, unveiledness, visibility or visibleness,n.)

56. Not Disguised: aboveboard, bald, bare, barefaced, crude, uncamouflaged, uncloaked, undisguised, unmasked, unveiled,adj. (baldness, bareness, barefacedness, crudeness or

crudity, undisguise or undisguisedness, unveiledness,n.)

57. To Remove the Disguise or Mask from:
expose, uncloak, undisguise, unmask,v. (exposure or exposal,n.)

58. To Remove One's Disguise or Mask,
Figuratively: expose oneself, undisguise, unmask,v.

59. To Remove One's Mask or Disguise at a
Masquerade Party, etc.: unmask,v. (un-
masker,n.)

971. SECRECY

1. Secret: arcane or arcanal, backdoor, backstairs or backstair, closet, confidential, covert,
cryptic or cryptical, dark, esoteric or esoterical, hush-hush, occult, private, snug, subterranean or subterraneous, under cover or undercover, underground,adj. (confidentialness
or confidentiality, covertness, darkness,
privateness or privacy, snugness,n.)

2. Secret in the Sense of Known Only to a
Few, or Only to Those Initiated into Mysteries, Special Doctrines or Understanding,
etc.: cabalistic, cabalistical, or cabalic; esoteric, mystic or mystical, occult, orphic or
Orphic, recondite,adj. (mysticity or mysticalness, occultness, reconditeness,n.)

3. Such Study, Teachings, Doctrines, etc.:
cabala, cabalism, cabbala, kabala, or kabbala;
esoterism or esotericism, occultism,n. (cabalist, esoterist, occultist,n.)

4. Something Secret in this Sense: occult,
n.

5. Such Secret Practices: esoterism, esotericism,n.

6. To Practice Such: esoterize,v. (esoterist,
n.)

7. Writings of This Nature: esoterica or eso-
terics,n. (esoteric,sing.n.)

8. Descr. of Language or Speech That Is
Secret in This Manner: orphic or Orphic,
adj.

9. Having a Secret or Hidden Meaning:
cryptic or cryptical, mystic or mystical,adj.
(mysticity or mysticalness,n.)

10. Secret in Actions, Procedures, Arrangements, Movement, etc., Often from Fear
of Detection: backdoor, backstairs or backstair, catlike, clandestine, covert, feline, furtive, hangdog, insidious, secretive, sly,
sneaky, stealthy, surreptitious, thievish, under
cover or undercover, underhand or underhanded,adj. (clandestineness, covertness,
felineness or felinity, furtiveness, insidiousness, secretiveness, slyness, sneakiness,
stealth or stealthiness, surreptitiousness,
thievishness, underhandedness,n. hangdog,
sneak,n.)

11. Operating in a Hidden, Obscure, Inconspicuous, or Secret Manner: insidious,
sly, subtle,adj. (insidiousness, slyness, subtlety or subtleness,n.)

12. Operating or Continuing in a Hidden or
Inconspicuous Manner, but Finally Having
Serious Effects, Consequences, etc.: insidi-
ous,adj. (insidiousness,n.)

13. Done, Made, Gotten, Used, etc., in a
Secret Manner and out of Fear of Detection: furtive, sly, sneaky, stealthy, surreptitious, under cover or undercover,adj.
(furtiveness, slyness, sneakiness, stealth or
stealthiness, surreptitiousness,n. sneak,n.)

14. Having a Facial Expression Indicative of
Such Secret Doing, etc.: furtive,adj. (furtiveness,n.)

15. To Act Secretly; To Remain or Move in
or around a Place Secretly: couch, lurk,
skulk, sneak,v. (skulk,n. coucher, lurker,
skulk or skulker, sneak or hangdog,n.)

16. To Exist Secretly, Unsuspected, or Unseen: lurk,v.

17. With One's True Identity Kept Secret or
Hidden, as under an Assumed Name: incognito,adj. (incognito,n. incognito,adv.)

18. One Whose Identity Is So Secret or Hidden: incognito,n.

19. Demanding the Greatest Secrecy from
Those Who Know about It, as Government
Information, Documents, etc.: classified, re-
stricted, top-secret,adj.

20. To Put a Label, Identification, etc., of
Such Secrecy on (Government Information, Documents, etc.): classify,v.

21. Secretly: confidentially, covertly; entre
nous (French); in camera (Latin); in privacy,
in private, privately, privily; sotto voce—
Italian (i.e., in a low or whispered tone, so
as not to be overheard); sub rosa (Latin);
under cover, underground,adv.

22. Secretly, in Order to Avoid Detection:
clandestinely, covertly, furtively, insidiously,
secretively, slyly, stealthily, surreptitiously,
thievishly, under cover, underhand, underhandedly,adv.

23. A Secret,n.
   1. arcanum—secret; so-called secret of
   nature sought by the alchemists (arcana,
   pl.n.)
   2. confidence—secret; something told or
   written to one as a secret

24. Secret and Marvelous Remedy of Great
Potency: arcanum,n. (arcana,pl.n.)

25. Hidden Secrets or Secret Things: penetralia,pl.n.

26. To Keep (Something) Secret: secrete,v.
(secretor,n.)

27. Keeping Secrets; Tending to Keep
Secrets: close-lipped, closemouthed, secretive,
sly,adj. (secretiveness, slyness,n.)

28. To Be Secretive: cover up,v.

29. Not Secretive: non-secretive,adj.

30. One Who Cannot Keep a Secret: sieve,n.

31. Descr. of Secrets; Said or Written as a
Secret; Given as a Secret: confidential,
private,adj. (confidentialness or confidentiality, privacy or privateness,n.)

32. As a Secret: confidentially, in confidence,
in privacy, in private, privately,adv.

33. To Tell a Secret or Secrets to; To Show
One's Trust in (a Person) by Telling a
Secret or Secrets to Him, Knowing There
Will Be No Violation of Secrecy: confide in,v.

34. To Tell (a Secret); To Tell (a Secret)
Knowing It Will Not Be Violated: confide,v.

35. One to Whom a Secret Is, or Secrets Are,
Told in Full Trust: confidant,n. (confidante,
fem.n.)

36. Having Knowledge of (Something Secret
or Confidential): privy to,adj.

37. Secret Organization or Group Fighting
or Opposing the Established Government;
Such a Secret Organization or Group Fighting or Opposing Fascist Governments in
Europe or Elsewhere during World War II:
underground,n.

38. Organization Whose Members Use
Secret Passwords, Gestures, Ceremonies,
etc.: secret society,n.

39. Government Organization Engaged in
Secret Investigations; Any Government
Agency of a Secret Character; U.S. Govern-

ment Agency Charged with Protecting the President from Bodily Harm and with Seeking Out Counterfeiters: secret service,n.

40. Secret Agent: spy, undercover agent,n.

41. Secret Enemy Agent: spy,n.

42. Not Secret: non-secret, overt,adj.

43. Lack of Secrecy: non-secrecy, unsecrecy, unsecretness,n.

44. To Carry or Take Away or Off, Remove, etc., Secretly or Mysteriously, or as if by Supernatural Agency: spirit away or off,v.

972. COVER

1. To Cover (Something, Someone, etc.),v.

1. **bank**—cover (a fire) with fuel, ashes, etc., so that it will burn slowly
2. **beset**—cover thickly (with something)
3. **blanket**—cover with, or as if with, a blanket
4. **bower, embower**—cover or shelter with leaves, foliage, etc.
5. **bury**—cover in order to hide; cover completely by falling on top of; cover with its mass; put in a hole in the ground and cover with earth
6. **canopy**—cover with some kind of roof or rooflike structure
7. **cap**—cover the top of; put a cover or lid on
8. **caparison**—cover (the harness, saddle, etc., of a horse) with richly ornamented material, etc.
9. **carpet**—cover with, or as if with, a carpet; cover thickly
10. **cloak**—cover with, or as if with, a coat, cloak, etc.; cover in order to conceal
11. **clothe (in)**, endue or indue (with)—cover (with, or as if with, a garment, clothing, etc.)
12. **coat**—cover with a layer or thin layer
13. **cowl**—cover with, or as if with, a hood or hood-shaped covering
14. **crown**—cover the highest part of
15. **crust, encrust, incrust**—cover with a hard or shell-like covering
16. **curtain**—cover (a window, opening, etc.) with a curtain; cover (anything else) with, or as if with, a cloth or curtain; cover in order to conceal
17. **daub**—cover or coat with something soft or sticky, as mud, plaster, paint, etc.
18. **deck**—cover by, or as if by, spreading over
19. **dome**—cover with, or as if with, an arched covering, top, roof, etc.
20. **drape**—cover with fabrics that hang in folds, as a window, opening, etc.; cover (anything) as if with such fabrics; cover as if in this manner
21. **encase, incase**—cover completely
22. **envelop, enswathe**—surround with a covering or wrapping, either literally or figuratively; cover completely
23. **fur**—cover with fur; coat with some substance put on as a deposit, esp. an unpleasant or foul deposit, as the tongue, etc.
24. **gild**—coat the surface of with a thin layer of gold, with gold leaf, or with an imitation of gold
25. **hood**—cover with a soft covering (esp. the head and neck); cover with a domed covering
26. **inundate**—cover (land) with water, as by overflowing it; cover completely with anything that flows, or that can be imagined as flowing
27. **invest**—cover the way clothing does; cover as if with garments or clothing
28. **lid**—cover (a box, container, etc.) with a top or movable top

29. **mantle**—cover with, or as if with, a loose cloak or coat; form a covering or coating over; overspread with a cover or coating
30. **muffle, muffle up**—cover or envelop (the person, or esp., the face and/or neck) with a scarf, strip of cloth, etc.; cover (a thing) with material that dulls or deadens sound
31. **overlay, lay over**—cover with a thing or substance; cover (with a thing or substance)
32. **overlie, lie over**—cover by lying upon; lie upon as a cover or covering
33. **overspread**—cover completely (with a thing or substance); cover by, or as if by, spreading over completely
34. **overwhelm**—cover completely with, or under, its mass
35. **pall**—cover with, or as if with, darkness or gloom, or with, or as if with, a dark and gloomy covering, literally or figuratively
36. **panoply**—cover completely with a rich, magnificent, or elaborate covering, garment, adornment, etc.
37. **perfuse**—cover completely with liquid, moisture, color, etc., as if spreading over
38. **roof**—cover (a house, etc.) with a roof; cover (something else) as if with a roof
39. **sheathe, sheath, ensheathe**—cover with a close-fitting or protective covering or layer of covering
40. **shelter**—cover and protect, either literally or figuratively, esp. from the weather, danger, etc.
41. **shroud, enshroud**—cover; cover like a garment, often figuratively
42. **shutter**—cover (a window or other opening) with a hinged, movable, or sliding blind, screen, covering, etc.
43. **smear**—cover or coat with something thick, greasy, or dirty
44. **smother**—cover completely or thickly; cover for purposes of concealing
45. **spread**—cover; cover with a thin layer of something
46. **strew, bestrew**—cover by sprinkling or scattering something on the surface of
47. **submerge, submerse**—cover with or as if with water; cover as water or liquid does; inundate
48. **swaddle**—wrap tightly with bandages, clothing, etc.; wrap (an infant) with strips of cloth
49. **swathe, enswathe, inswathe**—wrap around with, or as if with, bandages; wrap around completely; envelop in wrappings
50. **thatch**—cover (usually a roof) with straw, leaves, etc.
51. **top**—cover with a top; cover the top of
52. **tuck**—cover warmly, as by pushing the bedclothes around or under, etc.
53. **upholster**—cover (furniture, esp. seats) with material; cover (a room) with curtains, carpets, etc.
54. **vault**—cover with an arched roof or ceiling
55. **veil**—cover; cover (esp. the face) with a piece of gauzy or transparent material; cover in order to conceal or disguise
56. **veneer**—cover with a thin layer, usually of some fine material or quality; cover the surface of
57. **wrap, wrap up, enwrap, inwrap**—cover completely (with something); cover or envelop by winding or folding (something) around

2. To Cover Oneself; To Become Covered,v. *From Sec. 1:* fur (as the tongue, etc.), muffle up, wrap up

3. Act of Covering; State of Being Covered, n. *From Sec. 1:* burial, encrustation or incrustation, encasement or incasement, envelopment, inundation, investment or investiture, perfusion, submergence or submersion, enswathement or inswathement (inundatory, investitive, perfusive,adj.)

4. Covering; Cover; That Which Covers or Serves as a Cover,n. *From Sec. 1:* blanket, bower, canopy, cap, caparison, carpet or carpeting, cloak, clothing or clothes, coat or coating, cowl, crown; crust, encrustation, or incrustation; curtain, daub, dome, drape; envelopment, envelope, or envelop; furring, gilt or gilding, hood, lid, mantle, muffler, overlay, pall, panoply, roof or roofing, sheath or sheathing, shelter, shroud, shutter, swaddle or, for an infant, swaddling band, swathe, thatch or thatching, top or topping, upholstery, vault, veil, veneer or veneering; wrap, wrapping, wrapper, or wraps; *Also:*

1. **antimacassar**—cover over the back or arms of a chair, etc., to protect the upholstery against soil or oil from the hair
2. **bark**—outer covering of a tree, or of the woody stem, root, or branch of a plant
3. **bloom**—delicate and somewhat powderlike coating on some fruits and leaves; any surface coating like this
4. **bonnet**—cover; hood
5. **coverlet, coverlid**—cover; small cover
6. **cozy**—padded cover for a vessel or container, esp. a teapot
7. **hood**—cover for an automobile motor
8. **housing**—cover; covering; shelter
9. **hull**—outer covering, husk, shell, etc., of a fruit or seed; any covering, outer cover, etc.
10. **husk**—outer covering, esp. if dry; dry outer covering of an ear of corn or of other fruits or seeds
11. **integument, tegument**—external coating or covering (integumentary, tegumental, tegumentary,adj.)
12. **lid, eyelid**—cover of the eye
13. **peel**—outer covering, or skin, of fruit
14. **pod**—covering of the seeds of beans, peas, etc.
15. **rind**—thick outer covering, as of fruit, cheese, plants, certain animals, etc.
16. **robe**—piece of material, etc., used as a covering
17. **rug**—piece or stretch of floor carpeting, or something likened to it
18. **scarf**—long, ornamental cover of cloth for a table, bureau, etc.
19. **shell**—hard outer covering of an egg, animal such as an insect, turtle, mollusk, etc., fruit, seed, nut, etc., or any covering resembling this
20. **shuck**—hard outer covering of a nut, ear of corn, clam, oyster, etc.
21. **skin**—thin outer covering of the animal body, of fruit, etc.; external covering layer; outer coat
22. **spread**—story, article, advertisement, etc., covering one or usually more pages of a magazine, newspaper, etc.
23. **tegmen**—covering; cover; external coating or covering (tegminal,adj.)
24. **tegument, integument**—natural covering of an animal's body or any part of it, as the shell of a turtle, etc. (tegumental, tegumentary, integumentary,adj.)
25. **vagina**—sheath, or part like a sheath, in the body (vaginal,adj.)
26. **vestment**—that which covers the way a garment does (vestmental,adj.)

5. Covered,adj. *From Sec. 1:* banked, beset, blanketed, etc.; draperied; *From Sec. 4:* lidded, robed, vaginate; *Also:*

1. **blind**—covered, as an opening, ditch, etc.
2. **corticate, corticated, corticose, corticous**—covered with bark
3. **covert**—covered
4. **cucullate, cuculated**—covered with a cowl or hood
5. **foliate**—covered with leaves
6. **timbered, wooded**—covered with woods or growing trees
7. **tunicate**—having a coating or covering made up of several layers, as an onion or bulb (botany)

6. To Uncover, i.e., Remove the Cover or Covering from,v. *From Sec. 1:* unbank, unbury, uncap, uncloak, unclothe, uncoat, uncowl, uncurtain, undrape, ungild, unhood, unlid, unmantle, unmuffle, unroof, unsheathe, unshroud, unshutter, unswaddle, unswathe, unthatch, unveil, unwrap; *From Sec. 4:* bark, hull or unhull, husk or unhusk, peel or unpeel, pod, rind or unrind, shell or unshell, shuck, skin or unskin; *From Sec. 5:* decorticate, defoliate (decorication, defoliation, n.); *Also:* bare, decorticate, denude or denudate, expose, lay bare, strip, unbare (decortication, denudation, exposure or exposal, n.); *Also:*

1. **decorticate**—remove the peel, husk, outer covering, etc., from (decortication,n.)
2. **flay**—remove the outer covering, skin, etc., from
3. **pare**—remove the outer covering, outer coat, covering layer, etc., from (esp. fruits, vegetables, etc.) by cutting
4. **peel**—remove the outer covering, layer, skin, bark, rind, etc., from

7. Uncovered; With Its or One's Covering Removed,adj. *From Sec. 1:* unbanked, unblanketed, etc.; *From Sec. 4:* barked, hulled, etc.; *From Sec. 5:* decorticated or decorticate, defoliated; *From Sec. 6:* bare or bared; decorticated or decorticate; denuded, denudated, or denudate; exposed, laid bare, stripped, unbared (denudation, exposure,n.); decorticated or decorticate, flayed, pared, peeled; *Also:*

1. **bleak**—bare or exposed, swept by winds, and without inhabitants—of lands, places, etc. (bleakness,n.)
2. **naked, nude, stark**—bare; without coverings of any sort (nakedness, nudeness or nudity, starkness,n.)

8. To Remove (the Outer Covering, Coating, Layer, Skin, etc.): pare, pare away, pare off, peel, peel away, peel off, strip, strip away, strip off,v.

9. Piece of Such Outer Covering Removed: paring, peel or peeling, strip,n.

10. To Drop or Lose (Skins, Shells, Horns, Feathers, Fur, etc.)—of Animal Forms That Undergo This Periodic Process Preparatory to Growing New Skins, etc.: cast or cast off, exuviate, molt or moult, shed; slough or slough off (esp. of snakes or serpents in reference to the outer skin); throw off,v. (exuviation, molt or moult,n. molter or moulter, shedder,n.)

11. To Undergo This Process,v. *From Sec. 10:* exuviate, molt or moult, shed, slough,v. (exuviation, molt or moult,n. molter or moulter, shedder,n.)

12. The Skin, etc., Thus Dropped or Lost,n. *From Sec. 10:* exuviae, molt or moult, slough, n. (exuvial,adj.)

13. To Come or Drop Off—of Such Skin, etc., v. *From Sec. 10:* shed, slough,v.

14. To Come or Drop Off, etc.—of Skin in Scales or Layers, Hair, etc.: peel or peel off (skin only), shed; slough or slough off (dead skin or tissue),v.

15. To Come or Peel Off in Scales in the Course of a Disease or a Diseased Condition —of the Skin: desquamate,v. (desquamation, n. desquamative, desquamatory,adj.)

16. To Lose Layers or Scales of Skin, or Hair, by Natural Processes: peel (skin only), shed, v.

17. To Lose (Skin, Hair, etc.) by Natural Processes: shed,v. (shedder,n.)

18. Like, Similar to, or Shaped Like, a Cowl or Hood: cowled, cucullate,adj.

19. Drapes, Collectively: drapery,n.

20. The Business of Covering Furniture, etc., with Fabric: upholstery,n. (upholsterer,n.)

21. State of Being in or under a Protective Cover (from the Weather, etc.): shelter,n.

22. To Go into Such a Cover: shelter,v.

23. Without Such a Cover: shelterless,adj.

24. Cloth Covering or Cover for a Bed: bedcover, bedspread, blanket; comfort, comforter, or comfortable (quilted); counterpane, coverlet, quilt, spread,n.

25. Blanket: comforter, comfort, comfortable, or puff (quilted or tufted and containing feathers, down, wool, etc.); cover; crazy quilt (of patches sewed together in no particular pattern or design); eider down (filled with down, esp. from the eider duck); feather bed (filled with feathers); patchwork quilt (of patches of different colors, design, etc., sewed together); quilt (of two fabrics sewed together with wool, etc., between them),n.

26. Covers for a Bed, Including Sheets, Bedspreads, Blankets, etc.: bedclothes, bedding, n.

27. Cloth Covering for a Horse: blanket, body cloth, horsecloth,n.

28. Richly Ornamented Covering or Coverings for a Horse, esp. for Its Saddle, Harness, etc.: caparison, horsecloth, housing or housings, trappings,n.

29. Like, or Made of, Thatch: thatchy,adj.

30. Pert. to a Crust: crustaceous, crustal,adj.

31. Like, or of the Nature of, a Crust: crustaceous, crustlike,adj.

32. Having a Hard Crust or Coating: crustaceous,adj.

33. To Develop a Crust or Hard Covering; To Develop into a Crust: crust,v.

34. To Cover Her Young Chicks with Her Wings—of a Hen: brood,v.

35. To Become Covered Completely by, or as if by, Water or Other Fluid: submerge,v. (submergence,n.)

36. Able to Become Completely Covered by Water: submergible,adj. (submergibility,n.)

37. That Which Can Become So Covered: submergible,n.

38. Covering, or Acting, Serving, or Intended to Cover, a Whole Group or Category: blanket,adj. (as *blanket indictment,' rejection, endorsement,* etc.)

39. Acting as a Cover on a Vessel, Container, etc.; Acting or Serving as a Lid: tectiform, adj.

973. ROOF

1. Roof: housetop, roofing, top,n.; *Also:*
1. calash—roof of a horse carriage, of the type that can be pushed back
2. canopy—roof or rooflike structure over a bed, throne, etc., or held over a person or persons, as on sacred occasions; rooflike structure, often of cloth, over an entranceway; ornamental rooflike projection (canopied,adj.)
3. ceiling—roof of an enclosed room
4. cupola—rounded roof or ceiling
5. dome—roof of arched or hemispherical shape (domal, domical,adj.)
6. marquee—roof or rooflike structure over the entrance or entranceway of a theater, hotel, etc.

7. shed roof, pent roof, penthouse, penthouse roof—roof attached to the wall of a structure and inclining down from it
8. spire—tower roof that tapers to a point (spired,adj.)
9. terrace—flat roof on a house, esp. a house of Spanish or Oriental architecture
10. thatched roof—roof made of straw, leaves, etc.
11. vault—arched roof or ceiling (vaulted, adj.)

2. To Roof; To Put a Roof on or over,v. *From Sec. 1:* canopy, dome, vault

3. Roof as to Type: curb or gambrel roof (with a double slope); gable roof (with a double slope and ending in gables); hip roof (with sloping ends and sides); hip-and-valley roof (with both hips and valleys); lean-to roof (with only one slope); mansard roof or French roof (with a double slope on all sides, the lower slope sheerer than the upper),n.

4. Descr. of a Roof or Ceiling That Is Not Flat, but Inclines from the Top: inclined, pitched, sloped or sloping,adj.

5. Interior Part of a House Directly beneath the Roof: attic, garret, loft,n.

6. One of the Sloping Boards or Timbers Supporting a Roof: rafter,n.

7. Raised Edge Around a Roof Opening That Stops Water from Running Below: coaming,n.

8. Lower Edges of a Roof That Overhang the Structure: eaves,pl.n.

9. Similar to, or in the Form or Shape of, a Roof: rooflike, tectiform,adj.

10. Material for a Roof: roofing,n.

11. One Who Makes or Repairs Roofs: roofer, n.

974. CLOTHING; DRESS

1. Clothing; Dress: apparel, array, attire; bib and tucker (colloq.); clothes; duds (colloq.); garb, garments, garmenture, habiliment or, more commonly, habiliments; raiment (somewhat poetic); robes; togs or toggery (colloq.); toilet or toilette, trappings, vestment or vestments, wear, wearing apparel, n. (habilimental or habilimentary, vestmental,adj.); *Also:*
1. array, attire—richly ornamented, or rich or fine, clothing
2. canonicals, clericals—clergyman's official dress
3. caparison—dress and ornaments; richly ornamented dress
4. costume—special dress for an occasion, season, or place, or belonging to a certain period, age, profession, etc.; dress or clothing of another time or place, or of a profession, trade, character, etc., worn to a dance or party, on the stage, etc.
5. finery, frippery, gaudery—showy clothing
6. habit—clothing characteristic of a profession, calling, activity, etc.
7. livery—clothing or uniform of a male servant; characteristic dress, figuratively
8. mufti, plain clothes—civilian clothing worn by a member of the armed or uniformed forces; ordinary clothing worn by anyone whose occupation requires the wearing of a uniform while on duty
9. negligee—informal or casual dress, esp. of a female
10. panoply—complete suit of armor; complete and magnificent ornamental dress
11. regalia, robes—special dress; special dress of an office, rank, etc.
12. sackcloth—clothing worn in token of penitence

13. **smallclothes**—children's clothing
14. **sportswear, sport clothes, sports clothes** —clothing that allows freedom of movement and therefore is comfortable for wear while engaging in certain outdoor sports; clothing, esp. for women, that is not formal or dressy
15. **swaddling clothes**—long clothing for a baby
16. **togs**—clothing for a specific use, sport, activity, etc. (colloq.)
17. **toilette**—clothing for fashionable occasions
18. **trappings**—ornamental dress or clothing
19. **uniform**—special dress of members of the army, navy, police force, or other groups
20. **weeds, sackcloth**—clothing that indicates mourning
21. **wraps**—clothing for out-of-doors, esp. in cold weather

2. To Clothe, Dress, or Put Clothing on,v. *From Sec. 1:* apparel, array, attire, garb; garment (mostly in the past participle) ; raiment, robe; tog, tog out, or tog up; array, attire, caparison, livery, panoply, swaddle, uniform, wrap; *Also:* costume, deck, or deck out; endue (with) ; habilitate, habit, invest, suit, vest (enduement, habilitation, investiture or investment,n.) ; *Also:*
1. **attire**—dress for a formal, particular, or special occasion, party, etc.
2. **bedizen, dizen**—dress gaudily, showily, in finery, ornaments, etc. (bedizenment, dizenment,n.)
3. **bundle up**—dress warmly
4. **dandify**—dress (a man) in an excessively neat and foppish manner (dandification, n.)
5. **deck, habit**—dress in rich, ornamented, or fine clothing
6. **doll up**—dress in ornaments; dress showily; dress elegantly (colloq.)
7. **dress up**—dress in fine, rich, or elegant clothing; dress in clothing reserved for going out, special formal occasions, etc.
8. **invest**—dress or clothe in the badges and decorations of office, rank, etc. (investiture, investment,n.)
9. **outfit**—dress (a person) in a complete set of clothing; provide such a set for (a person)
10. **overdress**—dress in an extravagant fashion or beyond the bounds of good taste
11. **prank, prank up**—dress in a showy manner; put fine or rich, or richly ornamented, clothes on
12. **primp, prink**—dress in rich or fine clothing; dress carefully for showy attractiveness; dress with great care or fussiness
13. **spruce, spruce up**—dress for smart appearance
14. **titivate, tittivate**—dress up; spruce up (titivation, tittivation,n.)
15. **vest**—dress in church garments

3. To Dress, i.e., Dress Oneself, Put On One's Clothing, etc.,v. *From Sec. 2:* apparel oneself, array oneself, etc.; robe; bundle up, doll up, dress up, overdress, prank; primp or prink (esp. in front of a mirror) ; spruce up, titivate or tittivate (titivation or tittivation, n.) ; *Also:* get dressed, make one's toilet; *Also:*
1. **preen**—dress carefully with a view to looking pretty, attractive, etc.
2. **underdress**—dress less completely, carefully, or well than the occasion, weather, etc., demands

4. Clothed, Clad, or Dressed,adj. *From Sec. 1:* appareled, arrayed, garbed, garmented, habilimented, raimented, robed; togged, togged out, or togged up; toileted, vestmented; caparisoned, costumed, habited, liveried, panoplied, uniformed, wrapped; *From Sec. 2:* costumed, decked or decked out; endued (with) ; habilitated, habited, invested; attired, bediz-

ened or dizened, bundled up, dandified, dolled up, dressed up, invested, outfitted, overdressed, pranked or pranked up, primped, spruced or spruced up, titivated or tittivated, vested; *From Sec. 3:* underdressed

5. Dressed in a Garment Having a Low Neckline, with the Shoulders Bare—of Women: décolleté,adj.

6. Dressed with Careful Attention to Details of Personal Appearance: dapper, groomed; soigné, masc., or soignée, fem. (both French); spruce, well-groomed,adj. (dapperness, spruceness,n.)

7. With One's Clothing in Untidy Disorder: disheveled, unkempt,adj. (dishevelment,n.)

8. Disorder of Clothing: disarray, dishevelment,n. (disarrayed, disheveled,adj.)

9. State of Being Dressed in a Casual or Careless Fashion, or of Being Partly Undressed—Esp. Applied to Women: dishabille or deshabille, negligee,n. (in dishabille, in deshabille, in negligee,adv. phrase)

10. To Dress Oneself in (an Article of Clothing): don, draw on, get into, get on, pull on, put on, slip into, slip on,v.

11. To Dress Oneself in (Some Quality, Air, Attitude, etc.) as if It Were an Article of Clothing: assume, endue or indue, put on, take on,v. (assumption,n.)

12. Showy in One's Apparel; Fond of Clothing; of Clothing, Showy, Formal, or Stylish: dressy,adj. (dressiness,n.)

13. Pert. to Dress, Clothing, Garments, etc.: habilimental or habilimentary, vestiary, vestmental,adj.

14. Woman Who Models Clothes, i.e., Wears Them to Show Customers How They Look: manikin, mannequin, model,n.

15. The Entire Process of Dressing, Including Bathing, Fixing or Combing the Hair, etc.: toilet,n.

16. Such a Process as Applied Esp. to the Female: toilette,n.

17. Table at Which to Dress: dressing table, toilet, vanity,n.

18. Article or Substance, Other than Apparel, Used in Dressing or Grooming, as Brush, Comb, Liquid, or Other Preparation, etc.: toiletry,n.

**19. Such Articles or Substances, as toilet, toiletries, toilet set,n.

20. Case, Box, Bag, etc., Containing Such Articles and Substances, and Carried by the Female: vanity bag, vanity box, vanity case, n.

21. Light Box for Holding Hats, Collars, or Other Small Articles of Clothing: bandbox,n. (bandboxical, bandboxy,adj.—this is the reference for phrases like *stepped out of a bandbox*, etc., to indicate well-dressed, etc., appearance)

22. Articles of Men's Clothing, as Shirts, Ties, etc., and Sometimes Including Suits: haberdashery,n.

23. Man Who Pays an Inordinate Amount of Attention to, and/or Is Vain about, the Elegance or Attractiveness of His Dress and Appearance: beau, Beau Brummell, buck, coxcomb, dandy, dude, exquisite, fop; jack-a-dandy (if a small man) ; jackanapes, popinjay; toff (British),n. (beauism, buckishness, coxcombry or coxcombicality, dudishness or dudism, foppishness or foppery, jack-a-dandyism,n. beauish, buckish; coxcombical, coxcombic, or coxcomby; dandy, dandyish, dandiacal, or dandified; dudish, foppish,adj.)

24. Trait or Mannerism of Such a Person: coxcombry, foppery,n.

25. Manners or Behavior, etc., of Such a Person: beauism, coxcombry, dudism, foppery, jack-a-dandyism,n.

26. To Make into, or Cause to Be, Such a Person: dandify, dandyize,v. (dandification, n.)

27. Woman Who Is Likened to Such: coxcombess,n.

28. Person Dressed in High, or in the Latest, Fashion: dude (man) ; fashion plate (colloq.) ; swell; toff (British),n.

29. Room for Dressing: dressing room,n. (esp. for actors in the theater)

30. Room, etc., Where Church Garments and Sacred Objects Are Kept: sacristy, vestry,n.

31. Room, Piece of Furniture, etc., Where Clothing Is Kept: wardrobe,n.

32. Room, etc., Where Outdoor Clothes are Left Temporarily, as in a Restaurant, Theater, etc.: checkroom, cloakroom,n.

33. To Leave (Clothes) in Such a Room: check,v.

34. Department of a Royal or Other Ménage That Is in Charge of Clothing: wardrobe,n.

35. Garments as a Group, Set, or Collection, n.
1. **costume**—set of female clothing worn as a unit
2. **ensemble**—woman's outfit of clothing, the parts of which go together or harmonize in color, material, or some other way
3. **outfit, suit**—set of clothing for wear together
4. **trousseau**—bride's outfits of clothing and other personal possessions, as jewelry, linens, etc.
5. **wardrobe**—the sum of one's clothing; costumes, etc., of a theatrical company

36. Style of Dress: garb, guise,n.

37. Style of Dress, Characteristic of a Country, Age, Group, etc.: costume,n.

38. A Particular Garment, etc.,n.
1. **alb**—white garment for church service worn by a clergyman
2. **apron**—garment designed to protect the front of clothing during work, housework, etc.
3. **bathrobe**—robe worn before bathing, on arising in the morning, etc.
4. **bib, dickey, dicky**—article of clothing tied around the neck of a child to protect his clothing while he is eating; top part of an apron
5. **blouse**—loose upper garment worn by French and Russian peasants
6. **cap and gown**—academic hat (mortarboard) and long gown of dark color worn at commencement exercises, etc.
7. **cassock**—close-fitting garment, extending to the ground, worn by certain members of the clergy
8. **coveralls**—loose, one-piece garment, consisting of trousers and a top with sleeves, worn by mechanics, painters, etc., while working
9. **cowl**—garment with a hood worn by monks
10. **dolman**—long robe worn by Turks
11. **dressing gown**—garment worn when dressed casually, carelessly, incompletely, etc., or when getting dressed
12. **frock**—loose outer garment worn by workmen, peasants, monks, etc.
13. **gown**—loose-fitting and flowing garment of office, rank, profession, etc.

14. **kimono**—characteristic wide-sleeved outer garment of the Japanese
15. **jupon**—dresslike garment, richly decorated, worn over armor
16. **leotard**—tight-fitting garment worn by acrobats, dancers, etc.; the top has a low neckline, the bottom is in the form of tights
17. **pinafore, dickey, dicky**—child's apron covering most of the dress or undergarment
18. **robe**—long, loose outer garment; garment of office or rank
19. **sari**—chief outer garment of Hindu women, made of a single long piece of material, usually silk or cotton, and wound around the body with one end loose to cover the head; adaptation of this made into a modern dress or gown for women in the U.S. and elsewhere
20. **sarong**—principal garment of men and women in the Malay Archipelago, East Indies, etc.—worn wound around the lower part of the body (occasionally called, erroneously, a *pareu* or a *lavalava*)
21. **smock, duster, frock**—long loose garment worn over other clothes, usually to protect them while working
22. **suit**—garment of two or more pieces worn together, as jacket and trousers, jacket and skirt, etc.
23. **tog**—garment (colloq.)
24. **toga**—garment or robe of office or profession; distinctive or special garment; loose garment of the ancient Romans when making a public appearance
25. **tunic**—dresslike garment worn by both sexes in ancient Greece and Rome
26. **vest, waistcoat**—sleeveless garment worn under a man's coat, or a similar garment worn by a woman
27. **vestment**—garment; gown or robe, esp. an official or ceremonial gown or robe (vestmental,adj.)
28. **wrap**—garment wrapped, or to be wrapped, around the person
29. **wrapper**—long and loose-fitting garment

39. To Put the Indicated Garment On (a Person),v. *From Sec. 38:* apron, cowl, frock, gown, robe, smock or frock; tog, tog out, or tog up; wrap or wrap up

40. To Put the Indicated Garment On (Oneself),v. *From Sec. 38:* gown, robe

41. Dressed in the Indicated Garment,adj. *From Sec. 38:* aproned, cowled, frocked, gowned, robed, smocked or frocked; togged out, or togged up; togaed or togated, waistcoated, wrapped

42. One Who Wears a Gown or Robe as the Characteristic Dress of His Office, Profession, etc.: gownsman,n.

43. Garment Worn by Women while Getting Dressed, or when Incompletely, Casually, or Carelessly Dressed: dishabille or deshabille, dressing gown, duster, housecoat, house gown, kimono, morning dress, negligee, peignoir (literally, while combing the hair), robe; robe-de-chambre (French) ; wrapper,n.

44. Garment Worn in Bed; Sleeping Garment: bedgown, nightdress, nightgown, night robe, or, French, robe-de-nuit (these chiefly by women) ; nightshirt or shirt (knee-length, by men) ; pajamas or pyjamas (two-piece, with trousers),n.

45. Sleeping Garments, Collectively: night clothes, nightdress, nightwear,n.

46. Outer Clothing: outer dress, outer garments, outwear, overgarments, wraps,n.

47. Garment Worn over Others: outer garment, overdress, overgarment, wrap,n.

975. FORMAL DRESS

1. Clothes for Formal Wear, i.e., for the Theater, Opera, Evening Parties, Weddings, and Similar Formal Occasions: dinner clothes, dress clothes, evening dress, formal dress, formals, formal wear, full dress; *For men only:* soup-and-fish (slang), tails (colloq.),n.

2. Garment of Formal Wear for Men: cutaway (colloq.) or cutaway coat, dress coat, dress shirt, dress suit, full-dress suit, swallow-tailed coat or swallowtail, tail coat; tails (colloq.),n.

3. Such a Garment for Semi-Formal Wear: dinner coat or jacket, shell jacket (worn in the tropics in place of the tuxedo), tuxedo,n.

4. Formal Garment for Women: evening dress, evening gown, formal, formal dress, formal gown,n.

5. Semi-Formal Garment for Women: cocktail dress or gown, dancing dress, dinner dress or gown,n.

6. Semi-Formal Military or Naval Jacket: mess jacket,n.

7. Man's Shirt for Formal Wear: boiled shirt, dress shirt,n.

8. Man's White Bow Tie for Formal Wear: white tie,n.

976. COAT

1. Coat, i.e., Overcoat,n.
1. **balmacaan**—man's short overcoat with sleeves like those of a raglan
2. **burnoose, burnous**—cape or cloak, with a hood, worn by Moors, Arabs, etc.
3. **cape**—sleeveless cloak, fastened around the neck and hanging from the shoulders, worn by itself or attached to another coat
4. **capote**—cloak with a hood
5. **cardinal**—woman's cloak with a short hood
6. **chesterfield**—single-breasted overcoat with concealed buttons
7. **cloak, paletot**—loose-fitting coat
8. **coonskin**—coat made of raccoon skin
9. **dolman**—woman's capelike coat; woman's coat with sleeves wide at the armholes and narrower at the wrists
10. **frock coat, frock, Prince Albert**—closefitting, double-breasted man's coat, reaching to the knees
11. **greatcoat**—heavy overcoat
12. **mackinaw, Mackinaw coat**—short coat of thick wool and, often, plaid design
13. **manteau**—woman's cape or cloak; any cape or cloak
14. **mantelet, mantlet, mantilla**—short cape or cloak
15. **mantle, wrap**—cape; sleeveless cloak
16. **melton coat**—coat of heavy wool that has a smooth finish
17. **pea jacket, pea coat**—thick woolen coat, of short length, worn by sailors in winter weather
18. **pelisse**—long cloak with arm openings, worn by women; coat lined or decorated with fur
19. **raglan**—coat with sleeves that continue into the collar
20. **redingote**—woman's light, unlined coat worn open down the front; double-breasted long overcoat formerly worn by men
21. **spring coat, topcoat**—light coat worn in spring weather
22. **surcoat**—overcoat; coat worn over armor in medieval times
23. **surtout**—man's close-fitting overcoat
24. **ulster**—long, loose-fitted overcoat

2. Bottom of a Coat: skirt,n.

3. Raincoat: mackintosh or macintosh, oilskins, slicker, tarpaulin, waterproof,n.

4. Jacket; Short Coat,n.
1. **blazer**—bright-colored jacket worn, or similar to that worn, by a tennis player
2. **bolero**—short, vestlike jacket, ending above the waist or just coming to the waist, and worn open; may or may not have sleeves
3. **coatee**—close-fitted, short coat
4. **dolman**—hussar's gold-braided jacket
5. **doublet**—close-fitting jacket, with or without sleeves, formerly worn by men
6. **Eton jacket, Eton coat**—boy's or woman's waist-length jacket similar to those worn by the students at Eton College in England
7. **jerkin**—tight-fitting jacket, often sleeveless; such a jacket of leather worn in the 1500's and 1600's
8. **jumper**—loose jacket; loose jacket worn by sailors, workmen, etc.
9. **lumberjack**—jacket of wool, leather, etc., made to resemble those worn by woodcutters
10. **parka**—long woolen jacket with a hood; fur jacket worn in Alaska and in northeastern part of Asia; skiing jacket
11. **sack coat**—short, loose man's coat
12. **sacque, sack**—woman's or child's short, loose coat
13. **shrug**—woman's knitted jacket, covering the shoulders and back, and having a rounded, open front
14. **smoking jacket**—loose jacket, often trimmed with braid, worn by men around the house, while smoking, etc.
15. **spencer**—short woolen jacket
16. **sport jacket**—man's jacket, often of loud design or weave, that does not match the trousers
17. **tunic**—jacket of a military uniform (called *blouse* in the U. S. Army)
18. **windbreaker**—jacket, usually of leather, of close-fitting waist, cuffs, and collar

5. Garment Worn under a Jacket or Doublet: waistcoat,n.

6. Sweater: cardigan, cardigan jacket, or cardigan sweater; pull-over, slipover, or slip-on (one pulled over the head in donning),n.

977. NECKWEAR

1. Article of Clothing Worn as a Neck Adornment or Covering,n.
1. **bandanna, bandana**—large, colored handkerchief tied around the neck
2. **boa**—thin scarf of silk, feathers, etc., worn around the neck by women
3. **choker**—narrow fur piece, or other material, worn around the neck by women
4. **cravat, kerchief, neckcloth, neckerchief, neckpiece, necktie**—strip of material worn around the neck
5. **fichu**—woman's triangular kerchief worn around the neck, the ends crossed or otherwise brought together over the bosom
6. **guimpe, chemisette, jabot, tucker**—woman's neck adornment of lace, etc., worn with a dress having a low-cut neckline or openwork bodice
7. **muffler, comforter**—heavy neck scarf worn as protection against the weather
8. **neckband**—band worn around the neck by women
9. **ruff**—gathered material worn to adorn the neck
10. **scarf**—broad strip of material worn around the neck as adornment or covering
11. **tippet**—wool or fur scarf covering the

neck, or the neck and shoulders, and having hanging ends
12. **tucker**—piece of material worn by women around the neck and shoulders

2. Man's Necktie: ascot (tied with broad, flat ends hanging from the knot); bow tie (tied in a bow); cravat; foulard (of material with a small, printed design), four-in-hand (to be tied in a slip knot with the ends hanging); scarf (with hanging ends); Windsor tie (of soft silk or other material, tied in a loose double bow or tight double knot),n. (four-in-hand,adj.)

3. Articles of Clothing Worn around, or at, the Neck; Neckties, Collars, etc., Collectively: neckwear,n.

4. Collar,n.
1. **choker**—high collar (colloq.)
2. **dickey, dicky**—detachable collar for a woman's blouse
3. **Eton collar**—wide, stiff collar worn with a short jacket
4. **Peter Pan collar**—short collar with rounded ends on a woman's dress, blouse, etc.
5. **ruff**—collar of gathered material, popular in the 16th century
6. **stock**—collar fitting the neck like a band

5. Continuation of a Coat or Jacket Collar Turned Back: lapel, revere, revers,n.

6. Broad Strip of Material Worn over One Shoulder: sash,n.

7. Broad Piece of Material Worn by Women around the Shoulders: fichu (triangular in shape); shawl; stole (of fur or cloth); wrap,n.

978. GLOVES

1. Glove,n.
1. **gauntlet, gantlet**—long glove that partially covers the forearm; medieval armored glove
2. **kid glove**—glove made of leather from the skin of a goat or young goat
3. **mitt**—long glove, worn by women, covering the forearm and the main part of the hand, and extending, sometimes, over part of the fingers; baseball player's glove; boxer's glove (usually in pl.)
4. **mitten, mitt**—glove with special place for the thumb but without divided fingers
5. **mousquetaire glove, mousquetaire**—glove with a long, closed wrist

2. Thick Tube of Wool or Fur, etc., with an Opening for the Hands—Used as a Kind of Glove by Women: muff,n.

3. To Cover with, or as if with, a Glove; To Furnish Gloves to; To Act as a Glove for: glove,v.

4. Short Sleeve: armlet,n.

5. Very Short Sleeve, Continuous with the Shoulder of a Garment: cap sleeve,n.

6. Descr. of Other Types of Sleeves: balloon (puffed out); bouffant (full or puffed out); dolman (wide at the shoulder, narrow at the wrist, for women's clothing); puffed; raglan (continuing into the collar); set-in (with a seam at the shoulder),adj.

7. Part of the Sleeve That Covers the Wrist: wristband,n.

8. Band around the Wrist That Protects against Cold Weather, Usually Attached to the Underpart of the Sleeve: wristlet,n.

9. Opening or Hole in a Garment for the Arm to Go through: armhole,n.

10. Handkerchief: bandanna or bandana (of large size, with a gay pattern on a blue or red background); foulard (of light silk, rayon,

cotton, etc., with small printed pattern), kerchief,n.

979. FOOTWEAR

1. Articles for Covering the Feet, Esp. Shoes, Boots, etc.: footgear, footwear, shoeing,n.

2. Shoe,n.
1. **bed slipper**—slipper to wear on arising from bed
2. **blucher**—a kind of high shoe; a kind of half boot
3. **boot**—shoe with a top that reaches considerably up the leg, often to or above the knee
4. **bootee**—infant's cloth or knitted shoe; woman's half boot
5. **brogan, brogue**—strong, heavy, or coarse low or high shoe
6. **buskin**—high shoe reaching to the calf or beyond; half boot
7. **clog**—shoe with a thick, usually wooden, sole
8. **cothurnus, cothurn, buskin**—high shoe with a thick sole, worn by tragic actors in ancient Greece and Rome, and often considered a symbol of tragic drama
9. **gaiter**—shoe with elastic on the sides instead of laces or buttons; a kind of high shoe no longer worn
10. **hobnailed boot, hobnailed shoe**—boot or shoe with soles protected by short nails with large heads
11. **loafer, shuffler**—low shoe of soft leather and of slipperlike design
12. **moccasin**—soft leather shoe worn by the American Indians; any similar modern shoe
13. **mule**—woman's house slipper that leaves the back of the heel exposed
14. **oxford, Oxford shoe, Oxford tie**—low shoe with laces or buttons
15. **Prince Albert**—man's decorated house slipper with a low counter
16. **pump**—light low shoe, originally worn by dancers
17. **sabot**—wooden shoe worn in France, Holland, Belgium, etc.; European peasant's wooden shoe; leather shoe with a wooden sole
18. **saddle shoe**—low shoe with a flat heel, generally white in color, with a brown or black band across the instep
19. **sandal**—shoe consisting of little more than a sole, and fastened to the foot by thongs or straps
20. **scuff**—slipper without a heel or counter, for house wear
21. **slipper, pantofle, pantoffle**—light, low shoe that one slips one's foot into easily, often for wear indoors
22. **sneaker**—soft shoe worn in a gymnasium; similar shoe, with a soft sole, worn out of doors
23. **step-in**—woman's shoe or slipper with an open heel (usually in the pl.)
24. **wellington, Wellington boot**—man's boot with a loose top, the front of which is higher than the back; similar boot worn under the trouser leg

3. To Shoe, i.e., Put Shoes On, Provide with Shoes, etc.,v. *From Sec. 2:* boot, slipper

4. Shod, i.e., Having Shoes On, or Wearing Shoes,adj. *From Sec. 2:* booted, buskined, sandaled, slippered; *Also:* 1. **calced**—descr. of those members of religious orders who wear shoes

5. Coarse and Heavy Shoes: clodhoppers,n.

6. High Boots with Tassels in Vogue in England in the Early 1800's: Hessian boots,n.

7. One Who Polishes Shoes as an Occupa-

tion: bootblack, boots, shoeblack, shoeshine boy,n.

8. Shoes Worn over Regular Shoes in Wet or Snowy Weather: arctics, galoshes, overshoes, rubber boots or boots, rubbers; sandals (covering not much more than the soles of the shoes); snowshoes (for walking in deep snow without sinking in),n.

9. To Walk on, or Go by, Snowshoes: snowshoe,v. (snowshoer,n.)

10. Long Pieces of Wood Attached to the Shoes for Walking, Gliding, etc., Over Snow, Esp. as a Sport Down Hills: skis or skees,n. (skier,n. ski,v.)

11. Skiing Race Down a Winding Course: slalom,n.

12. To Strike with the Shoe or Foot; To Push, or Force to Move, by Using the Shoe or Foot: boot (colloq.), calcitrate, kick,v. (boot, calcitration, kick,n.)

13. Not Wearing Shoes: barefoot (or stockings); discalced or discalceate, shoeless, unshod, unshoed,adj.

14. Descr. of Those Members of Religious Orders Who Do Not Wear Shoes, or Who Go Barefoot: discalced or discalceate,adj.

15. Such a Member, as a Monk or Nun: discalceate,n.

16. A Stocking: anklet (reaching just above the ankle), hose; sock (covering only part of the leg to somewhere below the knee),n.

17. Stockings: hose, hosiery,n.

18. Embroidered or Woven Ornament, Rising from the Ankle, on Each Side of a Sock or Stocking: clock,n. (clocked,adj.)

19. To Embroider or Weave Such an Ornament On (a Sock or Stocking): clock,v.

20. A Covering over the Ankle and the Instep of the Shoe: gaiter, spat,n.

21. Coverings of the Legs Reaching, Usually, from the Ankle to the Knee: gaiters, gambados or gambadoes, leggings; overalls (waterproof); puttees (worn by soldiers, riders, etc.); spatterdashes (to protect the stockings, trousers, etc., in wet weather),n.

22. Armor for the Leg, from Ankle to Knee: greave, jamb, jambeau,n.

23. Armor for the Foot: solleret,n.

24. Mexican Sandals, Lately Popular in the U.S.: huaraches,pl.n.

980. TROUSERS

1. Trousers: breeches; britches (colloq. or dialectal); jeans, pants,n.; *Also:*
  1. bloomers, trouserettes—women's loose trousers, gathered at the knee, and worn for athletic exercises, etc.
  2. blue jeans—trousers of blue jean, blue denim, etc.
  3. buckskins—trousers made from the skin of a deer or buck
  4. cords, corduroys—corduroy trousers
  5. ducks—trousers made of plain, heavy cotton
  6. dungarees—work trousers, overalls, etc., made of coarse cotton
  7. flannels—trousers made of flannel
  8. hose—tight-fitting trousers formerly worn by men
  9. jeans—trousers made of a strong twilled cotton
  10. jodhpurs—riding trousers, fitting close around the ankles
  11. knickers, knickerbockers, knee breeches, knee pants—short trousers gathered below the knee

  12. Levi's—heavy trousers of blue denim with copper rivets (trade-marked name)
  13. overalls, jeans—work trousers with a part coming up over the chest, and fitted with shoulder straps
  14. pajamas, pyjamas—loose trousers, worn by both males and females in India and other Oriental countries, and usually made of silk or cotton
  15. pantaloons—trousers of various shapes and forms worn in earlier periods of time
  16. pedal-pushers—short trousers, ending usually below the knees, for children and women
  17. peg tops, peg-top trousers—trousers that are wide at the hips and that narrow considerably toward the ankles
  18. plus fours—wide knickers worn for sports, as golf, etc.
  19. rompers, jumpers—child's garment consisting of short trousers gathered at the thigh and an attached blouse or waist
  20. shorts—short trousers for sports, athletic exercises, etc.; knickers
  21. slacks—trousers not matched to a jacket; trousers for sportswear; women's trousers
  22. striped trousers—trousers with a broad silk stripe running down the outside of each leg, characteristic of diplomats
  23. tights—tight-fitting trousers worn by acrobats, dancers, etc., sometimes combined with a tight-fitting upper part

2. Covering Worn around the Buttocks, or Region of the Buttocks, and Hiding the Genitals: breechcloth; breechclout; dhoti or dhooti (worn by males in India); G string (worn by savages, or, when decorated in various fashions, by burlesque or strip-tease actresses); loincloth; pareu (of flowered pattern, worn in Polynesia); waistcloth,n.

3. Such a Covering for Infants: diaper,n.

4. To Put Such a Covering On (an Infant): diaper,v.

5. Baggy Flap Covering the Opening in the Front of Men's Trousers in the 15th and 16th Centuries: codpiece,n.

6. Band Going around the Waist, etc.: bellyband (around the belly, as on an infant, horse, etc.), belt; cummerbund or kummerbund (in India and other regions, or worn by diplomats, etc.); girdle, girth; Sam Browne belt (with a diagonal strap to the right shoulder, for military officers); sash (usually of silk); waistband (esp. as part of trousers or a skirt),n.

7. Belt Coming Diagonally from Shoulder to Hip for a Sword, Horn, Trumpet, etc.: baldric,n.

981. UNDERWEAR

1. Underwear: balbriggans (of knitted cotton); body clothes; flannels (of flannel); smallclothes, underclothes, underclothing, underdress, undergarments, underthings; undies (colloq.); woollies (of wool—colloq.),n.

2. Women's Underwear, Usually of Silk, Rayon, Nylon, Lace, etc.: lingerie,n.

3. An Undergarment,n.
  1. bloomers, trouserettes—female undergarment of loose trousers gathered at the knees
  2. brassiere; bra (colloq.); bandeau—undergarment that supports the female breasts
  3. briefs—male shorts or female panties that hug the crotch
  4. bustle—wire framework, cushion, etc., worn at one time by women to make the skirt stand out in the rear
  5. camisole—loose underbodice

6. **chemise**—a kind of slip or long under-shirt worn by women
7. **combination, union suit**—one-piece undergarment consisting of both top and drawers, or top and petticoat, etc.
8. **corset, corselet, foundation, girdle, stays**—woman's undergarment that supports and molds the figure
9. **corset cover**—undergarment, as a waist, etc., worn over the corset
10. **crinoline**—petticoat of stiff material worn under a full skirt
11. **drawers, shorts, underdrawers, under-pants**—undergarment in the style of short trousers
12. **pantalets, pantalettes**—women's drawers (humorous); drawers worn by women in the 1800's
13. **panties, step-ins**—woman's underdrawers
14. **petticoat, underskirt**—skirt, usually of cotton, silk, etc., worn by women under the outer skirt
15. **shift**—chemise (somewhat old-fashioned term)
16. **shimmy**—chemise (colloq.)
17. **shirt, undershirt, undervest**—undergarment for the upper part of the body
18. **slip**—woman's garment worn under the dress
19. **teddies**—woman's one piece undergarment, combining top and loose drawers
20. **underbodice**—undergarment, covering the waist and breasts, worn by women
21. **underwaist, waist**—undergarment worn by children, and to which other garments are buttoned
22. **unmentionable**—woman's undergarment (humorous)

4. To Put a Corset On (a Woman) or Fit (a Woman) with a Corset: corset,v.

5. Corsets, Collectively; Foundation Garments for Women, Including Brassieres, etc.: corsetry,n.

982. A WOMAN'S DRESS

1. A Woman's Dress: frock, gown,n.; *Also:*
1. **décolletage (French)**—dress with a low neckline
2. **dirndl**—dress with a full skirt and tight bodice
3. **habit**—riding dress
4. **hostess gown, housecoat, house gown**—long dress worn while entertaining guests at one's home
5. **house dress**—inexpensive cotton dress worn while doing housework
6. **jumper**—sleeveless dress, worn with a blouse, etc.
7. **mantua**—loose gown formerly worn by women
8. **Mother Hubbard**—full, loose dress
9. **pinafore**—sleeveless, apronlike dress
10. **princess dress**—close-fitting dress without a break at the waistline
11. **robe**—elaborate dress
12. **sheath**—close-fitting dress that hugs the lines of the body

2. To Put a Dress On (a Woman),v. *From Sec. 1:* frock, gown; robe

3. To Put On a Dress,v. *From Sec. 1:* gown; robe

4. Wearing, or Dressed in, a Dress,adj. *From Sec. 1:* frocked, gowned; décolleté, robed

5. Descr. of a Dress with a Low Neckline: décolleté,adj.

6. Low Neckline of a Dress: décolletage,n.

7. Descr. of Such a Neckline: plunging,adj.

8. Upper Part of a Woman's Dress, Esp. if Close-Fitting: bodice, corsage,n.

9. The Waist Part, or the Body, of a Woman's Dress: corsage,n.

10. Bottom Part of a Woman's Dress: skirt, n.

11. Skirt,n.
1. **culottes**—skirt made with trouserlike separations
2. **dirndl**—full skirt that has a tight waist
3. **hobble skirt**—woman's skirt so extremely narrow at the bottom as to impede walking
4. **hoop skirt, crinoline**—woman's skirt that flares out from the waist
5. **kilt, filibeg, philibeg**—short, plaited skirt worn by men in the Scottish Highlands
6. **lava-lava**—short skirt of printed calico worn in Samoa, etc.
7. **overskirt**—skirt worn over other skirts
8. **pannier**—puffed skirt
9. **pareu**—cotton skirt of flowered pattern worn in Polynesia, Tahiti, etc.
10. **peg-top skirt, peg tops**—skirt that is wide at the waist and narrows toward the bottom
11. **peplum**—short skirt attached to a jacket or waist
12. **underskirt**—skirt worn under other skirts

12. Fullness of Material, Bow, or Other Decoration at the Back of a Skirt below the Waist: bustle,n.

13. To Draw (One's Skirt) Up about Oneself: kilt,v.

14. Woman's Garment for the Upper Part of the Body: blouse; bodice (laced in front, and commonly worn with peasant dress); halter (leaving arms and back bare); middy blouse or middy (with a sailor collar); shirt, shirtwaist, T-shirt; tunic (falling over the skirt, and usually belted); waist,n.

15. The Bottom Part of Such a Garment Falling below the Waist to Cover the Hips, and Usually Flounced: peplum,n.

16. Woman's Detachable Blouse Front; Man's Detachable Shirt Front: dickey or dicky,n.

17. Woman's Sleeveless Vest, Worn over a Blouse or Dress, and Laced Tightly over the Bosom: bodice,n.

18. Man's Close-Fitting Collarless Shirt: basque shirt, polo shirt, T-shirt,n.

983. HAT

1. A Covering for the Head: cap, hat, head-cloth, headdress, headgear, headpiece,n.

2. A Hat, Cap, or Other Specific Head Covering,n.
1. **babushka**—scarf worn by women as a head covering, tying under the chin
2. **barret**—flat-shaped, small cap
3. **beanie**—round cloth or felt skullcap, usually worn by children; small, round hat without a brim
4. **beaver, castor**—flat, round hat made of beaver or other fur
5. **beret**—close-fitting, round, cloth hat without a visor
6. **biretta, birretta, beretta, berretta, barret**—cap of square shape, three projections on top, and a crowning tassel—worn by some Roman Catholic clergymen
7. **bonnet, capote**—woman's or child's hat that covers the hair and ties under the chin
8. **breton**—a kind of woman's hat having the brim turned up on all sides
9. **busby**—high fur hat worn by hussars, artillerymen, etc., in the British Army
10. **calash**—woman's bonnet or hood popular in the 1900's

11. cap—soft cloth hat without a brim; woman's head covering of lace or other material; head covering indicating profession, rank, etc.

12. cap and bells, fool's cap—cap with little bells, worn by a court jester

13. chapeau—hat

14. cloche—close-fitting woman's hat made somewhat in the shape of a bell

15. cocked hat—hat whose brim turns up on two or three sides

16. coif—close-fitting cap; cap in the shape of a hood, worn under a veil by nuns and others; kind of skullcap formerly worn by barristers

17. coonskin hat, coonskin cap—hat or cap made of the skin of a raccoon

18. cowl—hood; monk's hood; hood of a monk's garment

19. crush—soft felt hat so made as not to be hurt by crushing

20. derby; bowler (British); kelly (slang)—round hat made of stiff felt and having a narrow brim

21. dunce cap, dunce's cap, fool's cap—tall paper cap, shaped like a cone, for stupid or lazy students

22. fascinator—crocheted or lace scarf or shawl worn by women as a head covering

23. fedora—man's felt hat with a creased crown and snap brim

24. fez—Turkish felt cap in the shape of a cone with its top cut off, usually red in color, and having a long black tassel (fezzy,adj.)

25. garrison cap—military cap with a leather visor

26. helmet—medieval armored covering for the head; protective covering for the head, esp. as worn by soldiers, policemen, firemen, divers, etc.

27. Homburg—man's felt hat with a creased crown and rolled brim

28. hood—cloth covering for the head and neck, either attached to a cloak or coat or worn separately

29. kelly, Stetson—man's hat (slang)

30. kepi—French military cap with a flat, round top and a stiff, horizontal visor—often with a cloth hanging down the back of the neck, as in the French Foreign Legion

31. kerchief—cloth head covering used by women

32. lid—hat (slang)

33. mantilla—scarf or veil worn by women in Mexico, Spain, etc., over the head and shoulders

34. mobcap, mob—frilled cap formerly worn by women

35. mortarboard—academic cap with a flat top

36. nightcap, bedcap—cap worn in bed, or while asleep

37. overseas cap—small, soft, boat-shaped cap, without brim or visor, worn by U.S. soldiers

38. panama, Panama hat—hat made of the leaves of a palmlike plant

39. picture hat—woman's hat with a wide brim

40. pillbox—woman's short hat with a flat top, shaped like a box for pills

41. pith helmet, pith hat—hat made of spongy plant tissue and worn in tropical countries or elsewhere, esp. as protection against the sun

42. pork pie, porkpie—man's felt hat with a round, flat crown and snap brim

43. sailor—straw hat, the brim and crown of which are flat, worn by women

44. scarf—broad strip of material worn as head covering by women

45. shako—military cylindrical dress hat with a visor and flat top, and decorated with a plume or pompon; military dress hat of fur

46. shawl, wrap—piece of material worn by women over the head and shoulders

47. skimmer—man's straw hat (slang)

48. skullcap—small close-fitting cap of silk, velvet, etc., without a brim

49. snood—woman's hat in the form of a netlike bag, and worn on the back of the head to hold up the hair

50. sombrero—hat with a broad brim and high, usually tapering, crown, worn in Mexico, Spain, Southwestern U.S., and other places

51. southwester, sou'wester—seaman's waterproof hat with a broad back brim, worn as a protection against rain, water, spray, etc.

52. straw hat—hat, esp. a man's, made of woven straw

53. sunbonnet—large bonnet that shades the face and extends in back to below the neck

54. tam-o'-shanter, tam—cap of Scottish origin with a top that extends over the headband, and often decorated with a center tassel

55. tarboosh—Mohammedan man's cap of red cloth or felt, decorated with a long tassel; such a cap as the inner part of a turban

56. tiara—turban worn by the ancient Persians

57. toque—woman's hat with a soft crown and either very small brim or no brim at all

58. tricorn—three-cornered hat; hat with the brim bent to form a kind of triangle (tricorn,adj.)

59. tuque—Canadian knitted cap

60. turban—head covering worn by men of Eastern countries, consisting of material wound around the head or over a small cap; woman's brimless hat; woman's hat with the brim folded back against the crown

61. veil, veiling—transparent netted material worn by women over the head and/or face; part of a nun's headdress that covers the head, shoulders, and each side of the face

62. wimple—woman's head covering hiding the entire head, the chin, and the neck, formerly in general use, now used by nuns

3. To Hat; To Furnish with a Hat, or Put a Hat On (Someone); To Furnish with, or Put a Head Covering On,v. *From Sec. 2:* bonnet, cap, coif, cowl, helm, hood, scarf, shawl, turban, veil, wimple

4. Wearing a Hat or Head Covering,adj. *From Sec. 2:* bonneted, capped, coifed, cowled, fezzed, helmeted, or helmed, hooded, kerchiefed or kerchieft, scarfed, shawled, strawhatted, turbaned, veiled

5. To Unhat; To Remove the Hat, Cap, or Head Covering from,v. *From Sec. 2:* unbonnet, uncap, uncoif, uncowl, unhelmet or unhelm, unhood, unshawl, unveil (unveilment, n.); *Also:* 1. uncover—remove the hat or cap from (the head)

6. To Unhat, i.e., Take Off One's Hat, Cap, or Head Covering,v. *From Sec. 2:* unbonnet, uncap, unhelm, unshawl, unveil (unveilment, n.); *Also:* 1. uncover—remove one's hat or cap

7. Unhatted; Hatless; Without a Hat, Cap, or Head Covering,adj. *From Sec. 2:* unbonneted or bonnetless, uncapped or capless, uncoifed, uncowled, unhelmeted or unhelmed, unhooded or hoodless, unkerchiefed, unscarfed, unshawled, unturbaned or turbanless, unveiled or veilless, wimpleless; *Also:* bare-

headed or barehead, bare-skulled, uncovered (bareheadedness,n.)

8. To Remove the Hat or Cap from (the Head) as a Gesture of Respect: uncover,v.

9. To Remove One's Hat or Cap as a Gesture of Respect: bare the, or one's, head; unbonnet, uncap, uncover, unhat,v.

10. To Remove or Partly Remove (the Hat) in Greeting, or as a Gesture of Respect: doff, lift, raise, tip,v.

11. Man's Tall Hat, Worn on Formal or Dress Occasions, etc.: beaver, crush hat, high hat, opera hat; plug hat (slang); silk hat; stovepipe or stovepipe hat (colloq.) ; top hat; topper (colloq.) ,n.

12. Women's Hats, Collectively, or as a Class, Group, etc.: millinery,n.

13. Parts of a Hat or Cap,n.
 1. brim, hatbrim—projecting edge of a hat
 2. crown—top part of a hat
 3. hatband—band around the crown, just above the brim, esp. of a man's felt hat
 4. peak, visor—part of a cap that projects over the eyes

14. Place That Holds a Hat: hatbox, hat hook, hatrack, hatstand,n.

15. Helmet, i.e., Armor for the Head: casque (poetic), crest, headpiece,n.

16. Wearing a Helmet: casqued (poetic), crested, helmed, helmeted, adj.

17. To Remove the Helmet from: uncasque (poetic), uncrest, unhelmet or unhelm,v.

18. To Take Off One's Helmet: unhelm,v.

19. Not Wearing a Helmet: uncrested, unhelmeted or unhelmed,adj.

20. Shaped Like a Helmet: helmeted, helmet-like,adj.

21. Movable Front Part of a Helmet That Covers the Face, Esp. the Eyes: beaver, visor or vizor,n.

22. Piece of Armor, Attached to the Helmet, That Protects the Lower Part of the Face: beaver,n.

23. Piece of Armor Covering the Forehead or Face: frontal,n.

24. Decoration for the Head,n.
 1. aigrette, egret—plume of feathers worn as a head decoration
 2. circlet—decoration for the head in the shape of a large ring
 3. coronal—circular decoration for the head
 4. coronet—crownlike decoration for the head, often of flowers, or of precious metal and/or jewels
 5. crown—decoration for the head as a symbol of victory, honor, etc.; head covering or decoration worn by monarchs
 6. frontlet, frontal, tiara—ornamental band worn around the forehead
 7. garland, coronal—wreath of flowers or leaves worn on the head
 8. headband, bandeau, fillet—band worn around, or on, the head
 9. headdress—decoration for the head
 10. snood—headband or ribbon formerly worn around the hair by unmarried women, esp. in Scotland and Northern England
 11. tiara—jeweled or flowered crownlike decoration for the head, worn by women; decoration for the head worn by the ancient Persians

25. To Put Such a Decoration On,v. *From Sec. 24:* crown, garland, tiara

26. A Crown: coronal, diadem,n.

27. Small Crown Worn by a Member of Royalty Lower in Rank than a Monarch: coronal, coronet,n. (coronal,adj.)

28. Wearing, or Having the Right to Wear, Such a Crown: coroneted or coronetted,adj.

29. Pope's Triple Crown: tiara, triregnum,n.

30. Jeweled Headband Formerly Worn as a Crown by Eastern Monarchs, Esp. in Ancient Persia: diadem,n.

31. To Put a Crown On (Someone) as a Symbol of Sovereign Rank: crown, diadem,v.

32. Ceremony or Process of Crowning a Monarch: coronation,n.

33. Pert. or Relating to a Crown: coronal, coronary,adj.

34. Resembling a Crown: coronary,adj.

35. Something Resembling a Crown: corona, diadem,n. (coronal,adj.)

36. To Deprive of the Crown: discrown, uncrown,v. (uncrowned,adj.)

37. Not Having or Wearing a Crown; Not Having Been Crowned: uncrowned,adj.

38. Small Leather Case, Containing a Text from the Pentateuch, Worn by Jews on the Forehead during Prayer: frontlet, phylactery,n.

39. Such a Case Worn Also on the Left Arm: phylactery,n.

40. Bag of Net Worn by Women on the Back of the Head to Hold Up the Hair: snood,n.

41. To Hold Up (the Hair) with Such a Bag: snood,v.

42. Forked Pin for Keeping the Hair, or a Headdress or Hair Decoration, in Place: bobbie pin, hairpin,n.

43. Ornamental Clasp for Holding a Woman's or Girl's Hair in Place: barrette,n.

44. Ribbon for Decorating or Tying the Hair: hair ribbon,n.

984. UNDRESS

1. To Undress, i.e., Remove Clothing from: disarray, dismantle, disrobe, divest, strip, unattire, unbusk, unclothe, ungarment, unlace, unrobe, untruss,v. (divestment, divesture, or divestiture,n.)

2. To Undress, i.e., Remove One's Clothing: disrobe; peel (slang) ; strip, unbusk, unrobe,v. (disrober,n.)

3. Undressed: disrobed, stripped, unappareled, unarrayed, unattired, unclad, unclothed, ungarbed, ungarmented, undraped, unlaced, unrobed, untoileted, untrussed,adj.

4. State of Undress: dishabille or deshabille; divestment, divesture, or divestiture; negligee (chiefly of women) ; undress,n.

5. To Remove (a Piece of Clothing, or a Garment, etc.) from Oneself: divest oneself of, doff, draw off, get off, get out of, pull off, slip off, slip out of, take off,v.

6. To Remove (a Piece of Clothing, or a Garment, etc.) from (Someone): divest of, draw off; get (someone) out of; pull off, take off,v.

7. To Take Off a Garment or Garments and Put on Another or Others: change,v.

8. To Loosen the Clothing of: unlace,v.

9. To Remove (the Indicated Garment) from: uncloak, uncollar, unfrock, unglove, ungown, unmantle; unmuffle (a muffler) ; unrobe or disrobe,v.

10. To Remove the Indicated Garment from Oneself: uncloak, unmantle, unmuffle (a muffler), unrobe or disrobe,v.

11. Not Wearing the Indicated Garment or Clothing: coatless, trouserless, unbloused, uncaparisoned, uncloaked, uncollared, uncostumed, unfrocked, ungauntleted, ungloved, ungowned, unjacketed, unlivered, unmantled, unmuffled (a muffler), unpanoplied, unrobed, unshirted or shirtless, unskirted, untogaed, uninformed, unvested,adj.

12. To Take Off (What One Is Figuratively Wearing, as a Quality, Pretense, etc.): doff, v.

13. Actress in a Burlesque Show or in a Night Club Who Removes All or Most of Her Clothing, Piece by Piece, to the Accompaniment of Music: ecdysiast (coined, reputedly, by H. L. Mencken); stripper or stripteaser (colloq.); stripteuse (new coinage),n.

14. Such an Act or Performance: strip tease, n. (colloq.)

15. Place Where People Undressed Preparatory to Bathing in Ancient Greece and Rome: apodyterium,n.

16. With the Indicated Part of the Body Lacking Clothing or Covering: bare-ankled, bare-armed, barebacked, bare-chested, barefaced, bare-fingered; barefooted, barefoot, discalced or discalceate; barehanded, bareheaded or barehead, bare-kneed, barelegged, barenecked, bare-skulled, bare-throated, bare-toed,adj. (barefacedness, bareheadedness,n.)

17. One Whose Feet Are Bare: barefoot,n.

18. Naked: au naturel (French), bare or bared, bare-skinned; denuded, denudate, or denudated; exposed (of part of the body); in the altogether, buff, or raw (colloq.); in one's birthday suit (slang); nude, stark, stripped, uncovered, undraped,adj. (bareness, denudation, nudity or nudeness, starkness,n.)

19. A Naked Person or Thing: nude,n.

20. To Undress to the Point of Nakedness: strip,v.

21. To Make Naked: bare, denude or denudate; expose or uncover (by removing clothes from, as a part of the body, a limb, etc.); strip, undrape,v. (denudation, exposure,n.)

22. The Bare Skin: the buff,n. (colloq.)

23. Animal with Naked Feet: nudiped,n. (nudiped,adj.)

24. Practice of Going Naked as a Health Measure: nudism,n. (nudist,n. nudist,adj.)

985. PLANTS

1. Plant Life; Plants Collectively,n.
  1. **aborigines**—original plant life of a region (aboriginal,adj.)
  2. **benthos**—plant life at the bottom of a body of water (benthonic,adj.)
  3. **biota**—plant and animal life of a region
  4. **botany**—plant life of a region
  5. **flora**—plant life of a region or time, esp. as catalogued by species
  6. **greenery, verdure**—fresh-growing or green plant life or plants (verdurous,adj.)
  7. **haliplankton**—plankton of the ocean or sea
  8. **herbage, verdure**—green, non-woody, plant life or plants; such plants used for grazing animals (verdurous,adj.)
  9. **limnobios**—plant and animal life of fresh water
  10. **limnoplankton**—plankton of lakes and other bodies of fresh water
  11. **pasture, pasturage, grass**—green, non-woody plants or plant growths for grazing animals
  12. **plankton**—small plant life floating in the water and used as food by fish, marine life, etc. (planktonic,adj.)
  13. **vegetation**—plant life of a place, with no distinction as to species, etc.; plants collectively (vegetational,adj.)

2. The Greenness of Growing Plants: verdancy, verdure, verdurousness,n. (verdant, verdurous,adj.)

3. Descr. of Land or Ground Covered with, or Having, Green, Non-Woody Growing Plants: verdant, verdurous,adj. (verdancy, verdurousness,n.)

4. Descr. of Land or Ground Completely Lacking Such: verdureless,adj.

5. A Treatise or Other Work on the Plant Life of a Region or Time, Catalogued as to Species, etc.: flora,n. (floristic,adj.)

6. Selected Types of Plants,n.
  1. **alga**—type of plant comprising seaweeds and certain fresh-water plants (algae, pl.n. algal,adj.)
  2. **amphibian**—plant that can live both in water and on land (amphibious,adj.)
  3. **annual**—plant that lasts just one year or season
  4. **biennial**—plant that lasts two years, usually flowering the second year (biennial, adj.)
  5. **brake, bracken**—large fern
  6. **bramble**—rough, prickly, or spiny shrub
  7. **bryophyte**—plant of the group comprising liverworts and mosses (bryophytic, adj.)
  8. **bush**—low plant with spreading branches
  9. **cane**—plant with a long, woody, and jointed stem that may be either hollow or full of pith, as bamboo, rattan, etc.
  10. **cryptogam, cryptophyte**—plant that does not have true blossoms or seeds, as the ferns, mosses, thallophytes, algae, etc. (cryptogamic, cryptogamous,adj.)
  11. **diatom**—microscopic one-celled alga
  12. **epiphyte, air plant**—plant that grows non-parasitically on other plants, getting its nutrition from the air (epiphytic, epiphytical,adj.)
  13. **fern**—shrubby, non-flowering plant with fronds (ferny,adj.)
  14. **fungus, fungal**—plant of the group comprising mushrooms, molds, mildews, etc. (fungi,pl.n. fungal, fungous, fungus,adj.)
  15. **geophyte**—plant that grows in soil
  16. **herb**—plant with a non-woody stem that dies after each year's growth; such a plant that is valued for medicinal or seasoning properties (herbal, herbaceous, adj.)
  17. **hydrophyte**—plant growing in very wet soil (hydrophytic,adj.)
  18. **lichen**—thallophyte that grows in gray, black, yellow, or brown patches on rocks, tree bark, etc. (lichenous, lichenose, lichenaceous,adj.)
  19. **lithophyte**—plant that grows on rock surfaces (lithophytic,adj.)
  20. **liverwort**—mosslike plant that grows on the trunks of trees, in water, or in wet ground
  21. **microphyte**—microscopically small plant organism (microphytic, microphytal,adj.)
  22. **mildew**—parasitic fungus that forms a whitish coating on plants, paper, leather, cotton, linen, or other organic matter (mildewy,adj.)
  23. **mold**—fungus that forms a downy coating on organic matter, esp. in decay or dampness
  24. **moss**—plant that grows in velvety patches on rocks, trees, damp ground, etc.
  25. **mushroom**—fleshy, edible fungus of characteristic umbrella shape (mushroom, adj.)
  26. **organism**—any form of plant or animal life (organic,adj.)
  27. **perennial**—plant with a life cycle greater than two years (perennial,adj.)
  28. **phanerogam**—plant that has flowers and/or seeds (phanerogamic, phanerogamous,adj.)

29. **phycomycete**—algalike plant belonging to the most primitive subdivision of the fungi (phycomycetous,adj.)

30. **pteridophyte**—plant of the group comprising the ferns and allied types, horsetails, and club moss (pteridophytic, pteridophytous,adj.)

31. **rogue**—freak of nature in the plant world; non-typical, freakish, or inferior plant

32. **rust, rust fungus**—fungus that causes a plant disease characterized by spots on, and an unnatural reddish or brownish color of, the leaves and stems

33. **seaweed, kelp**—plant growing in the sea, esp. a marine alga

34. **seedling**—plant grown from a seed

35. **shrub**—short, woody, perennial plant or bush

36. **smut**—fungus that affects plants, esp. grains, and causes the parts to become black and powdery

37. **spermatophyte**—plant that produces seeds (spermatophytic,adj.)

38. **sport, mutation**—plant, plant part, or animal that shows exceptional deviation from the parent or normal form (mutational,adj.)

39. **thallophyte**—plant of the group comprising the algae, fungi, and lichens, and having no distinct leaves, stems, or roots (thallophytic,adj.)

40. **toadstool**—fleshy fungus with the characteristic umbrella shape, esp. the poisonous variety

41. **vegetable**—edible plant; any plant (vegetable, vegetal,adj.)

42. **wilding, wildling**—uncultivated plant, i.e., one that grows wild

43. **xerophyte**—plant that thrives with little or no moisture, as in the desert (xerophytic,adj.)

7. Such Plants Collectively; A Growth or Clump of Such Plants,n. *From Sec. 6:* bracken (from *brake*); bush, brush, or brushwood; canebrake, fernery, moss; seaweed, kelp, seaware, or sea wrack; shrubbery or scrub, vegetation

8. Plantlike; Resembling, or of the Nature of, a Plant,adj. *From Sec. 6:* algalike, etc.; brambly, bushy, ferny, fungoid or fungiform, herbaceous; lichenoid, lichenous, lichenose, or lichenaceous; mildewy, mossy, mushroom or fungiform, shrubby; vegetable, vegetal, vegetative, or vegetive; *Also:* **1.** phytoid—plantlike

9. Consisting of, Containing, Covered with, Abounding in, etc., Plants,adj. *From Sec. 6:* brambly, bushy or bosky, diatomaceous, ferny, fungous or fungus; lichened, lichenous, or lichenose; mildewed or mildewy, moldy, mossy, shrubby

10. To Cover with Such Plants,v. *From Sec. 6:* bush, mildew, mold, moss, shrub or shrubbery; *Also:* **1.** plant—cover, stock, or furnish (a place, ground, etc.) with plants

11. Such a Coating,n. *From Sec. 6:* mildew, mold

12. Plant Disease,n. *From Sec. 6:* mildew, rust, smut

13. To Affect with a Plant Disease,v. *From Sec. 6:* mildew

14. To Become Affected with a Plant Disease,v. *From Sec. 6:* mildew, smut

15. Affected with a Plant Disease,adj. *From Sec. 6:* mildewed or mildewy, rusty, smutty

16. To Make (a Chair, Furniture, etc.) Using the Jointed Stems of Cane: cane,v.

17. A Collector of, or Dealer in, Medicinal Herbs: herbalist,n.

18. Treatise or Book on Herbs: herbal,n.

19. Classified Collection of Dried Plants: herbarium or herbal,n.

20. To Become Coated with a Fungous Growth: mildew, mold,v.

21. Appearing as if Covered by Moss: mossy, adj.

22. Resembling a Mushroom in Rapid Growth; Growing Rapidly Like a Mushroom: mushroom,adj.

23. To Have, or Take On, the Flattened, or Umbrellalike, Shape of a Mushroom; To Grow or Spread Rapidly Like a Mushroom; To Gather Mushrooms: mushroom,v.

24. To Branch Out, or Spread, Like a Bush: bush,v.

25. To Plant or Protect (a Place) with Bushes: bush,v.

26. Body of a Plant without Distinct Leaves, Stems, or Roots: thallus,n.

27. Pert. or Relating to Plants: botanical or botanic, vegetable, vegetal, vegetational, or vegetative,adj.

28. Originating from Plants: organic (or from animals, rather than from non-living matter), phytogenic, phytogenous, vegetable, adj.

29. Drug Made from Some Part of a Plant: botanical,n.

30. Without Reasoning Power, Animal Response, etc., Like a Plant or Vegetable: vegetal, vegetant,adj. (vegetism,n.)

31. Existing in Great Passiveness, Like a Plant or Vegetable; Descr. of Such Existence: vegetative or vegetive,adj. (vegetativeness,n.)

32. To So Exist: vegetate,v. (vegetation,n.)

33. Pert. or Belonging to Selected Families of Plants,adj.
1. **agaricaceous**—of mushrooms, toadstools, and certain other fungi
2. **alliaceous**—of garlic, onions, and leek
3. **asclepiadaceous**—of milkweeds
4. **asteraceous, carduaceous**—of thistles, asters, goldenrod, etc.
5. **caprifoliaceous**—of honeysuckles
6. **convolvulaceous**—of morning-glories
7. **cornaceous**—of dogwood
8. **rosaceous**—of roses, blackberries, raspberries, strawberries, etc.
9. **tiliaceous**—of lindens
10. **urticaceous**—of nettles

34. Place for Plants; Place Where Plants Grow,n.
1. **aquarium**—tank of water for keeping and exhibiting aquatic plant and animal life; place where aquatic plant and animal life is exhibited
2. **botanical gardens**—public garden where plants are grown and exhibited
3. **brake**—area covered with bushes, brambles, etc.
4. **brush, brushwood**—area covered by a thick growth of bushes, small trees, etc.
5. **bush**—area covered with bushes
6. **fernery**—place, glass case, etc., where ornamental ferns are grown
7. **garden**—area, or public place, where useful and/or ornamental plants and trees are grown
8. **Garden of Eden, Eden**—garden that was the original abode of Adam and Eve
9. **grape arbor, grapery, vineyard**—area where grapevines are grown
10. **grapery**—building or enclosed area where grapevines are grown
11. **greenery**—place where green plants are kept and grown
12. **greenhouse, conservatory**—house or room with a glass top, for growing and exhibiting plants

13. **herbarium**—room or place where a collection of classified dried plants is kept
14. **hothouse**—heated building, with glass roof and/or walls, for the cultivation of young plants
15. **jungle**—area of wild and thickly growing vegetation
16. **nursery**—place or establishment where plants, young trees, etc., are grown for sale or to be transplanted
17. **rock garden, rockery**—garden among rocks or on rocky ground, or a collection of rocks and soil, where plants suitable to the environment grow or are grown
18. **scrub**—area overgrown with shrubs
19. **shrubbery**—place where shrubs are grown
20. **terrarium**—glass case, bottle, bowl, etc., containing small growing plants
21. **topiary**—ornamental garden containing trees and shrubs trained or trimmed into various decorative, odd, or fantastic shapes (topiary,adj.)
22. **vivarium**—indoor area in which plants are grown, such area simulating a natural environment

35. One in Charge of, or Who Owns or Runs, a Nursery: nurseryman,n.

36. Selected Plant Sciences,n.
1. **agrobiology**—of plant nutrition and growth, crop production, and soil control, all in relation one to the other
2. **agrostology**—of grasses
3. **algology, phycology**—of algae or seaweeds
4. **biochemistry**—of plants and animals in terms of chemistry
5. **biodynamics**—of the vital and active phenomena of plants and animals
6. **biology**—of plants and animals
7. **biophysics**—of plants and animals in terms of physics
8. **biophysiography**—of the description of plants and animals
9. **biostatics**—of the structure of plants and animals in relation to function
10. **botany**—of plants or plant life
11. **bryology**—of mosses and liverworts
12. **hydrobiology, limnobiology**—of the plant and animal life of fresh water, esp. of lakes or ponds
13. **lichenology**—of lichens
14. **microphytology**—of very tiny plants
15. **morphology**—of the form and structure of plant or animal organisms
16. **mycology, fungology**—of fungi
17. **paleobotany, paleophytology**—of plants of past geological periods
18. **phytogeography**—of plants in geographical relationships
19. **phytography**—of the classification or description of plants
20. **phytosociology**—of the relationship between the various plants of a region
21. **pteridology**—of ferns
22. **spermology**—of botanical seeds
23. **taxonomy**—of the classification of plants and animals

37. Pert. to, or Descr. of, a Plant Science, adj. *From Sec. 36:* agrobiological or agrobiologic, agrostological or agrostologic, etc.; biochemic or biochemical, biodynamic or biodynamical, biophysical, biostatic or biostatical, botanic or botanical, paleobotanic or paleobotanical, taxonomic or taxonomical

38. Student of a Plant Science,n *From Sec. 36:* agrobiologist, agrostologist, etc.; biochemist, botanist, paleobotanist, taxonomer or taxonomist; *Also:* **1. naturalist**—student of plant and animal life

39. To Study Plants Where They Grow; To Collect Plants for Study; To Explore (a Place) for the Purpose of Collecting and Studying Its Plants: botanize,v. (botanizer, n.)

40. History of the Origin and Development of a Plant or Plants: phytogenesis, phytogeny,n. (phytogenetic, phytogenetical,adj.)

986. GRASS

1. Grass,n.
1. **bamboo**—a kind of woody grass growing in hot climates
2. **bluegrass**—grass with bluish-green stems
3. **cereal, grain**—grass, or grassy plant, producing seeds used for food, as wheat, rice, rye, etc. (cereal,adj.)
4. **hay**—grass cut and dried for animal food
5. **pasture, pasturage**—grass grown for grazing animals
6. **reed**—a kind of tall grass with hollow and jointed stems (reed, collective n.)
7. **sedge**—grasslike plant that grows in moist places (sedgy,adj.)
8. **soilage**—grass or leaf-bearing plants raised as food for livestock

2. To Feed (an Animal) on Grass,v. *From Sec. 1:* pasture, soil; *Also:* grass, graze

3. To Feed on Grass (of Animals),v. *From Sec. 1:* pasture; *Also:* grass, graze

4. To Feed (Livestock) on Grass, Foliage, or Other Green Fodder in Order to Purge Them: soil,v.

5. Belonging to the Reed Family: arundinaceous,adj.

6. To Cover or Thatch with Reed: reed,v.

7. To Cut and Spread Out Grass to Dry for Animal Food: hay,v.

8. A Heap of Hay, Usually Piled Up Out of Doors to Dry: haycock, hayrick, haystack, n.

9. Hay Stored in a Barn: haymow,n.

10. Place in a Barn Where Hay Is Stored, Esp. an Upper Level: hayloft, haymow,n.

11. Like Grass: gramineous, grasslike, grassy, adj. (grassiness,n.)

12. Pert. to Grass: gramineous, grassy,adj.

13. Of the Color of Grass: grass-green, grassy, grassy-green,adj.

14. Belonging to the Grass Family: gramineous, poaceous,adj.

15. Land, Ground, or Stretch of Ground Covered with Grass: grassland, green; hayfield (of grass intended to be cut for hay); lawn (of fine grass, cultivated, trimmed, esp. around a house); lea; meadow or prairie (low or level, or one on which grass is grown for pasture or for hay); pasture or pasturage (for grazing animals); sward; terrace (around a house, or one built on various levels or slopes),n.

16. Grasslands of Russia: the Steppes,n.

17. Grasslands of South Africa, Containing Sparse Bushes and/or Trees: veld or veldt,n.

18. Grasslands of South America, Esp. Argentina: pampas,n. (pampean,adj.)

19. Surface of Ground or Soil Covered with Grass: greensward, sod, sward, turf,n.

20. Patch of Grass-Covered Soil Cut Out to Be Transplanted Elsewhere: sod,n.

21. To Cover or Plant (a Place or Ground) with Such: sod,v.

22. To Cover (Ground, etc.) with Grass: grass, sward, turf,v.

23. To Become Covered with Grass (of Ground, etc.): grass, sward.v.

24. Covered with Grass: grassy, turfy, verdant, verdurous,adj. (grassiness, turfiness, verdancy, verdurousness,n.)

25. Like Turf: cespitose, turflike, turfy,adj. (turfiness,n.)

26. A Growth of Grass: sward,n.

27. To Lay Out (Ground, etc.) in Grassy Slopes or Levels: terrace,v.

28. Capable of Growing or Producing Grass or Green Plants for Grazing Animals—of Land: pasturable,adj.

29. To Produce Grass—of Land: grass,v.

987. GRAIN

1. Selected Grains Used as Human Food: barley, buckwheat; corn (what the British call *wheat* and the Scots *oats*); maize (British); millet (chiefly for animals in the U.S., though used as human food in Europe and elsewhere); oats, rice, rye, wheat,n.

2. Rice; Rice Still Unmilled or in the Husk: paddy or padi,n.

3. Grain Ready for Grinding: grist,n.

4. Ground Grain: farina; flour (ground fine); grist; meal (usually excluding wheat), n. (floury, mealy,adj.)

5. To Grind (Grain): mill,v.

6. To Grind (Grain) into Flour: flour,v.

7. Like Flour; Covered with Flour; White because Covered with Flour: floury,adj.

8. Like, or Containing, Meal: farinaceous, mealy,adj. (mealiness,n.)

9. Made from, or Yielding, Meal or Flour: farinaceous,adj.

10. Covered with, or as if with, Meal: mealy, adj.

11. Machine or Building Where Grain Is Ground into Flour: flour mill, mill,n.

12. One Who Owns or Operates Such a Machine or Building: miller,n.

13. Breakfast Food Made of Grains: cereal,n.

14. Coat of the Seed of Cereal Grains when Separated Out: bran,n.

15. Resembling Bran: branlike, furfuraceous, adj.

16. Important Constituent of Wheat, Rice, and Other Grains, and of Various Vegetables: farina, starch,n.

17. Pert. to, Like, or of the Nature of, Starch: amylaceous, starchy,adj. (starchiness,n.)

18. Pert. to Grain: cereal,adj.

19. Bearing Grain: graniferous,adj.

20. Pert. to, or Resembling, Oats: avenaceous,adj.

21. Like, or Made from, Wheat or Other Grains: frumentaceous,adj.

22. Middle or Hard Parts of Wheat Grain, Used for Spaghetti, etc.: semolina,n.

23. Oat Kernels, Whole Wheat Grains, etc., Used as Food: groats,n.

24. Coarse-Ground Grain: grits,n.

25. A Single Hollow Stalk of Certain Grains, Esp. Barley, Wheat, Oats, or Rye, after It Has Been Cut and Dried—Used as Animal Food, in Mattresses, to Make Hats, etc.: straw,n. (straw, collective n.)

26. Pert. to, Made of, etc., Straw: stramineous, straw,adj.

27. Resembling Straw: stramineous, strawlike,adj.

28. Of the Yellowish Color of Straw: stramineous, straw-colored,adj.

988. TOBACCO

1. Tobacco: the weed,n. (colloq.)

2. A Kind of Kentucky Tobacco: burley or Burley,n.

3. Active Chemical Principle of Tobacco: nicotine,n.

4. Finely Ground Tobacco, Breathed in through the Nose: snuff,n.

5. Twist of Tobacco in Cylindrical Shape: roll,n.

6. Cigar,n.
  1. belvedere—type of cigar shorter than a corona
  2. cheroot—long, narrow type of cigar without pointed ends
  3. corona—type of long cigar with round, blunt ends
  4. Havana—cigar made of Cuban tobacco
  5. panatela—type of short, thin cigar with tapering ends
  6. perfecto—long cigar with narrow, pointed ends
  7. smoke—cigar
  8. stogie—thin cigar; cheap or inferior cigar
  9. weed—cigar (colloq.)

7. Cigarette: butt (colloq.); cubeb (of crushed berries, smoked to relieve catarrh); king-size cigarette (approx. 3¼ inches long); smoke; tailor-made (commercially packaged); weed (colloq.),n.

8. Types of Tobacco Pipes: brier, briar, brierroot or briarroot (made from a kind of woody root); calumet (smoked by North American Indians as a token of peace); clay pipe, corncob or corncob pipe; hookah or hooka (with a flexible tube, the smoke drawn through a vase of water); meerschaum or meerschaum pipe (the bowl made from a mineral of that name); narghile, nargile, or nargileh (Oriental, the smoke drawn through water),n.

9. Partially Smoked Tobacco Left in the Bottom of the Pipe Bowl: dottle or dottel,n.

10. Tobacco Products for Smoking, i.e., Cigars, Cigarettes, etc.: smokes,pl.n.

11. Dealer in Smoking Supplies, Cigarettes, Cigars, Tobacco, etc.: tobacconist,n.

12. Store for Such: cigar store, smoke shop, tobacconist's,n.

989. RUBBER

1. Pure Rubber: caoutchouc, crude or natural rubber, gum, gum elastic, India rubber,n. (India-rubber,adj.)

2. Milky Fluid from Which Rubber Is Made: latex,n.

3. Synthetic Rubber: buna, butyl rubber, neoprene,n.

4. Hard Rubber for Making Buttons, Combs, Electrical Insulation, etc.: ebonite, vulcanite,n.

5. Rubber in a Spongy Mass, Often with Large Air Openings, Used for Mattresses and Upholstery: foam rubber,n.

6. Rubberlike Substance from Certain Trees, Used in Dentistry, Golf Balls, Electric Insulation, etc.: gutta-percha,n.

7. Material or Fabric Made Flexible by Bands of Rubber Woven into It: elastic,n.

8. Band of, or Containing, Rubber: elastic, elastic band, rubber band,n.

9. Such Used to Hold Up the Stockings: garter,n.

10. To Fasten (Stockings, etc.) with Such: garter,v.

11. To Treat (Natural Rubber) with Sulphur in Order to Make It Stronger, Harder, More Elastic, etc.; To Treat (Other Substances) Similarly: vulcanize,v. (vulcanization,n.)

990. BRANCH

1. Branch of a Tree: bough, limb,n.

2. Branch of a Tree or Shrub after It Has Been Broken or Cut Off: stick,n.

3. Branch of Any Plant: ramus,n.

4. Small Branch: branchlet, branchling, sprig; twig (projecting off a larger one),n.

5. Young Branch: branchlet, branchling, shoot, sprig, sprout, switch, twig,n.

6. Young, Slender, and Pliable Branch or Twig: vimen,n. (vimineous,adj.)

7. Branch of a Tree or Plant Including the Leaves, Blossoms, Fruit, etc.; A Decoration Resembling This: spray, sprig,n.

8. To Decorate (Something) with an Adornment Resembling This: sprig,v.

9. Twig of a Willow Tree: osier, wicker, withe,n. (osier,adj.)

10. Descr. of Things Made of Such Twigs: osier, wicker,adj.

11. Strong, Thin, and Easily Bent Twig for Tying Things Together: wicker, withe, withy,n.

12. To Tie (Something) with Such Twigs: withe,v.

13. Made of, or Covered with, Such Woven Twigs: vimineous, wicker, withy,adj.

14. Resembling Such a Twig in Strength, Thinness, and Pliability: withelike, withy, adj.

15. Such Twigs Woven Together; Something, as a Basket, Chair, etc., Made of Such: wicker,n.

16. Articles Made of Such: wickerwork,n.

17. Small Wooden Branch That Has Fallen Off a Plant or Tree: twig,n.

18. Branches or Twigs That Have Broken Off a Tree or Plant: brush, brushwood,n.

19. Resembling a Twig: twiglike, twiggy,adj.

20. The Branches, Collectively, of a Tree: ramage,n.

21. Having Branches: branched, ramose, ramous,adj.

22. Having a Large Number of Small Branches or Twigs: ramulose, twiggy,adj.

23. Having a Large Number of Small Twigs: virgate,adj.

24. To Remove the Small or Young Branches or Twigs from: sprig,v.

25. Slender Long Branch Removed to Beat Someone or Something: switch,n.

26. To Beat or Whip (Someone or Something) with Such: switch, twig,v.

991. STEM

1. Stem of a Plant, etc.: axis; caulicle (small or rudimentary); caulis (esp. of a green or herbaceous plant); funicle or funiculus (of a seed); pedicel (small or subordinate, or bearing a single flower); pedicle (small); peduncle (of a flower or cluster of flowers); petiole (of a leaf); petiolule (of a small leaf or of a part of a compound leaf); shoot or sprout (young); stalk,n. (axial or axile, cauline, peduncular, petiolar,adj.)

2. Having a Stem; Stemmed, adj. *From Sec. 1:* funiculate, pedicellate; pedunculate, pe-

dunculated, or peduncled; petiolate or petiolated

3. Growing from, or on, a Stem,adj. *From Sec. 1:* cauline (the upper part), pedunculate or pedunculated, petiolar

4. Underground Rootlike Stem: rhizome,n.

5. Having Such: rhizomatous,adj.

6. Main Stem of a Tree: axis, bole, stem, trunk,n. (axial or axile,adj.)

7. Portion of a Tree Trunk when Cut or Otherwise Separate: log,n.

8. Woody Stem or Stems Used in Making Things: bamboo (screens, furniture, poles, etc.); cane (furniture, chairs, etc.); rattan or ratan (furniture, walking sticks, etc.); reed (arrows, mouthpiece attachments of musical instruments, etc.); rush (bottoms of chairs, baskets, mats, etc.); straw (hats, mattress stuffing, etc.),n.

9. Thin, Long Stem That Travels Along the Ground, Throwing Out Roots at Its Nodes, as of the Strawberry Plant, etc.: runner,n.

10. Having or Producing Such: sarmentose, adj.

11. Stem of a Plant That Creeps Along the Ground or Winds Around a Support, or the Plant Itself: vine,n.

12. Structure of Crossed Strips on Which Vines or Other Creeping Plants Climb: trellis,n.

13. To Train (Vines, etc.) on Such a Structure: trellis,v.

14. Any Similar Structure Used as a Screen, Gate, Window, Support, etc.: lattice, latticework, trellis,n.

15. Such Structures Collectively: latticing, latticework, trelliswork,n.

16. To Provide with Such a Structure or Structures: lattice, trellis,v.

17. To Form or Arrange (Strips of Metal, Wood, etc.) into Such a Structure: lattice, trellis,v.

18. A Trellis or Lattice for Training Plants, Shrubs, or Trees to Grow Flat; A Plant, Shrub or Tree So Trained: espalier,n.

19. To Train (a Plant, etc.) on Such, or Provide with Such: espalier,v.

992. ROOT

1. Very Small Root: radicel, radicle, rootlet,n.

2. A Root: radicle, radix,n. (radixes, radices, pl.n.)

3. Threadlike Root: fiber,n.

4. Fine Hair on the Young Root of Certain Plants: fibril,n. (fibrillar,adj.)

5. Of the Form of Such Hair: fibrilliform, adj.

6. Having Such Hairs: fibrillose,adj.

7. Rootlike Thread of Moss: rhizoid,n. (rhizoidal,adj.)

8. Pert. to a Root; Coming from a Root: radical,adj.

9. Resembling a Root: rhizoid, rhizomorphous, rootlike,adj.

993. LEAF

1. Leaf of Grass or Grain: blade,n.

2. Leaf of a Fern: frond,n.

3. Fronds Collectively: frondage,n.

4. Resembling a Frond: frondose,adj.

5. Shaped Like a Frond: frondiform,adj.

6. Having Fronds: frondiferous, frondigerous, frondose,adj.

7. Growing Mass of Leaves on a Plant or Tree: foliage, foliation, foliature, frondage, frondescence; greenery (when green) ; leafage, umbrage,n.

8. The Leaves and Stems of Non-Woody Plants: herbage,n.

9. Broad Part of a Leaf: blade,n.

10. Leafy Recess, Retreat, Shelter, etc.; Such Formed by Vines, Trees, Shrubs, etc.: arbor, bower,n. (bowery,adj.)

11. Arbor or Bower Formed by Vines Creeping Along an Archway of Crossed Strips of Wood or Metal: trellis,n.

12. Covered or Sheltered by Leaves: arbored, bowered, embowered,adj.

13. To Cover, Surround, or Shelter by Leafy Boughs: bower, embower,v.

14. Having Leaves; Covered with Leaves: foliate, leafy,adj. (foliation, leafiness,n.)

15. Having Broad Leaves: broad-leaved, latifoliate,adj.

16. Having the Stated Number of Leaves: monophyllous or unifoliate (one) ; diphyllous or bifoliate (two) ; trifoliate (three) ; quadrifoliate (four) ; quinquefoliate (five) ,adj.

17. Having No Leaves: aphyllous,adj.

18. To Sprout Leaves: foliate, frondesce,v. (foliation, frondescence,n. frondescent,adj.)

19. Pert. to Leaf Production: phyllogenetic, adj.

20. To Shape in the Form of a Leaf: foliate,v.

21. So Shaped: foliated,adj.

22. Resembling a Leaf or Leaves: foliate, leaflike, leafy, phylloid,adj. (leafiness,n.)

23. Of the Color, Form, or Texture of a Green Leaf: herbaceous,adj.

24. Leaf Arrangement on a Stem: phyllotaxy,n.

25. Circle of Intertwined Leaves: wreath,n.

26. To Strip the Leaves from; To Become Stripped of Leaves: defoliate,v. (defoliation, n.)

27. Fallen Leaves, Cut Grass, Straw, Loose Earth, etc., Spread Around the Roots of Plants as a Protection: mulch,n.

28. To Spread Such Around (Plant Roots): mulch,v.

29. Fiber from Palm Leaves, Used to Make Woven Baskets, Hats, etc.: raffia,n.

994. FLOWER

1. A Flower: bloom, blossom, inflorescence, posy,n.

2. A Small Flower: floret, floweret, flowerlet, flowret,n.

3. Flower Worn in the Buttonhole: boutonniere,n.

4. Wild Flower: wildling,n.

5. Flowers Collectively: flowerage, inflorescence,n.

6. Bunch of Flowers: bouquet; corsage (worn on a woman's dress, or at the waist, shoulder, etc.) ; nosegay, posy,n.

7. Cluster of Flowers: inflorescence,n.

8. Circle of Intertwined Flowers and Leaves: wreath,n.

9. To Flower: bloom, blossom, blow, effloresce, floreate,v.

10. State or Period of Flowering: bloom, blossom, blow, efflorescence, florescence, flowerage, inflorescence,n.

11. State or Period of Full Flowering: anthesis,n.

12. State or Period of Flowering Again: reflorescence,n. (reflorescent,adj.)

13. Flowering: blooming, blossoming, efflorescent, florescent, floriferous, inflorescent, adj.

14. Part of a Plant That Bears Flowers: inflorescence,n.

15. Arrangement of Flowers on a Stem or Axis: inflorescence,n.

16. Pert. to, or Consisting of, Flowers: floral, floreal,adj.

17. Resembling Flowers: anthoid, floral, floreal, flowerlike, flowery,adj. (floweriness, n.)

18. Bearing Flowers: floriferous,adj.

19. Covered with Flowers; Having an Abundance of Flowers: flowery,adj. (floweriness, n.)

20. Decorated with Designs or Ornaments of Flowers: floral; floriated, floriate, or floreated; flowery,adj. (floriation, floweriness,n.)

21. Floral Decoration or Ornament: floriation, flowerage, flower piece,n.

22. To Decorate with Flowers: floralize,v.

23. To Become Decorated with Flowers: floreate,v.

24. Having the Stated Number of Flowers: uniflorate (one) ; biflorate or biflorous (two); triflorate or triflorous (three) ; multiflorous (many) ,adj.

25. Having White Flowers: albiflorous, whiteflowered,adj.

26. Descr. of Flowers of Some Shade of Yellow: xanthic,adj.

27. Abounding in, Made from, or Consisting of, Roses: roseate,adj.

28. Parts of a Flower: anther, filament, ovary, ovule, petal, pistil, receptacle, sepal, stamen, stigma, style,n.

29. The Cultivation of Flowers, Plants with Decorative Flowers, etc., Esp. Under Glass: floriculture,n. (floriculturist,n. floricultural, adj.)

30. Art or Science of Growing Flowers, Fruits, and Vegetables: horticulture,n. (horticulturist,n. horticultural,adj.)

31. One Who Sells Flowers, or Who Grows Flowers for Sale: florist,n.

32. Large Ornamental Pot, Bowl, Receptacle, or Stand for Flowers or Other Decorative Plants: jardiniere,n.

33. Roman Goddess of Flowers: Flora,n. (Floral,adj.)

34. Writings about, or Description of, Flowers: anthography,n.

995. SEED

1. Edible Seed or Seeds of Grassy Plants Such as Wheat, Rye, Rice, etc.: grain,n.

2. Grass Seed Shaken out of Newly Cut Hay: hayseed,n.

3. Small Reproductive Body Produced by Mosses, Ferns, etc.: spore,n.

4. To Have or Develop Such: spore,v.

5. Bearing Such: sporiferous,adj.

6. Spore Case: sporanguim,n. (sporangia,pl. n. sporangial,adj.)

7. The Seed, i.e., Nut or Fruit, of the Oak Tree: acorn,n.

8. Pert. to Botanical Seeds: seminal,adj.

9. Producing or Bearing Such Seeds: seminiferous or seminiferal,adj.

10. To Produce Seeds after Ripening: seed,v.

11. To Shed Its Seeds after the Period of Flowering or Bearing: go to seed, seed,v.

12. To Remove the Seeds from: seed,v.

996. TREE

1. The Forest Trees of a Region: sylva or silva,n.

2. Low Trees, Collectively: scrub,n.

3. Term for a Tree in Botanical Nomenclature: arbor,n.

4. Selected Trees or Types of Trees,n.
　1. **ailanthus**—the type of tree alluded to in *A Tree Grows in Brooklyn* (ailanthic, adj.)
　2. **arboret**—small tree
　3. **arbuscle**—dwarf tree (arbuscular,adj.)
　4. **citrus**—tree that bears fruit, such as oranges, lemons, limes, grapefruit, etc. (citrus, citrous,adj.)
　5. **conifer**—tree that bears cones, such as evergreens, pines, firs, spruce, etc. (coniferous,adj.)
　6. **evergreen**—tree that remains green all year
　7. **forester**—tree that grows in a forest
　8. **hardwood**—tree yielding heavy, close-grained lumber
　9. **pollard**—tree with branches cut down to the trunk so that a thick growth of branches and foliage will result
　10. **sapling, tiller**—young tree
　11. **seedling**—tree grown from a seed; tree that has not yet attained a height of 3 feet
　12. **softwood**—tree yielding soft, easily sawed lumber; conifer
　13. **wilding**—apple tree that grows wild

5. To Cut the Branches of (a Tree) Back to the Trunk: pollard,v.

6. Bottom Part or End of a Tree Trunk or Other Plant from Which the Rest Has Been Cut Off: stump,n.

7. To Reduce (a Tree, etc.) to Such: stump, v.

8. Resembling Such; of Land Full of Such: stumpy,adj.

9. To Clear (Land) of Such: stump,v.

10. Standing Trees Suitable for Lumber, in Reference to Their Money Value; The Right to Cut Such on Another's Land; The Value of Such: stumpage,n.

11. Living in Trees: arboreal, arborean, arboreous, arboricole, arboricolous,adj.

12. Adapted for Climbing About in Trees, as the Limbs of Tree-Inhabiting Animals: arboreal,adj.

13. Growing on Trees: arboricoline,adj.

14. Living on Trees, as Certain Plants: arboricolous,adj.

15. Pert. or Relating to Trees: arboraceous, arboral, arborary, arboreal, arborean, arborical, arborous,adj.

16. Treelike: arboreal, arborean, arborescent or arboreous (esp. in size, structure, appearance, etc.); arboresque, arboriform or dendriform (in shape); arboroid (in shape or branching); dendroid, dendroidal, dendritic, or dendritical (in structure or branching), adj. (arborescence,n.)

17. To Give a Tree-Shaped Appearance to: arborize,v.

18. To Take On Such an Appearance: arborize,v.

19. Such an Appearance; A Figure of Such Appearance; The Outline of a Tree in a Fossil or Mineral: arborization,n.

20. Descr. of, or Designating, Trees, Shrubs, etc., Whose Leaves Fall Off Periodically: deciduous,adj. (deciduousness,n.)

21. Formed by Trees: arborous,adj.

22. With Trees on Both Sides: arbored, tree-lined,adj.

23. To Drive (a Hunted Person or Animal) Up a Tree: tree,v.

24. Belonging to the Elm Family of Trees: ulmaceous,adj.

25. Belonging to Other Families of Trees: betulaceous (birch or alder); fagaceous (beech, chestnut, and oak), adj.

26. Pert. to the Oak Tree: quercine,adj.

27. A Growth of Trees, Shrubs, Bushes, etc.: boscage or boskage (trees and/or shrubs); bosk (poetic), bosket or bosquet; brake (small trees, bushes, shrubs, etc.); brush or brushwood (small trees, bushes, shrubs, etc.); chaparral (evergreen oaks or any thickly growing small trees or shrubs—so called in the Southwestern U.S.); clump of trees, shrubs, or bushes; colonnade (long row); coppice or copse (small trees or bushes); forest (over a large area); grove (without underbrush); orchard (fruit and/or nut trees); plantation (planted and cultivated trees—chiefly British in usage); stand (growing in a particular place, or a particular type, species, etc.); thicket (small trees, shrubs, or bushes growing thickly); timber (esp. trees with usable wood); underbrush or undergrowth (small trees or shrubs growing beneath, or in the midst of, taller trees); woods or wood,n.

28. Groves or Thickets: boscage or boskage, n.

29. Place or Tract of Trees, Shrubs, Bushes, etc.,n. *From Sec. 27:* boscage or boskage, bosk, bosket or bosquet; brake, brush, chaparral, coppice or copse; forest, forest land, or forestry (usually somewhat wild and often containing game); grove (comparatively small, and often containing fruit or nut trees); orchard, thicket, timberland or timber; woods, wood, or woodland (less wild than a forest); *Also:* 1. arboretum (where trees or shrubs are grown for scientific purposes, study, exhibition, popular interest, etc.) 2. bush (trees and bushes) 3. island (in a prairie) 4. jungle (containing thickly growing trees, vines, and other vegetation, often somewhat swampy in character and usually located in tropical regions) 5. orangery (of orange trees, esp. a sheltered place or hothouse in cooler climates) 6. peachery (of peach trees) 7. pinery (of pine trees) 8. pinetum (of pine trees or other conifers grown for scientific study, exhibition, etc.) 9. scrub (overgrown with low or stunted trees, or with shrubs)

30. A Row of Closely Planted Bushes, Shrubs, Small Trees, etc.; A Boundary or Fence Formed of Such a Row: hedge, hedgerow,n.

31. To Surround, Enclose or Fence with, or Separate by, Such a Row or Rows: hedge, hedge about, hedge in, hedge off,v.

32. Forest Land Set Aside for the Use of All People by the U.S. Government: forest preserve, forest reserve,n.

33. To Convert (Land) into a Forest: afforest, forest,v. (afforestation, forestation,n.)

34. To Plant (an Area) Again with Forest Trees: reforest,v. (reforestation,n.)

35. The Care and Conservation of Forests; The Establishment and Management of Forests: forestation, forestry,n. (forester,n. forestral,adj.)

36. Pert. or Relating to Forests or Woods: bosky, forest, forestal, forestine, sylvan or silvan, sylvestral, woodland, woodsy, woody, adj.

37. Like, Characteristic of, or Suggestive of, a Forest or Woods: forestlike, foresty, sylvan or silvan, sylvestral, woodsy,adj. (sylvanity, n.)

38. Forest or Woodland Scenery or Scenes: sylvanry,n.

39. Growing in the Forest or Woods: wood, woodland,adj.

40. Living in the Forest or Woods: silvicolous (biology), sylvan or silvan, wood, woodland, woodsy,adj.

41. One Who Lives in the Forest or Woods: forester, sylvan, woodlander, woodman, woodsman,n.

42. Nymph or Supernatural Spirit of the Woods; Nymph Who Lives in Trees: dryad, hamadryad, wood nymph, wood spirit,n. (dryadic,adj.)

43. Forest Animal: forester,n.

44. Roman Goddess of the Woods: Diana,n.

45. One Who Frequents the Woods; One Who Is Accustomed to Living in the Woods or Forest and Is Skillful in Hunting, Trapping, etc.: woodsman,n.

46. Skill in Activities Relating to the Woods or Forests, as Exploring, Traveling, Hunting, Trapping, etc.: woodcraft,n.

47. One So Skilled: woodcraftsman,n.

48. Official Who Patrols, Guards, or Has Charge of a Forest: forester, forest ranger, forest warden,n.

49. Having Trees or Forests; Full of, or Covered with, Trees: arboreous, bosky, forested, sylvan or silvan, timbered, wooded,adj. (boskiness,n.)

50. Covered with, or Consisting of, Small or Stunted Trees, Shrubs, etc.: scrubby,adj. (scrubbiness,n.)

51. To Cover or Plant (Land) with Trees or Forests: forest, wood,v. (forestation,n.)

52. Manner of Growing, Habits, etc., of a Forest Tree: silvics,n. (silvical,adj.)

53. In Frigid Areas and on Mountains, That Line beyond Which Trees Do Not Grow: timber line,n.

54. To Clear of Trees or Forests: deforest, disafforest,v. (deforestation, disafforestation or disafforestment,n. deforester,n.)

55. The Cutting of Trees from a Stand so that the Remaining Trees Will Grow Rapidly: interlucation,n.

56. Lacking in Trees: treeless,adj. (treelessness,n.)

57. To Reduce the Legal Status of (Land) from That of a Forest to That of Ordinary Land: disafforest, disforest,v. (disafforestation or disafforestment, disforestation,n.)

58. The Cultivation of Fruit and Nut Trees, or of Trees Producing Food, as Sugar Maples, etc.: horticulture,n. (horticultural, adj.)

59. One Who Cultivates Such: horticulturist, orchardist, orchardman,n.

60. The Cultivation of Trees and Shrubs: arboriculture,n. (arboricultural,adj.)

61. Cultivator of Trees and Shrubs: arboriculturist, arborist,n.

62. The Cultivation of Forest Trees; Art of the Cultivation and Care of a Forest or of Forest Trees: silviculture or sylviculture,n. (silviculturist,n. silvicultural,adj.)

63. Worship of Trees: arborolatry, dendrolatry,n.

64. Selected Sciences of Trees or Forests,n.
  1. dendrography—of the description of trees
  2. dendrology—of trees and shrubs (dendrologic, dendrological, dendrologous, adj.)
  3. forestology—of forests
  4. forestry—of the planting and management of forests (forestral,adj.)
  5. paleodendrology—of fossil trees (paleodendrologic, paleodendrological,adj.)
  6. silvics—of the life of forest trees (silvical, adj.)

65. Student of Trees or Forests,n. *From Sec. 64:* dendrologist; forester (from *forestry*); paleodendrologist; *Also:* 1. arborist—student of trees

66. Device for Measuring the Height and Thickness of a Tree: dendrometer,n.

67. Device That Automatically Records the Growth in Thickness of a Tree: dendrograph,n. (dendrography,n.)

68. A Treatise Written about Trees: dendrology,n.

69. A Treatise Written about, or a Description of, the Trees in a Particular Area: silva or sylva,n.

70. A Treatise Written about Pine Trees: pinetum,n.

71. The Woody Part of Trees or Other Plants: xylem,n.

997. WOOD

1. Wood,n.
  1. hardwood—heavy, close-grained wood from a deciduous tree with broad leaves, as oak, maple, mahogany, walnut, etc.
  2. lumber—sawed or cut wood
  3. plank—timber sawed into pieces
  4. softwood—wood from a coniferous tree; wood that is easily sawed or cut, as pine, etc.
  5. timber—wood suitable for building

2. Inner Covering of Wood Boards or Other Material on the Outside Walls or on the Roof of a Frame Structure: sheathing,n.

3. Outer Covering of Wood Boards, Shingles, or Other Material on a Frame Structure: siding,n.

4. Line or Strips of Boarding at the Base of a Wall, Next to the Floor: baseboard,n.

5. Piece of Wood,n.
  1. baseboard—board that forms the bottom or base of something, as a wall, etc.
  2. beam—long, thick piece of timber, usually used for support
  3. billboard—large outdoor board or signpost on which notices, signs, advertisements, etc., are attached or painted
  4. board—long, thin, and wide piece of lumber; flat piece or sheet of wood for some specific purpose (boarding, collective n.)
  5. brand—partially burned piece of wood
  6. cinder—partially or completely burned piece of wood
  7. clapboard—thin board used, in overlapping design, to cover the outer walls of frame houses (clapboard,adj.)

8. **fagot**—piece of wood for a fire
9. **groundsill**—bottom horizontal timber of a structure lying in proximity to the ground
10. **lath**—narrow and thin strip of wood nailed to beams, studs, etc., as a base for plaster or tile; such a strip used in building a lattice or trellis (lathing, lath, lathwork, collective n.)
11. **list**—strip of wood
12. **panel**—thin, flat piece of wood or other material, generally attached as a decoration to a surface (paneling, collective n.)
13. **plank**—heavy piece of wood, thicker than a board (planking, collective n.)
14. **pole**—long, usually rounded, and thin piece of wood
15. **post**—strong piece of timber used as a place for displaying signs or notices, for nailing or attaching something to, etc.
16. **shingle**—one of the thin boards of wood or other material laid in overlapping design on the roof or exterior sides of a structure
17. **slab**—thick, flat piece of wood
18. **slat**—thin and narrow length of wood
19. **stave**—curved slat of wood forming the side of a barrel
20. **stick**—long and comparatively thin piece of wood
21. **stud, post**—length of timber used as an upright support in a building
22. **timber**—length of heavy wood that is, or is capable of being, part of the main structure of a building
23. **two-by-four**—piece of lumber, approximately two inches thick and four inches wide, used as a floor or wall support, or for other purposes
24. **wedge**—piece of wood pointed at the end

6. To Cover or Close with Sticks of Wood, v. *From Sec. 5:* board or board up, clapboard, lath, panel, plank, shingle

7. To Lay Planking On (a Floor, etc.): plank,v.

8. To Push or Propel (Something) with a Pole: pole,v.

9. To Split (Something) with a Wedge: wedge,v.

10. To Put a Notice or Announcement On (a Post, Wall, etc.): post,v.

11. Similar to a Lath; Tall and Slim, Like a Lath: lathy,adj.

12. A Knot in a Piece of Wood: knurl,n. (knurly, knurled,adj.)

13. Pert. to, or of the Nature of, Wood: ligneous,adj.

14. Resembling Wood: ligneous, ligniform (esp. in form or structure), woody, xyloid, adj. (woodiness,n.)

15. Containing, or Consisting of, Wood: wood, wooden, woody,adj. (woodiness,n.)

16. Made of Wood: wood, wooden,adj.

17. Built of Wood: timbered,adj.

18. Descr. of a Structure with a Wooden Framework: frame,adj.

19. Things Made of Wood; The Wooden Fittings of the Interior of a House, as the Baseboards, Window Ledges, etc.: woodwork, n.

20. Woody at the Base—of Certain Plant Stems: suffruticose, suffruticous,adj.

21. Becoming Partially Woody at Its Base— of Certain Plant Stems: suffrutescent,adj.

22. Destroying, Boring into, or Eating Wood —of Certain Insects, Mollusks, and Crustaceans: xylophagous; xylotomous (insects only),adj.

23. The Art of Cutting Extremely Thin Sections of Wood for Examination under a Microscope: xylotomy,n. (xylotomist,n.)

24. To Convert or Be Converted into Wood: lignify,v. (lignification,n.)

998. FARMING

1. Farming; Certain Sciences, Arts, Systems, etc., of Farming, Growing Plants, Managing the Soil, etc.,n.
1. **agriculture**—farming; cultivation of the land; the raising of crops, fruits, plants, trees, livestock, etc.; art or science of this
2. **agrology**—science of soil as applied in agriculture
3. **agronomics**—land and crop management as an art or science
4. **agronomy**—management of soil and production of crops as either a science or practice
5. **cultivation, culture**—art, action, or system of raising crops or growing plants in the soil
6. **gardening**—the raising of edible or decorative plants on a small plot of ground
7. **geoponics**—agriculture as an art or science
8. **horticulture**—art, science, or practice of growing edible, useful, ornamental, or flowering plants, or shrubs, fruit or nut trees, etc.
9. **husbandry**—farming; farming as a business; agriculture
10. **hydroponics**—system or practice of growing plants without soil, by keeping their roots immersed in water that contains all the required nutrients and minerals
11. **landscape gardening**—art of growing and arranging plants, trees, shrubs, and other garden ornamentation for decorative effect
12. **monoculture**—the raising of but one crop on the land
13. **pedology**—science of soil, soil classification, etc.
14. **tillage, or, literary, tilth**—art, act, or practice of growing crops on the land, or of getting the soil ready for planting
15. **topiary**—art or practice of trimming or training trees and shrubs into ornamental, odd, or fantastic shapes

2. To Farm, i.e., Engage in Farming or Other Pursuits Related to Growing or Arranging Plants, etc.,v. *From Sec. 1:* garden, landscape, till; *Also:*
1. **harvest, reap**—gather in the crop; cut grain and gather it in
2. **plow, plough**—engage in tilling the soil with an instrument (a plow or plough) that turns the soil up and cuts furrows in it in preparation for planting or sowing
3. **sow, seed**—plant or scatter seed in the ground for growth or for the production of a crop

3. To Farm (Land); To Plant (Land); To Plant (Something) in the Land to Grow,v. *From Sec. 1:* cultivate (land, soil, crops, etc.); garden (land, ground, etc.); till (land, soil, ground, etc.); *From Sec. 2:* harvest or reap (a crop, ripened grain, etc.); plow or plough (land or soil); sow (ground, land, or seed) or seed (ground or land); *Also:*
1. **grow, raise**—cause the land to produce, or aid the production and growth of (plants, trees, crops, etc.)
2. **harrow**—break up or level (soil, land, etc.) after plowing, using a toothed instrument (called a harrow) devised for that purpose

3. **plant**—place (seed, young trees or plants, etc.) in the ground to grow; place seeds, young trees or plants, etc., in (the ground) to grow

4. **subdue**—bring (land) under cultivation

4. Farmer; One Who Studies or Practices Farming or a Related Science, Art, Activity, etc.,n. *From Sec. 1:* agriculturist or agriculturalist, agrologist, agronomist, cultivator, gardener, horticulturist, husbandman, landscape gardener, pedologist, tiller; *From Sec. 2:* harvester, harvestman, or reaper; plower or plowman, sower or seeder; *From Sec. 3:* grower or raiser, planter; *Also:*

1. **clodhopper**—plowman
2. **farmerette**—female farmer, or a girl or woman who works on a farm (colloq.)
3. **farm laborer, farm hand, hired man, hired hand, plowman**—one who works on a farm
4. **gardener**—one employed to tend a garden, esp. of a home, estate, etc.
5. **granger**—farmer
6. **muzhik**—Russian peasant
7. **peasant**—one who works or tills the soil in Europe
8. **plowboy**—boy who leads the horses drawing a plow
9. **rancher, ranchman, or, in the Southwestern U.S., ranchero**—one who owns, manages, or works on a farm, esp. a farm devoted to the raising of livestock
10. **truck farmer, truck gardener**—one who raises vegetables, etc., for sale

5. Farming; Pert. to Farming, or to a Related Science, Art, Activity, etc.,adj. *From Sec. 1:* agricultural, agrologic or agrological, agronomic or agronomical, geoponic, horticultural, hydroponic, topiary; *Also:*

1. **agrarian**—pert. to farming or agriculture, or to the promotion of the interests of farm groups or communities
2. **georgic**—pert. to farming, agriculture, or the affairs or life of farm communities

6. Peasants Collectively; State of Being a Peasant: peasantry,n.

7. The Gathering of Crops, Ripened Cut Grain, etc.; The Time or Season for This: harvest,n.

8. A Treatise Written about Agriculture: geoponics,n.

9. To Respond to the Harrow or Plow in a Certain Way—of Soil or Land: harrow, plow, v.

10. Descr. of Land or Soil That Is Suitable for Farming, Cultivating, Tilling, etc.: arable, cultivable or cultivatable, tillable,adj. (arability, cultivability,n.)

11. Roman Goddess of Agriculture: Ceres,n.

12. A Farm: farmstead (with its buildings); grange (esp. with its buildings); plantation (for growing coffee, cotton, tobacco, or other tropical or semi-tropical products); ranch or rancho (esp. for raising and grazing livestock); truck farm or truck garden (for raising vegetables, etc., for sale),n.

13. Pert. to, or Used on, Farms: farming,adj.

14. House on a Farm: farmhouse,n.

15. Enclosure or Yard around Farm Buildings: farmyard,n.

16. Such around a Barn: barnyard,n.

17. Farm Building Where Grain, Hay, etc., Are Stored and Animals Stabled: barn,n.

18. Farmers' Group for Mutual Advancement, Welfare, etc., Established in the U.S. in 1867: Grange,n.

19. Member of this Group: Granger,n.

20. Farmers' Group for Selling Products, Buying Farm Supplies, etc.: farmers' co-operative,n.

---

999. SOIL

1. Soil: clay, clod, dirt, earth, ground, sod, n. (clayey, earthy,adj.); *Also:*

1. **alluvial**—gold-bearing soil deposited by flowing water, in Australia
2. **alluvium, alluvion, alluvial**—soil, mud, sand, gravel, clay, etc., deposited by flowing water, esp. in river valleys, etc. (alluvial,adj.)
3. **dust**—soil in fine, dry particles; a cloud of such in the air (dusty,adj.)
4. **headland**—unplowed soil at the border or fence of a field, esp. at the ends of plowed furrows
5. **loam**—loose, somewhat clayey or sandy soil, esp. such as is fertile (loamy,adj.)
6. **mold**—loose, soft soil rich with decayed organic matter
7. **muck**—soft, black soil that is extremely rich in organic matter (mucky,adj.)
8. **mud**—wet, soft soil (muddy,adj.)
9. **peat**—extremely organic soil containing partly decayed vegetation, cut and dried for fuel (peaty,adj.)
10. **silt, sullage**—fine soil or sand carried by rivers, streams, etc., and deposited as a sediment (silty,adj.)
11. **sod, sward, turf**—grass-covered soil (turfy,adj.)
12. **subsoil, substratum, underearth**—soil beneath the surface soil (substratal, substrative,adj.)
13. **terra firma**—solid earth; solid ground
14. **topsoil**—surface or upper soil

2. Pert. to Turf: cespitose,adj.

3. High Mound of Soil with Sloping Sides: terrace,n.

4. Made of Earth or Soil: earthen,adj.

5. To Fill or Clog Up (a Place) with Silt; To Become Filled or Clogged Up with Silt: silt,v.

6. To Bring to, Put on, or Come to the Ground, Land, or Shore: land,v.

7. To Place or Lay on the Ground; To Hit, or Fall to, the Ground: ground,v.

8. To Plow (Ground) in Such a Way as to Break Up the Subsoil: subsoil,v.

9. To Remove Topsoil from (the Ground or Land): topsoil,v.

10. Earth or Soil in the Poetic or Figurative Sense of the Substance from Which the Human Body Originates: clay,n.

11. Arising from, or Originating in, the Soil: telluric,adj.

12. Decomposed Vegetation, Manure, Lime, etc., Mixed Together and Used to Fertilize the Soil: compost,n.

13. Divination by Means of Examining the Pattern or Figure That Results when a Handful of Earth or Soil Is Thrown at Random on the Ground: geomancy,n. (geomancer,n. geomantic,adj.)

1000. MUD

1. Mud; Wet Soil,n.

1. **clay**—mud
2. **mire**—deep, spongy mud; soil that is wet and slimy to a considerable depth
3. **ooze**—soft, sticky mud; chalky mud that comes from small shell creatures and covers part of the ocean bottom
4. **slime**—soft, sticky mud
5. **slop, slosh, slush**—liquid, watery, or soft mud
6. **sludge**—mud; liquid, watery, or soft mud; deposit or sediment of mud; mire
7. **sullage**—mud deposited as a sediment by flowing water

2. Muddy, adj. *From Sec. 1:* clayey, miry, oozy, slimy, sloppy, slushy, sludgy (miriness, ooziness, sliminess, sloppiness, slushiness,n.); *Also:* **1.** squashy—muddy (squashiness,n.)

3. Muddy with Sediment Stirred Up from the Bottom; Cloudy, Thick, or Opaque with Mud or with Particles of Matter: muddled; riley (colloq.); roily or roiled, turbid (all descr. of water or liquid),adj. (turbidity or turbidness,n.)

4. To Make Muddy in This Fashion: muddle, muddy, puddle; rile (colloq.); roil,v.

5. Device to Measure the Turbidity of Water or Liquids: turbidimeter,n.

6. To Slosh Around or Wallow in Muddy or Dirty Water: puddle,v.

7. To Make or Cause to Be Muddy; To Splatter Mud Upon; To Dirty with Mud: muddy,v.

8. To Become Muddy or Soft, and Full of Indentations when Stepped or Walked on— of Ground or Land: poach,v.

9. To Push (Someone or Something) into Deep, Spongy Mud so that He or It Is Held Fast: mire,v.

10. To Sink into Mud, or into Soft, Deep, or Spongy Mud: mire; poach (while walking),v.

11. To Stick, or Stay Stuck, in Deep, Spongy Mud: mire,v.

12. Living in Mud: limicolous,adj.

13. A Hole, or Depression, as in a Road, That Is Filled with Mud: mudhole, slough,n. (sloughy,adj.)

14. Muddy or Wet Ground or Land,n.
 1. **bog**—wet and spongy ground; such ground the soil of which is composed largely of decayed vegetation; a stretch of such ground; small marsh or swamp
 2. **everglade**—expanse of low and swampy ground in the southern part of the United States containing growths of high grass and full of branching waterways
 3. **(the) Everglades**—swampland in southern Florida some thousands of square miles in area
 4. **fen**—low ground partly or completely covered by water; wet, spongy ground; marsh
 5. **marsh, marshland**—stretch of wet lowland; swamp (marshlander, marshman, n.)
 6. **mire**—soft, spongy, wet ground; a stretch of such; ground covered by deep and spongy mud
 7. **moor, moorland**—large tract of open, waste land (esp. in Britain) covered generally with peat, and so poorly drained as to be more or less wet most of the time
 8. **morass**—soft, wet, low ground; stretch of such ground; bog; swamp
 9. **ooze**—bog; marsh
 10. **peat bog**—bog containing peat
 11. **quagmire, quag**—stretch of soft, wet, spongy ground that sinks under the weight of a person walking on it
 12. **salt marsh, salina**—marsh overflowed with salt water
 13. **slough**—stretch of muddy, soft land; place where the mud is deep, or where the soil is muddy, or wet and spongy
 14. **swale**—low section in a stretch of land, or a low area in a meadow, that is wetter than surrounding, higher land and contains a luxuriant growth of vegetation
 15. **swamp, swampland, slough, slew, slue**—ground that is very wet and spongy; stretch of such ground; stretch of such ground that is not cultivable, though containing trees of a certain type
 16. **swampland**—land that is full of swamps

15. Like, or of the Nature of, Such Ground or Land, adj. *From Sec. 14:* boggy, fenny,

marshy, miry, moory or moorish, oozy, quaggy, sloughy, swampy or swampish (marshiness, miriness,n.); *Also:*
 1. paludal, paludine, plashy—marshy
 2. waterlogged—swampy

16. Pert. to Such Ground or Land, adj. *From Sec. 14:* marshy, swamp; *Also:* **1. paludal, paludine**—pert. to marsh or to other low ground that is partly or completely covered by water

17. Full of, or Containing or Consisting of, Such Tracts of Ground, adj. *From Sec. 14:* boggy, fenny, marshy, swampy

18. Living or Growing in Such Ground or Land, adj. *From Sec. 14:* fenny, swamp or swampy

19. To Sink or Become Stuck in, or as if in, Such Ground; To Cause to So Sink or Become Stuck, v. *From Sec. 14:* bog or bog down, swamp

20. Produced by Marshes, as Diseases or Poisonous or Harmful Exhalations or Germs: paludal,adj.

1001. DUST; POWDER

1. Cloud of Dust: pother, smother,n.

2. Fine Particles Deposited as Dust: grit,n. (gritty,adj.)

3. To Turn or Reduce, or Become Turned or Reduced, to Dust, as by Grinding, Crushing, Pounding, or Smashing, or by Being Ground, etc.: powder, pulverize,v. (pulverization,n.)

4. Capable of Being So Reduced: pulverable, pulverizable,adj.

5. That Which So Turns Something into Dust: pulverizer,n.

6. To Reduce, or Cause to Be Reduced, to Dust through the Process of Natural Decay: molder,v.

7. Crumbling, or Easily Crumbled, into Dust or Powder: friable, powdery, pulverulent,adj. (friability or friableness, powderiness, pulverulence,n.)

8. Consisting of, or Covered with, Dust or Powder: dusty, powdery, pulverulent,adj. (dustiness, powderiness, pulverulence,n.)

9. Of the Nature of Dust or Powder: dusty, powdery,adj. (dustiness, powderiness,n.)

10. To Remove or Wipe the Dust from; To Be Engaged in Such: dust,v. (duster,n.)

11. To Sprinkle or Daub with Dust or Powder; To Sprinkle in the Form of Dust or Powder: dust, powder,v.

12. Apparatus for Thus Sprinkling Dust or Powder: duster,n.

13. To Use Powder as a Cosmetic on the Face or Body: powder,v.

14. Pad for Such Use: powder puff,n.

15. Having the Grayish Color of Dust: dusty, adj. (dustiness,n.)

16. Jacket or Cover on a Book That Protects against Dust, Soil, etc.: book jacket, dust jacket,n.

17. Windstorm That Whirls Thick Masses of Dust into the Air: dust storm,n.

18. Region Subject to Such: dust bowl,n.

1002. CLAY

1. Like Clay: argillaceous, clayey, clayish, claylike,adj.

2. Containing a Large Amount of Claylike Substance: argillaceous,adj.

3. Containing Clay: argillaceous,adj.

4. Producing Clay; Containing Great Amounts of Clay: argilliferous,adj.

5. Clay; Clay Used by Potters: argil,n.

6. Made of Baked Clay: earthen,adj.

7. Clay, or a Combination of Clay and Sand, Waterproofed by Kneading while It Is Wet: puddle,n.

8. To Make (Clay) Waterproof by This Method: puddle,v.

9. Rectangular Block of Prepared, Baked Clay Used in Building, Pavements, etc.; Material for This; Such Blocks Collectively; A Similar Block of Any Kind: brick,n.

10. Place Where Bricks Are Made: brickyard, n.

11. Furnace Where Bricks Are Baked: brick-kiln,n.

12. Construction of Brick: brickwork,n.

13. To Lay Bricks On; To Build, Cover, Line, etc., with Bricks: brick,v.

14. One Whose Occupation Is Building with, or Laying, Bricks: bricklayer,n. (bricklaying, n.)

15. A Kind of Hard Brick or Mass of Fused Bricks: clinker,n.

1003. LAND

1. Continuous Portion or Piece of Land; Such a Portion (of Land): area, expanse, extent, stretch, sweep, tract,n. (areal,adj.)

2. Land; Tract or Piece of Land,n.
1. **bay**—level tract of land projecting into hills, woods, etc.
2. **border, borderland, frontier, march**—land, or tract of land, lying along the boundary of a country (frontier,adj.)
3. **cantle**—segment of land cut off from the rest
4. **continent**—one of the six main bodies of land in the world—Europe, Asia, Africa, Australia, North America, South America; large, unbroken tract of land (continental, adj.)
5. **(the) Continent**—mainland of Europe in distinction to the island of Great Britain (Continental,adj.)
6. **cove**—sheltered stretch of prairie between hills or forests
7. **downs**—open, high, and rolling land, esp. in southern or southeastern Britain
8. **farm land**—land devoted to, or suitable for, farming
9. **field**—small tract of land suitable for farming, grazing animals, etc.
10. **ground**—land; dry land
11. **grounds**—tract of land devoted to some special or specific use, or surrounding a building or buildings
12. **heath, moor**—tract of uncultivated, open land in Great Britain
13. **landscape**—section of country land, esp. as can be seen at one view
14. **lot**—separate piece of land; such as part of a district, city, etc.
15. **lowland**—land, or tract of land, lower than surrounding land (lowland,adj.)
16. **mainland, continent**—principal tract of land, in distinction to islands or peninsulas, etc. (continental,adj.)
17. **moor**—expanse of land in Great Britain kept for hunting game
18. **neck**—narrow stretch of land
19. **northland**—land in the north, or in the northern part of a country
20. **outland**—land lying outside the main area of a place (outland,adj.)
21. **paddy, padi**—rice field

22. **pampas**—grassy, treeless plains of South America, esp. Argentina (pampean,adj.)
23. **park**—tract of land set aside for public use, recreation, sports, etc.
24. **patch**—tract or piece of land or ground
25. **plain, level**—stretch or expanse of level land
26. **(the) Plains, the Great Plains**—expanse of level land stretching west from the Mississippi Valley
27. **plateau, highland, tableland, table**—high plain (highland,adj.)
28. **platform**—elevated and flat stretch of ground
29. **plot, plat**—small piece of ground or land
30. **prairie**—expanse or tract of level or somewhat rolling, treeless land in the Mississippi Valley
31. **preserve**—tract of land, or other place, where the game, fish, and other animal life are protected by the government
32. **purlieu**—land, or tract of land, bordering a forest
33. **region, area**—extended stretch or tract of land (regional, areal,adj.)
34. **ridge**—raised or elevated piece of land or ground
35. **slope, incline, grade**—piece of ground that inclines from the horizontal, i.e., is not level
36. **southland**—land in the south, or in the southern part of a country
37. **steppe**—vast, generally level and treeless, stretch of land, esp. in Southeastern Europe and in Asia
38. **terrain**—tract of land; tract of land thought of in reference to its physical features or military use
39. **terra incognita**—land still unexplored or otherwise unknown
40. **territory, terrene**—land; tract of land (territorial,adj.)
41. **tillage or, literary, tilth**—cultivated or tilled land
42. **tundra**—wide sweep of nearly level and treeless land in the arctic regions
43. **upland**—land or ground higher than surrounding land (upland,adj.)
44. **valley**—low land or ground between hills, mountains, or high lands
45. **waste, wasteland, wilderness**—tract of uncultivated or wild land
46. **wold**—land without forests; high plain; high, open tract of land

3. Inhabitant or Native of Land or of a Tract of Land,n. *From Sec. 2:* borderer or frontiersman, continental, Continental, lowlander, mainlander or continental, northlander or northerner, plainsman; highlander (from *plateau*); southlander or southerner, uplander; *Also:* 1. **groundling**—animal that lives, or plant that grows, close to the ground

4. To Touch Upon Another Land at the Boundary: border on or upon, march upon or with,v.

5. Consisting of, or Growing or Living on, Land: terrestrial,adj.

6. Pert. to Land: agrarian, terrestrial,adj.

7. Surface Features or Layout of a Land Region, Including Mountains, Hills, Valleys, Roads, Waterways, etc.: geography, topography,n. (geographic or geographical, topographic or topographical,adj.)

8. History of a Land Region as Evidenced by Such Surface Features; The Study of Such Features: topology,n. (topologic, topological,adj.)

9. Natural Features of Country Land: scenery,n. (scenic,adj.)

10. Descr. of Such Features when Beautiful, Picturesque, etc.: scenic,adj.

11. Land That Is Unproductive, etc.,n.

1. **Barren Grounds, Barren Lands**—stretch of wind-swept, relatively uninhabited, and naked land in Northern Canada
2. **barrens**—unproductive stretch of land; level tract of unproductive land with few trees and poor or sandy soil
3. **desert**—land, or stretch of land, so lacking in water that there is little or no vegetation; barren, dry area with no soil, usually covered by sand (desert,adj.)
4. **heath, moor**—wasteland covered by shrubs, in Great Britain
5. **waste, wasteland**—barren land or stretch of land

12. Fertile or Green Place in a Wasteland or Desert: oasis,n.

13. Land in Respect to Government Control, n.

1. **dominion**—territory governed by, or under the control of, a nation, or under single rule
2. **enclave**—foreign territory within, and surrounded by, the land of a specified country
3. **exclave**—territory belonging to a specified country but within, and surrounded by, foreign territory
4. **territory**—land under government control or under the control of a distant country; separate tract of land belonging to a state (territoriality,n. territorial,adj.)

14. To Make a Territory out of; To Reduce to the Status of a Territory: territorialize,v. (territorialization,n.)

15. State of Being So Made or Reduced: territorialization,n.

16. To Add New Territory to (a Place, etc.): territorialize,v. (territorialization,n.)

17. Land in Respect to Ownership, or as the Grounds Surrounding a Building or Buildings, Residence, etc.,n.

1. **campus**—grounds of an educational institution
2. **estate**—large piece of land with a residence or other buildings on it, esp. one belonging to a wealthy person or family
3. **freehold**—land owned for life with the privilege of bequeathal
4. **holding**—land, or piece of land, owned by someone
5. **lot**—portion or piece of owned land, esp. on which a house or other building stands, or suitable for building a house or other structure on
6. **manor**—British estate over which the owner still holds some feudal rights (manorial,adj.)
7. **parcel**—piece of land, esp. as put up for sale, purchased, etc.
8. **park**—grounds of a country estate
9. **plot**—small piece of ground on which a house or other structure is built
10. **real estate, real property, realty, property**—land, or land and its buildings and other improvements, etc., owned by a person, group, etc.
11. **terrace**—land area, whether paved, grassed, etc., at the front, back, or side of a residence
12. **yard**—grounds around, behind, or in front of, a residence or other building

18. Pert. to Land Ownership or Tenure: agrarian,adj.

19. Landowner: freeholder (of a freehold), landholder, landlord or, fem., landlady, squire,n.

20. Owning Land: landed, landowning,adj.

21. Landowner Who Rents Land, Buildings, Residences, Apartments, etc., to Others: landlord,n.

22. Practice, or Economic System, of Renting One's Lands to Tenants: landlordism, territorialism,n.

23. System in Which Landowners Have Predominant Power in a State: territorialism,n.

24. One Who Advocates Such a System, or Who Is a Landowner under Such a System: territorialist,n.

25. One Who Sells Land or Real Estate for Others: real estate agent, real estate broker, or, if a member of the national association in the United States, realtor,n.

26. Public Area in a City, Town, etc., Usually Planted with Grass, Trees, etc.: common, green, plaza, square,n.

27. Such an Area in New England Villages: village green,n.

28. Principles, Practices, Laws, or Agitation in Favor of Fair Distribution, or Fairer Redistribution, of Land: agrarianism,n. (agrarian,adj.)

29. One Who Favors These: agrarian,n.

30. Owning No Land: landless,adj.

1004. EARTH

1. The Earth: globe; planet (i.e., one of the celestial bodies revolving around the sun); terrene, world,n. (global, planetary, terrene, worldly,adj.)

2. A Little World; A World in Miniature; An Institution, Community, etc., That is a Miniature of the General World: microcosm,n. (microcosmic, microcosmical,adj.)

3. Central Mass, or Interior Part, of the Earth: barysphere, centrosphere,n.

4. Solid Portion of the Earth; The Earth's Crust: lithosphere,n.

5. Certain Zones or Areas of the Earth,n.

1. **(the) Antarctic, Antarctic Zone**—area around the South Pole, including the land mass and the ocean (antarctic,adj.)
2. **Antarctica**—the continent around the South Pole, uninhabited and ice-covered
3. **(the) Arctic, Arctic Zone**—region around the North Pole (arctic,adj.)
4. **equator**—imaginary belt around the earth that is equidistant between the North and South Poles (equatorial,adj.)
5. **Frigid Zone**—area or region from one of the poles to its polar circle—the North Frigid Zone around the North Pole, the South Frigid Zone around the South Pole
6. **hemisphere**—half of the earth, depending on how it is divided, i.e., Eastern or Western Hemisphere, or Northern or Southern Hemisphere (hemispherical, adj.)
7. **North Pole**—northernmost end of the earth; northern end of the earth's axis of rotation
8. **pole**—one of the ends of the earth's axis of rotation, i.e., the North Pole or the South Pole (polar,adj.)
9. **subtropics**—region near, or bordering on, the tropics (subtropical, subtropic, subtorrid,adj.)
10. **Temperate Zone**—either of the zones, i.e., North Temperate or South Temperate, between the tropics and a polar circle
11. **Torrid Zone, tropics**—region or zone on both sides of the equator, bounded by the Tropic of Cancer on the north and the Tropic of Capricorn on the south (tropic, tropical,adj.)
12. **ultima Thule, Thule**—northernmost regions of the habitable world, as conceived by people in ancient times, and probably referring to Norway, Iceland, etc.

6. Pert. to, at, or near, the North Pole: arctic,adj.

7. Pert. to, at, or near, the South Pole: antarctic,adj.

8. Pert. to, or Naming, the Tropical Regions of the New World, i.e., South America, West Indies, Tropical Parts of North America, etc.: Neotropical or Neotropic,adj.

9. Between the Tropics: intertropical, subsolar,adj.

10. Boundaries of the Zones of the Earth,n.
  1. Antarctic Circle—between the South Frigid and South Temperate Zones
  2. Arctic Circle—between the North Frigid and North Temperate Zones
  3. polar circle—either the Antarctic or the Arctic Circle
  4. Tropic of Cancer—between the North Temperate and Torrid Zones
  5. Tropic of Capricorn—between the South Temperate and Torrid Zones

11. Angular Distance North or South from the Equator: latitude,n. (latitudinal,adj.)

12. Angular Distance East or West on the Earth: longitude,n. (longitudinal,adj.)

13. North or South Divisional Circle of the Earth, Passing Through the Poles; Half Such Circle between the Poles: meridian,n. (meridian, meridional,adj.)

14. East or West Divisional Circle of the Earth's Surface: parallel,n.

15. Descr. of the Imaginary Line Near the Equator Where the Magnetic Needle Does Not React: aclinic,adj.

16. Pert. or Relating to the Earth or World: earthly, global, mundane; planetary (i.e., in the sense that the earth is one of the planets); subcelestial (i.e., beneath the heavens); sublunary or sublunar (i.e., beneath the moon); subsolar (i.e., beneath the sun); tellurian, telluric, terrene, terrestrial, worldly,adj.

17. Characteristic of the Earth: tellurian, telluric,adj.

18. Originating in, or Coming or Proceeding from, the Earth: earthborn, telluric,adj.

19. Not Pert. to, Not from or of, or Not Characteristic of, the Earth or This World: unearthly, unmundane, unterrestrial, unworldly,adj. (unearthliness, unworldliness,n.)

20. With the Earth as a Center; Pert. or Relating to, or Measured from, the Center of the Earth: geocentric, geocentrical,adj.

21. Pert. to Forces or Occurrences Inside the Earth: geodynamic, geodynamical,adj.

22. Such Forces, Occurrences, Processes, etc.: geodynamics,n.

23. Firmly Fixed in, or Rooted to, the Earth: earth-bound,adj.

24. Toward, or in the Direction of, the Earth: earthward, earthwards,adv. (earthward,adj.)

25. Going in the Direction of the Earth: earth-bound,adj.

26. Similar to, or Resembling, the Earth: geomorphic,adj.

27. Pert. to the Earth's Figure or Its Surface Form: geomorphic,adj.

28. Pert. or Relating to, Covering, Concerning, etc., the Entire World or Earth: earthwide, global, planetary, world-wide,adj.

29. Below, or Functioning or Operating below, the Earth's Surface: subsurface, subterranean, subterraneous, underearth, underground,adj.

30. The Inner Depths of the Earth: underearth,n.

31. An Inhabitant of the Earth, i.e., One Who Lives on This Planet: earth dweller, earthling, subcelestial, tellurian, terrestrial,n. (earth-dwelling, tellurian, terrestrial,adj.)

32. Belonging to, at Home in, or Being a Citizen of, the Entire World; Familiar with, or Relating or Pert. to, the Entire World of the Intellect, Commerce, Politics, Social Life, etc.: cosmopolitan,adj. (cosmopolitanism,n.)

33. A Person of Such a Sort: cosmopolitan, cosmopolite,n. (cosmopolitanism, cosmopolitism or cosmopolicy,n.)

34. Descr. of Plants or Animals Distributed Widely over the Entire World: cosmopolitan, adj. (cosmopolitanism,n.)

35. Such an Animal or Plant: cosmopolite,n. (cosmopolitism or cosmopolicy,n.)

36. Exhibition of Pictures of Places, Scenery, etc., in Various Parts of the World: cosmorama,n. (cosmoramic,adj.)

37. To Hide in a Hole in the Earth, as Certain Animals (Fox, etc.); To Chase (an Animal) into Such a Hole: earth,v.

38. Earthly in the Sense of Belonging or Relating to, Concerning, or Concerned with, This World or Worldly Affairs, Rather than Heaven, Spiritual Affairs, etc.: earthen, earthly, earthy, mundane, secular, subcelestial, sublunary or sublunar, subsolar, temporal, terrene, terrestrial, unspiritual, worldly, worldly-minded,adj. (earthiness, earthliness, secularity, temporality, unspirituality or unspiritualness, worldliness, worldly-mindedness,n.)

39. Not Earthly in This Sense: spiritual, unmundane, unsecular, untemporal, unterrestrial, unworldly,adj. (spirituality or spiritualness, unworldliness,n.)

40. Person Concerned with, or Interested in, the Affairs, Pleasures, etc., of This World: earthling, worldling,n.

41. Earthly, Rather than Religious or Sacred, etc.: profane, secular, worldly,adj. (profaneness or profanity, secularity, worldliness,n.)

42. To Make Earthly, Secular (in Any Sense), or Unspiritual: secularize,v. (secularization,n.)

43. Certain Sciences, etc., of the Earth,n.
  1. geochemistry—of the chemical composition of the earth's crust and of the chemical changes that occur in it (geochemist, n. geochemical,adj.)
  2. geognosy—of the make-up of the earth, bodies of water on it, air surrounding it, its interior, and its crust (geognost,n. geognostic, geognostical,adj.)
  3. geography—of the distribution of life, land masses, bodies of water, mountains, climate, etc., on the earth (geographer,n. geographic, geographical,adj.)
  4. geology—of the physical composition of the earth, changes past and present, its rocks and rock formations, etc.
  5. geomorphology, geomorphy, physiography—of the form, surface shapes, distribution of land and water, and the origin and development of the land masses of the earth (geomorphologist, geomorphist, physiographer,n. geomorphological, physiographic or physiographical,adj.)
  6. geophysics—of the relation between the earth and physical forces, and of such agencies and forces as modify the earth (geophysicist,n. geophysical,adj.)
  7. hydrogeology—of the modification or erosion of the earth by water (hydrogeological,adj.)

8. **paleogeology**—of showing geological conditions of earlier eras or periods of the earth's history (paleogeologic,adj.)

44. To Study Geology; To Examine (Land, Rocks, etc) from a Geological Point of View: geologize,v.

45. Descr. of Geological Formations Caused by the Action of Water: Neptunian or neptunian,adj.

46. Representation of Geographical Conditions on the Earth at Some Earlier Time in the Earth's History: paleogeography,n. (paleogeographic or paleogeographical,adj.)

47. Room, Enclosed Area, etc., in the Shape of a Globe, on the Walls of Which a Map of the Earth's Surface Is Drawn for Viewing by Spectators: georama,n.

48. Description of the General Phenomena of Nature: physiography,n. (physiographer,n. physiographic or physiographical,adj.)

49. Upward Thrust or Warping of the Earth's Crust: upheaval,n.

1005. EARTHQUAKE

1. A Trembling or Movement of Part of the Earth's Surface: convulsion, earthquake, quake; seaquake (under the sea or ocean); seism, temblor, tremor; upheaval (i.e., a rising up of the earth's crust), n. (seismic, seismical, seismal,adj.)

2. Such Trembling or Movement when Very Weak and Detectable Only by Special Instruments: microseism,n. (microseismic, microseismical,adj.)

3. Such when Very Severe: macroseism,n. (macroseismic,adj.)

4. The Violent Shake or Jar Caused by an Earthquake: shock,n.

5. Pert. to, or Indicating, Equal Intensity of Earthquake Shock: isoseismic,adj.

6. The Phenomena of Earthquakes: seismism,n.

7. Caused by an Earthquake; Subject to Earthquakes: seismal, seismic, seismical,adj. (seismicity,n.)

8. Science of Earthquakes,n.
1. **microseismology**—of earthquakes so mild as to be detectible only by special instruments
2. **seismology, seismography**—of earthquakes, earthquake detection and recording, and attendant phenomena (seismologist, seismographer,n. seismologic, seismological,adj.)

9. Instruments for Detecting, Measuring, etc., Earthquakes,n.
1. **macroseismograph**—for recording severe earthquakes
2. **microseismograph, microseismometer**—for measuring the direction, strength, and duration of very mild earthquakes (microseismometry,n.)
3. **microseismometrograph**—for recording with the greatest of sensitivity the movements of the ground during an earthquake
4. **seismochronograph**—for determining the exact moment of an earthquake shock
5. **seismograph**—for recording the shocks and other phenomena of earthquakes (seismography, seismographer,n. seismographic, seismographical,adj.)
6. **seismometer, seismometrograph**—for measuring the direction, strength, and duration of earthquakes, and the actual ground movements during an earthquake (seismometry,n. seismometric, seismometrical,adj.)

7. **seismoscope**—for recording the time and occurrence of earthquakes (seismoscopic, adj.)
8. **tromometer**—for detecting or measuring extremely slight tremors (tromometry,n. tromometric, tromometrical,adj.)

10. Record of an Earthquake Made on a Seismograph: seismogram,n.

11. A Description or List of Earthquakes: seismologue,n.

12. Scientific Description of Earthquakes and the Attendant Phenomena: seismography,n.

13. Producing Earthquakes: seismotic,adj.

14. Pert. to, or Indicating, Those Physical Features of the Structure of the Earth That Are Shown by, or Are Related to, Earthquakes: seismotectonic,adj.

1006. ROCK

1. Rock; A Rock; Rocklike Substance; A Structure of Rock,n.
1. **argillite**—claylike rock (argillitic,adj.)
2. **bedrock**—solid rock, usually under soil or fragments of other rock
3. **boulder**—a large, detached, rounded rock
4. **Carrara, Carrara marble**—white marble used in sculpture and otherwise, and coming from the mountains near the Italian city famous for its fine marble (Carraran, adj.)
5. **cement**—synthetic substance, often made of prepared clay and limestone, that hardens into a stonelike material
6. **chalk**—limestone that is easily pulverized (chalky,adj.)
7. **chalkstone**—lump, piece, or mass of chalk
8. **cliff, bluff, escarpment, scarp**—a high and steep rock, or the face of such a rocky mass
9. **cobblestone, cobble**—rounded stone used at one time to pave streets
10. **concrete**—synthetic, stonelike substance made from cement, sand, and broken stones, and used for the foundation or facing of structures, pavements, etc. (concrete,adj.)
11. **cornerstone, quoin, coin**—a stone where two walls come together; a stone laid at the corner of the foundation of a structure
12. **crag**—a steep or projecting rock; projecting rough part of a rock (cragginess,n. cragged, craggy,adj.)
13. **dornick**—a boulder; a stone
14. **flag, flagstone**—a flat piece of stone used in, or suitable for, paving (flagging, collective n. flaggy,adj.)
15. **flagstone**—rock that can be split into flags
16. **flint**—very hard stone, or a piece of it, that emits sparks when struck (flinty, adj.)
17. **gneiss**—rock of alternating layers of different minerals and having a coarse grain (gneissic,adj.)
18. **granite**—extremely hard grayish or pinkish rock (granitic,adj.)
19. **gravel**—mixture of pebbles and sand; pebbles; small stones (gravelly,adj.)
20. **lava**—molten or fluid rock that issues from a volcano; such rock when cooled and hardened
21. **ledge**—flat ridge of rock projecting from a cliff or slope; layer or mass of underground rock
22. **limestone**—rock that consists mainly of calcium carbonate—a source of building stones, lime, etc.
23. **marble**—limestone that has been crystallized by heat and pressure, capable of

taking a high polish, and used in building and sculpture; a piece of such

24. **masonry, stonework**—stone material used in building; product or products built of stone, brick, etc., esp. in or around structures

25. **megalith**—huge stone in prehistoric structures or monuments (megalithic, adj.)

26. **menhir**—upright prehistoric or archaeological single stone or monolith

27. **monolith**—huge stone used to fashion a statue, monument, or other architectural or sculptural product; statue, column, obelisk, etc., made from such a stone; stonelike substance used for floors (monolithic,adj.)

28. **mortar**—mixture of cement, sand, water, etc., for joining bricks, stones, etc.

29. **obelisk, shaft**—huge shaft of stone, tapering in shape, with four sides and, usually, a pyramidal top, erected as a monument (obeliscal,adj.)

30. **pebble**—small, rounded stone, usually one worn by the action of running water (pebbly, pebbled,adj.)

31. **precipice**—cliff that rises vertically or almost vertically; extremely steep cliff; cliff with an overhanging face; crag (precipitous,adj.)

32. **pyramid**—tremendous structure of stone with sloping sides meeting at a top point, esp. one built by the ancient Egyptians as a royal tomb (pyramidal, pyramidic, pyramidical,adj.)

33. **quarry**—a square piece of stone; a square tile

34. **riprap**—broken stones used for foundations, walls, etc.

35. **rubble**—rough, broken stones; rough stones direct from a quarry (rubbly,adj.)

36. **rubblework, rubble**—structure or structures of rough or irregular stones (rubbly, adj.)

37. **scar**—a projecting or isolated rock; submerged or low rock under the water of a sea or ocean; cliff

38. **schist, mica schist**—crystalline rock that can be split along parallel planes (schistic, schistose,adj.)

39. **scoria, cinders, slag**—a kind of loose lava (scoriae,pl.n. scoriaceous,adj.)

40. **shale**—a kind of rock formed by hardening clay or clayey substance—it is fine-grained and splits easily into thin layers

41. **shelf**—bedrock, esp. under deposits of soil or sand left by moving waters (term in mining)

42. **slab**—thick, broad, flat piece of stone

43. **slate**—a kind of hard rock with a fine grain—it splits naturally into thin, smooth layers; a piece or layer of this used as roofing material, or for writing on with chalk, slate

44. **stone**—piece of rock for a particular purpose; substance composed of rock (stoniness,n. stony,adj.)

45. **tile**—thin, shaped piece of stone, baked clay, or metal used for roofing, floors, wall covering, etc. (tile, collective n.)

46. **travertine, travertin**—a kind of limestone used for building and other purposes

47. **xenolith**—piece of a rock embedded in another rock of different type (xenolithic, adj.)

2. To Cover (a Road, Sidewalk, etc.) with a Hard Surface, i.e., One Made of Stone, Brick, Concrete, etc.: pave,v. (paver,n.)

3. A Road, Sidewalk, etc., So Covered; Material for Such Covering: pavement,n.

4. To Pave with a Kind of Rock,v. *From Sec. 1:* cobble or cobblestone, concrete, flag or flagstone, gravel, pebble; *Also:*

1. asphalt—pave (a road, etc.) with substances mixed with crushed rock

2. causeway—pave (a road, etc.) with cobblestones or pebbles

3. macadamize—pave (a road, etc.) with rolled layers of broken stones (macadamization,n.)

5. Pavement of Such,n. *From Sec. 4:* cobblestones, concrete, flagstones or flagging, gravel, pebbles; asphalt, macadam (asphaltic,adj.)

6. To Cover with a Kind of Rock,v. *From Sec. 1:* cement, concrete, gravel, mortar, pebble, slate, tile (cementation,n.)

7. Shaped Like a Pyramid: pyramidal, pyramidic, pyramidical, pyramidlike,adj.

8. To Build or Strengthen (a Foundation, Wall, etc.) with Broken Stones: riprap,v.

9. To Provide with a Cornerstone: quoin,v.

10. To Provide or Fit with Stones or Stonework: stone,v.

11. To Rub, Polish, Smooth, or Sharpen on, or with, a Stone: stone,v.

12. To Hit with Pebbles; To Throw Pebbles at: pebble,v.

13. To Join or Unite with Cement or Mortar: cement, mortar,v. (cementation,n.)

14. Descr. of Land, etc., Having Cliffs: cragged, craggy, cliffed, cliffy, clifty, precipiced, precipitous,adj. (craggedness, cragginess, precipitousness,n.)

15. Side of a Cliff: cliffside,n.

16. A Steep, Rocky Place: scar,n.

17. A Rocky Height: bluff, cliff, crag, escarpment, scar, scarp,n.

18. Sliding Mass of Rock, Rock Particles, Snow, Earth, Ice, etc.: avalanche, landslide, n.

19. Heap of Stones Erected as a Landmark or Memorial: cairn,n.

20. Circle of Stones Built in Prehistoric Times: cromlech,n.

21. Prehistoric Arrangements of Huge Stones in the Form of a Room or Enclosed Space, Used as a Tomb: dolmen,n.

22. Geological Layer of One Type of Rock: stratum,n. (strata,pl.n.)

23. Crack or Seam in Rock Filled with Mineral: streak, vein,n.

24. Such a Streak or Vein Containing Metallic Ore: lode,n.

25. Loose Particles Worn Away from Rocks: detritus,n.

26. Fine Debris or Grains of Rock: sand,n. (sandy,adj.)

27. Resembling Gneiss: gneissic, gneissoid, adj.

28. Resembling Granite: granitic, granitelike, granitoid,adj.

29. Resembling, or of the Structure of, Schist: schistic, schistoid, schistose, schistous,adj.

30. Descr. of Rock Produced by Volcanic Action: igneous; plutonic (solidified below the earth's surface); pyrogenic, volcanic,adj.

31. Pert. to Stones: lapidarian, lithic,adj.

32. Consisting of Rock or Stone: lithic, rocky, rupestral, rupestrian, stony,adj.

33. Resembling Rock or Stone: lithoid, lithoidal, petrosal, petrous, rocklike, rocky, stonelike, stony,adj. (rockiness, stoniness,n.)

34. Characteristic of, or Suggesting, Stone: stony,adj. (stoniness,n.)

35. Covered by, or Abounding in, Rock or Stone: rocky, stony,adj. (rockiness, stoniness,n.)

36. Pert. to, or Like, Marble: marble, marmoreal, marmorean,adj.

37. Like the Fine, White Marble of Paros: Parian,adj.

38. To Give the Mottled Color or Stain of Variegated Marble to: marble,v. (marbled, adj.)

39. Resembling or Containing Chalk: chalklike, chalky, cretaceous,adj. (chalkiness,n.)

40. Abounding in Chalk: cretaceous,adj.

41. Covered with Chalk: chalky,adj. (chalkiness,n.)

42. To Mark or Write with, Treat with, Mix with, etc., Chalk: chalk,v.

43. To Whiten with, or as if with, Chalk; Hence, to Make Pale: chalk,v.

44. Enclosed Piece of Slate for Writing on with Chalk: blackboard,n.

45. Growing on Rocks (of Plants); Living on or among Rocks (of Animals): rupestrine, rupicoline, rupicolous,adj.

46. Living under Rocks, as Certain Beetles: lapidicolous,adj.

47. Inscribed on Rocks: rupestral, rupestrian, adj.

48. Inscribed on Stone: lapidarian, lapidary, adj.

49. Pert. to Cutting, or Engraving on, Stones as an Art: lapidary,adj.

50. To Turn (Something) into Stone: lapidify, mineralize, petrify,v. (lapidification, mineralization, petrifaction or petrification,n. lapidific or lapidifical, petrifactive,adj.)

51. To Become So Converted: lapidify, petrify,v. (lapidification, petrifaction or petrification,n.)

52. To Turn or Change (Something) into a Hard, Stony Substance by the Deposit of Lime; To Become So Changed: calcify,v. (calcification,n.)

53. Place, as an Excavation, etc., from Which Stone of Various Sorts Is Cut, Blasted, etc.: quarry,n.

54. To Get, Cut, Blast, etc., (Stone) from Such a Place: quarry,v. (quarrier,n.)

55. To Make Such an Excavation, etc., in: quarry,v.

56. Place, Establishment, etc., Where Stone Is Cut or Shaped into a Form Suitable for Use in Building: stoneworks,n. (stoneworker, n.)

57. One Who Cuts Stone: lapicide, stonecutter,n.

58. One Who Builds or Constructs out of Stone, Bricks, or Similar Material: mason,n.

59. The Occupation of Such: masonry,n.

60. To Build, Construct, or Make Stronger with Stone, Brick, or Similar Material: mason,v.

61. One Who Lays Tile: tiler,n.

62. Pert. to, Resembling, Consisting of, or Arranged Like, Tile: tegular,adj.

63. Selected Sciences Dealing with Rocks,n.
   1. lithology—with the mineral composition of specimens of rock, or with the study of rocks (lithologist,n. lithologic, lithological,adj.)
   2. petrography—with the classification and description of rocks (petrographer,n. petrographic, petrographical,adj.)
   3. petrology—with the study, origin, structure, etc., of rocks (petrologist,n. petrologic, petrological,adj.)
   4. stratigraphy—with the classification, naming, arrangement, interpretation, etc., of layers of rock (stratigrapher, stratigraphist,n. stratigraphic, stratigraphical,adj.)

1007. SAND

1. Similar to, or of the Nature of, Sand: arenaceous, gritty, sabulous, sandlike, sandy, adj. (grittiness, sabulosity, sandiness,n.)

2. Growing in Sand: arenaceous,adj.

3. Living in Sand: arenicolous,adj. (zoology)

4. To Make the Sound of Sand Being Stepped on: grit,v.

5. Hard Particles of Sand or Stone: grit,n.

6. Like, or Containing, Such: gritty, sabulous,adj. (grittiness, sabulosity,n.)

7. Windstorm That Carries Great Clouds of Sand: sandstorm,n.

8. Sand Hill Made by the Wind, Generally at the Seashore or in Deserts: down, dune,n.

9. Tract or Region of Sand, or Chiefly of Sand: desert, sands,n. (desert,adj.)

10. Paper Containing Sand Particles, Used for Polishing, Smoothing, etc.: sandpaper, n.

11. To Smooth or Polish with Such: sandpaper,v.

12. To Smooth, Polish, Sprinkle, or Fill with Sand; To Add Sand to: sand,v.

13. One Who Works in Sand; Laborer Who Digs Sand: sand hog,n.

14. Like Sand, i.e., Not Firm or Steady: sandy,adj.

15. Mixture of Sand, Lime, Water, etc., for Covering Walls or Ceilings: plaster,n.

16. To Cover (Walls, Ceilings, etc.) with Plaster: plaster,v.

17. Plaster and Felt in Covered Sheets, Used as a Substitute for Wet Plaster for Walls: plasterboard,n.

18. Descr. of Construction Using Such: drywall,adj.

19. Powdery Material Like Plaster, Made of Gypsum, and Used for Casts or Molds in Sculpture, in Setting Broken Bones, etc.: plaster, plaster of Paris,n.

20. Piece of Sculpture Cast in Such; Cast for Broken Bones, etc., Made of Such: plaster cast,n.

1008. MINERALS

1. Selected Minerals,n.
   1. alabaster—white, marblelike, variety of pure gypsum, found mainly in Italy, and used in sculpture, ornaments, statuary, etc. (alabaster, alabastrine,adj.)
   2. calcite—common mineral, the chief component of chalk, limestone, and marble
   3. feldspar, felspar—a kind of crystalline and glassy mineral (feldspathic,adj.)
   4. gypsum—common mineral used to make ornaments, plaster of Paris, fertilizer, etc.
   5. hornblende—common mineral found in granite and other rock
   6. isinglass—transparent mica
   7. mica—a kind of mineral that crystallizes into thin, easily separable layers (micaceous,adj.)
   8. pitchblende—shiny brownish or blackish mineral containing radium and uranium
   9. quartz—brilliant mineral, usually found

in a colorless, transparent form or in various semi-precious stones

10. silica—hard mineral found in sand, opal, quartz, etc.—used in making glass, pottery, etc. (silicic, siliceous, silicious,adj.)

2. Smooth, White, and Marblelike, i.e., Resembling Alabaster: alabaster or alabastrine,adj.

3. Resembling, Containing, or Pert. to, Calcium Carbonate, Calcium, or Lime: calcareous,adj.

4. A Mineral Deposit in a Rock Fissure: lode,n.

5. Science of Minerals: mineralogy,n. (mineralogist,n. mineralogical,adj.)

6. To Change into Mineral; To Suffuse or Furnish with Minerals: mineralize,v. (mineralization,n.)

7. Neither Animal Nor Vegetable; Pert. to, or of the Nature of, a Mineral: inorganic, mineral,adj.

1009. GLASS

1. Section of Glass for a Window: light, panel, pane, window, windowpane,n.

2. Small Pane of Glass in the Shape of a Square or Diamond: quarry,n.

3. A Glass Section of a Window: light, pane, panel,n.

4. A Window: bay window (projecting, in somewhat the form of a semicircle, from the wall of a house or other structure); casement or casement window (opening outward on hinges); clerestory window (comparatively small and rectangular, and high on the wall, esp. of bedrooms in modern one-story houses); dormer or dormer window (upright, and built into a housing that projects from a slanting roof); picture window (large and stationary, and generally overlooking scenery); skylight (in the roof of a house or building or in the ceiling of a room); transom (above a doorway); wicket (small),n.

5. Possessing Such: casemented, dormered, transomed,adj.

6. Possessing Windows: fenestrated, windowed,adj.

7. The Housing Projecting from a Slanting Roof and Containing an Upright Window: dormer,n.

8. A Small Windowlike Opening in a Structure: fenestella,n.

9. Window Arrangement of a Structure: fenestration,n.

10. Frame for the Glass of a Window: sash, window sash,n.

11. Such a Frame That Opens Outward on Hinges: casement,n.

12. Bottom Protruding Edge, of Wood, etc., of a Window: sill, window ledge, window sill, n.

13. Vertical Post Forming the Side of a Window, Doorway, Fireplace, etc.: jamb or jambe,n.

14. Vertical Bar Separating the Panes of a Window: mullion,n.

15. To Furnish (a Window) or Separate (the Panes of a Window) with Such: mullion,v. (mullioned,adj.)

16. Crosspiece Serving as a Horizontal Division of a Window; Crosspiece Separating a Window from a Doorway: transom,n.

17. Sheet of Glass above the Dashboard of an Automobile: windshield,n.

18. One Who Repairs Windows by Substituting Whole Panes for Broken Ones: glazier,n.

19. The Work or Occupation of Such: glaziery,n.

20. The Arranging of the Show Windows of a Store in an Attractive Manner; The Arrangements or Display in Such Windows; Hence, by Extension, Actions, Behavior, or Statements That Are Not Genuine, True, or Sincere, but Are Intended Solely to Give a Favorable Impression: window dressing,n.

21. Person Whose Occupation Is the Dressing of Show Windows: window dresser,n.

22. To Look at, or Examine, Things in Store Windows without Buying Them or Intending to Buy Them: window-shop,v. (window-shopping,n. window-shopper,n.)

23. Window Covering: blind, curtain, drape; jalousie (with slats fixed at an angle); shade (able to be raised and lowered); shutter (movable, often of wood, with slats that open and close); venetian blinds, persiennes, or Persian blinds (with slats that open and close),n.

24. To Cover (a Window) with Such: curtain, drape, shutter,v.

25. A Clear, Highly Brilliant, and Transparent Glass or Mineral Having the Appearance of Ice: crystal,n.

26. Like Glass: glasslike, glassy, glazy; hyalescent (in appearance); hyaline, hyaloid, vitreal, vitrean, vitreous, vitric; vitriform (in form or appearance),adj. (glassiness, glaziness, hyalescence, vitreousness or vitreosity, n.)

27. Pert. to Glass: glass, vitreal, vitrean, vitreous, vitric,adj.

28. Of the Character or Nature of Glass: vitric,adj.

29. Obtained from Glass: vitreal, vitrean, vitreous,adj.

30. Descr. of Anatomical Tissue That Is Glassy: hyaloid,adj.

31. Becoming Glassy; Fairly or Somewhat Glassy: hyalescent,adj. (hyalescence,n.)

32. To Become Glassy: glaze,v.

33. Tending to Turn into Glass: vitrescent, adj. (vitrescence,n.)

34. Capable of Being Turned into Glass or Made Glassy: vitrescible, vitrifiable,adj. (vitrescibility, vitrifiability,n.)

35. To Convert, or Be Converted, into Glass; To Become, or Cause to Become, Glassy: vitrify,v. (vitrification or vitrifaction,n.)

36. That Which Has Undergone This Process: vitrification or vitrifaction,n.

37. To Remove, Destroy, or Eliminate the Glassy Properties of; To Cause (Glass) to Become Opaque, Crystalline, and Hard: devitrify,v. (devitrification,n.)

38. In Such a State: devitrified,adj. (devitrification,n.)

39. Made of Glass: glass,adj.

40. Articles Made of Glass: glassware, glasswork, vitrics,n.

41. Drinking Glasses Fashioned with a Stem and Base: stemware,n.

42. The Manufacture of Glassware or Glass: glassmaking, glasswork, vitrifacture,n.

43. The Art of Making and Decorating Glassware: vitrics,n.

44. The Art or Process of Blowing Glass into Objects, or, Using a Flame, of Fashioning Glass into Objects: glass blowing,n. (glass blower,n.)

45. Maker or Seller of Glass: glassman,n.

46. Place Where Glass Is Made: glasshouse, glassworks,n.

47. To Fit, Furnish, or Cover with Glass: glass, glaze,v.

48. Such Work: glasswork, glaziery, glazing, n.

49. One Whose Occupation Is Such: glassman, glazier,n.

50. To Put a Glassy or Shiny Surface On; To Give a Glassy or Shiny Surface to: glaze, v. (glazer,n.)

51. Thin, Glasslike Paper Used for Book Jackets, Window Envelopes, etc.: glassine,n.

52. Glass Formed when Molten Lava from a Volcano Undergoes Very Rapid Cooling: obsidian, volcanic glass,n.

1010. COAL

1. Coal,n.
  1. anthracite—hard coal (anthracitic,adj.)
  2. bituminous coal—soft coal
  3. cinder—partially or completely burned piece of coal
  4. lignite—coal that is imperfectly formed, often woody in texture (lignitic,adj.)

2. Coal Dust: culm,n.

3. Containing or Producing Coal: carboniferous,adj.

4. A Coal Mine and Subsidiary Buildings and Equipment: colliery,n.

5. One Who Mines Coal: coal miner, collier, n.

6. Pert. to, Resembling, or Containing, Coal: coaly,adj.

1011. SALT

1. Common Table Salt: sodium chloride,n.

2. A Strong Salt Solution: brine,n. (brinish, briny,adj.)

3. To Treat with, or Soak in, This, as for Pickling, etc.: brine,v.

4. To Add Salt to; To Season, Treat, Preserve, Cure, or Furnish with Salt: salt,v. (salter,n.)

5. Containing, or Tasting of Salt: brackish, briny; saliferous (containing); saline, salt, salty,adj. (salinity, saltiness,n.)

6. Like Salt: saline, saltlike,adj. (salinity,n.)

7. Producing Salt: saliferous,adj.

8. To Mix with Salt; To Combine with Salt, or Form a Salt with, by Chemical Action: salify,v.

9. Preserved or Pickled with Salt—of Food: salt, salted,adj.

10. Place, Establishment, or Building Where Salt Is Made: salina, saltern, saltworks,n.

11. Place, or Plot of Land, Where Sea Water Is Evaporated to Produce Salt: saltern,n.

12. One Who Makes or Sells Salt: salter,n.

13. Device to Measure the Amount of Salt in a Solution: salimeter, salinometer,n.

14. Salt or Salt Mixture That Neutralizes Acids; A Chemical Base That Neutralizes Acids and Forms a Salt with Them, and That Turns Red Litmus Paper Blue; Mineral Salt, or Mixture of Such, Found in Some Soils, That Is Harmful to Crops: alkali,n.

15. Pert. to, Containing, or Having the Qualities of an Alkali: alkaline,adj. (alkalinity,n.)

16. Somewhat, or Slightly, Alkaline: alkalescent,adj. (alkalescence,n.)

17. Resembling an Alkali: alkaline, alkaloid, alkaloidal,adj. (alkalinity,n.)

18. To Cause to Be Alkaline: alkalify, alkalize,v. (alkalization,n.)

19. To Become Alkaline: alkalify,v.

20. Condition in Which the Tissues and Blood Are Too Alkaline: alkalosis,n.

1012. METAL

1. Piece, Bar, etc., of Metal,n.
  1. casting—piece of metal formed by pouring into a mold to harden
  2. ingot—bar or other convenient shape or mass of metal formed by casting
  3. leaf—extremely thin sheet of metal
  4. paillette—thin piece of metal used in coating, gilding, or enameling
  5. paillon (French)—very thin sheet of metal used in coating, gilding, etc.
  6. plate—flat, thin sheet of metal; such used in printing; such, when polished, used for engraving or already engraved

2. To Make or Form (a Piece of Metal),v. *From Sec. 1:* cast, ingot

3. Metal in Flat, Thin Sheets: plate, sheet metal,n.

4. Extremely Thin Sheets of Metal; Such Used as the Backing of Glass to Produce a Mirror: foil,n.

5. To Cover, Coat, or Back with Such: foil, v.

6. Pliable Fabric Composed of Metal Rings Linked Together, Used to Make Defensive Armor: mail,n.

7. To Clothe or Arm with Such: mail,v. (mailed,adj.)

8. Substance, as Mineral or Rock, Containing Enough Metal to Make Mining Worth While: ore,n.

9. A Deposit Containing Ore: lode, vein,n.

10. To Transform (a Metal) into Ore: mineralize,v. (mineralization,n.)

11. Referring or Relating to Metal,adj.
  1. bimetallic—made up of, pert. to, or consisting of, two metals
  2. brassy—harsh and metallic in sound (brassiness,n.)
  3. metal—pert. to, or made of, metal
  4. metallic, metallical, metalline—pert. to, resembling (as in hardness, strength, etc.), consisting of, or of the character of, metal; having the sound of metal when struck (metallicity or metalleity,n.)
  5. metalliferous, metallic, metal-bearing—bearing, yielding, or containing metal
  6. metalloid—resembling a metal in appearance
  7. monometallic—pert. to, using, or consisting of, one metal only

12. A Substance Resulting from the Fusion of Two or More Metals, or, Less Frequently, of a Metal and a Non-Metal: alloy,n.

13. To Fuse (Such): alloy,v.

14. Alloy Used to Fuse Metals: solder,n.

15. A Chemical Element That Has Some of the Properties of Metals: metalloid,n. (metalloid,adj.)

16. Science, Study, etc., of Metals,n.
  1. metallography—study, under the microscope, of the structure of metals and alloys; science of the structure and alloys of metal (metallographist,n. metallographic,adj.)
  2. metallurgy—science, art, or process of separating or extracting metal from ore,

making alloys, shaping or working metal, etc. (metallurgist,n metallurgic, metallurgical,adj.)

17. Work with Metals,n.
1. brazing—the fusing or uniting of two metal substances with brass or other hard solder
2. casting—the shaping of metal by pouring it in a melted state into molds
3. forging—the shaping of metal by heating and hammering it
4. hydrometallurgy—the refining of ores, or the extraction of metals from ores, by the use of various chemical solutions or water processes (hydrometallurgical,adj.)
5. liquation—the separation of a metal from other metals, or from impurities, by heating and melting; the heating and melting of metals for such a purpose
6. metalworking, metalwork—the manufacture of metal objects
7. plating—the coating of metals, esp. of base metals with a finer or more precious metal
8. pyrometallurgy—the refining of ores by the use of heat
9. smelting—the obtaining or refining of metal by melting its ore; the melting of ore to obtain, or separate out, the metal
10. smithery—the work or occupation of one who works in metals
11. soldering—the fusing or uniting of two metal substances by means of a special alloy

18. A Worker with Metals,n. *From Sec. 17:* brazer, forger, metalworker or metalist, plater, smelter, smith, solderer

19. To Work with Metals,v. *From Sec. 17:* forge, metalwork, solder

20. To Do Something to or with (a Metal or Metals),v. *From Sec. 17:* braze, cast, forge, liquate, plate, smelt, solder; *Also:*
1. metal—cover or provide with metal
2. metalize, metallize—change into metal; give the characteristics or properties of metal to; treat or cover with metal (metalization,n.)

21. Place, Shop, etc., Where Work Is Done on or with Metals,n. *From Sec. 17:* metalworks, smelter or smeltery; smithy, smithery, or forge

22. Furnace Where Metal Is Heated Preparatory to Being Shaped: forge,n.

23. Heavy Iron Block on Which Heated Metals Are Hammered into Shape: anvil,n.

24. To Become Fused or United through the Use of a Special Alloy—of Metals: solder,v.

25. Objects Made of Metal: hardware or ironware (i.e., tools, implements, etc.), metalware, metalwork,n.

26. Objects of Metal, Esp. Cooking Vessels, etc., Covered by Enamel: enamelware,n.

27. Unit of Radium Emanation: curie,n.

28. Roman God of Fire and Metalworking: Vulcan,n. (Vulcanian,adj.)

29. Pert. to Metalworking: vulcanian,adj.

30. The Treatment of Disease by the Use of Metals or the Salts of Metals: metallotherapy,n.

31. Precious Metals: gold, iridium, osmium, palladium, platinum, rhodium, ruthenium, silver,n.

32. Science of the Production and Value of Precious Metals: chrysology,n.

1013. GOLD

1. Gold: aurum (chemistry),n.
2. Lump of Natural Gold: nugget,n.

3. Fine Particles of Gold: gold dust,n.
4. To Coat with Gold, Gold Leaf, or Similar Substance: gild,v.
5. The Gold or Other Substance Used in Such Coating: gilding, gilt, ormolu,n.
6. Metal So Gilded: ormolu,n.
7. The Surface So Produced: gilding,n.
8. Coated with Gold: aureate, gilded, gilt, adj.
9. Having Edges So Coated; Hence, by Extension, of the Best Quality: gilt-edged,adj.
10. Silver, Copper, or Bronze So Coated: vermeil,n. (vermeil,adj.)
11. To Plate (an Object) with Gold: goldplate,v. (gold-plated,adj.)
12. Pert. to Gold: auric, gold,adj.
13. Containing or Consisting of Gold: auric, auriferous, aurous,adj.
14. Of the Color of Gold: aureate, aureoline, aurulent, gilt, gold, golden,adj. (aureateness, n.)
15. To Give a Gold Color or Shine to: aureate,v.
16. Resembling Gold: aureate, gold, golden, adj. (aureateness,n.)
17. Shining Like Gold: aureate, gold,adj.
18. Bearing or Producing Gold: auriferous, aurific, gold-bearing,adj.
19. Made of Gold: gold, golden,adj.
20. Table Cutlery, Dishes, etc., Made of Gold: gold plate,n.
21. Descr. of Objects of Ancient Greece That Were Decorated with Gold and Ivory: chryselephantine,adj.
22. The Unique Qualities of Gold: aureity,n.
23. So-Called Science of the Middle Ages That Sought, among Other Things, to Change Base Metals into Gold: alchemy,n. (alchemic, alchemical,adj.)
24. Practitioner of Such: alchemist,n. (alchemistic, alchemistical,adj.)
25. To Change (Base Metals) into Gold or Silver: alchemize, transmute,v. (transmutation,n.)
26. To Change, or Become Changed, into Gold: aurify,v.
27. Substance Imagined, or Sought After, by Alchemists That Supposedly Had the Power to Transmute Base Metals into Gold: philosopher's stone,n.
28. Alchemist's Preparation for Accomplishing This, or for Extending Life: elixir,n.
29. A Common Yellow Mineral, Often Mistaken for Gold: fool's gold, iron pyrites, pyrite,n. (pyritic, pyritical,adj.)
30. One Who Makes Objects out of Gold; One Who Deals in Such: aurifex, goldsmith, n.
31. Working with or in Gold; The Filling of a Cavity in a Tooth with Gold: aurification, n.
32. Solvent for Gold, Made Up of Nitric and Hydrochloric Acids; Hence, a Test of True Gold: aquaregia,n.
33. Unit of Measurement That Expresses the Amount of Pure Gold in a Gold Alloy: karat,n. (pure gold is 24 karats)

1014. PLATINUM

1. Unrefined Platinum: platina,n.
2. To Coat with Platinum: platinize,v.
3. Resembling Platinum: platinoid,adj.

4. Any Metal Generally Associated with Platinum: platinoid,n.

5. Pert. to, Resembling, or Containing Platinum: platinic, platinous,adj. (chemistry)

6. Yielding Platinum: platiniferous, platinum-bearing,adj.

7. Native Alloy of Platinum and Iridium: platiniridium,n.

1015. SILVER

1. Silver: argent (poetic or archaic); argentine (or similar metal); argentum (chemistry); sterling (.925 pure),n.

2. Silver or Gold as a Mass or in Bars or Ingots: bullion,n.

3. Pert. to Silver: argental; argentic (chemistry); argentine, lunar, silver,adj.

4. Resembling Silver: argent, argental, argenteous, argentine, silver, silverlike, silvery,adj. (silveriness,n.)

5. With the Sound of Silver: silvery,adj. (silveriness,n.)

6. Of the Color of Silver: argent, silver, silvery,adj. (silveriness,n.)

7. Containing Silver: argentic or argentous, adj. (chemistry)

8. Yielding or Bearing Silver: argentiferous, silver, silver-bearing,adj.

9. Made or Consisting of Silver: silver,adj.

10. Coated with Silver: silver, silver-coated, silvered, silver-plated,adj.

12. To Coat with Silver; To Give the Color of Silver to: silver,v. (silverer,n.)

13. To Become the Color of Silver: silver,v.

14. Objects of Silver: flatware (table utensils or shallow vessels, whether of silver or other material); hollowware (table vessels of some depth, as sugar bowls, coffee or tea pitchers, etc.); silver plate (of plated silver); silverware; tableware (table utensils, vessels, etc., whether of silver or other material),n.

15. To Refine (Silver) in a Special Receptacle: cupel,v. (cupellation,n.)

16. Such a Receptacle; Receptacle for Separating Silver and Gold from Lead: cupel,n.

17. One Who Makes, or Sells, Objects of Silver: silversmith,n.

18. Elaborate Decoration on Silver, Esp. as a Border: gadroon or godroon,n. (gadrooned, adj.)

1016. COPPER

1. Copper: cuprum (chemistry),n.

2. Alloy of Copper,n.
  1. brass—of copper and zinc
  2. bronze—of copper and tin
  3. cupronickel—of copper and nickel
  4. German silver, albata—of copper, zinc, and nickel (resembles silver)
  5. ormolu—of copper and zinc made to imitate gold

3. One Who Works in or with Copper: coppersmith,n.

4. To Cover, Coat, Plate, etc., with Copper: copper,v.

5. Pert. to Copper: cupric (chemistry),adj.

6. Containing Copper: coppery; cupreous, cupric, or cuprous (chemistry); cupronickel (and nickel),adj.

7. Resembling Copper: copperlike, coppery, cupreous,adj.

8. Of the Color of Copper—copper-colored, coppery, cupreous,adj.

9. Bearing Copper: copper-bearing, cupriferous,adj.

10. Resembling, or Covered or Decorated with, Brass: brassy,adj. (brassiness,n.)

11. To Cover or Decorate with, or Make out of, Brass: braze,v.

12. Made of Brass: brass, brazen,adj.

13. Resembling Brass in Color, Strength, Sound when Struck, etc.: brazen,adj.

14. Worker in Brass: brazier or brasier,n.

15. Similar to Bronze: bronzy,adj.

16. To Give the Color or Appearance of Bronze to: bronze,v.

17. Made of Bronze: brazen,adj.

18. Green Film or Coating Produced on Old Bronze by Oxidation: patina,n.

19. Greenish or Bluish Film or Coating That Forms on Copper, Bronze, or Brass after Long Exposure to Air: verdigris,n.

1017. IRON

1. Iron,n.
  1. bloom—mass of iron coming from a forge or furnace; hammered iron or steel bar
  2. cast iron—hard pig iron containing carbon
  3. cast steel—steel made by pouring molten metal into a mold
  4. pig, pig iron—iron coming out of a blast furnace
  5. steel—iron treated by special processes
  6. wrought iron—iron with relatively little carbon

2. Relating or Referring to Iron or Steel, adj.
  1. ferric, ferrous—pert. to, or containing, iron (chemistry)
  2. ferriferous, ferruginous, iron-bearing—bearing, producing, or containing iron
  3. iron—made of iron
  4. ironlike, iron, irony—resembling iron, as in hardness, strength, color, etc.
  5. irony—containing, or consisting of, iron
  6. steel—pert. to, or made of, steel
  7. steely, steel—resembling steel, as in color, strength, or hardness; consisting of steel

3. Coat Forming on Iron or Other Metal when Exposed to Air and Moisture: rust,n.

4. Covered or Affected with Such: rubiginous, rusty,adj. (rustiness,n.)

5. To Affect, or Be Affected by, Such: rust,v.

6. Of the Color of Such: ferruginous, rubiginous,adj.

7. Plated or Bound with Iron: ironbound, ironclad, ironplated,adj.

8. Worker in or with Iron: blacksmith, ironsmith, ironworker, smith, steelworker (with steel),n.

9. Shop of Such: smithery, smithy,n.

10. Establishment Where Iron or Steel Is Fabricated: ironworks, steelworks,n. (ironworker, steelworker,n.)

11. Furnace and Forge Where Bars of Iron and Steel Are Hammered and Rolled: bloomery,n.

12. Articles of Iron or Steel: ironware, steelware,n.

13. To Convert (Iron) into Steel: acierate, v. (acieration,n.)

14. To Convert (Pig Iron) into Wrought Iron: puddle,v. (puddler,n. puddling,n.)

15. Pert. or Relating to Metals Other than Iron; Not Containing Iron: non-ferrous,adj.

1018. LEAD

1. Lead: plumbum (chemistry),n.

2. Relating or Referring to Lead,adj.
  1. **lead**—pert. to, containing, or made of, lead
  2. **leaden, plumbeous**—made of, containing, or consisting of, lead; resembling lead, as in color, heaviness, inertness, etc. (leadenness,n.)
  3. **plumbic, plumbous**—containing lead (chemistry)
  4. **plumbiferous, lead-bearing**—bearing or yielding lead
  5. **saturnine**—pert. to, or having a resemblance to, lead

3. To Cover, Line, Treat with, or Make Heavy with, Lead: lead,n.

4. Poisoning of the System Resulting from the Absorption of Lead or Its Salts: lead poisoning, plumbism, saturnism,n.

5. So Affected or Caused: saturnine,adj.

1019. ZINC

1. Pert. to Zinc: zincic, zincous,adj.

2. Like Zinc: zincky,adj.

3. Bearing or Yielding Zinc: zinc-bearing, zinciferous,adj.

4. To Coat or Impregnate (Iron, Steel, or Other Metal) with Zinc: galvanize, zincify, v. (galvanization, zincification,n.)

5. Art or Process of Etching on Zinc: zincography,n. (zincographer,n. zincographic, zincographical,adj.)

6. An Etched Zinc Plate, or a Print from Such: zincograph,n.

1020. TIN

1. Tin: stannum,n.

2. An Alloy of Tin and Various Other Metals: pewter,n.

3. Vessel, Utensil, Object, etc., Made of Such; Such Vessels, etc., Collectively: pewter,n.

4. Made of Such: pewter,adj.

5. One Who Makes Such: pewterer,n.

6. Made of Tin: tin,adj.

7. Work Done in Tin: tinwork,n.

8. Resembling Tin, as in Sound, Taste, etc.; Containing Tin: tinny,adj. (tinniness, n.)

9. Pert. to Tin, the Chemical Element: stannic,adj.

10. Containing Tin (Chemistry): stannic, stannous,adj.

11. Worker in or with Tin; One Who Makes Objects of Tin: tinman, tinner, tinsman, tinsmith, whitesmith,n.

12. One Who Mines Tin: tin miner, tinner,n.

13. Locality Where Tin Is Mined: stannary,n.

14. Objects Made of Tin Plate, Esp. Pots, Pans, etc.: tinware,n.

15. To Coat or Plate (Something) with Tin: tin, tin plate,v. (tin plater,n. tin-plated,adj.)

16. Steel or Iron in Thin Sheets So Coated: tin plate,n.

17. Place or Establishment Where Tin Is Treated, Smelted, Rolled, etc.: tinworks,n.

1021. MERCURY

1. Mercury: quicksilver,n.

2. To Add Mercury to: mercurate,v.

3. Pert. to, Caused by, Containing, etc., Mercury: mercurial,adj.

4. Containing Mercury (Chemistry): mercuric, mercurous,adj.

5. To Treat with Mercury or One of Its Compounds: mercurialize,v. (mercurialization,n.)

6. Pathological Condition of the System Caused by Mercury: mercurialism,n.

7. Drug Containing Mercury: mercurial,n.

1022. SUPPORT; HOLD UP

1. To Support; To Hold Up: base, bear; bolster up (something weak, esp. figuratively); brace (in order to make firm); bulwark; buoy or buoy up (esp. in order to keep from sinking in water, etc.); buttress, crutch; poise (in balance); prop or prop up; shore or shore up (in order to prevent sinking or sagging); stay; strut (a structure with oblique members); underlay (by placing something under); upbear, uphold,v. (upborne, upheld, adj.)

2. A Support; That Which Supports or Holds Up,n. *From Sec. 1:* base or basis, brace, bulwark, buttress; crutch (usually forked); prop, shore, stay, strut,n. (basal, basic,adj.); *Also:* bracket; column (of a structure); foundation, fulcrum, pedestal; point d'appui (French); stand, standard, substratum or substrate, underpinning, understratum (fulcrums or fulcra, substratums or substrata, understratums or understrata,pl.n. columnar, foundational, substratal or substrative,adj.); *Also:*
  1. **armrest, footrest, footstool, headrest, etc.**—support for the arm, foot, head, etc.
  2. **beam**—one of the horizontal supports of the floor or roof of a structure, deck of a ship, etc.
  3. **bedrock**—any type of strong, solid, or firm foundation
  4. **bipod**—two-legged support or stand for something
  5. **bracket, console**—triangular support, attached to a wall, for a shelf, etc.; projection from a wall that serves as a support for a statue, etc.
  6. **buttress**—masonry structure built against a wall as a support
  7. **cantilever, cantalever**—support projecting from a wall for a balcony, cornice, etc.; projecting support for a bridge
  8. **corbel**—projection from the face of a wall that acts as a support; horizontal piece of timber that supports a girder
  9. **crutch**—support used by the lame to facilitate walking or other motion; artificial support, figuratively
  10. **fulcrum**—support on which a lever turns in moving a body
  11. **girder**—chief supporting beam of a structure, laid horizontally; one of the supporting horizontal timbers under the joists of a floor
  12. **hurter**—supporting or strengthening part, piece, or member
  13. **joist**—one of the wooden beams in a structure that supports a floor or ceiling, i.e., to which floor boards or ceiling laths are nailed
  14. **lintel**—horizontal supporting member or crosspiece above a door or window
  15. **molding**—strip of wood or other material near the ceiling of a room for supporting pictures hung by wire, etc.
  16. **pedestal**—support, base, or foundation on which a statue, vase, etc., rests
  17. **pier**—heavy support for the spans of a bridge; support on which a gate or door is hung; square pillar; heavy vertical support

18. **pile**—heavy post, timber, pole, or similar structure of steel, concrete, etc., driven into dry ground or a river bed, etc., as a support for something built on it (piling, collective n.)

19. **pillar**—vertical support of stone, brick, wood, etc.

20. **post**—upright section of wood, steel, stone, concrete, etc., acting as a support

21. **riprap**—foundation or wall of broken stones

22. **shaft**—part of a candlestick that supports the branching arms

23. **shelf**—support for objects, fixed to a wall; any projection similar to this

24. **shore**—supporting beam, post, etc., placed obliquely against a structure, ship, etc. (shoring, collective n.)

25. **sill**—heavy horizontal wooden, concrete, stone, etc., member supporting the wall of a structure; such as the bottom part of the frame of a window, door, or other opening

26. **sling**—loop of rope, chain, etc., for supporting something to be raised, lowered, moved, etc.; loop of bandage or material supporting a sprained, lame, broken, etc., hand or arm and going around the neck

27. **stilt**—long pole, with a support for the foot, used in walking; high supporting post for a structure on dry ground, or for an arch, pier, etc.

28. **trestle**—horizontal board on spreading legs, used as a support

29. **tripod, trivet**—three-legged support or stand for an object (tripodal,adj.)

30. **trivet**—three-legged iron support or stand that holds cooking vessels over a fire; stand on short legs that holds hot platters or vessels on a dining table

31. **underpinning**—support under a finished wall

32. **unipod**—one-legged support or stand for an object (unipod,adj.)

33. **whatnot**—stand with shelves for small ornaments, objects of art, books, etc.

3. **To Support by Some Specific Means,v.**
From Sec. 2: bracket, buttress, corbel, pedestal, pile, pillar, shore, sling

4. **To Furnish with a Specific Support,v.**
From Sec. 2: bracket, corbel, joist, pedestal, pile, pillar, shelve

5. **To Nail Boards, Laths, etc., to Joists:** joist,v.

6. **To Put (Something) on a Shelf:** shelve,v.

7. **To Raise, Lower, or Move (Something) with, or Put (Something) in, a Sling:** sling,v.

8. **To Raise on Stilts:** stilt,v.

9. **Having Stilts, in Architecture**—stilted, adj.

10. **Machine for Driving Piles into the Ground:** pile driver,n.

11. **To Support with, or as if with, a Pillow or Pillows:** bolster, cushion, pillow,n.

12. **Such a Support:** bolster, cushion, pillow, n.

13. **To Form or Be the Support, Base, or Bases for, Literally or Figuratively:** underlie,v. (underlying,adj.)

14. **The Foundation of an Architectural Structure:** substruction, substructure, underbuilding,n. (substructural,adj.)

15. **Projecting Base, in Architecture, of a Foundation, Wall, Column, Pedestal, etc.:** footing,n.

16. **Supporting Members, Joined Together, of a Structure:** frame, framework, skeleton, n. (skeleton or skeletal,adj.)

17. **Such Supporting Members, or Frame-** work, Usually Triangular in Shape, for Bridges, Roofs, etc.: truss,n.

18. **To Support or Furnish with Such:** truss, v.

19. **Series of Wooden Supports for Cornices:** bracketing,n.

20. **Parts of a Pedestal, in Ascending Order:** base, dado, cap,n.

21. **A Foundation, Literal or Figurative:** base, basis, footing, grounds, groundwork, substructure,n. (basal, basic, substructural, adj.)

22. **Something Considered as a Firm Support:** anchor,n.

23. **Main or Chief Support, Usually Figurative:** Atlas, mainstay, stand-by,n.

24. **To Place on a Solid Support or Give a Basis or Foundation to, Esp. Figuratively:** base, found, ground,v.

25. **To Be So Placed or Given:** found, ground, v.

26. **Such a Solid Support:** base, basis, foundation, ground or grounding,n. (basal, basic, foundational,adj.)

27. **To Support (a Statement, Belief, etc.) with Details:** circumstantiate,v. (circumstantiation,n.)

28. **To Support with Proof:** sustain,v. (sustainment, sustentation or sustention,n. sustentative or sustentive,adj.)

29. **To Base (Statements, Actions, Beliefs, etc.) on:** predicate (on),v. (predication,n. predicative,adj.)

30. **To Support (a Person or Persons) Figuratively, as with Food, Clothing, Shelter, etc.:** aliment, maintain, subsist, sustain,v. (maintenance, subsistence; sustainment, sustentation, or sustention,n. alimentary, sustentative or sustentive,adj.)

31. **Such Support:** aliment, alimentation, maintenance, subsistence, sustenance, sustentation,n. (alimental,adj.)

32. **One Who Is Supported Economically or Emotionally:** dependent,n. (dependent,adj. dependency,n.)

33. **A Support for a Hernia or Rupture:** truss,n.

34. **A Support for the Male Genitals:** athletic supporter; dance belt (worn by professional dancers); jock strap, suspensory,n.

35. **Giving, Providing, or Lending Support:** supporting, supportive,adj.

36. **Capable of Supporting an Object in Fluid, i.e., Keeping It Afloat:** buoyant,adj. (buoyancy,n.)

37. **Capable of Being Supported:** supportable, adj.

38. **Without Figurative Support or Foundation:** baseless, footless, foundationless, groundless, unbased, unfounded, ungrounded, unsupported, unsustained,adj. (baselessness, foundationlessness, groundlessness, unbasedness, unfoundedness, ungroundedness, unsupportedness,n.)

1023. COLUMN

1. **column:** pillar, shaft,n.

2. **Series of Regularly Spaced Columns:** colonnade,n. (colonnaded,adj.)

3. **Arrangement of Columns in a Building; The Use of Columns in a Building:** columniation,n.

4. **Pert. to a Column or Columns:** columnar,adj.

5. Having Columns: columnar, columned, adj.

6. Having Columns at Each End: amphistylar,adj.

7. In the Form or Shape of a Column or Columns: columnar, columned, columniform, adj.

8. Rectangular Vertical Support Treated as an Architectural Column: pilaster,n.

9. Monument in the Form of a Column: pillar, shaft,n.

10. Parts of a Column: base, footstall, or pedestal (bottom); shaft (body); capital (top) ,n.

11. Lowest Part of the Base of a Column: plinth,n.

12. Parts Resting on a Column (in Ascending Order): architrave, frieze, cornice,n.

13. These Parts Considered as a Unit: entablature,n.

14. Style of a Column: order,n.

15. Pert. to, Descr. of, or Designating, Certain Orders of Columns: Composite (combining Corinthian and Ionic); Corinthian (Greek—with acanthus leaves, bell-shaped capital, and continuous frieze); Doric (simplest of the Greek orders); Ionic (Greek—of slim lines, with a decorated frieze and scrolled or curlicued capital); Tuscan (Roman—plain, with a circular capital) ,adj.

16. Without, or Not Having, Columns: astylar,adj.

1024. WALL

1. Wall; Part of a Wall,n.
  1. clerestory, clearstory—windowed wall of a church or other structure
  2. dado, wainscot—lower part of a wall when decorated differently from the upper part
  3. partition—partial wall separating one section of a room or space from another
  4. pier—part of the wall between doors or windows
  5. retaining wall, revetment—wall built to hold back the soil

2. To Separate (a Room, Space, etc.) with a Partial Wall: partition,v. (partitionment, n. partitioned,adj.)

3. Wood, Often Oak, or Other Material Used to Line an Interior Wall: paneling, wainscot or wainscoting,n.

4. To Line (a Wall) with Such: panel, wainscot,v.

5. Pert. to, Resembling, Done on, or Attached to, a Wall: mural,adj.

6. Outside the Walls, or, by Extension, the Limits or Boundaries of a Building, Town, Educational Institution, etc.: extramural, adj.

7. Inside Such Walls, Limits, or Boundaries: intramural,adj.

8. Shelf: bracket (on a triangular support); ledge (narrow) ; mantel or mantelpiece (above a fireplace) ,n.

9. Table: board (esp. for dining); console or console table (attached to a wall by brackets, or fitting close to a wall) ; corner table; counter or stand (on which merchandise is displayed, business transacted, etc.); drum table, end table, lamp table; refectory table (long and narrow, for dining) ; sawbuck table (for picnic grounds, outdoors, etc.) ; taboret (i.e., a kind of ornamental stand or small table for a lamp, etc.) ,n.

10. Pert. to the Table; Used or Done at the Table: mensal,adj.

11. Having a Table, i.e., a Flat Surface or Shape: tabular,adj.

12. To Place (Something) on a Table: table, v.

1025. FLOOR

1. Floor in the Sense of a Section of a Building, House, etc., at a Certain Height from the Ground: landing, level, story or storey,n.

2. The Rooms or Apartments on Such: floor, story or storey,n.

3. Having Such Floors or Stories: storied, adj.

4. A Half Floor or Story of Low Height, between Two Floors or Stories of Greater Height: entresol, mezzanine,n.

5. A Floor; Floors Collectively; Material Used to Make Floors: flooring,n.

6. A Smooth Floor for Roller Skating; The Building Containing Such: rink, skating rink,n.

7. A Smooth Floor of Ice for Skating; The Building Containing Such: ice-skating rink, rink, skating rink,n.

8. Floor Space; Space Taken by a Floor: floorage,n.

9. A Piece of Material for Washing or Wiping a Floor: floorcloth,n.

10. Covering for a Floor: carpet, carpeting, floorcloth; linoleum, asphalt tile, etc.; rug, or, from India, drugget,n.

11. To Cover (a Floor) with Such: carpet,v.

12. To Cover with Floors or a Floor; To Lay a Floor in: floor,v. (floorer,n.)

13. Floor of a Ship: deck,n.

14. To Provide (a Ship) with Such: deck,v.

15. To Knock (a Person) to the Floor or Ground: floor,v.

16. One Who, or Blow That, Does Such: floorer,n.

17. One Who Walks the Floor in a Store, Supervising the Salesclerks, Directing Shoppers, etc.: floorwalker,n.

18. Entertainment Provided on the Cleared Floor of a Restaurant, Night Club, etc.: floor show,n.

19. Architectural Plan of the Layout of Rooms on a Floor: floor plan,n.

20. Flooring of Small Pieces of Marble or Other Stone Set in Cement and Polished: terrazzo,n.

21. Flooring of Bark Used for Race Tracks, Horse Shows, Circus Floors, etc.: tanbark,n.

22. Raised Flooring for Public Speakers, Performers, or Other Activities: platform,n.

23. Platform: altar (for religious ceremonies); balcony or gallery (projecting from a high wall and protected by railings) ; dais, estrade, grandstand or stand (for viewing a public event, horse race, athletic contest, etc.) ; podium (for an orchestra leader) ; pulpit (for a clergyman while preaching); rostrum (for addressing an audience); scaffold or scaffolding (on which workmen stand while building, repairing, or decorating a building, on which a criminal is hanged, or where spectacles are exhibited) ; soapbox (for addressing a street audience, esp. on controversial topics) ; stage (in a theater, or for dramatic presentations, etc.) ; stoop (at the entrance to a house) ; stump (for political speechmaking, literally or figuratively),n. (rostrums or rostra,pl.n. rostral,adj.)

24. Material for Building a Scaffold: scaffolding,n.

25. To Support or Furnish with, or Place on, a Scaffold: scaffold,v.

26. To Use a Platform for Making Political Speeches: stump,v.

1026. WATER

1.Water,n.
1. aqua—water (pharmacy)
2. aqua pura—pure water (pharmacy)
3. bilge, bilge water—dirty or foul water that collects in the bottom of a ship
4. brine—very salty water
5. broth—water in which meat, vegetables, grains, or other substances have been cooked
6. dew—moisture in drops on any surface; such moisture condensed from the air at night and deposited on a cool surface, as grass, leaves, etc.
7. H₂O—water (chemical formula)
8. humidity—amount or degree of moisture in the atmosphere
9. hydrosphere—the water on the surface of the earth; the water vapor in the atmosphere; the water in the oceans or seas
10. liquid—water or any other substance in a form that flows easily but nevertheless retains its volume without change
11. mist—particles or globules of water in the atmosphere at or near the earth's surface
12. moisture, damp—water in small quantity; water or other liquid that causes a slight degree of dampness or wetness
13. soda, seltzer, club soda, vichy—artificially carbonated water
14. vapor—visible moisture in the air
15. Vichy, vichy, vichy water—naturally carbonated or mineral water

2. Watery,adj. *From Sec. 1:* briny or brinish, brothy, dewy, liquid, misty, vaporous or vapory (brininess, dewiness, liquidity or liquidness, mistiness, vaporousness or vaporosity, n.); *Also:*
1. aqueous—watery (aqueousness,n.)
2. serous—watery; thin and watery (serousness,n.)

3. Consisting of, Covered with, etc., Water, adj. *From Sec. 1:* dewy, misty, moist, vaporous or vapory (dewiness, mistiness, moistness, vaporousness or vaporosity,n.)

4. Containing Water: aqueous, fluid, hydrous, liquid,adj.

5. Carried or Supported by Water: water-borne,adj.

6. Smelling Like Bilge: bilgy,adj.

7. To Give Water to (Animals, etc.) for Drinking: water,v.

8. To Wet with Dew: dew,v.

9. A Drop of Dew: dewdrop,n.

10. To Become, or Cause to Become, Misty: mist,v.

11. Giving Off, Emitting, or Forming Vapor: vaporous, vapory,adj. (vaporousness, vaporosity,n.)

12. Made out of, with, or by Means of, Water: aqueous,adj. (aqueousness,n.)

13. A Compound Made Up of Water Chemically Combined with Some Other Substance: hydrate,n.

14. To Combine (a Substance) Chemically with Water: hydrate,v. (hydration,n. hydrator,n. hydrated,adj.)

15. Worship of Water by Primitive Peoples: hydrolatry,n.

16. Shaped Mass or Accumulation of Water or Other Liquid: lake; plash (small); pool; puddle (esp. dirty rain water),n.

17. A Stream of Excess Water: sluice,n.

18. A Trough or Channel for Carrying Water, Liquid, or Other Substances to a Lower Point: chute,n.

19. Concrete or Other Large Container Filled, or to Be Filled, with Water, for Swimming, Bathing, Diving, etc.: pool, swimming pool,n.

20. Descr. of Such if Unusually Large: Olympic,adj.

21. Source of Water: fount, fountain,n.

22. Operated by the Movement, Force, or Pressure of Water or Other Liquids; Hardening under Water, as Cement or Mortar, etc.: hydraulic,adj.

23. Relating or Referring to Water,adj.
1. amphibian, amphibious—living or growing on, belonging to, or capable of operating on, both land and water (amphibiousness,n.)
2. aquatic—pert. to, living or growing in, or performed in or on, water
3. hydroatmospheric—pert. or relating to both water and air
4. hydrothermal—pert. to hot, or heated, water, or to its actions or effects within, or in the surface of, the earth
5. limnetic—pert. to fresh water; living or growing in fresh water, as certain organisms
6. limnophilous, limnophile—living in fresh water, or in marshes, as certain animals
7. salt—growing in, or overflowed with, salt water

24. Animal or Plant That Lives or Grows Both on Land and in Water: amphibian,n.

25. Descr. of Animals That Live in Water during Early Stages, on Land during Later Stages: amphibiotic,adj.

26. Animal That Lives in, on, or Near the Edge of, Water: aquatic,n.

27. Plant That Grows in Water: aquatic, hydrophyte,n. (hydrophytic,adj.)

28. Sports Performed in or on Water: aquatics,n.

29. Consisting of Both Land and Water: terraqueous,adj.

30. Underwater; Overflowed with Water: awash, deluged, flooded, inundated, overflowed, submerged, submersed, swamped,adj.; *Also:*
1. subaqueous—living, located, happening, performed, used, etc., under water
2. submarine, undersea—living, located, happening, used, or functioning under the water of seas or oceans
3. submersed—descr. of plant life that grows, or is adapted for growing, under water; functioning under water
4. suboceanic—under the surface of the ocean
5. underwater—existing, living, happening, used, or to be used, under the surface of water

31. To Cause (Esp. Land) to Be under Water: deluge, engulf or ingulf, flood, inundate, overflow, submerge, submerse, swamp, whelm,v. (engulfment, inundation, submergence, submersion,n. submergible, submersible,adj. submergibility,n.)

32. To Go, Drop, Dive, Sink, etc., below the Surface of Water; To Become Covered with Water: submerge,v. (submergence,n.)

33. To Become Filled with Water and Sink, as a Vessel: swamp,v.

34. Able to Continue Functioning under Water: submersible,adj.

35. Under the Surface of the Sea or Ocean: undersea, underseas, adv.

36. Animal or Plant That Lives or Grows under the Waters of the Sea or Ocean: submarine, n.

37. Watertight Compartment Lowered under Water for Construction, etc.: caisson, n.

38. One Who Works on Underwater Tunnels: sand hog, n.

39. Science of Water, n.
   1. geohydrology—of underground water (geohydrologist, n.)
   2. hydrography—of the waters on the earth's surface, esp. their description, measurement, mapping, and navigability (hydrographer, n. hydrographic, hydrographical, adj.)
   3. hydrology—of the properties, laws, distribution, underground sources, etc., of water (hydrologist, n. hydrologic or hydrological, adj.)

40. Instrument or Device Used to Measure Water, n.
   1. bathometer, plumb, plumb line—depth of water or bodies of water
   2. drosometer—amount of dew on an object
   3. hydrolactometer—the percentage of water in milk
   4. sea gauge—depth of sea water

41. Electrical Device That Detects the Presence of Water, Shows or Controls the Height of Water in a Receptacle, or Prevents Explosions in, or Damage to, Steam Boilers from Low Water: hydrostat, n.

42. Device to Record the Height of Water; The Record of Such: hydrograph, n.

43. To Move About, Back and Forth, or Around in Water, Watery Substance, Mud, Slush, etc., with a Characteristic Sound, i.e., to Be in Such Movement: slosh, splash, v.

44. To Move or Stir (Something) Around, or Back and Forth, in Water or Liquid: slosh, swish, v.

1027. LIQUID

1. Liquid, n.
   1. aqua—liquid (pharmacy)
   2. blob—small mass of liquid
   3. broth—liquid in which bacteria are grown
   4. deliquescence—liquid resulting when something absorbs moisture from the air (chemistry)
   5. elixir—sweet and pleasant-smelling liquid containing a medicine or drug, or used as a medium for such
   6. fluid—liquid, gas, or other substance that can flow
   7. liquor—any liquid or liquid substance; liquid solution of a medicine or drug
   8. nectar—sweet liquid secreted by a plant
   9. slop, swill—liquid carelessly spilled
   10. smegma—liquid substance secreted by the sebaceous glands of the prepuce in the male, or of the clitoris and labia minora in the female
   11. soakage—liquid that has trickled out; absorbed liquid
   12. solution—homogeneous liquid mixture
   13. swill—liquid matter

2. Liquid; Pert. to a Liquid, adj. *From Sec 1:* fluid or fluidic, nectareous or nectarean, smegmatic

3. Liquidity, n *From Sec 1:* fluidity or fluidness

4. To Convert (Something) into a Liquid or Liquid State: dissolve; fuse (esp. under heat, as metals, etc.), liquefy; melt (as by heat or otherwise); render (fat); smelt (ore, to extract metal); thaw (from a frozen state, as ice, snow, etc.), v. (dissolution or solution, fusion, liquefaction, melt, thaw, n. liquefactive, adj.)

5. To Convert (Ice, Snow, etc.) to a Semiliquid State: thaw, v.

6. To Cause (Something, as a Solid, etc.) to Become Liquid or Dissolved: dissolvent, liquefactive, solvent, adj.

7. That Which Can Cause Such: dissolvent, dissolver, liquefacient, menstruum, solvent, n.

8. Able to Be Converted into a Liquid: dissoluble, dissolvable; fusible (esp. under heat, as metals, etc.); hydrosoluble (in water); liquefiable, meltable, soluble, solvable, solvent, adj. (dissolubility, dissolvability or dissolvableness, fusibility or fusibleness, meltability, solubility or solubleness, solvability or solvableness, solvency, n.)

9. To Give Such Property to: solubilize, v. (solubilization, n.)

10. Device That Converts Gas into a Liquid State: liquefier, n.

11. To Become Liquid or a Liquid: deliquesce (gradually, by absorbing moisture from the air—chemistry), dissolve; fuse (esp. under heat); liquefy; melt (as by heat or otherwise); thaw (from a frozen state, as ice, snow, etc.), v. (deliquescence, dissolution or solution, fusion, liquefaction, melt, thaw, n. deliquescent, adj.)

12. Becoming Liquid; Tending toward a Liquid State: liquescent, adj. (liquescence or liquescency, n.)

13. To Become Semiliquid from a Frozen State, as Ice, Snow, etc.: thaw, v. (thaw, n.)

14. Dissolved in a Solution: solute, adj.

15. Substance So Dissolved: solute, n.

16. Combination of One Thing Dissolved in Another, or of Several Things So Dissolved: solution, n.

17. To Become Dissolved Out and Washed Away by Water, as the Constituents of Soil or Other Substances: leach or leach out, v. (leach, n.)

18. To Dissolve Out and Remove the Constituents of: leach, v. (leach, n.)

19. To Get or Purify by Melting: render, v.

20. Amount Melted at a Time; That Which Is Melted: melt, meltage, n.

21. That Which Is Melted under Heat, as a Metal, etc.: fusion, n.

22. Temperature at Which Solids Melt: melting point, n.

23. Vessel in Which Metals, etc., Are Melted or Fused: crucible, melting pot, n.

24. To Melt (Metals or Other Substances) Together, under Heat: fuse, v.

25. That Which Is So Melted Together: fusion, n.

26. Able to Be So Melted Together: fusible, adj. (fusibleness, fusibility, n.)

27. Melted; Made by a Process of Melting: molten, adj.

28. Melting, i.e., in the Process or State of Becoming Melted: liquescent, adj. (liquescence or liquescency, n.)

29. Both, or Partially, Fluid or Liquid and Solid in Properties or Character: semifluid, semifluidic, semiliquid, adj. (semifluidity, semiliquidity, n.)

30. Substance That Is Such: semifluid, semiliquid, n.

31. Unable to Be Converted to a Liquid State: indissoluble or undissoluble, indissolvable or undissolvable; infusible or unfusible (under heat, as metals, etc.); insoluble or unsoluble, insolvable or unsolvable, unliquefiable, unmeltable,adj. (indissolubility or indissolubleness, indissolvability or indissolvableness, infusibility or unfusibleness; insolubility, insolubleness, or unsolubility; insolvability or unsolvableness, unmeltableness,n.)

32. Substance That Does Not Dissolve or Become Liquid: insoluble,n.

33. Selected Sciences of Liquids or Fluids, n.
   1. fluid mechanics—of the flow of liquids and gases
   2. hydraulics—of the motion and mechanics of liquids, including water, and of the application of such in engineering (hydraulic,adj.)
   3. hydrodynamics—of the motion, action, and mechanics of liquids and fluids, including water (hydrodynamic,adj.)
   4. hydrokinetics—of the motion, and laws of motion, of fluids and gases (hydrokinetic, hydrokinetical,adj.)
   5. hydromechanics—of the motion and equilibrium, and laws of motion and equilibrium, of fluids (hydromechanical, adj.)

34. Relating to the Motion of, or Forces in, Fluids; Pert. to, Originating in, or Operated by, Water or Other Fluids in Motion: hydrodynamic,adj.

35. Pert. to the Motions of Fluids or to the Forces Producing or Governing Such: hydrokinetic, hydrokinetical,adj.

36. Device to Measure or Indicate the Specific Gravity of Liquids: areometer, hydrometer,n. (hydrometric, hydrometrical, adj.)

37. The Measurement of Such with This Device: hydrometry,n. (hydrometric, hydrometrical,adj.)

38. Bead, Sphere, or Mass of Air- or Gas-Filled Liquid: blob, bubble,n. (bubbly,adj.)

1028. BUBBLE; FOAM

1. To Develop or Give Off Bubbles: boil, bubble, burble, effervesce, foam, seethe; simmer (gently, and with a quiet murmuring sound); sparkle,v.

2. Bubbling; Process or State of Bubbling: boiling, burble or burbling, ebullience, ebulliency, ebullition, effervescence, effervescency; gurgitation (usually violent); seethe; simmer (gently, and with a quiet, murmuring sound), n.

3. To Cause to Develop or Give Off Bubbles: boil, bubble, foam, sparkle,v.

4. To Come Off or Out or to Rise (from a Liquid) in Bubbles: effervesce,v. (effervescence, effervescency,n.)

5. To Bubble and Hiss: effervesce,v. (effervescence, effervescency,n.)

6. Bubbling: boiling, bubbly, burbling, ebullient, effervescent, foaming, foamy, seething, simmering,adj. (foaminess,n.)

7. Resembling, or Full of, Bubbles: bubbly, adj.

8. To Remain, or Cause to Remain, in a Condition Just Below Boiling: simmer,v. (simmer,n.)

9. Mass or Collection of Tiny Bubbles on the Surface of a Liquid; Saliva or Other Liquid in the Form of Such a Mass in the Mouth or around the Lips of a Person or Animal: foam, froth,n.

10. Mass of Tiny Bubbles of Sweat on the Skin of an Animal, Esp. a Horse: foam, froth, lather,n.

11. To Become Covered with Such: lather,v.

12. Foam: froth; lather (from soap and water); sea foam (of the sea); spume, suds, yeast,n.

13. Foam Made of Soap and Water: lather, suds,n. (lathery, sudsy,adj.)

14. To Develop Such a Foam—of Soap: lather, suds,v.

15. To Cover with Such; To Put Such On: lather, suds,v. (latherer,n.)

16. To Develop, Give Off, or Become Foam: cream, despumate, foam, froth, spume,v. (despumation,n.)

17. To Give Off As or Like Foam: despumate, froth, spume,v. (despumation,n.)

18. To Cause to Develop, Give Off, or Become Foam: foam, froth,v.

19. Full of, Covered with, Like, or Consisting of, Foam: barmy, foamy, frothy, spumescent, spumose, spumous, spumy, sudsy, yeasty,adj. (foaminess, frothiness, spumescence,n.)

20. To Cover with Foam: froth,v.

21. Foaming: foamy, frothing, spumescent, adj.

22. To Foam and Bubble: churn, seethe,v. (seethe,n. churning, seething,adj.)

23. To Produce (Foam) on by Shaking, Stirring, or Moving Violently: churn,v.

1029. BODY OF WATER

1. Body of Water,n.
   1. canal—man-made waterway; man-made body of water for irrigation
   2. inlet—strip of water extending inland, or lying between islands
   3. lake—large body of stationary water, fresh or salt, situated inland
   4. ocean—one of the several immense bodies of salt water covering the earth, such as the Atlantic, Pacific, etc.
   5. sea—large body of salt water, smaller than an ocean; any large body of water surrounded by land
   6. sound—long and fairly wide body of water between the mainland and an island; body of water connecting two larger bodies of water
   7. strait, straits, narrows, neck, channel—fairly narrow body of water connecting two wider bodies of water
   8. stream—body of moving water with a current and course
   9. swash—body of swift-moving water, esp. cutting through or behind a sand bar
  10. waterway—body of water that is, or can be, traveled upon to reach a destination

2. Description and History of the Bodies of Water on the Earth's Surface: hydrognosy,n.

3. To Build a Canal through or across (a Place): canal, canalize,v. (canalization,n.)

4. To Convert into a Canal: canalize,v. (canalization,n.)

5. System of Canals: canalization,n.

6. Stretch of Water: tract,n.

7. Stretch of Water Thickly Dotted with Small Islands: archipelago,n. (archipelagic, adj.)

8. Stretch of Water Encircled by a Coral Reef or by a Ring-Shaped Coral Island; Stretch of Shallow Sea Separated from the Main Body of Water by Sand Dunes: lagoon or lagune,n.

9. Stretch of Rough Water Caused by Opposing Currents or Tides: rip,n.

10. Water Subject to Tides; Water That Covers the Land at High Tide: tidewater,n.

11. Protected or Sheltered Portion of a Body of Water Large and Deep Enough for the Entrance of Vessels: basin; dock (artificial and esp. between piers or wharves); harbor, haven, marina, port, seaport,n.

12. Such Shelter for Watercraft: harborage, n.

13. To Come into, Bring into, or Keep in a Dock (of Watercraft): dock,v.

14. To Come or Go into the Shelter of a Harbor (of Watercraft): harbor,v.

15. City, Town, etc., Containing a Harbor, and Where Watercraft Load and Unload: port, seaport,n.

16. A Harbor Protected by a Great Stone Structure: mole,n.

17. The Motion of a Ship as It Goes through Water: seaway,n.

18. A Stream: bourn or bourne; canal (artificially improved for navigation); current; millstream (driving the mill wheel); river, watercourse; water system (with its branches); waterway (traveled upon to reach a destination),n.

19. Stream That Flows into a Larger Stream or Other Body of Water: affluent, branch, confluent, tributary,n. (affluent, confluent, tributary,adj.)

20. Upper Branches of a Stream or River: headwaters,n.

21. Small Stream: bayou (Southern U.S.); bourn or bourne, brook, brooklet, burn; creek (larger than a brook); rill (very small); rivulet; run (swift in motion); runlet, runnel; spring (formed by waters issuing from the earth); streamlet, watercourse,n.

22. River in Greek Mythology Whose Waters, When Drunk, Produced Forgetfulness: Lethe,n. (Lethean,adj.)

23. Anything That Flows Like a Stream: river, stream,n.

24. Pert. to Streams or Rivers: fluvial, fluviatile, riverine,adj.

25. Like a Stream or River: riverine, riverlike,adj.

26. Produced by a Stream or River, or by the Motion or Action of Such: fluvial. riverine, adj.

27. Growing in Streams or Rivers: fluvial, fluviatile,adj.

28. Located or Living at the Side of a River: riparian, riverine, riverside,adj

29. Formed by the Action of a Stream and the Sea, at the Place One Empties into the Other: fluviomarine,adj.

30. Characteristic of Streams or Rivers: fluviatile,adj.

31. Found in, or Close to, Streams or Rivers: fluviatile,adj.

32. Pert. to the Nile River, or to the Inhabitants of the Region Near It: Nilotic,adj.

33. Device That Measures the Height of the Waters of the Nile: Nilometer,n.

34. Pert. to the Rhine River or to Bordering Regions: Rhenish,adj

35. On the North Side of the River Po, i.e., in Reference to Rome: transpadane,adj.

36. Source of a Stream or River: fount, fountain, fountainhead, head. headspring, origin, riverhead, source, spring,n.

37. Natural Spring That Spouts Heated Water and Steam: geyser,n. (geyseral, geyseric, or geyserine,adj.)

38. Natural Spring of Hot Water: hot spring, thermal spring,n.

39. Spring Containing Natural Mineral Water: mineral spring, spa,n.

40. Portion of a Stream, River, or Other Body of Water,n.
  1. channel, fairway—deeper and more navigable portion of a river, harbor, or other waterway
  2. chute, chutes—steep fall in a river
  3. current—most rapidly moving portion of a stream
  4. estuary, firth, frith—mouth of a river, where the current meets the sea tide (estuarial,adj.)
  5. mouth, embouchure—portion of a river that empties into the sea
  6. narrows—narrow part of a river
  7. pool—deep, calm place in a river
  8. rapids, chute—portion of the river where the current is particularly fast and strong, esp. over a steep descent
  9. subsurface—portion of a stream, river, or other body of water below the surface

41. Occurring, Deposited, Formed, or Found in an Estuary: estuarine,adj.

42. Bottom of a Stream or River: bed, channel, race, river bed, river bottom, watercourse,n.

43. Ground Bordering a Stream or River: bank, riverbank, riverside, shore,n.

44. Pert. to Such Ground: riparian, riverside,adj.

45. One Who Owns Such Land: riparian,n. (legal)

46. Land Drained by a River or River System: basin, river basin; valley (low and extensive); watershed,n.

47. Other Land, etc., in Reference to a River, n.
  1. continental divide—ridge or high land separating rivers that flow into different oceans
  2. Continental Divide—ridge of the Rocky Mountains separating rivers that flow to the Atlantic or Arctic Ocean from those that flow to the Pacific Ocean
  3. delta—tract of land, often triangular in shape, formed by soil and sand deposited by the diverging branches of the mouth of some rivers; such in respect to the Nile River (deltaic,adj.)
  4. divide, watershed—ridge or high land dividing land areas that are drained by rivers or a river system

48. Water Falling Steeply or Perpendicularly, as over Rocks, etc.: cascade, cataract, chute, fall, waterfall,n. (cataractal, cataractine,adj.)

49. To Fall So: cascade, cataract,v.

50. Waterfall or Water Used, or Capable of Being Used, to Drive Machinery, etc.: water power,n.

51. Series of Small Waterfalls: cascade,n.

52. Pert. to Water Power: hydrodynamic,adj

53. Lake or Similar Body of Water,n.
  1. dam—body of water impeded or closed in by a protecting wall or other obstruction
  2. lagoon, lagune—shallow pond or lake, esp. one connecting with a larger body of water
  3. millpond, milldam—pond, formed by a dam, that provides the water to turn the mill wheel
  4. pond, basin—body of static water, smaller than a lake; such a man-made body, as by means of a dam, etc.
  5. pool—small body of static water; small pond

6. reservoir, basin—body of water stored for future use as a city's drinking supply

7. salina—pond or lake of salt water

8. sea—large lake

9. sluice—body of water confined or regulated by a gate in an artificial channel

10. spring—small lake or pool formed by waters issuing from the earth

11. tarn—small lake or pool in the mountains

54. Pert. to a Lake: lacustrine, laky,adj.

55. Like a Lake: laky,adj.

56. Descr. of Animals or Plants That Live or Grow in or on Lakes: lacustrine,adj.

57. Developed at the Bottom or Shore of a Lake: lacustrine,adj.

58. House, Shelter, etc., Built on Stilts over the Waters of a Lake, Esp. in Early or Prehistoric Times: lake dwelling,n. (lake dweller, n.)

59. Pert. to, Living, or Located on the Banks of a Lake, Other Body of Water, or Waterway: riparian,adj.

60. Growing in Ponds: fluvial, fluviatile,adj.

61. Device to Measure the Changes in the Level of a Lake: limnimeter, limnograph, or limnometer,n. (limnimetric,adj.)

62. Science of Lakes, Ponds, and Other Bodies of Fresh Water: limnology,n. (limnologist, n. limnologic, limnological,adj.)

63. An Inlet: arm; bay, basin, or bight (wide, and of a sea, lake, or any other body of water); bayou (Southern U.S.); canal (long and narrow, and extending inland to a considerable distance); cove (small and sheltered); fiord or fjord (narrow, of the sea, and surrounded by high banks or cliffs, esp. on the Norwegian coast); firth or frith (narrow, and of the sea, esp. on the coast of Scotland); gulf (wider than a bay, and extending inland for a considerable distance); slough, slew, or slue (of a river); sound (of a sea or ocean),n.

64. The Ocean or Sea: the brine; the deep or the briny deep (poetic); the hyaline (when calm or clear—poetic); Neptune; seaway (as a means of travel); surge (if rising and rolling); waste or wilderness (if turbulent or desolate),n.

65. The Open or Rough Sea: seaway,n.

66. Waters of the Ocean or Sea: the brine,n.

67. Salt Waters That Cover a Large Extent of the Surface of the Earth: oceans, Oceanus, sea, seas,n.

68. Agitation on the Ocean, Sea, or Other Large Body of Water, Caused by the Wind: sea,n.

69. A View of the Sea or Ocean: seascape,n.

70. A Route or Way Using the Sea: seaway,n.

71. Science of the Physical Geography of the Oceans: oceanography,n. (oceanographer,n. oceanographic, oceanographical,adj.)

72. Relating or Referring to the Ocean or Sea,adj.
1. **abyssal**—pert. or referring to the lowest depths of ocean waters
2. **aeromarine**—relating or referring to navigation in the air above oceans, as by planes, etc.
3. **bathic, bathyal**—pert. or referring to the deeper ocean waters
4. **bathybic**—pert. to, living, or growing in the deepest ocean or sea waters (biology)
5. **briny**—pert. or similar to the sea, esp. its salt waters (brininess,n.)
6. **deep-sea**—pert. to, or located, performed, or occurring in, the deeper ocean or sea waters
7. **landlocked**—without access to the sea, i.e., shut in by land

8. **marine**—pert. to, living or found in, or produced by, the ocean or sea

9. **maritime**—pert. to the ocean or sea; living or located close to the ocean or sea; referring to the ocean or sea in connection with shipping or sailing

10. **Neptunian**—pert. to the sea

11. **oceanic**—pert. or belonging to, living or found in, or produced by, the ocean; as vast as the ocean

12. **oceanlike, oceanic**—similar to an ocean

13. **pelagic**—pert. to the oceans or ocean, seas or sea, or to the surface or open waters of the ocean or sea; descr. of animals or plants that live or grow near, or on, the surface of the ocean; operating in the open waters of the ocean or sea, as ships, etc.

14. **sea-born**—produced or originating in the sea

15. **sea-borne**—carried by, or on, the sea

16. **seafaring, seagoing**—traveling by, or on, the sea; traveling the seas as one's occupation

17. **seagirt**—enclosed or surrounded by the sea

18. **seagoing**—made or designed for use on the open ocean or sea, as watercraft

19. **seaworthy**—of watercraft, capable of traveling on the open ocean or sea because strong, able to withstand rough weather, etc. (seaworthiness,n.)

20. **thalassic**—pert. to, living, found, or growing in, or produced by, the oceans or seas; pert. to inlets of the ocean or sea, or to smaller or inland seas

21. **transatlantic, transpacific**—across, beyond, on the other side of, or crossing, the Atlantic (or Pacific) Ocean

22. **transoceanic, overseas**—across, beyond, on the other side of, crossing, or extending over, the ocean

73. Traveling on or by Sea; The Occupation of Such, i.e., of Being a Sailor: seafaring,n.

74. One Who Travels on or by Sea; One Whose Occupation Is Such, i.e., a Sailor: seafarer,n.

75. Facing toward, or Going in the Direction of, the Sea or Open Sea: seaward,adj.

76. In the Direction of the Sea or Open Sea: seaward, seawards,adv.

77. That Direction toward the Sea and Away from the Land: seaward,n.

78. God of the Sea: Neptune (Roman); Oceanus (Greek, father of the ocean nymphs); Poseidon (Greek),n. (Neptunian,adj.)

79. Land Bordering the Ocean, Sea, or Other Body of Water: bank (rising); beach (sandy); coast, littoral, seaboard, seacoast, seashore, seaside, shore, strand; terrace (narrow and level, with a steep descent); tidewater, waterfront,n. (coastal, littoral, seaside,adj.)

80. Bordering on the Sea or Ocean: seaboard, seaside,adj.

81. To Border (a Body of Water): bank,v.

82. That Part of a City, Town, or Group of Buildings That Faces the Sea or Other Body of Water: sea front, waterfront,n.

83. Line Where the Land Meets the Water: seaboard, shore line, strand line,n.

84. Former Shore Line from Which the Sea, Ocean, or Lake Has Receded: strand line,n.

85. Outline of the Coast: coast line,n.

86. To Go Along the Coast of: coast,v.

87. Along the Coast: coastwise or coastways, adv.

88. Toward the Coast: coastward or coastwards,adv.

89. In the Direction of the Coast: coastward, adj.

90. Following the Coast: coastwise,adj.

91. Going, Running, etc., on or to the Shore (Esp. of a Vessel): aground, ashore,adv.

92. At a Distance, or Away, from the Shore: offshore,adv.

93. Situated or Working at a Distance from the Shore; Moving Away from the Shore: offshore,adj.

94. To Run (a Vessel) upon the Shore: beach, ground, land, strand,v.

95. To Be So Run or Driven: ground, land, strand,v.

96. On the Shore (Said of a Vessel, etc.): aground, ashore, beached, grounded, stranded, adj.

97. Living on or Along the Shore (Esp. in Reference to Certain Wading Birds, as the Plover, Curlews, Sandpipers, Snipes, etc.): limicoline,adj.

98. Land, Stretch of Land, etc., Jutting Out into the Sea, Ocean, or Other Water: cape, chersonese, head, headland, neck, peninsula, spit, tongue,n. (peninsular,adj.)

99. Point of High Land, or of Rock, Jutting Out into the Sea, Ocean, or Other Body of Water: head, headland, promontory,n.

100. Other Land or Ground in Reference to Water,n.
1. **bank**—shelf or shoal under the sea, some distance from the coast
2. **basin**—hollow or depression in the earth, whether natural or man-made, filled with water
3. **bed, channel**—land at the bottom of a body of water
4. **island**—body of land, smaller than a continent, entirely surrounded by water
5. **isthmus, neck**—narrow strip of land connecting larger bodies of land and surrounded on two sides by water
6. **ledge**—line or ridge of rocks in a body of water; reef
7. **mud flat,** flat—level stretch of land slightly below the surface of the water
8. **peninsula, chersonese**—land surrounded on three sides by water (peninsular,adj.)
9. **polder**—tract of lowland reclaimed from the sea, esp. in Holland
10. **race**—bed of any strong current
11. **reef, cay, key**—narrow chain of rocks or ridge of sand near, or at, the surface of the water
12. **shelf**—submerged bank of sand, or ridge of rock, in a sea or river
13. **shoal, shallow, sandbank, sand bar, mud flat,** flat—ridge or bar of sand in the bed of a sea or river, above water at low tide or low water (shoaly,adj.)
14. **spit**—long and narrow shoal extending from the land into the water
15. **swash**—ground over which the sea or other body of water washes or flows
16. **tideland, mud flat,** flat—land or ground covered by water when the tide is in

1030. ISLAND

1. Small Island: cay, isle, islet, key,n.

2. Low Island: cay, key,n.

3. Poetic Term for Island: isle,n.

4. Ring-Shaped Coral Island Surrounding a Lagoon: atoll,n.

5. Group of Small Islands Thickly Dotting a Stretch of Water: archipelago,n. (archipelagic,adj.)

6. Pert. to, Living or Situated on, Being, Forming, or Like, an Island or Islands: insular,adj. (insularity,n.)

7. Inhabitant or Native of an Island: islander,n.

8. Similar to, or Characteristic of, Such: insular,adj. (insularism,n.)

9. To Form into, Stud with, Cause to Be Like, or Place on, an Island, Literally or Figuratively: island,v.

10. To Form into, or Place on, a Small Island, Literally or Figuratively: isle,v.

11. To Live or Stay on a Small Island: isle,v.

12. The Islands of the Southern and Central Pacific Ocean: Oceania or Oceanica,n. (Oceanian,n.)

1031. WATER MOVEMENT

1. Movement of Water,n.
1. **billow, surge**—rolling and swelling of the sea or ocean, or of its waves
2. **crosscurrent**—current running in opposition to another current
3. **current, tide**—motion of a stream, river, or other body of water (tidal,adj.)
4. **eddy**—current of water, liquid, air, gas, dust, fog, etc., running against the main current, esp. in a circular, rotating, or whirling motion; small whirlpool
5. **flow**—movement of water, liquid, air, gas, etc., in one direction
6. **Maelstrom**—whirlpool found off the northwest coast of Norway
7. **millrace**—current that drives a mill wheel
8. **race**—very rapid current in a river or sea
9. **rip tide**—tide running in an opposite direction to another tide or tides, causing a violent disturbance in an area of water; undertow (esp. on the Pacific coast)
10. **seiche**—rhythmical, side-to-side motion or oscillation of the waters of a lake or inland sea
11. **stream**—steady movement or current of water, as in a river or sea, or of liquid, fluid, air, gas, etc.
12. **tidal wave**—rise of ocean or sea water along the shore, resulting from high winds; wavelike rise of ocean, sea, or other body of water resulting from the attraction of the moon and sun
13. **tide**—rhythmical and alternating rise and fall of ocean waters (tidal,adj.)
14. **torrent**—violent, rapid, or rushing flow or stream (torrential, torrent,adj.)
15. **undercurrent**—current beneath the surface
16. **underset**—current beneath the surface in an ocean
17. **undertow**—strong current beneath the surface of a body of water moving in an opposite direction to the surface current; backflow of water beneath the surface at a beach or shore, caused by the breaking of the waves
18. **whirlpool, maelstrom, vortex**—water swirling rapidly in a circle; current or eddy of such water (vortical, vorticose, adj.)

2. To Move Like or in the Motion of Water, etc.,v. *From Sec. 1:* billow or surge, eddy, flow, stream

3. Moving Thus,adj. *From Sec. 1:* billowy, billowing, surgy or surging; eddying, flowing, streaming, tidal; torrent, torrentful, torrential, or torrentuous; vortical, vorticose, or vortiginous (billowiness,n.)

4. To Cause to Move Thus,v. *From Sec 1:* surge, eddy, flow, stream

5. Resembling Such,adj. *From Sec. 1:* torrent or torrential, vortical or vorticose

6. Kinds of Tides: ebb tide (outgoing); flood tide (incoming); high tide (when in); low tide (when out); neap tide (in, but lower than usual); spring tide (in, and higher than usual),n.

7. To Move (of the Tide): ebb (out); flood or flow (in),v.

8. Having, Caused by, or Dependent on, Tides: tidal,adj.

9. Channel through Which the Tide Runs: tideway,n.

1032. OCEAN WAVE

1. An Ocean or Sea Wave: beachcomber (long and rolling); billow (large); breaker (becoming foamy upon hitting rocks, the shore line, etc.); comber (long and curling); decuman (very large); ripple (small); ripplet (still smaller); sea (large); surge (large and swelling, or sudden); swell (esp. if long and continuous); tidal wave (very destructive, and caused by an earthquake, etc.); water wave; wavelet (small); whitecap (the top broken into white foam),n.

2. To Move, Flow, Rise, or Roll in, or Like, Waves,v. *From Sec. 1:* billow, ripple, surge, swell (billow, surge, swell,n.)

3. To Cause (Water, etc.) to Move, Flow, Rise, or Roll So,v. *From Sec. 1:* ripple, surge

4. Moving, etc., So,adj. *From Sec. 1:* billowing or billowy, rippling or ripply, surging or surgy, swelling (billowiness,n.)

5. Full of, or Like, Such Waves,adj. *From Sec. 1:* billowy, ripply, surgy (billowiness,n.)

6. The Waves in Continuous Succession, or Collectively: sea, surf, swell,n.

7. Waves Breaking on Rocks, Shore, etc.; Line of Foam Caused by Such: surf,n.

8. Of Waves, To Hit upon (Shore, Rocks, etc.): break against, on, or upon; dash against, on, or upon,v.

9. The Breaking or Hitting of Waves, or the Sound So Caused or Made: swash,n.

10. Depression or Hollow between the Tops of Two Waves: trough,n.

11. The Progress of a Ship through the Waves: seaway,n.

12. Descr. of a Sea or Ocean, or Its Waters, Having Rough, Irregular, Short, and Broken Waves: chopping, choppy,adj. (choppiness,n.)

1033. WATER STRUCTURE

1. A Structure Built against, or to Confine, the Water,n.
 1. breakwater, pier—structure built out into the water to break or decrease the force of the waves
 2. dam—structure built against the water to hold back or impede its flow
 3. dike, dyke, embankment—bank or mound of earth or other material thrown up to confine the water of a sea, lake, river, etc.
 4. floodgate, sluice gate, sluice—gate or gatelike structure that holds back or regulates the flow of water, as in a stream, canal, etc., or, by extension, that holds back or regulates any flow, literally or figuratively
 5. jetty—structure of rock, wooden piles, etc., built out into water to deflect the current, tide, etc., or to protect a harbor
 6. levee—bank, mound, etc., of earth or other material erected to prevent a river from overflowing—so called in the Southern U.S.
 7. lock—structure in a canal, river, or other waterway, with a gate at each end, that raises or lowers a vessel from one level to another as it passes through

 8. milldam—dam built across a stream so that there will be a high enough level of water to furnish power for driving the mill wheel
 9. mole—great structure of stone or stones that acts as a breakwater
 10. sea wall—wall or embankment acting as a breakwater against the sea

2. To Furnish or Provide (Water) with Such a Structure,v. *From Sec. 1:* dam, dike, lock

3. To Confine, Restrict, or Enclose (Water) with Such a Structure,v. *From Sec. 1:* dam, dike, embank or bank (embankment,n.); *Also:* 1. bay—dam (water)

4. To Open the Floodgates or Sluice Gates of: sluice,v.

5. A Stone, Concrete, Cement, etc., Facing on an Embankment That Strengthens or Reinforces It against the Waters of a River, Sea, etc.: revetment,n.

6. To Put or Build Such on (an Embankment): revet,v.

7. To Be Engaged in Building Locks in a Canal, River, etc.: lock,v.

8. To Move (a Ship or Other Vessel) by Means of Locks: lock,v.

9. A Place to Anchor a Ship, etc., If Such a Place Is Protected by a Stone Structure Extending into the Water: mole,n.

10. Structure Built into or Alongside of the Water, at Which Ships, etc., Can Tie Up, Load and Unload, etc.: dock, jetty, landing; mole (built on or of stones); pier, quay, wharf,v.

11. Such Structures Collectively: quayage, wharfage,n.

12. To Furnish, Equip, or Provide (a Place) with Such: pier, wharf,v.

13. To Come into, and Tie Up at, Such a Structure—of Ships, etc.: dock, land,v. (dockage,n.)

14. To Bring (a Ship, etc.) into, and Tie Up at, Such: dock, land, wharf,v. (dockage, n.)

15. Accommodations, Facilities, or Space for Such: dockage, moorage, pierage, quayage, wharfage,n.

16. Fee Charged for Tying Up a Ship, etc., at Such: dockage, groundage, moorage, pierage, quayage, wharfage,n.

17. Wooden Structure Protecting a Pier: jetty,n.

18. The Use of a Wharf; Storage of Goods on or at a Wharf: wharfage,n.

19. To Put, Place, or Store (Goods) on a Wharf: wharf,v.

20. Structure into Which a Ship or Other Vessel Can Come for Repairs; If Floating, the Structure Can Be Raised Out of the Water, Otherwise the Water Can Be Drained from It: dry dock,n.

21. To Bring or Place, or Come into, Such: dock, dry-dock,v.

22. Passage or Structure, Artificial or Natural, through Which Water Flows, or Which Conveys Water: aqueduct (artificial, for conveying water from a distance); arroyo (with steep sides, generally dry except after heavy rains—term in Southwest U.S.); channel; culvert (of stone or pipe under a roadway, embankment, etc.); ditch, dike, dyke, gully, or trench (dug into the earth for draining or irrigating land); millrace or mill run (conveying the water that turns a mill wheel); race (of any strong current); runnel (small); sluice or sluiceway (artificial); spillway (for excess water of a reservoir); watercourse (natural or artificial); water gap (in a mountain ridge); waterway,n.

23. Pipe or Tube Carrying, or Carrying Off, Water or Liquid: channel, conduit, drain, drainpipe, duct, gully, gutter, trough; water main or main (i.e., the chief such pipe in a system),n.

24. System of Artificial or Natural Drains: drainage,n.

25. To Be Carried Along, or Flow, in or as if in Such Pipes or Tubes: gutter,v.

26. To Come, Flow, Pour, etc., through, or as if through, a Channel: drain, sluice,v. (drainage,n.)

27. To Let (the Water) Escape from, or Draw (the Water) Off from: dike, drain, sluice,v. (drainage,n.)

28. Pipe, Ditch, Channel, etc., for Carrying Surface Water from a Street or Road: gully, gutter,n.

29. Such for Carrying Rain Water from the Roof of a Building: downspout, gutter, trough,n.

30. To Furnish with Such: gutter,v.

31. Pipe Leading from the Gutter of a Roof to the Ground: leader,n.

32. Channel or Ditch Made by Running Water: gully, gutter,n.

33. To Make Such in: channel, gully, gutter, v.

34. Pipe, etc., for Carrying Off Waste Water and Other Waste: culvert, drain, drainpipe, sewer, sewer pipe,n.

35. System of Such Pipes, etc.: sewerage,n.

36. The Conveyance of Waste Water and Other Waste by Such: sewerage,n.

37. Waste Water and Other Waste So Carried Off: sewage, sewerage,n.

38. Hole Dug into the Ground to Reach Water; This Hole Plus the Water when Found: artesian well (drilled very deep, the water rising through underground pressure), well,n.

39. Device, Machine, etc., for Drawing, Raising, Driving, Emptying, Compressing, etc., Water or Other Fluids: pump,n.

40. To So Raise, etc. (Water or Other Fluids): pump,v.

41. To Drain Off Water by Means of Such: pump,v.

42. Upright Pump in the Street or Road for Drawing Water from Water Mains: hydrant, pump,n.

43. Device That Opens and Closes and Thus Controls, Stops, or Turns On and Off the Flow of Water or Other Liquid from a Pipe, etc.: cock, faucet; nozzle (at the end of a water hose); petcock, spigot, spout, tap,n.

44. Faucet through Which Rain Flows as It Drains Off a Roof: gargoyle (often in the shape of a grotesque human or animal head), rainspout, waterspout,n.

45. Any Hole, Pipe, Opening, etc., through Which Water Runs or Flows: spout, waterspout,n.

46. Structure Containing a Faucet or Faucets from Which Water Runs or Spouts: bubbler, drinking fountain, fount, fountain, water fountain,n.

47. Device in a Pipe for Turning On and Off the Flow of Gas: cock, petcock,n.

48. High Tank Used to Store Water: water tower,n.

49. Structure across or over Water or Other Places, and Erected and Used as a Passage: bridge,n.

50. To Erect a Bridge over: bridge, span,v.

51. To Extend across, as or Like a Bridge: bridge, span,v.

52. Kinds of Bridges: arch bridge (supported by arches); cantilever bridge (formed of cantilevers supported on piers); covered bridge (enclosed); drawbridge (able to be raised, lowered, or drawn aside), lift bridge, or bascule bridge (counterweighted to raise and lower easily); footbridge (narrow, for pedestrians only); gangplank, gangboard, or gangway (for boarding or leaving a vessel, from or to a dock, etc.); pontoon bridge, floating bridge or bateau bridge (supported on floats in the water); rope bridge (of rope, etc.); suspension bridge (supported by towers and suspended from cables or chains); swing bridge (able to swing in a horizontal plane so vessels can pass); trestle bridge (supported on a framework of upright or slanting beams, etc.); truss bridge (supported by a rigid framework of wood, metal, etc.); vertical lift bridge (lifting vertically to permit passage of vessels); viaduct (generally, carrying a road, railroad, highway, etc., over a valley, gorge, lower road, etc.),n.

53. Distance or Portion between the Supports of a Bridge: span,n.

1034. WETNESS

1. To Wet, i.e., Make Wet: bathe; imbue (with moisture); hose, wash, water,v. (imbuement,n.)

2. Wetted: bathed, hosed; imbued (with moisture); washed, watered,adj. (imbuement, n.)

3. That Which Wets: hose, wash,n.

4. To Wet (the Face) with Weeping: blubber,v.

5. To Wet Repeatedly: dabble,v.

6. To Make Somewhat, Partly, or a Little Wet: bathe, dabble, damp, dampen, moisten; humidify or humify (with water, moisture, or vapor),v. (humidification,n.)

7. To Become So: dampen, moisten,v.

8. So Wet: damp, moist, humid, irriguous, oozy,adj. (dampness or damp, moistness, humidity or humidness,n.)

9. So Wetted: bathed, dampened, moistened, humidified,adj.

10. Descr. of Air, Weather, or Atmosphere That Is Damp: humid,adj. (humidity or humidness,n.)

11. Device That Keeps Air Humid: humidifier,n.

12. Device to Regulate Humidity: humidistat, hygrostat,n.

13. Amount or Degree of Dampness or Moisture in the Air: humidity,n.

14. Average of Humidity and Heat at Any Particular Time: humiture,n. (new coinage)

15. Damp and Cold; Covered with a Cold and Sticky Dampness: clammy,adj. (clamminess,n.)

16. Disagreeably Damp: dank,adj. (dankness n.)

17. Disagreeably Damp or Humid and Warm, Close, or Oppressive (of Weather): muggy adj. (mugginess,n.)

18. Damp and Heavy (as Bread Poorly Baked, etc.): soggy,adj. (sogginess,n.)

19. To Wet by Flowing Over Completely—of Water, etc.; To Wet by Causing Water or

Other Liquid to So Flow Over, or by Covering or Surrounding with Such: bathe, deluge, flood, inundate, overflow,v. (inundation, n.)

20. So Wetted or Wet: awash, bathed, deluged, flooded, inundated, overflowed,adj. (inundation,n.)

21. To Wet Thoroughly: douse or dowse, drench; hose (with water or liquid issuing from a flexible tube); imbue (with moisture); saturate, soak; sodden (with water, moisture, or other liquid); sop, souse, steep,v. (drench, imbuement, saturation, soak or soakage,n. saturant,adj.)

22. That Which So Wets: drench, saturant,n.

23. To Become Thoroughly Wet: douse or dowse, sodden, sop,v.

24. To Be Thoroughly Wet: soak, sop, souse, v.

25. Thoroughly Wet or Wetted: doused or dowsed, drenched, dripping; imbued (with moisture); saturated, soaked, sodden, soggy; sopping, sopping wet, or soppy; waterlogged, wringing or wringing wet,adj. (imbuement, saturation, soak, soddenness, sogginess,n. saturability,n. saturable,adj.)

26. Saturated with Water and Therefore Heavy or Sluggish: waterlogged,adj.

27. To Lie in Water or Other Liquid and Become Thoroughly Wet: bathe, lave, soak; welter (esp. in blood),v.

28. To Wet, or Wet Thoroughly, with Blood or, Less Often, Any Staining Liquid; Of Blood, To Wet or Wet and Stain (Someone or Something): imbrue, imbue,v. (imbruement, imbuement,n.)

29. To Penetrate and Soak Through (Something): permeate,v. (permeation or permeance,n. permeative,adj.)

30. To Wet by Dashing or Scattering Water or Other Liquid Upon: bespatter, besplash, besplatter, bespray, besprinkle, dabble, plash, spatter, splash, splatter, spray, sprinkle, squirt,v.

31. So Wet or Wetted: bespattered, besplashed, besplattered, besprayed, besprinkled, plashed or plashy, spattered, splashed, splattered, sprayed, sprinkled, squirted,adj.

32. Wet and Soft: marshy,adj. (marshiness, n.)

33. Transparent or Translucent when Wet: hydrophanous,adj.

34. To Absorb (Liquid or Water): sop, sop up,v.

35. Causing Such Absorption: siccative,adj.

1035. DIP

1. To Dip, i.e., Push, Drop, or Plunge (Something or Someone) for a Short Time into Water or Other Liquid: bathe, douse or dowse, duck; dunk (bread, cake, etc., while eating); immerse (completely); sop (bread, cake, or other food or substance); souse, submerge or submerse,v. (immersion, submergence or submersion,n. dunker,n. submergible, submersible,adj.)

2. Bread, etc., So Dipped: sop,n.

3. To Dip, i.e., Be or Become Dipped: douse or dowse, souse, submerge,v.

4. State of Becoming or Being So Dipped: immersion, submergence, submersion,n.

5. To Dip Oneself in Water to Swim, Keep Cool, etc.: bathe, dip, lave,v. (bather,n.)

6. To Dip One's Body or Head under Water: duck,v. (ducker,n.)

7. Such an Act: duck,n.

9. Device with a Cuplike Bottom for Dipping Out Liquids: ladle,n.

9. To Dip (Liquid) from, with a Ladle: ladle, lave,v.

10. To Lift Out and Convey with, or as if with, a Ladle: ladle,v.

11. To Dip (Water or Liquid) from a Boat with a Pail, etc.: bail,v.

12. To Dip Water from (a Boat, etc.): bail,v.

13. To Dip Water from a Boat: bail,v. (bailer, n.)

14. Pail, etc., for This Purpose: bail, bailer,n.

15. To Dip (Something) In and Out and So Wet It: dabble,v.

16. To Fish by Letting the Bait Dip and Bob Gently in the Water: dib, dibble,v.

17. To Dip (Something) and Keep It in Water or Other Liquid: brine (in highly salted water, as for pickling, etc.); infuse (a plant, etc., in order to extract an essence, ingredient, etc.); pickle or souse (food in vinegar, salt water, etc.); seethe, soak; sop (esp. bread or similar food); steep (in order to soften, clean, or extract an essence from), v. (infusion, souse, steep,n.)

18. Liquid in Which Something Is So Dipped and Kept: brine, drench, pickle or souse, soak, steep,n.

19. To Lie So Dipped: soak, souse, steep,v. (soak, souse, steep,n.)

20. Something So Dipped and Kept: pickle; sop (esp. bread or similar food); souse (esp. parts of a pig),n.

21. The Extract or Essence Obtained by Soaking (a Plant, etc.): infusion,n.

1036. POUR

1. To Pour (Water, Liquid, or Other Substance Capable of Being Poured),v.
  1. circumfuse—pour around
  2. decant—pour off (liquor, etc.) slowly and carefully; pour from one vessel, bottle, container, etc., to another (decanter,n.)
  3. diffuse—pour forth or out, and spread
  4. discharge, effuse, flow, outpour, shed, teem—pour forth or out
  5. regurgitate—pour back
  6. shower—pour down in a large quantity or mass
  7. spill, slop—pour out (of a container, etc.) accidentally
  8. spout, spurt, jet—pour out suddenly and forcibly in a strong stream
  9. squirt—pour forcibly through a narrow opening
  10. strain—pour through a filter or sieve
  11. stream—pour forth or out in a steady flow
  12. superfuse—pour over or on something
  13. transfuse—pour from one vessel or container into another

2. To Pour, i.e., Come Pouring or Be Poured,v. *From Sec. 1:* discharge, effuse, or flow; regurgitate, shower; spill, spill over, slop, or slop over; spout, spurt, or jet; squirt, strain, stream, superfuse; *Also:*
  1. bubble (out)—pour (out) with an irregular sound
  2. cascade, cataract—pour down like a waterfall
  3. flush—pour with a rush; pour and spread suddenly
  4. gurgle—pour in a noisy and irregular stream
  5. gush, flood—pour with force, suddenness, or abundance
  6. teem—pour (of water)

3. A Pour; A Pouring,n. *From Secs. 1 and 2:* circumfusion, decantation, diffusion; discharge, effusion, flow, flowage, or outpour; regurgitation, shower; spill, spillage, spilth, or slop; spout, spurt, or jet; squirt, stream, superfusion, transfusion; *From Sec. 2:* cascade, cataract, gurgle, gush or flood; *Also:*
1. **affusion**—a pouring of water or liquid upon, as in baptism, etc.
2. **downpour**—a pouring down of water in heavy streams
3. **flood**—a heavy outpouring, as of water, lava, tears, words, etc.
4. **libation**—a pouring out of water, wine, etc., on the ground in some religious rites; the liquid so poured
5. **torrent**—violent and rushing downpour, outpour, stream, etc., of anything

4. Pouring,adj. *From Secs. 1 and 2:* circumfusing, diffusing, etc.; diffusive, transfusive; *From Sec. 3:* torrent, torrential; *Also:* 1. **profuse**—pouring forth abundantly or generously (profuseness,n.)

5. Instrument for Pouring Liquid Forcibly through a Narrow Opening: squirt, syringe, n.

6. The Sound of Pouring: gurgle,n.

7. To Pour (Water, Liquid, etc.) in Scattered Masses or Drops: dabble, plash, shed, slop, spatter, spill, splash, splatter, spray, sprinkle, swash,v.

8. To Pour (Tears) in Drops: shed,v.

9. To Come Pouring in Scattered Masses or Drops: plash, shower, spatter, spill, splash, splatter, spray, sprinkle, swash,v.

10. Such a Pour or Pouring: plash, shower, spatter, spill or spillage, splash, splatter, spray, sprinkle, swash,n.

11. Sound of Such a Pour or Pouring: plash, spatter, splash, splatter, swash,n.

12. Pouring So: plashy, showery, splashy,adj.

13. Device for Pouring or Ejecting Liquid in Fine Drops or Mist: atomizer, nebulizer, spray, sprayer, sprinkler, vaporizer,n.

14. To Change (Water or Liquid) into a Fine Spray or Mist: atomize, nebulize,v. (atomization, nebulization,n.)

15. To Pour Water, Liquid, etc., Upon (Someone or Something) in Scattered Masses or Drops: bespatter, besplash, besplatter, bespray, besprinkle, dabble, plash, shower, slop, spatter, splash, splatter, spray, sprinkle,v.

16. To Pour Water, Liquid, etc., upon, over, around, etc. (Someone or Something): douse or dowse (over); infuse (in, into, or upon); shower (upon); slop (upon); squirt (from a narrow opening and forcibly); suffuse (over or around); transfuse (in, into, or upon),v. (infusion, suffusion, transfusion, n. suffusive, transfusive,adj.)

17. To Pour (Light, Color, etc., or Something Likened to These) over or around (Someone or Something): suffuse with,v. (suffusion,n. suffusive,adj.)

18. To Pour Boiling Water upon or over: scald,v.

19. To Pour Water down (a Pump) to Get It to Work; To Pour Anything down or into (Something) for Like Purpose, Usually Figuratively: prime,v.

20. To Cover or Surround with Water or Other Liquid, or as if with This, Figuratively: bathe, circumfuse, deluge, flood, flow, flush, inundate, overflow,v. (flowage, inundation,n.)

21. To Cause or Let (Blood) Pour or Flow Out: shed, spill,v.

22. To Pour or Spray Water or Liquid through, over, or around (a Bodily Cavity, Canal, Wound, or Other Part): irrigate, flush, wash,v. (irrigation,n. irrigative,adj.)

23. To Supply (Land) with Water, as or with a Stream or River, or by Artificial Means, as or with a Canal, etc.: irrigate,v. (irrigation,n. irrigational or irrigative,adj.)

24. Irrigating; Serving to Irrigate: irrigative, irriguous,adj.

25. State of Being Irrigated: irrigation,n.

26. Able to Be Irrigated: irrigable,adj.

27. Well-Irrigated: irriguous,adj.

28. To Irrigate (Land) below the Surface: subirrigate,v. (subirrigation,n.)

1037. RAIN

1. To Rain: drizzle or mist (in fine or small drops); pour (heavily); shower (for a short period); sleet (in frozen or partly frozen particles, in particles that freeze as they fall, or combined with snow or hail); sprinkle (slightly); teem (very heavily),v.

2. A Rain; Rain,n. *From Sec. 1:* drizzle, pour, shower, sleet or ice rain, sprinkle (drizzly, showery, sleety,adj.); *Also:*
1. **cloudburst**—sudden and strong fall of rain
2. **deluge, flood**—extremely heavy fall of rain
3. **downpour**—heavy and steady fall of rain
4. **flurry**—light shower accompanied by gusts of wind
5. **precipitation**—rain, snow, sleet, hail, or other products of condensation in the atmosphere, or the dropping, falling, or depositing of such
6. **rainfall**—fall of rain
7. **rainstorm**—storm of rain, or including rain
8. **sun shower**—light fall of rain while the sun is shining
9. **thundershower**—shower accompanied by thunder and lightning
10. **torrent**—extremely strong and heavy, or violent, fall of rain (torrential,adj.)

3. Raining,adj. *From Sec. 1:* drizzling, drizzly or drippy; pouring, showering or showery, sleeting, sprinkling, teeming; *Also:* rainy

4. Rainy, i.e., Having, Full of, or Characterized by, Rain,adj. *From Sec. 1:* drizzly or drippy, showery, sleety; *Also:* damp, moist, moisty, pluvial, pluvious, soppy, wet

5. To Fall Like Sleet: sleet,v.

6. Pert. to Rain: pluvial, pluvious,adj.

7. Caused by, or Due to, Rain: pluvial,adj. (geology)

8. To Send Down (Rain, etc.), or Like Rain: rain,v.

9. Bringing, or Wet with, Rain: rainy,adj. (raininess,n.)

10. The Amount of Rain Dropped on the Ground: precipitation, rainfall,n.

11. The Amount of Hail, Snow, Sleet, etc., Dropped on the Ground: precipitation,n.

12. Icy Coating on the Streets, Electric Wires, Trees, etc., when Rain Freezes as, or after, It Falls: sleet,n. (sleety,adj.)

13. A Drop of Rain: raindrop,n.

14. Protected against, or Impervious to, Rain: rainproof,adj.

15. To Make So: rainproof,v.

16. Water That Has Fallen, or Is Falling, As Rain: rain water,n. (rain-water,adj.)

17. Stub of a Ticket to Be Used at a Future Time if an Outdoor Event Is Halted by

Rain; Hence, Figuratively, an Invitation or Opportunity at a Later Time: rain check,n.

18. God of Rain: rain god,n.

19. Roman God of Rain: Jupiter Pluvius,n.

20. Magician, Medicine Man, etc., in Tribal Society Who Claims the Power to Cause Rainfall: rain doctor, rain maker,n. (rain making,n.)

21. Instrument to Measure Rainfall: hyetometer, ombrometer, pluviometer, pluvioscope, rain gauge, udometer,n. (pluviometric or pluviometrical, udometric,adj.)

22. Automatic or Self-Registering Instrument to Measure Rainfall: hyetograph, hyetometrograph, ombrograph, udomograph,n.

23. Measurement of Rainfall; Science of Such Measurement: pluviometry, udometry, n. (pluviometric or pluviometrical, udometric,adj.)

24. Chart Indicating Average Yearly Fall of Rain: hyetograph,n.

25. Science of Rainfall: hyetography (of describing its geographical distribution), hyetology (of its quantity and other phenomena), n. (hyetographic or hyetographical, hyetological,adj.)

26. Arc of Color Appearing in the Heavens Following Rain; Anything Resembling This: iris, rainbow, sunbow; sundog (small or incomplete),n. (rainbowy,adj.)

27. To Cause to Be, or to Appear or Come Out, Like Such: rainbow,v.

28. Greek Goddess of the Rainbow: Iris,n.

29. Device to Protect a Pedestrian against Rain: bumbershoot (humorous), umbrella,n.

30. Having Very Little, or No, Rain: arid, droughty or drouthy, dry, rainless,adj. (aridity or aridness, dryness,n.)

31. A Long Period without Rain; Dry Weather; Lack of Rain: drought or drouth, n.

32. Ability of Certain Plants to Withstand Long Periods without Rain or Moisture, as in the Desert, etc.: xerophily,n. (xerophilous, xerophile,adj.)

33. A Plant with Such Ability: xerophile or xerophil, xerophyte,n. (xerophytism,n. xerophile, xerophytic,adj.)

1038. DRYNESS

1. To Dry, i.e., Make, or Cause to Be, Dry,v.
1. **dehumidify**—free from atmospheric or other moisture
2. **dehydrate, anhydrate**—remove water from (a chemical compound); remove water or moisture from (vegetables or other foods) for better keeping; cause to lose much or all water or moisture
3. **desiccate**—dry up completely; remove all moisture from (food) in order to preserve
4. **evaporate**—extract moisture from, as by heat, and thus make dry
5. **exsiccate**—dry completely; remove all moisture from, as by evaporation, etc.
6. **parch**—dry; dry up to an excess; dry by heat, hot wind, sun, excessive cold, etc.; make dry and hot; make a person extremely dry, i.e., thirsty, or dry and hot, or make his lips, throat, mouth, etc., very dry or dry and hot
7. **scorch**—parch or wither by heat
8. **sear**—dry up; wither
9. **stale**—make hard and dry, as bread
10. **torrefy, torrify**—dry with heat or fire
11. **towel**—dry, or rub or wipe dry, with a towel
12. **wipe**—dry by rubbing with the hand, a towel, a cloth, etc.

13. **wither, shrivel**—dry by exhausting or depriving of moisture; make dry and shrunken
14. **wizen**—dry up; make dry and shrunken, as a person, his face or body, etc.

2. To Dry, i.e., Become Dry, Lose Water or Moisture, etc.,v. From Sec. 1: dehydrate, desiccate, exsiccate, parch, sear, stale, wither or shrivel, wizen

3. A Making or Becoming Dry,n. From Secs. 1 and 2: dehumidification, dehydration or anhydration, desiccation, evaporation, exsiccation, torrefaction, wipe

4. Dried; Dry,adj. From Sec. 1: dehumidified, dehydrated or anhydrated, desiccated, exsiccated, parched, scorched; seared, sear, or, poetic, sere; stale, torrefied, wiped, withered or shriveled, wizened or wizen (staleness,n.); Also:
1. **adust**—dried by, or as by, heat; parched
2. **anhydrous**—lacking in water, esp. the water of crystallization (chemistry)
3. **arid**—dry; abnormally dry (as regions, land, etc.); lacking moisture; parched (aridity, aridness,n.)
4. **moistless, moistureless**—dry, i.e., lacking moisture
5. **thirsty**—dry or arid, as land or ground, etc. (thirstiness,n.)
6. **torrid**—dried by the heat of the sun, as regions, etc.; arid (torridity, torridness, n.)
7. **waterless**—dry; lacking in, or without, water

5. Drying, i.e., Causing or Tending to Cause Dryness, Loss of Moisture, etc.,adj. From Sec. 1: dehumidifying, dehydrating, etc.; desiccative or desiccatory, evaporative, exsiccative; Also: 1. siccative—drying; causing to dry

6. Drier or Dryer, i.e., Substance, Agent, etc., That Causes Drying,n. From Sec. 1: dehumidifier, dehydrator or dehydrant; desiccant, desiccator, or desiccative; exsiccative, towel, wiper; From Sec. 5: siccative (esp. one in paint); Also:
1. **sponge**—substance that freely absorbs water, hence is used to dry surfaces, etc.
2. **squeegee**—device for drying a surface by squeezing or pressing off water

7. Very Dry, i.e., Thirsty: parched,adj.

8. Abnormal Medical Dryness of Skin, Eyes, etc.: xerosis,n. (xerotic,adj.)

9. To Give Off Moisture: evaporate,v. (evaporation,n.)

10. Not Using or Containing Liquid or Fluid: aneroid,adj.

11. Not Using Water, as Pots or Pans in Cooking, or Other Devices: waterless,adj.

12. Tight against Water: stanch or staunch, watertight,adj. (stanchness or staunchness, n.)

13. Having Dry Shoes; Keeping the Shoes Dry: dry-shod,adj.

14. A Decay of Timber Causing It to Become Dry and Powdery; Disease of Vegetables Characterized by Extreme Dryness of the Dead Tissue; Hence, Figuratively, Hidden or Unsuspected Interior Decay: dry rot,n.

1039. SNOW

1. Snow in a Partially Melted or Watery State: slop, slosh, slush,n. (sloppy, sloshy, slushy,adj.)

2. To Splash Around in Such: slosh,v.

3. To Splash Such over or on (Someone or Something): slush,v.

4. Granular, Crystallized Snow Collected on High Mountains and Later Solidifying into Ice; A Field of Such: névé,n.

5. A Fall of Snow; The Amount That Falls at a Given Place in a Certain Period: precipitation, snowfall,n.

6. A Short, Light Fall of Snow or Rain: flurry (accompanied by gusts of wind), spit, n.

7. Storm Accompanied by a Fall of Snow: snowstorm,n.

8. Very Violent and Prolonged Snowstorm Accompanied by High, Cold Winds: blizzard, n. (blizzardly, blizzardy, blizzardous,adj.)

9. To Fall or Drop, or Let Fall or Drop, as or like Snow: snow,v.

10. To Cover, Obstruct, Bury, etc., with Snow: snow over, snow under, snow up,v.

11. Shut or Kept in by Snow: snowbound,adj.

12. A Field of Snow: snow field,n.

13. Mass of Snow Packed into Spherical Shape: snowball,n.

14. To Hurl Snowballs; To Hurl Snowballs at; To Increase, Grow Larger, or Accumulate at a Rapidly Accelerating Rate, like a Rolling Snowball: snowball,v.

15. Large Mass of Snow Driven Together, or Carried Along, by the Wind: snowdrift,n.

16. Large Mass of Snow Piled Up in One Place: snowbank, snow pile,n.

17. Single, Feathery Crystal of Snow: snowflake,n.

18. Blinded by the Reflection of the Sun Upon the Snow: snow-blind,adj. (snow blindness,n,)

19. Reflection from Snow Fields or Ice Fields: snowblink,n.

20. That Point, as on Mountains, etc., above Which the Snow Never Melts: snow limit, snow line,n.

21. Science Dealing with Snowfall, Rainfall, and Other Precipitation: hyetology,n. (hyetological,adj.)

22. As White As Snow: snow-white, snowy, adj. (snowiness,n.)

23. Having, Filled with, Characterized by, Pert. to, Like, or Suggestive of, Snow: snowy,adj. (snowiness,n.)

24. Covered with Snow: snow-clad; snowed over, under, or up; snowy,adj. (snowiness,n.)

25. With Snow on Its Top: snow-capped,adj.

26. Large Mass of Snow Falling down a Steep Bank: avalanche, snowslide,n.

27. Structure Erected as a Protection against Snow: snowshed,n.

28. Machine or Implement for Clearing the Snow from Streets, Roads, etc.: snowplow, snow shovel,n

1040. ICE

1. Particles of Ice, or Frozen Raindrops, That Fall during a Storm, Esp. a Thunderstorm: hail,n.

2. A Storm of Such: hail, hailstorm,n.

3. One Such Particle: hailstone,n

4. To Drop, Fall, or Pour as or Like Hail; To Drop or Pour Hail; To Drop (Something) Like Hail: hail,v

5. White, Non-Transparent Ice Formed from Frozen Slush: snow ice,n.

6. Field of Ice and Snow Moving Down Slowly from Mountains, or Outward from

the Point Where It Forms: glacier,n. (glacial,adj.)

7. Mass of Ice Detached from a Glacier and Floating in the Sea or Ocean: iceberg,n.

8. Caused by, or Associated with, the Action of Glaciers: glacial,adj.

9. Covered with Glaciers: glaciered,adj.

10. Under, at the Base of, or Pert. to the Base of, a Glacier: subglacial,adj.

11. One Who Studies Glaciers and Their Actions, or Who Believes that Specific Changes of the Earth's Surface Were Caused by Glaciers: glacialist,n.

12. To Cover with Glaciers; To Change or Affect by the Action of Glaciers: glaciate, v. (glaciation,n.)

13. Sheet of Artificial Ice for Skating: ice-skating rink, rink,n.

14. Place Where Such Is: glaciarium, ice-skating rink, rink,n.

15. To Skate on Ice: ice-skate,v.

16. Runner for Skating on Ice, Attached to One's Shoe; Shoe Fitted with Such a Runner: ice skate,n.

17. To Cover with Ice; To Cause to Form into Ice; To Make Look Like Ice: glaciate, ice,v. (glaciation,n.)

18. Covered with Ice: glaciated, iced, icy,adj. (iciness,n.)

19. Resembling, or Made of, Ice: icy,adj. (iciness,n.)

20. Pert. to Ice: ice,adj,

21. Pert to Sheets of Ice; Characterized by Ice in Sheets or Large Masses: glacial,adj.

22. Vast Sheet of Ice Floating in the Sea: ice field, ice floe, ice pack,n,

23. Vast Sheet of Ice over an Area: glacier, icecap, ice sheet,n. (glacial,adj.)

24. Boat That Sails on Ice: iceboat,n.

25. Ship That Breaks Paths through Ice: iceboat, icebreaker,n.

26. Confined, Shut In, or Surrounded by Ice: icebound,adj.

27. Brightness in the Sky, Caused by Reflection from an Expanse of Ice: blink, ice-blink,n

28. Tapering and Pointed Hanging Mass of Ice: icicle,n.

29. Covered with Such: icicled,adj.

30. To Remove Ice Formations from: deice,v.

31. Device or Contrivance That Removes or Prevents Ice Formations: deicer,n.

1041. FOG

1. Fog,n.
　1. brume—fog; mist; vapor
　2. haze—light fog; suspension or diffusion of tiny particles of vapor, smoke, and/or dust in the atmosphere near the surface of the earth
　3. mist—suspension of tiny particles of water in the atmosphere near the surface of the earth, less dense than fog
　4. smaze—combination of smog and haze (new coinage)
　5. smog—combination of fog and the industrial smoke of a city
　6. vapor—fog; mist; steamy mist rising into the air from water, moisture, or damp objects in contact with heat; visible particles of moisture suspended in the air

2. Foggy,adj. *From Sec. 1:* brumous, hazy, misty, vaporous or vapory (haziness, mistiness, vaporousness or vaporosity,n.); *Also:*

1. **murky, mirky**—containing thick haze or mist, as the atmosphere or the air (murkiness,n.)
2. **nubilous**—foggy; misty

3. **To Surround or Cover with, or as if with, Fog; To Become So Surrounded or Covered:** fog, fog up,v.

4. **To Become, or Cause to Become, Misty:** mist, mist up,v.

5. **Layer of Fog Visible from a Distance:** fog bank,n.

6. **Bright Spot in Such:** fogdog,n.

7. **Held Motionless because of Fog—of Ships:** fogbound,adj.

8. **Device to Sound Warning Signals on Ships during a Fog; A Deep Voice Having the Sound of Such:** foghorn,n.

1042. WIND

1. A Wind,n.
1. **Auster**—the south wind, a poetic personification
2. **Boreas**—the north wind, personified (boreal,adj.)
3. **bluster**—wind that is violent and full of noise
4. **breeze**—light or moderate wind, usually cool
5. **gale**—high, strong wind
6. **mistral**—strong, dry, cold wind from the north, esp. common in Southern France and bordering regions
7. **monsoon**—wind that comes at regular intervals in Southern Asia and the Indian Ocean, blowing in different directions at different seasons; any wind whose direction reverses at different seasons; wind that blows constantly between land and water
8. **northeaster**—wind blowing from the northeast
9. **norther**—north wind; sudden, strong, and stormy north wind, esp. around the Gulf of Mexico
10. **sea breeze, sea wind**—wind blowing from the cool ocean toward the warmer land
11. **simoom, simoon**—hot, dry, strong wind filled with sand, in the deserts of Southern Asia, Africa, etc.
12. **sirocco**—hot, dry wind filled with dust, from Northern Africa, blowing toward Southern Europe; warm and oppressive south or southeast wind, bringing rain, in this region; any hot and oppressive wind; hot wind of cyclonic source
13. **southwester, sou'wester**—wind blowing from the southwest
14. **trade wind**—ocean wind blowing toward the equator; wind that blows constantly in a regular course or in the same direction
15. **zephyr**—gentle, soft wind; west wind (zephyrean, zephyrian, zephyrous, zephyry,adj.)
16. **Zephyr, Zephyrus**—the west wind, a personification

2. Pert. to the Winds: Aeolian, Aeolic, Eolian, or Eolic,adj.

3. Pert. to the West Wind: favonian,adj.

4. A Quick, Short Wind: blast or blow (sudden and strong); breath, flatus, puff, waft, or whiff (very slight); flaw or windflaw (short but strong, often with rain or snow); flurry (sudden and strong); gust, waft, or whiff (sudden and strong); squall (sudden and extremely strong, often with rain, snow, or sleet),n.

5. Windy,adj. *From Sec. 4:* gusty, squally; *Also:* blowy; blustery, blusterous, or blustering (strongly and noisily so); breezy (lightly or moderately so)

6. **Windiness:** blowiness, breeziness, gustiness,n.

7. **Descr. of Wind That Is Full of Gusts:** flawy, gusty,adj.

8. **Descr. of Wind That Shifts or Changes Suddenly, Irregularly, etc.:** choppy, fluky or flukey,adj.

9. **Descr. of Winds or Air Currents That Move in an Upward Direction, or up a Slope:** anabatic,adj.

10. **Rainy Season when the Wind Blows from the Southwest in Southern Asia:** monsoon,n.

11. **To Move or Drift, i.e., Be in Motion, with the Wind at One's, or Its, Back:** rack,v.

12. **To Expose to the Wind or Air:** wind,v.

13. **Exposed, or Open to, or Swept by, the Wind or Winds:** bleak (cold winds), windswept, windy,adj. (bleakness, windiness,n.)

14. **Exposed, Open to, or Swept by, a Breeze or Breezes:** breeze-swept, breezy,adj. (breeziness,n.)

15. **Descr. of, or Pert. to, That Side or Part, Esp. of a Watercraft, That Is Exposed to the Wind:** weather,adj.

16. **The Side of a Watercraft That Is toward the Wind:** weatherboard,n.

17. **The Position of a Watercraft when It Is to the Windward of Another, Considered Advantageous; Hence, by Extension, Any Position of Advantage:** weather gauge,n.

18. **Atmospheric Disturbance Characterized by Strong and Unusual Winds, Often with Rain, Snow, Hail, or Thunder and Lightning; Heavy Rain, Snow, Hail, or Thunder and Lightning without Wind:** storm,n. (storminess,n. stormy,adj.)

19. **To Rain, Snow, Hail, Thunder, etc., with or without Wind:** storm,v.

20. **Shut In, Held Back, etc., by Storms or a Storm:** stormbound,adj.

21. **Stormy (of Weather, etc.):** rugged, tempestuous, turbulent, wintry or wintery,adj. (ruggedness, tempestuousness, turbulence or turbulency, wintriness,n.)

22. **Stormy or Windy Condition of the Atmosphere:** weather,n.

23. **Safe against Storms; Able to Withstand Storms; Protecting against Storms:** stormproof,adj.

24. **To Make So Safe, etc.:** stormproof,v.

25. **Door or Window That Gives Additional Protection against Storms, Cold, etc.:** storm door, storm window,n.

26. **Lacking in Storms:** stormless,adj.

27. **A Windstorm,n.**
1. **blizzard**—very violent windstorm, with dry and driving snow and extremely cold temperatures (blizzardly, blizzardous, blizzardy,adj.)
2. **bluster**—windstorm of some noise and violence
3. **dust devil**—whirlwind that scoops up dust, etc.
4. **cyclone**—violently whirling windstorm; windstorm rotating around a moving center of low atmospheric pressure, accompanied by heavy rain; tropical hurricane; hurricane in the Indian Ocean (cyclonic, cyclonical, cyclonal,adj.)
5. **equinoctial**—storm, such as a gale, etc., occurring at or about the beginning of spring or autumn
6. **gale**—windstorm characterized by winds moving up to 75 miles an hour

7. **hurricane**—violent and destructive storm with winds moving up to 100 miles an hour, until recently confined to tropical regions, and generally accompanied by heavy rain, thunder, and lightning; any phenomenon likened to a hurricane in speed or violence

8. **northeaster**—gale or other windstorm from the northeast

9. **southwester, sou'wester**—gale or other windstorm from the southwest

10. **squall**—sudden, violent windstorm not lasting very long, often accompanied by rain or snow (squally,adj.)

11. **tempest**—violent windstorm accompanied by rain, snow, or hail (tempestuous,adj.)

12. **tornado**—whirling windstorm of amazing speed, violence, and destructiveness, confined to a narrow path, and usually accompanied by a funnel-shaped cloud, esp. in the central states of the U.S.; any destructive windstorm; hurricane; whirlwind (tornadic,adj.)

13. **twister**—tornado, so called popularly in the U.S.

14. **typhoon**—tropical cyclone or hurricane of the China Sea area, Philippine Islands, or Western Pacific Ocean; tempest in India (typhonic,adj.)

15. **whirlwind**—rotating windstorm characterized by spiral motions of the air

28. **Subject to, or Having, Tempests:** tempestuous,adj. (tempestuousness,n.)

29. **Center of a Cyclone:** cyclone center, storm center,n.

30. **Central Region of a Hurricane, an Area of Low Pressure, Where the Skies Are Often Clear and the Air Is Calm:** eye,n.

31. **Instrument to Determine the Center of a Cyclone:** cyclonoscope,n.

32. **Instruments Used Together to Discover the Location and Motion of a Tropical Cyclone:** barocyclonometer and cyclonometer,n.

33. **The Atmospheric Conditions That Create a Cyclone or Other Windstorm, or Increase or Intensify the Actions of One Already in Existence:** cyclogenesis,n.

34. **Science Dealing with Cyclones:** cyclonology,n. (cyclonologist or cyclonist,n.)

35. **Underground Refuge from a Violent Windstorm, Esp. a Tornado:** cyclone cellar, storm cellar,n.

36. **Influence of the Wind in Changing the Direction of a Missile or Projectile; Amount of Such Change:** windage,n.

37. **Carried or Conveyed by the Wind:** windborne,adj.

38. **The Side Facing the Wind:** windward,n.

39. **Without Wind:** calm. windless,adj (calmness or calm,n)

40. **Science of, or Concerned with, the Wind:** anemology,n. (anemological,adj.)

41. **Measurement of Wind Force and Speed:** anemometry,n. (anemometric or anemometrical,adj.)

42. **The Recording, or Art of Recording, the Force and Speed of the Wind:** anemography, n.

43. **Device or Instrument Used on Wind:** anemograph (to record force or speed); anemometer (to measure force or speed); anemometrograph (to record speed, force, and direction); anemoscope (to indicate and record direction); vane, weather vane, weathercock, or wind vane (to indicate direction); weathercock (to indicate direction—in the shape of a cock or rooster), wind gauge (to

indicate force and direction),n. (anemographic, anemometrographic,adj.)

44. **To Furnish a Place with a Weather Vane:** weathercock,v.

45. **Something That, or a Person Who, Like a Weather Vane, Is Constantly Shifting or Changing; A Changeable, Fickle Person; One Who Trims His Opinions in Accord with the Fashion of the Time:** weathercock, n. (weathercockish, weathercocky,adj. weathercockism,n.)

46. **To So Act or Be:** weathercock,v.

47. **Greek God of the Wind:** Aeolus,n. (Aeolian, Aeolic, Eolian, or Eolic,adj.)

48. **Greek God of the North Wind:** Boreas, n. (Boreal,adj.)

1043. TO BLOW

1. **To Blow (of a Person Using His Breath, etc.):** huff, puff; whistle (by pursing the lips),v.

2. **The Sound of Such:** puff, whistle,n.

3. **To Blow Out (a Light, Flame, etc.):** puff out,v.

4. **To Blow Out, i.e., Come Blowing Out, as Smoke, Air, etc., in Jets or Small Bits:** puff, whiff,v. (puff, whiff,n.)

5. **To Blow (Something):** blast (a wind instrument); honk (a horn); insufflate (powder, vapor, air, etc.) into (a bodily cavity, esp. the lungs); puff, whiff, or whiffle (wisps of smoke, air, etc.); pump (air, etc., into a cavity or place); whistle (a tune, sound, etc.); wind (a horn, a blast, etc.),v.

6. **A Blowing on or of Something,n.** *From Sec. 5:* blast, honk, insufflation, puff, whiff, whistle

7. **Sound of a Horn Blowing:** honk,n.

8. **To Make Such a Sound—of the Horn or the Person Blowing It:** honk,v.

9. **To Give a Signal or Direction to, by Blowing a Horn:** honk, wind,v.

10. **To Blow (Something) Out or Away:** puff, whiff, whiffle,v.

11. **To Blow (Something) Up, as with Air, Gas, etc.; To Become So Blown Up:** inflate, pump up,v. (inflation,n. inflatable,adj.)

12. **To Reduce, or Be Reduced, from Such a State, when the Air or Gas Is Released:** deflate,v. (deflation,n.)

13. **To Blow (Some Substance) into or upon (a Thing or Place):** insufflate (the thing or place) with (the substance),v. (insufflation, n.)

14. **Device for Doing This:** insufflator,n.

15. **Device for Blowing Air:** bellows,n

16. **To Blow (of the Wind):** bluster (strongly, irregularly, and noisily); puff (in gusts); whiff (in gusts); whiffle (irregularly or in gusts). whistle (with a characteristic sound), v

17. **The Sound of Such:** bluster. puff, whistle,n.

18. **The Blowing of the Wind in Gusts:** blast,n

19. **Blowing (of the Wind):** blowy; blustering, blusterous, or blustery (noisily and strongly); breezy (lightly); gusty (suddenly and strongly): spanking (briskly or sharply),adj

20. **To Blow Suddenly and Violently (with the Impersonal Subject "It," Meaning the Wind, etc.):** squall, storm,v. (squally, stormy,adj.)

21. Blown About by the Wind: aeolian, wind-blown,adj.

22. Cut Short to Have the Appearance of Being Blown About by the Wind—of the Hair: wind-blown,adj.

23. Growing in a Particular Shape because Blown About by the Wind—of Trees: wind-blown,adj.

24. Mill or Machine Operated by the Blowing Wind: windmill,n.

25. A Watercraft Propelled Solely by the Blowing Wind, i.e., One with Sails Only: windjammer,n.

26. A Sailor on Such: windjammer,n.

27. Something Blown Down by the Wind: windfall,n.

28. Tight or Safe against the Passage of the Blowing Wind or Air: airtight, stormproof, windproof, windtight,adj.

1044. THUNDER; LIGHTNING

1. The Crashing Noise Accompanying Lightning: thunder, thundering,n.

2. Pert. to, or Resembling, Thunder and Lightning: fulminous,adj.

3. To Make the Sound of, or like, Thunder: peal, thunder, thunderpeal,v.

4. Producing, Full of, or Having the Sound of, Thunder: thundering, thunderous, thundery, thundrous,adj. (thunderousness,n.)

5. The Explosive Noise of Thunder: clap, crack, crash, peal, thunderblast, thunderclap, thundercrack, thunderpeal,n.

6. A Storm Accompanied by Thunder and Lightning: thunderstorm,n.

7. Such with Rain or Wind: thunder-gust (with wind); thundershower (with rain); thundersquall (with strong winds),n.

8. Lightning: heat lightning (near the horizon in summer); sheet lightning (appearing as a general illumination); wildfire (sheet lightning without thunder),n.

9. A Burst (of Lightning): bolt, flash, shaft, streak,n.

10. Flash of Lightning Accompanied by Thunder: bolt, thunderbolt, thunderstroke,n.

11. To Burst (of Lightning): flash, fulgurate, streak,v. (fulguration,n.)

12. To Burst (of Lightning—with the Impersonal Subject "It"): lighten, lightning,v.

13. Bursting (of Lightning): flashing, fulgurant, fulgurous,adj.

14. Resembling Lightning: fulgurant, fulgurous,adj.

15. Full of Lightning: fulgurous,adj.

16. To Flash Like Lightning: fulgurate,v. (fulguration,n.)

17. To Move Like Lightning, i.e., Very Fast and Suddenly: flash, streak,v.

18. Conductor Placed on a Structure to Divert Lightning by Providing a Means for It to Reach the Ground: lightning conductor, lightning rod,n.

1045. AIR

1. Air,n.
1. airflow—current caused by an object moving through air
2. atmosphere—the air, or envelope of air, surrounding the earth (atmospheric, atmospherical,adj.)
3. breeze, breath—light or gentle current of air

4. current, waft—air moving in a certain direction
5. draft, draught—current of air in an enclosed place
6. eddy—current of air running against the main current, or the movement of such (eddy,v.)
7. ozone—pure or refreshing air (colloq.)
8. vortex, whirlwind—whirling or rapidly rotating mass or eddy of air or wind, or the movement of such (vortical, vorticose, vortiginous,adj.)
9. waterspout—column of moisture-filled air, often shaped like a funnel, rotating rapidly as it descends from a storm cloud to a body of water (also called *twister* in parts of the U.S.)

2. Bit of Air, Smoke, or Vapor Suddenly Blown out of Something: blast or flow (forcible), puff, waft, whiff,n.

3. Forcible Rush of Air: blast,n.

4. Sound Carried on the Air: waft,n.

5. Odor Carried on the Air: waft, whiff,n.

6. Open to a Current of Air: airy, breezy, drafty or draughty (esp. of an enclosed place),adj. (airiness, breeziness, draftiness or draughtiness,n.)

7. To Expose or Open to Air, or Let Air Circulate through: aerate, aerify, air, ventilate,v. (aeration, aerification, airing, ventilation,n. aerator, ventilator,n. ventilative,adj.)

8. Pipe, Passage, etc., for Ventilating a Place, Room, etc.: ventiduct,n.

9. To Circulate through and Make (a Place) Fresh—of Air or Wind: ventilate,v. (ventilation,n. ventilative,adj.)

10. Out in the Air: alfresco, open-air, outdoor, out-of-door, out-of-doors,adj.

11. In the Open Air: alfresco, outdoors, out-of-doors,adv.

12. In the Open Air at Night: à la belle étoile, adv. (French)

13. The Open Air: the outdoors, the out-of-doors,n.

14. Relating, or Related, to Air,adj.
1. aerial—pert. to, in, growing in, living in, or frequenting, the air
2. aeriferous—carrying or conveying air
3. air-borne—carried by, or through, the air
4. airproof, airtight, hermetic—not permeable by air
5. airworthy—safe for flying in the air—of aircraft (airworthiness,n.)
6. airy—consisting of air; full of air or breezes
7. pneumatic—pert. to, operating or operated by means of, or containing, air; inflated or inflatable with compressed air, as a tire or tube

15. To Make Impermeable by Air: airproof, v.

16. To Dry by Means of Air: air-dry,v.

17. So Dried: air-dry,adj.

18. Like, or of the Nature or Quality of, Air: aerial, aeriform, airy,adj. (airiness,n.)

19. To Turn (Something) into, or Make Like, Air: aerify,v. (aerification,n.)

20. Selected Sciences, etc., Dealing with Air and Other Gases,n.
1. aerodynamics—with the motion of air and other gases (aerodynamic,adj.)
2. aeromechanics—with the action, movement, etc., of air and other gases (aeromechanic,adj.)
3. pneumatics, pneumodynamics, aerometry—with the pressure, density, and other mechanical properties of air and other gases (pneumatic, aerometric,adj.)

21. Devices Used in Measuring, etc., Air and Other Gases,n.

  1. aerometer—in measuring weight, density, etc., of air and other gases (aerometric, adj.)

  2. aeroscope—in collecting microscopic particles or objects from the air

  3. airometer, air meter—in measuring the speed of the flow of air

  4. pneumatometer—in measuring the amount of air absorbed or expelled in a single breath

22. Morbid Dread of Harmful Influences Carried by Air, or of Drafts of Air or Gas: aerophobia,n.

23. The Gulping In of Air Caused by Neurotic Stomach Disturbances (Psychiatry): aerophagia,n.

24. Sickness Resulting from Traveling through the Air in Planes, etc.: airsickness, n. (airsick,adj.)

25. Lacking in Freely Circulating, or Fresh, Air, as a Place, etc.; Descr. of Air That Is Not Fresh or Does Not Circulate Freely: airless, close, heavy, stale, stifling, still, stuffy,adj. (closeness, heaviness, staleness, stillness, stuffiness,n.)

26. Without, or Lacking in, Air: airless,adj.

1046. THE ATMOSPHERE

1. Description of the Atmosphere: aerography,n. (aerographer,n. aerographic, aerographical,adj.)

2. Atmospheric Phenomena, Forces, etc., as Wind, Rain, Snow, Hail, Weather, etc.: the elements,pl.n.

3. Pert. to Atmospheric Phenomena: meteoric, meteorologic, meteorological,adj.

4. An Atmospheric Phenomenon, as a Rainbow, Thunder, Hail, etc.: meteor,n.

5. Atmospheric Electricity or Other Disturbances That Cause Interfering Sounds on a Radio: static,n.

6. Condition of the Existence of Rain, Snow, Hail, Fog, Mist, Clouds, etc., in the Atmosphere, or the Influence of One or More of These: hydrometeor,n.

7. To Change, or Be Changed, as by Drying, Seasoning, Discoloring, Disintegrating, etc., as a Result of Exposure to the Atmosphere or the Air: weather,v.

8. So Changed: weather-beaten, weathered, weatherworn,adj.

9. Pressure of the Atmosphere: air pressure, atmospheric pressure,n.

10. Owing to, or Caused by, Atmospheric Pressure: aeolian,adj.

11. Pert. to the Pressure or Weight of the Atmosphere: baric,adj.

12. Line on a Weather Map Connecting Points Having the Same Atmospheric Pressure: isobar,n. (isobaric,adj.)

13. Having the Same Atmospheric Pressure: isobaric,adj.

14. Layers or Regions of the Atmosphere: troposphere (inner layer or region, below the stratosphere); substratosphere (below the stratosphere, but beyond 3½ miles from the earth); tropopause (top of the troposphere, i.e., between the troposphere and the stratosphere); stratosphere or isothermal region (outer region, beyond the troposphere); ionosphere (beyond the stratosphere),n. (stratospheric,adj.)

15. Plane Capable of Flying in the Stratosphere: stratocruiser,n.

16. Transmission of Television and of Frequency-Modulation Radio Programs from Planes Flying in the Stratosphere: stratovision,n.

17. Sciences Dealing with the Atmosphere,n.

  1. aerographics—with atmospheric phenomena

  2. aerology—with the properties of the atmosphere (aerologist,n aerological,adj.)

  3. climatology—with the weather, climate, or general condition of the atmosphere of a locality or region, including pressure, temperature, precipitation, etc. (climatologist,n. climatologic, climatological,adj.)

  4. meteorology—with the atmosphere and atmospheric phenomena, esp. in relation to climate or weather (meteorologist,n. meteorologic, meteorological,adj.)

  5. paleoclimatology—with the weather or climate of past geologic periods or eras (paleoclimatologist,n.)

  6. phenology—with the effects of climate on various phenomena of plant and animal life (phenologist,n. phenological,adj.)

18. Instruments or Devices for Registering, Recording, or Measuring Atmospheric Qualities or Changes,n.

  1. anemoscope—for indicating coming changes in weather

  2. aneroid, aneroid barometer—barometer containing a needle or pointer that is moved by changes in atmospheric pressure

  3. barograph—for automatically recording atmospheric pressure or the changes in it (barographic,adj.)

  4. barometer, weatherglass—for determining and measuring atmospheric pressure, in order to forecast weather, determine height, etc. (barometric, barometrical, or baric,adj.)

  5. baroscope—for indicating approximately the changes in atmospheric pressure (baroscopic, baroscopical,adj.)

  6. barothermograph—for recording atmospheric pressure and temperature

  7. barothermohygrograph—for recording automatically atmospheric pressure, temperature, and humidity

  8. hygrograph—for automatically recording the changes in atmospheric humidity

  9. hygrometer—for measuring atmospheric humidity (hygrometric, hygrometrical, adj.)

  10. hygroscope, weatherglass—for indicating changes in atmospheric humidity (hygroscopic, hygroscopical,adj.)

  11. hygrothermograph—for recording atmospheric humidity and temperature

  12. meteorograph—for recording automatically various atmospheric conditions

  13. statoscope—for registering small changes in atmospheric pressure

19. The Use of, or the Art of Using, the Barometer: barometry,n.

20. That Which, Figuratively, Records or Indicates Changes the Way a Barometer Does, as in Public Opinion or Other Conditions: barometer,n.

21. The Record Made by a Barograph: barogram,n.

22. Science of Atmospheric Humidity: hygrology,n.

23. Science of Determining or Measuring Atmospheric Humidity: hygrometry, hygrostatics,n. (hygrometric, hygrometrical,adj.)

1047. WEATHER

1. General Condition of the Atmosphere of a Locality or Region, Including Pressure, Temperature, Precipitation, etc.: climate; clime (poetic) ; weather,n.

2. Pert. to This: climatic, meteorologic or meterological,adj.

3. Region or Area Where Such Condition Prevails: climate; clime (poetic),n.

4. Pert. to the Climate or Weather of Past Geologic Periods or Eras: paleoclimatic,adj.

5. In Keeping with the Normal Weather of a Season: seasonable,adj. (seasonableness,n.)

6. Period of a Particular Kind of Weather: spell,n.

7. Descr. of Mild Climate, i.e., neither Very Hot nor Very Cold: moderate, temperate, adj. (moderateness, temperateness,n.)

8. To Expose (Something) to the Weather; To Withstand Such Exposure: weather,v.

9. Changed, Dried, Seasoned, Hardened, etc., by Such Exposure: weather-beaten, weathered, weatherworn,adj.

10. Able to Withstand Such Exposure: weatherproof,adj.

11. To Make So Able: weatherproof,v.

12. A Strip of Material Attached to the Joints of Windows or Doors to Make Tight against the Weather, i.e., the Cold, Wind, Rain, etc.: weather strip, weather stripping, n. (weather stripping, collective n.)

13. To Attach Such to: weather-strip,v.

14. Delayed or Held Back by Bad Weather: weather-bound,adj.

15. Map Showing Climatic or Weather Conditions over a Large Region: weather map,n.

16. To Predict Weather: forecast,v.

17. To Predict (Conditions of Weather): forecast,v.

18. Such a Prediction: forecast, weather cast, n.

19. The Making of Such Predictions: forecasting, weather casting,n.

20. One Who Makes Such, Esp. as an Occupation or Profession: forecaster, weather caster, weather forecaster, weatherman,n.

21. Skillful in Such; Hence, by Extension, Skillful in Predicting Any Changes, Reactions, Results, Public Opinion, etc.: weather-wise,adj.

22. Department of the U. S. Government Having Such Duties, etc.: Weather Bureau,n.

1048. GAS

1. Selected Gases or Gaseous Substances,n.
  1. atmosphere—gaseous substance surrounding the earth
  2. butadiene—gas used in making synthetic rubber
  3. chromosphere—envelope of gas surrounding the sun or a star
  4. damp—harmful mine gas
  5. effluvium—slight or invisible vapor; such that is harmful or unpleasant
  6. fluid—gas that can flow
  7. fume, fumes—gas or vapor, generally disagreeable or suffocating
  8. miasma—harmful or poisonous vapor supposed to arise from decaying matter and float in the air
  9. oxygen—chemical gaseous element, without color or odor, comprising about one fifth of the earth's atmosphere
  10. smoke—visible gaseous mixture given off when something burns, etc.
  11. steam, reek, vapor—water in the form of gas, as a result of heating, boiling, etc.
  12. vapor—gas; gaseous substance; gaseous

particles to be inhaled for medicinal purposes
  13. wind—gas in the stomach or bowels

2. Gaseous or Gas, i.e., Pert. to Gas, Gases, or a Gas,adj. From Sec. 1: atmospheric or atmospherical, chromospheric, effluvial, fluid or fluidic; miasmal, miasmic, or miasmatic; smoky, steam, vaporific; Also: pneumatic,adj.

3. Gaseous, i.e., Like, or in the Form of, Gas,adj. From Sec. 1: fumy or fumelike, smoky or smokelike, steamy; vaporific, vaporish, vaporlike, vaporous, or vapory (smokiness, steaminess, vaporousness or vaporosity, n.) ; Also: aeriform, gasiform, gassy,adj.

4. Giving Off or Producing Gas, Gases, or a Gas,adj. From Sec. 1: fuming or fumy; miasmal, miasmic, or miasmatic; smoky, steamy or reeky; vaporific (smokiness, steaminess,n.)

5. To Gas, i.e., Give Off Gas or a Gas,v. From Sec. 1: fume, smoke, steam or reek, vapor; break wind (from wind)

6. Full of Fumes: fumy,adj.

7. To Expose to, or Treat or Fill with, Fumes: fume, or, esp. to disinfect or kill the verminous animal life in, fumigate,v. (fumigation,n.)

8. Person or Device That Fumigates: fumigator,n.

9. Caused or Produced by Miasma: miasmal, miasmic, miasmatic,adj.

10. Science of Gas Measurement; Determination of the Amount of Gas in a Mixture: gasometry,n.

11. Process or Science of Chemically Measuring and Analyzing a Gas: eudiometry,n. (eudiometric, eudiometrical,adj.)

12. Device Used in Measuring Gas,n.
  1. eudiometer—in chemically measuring and analyzing a gas (eudiometric, eudiometrical,adj.)
  2. gas meter—in measuring the quantity of gas, esp. illuminating or heating gas, consumed
  3. gasometer, airometer—in measuring gas

13. Person Who Reads Gas Meters, to Determine and Record the Quantity Consumed: gasman,n.

14. Device to Hold or Store Gas: airometer; gas main (i.e., a large or main pipe, usually underground) ; gasometer, gas tank,n.

15. Full of, or Containing, Gas: gassy,adj.

16. To Convert (a Substance) into Gas or a Gaseous Form: aerify, gasify,v. (aerification, gasification,n.)

17. To Become So Converted: gasify,v. (gasification,n.)

18. Place or Establishment Where Illuminating or Heating Gas Is Manufactured: gashouse, gasworks,n.

19. Area of Slums, Tough Characters, etc., Suggestive of the Neighborhood of Such a Place or Establishment: gashouse,n.

20. Fixture Attached to a Gas Pipe, as for Lighting or Heating: gas fixture,n.

21. Ornamental Gas Fixture, with Branches, for Illumination: gaselier,n.

22. Such Hanging from the Ceiling: chandelier,n.

23. End or Point on a Gas Fixture from Which the Gas Issues to Be Lighted: gas burner, gas jet, gaslight,n.

24. The Flame of Gas Used in Illumination: gas jet,n.

25. The Light Produced by This: gaslight,n.

26. Descr., Characteristic, or Suggestive, of the Time When Light Was Produced by Gas, Rather than by Electricity: gaslight,adj.

27. Person Whose Occupation Is the Installation and Repair of Gas Fixtures: gas fitter, gasman,n. (gas fitting,n.)

28. Not Permeable by Gas: gastight,adj.

29. To Kill, Injure, or Attack with Gas; To Furnish with, or Expose to the Action of, Gas: gas,v.

30. An Attack with Gas, as in War: gas attack,n.

31. Device Worn Over the Face to Protect One from Inhaling Poison Gas: gas helmet, gas mask,n.

32. To Free (a Place or Thing) of Poison or Other Gas: decontaminate, degas, degasify, v. (decontamination, degasification,n.)

33. To Put Gas, Esp. Carbon Dioxide, into (Water or Other Liquid) in Order to Make It Effervescent, as in the Manufacture of Beverages, etc.: aerate, aerify, carbonate, charge,v. (aeration, aerification, carbonation,n.)

34. Containing Such Gas—of Beverages, etc.: aerated, carbonated, charged, effervescent, sparkling,adj.

35. To Expose to, or Treat with, Steam; To Emit, or Be Emitted, in the Form of Steam; To Go by Means of Steam: steam,v. (steamer,n.)

36. Heated or Heating by, Moved or Moving by, Operated or Operating by, or Conveying, Steam: steam,adj.

37. Full of, Covered with, or Consisting of, Steam: reeky, steamy,adj. (steaminess,n.)

38. Preventing the Leaking of Steam: steamtight,adj.

39. To Convert (a Substance) into Vapor: aerify, evaporate, vaporize,v. (aerification, evaporation, vaporization,n. evaporative,adj.)

40. Able to Be So Converted: evaporable, vaporizable,adj. (evaporability,n.)

41. To Become Converted into Vapor: evaporate, vaporize,v. (evaporation, vaporization, n. evaporative,adj.)

42. Able to Evaporate, or Evaporating, Quickly and Easily; Passing Off Quickly and Easily as, or in the Form of, Vapor: volatile, adj. (volatility, volatileness,n.)

43. To Become, or Cause to Be, So: volatilize, v. (volatilization,n. volatilizable,adj.)

44. To Cause To Pass Off or Rise as Vapor: evaporate, fume; transpire (from its cells—of plants); volatilize,v. (evaporation, transpiration, volatilization,n. evaporability,n. evaporative, transpiratory,adj. evaporable, volatilizable,adj.)

45. To Pass Off or Rise as Vapor: evaporate, fume, transpire, vapor, volatilize,v. (evaporation, transpiration, volatilization,n. evaporative, transpiratory,adj.)

46. An Opening in, or near, a Volcano, from which Vapor, Hot Gas, and Smoke Come Out: fumarole,n.

47. Place in Which Things Are Treated with Vapor, Smoke, or Fumes; Airtight Place in Which Plants Are Treated with Vapor for the Purpose of Destroying the Insects or Fungi on Them: fumatorium, fumatory,n.

1049. OXYGEN

1. Chemical Compound, Usually of Two Elements, One of Which Is Oxygen: oxide or oxid,n.

2. To Change (an Element) into Its Oxide: oxidate or oxidize,v. (oxidation, oxidization,n. oxidative,adj.)

3. To Combine (an Element, etc.) with Oxygen: oxidate, oxidize, oxygenate, oxygenize,v. (oxidation, oxidization, oxygenation, n. oxidative,adj.)

4. To Add Oxygen or Other Nonmetallic Element to: oxidate, oxidize,v. (oxidation, oxidization,n. oxidative,adj.)

5. To Treat with Oxygen: oxygenate, oxygenize,v. (oxygenation,n.)

6. To Cover with, or Become Covered with, the Characteristic Brownish-Red Coating Caused by Exposure to the Oxygen in Air —of Iron, etc.: oxidate, oxidize, rust,v. (oxidation, oxidization,n.)

7. So Covered or Coated: oxidated, oxidized, rusty,adj. (rustiness,n.)

8. To Combine Oxygen with (the Blood) by Breathing: aereate,v. (aeration,n.)

9. Able to Exist or Be Active in the Presence of Free Oxygen—of Organisms, etc.; Requiring Such Presence—of Tissues, etc.: aerobic,adj.

10. Microorganism So Able to Exist, etc.: aerobe or aerobium,n.

11. Absence or Deficiency of Oxygen, as in Bodily Tissues: anoxia,n. (anoxic,adj.)

12. Able to Exist or Be Active Only in the Absence of Free Oxygen—of Organisms, etc.; Requiring Such Absence—of Tissues, etc.: anaerobic,adj.

13. Microorganism So Able to Exist, etc.: anaerobe or anaerobium,n.

14. Caused by, or Pert. to, the Absence of Oxygen: anaerobic,adj.

15. To Remove Chemically Combined Oxygen from: deoxidize,v. (deoxidation,n.)

16. To Remove Free Oxygen from (Air, Water, etc.): deoxygenate or deoxygenize,v. (deoxygenation,n.)

17. Form of Oxygen with a Weak, Chlorine Odor: ozone,n. (ozonic, ozonous,adj.)

18. Containing Ozone: ozonic, ozoniferous, or ozonous,adj.

1050. SMOKE

1. Smoke; Smoke with a Pleasant Odor, as from Incense; Disagreeable Smoke: fume or fumes,n.

2. Thick Smoke from Slow or Suppressed Burning: smolder or smoulder,n.

3. Suffocating Smoke: fume or fumes; smother (very thick); smudge,n. (smothery, adj.)

4. A Bit of Smoke: puff, whiff, wisp,n.

5. A Bit of Tobacco Smoke Breathed In or Out: drag, puff, whiff,n.

6. To Smoke (a Cigarette, Cigar, Pipe, etc.) in Short Inhalations and Exhalations: drag on, puff, puff on, suck on,v.

7. To Breathe (Tobacco Smoke) In or Out: whiff,v.

8. To Be Engaged in Smoking a Cigarette, etc.: whiff,v.

9. To Draw Tobacco Smoke into the Lungs: inhale,v.

10. Car in a Train Where the Smoking of Tobacco Is Permitted: smoker, smoking car, n.

11. Party for Men Where They Smoke, Are Entertained, etc.: smoker,n.

12. To Give Off Smoke: fume, reek, smoke; smolder or smoulder (without flames),v.

13. To Give Off (Smoke, Fumes, etc.): reek, v.

14. To Give Off as Smoke: fume,v.

15. Giving Off or Producing Smoke: fumy or fuming, reeky or reeking, smoky or smoking; smoldering or smouldering (without flames), adj.

16. Like, or Suggestive of, Smoke: fuliginous, smoky,adj.

17. Pert. to Smoke: fuliginous, fumatory, smoky,adj.

18. Dark or Dark-Gray in Color, like Smoke: fuliginous, smoky, sooty,adj. (smokiness, sootiness,n.)

19. The Blackish Substance, Mainly Particles of Carbon, Rising in Smoke from Incomplete Combustion: soot,n.

20. To Cover or Stain with Such: soot,v.

21. Pert. to, Like, Covered or Stained with, or Full of, Soot: fuliginous, sooty,adj. (sootiness,n.)

22. To Treat with, or Expose to, Smoke: fume; fumigate (esp. to disinfect); reek, smoke; smudge (an orchard, etc., to protect against frost or insects),v. (fumigation,n. fumigator,n.)

23. Place Where Meat, Fish, etc., Are Treated or Cured with Smoke: smokehouse,n.

24. To Color or Stain with Smoke: smoke,v.

25. To Drive or Force Out, or Out of Hiding, by, or, Figuratively, as if by, Smoke: smoke out,v.

26. Protective or Concealing Screen of Smoke; Figuratively, Something Likened to This, Used for Concealing, Deception, etc.: smoke screen,n.

27. Structure for the Escape of Smoke, Combustion Gases, etc.: chimney,n.

28. Such in the Form of a Large Pipe, as on a Building, Steamship, Locomotive, etc.: smokestack,n.

29. Duct or Passage for the Smoke in a Chimney; Duct or Passage for, or for the Escape of, Air or Gases: flue,n.

30. Having, or Producing, Little or No Smoke: smokeless,adj.

1051. SKY; HEAVEN

1. The Sky: azure (blue or cloudless), the blue, canopy; empyrean (believed in ancient times to be the region of the purest fire or light); ether or aether, firmament, heavens; welkin (archaic, except in the phrase *let the welkin ring*, etc.); the wide blue yonder,in.

2. Pert. to the Sky or Skies,adj. *From Sec. 1:* empyrean or empyreal, ethereal or aethereal, firmamental, heavenly; *Also:* celestial, superlunary or superlunar, supernal, uranic,adj.

3. From, Coming from, or Being in, the Sky: supernal,adj.

4. As if out of the Sky; Hence, Unexpectedly: out of the blue,adv. phrase

5. The Sky as a Covering or Arch: arch or vault of heaven, firmament; welkin (archaic), n. (firmamental,adj.)

6. The Clear Sky; The Higher Regions of Air or Space: ether or aether,n. (ethereal or aetherial,adj.)

7. The Visible or Highest Heavens: empyrean,n. (empyrean or empyreal,adj.)

8. Very High, i.e., Figuratively As High As the Sky: sky-high,adj. or adv.

9. Apparent Boundary between the Earth and Sky, as Seen from a Distance: horizon, skyline,n. (horizontal,adj.)

10. Arc of the Horizon (Astronomy): azimuth,n. (azimuthal,adj.)

11. Outline of Figures, Esp. Buildings, Against the Sky: skyline,n.

12. In the Direction of the Sky: heavenward, heavenwards, skyward, skywards,adv. (heavenward, skyward,adj.)

13. The Action or Process of Writing in the Sky by Means of Smoke Released from Planes; The Writing or Words So Produced: skywriting,n.

14. Heaven: empyrean (the highest heaven); Olympus (i.e., the dwelling of the gods in Greek mythology); Nirvana (i.e., the state achieved, in Hinduism and Buddhism); paradise (i.e., as the dwelling of righteous people after death, or as a Mohammedan concept); seventh heaven (Talmudic concept, where God and the highest angels live); the sky; Zion or Sion,n.

15. Heavenly,adj. *From Sec. 14:* empyrean or empyreal, Olympian; paradisaic, paradisaical, paradisiac, or paradisiacal; *Also:* celestial, divine, ethereal or aetherial, superlunary or superlunar, supernal,adj.

16. Inhabitant of Heaven: celestial, Olympian,n.

17. From, Coming from, or Being in, Heaven: heavenly, supernal,adj.

18. Sent by Heaven: heaven-born, heaven-sent,adj.

19. Born in Heaven: heaven-born,adj.

20. Like, Suitable to, or Belonging to, Heaven: heavenly,adj. (heavenliness,n.)

21. The City of God in Heaven: Zion,n.

22. Paradise: Canaan (as a land of promise); Elysium (according to classical mythology, the abode of the righteous or good after death); empyrean (highest paradise as a poetic concept),n. (Canaanitic, Elysian, empyrean or empyreal,adj.)

23. Like, or Suitable to, Paradise: paradisaical, paradisaic, paradisiacal, or paradisiac,adj.

24. Place, According to Norse Mythology, Where the Souls of Heroes Killed in Battle Were Received; Hence, a Kind of Paradise or Heaven: Valhalla, Valhall, or Walhalla,n.

1052. UNIVERSE

1. The Universe: cosmos (as a harmonious and orderly system), macrocosm or macrocosmos, system, world,n. (cosmic, macrocosmic,adj.)

2. Pert. or Relating to the Universe: cosmic, macrocosmic, mundane, universal,adj.

3. Pert. to the Universe Exclusive of the Earth: cosmic,adj.

4. Description of the Universe: cosmography, macrocosmology,n. (cosmographer, n. cosmographic, cosmographical,adj.)

5. Origin of the Universe: cosmogony,n. (cosmogonic, cosmogonical,adj.)

6. Certain Theories of the Universe,n.
  1. cosmism—of the universe as a self-existent system
  2. cosmogony—of the origin of the universe (cosmogonist,n. cosmogonic, cosmogonical,adj.)
  3. cosmology—of the origin, nature, laws, elements, structure, etc., of the universe (cosmologic, cosmological,adj.)

7. Philosophy of the Evolution of the Universe: cosmism,n. (cosmist,n.)

8. Branch of Philosophy Dealing with the Nature, Origin, Structure, Elements, Laws, etc., of the Universe; Science of the Universe, Its Laws, Nature, Structure, etc.: cosmology,n. (cosmologist,n. cosmological, cosmologic,adj.)

9. Science of the Structure of the Entire Universe, Including the Heavens, Earth, etc.: cosmography,n. (cosmographer,n. cosmographic, cosmographical,adj.)

1053. HEAVENLY BODY

1. Heavenly Body: celestial body, celestial sphere, globe; luminary (esp. one that gives light); orb, sphere,n.; *Also:*

1. **asteroid, planetoid**—one of the minor planets, with an orbit between those of Mars and Jupiter (asteroidal, planetoidal, adj.)
2. **bolide**—large, bright meteor; such that explodes
3. **comet**—luminous, irregular body, usually with a nebulous train or tail, traveling in an orbit around the sun (cometary, cometic, cometical,adj.)
4. **fireball**—meteor that gives light, or that explodes
5. **meteor, shooting star, meteorite**—small heavenly body that enters, or passes through, the earth's atmosphere and, owing to friction with the air, becomes white-hot and luminous, and therefore visible (meteoric, meteoritic,adj.)
6. **meteorite**—meteoroid or meteor that has fallen to earth (meteoritic,adj.)
7. **meteoroid, meteor**—one of the small heavenly bodies that travel through outer space
8. **moon**—satellite of the earth (lunar,adj.)
9. **planet, globe, sphere**—solid heavenly body revolving around the sun; heavenly body that, according to astrology, influences a person's life (planetary,adj.)
10. **planetesimal**—comparatively small heavenly body of the solar system that travels in a planetary orbit (planetesimal,adj.)
11. **planetoid**—minor planet; planetlike heavenly body (planetoidal,adj.)
12. **satellite, moon**—small planet revolving around a major planet
13. **star**—self-illuminated heavenly body outside the solar system (stellar,adj.)
14. **sun**—globe of glowing gas, about 866,500 miles in diameter, about 93,000,000 miles from the earth; any self-illuminated heavenly body (solar,adj.)

2. Like a Comet: cometary, cometic, cometical,adj.

3. Like a Meteor: meteoric, meteorlike,adj.

4. Like a Planet: planetary, planetlike,adj.

5. Stricken by the Influence of the Planets: planet-stricken,adj.

6. Small Particles Falling to Earth from Outer Space: cosmic dust,n.

7. Streak of Fire or Light in the Sky Caused by a Meteoroid That Enters the Earth's Atmosphere: meteor,n. (meteoric,adj.)

8. Mass of Metal or Stone from Outside the Earth's Atmosphere That Has Fallen to Earth: meteorite,n. (meteoritic,adj.)

9. Major Planets: Earth, Jupiter, Mars, Mercury, Neptune, Pluto, Saturn, Uranus, Venus,n. (Jovian, Martian, Mercurial, Neptunian, Saturnian, Uranian, Venusian,adj.)

10. Supposed Inhabitant of Mars: Martian,n.

11. Venus, the Planet, So Called because It Is Often Visible in the Eastern Sky before

Dawn: daystar, Lucifer, morning star, Phosphor,n.

12. Considering the Planet Mars as a Center: areocentric,adj.

13. The Study or Science of Mars: areology, n. (areologist,n. areologic, areological,adj.)

14. Group of Heavenly Bodies: system,n.

15. Hypothesis of the Formation of the Planets through the Union of Planetesimals: planetesimal hypothesis,n.

16. The Accepted Theory or Doctrine that the Planets Revolve about the Sun and the Earth Turns on Its Axis: Copernican system,n. (Copernican,adj.)

17. The Sun and the Heavenly Bodies Revolving Around It: solar system,n.

18. Device to Illustrate, by Means of Balls, the Motions and Positions of the Heavenly Bodies in the Solar System: orrery, planetarium,n.

19. Model of the Solar System, or the Building or Place Where This Is Shown: planetarium,n.

20. Curved Path of a Heavenly Body about the Sun: orbit,n. (orbital,adj.)

21. Point at Which the Orbit of a Comet or Planet Is Most Distant from the Sun: aphelion,n.

22. Point at Which the Orbit of a Comet or Planet Is Nearest the Sun: perihelion,n.

23. Pert. to the Conjunction, or to Two Succeeding Conjunctions, of Heavenly Bodies, as a Planet and the Sun, etc.: synodic, synodical,adj.

24. Position or Grouping of the Planets and Stars at the Time of a Person's Birth, Supposed to Influence His Life or Fate; A Person's Fate So Influenced: constellation, horoscope,n. (horoscopic,adj.)

25. Imaginary Belt of the Heavenly Bodies, or a Circular Chart or Diagram of This, Used in Astrology: zodiac,n. (zodiacal,adj.)

26. Signs of the Zodiac: Aries (Ram), Taurus (Bull), Gemini (Twins), Cancer (Crab), Leo (Lion), Virgo (Virgin), Libra (Balance), Scorpio (Scorpion), Sagittarius (Archer), Capricorn (Goat), Aquarius (Water Bearer), Pisces (Fishes),n.

27. Chart of the Planets and Signs of the Zodiac by Which Astrologers Claim to Make Predictions: horoscope,n. (horoscopic,adj.)

28. To Draw Up Such a Chart: horoscope, or cast a horoscope,v. (horoscoper, horoscopist, n.)

29. To Draw Up Such for (a Person): horoscope,v.

30. The Art of Drawing Up Such: horoscopy, n.

31. Measurement of the Positions, etc., of Heavenly Bodies: astrometry, uranometry,n. (astrometrical, uranometrical,adj.)

32. The Mapping, Describing, or Charting of the Heavens and Heavenly Bodies: astrography,n. (astrographic,adj.)

33. Diagram, Chart, or List of Heavenly Bodies: uranometry,n. (uranometrical,adj.)

34. Instrument Formerly Used for Determining Altitude of the Sun and Stars, Solving Navigational Problems, etc.—Now Replaced by the Sextant: astrolabe,n. (astrolabical,adj.)

35. Instrument Used at Sea to Determine Position by Measuring the Angle between a Heavenly Body and the Horizon, or between Two Heavenly Bodies: sextant,n.

36. Science of the Heavens or of Heavenly Bodies,n.
1. astrolithology—of meteorite stones
2. astrology—of prediction, through studying the influence on human affairs of the relative positions of the heavenly bodies—a pseudo science (astrologer,n. astrological, astrologic,adj.)
3. astrometry—of the measurement of the position, movements, distances, etc., of heavenly bodies (astrometrical,adj.)
4. astronomy—of the stars and other heavenly bodies (astronomer,n. astronomic, astronomical, or uranic,adj.)
5. astrophysics—of the physical properties and phenomena of heavenly bodies (astrophysicist,n. astrophysical,adj.)
6. cosmography—of the structure of the heavens and earth, including description and mapping, and embracing astronomy, geology, and geography (cosmographer, n. cosmographic, cosmographical,adj.)
7. uranography, uranology—of describing and mapping the heavens, heavenly bodies, fixed stars, etc. (uranographer, uranographist,n. uranographic, uranographical, uranological,adj.)

37. Pert. to Chaldea, the Ancient Asiatic Region Noted for Its Astrology and Magic; Hence, Relating or Pert. to Astrology, Magic, and Other Occult Learning: Chaldean,adj.

38. One Versed in Astrology, Divination, Magic,etc.: Chaldean,n.

39. A Description of, or Treatise on, the Heavens and Heavenly Bodies: uranology,n. (uranological,adj.)

40. The Use of Photography in Astronomical Investigations: astrophotography,n. (astrophotographic,adj.)

1054. THE MOON

1. The Moon: luminary,n.

2. The Moon Personified: Cynthia, Diana, Phoebe,n.

3. The Moon in Its Various Phases: crescent (in its first or last quarter); full moon (completely illuminated); half-moon (half illuminated); harvest moon (full, about Sept. 22 or 23, the autumnal equinox); new moon (when invisible or, shortly thereafter, when a very slim crescent); old moon or waning moon (after fullness, as the area of illumination decreases); waxing moon (before fullness, as the area of illumination increases),n.

4. Shaped Like a Half-Moon: half-moon, semilunar,adj.

5. Shaped Like the Moon in Its First or Last Quarter: crescent, crescentic, crescentiform, crescentlike, crescentoid, crescentshaped, lunar, lunate, lunated, lunoid, mooned, moonlike, moon-shaped, moony, semilunar,adj.

6. Such a Shape: crescent,n.

7. To Decrease Periodically in Illumination after the Full Moon: wane,v. (wane,n waning,adj.)

8. To So Increase before the Full Moon: wax,v. (waxing,adj.)

9. Pert. to That Period when the Moon Is Invisible, between the Old and New Moon, About Four Days: interlunar,adj.

10. Period of the Complete Revolution of the Moon around the Earth: lunar month,n.

11. Period between One New Moon and the Next, About 29½ Days: lunar month, lunation, synodic month,n.

12. Twelve Such Periods, About 354 1/3 Days: lunar year,n.

13. Period of the New Moon: neomenia,n.

14. Descr. of the Moon When Over Half but Less than Full: gibbous or gibbose,adj. (gibbousness,n.)

15. Goddess of the Moon: Artemis, Cynthia, or Phoebe (Greek); Diana (Roman),n.

16. Supposed Dweller on, or Inhabitant of, the Moon: lunarian,n.

17. Pert. or Relating to the Moon: lunar, moony,adj.

18. Characteristic of the Moon: moonlike, moony,adj.

19. Resembling the Moon: lunar, moonish, moonlike,adj.

20. Resembling the Moon in Shape, i.e, Round: lunar, mooned, moonlike, moonshaped, moony,adj.

21. Decorated or Marked with Moons or Crescents: mooned,adj.

22. Having a Face As Round As the Moon: moonfaced,adj.

23. Beneath the Moon: sublunar, sublunary, adj.

24. Beyond or above the Moon: superlunar, superlunary,adj.

25. Point Where the Moon, in Its Orbit, Is Farthest from the Earth: apogee,n. (apogeal, apogean,adj.)

26. Point Where the Moon, in Its Orbit, Is Nearest the Earth: perigee,n. (perigeal,adj.)

27. Science of the Moon: selenography (esp. its physical features), selenology,n. (selenographer, selenographist, or lunarian; selenologist,n. selenographic or selenographical, selenological,adj.)

28. Picture of the Surface, or Extent of Surface, of the Moon: selenograph,n.

29. The Physical Features of the Moon: selenography,in.

30. Device to Observe the Moon: selenoscope, n.

31. Worship of the Moon: selenolatry,n.

32. Prediction or Divination by Means of Observing the Moon: selenomancy,n.

33. So Influenced by the Moon, Supposedly, as to Have a Disordered Mind, Be Dazed, or Be Otherwise Harmfully Affected: moonstricken, moon-struck,adj.

34. To Act as if So Influenced; Hence, to Wander or Gaze About Idly or Dreamily: moon,v. (mooning,n. mooning, moony,adj.)

35. One Who So Acts: mooncalf, mooner,n.

36. To Spend (Time) So: moon,v.

37. One Supposedly Influenced by the Moon, Hence a Born Fool or Idiot: mooncalf,n.

38. As Changeable or Fickle As the Moon: moonish,adj.

39. Gazing at the Moon; Hence, Absentminded: moon-gazing,adj. (moon-gazing,n.)

40. The Rising, or Time of Rising, of the Moon: moonrise,n.

41. The Setting, or Time of Setting, of the Moon: moonset,n.

42. Without a Moon: moonless,adj.

1055. THE SUN

1. The Sun: daystar (poetic), fireball, luminary; orb or orb of day (poetic), Phoebus (personified); Sol (familiar or personified),n.

2. Relating to, Produced, Influenced, or Determined by, or Operating by Means of the Heat or Light of, the Sun: solar,adj.

3. Pert. to, or Coming from, the Sun: solar, sunny,adj.

4. Directly under the Sun; Having the Sun at Its Highest Point in the Heavens: subsolar,adj.

5. Like the Sun: sunlike, sunny,adj. (sunniness,n.)

6. With the Sun as a Center: heliocentric, adj. (astronomy)

7. Devices, Instruments, etc., Used in Reference to the Sun,n.
  1. heliograph—for photographing the sun or for measuring the heat of sunlight (heliography,n. heliographic,adj.)
  2. helioscope—for looking at the sun without suffering eye injury (helioscopy,n. helioscopic,adj.)
  3. heliostat—for reflecting the rays of the sun in a certain direction (heliostatic, adj.)
  4. pyrheliometer—for measuring the heat and energy of the sun

8. Worship of the Sun: heliolatry,n. (heliolater,n. heliolatrous,adj.)

9. Science of the Sun: heliology,n. (heliologist,n.)

10. Science of the Heat of the Rays of the Sun: pyrheliometry,n. (pyrheliometric,adj.)

11. Seeming Path that the Sun Travels Yearly: ecliptic,n. (ecliptic, ecliptical,adj.)

12. Time When the Sun Crosses the Plane of the Equator, Twice a Year, When Night and Day Are of the Same Length: equinox,n. (equinoctial,adj.)

13. Such a Time at the Beginning of Spring, About March 21: vernal equinox,n.

14. Such a Time at the Beginning of Fall, About Sept. 21: autumnal equinox,n.

15. Time, Twice a Year, When the Sun is Farthest North or South of the Equator: solstice,n. (solstitial,adj.)

16. Such a Time at the Beginning of Summer, About June 21: summer solstice,n. (solstitial,adj.)

17. Such a Time at the Beginning of Winter, About December 22: winter solstice,n.

18. The Apparent Darkening of the Sun by the Intervention of the Moon between It and the Earth: eclipse, solar eclipse,n. (ecliptic, ecliptical,adj.)

19. The Apparent Darkening of the Moon by the Shadow of the Earth: eclipse, lunar eclipse,n. (ecliptic, ecliptical,adj.)

20. To So Darken (the Sun or Moon): eclipse,v.

21. To Expose to the Rays of the Sun; To Treat by Such Exposure: insolate, sun,v. (insolation,n.)

22. To Expose One's Body to the Rays of the Sun: sun, sun-bathe,v. (sunner, sun bather, n. sun bath,n.)

23. To Dry, Warm, Whiten, Tan, etc. (Something) by Means of the Sun's Rays: sun,v.

24. Cured by Such Drying, as Meat, etc.: sun-cured,adj.

25. Exposed, Dried, or Warmed by the Rays of the Sun: sunny,adj. (sunniness,n.)

26. A Room, etc., Exposed to the Sun's Rays: solarium, sun parlor, sunroom,n.

27. The Radiation from the Sun on or at a Certain Place: insolation,n. (meteorology)

28. To Affect by the Rays of the Sun: solarize,v. (solarization,n.)

29. Affliction Caused by the Exposure, or Excessive Exposure, of a Person to the Sun's Rays: insolation, sunstroke,n. (sunstruck,adj.)

30. Not Fading when Exposed to the Sun's Rays—of Colors, Fabrics, etc.: sunfast,adj.

31. Not Affected by the Rays of the Sun: sunproof,adj.

32. The Rising, or Time of Rising, of the Sun: aurora (personified), dawn, daybreak or break of day; dayspring (poetic); sunrise, sunup,n. (auroral or aurorean,adj.)

33. The Setting, or Time of Setting, of the Sun: sundown, sunset,n.

34. Seemingly Flat Surface of the Sun: disk, sun disk,n.

35. Dark Patch That Periodically Appears on Such: sunspot,n.

36. Grayish or Shadowy Outer Part of a Sunspot: penumbra,n. (penumbral,adj.)

37. Darker, Center Part of Such: umbra,n.

38. Period of Time Required for a Planet to Make a Complete Revolution around the Sun: solar year,n.

39. God of the Sun: Apollo (Greek and Roman); Helios or Phoebus (Greek),n. (Apollonian, Apollonic, or Apollonistic,adj.)

40. Goddess of the Dawn or Sunrise: Aurora (Roman); Eos (Greek),n.

41. The Interpretation or Explanation of Myths or Folklore by Reference to the Sun, or to the Sun as a Personification, Esp. When This Is Carried to an Extreme: solarism,n.

42. Toward the Sun: sunward,adj. (sunward or sunwards,adv.)

43. In the Circular Direction of the Path Seemingly Taken by the Sun, or of the Hands of a Clock: clockwise, sunwise,adv. (clockwise,adj.)

44. The Sudden Shining of the Sun through the Parted Clouds: sunburst,n.

45. Without a Sun: sunless,adj.

1056. STARS

1. A Star: celestial or heavenly body or sphere, luminary, sphere,n.

2. A Guiding Star: lodestar or loadstar, polestar,n.

3. The Bright Star Almost Directly over the Northern End of the Axis of the Earth: lodestar, North Star, Polaris, polestar,n.

4. A Star That Suddenly Becomes Dimmer; A New Star That Appears Suddenly and Goes through Such a Process: nova,n. (novae, novas,pl.n.)

5. Group of Stars: asterism,n.

6. Group of Fixed Stars to Which a Name Has Been Given: asterism, constellation,n.

7. To Group, or Be Grouped, As or Like Such Stars: constellate,v.

8. Region or Part of the Skies in Which Such a Group Appears: constellation,n.

9. Any Bright Group or Cluster, Likened to Such a Group of Stars; Hence, a Group of Related Ideas or Thoughts Brightly Clustered around a Central Theme (Psychology): constellation,n.

10. Group of Millions of Distant Stars Visible at Night as a Slightly Luminous Tract, Somewhat the Color of Milk, against the Dark Sky; A Similar but Smaller Group of Stars: galaxy, milky way,n. (galactic,adj.)

11. A Group or Gathering of Famous or Brilliant Persons, or Any Group of Things Brilliantly Arrayed, Likened to Such a Group of Stars: galaxy,n.

12. Group of Seven Bright Stars in Ursa Major, Seemingly Arranged Like a Dipper: Big Dipper or Great Dipper,n.

13. Such in Ursa Minor: Little Dipper,n.

14. Group of Stars Too Far Away to Be Individually Distinguishable by the Naked Eye: star dust,n.

15. Among, or Located among, the Stars, Generally Descr. of Space, etc.: intersidereal, interstellar, interstellary,adj.

16. Group or Patch of Stars in Cloudlike Form beyond the Solar System, Individually Indistinguishable: nebula,n. (nebulae,pl.n. nebular,adj.)

17. To Gaze at Stars or the Stars; Hence, Figuratively, to Be in a Dreamy Mood or Engage in Dreamy, Wandering Thoughts: stargaze,v. (stargazing,n. stargazer,n.)

18. One Who Gazes at Stars; Hence, an Astrologer, or, Humorously, an Astronomer: stargazer,n.

19. Without Stars: starless,adj.

20. Pert. to the Stars: astral, sidereal, star, starry, stellar,adj.

21. Coming from the Stars: astral, starry, adj.

22. Like, or of the Nature of, a Star or Stars: astral, sidereal, starlike, starry, stellar,adj. (starriness,n.)

23. Consisting of Stars: astral, starry, stellar,adj. (starriness,n.)

24. In the Shape of a Star: astroid, starlike, starry, star-shaped, stellate or stellated, stelliform; stellular (esp. if small),adj.

25. Property of Certain Crystallized Minerals of Showing a Star-Shaped Figure in Transmitted or Reflected Light: asterism,n.

26. Showing Such: asteriated,adj.

27. Determined by the Stars: sidereal,adj

28. Measured by the Seeming Movement of Fixed Stars: sidereal,adj.

29. Marked, Dotted, Ornamented, or Decorated with, a Star, Stars, or Star-Shaped Figures: starred, starry, star-spangled,adj.

30. To Mark, Ornament, or Decorate with a Star or Stars: star,v.

31. Full of, or Lighted by, Stars: starry,adj.

32. Covered with Little Stars, or Dotted with Starry Splashes of Color: stellular,adj.

33. Shiny or Shining with, or Like, Stars: sidereal, starlike, starry,adj.

34. Supposedly Influenced by the Stars: starred,adj.

35. Anything in the Shape of a Star, Esp. the Symbol in Printing or Writing Used Generally to Call Attention to a Footnote: asterisk, star,n.

36. To Mark (Material, a Word, etc.) with Such: asterisk, star,v.

37. Three Such, Placed in Triangular Shape before a Passage to Make It Conspicuous or to Call the Reader's Attention to It: asterism,n.

38. Symbol in the Form of a Six-Pointed Star: hexagram, pentacle,n (pentacular, adj.)

39. Symbol in the Form of a Five-Pointed Star: pentacle, pentagram, pentalpha, pentangle,n. (pentacular, pentagrammatic,adj.)

40. Five-Pointed Star Once Used as a Magic Charm or Symbol: pentacle,n. (pentacular, adj.)

1057. CLOUDS

1. Little Cloud: cloudlet,n.

2. Electrically Charged Storm Cloud That Produces Lightning and Thunder: thundercloud,n.

3. Main Cloud Forms: cirrus (icy formations); cumulus (lumpy); stratus (straight sheets),n.

4. Cloud Forms, Masses, or Layers: altocumulus (tight and lumpy or fleecy—over 12,000 feet); altostratus (high and grayish sheet—about 19,000 feet high); castellatus (altocumulus with turretlike projections); cirrocumulus or mackerel (very white and like rippled sand—over 20,000 feet); cirrostratus (solid white sheet of ice crystals—over four miles high); cirrus (thin, wispy, filmy, tufted, and white—20,000 to 40,000 feet high); cumulocirrus (small, white, and feathery); cumulocirrostratus (solid base with icy extensions, the rain cloud of a thunderstorm); cumulonimbus or thunderhead (mountainous mass of condensed vapor—starts at 5000 feet, with a head pushing up to 10,000 feet or more); cumulostratus (cumulus with a sheetlike base); cumulus, cauliflower, or woolpack (white, puffy—about 4000 feet high); cumulus congestus (floating cumulus, very large); cumulus humilis (floating cumulus in clear weather); fractocumulus (ragged cumulus); fractonimbus or scud (ragged nimbostratus drifting under a storm area); fractostratus (ragged stratus); lenticular (detached and in a double convex shape); mammatocumulus (cumulus with nipplelike projections); mare's-tail (spreading cirrus); nimbostratus (dense, shapeless mass of rain cloud—about 3000 feet high); rack (thin, flying, windswept, high, and broken mass); stratocumulus (high stratus, with large balls or rolls of dark formations—about 8000 feet high); stratus (dense sheet—about 1500 feet high),n.

5. Group or Formation of Floating or Drifting Clouds: cloud rack,n.

6. Like a Cloud or Clouds: cloudlike, cloudy, nebulous or nebulose,adj. (cloudiness, nebulousness or nebulosity,n.)

7. Cloudlike Bright Mass of Gaseous Matter beyond the Solar System: nebula,n. (nebulae,pl.n. nebular, nebulous,adj.)

8. Theory, Particularly Famous in the 19th Century, that Our Solar System Condensed into the Sun and Planets from a Nebula: nebular hypothesis,n.

9. Having Cloudlike Markings or Streaks: clouded, cloudy, nepheloid,adj. (cloudiness,n.)

10. Pert. to Clouds: cloudy,adj.

11. Full of, or Covered with, Clouds, as the Sky: clouded, cloudy, heavy, lowery or loury, nebulous or nebulose, nubilous, overcast, overclouded, skyless,adj. (cloudiness,n.)

12. A Covering or Spread of Clouds: overcast,n.

13. To Become Cloudy—of the Sky: cloud, cloud up, overcast, overcloud,v.

14. To Make (the Sky, etc.) Cloudy: cloud, overcast, overcloud,v.

15. Place or Region Figuratively in the Clouds, Hence Nonexistent, Only Dreamed of, etc.: cloudland, dreamland,n.

16. Without Clouds: azure, clear, cloudless, serene, unclouded, uncloudy,adj. (clearness, cloudlessness, serenity or sereneness, uncloudedness,n.)

17. To Clear, or Become Clear, of Clouds: uncloud,v.

18. Cloud of Particles, Dust, Smoke, or Similar Substance: mist, pother, smother,n.

19. Blowing Out Clouds of Tobacco Smoke: nepheligenous,adj.

20. Science of Clouds: nephology,n. (nephologist,n. nephological,adj.)

21. Scientific Examination or Observation of Clouds or of the Clouds: nephelognosy,n.

22. Instruments Related to Clouds or Cloudiness,n.
   1. **nephelometer**—for measuring the cloudiness of solutions, suspensions, etc. (nephelometry,n. nephelometric, nephelometrical,adj.)
   2. **nephelorometer**—for measuring the rate and direction of moving clouds
   3. **nepheloscope**—for exhibiting the formation of clouds
   4. **nephoscope**—for observing clouds, determining their height, the direction and speed of their motion, etc.

1058. COLDNESS

1. Cold: algid; bleak (as the wind); arctic (esp. of temperature or climate); chill, chilly; cutting (as the wind); freezing or frigid (extremely); frosty (of temperature or climate); gelid (extremely); glacial (extremely, i.e., like a glacier or like ice); hyperborean (of regions); ice-cold or icy (like ice); marmoreal or marmorean (i.e., cold and white or smooth, like marble—of things); stony (i.e., cold and stiff); wintry, winterly, or wintery (of climate or temperature),adj. (algidity, bleakness, chillness or chill, chilliness, frigidity or frigidness, frostiness, gelidity or gelidness, iciness, stoniness, wintriness,n.)

2. Unpleasantly Cold; Producing Such a Sensation: algid, chill, chilly; raw (i.e., cold and damp, as climate, temperature, a day or night, etc.),adj. (algidity, chillness or chill, chilliness, rawness,n.)

3. Somewhat Cold: cool,adj. (coolness,n.)

4. Unpleasantly Cool: chilly,adj. (chilliness, n.)

5. Pert. to the Colder Regions of the Temperate Zone: subtemperate,adj.

6. Feeling Cold: chilly; cool (pleasantly or somewhat); freezing or frozen (extremely), adj. (chilliness, coolness,n.)

7. A Feeling or Sensation of Unpleasant Cold: chill,n.

8. To Feel, or Cause to Feel, Cold: chill; freeze (extremely),v.

9. Sudden Sensation of Cold, Often Accompanied or Followed by Shivering: ague; algor (esp. at the beginning of a fever); chill or chills,n.

10. Loss of Bodily Heat (Physiology): thermolysis,n. (thermolytic,adj.)

11. To Become Cold: chill, cool; defervesce (i.e., lose heat),v. (defervescence,n.)

12. To Die of, or Kill by, Cold: freeze,v.

13. To Make Cold or Colder, Cool or Cooler: air-condition or air-cool (a room, place, etc., by cooling and drying the air); air-cool (machinery, etc., by a stream of air); chill, cool; ice (with ice, as drinks, food, etc.); quench (suddenly, by immersing in water, as steel, etc.); refrigerate (food, etc.); water-cool (by water or a stream of water),v.

14. Serving, or Acting, to Cool: air-conditioning, air-cooling, chilling, cooling; cutting (as the wind); frigorific; refrigerating, refrigerant, refrigerative, or refrigeratory; water-cooling,adj.

15. Cooled: air-conditioned, air-cooled, chilled, iced, refrigerated, water-cooled,adj.

16. Process of Cooling: air-conditioning, refrigeration,n.

17. Substance for Cooling: chiller, coolant, cooler, cryogen; freon (a gas); refrigerant, refrigeratory,n.

18. A Drink That Cools: cooler, febrifuge,n.

19. To Make and Keep (Foods, etc.) Cold: refrigerate,v. (refrigeration,n.)

20. Device for Keeping Water or Other Liquids Cool: cooler,n.

21. Cabinet for Keeping Foods, etc., Cold: icebox, ice chest, refrigerator,n.

22. Science of Refrigeration: cryogenics, cryogeny,n. (cryogenic,adj.)

23. Place Where Cooling Takes Place: refrigeratory,n.

1059. FREEZE

1. To Freeze (Something): glaciate or ice (i.e., turn it into ice),v.

2. Process or Act of Freezing Something: gelation (i.e., making it cold and solid); glaciation or icing (i.e., turning it into ice),n.

3. To Freeze or Almost Freeze (Foods): refrigerate,v. (refrigeration,n.)

4. To Freeze, i.e., Become Frozen: ice (i.e., turn to ice),v.

5. State of Being Frozen: frost,n.

6. Degree of Cold That Can Make Water Freeze: frost,n.

7. Frozen Dew, Vapor, Moisture, etc., as a Coating on a Surface: frost, hoar, hoarfrost; rime (from fog or vapor); white frost,n.

8. Covered or White with Such: frosted, frosty, rimy,adj. (frostiness,n.)

9. To Cover with Such: frost, rime,v.

10. To Give a Coating of Such to (Glass, Light Bulbs, etc.): frost,v. (frosting,n. frosted,adj.)

11. The Delicate Lines Formed on Glass, etc., by Frost; Similar Artificial Decoration on Objects: frostwork,n.

12. Consisting of, Attended by, Causing, or Like, Frost: frosty,adj. (frostiness,n.)

13. The Personification of Frost, i.e., Freezing-Cold Weather: Jack Frost,n.

14. To Kill or Injure (Trees, Plants, etc.) by Freezing-Cold Weather: freeze, frost,v.

15. To Injure (Tissues of a Bodily Part) by Freezing Cold: frostbite,v. (frostbite,n. frostbitten or frosted,adj.)

16. The Line beyond Which Frost Does Not Penetrate: frost line,n.

17. Freezing—of Weather: frosty,adj. (frostiness,n.)

18. Frozen: gelid; glacé (esp. foods, desserts, etc.); glacial (i.e., cold and hard, like ice or a glacier); iced; icy (i.e., turned into, or covered with, ice),adj. (gelidity, iciness,n.)

19. Point at Which Water or Liquid Freezes: freezing point,n.

20. Determination of Such for Various Liquids: cryoscopy,n. (cryoscopic,adj.)

21. Preparation of Sugar, etc., Resembling Frost, for Covering Cakes: frosting, icing,n.

22. To Cover (Cakes) with Such: frost, glacé, ice,v.

23. So Covered: frosted, glacé, iced,adj.

24. To Cover (Food) with an Icy Coating of Sugar Syrup: glacé, glaze,v. (glaze,n. glacé, glazed,adj.)

1060. HEAT

1. Hot, of the Weather, Climate, Air, etc.: boiling-hot (extremely); broiling or broiling-hot (extremely); burning or burning-hot (i.e., feeling like fire); muggy (i.e., hot, uncomfortable, and damp); roasting, scorching, scorching-hot, sizzling, or sizzling-hot (extremely); steaming or steaming-hot (i.e., as hot as, or seemingly as hot as, steam); sultry (i.e., oppressively hot, and often close and damp); sweltering (oppressively); torrid (oppressively or painfully); tropical (i.e., extremely, oppressively, or painfully hot, like the climate of the tropics); warm or warmish (somewhat),adj.

2. Such Heat: mugginess, sultriness, torridity or torridness, warmth or warmness,n.

3. Descr. of Heat or Hot Weather That Oppresses One: close, heavy, oppressive, stifling, adj. (closeness, heaviness, oppressiveness,n.)

4. Extremely Hot Day: scorcher or sizzler (chiefly colloq.),n.

5. Very or Extremely Hot—of Things Other than Weather, Climate, etc.: boiling-hot, burning or burning-hot; candent (i.e., white hot); fiery (i.e., like fire, as wind, sands, etc.); piping-hot (esp. foods); red-hot; scalding or scalding-hot (i.e., enough to burn painfully, as water, steam, etc., or something likened to it); scorching or scorching-hot (enough to burn); sizzling or sizzling-hot (as if just off the fire); steaming or steaming-hot (i.e., like, or full of, steam, as foods, etc.); white-hot,adj.

6. Such Heat: fieriness, white heat,n.

7. To Be Very Hot: sizzle,v. (colloq.)

8. Glowing with Heat: candent, candescent, glowing, incandescent,adj. (candescence, incandescence, or incandescency,n.)

9. To Be, Become, or Make So: incandesce, v.

10. To Be Hot Enough to Shine: glow,v.

11. To Give Off Heat: glow,v.

12. Extremely Hot Place, Room, etc.; Hence, a Place of Severe Test or Trial, or Such a Test or Trial Itself: furnace,n.

13. Moderately Hot: hypothermal, lukewarm, tepid, warm, warmish,adj.

14. Moderate Heat: lukewarmness, tepidity or tepidness, warmth or warmness,n.

15. To Become, or Cause to Become, So: tepefy, warm or warm up,v.

16. Warm or Hot, as Springs: thermal,adj.

17. To Make Hot or Hotter, or Warm or Warmer; To Subject to Heat: broil (by means of intense heat); calorify; chafe (by rubbing or friction, as a bodily part, etc., or by heating, as food, etc.); cook (food, etc.); fire, heat; irradiate (with radiant energy); parch (so as to make excessively dry, or so as to make a person hot and dry, or hot, dry, and thirsty); pasteurize (milk to about 140° F. in order to destroy certain microorganisms); roast; scald (to just below the boiling point); scorch (so as to dry up, shrivel, or wrinkle); toast (thoroughly, over a fire, or so as to brown, as bread, etc.); torrefy or torrify (so as to dry, as drugs, etc.); warm or warm up,v. (irradiation, pasteurization or pasteurism, torrefaction,n.)

18. To Become Heated, Warmed, etc.,v. *From Sec. 17:* broil, cook, heat, parch, scald, scorch, toast, warm or warm up,v.

19. Heating or Warming,adj. *From Sec. 17:* chafing, cooking, parching, etc.; *Also:* calefacient, calefactive, calefactory, calorific, irradiative,adj.

20. Heating by Coils or Pipes in the Walls or Ceilings of a Building: radiant heating,n.

21. To Heat and Cool Gradually (Glass, Metal, etc.) in Order to Prevent or Remove Brittleness, Internal Stress, etc.: anneal,v.

22. To Harden by Means of Heat: bake,v.

23. Producing Heat: calefactory; calorificient (foods, within the body); calorific, calorigenic, pyrogenic, pyrogenous, thermogenic, thermogenous,adj.

24. Production of Heat: calorification (esp. animal); diathermy or diathermia (in subcutaneous tissues, medically); pyrogenesis; thermogenesis (in the body),n. (diathermic, pyrogenetic, thermogenetic or thermogenic, adj.)

25. To Produce Heat in (Subcutaneous Tissues): diathermize,v.

26. Treatment by This Technique: diathermotherapy,n.

27. That Which Generates Heat: thermogenerator,n.

28. Serving to Communicate or Transmit Heat: calefactory, transcalent,adj. (transcalency,n.)

29. Permitting Heat Rays to Pass Through Freely: diathermanous, diathermic, diathermous, transcalent,adj. (diathermacy, diathermance, diathermancy, or diathermaneity; transcalency,n.)

30. Caused or Made by Heat: pyrogenic, pyrogenous, thermotic,adj.

31. Not Permitting the Passage of Heat Rays: adiathermal, adiathermanous, adiathermic, athermanous, athermous,adj. (adiathermancy, athermancy,n.)

32. Device or Appliance for Heating: boiler (for generating steam for heating, for heating and storing water, etc.); Bunsen burner (with a very hot, blue flame—used in chemistry laboratories, etc.); calefactor (small); fireplace; furnace (for central heating); heater, radiator,n.

33. Unit of Heat: British thermal unit (to raise, by one degree Fahrenheit, the temperature of one pound of water); caloric or calory (to measure the heat- or energy-producing capacity of a quantity of food, or, in physics, to measure the heat needed to raise the temperature of water); therm or therme (in physics, having various measurement applications,) n. (caloric,adj.)

34. Condition of Pleasant Bodily Heat: glow, n.

35. To Feel Hot: burn, glow,v.

36. To Feel Very Hot: broil, roast, sizzle,v. (colloq.)

37. Having a Sensation of Pleasurable Bodily Warmth, as from Excitement, Happiness, Liquor, Exercise, etc.: glowing,adj. (glow,n. glow,v.)

38. To Lie in, or Be Exposed to, the Pleasing Warmth of: bake in, bask in, toast in,v.

39. To Expose (Something) to Such Warmth: bake, bask, toast,v.

40. Warm and Comfortable: cozy, snug,adj. (coziness, snugness,n.)

**41. To Suffer from, Feel Oppressed by, Languish from, or Perspire Profusely because of, the Extreme Heat: swelter,v. (swelter,n. sweltering,adj.)

42. **To Cause to Suffer or Feel So—of the Heat:** swelter,v.

43. **To Make (a Person) Feel Hot or Feel the Sensation of Heat:** burn,v.

44. **Receiving Mental or Emotional Stimulation from Heat:** thermonous,adj.

45. **Substance or Agent Used Medically to Produce a Feeling of Heat when Applied Externally to the Body:** calefacient,n.

46. **Ability of the Body to Feel Heat, or to Feel Sensations of Heat and Cold:** thermesthesia,n.

47. **Pathological Condition in Which Such Ability Is Lost:** thermanesthesia,n.

48. **Heat:** caloric, temperature,n.

49. **Heat Caused by Rubbing or Friction, as in a Bodily Part, etc.:** chafe,n.

50. **Heated Condition or State:** calefaction,n.

51. **Growing Warm or Warmer:** calescent, incalescent,adj. (calescence, incalescence,n.)

52. **To Become Warm Enough So That Snow or Ice Will Melt—of the Weather:** thaw,v. (thaw,n.)

53. **Degree or Intenseness of Heat or Cold:** temperature,n.

54. **Pert. to Heat:** caloric, calorific or calorifical; chronothermal (i.e., to heat and time); hygrothermal (i.e., to heat and moisture); photothermic (i.e., to heat and light); thermal, thermic, thermotic, thermotical,adj.

55. **Pert. to, or Designating, the Heat Energy Released when the Nucleus of an Atom Is Split:** thermonuclear,adj.

56. **Without either Gain or Loss of Heat (Chemistry and Physics):** adiabatic,adj.

57. **Descr. of a Change Attended by Heat Absorption (Chemistry):** endothermic,adj.

58. **Descr. of a Change Attended by a Loss or Release of Heat (Chemistry):** exothermic, adj.

59. **Pert. to, or Designating, Equal Temperature:** isothermal,adj.

60. **Line Connecting Geographical Points Characterized by the Same Mean Temperature:** isotherm, isothermal, isothermal curve, isothermal line,n.

61. **Instruments, etc., to Measure or Indicate Heat or Temperature:** actinometer (of the sun's rays); calorimeter (quantitatively); cryometer (very low temperatures); pyrometer (very high temperatures); pyroscope (temperatures); telethermograph (changes in temperatures at a distance); telethermometer (temperature at a distance, electrically); thermometer (temperatures); thermoscope (changes in temperature),n. (actinometry, calorimetry, pyrometry, telethermometry, thermometry,n. telethermogram or telethermograph,n. actinometric or actinometrical, calorimetric or calorimetrical, pyrometric or pyrometrical, thermometric or thermometrical, thermoscopic or thermoscopical,adj.)

62. **Types of Thermometers:** centigrade or Celsius thermometer (with a scale of 0°, for the melting point of ice, to 100°, for the boiling point of water); clinical thermometer (for taking a person's temperature—if rectally, called a *rectal thermometer*), Fahrenheit thermometer or Fahrenheit (with a scale on which 32° indicates the freezing point, 212° the boiling point of water); thermograph (self-registering),n. (centigrade, Fahrenheit, adj.)

63. **Device to Regulate Temperature:** pyro-

stat (for high temperatures), thermostat,n. (thermostatic,adj.)

64. **Regulation of a Person's Bodily Temperature:** thermotaxis,n. (thermotaxic,adj.)

65. **Selected Sciences of Heat,n.**
　1. **calorifics**—of heat, or of heating
　2. **thermochemistry**—of chemical action and heat (thermochemist,n. thermochemical,adj.)
　3. **thermodynamics**—of heat and energy (thermodynamic, thermodynamical,adj.)
　4. **thermokinematics**—of heat in motion
　5. **thermology, thermotics**—of heat (thermological,adj.)
　6. **thermostatics**—of heat equilibrium

66. **Without, or Not Using, Heat:** athermic, heatless,adj.

1061. COOKERY

1. **To Cook (Food, etc.):** autoclave (under pressure); bake (in an oven, under hot coals, etc.); barbecue (under a fire in large pieces, as meat, or whole, as an animal, or in a pot, as meat or fish, with a highly seasoned sauce); boil (in water heated to 212°); braise (slowly, in very little liquid, as meat and vegetables); broil or grill (by direct heat or under, or exposed to, flames); brown (food, as meat, until brown); coddle (gently, as eggs or fruit, etc.); fry (in fat); griddle (in fat in a shallow pan, as pancakes, etc.); parboil or precook (partially, or for a short time, usually for later and longer cooking); poach (an egg, by breaking it into boiling water); roast (meat, etc., in an oven, or coffee beans until brown); rotisserie (on a portable electric grill, esp. one with a turning spit); sauté or pan-fry (in a small amount of fat); scald (in liquid kept just below the boiling point); sear (until the surface is cooked and the juices sealed in, as meat); simmer or stew (in liquid kept just below boiling, or boiling very gently),v. (broil, roast, simmer,n. sauté, adj.)

2. **To Cook, i.e., Be So Cooked or Cooking,** v. *From Sec. 1:* bake, boil, broil or grill, brown, fry, roast, scald, simmer or stew; *Also:* 1. sizzle—fry in hot fat, making a characteristic hissing sound

3. **The Sound of Food Frying in Hot Fat:** sizzle,n.

4. **A Party at Which Food Is So Cooked,**n. *From Sec. 1:* bake; barbecue (outdoors), fry, roast; *Also:* 1. cookout—party at which food is cooked outdoors

5. **Vessel in or on Which Food Is So Cooked,**n. *From Sec. 1:* autoclave or pressure cooker, boiler, broiler; fryer, fry pan, or frying pan; griddle, grill, roaster or roasting pan; *Also:*
　1. **baker**—small, portable oven placed, usually, over the burner of a gas range
　2. **chafing dish**—vessel in which food is cooked and kept hot, as over a candle, etc., at the table
　3. **cooker**—vessel in which food is cooked

6. **Place, Building, or Room Where Food Is So Cooked,**n. *From Sec. 1:* bakehouse or bakery (esp. for breads, cakes, rolls, etc.); grillroom, grill, or grille (i.e., restaurant, etc.); rotisserie (restaurant, etc.); *Also:* cookery, cookhouse, cuisine; galley (of a ship); kitchen,n.

7. **Something So Cooked,**n. *From Sec. 1:* barbecue, broil, grill, roast, sauté, stew

8. **Chicken Suitable for Such Cooking,**n. *From Sec. 1:* broiler, fryer or frier; roaster (also a pig, etc.)

9. Device for So Cooking,n. *From Sec. 1:* broiler, grill or gridiron; rotisserie, electric broiler, or electric grill; *Also:*
1. calefactor—small stove
2. oven—compartment in a stove, fireplace, etc., for baking or roasting
3. stove, cooker, cookstove, range—common appliance with burners on which food is cooked in vessels, and heated by various fuels, as coal, gas, electricity, etc.

10. One Who Bakes (Something, as Bread, etc.): baker,n.

11. Amount Baked at One Time: baking,n.

12. To Bake (Potatoes, Fish, or Other Food) in a Sauce; To Bake (Fish) in Scallop Shells: escallop or escalop,v. (escalloped,adj.)

13. Furnace or Oven in Which to Bake or Dry Bricks, Pottery, Lime, Grain, etc.: kiln, n.

14. To Bake (Such) in Such a Furnace or Oven: kiln,v.

15. To Dry (Such) in Such a Furnace or Oven: kiln-dry,v.

16. To Cook (Food, etc.) Too Much or Too Long: overcook, overdo,v.

17. Cooked Too Much or Too Long: overcooked, overdone,adj.

18. To Cook (Food) Too Little: undercook, underdo,v.

19. Cooked Insufficiently: rare, undercooked, underdone,adj. (rareness,n.)

20. Not Cooked Too Long: rare,adj. (rareness,n.)

21. Not Cooked at All: raw, uncooked,adj. (rawness,n.)

22. Cooked for a Long Time: well-cooked, well-done,adj.

23. Incompletely Baked: doughy, half-baked, adj.

24. One Who Cooks, Esp. Professionally: chef, cook, or, French, cusinier (masc.) or cuisinière (fem.),n.

25. Head Cook: chef,n.

26. Expert Cook: cordon bleu—French (humorous),n.

27. Art, Action, or Practice of Cooking: cookery,n.

28. Book with Recipes for Cooking: cookbook,n.

29. Pert. to, or Used in, Cooking or the Kitchen: culinary,adj.

30. Style or Manner of Cooking Food, or the Food So Cooked: cuisine,n.

31. Cooking Department or Quarters of a Hotel, Large House, etc.: cuisine,n.

32. Roman Goddess of Cooking, and of the Hearth and Hearth Fire: Vesta,n. (vestal, adj.)

1062. BREAD; CAKE; PIE

1. Bread: black or dark bread, corn bread; French toast (soaked in milk and egg, and fried); gluten bread, graham bread; hardtack (used by sailors and soldiers); Melba toast (small, thin, and dry); pizza (prepared with a cheese and tomato topping in Italian cookery); pumpernickel, raisin bread, rye bread, toast, white bread, whole-wheat bread,n.

2. Shaped Mass of Baked Bread, Cake, or Other Food: loaf,n.

3. Individual Shaped Mass of Baked Bread: bagel (ring-shaped, with a hole in the center), biscuit, brioche, bun, cracker; crouton (fried or toasted square, used in soups, etc.); crum-

pet; dumpling (steamed); English muffin; fritter (filled with apple, corn, etc., fried, and served hot); matzo (square of unleavened bread used during the Jewish Passover season —matzoth or matzos,pl.); muffin; pastry shell, pâté, patty, patty shell, timbale, or croustade (filled with cooked or creamed food of various sorts); popover; pretzel (shaped in the form of a loose knot, usually baked crisp, and salted); roll, rusk or zwieback, scone,n.

4. Pancake: crepe suzette (flavored with fruit, liqueur, etc., and served for dessert), flapjack, griddlecake, hot cake, wheat cake; waffle (with the characteristic indentations), n.

5. Device for Baking Waffles: waffle iron,n.

6. Cake: angel cake, cheesecake, coffee cake, coffee ring; cottage pudding (with sweet sauce); Danish pastry, devil's-food cake, French pastry or patisserie, fruit cake, gingerbread, jelly roll, layer cake, marble cake, pastry, pound cake, shortcake, spongecake, Stollen; torte (German); upside-down cake,n.

7. An Individual Small Cake: bun, cooky or cookie, cracker, cream puff, cruller, cupcake, doughnut or, slang, sinker, drop cooky, dumpling, éclair, French cruller, gingersnap, ladyfinger, lemon snap, macaroon, napoleon, petits fours (plural), shortbread, tart; tollhouse cooky (with chocolate bits); turnover, wafer,n.

8. Pie: Boston cream pie, chiffon pie, cream pie, fruit pie, lemon meringue pie, meat pie or pasty, mince pie, pumpkin pie; shoofly pie (with pecans),n.

9. Mixture of Flour, Eggs, Milk, etc., To Be Used in Baking: batter,n.

10. Such a Mixture in a Shaped Mass to Be Baked into Bread, Cake, Pie Shells, etc.: dough,n. (doughy,adj.)

1063. FEVER

1. Fever: ague (malarial, marked by fits of chills, sweating, etc.); calenture (tropical and violent, marked by delirium, and esp. attacking passengers on ships); febricula (not very high, of short duration, and usually of obscure origin); heatstroke (caused by great heat); hyperpyrexia (higher than normal for the disease); pyreticosis, pyrexia; remittent fever or remittent (abating and returning at regular intervals), temperature,n.

2. Pert. to Fever,adj. *From Sec. 1:* hyperpyrexial or hyperpyretic; pyrexial, pyrexic, pyrexical, or pyretic; *Also:* febrile, feverish, feverous,adj.

3. Fever or Ague Characterized by Attacks That Recur Every Stated Day, Counting Both the Day of Onset and of Abatement: tertian (third), quartan (fourth), quintan (fifth), octan fever (eighth),n. (tertian, quartan, quintan, octan,adj.)

4. Causing or Producing Fever: aguish or aguey, febrifacient, febriferous, febrific, feverish, feverous, pyretic, pyretogenic or pyretogenous, pyrogenic, pyrogenous,adj.

5. Substance That Causes Fever: febrifacient, pyrogen,n.

6. Having, or Affected by, Fever: aguish or aguey, febrific, febrile, fevered, feverish, feverous; hyperpyretic (i.e., by a fever that is higher than normal for the disease); pyretic, adj.

7. State of Being Affected with Fever: aguishness, febricity, febrility, feverishness, pyrexia,n.

8. To Affect with Fever: fever,v.

9. Resembling a Fever: aguish, aguey, or aguelike; feverish, feverous,adj. (aguishness, feverishness,n.)

10. Marked or Characterized by Fever, as a Disease, etc.: febrific, febrile,adj.

11. Indicating Fever: febrile, feverish, feverous,adj.

12. The Bodily Heat of Fever: cauma, fever heat,n. (caumatic,adj.)

13. Produced or Caused by Fever: pyretogenetic, pyretogenic, pyretogenous, pyrogenic, pyrogenous,adj. (pyretogenesis,n.)

14. Substance, Medicine, Agent, etc., That Reduces, etc., Fever: antipyretic (prevents, checks, or controls fever), defervescent (reduces fever); febrifuge (reduces or eliminates fever); refrigerant (reduces fever),n. (febrifugal,adj.)

15. So Reducing, etc., Fever: antipyretic, defervescent, febrifuge, refrigerant,adj.

16. To Begin to Lose Fever: defervesce,v. (defervescence,n. defervescent,adj.)

17. Lacking in, or Not Marked by, Fever: afebrile, apyretic, feverless, non-febrile,adj.

1064. FIRE

1. Fire,n.
  1. balefire—signal fire; bonfire
  2. beacon—signal fire
  3. blaze—fire burning hotly or brightly
  4. bonfire—large outdoor fire made for signaling or any other purpose
  5. conflagration, wildfire—large, intense, and destroying fire
  6. flame—fire, i.e., the burning gas or vapors of combustion
  7. hell-fire—the fire in, or of, Hell
  8. phlogiston—fire as a principle, in pre-scientific chemistry (phlogistic,adj.)
  9. smolder, smoulder—fire that burns or smokes without visible flames
  10. vortex—rapidly whirling mass of fire (vortical, vorticose, vortiginous,adj.)

2. Pert. to Hell-Fire: sulphurous or sulfurous,adj.

3. Darting Tongue of Fire: flame; flamelet (small); flicker,n.

4. Tiny Particle of Fire, or Glowing Bit Flying from a Fire: scintilla, spark, sparkle, n.

5. To Emit Such, or Come Out as Such: spark, sparkle,v.

6. Emitting Such when Struck, as Stones, etc.: ignescent,adj.

7. That Which Does So: ignescent,n.

8. Relating to Fire, adj.
  1. empyreal, empyrean—composed of pure or sublime fire
  2. fiery—containing, consisting of, resembling, coming with, marked by, flashing like, or suggestive of, fire (fieriness,n.)
  3. igneous—pert. to, characteristic of, or of the nature of, fire

9. To Set (Something) on Fire: fire, ignite; inflame (chiefly figuratively); kindle, light; rekindle (again); set fire to,v. (ignition, inflammation,n. igniter, kindler,n. inflammatory,adj.)

10. To Stir Up, Poke, Shake, and Feed Fuel to (a Fire); To Poke or Shake Up the Coals of (a Fire); To Take Care of a Fire or Furnace: stoke,v.

11. One Who Does This, Esp. as an Occupation: fireman, stoker,n.

12. To Take Care of the Fire in or of: fire, stoke,v.

13. To Light (a Fire): ignite, kindle; rekindle (again),v.

14. Device Used to Ignite: igniter, ignition,n.

15. The Malicious and Illegal Setting of a Building or Buildings or Other Property, Including One's Own, on Fire, to Collect Insurance, etc.: arson, incendiarism,n. (incendiary,adj.)

16. One Who Does So: arsonist, firebug, incendiary,n.

17. The Morbid Impulse to Set Fires for No Rational Purpose: pyromania,n. (pyromaniac or firebug,n. pyromaniacal,adj.)

18. Great Destruction of Life by Fire: holocaust,n. (holocaustic,adj.)

19. Able to Be Set Afire, or to Catch Fire: combustible, fiery, flammable; ignescent (figuratively, as an emotion, etc.); ignitable or ignitible, inflammable, piceous, tindery or tinderlike,adj. (combustibility or combustibleness, fieriness, flammability, ignitability or ignitibility, inflammability or inflammableness,n.)

20. Something That Catches Fire Easily: combustible, inflammable, tinderbox,n.

21. Substance That Catches Fire Easily: kindling (usually small pieces of dry wood); tinder (any dry substance, esp. such as can catch fire from a spark),n.

22. To Catch on Fire: fire, ignite; inflame (chiefly figuratively); kindle, light, take fire, v. (ignition, inflammation,n.)

23. To Burst into Fire: blaze or blaze up, flame or flame up, flare or flare up; inflame (chiefly figuratively),v.

24. Bursting into Flame: ignescent,adj.

25. That Which Does So: ignescent,n.

26. Catching on Fire Spontaneously: pyrophoric or pyrophorous,adj.

27. The Catching on Fire of Something without the Application of, or Contact with, Outside Heat or Flame: spontaneous combustion, thermogenesis,n. (thermogenetic, thermogenic,adj.)

28. On Fire: ablaze, afire, aflame, blazing, burning, conflagrant, fiery, flaming; flickering (unsteadily); glowing or candescent (without flames); smoldering or smouldering (without visible light or flame),adj. (candescence,n.)

29. To Be on Fire: blaze (brightly or rapidly), burn; flame (brightly or rapidly); flicker (unsteadily or weakly); glow (without flames); smolder or smoulder (without visible light or flame),v.

30. The State, Condition, or Fact of Being So on Fire: blaze, flicker, glow,n.

31. Act or Process of Burning, i.e., Being on Fire: combustion,n.

32. State of Burning with Rising or Darting Tongues of Light: flame or flames,n. (as in *flame* or in *flames*)

33. To Burn (Something), i.e., Partially or Completely Consume by Fire: ash (completely, i.e., to ashes); carbonize (until carbon is formed); cauterize (with a hot iron, flame, or caustic in order to cure or prevent infection in, as bodily tissue, etc.); char (either on the surface, or until black or like charcoal); cinder (to ashes); cremate (completely); incinerate (completely, or to ashes); parch (the surface of); scald (painfully, with boiling liquid or steam); scorch (slightly, or on the surface); sear (the surface of, as meat or other thing, or painfully, as a bodily member); singe (the surface or ends of, as hair),v. (carbonization, cauterization or cautery, cremation, incineration, singe,n. crematory,adj.)

34. To Burn, i.e., Become Burned,v. *From Sec. 33:* char, incinerate, scald, scorch (incineration,n.)

35. A Burn,n. *From Sec. 33:* scald, singe

36. Means, as a Hot Iron, etc., Used to Cauterize: cautery,n.

37. Charred Substance: char,n.

38. To Burn and Destroy Everything of Value in (a Region) before Retreating from the Advancing Enemy: scorch,v.

39. Policy of Doing This: scorched-earth policy,n.

40. Burned or Scorched; Parched, Dried, Dried Up, or Darkened by Heat or Fire: adust,adj.

41. To Subject to Fire or Flame: fire, flame; singe (to remove hair, down, feathers, nap, etc., from),v.

42. Something Burned or Burning,n.
1. brand—partially burned piece of wood; such a piece taken from the fire
2. burnt offering, holocaust—offering burnt as a sacrifice to gods (holocaustic,adj.)
3. charcoal, char—imperfectly burned wood or other substance
4. cinder—burned, or partially burned, coal, piece of wood, etc.; a still hot, but no longer flaming, coal (cindery,adj.)
5. ember—partially burned coal or piece of wood glowing in a fire, esp. a dying fire
6. firebrand—piece of wood or other material that is on fire

43. To Make Black with Charcoal; To Write or Draw (Something) with Charcoal: charcoal,v.

44. Powdery Remains when Something Is Completely Burned: ashes, cinders,n.

45. To Be Reduced to, or Become Formed into, Ashes: ash,v.

46. Like Ashes or Cinders: ashen, ashy, cindery, cinereous, cineritious,adj.

47. Containing, or Consisting of, Ashes or Cinders: ashen, ashy, cindery,adj.

48. Of the Grayish Color of Ashes: ash-colored, ashen, ashy, cinerous, cineritious,adj.

49. Covered with Ashes: ashy,adj.

50. As Pale As Ashes: ashen, ashy,adj.

51. Place for Keeping Ashes: ashery,n.

52. The Still Hot or Smoking Remains of a Fire; Ashes with Glowing Coals or Brands: embers,pl.n.

53. The Ruins Left by Destruction through Fire: ashes,pl.n.

54. The Remains of a Corpse after Being Cremated or Consumed by Fire: ashes,pl.n.

55. Place in Which to Burn Things or Make a Fire,n.
1. ashery—place where wood is burned until only ashes remain
2. cremator—incinerator for garbage, rubbish, etc.
3. fireplace, grate—structure of masonry, etc., in which a fire is made
4. furnace—chamber or compartment in which fuel is burned for heating a house, etc.
5. incinerator, cinerator—apparatus or compartment for burning things to ashes

56. One of a Pair of Metal Supports for the Wood or Logs in a Fireplace: andiron, firedog,n.

57. Screen Placed in Front of a Fireplace: fireguard, fire screen,n.

58. Board That Is Used for Closing a Fireplace: fireboard,n.

59. Brick or Stone Used to Line Fireplaces or Furnaces: firebrick, firestone,n.

60. Space around a Fireplace or Fire; Hence, by Extension, Figuratively, Home, Home Life, or Family Life: fireside, hearth, hearthstone,n. (fireside,adj.)

61. Substance to Be Burned, To Be Used in Making a Fire, etc.,n.
1. fagot—bundle of sticks, twigs, branches, etc., for making a fire
2. firewood—wood used to make fires
3. firing—substance to make or maintain a fire; fuel
4. fuel—inflammable and combustible material used to make a fire, as coal, charcoal, wood, oil, gasoline, etc.
5. funeral pile, funeral pyre, pyre—heap of wood on which a corpse is cremated
6. kindling—small pieces of dry wood, or other substance that is readily ignitable, used for starting a fire
7. peat—piece of organic soil used as fuel
8. pile—mass or heap of wood on which a person is burned to death, a sacrifice burned to the gods, or a corpse cremated

62. Pile or Collection of Peat: peat bog, peatery, peat stack,n.

63. Post to Which a Person Is Tied for Execution by Fire: stake,n.

64. Punishment or Execution by Being Burned to Death: the stake,n.

65. To Make, or Tie, into a Bundle of Sticks, etc., for a Fire: fagot,v.

66. To Furnish with Fuel: fire, fuel,v.

67. To Get, or Take In, Fuel: fuel,v.

68. Materials or Devices of a Combustible or Explosive Nature for Making a Display of Light and Noise, as for Signaling, Celebration of Holidays, etc.: fireworks,n.

69. One Such: firecracker,n.

70. Display Made by These: fireworks, pyrotechnics,n.

71. Pert. to, Like, or Suggestive of, Such: pyrotechnic, pyrotechnical,adj.

72. The Manufacture and Use, or the Art of Making and Using, Fireworks: pyrotechnics, pyrotechny,n. (pyrotechnist,n. pyrotechnic, pyrotechnical,adj.)

73. Fighting by Means of Fire: pyromachy,n.

74. One Who, as at Circuses, etc., Pretends to Eat Fire: fire-eater,n.

75. Alarm That Warns of Fire: fire alarm,n.

76. Device for This: fire alarm, fire-alarm box,n.

77. One Who Fights Fires: buff or fire buff (volunteer or auxiliary), fire fighter, fireman; firewarden or fireward (as in towns, forests, public buildings, etc.),n.

78. Group of Such: fire brigade, fire company, fire department,n.

79. City Bureau for Fighting and Preventing Fires: fire department,n.

80. Vehicle for Fighting Fires: fireboat (marine), fire engine, hook and ladder,n.

81. Place Where Fire Engines, etc., Are Kept: enginehouse, firehouse, fire station,n.

82. Other Devices or Contrivances Used in Fire Fighting, Prevention, etc.,n.
1. firebreak—strip of cleared land to control the spread of fire in a forest or prairie
2. fire drill—practice evacuation of a school or other public building; practice drill of a fire company
3. fire escape—structure erected outside a building for escape when the normal exits are blocked by fire
4. fire extinguisher—portable device for extinguishing a fire

5. **fire plug**—street hydrant to which a fire company attaches its hose
6. **fire tower**—tower erected in a forest as a lookout for detecting fire
7. **fire wall**—fireproof wall to prevent the spread of fire from one part of a building to another

83. Building Susceptible to Fires: firetrap,n.

84. Without Fire; Hence, Lacking in Liveliness or Animation: fireless,adj.

85. To Make (Something) Proof against Fire: fireproof,v.

86. Material Used for Such: asbestos, fireproofing,n. (asbestine,adj.)

87. Not Likely or Able to Burn or Catch Fire: fireproof; incombustible, uncombustible, or non-combustible; non-flammable, noninflammable, or uninflammable; non-ignitible, unignitable, or unignitible,adj. (incombustibility or incombustibleness, non-inflammability or uninflammability,n.)

88. That Which Is Not Able to Burn: incombustible, non-combustible,n.

89. Able to Be Burned, but Not Bursting into Flame: non-flammable,adj.

90. God of Fire and Metalworking: Hephaestus (Greek); Vulcan (Roman),n. (Vulcanian, adj.)

1065. LIGHT

1. Celestial or Atmospheric Light,n.
1. **afterglow**—light in the sky after the sun has set
2. **alpenglow**—light after sunset or before sunrise on the tops of mountains
3. **aurora australis, aurora**—streamers or bands of light sometimes visible at night in the sky of the Southern Hemisphere (auroral,adj.)
4. **aurora borealis, aurora, northern lights** —streamers or bands of light sometimes visible at night in the sky of the Northern Hemisphere, most prominent in arctic regions (auroral,adj.)
5. **crepuscular light**—faint light from a partly illuminated sky
6. **ignis fatuus** (Latin), **jack-o'-lantern, wildfire, will-o'-the-wisp**—light that moves or flits at night over marshes or swamps
7. **lightning**—light in the sky or atmosphere
8. **moonlight, moonglow, moonshine**—light from the moon (moonlight,adj.)
9. **skylight**—light in the sky
10. **starlight**—light from the stars (starlight, adj.)
11. **streamer**—band of light reaching up from the horizon, as at night
12. **sunlight, sunshine**—light from the sun (sunlight,adj.)
13. **twilight, candlelight, dusk, crepuscule, crepusculum**—faint light in the atmosphere just after sunset or before sunrise (twilight, dusky; crepuscular, crepusculine, or crepusculous,adj.)
14. **zodiacal light**—light sometimes seen in the eastern sky before sunrise, or in the western sky after sunset

2. Lighted by the Moon: moonlight, moonlighted, moonlit, moonshiny,adj.

3. Visionary, or Produced by the Imagination, in Allusion to the Effects of Moonlight: moonshiny,adj.

4. Like Moonlight: moonshiny,adj.

5. Occurring when the Moon Is Shining: moonlight,adj.

6. Lighted by the Sun: sunshiny, sunlit, sunny,adj. (sunniness,n.)

7. Lighted by the Stars: starlight, starlit, starry,adj. (starriness,n.)

8. Like the Light of the Stars: starlight,adj.

9. To Light (a Place) with Light from the Sky: skylight,v.

10. Lighted by, or as if by, Twilight; Dimly Lighted: twilit,adj.

11. Not Lighted by the Moon or Sun: moonless, sunless,adj.

12. Process of Using Sunlight to Synthesize Chemical Elements Needed in Growing or Developing (of Green Plants): photosynthesis,n. (photosynthetic,adj.)

13. To Be Engaged in This Process; To Produce (Such Chemical Elements) out of Sunlight: photosynthesize,v.

14. Penetrated by Sunlight: photic, sunlight, sunny,adj.

15. Attraction to the Light of the Sun: heliophilia,n. (heliophiliac,n. heliophiliac, heliophilous,adj.)

16. Pathological Dread of the Light of the Sun: heliophobia,n. (heliophobe,n. heliophobic,adj.)

17. Abnormal Sensitivity to the Rays of the Sun, as of the Skin: heliophobia,n. (heliophobic,adj.)

18. Referring, or Located in, That Depth of Ocean Waters Reached by Sunlight: photobathic,adj.

19. Instrument to Measure the Strength of the Rays of the Sun, or the Effect of X-Rays, Ultraviolet Rays, etc.: actinometer, n. (actinometry,n.)

20. Instrument to Measure Starlight: astrometer,n.

21. Light around a Heavenly Body: aureole or aureola (around the sun or moon, esp. as seen through a mist, etc.); corona (around the sun or moon, or such around the sun seen only during total eclipse); halo; photosphere (around the sun, composed of gas),n. (coronal, photospheric,adj.)

22. To Become Formed into a Halo: halo,v.

23. Bright Circular Spot of Light Sometimes Visible on the Halo of the Sun: parhelion, sundog,n. (parhelia,pl.n. parhelic, parheliacal,adj.)

24. Bright Spot on the Halo of the Moon: paraselene,n. (paraselenae,pl.n.)

25. Circle of Light around the Head, etc., of a Sacred Figure in a Painting or Picture: aureole or aureola, glory, halo; nimbus (also around sovereigns, as on pictures, medals, etc.),n.

26. To Surround with Such: halo,v.

27. Luminous Cloud Supposedly Surrounding a God or Goddess Who Came to Earth; Hence, Any Figurative Radiance Surrounding a Person or Thing, Esp. One of Glamour, Romance, Excitement, etc.: nimbus,n.

28. A Ray of Light: beam, blink; crepuscular ray (from the sun, esp. just following sunset); glance, gleam, glimmer, glint; moonbeam (from the moon); radiation or irradiation, shaft, streak, stream; sunbeam (from the sun); twinkle or twinkling (quick and short),n.

29. Other Light Rays: actinic rays (of short wave length); infrared rays (invisible and of great heat); ultraviolet rays (of very short wave length and invisible); violet rays (of very short wave length),n.

30. To Give Off Rays of Light: beam, blink, glance, gleam, glimmer, glint; radiate or irradiate (i.e., give off rays of light or heat); twinkle,v.

31. Giving Off Such: beaming, beamy, or beamish; gleaming or agleam, glimmering or aglimmer, glinting or aglint, radiant or irradiant, twinkling or atwinkle,adj. (radiance, radiancy, irradiance, or irradiancy,n.)

32. To Come, or Come Out, in Rays of Light or Heat: radiate, stream,v. (radiation,n.)

33. To Give Off (Something) in, as, or Like, Rays of Light: beam, radiate,v. (radiation, n.)

34. To Shed Rays of Light upon: irradiate,v. (irradiation,n. irradiative,adj.)

35. To Throw Back (Received Rays of Light, Heat, Sound, etc.); To Throw Back Such; To Be So Thrown Back: reflect,v. (reflection or reflexion,n. reflectional or reflective,adj. reflector,n.)

36. Throwing Back, or Able to Throw Back, Such: reflective,adj. (reflectiveness or reflectivity,n.)

37. To Bend or Change the Direction of (a Ray of Light): refract,v. (refraction,n. refractional or refractive,adj.)

38. Able to Do So: dioptric, dioptrical, prismatic, prismatical, refractive,adj. (refractiveness, refractivity,n.)

39. Instrument to Measure Refraction: refractometer,n.

40. Instrument to Measure the Index of Refraction: spectrometer,n.

41. That Which Refracts Light: refractor, prism,n. (prismatic, prismatical,adj.)

42. Capable of Being Refracted: refrangible, adj. (refrangibility or refrangibleness,n.)

43. Unit of Measurement of the Power of a Lens to Refract Light: diopter,n. (dioptral, dioptric, or dioptrical,adj.)

44. Instrument That Tests the Power of the Eye to Refract Light: dioptometer,n.

45. To Give, or Give Off, Light,v.
1. **beacon**—shine as a guiding or signal light
2. **bicker**—flicker; glitter; twinkle
3. **blaze**—burn or shine with, or give off, intense light, or intense light and heat; shine brightly
4. **blink**—shine in a faint, wavering, flickering, or unsteady fashion
5. **burn**—give off light; give off light; glow; glow like flames
6. **constellate**—shine in combined brightness, like the stars
7. **coruscate**—give off bright flashes, sparkles, gleams, or glitters of light
8. **effulge**—shine; shine brightly; flash; flash out
9. **flame**—give off the light of, or as of, fire or flames; emit light like that of a fire or flame
10. **flare**—burn or shine with a swaying or oscillating light or flame, or with a sudden burst of light or flame that does not last long; give off light to guide or warn
11. **flash**—give a sudden and short burst of light
12. **flicker**—burn or shine with an unsteady, weak, or wavering light; give off a weak dart of light or tongue of flame
13. **fluoresce**—produce or give off light when bombarded by a stream of particles, or when exposed to external radiation
14. **fulgurate**—flash like, or as, lightning
15. **glance**—flash
16. **glare**—shine or burn so brightly as to dazzle or hurt the eyes
17. **gleam**—give off a faint or subdued light; flash; glisten
18. **glimmer**—give off a faint, wavering, or unsteady light
19. **glint**—flash; gleam; glimmer
20. **glisten**—shine; shine with a faint, sparkling, or flickering light or glow

21. **glitter**—shine with, or give off, a bright and sparkling light or gloss
22. **glow**—shine with, or give off, bright light without flame; shine like something heated until it is luminous
23. **incandesce**—shine or glow when heated
24. **lighten**—flash like, or as, lightning; gleam; shine
25. **luminesce**—give off light without heat, i.e., a kind of cold light, as a firefly, phosphorus, etc.
26. **opalesce**—give off or reflect an iridescent or rainbowlike light or play of colors, or a milky and iridescent play of colors, like that of the opal
27. **outshine**—shine out or forth
28. **overshine, outshine**—shine more brightly than
29. **phosphoresce**—give off light without heat or burning, as phosphorus does
30. **radiate, irradiate**—shine; give off rays of light
31. **scintillate**—give off sparks of light; flash; gleam; sparkle
32. **shimmer**—shine with, or give off, a somewhat faint or subdued and flitting, trembling, dancing, vibrating, etc., light
33. **shine**—give off or cast light; glow with light, or with reflected light
34. **spangle**—shine or glitter like, with, or as with, bright metal disks or plates or similar shiny objects
35. **spark**—give, or give off, gleams or flashes of light, esp. such as are like the glowing particles thrown off by a fire
36. **sparkle**—give or give off, or shine with, a bright, twinkling light, like a gem, or like something wet shining in the sun
37. **twinkle, twink**—emit quick, short, and bright gleams of light; sparkle

46. To Cause to Give Off Light,v. *From Sec. 45:* blink, burn, flare, flash, flicker, glint, incandesce, lighten, shine, sparkle

47. To Emit (Light, or as Light),v. *From Sec. 45:* effulge, flash, scintillate, twinkle

48. A Giving Off of Light,n. *From Sec. 45:* blaze, coruscation, flash, flicker, flare, fluorescence, glare, gleam, glisten, glow, luminescence, opalescence; radiation, radiance, or irradiation; scintillation, shimmer, shine, sparkle, twinkle

49. A Light; Light,n. *From Sec. 45:* beacon, blaze, blink, coruscation, flame, flare, flash, flicker, fluorescence, glare, gleam, glimmer or glimmering, glint, glisten, glitter, glow, incandescence or incandescency, luminescence, phosphorescence; radiance, radiancy, or radiation; scintillation or scintilla, shimmer, shine, spark, sparkle; twinkle, twinkling, or twink; *Also:*
1. **afterglow**—glow left by the passing of something that shines
2. **aureole, aureola**—surrounding band of light or color
3. **blinker**—warning light that flashes on and off, as at a traffic intersection, etc.
4. **candlelight**—light from a candle; any artificial light
5. **coruscation**—play of light
6. **crepuscular light**—faint or dim light
7. **fire**—light likened to, or suggestive of, that from a fire
8. **firelight**—light from a fire
9. **flashlight**—flashing light; flash of light
10. **floodlight**—light giving a uniform illumination over a wide area
11. **gaslight**—light from illuminating gas
12. **lamplight**—light from a lamp
13. **luminary**—a synthetic or artificial light
14. **spotlight**—light focused on a single area, object, or person on the stage of a theater
15. **torchlight**—light from flaming torches

50. Bright; Giving, or Giving Off, Light; Shining or Shiny,adj. *From Sec. 45:* blazing or ablaze, blinking, burning, coruscating or coruscant, effulgent, flaming or aflame, flaring or aflare, flashing, flickering or aflicker, fluorescent, fulgurant or fulgurous, glancing; glaring, glary, or aglare; gleaming or agleam, glimmering or aglimmer, glinting or aglint, glistening; glittering, glittery, or aglitter; glowing or aglow, incandescent, luminescent, opalescent or opaline, phosphorescent, radiant or irradiant, scintillating or scintillant; shimmering, shimmery, or ashimmer; shining, shiny, or ashine; sparking, sparkling or asparkle; twinkling, twinkly, or atwinkle (blaze, effulgence, fluorescence, glitteriness, incandescence, luminescence, opalescence, phosphorescence; radiance, radiancy, irradiance, or irradiancy; scintillation, shininess, sparkle,n.); *From Sec. 49:* afire; *Also:* alight, ardent; argent (i.e., like silver); aureate (i.e., like gold); auroral; beaming, beamy, or beamish; bioluminescent, noctilucal, or noctilucent (of living matter, resulting from internal oxidation); bright, brilliant; candent or candescent (i.e., glowing with heat); cheerful (i.e., bright and pleasant, as a room or other place); circumfulgent (i.e., shining about or around); clinquant (i.e., glittering with, or as with, tinsel); dazzling (i.e., excessively or bewilderingly bright); fulgent (i.e., shining very brightly); fulgid (i.e., glittering); gemmy (i.e., glittering like a gem or precious stone); glossy (i.e., shiny, or shiny and smooth); interlucent (i.e., shining between); irradiate; lambent (i.e., shining softly or gently); lively (i.e., bright, as colors, light, etc.); lucent, lucid, or luciferous (i.e., giving light); luminiferous (i.e., producing or emitting light); luminous, lustrous or lustered, refulgent, relucent, resplendent; satiny (i.e., shining, or shining and smooth, like satin); sheeny (i.e., having a luster or shine); sleek, sleeky, or slick (i.e., having a gloss or shine, and smooth, as a surface, hair or fur, etc.); splendent (i.e., shining or gleaming, as a heavenly body; bright metal, marble, etc.); starry (i.e., shining like stars, as the eyes, etc.); translucent or translucid (i.e., shining through); vivid (i.e., sharply bright, as colors, light, etc.); waxen or waxy (i.e., having the luster or shine of wax),adj. (aureateness, bioluminescence or noctilucence, brightness, brilliance, brilliancy, or brilliantness; candescence, cheerfulness, dazzle, fieriness, fulgor, gemminess, gloss or glossiness, lambency, liveliness, lucence or lucency, lucidity or lucidness, luminosity or luminousness; luster, lustre, or lustrousness; refulgence, resplendence or resplendency, sheen, sleekness or slickness, starriness, translucence or translucency, vividness, waxiness,n.)

51. Vulgarly or Excessively Bright, as with Glaring Colors, etc.: garish, gaudy,adj. (garishness, gaudiness,n.)

52. Something That Shines: lambency (softly or gently), luminary, luminosity, shiner,n.

53. Flashing for a Short Time, or Extremely Brilliant or Bright for a Short Time, Like a Meteor (Figuratively): meteoric,adj.

54. To Make Bright or Shiny: brighten; buff (i.e., metal, etc., by rubbing or friction); burnish (i.e., make shiny and smooth, esp. by rubbing, polishing, or friction); furbish (i.e., by rubbing, polishing, scrubbing, scouring, etc.); gild (i.e., give a bright appearance to, esp. figuratively and often speciously); gloss (i.e., put a shine on the surface of); irradiate (i.e., by, or as if by, throwing light upon, often figuratively); kindle (i.e., make bright); light, light up, or lighten (with, or as with, light or color, or, figuratively, the face);

luster (i.e., by shining, polishing, etc.); planish (metal, etc., by hammering); polish (by rubbing); shine (by rubbing and polishing); sleek or slick (i.e., make smooth and shiny, as a surface, hair, etc.); varnish (i.e., make shiny or glossy in appearance, esp. with, or figuratively as with, varnish); wax (i.e., make shiny or bright by applying a surface coating of wax, or by rubbing wax upon),v. (irradiation,n.)

55. So Made or Become: brightened or bright, buffed, burnished, furbished, gilt, glossy; irradiated, irradiant, or radiant; lighted or lit, lustrous, planished, polished, shined or shiny; sleeked, slicked, sleek, sleeky, or slick; varnished; waxed, waxen, or waxy,adj.

56. Such a Condition of Brightness or Shine: brightness, burnish, gloss or glossiness; irradiance, irradiancy, radiance, or radiancy; luster, lustre, or lustrousness; polish, shine or shininess, sleekness or slickness, varnish,n.

57. Tool for So Brightening or Shining: buffer, buffing stick, or buffing wheel; burnisher, polisher, waxer,n.

58. Substance for Brightening or Shining: polish,n.

59. To Make (a Person) Bright or Radiant in Appearance: transfigure,v. (transfiguration,n.)

60. To Become Bright or Shiny: brighten, kindle, light or light up, lighten, shine,v.

61. To Grow Bright and Clear; To Begin to Become Light, as the Day: dawn,v.

62. Something That Shines: spangle (as a glittering disk of metal, used for decorating, etc., or any small, shiny particle, spot, drop, etc.); tinsel (shiny or glittering metallic substance or yarn),n. (tinsel,adj.)

63. To Decorate with Such: spangle, tinsel,v. (spangled, tinseled or tinsel,adj.)

64. A Sphere of Light: photosphere,n. (photospheric,adj.)

65. To Move Like a Flash of Light: flash, streak,v.

66. Formed of Pure Light: empyreal or empyrean,adj.

67. Pencil-Shaped Firework from Which Sparks Issue: sparkler,n.

68. Impression of Light Received by a Person from Pressure on the Eyeball when the Eye Is Closed, or from Excitation of the Retina: phosphene,n.

69. To Give Light to, Cast or Shed Light upon, etc.: floodlight (over a wide area), illuminate, illumine, irradiate, light, lighten, light up,v. (illumination, irradiation,n. illuminative, irradiative or irradiant,adj.)

70. To Become So Lighted: illuminate, illumine, light, lighten, light up,v. (illumination,n.)

71. To Give Light to, or Cast or Shed Light upon, Again: reillume, reilluminate, reillumine, relight; relume (poetic); relumine,v.

72. To Become So Lighted Again: relight,v.

73. To Cause to Light Up; To Become Lighted: kindle, light,v.

74. To Cause to Light Up Again; To Become Lighted Again: rekindle, relight,v.

75. To Make a Display of Lights, as at a Celebration, etc.—of a Place: illuminate,v. (illumination,n.)

76. To Decorate (a Place) with Lights; To Decorate (a Letter, Manuscript, Page, etc.) with Color or Gold in Such a Way as to Give the Effect of Light: illuminate,v. (illumination,n. illuminator,n.)

77. Amount, Strength, or Intensity of Light, Esp. at or on a Place or Surface: illumination,n.

78. To Dim or Overpower (a Person's Vision) or Bewilder or Confuse (a Person) with Excessive Brightness, Excessively Bright Light or Lights, or Bright and Moving Lights: daze, dazzle,v. (dazzle,n.)

79. To Be So Overpowered: dazzle,v.

80. Producing Light: luciferous, luminiferous; photogenic (biology); pyphoric, pyrophorous,adj.

81. Pert. to the Production of Light by Organisms: photic,adj.

82. Bringing Light: luciferous,adj.

83. A Source of Spiritual or Intellectual Light: lamp, torch,n.

84. One Who Is a Source of Figurative Light to Those around Him, i.e., a Famous Person of Great Mental Power: luminary,n.

85. Produced by Reflected Light: catoptric, catoptrical,adj.

86. Pert. to Reflected Light, or to a Mirror: catoptric, catoptrical,adj.

87. Reflecting Light: relucent,adj.

88. To Cause the Passage or Penetration of Light through (a Thing or Place); To Pass an Intense Light through (a Bodily Part or Organ) for Medical Diagnosis: transilluminate,v. (transillumination,n.)

89. To Light the Way for: beacon,v.

90. Admitting or Transmitting Light Incompletely or in Diffusion; Only Partially Transparent: lucent, translucent, translucid, semitransparent,adj. (translucence, translucency,n.)

91. Only Partially Translucent: semitranslucent,adj.

92. Admitting or Transmitting Light Completely, so that Objects Can Be Seen through It: transparent,adj. (transparence, transparency,n.)

93. That Which Does So, Esp. an Object Containing a Picture or Figure Visible when Held Up to the Light: transparency,n.

94. Not Admitting or Transmitting, or Unable to Admit or Transmit, Light, Sound, or Other Radiation: opaque,adj. (opacity, opaqueness,n.)

95. That Which Is Opaque: opacity, opaque, n.

96. Pert. to Light: luminary, photic,adj.

97. Pert. to the Chemical Effects or Action of Light: photochemical,adj.

98. Pert. to Light and Heat, or to the Heating Power or Influence of Light: photothermic,adj.

99. Requiring Light for the Continuance of Life: photobiotic,adj.

100. Reacting to Light: photosensitive,adj.

101. The Influence of Light on Organisms: photodynamics,n.

102. Selected Sciences of Light,n.
1. actinology—of the chemical effects of rays of light
2. catoptrics, catoptric—of the reflection of light, esp. by mirrors—a branch of optics (catoptric, catoptrical,adj.)
3. dioptrics—of the refraction of light through lenses—a branch of optics (dioptric, dioptrical,adj.)
4. optics—of light and vision (optical,adj.)
5. photics—of light
6. photochemistry—of light as a producer of chemical changes, as in photography, etc. (photochemical,adj.)
7. photodynamics—of the influence of light

on the movement of organisms, esp. plants
8. photometry—of the measurement of light intensity, or of the power of light to illuminate (photometrist,n. photometric, photometrical,adj.)

103. Instrument That Measures Intensity of Light or Illumination: photometer,n. (photometry,n. photometric, photometrical, adj.)

104. Unit of Measurement of the Flow of Light: lumen,n.

105. Unit of Illumination Equal to That of a Candle One Foot Away: candle-foot, foot-candle,n.

106. Illuminating Power Measured in Terms of Standard Candles: candle power,n.

107. Device, etc., That Gives Light,n.
1. astral lamp—oil lamp so designed that no shadow is cast on the illuminated surface
2. blinker—device that flashes on and off, generally for warning
3. bulb—glass sphere, globe, etc., screwed into an electric outlet and able to light up
4. candle—taper of wax burned to give light
5. chandelier, electrolier—contrivance suspended from the ceiling and holding a number of electric light fixtures
6. corona—chandelier of circular shape suspended from the ceiling of a church
7. flambeau—flaming torch, esp. one used for night parades, etc.
8. floodlight—device that projects light over a large area
9. fluorescent lamp, fluorescent light—lamp in which light is generated by passing electric current through a metallic gas or vapor
10. headlight, head lamp—lamp at the front of an automobile or other vehicle
11. hurricane lamp—lamp fueled by kerosene, oil, etc., rather than powered by electricity, and protected by a chimney
12. illuminator, illuminant—that which gives off light
13. klieg light—floodlight used in motion-picture studios
14. lamp—contrivance for giving light, whether by electricity, gas, kerosene, oil, etc.
15. lantern—lamp protected by a shade against the wind
16. luster—chandelier with hanging glass ornaments; one such ornament
17. neon lamp, neon light—orange-red tube, or tubular lamp, in which light is generated by passing electric current through the chemical element neon
18. searchlight, flashlight, torch—portable electric light, powered by batteries
19. spotlight—automobile light that focuses a strong beam on one place; device that projects a strong beam on a theater stage
20. stop light—device in the rear of an automobile that flashes a red light when the brakes are applied
21. taillight, tail lamp—lamp at the rear of an automobile or other vehicle
22. torch—portable, flaming stick of wood or other material; portable device for producing a hot flame, as in welding, etc.

108. Device That Projects Lighted Slides upon a Screen: lantern, magic lantern,n.

109. Structure, Tower, etc., Displaying a Light to Guide Ships: beacon, lighthouse,n. (lightkeeper,n.)

110. Ship Anchored at Some Spot in the Sea, etc., for This Purpose: lightship,n. (lightkeeper,n.)

111. Structure or Post Supporting a Street Light: lamppost,n.

112. A Signal that Lights Are to Be Extinguished, Esp. at Camp, in the Army, etc.: lights out,n.

113. Greek or Roman God of Light: Apollo, n.

1066. ELECTRICITY

1. Flow of Electricity: current, juice,n.

2. Electricity Produced by Chemical Means; Current Electricity: galvanism,n. (galvanic,adj.)

3. Electricity or Electric Power Derived from Falling or Other Moving Water: hydroelectric,n. (hydroelectric,adj.)

4. Units of Electricity: ampere (strength), coulomb (quantity), farad (capacitance), henry (inductance), ohm (resistance), volt (force), watt (power),n. (amperage, ohmage, voltage, wattage,n. faradic, ohmic, voltaic, adj.)

5. Negatively Charged Electrical Particle: electron,n. (electronic,adj.)

6. Electrical Poles: anode (positive), cathode or kathode (negative),n. (anodic, cathodic,adj.)

7. Electrical Conductor: electrode,n.

8. Pert. or Relating to Electricity: electric, electrical,adj.

9. Pert. to, Producing, or Produced by, Electric Current: electric, electrical, galvanic, voltaic,adj.

10. To Activate by, or as if by, Electric Current: galvanize,v. (galvanization,n.)

11. Pert. to Electricity in Motion: electrodynamic, electrodynamical,adj.

12. Pert. to Electricity Not in Motion: electrostatic,adj.

13. Pert. to the Flow of Electricity, or Producing Such: electromotive,adj.

14. Motion Produced by Electricity; Motion of a Current of Electricity: electromotion,n. (electromotive,adj.)

15. To Apply Electricity to, Charge with Electricity, Subject to the Action of Electricity, etc.: electrify, electrize,v. (electrification, electrization,n.)

16. To Prepare or Equip for the Use of Electricity: electrify,v. (electrification,n.)

17. One Who Works with Electricity, Repairs or Installs Electrical Devices, etc.: electrician,n.

18. Magnetism Produced by Electricity: electromagnetism,n. (electromagnetic,adj.)

19. Science of Electricity: electricity,n.

20. Selected Sciences Relating to Electricity, n.

　1. electrochemistry—to the chemical effects of electricity (electrochemist,n. electrochemical,adj.)

　2. electrodynamics—to electricity, electric current, and related magnetic forces (electrodynamic or electrodynamical,adj.)

　3. electrokinetics—to the motion of electricity (electrokinetic,adj.)

　4. electrometry—to the measurement of electricity (electrometric or electrometrical,adj.)

　5. electronics—to electrons in vacuums, vacuum tubes, gases, etc., or in radio or television (electronic,adj.)

　6. electrostatics—to electricity not in motion (electrostatic,adj.)

　7. galvanism—to electric currents (galvanist,n.)

　8. voltaism—to the production of electricity or currents of electricity, esp. by chemical means

21. Instrument Used in Measuring, Detecting, etc., Electricity,n.

　1. ammeter—for measuring strength of currents in terms of amperes

　2. cymometer—for measuring electromagnetic waves

　3. cymoscope—for detecting electrical waves

　4. electrometer—for detecting or measuring a difference of electrical potential between points, etc. (electrometry,n. electrometric, electrometrical,adj.)

　5. electroscope—for detecting the presence of minute charges of electricity (electroscopic,adj.)

　6. galvanometer—for detecting the presence, and measuring the strength and direction, of electrical currents (galvanometry,n. galvanometric,adj.)

　7. voltameter—for measuring the strength of a current, or the amount of electricity flowing through a conductor (voltametric, adj.)

　8. voltammeter, wattmeter—for measuring electrical force, power, or strength

　9. voltmeter—for measuring electrical force

22. Process of Making Electrical Measurements: electrometry,n. (electrometric, electrometrical,adj.)

23. Medical Treatment by Means of Electricity: electropathy, electrotherapeutics, or electrotherapy,n. (electrotherapeutist or electrotherapist,n. electropathic, electrotherapeutic, or electrotherapeutical,adj.)

24. The Use of Surgical Instruments Operated by Electricity: electrosurgery,n.

1067. CANDLE

1. A Candle: dip; tallow candle or tallow (made out of animal fat); taper (esp. if thin); wax candle (made of wax),n.

2. Holder for a Candle: candelabrum or candelabra (with branches), candleholder, candlestick; flambeau (large and ornamented); hurricane lamp (with a chimney); pricket (with one or more sharp metal points on which to stick a candle or candles),n. (candelabra or candelabras,pl.n.)

3. Holder for Candles with Several Branches, and Hanging from the Ceiling: chandelier,n.

4. Holy Candlestick with Seven Branches in a Jewish Temple: Menorah,n.

5. Wick of a Candle: candlewick,n.

6. One Who Manufactures or Sells Candles: chandler,n. (chandlery,n.)

7. Place Where Candles Are Stored: chandlery,n.

1068. WAX

1. Wax; Waxy Substance,n.

　1. adipocere—waxy, brownish substance that sometimes occurs in long-buried or long-immersed corpses (adipocerous,adj.)

　2. beeswax—wax secreted by bees

　3. ceresin, ceresine—a kind of white or yellow wax

　4. earwax, cerumen—waxy substance secreted within the ear (ceruminous,adj.)

　5. paraffin, paraffine—white, waxy substance used for making candles, rendering paper waterproof, sealing jars to preserve the contents, etc.

　6. paraffin wax—paraffin when solid

　7. spermaceti—waxy substance made from

the oil of a sperm whale, used in cosmetics, candles, ointments, etc.

2. To Cover, Coat, Fill, etc., with Paraffin: paraffin or paraffine,v.

3. To Treat, Polish, Shine, Rub, etc., (Something) with Beeswax or Other Wax: beeswax, wax,v.

4. Producing Wax: ceriferous,adj.

5. Like Wax: ceraceous, waxen, waxlike, waxy,adj. (waxiness,n.)

6. Covered with Wax: cerated, waxed, waxen, waxy,adj. (waxiness,n.)

7. Made of Wax: wax, waxen, waxy,adj.

8. The Art of Wax Modeling: ceroplastics,n. (ceroplastic,adj.)

9. Descr. of That Which Is Modeled from Wax: ceroplastic,adj.

1069. X-RAYS; RADIOACTIVITY

1. X-Ray: Roentgen ray or Röntgen ray,n.

2. Pert. to X-Rays: Roentgen, Röntgen, roentgen, or röntgen,adj.

3. Quantitative X-Ray Unit: roentgen or röntgen,n.

4. To Subject to, or Treat with, X-Rays: roentgenize, röntgenize, or X-ray,v. (roentgenization or röntgenization,n.)

5. To Treat with X-Rays for Therapeutic Purposes: roentgenize, röntgenize, or X-ray, v.

6. Such Treatment or Therapy: roentgenism or röntgenism, roentgenization or röntgenization, roentgenotherapy or röntgenotherapy, or X-ray therapy,n.

7. Pathological Condition of Tissues, etc., Caused by Too Much Exposure to, or Treatment by, X-Rays: roentgenism or röntgenism,n.

8. X-Ray Photograph: roentgenogram, roentgenograph, röntgenogram, or röntgenograph; tomogram (of a specific plane of the body),n. (roentgenography or röntgenography, tomography,n. roentgenographic or röntgenographic,adj.)

9. To Take an X-Ray Photograph of: roentgenograph, röntgenograph, or X-ray,v.

10. Impenetrable by X-Rays: roentgenopaque,adj.

11. Able to Be Seen by Means of X-Rays: roentgenoparent,adj.

12. Device by Which to Examine Objects, Including Parts of the Body, through Exposure to X-Rays or Other Radiation: fluoroscope, roentgenoscope or röntgenoscope, n. (fluoroscopy, roentgenoscopy or röntgenoscopy,n. fluoroscopic, roentgenoscopic or röntgenoscopic,adj.)

13. To Examine by This Device: fluoroscope, v.

14. To Examine by X-Rays: roentgenize, röntgenize, or X-ray,v. (roentgenization, röntgenization, roentgenism, or röntgenism, n.)

15. Device to Measure the Dosage of X-Rays in Medical Treatment: roentgenometer or röntgenometer,n. (roentgenometry or röntgenometry,n.)

16. Energy in the Form of Rays, as X-Rays, etc.: radiant energy, radiation,n.

17. Able to Give Off Such, as Radium, Uranium, or Thorium: radioactive,adj. (radioactivity,n.)

18. The Giving Off of Such: radiation,n.

19. To Expose to Such: irradiate,v. (irradiation,n.)

20. To Treat by Such: irradiate,v. (irradiation or radiation,n.)

21. Biology Dealing with the Effects of Such: radiobiology,n.

22. Chemistry Dealing with Such: radiochemistry,n.

23. Rays from Radioactive Material: alpha rays (of positively charged particles), Becquerel rays; beta rays (of electrons); gamma rays (similar to X-rays, but of shorter wave length and higher frequency, and more penetrating),pl.n.

24. Device That Detects and Measures Radioactivity: Geiger counter; Geiger-Müller counter (with amplifying system),n.

25. Radioactive Particles Measured by Such: Geigers,pl.n.

1070. DARKNESS; LACK OF LIGHT

1. Dark; Without Light: aphotic, black, blackish, caliginous, Cimmerian; darkling (poetic); darksome, lightless; murk or mirk (poetic); murky or mirky, obscure, opaque; sunless (i.e., without sunlight); unlighted or unlit,adj.

2. Darkness: blackness or black, caliginosity, dark, lightlessness, murk or mirk, murkiness or mirkiness; nigritude (very deep); obscure, obscurity, or obscureness; opacity or opaqueness, shade; shades (at the end of day); shadow; shadows (after the sun has set); tophet, topheth, Tophet, or Topheth (complete),n.

3. To Darken, i.e., Make Dark or Darker: becloud (with, or as with, clouds), bedim, blacken, cloud, dim, dusk; eclipse (by, or as by, casting a shadow upon, as the moon upon the sun, etc.); gloom, gray, obscure; overshadow (by, or as by, throwing a shadow over); shade, shadow,v. (obscuration,n.)

4. To Darken, i.e., Become Dark or Darker: blacken, darkle, dim, dusk, gloom, gray,v.

5. To Look, or Be, Dark and Threatening, as the Weather, Sky, Atmosphere, etc.: lower or lour,v.

6. Such an Appearance: lower or lour,n.

7. Dark and Gloomy: dismal, somber; Stygian or stygian (like, or suggestive of, the river Styx of the infernal regions); tenebrous, adj. (dismalness, somberness,n.)

8. Area of Darkness: dark, shade, shadow,n.

9. Descr. of Places Enveloped in Darkness: Cimmerian,adj.

10. One of a People Who, According to the Poet Homer, Lived in Continuous or Perpetual Darkness: Cimmerian,n. (Cimmerian, adj.)

11. Giving, or Receiving, No Light: lightless, adj.

12. Causing or Producing Darkness: tenebrific,adj.

13. Overtaken by Darkness, as in Traveling, etc.: benighted,adj.

14. Somewhat Dark: bleak (as the day, etc.), caliginous; cloudy (as the day, sky, etc.); darkish; darkling (poetic); darksome, dim; dismal (i.e., somewhat dark and gloomy); dreary or, poetic, drear (as the day, etc.); dusky, adusk, or dusk (i.e., like, or suggestive of, the darker period of twilight); gloomy (as a day, place, etc.); gray (as the day, atmosphere, etc.); ill-lighted; murk or mirk (poetic); murky or mirky, obscure; shadowy (i.e., covered with, or in, shadows); shady or shaded (i.e., protected from light); somber or sombre (i.e., somewhat dark and gloomy) ; twilight, crepuscular, crepusculine, or crepusculous (i.e., like, or suggestive of, twilight),adj. (bleakness, caliginosity, cloudiness, dimness, dismalness, dreariness, duskiness, gloom or gloominess, murk or mirk, murkiness or mirkiness, obscurity or obscureness, shadowiness, shadiness, somberness or sombreness,n.)

15. To Make (the Vision or the Eyes) Dim, as with Tears, etc.: blear, blur, cloud, dim,v.

16. To Become Dim, as the Vision: blur, dim,v.

17. Descr. of Such a Dim Condition of the Vision or Eyes: blear, bleared, bleary, blurred, blurry, clouded, cloudy,adj. (blear, bleariness, blur, blurriness, cloudiness,n.)

18. Condition of That Seen with Such Dim Vision: blur,n.

19. Having Eyes Dimmed with Tears, Watery Discharges, etc.: blear-eyed or bleary-eyed, adj.

1071. SHADOW

1. Partial Shadow Surrounding the Complete Shadow of the Sun or Moon in Eclipse; Any Partial Shadow around the Complete Shadow of a Body: penumbra,n. (penumbral,adj.)

2. Such a Shadow when Complete; Any Shadow: umbra,n.

3. Like a Shadow; Like a Shadow in Dimness, Slightness, Unrealness, Lack of Substance, etc.: shadowy,adj. (shadowiness,n.)

4. To Throw a Shadow over: adumbrate, overshadow, shade, shadow,v. (adumbration, n.)

5. Throwing a Shadow; Affording Shade: adumbral, adumbrative or adumbrating; bosky, bowery, overshadowing, shadowy or shadowing, shady or shading, umbrageous, umbriferous,adj. (boskiness, shadowiness, shadiness, umbrageousness,n.)

6. Throwing a Faint or Slight Shadow: adumbrant,adj.

7. To Be So Much Higher than as to Cast a Shadow over: overshadow,v.

8. That Which Affords Shadow or Shade: arbor or bower (of leaves, vines, etc., as on a trellis) ; canopy (overhanging) ; eyeshade (for the eyes) ; screen, shade; sunglasses (for the eyes) ; sunshade (against the sun) ; umbrage (the leaves of trees) ; umbrella, parasol, or, humorous, bumbershoot,n.

9. Tree Planted for Giving Shade: shade tree,n.

10. Shade: umbra,n.

11. In, or Enveloped by, Shadow or Shade: adumbral, bosky, bowery, shaded, shadowy, shady, umbrageous,adj. (boskiness, shadowiness, shadiness, umbrageousness,n.)

12. Shadow Picture Thrown, as on the Wall, by Shaping the Hands, etc.: shadowgraph, n.

13. Land or Place of Shadows, Hence of Uncertainty, Unreality, etc.: shadowland,n.

14. Lacking in Shade or Shadow: shadeless, shadowless, unshaded, unshady,adj.

15. Not Throwing a Shadow: shadowless, adj.

1072. DULLNESS; LACK OF SHINE

1. Dull, i.e., Not Shiny, Not Bright, etc.: dim, faded, lackluster, lusterless; mat or matted (in surface finish, esp. metals) ; ob-

scure (as appearance, color, etc.) ; opaque; tarnished (esp. metal or metallic surfaces or coatings, etc.) ; toned-down (i.e., made less bright—of colors) ; unglossy, unlustrous,adj. (dimness, lackluster, obscurity or obscureness, opacity or opaqueness, tarnish, unglossiness, n.)

2. To Make So Dull: dim, fade, obscure, tarnish, tone down,v. (obscuration,n.)

3. To Become So Dull: dim, fade, tarnish,v.

4. That Which Is Dull: lackluster, opaque or opacity,n.

5. A Dull Finish or Surface, i.e., One without Shine, on Metals: mat, tarnish,n.

6. To Give (Metals) Such a Dull Surface: mat,v.

7. Tool for Giving Such: mat,n.

8. Not Shined: unbrightened; unbuffed (esp. metals, etc.) ; unburnished, unfurbished, ungilded or ungilt, unglossed; unplanished (metal, etc.) ; unpolished, unshined, unvarnished, unwaxed,adj.

1073. GOVERNMENT; RULE

1. Government; Rule: administration, domination, dominion, empire, governance; regency (delegated) ; reign (of a monarch) ; sway,n.

2. System of Government: governance, polity, regime,n.

3. Specific or Descriptive Government, or System of Government,n.

1. absolutism, Caesarism, kaiserism—system in which the government or ruler possesses and exercises unrestricted or unlimited power (absolutist or absolutistic,adj.)

2. autarchy—government by absolute or unrestricted rule (autarchic or autarchical,adj.)

3. autocracy, Caesarism—government by one person who has supreme power (autocratic or autocratical,adj.)

4. autonomy, autarchy, self-government, self-rule—government by the group itself, rather than by an outside agency, group, country, etc.

5. benevolent despotism—despotism in which all acts of the government look to the good of the governed

6. coercion—government by force (coercionary,adj.)

7. collectivism—system of government in which the people as a whole, i.e., the state itself, owns the means of production and distribution, and controls all major economic activity (collectivist or collectivistic,adj.)

8. communalism, communism—system of government in which local communities are practically self-governing and independent, but are tied together in a loose national confederation (communalistic, adj.)

9. communism—system of government in which all but personal property is owned in common, i.e., by the state (communist or communistic,adj.)

10. communism, Bolshevism—currently, in Russia, etc., system of government in which economic and other activities are controlled by the state under totalitarian principles, and the reins of government are held tightly by a single, self-perpetuating group (communist or communistic, Bolshevik, bolshevik, Bolshevist, bolshevist, Bolshevistic, or bolshevistic, adj.)

11. czarism, tsarism, tzarism—autocratic or absolute government, or system of government, as or like that of Russia under the czars (czarist, tsarist, or tzarist,adj.)

12. **democracy**—government, or system of government, in which the ultimate power is in the people, and in which there are political and social equality, free elections, etc. (democratic or democratical, adj.)

13. **despotism**—government, or system of government, in which absolute rule is in the hands of a single ruler, often one who wields his authority tyrannically or oppressively (despotic,adj.)

14. **dictatorship**—government, or system of government, in which complete power is in one person, esp. a person who has taken such power without hereditary right or the consent of the governed

15. **fascism, Fascism, or, Italian, Fascismo**—system of government, as instituted in Italy in 1922, in which there is rigid control of production, etc., a strong one-party dictatorship, elements of racism, suppression of opposition, etc. (fascist, adj.)

16. **feudalism, feudal system**—system of government in medieval Europe—vassals lived on land owned by the lord, and in return owed him a certain amount of labor, military service, etc. (feudal or feudalistic,adj.)

17. **hierarchy, hierocracy**—government, or system of government, of a church by the clergy in descending ranks (hierarchal, hierarchic, or hierarchical; hierocratic or hierocratical,adj.)

18. **home rule**—self-government in respect to internal affairs of a colony, dependent country, dominion, etc.

19. **imperialism**—government, or system of government, by one country of another or others, or of colonies

20. **isocracy**—government, or system of government, in which everyone has equal political power (isocratic,adj.)

21. **matriarchate, matriarchy, matriarchal system, metrocracy**—government, or system of government, in certain primitive tribes, in which the mother was the head of the family or tribe, and descent was traced through her, rather than through the father (matriarchal, matriarchic, or metrocratic,adj.)

22. **monocracy**—government by one person, or by one person with supreme power (monocratic,adj.)

23. **nazism, naziism**—German fascism, or totalitarianism, esp. during Hitler's regime (nazi,adj.)

24. **oligarchy, oligarchism**—government, or system of government, by a few, i.e., by a special, small class or group, often for corrupt or self-seeking purposes (oligarchic, oligarchical, or oligarchal,adj.)

25. **papacy, Papacy, paparchy**—government, or system of government, of the Roman Catholic Church, the Pope being the head (papal or paparchical,adj.)

26. **paternalism**—system of government, whether of a country or other group, in which the ruler adopts a relationship to the governed like that of a father to his children (paternalistic or paternalist, adj.)

27. **patriarchate, patriarchy, patriarchalism, patriarchal system**—government, or system of government, in certain earlier social organizations, in which the father was the head of the family or tribe, and descent was traced in the male line

28. **republicanism**—government, or system of government, in which the power is vested in voting citizens and exercised by their elected representatives, and which, usually, provides for an elected

head, or president, rather than for a hereditary ruler (republican,adj.)

29. **socialism**—government, or system of government, in which the state owns and manages the means of production, distribution, communication, etc. (socialist or socialistic,adj.)

30. **sovietism**—government, or system of government, by councils or bodies of delegates, as in the Soviet Union, i.e., Russia (sovietist or soviet,adj.)

31. **terrorism**—government, or system of government, in which the people are kept in constant fear (terroristic,adj.)

32. **thearchy, theocracy, divine rule**—government by God or by a god (thearchic, theocratic, or theocratical,adj.)

33. **timocracy**—system of government in which (after Plato) the rulers are influenced by the love of honor and glory, or in which (after Aristotle) political power is in proportion to the amount of property owned (timocratic or timocratical,adj.)

34. **totalitarianism**—government, or system of government, in which all power is vested in one political group, all others being outlawed, as in Germany and Italy before World War II (totalitarian,adj.)

4. A State, Country, etc., under a Form or System of Government,n. *From Sec. 3:* autocracy, autonomy, democracy, despotism, dictatorship; empire (from *imperialism*); matriarchate (i.e., family or tribe); oligarchy, republic, timocracy (autonomous, autonomic, or autonomical; democratic, imperial, oligarchic, republican, timocratic or timocratical,adj.); *Also:*

1. **aristocracy**—a state in which the rule is vested in a nobility or upper class possessing special privileges (aristocratic or aristocratical,adj.)

2. **commonwealth**—self-governing country; a democracy or republic

3. **dominion**—territory or country governed by an outside state or by another country

4. **Dominion, Commonwealth**—self-governing country in the British Empire

5. **monarchy**—a state in which the rule is vested in a hereditary sovereign, as an emperor, empress, king, queen, etc.—called *absolute* or *despotic* if there are no limitations, as by laws or a constitution, on his rule, or *constitutional* or *limited* if there are such limitations (monarchic or monarchical,adj.)

6. **pantisocracy**—state or community of which all the members have equal political or governmental power—a utopian concept (pantisocratic or pantisocratical, adj.)

5. A or The Government,n. *From Sec. 3:* imperial government, oligarchy; *From Sec. 4:* aristocracy, monarchy; *Also:*

1. (the) **administration**—the constituted executive government of a land, esp. of the U.S. or of one of the states of the U.S.

2. (the) **federal government, the national government**—the government of the U.S. (federal,adj.)

3. (the) **Kremlin**—the government of Russia, i.e., the Soviet Union

4. (the) **Reich**—the government of Germany; under Hitler called the *Third Reich*

5. (the) **Vatican**—the government of the Pope, as distinguished from the *Quirinal*, the Italian civil government

6. **Whitehall**—the government, or the policies of the government, of the British Empire; the British Government

7. (the) **White House**—executive branch of the U.S. national government

8. (the) Wilhelmstrasse—the government, policies of the government, or foreign policy, of Germany

6. Theory, Principles, Policy, Practice, etc., of a System of Government,n. *From Sec. 3:* absolutism, collectivism, communalism, communism or Bolshevism, democracy, fascism, feudalism or feudality, hierarchism, home rule, imperialism or colonialism, matriarchalism, socialism; *From Sec. 4:* monarchism or royalism; *Also:*
  1. federalism—principle of centralized government, as in the U.S., with subdivisions of a country having less political power than, or subordinate political power to, that of the nation
  2. statism—principle or practice of concentrating political and economic control in the centralized government of a country, often at the expense of individual freedom

7. One Who Favors, Advocates, or Supports a Form or Principle of Government,n. *From Sec. 3:* absolutist, Caesarist, autonomist, coercionist, collectivist, communalist or communitarian, communist or Bolshevist; czarist, tsarist, or tzarist; democrat, fascist, feudalist, hierarchist, home ruler, imperialist, isocrat, matriarchist, monocrat, nazi, oligarchist, paternalist, republican, socialist, sovietist, terrorist, totalitarian; *From Sec. 4:* aristocrat; monarchist, monocrat, or royalist; pantisocrat or pantisocratist; *From Sec. 6:* federalist, statist

8. Favoring, Advocating, or Supporting a Form or System of Government,adj. *From Sec. 3:* collectivist or collectivistic, communist or communistic; czarist, tsarist, or tzarist; democratic, fascist or fascistic, imperialistic or imperialist, isocratic, matriarchist, monocratic; oligarchic, oligarchical, or oligarchal; paternalist or paternalistic, republican, socialist or socialistic (imperialism,n.); *From Sec. 4:* aristocratic or aristocratical; monarchist, monarchistic, monarchic, monarchical, or royalist; pantisocratic or pantisocratical (monarchism,n.); *From Sec. 6:* federalist, statist (statism,n.)

9. Person Living under a Form or System of Government,n. *From Sec. 3:* communalist or communitarian, communist; fascist (fascisti,pl.); nazi; *Also:* citizen, subject,n.

10. To Change or Convert (a Nation, etc.) to, or Bring under, a Form or Principle of Government,v. *From Sec. 3:* collectivize, communize or Bolshevize, democratize, feudalize, nazify, oligarchize, republicanize, socialize, sovietize (collectivization, communization or Bolshevization, democratization, feudalization, nazification, republicanization, socialization, sovietization,n.)

11. To Treat (the Governed People, whether of a Country or Other Group) in the Way a Father Treats His Children: paternalize,v.

12. To Become a Democracy; To Become Democratic: democratize,v. (democratization,n.)

13. To Become Bolshevik: Bolshevize,v. (Bolshevization,n.)

14. Governor or Ruler,n. *From Sec. 3:* autocrat or Caesar, benevolent despot; czar, tsar, or tzar; despot, dictator, hierarch; emperor (from *imperialism*); matriarch, oligarch; pope or Pope (from *papacy*); patriarch (autocratic or autocratical, despotic, dictatorial, imperial, matriarchal or matriarchic, papal, patriarchal or patriarchic,adj.); *From Sec. 4:* aristocrat, monarch (aristocratic or aristocratical; monarchal, monarchial, monarchic, or monarchical,adj.); *Also:*
  1. archon—ruler
  2. chief, chieftain—ruler, head, or leader of a clan or tribe

3. chief magistrate, first magistrate, magistrate—ruler or head of a state, whether a monarchy, empire, republic, etc.; head of a U.S. state or city (magisterial,adj.)

4. chief of state—governing head of a country

5. (the) crown, the throne—head of a monarchy, i.e., the king or queen

6. dynast—ruler; hereditary ruler, i.e., in a succession or line of monarchs, or, by extension, of an industrial empire, etc.

7. emperor, Caesar, czar, kaiser—ruler of an empire (imperial,adj.)

8. empress—female ruler of an empire (imperial,adj.)

9. gauleiter, Gauleiter—nazi political governor of a district

10. gerent—ruler

11. governor—ruler of a province, town, dependency, fort, etc.

12. governor general—governor who supervises subordinate or deputy governors

13. head—ruler

14. imperator—supreme ruler (imperatorial, adj.)

15. king—male monarch

16. kinglet—king of a small country or territory

17. lord—ruler

18. majesty—a royal person, i.e., king, queen, etc.; title used in addressing or referring to such

19. overking—king who has jurisdiction over lower kings or ruling princes

20. overlord—one of very high rank in a ruling or governmental system

21. Pharaoh—ruler of ancient Egypt (Pharaonic,adj.)

22. potentate—ruler; monarch; supreme ruler; prince

23. prince—ruler or monarch (historical); ruler with a rank or position below that of a king; ruler of a small country or territory

24. prince regent—prince who rules a country as a regent

25. princess—female monarch (historical)

26. queen—female monarch

27. queenlet—minor queen

28. regent—one who governs a country when, or because, the actual monarch is absent, too young, incapacitated, etc. (regental, adj.)

29. sovereign—monarch; monarch who has supreme power (sovereign,adj.)

30. suzerain—monarch or ruler of a nation that has political control of another nation (suzerain,adj.)

31. tetrarch—minor or subordinate ruler

32. vicegerent—one appointed by a sovereign or ruler to exercise the power of the sovereign or ruler, as in a certain place, etc. (vicegeral,adj.)

33. vice-regent—deputy regent (vice-regent, adj.)

34. viceroy—governor of a country, colony, or province as the representative or deputy of a monarch, emperor, etc. (viceregal, viceroyal,adj.)

15. Governors or Rulers as a Body or Group, or Collectively,n. *From Sec. 3:* hierarchy, oligarchy; papacy or papality (i.e., succession of popes); soviet, thearchy; *From Sec. 4:* aristocracy; *From Sec. 14:* chieftainry, crowned heads or royalty; magistracy or magistrature (from *chief magistrate*); dynasty, line, or succession; regency (dynastic or dynastical,adj.)

16. Rank, Position, or Office of a Governor or Ruler,n. *From Sec. 14:* archonship; chiefship, chieftainship, chieftaincy, or chieftainry; chief magistracy, magistrateship, magistracy, or magistrature; the crown or the throne; emperorship, czardom, or kaisership; governorship, governor-generalship;

kinghood, kingship, or royalty; lordship, overlordship; princedom, princehood, or princeship; queendom, queenship, queenhood, or royalty; regency or regentship, sovereignty, suzerainty, vicegerency; viceroyship, viceroyalty, or viceroydom

17. Authority, Power, etc., of a Governor or Ruler,n. *From Sec. 14:* chief magistracy, magistracy, or magistrature; crown or throne, empire, majesty, regency, sovereignty or regality, suzerainty, viceroyalty; *Also:* 1. royalty—authority, power, etc. of a monarch

18. Country, Territory, etc., Governed by a Ruler,n. *From Sec. 14:* chieftainry; magistracy or magistrature (from *chief magistrate*); kingdom, kingdomship, kingship, monarchy, realm, royalty, or regality; princedom or principality; queendom, kingdom, monarchy, or realm; regency, vicegerency, viceroyalty or viceroyship

19. The Rule or Reign, or Time or Period of Such, of a Governor or Ruler,n. *From Sec. 14:* chieftaincy; magistrature (from *chief magistrate*); dynasty, emperorship, governorship, governor-generalship, kingship, regency, sovereignty, vicegerency, viceroyalty

20. Serving or Acting as a Regent: regent, adj.

21. Relative, etc., of a Ruler,n.
1. crown prince, prince royal—eldest son of a monarch
2. crown princess—wife of a crown prince
3. empress—wife of an emperor
4. prince—son of a monarch
5. prince consort—husband of a reigning queen or empress
6. Prince of Wales—eldest son of a British monarch
7. princess—daughter of a monarch, or of a monarch's son; wife of a prince
8. princess royal—eldest daughter of a monarch
9. queen, queen consort—wife of a king
10. queen dowager—widow of a king
11. queen mother—widow of a king who is also the mother of a reigning king or queen
12. sultana—mistress or concubine of a king or prince
13. vicereine—wife of a viceroy

22. Pert. to a Monarch: kingly, monarchal, monarchial, monarchic, monarchical, princely, queenly, regal, regnal, royal, sovereign,adj.

23. Fit for, Characteristic of, Like, etc., a King, Queen, or Prince; Kinglike; Queenlike; Princelike: kingly, princely, queenly, regal, royal, sovereign,adj. (kingliness, princeliness, queenliness, regality or regalness, royalty, sovereignty,n.)

24. To Make (Someone) a King or Queen: crown, enthrone or inthrone, queen,v. (coronation, enthronement,n.)

25. Ceremony of Crowning a Monarch: coronation,n.

26. To Act or Play the King: king it,v.

27. To Rule (a Place) as Queen: queen,v.

28. To Act or Play the Queen: queen it (over),v.

29. Monarchs Collectively: crowned heads, royalty,n.

30. Palace of a Monarch; Reception Held by a Monarch: court,n.

31. Pert. to a Royal Court: aulic,adj.

32. Suitable for a Royal Court: courtly,adj (courtliness,n.)

33. Member or Frequenter of a Royal Court: courtier,n.

34. Principle of the Supremacy of Monarchs; Principle of Such in Church Matters: regalism,n.

35. Support of a Claim to a Monarch's Throne by Virtue of Direct Hereditary Descent: legitimism,n. (legitimist or legitimatist,n. legitimist, legitimistic,adj.)

36. Governor or Ruler of Certain Specific Countries, Regions, Places, etc.,n.
1. amir, ameer—ruler, prince, or member of the nobility of Mohammedan countries
2. Amir—title, formerly, of the ruler of Afghanistan
3. begum—Moslem female ruler or princess in India
4. bey—native ruler of Tunis; governor of a small Turkish province or district
5. caliph, calif, kaliph, khalif, khalifa—head of a Moslem state
6. czar, tsar, tzar—formerly Emperor of Russia or sovereign of certain other Slavic countries
7. czarina, czaritsa, tsarina, tsaritza, tzarina, tzaritsa—formerly Empress of Russia
8. dey—governor of Algiers before 1830; former ruler of Tunis or Tripoli
9. emir, emeer—Arabian ruler
10. exarch—ruler or governor of a remote province in the ancient Byzantine Empire
11. Gaekwar, Gaikwar—ruler of Baroda, in Western India
12. imperator—Roman emperor of early times (imperatorial,adj.)
13. Kaiser—ruler of Germany, 1871–1918, of Austria, 1804–1918, or of the Holy Roman Empire, 962–1806
14. khan—ruler of Turkish Mongol and Tatar tribes, and Emperor of China in medieval times
15. khedive—Turkish viceroy of Egypt, 1867–1914 (khedival, khedivial,adj.)
16. maharajah, maharaja—ruling Mohammedan ruler in India
17. maharani, maharanee—female Mohammedan ruler in India
18. mikado, Mikado—Emperor of Japan—term used by non-Japanese
19. Mogul—Mongol ruler of India from 1526 to 1857
20. nawab—deputy ruler or governor of the Mongol Empire in India
21. Nizam—ruler of Hyderabad, India
22. padishah, Padishah—former title of the Sultan of Turkey
23. rajah, raja—king or ruling prince in India, Java, Borneo, East Indies, etc.
24. rana—native ruler in India
25. rani, ranee—queen or ruling princess in India
26. sachem—chief or ruler of certain American Indian tribes
27. shah, padishah—ruler of Iran
28. sheik, sheikh—ruler or chief of an Arab or Mohammedan vilage, tribe, or family
29. shogun—military ruler in Japan up to 1868 (called *tycoon* by foreigners)
30. sultan—ruler in a Mohammedan country
31. Sultan—former monarch of Turkey
32. Tenno—Emperor of Japan

37. Rank, Position, or Office of Such a Ruler, n. *From Sec. 36:* caliphate or califate; czardom, tsardom, or tzardom; exarchate, kaisership, khanate, shogunate, sultanate or sultanship

38. Authority, Power, etc., of Such a Ruler, n. *From Sec. 36:* czardom, tsardom, or tzardom; emirate

39. Country, Territory, etc., of Such a Ruler, n. *From Sec. 36:* caliphate or califate; czardom, tsardom, or tzardom; emirate, exarchate, khanate, sheikdom or sheikhdom; sultanate

40. The Rule or Reign of Such a Ruler, n. *From Sec. 36:* emirate, shogunate, sultanate

41. Relative, etc., of Such a Ruler, n.
1. **czarevitch, tsarevitch, tzarevitch**—eldest son of a czar
2. **czarevna, tsarevna, tzarevna**—daughter of a czar; wife of the eldest son of a czar
3. **czarina, czaritza, tsarina, tsaritza, tzarina, tzaritza**—wife of a czar
4. **grand duke**—son, other than the eldest, of a czar
5. **maharani, maharanee**—wife of a maharajah
6. **rani, ranee**—wife of a rajah
7. **sultana**—mistress or concubine of a sultan
8. **sultana, sultaness**—wife, mother, sister, or daughter of a sultan

42. Government or Rule by a Specific Group, n.
1. **androcracy**—by men exclusively (androcratic,adj.)
2. **aristocracy, aristarchy**—by the best people, i.e., by those superior in intelligence, education, etc. (aristocratic, aristocratical,adj.)
3. **bureaucracy**—by government departments, often following inflexible rules or routine, involved in red tape, etc. (bureaucratic,adj.)
4. **demonocracy**—by demons or devils
5. **doulocracy, dulocracy**—by slaves
6. **ergatocracy**—by workers
7. **gerontocracy**—by old men
8. **gynarchy, gynecocracy, matriarchy, metrocracy**—by women (gynarchic, gynecocratic, gynecocratical, matriarchic, or metrocratic,adj.)
9. **hagiarchy**—by members of religious orders
10. **hagiocracy**—by holy people, or by those accepted as holy
11. **hierocracy**—by the clergy (hierocratic or hierocratical,adj.)
12. **mobocracy, mob rule, ochlocracy**—by the mob, or by the lower classes (mobocratic, mobocratical, ochlocratic, or ochlocratical,adj.)
13. **petticoat rule, petticoatism, petticoat government**—by women (usually derogatory)
14. **plutocracy**—by the wealthy (plutocratic or plutocratical,adj.)
15. **squirearchy**—by landed proprietors in England, esp. before 1832 (squirearchic, squirearchical, squirarchic, or squirarchical,adj.)
16. **stratocracy**—by military people, the army, etc. (stratocratic,adj.)
17. **technocracy**—by technical experts, engineers, etc. (technocratic,adj.)
18. **theocracy**—by the clergy claiming to be the representatives of God (theocratic or theocratical,adj.)

43. State, Country, or Place with Such a Government,n. *From Sec. 42:* aristocracy, plutocracy, stratocracy, theocracy

44. Member of the Ruling Group of Such a Government,n. *From Sec. 42:* aristocrat, bureaucrat, plutocrat; squire, squirearch, or squirarch; theocrat (aristocratic or aristocratical, bureaucratic, plutocratic or plutocratical,adj.)

45. Ruling Group or Body of Such a Government,n. *From Sec. 42:* aristocracy, bureaucracy, mobocracy, plutocracy, squirearchy

46. One Who Advocates or Favors Such Government or Rule,n. *From Sec. 42:* aristocrat, ergatocrat, gynecocrat, mobocrat or ochlocrat, stratocrat, theocrat (aristocratic or aristocratical; mobocratic, mobocratical, ochlocratic, ochlocratical,adj.)

47. Political Control by the Mob, or by the Lower Classes: mobocracy, mob rule, ochlocracy,n. (mobocratic, mobocratical, ochlocratic, or ochlocratical,adj.)

48. Leader of a Mob, Esp. One in Political Control: mobocrat,n.

49. Theory, Doctrines, or Political Movement of the Technocrats: technocracy,n. (technocratic,adj.)

50. A Subject or Citizen of a Theocratic Government: theocrat,n.

51. Government or Rule by a Specific Number of Persons: biarchy, diarchy, duarchy, duumvirate, or dyarchy (two); triarchy or triumvirate (three), tetrarchy or tetrarchate (four), pentarchy (five), hexarchy (six), heptarchy (seven), octarchy (eight),n. (diarchial, diarchic, or duumviral; tetrarchic or tetrarchical, pentarchical; heptarchal, heptarchic, or heptarchical,adj.)

52. Group of a Stated Number of Rulers: triarchy or triumvirate (three), tetrarchy (four), pentarchy (five), decemvirate (ten), n.

53. One of a Stated Number of Rulers: duarch (two), triumvir (three), tetrarch (four), pentarch (five), decemvir (ten),n. (triumviral, decemviral,adj.)

54. Country with Eight Rulers: octarchy,n.

55. Country Divided into Three or Four Governments: triarchy (three), tetrarchy (four), n.

56. Head of One of the Three Governments of a Country: triarch,n.

57. Group of the Stated Number of Associated States, Countries, etc., Each with Its Own Ruler: triarchy (three), pentarchy (five), hexarchy (six), heptarchy (seven), octarchy (eight),n.

58. Ruler of One of Seven Associated States or Countries: heptarch or heptarchist,n.

59. Harsh or Cruel Government or Rule: absolutism, autocracy, Caesarism, despotism, oppression, tyranny,n. (absolutist or absolutistic, autocratic or autocratical, despotic, oppressive; tyrannical, tyrannous, or tyrannic,adj.)

60. One Who Governs or Rules Harshly or Cruelly: autocrat, Caesar, czar, despot, kaiser, oppressor, tyrant or tyrannizer,n.

61. To Govern or Rule (a Place) Harshly or Cruelly: tyrannize or tyrannize over,v.

62. To Exercise Ruling Power Harshly or Cruelly: tyrannize,v.

63. To Govern or Rule: hold sway, reign,v. (reign,n.)

64. To Govern or Rule over (a Place, People, etc.): be at the head of, dominate, head, hold sway over, reign over, sway, wield power over, v. (domination, reign,n.)

65. To Bring (a People, etc.) under the Rule (of a Government, Conqueror, etc.): subject (to),v. (subjection,n.)

66. State or Condition of Being Brought under Such a Rule: subjection,n.

67. To Govern or Rule (a Place, People, etc.) Badly: misgovern, misrule,v. (misgovernment, misrule,n. misgovernor, misruler,n.)

68. Governing or Ruling: regnant (may also follow the noun, as in *the queen regnant*, etc.), reigning, sovereign,adj. (regnancy, sovereignty,n.)

69. Ruling in Place of a Monarch—Often Follows the Noun: regent,adj.

70. Time or Period in Which a Monarch Rules: reign, rule,n.

71. Pert. to, or Descr. of, Ruling, Reigning, or a Reign: regnal,adj.

72. Pert. to Government: civil, governmental, political,adj.

73. Pert. to the Government of a City, Town, etc.: municipal,adj.

74. Pert. to the Internal, Rather than the International, Affairs of a Government or State: domestic, municipal,adj.

75. Having Self-Government: autonomous; municipal (local) ; self-governing, self-ruling, adj. (autonomy, municipalism,n.)

76. City, Town, etc., Having Local Self-Government: municipality,n.

77. To Make Such out of (a Locality): municipalize,v. (municipalization,n.)

78. The Governing Body or Officials of Such: municipality,n.

79. Advocacy or Support of Local Self-Government: municipalism,n.

80. Advocate or Supporter of Such: municipalist,n.

81. The Right or Privilege of Participating in One's Government: political liberty,n.

82. Not Having Self-Government, i.e., Subject to External Rule, Government, Laws, etc.: heteronomous,adj. (heteronomy,n.)

83. Pert. to Government or Governmental Affairs Not Involved with, nor Influenced by, the Church, etc.: civil, secular, temporal, adj.

84. Power or Authority to Govern or Rule: crown (of a monarch), dominion; empire (supreme) ; scepter; sovereignty (supreme and independent),n. (sovereign,adj.)

85. Symbol of Such: crown, scepter,n.

86. Turkish or Moslem Political Power, or the Symbol of Such: crescent,n.

87. State, etc., That Has Supreme Ruling Power: sovereign or sovereignty,n.

88. State That Has Ruling or Political Power over Another: suzerain,n. (suzerainty, n. suzerain,adj.)

89. Territory, State, etc., under Rule or Government: domain, dominion, realm,n.

90. To Bring (Something, as an Industry, Land, or Other Property) under Governmental or Public Ownership or Control: collectivize; communalize or municipalize (of a city, town, etc.) ; communize, nationalize,v. (collectivization, communalization or municipalization, communization, nationalization, n.)

91. Exercising or Wielding Powers, as to Rule or Govern, etc., That Are Delegated by Another; Characterized by Such Delegated Powers: vicegerent,adj.

92. Capable of Being Governed: governable, rulable,adj. (governability or governableness, n.)

93. Incapable of Being Governed: ungovernable, unrulable, unruly,adj. (ungovernableness, unrulableness, unruliness,n.)

94. Supposed or Alleged Duty of White People to Govern the So-Called Backward, Ignorant, or Uncivilized Races or Peoples, or the Colored Races in Africa, etc., to Take Care of Them, Manage Their Affairs, Bring Them White Civilization, etc.—a Phrase Originated and Popularized by Rudyard Kipling in 1899 and Used by Apologists of Imperialism: white man's burden,n.

95. Time between Governments, Sovereigns, or Monarchs, or When a Country Has No Ruler or Government, or Only a Temporary One: interregnum,n. (interregnal,adj.)

96. Art of, or Skill in, Government: king-

craft (as a monarch), politics, statecraft, statesmanship,n. (political,adj.)

97. One Versed or Skilled in Government: politician, statesman,n.

98. Such Skill: statesmanship,n.

99. Like, or Characteristic of, Such Skill: statesmanlike or statesmanly,adj.

100. Shrewd, Cunning, or Crafty Skill in Government: statecraft,n.

101. Science of Government: political science, politics,n.

102. Governmental Organization of a Country, State, or Other Group; Condition of Being So Organized: polity,n.

103. Condition or State of Society in Which There Is Complete Lack of Government and/or Law; Political or Social Disorder or Violence Caused by Such: anarchy,n. (anarchic or anarchical,adj.)

104. Theory that a Lack of Direct Government Most Conduces to an Ideal State of Life and to Human Freedom: anarchism or anarchy,n. (anarchic, anarchical, anarchistic, or anarchist,adj.)

105. Advocate or Supporter of Such a Theory: anarch or anarchist,n. (anarchistic or anarchist,adj.)

106. Advocating Such a Theory: anarchic, anarchical, anarchistic, or anarchist,adj.

107. Similar to Anarchism or Anarchists: anarchistic or anarchist,adj.

108. Practices or Methods of Those Who Believe in Anarchy; Resistance, Often by Violence or Terror, to Constituted Government; Advocacy of the Overthrow of Constituted Government: anarchism,n. (anarch or anarchist,n. anarchistic or anarchist,adj.)

1074. FEUDALISM

1. Social Organization in Europe in the Middle Ages: feudalism or feudal system,n.

2. Principles, Theories, Practices, or Methods of Such: feudalism or feudality,n.

3. Pert. to Feudalism: feudal or feudalistic, adj.

4. Like, or Characteristic of, Feudalism: feudalistic,adj.

5. One Who Represents, Advocates, Supports, or Believes in, Feudalism: feudalist,n.

6. Inclined, Inclining, or Partial to Feudalism: feudalistic,adj.

7. To Convert to, or Bring under, Feudalism: feudalize,v. (feudalization,n.)

8. Land, Estate, etc., Held under the Feudal System from a Lord in Return for Services, etc.: fee, feod, feoff, feud, feudal benefice, feudality, feudatory, fief, vassalage,n.

9. The Right to Hold Such: fee,n.

10. Pert. to Land So Held: feudal,adj.

11. One Who Holds Such: feudatory, liege, liege man or liegeman, vassal,n. (vassal,adj. vassalage,n.)

12. Service, Homage, etc., Due a Lord from Such a Holder: vassalage,n.

13. Descr. of the Relationship between Vassal and Lord under Feudalism: feudatory, liege,adj.

14. Person Bound in Feudal Servitude to a Lord's Land, and Transferred with It: serf, n.

15. State or Fact of Being a Serf: serfage, serfdom, serfhood, or serfism,n.

16. Serfs Collectively: serfhood,n.

17. Feudal Ruler: liege, liege lord, lord; overlord (ranking above other lords); suzerain (i.e., a lord or overlord),n. (lordship, suzerainty,n. lordly, suzerain,adj.)

18. Minor or Petty Lord (Contemptuous): lording or lordling,n.

19. Japanese Feudal Lord: daimio or daimyo, n.

20. Such Collectively: daimio or daimyo,n.

21. Suitable for, Like, or Characteristic of, a Lord: lordly,adj. (lordliness,n.)

22. Power, Authority, etc., of a Lord: lordship,n.

23. To Act or Play the Lord: lord; lord it (over),v.

24. Territory or Domain of a Lord: lordship, manor,n. (manorial,adj.)

25. Woman with the Power of a Lord; Wife of a British Lord, i.e., of a Member of the British Nobility: lady,n.

1075. CITIZENSHIP

1. Citizen: citizeness (fem.); civilian (i.e., a private citizen, rather than a soldier, etc.); subject (i.e., of a government, enjoying its protection, owing it loyalty, etc.),n.

2. One Governed by a Ruler: liege (i.e., one who is loyal), subject,n.

3. Under the Rule of a Government or Monarch, etc.: subject,adj.

4. Citizens, Collectively: body politic, citizenry, commonwealth,n.

5. Pert. to, etc., a Citizen or Citizens: civic, civil, civilian, political,adj.

6. Condition of Being, or the Duties, Obligations, Rights, Privileges, etc., of, a Citizen: citizenship,n.

7. Good Citizenship; Principles and Ideals of Such: civism,n.

8. Science or Study of the Duties, Obligations, and Privileges of Citizenship, or of Civic, Municipal, Governmental, etc., Affairs: civics,n.

9. To Give the Status of a Citizen to: enfranchise, or, to an alien or immigrant, naturalize,v. (enfranchisement, naturalization,n.)

10. Country or Place Whose Citizens Come from Many Foreign Lands: melting pot,n.

11. Freedom of Opinion and Action of a Citizen, except Where Such Interferes with the Public Welfare: civil liberty,n.

12. Personal Rights of an American Citizen Guaranteed by the 13th and 14th Amendments to the Constitution: civil rights,n.

13. Such Rights Guaranteed by the First Ten Amendments to the U.S. Constitution: Bill of Rights,n.

14. To Deprive of the Rights and Privileges of Citizenship: denaturalize, disfranchise,v. (denaturalization, disfranchisement,n.)

15. Deprivation of Such Rights as a Result of Conviction of Treason: civil death,n.

1076. POLITICS

1. Political Affairs, Methods, Principles, Maneuvering, Artifice, Opinions, etc.; Profession or Practice of, or Participation in, Political Affairs; Art of Political Government: politics,n. (political,adj.)

2. Science of Political Government: political science, politics,n.

3. Person Engaged in Politics, in Seeking or Holding Political Office, etc.; Unprincipled Seeker after, or Holder of, Political Office: politician, politico,n.

4. To Engage or Participate in Politics: politic (colloq.), politicize,v.

5. To Talk or Discuss Politics; To Discuss from a Political Point of View; To Make Political; To Bring within the Realm of Politics: politicize,v.

6. Group Involved in Politics, Seeking Office, etc., as Opposed to Other Similar Groups: party, political party,n.

7. Politics from This Point of View: party politics,n.

8. Study or Application of Politics in Relation to Geography, International Problems, Expansion of Territory, etc.; Such as Practiced by the Nazis to Gain New Territory, World Domination, etc.: geopolitics,n.

9. Politics of All the Countries of the World, Esp. as They Affect International Affairs: cosmopolitics, international politics; Weltpolitik (German); world politics,n.

10. State or Community, or the People of Such, Organized under Political Government: body politic, polity,n.

11. Equality of Political Privileges or Rights: isonomy,n. (isonomic,adj.)

12. Member of a Political Party; Person with a Political View,n.
  1. Bolshevik, Bolshevist—extreme radical or progressive—contemptuous term (Bolshevik, Bolshevist,n. Bolshevistic,adj.)
  2. Communist, communist—member of the Communist party in Russia or elsewhere; one who holds similar political views (communist or communistic,adj.)
  3. Conservative, conservative—member of a party that opposes political change in a country's institutions; one who holds similar political views, or is moderate in his political thinking (conservative,adj.)
  4. democrat—person who supports political equality (democratic,adj.)
  5. Democrat—member of one of the two major parties in the U.S. (Democratic, adj.)
  6. Fabian, Fabianist—member of a British society advocating the gradual and peaceful spread of socialism; one who holds similar political views (Fabianist,adj.)
  7. Falangist—member of the Fascist party in power in Spain since the Spanish Civil War
  8. Fascist, fascist, Black Shirt—member of the political party in power in Italy under Mussolini, or of a similar party elsewhere; one who holds similar political views (fascist,adj.)
  9. independent, maverick, mugwump—one who has no blind loyalties to any political party, esp. to either of the two major U.S. political parties, in support, voting, etc.
  10. Jacobin—extreme political radical (Jacobinic or Jacobinical,adj.)
  11. Laborite, laborite—member of a British political party seeking the advancement of workers; member or supporter of a similar party elsewhere; or one holding similar political views
  12. leftist, left-winger—member of a radical or socialist political party; one who holds similar political views (leftist, left-wing, adj.)
  13. Leninist—supporter or advocate of the communist theories, principles, methods, etc., of Lenin, Premier of Soviet Russia from 1918–24 (Leninist,adj.)
  14. Liberal, liberal, liberalist—member of a political party favoring progress, reform, greater liberty, etc.; one who holds simi-

lar political views (Liberal, liberal, liberalist, or liberalistic,adj.)

15. Marxist, Marxian—one who holds the socialist and other political theories advanced by Karl Marx (Marxist or Marxian,adj.)

16. Menshevik, menshevik, Menshevist, menshevist—one who opposed, and was hostile to, the Russian Communist party and Government in and after 1917 (Menshevik, menshevik, Menshevist, or menshevist,adj.)

17. Moderate, moderate, moderatist—member of a political party advocating gradual reform or change; one who opposes the extreme politics of either the right or left

18. Nazi, brown shirt—member of the German political party in power under Hitler; one who holds similar political views (Nazi,adj.)

19. Progressive, progressive—member of a party advocating political and social improvement, reform, progress, etc.; one who holds similar political views (progressive,adj.)

20. Radical, radical—member of a party advocating extreme, sweeping, and drastic political and social reform, improvement of the lot of the lower classes, immediate remedies for social evils, etc.; one who holds similar political views (radical,adj.)

21. reactionary, reactionist, reactionarist—one who prefers, or advocates a return to, political processes of a past or earlier, and generally less liberal, time or era (reactionary or reactionist,adj.)

22. Republican—member of one of the two major U.S. political parties (Republican, adj.)

23. rightist, right-winger—conservative; reactionary (rightist or right-wing,adj.)

24. sans-culotte, sans-culottist—one who advocates extreme, radical, violent, or revolutionary political tactics to establish a republic or for other purposes (sans-culottic, sans-culottish,adj.)

25. Socialist, socialist—member of a political party advocating government ownership and control of industry, etc.; one who holds similar political views (socialist or socialistic,adj.)

26. Stalinist—supporter or advocate of the communist theories, methods, etc., of Stalin, Premier of Soviet Russia from 1941-53 (Stalinist,adj.)

27. syndicalist—one who advocates the theory or movement whereby control of government and society can be gained by trade unions through general strikes, violence, sabotage, terrorism or other illegal means (syndical, syndicalist, or syndicalistic,adj.)

28. Tory, tory—member of a British Conservative party; member of the group or party favoring Britain during the American Revolution; one who is a political conservative, or who opposes change or reform (Tory, tory,adj.)

29. Whig—member of an American political party about 1834-55; member of a British liberal party; member of such holding somewhat more conservative views than the rest of the party (Whig, Whiggish, adj.)

13. Such Members or Persons, Collectively, n. From Sec. 12: Fascisti, left or left wing, radicality, right or right wing; sans-culotterie

14. The Political Party of Such,n. From Sec. 12: Communist party or C.P., Conservative party, Democratic party, Fabian Society, Falange, Fascist party, Labor party or labor party; left, Left, or left wing (i.e., a party or section of a party); Liberal party, Nazi party, Progressive party, Radical party, Republican

party or G.O.P.; right or right wing (i.e., a party or section of a party); Socialist party

15. The Beliefs, Theories, Practices, Principles, Methods, or Attitudes, etc., of Such, n. From Sec. 12: bolshevism, communism, conservatism, democracy, Fabianism, fascism, Jacobinism, leftism, Leninism, liberalism, Marxism or Marxianism, Menshevism or menshevism, moderatism, nazism, progressivism, radicalism or radicality; reaction, reactionism, reactionarism, or reactionaryism; Republicanism, rightism, sans-culottism or sansculotterie, socialism, Stalinism, syndicalism, Toryism or toryism, Whiggery or Whiggism

16. To Convert (Someone, etc.) to Such a Party or Belief, etc.,v. From Sec. 12: bolshevize, communize, Jacobinize, liberalize, nazify, radicalize, sans-culotize (bolshevization, communization, liberalization, nazification, radicalization,n.)

17. To Become So Converted, Imbued, etc., v. From Sec. 12: bolshevize, liberalize, radicalize (bolshevization, liberalization, radicalization,n.)

18. Representing, or Relating to, Two or, in the U.S., Both Political Parties: bipartisan, adj. (bipartisanship,n.)

19. Not Involved with, Controlled by, Supporting, etc., Any Political Party: independent, non-partisan,adj.

20. A Communist: Bolshevik or Bolshevist; comrade (also used as a form of address), Red; tovarisch (title used by Russian communists),n. (Bolshevik, Bolshevist, or Bolshevistic; Red,adj.)

21. One Who Supports or Sympathizes with the Communist Party, though Not a Member: fellow traveler; Pink (colloq.); Pinko (slang),n. (pink,adj.)

22. Organization of the Communist Parties of European Nations: Cominform,n.

23. International Organization of Communist Parties, 1919-43: Comintern, Communist International, or Third International,n.

24. Committee of the Soviet Communist Party (up to 1952): Politburo,n.

25. Permanent Administrative Committee of Soviet Russia: Presidium,n.

1077. OFFICIAL; OFFICER

1. An Official or Officer of an Organization or of Government,n.

1. **amir, ameer**—Turkish official
2. **archon**—chief or presiding officer
3. **bureaucrat**—officious or pretentious government official (bureaucratic,adj.)
4. **burgomaster, burghmaster**—the opposite number of a U.S. mayor in a town or city in Holland, Germany, Austria, or Flanders
5. **chamberlain**—official of a royal court; official who manages a king's or noble's living quarters
6. **chancellor**—official of various sorts: president or chief administrative officer of a college or university, or honorary officer of a British university; officer who serves as secretary to a monarch, embassy, etc.; secretary or head of a department in the British Government; prime minister, as of Germany or Austria, etc.
7. **chief executive, chief magistrate**—highest executive officer of a governmental unit, such as the president of a republic or of the U.S., governor of a state in the U.S., etc.
8. **civil servant**—one employed in an official capacity by the government, esp. as a result of competitive examinations

9. **commissioner**—officer in charge of a government bureau or department
10. **coroner, medical examiner**—public officer whose duty it is to inquire into the death of anyone who, it is suspected, may not have died of natural causes
11. **deputy**—assistant to a public official (deputy,adj.)
12. **doge**—chief executive officer of Venice or Genoa, when these were independent republics
13. **executive**—official of a business corporation, etc.; highest public official of a governmental unit, as a president or governor, charged with enforcing the laws, administering the government, etc. (executive,adj.)
14. **functionary**—public or other official
15. **governor**—chief executive of a state of the U.S. (gubernatorial,adj.)
16. **governor**—official in charge of an institution or organization; official representing the British monarch in a colony or dependency
17. **incumbent, officeholder**—one who presently holds an office, as in the government, a business or other organization, etc.
18. **magistrate**—executive officer who administers the laws of a governmental unit (magisterial,adj.)
19. **mandarin**—public official of the former Chinese Empire
20. **marshal**—official in charge of parades, ceremonies, etc.; high officer in, or chief of, a fire department in some cities
21. **mayor**—chief executive officer of a city, village, municipality, etc. (mayoress,fem. n. mayoral,adj.)
22. **minister**—chief officer of a governmental department in Britain and certain other European countries (ministerial,adj.)
23. **panjandrum**—pretentious, pompous, important, or self-important official (ironic or contemptuous)
24. **president**—chief executive official of a republic; chief officer of a business or other organization, college, university, association, society, club, etc. (presidential, adj.)
25. **prexy**—president, esp. of a college or university (colloq.)
26. **prime minister, premier**—chief officer of certain governments, as in France, Britain, etc.
27. **secretary**—officer in charge of a government department (secretarial,adj.)
28. **selectman**—public official of various New England towns, villages, etc.
29. **sheik, sheikh**—officer of a Mohammedan religious organization
30. **syndic**—business manager, esp. of a university; public official (syndical,adj.)
31. **vice-chancellor**—officer next in rank to a chancellor; substitute or deputy chancellor
32. **vicegerent**—officer with delegated power (vicegeral,adj.)
33. **vice-president**—officer next in rank to a president, acting in his absence, etc.; officer in charge of a department in a corporation; (cap.) officer of the U.S. Government who succeeds the President on the latter's death, removal from office, etc., and who otherwise presides over the Senate (vice-presidential,adj.)

2. Position or Office of an Official or Officer, or the Period of Such Office,n. *From Sec. 1:* archonship, burgomastership, chancellorship or chancellery, commissionership, coronership, dogedom or dogeship, governship, incumbency, magistracy or magistrature, marshalcy or marshalship, mayoralty or mayorship, ministership or ministry, presidency, prime ministry or premiership, secretaryship, sheikdom or sheikhdom, vicegerency, vice-presidency; *Also:*
1. **administration**—period of office of executive officials
2. **(the) chair**—position of office or authority

3. Officials Collectively, or as a Body,n. *From Sec. 1:* civil service, board of governors, magistracy or magistrature, ministry; *Also:*
1. **administration**—executive officials of a government; executive branch of a government
2. **authorities**—law-enforcement officials
3. **brass**—high executives of a business or other organization (colloq.)
4. **bureaucracy**—officials of government departments (bureaucratic,adj.)
5. **cabinet**—officials advising a monarch or president or other chief executive; (cap.) officials in charge of the main departments of the U.S. Government (cabinet, adj.)
6. **council**—officials selected to act in executive capacity
7. **officialdom, officialism**—officials as a class, group, or body
8. **official family**—cabinet of the U.S. President

4. Office, Building, Room, or Department of an Official or of Officials,n. *From Sec. 1:* chancellery or chancery, secretariat or secretariate

5. The Employment or Work of Civil Servants: civil service,n.

6. To Appoint as a Deputy or Assistant Official: deputize,v.

7. Staff of the Secretary of a Government Department: secretariat or secretariate,n.

8. To Put in Office or in a Position of Authority: chair,v.

9. To Provide with Officers: officer,v.

10. To Perform the Duties of an Office: officiate,v. (officiation,n. officiator,n.)

11. Pert. to, or Holding, Office: official,adj.

12. Emanating from a Public Office or Officer, as a Statement, etc.: authoritative, magisterial, official,adj. (authoritativeness,n.)

13. Pert. to, Connected with, or Derived from, One's Office or Position: officiary,adj.

14. Having a Title, Rank, etc., That Is Descriptive of, or Derived from, One's Office: officiary,adj.

15. One Who Desires and Tries to Get a Public Office: office seeker,n.

16. To Try to Get (a Public Office) through Election: run for (office),v.

17. Excessive Attention to Official Methods, Routine, etc.: beadledom, bureaucracy, officialdom, officialism; red tape, red-tapedom, red-tapery, or red-tapism,n. (bureaucratic, red-tape, red-tapey, red-tapish,adj. bureaucrat, red-tapist,n.)

18. Unintelligent Display or Performance of Official Authority: beadledom, Bumbledom,n.

19. Official Delay and Formality: red tape,n.

20. The Position or Jurisdiction of Officials: officialdom,n.

21. To Function as an Official; To Bring under the Control of Officials; To Render Official: officialize,v. (officialization,n.)

22. Language Characteristic of Officials: officialese,n. (new coinage)

23. The Officer in Charge of a Meeting, Council, Committee, etc.: the chair, chairman or, fem., chairwoman, moderator, president, presider, presiding officer,n.

24. To Be, or Act as, Such an Officer: moderate, preside, take the chair,v.

25. To Act as Such an Officer at or over: moderate, preside at or over,v.

1078. POLICE

1. Police Officer; A Member or Official of the Police: arm of the law; bailiff (sheriff or assistant sheriff—executes legal papers, makes arrests, keeps order in court, etc.); bluecoat (colloq.); bobby or constable (in England); constable (esp. in England); deputy sheriff (assistant sheriff); gendarme (in France and Belgium; also, often humorously, elsewhere); marshal (police officer or chief of police in some cities, or a court officer of the U.S. or of some local governments, with duties similar to those of a sheriff); officer, officer of the law; patrolman (on foot); peace officer, police constable, policeman, police officer, policewoman or police matron; sheriff (of a county or other subdivision of a state of the U.S.); state trooper or trooper (of a state of the U.S.); tipstaff (British bailiff or constable); trooper (mounted),n. (constableship, marshalcy or marshalship, policemanship,n.)

2. The Police; Police Officers as a Body, Group, etc.,n.
  1. **constabulary**—constables of a region; police force organized along military lines; the police (humorous); state police (constabular or constabulary,adj.)
  2. **Gay-Pay-Oo, Ogpu**—Russian secret police from 1922–34
  3. **gendarmerie (French), gendarmery**—French police; the police elsewhere
  4. **Gestapo**—German secret police under nazism; any secret police
  5. **MVD, M.V.D.**—Russian secret police from 1946 on
  6. **NKVD, N.K.V.D.**—Russian secret police from 1934–46
  7. **police force**—body of police of a region, city, etc.
  8. **Polizei (German)**—the police

3. Pert. to a Constable or to Constables: constabular or constabulary,adj.

4. Pert. to a Sheriff: shrieval,adj.

5. Office, or District, of a Sheriff: shrievalty,n.

6. Area of Control, Power, or Jurisdiction of a Bailiff: bailiwick,n.

7. Unit or Division of a Police Force: platoon,n.

8. Group of Police: squad,n.

9. To Keep (a Place) Peaceful, Orderly, Regulated, etc., with, or as with, Police; To Keep (a Military Camp) Orderly and Clean: police,v.

10. To Govern (a Region) by Means of a Police Force: policize,v.

11. Ranking Officers of a Police Force, in Ascending Rank: sergeant, lieutenant, captain, inspector, chief,n.

12. Civilian Head of a Police Department: commissioner,n. (commissionership,n.)

13. Police Vehicle: Black Maria, paddy wagon, patrol wagon, or police van (each for transporting prisoners); police car, prowl car, squad car,n.

14. Building Housing the Police: police station, station house,n.

15. Building Housing the Executive Officers or Center of Operations of the Police, or Such Offices or Center: headquarters, police headquarters,n.

16. Other Persons Exercising Police Functions,n.

  1. **black shirt**—member of the Nazi *Schutzstaffel* (SS) or Elite Guard, used to police Germany and occupied countries, suppress opposition, etc.
  2. **brown shirt, storm trooper**—member of the Nazi *Sturm Abteilung* (SA), used to police party demonstrations, terrorize the populace, etc.
  3. **marshal**—court or judicial officer with duties similar to those of a sheriff (marshalcy, marshalship,n.)
  4. **proctor**—one who polices students taking examinations, keeps order in a college or university, etc. (proctorial,adj. proctorship,n.)
  5. **sergeant at arms**—officer of a legislative body or other assemblage whose duty it is to preserve order
  6. **vigilante**—member of a self-appointed and legally unauthorized committee of private citizens set up to punish criminals, maintain order, ferret out crime or wrongdoing, etc., usually when legal processes or protection have broken down or are nonexistent

17. Committee of Vigilantes: vigilance committee,n.

18. Activities, Principles, Practice, Methods, etc., of Vigilantes: vigilantism,n.

19. Group, Committee, Body, etc., of Men Who May Be, or Have Been, Called by a Peace Officer to Assist Him in Preserving Order, Pursuing Criminals, etc.: posse; posse comitatus (Latin),n.

20. Any Group of Men Invested with Legal Authority: posse,n.

1079. LAW

1. A Law: act; bylaw (i.e., a subsidiary law, or one adopted by an organization, corporation, society, etc.); canon (of, or pert. to, the church); commandment; curfew (that children or adults are to leave the streets after a certain hour); decree or edict (made by authority); ordinance (made by decree or authority, or for local purposes, etc.); regulation (aimed at control of behavior or activity); statute,n. (canonical; decretive, decretal, or decretory; edictal, statutory,adj.)

2. A Law Enacted by a Lawmaking Body: act, enactment, legislation, measure, statute, n. (statutory,adj.)

3. One Provision of a Law: enactment,n.

4. Unchangeable Law: law of the Medes and Persians,n.

5. Laws; Body, etc., of Law,n.
  1. **admiralty, admiralty law, maritime law**—laws relating to ships, the sea, naval affairs, etc.
  2. **blue laws**—puritanical laws; laws prohibiting certain activities, as gambling, drinking, dancing, the giving of entertainments, the conduct of business, etc., esp. on Sundays
  3. **canon, canon law**—church law (canonical,adj.)
  4. **case law**—laws established by court decisions
  5. **civil law**—body or system of law concerned with, or governing, private, noncriminal, affairs; laws, or system of law, derived from Roman law
  6. **code**—system of regulations or laws, of existing law, of the laws bearing on a subject, etc.
  7. **commercial law, law merchant**—laws governing the rights and duties of business transactions
  8. **common law**—laws, or system of law, derived from England; law based on court decisions or on custom (common-law,adj.)

9. **constitution**—the laws, or system of laws, by which a nation, state, corporation, society, etc., is governed; the document containing such (constitutional, adj.)
10. **corpus juris**—collection or body of laws of a nation, state, etc.
11. **criminal law**—body of laws relating to crimes
12. **dharma**—religious law, or conformity to such, in Hinduism or Buddhism
13. **equity, chancery**—system or body of laws or regulations serving to supplement common law or statutory law and superseding it, when necessary, for purposes of fair decisions (equitable,adj.)
14. **international law, law of nations**—law governing the conduct of nations to one another
15. **jurisprudence**—system or body of laws (jurisprudential,adj.)
16. **legislation**—laws enacted by a lawmaking body (legislative,adj.)
17. **pandect**—complete system or body of law
18. **penal code**—code of laws governing crimes and the punishments for them
19. **rule**—code of regulations followed by members of a religious group or organization
20. **statute law**—law, or body of laws, enacted by a lawmaking body
21. **unwritten law**—law based on court decisions, general customs of a people, etc., rather than on statutes, decrees, etc.

6. **To Arrange (Laws) into a System:** codify, v. (codification,n. codifier,n.)
7. **The Arrangement of Unwritten or Case Law into the Form of Statutes:** codification, n.
8. **Pert. or Relating to Law or Laws:** jural, juridic, juridical, jurisprudential, juristic, juristical, legal; legislative (of a lawmaking body); statutory,adj.
9. **Pert. to a Law or Statute That Establishes New Obligations and Rights:** enactory, adj.
10. **In Conformance with, Subject to, etc., the Laws as Stated in a Constitution:** constitutional,adj. (constitutionality,n.)
11. **Principles of Government by Authority of the Laws of a Constitution; Support for, or Adherence to, Such Principles; the Authority or Rule Laid Down by the Laws of a Constitution:** constitutionalism,n.
12. **One Who Supports, Advocates, Adheres to, Studies, or Writes about, a Constitution:** constitutionalist,n.
13. **Possessing the Authority or Power to Make or Alter a Constitution:** constituent, adj.
14. **Brought About by Law or Laws:** juristic or juristical,adj.
15. **Recognized under Law:** juristic or juristical, lawful, legal,adj. (lawfulness, legality, n.)
16. **Based on Law:** legal, nomothetic or nomothetical,adj.
17. **By Law:** de jure,adv. phrase (Latin)
18. **Authorized or Permitted by, or in Accordance with, Law or the Laws:** lawful, legal, legitimate, licit,adj. (lawfulness, legality or legalness, legitimacy or legitimateness, licitness,n.)
19. **To Make, Render, or Declare Legal or Lawful:** legalize; legitimate, legitimatize, or legitimize; validate,v. (legalization, legitimation or legitimization, validation,n. validatory,adj.)

20. **To Give Legal Power or Force to:** authorize, validate,v. (authorization, validation, n. validatory,adj.)
21. **To Give a Legal Organization or Form to (a Meeting, Court, etc.):** constitute,v. (constitution,n.)
22. **Having Legal Force; Legally Binding; Legally Proper or Sound:** valid,adj. (validity or validness,n.)
23. **Adherence to Law or Laws:** legality,n.
24. **Extremely Strict, Excessively Strict, or Extremely Literal Adherence to, or Observance of, Law, Laws, or a Law:** legalism,n. (legalist,n. legalistic,adj.)
25. **Such in Reference to Religion or Religious Law:** nomism,n. (nomistic,adj.)
26. **Obedient to, or Observant of, Law or the Laws:** law-abiding, lawful, legal,adj. (lawfulness, legality,n.)
27. **Science of Law or Laws:** jurisprudence, nomology,n. (jurisprudential, nomological, adj. jurisprudent, nomologist,n.)
28. **Pert. to a Science of Universal Law:** nomothetic or nomothetical,adj.
29. **One Skilled, Expert, or Versed in Law or Laws:** jurisconsult, jurisprudent, jurist, legalist, legist,n. (juristic or juristical,adj.)
30. **Scholar of, or Writer on, the Law or Laws:** jurist,n. (juristic or juristical,adj.)
31. **Skilled in Law or Laws:** jurisprudent,adj.
32. **Student of, or Expert in, Church Law; Student of Law in a Medieval University:** decretist,n.
33. **Textbook for a Law Student:** lawbook,n.
34. **Philosophy or Department of Law:** jurisprudence,n. (jurisprudential,adj. jurisprudent,n.)
35. **Equality of Laws:** isonomy,n. (isonomic, adj.)

1080. LEGISLATION

1. **To Make Laws:** legislate,v. (legislation,n. legislative,adj.)
2. **To Bring About (Attitudes, Actions, etc.) by Making Relevant Laws on the Subject:** legislate,v. (legislation,n.)
3. **To Make into a Law, as a Legislative Bill:** enact,v. (enactment,n. enactive,adj.)
4. **To Make (a Law or Laws):** constitute, enact, establish, pass, set up,v. (constitution, establishment, passage,n.)
5. **Having Such Powers or Functions:** constitutive, enactive, legislative,adj.
6. **Giving or Establishing Laws:** lawgiving, lawmaking, nomothetic or nomothetical,adj.
7. **The Making of Laws:** lawmaking, legislation,n. (legislative,adj.)
8. **One Who Makes Laws:** lawgiver (a code or system), lawmaker, legislator or, fem., legislatress; Solon (strictly, if wise),n. (legislatorial,adj.)
9. **Proposed Law Offered to a Legislature, but Not Yet Enacted:** bill, measure,n.
10. **Lawmaking Body:** assembly, chamber; congress (of a nation, esp. a republic); council; diet (of various foreign countries); legislature or legislative; parliament (of various foreign countries); senate,n. (congressional, legislative, parliamentary,adj.)
11. **Member of a Lawmaking Body:** councilman (esp. of a city) or councilor, legislator or, fem., legislatress, senator,n. (councilmanic, legislatorial, senatorial,adj. councilorship, senatorship,n.)

12. Lawmaking Body of Certain Countries, n.
1. Bundesrat, Bundesrath, Bundesversammlung—Switzerland
2. Congress—United States (Congressional, adj.)
3. Cortes—Portugal or Spain
4. Imperial Diet—Japan, when an empire
5. National Assembly—France
6. Parliament—England, etc. (parliamentary,adj.)
7. Reichstag—Germany
8. Rigsdag—Denmark
9. Riksdag—Sweden
10. States-General—Holland
11. Storting—Norway

13. Member of Such,n. *From Sec. 12:* Congressman or Congresswoman (the title generally refers, however, to a member of the lower house) ; parliamentarian or Member of Parliament (England),n.

14. Meeting Hall, House, etc., of a Lawmaking Body: chamber,n.

15. Person of Some Skill in Parliamentary Procedure or Debating: parliamentarian,n.

16. Having, or Consisting of, Two Legislative Houses or Chambers: bicameral,adj.

17. Having, or Consisting of, but One Such: unicameral,adj.

18. Upper Chamber or House of Certain Legislative Bodies,n.
1. Bundesrat, Bundesrath—Germany, when an empire
2. First Chamber—Holland
3. House of Lords—England
4. House of Peers—Empire of Japan
5. National Assembly—Portugal
6. Reichsrat, Reichsrath—Germany, under the Weimar Republic
7. Senate—U.S., Italy, France, Canada, South American countries, etc.
8. Ständerat—Switzerland

19. Member of Such,n. *From Sec. 18:* lord, peer, or peer of the realm (Britain), senator (senatorship,n. senatorial,adj.)

20. Lower Chamber or House of Certain Legislative Bodies,n.
1. assembly—various state or city legislatures in the U.S.
2. Chamber of Deputies—France and various other European countries
3. House of Commons, Commons—England, Canada, and certain other countries
4. House of Representatives—U.S. and some other nations
5. Nationalrat—Switzerland
6. Reichstag—Germany
7. Second Chamber—Holland

21. Member of Such,n. *From Sec. 20:* assemblyman, deputy, representative or, U.S., congressman or congresswoman

22. A Legislative, or, Sometimes, a Judicial or Executive Officer of Some Cities or Towns in the U.S.: alderman,n. (aldermanic or aldermanly,adj.)

23. The Rank or Office of an Alderman: aldermanate, aldermancy, aldermanry, or aldermanship,n.

24. Like, or Characteristic of, an Alderman: aldermanic, aldermanlike, or aldermanly,adj.

25. Body of Aldermen; Aldermen, Collectively: aldermanate, or, humorous, aldermanity,n.

26. Member of a Political Party in a Legislature Whose Function It Is to Keep Other Members in Line, Compel Attendance, etc.: whip or party whip,n.

27. Legislator Chosen by Other Legislators of His Political Party to Be Their Leader: floor leader,n.

1081. COURT OF LAW

1. The Court, Symbolically: the bar, the bench,n.

2. A Court: court of justice, court of law, judicatory, judicial tribunal, law court, tribunal,n.

3. Certain Law Courts,n.
1. admiralty, court of admiralty—court having jurisdiction over maritime or naval affairs, ships, etc.
2. appellate court, court of appeal, court of review—court that reviews decisions of other courts
3. court-martial—military or naval court trying those accused of offenses against army or naval law
4. court of chancery, court of equity—court that applies principles of fairness and of natural law to settle disputes
5. court of claims—court that settles claims against the government
6. court of domestic relations—court that settles marital or family disputes
7. kangaroo court—unauthorized court that makes a mockery of legal procedure and justice, as in a prison, frontier town, etc.
8. municipal court—court of a city, town, etc.
9. police court—court having jurisdiction over minor offenses
10. superior court—court having greater jurisdiction than lower courts; court of general jurisdiction in a state
11. supreme court—highest court of a state or nation

4. To Try (a Soldier, Sailor, etc.) by a Military or Naval Court: court-martial,v.

5. Such a Trial: court-martial,n.

6. System of Courts and Judges; Department of a Government Concerned with Such, or with the Administration of Justice: judiciary,n.

7. Building in Which Court Is Held: courthouse,n.

8. Room in Which Court Is Held: courtroom,n.

9. Railing in a Courtroom That Separates the Public or Spectators from Those Engaged in Court Business, as the Judge, Jury, Lawyers, etc.: bar,n.

10. Place Where the Prisoner Stands in a Courtroom: bar,n.

11. Days on Which a Court Sits, or Can Sit: juridical days,pl.n.

12. Court Sessions Held at Periodic Intervals in British Counties, or the Time or Place of Such: assizes,pl.n.

13. Decision of a Court or Judge: adjudication, authority, decree, judgment, ruling, verdict,n.

14. To Issue a Decision on (a Point, Matter, etc.)—of a Court or Judge: rule on,v.

15. Certain Court Orders,n.
1. brief—summoning a person to answer a legal action
2. injunction—to do, or more often, not to do something (injunctive,adj.)
3. subpoena—summoning a witness
4. summons, process—to appear in court
5. writ—to do or not to do something—issued also by a government, monarch, etc.

16. To Serve (a Person) with Such a Court Order,v. *From Sec. 15:* subpoena, summons,v.

17. One Who Serves Subpoenas, Summonses, Writs, and Other Legal Documents, Usually as an Occupation: process server,n.

18. Pert. or Relating to Law Courts: forensic, judicial, judiciary, juridic or juridical,adj.

19. The Administration of Justice or of the Law: judicatory, judicature, justice,n.

20. Pert. to the Administration of Justice: judicatory, judicial, judiciary, juridic or juridical, justiciary,adj.

21. The Power or Function of Administering Justice by Legal Trial: judicature,n.

22. The Application of, or Resort to, Principles of Fairness and Natural Law in the Settlement of Legal Disputes: chancery, equity,n.

23. Disobedience to the Orders of a Court or Congress; Disrespect Shown to a Court or Congress; Disorderly Conduct during the Session of a Court or of a Congressional Hearing—These Are All Legally Punishable Acts: contempt; contempt of court or contempt of congress,n.

1082. COURT CASE

1. Law Case: action, action at law, case, cause, lawsuit or suit, legal dispute, litigation, plea; proceeding, proceedings, legal proceeding, or legal proceedings,n. (litigious, adj.)

2. Furnishing Cause for, or Liable to, a Lawsuit: actionable,adj.

3. Ground or Basis for a Lawsuit, Legal Action, etc.: cause,n.

4. That Which Happens during a Legal Action or Proceeding: process or legal process,n.

5. The Matter to Be Judged in a Lawsuit, or by a Court: cause,n.

6. Famous Law Case, Legal Dispute, or Trial, or One That Attracts Wide Attention: cause célèbre,n. (French)

7. Examination in Court to Determine Guilt, Responsibility, etc.: trial,n.

8. To Examine and Determine (a Case), or the Guilt or Innocence of (a Person) in a Court of Law; To Sit as Judge in (Such a Case), or Be the Judge of (Such a Person), in a Court of Law: try,v.

9. To Hear and Render Judgment on, in a Court of Law: adjudge, adjudicate, judge,v. (adjudication, judgment,n. adjudicative,adj.)

10. To Sit or Act as Judge in a Court of Law: adjudicate (in, on, or upon), judge,v.

11. To Bring a Lawsuit: bring or take action or legal action; bring suit, go to law, institute or start legal action or proceedings, sue, take legal measures or steps,v. (suit,n.)

12. To Start and Carry On a Legal Action: prosecute,v. (prosecution,n.)

13. Person or Party Doing Such: prosecutor or prosecution,n.

14. To Start and Carry On Legal Action against (a Person, etc.): prosecute, sue,v. (prosecution, suit,n.)

15. To Carry On a Lawsuit: litigate,v. (litigation,n. litigious,adj.)

16. One Who Carries on a Lawsuit: litigant or litigator,n.

17. To Petition (a Court) for Justice or Legal Action: sue,v. (suit,n.)

18. To Try to Get or Enforce (Something) by Legal Action: prosecute,v. (prosecution, n.)

19. To Conduct Legal Proceedings in Court against (One Accused of Crime): prosecute, v. (prosecution,n.)

20. Officer Who Does So: prosecutor or prosecuting attorney,n.

21. To Dispute or Contest (a Case, etc.) at Law: litigate,v. (litigation,n. litigator,n.)

22. Engaged or Involved in a Lawsuit: litigant or litigating,adj.

23. One Engaged or Involved in a Lawsuit: litigant or litigator,n.

24. Person or Party against Whom a Legal Action or Suit Is Brought: defendant,n.

25. The Defendant and His Lawyer or Lawyers: defense,n.

26. The Arguments, Denials, etc., Used by a Defendant and His Lawyer or Lawyers in a Legal Action: defense,n.

27. One Who Brings a Legal Action or Suit: complainant, plaintiff,n.

28. Statement or Statements Made in a Lawsuit on Behalf of the Defendant and Plaintiff: plea or pleadings,n. (plead,v. pleader,n.)

29. Defendant's Answer to a Plaintiff's Claim; Defendant's Answer (i.e., Guilty, Not Guilty, etc.) to a Legal Accusation: plea,n. (plead,v. pleader,n.)

30. Prone, or Excessively Prone, to Bring Controversies or Disputes into Court, Start Lawsuits, etc.: litigious,adj. (litigiousness,n.)

31. Capable of Being Contested, Tried, Settled, etc., in a Law Case; Subject to Such Contesting, etc.: actionable, litigable, triable, adj.

32. Capable of Being Settled by a Judge in a Court of Law: judicable or judiciable,adj.

33. A Person Who, in a Legal Dispute, Favors Neither Side, but Clarifies a Point of Law without Prejudice, Gives Advice to the Court on the Matter, etc.: amicus curiae,n. (Latin)

34. A Trial or Court Case Dismissed or Ended because of the Commission of Some Legal Error; Trial or Court Case in Which No Conclusion Is Reached, as when a Jury Cannot Reach a Verdict, etc.: mistrial,n.

35. Persistent or Frequent Incitement or Bringing About of Lawsuits: barratry,n. (barratrous,adj.)

36. One Who Does So: barrator or barrater,n.

37. Doing So, or Inclined or Tending to Do So: barratrous,adj.

38. Illegal Act Whereby a Person Not Involved in a Lawsuit Agrees to Aid in the Prosecution, Pay the Costs, etc., in Return for a Share of the Gain if the Suit Is Successful: champerty,n. (champertous,adj.)

1083. A JUDGE

1. The Judge, Symbolically: the bench,n.

2. A Judge in a Court, etc.,n.
1. chancellor—judge in a court of chancery or equity
2. chief justice—head or presiding judge in a court of law in which there are several judges, as the U. S. Supreme Court, etc
3. jurist—learned and expert judge; by courtesy, any judge
4. justice—judge in a court of law
5. justice of the peace, justice—judge in a court trying minor civil or criminal cases
6. justiciary—judge of a superior court
7. magistrate—judge in a court trying minor civil or criminal cases, esp. in a city
8. police judge, police justice, police magistrate—judge in a court trying minor offenses

9. **surrogate**—judge in a court that rules on wills, estates, etc.

3. **Office, or Term of Office, of a Judge,**n. *From Sec. 2:* chancellorship or chancellery, justiceship; magistracy, magistrature, or magistrateship; surrogateship; *Also:* judgeship, judicature,n.

4. **Pert. to the Office of Judge:** juridical, justiciary,adj.

5. **Pert. to the Office of Magistrate:** magisterial, magistratic or magistratical,adj.

6. **Judges Collectively, or as a Body or Group:** judicature; judiciary (of the courts of a state, nation, etc.),n.

7. **Magistrates Collectively, or a Body of Such:** magistracy or magistrature,n.

8. **A Judge's Work, Function, Power, or Authority:** judicature,n.

9. **Pert. to a Judge or Judges:** judicial, judiciary,adj.

10. **Pert. to a Magistrate:** magisterial, magistratic or magistratical,adj.

11. **Like or Characteristic of a Judge or Judges:** judgelike, judicial,adj.

12. **Fitting for, or Proper to, a Judge or Judges:** judicial,adj.

13. **Fitting for, or Proper to, a Magistrate:** magisterial,adj.

14. **Authority or Legal Power of a Judge:** jurisdiction,n. (jurisdictional,adj.)

15. **Authority or Legal Power of a Magistrate:** magistracy, magistrature,n.

16. **Having the Rank of Magistrate:** magisterial, magistratic or magistratical,adj.

17. **The Function or District of a Magistrate:** magistracy, magistrature,n.

18. **Room or Place Where a Judge Hears Problems, Matters, Disputes, etc., Not Requiring Formal Court Action;** Private Office of a Judge: chamber, chambers, judge's chamber, or judge's chambers,n.

19. **A Judge, i.e., Person Who Judges (Other than a Member of the Judiciary or Court System),**n.
   1. **adjudicator**—person who gives or renders judgment, or acts as a judge, in a dispute or controversial matter
   2. **arbiter**—person with the power of judging and settling a dispute; person chosen to judge and settle a dispute or matter under controversy; person who has absolute and exclusive power of judging and deciding, or full authority to judge and decide (arbitral,adj.)
   3. **arbitrator**—person chosen by the opposing sides, as in industry and labor, etc., to judge and settle a controversy; arbiter
   4. **czar**—person appointed to be a chief arbitrator in a field, industry, etc.
   5. **judicator**—person who judges, acts as judge, passes judgment, sits in judgment, etc.
   6. **referee**—person to whom any controversy is referred for judgment and decision; person appointed by a court to hear matters and recommend judgment and decision; judge in boxing or other games or sports
   7. **umpire**—judge of the plays or rules in sports, as baseball and other games engaged in by teams; person selected to settle a controversy between opposing sides

20. **To Judge, i.e., Pass, Give, or Render Judgment or Decision on, or Act or Serve as Judge in Reference to,**v. *From Sec. 19:* adjudicate or adjudicate in, on, or upon, arbitrate; referee (a game or dispute); umpire

(adjudication, arbitration,n. adjudicative, arbitrative,adj.); *Also:* rule on,v.

21. **To Be, or to Act or Serve as, a Judge,**v. *From Sec. 19:* adjudicate (in, on, or upon), arbitrate, referee, umpire (adjudication, arbitration,n. adjudicative, arbitrative,adj.)

22. **The Hearing, Judging, and Settling of a Dispute by an Arbitrator:** arbitrament, arbitration,n. (arbitral, arbitrational,adj.)

23. **To Submit a Dispute to Arbitration; To Submit (a Controversial Matter or a Dispute) to Arbitration:** arbitrate,v.

24. **The Judgment or Decision of an Arbitrator:** arbitrament, award,n.

25. **Subject to Arbitration; Capable of Being Arbitrated:** arbitrable,adj.

26. **Office of an Arbitrator:** arbitratorship,n.

27. **Office, Authority, Judgment, or Decision of an Umpire:** umpirage,n.

28. **The Power to Judge, or to Render Judgments:** arbitrament,n.

29. **Power or Right to Judge and Settle Disputes:** authority,n.

30. **To Judge (a Person, Thing, etc.) Unfairly or Inaccurately; To Render Unfair or Inaccurate Judgments:** misjudge,v. (misjudgment,n.)

31. **To Judge (a Person, Matter, etc.) before Proper Investigation, before Learning All the Facts, etc.; To Judge (a Person or Matter) beforehand or Too Early:** prejudge,v. (prejudgment,n. prejudger,n.)

32. **A Judge of Excellence, Worth, Value,** etc.: arbiter elegantiae or arbiter elegantiarum (in matters of taste, etc.—Latin); authority (on matters or points in question); connoisseur (in the arts, fine arts, aesthetic fields, matters of taste, or, loosely, wine or food, etc.); critic or reviewer (esp. of literature, art, theater, etc.); gourmet (of food and drink),n. (critical,adj.)

33. **An Inferior Critic; Critic Who Shows No Competence or Skill in Judging:** criticaster,n.

34. **A Harsh Judge of Excellence, Worth, or Value:** critic,n.

35. **To Judge the Excellence, Worth, Value,** etc., of, Discussing the Good and Bad Points, etc.; To Engage in Such Judgments and Discussion: criticize,v. (criticism,n.)

36. **To So Judge (Literature, Art, Theater,** etc.): criticize, review,v. (criticism,n. critical,adj.)

37. **Art or Practice of So Judging Literature, Art, Theatrical Presentations, etc.:** criticism, critique,n. (critical,adj.)

38. **Essay, Article, etc., Rendering Such Judgments:** criticism, critique, review,n. (critical,adj.)

39. **Group Selected to Judge a Contest, Competition, etc.:** jury,n.

40. **Member of Such:** juror,n.

41. **Able to Judge, i.e., Exercise Judgment:** judicative,adj.

42. **Judging:** judicative,adj.

43. **Judging Worth, etc., Harshly or Severely:** critical,adj. (criticalness,n.)

44. **Rendering Judgments (of Behavior, Actions, etc.) Instead of Being Objective or Merely Descriptive:** judgmental,adj.

45. **Standard of Judgment or Judging:** canon, criterion, yardstick,n. (criteria,pl.n. criterional,adj.)

46. **Place of Judgment:** bar, tribunal,n.

47. Capable of Being, or Likely or Liable to Be, Judged: judicable, judiciable,adj.

1084. JURY

1. A Jury: blue-ribbon jury or blue-ribbon panel (of carefully chosen members); coroner's jury or jury of inquest (to determine the cause of someone's death, if other than natural causes are suspected); grand jury (selected to investigate alleged law violations and determine whether there is enough evidence to warrant a trial—composed of 12–23 members); petty jury, petit jury, or trial jury (listening to the evidence at a trial—usually 12 members, sometimes fewer),n.

2. Member of Such a Jury: grand juror or grand juryman, petty juror or petit juror,n.

3. One Who Serves on a Jury: juror, juryman, member of the jury,n.

4. Group of Persons Making Up a Jury: panel,n.

5. Chairman of a Jury: foreman,n.

6. Bystanders, Court Spectators, etc., Ordered to Serve on a Jury when the Jury List Is Exhausted: tales,pl.n.

7. One Bystander, Court Spectator, etc., So Ordered: tales or talesman,n.

8. Court Writ Ordering Such: tales,n.

9. Court Writ Ordering a Sheriff to Summon Qualified Persons to Serve on a Trial Jury: venire or venire facias,n.

10. Person So Ordered to Serve on a Trial Jury: venireman,n.

11. List of Persons Called for Jury Service: panel,n.

12. To Enter (a Person's Name or Persons' Names) on Such a List; To Choose (a Jury) from Such a List: impanel or empanel,v. (impanelment,n.)

13. One's Function as a Juror: jury duty, jury service,n.

14. A Decision or Finding of a Jury: verdict, n.

1085. LAWYER

1. Lawyer: advocate (i.e., one who pleads another's cause in court), attorney, attorney at law; corporation lawyer (engaged in the law work of business corporations); counsel, counselor or counselor-at-law (esp. one doing trial work), criminal lawyer or attorney; defense lawyer or attorney, or lawyer or attorney for the defense; mouthpiece (slang); plaintiff's lawyer or attorney, or lawyer or attorney for the plaintiff,n. (attorneyship, counselorship,n.) ; *Also:*

1. legal light—brilliant lawyer
2. pettifogger—one who conducts a law practice of no great value, or in a petty or tricky fashion
3. Philadelphia lawyer—lawyer who knows all the legal tricks and dodges, and is not averse to using them—a disparaging term (colloq.)
4. shyster—unethical or dishonest lawyer; pettifogger (colloq.)

2. To Act as Such,v. *From Sec. 1:* pettifog, shyster (pettifoggery,n.)

3. British Lawyer: barrister (court or trial lawyer); solicitor (one who does not engage in trial work, i.e., is not a member of the British bar),n.

4. Military or Naval Officer Who Presents a Case before a Court-Martial: judge advocate,n.

5. Law Officer of a Government: attorney general (chief national or state law officer); corporation counsel (of a city, i.e., of a municipal corporation); district attorney (within a local district); prosecutor or public prosecutor (conducts criminal cases on behalf of the community); public defender (defends accused people who cannot pay for legal aid); solicitor (of some cities, government departments, etc.); solicitor general (chief law officer of some states; national law officer next in rank to the attorney general),n.

6. Group or Body of Lawyers; Lawyers in a Case: counsel,n.

7. The Lawyers of a Community: the bar,n.

8. The Profession of Law: the bar, law, law practice, the practice of law,n.

9. To Follow Such: practice law,v.

10. To Engage in Arguing a Cause as a Lawyer, in Court; To So Argue (a Cause): plead,v.

11. The Spirit of Lawyers; A Characteristic or Typical Attitude, Action, etc., of Lawyers: legality,n.

12. Language Characteristic of Lawyers, etc.: legalese,n.

13. Like, or Characteristic of, Lawyers: lawyerlike or lawyerly,adj.

14. Legal Adviser: counsel or counselor,n.

15. Legal Adviser of an Embassy or Legation: counselor,n.

1086. STATEMENT UNDER OATH

1. To Give Sworn Statements or Evidence, as in a Court of Law, etc.: attest, bear witness, depone, depose, testify, vouch, witness, v. (attestation, deposition, testification,n.)

2. To State under Oath (that . . .); To Bear Witness to,v. attest (that . . .), attest to, certify to; depone or depose (that . . .); swear (that . . .); swear to; testify (that . . .); testify to, vouch, witness,v. (attestation, certification, deposition, testification,n.)

3. Statement, Statements, or Evidence Given under Oath: attest or attestation, deposition, testification, testimony, witness,n. (depositional, testimonial,adj.)

4. One Who Bears Witness, Gives Statements or Evidence under Oath, etc.: attestant, attester, or attestor; deponent, deposer, testifier, voucher, witness,n.

5. Attesting: attestant,adj.

6. To State in Writing under Oath: depone, depose,v. (deponent, deposer,n.)

7. Written Statement Made under Oath: affidavit, deposition,n. (depositional,adj.)

8. Sworn Testimony Given by a Witness in Writing, and Offered in Court when the Witness Cannot Be Present in Person: deposition,n. (depositional,adj.)

9. To Place (a Person) under Oath: administer the oath to, attest, swear, swear in, v. (attestation,n.)

10. One Who Administers an Oath to a Person: swearer, swearer-in,n.

11. The Stand from Which a Person Gives Sworn Statements, Evidence, etc., in Court: witness stand,n.

12. To Go upon Such: take the stand, take the witness stand,v.

13. To Call as a Witness; To Call to Witness: obtest,v. (obtestation,n.)

14. Solemn and Earnest Declaration that One Will Speak the Truth, Based on an

Appeal to God, etc.; The Words So Used: oath,n.

15. To Make Such: swear, take an oath, take the oath,v.

16. To Admit to Public Office by Placing under Oath: administer the oath of office to, swear in,v.

17. To Be So Admitted: take the oath of office,v.

1087. ILLEGALITY

1. Illegal, i.e., Contrary to, or in Violation of, Law, a Law, or Laws: bootleg; criminal (i.e., involving a crime); illegitimate, illicit, lawbreaking, lawless, unlawful, wrongful,adj.

2. Illegality: criminality, illegalness, illegitimacy, illicitness, lawlessness, unlawfulness, wrongfulness,n.

3. An Illegal Act: breach of law, crime, illegality, infraction or infraction of the law, infringement or infringement of the law, malfeasance, misdeed, offense or offense against the law; sin (i.e., against moral law); transgression or transgression of the law; trespass (against the person, property, or rights of another, committed by force); violation or violation of the law,n.

4. To Commit an Illegal Act: break the or a law; infract the or a law; infringe the law; offend; perpetrate or commit a crime, illegal act, etc.; sin (i.e., against moral law); transgress, or transgress the law; trespass; trespass upon or against (the person, property, or rights of another by force); violate the or a law, or commit a violation,v. (breach of law or lawbreaking, infraction, infringement, offense, perpetration or commission, transgression, trespass, violation,n. transgressive, violative,adj.)

5. One Who Commits Such an Illegal Act: lawbreaker, criminal, infractor, infringer, malfeasant, offender, perpetrator, sinner, transgressor, trespasser, violator,n.

6. Habitual Breaking of the Law: crime,n.

7. Illegal or Improper Conduct, Practice, Activities, etc.,n.
  1. malfeasance—illegal or improper conduct, esp. on the part of a public official (malfeasant,adj.)
  2. malpractice—wrong, illegal, or improper conduct on the part of a medical doctor in treating his patients, whether from gross and blameworthy ignorance, carelessness, etc., or from criminal design or purpose; such conduct in any professional or official capacity
  3. malversation—illegal, fraudulent, corrupt, or improper conduct or practice in public office or other position of trust
  4. misconduct—illegal conduct by a public official or by anyone, such as a lawyer, witness, juror, etc., connected with the administration of law or justice, or with the courts
  5. misfeasance—performance of an otherwise legal act in an illegal manner; illegal exercise of official power or authority
  6. misprision—illegal or improper conduct, or neglect of duty, by a public official; illegal neglect to give information about a serious crime, or about treasonous acts
  7. wrongdoing, malefaction—illegal, improper, or sinful conduct; the commission of illegal, criminal, or improper acts

8. One Who So Acts Illegally, Improperly, etc.,n. From Sec. 7: malfeasant, malpractitioner, misfeasor; wrongdoer, malefactor, or, fem., malefactress

9. One Who Scoffs at the Law, Stands in

Defiance of Law, Defiantly Commits Illegal Acts, etc.: scofflaw,n.

10. Defiance or Disregard of the Law: outlawry,n.

11. Descr. of a Place, City, Section, etc., Where the Laws Are Poorly if at All Enforced, Esp. the Laws against Gambling, Prostitution, Vice, etc.: wide-open,adj.

12. Wrongful Act, Other than Breach of Contract, That May Be Prosecuted by Civil Rather than Criminal Legal Action, Such as Willful Injury or Injustice to a Person's Property, Legal Rights, Reputation, etc.: tort, wrong,n. (tortious,adj.)

13. To Make, Transport, or Sell (Goods, etc.) Illegally: bootleg,v. (bootlegging,n. bootlegger,n.)

14. So Made, etc., Illegally: bootleg,adj.

15. To Bring In or Send Out (Goods, etc.) Illegally, without Payment of Taxes, Secretly, Surreptitiously, etc.; To Engage in Such Activities: smuggle,v.

16. One Who Does Such: contrabandist, smuggler,n.

17. Such Activities; Illegal Traffic in Goods, etc.: contraband, smuggling,n.

18. Goods Illegally Brought In or Sent Out: contraband,n. (contraband,adj.)

19. To Make or Declare Illegal: damn, illegalize, outlaw,v.

20. To Deprive of, or Declare without, Legal Force: damn, invalidate, outlaw,v. (invalidation,n.)

21. Without Legal Force: invalid,adj. (invalidity,n.)

22. To Deprive of the Protection of the Law: proscribe, outlaw,v. (proscription, outlawry,n. proscriptive,adj.)

23. To Remove from the Jurisdiction of the Law or Courts: outlaw,v. (outlawry,n.)

24. One Who Has Been Deprived of the Protection of the Law: outlaw,n.

25. To Declare to Be Such: outlaw,v. (outlawry,n.)

26. Without, or Not Governed by, Law or Laws: anarchic or anarchical, lawless,adj. (anarchy, lawlessness,n.)

27. Lawless Disorder: misrule,n.

1088. CRIME

1. A Crime: criminality (act, practice, or activity); felony (serious, i.e., murder, robbery, etc.); misdeed; misdemeanor (less serious, such as speeding in a motorcar, illegal parking, spitting on the sidewalk, etc., and punishable usually by a fine rather than by imprisonment); villainy,n.

2. One Who Commits a Crime or Crimes; A Criminal,n. From Sec. 1: felon, misdemeanant, villain; Also: gangster, malefactor or, fem., malefactress; malfeasant; Also:
  1. bandit, highwayman—one who commits crimes, such as armed robbery, etc., on the highway
  2. bravo—daring or desperate bandit or criminal
  3. brigand—bandit who roves with an armed band, as on the highways, in the mountains or forests, etc. (brigandish,adj.)
  4. desperado, bravo, resolute—desperate, dangerous, or reckless criminal
  5. gangster, mobster—member of a gang of criminals
  6. gunman—criminal who uses a gun, whether for murder or robbery
  7. hood—hoodlum (slang)

8. hoodlum, hooligan—petty or rough gangster (hooligan,adj.)

9. outlaw—habitual criminal; criminal fleeing from the police or law; notorious criminal

3. Criminals Collectively, or as a Group,n. *From Sec. 2:* banditti or banditry, brigandage, gang

4. The Activities, Practices, or Qualities of Criminals,n. *From Sec. 2:* banditry, brigandage or brigandism, gangsterism, hoodlumism or hooliganism

5. State of Being an Outlaw: outlawry,n.

6. Criminals as a Class: felonry, the underworld,n.

7. Group of Suspected Criminals Standing in Line for Inspection by the Police or Others; Such a Line: lineup or line-up,n.

8. Pert. to, Involving, or of the Nature of, a Serious Crime: felonious,adj. (feloniousness,n.)

9. Guilty of Crime: criminal, malfeasant, villainous,adj. (criminality, villainy,adj.)

10. Person Guilty of a Crime: criminal, culprit,n.

11. Person Found Guilty of, and under Sentence for, a Crime: convict, criminal,n.

12. To Find or Judicially Declare (a Person) Guilty of a Crime: convict,v. (conviction,n.)

13. Person Capable of Committing Crimes: villain,n.

14. One Believed Guilty of a Crime: suspect,n.

15. Person Charged in Court with Crime or Illegality: culprit,n.

16. (Caught) in the Actual Commission of a Crime or Other Offense: in flagrante delicto (legal phrase), red-handed,adj.

17. To Involve in, or Connect with, a Crime: criminate, incriminate, inculpate,v. (crimination, incrimination, inculpation,n. criminative or criminatory, incriminatory or incriminating, inculpatory,adj.)

18. One Who Is Guilty of Aiding Someone Who Commits a Serious Crime or Felony, though Not Present at Its Commission: accessory; accessory before the fact (before its commission); accessory after the fact (after its commission),n.

19. One Who Is Associated with Others or with Another in Crime or Criminal Acts: accomplice,n.

20. Science, or Study along Scientific Lines, of Crime and Criminals: criminology,n. (criminologist,n. criminological,adj.)

21. Crime or Offense against the Ruling or Sovereign Power of a Nation or State, or against the Sovereign Ruler or His Dignity; Loosely, and with Connotations of Irony or Contempt, Such against One's Superior or His Dignity: lese majesty, leze majesty, or, French, lèse-majesté,n.

1089. THE SOUL

1. The Soul: pneuma, psyche, spirit,n. (psychic or psychical, spiritual,adj.)

2. Soul of a Dead Person Living in Another's Body (Jewish Folklore): dibbuk,n.

3. Personification of the Soul (Greek Mythology): Psyche,n.

4. Selected Theories, Doctrines, Beliefs, or Philosophies about the Soul,n.

   1. animism—that objects or phenomena of nature, as rocks, trees, wind, rain, etc., including the universe itself, have souls

and are alive; that the soul is the principle of life and of bodily health; that the soul exists independently of matter; that life is produced by spiritual, rather than by physical, substances (animist,n. animistic,adj.)

2. creationism—that God creates a new soul for each newborn infant (creationist,n. creationistic,adj.)

3. infusionism—that the soul was in existence before the body, and was infused into it either at the moment of conception or at birth (infusionist,n.)

4. palingenesis—that the soul passes, at one's death, into a new body (palingenesist or palingenist,n. palingenetic or palingenesian,adj.)

5. pre-existentism—that the soul existed before the body (pre-existentiary,n.)

6. reincarnation, reincarnationism—that the soul passes, at one's death, into a new body or form and thus returns to earth (reincarnationist,n.)

7. traducianism—that the soul is procreated or conceived at the same moment as the body (traducian or traducianist,n. traducian or traducianistic,adj.)

8. transmigration, transmigrationism, transmigration of souls—that the soul passes successively, at each death, into another body, either human or animal (transmigrationist,n.)

5. The Passing of the Soul, at One's Death, into a New Body: metempsychosis, palingenesis, reincarnation, transmigration,n. (palingenetic or palingenesian, transmigratory,adj.)

6. To So Pass—of the Soul; To Cause (the Soul) to So Pass: transmigrate,v.

7. Existence of the Soul before It Joined the Body: pre-existence,n.

8. Without a Soul: brute, soulless,adj.

9. To Free (a Soul, Spirit, etc.) of Its Body or Bodily Existence: discarnate, disembody, v. (discarnation, disembodiment,n.)

10. The Theological Doctrine that Human Beings Are Composed of Two Principles, Soul and Body, or of Two Natures, Spiritual and Physical, or That There Are Two Opposing Principles in the Universe, Good and Evil: dualism,n. (dualist,n. dualistic,adj.)

11. Looking Deeply into One's Soul, Figuratively Speaking, as to Make a Decision, etc.: soul-searching,adj. (soul searching,n.)

1090. SPIRITUALITY

1. Spiritual in the Sense of Having No Body, or No Bodily or Material Existence: discarnate, disembodied, immaterial, incorporate, incorporeal, unfleshly,adj. (immateriality or immaterialness, incorporeality or incorporeity,n.)

2. To Make So Spiritual: dematerialize, discarnate, disembody, immaterialize,v. (dematerialization, discarnation, disembodiment,n.)

3. To Become So: dematerialize,v. (dematerialization,n.)

4. Spiritual in the Sense of Characterizing or Suggesting, or Being Characterized by, Delicate Refinement or Influence of the Spirit or Soul, Rather than of the Body or of Fleshly Interests: airy, ethereal, rarefied; spiritual, or, fem., spirituelle (French); supernal, unfleshly, unworldly,adj. (airiness, ethereality or etherealness, rarefaction, unworldliness,n.)

5. To Make, or Treat as, Ethereal: etherealize,v. (etherealization,n.)

6. To Make Spiritual: etherealize, spiritualize,v. (etherealization, spiritualization,n.)

7. To Make More Spiritual, Ethereal, Refined in Character, etc.: rarefy,v. (rarefaction,n.)

8. To Give a Spiritual Meaning or Sense to; To Understand or Interpret in Such a Sense: spiritualize,v. (spiritualization,n.)

9. Affectedly Spiritual in Language, Manner, or Attitude: unctuous,adj. (unctuousness, unctuosity, or unction,n.)

10. Spiritual in the Sense of Being Devoted to the Hereafter, Usually with Indifference to the Concerns of the Present or Actual World; Devoted to the World of the Intellect and Imagination Rather than to Practical Affairs; Pert. to a Person of Such Worlds: otherworldly,adj. (otherworldliness, n.)

11. Spiritual in the Sense of Seemingly Not of This World, or of Being Like, or Characteristic of, a Spirit, etc.: supersensible, supersensory, supersensual, unearthly, unworldly,adj. (unearthliness, unworldliness,n.)

12. State or Quality of Being Spiritual in Any Previously Designated Sense: spirituality, spirituosity,n.

13. Spiritual in the Sense of Containing No Sexual Element, as the Relationship between Members of Opposite Sexes: platonic, adj.

14. Such a Relationship: platonism, platonic love,n.

15. Practice or Theory of Such a Relationship: platonism,n.

16. Ill, Spiritually: soul-sick,adj. (soul-sickness,n.)

1091. ONE'S NATURE

1. One's Nature, etc.: character, constitution, crasis, disposition, make-up; mettle (i.e., nature that is characteristic of a person); personality, temper, temperament,n. (constitutional, temperamental,adj.)

2. Descr. of the Nature or Personality of a Person, According to Some Schools of Psychology: cerebratonic ("brain-minded"—interested in contemplation, intellectual matters and expression, etc.); somatotonic ("body-minded"—derives pleasure from bodily activities, movement, or action, athletically inclined, etc.); visceratonic ("stomach-minded" —derives pleasure from eating, the good-fellowship of the table, etc.),adj.

3. One's Moral Nature: character,n.

4. Nature or Disposition That Causes One to Be Contemptuous of, or Disinclined to Observe, Rules, Restraints, Control, etc.: temperament,n. (temperamental,adj.)

5. State of Mind: attitude (toward a person or thing), cheer, frame of mind, humor, mood, spirits, temper, tone,n. (attitudinal, adj.)

6. Attitude: disposition; habitude (habitual); outlook, sentiment, slant, standpoint, turn or bent of mind, viewpoint or point of view,n.

7. Character, Nature, or Quality That Distinguishes a Person or Thing: caliber, complexion; ethos (of a religious, political, occupational, social, racial, or other group); savor (of a thing); tone; vein (as shown in conduct, etc.),n.

8. Of the Same Nature: connatural,adj.

9. Associated in Nature or Quality: cognate, connate,adj. (cognation, connation,n.)

10. One Who or That Which Is So Associated with Another: cognate,n.

11. A Distinguishing or Distinctive Characteristic or Quality: attribute, cachet, character, distinction, feature, idiosyncrasy or idiocrasy, peculiarity, property, savor, streak, token, trait, vein,n. (idiosyncratic,adj.)

12. Characteristic: distinctive, distinguishing, peculiar, specific, typical or typic,adj.

13. Characteristic of a Region: local, regional, vernacular,adj.

14. An Odd or Unusual Characteristic of a Person: eccentricity, foible, idiosyncrasy or idiocrasy, kink, oddity, peculiarity, quirk,n. (idiosyncratic,adj.)

15. A Habitual Peculiarity in Manner, Action, Behavior, Speech, etc.: mannerism,n.

16. Having Such: mannered,adj.

17. Excessive Use of Such Peculiarities, or of Distinctive Characteristics, in Literature, Art, Speech, Action, Behavior, etc.: mannerism,n. (manneristic,adj.)

18. Person Addicted to or Employing Such, Esp. an Author or Artist: mannerist,n.

19. To Be a Characteristic of: characterize, v. (characterization,n.)

20. To Have Somewhat the Characteristics or Nature of: partake of (feelings, qualities, etc.),v.

21. To Have the Important Characteristics of: typify,v. (typification,n.)

22. To Have the Distinctive Characteristics of: savor of, smack of,v.

23. Having the Distinctive Characteristics, Qualities, Flavor, Taste, etc., of Something That Is Unspoiled, Genuine, etc.: racy,adj. (raciness,n.)

24. A Characteristic Trait of Certain Peoples, n.
  1. Americanism—of the people of the U.S.
  2. Anglicism—of the British
  3. Gallicism, gallicism—of the French
  4. Germanism, Teutonicism—of the Germans
  5. Hibernicism, Hibernianism—of the Irish
  6. Orientalism, orientalism—of Asiatics, Chinese, Japanese, and other Eastern peoples
  7. Sinicism, Sinism—of the Chinese

25. The Characteristics, Character, Culture, Institutions, etc., of Western Peoples, or of Europeans, in Contrast to Those or That of Asiatics: Occidentalism,n.

26. Student or Partisan of Such: Occidentalist,n. (Occidentalist,adj.)

27. Such of Eastern or Asiatic Peoples: Orientalism or orientalism,n.

28. The Study of Such: Orientalism,n. (Orientalist,n.)

29. The Characteristics, Character, Culture, etc., of Slavic Peoples: Slavicism or Slavism, n.

30. The Cardinal Humors, or Bodily Fluids, According to Old Physiology, That Determined, by Their Relative Proportions, a Person's Nature, Physical or Emotional Character, etc.: blood (cheerfulness, optimism, etc.); choler or yellow bile (irritability, etc.); melancholy or black bile (mental depression); phlegm (sluggishness or apathy),n.

31. Pert. to the Bodily Humors: humoral,adj.

1092. EMOTION

1. An Emotion; A Feeling: affect (psychology), affection, attitude, passion, sensation, sentiment,n. (affective, affectional, attitudinal, passional or passionary,adj.)

2. Emotion or Feeling as an Influence on a Mental State or on an Idea (Psychoanalysis): affect,n. (affective,adj.)

3. An Expression of One's Feeling or Emotion, as in Words, etc.: sentiment,n.

4. A Short and Quickly Passing Emotion or Feeling: flicker,n.

5. One's Emotional State: cheer, frame of mind, humor, mood, spirits,n.

6. Bearing or Air Indicative of One's Emotional State: attitude,n. (attitudinal,adj.)

7. The Emotional or Mental Reactions, Attitudes, Conditions, etc., of a Person or Group: psychology,n. (psychological,adj.)

8. Emotional or Mental State in Respect to Courage, Hope, Confidence, Discipline, Enthusiasm, Willingness to Undergo Hardships or Privations, etc.: morale,n.

9. Very Changeable in Mood or Emotional State; Characterized by, Expressive or Indicative of, or Resulting from, Such Changeableness: broody, moody,adj. (moodiness,n.)

10. Impulse; Emotion or Feeling, Often Sudden, That Stimulates to Action: afflatus (i.e., a supernatural or overwhelming impulse); compulsion (an irresistible and often pathological impulse to perform some act, often an illogical or irrational act); conatus (a natural impulse); estrus, estrum, oestrus or oestrum (a very strong or passionate impulse); motive, urge,n.

11. Having, or Characterized by, Impulses: compulsive, heady, hot-blooded, hotheaded, impetuous, impulsive, madcap,adj. (compulsiveness, headiness, hotheadedness, impetuousness or impetuosity, impulsiveness or impulsivity,n.)

12. One Having, or Acting under the Force of, Impulses: hothead; madcap (esp. a girl), n.

13. To Cause to React to Impulses: motivate, v. (motivation,n. motivational,adj.)

14. A Giving In or Surrender to, or an Unrestrained Following of, Natural Impulses or Feelings: abandon or abandonment,n.

15. Emotion, Feeling, Idea, Desire, etc., That Persistently Haunts or Besets a Person: idée fixe (French), obsession,n. (obsessional or obsessive,adj.)

16. State of Being Haunted or Beset by Such Emotions, etc.: obsession,n. (obsessional, adj.)

17. To Haunt or Beset (a Person)—of Such Emotions, etc.: obsess,v. (obsession,n. obsessive,adj.)

18. Underlying Emotions or Feelings of a Group, the Public, etc., Esp. on a Question or Subject: pulse,n.

19. General Trend of Emotions, Feelings, or Attitudes (in or of a Place): climate, spirit, tone,n.

20. Overwhelming Display of Public or Group Emotions or Feelings: tidal wave,n.

21. Expression of Emotion or Feeling through the Quality or Sound of the Voice: tone,n. (tonal,adj.)

22. Shade or Slight Difference of Emotion or Feeling: nuance,n.

23. Capacity for Emotion, or for the Finer or Higher Emotions: sensibilities,pl.n.

24. A Manifesting of Such Capacity; A Refined or Higher Emotion: sentiment,n. (sentimental,adj.)

25. Very Great Depth, Strength, or Intensity of Emotion or Feeling: ardency, ardor, de-

lirium, ecstasy, fervency, fervor, fire; fury (esp. of anger or similar emotion); heat, passion, perfervor, rage, rapture; ravishment (esp. pleasant emotion, as joy, etc.); transport, vehemence, violence, warmth, white heat, zeal,n. (delirious, ecstatic or ecstatical, passional or passionary,adj.)

26. Feeling, Characterized by, or Indicative of Very Great Depth, Strength, or Intensity of Emotion: ablaze (feeling such only, as *ablaze with anger, desire,* etc.), ardent; burning (with); carried away, delirious, ecstatic; enrapt or enraptured (feeling such); fervent, fervid, fiery, furious, heated or hot, hot-blooded, hotheaded, impassioned; inflamed (feeling such); intense, passionate, perfervid, possessed, rapturous or rapt; ravished (feeling such); sultry, torrid; transported (feeling such); vehement, violent; warm-blooded (feeling such); white-hot, zealous,adj.

27. State or Condition of Such,n. *From Sec. 26:* ardency, deliriousness, ecstasy, fervency, fervidness, fieriness, furiousness, hotness, hotheadedness, impassionedness, intenseness or intensity, passionateness, perfervidness or perfervidity, rapturousness, sultriness, torridness or torridity, warmness or warmth, zealousness

28. Means of Sustaining an Emotion or Feeling: fuel,n. (as in *add fuel to his anger,* etc.)

29. To Fill (a Person, etc.) with Deep, Strong, or Intense Emotion or Feeling: carry away, fire, heat, enrapture, impassion, inflame, possess, transport,v.

30. One Who Is Subject to Intense and, Often, Impulsive Emotions: hothead,n.

31. One Who Is Subject to Fits or Attacks of Intense or Deep Emotion: ecstatic,n.

32. To Have (Strong Emotions or Feelings): burn with (emotions or an emotion),v.

33. Marked or Characterized by Violent, Terrible, Unrestrained, or Base Passions, as Crimes, Stories, etc.: lurid,adj. (luridness, n.)

34. Descr. of Language, Poetry, etc., That Expresses Strong or Deep Emotion: lyrical, adj. (lyricism or lyricalness,n.)

35. Descr. of Language That Indicates or Expresses Heat or Intensity of Emotion: hot, sulphurous or sulfurous,adj.

36. Descr. of Language That Expresses Wild or Unrestrained Emotions: dithyrambic, rhapsodic or rhapsodical,adj.

37. Language, Speech, Song, Verse, Composition, Writing, etc., That Expresses Such: dithyramb or dithyrambic, rhapsody,n. (dithyrambic, rhapsodic or rhapsodical,adj.)

38. To Speak or Write in Such Language, etc.: rhapsodize,v. (rhapsodist,n.)

39. Venting Feelings, Emotions, or Opinions with Extreme or Excessive Passion or Violence: rabid,adj. (rabidness or rabidity,n.)

40. Deeply Religious Emotion or Ecstasy, as from Thinking about God, etc.: theopathy, n. (theopathic or theopathic,adj.)

41. Violent Display of Emotion, Emotional Reaction, etc.: outburst, scene, storm,n. (stormy,adj.)

42. Strong, Sharp, or Violent Attack of Emotion: paroxysm, spasm, throe,n. (paroxysmal, spasmodic or spasmodical,adj.)

43. Period of Emotion or Feeling That Begins Suddenly and Lasts Only a Short Time: spasm,n. (spasmodic or spasmodical,adj.)

44. To Feel, Experience, or Show, Emotion: throb,v.

45. Possessed or Carried Away by a Foolish, Blind, Unreasoning, etc., Passion, as of

Love, etc.: infatuated or infatuate,adj. (infatuation,n.)

46. Person So Carried Away: infatuate,n.

47. Such a Passion: infatuation,n.

48. To So Carry (a Person) Away: infatuate, v. (infatuation,n.)

49. To Become Hot or Excited by Passion, as the Feelings, Heart, etc.: inflame,v.

50. To Take Fire, Figuratively, as Feelings, Passions, etc.: blaze, inflame, kindle,v.

51. Violent Emotional State Caused by a Frenzied Passion or Desire for an Unattainable Thing or Ideal: nympholepsy,n. (nympholeptic,adj.)

52. One Afflicted with, or One in, Such a State: nympholept,n. (nympholeptic,adj.)

53. Warm in, or Showing Warmth of, Emotion or Feeling: affectionate, ardent; attached (to); cheerful (as *a cheerful welcome*, etc.); cordial, fervent, fervid, hearty; perfervid (extremely); spirited, tender, warm, warm-blooded, warmhearted,adj.

54. Warmth of Emotion or Feeling: affection, affectionateness, ardency or ardor; attachment (to); cheerfulness, cordiality or cordialness; fervency, fervidness, or fervor; heartiness, spiritedness, warmheartedness, warmness or warmth,n.

55. To Become, or Cause to Become, Warmer in Emotion or Feeling: melt, thaw,v.

56. Spirited or Lively Warmth of Emotion or Feelings: élan,n. (French)

57. Warmth of Emotion or Feeling in Respect to Religion: unction,n.

58. The Deepest Emotions: heartstrings,n.

59. Sudden or Strong Intensity (of an Emotion, Often, though Not Necessarily, a Painful or Unpleasant Emotion): agony,n.

60. Deeply or Sincerely Emotional: deep-felt, heartfelt,adj.

61. To Make (an Emotion, Esp. Anger, Rage, etc.) More Intense: add fuel to, fan,v.

62. Descr. of Language Suitable for Expressing or Transmitting Emotion: affective,adj. (affectivity,n.)

63. Expressing or Conveying Deep Emotion or Feelings: soulful,adj. (soulfulness,n.)

64. Overflowing with Lively Emotions: bubbling or bubbly, ebullient, effervescent,adj. (ebullience, ebulliency, or ebullition; effervescence or effervescency,n.)

65. To Show, or Overflow with, Such Emotions: bubble, effervesce,v.

66. Showing Emotions: emotional,adj. (emotionality,n.)

67. Disposed to Show One's Emotions or Feelings Openly: demonstrative, emotional, expansive, free, outgoing, spontaneous, uninhibited, unrepressed, unrestrained, unreticent,adj. (demonstrativeness, emotionality or emotionalism, expansiveness, freeness, outgoingness, unrestraint, spontaneity or spontaneousness,n.)

68. One So Disposed: emotionalist,n.

69. Pouring Out One's Emotions or Feelings Excessively or without Normal Reserve: bubbling or bubbly, effusive, exuberant, gushy, adj. (effusiveness, exuberance or exuberancy, gushiness,n.)

70. Language That Does Such: gush,n.

71. To Talk in Such Manner: gush,v.

72. To Interpret, Treat, React to, or Consider in, an Emotional Manner: emotionalize,v.

73. Tendency to Be Emotional, or to Consider or Interpret Things from an Emotional Viewpoint: emotionalism,n.

74. Mixed Emotions; Conflicting or Contrary Emotions or Feelings about a Person or Thing: ambivalence,n. (ambivalent,adj.)

75. Emotional Reaction: response,n. (responsive,adj. repsonsiveness,n.)

76. A Sharing of, Participation in, or Appreciation of, the Emotions or Feelings of Another or Others: empathy (as if projecting one's personality into that of another, often for a better understanding of his motives, psychology, etc.); identification (as if by putting oneself in his place, the process often being unconscious); sympathy (with a person or persons of similar personality, tastes, etc., or with any person or persons in distress, sorrow, etc.),n.

77. Characterized by, Exhibiting, or Indicating Such,adj. *From Sec. 76:* empathic or empathetic, sympathetic

78. Feeling, Sharing, Appreciating, etc., Such,adj. *From Sec. 76:* empathetic, sympathetic

79. To Share, etc., the Feelings of Another, v. *From Sec. 76:* empathize, identify, sympathize (identification,n. sympathizer,n.)

80. To Share, etc., the Feelings of (Another), v. *From Sec. 76:* emphathize with, identify with, sympathize with,v. (identification,n.)

81. Sympathetic Relationship in Feeling: rapport,n.

82. To Have Such (of Two or More Persons): be in or en rapport (with),v.

83. Descr. of Emotions or Feelings Enjoyed or Suffered by Someone Who Imagines He Is Undergoing the Experiences of Another: vicarious,adj. (vicariousness,n.)

84. The Ascribing to Inanimate Objects of Emotions or Feelings that Only People and Animals Are Capable of—a Literary Device: empathy, pathetic fallacy,n. (empathic,adj.)

85. To Ascribe Such Emotions or Feelings to (Inanimate Objects): empathize,v.

86. To Give a Seemingly External Reality to (an Emotion, Feeling, or Thought): project, v. (projection,n.)

87. To Ascribe to Others One's Own Emotions, Feelings, Impulses, or Ideas, Generally through Unconscious Processes, and Esp. when These Are Not Fully Acceptable to Oneself: project (upon),v. (projection,n.)

88. A Revival and Reliving of Forgotten or Repressed Childhood Emotions, Feelings, Impulses, Experiences, etc., in a New Relationship, Esp. toward One's Psychoanalyst, and on an Unconscious Level; An Intense Emotional Attachment under These Circumstances to the Analyst: transference,n. (transfer to,v.)

89. The Response of the Psychoanalyst to the Patient's Transference, when the Analyst's Unconscious or Repressed Feelings Are Stirred Up: countertransference,n.

90. The Transference of Emotions from the Original Object, Idea, or Cause to Some Illogical Object or Idea—This on the Unconscious Level: displacement,n.

91. History, as Given by a Patient to a Psychiatrist, Psychotherapist, or Psychoanalyst, of His Emotional Problems, Conflicts, Life in General, etc.: anamnesis,n.

92. The Unconscious Incorporation of Another's Emotional or Moral Attitudes into One's Own Personality, Esp. by a Child of the Parents' Attitudes; The Unconscious Incorporation of Another's Feelings, Experiences, etc., into One's Own Personality as if They Were Internal Rather than External: introjection,n. (psychoanalysis)

93. To So Incorporate (Attitudes, Feelings, etc.): introject,v.

94. To Provide (an Emotion) with an Outlet of Expression: canalize, channel,v. (canalization,n. channel,n.)

95. One Who Turns His Emotions, Interests, and Thoughts in the Stated Direction: ambivert (intermediate between an introvert and extrovert, or a combination of both); extrovert or extravert (to the outside world, toward other people and objects, rather than inward upon himself); introvert (toward himself, his own thinking and emotions, etc.), n. (ambiversion, extroversion or extraversion, introversion,n. extrovert or extravert, introvert,adj.)

96. Descr. of One So Constituted: extroverted or extraverted, introverted,adj.

97. To So Turn or Direct (the Emotions, Mind, Interests, etc.): extrovert, introvert,v. (extroversion, introversion,n.)

98. Tending to Examine One's Own Emotions, Feelings, Thought Processes, Motivations, etc.: introspective, subjective,adj. (introspectiveness, subjectiveness or subjectivity, n.)

99. To Engage in Such Examination: introspect,v. (introspection,n.)

100. A Feeling of Emotional Well-Being: euphoria; exaltation (esp. abnormal),n. (euphoric,adj.)

101. Capable of Emotions, Emotional Response, etc.: passible, responsive, sensitive, sentient,adj. (passibility, responsiveness, sensitiveness or sensitivity, sentience or sentiency,n.)

102. The Motivational or Causative Factors or Circumstances of Emotional Reactions, Activities, Behavior, etc.: psychodynamics,n. (psychodynamic,adj.)

103. The Study of Psychology from This Point of View: psychodynamics,n. (psychodynamic,adj.)

104. Pert. to the Emotions: affective, emotional, emotive, pathetic; psychic or psychical (i.e., pert. to the emotions or mind, rather than to the body); psychological (i.e., pert. to the mind or emotions),adj.

105. Pert. to, or Influenced or Affected by, One's Emotional Reaction, Background, Feelings, Temperament, etc.: subjective,adj. (subjectiveness or subjectivity,n.)

106. Originating in the Emotions or Mind, or Caused by Emotional Conflicts, as Ailments, Disorders, etc.: psychogenic or psychogenetic,adj. (psychogenesis,n.)

107. Designating, Denoting, or Descr. of, Physical or Bodily Ailments of Emotional Origin, or Those That Are Influenced or Aggravated by Emotional Conflicts, Problems, etc.: psychosomatic,adj.

108. Branch of Medicine Dealing with Such: psychosomatics or psychosomatic medicine,n.

109. Pert. to the Interrelationship or Interaction of the Mind and Body, the Psychic and the Physical, the Emotional and Bodily States, etc.: psychosomatic,adj.

1093. SENSITIVENESS

1. Sensitive, i.e., Having Sharp Emotional Sensibilities, Easily Moved, etc.: delicate (i.e., in feeling or perception); impressionable, impressible, or waxen (i.e., to outside effects, influences, impressions, etc.); suggestible (i.e., to outside suggestion or influence), temperamental; tender (i.e., to the distress or suffering of others); thin-skinned (esp. to insults, criticism, etc.); touchy,adj. (delicacy or delicateness; impressionability, impressionableness, or impressibility; suggestibility, temperamentalness, tenderness, touchiness,n.)

2. Not Emotionally Sensitive: anesthetic (to), blunt or blunted, indifferent, insensible, insensitive or unsensitive, obtuse; thick-skinned, pachydermatous, or pachydermous (i.e., esp. to insults, criticism, etc.); unfeeling; unimpressionable (i.e., to outside effects, influences, impressions, etc.); untemperamental,adj. (bluntness, indifference, insensibility or insensibleness, insensitiveness or insensitivity, obtuseness, unfeelingness, unimpressionability,n.)

3. One Who Is Not Sensitive, Esp. to Insults, Criticism, etc.: pachyderm,n.

4. To Make (Someone) Insensitive: blunt,v.

5. To Become Insensitive: blunt,v.

6. In or to the Sensitive, or Most Sensitive, Part of One's Feelings: to the quick,adv. phrase (hurt, cut, wounded, etc., to the quick)

7. Excessively or Abnormally Sensitive: hypersensitive, overstrung,adj. (hypersensitiveness or hypersensitivity,n.)

8. To Be Sensitive to the Beauty or Art of: appreciate,v.

9. Sensitive to Beauty or Art: appreciative, artistic, esthetic or aesthetic,adj. (appreciativeness,n.)

10. One Who Is Sensitive to Beauty or Art: esthete or aesthete,n.

1094. SENTIMENTALITY

1. Sentimental: bathetic (esp. to a degree that is excessive); gushy (excessively); lackadaisical (weakly); maudlin (weakly, foolishly, or tearfully, or as the result of alcohol); mawkish (weakly, nauseatingly, or in a sickening manner); melodramatic (i.e., exaggeratedly sentimental, sensational, and violent, as a story, behavior, attitude, etc.); mushy (weakly or effusively); namby-pamby, namby-pambical, or namby-pambyish (weakly or affectedly); slushy (in a weak or silly manner, esp. language, speech, writing, etc.); unctuous (affectedly),adj.

2. Such Sentimentality,n. From Sec. 1: bathos, gushiness, lackadaisicalness, maudlinness, mawkishness, melodrama, mushiness, namby-pambiness or namby-pambyism, slushiness; unctuousness, unctuosity, or unction

3. Language of Such Sentimentality,n. From Sec. 1: gush, melodrama, mush, namby-pamby, slush

4. To Talk with Excessive Sentimentality: gush,v.

5. Weakly or Affectedly Sentimental Prose, Verse, or Person: namby-pamby,n.

6. Such Behavior, Actions, etc.: namby-pambics,n.

7. Excessively Sentimental, Sensational, etc., Behavior: melodramatics,n.

8. Tendency toward Sentimentality; Sentimental Habit, Nature, or Character; Excess of Sentimentality over Reason or Thinking; Excessive Indulgence in Sentimentality; A Display or Expression of Sentimentality: sentimentalism,n.

9. Person Showing or Having Such; Sentimental Person: sentimentalist,n.

10. To Make, Render, or Cause to Be, Sentimental; To Treat, Consider, or Regard with, Sentimentality; To Be Sentimental about or over; To Indulge in Sentimentality, or Think or Act in a Sentimental Manner: sentimentalize,v.

11. Sentimental, or Foolishly or Weakly Sentimental, Person; One Easily Influenced by Sentimentality: softy,n. (colloq.)

12. A Sentimental Emotion; Person Causing Such: heartthrob,n.

13. Not Sentimental: unsentimental,adj. (unsentimentality,n.)

14. One Who Is Not Sentimental: unsentimentalist,n.

1095. ENTHUSIASM

1. Enthusiasm,n.
   1. **ardor, ardency**—intense and warm enthusiasm
   2. **ebullience, ebulliency, ebullition**—overflowing, seething, or bubbling enthusiasm
   3. **élan (French)**—lively and spirited enthusiasm
   4. **esprit de corps (French)**—enthusiasm of a group, or of a member or members for the group, including devotion to its ideals, etc.
   5. **fanaticism**—extreme, blind, or unreasoning enthusiasm, often in respect to religion or religious activities
   6. **fervency, fervidness, fervor**—eager, warm, and intense enthusiasm
   7. **fire**—burning enthusiasm
   8. **furor**—religious enthusiasm; general public exhibition of enthusiasm
   9. **heartiness**—sincere enthusiasm
   10. **mania**—persistent or excessive enthusiasm, as for a thing, activity, interest, etc.
   11. **monomania**—exaggerated and excessive enthusiasm in one direction only, often with attendant lack of enthusiasm or interest in other directions
   12. **overenthusiasm**—excessive enthusiasm
   13. **overzealousness**—excessive zeal
   14. **perfervor, perfervidness, perfervidity**—great, extreme, or excessive fervency
   15. **rabidness, rabidity**—extreme, blind, or unreasoning enthusiasm
   16. **rage**—extremely intense enthusiasm; height of enthusiasm
   17. **red heat**—extreme enthusiasm
   18. **verve**—enthusiasm and/or vigor or energy, as in expression of ideas in literature, art, etc.
   19. **wholeheartedness**—enthusiasm in doing or acting
   20. **zeal, zealousness**—warm and active enthusiasm, esp. in attaining or getting something
   21. **zealotry**—excessive, extreme, or unreasonable zeal

2. Enthusiastic,adj. *From Sec. 1:* ardent, ebullient, fanatic or fanatical, fervent or fervid, hearty, monomaniacal, overenthusiastic, overzealous, perfervid, rabid, red-hot, wholehearted or whole-souled, zealous or zealotic; *Also:*
   1. **crazy about, wild about**—extremely enthusiastic about (colloq.)
   2. **dithyrambic, rhapsodic, rhapsodical**—wildly or extravagantly enthusiastic; expressing wild enthusiasm
   3. **enthused**—enthusiastic (colloq.)

3. An Enthusiast,n. *From Sec. 1:* fanatic, monomaniac; zealot (from either *zeal* or *zealotry*)

4. An Enthusiasm, i.e., That Which Arouses Enthusiasm, or That about Which One Is Enthusiastic,n. *From Sec. 1:* furor, mania, monomania, rage; *Also:*
   1. **craze**—sudden and very popular enthusiasm, usually of short duration
   2. **fad**—temporary enthusiasm, as a thing,

activity, etc., of large numbers of people
3. **furor, furore**—that which creates great public enthusiasm

5. Like a Fad: faddish, faddy, or fadlike,adj.

6. Fond of, Given to, or Following, Fads: faddish or faddy,adj.

7. Person Who Is Fond of, or Given to, Fads, Follows Fads, or Has a Fad: faddist,n.

8. To Make (Someone) Enthusiastic: enthuse (colloq.), fire,v.

9. To Cause (Someone) to Show Enthusiasm; To Be Enthusiastic; To Show One's Enthusiasm: enthuse,v. (colloq.)

10. To Show One's Enthusiasm for a Team, Contestant, etc., as by Applauding, Yelling, etc.: cheer; root (colloq.),v. (rooter,n.)

11. To Make (Someone) a Fanatic; To Show Fanaticism or Act Fanatically: fanaticize,v.

12. To Shout (in Enthusiasm, Excitement, etc.): whoop,v.

13. A Shout (of Enthusiasm, Excitement, etc.): whoop,n.

14. Expressing Enthusiasm in Emotional or Poetic Language: dithyrambic, lyrical, rhapsodic or rhapsodical,adj.

15. Such Expression of Enthusiasm: lyricism or lyrism,n.

16. Wildly or Extravagantly Enthusiastic Composition, Song, Utterance (whether Written or Spoken), Language, etc.: dithyramb or dithyrambic, rhapsody,n. (dithyrambic, rhapsodic or rhapsodical,adj.)

17. To Write or Speak Such, or in Such a Manner: rhapsodize,v.

18. One Who So Speaks or Writes: rhapsodist,n. (rhapsodistic,adj.)

19. Intense Enthusiasm for Talking: furor loquendi,n. (Latin)

20. Such for Writing: furor scribendi,n. (Latin)

21. Like, or Characteristic of, a Zealot: zealot or zealotic,adj.

22. Behavior, Actions, Nature, etc., of a Zealot: zealotism or zealotry,n.

23. Lacking in Enthusiasm; Not Particularly Enthusiastic: chilly (to); cold (to); cool (to); frigid, heartless, lukewarm, nonchalant, tepid, unenthusiastic; unfanatical (i.e., not a victim of extreme, unreasoning, or blind enthusiasm); unfervent, unfervid, unzealous,adj. (chilliness, coldness, coolness, frigidity or frigidness, heartlessness, lukewarmness, nonchalance, tepidness or tepidity, unenthusiasm, unzealousness,n.)

24. To Lose Enthusiasm: chill, cool,v.

25. To Lose Religious Enthusiasm: backslide, v. (backslider,n.)

26. To Lower (Enthusiasm): chill, cool, dampen, discourage,v. (discouragement,n.)

27. That Which Does So: chill, damp, dampener, damper, discouragement,n.

28. To Destroy the Enthusiasm of (a Person): dampen, discourage, wet-blanket,v. (discouragement,n.)

29. One Who, or That Which, Does So: dampener, discouragement, discourager, wet blanket,n.

30. State or Condition of Having One's Enthusiasm Destroyed: discouragement,n.

1096. FRIENDLINESS

1. Friendly,adj.
   1. **affable**—friendly in the sense of welcoming approach, conversation, etc.

2. **amiable**—friendly in a pleasant and agreeable way, i.e., easy to get along with, etc.
3. **amicable**—characterized by friendliness, as relations, actions, attitudes, settlements, agreements, etc.
4. **boon**—friendly—found esp. in the phrase *boon companion*
5. **chummy**—friendly in the sense either of having a close friendship, as people, or of being sociable, as a time, etc.
6. **clubbable, clubable, clubby**—exhibiting friendliness; sociable
7. **companionable**—friendly, i.e., easy to be friends with; sociable
8. **congenial**—friendly, as a person, atmosphere, evening, etc.
9. **conversable**—friendly in the sense of being easy to approach and make conversation with
10. **convivial, jovial**—friendly in the sense of enjoying friends, good fellowship, eating and drinking together, etc.
11. **cordial**—friendly in a warm and sincere fashion
12. **debonair, debonaire, debonnaire**—friendly or affable and courteous
13. **familiar**—friendly, i.e., associated in close friendship
14. **genial**—friendly and cheerful, sympathetic, warm, kind, etc.
15. **gregarious**—friendly in the sense of being fond of companionship or company, or of preferring the company of others to being alone
16. **hearty**—sincerely friendly, as a greeting, person, etc.
17. **homey, homy**—friendly, i.e., characterized by friendliness or intimacy the way a home is, as a place, atmosphere, etc.
18. **intimate, bosom, close**—friendly, i.e., associated in very close and personal friendship or relations, as *an intimate, bosom, or close friend, to be intimate or close with,* etc.
19. **matey**—friendly (chiefly British)
20. **neighborly**—friendly, like a neighbor
21. **pally**—very friendly (with), i.e., like pals (colloq.)
22. **sociable, social**—friendly, i.e., pleasant to get along with in friendship or friendly relations; fond of or enjoying the friendship or company of others; characterized by pleasant friendliness, as a time, place, atmosphere, etc.
23. **thick**—very friendly or intimate (with), as people, companions, etc. (colloq.)

2. Friendliness,n. *From Sec. 1:* affability or affableness, amiability or amiableness, amicability or amicableness, chumminess, companionableness or companionability, congeniality, conversableness, conviviality, joviality, or jovialness; cordiality or cordialness, debonairness, familiarity, geniality or genialness, gregariousness, heartiness; intimacy, intimateness, or closeness; neighborliness; sociability, sociableness, sociality, or socialness; *Also:*
1. **amity**—friendliness and peace; friendliness and harmony; such between nations
2. **bonhomie, bonhommie**—pleasant, friendly, and affable manner
3. **comradeship, camaraderie, comradery**—friendliness and good spirit of the sort that exists between close companions, those who participate in the same cooperative activities, etc.
4. **friendship**—friendliness; friendly feeling, feelings, or disposition

3. A Friend,n. *From Sec. 1:* chum, familiar, intimate, matey, pal; *Also:*
1. **Achates**—loyal friend or companion (after the name of Aeneas's friend in Vergil's *Aeneid*)

2. **acquaintance**—slight or casual friend, i.e., with whom one is not close or intimate
3. **alter ego**—friend so close or inseparable as to be almost one's other self
4. **ami (masc.), amie (fem.)**—friend (French)
5. **amigo (Spanish)**—friend; native of Latin America friendly to Americans
6. **bon ami (masc.), bonne amie (fem.)**—good friend (French)
7. **buddy**—companion or comrade (colloq.)
8. **cater-cousin**—close or intimate friend
9. **cohort**—companion (loose usage)
10. **companion, comate**—friend who shares one's experiences, activities, or play
11. **compeer**—companion; comrade
12. **comrade**—friend who is closely associated with one in activity, experiences, play, interests, etc.
13. **confidant (masc.), confidante (fem.)**—intimate and trusted friend to whom one confides one's personal secrets or affairs
14. **crony**—intimate or good friend with whom one participates in various activities, games, etc.
15. **fellow**—companion; comrade
16. **good fellow**—sociable person; one who enjoys, and partakes of, the warm companionship of others in convivial activities, or who offers warm companionship, etc.
17. **mate**—companion; comrade

4. Friendship, i.e., State of Being, or Association as, A Friend or Friends,n. *From Sec. 1:* familiarity, intimacy; *From Sec. 3:* acquaintanceship, companionship; comradeship, camaraderie, or comradery; fellowship, good-fellowship or good-fellowhood; *Also:* company, society, sodality; solidarity (among a group, and arising from common interests, needs, etc.),n.

5. Friends, Collectively; A Group of Friends: circle or social circle; clique (small, exclusive, and often snobbish); companionship (of companions); company; coterie (small and select, esp. friends who gather frequently for social or other purposes); society, n.

6. Pert. to, Like, or Characteristic of, a Clique; Inclined to Form, or Stay in, a Clique: cliquish, cliquy, or cliquey,adj. (cliquishness,n.)

7. To Form a Clique; To Gather or Associate in a Clique: clique,v. (colloq.)

8. Like, Suitable to, or Characteristic of, a Comrade or Comrades: comradely,adj. (comradeliness,n.)

9. Pert. to, or Like, a Companion: companionate,adj.

10. Suitable for, or Characterized by, Social Friendliness: conversable,adj. (conversableness,n.)

11. Given to Social Pleasures or to a Life of Such; Hence, by Extension, Dissipated, Loose, Licentious, etc.: gay, primrose, rackety,adj.

12. Pert. or Relating to Friendly Relations: social,adj.

13. Loyalty among Friends: camaraderie, comradery,n.

14. Person Who Tries to Make Friends, or Tries to Get on Terms of Familiarity, with Well-Known, Influential, or Wealthy People: social climber,n. (social climbing,n.)

15. An Expression or Instance of Warm Friendliness: cordiality,n.

16. One Who Enjoys the Good-Fellowship of Others: convivialist,n.

17. Act or Remark That Shows Good-Fellowship: conviviality,n.

18. Act, Behavior, Attitude, or Speech, etc., That Is Excusable Only on the Ground of Very Close Friendship: familiarity, intimacy, n.

19. Undue or Excessive Instances of Such: familiarities, intimacies,pl.n.

20. To Make (Someone) Fit for Companionship with Others: socialize,v. (socialization, n.)

21. An Establishing of Friendly Relations, or a Re-establishing of Former Friendly Relations: rapprochement,n. (French)

22. To Be, or Associate, on Friendly Terms or in Friendship (with): associate (with); chum (with); comrade (with); fraternize (with); hobnob (with); neighbor (with); pal (with); socialize (with),v. (association, fraternization,n.)

23. To Be a Companion to: companion,v.

24. To Try to Get on Terms of Friendship with: cultivate, cultivate the friendship of,v. (cultivation,n.)

25. To Try to Promote (Friendship or a Friendship, Friendliness, etc.): cultivate,v. (cultivation,n.)

26. To Be Friendly to; To Be, or Act as, a Friend to: befriend,v.

27. To Regard with Friendliness; To Be Actively Friendly to: favor,v.

28. To Become Friendly, More Friendly, or Less Unfriendly: thaw, unbend,v.

29. To Seek the Friendliness of (a Person) by Insincere Flattery or Constant Attentions; To Engage in Such Activities for Such a Purpose: curry favor (with),v.

30. To Gain the Friendliness of (Someone) by Being Pleasant, Often Servilely or Insincerely Pleasant: ingratiate oneself with,v. (ingratiation,n. ingratiating or ingratiatory, adj.)

31. To Make (Someone) Friendly, More Friendly, or Less Unfriendly, by the Stated Means: appease (by giving in to the demands of, esp. political or economic demands, as of an aggressor); conciliate (by giving what is wanted, or by soothing, persuading, etc., and thus overcoming the hostility or distrust of); disarm (by removing the hostility, suspicion, or distrust of); mollify (by soothing the wounded feelings, anger, indignation, etc. of); placate (by quieting or allaying the anger of, by pleasing or satisfying, etc.); propitiate (by preventing or soothing the anger or hostility of); reconcile (i.e., cause to be friendly, or once again friendly, often to one another, as by settling points of controversy, differences, etc.); soothe (as a person, or his feelings, anger, resentment, etc., by kind or flattering talk, etc.); win over (by being pleasant, by persuasion, etc.),v. (appeasement, conciliation, mollification, placation, propitiation, reconciliation or reconcilement,n. conciliator, mollifier, placater, propitiator, reconciler, soother,n.)

32. Acting or Serving to Do Such,adj. *From Sec. 31:* appeasing or appeasive; conciliating, conciliative, or conciliatory; mollifying; placating, placatory, or placative; propitiating, propitiative, or propitiatory; reconciling or reconciliatory, soothing, winning (unconciliatory, unmollifying, unpropitiatory, unsoothing,neg.adj.)

33. Tending to Do Such,adj. *From Sec. 31:* conciliative or conciliatory, placative or placatory, propitiative or propitiatory, reconciliatory,adj.

34. Intended or Designed to Do Such,adj. *From Sec. 31:* conciliatory, placatory, propitiative or propitiatory, reconciliatory, soothing; *Also:* soft,adj. (as *a soft answer*, etc.)

35. That Which Does Such, or Is Offered or Given for Such Purpose,n. *From Sec. 31:* propitiation

36. Capable of Being Made Friendly, More Friendly or Less Unfriendly,adj. *From Sec. 31:* appeasable, conciliable, mollifiable, placable or pacable, propitiable, reconcilable,adj. (appeasableness, placability or placableness, reconcilability or reconcilableness,n.)

37. State of Being, or Having Been, Made So,n. *From Sec. 31:* appeasement, conciliation, mollification, propitiation, reconciliation,n.

38. One Who Has Been Made So,n. *From Sec. 31:* reconcilee,n.

39. Incapable of Being Made So,adj. *From Sec. 31:* unappeasable or inappeasable, unconciliable, unmollifiable; implacable, unplacable, or impacable; unpropitiable; irreconcilable, unreconcilable, or reconcileless; unsoothable or soothless,adj. (unappeasableness; implacability, implacableness, or impacability; irreconcilability, irreconcilableness, or unreconcilableness,n.)

40. One Who Cannot Be Reconciled: irreconcilable,n.

41. Without Friends: companionless, friendless, outcast, uncompanioned,adj.

42. Person without Friends or Home, Esp. a Child: waif,n.

43. Person Cast Out by Friends and Home; Friendless and Homeless Person: outcast,n.

1097. EMOTIONAL LACK, COLDNESS, INDIFFERENCE, ETC.

1. Incapable of Emotions or Feelings: impassible, insensible,adj. (impassibility or impassibleness, insensibility or insensibleness, n.)

2. To Make So: insensibilize,v. (insensibilization,n.)

3. Lacking in, or Devoid of, Emotions or Feelings; Having or Showing Little or No Emotion or Feeling; Emotionally Dull; Not Easily Aroused in or to Emotion: apathetic, bloodless, blunt or blunted; bovine (i.e., like a cow or ox); callous, calloused, or casehardened (esp. to the sufferings of others); cold, cold-blooded, coldhearted, cool, dispassionate, dull, feelingless; hardhearted or heartless (esp. to the sufferings of others); impassive or impassible, indifferent, insensate, insensible, insensitive, insentient, lethargic or lethargical, low-strung, marble; matter-of-fact, pragmatic, or pragmatical; obtuse, oscitant, passionless, phlegmatic or phlegmatical, rockhearted; rocky (of the heart, feelings, etc.); stoic or stoical (i.e., suppressing, or not showing, emotion, esp. in pain, distress, misfortune, etc.); stolid, stony, stonehearted, or stonyhearted; torpid, unemotional, unfeeling, unresponsive,adj. (apathy or apathism, bloodlessness, bluntness, bovinity, callousness or callosity, coldness, cold-bloodedness, coldheartedness, coolness, dispassion or dispassionateness, dullness or dulness, hardheartedness or heartlessness; impassiveness, impassivity, impassibleness, or impassibility; indifference, insensateness, insensibility or insensibleness, insensitiveness or insensitivity, insentience or insentiency, lethargy, obtuseness, oscitancy or oscitance, passionlessness; phlegmaticness, phlegmaticalness, phlegmatism, or phlegm; rockiness, stoicism or stoicalness, stolidity or stolidness, stoniness or stonyheartedness; torpor, torpidity, or torpidness; unemotionalism or unemotionalness, unfeelingness, unresponsiveness,n.)

4. One So Lacking, etc., in Emotions,n. *From Sec. 3:* apathist, insensate; phlegmatic, phlegmatist, or phlegmat; stoic (apathistical, adj.)

5. To Make (Someone) Unfeeling: blunt, brutalize, callous, caseharden, dull, indurate, insensibilize, lethargize, torpify,v. (brutalization, induration, insensibilization,n. indurative, torporific,adj.)

6. To Become Unfeeling: brutalize, callous, indurate,v. (brutalization, induration,n.)

7. Lacking Human Feelings, i.e., Like an Animal in This Respect: brutal, brutish, inhuman, inhumane,adj. (brutality, brutishness, inhumanity or inhumanness,n.)

8. One So Lacking: brute,n.

9. An Act Showing Such Lack: brutality, inhumanity,n.

10. To Make or Become So: brutalize, brutify,v. (brutalization,n.)

11. Lack of Spiritual Feeling, Esp. among Monks: acedia,n.

12. One So Lacking: acediast,n.

13. To Dull the Emotions, Mind, Senses, Reactions, etc., of (a Person): benumb; daze (as by a blow, shock, liquor, etc.); drug or narcotize (with drugs or narcotics); numb; shock (as by a blow, surprise, emotional trauma, etc.); stun (as by a blow, shock, surprise, unusual sight, etc.); stupefy (as by surprise, shock, liquor, narcotics, etc.); torpify, v. (narcotization, stupefaction,n. narcotic or narcotical, stupefactive or stupefacient, torporific,adj.)

14. In Such a State: benumbed, dazed, drugged or narcotized, numb or numbed, shocked, stunned; stupefied, stuporous, or stupid; torpid,adj.

15. Such a State: daze, narcosis, numbness, shock, stun; stupefaction, stupor, or stupidness; torpor, torpidness, or torpidity,n.

16. That Which Causes Such a State: drug or narcotic, shock, stun,n.

17. Indifferent: apathetic or apathetical, casual, disinterested; insouciant (esp. as a general frame of mind); lackadaisical, languid, languorous; Laodicean (esp. in matters of religion); lethargic or lethargical, listless, lukewarm, nonchalant, perfunctory; pococurante, pococurantic, or pococurantish; stoic or stoical (i.e., indifferent to both pleasure and pain); superior to (i.e., bravely or calmly indifferent to, as something painful or unfortunate); tepid, unconcerned,adj. (apathy or apathism, casualness, disinterest or disinterestedness, insouciance, lackadaisicalness, languidness, languor or languorousness, lethargy, listlessness, lukewarmness, nonchalance, perfunctoriness, pococuranteism or pococurantism, stoicism or stoicalness; superiority (to); tepidness or tepidity; unconcern, unconcernment, or unconcernedness,n.)

18. One Who Is Indifferent,n. *From Sec. 17:* apathist, Laodicean, pococurate, stoic,n.

19. To Make (Someone) Indifferent: alienate,v. (alienation,n.)

20. To Make (Someone) Lethargic: lethargize,v.

21. Systematic Indifference, Esp. to Religion: indifferentism,n. (indifferentist,n.)

22. Deliberate or Open Indifference, or Display of Such (to a Person): cold shoulder,n.

23. To Show Such to (a Person): cold-shoulder,v. (colloq.)

24. Characterized by, or Showing, Coldness of Feelings, Lack of Warmth, etc.: aloof, bloodless, chill, chilly, cold, coldhearted, cool, distant, frigid, frosty, icy, lukewarm, marble, nonchalant; offish, standoffish, or standoff; remote, rockhearted, spiritless, tepid, unaffectionate, uncordial, unfeeling, unfervent, unfervid, unhearty, wintry or wintery,adj. (aloofness, bloodlessness, chilliness, chilliness, coldness, coldheartedness, coolness, distantness or distance, frigidity or frigidness, frostiness, iciness, lukewarmness, nonchalance; offishness, standoffishness, or standoff; remoteness, tepidness or tepidity, uncordiality, unfeelingness, wintriness,n.)

25. To Make Cold in Emotions or Feelings: chill, cool,v.

26. That Which Makes So: chill,n.

27. To Make (Feelings, Desires, Passions, etc.) Cool; To Become So: quench,v.

28. Descr. of Feelings, Desires, Passions, etc., That Are Capable of Being Cooled: quenchable,adj. (quenchableness,n.)

29. Descr. of Feelings, etc., That Are Incapable of Being Cooled: quenchless, unquenchable,adj. (unquenchableness,n.)

30. Not Emotionally Demonstrative; Not Tending to Show or Express One's Feelings Openly or Freely: constrained, inhibited, reserved, restrained or self-restrained, reticent, self-controlled, shy, unaffectionate, undemonstrative, uneffusive, unemotional, unresponsive, unspontaneous,adj. (constraint, inhibition, reserve or reservedness, restraint or self-restraint, reticence or reticency, self-control, shyness, undemonstrativeness, unemotionalism or unemotionalness, unresponsiveness,n.)

31. Not Emotionally Involved; Showing a Lack of Emotional Involvement: detached, disinterested, dispassionate, impartial, indifferent, objective, unprejudiced,adj. (detachment, disinterest or disinterestedness, dispassion or dispassionateness, impartiality or impartialness, indifference, objectiveness or objectivity,n.)

32. Lacking Spontaneity of Feelings; Done without Feeling, Enthusiasm, Interest, etc.: mechanical, perfunctory,adj. (mechanicalness, perfunctoriness,n.)

33. Lacking in the Ability to Feel, Understand, See, etc., the Emotions of Others: imperceptive,adj. (imperceptiveness or imperceptivity,n.)

34. Having Such Ability: perceptive,adj. (perceptiveness or perceptivity,n.)

35. Having, or Showing, No Thought or Regard for the Feelings of Others: inconsiderate, indelicate, outrageous, tactless, thoughtless, unconsiderate, untactful, unthinking, wanton,adj. (inconsideration or inconsiderateness, indelicacy, outrageousness, tactlessness, thoughtlessness, unconsiderateness, untactfulness, unthinkingness, wantonness,n.)

36. Having, or Showing, Such Thought or Regard: considerate, delicate, regardful, tactful; tender (of); thoughtful,adj. (consideration or considerateness, delicacy, regardfulness, tact or tactfulness; tenderness (of); thoughtfulness,n.)

37. To Have or Show Such Thought for: consider, think of,v.

38. The Psychological Process Whereby a Feeling, Emotion, Impulse, etc., Is Held Back; an Emotional or Psychic Interference with Freedom of Action: inhibition,n.

39. To Affect with This Process: inhibit,v. (inhibitive or inhibitory,adj.)

40. To Undergo Such: inhibit oneself,v.

41. Held Back, or Generally Held Back, by Such a Process: inhibited,adj. (inhibition,n.)

42. To Force (an Unacceptable Impulse, Feeling, Emotion, Desire, etc.) into the Unconscious So That One Loses All Awareness or Memory of It, though It Nevertheless Influences Conscious Feelings or Behavior: repress,v. (repression,n. repressive,adj.)

43. An Impulse, etc., So Forced into the Unconscious: repression,n.

44. Affected by, Acting under, or Showing, Repressed Impulses, etc.: repressed,adj.

45. To Deliberately Push Out of Conscious Awareness (an Unacceptable Impulse, Feeling, Emotion, Desire, etc.), and Thus Escape Gratifying It: suppress,v. (suppression,n. suppressive,adj.)

46. Descr. of Such an Impulse, etc.: suppressed,adj.

47. An Impediment to Memory, Recognition, Thought Processes, etc., That Results from Repression or from Emotional Conflicts: block, emotional block,n.

1098. EMOTIONALLY HARDENED

1. To Harden (Someone) Emotionally or in Feelings: callous or caseharden (to the misery or suffering of others); harden, indurate; inure (to burdens, difficulties, painful circumstances, etc., as by repetition or habit); sear, steel, toughen,v. (induration, inurement,n. indurative,adj.)

2. To Become So Hardened: callous, harden, indurate, steel oneself, toughen,v. (induration,n.)

3. So Hard or Hardened: callous, calloused, or casehardened; hard, hardened, indurate, inured, steel, steeled, tough, toughened,adj. (callousness or callosity, hardness, inurement, toughness,n.); Also: cold-blooded, flinty, hardhearted, obdurate, rockhearted, stonehearted, stony, stonyhearted, unfeeling,adj. (cold-bloodedness, flintiness, hardheartedness, obduracy or obdurateness, stoniness, stonyheartedness, unfeelingness,n.)

4. To Toughen (the Mind): anneal,v.

5. To Harden (Something Abstract) Figuratively, i.e., Cause It to Set in a Rigid, Conventional, or Unchanging Form: ossify, v. (ossified,adj. ossification,n.)

1099. EMOTIONAL EFFECT

1. To Have an Emotional Effect upon: affect; exhilarate (i.e., produce gay, lively, or happy emotions in); impress, move, stir, touch,v. (exhilaration, impression,n.)

2. Having, or Serving or Tending to Have, Such an Emotional Effect: affecting or affective, exhilarating or exhilarative, impressive, moving, stirring, touching,adj. (affectivity, impressiveness,n.); Also: emotional, emotive, pathetic, sentimental,adj. (emotionality, emotiveness or emotivity, sentimentality,n.)

3. So Affected Emotionally: affected, exhilarated, impressed, moved, stirred, touched, adj. (exhilaration,n.)

4. Capable of Being Emotionally Affected: affectible or affectable, emotional, impressionable or impressible,adj. (affectibility, emotionality or emotionalism; impressionability, impressionableness or impressibility,n.)

5. One Capable of Being Emotionally Affected: emotionalist,n.

6. Easily Moved to Tender Emotions: kindhearted, soft, softhearted, tender, tenderhearted,adj. (kindheartedness, softness, soft-

heartedness, tenderness, tenderheartedness, n.)

7. One Easily Moved to Tender Emotions: softy (colloq.), tenderheart,n.

8. An Emotional Effect: impression or impress,n.

9. The Power or Ability to Affect the Emotions: appeal,n.

10. Not Moved or Affected Emotionally: unaffected, unimpressed, unmoved, unstirred, untouched,adj.

11. To Withstand or Be Untouched by (Emotional Effect or Appeal): resist,v. (resistance,n.)

12. To Affect Strongly; To Have a Strong Emotional Effect upon: arouse (as to anger or similar emotion); carry away, commove, excite, fire; impassion (i.e., with passion, etc.); inflame (to passion or violent feelings, or to anger or similar emotions); overpower (very strongly); overwhelm (so strongly as to be almost unendurable); penetrate (deeply); pierce (sharply); quicken (i.e., stir up, esp. the emotions, etc.); ravish (i.e., carry away with emotion, esp. joy, delight, or other pleasant feeling); rouse (i.e., stir up, as a person, emotion, etc., as if this had been sleeping); shock (i.e., with surprise, disgust, distress, etc.); stir or stir up; strike (forcibly, with a strong emotion); transport (i.e., carry away with a very strong or deep feeling or emotion),v. (arousal, excitement or excitation, inflammation, penetration, ravishment,n.)

13. Strongly Affecting, or Serving or Tending to Affect Strongly,adj. From Sec. 12: exciting, excitative, or excitatory; inflaming or inflammatory, overpowering, overwhelming; penetrating, penetrant, or penetrative; piercing, ravishing, rousing, shocking, stirring, striking, transporting or transportive, adj.; Also: 1. poignant—affecting the emotions strongly or painfully (poignancy or poignance,n.)

14. That Which Causes Such a Strong Emotional Effect,n. From Sec. 12: excitement, ravishment, shock

15. Strongly Affected Emotionally,adj. From Sec. 12: aroused, carried away, commoved, excited, fired, impassioned, inflamed, overpowered, overwhelmed, penetrated, pierced, quickened, ravished, roused, shocked, stirred or stirred up, transported

16. State of Being Strongly Affected,n. From Sec. 12: arousal, excitement or excitation, impassionedness, inflammation, ravishment, shock, transport

17. Easily Moved to Strong Emotion: excitable,adj. (excitability or excitableness,n.)

18. Capable of Being Strongly or Easily Moved to Passion, to Violent Feelings, or to Emotions Like Anger, etc.: inflammable,adj. (inflammability,n.)

19. To Be, or Become, Aroused—of Emotions, etc.: arouse, blaze, burn, fire, flame, inflame, quicken, rise, stir, surge or surge up, well or well up,v. (blaze, fire, rise, surge,n.)

20. To Increase the Strength of (a Feeling): fan, inflame,v.

21. To Increase the Strength of Emotion or Feeling in (a Person): inflame,v.

22. To Affect (Someone) with (a Feeling or Emotion): inspire (a feeling or emotion) in (a person), or inspire (a person) with (a feeling or emotion),v.

1100. EXCITEMENT

1. To Excite (a Person, Group, Feeling, etc.); To Have an Exciting Effect upon (a

Person, Group, Feeling, etc.): agitate (usually unpleasantly, so as to cause inner turmoil, etc.); commove; electrify or galvanize (as if by an electric shock); ferment (i.e., cause excitement in or among); fire (i.e., fill with great excitement); flurry (i.e., fill with sudden, nervous excitement); fluster or flustrate (i.e., fill with nervous excitement, or excite and confuse with alcohol); flutter (i.e., cause nervous excitement or agitation in); frenzy or phrensy (i.e., cause wild, violent, or uncontrollable emotional excitement in, or drive to this); inflame (extremely, esp. to passion, or to anger or similar emotion); intoxicate (to a condition resembling drunkenness or to a point beyond self-control); pique (as if by stinging or irritating, as *pique one's curiosity, interest,* etc.); provoke (to a feeling, or a feeling in, or to act or react); rouse or arouse (as to action, etc.); stimulate (as to action, or by alcohol); sting (sharply, esp. into action or reaction); thrill (very greatly, and usually pleasurably, as if causing to shake or shiver with excitement); tickle or titillate (pleasantly, agreeably, pleasurably, or so as to produce pleasure in); whet (the appetite, desires, etc.),v. (agitation, electrification or galvanization, fermentation or ferment, inflammation, intoxication, provocation, arousal [from *rouse* or *arouse*], stimulation, titillation,n.)

2. Exciting; Serving or Tending to Excite; Excitant, Excitative, or Excitatory,adj. *From Sec. 1:* agitating or agitative, commoving; electrifying, electric, galvanizing or galvanic; inflaming or inflammatory, intoxicating or intoxicant; piquant, racy, or salty; provoking or provocative; stimulating, stimulative, or stimulant; thrilling; tickling, titillating, or titillative,adj.; *Also:*

1. **breath-taking**—extremely exciting
2. **dramatic**—exciting in a way to stir the emotions or imagination; exciting in the manner of a play with its conflicts, etc.
3. **hair-raising**—so exciting or terrifying as to seem able to make one's hair stand on end
4. **heady**—exciting in the sense of causing extreme inner excitement; intoxicating
5. **hectic**—full of, or characterized by, excitement, as *hectic time, pleasures,* etc.
6. **lively**—exciting or full of excitement, as a tune, party, etc.
7. **lurid**—exciting or sensational, i.e., filled with violence, passion, crime, etc., as a story, life, etc.
8. **melodramatic**—sensational and, often, full of, or exhibiting, exaggerated emotionalism or sentimentality
9. **purple**—lurid or sensational, as writing, passage of prose, etc.
10. **rip-roaring, rip-roarious**—exciting and noisy, or hilariously exciting, as a period, time, party, etc. (colloq.)
11. **salty**—provocative in a pleasant manner, as writing, wit, language, etc.
12. **sensational**—exciting or thrilling; intended to produce or arouse great excitement, thrill, shock, etc., in the readers or viewers, as writing, a play, performance, etc.
13. **spine-tingling**—so exciting as to be capable of making one's spine tingle, as adventures, tales, performances, etc.
14. **stirring**—exciting, i.e., full of events or circumstances that excite the emotions
15. **woolly, wild and woolly**—characterized or marked by great excitement, as in the days of the western frontier of the U.S.
16. **yellow**—sensational in a cheap way, as newspapers, journalism, etc.
17. **zestful**—exciting in quality, character, etc.

3. Exciting Quality, n. *From Sec. 1:* thrill; *From Sec. 2:* piquancy, raciness, or saltiness;

provocativeness; drama, headiness, liveliness, luridness, melodrama, saltiness, zest or zestfulness

4. That Which Excites,n. *From Sec. 1:* intoxicant, provocation or provocative, stimulant or stimulus, sting; thriller (as a story, book, movie, etc.); titillant, titillator, or titillater; *Also:*

1. **excitant**—that which stimulates physiologically
2. **oestrus, oestrum, estrus, estrum**—something that stimulates or excites; stimulus

5. To Be Excited; To Show or Feel Excitement, or Be in a State of Excitement,v. *From Sec. 1:* ferment, fluster, flutter, thrill; *Also:*

1. **bubble, bubble over**—be happily excited
2. **effervesce**—show feelings of great and bubbling excitement
3. **rage**—rush around, move, talk, etc., in great excitement or agitation, as the winds or sea, or, of a person, in anger, violence, etc.
4. **rampage**—behave, act, move around, etc., in uncontrollable excitement or fury
5. **run amuck, run amok**—rush about in a destructive frenzy, killing people, smashing things, etc., having lost all self-control
6. **seethe**—be in a state of great excitement or agitation
7. **simmer**—be, remain, or continue in a state of controlled, suppressed, or subdued excitement or agitation
8. **storm**—rush around, move, talk, etc., in terrible excitement or fury, great passion, etc.
9. **throb**—feel, experience, or show great emotional excitement
10. **tingle**—feel thrills of excitement, as with love, fear, expectation, etc.
11. **twitter**—tremble or shiver with great excitement

6. Excited; Affected by, in a State of, or Manifesting, Excitement,adj. *From Sec. 1:* agitated, electrified or galvanic, fired or afire, flurried, flustered; fluttered, fluttery, fluttering, or aflutter; frenzied or phrensied, inflamed, intoxicated or drunk, piqued, provoked, roused or aroused, stimulated, stung, thrilled or athrill, tickled or titillated, whetted; *From Sec. 2:* hectic; *From Sec. 5:* bubbling or bubbly, effervescent, raging; rampaging, rampageous, or rampant; amuck or amok (from *run amuck*); seething, simmering, storming or stormy, throbbing; tingling, tingly, or atingle; twittering, twittery, or atwitter; *Also:*

1. **ablaze, afire, aflame**—highly excited; on fire with the excitement of an emotion
2. **agog**—extremely excited, esp. by curiosity, desire, eagerness, anticipation, expectation, or interest
3. **berserk**—in such a frenzy of excitement as to be destructive or violent
4. **beside oneself (with)**—so highly excited (with an emotion) as to be almost, or to seem, bereft of one's senses
5. **charged, emotionally charged**—filled with excitement, or with emotional excitement or tension, as atmosphere, a person, etc.
6. **delirious**—emotionally excited to an extreme or violent degree
7. **demoniac, demoniacal**—in frantic or frenzied excitement, as if possessed by a demon
8. **ebullient**—feeling, seething, or overflowing with, or manifesting, great emotional excitement
9. **ecstatic**—beside oneself with the excitement of a deep and powerful emotion; in a frenzy of poetic inspiration
10. **feverish, fevered, feverous, febrile**—in a

state of, or showing, intense nervous excitement

11. **frantic, frenetic, phrenetic, furibund**—wild with feelings of excitement, nervous excitement, or other violent or uncontrollable passions or emotions

12. **furious**—full of, or manifesting, violent or raging emotional excitement

13. **hysterical, hysteric**—full of, or manifesting, extreme, uncontrollable, and sometimes violent emotional or nervous excitement for no rational or sensible reason

14. **overwrought**—extremely, excessively, or unduly excited, as with nervousness, or with fear, anxiety, uneasiness, or similar emotions

15. **red-hot, white-hot**—full of great excitement

16. **wild**—full of, manifesting, or in a state of, violent and often uncontrollable excitement

17. **wrought-up, worked-up**—greatly excited, as with nervousness, or with fear, anger, anxiety, uneasiness, or similar emotions

7. Excitement; State, Condition, Feeling, or Manifestation of Excitement; Excited Behavior, etc.,n. *From Sec. 1:* agitation, electrification or galvanization, ferment or fermentation, fire, flurry; fluster, flustration, or flusteration; flutter, frenzy or phrensy, intoxication or drunkenness, provocation, stimulation, thrill, titillation; *From Sec. 2:* dramatics, melodramatics (both, behavior); *From Sec. 5:* effervescence or effervescency; rage (condition or behavior); rampage (behavior), rampageousness, or rampancy; amok (state of the person running amuck—so called by Malayans); seethe, simmer, storminess; tingle (state or feeling); twitter; *From Sec. 6:* delirium or deliriousness; ebullience, ebulliency, or ebullition; ecstasy; fever, feverishness, or febricity; franticness; fury or furiousness, hysteria or hysterics, red heat or white heat, wildness; *Also:*

1. **buck fever**—unsettling or unnerving excitement that attacks a new hunter when he sights game for the first time

2. **combustion**—great or violent excitement or agitation

3. **estrus, estrum, oestrus or oestrum**—wild, violent, or uncontrollable emotional excitement (estrous or oestrous,adj.)

4. **furor**—wild, uncontrollable excitement; such in relation to religion; general display, or popular demonstration, of excitement

5. **furor poeticus (Latin), furor**—wild and uncontrollable excitement of poetic inspiration

6. **hoopla**—great excitement, as in a place

7. **orgasm**—excessive, wild, or violent emotional excitement; fit or violent outburst of such (orgasmic or orgastic,adj.)

8. **racket**—excitement of social activity, revelry, etc.

9. **stir**—excitement, or state of noisy excitement, in a place, as *the city is in a stir over the crime;* excitement, as *to create a stir*

10. **tizzy, dither**—highly excited and therefore absent-minded state, often over a matter of little importance, as *to be in a tizzy or dither*—of persons

11. **to-do**—excitement, as in a place

12. **whirl**—state or condition of excitement marked by giddy alternation or succession of feelings and ideas, often contradictory, almost always confusing, as *to be in a whirl, his mind is in a whirl,* etc.

8. Excited Person,n. *From Sec. 6:* ecstatic (i.e., one subject to fits of ecstasy); frenetic or phrenetic (from *frantic, frenetic,* etc.); fury (from *furious*—esp. a woman); *Also:*

1. **maenad, menad**—wildly excited, raging, or frenzied woman (maenadic,adj.)

9. The Use of, or Addiction to Using, Literary or Other Material Intended to Produce Great Excitement, Shock, Thrill, etc., in Readers or Spectators: sensationalism,n. (sensationalist,n. sensationalistic,adj.)

10. A Fit or Attack of Extreme, Uncontrollable, or Violent Emotional or Nervous Excitement, Often Marked by Alternating Frantic Laughter and Weeping: hysterics,n.

11. Fond of, or Enjoying, the Excitement of Social Activity: rackety,adj.

12. Showing, or Marked or Characterized by, Outbreaks or Outbursts of Excitement: spasmodic or spasmodical,adj.

13. The Most Exciting Part (of Some Event, Plot, etc.); The Highest Point or Moment of Excitement: climax,n. (climactic or climactical,adj.)

14. Series of Events That Are As Exciting As the Conflict and Plot of a Play: drama,n. (dramatic,adj.)

15. Such if Exaggerated and Oversentimentalized: melodrama,n. (melodramatic,adj.)

16. To Consider, Interpret, or Present (Things, Events, Oneself, etc.) in a Highly Exciting Light, as if in a Play: dramatize,v. (dramatization,n.)

17. To Do Such in an Exaggerated and Oversentimentalized Fashion: melodramatize,v.

18. Charming, Attractive, and Exciting, as Events, Situations, People, Characters, Type of Work, etc.: glamorous, romantic,adj.

19. Such a Quality: glamour, romance,n.

20. To Invest with, or Consider as Having, Such a Quality: glamorize, romanticize,v.

21. One Who Constantly or Habitually Does So: romanticist,n.

22. Warrior of Scandinavian Mythology Who Fought with Terrible Frenzy, Strength, and Courage: berserker or baresark,n.

23. Excitable; Easily Excited: agitable (i.e., easily agitated); combustible; fiery (as a person, temper, nature, etc.); hot-blooded, hotheaded, inflammable, nervous, passionate; provokable or provocable (i.e., easily, or capable of being, provoked); vascular,adj. (combustibility or combustibleness, fieriness, hotheadedness, inflammableness or inflammability, nervousness, passionateness, provocability, vascularity,n.)

24. Given or Subject to Outbursts of Emotional Excitement: spasmodic or spasmodical,adj.

25. Not Excitable; Not Easily Excited: bovine, calm, cool, coolheaded, impassive, imperturbable, inexcitable; nonchalant (coolly so); passionless, phlegmatic or phlegmatical, placid, quiet, stolid, unexcitable, uninflammable, unnervous, unpassionate, unprovokable,adj. (bovinity, calmness, coolness, coolheadedness, impassiveness or impassivity, imperturbability or imperturbableness, inexcitability, nonchalance, passionlessness; phlegmaticness, phlegmaticalness, phlegmatism, or phlegm; placidity or placidness, quietness, stolidity or stolidness, unexcitability, uninflammability, unpassionateness, n.)

26. Unexcitable Person; Person of Unexcitable Temperament: phlegmatic, phlegmatist, or phlegmat,n.

1101. COMMOTION; DISTURBANCE

1. Commotion; Disturbance,n.

1. **ado**—commotion attended by excitement, noise, activity, talking, emotional reactions, etc.

2. **backwash**—commotion caused by something that has happened, passed, etc.
3. **ballyhoo**—noisy commotion (colloq.)
4. **bluster**—commotion and noise; noisy or boisterous commotion
5. **clatter**—noisy commotion or disturbance
6. **combustion**—violent commotion
7. **convulsion**—violent and extreme commotion or disturbance; violent and extreme disturbance, as of the earth's surface, i.e., an earthquake, or in social or living conditions or relations
8. **disorder**—public commotion or disturbance; disturbance of the peace of a community
9. **distemper**—civil or political commotion
10. **excitement**—commotion; bustling commotion
11. **ferment, fermentation, seethe, yeast**—commotion; state of commotion; state of commotion and agitation
12. **flurry**—commotion; sudden commotion; a sudden commotion or disturbance of prices in the stock market
13. **fracas**—disorderly and noisy disturbance
14. **fray**—a commotion; a noisy, excited commotion
15. **fuss, bother**—a commotion over trifles; an unnecessary commotion, as in *don't make such a fuss*, etc.
16. **hurly-burly**—noisy and excited commotion
17. **maelstrom**—dangerously turbulent commotion of affairs
18. **pandemonium**—wild and confused, or wild and lawless, commotion or disturbance, or the scene or place of such
19. **pother**—noisy commotion or fuss
20. **rabblement**—violent and noisy commotion or disturbance, as if made by a mob
21. **riot**—commotion; wild or violent commotion; commotion, or disturbance of the peace, caused by a number of people gathered together in a public place; such an illegal commotion or disturbance by three or more people gathered in a public place that terrorizes the populace (legal)
22. **rout**—commotion or disturbance created by three or more people for the purpose of starting a riot (legal)
23. **row**—a commotion or disturbance, as *create or start a row*, etc.
24. **ruction, ruckus**—noisy commotion or disturbance (colloq.)
25. **ruffle**—a commotion or disturbance, as one attended by arguing or fighting, or one that disturbs the peace, etc.
26. **rummage**—state of commotion and confusion, as *everything is in a rummage*, etc.
27. **rumpus**—noisy and disturbing commotion, as *start a rumpus*, etc.
28. **simmer**—state of controlled, subdued, or beginning commotion
29. **squall**—a noisy commotion or disturbance (colloq.)
30. **stir**—state of noisy commotion or disturbance in a place, as *the city is in a stir over the crime;* a commotion, as *create quite a stir*, etc.
31. **storm**—a violent commotion or disturbance of affairs, as in a home, city, country, social group, etc.; a commotion or disturbance of the earth's atmosphere
32. **tempest**—a violent or raging commotion, as *create a tempest*, etc.
33. **to-do**—commotion and excitement, often over trifles
34. **tumult**—commotion; a commotion; violent and noisy commotion; noisy commotion or disturbance created by a large number of people or by a crowd or mob; violent commotion and disorder, as in a place
35. **turbulence, turbulency**—state or condi-

tion of commotion, or violent and noisy commotion, disorder, or disturbance
36. **turmoil, moil**—state of commotion, confused commotion, or disturbance; a commotion
37. **upheaval**—sudden commotion or disturbance in social, domestic, or community affairs or relations
38. **uproar**—state of noisy and violent, or rowdy and disorderly, commotion or disturbance; such a commotion or disturbance
39. **welter**—commotion; confused commotion; commotion and confusion
40. **whir, whirr**—state of commotion and hurry
41. **whirl**—state of commotion, or of commotion and confusion, as *things are in a whirl*, etc.

2. To Be in a State of Commotion or Disturbance,v. *From Sec. 1:* ferment, seethe, or yeast; simmer

3. In a State of, or Characterized by, Commotion or Disturbance,adj. *From Sec. 1:* disorderly, fermenting or seething, hurly-burly, riotous, simmering, stormy, tempestuous, tumultuous or tumultuary, turbulent, uproarious (disorderliness, riotousness, storminess, tempestousness, tumultuousness or tumultuariness, turbulence or turbulency, uproariousness,n.)

4. To Take Part, or Engage in, a Riot: riot, v. (rioter,n.)

5. To Throw into Commotion; To Cause a Commotion or Disturbance in or among: disturb, stir up; tempest (i.e., cause a violent or raging commotion in); torment (as the waves, etc.); tumult (among); uncalm,v. (disturbance,n.)

6. To Cause or Make a Commotion by Being Disorderly: disturb the peace,v.

7. Causing Commotion, Disorder, or Disturbance: turbulent,adj. (turbulence or turbulency,n.)

8. One Who Makes or Causes Commotion, Confused Commotion, or Disturbance: turmoiler,n.

9. To Disturb Violently (a Peaceful or Calm Condition, etc.): shatter or, less violently, violate (the peace, quiet, calm, silence, etc.),v. (violation,n.)

10. To Disturb in Arrangement, Order, Condition, etc.: derange (i.e., in arrangement, condition, functioning, etc.), disarrange, disarray, discompose; disjoint (in order, continuity, etc.); dislocate, disorder, mess or mess up; muss or muss up (colloq.); throw into disorder, unsettle, upset,v. (derangement, disarrangement, dislocation,n.)

11. Disturbed in Arrangement, Order, Condition, etc.,adj. *From Sec. 10:* deranged, disarranged, disarrayed, discomposed, disjointed, dislocated; disordered, disorderly, unorderly, or unordered; messy or messed up, mussed up, thrown into disorder, unsettled, upset,adj.

12. To Become So Disturbed,v. *From Sec. 10:* disjoint, unsettle

13. Such Disturbed Arrangement or Condition,n. *From Sec. 10:* derangement, disarrangement, disarray, discomposure, disjointedness, dislocation, disorder or disorderliness, messiness

1102. HAPPINESS

1. Happy; Being Happy; Showing Happiness: beatific (showing pure, exalted, or blessed happiness); blissful (possessing, feeling, or showing supreme or exalted happiness); blithe, blitheful, or blithesome (in feelings or temperament, or showing such); cheerful (i.e., being in a mildly happy state, or showing such); content or contented (i.e., with what one possesses or is, and not desiring more or better); delighted (i.e., full of great joy, etc., or showing such); ecstatic (i.e., overwhelmed with happiness, beside oneself with joy or delight, or showing such); enchanted (i.e., delighted); enraptured (i.e., filled with the keenest happiness or delight); exalted (i.e., filled with joy, joy and pride, etc.); gay, glad, gleeful or gleesome; joyful or joyous (often in a less quiet, more expressive manner, showing such, or attended by such, as an occasion, etc.); jubilant (i.e., shouting with happiness, delight, joy, etc.); overjoyed (extremely happy, or overcome with happiness, joy, etc.); rapturous (i.e., filled with the most intense happiness or joy, or showing such); ravished (i.e., filled with transporting happiness or joy); rhapsodic or rhapsodical (i.e., showing, or expressive of, ecstasy); thrilled (feeling an extreme degree of excited happiness),adj.

2. Happiness; State or Condition of Being Happy; Expression or Display of Happiness, n. *From Sec. 1:* beatitude or beatification, bliss or blissfulness, blitheness or blithesomeness, cheerfulness or cheer; contentment, contentedness, or content; delight or delightedness, ecstasy, enchantment, exaltation; gaiety, gayety, or gayness; gladness; glee, gleefulness, or gleesomeness; joy, joyfulness, or joyousness; jubilance, jubilancy, jubilation, or jubilee; rapture or rapturousness, ravishment; *Also:* enjoyment (i.e., delight); eudemonia or eudaemonia (i.e., happiness, or state or condition of happiness); felicity; rejoicing or jubilee (i.e., feeling, display, or expression of happiness); well-being or welfare (i.e., general condition of happiness, health, etc.),n. (eudemonic, eudemonical, eudaemonic, or eudaemonical,adj.)

3. To Make Happy; To Cause or Produce Happiness in,v. *From Sec. 1:* blithen, cheer or cheer up, content, delight, enchant, enrapture, exalt, gladden, joy, ravish, thrill; *Also:* regale (i.e., delight, as with stories, gossip, good food, etc.); rejoice,v. (regalement,n.)

4. Causing or Promoting Happiness,adj. *From Sec. 1:* beatific, blissful, cheerful or cheery; delightful, delightsome, or delighting; enchanting, enrapturing, exalting, glad or gladsome, joyful or joyous; jubilant (as an occasion, etc.); ravishing, thrilling (blissfulness, cheerfulness or cheeriness, delightfulness or delightsomeness, gladness or gladsomeness, joyfulness or joyousness,n.); *Also:* Elysian, enjoyable; eudemonic, eudemonical, eudaemonic, or eudaemonical; felicific, happy, winsome,adj. (enjoyableness, winsomeness, n.)

5. Source of Happiness: cheer, delight, enchantment, felicity, joy, thrill,n.

6. Happy, Specifically over Accomplishment, Success, Triumph, or Victory, or over a Favorable Occurrence or Result, etc.: elated; exalted (often excessively, so); exultant, gleeful or gleesome, jubilant, triumphant,adj.

7. Such Happiness: elation or elatedness, exaltation or exaltedness; exultation, exultance, or exultancy; glee, gleefulness, or gleesomeness; jubilation, jubilance, or jubilancy; triumph,n.

8. To Feel or Show Such Happiness: crow, exult, jubilate, triumph,v. (exultation, jubilation,n.)

9. To Shout (in Exultation): whoop,v. (whoop,n.)

10. To Cause Such Happiness in: elate, exalt, v. (exaltation,n.)

11. To Feel, Express, or Show Happiness: crow (i.e., show or express happiness and pride; content oneself (with what one has, etc.); delight (in something, or to do something); enjoy (something or doing something); enjoy oneself (in); gloat over (i.e., gaze at, or think about, with malicious delight or joy); joy (i.e., be joyful); jubilate (i.e., express or show one's happiness); purr (i.e., express happiness or contentment in, or seemingly in, the way a cat does); rejoice (in or at); revel in (i.e., be most happy about or over); rhapsodize about or over (i.e., speak with ecstasy about); tread or walk on air (i.e., be very happy),v. (enjoyment, jubilation,n.)

12. Sound, or Figurative Sound, of Purring: purr,n.

13. To Say (Something) in Such Tones: purr,v.

14. To Become Happier: cheer up, soar,v.

15. To Be Glad to Get, Accept, Receive, etc.: welcome,v.

16. Descr. of, or Designating, That Which One Is Glad to Get, Accept, Receive, etc.: welcome,adj. (welcomeness,n.)

17. To Be Happy Together with, and Express Such Happiness to (a Person, Group, etc.), over His or Their Success, Good Fortune, etc.: congratulate, felicitate,v. (congratulation, felicitation,n. congratulant or congratulatory,adj.)

18. One Who Is Happy for or with Another or Others,n. *From Sec. 17:* congratulant or congratulator, felicitator

19. An Expression or Expressions of Such Happiness,n. *From Sec. 17:* congratulations, felicitations

20. To Wish Happiness to: felicitate,v. (felicitation,n. felicitator,n.)

21. To Greet with Happiness or Joy: acclaim, welcome,v. (acclaim or acclamation, welcome,n.)

22. Happiness That Comes from a Life Lived According to the Principles and Rules of Reason—an Aristotelian Concept: eudemonia or eudaemonia,n.

23. State or Place of Perfect, Absolute, Unalloyed, etc., Happiness: Eden, Elysium or Elysian fields, paradise, seventh heaven, Shangri-La, Utopia or utopia,n. (Elysian; paradisiacal, paradisiac, paradisaical, or paradisaic; Utopian or utopian,adj.)

24. One Who Believes in Such a State or Place: Utopian or utopian,n.

25. Delightful and Fertile Place, Region, Area, Spot, etc.: garden,n.

26. Time or Period of Great Happiness, Prosperity, Peace, etc.: golden age,n.

27. Time or Period When the Greatest Happiness and Peace Will Exist on Earth, When Christ Will Rule, etc.: millennium,n. (millennial or millenary,adj.)

28. Believer in Such a Time, etc.: millenarian, millenary, or millenarist,n.

29. Belief in Such a Time, etc.: millenarianism,n.

30. Descr. of a Time or Period When All Is Happy, Calm, Peaceful, Prosperous, etc.: Saturnian,adj.

31. Occasion When Great Happiness, Joy, etc., Is Displayed or Expressed: rejoicings,n.

32. Occasion or Season of Joy, Rejoicing, etc.: jubilee,n.

33. Joyful or Happy Celebration: jubilation, n.

34. Descr. of a Day That Is Especially Happy, or That Is Especially Productive of Happiness: red-letter,adj.

35. System of Ethics That Views Actions or Activities in the Light of Their Ability to Create Happiness: eudemonism, eudaemonism, eudemonics, or eudaemonics,n.

36. One Who Follows or Believes in Such a System of Ethics: eudemonist or eudaemonist,n. (eudemonistic, eudaemonistic, eudemonistical, or eudaemonistical,adj.)

37. Science of Happiness: eudemonics or eudaemonics,n. (eudemonic or eudaemonic, adj.)

1103. CHEERFULNESS

1. Cheerful; Being Cheerful; Showing Cheerfulness or Good Cheer: airy (i.e., with a heart light as air, or showing such, as a manner, act, attitude, etc.); beaming (as a person or face, etc.); blithe, blitheful, blithehearted, or blithesome (in feelings or temperament, or showing such); boon (as a companion, etc.); breezy (i.e., cheerful or gay and lively, as a tune, manner, etc.); bright (as a person, manner, spot, etc.); buoyant; carefree or insouciant (i.e., lighthearted, without care or anxiety, etc., as a person, manner, etc.); cheery; chipper (and, often, lively, as in mood, etc.); debonair, debonaire, or debonnaire; ebullient or effervescent (i.e., overflowing or bubbling with cheerfulness, high spirits, etc.); exhilarated, gay; genial (often in a sympathetic or friendly fashion); glad, good-natured or goodhumored; hilarious (and noisy); jaunty (i.e., without care or anxiety, and, often, lively, etc.); jocund, jolly; jovial (i.e., having, characterized by, or showing warm and goodhearted cheerfulness, playful spirits, good humor, etc.); lighthearted, lightsome; lively or sprightly (as a tune, manner, etc.); merry (i.e., full of lively or laughing cheerfulness, etc.); riant; roseate, rosy, or rose-colored (as views, expectations, anticipation, etc.); sunny; winsome (as a smile, face, etc.),adj.

2. Cheerfulness,n. *From Sec. 1:* airiness, blitheness or blithesomeness, breeziness, brightness, buoyancy; insouciance (from *carefree* or *insouciant*); cheeriness, debonairness; ebullience, ebulliency, or ebullition; effervescence or effervescency, exhilaration; gaiety, gayety, or gayness; geniality or genialness, gladness; good nature, goodnaturedness, good humor, or good-humoredness; hilarity or hilariousness, jauntiness, jocundity, jollity or jolliness, joviality or jovialness, lightheartedness, lightsomeness, liveliness or sprightliness; merriment or merriness, rosiness, sunniness or sunny nature, winsomeness; *Also:* bonhomie or bonhommie (of manner); good spirits, high spirits,n.

3. To Cheer or Cheer Up, i.e., Make Cheerful,v. *From Sec. 1:* blithen, brighten or brighten up, exhilarate, gladden (exhilaration,n.); *Also:* boost or raise the spirits of; buck up (colloq.); comfort or console (i.e., cheer up by relieving of grief, depression, sorrow, etc.); encourage, enliven, hearten, lighten; solace (i.e., cheer up by relieving of grief, depression, or sorrow),v. (consolation, encouragement, enlivenment, solacement,n.)

4. Cheering, i.e., Causing or Promoting Cheerfulness or Good Cheer,adj. *From Sec. 1:* brightening, cheery; exhilarating, exhilarant, exhilarative, or exhilaratory; genial (as atmosphere, surroundings, etc.); glad, gladsome, or gladdening; winsome (cheeriness, geniality or genialness, gladness or gladsomeness, winsomeness,n.); *From*

Sec. 3: comforting, comfortable, consoling, or consolatory; encouraging, enlivening, heartening, solacing

5. State of Feeling Cheered Up,n. *From Sec. 3:* exhilaration, comfort or consolation, encouragement, solace or solacement

6. That Which or One Who Cheers One Up,n. *From Sec. 1:* exhilarant (that which); *From Sec. 3:* comfort or consolation, encouragement, solace; solacer (one who)

7. To Show Lively Cheerfulness: effervesce, v.

8. To Become More Cheerful: brighten or brighten up, cheer up, take heart,v.

9. To Be Carefree: tread or walk on air,v.

10. That Which Brings Cheerfulness: cheer, n.

11. Able to Snap Back Easily into Cheerfulness or Good Cheer, to Recover Quickly from Misfortune or Depression, etc.: buoyant, elastic, resilient, supple,adj.

12. Such Ability: bounce, buoyancy, elasticity, resilience or resiliency, suppleness,n.

1104. MERRIMENT

1. Merry: convivial (esp. in or with company, while eating and drinking with others, etc.); festive (as of holiday occasions—descr. of atmosphere, pleasures, events, circumstances, moods, etc.); frolicking, frolicsome, frolicky, or frolic (i.e., full of fun, gaiety, high spirits, etc.); fun-loving; gay; gleeful or gleesome; hilarious (i.e., merry and noisy); jocular, jocund, jolly, jovial; larking, larksome, larkish, or skylarking (i.e., full of fun, merry pranks, etc.); mirthful (esp. when indulging in, or characterized or attended by, laughter, noise, etc.); riant; riotous (i.e., indulging in, or attended by, unrestrained merriment); rip-roaring or rip-roarious (i.e., attended by wild and noisy merriment, as a party, time, occasion, etc.); rollicking, rollicksome, or rollicky (i.e., behaving or acting in a merry and carefree manner, or attended by such behavior, as a time, occasion, etc.); saturnalian (i.e., merry, noisy, and uninhibited—descr. of behavior); sportful, sportive; sunny (in nature); winsome (in nature),adj.

2. Merriment; Merriness,n. *From Sec. 1:* conviviality, festivity or festiveness; gaiety, gayety, or gayness; frolic or frolicsomeness; glee, gleefulness, or gleesomeness; hilarity or hilariousness, jocularity, jocundity, jollity or jolliness, joviality or jovialness, larkishness, mirth or mirthfulness, riotousness or riot, rollicksomeness or rollick, sportfulness; sportiveness, sport, or fun; sunniness, winsomeness; *Also:* 1. levity—merriment or gaiety of manner or mood

3. To Engage in Merriment or Merry Behavior,v. *From Sec. 1:* frolic; jollify (colloq.); lark or skylark, riot, rollick (jollification, rollicking,n. frolicker, larker or skylarker, rioter, rollicker,n.)

4. A Merry Act or Remark: jocundity,n.

5. Like Shakespeare's Falstaff, a Fat, Jovial, Witty, and Brazen Boaster of Low Principles; Fat and Jolly, Brazen and Jolly, etc.: Falstaffian,adj.

6. Noisy and Rough in Merriment: boisterous, riotous, uproarious,adj. (boisterousness, riotousness, uproariousness,n.)

7. To Cause (Someone) to Be Merry: exhilarate; jollify (colloq.),v. (exhilaration, jollification,n. exhilarant,n.)

8. Causing Merriment: exhilarating, exhilarant, exhilarative, or exhilaratory; mirthful,adj. (mirthfulness,n.)

9. Merry Proceedings, Festivities, etc.: carnival (usually noisy); celebration, circus, festivity or festivities, frolic, fun, gaieties or gayeties; jollity, jollities, or jollification; jubilation, jubilee, merriment, merrymaking, revelry or revels, riot, rollick, sport,n. (celebratory, festive,adj.)

10. To Engage or Take Part in Merry Proceedings, Festivities, etc.: celebrate, frolic; jollify (colloq.); jubilate, make merry, revel, riot, rollick,v.

11. One Who Engages or Takes Part in Merry Proceedings, Festivities, etc.: celebrant, celebrater or celebrator; frolicker, merrymaker, reveler, rioter, rollicker,n.

12. Season or Occasion of Merry Festivity: jubilee,n.

1105. PLEASURE

1. Pleasure: amusement or entertainment; delectation; delight; enchantment; enjoyment; fruition (in possessing, attaining, etc.); fun; gratification; gusto (as in eating, drinking, doing, speaking, etc.—often in the phrase *with gusto*); joy; relish (as in eating or drinking, from the taste or flavor, or in any activity or action, often in the phrase *with relish*); titillation (i.e., pleasurable excitement); zest (i.e., gusto or relish—often preceded by *with*, or followed by *for*, as *with great zest, zest for living, etc.*),n.

2. A Pleasure, i.e., That Which, or, as Indicated, One Who, Affords or Gives, or Is a Source or Means of, Pleasure,n. *From Sec. 1:* amusement or entertainment; delight (or one who); enchantment, gratification; joy (or one who); relish; titillant, titillator, or titillater; zest; *Also:*
1. **ambrosia**—something exquisitely pleasurable or delightful to the taste or smell —from the food of the gods of Greek and Roman mythology
2. **luxury**—something that affords pleasure but is not a necessity; esp., such that is costly, rich, rare, hard to get, etc.
3. **nectar**—beverage exquisitely pleasurable in taste—from the drink of the gods of Greek and Roman mythology (nectareous or nectarean,adj.)
4. **spice, seasoning**—something that gives or adds a pleasurable and, often, exciting quality

3. To Pleasure, i.e., to Give or Afford Pleasure to (a Person),v. *From Sec. 1:* amuse or entertain, delectate, delight, enchant, gratify, relish, titillate or tickle (entertainment, gratification, titillation,n.)

4. Pleasurable or Pleasure-Giving, i.e., Giving or Affording Pleasure,adj. *From Sec. 1:* amusing, amusive, or entertaining; delectable; delightful, delightsome, or delighting; enchanting, enjoyable, gratifying, joyful or joyous, relishable, titillating, zestful or zesty; *From Sec. 2:* ambrosial or ambrosian, luxurious or silken, nectareous or nectarean, spicy or spiceful; *Also:*
1. **bittersweet**—both pleasurable and sad or painful; causing both pleasure and sadness or regret
2. **charming, charmful**—delightful; attracting with one's or its delightful quality
3. **delicious**—giving intense pleasure; giving or offering such to the senses, esp. those of taste and smell; delightful
4. **gay**—offering pleasures, esp. social pleasures
5. **pleasant, pleasing, pleasureful**—affording pleasure
6. **primrose**—affording pleasures, esp. sensual or fleshly pleasures

7. savory—exciting pleasure or enjoyment; giving pleasure to the sense of taste or smell
8. sensual—offering, promising, or catering to, the pleasures of the senses, esp. those involved in sexual activity
9. sensuous—affecting the senses, as those of hearing, seeing, etc., pleasurably, as *sensuous rhythms, poetry, music, spectacles,* etc.
10. sweet—affording pleasure or enjoyment
11. voluptuous—offering, promising, or catering to, pleasure, esp. of the senses; pleasurable to the senses
12. welcome—pleasurable
13. winsome—giving pleasure or delight, as a voice, appearance, personality, etc.

5. Pleasurableness; Pleasurable or Enjoyable Quality; Power to Give, Afford, Cause, or Excite Pleasure,n. *From Sec. 1:* amusingness, amusiveness, or entertainingness; delectableness or delectability, delightfulness or delightsomeness, enchantingness, enjoyableness, joyfulness or joyousness, relish, zest or zestfulness; *From Sec. 2:* luxury or luxuriousness, spice, or spiciness; *From Sec. 4:* charm, charmingness, or charmfulness; deliciousness; gaiety, gayety, or gayness; pleasantness or pleasingness, savor or savoriness, sensuality or sensualness, sensuousness, sweetness, voluptuousness, welcomeness, winsomeness

6. To Pleasure in, i.e., to Get or Derive Pleasure from, Find Pleasure in, etc.,v. *From Sec. 1:* delight in (something) or delight to (do something), enjoy or enjoy oneself in, joy in; relish (enjoyment,n.); *Also:*
1. **luxuriate in**—enjoy oneself wholeheartedly in (an activity, thing, feeling, etc.), as *luxuriate in self-pity, a warm bath,* etc. (luxuriation,n.)
2. **revel in, riot in**—get or take the keenest pleasure or delight in
3. **savor**—enjoy fully; give oneself over to the enjoyment of

7. To Pleasure, i.e., Take, Get, or Indulge in, Pleasure,v. *From Sec. 6:* enjoy oneself, joy, luxuriate (enjoyment, luxuriation,n.); *Also:*
1. **debauch**—indulge, esp. excessively, in sensual or orgiastic pleasure or pleasures (debauchery or debauch,n.)
2. **dissipate**—indulge, esp. excessively, in foolish, extravagant, unhealthy, sensual, wild, etc., pleasure or pleasures (dissipation,n.)
3. **racket**—indulge freely in, or be given over to, social pleasures, excitement, etc. (racket,n.)
4. **riot**—indulge in loose and wild pleasures

8. Given Over or Devoted to Seeking, or to Indulging in, Pleasure or Pleasures; Characterized by, Descr. of, or Pert. to, Pleasure or Pleasures,adj. *From Sec. 7:* debauched, dissipated or dissolute, rackety, riotous (debauchedness, dissipatedness or dissoluteness, riotousness,n.); *Also:*
1. **epicurean**—given over to, characterized by, or fond of, pleasures of the senses or appetites, luxury, etc. (epicureanism or epicurism,n.)
2. **fast**—given over to, characterized by, or descr. of, unrestrained, dissipated, or sexually loose pleasures, as a person, life, etc.
3. **gay**—given over to, characterized by, or descr. of, pleasure or pleasures, esp. social pleasures, as a *gay dog, gay life, gay season, gay round of parties,* etc.
4. **hedonic**—consisting of, pert. to, or having to do with, pleasure
5. **hedonistic, hedonist**—given over or devoted to pleasure as a way of life (hedonism,n.)

6. **pleasure-seeking**—seeking pleasure (pleasure seeking,n.)

7. **primrose**—given over or devoted to, or descr. of, pleasure or pleasures, esp. of the fleshly or sensual type, as activities, a life, a path, etc.

8. **saturnalian**—characterized by, or descr. of, loose, unrestrained, wild, etc., excesses of sensual pleasure or merrymaking

9. **sensual, sensualistic**—characterized by, pert., devoted, given over, or inclined to, or indulging in, the pleasures of the flesh, body, senses, appetites, sex, etc., generally in excess; unduly preoccupied with such pleasures (sensuality, sensualism, or sensualness,n.)

10. **sensuous**—keenly responsive to, fond of, or enjoying, the pleasures of the senses, as of seeing, hearing, touching, etc. (sensuousness,n.)

11. **sporty**—freely indulging in, or given over to, gay, fast, dissipated, or loose pleasures, as a person, life, etc. (sportiness,n.)

12. **sybaritic, sybaritical**—given over or devoted to, extremely fond of, or characterized by, pleasure, pleasure of the senses, or luxury (sybaritism,n.)

13. **voluptuary**—pert. to, characterized by, or descr. of, the pleasures of the senses or body, or luxury

14. **voluptuous**—given over or devoted to, full of, expressing, suggesting, arising or derived from, fond of, directed or inclined toward, or interested in, pleasures of the senses or flesh (voluptuousness,n.)

9. **One Who Indulges in, Is Given Over or Devoted to, Is Fond of, or Seeks, Pleasure or Pleasures,**n. *From Sec. 7:* debauchee, dissipater or dissipator, rioter; *From Sec. 8:* epicurean or, esp. in reference to eating and drinking, epicure; hedonist; pleasure seeker, pleasurer, or pleasurist; sensualist, sport, sybarite, voluptuary (from *voluptuous*)

10. **To Make Sensual:** sensualize,v. (sensualization,n.)

11. **To Look for Pleasure:** pleasure,v. (colloq.)

12. **To Eat or Drink (Food, Beverages, etc.) with Obvious Pleasure:** relish,v.

13. **To Make (Something) Pleasurable:** season, spice, zest,n.

14. **The Joy of Living; The Quality or Attitude of a Person Who Enormously Enjoys Life and Living:** joie de vivre (French), zest for life or living,n.

15. **Characterized by Such an Attitude:** zestful, zesty,adj. (zestfulness,n.)

16. **Lacking Such an Attitude:** zestless,adj.

17. **Excessive Indulgence in the Pleasures of Something:** jag (colloq.), orgy,n. (as *to go on a reading jag, an orgy of eating*, etc.)

18. **Time or Occasion of Unrestrained Sensual Pleasures:** saturnalia,n. (saturnalian, adj.)

19. **To Make a Murmuring Sound Indicating Pleasure; To Say with Such a Sound or Tone:** purr,v. (purr,n.)

20. **The Figurative Road of, or to, Pleasures, Esp. Sensual Pleasures; Life or World of Sensual or Fleshly Pleasures:** primrose path, n.

21. **Descr. of Music That Is Delightfully Sensuous, Soft, Sweet, etc.:** Lydian,adj.

22. **Ethical Theory that Sensual Pleasure or Gratification Is the Greatest Good in Life:** sensualism or sensationalism,n. (sensualist, n. sensualistic or sensationalistic,adj.)

23. **Philosophical Doctrine that Pleasure or Happiness Is the Greatest Good and Should Be the Principal Aim of Life or Activity:** hedonism,n. (hedonist,n. hedonic, hedonistic, or hedonist,adj.)

24. **Philosophy that Pleasure Tempered by Morality and Moderation, or the Absence of Pain, Is the Greatest Good or Goal in Life, as Formulated by the Greek Philosopher Epicurus; Devotion to, or Practice of, This Philosophy:** Epicureanism or Epicurism, n. (Epicurean,n. Epicurean,adj.)

25. **Branch of Psychology or of Ethics Studying, or Dealing with, Pleasurable and Painful Feelings or States of Mind:** hedonics,n. (hedonic,adj.)

26. **Psychological Doctrine that Pleasure Is the Chief Goal or Aim of Activity or Action:** hedonism,n. (hedonist,n. hedonistic, hedonist, or hedonic,adj.)

27. **Automatic or Instinctive Impulse to Seek Pleasure and Avoid Pain—a Concept in Psychoanalysis:** pleasure principle,n.

28. **A Ride in a Motorcar Purely for Pleasure, Esp. if the Vehicle Is Driven Very Fast and Recklessly, etc.:** joy ride,n. (joy riding, n. joy rider,n.—all colloq.)

29. **Lacking in, or Affording No, Pleasure:** charmless, delightless, joyless, pleasureless, savorless, spiceless, zestless; unamusing, uncharming, undelectable, undelicious, undelightful, undelighting, undelightsome, unenjoyable, unentertaining, ungratifying, unjoyful, unjoyous, unpleasant, unpleasing, unpleasurable, unsavory, unwelcome,adj.

30. **Lack of Pleasure:** unpleasure,n.

31. **Having Lost One's Enjoyment of, or Pleasure in:** tired of, weary of,adj.

32. **To Cause (One) to Lose Enjoyment of Pleasure:** tire, weary,v. (tiresome or tiring; wearial, wearisome, or wearying,adj.)

33. **Tired or Weary of, Bored with, or Indifferent to, Pleasure, Often Because of Overindulgence:** blasé, cloyed, jaded, pleasure-tired, pleasure-weary,adj. (jadedness,n.)

34. **To So Tire or Bore (a Person, His Senses, Appetites, etc.):** cloy, cloy on, jade,v.

35. **So Tiring:** cloying,adj. (cloyingness,n.)

36. **Not So Tired or Bored:** uncloyed or unjaded (of senses, appetites, etc.),adj.

37. **Not, or Never, So Tiring the Senses, Appetites, etc.:** uncloying,adj.

1106. TO PLEASE

1. **To Please by Being Satisfactory, Proper, etc.; To So Please (a Person):** suit,v.

2. **To Please (Someone) Greatly:** charm, delight, enchant, gratify, tickle,v. (gratification,n.)

3. **Pleasant; Pleasing:** affable (i.e., pleasant and polite, easy to talk to, etc.); agreeable; amiable (i.e., pleasant in personality); bland (as people, manner, personality, etc.); charming, delightful, delightsome, enchanting, or gratifying (i.e., exceedingly pleasant or pleasing); cheerful or cheery (i.e., pleasant, or pleasant and bright, as surroundings, atmosphere, etc.); companionable (i.e., pleasant to be with, as a person, etc.); complaisant; congenial (i.e., pleasant because suiting one's tastes or interests, as work, functions, surroundings, etc., or because similar in tastes, interests, or sympathies, as people); conversable (i.e., affable); delicate (i.e., pleasant because of its fine and subtle odor, taste, flavor, workmanship, etc.); delicious (i.e., exceedingly pleasant to the senses, esp. taste or smell, or in any other way); desirable (i.e., so pleasing in any way as to arouse desire of possession); dulcet (i.e., pleasing, pleasant, or agreeable to the feel-

ings or emotions); good-humored or good-natured (i.e., pleasant in mood, attitude, or disposition); gracious (i.e., pleasant and kindly, esp. to inferiors or those dependent on one); grateful (i.e., pleasant to the senses or mind, as wind, weather, etc.); likable or likeable (i.e., pleasing); lovely (i.e., highly pleasing or delightful, as people, things, places, time, etc.—colloq.); luscious (i.e., exceedingly pleasing to the senses, esp. those of taste or smell); mellow (i.e., pleasant in temper or personality, as people); palatable (i.e., pleasant or agreeable to the taste, feelings, or mind); savory (i.e., pleasing to the senses, esp. taste or smell, or to the mind, feelings, etc.); seemly (i.e., pleasing in appearance—somewhat archaic in flavor); suave or urbane (i.e., smoothly or blandly pleasant, as people, their speech, manner, etc.); sweet (i.e., pleasing in general, pleasing to the sense of taste or smell, or pleasant in personality or disposition); sweet-natured (i.e., pleasant in nature, disposition, or personality); unctuous (i.e., smoothly, sentimentally, or blandly pleasant, esp. to excess or as an affectation); welcome (i.e., pleasant because giving or offering what one wants or needs, as a breeze, relief, warmth, etc.); winsome (i.e., wholly delightful, as a child, manner, smile, voice, etc.),adj.

4. Pleasantness or Pleasingness,n. *From Sec. 3:* affability or affableness, agreeableness or agreeability, amiability or amiableness, blandness; charm, charmingness, delightfulness, delightsomeness, or enchantingness; cheerfulness or cheeriness, companionability or companionableness, complaisance, congeniality, conversableness, delicacy or delicateness, deliciousness, desirability or desirableness, dulcetness; good humor, good-humoredness, good nature, or good-naturedness; graciousness, likableness or likableness, loveliness, lusciousness, mellowness, palatability or palatableness, savoriness, seemliness; suavity, suaveness, urbanity, or urbaneness; sweetness; unctuousness, unctuosity, or unction; welcomeness, winsomeness; *Also:*
1. amenity—quality of being pleasant or agreeable
2. bonhomie, bonhommie—pleasant or good-natured manner or attitude

5. Fairly or Somewhat Pleasant, as a Time, etc.: tolerable,adj.

6. Pleasant Ways, Circumstances, Features, Actions, etc.: amenities,n.

7. Inclined or Disposed to Please—of a Person or His Manner: complaisant, complacent, compliable, compliant,adj. (complaisance, complacency or complacence, compliableness, compliancy or compliance,n.)

8. Descr. of Persons Who Act, without Sincerity, in a Way to Please Their Superiors; Descr. of the Actions, Personalities, Attitudes, etc., of Such People: courtly, obsequious,adj. (courtliness, obsequiousness,n.)

9. Pleasing in Appearance, or to the Eye or Sight: attractive; comely (esp. girls, women, etc.); presentable,adj. (attractiveness, comeliness, presentableness or presentability,n.)

10. Pleasing in Appearance or to the Eye or Sight, but Deceptive (as a Thing, Abstraction, etc.): plausible, specious,adj. (plausibility or plausibleness, speciousness or speciosity,n.)

11. That Which Is So Pleasing but Deceptive: speciosity,n.

12. Pleasant or Agreeable in Sound, or to the Ear: dulcet, musical, sweet,adj. (dulcetness, musicalness, sweetness,n.)

13. To Be Pleased to Get, Accept, Receive, etc.: welcome,v.

14. Hard to Please because of One's High Standards, etc.: fastidious; finical, finicking, finicky, or finikin; particular,adj. (fastidiousness, finicality or finicalness,n.)

15. Pleasing in Appearance, Form, Action, Movement, Attitude, Manner, etc.: graceful,adj. (grace or gracefulness,n.)

16. Graceful and Gay: debonair, debonaire, or debonnaire,adj. (debonairness,n.)

17. A Pleasing Quality, Property, Characteristic, etc.: grace,n.

18. Lacking Grace, Gracefulness, or Graceful Qualities, etc.: crude, graceless, ungraceful,adj. (crudity or crudeness, gracelessness, ungracefulness,n.)

19. A Graceful Act, i.e., Something One Does with Grace or Gracefulness: beau geste,n. (French)

20. To Make Pleasant or Agreeable, or More So: dulcify,v. (dulcification,n.)

21. To Make or Become Pleasant, Agreeable, or Sweet in Any Sense, as in Taste, Odor, Sound, Disposition, etc.: sweeten,v.

22. One Who, or That Which, Is Most Pleasant, Agreeable, or Sweet: sugar candy,n.

23. Least Pleasant: seamy,adj. (seaminess,n.)

1107. SATISFACTION

1. To Satisfy; To Satisfy (a Person, Desire, Demand, etc.),v.
1. appease—satisfy the demands of; bring to a state of satisfaction; satisfy (an aggressor, etc.) by giving in to his political or economic demands
2. assuage—satisfy (desires, etc.)
3. content—satisfy (a person); bring (a person) to a state of satisfaction with what he has or is
4. delight—give the keenest satisfaction to (a person, appetite, etc.)
5. fulfill—satisfy (desires, needs, conditions, etc.)
6. gratify—satisfy to the full (a person, desire, etc.)
7. indulge—satisfy (feelings, desires, whims, etc.); satisfy the feelings, desires, whims, etc., of (a person)
8. overindulge—indulge to excess
9. please—give satisfaction; give satisfaction to
10. sate—satisfy (desire) to the full
11. slake—satisfy (desire, anger, passion, etc.)
12. suffice—satisfy; satisfy (a person, etc.) by being adequate
13. suit—satisfy; satisfy (a person, purpose, need, etc.) by being appropriate, acceptable, etc.

2. Satisfaction, i.e., Act of Satisfying,n. *From Sec. 1:* appeasement, assuagement, fulfillment, gratification, indulgence or indulgency, overindulgence

3. Satisfied,adj. *From Sec. 1:* appeased, assuaged, content or contented, delighted, fulfilled, gratified, indulged, overindulged, pleased, sated, slaked, suited; *Also:*
1. complacent—satisfied; content; self-satisfied; smug
2. self-satisfied, self-complacent—satisfied with oneself, one's accomplishments, qualities, etc., or showing such satisfaction
3. smug—extremely or excessively satisfied with oneself, one's accomplishments, qualities, character, etc., or showing such satisfaction

4. **well-content**—greatly satisfied; completely content

4. Satisfaction or Satisfiedness, i.e., State or Condition of Being Satisfied,n. *From Sec. 1:* appeasement, assuagement, contentment or contentedness, delight, fulfillment, gratification; *From Sec. 3:* complacence or complacency; self-satisfaction, self-complacence, or self-complacency; smugness

5. Satisfactory; Satisfying,adj. *From Sec. 1:* appeasing, assuaging or assuasive, contenting; delighting, delightful, or delightsome; fulfilling, gratifying, indulgent or indulging, overindulgent or overindulging, pleasing, sating, sufficient, suitable

6. Satisfactoriness,n. *From Sec. 5:* delightfulness or delightsomeness, indulgence or indulgency, overindulgence, pleasingness, sufficiency, suitability or suitableness

7. A Satisfaction, i.e., That Which Satisfies,n. *From Sec. 1:* assuagement, fulfillment, indulgence

8. One Who Lives a Life of Unrealistic and Dreamy Contentment, Unaware of, or Indifferent to, the World Around Him: lotus-eater,n.

9. That Portion of Society Which Is Smugly Satisfied, Financially Well Off, and Sometimes, by Implication, Dull and Mediocre: villadom,n.

10. Capable of Being Satisfied: appeasable, gratifiable, satiable, satisfiable,adj. (appeasableness, satiability or satiableness,n.)

11. To Satisfy (a Person's Appetite, Hunger, or Thirst: appease, assuage, gratify, pacify; sate (to the full); slake or quench (thirst only),v. (appeasement, assuagement, gratification,n.)

12. To Become Satisfied—of Thirst: slake,v.

13. To Reduce the Pangs, etc., of (Hunger or Thirst): allay, alleviate, appease, quiet, relieve, still,v. (alleviation, appeasement, relief,n.)

14. Not to Be Satisfied—of Thirst: quenchless, unquenchable,adj. (unquenchableness,n.)

15. To Satisfy (a Person, His Desires, Appetite, etc.) to Excess or to the Point of Disgust or Nausea, Literally or Figuratively: cloy or cloy on (by an excess of sweetness, literally or figuratively, or of sentimentality, pleasure, food, etc.); glut; jade; pall or pall on or upon (by an excess of something good, pleasurable, too sweet, etc.); sate, satiate; surfeit (with food or drink),v. (glut, satiation,n.)

16. To Satisfy, i.e., Be Satisfying, to Such an Excessive Degree: cloy, pall,v.

17. So Satisfying to an Excessive Degree: cloying, glutting, jading, palling, sating, satiating, surfeiting,adj. (cloyingness,n.)

18. To Become So Satisfied to an Excessive Degree: pall,v.

19. So Satisfied to an Excessive Degree: cloyed, glutted, jaded, palled, sated, satiated or satiate, surfeited,adj.

20. State of Being So Satisfied to an Excessive Degree: glut, jadedness, satiety or satiation, surfeit,n.

21. Not, or Never, So Satisfying to an Excessive Degree: uncloying, unsatiating, unsurfeiting,adj.

22. Not So Satisfied to an Excessive Degree: uncloyed, unglutted, unjaded, unpalled, unsated, unsatiated, unsurfeited,adj. (unsatedness,n.)

23. To Eat to the Point of Excessive Satisfaction, Disgust, Nausea, etc.: glut,v.

24. To Eat or Drink to This Point: surfeit,v.

25. To Look upon, or Think about (Something) with Keen and Usually Malicious Satisfaction: gloat over,v.

26. To Engage in Such Looking or Thinking: gloat,v. (gloater,n. gloating,adj.)

27. To Satisfy One's Own Feelings, Desires, Whims, etc. (by Some Activity, etc.): indulge (in),v.

28. That Which Is Done, Taken, Eaten, Drunk, etc., for This Purpose: indulgence,n.

1108. TO INDULGE

1. To Indulge (a Person, His Appetites, Desires, Whims, etc.): baby (a person), cater to, cocker, coddle, cosher, cosset, dandle; gratify (appetite, whim, desire, etc.); humor (a person, esp. by giving in to, or satisfying, his moods, desires, caprices, etc.); mollycoddle (a person, esp. by relieving him of hardships, rigors of existence, etc.); pamper (appetites, desires, etc., or a person, esp. by satisfying him with every luxury, etc.); spoil (a person, esp. excessively, or in a way to weaken his character); spoon-feed (i.e., indulge excessively, as a person, etc., so that he has no chance to show initiative in, or independence of, thought or action, etc.),v.

2. Indulged,adj. *From Sec. 1:* babied, cockered, coddled, coshered, cosseted, humored, mollycoddled, pampered, spoiled, spoon-fed

3. Unindulged,adj. *From Sec. 1:* uncoddled, unhumored, unpampered, unspoiled

4. One Who Is Particularly Indulged: cosset, pet,n.

5. A Male Who Has Been Indulged, Pampered, etc., in Such a Way that He Is Unprepared for Hardships, the Rigors of Existence, etc.: mollycoddle,n.

6. To Indulge or Cater to the Vices, Evil or Base Passions, or the Low and Sensual Desires of (a Person, Group, etc.): pander to, v. (panderer or pander,n.)

7. To Treat, Take Care of, or Nurse (Someone) with Indulgent Consideration or Tenderness: coddle,v.

8. Habitually Indulging Another: indulgent, adj. (indulgence or indulgency,n.)

9. Indulgent to Inferiors or Those Dependent on One: gracious, kind,adj. (graciousness, kindness,n.)

10. Indulging Oneself, One's Desires, Feelings, Passions, Needs, etc.; Tending, or of a Nature or Disposition, to Do So: self-indulgent,adj. (self-indulgence,n.)

11. Not Doing So; Not of a Disposition to Do So: unself-indulgent,adj.

12. Not Indulgent: unindulgent,adj.

1109. TO LIKE

1. To Like: be fond of; dote on or upon (i.e., like extremely); enjoy; fancy, or have a fancy for; favor; prefer (i.e., like above another or others); relish (food or anything else),v. (fondness,n. fond, doting,adj.)

2. To Develop a Liking for: cotton to or with (colloq.), fancy,v.

3. A Liking (for): affection or attachment (i.e., a warm liking); affinity (i.e., a liking that is natural or instinctive, as for a person or thing); appetite, fancy, fondness, inclination; palate (i.e., a mental or intellectual liking); partiality (for or to); passion (i.e., an extremely intense liking, as for a person or thing); penchant, predilection, or propensity (i.e., a liking for a thing); preference (i.e., a liking for one or more above another or others); stomach (usually in the negative, as *no stomach for argument*, etc.); taste or relish (for something pleasurable); tooth (i.e., a liking for something edible),n.

4. Having a Liking for,adj. *From Sec. 3:* affectionate toward, or attached to; fond of; partial to (affectionateness, fondness, partiality,n.)

5. Broad, Tolerant, Liberal, etc., in One's Tastes, Likes, Interests, etc.: catholic,adj. (catholicity,n.)

6. Intellectually Fond of All Kinds and Sorts: omnivorous (as *an omnivorous reader*, etc.),adj. (omnivorousness,n.)

7. Mutual Liking (between People), Arising out of Similar Attitudes, Feelings, Interests, Experiences, etc.: sympathy,n. (sympathetic,adj.)

8. Of Such a Kind that One Can Have a Natural Liking for Him or It; Having Similar or Congenial Likings or Taste: simpatico, adj. (Spanish)

9. Wealthy Person of Low, Coarse, or Showy Likes, Taste, Manners, etc.: vulgarian,n.

10. Unrefined or Uncivilized Liking, Likes, Taste, or Tastes: barbarity,n.

11. Capable of Being Liked; Such as to Excite One's Liking: enjoyable; likable or likeable; preferable (i.e., above another or others); relishable,adj. (enjoyableness, likableness or likeableness, preferableness or preferability,n.)

12. Liked: doted on or upon; enjoyed; in favor; popular (i.e., liked by many people, or generally); preferred (i.e., liked above another or others),adj. (popularity,n.)

13. Liked (by Someone): in the good graces of (someone)

14. Period or Time of Popularity or of Being in Popular Favor: fashion, vogue,n.

15. Just Lately or Recently Popular or in Fashion or Vogue: newfangled, new-fashioned,adj.

16. No Longer Popular, etc.: old-fashioned, adj.

17. Woman or Girl Who Is Not Popular at a Dance, i.e., Is Not Sought as a Partner: wallflower,n. (colloq.)

18. Particularly or Specially Liked or in Favor: fair-haired, favored, favorite, pet; white-headed (Irish),adj.

19. The Showing of Particular or Special Liking for a Person: favoritism,n.

20. One Particularly or Specially Liked or in Favor: fair-haired boy; favorite; persona grata (Latin); pet; white-headed boy (Irish), n.

21. One Who Is Not Liked or Is in Disfavor: persona non grata,n. (Latin)

22. To Show Fondness or Affection (for a Person) in Its Characteristic Way—of a Dog: fawn (on),v.

23. To Attempt to Gain the Liking or Favor (of Someone) by Servile Attentions, Flattery, Exaggerated Regard, Deference, Submissiveness, etc.: fawn (on),v. (fawning, adj.)

24. One Who Tries to Gain Liking or Favor, as by Flattery, etc.: courtier, fawner,n.

25. To Insinuate or Establish Oneself into, or in, the Favor or Good Graces (of Another): ingratiate oneself (with),v. (ingratiation,n.)

26. Serving, Acting, or Intended to Accomplish This: ingratiating or ingratiatory, silken, soft,adj.

27. Ingratiatingly Pleasant or Sweet, to the Point of Alienating or Offending People of Acute Sensibilities: saccharine,adj. (saccharinity,n.)

1110. THANKS

1. Full of, Feeling, Showing, or Expressing, Thanks: appreciative, grateful, thankful,adj.

2. Thankfulness: appreciation, appreciativeness, gratefulness, gratitude,n.

3. To Express or Give Thanks to: thank,v.

4. To Express or Give Thanks for: acknowledge,v. (acknowledgment,n.)

5. A Giving of Thanks; Such to God: thanksgiving,n.

6. One Who Gives Thanks: thanksgiver,n.

7. To Be Thankful for: appreciate,v. (appreciation,n.)

8. Deserving of Thanks: thankworthy,adj. (thankworthiness,n.)

9. Letter of Thanks for Hospitality Received: bread-and-butter letter,n.

10. Not Thankful: thankless, unappreciative or inappreciative, ungrateful or ingrateful, unthankful,adj.

11. One Who Is Not Thankful, Grateful, etc.: ingrate,n.

12. Lack of Thankfulness: inappreciation, inappreciativeness, ingratefulness, ingratitude, thanklessness, unappreciation, unappreciativeness, ungratefulness, unthankfulness,n.

13. Not Getting Thanks: thankless, unappreciated, unthankful,adj. (thanklessness, unthankfulness,n.)

14. Not Fully or Sympathetically Appreciated: misunderstood (as a husband, wife, child, etc.),adj.

1111. TO LAUGH

1. To Laugh,v.

1. cachinnate—laugh loudly, noisily, excessively, as if hysterical, etc.
2. cackle—laugh in a noisy, high-pitched, and broken voice
3. chortle—laugh in triumph, victory, glee, etc.
4. chuckle—laugh quietly or to oneself, or to express amusement, satisfaction, delight, etc.
5. fleer—laugh in a coarse, crude, or mocking manner
6. giggle, twitter—laugh in an undignified, silly, embarrassed, or nervous manner, in an uncontrollable fashion, or in a high-pitched voice
7. guffaw—laugh loudly, in loud or coarse bursts, etc.
8. horselaugh—laugh loudly, coarsely, etc., esp. in derision, scorn, etc.
9. howl, howl with laughter—laugh very loudly; laugh loudly and contemptuously, derisively, scornfully, etc.
10. roar, roar with laughter—laugh with tremendous loudness and lack of restraint
11. scream, shriek, scream or shriek with laughter—laugh loudly, shrilly, hysterically, uncontrollably, etc.
12. snicker, snigger—laugh in a stifled or suppressed and somewhat disrespectful fashion; laugh slyly; giggle
13. titter, twitter—utter partially suppressed laughs; laugh in a low voice with some attempt at restraint, as from nervousness, embarrassment, inability to hide one's amusement, etc.

2. A Laugh,n. *From Sec. 1:* cackle, chortle, chuckle, fleer, giggle or twitter, guffaw or haw-haw, horselaugh, howl, roar, snicker or snigger, titter or twitter; *Also:* 1. **belly laugh** —an unrestrained, strong, hearty, or unashamed laugh (colloq.)

3. Laughter,n. *From Sec. 1:* cackling, chortling, etc.; cachinnation, chuckles, giggles, guffaws, horselaughter, howls or howls of laughter, roars or roars of laughter, screams or shrieks of laughter, snickers or sniggers, titters or twitters; *Also:*
1. **gelasmus, gelasma**—insane or hysterical laughter, esp. in spasms
2. **Homeric laughter**—loud, unrestrained, hearty laughter
3. **hysterics**—uncontrollable laughter
4. **mirth**—laughter caused or aroused by something funny, amusing, or absurd

4. Laugher,n. *From Sec. 1:* cachinnator, cackler, chortler, chuckler, giggler, snickerer or sniggerer, titterer or twitterer

5. To Say with a Laugh,v. *From Sec. 1:* chortle, chuckle, giggle, snicker or snigger, titter

6. Laughing,adj. *From Sec. 1:* cachinnating, cackling, chortling, chuckling, giggling, guffawing, roaring, screaming or shrieking, snickering or sniggering, tittering or twittering; *From Sec. 3:* hysterical; *Also:* riant,adj.

7. Full of Laughter and Gaiety: mirthful, adj. (mirthfulness,n.)

8. A Fit or Attack of Violent Laughter: convulsion, convulsions, or convulsions of laughter; hysterics,n. (convulsive, hysterical, adj.)

9. Loss of Self-Control Marked by Alternating Laughter and Weeping: hysteria, hysterics,n. (hysterical,adj.)

10. Disposed or Inclined to Laugh or Laughter; Having the Power or Faculty of Laughter: risible,adj.

11. Such Disposition, Inclination, Power, or Faculty: risibility or risibilities,n.

12. Inclined to Laugh in a Silly or Nervous Manner, or Given to Such Laughter: giggly, adj.

13. Pert. or Related to Laughter or to Laughing: gelastic, risible,adj.

14. Pert. to Loud, Noisy, or Excessive Laughter or Laughing: cachinnatory,adj.

15. Descr. of Robust, Hearty, Loud, etc., Laughter: sidesplitting,adj.

16. Utilized in Laughing: gelastic,adj.

17. Expressive of Laughter: risible,adj.

18. Sound, Esp. Loud Sound, of Laughter: ha-ha, haw-haw, he-he, ho-ho,n.

19. To Laugh at Contemptuously or Mockingly: deride, fleer, ridicule,v. (derision, fleer, ridicule,n. derider, ridiculer,n.)

20. Laughing Contemptuously or Mockingly; Characterized by Such Laughter: derisive or derisory,adj. (derisiveness,n.)

21. Exciting, or Worthy of, Contemptuous Laughter: derisible, ridiculous,adj. (ridiculousness,n.)

22. One Who, or That Which, Excites, or Is the Object of, Contemptuous Laughter: butt, derision, jest, jestingstock, joke, laugh, laughingstock,n.

23. To Cause (Someone) to Laugh: amuse; convulse (i.e., throw into violent laughter, or into a fit of such); tickle or titillate (either by light touches or strokes on sensitive parts of the body, or figuratively, as if using such); tickle the funny bone of (colloq.); tickle the risibilities of,v. (titillation,n.)

24. Causing Someone to Laugh,adj. *From*

Sec. 23: amusing, convulsing; tickling, titillating, or titillative (amusingness,n.); *Also:* funny, laughable, rib-tickling,adj. (funniness, laughableness,n.)

25. Caused to Laugh; Feeling a Desire to Laugh,adj. *From Sec. 23:* amused, convulsed, tickled or titillated,adj. (amusement, titillation,n.)

26. That Which Tickles or Titillates: tickler, titillant, titillator,n.

27. Sensitive to Tickling: ticklish,adj. (ticklishness,n.)

28. To Drive, Force, Put, Bring, etc. (Something or Someone) by Means of Laughter: laugh,v.

29. To Silence, Drown Out the Voice of, etc., with Contemptuous Laughter: howl down, laugh down,v.

30. To Send (Someone) Away from (a Place), by Scornful Laughter; To Reject the Argument of (Someone) by Such Laughter, etc.: laugh (someone) out of (a place),v.

31. To Ignore (Something Unpleasant) by Laughter: laugh away, laugh off,v.

32. To Change from Figurative Laughter, i.e., Delight, Glee, Joy, etc., to Sadness, Depression, Gloom, or Annoyance: laugh out of the other, or wrong, side of one's mouth,v.

33. To Have Cause to Laugh at the End, i.e., Be Successful, Triumphant, Victorious, etc., after All, despite Early Defeat or Failure: have the last laugh,v.

34. To Laugh to Oneself about Something; To Laugh in Secret: laugh in, or up, one's sleeve,v.

35. To Express Contempt for, or Amusement at (Someone or Something) with, or as with, a Laugh: laugh at,v.

36. Suggestive of Laughter because Delightful, Bright, Sunny, etc.: laughing,adj.

37. Something Not to Be Laughed at, i.e., Something Serious: no joke, no laughing matter,n.

38. Without, or Lacking in, Laughter or the Characteristics of Joy or Merriment Usually Expressed by Laughter, as a Person, His Face, Words, or Attitude, an Occasion, etc.: gloomy, grave, mirthless, serious, solemn, somber or sombre,adj. (gloom or gloominess, gravity or graveness, mirthlessness, seriousness, solemnity or solemnness, somberness or sombreness,n.)

1112. TO SMILE

1. To Smile,v.
1. **beam**—smile warmly or brightly; have a smiling look or expression on one's face, such indicating joy, delight, etc.
2. **fleer**—grin in derision or scorn, or in a mocking manner; grin at (someone) in such a manner
3. **grin**—smile broadly; smile in a way to show the teeth; smile in a way to show pleasure, gratification, amusement, etc.
4. **simper**—smile in a foolish, silly, artificial, affected, or self-conscious manner
5. **smirk**—smile in a silly, affected, self-satisfied, pretendedly pleasant, or excessively and offensively familiar, manner

2. A Smile,n. *From Sec. 1:* beam, fleer, grin, simper, smirk

3. Smiler,n. *From Sec. 1:* grinner, simperer, smirker

4. To Say with a Smile,v. *From Sec. 1:* grin, simper, smirk; *Also:* smile,v.

5. Smiling,adj. *From Sec. 1:* beaming or beamish, fleering, grinning, simpering, smirking; *Also:* riant,adj.

6. Inclined or Given to Smiling,adj. *From Sec. 1:* grinny, smirkish or smirky

7. To Express (Approval, Delight, etc.) with, or by Means of, a Smile: beam, grin, smile,v.

8. To Express Contempt for, or Amusement at (Someone or Something) with, or as with, a Smile: smile at,v.

9. To Look with Approval or Favor upon, as if with a Smile of Acceptance: smile on or upon,v. (smile,n.)

1113. FUNNY; LAUGHABLE

1. Funny, i.e., **Laughable:** absurd (i.e., because obviously illogical, contrary to reason, etc.); amusing or amusive (i.e., causing amusement, some light degree of laughter, etc.); antic (i.e., ludicrous in appearance or actions); comic or comical (i.e., exciting, or intend to excite, laughter, amusement, etc.); droll (i.e., funny or laughable in a quaint or odd fashion); farcical (i.e., because obviously illogical, nonsensical, ridiculous, absurd, ludicrous, etc.); hilarious (i.e., so funny as to send one into gales of merriment); humorous; ludicrous (i.e., because absurd, ridiculous, incongruous, preposterous, etc.); mirthful; ribtickling; ridiculous (i.e., because illogical, preposterous, absurd, etc.); risible (i.e., laughable, amusing, ludicrous, etc.); screaming (i.e., so funny as to cause great bursts of laughter); sidesplitting (i.e., so funny or laughable as to make one figuratively split one's sides laughing); slapstick (i.e., funny or laughable in a low, vulgar, rough, rough-and-tumble, etc., manner, as comedy, humor, etc.), adj.

2. Condition, Quality, or State of Being Funny, i.e., **Laughable; Funniness;** Laughableness,n. *From Sec. 1:* absurdity or absurdness, amusingness or amusiveness, comicality or comicalness, drollery or drollness, farcicality or farcicalness, hilariousness or hilarity, humor or humorousness, ludicrousness, mirthfulness, ridiculousness

3. That Which (as an Act, Action, Thing, Remark, etc.) Is Funny, i.e., **Laughable,**n. *From Sec. 1:* absurdity, drollery, farcicality or farce, rib tickler, the ridiculous, scream, slapstick

4. To Behave or Act in an Absurd, Ridiculous, Ludicrous, etc., Fashion: antic,v.

5. Such Behavior: antics,n.

6. Behavior That Is Droll, i.e., **Laughable and Quaint or Odd:** drollery,n.

7. The Laughable, Amusing, or Droll Part of Life or Art: comedy, the comic,n.

8. A Happening, or Group or Series of Happenings, of Laughable, Amusing, or Comical Character: comedy,n.

9. Descr. of That Which Is Both Serious and Funny: seriocomic or seriocomical,adj.

10. Funny Pictures in a Newspaper, Magazine, etc.: cartoons; comics; comic strip or strips; funnies (colloq.),n.

11. Ability to Appreciate Something Funny or Laughable: humor, sense of humor,n.

12. One's Responsiveness to Laughable Situations, Ideas, Sights, etc.: risibilities,n.

13. Unable to Appreciate Something Funny or Laughable: humorless,adj. (humorlessness,n.)

1114. HUMOR

1. Humorous (of Persons),adj.
  1. amusing—humorous in the sense of expressing oneself in a way to amuse, cause laughter or smiles, etc.

2. comical, comic—humorous in the sense of causing laughter, whether by speech, gestures, or actions

3. droll—humorous or amusing in a quaint or odd manner; waggish

4. facetious—humorous; humorous when seriousness is expected or required

5. funny—expressing oneself humorously

6. jocose, jocular—humorous in the sense of making jokes or jests rather than being serious; given to such humor

7. ribald—expressing oneself in coarse or vulgar humor

8. waggish—playfully, mischievously, or roguishly humorous

9. whimsical—humorous in a quaint, fanciful, curious, odd, etc., fashion

10. witty—humorous and clever, i.e., quick or skillful in saying clever things in an amusing or entertaining manner, sometimes at the expense of, or to the discomfort of, others

2. Humorous, i.e., **Characterized by Humor (as Things, Qualities, Statements, Remarks, etc.),**adj. *From Sec. 1:* amusing, comical or comic, droll, facetious, funny, jocose or jocular, ribald, waggish, whimsical, witty or salty; *Also:*
  1. Rabelaisian—characterized by coarse, gross, low, or robust humor
  2. slapstick—characterized by humor achieved through rowdy behavior, horseplay, etc.

3. Humorousness,n. *From Sec. 1 or 2:* amusingness, comicality or comicalness, drollness or drollery, facetiousness, funniness; jocosity, jocoseness, or jocularity; ribaldry, waggishness, whimsicality or whimsicalness, wittiness or saltiness; *Also:*
  1. levity—humorousness or facetiousness, esp. on solemn or serious occasions, or in circumstances calling for solemnity or seriousness
  2. pleasantry—jocularity in conversation

4. Humor,n. *From Sec. 1:* drollery, jocosity or jocularity, ribaldry, waggery, whimsy or whimsey; *From Sec. 2:* slapstick; *From Sec. 3:* levity; *Also:*
  1. esprit (French)—lively wit
  2. farce—broad and exaggerated humor
  3. pleasantry—good-natured humor in conversation
  4. repartee—humor or wit characterized by quick answers; humorous or witty conversation so characterized; skill in such humor or conversation

5. Humorous Person,n. *From Sec. 1:* comic or comedian, droll, ribald, wag, wit (waggish, adj.); *Also:*
  1. farceur (French)—humorous person; wag; humorist
  2. humorist—one who expresses himself humorously, whether in speaking, writing, or acting; one who does so professionally (humoristic,adj.)

6. Descr. of Humor or Wit That Is Expressed in a Poker-Faced, Quiet Manner: dry,adj. (dryness,n.)

7. Chief Comedian in a Burlesque Show: first banana or top banana,n. (theatrical slang)

8. Act, Action, Spirit, Language, or Manner of a Playfully, Mischievously, or Roguishly Humorous Person: waggery,n.

9. Having a Quick Wit and Graceful Mind: spirituel (masc.) or spirituelle (fem.),adj. (French)

10. Speech or Action Characterized by Quaint or Fanciful Humor: whimsicality,n.

11. Language or Speech Characterized by Coarse and Vulgar Humor: ribaldry,n.

12. To Season (Written Material, a Speech, Play, etc.) with (Bits of Wit, Jokes, Humor, etc.): farce, salt,v.

13. Play, Motion Picture, etc., with Humorous Treatment: comedy,n.

14. To Sparkle with Brilliant Wit or Humor: scintillate,v. (scintillation,n.)

15. To Treat, Consider, or Regard (Something) in a Humorous Fashion: humorize,v.

16. A Musical Composition of a Humorous, Capricious, or Fanciful Type or Nature, or Written in a Fanciful, Free, and Irregular Style: capriccio, caprice, humoresque,n.

17. Written So—of Music: capriccioso,adj.

18. Without, Lacking in, or Showing No, Humor: humorless, mirthless,adj. (humorlessness, mirthlessness,n.)

1115. JOKING

1. To Joke, i.e., Engage in Joking, Humor, etc.,v.

1. banter, chaff, josh—engage in, or exchange, talk or conversation characterized by good-natured joking or humor
2. droll—joke; engage in joking or jesting
3. fool—joke; jest; engage in playful joking, whether by speech or behavior
4. jest, jape—joke; talk in a joking manner; engage in joking instead of being serious; make jokes at someone's expense or for the purpose of ridiculing someone
5. kid, spoof—joke, banter, or jest (colloq.)
6. quip—make witty remarks; make witty and sarcastic remarks
7. wisecrack, crack wise—make humorous or witty remarks when seriousness is expected (slang)

2. Joking,n. *From Sec. 1:* banter, bantering, chaff, joshing, or josh; drollery, fooling; jest, jesting, or japery; kidding or spoofing, quipping, wisecracking or cracking wise; *Also:* jocosity, jocularity, pleasantry, waggery,n.

3. Joking,adj. *From Sec. 1:* bantering, bantery, chaffing, or joshing; jesting, kidding or spoofing; quippish, quippy, or quipsome; wisecracking (quippishness or quipsomeness, n.); *Also:* jocose, jocular, waggish,adj. (jocoseness or jocosity, jocularity, waggishness,n.); *Also:*

1. ribald—full of, or characterized by, coarse, robust, or vulgar joking (ribaldry, n.)
2. scurrilous—full of, or characterized by, coarse, indecent, obscene, or offensive jokes, joking, jests, etc. (scurrility or scurrilousness,n.)

4. Given to, or in the Habit of Using, Ribaldry: ribaldish,adj.

5. To Joke or Joke at (Someone),v. *From Sec. 1:* banter, chaff, or josh; jest, kid or spoof; *Also:* 1. pull the leg of—jest with (colloq.)

6. Joker, Jokester, or Jokist, i.e., One Who Jokes or Makes Jokes,n. *From Sec. 1:* banterer, chaffer, or josher; jester or japer, kidder, quipster or quipper, wisecracker; *From Sec. 3:* ribald; *Also:* farceur (French), wag,n.

7. A Joke; A Bit of Humor or Wit,n. *From Sec. 1:* banter, chaff, or josh; drollery; jest, jape, or japery; spoof, quip, wisecrack; *Also:* gag (colloq.), jocosity, jocularity,n.; *Also:*

1. bon mot—witty or humorous saying, remark, sentence, etc. (French; bons mots, pl.n.)
2. chestnut, wheeze—stale or old joke
3. drollery—quaintly funny remark; jest
4. jokelet—little joke
5. mot—witty remark or saying (French)

6. pleasantry—joke; humorous, funny, or jesting remark or act
7. quirk—clever and humorous remark
8. sally—witty or humorous remark or answer; a bit of repartee
9. squib—witty remark, often sarcastic; brief and witty piece of writing, usually sarcastic or satirical
10. waggery—playful or mischievous jest
11. witticism—witty or humorous remark

8. Humorous or Witty Remarks, Sayings, or Writings; Books That Are Humorous or Witty in a Coarse or Ribald Manner: facetiae,pl.n.

9. Intended or Suitable for Jokes, Joking, or Jesting: jocular,adj. (jocularity,n.)

10. Person Who Is Most Skillful or Clever in Using Wit to Make Jests; One Who Jests with Great Skill: picador,n.

11. Joke or Trick Consisting of Action, etc., Rather than Words: practical joke,n.

12. Practical Joke: jape or japery, lark, prank, trick, waggery,n.

13. To Play Practical Jokes: jape, lark, prank, v. (japery,n.)

14. Practical Joker: jester, larker, prankster, n.

15. To Play Practical Jokes on (Someone): jape,v.

16. Full of, Addicted to, or Characterized by, Practical Jokes: larksome; prankish, pranksome, or pranky; tricksome or tricksy, adj. (prankishness or pranksomeness,n.)

17. One Who Jokes, Plays Merry Tricks, etc., in a Circus, Theater, etc.; One Who Acts Like Such: clown,n.

1116. A CLOWN

1. Clown or Similar Person,n.

1. buffoon—absurd clown; one who amuses with merry tricks, jokes, coarse jests, horseplay, etc.
2. droll—buffoon
3. fool—professional jester once employed by kings, etc., for their amusement
4. gracioso—in Spanish comedies, a clown, buffoon, or comic character
5. harlequin—one who plays clownish tricks; buffoon
6. jester—clownish person kept by kings, etc., during the Middle Ages; one who plays clownish tricks
7. merry-andrew—clown; clownish person; jester
8. mime, mimer—clown; buffoon; jester
9. mountebank—tricky buffoon; one who sells wares, quack medicines, etc., by mounting a platform in a public place and acting clownishly, telling jokes, playing tricks, etc., to hold his audience
10. punchinello—clown; buffoon
11. scaramouch, Scaramouch—boastful buffoon who is, in actuality, a coward
12. zany—clown; absurd clown

2. Clownish; Like, or Characteristic of, a Clown or One Who Acts Like a Clown,adj. *From Sec. 1:* buffoonish or buffoon, zany or zanyish (buffoonishness,n.)

3. To Clown; To Behave or Act Like a Clown,v. *From Sec. 1:* buffoon, droll, fool, harlequin, mountebank

4. Clownery; Clowning; The Behavior, Actions, etc., of a Clown,n. *From Sec. 1:* buffoonery or buffoonism, drollery, fooling, harlequinade, mountebankery or mountebankism, zanyism

5. A Characteristic or Quality of an Absurd

Clown; An Absurd and Clownish Characteristic: zanyism,n.

6. Indulging in, or Characterized by, Coarse or Indecent Buffoonery, Clowning, etc.: scurrilous,adj. (scurrility or scurrilousness,n.)

1117. UNPLEASANTNESS

1. Unpleasant: disagreeable (in manner, mood, temperament, attitude, nature, character, quality, etc.); disobliging (i.e., unwilling to be pleasant); displeasing; distasteful; ill-natured (i.e., in disposition, temperament, etc., or showing such, as a remark, attitude, etc.); inaffable or unaffable (i.e., not pleasant and polite, hard to approach or talk to, etc.); inurbane or unurbane (i.e., not smoothly or blandly pleasant, as people, their speech, manner, etc.); jarring (as in sound, effect, etc., on the person, senses, or nerves); nasty (i.e., extremely disagreeable, as a person, action, duty, requirement, cold, etc.); objectionable (i.e., wholly disagreeable, engendering feelings of objection, dislike, etc.); obnoxious (i.e., extremely objectionable); odious (i.e., extremely, disgustingly, or repugnantly unpleasant); offensive (i.e., extremely or annoyingly unpleasant, or unpleasant to the senses, morals, etc.); painful (i.e., so unpleasant as figuratively to cause pain, as a time, duty, person, etc.); repellent, repugnant, repulsive, or revolting (i.e., causing the greatest distaste, disgust, etc., in one, acting so as to push one back or away, etc.); snuffy (esp. in appearance); sore (i.e., causing disagreeable or unpleasant feelings); ugly (as a person, his nature, actions, attitude, etc.; or in appearance, symptoms, general quality or nature, as weather, a cold, duty, etc.); unagreeable; unamiable (i.e., in personality, or showing such); unattractive, unappealing, or uninviting (i.e., in promise or prospect, or to the sight of desires); uncheerful or cheerless (i.e., not pleasant and bright, as surroundings, places, atmosphere, etc.); uncomfortable (as a person, duty, time, weather, i.e., causing discomfort or unpleasant feelings); uncompanionable (i.e., not pleasant to be with); uncomplaisant (i.e., descr. of a person who shows no effort to please, or descr. of the actions, attitudes, etc., of such a person); uncongenial (i.e., not suitable to one's tastes, temperament, or interests, as people, work, surroundings, etc.); unconversable (i.e., not suited or inclined to pleasant sociability); ungracious (i.e., generally unpleasant, unpleasant to one's inferiors, unpleasant because lacking in courtesy, etc.); ungrateful or unthankful (i.e., unpleasing, as weather, sounds, etc.); unlikable or unlikeable (i.e., not pleasing, as a person or thing); unlovely; unpalatable (i.e., unpleasant to the taste, feelings, or mind); unpleasing; unpresentable or uncomely (i.e., unpleasant in appearance or to the sight); unsavory (i.e., unpleasant to the senses, esp. taste or smell, or to the mind, morals, or feelings),adj.

2. Unpleasantness,n. From Sec. 1: disagreeableness, disobligingness, displeasingness, distastefulness, ill nature or ill-naturedness, inaffability, inurbanity or inurbaneness, nastiness, objectionableness or objectionability, obnoxiousness, odiousness, offensiveness, painfulness; repellence, repellency, or repulsiveness; snuffiness, ugliness, unagreeableness, unamiableness or unamiability, unattractiveness, uncheerfulness or cheerlessness, uncomfortableness, uncongeniality, unconversableness, ungraciousness, ungratefulness or unthankfulness, unlikableness or unlikeableness, unloveliness, unpalatableness

or unpalatability, unpleasingness; unpresentableness, unpresentability, or uncomeliness; unsavoriness,n.

3. To Be Unpleasant to, i.e., Be a Source of Unpleasantness or Displeasure to,v. From Sec. 1: disoblige, displease, jar, offend, repel, revolt (offense,n.)

4. To Be Unpleasant,v. From Sec. 1: displease, offend, repel

5. Displeased,adj. From Sec. 1: offended, repelled, revolted,adj.

6. State or Feelings of Being Displeased, n. From Sec. 1: displeasure, distaste, offense, repugnance or repugnancy, repulsion, revolt

7. To Feel the Greatest and Keenest Displeasure, Distaste, or Disgust for, from, etc.: revolt against, at, or from,v.

8. To Express One's Feelings of Displeasure about: object to, protest,v. (objection, protest,n.)

9. An Expression of Displeasure; A Cause of Such: objection,n.

10. To Express Displeasure on One's Face: frown (by contracting the brows); gloom; pout (by thrusting out the lips); scowl (by drawing down the eyebrows, wrinkling the forehead, etc.),v. (frowner, pouter, scowler, n.)

11. So Expressing Displeasure,adj. From Sec. 10: frowning, clouded, or cloudy; glooming or gloomy, pouting, scowling

12. Such a Facial Expression or Look,n. From Sec. 10: frown, glooming, pout, scowl

13. To Express (a Feeling, Reaction, Disapproval, etc.) with Such a Look,v. From Sec. 10: frown, scowl

14. A Mood of Displeasure: the pouts,n.

15. Easily Displeased: snuffy,adj. (snuffiness, n.)

16. To Cause Unpleasant Feelings in (a Person), as Food, Climate, etc.: disagree with,v.

17. An Unpleasant, Disagreeable, Tiresome, etc., Person: pill,n. (colloq.)

1118. OFFENSIVENESS

1. Offensive, i.e., Giving Offense: affronting (i.e., to a person by showing deliberate disrespect); blatant (owing to loudness, noisiness, conspicuousness, disregard for good taste, etc.—of people, things, or abstractions); displeasing; fulsome (i.e., to good taste because excessive, insincere, etc.—of abstractions, as praise, flattery, etc.); loud (i.e., in strength, vividness, conspicuousness, etc.—of abstractions other than sound); loudmouthed or thersitical (i.e., offensive or blatant in voice or speech); nasty (to taste or smell, or in any other way); noisome (to the senses, esp. the sense of smell); objectionable; obnoxious; obscene (to modesty, morals, or decency); odious (i.e., extremely or disgustingly offensive); offending; outrageous (i.e., offensive beyond belief or endurance, or to the sense of fairness, decency, etc.); revolting; scandalous (to one's sense of decency, or to the moral sense of the community); shocking (i.e., to one's sense of propriety, one's morals, etc.); ugly (to one's sense of morals, beauty, etc.); unsavory (in morals); vulgar (to good taste, good breeding, refinement, the higher feelings, etc.),adj.

2. Offensiveness,n. From Sec. 1: blatancy, displeasingness, fulsomeness, loudness, nastiness, noisomeness, objectionableness or objectionability, obnoxiousness, obscenity or obsceneness, odiousness, outrageousness, scandalousness, ugliness, unsavoriness; vulgarity, vulgarness, or vulgarism

3. To Offend (a Person, His Senses, etc.), v. *From Sec. 1:* affront, displease, outrage, scandalize, shock,v. (scandalization,n.)

4. Offended; Feeling Offended,adj. *From Sec. 1:* affronted, displeased, outraged, scandalized, shocked; *Also:* 1. **aggrieved**—feeling offended

5. Offense; Offendedness; A Feeling of Being Offended,n. *From Sec. 1:* displeasure, outrage

6. That Which Offends,n. *From Sec. 1:* affront (i.e., an act, etc.); obscenity (i.e., a thing or circumstance, etc.); outrage, scandal, shocker

7. A Word, Language, Expression, etc., That Is Offensive,n. *From Sec. 1:* affront, obscenity, vulgarism or vulgarity

8. Person Who Offends, or Who Is Offensive,n. *From Sec. 1:* affronter; loudmouth (colloq.); scandal or scandalizer, shocker, vulgarian

9. An Instance of Being Offensive,n. *From Sec. 1:* affront, outrage, vulgarity

10. To Make (a Person, etc.) Vulgar: vulgarize,v. (vulgarization,n.)

11. Making Remarks, Asking Questions, etc., That Are Offensive in the Sense of Violating One's Privacy, That Are of an Intimate or Disparaging Nature, etc.: personal,adj.

12. Descr. of Such Remarks or Questions: personal,adj.

13. Such Remarks: personalities,pl.n. (as in *engage in personalities, descend to personalities,* etc.)

14. Offensive Language,n.
1. **billingsgate**—foul or coarse and abusive language
2. **blasphemy**—language that offends the Deity, anything holy or sacred, etc.
3. **coprophemia**—foul and obscene speech
4. **obscenity**—language or speech that offends modesty, decency, etc.
5. **ordure**—offensive, foul, disgusting, etc., language
6. **scurrility**—coarse, offensive, indecent, obscene, abusive, etc., language

15. Offensive in Language; Using Offensive Language,adj. *From Sec. 14:* blasphemous, obscene, ordurous, scurrilous (blasphemousness, obscenity or obsceneness, scurrility or scurrilousness,n); *Also:*
1. **foulmouthed**—using offensive, foul, indecent, obscene, profane, disgusting, or abusive language (foulmouthedness,n.)
2. **thersitical**—using, or descr. of, language that is grossly offensive, foul, abusive, obscene, indecent, disgusting, coarse, vile, etc.

16. An Offensive, Coarse, Indecent, Obscene, Abusive, etc., Remark: scurrility,n.

17. To Use, or Indulge in, Blasphemy: blaspheme,v. (blasphemer,n.)

18. To Use Such against (God, Something Holy or Sacred, etc.): blaspheme,v.

19. The Use, to an Abnormal and Startling Extent, of Offensive, Foul, Disgusting, or Obscene Words in One's Speech: coprophrasia,n.

20. The Use of Offensive, Filthy, Disgusting, Foul, or Obscene Language; Constant and Repetitious Reference to Feces, Fecal Subjects or Processes, etc.—an Occurrence in Certain Types of Insanity: coprolalia,n. (coprolaliac,adj.)

1119. DISSATISFACTION

1. Dissatisfied: disaffected (i.e., discontented); discontented or discontent (i.e., generally dissatisfied with what one has or is, restlessly dissatisfied, etc.); disgruntled (i.e., dissatisfied and therefore in a bad humor, peevish, sulky, etc.); displeased; ennuied or, French masc., ennuyé, or French fem., ennuyée (i.e., discontented and bored or wearied, as from inactivity, lack of interest, etc.); envious (i.e., discontented because of, or over, another's possessions, successes, advantages, position, etc.); fretful, fretting, or fretted (i.e., discontented and irritable, resentful, etc.); jealous (i.e., envious and resentful, as of another who is successful, who has the advantages one desires, etc.); malcontent or malcontented (i.e, dissatisfied or discontented),adj.

2. Dissatisfaction,n. *From Sec. 1:* disaffection; discontent, discontentment, or discontentedness; disgruntlement, displeasure, ennui, enviousness or envy, fretfulness or fret, jealousy or jealousness; malcontentment, malcontent, or malcontentedness; *Also:*
1. **dysphoria**—state of pathological or morbid dissatisfaction (dysphoric,adj.)
2. **(the) grumbles**—a mood of mumbling or muttering discontent
3. **heartburn, heartburning**—discontent that burns or eats away at the heart, as it were, esp. from envy or jealousy; bitter, burning jealousy; envy
4. **unrest**—dissatisfaction or discontent combined with anger or agitation, a mood bordering on rebellion or revolt—of groups, etc.

3. To Be Dissatisfied; To Show or Express Dissatisfaction,v. *From Sec. 1:* envy (someone or something), fret; *Also:*
1. **begrudge, grudge**—envy (someone) the having of (something); be full of discontent that (someone) has (something), as *begrudge a person his good fortune,* etc.
2. **complain**—express one's dissatisfaction (complaint,n.)
3. **grumble**—murmur, mutter, or mumble in discontent; say in a discontented murmur or mutter (grumble,n.)
4. **repine (at)**—feel or express dissatisfaction or discontentment (over), esp. in an irritable or resentful manner
5. **snivel**—show one's discontentment or dissatisfaction whiningly and tearfully

4. One Who Is Dissatisfied, or Who Expresses Dissatisfaction,n. *From Sec. 1:* discontent, envier, fretter; malcontent (esp. habitually or by temperament); *From Sec. 3:* complainer, grumbler, sniveler

5. Expressing, or Expressive of, Dissatisfaction, etc.,adj. *From Sec. 1:* discontented, displeased, envious, fretful, jealous; *From Sec. 3:* begrudging or grudging, complaining, grumbly or grumbling, sniveling; *Also:* 1. **plaintive**—expressing, or expressive of, melancholy or mournful discontentment, as a song, words, manner, look, sigh, etc. (plaintiveness,n.)

6. Plaintive or Sorrowful (Music): doloroso, adj. (Italian)

7. To Dissatisfy (Someone); To Make (Someone) Dissatisfied,v. *From Sec. 1:* disaffect, discontent, disgruntle, displease

8. A Cause or Source of Dissatisfaction or Discontentment: complaint, dissatisfaction, n.

9. Dissatisfying: displeasing, dissatisfactory, adj. (displeasingness, dissatisfactoriness,n.)

10. One Who Tries, as by Discussion, etc., To Foment or Increase Dissatisfaction or

Discontent in Order to Bring About Changes: agitator,n.

11. To Do Such: agitate,v. (agitation,n.)

12. Political Agitator: malcontent,n.

13. One, Esp. a Political Speaker, Leader, or Official, Who Foments or Incites Social, Political, or Economic Dissatisfaction or Discontent among the Populace, Purely out of Selfish Motives, for Personal Gain, etc.: demagogue or demagog, rabble-rouser,n. (demagogic or demagogical, rabble-rousing, adj.)

14. Such Principles, Methods, Actions, Practices, Qualities, Character, Nature, etc.: demagoguery, demagogy, or demagogism,n. (demagogic or demagogical,adj.)

15. Demagogues as a Group: demagogy,n.

16. Dissatisfied or Discontented with the Government, Rule, etc.; Hence, Often, Disloyal to It: disaffected,adj. (disaffection,n.)

17. To Cause (Someone) To Be So Dissatisfied or Disloyal: disaffect,v.

18. So Dissatisfied or Discontented; Hence, Often, Rebellious: malcontent,adj. (malcontentism, malcontent, or malcontentment,n.)

19. One Who Feels So Dissatisfied or Rebellious: malcontent,n.

20. To Prevent (Someone) from Gratifying or Satisfying Conscious or Unconscious Desires, Impulses, or Needs: frustrate,v. (frustration,n.)

21. Feeling So Prevented or Unsatisfied: frustrated,adj. (frustration,n.)

22. Unsatisfied: unappeased or unassuaged (as desires, appetites, etc.); uncomplacent (esp. unsatisfied with oneself, one's accomplishments, etc.); uncontented or uncontent; unfulfilled (as desires, needs, conditions, or a person in respect to his desires or needs); ungratified; unpleased; unsated (as desires, etc.); unslaked (as thirst, desire, passion, anger, etc.),adj.

23. Unsatisfaction; State or Feeling of Being Unsatisfied,adj. From Sec. 22: unappeasedness, uncontentedness or uncontent, unfulfillment, unsatedness

24. Unsatisfying,adj. From Sec. 22: unassuaging, unfulfilling, ungratifying, unpleasing (unpleasingness,n.); Also: lame or thin (as an excuse, etc.); unsatisfactory; unsuitable,adj. (lameness, thinness, unsatisfactoriness, unsuitableness or unsuitability,n.)

25. Incapable of Being Satisfied: insatiable, unsatiable, or insatiate; unappeasable or inappeasable; unfulfillable (as demands, etc.); uncontentable; ungratifiable; unsatisfiable, adj.

1120. COMPLAINT

1. To Complain,v.
1. **beef, bellyache, kick**—complain (slang)
2. **bleat**—complain; make sounds or cries of complaint; talk in a complaining or whining tone of voice; say in complaint
3. **carp, cavil**—complain though there is no good or valid reason for complaint; complain peevishly or grumblingly or in a petty way
4. **clamor**—complain in loud tones; complain heatedly, noisily, or vigorously
5. **gripe**—complain; complain ceaselessly (colloq.)
6. **grumble**—complain angrily or peevishly, or by muttering or mumbling; say in tones of complaint
7. **nag** (at)—complain ceaselessly, tire-

somely, annoyingly, etc.; complain to (someone) in such a manner
8. **protest**—complain; complain about (the actions of another, etc.)
9. **pule**—whimper or whine, the way a dissatisfied or ill child might
10. **rail** (against, at)—complain bitterly or vehemently (about)
11. **remonstrate**—offer reasons in complaint; say (that . . .) in complaint
12. **snivel**—complain whiningly and tearfully
13. **squawk**—complain in loud and vehement tones or language (colloq.)
14. **storm**—complain in raging anger, fury, annoyance, etc.
15. **whimper**—complain weakly; whine; say in weak or whining complaint
16. **whine**—complain in a childish, ill-humored and somewhat nasal sounds of complaint; say in such tones of complaint
17. **yammer**—complain; carry on, or engage in, low, persistent, collective sounds or whines of complaint—of prisoners in a penitentiary; say in complaint or tones of complaint (all colloq.)

2. Complaint, i.e., a Complaining,n. From Sec. 1: beefing, bellyaching, or kicking; bleat or bleating; carping, caviling, or cavil; clamoring or clamor, griping, grumbling or grumble, nagging or nag; protesting, protest, or protestation; puling, railing; remonstrating, remonstration, or remonstrance; sniveling, squawking, whimpering or whimper, whining or whine, yammering or yammer

3. A Complaint,n. From Sec. 1: beef or kick, cavil, clamor, gripe, protest or protestation, remonstrance, squawk, whine; Also:
1. **grievance**—complaint against injustice or wrong
2. **jeremiad**—lengthy, mournful, and denouncing complaint or speech of complaint
3. **plaint**—complaint
4. **representation**—complaint; statement of complaint; protest
5. **round robin**—written complaint or protest, with the signatures in a circle so that no one can tell who signed first

4. Complainer,n. From Sec. 1: beefer or bellyacher, bleater, carper or caviler, griper, grumbler; nagger or, esp. a woman, nag; protester or protestant, railer, remonstrator or remonstrant, sniveler, whimperer, whiner, yammerer

5. Complaining,adj. From Sec. 1: bleating, carping or caviling, etc.; clamorous, grumbly, protestant, remonstrant or remonstrative, whiny; Also: petulant, querulous,adj. (petulance or petulancy, querulousness,n.)

6. Given to, or Habitually, Complaining,adj. From Sec. 1: grumbly, whiny; Also: petulant, querulous,adj. (petulance or petulancy, querulousness,n.)

7. Cause or Grounds for Complaint: complaint, dissatisfaction, grievance, quarrel,n.

8. A Wrong, Injustice, Offense, etc., about Which One Complains, or That Is Deemed Cause or Grounds for Complaint: grievance, n.

9. To Reason with (a Person) in Mild or Kindly Complaint about His Actions or Intended Actions; To Reason with a Person Earnestly but Kindly against Such Actions, i.e., Try to Talk Him Out of Them: expostulate with or remonstrate with (a person) about or on (the action),v. (expostulation, remonstration, or remonstrance,n. expostulatory, expostulative, remonstrative, or remonstrant,adj. expostulator, remonstrator, or remonstrant,n.)

1121. DISAPPOINTMENT

1. To Disappoint: balk; belie (as hopes, etc.); bilk, frustrate, let down,v. (frustration, n.)

2. A Disappointment: balk, blow, frustration, letdown,n.

3. Disappointed; Feeling Disappointed; Feeling Disappointment: balked, bilked, chagrined; chapfallen or chopfallen (i.e., disappointed and simultaneously annoyed, embarrassed, etc.); disgruntled (i.e., disappointed and therefore in bad humor); frustrated, let down,adj.

4. Disappointment, i.e., State or Feeling of Disappointment,n. *From Sec. 3:* chagrin, disgruntlement, frustration, letdown,n.

5. To Cause a Feeling of Disappointment in,v. *From Sec. 3:* chagrin, disgruntle,v.

6. A Feeling of Unhappy Disappointment: regret,n.

7. To Make a Show of Tearful, Often False, Disappointment: snivel,v. (snivel,n. sniveler,n.)

8. To Become Tired or Weak with Disappointment: droop,v. (drooping or droopy,adj. droopingness or droopiness,n.)

1122. PROMISE

1. To Promise, i.e., Make a Promise: bind oneself; commit oneself; engage or engage oneself; guarantee or guaranty (to do); give one's word, one's sacred word, one's word of honor, one's pledge, one's promise, etc.; obligate oneself; swear (solemnly, or by oath, to do); undertake (to do); vow (solemnly, esp. to do or not do); warrant (i.e., give a promise to, as a person),v. (commitment or committal, engagement,n.)

2. Promiser,n. *From Sec. 1:* guarantor, vower, warranter; *Also:* pledger; promisor (legal),n.

3. A Promise: assurance, commitment, engagement; guarantee or guaranty; obligation (i.e., a promise that is binding); parole (i.e., word of honor); pledge (i.e., solemn or sacred promise, as of secrecy, faithfulness, etc., or one made to God, a god, a saint, etc., as to do, give, become, etc.); vow; warrant or warrantee (i.e., a guarantee or assurance); word, sacred word, or word of honor,n.

4. Written Promise to Pay, Do, Not Do, etc.: bond,n. (legal)

5. Written Promise or Assurance by the Seller that Goods Are as Represented, etc.: guarantee, warranty,n.

6. Certificate Issued by a Corporation, Government, etc., Promising to Pay Money Borrowed by or on a Certain Date: bond,n.

7. One Who Owns Such: bondholder,n.

8. Written Promise to Pay: promissory note, n.

9. Duty Imposed by One's Promise: bond, obligation,n.

10. That Which Is, or Gives, a Promise, Pledge, or Indication of What Will Follow or May Be Expected: earnest, promise,n.

11. Done, Given, Offered, Dedicated, or Consecrated as a Fulfillment or Result of, or in Accordance with, a Promise, Pledge, or Vow: votary, votive,adj. (votiveness,n.)

12. Consecrated by a Promise or Vow: votary,adj.

13. Containing, of the Character or Nature of, or Having the Implication of, a Promise: promissory,adj.

14. Pert. to, or of the Character or Nature of, a Vow: votary,adj.

15. One to Whom a Promise Is Made, or to Whom Something Is Promised: promisee,n. (esp. legal)

16. That Which Is Promised: promise,n.

17. Quality, Condition, State, etc., of Offering a Promise of, or of Indicating, Future Excellence, Success, Achievement, Worth, etc.: promise,n.

18. So Offering or Indicating: promising,adj.

19. To Promise (Something or Some Act, etc.): forswear (i.e., promise earnestly or solemnly to give up, not do, etc.); guarantee or guaranty (i.e., promise the payment of, as another's debt in case of default, or the fulfillment of, as a contract, etc.); pledge (i.e., promise support, aid, secrecy, honor, etc.); plight (i.e., promise one's honor, faith, etc.); swear off (i.e., promise to give up or not do, as alcohol, drinking, or other activities); vow (i.e., promise something solemnly, to God or a saint, etc.); warrant (i.e., promise something),v.

20. To Give as a Pledge: mortgage, pledge, plight,v.

21. To Persuade (a Person) by Means of a Promise: assure,v. (assurance,n.)

22. To Promise to Pay or Donate Money to (a Fund, Drive, Charity, etc., or a Magazine to Be Received Periodically, etc.): subscribe to,v.

23. To Make Such a Promise: subscribe,v. (subscription,n.)

24. Such a Promise: subscription,n.

25. Such a Promiser: subscriber,n.

26. To Promise to Be Faithful, True, etc.: plight one's troth,v.

27. To Promise Solemnly to Give Up Alcoholic Beverages: take the pledge

28. To Promise to Join, or to Accept on Trial for Membership in, a Fraternity or Sorority: pledge,v.

29. One Who So Promises, or Is So Accepted: pledgee,n.

30. To Pledge (Something) to a Creditor as Security: hypothecate,v. (hypothecation,n.)

31. One Who So Pledges: hypothecator,n.

32. To Pledge (Property) as Security for a Loan: mortgage,v.

33. Such Pledging: mortgage,n.

34. The Deed or Document So Pledging: mortgage,n.

35. One Who So Pledges: mortgagor or mortgager,n.

36. One to Whom Property Is So Pledged: mortgagee,n.

37. To Deliver or Deposit (Possessions, etc.) as a Pledge against a Loan: hock (slang), pawn, pledge,v. (pawn or pawnage,n.)

38. State of Being So Delivered or Deposited: pawn (as *in pawn*), pawnage, pledge (as *in pledge*),n.

39. That Which Is So Delivered, Deposited, or Pledged: pawn, pledge,n.

40. One Who So Deposits: pawner or pawnor, pledgor or pledgeor,n.

41. One with Whom Such Is Deposited: pledgee,n.

42. One Who Lends Money on Such Possessions: pawnbroker; uncle (slang),n. (pawnbroking,n.)

43. Pert. to a Pawnbroker: avuncular,adj. (humorous)

44. Shop of a Pawnbroker: hockshop (slang), pawnshop,n.

45. To Pledge (Honor, etc.) as a Security: pawn,v.

46. That Which, or One Who, Is Given, Deposited, Delivered, etc., as Proof of Intention to Fulfill a Promise,n.

1. **bail, bond**—property or money deposited as security that a released prisoner will appear at the proper or appointed time
2. **collateral**—security deposited or pledged against a loan (collateral,adj.)
3. **earnest**—that which is given as a pledge or promise of the rest due, or as a promise of sincerity, action, fulfillment, etc.
4. **gage**—something deposited as a pledge of what one has promised; pawn; security
5. **guarantee**—that which is given as security
6. **hostage**—person given or held as security that a promise or pledge will be kept; any security or pledge
7. **pawn, pledge**—that which is deposited or left as a security against a loan; any thing or person serving or acting as a security; hostage
8. **security, surety, bond**—that which is given as proof of one's intention to fulfill a promise, pledge, duty, or loan, and to be forfeited if such is not fulfilled
9. **token payment**—partial payment as an indication of the earnestness of one's promise to pay the rest (of a debt, etc.)

47. One Who Deposits Bail for the Release of a Prisoner: bail, bond,n.

48. One Who Agrees to Make Payment for Another if the Latter Fails to Keep His Promise: bondsman, security, surety,n.

49. To Bind (Someone), or Place (Him) under a Duty, by a Promise: bind, commit, engage, obligate, oblige, pledge,v. (commitment or committal, engagement, obligation, n.)

50. One Bound by a Vow or Promise; One Bound by a Religious Vow to a Way of Life, as a Monk or Nun: votary or votarist,n. (votaress or votress,fem.n.)

51. To Keep a Promise: keep faith,v.

52. Keeping a Promise: faithful,adj. (faithfulness,n.)

53. To Break, or Go Back on, One's Promise, Word, etc.: break faith, forswear, renege,v. (forswearer, reneger,n.)

54. Not Keeping to, or Having Broken, One's Promise or Vow: faithless, unfaithful,adj.

55. Fact, State, or Condition of Having Broken One's Promise: faithlessness, infidelity, unfaithfulness,n.

1123. LOW SPIRITS; DEPRESSION

1. In Low Spirits; Indicative or Expressive of, or Characterized by, Low Spirits: abject; atrabilious or atrabiliar; black; bleak (i.e., utterly lacking in cheerfulness); blue, cast down; chapfallen or chopfallen; cheerless, crestfallen; dejected (temporarily, rather than in temperament); depressed (often in nature or temperament); despondent (i.e., completely dejected or depressed, often because all hope is gone and everything seems futile); disconsolate; discouraged (esp. because of lack or loss of hope or prospect of success); disheartened, dismal; dismayed (because of the prospect of danger, difficulty, or failure); dispirited, downcast, downhearted, gloomy; glum (and also, usually, painfully silent); heavyhearted, low, low-spirited; melancholy or melancholic; mopish or mopy

(i.e., dejected and listless, spiritless, sluggish, apathetic, etc.); soul-sick (i.e., spiritually dejected); spiritless, vaporish or vapory; wretched (i.e., deeply dejected or depressed), adj.

2. Low or Depressed Spirits,n. *From Sec. 1:* abjectness or abjection, atrabiliousness, blackness, bleakness, blueness, cheerlessness, crestfallenness, dejection or dejectedness, depression, despondency or despondence, disconsolateness or disconsolation, discouragement, disheartenment, dismalness, dismay, dispiritedness, downheartedness, gloom or gloominess, glumness, heavyheartedness, lowness, low-spiritedness, melancholy, mopishness, soul-sickness, spiritlessness; vaporishness or, somewhat old-fashioned or archaic, the vapors; wretchedness,n.; *Also:* damp; slough or slough of despond (i.e., of the deepest and most hopeless kind),n.

3. A Fit of Low Spirits or Depression: the blues or blue devils; the dismals (colloq.); the doldrums; the dumps (colloq.); the megrims; the mopes,n.

4. To Make, or Cause to Be, Low-Spirited or Depressed,v. *From Sec. 1:* cast down, deject, depress, discourage, dishearten, dismay, dispirit, gloom, mope,v. (discouragement, disheartenment,n.); *Also:* chill (the heart, spirits, mood, etc.),v.

5. Causing, or Productive of, Low Spirits or Depression,adj. *From Sec. 1:* abject, bleak, cheerless, depressing or depressive, disconsolate, discouraging, disheartening, dismal, dismaying, dispiriting, gloomy, melancholy (abjectness, bleakness, cheerlessness, depressingness or depressiveness, disconsolateness, dismalness, gloominess or gloom,n.); *Also:* chill, chilly, dreary or drearisome, somber or sombre, sullen; triste (French),adj. (chillness, chilliness, dreariness, somberness or sombreness, sullenness,n.)

6. To Be or Feel Low-Spirited or Depressed,v. *From Sec. 1:* despond, gloom, mope

7. One Who Is Low-Spirited or Depressed, n. *From Sec. 1:* mope or moper

8. To Look Low-Spirited or Depressed: gloom,v.

9. Descr. or Characteristic of, or Pert. to, Depression of Feelings or Low Spirits: depressive,adj.

10. In an Emotional State Marked by Low Spirits, General Unhappiness, and Feelings of Discouragement and Inadequacy: depressed,adj.

11. Such a State: depression,n.

12. Low or Depressed—Descr. of One's Spirits, Mood, Frame of Mind, etc.: abject, black, bleak, blue, cast down, cheerless, clouded, dampened, dark, dashed, dejected, downcast, droopy or drooping, melancholy, sagging,adj. (abjectness, blackness, bleakness, blueness, cheerlessness, darkness, dejectedness or dejection; droop, droopiness, or droopingness; sag,n.)

13. To Make (the Spirits, Mood, etc.) Low or Depressed: blacken, cast down, chill, cloud, dampen, darken, dash, deject, depress,v.

14. To Be, or Become, Low or Depressed—of the Spirits, etc.: droop, sag,v.

15. Given to Moods of Depression, Gloom, etc.; Arising from, or Expressive of, Such Moods: broody, moody,adj. (moodiness,n.)

16. Given to, or in the Habit of, Moping: mopish,adj. (mopishness,n.)

17. One Who Is Given to, or in the Habit of, Moping: mope,n.

18. Tendency to Be Depressed: melancholy, n.

19. Severe and Morbid Emotional Depression, Usually Accompanied by Anxieties about One's Health, Fantasies of Illness, etc.: hypochondria or hypochondriasis,n.

20. Sunk in, or Suffering from, Such: hypochondriac or hypochondriacal,adj.

21. One So Afflicted: hypochondriac,n.

22. Mental Illness Characterized by Extreme Depression, Gloom, Brooding, Moods of Anxious Foreboding, etc.: melancholia,n. (melancholic,adj.)

23. Afflicted by, or Suffering from, Such: melancholiac,adj.

24. One So Afflicted: melancholiac,n.

25. Sudden Letdown of Spirits, Very Intense but of Short Duration, Often Characterized by Morbid Ideas or Actions; Sudden, Sharp, and Temporary Psychic Depression: psycholepsy,n. (psycholeptic,adj.)

1124. GLOOM

1. Gloomy (of Persons, Temperament, Attitude, Feelings, etc., or Expressive of Such Feelings, as Looks, Face, Air, Manner, Tone, etc.): black or dark (as feelings, attitude, etc.); bleak, blue, cheerless; cloudy, clouded, overcast, overclouded, or overshadowed (i.e., darkened by gloom, as feelings, face, etc.); disconsolate, dismal, dour; dyspeptic or dyspeptical (i.e, exceedingly or morbidly gloomy, as if suffering from poor digestion); glum (i.e., gloomy and also, usually, painfully silent); melancholy or melancholic, mirthless, moody or broody; mopish or mopy (i.e., gloomy and listless, spiritless, sluggish, apathetic, etc.); morose (i.e., gloomy, gloomy and silent, gloomy and irritable or ill-humored, etc.); saturnine (esp. in temperament); somber or sombre, uncheerful,adj.

2. Gloom; Gloominess,n. *From Sec. 1:* blackness or darkness, bleakness, blueness, cheerlessness, cloudiness, disconsolateness or disconsolation, dismalness, dourness, glumness; melancholy (esp. if long-continuing or habitual); mirthlessness, moodiness, mopishness, moroseness, saturnineness or saturninity, somberness or sombreness, uncheerfulness

3. A Fit or Attack of Gloom: the blues or blue devils, the dismals, the mopes,n.

4. To Be Gloomy; To Look Gloomy: gloom, v.

5. To Make Gloomy: blacken or darken (mood, spirits, heart, countenance, etc.); cloud, overcast, overcloud, overshadow, or shadow (the face, mood, atmosphere, etc.); gloom,v.

6. To Be, or Make, Gloomy and Listless, Sluggish, Apathetic, etc.: mope,v.

7. One Who Is Gloomy and Listless, etc.: mope or moper,n.

8. To Clear (as the Face, etc.), or Become Clear, of Gloom or Depression: uncloud,v.

9. Gloomy, i.e., Causing Gloom: disconsolate, dismal, dreary or drearisome, melancholy, somber or sombre; triste (French),adj. (disconsolateness, dismalness, dreariness, somberness or sombreness,n.)

10. Gloomy (of Places, etc.): black, bleak, cheerless, dark, desolate; dismal, dreary, or drearisome (a place, day, etc.); forlorn (i.e., gloomy and deserted, as a place); funereal (the atmosphere of a place); sepulchral (i.e., reminding one of the grave, etc.); solemn (a

color); somber or sombre; sorry (an occasion); Stygian (i.e., suggestive of the river Styx in the infernal regions); sullen (the weather, sounds, tones, etc.); tenebrous; wintry or wintery (suggestive of winter, as a place, the atmosphere of a place, etc.),adj. (blackness, bleakness, cheerlessness, darkness, desolateness or desolation, dismalness, dreariness, forlornness, solemnness or solemnity, somberness or sombreness, sorriness, sullenness, wintriness,n.)

11. Making (a Place) Gloomy and Dark: tenebrific,adj.

12. To Grow or Become Gloomy—of a Place, etc.: darkle, gloom,v.

13. Something That Is Gloomy, Cheerless, etc.: dismal,n.

1125. SADNESS

1. Sad, i.e., Feeling, Full of, or Characterized by, Sadness: adust (i.e., melancholy, or pale and melancholy); aggrieved (i.e., full of sorrow or grief); atrabilious or atrabiliar (i.e., melancholy); brokenhearted or heartbroken (i.e., as if one's heart had been broken by sadness, grief, sorrow, disappointment, etc.); desolate or desolated (i.e., thoroughly and hopelessly unhappy, wretched, etc.); disconsolate or inconsolable (i.e., so sad as not to respond to cheering up, not to be comforted in one's grief or sorrow, etc.); distressed or distressful; doleful (usually, absurdly sad); dolorous; forlorn (i.e., unhappy or miserable in feeling or condition, or unhappy and friendless, forsaken, alone, lonely, etc.); grief-laden (i.e., burdened with grief); grief-stricken (i.e., afflicted or stricken with grief or sorrow); grieved (i.e., full of grief or sorrow); heartsick or sick at heart; heartsore; heart-stricken or heart-struck (i.e., deeply afflicted with grief or sorrow); heavyhearted; joyless (i.e., without joy, happiness, gladness, etc.); melancholy or melancholic (i.e., full of sadness, often a kind of thoughtful sadness); mirthless (i.e., without mirth, joy, merriment, etc.); miserable (i.e., pathetically or wretchedly unhappy); mournful; rueful; somber or sombre (i.e., sad, melancholy, etc.); sore or sore at heart; sorrow-burdened; sorrowclouded; sorrowful; sorrow-laden; sorrowstricken or sorrow-struck; sorrow-worn; sorry (i.e., full of sadness, as at seeing, hearing, or learning of, something sad); tragic or tragical (i.e., characterized by extreme sadness, as a day, occasion, look, appearance, etc.); triste (French); tristful; unhappy; woe-dejected; woeful or woful; woe-laden; woe-stricken or woe-struck; wretched (i.e., profoundly or miserably unhappy),adj.

2. Sadness,n. *From Sec. 1:* atrabiliousness; brokenheartedness, heartbreak, or heartbrokenness; desolateness or desolation; disconsolateness, disconsolation, inconsolableness, or inconsolability; distress or distressfulness; dolefulness; dolorousness or, poetic, dolor; forlornness, grief, grieving, heartsickness, heavyheartedness or heavy heart, joylessness; melancholy (esp. when long-continuing or habitual); mirthlessness, miserableness or misery, mournfulness, ruefulness, somberness or sombreness, sorrow or sorrowfulness, sorriness; tristesse (French); tristfulness, unhappiness, woe, woefulness or wofulness, wretchedness,n.; *Also:*

1. **heartache**—sorrow; deep or painful sorrow or grief
2. **tribulation**—deep and painful sorrow

3. Pretended or Hypocritical Grief or Sorrow: crocodile tears,n.

4. Sadness, Grief, Sorrow, or Sentimental Pessimism over the State of the World, etc.: Weltschmerz,n. (German)

5. Sudden and Sharp Feeling of Sadness, Grief, or Sorrow, as from Leave-taking, etc.: wrench,n.

6. Sad, i.e., Expressive of Sadness: brokenhearted or heartbroken (as cries, sobbing, etc.); dirgeful (i.e., mournful, or like a song or tune of mourning, as sounds, etc.); distressed or distressful; doleful (as in expression, sound, or appearance, usually absurdly so); dolorous; elegiac or elegiacal (i.e., expressive of grief, sorrow, or lamentation, as music, sounds, poetry, language, etc.); forlorn (as in appearance, etc.); funereal (i.e., sad or mournful, as in looks, expression, sound, etc., sometimes absurdly or ridiculously so); grievous (as a sound, appearance, etc.); joyless (in attitude, appearance, etc.); lugubrious (in sound, appearance, air, etc., esp. in a somewhat absurd, ridiculous, or pretended manner); melancholy (as air, tones, words, appearance, etc.); mirthless, miserable, moanful; mournful (as words, tones, air, etc.); plaintive or lamentatory (i.e., expressive of melancholy feelings, as tones, words, melodies, air, etc.); rueful; somber or sombre; sorrowful; tragic or tragical (i.e., expressive of pathetic sadness, as looks, demeanor, voice, sounds, etc.); tristful (as an air, countenance, tones, etc.); unhappy; wailful or wailsome (in sound or tone); wistful (i.e., expressive of melancholy, or of longing combined with melancholy); woebegone or wobegone (i.e., in looks, facial or other aspect, etc.); woeful or woful; wretched (in appearance),adj. (brokenheartedness or heartbrokenness, distressfulness, dolefulness, dolorousness, forlornness, grievousness, joylessness, lugubriousness, melancholy, mirthlessness, miserableness or misery, mournfulness, plaintiveness, ruefulness, somberness or sombreness, sorrowfulness, tragicalness, tristfulness, unhappiness, wistfulness, woebegoneness or wobegoneness, woefulness or wofulness, wretchedness,n.)

7. One Who Is Miserably Unhappy: wretch, n.

8. One Who Looks Sad, Miserable, or Wretched: woebegone,n.

9. To Become Sad: sadden,v.

10. To Feel Sadness, Grief, Sorrow, etc.: grieve (i.e., feel acute grief or sorrow and the mental suffering that results from such, enduring the pain in silence though expressing it in one's face, demeanor, etc.); lament; mourn (over the dead, or over any loss, unfortunate condition or fact, etc.); sorrow,v. (griever, lamenter, mourner, sorrower,n. grieving, lamentation or lamenting, mourning, sorrowing,n. grieving, lamenting, mourning, sorrowing,adj.)

11. Pert. to, or Descr. of, Lamentation: lamentational or lamentatory,adj.

12. Characterized by Lamenting: lamentatory,adj.

13. To Feel Sadness, Grief, Sorrow, etc., over or about (a Condition, Fact, Loss, etc.): deplore, lament, mourn,v. (lamentation,n. deplorer, lamenter, mourner,n.)

14. Such as to Excite Feelings of Sadness, Grief, Sorrow, etc.: deplorable, lamentable, rueful, tragic,adj. (deplorableness or deplorability, lamentableness, ruefulness,n.)

15. Lamentable Happening or Circumstance, or Sequence of Such Happenings or Circumstances: tragedy,n.

16. Sad, in the Sense of Poor, Unhealthy, Unsound, Very Bad or Inferior, etc., as in Condition or State, i.e., Such as to Excite Sadness or Pity in the Beholder: deplorable, grievous, lamentable, melancholy, miserable, mournful, pathetic, pitiable, pitiful, rueful, sorrowful, sorry, tragic, wailsome, woeful or woful, wretched,adj. (deplorableness or deplorability, grievousness, lamentableness, miserableness, mournfulness, pitiableness, pitifulness, ruefulness, sorrowfulness, sorriness, woefulness or wofulness, wretchedness,n.)

17. To Express Sadness, Grief, Sorrow, etc.: bemoan, bewail; keen (i.e., wail for, or utter wails or lamentations for, the dead—Irish); lament; moan (in prolonged sounds); mourn (i.e., express grief over the dead, or over any loss, unfortunate condition or fact, etc.); sigh (by audibly expelling the breath); wail (in prolonged, usually high-pitched, cries indicative of suffering),v. (bemoaner, bewailer, keener, lamenter, mourner, sigher, wailer,n. bemoaning, bewailing, keening, lamentation or lamenting, moaning, mourning, sighing, wailing,n. bemoaning, bewailing, keening, lamenting, moaning, mourning, sighing, wailing or wailsome,adj.)

18. An Expression of Sadness, Grief, or Sorrow,n. *From Sec. 17:* lament or lamentation, moan, sigh, wail

19. To Express Sadness, Grief, Sorrow over or about (a Condition, Fact, Loss, etc.),v. *From Sec. 17:* bemoan, bewail, keen, lament, moan, mourn, wail; *Also:* deplore,v.

20. That Which Expresses Sadness, Grief, or Sorrow,n.
  1. **(the) blues**—song of melancholy character, or expressive of the singer's sadness or melancholy
  2. **dirge**—tune, song, or musical composition that expresses mourning
  3. **elegy**—poem of grief or lamentation for the dead; song or musical composition that expresses sadness (elegiac or elegiacal,adj.)
  4. **jeremiad**—long speech or other expression of lamentation
  5. **keen**—a lamentation for the dead; a dirge (Irish)
  6. **lament**—poem or song of lamentation; dirge; elegy

21. To Express Sadness, Grief, or Sorrow over (a Person, Loss, etc.) in, or as in, an Elegy: elegize,v.

22. To Write an Elegy: elegize,v.

23. Writer of Elegies: elegist,n.

24. To Take On an Air or Expression of Sentimental or Wistful Sadness or Melancholy: languish,v. (languishing,adj.)

25. Such an Air or Expression: languishment, n.

26. To Make a Pretense or Show of Sadness, Grief, or Sorrow, Often Hypocritically: snivel,v. (snivel,n. sniveler,n.)

27. To Say or Utter in Tones of Sadness, Grief, or Sorrow: moan, mourn, sigh, wail,v.

28. To Dwell Constantly in Thought on (One's Unhappiness, Grief, Misfortunes, etc.): brood on or over,v.

29. To So Dwell on One's Unhappiness, etc.: brood,v. (brooder,n. brooding,adj.)

30. Given to Such Dwelling: broody,adj.

31. Sadly Thoughtful; Expressive of Sad Thoughtfulness; Engaged in Deep or Serious Thought about Sad or Melancholy Things: pensive, wistful,adj. (pensiveness, wistfulness,n.)

32. Suggestive or Remindful of, or Associated with, Sadness or Sorrow, as an Occasion, Day, Time, etc.: distressing or distressful, doleful, dolorous, dreary or drearisome, gloomy, melancholy, mournful, somber or sombre, sorry, tragic, woeful or woful,adj.

33. To Sadden, i.e., Cause Sadness, Grief, or Sorrow to: aggrieve (commonly in the passive voice); desolate, distress, grieve,v.

34. Saddening, i.e., Causing or Exciting Sadness, Grief, or Sorrow: cruel, deplorable, desolating, disconsolate, distressing or distressful, doleful, dolorous, dreary or drearisome, gloomy, grievous, heartbreaking, heartrending, lamentable, melancholy, miserable, mournful, poignant, somber or sombre, sore, sorry, wailsome, woeful or woful, wretched, adj. (cruelty or cruelness, deplorableness or deplorability, disconsolateness, distressfulness, dolefulness, dolorousness, dreariness, gloominess, grievousness, lamentableness, miserableness, mournfulness, poignancy, somberness or sombreness, soreness, sorriness, woefulness or wofulness, wretchedness,n.)

35. Cause or Source of Sadness, Grief, or Sorrow: cruelty (an act or action); distress, grief, heartache, misery; pity (as in *it's a pity*, etc.); sorrow, tribulation,n.

36. One Who Spoils or Destroys the Happiness, Joy, Enjoyment, Pleasure, etc., of Another or of Others: dampener, kill-joy, spoilsport, wet blanket,n.

37. To Spoil or Ruin the (Happiness, Joy, Enjoyment or Pleasure of): dampen, wetblanket,v.

38. To Weigh Heavily upon the Mind of—Said of Sadness, Grief, Sorrow, etc.: burden, crush, oppress,v. (oppression,n. burdensome, crushing, oppressing or oppressive,adj.)

39. Weighed Down (by Sadness, Grief, Sorrow, etc.)—of a Person, Mind, Heart, Spirit, etc.: burdened, crushed, oppressed,adj. (oppression,n.)

40. To Relieve the Sadness, Grief, or Sorrow of: cheer or cheer up, comfort, console, solace,v. (consolation, solacement,n.)

41. State or Feeling of Being Relieved of Sadness, Grief, or Sorrow: comfort, consolation, solace or solacement,n.

42. One Who Relieves Another's Sadness, Grief, or Sorrow: comfort or comforter, consolation or consoler, solacer,n.

43. That Which Is a Relief from Sadness, Grief, or Sorrow: comfort, consolation, solace or solacement,n.

44. Giving, or Tending to Give, Relief from Sadness, Grief, or Sorrow: cheering, comforting, consoling or consolatory, solacing or solaceful,adj. (consolatoriness,n.)

45. To Relieve (Sadness, Sorrow, or Grief): solace,v. (solacement,n.)

46. Capable of Being Relieved of One's Sadness, Grief, or Sorrow: consolable,adj. (consolableness,n.)

47. Incapable of Being Relieved of Sadness, Grief or Sorrow: disconsolate, inconsolable, unconsolable,adj. (disconsolateness or disconsolation, inconsolableness or inconsolability, n.)

48. Not Happy: blissless, cheerless, joyless, unblissful, uncheerful, unecstatic, unglad, ungleeful, unhappy, unjoyful, unjoyous,adj. (cheerlessness, joylessness, unbliss, uncheerfulness, ungladness, unhappiness, unjoyfulness, unjoyousness,n.)

49. Sadness over Something Done, Something One Has Done or Failed to Do, Something That Has Happened or Has Not Happened, Something or Someone Lost, Departed, etc.: regret or regrets,n.

1126. REGRET

1. Regretful, i.e., Full of, or Feeling, Regret: compunctious (i.e., for a wrong one has done, for an offense, sin, bad act, etc., and, often, suffering pangs of conscience as a result); contrite (i.e., sincerely regretful or remorseful over an offense, guilt, sin, etc.); penitent (i.e., sincerely sorry for misdeeds, sins, etc., and willing to atone); remorseful (i.e., suffering deep and painful regret over wrongdoing, etc.); repentant (i.e., feeling regret over any past action, or over wrongdoing, sin, misdeeds, etc.); rueful (about having done something one wishes one had never done, etc.); sorry (for what has happened, for what one has done or not done, said or not said, etc.),adj.

2. Regret; Regretfulness; A Feeling of Regret,n. *From Sec. 1:* compunction or compunctions, contrition or contriteness, penitence, remorse or remorsefulness, repentance, ruefulness, sorriness or sorrow,n.

3. To Be Regretful,v. *From Sec. 1:* repent, rue; *Also:* 1. **lament**—feel or express melancholy regret

4. To Regret, i.e., Feel Regretful about or over (Something),v. *From Sec. 1:* repent, rue; *Also:*
1. **deplore**—regret (something) sincerely or deeply
2. **lament, mourn**—feel or express melancholy regret over (something lost, gone, etc.)

5. Regretter, i.e., One Who Is Regretful,n. *From Sec. 1:* penitent or penitential, repenter, ruer; *From Sec. 4:* deplorer, lamenter

6. Regretful, i.e., Expressing or Indicating Regret,adj. *From Sec. 1:* contrite, penitent or penitential, remorseful, repentant, rueful

7. Caused by, or Arising From, Regret,adj. *From Sec. 1:* penitential, remorseful

8. Pert. to, or of the Nature of, Regret,adj. *From Sec. 1:* compunctious, penitential,adj.

9. Causing Regret,adj. *From Sec. 1:* compunctious

10. A Cause for Regret: pity, shame,n. (as in *it's a pity*, or *it's a shame*, etc.)

11. Lacking in Regret,adj. *From Sec. 1:* uncontrite, impenitent or unpenitent, remorseless or unremorseful, unrepentant, unrueful, unsorry (impenitence, impenitency, impenitentness, or unpenitentness; remorselessness, unrepentantness,n.); *Also:* regretless, unregretful,adj. (unregretfulness,n.)

12. One Who Does Not Regret His Misdeeds, Sins, etc., and Hence Has No Disposition to Make Atonement: impenitent,n.

13. Such as to Be Regretted, to Cause or Excite Regret, etc.: deplorable, lamentable, regrettable, unfortunate,adj. (deplorableness or deplorability, lamentableness, regrettableness, unfortunateness,n.)

14. Not Such as to Be Regretted: unregrettable,adj.

15. A Polite Expression of One's Feelings of Regretfulness: regrets,n.

16. Such an Expression when One Has Done Something Wrong: apology,n.

17. To Express Regret when One Has Done Something Wrong: apologize,v. (apologizer, n.)

18. Expressing Regretfulness when One Has Done Something Wrong; Feeling that One Should Express Such; Showing a Realization that One Should Express Such: apologetic,adj. (unapologetic,neg.adj.)

1127. TO WEEP

1. To Weep,v.
1. **bawl**—weep loudly, noisily, or as if in pain or anguish
2. **blubber**—weep; weep noisily or in such a way as to distort one's features or face
3. **cry**—weep, shedding tears, usually with inarticulate sounds or sometimes quietly, as in grief or mourning; make sounds of grief, pain, suffering, distress, etc., with or without tears
4. **dissolve in tears, break into tears, burst into tears**—weep; start to weep
5. **howl, yowl**—utter a prolonged mournful or distressed cry, or such cries, as in pain, rage, etc.
6. **mewl**—cry weakly or faintly, like a baby; cry in baby fashion; whimper
7. **pule**—cry in a thin, weak voice, like a sick or peevish child
8. **shed tears**—weep
9. **snivel**—weep, with or without vocal sounds, but with much drawing of air or mucus up the nose; weep in pretended grief; become tearful in grief, often hypocritically
10. **sob**—weep or cry with convulsive movements of the throat or chest, irregular breaking of the voice, or spasmodic catching of the breath
11. **squall**—cry loudly or in screams, as an infant
12. **wail**—cry in prolonged and usually high-pitched sounds of sorrow, grief, distress, pain, etc.
13. **whimper**—cry in a low, broken, often whining voice, as in complaint, distress, pain, discomfort, grief, etc.; do such, as a child or dog

2. Weeping,n. *From Sec. 1:* bawling, blubbering, crying, howling or yowling, mewling, puling, sniveling, sobbing, squalling, wailing, whimpering; *Also:* 1. **lachrymation**—weeping

3. A Cry; Instance, Fact, Fit, or Sound of Weeping or Crying,n. *From Sec. 1:* bawl, blubber, cry, howl or yowl, snivel, sob, squall, wail, whimper; *Also:* 1. **vagitus**—the cry of an infant just after birth (medical)

4. Fits of Bursting into Tears, or of Weeping: lachrymals or lacrimals,n.

5. A Weeper,n. *From Sec. 1:* bawler, blubberer, howler or yowler, mewler, puler, sniveler, sobber, squaller, wailer, whimperer; *Also:* 1. **lachrymist**—one who weeps

6. Weeping,adj. *From Sec. 1:* bawling, blubbering, crying, dissolved in tears, howling or yowling, mewling, puling, shedding tears, sniveling, sobbing, squalling, wailing or wailful, whimpering; *Also:* in tears, tearful, teary, weepy,adj. (tearfulness,n.)

7. To Say or Utter while Weeping or Crying,v. *From Sec. 1:* bawl, blubber or blubber out, howl or yowl, snivel, sob, squall, wail, whimper

8. Indicating, or Indicative of, Weeping: lachrymal, lacrimal, or lacrymal,adj. (lachrymalness,n.)

9. One in the Habit of Breaking Down and Crying Like a Baby, Esp. when Angry, Hurt, Offended, Dissatisfied, etc.: crybaby,n.

10. One in the Habit of Weeping: lachrymist, n.

11. To Distort (the Features or Face) with Weeping: blubber,v.

12. So Distorted—of the Features or Face: blubber or blubbered,adj.

13. To Bring Oneself to a State or Condition, Esp. Sleep, by Crying or Sobbing: cry or sob oneself to (sleep, etc.),v.

14. To Weep, Cry, Sob, etc., for a Long Time until Exhausted: weep, cry, sob, etc., one's eyes or heart out

15. Story or Account Told for the Purpose of Making One Weep, Figuratively, as with Pity, etc., or for the Purpose of Eliciting Pity: sob story,n. (colloq.)

16. Woman News Reporter Who Writes in a Mawkishly Sentimental Style Calculated to Make Readers Figuratively Weep with Pity for, or Sorrow over, the Plight of Those Whose Stories Are Told: sob sister,n. (colloq.)

17. Not Weeping; Not Able to Weep: dry-eyed, tearless,adj. (tearlessness,n.)

18. To Stop Weeping: dry one's eyes, dry one's tears,v.

1128. TEARS

1. A Tear: lachryma, teardrop,n.

2. A Little Tear: tearlet,n.

3. False, Pretended, or Insincere Tears: crocodile tears,n.

4. Having, or with, the Eyes Full of Tears: lachrymose, lacrimose, or lachrymosal; tearful, teary, weepy,adj. (lachrymosity, tearfulness,n.)

5. In the Habit of Shedding Tears: lachrymose or lacrimose,adj. (lachrymosity,n.)

6. Containing, or Full of, Tears—of the Eyes: moist (i.e., slightly tearful); tearful, teary, watery, wet,adj.

7. Causing or Bringing Forth Tears; Hence, Sad, Mournful, etc.: lachrymose or lacrimose, tearful, teary, weepy,adj. (lachrymosity, tearfulness,n.)

8. Accompanied by Tears, or by the Shedding of Tears, as a Story, etc.: tearful, teary, adj.

9. Producing or Secreting Tears, as Certain Glands; Characterized by Tears: lachrymal, lacrimal, or lacrymal,adj.

10. Such Glands: lachrymals, tear glands,n.

11. Substance That Causes the Shedding of Tears: lachrymator or lacrimator, lachrymatory, tear gas,n.

12. Pert. to Tears: lachrymal, lacrimal, or lacrymal; lachrymary, lachrymatory, teary, adj.

13. Like Tears: tearlike, teary,adj.

14. Shaped Like a Tear: lachrymiform, teardrop, tear-shaped,adj.

15. Causing the Flow or Shedding of Tears: lacrymatory or lacrimatory, lachrymogenic, tearful, tear-producing, teary,adj.

16. Of Tears, to Come Out: drop, flow,v.

17. Of Tears, to Come Out Abundantly: gush,v.

18. To Let (Tears) Drop, Flow, etc.: shed or weep (tears),v.

19. Small Vase with a Narrow Neck, Once Believed to Have Been Used to Receive the Tears of Friends of the Departed, Found in Tombs of Ancient Rome: lachrymal, lachrymal vase, lachrymary, or lachrymatory, n.

20. Story, Moving Picture, Play, etc., So Sad or Sentimentally Sad as to Cause, or Be Designed to Cause, the Shedding of Tears: tear-jerker,n. (colloq.)

21. Stained with Tears: tear-stained,adj.

22. Without, Free from, or Not Shedding, Tears: dry-eyed, tearless,adj. (tearlessness, n.)

1129. PITY; SYMPATHY

1. Feeling, Expressing, or Showing Pity or Sympathy: commiserating or commiserative (i.e., for the trouble, distress, or grief of another); compassionate (i.e., for the suffering, distress, or misfortune of another, often accompanied by a desire to help, or to alleviate the distress of, such a person); merciful; pitying or pitiful; rueful, soft, softhearted, sorry, sympathetic or sympathizing, tender, tenderhearted, warm, warmhearted,adj.

2. To Feel, Express, or Show Pity or Sympathy for,v. *From Sec. 1:* commiserate or commiserate with, compassion or compassionate; have mercy on; pity, or have or take pity on; sympathize with (commiseration,n. commiserator, sympathizer,n.); *Also:* **1.** bemoan —express pity for (a condition, state, etc., of another)

3. To Feel Pity or Sympathy: have mercy or pity; pity, sympathize, yearn

4. To Give In to Feelings of Pity; To Show or Feel More Pity, Compassion, etc.: relent, v.

5. Feelings of Pity or Sympathy,n. *From Sec. 1:* commiseration, compassion or compassionateness, mercifulness or mercy, pity, ruefulness, softness, softheartedness, sorriness, sympathy or sympatheticness, tenderness, tenderheartedness, warmth or warmness, warmheartedness

6. Given to Responding Easily or Quickly with Feelings of Pity or Sympathy,n. *From Sec. 1:* commiserative, compassionate, merciful, sympathetic (compassion or compassionateness, mercy or mercifulness, sympatheticness,n.); *Also:* softhearted, tenderhearted, warmhearted,adj. (softheartedness, tenderheartedness, warmheartedness,n.)

7. One So Given: softy (colloq.), tenderheart,n.

8. To Grieve in Sympathy with (One in Sorrow, Esp. One Who Has Lost Someone through Death): condole with,v.

9. An Expression of Such Sympathetic Grief: condolement, condolence, or condolences,n.

10. Expressing Such Grief: condolatory, condolent, or condoling,adj.

11. Feeling Such Grief: condolent or condoling,adj.

12. One Who Expresses or Feels Such Grief: condoler,n.

13. Evoking or Exciting Pity or Sympathy: affecting; bathetic (i.e., doing so falsely, insincerely, or excessively); heartbreaking, heart-rending, miserable, moving; pathetic (i.e., evoking pity or sympathy that is sometimes tinged with slight contempt); piteous; pitiable (i.e., evoking pity that is sometimes tinged with contempt); pitiful, poignant, rueful, touching,adj.

14. Quality or Condition of Evoking Pity or Sympathy,n. *From Sec. 13:* bathos, miserableness or misery, pathos or patheticalness, piteousness, pitiableness, pitifulness, poignancy, ruefulness,n.

15. To Evoke or Excite Pity in (a Person): move, touch, tug at the heart of, tug at the heartstrings of, wring the heart of,v.

16. To Evoke or Excite Pity in (the Heart, etc.): move, touch, tug at, wring,v.

17. Quality in Art, Esp. Literature or Music, That Evokes or Excites Pity or Sympathy: the pathetic, pathos,n. (pathetic,adj.)

18. Such a Quality when Overdone, Excessive, False, Insincere, etc.: bathos,n. (bathetic,adj.)

19. To Ask (Someone) for a Sympathetic Response: appeal to,v. (appeal,n.)

20. To Assume an Air of Tiredness, Melancholy, Sorrow, etc., in Order to Appeal for, or to Elicit, Sympathy: languish,v. (languishment,n. languisher,n. languishing,adj.)

21. Appealing for Pity, as a Look, Sound, etc.: languishing, piteous,adj. (piteousness, n.)

22. Without, Lacking in, or Feeling or Showing No, Pity or Sympathy: alien, aloof, coldblooded, coldhearted, cruel, hardened, hardhearted, heartless, inhuman, inhumane, merciless, obdurate, pitiless, relentless, remorseless, rockhearted or rocky, ruthless; stonehearted, stonyhearted, or stony; uncommiserating, uncompassionate or uncompassionating, unfeeling, unmerciful, unpitying, unsympathetic, unsympathizing,adj. (aloofness, cold-bloodedness, coldheartedness, cruelty or cruelness, hardheartedness, heartlessness, inhumanness, inhumanity, mercilessness, obduracy or obdurateness, pitilessness, relentlessness, remorselessness, ruthlessness, stonyheartedness, uncompassionateness, unfeelingness, unmercifulness, unpityingness, unsympathy,n.)

23. Act That Shows Lack of Pity or Sympathy: cruelty, inhumanity,n.

24. Not Giving In to Feelings of Pity or Sympathy: unrelenting,adj. (unrelentingness, n.)

25. To Become or Make Pitiless, Unsympathetic, or Unmerciful: harden,v.

1130. EMOTIONAL OR MENTAL SUFFERING

1. To Cause Emotional or Mental Suffering or Pain to or in (a Person, etc.): afflict; aggrieve (esp. in the passive); agonize (i.e., bring terrible suffering to); anguish (i.e., cause the most excruciating pain or suffering to); bedevil (maliciously or spitefully); chagrin (through humiliation, disappointment, failure, etc.); chasten (in order to make morally better); crucify (i.e., cause to suffer unbearably); devil (i.e., torment); distress; excruciate (i.e., cause the most intense mental suffering to); grieve (esp. by loss, misfortune, etc.); gripe; harass (as with cares, worries, troubles, debts, etc.); harrow (as by mistreating without cease, etc.); hurt, lacerate; martyr or martyrize (i.e., torment or torture, esp. for one's belief in, or pursuit of, a cause, principle, etc.); pain; persecute (in petty, mean ways); plague; prey on or prey upon (as fears, anxiety, etc., esp. on the mind); prick or prickle (as the conscience, etc., esp. with guilt or remorse); punish (for a wrong committed); rack; rend (the heart, etc.); rive (the heart, etc.); scourge; smite (as with a painful feeling, by the conscience, etc.); sting; torment (i.e., inflict with severe, almost unbearable, mental or emotional pain); torture (i.e., bring terrible suffering or pain to); trouble, try; twinge (i.e., cause a sudden and sharp mental or emotional pain to, as a person, the conscience, etc.); upset, vex; worry (with annoyances, troubles, etc.); wring (the heart, etc.),v. (crucifixion, excruciation, harassment, laceration, martyrization, persecution, punishment, torture,n.)

2. One Who Inflicts Such Emotional or Mental Suffering or Pain,n. *From Sec. 1:* afflicter, chastener, crucifier, harasser, harrier, persecutor, plaguer, punisher, tormentor or tormenter, torturer, troubler, vexer

3. Cause or Source of Emotional or Mental Suffering or Pain,n. *From Sec. 1:* affliction, agony, distress, grief, harassment, hurt, pain, plague, punishment, rack, scourge, sting, torment, torture, trial, trouble, vexation, worry or worriment; *Also:*

1. **cross**—affliction that tries one's endurance or patience; affliction patiently borne for the sake of Christ
2. **heartache**—source or cause of great emotional suffering or anguish
3. **sore**—cause or source of emotional or mental distress
4. **sorrow**—that which causes emotional or mental pain
5. **stinger**—remark, etc., that causes mental or emotional pain (colloq.)
6. **thorn**—cause of distress or mental pain
7. **tribulation**—that which causes distress, suffering, misery, etc.; great trouble
8. **visitation**—affliction considered as being an act of, or coming from, God
9. **woe**—that which causes great suffering, distress, or misery; affliction

4. Causing Emotional or Mental Suffering or Pain,adj. *From Sec. 1:* afflicting or afflictive, agonizing, anguishing, bedeviling, chagrining, chastening, crucifying, distressing or distressful, excruciating, griping, harassing, harrowing, harrying, hurtful, painful or paining, persecuting; plaguing, plaguy, plaguey, or plaguesome; preying; pricking, prickling, or prickly; punishing, racking; heart-rending (from *rend*); scourging, stinging, tormenting; torturing, torturous, or torturesome; troubling or troublesome, trying, upsetting, vexing or vexatious, worrying or worrisome (distressfulness, harrowingness, painfulness, plaguesomeness, prickliness, troublesomeness, tryingness, vexatiousness, worrisomeness,n.); *Also:* carking (poetic), cruel, dire, miserable, poignant, sore,adj. (cruelty or cruelness, direness, miserableness, poignancy, soreness,n.); *Also:*

1. **compunctious**—causing distress or pain of conscience or emotions
2. **dolorous**—causing distress or pain (dolorousness,n.)
3. **thorny**—emotionally or mentally painful (thorniness,n.)

5. To Cause, or Be the Cause of, Emotional or Mental Suffering or Pain: ache (as the heart); hurt, pain, prick; rankle (as unpleasant feelings, insults, slights, etc.); smart, sting,v.

6. Suffering; Emotional or Mental Pain,n. *From Sec. 1:* affliction, agony, anguish, bedevilment, chagrin, crucifixion, distress, excruciation, grief, gripe, harrassment, martyrdom, pain, persecution, rack, punishment, torment, torture or tortures, trouble, vexation, worry or worriment; *Also:*

1. **ache, aching**—emotional pain, as of the heart
2. **adversity**—condition or circumstances characterized or attended by distress, suffering, etc., though formerly circumstances were happy, prosperous, etc.
3. **anxiety, anxiousness**—emotional suffering or mental pain caused by fear over some ill, misfortune, or trouble that may occur in the future; distress of mind for which there is no rational cause
4. **compunction**—pain or distress of conscience or emotions
5. **heartache**—great emotional suffering; anguish
6. **misery**—great and wretched mental or emotional distress; distress or suffering caused by poverty or privation
7. **moil**—trouble
8. **remorse**—intense emotional suffering or pain caused by a feeling of guilt or by an attack of conscience
9. **remorse of conscience**—suffering or pain caused by an attack of conscience

10. **sorrow**—mental or emotional suffering caused by loss, disappointment, misfortune, etc.
11. **straits**—position or condition of distress or suffering
12. **travail**—distress, anguish, suffering, mental or emotional pain, etc., met or endured while accomplishing or achieving something
13. **trial**—the experiencing of mental pain and suffering
14. **tribulation**—great suffering, distress, misery, or trouble
15. **woe**—extreme distress, suffering, misery, or trouble
16. **wretchedness**—misery

7. Suffering; Subjected to Suffering; In a State of Emotional or Mental Suffering or Pain; Full of, Characterized by, or Showing, Such,adj. *From Sec. 1:* afflicted, aggrieved, agonized, anguished, bedeviled, chagrined, chastened, crucified, deviled, distressed or distressful, excruciated, grieved, harassed, harrowed, harried, hurt, lacerated, martyred or martyrized, pained, persecuted, plagued, preyed on or upon, pricked, punished, racked or on the rack, rent, riven, scourged, smitten, stung, tormented, tortured, troubled, tried, twinged, upset, vexed, wrung (distressfulness,n.); *From Sec. 6:* anxious, compunctious, miserable, remorseful, woeful or woful, wretched (anxiousness or anxiety, miserableness, remorsefulness, woefulness or wofulness, n.); *Also:* clouded or cloudy (i.e., full of, or darkened by, trouble, as a countenance, etc.); dolorous (i.e., full of, exhibiting, or expressing distress or pain); heartsore, sore at or of heart, or sore; heavy-laden (i.e., troubled, or burdened with troubles and cares); on the rack (i.e., in an extremely painful situation, or in terrible mental anguish); stricken (i.e., afflicted with distress, mental or emotional pain, etc., or expressive of such),adj. (dolorousness, soreness of heart or soreness,n.)

8. To Suffer; To Feel Emotional or Mental Pain: agonize (i.e., suffer or experience the most extreme mental or emotional pain or torture); anguish (i.e., experience excruciating mental or emotional pain or suffering); prick or prickle (as the conscience, etc.); smart (i.e., from insult, humiliation, slight, wounded feelings, etc.); sting or twinge (as the conscience, etc.); worry (i.e., feel emotional or mental distress, or torture oneself mentally, as over fears of future difficulties, disasters, etc.); writhe (i.e., suffer intense mental or emotional anguish, literally or figuratively squirming in distress, agony, etc.),v.

9. So Suffering; Showing Such Suffering, adj. *From Sec. 8:* agonizing or agonized, anguished, pricked, smarting, worrying or worried, writhing,adj.

10. Sufferer: martyr (i.e., one who suffers rather than give up principles, beliefs, etc., or one who suffers or undergoes distress or mental pain for a long and continuous period, generally without complaint); victim (i.e., from mental fears, worry, etc.); worrier (i.e., one who worries); wretch (i.e., one in great distress or misery),n.

11. A Mental or Emotional Pain: ache (as of the heart); compunction (as of conscience, for a slight wrong); gripe; hurt; pain; pang (i.e., a sudden and sharp emotional pain); prick (esp. of conscience); qualm (i.e., an emotional pain caused by uneasiness that what one is doing, or planning to do, is not proper, ethical, etc.; a sting of conscience); sting, twinge, or twitch (as of conscience); wrench (i.e., a sharp, painful feeling or emotion, as on leave-taking, etc.),n.

12. Characterized by, of the Nature of, or Causing, Such Pain,adj. *From Sec. 11:* compunctious, qualmish,adj.

13. To Shrink from, or under, Mental or Emotional Pain, Painful Circumstances, etc.: cringe, flinch, wince, writhe,v. (cringe, flinch, wince, writhe,n. cringer, flincher, wincer, writher,n.)

14. Not So Shrinking: unflinching, unwincing,adj.

15. To Make a Grimace Expressive of Mental or Emotional Pain: wince,v. (wince,n. wincer,n.)

16. An Experience That Causes, or Is Expected to Cause, Intense Mental or Emotional Suffering: ordeal,n.

17. Point, Moment, or Time for the Beginning of Such an Experience: zero hour,n.

18. A Troubling or Distressing Experience: trial, tribulation,n.

19. An Experience in Which One Suffers Terrible Mental or Emotional Distress or Anguish: Calvary (from the place of Jesus's crucifixion),n.

20. Place, Scene, or Occasion of Terrible Mental, Emotional, or Spiritual Suffering or Agony: Gethsemane or gethsemane (from the place of Jesus's betrayal and arrest),n.

21. Place of Great Suffering, Torment, Agony, Martyrdom, Sacrifice, etc.: Golgotha (from the place of Jesus's crucifixion),n.

22. Place, State, or Condition of Temporary Suffering, Expiation, or Remorse: purgatory, n. (purgatorial,adj.)

23. Involving, or Full of, Torture: torturous, adj.

24. Tending to Persecute: persecutive or persecutory,adj.

25. Pert. to, or Characterized by, Persecution: persecutional, persecutive, or persecutory,adj.

26. One Who Is Persecuted: persecutee,n.

27. Persecution by Means of, or with the Aid of, Troops, Soldiers, etc.: dragonnade,n.

28. Without, Free from, or Not Causing, Emotional or Mental Pain: painless, unpainful, or unpaining,adj. (painlessness,n.)

1131. ANXIETY; WORRY

1. To Cause (Someone) to Be Anxious or Worried: bother or pother, disquiet, distress, disturb; exercise (esp. in the passive, *exercised*); faze, feaze, or feeze (colloq.); fret; fuss or fuss up (usually over trifles or unnecessarily); perturb, trouble, upset, worry,v. (disturbance, perturbation,n.)

2. Causing Anxiety or Worry: carking (somewhat archaic or poetic); disquieting, distressing or distressful, disturbing; fazing, feazing, or feezing (colloq.); fretting, perturbing or perturbative, troubling or troublesome, upsetting, worrying or worrisome,adj. (distressfulness, troublesomeness, worrisomeness,n.)

3. A Cause or Source of Anxiety or Worry: anxiety, bother, care; cark (somewhat archaic or poetic); distress, disturbance, perturbation, thorn, torment, trouble, worry or worriment, n.

4. Thoughts That Cause Anxiety or Uneasiness: inquietudes,pl.n.

5. Causes of Anxiety: solicitudes,pl.n.

6. To Be Anxious: fret; fuss (esp. over trifles or unnecessarily); trouble; stew (colloq.); worry,v.

7. One Who Is Anxious: fretter; fusser, fuss, or, colloq., fussbudget; worrier,n.

8. Anxious; Worried: apprehensive, bothered; carking (of people—a somewhat archaic or poetic usage); concerned, disquieted, distressed, disturbed; dysphoric (i.e., pathologically or morbidly so); exercised (about or by something or someone); fazed, feazed, or feezed (colloq.); fretted; fussed, fussed up, or fussy (over trifles, or unnecessarily); nervous, perturbed, solicitous, troubled, uneasy, upset, wrought up,adj.

9. Anxiety; Anxiousness; Worry: apprehensiveness, apprehension, or apprehensions; care; cark (somewhat archaic or poetic); concern or concernment, disquietude, distress, disturbance of mind; dysphoria (i.e., pathological or morbid anxiety or worry); fret, fuss or fussiness, nervousness, perturbation, solicitude or solicitousness; stew (colloq., esp. in the phrase *in a stew*); trouble, uneasiness or unease, upset, worriedness, worriment,n.

10. Feelings or Emotions of Anxiety: solicitudes,pl.n.

11. Excessive Anxiety, Concern, or Care: solicitude,n.

12. Tending to Worry or Be Anxious: worrisome,adj. (worrisomeness,n.)

13. To Expect (Something Unpleasant) with Anxiety or Fear: apprehend,v. (apprehension,n. apprehensiveness,n. apprehensive,adj.)

14. Showing the Signs or Effects of Anxiety, Worry, or Trouble, as a Person, Face, etc.; Disturbed by Anxieties or Worry: careworn,adj.

15. Not Anxious; Not Worried: at ease, carefree, easy, insouciant, nonchalant, secure, unanxious, unapprehensive, unconcerned, undistressed, undisturbed; unfazed (colloq.); unfussed, unnervous, unperturbed, unsolicitous, untroubled, unupset, unworried,adj. (ease or easiness, insouciance, nonchalance, security, unanxiety or unanxiousness, unapprehensiveness or unapprehension; unconcern, unconcernment, or unconcernedness; undistress, undisturbedness or undisturbance, unperturbedness, unsolicitousness, untroubledness, unworriedness,n.)

16. To Reduce the Anxiety, Fears, Worry, Mental Distress, etc., of (a Person or the Mind); To Free (a Person or the Mind from Such): ease, relieve,v. (easement, relief,n.)

17. That Which Does So: easement, relief,n.

18. Freedom from the Worry, Anxiety, and Pain of the Outside World; The Quenching of the Heat of One's Passions; The Peace That Comes from Emotional Serenity, Achieved through the Avoidance of Disturbing Desires; Peace and Blessedness Attained by the Extinction of Desires and Passions (all Buddhist Concepts): nirvana,n.

1132. DISTURBANCE OF MIND OR EMOTION

1. To Disturb Mentally or Emotionally: agitate, ail, bother or pother, commove; convulse (i.e., with paroxysms of grief, sorrow, or pain); discomfit, discomfort, discompose, disconcert, discountenance or put out of countenance, disquiet, distemper, distract; exercise (chiefly in the passive, *exercised*); faze, feaze, or feeze (colloq.); flurry (i.e., throw into, or fill with, sudden emotional agitation, esp. as the result of haste or confusion); fluster, flusterate, or flustrate (i.e., make all upset, or upset and confused, by sudden orders, unexpected demands, unusual circumstances, etc.); flutter, fuss or fuss up, perturb; rattle (colloq.); roil, ruffle; shake, shock, jar, or jolt (very strongly); shatter (i.e., greatly disturb or damage in mind or emotions); trouble, uncalm, unhinge; unnerve (so that self-control, firmness, or courage, etc., is lost, or so as to paralyze emotionally); unsettle, unstring, upset, vex, worry,v. (agitation, botheration, discomfiture, disconcertion or disconcertment, distraction, perturbation, shatterment,n.)

2. Mentally or Emotionally Disturbing,adj. *From Sec. 1:* agitating, bothersome, commoving, convulsing, discomfiting, discomforting, discomposing, disconcerting, discountenancing, disquieting, distracting or distractive, flustering; perturbing, perturbative, or perturbatious; shaking, shocking, jarring, or jolting; shattering, troubling or troublesome, uncalming, unhinging, unnerving, unsettling, upsetting; vexing, vexatious, or vexatory; worrying or worrisome (vexatiousness,n.); *Also:* nerve-racking or nerve-wracking (i.e., most disturbing to the mind, mental composure, emotional equilibrium, or patience); uncomfortable or awkward; unquieting or unquiet,adj. (uncomfortableness or awkwardness,n.)

3. A Cause or Source of Mental or Emotional Disturbance,n. *From Sec. 1:* bother, discomfiter, discomfort, perturbation, ruffle; shock, jar, or jolt; trouble, vexation or vexer, worry or worriment

4. Mentally or Emotionally Disturbed; In, Manifesting, or Characterized by, a State of Mental or Emotional Disturbance,adj. *From Sec. 1:* agitated, bothered, convulsed, discomfited, discomfortable, discomposed, disconcerted, discountenanced or put out of countenance, disquieted, distracted; exercised about, by, or over (something or someone); fazed, flurried, flustered, fluttered, fussed or fussed up, perturbed, rattled, roiled, ruffled; shaken, shocked, jarred, or jolted; shattered, troubled, uncalm, unhinged, unnerved, unsettled, unstrung, upset, vexed, worried; *Also:* distraught (i.e., very greatly or deeply disturbed); ill at ease; in a stew (colloq.); inquiet; queasy (as the feelings, emotions, conscience, etc.); restive, restless; stormy, tempestuous, turbulent, tumultuary, or tumultuous (i.e., greatly disturbed, as the mind, feelings, or emotions, or characterized by such disturbance of mind, feelings, or emotions); uncomfortable, uneasy, unquiet, wrought-up, adj.

5. State, Condition, or Manifestation of Mental or Emotional Disturbance,n. *From Sec. 1:* agitation, bother or botheration, commotion, convulsion, discomfiture, discomposure or discomposedness; disconcertion, disconcertment, or disconcertedness; disquietude, distraction, flurry; fluster, flusteration, or flustration; flutter; fuss; perturbation, perturbedness, or perturbment; ruffle, shock, shatterment, trouble, uncalm, upset, vexation; worry, worriment, or worriedness; *From Sec. 4:* stew (from *in a stew*); inquietude or inquietness, queasiness, restiveness, restlessness; storm, storminess, tempestuousness, turbulence, turbulency, tumult, tumultuariness, tumultuousness, or turmoil; uncomfortableness, uneasiness or unease, unquietness; *Also:* ferment or fermentation; malaise (i.e., general physical discomfort combined with mental and emotional uneasiness); maelstrom (i.e., extreme agitation of mind or emotions); seethe (i.e., state of violent disturbance); trepidation (i.e., trembling or fearful agitation); unrest,n.

6. To Be in a State of Mental or Emotional Disturbance or Agitation: flutter, fuss, seethe; stew (colloq.); worry,v.

7. To Become Emotionally Disturbed: ruffle,v.

8. To Become Upset, or Upset and Confused or Bewildered, by Sudden Orders, Unexpected Demands, Unusual Circumstances, etc.: fluster,v.

9. Not Mentally or Emotionally Disturbed, adj. *From Sec. 1:* unagitated, unbothered, undiscomfited, undiscomposed, undisconcerted, undisquieted, undistracted, unexercised, unfazed, unflurried, unflustered, unfluttered, unfussed, unperturbed, unrattled, unruffled, unshaken, untroubled, unupset, unvexed, unworried (unagitatedness or unagitation, undistractedness, unperturbedness, untroubledness, unworriedness,n.); *From Sec. 4:* undistraught, untumultuous; *Also:* calm, undisturbed, unexcited,adj. (calmness or calm, undisturbedness or undisturbance,n.)

10. To Free of Trouble, Mental or Emotional Disturbance, etc.: calm, soothe, untrouble,v.

11. Able to Be Mentally or Emotionally Disturbed: agitable, perturbable, upsettable, vexable,adj. (perturbability,n.)

12. Not Easily Disturbed Mentally or Emotionally: bovine, calm, equable; evenminded, even-tempered, or even; impassive, imperturbable, nonchalant, passionless, phlegmatic or phlegmatical, placid, steady, stolid, undiscomfitable, undisturbable, unupsettable, adj. (bovinity, calmness, equableness or equability, evenmindedness or evenness, impassiveness or impassivity, imperturbability or imperturbableness, nonchalance, passionlessness; phlegmaticness, phlegmaticalness, phlegmatism, or phlegm; placidity or placidness, steadiness, stolidity or stolidness,n.)

13. One Who Is of Such a Temperament as Not to Be Easily Disturbed Mentally or Emotionally: phlegmatic, phlegmatist, or phlegmat,n.

14. To Disturb (the Mind or Emotions) with a Lasting Shock (Psychiatry): traumatize,v.

15. So Disturbing; Resulting from, or of the Nature of, Such a Shock: traumatic,adj.

16. A Lasting Shock to the Mind or Emotions: trauma,n. (traumas or traumata,pl.n.)

17. To Greatly Disturb or Damage (the Mind or Emotional Equilibrium): shatter,v. (shatterment,n. shattering,adj.)

1133. NERVOUSNESS; EMOTIONAL PRESSURE

1. Nervous: creepy (i.e., nervous and fearful); fidgety, flurried; flustered (i.e., nervous, or nervous and confused or excited, esp. because of sudden demands or orders, unusual circumstances, etc.); fussed-up (colloq.); high-strung; jittery (colloq.); jumpy, overstrung, overwrought, tense, uneasy, unstrung, adj.

2. Nervousness,n. *From Sec. 1:* creepiness, fidgetiness or the fidgets, flurry; fluster, flusteration, or flustration; fuss, jitteriness or the jitters, jumpiness; tenseness, tension, or tensity; uneasiness or unease

3. Fit or Attack of Nervousness or of Nerves: the fidgets; the jitters (colloq.); the willies (colloq.),n.

4. Abnormally Nervous State; Tendency or Disposition to Such a State: nervosity,n.

5. Nervousness on Appearing before a Public Audience, Esp. when Inexperienced in Such Activities: stage fright,n.

6. To Be Nervous, or Act Nervously: fidget, fluster, fuss; jitter (colloq.),v.

7. To Become Nervous: fluster, tense, tense up,v.

8. To Make Nervous: fidget, flurry; fluster, flusterate, or flustrate; fuss up (colloq.); string, tense, unstring,v.

9. Descr. of That Which Causes Nervousness and Fear: creepy,adj. (creepiness,n.)

10. Nervous Haste: flurry, hurry,n.

11. Not Nervous: calm, unnervous,adj. (calmness,n.)

12. To Remove or Reduce the Nervousness of: calm, relax, soothe,v. (relaxation,n.)

13. Emotional Pressure: strain, stress, tension,n.

14. Under, or Indicating, Emotional Pressure: high-strung, nervous, strained, overstrung, taut, tense,adj.

15. To Make Tense: string, tense,v.

16. To Become Tense: tense, tense up,v.

1134. RESTLESSNESS

1. Restless: dysphoric (medical), fidgety, fitful, inquiet, restive, uneasy, unquiet,adj.

2. Restlessness: dysphoria (medical), fidgetiness or the fidgets, fitfulness, inquietude or inquietness; jactitation or jactation (i.e., great restlessness and tossing of the body, a condition of certain diseases—medical term); restiveness, uneasiness, unquietness, unrest,n.

3. Fit of Restlessness: the fidgets,n.

4. One Who Behaves or Moves Restlessly: fidget or fidgeter,n.

5. To Behave, Act, or Move Restlessly: fidget, tittup,v.

6. Restless Behavior, Action, or Movement: fidget, the fidgets, tittup,n.

7. Behaving, Acting, or Moving Restlessly: fidgeting or fidgety, tittupy or tittuppy,adj. (fidgetiness,n.)

1135. EMOTIONAL OR PERSONALITY DISORDER

1. Selected Emotional or Personality Disorders,n.
  1. **ailment**—emotional disorder
  2. **breakdown, nervous breakdown, crack-up**—severe emotional disorder characterized by extreme depression and other abnormal symptoms
  3. **hospitalism**—emotional or personality disorder or deterioration in orphans, children of unwed mothers, etc., who are placed in institutions or hospitals in infancy and reared there for a considerable period—caused by impersonal atmosphere, lack of affection, etc.
  4. **hysteria**—severe emotional disorder or neurosis, characterized by violence of emotional outbursts, extreme anxiety, fits of laughing and weeping, disturbances of the motor, sensory, and other functions, apparent attacks of blindness, deafness or other physical ailments without organic cause, etc.—common esp. in young women (hysteric or hysterical,adj.)
  5. **maladjustment**—bad or poor emotional adjustment, or lack of such, to one's environment, work, family, the general phenomena of social living, etc.
  6. **neurasthenia, nervous prostration**—form of neurosis, most commonly caused by emotional conflicts, the symptoms of which are general lassitude, fatigue, depression, anxiety, aches and pains of no apparent organic origin, etc. (neurasthenic,adj.)
  7. **neurosis, psychoneurosis**—emotional or personality disorder characterized by anxiety, fear, compulsions, obsessions, phobias, various bodily symptoms, complaints, or ills of no apparent organic origin, etc. (neurotic, psychoneurotic, adj.)
  8. **psychasthenia**—form of neurosis characterized by compulsions, obsessions, fears, extreme anxieties, doubts, nervous movements, etc. (psychasthenic,adj.)
  9. **psychopathy, psychopathic personality, sociopathic personality**—emotional or personality disorder characterized by deceitfulness, perverse or criminal behavior, conceit, lack of social inhibitions or self-control, and the delusion of being beyond, or not subject to, restrictions or laws, so that any action, however culpable, may be committed without thought of punishment or sting of conscience (psychopathic, sociopathic,adj.)

2. Suffering from an Emotional or Personality Disorder or Disturbance,adj. *From Sec. 1:* hysteric or hysterical, maladjusted, neurasthenic, neurotic or psychoneurotic, psychasthenic, psycophathic or sociopathic

3. Sufferer from an Emotional or Personality Disorder or Disturbance,n. *From Sec. 1:* hysteric or hysteria, neurasthenic; neurotic, psychoneurotic, or neuropath; psychasthenic; psychopath, psychopathic personality, sociopath, or sociopathic personality

4. Similar to, or Resembling, Hysteria: hysteric, hysterical, hysteriform, hysteroid, or hysteroidal,adj.

5. Causing, Inducing, or Producing Hysteria: hysterogenic or hysterogenous,adj.

6. The Causing, Inducing, or Production of Hysteria, a Hysterical State, or an Attack of Hysteria: hysterogeny,n.

7. Pert. to, Designating, Descr. of, or Indicative of, Any Emotional or Personality Disorder or Neurosis: neurotic, psychoneurotic, psychopathic,adj.

8. Free from Emotional or Personality Disorders: adjusted, balanced, neurosis-free, unneurotic, well-adjusted, well-balanced,adj.

1136. INSANITY

1. Insanity; Mental Disorder; Lack of, or Deviation or Lapse from, Mental Health or Sound Mental Condition,n.
  1. **aberration**—mental disorder; lack of mental health
  2. **ailment, mental ailment**—mental disorder
  3. **alienation**—mental derangement or disorder; insanity; legal insanity
  4. **cachexia, cachexy**—lack of mental health (cachexic, cachectic, or cachectical,adj.)
  5. **catatonia**—form or phase of, or syndrome in, schizophrenia in which the patient seems to be in a stupor or trance, with speechlessness, muscular rigidity, and fixed posture; this condition often alternates with feverish outbursts, panic, hallucinations, etc. (catatonic,adj.)
  6. **cyclothymia**—condition similar to, but somewhat milder than, manic-depressive psychosis (cyclothymic,adj.)
  7. **deliration**—lack of mental health; mental disorders; delirium; insanity; madness
  8. **delirium**—mental disorder, temporary in nature, caused by high fever, intoxication, certain diseases or forms of insanity, etc., and characterized by wandering or incoherent speech, hallucinations, great restlessness and excitement, etc. (delirious,adj.)
  9. **delirium tremens, D.T.'s**—violent de-

lirium resulting from excessive alcoholic indulgence, and typically characterized by terrifying hallucinations, trembling, sweating, etc.

10. **dementia**—condition of mental illness or derangement characterized by deterioration or loss of the faculties, esp. memory, reasoning, will power, etc., and often attended by apathy or stupor, disorientation to the surroundings, and extreme confusion; acquired, rather than congenital, insanity, often of organic source

11. **dementia praecox**—form of insanity typically occurring in adolescence, and characterized by depressions, delusions, hallucinations, extremely eccentric behavior, withdrawal from associations with others, etc.

12. **derangement, mental derangement**—mental disorder; insanity; madness

13. **disorder**—mental disorder

14. **distemper**—mental derangement; mental disorder

15. **distraction**—mental derangement; insanity; madness

16. **frenzy, phrensy**—mental derangement; delirium that verges on insanity (frenzied, phrensied, frenetic or phrenetic, adj.)

17. **hallucinosis**—mental disorder, psychosis, or insanity characterized by the persistent seeing and hearing of nonexistent things and sounds

18. **hebephrenia**—form of schizophrenia, usually attacking young people at or just after puberty, in which there is a reversion to infantile behavior and thinking, silliness, unprovoked smiling or laughter, untidiness of person, masturbation, hallucinations, deterioration of emotional adjustments, etc. (hebephrenic, adj.)

19. **involutional melancholia**—psychosis marked by intense agitation and depression, and typically attacking people of advanced age

20. **lunacy**—unsoundness of mental health; insanity; legal insanity; madness (lunatic, adj.)

21. **lycanthropy**—form of insanity in which the victim thinks he is a wolf or other wild animal (lycanthropic, adj.)

22. **madness**—disorder of the mind; complete lack of mental health; insanity

23. **mania**—violent insanity; insanity attended by wild excitement; the manic phase of a manic-depressive psychosis (maniacal or manic, adj.)

24. **manic-depressive psychosis**—form of insanity in which there are alternating phases of wild exuberance, excitement, hilarity, etc. (the manic phase), and pathologically deep melancholia (the depressive phase)

25. **megalomania**—mental disorder chiefly characterized by delusions of grandeur, tremendous power, exaltation, or wealth, generally part of schizophrenia or other psychoses; loosely, the term is also used to describe a lopsided attachment or passion for, or for doing, things on a grand scale, or, as a natural concomitant, a tendency to wild exaggeration or conceit, with, of course, no implications of insanity (megalomaniac or megalomaniacal, adj.)

26. **mental imbalance**—lack of mental balance or health

27. **monomania**—insanity or mental disorder restricted to one area, category, idea, etc. (monomaniacal, adj.)

28. **neuropsychopathy**—mental illness based on, or showing itself in, symptoms and disorders of the nervous system (neuropsychopathic, adj.)

29. **neuropsychosis**—mental derangement caused by, or associated with, a disorder of the nerves; former term for psychosis

30. **paragraphia**—mental disorder, usually caused by injury to the cerebrum or other brain lesion, and characterized by one of the following: an inability to express ideas in writing; the use of scrambled letters; or the writing of letters or words other than those intended (paragraphic, adj.)

31. **paranoia**—form of insanity accompanied by systematized delusions of subjection to hostility and persecution, hallucinations of an auditory nature, and delusions of grandeur (paranoiac or paranoid, adj.)

32. **phrenitis**—intense or acute delirium (phrenitic, adj.)

33. **pixilation**—condition of being slightly, somewhat, or amusingly, unbalanced or disordered mentally

34. **psychopathy**—any mental disorder, ailment, or disease (psychopathic, adj.)

35. **psychosis**—severe or major mental disorder or illness in which the personality is seriously or totally disorganized or disoriented (psychotic, adj.)

36. **schizomania**—mental disorder showing aspects of both mania and schizophrenia

37. **schizophrenia**—psychosis characterized by deterioration of personality, loss of contact with reality, by disorientation, hallucinations, delusions of persecution, megalomania, etc. (schizophrenic or schizoid, adj.)

38. **schizothymia**—mental disorder that is a mild form of, or that resembles, schizophrenia (schizothymic, adj.)

2. Insane; Indicating Insanity; Mentally Disordered; Lacking in Mental Health, adj. *From Sec. 1:* cachectic or cachectical, catatonic, cyclothymic, delirious, demented, deranged, disordered, distempered, distracted; frenzied, phrensied, frenetic, or phrenetic; hebephrenic, lunatic or lunatical; mad or, less commonly, madding; maniac, maniacal, or manic; manic-depressive, megalomaniac or megalomaniacal, mentally unbalanced, monomaniacal, paranoiac or paranoid, pixilated, psychopathic, psychotic, schizophrenic or schizoid, schizothymic (deliriousness, dementedness, madness, n.); *Also:* balmy (colloq.); bughouse (slang); crackbrained; cracked (colloq.); crackpot; crazy or crazed; daffy (colloq.); daft, distraught, irrational; loco (colloq.); loony or luny (colloq.); moon-struck or moon-stricken; non compos mentis—Latin (legal); nutty (slang); out of one's mind or head; potty (i.e., slightly insane—colloq.); touched, or touched in the head (esp. somewhat or slightly insane); unbalanced; unhinged; unsettled (as the mind); unsound of mind, or of unsound mind; wild; zany (i.e., somewhat, slightly, or ludicrously insane), adj. (balminess, craziness, daffiness, daftness, irrationality or irrationalness, looniness, nuttiness, unsoundness of mind, wildness, zaniness, n.)

3. Insane Person; One Who Is Mentally Disordered, or Who Is Lacking in Mental Health, n. *From Sec. 1:* catatonic, cyclothymiac or cyclothymic, frenetic or phrenetic, hebephrenic, lunatic, lycanthrope, madman or madwoman, maniac, manic-depressive, megalomaniac, monomaniac, neuropsychopathic, paranoiac, psychopath, psychotic; schizophrenic, schizophrene, or schizoid (lunatic, maniacal, adj.); *Also:* bedlamite; crackbrain; crackpot; loony or loon (colloq.); nut (slang), n.

4. To Make (Someone) Insane; To Cause (Someone) to Become Mentally Disordered, v. *From Sec. 1:* dement, derange or derange the mind of, disorder, distemper, distract, frenzy or phrensy, madden (derangement, distraction,n.) ; *From Sec. 2:* craze, loco, unbalance or unbalance the mind of, unhinge or unhinge the mind of, unsettle the mind of, v.

5. Causing Insanity or Mental Disorder, adj. *From Sec. 4:* deranging, distracting; maddening or, less commonly, madding; unsettling

6. To Become Insane or Mentally Disordered: craze, madden,v.

7. To Be or Become Delirious: wander,v. (wandering,adj.)

8. To Speak in, or as in, Delirium: rave, wander,v. (raving, wandering,adj.)

9. Speech in, or as of, Delirium: deliration, raving or ravings, wanderings,n.

10. Descr. of One Who, That Which, a Case Which, etc., Is on the Line That Separates Sane from Insane: borderline,adj.

11. One Who, from Birth, Exhibits Mental Abnormality That Verges on, or Approaches, Insanity: mattoid,n.

12. For, Designed or Set Apart for, or Used by, the Insane: insane, lunatic,adj.

13. Fits of Insanity: lunes,pl.n.

14. Like, Resembling, or Related to, Paranoia: paranoiac or paranoid,adj.

15. Like, Resembling, or Related to, Schizophrenia: schizoid,adj.

16. Institution or Place for the Insane: asylum; bedlam; booby hatch (slang) ; bughouse (slang) ; insane asylum, institution, lunatic asylum, madhouse; nuthouse (slang) ; psychiatric or psychopathic ward (of a hospital) ; state hospital or institution,n.

17. Inmate of Such: bedlamite,n.

18. Held in Such: institutionalized,adj.

19. To Send (Someone) to Such: commit, institutionalize,v. (commitment, institutionalization,n.)

20. Sane: compos mentis (legal), lucid, rational; sound of, or in, mind, or of sound mind; uncrazed, underanged, undistempered, undistraught, unfrenzied, uninsane, well-balanced,adj.

21. Sanity: balance of mind, lucidness or lucidity, mental health or balance, rationality, saneness, soundness of mind,n.

1137. PAIN

1. To Pain (Someone, Some Bodily Part, or the Body); To Cause to Suffer Physically,v.
1. **afflict**—pain; cause physical pain to
2. **agonize**—torture with extreme or terrible pain
3. **ail**—affect with pain, or cause pain to, as in *what ails you?,* etc.
4. **anguish**—cause excruciatingly severe pain to
5. **bite**—cause to smart or sting, as the wind or an insect does to a bodily member, a sharp spice does to the tongue, etc.
6. **burn**—pain by extreme heat
7. **chasten**—cause to suffer pain in order to make morally better
8. **convulse**—shake or disturb the body with attacks of racking pain
9. **distress**—cause physical pain or suffering to
10. **excruciate**—cause the most intense or agonizing pain to; inflict such upon (excruciation,n.)
11. **hurt**—pain; be painful to
12. **prick**—pain sharply by, or as if by, puncturing or piercing (prick,n.)

13. **prickle**—affect with a pricking or tingling sensation
14. **punish**—subject to pain, or inflict pain upon, for committing a wrong, etc. (punishment,n.)
15. **rack**—pain to an extreme or excruciating degree
16. **scourge**—cause severe physical suffering to
17. **smart**—cause a sharp, often burning, pain in (a bodily part or member)
18. **sting**—pain sharply or burningly (sting, n.)
19. **torment**—cause intense bodily pain or suffering to
20. **torture**—subject to extreme pain or agonizing physical strain; do such as punishment, to extract a confession or information, or out of revenge or sheer cruelty (torture,n.)
21. **trouble**—be painful to, as a wound, illness, etc.
22. **twinge**—cause a sudden and sharp pain to, esp. in a specific area or part of the body

2. One Who Causes Someone to Suffer Physical or Bodily Pain,n. *From Sec. 1:* afflicter, chastener, punisher, tormentor or tormenter, torturer

3. Painful; Causing Physical or Bodily Pain or Suffering,adj. *From Sec. 1:* afflicting or afflictive, agonizing, anguishing, biting, burning, chastening, convulsing, distressing or distressful, excruciating, hurtful, pricking, prickling or prickly, punishing, racking, smart or smarting, stinging, tormenting; torturing, torturous, or torturesome (distressfulness, hurtfulness, prickliness,n.) ; *Also:*
1. **aching**—dully and continuously painful
2. **algetic**—painful; productive of physical pain
3. **cruel**—painful, as an action, etc. (cruelty or cruelness,n.)
4. **dire, grievous**—causing, productive of, or attended by, physical pain or suffering (direness, grievousness,n.)
5. **sore, tender**—painful, as a bodily part or spot, wound, etc. (soreness, tenderness,n.)
6. **splitting**—extremely painful, esp. a headache

4. Cause or Source of Physical or Bodily Pain or Suffering,n. *From Sec. 1:* affliction, agony, ailment, bite, burn, distress, punishment, rack, scourge, sting, torment, torture; *Also:* misery,n.

5. A Pain,n. *From Sec. 1:* prick, prickle, smart, sting, twinge or twitch; *Also:*
1. **ache**—a dull, continuous pain
2. **labor pain**—one of the periodic pains preceding childbirth
3. **lancination**—a piercing, stabbing, tearing, or penetrating pain
4. **pang**—a sudden and severe pain, though short or temporary
5. **throe**—a violent and sudden pain, though short or temporary
6. **tingle**—a slight stinging or prickling pain

6. Descr. of Sudden, Excruciating Pains That Stab or Pierce Like Lightning: fulgurant or fulgurating,adj. (medical)

7. An Attack of Pain: algospasm; convulsion of pain; paroxysm or spasm of pain; throe (a sudden and very sharp attack, but brief in duration),n. (algospastic,adj.)

8. Descr. of Pain That Comes in Attacks or Fits: convulsive, paroxysmal, spasmodic,adj.

9. To Be Physically Painful; To Cause Physical Pain,v. *From Sec. 1:* bite, burn, hurt, pain, prick, prickle, smart, sting; *Also:*
1. **ache**—be dully and continuously painful, as a bodily part, member, or area

2. **tingle**—cause slight stinging or prickling pain or pains

10. **Pain; Physical or Bodily Suffering,n.** *From Sec. 1:* affliction, agony, anguish, distress, excruciation, punishment, rack, smart, torment, torture or tortures; *Also:*
 1. **agony, death agony, throes**—final pain, suffering, or struggle before death
 2. **algesthesis**—physical pain (medical)
 3. **discomfort**—mild physical distress, suffering, or pain
 4. **dysphoria**—generalized and abnormal physical discomfort (dysphoric,adj.)
 5. **malaise**—vague and unlocalized physical or bodily discomfort, often occurring just before the outbreak of an illness or disease
 6. **misery**—extreme or acute physical discomfort, distress, suffering, or pain
 7. **pains, labor pains, throes**—suffering or pains attendant on childbirth
 8. **surfeit**—bodily discomfort from eating or drinking to excess
 9. **throes**—sharp, agonizing pain; agony
 10. **travail**—terrible suffering or pain

11. **To Be in, or Feel, Pain; To Suffer Physically,v.** *From Sec. 1:* agonize (as a person, etc.) ; ail (as a person, etc.) ; anguish (as a person, etc.) ; burn (as a bodily part) ; hurt (as a person, or a bodily member, organ, etc.) ; pain, prick, prickle; smart (as a bodily part or member) ; sting (as a bodily part or member) ; twinge (as a specific area or part of the body) ; *From Sec. 10:* surfeit, throe; *Also:*
 1. **ache**—have a dull, continuous pain, as a person, or a bodily part or member
 2. **tingle**—feel slight stinging or prickling pains, as a bodily part or member
 3. **travail**—suffer or experience the pains of labor, i.e., those preceding childbirth
 4. **writhe**—suffer such extreme pain as to squirm or twist in agony

12. **In Pain; Full of Pain; Suffering Pain; Suffering Physically; Exhibiting Such Suffering,adj.** *From Sec. 1:* afflicted, agonized or agonizing, anguished, chastened, convulsed, distressed or distressful, excruciated, punished, racked or on the rack, scourged, smarting, tormented, tortured, troubled, twinged (distressfulness,n.) ; *From Sec. 10:* uncomfortable (from *discomfort*), dysphoric, miserable, surfeited (uncomfortableness, miserableness,n.) ; *From Sec. 11:* aching or achy, tingling or tingly, travailing, writhing; *Also:*
 1. **crapulent, crapulous**—suffering physical discomfort from overindulgence in food or liquor (crapulence, crapulousness,n.)
 2. **painful**—afflicted with, or full of, pain, as a bodily member, part, or area (painfulness,n.)
 3. **sore**—feeling pain, or in pain, esp. localized pain, as a person or bodily part (soreness,n.)
 4. **tender**—painful, as a bodily part or member (tenderness,n.)

13. **To Figuratively Stab, Pierce, Rend, or Tear with Pain:** lancinate with pain,v. (lancination,n.)

14. **To Make (a Bodily Part, Spot, or Area) Sore through Rubbing or Friction:** chafe, gall,v.

15. **To Become So Sore:** chafe, gall,v.

16. **Such Soreness:** chafe,n.

17. **Such a Sore Spot:** chafe; gall (esp. on a horse) ; sore,n.

18. **Causing Movements That Are Attended by Pain:** algiomotor,adj.

19. **To Shrink from, or under, Pain:** cringe, flinch, wince,v. (cringe, flinch, wince,n. cringer, flincher, wincer,n.)

20. **Not Shrinking from, or under, Pain:** unflinching, unwincing,adj.

21. **To Make a Grimace of Pain:** wince,v. (wince,n. wincer,n.)

22. **The Sensation of Pain:** algesis,n. (algesic, adj.)

23. **The Perception or Feeling of Pain:** algesthesis,n.

24. **The Origin or Source of Pain:** algogenesis or algogenesia,n. (medical)

25. **Pert. to Pain:** algetic,adj.

26. **Unhealthy, Abnormal, or Morbid Enjoyment of, or Satisfaction from, One's Own Physical or Emotional Pain or Suffering; Such Enjoyment or Satisfaction from Being Hurt, Humiliated, Degraded, Insulted, etc., Whether as a Conscious or Unconscious Feeling:** masochism,n. (masochist,n. masochistic,adj.)

27. **Morbid Enjoyment of the Physical or Emotional Pain or Suffering of Others; Morbid Enjoyment from Inflicting Pain on Others:** cruelty, sadism,n. (sadist,n. cruel, sadistic,adj.)

28. **Tending to Inflict Physical or Emotional Pain or Suffering on Others:** cruel, sadistic, adj. (cruelty or cruelness, sadism,n. sadist,n.)

29. **An Act or Treatment That Inflicts Physical or Emotional Pain on Others:** cruelty,n.

30. **Sensitiveness to Pain:** algesia, soreness,n. (algesic, sore,adj.)

31. **Excessive Sensitiveness to Pain:** hyperalgesia or hyperalgia,n. (hyperalgesic,adj.)

32. **Excessive or Morbidly Increased Sensitiveness, or Excessively or Morbidly Increased Sensitiveness, to Pain, or to Heat, Cold, or Touch:** algesia, hyperesthesia,n. (algesic, hyperesthetic,adj.)

33. **Decreased Sensitiveness to Pain:** hypalgesia or hypalgia,n. (hypalgesic,adj.)

34. **Decreased, or Morbidly or Excessively Decreased, Sensitiveness to Pain, or to Heat, Cold, or Touch:** hypesthesia,n. (hypesthetic or hypesthesic,adj.)

35. **Power or Ability to Bear Pain, Suffering, Fatigue, etc.:** endurance, fortitude, stamina, n. (staminal,adj.)

36. **To Bear Pain, Suffering, Fatigue, etc.; To Bear (Such):** endure,v. (endurance,n.)

37. **To Make Partially or Totally Insensitive to Pain:** analgize; deaden; desensitize (esp. a bodily part),v. (desensitization,n.)

38. **To Make Partially or Totally Insensitive to Pain, or to Sensations of Heat, Cold, Touch, etc., as by Drugs, Hypnotism, Disease, Hysteria, Paralysis, etc.:** anesthetize; drug or narcotize (by narcotics),v. (anesthetization, narcotization,n.)

39. **Insensitiveness to Pain:** analgesia or analgia; anesthesia or anesthesis (or also to heat, cold, touch, etc.); impassibility or impassibleness,n. (analgesic, analgetic, or analgic; anesthetic,adj.)

40. **Insensitive to Pain:** anesthetic (as a bodily part, etc.) ; anesthetized (i.e., rendered so) ; desensitized (i.e., rendered so, esp. a bodily part); impassible,adj. (anesthetization, desensitization,n.)

41. **Causing or Producing Insensitiveness, or Partial Insensitiveness, to Pain:** analgesic, analgetic, analgic, or analgizing; anesthetic, anesthesiant, or anesthetizing; desensitizing, adj.

42. **Agent or Drug That Causes or Produces Partial or Total Insensitiveness to Pain:** analgesic or analgetic, anesthetic or anesthesiant, desensitizer,n.

43. Process of Producing Such Insensitiveness: anesthesia,n.

44. Lack of Pain: anodynia,n.

45. Remedy, Drug, or Agent That Relieves, Soothes, or Removes Pain: analgesic, anodyne, aspirin; balm (esp. an ointment, etc.); lenitive, mitigative, narcotic; opiate (derivative of opium); painkiller (colloq.); palliative, paregoric, sedative,n.

46. Relieving, Soothing, or Removing Pain: analgesic, anodyne, balmy, lenitive, mitigative, narcotic, opiate, palliative, paregoric, sedative,adj.

47. To Reduce, Relieve, or Soothe (Pain): allay, alleviate, assuage, deaden, decrease, diminish, dull, ease, lessen, lighten, mitigate, quiet, salve, soften, still,v. (alleviation, assuagement, diminution or diminishment, easement, mitigation,n.)

48. To Become Reduced, Relieved, or Soothed—of Pain: decrease, diminish, dull, ease, lessen,v.

49. To Reduce the Pain of (a Person): relieve; reprieve (temporarily),v. (relief, reprieve,n.)

50. To Lessen or Reduce the Pain or Symptoms of (a Disease, Ailment, Condition, etc.) without Curing It or Removing Its Cause: palliate,v. (palliation,n. palliating, palliative, or palliatory,adj. palliative or palliation,n.)

51. Instrument to Measure the Acuteness of the Sense of Pain, or of One's Sensitivity to Pain: algesimeter,n.

52. Such Measurement: algesimetry,n.

53. Instrument to Record the Amount of Pain a Person Suffers: algometer,n.

54. Causing Very Little Pain: indolent (medical),adj. (indolence,n.)

55. Lacking in, without, or Not Causing, Pain: indolent (medical), painless, unpainful, unpaining,adj. (indolence, painlessness, unpainfulness,n.)

56. Certain Specific Bodily Pains,n.
1. backache—pain or pains in the back
2. bellyache—colic (colloq.)
3. brachialgia—sharp or severe pain in the arm
4. Charley horse—painful cramp in the leg or arm muscles, resulting from overuse or strain
5. chiragra—pain of, or in, the hand
6. chiralgia—sharp pain along the course of the nerve or nerves in the hand
7. colic—spasmodic pain in the abdomen or bowels, caused by various conditions, as intestinal disturbances, appendicitis, nervousness, etc. (colic or colicky,adj.)
8. coxalgia, coxalgy, coxodynia—pain in the hip or hip joint (coxalgic,adj.)
9. cramp, algospasm—sudden muscular pain, caused by the involuntary contraction of the muscle as a result of chill, strain, etc. (crampy, algospastic,adj.)
10. cramps—pain or pains, usually spasmodic, in the intestines or bowels
11. crick, kink—painful spasm in the muscles, esp. of the back, neck, etc.
12. earache, otalgia, otodynia—pain in the ear (otalgic,adj.)
13. gastralgia—pain in the stomach; neuralgic pain or condition of the stomach
14. gout, podagra—excruciating pain around the joints of the feet and hands, esp. the big toe, or the disease characterized by this (gouty; podagric, podagral, podagrical, or podagrous,adj.)
15. gripe, gripes—sharp and sudden pain in the bowels or intestines (gripy,adj.)

16. headache—pain in the head, esp. the forehead, temples, etc.
17. heartburn, cardialgia, pyrosis—burning pain felt near or around the heart, caused by the backward flow of acids from the stomach to the esophagus
18. hemialgia—pain affecting one side of the body, but not the other
19. lumbago—pains in the lower part of the back, esp. of rheumatic nature (lumbaginous,adj.)
20. metralgia, metrodynia—pain in the uterus
21. myalgia—pain in the muscles, esp. of rheumatic nature (myalgic,adj.)
22. neuralgia—sharp pain in a nerve or nerves, or along the course of a nerve or nerves; the condition or ailment characterized by this (neuralgic,adj.)
23. ostalgia—pain in a bone or bones (ostalgic,adj.)
24. pedialgia, podalgia—pain in the foot
25. sciatica—ailment or condition characterized by spasmodic pain in the region of the hips and thighs
26. stitch—sharp, sudden, and brief pain in the side or back
27. stomach-ache, bellyache—pain in, or around, the stomach or belly (stomach-achy,adj.)
28. stomatalgia—pain in the mouth
29. toothache, odontalgia—pain in a tooth, or in several teeth (toothachy, odontalgic, adj.)
30. tormina—sharp pains in the abdomen, bowels, or intestines (torminal,adj.)
31. writer's cramp, writer's spasm, writer's palsy, graphospasm—painful muscular spasm in the fingers caused by their overuse in writing

57. Having, Affected by, or Suffering, Such Pains,adj. *From Sec. 56:* backachy, colicky, crampy; gouty, podagric, podagrical, podagral, or podagrous; gripy, headachy, neuralgic, stomach-achy, toothachy, torminous (goutiness,n.)

58. One Having, or Disposed to Having, Such Pains,n. *From Sec. 56:* neuralgiac; podagric (from *gout*),n.

59. Subject to Such Pains,adj. *From Sec. 56:* colicky, gouty (goutiness,n.)

60. Causing Such Pains,adj. *From Sec. 56:* backachy, colicky, crampy, gouty, gripy or griping, headachy or head-aching; *Also:*
1. algiomuscular—causing muscle pains
2. algogenic—causing nerve pains

61. To Cause Such a Pain in (a Person, Part, etc.),v. *From Sec. 56:* cramp, crick, gripe

62. To Feel a Sharp and Sudden Pain or Pains in the Bowels or Intestines: gripe,v.

63. Swollen or Deformed with Gout: gouty, adj. (goutiness,n.)

64. Pert. to Muscle Pains: algiomuscular,adj.

65. Headache: amphicrania (on both sides); cephalalgia, cephalalgy, or encephalalgia; hemialgia or hemicrania (on one side only); migraine, sick headache, or, formerly, megrim (a nervous headache, of unknown cause, generally affecting one side of head only),n. (cephalalgic, migrainous,adj.)

66. An Attack of Nervous Headache: migraine,n.

67. Like Migraine: migrainoid,adj.

68. Suffering from Migraine, or Subject to It: migrainous,adj.

1138. TORTURE

1. To Torture (Someone): crucify, excruciate, rack,v. *Also:*

1. **boot**—torture with an instrument of torture for the leg, once used to force confessions
2. **grill**—torture with extreme heat
3. **impale**—torture or punish by setting on a sharp stake thrust through the body
4. **martyr, martyrize**—torture or kill (a person) for his principles or beliefs
5. **rack**—torture by stretching the bodily joints of (a person) by means of an instrument devised for this purpose
6. **strappado**—torture (a person) by pulling him up high by means of a rope tied, generally, to his wrists, and then letting him plunge the full length of the rope—a practice in former times

2. Torture, i.e., Act of Torturing,n. *From Sec. 1:* crucifixion, excruciation; grilling, impalement, martyrization

3. Torture, i.e., a Form or Method of Torture,n. *From Sec. 1:* impalement, rack, strappado or estrapade; *Also:*
1. **third degree**—form of torture used by the police and others to extract a confession or information, as by beating, shining of bright lights in the victim's eyes, etc.
2. **torment**—torture (archaic)

4. Instrument of Torture,n. *From Sec. 1:* boot, rack, strappado; *Also:*
1. **Iron Maiden**—iron device in the form of a human body, opening up on hinges, and with the interior fitted with spikes—the victim was placed inside, the form was closed, and the spikes were thus thrust through his body
2. **scarpines**—instrument used by the Inquisition for torturing the lower legs
3. **thumbscrew**—instrument formerly used for torturing the thumbs by squeezing
4. **torment**—any instrument of torture (archaic)
5. **wheel**—circular frame on which a victim was stretched and his bones broken by an iron bar—used in the Middle Ages

5. State of Being Tortured,n. *From Sec. 1:* crucifixion, excruciation; grilling, martyrdom

6. One Who Tortures: crucifier, torturer,n.

7. Torturing; Full of Torture: crucifying, excruciating, torturesome, torturous,adj.

8. Involving Torture: torturous,adj.

9. One Who Prefers Torture or Death to Giving Up His Principles or Beliefs: martyr, n.

10. State of Being a Martyr: martyrdom,n.

11. To Become a Martyr: martyrize,v. (martyrization,n.)

12. To Make a Martyr of: martyr or martyrize,v. (martyrization,n.)

1139. TO CALM; TO SOOTHE

1. To Calm, i.e., Make Calm; To Soothe,v.
1. **abirritate**—soothe the irritation of (tissues, etc.—medical)
2. **allay**—calm or quiet (anger, fear, suspicion, anxiety, etc.)
3. **appease**—calm or quiet, esp., if a person, by giving in to his demands; bring to a calm state or condition (appeasement,n.)
4. **assuage**—calm (a person); calm (anger, passion, fierce feelings, etc.); make (such emotions) calm or calmer (assuagement, n.)
5. **attemper**—calm or soothe (anger, hurt feelings, etc.); calm; soothe
6. **becalm**—calm; make, or cause to be, calm, calmer, less violent, etc.
7. **comfort**—soothe (a person) in distress, grief, sorrow, misery, etc.
8. **compose**—calm, quiet, or free from unrest

or mental or emotional disturbance or agitation, as a person, the mind, the body, oneself, etc.
9. **conciliate**—calm or soothe the anger or hostility of (conciliation,n.)
10. **console**—soothe (a person) in grief, sorrow, or disappointment; comfort (consolation,n.)
11. **cool**—calm; allay
12. **ease**—soothe (fears, distress, anxiety, etc.); comfort
13. **lull**—calm; soothe; quiet; calm or soothe (fears, worries, etc.); soothe (to sleep); soothe (a person) into a condition by assurances, as *lull him into false security,* etc.
14. **mollify, dulcify**—calm, soothe, or pacify as a person, or his anger, rage, etc. (mollification, dulcification,n.)
15. **narcotize, drug**—soothe or calm (a person, the mind, etc.) to a point approaching sleep, stupor, unconsciousness, etc. (narcotization,n.)
16. **pacify, pacificate**—calm; quiet; calm or soothe (anger, hostility, etc.); calm the anger, wounded feelings, excitement, or agitation of (pacification,n.)
17. **placate**—calm the anger of (a person); appease; pacify (placation,n.)
18. **propitiate**—calm or quiet the anger or hostility of (a person, a god, etc.) and win his friendliness or good will; appease (propitiation,n.)
19. **put at rest**—calm or soothe (fears, anxiety, etc.)
20. **quell**—calm, quiet, or pacify (feelings, passion, sorrow, grief, etc.)
21. **quench**—calm or cool (passions, etc.)
22. **quiet**—calm, soothe, or pacify (a person, the mind, fears, anxieties, etc.); make (a person) mentally calm, i.e., free of mental or emotional disturbance, excitement, etc.
23. **salve**—calm or soothe (conscience, hurt feelings, pride, vanity, anger, etc.)
24. **sedate**—calm or soothe (a person) with medications or drugs, in order to relieve pain, excitement, etc., or to reduce activity (sedation,n.)
25. **smooth**—calm or soothe (distressed feelings, hurt, etc.)
26. **sober**—calm, i.e., convert from an excited or emotional state to one of calmness or self-control
27. **solace**—soothe (grief, sorrow, distress, etc.); soothe (a person) in grief, sorrow, or distress; comfort; console
28. **still**—calm or quiet (pain, anxiety, passion, excitement, disturbance, etc.); appease
29. **tranquilize**—calm; make calm or quiet; free from commotion, emotional or other disturbance, agitation, etc. (tranquilization,n.)
30. **unruffle**—calm; quiet; calm the emotional agitation of

2. Calming or Soothing; Acting, Tending, or Serving to Calm or Soothe,adj. *From Sec. 1:* abirritant (medical), allaying, appeasing or appeasive, assuaging or assuasive, becalming, comforting; conciliating, conciliative, or conciliatory; consoling or consolatory, easing, lulling, mollifying or dulcifying; narcotizing, narcotic, narcotical, or drugging; pacifying, pacific, or pacificatory; placating, placative, or placatory; propitiating, propitiative, or propitiatory; quenching, quieting, salving; sedative (generally, or by the use of drugs); sobering, solacing or solaceful, tranquilizing (conciliatoriness, mollifyingness, narcoticalness,n.); *Also:*
1. **anodyne**—soothing; soothing to the mind or feelings
2. **balmy**—soothing; having soothing qualities (balminess,n.)

3. **bland**—soothing or serving to soothe, as air, climate, words, manner, medicine, oil, etc. (blandness,n.)
4. **calmative**—calming; soothing; acting or serving as a medical sedative
5. **demulcent**—soothing, as a medication, esp. to inflamed, irritated, or abraded mucous membranes or other surfaces; soothing to the feelings
6. **dulcet**—soothing; soothing and sweet in sound
7. **emollient**—soothing; soothing to the skin; tending to soothe and soften the skin or other tissue
8. **irenic, irenical**—tending or serving to calm or soothe anger, hostility, etc.
9. **lenitive**—soothing; medically soothing; soothing to the skin or other tissue
10. **nervine**—medically calming or soothing to the nerves
11. **opiate**—soothing, calming, or quieting to the feelings, fears, anxieties, worries, etc.
12. **paregoric**—soothing; soothing medically, esp. to pain
13. **restful**—calming or soothing by inducing rest, relief from trouble or emotional disturbance, etc., as a place, surroundings, sounds, etc. (restfulness,n.)
14. **soothful**—soothing; gently soothing; full of a soothing quality; very soothing
15. **unctuous**—soothing and persuasive, or too smoothly so, as manner or speech, or a person in his manner or speech (unctuousness, unctuosity, or, in reference to speech only, unction,n.)

3. Not Calming; Not Serving to Calm; Unsoothing,adj. *From Sec. 1:* unassuaging, uncomforting, unconciliating or unconciliatory, unconsoling or unconsolatory, unmollifying, unnarcotic, unpropitiatory, unquieting, unsolacing; *From Sec. 2:* unirenic, unrestful (unrestfulness,n.)

4. Calmer or Soother, i.e., That Which Calms or Soothes; Soothing Agent or Substance,n. *From Sec. 1:* abirritant (medical), assuagement or assuager, comfort or comforter, consolation, mollifier, narcotic or drug, pacifier, propitiation, salve; sedative (a drug, etc.); solace, solacer, or solacement; soother; *From Sec. 2:* anodyne; balm (esp. to the mind, feelings, or temperament); calmative or calmant (medication); demulcent (medication); emollient (medication); lenitive; nervine or nerve tonic; opiate; paregoric (medication); *Also:*
1. **anodyne**—statement intended purely to calm or soothe, or to alleviate fear or worry, but not necessarily logical or truthful
2. **balm**—soothing ointment, oil, or lotion, as for the skin
3. **lotion**—liquid medication used for soothing, healing, or cleansing the skin
4. **lull**—soothing sound
5. **lullaby, cradlesong**—song used to soothe a child to sleep
6. **mitigative**—drug, medicine, or other remedy that is soothing or that is used to soothe
7. **pacifier**—sucking nipple used to soothe an infant
8. **petrolatum, petroleum jelly, Vaseline**—soothing jelly, derived from petroleum, applied to burns, wounds, sores, etc., or used as a base in salves or ointments
9. **placation**—something offered for the purpose of placating, conciliating, or propitiating
10. **placebo**—soothing, pacifying, or ingratiating statement, action, etc.
11. **salve, ointment, unguent, unction**—soothing and healing medicinal substance applied to wounds, burns, sores, etc. (unguentary, unctuous,adj.)

12. **sop**—something given or offered in order to soothe, calm, appease, or pacify
13. **sugar-tit, sugar-teat**—cloth dampened or impregnated with a sugar solution, and used to soothe or pacify an infant, who sucks on it
14. **unction**—that which soothes or comforts

5. Calmer or Soother, i.e., One Who Calms or Soothes,n. *From Sec. 1:* appeaser, assuager, comforter, conciliator, consoler, mollifier, pacifier, placater, propitiator, queller, quencher, quieter, smoother, solacer, tranquilizer; *Also:* 1. Job's comforter—one who, though intending or pretending to soothe, comfort, or console a person with words or sentiments, actually (whether unintentionally or spitefully) distresses, depresses, or discourages him

6. Calmed or Soothed,adj. *From Sec. 1:* allayed, appeased, assuaged, becalmed, comforted, composed or self-composed, conciliated, consoled, cooled, eased, lulled, mollified or dulcified, narcotized or drugged, pacified, placated, propitiated, put at rest, quelled, quenched, quieted, salved, sedated, smoothed, sobered, solaced, stilled, tranquilized

7. State of Being, or of Having Been, Calmed or Soothed,n. *From Sec. 1:* appeasement, assuagement, comfort, composure, conciliation, consolation, lull, mollification or dulcification, narcotization, pacification, propitiation, sedation, solace, tranquilization

8. Uncalmed or Unsoothed,adj. *From Sec. 1:* unallayed, unappeased, unassuaged, uncomforted, unconciliated, unconsoled, uneased, unmollified, unpacified, unplacated, unpropitiated, unquelled, unquenched, unquieted, unsalved, unsmoothed, unsolaced, unstilled, untranquilized (unappeasedness, unconciliatedness, unpacifiedness, unpropitiatedness,n.)

9. Capable of Being Calmed or Soothed,adj. *From Sec. 1:* appeasable, conciliable, consolable, mollifiable, pacifiable, placable or pacable, propitiable, quenchable, quietable,adj. (appeasableness, consolableness, placableness or placability, quenchableness,n.)

10. Incapable of Being Calmed or Soothed; Unsoothable,adj. *From Sec. 1:* unallayable, unappeasable, unassuageable, unconciliable; inconsolable, unconsolable, or disconsolate; unmollifiable, unpacifiable; implacable, unplacable, or impacable; unpropitiable, unquellable, unquenchable or quenchless, unquietable, solaceproof (unappeasableness; inconsolability, inconsolableness, disconsolateness, or disconsolation; implacability, implacableness, or impacability; unquenchableness,n.); *Also:* soothless—not to be soothed; unsoothable

11. To Calm, or Calm Down, i.e., Become Calm,v. *From Sec. 1:* cool or cool down, compose oneself, ease, lull, quench, quiet, sober down, still, tranquilize, unruffle; *Also:*
1. **collect oneself, pull or get oneself together**—become calm, i.e., regain control of oneself
2. **subside**—become calm, quiet, or tranquil, esp. after activity (subsidence,n. subsiding or subsident,adj.)

12. To Lie or Be Calm, Calm and Quiet, etc., as a Person or Place: repose, rest,v. (repose, rest,n.)

13. To Rub Gently, as a Person's Forehead, Face, or Other Part, in Order to Soothe or Calm Him or His Feelings; To Rub (the Fur) Gently, in Order to Calm or Soothe an Animal: smooth, stroke,v. (stroke,n.)

14. To Be Soothing: soothe,v.

15. Calm,adj.
1. **at rest, at peace, in repose**—in a calm

state; calm in the sense of not agitated or restless, or not disturbed or distressed emotionally

2. **collected, self-collected**—calm; in calm control or command of one's faculties
3. **composed, self-composed**—calm; not agitated or disturbed emotionally; having a settled serenity, as a person
4. **cool**—calm though there might be cause for excitement or agitation; collected; unexcited; showing calmness or lack of agitation
5. **coolheaded**—calm in mind; not excited; showing calmness of mind
6. **dispassionate**—calm; unperturbed by emotions or passions; showing such calmness
7. **easeful**—calm and quiet, as a place, surroundings, etc.
8. **easy**—calm, i.e., free from emotional strain, embarrassment, or lack of poise, as manner, bearing, etc.; poised
9. **equable**—uniformly and unchangingly calm, tranquil, unruffled, etc., as the mind or temperament, or a person
10. **equanimous**—calm and even in mind and temperament; self-composed; self-possessed
11. **even**—possessing or showing calmness, lack of agitation or excitement, etc.
12. **even-tempered, evenminded**—calm in mind or temper; not excited, angered, or agitated
13. **halcyon**—calm, or calm and peaceful, as days, times, or periods, in allusion to the bird of the kingfisher family that in fable made its nest in the sea at about the time of the winter solstice and was thought to calm the waves
14. **impassive**—calm, placid, or serene, i.e., not feeling or exhibiting emotional agitation or excitement, as a person, voice, demeanor, words, etc.
15. **imperturbable**—feeling or showing calmness, serenity, or tranquillity, though there might be cause for excitement, embarrassment, agitation, anxiety, etc.
16. **in countenance**—calm, composed, or poised, as a person
17. **insouciant**—calm; unagitated
18. **levelheaded**—possessing or indicating good judgment and calmness of temper
19. **moderate**—calm; calm and reasonable; calm, as wind or weather
20. **nonchalant**—calm and cool, esp. in embarrassing circumstances; indicative of such calmness and coolness
21. **passionless**—calm, i.e., feeling or showing freedom from emotional agitation or excitement
22. **patient**—calm and uncomplaining while waiting, enduring hardships or annoyance, etc., or exhibiting such calmness
23. **peaceful, pacific**—calm, or calm and quiet, as times, periods, places, surroundings, etc.
24. **philosophical, philosophic**—calm and sensible in the face of adversity or unpleasant or trying circumstances, or exhibiting such calmness, as words, air, attitude, etc.
25. **phlegmatic, phlegmatical**—calm and poised; self-composed; calm though there is cause for agitation or excitement; abnormally calm or cool when agitation or excitement is expected or natural
26. **placid**—calm; agreeably calm; free of disturbance or agitation (as a person, waters, etc.); having, or indicating, an inner calmness or composure; serene
27. **pococurante, pococurantic, pococurantish, pococurantist**—nonchalant
28. **poised**—composed or self-possessed in new or unusual circumstances or surroundings; calm, i.e., lacking nervousness

or self-consciousness, in difficult or embarrassing circumstances

29. **quiet, still**—calm; free from disturbance, agitation, fuss or excitement, as a person, thing, place, atmosphere, waters, etc.
30. **reposeful, restful**—calm or quiet, as a place, surroundings, etc.
31. **sedate**—calm, undisturbed by emotion or excitement, composed, or quiet, as a person, his mind, character, judgment, thinking, etc.
32. **self-possessed**—calm, i.e., composed, poised, having presence of mind, etc.
33. **serene**—calm, i.e., undisturbed emotionally; calm, without disturbance or agitation, as water, air, regions, etc.; possessing an inner calm or composure, as a person; full of calmness, as a period, age, etc.
34. **settled**—calm, as weather
35. **slumberous, slumbering, slumbery, slumbrous**—calm or quiet, as a place, feelings, passions, etc., often with the implication that the calmness is temporary
36. **smooth**—calm or unagitated, as waters of a lake, sea, etc., or the lake, sea, etc.
37. **sober**—calm, i.e., not excited, or not influenced by emotions, emotional pressure, or passions, as a person, attitude, etc.; sedate, as a person
38. **staid**—calm, quiet, sedate, or sober, often in a rather settled or colorless fashion, as a person, behavior, etc.
39. **steady**—calm, or calm and controlled, i.e., free from emotional disturbance or agitation, as nerves
40. **stoical, stoic**—calm, i.e., undisturbed in times of stress, distress, misfortune, etc., as a person, temperament, etc., or indicating such calmness, as attitude, air, etc.
41. **stormless**—calm, as a life, the sea, sky, atmosphere, etc.
42. **tranquil**—calm, i.e., not disturbed by emotional agitation, as a person, character, temperament, etc.; calm or quiet, i.e., lacking in commotion or disturbance, as a life, period, age, time, place, surroundings, waters, air, etc.
43. **unagitated**—calm, i.e., free of agitation, as a person, mind, place, surface, etc.
44. **unexcited**—calm, i.e., free of excitement, as a person, manner, behavior, etc.
45. **unflurried**—calm, i.e., not agitated emotionally, despite the haste or confusion in the surroundings or atmosphere
46. **unflustered**—calm, i.e., not upset emotionally by sudden orders, unexpected demands, or unusual circumstances
47. **unfluttered**—calm, i.e., free of nervous or emotional excitement or agitation, as a person
48. **unrattled**—calm, i.e., not disturbed by circumstances, etc. (colloq.)
49. **unruffled**—calm, i.e., not excited, agitated, or disturbed, as a person, attitude, surface of the water, etc.
50. **windless**—calm, as the sea, sky, atmosphere, etc.

16. Calmness or Calm, i.e., Calm State or Condition,n. *From Sec. 15:* rest, peace, or repose; collectedness or self-collectedness; composure, composedness, self-composure, or self-composedness; coolness, coolheadedness, dispassion or dispassionateness, easefulness, ease or easiness, equableness or equability, equanimity or equanimousness, evenness, evenmindedness, impassiveness or impassivity; imperturbation, imperturbability, or imperturbableness; insouciance, levelheadedness, moderateness or moderation, nonchalance, passionlessness, patience, peacefulness or peace; phlegmaticness, phlegmaticalness, phlegmatism, or phlegm; placidity or placidness, pococuranteism or pococurantism; poise;

quiet, quietness, quietude, quietism, stillness, or still; reposefulness or restfulness; sedateness, self-possession, serenity or sereneness, smoothness, soberness or sobriety, staidness, steadiness, stoicalness or stoicism; tranquillity, tranquility, or tranquilness; unagitatedness or unagitation; *Also:*

1. **aplomb**—calm composure or self-possession, even under unusual, embarrassing, etc., circumstances; assured poise
2. **countenance**—calmness, composure, or poise, esp. in the phrases *in countenance* and *out of countenance*
3. **doldrums**—state of calm, i.e., lack of activity, as of business, etc.
4. **lull**—condition of calm, or, esp., temporary calm, as of weather, feelings, activities, etc.
5. **presence of mind**—calmness and alertness of mind in unusual circumstances or emergencies, or when taken by surprise; ability to keep one's composure and think clearly under such circumstances
6. **sang-froid (French)**—unusual calmness or composure, or lack of emotional or mental agitation or fluster, under embarrassing, distressing, or trying circumstances; ability to remain calm and unemotional under these circumstances

17. Days or Period of Calmness and Peacefulness; Days or Period of Calm Weather, Esp. during the Week before and after the Winter Solstice: halcyon days,n.

18. Region in the Ocean That Is Calm and without Winds; Such Region Near the Equator; Region Near the Equator Where There Is Dead Calm or Very Light and Changeable Winds; Such a Calm or Such Winds in This Region: doldrums,n.

19. Calm Person,n. *From Sec. 15:* philosopher; phlegmatic, phlegmatist, or phlegmat; pococurante or pococurantist, stoic

20. Uncalm; Not Calm,adj. *From Sec. 15:* unreposed, uncollected, uncomposed, uneaseful, uneasy, unequable or inequable, out of countenance, immoderate or unmoderate, impatient, unpeaceful, unphilosophical or unphilosophic, unphlegmatic, unplacid, unpoised, unquiet or unstill, unreposeful or unrestful, unsedate, unself-possessed, unserene, unsettled; unslumberous, unslumbering, or unslumbrous; unsmooth, unsober, unstaid, unsteady, unstoical or unstoic, stormy, untranquil, agitated, excited, flurried, flustered, fluttered, rattled, ruffled, windy

21. Uncalmness; Uncalm; Lack of Calmness, n. *From Sec. 15:* uncollectedness, uneasefulness, uneasiness or unease, unequableness; immoderateness, immoderation, or unmoderateness; impatience, unpeacefulness or unpeace, unphilosophicalness; unquietness, unquietude, or unstillness; unreposefulness, unrestfulness, or unrest; unsmoothness; unsoberness, insobriety, or unsobriety; unstaidness, unsteadiness, storminess, agitation, excitement or excitedness, flurry; fluster, flusteration, or flustration; flutter, ruffle, windiness

22. To Cause Uncalmness, or Lack of Calmness, in; To Uncalm,v. *From Sec. 15:* unsmooth, unsober, unsteady, unstoicize or unstoic, untranquilize, agitate, excite, flurry, fluster, flutter, rattle, ruffle

1140. PEACE

1. To Make Peaceful,v.
1. **appease**—bring to a peaceful state or condition (appeasement,n.)
2. **assuage**—make (a person) more peaceful (assuagement,n.)

3. **pacify, pacificate**—make peaceful; bring (a nation, people, etc.) into a state or condition of peace (pacification,n.)
4. **placate**—make feel peaceful (placation, n.)
5. **quiet**—make peaceful
6. **tranquilize**—make peaceful (tranquilization,n.)

2. Acting or Serving to Make Peaceful or to Bring About Peace,adj. *From Sec. 1:* appeasing or appeasive, assuaging or assuasive; pacifying, pacific, or pacificatory; placating, placative, or placatory; quieting, tranquilizing; *Also:*
1. **irenic, irenical**—serving or tending to bring about peace or peacefulness; serving or tending to bring about peace within the church
2. **peacemaking**—serving or tending to bring about peace
3. **peacemongering**—attempting to bring about peace (contemptuous)

3. Not Acting or Serving to Make Peaceful or to Bring About Peace,adj. *From Sec. 1:* unassuaging, unpacific, unquieting; *From Sec. 2:* unirenic; *Also:* **1.** peaceless—not bringing about peace or peacefulness (peacelessness,n.)

4. One Who Causes Peacefulness or Who Makes Peace,n. *From Sec. 1:* appeaser, assuager, pacifier or pacificator, placater, quieter, tranquilizer; *Also:*
1. **peacemaker**—one who makes peace, esp. by calming or soothing those in dispute, settling their differences in a way satisfactory to all sides, etc. (peacemaking,n.)
2. **peacemonger**—one who attempts to bring about peace (contemptuous)

5. Made Peaceful,adj. *From Sec. 1:* appeased, assuaged, pacified, placated, quieted, tranquilized

6. Condition of Having Been Made Peaceful,n. *From Sec. 1:* appeasement, assuagement, pacification, tranquilization

7. Not Made Peaceful,adj. *From Sec. 1:* unappeased, unassuaged, unpacified, unplacated, unquieted, untranquilized (unappeasedness, unpacifiedness,n.)

8. Capable of Being Made Peaceful: appeasable, pacable, pacifiable, placable, quietable,adj. (appeasableness, placableness or placability,n.)

9. Incapable of Being Made Peaceful: impacable, implacable, unappeasable, unassuageable, unpacifiable, unplacable, unquietable,adj. (impacability, implacability or implacableness, unappeasableness,n.)

10. To Become Peaceful: quiet, tranquilize,v. (tranquilization,n.)

11. Peaceful: amicable (as a settlement, agreement, etc.); at peace; easeful (as a place or surroundings, etc.); halcyon (as times, periods, or conditions); irenic or irenical (as acts, words, measures, means, etc.); pacific or pacifical; peaceable; placid; quiet; restful (as place or surroundings, etc.); serene; tranquil,adj.

12. Peacefulness,n. *From Sec. 11:* amicableness or amicability, easefulness, peaceableness, placidity or placidness; quietness, quietude, or quiet; restfulness, serenity or sereneness; tranquillity, tranquility, or tranquilness

13. Unpeaceful,adj. *From Sec. 11:* unamicable, unirenic, unpacific, unpeaceable, unplacid, unquiet, unrestful, unserene, untranquil

14. Unpeacefulness,n. *From Sec. 11:* unpeaceableness, unquietness or unquietude, unrestfulness or unrest

15. Inclined or Disposed to, Fond of, or Wishing, Peace, as a Person or Group, etc.:

pacific or pacifical, peaceable, peaceful, peace-enamored, peace-loving, quiet, unbellicose, unbelligerent, unmilitant, unmilitaristic, unpugnacious, unwarlike,adj. (peaceableness, peacefulness, quietness, unwarlikeness,n.)

16. **Not Inclined or Disposed to, Fond of, or Wishing, Peace:** bellicose, belligerent, combative, martial, militant, militaristic, pugnacious, unpacific, unpeaceable, unpeaceful, unquiet, warlike,adj. (bellicoseness or bellicosity, belligerence or belligerency, combativeness, militancy, pugnaciousness or pugnacity, unpeaceableness, unpeacefulness, unquietness, warlikeness,n.)

17. **Person Who Is Peaceable; Esp. a Cuban or Filipino Who Did Not Take Part in the Revolts against Spain:** pacifico,n. (Spanish)

18. **Condition or General Feeling, Opinion, or Temper, as of the Populace or of a Group, That Conduces to Peace or Peacefulness:** irenicism,n.

19. **A Suggestion or Idea for Bringing About Peace; Such for Bringing About Peace within the Church:** irenicon,n.

20. **That Which Is Offered or Given as a Token of a Desire for Peace:** olive branch, peace offering,n.

21. **A Number or Collection of Peace Offerings:** pacifics,pl.n.

22. **Belief, Principle, or Policy that International Disputes Can and Should Be Settled Peacefully, by Negotiation, without Recourse to War, etc.; Opposition to War:** pacifism,n. (pacifist,n. pacifist or pacifistic, adj.)

23. **Peace:** amity (i.e., peace and friendship, as between groups, countries, etc.), quiet, repose, serenity, tranquillity,n.

24. **Peaceful Relations between Groups, Countries, etc.:** amity,n.

25. **Inner Peace:** peace of mind, peace of soul, repose, rest, serenity, tranquillity,n.

26. **Heavenly Inner Peace—a Buddhist Concept:** nirvana,n.

27. **Symbol of Peace:** dove, olive branch,n.

28. **One Who Advocates or Urges Peace:** peaceman; peacemonger (contemptuous),n. (peacemongering,adj.)

29. **A Time of Peace:** peacetime,n. (peacetime,adj.)

30. **Agreement between Nations to Be at Peace, End a War, etc.:** peace treaty,n.

31. **Conference to Draw Such Up:** peace conference,n.

32. **A Temporary Peace; a Temporary Cessation of War or Fighting; Such as a Preliminary to the Signing of a Peace Treaty:** armistice, truce,n.

33. **Similar to, or Suggestive of, Peace:** peacelike,adj.

34. **To End Warfare, Hostility, Fighting, etc. (with):** make peace (with), make one's peace with,v.

35. **To Prevent, or Avoid, the Rupture of Peacefulness in a Community, etc., as by Not Breaking, or by Preventing the Breaking of, the Law, or by Avoiding or Preventing Disorderly Conduct, etc.:** keep the peace, v.

36. **Pert. to Peace; Tending to Bring Back Peace:** pacific or pacifical,adj.

37. **Breaking or Violation of Peace; Violation of the Peace of a Community, as by Disorderliness, etc.:** peacebreaking,n.

38. **One Who So Breaks or Violates the Peace:** peacebreaker,n.

39. **Lack of Peace:** peacelessness; unpeace; unrest (within a country),n.

40. **Lacking in Peace:** peaceless,adj.

1141. COMFORT

1. **Comfortable, i.e., Producing, or Conducive to, Comfort:** convenient (i.e., for use, etc.); cozy, cozey, cosy, cosey, cozie, or cosie (i.e., comfortable and warm, as a place, bed, corner, etc.); easeful; easy (as a chair, etc.); restful; snug (i.e., permitting one to be comfortable or to live comfortably, as *a snug inheritance, income, or fortune;* or comfortable, warm, and, often, small, as a place, room, bed, environment, etc.),adj.

2. **Such Comfortableness or Comfort,n.** *From Sec. 1:* convenience, coziness, easefulness, restfulness, snugness,n.

3. **A Comfort, i.e., That Which Is Productive of, or Conducive to, Comfort:** convenience, easement,n.

4. **Something That Produces, or Conduces to, Bodily or Physical Comfort:** creature comfort,n.

5. **A Comfortable, or Warm and Comfortable, Room, Place, Position, etc.:** snuggery,n.

6. **Comfortable, i.e., Being in Comfort, as a Person:** cozy, cozey, cosy, cosey, cozie, or cosie (i.e., being comfortable and warm); easy (in mind); snug (i.e., comfortable and warm, protected from the elements or cold, etc.),adj.

7. **Comfortableness or Comfort,n.** *From Sec. 6:* coziness, ease, snugness; *Also:* cheer, ease, well-being,n.

8. **To Make (a Person, etc.) Comfortable:** comfort,v.

9. **To Make Comfortable and Warm:** snug, v.

10. **Not Comfortable:** discomfortable, uncomfortable,adj. (uncomfortableness,n.)

11. **To Make Uncomfortable, Esp. in Mind:** discomfort, uncomfort,v.

12. **Lack of Comfort:** discomfort, uncomfort, uncomfortableness,n.

13. **Causing Discomfort; Unproductive of, or Lacking in, Comfort:** awkward; cheerless (as a place, room, environment, etc.); inconvenient; strange (as circumstances, surroundings, etc.); uncomfortable,adj. (awkwardness, inconvenience, strangeness, uncomfortableness,n.)

14. **That Which Causes Discomfort:** discomfort, inconvenience,n.

15. **Not Feeling Comfortable:** awkward or strange (in new circumstances or surroundings, etc.); uncomfortable; uneasy (in mind or emotions),adj.

16. **Lack of Comfortable Feelings,n.** *From Sec. 15:* awkwardness or strangeness, uncomfortableness, uneasiness or unease; *Also:* discomfort, uncomfort,n.

1142. RELIEF; REDUCTION OF SEVERITY OR INTENSITY

1. **To Relieve; To Reduce (Something, Some Abstraction, Force, etc.) in Severity or Intensity,v.**
  1. abate—make less, or gradually less, severe or intense (abatement,n. abater,n.)
  2. allay—lessen, soften, or make easier to bear, as pain, hunger, suffering, grief, anxiety, fear, etc. (allayer,n.)
  3. alleviate—lighten, lessen, soften, make

easier to bear, or reduce the discomfort of, as punishment, pain, sorrow, suffering, etc. (alleviation,n. alleviator,n.)

4. **assuage**—make less severe or more mild; lighten or soften, as anger, sorrow, pain, suffering, etc. (assuagement,n. assuager, n.)

5. **attemper**—make less severe or harsh; soften

6. **cool**—lessen the emotional heat, passion, or intensity of; allay

7. **deaden, dull**—reduce the intensity or force of

8. **diminish**—lessen in degree or severity (diminution or diminishment,n.)

9. **ease**—lessen or reduce the severity of (pain, fear, anxiety, distress, etc.); make (something, as a burden, etc.) less painful; relieve of discomfort or distress (easement,n.)

10. **lessen, decrease, reduce**—make less severe or harsh, as punishment, pain, etc.; make less intense, as in force, etc. (reduction,n. lessener, reducer,n.)

11. **lighten**—reduce in harshness, severity, or burdensomeness, as pain, punishment, etc.

12. **melt**—soften in feelings, as the heart, etc.

13. **mitigate**—reduce in severity, intensity, or harshness, as pain, punishment, distress, etc.; make less in force or intensity, as heat, cold, harshness, anger, pain, etc.; soften; make milder; make less painful or rigorous; make more bearable (mitigation,n. mitigator,n.)

14. **moderate**—make less severe, intense, harsh, rigorous, or violent; make mild or milder

15. **mollify**—make less severe, intense, or violent, as anger or rage (mollification,n. mollifier,n.)

16. **palliate**—reduce the severity, intensity, or harshness of; lighten; make easier to bear; soften the seriousness of, as a fault, crime, etc. (palliation,n. palliator,n.)

17. **qualify**—lessen the severity, unpleasantness, or violence of; make milder; soften (qualification,n.)

18. **quell**—allay, or reduce the severity of, as feelings, passions, sorrow, grief, etc. (queller,n.)

19. **relax**—reduce or soften the severity or strictness of, as rules, discipline, etc.; lessen the force or intensity of, as attention, effort, etc.; make milder (relaxation, n. relaxer,n.)

20. **relieve**—lighten, reduce the intensity of, or ease, as pain, anxiety, fears, suffering, distress, etc.; lighten or reduce the pain, anxiety, fears, distress, etc., of, as a person (relief,n. reliever,n.)

21. **remit**—lessen in force, degree, or intensity, as care, watchfulness, efforts, diligence, etc. (remission or remittal,n.)

22. **reprieve**—relieve (a person) temporarily, as from pain, distress, or punishment (repriever,n.)

23. **respite**—give relief, or a period of relief, to (a person) from something painful, uncomfortable, vexing, distressing, etc.

24. **season**—make less severe or harsh; soften; make milder (as *season demands with courtesy, discretion,* etc.)

25. **slacken, slack**—make less severe or intense; lessen or reduce the intensity of (discipline, efforts, speed, toil, etc.); relax

26. **soften**—make less harsh or severe, or more mild, as demands, feelings, anger, burden, conditions, etc.

27. **solace**—alleviate, lighten, lessen, or relieve, as distress, sorrow, grief, etc. (solacer,n.)

28. **soothe**—alleviate, allay, lessen, or relieve, as pain, grief, doubt, fears, or similar feelings (soother,n.)

29. **sweeten**—make less harsh or severe; make mild or milder

30. **tame, tame down**—soften; soften or tone down the severity, harshness, or intensity of

31. **temper**—reduce in severity, intensity, harshness, force, or violence; soften; tone down

32. **tone down**—make less severe, intense, strong, harsh, rigorous, or violent; soften

33. **unsteel**—soften, as a person, his heart, temperament, attitude, etc.

34. **weaken**—reduce the intensity, force, or strength of

2. Relieving; Acting, Tending, or Serving to Cause Reduction of Severity or Intensity,adj. *From Sec. 1:* allaying; alleviating, alleviative, or alleviatory; assuaging or assuasive, cooling, deadening or dulling, easing; mitigating, mitigative, mitigatory, or mitigant; moderating, mollifying; palliating, palliative, or palliatory; qualifying or qualificative, relaxing or relaxative, relieving, reprieving, softening or soft, solacing or solaceful, soothing, sweetening, taming, weakening (mollifyingness,n.)

3. Not Relieving; Not Acting, Tending, or Serving to Cause Reduction of Severity or Intensity,adj. *From Sec. 1:* unassuaging, unmitigative, unmollifying, unqualifying, unrelaxing, unsoftening, unsolacing, unsoothing

4. Reliever; That Which Relieves, or Which Reduces, or Acts, Tends, or Serves to Reduce, the Severity or Intensity of Something,n. *From Sec. 1:* allayer; alleviation, alleviator, or alleviative; assuagement or assuager, easement, lessener or reducer; mitigation, mitigator, or mitigative; moderant or moderator, mollifier, palliation or palliative, relaxative or relaxer, relief or reliever, repriever; solace, solacement, or solacer; soother

5. Relieved; Reduced in Severity or Intensity,adj. *From Sec. 1:* abated, allayed, alleviated, assuaged, cooled; deadened, dulled, or dull; diminished, eased; lessened, less, decreased, or reduced; lightened or light, melted, mitigated, moderated or moderate, mollified, palliated, qualified, quelled, relaxed, relieved, reprieved, slackened, softened or soft, sweetened or sweet, tamed or tame, tempered, toned down, unsteeled, weakened or weak

6. State of Being Reduced in Severity or Intensity,n. *From Sec. 1:* alleviation, assuagement, diminution or diminishment, easement, decrease or reduction, mitigation, moderateness, palliation, qualification, relaxation, relief, softness, sweetness, tameness

7. Unrelieved; Not Reduced in Severity or Intensity,adj. *From Sec. 1:* unabated, unallayed, unalleviated, unassuaged, uncooled, undeadened, undulled, undiminished; unlessened, undecreased, or unreduced; unlightened, unmelted, unmitigated, unmollified, unpalliated, unqualified, unquelled, unrelaxed, unrelieved, unreprieved, unslackened, unsoftened, unsweetened, untamed or untame, untempered, unweakened (unalleviation, unmitigatedness, unqualifiedness or unqualification, unrelief, untamedness or untameness, n.)

8. Relievable; Capable of Being Reduced in Severity or Intensity,adj. *From Sec. 1:* abatable, allevible, diminishable, reducible, mitigable, mollifiable, qualifiable, relaxable, relievable, remissible, tamable (diminishableness, reducibleness or reducibility, tamableness or tamability,n.)

9. Unrelievable; Incapable of Being Reduced in Severity or Intensity,adj. *From Sec. 1:* unabatable, unallayable, unalleviable, undiminishable, unreducible or irreducible, unmitigable or immitigable, unmollifiable, unpalliable, unqualifiable, unquellable, unrelaxable, unrelievable, unremissible, unreprievable, untamable (unreducibleness, irreducibleness, or irreducibility; immitigability, unrelievableness, untamableness,n.)

10. To Reduce, i.e., Become Reduced, in Severity or Intensity,v. *From Sec. 1:* abate, cool or cool down, diminish, dull, ease; lessen, decrease, or reduce; melt, mitigate, moderate, relax, remit, slacken or slack, soften, sweeten, temper, tone down, weaken (abatement, diminution or diminishment, easement, decrease or reduction, mitigation, relaxation, remission,n.) ; *Also:*
   1. **relent**—become softer in attitude or feelings; become milder (relentment,n.)
   2. **subside**—become less severe, intense, violent, etc. (subsidence,n.)

11. Becoming Reduced in Severity or Intensity,adj. *From Sec. 1:* abating, cooling, diminishing, dulling, easing; lessening, decreasing, or reducing; melting, mitigating, moderating, relaxing, remitting or remittent, slackening or slacking, softening, sweetening, tempering, weakening (remittence or remittency,n.) ; *From Sec. 10:* relenting, subsiding or subsident

12. Not Becoming Reduced in Severity or Intensity,adj. *From Sec. 1:* unabating, undiminishing, unlessening or undecreasing, unmoderating, unrelaxing, unremitting, unslackening or unslacking, unsoftening, untempering, unweakening (unremittingness,n.) ; *From Sec. 10:* unrelenting or relentless, unsubsiding or unsubsided (unrelentingness or relentlessness,n.)

13. One Who Does Not Become Softer or Milder in Attitude or Feelings; One Who Is Relentless; One Who Never Gives In or Gives Up; One Who Cannot Be Softened or Soothed in Feelings or Attitude: unrelentor, n.

14. That Which Relieves Serious Irritation (as in an Area of the Skin or Elsewhere in the Body) by Producing a Slighter Irritation in Some Other Area or Part (Medical); That Which, Figuratively, Acts by a Similar Process, as in Human Relations, etc.: counterirritant,n.

15. So Doing: counterirritant,adj.

16. The Relieving of Inner Conflicts, Psychic Problems, Emotional Tensions, etc., by a Process of Bringing Repressed or Forgotten Material or Incidents to Consciousness and Discussing Them, Working Them Through, Reliving Them, etc., with the Psychoanalyst, Thus Gaining Insight into the Incidents and into One's Own Personality: abreaction; catharsis or katharsis,n. (cathartic, cathartical, or kathartic,adj. catharticalness,n.)

17. The Relieving of Emotions by Means of Art (including Literature, etc.) or the Production of Art: catharsis or katharsis,n. (cathartic, cathartical, or kathartic,adj. catharticalness,n.)

18. A Relief; Relief: reprieve (i.e., temporary relief, as from pain, distress, punishment, etc.); respite; rest (i.e., relief from something disturbing, fatiguing, or annoying); solace; truce (i.e., relief, or temporary relief, from pain, distress, cares, etc.),n.

19. Period of Relief: respite,n.

1143. MILDNESS

1. Mild,adj.
   1. **affable**—mild, or graciously mild, in face, countenance, or bearing

   2. **balmy**—mild and soothing, or mild and refreshing, as wind, weather, climate, etc.
   3. **benign**—mild, as climate, winds, sun, etc.
   4. **benign, benignant**—mild rather than malignant, i.e., not particularly, if at all, harmful, as a tumor or other medical condition
   5. **bland**—mild, i.e., not irritating or stimulating, as food, diet, medicines, climate, air, etc.
   6. **clement**—mild, or mild and pleasant, as weather, climate, etc.; mild, or mild and merciful, as a person or attitude
   7. **delicate**—pleasingly mild, rather than strong or heavy, as an odor, flavor, color, etc.
   8. **favonian**—mild, i.e., like the west wind
   9. **gentle**—mild, rather than severe, harsh, rough, violent, etc.; mild—of winds moving at a rate under 12 miles an hour; tame—of animals
   10. **lenient**—mild, rather than harsh or severe, as in tendency, attitude, spirit, treatment, etc.; clement
   11. **moderate**—mild, as wind, climate, temperature, weather, sun, etc.; mild, rather than severe or harsh, as reactions, treatment, pain, punishment, etc.
   12. **placable**—mild, as temperament or nature
   13. **temperate**—mild, as climate, etc.; mild in climate, as regions, areas, etc.

2. Mildness,n. *From Sec. 1:* affableness or affability, balminess; benignancy (from No. 4) ; blandness, clemency, delicacy or delicateness, gentleness; leniency, lenience, or lenity; moderateness, placableness, temperateness; *Also:* 1. **mansuetude**—mildness

3. Not Mild,adj. *From Sec. 1:* inaffable or unaffable, unbenign, inclement, ungentle, unlenient, immoderate, implacable, intemperate or untemperate (inaffability, unbenignity, inclemency or inclementness, ungentleness, immoderateness or immoderation, implacableness, intemperateness or untemperateness,n.)

4. An Act Showing Mildness and Mercy or Forgiveness: clemency,n.

5. An Act Showing, or Arising from, Mildness of Attitude, Spirit, etc.: lenity or leniency,n.

1144. GENTLENESS

1. Gentle,adj.
   1. **benign**—gentle in nature or temperament; gentle and kind; indicative of gentleness, or of gentleness and kindness
   2. **bland**—gentle, or gentle and pleasant, as a person, disposition, nature, smile, etc.
   3. **favonian**—gentle, i.e., like the west wind
   4. **lenient**—gentle, as in tendency, attitude, spirit, treatment, etc.
   5. **mild**—pleasantly gentle in attitude toward, or treatment of, another, as a person; showing such gentleness, as attitude, manner, behavior, treatment, speech, etc.; gentle in effect, result, force, etc.
   6. **moderate**—gentle, as wind, weather, climate, temperature, sun, etc.
   7. **quiet**—gentle, as manner, speech, etc.
   8. **soft**—gentle, or gentle and musical, in sound; gentle in touch or feel
   9. **tame**—gentle—of animals
   10. **tender**—gentle in touch; gentle, as in treatment of another

2. Gentleness,n. *From Sec. 1:* benignity, blandness; leniency, lenience, or lenity; mildness, moderateness, quietness, softness, tameness, tenderness; *Also:*
   1. **douceur (French)**—gentleness of manner, nature, etc.
   2. **mansuetude**—gentleness; tameness

3. A Gentle, Innocent, and Lovable Person, Child, Girl, Woman, etc.: dove,n.

4. To Make Gentle: sleeken; soften (as in sound, appearance, touch, etc.); tame or gentle (an animal, person, the wind, etc.),v.

5. Able to Be Tamed: tamable,adj. (tamability or tamableness,n.)

6. Unable to Be Tamed: untamable,adj. (untamableness,n.)

7. Not Tamed: untamed,adj. (untamedness, n.)

8. Ungentle; Not Gentle,adj. *From Sec. 1:* unbenign, unlenient, immoderate, untame, untender (unbenignity, immoderateness or immoderacy, untameness, untenderness,n.)

INDEX

A

aardvark,n.
of ~s, 403.11(4)
abacus,n.
user of an ~, 942.14
abandon,v., 236.1
abandoned,adj., 236.6
free, 309.15; 309.15(5,10,14,16, 20,24,27,30–33)
state of being ~, 236.7
abandonment,n., 236.2
freedom, 309.14(1,7,8,11–14, 17,20,21,23,24)
abdicate,v., 236.1(25)
abdication,n., 236.2(1)
abdomen,n., 347.1,5; see also belly,n.
pert. to the cavity of the ~, 347.4
aberration,n., 539.3
sexual ~, 710.31–35
abhor,v., 880.1
ability,n., 7.1; see also skill,n.
area of ~, 7.4
deprive of ~, 13.1(2,5,8)
intelligence and ~, 7.1(62)
lacking in ~, 13.3(2)
natural ~, 7.1(37,39,41,47,62, 66)
physical ~, 7.1(37)
potential ~, 7.1(21,23)
requiring ~, 7.8
show ~, 7.5
varied ~, 7.1(65)
able,adj., 7.2; see also skillful, adj.
make ~, 7.11
~ person, 7.3
abnormal,adj.
contrary to nature, 811.9,10
unusual, 536.4,5; see also un-usual,adj.
mentally ~ person, 1136.11
abode,n., 753.1; see also home, house,n.
aboriginal,adj., 720.18
abortion,n., 714.18
cause the ~ of, 714.21
causes ~, 714.19
causing ~, 714.20
performer of illegal ~, 714.23
undergo ~, 714.22
above,adv.
lying ~, 65.3(16)
abrade,v., 801.25,26
abrasion,n., 801.27–32
abscess,n., 383.2
abscessed,adj., 383.3
absence,n., 42.1
~ from school without per-mission, 42.1(4,10)
~ from work, office, duty, etc., 42.6
habitual ~, 42.1(1)
leave of ~, 42.1(3,5–7,9)
military leave of ~, 42.1(5)
naval leave of ~, 42.1(7)
~ with permission, 42.1(3,5, 6,7,9)
~ without permission, 42.1(2, 4,10)
absent,adj., 42.2
act of being ~, 42.4
~ person, 42.5
be ~, 42.3
while ~, 42.7
absent-minded,adj., 581.1; 1054.39
~ and excited state, 1100.7(10)
~ state, 581.2
absolute,adj.
certain, 641.1,6
complete, 328.1

free of control, 309.15; 309.15(6,14,16,18,20,25,28, 29,30,33,34,38)
unqualified, 309.15(8,25,34) ; 925.15
unrestricted in power, 5.5(6)
~ government, 1073.3(1–3,11, 13,14,22,34)
absolve,v., 897.24
absorb,v., 134.1
ability to ~, 134.3
able to ~, 134.2
~ (liquid or water), 1034.34, 35
tendency to ~, 134.3
absorbed,adj.
become ~, 134.9
absorber,n., 134.8
absorption,n.
causing ~, 1034.35
abstain,v., 74.1–3
absurd,adj., 608.5; 1113.1; see also laughable, nonsensi-cal,adj.
laughable, 1113.1
nonsensical, 608.5
~ act, 52.5(3)
act or behave ~ly, 608.11
~ behavior, 55.3(1)
~ characteristic, 1116.5
improbable and ~ situation, 608.13
~ language, use of, 665.9(24)
treatment that makes ~, 608.15
absurdity,n., 608.6,9; 1113.2
nonsensicality, 608.6,9
display of ~, 608.12
reduction to ~, 608.14
abundance,n., 915.1,2
abundant,adj., 915.4; 919.3
not ~, 917.27,30
abuse,n., 561.9
expose to ~, 561.5
object of ~, 561.6
word of ~, 666.3(20)
wordy ~, 561.2
abuse,v.
~ in words, 561.1
abused,adj.
state of being ~, 561.7
abusive,adj., 561.4
~ in language, 561.9; 1118.15
~ in words, 561.4,9
~ language, 1118.14
~ remark, 1118.16
~ woman, 708.14(2,9,14,15,18, 19,23)
~ word, 561.10
abyss,n., 170.9; 298.9
accent,n.
Irish ~, 670.4(4)
local ~, 670.4(4)
metrical ~, 689.25
southern ~, 670.4(6)
syllable ~, 670.4(1,14)
accept,v., 245.1; see also get, take,v.
bear, 246.1
bitter to ~, that which is, 245.9
~ in a college, 623.10
~ into a club, 245.1(8)
~ on trial in fraternity or sorority, 1122.28,29
ready to ~, 245.8
~ something bitter, 877.7
willing to ~, 245.8
acceptable,adj., 245.5
~ in quality, 831.6
acceptance,n., 245.2
descr. of ~, 245.4
accepted,adj.
generally ~, 245.6
no longer ~, 245.7

that which is ~, 245.3
accident,n., 29.6(2,13,21,40)
accidental,adj., 34.4; 45.14
accompanier,n., 131.3
accompaniment,n., 131.2,5
chaperon's ~, 131.8
involve as necessary ~, 131.7
musical ~, 131.5(4)
accompany,v., 131.1
~ as a result, 16.3(2)
~ as protection, 568.8
~ to a seat, 131.1(3,9)
~ to protect, 131.1(4,5,8)
accompanying,adj., 131.6
~ but less important, 848.38
~ group, 131.4
~ musician, 131.3(1
~ sound, 131.5(4)
~ thing, 131.5
accomplish,v., 49.1
accomplished,adj.
~ fact, 814.1(2)
something already ~, 814.1(2)
accomplishment,n., 49.6
final ~, 792.23(6)
account,n., 613.20,25
report, 613.1,8,17
story, 685.1
accurate,adj., 815.1; see also correct,adj.
correct, 815.1,5
claim to be ~, 812.12
declare ~, 812.12
prove ~, 812.15
accursed,adj., 882.8
accusation,n., 892.2,5
~ against one's accuser, 892.17
~ by a grand jury, 892.10
free from ~ of guilt, etc., 897.29
free of ~, 309.11(3,12,24)
injurious ~, 891.18
involve in an ~, 892.18
make ~s, 892.13
make an ~ in court, 892.7
~ of crime, etc., 892.9,20
wipe out ~ of guilt by atone-ment, 897.23
accusatory,adj., 892.6
accuse,v., 892.1,22,23
~ maliciously, 891.17
~ of crime, etc., 892.8,19
~ of fault, etc., 892.22
~ of lying, 821.12
~ of misconduct, 892.11
~ one's accuser, 892.15,16
~ reproachfully, 892.14
accused,adj.
~ person, 892.21
person ~ in court, 1082.24,25
person ~ of crime or illegal acts, 1088.15
accuser,n., 892.3
pert. to an ~, 892.4
accustom,v., 629.23
accustomed,adj., 535.1,2; 629.24
become ~ to, 629.19,20
make ~, 629.23
achieve,v., 49.1
achievement,n., 49.6
acidity,n.
medication for ~, 398.6(1)
acquaint,v., 613.28
acquaintance,n.
friend, 1096.3; see also friend,n.
knowledge, 611.1
acquire,v., 240.1; see also get,v.
acquit,v., 897.24
acquittal,n., 897.24,29,30
acrobat,n., 103.4
acrobatics,n., 103.1–5
across,adv., 121.9
going ~, 121.8

lying ~, 121.8
act,n., 52.5; see also action,n.
  absurd ~, 52.5(3)
  additional ~, 52.5(13)
  brave ~, 52.5(26,27,37,39,41)
  brilliant ~, 52.5(19)
  careless ~, 52.5(25,30)
  charitable ~, 52.5(10)
  chivalrous ~, 52.5(31)
  considerate ~, 52.5(21)
  contemptuous ~, 52.5(29)
  cruel ~, 52.5(4,5)
  dangerous ~, 52.5(41)
  extreme ~, 922.26
  final ~, 52.5(20)
  foolish ~, 52.5(28)
  formal ~, 52.5(15)
  glorious ~, 52.5(23)
  graceful ~, 52.5(7)
  gracious ~, 52.5(11)
  habitual ~, 52.5(22)
  illegal ~, to overthrow gov-
    ernment, 22.37
  insulting ~, 52.5(18,29)
  involuntary ~, 52.5(36)
  irrational ~, 52.5(14,24)
  kind ~, 52.5(8,9,11,12,17,21);
    842.2
  ~ of strength, 52.5(39)
  pleasing ~, 52.5(2)
  reckless ~, 52.5(25)
  rough ~, 52.5(3)
  savage ~, 4.29
  skillful ~, 7.7; 52.5(27,39,40)
  successful ~, 52.5(19)
  ~ to attract attention,
    52.5(39)
  ~ to avoid danger, 52.5(34)
  ~ to avoid failure, 52.5(34)
  unexpected ~, 52.5(19)
  unprovoked ~, 52.5(1)
  unusual ~, 52.5(27)
  violent ~, 52.5(33)
act,v., 52.1
  ~ absurdly, 52.1(2)
  ~ as, 969.6
  ~ as circumstances dictate,
    52.1(18)
  ~ as time dictates, 52.1(18)
  ~ briskly, 52.1(13)
  cause to ~, 52.9
  cause to ~ faster, 95.8
  excite to ~, 52.9
  ~ (in a theater), 969.5
  ~ in a part, 969.6
  ~ in opposition, 52.1(14)
  inability to ~, 585.10
  influence to ~, 52.9
  ~ noisily, 4.13; 52.1(4,5,15)
  ~ out, 969.6
  ~ rapidly, 95.6
  ~ reciprocally, 52.1(8,14)
  ~ secretly, 971.15
  ~ slower, 100.3–5
  ~ slowly, 100.1.2
  stimulate to ~, 52.9
  tending to ~, 52.3
  ~ together, 51.1
  ~ together illegally, 51.1(4,8)
  ~ together secretly, 51.1(4,7,
    8)
  ~ to influence preceding
    events, 52.1(14)
  ~ toward, 53.1
  ~ violently, 4.4,13
  ~ without control, 52.1(16)
  ~ without preparation,
    48.9(2)
  ~ without seriousness,
    52.1(19)
acting,adj., 52.3
  ~ in a group, 51.3(1)
  ~ properly, 818.7
  ~ suddenly, 52.3(1,2)
  ~ together, 51.2,3

  ~ together illegally, 51.2(3)
  ~ with violence, 4.1
acting,n. 969.2.21
  art of ~, 969.23
  exaggerated ~, 969.22
  pert. to ~, 969.9
  profession of ~, 969.24
action,n., 52.2,5; see also act,n.
  become excited to ~, 52.10
  center of ~, 137.1(11–13,24)
  continuous ~. 754.4
  demanding immediate ~,
    274.4(2,4,5)
  descr. of ~, 52.3
  direction of ~, 179.1(4,5,7,8,
    13–17)
  emotional stimulus to ~,
    1092.10,11
  energy of ~, 2.2
  excite to ~, 52.9
  extent of ~, 787.3
  follow a course of ~, 52.7
  free in ~, 309.15(21)
  freedom of ~, 309.14(22)
  harmful ~. 52.2(3)
  natural instinct, ~ from,
    810.11
  old-fashioned ~, 631.16
  out-of-date ~, 631.16
  place of ~, 782.2
  reciprocal ~, 52.2(2)
  rough ~, 52.2(3) ; 865.3
  rough in ~, 865.1(1)
  scene of ~, 783.4(1,5–7)
  self–~, 52.2(1)
  series of ~s. 173.9(8,14)
  serving to excite ~, 52.14
  space for ~, 787.2
  stimulate to ~, 52.9
  stimulator of ~, 52.13
  stimulus to ~, 52.12
  ~ that represents a change,
    539.15
  ~ that takes advantage,
    836.13
  time allowing for ~, 762.1(6)
  unfair ~, 635.4
  violence of ~, 4.2
  violent ~, 4.3
active,adj., 57.2,4; see also
    lively,adj.
  lively, 752.1
  aggressive and ~, 57.4(13)
  aggressively ~, 57.4(13)
  ~ at night, 778.5
  ~ at twilight, 777.5
  be ~, 57.3
  become ~, 57.7
  become ~ again, 57.7(3,4)
  become less ~, 58.6
  become more ~, 57.7(2)
  becoming less ~, 58.7
  cause to be ~, 52.9(1,8,15,29–
    32)
  graceful and ~, 57.4(10)
  ~ in motion, 57.4(2,6,8–11,14,
    17,19,20,23,24)
  quick and ~, 57.4(3,6,9,10,11,
    14,17,20)
  small and ~, 57.4(7) ; 909.1(3)
  state of being ~, 57.5
  strong and ~, 57.4(22,24)
activity,n., 57.1,5
  an ~, 57.9
  area of ~, 57.6
  be filled with ~, 57.1(3)
  ~ caused by light, 57.1(9)
  center of ~, 57.6(2,3)
  cessation of ~, 58.10
  continuing ~, 57.4(4)
  continuous or continued ~,
    754.5,6
  criminal ~, 1088.4
  decreased ~. spend the sea-
    son in, 770.11(1,2)
  disposition toward ~, 57.8

  filled with ~, 57.1(2)
  illegal ~, 1087.7
  improper ~, 1087.7
  ~ involving research, 57.9(1)
  of a bodily part, 57.1(14)
  place of ~. 782.2
  ~s for advantage or success,
    57.10
  speed, ~ combined with,
    57.5(1)
  stimulate to ~, 52.9
  suspension of ~, 58.11
  tendency toward ~, 57.8
  unimportant ~, 57.1(8)
  useless ~, 57.1(13)
actor,n. 969.3
  choose ~s, 969.47
  chosen ~s, 969.48
  comic ~, 969.3(1,8)
  crowd, ~ as member of,
    969.3(3,9)
  experienced ~, 969.3(10)
  group of ~s. 969.15
  group of ~s in Greek or
    Roman tragedy, 969.15(1)
  group of traveling ~s,
    969.15(4)
  leading ~, 969.1(4,6,7)
  motion-picture ~, 969.3(3)
  pantomime ~, 102.3(1)
  pert. to an ~, 969.9
  profession of ~, 969.24
  substitute ~, 324.4(16) ;
    969.3(11)
  travel as ~s, 969.17
  traveling ~, 969.3(10) ; 969.18
  ~ who delivers prologue,
    969.35
  wishing to become an ~,
    969.12
actress,n., 969.4
  burlesque ~ who strips,
    984.13
  decorative ~, 969.4(3)
  leading ~, 969.4(2)
  ~ taking flirtatious parts,
    969.4(4)
  ~ taking young parts,
    969.4(1)
  ~ who undresses publicly,
    984.13
  young ~, 969.4(5)
actual,adj., 807.1,4; see real,adj.
actuality,n., 807.1.2,4,5; see
    reality,n.
  in ~, 807.8
Adam,n.
  existing before ~, 759.1(14)
  one who lived before ~, 759.8
Adam and Eve,n.
  original home of ~, 984.34(8)
adapt,v., 539.1(1–3,50,51,53)
  ~ to social needs, 539.1(50)
adaptation,n., 539.3
add,v., 908.1,35
  ~ amounts, 908.35
  ~ as a syllable at the begin-
    ning of a word, 908.7
  ~ at the beginning, 908.7
  ~ at the end, 908.15
  ~ by mixing in, 908.32
  ~ finishing touches to, 908.11
  ~ in addition, 908.9
  ~ land, territory, etc., 908.28
  ~ numbers, 908.35
  serving to ~, 908.43
  ~ (something), 908.1
  ~ syllable at the end of a
    word, 908.17
  ~ to (something) to make
    enough, 908.12
  ~ to in speech, 908.10
  ~ unnecessary thing, etc.,
    908.9
  ~ up to, 908.36
added,adj., 908.40

able to be ~, 908.44
amount ~, 914.1(9)
be ~, 908.42
~ from the outside, 908.41
~ to make enough, 908.13
addiction,n.
~ to liquor, 749.41–45
~ to narcotics, 399.12
addition,n., 908.2
allowing ~, 908.42
an ~, 908.3,4
~ at the beginning of a word, 908.8
~ at the end, 908.16
~ by growth or increase, 908.4
~ by mixing, 908.33
~ by scientific discovery, 908.27
come as an ~, 908.45
coming as an ~, 908.46
disfiguring ~, 908.5
number in ~, 908.38; 927.1(2, 3,28)
number resulting from ~, 927.1(28)
numbers in ~, 908.39
~ of land, 908.29
~ of land, favorer of, 908.30
of the nature of ~, 908.42
resulting from ~, 908.42
strengthen by ~, 1.29(13)
~ stretching out from main part, 908.6
~ to a book, 908.22,23
~ to a document, 908.21,23,25
~ to a magazine, 908.24
~ to a mixture, 908.34
~ to a newspaper, 908.24
~ to a treaty, 908.21
~ to a will, 908.25
~ to knowledge, 908.27
~ to make enough, 908.14
~ to property, 908.26
additional,adj., 908.40
~ act, 52.5(13)
come as ~, 908.45
coming as ~, 908.46
address,n., style of ~, 699.2(2,7)
address,v.
talk to, 671.8
adequate,adj., 919.1
adhere,v., 302.16
adhesive,adj., 302.18
adhesive,n., 302.14
adjacent,adj., 790.17
adjoin,v., 790.20,21
adjoining,adj., 790.17
adjourn,v., 768.8; see also delay,v.
adjournment,n., 768.9; see also delay,n.
~ without decision when to meet again, 768.13
administer,v., 8.14
administrative,adj., 8.17
administrator,n., 8.16
admirable,adj., 855.8
excellent, 831.1
admiration,n., 855.2
affected with ~, 855.5
causing ~, 855.11
excite ~ in, 855.10
indication of ~, 855.9
object of ~, 855.7
place that causes ~, 782.1(36)
self-~, 855.6
worthy of ~, 855.8
admire,v., 855.1
admirer,n., 855.3
devoted ~, 657.4(3)
loyal ~, 658.3(2)
admiring,adj., 855.4
admission,n.
entrance, 133.2,9
descr. of ~, 675.3

implying an ~, 675.4
~ of belief or faith, 675.2(2)
~ of guilt, 884.24
~ of sin, 884.24
~ of truth, 675.2
pert. to ~, 675.3
admit,v.
~ about oneself, 675.1(11)
~ as genuine, 675.1(2)
~ as lost, 675.1(13)
~ as true, 675.1
~ authorship of, 675.1(2)
~ for argument, 675.1(10)
~ guilt, 675.1(2,8,9); 884.23
~ openly, 675.1(10)
~ ownership of, 675.1(2)
~ sin, 884.23
admittance,n.
entrance, 133.9
gives ~, that which, 133.10
adopt,v., 245.1; 247.1; see accept, take,v.
adult,adj., 732.1; see mature, adj.
adulterant,n., 839.22
adulterate,v., 805.1(1); 839.21; 883.16; 905.1
make impure, 905.1
spoil, 805.1(1)
adulterated,adj., 883.14; 905.3
adulteration,n., 839.21; 883.12; 905.1,3
pert. to ~, 905.4
resulting from ~, 905.4
adultery,n., 710.1(4,6,10)
commit ~, 710.2(4)
committer of ~, 710.3
committing ~, 710.4
man whose wife commits ~, 710.5
symbol of ~, 710.10
adulthood,n., 731.9(4,12,13,15, 16); see also maturity,n.
period preceding ~, 731.9(1)
advance,n., 174.2
line of ~, 174.4
advance,v., 174.1
~ suddenly to attack, 560.5,6
advantage,n., 831.13; 836.1
action that takes ~, 836.13
activities followed to gain ~, 57.10
come by way of ~, 836.4
condition of ~, 836.7
conducive to ~, 836.6
gain an ~ over, 833.17
~ gained from position or condition, 836.8
give ~ to, 833.7
looking for ~, 836.14
Northerner who took ~, 836.15
person used for one's ~, 279.15
position of ~, 836.7; 1042.17
regard for ~, 836.12
take ~ of, 836.9,10
taking ~, practice of, 836.12
~ that belongs to an office, 256.3(1)
thing used for one's ~, 279.16
unfair ~, taking, 836.11
use to one's own ~ only, 279.1(10)
advantageous,adj., 831.11; 836.2,6
be ~ to, 836.3
advertisement,n.
~ in a magazine or newspaper, 972.4(22)
~ of praise, 851.5
advertising,n.
booklet for purposes of ~, 687.1(8)

word or phrase in ~, 666.3(43); 666.6
advice,n., 278.3
give ~, 278.1(4,6)
~ on moral behavior, 843.13, 15
tedious ~ on moral behavior, 843.14
too ready to offer ~, 237.4
advise,v., 278.1
~ against, 278.1(2,3)
~ moral actions, 278.1(7)
adviser,n., 278.5
legal ~, 278.5(4,5); 1085.14,15
wise old ~, 278.5(7)
advising,n., 278.2
advisory,adj., 278.4
member of ~ group, 278.5(2,3, 5)
aeon,n., 769.4
affect,v., 9.1
~ emotionally, 1099.1,12
~ with (an emotion), 1099.22
affected,adj.
unnatural, 811.1
emotionally ~, 1099.3,15,16
not ~, 810.1
affecting,adj.
emotionally ~, 1099.2,13
affection,n.
liking, 1109.3; see liking,n.
love, 700.1; see love,n.
cause to appeal to one's ~s, 700.17,18
expressive of ~, 700.22
feel ~, 700.3
for specific things, places, people, etc., 700.30–32
affectionate,adj., 700.2,21,22
~ term, word, or action, 700.19
treat ~ly, 700.4
affirmative,adj., 541.4; see also yes,n.
be ~, 541.1
gesture ~ly, 102.1(6); 541.1(8)
Afghanistan,n.
ruler of ~, 1073.36(2)
afraid,adj., 576.1; see frightened,adj.
be ~, 576.3; see fear,v.
Africa,n., 784.9(7)
Dutch dialect of South ~, 664.4(1)
African,n.
South ~, 784.15(2)
afterbirth,n., 287.3(4)
afternoon,n., 775.9
middle of the ~, 775.11
pert. to the ~, 775.10
again,adv., 674.29
against,adv., 544.3; see opposed,adj., opposition,n.
age,n.
period, 769.1,4
ancient ~s, 769.9(1–3,5,6,9–12, 14)
caused by old ~, 759.15
depraved ~ of the world, 769.9(4,6)
ignorant ~ of the world, 769.9(4)
mankind, ~s of, 769.9
middle ~, 759.2(2,6)
Middle ~s, 769.9(4,7,13)
not showing signs of ~, 759.12
old ~, 759.2
~ over twenty-one, 758.1(2)
person as to ~, 758.2
person's ~, 758.1
pert. to old ~, 759.14
same in ~, 758.3,4
science or study of old ~, 759.25
Stone ~, 769.9(3,5,9,10,12)
~ under twenty-one, 758.1(3)

aged,adj., 759.1; see old,adj.
agile,adj.
  fast in movement, 94.3,8
  smooth of movement, 90.3
agitate,v.
  ~ emotionally or mentally,
    1132.1
agitation,n.
  excitement, 1100.7
  emotional or mental~, 1132.5;
    see disturbance,n.
agnosticism,n., 654.12(9)
agree,v., 541.1,10,17
  cause to ~, 541.21–24
  one who ~s, 541.3
  refuses to ~, one who, 542.8
  ~ to buy, 695.9
  ~ to pay, 695.9
  willing to ~, 541.5
  ~ with and approve of, 850.8
agreeable,adj.
  in agreement, 541.19
  pleasing, 1106.3; see pleas-
    ant,adj.
  showing agreement, 541.4
  make ~ or harmonious,
    541.28–31
agreeing,adj., 541.4,14,19
agreement,n., 541.2,11,13,18,20
  ~ among many, 541.6
  an ~, 541.13
  arranged by ~, 541.25
  bring into ~ or harmony,
    541.28–31
  cause ~ among or between,
    541.21–24
  come to an ~, 541.10–12
  descr. of an ~, 541.15
  done by ~, 541.7
  feel ~ with, 541.9
  give ~, 541.1
  giving ~, 541.2,4
  in ~, 541.4,14,19
  lack of ~, 541.1; see disagree-
    ment, dispute,n.
  make an ~, 541.10–12
  ~ of sounds, 541.20
  show ~, 541.1
  showing ~, 541.2,4
  try to cause ~ among or be-
    tween, 541.26,27
  try to come to an ~, 541.16
  unable to be brought into ~,
    542.5,7
agricultural,adj., 998.5
  ~ products, 745.21
agriculture,n., 998.1; see farm-
    ing,n.
ague,n.
  recurring ~, 1063.3
ahead,adv.
  move ~, 174.1–3
aid,n, 556.2; see help,n.
aid,v., 556.1; see help,v.
ailment,n., 389.1; see disease,
    illness,n.
aim,v.
  point or direct, 567.1–8
air,n., 1045.1
  able to live in ~, 1049.9
  blown-out ~, 1045.2
  carried by ~, 1045.14(3)
  carrying ~, 1045.14(2)
  change by exposure to ~,
    1046.7
  changed by exposure to ~,
    1046.8
  collect particles from the ~,
    instr. to, 1045.21(2)
  consisting of ~, 1045.14(6)
  containing ~, 1045.14(7)
  convert into ~, 1045.19
  current of ~, 1045.1(1,3–6,8,9)
  duct for ~, 1050.29
  escape of ~, duct for, 1050.29
  expose to ~, 1042.12; 1045.7

fear of ~, 1045.22
full of ~, 1045.14(6)
gulping in of ~, 1045.23
illness from ~ travel, 1045.24
inflated with ~, 1045.14(7)
lack of ~, requiring, 1049.12
let ~ in or through, 1045.7
light as ~, 949.1(1,2,4)
like ~, 1045.18
like ~, make, 1045.19
living or growing in the ~,
  1045.14(1)
measurement of ~, device
  for, 1045.21
microorganism living in ~,
  1049.10
movement of ~, 1031.1(4,5,
  11)
moving ~, 1045.1(1,3–6,8,9)
navigation in ~ above sea,
  1029.72(2)
odor carried on ~, 1045.5
open–~, 1045.13
open to ~, 1045.6,7
operating by ~, 1045.14(7)
out in the ~, 1045.10,11
out in the ~ at night, 1045.12
pert. to the ~, 1045.14(1,7)
protect against ~, 1045.15
protected against ~, 1043.28;
  1045.14(4)
relating to water and ~,
  1026.23(3)
requiring ~, 1049.9
rush of ~, 1045.3
safe in the ~, 1045.14(5)
science of ~, 1045.20
sound carried on ~, 1045.4
sounds of ~, 461.1–6
tight against ~, 1043.28;
  1045.14(4); 1045.15
upward ~ current, descr. of,
  1042.9
without ~, 1045.26
without ~, able to live or be
  active, 1049.12
without fresh ~, 1045.25
aircraft,n., 98.1
  flier of or in ~, 98.2
  pert. to ~, 98.3
  shed for ~, 98.5
airplane,n., 98.1; see also air-
    craft,n.
  control an ~, 8.1(19)
  ~ flying in stratosphere,
    1046.15
  motion of ~ out of control,
    167.2(8)
  pert. to flight in ~, 97.7(2)
  science of handling ~, 97.8
  tricks, etc., by an ~, 97.7(1);
    97.9
airport,n., 98.4
aisle,n., 122.1
  arranged like church ~s,
    311.4(3)
alabaster,n.
  like ~, 1008.2
Alaska,n., 784.9(19)
alchemy,n.
  practitioner of ~, 1013.25
  preparation used in ~,
    1013.28
  secret sought by ~, 971.23(1)
  substance sought in ~,
    1013.27
alcohol,n., 749.9
  liquor, 749.1; see liquor
    (alcoholic),n.
  kinds of ~, 749.10
  measurement of ~, device
    for, 749.14
  pert. to ~, 749.15
  preparation made with ~,
    749.11
  treat with ~, 749.16

unit of strength of ~, 749.13
alcoholic,adj., 749.15
  addicted to liquor, 749.42
  ~ drink, 748.15; 749.1–7; see
    also liquor (alcoholic),n.
  ~ quality, 749.12
  ~ strength, 749.12
alcoholic,n.
  alcoholic person, 749.43
  group of former ~s, 749.69
alcoholism,n., 749.41
alder,n.
  of the ~ family, 996.25
alderman,n., 1080.22–25
ale,n., 749.6(10); 749.7; see also
    beer,n.
alga,n., 985.6(10,11,39)
  science of ~, 985.36(3)
algebra,n.
  branch of ~, 942.1(7)
  expression in ~, 943.4
Algiers,n.
  ruler of ~, 1073.36(8)
alike,adj., 529.1; see also same,
    similar,n.
alive,adj., 750.3; see also liv-
    ing,adj.
  ability to stay ~, 750.13
  able to stay ~, 750.12
  be ~, 750.1
  being ~, 750.2
  born ~, 720.9(14)
  come ~, 751.19–21
  make ~, 751.16
  make ~ again, 751.17,18
  no longer ~ (of a business,
    periodical, etc.), 794.44
  no longer ~ (of a race,
    species, etc.), 794.45
  one who is ~, 750.4
  remain ~, 750.1
  something ~, 750.4
alkali,n.
  like an ~, 1011.15–17
alkaline,adj., 1011.17
  become ~, 1011.19
  ~ condition, 1011.20
  make ~, 1011.18
  slightly ~, 1011.16
all-inclusive,adj., 259.3,4
  ~ in sympathies, 259.5
allegory,n., 685.1; see also
    story,n.
  ~ on animals, 685.1(3,9)
allergy,n., 389.9–11
  pollen ~, 363.20(3)
alley,n., 122.1
alligator,n.
  characteristic of the ~,
    425.3
  descr. of the ~, 425.2
  pert. to the ~, 425.2
  resembling the ~, 425.3
allow,v., 554.1; see permit,v.
allude,v.
  ~ to, 673.1
allusion,n., 673.1,4
  derogatory ~, 673.3
almond,n.
  ~-shaped, 507.17(7)
almost,adv., 919.9
alone,adj., 330.1
  ~ and without money,
    330.1(2,30)
  cause to be ~, 330.3,4
  condition of being ~, 330.2
  doing ~, 330.1(26,27,33,34)
  kept ~, 330.1(12–14,20,22–24,
    36)
  leave ~, 330.3,4
  left ~, 330.1(1,3,6–10,19)
  life ~, 330.8
  living ~, 330.1(21)
  one left ~, 330.5
  one who is ~, 330.5
  one who lives ~, 330.7

place of living ~, 330.10
preferring to be ~, 330.6
unhappy at being ~, 330.1(9, 14,16,17,18,28,29)
aloneness,n., 330.2
along,adv.
get ~, 750.16
alphabet,n., 679.4
change to a different ~, 679.18
Egyptian ~, stone that helped decipher, 679.15
English ~, pert. to, 679.14
express by an ~, 679.12
expressed by an ~, 679.11
French ~, pert. to, 679.14
Slavic ~, pert. to, 679.13
alphabetic,adj., 679.10,11
put in ~ order, 679.9
Alps,n.
beyond the ~, 166.4(6)
other side of the ~, 166.4(4,5)
other side of the ~, inhabitant of, 166.5
alter,v., 539.1,2; see change,v.
altitude,n., 164.2; see height,n.
amaze,v., 271.2
amazed,adj., 271.4
amazing,adj., 271.1
ambassador,n., 523.6
~ and staff, 523.7
office of the ~, 523.9
residence of the ~, 523.9
ambiguity,n., 607.12-14
ambiguous,adj., 593.16
~ answer, 626.1(3)
~ in meaning, 607.11
talk ~ly, 671.1(32,44,73)
use ~ language, 603.9
~ use of words, 607.13,14
~ statement, 674.9(31)
~ word or expression, 607.12
ambition,n., 265.2,20
ambitious,adj., 265.3,19; 274.4
ambush,n., 244.3
ambush,v., 244.1
amends,n.
make ~ for, 845.20,22; see also make up for,v.
America,n.
inhabitant of arctic ~, 784.15(19)
pert. to arctic ~, 784.16
American,adj.
~ characteristic, 1091.24(1)
make ~, 784.10(1)
ammunition,n.
~ chest, 261.1(8)
storage place for ~, 262.3(18)
amnesia,n., 628.1(4)
amoral,adj., 818.15
amount,n., 914.1
added ~, 917.7
~ added, 914.1(9)
~ available, 914.1(15)
be too large in ~, 916.25,27
enough in ~, 916.13
excess ~, 920.6
excessive ~, 916.3,26; 921.5
excessive in ~, 921.1(2,3,13)
exist in large ~s, 916.17,24
full ~, 914.1(4)
greater ~, 914.1(3)
have large ~s of, 916.19
have large ~s of (undesirables), 916.23
having large ~s of, 916.20
inadequate ~, 919.12
~ kept for future, 914.1(1)
~ lacking, 919.15
large ~, 916; 916.1,2,4
large in ~, 916.12,14,15,16
largest possible ~, 916.8
~ less than half, 914.1(11)
measurement of ~, 946.50
~ more than half, 914.1(10)

~ of contribution, small, 917.10
~ of decrease, 914.1(6)
~ of different things, 914.1(16)
~ of drink, small, 917.8
~ of increase, 914.1(9)
~ of loss, 914.1(6)
~ of money, small, 917.9
~ of waste, 914.1(6)
~ per head, person, or unit, 914.6
pert. to ~, 914.3
scattered ~, 917.3
slight ~, 917.1,3
small ~, 917; 917.1,3,6,16,17
small ~ added to a mixture, 908.34
small ~ cut off, 917.4
small in ~, 917.19,21,22,23,24
small ~ in drops, 918.7
smaller ~, 917.12
smaller in ~, 917.26
smallest ~, 917.13,14
smallest in ~, 917.25
smallness of ~, 917.20
spring up in large ~, 916.18
sufficient ~, 919.2
~ that completes, 914.1(4)
~ that is enough, 919.2
~ to which numbers add up, 908.37
total ~, 914.4
amount,v.
~ to, 914.7
amphibian,n., 424.1
science of ~s, 403.26(1)
ample,adj., 919.3
amuse,v., 200.1; 1111.23
~ oneself, 200.7
amused,adj., 1111.25
amusement,n., 200.2,4,5; see also entertainment,n.
building for ~s, 727.12(4)
place for ~, 782.1(26)
place of ~, 200.9
room for ~s, 787.7(12)
~s, 200.6
spend (time) in ~, 200.8
traveling ~ devices, 200.10
amusing,adj., 200.3; 1111.24; see also laughable,adj.
analgesia,n., 1137.39,41,42
anatomy,n., 338.10
animal ~, 338.10(7)
bird ~, 338.10(5)
fish ~, 338.10(4)
horse ~, 338.10(3)
human ~, 338.10(1)
regional ~, 338.10(6)
reptile ~, 338.10(2)
ancestor,n., 723.8; see also descendant,n.
animal's ~, 723.8(9,10)
biological ~, 723.8(2,9)
horse's ~, 723.8(10)
pert. to ~s, 723.2,9
pert. to an ~, 722.7(1); 723.2,9
ancestral,adj., 723.2,9
biological ~ form, 723.8(9)
reappearance of ~ characteristics, 723.10,11
ancestry,n., 723.1; see also descent,n.
animal ~, 723.7
animals of common ~, 719.8
distinguished ~, 723.3
of mixed ~, 728.15(3)
pert. to ~, 723.2,9
study of ~, 723.12
study one's ~, 723.13,14
anchor,n.
put a ship at ~, 323.1(5)
anchor,v.
~ a ship, 302.28(32)
fee for ~ing, 1033.16

place to ~ a ship, 1033.9
ancient,adj., 759.1; see also old,adj.
science of ~ times, 759.26
student of ~ times, 759.27
~ times, 769.9(1-3,5,6,9-12,14)
and,n.
symbol for ~, 679.1(1)
anecdote,n.
collection of ~s, 682.19(1,6)
anesthesia,n., 435.1; 1137.39-43
partial ~, 435.1(27)
anesthetic,n., 435.5
administers ~s, one who, 401.2(6)
anesthetize,v., 435.2; 1137.38
angel,n., 655.1,3,4
chief ~, 655.2
like an ~, 655.6
pert. to ~s, 655.5
anger,n., 878.11
answer in ~, 878.6(19)
arouse to ~, 878.1
banish the ~ of, 878.20
cause to turn red with ~, 878.4
cause (~) to become sharper or more bitter, 878.5
causing ~, 878.3
disposed to ~, 878.18
~ disposing to hostile acts, 878.11(1)
expression of ~, 878.9
extreme ~, 878.11(7)
extreme in ~, 922.8
feel ~, 878.6(16,17,24)
feel ~ over insult, hurt, etc., 878.6(17,20)
feeling of ~ and offense, 868.5(1)
fit of ~, 560.24(4,5,16,17,23); 878.12
fit of silent ~, 878.13
look of ~, 878.7
make sounds of ~, 878.6(12, 20,21)
mood of ~, 878.12,15
~ over insult, hurt, etc., 878.11(1,4,5,6,9)
person disposed to ~, 878.17
prone to ~, 878.18
reduce the ~ of, 878.20
say in ~, 878.6(1,12,19,20,21, 22)
show ~, 878.6; 951.23
show (suppressed) ~, 951.22
show ~ by gesture, 878.6(4,7, 8,10,13,15,18,20)
show of ~, 878.8
showing ~, 878.10
slight ~, 878.2
sounds of ~, 468.1(7,13,19)
stare in ~, 878.6(10)
strengthen (~), 1092.61
talk in ~, 671.1(4,10,40,41,57, 78,109); 878.6(1,12,19,20)
weak ~, 878.11(3)
anger,v., 878.1,6
angered,adj., 878.2
easily ~, 878.18; 1099.18
person easily ~, 878.17
angering,adj., 878.3
angle,n., 944.1
90° ~, descr. of, 944.7
180° ~, 944.15
bent at an ~, 152.5(4,5)
eight ~d, 944.5(6)
equal ~d, 944.6
five ~d, 944.5(7)
four ~d, 944.5(8)
having ~s, 944.3,4,5
having equal ~s, 534.9
less than 90° ~, 944.13
mathematics of ~s and sides, 943.1(9)
measurement of ~s, 944.18

measurement of ~s of the head, 944.19
measuring ~s, device for, 944.20
more than 180° ~, 944.16
more than 90° ~, 944.14
not forming an ~, 944.17
not 90° ~, 944.12
outside ~ of building or wall, 944.2
right ~s, meeting at, 944.10
right ~s, pert. to, 944.11
right ~d, 944.8,9
seven ~d, 944.5(4)
six ~d, 944.5(5)
ten ~d, 944.5(2)
three ~d, 944.5(9)
twelve ~d, 944.5(3)
two ~d, 944.5(1)
angry,adj., 878.10
~ and bitter, 877.1(1); 878.10(1)
~ and silent person, 878.16
be ~, 878.6
be extremely ~, 878.6(2,6,9,16, 22)
be silently ~, 878.6(11,15,23)
become ~, 878.6
becoming ~, 878.19
bitterly ~, 878.10(1)
feel ~, 878.6(16,17,24)
feel ~ over insult, hurt, etc., 878.6(17,20)
insanely ~, 878.10(3)
look ~, 484.1(10,12,16,36); 878.6(8,10,13,15,18); 878.7
looking ~, 484.4(1)
make ~, 878.1
make less ~, 878.20
~ over injustice, insult, or hurt, 878.10(4,7,8)
silently ~, 878.10(2,5)
angular,adj.
~ shape, 507.1(1)
animal,adj.
both ~ and human in form, 662.28
disgusting ~ life, 881.9
like an ~ in emotions, 1097.7–10
animal,n., 403–28
allegory on ~s, 685.1(3,9)
anatomy of ~s, 338.10(7)
~ as to feet, 346.13
become like an ~, 429.14
big ~, 906.18
biological category of ~s, 318.8
breed ~s, 719.1,3–10
breeding ~s, 403.4(4)
breeding of ~s, 403.30
building for domestic ~s, 403.22(4,10,11,39)
chewing ~, 735.14
confine ~s in a place, 403.23
covering of ~, 972.4(15,21,24)
description of ~s, 403.29
domesticated ~s, 403.4(1,3)
enclosure for ~s, 300.7(3–5,7, 8,10,11); 403.22(9,14,21,29–32,34,40,43)
exhibition of ~s, 951.3(4,7)
fattened ~, 403.7(5)
fondness for ~s, 700.30(23, 28); 700.31,32
forest ~, 996.43
gnawing ~, 735.5
god of ~s in flocks, 662.26(9)
god of wild ~s, 662.26(9)
ground ~, 1003.3(1)
group of ~s, 403.5
group of newborn ~s, 403.5(44)
group of three ~s, 932.7
hornless ~, 403.7(11)
horrible ~, 403.7(7,8)

hunted ~s, 403.4(2); 486.7
~ in a zoo, 301.5(2)
infested with ~s, 403.18–20
land and water ~, 1026.24,25
large and strong ~, 403.7(3,7)
~ life, 403.1
like an ~, 403.8,9
like an ~ in form, 507.17(78)
live in ~ quarters, 403.25
~ living on water's edge, 1026.26
living quarters of ~s, 403.22
lost ~, 264.8(1,2)
make ~-like, 429.13
male ~, 707.1
marine ~s, 422–23
medical treatment of ~s, 401.1(102,108)
mythical ~s, 662.24–29
~ nature of a human, 429.15
neither ~ nor vegetable, 1008.7
newborn ~s, 403.14–17
non-typical ~, 403.7(12,13)
of ~s as to category, 403.6,11
of ~s as to habitat, 403.10
of crossbred ~s, 403.6(9,12,18)
of four-footed ~s, 403.6(3,24)
of hoofed ~s, 403.11(13,14,16)
of many-footed ~s, 403.6(22)
~ of mixed breed, 719.5
of one-footed ~s, 403.6(19)
~ of pure breed, 719.5(2,3)
~ of stunted growth, 909.4(1, 5,7)
of two-footed ~s, 403.6(4)
pet ~, 403.7(4)
place for ~s, 403.22
place of exhibition of ~s, 951.28(2,4,9)
playful ~, 199.5
powerful ~, 906.18(1)
prematurely born ~, 403.14
~ produced by breeding, 719.5
protection of ~s, place for, 1003.2(31)
~ raised as a pet, 403.31
~s of common ancestry, 719.8
savage, like an ~, 4.26
science of ~ classification, 985.36(23)
science of ~ life of lakes, 985.36(12)
science of ~s, 403.26; 985.36(4–9,12,15,23)
science of ~s, pert. to, 403.28
small ~, 909.4
small and unimportant ~, 403.7(15)
sounds of ~s, 456.1–3; see also sound,n.
student of ~s, 403.27; 985.38
stuffing ~s, art of, 403.30(7)
~ subsisting on specific foods, 734.28–31
~ that will eat a human, 734.30
treatise on ~ life, 403.2
underwater ~, 1026.36
water ~, 422.1–7; 423.1–10
wild ~, 403.7(16)
~ with a cut tail, 911.11
~ with naked feet, 984.23
~ without coloring, 403.7(1)
worker with ~s, 205.1
world of ~s, 403.3
world, ~ found all over the, 1004.34,35
worship of ~s, 656.15(28)
year-old ~, 403.7(17)
animalcule,n., 403.21
animated,adj., 752.1; see lively, adj.
animation,n., 752.2; see liveliness,n.
suspended ~, 794.24–26
ankle,n., 345.24

~bone, 345.25
covering for the ~, 979.20
anniversary,n., 781.13
announce,v., 613.1,12
announcement,n., 613.2,4,13,14
an ~, 613.14
pert. to ~, 613.7,16
put an ~ on, 997.10
tentative ~, 19.1(15)
announcer,n., 613.5,15
court ~, 613.15(1)
~ of guests' names, 694.17
announcing,adj., 613.6,16
annoy,v., 874.1
~ by attacks, 874.1(2,6,7,25)
~ by complaints, 874.1(14)
~ by jests, 874.1(23)
~ by physical contact, 874.1(13)
~ by questions, requests, etc., 874.1(8,10,12,14,18,23)
~ by repeated attacks, 874.1(2,6,7,25)
~ by words, 874.1(2,8,9,15)
continue to ~, 874.7,8
~ in great numbers, 874.1(11, 19)
~ in petty ways, 874.1(2,17)
~ (of dogs or other animals), 874.1(25)
one who ~s, 874.5
set dogs on to ~, 874.1(2)
annoyable,adj., 874.10
~ person, 874.11
annoyance,n., 874.2,3,5
act of ~, 874.2
an ~, 874.5
cranky ~, 874.3(2)
facial expression of ~, 365.2(4–6,8–10)
feeling of ~ and offense, 868.5(2)
gesture in ~, 102.1(10)
show ~, 874.13
show ~ by contracting brows, 874.14
source of ~, 874.1
state of ~, 874.3
annoyed,adj., 874.6
be ~, 874.12
become ~, 874.12
easily ~, 874.10
person who is easily ~, 874.10
annoyer,n., 874.5
annoying,adj., 874.4
continue to be ~, 874.8
~ demands, requests, etc., 874.9
~ person, 874.5
annual,adj., 781.8
anoint,v., 438.2(6)
anonymous,adj., 694.18; see nameless,adj.
answer,n., 626.1,3
accusing ~, 626.1(8)
affirmative ~, 626.1(12)
ambiguous ~, 626.1(3); 626.7
angry ~, 626.1(8,10)
authoritative ~, 626.1(3)
call on for an ~, 625.1(2)
clever ~, 626.1(5,10,11)
divine ~, 626.1(3); 626.7
humorous ~, 1115.7(8)
negative ~, 626.1(2)
pert. to an ~, 626.6
quick ~, 626.1(10)
reflected ~, 626.1(1)
retaliatory ~, 626.1(8,10)
search for ~s, 625.13
sharp ~, 626.1(8,10)
sharp in ~, 626.8
use of torture to force ~s, 625.14
wise ~, 626.1(3)
witty ~, 1115.7(8)
answer,v., 626.2

~ in anger, 878.6(19)
answerer,n., 626.4
answering,adj., 626.5
  ~ aloud and all together,
    626.9
answering,n., 626.3
  pert. to ~, 626.6
ant,n., 428.3; 428.3(5)
  be infested with ~s, 403.20(1)
  eating ~s, 734.27(19)
  group of ~s, 403.5(12)
  imaginary sensation of crawl-
    ing ~s, 434.1(4)
  like an ~, 428.2
  nest of an ~, 403.22(16)
  of ~s, 428.1(7)
  science of ~s, 403.26(27)
anteater,n.
  of ~s, 403.11(4)
antelope,n., 410.8
  of ~s, 403.11(2,12)
anthology,n., 682.19
anthropomorphism,n., 429.12
antidote,n., 800.24
  science of ~s, 800.26
  serving as an ~, 800.25
antique,adj., 759.1; see old,adj.
antique,n., 759.4,7
  admirer of ~s, 759.6
  collector of ~s, 759.6
  ~s, 759.5
  science or study of ~s,
    759.26(1–4,6)
  student of ~s, 759.27
antiquity,n.
  periods of ~, 769.9(1–3,5,6,9–
    12,14)
  science or study of ~, 759.26
  student of ~, 759.27
antler,n.
  point of an ~, 335.1(20)
anus,n.
  dilatation of viens at the ~,
    347.12(6)
  tubal passage from mouth to
    ~, 347.11
anxiety,n., 1131.9; see also ner-
    vousness,n.
  ~ about the hair, 369.22
  cause ~ in, 1131.1
  cause or source of ~, 1131.3
  causes of ~, 1131.5
  causing ~, 1131.2
  excessive ~, 1131.11
  feelings of ~, 1131.10
  foresee with ~, 772.13
  freedom from ~, 1131.18
  reduce ~ of, 1131.16,17
  showing ~, 1131.14
  thoughts that cause ~, 1131.4
anxious,adj., 1131.8; see also
    nervous,adj.
  be ~, 1131.6
  not ~, 1131.15
  ~ person, 1131.7
  tending to be ~, 1131.12
apart,adv.
  able to be torn ~, 337.9
  break ~, 802.1(1,10,11); 802.21,
    23; see also break, burst,
    explode,v.
  come ~, 325.2
  cut ~, 332.1(8,9,18,44,63); see
    also cut,v.
  held ~, 330.1(12–14,20,22–24,
    36)
  not tell ~, 605.10
  pull ~, 193.18(17,19)
  push ~, 197.1(4)
  set ~, 325.12
  set ~ by special differences,
    540.20,21
  take ~, 325.1
  tear ~, 337.1(4,5,11,13,15,17)
  tell ~, unable to, 540.19
apartment,n., 753.1(3,19,38,48);

see also home, house,
    room,n.
ape,n., 420.1,3
  group of ~s, 403.5(62)
  like an ~, 420.7
  pert. to ~s, 420.2,4,7
  science of ~s, 403.26(2)
aphid,n., 428.3
  of ~s, 428.1(11)
apologetic,adj., 898.11
apology,n.
  formal ~, 898.9
  full ~, 898.10
  full of ~, 898.11
  humble and formal ~, 898.9
apoplexy,n.
  attack of ~, 560.25
apothecaries' weight,n.
  unit of ~, 947.32,33
apparatus,n., 280.1,6; see
    equipment,n.
apparent,adj., 504.8
  evident, 598.13
  concerned with what is ~,
    598.15
  ~ without proof, 598.14
appear,v.
  be visible or seen, 483.3–6
  act of ~ing, 483.4
  ~ again, 483.3(8,9)
  ~ and vanish, 483.3(10)
  ~ in bodily form, 483.3(6)
  ~ repeatedly, 483.3(9)
  ~ to be, 504.9
appearance,n., 504.1
  change in ~, 504.5,6
  conceited about his ~, man
    who is, 974.23–27
  deceptive ~, 504.7; 823.6
  deceptive in ~, 823.9
  exact ~, 504.3
  external ~, 504.2
  false ~, 504.7
  ghostly ~, 483.8(2,3,17); 662.20
  give a deceptive ~ to, 823.5
  have the ~ of, 504.10
  having an ~ of distinction or
    importance, 848.24
  having the ~ of, 504.8
  improve the ~, agent to,
    505.11,12
  light in ~, 949.1
  mar the ~ of, 805.2–5
  mean in ~, 887.1
  netlike ~, 504.4
  on first ~, 483.7
  one's general ~, 504.11
  spoil the ~ of, 805.2–5
  surface ~, 504.2
  unexpected ~, 483.8(2,3)
  unnatural in ~, 811.6–8
  unreal ~, 483.8(2,3)
appease,v., 1096.31
appendage,n., 345.12
  having two ~s, 345.13
appendix,n., 347.9(2)
  inflammation of the ~,
    347.12(1)
appetite,n., 737.2; see hunger,n.
  good ~, 737.2(3)
  lack of ~, 737.9
  pert. to bodily ~, 338.8
  satisfy (~), 1107.11
  satisfy (~) to excess, 1107.15–
    22
  tempting the ~, 738.8
appetizer,n., 740.15(1,2)
appetizing,adj., 446.13
applaud,v., 851.1; 853.1,2
  ~ a person or side in a con-
    test, 853.3
applauder,n., 853.3
  paid ~s, 853.8
applauding,adj., 853.9
applause,n., 851.2; 853.4
  descr. of ~, 853.9

enthusiastic ~ from a group,
    853.5
  round of ~, 853.6,7
apple,n.
  bearing fruit of the ~ family,
    745.13
  crushed ~ substance, 745.4
  fruit of the ~ family, 745.1(7)
  juice of ~s, 745.3
  ~ tree, 994.6(13)
appliance,n., 180.6
appoint,v., 253.1
  ~ as assistant officer, 1077.6
  having the power to ~, 253.6
  ~ to the clergy, 253.1(8)
appointed,adj.
  ~ but not yet in office, 253.7
  ~ group, 253.4
  ~ person, 253.3
appointing,n., 253.2
  descr. of ~, 253.5
appreciate,v.
  know, 612.1
  rise in value, 839.11
appreciation,n.
  knowing, 612.1
  rise in value, 839.11
  thankfulness, 1110.2
appreciative,adj.
  aware, 611.1
  grateful, 1110.1
approach,n., 132.2
  means of ~, 50.1(3); 132.4;
    see also road,n.
approach,v., 132.1
  ~ and talk to, 132.1(1)
  cause to ~, 132.6
  ~ secretly, 132.1(5)
  ~ with sexual proposals,
    709.15,26
approachable,adj., 132.7
  not ~, 132.8
approacher,n., 132.3
approaching, adj., 132.5
appropriate,adj.
  proper, 818.1
  suitable, 817.1
approvable,adj., 850.19
approval,n., 850.2
  express (~), 1112.7
  expression of ~, 850.7
  give ~, 850.9
  help by ~, 850.10
  mention with ~, 850.6
  official ~ to print or publish,
    850.12
  paper showing ~, 850.13
  self-~, 850.11
  shout ~, 850.5
  show ~, 850.5
  sign of ~, 850.14
  speak of with ~, 850.6
  statement of ~, 850.13
  subject to ~, 850.18
  worthy of ~, 850.19
approve,v., 850.1,9; 1112.9
  ~ of, 850.1
  ~ of and agree with, 850.8
approved,adj.
  cause to be generally ~, 850.16
  generally ~, 850.15
  ~ in speech or language,
    850.17
  no longer ~, 894.12
approver,n., 850.4
approving,adj., 850.3
approximately,adv.
  ~ (of dates), 774.11
apron,n.
  child's ~, 974.38(17)
  top of an ~, 974.38(4)
aptitude,n., 7.1
arbitrary,adj., 8.11
arbitration,n.
  subject to ~, 1083.25
  submit dispute to ~, 1083.23

arbitrator,n., 1083.19
  authority of an ~, 1083.27
  decision of an ~, 1083.24,27
  judgment of an ~, 1083.24,27
  office of an ~, 1083.26,27
  settlement by ~, 1083.22
  submit dispute to an ~, 1083.23
arc,n., 508.16
  measure ~s, device to, 508.18
arch,n., 509.1,4
  become an ~, 509.6
  cover with an ~, 509.5
  form like an ~, 509.5
  pointed ~, 509.3
  series of ~es, 509.2
  shaped like an ~, 509.7
archaeologist,n., 759.27
archaeology,n., 759.26
archaic,adj., 759.1; see **old,**adj.
archbishop,n., 646.1; see **clergyman,**n.
arched,adj., 509.7
  ~ building, 727.12(2,13)
  ~ ceiling, 509.1; 973.1(11)
  ~ passage, 122.1(6,10,36)
  ~ roof, 509.1; 973.1(5,11)
  ~ space, 509.4; 787.1(25)
  ~ structure, 509.1
archery,n.
  study of, or enthusiasm for, ~, 566.19
architect,n., 727.3
architecture,n., 727.5
  construction, 727.2
  art of ~, 965.6(2)
  church ~, science of, 645.8
  ornamental ~, 959.8(1,10)
  resembling ~, 727.7
  science of ~, 727.10
  skill in ~, 727.8
  stone for ~, 1006.1(27)
  style of ~, 727.6
  styles of ~, 727.11
arctic,adj., 784.16
  ~ land, 1003.2(42)
arctic,n.
  inhabitant of the ~, 784.15(19,31)
area,n.
  place, 782.1; see **place,**n.
  space, 787.1; see **space,**n.
  ~ of land, 946.39
  restricted or limited ~, 558.6
arguable,adj., 542.13
argue,v.
  debate, 543.1
  dispute, 542.11; see **dispute, quarrel,**v.
  ~ for, 274.7
  ~ lawsuits, 1085.10
argument,n.
  debate, 543.2; see **debate,**n.
  dispute, 542.10; see **dispute, quarrel,**n.
  hatred of ~, 880.17(7)
  offer in ~, 237.1(1)
  persuasive ~, 638.4
  point made in an ~, expression when, 542.24
  ~s in court, lawsuit, etc., 1082.26,28,29
  summarizing of ~ in law court, 912.6
  ~ without weak points, descr. of, 1.24
argumentative,adj., 542.17
Aristotle,n.
  philosophy of ~'s disciples, pert. to, 807.14
arithmetic,n., 943.2
  calculate by ~, 942.1(1)
arm,n., 339.1,4
  hold the ~s of, 13.1(9)
  pain in the ~, 1137.56(3)
  pert. to the ~, 339.2,5

sign on the ~, 951.4(6)
armadillo,n.
  of ~s, 403.11(4)
armchair,n., 63.1(1,4,5,9)
armor,n., 568.22
  ~ attached to the helmet, 983.22
  clothe with ~, 1012.7
  ~ for the face or forehead, 983.23
  ~ for the foot, 979.23
  ~ for the head, 983.15
  ~ for the leg, 979.22
  garment over ~, 974.38(15)
  metal fabric for ~, 1012.6
  suit of ~, 974.1(10)
armpit,n.
  pert. to the ~, 339.3
army,n., 564.3,5
  enroll into ~, 564.16,17
  force into the ~, 3.3(8,13,15)
  front part of ~, 564.5(34)
  German ~, 564.5(35)
  government by the ~, 1073.42(16)
  ~ group, 564.3–5,15
  officers in ~, 564.8–13
  pert. to the ~, 564.6
  rank in the ~, 564.7,8,14
  rank of officer in the ~, 564.7
  service in the ~, 564.18
  treatise on the ~, 682.15(24)
arouse,v., 52.9
aroused,adj.
  be or become ~ (of emotions), 1099.19
arrange,v., 311.2
  ~ as in a theater, 311.2(5)
  ~ by time, 762.11
  ~ dishonestly, 311.2(3,4)
  ~ for in advance, 275.10(2,5,6)
  ~ in alternation, 311.2(7)
  ~ in layers, 311.2(9); 315.4(2)
  ~ in rows, 311.13
  ~ in stripes, 311.2(1)
arranged,adj., 311.4
  ~ in circles, 311.4(2,4)
  ~ in rows, 311.12
  ~ in rows, be or become, 311.14
  ~ like aisles, 311.4(3)
  ~ like tiles, 311.4(5)
arrangement,n., 311.1,3
  balanced ~, 311.1(42)
  ~ beforehand, 311.1(29)
  ~ by turns, 311.1(2)
  calendar ~ of saints, 311.1(19)
  checkered ~, 311.1(26,45)
  decorative ~, 311.1(27)
  descr. of ~, 311.4
  different ~, 311.1(30,33,34)
  disturb ~ of, 1101.10–13
  ~ in a line, 311.1(1)
  ~ in a picture, 311.1(9,13)
  ~ in layers, 311.1(40)
  ~ in lists, 311.1(5,44)
  ~ in order, 311.1(4,8)
  ~ in rows, 311.1(38); 311.13
  ~ in steplike form, 311.1(15)
  ~ in time, 311.1(6)
  ~ into a system, 311.1(7,16,17,20,21,23,27,36)
  massed ~, 311.1(28)
  new ~, 311.1(30,33,34)
  ~ of books, pert. to, 311.4(1)
  ~ of crossing lines, 311.1(12,22,26,35,45)
  ~ of parts, 311.1(9,10,13,25,41,46)
  ~ of print, 311.1(47)
  ~ of reading material in lines, 311.1(39)
  ~ of the world, 311.1(11)

  ~ of threads, 311.1(46)
  orderly ~, 311.1(7,16,17,20,21,23,27,31,32,36,37,42,43)
  pert. to ~, 311.4
  place for ~, 311.6
  place for ~ of papers, 311.7
  similarity in ~, 311.1(18)
  structural ~, 311.1(3)
  time ~, 762.10
arranger,n., 311.5
arrest,v.
  ~ legally, 247.6(2)
arrival,n., 118.2,3
  new ~, 118.3(1)
arrive,v., 118.1–3
arrogant,adj., 871.1; see **proud,** adj.
arrow,n., 566.6
  art of bow and ~, 566.18
  bows and ~s, 566.20
  container for ~, 261.1(38)
  distance ~ is hurled, 566.4
  enthusiasm for bow and ~, 566.19
  like an ~, 566.11
  maker of ~s, 566.13
  pert. to an ~, 566.10
  point of an ~, 566.9
  ~s, 566.7
  shaped like an ~, 507.17(67)
  shaped like an ~head, 507.17(67,68)
  shoot an ~, 566.14
  stem of an ~, 566.8
  study of bow and ~, 566.19
  use of bow and ~, 566.16,19
  user of bow and ~, 566.15,20
arrowhead,n.
  like an ~, 566.12
  pert. to an ~, 566.10
  shaped like an ~, 507.17(67,68)
arsenic,n., 800.2
  poisoning from ~, 800.18(1)
art,n., 965; see also **painting, picture,**n.
  century in reference to Italian ~, 965.34
  church ~, science of, 645.8
  collection of efforts in ~, 965.31
  discriminating taste in the fine ~s, 965.40–42
  effect in ~, 965.21
  elements of an ~, 965.27
  exhibition of ~, place of, 965.10
  fidelity to reality in ~, 807.11
  final work of ~, 792.23(6)
  fine ~, 965.6(2)
  free imagination in ~, 807.12
  in accord with ~, 965.20
  industrial or mechanical ~s, pert. to, 965.29
  interested in the fine ~s, 965.40–42
  liberal ~s of Middle Ages, 623.16
  methods of ~, 965.39
  movements in ~, 965.39
  object of ~, 964; see **object of art,**n.
  objects of ~, 964.1–5
  obscene ~, 713.5
  patron of the ~s, 568.21
  person contemptuous of ~, 863.4
  pert. to ancient Greek or Roman ~, 784.16(2)
  pert. to ~, 965.8
  place of exhibition of ~, 951.28(5,6); 951.29,30
  practice of ~, 965.22
  principles of ~, 965.39
  quality in ~, 965.21

represent by ~, 953.1(1,2,3, 4,6)
schools of ~, 965.39
sensitive to ~, 1093.8-10
skill in ~, 965.21,28
styles of ~, 965.39
the ~s, 965.6
theories of ~, 965.39
theory of the truthful in ~, 813.5
work of ~, 965.1
work of ~ borrowed from masters, 965.31
work of Italian ~ of 16th century, 965.35
works of ~, 965.9
artery,n.
  ~ disorders or diseases, 353.7
article,n.
  piece of writing, 682.16
  thing, 808.1
  useful ~s, 808.2
artificial,adj.
  affected, 811.1; see unnatural, adj.
  not made by nature, 811.4
  caused ~ly, 811.5
  not ~, i.e., natural, 810.1,3,5; see also genuine, natural, sincere,adj.
  of an ~ standard, 811.5
artist,n., 965.7
  early ~, 965.7(3)
  imaginative ~, 807.12
  Italian ~, 965.33
  modern ~, 761.15
  name of ~ on picture or painting, 965.32
  name of ~ on sculpture, carving, engraving, etc., 966.12
  pert. to an ~, 965.23
  realistic ~, 807.11
  skillful ~, 965.7(2)
  symbolic ~, 954.14
  ~ using colors, 965.7(1)
artistic,adj.
  ~ creation, 726.21
  ~ skill, 7.1(67)
artistry,n., 7.1
ascetic,n., 330.7
  ~ existence, 330.8
  pert. to an ~, 330.9
ascribe,v., 256.5; 893.7
  ~ emotions to inanimate objects, 1092.84,85
  ~ one's emotions, impulses, or ideas to others, 1092.87
  ~ to as author, 686.6
  ~ to unreasonably, 893.8
ashamed,adj., 868.12; 884.12
ashes,n., 1064.44
  become ~, 1064.45
  containing ~, 1064.47
  covered with ~, 1064.49
  gray, like ~, 1064.48
  like ~, 1064.46
  pale as ~, 1064.50
  place for ~, 1064.51
  place for ~ of the dead, 798.5-7
  ~ with glowing coals, 1064.52
Asia,n.
  countries of ~, 784.4(3)
Asiatic,adj., 784.16
  become ~, 784.13
  ~ characteristic, 1091.24(6)
  ~ characteristics, culture, institutions, etc., 1091.27
  make ~, 784.10(7)
  study of ~ characteristics, etc., 1091.28
Asiatic,n., 784.15(45)
aside,adv.
  push ~, 197.1(7,40,45)
  put ~, 323.16

set ~, 323.16
ask,v., 274.1
  ~ a question, 625.10; see also question,v.
  ~ and force to give, 274.1(17)
  ~ as a condition, 274.1(39)
  ~ as a price, 274.1(10)
  ~ for, 274.1
  ~ for help, 274.1(38)
  ~ for information, 274.1(13)
  ~ for justice or legal action, 1082.17
  ~ for opinions, 274.1(29)
  ~ for payment, 274.1(15)
  ~ questions, 625.1; see also question,v.
  ~ the return of, 274.1(32)
  ~ to come, 274.1(9,23)
  ~ to come back, 145.6; 274.1(31)
  ~ to return, 145.6; 274.1(31)
asker,n., 274.3
asleep,adj., 67.3; see also sleep,n.
  act of falling ~, 67.6
  descr. of the process of falling ~, 67.21
  falling ~, 67.21
  lying ~, 65.3(6)
  state or condition of lying ~, 67.4
asphyxia,n., 794.25,26
ass,n., 409.1
  cross between horse and ~, 409.1(4,8)
  group of ~es, 403.5(50)
  like an ~, 409.2
  of ~es, 403.11(13,14)
  worship of ~es, 656.15(17)
assent,n., 541.2; 554.2
assent,v., 541.1,3; 554.1
assenting,adj., 541.4; 554.3
assist,v., 556.1; see help,v.
assistance,n., 556.2; see help,n.
assistant,n., 556.3
associate,n., 524.5
associate,v., 524.1,2
  ~ in exclusive groups, 1096.7
  ~ in friendship with, 1096.22
  one who ~s, 524.5
  tending to ~ with own group, 524.8
associated,adj., 524.6
association,n., 524.3
  an ~, 524.4,9
  bring into ~, 524.2
  come into ~ with, 524.1
  form an ~ with, 524.1
  member of an ~, 524.5
  pert. to ~, 524.7
assume,v., 632.1(8)
  ~ an attitude, air, etc., 826.7
  ~ as a reality, 807.9
  ~ (quality, air, attitude, etc.), 974.11
assurance,n.
  written ~ by seller, 1122.5
assure,v., 641.4
aster,n.
  of the ~ family, 985.33(4)
astonish,v., 271.2
astonished,adj., 271.4
astonishing,adj., 271.1
astray,adv.
  go ~, 827.10
  led ~ by mischievous fairies, 662.13
astrologer,n., 1056.18
astrology,n.
  chart used in ~, 1053.25-30
  expert in ~, 1053.36(2); 1053.38
  pert. to ~, 1053.36(2); 1053.37
astronomer,n., 1056.18
astronomy,n., 1053.36

measurement unit in ~, 946.26(11,16)
asylum,n.
  ~ for parentless children, 721.15(4)
  ~ for prostitutes, 711.19
  ~ for the insane, 1136.16
  held in insane ~, 1136.18
  inmate of insane ~, 1136.17
  send to insane ~, 1136.19
atheism,n., 654.12(10)
Athenian,adj., 784.16
Athenian,n., 784.15(4)
athletic,adj.
  ~ competition, 20.2(2,3,5,6,9, 13)
athletics,n., 103.1-5; see also exercise, sports,n.
  club for ~, 524.9(17)
Atlantic Ocean,n.
  across ~, 1029.72(21)
atmosphere,n.
  ~ around a person or thing, 300.4(1)
  light in ~, 1065.1
  ~ under the surface, 970.54
atom,n.
  energy from ~, 1060.55
  splitting of the ~, 332.2(2)
atonable,adj., 222.4; 845.21
atone,v., 222.1
  ~ for, 845.20
atonement,n., 222.2
  condition, state, or place of ~, 845.25
  descr. of ~, 222.3
  of the nature of ~, 845.23
  temporary state after death for purposes of ~, 845.24
attach,v., 302.1,4,12,28,30
  animal organ that ~es, 302.3(2)
  ~ as a result, 302.1(3,38)
  ~ by fastening, 302.1,4
  ~ by sticking together, 302.12, 16
  ~ by tying, 302.28,30
  ~ metals, 302.12(3,13)
  plant's part that ~es, 302.3(1,2)
attached,adj., 302.8
  become ~, 302.4,16,30
  become ~ by sticking, 302.16
  become ~ by tying, 302.30
  permanently ~ (of animal forms), 302.9
  state of being ~, 302.5
  ~ thing, 302.8
attachment,n., 302.2,13,29
  an ~, 302.6
  ~ by sticking together, 302.13
  ~ by tying, 302.29
attack,n., 560.2,24
  a fit, 560.24; see fit,n.
  advance in ~, 560.5,6
  annoy by repeated ~s, 874.1(2,6,7,25)
  answering ~, 560.2(2)
  come down in a sudden ~, 560.7
  gas ~, 1048.30
  give means of ~ to, 560.18
  ~ in words, 561.2
  means of ~, 560.13
  merciless in ~, 889.11
  move forward in ~, arms raised, 174.1(9)
  object of ~, 560.14
  object of legal ~, 560.15
  ~ of a disease, 560.24,25
  ~ of apoplexy, 560.25
  ~ of epilepsy, 560.25
  ~ on cherished beliefs, 561.2(4)
  open to ~, 560.20

pert. to ~, 560.11
pert. to attack for seizing, 560.19
plundering ~, 560.2(9)
position for ~, 560.16
spot open to ~, 560.21
time when ~ begins, 560.17
used in ~, 560.11
attack,v., 560.1,5–8
advance to ~, 560.5,6
come down to ~, 560.7
conceal oneself waiting to ~, 970.33
enter in order to ~, 560.8,9
~ imaginary opponents, 560.1(30)
~ in answer, 560.1(10)
~ in order to annoy, 560.1(18)
~ in order to plunder, 560.1(12,14,16,20,21)
~ in order to rob, 560.1(17,33)
~ in order to seize (a place), 560.1(7,25,26)
~ in pretense, 560.1(13)
~ in words, 561.1
~ language that ~s through ridicule, 561.11
~ lie in concealment waiting to ~, 970.33
~ (of a disease), 560.22,23
~ (of dogs), 560.1(5,24)
prepared to ~, 560.12
~ savagely, 4.31
set dogs on to ~, 560.1(24)
~ the reputation or character of, 891.17
threaten to ~ bodily, 560.10
try to ~ bodily, 560.10
wait for in order to ~, 272.1(12)
~ with gas, 1048.29
~ with harsh criticism, 894.10
~ with the horns, 560.1(15)
attacker,n., 560.3
~ in words, 561.3
attacking,adj., 560.4
~ in words, 561.4
attain,v., 240.1; see get,v.
attainment,n., 240.2,3
object of ~, 18.7
attempt,n., 18.2
anguished ~, 18.2(13)
bold ~, 18.2(12)
descr. of ~, 18.4
~ doomed to failure, 18.2(16)
successful ~, 18.2(12)
~ to commit a crime of violence, 18.2(2)
~ to gain possession, 18.2(11)
~ to get by flattery, 18.2(3)
attempt,v., 18.1
attempter,n., 18.3
attendant,n., 131.3; 178.1(20)
group of ~s, 131.4; 178.5(2–4)
attention,n., 579.2,5; see also attentiveness,n.
able to pay ~ to one thing only, 579.19
act to attract ~, 52.5(39)
attack with ~s, 561.1(7)
attract ~, done to, 579.23
attracting ~, 579.24
call ~ to, 579.20–22; 951.1(2,9,15,22–24,31,33,39,43)
calling ~ to oneself, 579.21(2)
calling for ~, 952.5
center of ~, 137.1(11); 579.30–32
compelling ~, 579.25
demanding ~, 579.25
demanding immediate ~, 274.4(2,4,5); 579.25,26
done with ~ to detail, 579.13,14

draw one's ~ away, 581.4,15–17
Hindu system of deep ~, 579.27–29
lack of ~, 581.2; see inattention,n.
not paying ~, 581.1; see inattentive,adj.
occupy the ~ of, 579.6
pay ~, 579.1,7
pay no ~ to, 581.6
paying ~, 579.4
requiring immediate ~, 274.4(2,4,5); 579.25,26
~s in courtship, 579.3
self-~, 579.16,18
~ turned inward, 579.16,18
~ turned outward, 579.17
attentive,adj., 579.4,8
be ~ to, 579.7
courteously ~ to women, 579.8(2); 579.10–12
externally ~, 579.17
insincerely ~, 579.8(3)
inwardly ~, 579.16,18
servilely ~, 579.8(3)
attentiveness,n., 579.5,9; see also attention,n.
~ for sexual favors, 579.12
attic,n., 787.7(4,26)
attitude,n., 1091.5,6
assume an ~, 974.11
change ~, 539.1(39,41); 539.2(10)
concealed ~, 970.53,54
drop an ~, 984.12
emotional ~s, 1092.7
habitual ~, 629.4
incorporation of moral or emotional ~s of another, 1092.92,93
invest with intellectual ~, 584.18
old-fashioned ~, 631.16
out-of-date ~, 631.16
similar ~s, 1109.7
stale or trite ~, 759.30
trend of ~s in a place, 1092.19
~ under the surface, 970.54
attract,v., 196.1
one who ~s, 196.4
that which ~s, 196.3
~ to wrong, sin, etc., 196.1(1,4,12,15,16,18,19,21)
try to ~, 18.1(3)
attracted,adj.
be ~ to, 196.10
person to whom one is ~, 196.4(1)
state of being ~, 196.8
strongly ~, 196.9
attraction,n., 196.2,3,8
center of ~, 196.11
scientific ~, 196.12,13
attractive,adj., 196.5
exciting and ~, 1100.18–21
~ in appearance, 505.1
not ~, 196.7
~ quality, 196.6
attractiveness,n., 196.6
attribute,v., 256.5; 893.7; see also ascribe,v.
~ to as author, 686.6
~ to unreasonably, 893.8
auction,n., 212.8
audible,adj., 454.13
August,n.
pert. to ~, 780.7
Austria,n.
ruler of ~, 1073.36(13)
author,n., 685.5; 686.1; 687.2,5; see also writer,n.
literary person, 688.3
admit to being ~ of, 675.1(2)

ancient Greek or Roman ~s, 686.11
attribute to as ~, 686.6
be the ~ of, 686.2
consider as the ~ of, 893.7
descr. of writing in ref. to an ~, 686.8
excellent ~, 686.1(2)
famous ~, 615.5
imaginative ~, 807.12
inferior ~, 686.1(6)
line denoting the ~, 686.4,5
list of ~'s works, 311.19(1)
modern ~, 761.15
~ of memoirs, 627.28
~ of music, 686.1(5)
pert. to an ~, 686.3
piece of writing by unknown ~, 682.16(2)
realistic ~, 807.11
unknown ~, 686.1(1)
use of a man's name by a woman ~, 694.4
authoritative,adj., 5.5
authority,n., 5.4
based on ~, 5.14
be cruel in exercise of ~ or power, 889.7
be superior in ~, 833.16
cruel in exercise of ~ and power, 889.1(9)
display of official ~, 1077.18
document giving ~, 5.5(4)
exceeding legal ~, 5.21
exercise ~, 5.6
~ for an act, 5.15(2)
give ~, 5.7,12
give ~ to act for another, 5.12
give legal ~, 5.7(4)
go to a higher ~, 159.8
group with legal ~, 1078.20
harsh in exercise of ~ or power, 890.4
have ~, 5.6
having full and unrestricted ~, 5.5(6)
illegal exercise of official ~, 1087.7(5)
independent ~, 5.4(4)
king's ~, 1073.17(1)
lacking in ~, 10.1(19,27)
legal ~, 5.4(13)
means of ~, 5.15
~ of judge, 5.4(13)
~ of officials, 1077.20
~ of ruler, 1073.17,38
~ of the Pope, 5.4(25,26)
official ~, 5.4(5,14)
one who upholds ~, 5.17
opponent of ~, 544.4(3)
opposition to ~, 544.2(7,9,13,15,16,21); see also disobedience,n.
person who has ~ to act for another, 5.10
person with ~, 5.8
pert. to ~, 5.9
place or region of ~, 5.19; 782.6
position of ~, 1077.2(2)
proof of ~, 812.17
put in position of ~, 1077.8
reduce in ~, 10.5(11)
region of ~, 5.19; 782.6
source of ~, 5.15
symbol of ~, 5.16; 954.1(9)
~ to act for another, 5.11
~ to govern, 5.4(13); 1073.84
~ to make laws, 5.4(13)
~ to practice a profession, 5.4(14)
unfair in the exercise of ~, 635.6
written ~, 5.4(5,7)
authorize,v., 5.7,12

authorship,n.
ascription of false ~, 686.7
autointoxication,n., 800.18(2)
automaton,n., 429.4,5
automobile,n., 192.6
cover for ~ motor, 972.4(4,7)
drive an ~, 192.7
driver of an ~, 192.8
police ~, 1078.13
ride in an ~, 192.7
rider in an ~, 192.8,28
autumn,n., 770.1
beginning of ~, 1055.14
like ~, 770.8
middle of ~, 770.2
pert. to ~, 770.7
auxiliary,adj., 908.13,40
avarice,n., 265.17; see also
greed,n.
avaricious,adj., 265.3(3,6,8–10);
265.16(8,11); see also
greedy,adj.
~person, 265.18(2)
avenge,v., 221.1(1,4–8)
avenging,adj., 896.4
~ spirits, 896.31
average,adj., 535.1
aversion,n., 880.2
~ to specific things, 880.17
avoid,v., 76.1–4
act to ~ danger, 52.5(34)
act to ~ failure, 52.5(34)
swear to ~, 76.5
avoidable,adj., 76.7
avoidance,n., 76.2
avoirdupois weight,n.
unit of ~, 947.32,35
awake,adj., 72.11
a staying ~, 72.8
fully ~, 72.10
keeping ~, 72.9
awake,v., 72.1–6
aware,adj., 611.1
awful,adj., 883.7
awkward,adj., 14.1; see clumsy,
adj.
be ~, 14.4
~ person, 14.3
awkwardness,n., 14.2
ax,n., 332.13

B

baby,n., 721.1,3; see child,n.
baby carriage,n., 192.16
Bacchus,n., 749.21
devotee of ~, 748.14(1)
female attendants of ~,
749.23
festival to ~, 749.25
follower of ~, 749.24
priest of ~, 749.22
votary of ~, 749.22
bachelor,n., 706.1
advocating the ~ state,
706.6,7
like a ~, 706.5
one who had long been a ~,
703.1(1)
pert. to a ~, 706.4
state of a ~, 706.3
back,adj., 184.2
~ part, 184.1
~ part of a picture, 184.1(1)
~ side, 186.1(2,9)
back,adv.
being pushed ~, 197.9
bend ~, 152.1(12,13)
bending ~, 152.3(4)
bent ~, 152.5(7)
bring ~, 191.1
call ~, 693.1(13)
calling ~, 693.3(1)
come ~, 145.1
draw ~, 193.8–10

get ~, 240.12–14
give ~, 234.1–4
go ~, 145.1
hold ~, 558.1–6
jump ~, 110.1(8,22–24)
keep ~, 558.1–6
move ~, 145.1
move ~ and forth, 146.1–4;
see also sway, swing,v.
one ~ of the other, 184.4
pull ~, 193.8–10
push ~, 197.1(38,41,42)
put ~, 323.15
throw ~, 187.1(41,42)
throw ~ and forth, 187.1(1,
59,61)
turn ~, 148.1(18,19); 148.6(9,
10)
turn ~ward, 148.1(17);
148.6(11,12)
turning ~, 148.2(5)
back,n., 184.1
animal's ~, 184.8
at or near the ~ of the body,
184.11
bodily region of the ~ and
sides, 345.19
highest part of animal's ~,
184.9
lying on one's ~, 65.3(10,11,
13,17)
moving toward the ~, 184.7
one in ~ of the other, 184.4
pain in the ~, 1137.56(1,19,
26)
person's ~, 184.8
raise (~) in rounded shape,
958.12
to the ~, 184.5
top of animal's ~, 165.1(17)
toward the ~, 184.5
toward the ~ of a ship, 184.6
toward the ~ of the body,
184.10
turn the ~, 184.12
with the ~ in front, 184.3
backbone,n., 354.8
curvature of the ~, 354.17(1,
3,4,6,7,11); 354.18,19
cut through the ~, 332.1(5)
having a ~, 354.11
inflammation of the ~,
354.17(10)
pert. to the ~, 354.9
without a ~, 354.12
backward,adj.
~ flow, 112.2(23,24)
bacon,n.
side of ~, 186.1(6)
bacteria,n., 403.21
checking growth of ~, 398.10
liquid for growing~, 1027.1(3)
science of ~, 403.26(4)
substance that destroys ~,
398.8(2–7,9,10,12)
bad,adj.
evil, 883.22; see also sinful,
adj.
poor in quality, 883.1
wicked, 883.22; see also sinful,adj.
a doing of ~ acts, 883.28
~ act, 883.24
~ acts, 883.26
behave ~ly, 883.30
behaving ~ly, 883.31
~ behavior, 55.3(11,12)
conspicuously ~ly, 883.8
constructed ~ly (of literary
work), 726.28
doer of ~ acts, 883.29
extremely ~ly, 883.7,9
in ~ condition, 883.10
make less ~ than seemingly,
883.21

of ~ quality, 883.1
~ repair, 883.12(6)
represent as less ~, 883.21
treat as less ~, 883.21
bad luck,n., 36.1
attended by ~, 36.3
cause ~ to, 36.6
cause of ~, 36.5
doomed to ~, 36.3(4,14)
having ~, 36.3
one who incurs ~, 36.4
one who meets ~, 36.4
piece of ~, 36.2
stroke of ~, 36.2
bad temper,n., 876.2,10
be in a silent ~, 876.16
display of ~, 876.8
display of violent ~, 876.8
fit of ~, 876.6
fit of violent ~, 876.7
talk in a ~, 876.18
badge,n., 951.4(6,10,11,15,23);
see also emblem,n.
badger,n.
group of ~s, 403.5(8)
of ~s, 403.11(8,10)
bad-mannered,adj., 860.1; see
impolite
badness,n., 883
wickedness, 883.23
bad-tempered,adj., 876.1
~ and dissatisfied, 876.1(1,5)
~ and rough, 865.1(3)
~ and silent, 876.1(6,7)
~ and unfriendly (of ani-
mals), 879.13(5)
~ and untidy, 903.1(11)
~and worthless person,
888.5(3)
be ~, 876.14
be ~ and silent, 876.16
become ~, 876.15
~ female, 876.3(1)
~ girl, 876.4
humor determining ~ness,
1091.30
look ~ and silent, 876.17
make ~, 876.11
make ~ and silent, 876.13
make ~ by displeasing, 876.12
~ person, 876.3
~ wife, 876.5
~ woman, 876.4
bag,n., 261.15
~ carried on back while traveling, 261.16(11,14,19)
golf ~, 261.15(1)
~like bodily part, 350.1; see
sac,n.
money ~, 261.15(2,4,6,9)
~ to hold up the hair, 983.40
traveling ~, 261.16
traveling ~s, 261.16
woman's ~, 261.15(2,6,7)
baggage,n., 261.17
bagpipe,n.
player of a ~, 479.9(21)
sound of Scottish ~s,
465.1(10)
bail,n., 1122.46(1)
depositor of ~, 1122.47
bailiff,n., 1078.1
area of authority of a ~,
1078.6
bake,v., 1061.1,2; see also
cook,v.
amount ~d, 1061.11
~ bricks, 1061.14
compartment for ~ing,
1061.9(2)
~ in a sauce or shells, 1061.12
mixture used in ~ing, 1062.9,
10
one who ~s, 1061.10
~ pottery, 1061.14

baked,adj.
  incompletely ~, 1061.23
baking,n.
  method of ~, 50.1(24,25)
balance,n., 950.1
  a ~ against, that which is,
    950.13
  act as a ~ against, 950.12
  ~ and correspondence on
    both sides, 950.2
  be in ~, 950.7
  be in ~ with, 950.8
  bring into ~, 950.4
  in ~, 950.6
  keep in ~, 950.4
  lack of ~, 950.16
  lacking ~, 950.16,18
  lose one's ~, 168.1,4
  lose one's ~, cause to, 168.3
  loss of ~, cause, 950.17
  moving to a state of ~, 950.10
  science of ~, 950.15
  science of forces in ~, 3.10(5)
  state of ~, 950.1
  vibrate like a ~, 950.9
  vibrating to a state of ~,
    950.10
  without ~, 950.16,18
balance,v., 950.4,7,12
  ~ (one thing against an-
    other), 950.14
balanced,adj., 950.6
  not ~, 950.18
balancer,n., 950.11
  ~ on a tightrope, 950.11
balancing,n.
  act as a ~ weight, 947.14
  ~ weight, 947.12,13
bald,adj., 371.11
  ~ condition, 371.12
  ~ person, 371.13
ball,n., 508.8
  like a ~, 508.1(7)
ballet,n., 109.4(1)
  ~ dancer, 109.6(2,3,6,7)
  ~ enthusiast, 109.12
  leader of ~, 109.6(6)
  pert. to ~, 109.10(1)
  writing of ~, 109.11
ban,n., 555.2
ban,v., 555.1; see forbid,v.
banal,adj., 535.5
  ~ action, 535.6
  ~ expression, 535.6
  ~ person, 535.7
  ~ phrase, 535.6
  speak in ~ terms, 535.8
banana,n.
  belonging to the ~ family,
    745.22(9)
band,n., 502.1
  orchestra, 479.17
  ~ around the waist, 980.6
  diplomat's ~ around the
    waist, 980.6
  ~ of jewelry, 961.1
bandage,n., 302.32(5)
  loop of ~ for support,
    1022.2(26)
bandage,v., 302.28(7,41)
bandicoot,n.
  pert. to the ~, 418.3
banish,v., 144.1(1,3,5,17,19,22)
bankrupt,adj., 218.14
  announce as ~, 218.15
bar,n.
  frequenter of ~s, 749.54
  liquor ~, 749.37(2); 749.38,39
barber,n., 369.19
  pert. to a ~, 369.20
bare,adj., 972.7
barefoot,adj.
  ~ person, 984.17
bargain,n., 211.8(2,5)
bargain,v., 223.9,10

bark,n.
  covered with ~, 972.5(2)
  dog's ~, 456.1(2,80)
barking,n., 456.1(45)
barn,n.
  place for storage of hay in ~,
    986.10
  yard or enclosure around a ~,
    998.16
barnacle,n., 422.3
  of ~s, 422.1(13)
Baroda,n.
  ruler of ~, 1073.36(11)
barometer,n.
  use of the ~, 1046.19
barrel,n.
  maker of ~s, 261.4
  metal ~, 261.1(20)
  repairer of ~s, 261.4
  rounded part of a ~, 261.2
  ~-shaped vessel, 261.7(11,37)
  side of a ~, 997.5(19)
  small ~, 261.1(3,21,33)
  strip forming side of a ~,
    261.3
barrier,n.
  fence, 300.8
barroom,n., 749.37
bartender,n., 749.40
base,adj., 886.1; see corrupt,
  immoral,adj.
base,n., 169.4(4,5,10-12); 1022.21
  figurative ~, 1022.21,26
  ~ for a statue, 1022.2(16)
  give a ~ to, figuratively,
    1022.24
  ~ of a column, 1023.11
  projecting ~ (architecture),
    1022.15
  without figurative ~, 1022.38
base,v.
  ~ (actions or statements) on,
    1022.29
baseless,adj., 1022.38
basement,n., 787.7(13,39,41)
bashful,adj., 873.10,14
  ~ and lacking confidence,
    873.14(4,13,14)
  awkwardly ~, 873.11
  ~ person, 873.15
  pretendedly ~, 873.16
basin,n.
  ~ for washing, 899.37(1,3,4)
basis,n., 1022.21,26
  give a ~ to, 1022.24
  without ~, 1022.38
basket,n., 261.1(23,37); see also
  container,n.
bastard,adj., 720.10
bastard,n., 720.11
  declare a ~, 720.12
  procreation of a ~, 717.12(3)
  prove a ~, 720.12
bastardy,n.
  sign of ~, 951.4(4,5)
bat (animal),n., 404.1
  like a ~, 404.2
bath,n., 899.49
  ~ by sitting in hot water,
    899.49(2)
  foot ~, 899.49(1)
  ~ in hot room, 899.49(3)
  pert. to a ~, 899.56
  ~s to cure illness, use of,
    899.58
  sun ~, place for, 899.55
  sweat ~, place for, 899.53
  take a ~, 899.48
  ~ to cure illness, science of,
    899.59
  warm ~, a room for, 899.54
  writing about ~s, 899.57
bathe,v., 899.48
  room in which to ~, 295.1(1,
    9,16); 899.54

bathing,n., 899.52
  act of ~, 899.52
  apparatus, etc., for ~, 899.50
  place for ~, 295.1(1,9,16);
    899.51,53-55
  science of ~, 899.59
  writing about ~, 899.57
battle,n., 562.1; see fight,n.
  power in ~, 5.1(4)
  scene of ~, 562.8
battle,v., 562.2; see fight,v.
battlement,n., 568.30
  furnish with ~s, 568.32
  open spaces in a ~, 568.33,35
  solid part of a ~, 568.34
battler,n., 562.4; see fighter,n.
battling,adj., 562.5
battling,n., 562.3; see fighting,n.
bay (water),n., 1029.63
be,v.
  exist, 39.1
  live, 750.1
  remain, 757.1
bead,n.
  jewelry, 961.1
  prayer ~s, 961.1(23)
bean,n., 745.20
  ~ covering, 972.4(14)
  pert. to, or like, ~s, 745.22(6)
bear,n., 416.1,4
  baby ~, 416.2
  group of ~s, 403.5(66)
  like a ~, 416.3
  pert. to a ~, 416.3
  toy ~, 416.4
bear,v.
  carry, 190.1
  tolerate, 246.1-3
  ability to ~ or endure, 246.8
  able to ~ or endure, 246.9
  hard to ~, 246.7
  ~s the brunt, that which,
    246.11
  ~ up under, 246.1-3
bearable,adj., 246.4
beard,n., 370.1
  cultivation of ~s, 370.5
  cutting of the ~, 370.8
  excessive growth of ~, 370.7
  ~ in a woman, 370.7
  like a ~, 370.4
  relating to a ~, 370.4
  study of ~s, 370.6
  treatise on ~s, 370.6
  without a ~, 370.3
bearded,adj., 370.2
bearing,n.
  way of carrying oneself,
    504.11
beat,n.
  rhythmical ~, 105.4
beat,v.
  hit, 437.1; see also hit,v.
  ~ eggs, etc., 437.1(110)
  ~ rhythmically, 105.3,5
Beau Brummell,n., 974.23-26
  woman like a ~, 974.27
beautiful,adj., 505.1
  ~ and delicate, 11.1(3)
  ~ girl, 505.4
  lightly and gracefully ~, 949.6
  make ~, 505.10
  ~ sight, 483.3(27)
  ~ woman, 505.4
  ~ woman who is dangerous,
    572.10(1)
beautify,v., 505.10
  art of ~ing, 505.13
  intended to ~, 505.12
  person who gives ~ing treat-
    ments, 505.14
  substance used to ~, 505.11
beauty,n., 505.2
  facial ~, 505.2(2)

glow of ~, 505.3
god of manly ~, 505.20
goddess of ~, 505.19; 700.27(3)
ideal ~, 505.2(1)
importance of artistic ~, belief in, 505.18
love of ~, 505.17
lover of ~, 700.30(18) ; 700.31,
  32
obsession with ~, 505.15
pert. to ~, 505.6
pert. to complexion ~, 505.7
philosophy of ~, 505.16
place of ~, 816.9
science of ~, 505.16
sensitive to ~, 505.8,9; 1093.8-
  10
study of ~, 505.16
beauty parlor,n.
  worker in a ~, 505.14
beaver,n.
  home of ~s, 403.22(25)
bed,n., 69.1
  convertible ~, 63.1(18)
  cover in ~, 972.1(52)
  covering for a ~, 69.2; 972.24-
  26
  ~ garment, 974.44
  go to ~, 67.1(1,6)
  kept to ~, 58.1(3)
  not kept to ~, 107.7
  roof over a ~, 973.1(2)
  ~-wetting, 294.7(2,4)
bedbug,n., 428.3
  infested with ~s, 403.18(7)
  of ~s, 428.1(8)
  science of ~s, 403.26(17)
bedding,n., 69.1-3; 972.24-26
bedroom,n., 787.7(6)
  child's ~, 787.7(27)
  ship's ~, 787.7(9,36)
bedspread,n., 69.2; 972.24
bed-wetting,n., 294.7
bee,n.
  eating ~s, 734.27(2)
  eggs of ~s, 428.4(2)
  group of ~s, 403.5(1,12,35,72)
  keeper of ~s, 403.24
  place for ~s, 403.22(1,2,5,19)
  raising of ~s, 403.30(2)
  young of ~s, 428.4(2)
beech,n.
  of the ~ family, 996.25
beehive,n., 403.22(1,2,5,19)
beer,n., 749.6(10) ; 749.7
  drunk from ~, 749.50(2)
  ~ glass, 261.8(14,18,20,21)
  make ~, 749.28(1,3)
  making ~, chemistry of,
  749.36(2)
  making ~, place for, 749.26(1)
  obtain ~, place to, 749.37(1,5,
  15,18)
beetle,n., 428.3(7)
  like a ~, 428.2
  of ~s, 428.1(12)
  young of ~s, 428.4(4)
before,adv.
  ~ (in time), 771.14,15
before,prep.
  ~ (in time), 771.13
beg,v., 276.1
  ~ in the streets, 276.1(16)
beggar,n., 276.3
  gift to a ~, 276.10
  ~ in Naples, 209.9(1)
  leprous ~, 276.3(2)
  like a ~, 276.11
  Mohammedan ~, 276.3(1)
  ~s, collectively, 276.7
begging,adj., 276.4
  ~ and crying for mercy,
  276.4(2)
begging,n., 276.2
  descr. of ~, 276.4

expressive of ~, 276.4(1)
live by ~, 276.1(6,22)
pert. to ~, 276.6
practice of ~, 276.5
quality of ~, 276.5
try to get by ~, 276.1(21,27)
begin,v., 729.1,7; see also introduce,v.
  ~ again, 729.5; 729.7(9)
  ~ and continue, 729.6
  ~ (doing), 729.4
  ~ doing again, 49.1(32)
  one who ~s something, 729.1,
  17
  ~ to develop, 729.7(7,11) ;
  731.1
  ~ to form, 729.7(3)
  ~ to grow, 729.7(7,11) ; 731.1
  willingness to ~ something
  new, 729.20
beginner,n., 729.17
  period of being a ~, 729.18
  state of being a ~, 729.18
beginning,adj., 729.15
  in the ~ stages, 729.15
  ~ principles, 729.13
  ~ to develop, 729.9; 729.15(4,
  11) ; 731.2
  ~ to grow, 729.9; 729.15(4,11) ;
  731.2
beginning,n., 729.2,8,11; see
  also origin, source,n.
  add at the ~, 908.7
  come at the ~ of, 730.1(5,6,8)
  dealing with ~s, 729.15
  existing at the ~, 729.15(13)
  from the ~, 729.19
  give a ~ to, 729.1
  have a ~, 729.7
  manner of ~, 729.14
  ~ of a biological organ,
  729.11(23)
  ~ of a career, 729.11(8)
  place of ~, 728.4
  point of ~, 729.12
begun,adj.
  just ~, 729.16
  recently ~, 729.16
behave,v., 55.2,4
  ~ badly, 883.30
  ~ noisily, 4.13
  ~ with violence, 4.4,13
  ~ wrongly, 883.30
behaving,adj.
  ~ badly, 883.31
  manner of ~, 55.1
  ~ properly, 818.7
behavior,n., 55.1,3
  a formality of ~, 819.10(3)
  a saying on moral ~, 843.16
  absurd ~, 55.3(1)
  advice on moral ~, 843.13
  advice on moral ~ in a story,
  or from an experience,
  843.15
  advocate moral ~, 843.12
  analysis of ~, 55.5(5)
  bad ~, 55.3(11,12)
  basing of ~, or religious ~,
  on moral law, 843.5
  belief about purpose of ~,
  831.22(1,3)
  care in observing principles
  of ~, 56.5
  chivalrous ~, 55.3(9)
  compulsive ~, 55.3(16)
  correct in ~, 815.1(3)
  correctness of ~, 815.2(1)
  customs of proper ~, 56.3;
  818.5
  daring ~, 55.3(5,6)
  established ~, 55.3(17)
  excessively strict in moral ~,
  843.21
  express thinking about moral

~ or duty, 843.8-10
expressing truths about moral
  ~, 843.7
foolish ~, 55.3(8)
formal ~, 55.3(2)
frivolous ~, 55.3(10)
illegal ~, 1087.7
improper ~, 1087.7
improper in ~, 828.12
measurement of ~, 55.5(5)
moral ~, 843.31
moral in ~, 843.17
observant of moral ~, 843.17
pert. to ~, 55.6
pert. to properness of ~, 818.4
polite ~, 55.3(2,7)
principles of ~, 56.3
proper ~, 55.3(3,4,14) ; 818.8
proper ~, demand for, 818.12
proper ~, sense of, 818.9
proper in ~, 818.10
psychological doctrine of ~,
  55.7
reflections on moral ~, 843.13
reflexive ~, 55.3(17)
rigid ~, 55.3(16)
rough ~, 865.3
rough in ~, 865.1(1,9)
rules of proper ~, 56.3; 818.5
science of ~, 55.5
science of moral ~, 843.4
sinful ~, 55.3(11)
study of ~, 55.5
tedious advice on moral ~,
  843.14
treatise on moral ~, 843.6
unsuitable ~, 55.3(10)
violent ~, 4.3; 55.3(15)
behead,v., 796.15
  device for ~ing, 796.16
behind,adj., 184.2; see back,adj.
behind,n.
  back, 184.1; see back,n.
  buttocks, 348.1; see buttocks, n.
being,n.
  existence, 39.3
  human being, 429.3
  person, 431.1
belch,v., 288.1-7
Belgian,adj.
  language, 664.4(19)
Belgian,n.
  south ~, 784.15(62) ; 784.16
Belgium,n.
  pert. to south ~, 784.16
belief,n., 632.6
  adjustment of ~s, 632.12
  attack on cherished ~s,
  561.2(4)
  based on ~, 632.13; 632.15
  ~ based on little evidence,
  632.7(9,11)
  body of ~s, 632.8
  causing false ~, 632.16
  change in one's ~, 632.5
  convert to a political ~,
  1076.16,17
  destroy ~ in, 639.14
  documents that cause ~,
  632.28
  entitled to ~, 632.24,25
  entitling to ~, 632.26
  ethical ~s, 632.8(2)
  false ~, 632.6(12) ; 632.7(2)
  false ~s, treatise on, 682.15(5)
  foolish ~, 632.7(5)
  free of false ~s, 309.11(9)
  fundamental ~, 632.8(3)
  giving grounds for ~, 632.15
  have ~ in, 632.2
  have a false ~, 632.3
  holding acceptable ~s,
  632.18(8)

holding unacceptable ~s, 632.18(5,12)
~ in God, 632.6
~ in magic, 632.6(15)
~ in the supernatural, 632.6(15)
~ in unreality, 632.6(11)
lack of ~, 639.4
lacking in ~, 639.3
not worthy of ~, 639.12
~ of members of a sect, organization, etc., 632.7(10)
officially approved ~, 632.6(13)
officially unapproved ~, 632.6(9,10,17)
one's ~, 632.7
opposing ~ (religion, science, etc.), 632.6(9,10,12,17)
pert. to ~, 632.9
political ~s, 1076.15
reconciliation of ~s, 632.12
rejecting accepted ~s, 639.3(13,14)
religious ~, 632.7(1); 642.1(1)
religious ~s, 632.8(1)
return to former ~, 145.1(24)
~s, 632.8
~s from the past, 632.8(5)
spread ~s, 632.17
summary of ~s, 632.8
superstitious ~, 632.7(8)
systematically spread ~s, 632.8(4)
unfounded ~, 632.6(15)
unyielding in ~s, 632.18(6, 12); 632.19
vague ~, 632.7(4)
worthy of ~, 632.25
believable,adj., 632.22–26
believe,v., 632.1
~ falsely, 632.3
hard to ~, 639.10
hesitating to ~, 639.3(8,9)
~ in, 632.2
~ in a false religion, 632.4
refusal to ~, 639.2
tending to ~, 632.18
believed,adj.
commonly ~, 632.29
believer,n., 632.10
~ of falsehoods, 632.20
unyielding ~, 632.19
believing,adj., 632.18
believing,n.
state of ~, 632.6
belittle,v., 840.1
word that ~s, 666.3(35)
belittling,adj., 840.2
bell,n., 458.6
alarm ~, 458.6(8)
art of ~ ringing, 458.11
evening ~, 458.6(9)
part by which a ~ is hung, 458.8
pert. to ~s, 458.7
reverberating like ~s, 471.5(1)
ring a ~, 458.3
ring of a ~, 458.2
ringing of a ~, 458.4
~s, 458.6
science of ~s, 458.11
~-shaped, 507.17(13)
signal ~, 956.6(1)
signal by ~s, 956.1(13,14)
sounds of ~s, 458.1–7
tongue of a ~, 458.9
tower for a ~, 458.10
bellowing,n., 456.3(1)
belly,n., 347.1,5; see also **abdomen**,n.
big ~, 510.7
big of ~, 510.6
pain in the ~, 1137.56(2,7,10, 13,15,27,30)

pert. to the ~, 347.2
protuberant ~, 347.1(7)
belly button,n., 347.13
like a ~, 347.14
meditation while contemplating the ~, 585.14
shaped like a ~, 507.17(82)
belong,v., 256.1
advantage that ~s, 256.3(1)
that which ~s, 256.3
that which ~s to someone, 255.10
belonging,adj., 256.2
consider as ~, 256.5
not ~, 256.6
specially ~, 256.2(1,4,5)
~ to a group, 256.2(2,4,5)
~ to a place, 256.2(2)
~ to the nature of a thing, 256.2(3)
belonging,n.
a possession, 255.10
below,adv.
lying ~, 65.3(18)
belt,n., 980.6
diagonal ~, 980.6,7
~ for a horn, 980.7
~ for a sword, 980.7
~ for a trumpet, 980.7
bench,n., 63.1(7,17,18,19)
bend,n., 152.3
bend,v., 152.1,2
able to ~, 152.7
~ back, 152.1(12,13)
~ forward, 152.1(11,16)
~ in fear, 152.1(3)
~ in the middle, 152.1(14)
~ low, 152.1(3)
~ the head, 152.1(1,8,11,15)
~ the knee, 152.1(7,9)
~ the upper body, 152.1(1,8, 15)
bending,adj., 152.4
bending,n., 152.3
~ back, 152.3(4)
~ back of body organ, 152.3(3)
beneficial,adj., 556.4; 831.11; 836.2
benefit,n., 556.2; 831.13; 836.1
benefit,v., 556.1; 831.14; 836.3
bent,adj., 152.5
~ at an angle, 152.5(4,5)
~ back, 152.5(7)
~ down, 152.5(7)
easily ~, 152.7
~ in a spiral, 152.5(3)
~ like a hook, 152.5(6,8)
~ like the knee, 152.5(5)
state of being ~, 152.6
~ twice, 152.5(1,2)
bequeath,v., 242.4–6
bequest,n., 242.8
berries,n.
bearing ~, 745.14
eating ~, 734.27(3)
berry,n., 745.1(1); see also **fruit**,n.
like a ~, 745.22(2)
best,adj., 834.1
chosen as ~, 834.2
~ group, 318.1(51)
~ in quality, 164.6(2,4–8); 1013.8
one who is ~, 834.3
one who is ~ in sports, 834.4
~ part, 326.1(27); 834.6
those who are ~, 834.5
better,adj., 833.1; see also **superior**,adj.
be ~ in quality, excellence, etc., 924.8
be ~ than, 833.15
become ~, 835.1; see also **improve**,v.

belief that the world can be made ~, 831.22(2)
do ~ than, 833.11
do ~ than, in a contest, 833.14
make ~, 835.2; see **improve**,v.
match with something ~, 833.13
represent as ~, 833.18
try to do ~, 18.1(13,25)
try to do ~ than, 833.12
better,n.
get the ~ of, 833.17
beverage,n., 748.5; see also **drink**,n.
alcoholic ~, 749.1–8; see **liquor (alcoholic)**,n.
brewed ~, 749.7(4)
charge (~) with carbon dioxide, 1048.33
containing carbon dioxide—of ~s, 1048.44
~s, 748.6
beware,v., 577.9
bewilder,v., 605.1; see **confuse**,v.
bewildered,adj., 605.5
bewildering,adj., 604.1; 605.4
bewilderment,n., 605.2,3,18
bewitch,v., 663.12–15
beyond,adv.
go ~, 130.1–4
bias,n.
prejudice, 634.1
Bible,n., 648.1
accepts only the ~, one who, 648.6
book of ~ manuscripts, 687.1(9)
books of the ~, 648.1
Catholic ~, 648.1(21)
destruction of the ~, 687.24
~ expert, 648.5(1)
explanation of the ~, 599.2(3)
false ~, 648.4
Hindu ~, 648.1(19,20)
index of words in the ~, 687.9(5)
index to words of the ~, 648.3
Mohammedan ~, 648.1(11)
passage from the ~, 682.20(1)
pert. to explanation of the ~, 599.14
~ scholar, 648.5
spurious passages from the ~, 682.19(12)
strict adherence to the ~, 648.7
worship of the ~, 656.15(2)
Biblical,adj.
false ~ writings, 682.19(12)
bicycle,n., 192.17; see **cycle**,n.
big,adj., 906.3
abnormally ~, 906.10
amazingly ~, 906.12,13
~ amount, 916
~ and clumsy, 14.1(42); 14.5; 906.3(1); 906.15
~ and dignified, 906.6
~ and healthy, 906.3(4)
~ and heavy, 906.3(2)
~ and lasting, 906.3(3)
~ and rough, 906.14
~ and solid, 906.3(2)
~ and strong, 1.1(1,2); 906.8
~ and stupid, 906.3(1)
~ animal, 906.18
become ~ger, 907.4
becoming ~ger, 907.2
~ enough, 906.16
excessively ~ in growth, 906.11
extremely ~, 906.12,13

extremely ~ in extent, 906.17
~, hence impressive, 906.6
~, hence unmanageable, 906.5
~ like a statue, 906.7
~ like the ocean, 1029.72(11)
make ~ger, 907.1
make abnormally or unnaturally ~, 906.23
make seem ~, through a microscope or lens, 906.22
make seem ~ger than in actuality, 906.19
~ number, 916
~ (of crops, yields, etc.), 906.9
~ (of face, head, or forehead), 906.4
~ person, 906.18
~ quantity, 916
seem ~, 906.24
~ thing, 906.18
unusually ~, 906.10
very ~, 906.12,13
bigamy,n., 702.15
bigotry,n., 634.1
bile,n., 287.8(5)
carrying ~, 287.9
ox ~, 287.8(5)
bill,n.
~ of fare, 740.8
bill (for a debt),n., 218.5
billow,v., 93.1–3
bind,v., 302.28
binding,n.
books as to ~, 687.6
biological,adj.
~ classification or group, 318.8
doctrine of ~ reasoning, 751.14
~ movement, 101.1
biology,n., 403.26; 985.36
~ of radioactivity, 1069.21
birch,n.
of the ~ family, 996.25
bird,n., 405.1
anatomy of the ~, 338.10(5)
baby ~s, 405.5
caged ~, 405.1(3)
domesticated ~, 405.1(1–3,5,6)
drive ~s out of cover, 970.40
~ driven out of cover, 106.7
edible domestic ~s, 405.6
female ~, 405.3
full of ~s, 916.21
group of ~s, 403.5(2,4,6,9,14,15,21–24,27,28,30,45–47,49,52,54,55,60,64,68,70,74,78–80)
group of newborn ~s, 403.5(7,11,33)
~ life, 403.1(3,9)
like a specific ~, 405.10
living along shore (of ~s), 1029.97
male ~, 405.2
migratory ~, 405.1(12)
mythical ~, 405.1(8)
mythical creature, part ~, part woman, 662.26(3,5,11)
mythical immortal ~, 755.10
nest of ~s, 405.11
of ~s as to habits, 405.8
of ~s of prey, 405.8(1,10)
of domestic ~s, 405.8(2,3)
of non-migrating ~s, 405.8(12)
of perching ~s, 405.8(4,7)
of scratching ~s, 405.8(11)
of singing ~s, 405.8(6,7)
of specific ~s, 405.9
one who keeps ~s, 405.12
pert. to ~s, 405.7–9
place for ~s, 405.11

procreative instinct of ~s, 717.16
raising of ~s, 403.30(3)
science of ~s, 403.26(30,33)
singing ~, 405.1(7,10,13)
young ~, 405.4
young ~s of prey, 405.5(1)
birth,n., 720.1; see also childbirth, rebirth,n.
able to give ~, 715.1; see fertile,adj.
about to give ~, 718.7
after ~, 720.5(5)
before ~, 720.5(6)
child ~, 718.1–20; see childbirth,n.
Christ's ~, 720.3
day of ~, 720.6; see birthday,n.
give ~ from eggs, 717.14(1,11)
give ~ prematurely (of animals), 717.14(3,16)
give ~ to, 717.1
give ~ to animal young, 717.14
give ~ to young, 717.2–5
giving ~, 717.17
giving ~ from eggs, 717.17(2,6,7)
giving multiple ~, 717.17(1,5)
giving ~ to freaks, 537.8
happening, etc., at ~, 720.5(1)
multiple ~, child of, 721.5
new ~, 720.2
~ of a dead fetus, 720.4
of high ~, 720.9(10,15)
of low ~, 720.9(2,5)
of royal ~, 720.9(10)
period of giving ~, 718.3
pert. to ~, 720.5(2)
pert. to place of ~, 720.5(4)
power to cause ~, 5.1(12,17)
rate of ~, 720.15
unable to give ~, 716.1; see sterile,adj.
birthday,n.
pert. to ~s, 720.6
stars on one's ~, pert. to position of, 720.6
birthmark,n., 503.1(2)
birthstone,n., 961.16
bishop,n., 646.1; see also clergyman,n.
assistant ~, 556.3(11)
officiate as a ~, 646.10
remove as ~, 144.4(18)
bit,n.
a ~ cut off, 917.4
choice or pleasing ~, 917.2
disconnected ~ heard, 917.5
small ~, 917.15
smallest ~, 917.13
bite,n., 735.2
bite,v., 735.1
jump forward to ~, 735.8
try to ~, 735.8
biting,adj., 735.3,4
biting,n.
annoy by ~, 735.9
given to ~, 735.7
bitten,adj.
~ off, 735.10
~-off piece, 326.10(1)
bitter,adj.
~ and angry, 877.1(1); 878.10(1)
~ and sharp in manner, speech, or temper, 877.1(1)
~ and warped in judgment, prejudiced, etc., 877.1(2)
cause to be or feel ~, 877.3
~est part, 326.1(12)
~ from envy, hate, cynicism, etc., 877.1(2)

~ in attitude, 877.1
~ in feelings, 877.1
~ in language, 877.6
~ in smell, 445.10(1)
~ in taste, 452.11(2)
~ like wormwood, 452.11(1)
~ remark, 877.4
scornfully ~, 877.1(3)
something ~ to accept or endure, 877.7
something figuratively ~, 452.12
bitterness,n.
figurative ~, 452.13; 877.2,5
~ of feeling, 877.2
~ of spirit, 877.2(2)
~ of temper, 877.2(1)
prejudiced by ~, 877.1(2)
warped in judgment by ~, 877.1(2)
black,adj., 490.1
~ and blue, 490.7
mottled white and ~, 499.1(14)
~ of hair, 369.12(9,10);
369.13–15
~ pigment, 384.6
something ~, 490.6
black,n., 490.3
blackberry,n.
of the ~ family, 985.33(8)
blacken,v., 490.4,5
~ with charcoal, 1064.43
blackhead,n., 382.17
blackness,n., 490.2
blacksmith,n., 205.1(1); 1017.8
shop of a ~, 205.3
work of a ~, 205.2
bladder,n., 350.1(3,9,10)
disorders of the ~, 350.5
gall ~, pert. to the, 350.4
like a ~, 350.3
~-shaped, 507.17(6,29)
urinary ~, 350.1(9)
blame,n., 893.2
~ by the public, 893.3
deserving ~, 893.4,5
free from ~, 897.24,28
free of ~, 309.11(1,3); 845.6
person free of ~, 845.7
worthy of ~, 893.4,5
blame,v., 893.1
blamed,adj.
one ~ for the acts of others, 893.6
blameless,adj., 845.6
~ person, 845.7
blameworthy,adj., 893.4,5
blanket,n., 972.25
blaspheme,v., 861.11,12
blasphemous,adj., 861.8
blasphemy,n., 861.9,10
blaze,v., 1064.23,29
bleed,v., 352.7; see also blood,n.
bleeding,n., 352.8; see also blood,n.
abnormal ~, 352.23(8,9)
check ~, agent to, 352.15
checking ~, 352.14
medication to stop ~, 398.6(7,8)
blemish,n., 805.5
~ from healed burn or wound, 805.6
blemish,v., 805.2
blessing,n., 842.11
box containing ~s, 267.21
blind,adj., 481.2; 481.2(2,4)
become ~, 481.7
~ from snow reflection, 1039.18
make ~, 481.5,6,8
nearly ~, 481.2(1)
printing system for the ~, 690.6

spiritually or morally ~, 481.9(2)
totally ~, 481.2(3)
blindness,n., 481.1(1,2,5,10,32)
  beginning of ~, 481.1(3)
  color-~, 481.1(9,11)
  partial ~, 481.1(29)
  science of ~, 481.4
  word-~, 692.13(1)
blister,n., 382.24
  causing ~s, 382.27
  having ~s, 382.25
blister,v., 382.26
block,v., 557.1; 558.1
blockade,v., 296.8–10
blond,adj., 500.2(5,9)
  ~ of hair, 369.12(3,4,7,11–13) ; 369.13–15
blood,n., 352.1; see also **bleed**-**ing**,n.
  active circulation of ~, having, 352.3(13)
  carrying ~, 352.3(12)
  ~ cells, 352.2(5,6,8,10)
  clotted ~, 352.1(2,3)
  clotting element of ~, 352.2(12)
  clotting of ~, pert. to or causing, 352.3(19)
  containing ~, 352.3(1,4,14–16)
  covered with ~, 352.4
  cut off ~ supply from, 352.16
  cut off ~ supply to, 198.1(27)
  deficiency of red ~ cells, 352.23(1,3,6,13,18)
  deficient in red ~ cells, 352.18(1,2)
  descr. of ~, 352.3(10)
  destruction by white ~ corpuscles, 352.6(5)
  disorders of the ~, 352.23–25
  draw ~, 352.7–9
  eating ~, 734.27(29)
  excess of ~, 352.23(10,14)
  excess of white ~ corpuscles, 352.23(11,12)
  fluid part of the ~, 352.1(4)
  formation of ~, 352.6(4)
  full or ~, 352.3(1,4,7,14–16)
  high ~ pressure, 352.26(1,2)
  let ~, 352.7–9
  let (~) flow, 1036.21
  lie in ~, 1034.27
  like ~, 352.3(1,6,9)
  living in ~, 352.3(11)
  living on ~, 652.3(17)
  low ~ pressure, 352.26(3,4)
  mixed ~, person of, 430.6
  movement of ~, 352.6(1)
  of the color of ~, 352.3(4)
  pert. to ~, 352.3(1–4,8,14)
  ~ poisoning, 352.23(15,16,20, 21)
  ~ pressure, instr. to measure, 198.6(3) ; 352.20
  produced by ~, 352.3(5)
  producing ~, 352.3(5)
  red, like ~, 495.2(3,9)
  science of the ~, 401.1(28,29)
  shed ~, eager to, 889.9
  shedding of ~, pert. to, or at- tended by, 352.4(1,6,7)
  soft mass of ~, 352.1(1)
  stain with ~, 904.24; 1034.28
  stained by ~, 352.3(1) ; 352.4(5)
  ~sucker, 352.10; 662.7(27,45)
  ~sucking, 352.10
  ~ test, 401.10(7)
  thickening of ~, 352.6(2,3)
  tinged with ~, 352.4(3)
  transfer of ~, 352.12
  veins, descr. of ~ in, 352.3(19)
  ~ vessel system, 352.22
  ~ vessels, pert. to, 352.21

warm ~, having, 352.17
wet with ~, 1034.28
bloodied,adj., 352.4
bloodless,adj., 352.18
bloodshed,n.
  scene of ~, 562.8(1) ; 796.19(1)
bloodsucker,n., 352.10; 662.7(27, 45)
bloodsucking,adj., 352.11
bloody,adj., 352.4
bloody,v., 352.4(2,5)
bloom,v., 994.9; see **flower**,v.
blossom,v., 994.9; see **flower**,v.
blotch,n., 501.3
blotch,v., 501.2
blotchy,adj., 501.1
blouse,n., 982.14
  ~ front, 982.16
blow,n.
  a hit or hitting, 437.2
  blow for ~, 437.3
  death~, 437.2(1,2)
  finishing ~, 437.2(1,2,6)
blow,v., 1043.1,5,16,20
  ~ away, 1043.10
  device for ~ing, 1043.14,15
  ~ into, 1043.13
  ~ (of the wind), 1043.16
  ~ out, 1043.3,4,10
  ~ out, i.e., burst, 802.9,10; see **burst**,v.
  sound of ~ing, 1043.2
  sound of ~ing a horn, 1043.7, 8
  sound of wind ~ing, 1043.17
  ~ suddenly and violently (of the wind), 1043.20
  the ~ing of the wind, 1043.18
  to signal by ~ing a horn, 1043.9
  ~ up, 1043.11
  ~ up, i.e., explode, 802.9,10; see **explode**,v.
  ~ upon, 1043.13
  ~ with the breath, 1043.1
blowing,adj.
  ~ (of the wind), 1043.19
  ~ out clouds of tobacco smoke, 1057.19
blowing,n.
  sounds of ~, 461.1–3; 461.4(2, 3,6) ; 461.5
blown,adj.
  ~ about by the wind, 1043.21
  air, smoke, or vapor ~ out, 1045.2
  ~ down by the wind, 1043.27
blowout,n., 802.11
blowup,n., 802.11
blowy,adj., 1043.19
blue,adj.
  color, 492.1–13
  sad, 1123.1; 1124.1
  abnormally ~ skin, 384.2
  black and ~, 490.7
  ~ coating on brass, copper, or bronze, 1016.18,19
blush,v., 384.21(2–4,6,7)
  cause to ~, 384.22
blushing,adj., 384.23
boar,n., 419.7
  group of ~s, 403.5(63)
board,n., 997.5
  nail ~s to joists, 1022.5
  ~ ridden on water, 192.5
board,v.
  ~ a ship, 115.8
boardinghouse,n., 753.14; see **hotel**,n.
boast,n., 872.15
boast,v., 872.1
  ~ about, 872.2
  ~ extravagantly, 872.4
  ~ noisily, 872.3
  ~ wildly, 872.4

boasted,adj.
  descr. of thing ~ about, 872.26
  thing or person ~ about, 872.25
boaster,n., 872.16
  ~ and bully, 872.21
  empty ~, 872.20
  extravagant ~, 872.18
  noisy ~, 872.17
  wild ~, 872.18
boastful,adj., 872.23
  act the ~ daredevil, 872.5
  act the ~ ruffian, 872.5
  act the ~ soldier, 872.5
  act the ~ swordsman, 872.5
  ~ daredevil, 872.19
  ~ defiance, 872.14
  ~ language, 665.9(58,61)
  merry and ~, 1104.5
  noisily ~, 872.74
  ~ pretender or deceiver, 823.21; 872.22
  ~ ruffian, 872.19
  ~ soldier, 872.19
  ~ swordsman, 872.19
boastfully,adv.
  place ~, 872.6
  push forward ~, 872.6
  put ~, 872.6
  show ~, 951.1(23,24,31,39) ; 951.32
boasting,adj., 872.23; see **boast**-**ful**,adj.
boasting,n., 872.7
  ~ about accomplishments, 872.8
  ~ about one's country, 784.8(1,6)
  ~ about oneself, 872.8
  empty ~, 872.11
  extravagant ~, 872.10
  false ~, 872.13
  ~ hiding reluctance to fight, 872.14
  noisy ~, 872.9
  proud ~, 872.12
  wild ~, 872.10
boat,n., 115.3; see also **ship**,n.
  board towed behind motor~, 192.5
  carry by ~, 115.5
  Chinese ~, 115.3(12) ; 115.20(8)
  Eskimo ~, 115.3(9,17)
  go by ~, 115.4,25
  group of ~s, 115.22
  Japanese ~, 115.3(12)
  ~ race, 20.2(10)
  ride in a ~, 115.4
  ~s, 115.2,22
  sail~, 115.20
  ~-shaped, 507.17(50,69)
  skill in ~s, 115.6
bodiless,adj., 338.16
body,n., 338.1,2
  ~ and soul, doctrine of, 1089.10
  appear in form of a ~, 483.3(6)
  applied to a limited area of the ~, 782.16
  artificial member or part, ad- dition of to the ~, 400.6(36)
  bend the ~ in gesture, 102.1(2, 3,8)
  bend the upper ~, 152.1(1,8, 15)
  cause to become part of the ~ of, 326.46
  clean the ~, 899.48
  dead ~, 794.34; see **dead body**,n.
  deducing character from shape of ~, 365.4
  deprive of a ~, 338.17

deprive of existence as a ~, 338.17

discharge from or in the ~, 287.1–11

division into ~, soul, and spirit, 325.3(9) ; 932.23

figure of the ~, 338.4

fluids of the ~, or humors, 1091.30

growth on or in the ~, 731.21(3–5,8–13,16,18,20) ; see also **cancer, tumor,**n.

having a ~, 338.13–15

in the form of a ~, 338.13–15

legal ~, 338.6

main ~, 338.5

~-minded, 1091.2

motion of the ~, pert. to, 79.27(3) ; 102.11

of ~ and mind or emotions, 1092.109

opening in the ~, 298.8

pain to the ~, 1137

person as to ~ type, 338.12

pert. to mind and ~, 338.7(6)

pert. to passions of the ~, 338.8

pert. to the ~, 338.7

position of the ~, 60.1

power of the ~, 5.1(7,17)

sciences of the ~, 338.18

sexual interest in part of the ~, 710.33(12)

shape of the ~, 338.9(3,4)

show one's ~ in public, tendency to, 951.31

small area of the ~, 338.3

soil as origin of human ~, 999.10

sounds made by the ~, 460.1–4; see **sound,**n.

structure of the ~, 338.9(1,2, 4) ; see **anatomy,**n.

~ types, descr. of, 338.11

undeveloped part of the ~, 338.1(6)

without ~ form, 338.16

without a ~, 338.16

body of water,n., 1029

bodyguard,n., 568.5

British king's ~, 564.1(6,56)

boil,n.

~ on the skin, 382.16

boil,v., 1028.1 ; 1061.1,2; see **cook,**v.

boiler,n., 261.10

boiling,adj., 1028.6

boiling,n., 1028.2

keep below ~, 1028.8

remain below ~, 1028.8

vessel for ~, 261.10

boisterous,adj., 865.1(5,6) ; see **noisy,**adj.

bold (brave),adj., 575.1; see **brave,**adj.

bold (forward), adj., 862.1

~ act, 862.8

be so ~ as to, 862.10

cause to be ~, 862.12

contemptuously or scornfully ~, 862.3

~ girl, 862.6

~ person, 862.4

~ speech, 862.8

~ woman, 862.7

~ young person, 862.5

boldly (impudently),adv.

act ~, 862.9

face ~, 862.11

boldness (forwardness),n., 862.2

bomb,n., 565.10

drop ~s on, 565.3(2)

throw ~s at, 565.3(2,3,13,16)

bond,n.

---

floating of ~s, 113.7

stocks and ~s, 255.10(8)

bondage,n., 310.2,4; see **slavery,**n.

bone,n., 354.1

arm ~, 354.1(7,11)

breast~, 354.1(9)

cast for broken ~s, 1007.20

change into ~, 354.4

chest~, 354.1(9)

collar~, 354.1(2)

disorders of the ~s, 354.16

ear ~, 354.1(4)

formation of ~, 354.5

leg ~, 354.1(3,8)

like ~, 354.2(1–4)

~ marrow, pert. to, 354.10

~ pain, 1137.56(23)

pert. or relating to ~, 354.2

producing ~, 354.6

science dealing with the ~s, 401.1(60,61,64,65)

structure where ~s of corpses are piled, 797.10(1,6)

~ structure, 354.7

tooth ~, 354.1(1)

bonus,n., 219.3; 219.3(6,15,34, 38,39)

bony,adj.

make ~, 354.3

book,n., 687.1; see also **literature, story,**n.

additional matter at end of a ~, 687.9(1,2) ; 908.22

animal skin for ~binding, 382.1(20)

arrangement of ~s, pert. to, 311.4(1)

~ as to binding, 687.6

~ as to format, 687.1(11)

blank ~, 687.1(1)

~ by unknown author, 687.1(3)

~ carried around, 687.1(23)

censor ~s, 899.17

censor of ~s, 899.18

cover of a ~, 1001.16

design on title page of ~, 311.8(12)

desire for ~s, 687.10

destroyer of ~s, 687.25

destruction of ~s, 687.24; 801.2(1)

eating ~s, 734.27(5)

exciting ~, 1100.4

expert in ~s, 687.11,13

familiar with ~s, 692.10

famous ~, 615.5

guide ~, 177.4(1) ; 687.1(5,12, 14)

illustration opposite title page in a ~, 687.9(7)

~ in two languages, 687.1(10)

index of words in a ~, 687.9(5)

inscription in a ~, 687.9(4)

instructional ~, 687.1(12,14, 16,18–20,23)

large ~, 687.1(21)

lines in a ~, instr. to measure, 687.23

list of ~s on a subject, 687.12–14

list of what is in a ~, 687.9(6,8)

love for ~s, 700.30(2) ; 700.31, 32

mark chapters, etc., of a ~ in red, 495.9–12

obscene ~, 709.33

~ of an opera or musical comedy, 687.1(15)

~ of chronological events, 774.7(1)

~ of daily record, 774.7(7)

~ of different versions, 687.1(24)

~ of manuscripts, 687.1(9)

~ of the Scriptures, 687.1(9)

~ on religious subject, 687.1(22)

parts of a ~, 687.9

place for ~s, 687.15,16

prayer ~, 687.1(7)

production of ~s, 687.17

prohibited ~, 899.21

~ published as propaganda, 687.1(17,22)

publisher's emblem in a ~, 687.9(4)

ribald ~s, 1115.8

~s printed before 1500, 687.4(1)

seller of ~s, 687.18,20

selling of ~s, 687.19,20

series of ~s, 173.9(18)

series of four ~s, 687.4(2)

series of three ~s, 687.4(3)

sex ~s, 709.32,33

small ~, 687.1(6,8,17,22)

steal ~s, desire to, 687.21

story about ~s, 687.22

uncensored ~s, 899.22

unclean ~s, 899.22

~ under another's name, 687.1(2)

~ under one's own name, 687.1(4)

unfamiliar with ~s, 692.11

~ with editors' notes, 687.1(24)

worship of ~s, 656.15(2)

writer of a ~, 687.2,5; see also **author, writer,**n.

~ written for money only, 965.1(44)

bookbinder,n., 687.8

bookbinding,n.

art of ~, 687.7

bookseller,n., 687.18

pert. to a ~, 687.20

boot,n., 979.2; see **shoe,**n.

high ~s, 979.6

~s, collectively, 979.1

boot,v., 979.3

booth,n.

~ for horses or cattle, 787.7(35)

~ for study, 787.7(11,17)

bootlicker,n., 852.9

booty,n., 247.9; 248.5; 250.5

border,n.

boundary, 793.1; see **boundary,**n.

edge, 793.20; see **edge,**n.

limit, 793.13,14; see **limit,**n.

~land, 1003.2(2)

ocean ~, 1029.79

river ~, 1029.43–45

border,v.

~ on land, 1003.4

~ on water, 1029.81

bore,n.

boring person, 583.2,3

boring persons, 583.4

bore,v.

be boring, 583.7

bored,adj.

uninterested, 583.8

be ~ with, 583.10

tired and ~, 12.1(22)

~ with pleasure, 1105.33–37

boredom,n., 583.9

twist around in ~, 156.1(26, 35)

boring, adj., 583.1

be, or become ~, 583.7

find ~, 583.10

~ly unchanging, 531.3

~ person, 583.3

~ routine, 583.5
~ thing, 583.2
born,adj., 720.9; see also **native,
reborn,**adj.
~ again, 720.23
~ alive, 720.9(14)
be ~, 720.7
be ~ again, 720.21
be ~ from egg, 720.7(2,3)
being ~, 720.8
Christ was ~, reproduction of
stable where, 720.16
~ dead, 720.9(12)
eldest ~, being the, 759.23
humbly ~, 720.9(2,5)
~ in heaven, 1051.19
~ in wedlock, 720.9(6)
just ~, 720.9(9,16)
not yet ~, 720.14
~ of high rank, 720.9(10,15)
~ on or of the earth,
720.9(13)
~ out of wedlock, 720.10; see
bastard,adj.
people ~ at about same time,
720.13
prematurely ~ animal, 403.14
~ together, 720.9(4)
~ too soon, 720.9(1,11)
unfortunately ~, 720.9(7)
Borneo,n.
ruler of ~, 1073.36(23)
bosom,n., 360.1; see **breast,**n.
both,pron.
shared by ~, 931.18
bottle,n., 216.7(2,4,8–10,20,27,31,
41,42)
liquor ~, 261.7(19,20,22,25,29)
medicine ~, 261.7(31,41)
perfume ~, 261.7(12)
vinegar ~, 261.7(17)
wine ~, 261.7(19,20,29)
bottom,adj., 169.3
bottom,n., 169.4
bring up from ~, 163.3
fall to the ~, 167.1(28,30,38)
~ of the sea or ocean, 169.4(1,
6,8)
~ of a ship, 169.4(7)
~ of water, 1029.100(3,10)
part on the ~, 326.1(7,36,37)
river ~, 1029.42; 1029.100(10)
what settles to or at the ~,
757.11
bought,adj.
that which is ~ and sold,
212.4(1)
bounce,v., 110.1; see also
jump,v.
bound,adj.
limited, 793.17
~ by curved lines, 793.11
bound,v.
jump, 110.1; see **jump,**v.
limit, 793.8,15
boundary,n., 793; see also
bounds,n.
limit, 793.13,14; see **limit,**n.
be at the ~ of, 1003.4
be on the ~ of, 793.8
~ between earth and sky,
1051.9
beyond the ~, 793.12
circular space or object, ~
of, 793.5(1)
enclosed by curved ~, 300.5
enclosing ~, 793.1(2,5)
extreme ~, 922.16
inside the ~ of, 1024.7
~ line, 793.6
marked as a ~, 793.9
marker of a ~, 793.7
measurement around the
outer ~, 946.33
name the ~ of, 694.6(4)

nation's ~, 793.2,3
~ of an object, 793.5
~ of earth zones, 1004.10
~ of trees, bushes, or shrubs,
996.30
outside the ~ of, 1024.6
pert. to a ~, 793.9
place around a ~, 782.1(3)
placed at a ~, 793.9
set the ~ of, 793.15,16
sharing a ~, 793.10
boundless,adj., 755.3; 906.17
bounds,n.
limits, 793.13,14; see **limit,**n.
set the ~ of, 793.15,16
without ~, 755.3,5
without clear ~, 755.6
bovine,adj., 410.4,5
bovine,n., 410.1–6
male ~, 410.1(2,3,6,9,10)
young ~, 410.2
bow (gesture),n., 855.9(1,2,4–6)
bow,n.
weapon, 566.1
art of ~ and arrow, 566.18
enthusiasm for ~ and arrow,
566.19
parts of a ~, 566.2,3
~s and arrows, 566.21
study of ~ and arrow, 566.19
use of ~ and arrow. 566.16,19
user of ~ and arrow, 566.15,20
bow,v.
gesture in respect, 855.10
bowels,n., 347.9; see **intestine,**n.
feel sharp pain in the ~,
1137.62
pain in the ~, 1137.56(2,7,10,
13,15,27,30)
bowl,n., 261.9
~ for porridge, 261.9(8)
~ for serving soup, 261.9(10)
full ~, 925.11
bowlegged,adj., 345.7(1,3,8,9)
~ condition, 345.8
~ person, 345.9
box,n., 261.1(10,12,13,16,27,32) ;
see **container,**n.
cylindrical ~, 261.1(20)
~ for cigar or tobacco storage, 262.3(15)
~ for implements while traveling, 261.16(10)
~ for traveling, 261.16(17)
fruit or vegetable ~,
261.1(18)
box,v.
fight, 562.2; 562.2(6,7) ; see
fight,v.
boxer,n., 562.4; see **fighter,**n.
professional ~, 562.4(1)
weight of a ~, 947.47
boxing,n., 562.3; see **fighting,**n.
boy,n., 760.5
feminine ~, 707.11
mischievous ~, 202.3(10) ;
760.5(8)
street ~, 760.5(1,6)
bracelet,n., 961.1(1–3,7,9,12)
brag,n., 872.15; see **boast,**n.
brag,v., 872.1; see **boast,**v.
bragger,n., 872.16; see
boaster,n.
bragging,n., 872.7; see **boasting,**n.
brain,n., 357.1
activity of the ~, 357.7
disorders or diseases of the ~,
357.10
~ fever, 357.10(16)
inflammation of the ~,
357.10(1,4,6,7,15,18)
like the ~, 357.6
membranes of the ~, 387.1(1,
3,7,13)

~-minded, 1091.2
~ parts, 357.5
pert. to the ~, 357.4
science of the ~, 401.1(14,49)
small ~, 357.2,3
waves of the ~, instrument
to trace, 357.9
X-ray of the ~, 357.8
brainy,adj., 594.1; 595.1
bran,n.
like ~, 987.14
branch,n.
plant part, 990; see also
twig,n.
beat with a ~, 990.26
cut the ~es of a tree, 996.5
fallen ~, 990.17
fallen ~es, 990.18
fire, ~es for a, 1064.61(2,6)
~ for beating, 990.25
having ~es, 990.21,22
hit with a ~, 990.26
remove the ~es from, 990.24
small ~, 990.4
tree ~, 990.1,2,7,20
young ~, 990.5,6
brandy,n., 749.6; see also **liquor (alcoholic),**n.
brass,n.
cover with ~, 1016.11
covered with ~, 1016.10
decorate with ~, 1016.11
fuse with ~, 302.12(3)
green or blue coating on old
~, 1016.19
like ~, 1016.10
like ~ in color, sound, or
strength, 1016.13
made of ~, 1016.12
make out of ~, 1016.11
ornamented with ~, 1016.10
worker in ~, 1016.14
brassiere,n., 981.3(2)
brave,adj., 575.1
~ act, 52.5(26,27,37,39,41) ;
575.7
~ actions, 575.8,9
be ~, 575.4
~ behavior, 575.8
make ~, 575.10
~ person, 575.3
~ undertaking, 575.7(5)
~ when drunk, 575.1(33)
bravely,adv., 4.24
bravery,n., 575.2
call upon one's ~, 575.11
display of ~, 951.3(3)
literary piece about ~,
682.16(11)
perseverance and ~, 575.2(2)
poem about ~, 689.2(9)
pretended ~, 575.5,6
pretense of ~, 826.10(1)
show ~, 575.4
story of ~, 685.1(26)
token of ~, 951.8
bread,n., 1062.1–3
~ dipped into liquid, 1035.2
eating ~, 734.27(24)
mixture for ~, 1062.9,10
morsel of ~ topped with food,
740.15(2)
piece of ~, 326.10(7)
shaped mass of ~, 1062.2
shaped mass of ~, individual,
1062.3
break,n., 802.3,8
break,v.
~ apart, 802.1(1,10,11) ; 802.21,
23; see also **burst, ex-
plode,**v.
~ blood vessels, etc., 802.1(10)
~ bones, etc., 802.1(7)
cause to ~, 802.2
~ down (a structure), 802.24

~ down into partial ruin, 802.26
~ holes into, 802.1(16)
~ in sides of, 802.1(16)
~ into layers, 802.1(15)
~ into parts, 326.12
~ into pieces, 326.12,13,19–21; 802.1(1,2,5,6,8,9,12–14)
~ laws, 802.29–32
~ off, 802.1(2) ; 802.2(3)
~ off a part or piece, 326.12
~ off the hair, desire to, 371.9
~ open, 802.1(11) ; 802.2(1)
~ promises, 802.29
~ rules, 802.29
~ up, 802.21,23
~ up into parts, 802.25
breakable,adj., 802.4,5,7
~ and delicate, 11.1(5)
hard but ~, 802.6
breakage,n., 802.3
cause ~ in, 802.2
undergo ~, 802.1
breakdown,n.
have a mental, moral, or physical ~, 802.28
breakfast,n.
combined ~ and lunch, 740.16(5)
eat ~, 734.1(6)
time for ~, 740.19
breaking,n., 802.3
~ of the peace, 802.32,33
~ up of ice on river, 802.22
breakwater,n., 1033.1
breast,n., 360.1
excessive growth of the ~s, 360.6,7
false ~, 823.19
having ~s, 360.5
having beautiful ~s, 360.5(4)
having prominent ~s, 360.5(3)
having two ~s, 360.5(2)
like a ~, 360.3,4
more than two ~s, 360.8
~ pad, 823.19
pert. to the ~, 360.2
separation between female ~s, 325.7(2)
~-shaped, 507.17(48)
small ~s, 360.9
drink from the ~, 360.13
feed at the ~, 360.11–13
inflammation of the ~, 360.10
stop feeding at the ~, 360.14
breastbone,n., 354.1(9)
deformity of the ~, 354.16(4)
breath,n., 376.3,9
catch the ~, 376.1(5,6)
foul ~, 376.10
holding one's ~ in expectation, 268.10
holding one's ~ in wonder, 271.6
let out a long ~, 376.1(14)
measurement of air in ~, 1045.21(4)
offensive ~, 376.10
out of ~, 376.7(3,4,6)
take a long ~, 376.1(22)
breathe,v., 376.1
~ in, 376.1(8–10,15–17,20–22)
medication ~d in, 376.12(3,4)
~ noisily, 376.1(5,6,11,12, 14–19,21–23)
~ noisily in sleep, 376.1(18)
~ out, 376.1(2–4,7,11,12,14,19, 22,24)
~ oxygen into the blood, 1049.8
~ quickly, 376.1(11)
something ~d out, 376.11
~ tobacco smoke, 1050.7,9

~ tobacco up the nose, 376.1(20)
unable to ~, be, 376.17–19
unable to ~, make, 376.16, 18–20
~ with difficulty, 376.1(5,6,11, 12,16,17,21,23)
breathed,adj.
~ sound, 670.14(1)
breathing,adj., 376.4,5
~ abnormally, 376.7
~ hoarsely, 376.7(5)
~ with difficulty, 376.7
breathing,n., 376.2
abnormal ~, 376.2(1)
cut off ~, 376.16–20
descr. of ~, 376.4
devices used in ~, 376.12(3,5, 7,8)
inflammation of ~ tract, 376.8
medication to help ~, 376.12(3, 4)
normal ~, 376.2(2)
organs of ~, 376.12(1,2,6) ; see also **gill**, **lung**,n.
pert. to ~, 376.4
rapid ~, 376.2(3,5)
science of ~ organs, 376.15
sound of ~, 376.6
stop ~, 376.17–19
bred, adj.
cross~, 719.6
pure~, 719.6
breed,n., 719.7
ancestry, 723.1; see **ancestry**,n.
breed,v., 717.1,6,7; 719.1,2
place where animals ~, 403.22
place where birds ~, 405.11; see also **nest**,n.
~ with another race, 719.2(1)
breeder,n.
~ of animals or plants, 719.4
~ with another race, 719.4
breeding,n.
act of ~ animals, plants, etc., 719.3
animal ~, 403.30(1–6)
animal or plant produced by ~, 719.5
animals kept for ~, 403.4(4) ; 403.7(14)
kept for ~, 719.9
~ place, 403.22
place for ~ birds, 405.11; see also **nest**,n.
science of ~ animals or plants, 719.10
brewing,n.
chemistry of ~, 749.36(2)
bribable,adj., 220.6
bribe,n., 220.7
money for a ~, 220.5(1,3,5)
take a ~, 220.7
bribe,v., 220.1
serving to ~, 220.4
try to ~, 220.1(3)
briber,n., 220.3
bribery,n., 220.2
cause commission of crime by ~, 220.1(6)
guiltless of ~, 845.14
not open to ~, 845.13
open to ~, 220.6
brick,n.
build, cover, line, etc., with ~, 1002.13
build with ~, 1006.60
builder with ~, 1006.58
cement for joining ~s, 1006.1(28)
construction of ~, 1002.12
fireplace ~, 1064.59
furnace ~, 1064.59

hard ~, 1002.15
mass of fused ~s, 1002.15
place where ~s are made, 1002.10,11
product made of ~, 1006.1(24)
put ~s on, 1002.13
strengthen with ~, 1006.60
worker with ~s, 1002.14
bride,n.
garments of a ~, 974.35(4)
personal possessions of a ~, 974.35(4)
bridge,n., 1033.52
build a ~ over, 1033.50
builder of ~s, 727.3(2)
distance between supports of a ~, 1033.53
extend across, like a ~, 1033.51
kinds of ~s, 1033.52
part between supports of a ~, 1033.53
science of building ~s, 727.10(1–3)
space for passage under a ~, 787.1(11)
support for a ~, 1022.2(7,17) ; 1022.17
brief,adj., 911.1; see **short**,adj.
brief case,n., 261.16(3,12)
bright (lighted),adj., 1065.50
become ~, 1065.60,61
clear and ~, 598.3
excessively ~, 1065.51
extremely ~ for a short time, 1065.53
grow ~ and clear, 1065.61
make ~, 1065.54
make (a person) ~ in appearance, 1065.59
not ~, 1072.1
showy and ~, 951.34(3,5)
~ spot in fog, 1041.6
~ thing, 1065.52
vulgarly ~, 1065.51
brighten,v., 1065.54,60
substance for ~ing, 1065.58
tool for ~ing, 1065.57
brightened,adj., 1065.55
brightness (lightness),n., 1065.56
~ around king's picture, 1065.27
bewilder or confuse with ~, 1065.78
dim (vision) with ~, 1065.78
overpower with ~, 1065.78
restore to ~, 832.5
surrounding ~, 1065.27
brilliance,n.
display of ~, 951.3(3)
brilliant,adj.
~ act, 52.5(19)
group of ~ people or things, 1056.11
brim,n., 793.20
bring,v.
~ about, 15.1
~ about by trickery, 15.1(14)
~ back, 191.1
~ back after getting, 240.1(17)
~ back to good condition, 191.1(2)
~ back to usefulness, 191.1(2)
~ by laughter, 1111.28
~ in, 135.1–3
~ in illegally, 1087.15–18
~ in secretly, 1087.15–18
~ near, 790.11,13
~ on unexpectedly, 269.4
~ together in a collection, 319.1
~ together in a crowd, 318.11

~ together toward a point, 322.11
~ up a child, 721.16; see also upbringing,n.
~ up from bottom, 163.3
brink,n., 793.20
be on the ~ of, 793.25
bristle,n.
~-shaped, 507.17(72)
Britain,n.; see England,n.
British,adj.; see English,adj.
Brittany,n.
inhabitant or native of ~, 784.15(7,11)
pert. to ~, 784.16
broad,adj.
low and ~, 169.1
broad-minded,adj., 636.1,5
~ person, 636.6
broadness,n.
~ of attitudes, sympathies, point of view, etc., 636.4
broil,v., 1061.1,2; see cook,v.
broken,adj.
become ~, 802.1
~ down, 802.27
easily ~, 802.4–7
~ part or piece, 326.10
~ place, 802.8
bronze,n.
give the color or appearance of ~ to, 1016.16
gold-coated ~, 1013.10
green or blue coating on old ~, 1016.18,19
like ~, 1016.15
made of ~, 1016.17
Brooklyn,n.
tree that grows in ~, 996.4(1)
broom,n., 899.33
small ~ for clothes, 899.34
brothel,n., 711.9
keeper of a ~, 711.10
region of ~s, 711.11
region of ~s in Japan, 711.12
brother,n., 722.11
like a ~, 722.7(3)
pert. to a ~, 722.7(3,6)
~s, 722.12
younger ~, 722.11(4)
brotherhood,n., 722.13
brown,adj., 497.2
become ~, 497.3
~ like copper, 1016.8
make ~, 497.3
~ of hair, 369.12(2,5,9); 369.13–15
brown,n., 497.1
bruise,n., 803.2; see injury,n.
bruise,v., 803.1; see injure,v.
brunette,adj., 369.12(2,9,10); 369.13,14
brunette,n., 369.15
brush,n.
~ for clothes, 899.34
brush,v.
~ clean, 899.1(2,16); 899.32
brushed,adj.
neatly ~ or combed, 902.1(3)
bubble,n., 1027.38; 1028
come out or off in ~s, 1028.4
develop ~s, 1028.1
full of ~s, 1028.7
give off ~s, 1028.1
like ~s, 1028.7
mass of small ~s, 1028.9
rise in ~s, 1028.4
~s of liquid, 1028.9
~s of saliva, 1028.9
~s of sweat, 1028.10,11
bubble,v., 1028.1
~ and foam, 1028.22
~ and hiss, 1028.5
cause to ~, 1028.3
bubbling,adj., 1028.6

bubbling,n., 1028.2
sound of ~, 469.1(9,10);
469.2(1)
buffalo,n.
wild ~, 410.7
buffoon,n., 1116.1
bug,n., 428.3
like a ~, 428.2
of ~s, 428.1
science of ~s, 403.26(15,17)
young of ~s, 428.4
bugle,n.
signal by ~, 956.1(11,12)
build,v., 727.1
make, 726.1
~ a foundation, 1006.8
~ a nest, 727.1(6)
~ a wall, 1006.8
~ on top, 727.1(9)
~ over, 727.1(8,9)
~ poorly, 727.1(5)
~ with brick, 1006.60
~ with stone, 1006.60
builder,n., 727.3
maker, 726.2
~ of bridges, 727.3(2)
~ of roads, 727.3(2)
building,n.
something made, 726.3
a ~, 727.4,12; see also structure,n.
act of ~, 727.2
additional ~, 727.13
angle of a ~, 944.2
arched ~, 727.12(2,13)
circular ~, 727.12(13)
custodian of a public ~, 8.16(3,4)
design of ~, 727.6
designer of ~s, 727.3(1)
fortified ~, 727.12(5); see castle,n.
given to ~, 727.9
~ in which to live, 753.1; see home, house,n.
legislature's ~, 727.12(3)
manner of ~, 727.6
parts of a ~, 727.15
pert. to ~, 727.5
science of ~, 727.10
skill in ~, 727.8
space surrounded by ~s, 787.1(14)
square space, ~s around a, 727.16
storage ~, 727.12(8,14)
tall ~, 727.12(15)
tombs, a ~ for, 727.12(11)
wing of a ~, 727.15
bull,n., 410.1(3,6,9,10)
castrated ~, 410.1(6,9)
mythical creature, half ~, half man, 662.26(8)
of ~s, 410.4(3,4)
part ~, part human, 662.28(2)
young ~, 410.2(1,5)
bullet,n., 565.10
container for ~s, 565.15
pert. to ~s, 565.12
~s, 565.11
science of ~ flight, 565.7,16
sound of a ~, 469.7(21)
bullfight,n., 562.17
favoring ~s, 562.18
pert. to ~s, 562.18
bullfighter,n., 562.15
bullfighting,n., 562.16
bully,n., 8.10
~ and boaster, 872.21
bundle,n., 318.18
burden,n., 948.14; see also weight,n.
something carried, 190.9
additional ~, 948.14(13)

become free of ~, 309.21(1)
carrier of a ~, 948.15
carrying a heavy ~, 948.17
excessive ~, 948.14(9,10,13)
feeling of ~, 948.16
free of ~, 309.11(11,12,15,28);
309.15(19)
free of a ~, 948.19
get rid of a ~, 948.20
heavy ~, 948.14(6,8,11)
lift the ~ of, 948.21
~ of cost, 948.14(13)
~ of debt, 948.14(3)
~ of demand, 948.14(14)
~ of duty, 948.14(3,12,14)
~ of legal obligation, 948.14(3)
~ of requirement, 948.14(14)
oppressive ~, 948.14(4,8)
burden,v., 948.8
~ cruelly, 948.9
~ excessively, 948.11
~ with debt, 948.10
~ with legal obligations, 948.10
burdened,adj., 948.17
~ by sadness, etc., 1125.39
excessively ~, 948.18
over~, 948.18
feeling of being ~, 948.16
state of being ~, 948.16
burdensome,adj., 948.13
hard to carry, 190.10
~ and uncomfortable, 948.12(4,6)
~ and unpleasant, 948.12(5)
be too ~ for, 948.12
excessively ~, 948.13(7)
make less ~, 948.21
burdensomeness,n.
cruel ~, 948.16
burglar,n., 250.3
burglary,n., 250.2; see stealing,n.
burial,n., 797
~ alive, 797.4
dig up from ~, 171.1(5–7,12, 19); 797.22
~ grounds, 797.6; see cemetery,n.
like a ~ place, 797.12
monument, with ~ elsewhere, 797.14
~ of a corpse, 797.2
pert. to ~, 797.3
place for ~, 797.10; see also cemetery, grave, tomb,n.
prepares a corpse for ~, one who, 799.3
superintendent of ~s, 797.15; 799.3
wrap for ~, 797.5
wrappings for a corpse for ~, 797.20
burial place,n.
Egyptian ~, 1006.1(32)
mound over ~, 166.1(28)
prehistoric ~, 1006.21
burlesque,n., 869.3
comedian in ~, 1114.7
woman who undresses in ~, 984.13
burn,n., 1064.35
blemish left by a ~, 805.6
burn,v., 1064.33,34
give off light, 1065.45
~ a corpse to ashes, 798.1; see cremation,n.
destroy and ~ before retreating, 1064.38,39
not likely to ~, 1064.87,88
~ (something), 1064.33
~ the portrait of, 966.22
~ the statue of, 966.22
unable to ~, 1064.87,88

~ without flame, 1064.29
burned,adj., 1064.40
  able to be ~, 1064.89
  ~ coal, 1064.42(4,5)
  ~ offering, 1064.42(2)
  ~ piece of wood, 1064.42(1,3–6)
  ~ substance, 1064.37;
    1064.42(3,4)
burning,adj., 1064.28
  be ~, 1064.29
  ~ coal, 1064.42(4,5)
  ~ piece of wood, 1064.42(1,5,6)
burning,n.
  act of ~, 1064.31
  death by ~, 1064.64
  fact of ~, 1064.30
  heap of wood for ~ a person
    to death, 1064.61(8)
  malicious ~, 1064.15,16
  means of ~, 1064.36
  place for ~, 1064.55
  process of ~, 1064.31
  result of ~, 1064.44
  soil used for ~, 1064.61(7)
  spontaneous ~, 1064.27
  state of ~, 1064.30,32
  substance for ~, 1064.61
burst,n., 802.11
burst,v., 802.9,10; see also
  explode,v.
  cause to ~, 802.10
  ~ forth, 802.9(1)
  ~ inward, 802.9(3)
bursting,adj., 802.11
bursting,n., 802.11
bury,v.
  ~ (a corpse), 797.1
  ~ with snow, 1039.10
bus,n., 192.6(6,17)
  driver of a ~, 192.7
  rider in a ~, 192.8
bush,n.
  a growth of ~es, 996.27,28
  area covered by ~es,
    985.34(3,4,5,18)
  boundary of ~es, 996.30
  enclose with ~es, 996.31
  fence of ~es, 996.30
  fence with ~es, 996.31
  place or tract of ~es, 996.29
  row of ~es, 996.30
  short ~, 985.6(35)
  surround with ~es, 996.31
business,n., 210.1
  ~ cycle, phases of, 210.8
  ~ dealing, 210.1
  devotion to ~, 210.6
  do ~, 210.2
  god of ~, 210.11
  have ~ relations, 523.2
  important person in ~, 848.22
  interested only in ~, 214.1(6)
  ~ involving risk, 572.8
  make into a ~, 210.5
  ~man, 210.4
  ~ organization, 210.7
  person in ~, 210.4
  pert. to ~, 210.3
  ~ practice, 210.6
  reckless ~ practices, engage
    in, 210.9
  refusal to do ~ with, 581.12
  ~ relations, 523.1(3,6)
  ~ theory, 210.6
  traveling on ~, 107.4(4,7)
  try to get ~, 18.1(16,23)
busy,adj., 208.1
  be ~, 208.2
  being ~, 208.3
  cause to be ~, 208.4
  keep ~, 208.2,4
butter,n., 510.8
  referring to ~, 510.9(3,4)

vessel for making ~,
  261.7(14)
butterfly,n., 428.3
  like a ~, 428.2
  of the ~, 428.1(15,17,19,20)
  science of the ~, 403.26(22)
  student of the ~, 403.27(3)
  young of the ~, 428.4(1,3,9)
buttocks,n., 348.1
  animal's ~, 348.3
  beautiful ~, having, 348.6
  covering for the ~, 980.2,3
  fat ~, having, 348.7
  horse's ~, 348.2
  one of the two ~, 348.5
  pert. to the ~, 348.4
  region of the ~, 348.4,8
buy,n., 211.8
buy,v., 211.1
  ~ and sell, 211.1(2,11–13)
  ~ back, 211.1(9)
  ~ the freedom of, 211.1(8)
buyer,n., 211.4
  ~s, 211.5
Byron,n.
  descr. of writing like ~'s,
    686.8(1)

C

C(the letter),n.
  mark placed under a ~,
    680.1(8)
cabaret,n., 749.37(9,16)
cable,n.
  measurement unit of ~s,
    946.26(3,7)
café,n., 749.37(8)
cage,n.
  confine in a ~, 301.1(2,9)
  small ~, 301.4(11)
cake,n., 1062.6
  individual small ~, 1062.7
  mixture for ~, 1062.9,10
  shaped mass of ~, 1062.2
  store for French ~s, 741.5
calamity,n., 37.1
calculable,adj., 942.4
calculate,v., 942.1
  ~ (a score), 942.1(9)
  ~ by adding, 942.1(8)
  ~ incorrectly, 942.1(6)
  ~ the total of, 942.1(8)
calculation,n., 942.2
  approximate ~, based on,
    942.7
  art of ~, 942.10
  device or machine used in ~,
    942.13
  pert. to ~, 942.6
  special method or process of
    ~, 942.11,12
  unit in ~, 942.9
calculator,n., 942.3,13
  ~ of insurance risks, 942.8
calendar,n.
  ~ arrangement of saints,
    311.1(19)
  insert in the ~, 774.9
  inserted in the ~, 774.8
  ~ of months, 774.7(8)
  ~ of saints, 651.9
  period of time added to a
    ~, 769.8(4)
calf,n.
  young animal, 410.2
  like a ~, 410.5
  motherless ~, 410.2(3)
  of a ~, 410.4(6)
  prematurely born ~, 410.2(4)
caliph,n., 1073.36(5)
calisthenics,n., 103.1–5
call,n., 693.2
  animal's ~, 456.1; see
    sound,n.

pert. to a ~, 693.3
call,v., 693.1
  ~ after, 693.1(9)
  ~ back, 693.1(13)
  ~ by a warning name, 694.26
  ~ by magic, 663.8
  ~ by name, 694.6(2)
  ~ forth, 693.1(5,8,10,11,15)
  ~ to come, 693.1(3,4,15,16)
  ~ to court, 693.1(4,6,14)
  ~ to duty, 693.1(15)
  ~ together, 693.1(2,6,7,11,12)
  ~ upon by prayer, 649.5;
    693.1(10)
  ~ upon for a decision,
    693.1(1)
caller,n., 693.4
  ~ of spirits, 693.5
calling,adj., 693.3
  ~ back, 693.3(1)
calling,n.
  act of ~, 693.2
  act of ~ by name, 694.7(1)
  pert. to ~, 693.3
callous,adj., 1098.3
callous,v., 1098.1,2
calm,adj., 1139.15
  not excitable or excited,
    1100.25
  be ~, 1139.12
  become ~, 1139.11
  ~ condition or state, 1139.16
  emotionally ~, 1139.15
  ~ geographical region,
    1139.18
  happy, peaceful, and ~,
    1102.30
  not ~, 1139.20
  period of ~ weather, 1139.17
  ~ person, 1139.19
calm,n., 1139.16
  emotional ~, 1140.25,26
calm,v., 1139.1
  ~ medically, 1139.1(24)
  rub in order to ~, 1139.13
calmed,adj., 1139.6,7
  able to be ~, 1139.9
  not ~, 1139.8
  unable to be ~, 1139.10
calmer,n.
  one who calms, 1139.5
calming,adj., 1139.2
  ~ agent, 1139.4
  not ~, 1139.3
calmness,n., 1139.16
  disturb the ~, 1101.9
  cause lack of ~, 1139.22
  period of ~ and peace,
    1139.17
Cambridge,n.
  graduate of ~, 623.12(4)
  inhabitant of ~, 784.15(8)
  pert. to ~, 784.16
  student at ~, 622.5(6)
camel,n., 414.1
  animal allied to the ~,
    414.1(3)
  ~ driver, 205.1(3,4)
  of ~s, 403.11(12)
camera,n., 967.5
  motion-picture ~, 968.5
camp,n., 753.17,18
  put into ~, 323.1(8)
  setting out of a ~, 753.19
  setting out of a military ~,
    323.8
camp,v.
  ~ temporarily without tents,
    757.1(2)
can,n.
  container, 261.1(9–11,36,44);
    see also **container,n.**
Canadian,n.
  French ~, 784.15(9)
canal,n.

build a ~, 1029.3
convert into a ~, 1029.4
system of ~s, 1029.5
cancel,v., 17.5
cancer,n., 390.3,6
cause of ~, 390.9
causing ~, 390.8
having ~, 390.4
like ~, 390.5
origin of ~, 390.7
spreading of a ~, 390.10
candid,adj., 807.3; 813.6,7
candidate,n.
name as ~, 694.6(19)
person named as a ~, 694.11(4)
candle,n., 1067.1
~holder, 1067.2–4
light from a ~, 1065.49(4)
manufacturer or seller of ~s, 1067.6
point for holding a ~, 335.1(11)
seller of ~s, 212.3(3)
storage place for ~s, 1067.7
wick of a ~, 1067.5
candlestick,n., 1067.2,4
support for arms of a ~, 1022.2(22)
candor,n., 807.3; 813.6,8
candy,n., 450.1
manufacture or sale of ~, 450.2–4
cannibal,adj., 734.27; 734.27(1, 15)
cannibal,n., 734.28
~s, 734.29
cannibalism,n., 734.26(1)
cannon,n., 565.1(2,4,8,9,13,15, 17)
ancient or medieval ~, 565.18
art of shooting ~, 565.8
charge in a ~, 565.14
~s, 565.2(3–8)
science of ~, 565.7
shoot ~, 565.3(1–4,7,12–14,16)
shooting of ~, 565.4; 565.4(1–3,6); 565.8
soldier shooting ~, 564.1(3,4, 10,26)
soldiers shooting ~, 564.5(4, 6)
cap,n.
hat, 983.2; see also hat,n.
academic ~, 983.2(35)
Canadian ~, 983.2(59)
close-fitting ~, 983.2(3,16,48)
flat ~, 983.2(2)
~ for stupid or lazy students, 983.2(21)
jester's ~, 983.2(12)
military ~, 983.2(9,11,25,26,30, 37,45)
Mohammedan ~, 983.2(55)
nun's ~, 983.2(16,61,62)
~ of Eastern countries, 983.2(60)
Persian ~, 983.2(56)
projecting part of a ~, 983.13(4)
put on a ~, 983.3
Scottish ~, 983.2(54)
skull~, 983.2(3,6,24,48,55)
skull ~ worn by barristers, 983.2(16)
sleeping ~, 983.2(36)
Turkish ~, 983.2(24)
wearing a ~, 983.4
without a ~, 983.7
~ worn in bed, 983.2(36)
capability,n., 7.1; see skill,n.
capable,adj., 7.2; see skillful, adj.
be ~, 7.9
make ~, 7.11

~ person, 7.3
capacity,n.
~ in tons, 947.39
measurement of ~, 946.50
measurement unit of ~, 946.48,49
cape,n.
coat, 976.1(2,9,13,14,15)
land, 1029.98
Arab or Moorish ~, 976.1(2)
capital,n.
city, 785.1(7)
money, 213.4; 216.3; see also wealth,n.
capitalism,n.
pert. to ~, 255.12
supporter of ~, 255.13
capless,adj.
hatless, 983.7
caprice,n., 265.2(6,7,10,11,18,26, 28)
capricious,adj., 539.21
~ person, 539.22
capsule,n.
~-shaped, 507.17(14)
captain,n.
ship ~, 176.3(17)
captive,n., 247.9; 301.5
captivity,n., 301.3
captor,n., 247.8
capture,n., 247.7
open to ~, 247.13
capture,v., 247.6; see seize,v.
try to ~, 247.14
car,n.
automobile, 192.6; see automobile,n.
dining ~ of a train, 741.1(9)
carbon,n.
particles of ~, 1050.19
carbon dioxide,n.
charge (beverage) with ~, 1048.33
containing ~ (of beverages), 1048.44
card,n.
~ of five pips, 934.2
~ of four pips, 933.14
~ of three pips, 932.10,11
~ of two pips, 931.27
playing ~, 199.13
room for playing ~s, 787.7(12)
series of playing ~s, 173.9(20)
single playing ~, 930.24
spot on playing ~, 501.3(5)
visiting ~, 125.5
care,n.
carefulness, 577.2; see also carefulness,n.
protection, 568.2,3; 570.4; see protection,n.
advise ~, 577.10,11
done with ~, 577.5,7
excessive ~, 1131.11
give ~ and thought to, 577.8
one taken ~ of, 570.8
one who takes ~ of another, 570.2,10
patronage and ~, 570.5
protection and ~ of a guardian, 570.6
requiring ~, i.e., carefulness, 577.12
showing ~ for, 570.7
take ~ of, 570.1
take ~ of a child, 738.1(4)
take under one's ~, 568.10
urge ~, 577.10,11
care,v.
~ for, i.e., take care of, 570.1
~ for indulgently, 1108.7
carefree,adj., 1131.15
be ~, 1103.9
careful,adj., 577.1

~ about details, 577.1(32)
be ~ of, 577.9
done after ~ thinking, 577.6
~ in speaking, 577.1(8,26)
thoughtful and ~, 577.1(31)
~ to be on time, 577.4
~ to observe precise rules of conduct, 56.4
carefulness,n., 577.2; see also care,n.
~ as to probabilities, 577.3
done with ~, 577.5,7
requiring ~, 577.12
careless,adj., 578.1,2
~ about time, appointments, etc., 578.7
~ act, 52.5(25,30); 578.5
act ~ly, 578.4
be ~, 578.4
done ~ly, 578.2
~ person, 578.6
carelessness,n., 578.3
caress,n., 701.2
pert. to a ~, 701.4
caress,v., 701.1
tending to ~, 701.5
caressible,adj., 701.3
caretaker,n., 8.16
cargo,n., 190.9
carpenter,n., 205.9(1–3,6,7)
carpet,n., 1025.10
carriage,n.
baby vehicle, 192.16
horse-drawn vehicle, 192.12; see below
way of carrying oneself, 504.11
carriage (horse-drawn),n., 192.12
drive a ~, 192.13
driver of a ~, 192.14
pert. to ~s, 192.15
ride in a ~, 192.13
rider in a ~, 192.14
roof of a ~, 973.1(1)
carried,adj.
able to be ~, 190.5
act of being ~ across, 190.6
~ by air, 1045.14(3)
~ by sea or ocean, 1029.72(15)
~ by wind, 1042.37
something ~, 190.9
carrier,n.
one who, or that which, carries, 190.3,4
carrot,n.
belonging to the ~ family, 745.22(1)
carry,v., 190.1
able to ~, 190.8
act of ~ing, 190.2
~ away secretly, 971.44
~ by boat, 115.5
~ by ship, 115.13
hard to ~, 190.10,11
~ illegally, 1087.13
~ing the young in pouch, 190.7
means for ~ing, 190.4
~ on (continue), 754.19; see continue,v.
carrying,n.
flat container for ~, 261.5
way of ~ oneself, 504.11
Carthage,n.
inhabitant of ~, 784.15(10)
pert. to ~, 784.16
carve,v., 332.1(7,25,46,50,70); 966.1; see also cut,v.
carved,adj., 966.6
~ design, figure, or object, 966.5
~ letter or figure from antiquity, 966.5(1)
carver,n., 966.4

carving,n., 966
  a ~, 966.5
  art or process of ~, 966.3
  artist's name on ~, 966.12
  ~ from ancient times,
    966.5(1)
  pert. to ~, 966.7
  projection of ~ from back-
    ground, 966.8
  relief in ~, 966.8
cash,n., 213.1; see money,n.
cashier,n., 213.13
castle,n., 568.26(5); 727.12(5)
  built like a ~, 727.14
  head of a ~, 568.27
castoff,adj.
  ~ skins, shells, etc., 285.1(8,
    34)
castoff,n., 285.1
castrate,v., 710.38
  ~ cats, 710.38(1)
  ~ horses, 710.38(6)
  ~ roosters, 710.38(3)
castrated,adj.
  ~ male, 710.40-42
castration,n., 710.39
cat,n., 406.1-10
  domestic ~, 406.1
  female ~, 406.1(2)
  group of ~s, 403.5(41)
  like a ~, 406.12
  like a ~ in form, 507.17(36)
  male ~, 406.1(8)
  member of ~ family, 406.3,4
  pert. to a ~, 406.11
  young ~, 406.2
catastrophe,n., 37.1
catch,v., 244.1
  hard to ~, 244.8
  ~ in a trap, 244.1
  serving to ~, 244.5
  that which ~es, 244.4
  ~ up to, 244.9
catching,adj.
  acting, tending, etc., to
    catch, 244.5
  contagious, 389.21,22
catching,n., 244.2
category,n., 312.1; see also
  kind,n.
  intended to cover a ~, 972.38
cater,v.
  ~ to, 1108.1; see indulge,v.
Catholic,adj.
  book of Roman ~ rites, 819.14
  Roman ~, 642.11
Catholic,n.
  Roman ~, 642.13
Catholicism,n.
  conform to Roman ~, 642.14
  convert to Roman ~, 642.8(3)
  doctrines, etc., of Roman ~,
    645.10
  Roman ~, 642.12
cattle,n., 410.3
  dealer in ~, 205.1(7)
  group of ~, 403.5(20,34)
  like ~, 410.5
  of ~, 410.4(1,2,4)
caught,adj.
  situation in which ~, 244.7
causation,n., 15.2
causative,adj., 15.3
cause,n., 15
  a ~, 15.4
  consider as the ~ of, 893.7
  consider to be the ~ of, 15.5
  indicative of ~, 15.8(1)
  pert. to ~, 15.8
  producing a ~, 15.3
  relation of ~ and effect, 15.9
  science of ~s, 15.11
  statement of ~s, 674.9(1)
cause,v., 15.1
  ~ by laws, 1080.2

~ something unpleasant,
  15.1(10,12)
~ to act, 52.9
~ to happen, 15.1(18)
~ to happen, 15.1(21)
~ to happen artificially,
  15.1(19)
~ to happen at the same
  time, 15.1(20); 764.7
~ to happen by external control, 15.1(19)
~ to happen faster, 15.1(15)
~ to happen too soon,
  15.1(15)
~ to happen unexpectedly,
  15.1(15)
caused,adj.
  ~ by external factors, 15.7
  ~ by internal factors, 15.6
caution,n., 577.2; see carefulness,n.
  lacking in ~, 578.1; see care-
    less,adj.
cautious,adj., 577.1; see careful,adj.
cave,n., 298.10
  dweller in ~s, 298.13
  exploration of ~s, 298.15
  explorer of ~s, 298.16
  formation in a ~, 298.18
  full of ~s, 298.11
  living in ~s, 298.14
  pert. to ~s, 298.12
  science of ~s, 298.17
  spirit who lives in ~s,
    662.7(43)
cavity,n.
  a hole, 298.20
  a hollow, 299.1
  an opening, 298.4
  anatomical ~, 298.8
  containing ~s, 298.5
  full of ~s, 298.5
cease,v.
  come to an end, 792.2
  stop, 791.1,2; see stop,v.
ceaseless,adj., 755.1,2
ceiling,n.
  arched ~, 509.1; 973.1(11)
  inclined ~, descr. of, 973.4
  rounded ~, 973.1(4)
celebrate,v., 201.3; 1104.10
  ~ in hymns, 477.9
celebration,n., 201.1,2; 1104.9
  activities of a ~, 201.14
  anniversary ~, 781.13
  gaiety of ~s, 201.13
  happy ~, 1102.33
  ~ in the memory of, 627.34(3,
    4)
  intended for ~s, 201.10
  kept separate for ~s, 201.10
  like a ~, 201.8
  merry ~, 1104.9
  merry ~s, season or time of,
    1104.12
  suitable for a ~, 201.8
  take part in a ~, 201.3;
    1104.10
celebrator,n., 201.4; 1104.11
celebrity,n.
  person treated as a ~, 848.26
  treat as a ~, 848.25
celibacy,n.
  avoidance of marriage,
    706.1-7
  avoidance of sex, 710.47-50
cell (biological),n.
  components of a ~, 381.3
  containing ~s, 381.11
  destruction by white blood
    ~s, 801.2(4)
  destruction of ~s, 381.7;
    801.2(3)
  disintegration of a ~, 381.6

  divided into two ~s, 381.10
  division of a ~, 381.4
  having one ~, 381.8
  having two ~s, 381.9
  living substance of ~s, 751.12
  originating from a single ~,
    728.13(6)
  pert. to ~s, 381.11
  reproductive ~, 379.6
  science of ~s, 381.12
  small ~, 381.1
  structure, etc., of a ~, 381.5
cellar,n., 787.7(13,39,41)
cement,n., 1006.1(28)
  join with ~, 1006.13
cemetery,n., 797.6
  like a ~, 797.9
  pert. to a ~, 797.9
  public ~, 797.8
  underground ~, 797.7
censor,n., 899.18
  the self as ~, 228.1(6)
censor,v., 286.1(4,5,29);
  539.1(10-12)
  ~ books, writing, etc., 899.17
censored,adj.
  ~ books, writing, etc., 899.19
censorship,n., 286.2; 539.3
  free of ~, 309.11(36,38)
  ~ of books, writing, etc.,
    899.17
censurable,adj., 894.7
censure,n., 894.3; 895.3
  deserving ~, 894.7
  god of ~, 869.14
censure,v., 894.1; 895.1
census,n., 941.4
center,n., 137.1
  away from the ~, 137.14-16
  ~ between extremes, 137.1(8,
    14,15,17-20)
  ~ between numbers, 137.1(17,
    18)
  bring to the ~, 137.4
  come to the ~, 137.5
  coming to a ~, 137.7
  different ~s, having, 137.11
  distance from the ~, 788.1(8)
  distance through the ~,
    788.1(3)
  earth as ~, 1004.20
  in the ~, 137.2
  ~ line, 137.1(1)
  ~ of action, 137.1(11-13,24)
  ~ of attention, 137.1(11)
  ~ of earth, 137.1(6)
  ~ of electricity, 137.1(5)
  ~ of fruit, 137.1(9,12)
  ~ of gravity, 137.1(2)
  ~ of stars, 137.1(5)
  ~ of target, 137.1(3)
  ~ of turning, 137.1(25)
  ~ of wheel, 137.1(13)
  pert. to the ~, 137.2
  remove from the ~, 249.1(4)
  same ~, have, 137.9,10
  same ~, having, 137.8
  sun as ~, 1055.6
  toward the ~, 137.6
  without a ~, 137.12
center,v., 137.4,5
  not ~ed, 137.13
central,adj., 137.2
  ~ part, 326.33-35
centrality,n., 137.3
centrifugal,adj., 137.14-16
centripetal,adj., 137.6,7
century,n.
  ~ in ref. to Italian art or lit-
    erature, 965.34
ceramics,n., 261.14; see earthenware,n.
  art of ~, 965.6(2)
ceremonial,adj.
  ~ cleanness, 845.3,5

~ impurity, incapable of, 845.4
~ purity, 845.3,5
~ uncleanness, incapable of, 845.4
ceremonious,adj., 819.1; see also formal,adj.
showy and ~, 951.38
ceremony,n., 819.3
~ official, 1077.1(20)
certain (sure),adj., 641.1,6
be ~ of, 641.8
cause to feel ~, 641.9
inclined to be ~ in one's statements, 674.11,12
make ~, 641.4
certainty,n., 641.2,7
a ~, 641.3
feelings of ~, 641.7
certificate,n.
~ conferring scholastic honor, 857.11
~ granting delay in punishment, 897.21
~ of forgiveness, 897.17
~ on graduation, 857.11
Ceylon,n.
inhabitant of ~, 784.15(54)
pert. to ~, 784.16
chain,n., 302.32(8,23)
loop of ~ for support, 1022.2(26)
chair,n., 631.1; see also seat,n.
cover on ~ to protect against soil or hair oil, 972.4(1)
make a ~ out of stems, 985.16
chairman,n., 1077.23
be, or act as, ~, 1077.24,25
chalk,n.
containing ~, 1006.39,40
covered with ~, 1006.41
like ~, 1006.39
lump of ~, 1006.1(7)
mark or write with, treat with, mix with, etc., ~, 1006.42
slate for writing on with ~, 1006.44
whiten with ~, 1006.43
challenge,n., 545.2
~ to a duel, 545.3
challenge,v., 545.1
~ as false, 820.23
champagne,n., 749.6(10); 749.17; see wine,n.
champion,n., 834.4
chance,n., 34.1
allow to depend on ~, 34.12
attended by dangerous ~, 34.7
by ~, 34.4
dangerous ~, 34.2
even ~, 34.3
expose to ~, 34.12
full of ~, 34.7
full of ~ but promising profit, 34.8
happening by ~, 34.4
happening by ~ and successful, 34.5
something full of ~, 34.9
subject to ~, 34.6
subject to dangerous ~, 34.7
take a ~, 34.11
take a ~ in business, 34.13
theory of ~, 34.10
chandelier,n., 1065.107(5,6,16)
change,n., 539.3
action that represents a ~, 539.15
beyond ~, 531.9
favoring extreme ~, 539.18,20
full of ~, 539.21
hatred of ~, 880.17(8)
~ in disease, 539.3(11)
indicator of ~s, 1046.20

influence toward ~, 9.2(6); 539.17
introduce ~s, 730.1(4)
letter ~, 539.3(5)
~ of mind, 539.3(3,14,17)
opposition to ~, 544.8–10
period between ~s, 769.8(13, 15)
pert. to ~, 539.8
point of ~, 539.16
power to produce ~, 5.1(9)
prediction of ~s, skillful in, 1047.21
rate of ~, 99.1(2)
reversing ~, 539.3(1,15,17)
sound ~, 539.3(5)
subject to ~, 539.24
sudden ~, 539.15
suggest ~s, 238.1(5)
syllable ~, 539.3(5)
time of ~, 539.16
~ to misfortune, 539.3(8)
with the necessary ~s, 539.11
without ~, 531.1–10
change,v., 539.1,2
~ alphabet, 539.1(60)
~ and thus spoil, 539.1(9,54)
~ attitude, 539.1(39); 539.2(10)
~ biologically, 539.1(2,8,30, 51); 539.2(4)
~ by exposure to air or atmosphere, 1046.7
causing to ~, 539.6
~ conveyance, 539.1(64)
~ direction, 539.1(15,16,23); 539.2(8,9,13)
~ document, 539.1(24)
~ for another, 539.1(22); 539.12
~ gears, 539.1(49)
~ in substance, 539.1(62,65)
~ into gold, 539.1(62)
language or wording of ~, 539.1(6,10–12,20,21,24,25,40, 46,59,60)
~ letters, 539.1(60)
~ mind, opinions, etc., 539.2(5,7,10,12,14,15)
~ music, 539.1(7)
~ one language to another, 539.1(59,60)
one who ~s, 539.4,5
~ opinions, mind, etc., 539.2(5,7,10,12,14,15)
~ position or order, 539.1(5, 14,29,33–35,48,49,52,56,59,63)
~ quantity, 539.1(38)
~ ridiculously, 539.1(61)
~ sound of voice, 539.1(27,32)
tending to ~, 539.7
that which ~s, 539.4,5,10
that which does not ~, 531.10
~ to abnormal, 539.1(36,70); 539.2(2)
~ to better, 539.1(41)
~ to new environment, 539.1(2)
~ to new use, 539.1(1,2,51)
~ to opposite, 539.1(45,67)
~ topics, 539.1(16); 539.2(1, 3)
willing to ~, 539.21(2,11)
~ wording of, 539.1(6,10–12, 20,21,24,25,40,46,59,60)
changeable,adj., 539.9,21,23,24
act or be ~, 1042.46
~ as the moon, 1054.38
emotionally ~, 1092.9
~ person, 539.22; 1042.45
changed,adj.
able to be ~, 539.9
~ by exposure to air or atmosphere, 1046.8
~ by weather, 1047.9

unable to be ~, 531.8,9
changing,adj., 539.7
constantly ~, 539.21,23
constantly ~ scene, 783.4(2–4)
suddenly ~, 539.21
channel,n.
~ for water, 1026.18
chaos,n., 605.13
chaotic,adj., 605.14
chaperon,n., 131.3; 131.3(6)
accompaniment of a ~, 131.8
protection of a ~, 131.8
chaperon,v., 131.1(6)
character,n.
nature, 1091.1; see also nature (character),n.
written symbol, 679.1; see also letter,n.
attack the ~ of, 891.17
deducing ~ from face or body, 365.4
distinctive or distinguishing ~, 1091.7,11
essential ~ of a thing, 808.8–10
main ~ in a story, etc., 848.22(4)
of two different or opposing ~s, 931.3
paper or statement certifying the good ~ of, 850.13
science of moral ~, duty, or behavior, 843.4
strength of ~, 1.22
weakness of ~, 10.14
characteristic,adj., 1091.12
~ spirit, etc., of a time, 762.8
characteristic,n., 1091.11
be a ~ of, 1091.19
distinctive or distinguishing ~, 1091.11
excessive use of distinctive ~s, 1091.17,18
habitual ~, 1091.15,16
have the ~s of, 1091.20–22
odd ~, 1091.14
~ of a region, 1091.13
~ of Americans, 1091.24(1)
~ of Asiatics, 1091.24(6)
~ of the British, 1091.24(2)
~ of the Chinese, 1091.24(6,7)
~ of the French, 1091.24(3)
~ of the Germans, 1091.24(4)
~ of the Irish, 1091.24(5)
~ of the Japanese, 1091.24(6)
origin of a ~, 728.8
~s of Asiatics, 1091.27,28
~s of Europeans, 1091.25,26
~s of Western people, 1091.25,26
Slavic ~, 1091.29
unusual ~, 1091.14
charge,n.
cost, 223.1; see also cost, price,n.
~ for anchoring, 223.2(7,8,10, 14)
~ for entering, 223.2(1)
~ for opening liquor bottles, 298.7
~ for transportation, 223.2(3–6)
free of ~, 223.12
one in ~, 8.16
specific ~s, 223.2
charitable,adj.
generous, 229.1; see generous, adj.
~ act, 52.5(10); 232.8
~ gift, 232.4
charity,n., 232.4; see also generosity, kindness,n.
act of ~, 232.8
gift of ~, 232.4
give in, or to, ~, 232.1

giver to, or of, ~, 232.3
giving in, or to, ~, 232.2
lives on ~, one who,
  232.7(2,3)
pert. to ~, 232.5
place where ~ is given, 232.6
receiver of ~, 232.7(1)
charlatan,n., 826.15
  play the ~, 826.16
charm,n.
  attraction, 196.2,3
  attractiveness, 196.6
  a ~, 663.11
  good-luck ~, 35.5
  magic ~, 1056.40
charm,v.
  attract, 196.1
  delight, 1102.3; 1105.3
  please, 1106.2
charmer,n., 196.4
charming,adj.
  attractive, 196.5
  delightful, 1102.4; 1105.4
  pleasing, 1106.3
  simple and ~, 960.1(4)
chase,n., 173.13
chase,v., 173.12
  ~ into a hole, 1004.37
chasm,n., 298.9
chaste,adj.
  pure, 845.1,10; see pure,adj.
  virginal, 710.47; 845.11
  ~ person, 710.48
  remain ~, 710.49
chastity,n.
  avoidance of sex, 710.47
  purity, 845.1,10; see purity,n.
  sexual fidelity, 845.11
  symbol of ~, 710.50; 845.12
cheap,adj.
  inexpensive, 223.15
  worthless, 888.1
  ~ showiness, 951.42
  showy and ~, 951.41
  showy and ~ thing, 951.36(1)
cheat,n., 825.9; see cheater,n.
cheat,v., 825.1,2
  ~ after luring to a place,
  825.5
  ~ by giving too little, 825.3
  ~ by not paying gambling
  debts, 825.4
  ~ in petty ways, 825.6
cheated,adj.
  one easily ~, 825.13
  one who has been ~, 825.14
cheater,n., 825.9
  ~ at cards, 825.10,11
  clever ~, 796.3(4)
  ~ in games, 825.10–12
cheating,n., 825.7
  engage in ~, 825.2
  method of ~ by gaining
  confidence, 825.8
check,n.
  ornament with ~s, 959.1(29)
checkered,adj.
  ~ arrangement, 311.1(26,45)
cheek,n., 366.13
  coloring matter for the ~s,
  488.22(7)
  low-hanging ~, 366.13,14
  pert. to the ~s, 366.15
cheer,n.
  college ~, 464.1(26)
  good ~, 1103.2; see cheerfulness,n.
  without ~, 1123.1; 1125.48
cheer,v.
  applaud, 853.3
  become cheerful, 1103.8
  make cheerful, 1103.3;
  1125.40
  person who ~s in a contest,
  853.3

person who ~s one up, 1103.6;
  1125.42
that which ~s one up, 1103.6;
  1125.43
cheered,adj.
  able to be ~, 1125.46
  state of feeling ~, 1125.41
  unable to be ~, 1125.47
cheerful,adj., 1103.1; see also
  happy, merry,adj.
  ~ and suggestive of laughter,
  1111.36
  become more ~, 1103.8
  lively and ~, 752.5
  make ~, 1103.3; 1125.40
cheerfulness,n., 1103.2,5; see
  also happiness, merri-
  ment,n.
  causing ~, 1103.4; 1125.44
  humor determining ~, 1091.30
  show ~, 1103.7
  showing ~, 1103.1
  snap back into ~, able to,
  1103.11,12
  source of ~, 1103.6,10;
  1125.42,43
cheering,adj., 1103.4; 1125.44;
  see also cheerful,adj.
cheerless,adj., 1123.1; 1125.48;
  see also gloomy, sad, unhappy,adj.
cheers,n.
  burst of ~ from a group,
  853.7
cheese,n.
  covering of ~, 972.4(15)
  peel of ~, 972.4(15)
  skin of ~, 972.4(15)
cheesy,adj., 744.7
  become or make ~, 744.8
chef,n., 1061.24; see cook,n.
chemical,adj.
  ~ action, 808.14
  ~ properties, 808.15
  science of ~ action and heat,
  1060.65(2)
chemical,n.
  stimulation by a ~, 101.1(2,3)
  ~ that takes part in reactions, 54.10
chemistry,n.
  life explainable by ~, theory
  of, 751.9
  ~ of electricity, 1066.20(1)
  ~ of fermentation, 749.36(2)
  ~ of light, 1065.102(6)
  ~ of organic raw materials,
  808.12(2)
  ~ of radioactivity, 1069.22
cherish,v.
  treat lovingly, 700.4
cherished,adj.
  loved, 700.5
cherry,n., 745.1(5)
  ~ in syrup, descr. of,
  745.22(7)
  pert. to, or like, the ~,
  745.22(5)
chessboard,n.
  row on a ~, 311.11(2,6)
chest,n.
  body part, 388.1(4)
  container, 261.1(14,26,32);
  see container,n.
  abnormal sound in the ~,
  376.6(2,3)
  ~ cavity, 388.1(4)
  ~ for ammunition, 261.1(8)
  ~ for valuables, 261.1(17)
  pert. to the ~, 388.2(8)
chestbone,n., 354.1(9)
chestnut,n.
  of the ~ tree family, 996.25
chevrotain,n.
  of ~s, 403.11(12)

chew,n., 735.13
chew,v., 735.12
  animal that ~s the cud,
  735.14
chewing,n., 735.13
  portion of food for ~,
  740.15(13)
chicken,n., 405.1(1,2,5,6)
  baby ~s, 405.5(2,3)
  female ~, 405.3(1,3,5)
  ~ for cooking, 1061.8
  group of newborn ~s,
  403.5(7,11,33)
  house for ~s, 403.22(8) ;
  405.11(10)
  male ~, 405.2(1,2,4,7) ;
  405,4(3)
  of ~s, 405.8(2)
  place for ~s to sit, 405.11(10)
  young ~, 405.4(2,3,11–13)
  young male ~, 405.4(3)
chicken pox,n., 382.11(53)
  resembling ~, 382.14
chief,n., 176.3
  Arab ~, 1073.36(28)
  fire ~, 1077.1(20)
  Indian ~, 1073.36(26)
  Mohammedan ~, 1073.36(28)
  ~ of a tribe or clan,
  1073.14(2)
child,n., 721.1,3; see also children,n.
  art of bringing up a ~, 721.21
  attitude of a ~ to parent,
  721.14
  ~ born dead, 721.3(30)
  bring up a ~, 721.16; see also
  upbringing,n.
  deserted ~, 721.3(12)
  destruction of unborn ~,
  714.18; see abortion,n.
  foster ~, 721.3(11)
  friendless ~, 1096.42
  homeless ~, 721.3(35) ; 1096.42
  illegitimate ~, 720.11; see
  bastard,n.
  Indian ~, 721.3(22)
  like a ~, 721.10; see childish,adj.
  lost ~, 264.8(1) ; 721.3(35)
  mischievous ~, 721.4
  Negro ~, 721.3(23)
  newborn ~, 721.3(17)
  no longer a ~, 760.1(1,7,11)
  noisy and unmanageable ~,
  463.8
  ~ of mixed races, 721.3(16)
  ~ of multiple birth, 721.5–7
  parentless ~, 721.3(21)
  place for a ~, 721.15
  playful ~, 199.5
  premature ~, place for a,
  721.15(2)
  relationship of ~ to parents,
  722.3(2)
  science of bringing up a ~,
  721.20
  secretly changed ~, 721.3(3)
  sexual desire toward a ~,
  710.33(26)
  small ~, 909.3(17)
  take care of a ~, 721.19
  training of a ~, 721.22
  unborn ~, 721.8; see fetus,n.
  unmanageable and noisy ~,
  463.8
childbirth,n., 718.1; see also
  birth,n.
  after ~, 718.17
  assist (the woman) in ~,
  718.5
  assistance in ~, types of,
  718.6
  be in ~, 718.2
  before ~, 718.16

disease of ~, 718.18
doctor, etc., assisting in ~, 401.2; 401.2(1,2)
father's custom during ~, 718.20
goddess of ~, 718.19
medication to induce ~, 398.6(11)
period following ~, 718.4
period of ~, 718.3
pert. to ~, 718.15
science dealing with ~, 401.1(39,45,53,103)
woman in ~, 718.9
woman in relation to number of ~s, 718.11–14
woman just after ~, 718.10
woman's condition relative to ~, 718.8
childhood,n., 721.2
  period following ~, 731.9(1, 2); 760.2
  regression to ~, 731.30(3)
childish,adj., 721.10
  immature, 733.1
  adult's ~ behavior, 721.12
  anatomically ~, 721.11
childlike,adj., 721.10; see childish,adj.
children,n., 721.9
  breed ~ with another race, 719.2(1)
  correction of emotional or nervous ailments of ~, pert. to, 398.14(4)
  fondness for ~, 700.31(2)
  fondness for one's ~, 700.31(4)
  group of ~ in a family, 318.1(57)
  hatred of ~, 880.17(9)
  hospital for deserted ~, 721.15(1)
  institution for parentless ~, 721.15(4)
  medical specialty dealing with ~, 401.1(70)
  mother as to number of ~, 718.11–14
  one of ~ from same birth, 721.5–7
  place for ~, 721.15
  produce ~, 717.1–17
  unproductive of ~, 716.1; see sterile,adj.
chimpanzee,n., 420.6
chin,n.
  double ~, 366.16
  pert. to the ~, 366.17
China,n., 784.4(3); 784.9(4,5)
  make conform to customs of ~, 784.10(7,8)
  official of empire of ~, 1077.1(19)
  ruler of ~, 1073.36(14)
china (earthenware),n. 261.12; see earthenware,n.
Chinese,adj., 784.16; see also Oriental,adj.
  become ~, 784.13
  ~ characteristic, 1091.24(6,7)
  make ~, 784.10(7,8); 784.12
Chinese,n., 784.15(12,45)
  knowledge about the ~, 430.16
  science of the ~, 430.17
chiropody,n., 401.1(76)
chivalrous,adj., 858.5
  ~ act, 52.5(31)
  ~ acts, 858.7
  ~ behavior, 55.3(9)
  extravagantly ~, 858.9
  extravagantly ~ act, 858.10
  extravagantly ~ actions, 858.11

~ man, 858.6
chivalry,n., 858.5
  Japanese code of ~, 858.8
chocolate,n.
  flavoring of ~ and coffee, 747.3; see candy,n.
choice,adj., 252.10
  ~ part, 252.14
choice,n., 252.2,5; see also selection,n.
  allow no ~, 252.18
  allowing no ~, 252.17–19
  ~ between two, 252.5(1)
  careful in ~, 252.15
  difficult ~, 252.5(4,14)
  excess of ~, 920.21
  ~ for elimination, 252.5(3)
  having no ~, 252.16
  indicate a ~, 254.4; see vote,v.
  left to one's ~, 252.12(3,4)
  nominal but not actual ~, 252.5(9)
  ~ of government by voting, 254.5(2)
  state of ~, 252.7
  suitable for ~, 252.12
  wide range of ~, 252.6
choke,v., 376.16–20
choose,v., 252.1
  ~ actors, 969.47
  ~ as better, 252.1(9)
  freedom to ~, 252.9
  power to ~, 252.9
  right to ~, 252.9
  tending to ~ from various sources, 252.15(4)
chooser,n., 252.3
choosing,adj., 252.4
  ~ freely, 252.4(2,3)
  ~ from all systems, 252.4(1); 252.15(4)
choosing,n.
  act of ~, 252.2
  descr. of ~, 252.4
choosy,adj., 252.15
chop,v., 332.1(6,14,31,32); see cut,v.
chopped,adj.
  ~-off piece, 326.10(3)
chopping,n.
  sound of ~, 469.7(12)
chord,n.
  ~ of three tones, 932.9
chosen,adj.
  able to be ~, 252.12
  ~ as best, 252.10; 834.2
  ~ as best, those who are, 252.13
  ~ but not yet in office, 252.11
  specially ~, 252.10
  suitable to be ~, 252.12
  what is ~, 252.5; see also choice, selection,n.
Christ,n., 653.1
  beliefs or doctrines about ~, 653.10
  birth of ~, 720.3
  denies ~, one who, 653.5
  doctrine of ~, 653.6
  enemy of ~, 653.5
  false ~, 653.5
  image of ~ on the cross, 653.3
  infant ~ in art, 653.2
  non-divinity of ~, 653.10(4)
  pert. to ~, 653.1,4
  picture of ~, 965.1(25)
  redemption through ~, 653.8
  rising of ~ from death, 751.23
  ~'s return to earth, 653.10(1–3)
  salvation announced by ~, 653.7
  stable where ~ was born, reproduction of, 720.16
  story of ~, 653.9

time when ~ will rule, 1102.27–29
Christian,adj., 642.4
  ~ rather than Jewish, 642.4(1)
  ~ revelation, 642.15
Christian,n., 642.5; 642.5(2,4)
  early ~, 642.5(4)
  Jewish ~s, 188.2
  ~s, 642.7
Christianity,n., 642.3(3,16)
  a convert to ~, 642.10(1–3)
  convert to ~, 642.8; 642.8(1, 3); 642.9
  defense of ~, 854.17
  person sent to foreign country to convert natives to ~, 638.11
  theology dealing with defense of ~, 854.18
Christmas,n., 209.14
  ~ carol, 476,4(32)
chronology,n., 774.7; see also time,n.
  error in ~, 774.12,15
chubby,adj., 510.1; see fat,adj.
church,n., 645.1
  a meeting for ~ policy, 322.1(36)
  beliefs of Roman Catholic ~, 645.10
  cut off from the ~, 296.1(6); 296.5,7
  deprive ~ of support by state, 247.23(8); 247.28
  descr. of a ~, 645.2
  devotion to the ~, 645.7
  doctrines of Roman Catholic ~, 645.10
  government not involved with, or influenced by, the ~, pert. to, 1073.83
  government of a ~, 1073.3(17)
  government of the Roman Catholic ~, 1073.3(25)
  group dissenting from a ~, 642.18
  hater of ~ fathers, 880.18(5)
  holder of a position of honor or dignity in a ~, 857.14
  Jewish ~, 645.1(12,14)
  member of a ~, 645.3,5
  members of a ~, 645.4
  new member of a ~, 645.5
  not controlled by the ~, 207.3(1)
  officer of a ~, 646.1,14
  opposed to ~ influence, 645.12
  part of the ~ for the clergy, 646.7
  people not connected with the ~, 207.4–5
  people of a ~ district, 431.3(9)
  pert. to a ~, 645.2
  place served by a ~, 782.1(17)
  practices of a ~, 645.9
  practices of Roman Catholic ~, 645.10
  principles of a ~, 645.9
  principles of Roman Catholic ~, 645.10
  probation as member of the ~, 645.6
  refusal to attend Anglican ~, 645.14
  refusal to conform to ~ principles, 645.13
  room in a ~ for non-religious activities, 787.7(42)
  science of ~ antiquities, 645.8
  science of ~ architecture, 645.8
  science of ~ art, 645.8

science of ~ ornamentation, 645.8
selling of ~ positions, 212.9
spirit of a ~, 645.9
supremacy of monarchs in ~ matters, 1073.34
uncontrolled by the ~, 645.11
unrelated to the ~, 645.11
worship of ~es, 656.15(5)
worshipers in a ~, 645.4
cicada,n., 428.3
  of ~s, 428.1(11)
cider,n.
  brandy from ~, 749.6(1)
  substance used to make ~, 745.4
cigar,n., 988.6
  box for ~ storage, 262.3(15)
  container for ~s, 261.1(30)
  dealer in ~s, 988.11
  ~ store, 988.12
cigarette,n., 988.7
  dealer in ~s, 988.11
  ~ store, 988.12
cinema,n., 968.1; see **motion pictures**,n.
circle,n., 508.12
  arranged in ~s, 311.4(2,4)
  distance from center of ~, 788.1(8)
  distance around a ~, 788.1(2)
  distance through a ~, 788.1(3)
  earth's ~s, 1004.13,14
  earth's central ~, 508.12(5)
  flattened ~, 155.2(5) ; 508.10
  having ~s, 508.14
  like a ~, 508.3-6,11
  measure arcs of ~s, device to, 508.18
  measurement around ~, 946.30
  measurement from center of ~, 946.32
  measurement through center of ~, 946.31
  measurement unit of ~, 946.44,45
  move in ~s, 508.19
  ~ of flowers and leaves, 994.8
  ~ of leaves, 993.25
  ~ of people or things surrounding a place, 300.4(2)
  parts of a ~, 508.16
  pert. to a ~, 508.17
  prehistoric ~ of stone, 1006.20
circle,v.
  move in a circle, 508.19
  surround, 300.1; see **surround**,v.
circular,adj., 508.3
  almost ~, 508.6
  flat and ~, 508.4
  move in ~ path, 508.19
circulate,v.
  ~ air through, 1045.7
  ~ through (of air or wind), 1045.9
circumstance,n.
  difficult ~, 25.9
  ~ indicating what will follow, 951.4(20)
  superior ~, 833.6
citizen,n., 1075.1
  country whose ~s are from foreign lands, 1075.10
  duties, conditions, etc., of a ~, 1075.6
  freedom of a ~, 1075.11
  make a ~ of, 1075.9
  ~ of a government by the clergy, 1073.50
  rights of American ~, 1075.12,13

~s collectively, 1075.4
~s trained as soldiers, 564.5(22,23)
world ~, 1004.33
citizenship,n.
  deprivation of ~ for treason, 1075.15
  deprive of ~, 1075.14
  give ~ to, 1075.9
  good ~, 1075.7
  restore to ~, 832.8
  science of ~, 1075.8
city,n., 785.1
  between one ~ and another, 785.9
  characteristic of a large ~, 785.8
  chief ~, 785.1(3,7)
  combining ~ and country living, 786.10
  ~ containing a harbor, 1029.15
  district of a ~, 782.1(34)
  executive of ~, 1077.1(21)
  give self-government to a ~, 1073.77
  governing body of a ~, 1073.78
  head ~, 785.1(3,7)
  inhabitant of a ~, 785.2
  inhabitants of a ~, 784.17(2)
  like a ~, 785.5,8
  living in the ~, 750.3(10)
  make into a ~, 785.6
  make like a ~, 785.6
  outlying section of a ~, 785.1(9)
  pert. to a ~, 785.3
  pert. to the government of a ~, 785.7; 1073.73
  science of ~ affairs, 1075.8
  self-government of a ~, advocacy of, 1073.79,80
  ~ with self-government, 1073.76
  within a ~, 785.10
civet,n.
  like a ~, 403.12
  like a ~ in form, 507.17(92)
  of ~s, 403.11(17)
civilian,n.
  ~ in wartime, 562.13
civilization,n.
  lacking in ~, 866.1
clad,adj., 974.4; see **clothed**,adj.
claim,n.
  demand, 274.1
  statement, 674.9
claim,v.
  demand, 274.1
  say, 674.8(3,5,7,9,10,12,13,31, 38,55,61,69,76,104,113,119)
  ~ to be true, 812.2
clam,n., 422.3; 422.3(4)
  covering of ~s, 972.4(20)
  of ~s, 422.1(5,6,25,27)
  science of ~s, 403.26(11,23)
clan,n., 722.4
  pert. to a ~, 722.5(1)
clarify,v., 598.7,10
clarifying,adj., 598.12
clarity,n., 598.6; see **clearness**,n.
class,n.
  kind, 312.1; see **kind**,n.
  rank, 313.1; see **rank**,n.
  biological ~, 318.8
  social ~, 314.1; see **social class**,n.
  working ~, 314.2(17,20)
classification,n., 312.1; see also **kind**,n.
  biological ~, 318.8
  ~ of books, 312.5(1)
  ~ of diseases, 312.4(1)

pert. to ~, 312.5
science of ~, 312.4
science of animal ~, 985.36(23)
science of plant ~, 985.36(19, 23)
classify,v., 312.2,3
claw,n., 344.11
  having ~s, 344.12
  like a ~, 344.13
  pert. to a ~, 344.13
  ~-shaped, 507.17(15)
clay,n., 1002.5,7
  block of ~, 1002.9
  containing ~, 1002.2,3,4
  eating of ~, 734.26(4)
  like ~, 1002.1
  made of ~, 1002.6
  potter's ~, 1002.5
  producing ~, 1002.4
  rock formed by hardening ~, 1006.1(40)
  rock that is like ~, 1006.1(1)
  thin piece of baked ~, 1006.1(45)
clean,adj., 899.26,29; 904.6,7
  unstained, 899.29
  absolutely ~, 899.23
  ~ and neat, 902.1(5)
  ~ and tidy, 899.24
  become ~, 899.9
  brush ~, 899.1(2,16)
  ceremonially ~, 845.3
  ~ in habits, 899.25
  keep a place ~, 1078.9
  ~ of germs, microorganisms, etc., 899.11
  render ceremonially ~, 845.5
  rub ~, 438.1(5,10,13,20,22,27, 29,30,33) ; 899.1(1,2,5,7,8,9, 12,13,14,15,16,19)
  spotlessly ~, 899.23
  surgically ~, 899.11
  wash ~, 899.35
  wipe ~, 899.1(1,2,5,7,8,12,13, 14,15,16)
clean,v., 899.1; see also **wash**,v.
  ~ a ship's deck, 899.1(15)
  ~ a wound, etc., 899.1(4,5)
  able to be ~ed, 899.28
  agent, substance, etc., for ~ing of germs or microorganisms, 899.15
  ~ books, writing, etc., of objectionable material, 899.17
  ~ by brushing, 899.1(2,16) ; 899.32
  ~ by destroying germs, 899.10,13
  ~ by rubbing, 899.1(1,2,5,7,8, 9,12,13,14,15,16,19)
  ~ by washing, 899.35
  ~ by wiping, 899.1(1,2,5,7,8, 12,13,14,15,16)
  ~ clothing, etc., 899.1(6,19)
  instrument, etc., that ~s, 899.5
  liquid that ~s in religious ceremony, 899.5(1)
  one who ~s, 899.4
  person who ~s clothes, 899.39
  power to ~, 899.6
  ~ rugs, 899.1(6,17)
  serving to ~, 899.3
  ~ streets, 899.1(11)
  ~ surgically, 899.1(4,5)
  ~ the body, 899.48
cleanable,adj., 899.28
cleaner,n.
  cleaning agent, 899.5; see **cleanser**,n.
  one who cleans, 899.4
  street ~, 899.30

cleaning,n., 899.2
  act of ~, 899.2
  ~ as a religious ceremony,
    899.2(1)
  ~ of the emotions, 899.2(2)
  street ~, dept. of, 899.31
cleanness,n.
  quality of ~, 899.27
  restore to ~, 832.5
cleanser,n., 899.5
  ~ for clothes, 899.5(7) ; 899.34
  ~ for dishes, 899.5(4)
  ~ for the ear, 899.5(2)
  ~ for the skin, 899.5(5)
  ~ for the teeth, 899.5(3)
  ~ of germs, etc., 899.15
cleansing,adj., 899.3
  ~ surgically, 899.14
clear,adj.
  evident, 598.13; see evident,
    adj.
  not cloudy or muddy, 598.1
  understandable, 598.16; see
    understandable,adj.
  become ~, 598.7,11
  become ~ to the mind, 598.11
  become ~er to the mind,
    598.11
  bright and ~, 598.3
  calm and ~, 598.3
  grow ~ and bright, 1065.61
  ~ in meaning, 598.8,16; 607.7;
    607.9(9,10)
  ~ in sound, 598.5
  make ~, 598.7,10
  make ~ to the mind, 598.10,
    12
  make ~er, 598.10
  making ~ or ~er, 598.12
  sharp and ~ (of weather,
    etc.), 598.2
  ~ to the hearing, 598.5
  ~ to the mind, 598.8,13,16
  ~ to the senses, 598.4
  ~ to the sight, 598.5
  ~ to the understanding,
    598.8,13,16
clearly,adv.
  show ~, 951.1(10,17,18,27)
clearness,n.
  ~ in meaning, 598.9
  lack of ~, 603.2; 604.2; see
    mystery, unclearness, n.
  ~ of appearance, 598.1,3,6
  ~ of sound, 598.6
clergy,n., 646.4
  appoint to the ~, 253.1(8)
  government by the ~,
    1073.42(11,18)
  one not in the ~, 207.1(4) ;
    207.2–5
  opposed to the ~, 646.13
  opposer of the ~, 749.58
  part of the church for the
    ~, 646.7
  remove from the ~, 144.4(3,
    10,17,18)
clergyman,n., 646.1
  army ~, 646.1(7)
  divinity of ~'s office, believ-
    ing in, 646.9
  ~ group, 646.4
  ~ in a position of honor or
    dignity, 857.14
  Jewish ~, 646.1(32)
  ~ of an institution, 646.1(7)
  office or rank of ~, 646.2
  pert. to or descr. of a ~,
    646.3
  profession, etc., of a ~, 646.8
  residence of a ~, 646.6
  territory or jurisdiction of a
    ~, 646.5
clerk,n., 682.5(1–6)
clever,adj., 595.1,2

be ~er than, 595.6
  done ~ly, 595.2(1)
  made ~ly, 595.2(1,2)
  ~ person, 595.4
cleverness,n., 595.3
  use ~ to get, 595.5
clew,n., 601.11
cliché,n., 535.6; 759.30
client,n., 211.4
  ~s, 211.5
  without ~s, 211.6
cliff,n., 166.1(3,10,20,25) ;
  1006.1(8,12,31,37)
  ~ climber, 159.9(2)
  having ~s, 1006.14
  side of a ~, 1006.15
climate,n., 1047; see weather,n.
  adapted to changes in ~,
    770.14
climb,n., 159.2
climb,v., 159.1(3,6,11,20,22,28)
  crawl and ~, 159.1(6,21)
  ~ to the top of, 159.1(15,36)
climber,n., 159.3,9
climbing,adj., 159.4
climbing,n., 159.2
  adapted for tree ~, 996.12
  adapted to ~, 159.5
  ~ irons, 159.12
  mountain ~, 159.10
  stick used in mountain ~,
    159.11
cling,v., 302.16
  one who ~s, 302.22
clique,n., 318.1(18,26,84) ;
  1096.5–7
clitoris,n.
  substance secreted by the ~,
    1027.1(10)
cloak,n.
  coat, 976.1(3,13,14,15,18)
  Arab ~, 976.1(2)
  Moorish ~, 976.1(2)
  ~ with a hood, 976.1(2,4,5)
clock,n., 774.2–6; see timepiece,n.
  in the direction of ~ hands,
    148.2(2,3) ; 179.8(2) ; 1055.43
  in the direction opposite to
    ~ hands, 179.8(3)
  sound of a ~, 469.7(38)
  ~ weight, 947.15(3)
clockwise,adv.
  turning ~, 148.2(2,3)
clog,v., 558.1
  ~ with mud, 558.1(23)
  ~ with sand or earth, 757.12
close,adj.
  near, 790.1; see near,adj.
  be ~ to, 790.9
  be ~ to, figuratively, 793.25
  bring ~, 790.11,13
  come ~ to, 790.10
  conveniently ~, 790.3
  situated ~ together, 790.2
close,v., 297.1,2
  ~ and open, 297.1(10) ; 297.11
  ~ and open (the eyes), 297.12
  that which ~s, 297.4
  ~ up an opening, 297.8,9
closed,adj., 297.3,10
  state of being ~, 297.6
closet,n., 787.7(18,28)
closing,n., 297.5
  ~ down of a factory, etc.,
    297.7
  sound of ~, 469.7(33)
cloth,n.
  inferior ~, 883.4
  measurement unit of ~,
    946.26(2,6)
  metal ~ for armor, 1012.6
  ~ of rubber, 989.7
clothe,v., 974.2,39

~ in church garments,
  974.2(15)
  ~ in decorations of office or
    rank, 974.2(8)
  ~ oneself, 974.3,40
  ~ oneself in, 974.10
  ~ oneself in (quality, air,
    attitude, etc.), 974.11
  ~ showily, 974.2(2,4,5–7,11,12–
    14)
  ~ with armor, 1012.7
clothed,adj., 974.4,41
  carefully ~, 974.6,21
  carefully ~ man, 974.23–26
  carefully ~ woman, 974.27
  carelessly or casually ~,
    974.9
  fashionably ~ person, 974.28
  ~ in low neckline, 974.5
  untidily ~, 974.7
clothes,n., 974.1; see clothing,n.
  ~ washer, 899.39
clothing,n., 974.1; see also
  garment,n.
  ~ and ornaments, 974.1(3)
  army, navy, police, etc., ~,
    974.1(19)
  articles of men's ~, 974.22
  ~ as a set or collection, 974.35
  baby ~, 974.1(15)
  bride's ~, 974.35(4)
  casual ~ of female, 974.1(9,
    14)
  characteristic ~, 974.1(7)
  children's ~, 974.1(13)
  church ~, room for storage
    of, 787.7(42)
  civilian ~, 974.1(8)
  clergyman's ~, 974.1(2)
  container for articles of ~,
    974.21
  department in charge of ~,
    974.34
  disorder of ~, 974.8
  evening ~, 975.1
  fashionable in ~, 974.12
  fine ~, 974.1(1)
  fond of ~, 974.12
  ~ for fashionable occasions,
    974.1(17)
  ~ for men, 975.2
  ~ for penitence, 974.1(12)
  ~ for special activity,
    974.1(6)
  ~ for special occasions,
    974.1(4)
  formal ~, 975.1–8
  formal (of ~), 974.12
  formal ~ for women, 975.4
  furnish with ~, 233.1(2,9,13)
  furniture for ~, 974.31
  ~ instead of uniform,
    974.1(8)
  loosen the ~ of, 984.8
  maker of ~, 205.5(1,4,5,13,14,
    17)
  men's ~, dealer in, 205.5(9)
  men's ~, shop of dealer in,
    205.8
  ~ model, 974.14
  mourning ~, 974.1(20)
  navy ~, 974.1(19)
  ~ of a profession, 974.1(4,6)
  ~ of actors, 974.35(5)
  ~ of office or rank, 974.1(11)
  ~ of past periods, 974.1(4)
  ornamented ~, 974.1(1,3,10,
    18)
  outdoor ~, 974.1(21)
  outer ~, 974.46,47
  pays great attention to his
    ~, man who, 974.23–27
  pert. to ~, 974.13
  police ~, 974.1(19)

presser and cleaner of ~, 205.5(18)
put ~ on, 974.2,3,39
put ~ on oneself, 974.3,40
remove ~, 984.1,2,5–7,9,10
remove figurative ~, 984.12
rich ~, 974.1(1)
room for ~, 974.31,32
room for church ~, 974.30
seller of ~, 205.5(1,4,9,12)
semi-formal ~ for men, 975.3
semi-formal ~ for women, 975.5
servant's ~ (male), 974.1(7)
servant who takes care of man's ~, 205.14(16)
sewer of ~, 205.5(14)
sexual interest in ~, 710.33(12)
showy ~, 974.1(5)
showy in ~, 974.12
special ~, 974.1(11,16,19)
sports ~, 974.1(14,16)
style of ~, 974.36,37
supplier of ~ to army, 233.4(2)
untidiness of ~, 974.8
wearing of ~ of opposite sex, 710.33(8,31,34)
without ~, 984.16,18
without specific ~, 984.11
worker on ~, 205.5

cloud,n., 1057
a covering of ~s, 1057.12
blowing out ~s of tobacco smoke, 1057.19
clear of ~s, 1057.17
covered with ~s, 1057.11
examination or observation of ~s, 1057.21
exhibition of ~ formations, instrument for, 1057.22(3)
existence of ~, 1046.6
forms, formations, masses, or layers of ~s, 1057.3–5
full of ~s, 1057.11
gaseous matter like a ~, 1057.7
like a ~, 1057.6
little ~, 1057.1
luminous ~ around a god, 1065.27
~ of particles, dust, smoke, etc., 1057.18
pert. to ~s, 1057.10
rate and direction of ~s, instrument to measure, 1057.22(2)
region of the ~s, 1057.15
science of ~s, 1057.20
storm ~, 1057.2
without ~s, 1057.16
cloud,v., 1057.14
~ up, 1057.13
cloudlike,adj., 1057.6
cloudy,adj., 1057.6
become ~, 1057.13
~ in markings, 1057.9
make ~, 1057.14
~ qualities, instrument to measure, 1057.22(1)
clown,n., 1116.1
behavior, actions, etc., of a ~, 1116.4
quality of an absurd ~, 1116.5
clown,v., 1116.3
clowning,n., 1116.4
coarse and obscene ~, descr. of, 1116.6
clownish,adj., 1116.2
~ characteristic, 1116.5
club,n.
a society or group, 524.9
weapon, 437.5
policeman's ~, 437.5(3,23)

~-shaped, 507.17(16)
clubfoot,n., 346.12; 346.12(2)
clubfooted,adj., 346.11(4)
clue,n., 601.11
clumsiness,n., 14.2
clumsy,adj., 14.1
~ animal, 906.18(8)
be ~, 14.4
big and ~, 14.1(40,42) ; 14.5; 906.3(1) ; 906.15
heavy and ~, 14.1(43)
ill-mannered and ~, 14.1(14)
~ in action, 14.1(65,73,74)
~ in attempting to do or find, 14.1(18)
~ in both hands, 14.1(2,3)
~ in management of affairs, 14.1(26)
~ in movement, 14.1(15,16,20, 21,48,63,65,75)
~ in social contacts, 14.1(19, 41,51,53,59,60,70,71)
mentally ~, 14.1(41)
~ person, 14.3; 906.18(8)
~ player, 14.3(4)
stupid and ~, 14.1(6,20,21)
~ thing, 906.18(8)
~ to handle, 14.5
~ with the hands, 14.1(58,66)
~ worker, 14.3(2,3,12)
~ young man, 14.3(6)
cluster,n.
grow in ~s, 731.3(8)
growing in ~s, 731.5(1,8)
co-operate,v., 51.1; 203.1(29)
~ secretly, 203.1(7)
co-operation,n., 51.2; 203.3(1–3)
done in ~, 51.5
~ of drugs, 203.3(2)
coachman,n., 192.14
coal,n., 1010.1
ashes with glowing ~s, 1064.52
burned ~, 1064.42(4,5)
burning ~, 1064.42(4,5)
containing ~, 1010.3,6
container for ~s, 261.6
~ dust, 1010.2
like ~, 1010.6
~ mine, 1010.4
~ miner, 1010.5
pert. to ~, 1010.6
producing ~, 1010.3
coarse,adj.
not smooth, 440.1–3
~ act, 864.3
become ~, 864.5
cause to become ~, 864.6
figuratively ~, 864.1
~ jokes, full of, 1115.3(1,2) ; 1115.4
~ language, 1118.14,15
~-looking, red-faced, and fat, 864.7
~ly human, 864.8
~ly humorous remarks, sayings, books, etc., 1115.8
offensively ~, 864.9
~ person, 864.4
~ remark, 1118.16
~ woman, 708.14(5)
coarseness,n.
figurative ~, 864.2
coast,n., 1029.79; see **shore**,n.
curve in a ~ line, 155.2(2)
outline of ~, 1029.85
sea~, 1029.79
coat,n.
jacket, 976.4
overcoat, 976.1
bottom of a ~, 976.2
garment under a ~, 974.38(26)
rain~, 976.3

short ~, 976.4
coat,v.
~ the tongue, 972.1(23)
coating,n., 972.4; see also cover, covering,n.
external ~, 972.4(11,21,23)
frozen ~, 1059.7–9; see also frost,n.
fungus ~, 985.11,20
having a ~, 972.32
~ on copper, brass, or bronze, 1016.18,19
~ on fruits or leaves, 972.4(3)
~ on iron or other metal, 1017.3,4
remove the ~ from, 972.6; 972.6(1–4)
surface ~, 972.4(3)
coax,v., 638.1(3–5,19)
coaxing,n.
lead by ~, 176.1(8)
cobweb,n., 308.1(1,2,10)
able to make a ~, 308.6
like a ~, 308.1(3)
cock,n.
male bird, 405.2
young ~, 405.4(3)
cockfight,n.
place of a ~, 20.7(2)
cockroach,n., 428.3; see roach,n.
of ~es, 428.2(16)
cocktail,n., 749.5
coconut,n.
dried ~ meat, 745.1(3)
codfish,n.
young ~, 422.4(2)
coffee,n., 747.1
chemical in ~, 747.4
flavoring of chocolate and ~, 747.3
pot for ~, 261.10(13)
small cup of ~, 747.2
coffin,n.
~ and stand, 797.18
cloth thrown over a ~, 797.21
frame for a ~, 797.19
stone ~, 797.17
walks with the ~, one who, 799.4
coin,n., 213.2(4,7,8,12)
containing ~s, 213.12(4)
descriptions of ~s, 213.21
make ~s, 213.16
making ~s, place of, 213.17
~ of small value, 917.11
pert. to ~s, 213.12(3–5)
~s, 213.2(2,4,9,10)
science of ~s, 213.20(1,4,5)
~-shaped, 507.17(52)
sides of a ~, 186.1(7,9)
coin,v.
create, 726.17; see create,v.
coincidental,adj., 764.4
cold,adj., 1058.1; see also cool, frozen,adj.
without heat, 1060.66
become ~, 1058.11
damp and ~, 1034.15
disagreeably ~, 1058.2
emotionally ~, 1097.3–6,24
~er regions of temperate zone, 1058.5
feel ~, 1058.8
feeling ~, 1058.6
freezing ~ (of weather), 1059.17
make ~, 1058.8,13; see also cool, freeze,v.
make ~ in emotions, 1097.25, 26
make and keep (foods, etc.) ~, 1058.19; see also cool, freeze,v.
slightly ~, 1058.3

~ weather, 1059.13
cold,n.
  illness, 363.17–19
  insensitive to ~, 1137.38
  insensitiveness to ~, 1137.39
  protection against ~, 1047.12, 13
  sensitiveness to ~, 1137.32
  sensitiveness to ~, decreased, 1137.34
  shake with ~, 111.1(23)
cold-blooded,adj., 1098.3; 1129.22
  make ~, 1129.25
coldness,n., 1058
  degree of ~, 1059.6; 1060.53
  die of ~, 1058.12
  feel ~, ability to, 1060.46
  feel ~, inability to, 1060.47
  feeling of disagreeable ~, 1058.7
  harm by ~, 1059.15
  kill by ~, 1058.12
  sudden feeling of ~, 1058.9
collar,n., 977.4
  container for ~s, 974.21
  continuation of a ~, 977.5
  iron ~ for strangling, 796.14
  ~s, collectively, 977.3
collarbone,n., 354.1(2)
collect,v., 319.1,2
  ~ for armed forces, 319.1(32)
  ~ for war, 319.1(34)
  ~ in a crowd, 318.10
  ~ into a crowd, 318.11
  ~ into a group, 318.4
  ~ literary material, 319.1(13)
  ~ money, 319.1(32)
collected,adj., 319.6
  ~ by the government, that which is, 318.17
collection,n., 319.3
  a ~, 318.16
  bring together in a ~, 319.1
  descr. of ~, 319.5
  formed by ~, 319.6(1)
  put together in a ~, 319.1
collector,n., 319.4
college,n., 623.1; see school,n.
  accept into a ~, 623.10
  enroll in a ~, 623.9
  graduate of a ~, 623.12
  president of a ~, 1077.1(6,25)
collide,v., 436.1(11,17,18,28)
collision,n., 436.2; 436.2(4)
  shock of ~, 436.4
  sounds of ~, 469.7–10
colony,n.
  government of a ~, 1073.3(19)
color,n., 488.1
  agree in ~, 488.16(1,2)
  arc of ~ after rain, 1037.26,27
  art of combining ~s, 488.11
  artist using ~, 965.7(1)
  artist's ~s, 488.5
  band of ~s, 488.6
  ~ blindness, 481.1(9,11)
  categories of ~, 488.14
  change in ~, 488.15–17,19
  change of ~, 488.18,19
  changeable in ~, 488.8(37)
  changed in ~, 488.21
  cover with ~, 972.1(37)
  deficient in ~, 489.1(1)
  deficient in ~, person, animal, or plant that is, 489.6
  determine ~s, device to, 488.26(2)
  display of ~, 951.3(20)
  distinct (of ~), 1.20
  effect of ~ in a picture, 488.7
  full of ~, 488.8; 925.1(12,24)
  give ~ to, 488.15,19
  give off rainbowlike ~s, 1065.45(26)

glaring in ~, 1065.51
golden in ~, 1013.14,15
hair ~, 369.12–15
having ~, 488.8
having ~, state of, 488.10
having no particular ~, 488.12
horse, ~ of, 408.8
horse as to ~, 408.7
~ in a pearl, 963.2
lack of ~, 489.2
lacking ~, 489.1
like brass in ~, 1016.13
like copper in ~, 1016.8
like iron or steel in ~, 1017.2(4,7)
like lead in ~, 1018.2(2)
lose ~, 489.3
measure ~s, device to, 488.26(2)
milky in ~, 744.4(5,6,10)
of the ~ of blood, 352.3(5)
ornament with ~, 1065.76
perception of ~, device to test, 488.26(1)
pert. to ~, 488.13
picture of one ~, 488.9
play of ~s, 488.4
pour ~ over, 1036.17
quality of ~, 488.2
reduce the ~, 10.5(21)
remove ~ from, 489.4,5
rusty in ~, 1017.6
science of ~, 488.24
separate light into ~s, device to, 488.26(3)
show bright ~s, 488.23
silver in ~, 1015.12,13
skin ~, 384.1–26; see complexion,n.
smoky ~, 1050.18
softening of ~, 488.3
starry splashes of ~, 1056.32
strengthen (a ~), 1.29(9,17)
strong (of ~s), 1.20
surrounding band of ~, 1065.49(2)
take on a ~, 488.16(2)
treatise on ~s, 488.25
unhealthy in ~, 352.18(3)
variegated in ~, 1006.38
weak in ~, 10.1(64)
wine ~, having, 749.19(3)
without ~, 489.1
color,v., 488.15–17,19
  ~ like bronze, 1016.16
  ~ like marble, 1006.38
  ~ silver, 1015.12
  substances used to ~, 488.22
  ~ with smoke, 1050.24
coloration,n., 488.1,17
colored,adj., 488.8
  flesh-~, 488.8(14)
  ~ person, 430.9; see Negro,n.
  rainbow-~, 488.8(15,37)
colorful,adj., 488.8; 925.1(12,24)
  be showy and ~, 951.37
coloring,n., 488.1
  substances for ~, 488.22
colorless,adj., 489.1
colt,n.
  group of ~s, 403.5(56)
column,n.
  architectural ~, 1023.1
  arrangement of ~s, 1023.3
  base of a ~, 1023.11
  having ~s, 1023.5,6
  lowest part of ~, 1023.11
  monument in the form of a ~, 1023.9
  parts of a ~, 1023.10
  parts resting on a ~, 1023.12, 13
  pert. to a ~, 1023.4
  series of ~s, 1023.2
  shaped like a ~, 1023.7

stone ~, 1006.1(27)
style of a ~, 1023.14,15
support treated as a ~, 1023.8
use of ~s, 1023.3
without ~s, 1023.16
comb,n.
  bird's ~, 385.1(1–3)
combed,adj.
  neatly ~, 902.1(3)
combination,n., 320.3,4
  pert. to ~, 320.8
combine,v., 320.1,2
  ~ with water, 1026.14
combining,adj.
  ~ into a mass, 320.9
combustible,adj., 1064.19
combustion,n.
  spontaneous ~, 1064.27
come,v., 118
  ~ after, 173.1
  ~ apart, 325.2
  ~ as a result, 16.3
  ask to ~, 274.1(9,23)
  ask to ~ back, 274.1(31)
  ~ at the beginning of, 730.1(5,6,8)
  ~ away, 141.1; see depart,v.
  ~ back, 145.1–6
  ~ before, 175.1–5; see precede,v.
  ~ between, 118.1(11)
  ~ by pushing, 197.2
  call to ~, 693.1(3,4,15,16)
  ~ close to, 790.10
  ~ down, 167.1–3; see fall,v.
  ~ down in a sudden attack, 560.7
  ~ forth, 140.1–6
  ~ from, 118.1(9)
  ~ in or into, 133.1; see enter,v.
  ~ into being, 729.7; see begin,v.
  ~ into sight, 118.1(2)
  ~ last, 118.1(5)
  let ~ out in drops, 918.10
  ~ near to, 790.10
  ~ near to each other, 790.12
  ~ next, 173.1
  ~ off, 167.1(33)
  one who ~s, 118.3
  order to ~, 275.1(14)
  order to ~ to court, 275.1(13); 275.2(11)
  ~ out as particles of fire, 1064.5
  ~ out in drops, 918.9
  ~ out in rays of light, 1065.32
  ~ out or off in bubbles, 1028.4
  ~ out, 140.1–6
  ~ out (of tears), 1128.16,17
  ~ quickly, 118.1(16,17)
  ~ secretly, 118.1(19)
  ~ slowly, 118.1(19)
  ~ to (a place) in large numbers, 916.27
  ~ to ground, 999.6
  ~ to see, 118.1(23)
  ~ together, 321.2; see connect,v.
  ~ together in a collection, 319.2
  ~ together in a combination, 320.2
  ~ together in a crowd, 318.10
  ~ together in a group, 318.5
  ~ together toward a point, 322.10
  ~ up, 159.1; see rise,v.
  ~ up on the shore, 1029.94
  ~ where unwelcome, 118.1(10, 12,13)
  ~ with, 131.1; see accompany,v.
comedian,n., 1114.5

burlesque ~, 1114.7
Spanish ~, 1116.1(4)
comet,n., 1053.1; see also **heavenly body,n.**
  group of ~s, 318.1(55)
  like a ~, 1053.2
  orbit of ~, 1053.21,22
  point of ~ farthest from earth, 165.1(3)
comfort,n., 1141.2,7
  a ~, 1141.3,4
  conducive to ~, 1141.1
  curl up in ~, 156.7
  lack of ~, 1141.12,16
  press close for ~, 198.1(11,14, 18,19,22)
  without ~, 1141.13
comfortable,adj., 1141.1,6
  make ~, 1141.8,9
  not ~, 1141.10,15
  ~ place, 782.1(4) ; 1141.5
  ~ position, 1141.5
  ~ room, 1141.5
  warm and ~, 1060.40
comic,adj., 1113.1; see **laughable,adj.**
coming,adj.
  ~ soon, 765.12
coming,n.
  a ~, 118.2
command,n., 275.2; see **order,n.**
command,v., 275.1; see **order,v.**
commandment,n.
  Ten ~s, 648.2
commemorate,v., 627.30(5,6)
commemoration,n., 627.31,34
commemorator,n., 627.33
commence,v., 729.1,4,7; see **begin,v.**
commencement,n., 729.2,8,11; see **beginning,n.**
commend,v., 851.1
commendable,adj., 850.19; 851.8
commendation,n., 851.2
comment,n.
  statement, 674.9
comment,v., 674.8; see **say,v.**
commerce,n., 210.1; see **business,n.**
  pert. to ~, 210.3; 210.3(1)
committee,n.
  officer of ~, 1077.23–25
common,adj.
  undistinguished, 535.10–12
  usual, 535.1–3
  without originality, freshness, or imagination, 535.5–9
  be ~ or usual, 535.4
  make ~, 535.13
  ~ people, 431.6–9
commonplace,adj., 535.1,5,10
commonplace,n., 535.3,6,11
commotion,n., 1101.1
  agitation and ~, 1101.1(11)
  be in ~, 1101.2
  ~ by a mob, 1101.1(20–22,34)
  cause a ~, 1101.5,6
  causes ~, one who, 1101.8
  causing ~, 1101.7
  civil ~, 1101.1(9)
  confused ~, 1101.1(18,26,36, 39,41)
  hurry and ~, 1101.1(40)
  in ~, 1101.3
  ~ in social conditions, 1101.1(7,31,37)
  noise and ~, 1101.1(3–5,13,14, 16,19,24,27,29,30,34,35,38)
  ~ of prices in stock market, 1101.1(12)
  political ~, 1101.1(9)
  subdued ~, 1101.1(28)

take part in a ~, 1101.4
  ~ that disturbs the peace, 1101.1(8,21,22,25,34,35,38)
  throw into ~, 1101.5
communicate,v., 613.1,17; see also **tell,v.**
  ~ with, 613.28
communication,n., 613.2–4
  ~ at a distance, 613.29(2)
  ~ between people, 613.29(1)
  ~ by fingers, 664.11(3)
  delivered ~, 613.30(5,6)
  extrasensory ~, 433.12
  ~ of thought by psychic means, 613.29(3)
  ~ with the dead, 794.41
communicative,adj., 613.7
communicator,n., 613.5
communist,adj.
  ~ group, 318.1(24)
communist,n., 1076.20
  opposer of Russian ~s, 1076.12(16)
  supporter of ~s, 1076.21
  ~ sympathizer, 1076.21
Communist party,n., 1076.22–24
  supporter of ~, 1076.21
community,n.
  interest in welfare of one's ~, 784.8(4)
  religious ~, 644; see **convent,** **monastery,n.**
companion,n., 131.3(9) ; see also **friend,n.**
comparable,adj., 530.2
compare,v., 529.12
  able to be ~d, 530.2
  unable to be ~d, 530.3
  ~ with a standard, 530.5
comparison,n.
  basis of ~, 530.4
  ~ of differences, 530.1
  without basis for ~, 540.1(18, 19)
compartment,n., 787.7; see also **room,n.**
  covered ~, 787.7(7)
  ~ for horses or cattle, 787.7(35)
  temporary ~, 787.7(7)
  voting ~, 787.7(7)
compass,n.
  directions of the ~, 179.5,6
  stand for a ~, 179.7
compel,v.
  allow no choice, 252.18
  force, 3.3
compensate,v., 222.1
compensation,n., 222.2
  descr. of ~, 222.3
competence,adj., 7.1; see **ability,n.**
competent,adj., 7.2; see **able,** adj.
  be ~, 7.9
competition,n., 20.2
  athletic ~, 20.2(2,3,5,6,9,13)
  judges of a ~, 1083.39,40
  place in ~, 20.6
  place of ~, 20.7
  region of ~, 782.1(1)
  state of being in ~, 20.4
competitive,adj., 20.5
competitor,n., 20.3
complain,v., 468.2; 1120.1
  ~ (of prisoners), 1120.1(17)
complainer,n., 1120.4
complaining,adj., 468.3; 1120.5, 6
  habitually ~, 1120.6
  ~ woman, 708.14(9,15,23)
complaint,n., 1120.2
  a ~, 1120.3
  ~ against injustice, 1120.3(1)

cause or grounds for ~, 1120.7, 8
  offer reasons in ~, 1120.1(11)
  reason with in mild ~, 1120.9
  say in ~, 1120.1(2,6,11,15,16)
  sounds of ~, 468.1(1,2,7–9,15, 18)
  written ~ with signatures in a circle, 1120.3(5)
complete,adj., 328.1; 925.15
  make ~, 328.3
  making ~, 328.5
complete,v., 328.3
  one who ~s, 328.6
  that which ~s, 328.6
completeness,n., 328.2
  necessary to ~, 328.7
completion,n., 328.4
complex,adj.
  difficult, 25.1(4,9,15,16)
  hard to understand, 604.1–5
  not simple, 25.1(4,5,8–10,15, 16,20,25)
  ~ problem, 25.2(1)
complexion,n.
  blueness of ~, 384.2
  dark of ~, 384.3–5
  light of ~, 384.7–10
  pale of ~, 384.11–14
  pert. to beauty of ~, 505.7
  red of ~, 384.17–23
  sickly yellow of ~, 384.15,16
  sunburned of ~, 384.24,25
complicated,adj.
  difficult, 25.1(3,5,8–10,15,16, 20,25)
  hard to understand, 604.1–5
  not simple, 25.1(3,5,8–10,15, 16,20,25)
  ~ situation, etc., 25.9(2,7,18)
complication,n.
  free of ~, 309.11(41)
compliment,n., 851.2; 851.2(6)
  empty ~, 852.2(2)
compliment,v., 851.1; 852.1
composition,n.
  piece of writing, 682.16
comprehend,v., 593.1; see **understand,v.**
comprehension,n., 593.2; see **understanding,n.**
compressibility,n.
  measurement of ~, 198.7
compulsion,n., 3.4,6; 252.19
compulsive,adj., 3.5
  ~ behavior, 55.3(16)
compulsory,adj.
  allowing no choice, 252.17–19
  using force, 3.5
  ~ by official order, 3.5(1)
compute,v., 942.1; see **calculate,v.**
concave,adj., 155.4(5,9,11)
conceal,v., 970.1
  ~ by false appearance, 970.13
  ~ by wrapping, 970.8
  ~ character of, 970.18
  cover to ~, 972.1(5,10,16,44, 55)
  ~ crimes, 970.11
  ~ faults, 970.11
  ~ feelings, 970.19,21
  ~ illegal thing or act, 970.7
  ~ in a secret place, 970.4,5
  ~ in one's hand, 970.9
  ~ information, 970.10
  ~ motives, 970.19,21
  ~ oneself, 970.30–37
  ~ oneself aboard ship, 970.37
  ~ oneself for evil purpose, 970.32
  ~ oneself in a hole in the earth, 1004.37
  ~ oneself in sneaky fashion, 970.35

~ oneself waiting to attack, 970.33
screen used to ~ woman, 708.13
~ the face of, 970.6
concealed,adj., 970.42; see also secret,adj.
false in appearance, 970.51
not shown, 970.48
not told or not known, 970.49
~ atmosphere, 970.54
~ attitude, 970.53,54
be ~, 971.16
~ but present, 970.45
~ condition, 970.54
~ feeling, 970.53,54
~ food, 970.52
~ in identity, 971.17
~ in meaning, 971.9
~ in operation, 971.11
keep (information) ~, 970.50
keep (something) ~, 970.44
not ~, 970.55
~ opinion, 970.53
purposely ~, as plans, motives, etc., 970.47
~ supplies, 970.52
~ tendency, 970.53
~ valuables, 970.52
concealment,n., 970.2
~ by false appearance, 970.14
~ by smoke, 1050.26
drive out of ~, 144.1(8); 970.39; 1050.25
drive (birds) out of ~, 970.40
in ~, 970.36
lie in ~, 970.32
lie in ~ for evil purpose, 970.32
means of ~, 970.3,15; 1050.26
military ~, 970.16
~ of insanity, 970.22
~ of purpose, 970.20
place of ~, 970.41; see hiding place,n.
soldiers in ~, 970.34
wait in ~, 272.1(9)
wrap for ~, 970.8
conceit,n., 871.2; 871.2(9)
feel ~, 871.3
show ~, 871.3
show with ~, 871.9
talk with ~, 871.9
tendency to wild ~, 1136.1(25)
conceited,adj., 871.1(4,5,7–9,12, 14,27,28,30,31,41,45–49)
~ about his clothing or dress, one who is, 974.23–27
~ person, 871.5
~ woman, 871.5(2)
~ young man, 871.5(3)
concentrate,v.
pay attention, 579.1
unable to ~, 581.1(15); 581.3
concentrated,adj.
not diluted, 1.25,26
concentrating,adj.
attentive, 579.5
concentration,n.
attention, 579.2,5
Hindu system of deep ~, 579.27–29
concert,n.
give or manage ~s, 479.6
manager of ~ company, 8.16(7)
musical ~, 479.4
conciliate,v., 1096.31
concise,adj., 911.1(5,7,8,14,15, 19)
conclude,v.
end, 792.1,2; see end,v.
form an opinion, 633.1
think, 585.1; 589.1

concluding,adj., 792.15; see also final, last,adj.
~ number or section of entertainment, 792.23(2)
~ parts, 792.23
~ speech, 792.23(1,4,5)
~ things, 792.23
conclusion,n.
end, 792.36; see end,n.
opinion, 633.8
result of reasoning, 589.2,3
thinking, 585.2
arrive at a ~, 589.1; see reason,v.
concubinage,n., 702.22
concubine,n., 702.23,24; 710.19–21
mistress, 710.19–21
~ in a harem, 710.23
condemn,v.
disapprove of, 894.1
~ as inferior, 883.5
condemnation,n.
disapproval, 894.3
condense,v.
shorten, 911.2
condensed,adj.
shortened, 911.1
undiluted, 1.25,26
be a ~ symbol of, 911.4
~ symbol, 911.5
condiment,n., 446.17
condition,n.
provision, 525.1
state, 44.1
ask as a ~, 274.1(39)
combination of ~s, 44.2
difficult ~, 25.9
existing ~, 44.1(9)
favorable ~, 44.1(2)
~ of advantage, 836.7
~ of affairs, 44.1(8)
~ of circumstances, 44.1(8)
present ~, 44.1(9)
return to previous ~, 145.1(1, 15,21,22,24)
return to primitive ~, 145.2(1, 3)
~s, 44.2
state as a ~, 525.3
superior ~, 833.6
~ under the surface, 970.54
unfortunate ~, 44.1(6)
condition,v.
provide, 525.3
conditional,adj., 525.2
condolence,n., 1129.8–12
condone,v., 897.11
conduct,n., 55.1,3; see behavior,n.
conduct,v.
lead, 176.1; see lead,v.
~ oneself, 55.2; see behave,v.
confer,v.
discuss, 672.1; see discuss,v.
conference,n.
discussion, 672.2; see discussion,n.
confess,v., 675.1(2,9)
confesser,n., 675.5,6; 884.26,27
confession,n., 675.2
descr. of or pert. to ~, 675.3
~ of guilt or sin, 675.2(1)
place of ~, 884.29
priest who hears ~, 884.28
use of torture to force a ~, 625.14
confessor,n., 675.5; 884.26–28
confide in,v., 632.2
confidence,n.
belief, 632.6
certainty, 641.7
secret, 971.23
based on ~, 632.14

documents that cause ~, 632.28
entitling to ~, 632.26
not worthy of ~, 639.12
self~, 641.7; 641.7(1,2,4)
worthy of ~, 632.25
confident,adj.
believing, 632.18
certain, 641.6
cause to feel ~, 638.1; 641.9
over~, 641.6(3,8,11)
self~, 641.6(3,8,9,13)
confidential,adj., 971.1
confine,v., 301.1; see also imprison,v.
~ animals, 403.23
confined,adj.
~ animal, 301.5(2)
~ by illness, one who is, 301.6
closely ~, 301.11
~ in space, 301.20
~ indoors, 301.12
~ person, 301.5
confinement,n., 301.2,3; see also imprisonment, prison,n.
kept in solitary ~, 301.10
place of ~, 300.7; 301.4
solitary ~, 301.3(6)
conflict,n., 542.10; see dispute, quarrel,n.
a fight or battle, 562.1; see fight,n.
emotional ~s, caused by, 1092.106–8
state of ~, 542.1
confound,v.
confuse, 605.1; see confuse,v.
confuse,v., 605.1,11
not tell apart, 605.10
~ as to direction, 605.1(6,11, 18,25)
~ with brightness, 1065.78
~ with drugs, 605.1(7,24)
~ with lights, 1065.78
~ with liquor, 605.1(7,8,24,26)
confused,adj., 605.5,14
act ~, 605.8
become ~, 605.7
~ by liquor, 605.5(5)
~ by moon's influence, 1054.33,34
excited and ~ state, 1100.7(12)
feel ~, 605.9
make ~, 605.1,11
mentally ~, 605.5(1–5)
noisy and ~, 605.14
~ state, 605.3,13
talk ~ly, 671.1(91,92)
~ talk, 671.2(19)
confusing,adj., 605.4
hard to understand, 604.1
~ mass or collection, 605.19
~ state of things, 605.18
confusion,n., 605.2,3,12,13
be in great ~, 605.15
cause of ~, 605.6
commotion and ~, 1101.1(18, 26,36,39,41)
eliminate the ~ of, 598.10
in ~, 605.21
in ~ and haste, 95.5(4)
mental ~, 605.13
noisy ~, 605.13(2,4–6,11,14,15, 23)
~ of languages, 605.13(2); 664.3
~ of passageways, 605.17
~ of roads, 605.17
~ of sounds, 605.13(2,4–6,11, 14,15,23)
~ of voices, 605.13(2)
place of ~, 605.16

place of killing and ~, 605.16(5)
place of noise and ~, 473.4
reduce the ~ of, 598.10
reduce to ~, 605.1,11
scene of ~, 605.16
sounds of ~, 473.1-3
state of ~, 605.3,13
throw into ~, 605.1,11
time of ~ between governments, 605.20
twist around in ~, 156.1(26, 35)
congratulate,v., 1102.17-19
congress,n., 1080.10; see legislature,n.
disobedience or disrespect to ~, 1081.23
connect,v., 321.1,2
connected,adj., 321.8
logically ~, 590.5
one who is ~, 321.6
that which is ~, 321.6
connecting,adj., 321.9
~ word, 321.5(1-3)
connection,n., 321.3,4
causes ~, that which, 321.5
causing ~, 321.9
pert. to ~, 321.10
place of ~, 321.7
connective,adj., 321.9
connective,n., 321.5
connector,n., 321.5
conquer,v., 22.43
conquerable,adj., 22.48
~ by attack, 22.50
conquered,adj.
able to be ~, 22.48
state of being ~, 22.45
unable to be ~, 22.49
conqueror,n., 22.46
conquest,n., 22.44
~ and domination, 22.44
leader of the Spanish ~, 22.47
conscience,n.
be unwilling because of ~, 885.6
conforming to ~, 885.3
controlled by ~, 885.2
following one's ~, 885.8
free from ~, 309.15(11,27)
hesitate because of ~, 885.6
pain of ~, 885.4
psychoanalytic term for ~, 885.1
showing no ~, 885.9
stung by ~, 885.7
the self as ~, 228.1(6)
uneasiness of ~, 885.5
uneasy because of ~, 885.7
unrestricted or unguided by ~, 885.9
without ~, 885.10
conscious,adj.
able to have sensations, 432.16
deliberate, 45.12
having knowledge, 611.1
on purpose, 45.12
consciousness,n., 432.17; 611.1
above ~, 584.7; 612.13
below ~, 584.8
bring back to ~, 435.8
come back to ~, 435.9
consecrated,adj., 650.1; see sacred,adj.
consent,n., 541.2; 554.2
existing by mere ~, 541.8
consent,v., 541.1; 554.1
consenter,n., 541.3
consenting,adj., 541.4; 554.3
consequence,n.
importance, 848.2
result, 16.1
consequent,adj., 16.4

conservative,adj.
opposed to change, 544.8-10
~ beliefs, etc., 1076.15
~ in politics, 1076.12(17,23,28, 29)
~ political party, 1076.14
consider,v.
show regard for feelings, 1097.37
think, 585.1
~ as caused by, 15.5
~ as the cause of, 15.5
considerate,adj., 1097.36
~ act, 52.5(21)
not ~, 1097.35
consideration,n., 1097.36
consist of,v., 326.51
consistent,adj., 531.1,2; see unchanging, uniform,adj.
consolable,adj., 1125.46
not ~, 1125.47
consolation,n., 1125.41-43
console,v., 1125.40
consoler,n., 1125.42
consoling,adj., 1125.44
consonant,n., 670.14(2-4,6-8,10, 13)
conspicuous,adj., 952.1,5
be ~, 952.4
~ because unusual or strange, 952.6
~ by contrast, 952.1(2)
make ~, 952.3
most ~, 952.8
not ~, 952.9
offensively ~, 952.1(1)
~ part, 326.1(15)
show ~ly, 951.1(2,9,15,16,22, 23,24,31,33,38,39,43,45,55)
conspicuousness,n., 952.2
constable,n., 1078.1
pert. to a ~, 1078.3
constant,adj., 531.1,2; see unchanging, uniform, adj.
constipate,v., 293.22
constipated,adj., 293.24
constipating,adj., 293.23
constipation,n., 293.21
constitution,n.
bodily structure, 338.9
laws, 1079.10-13
make-up, 326.49
construct,v.
build, 727.1; see build,v.
make, 726.1; see make,v.
construction,n.
something made, 726.3
a ~, 726.3; 727.4
act of ~, 727.2
design of ~, 727.6
given to ~, 727.9
manner of ~, 727.6
pert. to ~, 727.5
poor in ~ (of literary work), 726.28
science of ~, 727.10
skill in ~, 727.8
constructor,n.
builder, 727.3
maker, 726.2
consul,n., 523.6; see diplomat,n.
contact,n., 436.2
come in ~ with, 436.1; see touch,v.
pert. to ~, 436.6(1)
sounds of ~, 469.7-10
contagious,adj., 389.21,22
contain,v., 260.1
ability to ~, measurement of, 260.9
ability to ~ quantity, 260.7,8
able to ~, 260.6
be able to ~, 260.4
contained,adj.

amount ~, 260.3
what is ~, 260.2
container,n., 261.1-17; see also vessel,n.
ammunition ~, 261.1(8)
arrow ~, 261.1(38)
cigar ~, 261.1(30)
close-fitting ~, 261.1(42)
coal ~, 261.6
cover for ~, 972.4(6)
dagger ~, 261.1(41,42)
drug ~, 261.1(22)
flat ~ for carrying, 261.1(45); 261.5
~ for articles of clothing, 261.16; 974.21
~ for collars, 974.21
~ for dressing articles or substances, 974.20
~ for hats, 974.21
~ for keeping things moist, 261.1(30)
~ for liquids, 261.7
~ for sacred thing, 261.1(40, 43)
~ for sewing implements, 261.1(29,31)
~ for traveling, 261.16
~ for valuables, 261.1(17)
gunpowder ~, 261.1(28)
hay or feed ~, 261.1(19,34)
incense-burning ~, 261.1(15)
~ in which to beat materials, 261.1(35)
medicine ~, 261.1(22)
metal ~, 261.1(9-11,36,44)
pistol ~, 261.1(25)
round ~, 261.1(2,3,7,21,36,46, 47)
serving as a cover on a ~, 972.39
storage ~, 261.1(5)
sword ~, 261.1(41,42)
contamination,n.
free of ~, 900.6
contemporary,adj., 764.1,4
be ~, 764.2
contemporary,n., 764.3
contempt,n., 870.2
bitter ~, 870.3(7)
bring into ~, 870.6
expose to ~, 870.7
express ~ (for), 870.1; 1111.35; 1112.8
facial expression of ~, 365.2(3,12,13)
feel ~ (for), 870.1
~ for God, 882.4
laugh at in ~, 1111.19
object of ~, 870.11-16; 1111.22
shame that brings ~, 868.16
shameful act or behavior that brings ~, 868.16
show ~ (for), 870.1
treat with ~, 870.1
with ~, 870.5
worthy of ~, 870.8,9
contemptible,adj., 870.8
act in a ~ manner, 870.10
laughable and ~, 1111.21,22
~ people, 870.15
~ person, 870.11,12,16
small and ~ thing, 909.5(10)
~ woman, 708.14(11,21); 870.13,14
contemptuous,adj., 870.3
~ act, 52.5(29); 870.2
be ~ of, 870.1
bitterly ~, 870.3(7)
~ facial expression, 870.2(3)
~ language, 870.2(1)
~ of control, 870.3(11)
~ of convention, 870.3(1)
~ of dignity, 870.3(1)
~ of law, 870.3(1)

~ of religion, 870.3(1)
~ of rules, 870.3(11)
person ~ of rules, control, etc., 870.4
~ remark, 870.2
~ treatment, 870.2(1)
content,adj., 1107.3; see **satisfied**,adj.
contentment,n., 1107.4; see **satisfaction**,n.
dreamy or unrealistic ~, one who lives in, 1107.8
live in ~, 750.1(30)
sound of ~, 467.1(8)
contents,n., 260.7
alphabetical list of ~, 311.19(3)
cubic ~, 260.8
cubic ~ measurement, 260.9
list of ~, 311.19(3,8)
measurement of ~, 946.48–50
contest,n., 20.2
athletic ~, 20.2(2,3,5,6,9,13); 322.1(37)
easily won ~, 20.2(15)
engage in a ~, 20.1
loser in a ~, 20.9
one entered in a ~, 20.3(4,5)
person second in a ~, 20.8
region of ~, 782.1(1)
running ~, 96.5,6
substitute falsely entered in a ~, 324.4(13)
contestant,n., 20.3
group of ~s, 318.1(89,93)
main ~, 20.3(6)
continual,adj., 754.3
continuation,n., 754.2
continue,v., 754.1
ability to ~, 754.22
~ a course of action, 52.7(1,3)
cause to ~, 754.9
causing to ~, 754.8
~ doing, 49.1(13,23,24,41); 754.19
~ in one's belief, 754.21
~ in one's demand, 754.21
~ in one's position, 754.21
~ in time, 762.12
~ longer than, 754.1(5,12)
tending to ~, 754.20
time during which something ~s, 754.10; 769.7
~ with, 754.19
continued,adj.
~ activity, 754.5,6
having ~ a long time, 754.12
continuing,adj., 754.3,20; 755.2; see also **continuous**,adj.
~ for a long time, 754.11
~ for a short time, 756.1; see **temporary**,adj.
~ for a stated time, 754.13
~ for centuries, 754.14
~ forever, 754.15–18
~ indefinitely, 754.3(1); 754.11; 755.1–3
~ unchanged, 754.3(10)
continuous,adj., 754.3,20; 755.2; see also **continuing**, adj.
~ action, 754.4,6
~ activity, 754.5,6
~ thing, 754.6,7
contract,n., 541.13
contract,v.
agree, 541.10; see **agree**,v.
decrease, 910.1,2; see **decrease**,v.
~ rhythmically, 910.16
contracting,adj.
~ and dilating, as the heart, 910.15
~ rhythmically, 910.4(2)
contraction,n.

agreement, 541.11; see **agreement**,n.
decrease, 910.3; see **decrease**, n.
cause ~, able to, 910.7
descr. of ~ and dilation of heart, 910.15
~ of bodily tissues, causing, 910.12
~ of bodily tissues, that which causes, 910.13
~ of the heart, 910.3(6)
unhealthy ~ of bodily part, 910.3(5)
contradict,v., 544.1(12,22–25, 27); 546.4
contradiction,n., 544.2; 546.2, 3
contradictory,adj., 544.3; 546.1
contrariness,n., 546.2
contrary,adj., 546.1
be ~, 546.4
contrary,n., 546.3
on the ~, 546.6
contrast,n., 540.2–4
conspicuous by ~, 952.1(2)
different by ~, 540.1(2,6,8)
express ~ of ideas, 540.23
full of ~s, 540.1(5)
contrast,v., 540.3
contrasting,adj., 540.1(2,6)
~ person or thing, 540.7
contribute,v., 230.1; see **give**,v.
contribution,n., 230.2,6; see **giving**, **gift**,n.
one-tenth part as ~, 938.14
small amount of ~, 917.10
control,n., 8.2
a ~, 8.4
act free of ~, 309.21(4)
bring under ~ of officials, 1077.21
bring under main ~, 8.23
contempt for ~, 1091.4
deprive of ~, 8.25
descr. of ~, 8.5
exercise ~ over, 8.1
free of ~, 309.11(5,32,35–39, 42,46); 309.15(1,4–8,10–16,18, 20–38)
freedom from ~, 309.14(1,2,4, 5,7,8,10–18,24)
give ~, 8.22
go beyond ~, 159.1(33)
harsh ~, 8.9
hold under ~, 257.1(19)
live free of ~, 309.21(4)
loss of ~, 8.26
means of ~, 8.4,21
~ of an industry, 8.2(5)
one subject to ~ by another, 8.19
one subject to hypnotic ~, 8.19(4)
pert. to ~, 8.5
political ~ by the mob, 1073.47,48
position of ~, 8.20; 177.6(3)
power of ~, 5.4(11)
region of ~, 782.6
remove from main ~, 8.24
self-~, 77.1–4
without ~, 8.27
control,v., 8.1
~ an airplane, 8.1(19)
~ a ship, 8.1(19)
~ by fear, 8.1(1,8)
~ cruelly, 8.8
~ exclusively, 8.1(18)
~ fraudulently, 8.1(16)
~ harshly, 8.8
~ secretly, 8.1(21)
that which ~s, 8.4
that which ~s a machine, 8.4(2,3,5,6)

~ the affairs of, 8.14
~ the mind or actions of, 8.1(15)
controllable,adj., 8.7
controlled,adj., 8.6
~ by government, 8.6(3)
~ by males, 8.6(1)
~ by outside agency, 8.6(3)
controller,n., 8.3
cruel ~, 8.10
harsh ~, 8.10
controlling,adj., 8.5
~ influence, 9.2(1)
convenience,n.
things that make for ~, 27.2
convenient,adj., 27.1
~ and spacious, 27.1(3)
~ to get to, 27.1(1,2,4)
~ to use, 27.1(1,4)
convent,n., 644.1
candidate for a ~, 644.9
head of a ~, 644.2,3
member of a ~, 644.5,10
not belonging to a ~, 644.12
probation in a ~, 644.11
convention,n.
custom, 629.1; see also **custom**,n.
proper conduct, 818.5
adherence to ~, 56.5(1); 629.6
adhering to ~, 629.5
adhering to religious ~, 629.5(7,8)
conformer to ~, 629.7
conforming to ~, 629.5
conformity to ~, 629.6
contrary to ~, 629.3
freedom from ~, 309.14(7)
make conform to ~, 629.8
precise detail of ~, 629.9
restricted by ~, 310.15
violating ~, 629.3,10
conventional,adj., 50.5; 629.2,5
become set in a ~ pattern, 629.21
cause to set in ~ form, 1098.5
make ~, 629.8
~ model, 317.1(30)
conventionalism,n., 50.5; 629.6
conversation,n., 671.2; 671.2(9, 11,15,22,26,28,32,39,40)
~ between two, 671.2(11,15, 40)
disinclined to ~, 671.20(1,3–8)
formal ~, 671.2(9,11,15)
~ in a play, novel, etc., 671.2(11,15)
informal ~, 671.2(7)
light ~, 671.2(28,39)
open as a topic of ~, 671.5(3)
pert. to ~, 671.4
private ~ between two, 671.2(40)
witty ~, 671.2(32)
words used in ~, 666.3(13,49)
conversational,adj., 671.4
~ language, 664.1(27); 665.9(14)
converse,v., 671.1(15,17,21–24, 63)
~ secretly, 671.1(20)
converser,n., 671.3
convert,n.
~ to a religion, 642.10
convert,v.
change, 539.1,2
change religious beliefs, 642.8,9
change to a belief, 638.1
~s natives to Christianity, one who, 638.11
~ to a religion, 642.8,9
convex,adj., 155.4(6,10–12)

conveyance,n.
carrier, 190.3,4
carrying, 190.2
vehicle, 192
convict,n., 301.5
~s, 301.7
convince,v., 638.1; see persuade,v.
cook,n., 1061.24
expert ~, 1061.26
head ~, 1061.25
cook,v., 1061.1,2
~ too little, 1061.18
~ too long, 1061.16
cooked,adj.
~ food, 1061.7
~ for a long time, 1061.22
~ not at all, 1061.21
~ not too long, 1061.20
party with ~ food, 1061.4
~ too little, 1061.19
~ too long, 1061.17
cooking,n.
~ appliance, 1061.9
art, practice, or act of ~,
1061.27
book with recipes for ~,
1061.28
chicken suitable for ~, 1061.8
~ department, 1061.31
goddess of ~, 1061.32
methods of ~, 50.1(24,25)
pert. to ~, 1061.29
place for ~, 1061.6,31
room or building for ~, 1061.6
style of ~, 1061.30
vessel for ~, 261.10; 1061.5
cooky,n., 1062.7
cool,adj., 1058.1; see also **cold**,
adj.
make ~, 1058.13
unpleasantly ~, 1058.4
cool,v., 1058.13; see also
freeze,v.
device for ~ing, 1058.20,21
drink that ~s, 1058.18
~ emotions, desires, etc.,
1097.27-29
heat and ~ gradually, 1060.21
place for ~ing, 1058.23
process of ~ing, 1058.16
science of ~ing, 1058.22
serving to ~, 1058.14
substance for ~ing, 1058.17
cooled,adj., 1058.15; see also
frozen,adj.
copied,adj.
original from which ~, 728.9
something ~, 533.5
~ word for word, 533.6
copier,n., 533.4; 682.5(1,5)
copious,adj., 915.4; 919.3
copper,n., 1016.1
alloy of ~, 1016.2
coat, cover, etc., with ~, 1016.4
containing ~, 1016.6
gold-coated ~, 1013.10
green or blue coating on old
~, 1016.19
~ in color, 1016.8
like ~, 1016.7
pert. to ~, 1016.5
worker in ~, 1016.3
yielding ~, 1016.9
copy,n., 533.2
imitation, 532.2
someone or something similar or same, 529.3
instr. to make a duplicate ~,
677.14(3)
make four ~s of, 933.15
make three ~s of, 932.34,35
one ~ of four, 933.16
one ~ of three, 932.33
copy,v., 533.1

imitate, 532.1
act of ~ing, 533.3
one who engages in ~ing,
533.4; 682.5(1,5)
that which is used for ~ing,
533.4
coquette,n., 700.12
coquette,v., 700.11
coquettish,adj., 700.13
coral,n., 422.3
island of ~, 1030.4
of ~s, 422.1(1,2,11)
cord,n., 302.32; see also **rope,n.**
metal ~, 302.32(27)
strong ~, 302.32(26)
thin ~, 302.32(11,22)
~ to hold a dog, 302.32(15)
twisted ~, 302.32(25)
cork,n., 297.9
cork,v., 297.8
corn,n.
covering of ~ ear, 972.4(10,
20)
corn,v., 263.1
corner,n., 783.5
chimney ~, 783.5(1)
cozy ~, 783.5(2)
fire, ~ by the, 783.5(1)
having ~s, 783.6
having three ~s, 783.7
sheltered ~, 783.5(2)
cornerstone,n., 1006.1(11)
provide with a ~, 1006.9
corporation,n.
officer of a ~, 1077.1(13)
corpse,n., 794.34; see **dead
body,n.**
correct,adj., 815.1,5
claim to be ~, 812.12
declare ~, 812.12
~ in action, 815.1(3)
~ in behavior, 815.1(3)
~ in judgment, 815.1(1)
~ in legal form, 815.1(4)
~ in taste, 815.1(1)
nearly ~, 815.6
prove ~, 812.15; see **prove,v.**
correct,v., 815.7
~ errors of (a person),
815.7(1)
~ false ideas of (a person),
815.7(1)
that which serves to ~, 815.10
~ the damage of or injury to,
815.7(3)
correctible,adj., 815.11
correction,n., 815.8
correctional,adj., 815.9
corrective,adj., 815.9
correctness,n., 815.2
demander of ~ in language,
815.14(3)
demander of ~ in rule or
form, 815.14
demander of ~ in scholar-
ship, 815.14(1)
demander of ~ in teaching,
815.14(1)
deviating from ~, 827.4
devised for extreme ~, 815.13
~ in observation of rule or
form, 815.14
~ of action, 815.2(2)
~ of behavior, 815.2(1)
~ of decision, 815.2(2)
~ of manners, 815.2(1)
requiring ~, 815.15
showing ~ of form, 815.15
correspondence,n.
letter writing, 678.1-11
similarity, 529.2
balance and ~, 950.2
correspondent,n., 678.8
corrode,v.
be eaten away, 801.21

eat away, 801.20
corrupt,adj., 886.1
~ act, 886.3
become ~, 886.22
indulge in ~ pleasure, 886.21
~ influence, 886.12
~ influence on a court or
jury, attempt to exert, 9.13,
14
~ person, 886.4
~ place, 886.11
corrupt,v., 886.22,24,26
~ by sexual intercourse,
710.17
~ into sexual looseness, 712.6
corruption,n., 886.2
corruptness,n., 886.2
corset,n., 981.3(8)
maker of ~s, 205.5(3)
put a ~ on, 981.4
~s, collectively, 981.5
cost,n., 223.1,2; see also **charge,**
price,n.
amount added to ~, 223.7
burden of ~, 948.14(13)
~ of operation, 223.4,5
costume,n., 974.35
~s of actors, 974.35(5)
cottage,n., 753.1; see also **home,**
house,n.
rustic ~, 753.1(7)
Swiss-style ~, 753.1(11)
couch,n., 63.2
cough,n., 364.7
caused by a ~, 364.10
disorders marked by a ~,
364.12
evidenced by a ~, 364.9
gasping sound after a ~,
364,11; 376.6(6)
pert. to a ~, 364.9,10
spasm after a ~, 364.11
cough,v., 364.8
~ up and spit out, 289.1(4);
364.8(1)
count (numbers),n., 941.9
official ~ of people, 941.4
count,v., 941.1
art of ~ing by fingers, 941.5
compulsion to ~, 941.10
decimal system of counting,
941.6
~ one by one, 941.2
countable,adj., 941.7
not ~, 941.8
counted,adj.
number of things ~, 941.9
counter,n.
~ for mixing drinks, 749.38,39
counterclockwise,adv.
turning ~, 148.2(7)
counterfeiter,n., 213.18
government agency against
~s, 971.39
counting,adj., 941.3
countless,adj., 941.8
countrified,adj., 786.1
become ~, 786.3
~ existence, 786.2
make ~, 786.3
state of being ~, 786.2
country (nation),n., 784.1
Asiatic ~s, 784.4(3)
~ at war, 563.4
between ~s, 784.5
~ between rival nations,
784.1(1)
boasting about one's ~,
784.8(1)
customs or culture of a ~,
784.10-14
democratic ~, 784.1(4)
eastern ~s, 784.4(3)
European ~s, 784.4(2)

~ governed from outside, 1073.4(3)
group of ~s, each with own ruler, 1073.57
inhabitant of a ~, 784.3,15
inhabitants of a ~, 784.17(2)
interest in the welfare of one's ~, 784.8(4)
internal affairs of a ~, pert. to, 1073.74
love of ~, 784.8; see also **patriotism**,n.
loyalty to one's ~, 784.8(3); see **patriotism**,n.
management of relations between ~s, 523.4–9
Mediterranean ~s, 784.4(1)
native ~, 784.1(2,3)
native of a ~, 784.3,15
Northern European ~s, 784.4(4)
~ of four governments, 1073.55
~ of supreme power, 1073.87
~ of three governments, 1073.55
origin, ~ of, 784.1(3)
outside the ~, 138.1(16)
person from the same ~, 784.7
pert. to a ~, 784.2
pert. to a specific ~, 784.16
self-governing ~, 1073.4(2,4)
substitute names for specific ~s, 784.9
~ under a government, 1073.4, 43,89
~ under a ruler or governor, 1073.18,39
~ under political government, 1076.10
Western ~s, 784.4(2)
~ with citizens from foreign lands, 1075.10
~ with eight rulers, 1073.54
~ with power over another, 1073.88
within a ~, 784.6
country (rural area),n.
banish to the ~, 786.5
combining ~ and city living, 786.10
existence in the ~, characteristic of, 786.1; see also **countrified**,adj.
go into the ~, 786.4
go to the ~ as punishment, 786.4
inhabitant of the ~, 786.6
inhabitants of the ~, 784.17(3); 786.7
like the ~, 786.1; see also **countrified**,adj.
live in the ~, 786.4
music about ~ life, 786.8(3,4)
natural features of ~ land, 1003.9,10
outside the ~, 138.1(16)
~ person, 786.6
poem of ~ life, 689.2(4); 786.8
prose composition on ~ life, 786.8(3,4)
~ region, 782.1(22)
spend time in the ~, 786.4
stay in the ~, 786.4
writer on ~ life, 786.9
courage,n., 575.2; see **bravery**,n.
courageous,adj., 575.1; see **brave**,adj.
court (of law),n., 1081.1–3
able to be settled in a ~, 1082.32
accused person in ~, 1082.24, 25
act against in ~, 1082.19,20

administration of ~s, 1081.19–21
adviser of the ~, 1082.33
arguments in ~, 1082.26,28,29
ask ~ for justice or legal action, 1082.17
bring disputes into ~, prone to, 1082.30
~ building, 1081.7
call to ~, 693.1(4,6,14)
~ case, 1082; see **lawsuit**,n.
~ days, 1081.11
decision of the ~, 1081.13,14
determine guilt or innocence in ~, 1082.8
disobedience to the ~, 1081.23
disrespect to the ~, 1081.23
examination in ~, 1082.7
examine in ~, 1082.8
friend of the ~, 1082.33
government department concerned with ~s, 1081.6
matter judged by the ~, 1082.5
~ officer, 1078.1; 1078.16(3)
~ order, 1081.15
~ order, serve with, 1081.16,17
order to come to ~, 275.1(13); 275.2(11)
pert. to ~s, 1081.18
prisoner in ~, place for, 1081.10
~ railing, 1081.9
remove from jurisdiction of the ~s, 1087.23
~room, 1081.8
~ sessions in England, 1081.12
sworn statement in a ~, 1086
system of ~s, 1081.6
try by military or naval ~, 1081.4,5
try to get or enforce in ~, 1082.18
unauthorized ~, 1081.3(7)
court (royal),n.
member of the ~, 1073.33
official of the ~, 1077.1(5)
pert. to a ~, 1073.31
suitable for a ~, 1073.32
court,v.
make love to, 700.7
courteous,adj., 858.1; see **polite**,adj.
courtesy,n., 858.2; see **politeness**,n.
court-martial,n.
officer presenting a case before a ~, 1085.4
courtship,n.
action in ~, 52.5(5)
attentions in ~, 579.3
chivalrous acts in ~, 858.7
cousin,n., 722.1(2,7,8)
cover,n., 972.4; see also **covering**,n.
~ for a bed, 972.24,25,26
~ for a horse, 972.27,28
~ for automobile motor, 972.4(4,7)
~ for furniture, 972.4(18)
~ for teapot or other container, 972.4(6)
~ of a book, 1001.16
~ of the eye, 972.4(12)
~ on chair to protect against soil or hair oil, 972.4(1)
outer ~, 972.4(9,11,23)
protective ~, 972.21
remove the ~ from, 972.6,8
serving as a ~ on a container, etc., 972.39
small ~, 972.4(5)
without ~, 972.7
without protective ~, 972.23
cover,v., 972.1

~ a fire, 972.1(1)
~ a horse, 972.1(8)
~ a roof, 972.1(50)
~ a window, 972.1(16,20,42); 1009.24
~ and protect, 972.1(40)
~ by lying upon, 972.1(32)
~ chicks with wings, 972.34
~ furniture, 972.1(53)
~ in bed, 972.1(52)
~ oneself, 972.2
serving or intended to ~ a group or category, 972.38
~ the face, 972.1(30,55)
~ the floor, 972.1(9)
~ the surface, 972.1(56)
~ the tongue, 972.1(23)
~ to conceal, 972.1(5,10,16,44, 55)
~ to disguise, 972.1(55)
~ to dull sound, 972.1(30)
~ with a glove, 978.3
~ with a layer, 972.1(12,23,24, 31,45,56)
~ with a roof, 972.1(6,19,25, 38,54)
~ with color, 972.1(37)
~ with darkness, 972.1(35)
~ with earth, 972.1(5)
~ with gloom, 972.1(35)
~ with gold, 972.1(24)
~ with leaves, 972.1(4,50)
~ with shell-like material, 972.1(15)
~ with straw, 972.1(50)
~ with water or liquid, 972.1(26,37,47)
covered,adj., 972.5
able to be ~ by water, 972.36
become ~ by water, 972.35
state of being ~, 972.3
~ with a hood, 972.5(4)
~ with bark, 972.5(2)
~ with layers, 972.5(7)
~ with leaves, 972.5(5)
~ with trees, 972.5(6)
covering,n., 972.4; see also **cover**,n.
act of ~, 972.3
deceptive ~, 823.13(1)
~ for a bed, 69.2
~ for a floor, 972.4(17)
~ for a shoe, 979.20
~ for the ankle, 979.20
~ for the buttocks, 980.2,3
~ for the leg, 979.21
~ of animals, 972.4(15,21,24)
~ of beans, 972.4(14)
~ of cheese, 972.4(15)
~ of clams, 972.4(20)
~ of corn ear, 972.4(10,20)
~ of egg, 972.4(19)
~ of fruit, 972.4(9–11,13–15, 19–21,23)
~ of insects, 972.4(19)
~ of nuts, 972.4(19,20)
~ of oysters, 972.4(20)
~ of peas, 972.4(14)
~ of plant, 972.4(2,15)
~ of seed, 972.4(9–11,13–15, 19–21,23)
~ of tree, 972.4(2)
~ of turtles, 972.4(19,24)
~ of vegetable, 972.4(14)
remove the ~ from, 972.6,8
window ~, 1009.23
without ~, 972.7
cow,n., 410.1
booth for a ~, 787.7(35)
dealer in ~s, 205.1(7)
derived from ~s, 410.6
like a ~, 410.5
of ~, 410.4
place for ~s, 403.22(7,11)
~s, collectively, 410.3

small ~, 410.1(8)
worker with ~s, 205.1(5-7)
young ~, 410.2
coward,n., 576.5
cowardice,n., 576.2; see fear,n.
show ~, 576.3; see fear,v.
streak of ~, 576.2(10)
symbol of ~, 576.9
cowardly,adj., 576.1; see frightened,adj.
be ~, 576.3; see fear,v.
cowboy,n., 205.1(5)
cowpox,n., 382.11(52)
crab,n., 422.3
eating ~s, 734.27(6)
like a ~, 422.2(1)
of ~s, 403.6(1) ; 422.1(7,13,34)
science of ~s, 403.26(10,12)
crack,n., 802.8,17
full of ~s, 830.8
having ~s (of pottery), 802.19
~ in rock, 1006.23,24
make ~s in, 802.16
make ~s in (pottery),
802.16(2)
network of ~s in porcelain,
802.18
crack,v., 802.15,16
cracked,adj.
become ~, 802.15
cracker,n., 1062.7
~ topped with food, 740.15(2)
cramped,adj.
~ and small, 909.1(19)
crave,v., 265.1; see desire,v.
crawl,v., 81.1-4
climb and ~, 159.1(6,21)
crazy,adj., 1136.2
cream,n., 510.8
referring to ~, 510.9(5)
remove ~, 249.2(5,6)
crease,n., 157.4; 158.4
crease,v., 157.1,2; 158.1,2
create,v., 726.17
make, 726.1
produce, 726.8
able to ~, 726.26,27
created,adj.
first ~, 729.15(13)
creation,n., 726.3,9,18,20
something created, 726.20
something made, 726.3
artistic ~, 726.21
before ~, 766.6(11)
earliest in ~, 766.6(9)
God's ~ of universe, 726.23-25
literary ~, 726.21
musical ~, 726.21
one's best ~, 726.21(1,4,5)
pert. to ~, 726.22
unimportant artistic ~,
726.21(8)
creative,adj., 726.22,27
all-~, 726.27(7)
creator,n., 726.2,10,19
~ of a real or imaginary
world, 726.19(3)
credit,n.
~ with, 893.7
creditor,n., 218.8
greedy ~, 218.8(4) ; 265.18(4)
credulous,adj., 632.18
creep,v., 81.1-4
creeping,adj.
~ like a worm, 427.16
cremation,n.
advocate of ~, 798.2
furnace for ~, 798.3
pile of wood for ~, 798.8
place for ~, 798.4
remains after ~, 1064.54
results of ~, place for, 798.5-7
wood for ~, 1064.61(5,8)
crescent,n.
ornamented with ~s, 1054.21

~-shaped, 507.17(10,46) ;
1054.5
cricket,n., 428.3
of ~s, 428.1(16)
science of ~s, 403.26(31)
crime,n., 1087.3; 1088.1
~ against ruler, nation, etc.,
1088.21
atone for a ~, 845.20
caught in a ~, 1088.16
commit a ~, 1087.4
connect with a ~, 1088.17
declare guilty of ~, 1088.12
guilty of ~, 1088.9
helps commit a ~, one who,
1088.18,19
involve in a ~, 522.1(3-5) ;
1088.17
involvement in a ~, 522.3
make amends for a ~, 845.20,
22
neglect to inform of ~,
1087.7(6)
~ of violence, attempt at,
18.2(2)
person accused of ~, 1088.15
person capable of committing
~s, 1088.13
person guilty of a ~, 884.38;
1088.10,11
person suspected of a ~,
1088.14
pert. to serious ~, 1088.8
relapse into ~, 145.1(1,15)
return to ~, 145.2(2)
science of ~, 1088.20
criminal,n., 1087.5,8,9; 1088.2,
10,11
activities or practices of ~s,
1088.4
class of ~s, 1088.6
dangerous ~, 1088.2(2,4)
desperate ~, 1088.2(2,4)
fleeing ~, 1088.2(9)
group of suspected ~s on
inspection, 1088.7
habitual ~, 1088.2(9)
highway ~, 1088.2(1,3)
pictures of ~s, 965.9(3)
qualities of ~s, 1088.4
~s, collectively, 1088.3
science of ~s, 1088.20
cripple,v., 13.1
crippled,adj., 346.11(6) ; see
lame,adj.
crisis,n., 539.16
critic,n., 894.5; 894.5(1) ; 1083.32
inferior ~, 1083.33
petty ~, 894.5(2)
critical,adj., 894.4
excessively ~, 894.4(4,6,8)
extremely ~, 894.4(2,4,6,8)
~ in petty ways, 894.4(1,2,3)
~ language or speech, 894.3(3)
~ remark or comment,
894.3(6)
self-righteously ~, 894.4(5)
criticism,n., 894.3
art or practice of ~, 1083.37
attack with harsh ~, 894.10
disposed to ~, 894.4
engage in ~, 894.2
engage in ~ of, 894.1
essay of ~, 1083.37
sharp ~, 894.3(7)
wound with harsh ~, 894.9
criticize,v., 894.1
criticizer,n., 894.5; 1083.32; see
also critic,n.
crockery,n., 261.12; see earthenware,n.
crocodile,n., 425.1; see also
reptile,n.
like a ~, 425.3,20
pert. to ~s, 425.2,20

crooked,adj., 181.1
crop,n.
gather in the ~, 998.2(1)
gathering of ~s, 998.7
grow ~s, 731.22(1,5) ; 998.2
growing of ~s, 731.23; 998.1
raising of only one ~, 998.1
(12)
science of ~ production, 985
.36(1)
cross,adj., 876.1; see bad-
tempered,adj.
cross,n., 652.2
carrier of a ~ in religious
parades, 652.4
Christ on the ~, image of,
653.3
Christian ~, 652.1
form of a ~, in the, 507.17(25,
26)
heraldic ~, 652.2
nail to the ~, 652.3
shaped like a ~, 507.17(25,
26)
worship of the ~, 656.15(24)
cross,v.
go across, 121.1-6
able to be ~ed, 121.4
~ like an X, 121.1(6)
roads ~, place where, 123.5
unable to be ~ed, 121.5
crossbow,n., 566.1
missile from a ~, 566.5
user of a ~, 566.17
cross-eye,n., 481.1(31) ; 361.6;
361.6(1)
cross-eyed,adj., 361.5(4,20,22)
~ condition, 361.6; 361.6(1) ;
481.1(31)
opposite of ~, 361.5(23)
crossing,adj.
~ lines, 311.1(12,22,26,35,45)
crouch,n., 64.2
crouch,v., 64.1
~ on the heels, 64.1(4)
crouching,adj., 64.3
crow,n.
like a ~, 405.10
of ~s, 405.9(6)
crowd,n., 318.9
be in a ~, 318.10
bring together into a ~, 318.11
collect in a ~, 318.10
collect into a ~, 318.11
move in a ~, 318.10
crowd,v., 318.10,11
~ around, 318.10(1)
crowded,adj., 318.12
be ~, 318.13
dirty and ~ area, 1048.19
dirty, poor, and ~, 904.1(20)
dirty, poor, and ~ place,
904.15
~ place, 318.14
crown,n., 983.26,27,30
like a ~, 983.34,35
~ of ancient Persia, 983.30
pert. to a ~, 983.33
Pope's ~, 983.29
put a ~ on, 983.31
take away the ~, 983.36
wearing a ~, 983.28
without a ~, 983.37
crown,v., 983.31
ceremony or process of ~ing,
983.32
~ with laurel, 857.4
cruel,adj., 889.1
~ act, 52.5(4,5) ; 889.4
be ~ in exercise of power or
authority, 889.7
be ~ to, 889.6
fierce and ~, 4.21
~ government, 1073.59

greedy and ~, 265.16(20,21) ; 889.1(11)
~ in exercise of power or authority, 889.1(9)
lawless and ~, 889.1(7)
make ~, 889.5
~ person, 4.23; 889.3
rough and ~, 865.1(4,10–12) ; 889.1(7)
ugly and ~ man, 506.3
ugly and ~ woman, 506.2(3)

cruelly,adv.
treat ~, 53.1(2,6,7,10,11,13) ; 889.6
treated ~, 889.8

cruelty,n., 889.2

crumble,v.
break, 802.1,2; see also break,v.
fall apart, 802.21

crumbling,adj.
~ easily, 802.7
~ into dust, 1001.7

crumbly,adj., 802.7

crush,n., 198.2

crush,v., 198.1(9,17,23,24,30–32)

crushable,adj.
~ thing, 443.5

crusher,n., 198.5

crushing,n.
sound of ~, 469.1(4–7)

crust,n.
develop a ~, 972.33
having a ~, 972.32
like a ~, 972.31
pert. to a ~, 972.30
scaly ~, 355.7,9

crustacean,n.
science of ~, 403.26(10,12)

cry,n., 1127.3
animal's ~, 456.1; see sound,n.
~ of a newborn infant, 1127.3(1)

cry,v.
weep, 1127.1; see weep,v.
~ in pain, 1127.1(1,5,6,12,13)

crystal gazing,n., 772.20(19)

Cuban,n.
~ who did not revolt against Spain, 1140.17

cube,n., 945.13
cut into ~s, 332.1(14)
shaped like a ~, 945.14,15

cubic,adj.
~ contents, 260.8
~ measurement, 260.9
~ space, 787.1(26)

cucumber,n.
~-shaped, 507.17(27)

cud,n., 740.7

cue,n., 239.2

cue,v., 239.1

cult,n., 631.1

cultivate,v., 998.3
~ the land, soil, etc., 998.2

cultivation,n.
~ of the land, soil, etc., 998.1

culture,n.
Asiatic ~, 1091.27,28
European ~, 1091.25,26
make conform to ~ of a country, 784.10–14
person contemptuous of ~, 863.4
pert. to Greek or Roman ~, 784.16(1–3)
Slavic ~, 1091.29

cuneiform,n.
art of ~, 679.6
character in ~, 679.7

cup,n.
drinking ~, 261.8
drinking ~ in religious ceremonies, 261.8(5)

full ~, 925.11
small coffee ~, 261.8(8)

curable,adj., 398.16

cure,n., 398.2,4
baths as a ~, writing about, 899.57
baths to ~, use of, 899.58
~ for social problems, 398.4(8) ; 398.11,12
pert. to medicinal ~s, 398.5
specific medicinal ~s, 398.6,8
universal ~, 398.11,12

cure,v., 398.1; see also heal,v.
preserve, 263.1–4
power to ~, 398.15

curing,adj., 398.3

curing,n., 398.2
pert. to ~, 398.14

curious,adj.
eager to find out, 624.15
inclined to question, 625.11
odd, 536.1

curl,n., 156.3
fancy ~, 156.3(1)
full of ~s, 156.5; 156.5(5)

curl,v., 155.1,8; 156.1,2
~ up in comfort, 156.7

curliness,n., 155.5; 156.6

curly,adj., 155.4; 156.5; 156.5(5)
~-haired, 369.11(2,3,7,8)
~ (of hair), 369.18(1–3,5–8)

current,n.
water ~, 1031.1

curse,n., 861.13; 882.1
language containing ~s, 882.2
statement containing ~s, 882.3
~ word, 666.3(23)
worthy of a ~, 882.9

curse,v., 861.11,12; 882.5,6
disposed to ~, 882.7

cursed,adj., 882.8

curser,n., 882.5

cursing,adj., 882.4

cursing,n., 861.10

curtain,n.
window covering, 1009.23
ornament with ~s, 959.1(22)

curve,n., 155.2
coast-line ~, 155.2(2)
flat circular ~, 155.2(5)
full of ~s, 155.4; 155.4(17,18)
inner surface of a ~, 155.10
outer surface of a ~, 155.11
outline of ~s, 155.9

curve,v., 155.1,8
act of ~ing, 155.7
cause to ~, 155.8
~ inward, 155.1(4)
~ like a spiral, 155.1(7,8,12)
~ outward, 155.1(3,5)

curved,adj., 155.4
abnormally ~, state of being, 155.5(1)
~ inward, 155.4; 155.4(1)
~ like a hook, 155.4(19)
~ like the letter S, 155.4(15, 16)
~ outward, 155.4; 155.4(4)
~ part, 155.6

curviness,n., 155.5

curving,adj., 155.3,4

curving,n., 155.7
measure ~, instrument to, 155.13

curvy,adj., 155.4

custom,n., 629.1; see also convention, habit, n.
American ~, 629.11(1)
Chinese ~s, 629.11(6,7)
conformer to ~, 629.7
conforming to ~, 629.5
conformity to ~, 629.6
contrary to ~, 629.3
formality of ~, 819.10(2)

French ~, 629.11(2)
Greek ~s, authority or expert on, 784.14
Irish ~, 629.11(3)
make conform to ~, 629.8
make conform to ~s of a country, 784.10
monks' ~s, 629.11(4)
Oriental ~s, 629.11(6)
Slavic ~s, 629.11(8)
Western ~s, 629.11(5)

customary,adj., 535.1,2; 629.2; see also habitual,adj.
be ~, 629.12
become set in a ~ pattern, 629.21
not ~, 629.3

customer,n., 211.4
~s, 211.5
try to get ~s, 18.1(16,23)

cut,adj., 332.7
able to be ~, 332.19
~ into many parts, 332.7(3)
~ into two equal lobes, 332.7(1)
~ into two equal parts, 332.7(1)
~ low (of a dress, etc.), 332.7(2)
neatly ~, 332.20
~-off part or piece, 326.10
small amount ~ off, 917.4
~ state, 332.4
that which is ~, 332.8

cut,n., 332.3
surgical ~, 402.1(10)

cut,v., 332.1
~ across, 332.1(27,65)
~ and gather grain, 998.2(1)
~ apart, 332.1(8,9,18,44,63)
~ away, 332.1(45,67)
~ (designs, figures, etc.), 996.1
~ down, 332.1(33,45)
~ fine, 332.1(32)
~ (hair) short, 911.13
~ in a V, 332.1(36)
~ in an X, 332.1(13)
~ in half, 332.1(2)
~ into cubes, 332.1(14)
~ into parts, 326.12,13; 332.1(2,15,68)
~ into pieces, 326.12,13; 332.1(4,8,14,18,32,51,53)
~ into portions, 332.1(4,51,58)
~ into shares, 332.1(4,51,58)
~ into slices, 332.1(4,53,58)
~ into three parts, 332.1(68)
~ into two parts, 332.1(2,15)
~ off, 332.1(1,11,30,34,35,37,40, 41,43,45,52,54,56,67,69)
~ off a part, 326.12
~ off a piece, 326.12; 332.1(6)
~ off at the neck, 332.1(12)
~ off the head of, 796.15,16
one who ~s, 332.5
~ open, 332.1(29,52,61)
~ out, 332.1(20)
~ out the intestines of, 332.1(17)
~ short, 332.1(3,10,11,19,22,40, 69)
~ short the tail of, 911.8
~ surgically, 402.2,6
that which ~s, 402.9,10,13–17; 402.13
~ the branches of a tree, 996.5
~ the hair, 371.1(1,3,4)
~ through, 332.1(38,39,64)
~ through the backbone, 332.1(5)
with the tail ~ short, 911.12

cutlery,n.
gold ~, 1013.20

silver ~, 1015.14
cutter,n.
  instrument for cutting,
    332.9,10,13–17; 402.13
  one who cuts, 332.5
cutting,adj., 332.6
  ~ instruments, maker or
    seller of, 332.12
  ~ instruments or imple-
    ments, 332.9,10,13–17
  ~ part, 332.11
cutting,n., 332.2,8
  act of ~, 332.2
  act of ~ off, 332.2(1)
  hair ~, pert. to, 371.7
  instruments for ~, 332.9,10,
    13–17
  instruments for surgical ~,
    402.13
  surgical ~, 402.1,5
cuttlefish,n.
  of ~, 422.1(9,27)
cycle,n.
  vehicle, 192.17
  drive or ride a ~, 192.18
  driver or rider of a ~, 192.19
cyclist,n., 192.19
cyclone,n., 1042.27; see also
    hurricane, tornado, wind-
    storm,n.
  center of a ~, 1042.29
  center of a ~, instrument to
    determine, 1042.31
  create a ~, conditions that,
    1042.33
  discover a ~, instrument to,
    1042.32
  science of ~s, 1042.34
cylinder,n., 508.9
cylindrical,adj., 508.1
cynicism,n.
  prejudiced by ~, 877.1(2)
czar,n., 1073.36(6)
  daughter of a ~, 1073.41(2)
  son of a ~, 1073.41(1,4)
  wife of a ~, 1073.41(3)
  wife of a ~'s son, 1073.41(2)

D

dagger,n., 332.14
  holder for a ~, 261.1(41,42)
dam,n.
  lake, etc., 1029.53
  structure, 1033.1
dam,v., 558.1
damage,n., 803.2; see harm,n.
damage,v., 803.1; see harm,v.
damaging,adj., 803.3; see
    harmful,adj.
damp,adj., 1034.8
  become ~, 1034.7
  cold and ~, 1034.15
  disagreeably ~, 1034.16,17
  heavy and ~, 1034.18
  make ~, 1034.6
  ~ (of air or weather), 1034.10
  sticky and ~, 1034.15
  warm and ~, 1034.17
dampen,v., 1034.6
dampened,adj., 1034.9
dampness,n., 1034.8
  ~ in the air, 1034.13
dance,n., 109.1,5
  ~ enthusiast, 109.12
  holding of a ~, 109.5
  mad ~, 109.8
  steps in a ~, 109.3
  type of ~, 109.1
  writing of ~s, 109.11
dance,v., 109.2
  compulsion to ~, 378.11(8)
  room in which to ~, 787.7(12)
  uncontrollable desire to ~,
    109.13

dancer,n., 109.6
  group of ~s, 109.7
  pert. to ~s, 109.10(1)
dancing,adj., 109.9
dancing,n., 109.4
  art of ~, 965.6(2)
  ballet ~, 109.4(1)
  building for ~, 727.12(4)
  jump in ~, 110.1(7)
  muse of ~, 109.15
  pert. to ~, 109.10
  representation of ~ by sym-
    bols, 109.14
dandruff,n., 369.25
dandy,n., 974.23–27
Dane,n., 784.15(41,42,56)
danger,n., 572.2,3
  a ~, 572.3
  accept ~, 572.5
  accept the ~ of, 572.5
  act to avoid ~, 52.5(34)
  business involving ~ or loss,
    572.8
  expose to ~, 572.4
  indifferent to ~, 575.1; see
    brave,adj.
  lead into ~, 176.1(2,6)
  save from ~, 571.1
  set free from ~, 309.1(3,15,17)
  threaten ~, 573.2; see
    threaten,v.
  threatening ~, 573.1; see
    threatening,adj.
  time of ~, 572.6
dangerous,adj., 572.1
  ~ act, 52.5(41); 572.9
  looking ~, 572.7; 573.1
  ~ person, 572.10
  ~ undertaking, 572.9
  ~ woman, 572.10(1)
dangerousness,n., 572.2
Danish,adj., 784.16
Dante,n.
  descr. of writing like ~'s,
    686.8(2)
daredevil,n., 575.3
  act the boastful ~, 872.5
  boastful ~, 872.19
daring,adj., 575.1; see brave,
    adj.
  ~ behavior, 55.3(5,6)
dark,adj.
  without light, 1065.11;
    1070.1,11
  ~ and gloomy, 1070.7
  ~ and threatening appear-
    ance, 1070.6
  become ~, 1070.4
  ~-haired, 369.12(5,9,10)
  ~ in color, 491.1,2
  ~ in color, like smoke, 1050.18
  look or be ~ and threaten-
    ing, 1070.5
  make ~, 1070.3
  ~ of hair, 369.12(5,9,10)
  ~ of skin, 384.3
  person of ~ hair, 369.15
  person of ~ skin, 384.5
  ~-skinned, 384.3
darken,v., 491.2; 1070.3,4
  ~ (the sun or moon), 1055.20
darkened,adj.
  ~ by heat or fire, 1064.40
darkness,n.
  color, 491.1
  lack of light, 1070.2
  area of ~, 1070.8
  causing ~, 1070.12
  cover with ~, 972.1(35)
  enveloped in ~, 1070.9
  inhabitant of ~, 1070.10
  ~ of hair, 369.14
  ~ of skin, 384.4
  overtaken by ~, 1070.13
date,n.

approximately (of ~s), 774.11
  error in ~s, 774.12,15
  give incorrect ~ to, 774.15
  investigator of ~s, 774.10
  out of ~, 631.12
  out-of-~ thing, 631.16
  out of ~ with surrounding
    events, 774.13,14
  science of proper ~s, 774.1(2)
daughter,n., 721.3
  acting like a ~, 721.13
  attitude of a ~, 721.14
  prince's ~, 1073.21(7)
  psychological situation be-
    tween ~ and father, 724.5
  ~s, 721.9
dawn,n., 1055.32
  goddess of ~, 1055.40
day,n.
  by the ~, 776.6(1,4,6)
  end of the ~, 776.5
  equal ~ and night, 1055.12–14
  every ~, 776.6(1,2,6)
  every five ~s, 776.6(5)
  every seven ~s, 776.6(3);
    779.4(3,6)
  forty ~s, 776.11
  ~ in the middle of week, 776.1
  leap year, extra ~ in, 776.7
  middle of the ~, 776.3,4
  night and ~, 776.8
  pert. to each ~, 776.6(1)
  pert. to the dog ~s, 780.7
  religious ~, 776.9; see Sun-
    day,n.
  ~s at the end of week, 776.2
  seven ~s, consisting of, 779.2
  twice a ~, 776.6(7)
daydream,n., 71.6
  full of ~s, 71.8
  given to ~s, 71.7
daydreamer,n., 71.9
daze,n.
  numbness, 435.1
  state of confusion, 605.3
  stupefied condition, 597.22
daze,v.
  confuse, 605.1
  numb, 435.2
  stupefy, 597.20
dazed,adj.
  confused, 605.5
  numbed, 435.3
  stupefied, 597.21
  causing a ~ condition, 597.23
dead,adj., 794.42–48
  a meeting for communication
    with the ~, 322.1(32)
  animal that feeds on ~ mat-
    ter, 734.31
  ~ body, 794.34; see dead
    body,n.
  born ~, 720.9(12); 794.46
  child born ~ 721.3(30)
  communication with the ~,
    662.4(4)
  communication with the ~,
    belief in, 794.41
  communicator with the ~,
    662.5(1,2)
  dwelling place of the ~,
    794.37
  eating ~ flesh, 734.27(9,20,30)
  ferryman of the souls of the
    ~ across river Styx,
    662.29(1)
  figuratively ~, 794.44
  fond of the ~, one who is,
    700.30(12)
  ghost of the ~, 662.19(9,10,14,
    16)
  list of the ~, 794.39
  ~ person, 794.34; see dead
    body,n.
  pert. to the ~, 794.35

song for the ~, 476.4(19,31,41, 46)
sorrow for the ~, exhibition of, 799.7
summon spirits of the ~, one who can, 662.5(1,2)
worship of the ~, 656.15(16)
dead body,n., 794.34
~ after cremation, 1064.54
animal's ~, 794.34(1)
ashes of cremated ~, place where kept, 798.5–7
attraction to a ~, 794.40
box for a ~, 797.16–21; see **coffin**,n.
burn a ~ to ashes, 798.1; see **cremation**,n.
feeds on a ~, demon that, 797.25
like a ~, 794.36
place for a ~, 794.38, 797.10; see also **grave, tomb**,n.
prepares a ~ for burial, one who, 799.3
preserve a ~, 263.1(6,9)
preserved ~, 794.34(5)
robber of a ~, 797.23–25
sexual violation of a ~, 710.33(24)
sitting with a ~, 62.6
vehicle for the ~ in a funeral, 799.2
wrap ~ for burial, 797.5
wrappings for a ~, 797.20
dead end,n., 122.1(8,13,15,23)
deadly,adj., 794.14; 796.4
~ in influence, 796.6
deaf,adj., 454.23
~-and-dumb person, 454.24
instrument to aid the ~, 454.21
make ~, 454.25
slightly ~, 454.23(1)
deaf-and-dumb,adj.
~ language, 664.11(3); 951.15
~ person, 454.24
state of being ~, 454.22(1)
deaf-mute,n., 454.24
language of ~s, 664.11(3); 951.15
state of being a ~, 454.22(1)
deafness,n., 454.22(1,3,5)
dealer,n., 212.3; see **seller**,n.
dear,adj.
expensive, 223.14
loved, 700.5
hold ~, 700.4
death,n., 794.1
after ~, 794.12(7–9); 794.13
apparent ~, 794.24,25
before ~, 794.12(1)
bodily tissue or organ, ~ of, 794.7–11
by accident, 794.2
~ by fire, 1064.18,64
~ by fire, wood for, 1064.61(8)
~ by hanging, 794.6
cause ~, able to (of illness), 389.3(1,5,7)
causes ~, that which, 796.10, 27; see also **poison**,n.
causes of ~ by starvation, 737.10
causing ~, 796.4
causing ~ (of illness), 389.3(1, 5,7)
dance of ~, pert. to or suggestive of, 794.12(3)
desire for ~, 794.19
dissection to determine cause of ~, 402.1(5)
final pain, struggle, or suffering before ~, 1137.10(1)
~ for beliefs, 1138.5

ghost who warns of ~, 662.19(2)
goddess associated with ~, 654.2(14)
having lost through ~, 264.5(1); 264.6
heap of wood for burning to ~, 1064.61(8)
~ instinct, 794.18
intangible, ~ of an, 794.3
large numbers, ~ of, 794.5
life after ~, 751.1(1)
like ~, 794.14
live on after ~, 750.1(18)
loss through ~, 264.2(1)
near ~, 922.18
~ notice, 794.18
one who or that which demands ~, 236.8(2)
pert. to ~, 794.12(2–6)
population, ~ in relation to, 794.5
prefers ~ to giving up beliefs, 1138.9
public official concerned with ~s, 1077.1(10)
punishable by ~, 794.22
punishment by ~, 794.23
put to ~, 796.1; see **kill**,v.
race, species, group, etc., ~ of, 794.4
rate of ~, 794.15
reminder of ~, 627.34(7)
returner after ~, 145.4(1)
rise from ~, 159.1(18)
rising of all humans from ~, 751.24
rising of Jesus from ~, 751.23
science of causes of ~, 401.1(69)
state after ~, 794.20
suggestive of ~, 794.12(3)
temporary state after ~ for expiating sin, 845.24
thinking about ~, 585.20
time after ~, 762.1(2)
warning sound of approaching ~, 468.1(10)
world beyond ~, 794.21
worship of ~, 656.15(16)
theological doctrine of ~, 792.26
deathless,adj., 755.7,8; see also **immortal**,adj.
debase,v., 868.27
~ oneself, 868.28
debatable,adj., 542.13
debate,n., 543.2
art of ~, 543.9,10
ending of ~ and bringing to a vote, 791.12
expert in legislative ~, 1080.15
logical ~, 543.7,8
not subject to ~, 542.14
pert. to public ~, 543.6
statement subject to ~, 674.9(27)
subject to ~, 542.13
debate,v., 543.1
~ noisily, 543.5
debater,n., 543.2
clever ~, 543.4
skillful ~, 543.4,10
debt,n., 218.1
able to pay ~s, 218.13
acknowledgement of payment of ~, 218.6
be in ~, 218.4
bill for a ~, 218.5
burden of ~, 948.14(3)
burden with ~, 948.10
departure without paying ~s, 141.2(5)
evade a ~, 76.1(29)

fail to pay ~s, 218.16
failed to pay ~s, having, 218.19
fails to pay ~s, one who, 218.18
failure to pay ~s, 218.17
faith in ability to pay ~s, 632.6(7)
one in ~, 218.7
one to whom ~ is owed, 218.8
part of a ~, 326.1(17)
place under a ~, 218.2
placed under a ~, 218.3
record of a ~, 218.5
~s, 218.1(1,4,5)
unable to pay ~s, 218.14
unable to pay ~s, announce as, 218.15
unpaid (of a ~), 218.20
debtor,n., 218.7
debutante,n., 760.6(2)
decay,n., 806.3
aesthetic ~, 883.12(4); 883.15
cause of ~, 806.11,20,21
caused by vapors of ~, 1048.9
causing ~, 806.10
changes caused by ~, 806.15
coming from ~, 806.13
fall into ~, 806.1(4)
~ from malnutrition, 806.3(3, 5)
~ from old age, 806.3(3,5)
hidden ~, 1038.14
indicating ~, 806.14
insect that causes ~, 806.21
intellectual ~, 883.12(4); 883.15
living on ~ (of plants), 739.8(7); 739.9
moral ~, 806.3(4)
~ of vegetables, 1038.14
~ of wood, 1038.14
organism that causes ~, 806.21
period of ~, 731.9(4,16); 731.18(3)
pert. to ~, 806.12
plant disease that causes ~, 806.20
preserve against ~, 263.1–4; see **preserve**,v.
producing ~, 806.10,11
smelling like ~, 806.18
smelling of ~, 445.10(4,14,17–19,21)
social ~, 806.3(4); 883.12(4); 883.15
source of ~, 806.11,20,21
spiritual ~, 806.3(4)
subject to ~, 806.8
tasting ~, 446.13(16)
tooth ~, 806.3(2)
unsuspected ~, 1038.14
vapor from ~, 1048.1(8)
decay,v., 806.1,2
~ and disappear, 806.1(5)
cause to ~, 806.2
food that may ~, 806.9
tending to ~, 806.7,8
~ to dust, 1001.6
decayed,adj., 806.4
become ~, 806.1
becoming ~, 806.5
morally, socially, spiritually, aesthetically, or intellectually ~ person, 806.6; 883.15
decaying,adj.
eating ~ matter, 734.27(9,20, 30)
~ flesh, 806.16,17
study of ~ stages, 806.22
deceit,n., 823.13; see **deception**,n.
lack of ~, 813.6,8

without ~, 812.4; 813.6,7
deceivable,adj., 823.23
  one who is ~, 823.24
deceive,v., 823.1,2
  ~ by giving something fake
    or inferior, 823.3
  easy to ~, 823.23
  ~ in order to lead into (an
    act), 823.4
  ~ with artful flattery, 852.7
deceived,adj.
  one who is ~, 823.25
deceiver,n., 823.20
  boastful ~, 823.21; 872.22
  ~ who sells quack remedies,
    823.22
decency,n., 873.7
  violation of ~, 802.30
decent,adj., 873.6
deception,n., 823.13
  ~ for illegal gain, 823.14
  lead by ~, 176.1(8)
  means of ~, 1050.26
  nonsensical talk during ~,
    607.28
  practice ~, 823.2
  skill in ~, 7.1(27)
  use ~, 823.2
  ~ used by magicians,
    823.13(3)
deceptive,adj., 823.7,10
  ~ and ruinous thing, 823.18
  ~ appearance, 823.6
  ~ by siding with both oppos-
    ing parties, 823.12
  ~ condition, 823.13(1)
  ~ covering, 823.13(1)
  ~ force, 823.17
  give a ~ appearance to, 823.5
  ~ idea, 823.17
  ~ image, 483.8(9,11,14,16)
  ~ in appearance, 823.9
  ~ly easy, 823.11
  ~ly pleasant, 823.11; 1106.10
  ~ly polite, 823.11
  ~ly safe, 823.10
  ~ly simple, 823.8
  ~ly smooth, 823.11
  ~ manner, 823.13(1)
  ~ person, 823.20
  ~ practice, 823.13
  ~ thing, 823.15-19
decide,v., 592.1
  ~ against, 592.1(6)
  ~ beforehand, 592.1(7,8)
  ~ by law, 592.1(1,2,5)
  one who ~s, 592.4; see also
    judge,n.
decided,adj.
  ~ by a judge, 592.12
  ~ by an authority, 592.12
  previously ~, 592.5
decimal system,n.
  make into a ~, 938.5
  ~ of counting, 941.6
  ~ of measurements, 946.21
decision,n., 592.2,3
  able to make ~s quickly,
    592.7
  arbitrator's ~, 1083.24,27
  call upon for a ~, 693.1(1)
  court's ~, 1081.13
  divine ~, 592.3(1)
  firm in ~, 592.10
  free from any previous ~,
    309.15(9)
  issue a ~, 1081.14
  judge's ~, 592.3(2); 1081.13
  jury's ~, 592.3(2); 1084.14
  make a ~, 592.1; see decide,v.
  make an unalterable ~, 592.6
  make ~s through mind
    power, 592.1(12)
  power of the mind to make
    ~s, 592.9

state of ~, 592.11
  wise ~, 592.3(1)
decisive,adj., 592.7,8
  take a ~ step, 592.6
declaration,n.
  statement, 674.9; see state-
    ment,n.
  solemn ~ of truth, 812.13; see
    oath,n.
declare,v.
  say, 674.8; see say,v.
  ~ true, accurate, genuine,
    etc., 812.12
decompose,v.
  decay, 806.1; see decay,v.
decomposition,n.
  decay, 806.3; see decay,n.
  chemical ~, 806.3(1)
decorate,v., 959.1; see also or-
    nament,v.
  ~ with flags, 957.9
decorated,adj., 959.8; see orna-
    mented,adj.
decoration,n., 959.2,3; see or-
    namentation,n.
  interior ~, 959.3(6)
  ~ of varicolored stone,
    965.1(34)
  ~s of office, rank, member-
    ship, etc., 959.4(2)
decorative,adj., 959.17; see or-
    namental,adj.
decreasable,adj., 910.6
decrease,n., 910.3
  amount of ~, 914.1(6)
  cause of ~, 910.8,9
  causing ~, 910.5
  gradual ~, 910.3(2,4)
  ~ of sound, 910.3(4)
decrease,v., 910.1,2
  ~ a little, 910.1(33)
  able to be ~d, 910.6
  ~ expenses, 910.11
  ~ (expenses), 910.1(31)
  ~ gradually, 910.1(17,39,40);
    910.2(6)
  ~ in quality, excellence, vigor,
    etc., 883.11
  ~ in severity, force, strength,
    etc., 1142.1,10; see also
    weaken,v.
  ~ in size when air or gas is
    lost, 1043.12
  ~ in value, 839.17
  ~ periodically (of the moon),
    1054.7
  ~ the fullness of, 925.28
  ~ the value of, 839.19
  ~ to half, 910.1(19)
  ~ to smallest possible
    amount, degree, etc.,
    910.1(24)
decreasing,adj., 910.4
  ~ temporarily, 910.4(1)
decree,n., 275.2; 275.2(3)
  church ~, 275.2(3,4)
  court ~, 275.2(13)
  fixed by ~, 275.5(1)
  governed by ~, 275.6
  official ~, 275.2(12)
  pert. to a ~, 275.4
  pope's ~, 275.2(2)
decree,v., 275.1
dedicate,v., 657.2
dedicated,adj., 657.6
dedication,n., 657.1
  ~ in a book, etc., 682.3(6)
deduct,v., 247.20
deduction,n., 247.21
deed,n.
  action, 49.6
  brave ~, 49.6(3,6,14,19)
  dangerous ~, 49.6(3,19)
  remarkable ~, 49.6(1,2,4,7,15,
    16)

~ that shows strength,
    49.6(16)
  ~ to gain attention, 49.6(15)
  ~ to ward off danger of fail-
    ure, 49.6(10)
deep,adj., 170.1
  ~ enough for sailing, 116.13
  ~ in sound, 462.3
  not ~, 170.11
  ~ (of sleep), 170.1(10)
  ~ part, 170.9
  ~ part of water, 170.9(7)
  ~ place, 170.9
  ~ place between hills,
    170.9(12)
  ~-rooted, 323.23
  ~-seated, 323.23
  ~ sounds, 462.1,2
  ~ space, 170.9
deepen,v., 170.3-5
deer,n., 413.5
  female ~, 413.2
  like a ~, 413.6
  male ~, 413.1
  of ~, 403.11(12)
  pert. to a ~, 413.6
  small ~, 413.3
  young ~, 413.4
deface,v., 805.2
defacement,n., 805.2,5
defamation,n., 891.18,19
  ~ for political purposes,
    891.19
defamatory,adj., 891.19
defame,v., 891.17
defeat,n., 22.2
  complete ~, 22.4
  decisive ~, 22.6
  thorough ~, 22.4
defeat,v., 22.1
  ~ by deception, 22.8
  ~ completely, 22.3
  ~ decisively, 22.5
  ~ in a contest, 22.7
  ~ thoroughly, 22.3
  ~ unfairly, 22.9
defeated,adj.
  capable of being ~, 22.21
  having ~ an opponent, 22.11
  incapable of being ~, 22.22
defeater,n., 22.10
defecate,v., 293.1
  ~ frequently, 293.4
  unsuccessful urge to ~, 293.25
defecation,n., 293.2
  cause ~, 293.13-15
  causes ~, agent that, 293.16
  causing ~, 293.17
  control ~, ability to, 293.26
  control ~, inability to, 293.27
  difficulty in ~, 293.19,21; see
    constipation,n.
  ~ of loose matter, 293.5
  pert. to ~, 293.3
  place for ~, 295.1
defect,n., 830.1; see fault,n.
  free of ~, 816.3
defend,v.
  come to support of, 854.15
  protect, 568.1; see protect,v.
defender,n.
  protector, 568.5
  supporter, 854.5
  ~ for the sake of argument,
    854.19
  insincere ~, 854.19
defense,n.
  protection, 568.2-5; see pro-
    tection,n.
  support, 854.16
  come to the ~ of, 854.15
  give means of ~ to, 568.17
  Japanese art of self-~, 568.13
  ~ of a cause, 854.16
  ~ of Christianity, 854.17

systematic ~ in argument, 854.17
defensive,adj.
  protective, 568.6
defiance,n., 544.2
  boastful ~, 872.14
  walk with ~, 871.3(7)
deform,v., 805.2–4
deformed,adj., 507.14
  ~ witn gout, 1137.63
deformity,n., 805.3,5
  backbone ~, 354.17(1,3,4,6,7, 11) ; 354.18,19
  breastbone ~, 354.16(4)
  physical ~, 507.15
defy,v., 544.1(1,8,19,31,33)
degradation,n., 886.2
degrade,v., 868.27
  ~ oneself, 868.28
degraded,adj., 886.1
  one who lives in ~ circumstances, 750.4(14)
  ~ person, 886.4; 886.4(1)
degree,n.
  greatness, 924.1–8; see also amount,n.
  college ~, 623.13
  greatest possible ~, 924.3
  greatest possible in ~, 924.2
  recipient of a college ~, 623.12
  very great in ~, 924.1
deity,n., 654.1,2; see God (god),n.
delay,n., 768.2,9
  cause a ~ in, 768.8
  causing ~, for the purpose of, 768.10
  engage in tactics of ~, 768.1(2,7,9)
  given to ~, 768.4
  ~ in punishment, 897.20
  official ~, 1077.19
  period of ~, 768.5,6
  pert. to ~, 768.7
  unwilling to accept ~, 265.26(8) ; see impatient, adj.
  willing to accept ~, 265.23(8) ; see patient,adj.
  without ~, 766.14–17
delay,v., 768.1,8
  ~ consideration of, 768.8(18)
  ~ discussion of, 768.8(16)
  ~ eating a meal, 768.8(17)
  legislature, ~ the meeting of a, 768.8(7)
  period when one may ~ payment, 768.5,6
  ~ progress of, 768.8(12)
  ~ punishment of, 768.8(9) ; 897.19
  ~ (someone), 768.8(3,4)
  tending to ~, 768.4
delayed,adj., 768.11
  ~ by bad weather, 768.12; 1047.14
  cause to be ~, 768.8
delayer,n., 768.3
deliberately,adv., 45.13
delicacy,n., 11
delicate,adj., 11.1
  affectedly ~, 11.1(8,10)
  ~ and beautiful, 11.1(3)
  ~ and breakable, 11.1(5)
  ~ and elusive, 11.1(12)
  ~ and thin, 11.1(4)
  ~ and weak, 11.1(5,6,11)
  ~ in touch, 949.11
  light and ~, 949.1(4)
  ~, small, and thin, 11.1(4) ; 909.1(6)
delicious,adj., 446.13
delight,n.
  happiness, 1102.2; see happiness,n.

pleasure, 1105.1; see pleasure,n.
delight,v., 1102.3; 1105.3
delightful,adj., 1102.4; 1105.4
  ~ and fertile place, 1102.25
delirious,adj., 1136.2
delirium,n., 1136.1(7)
  acute or intense ~, 1136.1(32)
  as in ~, 809.1(20)
  ~ from intoxication, 1136.1(8, 9)
  speak in ~, 1136.8
  speech of ~, 1136.9
  suffer from ~, 1136.7
  ~ verging on insanity, 1136.1(16)
delusion,n., 632.7(2)
  mental derangement marked by ~s, 1136.1(5,8,9,11,17,18, 21,25,31,37,38)
demagogue,n., 1119.13–15
demand,n., 274.2; see also request,n.
  annoying ~s, 874.9
  attack with ~s, 561.1(7)
  final ~, 274.2(4)
  make excessive ~s on, 274.1(1)
  make great ~s on, 274.1(42)
  make repeated ~s on, 274.1(8, 20)
  make unreasonable ~s on, 274.1(21)
  making great ~s, 274.4(1,2)
  strictness in ~s, 890.9
demand,v., 274.1; see also order,v.
  ~ and force to give, 3.3(11)
demander,n., 274.3
demanding,adj., 274.4
  arrogantly ~, 274.4(3)
  ~ immediate attention or action, 274.4(2,4,5)
demeanor,n., 504.11
dement,v., 1136.4
demented,adj., 1136.3
democracy,n., 1073.3(28) ; 1073.4(2,6)
  become a ~, 1073.12
democratic,adj.
  become ~, 1073.12
  ~ country, 784.1(4)
demon,n., 660.1; see devil, spirit,n.
  female ~ that has sexual intercourse with men, 65.2(2)
  ~ that ravishes women, 65.2(1)
demonstration,n., 951.2,3
demonstrative,adj.
  emotionally ~, 1092.67
demoralize,v., 886.24
denial,n., 547.2
  self-~, 77.1–4
Denmark,n., 784.4(4)
  inhabitant of ~, 784.15(16,41, 42,56)
  pert. to ~, 784.16
denomination,n.
  religious ~, 642.17
dense,adj., 517.7
  become ~, 517.8
  make ~, 517.8
density,n.
  measure ~, device to, 517.9,10
  measurement of ~, 947.26
dentistry,n.
  branches of ~, 401.1(20,54,59, 71,72,80,81,90)
deny,v., 547.1
denying,adj., 547.3
depart,v., 141.1; see also leave,v.
  cause to ~, 144.1
  force to ~, 144.1
  ~ secretly, 141.1(3,8,36)

tendency to ~, 141.5
departer,n., 141.3
departing,adj., 141.4
departure,n., 141.2
  forbid ~ of ships, 555.6
  ~ from office, 141.2(2)
  means of ~, 140.5
  privilege of ~, 140.6
  sadness on ~, 1125.5
  sadness over ~, 1125.49
  secret ~, 141.2(5)
  ~ without paying debts, 141.2(5)
depend,v.
  ~ mutually, 526.2
  ~ on, 526.1
  ~ on for support, 526.3
  that which one ~s upon, 526.8
dependable,adj., 526.6
  ~ person or thing, 526.7
dependence,n.
  free of ~, 309.11(2)
dependent,adj.
  one ~ on the will of another, 526.5
  ~ person, 526.4
depending,adj.
  ~ on something uncertain, 29.5
depopulate,v., 750.26,27
deport,v., 144.1(1,3,5,17,19,22)
deposit,n., 323.2,3
deposit,v., 323.1
  ~ as sediment, 323.14
depraved,adj., 886.1
depravity,n., 886.2
depreciate,v.
  belittle, 840.1; see belittle,v.
depress,v.
  make unhappy, 1123.4,13
depressed,adj.
  low-spirited, 1123.1,12; see also gloomy, sad,adj.
  be ~, 1123.6,14
  become ~, 1123.14
  feel ~, 1123.6
  look ~, 1123.8
  make ~, 1123.4,13
  ~ person, 1123.7
depression,n.
  gloom, 1123.2; see also gloom, sadness,n.
  hollow, 299.1; see hollow,n.
  causing ~, 1123.5
  clear of ~, 1124.8
  fit of ~, 1123.3
  given to moods of ~, 1123.15–17
  in a ~, 1123.1
  mental illness characterized by ~, 1123.22; 1136.1(6,11, 19,24)
  morbid ~ accompanied by anxiety about health, 1123.19–21
  pert. to ~, 1122.9
  recover from ~, able to, 1103.11,12
  sudden, sharp, and temporary ~, 1122.25
  tendency to ~, 1123.18
deprive,v., 247.23
depth,n., 170.9
  art of showing ~, 965.6(5)
  constant in ~, 170.2
  earth ~s, 1004.30
  lack of ~, 170.12
  lacking ~ of mind, 597.7
  lacking ~ of thought, 597.8
  lowest ~s, 169.4(1)
  measure ~, instrument to, 170.8; 1026.40(1,4)
  measure of ~, 170.6
  object with illusion of ~, 965.30

ocean ~s, 170.9(3,4)
~ of water, device to measure, 1026.40(1,4)
~ of water, measurement unit of, 946.26(7)
picture in ~, 965.1(15)
picture with illusion of ~, 965.1(15,52,53)
water ~s, pert. to, 1029.72(1, 3,4,6)
weight to measure ~ of water, 947.15(4) ; 947.17
without ~, 170.11
derby,n.
hat, 983.2(20)
derogate,v., 840.1
derogatory,adj., 840.2
~ allusion, 673.3
~ remarks, 674.9(16)
~ suggester, 238.3(1)
~ suggestion, 238.2(1,2)
~ word, 840.4
descend,v., 167.1; see fall,v.
~ in a sudden attack, 560.7
descendant,n., 723.15
indirect ~, 723.16
~s, 723.17
~ who is a throwback, 723.11
descent,n., 167.2
gods' ~, 728.7
line of family ~, 723.1-6; see also ancestry,n.
describe,v., 617.1
hard to ~, 617.6
~ in detail, 617.1(9)
one who ~s, 617.3
~ the earth, 617.1(5)
unable to be ~d, 665.7(1-4)
description,n., 617.2
~ of a region, 617.2(1,2)
~ of a specific subject, 682.15; see also under the specific subject
pert. to ~, 617.5
short ~, 617.2(4)
descriptive,adj., 617.4
desecrate,v., 650.9
desensitize,v., 1137.37
desert,n.
fertile land in a ~, 1003.12
fertile or green place in ~, 1003.12
~ plant, 1037.33
desert,v., 142.1; 330.3
~ a cause, party, etc., 142.1(2,4,9)
~ a person, 142.1(1,3,5-8)
~ a religion, 142.1(2)
deserted,adj., 330.1
~ by the mother (of animals), 403.31
~ person, 330.5
deserter,n., 142.3
pert. to a ~, 142.4
desertion,n., 142.2; 330.2
pert. to ~, 142.4
deserve,v., 841.1
deserved,adj., 841.8
according to what is ~, 841.9
not ~, 841.10
that which is ~, 841.7
deserving,adj., 841.2; see worthy,adj.
~ praise, 851.8
design,n., 311.8
arrangement, 311.1
burning ~s into a surface, art of, 311.10
changing ~, 311.8(5)
~ in a book, 311.8(12)
~ of building, 727.6,11
~ of initials of name, 694.27
~ pricked into the skin, 311.8(10)
structural ~, 311.1(3)

desirable,adj., 265.14; 1106.3
~ thing, 265.7
desire,n., 265.2
anxious ~, 265.2(23)
arising out of sudden ~, 265.8(3,4)
arousal of ~, 265.13
arouse ~, 265.12
arouse sexual ~ in, 709.19
arousing ~, 265.14
arousing sexual ~, 709.18
based on one's own ~, 265.8(1,2)
cause of ~, 265.15
cause of sexual ~, 709.17
caused by natural ~, 265.8(4)
demon of ~, 662.7(29)
expressive of ~, 265.9,10
faint ~, 265.2(27)
~ for home, 265.2(17)
~ for the past, 265.2(17)
~ for the unattainable, 265.2(19) ; 1092.51,52
force ~ into the unconscious, 1097.42-46
fulfilling ~s, 265.11
haunt with ~, 265.12(4)
have sexual ~s, 709.14
object of ~, 18.7; 265.7
persistent and besetting ~, 1092.15-17
pert. to ~, 265.10
pert. to bodily ~s, 338.8
sexual ~, 709.7
sexual ~, lack of, 710.43-45
sexual ~, unnatural, 710.31-35; see sexual aberration,n.
sexual ~ in female mammals, 709.7(17,34,39) ; 709.13
sinful ~ 265.2(29)
source of ~, 265.15
strange ~, 265.2(6,7,10,11,18, 26,28)
strange ~s, full of, 265.3; 265.3(5)
uncontrollable ~, 265.2(5,6,12, 15,21)
desire,v., 265.1
expect and ~, 268.12
desired,adj.
~ thing, 265.7
desirer,n., 265.5
desirous,adj., 265.3
~ of being, 265.3(12)
~ of possessions, 265.3(1,3,6, 8-10)
~ of power, 265.3(1)
sexually ~, 709.8,9
desirousness,n., 265.4
despair,n., 267.9
despair,v., 267.12
desperately,adv., 4.24
despicable,adj., 870.8
despot,n., 8.10; 635.6; 890.4; 1073.60
despotic,adj., 8.11; 635.6; 890.4; 1073.59
despotism,n., 8.9,12; 635.6; 890.4; 1073.59
despotize,v., 8.8; 635.6; 890.4; 1073.61
dessert,n., 740.15(3,8)
destine,v., 33.5
~ beforehand, 33.5(3-6)
destined,adj., 33.7
destiny,n., 33.1
unhappy ~, 33.1(2)
destroy,v., 801.1
eat away, 801.20-24
wear away, 801.25-32
~ a place, 801.11
~ a ship at sea, 801.1(9)
~ by fire, 1064.33
~ completely, 801.15
~ figuratively, 801.12

~ financially, 801.12(3)
~ gradually, 801.14
~ maliciously, 801.1(12)
privilege to ~, 6.1(1)
~ reputation, etc., 801.12(1)
~ unity of, 801.1(3)
destroyed,adj., 801.34
able to be ~, 801.35
be ~, 801.33
be gradually ~, 801.33(3)
become ~, 801.33
person who has been ~, 801.39
that which can be ~, 801.36
unable to be ~, 801.37
destroyer,n.
one who destroys, 801.4
~s in wartime, 801.5
destructible,adj., 801.35
destruction,n., 801.2
Bible ~, 687.24
book ~, 687.24,25
~ by fire, 1064.18,33
~ by fire, ruins from, 801.38; 1064.53
~ by white blood cells, 801.2(4)
cause of ~, 801.4
complete ~, 801.16
figurative ~, 801.13
left after ~, what is, 801.38; 1064.53
~ of books, 801.2(1)
~ of cells, 801.2(3)
~ of insects, place for, 899.16
philosophy of ~, 801.10
policy of ~, 801.6,7
self-~, 795.1; see suicide,n.
source of ~, 801.4
destructive,adj., 801.3
~ and forcible, 3.2(16)
~ frenzy, in a, 1100.6(3)
~ insect, 801.4(2)
~ to crops, 801.8
desultory,adj., 46.13; 110.3(3)
detach,v., 302.7
detail,n., 327.1
careful about ~s, 577.1(32)
describe in ~, 617.1(9)
done with attention to ~s, 577.7
give ~s, 327.4
enlarge the ~s of, 907.12
in ~, 327.6
list of ~s, 311.19(4,6,8) ; 327.3
minor ~s, 327.2
small ~s, 327.2
special ~, 540.28
support with ~s, 1022.27
tell about in ~, 613.23(2,6-8)
tell in ~, 613.17(6-8)
unimportant ~s, 327.2
with attention to ~s, 579.13, 14
detailed,adj., 327.6
detect,v.
find, 487.1
find out, 624.1; see discover,v.
detectable,adj., 487.4
detected,adj.
easily ~, 624.6
detection,n.
finding, 487.2
finding out, 624.2
detective,n.
finder, 487.3
one who finds out, 624.4
searcher, 486.4
seeker of criminals, 486.4(4)
act like a ~, 486.1(36)
play the ~, 486.1(36)
detector,n.
finder, 487.3
one who finds out, 624.4
deterioration,n., 883.12

belief in world ~, 883.19
determination,n., 45.1; 624.2
determine,v.
　find out, 624.1
　have as one's purpose, 45.2
　~ not to sin, 45.3
determined,adj., 45.4
develop,v.
　grow, 731.3,22,27; see grow,v.
　happen, 29.1; see happen,v.
　begin to ~, 729.7(3,7,11)
　beginning to ~, 729.9;
　729.15(4,11) ; 731.2
　~ faster, cause to, 95.8(1,2,4–
　9)
developed,adj.
　excessively ~, 732.8,9
　poorly ~, 733.7,10,11
　poorly ~ organ, 733.8
developing,adj., 731.5; see
　growing,adj.
development,n.
　growth, 731.4,23; see also
　growth,n.
　happening, 29.2,6; see hap-
　pening,n.
　arrested ~, 731.30
　arrested in ~, 731.28,29
　capable of ~, 731.19,20
　earliest stages of ~, in the,
　733.9
　early in ~, 766.1(2)
　encourage the ~ of, 731.27
　history of individual ~,
　731.16,(1)
　history of race ~, 731.16(2)
　lack of repetition of race ~
　in individual growth, 731.14
　~ outside the body, 731.4(6)
　period in ~, 769.8(15)
　period of ~, 731.18
　period of greatest ~,
　731.18(1)
　period of incomplete ~,
　731.18(2)
　racial ~, 731.4(7)
　repetition of race ~ in in-
　dividual growth, 731.13
　retarded ~, 731.30
　retarded in ~, 731.28,29
　slow the ~ of, 731.28
　stop the ~ of, 731.28
　student of ~, 731.17
deviate,n., 539.5
　sexual ~, 710.32,34
deviate,v., 539.1,2
deviation,n., 539.3
　sexual ~, 710.31,33; see sex-
　ual aberration,n.
device,n.
　a saying, 676.1
　piece of equipment, 280.6
devise,v.
　invent, 726.17
　make, 726.1
devil,n., 660.1
　belief in ~s, 660.8
　government by ~s, 1073.42(4)
　influence by ~s, 660.20
　inspired as if by a ~, 660.15
　intercourse with the ~, 660.6,
　7
　like the ~, 660.2
　little ~, 660.1(9)
　~ of desire, 662.7(29)
　pert. to the ~, 660.2
　possess by a ~, 660.16
　possessed by a ~, 660.14
　possessed by a ~, one who is,
　660.16
　possession by ~s, 660.19
　power from, or to control, ~s,
　660.4(2,8,9)
　realm of ~s, 660.9
　represent as a ~, 660.21

sea ~, 660.1(6)
sign of the ~, 660.4
study of ~s, 660.8(2–7)
turn (someone) into a ~,
　660.13
victim of a ~, 660.18
worship of ~s, 660.10–12
devilish,adj., 660.2
　~ actions, 660.3
　~ art, 660.3(1,2)
　~ magic, 660.3(1,2) ; 663.1(2,
　4–7,10,13–16)
　~ nature, 660.3
　represent as ~, 660.21
devilishness,n., 660.3
　sign of ~, 660.4
devote,v., 657.2
devoted,adj., 657.6
　~ admirer, 657.4(3)
　be ~ to, 657.3
　~ follower, 657.4(3)
　~ person, 657.4
devotion,n., 657.1
　~ and loyalty, 657.1(2)
　blind ~ and worship,
　657.1(13)
　given in ~, 657.8
　object of ~, 657.7
　pert. to ~, 657.5
　~ to country or ruler,
　657.1(2)
devour,v., 734.1; see eat,v.
devouring,adj.
　figuratively ~ everything,
　734.9
dew,n.
　amount of ~, device to meas-
　ure, 1026.40(2)
　drop of ~, 1026.9
　frozen ~, 1059.7–9
diabetes,n.
　hormone for ~, 287.8(7)
diagnose,v., 624.1
diagnosis,n., 624.2
diagnostic,adj., 624.3; 624.3(1)
dialect,n., 664.1(8,11,12,15,27)
　Athenian ~, 664.4(2)
　Dutch ~, 664.4(1)
　French ~, 664.4(5)
　London ~, 664.4(2)
　~ of English in Far East or
　South Seas, 664.4(14)
　~ of India, 664.4(9,18)
diamond,n., 962.1
　a ~ as to cut, 962.4
　bearing ~s, 962.11
　~-bearing rock, 962.12
　containing ~s, 962.11
　cut of a ~, 962.5
　foreign body in a ~, 962.7
　former name for a ~, 962.2
　hard like a ~, 962.8
　made of ~s, 962.9
　ornament with ~s, 962.18
　parts of a ~, 962.6
　qualities of a ~, 962.3
　set with ~s, 962.10
　~-shaped, 507.17(65)
　shiny like a ~, 962.8
　single ~, 962.1(10)
diaphragm,n., 388.1(2)
　pert. to the ~, 388.2(2,9)
diarrhea,n., 293.5
diary,n., 774.7(7)
Dickens,n.
　descr. of writing like that of
　~, 686.8(3)
dictate,v., 275.1
dictatorial,adj., 8.11; 275.4
　one who is ~, 8.10; 275.3
　~ quality, 8.12
dictionary,n., 666.19
　art of the ~, 666.20
　~ editor, 666.20
die,n.

~ of five pips, 934.2
~ of four pips, 933.14
~ of three pips, 932.10,11
~ of two pips, 931.27
die,v., 794.27
　~ before (someone else),
　794.28
　~ from lack of air, 794.29
　~ from lack of food, 794.30
　~ of cold, 1058.12
　~ of hunger, 737.6
　one who ~s for a belief or
　cause, 1138.9; see martyr,n.
diet,n., 740.2(6,14) ; 740.10–13
　go on a ~, 734.1(12) ; 734.23–
　25
　treatise on ~s, 682.15(1,23)
dietetics,n., 734.19
differ,v., 540.3
difference,n., 540.2; see also
　distinction,n.
　arrange to note ~s, 540.17
　arrange to point up ~s,
　540.22
　comparison of ~s, 530.1
　degree of ~, 540.12,13
　examine to note ~s, 540.17
　find ~s, 540.14
　give special ~s to, 540.24
　~ in feelings or interests,
　540.2(1,5)
　note ~s, able to, 540.15
　note ~s in, 540.14
　referring to ~s, 540.11
　set apart by special ~s,
　540.20,21
　unable to see ~s in, be, 540.19
different,adj., 540.1
　be ~, 540.3
　become ~, 539.2; see
　change,v.
　~ form, 540.10
　~ in form, 540.1(17,36)
　make ~, 539.1; see change,v.
　many and ~, 540.1(21) ; 916.10
　new and ~, 540.1(25,26) ;
　761.1(9–11,16)
　of ~ forms, 540.9
　of ~ kinds, 540.9
　of two ~ natures or char-
　acters, 931.3
　pair ~ people or things, 540.8
　people who are ~, 540.5
　person who is ~, 540.4
　something ~, 540.4
　things that are ~, 540.5,6
　~ when compared, 540.1(2,
　6,8)
difficult,adj., 25.1
　~ and uncertain, 25.1(12)
　be too ~, 25.3
　~ circumstance, 25.9
　~ condition, 25.9
　make ~, 25.4
　~ position, 25.9
　~ situation, 25.9
　~ situation having no escape
　or solution, 25.9(5,14)
　~ to do, 25.1(1)
　~ to solve, 25.1(2–5,17,23–25)
　~ to understand, 25.1(2–5, 7–
　10,20,22,24,25)
difficulties,n.
　cause ~ in, 25.4
　eliminator of ~, 25.8
　finder of ~, 25.8
　full of the ~ of life, 25.1(28)
　herald of ~, 25.7
　one who causes ~, 25.5,6
difficulty,n., 25.2
　free of ~, 309.11(25,41)
　~ that traps one, 25.2(3)
dig,v., 171.1
　~ into rock, 1006.55

~ up from burial, 171.1(5–7, 12,19) ; 797.22

digestion,n.
able to undergo ~, 739.15
good ~, 739.17,18
incorporation of food after ~, 739.23
passage of food after ~, 739.22
pert. to ~, 739.10,11
poor ~, 739.19–21
promoting ~, 739.13,14
unable to undergo ~, 739.16

digestive,adj.
~ passage, 347.11

digger,n., 171.3
grave~, 797.15
~ in sand, 1007.13

digging,n., 171.2
adapted for ~, 171.5
instrument for ~, 171.4
machine for ~, 171.4(1)

dignified,adj., 846.1
excessively ~ in language, 951.49
large and ~, 846.4; 906.6
ostentatiously ~, 846.3; 951.49
respectable and ~, 855.19

dignify,v., 846.5

dignity,n., 846.2
below one's ~, 867.6
falling off in ~, 846.6
give ~ to, 846.5
hurt the ~ of, 868.1(1)
lower in ~, 868.27
lower oneself in ~, 868.28
lower the ~ of, 868.10
offense against ~, 1088.21
position of ~, one holding a, 857.14
positions of ~, those holding, 857.15

digress,v., 128.1(3,4,12,17)
digression,n., 128.2; 128.2(2)
digressive,adj., 128.4
dilemma,n., 602.1(6)
diligence,n., 577.2; see **carefulness**,n.
diligent,adj., 577.1; see **careful**, adj.
dilute,v., 10.5(39)
dim,adj., 1070.14
become ~, as the vision, 1070.16
~ like a shadow, 1071.3
make (vision or eyes) ~, as with tears, 1070.15
~ of eyes, as with tears, 1070.19
~ (of eyes or vision), 1070.17
dim,v., 1070.3,4,15,16
~ (vision) with brightness, 1065.78
dimension,n.
having three ~s, 946.36
having two ~s, 946.35
measurement in three ~s, 946.50
diminish,v., 910.1,2; see **decrease**,v.
dine,v., 734.1; see **eat**,v.
dinner,n., 740.16(20)
after–~, 740.20(1,5)
before–~, 740.20(7)
eat ~, 734.1(13,32)
frequent visitor for ~, 734.3(1)
pert. to ~, 740.20(6)
seafood ~, 740.16(18)
time for ~, 740.19
dinosaur,n., 426.1,2
pert. to, or descr. of, ~s, 426.3
dip,v., 1035.1,3
~ and soak, 1035.17

~ body or head under water, 1035.6,7
device for ~ping out liquids, 1035.8
~ in and out, 1035.15
liquid for ~ping and preserving, 1035.18
~ liquid out, 1035.9
~ oneself in water, 1035.5
~ (water, etc.) from a boat, 1035.11,12
diphtheria,n.
test of immunity to ~, 401.10(6)
diploma,n.
recipient of a ~, 623.12; 857.12
diplomacy,n., 523.4
art of ~, 523.5
rules of conduct in ~, 56.3(8)
diplomat,n., 523.6
office or residence of a ~, 523.9
~'s band around the waist, 980.6
~'s trousers, 980.1(22)
dipped,adj.
be or become ~, 1034.3
state of being ~, 1034.4
dipsomania,n., 749.41
dipsomaniac,n., 749.43
dipsomaniacal,adj., 749.42
direct,adj., 182.1
~ and prompt, 182.1(9)
~ and to the point, 182.1(2)
not ~, 183.1–3
direct,v.
control, 8.14
guide, 177.1
order, 275.1
direction,n., 179.1
control, 8.15
order, 275.2
~ away from the wind, 179.1(18)
change in ~, 539.1(15,16,23) ; 539.2(8,9,13)
determine the ~ of, 179.4
general ~, 179.1(4,5,7,8,14–17)
go in a ~, 179.2
in a ~, 179.8
in an opposite ~, 179.8(8)
in four ~s, 179.8(7)
in the ~ away from the wind, 179.8(10)
in the ~ of clock hands, 179.8(2)
in the ~ of the wind, 179.8(5)
in the ~ opposite to clock hands, 179.8(3)
in the same ~, 179.8(6,9)
in two ~s, 179.8(1)
make lose sense of ~, 605.1(6, 11,18,25)
~ of action, 179.1(4,5,7,8,13–17)
~ (control) of natural and social forces, 8.15(1)
place so as to face a ~, 179.3
point in a ~, 179.2
~s of the compass, 179.5,6
~s to the reader, 680.3
~ toward the wind, 179.1(9)
directive,adj., 8.17; 275.4
director,n., 8.16; 275.3
directorial,adj., 8.17; 275.4
dirt,n.
earth, 999.1
filth, 904.3
dirtiness,n., 904.2
dirty,adj., 904.1
~ and mean, 887.5
~ and shabby, 903.9
~ and tired, 12.1(1)

~ and untidy person, 903.4; 903.4(1–4)
~ and untidy woman, 903.4; 903.4(1–4)
~ and untidy, 903.1(2,8–10,12, 18,20–23)
~ and wet, 904.1(2)
become ~, 904.8
crowded and ~ area, 1048.19
~, crowded, and poor, 904.1(20)
~, crowded, and poor place, 904.15
disgustingly ~, 904.1(5,6,9,12–15,17,28,29,31)
~ in habits, 904.13
~ language, 904.16; 1118.14,15, 19,20
make ~, 904.5,11
~ mark, streak, etc., 904.4
not ~, 904.6,7; see **clean**,adj.
~ place, 904.14
~ with germs, 904.10
~ with mud, 1000.7
~ word, 713.3; 863.8
dirty,v., 904.5,8
tending to ~, 904.12
disability,n., 13.4
disable,v., 13.1
~ by holding the arms, 13.1(9)
disabled,adj., 13.3
~ from fighting, 13.3(1)
~ from struggling, 13.3(1)
disablement,n., 13.2
disadvantage,n., 836.16
one at a ~, 836.18
subject to ~, 836.17
sustain ~, 803.22
disagree,v., 542.3,11
inclined to ~, 542.17
disagreeable,adj., 1117.1; see **unpleasant**,adj.
disagreement,n., 542.1,10
a ~, 542.10; see **dispute**, **quarrel**,n.
be in ~, 542.3,11
caused by group ~, 542.9
causing ~s, 542.21
group in ~ with the rest, 326.6(13)
in ~, 542.2
not open to ~, 542.14
open to ~, 542.13
settle a ~, 541.21
show ~, 542.3,11
shows ~, one who, 542.4
state of ~, 542.1
try to settle a ~, 541.26
disappear,v., 143.1–3
appear and ~, 483.3(10)
decay and ~, 806.1(5)
disappoint,v., 1121.1
disappointed,adj., 1121.3
disappointment,n., 1121.1,3
a ~, 1121.2
become tired or weak with ~, 1121.8
cause ~ in, 1121.5
feeling ~, 1121.3
feeling of ~, 1121.4
feeling of unhappy ~, 1121.6
show tearful ~, 1121.7
disapproval,n., 894.3
cry of ~, 468.1(3)
descr. of ~, 894.4
deserving ~, 894.7
express ~, 894.2
express ~ of, 894.1
facial expression of ~, 365.2(4–6,10)
incur the ~ of, 894.13
not deserving ~, 894.8
one who expresses or shows ~, 894.5

sign of ~, 894.11
subject to approval or ~, 850.18
worthy of ~, 894.7
disapprove,v., 894.1,2
~ of, 894.1
one who ~s, 894.5
disapproved,adj.
state of being ~ of, 894.6
disapprover,n., 894.5
disapproving,adj., 894.4
disaster,n., 29.6(6,8,9,15) ; 37.1
disband,v., 144.1
~ troops, 325.1(16)
disbelief,n., 639.2,4
having no ~, 639.7
maintaining that ~ is necessary, 639.3(1)
show or express ~ about, 639.13
showing no ~, 639.7
with ~, 639.9
disbelieve,v., 639.1
tending to ~, 639.3(8,9,11,14–17,20–23)
disbeliever,n., 639.5
~ in the true religion, 639.5(2)
disbelieving,adj., 639.3
cause someone to be ~, 639.6
~ everything, 639.3(14)
~ in honesty, 639.3(3)
~ in nobility, 639.3(3)
~ in orthodox doctrine, 639.3(10,25)
~ in religious matters, 639.3(10,20,23,25)
~ in the future, 639.3(2)
~ in virtue, 639.3(3)
totally ~, 639.3(14)
discard,n., 285.1; 286.3
discard,v., 286.1
~ (a lover), 286.1(35)
discarded,adj.
able to be ~, 286.5
~ skins, shells, etc., 285.1(8,34)
~ thing or things, 285.1; 286.3
~ things from a sinking ship, 285.1(10,11)
unable to be ~, 286.6
discharge,n.
bodily ~, 287.2–4
bodily organ of ~, 287.5
fluid ~, 287.2(3)
~ from the vagina, 287.2(4) ; 287.3(1,3,4) ; 292.1
~ of mucus, 287.2(1,5)
pert. to bodily ~, 287.4
discharge,v.
~ from a position or office, 144.4
~ from or in the body, 287.1
~ from the mouth, 287.1(4,16) ; 289.1
~ from the throat, 287.1(4) ; 289.1
~ gas from the body, 287.1(1,2) ; 288.1–7
disciplinary,adj., 896.4
discipline,n., 896.2
self-~, 77.1–4
discipline,v., 896.1
disclosure,n., 951.2,3
discolor,v., 488.15–17
discoloration,n., 488.17,20
skin ~, 488.20(1)
discolored,adj., 488.21
discomfort,n., 1141.12,16
cause of ~, 1141.14
causing ~, 1141.13
~ from excessive eating or drinking, 1137.10(8)
in ~ from eating or drinking, 1137.12(1)

physical ~, 1137.10(4–6)
discontented,adj., 1119.1; see dissatisfied,adj.
discourage,v., 267.14; 1095.26,28
discouraged,adj., 267.10
discouragement,n., 267.9,17; 1095.27,29,30
feelings of ~ and inadequacy, 1123.10,11
discourager,n., 267.15; 1095.29
discouraging,adj., 267.16
discourteous,adj., 860.1; see impolite,adj.
discourtesy,n., 860.2; see impoliteness,n.
discover,v.
find, 487.1
find out, 624.1
attempt to ~, 624.8,9
~ disease type, 624.1(9)
eager to ~, 624.15
discoverable,adj., 487.4; 624.5
discoverer,n., 487.3; 624.4
discovery,n., 487.2,6–8; 624.2
scientific ~, 908.27
serving to ~, 624.3
discus,n.
~ thrower, 187.7
discuss,v., 672.1
able to be ~ed, 672.11
~ and settle, 672.1(11)
~ with African natives, 672.1(9)
~ with the enemy, 672.1(10)
discussion,n., 672.2,3
a meeting for ~, 322.1(17,24) ; 672.2(4)
art of ~, 672.8
delay the ~ of, 768.8(16,18)
ending of ~ and bringing to a vote, 791.12
~ group, 672.6
hatred of ~, 880.17(7)
leader of a ~, 176.3(4,5,10)
offer for ~, 237.1(5)
open to ~, 672.9–11
pert. to ~, 672.4
place for ~, 672.7
presider at a ~, 672.5
statement subject to ~, 674.9(27)
stimulate public ~, 52.9(3)
suggest for ~, 238.1(3)
discredit,n., 891.12
discredit,v., 891.11
disease,n., 389.1; see also illness,n.
artery ~s, 353.7
attack of a ~, 560.22–25
bladder ~s, 350.5
blood ~s, 352.23–25
bone ~s, 354.16
brain ~s, 357.10
bronchial ~, 375.5
cancerous ~, 390.3–10
cause ~, 389.4
cause of ~, 389.17
caused by ~, 389.19
causing ~, 389.18
~ characterized by enlargement of the body, 907.13
childbirth ~, 718.18
classification of ~s, 312.4(1)
coughing ~s, 364.12
ear ~s, 354.16(1) ; 362.7,8
eye ~s, 361.6
eyelid ~s, 361.6(3,10) ; 361.17
find out type or cause of ~, 624.1(9)
foot ~s, 346.12; 1137.56(14)
~ from fleas, 396.1(31)
~ from lice, 396.1(31)
~ from mosquitoes, 396.1(4,20,22,35,36)

~ from pork, 396.1(28)
~ from raw milk, 396.1(6,33)
genital ~s, 379.9,10
get a ~, 240.1(13)
give a ~, 230.1(12,34)
gradual end of a ~, 389.26
gum ~, 368.23
hair ~, 369.24
hand ~, 1137.56(14)
heart ~s, 351.6,7
hip ~, 345.21; 1137.56(25)
imitation of ~, 389.8
intestinal ~s, 347.12
irregularity accompanying ~, 536.6
joint ~s, 377.9(1,3,13,24) ; 377.10,11
kidney ~s, 388.3
liver ~s, 388.4
lung ~s, 374.4,6,8,14
lymph ~s, 388.5,6
mark of ~, 503.1(12)
mental, concept of ~ as, 400.6(8)
mental ~, 1136.1; see insanity,n.
miscellaneous ~s, 396.1–4
mouth ~s, 367.9
muscular ~s, 377.9–11
neck ~, 359.6,7
nerve ~s, 378.11–14; 1137.56(22)
nose ~s, 363.17–20
observable course of a ~, pert. to 955.11
observable in a ~, 389.7
onset of ~, 389.20
origin of ~, 389.20
ovary ~, 379.9(9)
pituitary ~s, 394.2; 907.13(3)
place of epidemic ~, 389.24
plant ~, 389.1(5) ; 985.12–15
poisons, ~s caused by, 800.12–18
prediction of the course of a ~, 772.12
prevention of ~, 397.12
prevention of ~, art of, 569.13
prostate ~, 379.9(11)
protect against ~, 569.1–13
relating to ~, 389.3
respiratory ~s, 363.17–20; 376.8
scalp ~, 369.25
science of ~s, 401.1(52,69)
sexual ~s, 379.9,10
skin ~s, 382.11–14,16–27
source of ~, 389.17
spread of ~, 389.21,22
stomach ~, 347.12(4)
tendency to ~, 389.13,14
tendon ~s, 377.9(24,29) ; 377.10,11
testicle ~, 379.9(8)
thigh ~, 1137.56(14)
throat ~s, 364.13
thyroid ~s, 394.1
time for ~ to develop, 389.23
toe ~, 1137.56(14)
tooth ~s, 368.20,21
treatise on ~s, 682.15(13)
treatment of ~, 400.2,6; 401.1; see medical science, therapy,n.
turning point in a ~, 389.25
unable to resist a ~, 552.10
urinary ~s, 294.8
uterus ~, 379.9(7)
vein ~s, 353.7
venereal ~s, 379.9,10
vitamin deficiency ~s, 395.1
windpipe ~s, 375.4,5
diseased,adj., 389.2; see ill,adj.
mentally ~, 1136.2
disembodied,adj., 338.16

disembody,v., 338.17
disfavor,n., 880.2,11; 894.3
  person in ~, 1109.2
disfavor,v., 880.1(6) ; 894.1
disfavored,adj., 880.10
disfigure,v., 805.2
disfigurement,n., 805.2,5
disgrace,n., 891.5
  ~ attendant on hateful acts,
    880.15
  bring ~ upon, 891.1,11
  bringer of ~, 891.8
  bringing ~, 891.6
  cause of ~, 891.7,8
  causing ~, 891.6
  expose to ~, 891.2
  mark of ~, 503.1(4,11,12) ;
    891.4
  mark with ~, 891.3
disgrace,v., 891.1,11
disgraceful,adj., 891.6
  ~ act, action, or happening,
    891.9
disguise,n., 826.9; 970.14,15
  remove the ~ from, 970.57–59
disguise,v., 970.13
  cover to ~, 972.1(55)
  ~ oneself, 970.17
disguised,adj., 970.51
  not ~, 970.56
disgust,n., 881.7
  drink to the point of ~,
    1107.23,24
  eat to the point of ~, 1107.23,
    24
  facial expression of ~,
    365.2(3,5)
  feel ~, 881.3
  feel ~ and hate, 880.1(1,2,7,8,
    9)
  feel ~ at, 881.5
  feeling of ~, 881.7
  satisfy to the point of ~,
    1107.15–22
  to the point of ~, 881.3
disgust,v., 881.1
disgusted,adj., 881.6
  easily ~, 881.11
  feel ~, 881.4
  feel ~ by, 881.5
  state of being ~, 881.7
disgusting,adj., 881.2
  ~ animal life, 881.9
  ~ because of insincerity,
    881.2(1)
  ~ in odor, 445.10; 445.10(7,
    9,15,17–19,21,23) ; 881.2(4)
  infested with ~ animal life,
    403.18–20
  ~ language, 1118.14; 1118.15(1,
    2) ; 1118.19,20
  ~ people, 881.9
  ~ sight, 881.10
  ~ thing, 881.8
  ~ to the moral sense, 881.2(3)
dish,n., 261.9
  gold ~es, 1013.20
disharmony,n., 542.1; see disagreement,n.
dishonest,adj., 822.1
  ~ and tricky, 822.5
  ~ and tricky act, 822.7
  ~ and tricky person, 822.6
  ~ and tricky practice, 822.7
  arrange ~ly, 311.2(3,4)
  ~ method of operation, 822.4
  ~ person, 822.3
dishonesty,n., 822.2
dishonorable,adj., 886.1
disinfect,v., 899.10
disinter,v., 171.1(5–7,12,19)
disinterested,adj., 636.1
dislikeable,adj., 880.4
dislike,n., 880.2
  arouse ~ in, 880.16

causing ~, 880.4; 880.4(1,2,3)
  gesture in ~, 102.1(10)
  ~ over insult, injury, etc.,
    880.2(6)
dislike,v., 880.1(3,6)
  ~ the taste of, 880.12
disliked,adj., 880.10
  person who is ~, 880.5(4,5) ;
    1109.21
  state of being ~, 880.11
disloyal,adj., 659.1
  be ~ to, 659.3
  ~ person, 659.4
  ~ to country, 659.1(4,7–10)
  ~ to government, 1119.16
  ~ to marriage vows, 659.1(11,
    12)
  ~ to one's promise or trust,
    659.1(3,11,12)
disloyalty,n., 659.2
  cause ~ to government,
    1119.17
  incitement to ~, 659.5
  ~ to marriage vows, 659.2(4)
dismay,n., 576.2
dismay,v., 576.6
dismayed,adj., 576.1
  be ~, 576.3
dismiss,v., 144.1
  ~ from a position, 144.4
  ~ from clergy, 144.4(3,10,17,
    18)
  ~ from membership, 144.4
  ~ from office, 144.4
dismissal,n., 144.2,4
  signal for ~, 956.1(14)
disobedience,n., 549.2
  act of ~, 549.4
  ~ to court or congress,
    1081.23
disobedient,adj., 549.1
  ~ person, 549.5
disobey,v., 549.3
  one who ~s, 549.5
disorder,n.
  confusion, 605.13; see con-
    fusion, disturbance,n.
  untidiness, 903.2
  causing ~, 1101.7
  crowd's violence and ~, 4.16
  free from ~, 1135.8
  ~ from lack of government or
    law, 1073.103
  in ~, 903.1
  indicative of ~, 1135.7
  lawless ~, 1087.27
  mental ~, 1136.1; see insan-
    ity,n.
  ~ of clothing, 974.8
  personality ~, 1135.1
  pert. to ~, 1135.7
  sufferer from a personality
    ~, 1135.3
  suffering from a personality
    ~, 1135.2
  throw into ~, 605.11
  throw (things) around in ~,
    903.5
disorder,v., 605.11
disordered,adj.
  confused, 605.14
  untidy, 903.1; see untidy,adj.
  mentally ~, 1136.2
disorderly,adj.
  unruly, 550.1; see unruly,adj.
  untidy, 903.1; see untidy,adj.
  ~ and rough, 865.1(8,12)
  avoid or prevent ~ conduct,
    1140.35
  ~ conduct, 1140.37
  ~ conduct in court or con-
    gress, 1081.23
  ~ in habits, 903.6
disparage,v., 840.1
disparagement,n., 840.1

laugh at in ~, 840.5
disparaging,adj., 840.2; see also
  derogatory,adj.
display,n., 951.2,3; see also
  exhibition, exposure,
  show,n.
  ~ by gesture, 951.3(5)
  empty ~, 951.3(9,11,13–16,18,
    23,24)
  false ~, 951.3(24)
  ~ of brilliance, 951.3(3)
  ~ of color, 951.3(20)
  ~ of courage, 951.3(3)
  ~ of emotions, 951.3(10,19,21,
    22) ; 951.17
  ~ of lights, 1065.75
  ostentatious ~, 951.40
  pleasing but false ~,
    951.3(24)
  public ~ for political pur-
    poses, 951.19
  public ~ of emotions, 951.17
  public ~ of military power,
    951.18
  showy ~, 951.40
  spectacular ~, 951.3(15,16,18–
    20,22)
  ~ to impress others, 951.40
display,v., 951.1; see show,v.
displease,v., 1117.3,4
displeased,adj., 1117.5; 1119.1
  easily ~, 1117.15
  state of being ~, 1117.6
displeasing,adj., 1117.1; see
  unpleasant,adj.
displeasure,n., 1117.6
  be a source of ~ (to), 1117.3,4
  express ~ about, 1117.8
  express ~ on the face,
    1117.10,11,13
  expression of ~, 1117.9
  facial expression of ~,
    365.2(4–6,8–10) ; 1117.12
  feel ~ for, 1117.7
  mood of ~, 1117.14
disproof,n., 820.19
disproportional,adj., 520.11
disprove,v., 820.19
disputable,adj., 542.13
dispute,n., 542.10; see also
  quarrel,n.
  bringing ~s into court,
    1082.30
  causing ~s, 542.17,21
  engaged in a ~, 542.15
  involve in a ~, 542.20
  legal ~, 1082.1; see lawsuit,n.
  not open to ~, 542.14
  open to ~, 542.13
  power to settle ~s, 1083.29
  public ~, 542.10(17) ; see de-
    bate,n.
  settle a ~, 541.21–24
  settlement of ~ by arbitrator,
    1083.22–24
  situation marked by ~,
    542.16
  submit a ~ to arbitration,
    1083.23
  suitable for ~, 542.23
  try to settle a ~, 541.26,27
dispute,v., 542.11; see also
  quarrel,v.
  ~ about price, 542.11(2)
  inclined to ~, 542.17
disputer,n., 542.12
disregard,v., 581.6,14; 582.1
  able to be ~ed, 581.13
disreputable,adj., 891.13
disrepute,n., 891.12
disrespect,n., 861.2
  feel ~ for, 861.5
  show ~ for, 861.6
  ~ to court or congress,
    1081.23

treat (the sacred) with ~,
  861.14
disrespectful,adj., 861.1
  ~ act, behavior, statement,
    thing, etc., 861.4
  ~ language, 861.4,10
  ~ language to God, 861.10
  ~ language to or about holy
    or sacred people or things,
    861.10
  ~ person, 861.3
  ~ to God, 861.8
  ~ to parents, 861.7
  ~ to sacred things or persons,
    861.8
  use ~ language to God or
    about holy or sacred people
    or things, 861.11
dissatisfaction,n., 1119.2
  cause ~ in order to bring
    about change, 1119.11
  cause of ~, 1119.8
  cause ~ with government,
    1119.17
  causes ~, one who, 1119.10,12,
    13
  express ~, 1119.3
  expressive of ~, 1119.5
  facial expression of ~,
    365.2(4–6,8–10)
  ~ from envy, 1119.2(3)
  group or political ~,
    1119.2(4) ; 1119.16
  incitement to ~ with govern-
    ment, 549.10
  say in ~, 1119.3(3)
  show ~, 1119.3
  source of ~, 1119.8
  weep in ~, 1119.3(5)
  whine in ~, 1119.3(5)
dissatisfactory,adj., 1119.24;
  see **unsatisfactory**,adj.
dissatisfied,adj., 1119.1; see also
  unsatisfied,adj.
  be ~, 1119.3
  make ~, 1119.7
  ~ person, 1119.4
  person ~ with the govern-
    ment, 1119.19
  ~ with the government,
    1119.16–19
dissatisfy,v., 1119.7
dissatisfying,adj., 1119.9; see
  also **unsatisfying**,adj.
dissection,n.
  ~ of corpses, 402.1(3,7,12,17)
dissimilar,adj., 540.1; see different,adj.
dissipate,v., 225.1
  indulge in pleasure, 1105.7
dissipated,adj., 886.1; 1096.11
  given over to pleasure, 1105.8
dissipation,n., 225.1; 886.2
  sexual ~, 709.7
  sexual ~, one engaging in,
    710.18
dissolvable,adj., 1027.8
dissolve,v., 1027.11
  cause of ~ing, 1027.7
  ~ out, 1027.18
dissolved,adj.
  become ~ and washed away
    by water, 1027.17
  causing ~ state, 1027.6
  combination of ~ substances,
    1027.16
  ~ in a solution, 1027.14
  ~ substance, 1027.15
  unable to be ~, 1027.31,32
distance,n., 788.1
  ~ around, 788.1(1,2)
  ~ arrow is hurled, 566.4
  art of showing ~, 965.6(5)
  astronomical ~, 788.1(6)
  be a ~ from, 788.2

center, ~ from, 788.1(8)
center, ~ through, 788.1(8)
distribution, ~ of, 788.1(9)
equal ~, 788.1(4)
having equal ~s around,
  534.11
horse's step, ~ of, 788.1(13)
measure ~ in walking, instrument to, 107.10
measurement of ~, devices
  for, 788.3
measurement unit of ~ in
  walking, 946.26(15)
~ north or south of the equator, 1004.11
object with illusion of ~,
  965.30
step, ~ of a, 788.1(13)
supports, ~ between,
  788.1(11)
thumb and little finger, ~ between, 788.1(11)
~ traveled by light, 946.26(11,
  16)
unit of ~, 946.26
water ~, unit of, 946.26(14)
distant,adj., 789.1; see also **far**,
  adj.
  more ~, 789.2; see **farther**,
    adj.
  most ~, 789.3–6; see **farthest**,
    adj.
  sea, ~ part of, 788.1(7)
distaste,n., 1117.6
  feel ~ for, 1117.7
distend,v., 518.1,2
distended,adj., 518.4; see **swollen**,adj.
  able to be ~, 518.9
distention,n., 518.3; see also
  swelling,n.
distill,v., 749.28–30
distinct,adj., 598.5,8
  ~ (of colors), 1.20
distinctness,n., 598.6,9
distinction,n., 540.2; see also
  difference,n.
  fine ~s in discussion, 540.16
  having an air or manner of
    ~, 848.24
  make ~s, 540.14
  make ~s, able to, 540.15
  make ~s, unable to, 540.18
  not making ~s, 540.18
distinctive,adj., 1091.12
distinguished,adj., 615.1; see
  famous,adj.
distress,v.
  ~ emotionally, 1130.1
  ~ physically, 1137.1
distribute,v., 231.1; see also
  give,v.
distributed,adj.
  that which is ~, 231.3
distribution,n., 231.2
  distance of ~, 788.1(9)
  fair ~ of land, principles of,
    1003.28,29
district,n., 782.1; see **place**,n.
distrust,n., 639.4
  with ~, 639.9
distrust,v., 639.1
distrustful,adj., 639.3(2,12,23)
  ~ of one's ability, etc.,
    639.3(4)
  ~ of the future, 639.3(2)
disturb,v.
  cause a commotion in,
    1101.5
  ~ emotionally or mentally,
    1132.1,14,17
  ~ in arrangement, order, or
    condition, 1101.10–13
  ~ peace or calm, 1101.9
disturbance,n.

commotion, 1101.1; see also
  commotion, confusion,
  disorder,n.
emotional agitation, 1132.5;
  see also **anxiety, nervousness**,n.
be in a state of emotional ~,
  1132.6
cause or source of emotional
  ~, 1132.3
correction of emotional ~s in
  children, 398.14(4)
emotional or mental ~ on returning home, 753.13
~ of the peace, 1101.1(8,21,22,
  25,34,35,38)
produced by emotional ~,
  809.1(20,21)
radio ~, 1046.5
remove the emotional ~ of,
  1132.10
science dealing with emo-
  tional ~s, 401.1(2,36,44,62,
  82–86)
surgery to correct emotional
  ~, 402.1(18) ; 402.5(23,27,28,
  41)
treatment of emotional ~s,
  400.2(1) ; 400.6(3,16,21,29,37–
  39)
without emotional ~, 1132.9
disturbed,adj.
  able to be emotionally ~,
    1132.11
  be emotionally ~, 1132.6
  become emotionally ~, 1132.7,
    8
  emotionally or mentally ~,
    1132.4; see also **anxious,
    nervous**,adj.
  not easily ~ emotionally,
    1132.12,13
disturbing,adj.
  emotionally or mentally ~,
    1132.2
disuse,n., 284.4
  cause to be in ~, 284.5
  fall into ~, 284.1
  falling into ~, 284.2
  in ~, 284.8–11
ditch,n., 299.1(21,35)
  ~ made by water, 299.1(6,7,21,
    22)
  narrow ~, 299.1(6,7)
  protective ~, 568.30(7,13)
  water-filled ~ for protection,
    568.30(7)
dive,v., 170.16
  ~ for pearls, 963.11
diver,n.
  ~ for pearls, 963.12
diversion,n., 200.2,4,5; see
  amusement,n.
divide,v.
  separate, 325.1,2; see sepa-
    rate,v.
  ~ in half, 929.2
  ~ into five, 934.4
  ~ into four, 933.8
  ~ into parts, 326.8,28
  ~ into pieces, 326.16,19
  ~ into small parts, 326.28
  ~ into three parts, 932.20
  ~ into two parts, 931.8
divided,adj.
  separate or separated, 325.8;
    see separated,adj.
  ~ in half, 929.3
  ~ into eight parts, 937.7
  ~ into five parts, 934.5
  ~ into four, 933.6
  ~ into many parts, 326.53(2)
  ~ into seven parts, 936.6
  ~ into six parts, 935.5
  ~ into ten parts, 938.3

~ into three lobes, 932.21
~ into three parts, 326.53(3);
    932.19
~ into twenty parts, 939.3
~ into two lobes, 931.9
~ into two parts, 931.7
divination,n., 772.3,5,20; see
    prediction,n.
divine,adj., 654.4
both human and ~, 429.8;
    654.4(7)
from ~ power or intervention,
    654.4(6)
science of ~ things, 654.15
divine,v., 772.1,2; see predict,v.
diviner,n., 772.6; see predic-
    tor,n.
divining,n., 772.3,5,20
~ rod, 486.5
divinity,n., 654.5
~ of priestly office, believing
    in, 646.9
speculate about ~, 654.16
division,n.
group, 318.1; see group,n.
part, 326.6,10; see part,n.
separation, 25.3,7; see sep-
    aration,n.
even part in ~, 927.6
full of ~s, 25.1(15)
number in ~, 927.1(7,9–11,20,
    22,24,27)
number remaining after ~,
    927.1(25)
number resulting from ~,
    927.1(24)
~ of closed space, 326.6(2)
~ of man's nature into three
    elements, 932.23
~ sent on special mission,
    326.6(4,5)
uneven part in ~, 927.5
divisional,adj., 318.2; 326.7
divorce,n., 705.1
causing ~, 705.6
~ decrees, 705.7
one named in a ~ action,
    705.8
payment during or after ~,
    219.3(1)
woman in process of ~, 705.5
divorced,adj.
~ person, 705.4
dizziness,n., 606.1
causing ~, 606.2
dizzy,adj., 606.1
be ~, 606.3
become ~, 606.4
feel confused and ~, 606.5
make ~, 606.6
~ woman, 606.7
do,v., 49.1
~ a favor for, 842.9
~ again and again, 49.1(13,23,
    24,27,28,30,32,41)
~ as a business, 49.1(13)
~ as a habit, 49.1(23)
~ as a profession, 49.1(13)
~ as a regular practice,
    49.1(13)
~ awkwardly, 14.4
~ beforehand, 49.1(4)
~ better than, 833.11
~ business, 49.1(38)
~ carelessly, 49.1(33)
~ clumsily, 14.4; 24.1(7)
~ completely, 49.1(6,10–12,14–
    16,21)
~ easily, 26.5
expect to ~, 49.1(3,39)
fail to ~, 73.1; 74.1; 76.1
~ faster than, 95.7
~ hastily, 49.1(33)
~ in a different form, 49.1(27)
~ in anger, 49.1(43)

~ in excess of, 920.10
~ in return, 49.1(31)
~ less than one should,
    49.1(34)
~ more than, 920.16
~ more than duty demands,
    920.15
~ more than necessary,
    49.1(36)
not ~, 73.1; 74.1; 76.1
~ poorly, 49.1(35)
~ quickly, 49.1(11,15)
~ rapidly, 95.6
~ slower, 100.3–5
~ slowly, 100.1,2
~ successfully, 23.9; 49.1(1,2,
    16,41)
~ superficially, 49.1(9)
~ together, 51.1
~ together illegally, 51.1(4,8)
~ together secretly, 51.1(4,7,
    8)
~ too much, 49.1(19,20)
~ unskillfully, 14.4
~ unsuccessfully, 14.4(1);
    24.1(7)
~ what is helpful for, 49.1(17)
~ what is necessary for,
    49.1(17)
~ without delay, 49.1(15)
~ without preparation, 48.9
do away with,v., 286.1; see
    eliminate,v.
dock,n., 1033.10,11,15,17; see
    also wharf, wharves,n.
anchor a ship at a ~, 323.1(5)
fee for tying up at a ~,
    1033.16
doctor,n., 401.2
~ accepted as a specialist,
    623.12(6)
art of the ~, pert. to, 401.5
ear ~, 401.2(7)
eye ~, 401.2(19)
~ for childbirth, 401.2(1,2)
horse ~, 401.2(9)
illegal or improper conduct of
    a ~, 1087.7(2)
~ in legal aspects of insanity,
    401.2(4)
nerve ~, 401.2(18)
oath of a ~, 401.9
prescribed by a ~, 401.6
symbol of a ~, 401.7
unskillful ~, 401.2(21,22)
doctoring,n., 400.2,6; 401.1; see
    medical science, therapy,n.
doctrine,n., 56.1
document,n., 684.4
addition to a ~, 908.21,23,25
ancient ~, 684.4(2)
ancient ~s, science of,
    682.14(1–5)
art of writing legal ~s,
    682.14(6)
~ certifying quality, value,
    good character, etc., 850.13
false ~, 820.15
forged ~, 820.15
~ giving authority, 5.15(4)
handwritten ~, 684.4(1)
~ of approval, 850.13
~ of permission, 554.8
~s that cause confidence or
    belief, 632.28
doer,n., 49.3; 52.4
leading ~, 51.6
superficial ~, 49.3(1)
~ with others, 51.4
dog,n., 407.1
attack (of ~s), 560.1(5,24)
baby ~, 407.4
female ~, 407.2
group of ~s, 403.5(40,51)
group of three ~s, 932.7

house for ~s, 403.22(23)
hunting ~, 407.6
kindness to ~s, 407.8
like a ~, 407.7
member of ~ family, 407.9–17
~ of mixed breed, 407.3
pert. to ~s, 407.7
rat-catching ~, 407.5
set ~s on, 560.1(24)
set ~s on to annoy, 874.1(2)
small ~, 909.4(8)
three-headed mythical ~,
    568.5(3)
young ~, 407.4
dogmatic,adj., 633.17
dogwood,n.
of the ~ family, 985.33(7)
doing,adj.
~ together, 51.3
doing,n., 49.2
act of ~ somethng in the fine
    arts, 49.2(1)
continue ~, 754.19
descr. of ~, 49.4
~ together, 51.2
doll,n.
~ used in performance, 969.40
dollar,n., 213.1,2; see money,n.
thousand ~s, 940.30
dolphin,n., 423.5
dome,n., 973.1; see roof,n.
~-shaped, 507.17(34)
dominate,v.
be higher or taller than,
    164.7; 515.4; 1071.7
control, 8.1
have power over, 5.6
dominated,adj.
state of being ~, 22.45
domination,n.
control, 8.2
power, 5.4
bring under ~, 22.43
conquest and ~, 22.44
domineer,v., 8.8
domineering,adj., 8.11
domino,n.
~ of four pips, 933.14
~ of three pips, 932.10,11
~ of two pips, 931.27
done,adj., 49.9
~ after some other act, 49.8
~ by both parties, 51.5(1,4,
    5,7)
~ by many together, 51.5(2,
    4–8)
~ by three together, 51.5(8)
capable of being ~, 49.5
~ in co-operation, 51.5
that which has been ~, 49.6;
    814.1(2)
that which is ~, 49.6
things to be ~, 49.10(7)
~ together, 51.5
~ without preparation, 48.10
donkey,n., 409.1
like a ~, 409.2
door,n., 133.7
crosspiece between window
    and ~way, 1009.16
~keeper, 133.8
~ opener, 133.10
doorway,n.
side of a ~, 1009.13
dot,n., 501.3
~ over a letter, 680.1(26)
dot,v., 501.2
dotted,adj., 501.1
double,adj., 931.14
double,n.
similar person or thing,
    529.3
ghostly or fictional ~,
    529.3(4)
double,v., 931.12,13

doubt,n., 639.2,4
  a feeling of ~, 640.6(1)
  condition or situation of ~, 640.10
  express or show ~ about, 639.13
  expressing ~, 639.8
  gesture of ~, 102.1(10)
  indicating ~, 639.8
  open to ~, 639.10
doubt,v., 639.1,13
doubter,n., 639.5
doubtful,adj., 639.3,10; 640.1,5
dove,n., 405.1(4)
  like a ~, 405.10
  of ~s, 405.9(5)
  shelter for ~s, 405.11(4–6)
down,n.
  hair, 369.1(18,21); see hair,n.
  covered with ~, 369.6(4,9,12–15,20,21)
  having hair like ~, 369.11(3)
  like ~, 369.10(4,5)
down,adv.
  come ~, 167.1
  get ~ from, 167.10
  get ~ off, 167.10
  go ~, 167.1
  lying ~ in rest, 65.3(12)
  lying face ~, 65.3(9–11)
  move ~, 167.1
  move up and ~, 162.1,2
  press ~, 198.1(2,12)
  push ~, 197.1(7,29,37,53)
  slope ~, 154.1(6–10,13)
  sloping ~, 154.4(2,4,5)
  straight up and ~, 180.1(5–8,13)
  throw ~, 187.1(38)
downward,adj.
  ~ slope, 154.3(2–4,6)
downy,adj., 369.6(4,7,9,12,13,14, 15,20,21); 369.10(5,7)
dowry,n.
  furnish a ~ to, 233.1(6)
dozen,n., 940.1; see twelve,n.
  twelve ~, 940.26
  one hundred forty-four ~, 940.39
draft,n.
  piece of writing, 682.3
  sketch, 965.1
  rough ~ in writing, 682.3(19)
draft,v.
  force into armed services, 3.3(13,15)
  sketch, 965.2
  write, 682.1
drafting,n.
  sketching, 965.4,13
  skill in ~, 965.13
drag,v., 193.1; see pull,v.
drama,n., 969.1,2; see also performance (theatrical),n.
  actor in a ~, 969.3
  amateur ~, 969.26
  art of producing ~, 969.20
  art of the ~, 965.6(2)
  art of writing ~, 969.19
  ~ as a display of talent, communication of theme or idea, etc., 969.1(49)
  category of ~, 969.2
  descr. of horror ~, 969.9(1)
  interval between acts of a ~, 969.13
  musical ~, 969.1(11,25–30,38, 48)
  part in a ~, 969.10,14
  parts or divisions of a ~, 969.34
  performance of ~, 969.1
  pert. to ~, 969.9
  presentation of ~, 969.1
  ~s put on, 969.16

science of writing ~, 969.19
sensational or **excessively sentimental** ~, 969.1(19)
  travel to put on ~s, 969.17
  words of a ~, 969.14
  writer of ~, 969.8,19
dramatic,adj., 969.9
  ~ part, 969.10,11,14
  ~ productions by amateurs, 969.26
  ~ works, 969.25
dramatist,n., 685.5; 969.8,19
dramatize,v., 969.7
drape,n.
  ornament with ~s, 959.1(22)
  ~s, collectively, 972.19
draw,v.
  ~ in a contest, 20.10
draw,v.
  pull, 193.1; see pull,v.
  ~ a line around, 965.37
  ~ (a picture, etc.), 965.2,3
  ~ a sword, knife, etc., 193.18(24)
  ~ back, 145.1
  ~ back in fear, 145.1(3,4,6–9, 11,17,19,25,27,28)
  ~ back in pain, 145.1(7)
  ~ forth, 193.18(8,9,26)
  ~ near to each other, 790.12, 13
  ~ off, 193.18(1,8,11,12,20)
  ~ out, 193.18
  ~ tight, 193.18(21,22)
  ~ together, 193.13
  ~ up, i.e., write, 682.1; see write,v.
  ~ with charcoal, 1064.43
drawing,n.
  a ~, 965.1(6,7,12–14,17,27,28, 39,50,56); see also picture,n.
  amusing ~, 965.1(7)
  amusing ~s in newspaper or magazine, 965.38
  animated ~s in motion pictures, 968.13
  art of ~, 965.6; 965.6(2–4)
  art of ~ with chalk, crayons or soft paste, 965.6(1)
  ~ by copying, 965.1(56)
  ~ of the lines of something, 965.1(56)
  ~ on metal, 965.1(21)
dread,n., 576.2; see fear,n.
dreadful,adj., 576.7
dream,n., 71.1
  a place in a ~, 1057.15
  as in ~s, 809.1(20)
  day–~, 71.6–9
  frightening ~, 71.2
  interpreter of ~s, 607.20(2)
  like a ~, 71.3
dreamy,adj., 71.3,4
  be in a ~ mood, 1056.17
  lost in ~ thought, 585.4(1–4)
  ~ state, 71.5
  ~ thinking, 585.15
dress,n., 974.1; see also clothing,n.
  bottom of a ~, 982.10
  close-fitting ~, 982.1(12)
  ~ for entertaining at home, 982.1(4)
  ~ for evening wear, 975
  ~ for masked party or dance, 970.28
  formal ~, 975.1,2,4,7,8
  low neckline of a ~, 982.6
  put a ~ on, 982.2,3
  riding ~, 982.1(3)
  semi-formal ~, 975.3,5,6
  torn and ragged ~, person in, 903.12
  untidy ~, 903.1(1,2,5,6,8–12,

15,16–18,20,21,23–25)
  upper part of a ~, 982.8
  waist of a ~, 982.9
  wearing a ~, 982.4
  ~ with low neckline, descr. of, 982.5,7
  ~ with low neckline, 982.4(1)
  woman's ~, 982.1
  work ~, 982.1(5)
dress,v., 974.2; 982.2,3; see clothe,v.
  article or substance used in ~ing, 974.18,19
  container for ~ing articles or substances, 974.20
  garment worn while ~ing, 974.43
  ~ oneself, 974.3
  ~ oneself in, 974.10,40; 982.3
  ~ oneself in (quality, air, attitude, etc.), 974.11
  process of ~ing, 974.15,16
  room for ~ing, 787.7(8); 974.29
  table for ~ing, 974.17
dressed,adj., 974.4; see clothed, adj.
dressmaker,n., 205.5(4,5)
dried,adj., 1038.4
  ~ by air, 1045.17
  ~ by heat or fire, 1064.40
  ~ by weather, 1047.9
drink,n., 748.4,5
  able to be filled with ~, as a person, 925.24
  alcoholic ~, 748.15; 749.3,4; see also liquor (alcoholic),n.
  ~ and play, 748.16
  be entertained with ~, 734.6
  bedtime ~, 748.5(5)
  brewed ~, 749.7(4)
  cooling ~, 1058.18
  delicious ~, 748.5(4)
  fill (a person) with ~, 925.22
  fill (oneself) with ~, 925.23
  filled with ~, as a person, 925.20
  fruit ~, 748.5(9)
  full of ~, as a person, 925.20
  gas, containing (of ~s), 1048.34
  gas into ~s, put, 1048.33
  give a ~ to animals, 1026.7
  gods' ~, 748.5(4)
  lime ~, 748.5(8)
  liquor, ~ following, 748.5(3)
  ~ of liquor, 748.15; 749.3,4
  ~ of magic effect, 748.5(6)
  ~ of medicine, 748.5(6)
  ~ of poison, 748.5(6)
  ~s, 748.6
  small amount of ~, 917.8
  stimulating ~, 748.5(2)
  ~ that gives strength, 1.34
  unable to be filled with ~, as a person, 925.25
drink,v., 748.1
  ~ a toast to, 748.1(13); 748.12(15,18); 856.11
  ~ alcoholic beverages, 748.12
  ~ from the breast, 360.13
  ~ to excess, 1107.24
  ~ to point of nausea or disgust, 1107.24
  ~ to the health or success of, 748.1(13); 748.12(15,18)
  ~ with pleasure, 1105.12
drinkable,adj., 748.7
drinker,n., 748.3
  liquor ~, 748.14
drinking,n., 748.2
  ~ bout, 748.17
  ~ cup, 261.8
  fountain for ~, 748.8; 1033.46

~ glass, 261.8
hatred of ~, 880.17(1)
immoderation in ~ liquor, 748.18
moderate in ~ or eating, 923.1(1)
~ of liquor, 748.13
~ party, 748.17
pert. to ~ with others, 734.16
social ~, disposition toward, 748.19
social ~, pert. to, 748.20
toasts made in ~, 748.21
drive,v., 106.1; see also push,v.
~ a carriage, 192.13
~ a cycle, 192.18
~ a motor vehicle, 192.7
~ a ship onto the shore, 1029.94
~ a sled, 192.21
~ a taxi, 192.7
~ away, 144.1
~ (birds) out of concealment, 970.40
~ by laughter, 1111.28
~ forward, 106.1(8,9)
~ into piles, 106.1(3)
~ out, 106.1(2,4); 144.1
~ out of a country, 144.1(1,3, 5,17,19,22)
~ out of hiding, 144.1(8); 970.39; 1050.25
~ out with smoke, 1050.25
pert. to ~ing, 192.29
~ up a tree, 996.23
driven,adj.
be ~ along, 106.5,6
bird ~ out of cover, 106.7
driver,n.
automobile ~, 192.8
camel ~, 205.1(3,4)
carriage ~, 192.14
cycle ~, 192.19
elephant ~, 205.1(10)
fast ~, 192.27
motor-vehicle ~, 192.8
mule ~, 205.1(11)
~ of a ferry, 115.10
sled ~, 192.22
streetcar ~, 192.11
taxi ~, 192.8
train ~, 192.26
truck ~, 190.3; 192.8
driving,adj., 106.3
~ force, 106.2,4
drop,n., 918.1
blowing ~s, 918.4
come out in ~s, 918.9
fall in ~s, 167.1(12–14,35–37, 43,45); 918.9
fall of ~s, 167.2
falling ~, 918.2
falling ~s, 918.4
fine ~s of rain, 918.8
flow in ~s, 918.9
let fall, flow, or come out in ~s, 918.10
liquid in ~, 918.5
~ of liquid, etc., 918.1
~ of rain, 1037.13
pour in ~s, 1036.7,9,15
pouring in ~s, 1036.10,12
rain in ~s, 918.12
sound of ~s, 918.11
splashed ~s, 918.3
spraying fine ~s, instrument for, 1036.13
that which comes, falls, etc., in ~s, 918.6,7
drop,v.
come down, out, etc., in drops, 918.9
decrease, 910.1,2; see decrease,v., 910.1,2
fall, 167.1; see fall,v.

fall or flow in drops, 918.9
cause to ~, 167.4
let ~, 167.4
~ like ice particles, 1040.4
~ like rain, 1037.8
~ like snow, 1039.9
~ off, 167.1(33)
dropping,adj., 167.3
dropping,n., 167.2
~ a ~ of a bodily part, 167.2(6)
dropsy,n., 396.1(10)
drowning,n.
slaughter by ~, 796.2(10)
drug,n., 398.4; 399.7; see also cure, medication, medicine, narcotic,n.
~ addict, 399.13
addiction to ~s, 399.12
art of compounding ~s, 399.1(1,6)
book of ~s, 399.6
container for ~s, 261.1(22)
~ from a plant, 985.29
illness from ~s, 399.15
kept in stock (of a ~), 399.4
liquid medium for ~s, 1027.1(5)
liquid solution of a ~, 1027.1(7)
measurement of ~s, 946.20
method for compounding ~s, 50.1(25)
pert. to ~s, 398.5(2); 399.2
place where ~s are kept, 399.5
science of ~s, 399.1(2–5)
slavery to ~s, 629.27
specific ~s, 398.6,8
student of ~s, 399.3
weight in ~s, 947.32,33
weight system in ~s, 947.31(1)
drug,v., 399.9
drugged,adj., 399.11
~ state, 399.10
druggist,n., 399.3
kept in stock by a ~, 399.4
drugstore,n., 399.5
drum,n.
musical instrument, 479.8(3, 26–32); 479.11(2)
play a ~, 479.10
player of ~s, 479.9
signal on ~s, 956.1(11,12)
sounds of beating a ~, 469.7(16,25,27,29,30,37,39)
drunk,adj., 749.46,50
brave when ~, 575.1(3)
make ~, 749.51
not ~, 749.61
one who is ~, 749.48
one who is habitually ~, 749.49
drunkard,n., 749.49
drunkenness,n., 749.47
~ from sleep, 67.14
dry,adj., 1038.4,12
become ~, 1038.2
having ~ shoes, 1038.13
~ in weather, 1037.30
make ~, 1038.1
~ weather, 1037.31
dry,v., 1038.1,2
~ and shrink, 1038.1(8,13,14)
~ bricks, pottery, etc., 1061.15
~ by air, 1045.16
~ by sunlight, 1055.23
drying,adj., 1038.5
drying,n., 1038.3
agent for ~, 1038.6
cause of ~, 1038.6
dryness,n.
agent that causes ~, 1038.6
causing ~, 1038.5
~ of skin, eyes, etc., 1038.8
duck,n.
female ~, 405.3(2)

group of ~s, 403.5(64,68,70)
male ~, 405.2(5)
walk like a ~, 107.1(58)
young ~, 405.4(5)
duel,n., 562.1(1,19,28)
challenge to a ~, 545.3
first crossing of swords in ~, 562.3(1)
rules for ~s, 562.6
duel,v., 562.2(3); see fight,v.
dueler,n., 562.4
dull,adj., 336.1
not sharp, 336.1
not shiny, 1072.1,8
stupid, 597.1; see stupid,adj.
uninteresting, 583.1; see uninteresting,adj.
~ and lifeless, 794.49
become ~, 1072.3
emotionally ~, 1093.2; 1097.3
~ finish, 1072.5
~ in flavor, 446.18,19
make ~, 336.2; 1072.2
mentally ~, 597.1
~ of understanding, 597.6
~ sounds, 462.13,14
~ statement, 674.9(3,5,7,8,11, 18,28,30)
~ surface, 1072.5
~ thing, 1072.4
dull,v., 336.2; 1072.2
~ the emotions, senses, or reactions, 1097.13
~ the mind, 597.20; 1097.13
dulled,adj.
mentally ~, 597.21
dullness,n.
~ of mind, 597.2,4,18,22
~ of the senses, 435.1
dumb,adj.
mute, 454.23; 475.1; 671.21; see also silent,adj.
stupid, 597.1,6,10,19; see stupid,adj.
unspoken, 475.1(18,21,22); 475.8,10; 607.6
dupe,n., 823.24,25
dust,n.
cloud of ~, 1001.1; 1057.18
consisting of ~, 1001.8
cover that protects book against ~, 1001.16
covered with ~, 1001.8
crumbling into ~, 1001.7
decay to ~, 1001.6
grind to ~, 438.8(2,6)
like ~, 1001.9
of the color of ~, 1001.15
particles of ~, 1001.2
speck of ~, 501.3(4)
sprinkle with ~, 1001.11
suspension of ~ in air, 1041.1(2)
turn to ~, 1001.3,6
whirlwind of ~, 1042.27(3)
windstorm of ~, 1001.17,18
wipe the ~ from, 1001.10
Dutchman,n., 784.15(17)
dutiful,adj., 528.5
duty,n., 528.1
be necessary as a ~, 273.7
burden of ~, 948.14(3,12,14)
call to ~, 693.1(15)
do more than ~ demands, 920.15
express thinking about moral ~ or behavior, 843.8,9
failure in one's ~, 528.6
failure to meet financial ~, 528.8
free of ~, 309.11(1,22,23,26–28)
freedom from ~, 309.14(14)
from a sense of ~, 528.4
~ imposed by promise, 1122.9

more than ~ demands, 920.14
neglect of ~, 528.6,7
neglect of official ~, 1087.7(6)
place of ~, 782.1(19,30)
place under ~ by promise, 1122.49
required by ~, 528.2
resting on one as a ~, 528.3
science of ~, 528.9
science of moral ~, 843.4
theory of ~, 528.9
dwarf,n., 909.3(3,4,6,7,12,16)
make into a ~, 909.6(1,4)
dwell,v., 750.1; see live,v.
dweller,n., 750.4; see inhabitant,n.
dwelling,n., 753.1; see home, house,n.
dye,n., 488.22
dye,v., 488.15,16
dyeing,n.
pert. to ~, 488.19
dying,adj., 794.33
~ eventually, 794.31
never ~, 755.7,8; see also immortal,adj.
~ together, 794.32
dying,n., 794.1; see death,n.
keep from ~ out, 755.12
dynamite,n., 802.12
user of ~, 802.14
dynamite,v., 802.10

E

eager,adj., 265.19
anxiously ~, 265.19(9)
~ expectation, 268.6
~ expectation, be in a state of, 268.11
make ~, 265.22
~ person, 265.21
ready and ~, 265.19(8)
sincere and ~, 265.19(14)
~ to taste, 265.19(7)
eagerness,n., 265.20
eagle,n.
like an ~, 405.10
nest of an ~, 405.11(1)
of ~s, 405.8(1,10); 405.9(3)
young ~, 405.4(6)
young ~s, 405.5(1)
ear,n., 362.1
around the ~, 362.3(10)
cause ~s to stick out, 958.10
cleanser for the ~, 899.5(2)
combination of symptoms in the middle ~, 955.3
different effect on each ~, having, 362.3(5)
~ doctor, 401.2(7)
external parts of the ~, 362.2
having ~s, 362.4
having droopy ~s, 362.4(4)
having two ~s, 362.4(3)
inflammation of bone behind the ~, 354.16(1)
inflammation of the ~, 352.7
middle ~, 362.6
near the ~, 362.3(9)
originating in the ~, 362.3(8)
pain in the ~, 1137.56(12)
pert. to both ~s, 362.3(4)
pert. to the ~, 362.3(1,2,6,7)
science of the ~, 401.1(66–68)
~ trumpet, 454.21
use of two ~s, involving, 362.3(3)
eardrum,n.
inflammation of the ~, 362.8
earlier,adj.
exist ~, 766.4,5
make ~, 766.3
earliest,adj., 766.6

in ~ stage of development, 733.9
in the ~ stages, 729.15
pert. to ~ growth, 731.11
early,adj., 766.1
assigning dates that are too ~, 774.12,15
~ growth, 731.9(1,7,11,14)
~ in development, 766.1(2)
~ in history of a movement, art, science, etc., 766.1(3)
in the ~ stages, 729.15
~ morning, 775.2–5
too ~, 29.3(68); 765.7
early,adv., 766.2
earnest,adj., 610.1; see serious, adj.
earth,n.
soil, 999.1; see also soil,n.
the planet, 1004.1; see also world,n.
below surface of the ~, 1004.29
born on or of the ~, 720.9(13)
boundary between ~ and sky, 1051.9
center, the ~ as, 1004.20
center of the ~, 137.1(6)
characteristic of the ~, 1004.17
coming from the ~, 1004.18
cover with ~, 972.1(5)
crust of the ~, 1004.4
depths of the ~, 1004.30
description of ~ phenomena, 1004.48
distance east on the ~, 1004.12
distance north on the ~, 1004.11
distance south on the ~, 1004.11
distance west on the ~, 1004.12
earliest days of the ~, 762.1(4) ; 763.1,2
east circle of the ~, 1004.14
eating of ~, 734.26(4)
fine ~ deposited as sediment, 757.11(4)
forces inside the ~, 1004.21,22
~ formations caused by water action, 1004.45
gas around the ~, 1048.1(1)
half of the ~, 1004.5(6)
inhabitant of the ~, 1004.31
interior of the ~, 1004.3
like the ~, 1004.26
map of ~'s surface, room for viewing, 1004.47
mathematics of ~'s surface, 943.1(3)
north circle of the ~, 1004.13
not of the ~, 1004.19
occurrences inside the ~, 1004.21,22
opening in the ~, 298.9
opposite ends of the ~, 792.8
outside the ~, 138.1(13)
pert. to the ~, 1004.16
pert. to the whole ~, 1004.28
representation of early conditions of the ~, 1004.46
rooted to the ~, 1004.23
science of the ~, 1004.43; 1053.36(6)
solid ~, 999.1(13)
solid part of the ~, 1004.4
south circle of the ~, 1004.13
surface form or figure of the ~, 1004.27
thrust of the ~'s crust, 1004.49
toward the ~, 1004.24,25
west circle of the ~, 1004.14

zones of the ~, 1004.5,10
earthenware,n., 261.11
art of making ~, 261.14
fragment of ~, 326.10(17,22)
manufacture of ~, 261.12,13
pert. to ~, 261.13
~ with fine cracks, 802.20
earthly,adj., 1004.38,41
make ~, 1004.42
not ~, 1004.39
~ rather than religious or sacred, 1004.41
earthquake,n., 1005.1; 1101.1(7)
caused by ~, 1005.7
causing ~s, 1005.13
description of ~, 1005.11,12
earth features related to ~s, pert. to, 1005.14
equal strength of ~s, pert. to, 1005.5
instrument to measure or detect ~s, 1005.9
jar caused by ~s, 1005.4
list of ~s, 1005.11
phenomena of ~s, 1005.6
record of ~, 1005.10
science of ~s, 1005.8
strong ~, 1005.3
subject to ~s, 1005.7
treatise on ~s, 682.15(21)
weak ~, 1005.2
earthworm,n., 427.1
ease,n., 26.3
careless ~, 26.3(1)
~ of action, 26.3(3)
~ of movement, 26.3(3)
~ of touch, 26.3(3)
ease,v., 1142.1,10; see also weaken,v.
east,adj.
~ circle of earth, 1004.14
~ distance on earth, 1004.12
east,n.
countries of the ~ or Far East, 784.4(3)
face the ~, 179.2(1)
inhabitant of the ~, 179.13
inhabitant of the Far ~, 784.15(45)
place so as to face the ~, 179.3
point to the ~, 179.2(1)
turn to the ~, 148.1(14)
East Indies,n.
ruler of ~, 1073.36(23)
Easter,n., 209.16
pert. to ~, 209.17
eastern,adj., 179.12
~ direction, 179.14
~ inhabitant, 179.13; 784.15(45)
Easternize,v., 784.10(7)
easy,adj., 26.1
deceptively ~, 823.10
~ in movements, 90.3,4
~ job, 26.4
makes (something) ~, 26.2
~ movements, 90.1,2
easygoing,adj., 890.12
eat,v., 734.1
~ away, 801.20
~ grass, 734.4
~ greedily, 734.1(2,11,15,16–20,29,36)
not ~, 734.21–25
place where people ~, 741.3
~ sparingly, 734.1(12) ; 734.23–25
~ to excess, to point of disgust or nausea, 1107.23,24
~ with pleasure, 1105.12
eatable,adj., 734.17
eatable,n., 740.1; see food,n.
eaten,adj.
worm-~, 427.17

eater,n., 734.3
greedy ~, 734.3; 734.3(1)
~ of dead flesh, matter, etc.,
734.31
~ of humans, 734.30
~ of specific foods, 734.28
~ of vegetables and milk
only, 734.28(1)
~s of specific foods, 734.29
eating,adj.
~ ants, 734.27(19)
~ bees, 734.27(2)
~ berries, 734.27(3)
~ blood, 734.27(29)
~ books, 734.27(5)
~ bread, 734.27(24)
~ crabs, 734.27(6)
~ dead or decaying flesh,
734.27(9,20,30)
~ decaying matter, 734.27(9,
20,30)
~ everything, 734.9
~ fish, 734.27(26)
~ frogs, 734.27(4)
~ fruits, 734.27(8,11)
~ grains, 734.27(13,14)
~ grasses, 734.27(12)
~ horseflesh, 734.27(10)
~ human flesh, 734.27(1,15)
~ insects, 734.27(17)
~ lizards, 734.27(31)
~ many foods, 734.27(27)
~ meat, 734.27(7,22)
~ nuts, 734.27(21)
~ plants, 734.27(14,22,25)
~ roots, 734.27(28)
~ seeds, 734.27(13,32)
~ serpents, 734.27(23)
~ sparingly, 734.24,25
~ specific foods, 734.27; see
also under eating,n., below
~ with others, 734.12
~ wood, 734.27(16,18,34)
~ worms, 734.27(33)
eating,n., 734.2
art of good ~, 734.19(2)
aversion to ~, 737.9
enjoyer of ~, 734.13
enjoyment of ~, 734.15
excessive ~, 734.2(4)
fit for ~, 734.17
fond of ~, 734.14
fondness for ~, 734.15
greedy in ~, 734.8
illness from excessive ~,
734.11
immoderate in ~, 734.10
implements used in ~, 332.10
interested in ~, 737.1(4); see
also hungry,adj.
moderate in ~, 923.1(1)
~ of a god, 734.26(10)
~ of earth or clay, 734.26(4)
~ of feces, 734.26(3,9)
~ of filth, 734.26(9)
~ of fish, 734.26(6)
~ of hair, 734.26(11)
~ of horseflesh, 734.26(5)
~ of human flesh, 734.26(1,2)
~ of one's own species,
734.26(2)
~ of plant life or vegetables
exclusively, 734.26(12)
~ of plants, 734.26(8)
~ of raw flesh, 734.26(7)
~ of specific foods, 734.26–
29; see also under eating,
adj., above
~ of vegetables, 734.26(12)
pert. to ~ with others, 734.16
place for ~ in a monastery or
convent, 741.3(8)
pleasures of ~, devoted to,
1105.8(1)
rapid ~, 734.2(5)

refrain from ~, 734.21–25
science of ~, 734.19,20
system of ~ to improve
health, 740.10–13
time of ~ and celebration,
734.7
treatise on ~, 682.15(23)
unfit for ~, 734.18
eccentric,adj., 536.1,4
~ person, act, etc., 536.2,5
eccentricity,n., 536.2
echo,n., 471.1
echo,v., 471.2,3
echoing,adj., 471.5
echoing,n., 471.4
eclipse,n.
~ of moon, 1055.19
~ of sun, 1055.18
economical,adj., 226.1
be ~, 226.3
spend ~ly, 224.1(4)
use ~ly, 279.1(20)
economics,n., 216.10
economize,v., 226.3
economy,n., 226.2
~ of language, 665.9(8,15,16,
39,48,51,53)
edge,n., 793.20
be on the ~ of, figuratively,
793.25
cup's ~, 793.20(1)
decorative ~, 793.20(4)
dish ~, 793.20(1)
fabric's ~, 793.20(5)
form an ~, 793.23
hat's ~, 793.20(1)
having an ~, 793.21
lower ~ of a roof, 973.8
ornament the ~ of, 959.1(23,
26)
ornamental ~ on silver,
1015.18
provide with an ~, 793.24
raised ~ around roof opening, 973.7
road's ~, 793.20(6)
rough ~, 793.20(3)
scallop-shaped (of ~s),
507.17(22)
sharp ~ of, 334.1(9,12,20)
top ~, 793.20(1,2)
edible,adj., 734.17
edible,n., 740.1; see food,n.
edit,v., 682.9
editor,n., 691.4
educate,v., 621.1; see teach,v.
educated,adj., 621.11
learned, 622.14; see learned,
adj.
well-~ class, 621.14
education,n., 621.3,4; see also
teaching,n.
get practical ~ in, 622.1(8)
one's ~, 621.4
outdoor adult ~, 621.17
pert. to ~, 621.6
pert. to adult ~, 622.4(2,5)
pert. to higher ~, 621.6(1)
system of spiritual ~, 621.15
educational,adj., 621.5,6
educator,n., 621.7; see also
teacher,n.
eel,n.
like an ~, 422.2(2)
eerie,adj., 662.1; see also
ghostly, supernatural,adj.
mysterious, 604.1(32,39,52,55)
strange, 536.1
supernatural, 662.1
unnatural, 811.11
effect,n., 16.1
doctrine of ~, 15.10
dropping in ~, 17.1(1,2)
emotional ~, 1099
emotional ~, cause of, 1099.14

extent of ~, 787.3
in ~ but not in fact, 16.21
lacking in ~, 17.1
pert. to ~, 15.8
power to produce ~, 5.1(5,6,
8,19)
powerful in ~, 16.13
producing desired ~, 16.11
productive of ~, 16.11
put into ~, 16.23,25
serious in ~, though in-
conspicuous, hidden, etc.,
971.12
effective,adj., 16.11
capable of becoming ~, 16.19
make ~, 16.22
provide the means to make ~,
50.8(2)
effectiveness,n., 16.12
lose ~, 17.4
that which falls off in ~, 17.3
effectual,adj., 16.11; see effective,adj., above
effeminacy,n., 707.10
effeminate,adj., 707.9
become ~, 707.13
make ~, 707.12
~ man or boy, 707.11
efficiency,n., 7.1; see also
skill,n.
Russian, system of ~, 726.7
efficient,adj., 7.2; see also
skillful,adj.
make ~, 7.12
effort,n., 18.2; see also
attempt,n.
violent and sudden ~, 4.10
egg,n., 380.1
be born from an ~, 720.7(2,3)
bee's ~s, 428.4(2)
carrying ~s, 380.8
covering of ~, 972.4(19)
developed from one ~, 721.6
developed from two ~, 721.7
discharge of ~ from ovary,
380.9
examine ~s, 380.11
fertilized ~, 380.1(1,2,4)
fish ~s, 380.2(3,4); 422.6
give birth from ~s, 717.14(1,
11,12,17)
insect ~, 380.1(3)
~-laying organ of insects,
379.1(14)
like an ~, 380.7
louse ~, 380.1(3)
oyster ~s, 422.6
place where ~s are hatched,
403.22(17)
production of an ~, 380.9
~s, 380.2
~s in a nest, 380.2(2)
science of bird's ~s, 380.10
shaped like an ~, 380.6;
507.17(54)
sturgeon ~s, 380.2(1)
tube carrying ~s, 379.1(13)
white of an ~, 380.3
yellow of an ~, 380.4,5
egoism,n., 228.3
egotism,n., 228.3
Egypt,n.
ruler of ancient ~,
1073.14(21); 1073.36(15)
science of ancient ~, 759.26
27
Egyptian,adj.
key to ~ hieroglyphics, 601 9
science of ancient ~ writings
or inscriptions, 682.14(4)
treatise on ancient ~ writings or inscriptions,
682.15(7)
eight, n. or adj., 937.1
consisting of ~, 937.4

consisting of ~ parts, 937.7
divided into ~ parts, 937.7
group of ~, 937.3
happening every ~ days, 937.6
in groups of ~, 937.5
multiply by ~, 937.10
of ~ elements or units, 937.8
pert. to the number ~, 937.2
the number ~, 937.1
~ times as great, 937.12
eightfold,adj., 937.9
increase ~, 907.9(4)
eighty,n., 940.18
~-year-old person, 758.2(5)
elastic,adj., 110.5-7
elbow,n., 339.8
with the ~s pointing outward, 60.7
elder,adj., 759.20; see older,adj.
elderly,adj., 759.1; see old,adj.
eldest,adj., 759.22; see oldest, adj.
elect,v., 252.8; see also choose,v.
having the power to ~, 252.8
election,n., 252.2,5; see also choice,n.
electrical,adj., 1066.9
center of ~ charge, 137.1(5)
~ conductor, 1066.7
~ pole, 1066.6
~ power from water, 1066.3
electricity,n., 1066
activate by ~, 1066.10
apply ~ to, 1066.15
atmospheric ~, 1046.5
chemical ~, 1066.3
equip with ~, 1066.16
flow of ~, 1066.1
~ from water, 1066.3
magnetism by ~, 1066.18
measurement of ~, 1066.22
measurement of ~, instrument for, 1066.21
movement by or of ~, 1066.14
negative particle of ~, 1066.5
pert. to ~, 1066.8
pert. to flow of ~, 1066.13
pert. to ~ in motion, 1066.11
pert. to ~ not in motion, 1066.12
pole of ~, 1066.6
produced by, or producing, ~, 1066.9,13
science of ~, 1066.19,20
surgery by ~, 1066.24
therapy by ~, 1066.23
time before ~, 1048.26
unit of ~, 1066.4
worker with ~, 1066.17
elegy,n., 689.2; see poem,n.
express sadness in an ~, 1125.21
write an ~, 1125.22
writer of an ~, 1125.23
elephant,n., 417.1
baby ~, 417.3
driver of an ~, 205.1(10)
group of ~s, 403.5(34)
keeper of ~s, 205.1(10)
like an ~, 417.4,6
male ~, 417.2
of ~s, 403.11(16)
of the ~ order, 417.5
pert. to ~s, 417.6
prehistoric ~, 417.1(1,2)
elevate,v., 163.1; see raise,v.
elevation,n., 163.1; 164.2; see height,n.
elevator,n., 163.4
~ car, 163.5
~ passage, 122.1(22,32)
elf,n., 662.7; see fairy,n.
eliminate,v., 286.1
~ by biting, 735.6

~ from or in the body, 287.1
~ written matter, 286.1(4,5, 13–15,23,25,29,38,44,55,59); 286.7
eliminated,adj.
able to be ~, 286.5
something ~, 286.3
unable to be ~, 286.6
elimination,n., 286.2
~ from the body, 287.2
~ through psychoanalysis, 286.2(1)
eliminative,adj., 286.4
elk,n.
group of ~, 403.5(32)
ellipse,n.
shaped like an ~, 508.11
elm,n.
of the ~ family, 996.24
elocution,n., 671.14–16; see also speech,n.
elusive,adj., 244.8
~ and delicate, 11.1(12)
embarrass,v., 868.10,19
embarrassed,adj., 868.12,20–22, 25
embarrassing,adj., 868.14,24,25
~ happening, 29.6(14)
~ situation, 25.9(4); 542.16
embarrassment,n., 868.11,15,23
cause ~, 868.10,19
cause of ~, 868.15,26
causing ~, 868.14,24,25
free of ~, 309.11(13)
showing ~, 868.12,20–22,25
source of ~, 868.26
turn red from ~, 873.9
twist around in ~, 156.1(26, 35)
embezzle,v., 250.1(12); see also steal,v.
embezzled,adj.
~ goods at sea, 250.5(4)
embezzlement,n., 250.2
~ at sea, 250.2(10)
embezzler,n., 250.3
emblem,n., 951.4(2,6,11,15,23)
description of ~s, 951.11
designer of ~s, 951.10
Indian ~, 954.1(13)
primitive ~, 954.1(13)
producer of ~s, 951.10
publisher's ~ in a book, 687.9(4)
represent by ~, 953.2
~s of office, rank, etc., 951.9
~s of royalty, 951.9
study of ~s, 951.11
embodied,adj., 338.13
embodiment,n., 338.14,15
embody,v., 338.15
embrace,v.
hug, 257.1(3,5,8,14)
include, 259.1; see include,v.
embryo,n., 721.8
germ layers of an ~, 315.2
science of ~s, 751.13(6)
eminent,adj., 615.1; see famous,adj.
emotion,n., 1092.1,2
affect the ~, power to, 1099.9
affect with (an ~), 1099.22
animal-like in ~s, 1097.7–10
appreciation of ~s of others, 1092.76–78
ascribe one's ~ to others, 1092.87
ascription of ~ to inanimate objects, 1092.84,85
attack of ~, 560.24(1,15)
base ~s, marked by, 1092.33
be or become aroused (of ~s), 1099.19
become excited (of ~s), 1092.50

become excited by ~, 1092.49
capable of ~, 1092.101
capacity for ~, 1092.23
carried away by ~, 1092.26; 1099.15
carried away by a foolish ~, 1092.45
carry away with ~, 1092.29; 1099.12–14
carry away with a foolish ~, 1092.48
changeable in ~s, 1092.9
cleansing of the ~s, 899.2(2)
coldness of ~s, 1097.3–6,24
concealed ~, 970.53,54
conflicting ~s, 1092.72
considerate of ~s of others, 1097.36,37
deepest ~s, 1092.58
depth of ~, 1092.25–27
difference of ~, slight, 1092.22
display of ~, 951.3(10,19,21, 22)
display of public ~s, 1092.20
done without ~, 1097.32
dull of ~, 1097.3
dull the ~s of, 1097.13–16
engrossed with one's ~s, 579.16,18
excited by ~, 1092.26,27
excitement of ~s, 1100.1,7; see excitement,n.
express ~s, 665.1(9,12–14)
expressing ~, suitable for, 1092.62
expressing deep ~, 1092.63
expression of ~, 665.2,4; 1092.3
expression of ~ through the voice, 1092.21
expressive of ~, 665.3(3,10–14)
feel ~, 1092.44
fill with ~, 925.18
fill with deep or strong ~, 1092.29; 1099.12
filled with ~, 925.17
fit of ~, 560.24
foolish ~, 1092.47
force unacceptable ~ into the unconscious, 1097.42,45
~ from another's experience, 1092.83
give external reality to ~s, 1092.86
have strong ~s, 1093.32
hold back ~s, 77.4
holding back of ~s, 77.1; 1097.38
humors determining ~, 1091.30
incapable of ~s, 1097.1,2
incorporation of the ~s of another, 1092.92,93
increase the strength of an ~, 1099.20,21
influence ~s, 9.1(2,3,5,6,8–10,12,14)
influence upon ~s, 9.1(12); 9.2(12)
influence by the ~s, 584.15; 1092.105
injury to the ~s, 803.20
lack of ~, 1097
lack of spiritual ~s, 1097.11, 12
medical science of ~s and illness, 1092.108
mixed ~s, 1092.74
originating from or in the ~s, 728.13(8); 1092.106–8
outlet for ~s, 1092.94
overflow with lively ~s, 1092.65
overflowing with lively ~s, 1092.64

persistent and besetting ~, 1092.15–17
pert. to ~s, 1092.104
public display of ~, 951.17
purification of the ~s, 900.8
refined ~, 1092.24
religious ~, 1092.40
rerouting of ~s, 77.1(30)
revival of childhood ~s, 1092.88
science of the ~s, 584.21
share ~s, 1092.79–82
shared with another (of ~s), 1092.83
sharing of ~s of others, 1092.76
show ~, 1092.44
show (suppressed) ~, 951.22
show ~s openly, disposed to, 1092.67,68
show lively ~s, 1092.65
showing ~, 1092.66
similar ~s, 1109.7
state of the ~s, 1091.5,6; 1092.5,6,8
stimulating ~, 1092.10
strength of ~, 1092.25–27
strengthen (an ~), 1092.61
strong ~, easily moved to, 1099.17
study of the ~s, 584.22
support for an ~, 1092.28
surrender to ~s, 1092.14
sympathetic relationship of ~, 1092.81,82
sympathy of ~s, 1092.76–78, 81,82
talk in unrestrained ~, 1092.71
temporary ~, 1092.4
temporary period of ~, 1092.43
tender ~s, 700.1(30)
tender ~s, easily moved to, 1099.6,7
transference of ~s illogically, 1092.90
treating phenomena without reference to one's ~s, 138.1(18)
trend of ~s in a place, 1092.19
~ under the surface, 970.54
underlying ~s of a group, 1092.18
understand the ~s of others, able to, 1097.34
understand the ~s of others, unable to, 1097.33
unfavorable ~, 838.2
uninfluenced by the ~s, 584.16
unrestrained in ~s, 1092.69–71
violence of ~, 1092.25,27,59
violent ~, easily moved to, 1099.18
violent ~s, marked by, 1092.33
violent and sudden ~, 4.10
violent attack of ~, 1092.42
violent display of ~, 1092.41
violent in ~s, 4.12; 1092.26
warm in ~, 1092.53
warmer in ~, become or make, 1092.55
warmth of ~, 1092.54,56
warmth of religious ~, 1092.57
without ~s, 1097.3
without consideration for ~s of others, 1097.35
without human ~s, 1097.7–10
without spontaneous ~s, 1097.32
word that expresses ~, 666.3(22,23,25)
emotional,adj., 1099.2,4

~ activities, factors of, 1092.102
affect ~ly, 1099.1,12
affected ~ly, 1099.3,15
affected ~ly, capable of being, 1099.4–7,17,18
affecting ~ly, 1099.2,13
~ ailment, 1135.1
~ attachment to a psychoanalyst, 1092.88
~ attitudes, 1092.7
~ behavior, factors of, 1092.102
~ breakdown, 802.28
capable of ~ response, 1092.101
cold ~ly, 1097.3–6, 24–26
~ condition, 1091.5,6; 1092.5, 6,8
~ conditions, 1092.7
~ conflicts, caused by, 1092.106–8
consider ~ly,1092.72
correction of ~ ailments of children, 398.14(4)
deeply ~, 1092.26,27,60,63
deeply or strongly ~ (of language or poetry), 1092.34
detached ~ly, 1097.31
~ disorder, 1135.1
~ disturbance, 1132.5
dull ~ly, 1097.1–6,13
~ effect, 1099.8
~ effect, cause of, 1099.14
effective ~ly, 1099.2
excessively ~, 1092.69–71
~ excitement, 1100; see **excitement,n.**
harden ~ly, 1098.1
hardened ~ly, 1098.3
held back ~ly, 1097.30
~ history of a patient, 1092.91
hotly ~ (of language), 1092.35
incorporation of ~ attitudes of another, 1092.92
~ indifference, 1097.1,3
Z interference, 1097.38–41,47
interpret ~ly, 1092.72
~ language, 1092.37,38,70
of ~ and bodily states, 1092.109
openly ~, 1092.67,68
~ peace, 1140.25,26
~ person, 1092.30,31
~ poetry, 1092.37,38
~ pressure, 1133.13–16
psychoanalyst's ~ response to a patient, 1092.89
~ reactions, 1092.7,75
~ reactions, factors of, 1092.102
restrained ~ly, 1097.30
science dealing with ~ disturbances, 401.1(2,36,44,62, 82–86)
~ shock, 1132.14–17
sincerely ~, 1092.60
~ song, 1092.37,38
~ speech, 1092.37,38
strongly ~, 1092.26,27,60,63
surgery to correct ~ disturbances, 402.1(18); 402.5(23, 27,28,41)
tendency to be ~, 1092.73
test of ~ attitudes, 401.10(3, 5)
testing of ~ reactions, 19.9(4)
treatment of ~ disturbances, 400.2(1); 400.6(3,16,21,29,37–39)
turned inward ~ly, 1092.95–99
turned outward ~ly, 1092.95–97
unaffected ~ly, 1099.10

uninvolved ~ly, 1097.31
violent ~ state caused by desire for the unattainable, 1092.51,52
violently ~, 1092.39
~ well-being, 1092.100
wildly ~ (of language), 1092.36
withstand ~ effect or appeal, 1099.11
empathy,n., 1092.76–78
emperor,n.
~ of China, 1073.36(14)
~ of Holy Roman Empire, 1073.36(13)
~ of Japan, 1073.36(18,32)
~ of Russia, 1073.36(6)
Roman ~, 1073.36(12)
wife of an ~, 1073.21(3)
emphasis,n., 848.30
~ on a syllable, 670.4(1,16)
emphasize,v., 848.30
employer,n.
strict ~, 203.23(2)
empress,n.
husband of an ~, 1073.21(5)
~ of Russia, 1073.36(7)
emptied,adj., 926.22
able to be ~, 926.24
unable to be ~, 926.25
emptiness,n., 926.1,2
figurative ~, 926.3,9–12
~ from blood loss, 926.26
in or into ~, 926.17,18
infinite ~, 926.16
~ left by death or departure, 926.19
empty,adj., 926.1
without incumbent, 926.7
without occupant, 926.6
become ~, 926.22
cause to be or become ~, 926.21
containing ~ space, 926.8
figuratively ~, 926.5,9–12
~ in facial expression, look, stare, etc., 926.11
in or into ~ space, 926.17,18
~ in speech, 926.5
nearly ~, 926.4
~ of, 926.2
~ of face, 926.11
~ of ideas, intelligence, etc., 926.12
~ office or position, 926.20
~ place, 926.20
~ space, 926.13,15
~ thing, 926.14
with ~ hands, 926.28
empty,v., 926.21,29
~ a place, 926.21(1,6,7,8,11)
~ a ship, 926.21(3,9,10)
~ bodily organs, 926.21(2,3,5, 6,12)
~ of contents, 926.21(1,2,3,5,7, 8,9,10)
~ of fluid, 926.21(2,3,4,5,12)
~ of inhabitants or people, 926.21(1,6,11)
~ of strength or energy, 926.21(2,5,7)
~ water, 1033.41
~ (water) from a boat, 1035.11,12
~ waters of a river, 926.21(4)
enchant,v., 663.12
attract, 196.1
enchanter,n., 663.13
encircle,v., 300.1; see **surround**,v.
enclose,v.
put in, 323.1; see **put**,v.
surround, 300.1; see **surround**,v.
~ water, 1033.3

~ with bushes, shrubs, or trees, 996.31
enclosed,adj.
~ by curved lines, 300.5
~ place or space, 300.7
enclosure,n.
place where something is put, 323.4,7
putting in, 323.2
surrounding, 300.2
that which is put in, 323.3
that which surrounds, 300.4, 7
barn ~, 998.16
farm ~, 998.15
~ for animals, 300.7
~ for people, 300.7; 301.4
~ for slaves, 301.4(1)
encourage,v.
give hope to, 267.5
urge, 277.1
~ in wrongdoing, 277.1(1,3)
encouragement,n., 267.2; 277.2
protection, support, and ~, 568.20
encouraging,adj., 267.6; 277.3
encroach,v., 130.1–4
end,n., 791.3; 792.6,10
a bringing to an ~, 792.1
a coming to an ~, 792.3
bitter ~, 922.14
bring to an ~, 791.1; 792.1
come to an ~, 792.2,4
coming at the ~, 792.19
disastrous ~, 792.6(1)
draw to an ~, 792.5
happening at the ~, 29.3(15, 67) ; 792.19
having an ~, 792.14
loose ~, 792.10(5)
meeting's ~, 792.6(3)
omission of ~, 911.1(11)
opposite ~s of the earth, 792.8
part at the ~, 792.7,10,23
place's ~, 792.10(6) ; see also edge,n.
pointed ~, 792.11; see also point,n.
put an ~ to, 791.10–12
railroad, etc., line's ~, 792.9
resulting ~, 792.6(4)
short ~, 792.10(3,4)
stand something on its ~, 61.5
story's ~, 792.6(2) ; 792.23(1, 2,7)
thicker ~, 792.10(1,3,4)
thing's ~, 792.10; see also edge,n.
torn ~, 792.10(5)
without ~, 755.1–3
end,v., 792.1,2,4
put an end to, 791.10
stop, 791.1,2; see stop,v.
~ a meeting, 791.1(2)
cause to ~, 791.1
endanger,v., 572.4
endeavor,n., 18.2; see attempt,n.
place of ~, 18.5
endeavor,v., 18.1
ended,adj., 792.12
able to be ~, 792.13
ending,n., 791.3; 792.6,23
endless,adj., 755.1–3
~ly, 755.4
~ period of time, 769.5
~ time, 762.3
endurable,adj., 246.4
endurance,n., 246.2,8; 754.2,22; see also tolerance,n.
descr. of ~, 246.3
lacking in ~, 10.1(65)
lacking in moral ~, 10.1(65)

lacking in physical ~, 10.1(65)
endure,v.
continue, 754.1; see continue,v.
tolerate, 246.1; see also bear, tolerate,v.
ability to ~, 754.22
able to ~ or bear, 246.9
one who can ~ hardships, 246.10
~ something bitter, 877.7
enema,n., 293.16(3)
enemy,n., 879.4
chief ~, 879.4(1)
~ in war, 879.4(4)
secret sympathizers with the ~, 801.5
energetic,adj., 2.8,9,10
~ person, 2.11
energy,n., 2.1; see also force,n.
active ~, 2.3
available ~, 2.6
deprive of ~, 10.5(28)
direct one's ~ to, 2.14
empty of ~, 926.21(2,5,7)
exert ~ in attempting, 18.1(11,22,24)
exertion of ~, 2.16
expend ~, 2.15
expenditure of ~, 2.16
expenditure of ~, pert. to, 2.22
focusing of ~ on an idea, 2.30
~ from atom, 1060.55
full of ~, 2.8,10
give ~, 2.18,19
give nervous ~, 2.20
impression of ~, 2.12
invest with sexual ~, 709.21
lacking ~, 10.1
lose ~, 10.8
machine that converts ~, 2.23
measuring device for ~, 2.25
nervous ~, 2.5
not losing ~, 2.13
~ of action, 2.2
~ of motion, 2.2
painful ~, 2.15(5,6)
path of ~, 2.29
person full of ~, 2.11
pert. to ~, 2.21
place where ~ is exerted, 2.26
potential ~, 2.17
psychic ~, 2.30
put forth ~, 2.15
radioactive ~, 1069.16–18
requiring ~, 2.17
science of ~, 2.28
science of heat and ~, 1060.65(3)
sexual ~, 709.10
spend ~, 2.15
theory of ~, 2.27
~ to start something new, 2.4
unit of ~, 2.24
unit of ~ production of food, 1046.33
violent and sudden ~, 4.10
without ~, 10.1
X-ray ~, 1069.16
enforce,v., 3.3; 16.25
enforceable,adj., 16.26
legally ~, 3.8
enforced,adj.
sternly ~, 551.8
engage,v.
attach, 302.1,4,12,16; see attach,v.
promise in marriage, 704.2,3
engaged,adj.
promised in marriage, 704.4
~ person, 704.5
engagement,n.

attachment, 302.2,5,13,17; see attachment,n.
promise of marriage, 704.1
ceremony of ~, 704.7
engine,n.
sound of ~ exhaust, 461.4(3)
engineer,n., 727.3
engineer,v.
build, 727.1; see build,v.
engineering,n., 727.2,10
England,n., 784.9(21)
fondness for ~, 700.30(1) ; 700.31,32
government of ~, 1073.5(6)
make conform to customs of ~, 784.10(2)
party favoring ~ during American Revolution, 1076.12(28)
English,adj., 784.16
~ characteristic, 1091.24(2)
in ~ style, 784.19
make ~, 784.10(2)
English,n.
dialect of ~, 664.4(2,14)
make conform to ~ language, 664.6
study of ~ language, 664.11(2)
Englishman,n., 784.15(18,37)
engrave,v., 966.1
pert. to ~ing of stones, 1006.49
engraved,adj., 966.6
engraver,n., 966.4
engraving,n., 966.5
art of ~, 965.6(2,3) ; 966.3
artist's name on ~, 966.12
pert. to ~, 966.7
process of ~, 966.3
enjoy,v., 1105.6,7
enjoyable,adj., 1105.4; see pleasurable,adj.
enjoyment,n., 1105.1; see pleasure,n.
enlarge,v., 907.1,2
enlargement,n., 907.3
bodily ~, abnormal, 907.13
~ of a bodily organ or cavity, 907.3(5)
~ of the heart, 907.3(4)
enmity,n.
hostility, 879.2; see hostility,n.
opposition, 544.2(10,12,20)
enormous,adj., 906.12; see also big,adj.
enough,adj., 919.1
added to make ~, 908.13
amount that is ~, 919.2
barely ~, 919.5
be ~, 919.7,8
big ~, 906.16
fully ~, 919.3
make ~ by addition, 908.12
more than ~, 919.6
not ~, 919.10
not have ~, 919.13
~ to be seen, 919.4
enroll,v., 695.6,9
~ in a college, 623.9
enslave,v., 310.1
entangle,v., 156.1(8)
entanglement,n., 156.3
become free of ~, 309.21(2)
free of ~, 309.11(13,17,25,41)
enter,v., 133.1,6
able to be ~ed, 133.14
forbid to ~, 555.5
~ late or later, 767.4
opens a way to ~, that which, 298.6
permission to ~, 133.9; 554.7
permit to ~, 554.7
right to ~, 133.9

~ to attack, 560.8,9
unable to be ~ed, 133.15
entering,adj., 133.4,5
entertain,v., 200.1; see
amuse,v.
be ~ed with food and drink,
734.6
entertainer,n.
actor, 969.3; see actor,n.
actress, 969.4; see actress,n.
traveling group of ~s, 200.10
entertainment,n., 200.2,4,5; see
also amusement, party,n.
an ~ by dancing girls,
200.5(2)
~ in a restaurant, night club,
etc., 1025.18
~s, 200.6
enthusiasm,n., 1095.1
an ~, 1095.4
cause of ~, 1095.4
expressing ~, 1095.14
expression of ~, 1095.15
~ for talking, 1095.19
~ for writing, 1095.20
lose ~, 1095.24
lose religious ~, 1095.25
reduce ~, 1095.26–30
shout in ~, 1095.10,12
shout of ~, 1095.13
show ~, 1095.9–15
talk in wild ~, 1095.17,18
without ~, 1095.23; 1097.32
write in wild ~, 1095.17,18
enthusiast,n., 1095.3
enthusiastic,adj., 1095.2
be ~, 1095.9
make ~, 1095.8,9,11
wildly ~ language, song, or
writing, 1095.16
entire,adj., 328.1; see complete,
adj.
entirety,n., 328.2
entity,n., 930.2
entrails,n., 347.9; see intestine,n.
entrance,n., 133.2,7
ease of ~, 133.11
forbid ~ of ships, 555.6
gives ~, that which, 133.10
~ hall, 122.1(11,21,25,37);
133.7(14,20)
~ into society, 133.2(2)
~ keeper, 133.8
means of ~, 50.1(3); 133.7;
298.6
permit ~, 133.13
price for ~, 133.12
roof over an ~, 973.1(2,6)
entrant,n., 133.3
entreat,v.
ask, 274.1; see also ask,v.
beg, 276.1; see also beg,v.
entreaty,n., 274.2; 276.2; see
also begging, demand,n.
responsive to ~, 276.8
unresponsive to ~, 276.9
envelop,v., 300.1; see surround,v.
environment, n., 783.1; see also
surroundings,n.
science of ~, 751.13(5)
science of biological ~,
783.2(2)
science of improvement of ~,
783.2(3)
science of race and ~, 783.2(1,
3)
environs,n., 783.1; 790.8
envoy,n., 523.6
group of ~s, 523.8
envy,n., 265.2
bitter ~, 1119.2(3)
causing ~, 265.14(1)

dissatisfaction from ~,
1119.2(3)
prejudiced by ~, 877.1(2)
with ~, 265.6
envy,v., 265.1(3,9); 1119.3(1)
eon,n., 769.4
epilepsy,n., 378.11(3,6)
attack of ~, 560.25
resembling ~, 378.14
epoch,n., 769.1,8
equal,adj., 534.1
at an ~ pace, 534.8
be ~ in measurement, 946.16
be of ~ weight, 947.8
having ~ distances around,
534.11
having ~ angles, 534.9; 944.6
having ~ sides, 534.10
~ in measurement, 946.17
~ in weight, 947.10
make ~, 534.5
make ~ in measurement,
946.16
make ~ in weight, 947.9
one who is ~, 534.3
that which is ~, 534.3
to an ~ extent, 534.8
~ weight, 947.12
equal,n.
an ~, 534.3
one's ~, 534.3
person or thing without an ~,
534.15
without ~, 534.13,14
equal,v., 534.4
try to ~, 18.1(13); 534.6
equality,n., 534.2
doctrine of ~, 534.12
mathematical ~, statement
of, 534.7
~ of laws, 1079.35
~ of measurement, 946.18
~ of weight, 947.7
political ~, 1076.11; 1076.12(4)
political ~, supporter of,
1076.12(4)
equator,n.
calm region near ~, 1139.18
distance north or south of the
~, 1004.11
line near the ~, descr. of the,
1004.15
sun crosses ~, 1055.12–14
sun farthest from ~, time
when, 1055.15–17
equiangular,adj., 534.9; 944.6
equilibrium,n., 950.1; see balance,n.
equipment,n., 280.1,3
bride's ~, 280.1(23)
having good ~, 280.5
home ~, 280.1(3,5,8,9,17)
infant's ~, 280.1(12)
military ~, 280.1(1,4,14)
piece of ~, 280.6
place to get ~, 280.4
ship's ~, 280.1(10,18,19,21)
worker's ~, 280.1(11,20)
equivalent,adj., 534.1; see
equal,adj.
era,n., 769.1,8
eradicate,v., 286.1; see eliminate,v.
erase,v., 286.1; see eliminate,v.
erect,adj., 180.1(5,12)
erection,n.
penis ~ without sexual desire, 379.9(10)
ermine,n., 403.13(2)
of ~s, 403.11(10)
erode,v., 801.25,26
erosion,n., 801.27–32
errand,n., 189.5
erratic,adj., 539.21,23
~ person, 539.22

error,n., 829.1; see mistake,n.
escape,n., 141.2
means of ~, 141.7
no ~, 141.9
provide means of ~, 141.6
escape,v., 141.1; see also depart,v.
let ~, 309.1; see free,v.
escaper,n., 141.3
escort,n., 131.3; 131.3(3,4,7)
escort,v., 131.1
Eskimo,adj., 784.16
~ home, 753.1(33)
~ language, 664.4(10)
Eskimo,n., 784.15(19)
esophagus,n., 347.6–8
esperanto,n., 664.7
essay,n.
attempt, 18.2; see attempt,n.
piece of writing, 682.16
essay,v., 18.1
essence,n., 808.7
concentrated ~, 808.9
~ of a thing, 808.8
unchanging ~, 808.10
essential,adj., 273.6; see necessary,adj.
establish,v.
give a beginning to, 729.1(2,
6,11,20); 729.2
place, 323.1
established,adj.
deep-seated, 323.23
establishment,n.
beginning, 729.2
business organization, 210.7
placing, 323.2
estate,n.
condition, 44.1
inheritance, 241.4
one who settles an ~, 241.11
esteem,n.
admiration,n., 855.2; see admiration,n.
respect, 856.2; see respect,n.
lower oneself in ~, 868.28
reduce in ~, 868.27
esteem,v.
admire, 855.1; see admire,v.
respect, 856.1; see respect,v.
etching,n.
zinc ~, 1019.5,6
eternal,adj.
continuing forever, 754.15,16
endless, 755.1,2
immortal, 755.7; see im-
mortal,adj.
equally ~, 754.18
make ~, 755.11
~ quality, 755.8
ethical,adj., 818.3,4; 843.17
cause to be ~, 818.6
consider as ~, 818.6
treat as ~, 818.6
ethicalness,n., 843.18
ethics,n., 528.9; 818.5
~ in relation to happiness,
1102.35,36
~ of pleasure and pain,
1105.25
science of ~, 528.9(1)
theory of ~, 528.9(3)
etiquette,n.
convention, 629.1
formality, 819.3
proper conduct, 818.8
a formality of ~, 819.10(1)
necessary for ~, 273.6(6)
eunuch,n., 710.40
like a ~, 710.41
Europe,n., 1003.2(5)
countries of ~, 784.4(2,4)
make conform to customs of
~, 784.10(4,6)
European,adj.

~ characteristics, culture, institutions, etc., 1091.25
make ~, 784.10(4,6)
South ~, 784.16
European,n.
Southern ~, 784.15(39)
evade,v.
avoid, 76.1; see avoid,v.
escape, 141.1; see escape,v.
evaporate,v., 1048.39–45
evasion,n.
avoidance, 76.2
escape, 141.2; see escape,n.
even,adj., 531.1,2
evening,n., 777.1,4,6; see also night,n.
active, etc., in the ~, 777.5
~ before an event, 777.2
middle of the ~, 777.3
event,n., 29.6; see happening,n.
evidence,n., 483.1; 812.16
~ in court, 1086.3,11,12
evident,adj., 483.1; 598.5,8,13
concerned with what is ~, 598.15
~ without proof, 598.14
evil,adj., 883.22; 886.1
a doing of ~, 883.28
~ act, 883.24
~ action, 883.27
~ acts, 883.26
doer of ~ acts, 883.29
interpreting innocent things, actions, or words in an ~ manner, 883.40
part for ~ purposes, 326.1(40)
~ spirit, 660.1; see also devil,n.
~ thing, 883.32
evil,n., 883.32
afflict with ~, 883.33
area where ~ flourishes, 883.36
box containing human ~s, 267.21
cause of ~, 883.35
explanation why God permits ~, 599.2(5)
good and ~, doctrine of, 1089.10
indicative of coming ~, 773.5
place favorable to the rapid growth of ~, 883.38
place of ~, 883.37
predict ~, 772.18
predictor of ~, 772.17
reputation for ~, 883.34
temptation to ~, sign of, 660.4
evildoer,n., 883.29
evildoing,n., 883.28
evilness,n., 883.23
exact,adj., 815.1
exaggerate,v., 906.19
~ in drawing or description, 906.21
exaggerated,adj., 906.20
~ picture, 965.1(6)
exaggeration,n., 906.19
~ for effect, 669.3(16)
tendency to wild ~, 1136.1(25)
examination,n., 485.2
test, 19.1,3; see test,n.
instrument used in medical ~s, 485.7
medical ~s, 485.5
examine,v., 485.1
test, 19.2; see test,v.
~ by X-ray, 1065.12–14
~ medically, 485.9
~ to learn about, 624.8(7)
examiner,n., 485.3
tester, 19.4
news ~, 485.3(1)
examining,adj., 485.5

testing, 19.5
example,n., 317.1
for ~, 317.7
~ for future acts or events, 317.1(23)
give ~s of, 317.5,6
illustrative ~, 317.1(5,10,14, 16)
perfect ~, 317.1(26)
pert. to an ~, 317.2
serve as an ~, 317.3
serving as an ~, 317.2
typical ~, 317.1(7,11,12,26,27, 28,31)
unique ~, 317.1(17)
excel,v., 833.11,15
excellence,n., 831.2
lose ~, 883.11
model of ~, 317.1(20); 831.3
~ of character, 831.4
reduce the ~ of, 883.16
reducer of ~, 883.18
excellent,adj., 831.1
~ character, person of, 830.5
~ condition, 831.9
in ~ condition, 831.7
exceptional,adj., 536.4,5
excerpt,n., 252.5
excerpt,v., 252.1
excess,n., 916.26; 920.2,6
be in ~, 920.9
do in ~, 920.10
go in ~ of, 920.10
in ~, 920.1
~ matter, 920.5
~ of a good thing, 920.20
~ of choice, 920.21
~ person, 920.7,8
possessed of an ~, 915.12
~ thing, 920.3,4
~ worker, 920.8
excessive,adj., 921.1
~ action, 921.4
~ amount, 916.3,26; 921.5
be in ~ supply, 915.10
~ degree, 921.5
~ feeling, 921.4
~ in amount, 921.1(2,3,13)
~ in appetite, 921.1(7)
~ in price, 921.1(2,3,9,13)
~ in spending, 921.1(3)
not ~, 921.3; 923.1
~ opinion, 921.4
~ supply, 915.8,9
excessively,adv., 921.8
excessiveness,n., 921.2
exchange,n., 539.13
~ of witty remarks, 539.14
exchange,v., 539.12
excitable,adj., 1100.23
excitation,n., 1100.1
~ to act, 52.11
excite,v., 1100.1
one who ~s to action, 52.13
~ sexually, 709.19
that which ~s, 1100.4
that which ~s to action, 52.12
~ to action, 52.9
~ with emotion, 1092.29
~ with love, 700.14
excited,adj., 1100.6
~ and absent-minded state, 1100.7(10)
be ~, 1100.5
become ~ (of passions or emotions), 1092.50
become ~ by passion or emotion, 1092.49
become ~ to action, 52.10
~ behavior, 1100.7
~ by emotion, 1092.26
confused and ~ state, 1100.7(12)
easily ~, 1100.23
feel ~, 1100.5

not easily ~, 1100.25
~ person, 1100.8
sexually ~, 709.8,9
~ state, 1100.7
~ woman, 1100.8(1)
excitement,n., 1100.7
be in a state of ~, 1100.5
feel ~, 1100.5
fit of violent ~, 1100.10
fond of social ~, 1100.11
given to outbursts of ~, 1100.24
highest point of ~, 1100.13
in a state of ~, 1100.6
~ in hunting, 1100.7(1)
marked by outbursts of ~, 1100.12
mental derangement marked by ~, 1136.1(5–9,23,24,36)
~ of poetic inspiration, 1100.7(5)
~ of social activity, 1100.7(8)
public ~, demonstration of, 1100.7(4)
religious ~, 1100.7(4)
rush about in ~, 1100.5(3–5,8)
sexual ~, 709.7
shake with ~, 111.1(29); 1100.5(11)
show ~, 1100.5
showing ~, 1100.6
spit in ~, 289.1(9)
techniques to produce ~, use of, 1100.9
~ to act, 52.11
violent ~, 1100.7(7)
violent with ~, 1100.6(3,7,11, 13,16)
warmth from ~, 1060.37
wild ~, 1100.7(4,7)
wild with ~, 1100.6(11)
exciting,adj., 1100.2
adds an ~ quality, that which, 1105.2(4)
attractive and ~, 1100.18–21
consider, interpret, or present in ~ light, 1100.16,17,20
~ events, 1100.14,15
most ~ part, 1100.13
~ quality, 1100.3
sexually ~, 709.18
~ to action, 52.14
exclude,v., 296.1
~ from human relationship, 296.1(9)
~ from membership, 296.1(2)
~ from the church, 296.1(6)
exclusion,n., 296.2,3
advocate of ~, 296.4
exclusive,adj., 296.7
~ in friendship, 1096.6
excrete,v., 287.1; 293.1; 294.1
excretion,n., 287.2,3; 293.2; 294.3
~ in disease, 287.2(2)
organ of ~, 287.5
pert. to ~, 287.4
science of ~s, 287.15(1)
excusable,adj., 897.9,16
excuse,n., 898.1
argument of ~, 898.1
~ for absence, 898.7
~ for deception, 898.1(3,6)
~ for delay, 898.1(5)
make ~s, 898.3
make an ~ for, 898.2
offer ~s, 898.3,8
offer ~s for, 898.8
offer as an ~, 898.5
speech of ~, 898.4
statement of ~, 898.6
unconscious ~, 898.1(4)
urge as an ~, 898.5
excuse,v., 897.1,6,12,24; 898.2; see also forgive,v.

execute,v.
  do, 49.1; see do,v.
  kill, 796.1; see kill,v.
  ~ by electricity, 796.1(7)
  ~ by hanging, 796.1(10)
execution,n.
  doing, 49.2
  killing, 796.2; see killing,n.
  ~ of a heretic, 796.2(1)
executioner,n., 796.3
executive,adj., 8.17
executive,n., 8.16; 49.3
exemplary,adj., 317.2
exemplify,v., 317.3
exercise,n.
  bodily ~, 103.1,2
  club for athletic ~s, 524.9(17)
  pert. to ~, 103.3
  warmth from ~, 1060.37
exercise,v.
  one who ~s, 103.4
  ~ the fingers, instrument to,
    103.5
exert,v., 2.15
exertion,n., 2.16
exhaust,v.
  empty, 926.21; see empty,v.
  fatigue,v., 12.3,6
exhausted,adj.
  emptied, 926.21
  fatigued, 12.1
exhaustion,n.
  emptying, 926.21,23
  fatigue, 12.2
  ~ from blood loss, 926.26
exhibit,v., 951.1; see also
  show,v.
exhibition,n., 951.3; see also
  display, exposure, show,n.
  animals, ~ of, 951.3(4,8)
  animals, place of ~ of,
    951.28(2,4,9)
  art, science, etc., ~ of,
    951.28(5,6) ; 951.29,30; 965.10
  cloud formations, instrument
    for ~ of, 1057.22(3)
  farm products, ~ of, 951.3(8) ;
    951.28(3)
  ~ of world scenery, 1004.36
  paintings, ~ of, 965.10
  pictures, ~ of, 965.10
  place of ~, 951.28
  plants, flowers, ~ of, 951.28(1)
  wax figures, ~ of, 951.28(8) ;
    951.30
exhort,v.
  advise, 279.1
  urge, 277.1
  serving to ~, 277.3(1)
exhortation,n., 277.2,4; 279.2
exile,n., 144.2,3
exile,v., 144.1(1,3,5,17,19,22)
  ~ to the country, 786.4
exist,v., 39.1
  live, 750.1
  ~ at the same time, 39.1(1) ;
    764.2,3
  ~ before, 766.4,5
  continue to ~, 39.1(5,7)
  ~ earlier, 39.1(4) ; 766.4,5
  ~ in large amounts, 916.17,24
  ~ in many places, 39.1(5)
  ~ longer than, 39.1(3)
  ~ previously, 39.1(4)
  ~ secretly, 971.16
  ~ together, 39.1(1)
  ~ unsuspected, 971.16
  ~ within, 39.1(6)
  ~ without visible signs,
    39.1(6)
existence,n., 39.3
  living, 750.2
  bring into ~, 729.1; see
    begin,v.
  burst into ~, 118.1(7)

come into ~, 729.7; see
  begin,v.
  having real ~, 807.4
  individual, ~ as, 930.14
  place of ~, 782.1(27)
  scene of ~, 783.4(5)
  something with a real ~,
    807.5
existent,adj., 39.2
  alive, 750.3
existing,adj., 39.2
  living, 750.3
  ~ at the same time, 764.1
  ~ in space and time, 787.6
exit,n., 140.5
  passage without ~, 122.1(8,
    13,15,23) ; 141.8
  place without ~, 141.8
  road without ~, 123.1(7,20,21,
    29)
exonerate,v., 897.24
expand,v., 907.1,2
expanding, 907.4,5
  capable of ~, 907.7
expanse,n.
  space, 787.1; see space,n.
expansible,adj., 907.6
expansion,n., 907.3
  policy of ~, 907.8
expect,v., 268.1
  desire and ~, 268.12
  ~ erroneously, 268.14
  ~ to get, 268.13
expectant,adj., 268.4
  ~ state, 268.5,6
expectation,n., 268.2,5
  be in a state of eager ~,
    268.11
  eager or anxious ~, 268.6
  holding one's breath in ~,
    268.10
expected,adj., 268.7
  more than ~, 920.13
  reasonably ~, 268.8
  what is ~, 268.9
expecter,n., 268.3
expedient,adj.
  advantageous, 836.2
  suitable, 817.1
expedient,n.
  advocate or user of ~s,
    596.10
expenditure,n., 224.2,3
expense,n., 224.2,4
  agree to pay ~s of, 219.6
expensive,adj., 223.14
  not ~, 223.15
experience,n., 619.2
  account of remembered ~s,
    627.27
  an ~, 32.1
  difficult ~, 32.1(5)
  exciting ~, 32.1(1)
  force to undergo ~, 3.3(17)
  force to undergo unpleasant
    ~, 32.3
  frightening ~, 32.1(4)
  learner by practical ~,
    622.5(3)
  mystical ~, 32.5
  one who relies entirely on
    practical ~, 621.13(1)
  one's complete ~, 619.6
  painful ~, 32.1(5) ; 1130.16,
    18,19
  pleasurable ~, 32.1(3)
  relating to ~, 619.8
  reliance on ~, 619.7
  revival of childhood ~s,
    1092.88
  theory of knowledge from ~,
    611.9
  unpleasant ~, 32.1(5)
  unusual ~, 32.1(1)
  wild ~, 32.1(2)

experience,v., 32.2; 433.4
  cause to ~, 32.3
  ~ emotion, 1092.44
experienced,adj., 619.1
  become ~, 619.3
  make ~, 619.4
  ~ person, 619.5
experiment,n., 19.1
  based on ~, 19.8
  by way of ~, 19.5(3)
  dependent on ~, 19.8
  place for ~, 19.10
  theory or practice of relying
    on ~, 19.9(3)
experiment,v., 19.2
experimenter,n., 19.4
expert,adj., 7.2
expert,n., 7.3
expertness,n., 7.1
expiable,adj., 222.4; 845.21
expiate,v., 222.1; 845.20
expiation,n., 222.2; 845.20
  condition, state, or place of
    ~, 845.25; 1130.22
  of the nature of ~, 845.23
  state after death for ~,
    845.24
expiatory,adj., 222.3; 845.23
explain,v., 599.1
  hard to ~, 599.9,10
  ~ incorrectly, 599.16
  ~ the meaning of, 607.17
  ~ the text of, 965.14
explainable,adj., 599.6
explainer,n., 599.4
  ~ of meaning, 607.20
  ~ of mysteries, 599.4(3,4)
  ~ of news events, 599.4(1)
explanation,n., 599.2,3
  ask for an ~, 599.12
  call on for an ~, 625.1(2)
  later ~, 599.3(1)
  ~ of evil, 599.2(5)
  ~ of meaning, 607.18
  ~ of the Bible, 599.2(3)
  ~ of words, 599.2(2) ; 599.3(9)
  offer as ~, 237.1(6)
  pert. to ~s, 599.15
  requiring ~, 599.11
  science of ~, 599.13
  science of Bible ~, 599.14
explanatory,adj., 599.5
  ~ notes, 599.3; 599.3(2,4–7,
    10)
  ~ notes, provide with,
    599.1(2,10)
  ~ of meaning, 599.3
  ~ remarks, 599.3(4,5,8)
  ~ word, 666.3(33)
  ~ writings, 599.3(5,8)
explode,v., 802.9,10; see also
  burst,v.
  substance that ~s, 802.12
  ~ violently, 802.9(2)
exploration,n., 486.2
  ~ of caves, 298.15
explore,v., 486.1; see also
  search,v.
  ~ for plants, 985.39
explorer,n., 486.4
  cave ~, 298.16
explosion,n., 802.11
  device that causes ~, 802.12,
    13
  sounds of ~, 461.4–6
explosive,adj., 802.11
  ~ liquid, 802.12(2)
explosive,n., 565.17; 802.12
  amount of ~s set off, 565.13,
    14
  container for ~s, 565.15
expose,v.
  make known, 613.1,8
  show, 951.1; see show,v.
exposure,n.

making known, 613.2
showing, 951.2; see also display, exhibition, show,n.
~ of corruption, 951.21
~ of crime, wickedness, etc., 951.20
express,v., 665.1
able to be ~ed, 665.6
~ by gesture, 102.1
~ed in words, 666.17
~ feelings, 665.1(9,12–14)
unable to be ~ed, 665.7
expression,n.
word or phrase, 666.1,2
art of ~, 665.5
Cockney ~, 666.7(4)
facial ~, 365.2; 1117.12
having a facial ~ indicative of secrecy, 971.14
~ in language, 665.2
manner of ~, 665.8–10; see also language, speech,n.
~ of feelings, 665.2,4
~ peculiar to England, 666.7(1,3,4)
~ peculiar to French, 666.7(5)
~ peculiar to Greece or Athens, 666.7(2,6)
~ peculiar to Irish, 666.7(7)
expressive,adj., 665.3
~ of complex ideas, 665.3(7)
extend,v., 193.18; 194.1; see pull, draw, stretch,v.
~ across, 1033.51
extent,n., 194.2
space, 787.1; see space,n.
large in ~, 906.17
of wide ~, 194.4
exterior,adj., 138.1; see outside,adj.
exterior,n., 138.2; see outside,n.
external,adj., 138.1; see outside,adj.
caused by ~ factors, 15.7
treating phenomena as ~, 138.1(18)
extinguish,v.
~ a fire, flame, etc., 801.17
~ a light, 801.18
extract,n.
choice, 252.5
~ from soaking, 1035.21
extract,v.
draw out, 193.18
select, 252.1
extracurricular,adj., 623.5,6
extraordinary,adj., 536.1; see unusual,adj.
~ person, act, etc., 536.2
extravagant,adj., 225.2,3
be ~, 225.1
~ person, 225.4
spend ~ly, 224.1(3,6,7,10,11)
extreme,adj., 922.1–3,8
~ act, 922.26
~ actions, 922.15
advocacy of ~ principles, 922.24
advocate of ~ principles, 922.20
be ~, tendency to, 922.19
~ boundary, 922.16
~ degree, extent, etc., 922.9
~ in anger, 922.8
~ in change, 922.4
~ in morality, 922.5
~ in reforming, 922.4
~ in religion, 922.5
~ limit, 922.10,16
~ need, suffering, misfortune, etc., 922.17,18
not ~, 922.28; 923.1
~ opinion, 922.26
~ part, 922.16
~ people, 922.22

~ person, 922.21
~ point, 922.16
~ practices, 922.25
~ principles, 922.25
situated at ~ point, 922.11
extreme,n., 922.13
advocacy of ~s, 922.24
center between ~s, 137.1(8,14, 15,17–20)
going to ~s, 922.3,19,21,22
to an ~, 922.12
extremely,adv., 922.27
extremity,n.
greatest ~, 922.14
last ~, 922.14
exult,v., 1102.8
exultant,adj., 1102.6
make ~, 1102.10
exultation,n., 1102.7
shout in ~, 1102.9
eye,n., 361.1
condition of the ~s, 361.6
contraction of the ~s, drug for, 398.6(10)
cover of the ~, 972.4(12)
deep-set (of the ~s), 361.9
descr. of ~ condition or appearance, 361.5
dilation of ~s, drug for, 398.6(9)
disorder of the ~s, 361.6; see also vision,n., disorders of
~ doctor, 401.2(19)
dryness of the ~s, 1038.8
for one ~ only, 361.10
for two ~s, 361.11
having bulging ~s, 361.5(6, 8,16)
having contracted ~s, 361.5(14)
having crossed ~s, 361.5(4,20, 22)
having dark ~s, 361.5(3)
having dilated ~s, 361.5(13)
having diverging ~s, 361.5(23)
having fierce ~s, 361.5(23)
having large ~s, 361.5(9)
having one ~, 361.5(10,11)
having piercing ~s, 361.5(7)
having plum-shaped ~s, 361.5(19)
having red and sore ~s, 361.5(2)
having round ~s, 361.5(12,17)
having shining ~s, 361.5(21)
having staring ~s, 361.5(8, 16,23)
having twitching ~balls, 361.5(15)
inflame the ~s, 361.7
intersection of the ~ nerves, 361.12
looking to the side, with the ~s, 361.8
movements of the ~s in reading, 692.14
mucus from the ~s, 287.13(3)
near the ~, 361.3
parts of the ~, 361.4
person as to ~s, descr. of a, 361.5
pert. to the ~, 361.2
science dealing with the ~s, 401.1(56,57,63)
~ shade, 1071.8
shut the ~s of, 481.8
signal by the ~, 956.1(17)
sore ~s, cause, 361.7
spot on cornea of the ~, 501.3(1)
squint of the ~s, 361.6(3)
using both ~s, 361.5(1)
using one ~, 361.5(10)
using the left ~, 361.5(18)

using the right ~, 361.5(5)
watery ~s, cause, 361.7
wrinkle at corner of the ~, 158.4(1)
eyebrow,n.
having thick and overhanging ~s, 361.14
lowering of the ~s, 365.2(4, 6,10)
pert. to the ~, 361.13
eyed,adj.
dim-~, 1070.17,19
eyeglasses,n., 480.16,17
maker or seller of ~, 480.20
eyelashes,n., 361.15
coloring matter for the ~, 488.22(5)
eyelid,n.
disorders of the ~s, 361.6(3, 10); 361.17
drooping of ~, 167.2(6)
membrane lining the ~, 361.4(1)
pert. to the ~s, 361.16

F

face,n.
appearance of the ~, 365.1(4, 5,7)
big of ~, 906.4
cover the ~, 972.1(30,55)
deducing character from shape of ~, 365.4
displeasure on the ~, expression of, 1117.12
empty of ~, 926.10,11
express displeasure on the ~, 1117.10,13
expression by the ~, 365.2
expressionless ~, 365.1(3)
expressionless of ~, 365.3
fat and innocent of ~, 510.3
having two ~s, 365.5
likeness of the ~, 365.1(6)
outline of the ~, 365.1(5,8);
507.20(8,10)
pale of ~, 384.11(14); 384.13
parts of the ~, 365.1(4,5)
round of ~, 1054.22
single part of the ~, 326.1(15)
~-to-face, 365.7
white spot on animal's ~, 501.3(2)
face,v., 365.6
~ boldly, 862.11
~ impudently, 862.11
place so as to ~ the east or other direction, 179.3
~ the east, 179.2(1)
facial,adj.
~ appearance, 365.1
~ expression or gesture, 365.2
having a ~ expression indicative of secrecy, 971.14
~ly expressionless, 365.3
make a ~ expression of pain, 1130.15
fact,n., 814.1
reality, 807.1,2,5; see reality, n.
accomplished ~, 814.1(2)
dealing with ~s, 814.2
in ~, 814.3
in accord with ~s, 814.2
~ indicating what follows, 951.4(20)
numerical ~, 814.1(3)
~s in a row, 311.16
science of numerical ~s, 814.4
special ~, 540.28
unadorned in ~s, 959.11
factory,n., 203.11(4); 726.5

fad,n., 631.1(2); 1095.4(1)
  follower of ~s, 1095.7
  following a ~, 631.4
  fond of ~s, 1095.6
  given to a ~, 631.4
  like a ~, 631.5; 1095.5
Faeroe Islands,n., 784.4(4)
fail,v., 24.1
  ~ a subject, 24.1(6)
  ~ a test, 24.1(6)
  ~ after just starting, 24.1(1)
  ~ after successful start, 24.1(4)
  ~ in business, 24.1(3)
  ~ someone in school, 24.5
  ~ to achieve a goal, 24.1(9)
  undertaking sure to ~, 267.18
failure,n., 24.2
  act to avoid ~, 52.5(34)
  indicating probable ~, 24.7
  indicative of ~, 951.5(3)
  likely to bring ~, 24.6
  person who is a ~, 24.4
faint,n., 435.1; see **unconscious**, adj.
  bring back from a ~, 435.8
  come back from a ~, 435.9
faint,v., 435.6
fainting,n.
  fit of ~, 560.24(18)
fair,adj., 637.1
  person who is ~, 637.3
  honest and ~ person, 813.4
fairly,adv.
  competing ~, 637.4
  playing ~, 637.4
fairness,n., 637.2
  application of ~ in legal disputes, 1081.22
fairy,n., 662.7(12,15,33,38,39)
  belief in ~s, 662.9
  evil ~, 662.7(20,32)
  helpful ~, 662.7(4)
  Irish ~, 662.7(28)
  led astray by mischievous ~s, 662.13
  living place of ~s, 662.12
  magic ~, 662.7(12)
  mischievous ~, 662.7(12,21, 22,28,32–35,39)
  nature of a ~, 662.11
  pert. to a ~, 662.8
  ~s, collectively, 662.10(1)
  story about ~s, 662.13
  ugly ~, 662.7(20,32)
  water ~, 662.7(31,44)
faith,n., 632.6
  based on ~, 632.14
  have ~ in, 632.2
  in good ~, 812.4; 813.7,9
  lacking in ~, 639.3(13–15,20, 24)
  worthy of ~, 632.25
faithful,adj., 658.1; see **loyal**, adj.
  promise to be ~, 1122.26
faithfulness,n., 658.2; see **loyalty**,n.
fall,n.
  autumn, 770.1
  dropping, 167.2
  loss of balance, 168.2
  rise and ~, 161.2
fall,v.
  drop, 167.1
  lose balance, 168.1,4
  about to ~ down, 167.8
  ~ apart, 802.21,23
  ~ back, 145.1
  begin to ~, 167.5; 168.4
  cause to ~, 167.4; 168.3
  ~ in drops, 167.1(12–14,35–37, 43,45); 918.9
  let ~, 167.4
  let ~ in drops, 918.10

let ~ like rain, 1037.8
let ~ like snow, 1039.9
~ like ice particles, 1040.4
~ like rain, 1037.8
~ like sleet, 1037.5
~ like snow, 1039.9
likely to ~ down, 167.7
~ of muscles, etc., 167.1(25)
~ of water, 1029.49
ready to ~ down, 167.9
rise and ~, 161.1
rise and ~ in horse saddle, 161.1(3)
rises and ~s, 161.4
~ to the bottom, 167.1(28,30, 38)
~ to the ground, 999.7
falling,adj., 167.3
  ~ off, 167.6
  ~ out, 167.6(2)
falling,n.
  sound of ~, 469.1(8,23)
falls,n.
  water ~, 1029.48–51
false,adj.
  imitating the genuine, 820.4
  not authentic, 820.5
  not based on fact or truth, 820.8
  not genuine, 820.1
  not true, 820.1
  ~ appearance, give a, 820.17
  ~ belief, 632.6(12); 632.7(2); 820.13
  ~ beliefs, treatise on, 682.15(5)
  challenge as ~, 820.23
  ~ character, 820.12
  conceal by ~ appearance, 970.13
  declare ~, 820.24
  declared ~, unable to be, 820.26
  ~ document, 820.15
  free of ~ beliefs, 309.11(9)
  ~ front, 823.13(1)
  have a ~ belief, 632.3
  ~ idea, 820.13
  ~ image, 483.8(8,9,11,14,16)
  ~ in impression, 820.10
  make ~, 820.17
  ~ nature, 820.12
  possibly ~, 820.11
  prove ~, 820.19,21,22
  proved ~, unable to be, 820.25
  something ~, 820.14
  ~ thinking, 820.13
  ~ though deceptively true, 820.2
  ~ writings, 820.6
falsely,adv.
  make ~, 820.18
  represent ~, 820.18
  testify ~, 638.1(17)
falseness,n., 820
  prefix to indicate ~, 820.9
falsify,v., 820.17
fame,n., 615.2
  bring back to ~, 615.6
famed,adj., 615.1; see **famous**, adj.
familiar,adj., 535.1,2
family,n., 722.4
  ancestry or descent, 723.1–5; see **ancestry**,n.
  at home, surrounded by ~, 753.5
  branch of a ~, 723.6
  group of ~s, 318.1(26)
  ~ in a home, 753.7
  ~ life, 1064.60
  of mixed ~, 728.15(3)
  one related by ~, 722.1
  ~ origin, 728.3

pert. to a ~, 722.5
related ~s, 722.4,6
related by ~, 722.2
relationship by ~, 722.3
study of ~ line, 723.12–14
famous,adj., 615.1
  ~ and intelligent person, 1065.84
  ~ book, author, etc., 615.5
  ~ for bad things, 615.1(3,13)
  ~ for poetry, 615.1(10)
  group of ~ people, 1056.11
  ~ in history, 771.20
  ~ in literature, 615.1(2)
  make ~, 615.4
  ~ person, 615.3
  ~ person, 615.3
fanatic,adj., 1095.2
  make ~, 1095.11
fanatic,n., 1095.3
fanaticism,n., 1095.1
  show ~, 1095.11
fanciful,adj., 809.1; see also **unreal**,adj.
fancy,adj., 959.17; see also **ornamental**,adj.
fang,n.
  centipede's poison ~, 800.7
far,adj., 789.1
  ~ from center, 789.1(3)
  ~ north, 789.7
  ~ regions, 789.9
  ~ south, 789.8
farewell,n., 127.1
  a saying ~, 127.3
  Hawaiian ~, 127.1(2)
  speech of ~, 127.2
  speech of ~, student who makes, 127.4
farm,n., 998.12
  ~ building, 998.17
  enclosure around a ~, 998.15
  exhibition of ~ products, 951.3(7); 951.28(3)
  house on a ~, 998.14
  pert. to ~s, 998.13
  pert. to interests of ~s, 998.5(1)
  pert. to life or affairs of ~s, 998.5(2)
  ~ worker, 998.4(2,3,9)
farm,v., 998.2,3
farmer,n., 998.4
  female ~, 998.4(2)
  Russian ~, 998.4(6)
  ~s' group, 998.18–20
farming,n., 998.1
  goddess of ~, 998.11
  land for ~, 1003.2(8,9)
  pert. to ~, 998.5
  student of ~, 998.4
  suitable for ~, 998.10
  treatise on ~, 998.8
farsightedness,n., 481.1(18,19, 28)
farther,adj.
  beyond the ~ side, 789.2
  on the ~ side, 789.2
farthest,adj., 789.3
  ~ away, 789.4
  ~ in specified direction, 789.6
  ~ in time, 767.5
  ~ point, 789.5
fascinate,v.
  attract, 196.1
  interest, 580.1
  occupy attention of, 579.6
fascinating,adj.
  attractive, 196.5
  interesting, 580.2
Fascist,n., 1076.12(8)
fashion,n., 631.1
  according to latest ~, 631.10
  addict of ~, 631.3
  addiction to ~, 631.2

follower of ~, 631.3
following of ~, 631.2
going out of ~, 631.15
out of ~, 631.12
people of ~, 631.11
world of ~, 631.11
fashionable,adj., 631.6
  ~ in appearance, 631.7
  ~ in dress, 631.7; 974.12
  neat and ~, 631.8
  newly ~, 1109.15
  ostentatiously ~, 951.45
  person ~ in dress, 974.28
  speedy and ~, 631.9
fast,adj., 95.1; see **rapid,adj.**
fast,adv., 95.5; see **rapidly,adv.**
fast,n.
  Lenten ~, 940.9
fasten,v., 302.1,4
  ~ by tying, 302.28,30
fastened,adj.
  become ~, 302.4,30
  state of being ~, 302.5
fastener,n., 302.3
fastening,n., 302.2,3,29
faster,adv.
  act ~, cause to, 52.9(6,32);
    54.12
  develop ~, cause to, 95.8
  do ~ than, 95.7
  go ~, cause to, 95.8
  happen ~, cause to, 95.8
  move ~, 94.6,7
  react ~, cause to, 54.12
  ~ than sound, 99.7(3)
fastidious,adj., 252.15
fat,adj., 510.1,6
  become ~, 510.5
  coarse-looking and ~, 864.7
  grow ~, 731.3(3)
  make ~, 510.5
  merry and ~, 1104.5
  ~ of face, 510.3
  ~ person, 510.4
  red-faced and ~, 864.7;
    903.1(2)
  untidy and ~, 903.1(2)
fat,n., 510.8; see also **oil,n.**
  causing use of ~, 510.10
  convert ~ into soap, 899.43
  dripping juices and ~ of
    meat, 447.4
  put ~ on, 510.12
  referring to ~, 510.9
  secreting ~, 510.11
  smear or cover with ~, 510.12
fatalistic,adj., 33.10
fate,n., 33.1
  ~ as influenced by stars,
    1053.24
  belief in ~, 33.8,11
  believer in ~, 33.9
  believing in ~, 33.10
  controlled by ~, 33.3
  ~ personified, 33.2
  pert. to ~, 33.4
  unhappy ~, 33.1(2)
fate,v., 33.5
fated,adj., 33.7
father,n., 724.1
  animal's ~, 724.1(9)
  custom of ~ during child-
    birth, 718.20
  government by a ~, 1073.3(26,
    27)
  having different ~, 725.7(1)
  having same ~, 725.7(2)
  like a ~, 724.2; see also
    fatherly,adj.
  pert. to a ~, 722.7(4,11,12);
    724.2; see also **fatherly,adj.**
  psychological situation in-
    volving ~ and daughter,
    724.5

relationship like that of a ~
  to a child, 724.7
treat as a ~ does, 724.9;
  1073.11
without a ~, 724.6
father,v., 717.6
fatherhood,n., 724.4
fatherly,adj., 724.2
  assume ~ responsibility for,
    724.3
  treat in a ~ manner, 724.9;
    1073.11
fatigue,n., 12.2
  bear ~, 1137.36
  bear ~, ability to, 1137.35
  ~ from blood loss, 926.26
  science of vocational ~,
    204.2
  sink from ~, 167.1(15)
  strength to endure ~, 1.16,
    17
  writer's ~, 12.7
fatigue,v., 12.3,6
fatigued,adj., 12.1; see also
  tired,adj.
fatiguing,adj., 12.4
fatness,n., 510.2
faucet,n., 1033.43
  gas ~, 1033.47
  rain ~, 1033.44
  water-~ structure, 1033.46
fault,n., 830.1
  containing a ~, 830.5
  find ~ with, 894.1
  free of ~, 816.3
  mark indicating a ~ in be-
    havior, 830.7
  moral ~, 830.3
  one without ~, 816.4
  person guilty of a ~, 884.38
  physical ~, 830.4
  show the ~s of, 951.1(21,40)
  slight ~, 830.2
faultfinder,n., 894.5
faultfinding,n., 894.3
  disposed to ~, 894.4
  engage in ~, 894.2
faulty,adj., 830.5
  be ~, 830.6
favor,n.
  support, 854.3
  a ~, 842.7
  do a ~ for, 842.9
  granted ~, 842.8
  in ~, 1109.18
  insinuate oneself into the ~
    of, 1109.25–27
  person in ~, 1109.20
  regard with ~, 854.14
  speak in ~ of, 854.12,13
  try to get the ~ of, 1109.23,24
  unwilling to do ~s, 265.26(5,
    16)
  willing to do ~s, 265.23(7)
  willing to do a ~, 842.10
favor,v., 854.1,14; 1112.9; see
  also **support,v.**
favorable,adj., 837.1
  ~ in disposition, 837.2
  ~ in inclination, 837.2
  providing ~ results, 837.3
favorably,adv.
  regard ~, 854.14
  speak ~ of, 854.12,13
favorer,n., 854.5; see also **sup-**
  porter,n.
favorite,adj., 1109.18
favorite,n., 1109.20
favoritism,n., 634.1
  ~ to relatives, 722.9,10
fear,n., 576.2
  a trembling from ~, 111.2(6)
  act of ~, 576.4
  ~ before an audience,
    576.2(6)

bend in ~, 152.1(3)
cause ~ to, 576.6
cause of ~, 576.8,10
cause to jump with ~,
  110.10(4)
causes ~, one who, 576.8
causing ~, 576.7; see **fright-**
  ening,adj.
causing ~ and nervousness,
  1133.9
crouch in ~, 64.1(1,2)
draw back in ~, 145.1(3,4,6–9,
  11,17,19,25,27,28)
feel ~, 576.3
foresee with ~, 772.13
full of silly ~s, 576.1(56)
government by ~, 1073.3(31)
having a specific ~, 576.12
jump with ~, 110.1(1,28,29)
move in ~, 83.1
movement of ~, 83.2; 576.4
object of ~, 576.10
  ~ of air, 1045.22
  ~ of aloneness, 576.11(14,51)
  ~ of animals, 576.11(87)
  ~ of babies, 576.11(66)
  ~ of bacteria, 576.11(15)
  ~ of bees, 576.11(10)
  ~ of being alone, 576.11(14,
    51)
  ~ of being hit, 576.11(72)
  ~ of being looked at,
    576.11(74)
  ~ of being poisoned,
    576.11(82)
  ~ of being seen, 576.11(74)
  ~ of being shut in, 576.11(22)
  ~ of being stared at,
    576.11(62)
  ~ of birds, 576.11(63)
  ~ of blood, 576.11(44)
  ~ of books, 576.11(18)
  ~ of British people, etc.,
    576.11(8)
  ~ of burial alive, 576.11(78)
  ~ of cats, 576.11(3)
  ~ of closed places, 576.11(22)
  ~ of colors, 576.11(21,31)
  ~ of confining places,
    576.11(22)
  ~ of contamination,
    576.11(52)
  ~ of corpses, 576.11(54)
  ~ of crowds, 576.11(22,59)
  ~ of darkness, 576.11(58)
  ~ of death, 576.11(54,80)
  ~ of defecation, 576.11(24)
  ~ of deformity or deformed
    people, 576.11(79)
  ~ of demons, 576.11(27)
  ~ of depths, 576.11(16)
  ~ of devils, 576.11(27)
  ~ of dirt, 576.11(52)
  ~ of disease, 576.11(20,26,50,
    57)
  ~ of dogs, 576.11(25)
  ~ of drinking, 576.11(28)
  ~ of eating, 576.11(76)
  ~ of elevators, 576.11(1)
  ~ of fear, 576.11(68)
  ~ of feces, 576.11(24)
  ~ of females, 576.11(32,41)
  ~ of fire, 576.11(71)
  ~ of fish, 576.11(48)
  ~ of food, 576.11(76)
  ~ of forests, 576.11(47)
  ~ of France, 576.11(33)
  ~ of French customs, etc.,
    576.11(33)
  ~ of frogs, 576.11(17)
  ~ of gases, 1045.22
  ~ of German people, ideas,
    etc., 576.11(36)
  ~ of Germany, 576.11(36)
  ~ of germs, 576.11(15)

~ of giving birth, 576.11(81)
~ of giving birth to freaks,
  576.11(79)
~ of gold, 576.11(13)
~ of Greek people, customs,
  etc., 576.11(39,43)
~ of hair, 576.11(83)
~ of heart disease, 576.11(20)
~ of hell, 576.11(42)
~ of high places, 576.11(1)
~ of insanity, 576.11(50)
~ of ladders, 576.11(1)
~ of leaving shelter, 576.11(2)
~ of light, 576.11(70)
~ of lightning, 576.11(11)
~ of love, 576.11(30)
~ of males, 576.11(6)
~ of marriage, 576.11(34)
~ of medicine, 576.11(67)
~ of men, 576.11(6)
~ of nakedness, 576.11(40)
~ of neglect of duty,
  576.11(65)
~ of Negroes, 576.11(55)
~ of newness, 576.11(56)
~ of noise, 576.11(69)
~ of open spaces, 576.11(2)
~ of pain, 576.11(4)
~ of people, 576.11(9)
~ of poison, 576.11(82)
~ of rabies, 576.11(50)
~ of railroad travel,
  576.11(75)
~ of red, 576.11(31)
~ of robbers or robbery,
  576.11(49)
~ of Russia, Russians, etc.,
  576.11(73)
~ of sex, 576.11(35)
~ of sexual disease,
  576.11(26)
~ of sexual intercourse,
  576.11(23)
~ of sexual love, 576.11(30)
~ of Slavic people, etc.,
  576.11(77)
~ of smells, 576.11(64)
~ of snakes, 576.11(61)
~ of stars, 576.11(12)
~ of strangers, 576.11(86)
~ of sunlight, 1065.16
~ of taste, 576.11(37)
~ of telling lies, 576.11(53)
~ of thirteen, 576.11(84)
~ of thunder, 576.11(19)
~ of thunderstorms,
  576.11(11)
~ of toads, 576.11(17)
~ of traveling, 576.11(45,75)
~ of vehicles, 576.11(5)
~ of wandering, 576.11(29)
~ of water, 576.11(46)
~ of winds, 576.11(7)
~ of women, 576.11(32,41)
~ of words, 576.11(60)
~ of worms, 576.11(85)
~ of writing, 576.11(38)
paralyzing ~, 576.2(1)
pathological ~s, 576.11
reduce the ~s of, 1131.16,17
show ~, 576.3
sign of ~, 576.4
sound of ~, 468.1(12)
symbol of ~, 576.9
tremble with ~, 111.1(17,19,
  23,24)
trembling with ~, 111.3(4)
victim of a specific ~, 576.13
without ~, 575.1; see **brave,**
  adj.
fear,v., 576.3
hate and ~, 880.1(1,7,9)
fearful,adj.
afraid, 576.1; see **frightened,**
  adj.

frightening, 576.7; see **frightening,**adj.
fearless,adj., 575.1; see **brave,**
  adj.
feast,n., 740.16(9,17)
drunken ~, 740.16(1)
drunken ~, pert. to, 740.20(2)
elaborate ~, 740.16(2)
imaginary ~, 740.16(3)
pert. to a ~, 740.20(3)
sumptuous ~s, descr. of,
  740.20(4)
feast,v., 734.1; see **eat,**v.
feat,n., 49.6
feather,n., 341.1
~ as head decorations,
  983.24(1)
~ for helmet, 959.3(5)
group of ~s, 341.2
grow ~s, 341.8,9
like ~s, 341.4
like a ~, 341.4,7
lose ~s, 972.10
ornament with ~s, 959.1(24)
parts of a ~, 341.6
put ~s on, 341.10
remove the ~s from, 341.12
shed ~s, 286.1(37) ; 341.13
smooth the ~s, 341.11
treatise on ~s, 682.15(20)
with ~s, 341.3
without ~s, 341.14
feathery,adj., 341.4
be or become ~, 341.5
feature,n., 1091.11; see **characteristic,**n.
facial ~s, 365.1(5,7)
February,n.
inserted in the calendar (of
  ~ 29th), 774.8,9
feces,n., 293.6
animal ~, 293.9
containing ~, 293.12
descr. of, 293.10
eating of ~, 734.26(3,9)
filthy with ~, 904.1(4)
fluid discharge of ~, 293.8
hardened ~, 293.7; 293.9(2)
inspection of ~, 293.32
interest in ~, 293.28
like ~, 293.12
living in ~, 293.30
pert. to ~, 293.10,11
reference to ~ in language,
  1118.20
sexual aberration relating to
  ~, 710.33(6)
study of ~, 293.31
talking about ~, 293.29
fee,n., 219.3; see **payment,**n.
feeble-minded,adj., 597.1,19;
  see also **stupid,**adj.
~ person, 597.17
~ state, 597.18; see also **stupidity,**n.
feed,n., 740.4
feed,v.
eat, 734.1; see **eat,**v.
give food to, 738.1
supply with food, 233.1(1,10,
  12,15,17,21,23,24)
able to ~ animals (of land),
  986.28
~ at the breast, 360.11–13
~ domestic animals, 738.6
~ grass to, 986.2
~ grass to livestock for purging, 986.4
~ less than enough to, 738.4
~ on certain foods, 734.26–29;
  see **eating,**n., **eating,**adj.
~ on grass, etc., 734.4; 986.3
place where animals ~,
  782.1(23)
~ too much to, 738.3

feeding,n.
animal's ~ grounds, 734.5
forced ~, 738.5
feel,v.
~ a sensation, 433.3
~ about with the hands,
  436.1(15)
~ emotion, 1092.44
~ with the hands, 436.1(16,22,
  24,31)
feeling,n.
emotional ~, 1092.1; see **emotion,**n.
have a ~ of coming misfortune, 37.8
hurt the ~s of, 868.1
hurt (the ~s), 868.4
injury to the ~s, 868.2
~ of coming disaster, 37.7
physical ~, 434.1–4; see **sensation,**n.
strengthen in ~, 1.29(5)
feet,n., 346.11; see also **foot,**n.
animal as to ~, 346.13
animal with naked ~, 984.23
care of the ~, 346.17,18
child's ~, 346.7
having ~, 346.11(10,11)
having ~ that grasp,
  346.11(2)
having ~ turned inward,
  346.11(12)
having divided ~, 346.11(3)
having flat ~, 346.11(5,15)
having four ~, 346.11(13)
having large ~, 346.11(7)
having many ~, 346.11(9)
having small ~, 346.11(8)
having three ~, 346.11(16)
having two ~, 346.11(1)
measurement in ~, 946.42
person as to ~, 346.12
sore of ~, 12.1(14)
without ~, 346.16
female,adj., 708.5; see also **feminine, womanly,**adj.
deprive of ~ qualities, 708.9
female,n., 708.1; see also **girl,
  woman, women,**n.
development of maleness in a
  ~, 707.5
group of animal ~s, 708.4
like a ~, 708.5,8; see also
  feminine,adj.
pert. to ~s, 708.5; see also
  feminine,adj.
~ qualities, 708.6
~s, collectively, 708.2
young ~, 760.6; see **girl,
  woman,**n.
feminine,adj., 708.5
both ~ and masculine organs,
  characteristics, etc., 710.36
~ habits, etc., in the male,
  710.33(8,31,34)
~ man, 707.2(1,3) ; 707.11
neither masculine nor ~,
  710.51
~ (of a man), 707.8–10,12–15;
  see **effeminate,**adj.
~ qualities, 708.6
~ qualities in a male, 707.10,
  14,15
femininity,n., 708.6
deprive of ~, 708.9
fence,n., 300.8
~ of trees, bushes, or shrubs,
  996.30
parts of a ~, 300.9
protective ~, 568.30(1,9,10,14)
fence,v., 300.1; see **surround,**v.
~ in, 301.1; see **confine,**v.
~ with trees, bushes, or
  shrubs, 996.31
ferment,v., 749.28,31,33

fermentation,n., 749.32
chemistry of ~, 749.36(2)
measure ~, device to, 749.35
relating to ~, 749.34
science of ~, 749.36
fern,n., 985.6(5,10,30)
having ~ leaves, 993.6
leaf of a ~, 993.2
~ leaves, 993.3
like a ~, 993.4
place for ornamental ~s, 985.34(6)
science of ~s, 985.36(21)
shaped like a ~, 993.5
ferocious,adj., 4.19; see **fierce**, adj.
ferociousness,n., 4.20
ferret,n.
group of ~s, 403.5(26)
of ~s, 403.11(10)
ferry,n.
driver of a ~, 115.10
ferryman,n., 115.10
~ of souls, 662.29(1)
fertile,adj., 715.1
be ~, 715.10
delightful and ~ place, 1102.25
end of female's ~ period, 716.5
figuratively ~, 715.9
~ land in a desert, 1003.12
make ~, 715.11
~ (of the female), 715.1
~ (of the soil), 715.7,8
~ soil, 999.1(5,6,7)
fertility,n.
symbol of ~, 954.1(2)
fertilizer,n.
soil ~, 999.12
fester,n., 383.2
fester,v., 383.4,7,9
festered,adj., 383.3
festering,adj., 383.11
fetus,n., 721.8
dead ~, birth of a, 720.4
destruction of a ~, 714.18; see **abortion**,n.
movement of a ~, 79.19
organ of attachment of ~, 379.1(16)
feud,n., 221.2
blood ~, 221.2(6)
feudal,adj., 1074.3
~ lord, 1074.17; see **lord**,n.
feudalism,n., 1074.1
convert to ~, 1074.7
land under ~, 1074.8–11
like ~, 1074.4
partial to ~, 1074.6
pert. to ~, 1074.3
principles of ~, 1074.2
ruler under ~, 1074.17–25
slave under ~, 1074.14–16
supporter of ~, 1074.5
fever,n., 1063.1
affect with ~, 1063.8
caused by ~, 1063.13
causes ~, substance that, 1063.5
causing ~, 1063.4
eliminates ~, that which, 1063.14
having ~, 1063.6
heat of ~, 1063.12
indicating ~, 1063.11
like a ~, 1063.9
lose ~, 1063.16
marked by ~, 1063.10
mental derangement caused by ~, 1136.1(8)
pert. to ~, 1063.2
preventive of ~, 1063.14,15
recurring ~, 1063.3

reduces ~, that which, 1063.14
reducing ~, 1063.15
without ~, 1063.17
feverish,adj., 1063.6
~ state, 1063.7
fiancé,n., 704.5
fiancée,n., 704.5
fiber,n., 306.1; see **thread**,n.
fickle,adj., 539.21
~ person, 539.22
fiction,n.
literature, 688.1
something imaginary, 809.3
story, 685.1; see **story**,n.
existing only in ~, 809.1(5,9, 15,17); see also **imaginary, unreal**,adj.
fictional,adj., 809.1; see also **imaginary, unreal**,adj.
~ double or counterpart, 529.3(4)
field,n., 1003.2
rice ~, 1003.2(21)
fiend,n., 660.1; see **devil**,n.
fierce,adj., 4.19
cruel and ~, 4.21
~ person, 4.22,23
fiercely,adv., 4.24
fife,n.
signal by ~, 956.1(12)
fifth,adj., 934.6
happening every ~ day, 934.6
fifty,n., 940.10
lasting ~ days, 940.11
~-year-old person, 758.2(5)
fight,n., 562.1
~ between angels, 562.1(3)
~ between dogs, 562.1(15)
~ between gods, 562.1(39)
~ between knights, 562.1(25, 40,41)
~ between two, 562.1(1,17,19, 28)
fist ~, 562.1(26,31)
~ for something, 562.1(32)
prize ~, 562.1(26)
Roman ~, 562.1(24)
rough ~, 865.7
sea ~, 562.1(29,30)
verbal ~, 562.1(14,25); see **dispute**,n.
~ with lances, 562.1(40)
fight,v., 562.2
~ against, figuratively, 562.2(4)
disguised reluctance to ~, 544.2(5)
inclined to ~, 562.11,12
refuses to ~ in wartime, one who, 562.14
reluctance to ~, 872.14
~ roughly and playfully, 865.9
~ with fists, 562.2(1)
~ with imaginary foe, 562.2(6,9)
~ with swords, 562.2(3)
fighter,n., 562.4
non-~, 562.13
Scandinavian ~ of mythology, 1100.22
fighting,adj., 562.5
take a ~ attitude, 562.7
fighting,n., 562.3
~ between knights, 562.3(3)
end ~, 1140.34
end of ~, temporary, 1140.32
engaged in ~, 562.5(1–3)
fond of ~, 562.11,12
instruments of ~, 562.9
scene of ~, 562.8
~ with fists, 562.3(2,4)
~ with imaginary foe, 562.3(5,6)

~ with swords, 562.3(1)
figure,n.
number, 927.1
geometric ~s, 945
~ of speech, 669.1–8
sculptured ~, 966.18
figure,v.
calculate, 942.1; see **calculate**,v.
~ results of, 16.27
figure of speech,n., 669.1–8
ornamented by ~, 951.48
filament,n., 306.1; see **thread**,n.
Filipino,n.
~ who did not revolt against Spain, 1140.17
fill,v., 925.2,8
~ (a person) with food or drink, 925.22
act of ~ing, 925.3
~ again, 925.2(5,6)
~ figuratively, 925.18
~ hole with dirt, 925.5(8)
~ (oneself) with food or drink, 925.23
~s and unloads ships, one who, 925.14
~ ship, 925.2(2)
~ ship with water, 925.5(7)
~ with a quality, 925.18
~ with emotion, 925.18
~ with rubbish, 925.2(3)
fillable,adj., 925.2
filled,adj., 925.1
able to be ~ with food or drink, 925.24
be ~, 925.7,19
become ~, 925.8,19
figuratively ~, 925.17
unable to be ~ with food or drink, 925.25
~ with a quality, 925.17
~ with emotion, 925.17
~ with food or drink, 925.20
filler,n., 925.5
filling,adj., 925.6
film,n.
~ of waste matter, 285.1(16, 29)
~ on brass, bronze, or copper, 1016.18,19
filth,n., 904.3
causing or caused by ~, 904.9
eating of ~, 734.26(9)
filthy,adj., 904.1,10; see also **dirty**,adj.
become ~, 904.8
~ language, 904.16
make ~, 904.5
~ place, 904.14
quality of being ~, 904.2
~ with feces, 904.1(4)
~ with impurities, 904.1(4)
~ with insect larvae, 904.1(9)
~ word, 713.3; 863.8
fin,n., 342.1
final,adj., 792.15; see also **concluding, last**,adj.
~ accomplishment, 792.23(6)
~ act, 52.5(20)
~ artistic work, 792.23(6)
doctrine of ~ things or states, 792.26
in ~ and fixed form, 792.18
~ parts, 792.23
~ point, 792.23(11)
~ speech, 792.23
~ things, 792.23
find,n., 487.6
valuable ~, 487.7,8
find,v., 487.1; see also **found**, adj.
~ and use, 279.1(18)
attempt to ~ out, 624.8–14
eager to ~ out, 624.15

hard to ~, 487.5
~ out, 624.1–5; see **discover**,v.
finder,n., 487.3
finding,n., 487.2
fine,n., 896.2(1,4)
  impose a ~ on, 896.15
fine,v., 896.1(1,16)
finger,n., 344.1
  able to touch each ~ (of the thumb), 436.10
  communication by ~s, 664.11(3)
  condition of ~s, 344.7
  exercise the ~s, instrument to, 103.5
  grasping ~s, 247.16
  having ~s, 344.6(2–6,8–10)
  having fast or light ~s, 344.6(9)
  having skillful ~s, 949.10
  ~ language, 951.15
  like ~s, 344.5(2,4)
  pain in the ~s from writing, 1137.56(31)
  pert. to ~s, 344.5(1,3)
  ~-shaped, 507.17(30,33)
  with the ~s, 344.5(3)
fingernail,n., 344.12(4,5)
  care of the ~s, 343.18
  sensitive flesh under ~, 385.1(6)
  skin around ~, 382.1(1,4,9)
fingerprint,n., 344.9
  classification of ~s, 344.10
  identification by ~s, 344.10
  science of ~s, 344.10
finish,n., 792.6
finish,v.
  complete, 328.3
  end, 792.1,2,5
finished,adj., 328.1; see **complete**,adj.
finishing,adj., 792.15; see **final**, adj.
  ~ blow, 437.2(1,2,6)
  ~ stroke, 792.20
Finland,n., 784.9(15)
fire,n., 1064.1
  alarm that warns of ~, 1064.75,76
  building susceptible to ~s, 1064.83
  burst into ~, 1064.23
  bursting into ~, 1064.24,25
  catch ~, able to, 1064.19
  catch on ~, 1064.22
  catches ~ easily, that which, 1064.20,21
  catching on ~ spontaneously, 1064.26,27
  come out as particles of ~, 1064.5
  composed of pure ~, 1064.8(1)
  consume by ~, 1064.33
  containing ~, 1064.8(2)
  corner by the ~, 783.5(1)
  death by ~, 1064.18
  death by ~, heap of wood for, 1064.61(8)
  death by ~, post for, 1064.64
  destroy by ~, 1064.33
  destruction by ~, 1064.33
  destruction of life by ~, 1064.18
  eater of ~, 1064.74
  fighter of ~, 1064.77,78
  fighting by ~, 1064.73
  ~-fighting, 1064.82
  ~-fighting vehicle, 1064.80,81
  flameless ~, 1064.1(9)
  give off particles of ~, 1064.5
  giving off particles of ~ when struck, 1064.6
  go out (of a ~), 801.19
  god of ~, 1012.28; 1064.90

goddess of the hearth ~, 1061.32
hell-~, 1064.1(7) ; 1064.2
killing by ~, 796.2(7)
light a ~, 1064.13
light a ~, device to, 1064.14
light from ~, 1065.49(7,8)
like ~, 1064.8(2,3)
not bursting into ~, 1064.89
officer of ~ dept., 1077.1(20)
on ~, 1064.28–31
particle of ~, 1064.4
pert. to ~, 1064.8(3)
place to make a ~, 1064.55
prevention of ~, 1064.82,85,86
put out (a ~), 801.17
relating to ~, 1064.8
remains of a ~, 1064.44,52
ruins from destruction by ~, 1064.53
set ~s, morbid impulse to, 1064.17
set on ~, 1064.9
setting of ~s, malicious, 1064.15,16
signal ~, 956.1(2) ; 1064.1(1, 2,4)
soil used for a ~, 1064.61(7)
something on ~, 1064.42
space around a ~, 1064.60
sticks for a ~, 1064.61(2,6)
stir up, poke, shake, etc., a ~, 1064.10,11
streak of ~ in the sky, 1053.7
subject to ~, 1064.41
substance for a ~, 1064.61
take care of a ~, 1064.10–12
tie into a bundle for a ~, 1064.65
tongue of ~, 1064.3
unable to catch ~, 1064.87,88
without ~, 1064.84
wood for a ~, 1064.61(2,6)
worship of ~, 656.15(22)
fire,v.
  catch on fire, 1064.22
  set on fire, 1064.9,41
  shoot, 565.3; see **shoot**,v.
firearm,n., 565.1; see **gun**, **cannon**,n.
  ~s, 565.2
fireman,n., 1064.11,77
firemen,n., 1064.78
fireplace,n., 1064.55(5)
  board for closing a ~, 1064.58
  brick or stone for a ~, 1064.59
  screen for a ~, 1064.57
  side of a ~, 1009.13
  space around a ~, 1064.60
  supports in a ~, 1064.56
fireproof,adj., 1064.85–88
firework,n., 1064.69
  ~ that sparkles, 1065.67
fireworks,n.
  display of ~, 1064.70
  like, or pert. to, ~, 1064.71
  manufacture, use, or art of ~, 1064.72
firm,adj.
  steady, 88.1; see **steady**,adj.
  stiff, 442.1
  built ~ly, 88.5
firmness,n.
  steadiness, 88.2
  stiffness, 442.2
  degree of ~, 442.6
  lacking ~, 443.1(4,6,8,11,13) ; 443.2; 444.1
first,adj.
  beginning, 729.15; see **beginning**,adj.
  coming first, 766.7
  ~ created, 729.15(13)
  dealing with ~ things, 729.15

~ in rank, 313.9
one who is ~ in his class, etc., 766.8
~ part, 326.1(27,29)
those who are ~, 766.9
fish,n., 422.3
  anatomy of the ~, 338.10(4)
  avoidance of ~, 76.2(2)
  eating ~, 734.27(26)
  eggs of ~, 422.6
  full of ~, 422.7
  group of ~, 403.5(59,61)
  ~ life, 403.1(7,10)
  like ~, 422.2,3
  male ~, 422.3(3)
  mythical creature, part ~, part human, 662.26(6,7,11, 13)
  of ~, 422.1(3,10,19,24,29)
  place for ~, 403.22(3,33)
  place where ~ are caught, 403.22(13)
  raising of ~, 403.30(5)
  science of ~es, 403.26(20,21)
  science of shell~, 403.26(23)
  ~-shaped, 507.17(43,60)
  shell~, 422.1(5,6,13,20,25,27, 33) ; 422.3
  small ~, 422.3(2)
  treatise on ~, 682.15(12)
  worship of ~, 656.15(10)
fish,v., 486.13
  ~ by letting bait dip, 1035.16
  ~ for pearls, 963.11
  right to ~, 486.18
fisherman,n., 486.14
fishing,n.
  gear for ~, 486.15,16
  pert. to ~, 486.20
  place for ~, 486.17
  science of ~, 486.19
fist,n.
  tighten the ~, 302.10(3)
fit,n.
  attack, 560.24
  ~ of anger, 878.12,13
  ~ of bad temper, 876.6,7
  ~ of laughter and weeping, 1100.10
  ~ of nervousness, 1133.3
  ~ of resentment, 878.15
  ~ of weeping or tears, 1127.3, 4
  violent ~ of emotion, 1092.42
fit,v., 817.5,6
fitting,adj., 817.1
five, n. or adj., 934.1
  a number ~ times greater, 934.12
  arranged in ~s, 934.7
  card or die of ~ pips, 934.2
  consisting of ~, 934.7
  consisting of ~ parts, 934.5
  divide into ~, 934.4
  divided into ~ parts, 934.5
  group of ~, 934.3
  happening every ~ days, 934.6
  multiply by ~, 934.10
  thing of ~ parts, 934.8
fivefold,adj., 934.9
  increase ~, 907.9(6)
flag,n., 957.1
  British ~, 957.5
  ~ carrier, 957.2
  cloth used for ~s, 957.8
  Confederate ~, 957.4
  decorate with ~s, 957.9
  device on ~, 957.17
  French ~, 957.6
  ~ indicating surrender, etc., 957.11
  lower the ~, 957.12
  mourning, position of ~ in, 957.13

pirate ~, 250.11
~pole, 957.16
put a ~ on, 957.9
~s, collectively, 957.7
~s for decoration, 957.8
~s of a ship, 957.7
signal by ~, 956.1(15,16) ;
   956.2(1,2)
trap (game) by waving ~,
   957.10
trouble at sea, ~ as signal of,
   957.15
U.S. ~, 957.3
unity, device on ~ to indicate, 957.17
~ with points, 957.18
flame,n., 1064.3; see also **fire,n.**
gas ~, 1048.24
not bursting into ~, 1064.89
subject to ~, 1064.41
flame,v., 1064.29; 1065.45(10,12)
~ing stick of wood, etc.,
   1065.107(7,22)
flammable,adj., 1064.19
flash,v., 1065.45
~ like lightning, 1044.16
flashing,adj., 1065.50
~ for a short time, 1065.53
flashlight,n., 1065.107(18)
flask,n., 261.7(22,25)
~-shaped, 507.17(6)
flat, adj., 519.1
become ~, 519.3
become ~ like a mushroom,
   985.23
circular and ~, 508.4
~ in flavor, 446.18,19
~ in shape or surface, 1024.11
low and ~, 169.1
lying ~, 65.3(10,11)
make ~, 519.4
~ ornament, 959.3(15)
~ surface, 519.2
flatfoot,n., 346.12; 346.12(2)
flat-footed,adj., 346.11(5,15)
flatter,v., 851.1; 852.1,5
~ excessively, 852.1(1,2,5)
~ obsequiously, 852.1(1) ;
   852.8
~ obviously, 852.6
~ offensively, 852.6
~ servilely, 852.1(1) ; 852.8
flatterer,n., 852.4
group of ~s, 318.1(27)
obsequious ~, 852.9
self-seeking ~, 852.9,10
servile ~, 852.9
flattering,adj., 852.3
flattery,n., 851.2; 852.2
deceive with artful ~, 852.7
engage in ~, 852.5,6
full of ~, 852.3
seek friendliness by ~,
   1096.29
self-seeking ~, 852.2(3) ;
   852.8,10
servile ~, 852.8,10
treat with ~, 852.1(3)
flatworm,n., 427.12,13
flavor,n., 446.10
descr. of ~, 446.13,18
dull of ~, 446.18,19
full of ~, 446.13
give or add ~ to, 446.14
giving or adding a ~, 446.16
have ~, 446.11
have the ~ of, 446.12
improve ~ of, 446.15
improves or adds ~, that
   which, 446.17
lack of ~, 446.19,20
without ~, 446.18,20
flavor,v., 446.14
flavorless,adj., 10.1(30) ; 446.18,
   19

make ~, 446.20
flavorsome,adj., 446.13
flaw,n., 830.1; see **fault,n.**
full of ~s, 830.8
flea,n.
disease caused by ~s,
   396.1(31)
infested with ~s, 403.18(7)
flee,v., 141.1; see **depart,v.**
flesh,n., 385.1; see also **skin,n.**
~-colored, 385.4; 488.8(14) ;
   495.13(1)
decaying animal ~, 806.16,17
fold of ~ on animal, 385.1
in the ~, 385.6
invest with ~, 385.5
pert. to ~, 385.2
sensitive ~ under fingernails,
   385.1(6)
turn into ~, 385.7
~ under lower jaw, 385.1(5)
fleshy,adj., 385.3
become or make ~, 385.7
flexible,adj., 152.7
flight,n., 97.2; see also **departure, flying,n.**
~ during amnesia, 141.2(6)
~ from Mecca, 141.2(7)
put to ~, 144.1(11,27,28)
flighty,adj., 606.1; see **dizzy,
adj.**
~ woman, 606.7
flimsy,adj., 909.11,12
flirt,n., 700.12
silly ~, 608.21
flirt,v., 700.11
flirtatious,adj., 700.13
~ woman, 700.12
float,v., 113.1,2
ability to ~, 113.10,11
able to ~, 113.11
keep things ~ing, able to,
   1022.36
floater,n., 113.13,14
floating,adj., 113.8
~ matter, 113.12
~ on the waves, 113.8(2)
floating,n., 113.3–6
art of ~, 113.9
~ of bonds or stocks, 113.7
flock,n.
living in ~s, 750.3(4,9)
flood,n., 112.2,7,8
after the Biblical ~, 112.10
before the Biblical ~, 112.11
descr. of a ~, 112.9
one who lived before the ~,
   759.9
flood,v., 112.1; 1034.19
~ the land, 1026.31
flooded,adj., 112.6; 1026.30;
   1034.20
~ with salt water, 1026.23(7)
~ with water, 1026.30
floodlight,n., 1065.107(13,19)
~ in motion-picture studios,
   1065.107(13)
floor,n., 1025.5
cloth for a ~, 1025.9
cover the ~, 972.1(9) ; 1025.11
cover with a ~, 1025.12
covering for a ~, 972.4(17) ;
   1025.10
~ for race tracks, horse
   shows, circuses, etc.,
   1025.21
~ for skating, 1025.6,7
lay planking on (a ~), 997.7
material for ~s, 1025.5
~ of a building (height),
   1025.1,4
plan of rooms on a ~, 1025.19
polished ~ of marble, etc.,
   1025.20
raised ~, 1025.22,23

rooms or apartments on a ~,
   1025.2
~s, 1025.5
ship's ~, 1025.13
~ space, 1025.8
flour,n., 987.4
~ etc., used in baking,
   1062.9,10
like ~, 987.7
made from ~, 987.9
shaped mass of ~ for baking,
   1062.10
yielding ~, 987.9
flow,n., 112.2
sound of a ~, 469.1(12)
stop the ~ of, 791.6
flow,v., 112.1; see also **pour,v.**
able to ~, 112.5
~ in drops, 918.9
~ in waves, 1032.2–4
let ~ in drops, 918.10
let (blood) ~, 1036.21
that which ~s, 112.4;
   1027.1(6) ; 1029.23
flower,n., 994.1
arrangement of ~s, 994.15
bearing ~s, 994.18,19,24
bearing white ~s, 994.25
bears ~s, part that, 994.14
bunch of ~s, 994.6
circle of ~s and leaves, 994.8
cluster of ~s, 994.7
consisting of ~s, 994.16
covered with ~s, 994.19
cultivation of ~s, 994.29
decorate with ~s, 994.22
decorated with ~s, 994.20
decorated with ~s, become,
   994.23
description of ~s, 994.34
exhibition of ~s, 951.28(1)
goddess of ~s, 994.33
grow ~s, 731.22(1,5)
grower of ~s, 994.29–31
having or producing ~s,
   994.13
~ in buttonhole, 994.3
like ~s, 994.17
ornament of ~s, 959.3(9) ;
   994.21
parts of a ~, 994.28
pert. to ~s, 994.16
pot, stand, etc., for ~s, 994.32
~s, collectively, 994.5
science of growing ~s, 994.30
seller of ~s, 994.31
small ~, 994.2
sprout ~s, 994.9
wild ~, 994.4
yellow ~s, descr. of, 994.26
flower,v., 994.9
flowering,adj., 994.13
~ at evening, 777.5(20)
~ at night, 778.5(2)
~ part, 994.14
flowering,n.
state of ~, 994.10–12
time of ~, 762.1(1) ; 994.10–12
flowing,adj., 112.3
flowing,n., 112.2
fluency,n., 665.9(59)
fluent,adj., 665.3
fluid,adj., 1027.2
fluid,n., 1027.1; see also **liquid,n.**
device for drawing in and
   ejecting ~s, 193.12
force of ~s, pert. to, 1027.34,
   35
measurement unit of ~s,
   946.46
operated by ~s in motion,
   1027.34
pert. to the motion of ~s,
   1027.34,35

science of ~s, 1027.33
flute,n.
  early ~, 479.8(22)
  player of a ~, 479.9(10)
fly,n., 428.3
  of the ~, 428.1(6)
  science of the ~, 403.26(13)
fly,v., 97.1
  ability to ~, 97.6
  able to ~, 97.5
  disposed to ~, 97.4
flying,adj., 97.3
  ~ in the evening, 777.5(2)
flying,n., 97.2
  pert. to ~, 97.7
  science of ~, 97.8
  tricks, etc., in ~, 97.9
foam,n., 1028.12
  become ~, 1028.16
  cover with ~, 1028.20
  cover with soapy ~, 899.47
  covered with ~, 1028.19
  develop ~, 1028.16
  full of ~, 1028.19
  give off ~, 1028.16
  give off as or like ~, 1028.17
  like ~, 1028.19
  ~ of waves, 1032.7
  produce (~) by shaking or
    stirring, 1028.23
  soapy ~, 899.44; 1028.13
foam,v., 1028.16-18
  ~ and bubble, 1028.22
  cause to ~, 1028.18
foaming,adj., 1028.21
foamy,adj., 1028.19,21
fodder,n., 740.4
fog,n., 1041.1
  bright spot in ~, 1041.6
  condition of ~, 1046.6
  cover or surround with ~,
    1041.3
  layer of ~, 1041.5
  motionless because of ~,
    1041.7
  smoke and ~, 1041.1(5)
  smoke, haze, and ~, 1041.1(4)
  warning signal during ~,
    1041.8
foggy,adj., 1041.2
fold,n., 157.4
  easily contracting into ~s,
    157.6
  having ~s, 157.5
  ~ of skin, 157.8
fold,v., 157.1-3
folded,adj., 157.5
  ~ part, 157.7; 326.1(25)
folklore,n.
  interpretation of ~, 1055.41
follow,v.
  come after, 173.1-3
  come next, 173.1-3
  pursue, 173.12-17; see
    pursue,v.
  ~ a course of action, 52.7
  ~ as a result, 16.3(2);
    173.1(2)
  things that ~ one another,
    173.9; 914.1(14); see also
    series,n.
follower,n., 178.1
  pursuer, 173.14
  be a ~ of, 178.2
  devoted ~, 657.4(3)
  group of ~s, 178.5
  loyal ~, 658.3(2)
  pert. to a ~, 178.4
  ~s, 178.5
  servile ~, 178.1(3,9,12,13,18,21,
    23)
  state of being a ~, 178.3
  tending to be a ~, 178.6
  undesirable ~, 178.1(4,10,16)
following,adj., 173.4

pursuing, 173.12,15
  ~ as a result, 173.4(2,4-6,12,
    13)
  ~ circumstance or event,
    173.6
  ~ in implication, 173.8
  ~ in meaning, 173.8
  ~ logically, 173.4(5,11); 173.8
  ~ thing, 173.6
  ~ things, 173.6(8)
following,n.
  coming after or next, 173.2
  pursuit, 173.13
  order of ~, 173.7
following,prep., 173.5
fond,adj.
  loving, 700.2,21,22
  be ~ of, 1109.1
  feel ~ of, 700.3
  intellectually ~ of all sorts,
    1109.6
  ~ of, 1109.4
fondle,v., 701.1; see **caress**,v.
fondness,n., 1109.3; see
    liking,n.
  love, 700.1; see **love**,n.
  develop a ~ for, 1109.2
  expressive ~ of, 700.22
  ~ for specific things, places,
    people, etc., 700.30-32
  show ~ (of a dog), 1109.22
food,n., 740.1,2; see also **meal**,n.
  able to be filled with ~, as a
    person, 925.24
  allotment of ~, 740.2(5,6,14);
    see also **diet**,n.
  aversion to ~, 737.9
  avoidance of certain ~s,
    734.23-25
  ball of ~, 740.15(11)
  be entertained with ~, 734.6
  breaking down of ~, 739.10;
    see **digestion**,n.
  ~ chewed by cow, etc., 740.7
  choice ~, 740.2(21)
  coarse ~, 740.2(17)
  cold ~, 740.2(4)
  concealed ~, 970.52
  connoisseur of ~s, 734.13(3,4,
    6)
  cooked ~, 1061.7
  decay, ~ subject to, 806.9
  delight with ~, 738.2
  desire for ~, 737.2; see
    hunger,n.
  desiring ~, 737.1; see **hungry**,
    adj.
  eating certain ~s, 734.26-29;
    see **eating**,n.
  elements in ~, 740.21
  energy-producing unit of ~,
    740.22
  enjoyer of ~, 734.13
  entertain with ~, 738.2
  fill (a person) with ~, 925.23
  fill (oneself) with ~, 925.23
  filled with ~, as a person,
    925.20
  ~ for domestic animals, 740.4-
    6
  ~ for hogs, 285.1(33,40)
  ~ for livestock, 986.1(8)
  ~ for pigs, 740.5
  full of ~, as a person, 925.20
  fullness of ~, in respect to a
    person, 925.21
  give ~ to, 738.1; see **feed**,v.
  grain ~s, 987.13
  half-digested ~, 740.2(3)
  heat-producing unit of ~,
    740.22
  incorporation of ~, 739.23
  infants' ~, 740.2(11)
  lack of ~, 737.10
  light ~, 740.2(15,16,18)

list of ~, 740.8-10
  miraculously supplied ~,
    740.2(8)
  needed ~, 740.2(8)
  ornament ~, 959.1(19)
  passage of ~ after digestion,
    739.22
  pert. to ~ from animals,
    743.5
  piece of ~, 326.10(7)
  place to buy or get ~, 741.4
  place where ~ is served, 741.3
  poor ~, 740.2(20)
  portion of ~, 740.15
  provide with ~ and sleeping
    quarters, 740.18
  regulate the ~ of, 740.14
  science of ~, 734.19,20
  seller of ~, 233.4(1,3,4)
  sleeping quarters and ~,
    740.17
  soaked ~, 740.2(19)
  soft ~, 740.2(11)
  special ~s, 740.2(5)
  storage place for ~, 262.3(16,
    19)
  strained ~, 740.2(13)
  style of cooked ~, 1061.30
  supplier of ~ to army,
    233.4(2)
  supply ~, 233.1(5)
  supply of ~, 740.3
  supply with ~, 233.1(1,10,12,
    15,17,21,23,24)
  treatise on ~s, 682.15(23)
  unable to be filled with ~, as
    a person, 925.25
  unit of ~ energy, 740.22
  vessel for ~, 261.9
fool,n., 608.16,19
  born ~, 1054.37
  cowardly ~, 608.18
  professional ~, 1116.1; see
    clown,n.
  treat as a ~, 608.25
foolish,adj.
  nonsensical, 608.5
  unwise, 596.5
  ~ act, 52.5(28); 596.7; 608.10
  act or behave ~ly, 608.11
  ~ and flirtatious woman,
    608.21
  ~ behavior, 55.3(8)
  ~, conceited, and talkative
    person, 608.20
  given to ~ ideas, 608.23
  make ~, 608.24
  ~ people, 608.22
  ~ person, 596.8; 608.16,19
  state of being ~, 596.6
  ~ talk, 671.2(1,6,10,14,17-19,
    29,34)
  talk ~ly, 671.1(2,7-9,31,37,38,
    53,69,70,77,78,83,99,102,109)
  talking ~ly, 671.4(1)
  ~ young man, 608.17
foolishness,n.
  nonsense, 608.1,3,4
  nonsensicality, 608.6,9
  unwisdom, 596.6
foot,n., 346.1; see also **feet**,n.
  amoeba's ~, 346.3
  armor for the ~, 979.23
  beat, strike, or scrape with
    the ~, 346.2
  bottom of the ~, 346.8,10
  covering for the ~, 979.1
  disease of the ~ joints,
    1137.56(14)
  drawing back of the ~ in
    respect, 855.9(7)
  hit with the ~, 979.12,23
  medical condition of the ~,
    346.11-14
  pain in the ~, 1137.56(14,24)

pert. to the ~, 346.9
push with the ~, 979.12
science of the ~, 401.1(8,76, 77)
shaped like a ~, 507.17(56)
sore of ~, 12.1(14)
footnote,n., 680.3
symbols referring to a ~, 680.1(3,11,20)
footprint,n.
fossil ~, 757.9
~ left by person or animal, 757.7
~s, 757.8
study of fossil ~s, 757.10
footstep,n., 108.4(1,3,5,6); see also step,n.
sound of ~s, 469.5,6
footstool,n., 63.3
footwear,n., 979; see also shoe, etc.
fop,n., 974.23-26
woman like a ~, 974.27
forbid,v., 555.1
acting to ~, 555.3
~ entrance or departure of ships, 555.6
~ to enter, 555.5
forbiddance,n., 555.2
forbidden,adj., 555.4
~ for trade, import, or export, 555.4(1)
force,n., 3.1
active ~, 3.1(1)
balancing ~, 3.1(4,5)
cause to lose ~, 17.5(43,45)
concentrated ~, 3.1(11)
device for measuring ~, 3.12
driving ~, 3.1(2,8); 106.2,4
earth interior ~s, 1004.21,22
fluid ~, pert. to, 1027.34,35
get by ~, 3.3(3,11)
government by ~, 1073.3(6)
lose ~, 10.8
main ~, 3.1(3)
measurement of ~s, 3.11
move by ~, 79.17
neutralizing ~, 3.1(4,5)
~ of movement, 3.1(10)
opposing ~, 3.1(4,5,15)
painful ~, 3.1(15)
pert. to physical ~s, 3.9
physical ~, 3.1(15)
put into ~, 16.23,25
reduce in ~, 10.5; 1142.1,10; see also weaken,v.
reduces ~ of a blow, 10.13
science of ~s, 3.10
spiritual ~, 3.1(13)
sudden ~, 4.10
tensional ~, 3.1(14)
theory of ~s, 3.13
unlawful use of ~, 3.4(3)
use ~, 3.3
use ~ to balance or neutralize, 3.3(5,6)
use of ~, 3.4
using ~, 3.5
violent ~, 4.10
with great ~, 3.7
without ~, 10.1(1,44,46,75); 17.1(17,26)
force,v., 3.3
~ by duty, 3.3(14)
~ by laughter, 1111.28
~ by oppression, 3.3(9)
~ by persecution, 3.3(9)
~ by promise, 3.3(14)
~ by threats, 3.3(1)
~ into armed service, 3.3(8, 13,15)
~ into duty, 3.3(15)
~ into naval service, 3.3(13, 15)
~ into service, 3.3(15)

~ into the unconscious, 1097.42-46
~ obedience, 3.3(2,10)
~ out, 3.3(21); 144.1
~ out of hiding, 3.3(7)
~ out of shape, 3.3(18)
~ to give, 3.3(11,12,20,21)
~ to undergo, 3.3(17)
forced,adj.
state of being ~, 3.6
forceful,adj., 3.2
~ in movement, 91.3
move ~ly, 91.1
~ movement, 91.2
forcible,adj., 3.2
forebear,n., 723.8; see ancestor,n.
forecast,n., 772.3,5; see prediction,n.
forecast,v., 772.1,2; 773.1; see also predict,v.
forefather,n., 723.8; see ancestor,n.
forehead,n., 358.5
big of ~, 906.4
pert. to the ~, 358.6
side of the ~, 358.7
wrinkle the ~, 158.1(2)
foreign,adj., 538.1
~ but now a citizen, 538.2
fondness for ~ customs, things, etc., 700.31(5)
~ places, 782.1(15)
~ thing, plant, or word, 538.3
foreigner,n., 538.4
group of ~s, 318.1(33)
place or country whose citizens were ~s, 1075.1
prejudice against ~s, 634.1(12)
foresee,v., 482.5-7; 772.1; see also predict,v.
foresight,n., 482.6,7
foreskin,n., 379.1(17)
removal of ~, 402.5(7)
forest,n., 996.29
~ animal, 996.43
care, management, etc., of ~s, 996.35
clear of ~s, 996.54
convert from a ~, 996.57
convert into a ~, 996.33
cover with ~s, 996.51
cultivation and care of a ~, 996.62
establishment of ~s, 996.35
frequenter of the ~s, 996.45
god of the ~, 654.2(13); 662.26(9,10)
goddess of the ~, 996.44
~ guard, offical, etc., 996.48
growing in the ~, 996.39
having ~s, 996.49
inhabitant of the ~, 996.41,45
~ land, 996.32
land near a ~, 1003.2(32)
like a ~, 996.37
living in the ~, 996.40
~ nymph, 996.42
pert. to ~s, 996.36
plant with ~s, 996.51
~ scenery, 996.38
science of ~s, 996.64
skill in the ~, 7.1(69); 996.46
spirits of the ~, 996.42
student of ~s, 996.65
foretaste,n., 446.9
foretell,v., 772.1,2; 773.1; see also predict,v.
foreword,n., 730.4; see also introduction,n.
forge,v.
falsify, 820.16
make, 726.1

forget,v.
hard to ~, 627.19
forgetful,adj., 628.2
forgetfulness,n., 628.1; see also forgotten,adj.
cause of ~, 628.4
causing ~, 628.3
flight in a state of ~, 141.2(6)
river of ~, 1029.22
forgetting,n., 628.5
cause of ~, 628.4
forgivable,adj., 897.9,16
forgive,v., 897.1,6,12
~ for past offenses, 897.12
forgiveness,n., 897.2,7,40
an act of ~, 1143.4
certificate of ~, 897.17
~ for sin, 897.7(2)
generous in ~, 897.5
~ of punishment, 897.13
power to decide on ~ of punishment, 897.38
~ to enemy, 897.42
~ to opponent, 897.42
forgiver,n., 897.15
forgiving,adj., 897.4,8,14,39
not ~, 897.45
forgotten,adj.
able to be ~, 628.6
becoming ~, 628.8
place of being ~, 628.9
state of being ~, 628.7
fork,n., 148.2; 148.2(1)
point of a table ~, 335.1(13, 20)
fork,v., 148.1(2,10,11); 325.1(6, 7); 325.2(1,2,4)
form,n., 507.1; see also shape,n.
adherence to ~, 819.9
come into a definite ~, 507.3
give ~ to, 507.2
give a definite ~ to, 507.2(2)
give a new ~ to, 507.4
irregular in ~, 507.1(11)
netlike ~, 507.1(11); 507.17(64)
new ~, 507.1(10)
new and changed ~, 507.1(7)
observance of ~, 819.9
of many ~s, 507.12
of specific ~, 507.17
person correct in observation of ~, 815.14
person demanding correctness of ~, 815.14
purest ~, 507.1(9)
requiring correctness of ~, 815.15
rigid ~, 819.15
rough ~, 507.1(13)
showing correctness of ~, 815.15
take on a new ~, 507.3
vague ~, 507.1(14)
wavelike ~, 507.1(12)
form,v.
give form or shape to, 507.2
make, 726.1
formal,adj., 819.1
~ act, 52.5(15)
act ~, 819.8
be ~, 819.8
~ behavior, 755.3(2)
~ dress, 975
~ in clothing, 974.12
~ language, 665.9(7)
make ~, 819.6
showy and ~, 951.38
stiffly ~, 819.2
formalism,n., 50.5; 819.9; see also conventionalism, formality,n.
formalities,n.
polite ~, 858.18

prescribed ~ of procedure, 819.13
system of ~, 819.11
formality,n., 50.5; 819.3
a ~, 819.10
adherence to ~, 50.5; 819.9
adherence to ~ in art, 819.9(1)
adherence to ~ in literature, 819.9(1)
adherence to ~ in religion, 819.9(2,4)
adherence to ~ of office, 819.9(3)
done as a ~, 583.12
empty ~, 819.5
hypocritical ~, 819.5
meaningless ~, 819.4
observance of ~, 819.9
observe with ~, 819.7
official ~, 1077.19
ridiculous ~, 819.5
useless ~, 819.5
without ~, 819.17
former,adj., 771.12
formless,adj., 507.16
fort,n., 568.26
head of a ~, 568.27
fortification,n., 568.26,30
furnish with ~s, 568.28,32
parts of ~s, 568.30, 33–35
fortified,adj., 568.31
~ place, 568.26
fortify,v., 568.28
fortitude,n., 246.8
fortress,n., 568.26
head of a ~, 568.27
fortuneteller,n., 772.6
forty, n. or adj., 940.8
consisting of ~, 940.9
forward,adj.
bold, 861.1; see bold,adj.
~ flow, 112.2(2)
~ jump, 110.2(2)
~ movement, 91.2(5,6); 174.2
forward,adv.
bend ~, 152.1(11,16)
drive ~, 106.1(8,9)
go ~, 119.1(2,6,32,60)
move ~, 89.1(20); 174.1–3
move ~ slowly, 100.1(5,8)
push ~, 197.1(6,9,13,26,33,35, 57)
running ~, 96.3(2)
throw ~, 187.1(39)
turn limbs ~, 148.6(8)
forwardness,n.
boldness, 862.2
fossil,n., 757.4
~ footprint, 757.9
~ remains, 757.4(11)
science of ~s, 759.26(5,7)
study of ~ footprints, 757.10
treatise on ~s, 682.15(15)
found,adj.
able to be ~, 487.4
able to be ~ out, 624.5
something ~, 487.6–8
unable to be ~, 487.5
foundation,n., 1022.2,21
build a ~, 1006.8
figurative ~, 1022.21,26
~ for a statue, 1022.2(16)
give a ~ to, figuratively, 1022.24
~ of a building, 1022.14
~ of broken stones, 1022.2(21)
strengthen a ~, 1006.8
strong ~, 1022.2(3)
without figurative ~, 1022.38
fountain,n., 1033.46
four, n. or adj., 933.1
arranged in ~, 933.7
card, die, domino, etc., of ~ pips, 933.14

consisting of ~, 933.6,9
divide into ~, 933.8
divided into ~, 933.6
group of ~, 933.2
happening every ~ days, 933.17
involving ~, 933.13
make ~ copies of, 933.15
multiply by ~, 933.10
one of ~, 933.12
participated in by ~, 933.13
set of ~ parts, 933.3
fourfold,adj., 933.4
~ in character, nature, or shape, 933.4
increase ~, 907.9(5)
four hundred,n.
consisting of ~, 940.27
fourth,adj.
happening every ~ day, 933.17
fourth,n.
relating to the ~, 933.17
fowl,n., 405.1–8; see chicken,n.
of ~, 405.8(2)
fox,n.
female ~, 407.12
group of ~es, 403.5(65)
hole of a ~, 403.22(6,20)
like a ~, 407.15
pert. to a ~, 407.13,14
young ~, 407.17
fraction,n.
bottom number of ~, 927.1(7)
top number of ~, 927.1(20)
fragment,n.
part, 326.1,10,23; see part,n.
~ of earthenware, 326.10(17, 22)
~ of something heard, 326.10(30)
France,n.
fond of ~, one who is, 700.30(6)
inhabitant of ~, 784.15(21)
inhabitant of Southern ~, 784.15(39)
make conform to customs of ~, 784.10(3)
pert. to ~, 784.16
pert. to Southern ~, 784.16
frank,adj., 807.3; 813.6,7
~ as a child, 813.6(3)
excessively ~, 813.6(2)
honest and ~ person, 813.4
tactlessly ~, 813.6(2)
talking ~ly, 671.4(5)
frankfurter,n., 743.2
frankness,n., 807.3; 813.6,8
fraternity,n.
brotherhood, 722.13
accept on trial in a ~, 1122.28,29
promise to join a ~, 1122.28, 29
freak,n., 536.5
causing ~s, 537.8
condition of being a ~, 537.6
full of ~s, 537.5
giving birth to ~s, 537.8
human ~s, 537.10
like a ~, 537.4,7
~ of nature, 537.1
~ plant, 537.2; 985.6(31,38)
~s, 537.3
science of human ~s, 537.9
three-headed ~, 358.16; 537.10(4,7)
two-headed ~, 358.14; 537.10(1,5,6)
freakish,adj., 536.4; 537.5
freckle,n., 384.26
freckled,adj., 501.1(8)
free,adj., 309.15
without cost, 223.13

act ~ of control, 309.21(4)
be ~, 309.21
become ~, 309.21
become ~ of burden, 309.21(1)
become ~ of care, 309.21(3,6)
become ~ of entanglements, 309.21(2)
become ~ of manner, 309.21(3, 5,6)
become ~ of worry, 309.21(3, 6)
~ from conscience, 309.15(11, 27)
~ from previous decision, 309.15(9)
live ~ of control, 309.21(4)
~ of a condition, 309.15
~ of action, 309.15(21)
~ of burden, 309.15(19)
~ of cost, 223.13
~ of control, 309.15(1,4–8,10–16,18,20–38)
~ of hindrance, 309.15(21–23, 26,35–37)
~ of love, 309.15(2)
~ of qualifications, 309.15(28)
~ person, 309.5,16
set ~, 309.1
set or make ~ of, 309.11
setting ~, 309.2,7,13
free,v., 309.1
~ a prisoner, 309.1(6,8,13–16, 28,32)
~ for other uses, 309.11(30)
~ from foot shackles, 309.1(24,27,35)
~ from handcuffs, 309.1(24,26, 31)
~ from slavery, 309.1(1,5,6,10, 12)
~ of a condition, 309.11
~ of accusation, 309.11(3,12, 24)
~ of army control, 309.11(7)
~ of blame, 309.11(1,3)
~ of burden, 309.11(11,12,15, 28); 948.19
~ of censorship, 309.11(36,38)
~ of complication, 309.11(41)
~ of contamination, 309.11(3, 4)
~ of control, 309.11(5,32,35–39,42,46)
~ of dependence, 309.11(2)
~ of difficulties, 309.11(25, 41)
~ of duty, 309.11(1,22,23,26–28)
~ of embarrassment, 309.11(13)
~ of entanglement, 309.11(13, 17,25,41)
~ of false belief, 309.11(9)
~ of false ideas, 309.11(9)
~ of gas, 1048.32
~ of guilt, 309.11(1,3,24)
~ of habit, 309.11(10)
~ of hardship, 309.11(24)
~ of high regard for, 309.11(14,18)
~ of hindrance, 309.11(13,25, 27,31,46)
~ of illusions, 309.11(14,18)
~ of impurities, 309.11(3,4)
~ of infection, 309.11(19)
~ of insects, 309.11(20)
~ of involvement, 309.11(16)
~ of liability, 309.11(23)
~ of lice, 309.11(6,20)
~ of obligation, 309.11(1,2,16, 21–24,26,27)
~ of obstruction, 309.11(8,31, 33,34,40,44,45)
~ of oppression, 309.11(11,12)

~ of poison gas, 1048.32
~ of rats, 309.11(20)
~ of requirements, 309.11(23, 26)
~ of responsibility, 309.11(1)
one who ~s, 309.4
~ oneself, 309.21
~ oneself of burden, 948.20
serving to ~, 309.7,13
that which ~s, 309.6
freed,adj.
~ person, 309.5
freedom,n., 309.3,14
abuse of ~, 309.18
advocate of ~, 309.17
buy the ~ of, 211.1(8)
citizen's ~, 1075.11
deprive of ~, 310.1
desire for ~, 309.19
destruction of ~, 801.13(1)
economic ~, 309.14(3)
emotional interference with ~, 1097.38–41
~ from a condition, 309.14
~ from conscience, 309.14(7, 12–14,21,23)
~ from control, 309.14(1,2,4,5, 7,8,10–18,24)
~ from convention, 309.14(7)
~ from duty, 309.14(14)
~ from government, 309.14(2)
~ from inhibitions, 309.14(8)
~ from law, 309.14(12,13)
~ from loss, 309.14(9)
~ from moral restraint, 309.14(7,12–14,21,23)
~ from obligation, 309.14(14)
~ from outside government, 309.14(4,5,10,18)
~ from punishment, 309.2(1); 309.14(9)
~ from work, 209.12
lack of ~, 310.2–4
lacking in ~ from conventions, 310.15
~ of action, 309.14(22)
political ~, 309.14(4,5,10,18)
political ~, movement toward, 309.20
freeing,adj., 309.7,13
freeing,n., 309.2,12
~ from punishment, 309.2(1)
freeze,v., 1059.1,3,4; see also frost,n.
act of ~ing, 1059.2
degree of coldness that ~s water, 1059.6
~ing point, determination of, 1059.20
point at which water ~s, 1059.19
process of ~ing, 1059.2
freezing,adj.
~ weather, 1059.13
French,adj., 784.16
~ Canadian, 784.15(9)
~ characteristic, 1091.24(3)
hating the ~, 880.19(1)
in ~ style, 784.18
~ language, 664.4(5,16)
make ~, 784.10(3)
~ person born in a colony, 784.15(15)
frenzy,n., 1100.7; see excitement,n.
fresh,adj., 761.8
impudent,860.1; 861.1; 862.1; see also bold,disrespectful, impolite, impudent,adj.
new, 761.1; see new,adj.
be ~, 1.11
becoming again ~, 761.11
no longer ~, 759.28–30
freshen,v., 761.10
freshness,n., 761.9

impudence, 860,2; 861.2; 862.2
newness, 761.2
deprive of ~, 10.5(43)
lacking ~, 535.5–9
symbol of ~, 761.12
friction,n.
disagreement, 542.1
rubbing, 438.2
make sore by ~, 438.7
friend,n., 1096.3
act as a ~ to, 1096.26
be a ~ of, 1097.23
be a ~ to, 1096.26
group of ~s, 1096.5
like a ~, 1096.8,9
loyal ~, 658.3(1)
loyalty among ~s, 1096.13
pert. to a ~, 1096.8,9
~s, collectively, 1096.5
tries to make ~s with wealthy or important people, one who, 1096.14
without ~s, 330.1(5,8,11); 1096.41
friendless,adj., 330.1; 1096.41
~ child, 1096.42
~ person, 1096.42,43
friendliness,n., 1096.2; see also friendship,n.
~ and peace, 1096.2(1)
characterized by social ~, 1096.10
discourage ~, 879.15
enjoys ~, one who, 1096.16
expression of ~, 1096.15
gain the ~ of by being pleasant, 1096.30
regard with ~, 1096.27
seek the ~ of by flattery, 1096.29
suitable for social ~, 1096.10
friendly,adj., 1096.1
able to be made ~, 1096.36
~ act, 1096.17
be ~ to, 1096.26,27
be ~ with, 1096.22
become ~, 1096.28
establishment of ~ relations, 1096.21
make (someone) ~, 1096.31–39
pert. to ~ relations, 1096.12
pleasant and ~, 858.4
polite and ~, 858.4
~ remark, 1096.17
try to become ~ with, 1096.24
unable to be made ~, 1096.39, 40
friendship,n., 1096.4; see also friendliness,n.
associate in ~ with, 1096.22
exclusive in ~, 1096.6
excusable because of ~, action, 1096.18,19
~ gift, 230.6(8,16)
sign of ~, 951.4(26)
try to promote (~), 1096.25
fright,n., 576.2; see fear,n.
frighten,v., 576.6
~ in order to control, 8.1(1,8)
one who ~s, 576.8
frightened,adj., 576.1
be ~, 576.3; see fear,v.
become ~, 576.3; see fear,v.
person who is ~, 576.5
~ state, 576.2; see fear,n.
frightening,adj., 576.7
~ and unnatural, 576.7(4,17, 18)
~ but imaginary, 576.7(2)
~ by threatening danger, 573.1(13–15)
frivolous,adj., 609.1
~ act, 609.8
act ~ly, 609.7

~ behavior, 55.3(10)
~ girl, 760.6(10)
~ language, 665.9(31)
~ person, 609.3
talk ~ly, 609.9,10
treat ~ly, 53.1(14); 609.10
~ woman, 609.4–6
frivolousness,n., 609.2
frog,n., 424.1
eating ~s, 734.27(4)
immature ~, 424.2
like the ~, 424.4
of ~s, 403.11(1)
pert. to ~s, 424.3
place for ~s, 403.22(35)
science of ~s, 403.26(1)
frond,n.
having ~s, 993.6
like a ~, 993.4,5
~s, collectively, 993.3
front,adj., 185.2
~ part, 185.1
~ part of a group, 185.1(10, 11)
~ part of a picture, 185.1(6)
~ position, 185.6
~ side, 186.1(7)
~ surface, 193.1(4)
~ view, 185.6
front,n., 185.1
building ~, 185.1(2,7,8)
false ~, 185.1(2); 823.13(2)
group in ~, 176.3(19); 185.1(10,11); 185.3
in ~, 185.2
~ of the body, 185.1(1,3)
on the ~, 185.2
person in ~, 185.3
pert. to the ~, 185.2
put in ~ of, 323.1(3,12)
ship's ~, 185.10–12
size of the ~, 185.7
to the ~, 185.4
toward the ~, 185.2,4
toward the ~ of the body, 185.5
with the back in ~, 184.3
with two ~s, 185.9
frontier,n., 793.2,3
inhabitant of the ~, 793.4
frost,n., 1059.7
causing ~, 1059.12
cover with ~, 1059.9
cover (glass, etc.) with ~, 1059.10
covered with ~, 1059.8
harm by ~, 1059.14
kill by ~, 1059.14
like ~, 1059.12
~like coating for foods, 1059.21–24
line beyond ~, 1059.16
~ lines, 1059.11
~ ornamentation, 1059.11
personification of ~, 1059.13
white with ~, 1059.8
frosting,n., 1059.21
cover with ~, 1059.22
covered with ~, 1059.23
frown,n., 365.2(6,10)
frozen,adj., 1059.18
become ~, 1059.4
~ coating, 1059.7–9; see also frost,n.
state of being ~, 1059.5
frugal,adj., 226.1
be ~, 226.3
frugality,n., 226.2
fruit,n., 745.21
bear ~, 745.11
bear ~, make able to, 745.12
bearing ~, 745.9,10,13,14
belonging to a family of ~s, 745.22

center of ~, 137.1(9,12); 326.34
certain ~s, 745.1
coating on ~, 972.4(3)
covering of ~, 972.4(9,10,11, 13,14,15,19,20,21,23)
descr. of certain ~s, 745.22(4, 7)
~ drink, 748.5(9)
eating ~s, 734.27(8,11)
flavor of various ~s, 745.6
growing or raising of ~, 745.25
like ~, 745.7,8
mixture of ~s, 745.6
peel of ~, 972.4(13)
pert. to certain ~s, 745.22
pit of ~, 748.18
science of ~s and seeds, 745.24
science of growing ~, 994.30
seller of ~, 745.23
skin of ~, 972.4(9,10,11,13,14, 15,19,20,21,23)
stewed ~, dish of, 745.5
~ tree, 996.4(4,13)
~ trees, cultivation of, 996.58
unproductive of ~, 745.17
fruiterer,n., 745.23
fruitful,adj., 831.11
fertile, 715.1,7,9; see **fertile**, adj.
successful, 23.2; see **success-ful**,adj.
fruitless,adj.
ineffective, 17.1; see **ineffec-tive**,adj.
sterile, 716.1; see **sterile**,adj.
unsuccessful, 24.3
frustrate,v.
hinder, 557.1
make ineffective, 17.5
fry,v., 1061.1,2; see **cook**,v.
pan for ~ing, 261.10(11,12)
sound of ~ing, 1061.3
~ with a hissing sound, 1061.2(1)
fuel,n., 1064.61
furnish with ~, 1064.66
get, or take in, ~, 1064.67
fugitive,n., 141.3
full,adj., 925.1
without qualification, 925.15
become ~, 925.8
~ bowl, 925.11
condition of being ~, 925.4
~ cup, 925.11
deceptively ~ (of language), 926.5
~ glass, 925.11
~ in sound, 467.3(6,7,9)
less ~, make, 925.28
make ~, 925.2
~ of color, 925.1(12,24)
~ of food or drink, as a per-son, 925.20
~ of liquid, 925.1(12,24)
~ of soft material, 925.1(19, 23)
~ of tears, 925.1(24)
~ of thoughts, 925.26,27
~ of words, 925.26,27
over~, 925.1(2,4,5,8,9–11,15–18,20–23,25)
space that is ~, 787.1(13); 925.10
very ~, as clothing, drapes, etc., 925.16
fullness,n., 925.4
causing ~, 925.6
decrease the ~ of, 925.28
~ of food or drink, in regard to a person, 925.21

top ~, 925.12
fume,n.
give off ~s, 1050.13
treatment with ~s, place of, 1048.47
fumigate,v., 1048.7
person or device that ~s, 1048.8
place for ~ing, 1048.47
~ with smoke, 1050.22
fun,n., 200.4; see also **amuse-ment**, **pleasure**,n.
full of ~, 1104.1
make ~ of, 869.1,9,10
making ~ of, 869.5,12
funeral,n.
attender at a ~, 799.6
manager of a ~, 799.3
pert. to a ~, 799.5
rites of a ~, 799.1
~ song, 476.4(19,31,41,46)
vehicle for the corpse in a ~, 799.2
walks with the coffin at a ~, one who, 799.4
fungus,n., 985.6(22,23,25,29,32, 36,39,40)
become coated with ~, 985.20
coating of ~, 985.11
destroyer of ~, 398.8(8)
of the ~ family, 985.33(1)
science of the ~, 985.36(16)
funnel,n.
~-shaped, 507.17(44)
funny,adj.
laughable, 1111.24; 1113.1,2; see **laughable**,adj.
odd, 536.1
fur,n., 369.1(8,27,49)
covered with ~, 369.6(8)
dealer in ~s, 205.5(6)
like ~, 369.10(6)
lose ~, 972.10
maker of ~ garments, 205.5(6)
shed ~, 286.1(37)
worker on ~s, 205.5(6)
furnace, n., 1060.32; 1064.55
cremation ~, 798.3
~ for bricks, pottery, etc., 1061.13
iron ~, 1017.11
metal ~, 1012.22
steel ~, 1017.11
stone for a ~, 1064.59
take care of a ~, 1064.10,11
furnish,v., 233.1; see **supply**,v.
furniture,n., 280.1(3,5,8,9,17)
cover ~, 972.1(53)
cover for ~, 972.4(18)
covering ~, business of, 972.20
make ~ out of stems, 985.16
matching set of ~, 529.10
furrow,n., 157.4; 158.4
furthest,adj., 789.3; see **far-thest**,adj.
fussy,adj.
choosy, 252.15
futile,adj., 17.1
futility,n., 17.2
attitude of ~, 552.6
philosophy of ~, 17.8; 267.19; 552.6
future,n., 771.21
be in the ~, 29.22
event in the ~, 771.24
~ generations, 771.22
give to the ~, 230.1(8,30,49)
in the ~, 771.26
indicate the ~, 773.1–6
indicative of the ~, 951.5(1)
people of the ~, 771.22
pert. to the ~, 771.25

prediction of the ~, 772.1–21; see **prediction**,n.
promise of the ~, 1122.10
sign of the ~, 773.1–6; 951.4(1, 9,18,20)
~ state, 771.23
without a ~, 771.27

G

G(the letter),n.
incorrect pronunciation of ~, 670.7(1)
~ sound, 670.14(13)
gain,n., 240.2,3
derive ~, 240.1(24)
unexpected ~, 240.3(1)
gain,v., 240.1; see **get**,v.
try to ~, 18.1(7)
try to ~ possession of, 18.2(11)
gait,n.
manner of walking, 107.2
horse ~, 104.1
gale,n., 1042.27
galley,n.
boat, 115.14
gallows,n., 172.5(2,5)
gamble,n., 34.14
gambler,n.
cheating ~, 825.10–12
gambling,adj.
~ scheme, 34.14
gambling,n.
building for ~, 727.12(4)
fail to pay ~ debts, 218.16(4)
full of ~, 1087.11
room for ~, 787.7(12)
game,n.
outdoor ~s, participator in, 199.9
water ~s, 1026.28; 114.7
gangrene,n., 794.7
causing ~, 794.11
gangrene,v., 794.8
gangrenous,adj., 794.9,10
gap,n., 787.4
garbage,n., 285.1
garden,n.
~ of Adam and Eve, 985.34(8)
~ of ferns, 985.34(6)
~ on rocky ground, 985.34(17)
ornamental ~ with plants in odd shapes, 985.34(21)
gardening,n., 998.1
ornamental ~, 998.1(8,11,15)
soilless ~, 998.1(10)
garlic,n.
of the ~ family, 985.33(2)
smelling of ~, 445.10(2)
garment,n., 974.38; see also **clothing**,n.
academic ~, 974.38(6)
acrobat's ~, 974.38(16)
bed ~, 974.44
bride's ~s, 974.35(4)
clergyman's ~, 974.38(1,7)
dancer's ~, 974.38(16)
dressed in a ~, 974.41
East Indian ~, 974.38(20)
French ~, 974.38(5)
Greek ~, 974.38(25)
Hindu ~, 974.38(19)
Japanese ~, 974.38(14)
Malay ~, 974.38(20)
monk's ~, 974.38(9,12)
neck ~, 977.1
~ of office or profession, wearer of, 974.42
~ of office, rank, or profes-sion, 974.38(13,18,24,27)
outer ~s, 974.46,47
~ over armor, 974.38(15)
peasant's ~, 974.38(12)

protective ~, 974.38(2,4,8,11,
  12,17,21,28,29) ; 980.1(6)
put a ~ on, 974.39,40
Roman ~, 974.38(24,25)
Russian ~, 974.38(5)
set of ~s, 974.35
shoulder ~, 977.6,7
sleeping ~s, 974.44,45
Turkish ~, 974.38(10)
under~s, 981
~ under a coat, 974.38(26)
~ under a jacket, 974.38(26)
~ while dressing, 974.43
without a specific ~, 984.11
work ~, 974.38(2,8,12,21) ;
  980.1(6)
garret,n., 787.7(4,26)
garrison,n.
  pert. to a ~, 568.16
  place protected by a ~,
    568.26(14,20)
  protected by a ~, 568.7(4)
gas,n., 1048.1
  ~ around sun or star,
    1048.1(3)
  ~ around the earth, 1048.1(1)
  attack with ~, 1048.29,30
  ~ beyond solar system,
    1057.7
  containing ~ (of beverages),
    1048.34
  convert ~ to liquid, device to,
    1027.10
  convert into ~, 1048.16,17
  disagreeable ~, 1048.1(7)
  duct for ~es, 1050.29
  escape of ~, structure for,
    1050.27–29
  expose to ~, 1048.29
  ~ faucet, 1033.47
  fear of ~es, 1045.22
  ~ fixtures, 1048.20–23
  ~ fixtures, worker on, 1048.27
  flame of ~, 1048.24
  flowing ~, 1027.1(6)
  ~ for synthetic rubber,
    1048.1(2)
  free of ~, 1048.32
  free of poison ~, 900.6;
    1048.32
  full of ~, 1048.15
  furnish with ~, 1048.29
  give off ~, 1048.5
  giving off ~, 1048.4
  harm with ~, 1048.29
  hold or store ~, device to,
    1048.14
  ~ in bowels, 1048.1(13)
  ~ inhaled for medicinal pur-
    poses, 1048.1(12)
  kill with ~, 1048.29
  light from ~, 1048.25;
    1065.49(11)
  like ~, 1048.3
  manufacture of ~, place for,
    1048.18
  measurement of ~es, device
    for, 1045.21(1) ; 1048.12
  ~ measurement, science of,
    1048.10,11
  ~ meters, one who reads,
    1048.13
  mine ~, 1048.1(4)
  movement of ~, 1031.1(4,5,11)
  pert. to ~, 1048.2
  protection against poison ~,
    1048.31
  put ~ into beverage, 1048.33
  science of ~es, 1027.33(1,4) ;
    1045.20
  suffocating ~, 1048.1(7)
  tight against ~, 1048.28
  water in form of ~, 1048.1(11)
gas,v., 1048.5
gaseous,adj., 1048.2,3

gasp,n., 376.3; see **breath,**n.
  ~ after a cough, 376.6(6)
gasp,v., 376.1(6) ; see **breathe,**v.
gassy,adj., 1048.3
gate,n., 133.7
  ~keeper, 133.8
  ~ of crossed strips, 991.14,15
gather,v., 319.1,2; see **collect,**v.
  cut and ~ grain, 998.2(1)
  ~ in the crop, 998.2(1)
gatherer,n., 319.4
gathering,n.
  ~ of crops, 998.7
  ~ of cut grain, 998.6
gay,adj.
  cheerful, 1103.1; see **cheer-
    ful,**adj.
  happy, 1102.1; see **happy,**adj.
  merry, 1104.1; see **merry,**adj.
gaze,v., 484.1
gazer,n., 484.3
geese,n.
  group of ~, 403.5(30,64) ; see
    also **goose,**n.
  like ~, 405.10
  of ~, 405.9(2)
gelatin,n.
  like ~, 746.6
  pert. to ~, 746.5
gem,n., 961.10–21
  artificial ~, 961.20
  birth ~, 961.15,16
  cut of a ~, 962.5
  cutter of ~s, 961.24,25
  cutting of ~s, pert. to, 961.26
  engraved ~, 961.13,14
  engraved ~s, description of,
    961.30
  engraved ~s, study of, 961.29
  engraving ~s, art of, 961.28
  engraving of ~s, pert. to,
    961.27
  expert in ~s, 961.24
  mythical ~, 961.21
  ornament with ~s, 959.1(9) ;
    961.4
  producing ~s, 961.23
  science of ~s, 961.22
  set with ~s, 961.5
  surface of a ~, 139.1(3)
  treatise on engraved ~s,
    682.15(2)
  weight system of ~s,
    947.31(4)
  weight unit of a ~, 947.32,34,
    43,44
  ~ with facets, 961.17
gender,n.
  descr. of ~, 709.3
genera,n.
  of two ~, 312.10(3) ; 312.11
general,adj., 41.1; 535.1,2; see
    also **universal,**adj.
generate,v.
  procreate, 717.6
  produce, 726.8; see **pro-
    duce,**v.
generation,n.
  procreation, 717.6
  production, 726.9
  future ~s, 771.22
generosity,n., 229.2
  act of ~, 229.5
generous,adj., 229.1
  ~ act, 229.5
  be ~ with, 229.4
  ~ in forgiving, 229.1(15)
  ~ person, 229.3
  ~ to guests or strangers,
    229.1(12) ; 842.1(5)
genital,adj., 717.8,9
genitals,n., 379.1
  calling attention to one's ~,
    579.21(2)
  covering for the ~, 980.2,5

diseases of the ~, 379.9
liquid secreted by the ~,
  1027.1(10)
looking at ~, 484.8
medical science of diseases of
  ~, 401.1(99,107)
medical science of the ~,
  401.1(3,26,27,106)
pert. to ~ and urinary
  organs, 379.1(2)
region of the ~, 379.1(19)
small ~, 379.5
support for male ~, 1022.34
genius,n.
  ability, 7.1
  able person, 7.3
Genoa,n.
  chief official of ~, 1077.1(12)
gentle,adj., 1144.1
  ~ and innocent person, 1144.3
  made ~, 1144.5–7
  made ~ by maturity, 732.7
  not ~, 1144.8
  ~ of voice, 462.4
gentleman,n., 858.22
  Spanish ~, 858.23
gentleness,n., 1144.2
  talking, or spoken, with ~,
    671.4(6)
genuine,adj.
  real, 807.1,3; see **real,**adj.
  true, 812.1; see **true,**adj.
  admit as ~, 675.1(2)
  claim to be ~, 812.12
  declare ~, 812.12
  falsely substituted for the ~,
    324.8
  having the characteristics of
    something ~, 1091.23
  prove ~s, 812.19
genuineness,n., 807.1,3; 812.1
  pretended ~, prefix to in-
    dicate, 820.9
genus,n.
  of the same ~, 312.8,9
geography,n., 617.2; 1053.36(6)
  ocean ~, 1029.71
  politics and ~, 1076.8
geologic,adj.
  divisions of ~ time, 763.1
  ~ eras, 763.2
  pert. to ~ time before life,
    763.3
  pert. to early ~ time, 763.4
  pert. to recent ~ time, 763.5
geology,n., 1004.43; 1053.36(6)
  study ~, 1004.44
geometric,adj.
  ~ figure, 945.1–6; see also
    polygon,n.
  ~ solid, 945.11–17
geometry,n., 943.1(6,8)
  non-Euclidean ~, 943.1(6)
germ,n.
  breeding place of ~s,
    403.22(28)
  clean of ~s, 899.10,13
  cleanser of ~s, 899.15
  destroy ~s in, 796.17; 899.10
  destroys disease ~s, sub-
    stance that, 398.8(2,7,9,10,
    12)
  dirty with ~s, 904.10
  disease ~s, 403.21
  free of ~s, 309.11(19)
  grow ~s, 731.22(2)
  growth of ~s, 731.21(7)
  make impure with ~s, 904.15
  poisonous ~s in the at-
    mosphere, 800.1(5)
  without ~s, 899.11
German,adj., 784.16
  ~ characteristic, 1091.24(4)
  ~ superiority, 833.10
German,n., 784.15(6,23,30,56)

Germany,n., 784.9(22)
fondness for ~, 700.30(7) ; 700.31,32
government of ~, 1073.3(23) ; 1073.5(4,8)
political party in ~ under Hitler, 1076.12(18)
ruler of ~, 1073.36(13)
gestural,adj., 102.4
gesture,n., 102.2
art of ~, 102.7,8
communication by ~, science of, 102.9
display by ~, 951.3(5)
~ of pride, 871.3(1)
~ of respect, 856.9
~ of respect while drinking, 856.9(8)
~ of submission, 552.7
~ of the arms, hand, head, etc., 956.1(7,10,15)
performance by ~s, 969.1(18, 20,32)
show anger by ~, 878.6(4,7,8, 10,13,15,18,20)
show by ~, 951.1(42,43,44)
signal by ~, 956.1(7,10,15,16)
summoning ~, 956.1(3)
gesture,v., 102.1
~ in respect, 856.10,11
gesturer,n., 102.3
gesturing,adj., 102.5
get,v., 240.1
~ a disease, 240.1(13)
~ a part of, 240.1(22,31)
~ along, 750.16
~ as a result, 240.1(18,27)
~ as a result of effort, 16.7
~ away, 141.1; see **depart**,v.
~ back, 240.12–14
~ back losses, 240.14
~ back previous position, 240.14
~ back property, 240.13
be happy to ~, 1102.15,16
be pleased to ~, 1106.13
~ by begging, 240.1(19)
~ by figuring, 240.1(33)
~ by magic, 663.8
~ down from, 167.10
expect to ~, 268.13
go for and ~, 240.1(17)
~ new members, 240.1(28)
~ off, 167.10
one who ~s, 240.4
~ strength, 240.14
~ the better of, 833.17
try to ~, 18.1(2,3,5,7,8,12,14, 16,23,26) ; 240.11
try to ~ by flattery, 18.2(3)
~ upon, 159.1(7,15,35)
getting,n., 240.2
ghost,n., 662.19
belief in ~s, 662.22
bloodsucking ~, 662.19(16)
inhabited or visited by ~s, 662.23
like a ~, 662.21; 1090.11
noisy ~, 662.19(8)
~ of a dead person, 662.19(9, 10,14,16)
terrifying ~, 662.19(1,2,6,12, 16)
visible ~, 662.19(1,2,6,12,16)
~ who warns of death, 662.19(2)
worship of ~s, 656.15(6)
ghostly,adj., 662.21; see also **supernatural**,adj.
~ appearance or image, 483.8(2,3,7,17) ; 662.20
~ double or counterpart, 529.3(4)
giant,n., 906.18(5,7,13,14)
befitting a ~, 662.17

custom or characteristic of ~s, 662.15
good-humored ~, 906.18(5,13)
one-eyed ~, 662.29(2) ; 906.18(4)
pert. to a ~, 662.8
race of ~s, 662.10(2)
satirical ~, 906.18(13)
stories about ~s, 662.16
strong ~, 1.39
terrifying ~, 662.29(6)
ugly ~, 662.7(43) ; 662.29(6)
gift,n.
aptitude, 7.1; see **ability**,n.
something given, 230.6
charitable ~, 232.4
conciliatory ~, 230.6(13)
~ for clergyman, 230.6(2)
friendship ~, 230.6(8,16) ; 627.34(5)
~ in respect, 230.6(17)
~ in thanks, 230.6(17)
love ~, 230.6(1)
receiver of a ~, 230.4
slight ~, 230.6(16,18)
~ to a beggar, 276.10
~ to a church, 230.6(10,11)
~ to a customer, 230.6(9)
~ to the poor, 213.3(6) ; 230.6(12) ; 232.4; see also **charity**,n.
gigantic,adj.
pert. to a giant, 662.8
very big, 906.12
rough and ~, 906.14
Gilbert and Sullivan,n.
admirer of ~, 479.21
anyone connected with ~, 479.21
gill,n.
below the ~s, 376.14
having ~s, 376.13
~s, 376.12(1)
gin,n., 749.6; see **liquor (alcoholic)**,n.
giraffe,n., 415.1
of ~s, 403.11(12)
girdle,v., 300.1; see **surround**,v.
girl,n., 760.6
female, 708.1; see also **female**, **woman**, **women**,n.
boyish ~, 760.6(12,24)
~ entering social life, 760.6(2, 6)
fascinating ~, 760.6(27)
giddy ~, 760.6(10)
homeless ~, 760.6(23)
innocent ~, 760.6(13)
mischievous ~, 202.3(5,6) ; 760.6(12,18)
noisy ~, 760.6(12,21,24)
~ of Mohammedan paradise, 760.6(11)
Parisian shop ~, 760.6(17)
pert. to a ~, 708.5; see also **feminine**,adj.
~s, collectively, 708.2
saucy ~, 760.6(3,9,12,18)
unconventional ~, 760.6(9)
unmarried ~, 760.6(5,16,25)
girlish,adj., 708.5; see also **feminine**,adj.
gist,n., 586.11; 607.3
give,v., 230.1; see also **supply**,v.
~ a disease, 230.1(12,34)
~ a part of, 230.8
~ a privilege, 230.1(13,19,51)
~ a quality, 230.1 (12,25–27, 33,50)
~ a share of, 230.8
~ after death, 230.1(8,36)
~ back, 234.1–4
~ by will, 242.4–6
continue to ~, 230.1(38)
~ for protection, 230.7

~ for safekeeping, 230.7
~ forth, 235.1–4
~ in, 552.1; see **submit**,v.
~ in, one who does not, 1142.13
~ in charity, 232.1
~ in marriage, 230.1(9)
~ in return, 234.5
~ in shares, 231.1
~ in a superior manner, 230.1(14,51)
~ off, 235.1–4
~ off like or as rays of light, 1065.33
~ one's disease, 230.1(12)
~ pain, 230.1(34) ; see also **pain**,v.
~ punishment, 230.1(34) ; see also **punish**,v.
~ through heredity, 230.1(8, 30,49)
~ to charity, 232.1
~ to the future, 230.1(8,30, 49)
~ up, 236.1–6
~ up, one who does not, 1142.13
given,adj.
~ in devotion, 657.8
one to whom ~, 230.4
what is ~, 230.6; see **gift**,n.
giver,n., 230.3
~ by will, 242.6
~ to charity, 232.3
giving,n., 230.2
continue ~, 230.1(38)
~ for human benefit, 230.2(4)
pert. to ~, 230.4
~ to charity, 232.2
~ to the poor, 230.2(1,2,4) ; see also **charity**,n.
glacier,n.
affect by ~s, 1040.12
base of a ~, pert. to, 1040.10
caused by ~s, 1040.8
cover with ~s, 1040.12
covered with ~s, 1040.9
~ in the sea, 1040.7
student of ~s, 1040.11
glad,adj.
cheerful, 1103.1; see **cheerful**,adj.
happy, 1102.1; see **happy**,adj.
gladiatorial,adj.
~ contest, 562.1(24)
glass,n., 1009
articles of ~, 1009.40,41
beer ~, 261.8(14,18,20,21)
cover with ~, 1009.47,48
drinking ~, 261.8; 1009.41
fit with ~, 1009.47,48
from ~, 1009.29
~ from molten lava, 1009.52
full ~, 925.11
furnish with ~, 1009.47,48
icelike ~, 1009.25
like ~, 1009.26,28,30
made of ~, 1009.39
make (~) opaque, 1009.37
manufacture of ~, 1009.42
manufacture of ~, place of, 1009.46
manufacture of ~ articles, 1009.42–44
manufacturer of ~, 1009.45
pane of ~, 1009.2
pert. to ~, 1009.27
~ section for, or in, a window, 1009.1,3
seller of ~, 1009.45
sound of ~ making contact, 469.7(3)
turn into ~, 1009.35,36
turn into ~, tending to, 1009.33

turned into ~, able to be,
1009.34
worker with ~, 1009.44,45,49
glassy,adj., 1009.26
~ (anatomical tissue),
1009.30
become ~, 1009.32,35
becoming ~, 1009.31
made ~, able to be, 1009.34
make ~, 1009.35
make ~ of surface, 1009.50
~ paper, 1009.51
remove ~ properties, 1009.37
something made ~, 1009.36
somewhat ~, 1009.31
glide,v., 90.1,2
gloom,n., 1124.2; see also
depression, sadness,n.
causing ~, 1124.9
clear of ~, 1124.8
cover with ~, 972.1(35)
fit of ~, 1124.3
given to moods of ~, 1123.15
gloomy,adj., 1124.1,9,10; see
also **depressed, sad**,adj.
be ~, 1124.4,6
become ~, 1124.12
dark and ~, 1070.7
look ~, 1124.4
make ~, 1124.4,6
making (a place) ~ and
dark, 1124.11
open to ~ influences, 9.9(5)
~ person, 1124.7
~ thing, 1124.13
glorification,n., 847.7; 851.2
~ into object of worship,
656.7
glorify,v., 847.7; 851.1
glorious,adj., 847.1
~ act, 52.5(23)
make ~, 847.7
glory,n., 847.2
government influenced by ~,
1073.3(33)
invest with ~, 847.7
~ surrounding idealized
thing, 847.6
gloss,n., 1065.56
glossy,adj., 1065.50,55
make ~, 1065.54
glove,n., 978.1
act as a ~ for, 978.3
cover with a ~, 978.3
dealer in ~s, 205.5(8)
furnish ~s to, 978.3
maker of ~s, 205.5(7)
tube used as ~s, 978.2
glow,v., 1064.29; 1065.45
glue,n., 302.14,26
like ~, 302.24
glue,v., 302.12
gluey,adj., 302.24
gluttony,n., 734.8; 737.2
gnat,n., 428.3
of ~s, 428.1(6)
science of ~s, 403.26(13)
gnaw,v., 735.1
gnawing,adj., 735.4
~ animal, 735.5
gneiss,n.
like ~, 1006.27
go,v., 119.1
~ about in search of pleasure, 700.9
~ across, 121.1
~ ahead, 174.1
~ along the shore of, 1029.86
~ and get, 240.1(30)
~ around, 119.1(7–10,16,30)
~ around to guard, 568.9
~ away, 141.1; see **depart**,v.
~ back, 145.1

~ back and forth, 119.1(54) ;
146.1–4; see also **sway,
swing**,v.
~ before, 175.1–5; see **precede**,v.
~ beyond, 130.1–4
~ by boat, 115.4
~ by pushing, 197.2
~ by ship, 115.25
~ by steam, 1048.35
~ by water, 115.26
~ down, 167.1; see **fall**,v.
~ faster, cause to, 95.8
~ for and get, 240.1(17)
~ forth, 140.1–6; see also **depart**,v.
~ forward, 119.1(2,6,32,60) ;
174.1
~ high, 159.1
~ higher, 159.1
~ in a direction, 119.1(20,49,
55) ; 179.2
~ in excess of, 920.10
~ in or into, 133.1; see **enter**,v.
~ instead of, 119.1(47)
~ into uncivilized country
first, 175.1(10)
let ~, 309.1; see **free**,v.
~ lower, 167.1; see **fall**,v.
~ often, 119.1(34)
~ on, 754.1; see **continue**,v.
~ on board, 133.6
~ on in time, 762.12
~ on with, 754.19
~ out, 140.1–6; see also **depart**,v.
~ out (of a fire, etc.), 801.19
~ out in a row, 311.18
~ over, 121.1
~ over the head of, 159.8
permission to ~, 554.2(4,5)
place to which one is ~ing,
782.14
place to which people ~,
782.13
~ rapidly, 95.6; 119.1(19,21–
23,35–40,45,63)
~ secretly, 119.1(4,44)
~ slower, 100.3–5
~ slowly, 100.1,2; 119.1(15,52)
~ through, 121.1; see also
pierce,v.
~ through (of air or wind),
1045.9
~ through in search,
121.1(17)
~ to another country, place,
etc., 119.1(27,53)
~ to see, 119.1(58)
~ to the country, 786.4
~ too far, 130.1–4
~ under water, 119.1(46) ;
1026.32
~ up, 159.1; see **rise**,v.
~ where unwelcome, 119.1(24,
25,29)
~ with, 131.1; see **accompany**,v.
goal,n., 45.1(3,6)
final ~, 45.1(18)
~ of many people, 45.1(11)
goat,n.
female ~, 412.3
group of ~s, 403.5(74)
hornless ~, 412.4
like a ~, 412.7
male ~, 412.2
mythical ~, half stag, 412.6
mythical god, partly a ~,
662.26(9,10)
of ~s, 403.11(2,12)
pert. to a ~, 412.7
smelling like a ~, 412.7;
445.10(12)

~ that leads sheep to slaughter, 176.3(14)
wild ~, 412.1
young ~, 412.5
goblin,n., 662.7(2,3,22,32)
class of ~s (Hindu), 662.10(4)
God (god),n., 654.1,2
a ~, 654.2
action of ~ or a ~, 654.10
ancestral spirits considered
~s, 662.10(3)
appearance of ~ or a ~ on
earth, 654.9
belief about ~ or ~s, 654.12
belief in many ~s, 654.12(4,6,
8,12,16,17)
belief in one ~, 654.12(14)
church of ~, 645.1(15)
City of ~, 1051.21
contempt for ~, 882.4
create in the image of ~,
654.7
devotion to ~, 657.1(6,17)
disbelief in ~ or a ~,
643.12(1–3,10) ; 654.12(5,11)
eating of a ~, 734.26(10)
explanation why ~ permits
evil, 599.2(5)
false ~, 654.2(1)
falseness to ~, 659.2(6)
government by ~ or a ~,
1073.3(32)
Greek ~, partly animal,
662.26(9,10,13)
head ~ of Greek mythology,
654.2(16)
head ~ of Roman mythology,
654.2(9)
household ~s, 654.3(1,3)
knowledge of ~, 654.14
lascivious ~ of the woods,
654.2(13)
like ~ or a ~, 654.6
love for ~, 700.30(22)
luminous cloud around a ~,
1065.27
minor ~, 654.2(5,8)
~ of Hell, 660.1
origin and descent of the ~s,
728.7
partly human ~, 654.2(5)
pert. to ~ or ~s, 654.4
proceeding from ~, 654.4(6)
protective ~ of Greek my-
thology, 654.2(3)
~s, 654.3
~s of the underworld, 660.5
~s of the underworld, pert.
to the, 660.2(1)
science of ~, 654.13,15
speculate about ~, 654.16
status of a ~, 654.5
symbol of a ~, 954.1(14)
talk about ~, 671.1(71,81)
theory of ~, 45.19
thinking about ~, 643.5
treat like, or make into, a
~, 654.11
union of Father, Son, and
Holy Ghost into ~, 654.8
~ who originated evil,
654.2(6)
without ~, 643.12(2,10)
without reverence for ~,
643.12(5,11)
worship false ~s 656.1(2,12)
worship of ~, 656.2
worship of all ~s, 656.15(19)
worship of different ~s,
656.15(27)
worship of one ~, 656.15(15)
goddess,n., 654.2
~ associated with death,
654.2(14)

minor ~, 654.2(12,14) ; 654.19;
  see **nymph**,n.
minor Greek ~, partly bird-
  like, 662.26(11)
~ of inspiration, 654.2(10) ;
  654.17; see **muse**,n.
godfather,n., 724.1(3,10)
godfather,v., 724.3
godlike,adj., 654.6
godliness,n., 654.5
godly,adj., 654.4; see **divine**,adj.
godmother,n., 725.1(3,12)
godmother,v., 725.3
goiter,n., 394.1(9)
gold,n., 1013.1
  bars of ~, 1015.2
  bearing or yielding ~,
    1013.18
  ~-bearing soil, 999.1(1)
  bronze coated with ~, 1013.10
  change into ~, 539.1(62) ;
    1013.23,25
  coat with ~, 1013.4
  ~-coated, 1013.8
  ~-coated edges, having,
    1013.9
  ~-coated metal, 1013.6
  ~-colored, 1013.14
  containing ~, 1013.13
  copper coated with ~,
    1013.10
  cover with ~, 972.1(24) ;
    1013.4
  decorated with ~ and ivory,
    1013.12
  dishes of ~, 1013.20
  filling of tooth with ~, 1013.31
  inferior to ~, 883.2
  like ~, 1013.16
  lump of ~, 326.15(2) ; 1013.2
  made of ~, 1013.19
  maker or seller of ~ objects,
    1013.30
  metal coated with ~, 1013.6
  mineral mistaken for ~,
    1013.29
  ornament with ~, 1065.76
  particles of ~, 1013.3
  pert. to ~, 1013.12
  plate with ~, 1013.11
  qualities of ~, 1013.22
  refining vessel for ~, 1015.16
  science of production of ~,
    213.20(1)
  shining like ~, 1013.17
  silver coated with ~, 1013.10
  solvent for ~, 1013.32
  ~ surface, 1013.7
  tableware of ~, 1013.20
  test of true ~, 1013.32
  unit of ~ measurement,
    1013.33
  ~ used in coating, 1013.5
  working with ~, 1013.31
golden,adj., 1013.14,16
  ~ in color, 1013.14
  make ~ in color, 1013.15
goldenrod,n.
  of the ~ family, 985.33(4)
goldfinch,n.
  group of ~es, 403.5(9)
gonorrhea,n., 379.9(1,3,12,17)
  germ causing ~, 403.21(7)
good,adj., 831.1
  be ~ enough, 831.17,18
  be ~ for, 831.14
  be morally ~, 843.20
  belief about what is ~, 831.22
  belief that the useful is ~,
    831.22(1,3)
  ~ enough, 831.19,20
  excess of a ~ thing, 920.20
  ~ for one, 831.11
  ~ for one's morals, 843.23
  ~ for the mind, 831.12

in ~ condition, 831.7,9
moderately ~, 831.20
morally ~, 843.17
neither ~ nor bad, 831.21
supply of ~ things, 915.3
that which is ~ for one,
  831.13
~ thing, 831.15
good,n.
  ~ and evil, doctrine of,
    1089.10
  highest ~, 831.16
  productive of ~, 831.11
good-by,n., 127.1,5
  song of ~, 476.4(3)
goodness,n.
  excellence, 831.2
  moral ~, 843.18,23
  promoting moral ~, 843.23
goose,n.
  female ~, 405.3(4) ; see also
    geese,n.
  like a ~, 405.10
  male ~, 405.2(6)
  young ~, 405.4(8)
gorilla,n., 420.6
gossip,n.
  rumor, 616.3; see **rumor**,n.
  spreader of rumors, 616.10
gossip,v., 616.5; 671.1(49)
gotten,adj.
  able to be ~, 240.5
  ~ by corrupt purchase, 240.8
  ~ by wickedness, trickery,
    etc., 240.7
  ~ from the outside, 240.6
  that which is ~, 240.3
gout,n., 1137.56(14)
  swollen or deformed with ~,
    1137.63
govern,v., 1073.63,64
  ~ as queen, 1073.27
  authority to ~, 5.4(13) ;
    1073.84
  ~ badly, 1073.67
  ~ by a police force, 1078.10
  ~ cruelly or harshly, 1073.61,
    62
  duty of white people to ~,
    1073.94
  pert. to ~ing, 1073.71,72
  power to ~, 5.4(13) ; 1073.84
governed,adj., 1075.3
  able to be ~, 1073.92
  ~ by a ruler, one who is,
    1075.2
  ~ by decree, 275.6
  unable to be ~, 1073.93
governing,adj., 1073.68
  self-~, 1073.75
  ~ substitute for monarch,
    1073.69
government,n., 1073.1,3,5;
    1073.5(1,2)
  a ~, 1073.5
  ~ according to ownership of
    property, 1073.3(33)
  ~ affairs not involved with
    the church, 1073.83
  art of ~, 1073.96
  art of political ~, 1076.1
  autocratic ~, 1073.3(1–3,5,11,
    13–15,22) ; 1073.59
  bring (people) under ~,
    1073.65,66
  bring under ~ ownership or
    control, 1073.90
  British ~, 1073.5(6)
  ~ by a father, 1073.3(26,27)
  ~ by a group, 1073.42
  ~ by a king, queen, etc.,
    1073.4(5)
  ~ by a specific number of
    rulers, 1073.51
  ~ by demons or devils,

1073.42(4)
~ by departments, 1073.42(3)
~ by engineers, 1073.42(17)
~ by fear, 1073.3(31)
~ by force, 1073.3(6)
~ by God or a god, 1073.3(32)
~ by holy people, 1073.42(10)
~ by influence of honor or
  glory, 1073.3(33)
~ by landowners in England,
  1073.42(15)
~ by men, not women,
  1073.42(1,7)
~ by monks, 1073.42(9)
~ by nobles, 1073.4(1)
~ by nuns, 1073.42(9)
~ by slaves, 1073.42(5)
~ by technical experts,
  1073.42(17)
~ by the army or military
  people, 1073.42(16)
~ by the clergy, 1073.42(11,
  18)
~ by the few, 1073.3(24)
~ by the lower classes,
  1073.42(12)
~ by the mob, 1073.42(12)
~ by the mother, 1073.3(21)
~ by the old, 1073.42(7)
~ by the people, 1073.3(12,
  28) ; 1073.4(2,6)
~ by the superior, 1073.42(2)
~ by the wealthy, 1073.42(14)
~ by violence, 4.18(3)
~ by women, 1073.42(8,13)
~ by workers, 1073.42(6)
centralized ~, 1073.6(1)
centralized ~ reducing individual freedom, 1073.6(2)
church ~, 1073.3(17,25)
civil ~, pert. to, 1073.83
colonial ~, 1073.3(19)
community under political ~,
  1076.10
control of ~ by trade unions,
  advocate of, 1076.12(27)
controlled by ~, 8.6(3)
convert to a form of ~,
  1073.10
country under ~, 1073.4,43,89
cruel ~, 1073.59
delegated ~ power, exercising, 1073.91
executive ~, 1073.5(1)
executive branch of the ~,
  1077.3(1)
external ~, dependent on,
  1073.82
freedom from ~, 309.14(2)
freedom from outside ~,
  309.14(4,5,10,18)
German ~, 1073.5(4,8)
German system of ~,
  1073.3(23)
harsh ~, 1073.59
internal affairs of a ~, pert.
  to, 1073.74
Italian civil ~, 1073.5(5)
lack of ~, 1073.103
lack of ~, theory about,
  1073.104–7
medieval ~, 1073.3(16) ; see
  feudalism,n.
Moslem ~ power, symbol of,
  1073.86
~ of a ruler, 1073.19
~ of equal political power,
  1073.3(12,20,28)
~ of the Pope, 1073.3(25) ;
  1073.5(5)
~ official, 1077.1
opposition to ~, 544.2(18)
opposition to ~, secret organization in, 971.37
organization of ~, 1073.102

overthrow of ~, advocacy of, 1073.108
participation in ~, privilege of, 1073.81
people under political ~, 1076.10
person living under a form of ~, 1073.9
pert. to ~, 1073.72,73
pert. to city ~, 785.7
policy of ~, 1073.6
power of ~, 5.4(11)
practice of ~, 1073.6
principles of ~, 1073.6
resistance to ~, 4.18(1); 971.37; 1073.108
Russian ~, 1073.5(3)
Russian system of ~, 1073.3(10,11,30)
science of ~, 1073.101
science of political ~, 1076.2
self-~, 1073.3(4,8,18); 1073.4(2)
self-~, advocacy of, 1073.79,80
self-~, city with, 1073.76
self-~, having, 1073.75
self-~, without, 1073.82
skill in ~, 1073.96,100
skilled person in ~, 1073.97–99
state under political ~, 1076.10
supporter of a form of ~, 1073.7,46
supporting a form of ~, 1073.8
symbol of ~, 1073.85,86
system of ~, 1073.2,3
temporary ~, period of, 1073.95
territory under ~, 1073.89
the ~, 1073.5
theory of ~, 1073.6
time between ~s, 1073.95
totalitarian ~, 1073.3(10,14,15, 23,34)
Turkish ~ power, symbol of, 1073.86
under a ~, 1075.3
U.S. executive ~, 1073.5(7)
violence against ~, 4.18
~ with state ownership, 1073.3(7,9,29)
without ~, period, 1073.95
governor,n., 1073.14; see **ruler**,n.
~ of a U.S. state, 1077.1(7,13)
gown,n., 974.38; see also **dress**, **garment**,n.
dressing ~, 974.43
night~, 974.44
grab,v., 247.6; see **seize**,v.
grace,n.
shapeliness, 507.13
obsession with beauty and ~, 505.15
without ~, 14.1(22,34)
graceful,adj.
shapely, 507.13
~ act, 52.5(7); 1106.19
beautiful and ~, 949.6
gay and ~, 1106.16
~ in humor, style, irony, etc., 949.12
~ in movement, 90.3; 949.7(2)
tall and ~, 515.1(4,7,11,14)
thin and ~, 513.1(9,26,27,30)
without ~ qualities, 1106.18
graceless,adj., 14.1
gracious,adj., 842.1
kind, 842.1
pleasing, 1106.3
~ act, 52.5(11)
gradation,n.
mark the ~s of, 946.13
gradual,adj., 100.11

gradually,adv., 100.13
gradualness,n., 100.12
doctrine of ~, 100.14
graduate,n.
Cambridge ~, 623.12(4)
certificate granted a ~, 623.14
college ~, 623.12(3,5–8)
degree conferred on a ~, 623.13
female ~, 623.12(1)
male ~, 623.12(2)
Oxford ~, 623.12(9)
graduation,n.
certificate on ~, 857.11
~ exercises, 623.15
~ with honors, 857.13
graft,v.
~ living tissue, etc., 323.1(18, 24,74)
grain,n.
food, 987.1,13,23
slight amount, 917.1,17
small particle, 917.15
bearing ~, 987.19
beat ~, 437.1(98)
constituent of ~, 987.16
cut and gather ~, 998.2(1)
eating ~s, 734.27(13,14)
~ for grinding, 987.3
~ for spaghetti, 987.22
gathering of cut ~, 998.6
grind ~, 987.5,6
ground ~, 987.4
~ ground coarse, 987.24
leaf of ~, 993.1
like ~, 987.21
machine or building for grinding ~, 987.11
made from ~, 987.21
pert. to ~, 987.18
seed of cereal ~, coating on, 987.14
stalk of ~, 987.25
stick for beating ~, 437.5(11)
storehouse for ~, 262.3(9,13, 14,24)
grainy,adj.
~ in form, 507.17(39)
grammar,n., 664.11
ambiguous construction in ~, 667.1(2)
error in ~, 667.3
error in ~, make, 667.5
parts of speech in ~, 666.28
student of ~, 664.12
word in ~, 666.3(27)
word relationship in ~, 666.13,14
grammatical,adj.
~ effects, 669.3–7
~ number, 927.16
~ time, 762.1(11)
grand,adj., 847.1
impressive and ~, 847.4
ostentatiously ~, 847.3
passion for ~ actions, 1136.1(25)
~ quality, 847.5
~ thing, 847.5
grandeur,n.
delusions of ~, 1136.1(25,31, 37,38)
grandfather,n., 724.10
grandmother,n., 725.10
grandness,n., 847.2
granite,adj.
like ~, 1006.28
grape,n., 745.1(1)
crop of ~s, 745.2
growing like ~s, 731.5(8)
like ~s, 745.22(13)
pert. to ~s, 745.22(13)
place where ~s grow, 985.34(9,10)

raising of ~s, 745.25(7,8)
shaped like a ~ cluster, 507.17(3,11)
grapefruit,n., 745.1(8)
cross between tangerine and ~, 745.1(9)
descr. of ~, 745.22(4)
raising of ~, 745.25(1)
grasp,v.
seize, 247.6; see **seize**,v.
understand, 593.1; see **understand**,v.
grasping,adj.
desirous, 265.3
greedy, 265.16
~ hands or fingers, 247.16
~ person, 265.5
grass,n., 986.1
able to grow ~ for animals (of land), 986.28
~-colored, 986.13
cover with ~, 986.21,22
covered with ~, 986.24
cut ~ for animal food, 986.7
eat ~, etc., 734.4
eating ~es, 734.27(12)
feed ~ to, 986.2
feed on ~, 986.3
feed (livestock) on ~, for purging, 986.4
growth of ~, 986.26
land covered with ~, 986.15–20
leaf of ~, 993.1
like ~, 986.11,25
of the ~ family, 986.14
patch of ~, 986.20
pert. to ~, 986.12
plant with ~, 986.21
produce ~, 986.29
science of ~es, 985.36(2)
surface covered with ~, 986.19
surface of ~, 139.1(14)
grasshopper,n., 428.3
of ~s, 428.1(16)
science of ~s, 403.26(31)
grassland,n., 986.15
~ of Russia, 986.16
~ of South Africa, 986.17
~ of South America, 986.18
grassy,adj., 986.12
lay out in ~ slopes, 986.27
~ level, 986.15
~ slope, 986.15
grateful,adj., 1110.1; see **thankful**,adj.
gratitude,n., 1110.2
grave,n., 797.10; see also **tomb**,n.
digger of ~s, 797.15
like a ~, 797.12
marker for a ~, 797.13
robber of a ~, 797.23–25
serve as a ~ for, 797.11
underground ~, 797.10(2)
gravedigger,n., 797.15
gravel,n.
swallowing ~, 736.4
gravity,n.
center of ~, 137.1(2)
stimulation by ~, 101.1(4,5)
gravy,n.
served in its ~, 447.5
gray,adj., 498.2
having ~ hair, 369.12(8)
~ like ashes, 1064.48
~ like dust, 1001.15
smoky ~, 1050.18
gray,n., 498.1
grease,n., 510.8; see **fat**, **oil**,n.
grease,v., 510.12,16,17
place to ~ cars, 510.18
greasy,adj., 510.9(9–11)
smooth of manner, etc.,

823.11; 859.10
great,adj.
  big, 906.3
  ~ in degree, 924.1
Great Britain,n., 784.9(21) ; see
  England,n.
greater,adj.
  be ~ in degree, 924.8
  become ~, 902.2
  become ~ in degree, 924.7
  ~ in number, 924.6
  ~ in position, 924.6
  ~ in value, 924.6
  make ~, 907.1
  make ~ in degree, 924.8
greatest,adj.
  ~ possible in degree, 924.2–5
Greece,n.
  expert on ~, 784.14
  fondness for ~, 700.30(8,17) ;
    700.31
  make conform to customs of
    ~, 784.10(5)
  pert. to ancient ~, 784.16(1–
    3)
  pert. to culture of ~,
    784.16(1–3)
greed,n., 265.17
  eat with ~, 734.1(2,11,15,16–
    20,29,36)
  neurotic ~ for wealth,
    265.17(1)
greedy,adj., 265.16
  ~ creditor, 265.18(4)
  cruel and ~, 265.16(20,21) ;
    889.1(11)
  ~ eater, 734.3
  ~ for food, 265.16(4,6,7,9,10,
    13,15,16,18,19,21)
  ~ for money, 265.16(1,2,11)
  ~ in eating, 734.8
  ~ person, 265.18
  stingy and ~, 265.16(2,11)
Greek,adj., 784.16; 784.16(1–4)
  ~ in style, 960.3
  ~ language, 664.4(2,15)
  make ~, 784.10(5) ; 784.11
Greek,n., 784.15(1,3,24)
  hater of ~s, 880.18(3)
green,adj., 493.1–10
  ~ coating on brass, copper, or
    bronze, 1016.18,19
  ~ like a leaf, 993.23
  ~ like grass, 986.13
  ~ with grass, 493.5
green,n., 493.1–10
greenness,n., 493.7
  ~ of plants, 985.2
greet,v., 126.1
  ~ with happiness, 1102.21
greeter,n., 126.3
greeting,n., 126.2
  express in ~, 126.4
  Hawaiian ~, 126.2(1)
  Japanese ~, 126.2(2)
  pert. to ~, 126.6
  public ~, 126.2(4)
  speech of ~, student who
    makes, 126.3(1)
  style of ~, 126.5
grief,n., 1125.2; see sadness,n.
  exhibition of ~ for the dead,
    799.7
grimace,n., 365.2
grimace,v., 365.2
  ~ with pain, 1130.15
grind,n., 438.9
grind,v., 438.8
  ~ grain, 987.5,6
  machine or building for ~ing
    grain, 987.11
  ~ (the teeth), 735.11(5)
  ~ to dust, 438.8(2,6)
  ~ to powder, 438.8(2,3,5–7)
grinding,n., 438.9

  ~ of the teeth, 735.11
  sound of ~, 469.1(7)
groan,n., 468.1
groan,v., 468.2
groceries,n.
  seller of ~, 233.4(1) ; 745.23
groin,n.
  region of the ~, pert. to,
    388.1(4)
groove,n., 157.4(11,16,22,28,30,
    33,36)
  having two ~s, 299.2(2)
gross,n.
  twelve ~, 940.39
grotesque,adj., 811.6
  ~ figure, 811.8
  ~ thing, 811.7
ground,n.
  below the ~, 1004.29
  below the ~, passage,
    122.1(32,33,35)
  below the ~, room that is,
    787.7(13,39,41)
  bring to the ~, 999.6
  come to the ~, 999.6
  fall to the ~, 999.7
  growing in muddy ~, 1000.18
  growing in or on the ~,
    731.5(11,21)
  hit the ~, 999.7
  lay on the ~, 999.7
  living in muddy ~, 1000.18
  muddy ~, 1000.14–17
  place on the ~, 999.7
  put on ~, 999.6
  ~s, 1003.17
  ~s of a country estate,
    1003.17(8)
  ~s of a school, 1003.17(1)
  solid ~, 999.1(13)
groundless,adj., 1022.38
group,n., 318.1
  accompanying ~, 318.1(41,53)
  administrative ~, 318.1(13,49)
  best ~, 318.1(51)
  biological ~, 318.8
  cause to form into a ~, 318.4
  collect into a ~, 318.4,5
  communist ~, 318.1(24)
  exclusive ~, 318.1(18,26,29,84)
  exclusive ~s, tending to form,
    318.6
  ~ in opposition, 318.1(98)
  leisure ~, 318.1(85)
  member of a ~, 318.3
  new member of a ~, 318.3(1)
  ~ of animals, 403.5
  ~ of children, 318.1(57)
  ~ of comets, 318.1(55)
  ~ of contestants, 318.1(89,93)
  ~ of families, 218.1(26)
  ~ of foreigners, 318.1(33)
  ~ of players, 318.1(89,93)
  ~ of students, 318.1(28)
  ~ of tests, 318.1(9)
  ~ of toadies, 318.1(27)
  ~ of women, 318.1(10,43,62)
  ~ of workers, 318.1(14,33,44,
    58,59,70,80,87,93,94)
  ~ of worshipers, 318.1(38,57)
  pert. to a ~, 318.2
  political ~, 318.1(11,12,15,35,
    65,68,72,98)
  prejudice in favor of a ~,
    634.1(25)
  racial ~, 318.1(68,94)
  religious ~, 318.1(68,73,94)
  ~ sent on a special mission,
    326.6(4,5)
  serving or intended to cover
    a ~, 972.38
  social ~, 318.1(18,26,29,42,84,
    94)
  ~ spirit, 318.7

  ~ to influence legislation,
    9.12
  transplanted ~, 318.1(33)
group,v., 318.4,5
  ~ like stars, 1056.7
grow,v., 731.3,22
  increase, 907.2; see in-
    crease,v.
  able to ~, 731.19,20
  ~ again, 731.3(26) ; 731.22(6)
  ~ along the ground, 731.3(33)
  begin to ~, 731.1
  beginning to ~, 729.9;
    729.15(4,11) ; 731.2
  ~ beyond, 731.3(21,22)
  cause to ~, 731.22
  ~ crops, plants, flowers, etc.,
    731.22(1,5)
  ~ faster than, 731.3(21,22)
  ~ fat, 731.3(3)
  ~ forth, 731.3(7)
  ~ germs, 731.22(2)
  ~ in groups, 731.3(8)
  ~ in population, 731.3(6)
  ~ irregularly, 731.3(25,28)
  ~ mature, 731.3(19,20,27)
  ~ rapidly, 985.23; 1039.14
  ~ ripe, 731.3(19,20,27)
  something that ~s, 731.21
  ~ strong, 1.30; 731.3(3,5,15,
    32)
  ~ together, 731.3(1,9,11,17)
growing,adj., 731.5
  increasing, 907.4
  ~ abnormally, 731.5(14,18)
  ~ in clusters, 731.5(1,8)
  ~ in or on the ground,
    731.5(11,21)
  ~ in pairs, 731.5(5)
  ~ irregularly, 731.5(16)
  ~ like grapes, 731.5(8)
  ~ mature, 731.5(2)
  ~ naturally, 731.5(19)
  ~ on, 731.5(20)
  ~ on trees, 731.5(4)
  ~ rapidly, 985.22
  ~ wild, 731.5(3,7,14,17,18)
growl,n., 468.1; 573.4; 878.9
growl,v., 468.2; 573.2; 878.6
growling,adj., 468.3; 573.1(7,8,
    21,24) ; 878.10
grown,adj., 732.1; see also ma-
    ture,adj.
  excessively ~, 732.8,9
  not fully ~, 733.1,7,9–11
  principal thing ~, 731.26
  ~-up, 732.1
growth,n., 731.4,21,23; see also
    development,n.
  increase, 907.3; see in-
    crease,n.
  a ~, 731.21
  abnormal ~, 731.4(8–10) ;
    731.21(3–5,8–13,16,18,20) ;
    see also cancer, tumor,n.
  area of ~, 731.15
  arrested ~, 731.30
  arrested in ~, 731.28,29
  capable of ~, 731.19,20
  causing ~, 731.24,25
  earliest ~, pert. to, 731.11
  earliest stages of ~, in, 733.9
  early ~, 731.9(1,7,11,14)
  encourage the ~ of, 731.27
  figurative ~, 731.4(13)
  full ~, 731.9(2–5,8,9,12,15,16)
  gland regulating ~, 731.6
  go through ~, 731.3
  held back in ~, 731.28,29
  highest point in ~, 731.9(3,5,
    6,8,9,12,16)
  history of individual ~,
    731.16(1)
  history of racial ~, 731.16(1)

~ into an individual, 731.4(11)
malignant ~, 731.21(4,11,12) ; see also cancer,n.
natural ~, 731.21(9)
~ of germs, 731.21(7)
~ on a tree, 731.21(2)
~ on or in the body, 731.21(3–5,8–13,16,18,20) ; see also cancer, tumor,n.
~ on the skin, 731.21(3,9)
period of or in ~, 731.7–9; 769.8(15)
physiological ~, 731.4(3,4,12)
place of rapid ~, 883.38
prevent the ~ of, 909.6(1,4)
reach full ~, 731.10
reach highest point of ~, 731.10
repetition of ~, 731.12
repetition of race history in ~ of individual, 731.13,14
retarded ~, 731.30
retarded in ~, 731.28,29
rough ~, 731.21(17)
seasonal ~, 731.21(6)
slow in ~, 100.6(1,15)
slow the ~ of, 100.5(2) ; 731.28
stop the ~ of, 731.28; 791.1(1, 3,8,15)
student of ~, 731.17
young ~, 731.21(1,15)
grudge,n.
holding a ~, 221.3
guarantee,n., 1122.3; see promise,n.
guarantee,v., 641.4; 1122.1; see promise,v.
guard,n., 568.4,5; see protection, protector,n.
guard,v., 568.1; see protect,v.
~ side of military troops, 568.24
guardian,n., 568.5
care and protection of a ~, 570.6
one under a ~, 568.19(3)
pert. to a ~, 568.15
state of being a ~, 568.14
guardianship,n., 568.2(6) ; 568.3(2)
guess,n., 588.1,4
pert. to a ~, 588.3
guess,v., 588.2
guessing,n., 588.4
part of science subject to ~, 612.26
pert. to ~, 588.3
guest,n.
place where ~s are received, 201.16
~s, collectively, 201.17
guidance,n., 177.2
pert. to ~, 177.5
without ~, 177.8
guide,n., 177.3,4
act as a ~, 177.1(6,7)
~book, 177.4(1) ; 687.1(5,14)
~ for sight-seers, 177.3(1)
~post, 177.4(5,7,11)
guide,v., 177.1
serving to ~, 177.5
~ spiritually, 177.1(14)
~ wrongly, 177.1(10,12)
guidebook,n., 177.4(1) ; 687.1(5, 14)
guiding,adj., 177.5
~ light, 177.4(2)
~ light for ships, 1065.109,110
~ position, 177.6(3)
~ signal, 177.4(2) ; 956.1(2)
~ spirit or fairy, 662.7(16,17)
~ star, 177.4(8,9) ; 1056.2
guilt,n.

admission of ~, 675.2; 675.2(1) ; 884.24
admit ~, 675.1(2,8,9) ; 884.23
arising from ~, 884.18
atone for ~, 845.20,22
be sorry for ~, 884.17
determine ~ in court, 1082.8
feeling of ~, 884.13
feeling of ~, arising from, 884.18
free from ~, 897.24,28
free of ~, 309.11(1,3,24) ; 845.6
free oneself of ~, 845.19
involved in ~, 884.30
make amends for ~, 845.20,22
showing ~, 884.16
wipe out ~, 884.23
without ~, 845.6; 884.15,22; see also guiltless,adj.
guiltless,adj., 845.6; 884.15,22; see also innocent,adj.
declare ~, 897.32
make morally ~, 845.15
~ of illicit sex, 845.11
~ person, 845.7
prove ~, 897.33
guilty,adj.
believe ~, 884.31
believed ~, 884.32
declare ~, 884.39
declare ~ of crime, 1088.12
feeling ~, 884.12,18
find ~, 884.36
not ~, declare, 897.32
not ~, prove, 897.33
~ of crime, 1088.9
~ of sin, 884.9
person ~ of a fault, crime or offense, 884.38
person ~ of crime, 1088.10,11
person believed ~, 884.34
person found ~, 884.37
proved ~, 884.35
gulf,n.
body of water, 1029.63
gullet,n., 347.6–8
gullible,adj., 823.23
gum,n.
dental science of ~s, 401.1(72)
inflammation of the ~s, 368.23
~s of the teeth, 368.22
gun,n., 565.1
art of shooting ~s, 565.8
hammer of a ~, 437.9(1)
holder for a ~, 261.1(25)
pull back hammer of a ~, 565.9
~s, 565.2
science of ~s, 565.7
shoot ~s, 565.3
shooting of ~s, 565.4
gunner,n., 564.1(3,4,10,11,38,45)
gunpowder,n.
container for ~, 261.1(28)
gut,n., 347.9; see intestine,n.
gutter,n., 299.1(6,7,14,16,21,35)
gypsy,n., 128.3; 129.1
associate of ~s, 129.2
~ language, 664.4(17)
like a ~, 129.3
pert. to ~s, 129.3

H

H (the letter),n.
pronunciation with ~, 670.4(3)
sound of ~, 670.14(1)
habit,n., 629.1; see also custom,n.
adherence to ~, 629.6
adhering to a ~, 629.5

be in the ~ of, 629.18
coarse ~, 629.1(19)
conformer to ~, 629.7
conforming to ~, 629.5
conformity to ~, 629.6
contrary to ~, 629.3
free of a ~, 309.11(10)
give oneself over to a ~, 629.26
having a drug ~, 629.5(2)
of bad ~s, 629.17
of good ~s, 629.16
relapse into former, bad, or criminal ~s, 145.1(1,15,24) ; 145.2(2) ; 629.22
~s, 629.1
slavery to a drug ~, 629.27
strengthen in ~, 1.29(5)
strengthened by ~, 629.13
strengthened in one's ~s, 629.14,15
undesirable ~, 629.1(18)
unnatural ~, 629.1(10)
habitable,adj., 750.8
habitat,n., 753.1; see home,n.
habitation,n., 753.1; see home, house,n.
habitual,adj., 535.1,2; 629.2; see also customary,adj.
~ act, 52.5(22)
devote oneself ~ly to, 629.26
do ~ly, 629.18
~ mental attitude, 629.4
not ~, 629.3
habituate,v., 629.23
habituated,adj., 629.24; see accustomed,adj.
hackneyed,adj., 282.6
hagfish,n.
of ~es, 422.1(15)
hail,n.
amount of ~, 1037.11
condition of ~, 1046.6
particle of ~, 1040.3
storm of ~, 1040.2
hair,n., 369.1
animal's ~, 369.1(8,13,14,17–19,21,24,27,33,35,44–46,49)
anxiety about the ~, 369.22
bag to hold up the ~, 983.40
break off the ~, desire to, 371.9
bristling of the ~, 369.23
cavity from which ~ grows, 369.2
characteristic of ~, 369.5
color of ~, 369.12–15
covered with ~, 369.6
curly (of ~), 369.1(1–3,5–8)
cut ~ short, 911.13
cut short (of the ~), 1043.22
cut the ~, 371.1(1,3,4)
cutting of ~, pert. to 371.7
disease of the ~, 369.24
dresses ~, one who, 369.19
eating of ~, 734.26(11)
face ~, 369.1(3,46) ; see beard,n.
false ~, 369.1(48) ; see wig,n.
genital ~, 369.1(31)
genital ~ development, 369.9
having combed ~, 369.16
having curly ~, 369.1(2,3,7, 8)
having downy ~, 369.11(3)
having gray ~, 369.12(8)
having long ~, 369.11(4)
having short ~, 369.11(5)
having short, thick ~s, 369.11(1)
having unpigmented ~, 369.12(1)
having white or whitish ~, 369.12(1,12)
having woolly ~, 369.11(6,8)

knot in ~, 302.34
like ~, 369.10
lose ~, 972.14,16,17
loss of ~, 371.12
loss of ~, disease attended
  by, 371.14
ornament for the ~, 983.42–44
pert. to ~, 369.5
pin for the ~, 983.42
removal of ~, 371.2,5,6
remove the ~ of, 371.1
rise erect (of ~), 159.1(5)
root ~, 992.4
science of the ~, 401.1(105)
sensation when the ~ is
  touched, 434.1(14)
shaped like a ~, 507.17(59,72)
short ~, 911.14
specks in the ~, 369.25
straight (of the ~), 369.18(4)
style of ~, 369.17,18
substance for the ~, 369.21
tearing out of one's ~, 371.10
uncombed ~, 903.13
untidy (of the ~), 903.1(1,6,
  17,24,25)
untidy of ~, 903.1(1,6,17,24,
  25)
unusual growth of ~, 369.3,4
wash the ~, 899.35(7)
wavy (of ~), 369.18(7,8)
without ~, 371.11; see bald,
  adj.
hairdresser,n., 369.19
  pert. to a ~, 369.20
hairiness,n., 369.7
  abnormal ~, 369.7; 369.7(1,2)
hairy,adj., 369.6
  ~ growth, 369.1
  make ~, 369.8
  unusually ~, 369.6(10)
half,n., 929.1
  decrease to ~, 910.1(19)
  divide in ~, 929.2
  divided in ~, 929.3
  less than ~, 914.1(11)
  more than ~, 914.1(10);
  920.12
half-breed,n., 430.6
hall,n., 122.1(6,10,11,17,21,25,37)
  entrance ~, 122.1(11,21,25,
  37); 133.7(14,20)
hallucination,n., 483.8(2,3,9,11,
  14,16); 809.3
  hearing ~, 454.22(3,4,6)
  mental derangement marked
  by ~s, 1136.1(5,8,9,11,17,18,
  31,37,38)
  of the nature of ~, 809.1
halo,n., 1065.21,25,27
  ~ around a king, etc., 1065.25
  become a ~, 1065.22
  spot on ~ of moon, 1065.24
  spot on ~ of sun, 1065.23
halt,v., 791.1,2; see stop,v.
hammer,n., 437.9
  gun's ~, 437.9(1)
  pull back gun ~, 565.9
hand,n., 343.1
  both ~s well, able to use,
  343.15
  care of the ~s, 343.18
  clenched ~, 343.2
  disease of the joints in the
  ~, 1137.56(14)
  grasping ~s, 247.16
  increase in size of the ~,
  343.20
  inside of the ~, 343.5,6
  left ~, preferring the, 343.14
  pain in the ~, 1137.56(5,6,14)
  pert. to the ~, 343.3
  pert. to the right ~, 343.4
  right ~, preference for the,
  343.13

right from the left ~, able
  to tell, 343.16
  ~s on hips, 60.7
  shaped like a ~, 507.17(55)
  skill in using ~s, 7.1(6,7,28,
  30,43,44)
  sleight of ~, 663.18
  study of the ~, 343.19
  two ~s, done with, 343.17
handcuffs,n., 558.3(6)
  free from ~, 309.1(24,26,31)
  put ~ on, 558.1(36)
handed,adj.
  both right- and left-~, 343.15
  four-~, 343.7(3)
  left-~, 343.11,12
  left-~ person, 343.13
  many-~, 343.7(2)
  right-~, 343.8,9
  two-~, 343.7(1)
handiness,n., 7.1
handerchief,n., 978.10
  neck ~, 977.1(1,4,5)
handle,n., 258.1
  having a ~, 258.2
handle,v., 436.1(13,22)
  ~ clumsily, 14.4(3)
  clumsy to ~, 14.5
handsome,adj., 505.1; see also
  beautiful,adj.
  ~ man, 505.5
handsomeness,n., 505.2
handwriting,n., 677.1; see also
  writing,n.
  analysis of ~, 677.12,13
  art of ~, 677.5
  art of small ~, 677.5(2)
  bad ~, 677.1(2)
  character in flowing ~,
  679.1(6)
  composition in ~, 682.3(11)
  curved shape in ~, 677.10
  decoration in ~, 677.11
  descr. of ~, 677.2
  document in ~, 684.4(1)
  easy-to-read ~, 677.2(5)
  fancy shape in ~, 677.11
  fancy twist in ~, 156.3(1,3)
  flowing (of ~), 96.3(2);
  677.2(2,6)
  hard-to-read ~, 677.1(6,7,14–
  16); 677.2(1,3,4)
  imitation of another's ~,
  677.8
  incorrect ~, 677.1(2)
  manuscript in author's ~,
  684.1(2)
  materials or instruments for
  ~, 677.14
  one's own ~, 677.1(1)
  ornament ~, 959.1(13); 959.14
  pert. to ~, 677.2
  rapid ~, 677.7
  running (of ~), 96.3(2);
  677.2(6)
  small (of ~), 677.2(1)
  small ~, 677.1(11); 677.6
  small ~, instrument for,
  677.14(2)
  taking down a speech in ~,
  677.9
  turn of the pen in ~, 148.2(6)
  write by ~, 677.3,4
hang,v., 172.1,2
  kill by hanging, 796.1(10,13)
  cause to ~, 172.2
  let ~, 172.2
  let tongue ~ out, 172.2(2)
  ~ on gallows, 172.2(1)
  ~ over, 172.1(1,2,7,10–12,16)
  ~ the picture of, 966.22
  ~ the statue of, 966.22
hanging,adj., 172.4
  ~ loose, 304.1(2,5)

~ loosely and untidily,
  903.1(1,6,17,24,25)
  ~ ornament, 172.7; 959.3(14)
  ~ part, 326.1(39)
  ~ piece, 326.18
  ~ thing, 172.6
  ~ weight, 947.15(2,4); 947.17
hanging,n., 172.3
  death by ~, 794.6
  device for ~, 172.5
  device for ~ criminals,
  796.19(2)
  loop of rope for ~ a victim,
  302.33
hangover,n., 749.53
haphazard,adj., 46.13
happen,v., 29.1
  about to ~, 29.16,17
  ~ after inactivity, 29.1(21)
  ~ again, 29.1(17,18,21,22)
  ~ as a possibility, 29.1(12)
  ~ as a result, 16.3; 29.1(11,12)
  ~ as an accident, 29.1(12)
  ~ at the end, 29.1(13,27)
  ~ at the same time, 29.1(1,8,
  9,25); 764.5,6
  be about to ~, 29.18,20
  ~ before (something else),
  29.1(2,19)
  ~ between other occurrences,
  29.1(14)
  ~ by turns, 29.1(2)
  ~ by way of help, 29.1(23)
  ~ by way of relief, 29.1(23)
  cause to ~ at the same time,
  764.7
  cause to ~ faster, 95.8
  certain to ~, 29.21
  expected to ~, 29.28
  ~ faster, cause to, 95.8
  ~ finally, 29.1(10,13)
  ~ in addition, 29.1(24)
  likely not to ~, 29.27
  likely to ~, 29.23–25,27
  ~ more often, 29.1(20)
  prepare to ~, 29.19
  ~ repeatedly in the mind,
  29.1(17)
  threatening to ~, 29.26
  ~ unexpectedly, 29.1(24)
  ~ unnecessarily, 29.1(24)
  what is likely to ~, 29.29,30
  what will ~, 29.9
happened,adj.
  not having ~ before, 29.4
happening,adj., 29.3
  ~ again, 29.3(54,55)
  ~ again after inactivity,
  29.3(52)
  ~ again and again, 29.3(37,
  43,45)
  ~ as a result, 29.3(26)
  ~ at a certain time, 29.3(13)
  ~ at once, 29.3(31,34,65)
  ~ at sunset, 29.3(2)
  ~ at the same time, 29.3(41)
  ~ at the end, 29.3(15,67);
  792.19
  ~ at the right time, 29.3(41,
  57)
  ~ at the same instant, 764.8
  ~ at the same time, 29.3(16–
  20,66); 764.4,5
  ~ at the wrong time, 29.3(68)
  ~ before the Civil War,
  29.3(7)
  ~ before the war, 29.3(7)
  ~ by chance, 29.3(1,3,12,14,23,
  28,30,32,33,51)
  ~ by itself, 29.3(61,62)
  ~ by turns, 29.3(5)
  ~ by way of help, 29.3(63)
  ~ by way of relief, 29.3(63)
  ~ earlier, 29.3(8,46)
  ~ every eight days, 937.6

~ every fifth day, 934.6
~ every fourth day, 933.17
~ every seven days, 936.10
~ every third day, 932.36
~ for a moment, 29.3(34)
~ in addition, 29.3(64)
~ in many places, 29.3(49,69)
~ in scattered places, 29.3(59, 62)
~ in the dark, 29.3(25)
~ irregularly, 29.3(10,30,33, 35,39,51,52,60,62)
~ later, 29.3(26,27)
~ now, 29.3(42)
~ often, 29.3(24,29,37,47,56)
~ one after the other, 29.3(21)
~ regularly, 29.3(22,36,43)
~ repeatedly in the mind, 29.3(44)
~ seldom, 29.3(39,52,58)
~ suddenly, 29.3(65)
~ together, 29.3(18,19,20,32)
~ too soon, 29.3(48,68)
~ unexpectedly, 29.3(23,64)
~ unnaturally, 29.3(38,50)
~ unnecessarily, 29.3(64)
~ while walking, 29.3(6)
~ with diminished importance, 29.3(9,11)
~ with something more important, 29.3(14,32)
~ without warning, 29.3(65)
happening,n., 29.6
absurd ~s, 29.7(4)
accidental ~, 29.6(13,21)
act of ~, 29.2
added ~, 29.6(40)
~ as an authorization, 29.6(5, 33)
~ as an example, 29.6(5,33)
book, chart, etc., of ~s, 774.7(1,7)
combination of ~s, 29.7
embarrassing ~, 29.6(14)
final ~, 29.6(11,16)
full of important ~s, 29.11
future ~, 771.24
group of ~s, 29.7
important ~, 29.6(19,24)
~ in a novel, 29.6(18)
~ indicating what will follow, 951.4(20)
instrument to examine simultaneous ~s, 29.15
lack of ~s, 926.3
less important ~, 29.6(4,22)
list of ~s, 311.19(4,6) ; 774.7(6, 9)
main ~, 326.31
most important ~, 29.6(11)
observed ~, 29.6(31)
past ~s, 771.7,16
period between ~s, 769.6; 769.8(10–13)
pert. to the ~s of the day or time, 29.8
place of ~, 29.14; 782.7,8
possible ~, 29.6(13,20)
precedes a ~, period that, 769.8(7)
presenting ~s to show relationship, 520.8
previous ~, 29.6(3)
range of ~, 29.13
record of ~s, 774.7(1,2,4,7)
resulting ~s, 29.7(11)
~s, 29.7
~s that follow, 173.6
sad ~, 29.6(42)
sad and comical ~, 29.6(43)
separate ~, 29.6(18)
sequence of ~s, 173.6(1)
series of ~s, 173.9(5,22)
set of ~s, 29.7

simultaneous ~, 29.6(12,39, 41)
simultaneous ~s, 29.7(7)
terrible ~, 29.6(42)
~ that causes changes, 29.6(8,9)
~ that follows, 29.6(38) ; 173.6
~ that indicates future misfortune, 29.6(32)
uncertain ~, 29.6(13)
unexpected ~, 29.6(1,2,13,40)
unfavorable ~, 29.6(14)
unfortunate ~, 29.6(1,5,7–9,17, 26–28,42,43)
unimportant ~, 29.6(23)
unnatural ~, 29.6(25,35)
unnecessary ~, 29.6(40)
unplanned ~, 29.6(1)
unusual ~, 29.6(31,36) ; 536.2, 5
without important ~s, 29.12
without unusual ~s, 29.12
happiness,n., 1102.2,7; see also cheerfulness, merriment, pleasure,n.
believer in perfect ~, 1102.24
cause ~ in, 1102.3
causing ~, 1102.4; see also pleasurable,adj.
destroy the ~ of, 1125.37
destroyer of ~, 1125.36
display of ~, 1102.2
ethics in relation to ~, 1102.35,36
express ~, 1102.8,11
express ~ over another's success, etc., 1102.17–19
expression of ~, 1102.2
expression of ~s, time of, 1102.31,32
feel ~, 1102.8,11
~ over accomplishments, etc., 1102.7
~ from life of reason, 1102.22
greet with ~, 1102.21
perfect ~, 1102.23,24
place of perfect ~, 816.9; 1102.23,24
say in ~, 1102.13
science of ~, 1102.37
season of ~, 1102.32
shout in ~, 1102.9
show ~, 951.23; 1102.8,11
showing ~, 1102.1
sounds of ~, 1102.12
source of ~, 1102.5; see also pleasure,n.
theory of ~ as aim of life, 1105.23
time of great ~, 1102.26–34
warmth from ~, 1060.37
wish ~ to, 1102.20
without ~, 1111.38; 1125.48
happy,adj., 1102.1,6; see also cheerful, merry,adj.
be ~, 159.1(24) ; 1102.11
be ~ for another, 1102.17–19
be ~ to get, 1102.15,16
become ~er, 1102.14
calm, peaceful, and ~, 1102.30
~ celebration, 1102.33
feel ~, 159.1(24) ; 1102.11
make ~, 1102.3,10
not ~, 1125.48
~ over success, favorable occurrence, etc., 1102.6
harangue,n., 671.2
pert. to ~s, 671.4(2)
harangue,v., 671.1,8
haranguer,n., 671.3
harbor,n., 1029.11
city containing a ~, 1029.15
deeper part of ~, 1029.40
~ protected by a stone structure, 1029.16

hard,adj., 441.1
difficult, 25.1; see difficult, adj.
~ as metal, 1012.11(4)
~ but breakable, 802.6
emotionally ~, 1097.3; 1098.3; 1129.22
~ like iron or steel, 1017.2(4, 7)
~ like a diamond, 962.8
something ~, 441.6
~ to overcome, 22.33
harden,v., 441.3,4
~ by heat, 1060.22
~ emotionally, 1098.1,2
~ figuratively, 1098.5
~ (the mind), 1098.4
hardened,adj., 441.1
~ by weather, 1047.9
hardening,adj.
~ under water, 1026.22
hardhearted,adj., 1097.3; 1098.3; 1129.22
become ~, 1097.6; 1098.2; 1129.25
make ~, 1097.5; 1098.1; 1129.25
hardness,n., 441.2
measure ~, instrument to, 441.7
hardship,n.
free of ~, 309.11(24)
full of the ~s of life, 25.1(28)
one not used to the ~s of nature, 10.4(1)
one who can endure ~s, 246.10
hard-working,adj., 203.20
hare,n., 421.2; see also rabbit,n.
group of ~s, 403.5(17)
group of three ~s, 932.7
home of a ~, 403.22(15)
pert. to ~s, 421.4,5
young ~, 421.3
harem,n., 710.22
concubine in a ~, 710.23
harlot,n., 711.1; 712.4
harlotry,n., 711.5
harm,n., 803.2; see also injury,n.
cause or source of ~, 803.13, 14
reduce the ~ of, 804.4
sustain ~, 803.22
threaten ~ to, 803.9
threatening ~, 803.8
wishing ~ to someone, 803.12
harm,v., 803.1
ask God to ~, 803.11
~ by cold, 1059.15
~ by frost, 1059.14
inclined to ~, 803.10
not ~, 804.2
untouched by what might ~, 436.13
walk on and ~, 107.1(51)
~ with gas, 1048.29
harmed,adj.
able to be ~, 803.24
easily ~, 803.23
not ~, 804.1
one who is ~, 803.25
unable to be ~, 804.3
harmful,adj., 803.3
~ action, 52.2(3)
forcible and ~, 3.2(16)
~ in influence, 803.3(2)
known to be ~ as a medication, 803.5
make less ~, 804.4
~ medication, 803.5–7
not ~, 804.5,6
rough and ~, 865.1(13)
spreading ~ ideas, practices, etc., 803.4

~ thing, 803.13,14
~ to crops, 803.3(8)
~ to heredity, 803.3(4)
~ to morality, 886.13
~ to morals, 803.3(6,7,9)
~ to peace, 803.3(6)
~ to the community, 803.3(1, 6)
~ to the mind, 803.3(5)
treat ~ly, 53.1(15)
harming,n., 803.2
harmless,adj., 804.5,6
harmonious,adj.
in agreement, 541.19
musical, 467.3
make ~, 541.28–31
harmony,n.
agreement, 541.18,20,29
be, act, do, etc., in ~, 541.17–20
bring into ~, 541.28–31
in ~, 541.19
internal ~, 541.20(3)
lack of ~, 542.1–7
not in ~, 542.2,6,7
harp,n., 479.8(7,17)
pert. to a ~, 479.16
player of a ~, 479.9; 479.9(12)
harsh,adj.
~ and metallic in sound, 1012.11(2)
~ and repelling approach, 890.3
~ government, 1073.59
~ in attitude, 890.1
~ in authority, 890.4
~ in feeling, 890.1
~ in killing, 889.12
~ in manner, 890.1
~ in power, 890.4
~ in sound, 466.3
~ sounds, 466.1,2,4
harshly,adv.
treat ~, 53.1(12,13) ; 890.5
treated ~, 53.5
harshness,n.
~ of attitude, 890.2
~ of feeling, 890.2
~ of manner, 890.2
reduce in ~, 1142.1,10; see also weaken,v.
hasten,v., 94.1–7; see also run,v.
hasty,adj., 95.1; see rapid,adj.
careless and fast, 578.1; see careless,adj.
hat,n., 983.1,2; see also cap,n.
armored ~, 983.2(26)
~ as protection against sun, 983.2(41,53)
bell-shaped ~, 983.2(14)
box for a ~, 983.14
cause ~ to stick out, 958.10
clergyman's ~, 983.2(6)
container for ~s, 974.21
derby ~, 983.2(20)
diver's ~, 983.2(26)
edge of a ~, 793.20(1)
fireman's ~, 983.2(26)
high ~, 983.11
~ indicating rank or profession, 983.2(11)
maker or seller of ~s, 205.5(10)
Mexican, Spanish, etc., ~, 983.2(50)
military ~, 983.2(9,11,25,26,30, 37,45)
part of a ~, 983.13
place for a ~, 983.14
police ~, 983.2(26)
protective ~, 983.2(26,41)
put a ~ on, 983.3
remove one's ~, 983.6
remove the ~ from, 983.5

remove the ~ in greeting, 983.10
remove the ~ in respect, 983.8–10
straw ~, 983.2(43,47)
tall ~, 983.11
~ to hold up hair, 983.2(49)
triangular ~, 983.2(58)
waterproof ~, 983.2(51)
wearing a ~, 983.4
without a ~, 983.7
women's ~s, 983.12
hat,v., 983.3
hatable,adj., 880.4
hate,n., 880.2; see also hatred,n.
act of ~, 880.14
arouse ~ in, 880.16
causing ~, 880.4
disgust and ~, 880.2(7)
feel ~ and contempt, 880.1(4)
feel ~ and disgust, 880.1(1,2, 7,8,9)
feeling ~, 880.3
fill with ~, 880.16,19
object of ~, 880.5
prejudiced by ~, 877.1(2)
showing ~, 880.3
worthy of ~, 880.4
hate,v., 880.1
cause to ~ mankind, 880.20
fear and ~, 880.1(1,7,9)
~ mankind, 880.20
hated,adj., 880.4
state of being ~, 880.13
hateful,adj., 880.4
disgrace attendant on ~ acts, 880.15
hater,n., 880.18
~ of church fathers, 880.18(5)
~ of Greeks, 880.18(3)
~ of mathematics, 880.18(4)
~ of people, 880.18(1)
~ of priests, 880.18(5)
~ of tobacco smoke, 880.18(2)
~ of wine, 880.18(6)
hating,adj., 880.19
~ French people, 880.19(1)
~ war, 880.19(2)
hatless,adj., 983.7
hatred,n., 880.2; see also hate,n.
~ of argument, 880.17(7)
~ of change, 880.17(8)
~ of children, 880.17(9)
~ of discussion, 880.17(7)
~ of drinking, 880.17(1)
~ of Jews, 880.17(2)
~ of knowledge, 880.17(7)
~ of life, 880.17(13)
~ of male sex by women, 880.17(3)
~ of mankind, 880.17(4)
~ of marriage, 880.17(5)
~ of newness, 880.17(8)
~ of new things, 880.17(8)
~ of people, 880.17(4)
~ of strangers, 880.17(12)
~ of tyranny, 880.17(11)
~ of wisdom, 880.17(10)
~ of women, 880.17(6)
haughty,adj., 871.1; see proud, adj.
have,v.
contain, 260.1
possess, 255.1
Hawaiian,n., 784.15(25)
hawk,n.
like a ~, 405.10
of ~s, 405.8(1,10) ; 405.9(1)
hay,n.
heap of ~, 986.8
~ in a barn, 986.9,10
hay fever,n., 363.20(3)

hazardous,adj., 572.1; see dangerous,adj.
haze,n., 1041.1
smoke, fog, and ~, 1041.1(4)
hazy,adj., 1041.2
head,n., 358.1
amount per ~, 914.6
armor for the ~, 983.15
back of the ~, 358.4(2,4)
bend the ~, 152.1(1,8,11,15)
big of ~, 906.4
by the ~, 358.11
covering for the ~, 983.1,2
cut off the ~ of, 796.15,16
figured by the ~, 358.11
freak with three ~s, 537.10(4, 7)
freak with two ~s, 537.10(5,6)
front of the ~, 358.4(1,5) ; 358.5
gesture with the ~, 102.1(1,6)
go over the ~ of, 159.8
having a ~, 358.12
having a broad ~, 358.17,18
having a large ~, 358.19,20
having a short ~, 358.17,18
having a small ~, 358.21,22
having three ~s, 358.15,16
having two ~s, 358.13,14
like a ~, 358.9,10
measure the ~, instrument to, 358.24
measurement of angles of the ~, 944.19
membrane covering infant's ~, 387.1(2)
move the ~ to the side, 186.8(2)
nun's covering for the ~, 983.2(61,62)
ornament for the ~, 983.24
pain in the ~, 1137.56(16) ; 1137.65–68
pert. to the ~, 358.2
pert. to the ~ and tail, 358.3
science of the ~, 358.25
shake the ~, 111.5(7)
shave the ~, 371.1(4)
shaven ~, 371.3,4
side of the ~, 358.7,8
top of the ~, 358.4(3,6)
top of the ~, skin on, 382.1(18)
unnatural position of the ~, ailment causing, 359.6,7
wearing a covering for the ~, 983.4
without a ~, 358.23
headache,n., 1137.65–68
attack of nervous ~s, 1137.66
headband,n.
jeweled ~, 961.2
heading,n., 699.11
~ in a newspaper, 699.11(1,4)
~ of a law, 699.11(5)
~ of a page, chapter, etc., 699.11(2,5)
~ of a topic, 699.11(7)
headline,n., 699.11(1,6)
heal,v., 398.1; see also cure,v.
~ing agent, 1139.4(3,11)
power to ~, 398.15
serving to ~, 398.3
healed,adj.
able to be ~, 398.18
become ~, 398.19,20
healer,n., 401.2
~ by magic, 401.2(23)
healing,adj., 398.3
~ substance or agent, 398.4
healing,n., 398.2
art or science of ~, 401.1(43, 74) ; see medical science,n
mark left by ~, 503.1(8)
pert. to ~, 398.14

health,n., 397.2
anxiety about one's ~,
  1123.19–21
bring back to ~, 398.1; see
  cure, heal,v.
come back to ~, 398.21
concerned about one's ~,
  397.10
goddess of ~, 397.11
good ~, 397.2
lack of ~, 389.1; see **disease,
  illness**,n.
lack of mental ~, 1136.1; see
  insanity,n.
pert. to ~, 397.5
poor ~, 389.1; see **disease,
  illness**,n.
promoting ~, 397.6,8
~ resort, 397.9
restoration of ~, 400.2,6;
  401.1; see **medical science,
  therapy**,n.
science of ~, 397.7
time of greatest ~, 397.4
healthful,adj., 397.6
healthy,adj., 397.1
become ~ again, 398.21
big and ~, 906.3(4)
looking ~, 397.3
strong and ~, 1.5
heap,n., 318.18
heap,v., 318.20,21; 319.1
hear,v.
easy to ~, 454.16
hard to ~, 454.17
inability to ~, 454.22(1,2)
~ incorrectly, 454.5
make hard to ~, 454.15
one who ~s, 454.8
those who ~, 454.9
unable to ~, 454.23–25
~ unintentionally, 454.6
unwillingness to ~, 454.22(2)
heard,adj., 454.11
able to be ~, 454.13
chance to be ~, 454.10
easily ~, 454.16
not easily ~, 454.17
small part of something ~,
  326.27
unable to be ~, 454.14,15
what is ~, 454.12
hearing,n.
act of ~, 454.1
aiding ~, 454.4
defect of ~, 454.22–25
defective in ~, 454.23
deriver of sexual pleasure
  from ~, 710.34(1)
false or imaginary ~,
  454.22(3,4,6) ; see also **hallucination**,n.
instrument for ~, 454.20
instrument for ~ medically,
  454.20(2,6)
instrument that aids ~,
  454.21
~-minded, 454.18
pert. to ~, 454.2
pert. to sight and ~, 454.3
power of ~, 454.1
science of ~, 454.19
sense of ~, 454.1,2
hearing aid,n., 454.21
heart,n.
abnormal sound in the ~,
  376.6(1)
action of the ~, instrument
  to trace, 351.5
chamber of the ~, 351.2
contract and expand (of the
  ~), 910.16
contracting and dilatating (of
  the ~), 910.15

contraction of the ~,
  351.1(3); 910.3(6)
dilation of the ~, 351.1(1)
disorders of the ~, 351.6
enlargement of the ~,
  907.3(4)
medication for the ~, 398.6(5)
membranes of the ~, 387.1(4,
  11)
pain near the ~, 1137.56(17)
pert. to the ~, 351.3
rapid beating of the ~,
  351.1(2,4)
science of the ~, 401.1(7)
~-shaped, 507.17(21)
sufferer from ~ disorder,
  351.7
within the ~, 351.4
heartbeat,n., 105.4
rapid ~, 351.1(2,4)
hearth,n., 1064.60
goddess of the ~, 1061.32
heartless,adj., 1097.3; 1098.3;
  1129.22
become ~, 1097.6; 1098.2;
  1129.25
make ~, 1097.5; 1098.1;
  1129.25
heat,n., 1060.30
caused by ~, 1060.30
change attended by ~ ab-
  sorption, 1060.57
change attended by ~ loss,
  1060.58
come out in rays of ~, 1065.32
degree of ~, 1060.53
~ energy from atom, 1060.55
extreme ~, 1060.6
feel ~, ability to, 1060.46
feel ~, inability to, 1060.47
~ from rubbing, 1060.49
generator of ~, 1060.27
give off ~, 1060.11
glow with ~, 1060.9,10
glowing with ~, 1060.8
harden by ~, 1060.22
impervious to ~ rays, 1060.31
insensitive to ~, make,
  1137.38
insensitiveness to ~, 1137.39
lose ~, 1058.11
loss of bodily ~, 1058.10
made by ~, 1060.30
measure or indicate ~, instrument to, 1060.61,62
moderate ~, 1060.14
~ of fever, 1063.12
~ of weather, climate, air,
  etc., 1060.2
oppressive ~, 1060.3
pert. to ~, 1060.54
pleasant bodily ~, 1060.34
produce ~ in (tissues),
  1060.26
producing ~, 1060.23
production of ~, 1060.24
regulate ~, device to, 1060.63
regulation of bodily ~, 1060.64
science of ~, 1060.65
science of ~ and energy,
  1060.65(3)
sensitiveness to ~, 1137.32
sensitiveness to ~, decreased,
  1137.34
stimulated by ~, 1060.44
stimulation by ~, 101.1(14)
subject to ~, 1060.17
suffer from ~, 1060.41,42
sweat from ~, 1060.41,42
therapy by ~, 1060.26
throw back rays of ~, 1065.35,
  36
transmitting ~, 1060.28,29
unchanging under ~, 531.6
unit of ~, 1060.33

without ~, 1060.66
without ~ gain or loss,
  1060.56
heat,v., 1060.17,18
~ and cool gradually, 1060.21
~ by sunlight, 1055.23
heated,adj.
~ by steam, 1048.36
~ by the sun, 1055.2
heathen,adj., 643.12–14
heating,adj., 1060.19,23,28,29
heating,n.
~ by coils, 1060.20
device or appliance for ~,
  1060.32,45
science of ~, 727.10(3);
  1060.65(1)
vessel for ~, 261.10
heaven,n., 1051.14,24; see also
  heavens, sky,n.
born in ~, 1051.19
City of God in ~, 1051.21
concerned with ~, 1004.39
inhabitant of ~, 1051.16
like ~, 1051.20
loss of possibility of ~,
  264.2(5)
sent by ~, 1051.18
sent to ~, 1051.15,17
unconcerned with ~, 1004.38
heavenly,adj., 1051.15
heavenly body,n., 1053.1; see
  also **moon, planet, star,
  sun**,n.
a meeting of ~s, 322.1(14)
conjunction of ~s, pert. to,
  1053.23
diagram of ~, 1053.33
group of ~s, 1053.14
light around a ~, 1065.21
list of ~s, 1053.33
mapping of ~s, 1053.32
position of a ~, instrument
  to determine, 1053.34,35
positions of ~s, measurement
  of, 1053.31
place for viewing the ~s,
  480.13(3)
prediction by ~s, 1053.36(2)
science of ~s, 1053.36
treatise on ~s, 1053.39
heavens,n., 1051.1,5–7; see also
  heaven, sky,n.
body in the ~, 1053.1
mapping of the ~, 1053.32
overhead point of the ~,
  165.1(24)
place for viewing the ~,
  480.13(3)
science of the ~, 1053.36
treatise on the ~, 682.15(25) ;
  1053.39
heavily,adv.
suddenly and ~, 948.5
heaviness,n., 948.2
amount of ~, 948.3
heavy,adj., 948.1
be too ~ for, 948.7,12
~ because soaked, 1034.26
big and ~, 906.3(2) ; 948.1(5,
  6)
~ by poor baking or cooking,
  948.4
clumsy and ~, 14.1(43) ;
  948.1(5,6)
damp and ~, 1034.18
excessively ~, 948.6
~ like lead, 1018.2(2)
~ movement, 86.1–3
put a ~ burden or weight
  upon, 948.8
wet and ~, 948.1(7) ; 948.4
Hebrew,adj., 642.4
Hebrew,n.
the **language**, 664.4(7,12)

the person, 642.5
height,n., 164.2; 166.1
　measure ~, instrument to,
　　164.9; 1046.18(2,4)
　measure distance and ~ in
　　surveying, device to,
　　788.3(5)
　measurement of ~s, 164.8
　rocky ~, 166.1(4,24) ; see also
　　cliff,n.
heir,n., 241.5
　privileges of an ~, 241.7
held,adj.
　able to be ~, as a position,
　　257.7
hell,n., 661.1,3
　a place like ~, 661.5
　any part of ~, 661.4
　god of ~, 660.1
　like ~, 661.2
　pert. to ~, 661.2
helmet,n., 983.15
　armor attached to the ~,
　　983.22
　~ as sun protection, 983.2(41)
　front part of a ~, 983.21
　remove one's ~, 983.18
　remove the ~ from, 983.17
　~-shaped, 507.17(37) ; 983.20
　wearing a ~, 983.16
　without a ~, 983.19
help,n., 556.2
　ask for ~, 274.1(38)
　call for ~, 556.9
　needing ~, 556.11,14–16
　not needing ~, 556.12,13
　person appealed to for ~,
　　274.6
　request for ~, 274.2(2)
　source of ~, 728.4(15)
　~ to the poor, 213.3(6) ;
　　230.6(12)
　too ready to offer ~, 237.4
　turn for ~ to, 556.7,8
　where one turns for ~, 556.6
　without ~, 330.1(26,27,28,33,
　　34)
　worthy of ~, 841.3
help,v., 556.1
　~ by approval, 850.10
　fail to ~, 556.10
　willing to ~, 265.23(1) ; 556.5
helper,n., 556.3
helpful,adj., 556.4
　~ fairy, 662.7(4)
helping,adj., 556.3
helpless,adj., 13.3(2)
　become ~, 556.16
　leave in a ~ condition,
　　323.1(46)
　left ~ and alone, 330.1(19)
　make ~, 10.5(17) ; 556.15
　place for ~ people, 568.26(3)
　weak and ~, 10.1(18,48) ;
　　556.14
hen,n., 405.3
　young ~, 405.4(11,13)
herald,n., 175.5 ; 175.5(3,9)
herd,n.
　living in ~s, 750.3(4,9)
heredity,n.
　bad for ~, 243.4 ; 803.3(4)
　beneficial to ~, 243.3
　deterioration of ~, study
　　of, 243.1(1)
　factors in ~, 243.5
　give through ~, 230.1(8,30,49)
　improved ~, science of,
　　243.1(2)
　quality in ~, 243.6
　science of ~, 243.1(3,4)
　support of claim to throne by
　　~, 1073.35
　theories of ~, 243.2
heresy,n., 632.6(10,12,17)

treatise on ~, 682.15(5)
heretic,n., 632.10
　leader of ~s, 632.11
hermaphroditism,n., 710.36
hermit,adj., 330.9
hermit,n., 330.7
　life of a ~, 330.8
　pert. to a ~, 330.9
　place of living of a ~, 330.10
hernia,n., 391.1–4
　science of ~s, 401.1(30)
　support for a ~, 1022.33
hero,n., 575.3
heroic,adj., 575.1; see **brave**,adj.
heroine,n., 575.3
heron,n.
　group of ~s, 403.5(60)
herring,n., 422.3
　like the ~, 422.2
　of ~, 422.1(10)
　~-shaped, 507.17(17)
hesitant,adj., 75.4
hesitate,v., 75.1
　~ because of conscience, 885.6
　cause to ~, 75.5
hesitation,n., 75.2
　feeling of ~, 75.3
hidden,adj., 970.42; see **con-**
　cealed,adj.
hide,v., 970.1,30–33,35; see also
　conceal,v.
hiding,n., 970.2; see also **con-**
　cealment,n.
　force out of ~, 3.3(7)
　place of ~, 970.41
hieroglyphics,n.
　key to Egyptian ~, 601.9
high,adj., 164.1
　~ and rocky place, 1006.16,17
　~ as the sky, 1051.8
　be ~, 164.7; 515.4; 1071.7
　~ in rank, 313.5
　~ land, 166.1
　~ place, 166.1
　~ point, 165.1; see **top**,n.
　~ rank, 313.4
　~-ranking person, 313.14
　~-ranking persons, too many,
　　313.15
high,adv., 164.3
highball,n., 749.4
higher,adj., 164.4
　be ~, 164.7
　be ~ than, 164.7; 515.4;
　　1071.7
　going ~, 164.5
　~ in rank, 313.7
　make ~, 163.1; see **raise**,v.
　~ ranks, 313.6
highest,adj., 164.6
　~ in rank, 164.6(2,4–6) ; 313.9
　~ point, 165.1; see **top**,n.
　~ point of progress, 165.1
　reach the ~ point, 165.2
high-pitched,adj., 465.3
　~ sounds, 465.1,2
highway,n., 123.1
hill,n., 166.1
　high ~, 166.1(19)
　measurement of ~s, 164.8
　~ of lava, 166.1(30)
　pert. to a ~, 166.2
　range of ~s, 166.1(22)
　rocky ~, 166.1(17)
　sand ~, 1007.8
　small ~, 166.1(13,14,16,18,28)
　wooded ~, 166.1(15)
hilly,adj., 166.3
hinder,v., 557.1
　attempt to ~ progress, 557.7
　serving to ~, 557.4
　~ with foot shackles,
　　557.1(15,19,23,26)
　~ with snow, 1039.10
hindrance,n., 557.2,3

emotional ~, 1097.47
free of ~, 309.11(13,25,27,31,
　46) ; 309.15(21–23,25,26,35–
　37)
　~ that deflects gases, sounds,
　　etc., 557.3(1)
　the ~ of legislation, 557.6
　the ~ of progress, 557.2(1) ;
　　557.6
　~ to progress, 557.3(2,3,5,6,12,
　　13)
hint,n., 239.2
　give a ~, 239.1
　slight ~, 239.2(1,4)
　useful ~, 239.2(6,7)
hint,v., 239.1
hip,n., 345.15
　~ ailment, 1137.56(25)
　disease of the ~, 345.21
　hands on ~s, 60.7
　in the ~ region, 345.18
　~ joint, 345.16
　~ pain, 1137.56(8,25)
　part around the ~, 345.17
　pert. to the ~, 345.18
　region between the ~bone
　　and the so-called false ribs,
　　345.19
hippopotamus,n.
　like a ~, 417.6,7
　pert. to the ~, 417.6,7
hiss,n., 472.1
hiss,v., 472.2
　bubble and ~, 1028.5
　~ (of a snake), 456.2(1)
　~ while frying, 1061.2(1)
hissing,adj., 472.3
historian,n., 771.17
　~ of the Middle Ages,
　　759.27(2)
historical,adj., 771.20
　~ records, 771.16(1,2)
history,n., 771.16,19
　before recorded ~, 766.6(3,11)
　famous in ~, 771.20
　periods in ~, 769.9
　pert. to ~, 771.20
　regional ~, 771.16(4)
　student of ~, 771.17
　work of ~, 771.19
　writer of ~, 771.17
　writing of ~, 771.18
hit,n., 437.2; see **blow**,n.
hit,v., 437.1
　~ a person to the floor or
　　ground, 1025.15
　~ as punishment, 896.1(3,5–7,
　　9,11,13,22,28)
　that which one tries to ~,
　　437.4
　~ the ground, 999.7
　~ to bring back sensation,
　　437.1(106)
　~ upon rocks or shore (of
　　waves), 1032.8
　~ with a branch, 990.26
　~ with stones, 1006.12
　~ with strip of hide, 387.17
　~ with the foot, 979.12
　~ with the paw, 346.2
　~ with the shoe, 979.12
hitting,n., 437.2
　sounds of ~, 469.7–10
　stick used for ~, 437.5
hive,n., 403.22(1,2,5,19)
hives,n., 382.11(50,51)
hoarse,adj., 460.4
　breathing ~ly, 376.7(5)
hobby,n., 200.11
　follower of a ~, 200.12
　following a ~, 200.13,14
hog,n., 419.1–9; see also **pig**,n
　food for ~s, 285.1(33,40)
　kinds of ~s, 419.7
hold,n., 257.2

firm ~ when lifting or pushing, 257.2(1)
lay ~ of, 257.1(21) ; see
  seize,v.
hold,v., 257.1
  contain, 260.1
  ~ a place, 257.1(18,19)
  ability to ~ quantity, 260.7
  able to ~, 257.6
  able to ~ a lot, 260.6
  acting to ~, 257.5
  ~ and defend, 257.1(16)
  ~ and twist, 257.1(26)
  ~ and use, 257.1(25)
  ~ back, 74.1; 558.1
  ~ back emotions, impulses,
    etc., 1097.38–41
  ~ back the growth of, 731.28
  be able to ~, 260.4
  ~ close for comfort, 257.1(9)
  implement that ~s, 257.4
  ~ in, 558.1
  ~ in fighting or wrestling,
    257.1(4,5,10)
  ~ in one's possession,
    257.1(15,16,19,20)
  ~ in place, 257.1(22)
  ~ in place as if hanging,
    257.1(22)
  ~ in the mind, 257.1(2,17) ;
    see also remember,v.
  one who ~s, 257.3
  part for ~ing, 258.1
  tending to ~, 257.5
  that which ~s, 257.4
  that which ~s things to-
    gether, 302.11
  ~ things together, 302.10
  try to ~, 18.1(7)
  try to ~ onto, 257.8
  unable to ~ onto, 257.9
  ~ under control, 257.1(19)
  ~ up, 1022.1; see support,v.
  ~ within one's arms, 257.1(3,
    5,7,9,14)
holder,n., 257.3,4; see also
  container,n.
  dagger ~, 261.1(41,42)
  pistol ~, 261.1(25)
  sword ~, 261.1(41,42)
holding,adj., 257.5
  ~ (an opinion, idea, etc.)
    stubbornly in the mind,
    257.5(2,3)
  ~ moisture, 257.5(1)
  ~ stubbornly in the mind,
    257.5(2,3)
holding,n., 257.2
  period of ~, 769.8(16)
hole,n., 298.20; see also hollow,
  opening,n.
  animal's ~, 298.20(1,9)
  bottomless ~, 170.9(2)
  break ~s into, 802.1(16)
  containing ~s, 298.5
  ~ for flowing water, 1033.45
  full of ~s, 298.5
  make ~s in, 298.19
  make a ~ larger, 298.22
  making ~s, instrument for,
    298.21
  mud ~, 1000.13
  ~ to reach water, 1033.38
holiday,n., 209.12
  honor a ~, 857.2
  like a ~, 209.13
  pert. to a ~, 209.13
  suitable for ~s, 209.13(3)
Holland,n.
  inhabitant of ~, 784.15(17)
  pert. to ~, 784.16
  reclaimed lowland in ~,
    1029.100(9)
hollow,adj., 299.2
  ~ like a pipe, 299.2(5)

make ~, 299.4
  ~ on both sides, 299.2(3)
  ~ on one side, 299.2(4)
  ~ part, 299.1
  ~ place, 299.1
hollow,n., 299.1; see also hole,
  opening,n.
  ~ between waves, 1032.10
  having ~s, 269.2(1,2,7)
  water-filled ~, 1029.100(2)
hollow,v., 299.4
hollowness,n., 299.3
holy,adj., 650.1; see sacred,adj.
home (living quarters),n.,
  753.1; 1064.60; see also
  house,n.
  ~ and grounds, 753.1(28)
  animal's ~, 753.1
  animal's ~ in the ground,
    298.20(1)
  at ~, surrounded by family,
    753.5
  bird's ~, 405.11
  concubines' ~, 753.1(24)
  country ~, 753.1(7,12,23,49)
  desire for ~, 265.2(17)
  devoted to the ~, 753.4
  earliest ~, 753.1(15)
  Eskimo ~, 753.1(33)
  expelled from ~, person,
    753.10
  give a ~ to, 753.2
  hermit's ~, 753.1(26)
  inferior ~, 753.1(31,32,44,45)
  king's ~, 727.12(1,10) ;
    753.1(37)
  ~ life, 1064.60
  longing for ~, 753.12
  management of a ~, 753.8
  normal ~ of animal or plant,
    753.1(21)
  occupants of a ~, 753.6,7; see
    also inhabitant,n.
  of animals as to ~, 403.10
  ~ of living organisms,
    753.1(6)
  ~ of the dead, 794.37
  outside the ~, 138.1(16)
  one-story ~, 753.1(8)
  pert. to ~, 753.3
  precede to secure a ~ for
    others, 175.1(5)
  rented ~, 753.1(3,35,48)
  returning to the ~, mental
    disturbance on, 753.13
  roof ~, 753.1(38)
  soldier's ~, 753.1(4)
  temporary ~, 753.1(29,34,39,
    47,50) ; 753.14,16,17,18; see
    also hotel, tent,n.
  transient ~, 753.1(29) ; 753.14,
    16,17,18; see also hotel,
    tent,n.
  two-story ~, 753.1(19)
  vile ~, 753.1(18)
  wander from ~, desire to,
    128.6
  without a ~, 753.9; see also
    homeless,adj.
  without a ~, person who is,
    113.13,14; 128.3; 753.10,11;
    1096.42,43
  wives' ~, 753.1(24)
homeless,adj., 128.4; 753.9
  ~ beggar in Naples, 209.9(1)
  ~ boy, 760.5(6)
  ~ child, 1096.42
  ~ girl, 760.6(23)
  ~ person, 113.13,14; 128.3;
    753.10,11; 1096.42,43
homely,adj., 506.1
homemaking,n., 753.8
Homer,n.
  descr. of writing like ~'s,
    686.8(4)

homesickness,n., 265.2(17) ;
  753.12
homosexual,n., 710.34
  ~s, 710.35
homosexuality,n., 710.33(4,17–
  19,22,25,28,32,35)
honest,adj., 813.1
  frank, 813.6
  fair and ~ person, 813.4
  frank and ~ person, 813.4
  morally ~, 813.3
honesty,n., 813.2
  of questionable ~, 822.8
honey,n., 451.1
  diluted ~, 451.2
  fermented ~, 451.3
  like ~, 451.5
  producing ~, 451.4
  sweetened with ~, 448.1(8)
honeycomb,n.
  like a ~, 299.2(1)
  ~-shaped, 507.17(5)
honeysuckle,n.
  of the ~ family, 985.33(5)
honor,n., 857.8
  avenging of ~ by killing
    seducer, 896.29
  bringer of ~, 857.19
  bringing ~, 857.18
  certificate conferring scholas-
    tic ~, 857.11
  gesture of ~, 102.1(9)
  government influenced by ~,
    1073.3(33)
  graduation with ~s, 857.13
  increase the ~ of, 857.20
  indicating ~, 857.10
  mention as worthy of ~,
    857.7
  position held as an ~, 857.17
  position of ~, holder of,
    857.14
  positions of ~, those holding,
    857.15
  raise in ~, 163.1(5)
  rank held as an ~, 857.17
  symbol of ~, 857.9
  title held as ~, 857.17
  worthy of ~, 857.18
honor,v., 857.1
  ~ a holiday, 857.2
  ~ in song, 857.3
  ~ with a medal, 857.6
  ~ with a ribbon, 857.6
  ~ with entertainment, 857.5
  ~ with laurel, 857.4
honorable,adj., 857.18
honored,adj., 856.13
  not ~, 857.21
  ~ owing to age, 856.14
  ~ owing to time, 856.14
  person ~ with a medal, 857.16
hood,n., 983.2(10,16,18)
  cape or cloak with a ~,
    976.1(2,4,5)
  jacket with a ~, 976.4(10)
  like a ~, 972.18
  monk's ~, 983.2(18)
hood,v., 972.1(13)
hoof,n., 346.4
  having ~s, 346.6
  having split ~s, 346.11(3)
  like a ~, 346.5
  of animals with ~s, 403.11(13,
    14,16)
  ~-shaped, 507.17(85)
  sound of horse's ~s, 469.7(12)
hook,n., 155.12
  bent like a ~, 152.5(6,8)
  curved like a ~, 155.4(19)
  instrument with a ~, 155.12
  ~-shaped, 507.17(83)
hookworm,n.
  ~ disease, 396.1(2,32)
hope,n., 267.2

box containing ~ and other
  blessings, 267.21
give ~ to, 267.5
give up ~, 267.12
giving ~, 267.6
lack of ~, 267.9; see **hopelessness,n.**
lose ~, 267.12
remover of ~, 267.15
robbing of ~, 267.16
robs of ~, that which, 267.17
take ~ from, 267.14
useless ~, 267.18
without ~, 267.10,13; see
  hopeless,adj.
hoped,adj.
~ for, 267.7
what is ~ for, 267.8
hopeful,adj.
~ person, 267.3
hopefulness,n., 267.2
humor determining ~, 1091.30
hopeless,adj., 267.10
cause of ~ feelings, 267.17
causing ~ feelings, 267.16
make feel ~, 267.14
makes feel ~, one who, 267.15
person who feels ~, 267.11
~ undertaking, 267.18
hopelessness,n., 267.9
~ about the world, 267.9
attack of ~, 267.20
philosophy of ~, 267.19
horizon,n., 1051.9
arc of the ~, 1051.10
parallel to the ~, 179.8(4)
straight with the ~, 180.1(4)
hormone,n., 287.8
~ for diabetes, 287.8(7)
sex ~s, 287.12
horn,n.
animal without ~s, 403.7(11)
animal's ~, 355.1
attack with the ~s, 560.1(15)
belt for a ~, 980.7
branch of deer's ~, 355.1(3)
buck's ~, 355.1(2)
deer's ~, 355.1(1)
having ~s, 355.2
lose ~s, 972.10
projecting part of deer's ~s,
  335.1(20)
~-shaped thing, 507.18
sounds of a ~, 461.1(2,6–8) ;
  1043.7
stag's ~s, 355.1(2)
horny,adj., 355.3(1–3,5–7)
horoscope,n., 1053.24–30
horrible,adj., 880.4,8; 883.7
enjoying the ~, 880.9
horrified,adj., 880.3
horrify,v., 880.16(2,5,7,8)
horrifying,adj., 880.4,8
horror,n., 880.2
arousing ~, 880.8
drama of ~, 969.9(1)
filled with ~, 880.3
shake with ~, 111.1(17,24)
horse,n., 408.1–18
anatomy of the ~, 338.10(3)
ancestor of a ~, 723.8(10)
~ and vehicle, 408.10
baby ~, 408.4
booth for a ~, 787.7(35)
breaker of ~s to the saddle,
  205.1(2)
breeding ~, 408.2(5) ; 408.3(1)
breeding ~s, 408.9(3)
castrated male ~, 408.2(2)
color of a ~, 408.8
cover a ~, 972.1(8)
cross between ass and ~,
  409.1(4,8)
cross between zebra and ~,
  408.18

doctor of ~s, 401.2(9)
eating ~flesh, 734.27(10)
eating of ~flesh, 734.26(6)
father of a ~, 724.1(9) ;
  408.2(3)
female parent of a ~, 408.3(2)
flying ~, 408.12
fond of ~s, 700.32(2)
fondness for ~s, 700.30(9)
gait of a ~, 104.1
god with tail and ears of a ~,
  662.26(10)
group of ~s, 403.5(56,71,73) ;
  408.9
harnessed ~s, 408.9(4,5)
height of ~, measurement
  unit of, 946.26(9)
jump (of a ~), 110.1(4,7,10)
leap of a ~, 104.1(3)
like a ~, 408.17
losing race ~, 20.3(1)
maker of, or dealer in, ~
  equipment, 205.1(12)
male ~, 408.2
male parent of a ~, 724.1(9) ;
  408.2(3)
medical treatment of ~s,
  401.1(102,108)
mother of a ~, 408.3(2)
movements of a ~, 104.1
mythical ~, 408.12–14
mythical creature, half ~,
  half man, 662.26(2)
of ~, 403.11(13,14,16)
on a ~, 408.25,26
pert. to a ~, 408.16
primitive ~, 408.15
purebred ~, 719.5(3)
~ race, 20.2(4,6,11,12) ; see
  horse race,n., below
race ~s, 408.9(1,2)
~ racing, 20.11
rider of a ~, 408.19,20,23
riding ~s, academy of, 408.27
riding ~s, art of, 408.24
riding ~s, pert. to, 408.21
riding ~s, skill in, 408.22
school of ~ riding, 623.1(13)
science of ~s, 403.26(19)
soldier on ~, 564.1(11–13,15,
  16,18,29,50,53)
soldiers on ~, 564.5(8,32)
type of ~, as to activity, 408.6
type of ~, as to breed, 408.5
type of ~, as to color, 408.7
type of ~, as to quality, 408.6
type of ~, as to use, 408.6
war ~ of Alexander, 408.11
worker with ~s, 205.1(2,8)
young ~, 408.4
horse race,n., 20.2(4,6,11,12)
place for a ~, 20.12
winner of a ~, 20.14
horse racing,n., 20.11
pert. to ~, 20.13
horseshoe,n.
fit ~s on, 205.4
fitting or making ~s, 205.2
maker or fitter of ~s, 205.1(1)
shop for fitting or making ~s,
  205.3
hospital,n., 400.5
~ for deserted children,
  721.15(1)
~ for lepers, 382.15
~ for prostitutes, 711.19
host,n.
secret ~, 201.19
unknown ~, 201.19
hostage,n., 1122.46(7)
hostile,adj., 879.1
opposed, 544.3
act ~, 879.8
~ act or action, 879.5

~ act or action, unprovoked,
  879.6
anger disposing to ~ acts,
  878.11(1)
be ~, 879.8
cause to be ~, 879.10
~ course of action, 879.7
deliberately ~, 879.1(3)
feel ~, 879.8
~ person, 879.4
slyly ~, 879.1(2)
~ spirit, 879.2(2)
~ without provocation,
  879.1(1)
hostility,n., 879.2; see also **ill
  will,n.**
opposition, 544.2(8,12,20)
arouse or cause ~ in, 879.10
arousing ~, 879.11
~ between nations, 879.3
eliminate the ~ of, 878.20
end ~, 1140.34
feel ~, 879.8
~ following affection or
  friendliness, 879.2(6)
~ over insult, 879.2(7)
reduce the ~ of, 878.20
say in ~, 879.8(4)
secret ~, 879.2(8)
show ~, 879.8
sounds of ~, 468.1(7,13,19) ;
  879.8(4)
hot,adj., 1060.1,3,5; see also
  warm,adj., heat,n.
be ~, 1060.9–11
be very ~, 1060.7
become ~, 1060.9,15,18,48,50
become moderately ~, 1060.15
~ condition, 1060.2,3,6,8,14
extremely ~, 1060.3,5
extremely ~ day, 1060.4
extremely ~ place or room,
  1060.12
feel ~, 1060.35,36
make ~, 1060.9,15,17,42,43
make moderately ~, 1060.15
moderately ~, 1060.13
~ (of air, climate, or
  weather), 1060.1
~ (of springs), 1060.16
oppressively ~, 1060.3
vessel for keeping food ~,
  1061.5(2)
hotel,n., 753.14
keeper of a ~, 753.15
hotness,n., 1060; see **heat,n.**
hot-tempered,adj., 876.1,20
~ female, 876.3(1) ; 876.21
~ girl, 876.4
~ person, 876.3,21
~ wife, 876.5
~ woman, 876.4
hound,n.
group of ~s, 403.5(51)
hourglass,n., 774.2(17)
house,n., 753.1; see also **cottage, home,n.**
country ~, 753.1(7,12,23,49)
elegant ~, 753.1(36,37,49)
Eskimo ~, 753.1(33)
farm~, 998.14
~ for hunting or fishing,
  753.1(34)
~ for undressing, 753.1(9)
inferior ~, 753.1(31,32,44,45,
  50)
king's ~, 727.12(1,10) ;
  753.1(37)
occupant of a ~, 753.6
occupants of a ~, 753.7
one-story ~, 753.1(8)
opposition to living in ~s,
  749.55(4)
pert. to a ~, 753.3
provide a ~ for, 753.2

row of ~s, 753.1(4)
small ~, 753.1(9–11,13,14,31,
  32,44,45,50)
summer ~, 753.1(7)
two-family ~, 753.1(19)
two-story ~, 753.1(19)
~ with rented rooms, 753.14;
  see also hotel,n.
without a ~, 753.9; see also
  homeless,adj.
housekeeping,n., 753.8
hover,v., 172.1(2)
howl,n., 456.1; 468.1
howl,v., 456.2; 468.2
howling,n., 456.1(73)
huckleberry,n.
belonging to the ~ family,
  745.22(12)
hug,n., 198.2; 257.2; 701.2
hug,v., 198.1(25) ; 257.1(3,5,8,9)
~ as a caress, 701.1(8,15)
huge,adj., 906.12; see big,adj.
human,adj.
ascription of ~ characteristics, 429.12
automaton in ~ form, 429.5
become ~, 429.11
both animal and ~ in form,
  662.28
both divine and ~, 429.8;
  654.4(7)
deprive of ~ characteristics,
  429.13
eater of ~ flesh, 734.28–30
eating ~ flesh, 734.27(1,15)
eating of ~ flesh, 734.26(1,2)
lose ~ characteristics, 429.14
make ~, 429.10
more than ~, 429.9
~ origin, 429.20,21
~ welfare, interest in, 429.18
human,n., 429.3; see also man,
  mankind,n.
animal-like ~, 429.3(3)
animal like a ~, 403.7(6)
animal nature of a ~, 429.15
biological category of ~s,
  429.2
center of universe, theory of
  ~s as, 429.17
coarse ~, 864.8
like a ~, 429.7
mechanical ~, 429.2(2,13)
mythical ~s, 666.26,28,29
mythical ~s, part animal,
  662.26–29
~s, 429.1
~s no better than animals,
  429.16
worship of a ~, 656.15(1)
humanity,n., 429.1; see also
  human, man, mankind,n.
origin of ~, theories of,
  728.17(5–9)
time before ~, 762.1(4) ;
  763.1–5
humble,adj., 873.1,5
act ~, 873.3
be ~, 873.3
cause to feel ~, 868.27; 873.4
contemptibly ~, 873.2
make ~, 868.27; 873.4
humble,v., 868.27; 873.4
~ oneself, 868.28
humbleness,n., 873.1
crouch in ~, 64.1(2,3)
lie face downward in ~,
  65.1(6)
humid,adj., 1034.8
disagreeably ~ and warm,
  1034.17
keep air ~, device to, 1034.11,
  12
made ~, 1034.9
make ~, 1034.6

humidity,n.
average of ~ and heat,
  1034.14
instrument to measure ~,
  1046.18(7–11)
science of atmospheric ~,
  1046.22,23
humiliate,v., 868.10
humiliating,adj., 868.14,18
~ action, insult, language, or
  treatment, 868.17
humiliation,n., 868.11
cause ~, 868.10
cause of ~, 868.15
causing ~, 868.14
enjoyment of one's own ~,
  1137.26
hummingbird,n., 405.1(11)
of ~s, 405.9(10)
humor,n., 1114.3,4; see also
  joke, joking,n.
bodily fluid, 1091.30
bit of ~, 1115.7
combining seriousness and ~,
  610.4
descr. of quiet ~, 1114.6
engage in ~, 1115.1
season with ~, 1114.12
show ~, 951.23
sparkle with ~, 1114.14
without ~, 1114.18
humor,v., 1108.1
humorist,n., 1114.5; 1115.6
humorous, adj., 1114.1,2; see
  also laughable, witty,adj.
~ answer, 1115.7(8)
be ~, 1115.1
~ books, 1115.8
coarsely ~ language or
  speech, 1114.11
collection of ~ writings,
  682.19(1,6)
gracefully ~, 949.12
lightly ~, 949.12
~ musical composition,
  1114.16,17
~ person, 1114.5; 1115.6
~ play, motion picture, etc.,
  1114.13
playfully ~ action, spirit,
  language, etc., 1114.8
quaintly ~ action or speech,
  1114.10
~ remark, 1115.7
~ remarks, 1115.8
~ sayings, 676.2(1) ; 1115.8
skillfully ~, 949.12
~ story, 685.1(3,6)
treat ~ly, 1114.15
~ writings, 1115.8
humorousness,n., 1114.3
humpback,n., 354.17(3,4,6) ;
  354.19
humpbacked,adj., 354.18
~ person, 354.19
hunchback,n., 354.17(3,4,6) ;
  354.19
hunchbacked,adj., 354.18
~ person, 354.19
hundred, n. or adj., 940.21
multiply by a ~, 940.25
number a ~ times greater,
  940.24
~-year-old person, 758.2(1)
hundredfold,adj., 940.23
increase by a ~, 907.9(1)
hundred forty-four,n., 940.26
hundredth,adj., 940.22
hundredth,n.
pert. to ~s, 940.22
hunger,n., 737.2
die of ~, 737.6
exciting ~, 737.8
kill by ~, 737.7

lack of ~, 737.9
morbid ~, 737.2(2,4–6)
reduce (~), 1107.13
satisfy (~), 1107.11
satisfy (~) to excess, 1107.15–
  22
weaken by ~, 737.7
hunger,v.
be hungry, 737.3
desire, 265.1
hungry,adj., 737.1
be ~, 737.3
excessively ~ from disease or
  insanity, 737.1(2)
make ~, 734.4
~ person, animal, or plant,
  737.5
hunt,n., 486.2
animal ~, 486.10
hunt,v., 486.1; see also search,v.
~ animals, 486.9
~ wolves, 486.9(6)
hunted,adj.
animals ~ for, 486.7
something ~ for, 486.7
hunter,n., 486.4
animal ~, 486.11
female ~, 486.11(2,4)
seal ~, 486.11(8)
skilled ~, 486.11(11) ; 996.45,
  47
wolf ~, 486.11(9)
hunting,n., 486.2
animal ~, 486.10
art of ~, 486.10(1,4)
excitement in ~, 1100.7(1)
fond of animal ~, 486.12
land for ~, 1003.2(17)
pert. to animal ~, 486.12
seal ~, 486.10(3)
skill in ~, 7.1(69) ; 996.46
hurricane,n., 1042.27; see also
  cyclone, windstorm,n.
calm center of a ~, 1042.30
hurry,n., 94.4
commotion and ~, 1101.1(40)
hurry,v., 94.1,5,6,7; see also
  run,v.
hurt,adj.
easily ~ in feelings, 868.9
feel ~, 868.7
feel ~ by, 868.8
hurt,n.
harm, 803.2; see harm,n.
pain, 1130.6,11; 1137.10; see
  pain,n.
angry over ~, 878.10(4,7,8)
feeling of ~, 868.5
fit over ~, 878.11(1,4–6,9)
hurt,v.
harm, 803.1; see harm,v.
injure, 803.1; see injure,v.
pain, 1130.1,5; 1137.1,9; see
  pain,v.
~ emotionally, 1130.1,5
~ physically, 1137.1,9
~ (the feelings), 868.4
~ the feelings of, 868.1
~ the pride of, 868.1(4) ;
  868.10
~ the vanity of, 868.1(4)
hurtful,adj., 803.3; see harmful,adj.
husband,n., 703.1
excessive love for ~, 700.1(16)
living together as ~ and wife,
  702.20,22
new ~, 703.1(1,4,11)
pert. to one's ~, 703.4
queen's ~, 703.1(13) ;
  1073.21(5)
relationship between ~ and
  wife, pert. to, 703.6
white ~ of Indian woman,
  703.1(16)

woman whose ~ has died, 706.8
hut,n., 753.1; see **house**,n.
hybrid,adj., 719.6
hybrid,n., 430.6; 719.5
Hyderabad,n.
   ruler of ~, 1073.36(21)
hydrophobia,n., 396.1(26)
hygienic,adj., 899.11
hymen,n., 379.1(6)
hymn,n., 476.4(2,12,17,38,41,49) ; 477.1–14
   treatise on ~s, 682.15(11)
   writing of ~s, 476.8
hypnosis,n., 70.10–15
   psychoanalysis under ~, 400.6(21)
   study of ~, 70.16
hypnotic,adj., 70.4
   one subject to ~ control, 8.19(4)
   ~ power, 5.1(3) ; 70.9
   ~ sleep, 67.2(1,4,7)
   ~ state, 70.10–15
hypnotism,n., 70.1
   like ~, 70.6
   pert. to ~, 70.5
   resulting from ~, 70.7
   therapy through ~, 584.27
hypnotist,n., 70.3
hypnotize,v., 70.2
hypocrisy,n., 826.21,23
hypocrite,n., 826.20
   speak like a ~, 826.22
hypocritical,adj., 826.21
   ~ but smooth and soft-spoken, 826.24
   ~ in smoothness of manner or speech, 859.9
hysteria,n.
   causing ~, 1135.5,6
   like ~, 1135.4

I

ice,n., 1040
   breaking up of ~ on river, 802.22
   boat for ~, 1040.24
   coating of ~, 1037.12
   convert ~ to liquid, 1027.5
   cover with ~, 1040.17
   covered with ~, 1040.18
   drop like ~ particles,1040.4
   field of ~ on high mountains, 1039.4
   form into ~, 1040.17
   ~ from slush, 1040.5
   glass or mineral like ~, 1009.25
   hanging particle of ~, 1040.28,29
   ~ in the sea, 1040.7,22
   like ~, 1040.19
   made of ~, 1040.19
   moving ~ field, 1040.6–12; see **glacier**,n.
   particle of ~, 1040.3
   particles of ~, 1040.1
   pert. to ~, 1040.20
   reflection from ~, 1039.19; 1040.27
   remove ~ from, 1040.30,31
   sheet of ~, 1040.21,23
   ship that breaks ~, 1040.25
   shut in or surrounded by ~, 1040.26
   skate on ~, 1040.15
   skating, ~ for, 1025.7; 1040.13
   ~-skating place, 1040.14
   sliding mass of ~, 1006.18
   ~ storm, 1040.2
Iceland,n., 784.4(4)
icing,n.
   ~ on cake, etc., 1059.21–24
icon,n.

study of ~s, 965.18
idea,n., 586.1; see also **thought**,n.
   ability to have ~s, 586.17,18
   ascribe one's ~s to others, 1092.87
   existing only in ~s or as an ~, 586.10
   expressing ~s in a single word, 586.4
   expressing abstract ~s, 586.5
   expression of ~s in psychoanalysis, 586.9
   expressive of complex ~s, 665.3(7)
   form ~s, 586.14
   form an ~ of, 586.12
   form an ~ of beforehand, 586.13
   form in ~, 586.15
   free of false ~s, 309.11(9)
   full of ~s, 586.2,3
   have ~s, 586.14
   ~ influencing personality, 586.8
   main ~, 586.11
   object of which an ~ is formed, 586.16
   old ~s in new form, with, 761.1(13)
   physical representation of an ~, 953.9
   picture ~s, 586.6; see also **image**,n.
   psychological group of ~s, 1056.9
   relating to an ~, 586.2
   series of ~s, 173.9(4,6,22) ; 586.7
   stale ~, 759.30
   trite ~, 759.30
   uncontrolled association of ~s, 585.13
   word expressive of an ~, 666.3(40)
ideal,adj., 816.1
   ~ but impractical, 284.21(3)
ideal,n.
   unattainable ~, desire for, 1092.51,52
idealistic,adj.
   impractical and ~, 284.21(1)
identification,n.
   mark of ~, 503.1(5)
identity,n.
   proof of ~, 812.17
idiocy,n., 597.2,4,18
idiom,n., 666.3
   British ~, 666.7(1,3)
   Cockney ~, 666.7(4)
   French ~, 666.7(5)
   Greek ~, 666.7(2,6)
   Irish ~, 666.7(7)
idiot,n., 597.3,17
   born ~, 1054.37
idiotic,adj., 597.1,19
idle,adj., 209.1
   worthless and ~ person, 888.5(2)
idle,v., 209.4,5,7
   ~ away time, 762.17,18
idleness,n., 209.2
   spend time in ~, 762.17,18
idly,adv.
   spend time ~, 762.17,18
idol,n., 656.8(1) ; 657.7
   worship ~s, 656.1(2,7,8,12)
ignorance,n., 611.3
   doctrine of human ~, 611.6
   pretended ~, 611.5
   resulting from moral ~, 843.25
ignorant,adj., 611.3
   ~ about the world, 611.3(4,7)
   ~ age of mankind, 769.9(4)

~ of morality, 611.3(2) ; 843.24
   ~ person, 611.4
ignore,v., 581.6,14
   able to be ~d, 581.13
   ~ by laughter, 1111.31
   ~ faults, 897.11
   instance of ~ing, 581.8
   ~ offenses, 897.11
   one who ~s, 581.7
   ~ a person, 1097.23
   state of being ~d, 581.9
ill,adj., 389.2
   be ~, 389.5(1)
   become ~, 389.5(2–7)
   become ~ again, 145.1(15)
   falling ~ easily, 389.15
   looking ~, 389.16
   make ~, 389.4
   mentally ~, 1136.2; see **insane**,adj.
   person who is ~, 389.6
   spiritually ~, 1090.16
   thin and ~, 389.2(1)
ill-at-ease,adj., 868.20; 1132.4
illegal,adj., 1087.1
   ~ act, 1087.3
   ~ activities, 1087.7
   ~ activities, place of, 1087.11
   ~ acts, 1087.6
   bring in ~ly, 1087.15–18
   caught in ~ act, 1088.16
   commit ~ act, 1087.4
   committer of ~ acts, 1087.5,9
   ~ conduct, 1087.7
   declare ~, 1087.19–25
   hires himself out for ~ activities, one who, 796.3(4)
   make ~, 1087.19–25
   make ~ly, 1087.13
   person accused of ~ acts, 1088.15
   ~ practice, 1087.7
   sell ~ly, 1087.13
   send out ~ly, 1087.15–18
   ~ traffic in merchandise, 1087.17,18
   transport ~ly, 1087.13
illegality,n., 1087.2
ill fame,n., 891.12
ill-mannered,adj., 860.1
   clumsy and ~, 14.1(4)
illness,n., 389.1; see also **dis-ease**,n.
   cause ~, 389.4
   cause or source of ~, 389.17
   causing ~, 389.18
   emotional ~, 1135.1
   ~ from air travel, 1045.24
   ~ from alcoholic indulgence, 749.53
   ~ from narcotics or drugs, 399.15
   ~ from tobacco, 399.15(8)
   imaginary ~es, having, 397.10
   mental ~, 1136.1; see **insanity**,n.
   reaction of ~ to food, etc., 389.9–11
   relating to ~, 389.3
   shake with ~, 111.1(23)
   sunlight, ~ caused by, 1055.29
   treatment of ~, 400.2,6; see **therapy**,n.
illogical,adj., 591.1,6,7
   seeming ~, 591.2,3
   something ~, 591.4,5
illogicality,n.
   ~ in expression, 665.9(29)
ill-omened,adj., 36.3
ill repute,n., 891.12
illuminate,v., 1065.54,69–71
illumination,n., 1065.69
   measurement of ~, 1065.103
   ~ power, 1065.106

science of ~, 1065.102(8)
unit of ~, 1065.104,105
illusion,n., 632.6(12) ; 632.7(2)
  free of ~s, 309.11(14,18)
  freed from pleasant ~s,
    639.3(5,6)
ill will,n., 879.2
  arousing ~, 879.11
  feel ~, 879.8
  feeling ~, 879.1
  show ~, 879.8
  showing ~, 879.1
image,n., 483.8; 965.1(25,47)
  beautiful ~, 483.8(27)
  deceptive ~, 483.8(9,11,14,16)
  false ~, 483.8(8,9,11,14,16)
  form a mental ~, 482.2,5
  formation of mental ~s, 482.3
  ghostly ~, 483.8(2,3,7,17)
  god's ~, 965.1(26,59)
  insubstantial ~, 483.8(7)
  later ~, 483.8(1,18)
  memory of mental ~s, pert.
    to, 627.5(1)
  mental ~, 483.8(5,7,17,26,27)
  mental ~s, 482.1
  pert. to mental ~s, 482.8
  power of forming mental ~s,
    482.4,7
  recalls mental ~s vividly, one
    who, 627.9
  sacred ~, 965.1(25)
  science of mental ~s, 482.9
  study of ~s, 965.18
  sudden ~, 483.8(2,3)
  unreal ~, 483.8(2,3,8,11,14,16)
  vague ~, 483.8(7,17)
  vivid mental ~s, one who has,
    482.10
  worship, ~ for, 965.1(26)
  worship of ~s, 656.15(10,11)
imagery,n.
  mental ~, 482; 965.26
imaginary,adj., 809.1; 1065.3;
  see also unreal,adj.
  ~ animals, 662.24-29
  ~ being, 662.7
  ~ condition, 809.2
  creator of ~ world, 726.19(3)
  ~ creatures, part human,
    part animal, 662.26-30
  ~ hearing, 454.22(3,4,6) ; see
    also hallucination,n.
  ~ land, 809.4
  ~ place, 809.4; 816.9; 1057.15
  ~ quality, 809.2
  ~ reptiles or serpents, 662.25
  ~ sensation, 434.1(4,7,10,11)
  something ~, 587.3; 809.3
imagination,n., 587.7
  appealing to the ~, 587.9
  derived from the ~, 587.4
  devoted to world of the ~,
    1090.10
  free ~ in literature or art,
    807.12
  having ~, 587.6,7
  lacking ~, 535.5-9
  make perceptible to the ~,
    587.5
  power of seeing in the ~,
    587.8
  produced by the ~, 809.1;
    1065.3; see imaginary,adj.
  product of the ~, 587.3; 809.3
  showing ~, 587.6
  stimulating the ~, 587.9
  using the ~, 587.6
imaginative,adj., 587.6
imaginativeness,n., 587.7
imagine,v., 587.1
  ~ beforehand, 587.2
  power to ~, 587.8
imbalance,n., 950.16
imbalanced,adj , 950.18

imbecile,n., 597.3,17
imbecilic,adj., 597.1,19
imbecility,n., 597.2,4,18
imitate,v., 532.1
imitated,adj.
  able to be ~, 532.6
  unable to be ~, 532.7
imitation,n., 532.2
  art of ~, 532.8
  picture in ~ of style,
    965.1(40)
  worthy of ~, that which is,
    532.9
imitative,adj., 532.4,5
imitator,n., 532.3
immature,adj., 733.1,3,9-11
  ~ animal, 733.5
  biologically ~, 733.7
  ~ person, 733.4; 760.3(1)
  ~ thing, 733.4
  young and ~ person, 760.3(1)
immaturity,n., 733.2
  period of ~, 733.6
immeasurable,adj., 946.5; see
  unmeasurable,adj.
immediate,adj., 766.14,17
immediately,adv., 766.16,17
immediateness,n., 766.15
immense,adj., 906.12,17; see
  big,adj.
immerse,v.
  ~ into holy water, 845.17
immigrant,n.
  prejudice against ~s,
    634.1(12)
immobile,adj., 59.5
  cause to be ~, 59.7
immoderate,adj., 923.3
immodest,adj., 873.17
immoral,adj., 828.11; 886.1
  ~ act, 886.3
  become ~, 886.17
  becoming ~, 886.18
  ~ custom, 886.8
  given to ~ pleasures, 1096.11
  ~ habit, 886.8
  having become ~, 886.19
  ~ in principle, 886.9
  indulge in ~ pleasure, 886.21
  ~ person, 886.4
  ~ practice, 886.8
  sexually ~, 712.1
  sexually ~ man, 712.3
  sexually ~ woman, 712.4
immorality,n., 886.2
  freedom from moral re-
    straint, 309.1(7,12-14,21,23)
  advocacy of ~, 886.15
  cause of ~, 886.28
  indulge in sexual ~, 712.5
  place of ~, 886.27
  place where laws against ~
    not enforced, 711.14
  region of ~ and vice, 711.13
  seduce into sexual ~, 712.6
  sexual ~, 712.2
  time of general ~, 886.16
immortal,adj., 755.7
  make ~, 755.11
  ~ person, 755.9
immortality,n., 755.8
  symbol of ~, 755.10
  theological doctrine of ~,
    792.26
immovable,adj., 59.1
immunity,n., 569.9
  gradual ~ against poison,
    569.10
  reduction or loss of ~, 569.11
  science of ~, 569.12
immunization,n., 569.2
  pert. to ~, 569.5
  rapid ~, 569.2(1)
immunize,v., 569.1
  ~ against disease, 569.1

~ against smallpox, 569.1(3,4)
  one who ~s, 569.3
  substance used to ~, 569.4
impact,n., 436.2; 437.2
  sounds of ~, 469.7-10
  sudden ~, 437.2(7)
impair,v.
  spoil, 805.1
  weaken, 10.5
impartial,adj., 636.1
impassive,adj., 1132.12
impatience,n., 272.11
impatient,adj., 272.10
  angrily ~, 272.10(2)
  be ~, 272.12
  become ~ with, 272.13
impede,v., 557.1; see hinder,v.
impediment,n., 557.3; see hindrance,n.
impenetrable,adj., 133.15;
  332.27
  ~ by X-rays, 1069.10
impenitent,adj., 884.15
imperative,adj., 273.6; 848.4
imperfect,adj., 830.5
imperfection,n., 830.1,5
imperious,adj., 8.11
impermanent,adj., 756.1; see
  temporary,adj.
impersuadable,adj., 638.13
impertinent,adj., 860.1; 861.1;
  862.1
imperturbable,adj., 1132.12
impetuous,adj., 1092.11
  ~ person, 1092.12
implement,n., 280.6(11,16,17)
  ancient stone ~, 280.6(14)
  kitchen ~, 280.6(17)
  science of making ~s,
    727.10(4)
  worker's ~s, 280.1(11,20)
implication,n., 238.2; 238.2(1-
  3)
  by ~, 238.5
implied,adj., 238.5
implore,v.
  ask, 274.1
  beg, 276.1
imply,v., 238.1(8,9,13,14)
implying,adj., 238.4
impolite,adj., 860.1,8
  ~ act, 860.6,9
  ~ behavior, 860.6,9
  contemptuously ~, 860.3
  ~ girl, 860.5
  ~ in manner, 860.13
  ~ in speech, 860.13
  ~ language, 860.6,9
  man who is ~ to women,
    860.11
  ~ person, 860.4
  scornfully ~, 860.3
  ~ to elders, 860.16; see also
    disrespectful,adj.
  ~ to inferiors, 860.12
  ~ to women, 860.10
  ~ treatment, 860.6
  unfriendly and ~, 860.7;
    879.13(3)
  ~ woman, 708.14(10,13) ;
    860.5
impolitely,adv.
  make fun of ~, 860.15
  speak ~, 860.14
impoliteness,n., 860.2
importance,n., 848.2
  falling off in ~, 848.39
  feeling of ~, 848.33
  greater ~, 848.20
  indicate ~, 848.30
  lack of ~, 849.1
  of little ~, 887.2
  ~ of rank, 848.3
  place ~ on, 848.30

self-~, action, speech, or
manner of, 848.32
superior in ~, 833.3
important,adj., 848.1
acting ~, 848.31
~ and indispensable person,
848.15
~ and indispensable thing,
848.14
~ at this instant, 848.4
be most ~, 848.7
become ~, 848.23
~ character in a story, novel,
play, etc., 848.22(4)
consider ~, 848.30
~ crop or thing produced,
848.6
decisively ~, 848.8
decisively ~ point, 848.10
decisively ~ thing, 848.9
decisively ~ time, 848.11
equally ~, 848.17
feeling ~, 848.31
less ~, 848.35,38,39
less ~, become, 848.41
less ~, treat as, 848.40
less ~ part, 326.1(1)
less ~ rank, holder of, 848.37
less ~ thing, etc., 848.36
more ~, 848.18
more ~, be 848.19,21
most ~, 848.5
~ part, 326.29,31
~ person, 848.22
~ person in business or industry, 848.22
~ person or character in a
struggle, conflict, activity,
etc., 848.22(4)
person treated as ~, 848.26
~ person, having the air,
manner, or appearance of,
848.24
~ point in progress, 848.12
powerful and ~ person,
5.8(2)
seem ~, 848.23
self-~ and showy, 951.38
self-~ and small person,
848.34(1)
self-~ and young person,
848.34(2)
self-~ official, 1077.1(23)
self-~ person, 848.34
so ~ as to be indispensable,
848.13
~ to execution, 848.16
~ to success, 848.16
~ to war, 848.16
treat as ~, 848.25
impotent,adj., 13.3(2)
impractical,adj., 284.21; 1090.10
ideal but ~, 284.21(3)
idealistic and ~, 284.21(1)
theoretical and ~, 888.4
imprison,v., 301.1; see also **confine**,v.
imprisoned,adj.
~ person, 301.5; see also
prisoner,n.
imprisonment,n., 301.2,3; see
also **confinement**,n.
kept in solitary ~, 301.10
period of ~, 301.9
person sentenced to ~,
301.5(1)
place of ~, 301.4; see
prison,n.
solitary ~, 301.3(6)
improbable,adj.
absurd and ~ situation,
608.13
improper,adj., 828.1,5,6,9
incorrect, 827.1,4; see **incorrect, wrong**,adj.

~ act, 828.3
acting in an ~ manner,
828.12
~ and unnecessary, 828.4
be ~, 828.10
behaving in an ~ manner,
828.12
cause to be ~, 828.7
~ conduct, practice, or activities, 1087.7
morally ~, 828.11
something ~, 828.3
~ usage, 828.3
~ word, 667.4
~ word usage, 667.3
improperness,n., 828.2
impropriety,n., 828.2
improvable,adj., 835.4
improve,v., 835.1,2
~ by addition, 835.2(4,6)
~ by changing, 835.2(7)
~ by changing habits,
835.1(2)
~ by discipline, 835.2(2)
~ by practice, 835.2(3)
~ by punishment, 835.2(2);
896.30
~ by teaching, 835.2(3)
~ by training, 835.2(3)
~ by variety, 835.2(4,6)
campaign to ~ conditions,
835.6
~ in value or worth, 835.1(1)
~ morally, 835.1(3,8)
~ spiritually, 835.1(3,8)
improvement,n., 835.3
system of spiritual self-~,
621.15
improver,n., 835.5
impudent,adj., 860.1; 861.1;
862.1
~ act, 862.8
cause to be ~, 862.12
~ girl, 862.6
~ person, 862.4
~ speech, 862.8
~ woman, 862.7
~ young person, 862.5
impudently,adv.
face ~, 862.11
impulse,n., 1092.10
ascribe one's ~s to others,
1092.87
cause to react to ~s, 1092.13
characterized by ~s, 1092.11
force an ~ into the unconscious, 1097.42–46
haunt with an ~, 265.12(4)
holding back of ~s, 1097.38–41
revival of childhood ~s under
psychoanalysis, 1092.88
surrender to ~s, 1092.14
impulsive,adj., 1092.11
~ person, 1092.12
impure,adj.
~ because of contact, 905.8
become ~, 905.12
ceremonially ~, 886.25,29
incapable of being made ceremonially ~, 845.4
make ~, 905.10
make ~ by contact, 905.7
make ~ by mixing, 905.1
make ~ with germs, 905.15
make ceremonially ~, 886.26,
30
make metal ~, 905.5
make morally ~, 886.26
make water ~, 905.6
morally ~, 886.25
~ quality, 905.13
~ thing, 905.13
~ through mixture, 905.3
impurity,n., 905.1,3,7
~ because of contact, 905.9

cause of ~, 905.13
trace of ~, 905.11
impute,v., 256.5
~ to, 893.7
in,adv.
draw ~, 193.8–10
hold ~, 558.1–6
keep ~, 558.1–6
pull ~, 193.8–10
push ~, 197.1(6,15,16,29–31,44,
53,56,58) ; 197.2(1,5)
put ~, 323.1
inaccurate,adj., 827.1; see **incorrect**,adj.
inactive,adj., 58.1
be ~, 58.8
be temporarily ~, 58.8(3)
become ~, 58.6
becoming ~, 58.7
emotional shock, ~ from,
58.1(14,28,33)
emotionally ~, 58.1(14,17,28,
33)
fatigue, ~ from, 58.1(14,28,33)
illness, ~ from, 58.1(3,14,28,
33)
less ~, 58.1(24)
make ~, 58.3
plant, ~ like a, 985.31
present, but ~, 38.1(2) ;
58.1(12,18)
state of being ~, 58.2
temporarily ~, 58.1(1,19,27,
36)
inactivity,n., 58.2
cause ~ in, 58.3
cause of ~, 58.4
condition of ~, 58.2
humor causing ~, 1091.30
live in ~, 58.8(5)
period of ~, 58.9
reducing bodily ~, 58.5
state of ~, 58.2
summer ~, 58.8(1)
warm weather ~, 58.12
winter ~, 58.8(2)
inadequacy,n., 919.11
inadequate,adj., 919.10
inattention,n., 581.2,8
done through ~, 581.5
gesture of ~, 102.1(6)
instance of ~, 581.8
inattentive,adj., 581.1
be ~ to, 581.6
become ~, 581.4
make ~, 581.4,15
~ person, 581.3
inaudible,adj., 454.14
almost ~, 454.17
make ~, 454.15
inborn,adj., 720.17
incalculable,adj., 942.5
incapable,adj., 14.1
incense,n.
substance used in making ~,
445.17
vessel for burning, 261.1(15)
inch,n.
eighteen to twenty-two ~es,
946.26(5)
four ~es, 946.26(9)
nine ~es, 946.26(20)
incite,v., 52.9
inclination,n.
bending, 152.3
leaning, 153.3
slant, 154.3
tendency, 630.1
incline,v.
bend, 152.1,2
lean, 153.1
slant, 154.1,2
tend, 179.2; 630.3
inclined,adj.
bent, 152.5

leaning, 153.4
slanting, 154.4
sloping, 154.4
tending, 630.2
be ~, i.e., tend, 630.3
cause to be ~, 630.4
include,v., 259.1
contain, 260.1
inclusion,n., 259.2
inclusive,adj., 259.3
all—~, 259.3,4
all—~ in sympathies, 259.5
incognito, adj., adv., 694.22–25
incoherent,adj., 591.7
~ in speech, 671.24,25
incomparable,adj., 530.3
incompetent,adj., 14.1
incomplete,adj., 329.1
incompleteness,n., 329.2
inconsiderate,adj., 1097.35
inconsistent,adj., 539.22
inconspicuous,adj., 952.9
~ in operation, 971.11
~ in operation, but serious in
effects, 971.12
~ position, 952.10
inconstant,adj., 531.21
~ person, 531.22
inconvenient,adj., 28.1
~ to get to, 28.5
~ to handle, 28.4
~ to manage, 28.4
incorrect,adj., 827.1,4; see also
wrong,adj.
~ thing, 827.2
~ word, 667.4
~ word usage, 667.3
incorrectly,adv.
act ~, 827.9
conceived ~, 827.5
done ~, 827.5
represent ~, 953.4
understand ~, 827.6
understood ~, 827.5
use words ~, 667.5
incorrectness,n., 827.1,4
incorrigible,adj., 815.12
increasable,adj., 907.6
increase,n., 907.3
abnormal ~, 907.3(6)
amount of ~, 914.1(9)
capable of ~, 907.6
come as an ~, 907.15
periodic ~, 907.3(7)
pert. to ~, 907.5
regular ~, 907.3(7)
increase,v., 907.1,2,9,10
~ details in speaking or writing, 907.12
~ eightfold, 907.9(4)
~ fivefold, 907.9(6)
~ fourfold, 907.9(5)
~ hundredfold, 907.9(1)
~ (of the moon), 1054.8
~ rapidly, 985.23; 1039.14
~ sevenfold, 907.9(7)
~ sixfold, 907.9(8)
~ tenfold, 907.9(2)
~ threefold, 907.9(9)
~ twofold, 907.9(3)
increasing,adj., 907.4
incredible,adj., 639.10
incredulous,adj., 639.3
incurable,adj., 398.17
indebt,v., 218.2
indebted,adj., 218.3
indecent,adj.
immodest, 873.17
immoral, 828.11
obscene, 713.1
indefinite,adj.
uncertain, 640.1,5; see uncertain,adj.
unclear, 603.1; see unclear,
adj.

indelicate,adj., 1097.35
sexually ~, 713.1
independence,n., 309.3,14; see
freedom,n.
economic ~, 309.14(3)
political ~, 309.14(4,5,10,18)
independent,adj., 309.15; see
free,adj.
independent,n.
political ~, 309.15(6);
1076.12(9)
indescribable,adj., 617.6;
665.7(1–4)
indestructible,adj., 801.37
India,n., 784.4(3)
fondness for ~, 700.30(10)
inhabitant of ~, 784.15(28,45)
language of ~, 664.4(8,9,18)
pert. to ~, 784.16
ruler of ~, 1073.36(19,20,23–
25)
Indian,n.
American ~, 430.11
female American ~, 430.11(3)
part ~, 430.6(2,5,7–16,18,23,
24)
ruler of a tribe of American
~s, 1073.36(26)
Indiana,n.
inhabitant of ~, 784.15(29)
pert. to ~, 784.16
indicate,v., 951.1; see show,v.
indication,n., 951.4; see also
show, sign,n.
as an ~ of, 951.7
~ left by passing, 757.6
~ of the future, 773.1–6
indicative,adj., 951.5
~ of failure, 951.5(3)
~ of secrets, 951.5(6)
~ of success, 951.5(2)
~ of the future, 773.4,5;
951.5(1)
indicator,n., 951.4; see also
sign,n.
indifference,n., 1097.17
deliberate ~ to a person,
1097.22,23
gesture of ~, 102.1(10)
systematic ~, esp. to religion,
1097.21
indifferent,adj., 1097.17
contentedly ~ to the world,
one who is, 1107.8
make ~, 1097.19,20
~ person, 1097.18
indigestion,n., 739.19–21
indirect,adj., 183.1
~ language, 665.9(11,38)
~ manner, 183.3
~ means, 183.3
indirectness,n., 183.2
indispensable,adj., 273.6; 848.13
~ person, 848.15
~ thing, 848.14
indisputable,adj., 542.14
indistinct,adj., 603.1; see unclear,adj.
individual,adj., 930.3,4,8; see
also one,adj.
give ~ character to, 930.10
make ~, 930.10
~ quality, 930.13
individual,n., 930.2; see also
one, person,n.
development of the ~,
731.16(1)
existence as an ~, 930.14
growth into an ~, 731.4(11)
repetition of racial development in an ~, 731.13,14
individuality,n., 930.2,8,13,22
individualize,v., 930.10
individually,adv., 930.15
consider ~, 930.12

pert. ~ to each, 930.9
treat ~, 930.12
indulge,v., 1107.1; 1108.1
~ excessively, 921.7;
1107.1(9); 1108.1
~ in pleasure, 1105.7
~ the vices of, 1108.6
indulged,adj., 1107.3; 1108.2,7
male who has been ~, 1108.5
one who is ~, 1108.4
indulgence,n., 1107.2,6
alcoholic ~, 921.1(7); 923.1(5)
excessive ~ in the pleasures
of something, 1105.17
excessive alcoholic ~, 921.1(7)
excessive in ~, 921.1(7)
moderate alcoholic ~,
923.1(5)
indulgent,adj., 1107.5
not ~, 1108.12
~ to inferiors, etc., 1108.9
treat, take care of, or nurse
~ly, 1108.7
indulger,n.
~ in pleasure, 1105.9
indulging,adj.
habitually ~ another, 1108.8
~ in pleasure, 1105.8
not ~ oneself, 1108.11
~ oneself, 1108.10
industrial,adj., 210.3
~ arts, 210.10
~ executive, 210.4; 210.4(2,6)
~ management science,
210.10
pert. to ~ arts, 965.29
Russian system of ~ output,
726.7
~ science, 210.10
industrialist,n., 210.4
important ~, 210.4(6);
848.22(2)
powerful ~, 5.8(1); 210.4(6)
ruling ~, 1073.14(6)
industrious,adj., 203.20
industry,n.
business, 210.1; see business,n.
hard work, 203.20
control of ~, give, 8.22(1)
important person in ~,
848.22(2)
ruler of ~, 1073.14(6)
inedible,adj., 734.18
ineffective,adj., 17.1
make ~, 17.5
making ~, 17.6,7
inequality,n., 534.17
inert,adj., 58.1
~ like lead, 1018.2(2)
inevitable,adj., 29.21; 76.9
inexcusable,adj., 897.10
inexpensive,adj., 223.15
~ thing, 223.16
inexperience,n., 620.1
sexual ~, 710.47
inexperienced,adj., 620.1
~ person, 620.2
sexually ~, 620.1(4,12)
sexually ~ person, 620.2(4);
710.48
time of youthful ~, 620.3
inexpiable,adj., 222.5
inexpressible,adj., 665.7
infant,n., 721.1,3; see also
child,n.
sounds of ~s, 457.1,2
infantile,adj., 721.10; see
childish,adj.
infantile paralysis,n., 354.17(9)
infect,v., 904.11
infected,adj., 904.10
make ~, 904.11
infectious,adj., 389.21,22

inferior,adj., 883.1; 1125.16; see also **worse**,adj.
~ articles, 883.4
become ~, 883.11–14
~ cloth, 883.4
condemn as ~, 883.5
gold, ~ to, 883.2
make ~, 883.16,17
~ person claiming superiority, 883.4
precious metal, ~ to, 883.2
probably ~, 883.6
showy and ~ thing, 951.36(3)
showy but ~, 951.34(1)
silver, ~ to, 883.2
~ things, 883.4
infertile,adj., 716.1
infested,adj.
be ~, 403.20
~ with animal life, 403.18,19
infinite,adj., 755.1,3; 906.17
~ time, 762.3
infinity,n., 755.1,3,5; 762.3
inflame,v.
anger, 878.1
cause intense emotion in, 1092.29
swell, 518.1,2
inflamed,adj.
angered, 878.2
impassioned, 1092.26
swollen, 518.4
inflammable,adj.
easily angered, 878.18
easily set on fire, 1064.19
inflammation,n., 392.1–5; 518.3; see also under part involved, as **hand**, etc.
~ of hands and feet, 392.1(2)
influence,n., 9.2
ability, ~ from, 9.2(11)
accomplishments, ~ from, 9.2(11)
act as an ~ against, 9.5,6
be greater in ~, 9.4
change, ~ toward, 9.2(6)
controlling ~, 8.1(20,29); 9.2(1)
corrupt ~, 886.12
emotional ~, 9.2(12); 1099.8
exert an ~ upon, 9.1; see influence,v.
exert an emotional ~ upon, 1099.1,12
exert controlling ~, 8.1(20,29)
exert secret ~, 9.7
exerting ~, 9.3
exerting an emotional ~, 1099.2
foul ~, 9.2(9)
good in ~, 9.3(1)
greater in ~, 833.3
greatest in ~, 9.3(2)
irresistible ~, 9.2(15)
magic ~, 9.2(14)
mental ~, 9.2(8)
nation's ~, 9.2(5)
~ of planets or stars, 1053.24
open to ~, 9.9
sphere of ~, 9.8; 782.10
subject to ~, 9.9
subject to controlling ~, 8.6(4)
superficial ~, 9.2(14)
supernatural ~, 662.4(8)
surrounding ~, 9.2(2); 783.1(1,6,8)
~ toward change, 539.17
under the ~ of, 9.10,11
influence,v., 9.1
~ beforehand, 9.1(11,12)
~ by devils, 660.20
~ emotionally, 9.1(2,3,5,6,8–10,12,14); 1099.1,12
~ preceding events, 52.1(14)

~ to act, 52.9
influenced,adj.
able to be ~, 9.9
~ by moon, 1054.33
~ by planets, 1053.5
~ by stars, 1056.34
emotionally ~, 1099.3
influential,adj., 9.3
be ~, 9.4–7
be more ~, 9.4
more ~, 833.3
most ~, 9.3(2)
inform,v., 613.28,29
~ on, 613.10
one who ~s on another, 613.11
informal,adj., 819.16,17
~ language, 664.1(27,28)
informant,n., 613.31
information,n., 613.30; see also **knowledge**, **report**,n.
~ about happenings, 613.30(4, 7,10,12)
claim to special ~, 613.41,42
collection of ~ about a person or thing, 613.30(3)
~ delivered by someone, 613.30(5,6)
descr. of ~ suitable for all, 613.38
eager to gain ~, 624.15
gain ~, 624.1,7
gain ~ by observing an area, 624.7
give ~ about, 613.1–7, 23–27; see **tell**,v.
give ~ on a horse race, 613.34, 35
give false ~ to, 613.28(10)
give incriminating ~ about, 613.10,11
give secret ~ to, 613.28(13)
giver of ~, 613.31
giver of ~ for gambling, 613.31(2)
inclined to give ~, 613.33
looking for ~, 486.3
make ~ known, 613.1
official ~, 613.30(2)
one to whom confidential ~ is given, 613.37
origin of ~, 613.36
seek ~, 486.1; 624.8
seeker of ~, 624.10
seeking ~, given to, 624.11
seeking ~, pert. to, 624.12
seeking of ~, 624.9
~ sent by messenger, 189.6
storehouse of ~, 262.3(29,31)
try to gain ~, 624.8
unwilling to give ~, 671.20(1, 7,8)
informative,adj., 613.32
informed,adj., 611.1
state of being ~, 613.39,40
informer,n., 613.11,31
ingratitude,n., 1110.12
inhabit,v., 750.1; see also **live**,v.
inhabitable,adj., 750.8
inhabitant,n., 750.4; see also **native**,n.
deprive of ~s, 750.26,27
earliest ~, 750.4(1,8)
evacuated ~, 926.27
few ~s, place of, 782.1(2,23)
full of ~s, 750.7(2)
~ of a city, 784.15(13); 785.2
~ of a cottage, 750.4(3)
~ of a nation, 784.3
~ of a state, 784.15(13)
~ of a town, 785.2
~ of a village, 785.2
~ of an institution, 750.4(7)
~ of arctic regions, 784.15(31)

~ of arctic America, 784.15(19)
~ of Asia, 784.15(45)
~ of Athens, 784.15(4)
~ of Belgium (south), 784.15(62)
~ of Brittany, 784.15(7,11)
~ of Cambridge, 784.15(8)
~ of Carthage, 784.15(10)
~ of caves, 298.13
~ of Ceylon, 784.15(54)
~ of China, 784.15(12,45)
~ of country regions, 786.6
~ of darkness, 1070.10
~ of Denmark, 784.15(16,41, 42,56)
~ of England, 784.15(18,37)
~ of Europe (south), 784.15(39)
~ of Far East, 784.15(45)
~ of forests, 996.41,45
~ of France, 784.15(21)
~ of France (south), 784.15(39)
~ of French Canada, 784.15(9)
~ of Germany, 784.15(6,23,30, 56)
~ of Greece, 784.15(1,3,24)
~ of Hawaii, 784.15(25)
~ of heaven, 1051.16
~ of Holland, 784.15(17)
~ of India, 784.15(28,45)
~ of Indiana, 784.15(29)
~ of Ireland, 784.15(11,22,33, 48)
~ of Isle of Man, 784.15(22,38)
~ of Israel, 784.15(34)
~ of Japan, 784.15(35,45)
~ of Jerusalem, 784.15(26)
~ of London's East End, 784.15(14)
~ of Mars, 1053.10
~ of Mediterranean countries, 784.15(36)
~ of Michigan, 784.15(65)
~ of Moscow, 784.15(40)
~ of North Carolina, 784.15(60)
~ of Norway, 784.15(41–43,56)
~ of Oxford, 784.15(47)
~ of Peiping, 784.15(49)
~ of Peking, 784.15(49)
~ of Peru, 784.15(50)
~ of Philippine Islands, 784.15(20)
~ of Portugal, 784.15(32,51)
~ of rooms, 750.4(11)
~ of Russia, 784.15(40)
~ of Russia (west), 784.15(64)
~ of Scandinavia, 784.15(41, 42,56)
~ of Scotland, 784.15(11,22,27, 52)
~ of Siam, 784.15(53)
~ of South Africa, 784.15(2)
~ of southern lands, 784.15(39)
~ of Spain, 784.15(32,55)
~ of Sweden, 784.15(41,42,56, 57)
~ of Switzerland, 784.15(58)
~ of Tangier, 784.15(59)
~ of the earth, 750.4(5,12); 1004.31
~ of the east, 179.13
~ of the frontier, 793.4
~ of the interior, 136.4
~ of the land, 1003.3
~ of the moon, 1054.16
~ of the north, 179.11
~ of the other side of the Alps, 166.5
~ of the other side of the mountains, 166.5

~ of the south, 179.16
~ of the suburbs, 785.2,4
~ of the west, 179.19
~ of Turkey, 784.15(46)
~ of Venice, 784.15(61)
~ of Wales, 784.15(11,63)
~ of Western world, 784.15(44)
~ of Wisconsin, 784.15(5)
original ~, 750.4(1,8)
~s, 750.5,6
~s of a city, 784.17(2)
~s of a nation, 784.17(2)
~s of a state, 784.17(2)
~s of country regions, 784.17(3) ; 786.7
~s of Isle of Man, 784.17(4)
~s of Peiping, 784.17(5)
~s of Peking, 784.17(5)
~s of suburbs, 785.4
~s of Switzerland, 784.17(6)
~s of tropics, 784.17(1)
~s of Wales, 784.17(7)
temporary ~, 750.4(13)
without ~s, 750.24; 972.7(1)
without ~s, place, 750.25
inhabitation,n., 750.2
inhabiting,adj., 750.3
inharmonious,adj., 542.2
inherit,v.
entitled to ~ throne, title, or position, 6.5
inheritable,adj., 241.10
inheritance,n., 241.4; see also **heredity**,n.
cut off from ~, 242.14
joint ~, 241.2
right of ~, 241.6
system of ~, 241.3
person appointed to settle an ~, 241.11
pert. to, or derived from, ~, 241.8,9
inherited,adj.
able to be ~, 241.10
inheritor,n., 241.5
privileges of ~, 241.7
inhibit,v., 558.1
inhibited,adj., 558.5; 1097.30
inhibiting,adj., 558.4
inhibition,n., 558.2,3
freedom from ~s, 309.14(8)
inhuman,adj.
become ~, 429.14
make ~, 429.13
injure,v., 803.1; see **harm**,v.
~ feelings, 868.1,4
injured,adj.
able to be ~, 803.24
easily ~, 803.23
~ in one's rights, 803.21
not ~, 804.1
one who is ~, 803.25
unable to be ~, 804.3
injurious,adj., 803.3; see **harmful**,adj.
injury,n., 803.3; see also **harm**,n.
defacing ~, 805.5
endure ~, strength to, 1.16,17
mark left by an ~, 805.5,6
mark of ~, 803.15,20; 805.5,6
marks of ~, show, 803.19
penetrating ~, 803.18
surface ~ to the skin, 803.16, 17
sustain ~, 803.22
~ to feelings, 803.20
~ to reputation, 803.20
injustice,n., 635.2; 828.11
angry over ~, 878.10(4,7,8)
ink,n.
stain of ~, 904.23
ink-blot test,n., 401.10(5)
inlet,n., 1029.63

ocean ~s, pert. to, 1029.72(20)
inn,n., 753.14; see **hotel**,n.
innate,adj., 720.17
inner,adj., 136.1; see also **interior**,adj.
~most part, 326.1(9)
~ place, 782.1(25)
~ space, 787.1(2,7)
innocence,n., 845.1,6
determine ~ or guilt in court, 1082.8
swearer to another's ~, 897.31
innocent,adj., 845.1,6; see also **guiltless**,adj.
fat and ~ of face, 510.3
~ girl, 760.6(13)
inoculate,v., 569.1; see **immunize**,v.
inopportune,adj., 765.4,6,7
inquire,v., 625.1,10; see also **question**,v.
eager to ~, 624.15
~ into, 624.8
inquirer,n., 624.10; 625.5,12
inquiry,n., 624.9; 625.2-4
making offensive or searching ~, 624.14
inquisitive,adj., 625.11
~ person, 625.12
inquisitor,n., 624.10; 625.5
pert. to an ~, 624.13
insane,adj., 1136.2
asylum for the ~, 1136.16-18
become ~, 1136.6
for the ~, 1136.12
~ from the moon, 1054.33
make ~, 1136.4
~ person, 1136.3,17
send to an ~ asylum, 1136.19
insanity,n., 1136.1
acquired ~, 1136.1(10)
adolescent ~, 1136.1(11,18)
amusing ~, 1136.1(33)
~ associated with nerve disorders, 1136.1(28,29)
between sanity and ~, 1136.10
~ caused by fever, 1136.1(8)
causing ~, 1136.5
~ characterized by depression, 1122.22,24; 1136.1(6,11, 19,24)
concealment of ~, 970.22
delirium verging on ~, 1136.1(16)
fits of ~, 1136.13
doctor of legal aspects of ~, 401.2(4)
~ from cocaine, 399.15(2)
~ in one area only, 1136.1(27)
indicating ~, 1136.2
legal ~, 1136.1(3,20)
like ~, 1136.14,15
~ marked by delusions of grandeur, 1136.1(18,25,31)
~ marked by delusions of being a wolf, 1136.1(21)
~ marked by delusions of persecution, 1136.1(18,31,37, 38)
~ marked by desire to kill, 796.20
~ marked by excitement, 1136.1(5-9,23,24,36)
~ marked by hallucinations, 1136.1(5,8,9,11,17,18,31,37, 38)
medical science dealing with ~, 401.1(1,36,44,51,62,82,84, 85)
~ of old age, 1136.1(19)
person verging on ~ from birth, 1136.11
slight ~, 1136.1(33)

surgery to correct ~, 402.1(18) ; 402.5(23,27,28,41)
temporary ~, 1136.1(8,32)
temporary ~ from alcoholic indulgence, 1136.1(9)
treatment of ~, 400.6(13,23, 28,37)
violent ~, 1136.1(23)
insatiable,adj., 1119.25
inscribe,v., 682.1; see **write**,v.
inscription,n., 682.2,3; see also **writing**,n.
ancient ~s, science of, 682.14(3,4)
~ at end of a book, 687.9(4)
Egyptian ~s, science of, 682.14(4)
Egyptian ~s, treatise on, 682.15(7)
~ in a book, etc., 682.3(5,6) ; 687.9(4)
~ on a coin, 682.3(4,10)
~ on a gravestone, etc., 682.3(9)
~ on a medal, 682.3(4,10)
~ on a monument, building, etc., 682.3(7)
~ on a picture, badge, etc., 682.3(10)
publisher's ~ in a book, 687.9(4)
science of ~s, 682.14(3)
insect,n., 428.3
covering of ~s, 972.4(19)
destruction of ~s, place for, 899.16
destructive ~, 428.3(4) ; 801.4(2)
eating ~s, 734.27(17)
free of ~s, 309.11(20)
group of ~s, 403.5(39,72)
infested with ~s, 403.18(4)
like an ~, 428.2
of ~s, 403.6(1) ; 428.1
place for live ~s, 403.22(22, 27,28)
plant disease ~, 428.3(1)
repellent of ~s, 428.5,6
science of ~s, 403.26(13,15,31)
withering of plants, ~ that causes, 806.21
young of ~s, 428.4
insensitive,adj., 435.3
become emotionally ~, 1093.5
emotionally ~, 1093.2
emotionally ~ person, 1093.3
make emotionally ~, 1093.4
make ~ to pain, heat, cold, or touch, 1137.37,38
~ to pain, 1137.39,40
~ to touch, heat, cold, 1137.39
insensitiveness,n., 435.1; 1093.2
causing ~ to pain, 1137.41
drug or agent that causes ~ to pain, 1137.42
production of ~ to pain, 1137.43
inseparable,adj., 325.10
~ part, 326.43
insert,v., 323.1
~ at a later time, 323.1(36)
~ words, etc., 323.1(30,37,39, 40)
insertion,n., 323.2
~ of a unit of time, 323.9
inside,adj., 136.1; see also **interior, internal**,adj.
~ a place, 1024.7
soft ~ part, 443.6
inside,n., 136.2; see also **interior**,n.
originating from the ~, 728.13(1,2)

insight,n., 593.2; see also understanding,n.
belief in spiritual ~, 593.7,8
special ~ into God's nature, 593.2(12)
insincere,adj., 826.23
~ actions, behavior, or statements, 1009.20
be ~ with, 826.26
~ language, 664.1(3,16); 665.9(57)
offensive because ~, 826.27
~ statements, 674.9(10,32)
talk ~ly, 671.4(3)
~ talk, 671.2(5,8)
insincerity,n., 826.23
act with ~, 826.25
insist,v., 274.1
insistent,adj., 274.4
insolent,adj., 860.1; 861.1; 862.1; see also impudent, adj.
insoluble,adj.
unsolvable, 601.6
inspect,v., 484.1; 485.1
inspection,n., 484.2; 485.2
inspector,n., 484.3; 485.3
inspiration,n., 52.11
~ by the muses, pert. to, 654.18
excitement of poetic ~, 1100.7(5)
frenzy of ~, in a, 1100.6(9)
goddess of ~, 654.2(10); 654.17
poetic ~, 689.10
without ~, 14.1(30)
inspire,v., 52.9
inspired,adj.
~ as if by a devil, 660.15
instant,n., 769.3
happening at the same ~, 764.8
instead of,prep., 782.19
instill,v., 323.1
~ figuratively, 323.22
instinct,n.
action from natural ~, 810.11
institute,v., 729.1,7
institution,n.
beginning, 729.2
Asiatic ~s, 1091.27,28
European ~ s, 1091.25,26
female supervisor of an ~, 8.16(8)
instruct,v.
order, 275.1
teach, 621.1; see teach,v.
instruction,n.
ordering, 275.2
teaching, 621.3,5,6; see teaching,n.
instructive,adj., 621.5
instructor,n., 621.7; see teacher,n.
insubstantial,adj., 513.12; 909.11,12
light and ~, 949.1(2,4,6,7)
~, like a shadow, 1071.3
insufficient,adj., 919.10
insult,n., 867.2
angry over ~, 878.10(4,7,8)
attack with ~s, 561.1
humiliating ~, 868.17
insult,v., 867.1
insulted,adj.
enjoyment from being ~, 1137.26
insulting,adj., 867.3
~ act, 52.5(18); 867.2(3)
~ attitude, 867.2(5)
~ behavior, 867.2(5)
~ language, 867.2(2,5,7)
~ reference, 867.5

~ to one's dignity, 867.6
~ treatment, 867.2(2,4)
~ word, 867.4
insurance,n.
making certain, 641.5
calculator of ~ risks, 942.8
insure,v.
make certain, 641.4
intellect,n., 584.1
devoted to world of the ~, 1090.10
intellectual,adj., 584.2; 585.5
invest with ~ attitude, 584.18
source of ~ light, 1065.83,84
intellectual,n., 622.17
class of ~s, 594.10
intelligence,n., 594.3
ability and ~, 7.1(62)
~ from training, 594.7
native ~, 584.3
~ score, 594.14
subnormal in ~, 597.1,6,19; see feeble-minded, stupid,adj.
sudden display of ~, 594.8
testing ~, science of, 19.9(4)
testing of ~, 584.24
~ tests, 594.13
intelligent,adj., 594.1,2; see also clever, shrewd,adj.
abnormally ~ for age, 594.5,6
~ and famous person, 1065.84
~ person, 594.6,9–12
intelligible,adj., 598.16; see understandable,adj.
intemperate,adj., 923.3
~ in drinking, 748.18
intend,v., 45.2
intense,adj., 170.1
intensity,n., 170.1
reduce in ~, 10.5
intention,n., 45.1
good ~s, 45.10,11
intentional,adj., 45.12,15
intercourse,n.
sexual intercourse, 710.1; see sexual intercourse,n.
interest,n., 580.3
attention, 579.2,5
money, 219.3(13,46)
interesting quality, 580.3
ability to arouse ~, 580.5
all-consuming ~, 579.15
broad or liberal in one's ~s, 1109.5,6
center of ~, 579.30–33
done without ~, 583.12
exorbitant rate of ~, 218.12
holding one's breath in ~, 580.10
~ in welfare of country, community, etc., 784.8(4)
keen and happy ~, 580.9
object of ~, 580.11
pay ~, 219.1(25)
reawaken ~ in, 580.6
reawakening of ~ in religion, 580.7
sexual ~, 709.7
similarity of ~s, 529.7
sphere of ~, 580.13
subordinate ~, 580.12
temporary ~, dealing with topics of, 756.4
withdrawal from worldly ~s, 141.2(1)
without ~, 1097.32
interest,v., 580.1
interested,adj.
become ~, 580.8
sexually ~, 709.8,9
interesting,adj., 580.2
be ~ to, 580.1
being ~, 580.3

make ~, 580.4
interfere,v., 559.1
~ with, 557.1; see hinder,v.
interference,n., 557.2,3
hindrance, 557.2,3
~ by another nation, 559.5
emotional ~ resulting from conflicts, 1097.47
emotional ~ with freedom, 1097.38–41
interferer,n., 559.3,4
interfering,adj., 559.2
hindering, 557.4
interim,n., 769.6; 769.8(10–13)
interior,adj., 136.1; see also inside, internal,adj.
~ part of a country, 136.3
~ part or parts, 136.2
interior,n., 136.2
inhabitant of the ~, 136.4
intermission,n., 769.6; 769.8(10–13)
midday ~, 769.8(12)
internal,adj., 136.1; see also inside, interior,adj.
caused by ~ factors, 15.6
~ organs, 347.9
interpret,v., 607.17
understand,593.1; see understand,v.
~ emotionally, 1092.72,73
~ in exciting light, 1100.16,17, 20,21
interpretation,n., 607.18
understanding, 593.2
give a false ~, 607.21
science of ~, 607.22(1)
interpreter,n., 607.20
~ in the Far East, 607.20(1)
~ of dreams, 607.20(2)
interpretive,adj., 607.19
interrupt,v., 791.1
interrupted,adj., 29.3(35)
interruption,n., 791.3
~ in the rhythm of poetry or music, 791.3(3)
interval,n., 769.6; 769.8(10–13)
intestinal,adj., 347.10
intestine,n., 347.9
cut out the ~s of, 332.1(17)
disorders of the ~, 347.12
gas in the ~s, 1048.1(13)
remove the ~, 249.2(3)
science of the ~, 401.1(17,22, 58,95)
intimate,adj., 1096.1
intolerable,adj., 246.5
intoxicate,v.
excite, 1100.1
~ with liquor, 749.51
intoxicated,adj.
excited, 1100.6
~ with liquor, 749.46; see drunk,adj.
intoxication,n.
excitement, 1101.1
mental derangement from ~, 1136.1(8,9)
~ with liquor, 749.47
intricate,adj.
difficult, 25.1(10,16)
hard to understand, 604.1
winding, 156.5
~ problem, 25.2(1)
introduce,v., 730.1
~ changes, 730.1(4)
~ into office, 730.1(1,2)
~ new things, 730.1(4)
~ to someone, 730.1(7)
introducer,n., 730.3
~ of speakers, 730.9
introduction,n., 730.2,4
be an ~ to, 730.1(5,6)
deliver an ~, 730.6
musical ~, 730.4(3,15)

precede as an ~, 175.1(13,14)
tedious in ~, 730.7
write an ~, 730.6
writer of ~s, 730.8
introductory,adj., 730.5
be ~ to, 730.1(5,6)
~ part, 730.4
introspection,n., 228.3(1,12,15,
17)
invade,v., 133.1
invalid,n., 389.6
invariable,adj., 531.1,2
invasion,n., 133.2
sudden ~, 560.9
invent,v., 726.17
invention,n., 726.18,20
inventive,adj., 726.27
inventor,n., 726.19
investigate,v.
search, 486.1; see search,v.
try to find out, 624.8
investigation,n., 486.2,3; 624.9
making offensive or searching
~, 624.14
motivating further ~, 486.6
without further ~, 486.8
investigator,n., 486.4; 624.10
pert. to an ~, 624.13
invigorate,v., 1.29
invisible,adj., 483.12(2,7,8,9,11,
14,18)
~ as a symptom, 483.12(10)
invitation,n., 274.2
~ for another time, 1037.17
invite,v., 274.1
involuntary,adj., 265.26
~ act, 52.5(36)
involve,v., 522.1
~ as a result, 16.5
~ in a dispute, 542.20
~ in wrongdoing, 522.1(3–5) ;
522.3
involved,adj.
not simple, 25.1(3–5,8–10,15,
16,20,25)
winding, 156.5
~ as an essential part, 522.2
involvement,n., 25.2
free of ~, 309.11(16)
inward,adv.
curve ~, 155.1(4)
curved ~, 155.4
Iran,n.
ruler of ~, 1073.36(27)
Ireland,n., 784.9(8,9,11,14)
Irish,adj., 784.16
~ accent, 670.4(4)
~ characteristic, 1091.24(5)
Irishman,n., 784.15(11,22,33,48)
iron,n., 1017.1
instrument for ironing, 439.4
articles of ~, 1017.12
bar of ~, 1017.1(1)
~ block, 1012.23
coating on ~, 1017.3–6
convert ~, 1017.13,14
~ furnace, 1017.11
like ~, 1017.2(4)
not containing ~, 1017.15
of the color of rusty ~,
495.2(2,5,8)
of the color, strength, or
hardness of ~, 1017.2(4)
place of manufacture of ~,
1017.10
plated with ~, 1017.7
relating to ~, 1017.2
tin-coated ~, 1020.16
worker with ~, 1017.8
iron,v., 439.2(6)
ironworker,n., 1017.8
shop of an ~, 1017.9
irony,n., 868.2(2) ; 869.3(4)
bitter ~, 869.5(4)
graceful in ~, 949.12

light in ~, 949.12
polite ~, 869.3(1)
ridicule by ~, 869.1(7,8)
skillful in ~, 949.12
irrational,adj., 591.1
~ act, 52.5(14,24)
irregular,adj., 539.23
grow ~ly, 731.3(25,28)
growing ~ly, 731.5(16)
irregularity,n., 539.23
~ accompanying disease,
536.6
irrelevance,n., 521.7
irrelevant,adj., 521.6
something ~, 521.8
irreligious,adj., 643.12–14
become ~, 643.16
make ~, 643.15
~ person, 643.13
irrepairable,adj., 832.19
irreproachable,adj., 845.6
~ person, 845.7
irresistible,adj., 544.7
irresponsible,adj., 527.6
irrigate,v.
~ a bodily opening, cavity,
wound, etc., 1036.22
~ (land) below the surface,
1036.28
serving to ~, 1036.24
irrigated, adj.
able to be ~, 1036.26
state of being ~, 1036.25
well ~, 1036.27
irrigation,n.
water for ~, 1029.1(1)
irritable,adj., 874.10; 876.1; see
also annoyed, bad-tem-
pered,adj.
~ person, 874.11
irritate,v., 874.1; see annoy,v.
~ feelings of, 874.1(5)
~ hearing of, 874.1(5)
irritated,adj.
annoyed, 874.6
rubbed sore, 1137.14
be ~, 874.12
become ~, 874.12
irritating,adj., 874.4; see
annoying,adj.
irritation,n.
annoyance, 874.2,3
relieve medical ~, agent to,
1142.14,15
island,n., 1030
coral ~, 1030.4
form into an ~, 1030.9,10
group of small ~s, 1030.5
inhabitant of an ~, 1030.7,8
like an ~, 1030.6
live or stay on an ~, 1030.11
living on an ~, 1030.6
low ~, 1030.2
native of an ~, 1030.7,8
Pacific ~s, 1030.12
pert. to an ~, 1030.6
put on an ~, 1030.9,10
small ~, 1030.1
traffic ~, 148.15
water between ~s, 1029.1(2)
water thickly dotted with
small ~s, 1029.7
Isle of Man,n.
inhabitant of ~, 784.15(22,38)
inhabitants of ~, 784.17(4)
pert. to ~, 784.16
isolate,v.
leave alone, 330.3
set apart, 325.12
isolated,adj., 325.12
alone, 330.1(12,13,20,22–24,36)
~ existence, 330.8
~ person, 330.5,7
isolation,n., 325.12; 330.2,4
life of ~, 330.8

one who lives in ~, 330.7
place of ~, 330.10
put in ~, 323.1(46)
Israel,n.
inhabitant of ~, 784.15(34)
pert. to ~, 784.16
Italian,adj.
~ artist, 965.33
~ language, 664.4(16)
~ writer, 965.33
Italy,n.
government of ~, 1073.5(5)
political party in ~ under
Mussolini, 1076.12(8)
itch,v., 434.3
itching,adj., 434.4
itching,n., 434.1(1,2,4,6,9,15)
itinerant,adj., 107.4(7)
itself,pron.
by ~, 228.2
ivory,n.
decorated with gold and ~,
1013.12

J

jacket,n., 976.4
Alaskan ~, 976.4(10)
garment under a ~,
974.38(26) ; 976.5
hooded ~, 976.4(10)
hussar's ~, 975.6; 976.4(17)
military ~, 975.6; 976.4(8)
naval ~, 975.6
sailor's ~, 975.6; 976.4(8)
skiing ~, 976.4(10)
tennis ~, 976.4(1)
woodcutter's ~, 976.4(9)
workman's ~, 976.4(8)
jail,n., 301.4; see prison,n.
jail,v., 301.1; see also confine,
imprison,v.
jam,n.
fruit ~, 746.1
Japan,n., 784.4(3) ; 784.9(13,18)
feudal lord in ~, 1074.19,20
ruler of ~, 1073.36(18,29,32)
Japanese,adj., 784.16; see also
Oriental,adj.
become ~, 784.13
~ characteristic, 1091.24(6)
~ code of chivalry, 858.8
make ~, 784.10(7)
Japanese,n., 430.12,13;
784.15(35,45)
part ~, 430.12
jar,n.
vessel, 261.7(1,14,16,39)
jar,v., 111.5
jaundice,n., 396.1(18)
curing ~, 396.4
Java,n.
ruler of ~, 1073.36(23)
jaw,n., 366.1
descr. of the ~s, 366.9
flesh under the ~, 385.1(5)
having ~s of a certain kind,
366.9
pert. to the ~, 366.2,5
~s, 366.4
smallness of the ~s, 366.10
under the ~, 366.3
without ~s, 366.11,12
jawbone,n., 366.6,7
under the ~, 366.8
jay,n.
group of ~s, 403.5(4)
jealous,adj., 1119.1,5
be ~, 1119.3
~ person, 1119.4
jealousy,n., 1119.2; see also
envy,n.
jelly,n.
animal ~, 746.4
base for fruit ~, 746.2

become ~, 746.7
become like ~, 746.7
fruit ~, 746.1
like ~, 746.3,6
make into ~, 746.8
make like ~, 746.8
pert. to ~, 746.5
shaking like ~, 111.3(2)
jelly,v., 746.7,8
jellyfish,n., 422.3
group of ~, 403.5(67)
of ~, 422.1(11,14,22,23,26)
jerk,n., 89.2
jerk,v., 89.1
jerky,adj., 89.3
~ movement, 89.1–4
Jerusalem,n.
inhabitant of ~, 784.15(26)
pert. to ~, 784.16
jest,v., 1115.1
~ at, 1115.5
jester,n., 1115.6
court ~, 1116.1; see **clown**,n.
professional ~, 1116.1; see **clown**,n.
skillful ~, 1115.10
Jew,n., 642.5
colonize ~s in Palestine, movement to, 642.16
dispersed ~s, 188.2
dispersion of the ~s, 188.2
fond of ~s, 700.30(11)
hatred of ~s, 880.17(2)
place to which ~s were restricted, 558.6(1)
prejudice against ~s, 634.1(1)
savior of the ~s, 571.3(2)
~s, collectively, 642.7; 642.7(2)
slaughter of ~s, 796.2(11); 796.23
jewel,n., 961.1,10–21; see also **gem**,n.
like a ~, 961.8
ornament with ~s, 959.1(9); 961.4
set with ~s, 961.5
sun's rays, ~ in the form of, 959.3(20)
jeweler,n., 961.6
magnifying glass of ~s, 961.7
jewelry,n., 961.1,2,9
diamond ~, 962.1
headband of ~, 961.2
mineral used in ~, 961.12
ornament with ~, 959.1(9); 961.4
pearl ~, 963.1
piece of ~, 961.1
seller of ~, 961.6
stone used in ~, 961.10–21
weight in ~, 947.32,34
weight system in ~, 947.31(4)
Jewish,adj., 642.4
a convert to the ~ religion, 642.10(3)
~ instruction, place of, 645.1(12,14)
~ law, book of, 648.1(18)
not ~, 642.4(1)
student of ~ law, 648.5(3)
~ worship, place of, 645.1(12,14)
jinrikisha,n., 192.9(2,4)
job,n.
piece of work, 203.5
position, 205.18–22
jock strap,n., 1022.34
join,v., 321.1,2; see **connect**,v.
joint,n., 321.7
disease of the ~s, 377.9(1,3,13,24); 1137.56(14)
hip ~, 345.16
inflammation of the ~s, 377.9(3,13)

one who fits things together at the ~s, 321.11
put a bodily ~ out of place, 323.20
stiffness in a ~, 377.9(1)
weak in the ~s, 10.1(51)
joke,n., 1115.7
addicted to practical ~s, 1115.16
~ of action, 1115.11
play practical ~s, 1115.13,15
practical ~, 1115.12
season with ~s, 1114.12
joke,v., 1115.1
~ at, 1115.5
joker,n., 1115.6; 1116.1; see also **clown**,n.
practical ~, 1115.14
professional ~, 1115.17; see **clown**,n.
skillful ~, 1115.10
joking,adj., 1115.3
joking,n., 1115.2
intended for ~, 1115.9
jolly,adj., 1104.1
journalist,n., 691.4
occupation of a ~, 691.6,7
~s, 691.5
~ who writes to elicit pity, 1127.16
journey,n., 124.2
journey,v., 124.1; see **travel**,v.
jovial,adj., 1104.1
joy,n., 1102.2; see also **happiness, merriment**,n.
joyless,adj., 1105.29
judge,n., 1083.1,2,19,32
able to be settled by a ~, 1082.32
act or serve as a ~, 1083.21
authority of a ~, 5.4(13); 1083.8,14,15,17
be a ~, 1083.21
contest ~s, 1083.39,40
court ~, 1083.1
decision of a ~, 1081.13,14
fitting for a ~, 1083.12,13
function of a ~, 1083.8,14,15,17
harsh ~, 1083.34
like a ~, 1083.11
~ of art, literature, theater, etc., 1083.32
~ of excellence, worth, or value, 1083.32
~ of food, drink, wine, etc., 1083.32
~ of sports, 1083.19(6,7)
~ of taste, 1083.32
office of ~, 1083.3
~ on legal wills, estates, etc., 1083.2(9)
period of being a ~, 1083.3
pert. to a ~, 1083.9,10
pert. to office of ~, 1083.4,5
power of a ~, 1083.8,14,15,17
private office of a ~, 1083.18
rank of ~, having, 1083.16
~s, collectively, 1083.6,7
settlement of a dispute by a ~, 1083.22
sit as a ~, 1082.8–10
system of ~s and courts, 1081.6
judge,v., 633.1; 1083.20,21
able to ~, 1083.41
art of ~ing, 1083.37
~ before knowing facts, 633.1(13)
~ beforehand, 1083.31
~ excellence, worth, or value, 1083.35,36
hear and ~ in court, 1082.8–10
one who ~s, 1083.19

power to ~, 1083.28,29
right to ~, 1083.29
standard of ~ing, 1083.45
~ unfairly, 1083.30
~ value of, 839.14
judged,adj.
able to be ~, 1083.47
likely to be ~, 1083.47
position from which things or ideas are ~, 782.23
judging,adj., 1083.42
~ harshly, 1083.43
~ instead of being objective, 1083.44
judgment,n., 633.8
able to exercise ~, 1083.41
arbitrator's ~, 1083.24,27
call upon for a ~, 693.1(1)
essay rendering ~, 1083.38
good ~, 596.3
good ~, having or showing, 596.1,2
habit of writing in ~ of, 682.8
harsh in ~ of worth, 1083.43
incorrect ~, 633.8(9)
lenient in ~ of others, 890.15
liable to ~, 1083.47
place of ~, 1083.46
poor ~, 596.6
poor ~, having or showing, 596.5
render ~s, 1083.20,21,35–38
rendering ~s, instead of being objective, 1083.44
standard of ~, 1083.45
strict in ~ of others, 890.10
talk in ~, 671.1(51,54,81,84)
unfavorable ~, 838.2
warped in ~, 877.1(2)
write in ~ of, 682.1(13)
jug,n., 261.7(21,32,35)
beer ~, 261.7(35)
juice,n.
apple ~, 745.3
meat ~s, 447.4
served in its ~s (of meat), 447.5
sour ~, 447.3
juicy,adj., 447.1
sweet and ~, 447.2
July,n.
pert. to ~, 780.7
jump,n., 110.2
characterized by ~s, 110.9
forward ~, 110.2(2)
~ of a whale, 110.2(1)
jump,v., 110.1
~ back, 110.1(18,22–24)
~ back into shape; able to, 110.5–7
cause to ~, 110.10
~ forward to the, 735.8
~ in dancing, 110.1(7)
~ in surprise, 110.1(28,29)
~ into, 110.1(20,30)
~ of a horse, 110.1(4,7,10)
~ over, 110.1(15,34)
tending to ~, 110.3
~ with fear, 110.1(1,28,29)
jumping,adj., 110.4
jumping,n., 110.2
adapted to ~, 110.8
characterized by ~, 110.9
jumpy,adj., 110.3(2)
junction,n., 321.7
junk,n.
boat, 115.20
trash, 284.20; 285.1
juror,n., 1084.2,3
jury,n., 1084.1,4
attempt illegal influence on a ~, 9.13,14
chairman of ~, 1084.5
choose a ~ from list, 1084.12

court order for ~ service, 1084.8,9
decision of a ~, 1084.14
enter name on ~ list, 1084.12
function on a ~, 1084.13
member of a ~, 1084.2,3
those ordered to serve on a ~, 1084.6,7,10,11

justice,n.
fairness, 637.2
administration of ~, 1081.19-21
ask for ~, 1082.17
fasting to obtain ~, 734.22
goddess of retributive ~, 896.32
government department of ~, 1081.6

justification,n., 898.1
justify,v., 898.2
jut,v., 958.1; see **stick out,v.**
juvenile,adj.
childish, 721.10; see **childish, adj.**
young, 760.1; see **young,adj.**

K

K(the letter),n.
incorrect pronunciation of ~, 670.7(1)
sound of ~, 670.14(13)
kangaroo,n., 418.1,2
bodily sac for ~ babies, 350.1(5,6)
pert. to the ~, 418.3
keep,v., 257.1(15,16,19,20)
~ back, 558.1-6
~ in, 301.1; 558.1; see also **confine,v.**
~ on, 754.1; see also **continue,v.**
~ on with, 754.19; see also **continue,v.**
~ out, 296.1-7; see **exclude,v.**
place to ~ things, 262.3; see **storehouse, storeroom,n.**
kettle,n.
large ~, 261.10(2)
Russian tea ~, 261.10(9)
tea ~, 261.10(13)
key,n.
private ~, 298.24
~ that opens all locks, 298.23
~ to a problem, 601.11
~ to hieroglyphics, 601.9
~ to secret writing, 601.8
keyboard,n.
piano or organ ~, 479.12
kidnap,v., 247.17
kidney,n.
above the ~s, 388.2(12)
diseases of the ~, 388.3
near the ~s, 388.2(1)
pert. to the ~, 388.2(5,10)
science of the ~s, 401.1(48, 106)
secretion of the ~, 287.8(1)
kill,v., 796.1
~ (a person) for his beliefs, 1138.1(4)
~ as sacrifice, 236.1(17)
~ by cold, 1058.12
~ by cutting off air, 796.11-14
~ by cutting off the head, 796.15,16
~ by frost, 1059.14
~ by hunger, 737.7
~ by strangling, 796.11-14
~ disease germs in, 796.17
~ figuratively, 796.8
~ in murderous frenzy, 1100.5(3)
insanity marked by desire to ~, 796.20

intending to ~, 796.7
not ~, 796.28
one who has been ~ed, 794.34(2,4,6)
tending to ~, 796.4
used to ~, 796.5
~ vermin, 1048.7
~ with gas, 1048.29
killer,n., 796.3,10,13,22
bug ~, 796.27(1,2)
Chinese ~, 796.3(4)
criminal ~, 1088.2(6)
fox ~, 796.26
hired ~, 796.3(1,4)
insect ~, 796.27(1,2)
rat ~, 796.27(2-4)
rodent ~, 796.27(2-4)
wife ~, 796.3(2)
killing,adj., 796.4
killing,n., 796.2
~ and robbery in India, 796.2(13)
~ by drowning, 796.2(10)
~ by fire, 796.2(7)
capable of ~, 796.7
characterized by ~, 796.4,7,9
descr. of ~ with heavy losses to all, 796.9
guilty of ~, 796.8
harsh in ~, 889.12
involving ~, 796.7
merciless in ~, 889.12
mercy ~, 796.2(5)
~ of a brother, 796.21(3)
~ of a child, 796.21(2,4)
~ of Christ, 796.21(1)
~ of a daughter, 796.21(2)
~ of a father, 796.21(7,8)
~ of a fox, 796.25
~ of a god, 796.21(1)
~ of a husband, 796.21(5)
~ of an infant, 796.21(4)
~ of Jews, 796.2(11); 796.23
~ of a king, 796.21(7,9)
~ of a mother, 796.21(6,7)
~ of an older member of family, 796.21(7)
~ of a parent, 796.21(7)
~ of a prophet, 796.21(13)
~ of a racial, religious, etc., group, 796.23
~ of a ruler, 796.21(7,9)
~ of a sister, 796.21(3,10)
~ of a son, 796.21(2)
~ of a tyrant, 796.21(11)
~ of a wife, 796.21(12)
~ of a wolf, 796.24
place of ~, 796.19
place of confusion and ~, 605.16(5)
self-~, 795.1; see **suicide,n.**
substance for ~, 796.27; see also **poison,n.**
used for ~, 796.5
kin,n., 722.4
kind,adj., 842.1
~ act, 52.5(8,9,11,12,17,21)
be ~ to, 53.1(3); 842.4
~ in judging, 842.1(2)
~ in not punishing, 842.1(3,6)
polite and ~, 842.1(4)
~ to dependents, 842.1(1,4)
~ to guests, 842.1(5)
~ to inferiors, 842.1(1,4)
~ to strangers, 842.1(5)
kind,n., 312.1
of different ~s, 312.10-12
of no particular ~, 312.6
of several ~s, 312.10-12
of the same ~, 312.7-10
purest ~, 312.1(24)
kindness,n., 842.2
act of ~, 842.6
expressive of ~, 842.5
God's ~, 842.2(2)

show ~ to, 842.4
~ to dogs, 407.8
king,n., 1073.14; 1073.14(5,6,16, 18,19,22,29,30); see also **ruler,n.**
act or play the ~, 1073.26
authority or power of a ~, 1073.17(1)
daughter of a ~, 1073.21(7,8)
fit for a ~, 1073.23
governing in place of a ~, 1073.69
government by a ~, 1073.4(5)
like a ~, 1073.23
make a ~ of, 1073.24,25
mistress of a ~, 1073.21(12)
mother of a ~, 1073.21(11)
palace of a ~, 1073.30
pert. to a ~, 1073.22
private room of a ~, 1073.21(15)
reception by a ~, 1073.30
residence of a ~, 727.12(1,10)
~s, collectively, 1073.29
~'s throne, support of claim to by heredity, 1073.35
skill as a ~, 1073.96
son of a ~, 1073.21(1,4)
son of the British ~, 1073.21(6)
supremacy of ~s, 1073.34
time or period of a ~, 1073.70, 71
under the rule of a ~, 1075.2,3
widow of a ~, 1073.21(10,11)
wife of a ~, 1073.21(9)
kiss,n., 701.7
pert. to a ~, 701.8
kiss,v., 701.6
kissing,adj., 701.10
kissing,n.
pert. to ~, 701.9
study of ~, 701.11
kitchen,n.
pert. to the ~, 1061.29
ship's ~, 787.7(21)
small room off the ~, 787.7(33)
kith,n., 722.4
kitten,n., 406.2
group of ~s, 403.5(41)
knee,n.
bend the ~, 152.1(7,9)
bent like the ~, 152.5(5)
pert. to the ~, 345.22
standing with ~s bent in, 61.4(2)
kneel,v., 152.1(7)
kneecap,n., 345.23
knife,n., 332.9
~ maker, seller, etc., 332.12
surgical ~, 402.13
knife,v., 332.1(28)
knight,n.
contest of ~s, 20.2(13)
knit,v., 302.28; 307.1
knob,n., 958.7(5,8,9)
a swelling, 518.6
saddle ~, 958.7(10)
sword handle ~, 958.7(10)
knobby,adj., 958.8
swollen, 518.5
knock-kneed,adj., 345.7(4,8)
~ condition, 345.8
~ person, 345.9
knot,n.
full of ~s, 302.35
~ in rope, hair, thread, etc., 302.34
~ in wood, 997.12
know,n.
one in the ~, 612.8
know,v., 612.1
~ beforehand, 612.3
~ on seeing again, 612.4
knowable,adj., 612.7

knowing,adj.
~ about, 611.1
~ secrets, 971.36
knowing,n., 612.5; see also
knowledge,n.
process of ~, 612.5
product of ~, 612.6
knowledge,n., 611.2; see also
information, knowing,n.
able to apply ~, 611.18
abstract ~, 611.2(13)
addition to ~, 908.27
advanced region of ~,
782.1(8)
beyond human ~, 612.16,17;
see unknowable,adj.
body of ~, 611.2(10)
digest of ~, 611.11
divine ~, 611.2(1)
division of ~, 611.13
doctrine that ~ is uncertain,
612.22
esoteric ~, 611.2(3)
extensive in ~, 194.4(1)
gain ~, 612.2
hatred of ~, 880.17(7)
have ~ of, 612.1; see know,v.
having ~, 611.1
instinctive ~, 611.2(6)
means of ~, 611.17; 613.4
methodical view of ~, 611.14
object of ~, 611.8
~ of man's nature, 611.2(2)
~ of sacred things, 650.6
one who has ~, 612.8
one who has ~ of the world,
612.9
one who has secret ~, 612.15
pert. to ~, 611.7
pretension to all ~, 611.10
previous ~, 611.2(5,8)
pursuit of ~ by experiment,
19.9(2)
range of ~, 611.12
science of ~, 611.16
sphere of ~, 782.9
spread ~, 611.15
summary of ~, 611.11
superficial ~, 611.2(11,12)
theory that ~ is gained from
experience, 611.9
unexplored region of ~,
782.1(8)
without ~, 611.3; see ignorant,adj.
known,adj.
able to be ~, 612.7
become ~, 612.10
generally ~, 612.11
make ~, 613.1,17; see also
tell,v.
make faults, crimes, etc., ~,
613.8
make secrets ~, 613.9
not well ~, 612.14,15
~ only to a few, 612.14,15
~ to the mind, 612.12,13
unable to be ~, 612.16–18; see
unknowable,adj.
well-~, 615.1; see famous,adj.
widely ~, 612.11

L

L(the letter),n.
incorrect pronunciation of ~,
670.7(3)
label,n., 698.2
label,v., 698.1
labor,n., 203.4; see also work,n.
childbirth, 718.1; see childbirth,n.
one involved in ~ relations,
206.2
~ relations, concepts in, 206.1

~ union, 206.1,2
labor,v., 203.1; see work,v.
laborer,n., 203.7; see worker,n.
laborious,adj., 203.20,21
labyrinth,n., 605.17
lace,v., 302.28; 307.1
lack,n., 43.1; 919.15
causing ~, 43.4
indicating ~, 43.4
~ of a word, 43.1(6)
~ of enough, 43.1(11)
~ of money required, 43.1(4)
~ of motion, 59.2
~ of necessary things, 43.1(2,
3,10,12,14)
~ of parts, 43.1(6)
~ of prejudice, 636.2
~ of proper action, 43.1(13)
~ of proper conduct, 43.1(13)
~ of proper function, 43.1(13)
~ of required amount,
431.1(3)
lack,v., 43.3; 919.13
lacking,adj., 43.2; 919.10
necessary but ~ in supply,
273.6(4)
ladder,n.
like a ~, 160.21
scored like ~ steps, 160.21
step of a ~, 160.2
lady,n., 708.1; see also female,
girl, woman, women,n.
lake,n., 1029.53
animal life of ~s, science of,
985.36(12)
changes in ~ level, instrument to measure, 1029.61
developed in ~ level, on, or near a
~, 1029.57
~ for water storage, 262.3(22)
growing in or on ~s, 1029.56
like a ~, 1029.55
line from which a ~ has receded, 1029.84
living in or on ~s, 1029.56
movement of a ~, 1031.1
on the border of a ~, 1029.59
pert. to a ~, 1029.54
science of ~s, 1029.62
science of plant life of ~s,
985.36(12)
shelter built over a ~, prehistoric, 1029.58
lamb,n., 411.5
lame,adj., 107.8; 346.11(6,14)
cause to be ~, 346.14
~ person, 346.13
walk ~ly, 107.1(10,12); 346.15
lame,v., 13.1; 346.14
lameness,n., 346.12
~ in horses, 346.12(1)
lament,n., 1125.18,20
lament,v., 1125.10,13,17,19
lamentable,adj., 1125.14
~ happenings or circum-
stances, 1125.15
lamentation,n., 1125.18
pert. to ~, 1125.12
lamp,n., 1065.107
lamprey,n., 422.3
of ~s, 422.1(15)
land,n., 1003.2; see also earth,
soil,n.
add new ~, 908.28; 1003.16
added ~, 908.28–30
animal living both on ~ and
in water, 1026.24,25
arctic ~, 1003.2(42)
area of ~, 946.39
~ as property, 255.10(8,14–16)
border~, 1003.2(2)
border on ~, 1003.4
~ bordering sea, 1029.79
building, ~ around,
1003.2(11); 1003.17

come to ~, 999.6
consisting of ~, 1003.5
consisting of ~ and water,
1026.29
continuous ~, 1003.1;
1003.2(33,38,40,42,46)
country ~, 1003.2(13)
cultivated ~, 1003.2(41)
cut-off ~, 1003.2(3)
~ drained by river, 1029.46
dry ~, 1003.2(10)
fair distribution of ~,
1003.28,29
farming ~, 1003.2(8,9)
fertile ~ in a desert, 1003.12
feudal ~, 1003.17(6); 1074.8
flat ~, 1003.2(16,22,25–28,30,
37,42)
forest, ~ near a, 1003.2(32)
forest ~, 996.32
government-controlled ~,
1003.13
grass~, 986.15–20
grassy, treeless ~ of South
America, 1003.2(22)
growing in muddy ~, 1000.18
growing on ~, 1003.5
high ~, 166.1; 1003.2(7,27,28,
34,43,46); 1029.47(1,4)
high ~ jutting out into water,
1029.99
hills, ~ between, 1003.2(44)
history of ~, 1003.8
holding of ~, pert. to,
1003.18
hunting ~, 1003.2(17)
imaginary ~, 809.4
~ in reference to water,
1029.100
inhabitant of a ~, 1003.3
~ jutting out into water,
1029.98
layout of ~, 1003.7
level ~, 1003.2(16,22,25–28,30,
37,42)
line between ~ and sea,
1029.83
living in muddy ~, 1000.18
living on ~, 1003.5
living on ~ and water,
1026.23(1)
low~, 1003.2(15,44)
low~ reclaimed from the sea,
1029.100(9)
main body of ~, 1003.2(4,16)
mathematics of ~, 943.1(3)
measurement unit of ~,
946.38,40,41
military use, ~ as to,
1003.2(38)
mountain ~, 166.1(12)
mountains, ~ between,
1003.2(44)
muddy ~, 1000.14
narrow ~, 1003.2(18)
narrow strip of ~,
1029.100(5,14)
native of a ~, 1003.3
natural features of country
~, 1003.9,10
north~, 1003.2(19)
occupancy of ~ in return for
services, 255.2(7)
operating on ~ and water,
1026.23(1)
~ outside the main area of a
place, 1003.2(20)
~ over which water flows,
1029.100(15,16)
owned ~, 1003.17
owner of ~, 255.3(2); 1003.19,
21
owners of ~, 255.4
ownership of ~, 1003.18
owning ~, 1003.20

owning no ~, 1003.30
pert. to ~, 1003.6
physical features, ~ as to, 1003.2(38)
piece of ~, 1003.2,17
plant living both on ~ and in water, 1026.24,25
protected ~, 1003.2(31)
public ~, 1003.2(23) ; 1003.26, 27
raised ~, 166.1
renting (of ~ to tenants, 1003.20
rising (of ~), 159.4(1)
river ~, 1029.46,47
seller of ~ for others, 1003.25
separate ~, 1003.17
separate piece of ~, 1003.2(3, 14,24,29)
sloping ~, 1003.2(35)
south~, 1003.2(36)
stretch of ~, 1003.1; 1003.2(33, 38,40,42,46)
study ~, 1004.44
supply ~ with water, 1036.23–28
surface features of ~, 1003.7,8
surrounded by ~, 1029.72(7)
surrounded by foreign ~, 1003.13(2,3)
~ surrounded by water, 1029.100(4) ; see also is-land,n.
~ surrounded on three sides by water, 1029.100(8)
~ surrounded on two sides by water, 1029.100(5)
touch another ~, 1003.4
tract of ~, 1003.1,2
treeless ~, 1003.2(22,46)
uncultivated ~, 1003.2(12,45)
underwater ~, 1029.100(1–3,6, 7,12,13–16)
unexplored ~, 1003.2(39)
uninhabited ~, 1003.11(1)
unknown ~, 1003.2(39)
unproductive ~, 1003.11
waste~, 1003.11
wild ~, 1003.2(45)
without ~, 1003.30
landlord,n., 255.3(2) ; 1003.19
power of ~s in a state, 1003.23
~s, collectively, 255.4
~ system, 1003.22
landmark,n.
stone ~, 1006.19
landowner,n., 255.3(2) ; 1003.19, 21; see also landlord,n.
~ of riverbank, 1029.45
language,n., 664.1; see also dialect, speech,n.
absurd ~, use of, 665.9(24)
abusive ~, 561.2,8; 1118.14,15
affected ~, 664.1(19)
appropriate ~, use of, 665.9(19)
approved in ~, 850.17
attack in ~, 561.1–11
bitter in ~, 877.6
boastful ~, 665.9(58,61)
book in two ~s, 687.1(10)
business ~, 664.1(3,4,9,11,12, 15,16,27)
coarse ~, 1118.14,15
common ~, 664.1(12)
commonplace ~, 665.9(2,9,24, 40)
confusion of ~s, 605.13(2) ; 664.3
conversational ~, 664.1(27) ; 665.9(14)
correct in ~, 815.14(3)
curses, ~ containing, 882.2
cutting ~, 868.2(2)

deaf-and-dumb ~, 664.11(3) ; 951.15
defamatory ~, 891.18
descr. of ~, 664.2
dignified in ~, 951.49
dirty ~, 713.3; 904.16; 1118.14
disconnected ~, 665.9(29)
disgusting ~, 1118.14; 1118.15(1,2) ; 1118.19,20
disrespectful ~ to God, 861.10
economy of ~, 665.9(8,15,16, 39,48,51,53)
elegant ~, 664.1(19) ; 665.9(6, 18,20,21,24,25,33,35,36,42,50, 54–56,58,61)
elegant in ~, 665.10(5)
emotional ~, 665.9(45) ; 1092.37,70
emotional in ~, 665.10(1)
empty ~, 665.9(58)
enthusiastic ~, 1095.16
esoteric ~, 665.10(4)
express in ~, 665.1
expressed in many ~s, 664.9
expression in ~, 665.2
expression in ~, art of, 665.5
expressive in ~, 665.3
figures of speech, ~ full of, 951.48
filthy ~, 713.3; 904.16; 1118.14
finger ~, 664.11(3) ; 951.15
fluency of ~, 665.9(59)
foreign ~, passages for learn-ing a, 682.20(1)
formal ~, 665.9(7)
frank ~, 665.9(10)
French ~, 664.4(16)
French ~ in Louisiana, 664.4(5)
frivolous ~, 665.9(31)
~ from Latin, 664.4(16)
~ full of sayings, 665.9(48)
Hebrew ~, 664.7(12)
humiliating ~, 868.17
illiterate ~, 664.1(15)
illogical ~, 665.9(29)
impolite ~, 665.9(26)
impressive ~, 665.9(25,33,50)
impressive in ~, 665.10(3)
~ in rhyme, 664.1(17)
inability to use or understand ~, 671.21,22
indirect ~, 665.9(11,38)
informal ~, 664.1(27,28)
insincere ~, 664.1(3,16) ; 665.9(57)
lawyer ~, 1085.12
libelous ~, 891.18
literary ~, 665.9(7)
lived in by people of many ~s, 750.7(1)
lofty ~, 665.9(25,33) ; 951.49
logical ~, 665.9(13)
meaningless ~, 607.24; 664.1(3,7) ; see also non-sense,n.
native ~, 664.1(13,27)
newspaper ~, 664.1(10)
obscene ~, 713.3; 904.16; 1118.14
~ of Belgium, 664.4(19)
~ of criminals, 664.1(3)
~ of Eskimos, 664.4(10)
~ of France, 664.4(16)
~ of Greece, 664.4(2,15)
~ of gypsies, 664.4(17)
~ of Hebrews, 664.7(12)
~ of India, 664.4(8,9,18)
~ of Italy, 664.4(16)
~ of Mediterranean ports, 664.4(11)
~ of Portugal, 664.4(16)
~ of Spain, 664.4(3,16)

~ of the arts, 664.1(23)
~ of thieves, 664.1(1,3)
~ of tramps, 664.1(1)
~ of Turkey, 664.4(13)
~ of varying tones, 664.5
~ of Wales, 664.4(6,20)
offensive ~, 868.2(2) ; 1118.14, 15,17–20
offensive in ~, 1118.15
official ~, 664.1(7) ; 1077.22
opposite meaning, ~ of, 868.2(2)
ordinary ~, 664.1(18,27,28)
original ~, 664.1(26)
ornamented ~, 951.48
ostentatious in ~, 951.48,49
parent ~, 664.1(26)
persuasive ~, 665.9(12,57)
pert. to ~, 664.2
picturesque ~, 665.9(28)
pretentious ~, 665.9(61)
pretentious in ~, 951.49
professional ~, 664.1(3,9,11,15, 16,27)
roundabout ~, 665.9(11,38)
sarcastic ~, 665.9(30)
scandalous ~, 891.18
science of ~, 664.11
scientific ~, 664.1(23)
secret ~, 664.1(3,5) ; 971.8
sentimental ~, 665.9(27,49) ; 1094.3
sharp in ~, 333.4(2,4–7) ; 334.1(1,6–8,12,22) ; 876.22
showy ~, 664.1(19,20) ; 665.9(50)
showy ~, use of, 665.9(6,18,20, 21,24,25,35–37,54–56,61)
showy in ~, 665.10(2,3,5) ; 951.48,49
sign ~, 951.12
simplified ~, 664.1(9,11)
skillful in ~, 7.2(3)
sounds of a ~, 670.10–14
speaker of many ~s, 664.10
speaking four ~s, 664.8(6)
speaking many ~s, 664.8(3–7)
speaking three ~s, 664.8(7)
speaking two ~s, 664.8(1,2)
special ~, 664.1(3,6,8,11,15,16, 21,27)
specific ~s, 664.4
spoken ~, 664.1(22,25,27,28)
stinging in ~, 333.4(2,4–7) ; 334.1(1,6–8,12,22) ; 876.22
strength of ~, 1.19
strictness in ~ correctness, 664.13
student of ~, 664.12
substandard ~, 664.1(21,28)
substandard ~, use of, 665.9(1)
synthetic ~s, 664.7
telegram ~, 664.1(24)
unacceptable ~, 664.1(21,28)
unclear ~, 665.9(34)
unending ~, 665.9(60)
unrefined ~, 664.1(21,28)
use ambiguous ~, 603.9
use of ~, 665.8–10
vile ~, 891.17
vulgar ~, 664.1(2)
wordy ~, 664.1(7) ; 665.9(32, 41,44,52,54,55)
lapel,n., 977.5
large,adj., 906.3; see also big, adj.
dignified and ~, 846.4
lariat,n., 302.32(14)
lark,n.
group of ~s, 403.5(2,6,22)
larva,n., 428.4
larynx,n.
inflammation of the ~, 364.13(1)

produced in the ~, 364.4
lascivious,adj., 709.8; 712.1;
  713.1
lasciviousness,n., 709.7; 712.2;
  713.2
lasso,n., 302.32(12)
last,adj., 792.15; see also **final**,
  adj.
  ~-mentioned, 792.17
  next to the ~, 792.21
  ~ possible, 792.16
  ~ possible thing, 792.23(9)
  preceding the next to the ~,
    792.22
  something ~, 792.23(3,9)
last,v., 754.1; see **continue**,v.
lasting,adj., 754.3; see **continuing**,adj.
  permanent, 754.11
  ~ for a short time, 756.1; see
    temporary,adj.
  not ~, 756.1; see **temporary**,
    adj.
late,adj., 767.1
  assigning dates that are too
    ~, 774.12,15
  be ~, 767.3
  come in ~, 767.4
  coming ~, 767.1(2)
  habitually ~, 767.1(3,6,7)
  stays up ~ at night, one who,
    778.6
latent,adj.
  becoming ~, 970.46
later,adj., 767.2
  come in ~, 767.4
  coming ~, 767.1(2)
  put off to a ~ time, 768.1,8;
    see **delay**,v.
  ~ time, 762.1(3)
latest,adj., 767.5
lather,n., 899.44
lather,v., 899.46,47
Latin,n.
  language from ~, 664.4(16)
laugh,n., 1111.2
  say with a ~, 1111.5
laugh,v., 1111.1
  ability to ~, 1111.11
  able to ~, 1111.10
  ~ at in contempt, 1111.20,21
  ~ at in disparagement, 840.5
  cause to ~, 1111.23,24
  caused to ~, 1111.25
  feeling a desire to ~, 1111.25
  not to be ~ed at, 1111.37
  ~ secretly, 1111.34
  ~ to oneself, 1111.34
  used in ~ing, 1111.16
laughable,adj., 1111.24; 1113.1;
  see also **comic, funny, humorous**,adj.
  ~ act, remark, thing, etc.,
    1113.3
  appreciation of what is ~,
    1113.11
  behave or act in a ~ manner,
    1113.4
  ~ behavior, 1113.5,6
  both serious and ~, 1113.9
  ~ happening, 1113.8
  ~ part of life or art, 1113.7
  ~ pictures, 1113.10
  responsiveness to what is ~,
    1113.12
  unappreciative of what is ~,
    1113.13
laughableness,n., 1113.2; see
  also **humor**,n.
laugher,n., 1111.4
laughing,adj., 1111.6
laughter,n., 1111.3
  alternating ~ and weeping,
    1111.9
  causing ~, 1111.24; 1113.1

change from ~ to sadness,
  1111.32
drive, force, put, or bring by
  ~, 1111.28
express contempt by ~,
  1111.35
expressive of ~, 1111.17
fit of ~ and weeping, 1100.10
fit of violent ~, 1111.8
full of ~, 1111.7
given to ~, 1111.10–12
given to nervous or silly ~,
  1111.12
hearty ~, descr. of, 1111.15
ignore by ~, 1111.31
object of contemptuous ~,
  1111.22
pert. to ~, 1111.13,14
reject argument of by ~,
  1111.30
send away by ~, 1111.30
silence with ~, 1111.29
sound of ~, 1111.18
suggestive of ~, 1111.36
without ~, 1111.38
worthy of contemptuous ~,
  1111.21
lava,n.
  glass from ~, 1009.52
  loose ~, 1006.1(39)
  mountain or hill of ~,
    166.1(30)
lavish,adj., 229.1; see **generous**,
  adj.
law,n., 1079
  a ~, 1079.1,2
  adherence to ~, 56.5(2,3) ;
    1079.23,24
  adherence to religious ~,
    1079.25
  administration of the ~,
    1081.19–21
  authority to make ~s, 5.4(13)
  based on ~, 1079.16
  behavior based on moral ~,
    843.5
  body of ~, 1079.5
  book of Jewish ~, 648.1(18)
  break a ~, 802.29–32
  ~ breaker, 1087.5
  ~ breaker, defiant, 1087.9
  breaking of the ~, habitual,
    1087.6
  brought about by ~, 1079.14
  by ~, 1079.17
  ~ case, 1082.1; see **lawsuit**,n.
  cause by ~s, 1080.2
  clarifies the ~ in court, one
    who, 1082.33
  constitutional ~, 1079.10–13
  contrary to ~, 1087.1; see
    illegal,adj.
  ~ court, 1081; see **court (of
    law)**,n.
  defiance of the ~, 1087.10
  deprive of the protection of
    the ~, 1087.22
  disregard of the ~, 1087.10
  ~-enforcement officers,
    1077.3(2) ; 1078.2; 1085.5;
    see **police**,n.
  equality of ~s, 1079.35
  expert in ~, 1079.29
  external ~, dependent on,
    1073.82
  freedom from ~, 309.14(12,13)
  ~-giving, 1080.6
  go to ~, 1082.11
  lack of ~, 1073.103
  make a ~, 1080.1,4,5
  make into a ~, 1080.3
  ~ maker, 1080.8
  ~ making body, 1080.10; see
    legislature,n.

~ making, 1080.6,7; see **legislation**,n.
natural ~, application of in
  legal disputes, 1081.22
not break the ~, 1140.35
obedient to ~, 1079.26
~ officers, 1077.3(2) ; 1078.2;
  1085.5; see also **police**,n.
opposition of ~s, 544.2(2)
opposition to ~s, 544.2(6)
permitted by ~, 1079.18
pert. to ~, 1079.8,9
philosophy of ~, 1079.34
poor enforcement of ~, descr.
  of place of, 1087.11
prevent ~ breaking, 1140.35
proposed ~, 1080.9
provision of ~, 1079.3
puritanical ~s, 1079.5(2)
recognized under ~, 1079.15
religious ~, 1079.5(12)
remove from authority of the
  ~, 1087.23
right to vote on ~s, 254.1(4)
~s, 1079.5
~s regulating government,
  1079.5(9)
scholar of the ~, 1079.30
science of ~, 1079.27
science of ~ and medicine,
  401.1(21,37,42)
science of universal ~, pert.
  to, 1079.28
skilled in the ~, 1079.31
student of the ~, 1079.32
student of church ~, 1029.32
student of Jewish ~, 648.5(3)
system of ~s, 1079.5
systematize the ~s, 1079.6,7
temperance ~s, 749.67,68
textbook of ~, 1079.33
unchangeable ~, 1079.4
voting as to ~s, 254.5(4)
without ~s, 1087.26
writer on ~, 1079.30
law court,n., 1081; see **court
  (of law)**,n.
lawful,adj., 1079.18,26; see
  legal,adj.
lawless,adj., 1087.1; see also **illegal**,adj.
  ~ area of a city, 883.36
  cruel and ~, 889.1(7)
  ~ disorder, 1087.27
  rough and ~, 865.1(4,10–12)
lawsuit,n., 1082.1
  able to be settled or tried in
    a ~, 1082.31,32
  application of natural law
    in ~s, 1081.22
  basis for a ~, 1082.3
  bring a ~, 1082.11
  dismissed ~, 1082.34
  dispute a ~, 1082.21
  famous ~, 1082.6
  furnishing cause for a ~,
    1082.2
  hear and render judgment on
    a ~, 1082.8,9
  illegal aid in the prosecution
    of a ~, 1082.38
  involved in a ~, 1082.22
  liable to a ~, 1082.2
  matter to be judged in a ~,
    1082.5
  persistent bringing of ~s,
    1082.35
  person against whom a ~ is
    brought, 1082.24
  person involved in a ~,
    1082.23
  person who brings a ~,
    1082.27
  person who persistently
    brings ~s, 1082.36

person who presses a ~,
1082.16
prone to bring ~s, 1082.30,37
start and carry on a ~,
1082.12,14
statements made in a ~,
1082.28,29
what happens in a ~, 1082.4
lawyer,n., 1085.1
act as ~, 1085.2
~ as adviser, 1085.14,15
body of ~s, 1085.6
British ~, 1085.3
~ for the accused, 1082.25
~ for the defendant, 1082.25
government ~, 1085.5
language of ~s, 1085.12
like ~s, 1085.13
military or naval ~, 1085.4
profession of ~s, 1085.8,9
~s in a case, 1085.6
~s of a community, 1085.7
spirit, attitude, etc., of ~s,
1085.11
lax,adj.
loose, 304.1
not strict, 890.12
laxative,n., 293.16(1,2,4-7,9-13)
take a ~, 293.18
treat with a ~, 400.1(4)
lay,adj., 207.3
lay,v., 323.1
layer,n., 315.1
arrange in ~s, 311.2(9) ;
315.4(2)
arrangement in ~s, 311.1(40)
be in ~s, 315.6
break into ~s, 315.3 ; 802.1(15)
cover with a ~, 972.1(12,23,24,
31,45,56)
cover with ~s, 315.4(1,3)
covered with ~s, 972.5(7)
external ~, 972.4(21)
form into ~s, 315.4(1,2) ; 315.5
germ ~s of an embryo, 315.2
having ~s, like rock, 1006.27,
29
~ of rock, 315.1(8,9)
~ of society, 315.1(9)
outer ~, 138.2(4)
split into thin ~s, 315.3
layman,n., 207.1
pert. to a ~, 207.3
state of being a ~, 207.2
laymen,n., 207.4
controlled by ~, 207.3(1)
put under the control of ~,
207.5
lazily,adv.
spend time ~, 762.17,18
laziness,n., 209.2
lazy,adj., 209.1
be ~, 209.4
~ person, 209.3
lead (metal),n., 1018.1
cover, line, treat, or weight
with ~, 1018.3
like ~, 1018.2(2,5)
of the color, heaviness, or
inertness of ~, 1018.2(2)
poisoning by ~, 1018.4,5
relating to ~, 1018.2
weight made of ~, 947.15(4) ;
947.17
lead,v., 176.1; see also guide,v.
~ by coaxing, 176.1(8)
~ by deception, 176.1(8) ;
823.4
~ into a trap, 176.1(6)
~ into danger, 176.1(2,6)
~ into error, 176.1(2,10,13)
~ into sin, 176.1(2,10,13)
serving to ~, 176.5
that which ~s, 176.4
leader,n., 176.3

discussion ~, 176.3(4,5,10)
false ~, 176.2(1)
German ~, 176.6(11,12)
group ~, 176.3(6-13,16,18,19)
inclined to follow a ~, 178.6
military ~, 176.3(3,6-8)
mob ~, 176.3(1)
nazi ~, 176.6(11,12)
~ of a tribe or clan,
1073.14(2)
~ of sheep, 176.3(1,14)
without a ~, 176.6
leadership,n., 176.2
false ~, 176.2(1)
nation's political ~, 176.2(2)
leading,adj., 176.5
~ participant, 51.6
leading,n., 176.2
false ~, 176.2(1)
pert. to ~, 176.5
leaf,n., 993; see also leaves,n.
~ arrangement, 993.24
broad part of a ~, 993.9
in the form of a ~, 507.17(42)
like a ~, 993.22
like a fern ~, 993.4
~ mass, 993.7
~ of a fern, 993.2
~ of grain, 993.1
~ of grass, 993.1
of the color, form, or texture
of a ~, 993.23
pert. to ~ production, 993.19
shape like a ~, 993.20
shaped like a ~, 993.21
shaped like a fern ~, 993.5
withering but not falling off
(of a ~), 806.18,19
leafy,adj., 993.22
~ shelter, 993.10,11
leak,n., 140.2,3
spring a ~, 140.7
leak,v., 140.1
lean,adj., 513.1; see thin,adj.
lean,v., 153.1
cause to ~, 153.2
leaning,adj., 153.4
leaning,n., 153.3
leap,n., 110.2; see also jump,n.
~ of a horse, 104.1(3)
leap,v., 110.1; see jump,v.
learn,v.
find out, 624.1; see discover,v.
study, 622.1
create a desire to ~ in, 622.12
eager to ~, 622.11
quick to ~, 594.4 ; 622.10
learned,adj., 622.14
~ people, 622.18
~ person, 622.17,19
~ teacher, 622.17(7)
~ woman, 622.17(5)
learnedness,n., 622.15
learner,n., 622.5; see also student,n.
beginning ~, 622.5(1)
~ by practical experience,
622.5(3)
fellow ~, 622.5(11)
~ in religion, 622.5(13)
new ~, 622.5(22)
~ of church doctrines,
622.5(7)
self-~, 622.5(4)
learning,n., 622.13
Babylonian ~, person versed
in, 622.19
excessive display of ~, 622.20
fondness for ~, 700.31(3)
indicative of ~, 622.16
institution of ~, 623.1; see
school,n.
occult ~, pert. to, 1053.37
pert. to ~, 622.16
pert. to occult ~, 622.16(1)

trait, expression, etc., showing off one's ~, 622.22
lease,v., 281.1
leather,n., 386.1
~ for bookbinding, 386.4
imitation ~, 386.14
like ~, 386.8
made of ~, 386.9
make into ~, 386.11,12
place for manufacture of ~,
386.10
soap for ~, 386.18
strip of ~, 302.32(3,10,15,21,
24) ; 386.6
untanned ~, 386.15
use ~, 386.13
leathery,adj., 386.8
leave,v., 141.1; see also depart,
desert,v.
~ a country, 141.1(16,19,23)
~ a group, 141.1(31,37)
~ (a place), 141.1
~ (a ship), 141.1(7,12)
~ (a train), 141.1(10)
~ an office, 141.1(2,27)
cause to ~, 144.1
cause to ~ the protection of,
144.1(29)
force to ~, 144.1
leave of absence,n., 42.1(3,5,6,7,
9)
military ~, 42.1(5)
naval ~, 42.1(7)
leaver,n., 141.3
leaves,n., 993.7; see also leaf,n.
~ and stems, 993.8
~ as food, 740.6
circle of ~, 993.25
coating on ~, 972.4(3)
cover with ~, 972.1(4,50)
cover, shelter, or surround by
~, 993.13
covered with ~, 972.5(5) ;
993.12,14
fallen ~ used to protect a
plant, 993.27
fern ~, 993.3
fiber from palm ~, for weaving, 993.29
having ~, 993.14-16
having fern ~, 993.6
like ~, 993.22
lose ~, 993.26
ornament with ~, 959.1(14)
protect with ~, 972.1(4)
remove ~ from, 993.26
roof of ~, 973.1(10)
shelter of ~, 993.10,11
sheltered by ~, 993.12
sound of ~ moving, 469.1(16,
18-20)
sprout ~, 993.18
without ~, 993.17
leaving,adj., 141.4
leaving,n., 141.2; see also departure,n.
means of ~, 50.1(3)
leavings,n., 757.4
lecher,n., 709.9; 712.3
lecherous,adj., 709.8; 712.1
lechery,n., 709.7; 712.2
lecture,n., 671.2
~ on foreign or unusual
places, 968.12
lecture,v., 671.1; see talk,
teach,v.
lecturer,n., 621.7(2) ; 671.3
leech,n., 427.8
like a ~, 427.10
of ~es, 427.9
raising of ~es, 403.30(4)
leek,n.
of the ~ family, 985.33(2)
left (direction),adj.

able to tell the right hand from the ~, 343.16
able to use the ~ or right hand equally well, 343.15
~-handed, 343.11
~-handed person, 343.13
~-handedness, 343.12
on the ~, 179.23(3)
pert. to the ~, 179.23(4)
preferring the ~ hand, 343.14
toward or pert. to the ~ of a ship, 179.23(1,2)
toward the ~, 179.23(3,4) ; 179.24
turning toward the ~, 148.2(7)
left (remaining),adj., 757.5; see also **remaining,adj.**
mark ~ by passing person, animal, or thing, 757.6
what is ~ after destruction, 801.38
what is ~ over, 757.4; see **remains,n.**
leg,n., 345.1; 345.12(3)
armor for the ~, 979.22
condition of ~s, 345.8
covering for the ~, 979.21
having crooked ~s, 345.7(1)
having inwardly curving ~s, 345.7(4,8)
having long ~s, 345.7(5,6)
having outwardly curving ~s, 345.7(1,3,8,9)
having three ~s, 345.7(7)
having two ~s, 345.7(2)
parts of the ~, 345.4
person's ~s, 345.3
person with bow~s, 345.9
person with ~s curved inward, 345.9
pert. to the ~, 345.5
pert. to the calf of the ~, 345.6
sit with the ~s spread apart, 62.1(13)
with one ~ on each side, 345.10
with the ~s crossed, 345.11
with the ~s far apart, 345.10
wooden ~, 345.2
legal,adj., 1079.15,16,18,22,26
~ adviser, 1085.14,15
arguments in a ~ action, 1082.26,28,29
ask for ~ action, 1082.17
bringer of a ~ action, 1082.27
carry on ~ action, 1082.15,16
declare ~, 1079.19
~ dispute, 1082.1; see **lawsuit,n.**
give ~ organization to, 1079.21
give ~ power to, 1079.20
having ~ force, 3.8
lacking in ~ force, 17.1(24) ; 1087.20,21
make ~, 1079.19
start and carry on ~ action, 1082.12–14
take ~ action, 1082.11
try to get or enforce by ~ action, 1082.18
legend,n.
story, 685.1(11,15) ; see also **myth,n.**
unreality, 809.3; see **unreality,n.**
collection of ~s, 682.19(7,9) ; 685.2
study or science of ~s, 685.7
teller or writer of ~s, 685.5
legendary,adj., 809.1; see also **mythical, unreal,adj.**

legislation,n., 1080; see also **law,n.**
hindrance of ~, 557.6
influence ~, 9.12
legislator,n., 1080.8,11,13,19,21, 22–25
~ in control of others in party, 1080.26,27
legislature,n., 1080.10
a meeting of the ~, 322.1(13, 21,27,33)
adjourning without decision to meet again (of a ~), 768.13
building in which the ~ sits, 727.12(3)
delay the meeting of a ~, 768.8(7)
engage in delaying in a ~, 768.1(2)
expert in procedures of a ~, 1080.15
having a ~ of one house, 1080.17
having a ~ of two houses, 1080.16
lower house of a ~, 1080.20
meeting place of a ~, 1080.14
member of a ~, 1080.11,13,19, 21,22–27
~ of Canada, 1080.18(7) ; 1080.20(3)
~ of Denmark, 1080.12(8)
~ of England, 1080.12(6) ; 1080.18(3) ; 1080.20(3)
~ of European countries, 1080.20(2,3)
~ of France, 1080.12(5) ; 1080.18(7) ; 1080.20(2)
~ of Germany, 1080.12(7) ; 1080.18(1,6) ; 1080.20(6)
~ of Holland, 1080.12(10) ; 1080.18(2) ; 1080.20(4)
~ of Japan, 1080.12(4) ; 1080.18(4)
~ of Norway, 1080.12(11)
~ of Portugal, 1080.12(3) ; 1080.18(5)
~ of South American countries, 1080.18(7)
~ of Spain, 1080.12(3)
~ of Sweden, 1080.12(9)
~ of Switzerland, 1080.12(1) ; 1080.18(8) ; 1080.20(5)
~ of U.S., 1080.12(2) ; 1080.18(7) ; 1080.20(4)
~ of U.S. state or city, 1080.20(1)
room in which a ~ sits, 787.7(14)
upper house of a ~, 1080.18
leisure,n., 209.12
~ group, 318.1(85)
lemon,n.
descr. of ~s, 745.22(4)
raising of ~s, 745.25(1)
~ tree, 996.4(4)
lend,v.
~ money, 218.11
~ property, 281.1
lender,n., 281.3
money~, 218.9; 1122.42
lending,n., 281.2; see **loan,n.**
length,n., 913; see also **distance, measurement, size,n.**
ancient unit of ~, 946.26(5)
continuous ~, 788.1(12)
time ~, 913.7,8
unit of ~, 946.26,27
lengthen,v., 913.1; see also **increase,v.**
~ tediously, 913.3
~ time, 913.1
~ undesirably, 913.2

~ unexpectedly, 913.2
~ unnecessarily, 913.3,4
lengthening,n., 913.1
syllable in poetry, ~ of, 911.16
leniency,n., 890.12; 1143.2; 1144.2
lenient,adj., 890.12; 1143.1; 1144.1
~ act, 897.36; 1143.4,5
~ in judgment, 890.15
~ in punishment, 897.35
~ treatment, 1143.4,5
lens,n., 480.16
big through a ~, 906.22
maker, seller, or grinder of ~es, 480.20
leopard,n.
group of ~s, 403.5(43)
leprosy,n., 382.11(23)
hospital for ~, 382.15
medication for ~, 398.6(4)
person with ~, 382.13
science of ~, 401.1(38)
Lesbian,n., 710.34
Lesbianism,n., 710.33(28,35) ; see also **homosexuality,n.**
less,adj.
become ~, 910.2
~ by subtraction, 910.19
make ~, 910.1
~ than natural, 910.18
lessen,v.
decrease, 910.1,2; see **decrease,v.**
decrease in force, harshness, severity, etc., 1142.1,10; see also **weaken,v.**
lessening,adj., 910.4; 1142.2,11
lesser,adj., 910.17
lesson,n., 622.3
practical ~ in a story or fable, 622.3(6)
let,v., 554.1; see **permit,v.**
lethargic,adj., 58.1; 1097.3,17
make ~, 1097.20
letter (communication),n., 678.1
added thought written at end of a ~, 682.3(14)
art of writing ~s, 678.11
contained in ~s, 678.9
love ~, 678.1(1)
Pope's ~, 678.1(3)
~s, 678.2
"thank you" ~, 1110.9
write ~s, 678.3,4
writer of ~s, 678.8
writing of ~s, 678.5–7,10
letter (written symbol),n., 679.1
antique ~, 966.5(1)
Assyrian ~s, 679.4(5) ; 679.6,7
capital ~, 679.1(14,20)
capital ~s, written in, 679.19
change into another kind of ~s, 679.18
consisting of four ~s, 679.16(3)
consisting of one ~, 679.16(2)
consisting of three ~s, 679.16(4)
consisting of two ~s, 679.16(1)
curved shape of a ~, 677.10
diacritical marks over ~s, 680.1
Egyptian ~, 679.1(7)
fancy shape of a ~, 677.11
first ~ of a word or name, 679.1(9)
~ in flowing handwriting, 679.1(6)
large ~, 679.1(2,14,20)
line at top or bottom of a

printed ~, 679.20
~ of speech sound, 670.21
omission of ~s, 666.22–24;
  911.1(1,6,16)
ornament a ~, 1065.76
Persian ~s, 679.4(5); 679.6,7
pert. to ~s, 679.5
pictorial ~, 679.1(8,17)
print in certain ~s, 679.2
representation by ~s, 679.3
~s, 679.4
secret ~, 679.1(5,7)
secret ~s, 679.4(2–4); 683.3–
  10
shorthand ~, 679.1(18)
slanting ~, 679.1(10)
small ~, 679.1(13,15)
sound, ~ standing for a,
  679.1(16)
syllable, ~ standing for a,
  679.1(16)
system of ~s, 679.4; see also
  alphabet,n.
Teutonic ~ (ancient),
  679.1(19)
the ~ &, 679.1(1)
the ~ Z, 679.1(11)
transposition of ~s, 679.17
vowel, use of a ~ as a, 679.8
wedge-shaped ~s, 679.4(5);
  679.6,7
word, ~ standing for a,
  679.1(12,16)
level,adj., 519.1; see flat,adj.
lever,n., 8.4
  support on which a ~ turns,
  1022.2(10)
lewd,adj., 709.8; 712.1; 713.1;
  see also obscene,adj.
lewdness,n., 709.7; 712.2; 713.2
liar,n., 821.4
  descr. of ~s, 821.11
libel,n., 891.18
libel,v., 891.17
libelous,adj., 891.19
liberal,adj.
  generous, 229.1
  unprejudiced, 636.1
  ~ arts of Middle Ages, 623.16
  become ~, 636.7
  make ~, 636.7
liberal (in politics),n.,
  1076.12(1,14,19)
liberate,v., 309.1,11; see free,v.
liberation,n., 309.2,3,14; see
  freedom, freeing,n.
liberator,n., 309.4
liberty,n., 309.3,14; see freedom,n.
  take undue ~, 862.1,9
librarian,n., 687.16
library,n., 687.15
  head of a ~, 8.16(3,4)
lice,n.
  infested with ~, 403.18(2,3,7)
  of ~, 428.1(18); see also
  louse,n.
license,n.
  document, 554.8
  freedom, 309.14
  permission, 554.2
  one who has a ~, 554.9
license,v., 554.1
lichen,n.
  science of ~s, 985.36(13)
lie (falsehood),n., 821.1
  a ~ to save another's
  feelings, 821.1(3)
  ~ about a political candidate,
  821.1(2)
  tell a ~, 821.2
  telling a ~, 821.3
  tremendous ~, 821.1(4)
  trivial ~, 821.1(1,3)
lie (recline),v., 65.1

~ along the boundary of,
  65.1(2,15)
~ along the edge of, 65.1(2,
  15)
~ calm, 1139.12
~ close, 65.1(5,9,10,16)
~ close to the ground,
  65.1(18)
~ down, moving limbs
  awkwardly, 65.1(17)
~ down to sleep, 65.1(13)
~ face downward, 65.1(6)
~ flat, 65.1(11)
~ in bed during courtship,
  65.1(3)
~ in blood, 1034.27
~ in concealment, 970.32
~ in concealment for evil
  purpose, 970.32
~ in concealment waiting to
  attack, 970.33
~ in humbleness, 65.1(6)
~ in the mud, 65.1(12)
~ in the warmth of, 65.1(1)
~ in water, 1034.27
~ lazily, 65.1(7,8)
~ next to, 790.17–21
~ relaxedly, 65.1(7)
~ soaked, 1035.19
~ soaking wet, 65.1(19)
~ spread out, 195.1
~ touching, 790.17–21
~ upon to cover, 972.1(32)
lie (tell a lie),v., 821.2
  compulsion to ~, 821.7
  ~ under oath, 821.2(5)
lied-about,adj., 821.10
life,n., 751.1
  ~ after death, 751.1(1)
  bring back to ~, 751.18
  come back to ~, 751.21
  come to ~, 751.19
  course of ~, 751.2
  easygoing ~, 751.1(2)
  everlasting ~, 751.1(3)
  explanation of ~, 751.9,10
  extension of ~, alchemist's
  preparation for, 1013.28
  fidelity to ~ in art or
  literature, 807.11,12
  ~ force, etc., 751.4
  full of ~, 1.12; 752.1; see
  also lively,adj.
  get new ~, 751.20
  give ~ to, 751.16
  give new ~ to, 751.17
  hatred of ~, 880.17(13)
  length of ~, 751.3
  length of ~, calculation of,
  751.15
  made up of two forms of ~,
  326.47(3)
  origin of ~, theories of,
  728.17(5–9)
  pert. to ~, 751.5
  philosophy of purpose of ~,
  751.10
  previous to ~ on earth, pert.
  to time, 763.3
  primitive ~, pert. to,
  751.8
  prolong ~, substance to,
  751.11
  resemblance to real ~,
  529.8
  rising to ~ from death,
  751.23,24
  sacrifice of one's ~, 795.1(2);
  795.7
  science of ~ and environment,
  751.13(5)
  science of social ~, 751.13(4,
  7)
  sciences of ~, 751.13
  similar to real ~, 751.6,7

simple ~, pert. to, 751.8
story of one's own ~,
  682.16(4,40)
story of someone's ~,
  682.16(6)
substance of ~, 751.12
take the ~ out of, 796.18
theories of ~, 728.17; 751.9;
  1089.4
theory of creation of ~,
  1089.4(1)
without ~, 794.42,43,45–48;
  see also dead, lifeless,adj.
lifeless,adj., 794.42,43,45–48
  dull and ~, 794.49
  figuratively ~, 794.44,48
lift,v., 163.1; see raise,v.
light,adj., 949.1
  able to move ~ly, 90.4
  ~ as air, 949.1(1,2,4)
  delicate and ~, 949.1(4)
  ~ fingers, 949.10
  graceful and ~, 949.6
  ~ in appearance, 949.1
  ~ in humor, 949.12
  ~ in irony, 949.12
  ~ in movement, 90.3; 949.7,8
  ~ in step, 949.7(5–7)
  ~ in style, 949.12
  ~ in touch, 949.11
  ~ in walk, 949.7(5–7)
  ~ in weight, 949.1
  insubstantial and ~, 949.1(2,
  4,6,7)
  ~ly moving thing, 949.9
  move ~ly, 90.1
  ~ movement, 90.2
  person ~ in weight, 949.3
  ~-skinned, 384.7–10
  unimportant and ~, 949.1(5)
light,n., 1065.49
  a ~, 1065.49
  admit ~, unable to, 1065.94,95
  admitting ~ completely,
  1065.92,93
  admitting ~ incompletely,
  1065.90
  admitting ~ when wet,
  1034.33
  amount or strength of ~,
  1065.77,106
  ~ around head of saint, etc.,
  1065.25
  ~ around heavenly body,
  1065.21–24
  ~ around moon, 1065.21–24
  ~ around sun, 1065.21–24
  artificial ~, 1065.49(4,13)
  atmospheric ~, 1065.1
  automobile ~, 1065.107(10,19–
  21)
  bewilder with ~s, 1065.78
  bringing ~, 1065.82
  candle ~, 1065.49(4)
  celestial ~, 1065.1
  chemical action of ~, pert.
  to, 1065.97
  chemistry of ~, 1065.102(6)
  device that gives ~, 1065.107
  dim ~, 1065.49(6)
  dim (vision) with ~s, 1065.78
  display of ~s, 1065.75
  distance traveled by ~,
  788.1(6); 946.26(11,16)
  effect of ~ and shade in a
  picture, 488.7
  electric ~, 1065.107
  fire ~, 1065.49(7,8)
  flash ~, 1065.107(18)
  flood ~, 1065.107(13,19)
  gas ~, 1048.25; 1065.49(11)
  give ~, 1065.45
  give ~ to, 1065.69,71,73,74
  give off ~, 1065.30,31,45,46
  give off as ~, 1065.47

give off ~, cause to, 1065.46
give off cold ~, 1065.45(25,29)
give off rainbowlike ~, 1065.45(26)
giving ~, 1065.50
giving off of ~, 1065.48
god of ~, 1065.113
guiding ~ for ships, 1065.109, 110
heating power of ~, pert. to, 1065.98
impression of ~ when eye is closed, 1065.68
~ in motion-picture studio, 1065.107(13)
influence of ~, 1065.101
intellectual ~, 1065.83,84
lack of ~, 1070.2; see dark-ness,n.
lamp ~, 1065.49(12)
marshes or swamps, ~ over, 1065.1(6)
measurement of ~, instrument for, 1065.103
moon~, 1065.1(8)
moon~, like, 1065.4
mountain tops, ~ on, 1065.1(2)
move like a flash of ~, 1065.65
ornament with ~, 1065.76
overpower with ~s, 1065.78
pass a ~ through (bodily part or organ), 1065.88
passage or penetration of ~, cause the, 1065.88
pert. to ~, 1065.96
pert. to heat and ~, 1060.54; 1065.98
picture in ~ and shade, 965.1(8)
play of ~, 1065.49(5)
pour ~ over, 1036.17
power of ~, 1065.77,106
producing ~, 1065.80
production of ~ by organisms, 1065.81
protective device against ~, 568.23
pure ~, formed of, 1065.66
put out (a ~), 801.18
~ ray, 1065.28,29; see ray (of light, etc.),n.
reacting to ~, 1065.100
reflected ~, pert. to, 1065.85, 86
reflecting ~, 1065.87
requiring ~, 1065.99
science of ~, 1065.102
science of ~ and vision, 1065.102(2–4)
search~, 1065.107(18)
sensitiveness to ~, 433.18(10, 11)
separate ~ into its colors, device to, 488.26(3)
shade and ~ in a picture, 965.36
signal ~, 956.1(2); 956.6(2)
signal of ~, 956.1(8,16)
signal to put out ~s, 1065.112
sky~, 1065.1
sphere of ~, 1065.64
spiritual ~, 1065.83,84
stage ~, 1065.49(14); 1065.107(19)
star~, 1065.1(10)
star~, instrument to measure, 1065.20
star~, like, 1065.8
stimulation by ~, 101.1(11, 12); 101.2
streak of ~ in the sky, 1053.7
street ~, structure for a, 1065.111
strength of ~, 1065.77,106

sun~, 1065.1(12); see sun-light,n.
surrounding band of ~, 1065.49(2)
throw ~ upon, 1065.69,71
throwing back ~, 1065.36,87
torch~, 1065.49(15)
unit of ~, 1065.105
unit of ~ flow, 1065.104
warning ~, 1065.49(3)
waves of ~, metric unit of, 946.28(1)
without ~, 1070.1,11; see dark,adj.
without ~ to guide, 177.8
light,v., 1065.54,69
~ again, 1065.71
~ by the sky, 1065.9
device for ~ing, 1065.107
~ the way for, 1065.89
light ray,n., 1065.28,29; see ray (of light, etc.),n.
lighted,adj.
become ~, 1065.70,73
become ~ again, 1065.72,74
~ by moon, 1065.2
~ by stars, 1056.31; 1065.7
~ by sun, 1055.2; 1065.6
~ by twilight, 1065.10
dimly ~, 1065.10
~ slides, projector of, 1065.108
lighter,adj.
make ~ in weight, 949.13
~ than average, 949.4
~ than normal, 949.4
~ than required, 949.4
lighting,n., 1065.69
science of ~, 727.10(3)
lightness,n., 949.2
~ of action, 26.3(3)
~ of movement, 26.3(3); 90.3
~ of touch, 26.3(3)
lightning,adj., 1044.13
lightning,n., 1044.8
burst of ~, 1044.9
flash like ~, 1044.16
flash of ~ with thunder, 1044.10
full of ~, 1044.15
like ~, 1044.14
like thunder and ~, 1044.2
move like ~, 1044.17
~ rod, 1044.18
sound accompanying ~, 1044.1
lightning,v., 1044.11,12
lights-out,n.,
signal for ~, 956.1(11)
likable,adj., 1106.3,15; 1109.11
naturally ~, 1109.8
like,adj., 529.1; see same, similar,adj.
like,v., 1109.1
liked,adj., 1109.12,13
capable of being ~, 1109.11
specially ~, 1109.18
specially ~ person, 1109.20
likelihood,n., 30.2,5
based on ~, 30.6
likely,adj., 30.1,2
be ~ to go in the direction of, 30.4
likes,n.
broad or liberal in one's ~, 1109.5,6
having similar ~, 1109.8
uncivilized or unrefined ~, 1109.10
wealthy person of coarse ~, 1109.9
liking,n., 1109.3; see also likes,n., above
develop a ~ for, 1109.2
get the ~ of, 1109.25–27

having a ~ for, 1109.4
mutual ~, 1109.7
show ~ (of a dog), 1109.22
special ~ for a person, 1109.19
try to get the ~ of, 1109.23,24
lily,n.
~-shaped, 507.17(24)
lime,n.
descr. of ~s, 745.22(4)
drink of ~ juice and water, 748.5(8)
resembling calcium or ~, 1008.3
limestone,n., 1006.1(6,23,46)
soft ~, 1006.1(6)
limit,n., 558.3; 793.13,14
extreme ~, 922.16
having ~s, 793.17
having the same ~s, 793.18
inside the ~s of, 1024.7
lowest possible ~s, at or near, 793.19
outside ~s, 138.2(1)
outside the ~s of, 1024.6
~s, 793.13
set the ~s of, 793.15
without ~, 755.4
without ~s, 755.3
without clear ~s, 755.6
limit,v., 558.1; 793.15
serving to ~, 793.16
limitation,n., 558.2,3
limited,adj., 558.5; 793.17
~ area, 559.6
~ in supply, 917.30
~ in time, 558.5(3)
limiting,adj., 558.4; 793.16
limitless,adj., 755.3; 906.17
limp,adj., 444.1
become ~, 444.3
make ~, 444.4
limpness,n., 444.2
linden,n.
of the ~ family, 985.33(9)
line,n., 316.1
arrangement in a ~, 311.1(1)
bring into ~, 316.4(1)
center ~, 137.1(1)
crossing ~s, 311.1(12,22,26,35, 45)
draw a ~ around, 965.37
enclosed by curved ~s, 300.5
form a ~, 316.4(1,4)
forming a straight ~, 180.3
~ from the center of a circle, 946.32
frost ~s, 1059.11
interlacing ~s, 959.3(21)
lead weight and ~, 947.17
lying in a straight ~, 180.2
mark a ~ under, 316.4(5)
mark between the ~s, 316.4(2)
mark with ~s, 316.4(3)
marked with wavy ~s, 502.2(2)
~ markings, 503.1(6,9)
measurement of ~s in a book, 687.23
moving in a straight ~, 180.3
number of ~s, 316.3
~ on top or bottom of a printed character, 679.20
~ of people or things surrounding a place, 300.4(2)
pert. to ~s, 316.2
poetic ~, 689.17–23,28,29,39–46
put between the ~s, 323.1(38)
reading matter in ~s, 311.1(39)
relating to ~s, 316.2
shape, ~ that indicates, 507.19

slanting ~ between words, 680.1(28)
~ through the center of a circle, 946.31
wait in ~, 272.1(10)
waiters on ~, 272.5

lion,n.
baby ~, 406.5
cross between tiger and ~, 406.8
female ~, 406.10
group of ~s, 403.5(53)
like a ~, 406.12,14
mythical creature, part ~, 662.26(12); 662.27
nickname for a ~, 406.6
pert. to a ~, 406.11,13
small ~, 406.7
young ~, 406.7

lip,n.
coloring matter for the ~s, 488.22(4,7)
having two ~s, 367.12
pert. to the ~s, 367.11
shapely line of the ~, 367.10
sound formed by the ~s, 670.14(2,7,8)

liqueur,n., 749.6(7); see **liquor (alcoholic),n.**

liquid,adj., 1027.2
become ~, 1027.13
become semi~, 1027.13
becoming ~, 1027.12
both ~ and solid, 1027.29
semi~ and sticky, 302.24(9,11, 12,14,16)

liquid,n., 1027.1; see also **fluid, water,n.**
absorb ~, 1034.34
absorbed ~, 1027.1(11)
bubbles of ~, 1028.9
channel for carrying ~, 1026.18
cleansing ~, 899.5
cleansing ~ (religion), 899.5(1)
compressibility of ~s, measurement of, 198.7
convert gas to a ~, device to, 1027.10
convert (ice or snow) into ~, 1027.5
convert into a ~, 1027.4
convertible into a ~, 1027.8
cover with ~, 1036.20
drops of ~, 918.5
explosive ~, 802.12(2)
flowing ~, 1027.1(6)
~ for dipping and preserving something, 1035.18
~ for growing bacteria, 1027.1(3)
~ for soups, 742.2
~ from moisture absorption, 1027.1(4)
full of ~, 925.1(12,24)
mass of ~, 1026.16; 1027.1(2)
mass of air- or gas-filled ~, 1027.38
~ matter, 1027.1(13)
~ medium for drug or medicine, 1027.1(5)
~ mixture, 1027.1(12)
move ~s, 1033.39,40
move (something) around in ~, 1026.44
movement of ~s, 1031.1(4,5,11, 14)
operated by ~ pressure, 1026.22
plant ~, 1027.1(8)
raising ~s, device for, 1033.39
science of ~s, 1027.33

secreted ~ of genitals, 1027.1(10)
~ solution of drug or medicine, 1027.1(7)
sounds of ~, 459.1–3
specific gravity of ~s, device to measure, 1027.36
specific gravity of ~s, measurement of, 1027.37
spilled ~, 1027.1(9)
surround with ~, 1036.20
sweet ~, 1027.1(5,8)
~ that has trickled out, 1027.1(11)
unable to be converted to a ~, 1027.31,32
without, or not using, ~, 1038.10

liquidity,n., 1027.3
causing ~, 1027.6,7

liquor (alcoholic),n., 749.1,2
addict of ~, 749.43; see also **drunkard,n.**
addicted to ~, 749.42; see also **drunk,adj.**
addiction to ~, 749.41,44,45
addicts to ~, group of former, 749.69
avoidance of ~, 749.55–58
charge for opening ~ bottles, 298.7
confuse with ~, 605.1(7,8,24, 26)
confused with ~, 605.5(5)
connoisseur of ~s, 734.13(3,4, 6)
containing ~, descr. of beverages, 749.8
counter for mixing or serving ~, 749.38,39
~ drink, 748.15; 749.3–5
drink ~, 748.12
drink taken after ~ drunk neat, 748.5(3)
drink ~ to the health or success of, 748.12(15,18)
drinker of ~, 748.14
drinking of ~, 748.13
excessively indulging in ~, 921.1(7)
excite with ~, 749.52
~ from cider, 749.6(1)
~ from pears, 749.6(16)
illness from ~, 749.53
immoderation in drinking ~, 748.18
laws against ~, 749.67,68
make ~, 749.28
making ~, device for, 749.27
making ~, place for, 749.26
malt ~, 749.7; see **beer,n.**
measurement unit in ~, 946.46(6)
mental derangement from indulgence in ~, 1136.1(8,9)
merry with ~, 749.50(1)
moderate in the use of ~, 749.59,60; 923.1(5)
obtain ~, place to, 749.37
opposed to sale of ~, 749.62, 64,65
opposition to use of ~, 749.64,65,68
party with ~, 748.17
promise to give up ~, 1122.27
seller of ~, 749.40
seller of ~ to army, 233.4(3,4)
server of ~, 749.40
~ shop, 749.37
social drinking of ~, 748.19,20
storage place for ~, 262.3(5)
stupefied with ~, 597.21(3)
stupefy with ~, 597.20(2,7)
toasts made in drinking ~, 748.21

types of ~, 749.6
undiluted (of ~), 1.26
unit of strength of ~, 749.13
warmth from ~, 1060.37

list,n., 311.19
arrangement in ~s, 311.1(5, 44)
long ~, 311.19(7)
maker of a ~, 311.22
~ of author's works, 311.19(1)
~ of books or writings, 687.12–14
~ of contents, 311.19(3,8)
~ of details, 311.19(4,6,8)
~ of events, 311.19(4,6)
~ of names, 695.5; 311.19(4,5)
~ of things in a book, 687.9(6, 8)
put a, or one's, name on a ~, 695.6–8
put on a ~, 311.21,22

list,v., 311.20

listen,v., 453.1
force to ~, 453.7
group that ~s, 453.5
~ medically, 453.1(4,11)
one who ~s, 453.4
place where people ~, 453.6
unwillingness to ~, 454.22(2)

listener,n., 453.4
~s, 453.5

listening,n., 453.2
device for ~, 454.20
device for ~ medically, 454.20(2,6)
pert. to ~, 453.3

lit,adj.
see **lighted,adj.**

literary,adj., 688.2
collection of ~ passages, 682.19; 682.20(1); 965.31
~ creation, 726.21
~ language, 665.9(7)
~ passage, 682.20
~ passages for learning foreign language, 682.20(1)
~ person, 688.3
poorly constructed (of ~ work), 726.28
~ sketch, 682.16(39)
successful ~ work, 23.8
~ urge, 682.21(1)
~ woman, 688.3(1)
~ writings, 682.16

literature,n., 682.16; 688.1; see also **literary,adj.**
ancient Greek or Roman ~, 688.1(2)
art of ~, 965.6(2)
borrowed ~, 965.31
century in ref. to Italian ~, 965.34
collection of efforts in ~, 965.31
contemptuous of ~, 863.4
fidelity to reality in ~, 807.11
free imagination in ~, 807.12
highest era of ~, 688.4
obscene ~, 709.33; 713.4
patron of ~, 568.21
pert. to ancient Greek or Roman ~, 784.16(2)
sexual ~, 709.32,33
theory of the truthful in ~, 813.5

little,adj., 909.1; see **small,adj.**

livable,adj., 750.8

live,v., 750.1
~ before, 750.1(19)
~ contentedly in, 750.1(30)
~ down, 750.1(27)
~ in quarters (of animals), 403.25
~ in the country, 786.4
~ like a plant, 985.32

~ longer than, 750.1(15,25)
~ next to or nearby, 790.5-7, 22
~ off another, 750.17-20
~ on after death of body, 750.1(18)
one who ~s, 750.4; see **inhabitant,n.**
~ passively, 750.1(28)
place to ~, 753.1; see **home, house,n.**
power to ~, 750.12,13
region where animals or plants ~, 782.5
~ richly, 750.1(13)
science of how people ~ together, 751.13(4,7)
that which ~s, 750.4
~ together, 750.1(4,5)
~ with, 750.1(29)
~ within, 750.1(8)
lived,adj.
fit to be ~ in, 750.8
~ in, 750.7
one ~ off by a parasite, 750.21
unfit to be ~ in, 750.9
liveliness,n., 752.2
show ~, 752.3
lively,adj., 752.1
able to move in ~ manner, 90.4
be ~, 752.3
cheerful and ~, 752.5
excessively ~, 752.6
~ in movement, 90.3
make ~, 752.4
move in ~ manner, 90.1
~ movement, 90.2
nervously ~, 752.6
not ~, 1064.84; 58.1; see **inactive,adj.**
~ woman, 708.14(4,8)
liver,n.
disorders of the ~, 388.4
lobster's ~, 388.1(5)
pert. to the ~, 388.2(3)
secretion of the ~, 287.8(2,5)
liverwort,n., 985.6(7)
science of ~s, 985.36(11)
living,adj., 750.3
~ a long time, 750.3(5,6)
~ a short time, 750.3(8)
~ again, 751.22
~ in cities, 750.3(10)
~ in communities, 750.3(9)
~ in herds, flocks, etc., 750.3(4,9)
~ in marshes, 1000.18
~ in mud, 1000.12,18
~ in swamps, 1000.18
~ in trees, 996.11
~ on land, 1003.5
~ on trees, 996.14
~ substance, 751.12
~ thing, 750.4(6,10)
living,n., 750.2
combining city and country ~, 786.10
enjoying ~ together, 750.11
make fit for ~ with others, 750.10
pert. to conditions of ~, 750.14
living quarters,n., 753.1; see **home, house,n.**
living room,n., 787.8
lizard,n., 425.1,12,13; see also **reptile,n.**
eating ~s, 734.27(31)
pert. to ~s, 425.2,14
loader,n.
ship ~, 925.14
loaf,v., 209.4,5
loafer,n., 209.3,9

loan,n., 281.2
deliver (possessions, etc.) as pledge against a ~, 1122.37
exorbitant interest for ~, 218.12
promise to repay ~, accepter of, 1122.41
loan,v., 218.11; 281.1; see **lend,v.**
lobe,n.
cut into two equal ~s, 332.7(1)
divided into three ~s, 932.21
divided into two ~s, 931.9
lobed,adj., 508.20
lobster,n., 422.3
of ~s, 403.6(1); 422.1(13)
science of ~s, 403.26(10,12)
local,adj., 782.15
locality,n., 782.1,3,7; see also **place,n.**
locate,v., 487.1
put or place, 323.1
location,n., 323.2,4
make one's ~ known, 613.1(26)
lock,n., 297.4
lock,v., 297.1,2
locked,adj., 297.3
lockjaw,n., 377.9(30,36)
locust,n., 428.3
group of ~s, 403.5(36)
of ~s, 428.1(16)
science of ~s, 403.26(31)
lofty,adj., 164.1
~ in language, 951.49
~ language, 664.1(19); 665.9(6,18,20,21,24,25,33,35, 36,42,50,54-56,58,61)
logical,adj., 590.1
connected ~ly, 590.5
following ~ly, 173.4(5,11); 173.8
~ in expression, 665.9(13)
seemingly ~, 590.2,3
loincloth,n., 980.2
loins,n.
pert. to the ~, 345.20
London,n.
dialect of ~, 664.4(2)
inhabitant of East End of ~, 784.15(14)
pert. to East End of ~, 784.16
loneliness,n., 330.2
lonely,adj., 125.6; 330.1(9,14,17, 18,28,29)
lonesome,adj., 125.6; 330.1(9,14, 17,18,28,29)
long,adj.
~ in appearance, 516.1,2
~ in time, 913.8
tediously ~, 913.9
longer,adj.
become ~, 516.5
become ~ in time, 913.5,6
~ in time, 913.7,8
make ~, 516.4
make ~ in time, 913.1,2,4
~ than wide, 516.3
longhand,n., 677.1; see **handwriting,n.**
look,n., 484.2
appearance, 504.1
facial expression, 365.1
angry ~, 878.7
displeased ~, 1117.12
look,v., 484.1
~ at, 484.1; see also **examine,v.**
~ at things in store windows, 1009.22
~ at with malicious satisfaction, 1107.25,26
~ back mentally, 484.1(32)

~ for, 486.1; see also **search,v.**
position from which things or ideas are ~ed at and judged, 782.23
something ~ed for, 486.7
something to ~ at, 483.8(21, 23,24,27)
try to ~, 484.1(39)
looking,n., 484.2; 486.2
a ~ back, 484.2(2)
descr. of ~, 484.4
sexual pleasure from ~, 710.33(29,36); 710.34(2)
loop,n.
~ in rope, 302.33
move, raise, lower, etc., with a ~, 1022.7
put in a ~, 1022.7
supporting ~, 1022.2(26)
loose,adj., 304.1
lax, 304.1
~ and shaky, 111.4(4); 304.1(6)
become ~, 304.4
billowing and ~, 304.1(1)
~ end, 792.10(5)
hanging ~, 304.1(2,5)
~-jointed, 304.1(6)
make ~, 304.3
making ~, 304.5
producing ~ state, 304.6
sexually ~, 712.1-6; see also **immoral,adj.**
~ state, 304.5
loosen,v.
become or make loose, 304.3, 4
relax, 1142.1,10
set free, 309.1; see **free,v.**
untie, 302.31
act of ~ing, 304.5
loosened,adj., 304.1
looseness,n., 304.2
causing or producing ~, 304.6
lord,n., 1074.17
act or play the ~, 1074.23
authority or power of a ~, 1074.22
Japanese ~, 1074.19,20
like a ~, 1074.21
petty ~, 1074.18
relationship between ~ and vassal, 1074.13
service or homage due a ~, 1074.12
suitable for a ~, 1074.21
territory of a ~, 1074.24
vassal of a ~, 1074.11
woman with the power of a ~, 1074.25
worship of ~s, 656.15(13)
Lord (God),n., 654.1; see **God,n.**
lose,v., 264.1
~ by fault or error, 264.1(1)
~ by forgetting location, 264.1(3,4)
~ feathers, 972.10
~ fur, 972.10
~ horns, 972.10
~ shells, 972.10
~ skins, 972.10-17
~ soluble parts, 264.1(2)
loser,n.
~ in a contest, 20.9
~ or ~s of a relative through death, 264.6
loss,n., 264.2
amount of ~, 914.1(6)
business involving ~, 572.8
freedom from ~, 309.14(9)
~ of one's soul, 264.2(5)
~ of possibility of heaven, 264.2(5)

sadness over ~, 1125.49
sustain a ~, 803.22
~ through death, 264.2(1)
lost,adj., 264.4
admit as ~, 675.1(13)
~ and puzzled, 264.4(2)
~ animal, 264.8(1,2)
~ child, 264.8(1)
having ~, 264.5
having ~ through death,
264.5(1)
one who has ~ through death,
264.6
~ person, 264.8(2)
place where one is ~,
782.1(32)
~ thing, 264.3; 264.8(2)
loud,adj., 463.3
be ~, 463.2
become ~er, 463.10
in a ~ voice, 463.5
make ~ sounds, 463.2; see
also shout,v.
make ~er, 463.9
person with a ~ voice, 463.6
~ sounds, 463.1; 464.1; see
also shout,n.
loudness,n., 463.4
Louisiana,n.
French dialect in ~, 664.4(5)
louse,n.
see also lice,n.
disease caused by a ~,
396.1(31)
of the ~, 428.1(18)
love,n., 700.1
a meeting for ~, 322.1(38)
action showing ~, 700.19
~ affair, 700.20
excessive ~ for one's husband, 700.1(16)
excessive ~ for one's wife,
700.1(26)
excite with ~, 700.14
feel ~ for, 700.3
feeling of ~, 700.1
foolish ~, 700.1(15,16,26)
foolish ~, one excited with a,
700.15
free of ~ commitment,
309.15(2)
full of ~, 700.2
~ gift, 230.6(1)
god of ~, 700.27(1,2)
goddess of ~, 505.19; 700.27(3)
in ~ with, 700.2(2,3)
inclined to making ~, 700.16
make ~ (to), 700.7; see also
caress,v., sexual inter-
course,n.
make ~ insincerely, 700.11-13
makes ~, one who, 700.23; see
lover,n.
meet to make ~, 700.10
non-sexual ~, 700.1(20)
object of ~, 700.6
~ of specific things, places,
people, etc., 700.31,32
offer ~ insincerely, 700.11-13
play at ~, 700.11-13
poem about ~, 689.2(11,15,16)
~ potion, 700.24
self-~, 700.1(5,7,18)
sexual ~, 700.1(15,19)
sexual ~, one interested in,
700.26
sexual ~, pert. to, 700.25
show ~ (of a dog), 1109.22
show one's ~, tending to,
700.21
showing ~, 700.22
song of ~, 476.4(6,45)
sound of ~, 467.1(2)
try to get the ~ of, 18.1(26);
240.11(2,5); 700.8

word showing ~, 700.19
writings about sexual ~,
682.16(12)
sing a ~ song to, 476.1(10)
love,v., 700.3,7
loved,adj., 700.5
one who is ~, 700.6
woman who is ~, 700.23(14)
lovely,adj.
attractive, 196.5
beautiful, 505.1
delightful, 1102.4
lover,n., 700.23
mistress or concubine,
710.19-23
cast aside a ~, 700.28,29
female ~, 700.23(14)
illicit ~, 710.18
insincere ~, 700.12
~ of a married woman,
700.23(6,7)
~ of specific things, places,
people, etc., 700.30
loving,adj., 700.2
treat ~ly, 700.4
low,adj.
~ and broad, 169.1
~ and flat, 169.1
cut ~ (of a dress, etc.),
332.7(2)
~ in rank, 313.16
~ in sound, 462.3,8,11,12
~ people, 887.7
~ sounds, 462.1,6,9,13
low spirits,n., 1123.2; see also
depression, gloom, sad-
ness,n.
humor causing ~, 1091.30
in ~, 1123.1; see also depressed, gloomy, sad,adj.
lower,adj., 169.2
become ~ in sound, 462.16
~ in rank, 169.2(1,2); 313.17
make ~ in sound, 462.15
person of ~ rank, 313.18
lower,adv.
go or move ~, 167.1
lower,v., 167.1,4
decrease, 910.1,2
~ a flag, 957.12
~ in dignity, 868.10,27,28
~ in esteem, 868.27,28
~ in pride, 868.10
~ in sound, 462.15,16
~ oneself from, 167.10
~ with a loop, 1022.7
lowest,adj., 169.3
~ depths, 169.4(1)
~ point, 169.4; see also bottom,n.
loyal,adj., 658.1
~ admirer, 658.3(2)
~ follower, 658.3(2)
~ friend, 658.3(1)
~ person, 658.3
stay ~ to, 658.5
~ to government during revolution, 658.1(70)
loyalty,n., 658.2
~ among friends, 1096.13
~ and devotion, 658.2(1)
bound by ~, 658.4
~ to country or ruler,
658.2(1); 784.8(3); see also
patriotism,n.
~ to the group, 658.2(2)
luck,n.
bad ~, 36.1
causing ~, 35.2
good ~, 35.1
have ~, 35.4
having ~, 35.3
indicating ~, 35.2
pert. to ~, 35.6
resulting from ~, 35.2,6

something relied on for ~,
35.5
something that brings ~,
35.5
something worn for ~, 35.5
unexpected ~, 35.1(1,3)
lucky,adj., 35.2,3
lucrative,adj., 219.7
luggage,n., 261.17
lump,n., 958.7
a swelling, 518.6
~ of gold, 326.15(2)
lumpy,adj., 958.8
swollen, 518.4
lunacy,n., 1136.1; see insanity,n.
lunatic,adj., 1136.2; see insane,
adj.
lunatic,n., 1136.3
lunch,n., 740.16(11,15,21)
combined breakfast and ~,
740.16(5)
eat ~, 734.1(22,33)
time for ~, 740.19
lung,n.
abnormal sound in the ~s,
376.6(1)
affecting the ~s, 374.1
gas or air in the ~ cavity,
374.14
having ~s, 374.3
inflammation of the ~s,
374.4-7
membrane around the ~,
387.1(14)
pert. to the ~s, 374.1,2
science of the ~s, 376.15
sufferer from ~ disease,
374.13
treatise on the ~s, 682.15(18)
tuberculosis of the ~s, 374.8-
12
lure,n., 196.2,3; see attraction,n.
lure,v., 196.1; see attract,v.
lust,n.
sexual ~, 709.7
luster,n.
magnificence, 847.2
shine, 1065.56
lustful,adj., 709.8
~ person, 709.9
lustrous,adj.
bright, 1065.55
magnificent, 847.1
lute,n.
maker of ~s, 479.13
player of a ~, 479.9(15)
luxurious,adj., 216.3; 223.14(12)
luxury,n., 216.2
devoted to ~, 1105.8(1,12,13)
weak from indulgence in ~,
10.1(16)
worn out from ~, 10.1(16)
lying (reclining),adj., 65.2
~ above, 65.3(16)
~ asleep, 65.3(6)
~ away from the main part,
323.13
~ below, 65.3(18)
~ down in rest, 65.3(12)
~ face downward, 65.3(9-11)
~ flat, 65.3(10,11)
~ nearby, 790.2
~ on, with downward pres-
sure, 65.3(7)
~ on one's back, 65.3(10,11,13,
17)
~ on top, 65.3(8,15,16)
~ over, 65.3(8,15)
~ under, 65.3(14,18)
lying (telling lies),n., 821.3
accuse of ~, 821.12
guilty of ~ under oath, 821.8
habit of ~, 821.5

pathological ~, 821.7
lying (untruthful),adj., 821.5,6
lymph,n.
  diseases of the ~, 388.5,6
lynx,n.
  pert. to a ~, 406.11,13
lyre,n.
  ancient ~, 479.8(7)
  pert. to a ~, 479.15
  play a ~, 479.10
  player of a ~, 479.9
  shaped like a ~, 479.16

M

machine,n., 280.6
  controls a ~, 8.4(2,3,5,6)
  energy, ~ for converting,
    2.23
  pert. to ~s, 280.7
  self-functioning ~, 280.6(5,
    15)
  starts a ~, 8.4(2,3,5,6)
  worker on ~s, 280.8
machinery,n., 280.1
  pert. to ~, 280.7
  use of automatic ~, 280.9
  worker on ~, 280.8
mad,adj.
  angry, 878.10; see angry,adj.
  insane, 1136.2; see insane,
    adj.
made,adj., 726.4; see also produced,adj.
  ~ by man, 811.4
  ~ of, 726.4(2)
  place where things are ~,
    726.5,6
  something ~, 726.3
madman,n., 1136.3
madness,n.
  anger, 878.11
  insanity, 1136.1; see in-
    sanity,n.
magazine,n.
  publication, 691.1; see pub-
    lication,n.
  storage place, 262.3
  addition to a ~, 908.24
magic,adj., 663.4
  ~ article, 663.11
  cast a ~ spell, 663.12–15
  ~ charm, 663.11; 1056.40
  drink of ~ effect, 748.5(6)
  ~ expression, 663.10
  ~ influence, 9.2(14)
  ~ ornament, 663.11
  ~ power, 7.1(20,21)
  ~ skill, 7.1(68)
  ~ spell, 663.16
  spirit or fairy of ~ power,
    662.7(12,14,15,16,26,33,38,
    39)
  ~ symbol, 1056.40
  ~ trick, 663.3
  ~ word, 663.10
magic,n., 663.1
  belief in ~, 632.6(15); 663.7
  believing in ~, 632.18(9)
  call by ~, 663.8
  call forth by ~, 693.1(5,10)
  caused by ~, 663.4(3)
  devilish ~, 660.3(1,2); 663.1(2,
    4–7,10,11,13–16)
  evil ~, 660.3(1,2); 663.1(2,4–7,
    10,11,13–16)
  get by ~, 663.8
  Negro ~, 663.1(7,13,14)
  perform ~, 663.5
  performance of ~, 663.1(3,
    12); 663.6
  pert. to ~, 663.4; 1053.37
  practice ~, 663.5
  practice of ~, 663.1(3,12);
    663.6

relating to ~, 663.4; 1053.37
send away by ~, 663.9
worship of ~, 656.15(26)
magician,n., 663.2; 1053.38
  pert. to a ~, 663.4
  rain-causing ~, 1037.20
magistrate,n., 1083; see
  judge,n.
magnetic,adj., 196.5
  ~ forces, device to measure,
    196.13
  tendency to turn toward ~
    pole, 148.16
magnetism,n., 196.2,3
  ~ by electricity, 1066.18
magnetize,v., 196.1
magnificence,n., 847.2,5
magnificent,adj., 847.1,4
  ostentatiously ~, 847.3
  ~ quality, 847.5
  ~ thing, 847.5
maharajah,n.
  wife of a ~, 1073.41(5)
main,adj., 848.5; see important,adj.
  ~ part, 326.29,31
maize,n., 605.17
majestic,adj., 844.1; 846.1;
  847.1; see dignified, magnificent, noble,adj.
make,v.
  create, 726.1,17; see create,v.
  manufacture, 726.1
  produce, 726.1
  ~ by mixing, 726.1(1,3,5–7,20)
  ~ by putting together,
    726.1(4,7,8,22)
  ~ falsely, 820.16,18
  ~ from parts, 327.52
  ~ illegally, 726.1(2); 1087.13
  ~ in imitation of the genuine,
    820.16
  ~ up, 726.17
  ~ without preparation, 48.9
make believe,v., 826.5; see pretend,v.
make-believe,n., 826.10; see
  pretense,n.
make fun of,v., 869.1
  ~ good-naturedly, 869.9,10
  ~ rudely, 860.15
make merry,v., 201.3; 1104.10
maker,n., 726.2,19
make-up,n., 326.49
  essential to the ~ of the
    whole, 326.44
  manner of ~, 326.49
  part essential to the ~ of the
    whole, 326.9,45
make up for,v., 222.1–5
making fun of,adj., 869.5
  ~ good-naturedly, 869.12
making merry,n., 201.1; see
  merrymaking,n.
malady,n., 389.1; see also disease, illness,n.
malaria,n., 396.1(22)
male,adj., 707.3; see also masculine,adj.
male,n., 707.1; see also boy,
  man,n.
  castrated ~, 710.40–42
  dominated by ~s, 8.6(1)
  female qualities in a ~,
    707.10,14,15
  hatred of ~s, 880.17(3)
  like a ~, 707.3(2)
  pert. to a ~, 707.3(8)
  revolving around the ~,
    707.3(1)
  state of being a ~, 707.4(1)
  young ~, 760.3,5
malicious,adj., 879.1
  deliberately ~, 879.1(2)
  ~ person, 879.4(2,6)

slyly ~, 879.1(2)
talk ~ly of, 891.17
mallard,n.
  group of ~s, 403.5(68)
mammal,n., 403.7
  aquatic ~, 423
  marine ~, 423
  of ~s, 403.6(15)
  science of ~s, 403.26(24,25)
  water ~, 423
  ~ with pouches for young,
    418.1–3
man,n., 429.3; 707.2; see also
  human, male, mankind,n.
  early ~, 429.6
  feminine (of a ~), 707.8,9;
    see also effeminate,adj.
  feminine ~, 707.2(1,3);
    707.11
  feminine qualities in a ~,
    707.10,14,15
  like a ~, 707.3(2,5–7)
  little ~, 707.2(5,6)
  made by ~, 811.4
  make into a ~, 429.10(7)
  mechanical ~, 429.4
  old ~, 759.17
  place where only a ~ may go,
    707.6
  rough ~, 707.2(2)
  sexually loose ~, 712.3
  state of being a ~, 707.4
  young ~, 760.3,5
manage,v., 8.14; see also control,v.
management,n., 8.15
  system of ~, 8.18
manager,n., 8.16
  business ~ of a college,
    1077.1(30)
managerial,adj., 8.17
manatee,n., 423.5
mandatory,adj., 252.17
mange,n., 382.11(42)
manhood,n.
  early ~, 707.4(2); 760.2(1)
mania,n.
  desire, 265.2
  madness, 1136.1; see also
    insanity,n.
  ~ for alcohol, 749.41
  ~ for sexual intercourse,
    709.7
  ~ of power, grandeur, etc.,
    1136.1(25)
  ~ restricted to one area,
    1136.1(27)
  ~ to set fires, 1064.17
  ~ to steal, 250.2
mankind,n., 429.1; see also
  human, man,n.
  ages or periods of ~, 769.9
  biological category of ~,
    429.2
  hate ~, 880.20
  hatred of ~, 429.19; 880.17(4)
  origin of ~, 429.21
  origin of ~, theories of,
    429.20
  races of ~, 430.1–19
  sciences of ~, 429.22
  student of ~, 429.23
manly,adj., 707.3(5,6,8–10); see
  also male, masculine,adj.
  deprive of ~ strength,
    10.5(14)
  make ~, 707.6
  ~ qualities, 707.4
  strong and ~, 1.1(4)
manner,n.
  attitude, 1091.6
  method, 50.1
mannerism,n., 1091.11
manners,n.
  bad ~, 860.2,8

correctness of ~, 815.2(1)
good ~, 858.2
showy or coarse ~, wealthy
  person of, 1109.9
skill in social ~, 7.1(2)
violating good ~, 860.8
manual,adj.
  ~ ability, 7.1(15)
  ~ capacity, 7.1(18)
  ~ skill, 7.1(6,7,28,30,43,44)
manufacture,n., 726.3
  place of ~, 726.5
manufacture,v., 726.1
manure,n., 293.9,11
manuscript,n., 684.1
  ancient ~, 684.1(4)
  ancient ~s, 684.3
  book of ~s, 687.1(9)
  both sides, ~ written on,
    684.1(3)
  both sides, the writing of ~s
    on, 684.2
  ornament a ~, 1065.76
  shorthand ~, 684.1(8)
  typed ~, 682.16(38) ; 684.1
  written and erased ~,
    684.1(5)
Manxman,n., 784.15(22)
many,adj., 916.9
  different and ~, 916.10
map,n., 618.1
  book of ~s, 618.2
  climate ~, 1047.15
  making of ~s, 618.3
  projection ~, 966.11
  room for viewing a ~, 1004.47
  spherical ~, 618.4
  weather ~, 1047.15
mapping,n.
  science of ~ surface waters,
    1026.39(2)
mar,n., 805.5
  harm or damage, 803.2; see
    harm,n.
mar,v.
  harm, 803.1; see harm,v.
  spoil, 805.1; see spoil,v.
  ~ the appearance of, 805.2,4
marble,n.
  colored like ~, 1006.38
  like ~, 1006.36,37
  mottle or stain like ~, 1006.38
  pert. to ~, 1006.36
  sculpture, ~ used for,
    1006.1(4)
march,n., 107.2
march,v., 107.1(7,8,18)
mare,n.
  group of ~s, 403.5(71)
marionette,n., 969.40; see
  puppet,n.
margin,n., 793.20,22; see also
  edge,n.
mark,n., 503.1
  birth~, 503.1(2)
  ~ burned on skin, on
    animals, or on criminals,
    503.1(4,11)
  characteristic ~, 503.1(1)
  circular ~, 503.1(7)
  defacing ~, 805.5
  diacritical ~s, 680.1
  dirty ~, 904.4
  ~ from healed wound or
    burn, 805.6
  identifying ~, 503.1(5)
  ~ left by healing, 503.1(8)
  ~ left by passing, 757.6
  ~ left by something or some-
    one, 503.1(15,16,18,19)
  ~ left by use, 503.1(10)
  long ~, 503.1(13)
  ~ of disease, 503.1(12)
  ~ of disgrace, 503.1(4,11,12) ;
    891.4

~ on a tree, 503.1(3)
~ on the skin, 503.1(12)
punctuation ~, 680.1
white ~ on animal's face,
  503.1(3)
wormlike ~s, 503.1(17)
mark,v., 503.2
  ~ gradations on, 946.13
  ~ with a star-shaped symbol,
    1056.36
  ~ with chalk, 1006.42
  ~ with disgrace, 891.3
marked,adj., 503.3
market,n., 212.7
marking,n., 503.1
  cloudy in ~s, 1057.9
  line ~s, 503.1(6,9)
marmalade,n., 746.1
marmot,n., 421.8
  like the ~, 421.10
  pert. to ~s, 421.9
marred,adj.
  become ~ in form or shape,
    805.3
marriage,n., 702.8; see also
  wedding,n.
  after ~, 702.27(8)
  arranger of a ~, 704.12,13
  become united through ~,
    702.3
  before ~, 702.27(9)
  bond of ~, 702.17
  ceremony or celebration of,
    702.26
  completion of a ~ by inter-
    course, 710.1(3)
  god of ~, 702.28(3)
  give in ~, 230.1(9)
  goddess of ~, 702.28(1,2,4)
  hatred of ~, 880.17(5)
  kinds of ~, 702.8
  living together in ~, 702.20
  living together without ~,
    702.22–24
  make love to with a view to
    ~, 700.7(1,3,5)
  mixed ~, one who favors,
    702.14
  notice of forthcoming ~,
    704.6
  offer ~, 237.1(9)
  offer ~ to, 704.14
  outside of ~, 702.27(3)
  ~ outside the race, 702.8(9,
    15,18) ; 702.14
  ~ outside the religion,
    702.8(9,18)
  person who practices a form
    of ~, 702.9
  pert. to ~, 702.10,27
  plural ~, 702.15
  practice plural ~, 702.16
  promise in ~, 704.2
  promise of ~, 704.1
  promised in ~, 704.4
  promised in ~, one who is,
    704.5
  related by ~, 722.2(1)
  relationship through ~, 702.5
  relatives by ~, 722.4(6)
  requirement about ~, 702.25
  second ~, 702.15(7)
  seeks wealth by ~, 214.3(1)
  ~ song, 476.4(9,16,23,26,37)
  state of ~, 702.19
  suitable for ~, 704.8
  take in ~, 702.1
  termination of ~, 705.1; see
    also divorce,n.
  third ~, 702.15(8)
  ~ to an inferior, 702.8(13,22) ;
    702.10(1)
  ~ to one female, 702.8(21)
  ~ to one male, 702.8(19)

~ to one person, 702.8(19–21) ;
  see also monogamy,n.
unite others in ~, 702.2
unite through ~, 702.4
united in ~, 702.6
unsuitable ~, 702.8(14,16,17)
void a ~, 705.2,3
  ~ within the group, 702.8(9)
woman under ~, state of a,
  702.21
write a song of ~, 476.7
marriageable,adj., 704.8
married,adj., 702.6
  ~ couple, 703.3,4
  ~ life, 702.18
  man about to be ~, 703.1(4)
  ~ person, 703.1; see also
    husband, wife,n.
  pert. to ~ state, 702.27(2,5)
  poorly ~, 702.7
  ~ relationship, pert. to, 703.6
  ~ state, 702.19
  woman about to be ~,
    703.1(3)
marry,v., 702.1,2
  ~ again, 702.1(8,9) ; 702.2(6,7)
  ~ outside the race, 702.1(6)
  ~ poorly, 702.1(7)
  promise to ~, 704.3
  refuse to ~, 704.15,16
  ~ unsuitably, 702.1(7) ;
    702.2(4,5)
Mars,n.
  inhabitant of ~, 1053.10
  science of ~, 1053.13
  with ~ as center, 1053.12
marsh,n., 1000.14; see also
  swamp,n.
  full of ~es, 1000.17
  growing in ~es, 1000.18
  light over ~es, 1065.1(6)
  living in ~es, 1000.18;
    1026.23(6)
  produced by ~es, 1000.20
marshy,adj., 1000.15–17
marten,n.
  group of ~s, 403.5(57)
  of ~s, 403.11(10)
martin,n.
  of ~s, 405.9(8)
martyr,n., 1138.9
  become a ~, 1138.11
  earliest ~, 236.3(2)
  first ~, 236.3(2)
  make a ~ of, 1138.12
  state of being a ~, 1138.10
martyrdom,n.
  place of ~, 1130.21
marvel,n., 271.10
marvel,v., 271.8
marvelous,adj.
  excellent, 831.1
  surprising, 271.1
Mary,n.
  the Virgin ~, 653.11
  worship of the Virgin ~,
    656.2(6) ; 656.15(14)
masculine,adj., 707.3; see also
  male, manly,adj.
  both ~ and feminine organs,
    characteristics, etc., 710.36,
    37
  development of ~ characteris-
    tics in women, 707.5
  neither ~ nor feminine,
    710.51
  ~ (of women), 707.3(4,7)
  ~ woman, 708.14(2,3)
mask,n., 970.3
  face ~, 970.23
  party with ~s, 970.27
  remove the ~, 970.57–59
mask,v.
  conceal, 970.1
  disguise, 970.13

mass,n., 318.19
  arrangement in a ~, 311.1(28)
  become a ~, 318.20
  combining into a ~, 320.9
  form into a ~, 318.20,21
  ~ of buildings, 318.19(24)
  ~ of water, 1026.16
  put into a ~, 318.21
  ratio of weight or ~, 947.23
mass,v., 318.20,21; 319.1
massage,n., 438.2; 438.2(2,4)
massage,v., 438.1; see rub,v.
massager,n., 438.5
masterpiece,n., 726.3(2);
  726.21(4)
masturbation,n., 710.27
  pert. to ~, 710.29
masturbator,n., 710.28
match,n., 20.2
match,v.
  make the same, 529.4
  make equal, 534.5
  ~ with something better,
    833.13
material,adj., 808.11
maternal,adj., 725.2; see
  motherly,adj.
mathematical,adj., 943.3
mathematician,n., 943.2
mathematics,n., 943.1
  branch of ~, 943.1
  ~ dealing with measurement,
    943.1(4,5,8,9)
  earth ~, 943.1(3)
  land ~, 943.1(3)
  hater of ~, 880.18(4)
  surface ~, 943.1(3)
  triangle ~, 943.1(9)
matrimony,n., 702.8; see
  marriage,n.
matter,n., 808.7; see also
  essence, thing,n.
  excess ~, 920.5
  minute part of ~, 326.25
  pert. to ~, 808.11
  science of ~, 79.28(4); 808.12
matter-of-fact,adj., 1097.3
mature,adj., 732.1; see also
  ripe,adj.
  become ~, 732.3
  becoming ~, 732.4
  grow ~, 731.3(19,20,27)
  growing ~, 731.5(2)
  make ~, 732.5
mature,v., 732.3,5
maturity,n., 732.2
  made gentle, etc., by ~, 732.7
  period of ~, 731.9(2–5,8,9,12,
    15,16)
  promoting ~, 732.6
  reach ~, 731.10
maximum,n., 920.18
mayor,n.
  ~ in Europe, 1077.1(4)
meal (food),n., 740.16; see also
  food,n.
  after a ~, 740.20(1,5)
  before a ~, 740.20(7)
  delay a ~, 768.8(17)
  elaborate ~, 740.16(2,9,17)
  evening ~, 740.16(8,20)
  informal ~, 740.16(14)
  light ~, 740.16(16,19)
  main dish of a ~, 740.15(12)
  morning ~, 740.16(4,5)
  noon or midday ~, 740.16(5,
    8,11,15,21)
  outdoor ~, 740.16(13)
  pert. to a ~, 740.20
  provide with ~s and sleeping
    quarters, 740.18
  restaurant ~ at a specific
    price, 740.16(21)
  seafood ~, 740.16(18)

  sleeping quarters and ~s,
    740.17
  sumptuous ~s, descr. of,
    740.20(4)
  time for a ~, 740.19
meal (grain),n., 987.4
  covered with ~, 987.10
  like or containing ~, 987.8
  made from ~, 987.9
  yielding ~, 987.9
mean,adj., 887.2
  low in rank, 887.3
  unimportant, 887.2
  valueless, 887.2
  dirty and ~, 887.5
  ~ in appearance, 887.1
  ~ in character, 887.1
  ~ in personality, 887.1
  ~ in quality, 887.1
  mercenary and ~, 887.8
  not ~, 887.9
  ~ people, 887.7
  ~ person, 887.6
  wicked and ~, 887.4
mean,v., 607.1
meaning,n., 607.2
  acceptance of literal ~ only,
    607.16
  become clear in ~, 598.11
  central ~, 607.3
  clarity of ~, 598.9
  clear in ~, 598.8,16; 607.7;
    607.9(9,10)
  descr. of ~, 607.10
  equal in ~, 607.5
  explain the ~ of, 598.10;
    599.1; 607.17
  explainer of ~, 607.20
  explanation of ~, 607.18
  explanatory of ~, 599.5;
    607.19
  false ~, give a, 607.21
  full of ~, 607.9
  give spiritual ~ to, 1090.8
  give the ~ of, 607.17
  giver of ~, 607.20
  have a ~, 607.1
  having ~, 607.9
  hidden ~, 607.2(2)
  logically following in ~, 173.8
  make clear in ~, 598.10; 599.1
  opposite ~, words of,
    666.12(1)
  opposite ~ to that stated,
    having the, 607.11(4,6)
  pert. to ~, 607.10
  same ~, words of the,
    666.12(10)
  science of ~, 607.22
  secret in ~, 604.1(12,15,32,37);
    607.9(1,3,6,8,15); 971.9; see
    also mysterious,adj.
  several ~s, having, 607.11
  several ~s, use of words with,
    607.13,14
  several ~s, word or expression
    of, 607.12
  shade of difference in ~,
    607.4
  signs, ~ of, 951.12
  spiritual ~ of words, 607.2(2)
  symbolic ~, 954.13
  threatening in ~, 607.9(7,11)
  twist the ~ of, 607.21
  unclear in ~, 603.1; 604.1
  understand a wrong ~ from,
    593.14,17
  understand the ~ of, 593.1;
    see understand,v.
  use language unclear in ~,
    603.9
  without ~, 607.23; 608.5; see
    meaningless,adj.
  wrong ~, give a, 607.21
meaningful,adj., 607.9

  become ~, 607.8
  seem ~, 607.8
meaningless,adj., 607.23; 608.5;
  see also nonsensical,adj.
  ~ language, 664.1(3,7);   see
    also nonsense,n.
  ~ sounds, 607.29
  ~ statements, 607.31
  ~ talk, 607.26,28,30; see also
    nonsense,n.
  talk ~ly, 607.27
  ~ thing, words, or language,
    607.24; see also nonsense,n.
  ~ words, 607.29; see also
    nonsense,n.
  ~ words, use of, 667.1(8)
means,n., 50.1
  established ~, 50.1(10)
  indirect ~, 50.1(7)
  ~ of advancing, 50.1(36)
  ~ of approaching, 50.1(3)
  ~ of entering, 50.1(3); 133.7
  ~ of leaving, 50.1(3); 140.5
  ~ of living, 50.1(21)
  provide the ~, 50.8
  skilled in ~, 50.2
  ~ to an end, 50.1(16)
meant,adj.
  ~ but not expressed, 607.6
measles,n., 382.11(17,28,40,41)
measurable,adj., 946.4
  not ~, 946.5
measure,v., 946.1
  ~ by the hand, 946.1(7)
  ~ cubic volume of, 946.53
  ~ distance by walking,
    946.1(4)
  ~ land, 946.1(8)
  ~ quantity, 946.1(6)
  ~ water depth, 946.1(5)
measurement,n., 946.2
  adapted for use in ~, 946.10
  alcoholic beverage ~,
    946.46(6)
  allow of ~, 946.14
  area ~, 946.37,43
  ~ around, 946.29,30,33
  ~ around circle, 946.38
  ~ around outer boundaries,
    946.33
  art of ~, 946.11
  astronomy ~, 946.26(11,16)
  British ~, 946.55
  cable ~, 946.26(3,7)
  capacity ~, 946.48,49
  circle, ~ from center of,
    946.32
  circle, ~ through center of,
    946.31
  circle ~, 946.44,45
  cloth ~, 946.26(2,6)
  decimal system of ~, 946.21
  density ~, 947.26
  device for ~, 946.3
  distance ~, 946.26
  drug ~, 946.20
  dry ~, 946.54
  equal in ~, 946.16,17
  fluid ~, 946.46
  horse-height ~, 946.26(9)
  land ~, 946.38,40,41,43
  length ~, 946.26–28
  length ~, ancient, 946.26(5)
  light-wave ~, 946.28(1)
  metric ~, 946.27,28,43,48,49
  printing ~, 946.26(1,17,18)
  square ~, 946.37,43
  standardized unit of ~,
    946.25
  surface ~, 946.43
  surveying ~, 946.26(4,12)
  time ~, 774.1–15
  walking ~, 946.26(15)
  water-depth ~, 946.26(7)

weight or density, ~ of, 947.26
whiskey ~, 946.46(6)
wine ~, 946.46(8,9) ; 946.47
wire ~, 946.26(13)
meat,n., 743.1–4
~ as to animal of origin, 743.1
avoidance of ~, 734.26(12) ; 734.28(1)
decaying ~, 806.16,17
~ dishes, 743.4
eating ~, 734.27(7,22)
kinds of ~, 743.1,4
opposer of use of ~, 734.27; 749.58
opposition to use of ~, 734.26(8,12)
pert. to animal ~, 743.5
sausage ~, 743.2
slice of ~, 743.3
mechanical,adj.
without enthusiasm, 1095.23; 1097.32
mechanical arts,n.
pert. to ~, 965.29
mechanics,n.
branches of ~, 3.10; 950.15
mechanism,n., 280.6
medal,n.
description of ~s, 219.14
engraver or designer of ~s, 219.16
honor with a ~, 857.6
honored with a ~, 857.16
large ~, 219.11(11)
ornament in shape of a ~, 959.3(12)
receiver of a ~, 219.13
science of ~s, 219.15
sides of a ~, 186.1(7,9)
meddle,v., 559.1
meddler,n., 559.3,4
meddlesome,adj., 559.2
medical,adj., 398.14
~ examinations, 485.5,6,8
examine ~ly, 485.9
instrument used in ~ examination, 485.7
~ science, 401.1; see below
~ symbol, 401.7
~ tests, 401.10
~ treatment, 400.2; see therapy,n.
medical doctor,n., 401.2; see doctor,n.
medical science,n., 401.1; see also doctoring, therapy,n.
god of ~, 401.8
~ of anesthesia, 401.1(4,5)
~ of animals, 401.1(102,108)
~ of the anus, 401.1(79)
~ of baths, 401.1(6)
~ of the bladder, 401.1(9,106)
~ of the blood, 401.1(28,29)
~ of the body, 401.1(93)
~ of the bones, 401.1(60,61,64, 65)
~ of the brain, 401.1(14,49)
~ of causes of death, 401.1(69)
~ of causes of disease, 401.1(19,69)
~ of childbirth, 401.1(39,45,53, 103)
~ of children, 401.1(70)
~ of correction by cutting, 401.1(60,61,97)
~ of diseases, 401.1(52,69)
~ of doses, 401.1(13,78)
~ of the ears, 401.1(66,68)
~ of emotional disorders, 401.1(2,36,44,62,82–86)
~ of emotions and bodily ailments, 1092.108

~ of endocrine glands, 401.1(16)
~ of epidemics, 401.1(18)
~ of the eyes, 401.1(56,57,63)
~ of fever, 401.1(87)
~ of the foot, 401.1(8,76,77)
~ of freaks, 401.1(100) ; 537.9
~ of functions of living organs, 401.1(75)
~ of the gums, 401.1(72)
~ of the hair, 401.1(105)
~ of healing, 401.1(43,74,101)
~ of the heart, 401.1(7)
~ of hernias, 401.1(30)
~ of horses, 401.1(102,108)
~ of immunity, 401.1(32)
~ of the internal organs, 401.1(33,95)
~ of the intestines, 401.1(17, 22,58,95)
~ of the kidneys, 401.1(48, 106)
~ of the larynx, 401.1(35)
~ of law and medicine, 401.1(21,37,42)
~ of leprosy, 401.1(38)
~ of local diseases, 401.1(15)
~ of malaria, 401.1(40)
~ of manipulation, 401.1(65)
~ of medications, 401.1(41, 101)
~ of mental disorders, 401.1(1,36,44,51,62,82,84, 85)
~ of the mind and body, 584.6; 1092.108
~ of the mouth, 401.1(96)
~ of the muscles, 401.1(46,60, 61)
~ of muscular movements, 401.1(34)
~ of the nervous system, 401.1(49–51)
~ of the nose, 401.1(47,68,89)
~ of old age, 401.1(24) ; 759.25
~ of the organs, 401.1(58)
~ of the pharynx, 401.1(73)
~ of poisons, 401.1(104)
~ of pregnancy; 401.1(39,45, 53,103)
~ of recognition of diseases, 401.1(12,33)
~ of the rectum, 401.1(79)
~ of remedies, 401.1(101)
~ of ruptures, 401.1(30)
~ of serums, 401.1(92)
~ of sex diseases, 401.1(99, 107)
~ of sex organs (female), 401.1(26,27)
~ of sex organs (male), 401.1(3,106)
~ of the skin, 401.1(11)
~ of the stomach, 401.1(17,22, 23)
~ of symptoms, 401.1(12,33, 91,98) ; 955.12
~ of syphilis, 401.1(99,107)
~ of the teeth, 401.1(10,20,54, 59,71,72,80,81,90)
~ of the throat, 401.1(35,66, 68,73)
~ of tissues, 401.1(31,69)
~ of the tongue, 401.1(25)
~ of tumors, 401.1(55)
~ of the urinary system, 401.1(106)
~ of viruses, 401.1(109)
~ of the vision, 401.1(56,57, 63)
~ of X-rays, 401.1(88,90)
pert. to a ~, 401.3
practice a ~, 401.4

~ restricted to a part, disease, etc., 401.1(94)
student or practitioner of a ~, 401.2
medical student,n., 401.2(17)
medical treatment,n., 400.2; see therapy,n.
medicate,v., 400.1
act of ~ing, 400.2
medication,n., 398.4,6,8; 400.2; see also cure, drug, medicine,n.
book of ~s, 399.6
compounding ~s, 50.1(25)
compounding ~s, art of, 399.1(1,6)
harmful ~, 803.5,6
healing ~, 1139.4(3,11)
morbid craving for ~, 398.7
pert. to ~s, 398.5
place where ~s are dispensed, 399.5
science of ~s or doses, 401.1(13,41,78,101)
soothing ~, 398.4(3,5,10,14,17, 19,23,24)
specific ~s, 398.6,8
standard ~, 398.4(9)
substance used in ~s, 398.13
~ to please a patient, 398.4(13)
medicine,n., 398.4,6,8; see also cure, drug, medication,n.
ball of ~, 398.4(2,6,11,12,23)
bottle for ~, 261.7(31,41)
compounding ~, 50.1(25)
compounding ~s, art of, 399.1(1,6)
container for ~, 261.1(22)
drink of ~, 748.5(6)
liquid ~, 1027.1(7)
liquid medium for ~, 1027.1(5)
pert. to ~, 398.5
practice of ~, 401.1; 401.1(43, 74) ; see also medical science,n.
pretends to cure, ~ that, 826.17
seller of quack ~, 826.19
soothing ~, 1139.4; 1139.4(2,3, 6,8,11)
strength-giving ~, 1.33,34
substance used in ~s, 398.13
medicine man,n., 401.2(23,24)
meditate,v., 585.1; see think,v.
meditation,n., 585.2; see thinking, thought,n.
Hindu system of deep ~, 579.27–29
~ while contemplating the navel, 585.14
Mediterranean,n.
countries on the Eastern ~, 784.4(1)
inhabitant of an Eastern ~ country, 784.15(36)
pert. to an Eastern ~ country, 784.16
medium,adj., 137.2(6)
medium (spiritualism),n., 662.5(2)
meet,v., 322.3,9
~ again, 322.3(2)
agreement to ~, 322.7
~ by chance, 322.3(1)
place where people ~, 782.1(26)
~ suddenly, 322.9(6)
tend to ~ at a point, 322.10
~ unexpectedly, 322.9(4)
meeting,n., 322.1
call a ~, 322.6
delay the ~ of a legislature, etc., 768.8(7)

disorderly ~, 322.1(31)
draw toward a ~ point, 322.10,11
end a ~, 791.1(2)
end of a ~, 792.6(3)
~ for church policy, 322.1(36)
~ for communication with the dead, 322.1(32)
~ for competition in sports, 322.1(37)
~ for discussion, 322.1(17,24)
~ for questions, 322.1(24)
~ for secret worship, 322.1(16)
~ for worship, 322.1(12,16,35)
hostile ~, 322.1(22,37)
legislative ~, 322.1(13,21,27, 33)
member of a ~, 322.4
members of a ~, 322.5
~ of celestial bodies, 322.1(14)
officer of a ~, 1077.23
pert. to a ~, 322.2
place of ~, 322.8
~ place of a legislature, 1080.14
political ~, 322.1(5,13,21)
records of a ~, 684.5(5)
romantic ~, 322.1(38)
room for ~s, 787.7(22,25)
sexual ~, 322.1(3,30,38)
melancholy,adj., 1125.1; see **sad**,adj.
melody,n., 478.1–7
melt,v.
become warm enough to ~, 1060.52
get by ~ing, 1027.19
made by ~ing, 1027.27
~ (metals, etc.) together, 1027.24
purify by ~ing, 1027.19
temperature at which solids ~, 1027.22
vessel for ~ing metals, 1027.23
melted,adj., 1027.27
amount ~ at a time, 1027.20
becoming ~, 1027.28
metal ~ under heat, 1027.21
~ substance, 1027.20
melting,adj., 1027.28
member,n.
decisions, ~s required for, 914.1(13)
get new ~s, 240.1(33)
membrane,n., 387.1
pass through a ~, 121.1(10); 121.2(1); 121.7
relating to a ~, 387.2,3
memoirs,n., 627.27
writer or teller of ~, 627.28
writing of ~, 627.29
memorable,adj., 627.19,20
memorandum,n., 627.34(1,8,9, 11)
memorial,n., 627.34(2,8,10,17, 19)
stone ~, 1006.19
memorize,v., 323.1(50)
memory,n., 627.2,4,6
account of experiences from ~, 627.27–29
aid to the ~, 627.15,34
aiding the ~, 627.14,31,32
beyond human ~, 627.36
bring back to ~, 627.1,30; see also **remember**,v.
by ~, 627.17
commit to ~, 627.13
committing to ~ without understanding, 627.16
contained in ~, 627.5(2)
disorders of the ~, 628.10,11
easily kept in ~, 627.19

from ~, 627.17
full of ~, 627.18
goddess of ~, 627.35
illusion of ~, 627.25,26
impediment to ~, 1097.47
improvement of ~, 627.23,24
increased ~, 627.4(1)
indulge in ~s, 627.10–12
keep in ~, 627.1(8)
lapse of ~, 628.1(2)
loss of ~, 628.1
period of ~, 627.8
persistent ~, 627.6(2)
person with a vivid ~, 627.9
pert. to ~, 627.5
pert. to the ~ of mental imagery, 627.5(1)
preservation of the ~ of, 627.31
preserve the ~ of, 627.30(2,5, 6)
preserver of the ~ of, 627.33
preserves the ~ of, that which, 627.34
preserving the ~ of, 627.32
prompt the ~, 627.30
prompter of the ~, 627.33,34
prompting the ~, 627.31,32
put away in the ~, 323.1(50)
reach back in ~, 627.10
something held in ~, 627.6
stir the ~, 627.30
structure to the ~ of, 727.17(4)
suggestive of the ~ of, 627.32(2,3)
unconscious ~ group, 586.8; 627.6(1)
weakened ~, 628.10(1)
men,n.
government by ~, not women, 1073.42(1,7)
mend,v.
improve, 835.1,2
repair, 832.9
sew, 305.1
menopause, 292.8
menstruation, 292.1
agent that causes ~, 292.5
be in a state of ~, 292.3
difficult ~, 292.1(2)
end of ~, 292.8
excessive ~, 292.1(3)
first ~, 292.6
in ~, 292.4
lack of ~, 292.7
painful ~, 292.1(2)
pert. to ~, 292.2
vaginal plug for ~, 297.9(1)
mental,adj., 584.2; see also **mind**,n.
~ derangement, 1136.1; see **insanity**,n.
description of ~ traits, 584.23
~ disease, 1136.1; see **insanity**,n.
~ disturbance, 1132
engage in ~ activity, 585.1; see **think**,v., **thought**,n.
~ faculties, 584.1; see also **intelligence**, **mind**,n.
~ illness, 1136.1; see **insanity**,n.
~ image, 482.1–10; 483.8(5,7, 17,26,27); see also **idea**, **image**,n.
~ life, 584.12
native ~ faculties, 584.3
numb the ~ faculties, 597.20–23
of the ~ faculties, 584.2
~ power, 584.10,11; see also **intelligence**,n.
~ processes, aware of, 584.7

~ processes, measurement of, 584.24
~ processes, unaware of, 584.8,9
~ processes influenced by the emotions, descr. of, 584.15
~ processes uninfluenced by emotions, descr. of, 584.16
rapid ~ activity, 585.19
science of ~ processes, 584.21
~ testing, 584.24
~ tests, 594.13
theory about ~ processes, 584.25
~ weakness, 597.2,18; see also **stupidity**,n.
~ weakness from old age, 597.27
mentality,n., 584.1; see also **intelligence**, **mind**,n.
of the ~, 584.2
mention,v.
say, 674.8
talk about, 671.5
~ as worthy of honor, 857.7
~ beforehand, 671.5(12)
~ in detail, 671.7
~ individually, 671.7
mentioned,adj.
commonly or frequently ~, 671.6
menu,n., 740.8
permitting choice from the ~, 740.9
mercenary,adj., 214.1
~ attitude, 214.2
mean and ~ person, 887.8
~ person, 214.3
merchandise,n., 212.4
merchant,n., 212.3
merciful,adj., 897.39; 1129.6
be ~ to, 842.3
disposed to be ~, 897.43
not ~, 897.45
merciless,adj., 889.10; 897.45; 1129.22
~ in attack, 889.11
~ in killing, 889.12
make ~, 1129.25
savage and ~, 4.27
mercury (metal),n., 1021.1
add ~ to, 1021.2
containing ~, 1021.4
drug containing ~, 1021.7
pert. to ~, 1021.3
~ poisoning, 1021.6
treat with ~, 1021.5
mercy,n., 897.40; 1129.5
act of ~, 897.44; 1143.4
begging and crying for ~, 276.4(2)
disposition to ~, 897.43
divine ~, 897.41
God's ~, 897.41
~ killing, 796.2(5)
little ~, 889.15
show ~ to, 842.3
~ to the enemy, 897.42
~ to the opponent, 897.42
mermaid,n., 662.26(11)
male counterpart of a ~, 662.26(7)
merriment,n., 1104.2,9; see also **cheerfulness**, **happiness**, **pleasure**,n.
causing ~, 1104.8
engage in ~, 1104.3
~ of parties or celebrations, 201.13
season of ~, 1104.12
time of ~, 1104.12
without ~, 1111.38
merry,adj., 1104.1; see also **cheerful**, **happy**,adj.
~ act or remark, 1104.4

~ and boastful, 1104.5
~ and fat, 1104.5
~ and noisy, 1104.6
~ and rough, 1104.6
~ and shameless, 1104.5
cause to be ~, 1104.7
~ celebration, 1104.9
engage in ~ behavior, 1104.3
~ festivities, 1104.10
~ festivity, season or time of, 1104.12
make ~, 201.3; 1104.10
~maker, 201.4; 1104.11
~making, 201.1,2,6; 1104.9; see **merrymaking**,n., below
~ proceedings, 1104.9
~ with liquor, 749.50(1)
merrymaker,n., 201.4; 1104.11
merrymaking,n., 201.1,2,6; 1104.9; see also **party**,n.
characterized by ~, 201.9
engage in ~, 201.3; 1104.10
engager in ~, 201.4; 1104.11
engaging in ~, 201.6
fond of ~, 201.11
given to ~, 201.11
like ~, 201.8
occasion of ~, 201.2
pert. to ~, 201.7
Roman ~, women who participated in, 201.5
suitable for ~, 201.8
those who engage in ~, 201.4
time or season of ~, 1104.12
turn (~) into drunken revelry, 201.12
wild ~, descr. of, 1105.8(8)
mesh,n., 307.3
message,n., 613.30
deliverer of a ~, 613.31; 613.31(1)
written ~, 613.30(6)
written ~ from a spirit, 682.3(17)
messenger,n., 189.2; 613.31(1)
sent by special ~, 189.3
metabolism,n.
factors in ~, 731.4(3,4)
metal,n., 1012; see also **copper, gold, iron**, etc.
bar of ~, 1012.1
change (~) into ore, 1012.10
chemical element like ~, 1012.15
combination of ~s, 1012.12
containing ~, 1012.11(3,5)
cooking vessels of ~, 1012.26
cover or coat with thin sheet of ~, 1012.5
deposit containing ~, 1012.9
fabric of ~ for armor, 1012.6
~ for a mirror, 1012.4
~ from the sky, 1053.8
~ furnace, 1012.22
fuse ~s, 302.12(3,13); 1012.13
fuse ~s, substance used to, 1012.14
god of ~working, 1012.28; 1064.90
gold-coated ~, 1013.6
hard as ~, 1012.11(4)
impure ~, 904.5
~ in thin sheets, 1012.3
inferior to precious ~, 883.2
iron block for hammering ~s, 1012.23
like ~, 1012.11(4,6)
made of ~, 1012.11(3)
make or form (a piece or bar of ~), 1012.2
medical treatment with ~s, 1012.30
melt ~s together, 1027.24
~ melted under heat, 1027.21

melting ~s, vessel for, 1027.23
mineral containing ~, 1012.8
objects of ~, 1012.25,26
pert. to ~, 1012.11
pert. to ~s other than iron, 1017.15
piece of ~, 1012.1
precious ~s, 1012.31
purification of ~s, 900.7
purity of ~s, 900.17
referring to one ~, 1012.11(6)
referring to two ~s, 1012.11(1)
refinement of ~s, 1012.17(8,9)
rock containing ~, 1012.8
science of ~s, 1012.16
science of production and value of ~, 1012.32
science of production of precious ~s, 213.20(1)
search for underground ~ ores, 486.1(8)
shop where ~s are worked on or with, 1012.21
small plate of shiny ~, 519.5(3)
sounds of ~, 469.7(3–6,10,17, 21,22,26); 1012.11(2,4)
stick for finding underground ~ ores, 486.5
strip of ~, 326.15(4)
strong as ~, 1012.11(4)
thin piece of ~, 1006.1(45)
thin sheet of ~, 1012.1(3–6); 1012.4
use of ~ for money, 213.19
weight system of ~s, 947.31(4)
weight unit of precious ~s, 947.34
work with ~s, 1012.19,20
worker with ~s, 1012.18
~working, 1012.17
yielding ~, 1012.11(3,5)
metalworking,n., 1012.17
engage in ~, 1012.19,20
god of ~, 1012.28; 1064.90
one engaged in ~, 1012.18
pert. to ~, 1012.29
~ shop, 1012.21
meteor,n., 1053.1; see also **heavenly body**,n.
like a ~, 1053.3
meter (poetic),n., 689.26; see also **metrical**,adj.
art or science of ~, 689.32
expert in ~, 689.5(1)
having the same ~, 689.20
lines as to ~, 689.39–43
mark off by ~, 689.28,29
put into ~, 689.4(1)
method,n., 50.1
adherence to ~, 50.5
adherence to mechanical ~, 50.5(7)
art of ~, 50.7
body of ~s, 50.1(33,38)
changed ~, 50.1(39)
conventional ~, 50.1(10,11)
devotion to ~, 50.5
established ~, 50.1(10,11,32)
excessive attention to official ~s, 1077.17
fast ~, 50.1(34)
give ~ to, 50.4
~ of acting, 50.1(20)
~ of compounding medicine, 50.1(25)
~ of doing, 50.1(20)
~ of living, 50.1(21)
~ of mixing ingredients, 50.1(24,25)
~ of treatment, 50.1(45)
~ of working, 50.1(20)

official ~, unnecessary and stupid, 50.1(4)
prescribed ~, 50.1(31)
principles and ~s, 50.1(43)
principles of ~, 50.7
rapid ~, 50.1(34)
regular ~, 50.1(30); 50.3
rigid ~, 50.1(26)
science of ~, 50.6
skilled in ~, 50.2
superiority of ~, 7.1(54)
thorough in ~, 50.3(4)
methodical,adj., 50.3
make ~, 50.4
metrical (poetry),adj., 689.27; see also **meter (poetic)**,n.
~ line of poetry, 689.21
~ stress or accent, 689.25
~ structure, 689.31
style of ~ composition, 689.30
~ units, 689.24,36–43
metric system,n.
area in ~, 946.43
capacity in ~, 946.48,49
length in ~, 946.27,28
units in ~, 946.27,28,43
weight in ~, 947.41,42
miasma,n.
caused by ~, 1048.9
Michigan,n.
inhabitant of ~, 784.15(65)
microorganism,n., 403.21
clean of ~s, 899.10,13
cleanser of ~s, 899.15
destroy ~s in, 899.10
without ~s, 899.11
microscope,n.
big through a ~, 906.22
midday,n., 775.8; 776.3; see also **noon**,n.
pert. to ~, 776.4
middle,n., 137.1; see **center**,n.
middle age,n., 759.2(2,6)
Middle Ages,n., 769.9(4,7,13)
student of the ~, 759.27(2)
midget,n., 909.3(9,16)
midnight,n., 778.2
midwife,n., 401.2; 401.2(1,2)
midwifery,n., 401.1(39,45,53, 103)
mien,n., 504.11
migraine,n., 1137.65–68
mild,adj., 1143.1
become ~er, 1142.10
~ in attitude, person who does not become, 1142.13
~ in climate, 1047.7
make ~er, 1142.1
not ~, 1143.3
~ treatment, 1143.4,5
mildness,n., 1143.2
an act showing ~, 1143.4,5
mile,n.
one-eighth ~, 946.26(8)
three ~s, 946.26(10)
water ~, 946.26(14)
military,adj., 564.2,6
display of ~ power, 951.18
enroll into ~ service, 564.16, 17
free of ~ control, 309.11(7)
~ group, 564.5,15
~ man, 564.1; see **soldier**,n.
~ men, 564.3–5
~ officers, 564.8–13
~ rank, 564.7,8,14
~ science, 564.18
~ service, 564.18
~ station, 782.1(19,21)
~ transportation and supply, science of, 190.12
treatise on ~ subjects, 682.15(24)
milk,n.

business of ~ or milk products, 744.6
color of ~, having the, 744.4(5,6,10)
curdled ~, 744.2
derived from ~, 744.4(2,7)
descr. of ~, 744.4(3,10,11)
disease from raw ~, 396.1(6, 33)
like ~, 744.4(4–6,10)
parts of ~, 744.1
pert. to ~, 744.4(2,4–7,10)
place where ~ is prepared, sold, etc., 744.5
secreting ~, 744.4(8,9)
secretion of ~, pert. to, 744.4(6)
sour ~, 744.3
vegetarian who drinks ~, 734.28(1)
water in ~, device to measure, 1026.40(3)
with ~, 744.4(1)
milkweed,n.
of the ~ family, 985.33(3)
milky,adj., 744.4(4–6)
becoming ~, 744.4(6)
mill,n.
current driving a ~, 1031.1(7)
water for a ~, 1029.53(3)
millennium,n., 1102.27–29
mind,n., 584.1; see also intelligence,n., mental,adj.
a shock to the ~, 1132.16
able to be grasped by the ~, 585.28
able to be pictured in the ~, 585.29
~ before impressions, 584.4
bring to ~, 584.20
come into one's ~, 584.19
development of the ~, 584.17
diseases of the ~, 1136.1; see insanity,n.
disturbance of ~, 1132
dull the ~ of, 1097.13–16
happening in the ~, 584.14
lacking depth of ~, 597.7
medical science of the ~, 584.21(2,3)
origin of the ~, 584.17
originating in the ~, 584.13; 1092.106
outside control of the conscious ~, 8.27
part of the ~ one is aware of, 584.7
part of the ~ one is unaware of, 584.8,9
pert. to body and ~, 584.5; 1092.109
pert. to the ~, 584.2
power of the ~, 5.1(7,17); 584.10,11; see also intelligence,n.
quick of ~, 594.1; see intelligent,adj.
~ reader, 584.26
science of the ~, 584.21
state of ~, 1091.5,6; 1092.5,8
study of ~ and emotions, 584.22
testing or measurement of the ~, 584.24
theory that ~ is the ultimate reality, 584.25
therapy involving ~ and body, 584.6
toughen (the ~), 1098.4
unable to make up one's ~, 640.5(5,8,18–20); 640.7
mind,v., 551.3; see obey,v.
mineral,n., 1008.1
change into ~, 1008.6
~ containing metal, 1012.8

~ deposit in a rock fissure, 1008.4
icelike ~, 1009.25
jewelry, ~s used in, 961.12
nacre, ~ in, 963.9
of the nature of ~, 1008.7
pearl, ~ in, 963.9
~ resembling gold, 1013.29
~ salt in soil, 1011.14
science of ~s, 1008.5
suffuse with ~s, 1008.6
minimum,adj., 909.2; 917.25
minimum,n., 917.14
minister,n., 523.6; 646.1; see ambassador, clergyman,n.
mink,n.
of ~s, 403.11(10)
minor,adj., 169.2; 910.17
miracle,n., 662.3
performance of ~s, 662.4(6,7)
miraculous,adj., 662.1; see supernatural,adj.
mirage,n., 483.8(8,9,14,16); 809.3; 823.15
mirror,n., 483.9
metal for a ~, 1012.4
pert. to a ~, 1065.86
reflection by ~s, 1065.102(2)
signal by ~, 956.1(8); 956.10
something seen through a ~, 483.8(10,20)
mirth,n., 1104.2
misbehave,v., 883.30
misbehavior,n., 883.30
official ~, 1087.7
miscarriage,n.
failure, 24.2
~ in pregnancy, 714.18; see abortion,n.
miscarry,v.
fail, 24.1
~ in pregnancy, 714.22
miscellaneous,adj., 540.9
~ articles, etc., 540.6
miscellany,n., 540.9
mischief,n., 202.2
mischievous,adj., 202.1
~ boy, 202.3(10); 760.5(8)
~ child, 202.3; 202.3(1,8–11)
~ fairy, 662.7(12,21,22,28,32–35,39)
~ girl, 202.3(5,6); 760.6(12,18)
~ness, 202.2
~ person, 202.3
~ person causing difficulties, 25.6
~ tricks, 202.2(1); 824.3–5
misconduct,n., 883.30
miser,n., 227.3
miserable,adj., 1125.1,6,16,34
miserly,adj., 227.1
misery,n., 1125.2,6,35
misfortune,n., 37.1
accompanied by ~, 37.2
cause ~ to, 37.6
cause of ~, 37.5
causing ~, 37.2
descr. of ~, 37.2
doomed to ~, 37.3
extreme ~, 922.17,18
feeling of coming ~, 37.7,8
full of ~, 37.2
incurs ~, one who, 37.4
indicating ~, 37.2
indicative of coming ~, 773.5
meets ~, one who, 37.4
pert. to ~, 37.2
piece of ~, 37.1
predict ~, 772.18
predictor of ~, 772.17
recover from ~, able to, 1103.11,12
sudden ~, 37.1(2,6)
that which, if disturbed, will cause ~, 267.21

think constantly about one's ~, 1125.28–30
unexpected ~, 37.1(8,13)
warning sound of imminent ~, 468.1(10)
misgovern,v., 1073.67
misinterpret,v., 607.21
mislay,v., 264.1(4)
misrepresent,v., 953.4
miss,v., 581.6
miss (title),n., 699.8
misshapen,adj., 507.14
missile,n., 565.10,19,21; see also bullet,n.
forked stick to hurl ~s, 565.20
~ from a crossbow, 566.5
military engine to hurl ~s, 565.18; see also cannon, gun,n.
pert. to throwing ~s, 565.12
~s, 565.11
sharp-pointed ~, 566.6(2)
missing,adj., 42.2; 264.4
mission,n., 189.5
performer of a ~, 189.2
misspelling,n., 681.1(1); 681.3
mist,n., 1041.1
change into a ~, 1036.14
condition of ~, 1046.6
sprayer of ~, 1036.13
mistake,n., 827.2; 829.1
absurd ~, 829.1(3,11)
careless ~, 829.1(2,6,21,23–25)
cause to make a ~, 829.9
containing ~s, 829.4
corrected, ~ to be, 829.1(4)
embarrassing ~, 829.1(10)
free from ~s, 815.1
having made a ~, 829.5
~ in behavior, 829.1(8,19,26)
~ in calculation, 829.1(14)
~ in dates, chronology, etc., 774.12,15
~ in identification, 829.6
~ in printing, 829.1(4,5,18,27)
~ in reasoning, 829.1(7)
~ in speech, 829.1(9,12,24)
~ in understanding, 829.1(13, 15–17,20)
~ in writing, 829.1(4,5,12,25)
incapable of ~s, 815.16
laughable ~, 829.1(3,11)
lead into a ~, 176.1(2,10,13)
list of ~s, 829.3
make a ~, 829.2
making no ~, 815.17
slight ~, 829.1(12,23)
social ~, 829.1(8,26)
stupid ~, 829.1(2,3)
without ~s, 815.1
mister,n., 699.10
mistranslate,v., 607.21
mistress,n.
lover, 710.19–23
title, 699.8
king's ~, 1073.21(12)
prince's ~, 1073.21(12)
sultan's ~, 1073.41(7)
mistrust,v., 639.1
misty,adj., 1026.2,3; 1041.2
become or make ~, 1026.10; 1041.4
misunderstand,v., 593.14,17
misunderstanding,n., 593.15
subject to ~, 593.16
misunderstood,adj.
able to be ~, 593.16
purposely made to be ~, 603.9
unable to be ~, 598.21,22
use language that can be ~, 603.9
misuse,n., 283.2
~ of words, 667.3–5
misuse,v., 283.1

mite (animal),n., 428.3
  like a ~, 428.3
  of ~s, 428.1(1,3,23)
mix,v., 320.1,2
  stir, 320.11
  ~ with people, tending to, 320.10
mixed,adj.
  able to be ~, 320.6
  ~ race, person of, 430.6
  unable to be ~, 320.7
mixer,n., 320.12
  ~ that reduces quality, 883.18
mixing,n., 320.3,4
  implement for ~, 320.12
mixture,n., 320.3,4
  in a disorderly ~, 320.5
  liquid ~, 1027.1(12)
  part of a ~, 326.9(7)
moan,n., 468.1; 1125.18
moan,v., 468.2; 1125.17
mob,n.
  ~ as a ruling class, 431.10
  disturbance by a ~, 1101.1(20–22,34)
  government by the ~, 1073.42(12)
  leader of a ~, 176.3(1); 1073.48
  political control by the ~, 1073.47
mock,adj., 826.11
mock,v., 869.1,2
model,n., 317.1
  clothing ~, 974.14
  conventional ~, 317.1(30)
  make a ~ of, 317.4
  ~ of excellence, 317.1(18,20)
  ~ of perfection, 317.1(18,20)
  original ~, 317.1(1,3,21,24,25,29)
  perfect ~, 317.1(4,9,13,26)
  pert. to a ~, 317.2
  represent by a ~, 953.1(9,10); 953.3
  serve as a ~, 317.3
  typical ~, 317.1(9,12,19,26)
moderate,adj., 921.3; 922.28; 923.1
  calm, 1139.15
  ~ in alcoholic indulgence, 923.1(5)
  ~ in drinking, 923.1(1,5)
  ~ in eating, 923.1(1)
  ~ in politics, 923.1(2)
  ~ in price, 923.1(4)
  make ~, 923.8
  not ~, 923.3
  ~ opinions, one who holds, 923.5
  ~ person, 923.5
moderate,v., 923.8
moderation,n., 923.2
  advocate of ~, 923.4,5
  cause of ~, 923.7
  ~ in action, 923.6
  ~ in opinions, 923.6
  ~ in principles, 923.6
modern,adj., 761.13
  extremely ~, 761.13(2,4,8)
  new and ~, 761.13(5)
  ~ person, 761.16
  something ~, 761.14
  ~ state or quality, 761.17,18
  ~ writer, artist, etc., 761.15
modest,adj.
  decent, 873.6
  free from pride, 873.1
  not elegant, 873.5
  unpretentious, 873.5
  affectedly ~, 873.10(2,5–8)
  excessively ~, 873.10,12
  ~ person, 873.12
  unnaturally ~, 873.10,12
modesty,n., 873.7

affected ~, 873.11
  exaggerated ~, 873.13
  excessive ~, 873.11
  goddess of ~, 873.8
  red from ~, 873.9
  unnatural ~, 873.11,13
  without ~, 873.17
Mohammedan,adj., 642.4
Mohammedan,n., 642.5; 642.5(5)
  ~s, collectively, 642.7(1)
Mohammedanism,n., 642.3(9,13,14)
moist,adj., 1026.3; 1034.8; see also **damp**,adj.
  become ~, 1034.7
  make ~, 1034.6
  sticky and ~, 302.24(3,10,12)
moisten,v., 1034.6
moistened,adj., 1034.9
moisture,n., 1026.1(6,8,11,12,14); see also **water**,n.
  frozen ~, 1059.7–9
  give off ~, 1038.9
  giving off visible ~, 1026.11
  ~ in the air, 1034.13,14
  liquid from ~ absorption, 1027.1(4)
  lose ~, 1038.2
  pert. to heat and ~, 1060.54
  retaining ~, 257.5(1)
  without ~, plant that lives, 1037.33
molasses,n., 449.1(24,25)
mole (animal),n.
  group of ~s, 403.5(42)
mollusk,n.
  science of ~s, 403.26(11,23)
moment,v., 769.3
monarch,n., 1073.14; see also **king, prince, queen, ruler**,n.
  female ~, 1073.14(25–27); see also **queen**,n.
  power of a ~, 5.4(4,9,21,22); 1073.17
  rank, position, or office of a ~, 1073.16
  ~s, collectively, 1073.15
monastery,n., 644.1
  Algerian ~, 330.10(1)
  candidate for a ~, 644.9
  head of a ~, 644.2,3
  heated room in a ~, 787.7(10)
  life in a ~, 644.4
  member of a ~, 644.5,10
  not belonging to a ~, 644.12
  probation in a ~, 644.11
money,n., 213.1–3
  amount of ~, 213.5
  ancient unit of ~, 213.2(11)
  artistic work done for ~ only, 965.1(44)
  British ~, 213.3(11)
  coin ~, 213.16
  collection of ~ at religious service, 213.11
  convert into ~, 213.16(4)
  decrease ~ in circulation, 910.1(13); 910.10
  deprive of ~ value, 213.27(1)
  dishonest ~, 213.3(7,12)
  earn ~, 213.7
  earner of ~, 213.8
  ~ for a bribe, 220.5(1,3,5)
  ~ for a journey, 213.3(14); 915.17
  ~ for the poor, 213.3(6)
  give value as ~, 213.25(1)
  have ~ for, 213.6
  having ~ value, 213.26
  ~ in coins, 213.2(2,4,7–10,12)
  interest in ~, 214.2
  interested in ~, 214.1
  lend ~, 218.11

lender of ~, 218.9; 1122.42–44
  make ~, 213.7
  management of ~, 213.22
  manufacture ~, 213.16
  manufacture ~ illegally, 213.16(2)
  means of earning ~, 213.9
  metal for ~, use of, 213.19
  paper ~, 213.2(1,5,6,13)
  payment for use of ~, 219.3(13,32)
  person dealing with ~, 213.13
  person in charge of ~, 213.13
  person interested in ~, 214.3
  person skilled in ~ exchange, 213.14
  pert. to ~, 213.12
  place for keeping ~, 213.15
  plots to get ~, 47.3(1)
  profit in ~, 215.1
  profitable in ~, 215.2
  ~ record, 213.23
  ~ records, keeping of, 213.24
  reduce value of ~, 213.27(2)
  ~ resources, 213.4
  restore to use as ~, 213.25(2)
  science of ~, 213.20
  supply with ~ for support, 233.1(7)
  ~ to be spent, estimate of, 213.10
  without ~, 217.1; see **poor (in money)**,adj.
  without ~ and alone, 330.1(2,30)
  writing, art, etc., produced only for ~, 682.16(25)
moneylender,n., 218.9; 1122.42–44
mongoose,n., 403.13(1)
  of ~s, 403.11(5)
monk,n., 644.5
  barefoot ~, 979.15
  ~ bound by a vow, 1122.50
  government by ~s, 1073.42(9)
  make ~like, 644.6
  new ~, 644.10
  shoeless ~, 979.15
monkey,n., 420.1,3,6
  like a ~, 420.7
  nickname for a ~, 420.5
  pert. to ~s, 420.2,4,7
monogamy,n., 702.8(19–21)
  favoring ~, 702.12,13
  practicing ~, 702.11
monotonous,adj., 583.1; see also **boring**,adj.
  ~ in sound, 470.3
  make a ~ sound, 470.2
  ~ sounds, 470.1
  ~ tone of voice, 470.1(1,4,5)
month,n., 780.1
  by the ~, 780.4
  calendar of ~s, 774.7(8)
  every ~, 780.3(4,5)
  every fourth ~, 780.3(6)
  every six ~s, 780.3(8); 781.11
  every three ~s, 780.3(7,11,12)
  every two ~s, 780.3(1–3)
  last ~, 780.6
  lasting a ~, 780.3(10)
  lasting two ~s, 780.3(2)
  lunar ~, 1054.10,11
  next ~, 780.5
  once a ~, 780.3(4,5)
  pert. to ~s of the dog days, 780.7
  six ~s, 780.2(2)
  three ~s, 780.2(3)
  twice a ~, 780.3(9)
  two ~s, 780.2(1)
monument,n.
  columnar ~, 1023.9
  stone ~, huge, 1006.1(27,29)

stone ~, prehistoric,
1006.1(25,26)
~ to one whose corpse is
buried elsewhere, 797.14
mood,n., 1091.5; 1092.5; see
also **emotion**,n.
changeable in ~, 1092.9
surrounding ~, 783.1(1,2)
moon,n., 1054.1–3
above the ~, 1054.24
between old and new ~s,
1054.9
beyond the ~, 1054.24
changeable as the ~, 1054.38
darken (the ~), 1055.20
decrease periodically (of the
~), 1054.7
descr. of the ~, 1054.14
eclipse of the ~, 1055.19
features of the ~, 1054.29
goddess of the ~, 1054.15
increase periodically (of the
~), 1054.8
influenced by the ~, 1054.33–
37
inhabitant of the ~, 1054.16
light around the ~, 1065.21–24
light from ~, 1065.1(8)
lighted by the ~, 1065.2
like the ~, 1054.18–20
like the light of the ~, 1065.4
new ~, period of the, 1054.13
observation of the ~, device
for, 1054.30
orbit of the ~, farthest point
of, 1054.25
orbit of the ~, nearest point
of, 1054.26
ornamented with ~s, 1054.21
pert. to the ~, 1054.17
phases of the ~, 1054.3
picture of the surface of the
~, 1054.28
prediction by the ~, 1054.32
ray of light from the ~,
1065.28
rising of the ~, 1054.40
science of the ~, 1054.27
setting of the ~, 1054.41
shadow of the ~, 1071.1,2
~-shaped, 507.17(10,23,46,47,
71) ; 1054.4–6,20
~ shines, occurring when the,
1065.5
spot on halo of the ~, 1065.24
staring at the ~, 1054.39
time between new ~s, 1054.11,
12
time for the ~ to revolve
around the earth, 1054.10
under the ~, 1054.23
without a ~, 1054.42
worship of the ~, 1054.31
moral,adj., 818.3; 843.17
advice on ~ behavior, 843.13–
15
advocate ~ behavior, 843.12
against ~ principles, 886.9
behavior based on ~ law,
843.5
characteristic ~ climate of a
time, 762.8
~ decay, 806.3(4) ; 806.4,6;
886.23
~ defiler, 886.14
excessively ~, 843.21
extremely ~, 843.22; 922.5
good, ~ly, 843.17
~ goodness, 843.18
~ ignorance, 843.24,25
~ impurity, 886.25,26
incorporation of ~ attitudes
of another, 1092.92,93
Japanese ~ code, 843.2

~ lethargy, 886.20
observant of ~ behavior,
843.17
pert. to ~ teaching, 621.6(4)
practice of ~ conduct, 843.3
~ principles, 843.1
promoting ~ goodness, 843.23
~ purity, 845.1,2
reflections on ~ behavior,
843.13,16
remove ~ stain from, 845.15
science of ~ duty, character,
or behavior, 843.4
~ stain, 891.22–25
strict in ~ behavior, 843.21
talk about ~ behavior or
duty, 843.7–10,13,16
teaching a ~ lesson, 621.5(1)
treatise on ~ behavior, 843.6
~ uncleanness, 886.25–28
urge ~ thinking or attitudes,
843.11
without ~ restraint, 886.1,2
without ~ scruples, 886.10
without ~ stain, 845.10
morality,n., 818.5; 843.1
extreme in ~, 843.22; 922.5
harmful to ~, 803.3(6,7,9) ;
886.13
stray from ~, 886.17
straying from ~, 886.18
talk about ~, 671.1(51,54,81,
84) ; 843.8,9,11
moralize,v., 843.8,11
~ annoyingly, 843.9
~ tediously, 843.9
moralizing,n.
habit of ~, 843.10
morals,n., 843.1
Buddhist ~, 843.18
good for one's ~, 843.23
harmful to ~, 803.3(6,7,9) ;
886.13
Hindu ~, 843.18
ignorance of ~, 843.24
low ~, 886.2
resulting from ignorance of
~, 843.25
without ~, 886.2
without reference to ~, 843.26
more, adj. or adv.
be ~ than, 920.17; see also
excess,adj.
become ~, 907.2
do ~ than, 920.16
do ~ than duty demands,
920.15
make ~, 907.1
~ than, 920.11
~ than duty demands, 920.14
~ than enough, 919.6
~ than expected, 920.13
~ than half, 920.12
morning,n., 775.1
early ~, 775.2–5
middle of the ~, 775.7
pert. to ~, 775.6
morning-glory,n.
of the ~ family, 985.33(6)
moron,n., 597.3,17
moronic,adj., 597.1,19
moronism,n., 597.2,18
mortgage,n., 1122.32–36
Moscow,n.
inhabitant of ~, 784.15(40)
pert. to ~, 784.16
Moslem,adj., 642.4
Moslem,n., 642.5; 642.5(5)
~s, collectively, 642.7(1)
symbol of political power of
~s, 1073.86
Moslemism,n., 642.3(9,12,14)
mosquito,n., 428.3
diseases caused by ~es,
396.1(4,20,22,35,36)

of ~es, 428.1(6)
repellant of ~es, 428.6
science of ~es, 403.26(13)
yellow-fever ~, 428.3(6)
moss,n., 985.6(7,10)
covered by ~, 985.21
root of ~, 992.7
science of ~es, 985.36(11)
most,n., 916.8; 920.18
moth,n., 428.3
like a ~, 428.2
of ~s, 428.1(9,15,21,22)
science of ~s, 403.26(22)
student of ~s, 403.27(1)
mother,n., 725.1
animal's ~, 725.1(1)
~ as to number of children,
718.11–14
government by the ~,
1073.3(21)
king's ~, 1073.21(11)
like a ~, 725.2; see also
motherly,adj.
pert. to a ~, 722.7(7,8,11) ;
725.2; see also **motherly**,
adj.
proud ~, 725.1(10)
psychological situation involving ~ and son, 725.6
queen's ~, 1073.21(11)
ruling ~, 725.1(6)
the same ~, having, 725.7
without a ~, 725.8
mother,v., 725.5
motherhood,n., 725.4
study of ~, 725.9
motherly,adj., 725.2
act in a ~ manner, 725.5
assume ~ responsibility for,
725.3
treat in a ~ manner, 725.5
motion,n., 79 et seq.; see **movement**,n.
motion picture,n., 968.1
animated ~, 968.13
art of the ~, 968.3
~ camera, 968.5
close-range ~, 968.10
exciting ~, 1100.4
humorous ~, 1114.13
~ industry, 968.2
make a ~ of, 968.4,7
~ of foreign or unusual
places, 968.12
outline for a ~, 685.1(27)
~ photograph for display,
968.11
~ projector, 968.6
science of the ~, 968.3
theater for ~s, 968.9
writer for ~s, 968.8
motionless,adj., 59.1
be ~, 59.3
make ~, 59.7
motionlessness,n., 59.2
motivate,v., 52.9
motivation,n., 52.11
relying on human ~, 52.15
motive,n., 52.12
concealed ~, 970.47
external ~, 52.12(1)
underlying ~, 52.12(2)
motto,n., 676.1; see **saying**,n.
mountain,n., 166.1
between ~s, 166.4(1)
beyond the ~s, 166.4(6)
~ climber, 159.9(1,3)
~ climbing, 159.10
development of ~s, 166.9
full of ~s, 166.3
high ~, 166.1(1)
~ land, 166.1(12)
light on ~tops, 1065.1(2)
lying at the base of a ~,
166.4(2,3)

measurement of ~s, 164.8
~ of lava, 166.1(30)
other side of a ~, 166.4(4,5)
other side of a ~, inhabitant of, 166.5
pert. to a ~, 166.2
~ range, 166.1(6,22,26)
science of ~s, 166.6
staff used in ~ climbing, 159.11

mourn,v., 1125.10,13,17,19
mourner,n., 1125.10
be sad with a ~, 1129.8–12
mournful,adj., 1125.1,6
~ sound, 468.3(2)
mourning,n., 1125.10,17
clothes for ~, 974.1(20)
signal of ~, 957.13
song, poem, etc., of ~, 1125.20(2,3,5,6)
sounds of ~, 468.1(10,11,14, 16)

mouth,n., 367.1
ailments of the ~, 367.9
fleshy process in back of the ~, 364.6
having a ~, 367.6
pain in the ~, 1137.56(28)
pert. or relating to the ~, 367.5
region of the ~, 367.2
river ~, 367.7; 1029.40(4,5)
roof of the ~, 367.3,4
science of the ~, 401.1(96)
shaping of the ~, 507.8
tubal passage from ~ to anus, 347.11
tube from ~ to stomach, 347.6–8

mouthpiece,n.
~ of musical instrument, 367.8

movable,adj., 79.26
move,v., 79 et seq.
able to ~, 79.25
able to be ~d, 79.26
~ about in water, 1026.43,44
~ about or around, 79.1,4
~ about secretly, 100.1(9)
~ ahead, 174.1–3
~ away, 89.1(23)
~ back and forth, 146.1–4; see also sway, swing,v.
~ back, 145.1–6
~ blindly, 86.1(3)
~ boastfully, 80.1(5)
~ by force, 79.17
~ circularly, 508.19; see also rotate,v.
~ clumsily, 86.1–3
~ continuously, 79.14,15
~ down, 167.1–3; see fall,v.
~ easily, 90.1–4
~ fast, 94.1–9; see also run,v.
~ fast and suddenly, 1044.17
~ faster, 94.6,7
~ forcefully, 91.1–3
~ forward, 89.1(20); 174.1
~ forward slowly, 100.1(5,8)
~ forward to attack, 560.5,6
~ from side to side, 89.1(30); 186.9; see also sway, swing, twist,v.
~ happily, 80.1(2,5,6)
~ heavily, 86.1–3
~ in a crowd, 318.10
~ in a row, 311.17
~ in circles, 508.19; see also rotate,v.
~ in confusion, 84.1,2
~ in fatigue, 85.1(5)
~ in fear, 83.1–3
~ in lively fashion, 80.1; 90.1–4
~ in mud, 1026.43

~ in numbers, 79.10
~ in snow, 1026.43
~ in water, 79.1(7)
~ in waves, 93.1–3; 1032.2–4
inability to ~, 59.6
~ irregularly, 79.8
~ jerkily, 89.1–4
~ lightly, 90.1–4
~ like light, 1065.65
~ like lightning, 1044.17
~ like water, 1031.2–4
~ liquids, 1033.39,40
~ lower, 167.1; see fall,v.
~ nervously, 83.1–4
~ noisily, 92.1
not ~, 59.3
~ (of the tides), 1031.7
~ on all fours, 81.1–3
~ on the ground, 79.11
~ on water surface, 79.11
~ on wheels, 79.16
~ out of the way, 79.4(2)
~ painfully, 85.1(4)
~ past, 79.7
~ playfully, 80.1
~ proudly, 80.1(5)
~ quickly, 94.1–9; see also run,v.
~ restlessly, 83.1–4; 1134.5,7
~ secretly, 82.1–4; 971.15
~ slightly, 79.5
~ slower, 100.3–5
~ slowly, 85.1(2,6); 100.1,2
~ smoothly, 90.1–4
~ suddenly, 83.1(1,4,6,7); 89.1,4
~ suddenly and fast, 1044.17
~ the head to the side, 186.8(2)
~ to one side, 89.1(10,21,24)
~ to the side, 186.8
unable to ~, 59.5
unable to ~ about freely (of animal forms), 302.9
unable to be ~d, 59.8
~ unsteadily, 86.1–3
~ up, 159.1; see rise,v.
~ up and down, 162.1,2
~ upward, 89.1(1,17,19,31); see also jump,v.
~ violently, 4.4; 91.1
~ water, 1033.39,40,42
~ weakly, 79.13
~ with a loop, 1022.7
~ with a sound, 92.1
~ with difficulty, 85.1
~ with effort, 85.1
~ with the wind, 1042.11
~ within one another, 79.12
movement,n., 79 et seq.
active in ~, 57.4(2,6,8–11,14, 17,19,20,23,24)
affected in ~, 79.24
biological ~, 101.1
bodily ~, pert. to, 102.11
~ by electricity, 1066.14
dainty in ~, 79.24
energy of ~, 2.2
forward ~, 174.2,3
frightened ~, 576.4
graceful in ~, 949.7(2)
horse ~s, 104.1
irregular ~, 79.9
light in ~, 949.7,8
light in finger ~s, 949.10
line of ~, 79.22
military ~s, 79.18
~ of air, 79.2(3); 1031.1(4,5, 11)
~ of electricity, 1066.14
~ of fetus, 79.19
~ of gas, 1031.1(4,5,11)
~ of liquids, 1031.1(4,5,11,14)
~ of plane out of control, 167.2(8)

~ of water, 79.2(3); 1031.1
painful ~s, causing, 1137.18
pert. to ~, 79.27
playful ~, 80.2
pleasing in ~, 1106.15
quick in ~, 949.7(1,4–8)
quick in finger ~s, 949.10
quickness of ~, 949.8
regular ~, 79.20
repeated ~, 79.21
restless ~, 1133.6
science of ~, 79.28
series of ~s, 173.9(8)
ship ~ through water, 1029.17
slight ~, 79.6
sounds of ~, 469.1–3
space for ~, 787.2
stop the ~ of, 59.4; 791.1(4,7, 8,17,19,20,22)
study of ~, instrument for, 79.29
~ to or from a stimulus, 101.1
unsteady ~, 86.2
violence of ~, 4.2
violent ~, 4.3
without ~, 59.1–8
movies,n., 968.1,2; see motion picture,n.
moving,adj.
~ about at night, 778.5(5,6)
balance, ~ into, 950.10
~ by steam, 1048.36
~ gracefully, 949.7(2)
~ lightly, 949.7,9
~ quickly, 949.7(1,4–8)
self-~, 79.23
slow-~, 100.6
~ step by step, 108.5
~ violently, 4.1
Mr.,n., 699.10
Mrs.,n., 699.9
mucus,n., 287.13
covered with ~, 302.24(9,11, 14)
descr. of ~, 287.14
discharge of ~, 287.2(1,5)
~ from the eyes, 287.13(3)
~ from the nose, 287.13(3–5)
full of ~, 287.14(2)
like ~, 287.14(1)
secreting ~, 287.14(1,3)
mud,n., 1000.1
clog with ~, 558.1(23)
dirty with ~, 1000.7
hole of ~, 1000.13
living in ~, 1000.12,18
move about in ~, 1026.43
push into ~, 1000.9,19
sink into ~, 167.1(23); 1000.10,19
splash ~ upon, 1000.7
stick in ~, 1000.11,19
muddy,adj., 1000.2,3,15–17
become ~ (of land), 1000.8
~ ground, 1000.14–17
growing in ~ land, 1000.18
~ land, 1000.8,14–17
living in ~ land, 1000.18
make ~, 1000.4,7
measure how ~ a liquid is, 1000.5
splash around in ~ water, 1000.6
mulatto,n., 430.6
mulberry,n.
belonging to the ~ family, 745.22(8)
mule,n., 409.1
~ driver, 205.1(11)
group of ~s, 403.5(5)
multiplication,n.
number in ~, 924.1(11,17–19, 23)
number resulting from ~, 927.1(23)

multiply,v.
~ by a hundred, 940.25
~ by a number, 907.11
~ by eight, 937.10
~ by four, 933.10
~ by six, 935.6
~ by ten, 938.9
~ by three, 932.29
~ by two, 931.12
mural,n., 965.1(16,51)
murder,n., 796.2; see **killing,n.**
capable of ~, 796.7
characterized by ~, 796.7
guilty of ~, 796.8
involving ~, 796.7
murder,v., 796.1; see also **kill,v.**
intending to ~, 796.7
murderer,n., 796.3; see **killer,n.**
murderous,adj., 796.4,7,8
murmur,n., 462.6
murmur,v., 462.7
murmuring,adj., 462.8
muscle,n., 377.1
band connecting a ~, 377.5
contract the ~s involuntarily, 377.14
fall down or forward (of ~s), 167.1(25)
having large ~s, 377.6
~ in the arm, 377.1(1,12)
~ in the buttocks, 377.1(5)
~ in the jaw, 377.1(7)
~ in the thigh, 377.1(1,8)
into ~, 377.4
~ pain, 1137.56(4,9,11,21); 1137.60(1)
pert. to ~, 377.3
quiver of a ~, 111.2(3)
~s, 377.2
science of ~s, 401.1(34,46,60, 61)
strained ~, 377.9(7)
~ system, 377.2
muscular,adj., 377.3,6
~ action, contraction, etc., 377.9(8,9,15,16,18,30,31,33–35); 377.10,11
~ disorders, 377.9–11
~ power, 5.1(15,16); 377.8
~ rigidity, 377.9(5,7); 377.10, 11
~ rigidity after death, 377.9(25)
~ spasms, 377.9(10–12,14,32); 377.10,11
muscularity,n., 377.7
muse,n., 654.17
pert. to the ~s, 654.18
worship of the ~s, pert. to, 654.18
museum,n., 951.28
head of a ~, 8.16(3,4)
London waxworks ~, 951.30
Paris art ~, 951.29
mushroom,n.
gather ~s, 985.23
like a ~ in rapid growth, 985.22
of the ~ family, 985.33(1)
music,n., 478.1; 479.1
accompanying ~, 131.5(4)
arrangement of ~, 479.19
art of ~, 965.6(2)
author of ~, 686.1(15)
~ borrowed from the masters, 965.31
~ box, 479.8(2,14,16,20)
collection of efforts in ~, 965.31
composition of ~, 479.19
concluding ~, 792.23(2)
country life, ~ about, 786.8(3, 4)
fanciful ~, 1114.16,17
florid style of ~, 479.18

humorous ~, 1114.16,17
introductory ~, 730.4(3,15)
lover of ~, 700.30(16); 700.31
sad ~, 1125.20(2,3,5,6)
science of ~, 479.22
shepherd life, ~ about, 786.8(4)
skill in ~, 7.1(67); 479.7; 965.28
sweet and soft ~, descr. of, 1105.21
time in ~, device to measure, 774.2(14)
varied sources, ~ from, 965.31
write ~, 479.23
writer of ~, 479.23
musical,adj., 467.3
~ composition, 479.1,2
~ creation, 726.21
~ district, 479.20
~ in sound, 467.3
~ instrument, 479.8; see **musical instrument,n.**, below
make a ~ sound, 467.2; 469.2
oscillating motion producing ~ sound, 469.4
~ passage, 478.1; 479.1
~ sounds, 455.1(3); 461.1; 467.1; 469.1(13,14,16,25,27, 30)
system of ~ sounds, 467.4
~ time, 762.1(9,10)
musical comedy,n., 969.1
book of a ~, 687.1(15)
musical instrument,n., 479.8
~ as to category, 479.11
play a ~, 479.3,10
player of a ~, 479.9
players of ~s, 479.17
playing of a ~, 479.4
pluck a ~, device to, 479.14
sounds of ~s, 461.1,2
musician,n., 479.5,9
accompanying ~, 131.3(1)
group of ~s, 479.17
mussel,n., 422.3
of ~s, 422.1(5,6,25)
mustache,n., 370.1(3,5,11); see also **beard,n.**
mute,adj., 454.23; 475.1; 671.21; see also **silent,adj.**
~ person, 454.24; 604.10; 671.22
muteness,n., 454.22(1); 475.2; 671.21
mutual,adj., 51.5; 931.18
mysterious,adj., 604.1,7
carry or take away ~ly, 971.44
~ person, 604.4,10
~ symbol, 604.3(4)
~ thing or condition, 604.2,3
mysteriousness,n., 604.2
mystery,n., 604.2,3
belief in ~, 604.6
doctrines of ~, 604.6
explainer of ~, 599.4(3,4)
expounder of ~, 604.8
one who initiates into ~, 604.9
one who is a ~, 604.4
study of ~, 604.6
thing that is a ~, 604.3
mystical,adj., 604.1
~ condition, 604.2
~ in meaning, 607.9(1,3,8,15)
~ use of words, 667.1(3)
mysticism,n., 604.6
mystification,n., 605.3
mystified,adj., 605.5
mystify,v., 605.1
mystifying,adj., 604.1

myth,n., 685.1(13); see also **legend,n.**
something unreal, 809.3
collection of ~s, 682.19(7,9)
interpretation of ~s, 1055.41
~s, 685.2
science of ~s, 685.7
turn into, or surround with, ~, 685.9
mythical,adj., 809.1; see also **imaginary, unreal,adj.**
~ animals, 662.24–29
~ animals, part human, 662.26
~ being, 662.24–30
~ bird, 662.26(6); 755.10
~ dog, 568.5(3)
~ fishlike human, 662.26(6,7, 11,13)
~ goat, 412.6
~ horse, 408.12–14
~ monster, 662.24–30
~ reptile or serpent, 662.25
~ stag, 412.6
mythological,adj., 809.1; see **mythical,adj.**

N

nacre,n.
covered with ~, 963.8
like ~, 963.7
lined with ~, 963.8
mineral constituent of ~, 963.9
pert. to ~, 963.7
nag,n., 274.3(1–3)
nag,v., 274.1(6)
nail,v.
~ boards to joists, 1022.5
naked,adj., 984.18
animal with ~ feet, 984.23
~ body, 965.1(36)
make ~, 984.21
~ person, 984.19
picture of the ~ body, 965.1(36)
practice of going ~, 984.24
sculpture of the ~ body, 965.1(36)
~ skin, 984.22
~ thing, 984.19
name,n., 694.1
affectionate ~, 694.1(17)
announcer of guests' ~s, 694.17
artist's ~ on picture or painting, 965.32
artist's ~ on sculpture, carving, engraving, 966.12
attack the good ~ of, 891.17
book written under another's ~, 687.1(2)
book written under one's own ~, 687.1(4)
call by ~, 694.6(2)
consisting of ~s, 694.2
descriptive ~, 694.1(7,18,43, 47); see also **title,n.**
design of initials of ~, 694.27
false ~, 694.1(3–5,29–31,35,38, 42)
false ~, having, using, or assuming a, 694.22–25
family ~, 694.1(10,13,23,39,44)
first ~, 694.1(12,21,36)
~ from a child, 694.1(33)
~ from a father, 694.1(34)
~ from a female ancestor, 694.1(25)
~ from a mother, 694.1(24)
general ~, 694.1(15)
give a ~ to, 694.6(3,6,7,9–12, 14,15,17,18,21–24)
give a new ~ to, 694.6(12)

having a ~, 694.13,14
in ~ only, 694.12
intimate ~, 694.1(2,10,11,13,
 17,27,28,41)
list of ~s, 311.19(4,5) ; 695.5
nick-~, 694.1(2,10,11,13,17,27,
 41)
nick-~s, of U.S. states, 694.29
pen ~, 694.1(30,38)
pert. to ~s, 694.2
piece of writing under another's ~, 682.16(1)
piece of writing under one's
 own ~, 682.16(5)
place ~, 694.1(37,48)
place ~s, 694.3
poem forming a ~, 689.2(20)
row of ~s, 311.11(4)
say the ~ of, 694.6(5)
science of ~s, 695.3
scientific ~, 694.1(32,48)
shortened ~, 694.1(17)
showing author's ~, 694.21
signed ~, 694.1(8,40) ; see
 signature,n.
source of a ~, 694.15,16
speak to by ~, 694.6(2,5)
stage ~, 694.1(31)
student of ~s, 695.2
study of ~s, 695.1
substitute ~, 694.1(2,10,11,13,
 17,27,28,41)
system of ~s, 695.4
trade ~, 694.1(43)
tribal ~, 694.1(9)
true ~, 694.1(9)
unit ~, 694.1(15)
unknown ~, person with,
 694.19
use of a man's ~ by a woman
 author, 694.4
without a ~, 694.18; see also
 nameless,adj.
write one's ~, 694.5; 695.9;
 see also sign,v.
write one's ~ on a list, 695.8
write the ~ of on a list, 695.6
write to by ~, 694.6(2)
wrong ~, 694.1(26)
wrong ~, give or call by,
 694.26
name,v., 694.6
 ~ as candidate, 694.6(19)
 ~ boundaries of, 694.6(4)
 ~ incorrectly, 694.26
 ~ one by one, 694.6(13,20)
named,adj., 694.9
 person ~ after another,
 694.11(1,3)
 person ~ as a candidate,
 694.11(4)
 person ~ to a post, 694.11(2)
 self-~, 694.10
nameless,adj., 694.18
 done by a ~ person, 694.20
 not ~, 694.21
 ~ person, 694.19
namely,adv., 694.28
namesake,n., 694.11(1)
naming,n.
 act of ~, 694.7
 pert. to ~, 694.8
narcotic,adj., 399.8
 ~ state, 399.10
narcotic,n., 399.7
 addict of ~s, 399.13
 addiction to ~s, 399.12
 illness from ~s, 399.15
 influence of a ~, 399.14
 insanity from ~s, 399.15(2)
 morbid desire for ~s, 399.16
 put under a ~, 399.9
 slavery to ~, 629.27
 stupor from ~s, 399.15(6,7)

unconsciousness from ~s,
 399.15(7)
under a ~, 399.11
narrow,adj., 512.1,2
narrow-minded,adj., 634.8
 make ~, 634.10
 ~ person, 634.9
narrow-mindedness,n., 634.7
nasty,adj., 904.1; 1117.1; 1118.1
nation,n., 784.1; see country
 (nation),n.
nationalism,n., 784.8(1) ; see
 also patriotism,n.
 extreme ~, 784.8(6)
native,adj., 720.18
 ~ country, 784.1(2,3)
native,n., 720.19
 ~ of a nation, 784.3
 ~ of a specific country, etc.,
 784.15; see inhabitant,n.
 prejudice toward ~s,
 634.1(12)
 workers, ~ in charge of,
 8.16(2)
natural,adj.
 as produced by nature,
 810.3,4
 in accord with nature,
 810.7,8
 not affected, 810.1
 not artificial, 810.1
 part of one's nature, 810.5
 action from ~ instinct, 810.11
 adherence to the ~, 810.10
 below what is ~, 810.14
 ~ condition, state, or quality,
 810.9
 ~ person, 810.2
 pert. to ~ laws, 810.6
nature (character),n., 1091.1
 associated in ~, 1091.9,10
 descr. of a person's ~, 1091.2
 distinguishing ~, 1091.7,11
 division of man's ~ into
 three parts, 932.23
 have the ~ of, 1091.20
 having two different or
 opposing ~s, 931.3
 humors determining ~,
 1091.30
 moral ~, 1091.3
 part of one's ~, 810.5
 same in ~, 1091.8
 Slavic ~, 1091.29
nature (physical phenomena,
 etc.),n.
 as produced by ~, 810.3,4
 bring into accord with ~,
 810.13
 contrary to ~, 811.9,10
 contrary to laws of ~, 811.11;
 see also supernatural,adj.
 imitating ~, 810.12
 no longer contrary to ~,
 810.7,8
 pert. to ~, 810.6
 phenomena of ~, 1004.48
 treatise on phenomena of ~,
 682.15(17)
 worship of ~, 656.15(3,21)
naughty,adj., 202.1; 549.1
nausea,n., 290.17
 ~ at sea, 290.18
 eat or drink to point of ~,
 1107.23,24
 fit of ~, 560.24(18)
 satisfy to point of ~, 1107.15-
 22
 to the point of ~, 290.13
nauseate,v., 290.12,16
nauseated,adj., 290.17
 easily ~, 290.19
nauseating,adj., 290.14
nautilus,n., 422.3
 of ~es, 422.1(9)

naval,adj.
 ~ officers, 564.21
 ~ rank, 564.7,21
 ~ soldier, 564.1(35)
 ~ soldiers, 564.5(20)
navel,n., 347.13
 like a ~, 347.14
navigate,v., 116.1
navigation,n., 116.2
 ~ along the coast, 116.2(1)
 art or science of ~, 116.12
 deep or wide enough for ~,
 116.13
 ~ in air above sea or ocean,
 1029.72(2)
 instrument to solve problems
 in ~, 1053.34,35
navigator,n., 116.3
navy,n.
 ~ engaged in operation,
 564.5(1)
 enroll (someone) in the ~,
 564.16,17
 force into the ~, 3.3(13,15) ;
 564.19
 officers of the ~, 564.21
 rank in the ~, 564.7,21
 ~ ship, 115.16
 ~ ships, 115.18
 unit of a ~, 564.5(13)
nazi,n.
 ~ ruler, 1073.14(9)
 ~ symbol, 954.1(11)
near, adj., adv., 790.1,2; see also
 nearby, adj., adv.
 be ~ to, 790.9
 be ~ to, figuratively, 793.25
 bring ~, 790.11,13
 come ~ to, 790.10
 conveniently ~, 790.3
 draw ~ to each other, 790.12,
 13
near,v., 790.10
nearby, adj., adv., 790.1,2; see
 also near, adj., adv.
 conveniently ~, 790.3
 living ~, 790.5-7
 people ~, 790.7
 person or thing ~, 790.6
 places ~, 790.8
nearest,adj., 790.14-16; see also
 next,adj.
nearness,n., 790.4
nearsightedness,n., 481.1(25,
 30)
neat,adj., 902.1,6
 become ~, 902.5
 clean and ~, 902.1(5)
 fashionable and ~, 631.8,9;
 902.1(1,6,9)
 ~ in dress, 902.1(1,3,6,8-10)
 ~ in habits, 902.1(7,8)
 make ~, 902.3
 make ~ by cutting, 902.3(4)
 make oneself ~, 902.4
 make stylish and ~, 902.3(2,
 3)
 not ~, 903.1
 speedy and ~, 631.9
 stiffly ~, 902.1(2)
 stylish and ~, 631.8,9; 902.1(1,
 6,9)
neaten,v., 902.3
neatness,n., 902.2
necessarily,adv., 273.9
necessary,adj., 273.6
 be ~ as a duty, 273.7
 be ~ for, 273.7
 ~ beforehand, 273.6(21)
 ~ but in short supply,
 273.6(4)
 ~ by official order, 273.6(14)
 consider ~, 273.1(3)
 ~ condition, 273.3(7)
 ~ for etiquette, 273.6(6)

involve as a ~ result, 522.1(1)
involved as a ~ part, 522.2
made ~, 273.6
make ~, 273.8
~ part, 273.3(4) ; 326.45
part ~ to the whole, 326.9,45
~ parts, 273.3(13) ; 326.32
something considered ~,
  273.3(3)
~ thing, 273.3; 848.14
~ to completeness, 273.6(12)
~ to life, 273.6(19,26)
~ to the whole, 326.44
~ to war, 273.6(24)
necessitate,v., 273.8
necessity,n., 273.2,3
by ~, 273.9
doctrine of ~, 273.10
neck,n., 359.1
adornment for the ~, 977.1
back of the ~, 359.3
garment for the ~, 977.1,3
having a thick ~, 359.5
part or organ like a ~, 359.2
pert. to the ~, 359.4
sever at the ~, 332.1(12)
twisting of the ~, ailment
  causing, 359.6,7
neckline,n.
low ~, 974.5; 982.5-7
necktie,n., 977.1
formal ~, 975.8
man's ~, 977.2
neckwear,n., 977.1-4
need,n., 273.2
a ~, 273.3
answer the ~, 279.19
extreme ~, 922.17,18
fulfilling ~s, 273.4
fulfills a ~ unexpectedly, that
  which, 273.3(5)
pert. to bodily ~s, 273.5
state of being in ~, 273.2(4-6)
need,v., 273.1
needed,adj., 273.6; see necessary,adj.
what is ~, 273.3
needle,n.
shaped like a ~, 507.17(2)
needless,adj., 273.11; see unnecessary,adj.
neglect,n., 582.2,4
condition of ~, 582.6
illegal ~ to inform of crime
  or treason, 1087.7(6)
~ of duty, 582.2(2-5) ;
  1087.7(6)
neglect,v., 582.1
neglected,adj., 582.7
able to be ~, 582.8
neglectful,adj., 582.3
~ of duty, 582.3(1,4)
~ person, 582.5
neglectfulness,n., 582.4
negligence,n., 582.4
negligent,adj., 582.3
~ person, 582.5
Negro,n., 430.7
fondness for ~es, 700.30(13) ;
  700.31
like a ~, 430.8
part ~, 430.6
prejudice against ~es,
  634.1(10)
segregation of ~es, 325.17,18
Negroid,n.
small ~, 909.3(11)
neighbor,n., 790.6
~s, 790.7
neighbor,v., 790.9,11,20,22
neighborhood,n., 790.4,8
neighboring,adj., 790.1,2,5,17
nephew,n., 722.1(10)
pert. to a ~, 722.7(9)

relationship between ~ and
  uncle, 722.3(1)
nerve,n.
~ activity, 378.9
~ cell, 378.6
~ center, 378.1
~ disease, 1137.56(22)
~ disorder causing dancing,
  378.11(8) ; 378.13
~ disorders or diseases,
  378.11-13
~ doctor, 401.2(18)
harmful to the ~s, agent or
  substance, 378.10
~ impulse, 378.7
mental illness associated with
  ~ disorders, 1136.1(28,29)
~ network, 378.3,4
~ pain, 1137.56(22) ;
  1137.60(2)
pert. to the ~s, 378.8
reacting on the ~s, 378.8(1)
science of the ~s, 401.1(49-
  51)
~ system, 378.5
~ tissue, 378.2
nervous,adj., 1133.1; see also
  anxious, disturbed,adj.
act ~ly, 1133.6
be ~, 1133.1
become ~, 1133.7
~ breakdown, 802.28; 1135.1
~ haste, 1133.10
make ~, 1133.8
make less ~, 1133.12
~ movement, 83.1-4
not ~, 1133.11
shake ~ly, 111.1(8,29)
~ state, 1133.2,4
nervousness,n., 1133.2; see also
  anxiety, disturbance,n.
causing ~ and fear, 1133.9
fit of ~, 1133.3
~ on public appearance,
  1133.5
remove or reduce the ~ of,
  1133.12
twist around in ~, 156.1(26,
  35)
nest,n.
ant's ~, 403.22(16)
build a ~, 727.1(6)
eagle's ~, 405.11(1)
~ of bird of prey, 405.11(1)
of birds in hanging ~s,
  405.8(8)
wasps' ~, 403.22(42)
net,n., 308.1; see also network,n.
armed with a ~, 308.7
fish ~, 308.1(6)
~ for wild game, 308.1(9)
having a ~, 308.7
like a ~, 308.9
like a ~ in form, 507.17(64)
open space of a ~, 308.10
pert. to ~s, 308.8
pert. to construction of ~s,
  308.8
spider's ~, 308.1(1,2,10) ; see
  cobweb,n.
nettle,n.
of the ~ family, 985.33(10)
network,n., 308.1; see also
  net,n.
fabric of ~, 308.5
form into a ~, 308.4
~ of interrelating parts, 520.6
~ of plotting, 308.1(1,10)
open space in ~, 308.10
spider's ~, 308.1(1,2,10) ; see
  cobweb,n.
structure in the form of a ~,
  727.17(5)
neurosis,n., 1135.1

neurotic,adj., 1135.2
neurotic,n., 1135.3
neutral,adj., 636.1
neutralize,v., 17.5; 544.1(13,14,
  16,17,28)
new,adj., 761.1; see also fresh,
  modern,adj.
~ and different, 761.1(9-11,
  16)
hatred of ~ things, 880.17(8)
made ~, 761.1(14,15)
make ~, 761.4
modern and ~, 761.1(3)
no longer ~, 759.28-30
old ideas in ~ form, with,
  761.1(13)
start ~ things, energy to,
  2.4,9
~ theories, disposed to, 761.6
~ thing, 761.3
~ way, 761.5
~ way, in a, 761.7
newness,n., 761.2
hatred of ~, 880.17(8)
news,n., 613.30(4,10,12)
analyzer of ~ events, 485.3(1)
full of ~, 613.32(1)
newspaper,n., 691.1; see also
  publication,n.
addition to a ~, 908.24
~s, 691.3
newt,n.
of ~s, 403.11(1)
science of ~s, 403.26(1)
next,adj., 173.4; 790.17
~ circumstance, 173.6
lie ~ to, 790.20,21
lies ~, that which, 790.18,19
live ~ to, 790.22
situated ~, 790.17,23,24
~ thing, 173.6
next,adv.
come ~, 173.1
nibble,v., 735.1
nickle,n.
~ and copper alloy, 1016.2(3)
~, copper, and zinc alloy,
  1016.2(4)
nickname,n., 694.1(2,10,11,13,
  17,27,41)
~s of U.S. states, 694.29
night,n., 778.1; see also
  evening,n.
active at ~, 778.5
all ~, 778.4
coming of ~, 778.8
comprising a sequence of day
  and ~, 776.8
equal ~ and day, 1055.12-14
every ~, 778.3(2)
flowering at ~, 778.5(2)
happening at ~, 778.3
like ~, 778.3(2)
middle of the ~, 778.2
moving about at ~, 778.5(5,6)
out in the air at ~, 1045.12
overtaken by ~, 778.7
pert. to ~, 778.3
powerful at ~, 778.5(4)
shining at ~, 778.5(3)
stays up late at ~, one who,
  778.6
walking at ~, 778.5(1)
walking by ~, 107.2(1)
wandering at ~, 128.2(3) ;
  778.5(5)
night club,n., 749.37(8,9)
nightingale,n.
group of ~s, 403.5(79)
nightmare,n., 71.2
like a ~, 71.3(3)
Nile River,n.
device to measure water
  height of ~, 1029.33
nimble,adj.

fast in movement, 94.3,8
smooth of movement, 90.3
nimbus,n., 1065.25,27
nine,n.
  consisting of ~, 937.13
  sets of ~, 937.15
ninefold,adj., 937.14
ninetieth,adj., 940.20
ninety, n. or adj., 940.19
  ~-year-old person, 758.2(3)
nipple,n., 360.15
  having ~s, 360.16
  inflammation of the ~, 360.18
  like a ~, 360.17
  soothing ~, 1139.4(7,13)
no,n.
  say ~, 547.1; 548.1; 555.1
  saying neither yes nor ~,
    554.6
  tendency to say ~, 544.2(13)
Noah,n.
  dating back to ~, 759.1(12)
nobility (nobleness),n., 844.2
nobility (class),n., 314.2
noble,adj., 844.1
  ~ in ideas, 844.5
  ~ in language, 844.5
  ~ in sentiment, 844.5
  make ~, 844.6
  ~ person, 844.3
  ~ quality, 844.4
  ~ thing, 844.4
noble,n., 314.7; see also
  nobleman,n., below
  government by ~s, 1073.4(1)
  Mohammedan ~, 1073.36(1)
  pert. to ~s, 314.14
  ~s, collectively, 314.13
  sign of the rank of a ~,
    951.4(7)
  wife of a British ~, 1074.25
nobleman,n., 314.7; see also
  noble,n., above
  below a ~ in rank, 314.16-21
  domain of a ~, 314.10
  pert. to a ~, 314.11
  rank of a ~, 314.9
  with the title of a ~, 314.15
noblemen,n., 314.13; see also
  noble, nobleman,n., above
  pert. to ~, 314.14
nobleness,n., 844.2
noblewoman,n., 314.8; see also
  noble,n., above
nod,n., 102.2(1) ; 152.3(2)
nodding,adj., 102.5(1)
noise,n., 463.1
  act with ~, 4.13
  behave with ~, 4.13
  commotion and ~, 1101.1(3-
    5,13,14,16,19,24,27,29,30,34,
    35,38)
  confused ~s, 473.1-3
  confusion and ~, 605.13(2,4-6,
    11,14,15,23)
  make ~, 463.2
  move with ~, 92.1
  place of confusion and ~,
    473.4
  talk with ~, 4.13
  violence and ~, 4.14
noisy,adj., 463.3
  be ~, 463.2
  ~ child, 463.8
  ~ girl, 760.6(12,21,24)
  merry and ~, 1104.6
  ~ person, 463.8
  rough and ~, 865.1(2,5,6) ;
    865.5
  ~ spirit or ghost, 662.7(34)
  violent and ~, 4.15
  ~ woman, 463.7
nomenclature,n., 695.4,5
non-believer,n., 639.5
nonexistent,adj.

unreal, 809.1; see **unreal,**adj.
  ~ place, 1057.15
  ~ thing, 809.3
non-partisan,adj., 636.1
non-professional,adj., 207.3
  ~ person, 207.1; see **lay-**
    man,n.
nonsense,n., 608.1,3,4,6
  ~ during deception, 608.2
  make ~ of, 607.25
  poem of ~, 689.2(1)
nonsensical,adj., 607.23; 608.5;
  see also **absurd, foolish,**
  silly,adj.
  act or behave ~ly, 608.11
  ~ action, 608.10
  given to ~ talk, 607.32
  ~ in actions, 608.7
  ~ in appearance, 608.7
  ~ in talk, 608.8
  ~ person, 608.16; see also
    fool,n.
  ~ situation, 608.13
  ~ sounds, 607.29
  ~ talk, 607.26,28,30
  talk ~ly, 607.27
  treatment that makes some-
    thing seem ~, 608.15
  ~ words, 607.29
nonsensicality,n., 607.23; 608.6
  instance of ~, 608.9
noon,n., 775.8
  after ~, 775.9-11
  before ~, 775.5
  intermission at ~, 769.8(12)
noose,n., 302.33
normal,adj., 535.1
  higher than ~, 536.9
  less than ~, 536.8
north,adj.
  ~ circle of the earth, 1004.13
  ~ distance on the earth,
    1004.11
  far ~, 789.7
north,n.
  equator, ~ of the, 1004.11
  inhabitant of the ~, 179.11
  land in the ~, 1003.2(19)
North Carolina,n.
  inhabitant of ~, 784.15(60)
northern,adj., 179.10
  ~ regions, 1004.5(12)
Northerner,n.
  ~ who took advantage of the
    South after the Civil War,
    836.15
North Pole,n.
  pert. to the ~, 1004.6
Norway,n., 784.4(4) ; 784.9(12)
Norwegian,adj., 784.16
Norwegian,n., 784.15(41-43,56)
nose,n.
  a cold in the ~, 363.17-19
  animal's ~, 363.3,4
  appearance of the ~, descr.
    of, 363.9-11
  bird's ~, 363.2
  bony part of the ~, 363.6
  coming from the ~, 363.13
  descr. of the appearance of
    the ~, 363.9
  elephant's ~, 363.5
  having a broad, short ~,
    363.10
  human ~, 363.1
  inflammation of membranes
    of the ~, 363.20
  mucus from the ~, 287.13(3-
    5)
  openings in the ~, 298.8(8,
    9) ; 363.7
  person with a broad, short
    ~, 363.11
  pert. to the ~, 363.12

pronunciation through the
  ~, 670.4(11)
  said through the ~, 363.13
  science of the ~, 401.1(47,68,
    89)
  tissue behind the ~, 363.8
  uttered through the ~, 363.13
nostalgia,n., 753.12
nostril,n., 298.8(8)
notable,adj., 615.1
notation,n.
  Arabic system of ~, 927.10
  specialized system of ~,
    927.11
note,n., 627.34
  explanatory ~s, 599.3;
    599.3(2,4-7,10)
  marginal ~s, 682.3(12)
noted,adj., 615.1; see **famous,**
  adj.
nothing,n., 928.1,4
  amounting to ~, 928.3
  bringing ~, 926.28
  reduce to ~, 801.15
  taking ~, 926.28
nothingness,n., 928.2
notice,n.
  announcement, 613.14
  looking, 484.2
  seeing, 480.2
  calling for ~, 952.5
notice,v., 480.1; 484.1
noticeable,adj., 483.1; 952.1
notify,v., 613.28
notoriety,n., 615.2(4); see also
  rumor,n.
notorious,adj., 615.1(3)
nourish,v., 738.1
nourishing,adj., 739.5
  something ~, 739.6
nourishment,n., 739.1,6; 740.1
  healthy ~, 739.3
  inadequate ~, 739.4
  obtaining ~, descr. of, 739.8
  pert. to ~, 739.2
  poor ~, 739.4
  science of ~, 734.19
  spiritual ~, 739.7
novel,adj.
  different, 540.1
  new, 761.1; see **new,**adj.
  unusual, 536.1; see **unusual,**
    adj.
novel,n., 685.1
  concluding part of a ~,
    792.23(1) ; 792.24,25
  ~ of real people in disguise,
    685.1(24)
  ~ of wandering and adven-
    ture, descr. of, 685.6
  ~s, 688.1
novelist,n., 685.5
novelty,n., 536.2; 540.2; 761.2,3
now,adv., 771.2
now,n., 771.1
nude,adj., 984.18; see **naked,**
  adj.
nuisance,n., 874.5
numb,adj., 435.3
number,n., 927.1
  amount or quantity, 914.1
  a ~, 927.1
  added ~, 927.1(2,3)
  addition, ~ resulting from,
    927.1(28)
  addition, ~s in, 908.39
  Arabic system of ~s, 927.10
  center between ~s, 137.1(17,
    18)
  come in large ~s, 914.27
  consisting of a ~, 927.1
  descr. of part of a ~ that
    divides evenly into it, 927.6

descr. of part of a ~ that does not divide evenly into it, 927.5
different things, ~ of, 914.1(16)
divided ~, 927.1(9,20,22)
division, ~ remaining after, 927.1(25)
division, ~ resulting from, 927.1(24)
divisor of a ~, 927.1(7,10,11)
enough in ~, 916.13
fact expressed in ~s, 814.1(3) ; 814.4
~ five times as great as another, 934.12
give a ~ to, 927.13
grammatical ~, 927.16
greater in ~, 833.5,16; 924.6
greater ~ of, 916.7
having ~s, 927.14
~ made a hundred times greater, 940.24
~ in addition, 908.38
interest in ~s, 927.17
large ~, 927.1(13,14) ; 940.41
large ~ in, 916.12,14,15
large ~ of, 916.4,6
largest possible ~, 916.8
~ less than one, 927.1(12)
morbid and compulsive interest in ~s, 927.17
multiplication, ~ resulting from, 927.1(23)
multiplied ~, 927.1(11,18)
multiplying ~, 927.1(17,19)
naming ~s, 927.8
naming by ~s, 927.9
~ of members, 914.1(13)
~ of things counted, 941.9
~ of things following, 914.1(14)
~ of things in a row, 914.1(14)
order, ~ indicating, 927.1(21)
pert. to ~, 914.2; 927.3
prophecy by ~s, 927.7
read a ~, 927.12
reading ~s, 927.8
row, ~s in a, 311.16
row of ~s, 311.11(1,4,10)
say a ~, 927.12
science of ~s, 927.7
study of ~s, 927.7
subtracted ~, 927.1(27)
subtracted, ~ from which, 927.1(16)
subtraction, ~ resulting from, 927.1(25)
succession, ~ indicating, 927.1(21)
superior in ~, 833.5; 924.6
system of ~s, 927.9–11
ten times greater ~, 938.8
thousand, ~ beyond a, 940.41
three times greater ~, 932.32
whole ~, 927.1(15)
without a ~, 927.15
without ~s, 927.15
word for a ~, 927.2
numbered,adj., 927.14
numerous,adj., 916.12
nun,n., 644.5
barefoot ~, 979.15
~ bound by a vow, 1122.50
government by ~s, 1073.42(9)
new ~, 644.10
shoeless ~, 979.15
nurse,n., 570.10
nurse,v., 570.1
nursery,n., 721.15
nut,n.
bearing ~s, 745.15
covering of ~s, 972.4(19,20)
eating ~s, 734.27(21)

flavor of ~s, having, 745.16
full of ~s, 745.16
~-shaped, 507.17(51)
shell of ~s, 972.4(20)
~ trees, cultivation of, 996.58
nutrition,n., 739.1; see nourishment,n.
science of ~, 734.19,20
nymph,n., 654.2,19

O

oak,n.
of the ~ family, 996.25
pert. to the ~, 996.26
seed, nut, or fruit of the ~, 995.7
oar,n., 117.3
like an ~, 117.8
oat,n.
kernel of ~s, 987.23
like ~s, 987.20
pert. to ~s, 987.20
oath,n.
curse, 861.13
admit, or be admitted, to public office by ~, 1086.16, 17
one who administers an ~ to a person, 1086.10
place under ~, 1086.9
statement under ~, 1086.3
obedience,n., 551.2; see also submission, submissiveness,n.
demanding ~, 551.9
entitled to ~, 551.4
force ~, 3.3(2,10) ; 551.6,7
means of compelling ~ to international law, 551.12
one who advocates ~, 551.5
one who demands ~, 551.5
power to compel ~, give, 551.10
teach ~ to, 551.11
~ to religious law, 551.2(2)
obedient,adj., 551.1; see also submissive,adj.
be ~, 551.3
make ~, 551.11
person who is ~, 551.13
teach to be ~, 551.11
obey,v., 551.3; see also submit,v.
force to ~, 551.6,7
willing to ~, 551.1; see obedient, submissive,adj.
willingness to ~, 551.2; see obedience, submissiveness,n.
obituary,n., 794.16
~ writer, 794.17
object,n., 808.1; see also thing,n.
purpose, 45.1
make into an ~, 808.3,4
treat as a material ~, 808.3,4
object,v., 1117.8
~ to, 544.1(6,27,30,33,34)
objectionable,adj., 1117.1; 1118.1
~ person, 880.5(4,5) ; 1117.17; 1118.8
objects of art,n., 964.1,2
collector of ~, 964.5
excellence of ~, 964.4
interest in ~, 964.3
knowledge of ~, 964.3
quality of ~, 964.4
student of ~, 964.5
taste for ~, 964.3
obligation,n., 252.19
debt, 218.1
duty, 528.1

free of ~, 309.11(1,2,16,21–24, 26,27)
freedom from ~, 309.14(14)
obligatory,adj., 252.17; 528.2
necessary, 273.6
oblige,v.
allow no choice, 252.18
do a favor for, 842.9
force, 3.3
obliging,adj., 556.5; 842.10
obscene,adj., 713.1
~ art, 713.4
~ books, 709.33
~ jokes, full of, 1115.3(1,2) ; 1115.4
~ language, expression, etc., 713.3; 1118.14,15,19,20
~ literature, 713.4
~ remark, 1118.16
study of ~ literature, 713.5
~ word or phrase, 666.3(23, 31)
~ writings, 682.16(24)
obscenity,n., 713.2,3
fondness for ~, 700.30(3)
obscure,adj.
unclear, 603.1; see unclear, adj.
unclear in meaning, 604.1; see also mysterious,adj.
become ~, 603.3; 604.6
~ in operation, 971.11
~ in operation but serious in effects, 971.12
make ~, 603.4; 604.5
~ person, 603.7; 604.4
~ thing, 603.7; 604.3
use ~ language, 603.9
obscure,v., 603.4; 604.5
one who ~s, 603.6
obscurity,n., 603.2,5; 604.2,3
bring from ~ into public notice, 615.6
eliminate or reduce the ~ of, 598.10
~ of mind, 603.8
one who causes ~, 603.6
observation,n., 484.2; 485.2
~ of signs or omens, 484.2(1)
region under ~, 782.1(31)
observe,v.
examine, 485.1; see examine,v.
honor, 857.2
look at, 484.1; see look,v.
observer,n., 484.3
obsolete,adj., 284.8,11
become ~, 284.1
becoming ~, 284.2
~ word, 666.3(5)
obstacle,n., 557.3
full of ~s, 25.1(23) ; 557.5
place ~s in the way of, 557.1,2,4
obstetrics,n., 401.1(39,45,53,103)
obstetrician,n., 401.2; 401.2(1,2)
obstinacy,n., 553.2
obstinate,adj., 553.1; see stubborn,adj.
continuing, 754.20
obstruct,v., 557.1; 558.1
obstruction,n., 557.2,3; 558.2,3
free of ~, 309.11(8,31,33,34,40, 44,45)
obstructive,adj., 558.4
obtain,v., 240.1; see get,v.
obvious,adj., 483.1; 535.5,10: 598.5,8,13,16
concerned with what is ~, 598.15
~ without proof, 598.14
occupancy,n., 247.2; 255.2; 750.2
~ in return for services, 255.2(7)

~ of office, 255.2(7)
~ under lease, 255.2(6)
occupant,n., 247.3; 255.3; 750.4
house ~s, 753.6,7
occupation,n., 247.2; 255.2;
750.2
work, 204.1; see also work,n.
science of fatigue in ~, 204.2
science of selection of ~,
204.2
occupied,adj., 750.7
occupy,v.
have possession of, 255.1
live in, 750.1
take possession of, 247.1
occur,v., 29.1; see happen,v.
occurrence,n., 29.2,6; see happening,n.
ocean,n., 1029.64; see sea,n.
octopus,n., 422.3
of ~es, 422.1(9,28)
odd,adj., 536.1
~ person, act, etc., 536.2
oddity,n., 536.2
odor,n., 445.9; see also smell,n.
breath with a bad ~, 376.10
~ carried on air, 1045.5
decay, having an ~ of, 806.14
detect ~s, instrument to
measure ability to, 445.22
effect of ~s, measurement of,
445.20,21
give an ~ to, 445.12
have an ~, 445.11
having an ~, 445.10
having an ~ of dirty water,
1026.6
having the ~ of a goat,
412.7; 445.10(12)
having the ~ of urine,
294.5(6)
inability to tolerate ~s,
445.23
~ left by person or animal,
757.6(1,3)
pleasurable in ~, 1105.4(3,7)
remove the ~ of, 445.25
science of ~s, 445.8
substance giving a pleasant
~, 445.13-16; see also perfume,n.
suggestive of an ~, 238.4(2)
without ~, 445.24
odorless,adj., 445.24
odorous,adj., 445.10
~ like a goat, 412.7;
445.10(12)
~ of garlic or onions,
445.10(2)
off,adv.
drop or fall ~, 167.1(33)
get ~, 167.10
offend,v., 868.1; 1118.3
person who ~s, 1118.8
that which ~s, 1118.6,7
offended,adj., 868.6; 1118.4
easily ~, 868.9
feel ~, 868.7,8
feeling ~, 868.6; 1118.4
feeling of being ~, 1118.5
offense,n., 868.2; 1118.5
~ against monarch, country,
one's superior, etc., 1088.21
avoid ~, word or phrase to,
666.3(21)
causing ~, 868.3
feelings of ~, 868.5
guilty of ~, 884.38
~ to dignity, 868.2(1)
~ to feelings, 868.2
~ to pride, 868.2(1)
wipe out ~, 897.23
offensive,adj., 868.3; 1118.1,12,
15
asking ~ questions, 1118.11

coarse and ~, 864.9
~ in language, 1118.15
insincere, hence ~, 826.27
instance of being ~, 1118.9
~ language, 1118.7,14
make ~, 1118.10
making ~ remarks, 1118.11
~ person, 1118.8
~ remark, 1118.7,16
~ remarks, 1118.13
~ thing, act, circumstance,
etc., 1118.6
~ to the feelings, 868.3
use ~ language, 1118.17,18
use of ~ language, 1118.19,20
~ word, 1118.7
~ words, use of, 1118.19,20
offensiveness,n., 1118.2
offer,n., 237.2
generous ~, 237.2(1)
offer,v., 237.1; see also suggest,v.
~ as explanation, 237.1(6)
~ as price, 237.1(2)
~ for discussion, 237.1(5)
~ in argument, 237.1(1)
keep ~ing, 237.1(4)
~ marriage, 237.1(9)
too ready to ~ services, advice, etc., 237.4
offerer,n., 237.3
offering,n., 237.2
burnt ~, 1064.42(2)
religious ~, 237.2(2)
office,n., 1077.2
position, 205.18
accept public ~, 1086.17
admit to public ~, 1086.16
coming from a public ~,
1077.12
decorations of ~, 959.4(2)
give an ~ to, 205.19,20
group of three people in ~,
932.5
holding ~, 1077.11
introduce into ~, 730.1(1,2)
perform the duties of ~,
1077.10
period of ~, 769.8(9,16);
1077.2
person named to an ~,
694.11(2)
pert. to ~, 1077.11
pert. to one's ~, 1077.13
position of ~, 1077.2(2)
previous holder of an ~,
175.5(2,5-7)
put into ~, 1077.8
seeker after ~, 265.5(2)
seeker after public ~, 1077.15
take the ~ left vacant by,
324.2(3)
three people in power or ~,
932.5
try for public ~, 1077.16
vacant ~, 926.20
with the title or rank of one's
~, 1077.14
officer,n., 1077.1; see also official,n., below
military ~s, 564.8-13
naval ~s, 564.21
rank of a military ~, 564.7,8,
14
rank of a naval ~, 564.7,21
official,adj., 1077.11,12
~ delay, 1077.19
excessive attention to ~
methods or routine, 1077.17
~ formality, 1077.19
~ misconduct, 1087.7
perform ~ duties, 1077.10
render ~, 1077.21
strictness in ~ duties, 890.11

unintelligent display of ~
authority, 1077.18
official,n., 1077.1
~ advising a monarch or
president, 1077.3(5,8)
appoint as an assistant ~,
1077.6
assistant ~, 1077.1(11)
authority of ~s, 1077.20
body of ~s, 1077.3
bring under control of ~s,
1077.21
building, room, etc., of an ~,
1077.4
chief ~, 1077.1(2)
coming from a public ~,
1077.12
corporation ~, 1077.1(13)
current ~, 1077.1(17)
executive ~, 1077.1(7,18,24)
executive ~ of city, 1077.1(21)
executive ~ of European governments, 1077.1(26)
executive ~ of government
dept., 1077.1(27)
executive ~s, 1077.3(1)
executive ~s of a government,
1077.3(1)
function as an ~, 1077.21
go to a higher ~, 159.8
government ~, 1077.1
government ~s, 1077.3(4,5,8)
high ~s, 1077.3(3)
jurisdiction of ~s, 1077.20
language characteristic of
~s, 664.1(7) ; 1077.22
law ~ of a government,
1085.5
law-enforcement ~s,
1077.3(2) ; 1078.1; see also
police,n.
legislative or executive ~ of
a city or town, 1080.22
Mohammedan ~, 1077.1(29)
~ of Chinese Empire,
1077.1(19)
~ of European government
department, 1077.1(22)
~ of fire dept., 1077.1(20)
~ of Genoa, 1077.1(12)
~ of meeting, council, or
committee, 1077.23
~ of New England towns,
1077.1(28)
~ of royal court, 1077.1(5)
~ of Venice, 1077.1(12)
parade ~, 1077.1(20)
police ~, 1078.1
position of an ~, 1077.2
position or jurisdiction of ~s,
1077.20
presiding ~, 1077.1(2)
pretentious ~, 1077.1(3)
provide with ~s, 1077.9
~ representing British king,
1077.1(16)
~s, collectively, 1077.3
self-important ~, 1077.1(23)
staff of a government ~,
1077.7
Turkish ~, 1077.1(1)
~ with delegated power,
1077.1(32)
work of civil ~s, 1077.5
offspring,n., 721.3,9; see child,
children,n.
oil,n., 510.13
~-covered place, 510.15
drill for ~, 510.19
hair ~, protection against,
972.4(1)
like ~, 510.14
purification of ~, place for,
900.7
referring to ~, 510.14

oil,v., 439.2(5); 510.16,17
oily,adj., 510.14
old,adj., 759.1
no longer new or fresh,
759.28
~ age, 759.2
become or make ~, i.e., no
longer new or fresh, 759.29
caused by ~ age, 759.15
fondness for ~ people,
700.31(1)
government by the ~,
1073.42(7)
grow ~, 759.10
growing ~, 759.11
like an ~ woman, 759.18
~ man, 759.17
medical science of ~ people,
401.1(24)
never growing ~, 760.10
not ~ enough, 760.8,9
period of ~ age, 731.9(4,13,15,
16)
~ person, 759.3,8,9,17,18
person in terms of how ~ he
is, 758.2
pert. to ~ age, 759.14
science or study of ~ age,
759.25
science or study of ~ things,
759.26
science or study of ~ times,
759.26
sexual attraction toward ~
people, 710.33(16)
student of ~ things or times,
759.27
~ thing, 759.4,7; see also
antique,n.
too ~, 759.13
ugly ~ woman, 759.18(3,8,11)
without signs of ~ age, 759.12
~ woman, 759.18
older,adj., 759.20
be ~ than, 759.16
~ member, 759.24
state of appearing ~, 759.21
oldest,adj., 759.22
being the ~ born, 759.23
~ member, 759.24
old-fashioned,adj., 631.12,17
~ action, 631.16
~ attitude, 631.16
become ~, 631.14
becoming ~, 631.15
make ~, 631.13
~ people, 631.17
~ person, 631.18
~ phrase, 631.16
~ thing, 631.16
~ word, 631.16
olive,n.
belonging to the ~ family,
745.22(10)
like an ~, 745.22(11)
~-shaped, 507.17(53)
omen,n., 773.2,3; 951.4
omen,v., 773.1
ominous,adj., 773.4,5
omission,n., 73.2
shorten by ~, 911.2
shortened by ~ of end,
911.1(11)
shortened by ~ of letters,
911.1(1,16)
shortened by ~ of parts,
911.1(10,12,13,17,18)
shortened by ~ of syllables,
911.1(16)
shortened by ~ of words,
911.1(2,10,12,17,18)
omit,v., 73.1
omnibus,n., 192.6(2,6); see
bus,n.
one, n. or adj., 930.2

able to be made ~, 930.20
~ at a time, 930.15
become ~, 930.21
count ~ by one, 941.2
less than ~, 927.1(12)
made ~, 930.19,20
make into ~, 930.18
more than ~, 916.11
number ~, 930.2
one by ~, 930.15
only ~, 930.5–7
pert. to ~ only, 930.4,8
state of being ~, 930.22,23
oneness,n., 930.22,23
onion,n.
of the ~ family, 985.33(1)
smelling of ~s, 445.10(2)
onlooker,n., 484.3
only,adj., 930.16
only,adv., 930.17
opaque,adj., 1065.94
make ~, 1009.37
~ thing or object, 1065.95
open,adj., 298.5
become ~, 298.2
break ~, 802.1(11); 802.2(1)
cut ~, 332.1(29,52,61)
slightly ~ (of doors), 298.5(1)
~ space, 787.4
spread ~, 195.6(3)
~ to the air, 1045.6
open,v., 298.1,2
cause to ~, 298.1
charge for ~ing liquor bottles, 298.7
close and ~, 297.1(10); 297.11,
12,13,14
~s a way, that which, 298.6
~ the mouth, 298.2(4,6,7)
~ to the air, 1045.7
opened,adj., 298.5
opening,n., 298.3,4; see also
hole,n.
an ~, 298.4
anatomical ~, 298.8
battlement or parapet ~s,
568.33,35
containing ~s, 298.5
~ for flowing water, 1033.45
full of ~s, 298.5
having only one ~, 298.5(2)
~ in a volcano, 1048.46
~ in the earth, 170.9(1,2,5,6,
10,11); 298.9,10; see also
cave,n.
make an ~ in, 298.1
windowlike ~, 1009.8
without an ~, 297.3,10
opera,n., 969.1(28–30)
book of an ~, 687.1(15)
manager of an ~ company,
8.16(7)
words of an ~, 666.9(2);
666.11
operate,v.
act, 52.1
work, 203.1,2
~ surgically, 402.2,6
operation,n.
action, 52.2
working, 203.3
surgical ~, 402.1,5
surgical ~, susceptible to,
402.10
operator,n.
surgeon, 402.3,7
worker, 203.7
opinion,n., 633.8
adjustment of ~, 633.18
admitting of ~, 633.15
ambiguous ~, 633.5
ask for ~s, 274.1(29)
based on ~, 633.13
based on one's own ~, 633.14

change ~s, 539.2(5,7,10,12,14,
15)
change in public ~, indicator
of, 1046.19
change of ~, 539.3(1,15,17)
~ changer, 1042.45,46
collection of ~s, 633.10
concealed ~, 970.53,54
debatable ~, 633.8(21)
display of popular ~, 633.3
division owing to difference
of ~, 325.3(6)
established ~, 633.8(6)
express an ~, 633.1
express an ~ ambiguously,
633.5
express a low ~ of, 840.1,4
express an unfavorable ~,
894.1
expressing an ~ of, 840.2
expression of ~ from a group,
633.2
expression of ~, means of,
633.4
extreme ~, 922.26
firm in ~, 633.17
fondness for ~s, 700.30(19);
700.32
form an ~, 633.1
formal ~, 633.8(5)
full of ~s, 633.16
group ~, 633.2
have an ~, 633.1
having the required ~, 633.6
incorrect ~, 633.8(9)
induced ~, 633.8(12)
low ~, 840.1,3,4
low ~, word that expresses,
840.4
means of expressing ~, 633.4
moderate ~, holder of, 923.5
moderation in ~s, 923.6
narrow in ~, 634.8
narrowness of ~, 634.7
not expressing an ~, 633.7
not permitted to express ~s,
475.7
personal ~, 633.8(17,19,20)
pert. to ~, 633.12
popular ~, 633.3; 633.8(17,18)
positive in ~, 633.17
praising ~, 851.5
preconceived ~, 633.8(13,14,
15)
prediction of public ~, skillful in, 1047.21
unfavorable ~, 838.2; 894.1,3
written ~, 633.9
wrong ~, 633.8(9)
opinionated,adj., 633.17
opossum,n.
bodily sac for ~ babies,
350.1(5,6)
pert. to the ~, 418.3
opponent,n., 544.4
~ of authority, 544.4(3)
~ of change, 544.10
~ of progress, 544.10
opportune,adj., 765.1; 837.1
opportunistic,adj.
~ action or procedure, 836.13
opportunism,n., 836.12
opposable,adj., 544.6
oppose,v., 544.1
one who ~s, 544.4
tendency to ~ authority,
544.2(7,9,13,15,16,21); see
also **disobedient**,adj.
that which ~s, 544.5
opposed,adj., 544.3
able to be ~, 544.6
~ to change, 544.8
~ to progress, 544.8
unable to be ~, 544.7
opposer,n., 544.4,5

opposing,adj., 544.3
  act as ~ weight, 947.14
  ~ weight, 947.13
opposite,adj., 546.1
  be ~, 546.4
  ~ in meaning, 546.1(5)
  of two ~ characters, 931.3
  of two ~ natures, 931.3
opposite,adv., 546.5
  able to be placed ~, 323.7
  put ~, 323.1(3)
opposite,n., 546.3
oppositeness,n., 546.2
opposition,n., 544.2
  act in ~, 544.1
  be in ~, 544.1
  boastful ~, 544.2(5)
  crushing ~, 22.30
  in ~, 544.3
  ~ of law or rule, 544.2(2)
  passive ~ to laws, 544.2(6)
  say in ~, 544.1(4,6,9,11,12,22–
    25,27,29,30,33,34,37) ; see
    also **dispute, quarrel**,v.
  show ~, 544.1
  ~ to authority, 544.2(7,9,13,
    15,16,21) ; see also **disobedi-
    ence**,n.
  ~ to change, 544.9
  ~ to government, 544.2(18) ;
    1073.108
  ~ to law, 544.2(6)
  ~ to progress, 544.9
  ~ to tradition, 544.2(11)
  ~ to war, 544.2(14)
  ~ to worship, 544.2(11)
  group in ~, 318.1(98)
oppress,v., 889.6,7; 890.4
oppressed,adj., 8.13; 889.8
oppression,n., 889.7; 1073.59
  force by ~, 3.3(9)
  free of ~, 309.11(11,12)
oppressive,adj., 889.6,7; 890.4;
  1073.59
optimism,n., 267.2
optimist,n., 267.3
optimistic,adj., 267.1
option,n., 252.9(1)
optional,adj., 252.12(3)
orange,n.
  color, 500.1
  descr. of ~s, 745.22(4)
  raising of ~s, 745.25(1)
  ~ tree, 996.4(4)
  ~ trees, 996.29(5)
  ~-type fruit, 745.1(10)
oration,n., 671.2
orator,n., 671.3; 671.3(2)
oratory,n., 671.2
orbit,n., 123.4
  ~ of comet, 1053.21,22
  ~ of moon, 1054.25,26
  ~ of planet or comet, farthest
    point in, 1053.21
  ~ of planet or comet, nearest
    point in, 1053.22
  ~ of sun, 1055.11
orchestra,n., 479.17
order (arrangement),n., 311.1;
  see also **arrangement**,n.
  bring back to ~, 902.9
  disturb the ~ of, 1101.10–13
  in good ~, 902.6
  ~ of following, 173.7
  second in ~, 931.21
  superior in position, ~, or
    rank, 833.4
  third in ~, 932.17
  without ~, 903.1(3–5,7,13–15)
order (command),n., 275.2
  ~ by the church, 275.2(3,4)
  ~ by the Pope, 275.2(2)
  containing an ~, 275.4
  court ~, 275.2(11,13) ; 1081.15–
    17

  ~ demanding presence in
    court, 275.2(11)
  issue a revoking ~, 275.9
  one who gives an ~, 275.3
  pert. to an ~, 275.4
  put in an ~ for services,
    275.10
  right to give ~s, 275.7
order (command),v., 275.1
  put in an order for, 275.10
  ~ by law, 275.1(1)
  ~ for treatment, 275.10(4)
  ~ in advance, 275.10(1,2,5,6)
  ~ not to, 275.8; see **forbid**,v.
  one who ~s, 275.3
  ~ (someone) about, 275.1(9)
  ~ the services of, 275.10(3)
  ~ to come, 275.1(14)
  ~ to come to court, 275.1(13)
  ~ with authority, 275.1(1,5)
ordered (commanded),adj.,
  275.5
orderly,adj.
  obedient, 551.1; see **obedient**,
    adj.
  neat, tidy, 902.6; see also
    neat, tidy,adj.
  compulsively ~, 902.8
  excessively ~, 902.8
  ~ in habits, 902.7
  keep a place ~, 1078.9
  make ~, 551.11; 902.9
ordinary,adj., 535.1–3,10–12
  be ~, 535.4
organ (musical instru-
  ment),n.
  keyboard of an ~, 479.12
  player of an ~, 479.9;
    479.9(18)
  street ~, 479.8(2,14,16)
organ (part of the body),n.
  internal ~s, 347.9
  pert. to a bodily ~, 388.1(6)
organism,n.
  animal ~s, 403.21
organize,v.
  arrange, 311.2
  begin, 729.1
organization,n.
  arrangement, 311.1,3
  start, 729.2
  business ~, 210.7
orgasm,n., 710.24
  attain ~ by manipulation,
    710.26–29; see also **mastur-
    bation**,n.
  ~ from rubbing, 710.33(15)
  inability to reach ~, 710.30
  ~ produced by tongue, etc.,
    710.33(2,7,11,21,30)
  withdrawal of penis before ~,
    710.25
orgies,n.
  addiction to drunken ~,
    749.45
orgy,n., 1105.17
  merrymaking, 201.1,2
oriental,adj.
  become ~, 430.18; 784.13
  knowledge of ~ languages,
    customs, etc., 430.16
  make ~, 430.18; 784.10(7,8)
  ~ trait, custom, etc., 430.19
origin,n., 728.1,4; 729.11; see
  also **beginning, source**,n.
  acting as ~, 728.5
  an ~, 728.4
  ~ and survival of species,
    theory of, 728.17(5)
  be the ~ of, 728.18
  consider as the ~ of, 893.7
  country of ~, 784.1(3)
  doctrines of ~, 728.17
  earliest in ~, 766.6(9)
  family ~, 728.3

  from an ~, 728.13; see **orig-
    inating**,adj., below
  give ~ to, 728.18
  gods' ~ and descent, 728.7
  have an ~, 729.7
  national ~, 728.2
  ~ of a trait, 728.8
  of common ~, 728.16
  ~ of humanity, theories of,
    728.17(5–9)
  of irregular ~, 728.14
  ~ of life, theories of,
    728.17(1–3,6,10)
  of mixed ~, 728.15
  of the same ~, 728.16
  ~ of the world, theory of,
    728.17(4)
  place of ~, 728.4
  that which is an ~, 728.4
  theories of ~, 728.17
  words of common ~, 666.12(2,
    4,9)
  world's ~, 728.6
original,adj., 728.10; 726.27;
  761.1
  in ~ state or form, 728.11
  ~ in growth, 728.12
original,n., 726.20; 761.3
  ~ from which copied, 728.9
  ~ from which derived,
    728.4(20)
originality,n., 726.27; 761.2
  lacking ~, 535.5–9
originate,v., 728.18; 729.1,7; see
  also **begin**,v.
  create, 726.17
originating,adj.
  ~ from a single cell, 728.13(6)
  ~ from a single parent,
    728.13(7)
  ~ from emotions, 728.13(8)
  ~ from within, 728.13(1,2)
  ~ from without, 728.13(3–5,9)
origination,n., 726.18; 728.1;
  729.2,8; see also **origin, be-
    ginning, source**,n.
originator,n., 726.19; 728.18;
  729.3
  consider as the ~ of, 893.7
ornament,n., 959.3; see also
  decoration,n.
  addiction to ~, 959.21
  body, ~ worn on the, 961.1
  cheap ~, 959.5
  church ~s, science of, 645.8
  clothing and ~s, 974.1(3)
  dress ~, 959.3(10,17)
  flat ~, 959.3(15)
  floral ~, 959.3(9) ; 994.21
  garment ~, 959.3(10,17)
  hair ~, 983.42–44
  hanging ~, 172.7; 959.3(14)
  head ~, 959.3(4) ; 961.2;
    983.24
  helmet ~, 959.3(5)
  inappropriate ~, 959.3(16)
  jeweled ~, 961.1
  jeweled head ~, 961.2
  lack of ~, 959.10
  luck ~, 35.5
  magic ~, 663.11
  medal-shaped ~, 959.3(12)
  military ~, 959.3(1,7)
  naval ~, 959.3(1,7)
  office, ~s of, 959.4(2)
  pert. to ~, 959.16
  projecting ~, 958.7(13)
  rank, ~s of, 959.4(2)
  ~s, collectively, 959.4
  shiny ~, 1065.62
  shoulder ~, 959.3(7)
  showy ~, 959.6
  showy ~s, 951.46; 959.6
  small ~, 959.3(22)

sun's rays, ~ in shape of,
  959.3(20)
superfluous ~, 959.3(16)
table ~, 959.3(3,8)
tree branch ~, 959.3(19) ;
  990.7
triangular ~, 945.4
use of ~s, 959.20,21
used for ~, 959.17
wax ~s, 959.4(4)
without ~s, 959.9
worthless ~, 959.5
ornament,v., 959.1
~ dress, 959.1(4,12,15–17,23,26,
  30)
~ edge of, 959.1(23,26)
~ excessively, 959.1(1,21)
~ food, 959.1(19)
~ garments, 959.1(4,12,15–17,
  23,26,30)
~ handwriting, 959.1(13) ;
  959.14; 1065.76
~ head, 959.1(5)
~ letter with color, 1065.76
~ manuscript with color,
  1065.76
~ page with color, 1065.76
serving to ~, 959.17
~ skin, 959.1(28)
~ text with pictures, 965.14
~ with a star, 1056.30
~ with checks, 959.1(29)
~ with curtains, 959.1(22)
~ with diamonds, 962.18
~ with drapes, 959.1(22)
~ with feathers, 959.1(24)
~ with flowers, 959.1(18) ;
  994.22
~ with gems, 959.1(9) ; 961.4
~ with jewels, 959.1(9) ; 961.4
~ with leaves, 959.1(14)
~ with light, 1065.76
~ with pearls, 963.17
~ with pictures, 965.14
~ with projections, 959.1(27)
~ with sculpture, 966.14
~ with shiny things, 1065.63
~ with tree branch, 990.8
ornamental,adj., 959.17
~ articles, 959.4(1)
make ~, 959.18
not ~, 959.22
~ plant, 959.3(13)
ornamentation,n., 959.2,3; see
  also decoration, orna-
  ment,n.
architectural ~, 959.8(1)
cheap ~, 959.7
church ~, science of, 645.8
frost ~, 1059.11
heraldic ~, art of, 959.12
inappropriate ~, 959.13
interlaced lines, ~ by,
  959.3(21)
lack of ~, 959.10
~ on silver, 1015.18
showy ~, 959.7
skin ~, 959.15
superfluous ~, 959.13
vulgar ~, 959.7
without ~, 959.9
ornamented,adj., 959.8
~ by stars, 1056.29
conspicuously ~, 959.8(5)
excessively ~, 959.8(5,10)
gracefully ~, 959.8(3)
highly ~, 959.8(1,3,5,7–10)
inappropriately ~, 959.13
showily ~, 959.8(1)
tastelessly ~, 959.8(1,10)
unable to be ~, 959.23
unnecessarily ~, 959.13
vulgarly ~, 959.8(1)
~ with flowers, 959.8(6) ;
  994.20,23

~ with moons, 1054.21
~ with pearls, 963.16
ornamenter,n., 959.19
ornate,adj., 959.8(1,3,5,7,8,10)
orphan,n.
place for ~s, 568.26(3)
oscillate,v., 147.1,4; see also
  sway, swing,v.
ostentation,n., 951.35; see
  showiness,n.
ostentatious,adj., 951.34; see
  showy,adj.
ostracism,n., 296.2,3; 581.8,9,12
ostracize,v., 296.1; 581.6,11,12
~d person, 581.10
instance of ~ing, 581.8
state of being ~d, 581.9
otter,n.
of ~s, 403.11(7,10)
out,adv.
able to be pushed ~, 197.8
come ~, 140.1
draw ~, 193.18–22,24
drive ~, 144.1
go ~, 141.1; see depart,v.
go ~ (of a fire, etc.), 801.19
press or squeeze ~, 198.1(13)
pull ~, 193.18–22,24
push ~, 197.1(7,8,10–12,26–28,
  36,39,50,59) ; 197.2(2)
pushed ~, 197.10
put ~ (a fire, flame, etc.),
  801.17
put ~ (a light), 801.18
send ~, 189.1(2,8,15)
stretch ~, 194.1(1–10)
outcome,n., 16.1
outdoor, adj., adv., 138.1(1,19) ;
  1045.10–12
outer,adj., 138.1; see also outside,adj.
~ places, 782.1(15)
outlaw,n., 1088.2
outlaw,v., 1087.22–25
outlet,n., 140.5; 141.7
outline,n., 507.20; 912.1(3,4,6,
  14)
~ against the sky, 1051.11
blacked-in ~, 507.20(10)
book for rough ~s, 965.17
facial ~, 507.20(8)
give an ~ to, 507.21
instrument to make ~s,
  677.14(1)
~ of a story, 685.1(27)
~ of curves, 155.9
picture of the ~s of something, 965.1(56)
plan the ~ of a story, etc.,
  46.1(5)
rough ~, 965.16
outline,v., 507.21; 912.2
out-of-date,adj., 631.12
~ action, 631.16
~ attitude, 631.16
become ~, 631.14
becoming ~, 631.15
make ~, 631.13
~ person, 631.18
~ phrase, 631.16
~ thing, 631.16
~ word, 631.16
outside,adj., 138.1
~ a place, 1024.6
cause to be ~, 138.3
~ layer, 138.2(4)
~ limits, 138.2(1)
~ part, 138.2
~ parts, 138.2(2,3)
~ surface, 139.1(7)
~ the consciousness, 138.1(7,
  8)
~ the country, 138.1(16)
~ the earth, 138.1(13)
~ the home, 138.1(1,19)

~ the limits of territory,
  138.1(14)
~ the self, 138.1(2)
~ the solar system, 138.1(12)
~ the walls, 138.1(10)
~ the world, 138.1(9,13)
outside,n., 138.2
originating from the ~,
  138.1(3,4,11,13,15) ;
  728.13(3–5,9)
pert. or relating to the ~,
  138.1
outward,adv.
curve ~, 155.1(3,5)
curved ~, 155.4
turned ~, 148.10(3)
ovary,n., 379.1(5,12)
discharge of egg from the ~,
  380.9
inflammation of the ~,
  379.9(9)
tube from the ~, 379.1(13)
oven,n., 1061.9
~ for bricks, pottery, etc.,
  1061.13
portable ~, 1061.5(1)
over,adv.
jump ~, 110.1(15,34)
lying ~, 65.3(8,15,16)
overburdened,adj., 948.18
overcome,adj.
be ~, 22.26
capable of being ~, 22.31
incapable of being ~, 22.32
overcome,v., 22.23
~ by greater strength, 22.29
~ completely, 22.24
~ difficulties of, 22.28
~ difficulty, 22.27
~ feelings of, 22.25
hard to ~, 22.33
means of ~ing opposition,
  22.30
~ mind of, 22.25
~ obstacle, 22.27
~ obstacles of, 22.28
~ physically, 22.29
~ problems of, 22.28
overdo,v., 49.1(19,20)
overestimate,v., 839.16
overflowed,adj., 1034.20
~ by water, 112.6
overhang,v., 172.1(1,2,7,10–12,
  16)
overlook,v.
ignore, 581.6
neglect, 582.1
overpower,v., 22.23–25
~ emotionally, 1099.12
~ with lights or brightness,
  1065.78,79
overpowering,adj.
emotionally ~, 1099.13
overshadow,v., 1071.4
overshoes,n., 979.8
overstep,v., 130.1
overthrow,n., 22.35
overthrow,v., 22.34
acting to ~, 22.36
advocacy of ~ing the government, 1073.108
illegal act to ~ government,
  22.37
~ opposition, 22.39
~ revolt, 22.39
tending to ~, 22.36
overthrown,adj.
capable of being ~, 22.40
incapable of being ~, 22.41
overtired,adj., 12.1(24–26)
overused,adj., 282.6
overvalue,v., 839.16
overwhelm,v., 22.23–25
owe,v.

one to whom a debt is ~d, 218.8
one who ~s, 218.7

owl,v.
young ~, 405.4(10)

own,v.
admit, 675.1
have, 255.1; see **possess,v.**

owned,adj.
~ by two or more, 255.7
exclusively ~, 255.9
privately ~, 255.9
something ~, 255.10

owner,n., 255.3
land~, 255.3(2); 1003.19,21, 24
land~s, 255.4
property ~, 255.3(1)
~s, collectively, 255.4

ownership,n., 255.2
admit ~ of, 675.1(2)
common ~, 255.2(1)
give into common ~, 255.8
government according to ~ of property, 1073.3(33)
joint ~, 255.2(2-4)
land ~, pert. to, 1003.18
summary of previous ~, 912.1(1)

owning,adj.
land~, 1003.20

ox,n.
mythical creature, half ~, half man, 662.26(1)
small ~, 410.1(8)

oxen,n.
group of ~, 403.5(73)
of ~, 403.11(2,12)
wild ~, 410.7

Oxford,n.
graduate of ~, 623.12(9)
inhabitant of ~, 784.15(47)
student at ~, 622.5(15)

oxygen,n., 1049
able to live or be active in ~, 1049.9
add ~ to, 1049.4
breathe ~ into the (blood), 1049.8
change into ~ compound, 1049.2
combine with ~, 1049.3
compound of ~, 1049.1
lack of ~, 1049.11
lack of ~, caused by or pert. to, 1049.14
lack of ~, requiring, 1049.12
microorganism able to live in absence of ~, 1049.13
microorganism living in ~, 1049.10
remove ~ from, 1049.15,16
requiring ~, 1049.9
treat with ~, 1049.5
~ with odor of chlorine, 1049.17
without ~, able to live or be active, 1049.12

oyster,n., 422.3; 422.3(1)
covering on ~s, 972.4(20)
crop of ~s, 422.5
eggs of ~s, 422.6
of ~s, 422.1(5,6,25,27)
science of ~s, 403.26(11,23)
young ~, 422.4(7,8)

ozone,n.
containing ~, 1049.18

P

Pacific Ocean,n.
across the ~, 1029.72(21)

pack,n., 318.1,16,18

pack,v., 319.2,7
closely ~ed, 319.8

instrument for ~ing down, 319.9

package,n., 318.18
small ~, 318.18(14,15)

pact,n., 541.13

pad,n.
~ of paper, 684.10(9)

pagan,adj., 642.4; 642.4(1); 643.12

pagan,n., 642.5; 643.13

paganism,n., 642.3(7)

page,n., 684.13
usher, 131.3
bind in ~s, 684.16
~-by-page, 684.20
consisting of ~s, 684.19
figures by which ~s are numbered, 684.18
inner part of a ~, 684.14
number ~s, 684.15
number of ~s in a book, 684.17
ornament a ~, 1065.76
pert. to ~s, 684.19
~s in a book, 684.12

paid,n.
person ~, 219.5

pail,n., 261.1(7); see **container,n.**
~ for emptying boat, 1035.14

pain,n., 1130.6,11; 1137.5,10,56; see also **torture,n.**
a ~, 1130.11; 1137.5,56
attack of ~, 560.24(5,7,8,14,15, 18,21,25); 1137.7
be in ~, 1137.11
bear ~, 1137.36
bear ~, ability to, 1137.35
bodily ~s, cause, 1137.61
bodily ~s, causing, 1137.60
bodily ~s, specific, 1137.56
cause ~, 1130.1,5; 1137.9
cause a burning ~ to, 1137.1(5,6,17,18)
cause a sharp ~ to, 1137.1(5, 6,12,13,17,18)
cause bodily ~, 1137.61
cause or source of ~, 1130.2, 3; 1137.2,4,24,29
cause ~ to, 1137.1,61
causes ~, experience that, 1130.16-19
causing ~, 1130.4,12; 1137.3, 60
causing bodily ~s, 1137.60
causing very little ~, 1137.54
conscience ~, 885.4
cry in ~, 1127.1(1,5,6,12,13)
draw back in ~, 145.1(3,7,9, 25,27); 1130.13; 1137.19
drug that relieves ~, 1137.45
enjoyment from inflicting ~, 1137.27
enjoyment of another's ~, 1137.27
enjoyment of one's own ~, 1137.26
ethics of pleasure and ~, 1105.25
extreme ~, 922.17
facial expression of ~, 365.2(5); 1130.15; 1137.21
feel ~, 1130.8; 1137.11
feel ~ in the bowels, 1137.62
feeling of ~, 1137.22,23
final ~ before death, 1137.10(1)
freedom from ~, 1131.18
full of ~, 1137.12
give ~, 230.1(34)
giving ~, 1137.28
grimace with ~, 1130.15; 1137.21
in ~, 1130.7,9; 1137.12,57,59
in extreme ~, 922.18

~ in arm, 1137.56(30)
~ in back, 1137.56(1,19,26)
~ in belly, 1137.56(2,7,10,13, 15,27,30)
~ in bone, 1137.56(23)
~ in bowels, 1137.56(2,7,10,13, 15,27,30)
~ in ear, 1137.56(12)
~ in fingers from writing, 1137.56(31)
~ in foot, 1137.56(14,24)
~ in hand, 1137.56(5,6,14)
~ in head, 1137.56(16); 1137.65-68
~ in hip, 1137.56(8,25)
~ in mouth, 1137.56(28)
~ in muscles, 1137.56(4,9,11, 21)
~ in muscles, causing, 1137.60(1)
~ in nerve, 1137.56(22)
~ in nerve, causing, 1137.60(2)
~ in one side of body, 1137.56(18)
~ in side, 1137.56(26)
~ in stomach, 1137.56(2,7,10, 13,15,27,30)
~ in thigh, 1137.56(25)
~ in toe, 1137.56(14)
~ in uterus, 1137.56(20)
inflict ~, tending to, 1137.28
insensitive to ~, 1137.40
insensitive to ~, make, 1137.37,38
insensitiveness to ~, 1137.39
insensitiveness to ~, causing, 1137.41
insensitiveness to ~, drug or agent that causes, 1137.42
insensitiveness to ~, process of producing, 1137.43
lack of ~, 1137.44
measurement of ~, 1137.51, 53
~ near the heart, 1137.56(17)
occasion of ~, 1130.20
origin or source of ~, 1130.2, 3; 1137.2,4,24,29
person in ~, 1130.10; 1137.58
pert. to ~, 1137.25
place or scene of ~, 1130.20-22
psychology of pleasure and ~, 1105.25
reduce the ~ of, 1131.16,17; 1137.49,50
reduced sensitiveness to ~, 1137.33,34
relieve ~, 1137.47,49
relieve ~ without curing, 1137.50
relieve or remove ~, drug or agent to, 1137.45; 1139.1(24)
relieved of ~, become, 1137.48
relieving or removing ~, 1137.46
sensitiveness to ~, 433.18(1, 12); 1137.30-32
sensitiveness to ~, decreased, 1137.33,34
sexual aberration relating to ~, 710.33(1,23,27)
shrink from ~, 1130.13; 1137.19
shrink in ~, 145.1(3,7,9,25,27)
shrinking from ~, not, 1130.14; 1137.20
soothe ~, 1137.47; 1139.1(24)
sounds of ~, 468.1(1,4-6,9,11, 14,15-17)
source of ~, 1130.2,3; 1137.2, 4,24,29

stab, pierce, or tear with ~, 1137.13
sudden ~s that stab like lightning, descr. of, 1137.6
temporary ~, place or condition of, 1130.22
~ that comes in attacks, descr. of, 1137.8
without ~, 1130.28; 1137.55
pain,v.
~ emotionally or mentally, 1130.1,5; see also torture,v.
~ physically, 1137.1,9; see also torture,v.
painful,adj.
emotionally or mentally painful, 1130.4
physically painful, 1137.3,12
be emotionally ~, 1130.1,5
be physically ~, 1137.9
causing ~ movements, 1137.18
make physically ~ from rubbing, 1137.14–17
~ to a bodily part, 1137.60
paint,v., 965.2,3
painter,n., 965.7; see also artist,n.
painting,n., 965.1,4–6; see also art, drawing, picture, portrait, sketch,n.
a ~, 965.1
art of ~, 965.6
artist of the past, a ~ by, 965.1(32)
artist's name on a ~, 965.32
exhibition of ~s, 965.10
masters, a ~ borrowed from, 965.31
movements in ~, 965.39
oil ~, 965.1(5)
pert. to ~, 965.8
plaster, ~ on wet, 965.1(23)
principles of ~, 965.39
process of ~, 965.5
~s, collectively, 965.9
schools of ~, 965.39
small ~, 965.9(4); 965.1(33)
small ~, art of, 909.10
theories of ~, 965.39
unskillful ~, 965.1(10)
varied sources, ~ of, 965.31
wall ~, 965.1(16,35,51)
water-color ~, 965.1(2,3,24, 58)
pair,n., 931.1
growing in ~s, 731.5(5)
pair,v., 931.11
~ unlike things or people, 540.8
palace,n., 727.12(1)
pert. to a ~, 753.3
royal ~, 1073.30
pale,adj., 384.11; 488.8(25); 489.1
~ as ashes, 1064.50
~ animal, 489.6
become ~, 384.14; 489.3
~ in color, 488.8(25); 489.1
~ in complexion, 384.11
make ~, 384.14; 489.4
make ~, like chalk, 1006.43
~ person, 384.13; 489.6
~ plant, 489.6
paleness,n., 384.12; 489.2
pallor,n., 384.12; 489.2
palm (of hand),n., 343.5
pert. to the ~, 343.6
palm (plant),n.
~ fiber for weaving, 993.29
palmistry,n., 772.20(44)
pamper,v., 1108.1
pamphlet,n., 687.1(22)
seller of religious ~s, 687.17(2)

selling of religious ~s, 687.18
write ~s, 687.3
writer of ~s, 687.2
pan,n., 261.10; see also pot,n.
frying ~, 261.10(11,12)
pancake,n., 1062.4
pancreas,n.
pert. to the ~, 388.1(7)
secretion of the ~, 287.8(7)
pangolin,n.
of ~s, 403.11(4)
panther,n.
female ~, 406.10
like a ~, 406.12,14
pert. to a ~, 406.11,13
pantomime,n.
actor in a ~, 102.3(1)
art of ~, 102.7
author of a ~, 102.6
play in a ~, 102.10
pants,n., 980.1; see trousers,n.
paper,n., 684.10
ancient ~, 684.10(3)
book ~, 684.12
glassy ~, 1009.51
like ~, 684.11
page of ~, 684.13
roll of ~, 684.10(7)
sheets of ~, 684.10(2,5,6,9)
sound of ~, 469.1(4–7,16)
strips of ~, 684.10(1)
parade,n., 318.15
~ official, 1077.1(20)
paradise,n., 1051.14,22,24
girl of Mohammedan ~, 760.6(11)
like ~, 1051.23
pert. to ~, 1051.15
paraffin,n., 1068.1(5,6)
parallel,adj.
make ~, 179.9
~ to the horizon, 179.8(4)
parallelogram,n., 945.7
paralysis,n., 377.15
attack of ~, 560.24(24)
~ from emotion, 377.15(1,9–11)
infantile ~, 354.17(9)
~ of speech muscles, 377.15(4)
paralytic,n., 377.17
paralyze,v., 377.18
paralyzed,adj., 377.16
~ person, 377.17
paralyzing,adj., 377.19
paranoia,n.
like ~, 1136.14
parapet,n., 568.30
openings in a ~, 568.35
parasite,n., 750.17
be a ~, 750.20
destroyer of ~s, 398.8(11)
infested with ~s, 403.18(7)
multiplication of animal ~s, 717.12(7)
science of animal ~s, 403.26(35)
victim of a ~, 750.21
parasitic,adj., 750.19
living on or in, but not ~, 750.22,23
parasitism,n., 750.18
parchment,n.
manuscript, 684.1; see manuscript,n.
~ of animal skin, 382.1(20)
pardon,n., 897.2,7; see forgiveness,n.
pardon,v., 897.1,6,12; see forgive,v.
pardonable,adj., 897.9,16
parent,n., 724.1; 725.1; see father, mother,n.

originating from a single ~, 728.13(7)
parental,adj., 724.2; 725.2
parish,n.
pert. to a ~, 782.1(17)
parliament,n., 1080.12; see legislature,n.
parlor,n., 787.8
parrot,n.
like a ~, 405.10(2)
parrot fever,n., 396.1(23,24)
part,n., 326.1,6,9,10; see also division, piece,n.
arrangement of ~s, 311.1(9, 10,13,25,41,46)
~ as a share, 326.1(24,26,33)
be a ~ of, 326.41
be a typical ~ of, 326.41(4)
be made up of (~s), 326.51
become ~ of the body of, cause to, 326.46
being a ~ of, 326.42
being an essential ~ of the whole, 326.44
belong as a ~ of, 326.41(1)
best ~, 326.1(27)
bitterest ~, 326.1(12)
bottom ~, 326.1(7,36,37)
break into ~s, 326.12,13
break off a ~, 326.12
break up into its ~s, 802.25
broken ~, 326.10
central ~, 326.33
central ~ of a fruit, 326.34
central ~ of a tree, 326.34
central ~ of a wheel, 326.35
conspicuous ~, 326.1(15)
cut into ~s, 326.12,13; 332.7(3)
cut into three ~s, 332.1(68)
cut into two ~s, 332.1(15)
cut into two equal ~s, 332.1(2); 332.7(1)
cut-off ~, 326.10
cut off a ~, 326.12
descr. of a ~, 326.2,7,11
divide into ~s, 326.8
divide into small ~s, 326.28
divided into many ~s, 326.53(2)
divided into three ~s, 326.53(3)
divisional ~, 326.6
essential ~, 326.29,45
essential ~, 326.32
essential ~ to the whole, 326.9,45
evil ~, 326.1(40)
extended ~, 326.1(5,20,28,36, 40)
facial ~, 326.1(15)
first ~, 326.1(27,29)
folded ~, 326.1(25)
~ for feeling or touching, 326.1(40)
hanging ~, 326.1(39)
having many ~s, 326.53(2)
having three corresponding ~s, 326.53(3)
having two corresponding ~s, 326.53(1)
important ~, 326.29,31
~ in disagreement with the rest, 326.6(13)
incomplete ~, 326.1(8,16,32)
innermost ~, 326.1(9); 326.33
inseparable ~, 326.43
involved as a necessary ~, 522.2
larger ~, 326.1(6)
least ~, 326.26
less important ~, 326.1(1)
made up of distinct or different ~s, 326.47(2,6,7,9, 22)

made up of non-correspond-
ing ~s, 326.47(1)
made up of ~s, 326.47
made up of ~s from over the
world, 326.47(16)
made up of ~s of two kinds,
or of two forms of life,
326.47(3)
made up of three ~s,
326.47(26,27)
made up of two ~s, 326.47(17)
main ~, 326.29,31
make up from ~s, 326.52
make-up of ~s, 326.49
minute ~ of matter, 326.25
not a ~ of, 326.54
~ of a debt, 326.1(17)
~ of a mixture, 326.9(7)
~ of a story, 326.1(17)
~ of an organization,
326.6(13)
~ on which others depend,
326.30
one of two equal ~s, 326.1(21)
outer ~, 138.2
outer ~s, 138.2(2,3)
permanent ~, 326.43
pert. to a ~, 326.2,7,11
~ productive of result,
326.9(6)
projecting ~, 326.1(28,36,40)
related ~s, 326.4,5
remaining ~, 326.1(36,37) ;
326.24
sectional ~, 326.6
separate into ~s, 326.3
shaved-off ~, 326.10(15,23)
simplest ~, 326.9(5)
small ~, 326.23–27
small ~ of something heard,
326.27
small remaining ~, 326.24
soft inner ~, 443.6
split-off ~, 326.10(24,32)
sum of ~s, 328.8
surrounding ~s, 783.1(4,6,13)
tear into ~s, 326.12,13
tear off a ~, 326.12
thin ~, 326.1(34,35)
torn ~, 326.10(19,25,33)
~ typical of the whole,
326.1(13)
unimportant ~, 326.1(10)
worst ~, 326.1(12)
partial,adj.
favorably inclined, 837.2
having a liking for, 1109.4
incomplete, 329.1
prejudiced, 634.2
participant,n., 51.4
leading ~, 51.6
participate,v., 51.1
participated,adj.
~ in by four, 933.13
~ in by three, 932.24
~ in by two, 931.16,17
participation,n., 51.2
particle,n., 326.17; see **piece**,n.
cloud of ~s, 1057.18
small ~, 917.15
particular,adj.
choosy, 252.15
separate, 325.8
single, 930.3
special, 540.25
particular,n., 327.1; see **detail**,n.
partridge,n.
group of ~s, 403.5(6,15)
of ~s, 405.9(9)
party (entertainment),n.,
201.2; see also **merry-
making**,n.
activities of a ~, 201.14
attend a ~, 201.3

drinking ~, 748.17
engaging in a ~, 201.6
excitement of ~s, 1100.7(8)
fond of a ~, 1100.11
~ for men, 1050.11
~ for smoking, 1050.11
gaiety of a ~, 201.13
giver of a ~, 201.18
like a ~, 201.8
masked ~, 970.27
merry ~s, 1104.9–11
merry ~s, season or time of,
1104.12
pert. to a ~, 201.7
place for ~s, 201.16
pleasure of a ~, 201.13
rapid round of ~s, 201.15
suitable for a ~, 201.8
those who attend a ~, 201.4
~ to the memory of someone,
627.34(3,4)
~ with cooked food, 1061.4
party (political),n., 1076.14;
see **political party**,n.
pass,v., 120.1
able to be ~ed through, 121.4
~ on (judge) written material, 8.1(3)
~ over, 121.1
permit to ~, 554.7
~ through, 121.1
~ through a membrane,
121.1(10) ; 121.2(1) ; 121.7
~ through a river mouth,
121.1(7)
~ time, 762.13–20
unable to be ~ed through,
121.5
passage,n., 122.1; see also
road,n.
a passing, 120.2
arched ~, 122.1(6,10,36)
~ closed at one end, 122.1(8,
13,15,23)
confusion of winding ~ways,
605.17
elevator ~, 122.1(22,32)
~ for water, 1033.22,32
underground ~, 122.1(32,33,
35)
passion,n., 1092.25,27
become excited (of ~s),
1092.50
become excited by ~, 1092.49
carried away by ~, 1092.26,27
carried away by a foolish ~,
1092.45,46
carry away with a foolish ~,
1092.48
easily moved to ~, 1099.18
foolish ~, 1092.47
pert. to bodily ~s, 338.8
quenching of ~s, 1131.18
violent or base ~s, marked
by, 1092.33
wild with ~, 1100.6(11)
passionate,adj., 1092.26
extremely ~, 1092.39
passionateness,n., 1092.27
passive,adj., 58.1; 552.3; see
inactive,adj.
passport,n.
signature of approval on a
~, 696.2(2)
password,n., 666.3(16,52)
secret ~, 956.1(4)
past,adj., 771.8,10–12
past,n., 771.4,5
belonging to the ~, 759.1; see
also **old**,adj.
descr. of, or relating to, the
~, 771.8,10–12
descr. of the ~, before
electricity, 1048.26
desire for the ~, 265.2(17)

distant ~, 771.5,6
events of the ~, 771.7; see
also **history**,n.
in the ~, 771.8,9,12
in the distant ~, 771.11
in the recent ~, 771.10
object associated with the
~, 759.4,5,7
recent ~, 771.4
remains from the ~, 757.4(5,
13,18–20) ; see also **fossil**,n.
science or study of the ~,
759.26
sign of the ~, 951.4(27)
student of the ~, 759.27
paste,n., 302.14,26
like ~, 302.24(4,13)
paste,v., 302.12
pastime,n., 200.5; see **amusement**,n.
pastor,n., 646.1; see **clergyman**,n.
pastry,n., 1062.6
store for French ~, 741.5
paternal,adj., 724.2; see
fatherly,adj.
paternity,n., 724.4
path,n., 122.1; 123.1; see also
passage, road,n.
confusion of winding ~s,
605.17
~ of a comet, 1053.21,22
~ of a curve, 123.4(1)
~ of a moving body, 123.4
~ of a planet, 1053.21,22
~ of a point, 123.4(1)
~ of energy, 2.29
~ of planets, 1053.20
~ of the moon, 1054.25,26
~ of the sun, 1055.11
winding ~s, 123.3
pathetic,adj., 1125.16; 1129.13
unsuccessful in ~ effect,
17.1(2)
patience,n., 272.8
tolerating with ~, 246.2(1,2)
lose ~ with, 272.13
patient,adj. 246.3; 272.7
be ~, 272.9
bear ~ly, 246.1(1,2,5)
~ in pain, hardship, etc.,
272.7(3–6)
patient,n., 389.6
patriotism,n., 784.8
exaggerated ~, 784.8(1,2,5,6)
extreme ~, 784.8(6)
offensive ~, 784.8(1,2)
patron,n., 211.4
~ of the arts or literature,
568.21
patronage,n., 211.2
support for artists, 568.20
care and ~, 570.5
pattern,n., 311.8; see **design**,n.
pause,n., 791.3; see also **stop**,n.
~ in hostilities, etc., 791.3(1)
~ in poetry or music rhythm,
791.3(3)
pause,v., 791.2; see also **stop**,v.
pave,v., 1006.4
pavement,n., 1006.5
stone for ~, 1006.1(9,10,14,15)
pawn,v., 1122.37,38
something ~ed, 1122.39,41
pawnbroker,n., 1122.42
pert. to a ~, 218.10; 1122.43
shop of a ~, 1122.44
pawner,n., 1122.40
pay,n., 219.3; see **payment**,n.
pay,v., 219.1
agree to ~ the expenses of,
219.6
~ attention, 579.1; see **attention**,n., **attentive**,adj.

~ back, 219.1(17,18,22–24) ; 221.1
~ back for injury, wrong, etc., 221.1(1,4–8)
~ back in kind, 221.1
~ for damage or injury, 219.1(4,9,15,24) ; 222.1(2,6,7, 10)
~ for loss, 219.1(4,9,15,24) ; 222.1(2,5–7,10)
~ing well, 219.7
not ~ debts, 218.16
promise to ~, 1122.4–6,8,22,24
payment,n., 219.2,3
additional ~, 219.3(6,15,34,38, 39) ; 219.8
anchoring or tying up ship, ~ for, 219.3(33) ; 1033.16
ask for ~, 274.1(15)
attack, ~ to avoid, 219.3(60) ; 223.8
author, ~ to, 219.3(47)
bravery, ~ for, 219.11(10)
damage, ~ for, 222.2
delay ~, period when one may, 768.5,6
divorce, ~ during or after, 219.3(1)
evade ~ of, 76.1(3,29)
excellence, ~ for, 219.11
government ~, 219.3(7,28,53)
group, yearly ~ to a, 219.3(58)
~ in kind, 221.2,3
injury, ~ for, 219.3(3,45,50) ; 222.2
interest ~, 219.3(13,46)
loss, ~ for, 222.2
newcomer, ~ from a, 219.3(26)
non-~ of debts, 218.17
part ~, 219.3(19,31,55)
pert. to ~, 219.4
poor, ~ to the, 219.3(14,43)
pound, ~ per, 219.3(57)
punishment, ~ as, 219.3(25)
receipt for ~, 240.10
release of animal, ~ for, 219.3(37)
religious organization, ~ to, 219.3(54)
rescue of ship, ~ for, 219.3(49)
respect, ~ out of, 219.3(60)
ride, ~ for a, 219.3(23)
salary ~, 219.3(20,21,30)
sale, ~ from, 219.3(42)
seal a bargain, ~ to, 219.3(19)
services, ~ for, 219.3(8,10,11, 15,17,20,21,24,29,34,48,51,52, 61)
small ~, 219.3(35)
thanks, ~ out of, 219.3(60)
tip, ~ as a, 219.8
ton, ~ per, 219.3(57)
towing, ~ for, 219.3(59)
transportation, ~ for, 219.3(9,16,22,23,27)
unwilling ~, 219.3(60)
use of money, ~ for, 219.3(13, 32)
use of property, ~ for, 219.3(44,47) ; see also rent,n.
winner, ~ to, 219.3(40) ; 219.11
work, ~ for, 219.3(8,10,11,17, 20,21,24,29,34,48,51,52,61)
yearly ~, 219.3(4,30,58)
pea,n., 745.20
covering of ~s, 972.4(14)
pert. to, or like, ~s, 745.22(6)
peace,n., 1140.12,23; see also peacefulness,n., below
advocate of ~, 1149.28
~ agreement, 1140.30,31

bring back ~, tending to, 1140.36
bringing about ~, 1140.2
condition leading to ~, 1140.18
disturb the ~, 1101.4,5,9
disturbance of the ~, 1101.1(8,21,22,25,34,35,38)
emotional ~, 1131.18 ; 1140.25, 26
friendliness and ~, 1096.2(1)
~ from emotional serenity, 1131.18
harmful to ~, 803.3(6)
inclined to ~, 1140.15
inner ~, 1131.18 ; 1140.25,26
lack of ~, 1140.14,39
like ~, 1140.33
~maker, 1140.4
not bringing about ~, 1140.3
~ offering, 1140.20,21
period of ~ and calmness, 1139.17
pert. to ~, 1140.36
suggestion for ~, 1140.19
symbol of ~, 1140.27
temporary ~, 1140.32
time of ~, 1102.26,27; 1140.29
uninclined to ~, 1140.16
violation of the ~, 802.32; 1101.1(8,21,22,25,34,35,38) ; 1140.37
without ~, 1140.40
peaceful,adj., 1140.11
able to be made ~, 1140.8
become ~, 1140.10
belief in ~ negotiations, 1140.22
breach of ~ relations, 802.33
happy, calm, and ~, 1102.30
made ~, 1140.5,6
make ~, 1140.1
making ~, 1140.2
not ~, 1140.13,14
not made ~, 1140.7
not making ~, 1140.3
~ person, 1140.17
~ relations, 1140.24
unable to be made ~, 1140.9
peacefulness,n., 1140.12,23; see also peace,n., above
avoid rupture of ~, 1140.35
disturb ~, 1101.9
lack of ~, 1140.14,39
prevent rupture of ~, 1140.35
peach,n., 745.1(5)
pert. to, or like, ~es, 745.22(5)
smooth-skinned ~, 745.1(6)
~ trees, 996.29(6)
peacock,n.
group of ~s, 403.5(46)
pear,n.
liquor from ~, 749.6(16)
~-shaped, 507.17(62)
pearl,n., 963.1
appearance of a ~, 963.3
color in a ~, 963.2
containing ~s, 963.16
dive for ~s, 963.11
diver for ~s, 963.12
fish for ~s, 963.11
like a ~, 963.10,15
like ~ substance, 963.7,8
mineral constituent of a ~, 963.9
ornament with ~s, 963.17
ornamented with ~s, 963.16
pert. to a ~, 963.15
pert. to ~ substance, 963.7,8
ship for ~ fishing, 963.14
small ~, 963.1(9)
substance of a ~, 963.4–6
surface appearance of a ~, 963.3

types of ~s, 963.1
weight in ~s, 947.45
peasant,n., 786.6,7
~ bound to the land, 310.9
Russian ~, 998.4(6)
~s, collectively, 998.6
state of being a ~, 998.6
peat,n.
pile of ~, 1064.62
pebble,n.
hit with ~s, 1006.12
sand and ~s, 1006.1(19)
throw ~s at, 1006.12
peculiar,adj.
characteristic, 1091.12; see characteristic,adj.
odd or unusual, 536.1
~ person, act, etc., 536.2
~ to a region, 1091.13
peculiarity,n.
characteristic, 1091.11,14; see characteristic,n.
oddity, 536.2
habitual ~, 1091.15
pedant,n., 622.20
act like a ~, 622.21
peddle,v., 212.1(3,4,6,7)
peddler,n., 212.3(4,8,12,14)
~ of religious articles, 212.3(5)
pedestal,n.
parts of a ~, 1022.20
peel,n.
cheese ~, 972.4(15)
fruit ~, 972.4(13)
remove ~ from, 972.6,8
peel,v., 972.6,8
Peiping or Peking,n.
inhabitant of ~, 784.15(49) ; 784.17(5)
penalize,v., 896.1; see punish,v.
penalty,n., 896.2; see also punishment,n.
delay death ~ of, 897.19
delay in death ~ of, 897.20
pendulous,adj., 172.4
penetrable,adj., 133.14; 332.26
not ~, 133.15
penetrate,v., 121.1; 332.22
penetrating,adj., 121.3; 332.25
penetration,n., 121.2; 332.23,24
peninsula,n., 1029.98
penis,n., 379.1(15)
erection of the ~ without sexual desire, 379.9(10)
female organ like the ~, 379.1(1)
head of the ~, 379.1(4)
skin covering the ~, 379.1(17)
surgery on the ~, 402.5(7)
swell (of the ~), 518.1(10)
symbol of the ~, 379.4
withdrawal of the ~, 710.25
worship of the ~, 656.15(20)
penitence,n., 884.13
clothing for ~, 974.1(12)
penitent,adj., 884.12
penitent,n., 884.14
penmanship,n., 677.1
pennant,n., 957.1
people,n., 431.3; see also human, man, mankind, person,n.
common ~, 431.6,8
facts about ~, 431.15
few ~, place of, 782.1(2,23)
fond of ~, 700.32(3)
fondness for ~, 700.30(4)
full of ~, 431.5
future ~, 771.22
government by the ~, 1073.3(12,28) ; 1073.4(2,6)
hatred of ~, 880.17(4)
low-class ~, 431.8,9
referring to ~, 431.4

science of ~, 431.13
~ under political govern-
ment, 1076.10
white ~, 430.10
working ~, 431.11
people,v., 750.1
perceivable,adj., 433.8,9
~ by taste, 446.5
~ by touch, 436.11
not ~, 433.10,11
quality ~ by touch, 436.7
something barely ~, 483.8(22)
perceive,v., 433.4
able to ~, 433.2
perceived,adj.
ability to be ~, 433.9
able to be ~, 433.8
inability to be ~, 433.11
unable to be ~, 433.10
what is ~, 433.7
perceiver,n., 433.5
perceiving,adj., 433.2
perceiving,n., 433.1; see perception,n.
perceptible,adj., 433.8,9; see
perceivable,adj.
perception,n., 433.1
abnormal ~, 433.12–17
beyond ~, 433.10
extrasensory ~, 433.12–17
object of ~, 433.7
organs of ~, 433.6
pert. to ~, 433.3
powers of ~, 433.6
~ through the senses, 433.1
perch,n., 63.1; see seat,n.
sitting on a ~, 62.7
perch,v., 62.1; see sit,v.
percussion,n., 437.2
~ cap, 802.13
perfect,adj., 816.1,3
capable of becoming ~, 816.6
make ~, 816.7
perfection,n., 816.1
belief in human ~, 816.8
demander of ~, 816.5
example of ~, 816.2
model of ~, 317.1(18,20) ;
816.2
place of ~, 816.9
raise to ideal ~, 816.10
perform,v., 49.1
~ dramatic part, 49.1(29)
~ duties of office, 49.1(18)
~ music, 49.1(29)
performance,n., 49.2,6
performance (theatrical),n.,
969.1,2; see also drama,n.
~ between the acts of a play,
969.1(10)
~ by gestures, 969.1(18,20,32)
~ by imitation, 969.1(14)
~ by one person, 969.1(43)
~ by puppets, 969.41,42
~ by reading, 969.1(7)
~ by two actors, 969.1(6)
doll used in ~s, 969.40
elaborate ~, 969.1(11,31,44)
first ~, 969.1(35)
~ in mask or disguise,
969.1(24)
~ in or on water, 969.1(1)
~ of a historical nature,
969.1(31)
~ of swimming, 969.1(1)
~ of undressing, 984.14
part in a ~, 969.10,11,14
pert. to a ~, 969.9
~ seen through an opening,
969.46
slight ~, 969.1(40,41)
therapy by ~, 969.37
travel to give a ~, 969.17
performer,n., 49.3; 969.3
leading ~, 49.3(3)

prominent ~, 49.3(3)
perfume,n., 445.15
bottle for ~, 261.7(12)
maker or seller of ~, 445.19
place where ~ is made, sold,
etc., 445.18
substance used in ~, 445.17
perfume,v., 445.12
perilous,adj., 572.1; see dangerous,adj.
period (time),n., 769.1,8
menstruation, 292.1
appointed ~, 769.8(17)
calendar, ~ added to a,
769.8(4)
changes, ~ between, 769.8(13,
15)
endless ~, 769.5
fixed ~, 769.8(17)
growth, ~ in, 769.8(15)
holding, ~ of, 769.8(16)
intervening ~, 769.6;
769.8(10–13)
lasts, ~ that something, 769.7
limited ~, 769.2
long ~, 769.4
mankind, ~s of, 769.9
office, ~ of holding, 769.8(9,
16)
pause, ~ for, 769.8(10–12)
precedes an event, ~ that,
769.8(7)
progress, ~ of, 769.8(15)
rest, ~ for, 769.8(10–12)
short ~, 769.2,3
year, one of the four ~s of
the, 769.8(14) ; see season,n.
periodical,n., 691.1; see publication,n.
~s, 691.2
permanent,adj., 754.11,15
permeate,v., 121.1
permeating,adj., 121.3
permeation,n., 121.2
permission,n., 554.2
document giving ~, 554.8
~ to enter, 133.9
~ to go ashore, off duty, etc.,
554.2(4,5)
~ to publish, 554.2(3)
with or without ~, 554.12
permissive,adj., 554.3
permit,n., 554.8
one who has a ~, 554.9
permit,v., 554.1
~ to enter or pass, 554.7
permitted,adj.
~ for consideration, 554.11
freely ~, 554.10
~ in court as evidence, 554.11
perpendicular,adj., 180.1;
944.10
perpetual,adj., 754.15; 755.1,2
make ~, 754.17
~ thing, 754.16
perpetuate,v., 754.17
perplex,v., 605.1; see confuse,v.
perplexed,adj., 605.5
perplexing,adj., 604.1; 605.4
perplexity,n., 604.3; 605.3,18
persecute,v., 1130.1
tending to ~, 1130.24
persecuted,adj.
~ person, 1130.26
persecution,n., 1130.6
~ by means of soldiers, etc.,
1130.27
delusions of ~, 1136.1(18,31,
37,38)
force by ~, 3.3(9)
pert. to, or characterized by,
~, 1130.25
perseverance,n., 553.2; 754.2
courage and ~, 575.2(2)
persevere,v., 553.4; 754.1

persist,v., 553.4; 754.1
persistence,n., 553.2; 754.2
person,n., 431.1; see also human, man, mankind, peo-
ple,n.
amount per ~, 914.6
authoritative ~, 5.8
~ by person, 431.2
colored ~, 430.7; see Negro,n.
importance of a ~, doctrine
of, 431.12
important ~, 848.22
white ~, 430.9
personal,adj., 331.1; 930.8
have ~ relations, 523.2
~ relations, 523.1(5)
personality,n., 1091.1; see nature,n.
~ disorder, 1135.1; 1136.1; see
also insanity,n.
personification,n., 338.14,15
personified,adj., 338.13
personify,v., 338.15
perspire,v., 291.1; see sweat,v.
persuadable,adj., 638.9
persuade,v., 638.1
able to ~, 638.7
attempt to ~, 638.10
~ by promise, 1122.21
~ into wrongdoing, 638.1(16,
17)
~ not to, 638.1(10)
person sent out to ~, 638.11
~ to change beliefs, 638.1(7,
15)
~ to join, 638.1(1,11)
~ to support, 638.1(1,11)
~ to testify falsely, 638.1(17)
unable to ~, 638.15
persuaded,adj., 638.9
able to be ~, 638.9
cannot be ~, one who, 638.14
has been ~, one who, 638.6
unable to be ~, 638.13
persuader,n., 638.4,5
persuading,n.
art of ~ a god or supernatural being, 638.12
persuasion,n., 638.2
persuasive,adj., 638.7
~ and soothing, 1139.2(15)
~ argument, 638.4
~ in language, 638.7
~ language, 665.9(12,57)
~ talk, 638.4
pertain,v., 521.3
pertinence,n., 521.2
pertinent,adj., 521.1
~ in time, 521.5
legally ~, 521.4
not ~, 521.6
not ~, that which is, 521.8
not ~ in time, 521.9
Peru,n.
inhabitant of ~, 784.15(50)
pert. to ~, 784.16
perversion,n., 539.3; 811.9;
886.2,24
~ of nature, 811.10
sexual ~, 710.31,33; see sexual aberration,n.
pervert,n., 886.4
sexual ~, 710.32,34
pervert,v., 176.1; 539.1; 886.24
perverted,adj., 811.9; 886.1
pessimism,n., 267.9,19
~ about the world, 267.9(13) ;
1125.4
pest,n.
disease, 393.1
nuisance, 274.3; 874.5
pester,v., 274.1; 874.1
pet,n.
animal as a ~, 403.7(10)
brought up as a ~, 403.31

pet,v., 701.1; see caress,v.
petition,n., 274.2
~ with signatures in a circle, 274.2(3)
petition,v., 274.1; 276.1
petitioner,n., 274.3; 276.3
petroleum,n., 510.13
petticoat,n., 981.3(10,14)
petty,adj., 887.1,2
phantom,n., 662.19; 809.3
pharynx,n.
    inflammation of the ~, 364.13(2)
phase,n.
    appearance, 504.1
    period, 769.8
pheasant,n.
    group of ~s, 403.5(23,49)
    like a ~, 405.10(1)
    young ~, 405.4(12)
phenomenon,n., 29.6
Philippine Islands,n.
    inhabitant of the ~, 784.15(20)
    pert. to the ~, 784.16
philosopher,n.
    modern ~, 761.15
philosophical,adj.
    ~ theories of reality, 807.17
philosophy,n.
    ~ based on intuition or thinking, 807.16
    branch of ~ dealing with reality, 807.13(1)
    pert. to ~ of Aristotle's disciples, 807.14
    pert. to ~ of Plato, 807.15
phlegmatic,adj., 1097.3; 1100.25; 1132.12
    ~ person, 1097.4; 1100.26; 1132.13
phonetic,adj., 474.2
phonograph,n., 455.9(4,16)
photograph,n., 967.1
    mounted ~s, 967.7
    ~ displayed outside a theater, 968.11
    unposed ~, 967.9
    X-ray ~, 1069.8,9
photograph,v., 967.2
    ~ with motion-picture camera, 968.4
photographer,n., 967.3
photographic,adj., 967.6
photography,n., 967.4
    art of ~, 965.6(3)
    attractive in ~, 967.8
    camera used in ~, 967.5
    ~ in astronomy, 1053.40
    process in ~, 967.4
    suitable for ~, 967.8
phrase,n., 666.2
    abstract ~, 666.3(1)
    abusive ~, 666.3(20)
    affected ~, 666.3(14)
    ~ as a motto, 666.3(43); see also saying,n.
    commonly used ~, 666.3(48, 49)
    conversational ~, 666.3(13,49)
    explanatory ~, 666.3(33)
    fanciful ~, 666.3(14)
    favorite ~, 666.3(10)
    favorite ~ of a group, 666.3(11)
    ~ formed by rearranging letters, 666.3(4,44)
    ~ in advertising, 666.3(43)
    ~ in drinking, 666.3(47)
    local ~, 666.3(26,38,49)
    native ~, 666.3(49)
    new ~, 666.3(29)
    obscene ~, 666.3(31)
    ~ of ignorant speakers, 666.3(51)

old-fashioned ~, 631.16
out-of-date ~, 631.16
~ peculiar to a language, 666.3(24)
pert. to ~s, 666.10
sarcastic ~, 666.3(7)
sharp ~, 666.3(7)
special ~s of a subject, 666.9(7)
stale or trite ~, 759.30
substandard ~, 666.3(8)
technical ~, 666.3(45)
~ to avoid offense, 666.3(21)
~ unchanged when read backward, 666.3(32)
unnecessary ~, 666.3(36)
physic,n.
    doctoring,n., 401.1; see medical science,n.
    laxative,n., 293.16
physical,adj., 338.7
    ~ breakdown, 802.28
    humors determining ~ character, 1091.30
    ~ sensation, 434.1–4
    spiritual and ~ natures, doctrine of, 1089.10
physician,n., 401.2; see doctor,n.
physics,n., 3.10; 808.12
    caused by the operation or forces of ~, 808.16
    theory that life is explainable by ~, 751.9(1)
pianist,n., 479.9
    finger exerciser for ~s, 103.5
piano,n., 479.8(5,8,9,15,18,21); 479.11(2)
    keyboard of a ~, 479.12
    player of a ~, 479.9; 479.9(19)
pick,v.
    choose, 252.1
pickle,v., 263.1–4
pickpocket,n., 250.3(3)
pictorial,adj., 965.8
picturable,adj., 965.12
picture,n., 965.1; see also art, drawing, painting, photograph, portrait, sketch,n.
    action, ~ of, 965.1(48,55,57)
    amusing ~, 965.1(7)
    amusing ~s in newspaper or magazine, 966.18
    art of making ~s, 965.6
    artist's early ~s, 965.1(45)
    artist's name on a ~, 965.32
    back part of a ~, 184.1(1)
    body, ~ of the, 965.1(4,22,36)
    book, ~ opposite title page of, 687.9(7)
    burn the ~ of, 966.22
    camera, ~ by a, 965.1(41)
    Christ, ~ of, 965.1(25)
    circular wall ~, 965.1(9)
    collection of ~s, 965.9
    copied ~, 965.1(56)
    criminals' ~s, 965.9(3)
    depth illusion, ~ with, 965.1(15,52,53); 965.30
    distance illusion, ~ with, 965.30
    exaggerated ~, 965.1(6)
    exhibition of ~s, 965.10
    front part of a ~, 185.1(6)
    funny ~s, 1113.10
    god in animal form, ~ of, 965.1(59)
    Greek vase, ~ on, 965.1(19)
    hang the ~ of, 966.22
    heraldic shield, ~ on, 965.1(20)
    ideas in ~s, 586.6; see also image,n.
    imitation of artist, ~ in, 965.1(40)

language full of ~s, 665.9(28)
light and shade, ~ in, 965.1(8)
light and shade in a ~, 965.36
like a ~, 965.25
literary style that presents ~s to the mind, descr. of, 965.26
make a ~, 965.2,3
metal, ~ on, 965.1(21,33)
miniature, ~ in, 965.1(15)
money only, ~ made for, 965.1(44)
motion ~, 968.1
naked body, ~ of, 965.1(36)
objects, ~ of, 965.1(54)
one color, ~ of, 488.9
outlines, ~ of, 965.1(56)
person's ~, 965.1(12,22,28,30, 33,36,42,47)
pert. to ~s, 965.8
printing, ~ for, 965.1(35)
Renaissance, ~ before, 965.1(45)
represent by ~, 965.2
ridicule of artist, ~ in, 965.1(40)
~s, collectively, 965.9
scenery, ~s of, 965.1(29,38,46, 48,49,57); 965.15
sexual excitement from ~s, 710.33(20)
shadow ~, 1071.12
small ~, 965.1(15,33)
study of ~s, 965.18
suggestive of a ~, 965.25
suitable for a ~, 965.24
supernatural being in animal form, ~ of, 965.1(59)
varicolored stone or glass, ~ of, 965.1(34)
wall ~, 965.1(9,16,35,51), 666.3(40)
word expressive of a ~, 666.3(40)
picture,v., 965.2,3
    serving to ~, 965.11
pictured,adj.
    able to be ~, 965.12
pie,n., 1062.8
piece,n., 326.10,15; see also part,n.
    bitten-off ~, 326.10(1)
    break into ~s, 326.12,13,19–21; 802.1(1,2,5,6,8,9,12–14)
    break off a ~, 326.12
    broken ~, 326.10
    chopped-off ~, 326.10(3)
    cut into ~s, 326.12,13; 332.1(4, 8,14,18,32,51,53)
    cut-off ~, 326.10
    cut off a ~, 326.12; 332.1(6)
    descr. of a ~, 326.11
    divide into ~s, 326.16,19
    hanging ~, 326.18
    in or into ~s, 337.1(1,2,14,16)
    irregularly shaped ~, 326.15(1,2)
    large ~, 326.22
    ~ of bread, 326.10(7)
    ~ of food, 326.10(7)
    pert. to a ~, 326.11
    small ~, 326.17
    tear into ~s, 326.12,13
    tear off a ~, 326.12
    thick, flat ~, 326.15(3)
    thin ~, 326.10(29,32); 326.15(4,5)
    torn ~, 326.10(19,25)
pier,n., 1033.1,10–19
    fee for tying up at a ~, 1033.16
pierce,v., 121.1; 332.22
    ~ with figurative pain, 1137.13

pierced,adj., 332.28
 able to be ~, 121.4; 332.26
 not ~, 332.29
 ~ state, 332.24
 unable to be ~, 121.5; 332.27
piercing,adj., 121.3; 332.25
piercing,n., 121.2; 332.23
piety,n., 643.2
pig,n., 419.1
 baby ~, 419.4
 castrated ~, 419.2
 female ~, 419.3
 ~ for roasting, 1061.8
 group of ~s, 403.5(19,20,25, 69)
 like a ~, 419.9
 litter of ~s, 419.6
 male ~, 419.2
 parts of a ~ in vinegar, etc., 1035.20
 pert. to the ~ family, 419.8
 place for ~s, 403.22(30,31,40)
 ~s, 419.5
 side of a ~, 186.1(6)
 small ~, 419.4
 wild ~, 419.7
 young ~, 419.4
pigeon,n., 405.1(5)
 house for ~s, 405.11(4)
 of ~s, 405.9(4)
 young ~, 405.4(15)
pigment,n., 488.1,22
 black ~, 384.6
 deficient in ~, person, animal, or plant, 489.6
 yellow ~, 500.5
pigmentation,n., 488.1
pigmented,adj., 488.8
pile,n., 318.18
pile,v., 318.20,21; 319.1
pilgrimage,n., 124.2
 ~ to Mecca, 124.2(4)
pill,n., 398.4(2,6,11,22,23)
pillar,n., 1022.2; 1023.1
pillow,n., 69.3; 1022.12
 covering for a ~, 69.3(3)
 support with a ~, 1022.11
pimp,n., 711.16
pimp,v., 711.15
pimple,n., 382.17,18
 causing ~s, 382.23
 condition of ~s, 382.11(1–3,14, 20,32–34,37)
 eruption of ~s, 382.22
 having ~s, 382.20
 pert. to a ~, 382.19
pimple,v., 382.21
pimpled,adj., 382.20
pimply,adj., 382.20
pin,n.
 ~ for roasting meat, 437.8
pin,v., 302.1
pinch,n., 198.2
pinch,v., 198.9
pine,n.
 treatise on ~ trees, 996.70
 ~ tree, 996.4(5,6,12)
 ~ trees, 996.29(7,8)
pineapple,n.
 belonging to the ~ family, 745.22(3)
pink,adj., 496.2,4
 make ~, 496.3
 turn ~, 496.6
pink,n., 496.1,5
pious,adj., 643.1
piousness,n., 643.2
pipe,n.
 ~ for waste water, 1033.34–36
 ~ for water, 1033.23–31,45
 hollow, like a ~, 299.2(5)
 tobacco ~, 988.8
 ventilating ~, 1045.8
piracy,n.
 commit ~, 250.8

pert. to ~, 250.9
pirate,n., 250.6,7
 act or play the ~, 250.8
 ~ flag, 250.11
 like a ~, 250.10
 pert. to a ~, 250.9
 ~ ship, 115.15
pistol,n., 565.1; see **gun**,n.
pit,n.
 fruit ~, 745.18
 remove ~s, 249.2(4,7)
pitch,v., 187.1; see **throw**,v.
pitcher,n.
 container, 261.7(21,28,35)
 beer ~, 261.7(35)
pitiful,adj., 1125.16; 1129.1,13
pitiless,adj., 889.10; 1129.22,24;
 see also **cruel**,adj.
 ~ act, 1129.23
 become ~, 1129.25
 ~ in killing, 889.12
 make ~, 1129.25
pituitary,adj.
 ~ disease, 907.13(3)
 disorders of the ~ gland, 394.2
 overactivity of the ~ gland, 907.13(3)
pity,n., 1129.5
 artistic quality that excites ~, 1129.17,18
 asking for ~, 1129.21
 excite ~, 1129.15,16
 exciting ~, 1125.16; 1129.13
 express ~, 1129.2
 expressing ~, 1129.1,6
 feel ~, 1129.2–4
 feeling ~, 1129.1,6
 feels ~, one who, 1129.7
 give in to ~, 1129.4
 journalist who writes to elicit ~, 1127.16
 not giving in to ~, 889.10; 1129.22,24
 show ~, 1129.2,4
 showing ~, 1129.1,6
 story told to elicit ~, 1127.15
 without ~, 889.10; 1129.22,24
 without ~, cause to be, 1129.25
placate,v., 1096.31
place,n., 782.1,3; see also
 position,n.
 action, ~ of, 782.2
 activity, ~ of, 782.2
 administration, ~ of, 782.6
 admiration, ~ that causes, 782.1(36)
 amusement, ~ of, 782.1(26)
 animals feed, ~ where, 782.1(23)
 assigned ~, 782.1(19,30)
 authority, ~ of, 5.19; 782.6
 body, applied to a ~ on the, 782.16
 boundary, ~ around a, 782.1(3)
 church, ~ served by a, 782.1(17)
 contest or competition, ~ of, 782.1(1)
 country ~, 782.1(22)
 cozy ~, 782.1(4)
 duty, ~ of, 782.1(19,30)
 empty ~, 926.20
 existence, ~ of, 782.1(27)
 far ~s, 789.9
 fixed ~, 782.1(29,37)
 foreign ~s, 782.1(14)
 from that ~, 782.18
 from this ~, 782.17
 geographical ~, 782.1(10); 782.3
 go, ~ where people, 782.13

going to, ~ where one is, 782.14
 imaginary ~, 809.4; 816.9
 in ~ of, 782.19
 indented ~ in a wall, 782.1(25)
 influence, ~ of, 782.10
 inner ~, 782.1(25)
 limited ~, 782.1(16,20,37)
 living, ~ of, 782.5
 lost, ~ where one is, 782.1(35)
 marked-off ~, 782.1(37)
 meeting, ~ of, 782.1(26)
 natural ~, 782.4,5
 nearby ~s, 790.8
 nonexistent ~, 1057.15
 observation, ~ under, 782.1(31)
 occurrence, ~ of, 782.7,8
 operation, ~ of, 782.1(32)
 out of ~, 323.21
 out-of-the-way ~, 782.1(4,25)
 outer ~s, 782.1(15)
 particular ~, pert. to a, 782.15
 power, ~ of, 5.19
 put, ~ where something is, 323.4
 put in ~ of, 324.1
 put out of ~, 323.17–20
 quiet ~, 782.1(4,25)
 restricted ~, 558.6
 rule, ~ of, 782.6
 safekeeping, ~ for, 782.1(5)
 sea, ~ beyond the, 782.1(14)
 secluded ~, 782.1(4,25)
 sheltered ~, 782.1(4,25)
 soldier is stationed, ~ where, 782.1(19,21)
 standing, ~ of, 782.1(29,30)
 story, etc., occurs, ~ where, 782.8
 surrounding ~s, 783.1
 take the ~ of, 324.2
 thinly populated ~, 782.1(2, 23)
 to that ~, 782.19
 to this ~, 782.17
 traveled over, ~ repeatedly, 782.12
 traveling to, ~ where one is, 782.14
 visited, ~ frequently, 782.11, 12
 wonder, ~ that causes, 782.1(36)
place,v., 323.1; see also **put**,v.
 ~ boastfully, 872.6
 ~ on the ground, 999.7
placid,adj., 1132.12; 1139.15;
 see also **calm**,adj.
placing,n., 323.2
 ~ after, 323.11
 bad ~, 323.10
 ~ before, 323.12
 pert. to ~, 323.6
plague,n.
 disease, 393.1
 nuisance, 874.5
plain,adj.
 homely, 506.1
 unornamented, 959.9
 ~ in a countrylike way, 959.9(5)
 ~ in manner, 959.9(1–3)
 ~ in style, 959.9(1–3)
 ~ (of facts, statements, truths), 959.11
 primitively ~, 959.9(5)
 roughly ~, 959.9(5)
 severely ~, 959.9(1,6)
 simple and ~, 960.1(3)
plain,n., 1003.2(1,6,25,26,30)
 arctic ~s, 1003.2(42)
 Asian ~s, 1003.2(37)

European ~s, 1003.2(37)
high ~, 1003.2(27,46)
South American ~s, 1003.2(22)
plainness,n.
homeliness, 506.1
lack of ornamentation, 959.10
plaintive,adj., 1119.5; 1125.6
~ (of music), 1119.6
plan,n., 46.3
deceptive ~, 46.3(1)
having high ~s, 46.8
impractical ~, 46.3(2)
~ of activities, 46.3(3-5)
one who spoils a ~, 559.4
pert. to a ~, 46.5
without a ~, 46.13
plan,v., 46.1
able to ~ for the future, 46.9
~ beforehand, 46.1(6)
~ cleverly, 46.1(3)
~ illegally, 46.1(5,7); see also plot,v.
~ secretly, 46.1(5,7); see also plot,v.
tending to ~ wisely, 46.6
~ together, 46.1(2)
planet,n., 1053.1; see also heavenly body,n.
conjunction of ~ and sun, 1053.23
illustrate ~s, device to, 1053.18
influenced by the ~s, 1053.5
like a ~, 1053.4
major ~s, 1053.9
orbit of a ~, 1053.21,22
path of a ~, 1053.20
point of a ~ farthest from earth, 165.1(3)
position of ~s as influence on life, 1053.24
revolution of ~ around the sun, 1055.38
science of ~s, 1053.36
sun and its ~s, 1053.17
theory of ~s, 1053.16
theory of formation of ~s, 1053.15
planless,adj., 46.13
planned,adj., 46.11
planner,n., 46.4
planning,adj.
~ for the future, 46.7
planning,n., 46.2
done after careful ~, 577.6
~ of natural and social forces, 46.2(4)
~ of war, 46.2(3)
pert. to ~, 46.5
poor in ~, 46.10
skillful ~, 46.2(2)
wise ~, 46.2(1)
plant,n., 985
able to grow ~s for animals (of land), 986.28
area of wild ~s, 985.34(15)
biological category of ~s, 318.8
body of a ~, 985.26
breed ~s, 719.1,3-10
collect ~s, 985.39
cover with ~s, 985.10
covering of ~s, 972.4(2,15)
creeping ~s, structure for, 991.12,14,15
~ deficient in color, 489.6
desert ~, 985.6(43); 1037.33
~ disease, 985.12-15
dried ~s, collection of, 985.19
drug from a ~, 985.29
eating ~s, 734.27(14,22,25)
eating of ~s, 734.26(8,12)
edible ~, 985.6(41)

exist like a ~, 985.32
explore in order to collect ~s, 985.39
flat-trained ~, 991.18
foreign ~, 538.3
freak ~, 537.2; 985.6(31,38)
~ from a seed, 985.6(34)
greenness of ~s, 985.2
ground ~, 1003.3(1)
grow ~s, 731.22(1,5); 998.1,2
growth of ~s, 985.7
having ~s, 985.3,9
history of ~s, 985.40
~ in reference to nourishment, 739.8,9
inferior ~, 985.6(31)
land and water ~, 1026.24,25
~ life, 985.1
like a ~, 985.8
medicinal ~, 985.6(16)
medicinal ~s, collector of or dealer in, 985.17
medicinal ~s, treatise or book on, 985.18
of a ~ family, 985.33
originating from ~s, 985.28
ornamental ~, 959.3(13)
pert. to ~s, 985.27
place for ~s, 985.34
place of exhibition of ~, 951.28(1)
place where ~s grow, 985.34
poisonous ~s, 800.3
pot for ~s, 994.32
~ produced by breeding, 719.5
protection around a ~, 993.27
raise ~s, 998.1,2
~ raised as food for livestock, 986.1(8)
~s, collectively, 985.1,7
science of ~ classification, 985.36(19,23)
science of ~ life of lakes, 985.36(12)
science of ~s, 985.36
science of ~s and animals, 403.26(5-7,9,14,26,32,36,38)
science of tiny ~s, 985.36(14)
soilless ~ raising, 998.1(10)
stand for ~s, 994.32
student of ~s, 985.38
study ~s, 985.39
~ that lives without rain or moisture, 1037.33
treatise on ~s, 985.5
types of ~s, 985.6
underwater ~, 1026.36
water ~, 1026.27
wild ~, 985.6(42)
withered leaves, ~ with, 806.19
withering disease of ~s, 806.20
without ~s, 985.4
woody part of a ~, 996.71
world ~, 1004.34,35
plant,v., 998.3
~ bushes, 985.25
~ grass, 986.21
~ living tissue, 323.1(18,23,24, 74)
~ seed, 998.2(3)
~ with trees, 996.34,51
plaster,n.
cover with ~, 1007.16
~ for sculpture, setting broken bones, etc., 1007.19
~ in sheets, 1007.17
plate,n., 519.5
dish, 261.9
~ for porridge, 261.9(8)
platform,n., 1025.23
platinum,n., 1014
alloy of ~ and iridium, 1014.7

coat with ~, 1014.2
containing ~, 1014.5
like ~, 1014.3,5
metal associated with ~, 1014.4
pert. to ~, 1014.5
unrefined ~, 1014.1
yielding ~, 1014.6
platitude,n., 665.9(2,9,24,40)
Plato,n.
pert. to ~ or his philosophy, 807.15
play,n., 199.3
done in a spirit of ~, 199.6
drink and ~, 199.3(1)
outdoor ~, participator in, 199.9
spend (time) in ~, 199.7
play (drama),n., 969.1; see also drama, performance (theatrical),n.
part in a ~, 969.10,11
~s put on, 969.16
words of a musical ~, 666.9(2)
play,v., 199.1
~ a musical instrument, 479.3,10
~ at, 199.11
~ in (water), 199.1(1)
~ more skillfully than, 199.8
one who ~s, 199.2
~ roughly but kindly, 865.8
~ with, 199.1(12,13); 199.10
~ with (a child), 199.1(3)
player,n., 199.2
group of ~s, 318.1(89,93)
playful,adj., 199.4
~ animal, 199.5
~ child, 199.5
~ movement, 80.1,2
plaything,n., 199.12
playwright,n., 685.5
plea,n., 274.2; 276.2
plead,v.
ask, 274.1; see ask,v.
beg, 276.1; see beg,v.
~ on someone's behalf, 276.1(13)
pleasant,adj., 1106.3
be ~, 1106.2
be ~ to gain friendliness, 1096.30
become ~, 1106.21
~ characteristic, property, or quality, 1106.17
~ circumstances, features, actions, etc., 1106.6
deceptively ~, 823.11; 1106.10
excessively ~, 1109.27
fairly ~, 1106.5
friendly and ~, 858.4
~ in appearance, 1106.9,15
~ in appearance, but deceptive, 1106.10
~ in attitude, 1106.15
~ in movement, action, manner, etc., 1106.15
~ in sound, 467.3; 1106.12
insincerely ~, 1106.8
least ~, 1106.23
made ~ by maturity, 732.7
make ~, 1106.20,21
make more ~, 1106.20
~ person, 1106.22
polite and ~, 858.4
somewhat ~, 1106.5
~ sounds, 467.1,2
~ thing, 1106.22
unwilling to be ~, 265.26(5)
pleasantness,n., 1106.4
please,v., 1106.1,2,4; 1107.1; see also satisfy, suit,v.
~ by being satisfactory, 1106.1

~ greatly, 1106.2
hard to ~, 1106.14; see also
   choosy,adj.
inclined to ~, 1106.7
pleased,adj., 1107.3; see also
   satisfied,adj.
be ~ to get, 1106.13
pleasing,adj., 1106.3; 1107.5; see
   also pleasant, satisfactory,
   suitable,adj.
~ act, 52.5(2)
be ~, 1106.2; 1107.1; see also
   satisfy, suit,v.
pleasingness,n., 1106.4; 1107.6
pleasurable,adj., 1105.4
~ and painful, 1105.4(1)
~ and sad, 1105.4(1)
~ in sound, 1105.4(9); 1105.21
make ~, 1105.13
~ quality, 1105.5
sensually ~, 1105.4(6)
sexually ~, 1105.4(6,8,11)
socially ~, 1105.4(4)
sweet, soft, and ~ in sound,
   1105.21
~ to the sense of smell,
   1105.4(3,7)
~ to the senses, 1105.4(3,6-9,
   11)
~ to the taste, 1105.4(3,7)
~ to the vision, 1105.4(9)
pleasurableness,n., 1105.5
pleasure,n., 1105.1,2; see also
   happiness,n.
bored with ~, 1105.33-37
causing ~ and regret,
   1105.4(1)
denial of ~, 77.1
desire for sexual ~, 709.7
destroy the ~ of, 1125.37
destroyer of ~, 1125.36
devoted to ~, 1105.8
devoted to ~ as a way of life,
   1105.8(5)
devoted to ~ of the senses,
   1105.8(1,9,10,12-14)
devoted to ~s of eating,
   1105.8(1)
devoted to sensual ~,
   1105.8(2,7-10,12-14)
devoted to sexual ~, 1105.8(2,
   7-9,11,14)
devoted to social ~s,
   1105.8(3)
drink with ~, 1105.12
eat with ~, 1105.12
ethics of ~ and pain, 1105.25
excessive indulgence in the
   ~s of, 1105.17
facial expression of ~,
   365.2(11)
fond of ~, 1105.8
get ~, 1105.7
get ~ from, 1105.6
give ~ to, 1105.3
given to immoral ~s, 1096.11
given to social ~s, 1096.11
giving ~, 1105.4
go about in search of ~, 700.9
indifferent to ~, 1105.33-37
indulge in ~, 1105.7
indulge in sensual ~, 1105.7(1,
   2,4)
indulge in sexual ~, 1105.7(1,
   2,4)
indulge in social ~, 1105.7(3)
indulge in wild ~, 1105.7(2,4)
indulger in ~, 1105.9
indulging in ~, 1105.8
lack of ~, 1105.30
life of sensual ~s, 1105.20
lose ~, cause to, 1105.32
lost ~ in, having, 1105.31
means of ~, 1105.2
murmur with ~, 1105.19

~ of celebrations, 201.13
~ of living, 1105.14,15
~ of merrymaking or parties,
   201.13
pert. to ~, 1105.8
power to give ~, 1105.5
psychology of ~ and pain,
   1105.25
pursuer of sexual ~, 709.9
pursuing sexual ~, 709.8
pursuit of sexual ~, 709.7,16
responsive to ~s of the
   senses, 1105.8(10)
~ ride, 1105.28
road to sensual ~s, 1105.20
say in ~, 1105.19
seek ~, 1105.11
seek ~ and avoid pain,
   impulse to, 1105.27
~ seeker, 1105.9
sexual ~, 709.12
sound of ~, make, 1105.19
source of ~, 1105.2
theory of ~, 1105.23,24,26
theory of sensual ~, 1105.22
time of unrestrained sensual
   ~s, 1105.18
tired of ~, 12.1(2,17); 1105.33
~ to the sense of smell,
   1105.2(1)
~ to the taste, 1105.2(1,3,4)
without ~, 1105.29
without ~ of living, 1105.16
world of sensual ~s, 1105.20
world's ~s, person concerned
   with, 1004.40
pleasure,v., 1105.3,6,7
pleasureless,adj., 1105.29
pledge,n., 1122.3; see promise,n.
pledge,v., 1122.19,20; see
   promise,v.
plentiful,adj., 919.3
plenty,adj., 919.3
plenty,n., 919.1,2
pleurisy,n., 374.6,7
pliable,adj., 152.7; 552.3
   strong and ~, 990.14
plot,n., 47.2
   artificial aid in solving
      problems of a ~, 601.13
   one who spoils a ~, 559.4
plot,v., 47.1
~ evil, 47.1(3,4,7,14)
~ secretly, 47.1(3,11,13)
   tending to ~, 47.5
~ together, 47.1(3,4,6,7,9)
plotter,n., 47.3
   political ~s, 47.4(1)
~s, 47.4
plotting,adj., 47.5
plotting,n.
   network of ~, 308.1(1,10)
plover,n.
   group of ~, 403.5(14)
plow,v., 998.3; 999.8
plowman,n., 998.4(1,3,7,8)
pluck,n.
   courage, 575.2; see bravery,n.
   pull, 193.2; see pull,n.
pluck,v., 193.1; see pull,v.
~ a musical instrument,
   193.1(14)
plug,n., 297.9; 558.3
   medical ~, 297.8(1)
   vaginal ~, 297.9(1)
plug,v., 297.8; 558.1
plum,n., 745.1(5)
   pert. to, or like, ~s, 745.22(5)
plumage,n., 341.2; see
   feather,n.
plump,adj., 510.1; see fat,adj.
plunder,n., 248.2,5
   commit ~, 248.1
   committing ~, 248.4,9

living off ~, 248.9,10
search for ~, 248.6,7
plunder,v., 248.1
   attack in order to ~, 560.1(12,
      14,16,20,21)
   tending to ~, 248.4,9
plunderer,n., 248.3
plundering,adj., 248.4,9
plunge,v.
   dive, 170.16
   fall, 167.1
   jump, 110.1
   push, 197.1,2
   throw, 187.1
Pluto,n., 660.1; see devil,n.
pneumonia,n., 374.4,5
   germ causing ~, 403.21(15)
pocketbook,n., 261.15; see
   purse,n.
poem,n., 689.2,13; see also
   poetry,n.
~ about country life,
   689.2(4); 786.8
~ about heroes, 689.2(9)
~ about sexual love, 689.2(11)
~ about shepherds, 689.2(4);
   786.8(2,4)
   collection of ~s, 682.19(3)
   concluding part of a ~,
      792.23(1)
   famous ~, 615.5
~ forming a name, 689.2(20)
~ in praise, 689.7(12)
   love ~, 689.2(15,16)
   marriage ~, 689.2(10)
   mourning ~, 689.2(8)
   musical ~, 689.2(5,7,12,14-17)
   narrative ~, 689.2(2)
   nonsense ~, 689.2(1)
~ of mourning, 1125.20(2,3,5,
   6)
~ of retraction, 689.2(18)
~ of specific number of lines,
   689.13
   religious ~, 689.2(12,19)
   sad ~, 689.2(8); 1125.20(3,6)
   write ~s, 689.3
   writer of ~s, 689.5; see
      poet,n., below
poet,n., 689.5
   inferior ~, 689.7
   Italian ~, 689.6
   part of a ~, 689.12
   pert. to ~s, 689.11
~ who writes couplets, 689.14
~ who writes sonnets, 689.15
poetic,adj., 689.11
   excitement of ~ inspiration,
      1100.7(5)
~ inspiration, 689.10
~ inspiration, in a frenzy of,
   1100.6(9)
~ time, 762.1(10)
poetry,n.
   addiction to writing ~, 689.9
   art of writing ~, 689.9
   art or science of ~, 689.32
   compose ~, 689.3
   emotional ~, 1092.37,38
   half a line of ~, 689.22
   inferior ~, writing of, 689.8
   kinds of ~, 689.1(1-5)
   line of ~, 689.17,21,23,39,40,43,
      45,46
   literary criticism of ~, 689.35
   mark off lines of ~, 689.28,29
   metrical unit of ~, 689.24,36-
      38
   pause in a line of ~, 689.44,45
   pert. to ~, 689.11
   repeated sounds in ~, 689.19
   rhythm in ~, 689.26
   rules of ~, 689.33
   theory of ~, 689.34
   two lines of ~, 689.18

treatise on ~, 682.15(19)
turn or put into ~, 689.4
point,n., 335.1
 antler ~, 335.1(20)
 central ~ or gist, 607.3
 come to a ~, 335.3
 decisively important ~, 848.10
 deeply forked ~s, having, 957.18
 extreme ~, 922.16
 ~ for a candle, 335.1(12)
 fork ~, 335.1(13,20)
 get more ~s than, 833.14
 having three ~s, 335.2(13–15)
 having two ~s, 335.2(7)
 highest ~, 335.1(1,8,22)
 important ~ in progress, 848.12
 mathematical ~, pert. to, 335.5
 metal ~, 335.1(10,11,15)
 ~ of change, 539.16
 ~ of view, 480.12
 ~ on a plant, 335.1(12,16,19)
 ~ on a porcupine, 335.1(14, 16)
 ~ on an animal, 335.1(14,16)
 pen ~, 335.1(7,9)
 pyramid ~, 335.1(22)
 sharp ~, 335.1(5,17–20)
 to the ~ (direct), 182.1
 to the ~ (concise, etc.), 911.1(5,7,8,14,15,17,19)
 to the ~, quality of being (conciseness, etc.), 665.9(8, 15,16,39,48,51,53)
 triangle ~, 335.1(22)
 turning ~, 539.16
point,v., 567.1
 ~ in a direction, 179.2
 ~ to the east, 179.2(1)
pointed,adj., 335.2
 ~ end, 335.1; 792.11
 ~ part, 335.1
 sharply ~, 335.2
pointy,adj., 335.2; see **pointed,** adj., above
poison,n., 800.1
 caused by ~, 800.5
 centipede's ~ fang, 800.7
 common ~, 800.2
 desire to take ~, 800.21
 diseases caused by ~, 800.12–18
 drink of ~, 748.5(6)
 free of ~, 800.23
 free of ~ gas, 900.6; 1048.32
 gland for secretion of ~, having a, 800.6
 habit of eating ~, 800.22
 ~ in the atmosphere, 800.1(5)
 insect, etc., ~, 800.1(10,14)
 intellectual ~, 800.4
 like ~, 800.8
 moral ~, 800.4
 neutralizer of ~, 800.24
 neutralizing ~, 800.25
 pert. to ~, 800.5
 producing ~, 800.10
 protect against ~, 569.1(1); see **immunize,**v.
 protection against ~, 569.2,9, 10; see **immunity,**n.
 rat ~, 800.1(6)
 science of ~s, 800.26
 snake ~, 800.1(10,13,14)
 tablet of ~, 800.1(11)
poison,v., 800.11
poisoned,adj.
 become gradually more ~, 800.20
 ~ state, 800.14–16,18
poisoning,n., 800.17
 arsenic ~, 800.18(1)
 blood ~, 800.18(5,8–11)

lead ~, 800.18(6); 800.19; 1018.4,5
 mercury ~, 1021.6
 self-~, 800.18(2)
 specific ~s, 800.18
poison ivy,n., 800.3
 oil from ~, 800.1(9)
poisonous,adj., 800.9
 able to inflict a ~ bite, 800.6
 free of ~ gas, 900.6; 1048.32
 ~ germs in the atmosphere, 800.1(5)
 make ~, 800.11
 ~ oil from poison ivy, 800.1(9)
 ~ plants, 800.3
 ~ protein, 800.1(7)
 ~ substance, 800.1
 ~ vapor, 1048.1(8)
 ~ vapor, caused by, 1048.9
poke,v., 197.1; see **push,**v.
pole,n., 437.7; see **stick,**n.
 ~ as a weapon, 437.5(17)
polecat,n.
 of ~s, 403.11(10)
police,n., 1078.2
 ~ as law-enforcement officials, 1077.3(2)
 ~ automobile, 1078.13
 body or group of ~, 1078.2,8
 ~ building, 1078.14,15
 civilian head of ~, 1078.12
 committee of citizens taking over ~ functions, 1078.17,18
 French ~, 1078.2(3)
 German secret ~, 1078.2(4)
 govern by a ~ force, 1078.10
 group deputized to assist the ~, 1078.19
 Nazi ~, 1078.16(1,2)
 ~ officer of a legislature or of a meeting, 1078.16(5)
 ~ officer or official, 1078.1
 ~ officers, 1077.3(2); 1078.11
 person with ~ functions, 1078.16
 pert. to the ~, 1078.3,4
 private citizen taking over ~ functions, 1078.16(6)
 Russian secret ~, 1078.2(2,5, 6)
 secret ~, 1078.2(2,4,5,6)
 unit of ~, 1078.7
 ~ vehicle, 1078.13
policeman,n., 1078.1
 ~'s club, 437.5(3,23)
policer,n., 1078.16
 ~ in a college, 1078.16(4)
 ~ of examinations, 1078.16(4)
polish,n.
 refinement, 859.3
 shine, 1065.56
 substance for rubbing, 438.4
polish,v., 438.1(6,7,10,17,24,25, 32); 1065.54; see also **rub,**v.
 refine, figuratively, 859.4
 ~ on or with stone, 1006.11
 tool for ~ing, 1065.57
 ~ with sand, 1007.11,12
 ~ with wax, 1068.3
polished,adj., 859.1,8; 1065.55
polite,adj., 858.1; see also **chivalrous,**adj.
 ~ act, 858.19,21
 ~ acts, due or expected, 858.20
 ~ behavior, 55.3(2,7)
 deceptively ~, 823.11
 ~ formalities, 858.18
 formally ~, 858.12
 friendly and ~, 858.4
 ~ in speech, 858.14
 kind and ~, 842.1(4); 858.3
 knowledge of ~ society, 858.17

obsequiously ~, 858.16
 ~ person, 858.22,23
 pleasant and ~, 858.4
 servilely ~, 858.16
 slavishly ~, 858.16
 smoothly ~, 858.15
 speak ~ly, 858.14
 ~ society, knowledge of, 858.17
 ~ society, training in, 858.17
 stiffly ~, 858.12
 ~ to women, 858.5; see **chivalrous,**adj.
 training in ~ society, 858.17
politeness,n., 858.2; see also **chivalry,**n.
 formal ~, 858.13
 gesture in ~, 102.1(2,3)
political,adj.
 ~ affairs, etc., 1076.1
 art of ~ government, 1076.1
 ~ beliefs, principles, etc., 1076.15
 convert to a ~ belief, 1076.16,17
 ~ equality, 1076.11; 1076.12(4)
 ~ freedom, 309.14(4,5,10,18); 309.20
 give ~ power, 5.7(2)
 ~ government, people under, 1076.10
 ~ group, 318.1(11,12,15,35,65, 68,72,98); 1076.6
 holder of ~ office, 1076.3
 holder of ~ views, 1076.12
 ~ independence, 309.14(4,5,10, 18)
 ~ independent, 309.16(1)
 involving two ~ parties, 931.17
 make ~, 1076.5
 ~ meeting, 322.1(5,13,21)
 member of a ~ party, 1076.12
 opposer of ~ change, 1076.12(17,23,28,29)
 science of ~ government, 1076.2
 seeker of ~ office, 1076.3
 seekers of ~ office, 1076.6
 statement in a ~ platform, 674.9(17)
 supporter of a ~ party, 1076.12
 symbol of ~ power, 5.16
 symbol of Turkish or Moslem ~ power, 1073.86
 U.S. ~ party, member of, 1076.12(5,22)
 ~ violence, 4.18
political party,n., 1076.14
 Communist ~, 1076.22–24
 convert to a ~, 1076.16
 German ~ under Hitler, 1076.12(18)
 Italian ~ under Mussolini, 1076.12(8)
 member of a ~, 1076.12,13
 representing two ~s, 1076.18
 Russian ~, member of, 1076.12(1,2,13,15,26)
 Spanish ~, 1076.12(7)
 supporter of a ~, 1076.12
 uninvolved with a ~, 1076.12(9); 1076.19
 U.S. ~, member of, 1076.12(5, 22)
politics,n., 1076
 a conservative in ~, 1076.12(17,23,28,29)
 a group in ~, 318.1(11,12,15, 35,65,68,72,98); 1076.6
 a liberal in ~, 1076.12(1,14,19)
 a person in ~, 1076.3
 a radical in ~, 1076.12(1,10, 12,24)

a reactionary in ~, 1076.12(21,23)
a socialist in ~, 1076.12(6,12, 15)
an independent in ~, 1076.12(9)
engage in ~, 1076.4
geography and ~, 1076.8
moderate in ~, 923.1(2)
Nazi ~, 1076.8
~ of the world, 1076.9
opposer of change in ~, 1076.12(17,21,23,28,29)
talk or discuss ~, 1076.5
polliwog,n., 424.2
polygamy,n., 702.15
practice ~, 702.16
polygon,n., 945.2
eight-sided ~, 945.2(6)
fifteen-sided ~, 945.2(9)
five-sided ~, 945.2(7)
four-sided ~, 945.2(8); 945.7, 8
nine-sided ~, 945.2(5)
seven-sided ~, 945.2(3)
six-sided ~, 945.2(4)
ten-sided ~, 945.2(1)
three-sided ~, 945.2(10)
twelve-sided ~, 945.2(2)
polyp,n., 422.3
like the ~, 422.2
of ~s, 422.1(11,22,23,30)
pond,n., 1029.53; see also lake,n.
growing in ~s, 1029.60
science of ~s, 1029.62
pool,n., 1029.53; see also lake,n.
poor (in money),adj., 217.1
cause to be ~, 217.3
~ people, 217.5
~ person, 217.4
~ person living on charity, 232.7
place for the ~, 232.6
state of being ~, 217.2
poor (in quality),adj., 883.1,3
poor (lacking),adj., 43.2
pop,v., 802.9,10; see also burst, explode,v.
Pope,n., 646.1(24)
adherent of the ~, 646.11
authority of the ~, 5.4(25,26)
favoring supremacy of the ~, 646.12
government of the ~, 1073.3(25); 1073.5(5)
jurisdiction of the ~, 646.5(3)
office of the ~, 646.2(2)
officiate as a ~, 646.10
power of the ~, 5.4(25,26)
prejudice in favor of the ~, 634.1(13)
representative of the ~, 523.6(6,9)
residence of the ~, 646.6(3)
supporter of the ~, 854.6
popular,adj., 279.10; 535.1; 1109.12; see also liked,adj.
newly ~, 1109.15
no longer ~, 1109.16
specially ~, 1109.18
specially ~ person, 1109.20
popularity,n.
period of ~, 1109.14
restore to ~, 832.7
populate,v., 750.1
populated,adj., 750.7
~ by people of different languages, 750.7(1)
thickly ~, 750.7(2)
population,n., 431.3; see also people,n.
facts about ~, 431.15
grow in ~, 731.3(6)

science of ~, 431.13
student of ~, 431.14
porch,n., 727.21
porcupine,n.
pointed process of a ~, 335.1(14,16)
pore,n., 298.8(10)
pork,n.
disease from ~, 396.1(28)
infected (of ~), 396.3
porous,adj., 298.5(3,4,7)
porpoise,n., 423.5
group of ~s, 403.5(61)
pert. to ~s, 423.6
porridge,n.
bowl for ~, 261.9(8)
port,n., 1029.11
portion,n., 326.1; see also part,n.
~ cut from the whole, 326.10(8)
cut into ~s, 332.1(4,51,58)
~ of food, 740.15
portrait,n., 965.1(12,22,28,30,33, 36,42,47); see also picture,n.
burn or hang the ~ of, 966.22
~ on metal, 965.1(33)
small ~, 965.1(33)
study of ~s, 965.19
Portuguese,n., 784.15(32); 784.16
~ language, 664.4(16)
pose,n., 60.1; 826.7
hold a ~, 60.3
pose,v., 60.3,5; 826.7,10
poser,n.
pretender, 826.7,12
position,n.
job, 205.18
place, 782.1,20; see also place,n.
posture, 60.1; see also posture,n.
rank, 313.1; see also rank,n.
abstract ~, 782.25
accept a ~ (job), 205.22
advantageous ~, 836.7; 1042.17
~ after, 323.11; 782.22
bad ~, 323.10; 782.21
~ before, 323.12
bodily ~ close to ground, 60.6
comfortable bodily ~, 1141.5
difficult ~, 25.9
empty ~, 926.20
entitled to inherit ~, 6.5
give a ~ (job) to, 205.19,20
greater in ~, 833.4,6; 924.6
honor, descr. of ~ of, 857.17
inconspicuous ~, 952.10
~ of affairs, 782.24
~ of judging, 782.23
~ of viewing, 782.23
place in a bodily ~, 60.5
social ~, 314.1; see social class,n.
superior in ~, 833.4,6; 924.6
positive,adj., 633.17; 641.1,6
possess,v., 255.1; see also own,v.
~ again, 255.1(5)
possession,n., 255.2,10; see also ownership, property,n.
a ~, 255.10
bride's personal ~s, 974.35(4)
descr. of ~, 255.5
family ~s, 255.10(9)
hold in one's ~, 257.1(15,16, 19,20)
household ~s, 255.10(9)
~ of a place, 255.2(6)
~ of land in return for services, 255.2(7)
pass into the ~ of, 256.4

period of ~, 255.6
personal ~s, 255.10(5,6,10–12, 18)
right of ~, 255.6
troublesome ~, 255.10(19)
valuable ~s, 255.10(2,13,17)
possessor,n., 255.3; see also owner,n.
consider as the ~ of, 893.7
descr. of a ~, 255.5
possibility,n., 31.2
figure the ~ of, 31.3
~ of happening, 29.31
unknowable ~, 612.19
possible,adj., 31.1
post office,n.
to be held at the ~, 678.12
posterity,n., 723.17
postpone,v., 768.8
postponement,n., 768.9
postscript,n., 682.3(1)
~ to a poem, etc., 682.3(6)
posture,n., 60.1
pretense, 826.7,10
hold a ~, 60.3
~ in painting, 60.4
~ in sculpture, 60.4
pert. to ~, 60.2
place in a ~, 60.5
strike a ~, 60.3; 826.7
posture,v., 826.7
pot,n., 261.10
~ for coffee, 261.10(13)
~ for distilling, 261.10(8)
~ for melting metals, 261.10(3)
~ for tea, 261.10(9,13)
metal ~s, 1012.26
repair ~s, 832.16
~s and pans of tin plate, 1020.14
potion,n.
love ~, 700.24
pottery,n., 261.11; see earthenware,n.
~ with fine cracks, 802.20
pouch,n., 350.1; see sac,n.
carrying the young in a ~, 190.7
poultry,n., 405.6; see also chicken,n., etc.
pound,n.
enclosure, 300.7; see enclosure,n.
payment per ~, 219.3(37)
pound,v., 437.1; see hit,v.
instrument for ~ing to a powder, 437.5(15)
pour,v., 1036.1,2; see also flow, scatter,v.
~ around, 1036.16
~ boiling water on or over, 1036.18
~ (color) over, 1036.17
~ in drops or scattered masses, 1036.7,9,15
let (blood) ~ out, 1036.21
~ (light) over, 1036.17
~ like frozen raindrops, 1040.4
~ over, 1036.16
~ (tears), 1036.8
~ upon, 1036.16
~ water down a pump, 1036.19
pouring,adj., 1036.4
~ in drops or scattered masses, 1036.12
pouring,n., 1036.5
device for ~ through a narrow opening, 1036.5
~ in drops or scattered masses, 1036.10
instrument for ~ in a mist or in fine drops, 1036.13

poverty

sound of ~, 469.1(9) ;
469.2(1) ; 1036.6
sound of ~ in drops or scattered masses, 1036.11
poverty,n., 217.2
scarcity, 917.28; see scarcity,n.
reduce to ~, 217.3
~-stricken, 217.1; see poor,
adj.
powder,n., 1001.1
consisting of ~, 1001.8
covered with ~, 1001.8
crumbling into ~, 1001.7
grind to ~, 438.8(2,3,5–7)
instrument for pounding into
a ~, 437.5(15)
like ~, 1001.9
perfumed ~, 445.16
red ~ used as a cosmetic,
488.22(7)
rub into ~, 438.1(31)
sprinkle with ~, 1001.11
use ~ as a cosmetic, 1001.13
powdery,adj., 1001.8
become ~, 438.10; 1001.3
make ~, 1001.3
power,n., 5.1; see also authority,n.
act for another, ~ to, 5.11
based on legal ~, 5.14
battle, ~ in, 5.1(4)
be beyond the ~ of, 10.12
bodily ~, 5.1(7,10,17)
change, ~ to, 5.1(9)
controlling ~, of, 5.4(11)
cruel in exercise of ~,
889.1(9) ; 889.7; 890.4
delegated ~, exercising,
1073.91
delusions of ~, 1136.1(18,25,
31,37,38)
deprive of ~, 13.1(2,5,8)
deprive of controlling ~,
8.25
exceeding legal ~, 5.21
exercise ~, 5.6
extent of ~, 787.3
feeling of abnormal ~, 5.20
full of ~, 5.2
give ~, 5.7,12
give ~ to act for another,
5.12
govern, ~ to, 1073.84
governmental ~, 5.4(11)
group of three in ~, 932.5
harsh in exercise of ~,
889.1(9) ; 889.7; 890.4
have ~, 5.6
having ~, 5.2,5; see powerful,
adj., below
having unrestricted ~, 5.5(6)
hypnotic ~, 5.1(3)
increase ~ of, 5.13
king's ~, 5.4(9) ; 1073.17(1)
landlord's ~, 1003.23
lose ~, 10.8
magic ~, 5.1(20,21)
means of ~, 5.15
measure ~, 5.22
mental ~, 5.1(7,17)
mother's ~, descr. of, 5.18
muscular ~, 5.1(15,16)
~ over, 5.4
person who has risen to ~,
5.8(5)
person with delegated ~, 5.10
pert. to ~, 5.9
physical ~, 5.1(7,10,17)
place of ~, 5.19
political ~, 5.4(12,21,22) ;
5.7(20) ; 1073.17,38
Pope's ~, 5.4(25,26)
produce effect, ~ to, 5.1(5,6,
8,19)

reduce in ~, 10.5
region of ~, 5.19; 782.6,10
ruler's ~, 1073.17,38
royal ~, 5.4(9) ; 1073.17(1)
sexual ~, 5.1(12,17)
source of ~, 5.15
superior in ~, 833.3,16
supernatural ~, 5.1(20)
supreme ~, 5.4(10–12,15,17,18,
20–23)
symbol of ~, 5.16; 954.1(9)
Turkish or Moslem political
~, symbol of, 1073.86
unfair in exercise of ~, 635.6
wealth, ~ of, 5.4(16)
without ~, 10.1(1,19,27,28,47) ;
13.3; see also weak,adj.
powerful,adj., 5.2,5
~ animal, 906.18(1)
~ at night, 778.5(4)
~ in effect, 16.13
~ in result, 16.13
most ~, 5.5(8,9)
~ person, 5.3,8; 906.18(1,9,14)
simple but ~, 960.5
~ thing, 906.18(9,14)
powerless,adj., 13.3; see also
weak,adj.
make ~, 10.5(4) ; 13.1; see also
disable, weaken,v.
make ~ with confusion,
10.5(4)
practical,adj.
sensible, 596.1
useful, 279.17
action that is ~, 596.9
concern with ~ results, 16.28;
279.23
~ in use, 279.5
~ joke, 1115.12–16; see also
joke,n.
practicality,n.
sensibleness, 596.3
usefulness, 279.18
practice,n., 7.1; 49.2; 279.2;
629.11
practice,v., 49.1; 279.1
prairie,n., 1003.2(6)
praise,n., 851.2
advertisement expressing ~,
851.5
claim to ~, 851.11
descr. of, 851.4
deserves ~, that which,
851.10
deserving ~, 851.8
elicits ~, one who or that
which, 851.9
expressive of ~, 851.4
opinion expressing ~, 851.5
poem of ~, 689.2(12)
showing ~, 851.4
song of ~, 851.6
worthy of ~, 851.8
praise,v., 851.1
~ in hymns, 477.9
~ insincerely, 851.1(6)
~ too highly, 851.1(6,8,10)
praiser,n., 851.3
praiseworthy,adj., 851.8
praising,adj., 851.4
prank,n., 824.3
pray,v., 276.1
one who ~s for another,
649.6
prayer,n., 649.1
beads for ~s, 961.1(23)
book of ~s, 687.1(7)
call upon by ~, 693.1(10) ;
649.5
case worn by Jews during ~,
983.38,39
night of ~, 649.4
place for ~, 645.1; see
church,n.

~s, 649.2
signal for ~, 956.6(1)
time for ~s, 649.3
ward off by ~, 76.6
preach,v., 647.1
preacher,n., 647.4; see also
clergyman,n.
habit, etc., of ~s, 647.9
pert. to a ~, 647.5
talk like a ~, 647.10
preaching,adj., 647.6
preaching,n., 647.2
a ~, 647.3
addicted to ~, 647.7
art of ~, 647.8
habit, etc., of ~, 647.9
pert. to ~, 647.5
supply with ~, 647.12
preachingly,adv., 647.11
precaution,n., 577.2
precede,v., 175.1; see also
introduce,v.
~ as a sign or announcement,
175.1(3,5,7,8,12,15)
~ as an introduction,
175.1(13,14)
one who ~s others, 175.5
period that ~s an event,
769.8(7)
that which ~s others, 175.5
~ to get living quarters for
others, 175.1(5)
precedence,n., 175.2,4
precedent,n., 29.6(5)
preceder,n., 175.5
~ in a position, 175.5(2,5–7)
preceding,adj.
coming before, 175.3
introductory, 730.5; see introductory,adj.
~ in place, 175.3(3,7)
~ in speech or writing,
175.3(1,2,4,6)
~ in time, 175.3(3,5,7–14)
~ the main part, 175.3(8,9,13,
14)
precious,adj.
artificial, 811.1
loved, 700.5
valuable, 839.2
precipice,n., 1006.1(8,12,31,37) ;
see also cliff,n.
predator,n., 248.11
predatory,adj., 248.4,9
predestine,v., 33.5(3–6)
predicament,n., 25.9
predict,v., 772.1
~ evil, 772.18
~ from signs or symptoms,
772.11
~ misfortune, 772.18
~ the future, 772.2
~ the weather, 1047.16
~ with anxiety, 772.13
~ with fear, 772.13
prediction,n., 772.3,5,20
a ~, 772.5
action, ~ to determine time
for, 772.16
art of ~, 772.4
~ by air, 772.20(1)
~ by animals, 772.20(57)
~ by arrows, 772.20(10)
~ by atmosphere, 772.20(1)
~ by ax movements, 772.20(9)
~ by Bible, 772.20(11)
~ by birds, 772.20(43)
~ by books, 772.20(11,55)
~ by cake dough, 772.20(18)
~ by claws, 772.20(41)
~ by cock and corn, 772.20(2)
~ by communication with the
dead, 772.20(36,53)
~ by crystal ball, 772.20(19)
~ by dreams, 772.20(39)

~ by entrails, 772.20(4,26)
~ by evil spirits, 772.20(53)
~ by feces, 772.20(51)
~ by figures, 772.20(23)
~ by finger rings, 772.20(20)
~ by fire, 772.20(48,50)
~ by fish, 772.20(31)
~ by flames, 772.20(48)
~ by flight of birds, 772.20(7, 43)
~ by flour, 772.20(3)
~ by footprints, 772.20(30)
~ by fountains, 772.20(46)
~ by hands, 772.20(44)
~ by head, 772.20(14)
~ by heavenly bodies, stars, etc., 772.20(5,6,22,28); 1053.36(2); 1054.32
~ by lead, 772.20(34)
~ by letters of a name, 772.20(40)
~ by letters of the alphabet, 772.20(37,40)
~ by lines, 772.20(23,55)
~ by lines in a book, 772.20(55)
~ by liquids, 772.20(29)
~ by lots, 772.20(16,54)
~ by mice, 772.20(35)
~ by moon, 772.20(5,28); 1054.32
~ by nails or claws, 772.20(41)
~ by numbers, 927.7
~ by oracles' answers, 772.20(56)
~ by palm lines, 772.20(44)
~ by pebbles, 772.20(47)
~ by planets, 772.20(28); 1053.36(2)
~ by plants, 772.20(12)
~ by rods, 772.20(49)
~ by sacrificial objects, 772.20(27)
~ by salt, 772.20(25)
~ by sea tides, 772.20(29)
~ by serpents, 772.20(42)
~ by shoulder blades, 772.20(50)
~ by sieve motions, 772.20(17)
~ by signs, 772.20(7)
~ by smoke, 772.20(13)
~ by soil, 999.13
~ by soles of the feet, 772.20(45)
~ by south wind, 772.20(8)
~ by stars, 772.20(5,6,22,28)
~ by stones or stone charms, 772.20(33)
~ by straws, 772.20(52)
~ by thunder, 772.20(32)
~ by ventriloquism, 772.20(21)
~ by walking in a circle, 772.20(24)
~ by wands, 772.20(49)
~ by water, 772.20(29)
~ by wax, 772.20(15)
~ by wine, 772.20(38)
diagram of stars and planets for ~, 772.21
disease, ~ of the course of, 772.12
engage in ~s, 772.2
expert in ~, 1053.38
inspection of feces for ~, 293.32
power of ~, claiming, 772.10
power of ~, gifted with, 772.9
skillful in ~ of change, 1047.21
skillful in ~ of public opinion, 1047.21

skillful in ~ of results, 1047.21
weather ~, 772.14; 1047.18,19
weather ~, instrument for, 1046.18
predictive,adj., 772.8
predictor,n., 772.6,20
ancient Roman ~, 772.19
female ~ of evil or misfortune, 772.17
pert. to ~s, 772.7
unbelieved ~, 772.17
weather ~, 772.15; 1047.20
preface,n., 730.4; see also introduction,n.
writer of ~s, 730.8
prefatory,adj., 730.5
prefer,v., 252.1; 1109.1
preference,n., 252.5(12); 1109.3
prefix,n., 908.8,20
prefix,v., 908.19
pregnancy,n., 714.2
abortion or miscarriage in ~, 714.18; see abortion,n.
beginning of ~, 714.10(1)
carry during ~, 714.5
end of ~, 714.10(6)
events in ~, 714.10,11
false ~, 714.12(3)
incapable of ~, make, 710.38(8,9)
male cell causing ~, 379.6(7)
male fluid causing ~, 379.7
period of ~, 714.10(2)
prevention of ~, 714.16,17
science dealing with ~, 401.1(39,45,53,103)
test for ~, 401.10(1,4)
types of ~, 714.12
pregnant,adj., 714.1
meaningful, 607.9
become ~, 714.3,4
make ~, 714.6–9
woman ~ the first time, 714.13
woman ~ the second or later time, 714.14,15
prejudice,n., 634.1,7
~ against foreigners, 634.1(12)
~ against immigrants, 634.1(12)
~ against Jews, 634.1(1)
~ against Negroes, 634.1(10)
cause ~ in, 634.4
directed to one's ~, 634.6
feel ~, 634.5
~ in favor of group, 634.1(25)
~ in favor of natives, 634.1(12)
~ in favor of one's district, 634.1(26)
~ in favor of Pope, 634.1(13)
~ in favor of race, 634.1(22–24)
~ in favor of religious sect, 634.1(25)
lack of ~, 636.2
racial ~, 634.1(22–24)
show ~, 634.5
showing ~, 634.2
prejudice,v., 634.4
prejudiced,adj., 634.2
~ by bitterness, 877.1(2)
~ by cynicism, 877.1(2)
~ by envy, 877.1(22)
~ by hate, 877.1(2)
cause to be ~, 634.10
~ person, 634.3,9
state of being ~, 634.1
preliminary,adj.
introductory, 730.5; see introductory,adj.

preceding, 175.3(8,13,14); see preceding,adj.
prelude,n., 730.4; see also introduction,n.
premature,adj., 765.4,7
prematurity,n., 765.5,7
premonition,n., 37.7; 773.3
premonitory,adj., 37.2; 773.5
preparation,n., 48.3; 726.3
a ~, 48.4
pert. to ~, 48.7
without ~, 48.9,10
prepare,v., 48.1,2; 726.1
~ against attack, 48.1(1,7)
~ against danger, 48.1(1,7)
~ against threat, 48.1(7)
~ and give, 48.1(5)
~ beforehand, 48.1(7,9,11)
~ by giving information to, 48.1(8)
~ food for keeping, 48.1(40)
~ for action, 48.1(12)
~ for winter, 48.1(13)
~ leather for keeping, 48.1(4)
~ meat for keeping, 48.1(4)
~ on little notice, 48.1(6)
prepared,adj., 48.5
~ hastily, 48.12
~ on the spur of the moment, 48.12
~ suddenly, 48.12
preparedness,n., 48.6
prepuce,n., 379.1(17)
~ liquid, 1027.1(10)
prescribe,v., 252.18; 275.1
prescribed,adj., 252.17
prescription,n., 275.2
presence,n., 38.2
make one's ~ known, 643.1(26)
present,adj., 38.1
be ~ at, 38.4
concealed but ~, 970.45
everywhere ~, 38.1(3,4)
inactive but ~, 38.1(2)
person who is ~, 38.3
present,n.
gift, 230.6
now, 771.1
present,v.
introduce, 730.1
offer, 237.1
show, 951.1
~ in an exciting light, 1100.16,17,20,21
presentation,n.
introduction, 730.2
offer, 237.2
show, 951.2
comprehensive ~ of a subject, 951.3(17)
presently,adv., 766.11
preserve,v.
pickle, etc., 263.1
protect, 568.1
~ a corpse, 263.1(6,9)
liquid for ~ing, 1035.18
~ with salt, 1011.3,4,9
preside,v., 1077.24
president,n., 1077.1
~ of a college, 1077.1(6,25)
~ of a republic, 1077.1(7)
~ of the U.S., 1077.1(7,13)
protects U.S. ~, organization that, 971.39
press,v., 198.1; see also push,v.
~ close for comfort, 198.1(11, 14,18,19,22)
~ down, 198.1(2,12)
one who ~es, 198.4
~ out, 198.1(13)
serving to ~, 198.3
that which ~es, 198.5
~ the throat to stop breathing, 198.1(3,26,27,29)

~ to cut off blood circulation, 198.1(27)
~ with the nose, 198.1(19)
pressing,adj., 198.3
urgent, 274.4
pressure,n., 198.2
atmospheric ~, 1046.9–11
blood ~, instrument to measure, 198.6(3)
emotional ~, 1133.13
~ in a struggle, 198.2(1)
lying on with ~, 65.3(7)
measure ~, instrument to, 198.6
remove ~ from, 198.8
~ upon endurance, 198.2(2,3)
prestige,n., 615.2; see **fame**,n.
pretend,v., 826.1,2,4–9
~ ability, 826.5(1) ; 826.8
~ an attitude, 826.7
~ characteristics, 826.1,4
~ conditions, 826.1,4
~ disability, 826.5(2)
~ feelings, 826.1,4
~ illness, 826.5(2)
~ing to be, 826.3
~ medical skill, 826.8
~ not to have a condition, 826.9
~ not to have a feeling, 826.9
~ not to have a quality, 826.9
~ not to see, 826.6
~ qualities, 826.1,4
~ to attack, 560.1(13)
~ to be, 826.2
~ to have a feeling, 826.4
pretended,adj., 826.11
pretender,n., 826.12
boastful ~, 872.22
~ to excellence, 826.12(2)
~ to goodness, 826.12(4)
~ to influence, 826.12(3)
~ to medical skill or knowledge, 826.15
~ to power, 826.12(3)
~ to virtue, 826.12(4)
~ to wealth, 826.12(3)
pretense,n., 826.10
characterized by ~, 826.11,14
drop a ~, 984.12
full of ~, 826.11
lack of ~, 807.3; 813.6,8
make a ~, 826.5
~ of ability, 826.10(2)
~ of being someone else, 826.10(4)
~ of bravery, 826.10(1)
~ of excellence, 826.10(6)
~ of feelings, 826.10(3)
~ of goodness, 826.10(2)
~ of knowledge, 826.10(2)
~ of medical skill or knowledge, 826.10(5)
~ of piety, 826.10(13)
~ of skill, 826.10(2)
~ of spirituality, 826.14
~s, 826.13
pretentious,adj., 826.11,14
~ in language, 951.49
~ in style, 951.49
~ language, 665.9(61)
pretty,adj., 505.1; see **beautiful**,adj.
make ~, 505.10(5)
prevail,v.
be prevalent, 40.3
be stronger, 1.27
be superior, 833.16
prevalence,n., 40.2
prevalent,adj., 40.1; 279.10; 535.1
be ~, 40.3
prevent,v., 78.1
try to ~, 78.5

prevention,n., 78.2
art of disease ~, 569.13
preventive,adj., 78.4
preventive,n., 78.3
prey,n., 247.9; 248.13
living off ~, 248.9,10
search for ~, 248.6,7
prey,v., 247.23(19) ; 248.12
tending to ~, 248.9
preyer,n., 247.25; 248.11
preying,n., 248.10
price,n., 223.1,2; see also **charge**, **cost**,n.
argue about ~, 542.11(2)
commotion in ~s in stock market, 1101.1(12)
~ control, 223.12
discuss ~, 223.9
discussion of ~, 223.10
estimated ~, 223.6
excessive in ~, 921.1(2,3,9,13)
~ for avoiding attack, 223.8
high in ~, 223.14; see also **expensive**,adj.
list of ~s, 223.3
low in ~, 223.15,16; see also **inexpensive**,adj.
moderate in ~, 923.1(4)
offer a ~, 223.11
offer as a ~, 237.1(2)
~ per ton, 947.39
prickle,n., 333.3; 335.1
animal's ~, 335.1(14,16)
developing ~s, 335.4
full of ~s, 335.1(4,8,9)
like a ~, 335.1(1)
plant's ~, 335.1(16,19)
shaped like a ~, 507.17(1)
prickly,adj., 334.1; 335.2
pride,n., 871.2; see also **proud**, adj.
cause ~ in, 871.4
exhibition of ~, 871.2(1)
hurt the ~ of, 868.1(4) ; 868.10
lower the ~ of, 868.10
self-~, 871.2(2,3)
show ~, 871.3
show of ~, 871.2(7)
show with ~, 871.9
talk with ~, 871.9
treat with ~, 871.7,8
walk with ~, 871.3(6,7)
priest,n., 646.1; see **clergyman**,n.
boy who helps a ~, 556.3(3)
hater of ~s, 880.18(5)
primary,adj.
early, 766.7
important, 848.5,13
primitive,adj.
earliest, 766.6
uncivilized, 866.1
belief in ~ culture, 866.6
living in ~ circumstances, 750.4(14)
pert. to ~ social life, 751.8
return to ~ type, 145.2(1,3)
reversion to ~ stage, 866.9
reversion to ~ state, 866.8
reversion to ~ type, 145.2(1, 3) ; 866.8
study of ~ people, 866.5
unconscious ~ forces, 866.7
prince,n.
daughter of a ~, 1073.21(7)
mistress of a ~, 1073.21(12)
petty ~, 314.12
wife of a ~, 1073.21(2,7)
principal,adj., 848.5
principal,n., 848.3
school ~, 623.7(2)
principle,n., 56.1
abstract ~s, 56.1(30)
art, ~s of an, 56.1(30)

beginning ~s, 729.13
behavior, ~s of, 56.3; 843.1
body of ~s, 56.1(16)
care in observing ~s of behavior, 56.5
conduct, ~s of, 56.3; 843.1
essential ~, 56.1(15,21)
established ~, 56.1(2)
explanatory ~s, 56.1(30)
extreme ~s, 922.25
first ~, 56.1(26)
fundamental ~, 56.1(3,4,11,14, 21)
fundamental ~s, 56.1(3,4,11, 13–15,21,26)
general ~, 56.1(30)
government ~s, 56.1(27)
guiding ~, 56.1(10,14,20)
important ~, 56.1(10,12)
lay down ~s, 56.2
moral conduct, ~s of, 843.1
observant of moral ~s, 843.17
philosophy, ~s of, 56.1(8,27)
politics, ~s of, 56.1(8,19)
proved, ~ to be, 56.1(29)
rational ~ of the universe, 56.1(17)
religion, ~s of, 56.1(6,8,9,12, 27)
~s, 56.1
science, ~s of, 56.1(30)
subject, ~s of, 56.1(1,18)
true and acceptable ~, 56.1(28)
print,n.
arrangement of ~, 311.1(47)
row of ~, 311.11(1)
print,v.
~ in certain letters, 679.2
~ incorrectly, 682.11
official approval to ~, 850.12
printer,n., 690.2
master ~s, 690.3
~s, 690.3
printing,n., 690.1
appearance of ~, 690.7
art of ~, 690.4
incorrect ~ of words, 682.2(2)
measurement unit in ~, 946.26(1,17,18)
picture for ~, 965.1(35)
processes of ~, 690.1
~ similar to handwriting, 690.5
~ system for the blind, 690.6
prism,n., 945.16
six-sided ~, 945.17
prison,n., 301.4
convicts of a ~, 301.7
~ for rehabilitation, 301.4(19)
~ for young criminals, 301.4(19)
head of a ~, 301.17
military ~, 301.4(5,14)
~ on a warship, 301.4(5)
period in ~, 301.9
person sentenced to ~, 301.5(1)
science of ~ management, 301.19
section of a ~, 301.18
send back to ~, 301.8
set free from ~, 309.1(6,8,13–16,28,32)
small room in a ~, 301.4(8,9)
underground ~, 301.4(3,12,15, 16)
prisoner,n., 301.5
held as a ~, 301.15
keep as a ~, 301.16
make a ~ of, 301.13
place for ~ in a court, 1081.10

~'s return, promise of,
1122.46(1)
state of being a ~, 301.14
privacy,n., 331.2
private,adj., 331.1
~ place, 331.3
~ room, 787.7(8,9,15,18,19,32,
38)
privately,adv., 331.4
privilege,n., 6.1
claimer of ~, 6.3
destroy property, ~ to, 6.1(1)
equality of political ~s,
1076.11
give ~, 6.2; 230.1(13,19,51)
government, ~ granted by,
6.1(6)
holder of ~, 6.3
minor ~, 6.1(2)
royal ~, 6.6
scholastic ~, certificate conferring, 857.11
specially acquired ~, 6.1(5)
take away ~, 6.7
take property, ~ to, 6.1(1)
~ to enter, 133.9
unique ~, 6.1(8)
use property, ~ to, 6.1(1)
prize,n., 219.11
give a ~ to, 219.12
receiver of a ~, 219.13
probability,n.
based on ~, 30.6
probable,adj., 30.1
problem,n., 602.1
complex ~, 25.2(1) ; 602.1(3)
full of ~s, 25.1(12,23)
of the nature of a ~, 602.2
procedure,n., 50.1(5,23,30) ;
174.2
~ that takes advantage,
836.13
proceed,v., 174.1
procrastinate,v., 768.1; see delay,v.
procrastination,n., 768.2; see
delay,n.
given to ~, 768.4
procrastinator,n., 768.3
procreate,v., 717.7; see reproduce,v.
procure,v., 240.1; see get,v.
produce,n., 726.3,11; see also
product,n.
produce,v., 726.8
create, 726.17; see create,v.
make, 726.1; see make,v.
~ a result, 16.9
able to ~ abundantly, 726.12;
see also fertile,adj.
~ as a result, 16.8
produced,adj., 726.4
~ by living matter, 726.16
principal thing ~, 731.26
self-~, 726.15
that which is ~, 726.3,11,20,21
the total ~, 726.13
producer,n., 726.10
creator, 726.19
maker, 726.1
product,n.
something created, 726.20,21
something made, 726.3
something produced, 726.11
agricultural ~s, 745.21
artificial ~, 726.3(1)
artistic ~, 726.21
best ~, 726.3(2,3)
human ~, 726.3(1)
primitive ~, 726.3(1)
secondary ~, 726.11(1)
the total ~, 726.13
production,n., 726.3,9,11,18,20
an artistic ~, 726.21
Russian system of ~, 726.7

self-~, 726.14
productive,adj.
effective, 16.11; see effective,
adj.
fertile, 715.7,9; see fertile,adj.
be ~, 715.10
make ~, 715.11
not ~, 716.1; see sterile,adj.
not very ~, 716.2,3
productivity,n., 715.7,9
symbol of ~, 954.1(2)
profane,adj., 650.9,11; 861.8
set apart as ~, 325.12(15)
~ word, 666.3(23)
profane,v., 650.9; 861.14; 886.30
profaned,adj., 886.29
profanity,n., 861.9,10
profess,v.
admit, 675.1
pretend, 826.1
profession,n.
admission, 675.2
occupation, 204.1
authority to practice a ~,
5.4(14)
one not in a ~, 207.1
people not connected with a
~, 207.4
person engaged in a ~,
203.7(30)
professor,n., 621.7; see
teacher,n.
professorial,adj., 621.10
professorship,n., 621.9
proficiency,n., 7.1; see skill,n.
proficient,adj., 7.2; see skillful,adj.
profit,n., 240.3
financial ~, 215.1
make exorbitant ~s, 215.3
profit,v., 240.1
profitable,adj., 215.2; 219.7
progress,n., 174.2
attempt to hinder ~, 557.7
delay the ~ of, 768.8(12)
highest point of ~, 165.1
hindrance of ~, 557.2(1) ;
557.6
hindrance to ~, 557.3(2,3,5,6,
12,13)
important point in ~,
848.12
line of ~, 174.4
opposition to ~, 544.9
period of ~, 769.8(15)
place, condition, etc., where
~ is slowed, 557.3(3)
slow in ~, 100.6
slow the ~ of, 100.5(1,2)
progress,v., 174.1
prohibit,v., 555.1; see forbid,v.
~ from entering, 555.5,6
prohibited,adj., 555.4
~ book, 899.21
prohibition,n., 555.2
prohibitive,adj., 555.3
project,v.
stick out, 172.1(1,7,10,12) ;
958.1–3; see also stick out,v.
throw, 187.1; see throw,v.
land ~ing into water,
1029.98,99
projectile,adj., 187.3; 958.4
projectile,n., 187.4; 565.10,19,
21; see also bullet, mis-
sile,n.
pert. to throwing ~s, 565.12
science of ~s, 565.7,16
~s, collectively, 565.11
projecting,adj., 172.4; 958.5,6
~ part, 326.1(28,36,40) ; 958.7
projection,n.
act of sticking out, 958.1,3
act of throwing, 187.2

that which sticks out,
958.7
carved ~, 966.8
full of ~s, 958.8
map showing ~s, 966.11
ornament with ~s, 959.1(27)
rooflike ~, 972.1(2)
roundness of ~, 958.8
sculptured ~, 966.8
projector,n.
slide ~, 1065.108
prologue,n., 730.4
actor who delivers a ~,
969.35
deliver a ~, 969.36
promise or pledge,n., 1122.3
accepter of a ~ against a
loan, 1122.41
~ against a loan, 1122.39;
1122.46(2,4,5,7,8)
bind by a ~, 1122.49
bound by a ~, one who is,
1122.50
break one's ~, 802.29; 1122.53
broken one's ~, having,
1122.54,55
consecrated by a ~, 1122.12
containing a ~, 1122.13
disloyal to one's ~, 659.1(3,
11,12)
done, etc., in accordance with
a ~, 1122.11
duty imposed by one's ~,
1122.9
give as a ~, 1122.20
guarantees the ~ of another,
one who, 1122.48
keep a ~, 1122.51
keeping a ~, 1122.52
like a ~, 1122.14
make a ~, 1122.1,19
moneylender against a ~,
1122.42
~ of prisoner's return,
1122.46(1)
~ of the future, 1122.10
one to whom a ~ is made,
1122.15
person deposited against a ~,
1122.46(6,7)
persuade by a ~, 1122.21
pert. to a ~, 1122.14
place under duty by a ~,
1122.49
property, money, or thing deposited as a ~, 1122.46
religious ~, one who is bound
by, 1122.50
security against a ~, 1122.46
~ to pay, 1122.4,6,8,24
written ~, 1122.4–6,8
promise or pledge,v., 1122.1,19
~ as security to a creditor,
1122.30,32
~ (honor) as a security,
1122.45
one who ~s to pay for an-
other, 1122.48
~ to be faithful, 1122.26
~ to give up alcholic beverage, 1122.27
~ to join a fraternity or sorority, 1122.28
~ to pay, 1122.22
promised,adj.
something ~, 1122.16,39,46
promiser,n., 1122.2
~ for another, 1122.47,48
prompt,adj., 766.10
prompt,n.
hint, 239.2
reminder, 627.34
reminding, 627.31
prompt,v.
excite to act, 52.9

hint, 239.1; see hint,v.
remind, 627.30; see remind,v.
prompter,n., 239.3; 627.33
prone,adj.
  lying flat, 65.3
  tending, 630.2
prong,n., 335.1; see point,n.
pronounce,v., 670.2,5
  ~ a speech sound, 670.15
  unable to be ~d, 665.7(8)
pronunciation,n., 670.1
  childish ~, 670.4(10)
  clear ~, 670.4(2,8)
  correct ~, 670.3,9
  identical in ~, 670.8
  incorrect ~, 670.6,7
  indistinct ~, 670.4(7,15)
  Irish ~, 670.4(4)
  manner of ~, 670.1,4
  ~ of S, 670.4(13,14)
  science of ~, 670.9,25
  shortened in ~, 911.1(16)
  slow ~, 670.4(6)
  slurring ~, 670.4(7)
  sounds in ~, 670.10,11,13,14
  southern ~, 670.4(6)
  ~ through the nose, 670.4(11)
  vibration of R in ~, 670.4(12, 19)
  ~ with H, 670.4(3)
proof,n., 812.16; see also prove,v.
  capable of ~, 812.21
  give or present ~ of, 812.18
  ~ of authority, right, identity, etc., 812.17
  pert. to ~, 812.22
  serving as ~, 812.20
  support by ~, 812.18; 1022.28
propaganda,n., 613.30
  book published as ~, 687.1(17, 22)
propagate,v., 717.7; see reproduce,v.
propagation,n., 717.7; see reproduction,n.
  worship of ~, 656.15(20)
propensity,n., 630.1
proper,adj., 818.1
  be ~ for, 818.15
  ~ behavior, 55.3(3,4,14); 818.4,5,8,9,12
  customs of ~ behavior, 818.5
  demand for ~ behavior, 818.12
  deviate from ~ course, 828.5–7
  excessively ~, 818.10,11
  judgment of ~ and improper, 818.16
  morally ~, 818.3
  no concept of ~ and improper, 818.15
  not concerned with ~ and improper, 818.15
  not involving ~ and improper, 818.15
  off the ~ course, 828.8
  rules of ~ behavior, 818.5
  sense of ~ behavior, 818.9
  stiffly ~, 818.10,11
properness,n., 818.2
  acting with ~, 818.7
  behaving with ~, 818.7
  judgment of ~, 818.16
  no concept of ~, 818.15
  not concerned with ~, 818.15
  not involving ~, 818.15
property,n., 255.10; see also possession,n.
  addition to ~, 908.26
  economic system based on ~, 255.11–13
  get back ~, 240.13

~ inherited, or to be inherited, 241.4; 255.10(7)
personal ~, 255.10(5,6,10–12, 18)
real ~, 255.10(8,14–16)
total ~, 255.10(4,7)
prophecy,n., 772.3,5; see prediction,n.
prophesy,v., 772.1,2; 773.1; see predict,v.
prophet,n., 772.6; see also predictor,n.
  pert. to ~s, 772.7
prophetic,adj., 772.7,8; 773.4
proportion,n.
  in ~, 520.10
  not in ~, 520.11
proportional,adj., 520.10
propriety,n., 818.2; see properness,n.
prosper,v.
  grow, 731.3
  succeed, 23.1
prosperity,n.
  success, 23.4
  wealth, 216.2
  time of ~, 1102.26
prosperous,adj.
  financially profitable, 215.2
  growing, 731.5
  successful, 23.2
  wealthy, 216.1; see wealthy, adj.
prostate,n.
  inflammation of the ~, 379.9(11)
prostitute,n., 711.1
  associate with ~s, 711.6
  get customers for a ~, 711.15,16
  invite men (of a ~), 711.17
  lover of ~s, 700.30(21)
  make a ~ of, 711.7
  public ~, 711.3
  refuge for ~s, 711.19
  region where Japanese ~s live, 711.12
  worn-out ~, 711.2
  writing about ~s, 711.18
prostitution,n., 711.5
  full of ~, 1087.11
  house of ~, 711.9; see brothel,n.
  place where laws against ~ are not enforced, 711.14
  seducer into ~, 711.8
  woman forced into ~, 711.4
  writing about ~, 711.18
protect,v., 568.1,11
  take care of, 570.1; see care,n.
  ~ a military installation, 568.28
  ~ a place, 568.28
  accompany to ~, 131.1(4,5,8); 568.8
  ~ against air, 1045.04
  ~ against disease, 569.1,3; see immunize,v.
  ~ against poison, 569.1(1); see immunize,v.
  ~ against rain, 1037.15
  ~ against weather, 1047.11,13
  cover and ~, 972.1(40)
  go around to ~, 568.9
  ~ side of military troops, 568.24
  ~ with bushes, 985.25
  ~ with leaves, 972.1(4)
protected,adj., 568.7
  ~ against air, 1043.28; 1045.14(4)
  ~ against rain, 1037.14
  ~ against weather, 1047.10
  ~ against wind, 1043.28

~ by a garrison, 568.7(4)
~ (of a place), 568.31
~ person, 568.19
~ place, 568.26
protection,n., 568.2–4
  care, 570.4; see care,n.
  ~ against cold, 1047.12,13
  ~ against disease, 569.2,4,5; see immunity,n.
  ~ against poison, 569.2; see immunity,n.
  ~ against poison gas, 1048.31
  ~ against rain, 1037.29; 1047.12
  ~ against storms, 1042.23–25
  ~ against water, 1033.1,5
  ~ against weather, 1047.12
  ~ against wind, 1047.12,13
  ~ by smoke, 1050.26
  device for ~ against attack, 568.22
  device for ~ against light, sun, or rain, 568.23
  ~ for a place, 568.30
  give for ~, 230.7
  give means of ~ to, 568.17
  give place of ~ to, 568.11
  guardian's ~, 568.2(3,6); 568.3(2)
  Japanese art of self-~, 568.13
  leave the ~ of, cause to, 144.1(29)
  means of ~, 568.4
  ~ of a chaperon, 131.8
  ~ of a place, 568.29
  one under ~, 568.19
  person appealed to for ~, 274.6
  pert. to ~, 568.6
  place for ~ of animals, 1003.2(31)
  place of ~, 568.26
  request for ~, 274.2(2)
  source of ~, 568.4(10); 568.5(14)
  ~, support, and encouragement, 568.20
  take under one's ~, 568.10
  turning for ~, 568.18
protective,adj., 568.6
  ~ covering against attack, 568.22
  ~ device against light, rain, sun, etc., 568.23
  ~ screen of artillery fire, 568.25
  ~ spirit or fairy, 662.7(6)
protector,n., 568.4,5
  ~ of swimmers, 568.5(10)
  pert. to a ~, 568.6
  ~s, 568.5
protest,n., 1120.2,3; see complaint,n.
protest,v., 1120.1; see complain,v.
proud,adj., 871.1; see also pride,n.
  be ~, 871.3
  be ~ of, 871.10
  ~ in bearing, 871.1(30)
  ~ in speech, 871.1(28)
  ~ in walk, 871.1(28)
  make ~, 871.4
  ~ of accomplishments, 871.1(4,5,7–9,12,14,27,28,30, 31,41,45–49)
  ~ of appearance, 871.1(4,46)
  ~ of authority, 871.1(23)
  ~ of importance, 871.1(37)
  ~ of power, 871.1(23)
  ~ of wealth, 871.1(35,36)
  ~ people, 871.6
  ~ person, 871.5
prove,v., 812.15; see also proof,n.

~ genuineness of, 812.19
serving to be ~, 812.20
proved,adj., 812.23
able to be ~, 812.21
proverb,n., 676.1; see saying,n.
provide,v.
produce, 726.8; see pro-
duce,v.
supply, 233.1; see supply,v.
provided,adj.
that which is ~, 233.3
provision,n.
condition, 525.11
production, 726.9
supply, 233.3
supplying, 233.2
seller of ~s, 233.4(1,3,4)
state as a ~, 525.3
provisional,adj., 525.2
prude,n., 873.12
prudery,n., 873.11
prudish,adj., 873.10
prudishness,n., 873.11
psalm,n., 476.4(2,12,17,27,41,
49); see also hymn,n.
writing of ~s, 476.8
psychiatrist,n., 400.7; 401.2;
401.2(4); 584.21
psychiatry,n., 400.2(1); 400.6(3,
13,16,21,22,28,29,38,39);
401.1(1,2,36,51,62,83–86);
584.21
psychoanalysis,n., 400.2(1);
400.6(3,16,21,22,29,37,39);
401.1(2,36,51,62,82,84–86);
584.21
expression of ideas in ~, 586.9
revival of childhood emotions,
impulses, experiences, etc.,
under ~, 1092.88
psychoanalyst,n., 400.7; 401.2;
584.21
emotional attachment to the
~, 1092.88
emotional response of the ~
to the patient, 1092.89
psychological,adj., 584.2,21
~ result, 16.1(6)
psychology,n., 584.21
psychoneurosis,n., 1135.1
psychoneurotic,adj., 1135.2
psychoneurotic,n., 1135.3
psychosis,n., 1136.1; see insanity,n.
psychotherapist,n., 400.7
psychotherapy,n., 400.6(3,16,21,
22,29,37)
psychotic,adj., 1136.2
psychotic,n., 1136.3
puberty,n.
arriving at ~, 709.29
in ~, 709.29
person in ~, 709.30
pert. to ~, 709.28
public,adj., 431.4
bring under ~ control or
ownership, 1073.90
public,n., 431.3; see people,n.
public speaking,n., 671.16; see
speech,n.
manner of ~, 671.14,15
publication,n., 691.1; see also
publish,v.
act of publishing, 691.12
copies of a ~ sold, 691.8
occupation connected with
~s, 691.6,7
organization selling to ~s,
691.9
person conected with ~s,
691.4,5
place where ~s are kept,
687.15,16
prepare writing for ~, 682.9
~s, 691.2

publicity,n., 614.1
bad ~, 614.1(2); 615.2(4); see
also rumor,n.
business of ~, 614.4,5
give ~ to, 614.2; 615.4(1);
615.6
seeking of ~, 614.3
publish,v.
~ a periodical, book, etc.,
691.10
act of ~ing, 691.12
approval to ~, 850.12
be ~ed, 691.11
permission to ~, 554.2(3)
publisher,n., 691.4,5
emblem of a ~, 687.9(4)
pucker,v., 157.1(1,17); 157.2;
158.1
puckered,adj., 157.5; 157.5(1)
pull,n., 193.2
~ on oars, 193.2(2)
pull,v., 193.1; see also draw,v.
~ apart, 193.18(17,19)
~ away, 193.18(17,26,27)
~ back, 145.1; 193.8
~ back (claws), 193.8(5)
~ back (gun hammer), 565.9
~ back in fear, 145.1(3,4,6–9,
11,17,19,25,27,28)
~ back in pain, 145.1(3,7,9,25,
27)
~ down (a structure),
802.24
~ forth, 193.18(8,12)
~ in, 193.8
~ in with the mouth, 193.8(1,
6)
~ off, 193.18(1,5,15,17,20)
~ out, 193.18(1,3,6–10,12–14,
16,23,25,26)
that which ~s, 193.3
~ tight, 193.18(21,22)
~ together, 193.13
pulled,adj.
able to be ~ back, 193.11
able to be ~ in, 193.11
be ~ along behind, 193.7
that which is ~ along behind,
193.6
pulling,adj., 193.4
pulling,n., 193.2
condition caused by ~, 193.5
descr. of ~, 193.4
device for ~ in and ejecting
fluids, 193.12
~ out of teeth, 402.5(22)
~ to pieces, 193.19(1)
vehicle for ~, 192.6(26)
pulpit,n.
supply with a ~, 647.12
without a ~, 647.13
pulsate,v., 105.3
pulse,n., 105.4; 351.8
like the ~, 351.9
measure the ~, instrument
to, 351.10
pulse,v., 105.3
pumice,n.
pert. to ~, 899.7
pump,n.
pour water down a ~,
1036.19
street ~, 1033.42
pun,n., 607.12(1–4); 667.10
making ~s, 667.11
pert. to a ~, 607.15
question to which the answer
is a ~, 625.3(1,4)
punctuate,v., 680.2
punctuation,n.
~ mark, 680.1
use a ~ mark on, 680.2
punish,v., 896.1
~ by a fine, 896.1(1,12,16)

~ by hitting, 896.1(3,5–7,9,11,
13,22,28)
~ by pain, 896.1(8,26)
~ by ridicule, 896.1(19)
desiring to ~, 896.5
~ for one's religion, 896.1(18)
~ in a cruel manner, 896.1(3,
8,10,14,15,25,26)
~ in petty ways, 896.1(18)
not ~, 897.37
not wish to ~, 896.33
promise to ~, 896.27
uninspired by desire to ~,
897.34
punishable,adj., 896.7
~ by death, 794.22
punisher,n., 896.3
punishing,adj., 896.4
lightly ~, 897.35
~ spirits (Greek religion),
896.31
punishment,n., 896.2
a freeing from ~, 309.2(10)
~ after death, 896.2(9);
896.17
advocate of ~, 896.22,23
banish to the country as ~,
786.5
bodily ~, 896.2
book of rules for ~, 896.2(1)
~ by a fine, 896.2(1,4)
~ by burning to death,
1064.64
~ by death, 794.23
~ by God, 896.2(11,12)
~ by heaven, 896.2(11)
~ by hitting, 896.2(2,5)
~ by imprisonment, 896.2(7)
change to lighter ~, 896.28
come as ~, 896.13
corporal ~, 896.2
cruel and unusual ~, 896.2
delay ~, 768.8(9); 897.19
delay in ~, 897.20,21
descr. of ~, 896.6
deserved ~, 896.2(3,6,9,12);
896.26
deserving ~, 893.5; 896.7,24,
25
device for ~, 896.8
eternal ~, 896.16–18
forgiveness of ~, 897.13
free from ~, 897.12
free (witness) from ~,
897.12(1)
freedom from ~, 309.2(1);
309.14(9); 897.13,14
give ~, 230.1(34)
give as ~, 896.12,15
go to the country as ~, 786.4
goddess of ~, 896.32
immunity from ~, 897.13
improve by ~, 896.30
means of ~, 896.8
merciless ~, 896.2(10)
payment as ~, 219.3(25)
place of ~, 896.19
power to decide on ~, 897.38
pronounce ~ upon, 896.11
purification of souls by ~,
896.20
quick ~, 896.2(10)
refrain from ~, 897.37
restrain by ~, 896.30
seducer's killer, light or no
~ for, 896.29
sin, ~ for, 896.2(8)
state of ~, 896.19
unusual ~, 896.2
worthiness of ~, 841.5
punning,n., 607.14
pert. to ~, 607.15
pupil,n.
student, 622.5; see student,n.
puppet,n., 969.40

art of ~ shows, 969.43
manipulator of ~s, 969.44
performance of ~s, 969.42
~s, 969.41
~ show, 969.45
~ shows, 969.41
purchase,n., 211.2; see buy, buying,n.
purchase,v., 211.1; see buy,v.
pure,adj., 900.10
become ~, 900.9
ceremonially ~, 845.3,5
~ in artistic or literary style, 900.14
~ in style, 900.14,15
make ~, 900.1
make ceremonially ~, 845.5
make ~ in style, 900.16
morally ~, 845.1,2,10,11
sexually ~, 710.47; 845.11
sexually ~ person, 710.48
~st form, 507.1(9)
still ~, 900.13
purification,n., 900.1,9
~ of emotions, 900.8
place for ~ of metals, oil, sugar, etc., 900.7
place for ~ of souls, 896.20
washing as means of ~, 899.36(1)
purified,adj., 900.11
purifier,n., 900.1
figurative ~, 900.2
purify,v., 309.11(3,4) ; 900.1,9
~ by melting, 900.3; 1027.19
~ character of, 845.18
~ in style, 900.16
~ morally, 845.15-18
~ of harmful qualities or things, 900.5
~ with air, 900.4
purity,n., 900.10
moral ~, 845.1-3,10,11
of original ~, 900.13
relative ~ of metals, 900.17
sexual ~, 710.47; 845.11
symbol of sexual ~, 845.12
purple,adj., 494.2
become ~, 494.6
becoming ~, 494.4
color ~, 494.5
purple,n., 494.1
purplish,adj., 494.3
purpose,n., 45.1
adapted to the ~, 45.7
concealed ~, 970.47
conscious ~, 45.7
deliberate ~, 45.1(4,5,7,10,14,17)
doctrine of ~, 45.19
done on ~, 45.12
final ~, 45.1(6,9,16,18)
fixed in ~, 45.4
for a certain ~ only, 45.16
for this ~ only, 45.16
full of ~, 45.5
have as one's ~, 45.2
having but one ~ in mind, 45.8
hidden ~, 45.1(2,5)
life ~, 45.1(12)
not on ~, 45.14
on ~, 45.13
one who spoils a ~, 559.4
particular ~, 45.1(13)
pert. to ~, 45.7
preconceived ~, 45.9
said on ~, 45.12
secret ~, 45.1(2,5)
serious ~, 45.6
serve a ~, something to, 279.22(1,5-7,9-12)
serve the ~, 279.19
suiting one's ~, 45.17
theory of ~, 45.19

unchanging in ~, 531.5
without ~, 45.20-22,24
without intellectual ~, 45.23
purpose,v., 45.2
purposeful,adj., 45.5
purposeless,adj., 45.20-22
act in a confused and ~ manner, 605.8
~ person, 45.22,24
purposely,adv., 45.13
purse,n.
man's ~, 261.15(9)
~-shaped, 507.17(12)
small ~, 261.15(4)
woman's ~, 261.15(2)
pursue,v., 173.12
~ secretly, 173.12(3,5,7)
tending to ~, 173.15
pursuer,n., 173.14
pursuit,n., 173.13
eager ~ of desired thing, 173.17
pus,n., 383.1
accumulation of ~, 383.2
condition of ~, 383.8
discharge ~, 383.9
discharge of ~, 383.10
discharging ~, 383.11
generate ~, 383.4
generating ~, 383.6
generation of ~, 383.5
like ~, 383.12
~ sore, 383.2
push,n., 197.4
descr. of a ~, 197.5
push,v., 197.1,2
~ against, 197.1(3,17,20,24,25,30-32,34,45,46,51)
~ apart, 197.1(49)
~ around roughly and playfully, 865.9
~ aside, 197.1(7,40,45)
~ away, 197.1(7,38,40,45)
~ back, 197.1(38,41,42)
~ down, 197.1(7,29,37,53)
~ forward, 197.1(6,9,13,26,33,35,57)
~ forward boastfully, 872.6
~ in, 197.1(6,15,16,29-31,44,53,56,58) ; 197.2(1,5)
~ into mud, 1000.9,19
~ itself, 197.2
one who ~es, 197.6
~ oneself, 197.2
~ out, 197.1(7,8,10-12,26-28,36,39,50,59) ; 197.2(2)
that which ~es, 197.7
~ up, 197.1(1)
~ with a pole, 997.8
~ with head lowered, 197.1(2,4,5)
~ with the shoe, 979.12
pushed,adj.
able to be ~ out, 197.8
being ~ back, 197.9
~ out, 197.10
pusher,n., 197.6,7
pushing,adj., 197.5
pushing,n., 197.3
descr. of ~, 197.5
pussy,adj., 383.3
become ~, 383.4
becoming ~, 383.6
~ condition, 383.8
make ~, 383.7
put,v., 323.1
~ a ship at anchor, 323.1(5)
able to be ~ down, 22.40,41
able to be ~ opposite, 323.7
~ aside, 323.16
~ away, 323.1(58)
~ away in memory, 323.1(50)
~ back, 323.15
~ back from the surface, 323.1(57)

~ between the lines, 323.1(38)
~ down, 323.1(13,15,43,51,53-55)
~ down opposition, 22.39
~ down revolt, 22.39
~ forward boastfully, 872.6
~ in, 323.1
~ in, figuratively, 323.22
~ in a helpless position, 323.1(46)
~ in an isolated place, 323.1(46)
~ in a safe place, 323.1(15,20,45,58)
~ in front of, 323.1(3,12)
~ in place of, 323.1(69) ; 324.1
~ into camp, 323.1(8)
~ living tissue into a site, 323.1(18,23,24,74)
~ off, i.e., delay, 768.1,8; see delay,v.
~ on, 323.1(1,2,14,25)
~ on (clothing), 974.2,3,39
~ on the ground, 999.6
~ on top of, 323.1(70,72,73)
~ opposite, 323.1(3)
~ out (a light), 801.18
~ out (fire, flame, etc.), 801.17
~ out of place, 323.17-20
place where something is ~, 323.4
~ side by side, 323.1(3,10,42)
that which is ~, 323.3
~ together, 321.1; see connect,v.
~ together in a collection, 319.1
~ together in a combination, 320.1
~ together into a group, 318.4
~ under water, 323.1(68)
~ up with, 246.1-3
putrefaction,n., 806.3; see decay,n.
putrefied,adj., 806.4; see decayed,adj.
putrefy,v., 806.1,2; see decay,v.
putrid,adj., 806.4,7,12-14; see also decayed,adj.
putting,adj., 323.5
putting,n., 323.2
pert. to ~, 323.6
puzzle,n., 602.1; 604.3,4; 605.3,6
puzzle,v., 605.1
puzzled,adj., 605.5
puzzlement,n., 605.3,6
puzzling,adj., 604.1; 605.4
~ person, 604.4,10
pyramid,n.
like a ~, 1006.7
point opposite base of ~, 335.1(22)
~-shaped, 507.17(61)

Q

quack,n., 826.15
play the ~, 826.16
quadrilateral,n., 945.7
quail,n.
group of ~, 403.5(6,15)
of ~, 405.9(9)
quaint,adj., 536.1
~ person, act, etc., 536.2
quality,n.
acceptable in ~, 831.6
assume a ~, 974.11
bad in ~, 883.1
best in ~, 1013.8
certificate of ~, 850.13
distinctive or distinguishing ~, 1091.7,11
drop a ~, 984.12

fill with a ~, 925.18
filled with a ~, 925.17
good in ~, 831.1; see excellent,adj.
lose ~, 883.11
physical representation of a
~, 953.9
poor in ~, 883.1,3,6
reduce the ~ of, 883.16,18
strengthen in ~, 1.29(9)
quandary,n., 25.9; 602.1(2) ;
640.10
quantity,n., 914.1; see
amount,n.
quarrel,n., 542.10; see also dispute,n.
causes ~s, one who, 542.22
engaged in a ~, 542.15
situation marked by ~s,
542.16
quarrel,v., 542.11; see also dispute,v.
inclined to ~, 542.17
~ like cats, 542.11(1)
person inclined to ~, 542.18
woman inclined to ~, 542.19
quarreler,n., 542.12
quarrelsome,adj., 542.17
~ person, 542.18
~ woman, 542.19
quarters,n., 753.1; see also
home, house,n.
animals' ~ in the ground,
298.20(1)
~ of the dead, 794.37
queen,n., 1073.14(5,6,8,18,25) ;
see also ruler,n.
act or play the ~, 1073.28
fit for a ~, 1073.23
government by a ~, 1073.4(5)
govern as ~, 1073.27
husband of a ~, 1073.21(5)
like a ~, 1073.23
make a ~ of, 1073.24,25
minor ~, 1073.14(27)
Moslem ~ in India, 1073.36(3)
mother of a ~, 1073.21(11)
~ of India, 1073.36(25)
pert. to a ~, 1073.22
~s, collectively, 1073.29
queer,adj., 536.1
~ person, act, etc., 536.2
question,n., 625.3
annoy by ~s, 874.1(8,10,12,14,
18,23)
ask a ~, 625.10
ask ~s, a meeting to,
322.1(24)
attack with ~s, 561.1(4,7,11)
book of ~s and answers in
religious teaching, 621.19(1)
call into ~, 639.13
eager to ask ~s, 625.11,12
~ for effect, 625.3(3)
inclined to ask ~s, 625.11,12
keep asking ~s, 625.1(11)
offensive ~s, asking, 1118.11
pert. to ~, 625.7
puzzling ~, 625.3(2)
rapid fire of ~s, 625.4(1)
series of ~s, 173.9(2) ; 625.4
set of ~s and answers, 625.8
subtle ~s in pretended ignorance, 611.5
~ to which answer is a pun,
625.3(1,4)
use of ~s to help thinking,
625.9
written ~s, 625.4(3)
question,v., 625.1
authorized to ~ witnesses,
625.15
~ by means of torture, 625.14
eager to ~, 625.11,12
person ~ed, 625.6

serving to ~, 625.7
~ to test, 625.1(5,15,17)
questioner,n., 625.5
questioning,n., 625.2
pert. to ~, 625.7
quick,adj., 94.8; 95.1; see
rapid,adj.
quicken,v., 94.6,7; see also
faster,adv.
~ the action of, 52.9(6,32) ;
94.5,7; 95.8
~ the reaction of, 54.12
quickly,adv., 95.5; see faster,
rapidly,adv.
quickness,n., 95.2; see rapidity,n.
quiet,adj.
calm, 1139.15; see calm,adj.
gentle, 1144.1; see gentle,adj.
inactive, 58.1; see inactive,
adj.
not moving, 59.1; see mo-
tionless,adj.
silent, 475.1; see silent,adj.
unvisited, 125.6
~ person, 475.3
~ place, 782.1(4,25)
serious and ~, 610.3
quiet,v.
become inactive, 58.6
become peaceful, 1140.10
become silent, 475.6
calm, 1139.1
make inactive, 58.3
make peaceful, 1140.1
silence, 475.5
quietness,n.
calmness, 1139.16
gentleness, 1144.2
inactivity, 58.2
lack of motion, 59.2
peacefulness, 1140.12
silence, 475.2
quiver,n., 111.2
muscular ~, 111.2(3)
quiver,v., 111.1; see shake,v.
quote,v., 674.20
~ as proof, 674.20
~ incorrectly, 674.21
quotation,n.
brief ~, 674.22
disconnected ~s, 674.23
end a ~, 674.24

R

R(the letter),n.
incorrect pronunciation of ~,
670.7(2,3)
vibration of ~, 670.4(12,19)
rabbit,n., 421.2; see also hare,n.
enclosure for ~s, 300.7(8) ;
403.22(21,44)
group of ~s, 403.5(17,38,48)
hole of a ~, 403.22(6,20)
home of ~s, 403.22(44)
one who keeps or breeds ~s,
403.24
pert. to ~s, 421.4
rabbit fever,n., 396.1(25,29)
rabies,n., 396.1(17)
raccoon,n.
of ~s, 403.11(11)
race (contest),n., 2.2
boat ~, 20.2(10)
rowing ~, 20.2(10)
skiing ~, 979.11
substitute falsely entered in a
~, 324.4(13)
race (racial stock),n., 430.1
breed with member of an-
other ~, 719.2(1)
degeneration of ~, 430.4
degeneration of ~, science
of, 429.22(8)

development of a ~, 731.4(7) ;
731.16(2) ; 731.17,18
group of the same ~, 318.1(68,
94) ; 722.4(12)
history of a ~, 430.5
human ~, 429.1
improvement of ~, science of,
429.22(12)
mixed ~, person of, 430.6;
719.5
of mixed ~, 728.15(3)
of the ~s of man, 430.2
pert. to a ~, 722.5
prejudice for or against ~,
634.1(22-24)
repetition of ~ history in individual growth, 731.13,14
science of ~, 429.22
science of environment and
~, 783.2(1,3)
segregation of ~s, 325.17,18
student of ~, 429.23
superiority of ~, belief in,
634.1(22,24)
threat to the white ~, 573.5
white ~, person of, 430.9,10
yellow ~s, pert. to, 430.15
racial,adj., 430.3
~ group, 318.1(68,94) ;
722.4(12)
~ segregation, 325.17,18
radiance,n., 1065.56
radiant,adj., 1065.50,55
make (a person) ~, 1065.59
radical (in politics),n.,
1076.12(1,10,12,24)
radio,n.
disturbance on the ~, 1046.5
transmission of ~ programs
through the stratosphere,
1046.17
radioactive,adj.
~ particles, 1069.25
~ rays, 1069.1,23
radioactivity,n., 1069; see also
X-ray,n.
biology of ~, 1069.21
chemistry of ~, 1069.22
free of ~, 900.6
measure or detect ~, device
to, 1069.24
radium,n.
unit of ~ emanation, 1012.27
raid,n., 560.2
raid,v., 560.1
railing,n.
staircase ~, 160.14
railroad,n.
end of a ~ line, 792.9
~ station, 782.1(6)
rain,n., 1037.2
amount of ~, 1037.10
arc of color after ~, 1037.26,
27
~ as atmospheric phenom-
enon, 1046.2
bringing ~, 1037.9
caused by ~, 1037.7
condition of ~, 1046.6
deficient in ~, 1037.30
drop of ~, 1037.13
drops of ~, 918.8
faucet for ~ to flow through,
1033.44
frozen ~, 1037.12; 1040.1
frozen ~, storm of, 1040.2
god of ~, 1037.18,19
lack of ~, 1037.31
magician who causes ~,
1037.20
pert. to ~, 1037.6
protect against ~, 1037.15
protected against ~, 1037.14
protective device against ~,
568.23; 1037.29; 1047.12

season of ~ in Asia, 1042.10
send down ~, 1037.8
stub of a ticket in case of ~, 1037.17
thunder with ~, 1044.7
wet with ~, 1037.9
without ~, 1037.30
without ~, ability to do, 1037.32
without ~, period, 1037.31
without ~, plant that lives, 1037.33
rain,v., 1037.1
~ in drops, 918.12
~ in frozen drops, 1040.4
rainbow,n., 1037.26,27
~ as atmospheric phenomenon, 1046.4
give off ~like light or color, 1065.45(26)
goddess of the ~, 1037.28
like the ~ in color, 488.8(15, 37)
raincoat,n., 976.3
raindrop,n.
frozen ~s, 1040.1,2
rainfall,n.
chart of ~, 1037.24
light ~, 1039.6
measure ~, instrument to, 1037.21,22
measurement of ~, 1037.23
science of ~, 1037.25
treatise on ~, 682.15(10)
raining,adj., 1037.3
rainspout,n., 1033.44
rainy,adj., 1037.4
raise,v., 163.1
car that ~s, 159.7
device for ~ing, 163.4
~ in honor, 163.1(5)
~ in rank, 163.1(5) ; 313.10,12
land that is ~d, 166.1
~ liquids, 1033.39,40
~ on supports, 1022.8
~ (the back) in rounded shape, 958.12
~ the head, 163.1(11)
~ to judge weight, 163.1(7)
~ water, 1033.39,40,42
~ with a loop, 1022 7
raisin,n.
seedless ~, 745.1(4)
rajah,n.
wife of a ~, 1073.41(6)
random,adj., 46.13
range (extent),n., 194.2
of wide ~, 194.4
rank,n., 313.1
emblem of ~, 951.9
first in ~, 313.9
having a ~ descriptive of one's office, 1077.14
high ~, 313.4
high ~, having too many persons of, 313.15
high ~, person of, 313.14
high in ~, 313.5
higher ~s, 313.6
higher in ~, 164.4; 313.7; 833.4
highest in ~, 164.6(2,4–6) ; 313.9
hold a ~, 313.3
hold a higher ~ than, 313.8
honorary ~, 857.17
importance of ~, 848.3
~ in school, 313.1(1,5)
less important ~, holder of, 848.37
low in ~, 313.16; 887.3
lower ~, person of, 313.18
lower in ~, 169.2(1,2) ; 313.17
military ~, 564.7–15
naval ~, 564.7,21

~ of command, 313.1(3)
raise in ~, 163.1(5) ; 313.10,12
reduce in ~, 313.19
rise in ~, 313.11,13
second in ~, 931.21
social ~, 314.1; see **social class**,n.
third in ~, 932.17
woman of ~, 708.14(6)
worship of high ~, 656.15(13)
rank,v., 313.2,3
rape,n., 710.14
rape,v., 710.13
rapid,adj., 94.8; 95.1
active and ~, 57.4(3,6,9–11,14, 17,20)
~ and smart in appearance, 94.9
~ in finger movements, 949.10
~ (in music), 95.11,12
~ in movement, 94.3,8,9; 949.7(1,4–8)
make the action of more ~, 52.9(6,32)
make the reaction of more ~, 54.12
move ~ly, 94.1,5
~ movement, 94.2
too ~ly, 765.7
violent and ~, 4.6
rapidity,n., 95.2
activity combined with ~, 57.5(1)
burst of ~, 95.4
cause of ~, 95.9,10
give ~ to, 94.5
nervous ~, 1133.10
~ of movement, 94.4; 949.8
skill and ~, 7.1(51)
rapidly,adv., 95.5; see also **faster**,adv.
able to move ~, 94.8
act ~, 95.6
come ~, 118.1(16,17)
do ~, 95.6
go ~, 95.6; 119.1(19,21–23,35– 40,45,63)
~ (in music), 95.11
make go, act, happen, react, etc., ~, 52.9(6,32) ; 54.12; 94.5,7; 95.8
move ~, 94.1,5–7; 95.6,8
rare,adj., 536.1; 917.27
rarity,n., 536.2; 917.27
rascal,n., 886.5
rascally,adj., 886.6
~ act, 886.7
rash,adj.
indifferent to danger, 575.1; see **brave**,adj.
without caution, 578.1; see **careless**,adj.
rash,n., 382.11(14,17,28,32,39,43, 44)
rat,n., 421.1,6; see **rodent**,n.
free of ~s, 309.11(20)
rate,n., 99.1
measure ~, instrument to, 99.3
measurement of ~, 99.4
measurement of ~, science of, 99.6
~ of change, 99.1(2)
~ of sound, 99.7
~ per thousand, 99.1(4)
record of ~, 99.5
~ setter, 99.2
ratio,n., 520.1
raven,n.
place for ~s, 405.11(8)
young ~, 405.4(14)
ravine,n., 170.10
ray (fish),n., 422.3
of ~s, 422.1(18)

ray (of light, etc.),n., 1065.28, 29
arranged in ~s, 508.21
bend a ~, 1065.37–44
biology of radioactive ~s, 1069.21
chemistry of radioactive ~s, 1069.22
come out in ~s, 1065.32
effect of ~s, instrument to measure, 1065.19
energy in the form of radioactive ~s, 1069.16; see also **radioactivity**,n.
expose to radioactive ~s, 1069.19
~ from the moon, 1065.28
~ from the sun, 1065.28
give off ~s, 1065.30
give off like or as ~s, 1065.32
giving off ~s, 1065.31
having ~s, 508.21
like a ~, 508.22
radioactive ~, 1069.23; see also **radioactivity**,n.
science of ~s, 1065.102(1)
shed ~s upon, 1065.34
throw back ~s, 1065.35
throwing back ~s, 1065.36,87
treat by radioactive ~s, 1069.20
X-~, 1069.1; see **X-ray**,n.
rayed,adj., 508.21
reach,n., 194.2
reach,v., 194.1
~ across, 1033.51
react,v., 54.2
cause to ~ to impulses, 1092.13
inability to ~ to surroundings, 59.6(1)
power to ~, 54.6
tending to ~, 54.4
~ to emotionally, 1092.72,73
reacting,adj., 54.3
~ emotionally, 1092.75
reaction,n., 54.1,9
bodily ~, 54.1(7–9)
characterized by ~, 54.4
chemical ~ with water, 54.1(2)
chemical in a ~, 54.10
descr. of ~, 54.5
dull the ~s of, 1097.13–16
emotional ~s, 1092.7,75
harmful ~, 54.1(1)
indirect ~, 54.1(3)
pert. to ~, 54.5
physical ~ to some special factor, food, etc., 389.9
prediction of ~s, skillful in, 1047.21
resulting from ~, 54.4
science of human ~, 54.7
speed up the ~ of, 54.12
stimulation, ~ to, 54.1(4)
sudden ~, 54.1(6)
violent ~, 54.1(6)
reactionary,adj., 544.8
reactionary,n., 544.10; 1076.12(21,23)
reactor,n., 54.8
psychological experiment, ~ in, 54.11
read,adj.
able to be ~, 692.6
having ~ a lot, 692.10
not having ~ much, 692.11
unable to be ~, 692.7
read,v., 692.1
able to ~, 692.8
~ and accept, change, etc., 692.1(2)
easy to ~, 692.6
hard to ~, 692.7

inability to ~, 692.12,13
~ incorrectly, 692.3
~ or say a number, 927.12
unable to ~, 692.12
reader,n., 692.2
reading,n.
~ aloud, 692.4
body of ~ material, 692.5
~ disabilities, 692.13
eye movements in ~, 692.14
fond of ~, 692.9
~ in lines, 311.1(39)
~ room, 787.7(20,24,38)
~ stand, 692.16
use of phonetics to teach ~, 692.15
ready,adj., 48.5
be ~ for, 48.8
eager and ~, 48.5(3); 265.19(8)
real,adj., 807.1,3,4
become ~, 807.7
having ~ existence, 807.4
make ~, 807.6
real estate,n., 1003.17(10)
~ agent, 1003.25
reality,n., 807.1-5
appearance of ~, 812.10
assume as a ~, 807.9
escape from ~, 76.2(1)
fidelity to ~ in art or literature, 807.11,12
give external ~ to an emotion or thought, 1092.86
in ~, 807.8
interested in ~, 807.10
sciences of ~, 807.13
theories or doctrines of ~, 807.17
theory that mind is the ultimate ~, 584.25
turn into ~, 807.6,7
realization,n.
getting, 240.2
knowledge, 611.2; see knowledge,n.
understanding, 593.2; see understanding,n.
realize,v.
gain, 240.1; see get,v.
know, 612.1; see know,v.
understand, 593.1; see understand,v.
rear,adj., 184.2; see back,adj.
rear,n., 184.1; see back,n.
rear,v.
~ a child, 721.16; see also upbringing,n.
~ up, 159.1(7,17,34)
rearing,n.
child ~, 721.17; see also upbringing,n.
reason,n.
a ~, 600.1
basic ~, 600.1(7)
find ~s for, 600.5
~ for being excused, 600.1(3)
~ for existence, 600.1(6)
give ~s against, 1120.9
give ~s for, 600.2
give ~s in complaint, 1120.1(11); 1120.9
give as a ~, 600.4
make conform to ~, 589.14
making one's conduct conform to ~, 56.5(4)
satisfactory ~, 600.1(4,5,8)
statement of ~s, 674.9(1)
without good ~, 600.6
reason,v., 585.1; 589.1
~ falsely, 589.1(7,10)
one who ~s, 589.5; see reasoner,n.
~ with (a person) against his actions, 1120.9

~ with (a person) in complaint, 1120.1(11); 1120.9
reasonable,adj., 590.1
made ~ by maturity, 732.7
make ~, 590.4
seemingly ~, 590.2,3
reasoner,n., 589.5
false ~, 589.17
pert. to ~s by similarities, 589.6
reasoning,adj., 585.4,6
reasoning,n., 585.2; 589.2
art of ~, 589.15
based on ~, 589.12
basic ~, 589.8
basis of ~, 589.11
chain of ~, 173.9(6); 589.7
derive by ~, 589.1
error in ~, 589.19-21
explanation of the supernatural by ~, 589.9
false ~, 589.16,19-21
find the ~ behind, 589.13
incapable of human ~, 597.12
instance of ~, 589.3
logical ~, 589.10
make conform to ~, 589.14
pert. to ~, 585.5; 589.4
result of ~, 589.3
science of ~, 589.15
sharp in ~, 334.1(14,15,21)
rebel,n., 549.5; 1119.19
rebel,v., 549.3
one who ~s, 549.5
rebellion,n., 549.2,4
advocacy of ~, 549.7
incitement to ~, 549.10
pert. to ~, 549.6
spirit of ~, 549.9
rebellious,adj., 549.1; see also disloyal,adj.
~ person, 549.5; 1119.19
~ to government, 1119.18
rebelliousness,n., 549.2; 1119.18
rebirth,n., 720.20
give ~ to, 720.22
reborn,adj., 720.23
be ~, 720.21
rebuke,n., 895.3
rebuke,v., 895.1
recall,v., 627.1; see remember,v.
recant,v., 251.1(2,3)
recede,v., 145.1
receipt,n., 218.6; 240.2,10
receive,v., 134.1; 240.1; 245.1
able to be ~d, 240.5; 245.5
~ by a will, 240.1(20)
~ from a predecessor, 240.1(20)
~ from an ancestor, 240.1(20)
room in which to ~ visitors, 787.7(14)
that which is ~d, 240.3; 245.3
receiver,n., 240.4
~ by inheritance or will, 240.4(1,3); 242.7
~ of benefit, etc., 240.4(1)
~ of charity, 232.7
~ of gift, 230.4; 240.4(1)
~ of stolen goods, 240.4(2)
~ of visitors, customers, etc., 240.4(4)
receiving,n., 240.2; 245.2
ceremony or manner of ~ visitors, 240.9
paper acknowledging ~, 240.10
recent,adj., 771.10
receptacle,n., 261.1; see container, holder,n.
~ for refuse or waste, 285.2
reception,n., 240.2; 245.2; see receiving,n.
receptive,adj., 134.2; 245.4,8

recess (hollow),n., 299.1(29);
see also hollow,n.
cavelike ~, 299.1(19)
deep ~, 299.1(24)
~ for a statue, 299.1(25)
recess (rest),n., 66.7; 209.12;
769.8(10-12); 1142.18,19
reciprocal,adj., 221.3; 234.4;
520.4; 931.18
reciprocate,v., 221.1; 234.2,5
reckless,adj.
indifferent to danger, 575.1;
see brave,adj.
without caution, 578.1; see careless,adj.
~ act, 52.5(25)
recline,v., 65.1; see lie (recline),v.
recliner,n., 65.2
reclining,adj., 65.3
recluse,n., 330.7
existence as a ~, 330.8
recognition,n., 627.2
recognize,v., 627.1
recollect,v., 627.1; see remember,v.
recollection,n., 627.2,6
recommend,v., 238.1(4,12,15)
recommendation,n., 238.2;
238.2(4)
recompense,n., 219.2,3; 221.2;
222.2
recompense,v., 219.1; 221.1;
222.1
descr. of ~, 222.3
reconcile,v.
make agree, 541.21
make friendly, 1096.31
able to be ~d, 541.24; 1096.36
one who cannot be ~d, 1096.40
one who has been ~d, 1096.38
~ oneself to, 245.1
reconciliation,n., 245.2; 541.21,
22; 1096.31
record,n., 684.5
book of phonograph ~s, 684.22
court of public ~s, 684.8
daily ~, 684.5(3)
historical ~s, 771.16(1,2)
historical ~s, writer of, 771.17
keeper of ~s, 684.6
~ of events, 774.7(1,2,4,7)
official ~s, 684.5(2)
phonograph ~, 684.21
place for public ~s, 684.7
~ player, 455.9(4,9,16)
public ~s, 684.5(2)
~s of a meeting, 684.5(6)
~s of memorable things, 684.5(4)
time ~, 774.7
~ to aid memory, 684.5(6)
writer of ~s, 684.6; 771.17
yearly ~s, 684.5(1)
recording,n.
make a ~ of, 684.9
recreation,n., 200.4,5; see amusement,n.
land for ~, 1003.2(23)
rectangle,n., 945.7(1,5)
figure in the shape of a ~, 945.9
in the form or shape of a ~, 945.10
rectum,n.
opening at the end of the ~, 298.8(2); 347.9(1)
science of the ~, 401.1(79)
red,adj., 495.2,14
become ~, 495.4
become ~, hot, and swollen, 518.1(14)

becoming ~, 495.5
blue ~, 495.17
~ cosmetics for lips or
cheeks, 488.22(4,7)
~-faced and coarse-looking,
864.7
~-faced and fat, 864.7;
903.1(2)
~-faced and untidy, 903.1(2)
~ like copper, 1016.8
make ~, 495.6
~ of complexion, 384.17,23
~ of hair, 369.12(6); 369.13
turn ~ from modesty or embarrassment, 873.9
turn ~ with anger, 878.4
yellow or yellowish ~, 495.19
red,n., 495.1,13
blue ~, 495.17
colored in ~, 495.10
mark a book in ~, 495.11,12
marked with ~, 495.9,10
ornament with ~, 495.6(6)
printed in ~, 495.10
tinged with ~, 495.16
yellow ~, 495.18
red tape,n., 1077.17
redden,v., 495.4,6
reddishness,n., 495.15
redness,n., 495.3
causing ~, 495.7,8
reduce,v., 910.1; see also decrease,v.
~ excellence, 883.16,18
~ force, 10.5
~ money value, 839.23,24
~ power, 10.5
~ quality, 883.16,18
~ rank of, 313.19
~ strength, 10.5
~ value, 883.16,18
reduction,n., 910.3; see decrease,n.
reed,n.
cover with ~, 986.6
of the ~ family, 986.5
sounds of a ~ instrument,
461.1(5); 461.3
refer,v.
~ to, 673.1
~ to continually, 673.1(3)
referee,n., 1083.19; see arbitrator,n.
reference,n., 673.1
a hint by indirect ~, 673.4
derogatory ~, 673.3
indirect ~, 673.2
insulting ~, 867.5
~ symbols, 680.1(3,11,20)
~ notes, 680.3
refine,v.
improve, 835.2; see im-
prove,v.
purify, 900.1,9; see purify,v.
~ figuratively, 859.4
refined,adj.
purified, 900.11
spiritual, 1090.4
affectedly ~, 859.6
figuratively ~, 859.1
highly ~, 900.12
~ in manner, 859.8
~ in speech, 859.8
make more ~ in character,
1090.7
~ (of literary or artistic
style), 859.2
too ~, 859.7; 900.12
refinement,n.
improvement, 835.3; see improvement,n.
purification, 900.9
purity, 900.10; see purity,n.
a ~ of living, 859.5
figurative ~, 859.3

lack of ~, 863.2; see unrefinement,n.
person contemptuous of ~,
863.4
person without ~, 863.3
reflection,n.
blinded by snow ~, 1039.18
~ from ice, 1039.19; 1040.27
~ from snow field, 1039.19
science of ~ by mirrors,
1065.102(2)
reflexive,adj., 266.9
~ behavior, 55.3(17)
refract,v.
able to ~, 1065.38
refraction,n., 1065.37–44
eye ~, instr. to measure,
480.19
measure ~, instrument to,
1065.39,40
science of ~, 1065.102(3)
unit of ~, 1065.43
refractor,n., 1065.41
refrain,v., 74.1
refreshment,n.
food, 740.2(15,18)
refrigerate,v., 1058.13; see cool,
freeze,v.
refrigeration,n.
science of ~, 1058.22
refrigerator,n., 1058.21
refuge,n., 568.26
give ~ to, 568.11
place of ~, 568.26
refugee,n., 141.3
refusal,n., 548.2
refuse,v., 285.1; see also
waste,n.
brewery ~, 285.1(5)
kitchen ~, 285.1(9,13,14,33,40)
liquid ~, 285.1(33,40)
street ~, 285.1(37)
refuse,v., 548.1
refute,v., 820.19
attempt to ~, 820.22
ideas that ~, 820.21
statements that ~, 820.21
regal,adj., 1073.22,23; see
royal,adj.
regent,n., 5.10; 1073.14(24,32–
34)
acting as ~, 1073.20
region,n., 782.1; see place,n.
~ of influence, 782.9
~ of knowledge, study, etc.,
782.9
regional,adj., 782.15
regret,n., 1126.2
cause for ~, 1126.10
caused by ~, 1126.7
causing ~, 1126.9
causing pleasure and ~,
1105.4(1)
express ~, 1126.17
expressing ~, 1126.6,18
expression of ~, 1126.15,16
indicative of ~, 1126.6,18
like ~, 1126.8
offer ~s, 898.8
pert. to ~, 1126.8
without ~, 1126.11,12
regret,v., 1126.4
regretful,adj., 1126.1,6
be ~, 1126.3
regrettable,adj., 1126.13
not ~, 1126.14
regretter,n., 1126.5
regular,adj., 529.1; 531.2,4;
535.1,2
regularity,n., 529.2; 531.2,4
rehearsal,n., 48.3; 613.18; 613.24
rehearse,v., 48.1; 613.17; 613.23
rehearsed,adj., 48.5(2,4)
reign,v., 1073.63,64
reincarnate,v., 1089.6

reincarnation,n., 1089.4(4,6,8);
1089.5
reject,v., 548.1
~ because of sin, 884.11
~ by laughter, 1111.30
rejection,n., 548.2
power of ~ of laws, 548.6
sign of ~, 548.5
rejoice,v., 1101.3,11; see happy,
adj., happiness,n.
relapse,n., 145.2
relapse,v., 145.1(1,15,21,22,24)
related,adj., 520.4
be ~, 520.2
~ by blood or family, 722.2
~ by marriage, 722.2(1)
consider as ~, 520.3
network of ~ parts, 520.6
~ people, 722.4
~ person, 520.5; 722.1
pert. to ~ people, 722.5
~ thing, 520.5
relations,n., 523.1
~ between nations, management of, 523.4
business ~, 523.1(3,6)
have ~, 523.2
have social ~, 523.2
personal ~, 523.1(5)
science of human ~, 523.3
social ~, 523.1(1–4,6)
relationship,n., 520.1
blood or family ~, 722.3
bring into ~, 520.3
bring into proper ~, 520.9
have a ~, 520.2
in close ~ with one's family,
520.7
presenting events to show ~,
520.8
relative,n.
blood or family ~, 722.1
favoritism to ~s, 722.9,10
pert. to ~s, 722.5
pert. to, or like, a specific ~,
722.7
~s, 722.4
relax,v., 10.5,8; 304.3,4; 309.21;
1142.1,10; see also loosen,
weaken,v.
relaxation,n., 10.6,7,9; 304.2;
1142.6,10
release,n., 309.2,12,14; see also
freedom,n.
pay for ~ of, 219.1(13)
payment for ~, 219.3(37)
release,v., 309.1,11; see free,v.
relevance,n., 521.2
relevant,adj., 521.1
reliable,adj., 526.6
relief,n., 309.12,14; 1142.6,18
~ for sadness, 1125.43
~ from sadness, 1125.41
~ in sculpture or carving,
966.8,9
~ of emotional conflicts, etc.,
in psychoanalysis, 1142.16
~ of emotions by art, 1142.17
period of ~, 66.7; 209.12;
769.8(10–12); 1142.19
source of ~, 728.4(15)
relievable,adj., 1125.46; 1142.8
relieve,v., 309.11; 1142.1; see
also free, weaken,v.
~ pain, 1137.45–50
~ sadness, 1125.40,44,45
relieved,adj., 309.15; 1142.5
able to be ~, 1142.8
able to be ~ (of sadness),
1125.46
become ~, 1142.10
become ~ of pain, 1137.48
becoming ~, 1142.11
not ~, 1142.7
not becoming ~, 1142.12

unable to be ~, 1142.9
unable to be ~ (of sadness), 1125.47
reliever,n., 1142.4
irritation ~, 1142.14
~ of another's sadness, 1125.42
pain ~, 1137.42,45
relieving,adj., 1142.2
~ agent, 1142.4
~ agent for irritation, 1142.14
~ agent or drug for pain, 1137.42,45
~ irritation, 1142.15
not ~, 1142.3
~ pain, 1137.41,46
~ sadness, 1125.44
religion,n., 642.1,3
a convert to ~, 642.10
Asian ~, 642.3(2)
~ based on concept that disease is mental, 400.6(8)
Catholic ~, 642.3(4); 645.10
Chinese ~, 642.3(2,5,19)
Christian ~, 642.3(3,4,6,16)
convert to a ~, 642.8,9
devotion to ~, 657.1(9,14,16)
extreme in ~, 922.5
false ~, 642.1(4)
formality in ~, 819.9(2,4); 819.10(4)
Greek or Roman ~, ancient, 642.3(7,15)
group dissenting from a ~, 642.18
group in a ~, 642.17
Hindu ~, 642.3(1,8)
Indian ~, 642.3(1,8,10,18)
indifference to ~, 1097.21
Japanese ~, 642.3(17)
Jewish ~, 642.3(11)
like a ~, 642.6
member of a ~, 642.5
member of a different ~, 642.5(3)
member of the same ~, 642.5(1)
members, collectively, of a ~, 642.7
moral law and ~, 843.5
~ of human and animal gods, 642.3(20)
~ of India, 642.3(1,8,10,18)
Mohammedan ~, 642.3(9,12-14)
Persian ~, 642.3(21)
pert. to ~, 642.2,4
practice ~ strictly, 643.4
prejudice toward a ~, 634.1(25)
reawakening of interest in ~, 580.7
rites in ~, book of, 819.14
Roman Catholic ~, 645.10
science of ~, 642.20
science of comparative ~, 642.21
specific ~, 642.3
system of ~, 642.19
talk about ~, 671.1(71,81)
treatise on ~, 682.15(6)
true ~, 642.1(2)
unrelated to ~, 643.17
without a ~, 643.12-14
religious,adj., 643.1
~ community, 644.1; see also convent, monastery,n.
earthly, rather than ~, 1004.41
~ ecstasy, 1092.40
education without ~ element, 643.19
~ excitement, 1100.7(4)
~ fanatic, 643.3(1)

fits of ~ mania, one who has, 643.6
~ group, 318.1(38,57,68,73,81, 94)
~ in motive, 643.7
insincerely ~, 643.10,11
~ law, 1079.5(12)
~ law, adherence to, 1079.25
not ~, 643.12,17
not ~, person who is, 643.13
~ observance of Sunday, 643.8,9
~ order, 644.1; see also convent, monastery,n.
~ order not wearing shoes, descr. of, 979.14
~ order not wearing shoes, member of, 979.15
~ order wearing shoes, descr. of, 979.4(1)
~ person, 643.3
~ poem, 689.2(12,19)
political rejection of ~ worship or element, 643.18, 19
~ promise, bound by, 1122.50
warmth of ~ emotion, 1092.57
~ way of life, person bound to, 644.7
women united in a ~ faith or organization, 644.8
~ worship, place of, 645.1; see church,n.
religiousness,n., 643.2
reluctance,n., 265.27
reluctant,adj., 265.26
rely,v.
~ on, 526.1
that which one has to ~ on, 526.8
remain,v., 757.1
~ about a place secretly, 971.15
~ for the night, 757.1(8)
let it ~ (note to the printer), 757.2,3
~ near, 757.1(3,4)
what ~s, 757.4,6; see re-mains,n., below
~ with for a short time, 757.1(12)
remaining,adj., 757.5
~ mark, 757.6
~ part, 326.1(36,37); 326.24
~ thing, trace, etc., 757.4
remains,n., 757.4,6
~ after destruction, 801.38
fossil ~, 757.4(11)
~ left by passing animal, person, or thing, 757.6
~ of the past, 757.4(5,13,18-20)
science of ~ of the past, 759.26
~ settling to the bottom, 757.11
student of ~ of the past, 759.27
worst ~, 757.4(4)
remark,n., 674.9; see state-ment,n.
remark,v.
notice, 480.1; 484.1
say, 674.8
remarkable,adj.
conspicuous, 952.1
unusual, 536.1
remediable,adj., 815.11
remedial,adj., 398.3; 815.9
remedy,n., 398.4; 815.8; see also cure, drug,n.
pretended ~, descr. of, 826.17
pretended ~, seller of, 826.19
pretended ~, treat with, 826.18

secret ~, 971.24
specific ~ or drug, 398.6,8
remedy,v., 398.1; 815.7; see correct, cure,v.
remember,v., 627.1; see also memory,n.
ability to ~, 627.4
able to ~, 627.4
act of ~ing, 627.2; see remembering,n., below
easy to ~, 627.19
inability to ~, 628.10,11
~ incorrectly, 627.7
cause to ~, 627.30
causes to ~, one who, 627.33
causing to ~, 627.31,32
~ past experiences, 627.1(6,9)
remembered,adj.
account of ~ experiences, 627.27
cause to be ~, 627.30
something ~, 627.6
remembering,n., 627.2; see also memory,n.
illusion of ~, 627.25,26
pert. to ~, 627.5
worth ~, 627.20-22
remembrance,n., 627.2,4,6,34; see also memory,n.
pert. to ~, 627.5
remind,v., 627.30
~ in order to ridicule, 627.30(12)
reminder,n., 627.31,33,34
~ of death, 627.34(7)
~ of friendship, 627.34(5)
remindful,adj., 627.32
reminisce,v., 627.1(9); 627.10; see also remember,v.
reminiscence,n., 627.2,6
pert. to ~, 627.5
~s, 627.27
reminiscent,adj., 627.32
remnant,n., 757.4; see re-mains,n.
remorse,n., 884.13; 1126.2
without ~, 884.15; see also remorseless,adj., below
remorseful,adj., 884.12,18; 1126.1,7
remorseless,adj.
without guilt, 884.15
without pity, 889.10; 1129.22
without regret, 1126.11
remote,adj., 521.6
foreign, 538.1
unvisited, 125.6
removal,n., 247.2
surgical ~, 402.1(1,6,8,9,15,19)
remove,v., 247.1; 249.1,2
get rid of, 286.1
~ coating from, 972.6; 972.6(1-4)
~ cover from, 972.6,8
~ covering from, 972.6,8
~ cream, 249.2(5,6)
~ disguise from, 970.57-59
~ from bishop's position, 144.4(18)
~ from center, 249.1(4)
~ from clergy, 144.4(3,10,17, 18)
~ from office, 144.4
~ from the top, 249.2(6)
~ mask from, 970.57-59
~ objectionable material from books, writing, etc., 899.17
~ peel from, 972.6; 972.6(1,3, 4); 972.8
~ pits, 249.2(4,7)
~ secretly, 971.44
~ shell from, 972.6
~ the top from, 249.2(8)

~ tissue and regrow elsewhere, 249.1(17)
~ viscera from, 249.2(3)
Renaissance,n., 720.20
a picture painted before the ~, 965.1(45)
rent,n.
occupancy by paying ~, 255.2(6)
rent,v., 281.1
one who ~s from another, 281.4
one who ~s to another, 281.3
renting,n., 281.2
system of ~ land, 1003.22
repair,n., 815.8
capable of ~, 832.18
incapable of ~, 832.19
ship ~, place of, 1033.20,21
repair,v., 815.7; 832.9
~ broken, torn, worn, etc., thing, 832.13
~ by sewing, 832.13
~ coarsely, 832.11
~ completely, 832.10
~ hastily, 832.11
~ pots, 832.16
~ shoes, 832.14
~ unskillfully, 832.12
repairable,adj., 815.11; 832.18
repairer,n.
shoe ~, 832.15
repairing,adj., 815.9; 832.17
reparation,n., 222.2
capable of ~, 222.4
incapable of ~, 222.5
making ~, 222.3
repeat,v., 49.1(23,28,30,32) ; 674.13
direction, in music, to ~, 674.28
~ for practice, 674.13(8,14)
~ from memory, 674.13(11)
~ ideas, 674.13(4,10,12,13,17, 18)
~ monotonously, 674.13(2)
morbid condition causing one to ~, 674.18
~ sounds, 674.13(14,12,13)
~ unnecessarily, 674.13(18)
~ without understanding, 674.13(7)
~ words, 674.13(4,9,12,13,16, 18)
repeated,adj.
~ series, 674.25
~ sound, phrase, verse, etc., 674.26
repeater,n., 674.16
repent,v., 884.17; 1126.3,4
repentance,n., 884.13,17; 1126.2
repentant,adj., 884.12,18; 1126.1,6
repetition,n., 674.14
~ for emphasis, 674.19
full of ~s, 674.17
impress on the mind with ~s, 674.13(3)
~ of a song, performance, etc., 674.27
symbol to indicate ~, 680.1(15)
unnecessary ~, 674.14; 674.14(1)
~ without understanding, 674.14(2)
repetitive,adj., 674.15
report,n., 613.4,20,24,25; see also information,n.
false ~, 613.20(3,6)
government ~, 613.20(8)
~ of happenings, 613.20(4)
~ to injure the reputation, 613.20(3,6)
report,v., 613.1,8,17,23; see also tell,v.

~ to a teacher, 613.23(6)
reporter,n., 613.19,26
pert. to a ~, 613.22
young ~, 691.4(1)
represent,v., 953.1
~ accurately, 953.1(1)
~ as better, 833.18
~ as less bad, 883.21
~ as less serious, 883.21
~ beforehand, 953.3
~ by art, 953.1(1-4,6)
~ by emblem, 953.2
~ by model, 953.1(9,10) ; 953.3
~ by picture, 965.2,3
~ by symbol, 953.1(9,10) ; 953.3
~ by type, 953.1(9,10) ; 953.3
~ falsely, 820.18
~ in the theater, 953.1(7,8)
~ in words, 953.1(6)
~ inaccurately, 953.4
~ incorrectly, 953.4
~ on the stage, 953.1(7,8)
~ unfairly, 953.4
~ vaguely, 953.5
~ vividly, 953.1(2)
representation,n., 953
art, ~ in, 953.8
art of ~, 965.6
costume, ~ in, 953.7
depth, ~ in, 965.6(5)
depth illusion, ~ with, 965.30
distance, ~ in, 965.6(5)
distance illusion, ~ with, 965.30
geographical conditions, ~ of, 1004.46
idea, physical ~ of an, 953.9
pert. to ~, 965.8
pictorial ~, 965.1,4
quality, physical ~ of a, 953.9
sea, ~ of the, 965.1(49)
small ~, 909.5(4)
syllables, ~ of by pictures, 953.6
symbolic ~, 953.10
words, ~ of by pictures, 953.6
written symbols, ~ by, 679.3
repress,v., 558.1
repression,n., 558.2
emotional interference from ~, 1097.47
psychological ~, 1097.42-46
reproach,n., 894.3; 895.3
reproach,v., 894.1; 895.1
reproachful,adj., 894.4
reproduce,v., 717.7
copy, 533.1
able to ~, 715.2-6
reproduction,n., 717.7
copy, 533.2
make incapable of sexual ~, 710.38
male power of ~, 717.11
~ of dissimilar offspring, 717.13
pert. to ~, 717.8
pert. to organs of ~, 717.9; see also genitals,n.
specific forms of ~, 717.12
symbolic seat of ~, 717.10
reproductive,adj., 715.2; 717.8,9
~ cell, 379.6
decrease of male's ~ power, 716.6
diseases of ~ organs, 379.9,10
~ glands of fishes, 379.1(9)
~ instinct of birds, 717.16
lack of male ~ power, 716.1
~ organs, 379.1; see genitals,n.
reproof,n., 895.3
reprove,v., 895.1
reptile,n., 425.1,7,8; see also snake,n.

anatomy of ~s, 338.10(2)
description of ~s, 425.6
habits, etc., of ~s, 425.4
like a ~, 425.3,5
mythical ~s, 662.25
pert. to ~s, 425.2
science of ~s, 403.26(18,29)
repulsive,adj., 197.5; 880.4; 881.2
reputable,adj., 856.13
reputation,n., 615.2
bad ~, 891.12,13; see also disgrace,n.
evil, ~ for, 883.34
injure the ~, 891.11,17,22
injury to the ~, 803.20
lessen the ~ of, 891.21
stain on the ~, 891.23
stain the ~ of, 891.22
repute,n., 616.1
request,n., 274.2; see also demand,n.
annoy by ~s, 874.1(8,10,12,14, 18,23)
annoying ~s, 874.9
~ for help, 274.2(2)
~ for protection, 274.2(2)
pert. to an earnest ~, 274.5
request,v., 274.1; see ask, demand,v.
require,v.
allow no choice, 252.18
demand, 274.1
force, 3.3
need, 273.1
order, 275.1
required,adj., 252.17
necessary, 273.6
requirement,n.
demand, 274.2
necessity, 273.3
order, 275.2
that which allows no choice, 252.19
use of force, 3.4
free of ~s, 309.11(23,26)
strictness in ~s, 890.9
rescue,n., 309.2; 571.2
rescue,v., 309.1(3,15) ; 571.1
rescuer,n., 309.4; 571.3
research,n., 486.2; 624.9
activity involving ~, 57.9(1)
research,v., 486.1
~ into, 624.8
researcher,n., 486.4; 624.10
resemblance,n., 529.2; see also similarity,n.
~ to real life, 529.8
~ to surroundings (of animals), 529.9
~ to truth, 529.8
resemble,v., 529.4
resembling,adj., 529.1; see similar,adj.
resent,v., 868.6; 878.6(24)
resentful,adj., 868.6; 878.10
resentment,n., 868.5; 878.11(1, 4-6,9)
eliminate ~, 878.20
fit of ~, 560.24(9) ; 878.15
reduce ~, 878.20
reside,v., 750.1; see live,v.
residence,n., 750.2; 753.1; see home, house, living,n.
resident,n., 750.4; see inhabitant,n.
residue,n., 757.4; see remains,n.
resist,v., 544.1; see also oppose,v.
unable to ~, 552.3(13,17)
unable to ~ a disease, 552.10
resistance,n., 544.2; see also opposition,n.

not offering ~, 10.1(21); see also **obedient, submissive,** adj.
~ to government, 4.18(1)
resistant,adj., 544.3; see **opposed,**adj.
resisted,adj.
able to be ~, 544.6
unable to be ~, 544.7
resister,n., 544.4,5
resistible,adj., 544.6
resolution,n.
decision, 592.2
purpose, 45.1
separation, 325.3
resolve,v.
decide, 592.1
have as a **purpose,** 45.2
separate, 325.1,2
~ not to sin, 45.3
respect,n., 856.2
advancement in ~, 856.20
arousing ~, 856.18
commanding ~, 856.18
degree of ~, 856.3
gesture in ~, 102.1(2–4,8,9); 102.2(2)
gesture of ~, 856.9
indication of ~, 856.9
lack of ~, 861.2
lower self-~ of, 868.10
popular ~, 856.4
public ~, 856.7
worthy of ~, 856.15
respect,v., 856.1
~ servilely, 856.5
respectable,adj., 856.13,15,19
~ people, 856.16
~ things, 856.17
respected,adj., 856.13,14
respectful,adj., 856.6
~ act, 856.8
respond,v.
answer, 626.2
react, 54.2
response,n.
answer, 626.1
reaction, 54.1
responsibility,n., 526.6; 527.1
free of ~, 309.11(1,23)
give an unbearable ~ to, 527.4
place the ~ on, 527.2
shift one's ~, 527.5
responsible,adj., 526.6
be ~ for, 527.3
hold ~ for, 893.7
responsive,adj., 1092.101
rest,n.
remainder, 757.4
repose, 66.7; 1142.18,19
midday ~, 66.7(6)
pain, ~ from, 66.7(8); see also **relief,**n.
period of ~, 66.7; 209.12; 769.8(10–12); 1142.18,19
pert. to ~ from work, 66.6
place for ~, 66.2
science of bodies at ~, 66.5
state of ~, 66.3
suffering, ~ from, 66.7(8)
rest,v., 66.1
~ lazily, 66.1(3)
lying down to ~, 65.3(12)
~ on fluid, 66.1(1)
~ on knees, 66.1(2)
~ on water, 66.1(1)
restaurant,n., 741.1,3
owner or manager of a ~, 741.2
server in a ~, 205.11–13
resting,adj., 65.3
resting,n.
state of ~, 66.3
state of ~ on the surface, 66.4

restless,adj., 1134.1
act or behave ~ly, 1134.5
~ action or behavior, 1134.6
move ~ly, 83.1,4; 1134.5
moving ~ly, 83.3; 1134.7
~ person, 1134.4
restlessness,n., 1134.2
fit of ~, 1134.3
restoration,n.
~ after destruction, 832.2
capable of ~, 832.3,4
pert. to ~, 832.4
restore,v., 832.1
serving to ~, 832.4
~ to brightness, 832.5
~ to citizenship, 832.8
~ to cleanness, 832.5
~ to good condition, 832.1
~ to healthy condition, 832.1
~ to popularity, 832.7
~ wasteland, 832.6
restrain,v., 558.1
~ by punishment, 896.30
restrained,adj., 558.5
emotionally ~, 1097.30
restraining,adj., 558.4
restraint,n., 558.2,3
self-~, 77.1
restrict,v., 558.1
restricted,adj., 558.5
~ place or area, 558.6
restriction,n., 558.2,3
contempt for ~s, 1091.4
lacking in freedom from conventional ~s, 310.15
restrictive,adj., 558.4
~ device on dog's mouth, 557.3(8)
result,n., 16.1
able to bring about ~s, 16.14
attach as a ~, 302.1(3,38)
concern with practical ~s, 16.28
contrary ~s, 16.2(1)
contribute to a ~, 16.10
doctrine of ~s, 16.29
element that helps produce a ~, 326.9(6)
figure the ~s of, 16.27
final ~, 16.1(3)
follow as a ~, 173.1(2)
following as a ~, 173.4(2,4–6,12,13)
follows as a ~, that which, 173.6(2,5–7)
get as a ~, 240.1(18,27)
have contrary ~s, 16.6
help to produce a ~, 16.10
indirect ~, 16.1(9)
indirect ~s, 16.20
involve as a ~, 16.5
involve as a necessary ~, 522.1(1)
involving ~s, 16.17
later ~, 16.1(1)
natural ~, 16.1(4)
~ of a complicated situation, 16.1(5)
~ of actions, 16.1(7,9,10); 16.2(2)
~ of efforts, 16.1(7); 16.2(2)
prediction of ~s, skillful in, 1047.21
produce a ~, 16.9
produce as a ~, 16.8
productive of ~, 16.11,15,16,18
providing favorable ~s, 837.3
psychological ~, 16.1(6)
reciprocal ~, 16.1(9)
~s, 16.2
unfavorable ~, 838.4
unfortunate ~s, 16.2(1)
unintended ~, 16.1(2)
without ~, 16.1
without important ~s, 849.3
result,v., 16.3

resulting,adj., 16.4
~ from luck, 16.4(2)
logically ~, 16.4(1)
naturally ~, 16.4(1,4)
retaliate,v., 221.1(1,4–8)
retaliation,n., 221.2
retaliatory,adj., 221.3
retire,v.
go away, 141.1(2,26,27)
go to sleep, 67.1
move back, 145.1
not work, 209.5
~ from office, 236.1(2,25)
retired,adj., 209.6
~ person, 209.9
retreat,n., 145.2
place of ~, 568.26(4)
retreat,v., 145.1
retribution,n., 221.2,3
return,n., 145.2; 234.2,3; 626.1
give in ~, 234.5
~ to bad habits, 145.2(2)
~ to crime, 145.2(2)
~ to primitive type, 145.2(1, 3)
~ to sin, 145.2(2)
return,v.
answer, 626.2
give back, 234.1,5
go or come back, 145.1
ask to ~, 145.6
cause to ~, 145.6
person inclined to ~, 145.5
~ to previous condition, 145.1(1,15,21,22,24)
returner,n., 145.4
returning,adj., 145.3
reveal,v.
make known, 613.1,17; see also **tell,**v.
show, 951.1(6,8,14,26,51–54, 56)
revealer,n., 613.5; 951.4
revealing,adj., 613.6
revel,v., 201.3; 1104.10
revelation,n., 613.2,3; 951.2,3
giving a ~, 951.5(1)
pert. to ~, 613.7
reveler,n., 201.4; 1104.11
revelry,n., 201.1; see **merry-making, merriment,**n.
revenge,n., 221.2,3; 896.2
uninspired by ~, 897.3
revenge,v., 221.1(1,4–8); 896.1(2, 20)
revengeful,adj., 221.3; 896.4
revenging,adj., 896.4
reversion,n., 145.2; see also **return,**v.
~ to primitive stage, 866.8,9
revert,v., 145.1; see also **return,**v.
revise,v., 539.1,2; see **change,**v.
revision,n., 539.3
revival,n., 751.18,21
~ of all humans, 751.24
~ of Jesus, 751.23
revive,v., 751.18,21
revived,adj., 751.22
revolt,n., 549.4; see **rebellion,**n.
revolt,v., 549.3; see **rebel,**v.
revolution,n., 549.2
change, 539.3
rebellion, 549.2; see **rebellion,**n.
rotation, 150.3; see **rotation,**n.
advocate of the American ~, 549.8
revolutionary,n., 549.5
~ who uses dynamite, 802.14
revolve,v., 150.1,2; see **rotate,**v.
reward,n., 219.11
receiver of a ~, 219.13
that which deserves ~, 219.17

worthiness of ~, 841.6
reward,v., 219.12
rhetoric,n., 664.1
rhetorical,adj., 664.2
~ effects, 669.3; see **figure of speech,**n.
rheumatism,n.
resembling ~, 377.12
rhinoceros,n.
group of ~es, 403.5(16)
like a ~, 417.6
of ~es, 403.11(16)
pert. to the ~, 417.6
rhyme,n., 689.1,2; see **poem, poetry,**n.
rhythm,n., 105.1
poetic ~, 689.25,26
unit of poetic ~, 689.24,36–43
rhythmical,adj., 105.2
~ beat, 105.4
beat ~ly, 105.3
poetically ~, 689.27
~ unit in poetry, 689.24,36–43
rib,n., 354.13
between the ~s, 354.14
ribald,adj., 1115.3(2)
obscene, 713.1; see **obscene,** adj.
~ book, 1115.8
ribaldry,n., 1115.3(2)
obscenity, 713.2; see **obscenity,**n.
given to ~, 1115.4
ribbon,n.
honor with a ~, 857.6
rice,n., 987.2
constituent of ~, 987.16
~ field, 1003.2(21)
rich,adj.
abundant, 915.4
fertile, 715.7
wealthy, 216.1; see **wealthy,** adj.
~ in sound, 467.3(6,7,9)
riches,n., 216.2,3; see **wealth,**n.
rickets,n., 354.16(5)
medication for ~, 398.6(2)
rickshaw,n., 192.9(2)
rid,adj.
free, 309.15; see **free,**adj.
get ~ of, 286.1; see **eliminate,**v.
rid,v.
eliminate, 286.1; see **eliminate,**v.
free, 309.11; see **free,**v.
riddance,n.
a freeing, 309.12
elimination, 286.2; see **elimination,**n.
riddle,n., 602.1(1,4,5,8)
offer ~s, 602.3
ride,n.
~ for pleasure, 1105.28
payment for a ~, 219.3(23)
ride,v.
~ a cycle, 192.18
~ a sled, 192.21
~ downhill, 192.25
~ in a boat, 115.4
~ in a carriage, 192.13
~ in a motor vehicle, 192.7
~ in a taxi, 192.7
~ in an automobile, 192.7
rider,n.
bus ~, 192.8
cycle ~, 192.19
horse ~, 408.19,20,23
~ in a carriage, 192.14
~ in an automobile, 192.8,28
~ in any vehicle, 192.28
sled ~, 192.22
ridicule,n., 869.3
beliefs, ~ of, 869.3(2)

engage in ~, 869.2; see **ridicule,**v., below
expose to ~, 869.7
exposure to ~, 869.8
god of ~, 869.14
good-natured ~, 869.11
language of ~, 869.3
language that attacks through ~, 561.11
laugh at in ~, 1111.20,21
object of ~, 869.13
personification of ~, 869.14
picture in ~ of an artist, 965.1(40)
traditions, ~ of, 869.3(2)
words of ~, 869.3
ridicule,v., 869.1,2
~ by exaggeration, 869.1(2)
~ by imitation, 869.1(1,9)
~ by imitation of style, 869.3(5)
~ by irony, 869.1(7,8)
~ by sarcasm, 869.1(7,8)
~ good-naturedly, 869.9,10
ridiculer,n., 869.4
ridiculing,adj., 869.5
good-naturedly ~, 869.12
ridiculous,adj.
laughable, 1113.1; see **laughable,**adj.
nonsensical, 608.5; see **absurd, nonsensical,**adj.
riding,n.
~ horses, 408.21,22,24
school of horse ~, 623.1(13)
rifle,n., 565.1; see **gun,**n.
right,adj.
correct, 815.1; see **correct,** adj.
proper, 818.1; see **proper,**adj.
suitable, 817.1; see **suitable,** adj.
right (direction), adj. or n.
able to tell ~ from left hand, 343.16
able to use ~ or left hand, 343.15
~-handed, 343.8,9
on the ~, 179.21
pert. to the ~, 179.21
pert. to the ~ hand, 343.4
preference for the ~ hand, 343.10
toward, or pert. to, the ~ of a ship, 179.21(3)
toward the ~, 179.22
turning toward the ~, 148.2(2,3)
right,n., 6.1; see also **privilege,**n.
~ and wrong of something, 818.17
having no concept of ~ and wrong, 818.15
judgment of ~ and wrong, 818.16
private ~s, pert. to, 6.4
that which serves as proof of a ~, 812.17
right away,adv., 766.16,17
righteous,adj., 843.17
righteousness,n., 843.18
rigid,adj., 442.1; see also **stiff,** adj.
~ behavior, 55.3(16)
set in ~ form, 1098.5
something to hold things ~, 442.5
rigidity,n., 442.2
lacking in ~, 443.1(4,6,8,11,13); 444.1
ring,n.
bell sound, 458.1
circle, 508.12
jewelry, 961.1
formation into ~s, 508.15

having ~s, 508.14
in the form of a ~, 508.13
ring,v.
sound like a bell, 458.2,3
surround, 300.1
ringing,n., 458.4
art of bell ~, 458.11
sounds of ~, 458.1,4
ringworm,n., 382.11(49)
riot,n., 309.14; 550.2; 605.13; 1101.1; 1104.2,9
riot,v., 1104.3,10; 1105.7
riotous,adj., 309.15; 550.1; 605.14; 1101.3; 1104.1,6; 1105.8
ripe,adj., 732.1; see **mature,**adj.
grow ~, 731.3(19,20,27); see **mature,**v.
ripen,v., 731.3(19,20); 732.3,5
ripeness,n., 732.2; see also **maturity,**n.
ripening,adj., 732.4,6
rise,n., 159.2
~ and fall, 161.2
figurative ~, 159.2(1)
~ of earth's crust, 159.2(2)
rise,v., 159.1
~ above, 159.1(9,16,27,31,32, 33)
~ again, 159.1(18)
~ and fall, 161.1
~ and fall in horse saddle, 161.1(3)
~ as vapor, 1048.45
~ beyond control, 159.1(33)
~ beyond the understanding, 159.1(33)
cause to ~ as vapor, 1048.44
~ erect (of hair), 159.1(5)
~ from death or destruction, 159.1(18)
~ in bubbles, 1028.4
~ in rank, 313.11,13
~ in rounded projection, 958.12
~ in spirits, 159.1(24)
~ in value, 839.11
~ in waves, 159.1(4,26, 37); 1032.2,3
make ~, 163.1(10); see also **raise,**v.
make ~ in value, 839.12
make (hair) ~, 163.1(2)
~ on hind legs, 159.1(7,17,34)
~s and falls, that which, 161.4
riser,n., 159.3
rising,adj., 159.4
~ above water surface, 159.4(2)
~ and falling, 161.3
~ (of land), 159.4(1)
~ on hind legs, 159.4(4)
rising,n., 159.2
magic trick of ~ in air, 663.3(1)
means of ~, 159.6
step for ~, 160.1,2
risk,n., 572.3; see also **danger,**n.
willingness to assume ~s of new venture, 729.20
risk,v., 34.12; 572.5
something ~ed, 572.11
risky,adj., 34.7; 572.1
risqué,adj., 713.1
rite,n., 819.10,12
ritual,adj., 819.1
ritual,n., 819.10–12
ritualism,n., 50.5; 819.9
rival,n., 20.2; 534.3
rival,v., 534.6
river,n., 1029.18
action of a ~, formed by, 1029.29
bank of a ~, 1029.43
bank of a ~, at the, 1029.28

border of a ～, 1029.43
border of a ～, at the, 1029.28
bottom of a ～, 1029.42;
  1029.100(3,10)
calm place in a ～, 1029.40(7)
caused by a ～, 1029.26
characteristic of ～s, 1029.30
close to ～s, 1029.31
deep place in a ～, 1029.40(7)
forgetfulness, ～ of, 1029.22
formed by action of a ～,
  1029.29
found in ～s, 1029.31
growing in ～s, 1029.27
land drained by a ～, 1029.46
land in reference to a ～,
  1029.47
like a ～, 1029.25
living at the side of a ～,
  1029.28
located at the side of a ～,
  1029.28
mouth of a ～, 367.7;
  1029.40(4,5)
movement of a ～, 1031.1
narrow part of a ～,
  1029.40(6)
Nile ～, pert. to, 1029.32
pass through the mouth of
  the ～, 121.1(7)
pert. to ～s, 1029.24
Po ～, on the north side of,
  1029.35
portion of a ～, 1029.40
produced by the motion of a
  ～, 1029.26
Rhine ～, pert. to, 1029.34
side of a ～, living or located
  at the, 1029.28
small ～, 1029.21
source of a ～, 1029.36
upper branches of a ～,
  1029.20
waterfall in a ～, 1029.40(2,
  8) ; 1029.48-51
roach,n., 428.3
infested with ～es, 403.18(7)
of ～es, 428.1(16)
science of ～es, 403.26(31)
road,n., 123.1
～ along canal, 123.1(52)
builder of ～s, 727.3(2)
by means of a ～, 123.9
confusion of winding ～s,
  605.17
cover ～ with stone, 1006.2
descr. of ～s that lead in four
  directions, 123.8
direct ～, 123.1(44)
edge of a ～, 123.6; 793.20(6)
～ for walking, 123.1(1,2,5,9,
  11-14,16,17,24,31,35-38,42,47,
  50,52-54,58)
having four ～s meeting, 123.7
indirect ～, 123.1(10,22)
pert. to a ～, 123.2
piece of ～, 917.6
～s cross, place where, 123.5
science of building ～s,
  727.10(2,3)
side ～, 123.1(10-14,45)
stone ～, 1006.3
～ to avoid tolls, 123.1(45)
toll ～, 123.1(55)
～ without exit, 123.1(7,20,21,
  29)
roast,v., 1061.1,2; see cook,v.
compartment for ～ing,
  1061.9(2)
rob,v., 250.1; see steal,v.
～ at sea, 250.1(15)
attack in order to ～,
  560.1(17,33)
robber,n., 250.3
grave ～, 797.23,25
sea ～, 250.6; see pirate,n.

robbery,n., 250.2; see stealing,n.
living by ～, 248.10(1)
murder and ～ in India,
  796.2(13)
robe,n., 974.38; see dress, garment,n.
rock (or stone),n., 1006.1
a ～ for architecture,
  1006.1(27)
a ～ in prehistoric structures
  or monuments, 1006.1(25,
  26)
a ～ where walls meet,
  1006.1(11)
be in layers (of ～), 315.6
broken ～s, 1006.1(35)
broken ～s for walls or
  foundations, 1006.1(34)
build with ～, 1006.8,60
builder with ～, 1006.58
building with ～, 1006.59
claylike ～, 1006.1(1)
classification of ～s, 1006.63(2,
  4)
consisting of ～, 1006.32
～ containing metal, 1012.8
cover with ～, 1006.6
cover (a road) with ～, 1006.2
covered with ～, 1006.35
crack or seam in ～ filled with
  metal, 1006.24
crack or seam in ～ filled
  with mineral, 1006.23
cutter of ～, 1006.57
cutting or engraving ～s, pert.
  to, 1006.49
diamond-bearing ～, 962.12
dig into (～), 1006.55
Egyptian tomb of ～,
  1106.1(32)
face of ～, 1006.1(8)
fireplace ～, 1064.59
flat piece of ～, 1006.1(42)
～ for building, 1006.1(24)
～ for corner or foundation,
  1006.1(11)
～ for floors, 1006.1(27,45)
～ for paving, 1006.1(9,10,14,
  15) ; 1006.3
～ for roads, 1006.1(9,10,14,
  15) ; 1006.3
～ for roofs, 1006.1(43,45)
～ for sculpture, 1006.1(4,27)
～ for wall coverings,
  1006.1(45)
～ for writing on, 1006.1(43)
～ from the sky, 1053.8
full of ～, 1006.1(47)
get (～) by cutting, blasting,
  etc., 1006.54
growing on ～s, 1006.45
grains of ～, 1006.25
hard ～, 1006.1(16,18)
high ～, 1006.1(8,12,31,37)
high face of ～, 166.1(4)
hit with small ～s, 1006.12
large ～, 1006.1(3,13)
～ landmark, 1006.19
layer of ～, 315.1(8,9) ; 1006.22
like ～, 1006.33,34
like specific ～, 1006.27-29,36,
  37
line of ～s in water,
  1029.100(6,11,12)
living on or among ～s,
  1006.45
living under ～s, 1006.46
melted or fluid ～, 1006.1(20)
～ memorial, 1006.19
mixture for joining ～s,
  1006.1(28)
monument of ～, 1006.1(27,
  29) ; 1006.19
～ over a grave, tomb, etc.,
  797.13

particles of ～, 1007.5
particles of ～, containing or
  like, 1007.6
particles worn away from ～,
  1006.25
pave with ～, 1006.4
pert. to ～s, 1006.31
place where ～ is cut, blasted,
  etc., 1006.53,56
polish on, or with, ～, 1006.11
prehistoric circle of ～,
  1006.20
prehistoric ～ structure,
  1006.1(25,26) ; 1006.20,21
product built of ～, 1006.1(24)
projecting ～, 1006.1(12,21,37)
provide with ～s or stone-
  work, 1006.10
pyramidal shaft of ～,
  1006.1(29)
road covered with ～, 1006.3
rub on, or with, ～, 1006.11
science of ～s, 1004.43(4) ;
  1006.63; 1053.36(6)
sharpen with ～, 1006.11
sidewalk covered with ～,
  1006.3
sliding mass of ～, 1006.18
sloping structure of ～,
  1006.1(32)
small ～, 1006.1(19)
small, round ～, 1006.1(30)
smooth on, or with, ～,
  1006.11
solid ～, 1006.1(2)
square piece of ～, 1006.1(33)
strengthen with ～, 1006.8,60
structure of rough ～s,
  1006.1(36)
study ～s, 1004.44
substance like ～, 1006.1(5,10,
  28)
swallowing ～s, 736.4
～ that sparks when struck,
  1006.1(16); 1064.7
～ that splits into layers,
  1006.1(15,17,40,43)
throw small ～s at, 1006.12
turn into ～, 1006.50-52
underground ～, 1006.1(2,21,
  41)
underwater ～, 1006.1(37)
volcanic ～, 1006.1(20)
volcanic ～, loose, 1006.1(39)
volcanic action, descr. of ～
  produced by, 1006.30
water, ～s in, 1029.100(6,11,
  12)
～ within another rock,
  1006.1(47)
～ worker, 1006.58
worship of ～s, 656.15(12)
written on ～, 1006.47,48
rock (movement),n., 146.2;
  147.2
rock,v., 146.1,3; 147.1,4
rocking,adj., 146.4; 147.3
rocky,adj., 1006.33,35
rocking, 146.4; 147.3
～ height, 166.1(4,24) ; 1006.16,
  17; see also cliff,n.
～ hill, 166.1(17)
rod,n.
stick, 437.7; see stick,n.
divining ～, 486.5
five and one-half to eight ～s,
  946.26(19)
～-shaped, 507.17(9,90,91)
rodent,n., 421.1,6
free of ～s, 309.11,20
like a ～ in form, 507.17(38)
pert. to ～s, 421.7
roe,n.
group of ～s, 403.5(6)
role,n., 969.10,14
double ～, 969.11

roll,n.
  bread, 1062.3
  rolling movement, 146.2;
    147.2; 149.3; 150.3; 151.2
  full of ∼s, 151.5
roll,v., 146.1,3; 147.1,4; 149.1,2;
    150.1,2; 151.1
  ∼ about, 151.1(11,12)
  ∼ about in sin, 151.1(12)
  ∼ back and forth, 151.1(7,10)
  ∼ in waves, 93.1; 151.1(1);
    1032.2
  ∼ nervously, 83.1(9); 151.1(8)
  tending to ∼, 151.4
  ∼ tightly, 151.3
rolling,adj., 146.4; 147.3; 150.4
  ∼ easily, 151.4
Roman,adj., 784.16(1,2)
  ∼ in style, 960.3
Rome,n.
  pert. to ancient ∼, 784.16(1,2)
  pert. to culture of ancient ∼,
    784.16(2)
romp,n., 80.2; 199.3
romp,v., 80.1; 199.1
roof,n., 973.1
  apartment on the ∼,
    753.1(38)
  arched ∼, 509.1; 973.1(5,11)
  bed ∼, 973.1(2)
  carriage ∼, 973.1(1)
  cover a ∼, 972.1(50)
  cover with a ∼, 972.1(6,19,25,
    38,54)
  entrance, ∼ over, 973.1(2,6)
  hotel entrance, ∼ over,
    973.1(6)
  inclined ∼, 973.1(7)
  inclined ∼, descr. of, 973.4
  kind of ∼, 973.3
  leaves, ∼ of, 973.1(10)
  like a ∼, 973.9
  lower edge of ∼, 973.8
  maker of ∼s, 973.11
  material for a ∼, 973.10
  ∼ on columns, 727.21(6)
  put a ∼ on or over, 973.2
  raised edge around ∼ open-
    ing, 973.7
  repairer of ∼s, 973.11
  room, ∼ of a, 973.1(3)
  rooms below the ∼, 787.7(4,
    26)
  rooms on a ∼, 753.1(38)
  rounded ∼, 973.1(4)
  space under the ∼, 973.5
  straw ∼, 973.1(10)
  structure on a ∼, 727.17(2,3,
    6,7)
  support for a ∼, 973.6
  theater entrance, ∼ over,
    973.1(6)
  throne, ∼ over, 973.1(2)
  tower ∼, 973.1(8)
  type of ∼, 973.3
roof,v., 972.1(6,19,25,54); 973.2
room,n.
  space, 787.1; see **space,**n.
  a ∼, 787.7
  amusement ∼, 787.7(12,25)
  card∼, 787.7(12)
  child's ∼, 721.15(3); 787.7(27)
  church ∼ for non-religious
    activities, 787.7(42)
  church garments, storage ∼
    for, 787.7(42)
  circular ∼, 787.7(30)
  comfortable ∼, 1141.5
  cooking ∼, 787.7(21,23);
    1061.6
  dancing ∼, 787.7(12)
  dressing ∼, 787.7(8)
  eating ∼, 787.7(20,29)
  furnish ∼ for, 787.14
  gambling ∼, 787.7(12)
  game ∼, 787.7(12)

  have ∼ for, 260.1(1); 787.13
  heated ∼, 787.7(10); 1060.12
  infant's ∼, 721.15(3);
    787.7(27)
  king's private ∼, 787.7(15)
  legislature ∼, 787.7(14)
  living ∼, 787.8
  meeting ∼, 787.7(22,25)
  monastery, heated ∼ in a,
    787.7(10)
  partitioned ∼, 787.7(7,16,17,
    35)
  plan of ∼s, 1025.19
  private ∼, 787.7(8,9,15,18,19,
    32,37,38)
  reading ∼, 787.7(20,24,38)
  reception ∼, 787.7(14)
  recessed part of a ∼, 787.9
  rented ∼s, 753.1(3,35,48)
  roof, ∼s below the, 787.7(4,
    26)
  roof, ∼s on a, 753.1(38)
  ∼s on a floor, 1025.2
  ∼s on roof, 753.1(38)
  separate a ∼ with partial
    wall, 1024.2
  series of ∼s, 173.9(21);
    753.1(3); 787.10
  ship's sleeping ∼, 787.7(9,36)
  sleeping ∼, 787.7(6,9,27,36)
  small ∼, 787.7(1,2,7,8,11,15–
    18)
  storage ∼, 787.7(15,28,33,42)
  study ∼, 787.7(11,17,38)
  suite of ∼s, 753.1(3); 787.10
  sun∼, 787.7(34,40); 1055.26
  supply with ∼, 233.1(1)
  train, ∼ on a, 787.7(16)
  underground ∼, 787.7(13,39,
    41)
  upper ∼, 787.7(4,26)
  voting ∼, 787.7(7)
  waiting ∼, 787.7(2)
  washing ∼, 787.7(5)
  working ∼, 787.7(37,38)
roominess,n., 787.12
roomy,adj., 260.6; 787.11
rooster,n., 405.2(1,2,4,7)
  castrated ∼, 405.2(1)
  young ∼, 405.4(3)
root,n., 992.2
  coming from a ∼, 992.8
  eating ∼s, 734.27(28)
  hair on a ∼, 992.4
  like a ∼, 992.9
  moss ∼, 992.7
  pert. to a ∼, 992.8
  protection around ∼s, 993.27
  small ∼, 992.1
  threadlike ∼, 992.3
rooted,adj.
  deep-∼, 323.23
rope,n., 302.32; see also **cord,**n.
  ∼ for a dog, 302.32(15)
  ∼ for catching animals,
    302.32(12,14)
  ∼ for tying animal to a place,
    302.32(23)
  knot in a ∼, 302.34
  loop in a ∼, 302.33
  loop of ∼ for support,
    1022.2(26)
  metal ∼, 302.32(8,9,27)
  ∼ of untanned hide, 386.16
  parts of a ∼, 302.33
  ∼ tension, pert. to, 193.23
  twisted ∼, 302.32(20,25)
rose,n.
  having ∼s, 994.27
  made of ∼s, 994.27
  of the ∼ family, 985.33(8)
rot,n., 806.3; see **decay,**n.
rot,v., 806.1,2; see **decay,**v.
rotate,v., 150.1,2
  ability to ∼, 150.5

  something that ∼s, 150.6,8
  tendency to ∼, 150.5
rotating,adj., 150.4
rotation,n., 150.3
  science of ∼, 150.7
rotten,adj., 806.4; see also **de-
    cayed,**adj.
  become ∼, 806.1
  become ∼ (of eggs), 806.1(1)
  ∼ (of eggs), 806.4
rough,adj.
  not complete, 329.1
  not smooth, 440.1
  violent, 4.1; 865.1
  ∼ act, 52.5(33)
  ∼ action, 865.4
  area of ∼ people, 1048.19
  bad-tempered and ∼, 865.1(3)
  become ∼, 440.3; 865.5
  ∼ behavior, 865.4
  big and ∼, 906.14
  cruel and ∼, 865.1(4,10–12);
    889.1(7)
  disorderly and ∼, 865.1(8,12)
  ∼ edge, 793.20(3)
  ∼ fight, 865.7
  ∼ growth, 731.21(17)
  harmful and ∼, 865.1(13)
  ∼ in action, 52.2(3); 865.1
  ∼ in behavior, 865.1
  ∼ in falling, 865.6
  ∼ in fighting, 865.6
  ∼ in manner, 865.1
  ∼ in movement, 865.6
  lawless and ∼, 865.1(4,10–12)
  make ∼, 440.3
  man ∼ with women, 707.2(2)
  merry and ∼, 1104.6
  noisy and ∼, 865.1(2,5,6)
  ∼ person, 796.3(4); 865.3
  ∼ shape, 507.1(13)
  ∼ spot on skin, 440.4
  ∼ struggle, 865.7
  strong and ∼, 865.1(13)
roughly,adv.
  treat ∼, 53.1(7–10,15)
  treated ∼, 53.5
roughness,n., 4.2; 440.2; 865.2,4
round,adj., 508.1
  almost ∼, 508.2
  ∼ like the moon, 1054.20
  ∼ objects or forms, 508.9
  ∼ of face, 1054.22
roundabout,adj., 183.1
  ∼ manner, 183.3
  ∼ means, 183.3
roundness,n., 508.1
  ∼ of projection, 958.12
  ∼ of the back, 958.12
roundworm,n., 427.11,13
route,n., 123.1; see also **road,**
    means,n.
  ∼ by sea, 1029.70
  direct ∼, 123.1(44)
  habitual ∼, 123.1(43)
  indirect ∼, 123.1(10,22)
  ∼ of a journey, 123.1(30)
  shortest ∼, 123.1(6,44)
routine,adj., 50.3
routine,n., 50.1; see also
    means, method,n.
  adherence to ∼, 50.5
  adherence to ∼ of office,
    819.9(3)
  devotion to ∼, 50.5
  excessive attention to official
    ∼, 1077.17
row,n.
  line, 311.11
  arrange in ∼s, 311.13
  arranged in ∼s, 311.12
  arrangement in ∼s, 311.1(38);
    311.13
  be or become arranged in ∼s,
    311.14

~ cut by a scythe, etc., 311.11(9)
facts in ~s, 311.16
figures in ~s, 311.16
go out in a ~, 311.18
military ~, 311.11(6)
move in a ~, 311.17
numbers in ~s, 311.16
~ of bushes, 996.30
~ of names, 311.11(4)
~ of numbers, 311.11(1,4,10)
~ of print, 311.11(1)
~ of shrubs, 996.30
~ of things, 311.15; 914.1(14)
~ of trees, 996.30
~ of words, 311.11(4)
~ on a chessboard, 311.11(2,6)
~ swept by wind, 311.11(12)
~s, 311.15
row (quarrel),n., 542.10
row,v.
  paddle, 117.1,2
  art of ~ing, 117.7
  skill in ~ing, 117.6
row (quarrel),v., 542.11
rowdy,adj., 865.1(8,12)
rowdy,n., 865.4; see also ruffian,n.
rower,n., 117.4
  ~s, 117.5
rowing,adj.
  ~ race, 20.2(10)
royal,adj., 1073.22,23
  of ~ birth, 720.9(10)
  possessing ~ privilege, 6.6
  ~ power, 5.4(9)
royalty,n., 1073.15–18,23
  emblems of ~, 951.9
  signs of ~, 951.9
rub,v., 438.1
  ~ clean, 899.1(1,2,5,7–9,12–16,19)
  ~ into powder, 438.1(31)
  ~ on or with stone, 1006.11
  one who ~s, 438.5
  ~ out, 286.1
  ~ the body, 438.1(12)
  ~ the skin, 438.1(1–3,8,9,12,28)
  ~ to calm or soothe, 1139.13
  ~ with oil, 438.1(2)
  ~ with wax, 1068.3
rubbed,adj.
  causing a ~ place, 438.6
  ~ place, 438.3
rubber,n., 989.1
  one who rubs, 438.5
  band of ~, 989.8
  band of ~ for holding up, 989.9
  fabric of ~, 989.7
  gas for synthetic ~, 1048.1(2)
  hard ~, 989.4
  ~like substance, 989.6
  pure ~, 989.1
  source of ~, 989.2
  spongy ~ used in mattresses, 989.5
  synthetic ~, 989.3
  treat ~, 989.11
rubbing,n., 438.2
  make sore by ~, 438.7
  orgasm from ~, 710.33(15)
  sound of ~, 469.7(14,15,24,31,32,34)
  substance or thing used for ~, 438.4
rubbish,n., 284.20; 285.1; see also waste,n.
ruffian,adj., 865.1(4,10–12)
ruffian,n., 865.4
  act the boastful ~, 872.5
  boastful ~, 872.19

rug,n., 1025.10
ruin,n., 801.2,13,33; see also destruction,n.
  break down into partial ~, 802.26
  complete ~, 801.16
  in partial ~, 802.27
ruin,v., 801.1,12,33
  ~ completely, 801.15
ruined,adj., 801.34; see also destroyed,adj.
  able to be ~, 801.35
  be or become ~, 801.33
  unable to be ~, 801.37
ruiner,n., 801.4; see destroyer,n.
ruinous,adj., 801.3; see destructive,adj.
ruins,n., 801.38
  ~ from fire, 1064.53
rule (govern),v., 1073.63,64; see govern,v.
  place where one ~s, 782.6
rule (government),n., 1073.1; see government,n.
  symbol of ~, 954.1(9)
rule (principle),n., 56.1; see also principle,n.
  adherence to ~, 56.4,5
  break a ~, 802.29
  careful about ~s, 56.4; 815.14; 843.17
  conforming to ~, 815.4
  contempt for ~s, 1091.4
  lay down ~, 56.2
  moral ~s, 843.1,17
  ~s, 56.1
  ~s of honor, 56.1(23)
  ~s of order, 56.1(23)
  ~s of rank, 56.1(23)
  set of ~s, 56.1(5,16,23)
ruler (governor),n., 1073.14,36,44,53
  Afghanistan ~, 1073.36(2)
  Arabian ~, 1073.36(9)
  authority or power of a ~, 1073.17,38
  bad ~, 1073.67
  body of ~s of a city, 1073.78
  body or group of ~s, 1073.15,45,52
  country or territory under a ~, 1073.18,39
  cruel or harsh ~, 1073.60
  feudal ~, 1074.17–20,25
  governed by a ~, one who is, 1075.2
  hereditary ~, 1073.14(60)
  military ~ in Japan, 1073.36(29)
  minor or subordinate ~, 1073.14(31)
  Mohammedan ~, 1073.36(1,5,30)
  Mohammedan ~ in India, 1073.36(16)
  Mohammedan ~ (female) in India, 1073.36(17)
  Moslem ~, 1073.36(5)
  Moslem female ~ in India, 1073.36(3)
  nazi ~, 1073.14(9)
  ~ of a clan or tribe, 1073.14(2)
  ~ of a monarchy, 1073.14; see king, queen,n.
  ~ of a territory, 1073.14(23)
  ~ of Algiers, 1073.36(8)
  ~ of American Indian tribes, 1073.14(2); 1073.36(26)
  ~ of an empire, 1073.14(7,8)
  ~ of Arab village, tribe, or family, 1073.36(28)
  ~ of Austria, 1073.36(13)

  ~ of Baroda (India), 1073.36(11)
  ~ of Borneo, 1073.36(23)
  ~ of Byzantine province, 1073.36(10)
  ~ of China, 1073.36(14)
  ~ of East Indies, 1073.36(23)
  ~ of Egypt (ancient), 1073.14(21)
  ~ of Egypt (Turkish), 1073.36(15)
  ~ of Germany, 1073.36(13)
  ~ of Holy Roman Empire, 1073.36(13)
  ~ of Hyderabad, India, 1073.36(21)
  ~ of India, 1073.36(19,20,23–25)
  ~ of industry, 1073.14(6)
  ~ of Iran, 1073.36(27)
  ~ of Japan, 1073.36(18,32)
  ~ of Java, 1073.36(23)
  ~ of Mohammedan village, tribe, or family, 1073.36(28)
  ~ of one of seven associated countries, 1073.58
  ~ of one of three governments of a country, 1073.56
  ~ of Russia, 1073.36(6,7)
  ~ of small country, 1073.14(23)
  ~ of Tripoli, 1073.36(8)
  ~ of Tunis, 1073.36(4,8)
  ~ of Turkey, 1073.36(22,31)
  ~ of Turkish province, 1073.36(4)
  ~ of Turkish tribes, 1073.36(14)
  office, position, or rank of ~, 1073.16,37
  reign of a ~, 1073.19,40
  relative of a ~, 1073.21,41
  Roman ~, 1073.36(12)
  ~s collectively, 1073.15,45,52
  Slavic ~, 1073.36(6)
  substitute ~, 1073.14(24,28,32–34)
  substitute ~, acting as, 1073.20
  supreme ~, 1073.14(29)
  symbol of ~, 954.1(9)
  temporary ~, period of, 1073.95
  time or period of a ~, 1073.19,40
  without a ~, period, 1073.95
ruling,n.
  court ~, 1081.13
rum (liquor),n., 749.1,6; see liquor (alcoholic),n.
rumor,n., 616.1
  a ~, 616.2
  filled with ~, 616.9
  idle ~, 616.3
  like a ~, 616.9
  malicious ~, 616.3,4
  pert. to a ~, 616.9
  spread ~, 616.5,6
  spread by ~, 616.6
  spreader of ~s, 616.10
  spread false ~s, 891.17(1,6,10,12,13,16,17)
  spreading ~s, 616.8
rumor,v., 616.6
rumored,adj., 616.9
run,n., 94.2; 96.2
run,v., 94.1; 95.6; 96.1
  ~ away, 141.1; see also depart,v.
  turn the back to ~ away, 184.12
running,adj., 94.3; 96.3
  ~ forward, 96.3(2)
  ~ (of handwriting), 96.3(1)
running,n., 94.2; 96.2

adapted to ~, 96.4
~ contest, 96.6
participate in a ~ contest, 96.5
rupture,n.
break, 802.3
hernia, 391.1; see hernia,n.
rupture,v.
break, 802.1,2; see break,v.
herniate, 391.4
rural,adj., 786.1; see countrified,adj.
rush,n., 91.2; 94.2
rush,v., 91.1; 94.1; 95.6,8; 96.1
~ about in excitement, 1100.5(3–5,8)
rushing,adj., 91.3; 94.3
Russia,n., 784.9(17)
administrative committee of Soviet ~, 1076.25
Empress of ~, 1073.36(7)
fondness for ~, 700.30(24)
government of ~, 1073.3(10, 11,30); 1073.5(3)
political groups of ~, member of, 1076.12(1,2,13,15,16, 26)
ruler of ~, 1073.36(6,7)
Russian,adj., 784.16
Russian,n., 784.15(40)
West ~, 784.15(64)
rust,n.
colored like ~, 1017.6
cover with ~, 1049.6
covered with ~, 1017.4; 1049.7
rust,v., 1049.6
rustic,adj., 786.1; see countrified,adj.
rustic,n., 786.6
rusty,adj., 1017.4,6; 1049.7
ruthless,adj., 889.1,10; 1129.22; see also cruel, pitiless,adj.

S

S(the letter),n.
curved like ~, 155.4(15,16)
incorrect pronunciation of ~, 670.7(4)
pronunciation of ~, 670.4(13, 14)
~ sound, 670.14(10)
sounds of ~, 472.1
sabotage,n., 801.2
policy of ~, 801.6,7
sabotage,v., 801.1
saboteur,n., 801.4
secret ~s, 801.5
sac,n., 350.1
external ~ for carrying young, 350.1(5,6)
~-shaped, 507.17(12)
small ~, 350.1(2,4,8)
sack,n., 261.15
sacred,adj., 650.1
container for a ~ thing, 261.1(40,43)
declare ~, 650.2
devotion to ~ things, 657.1(6)
falsely ~ writings, 648.4
knowledge of ~ things, 650.6
made ~ by a vow, 1122.12
make look ~, 650.3
not ~, 650.11; 1004.41
~ piece of writing, 648.1; 682.16(31)
~ place, 650.8
room for ~ objects, 974.30
selling of ~ objects, 212.9
set apart as ~, 325.12(11,15); 325.13; 650.2
treatise on ~ subjects, 682.15(6)
~ writings, 648.1; 682.16(31)

~ writings, history of, 650.5
writings on ~ subjects, 650.7
sacredness,n., 650.1
pretense of ~, 650.4
remove the ~ of, 650.10
violate the ~ of, 650.9
sacrifice,n., 236.2,5
~ of many victims, 236.2(3)
~ of one's life, 795.1(2) ; 795.7
one who or that which demands ~ of life, 236.8(2)
place of ~, 1130.21
self-~, 77.1; 236.2(4)
~ to the gods by fire, 1064.42(2)
wood for ~ to gods, 1064.61(8)
sacrifice,v., 236.1(17)
~ to the gods, 236.1(17)
worth ~ing, 236.9
sacrificed,adj.
that to which one is ~, 236.8(1)
that which is ~, 236.5
sacrificer,n., 236.3(1,2)
sad,adj., 1125.1,6; see also depressed, gloomy,adj.
causing tears or weeping, 1128.7
poor, inferior, etc., 1125.16
be ~, 1125.10,13
be ~ in sympathy with (a mourner), 1129.8–12
~ because alone, 330.1(9,14, 16,17,18,28,29)
become ~, 1125.9
both ~ and pleasurable, 1105.4(1)
~ circumstances, 1125.15
feel ~, 1125.10,13
~ happenings, 1125.15
influenced by ~ things, 9.5(5)
look ~, 1125.24
look ~ to elicit sympathy, 1129.20
make ~, 1125.33
miserably ~ person, 1125.7,8
~ music, 1125.20(2,3,5,6)
~ (of music), 1119.6
~ poem, 1125.20(3,6)
~ song, 1125.20(1–3,5,6)
~ story, etc., 1128.20
thoughtful and ~, 1125.31
sadden,v., 1125.33
saddening,adj., 1125.14,16,34
sadness,n., 1125.2; see also depression, gloom,n.
air of ~, 1125.25
associated with ~, 1125.32
assume air of ~, 1125.24
cause or source of ~, 1125.35
causing ~, 1125.14,16,34
change from laughter to ~, 1111.32
express ~, 1125.17,19,21–23
expression of ~, 1125.18,20,25
expressive of ~, 1125.6
~ on departure, 1125.5,49; see also regret,n.
~ over the past, loss, etc., 1125.49; see also regret,n.
~ over the world's state, 1125.4
pretend ~, 1125.26
pretended ~, 1125.3
relief for ~, 1125.43
relief from ~, 1125.41
relieve (~), 1125.45
relieve of ~, 1125.40
relieved of ~, able to be, 1125.46
relieved of ~, unable to be, 1125.47
reliever of another's ~, 1125.42
relieving of ~, 1125.44

say in ~, 1125.27
sounds of ~, 468.1–3
suggestive of ~, 1125.32
think constantly about one's ~, 1125.28–30
weigh heavily upon one (of ~), 1125.38
weighed down by ~, 1125.39
safe,adj., 568.7
falsely seeming ~, 572.1(12, 16,21); 823.10
~ in the air, 1045.14(5)
keep ~, 568.1; see protect,v.
make ~, 568.1; see protect,v.
~ place, 568.26
put in a ~ place, 323.1(15,20, 45,58)
safebreaker,n., 250.3(2,11,12)
safeguard,n., 568.4; see protection,n.
safeguard,v., 568.1; see protect,v.
safekeeping,n., 568.2; see also protection,n.
give for ~, 230.7
place of ~, 262.3; 568.26(9, 23) ; 782.1(5); see also storehouse, storeroom,n.
put away for ~, 323.1(15,20, 45,58)
safety,n., 568.2; see also protection,n.
means of ~, 568.4
place of ~, 568.26
source of ~, 568.4(10)
said, adj. or v., 674.3–5; see also say,v.
beyond what is ~, 475.9
~ clearly, 674.5(1–3)
not ~, 475.8
~ previously, 674.6
something ~, 674.9; see statement,n.
~ through mouth and nose, 674.5(4)
unable to be ~, 665.7(4–8)
~ without preparation, 48.10
sail,v., 116.1
sailing,n., 116.2
art or science of ~, 116.12
deep or wide enough for ~, 116.13
pert. to ~, 116.11
sailor,n., 116.3
life, etc., of a ~, 116.9
like a ~, 116.8
occupation of a ~, 1029.73
~ on a sailing ship, 1043.26
~ on the seas, 1029.74
pert. to ~s, 116.7
work of a ~, 116.9,10
saint,n.
befitting a ~, 651.1
calendar arrangement of ~s, 311.1(19)
calendar of ~s, 651.9
catalogue of a ~, 651.7
character of a ~, 651.2
declare a ~, 651.5
former possession of a ~, 656.8(4)
light around the head of a ~, 1065.25
like a ~, 651.1
not befitting a ~, 651.11
remove status of a ~, 651.12
~s, collectively, 651.3
state of a ~, 651.2
treatise on lives of ~s, 682.15(3)
worship of ~s, 656.2(5) ; 656.15(8)
writings about ~s, 651.8
sainthood,n.
degrees of ~, 651.6

saintliness,n.
  pretense of ~, 651.4
saintly,adj., 651.1
salable,adj., 212.6
salamander,n.
  of ~s, 403.11(1)
  science of ~s, 403.26(1)
salary,n., 219.3(20,21,30,35,61)
sale,n., 212.2; see also **selling**,n.
  articles for ~, 212.4
salesman,n., 212.3; see **seller**,n.
saliva,n., 289.3; see **spit**,n.
salmon,n.
  small ~, 422.3(5)
  two-year ~, 422.3(6)
  young ~, 422.4(4–6)
saloon,n., 749.37
  frequenter of ~s, 749.54
salt,n., 1011.1
  containing ~, 1011.5
  like ~, 1011.6
  maker or seller of ~, 1011.12
  measure ~, device to, 1011.13
  mineral ~ in soil, 1011.14
  mix or combine with ~, 1011.8
  pickle with ~, 1011.3
  pickled with ~, 1011.9
  place where ~ is made, 1011.10,11
  preserve with ~, 1011.4
  preserved with ~, 1011.9
  producing ~, 1011.7
  season with ~, 1011.4
  ~ solution, 1011.2
  table ~, 1011.1
  tasting of ~, 1011.5
  ~ that neutralizes acids, 1011.14
saltworks,n., 1011.10
salty,adj., 1011.5
salvation,n., 571.2,4
  announced by ~, 653.7
same,adj., 529.1; 531.1–3; see also **similar**,adj.
  be the ~, 529.4
  become the ~, 529.4
  make the ~, 529.5; see also **copy**, **imitate**,v.
  one who is the ~, 529.3
  that which is the ~, 529.3
  two exactly the ~, 529.11
sameness,n., 529.2; see also **resemblance**, **similarity**,n.
sanctuary,n., 568.26; 650.8
sand,n., 1007
  ~ bar in water, 1029.100(1,6, 11,12–14)
  cement, water, and ~, 1006.1(28)
  ~ deposited as sediment, 757.11,12
  digger in ~, 1007.13
  fill with ~, 1007.12
  growing in ~, 1007.2
  ~ hill, 1007.8
  like ~, 1007.1,14
  like particles of ~, 1007.6
  ~, lime, and water mixture, 1007.15
  living in ~, 1007.3
  paper containing ~, 1007.10
  particles of ~, 1007.5
  pebbles and ~, 1006.1(19)
  polish with ~, 1007.11,12
  smooth with ~, 1007.11,12
  sound like stepped-on ~, 1007.4
  sprinkle with ~, 1007.12
  tract of ~, 1007.9
  windstorm of ~, 1007.7
  worker in ~, 1007.13
sandal,n., 979.2; see also **shoe**,n.
  Mexican ~s, 979.24

sandy,adj., 1007.1
sane,adj., 1136.20
sanitary,adj., 899.11
  make ~, 899.13
sanity,n., 1136.21
  between ~ and insanity, 1136.10
Santa Claus,n., 209.15
sarcasm,n., 869.3(6); 869.5(1,3, 4)
  light ~, 665.9(30); 869.3(3)
  ridicule by ~, 869.1(7,8)
sarcastic,adj., 869.5(1,3,4)
  ~ remark, 674.9(4,12); 1115.7(9)
  ~ word, 666.3(7)
  ~ writing, 1115.7(9)
sardine,n., 422.3
  like the ~, 422.2
  of ~s, 422.1(10)
Satan,n., 660.1; see **devil**,n.
satiate,v., 1107.15,16
satiated,adj., 1107.19
satiating,adj., 1107.17
satiation,n., 1107.20
satiety,n., 1107.20
satire,n., 869.3
  art or practice of ~, 869.6
satiric,adj., 869.5
  ~ piece of writing, 532.2(3); 1115.7(9)
satirize,v., 532.1(2,3,11); 869.1,2
satirizer,n., 869.4
satisfaction,n., 1107.2,4,7
  capable of ~, 1107.10
  drink to point of excessive ~, 1107.24
  eat to point of excessive ~, 1107.23,24
  excessive ~, 1107.20
  incapable of ~, 1119.25
  look upon with malicious ~, 1107.25,26
  prevent the ~ of a desire, need, or impulse, 17.5(6–8, 15,21,22,41); 1119.20
  think about with malicious ~, 1107.25,26
satisfactoriness,n., 1107.6
satisfactory,adj., 1107.5
satisfied,adj., 1107.3
  able to be ~, 1107.10
  become ~ (of thirst), 1107.12
  become ~ to excess, 1107.18
  not ~ to excess, 1107.22
  self–~, 1107.3(1–3)
  self–~ group, 1107.9
  ~ to excess, 1107.19
  unable to be ~, 1119.25
  unable to be ~ (of thirst), 1107.14
satisfy,v., 1107.1
  ~ (hunger, thirst, or appetite), 1107.11,13
  ~ one's own desires, etc., 1107.27
  that which ~, 1107.7
  ~ to excess, 1107.15,16
satisfying,adj., 1107.5
  ~ to excess, 1107.16
satisfyingness,n., 1107.6
sausage,n., 743.2
savage,adj., 4.19,25,26; 866.1
  ~ act, behavior, or character, 4.29; 866.4
  attack ~ly, 4.31
  ~ like a beast, 4.26
  merciless and ~, 4.27
  ~ people, 866.3
  ~ person, 4.28; 866.2
  treat ~ly, 4.30
savage,n., 4.28; 866.2
  ~s, 866.3
savageness,n., 4.20,25; 866.1

save,v.
  protect, 568.1; 571.1; see also **protect**,v.
  store up, 262.1; see **store**,v.
  ~ a ship at sea, 571.1(3)
  ~ from capture, 571.1(1,2)
  ~ from danger, 571.1
  ~ money, 262.1(1)
  state of being ~d, 571.4
savior,n., 568.5; 571.3
  ~ of the Jews, 571.3(2)
savory,adj., 446.13
saw,n., 332.12(4,7)
say,v., 674.1,8
  ~ again, 674.13; see **repeat**,v.
  ~ in addition, 908.10
  ~ in anger, 878.6(1,12,19–22)
  ~ in complaint, 1120.1(2,6,11, 15,16)
  ~ in detail, 674.2
  ~ in dissatisfaction, 1119.3(3)
  ~ in happiness, 1102.13
  ~ in hostility, 879.8(4)
  ~ in opposition, 544.1(4,6,9, 11,12,22–25,27,29,30,33,34); see also **dispute**, **quarrel**,v.
  ~ in pleasure, 1105.19
  ~ in sadness, 1125.27
  ~ in warning, 574.1
  ~ incorrectly, 674.8(63)
  ~ no, 547.1; 548.1; 555.1
  not ~, 674.7
  ~ numbers, 927.12
  ~ under oath, 1086.1,2
  ~ while weeping, 1127.7
  ~ with a laugh, 1111.5
  ~ with a smile, 1112.4
  ~ without preparation, 48.9(2)
  ~ yes, 541.1; 554.1; see **yes**,n.
saying,n., 674.9; 676.1
  a ~, 676.1
  act of ~, 674.9; see **statement**,n.
  containing ~s, 676.3
  given to using ~s, 676.4
  humorous ~, 676.1(8,14,19, 20); 1115.7(1,5)
  humorous ~s, 676.2(1); 1115.8
  humorous ~s, use of, 676.7
  language full of ~s, 665.9(48)
  liquor, a ~ when drinking, 676.1(25)
  ~ on moral behavior, 843.16
  pert. to a ~, 674.10
  pert. to ~s, 676.3
  ~s, collectively, 676.2
  speak in ~s, 676.5,6
  talk full of ~s, 671.2(20)
  trite ~, 676.1(28)
  witty ~, 676.1(8,14,19,20); 1115.7(1,5)
  witty ~s, 676.2(1); 1115.8
  witty ~s, use of, 676.7
  write ~s, 676.5,6
scale (shell),n.
  arrangement of ~s, 355.4
  covered with ~s, 355.3(4,5–8)
  ~s of animal skin, 355.8
scallop,n., 422.3
  of ~s, 422.1(27)
  ~-shaped, 507.17(22)
scalp,n.
  disease of the ~, 369.25
scaly,adj., 355.3(4,5–8)
  covered by ~ material, 355.6
  ~ crust, 355.7,9
  ~ material, 355.5
scandal,n., 616.3; 891.5,7–9,16,18
  given to ~, 891.10
scandalous,adj., 881.12; 891.6, 19
Scandinavian,n., 784.15(41,42, 56); 784.16

scar,n.
 cliff, 1006.1(8,12,31)
 injury to feelings or reputation, 803.20
 mark, 503.1; 803.15; 805.5,6
 mark of disgrace, 891.4
 moral stain, 891.23
 rocky height, 166.1
 ~ from smallpox vaccination,
  569.6
scar,v.
 mark, 503.2
 mark with disgrace, 891.3
 spoil, 805.1,2
 stain morally, 891.22
scarce,adj., 917.27,30
scarcity,n., 917.28,29
scare,n., 576.2; see fear,n.
scare,v., 576.6
scared,adj., 576.1; see frightened,adj.
 be ~, 576.3; see fear,v.
scarf,n., 977.1
 head ~, 983.2(1,22,31,33,46,61,
  62)
scarlet fever,n., 382.11(43)
 test for susceptibility to ~,
  401.10(2)
scatter,v., 188.1
 spread, 195.1
 throw, 187.1
 ~ing of the Jews, 188.2
 ~ seed, 998.2(3)
scene,n., 783.4
 action, ~ of, 783.4(1,5-7)
 changing ~, 783.4(2-4)
 contest, ~ of, 783.4(1)
 existence, ~ of, 783.4(5)
 important happenings, ~ of,
  783.4(7)
 miniature ~, 483.8(6)
 striking ~, 483.8(25)
scenery,n.
 exhibition of world ~,
  1004.36
 ~ of a play, 783.3
 picture of ~, 965.1(29,38,46,
  48,49,57)
 pictures of ~, 965.15
scent,n., 445.9; see odor,n.
scheme,n., 47.2; see also plot,n.
 deceptive ~, 47.2(3,4)
 dishonest ~, 47.2(1)
 gambling ~, 34.14
scheme,v., 47.1; see also plot,v.
schemer,n., 47.3
 ~s, 47.4
scheming,adj., 47.5
schist,n.
 like ~, 1006.29
schizophrenia,n., 1136.1; see
  insanity,n.
 like ~, 1136.15
scholar,n.
 learned person, 622.17
 student, 622.5; see student,n.
school,n., 623.1
 boarding ~, 623.1(15)
 elementary ~, 623.1(7,17,18)
 ~ for clergy, 623.1(20)
 ~ for college preparation,
  623.1(16)
 ~ for girls, 623.1(6,20)
 ~ for higher learning,
  623.1(1-3,9,10,12,14,20,21)
 ~ for teachers, 623.1(14)
 head of a ~, 623.7,8
 high ~, 623.1(1,11,18)
 ~ of art, 623.1(4)
 ~ of horse riding, 623.1(13)
 ~ of music, 623.1(4)
 pert. to ~, 623.2,3
 pert. to ~ activities other
  than studies, 623.4-6
 private ~, 623.1(16,20)

scissors,n., 332.9(12)
 maker or seller of ~, 332.12
scold,n., 876.4; 895.7
scold,v., 894.1,2; 895.1,2
 disposed to ~, 895.6
scolder,n., 894.5; 895.4,7,8
scolding,adj., 894.4; 895.5
 ~ disposition, 895.6
 ~ wife, 876.5; 895.8
 ~ woman, 895.7
scolding,n., 894.3; 895.3
 ~ by a wife, 895.3(2)
scorn,n., 870.2; see also contempt,n.
scornful,adj., 870.3; see also
  contemptuous,adj.
scorpion,n., 428.3
 like a ~, 428.2(1)
 of ~s, 403.6(1); 428.1(3,4)
 science of ~s, 403.26(3)
Scotch,adj., 784.16
Scotland,n., 784.9(2)
Scotsman,n., 784.15(11,22,27,
  52)
scoundrel,n., 886.5
scoundrelly,adj., 886.6
 ~ act, 886.7
scowl,n., 365.2(4,6); 874.14;
  878.7; 1117.12
scowl,v., 874.14; 878.6(8,10,13);
  1117.10,13
scrape,v., 438.1; see rub,v.
 ~ with the foot, 346.2
scratch,n., 332.31
scratch,v., 332.30
scratching,adj.
 habituated to ~ the ground
  for food, 332.32
scream,n., 463.1; 464.1; 465.1
scream,v., 463.2; 464.2; 465.2
screech,n., 463.1; 464.1; 465.1
screech,v., 463.2; 464.2; 465.2
screen,n., 568.4,23; 970.3
 ~ of crossed strips, 991.14,15
screen,v., 312.2; 568.1; 970.1
scrub,v., 438.1(11,18-21)
sculptor,n., 966.4
 ~ of statues, 966.17
 word after ~'s name, 966.12
sculpture,n., 966.5,18
 art of ~, 965.6(2); 966.3
 artist's name on ~, 966.12
 ~ cast in plaster, 1007.20
 like a piece of ~, 966.13
 ~ of figures in the round,
  966.16
 ~ of naked body, 965.1(36)
 ornament with ~, 966.14
 plaster for ~, 1007.19
 process of ~, 966.3
 projection of ~, 966.8,9
 relief in ~, 966.9
 stone for ~, 1006.1(4,27)
sculpture,v., 966.1(8-11)
sculptured,adj., 966.6
scurrilous,adj.
 abusive, 561.9; 1118.15
 obscene, 713.1
scurvy,n.
 medication for ~, 398.6(3)
sea (ocean),n., 1029.64,67
 across the ~, 1029.72(22)
 across the Atlantic ~,
  1029.72(21)
 across the Pacific ~,
  1029.72(21)
 ~ animal, 422.3,4; 423.1,3,5,7,
  10
 animal living under the ~,
  1026.36
 away from the ~, 1029.72(7)
 big as the ~, 1029.72(11)
 ~ border, 1029.79
 bordering on the ~, 1029.80
 bottom of the ~, 169.4(1,6,8)

carried by, or on, the ~,
  1029.72(15)
coast of the ~, 1029.79
 ~ depths, 170.9(3,4)
depths of ~ water, pert. to,
  1029.72(1,3,4,6)
 ~ devil, 660.1(6)
direction toward the ~,
  1029.77
god of the ~, 1029.78
growing in the ~, 1029.72(4,
  8,9,11,13,20)
inlets of the ~, pert. to,
  1029.72(20)
land bordering the ~, 1029.79
land jutting out into the ~,
  1029.98,99
land over which the ~ flows,
  1029.100(15,16)
like a ~, 1029.72(12)
line between the ~ and land,
  1029.83
line from which the ~ has
  receded, 1029.84
living in the ~, 1029.72(4,8,9,
  11,13,20)
movement of the ~, 1031.1
navigation in the air above
  the ~, 1029.72(2)
open ~, 1029.65
operating in the ~, 1029.72(9,
  13)
originating in the ~,
  1029.72(14)
outline of the ~ coast, 1029.85
part of a city that faces the
  ~, 1029.82
pert. or relating to the ~,
  1029.72
place beyond the ~, 782.1(14)
plant growing under the ~,
  1026.36
produced by the ~, 1029.72(14,
  20)
rises and falls like the ~,
  that which, 161.4
rough ~, 1029.65
roughness of the ~ caused by
  wind, 1029.68
route by the ~, 1029.70
science of the ~s, 1026.39(2);
  1029.71
shore of the ~, 1029.79
 ~ spirit, 662.7(7)
surrounded by the ~,
  1029.72(17)
toward the ~, 1029.75,76
traveler by ~, 1029.74
traveling by ~, 1029.72(16,18,
  19); 1029.73
under the ~, 1026.30; 1026.35
view of the ~, 1029.69
waters of the ~, 1029.66
 ~ waters reached by sunlight,
  referring to, 1065.18
 ~ wave, 1032.1; see wave,n.
sea anemone,n., 422.3
 of ~s, 422.1(1,2,11)
sea cucumber,n., 422.3
 of ~, 422.1(21)
sea lily,n., 422.3
 of the ~, 422.1(12)
sea urchin,n., 422.3
 like the ~, 422.2
 of ~s, 422.1(7,16)
seal (animal),n., 423.5,7
 baby ~, 423.10
 breeding place of ~s,
  403.22(36)
 group of ~s, 403.5(52,59,75)
 like the ~, 423.9
 pert. to ~s, 423.8
 place where ~s are hunted,
  403.22(37)
seal (on document),n., 697.1

seal

impress a ~ on, 697.2
impression made by a ~, 697.1(4)
science of ~s, 697.3
seal,v., 297.1,2; 302.1,12
seaport,n., 1029.11
search,n., 485.2; 486.2
~ for plunder, 248.7
~ for prey, 248.7
useless ~, 486.2(4)
search,v., 485.1; 486.1
~ for metals or water, 486.1(8)
~ for plunder, 248.6
~ for prey, 248.6
go through to ~, 121.1(17)
something ~ed for, 486.7
searcher,n., 485.3; 486.4
~ for plunder, 248.8
~ for prey, 248.8
searching,n., 485.4; 486.3
descr. of ~, 486.3
searchlight,n., 1065.107(18,22)
seasickness,n., 290.18
season,n., 770.1
adapted to ~s, 770.14
depending on ~s, 770.13
four ~s, 770.1
in keeping with the ~, 770.12
middle of a ~, 770.2
pert. to ~s, 770.3,5,7,9,13
rainy ~ in Asia, 1042.10
spend the ~, 770.11
season,v.
accustom, 629.23
make experienced, 619.4
spice, 446.14
seasoning,n.
experience, 619.2
spice, 446.17
seat,n., 63.1
accompany to a ~, 131.1(3,9)
armless ~, 63.1(2,6,7,11,13,18, 19,21,22,23)
arms, ~ with, 63.1(1,4,5,9)
authority, ~ of, 63.1(3)
backless ~, 63.1(2,11,22,23)
bed, ~ convertible to, 63.1(18)
church ~, 63.1(20)
church ~s, 63.4(4)
circular ~, 63.1(13)
elephant, ~ on back of, 63.1(18)
elevated ~, 63.1(12,15)
horse, ~ on a, 63.1(16)
king, ~ for a, 63.1(24)
structure of ~s, 63.4
teacher, ~ of a, 63.1(3)
theater ~s, 969.33
seated,adj., 62.4
deep-~, 323.23
seaweed,n., 985.6(1,10)
science of ~s, 985.36(3)
treatise on ~s, 682.15(16)
seclude,v., 330.3
secluded,adj., 330.1
~ place, 782.1(4,25)
seclusion,n., 330.2,4
life of ~, 330.8
one who lives in ~, 330.7
place of ~, 330.10
second,adj.
order, ~ in, 931.21
~ power (math.), 931.22
rank, ~ in, 931.21
secrecy,n., 971.1,2
lack of ~, 971.43
not tending to ~, 971.29
tending to ~, 971.27
secret,adj., 970.48,49; 971.1,2,8, 10,13; see also **secretly**,adv.
~ agent, 971.40,41
conceal in a ~ place, 970.4,5
~ doctrines, 971.3

~ facial expression, having a, 971.14
fear, ~ because of, 971.10,13
give ~ information to, 613.28(13); 613.34
giver of ~ information for gambling, 613.31(2); 613.35
~ government organization, 971.39
~ in actions, 971.10,13
~ in identity, 971.17
~ in meaning, 604.1(12,15,32, 37); 607.9(1,3,6,8,15); 971.9; see also **mysterious**,adj.
~ in movement, 82.3
~ in name, 971.17
~ in operation, 971.11,12
keep ~, 970.50; 971.26
key to ~ writing, 601.8,9
~ language, 664.1(3,5)
~ letters, 679.4(2-4)
~ movement, 82.2
not ~, 970.55,56; 971.42
~ (of government documents, etc.), 971.19
~ (of language), 971.8
~ (of speech), 971.8
~ organization, 971.38
~ organization opposing the government, 971.37
~ practices, 971.5
~ remedy, 971.24
solve ~ writing, 601.7
~ study, 971.3
~ symbol, 604.3(4); 954.1(3)
~ symbols, 683.3
~ teachings, 971.3
~ word, 666.3(16,34,42,52)
~ words, 683.2
~ writing, 683.1
~ writings, 971.7
~ written symbol, 679.1(5,7)
secret,n., 971.4,23
alchemists, ~ sought by, 971.23(1)
as a ~, 971.32
cannot keep a ~, one who, 971.30
descr. of ~s, 971.31
given as a ~, 971.31
hidden ~s, 971.25
in ~, 971.21,22; see **secretly**, adv.
keep ~s, 971.26,28
keeping ~s, 971.27
knowing (a ~), 971.36
~ of nature, 971.23(1)
one to whom ~s are told, 613.37; 971.35
said as a ~, 971.31
tell ~s, 613.1(5,6,9,14,17,18,28, 30,31,35); 971.33,34
tell the ~s of, 613.9
telling ~s, 971.31
written as a ~, 971.31
secretarial,adj., 682.6
~ group, 318.1(80)
secretary,n., 682.5(1-6)
~ of government department, staff of a, 1077.7
secrete,v., 970.1,4,5; see **conceal**,v.
~ in the body, 287.1
secreting,adj., 287.4
~ internally, 287.7
~ organ, 287.5
~ through the skin, 287.10
secretion,n., 287.2,3,6,8
increase in ~ by the skin, 287.11
~ of the kidneys, 287.8(1)
~ of the liver, 287.8(2,5)
~ of the pancreas, 287.8(7)
~ of the skin, 287.8(8); 291.3; see also **sweat**,n.

~ of the thyroid, 287.8(10)
organ of ~, 287.5
pert. to ~, 287.4
science of ~s, 287.15
secretive,adj., 971.10,27
secretly,adv., 971.21,22
act ~, 971.15
approach ~, 132.1(5)
bring in ~, 1087.15-18
carry or take away ~, 971.44
come ~, 118.1(19)
exist ~, 971.16
go ~, 119.1(4,44)
move ~, 82.1; 971.15
move about ~, 100.1(9); 971.15
remain ~, 971.15
send out ~, 1087.15-18
talk ~, 671.1(20)
wait ~, 272.1(9)
secretory,adj., 287.4
sect,n., 642.17
section,n.
class, 312.1; see **class**,n.
division, 326.1
group, 318.1; see **group**,n.
part, 326.6; see **part**,n.
place, 782.1; see **place**,n.
~ of closed space, 326.6(2)
~ sent on special mission, 326.6(4,5)
section,v.
classify, 312.2
cut, 332.1
divide, 326.3
separate, 325.1
~ into parts, 326.8
sectional,adj., 318.2; 326.2,7; 332.7; 782.15
sectionally,adv., 318.2
secular,adj., 643.17; 645.11; 1004.38,41
make ~, 1004.42
secure,adj.
certain, 641.1
safe, 568.7
secure,v.
assure, 641.4
attach, 302.1,4
get, 240.1
protect, 568.1
security,n.
certainty, 641.2
proof to fulfill a promise, 1122.46
protection, 568.3
acts as ~ for another, 1122.48
sediment,n., 757.11
clog with ~, 757.12
seduce,v., 886.24,26
attract, 196.1
persuade, 638.1
~ into sexual looseness, 712.6
~ sexually, 710.15
seducer,n.
attracter, 196.4
persuader, 638.5
sexual ~, 710.15; 712.6
seduction,n., 886.24,26
attraction, 196.2
persuasion, 638.2
sexual ~, 710.15; 710.18(2,5); 712.6
seductive,adj., 886.24,26
see,v., 480.1
able to ~, 480.10
easy to ~, 483.1; see also **conspicuous, evident, obvious, visible**,adj.
hard to ~, 483.12; see also **inconspicuous**,adj.
hard to ~, something that is, 483.8(22)
impossible to ~, 483.12; see also **invisible**,adj.

inability or partial inability
to ~, 481.1; see also **blindness,n.**
one who ~s, 480.3
unable to ~, 481.2; see also
blind,adj.
seed,n., 995
bearing ~s, 995.9
cereal ~, coating on, 987.14
covering of a ~, 972.4(9–11,
13–15,19–21,23)
eating ~s, 734.27(13,32)
fern ~, 995.3
grass ~, 995.1,2
moss ~, 995.3
oak ~, 995.7
pert. to ~s of plants, 995.8
plant a ~, 998.2(3)
produce ~s, 995.10
remove ~ from, 995.12
scatter ~, 998.2(3)
science of ~s, 985.36(22)
science of fruits and ~s,
745.24
shed ~s, 995.11
seeing,n., 480.2; see also **sight,
view, vision,n.**
devices,for ~, 480.16,17
devices for ~, maker or seller
of, 480.20
pert. to ~, 480.6,8
place for ~, 480.13
power of ~, 480.5
sensation of later ~, 480.9
sense of ~, 480.4
worth ~, something that is,
483.8(21,23,24,27)
seek,v., 486.1; see **search,v.**
seeker,n., 486.4
water ~, 486.4(2)
seeking,adj., 486.3
seeking,n., 486.2
seem,v., 504.9
seen, adj., v.
able to be ~, 483.1; see
visible,adj.
able to be ~ through, 483.10
be ~, 483.3–6
beyond what is directly ~,
483.12(13)
something ~, 483.8
unable to be ~, 483.12; see
invisible,adj.
segment,n.
part, 326.1,6,10; see **part,n.**
segregate,v., 325.12; 330.3
segregated,adj., 330.1
segregation,n., 325.3,12; 330.2,4
~ of Negroes, 325.17,18
racial ~, 325.17,18
seize,v., 247.1,6
attack in order to ~, 560.1(7,
25,26)
~ legally, 247.1(12,14,16,27);
247.6(2,3,15,22)
tendency to ~, 247.10
try to ~, 18.1(15,17); 247.14
seized,adj.
one who is ~, 247.9
that which is ~, 247.9; 248.5
seizer,n., 247.8
seizure,n., 247.2,7
a fit, 560.24
adapted for ~, 247.11,12
habit of ~ by force, 247.10
instrument for ~, 247.15
open to ~ through attack,
247.13
select,v., 252.1; see **choose,v.**
selection,n., 252.2,5; see also
choice,n.
~ for learning foreign
language, 252.5(2)
~ from writing, 252.5(2,6,7)

make an unfair ~ of material,
252.1(6)
~s of writings, i.e., collection,
682.19
unfair ~ from writing,
252.5(8)
self,n., 228.1
~ as censor, 228.1(6)
~ as conscience, 228.1(6)
~-interest, 228.3; see **self-
interest,n.**
~-interested person, 228.5
love of ~, 700.1(5,7,18,23)
other ~, 228.1(1,2)
outside the ~, 138.1(2)
uninhibited ~, 228.1(4)
self-admiration,n., 855.6
self-approval,n., 850.11
self-assertive,adj.
offensively ~, 674.12
self-assurance,n., 641.7;
641.7(1,2,4); see **self-confidence,n.**
self-assured,adj., 641.6(3,8,9,
14)
self-confidence,n., 641.7;
641.7(1,2,4)
cause a male to lose ~, 640.9
cause to lose ~, 640.8; see
also **embarrass,v.**
self-confident,adj., 641.6(3,8,9,
13)
self-control,n., 77.1
exercise ~, 77.4
exercising ~, 77.2
one who exercises ~, 77.3
self-defense,n.
Japanese art of ~, 568.13
self-denial,n., 77.1
exercise ~, 77.4
exercising ~, 77.2
one who exercises ~, 77.3
self-destruction,n., 795.1
self-discipline,n., 77.1
exercise ~, 77.4
exercising ~, 77.2
one who exercises ~, 77.3
self-generated,adj., 726.15
self-government,n., 1073.3(4,8,
18); 1073.75
advocacy of local ~, 1073.79,
80
city with ~, 1073.76
country with ~, 1073.4(2)
give ~ to a city, 1073.77
having ~, 1073.75
not having ~, 1073.82
without ~, 1073.82
self-importance,n.
action, manner, or speech of
~, 848.32
self-important,adj., 848.31
~ official, 1077.1(23)
~ person, 848.34
showy and ~, 951.38
small and ~ person, 848.34(1)
young and ~ person,
848.34(2)
self-interest,n., 228.3
based on ~, 228.6
person consumed with ~,
228.4
pert. to ~, 228.4
selfish,adj., 227.4
woman bent on ~ gain,
227.5
self-moving,adj., 79.23
self-named,adj., 694.10
self-pride,n., 871.2(2,3)
self-produced, 726.15
self-production,n., 726.14
self-respect,n.
lower the ~ of, 868.10
self-restraint,n., 77.1
exercise ~, 77.4

exercising ~, 77.2
one who exercises ~, 77.3
self-sacrifice,n., 77.1
self-satisfied,adj., 1107.3(1–3)
~ group, 1107.9
sell,v., 212.1
buy and ~, 212.1(5,16–18)
~ illegally, 1087.13
seller,n., 212.3
~ of food, 233.4(1,3,4)
~ of groceries, 233.4(1)
~ of liquor to army, 233.4(3,
4)
~ of provisions, 233.4(1,3,4)
~ of quack remedies, 823.22;
826.19
supervisor of ~s in a store,
1025.17
traveling ~, 212.3(1,4,6–8,12,
14,15)
selling,n., 212.2
~ at auction, 212.8
booklet for ~ purposes,
687.1(8)
buying and ~, 212.2(1)
~ of church positions, 212.9
~ of sacred objects, 212.9
place of ~, 212.7
semantics,n., 607.22(3–6)
semen,n., 379.7
producing ~, 379.8
tube carrying ~, 379.1(22)
semicircular,adj., 508.5
senate,n., 1080.10,18; see **legislature,n.**
senator,n., 1080.11,19
send,v., 189.1; see also **sent,adj.**
~ away, 144.1
~ away by laughter, 1111.30
~ back to prison, 301.8
~ by ship, 115.13
~ down like rain, 1037.8
~ for, 189.1(14)
~ out, 144.1; 189.1(2,8,9,15)
~ out illegally, 1087.15
~ out secretly, 1087.15
sensation,n., 433.1; 434.1; see
also **perception,n.**
emotion, 1092.1
ability to have ~s, 432.17
able to have ~s, 432.16
bring back ~, 435.8
causing ~s, 434.4
causing the ~ of touching,
436.9
descr. of ~, 433.3; 434.2
dull the ~s, 435.2; 1097.13
dullness of ~, 435.1; 1097.15
dullness of ~, cause, 435.2
feel a ~, 434.3
feeling a ~, 434.2
hair ~, 434.1(14)
imaginary ~, 434.1(4,7,10,11)
imaginary ~ of ants crawling, 434.1(4)
itching ~, 434.1(1,2,4,6,9,15)
lack of ~, 435.1; 1097.15
lack of ~, cause, 435.2;
1097.13
lack of ~, cause of, 435.5;
1097.16
lack of ~, causing, 435.4
lacking ~, 435.3; 1097.14
lose ~, 435.6
loss of ~, 435.1; 1097.15
loss of ~, cause, 435.2;
1097.13
loss of ~, cause of, 435.5;
1097.16
loss of ~, causing, 435.4
numb ~s, 435.2; 1097.13
numbness of ~, 435.1; 1097.15
physical ~, 434.1
skin ~, 434.1(1–9,12,13,15)
stinging ~, 434.1(7,8,13,15)

touch ~, 434.1(3,5,12–14)
sensational,adj.
exciting, 1100.2
pert. to sensation, 433.3
~ behavior, 1094.7
use of ~ techniques, 1100.9
sense,n.
common sense, 596.3
good sense, 596.3
intelligence, 594.3; see intelligence,n.
meaning, 607.2; see mean-
ing,n.
sensation, 433.1; 434.1; see
also perception, sensa-
tion,n.
wisdom, 596.3; see wisdom,n.
apparatus of the ~s, 432.14
beyond the ~s, 433.10
common ~, 596.3
dull the ~s of, 435.2; 1097.13
dulling the ~s, 435.4
dullness of the ~s, 435.1;
1097.15
dulls the ~s, that which,
435.5; 1097.16
good ~, 596.3
good ~, having or showing,
596.1,2
individual ~s, 432.3–7
~ of hearing, 432.3
~ of hearing, pert. to,
432.8,13
~ of seeing, 432.6
~ of seeing, pert. to, 432.11,13
~ of smell, 432.5
~ of smell, pert. to, 432.10
~ of taste, 432.4
~ of taste, pert. to, 432.9
~ of touch, 432.7
~ of touch, pert. to, 432.12
operation of the ~s, 432.15
perception through the ~s,
433.1
pert. to the ~s, 432.2,9–13
poor ~, 596.6
poor ~, having or showing,
596.5
sixth ~, 433.12
use of the ~s, 432.1
senseless,adj.
of poor sense, 596.5
stupid, 597.1; see stupid,adj.
unconscious,adj., 435.3; see
unconscious,adj.
~ statement, 607.31; 674.9(11,
23,30)
sensible,adj.
able to be perceived, 433.8
able to feel, 432.16
aware, 611.1
intelligent, 594.1,2; see intelligent,adj.
wise, 596.1,2; see wise,adj.
sensitive,adj., 432.16; 433.19;
868.9; 1092.101; 1093.1
be ~ to beauty or art of,
1093.8
excessively ~, 1093.7
in or to the ~ part of the
feelings, 1093.6
make ~, 433.20,21
~ to art, 1093.9
~ to beauty, 1093.9
~ to beauty or art, one who
is, 1093.10
sensitiveness,n., 432.17; 433.18;
868.9; 1092.101; 1093.1
abnormal ~, 433.18(2–6)
decreased ~, 1137.33,34
reduce or eliminate ~, 433.22
~ to heat, cold, touch, etc.,
1137.32
~ to light, 433.18(10,11)

~ to pain, 433.18(1,12);
1137.30–32
sensory,adj., 433.3
sensual,adj.
devoted to pleasures of the
senses, 1105.8
pert. to sensation or the
senses, 432.2; 433.3
pert. to sex, 709.4
pleasurable, 1105.4
sexually desirous, etc., 709.8
~ gratification, arising from,
709.11
indulge in ~ pleasure,
1105.7(1,2,4)
indulge the ~ desires of,
1108.6
life of ~ pleasures, 1105.20
~ly pleasurable, 1105.4(6)
make ~, 1105.10
~ person, 709.9; 1105.9
road to ~ pleasures, 1105.20
time of ~ pleasures, 1105.18
world of ~ pleasures, 1105.20
sensuous,adj.
devoted to pleasures of the
senses, 1105.8
pert. to the senses, 432.2
pleasurable, 1105.4
sent,adj.
~ by heaven, 1051.18
~ by special messenger, 189.3
group ~, 189.2
one ~, 189.2
place to which ~, 189.4
sentence,n.
explanatory ~, 666.3(33)
~ parts, 667.13
types of ~s, descr. of, 667.12
~ unchanged when read
backward, 666.3(32)
sentimental,adj., 1094.1
affectedly or weakly ~ person, writing, 1094.5,11
affectedly or weakly ~ behavior, etc., 1094.5–7
be ~, 1094.10
~ behavior, actions, etc.,
1094.6,7
~ emotion, 1094.12
~ habit, nature, etc., 1094.8
~ language, 1094.3
make ~, 1094.10
~ person, 1094.5,9,11
~ prose, 1094.5
talk ~ly, 1094.4
~ verse, 1094.5
sentimentality,n., 1094.2
excessive ~, 1094.8
tendency to ~, 1094.8
separable,adj., 325.9
separate,adj., 325.8
make into a ~ entity, 325.15
make into a ~ substance,
325.16
one who is ~, 325.9
regard as a ~ substance,
325.16
show the ~ness of, 325.14
that which is ~, 325.6
separate,v., 325.1,2
cut apart, 332.1(8,9,18,44,63);
see also cut,v.
tear apart, 337.1(4,5,11,13,15,
17)
~ by special differences,
540.20
~ by trees, bushes or shrubs,
996.31
~ from anchorage, 325.1(75)
~ into parts or sections,
328.8
one who ~s, 325.4
that which ~s, 325.4
~ with a wall, 1024.2

separated,adj., 325.8; see also
divided,adj.
able to be ~, 325.9
that which has been ~, 325.6
unable to be ~, 325.10
separation,n., 325.3,7; see also
division,n.
~ between female breasts,
325.7(2)
causing ~, 325.5
inclined to ~, 325.5
~ into body, soul, and spirit,
325.3(9)
pert. to ~, 325.11
wide ~, 325.7(1)
serf,n.
~s collectively, 1074.16
state of being a ~, 1074.15
series,n., 173.9
form into a ~, 173.10
forming a ~, 173.11
~ of actions, 173.9(8,14)
~ of books, 173.9(18)
~ of happenings, 173.9(5,22)
~ of ideas, 173.9(4,6,22)
~ of motions, 173.9(8)
~ of playing cards, 173.9(20)
~ of questions, 173.9(2)
~ of rooms, 173.9(21)
~ of statements, 173.9(2)
one of a ~, 173.6(7)
repeated ~, 674.25
united in a ~, 173.11
serious,adj., 610.1
both ~ and comic, 1113.9
~ in appearance, 610.2
inconspicuous but ~, 971.12
less ~, 883.21
make ~, 610.5
make more ~, 610.6
not ~, 609.1; see frivolous,
adj.
obscure but ~, 971.12
quiet and ~, 610.3
secret but ~, 971.12
something ~, 1111.37
treat ~ly, 610.5
seriousness,n., 610.1
combining ~ and humor,
610.4
sermon,n., 647.3
deliver a ~, 647.1
pert. to teaching by ~s,
621.6(4)
serpent,n., 425.7; see also reptile, snake,n.
eating ~s, 734.27(23)
mythical ~s, 662.25
mythical creature, part ~,
part woman, 662.26(4)
science of ~s, 403.26(18,29)
servant,n., 205.14
be a ~ to, 205.15
household ~, 205.14
man's personal ~, 205.14(16)
set,n., 318.1
set,v., 323.1; see put,v.
set apart,v., 325.12
set aside,v., 323.16
~ as sacred, 650.2
setting,n.
surroundings, 783.1
~ of a play, 783.3
settle,v.
drop, 167.1
establish, 323.1
live, 750.1,15
make agree, 541.10,21
~ a disagreement, dispute,
etc., 541.21
~ on land, 750.15
power to ~ disputes, 1083.29
try to ~ a disagreement, etc.,
541.26,27
what ~s to the bottom, 757.11

settlement,n.
   agreement, 541.11
   dropping, 167.2
   establishment, 323.2
   living, 750.2
   ~ by arbitrator, 1083.22,24
seven, n. or adj., 936.1
   consisting of ~ parts, 936.6
   divided into ~ parts, 936.6
   group of ~, 936.4
   happening every ~ days, 936.10
   multiply by ~, 936.8
   number ~, 936.1,2
   times ~, 936.9
   total of ~, 936.3
sevenfold,adv., 936.7
   increase ~, 907.9(7)
seventy,n., 940.16
   consisting of ~, 940.17
   ~-year-old person, 758.2(6)
severe,adj., 890.1,6,16; see also **strict,**adj.
   more ~, 890.17,18
   sharp and ~, 334.1(5)
severity,n., 890.2,6
   reduce in ~, 1142.1,10; see also **weaken,**v.
sew,v., 305.1
   one who ~s, 205.5(4,5,13,14,17); 305.3
   ~ surgically, 305.1(8)
sewer (for refuse),n., 285.2(2–4)
   waste carried by ~s, 285.1(30,38)
sewing,n.
   container for ~ implements, 261.1(29,31)
sex,n.
   avoid ~, 710.49
   avoidance of ~, 710.47
   between the ~es, 709.1(4)
   both ~es, attraction to, 710.33(4)
   combination of both ~es, 710.36,37
   common to both ~es, 709.1(2)
   deprive of ~, 710.38; see also **castrate,**v.
   detour ~ drives, 77.1(30); 710.46
   emphasis on ~, 709.20,22–24
   go about with opposite ~, 700.9
   grammatical ~, 709.2
   grammatical ~, descr. of, 709.3
   guiltless of illicit ~, 845.11
   ~ hormones, 287.12
   indifference to ~, 710.43
   ~ life, 709.6
   literature devoted to ~, 709.32,33
   ~ organs, 379.1; see **genitals,**n.
   own ~, attraction to one's, 710.33
   pert. to ~, 709.1(5); 709.4
   pert. to both ~es, 709.1(1,3)
   pert. to one ~, 709.1(6)
   pursuit of ~, 709.7,16
   rerouting of ~ desire, 77.1(30)
   science of ~, 709.31
   unrelated to ~, 710.51
   without ~, 710.51
   writings about ~, 682.16(12,24)
sexless,adj., 710.51; 1090.13
sexual,adj., 709.1,4
   ~ aberration, 710.31,33; see **sexual aberration,**n.
   ~ ability, period of, 709.27; see **puberty,**n.

abnormal ~ activity, 710.31,33; see **sexual aberration,**n.
~ activities, pert. to, 709.4
~ appetites, pert. to, 709.4
approach with ~ proposals, 709.15,26
area responding to ~ stimulation, 379.3
arresting of ~ development, 710.33(12,13)
attentiveness for ~ favors, 579.12
~ character, 709.5
~ curiosity, 709.7(37)
~ desire, 709.7,10
~ desire, agent that causes, 709.17
~ desire, causing, 709.18
~ desire, lack of, 710.43
~ desire, unnatural, 710.31,33; see **sexual aberration,**n.
~ desire in, cause, 709.19
~ desire in female mammals, 709.7(17,34,39); 709.13
~ deviation, 710.31,33; see **sexual aberration,**n.
devoted to ~ pleasure, 1105.8(2,7–9,11,14)
~ energy, 709.10
~ excitement, 709.7
~ excitement, causing, 709.18; 1105.4(6,8,11)
~ excitement of male elephants, 709.7(31)
~ feeling aroused by one's own body, 709.7(32)
god of ~ love, 700.27(2)
~ gratification, arising from, 709.11
have ~ desires, 709.14
~ immorality, 712.2; see also **immoral,**adj.
~ immorality, indulge in, 712.5
~ immorality, lead into, 712.6
indulge in ~ pleasure, 710.2; 1105.7(2,4)
inexperienced ~ly, 620.1(4,12); 620.2(4)
~ instinct, energy from the, 709.10
~ intercourse, 710.1; see **sexual intercourse,**n.
~ interest, 709.7
~ interpretation, 883.40
invest with ~ quality, 709.21,24
~ life, 709.6
~ looseness, 712.2; see also **immoral,**adj.
~ looseness, indulge in, 712.5
~ looseness, lead into, 712.6
~ love, 700.1(15,19)
~ly desirous, 709.8
~ly desirous person, 709.9
~ly excited, 709.8
~ly excited person, 709.9
~ly exciting, 709.18; 1105.4(6,8,11)
~ly exciting literature or art, 713.4; see also **obscene,**adj.
~ly exciting literature or art, study of, 713.5
~ly immoral, 1096.11
~ly immoral man, 712.3
~ly immoral woman, 712.4
~ly interested, 709.8
~ly loose, 712.1; 1096.11; see also **immoral,**adj.
~ly loose man, 712.3
~ly loose woman, 712.4
~ nature, 709.5

non-~ love between man and woman, 700.1(20)
one interested in ~ love, 700.26
pert. to ~ love, 700.25
~ perversion, 710.31,33; see **sexual aberration,**n.
~ pervert, 710.32,34
pleasurable ~ly, 709.18; 1105.4(6,8,11)
~ pleasure, 709.12
~ pleasure from animals, 710.33(9,38,39)
~ pleasure from looking at genitals, 484.8; 710.33(29,36)
~ pleasure, pursuit of, 709.16
~ power, 5.1(12,17); 709.25
~ relationship without marriage, 710.8,9
restore ~ power to, 760.14
~ sounds of animals, 456.1(3,11,49,68)
~ striving, 709.10
~ weakness, 10.1(27)
without a ~ element, 710.51; 1090.13
sexual aberration,n., 710.31
one possessing a ~, 710.32,34
specific ~s, 710.33
sexual intercourse,n., 710.1
a meeting for ~, 322.1(3,30,38); 710.11,12
adulterous ~, 710.1(1,4,6,10)
against ~, one who is, 749.58
avoid ~, 710.49
avoidance of ~, 710.47
avoider of ~, 710.48
~ before marriage, 710.1(17)
~ between animals, 710.1(14,15)
~ between blood relatives, 710.1(9)
completion of a marriage by ~, 710.1(3)
corrupt by ~, 710.17
culmination of ~, 710.24; see **orgasm,**n.
deprive of virginity through ~, 710.16
disease from ~, 379.9(1–3,5,6,12,13,17)
entice into ~, 710.15
evil spirit that has ~ with men, 65.2(2); 662.7(40)
evil spirit that has ~ with women, 65.2(1); 662.7(25,30)
force ~ on (the female), 710.13,14
have ~, 710.2
have ~ for money, 710.2(11); 711.6
have ~ (of animals), 710.2(3)
have ~ with prostitutes, 710.2(10,11)
having ~, 710.4
inability to engage in ~, 710.43(3)
insatiable desire for ~, 709.8,9
insatiable desire for ~ by a man, 709.7(16,36)
insatiable desire for ~ by a woman, 709.7(2,33)
invite men to have ~, 711.17
man whose wife has ~ with others, 710.5,6
money, ~ for, 710.1(18); 711.5; see **prostitution,**n.
money, have ~ for, 710.2(10,11); 711.6
non-indulgence in ~, 710.47

one who has ~, 710.3,8,9,13,15, 18–21; 711.1; see also **prostitute**,n.
pert. to ~, 710.7
watches ~, one who, 484.3(4); 710.34(2)
watching ~, pleasure from, 710.33(29,36)
~ with animals, 710.33(3,5, 33,37)
~ with prostitutes, 710.1(20)
sexy,adj.
obscene, 713.1; see **obscene**, adj.
sexually exciting, 709.18; 1105.4(6,8,11)
shabby,adj., 903.8
mean, 887.2,3; see **mean**,adj.
dirty and ~, 903.9
~ in dress, 903.10
~ person, 903.11,12
shack,n., 753.1; see **house**,n.
shackle,n., 557.3; 558.3
foot ~s, 558.3(1,3)
hand ~s, 558.3(5,6)
hinder with foot ~s, 557.1(15, 19,23,26)
leg ~s, 558.3(4)
shackle,v., 557.1; 558.1
shade,n.
ghost, 662.19; see also **ghost**,n.
shadow, 1071.10; see also **shadow**,n.
affording ~, 1071.5
effect of light and ~ in a picture, 488.7
eye~, 1071.8
in the ~, 1071.11
provider of ~, 1071.8
tree for ~, 1071.9
window ~, 1009.23
without ~, 1071.14
shade,v., 1071.4
shaded,adj., 1071.11
shadow,n., 1071.2; see also **shade**,n.
complete ~, 1071.2
in the ~, 1071.11
like a ~, 1071.3
partial ~, 1071.1
~ picture, 1071.12
place of ~s, 1071.13
provider of ~, 1071.8
throw a ~ over, 1071.4,7
throwing a ~, 1071.5,6
without a ~, 1071.14,15
shadow,v., 1071.4
shadowy,adj., 1071.11
shady,adj., 1071.5,11
of bad reputation, 891.13
shake,n., 111.2
shake,v., 111.1,5
~ nervously, 111.1(8,29)
~ the head, 111.5(7)
~ with cold, 111.1(23)
~ with excitement, 111.1(29); 1100.5(11)
~ with fear, 111.1(17,19,23,24)
~ with horror, 111.1(17,24)
~ with illness, 111.1(23)
~ with the teeth, 111.5(11)
shaking,adj., 111.3
~ like jelly, 111.3(2)
shaking,n., 111.2
signal by ~, 956.1(15,16)
shaky,adj., 87.1; 111.4; see also **unsteady**,adj.
~ and loose, 111.4(4); 304.1(6)
shallow,adj., 139.2; 170.11
become ~, 170.14
make ~, 170.14
~ (of sleep), 170.11(7)
~ place in water, 170.13

shallowness,n., 170.12
shame,n., 868.11; 884.13; 891.5
cause ~, 868.10; 891.1
cause of ~, 868.15; 891.7,8
causing ~, 868.14; 891.6
extreme ~ that brings contempt, 868.16
feel ~, 868.13
lack of ~, 873.18
lacking ~, 873.17
public ~ that brings contempt, 868.16
showing ~, 868.22
without ~, 873.17
shame,v., 868.10; 891.1
shamed,adj., 868.12
shameful,adj., 868.14; 891.6
~ act, 868.16; 891.9
~ behavior, 868.16
shameless,adj., 873.17
merry and ~, 1104.5
~ person, 873.19
shape,n., 507.1; see also **form**,n.
angular ~, 507.1(1)
bodily ~, 338.9(3,4)
change its ~, able to, 507.10(3)
correspondence of ~, 507.6
force out of ~, 3.3(18)
give ~ to, 507.2
hammered into ~, 507.11
irregular ~, 507.1(6)
irregular in ~, 507.14
line indicating ~, 507.19
mar or spoil the ~ of, 805.2–4
of many ~s, 507.12
of specific ~, 507.17
pert. to ~, 507.9
plastic mold of the ~, 507.7
regaining ~ easily, 110.5–7
regular in ~, 507.13
rough in ~, 507.14(9)
twist out of ~, 156.1(7,30); 156.2(4,7–9,15)
twisted out of ~, 156.5; 156.5(6,12,22)
unnatural in ~, 811.6,7
unpleasant in ~, 507.14
shape,v., 507.2
shaped,adj.
able to be ~, 507.10
~ like a specific thing, animal, etc., 507.17
place where something is figuratively ~, 726.6
shapeless,adj., 507.16
shapely,adj., 507.13
small and ~, 909.1(17)
shaping,n.
~ of the mouth, 507.8
share,n., 326.36
by ~, 326.39
by equal ~s, 326.40
cut into ~s, 332.1(4,51,58)
~ due from or to each, 326.37
give a ~ of, 230.8
give in ~s, 231.1
one's ~, 326.38
share,v., 230.8; 231.1
~ emotions, 1092.79,80
shared,adj.
that which is ~, 231.3
sharing,n.
~ of other's emotions, 1092.76
shark,n., 422.3
of ~s, 422.1(18)
young ~, 422.4(3)
sharp,adj., 334.1
~ in answer, 626.8
~ in language, 333.4(2,4–6); 334.1(1,6–8,12,22); 876.22; 877.1(1)
~ in manner, 877.1(1)
~ in smell, 445.10(1)

~ in speech, 877.1(1); see also ~ in language, above
~ in taste, 446.13(2,10,13,14, 22,25,29)
~ in temper, 334.1(1); 876.1, 20; 877.1(1); see also **sharp-tempered**,adj.
make ~, 334.2
~ of edge, 334.1(9,12,20)
~ (of pain), 334.1(13)
~ (of reasoning), 334.1(14,15, 21)
~ (of wind), 334.1(7)
~ point, 335.1(5,17–20)
~ point, with a, 334.1(2,4,6, 16–18)
~ phrase, 666.3(7)
~ remark, 674.9(4,15,25)
severe and ~, 334.1(5)
~ statement, 876.23
stinging and ~, 334.1(18)
sudden and ~, 334.1(5)
~ temper, 876.2
~ word, 666.3(7); 876.23
sharpen,v., 334.2
implement for ~ing, 334.3
~ on or with stone, 334.2(2); 1006.11
sharpness,n., 334
~ of feelings, 876.2(1)
talk with ~, 876.18
sharp temper,n., 876.2
sharp-tempered,adj., 334.1(1); 876.1,20; 877.1(1); see also **angry, bad-tempered, sharp**,adj.
~ female, 876.3(1); 876.4,21
~ girl, 876.4
~ person, 876.3,4,5,21
~ wife, 876.5
~ woman, 876.4
shave,v., 332.1(37,43,56); see also **cut**,v.
~ the head, 371.1(4)
Shaw,n.
admirer of ~, 686.10
descr. of ~'s work or theories, 686.9
descr. of writing like ~'s, 686.8(5)
shawl,n., 977.7
head ~, 983.2(1,22,31,33,44,46, 61,62)
sheath,n., 261.1(41)
bodily ~, 972.4(25)
shed,v., 286.1; see also **eliminate**,v.
~ feathers or fur, 286.1(37)
~ skin or covering, 286.1(33, 37,53)
sheep,n., 411.1,6
castrated ~, 411.2(4)
enclosure for ~, 300.7(7); 403.22(14)
female ~, 411.3
group of ~, 403.5(29)
herder of ~, 205.1(13)
hornless ~, 411.4
leader of ~, 176.3(1,14)
like ~, 411.7
male ~, 411.2
male ~ with a bell, 176.3(1)
of ~, 403.11(2,12)
pert. to ~, 411.7
shed for ~, 403.22(10)
young ~, 411.5,6
shelf,n., 1024.8
put on a ~, 1022.6
undersea ~, 1029.100(1)
shell,n., 355.10
cover with a ~-like material, 972.1(15)
discarded ~s, 285.1(8); 355.13
~fish, 422.1(5,6,13,20,25,27, 33); 422.3

~fish, science of, 403.26(23)
fruit ~, 972.4(9–11,13–15,19,
 21,23)
having a ~, 355.12
like a ~, 355.11(1)
like a tortoise ~, 425.19
like a turtle ~, 355.11(4,5)
lose ~s, 972.10
nut~, 972.4(20)
pert. to ~s, 355.11(1–4)
pert. to a turtle ~, 355.11(4)
remove ~, 972.6.8
science of marine ~s, 355.14
seed ~, 972.4(9–11,13–15,19,
 20,23)
shaped like a snail's ~,
 507.17(19,41)
turtle ~, 355.10(1) ; 972.4(24)
shelter,n., 568.3,4; 972.4; see
 also **protection, cover,n.**
living quarters, 753.1; see
 home, house,n.
~ for animals, 300.7
~ for ships, etc., 1029.11,12
~ of leaves, shrubs, vines, or
 trees, 993.10,11
temporary ~s, 753.18
sheltered,adj., 568.7(5)
~ place, 782.1(4,25)
shepherd,n.
music about ~ life, 786.8(4)
poem about ~s, 689.2(4) ;
 786.8(2,4)
prose composition on ~ life,
 786.8(4)
writer on ~ life, 786.9
sheriff,n., 1078.1
office of a ~, 1078.5
pert. to a ~, 1078.4
shield,n., 568.4,5,22
~-shaped, 507.17(18,57,70)
shield,v., 568.1
shinbone,n., 354.1(8)
shine,n., 1065.56
lack of ~, 1072.1
sky ~ from ice, 1040.27
shine,v., 1065.45,54,60
~ing of the sun through
 parted clouds, 1055.44
make ~ like gold, 1013.15
substance for ~ing, 1065.58
tool for ~ing, 1065.57
~ with heat, 1060.9,10
~ with wax, 1068.3
shined,adj., 1065.55
shining,adj., 1065.50
~ at night, 778.5(3)
~ thing, 1065.22,62
~ with heat, 1060.8
shiny,adj., 1065.50
~, like gold, 1013.17
become ~, 1065.60
black and ~, 490.1(13)
make ~, 1065.54
~ ornament, 1065.62
ornament with ~ things,
 1065.63
put a ~ surface on, 1009.50
round and ~, 508.1(1)
rub until ~, 438.1(6,7,10,16,17,
 24,25,32)
small plate of ~ metal,
 519.5(3)
soft and ~, 443.1(12,14)
~ thing, 1065.62
~ with, or like, stars, 1056.33
ship,n., 115.1,7; see also **boat,n.**
advantageous position of a
 ~, 1042.17
armed ~, 115.16–18
back of a ~, toward the,
 184.6
back part of a ~, 184.1(5)
bedroom on a ~, 787.7(9,36)
board a ~, 115.8

bottom of ~, 169.4(7)
builder of ~s, 115.11,12
carry by ~, 115.13
Chinese ~, 115.20(8)
control a ~, 8.1(19)
destroy a ~ at sea, 801.1(9)
diving ~, 115.7(4)
floating wreckage of a ~,
 113.12(6)
~ for ice breaking, 1040.25
~ for ice sailing, 1040.24
front part of a ~, 185.10–12
go by ~, 115.25; see sail,v.
group of ~s, 115.22
group of merchant ~s,
 115.22(1,2)
group of naval ~s, 115.18
group of war~s, 115.18
left side of a ~, 179.23(1,2)
loader of ~s, 925.14
movement of a ~, 1029.17
naval ~, 115.16,18
officer of a ~, 116.6
pearl-fishing ~, 963.14
personnel of a ~, 116.4,5
pert. to ~s, 115.23,24
pirate ~, 115.15
position for a ~, instrument
 to determine, 1053.34,35
~ repair, place of, 1033.20,21
right side of a ~, 179.21
~'s rate, record of, 99.5(1)
~s, 115.2
sailing ~, 115.20; 1043.25
science of building ~s,
 727.10(4)
seal-hunting ~, 486.11(8)
seller of ~s, 115.11
send by ~, 115.13
slow ~, 100.9
space for a ~ to move,
 787.1(3)
unloader of ~s, 925.14
war~, 115.16,18
war~s, group of, 115.18
war~s, pert. to, 115.19
~ with a guiding light,
 1065.110
worker on a ~, 115.11; see
 also sailor,n.
shipwrecked,adj.
~ person, 330.7(6)
shirk,v., 76.1(4)
shirker,n., 76.3(1)
shirt,n.
collarless ~, 982.18
formal ~ for men, 975.7
front of a ~, 982.16
maker of a ~, 205.5(15)
men's ~s, 974.22
shiver,n., 111.2; 576.4
shiver,v., 111.1; 576.3; see also
 fear, shake,v.
shivers,n., 576.2
shoal,n., 170.13; 1029.100(1,12–
 14,16)
full of ~s, 170.15
shock,n., 1097.15,16; 1132.16
blow, 437.2
fear, 576.2
surprise, 271.3
~ of collision, 436.4
produce ~, use of techniques
 to, 1100.9
shock,v., 22.25; 881.1(6) ;
 1097.13; 1132.17
surprise, 271.2
frighten, 576.6
shocked,adj., 1097.14
frightened, 576.1
surprised, 271.4
shocking,adj., 881.12; 1132.15
frightening, 576.7
surprising, 271.1
use of ~ techniques, 1100.9

shod,adj., 979.4
shoe,n., 979.2
baby's ~, 979.2(4)
coarse ~s, 979.5
covering for a ~, 979.20
dry ~s, having, 1038.13
heavy ~s, 979.5
hit with the ~, 979.12
Indian ~, 979.2(12)
maker of ~s, 205.5(16)
Mexican ~s, 979.24
polisher of ~s, 979.7
push with the ~, 979.12
put ~s on, 979.3
rain ~s, 979.8
repair ~s, 832.14
repairer of ~s, 205.5(2,16) ;
 832.15
~s, collectively, 979.1
snow ~s, 979.8
tragic drama, ~ as symbol
 of, 979.2(8)
wearing ~s, 979.4
without ~s, 979.13
wooden ~, 979.2(17)
shoe,v., 979.3
shoeless,adj., 979.13
shoot,v., 565.3
~ an arrow, 566.14
~ from a bow, 565.3(5,17)
shooter,n., 565.6
shooting,n., 565.4,8
art of ~, 565.8
science of ~, 565.7
shop,n., 203.11; 212.7
shop,v., 211.1
shopper,n., 211.4
shopping,n., 211.2
addiction to ~, 211.7
shore,n., 1029.43,79
along the ~, 1029.87
away from the ~, 1029.92,93
come to ~, 999.6
come up on the ~, 1029.94
following the ~, 1029.90
go along the ~ of, 1029.86
~ line, 1029.83
~ line, former, 1029.84
living along the ~ (of birds),
 1029.97
on the ~, 1029.91,96
outline of the ~, 1029.85
river ~, 1029.43
river ~, owner of, 1029.45
river ~, pert. to, 1029.44
run or drive (a ship) up on
 the ~, 1029.94
toward the ~, 1029.88,89
short,adj., 514.1; 911.1
~ and to the point, 911.1(5,7,
 8,14,15,17,19)
become ~er, 911.6
cut (hair) ~, 911.13
cut ~ (of the hair), 1043.22
cut the tail ~, 911.8,12
~ end, 792.10(3,4)
~ in appearance, 514.1
make ~er, 911.2
~ person, 514.2
shorten,v., 911.2
decrease, 910.1,2
~ a word, 911.2(2)
~ an account or story,
 911.2(1–3,5,6)
~ material, 911.2(1–3,5,6)
shortened,adj., 911.1
~ by omission of end,
 911.1(11)
~ by omission of letters,
 911.1(1,6,16)
~ by omission of parts,
 911.1(3,4,6,10,12,13,17,18)
~ by omission of syllables,
 911.1(16)

~ by omission of words,
911.1(2,10)
~ form, 911.3
~ in pronunciation, 911.1(16)
~ version, 911.3
shortening,n.
~ of a syllable in poetry,
911.15
shorthand,n., 682.12(4–8) ; see
also stenography,n.
manuscript in ~, 684.1(8)
something written in ~,
682.13
shortsighted,adj., 481.9
shot,n., 565.5,10,11
sound of ~s, 463.1(33)
sound of a ~, 463.1(28)
shoulder,n.
~ blade, 339.7
garment around the ~s,
977.6,7
gesture with the ~s, 102.1(10)
pert. to the ~, 339.6
shout,n., 463.1; 464.1
~ of excitement or enthusiasm, 1095.13
shout,v., 463.2; 464.2
~ approval, 850.5
~ enthusiastically, 1095.10,12
~ in excitement, 1095.12
~ in exultation, 1102.9
shouting,n., 464.1
descr. of ~, 464.3
show,n., 951.2,3; see also display, exhibition, expo-
sure,n.
drama, entertainment, etc.,
969.1; see drama, performance (theatrical),n.
empty ~, 951.3(9,11,13–16,18,
23,24)
fine ~, 951.47
mere ~, 951.50
place for a ~, 951.28
show,v., 951.1
~ accidentally, 951.1(8) ;
951.25
~ anger, 878.6; 951.22,23
~ as a result, 951.1(5)
~ boastfully, 951.1(23,24,31,
39) ; 951.32,33
~ body publicly, 951.31
~ by example, 951.1(19)
~ by gesture, 951.1(24,42,43)
~ by waving, 951.1(24)
~ clearly, 951.1(10,17,18,27)
~ conspicuously, 951.1(2,9,15,
16,22–24,31,33,38,39,43,45,
55)
~ emotion (suppressed),
951.22
~ faults of, 951.1(21,40)
~ gradually, 951.1(13,53)
~ happiness, 951.23
~ humor, 951.23
~ image of, 951.1(29,37)
~ in advance, 951.1(1,35)
~ incompletely, 951.1(1)
~ indirectly, 951.1(47)
~ itself suddenly, 951.24
~ obscurely, 951.1(1,47)
~ off, 951.1(2,15,20,21,23,24,31,
33) ; 951.32
~ off, tendency to, 951.31
~ off, walk up and down to,
951.33
~ oneself by walking, 951.33
~ points of interest, 848.29
~ presence of, 951.1(5,7,25,28,
37,41,42,44,48,50)
~ publicly, 951.1(15,20,30,34,
35,38,46,56)
~ secrets, 951.1(6,8,14,21,26,
38,40,51,52,54,56)
serving to ~, 951.5

~ symbolically, 954.8
~ symptomatically, 951.1(25)
showily,adv.
~ ornamented, 959.8(1)
showiness,n., 951.35
cheap or vulgar ~, 951.42
showing,adj., 951.5; see indicative,adj.
showing,n., 951.2
place of ~, 951.28
shown,adj.
able to be ~, 951.6
be ~, 951.26
that which is publicly ~,
951.16
wordlessly ~, 951.27
showy,adj., 951.34
be ~, 951.37
bright and ~, 951.34(3,5)
ceremonious and ~, 951.38
cheap, ~ ornamentation,
959.7
cheap and ~ thing, 951.36(1)
cheaply ~, 951.41
cheaply ~ person, 951.43
~ display, 951.40
formal and ~, 951.38
~ in clothing or dress, 974.12
~ in language, 665.10(2,3,5) ;
951.48,49
~ in style, 951.48,49
~ in writing, 951.48,49
inferior and ~, 951.34(1)
inferior and ~ thing,
951.36(3)
~ language, 664.1(19,20)
~ language, use of, 665.9(6,18,
20,21,24,25,35–37,54–56,61)
make ~, 951.44
~ ornament, 959.5
~ ornaments, 951.46; 959.6
~ person, 951.39,43
self-important and ~, 951.38
stylish and ~, 951.45
~ things, 951.36
vulgar, ~ ornamentation,
959.7
vulgarly ~, 951.41
vulgarly ~ person, 951.39,43
wealthy person of ~ tastes,
1109.9
worthless and ~, 888.2;
951.34(1,4)
worthless and ~ thing,
888.10; 951.36(1,3)
shrew (animal),n.
like a ~, 403.12
of the ~s, 403.11(15)
shrew (woman),n., 876.4; 895.7
shrewd,adj., 595.1,2
be ~er than, 595.6
~ person, 595.4
shrewdness,n., 595.3
without ~, 595.7
shrewish,adj., 876.1; 895.6
shriek,n., 464.1; 465.1
shriek,v., 464.2; 465.2
shrill,adj., 332.25; 465.3
shrimp (animal),n., 422.3
of ~, 403.6(1) ; 422.1(13)
science of ~s, 403.26(10,12)
shrink,v., 910.1,2
dry and ~, 1038.1(8,13,14)
~ in fear, 145.1(3,4,6–9,11,17,
19,25,27,28) ; 576.3
~ in pain, 145.1(3,7,9,25,27) ;
1137.19
shrivel,v.
decay, 806.1,2
dry, 1038.1,2
wrinkle, 158.1,2
shrub,n., 985.6(6)
area of ~s, 985.34(18,19)
boundary of ~s, 996.30
covered with ~s, 996.50

cultivation of ~s, 996.60
enclose with ~s, 996.31
fence of ~s, 996.30
fence with ~s, 996.31
grow ~s, 998.1(8,11,15)
growth of ~s, 996.27,28
place or tract of ~s, 996.29
raise ~s, 998.1(8,11,15)
row of ~s, 996.30
science of ~s, 996.64(2)
shelter of ~s, 993.10,11
surround with ~s, 996.31
trained ~s, 991.18
training ~s, 998.1(15)
shudder,n., 111.2; 576.4
shudder,v., 111.1; 576.3
shut,adj., 297.3
shut,v., 297.1,2; see also close,v.
~ in, 301.1; see confine,v.
~ off, 296.8
~ out, 296.1; see exclude,v.
~ out from social or other
relations, 296.1(9) ;
581.6(8) ; 581.11,12
~ out of sight, 296.1(3)
~ the eyes of, 481.8
shy (bashful),adj., 873.14
~ person, 873.15
pretendedly ~, 873.16
Siam,n., 784.9(16,20)
Siamese,adj., 784.16
Siamese,n., 784.15(53)
Sicily,n.
pert. to ~, 784.16(5)
sick,adj., 389.2; see ill,adj.
sickly,adj., 389.2; see ill,adj.
~ of complexion, 384.15
sickness,n., 389.1; see disease,
illness,n.
sickroom,n.
pert. to a ~, 389.12
side,n., 186.1
animal's ~, 186.1(5,6)
back ~, 186.1(2,9)
bodily region of the back and
~s, 345.19
figurative ~, 186.1(1,4)
flat ~, 186.1(8)
front ~, 186.1(7)
guard the ~ of, 568.24
having ~s, 186.5
having equal ~s, 534.10
hog's ~, 186.1(6)
involving one ~ only, 186.6
involving two ~s, 186.7
move from ~ to side, 186.9;
see also sway, swing,v.
move the head to the ~,
186.8(2)
move to the ~, 186.8
~ of a window, doorway, fireplace, etc., 1009.13
~ of bacon, 186.1(6)
~ of a coin with main design,
186.1(7)
~ of a medal with main design, 186.1(7)
on the farther ~, 789.2
pain in the ~, 1137.56(26)
pert. to the ~, 186.2
principal ~, 186.1(3)
situated at the ~, 186.3
turned to one ~, 148.10(1,2)
side-by-side,adj., 186.4; 790.23
put ~, 323.1(3,10,42) ; 790.24
-sided,adj., 186.5
equal-~, 186.5(2)
four-~, 186.5(6,7)
many-~, 186.5(3–5)
one-~, 186.5(9)
three-~, 186.5(8)
two-~, 186.5(1)
siege,n., 300.2; 560.2
pert. to a ~, 300.6; 560.19
siege,v., 300.1(2,5) ; 560.1(7,26)

sigh,n., 376.3(1)
  sound of a ~, 376.6(4)
sigh,v., 376.1(22)
  ~ for, 265.1; see desire,v.
sight,n., 480.2,4; see also see-
    ing, view, vision,n.
  a ~, 483.8
  catch ~ of, 480.1
  clear to the ~, 483.1
  lost to the ~, 483.12(9)
  obtained through ~, 480.7
  power of ~, 480.5
  shut out of ~, 296.1(3)
sight-seeing,n.
  bus for ~, 192.6(6)
  guide for ~, 177.3(1)
sign,n., 951.4; see also signal,n.
  analysis of ~s, 951.14
  approval, ~ of, 850.14
  arm, ~ on the, 951.4(6)
  art of ~s, 951.13
  art of ~s by fingers, 951.15
  as a ~ of, 951.7
  bad ~s, under, 36.3(4–6,10,14)
  bastardy, ~ of, 951.4(4,5)
  be a ~ of, 951.1(5,11,25,27,37,
    41–44,48–50)
  belief, ~ of, 951.4(3)
  characteristic ~, 951.4(14)
  description of ~s, 951.14
  disease, ~ of, 951.4(24)
  external ~, 951.4(2,10,17,26)
  favorable ~, 951.4(1)
  fear, ~ of, 576.4
  friendship, ~ of, 951.4(26)
  future, ~ of the, 773.2,3,6;
    951.4(1,9,18,20)
  future, give or be a ~ of the,
    773.1
  give ~s of, 951.1(7,28,49,50)
  give ~s of the future, 773.1
  giving ~s of the future,
    773.4,5
  identifying ~, 951.4(8,10,16,
    17)
  language of ~s, 951.12
  language of ~s, pert. to,
    664.2(3)
  luck, ~ of, 951.4(18)
  meaning of ~s, 951.12
  membership, ~ of, 951.4(2,6,
    10,11,15,16,23)
  name, ~ for one's, 951.4(17)
  noble rank, ~ of, 951.4(7)
  office, ~ of, 951.4(2,6,10,11,15,
    16,23); 951.9
  past, ~ of the, 951.4(27)
  pert. to ~s, 951.12
  precede as a ~, 175.1(3,5,7,8,
    12,15)
  profession, ~ of, 951.4(22)
  quality, ~ of, 951.4(12)
  rank, ~ of, 951.4(15); 951.9
  royalty, ~s of, 951.9
  science of ~, 951.13
  secret, ~ of a, 951.4(25)
  tell by ~s, 613.17(12)
  threatening ~, 573.4
  warning ~, 574.2; 574.6(6)
  worth, ~ of, 951.4(2)
sign,v., 696.1; see also signa-
    ture,n.
  ~ another's name illegally,
    696.1(6)
  ~ as witness, 696.1(1,9)
  ~ on the back of, 696.1(5)
  ~ one's name, 696.1
signal,n., 956.1; see also sign,n.
  arms, ~ with, 956.1(7)
  art of ~s, 951.13
  ~ bell, 956.6(1)
  bells, ~ by, 956.1(13,14)
  bugle, ~ on, 956.1(11,12)
  dismissing ~, 956.1(14)

dots and dashes, system of
    ~s by, 956.11
  drums, ~ on, 956.1(11,12)
  eye, ~ by, 956.1(17)
  fife, ~ on, 956.1(12)
  ~ fire, 956.1(2) ; 1064.1(1,2,4)
  fire, ~ from, 956.6(3)
  flag, ~ by, 956.1(15,16)
  flags, system of ~s by,
    956.9,12
  gesture, ~ by, 956.1(7,10,15,
    16)
  guiding ~, 956.1(2)
  hands, ~ with, 956.1(7)
  head, ~ with, 956.1(7)
  ~ light, 956.1(2,8,16) ; 956.6(2)
  lights out, ~ for, 956.1(11) ;
    1065.112
  mirror, ~ by, 956.1(8)
  mirror, system of ~s by,
    956.10
  mourning, ~ of, 957.13
  passing, secret ~ for,
    956.1(4)
  prayer, ~ for, 956.6(1)
  sea, ~ of trouble at, 957.15
  shaking, ~ by, 956.1(15,16)
  sound, ~ by, 956.6(5)
  streets, ~ to clear, 956.1(5)
  summoning ~, 956.1(3,14)
  summoning ~ for soldiers,
    956.1(12)
  surrender, ~ of, 957.11
  system of ~s, 956.8
  system of ~s by dots and
    dashes, 956.11
  system of ~s by flags, 956.9,
    12
  system of ~s by mirror,
    956.10
  system of ~s in telegraphy,
    956.11
  telegraphy, system of ~s in,
    956.11
  waken, ~ to, 956.1(9)
  warning ~, 574.6; 956.1(1,2,6,
    13) ; 956.6(5)
  warning ~ in fog, 956.1(6) ;
    1041.8
signal,v., 956.2–4
  ~ by blowing, 1043.9
  ~ by flag, 956.2(1,2)
  ~ by sound, 956.3(1)
signaler,n., 956.6,7
signaling,n., 956.5
  act of ~, 956.5
  device for ~, 956.6
signature,n., 696.2; see also
    sign,v.
  copy another's ~ illegally,
    696.1(6)
  document written by another,
    pert. to someone's ~ on,
    696.4(1)
  passport ~, 696.2(2)
  ~s in a circle, complaint
    with, 1120.3(5)
signer,n., 696.3
signing,adj., 696.4
signing,n., 696.1
  pert. to ~, 696.4
signpost,n., 997.5(3,15)
silence,n., 475.2
silence,v., 475.5
silent,adj., 475.1
  unspoken, 475.1(18,21,22) ;
    475.8,10; 607.6
  angry and ~, 475.1(16,17) ;
    878.10(2,5)
  angry and ~ person, 878.16
  become ~, 475.6
  make ~, 475.5
  ~ person, 475.3; 604.10; 671.22
  tending to be ~, 475.4
silk,n.

like ~, 373.4
  pert. to ~, 373.3
  production of ~, 373.5
  sound of ~, 469.1(16,18–20,22)
silkworm,n.
  raising of ~s, 403.30(6)
silky,adj., 373.4
silly,adj.
  nonsensical, 608.5; see ab-
    surd, foolish, nonsensical,
    adj.
  stupid, 597.1; see stupid,adj.
  ~ and flirtatious woman,
    608.21
  conceited, ~ person, 608.20
  ~ people, 608.22
  ~ person, 608.16
  ~ talk, 607.26,28–31
  ~ talk, given to, 607.32
silver,n., 1015.1
  become ~ in color, 1015.13
  change into ~, 1013.25
  coat with ~, 1015.10
  coated with ~, 1015.10
  containing ~, 1015.7
  give a ~ color to, 1015.12
  gold-coated ~, 1013.10
  ~ in bars, 1015.2
  ~ in color, 1015.6
  ~ in sound, 1015.5
  inferior to ~, 883.2
  like ~, 1015.4
  made of ~, 1015.9
  maker or seller of ~, 1015.17
  metal resembling ~, 1016.2(4)
  objects of ~, 1015.14
  of pure ~, 1015.11
  ornamentation on ~, 1015.18
  pert. to ~, 1015.3
  pure ~, 1015.1
  refine ~, 1015.15
  refining vessel for ~, 1015.16
  science of production of ~,
    213.20(1)
  yielding ~, 1015.8
similar,adj., 529.1; see also
    same,adj.
  be ~, 529.4; see also copy,
    imitate,v.
  become ~, 529.4
  made up of ~ things or peo-
    ple, 529.6
  make ~, 529.5; see also copy,
    imitate,v.
  one who is ~, 529.3
  that which is ~, 529.3
similarity,n., 529.2; see also
    resemblance,n.
  find points of ~, 529.12
  ~ of interests, 529.7
  show points of ~, 529.12
simple,adj., 960.1,4
  countrified, 960.1(5)
  easy, 26.1
  not complex or compound,
    960.4
  not elaborate, 960.1
  primitive, 960.1(5)
  rough, 960.1(5)
  unfinished, 960.1(5)
  unornamented, 959.9
  advocate of ~ life, 960.8
  charming and ~, 960.1(4)
  deceptively ~, 823.8
  ~ in literary or artistic style,
    960.3
  ~ (of facts, truths, state-
    ments), 959.11
  plain and ~, 960.1(3)
  powerful and ~, 960.5
  severely ~, 960.1(1,6)
simplest,adj.
  ~ part, 326.9(5)
simplicity,n., 960.2,4
  advocate of ~, 960.8,9

pretense of ~, 960.7
simplify,v., 960.6
simultaneous,adj., 764.4
sin,n., 884.2
  admission of ~, 884.24
  admit ~, 884.23
  atone for ~, 845.20,22
  feeling of ~, 884.12–14,18
  free of ~, 845.6–9,17; 884.15;
    897.24,28
  free of moral ~, 845.15
  free oneself of ~, 845.19
  guilty of ~, 884.9
  involve in ~, 522.1(3–5)
  involvement in ~, 522.3
  lead into ~, 176.1(2,10,13)
  make amends for ~, 845.20,22
  not liable to ~, 845.7
  place of ~, 883.37
  punishment, ~ that brings,
    884.5
  reject because of ~, 884.11
  relapse into ~, 145.1(1,15)
  return to ~, 145.2(2)
  roll about in ~, 151.1(12)
  seven deadly ~s, 884.4
  slight ~, 884.3
  sorry for ~, 884.17
  tempted by ~, 884.8
  uneasiness over ~, 884.18
  wash away ~, 845.17
  without ~, 845.1,6,9
  without feeling of ~, 884.15,22
sin,v., 884.1
  determine not to ~, 45.3
  liable to ~, 884.8
sincere,adj., 807.3; 813.7
  eager and ~, 265.19(14)
sincerely,adv., 813.9
sincerity,n., 807.3; 813.8
sinful,adj., 883.22; 884.10; see
  also **immoral,**adj.
  ~ behavior, 55.3(11);
    1087.7(7)
  desire ~ly, 265.1(4,15)
  ~ desire, 265.2(29)
  ~ly desirous, 265.3(7)
sing,v., 476.1; see also **song,**n.
  ~ praises of, 851.1(1,7,9)
  ~ without preparation,
    48.9(2)
singer,n., 476.3,22
  group of ~s, 476.19
  leader of ~s, 476.20
  melody ~, 478.6
  voice of a ~, 476.21
singing,n., 476.2; see also
  song,n.
  art of ~, 476.11,12
  pert. to ~, 476.13–15
  ~ voice, 476.21
  ~ voice, descr. of a, 476.23
single,adj., 930.3
sink,v., 167.1; see also **fall,**v.
  cause to ~, 167.4
  ~ from fatigue, 167.1(15)
  ~ in the middle, 167.1(27)
  ~ in water, 167.1(39)
  ~ into mud, 167.1(23);
    1000.10,19
  ~ (nail, etc.) below surface,
    167.4(1)
  ~ to the bottom, 167.1(28,38)
sinless,adj., 845.1,6,9
  make ~, 845.15
  ~ person, 845.7
sinner,n., 884.6
sinning,adj., 884.7
sip,v., 748.1; see **drink,**v.
sister,n., 722.11
  like a ~, 722.7(13)
  pert. to a ~, 722.7(13,14)
sit,v., 62.1
  babies, ~ with, 62.1(1)
  bar, ~ on a, 62.1(8,9)

bird, ~ like a, 62.1(8,9)
  ~ close, 62.1(7)
  eggs, ~ on, 62.1(3–5,10)
  floor, ~ on the, 62.1(12)
  legs spread, ~ with, 62.1(13)
  pole, ~ on a, 62.1(8,9)
sitter,n., 62.3
sitting,adj., 62.4
sitting,n.
  a ~, 62.5,6
  a ~ with a corpse, 62.6
  accustomed to ~, 62.9
  adapted for ~ on a perch,
    62.7
  characterized by ~, 62.8
  manner of ~, 62.2
  pert. to ~, 62.8
  pert. to ~ on a perch, 62.7
  requiring ~, 62.8
situate,v., 323.1
situated,adj.
  ~ at extreme point, 922.11
  ~ away from the main part,
    323.13
situation,n., 323.2,4
  job, 203.11; 205.18
  position, 782.3,20
  state, 44.1
  complicated ~, 25.9(2,7,18)
  difficult ~, 25.9
  embarrassing ~, 25.9(4)
  ~ in which one is caught,
    244.7
  unpleasant ~, 25.9(11,13)
six, n. or adj., 935.1
  consisting of ~ parts, 935.5
  divided into ~ parts, 935.5
  group of ~, 935.3
  multiply by ~, 935.6
  number ~, 935.1,2
  ~ times as great, 935.8
six hundred,n.
  pert. to ~, 940.28
sixfold, adj. or adv., 935.4
  increase ~, 907.9(8)
sixty, n. or adj., 940.12
  based on ~, 940.14
  by ~, 940.15
  consisting of ~, 940.15
  pert. to ~, 940.13
  ~-year-old person, 758.2(7)
sizable,adj., 906.3
size,n., 906.1
  land ~, 946.39
  measurement of ~, 946.50
  space, ~ that occupies,
    906.2
skate,v.
  floor or building for ~ing,
    1025.6,7
  ~ on ice, 1040.15
skating,n.
  ice-~ place, 1040.14
  ice for ~, 1040.13
skeptic,n., 639.5
skeptical,adj., 639.3
skepticism,n., 639.4
  with ~, 639.9
sketch,n., 965.1(6,12,17,56); see
  also **drawing, picture,**n.
sketch,v., 965.3
  book in which to ~, 965.17
skiing,n.
  ~ race, 979.11
skill,n., 7.1
  act requiring ~, 7.7(4)
  act showing ~, 7.7
  area of ~, 7.4
  artistic ~, 7.1(67); 965.28
  boats, ~ in, 115.6
  creative ~, 7.1(45)
  deception, ~ in, 7.1(27)
  difficult situations, ~ in,
    7.1(6,12,38,57)
  doing, ~ in, 7.1(59)

done with ~, 7.6
  field, ~ in a, 7.1(49)
  finger ~, 949.10
  forest ~, 7.1(69)
  hand ~, 7.1(6,7,15,18,28,30,43,
    44)
  hunting ~, 7.1(69)
  instinctive ~, 7.1(8)
  inventive ~, 7.1(45)
  lack of ~, 14.2
  made with ~, 7.6
  magic ~, 7.1(68)
  management ~, 7.1(55)
  manual ~, 7.1(6,7,15,18,28,30,
    43,44)
  many directions, ~ in,
    7.1(65)
  music ~, 7.1(67); 965.28
  natural ~, 7.1(9,16,34,66)
  new things, ~ in, 7.1(45,46)
  people, ~ with, 7.1(29,31,32,
    61)
  performance ~, 7.1(67)
  physical ~, 7.1(51)
  planning ~, 7.1(59)
  requiring ~, 7.8
  saying proper thing, ~ in,
    7.1(29,58,61)
  show ~, 7.5
  showing ~, 7.6
  social manners, ~ in, 7.1(2)
  speed and ~, 7.1(51)
  structural ~, 7.1(11); 727.8
  subject, ~ in a, 7.1(49)
  token of ~, 951.8
  touch, ~ of, 7.1(29)
  trapping ~, 7.1(69)
  wood, ~ with, 7.1(69)
  worker's ~, 7.1(70)
skillful,adj., 7.2
  ~ act, 52.5(27,39,40)
  become ~, 7.10
  ~ in humor, 949.12
  ~ in irony, 949.12
  ~ in language, 7.2(3)
  ~ in stealing, 7.2(4)
  ~ in style, 949.12
  ~ in touch, 949.11
  make ~, 7.11
  ~ manager, 7.3(7)
  ~ maneuverer, 7.3(7)
  ~ person, 7.3
  practice, ~ through, 7.2(8)
skin,n., 382.1; see also **flesh,**n.
  animals' ~s, 382.1(10,15,20);
    382.3(2); 386.1–5,15; see
    also **leather,**n.
  appearance of the ~, 384.1
  ~ around fingernail, 382.1(1,
    4,9)
  art of stuffing animal ~s,
    382.10
  between layers of ~, 382.7
  blueness of ~, 384.2
  broken or bruised ~, 382.11(2,
    3,14,18,32,33,37,39,48)
  brownish-yellow spot on the
    ~, 384.26
  bruise on the ~, 803.16,17
  cheese ~, 382.1(17); 972.4(15)
  color of ~, 384.1; see **com-
    plexion,**n.
  design pricked into the ~,
    311.8(10)
  discarded ~s, 285.1(8,34)
  diseases of, or affecting, the
    ~, 382.11,16–18,22,24
  dryness of ~, 382.11(29,56);
    1038.8
  fold of ~, 157.8; 382.4
  ~ for bookbinding, 382.1(20)
  ~ for parchment, 382.1(20)
  fruit ~, 382.1(13); 972.4(9–11,
    13–15,19–23)
  growth on the ~, 731.21(3,9)

hardness of ~, 382.11(4,5,7, 13,21,30,45)
injury on the ~, 803.16,17,19
injury penetrating the ~, 803.18
itchiness of the ~, 382.11(12, 22,34,35,42)
like ~, 382.6
lose ~, 286.1(33,37,53) ; 972.10,11
lost ~, 382.1(19) ; 382.3(1) ; 972.12
mark burned on the ~, 503.1(4,11)
mark on the ~, 503.1(12)
mark on the ~ from birth, 503.1(2)
naked ~, 984.22
~ on top of head, 382.1(18)
opening in the ~, 298.8(11)
ornament the ~, 959.1(28)
pert. to the ~, 382.2
rash on the ~, 382.11(14,17, 28,32,39,40,43,44)
remove the ~ from, 972.6,8
scales of animal ~, 355.8
scales of dead ~, 382.5
science of the ~, 401.1(11)
seed ~, 972.4(9–11,13–15,19–23)
sensation on the ~, 434.1(1–9, 12,13,15)
shed ~, 286.1(33,37,53) ; 972.10,11
spots on ~, 501.1(7,8) ; 501.3(3,6) ; 501.4
spotted by ~ disease, 501.1(12)
streak left on the ~, 502.1(10, 12–14)
thickness of ~, 382.11(4,5,7, 13,19,30)
tropical ~ disease, 382.11(16, 57)
under the ~, 382.8,9
wrinkle in ~, 158.4
skinny,adj., 513.1; see **thin**,adj.
skirt,n., 982.11
bow at back of ~, 982.12
decoration at back of ~, 982.12
draw one's ~ up, 982.13
fullness at back of ~, 982.12
man's ~, 982.11(5)
Polynesian ~, 982.11(9)
Samoan ~, 982.11(6)
Scotsman's ~, 982.11(5)
Tahitian ~, 982.11(9)
under~, 981.3(10,14)
skull,n., 356.1
base of the ~, pert. to, 356.3
having a ~, 356.4
measure the ~, instrument to, 356.8
opening in infant's ~, 356.6
opening in the ~, 298.8(1,14)
parts of the ~, 356.2
science of the ~, 356.7
study of ~ shape, 356.7(4)
unusual ~ conditions, 356.5
skullcap,n., 983.2(3,6,24,48,55)
barrister's ~, 983.2(16)
skunk,n.
of ~s, 403.11(9,10)
sky,n., 1051.1,5,6; see also **heaven, heavens**,n.
body in the ~, 1053.1
boundary between earth and ~, 1051.9
description of the ~, 682.15(25)
falling particles from the ~, 1053.6
from the ~, 1051.3
in the ~, 1051.3

light in the ~, 1065.1
outline against the ~, 1051.11
pert. to the ~, 1051.2
toward the ~, 1051.12
~writing, 1051.13
slander,n., 891.18
slander,v., 891.17
slanderous,adj., 891.19
slant,n., 154.3; see **slope**,n.
slant,v., 154.1,2; see **slope**,v.
slanting,adj., 154.4
~ down, 154.4(2,4,5)
in a ~ direction, 154.6
slate,n.
~ for chalk writing, 1006.44
slaughter,v., 796.2; see **kill**,ing,n.
slaughter,v., 796.1; see **kill**,v.
slaughterhouse,n., 796.19(3,4)
goat that leads sheep into a ~, 176.3(14)
slave,n., 8.19; 310.5,9
chained ~s, 310.10
feudal ~, 1074.14
fugitive ~, 310.6
government by ~s, 1073.42(5)
harem ~, 310.8
like a ~, 310.11
make a ~ of, 310.1
mental ~, 310.7
moral ~, 310.7
pert. to ~s, 310.11
slavery,n., 310.2,4
bonds of ~, 310.13
causing ~, 310.12
elimination of ~ in the U.S., 309.9
free from ~, 309.1(1,5,6,10,12)
mental ~, 310.3
moral ~, 310.3
symbol of ~, 310.13
Slavic,adj.
~ characteristics, character, culture, etc., 1091.29
fondness for ~ people, customs, etc., 700.30(25) ; 700.31
slay,v., 796.1; see **kill**,v.
slayer,n., 796.3; see **killer**,n.
sled,n., 192.20
drive or ride a ~, 192.21
driver or rider of a ~, 192.22
sleep,n., 67.2
cause of ~, 67.18
causing ~, 67.17
condition causing ~, 67.15
deep ~, 67.2(1,4,6,7)
disorder of ~, 67.16
driving ~ away, 72.13
~-drunkenness, 67.14
falling into ~, 67.21
garments for ~, 974.44,45
go to ~, 67.1(1,6)
god of ~, 67.22
hypnotic ~, 67.2(1,4,7)
hypnotic ~, science of, 67.19
like ~, 67.20
pert. to ~, 67.23
put oneself (to ~) by weeping, 1127.13
resembling ~, 67.20
science of ~, 67.19
short ~, 67.2(2,3)
song to put to ~, 476.4(7,29) ; 1139.4(5)
spirit who puts children to ~, 662.7(36)
state of ~, 67.2
state resembling ~, 67.5
unbroken ~, 67.7
~-walking, 107.3(1,2)
sleep,v., 67.1
furnish place to ~, 233.1(1)
inability to ~, 72.7

likes to ~, one who, 67.13
place to ~, 68.1
sleepiness,n., 67.9
cause of ~, 67.18
causing ~, 67.17
gesture in ~, 102.1(6)
unnatural ~, 67.12,14
sleeping,adj., 67.3
sleeping,n.
meals and ~ quarters, 740.17
plan of ~ to improve health, 740.13
provide with meals and ~ quarters, 740.18
room for ~, 787.7(6,9,27,36)
sleeping sickness,n., 357.10(7)
sleepy,adj., 67.8
be ~, 67.10
person who is ~, 67.13
unnaturally ~, 67.11
usually ~, 67.13
sleet,n.
fall like ~, 1037.5
sleeve,n.
short ~, 978.4,5
types of ~s, 978.6
upper opening of the ~, 978.9
wrist, part of ~ over the, 978.7,8
sleight of hand,n., 663.18
slender,adj., 513.1; see **thin**, adj.
slice,n., 326.10
cut into ~s, 332.1(4,53,58)
~ of meat, 326.10(18) ; 743.3
small ~, 326.10(5)
thick ~, 326.10(27)
transverse ~, 326.10(6)
slice,v., 326.12,13; 332.1(4,53) ; see also **cut**,v.
slide,n., 90.2; 167.2
projector of lighted ~s, 1065.108
slide,v., 90.1,2; 167.1
slight,adj.
~ in degree, 909.11,12
~ like a shadow, 1071.3
~ in size, 909.1
slight,n., 581.8; 867.2
slight,v.
ignore, 581.6
insult, 867.1
neglect, 582.1
slim,adj., 513.1; see **thin**,adj.
strong and ~, 1.1(9)
slimy,adj., 302.24(9–12,14)
slingshot,n., 565.20
missile from a ~, 565.21
slipper,n., 979.2(1,11–13,15,19–21,23)
slippery,adj., 439.5
make ~, 439.2(5,7)
~ place, 439.6
smooth and ~, 439.5(1)
~ surface, 139.1(10)
slogan,n., 676.1; see **saying**,n.
slope,n., 154.3
downward ~, 154.3(2–4,6)
grassy ~, 986.15
instrument to measure ~, 154.5
upward ~, 154.3(1,6–8,11,12)
slope,v., 154.1,2
~ down, 154.1(6–10,13)
~ up, 154.1(1)
sloping,adj., 154.4
~ down, 154.4(2,4,5)
sloth (animal),n.
of ~s, 403.11(3)
sloven,n., 903.4
slovenly,adj., 903.1(2,8–12,18,19)
~ person, 903.4
~ woman, 903.4
slow,adj., 100.6

~ (in music), 100.10
mentally ~, 100.6(23)
move ~ly, 85.1(2,6)
~ movement, 100.1,2
~-moving, 100.6
~ person, 100.8
~ ship, 100.9
~ vehicle, 100.9
slow,v., 100.3,5
~ the growth of, 100.5(2);
731.28
~ the progress of, 100.5(1,2)
slowed,adj., 100.6
slower,adj., 100.6
~ action, 100.4
~ movement, 100.4
~ than sound, 99.7(2)
slower, adv. or adj.
act, do, go, or move ~, 100.3
cause to be ~, 100.5
slowly,adv.
act ~, 100.1,2
come ~, 118.1(19)
do ~, 100.1,2
go ~, 100.1,2; 119.1(15,52)
~ (in music), 100.10
move ~, 100.1,2
stepping ~, 100.6(29)
slowness,n., 100.7
sluggish,adj., 58.1; see inactive,
adj.
~ because soaked, 1034.26
slumber,n., 67.2; see sleep,n.
slumber,v., 67.1; see sleep,v.
slur,n., 891.18
slur,v., 891.17
sly,adj.
clever, 595.1,2
deceptive, 823.7
secret, 971.10,11,13
small,adj., 909.1
abnormally ~, 909.1(1,4,5,9,
18,20–23,25,32)
active and ~, 57.4(7);
909.1(3)
~ amount, 917.1
~ animal, 909.4
become ~, 909.7
~ by contrast, 909.9
~ child, 909.3(17)
contemptible and ~ person,
909.3(14)
contemptible and ~ thing,
909.5(10)
cramped and ~, 909.1(19)
delicate and ~, 11.1(4);
909.1(6)
~ dog, 909.4(8)
extremely ~, 909.1(1,7,11,13–
16,28,29,33,34)
growth stoppage, ~ because
of, 909.1(22,23,27)
make ~, 909.6
make unimportant and ~,
909.6(2)
~ Negroid, 909.3(11)
~ (of a dog), 909.1(30)
~ painting, 909.5(4);
965.1(33)
~ painting, art of, 909.10
~ person, 909.3
~ portrait, 909.5(4);
965.1(33)
~ portrait, art of, 909.10
~ quantity, 917.1
~ representation, 909.5(4)
self-important and ~ person,
848.34(1)
shapely and ~, 909.1(17)
~ thing, 909.5
too ~ to be important,
909.1(8)
unimportant and ~ person,
909.3(14,15)

unimportant and ~ thing,
909.5(2,10)
unusually ~, 909.1(1,4,5,9,18,
20–23,25,32)
very ~, 909.1(1,7,11,13–16,28,
29,33,34)
weak and ~, 10.1(49);
909.1(20)
worthless and ~ thing,
909.5(1,13)
smaller,adj.
become ~, 910.2
make ~, 910.1
make seem ~, 909.8
smallest,adj., 909.2
smallpox,n., 382.11(54,55);
382.12,14
having pits like those of ~,
299.2(7)
inoculate against ~, 569.1(3,
4); see immunize, vacci-
nate,v.
scar from ~ inoculation,
569.6
smart,adj.
clever, 595.1,2; see clever,adj.
intelligent, 594.1,2; see intelligent,adj.
smash,v., 437.1; 801.1; 802.1
smear,v., 195.2,3; 972.1
smell,n., 445.9; see also odor,n.
disgusting in ~, 881.2(4)
pleasure to the sense of ~,
1105.2(1)
sense of ~, 445.3
sense of ~, lack of, 445.7
sense of ~, science of, 445.8
smell,v., 445.1,11
smelling,n.
act of ~, 445.2
smile,n., 1112.2
say with a ~, 1112.4
smile,v., 1112.1
smiler,n., 1112.3
smiling,adj., 1112.5,6
smoke,n., 1050.1
bit of ~, 1050.4
bit of tobacco ~, 1050.5
blowing out tobacco ~,
1057.19
blown-out ~, 1045.2
breathe tobacco ~, 1050.7,9
cloud of ~, 1057.18
color with ~, 1050.24
concealing screen of ~,
1050.26
dark, like ~, 1050.18
disagreeable ~, 1050.1
drive out with ~, 1050.25
escape of ~, structure for,
1050.27–29
expose to ~, 1050.22
fog and ~, 1041.1(5)
fog, haze, and ~, 1041.1(4)
fumigate with ~, 1050.22
give off ~, 1050.12,13
give off as ~, 1050.14
giving off ~, 1050.15
gray, like ~, 1050.18
like ~, 1050.16
of the color of ~, 1050.18
particles of ~, 1050.19
pert. to ~, 1050.17
producing ~, 1050.15
protective screen of ~,
1050.26
stain with ~, 1050.20,24
stained with ~, 1050.21
suffocating ~, 1050.3
suspended ~, 1041.1(2)
thick ~ from slow burning,
1050.2
treat with ~, 1050.22
treatment with ~, place of,
1048.47; 1050.23

~ with a pleasant odor,
1050.1
without ~, 1050.30
smoke,v.
~ a cigarette, cigar, pipe,
etc., 1050.6–9
party for ~ing, 1050.11
train where ~ing is permitted, 1050.10
smoky,adj., 1050.15–18
smooth,adj., 439.1
deceptively ~ of manner,
823.11
excessively ~ of manner or
speech, 859.10
hypocritically ~ of manner
or speech, 859.9
make ~, 439.2
~ movement, 90.1–4
~ of manner, 823.11;
859.8–10
~ of speech, 859.8–10
~ place, 439.3
rub ~, 438.1(6,7,10,16,17,24,
25,32)
sickeningly ~ of manner or
speech, 859.10
sounds that flow ~ly, 467.3(4)
~ surface, 139.1(10)
white and ~, 1008.2
smooth,v., 439.2
~ on or with stone, 1006.11
~ the feathers, 439.2(12)
~ with sand, 1007.11,12
smother,v., 376.16,17
die, 794.29
kill, 796.11–14
smuggler,n., 1087.16
snail,n., 422.3
of ~s, 422.1(20,27,33)
science of ~s, 403.26(23)
shaped like a ~'s shell,
507.17(19,41)
snake,n., 425.7,8; see also reptile,n.
fondness for ~, 700.30(14);
700.31
~-haired sisters of mythology, 662.29(4)
house for ~s, 403.22(38)
like a ~, 425.3,10
mythical ~s, 662.25
pert. to ~s, 425.2,9
science of ~s, 403.26(18,29)
~-shaped, 507.17(20,73,89)
suggestive of ~s, 425.11
worship of ~s, 656.15(18)
snarl,n., 468.1; 878.9
snarl,v., 468.2; 876.8; 878.6
snarling,adj., 876.19
snatch,v., 247.1,6,17
sneak,n., 82.2,4; 971.15
sneak,v., 82.1; 971.15
sneaky,adj., 82.3; 971.10,13
sneer,n., 870.2
sneer,v., 870.1
sneeze,n., 363.15
sneeze,v., 363.14
sneezing,n., 363.15,16
snipe,n.
group of ~s, 403.5(78,80)
snob,n.
~s, 871.6
snobbery,n., 871.2
snobbish,adj., 871.1
~ people, 871.6
snoring,adj.
~ deeply, 376.5(1)
~ sound, 376.6(3)
snoring,n., 376.2(4)
snow,n., 1039
amount of ~, 1037.11; 1039.5
~ as atmospheric phenome-
non, 1046.2

blinded by ~ reflection, 1039.18
bury with ~, 1039.10
clearing ~, machine for, 1039.28
condition of ~, 1046.6
convert ~ to liquid, 1027.5
cover with ~, 1039.10
covered with ~, 1039.24
crystal of ~, 1039.17
fall of ~, 1039.5,7
fall or drop as ~, 1039.9
falling ~, mass of, 1039.26
field of ~, 1039.12
filled with ~, 1039.23
hinder with ~, 1039.10
kept in by ~, 1039.11
like ~, 1039.23
mass of ~, 1039.13,15,16
melted ~, 1039.1
move about in wet ~, 1026.43; 1039.2
protect against ~, structure to, 1039.27
reflection from ~ field, 1039.19
shut in by ~, 1039.11
sliding mass of ~, 1006.18
* solid ~ on high mountains, 1039.4
splash around in watery ~, 1039.2
splash watery ~ over or on, 1039.3
topped by ~, 1039.25
unmelting ~, level of, 1039.20
watery ~, 1039.1
white as ~, 1039.22
snowball,n.
throw ~s, 1039.14
snowfall,n., 1039.5,7
great ~ with high winds, 1039.8
light ~, 1039.6
science of ~, 1039.21
snowshoe,n.
~s, 979.8
snowstorm,n.
great ~ with high winds, 1039.8
snug,adj., 1141.1,6
soak,v., 1034.21,24; 1035.17
dip and ~, 1035.17
extract from ~ing, 1035.21
~ through, 1034.29
soaked,adj., 1034.25
lie ~ in water or liquid (of substances), 1035.19
something ~ in water or liquid, 1035.20
soap,n.
become ~, 899.43
convert (fat) into ~, 899.43
cover with ~, 899.40
~ foam, 899.44; 1028.13
~ for leather, 386.18
form ~suds, 899.46
full of ~, 899.41,42
like ~, 899.41
pert. to ~, 899.42
rub ~ on, 899.40
soapy,adj., 899.41,42
cover with ~ foam, 899.47
~ foam, 899.44; 1028.13
~ water, 899.45
sob,n., 1127.3
sob,v., 1127.1,7
sobber,n., 1127.5
sober,adj.
moderate in drinking, 749.59,60
not drunk, 749.61
serious, 610.1; see **serious,** adj.

sociable,adj., 1096.1,10
social,adj., 1096.1
~ class, 314.1; see **social class,**n., below
cut off from ~ relations, 296.1(5,9); 581.6(8); 581.11, 12
~ decay, 806.3(4); 806.4,6
devoted to ~ pleasures, 1105.8(3)
~ forms, adherence to, 50.5(1)
given to ~ pleasures, 1096.11
~ group, 318.1(18,26,29,42,84, 94)
have ~ relations, 523.2
indulge in ~ pleasures, 1105.7(3)
make ~, 1096.20
~ position, one who plots to attain, 47.3(1)
~ relations, 523.1(1–4,6)
suitable for ~ friendliness, 1096.10
social class,n., 314.1
impressed by ~, 314.6
lower ~, 314.2(6,19,24)
member of a ~, 314.3
member of the upper ~, 314.7, 8,12,16
middle ~, 314.2(4)
new member of higher ~, 314.3(2)
pert. to ~, 314.4
plotter for ~, 47.3(1)
upper ~, 314.2(1–3,5,7,8,10,11, 15,16,18,21–23,26); 314.13, 18; see also **nobleman, noblewoman,**n.
socialist,n., 1076.12(6,12,15)
society,n., 314.2
a ~, i.e., club or association, 524.9
entrance into ~, 133.2(2)
girl entering ~, 760.6(2,6)
layer of ~, 315.1(9)
polite ~, knowledge of or training in, 858.17
soda (water),n., 1026.1(13,15)
sofa,n., 63.2
soft,adj.
not hard, 443.1
reduced in severity, 1142.5
become ~, 443.3; see **soften,**v., below
become ~ (of land), 1000.8
~ in sound, 462.3–5,8,11,12; 1105.21
~ inner part, 443.6
~ (of fruit), 443.1(9,10)
~ of voice, 462.4
shiny and ~, 443.1(12,14)
something ~, 443.5
~ sounds, 462.1,6,9,13
sweet and ~ in sound, 1105.21
wet and ~, 443.1(15–17); 1034.32
white and ~, 443.1(5)
woolly and ~, 443.1(7)
soften,v., 443.3
reduce in severity, 1142.1
~ in sound, 462.16
~ sound, 462.15
tending to ~, 443.4
softness,n., 443.2
reduction in severity, 1142.6
causing ~ (medical), 443.7
~ of appearance caused by time, 443.2(2)
~ of sound, 462.17
soil,n.
dirt, filth, 904.3; see also **dirt, filth, stain,**n.
earth, 999.1

~ as origin of human body, 999.10
farm the ~, 998.2(2)
fertile ~, 999.1(5,6,7)
~ fertilizer, 999.12
fill with ~, 999.5
gold-bearing ~, 999.1(1)
grassy ~, 999.1(11)
made of ~, 999.4
manage the ~, 998.2
management of the ~, 998.1
originating in ~, 999.11
prophecy by ~, 999.13
science of ~ control, 985.36(1)
science of the ~, 998.1(2,13)
sliding mass of ~, 1006.18
sloping ~, 999.3
student of ~, 998.4
under the ~, 999.1(12)
unplowed ~, 999.1(4)
upper or surface ~, 999.1(14)
wet ~, 999.1(8); 1000.1
without ~, raising of plants, 998.1(10)
soil,v., 904.5
tending to ~, 904.12
soiled,adj., 904.1(2,8,18,22–25, 27,30)
solar system,n.
beyond or outside the ~, 138.1(2)
gaseous mass beyond the ~, 1057.7
theory of origin of the ~, 1057.8
sold,adj.
able to be ~, 212.6
be ~ for, 212.5; see also **sell,**v.
that which is ~, 212.4
soldier,n., 564.1,17; see also **army, warrior,**n.
act the boastful ~, 872.5
Algerian ~, 564.1(50)
American ~, 564.1(17,19,23,42, 49,54)
Australian ~, 564.1(5)
boastful ~, 564.1(51); 872.19
British ~, 564.1(18,44,48,52)
British ~s, 564.5(15)
cannon ~, 564.1(3,4,10,26)
cannon ~s, 564.5(4,6)
citizens as ~s, 564.5(22,23)
concealed ~s, 970.34
Croatian ~, 564.1(29)
engineer ~, 564.1(47)
foot ~, 564.1(16,17,30,38)
foot ~s, 564.5(17,27)
fort ~s, 564.5(16)
French ~, 564.1(13,16,21,41, 50,57)
German ~, 564.1(7,28,32)
German ~s, 564.5(35)
Greek ~s, 564.5(27)
group of ~s, 564.3,4,5,15
guarding ~s, 568.5(4,8,13,15, 16)
horse ~, 564.1(11–13,15,16,18, 29,50,53)
horse ~s, 564.5(8,32)
Hungarian ~, 564.1(29)
Indian native ~, 564.1(48)
inferior ~, 564.1(37)
irregular ~, 564.1(25)
Islam ~, 564.1(34)
king's bodyguard ~, 564.1(6, 56)
naval ~, 564.1(35)
naval ~s, 564.5(20,24)
new ~, 564.1(43,46)
~ of fortune, 564.1(1,14,22,27, 36)
old ~, 564.1(9,54)
pert. to a ~, 564.2

place ～s in to protect, 568.28(5)
place protected by ～s, 568.26
raiding ～, 564.1(21,25)
Russian ～, 564.1(15)
～s, 564.3,4,5
～s in concealment, 970.34
station for ～s, 782.1(19,21)
treatise on ～s, 682.15(24)
Turkish ～, 564.1(31,39,50)
sole,n.
pert. to the ～, 346.10
solid,adj., 808.5
become ～, 808.6
big and ～, 906.3(2)
both ～ and liquid, 1027.29
make ～, 808.6
solid,n.
geometric ～, 945.11–13,16
solidity,n., 808.5
lacking in ～, 909.11
solitary,adj., 125.6; 330.1; see also alone,adj.
～ condition, 330.2
～ existence, 330.8
one who lives a ～ life, 330.7
～ person, 330.5
solitude,n., 330.2
condition of ～, 330.2
life of ～, 330.8
one who lives in ～, 330.7
one who prefers ～, 330.7
preferring ～, 330.6
soluble,adj.
dissolvable, 1027.8
solvable, 601.5
solution,n.
mixture, 320.4; see mixture,n.
solving, 601.2; see solving,n.
solvable,adj., 601.5
solve,v., 601.1
～ a complicated problem, 601.3
able to be ～d, 601.5
～ secret writing, 601.7
that which ～s, 601.11,12
unable to be ～d, 601.6
solvent,n., 1027.7
solving,n., 601.2
aid in ～, 601.11–13
aid in ～ Egyptian writing, 601.9
aid in ～ secret writing, 601.8
artificial aid in ～ a plot, 601.13
～ of a complicated situation, 601.10
result of ～, 601.4
somersault,v., 149.2(1)
son,n., 721.3
acting like a ～, 721.13
attitude of a ～, 721.14
psychological situation between ～ and father or mother, 725.6
relationship of ～ to father, 722.3(2)
～s, 721.9
younger ～, 721.3(2)
song,n., 476.4
poem for singing, 689.2(5,7, 12,14–17)
Christmas ～, 476.4(32)
collection of ～s, 476.9,10
emotional ～, 1092.37
enthusiastic ～, 1095.16
farewell ～, 476.4(3)
～ for the dead, 476.4(19,31,41, 46)
funeral ～, 476.4(19,31,41,46); 1125.20(2,3,5,6)
honor in ～, 857.3
like a ～, 476.16
love ～, 476.4(6,45)

marriage ～, 476.4(9,16,23,26, 37)
mourning ～, 476.4(19,31,41, 46); 1125.20(2,3,5,6)
muse of ～, 109.15
～ of praise, 851.6
～ of worship, 656.14
pert. to ～, 476.5
praise in ～, 851.1(1,7,9)
religious ～, 476.4(2,12,17,27, 38,44); see also hymn,n.
sacred ～, 476.4(2,12,17,27,38, 44); see also hymn,n.
sad ～, 1125.20(1–3,5,6)
sleep ～, 476.4(7,29)
soothing ～, 1139.4(5)
write ～ of marriage, 476.7
writer of ～s, 476.6
writing of religious ～s, 476.8
sonnet,n., 689.13(1)
write ～s, 689.16
writer of ～s, 689.15
soon,adv., 766.11
coming ～, 766.12
too ～, 765.7
soot,n.
cover with ～, 1050.20
full of ～, 1050.21
like ～, 1050.21
pert. to ～, 1050.21
stain with ～, 1050.20
stained with ～, 1050.21
soothe,v., 1139.1
～ medically, 1139.1(1,15,24)
～ pain, 1137.47–50
rub to ～, 1139.13
soothed,adj., 1139.6,7
able to be ～, 1139.9
not ～, 1139.8
unable to be ～, 1139.10
soother,n., 1139.5
soothing,adj., 1139.2
～ agent, 1139.4
be ～, 1139.14
～ in language, speech, etc., 638.7(4)
～ in sound, 467.3(3); 1139.2(6)
medically ～, 1139.2(2–5,7,9– 12)
～ medication, 398.4(1,3,5,10, 14,17,19,23,24); 1139.4; 1139.4(2,3,6,8,11)
～ nipple, 1139.4(7,13)
not ～, 1139.3
persuasive and ～, 1139.2(15)
～ song, 1139.4(5)
soothsayer,n., 772.5; see predictor,n.
ancient Roman ～, 772.19
soothsaying,n., 772.3,4; see prediction,n.
sophisticated,adj.
unnatural, 811.1; see unnatural,adj.
worldly wise, 596.1
make ～, 811.3
～ person, 811.2
sorcerer,n., 662.5; 663.2
sorcery,n., 662.4(8,9); 663.1(2,5, 6,11,13–16)
pert. to ～, 663.4
sore,adj.
angry, 878.10
in pain, 1137.12
become ～ from rubbing, 1137.15
make ～ by rubbing, 438.7; 1137.14
～ spot, 1137.17
with ～ feet, 12.1(14)
sore,n.
inflammatory ～, 392.1(1,2)
pus ～, 383.2

skin ～s, 382.11(2,3,14,18,32,33, 37)
sorority,n.
accept on trial in a ～, 1122.28,29
promise to join a ～, 1122.28, 29
sorrow,n.
regret, 1126.2; see regret,n.
sadness, 1125.2; see sadness,n.
sorrowful,adj., 1125.1; see sad, adj.
sorry,adj., 1126.1
be ～, 1126.3,4
be ～ for guilt or sin, 884.17
sort,n., 312.1; see kind,n.
sort,v., 312.2,3
soul,n., 1089.1,2
human being, 429.3; see human,n.
person, 431.1; see person,n.
beliefs about the ～, 429.12(2, 7); 1089.4
body as abode of the ～, 338.1(3)
division into body, ～, and spirit, 325.3(9); 932.23
doctrine of body and ～, 1089.10
ferryman of ～s of the dead, 662.29(1)
free (a ～) of bodily existence, 1089.9
influenced by the ～, 1090.4
live on after death of body (of the ～), 750.1(18)
looking deeply into one's ～, 1089.11
loss of one's ～, 264.2(5)
passing of the ～ into new body, 1089.5
personification of the ～, 1089.3
previous existence of the ～, 1089.7
saving of the ～, 571.2(1,2); 571.4
seizer of ～s, 662.26(3)
without a ～, 1089.8
sound,n., 455.1
accompanying ～, 131.5(4)
admit or transmit ～, unable to, 1065.94
air ～s, 461.1,4
amount of ～, 455.6(4,15)
angry ～s, 468.1(7,13,19); 878.9
angry ～s, make, 878.6(12,20, 21)
animal ～s, 456.1(33,43,57,59, 61,63–65,68,73–75,81,84)
ass ～, 456.1(8)
bee ～s, 456.1(9,35,44)
beetle ～s, 456.1(7,35,44)
bell ～s, 458.1,4
bell ～s, make, 458.2
bird ～s, 456.1(10,12–27,30–32, 34,36,40–42,52,53,55,58–60, 63–65,70–73,78,79); 456.2(2– 4); 469.1(15,27)
blackbird ～s, 456.1(53,78)
blowing ～s, 461.1; 461.4(2,3, 6); 1043.2,17
blowing ～s, make, 461.2,5
body ～s, 460.1
brassy in ～, 1016.13
break with a ～, 802.1(3,4); 802.2(2)
breathed ～s, 376.6; 670.14(1)
breathing, ～s of, 376.6
brushing ～, 469.1(22)
bubbling ～s, 469.1(9,10); 469.2(1)
buck ～s, 456.1(3,68)

bull ~s, 456.1(3,4,57) ; 456.3(1)
bullet ~, 469.7(21)
calf ~s, 456.1(5,6)
~ carried on air, 1045.4
cat ~s, 456.1(11,47–49,54,84) ;
 456.2(2)
character of ~, 455.6
chest ~s, 376.6(2,3)
chopping ~, 469.7(12)
cicada ~s, 456.1(16,67)
clock ~, 469.7(38)
closing, ~ of, 469.7(33)
cock ~s, 456.1(24–26,32,36,64)
cockchafer ~s, 456.1(21)
coins, ~ of, 469.7(3)
collision ~s, 469.7
complaining ~s, 468.1(1,2,7–9,
 15,18) ; 468.2(1) ; 468.3(1)
confused ~s, 473.1
confusion of ~s, 605.13(2,4–6,
 11,14,15,23)
contact ~s, 469.7
contented ~, 467.1(8)
cover to dull ~, 972.1(30)
cow ~s, 456.1(46,50) ; 456.3(1)
crack with repeated ~s,
 802.16(1)
crane ~s, 456.1(22,79)
cricket ~s, 456.1(15,17,18,19,
 28,67)
crow ~s, 456.1(12,30)
crushing ~s, 469.1(4–7)
cuckoo ~s, 456.1(34)
decrease ~, 462.15
decrease in ~, 462.16
decrease of ~, 462.17
decreasing in ~, 462.18
deep ~s, 462.1
deep in ~, 462.3
deer ~s, 456.1(3,68)
device used for ~, 455.9
different ~ to each ear,
 bringing, 362.3(5)
disapproving ~, 468.1(3)
dog ~s, 456.1(1,2,38,43,45,61,
 73,80–84)
donkey ~, 456.1(8)
dove ~, 456.1(27) ; 456.2(2)
drops, ~ of, 918.11
drum ~s, 469.7(16,25,27,29,30,
 37,39)
duck ~s, 456.1(55)
dull ~s, 462.13,15
eagle ~, 456.1(59)
echoing ~s, 471.1
elephant ~, 456.1(69)
engine exhaust ~, 461.4(3)
explosion ~, 461.4; 463.1(28) ;
 1044.5
falling ~s, 469.1(8,23)
faster than ~, 99.7(3)
flowing ~, 469.1(12)
footstep ~s, 469.5
fowl ~s, 456.1(10,19,20,23,36,
 64) ; 456.2(3)
fox ~s, 456.1(82,83)
frightened ~, 468.1(12)
frog ~, 456.1(30)
frying ~, 1061.3
full and rich in ~, 467.3(1,5–
 7,9)
gasping ~ after a cough,
 364.11; 376.6(6)
glasses, ~ of, 469.7(3)
gnat ~s, 456.1(44,69)
goat ~s, 456.1(6)
goose ~s, 456.1(10,20,22,31,36,
 40,41) ; 456.2(3)
grasshopper ~s, 456.1(16,29,
 67)
grinding ~, 469.1(7)
gun ~s, 463.1(28,33)
happy ~s, 1102.12
harsh ~s, 466.1
harsh in ~, 466.3

heart ~, 376.6(1) ; 460.1(5)
hen ~s, 456.1(10,19,20,23) ;
 456.2(3)
heron ~s, 456.1(7)
high-pitched ~s, 465.1
high-pitched in ~, 465.3
hissing ~s, 472.1
hitting ~s, 469.7
horn ~s, 461.1(2,6–8) ; 1043.7
horse ~s, 456.1(51,62,76,77)
horse's hoof ~, 469.7(12)
hostile ~s, 468.1(7,13,19) ;
 879.8(4)
identity of ~, 455.7(5,6)
impact ~s, 469.7
increase ~, 463.9
increase in ~, 463.10,11
increase in ~, tendency to,
 463.12
increasing gradually in ~,
 463.11
infant ~s, 457.1
insect ~s, 456.1(7,9,15,17–19,
 21,28,29,35,44,53,67,69)
interfering ~, 455.1(7)
jackal ~s, 456.1(73–75)
jarring ~s, 466.1
jarring in ~, 466.3
katydid ~, 456.1(67)
keep ~ out of, 462.19
lamb ~s, 456.1(5)
laughter, ~ of, 1111.18
leaves, ~ of, 469.1(16,18–20)
lightning, ~ accompanying,
 1044.1
like tin in ~, 1020.8
lion ~s, 456.1(3,38,57,61,81)
lip ~, 460.1(8)
liquid ~s, 469.1
loud ~, 463.1; 464.1; 1044.5
loud in ~, 463.3; 464.3; 1044.4
love ~, 467.1(2)
low ~s, 462.1,6,9,13
low in ~, 462.3–5,8,11,12
lung ~, 376.6(1) ; 460.1(5)
magpie ~s, 456.1(13)
make ~s, able to, 455.11(3,5)
making ~s, 455.11(1,2,4)
many ~s, 455.4
meaningless ~s, 607.29
metallic ~s, 469.7(3–6,10,17,
 21,22,26) ; 469.8–10;
 1012.11(2,4)
monkey ~, 456.1(13)
monotonous ~, 470.1
monotonous in ~, 470.3
mosquito ~s, 456.1(44,69)
mournful ~s, 468.1(10,11,14,
 16)
mournful in ~, 468.3(2)
mouse ~s, 456.1(14,65,66)
move with ~, 92.1
move with a ~, 92.1
movement ~s, 469.1(1,3,17,21,
 22,32,33)
murmuring ~s, 462.6
musical ~s, 455.1(3) ; 467.1;
 469.1(13–15,25–27,30) ; see
 also music,n.
musical ~s, system of, 467.4
musical in ~, 467.3; 469.3
nasal ~, 460.1(11)
nightjar ~s, 456.1(21)
nonsensical ~s, 607.29
ocean wave ~s, 459.1(4) ;
 459.3; 469.7(28) ; 1032.9
omission of word ~s,
 666.22(4–6)
owl ~s, 456.1(42,60,70,73,79)
pained ~s, 468.1(1,4–6,9,11,14,
 15–17)
paper ~s, 469.1(4–7,16)
partridge ~, 456.1(21)
pert. or relating to ~, 455.5
pheasant ~, 456.2(3)

pig ~s, 456.1(39,66)
pleasant ~, 467.1
pleasant in ~, 467.3; 1106.12
pleasurable in ~, 1105.4(9)
pleasure, make ~s of, 1105.19
pouring, ~s of, 469.1(9) ;
 469.2(1) ; 1036.6,11
rapid, light ~s, 455.3
raven ~s, 456.1(12,30,31) ;
 456.2(4)
reduce ~, 462.15
reduce in ~, 462.16
reducing in ~, 462.18
reduction of ~, 462.17
reed instrument ~s, 461.1(5) ;
 461.3
repeat ~s, 674.13(1,4,12,13)
representing the same ~,
 455.8
rhythmical ~, 105.1,4
rhythmical in ~, 105.2,5
rich in ~, 467.3(1,5–7,9)
ringing ~s, 458.1
ringing in ~, 458.5
rising and falling ~,
 463.1(31)
rooster ~s, 456.1(24–26,32,36,
 64)
rubbing ~s, 469.7(14,15,24,31,
 32,34)
rushing ~, 469.1(32)
s ~s, 472.1
same ~, words of, 666.12(7,8)
science of ~, 455.12
science of speech ~s, 670.25
Scottish bagpipe ~, 465.1(10)
sexual ~s of animals, 456.1(3,
 11,49,68)
sharp ~, 463.1; 465.1
sharp in ~, 334.1(19) ; 463.3;
 465.3
sheep ~, 456.1(6)
sigh, ~ of a, 376.6(4)
signal through ~, 956.1(1,6,
 9,11–14) ; 956.3(1) ; 956.6(5) ;
 see also signal,n.
silk, ~s of, 469.1(16,18–20,22)
silver in ~, 467.3(8) ; 1015.5
similarity of ~, 455.7
slower than ~, 99.7(2)
smoothly flowing in ~,
 467.3(4)
snake ~s, 456.1(40,56) ;
 456.2(1)
snipe ~s, 456.1(58)
soft ~s, 462.1,6,9,13
soft in ~, 462.3–5,8,11,12;
 1105.21
soften ~, 462.15
soften in ~, 462.16
softening in ~, 462.18
softening of ~, 462.17
soothing in ~, 467.3(3) ;
 1139.2(6)
speech ~s, 670.10,11,13,14
speech ~s, description of,
 670.23
speech ~s, representing,
 670.22
speech ~s, science of, 670.25
speech ~s, symbols of,
 670.21
speed of ~, 99.7
spitting ~s, 460.1(9,10)
stag ~s, 456.1(3,68)
stepping ~s, 469.5
stomach ~, 460.1(7)
striking ~s, of, 469.7
striking of ~ against the ear,
 455.2
sweet ~s, 467.1
sweet in ~, 467.3; 1105.21
threatening in ~, 573.1(1,6–
 9,21,22,24)
throaty ~s, 460.1(1–4,6)

throaty in ~, 460.3(1,2) ;
460.4
throw back rays of ~, 1065.35
thunder ~s, 463.1(26,42) ;
1044.5
thunder ~s, having, 1044.4
thunder ~s, make, 1044.3
transposition of ~s in a
word, 670.24
trumpet ~s, 461.1(1,3,4,6)
turkey ~s, 456.1(37,82,83)
unhappy ~s, 468.1
unhappy in ~, 468.3
unit of ~, 455.10
unpleasant ~s, 466.1
unpleasant in ~, 466.3
vibrating ~s, 469.1(1–3,13–15,
17,21,24–31,33–35)
voice, make ~s with the,
474.4
voice ~s, 474.3
walking ~s, 469.5
warning ~, 455.1(5) ;
468.1(10) ; 574.6
warning ~, device to make a,
574.4(1,4)
water ~s, 459.1
wave of ~, 455.1(9)
waves, ~ of, 459.1(4) ; 459.3;
469.7(28) ; 1032.9
weak in ~, 10.1(64)
weeping ~s, 1127.3
whispering ~, 462.9
whispering in ~, 462.11,12
whistle ~s, 461.1(7,8) ;
461.4(2)
wind ~s, 1043.17
wind instrument ~s, 461.1
wolf ~s, 456.1(43,73)
word as to its ~, 666.3(50)
sound,v., 456.2; 457.2; etc.; see
sound,n., above
~ a bell, 458.3
~ like sand, 1007.4
~ like thunder, 1044.3
make (a bell) ~, 458.3
~ (of a bell), 458.2
soup,n., 742.1
bowl for serving ~, 261.9(10)
liquid for ~, 742.2
sour,adj., 452.1
become ~, 452.5–7
~ in taste, 452.1
~ in temper, 876.1
make ~, 452.3,4,7
~ temper, 876.2
source,n., 728.1,4; see also
beginning, origin,n.
acting as ~, 728.5
from a ~, 728.13; see originating,adj.
~ of help, 728.4(15)
~ of relief, 728.4(15)
~ of supply, 728.4(15,21,22,
24)
~ of support, 728.4(15)
~ of water, 728.4(6,9,17,18)
rich ~, 728.4(8,11)
sourness,n., 452.2
~ of feelings or nature,
876.2(3)
~ of temper, 876.2
sour-tempered,adj., 876.1; see
also bad-tempered, sharp-
tempered,adj.
south,adj.
~ circle of the earth, 1004.13
~ distance on earth, 1004.11
far ~, 789.8
south,n., 179.17
distance north or ~ of the
equator, 1004.11
inhabitant of the ~, 179.16
land in the ~, 1003.2(36)
South African,n., 784.15(2)

southern,adj., 179.15
~ accent, 670.4(6)
South Pole,n.
pert. to the ~, 1004.7
souvenir,n., 627.34(5,6,13–15,18)
space,n., 787.1
action, ~ for, 787.2
action, ~ of, 787.3
arched ~, 787.1(25)
available ~, 787.1(17)
blank ~, 787.4(2,4)
bridge, ~ under, 787.1(11)
building, ~ surrounding a,
787.1(1)
buildings, ~ surrounded by,
787.1(14)
cells, ~ between, 787.4(4)
cleared ~, 787.1(5,11)
continuous ~, 787.1(8,10,16,
19–21,23,24)
cubic ~, 787.1(26)
effect, ~ of, 787.3
emptiness of infinite ~, 926.16
empty ~, 926.13; 926.15
enclosed ~, 787.1(4,17,18)
existing in ~ and time, 787.6
full ~, 787.1(13) ; 925.10
in or into empty ~, 926.17,18
inner ~, 787.1(2,7)
intervening ~, 787.4(6)
large ~, 787.1(8,10,12,16,19–
21,23,24)
~ left empty by death or
departure, 926.19
missing part, ~ indicating,
787.4(2,4)
movement, ~ for, 787.2
open ~ between, 787.4
open ~ in a net or network,
308.10; 787.4(5)
partitioned ~, 787.1(6)
pert. to ~, 787.5
power, ~ of, 787.3
section of closed ~, 326.6(2)
ship to move, ~ for, 787.1(3)
stage, ~ at side of, 787.1(27)
stretches, ~ that something,
787.1(2,7,9,15,16,19–21)
surrounding ~, 787.1(1)
total ~, 787.1(2)
wide ~, 787.1(8,10,16,19–21,23,
24)
spacious,adj., 787.11
~ and convenient, 27.1(3)
spaciousness,n., 787.12
spaghetti,n.
grain used for ~, 987.22
Spain,n.
fond of ~, 700.32(1)
inhabitant of ~, 784.15(32,55)
pert. to ~, 784.16
political party of ~, member
of, 1076.12(7)
Spaniard,n., 784.15(32)
Spanish,adj., 784.16
~ conquest, leader of, 22.47
~ gentleman, 858.23
~ language, 664.4(3,16)
~ person born in a colony,
784.15(15)
spank,v., 437.1; see hit,v.
spark,n., 1064.4; 1065.49
giving off ~s, 1064.6
stone that gives off ~s when
struck, 1064.7
spark,v., 1064.5; 1065.45
sparkle,n., 1064.4; 1065.48,49
sparkle,v., 1064.5; 1065.45,46
sparrow,n.
group of ~s, 403.5(74)
sparse,adj., 917.19,27
speak,v., 671.1; 674.1; see say,
talk,v.
~ about, 671.5
~ against, 671.9

~ to, 671.8
speak-easy,n., 749.37(7)
speaker,n., 671.3
~ for another, 671.3(1,3)
introducer of ~s, 730.9
~ of epilogues, 792.25
speaking,adj., 671.4; see talking,adj.
speaking,n., 671.2; see speech,
talk, talking,n.
spear,n., 332.15
stem of a ~, 332.16
special,adj., 540.25; see also
different,adj.
applied to this ~ case only,
540.27
~ detail, fact, etc., 540.28
make ~, 540.26
specialist,n.
medical ~, 401.2; see doctor,n.
medical ~ with advanced
degree, 623.12(6)
species,n., 312.29; 318.8
development of the ~,
731.16(2)
eating of one's own ~,
734.26(2)
of different ~, 312.10(4,7)
of the same ~, 312.8
period in the development of
the ~, 731.18
repetition of development of
the ~ in the individual,
731.13
repetition of development of
the ~ in the individual,
lack of, 731.14
specific,adj., 328.1; 540.25; 930.8
specific gravity,n.
determination of ~, 947.24
device to measure ~, 947.25;
1027.36
measurement of ~, 1027.37
specify,v., 327.4; 671.7; 930.10
specimen,n., 317.1
speck,n., 501.3
small amount, 917.1,17
small particle, 917.15
dust ~, 501.3(4)
speck,v., 501.2
specked,adj., 501.1
spectacle,n., 483.8
spectacles,n.
eyeglasses, 480.16
spectator,n., 480.3; 484.3
tennis match ~s, 484.5
specter,n., 662.7; see also
ghost, spirit (supernat-
ural being),n.
speech,n., 671.2; see also
language, talk, talking,n.
abusive ~, 561.2; 671.2(37)
~ ailment, 671.21,23
artistic ~, 665.9(46)
attacking ~, 561.2; 671.2(37)
authoritative ~, 671.2(3)
~ by one person, 671.2(23)
concluding ~, 671.2(16) ;
792.23(1,5)
concluding part of a ~,
792.23(4,5,7)
critical ~, 671.2(37)
delirium, ~ in, 1136.9
deliver a ~, 671.1(25–28,51,60,
66,71,72,79,81,88,89)
deliver a noisy, vehement ~
to, 671.8(7)
deliver vehement ~es, tending to, 671.12
descr. of a vehement ~,
671.13
~ difficulty, 671.21,23
directness of ~, 665.9(5)
emotional ~, 1092.37,38

empty in ~, 926.5
excessively smooth of ~ or manner, 859.10
figure of ~, 669.1,3; see **figure of speech,**n.
formal ~, 671.2(2,12,24)
frank and good-natured manner of ~, 665.9(4)
hypocritically smooth of ~ or manner, 859.9
~ impediment, 671.21
incoherent (of ~), 671.24
incoherent in ~, be, 671.25
locality, manner of ~ peculiar to a, 665.9(43)
long ~, 671.2(37)
make ~es to cause delay, 768.1(2)
manner of ~, 665.8,9
parts of ~, 666.28
pert. to ~, 671.4
pretentious ~, 665.9(6,18,20, 21,24,25,35–37,54–56,61)
public ~, 671.2(2,12,24)
quaint ~, 671.2(41)
rapid ~, 671.23
rapid manner of ~, 665.9(59)
refined of ~, 859.8
science of ~, 664.11(8,9)
secret language or ~, descr. of, 971.8
sickeningly smooth of ~ or manner, 859.10
smooth of ~, 859.8
~ sounds, 670.10,11,13,14
~ sounds, consisting of, 670.12
~ sounds, description of, 670.23
~ sounds, letter or symbol of, 670.21
~ sounds, pert. to, 670.12
~ sounds, representing, 670.22
~ sounds, science of, 670.24
~ sounds, transposition of, 670.24
strange ~, 671.2(41)
substandard ~, 665.9(1)
supporting ~, 854.16
taking down a ~ in longhand, 677.9
tedious ~, 671.2(30)
urgent ~, 671.2(3)
vehement ~, 671.2(13)
speechless,adj., 454.23; 475.1; 671.21; see also **silent,**adj.
~ person, 454.24; 671.22
speed,n.
rapidity, 94.4; 95.2; see **rapidity,**n.
rate, 99.1; see **rate,**n.
at full ~, 95.3; 95.5(1)
burst of ~, 95.4
cause of ~, 95.9,10
in full ~, 95.3
speed,v., 94.1,5,7; 95.6,8
speedily,adv., 95.5; see **faster, rapidly,**adv.
speedy,adj., 94.8; 95.1; see **rapid,**adj.
~ and smart in appearance (of ships), 94.9
spell,n.
fascination, 196.6
period of work, 203.12
cast a magic ~, 663.12
caster of a magic ~, 663.13
casting a magic ~, 663.14
like someone under a magic ~, 663.17
magic ~, 663.16
state of being under a magic ~, 663.15
spell,v.

~ incorrectly, 681.4
spelling,n., 681.1
~ according to sound, 681.1(3,4)
art of correct ~, 681.2
book to teach ~, 687.1(19)
correct ~, 681.1(2)
English ~ system, 681.1(1)
incorrect ~, 681.1(1); 681.3
same ~, words of, 666.12(5,6)
unacceptable usage in ~, 681.1(1)
spend,v., 224.1
~ economically, 224.1(4)
~ time, 762.13–20
~ time in the country, 786.4
~ wastefully, 224.1(3,6,7,10, 11)
spending,n., 224.2
cause of ~, 224.4
controlling ~, 224.5
economical in ~, 226.1
economical in ~, be, 226.3
economy in ~, 226.2
pert. to ~, 224.5
wasteful in ~, 225.2
wasteful in ~, be, 225.1
wasteful in ~, person who is, 225.4
spendthrift,n., 225.4
spent,adj.
that which is ~, 224.3
sperm,n., 379.6(7); 379.7
fluid containing ~, 379.7
organ for ripening of ~, 379.1(2)
producing ~, 379.8
tube carrying ~, 379.1(22)
sphere,n.
place, 782.1,3
region of action, 782.2; 787.3
region of influence, 9.8; 782.10; 787.3
region of knowledge, 782.9
region of power or authority, 5.19; 9.8; 782.6; 787.3
round object, 508.8,9
~ of living organisms, 753.1(6)
spherical,adj., 508.7
sphinx,n., 662.27
like the ~, 662.28(1)
spice,n.
interest, 580.3,5
seasoning, 446.17
spider,n., 428.3
like a ~, 428.2
of ~s, 403.6(1); 428.1(3)
science of ~s, 403.26(3)
web of a ~, 308.1(1,2,10); see **cobweb,**n.
spill,v., 1036 7,9,15
spin,n., 150.3; see **rotation,**n.
spin,v., 150.1,2; see **rotate,**v.
weave, 307.1
spinal cord,n.
inflammation of the ~, 354.17(2,5,7,9)
membranes of the ~, 387.1(1, 3,7,13)
pert. to the ~, 354.10
spine,n.
backbone, 354.8; see **backbone,**n.
pointed projection, 335.1(2,5, 12,14,19)
spinster,n., 706.1
like a ~, 706.5
pert. to a ~, 706.4
~ state, 706.3,6,7
spiny,adj., 335.2; see **pointed,** adj.
becoming ~, 335.4
spiral,adj., 155.4; 155.4(13); 156.5; 156.5(8,16,21)

spiral,n., 155.2; 156.3; 156.3(1); 156.4; 156.4(2)
bent in a ~, 152.5(3)
~-shaped, 507.17(40,41)
spiral,v., 155.1(7,8); 156.1(1,3, 10,17)
spirit,n.
alcohol, 749.1,9
courage, 575.2
liveliness, 752.2
mood, 1091.5; 1092.5
soul, 1089.1
supernatural being, 662.7; see below
division into body, soul, and ~, 325.3(9); 932.23
influenced by the ~, 1090.4
spirit (supernatural being),n., 662.7; see also **ghost,**n.
action of ~s, 662.4(3)
ancestral ~s considered gods, 662.10(3)
belief in ~s, 662.9
bloodsucking ~, 662.7(27,45)
characteristic of a ~, 1090.11
communications from ~s, instrument to record, 677.14(4)
diminutive ~, 662.7(11,12,14, 15,19,33,39,43)
enormous ~, 662.7(18,43)
evil ~, 660.1; 662.7(2,3,5,8–10, 20,23,25,27,30,32,35,40); see also **devil,**n.
evil ~s, class of (Hindu), 662.10(4)
evil ~ who has sexual intercourse with sleeping men, 662.7(40)
evil ~ who rapes women, 662.7(25,30)
good ~, 662.7(13)
guiding ~, 662.7(16,17)
intercourse with evil ~s, 660.6
intercourse with evil ~s, one who has, 660.7
like a ~, 1090.11
magic ~, 662.7(12,14,15,16,26, 33,38,39)
magic with the help of evil ~s, 663.1(2,5,6,11,15,16)
noisy ~, 662.7(34)
~ of desire, 662.7(29)
~ of the sea, 662.7(7)
pert. to a ~, 662.8
pert. to the ~s of the dead, 662.21(3)
power from, or to control, evil ~s, 662.4(2,8,9)
protective ~, 662.7(6)
~s and gods of the lower world, 660.5
~s, collectively, 662.10
summoner of ~s, 693.5
terrifying ~, 662.7(1,37,43); see also **ghost,**n.
the ~ world, 662.18
ugly ~, 662.7(2,3,20,22,32,43)
water ~, 662.7(31,44)
~ who inhabits the air, 662.7(41,42)
~ who lives in caves, 662.7(43)
~ who puts children to sleep, 662.7(36)
spiritual,adj., 1004.39; 1090.1,4, 10,11,13
affectedly ~, 1090.9
~ and physical natures, doctrine of, 1089.10
become ~, 1090.3
belief in ~ insight, 593.7,8
claim to special ~ information, 613.41,42

~ decay, 806.3(4)
give ~ meaning to, 1090.8
informed ~ly, state of being, 613.40
~ insight, 593.2(12)
lack of ~ feelings, 1097.11
make ~, 1090.2,5,6
make more ~, 1090.7
~ meaning of words, 607.2(2)
not ~, 1004.38
~ relationship, 1090.14,15
sick ~ly, 1090.16
source of ~ light, 1065.83,84
symbolic ~ly, 954.5
system of ~ education, 621.15
understand in ~ sense, 1090.8
~ use of words, 667.1(3)
spiritualism,n.
automatic writing in ~, 682.3(18)
spirituality,n., 1004.39; 1090.1, 4,10–12
spit (saliva),n., 289.3; see also spitting,n.
bubbles of ~, 1028.9
carrying ~, 289.6
cause a flow of ~, 289.9
causes ~, that which, 289.10, 11
causing flow of ~, 289.6,12
flow of ~, 289.8
let ~ flow, 289.1(2,3,6,7)
like ~, 289.7
pert. to ~, 289.4
pert. to ~ glands, 289.5
produce ~, 289.1(5) ; 289.9
secrete ~, 289.1(5)
smear ~ over, 289.1(6,7)
vessel for ~, 289.13
spit,v., 289.1; see also spitting,n.
cough up and ~ out, 289.1(4)
~ in excitement, 289.1(9)
~ while talking, 289.1(8,9)
spite,n., 879.2
spiteful,adj., 879.1
become ~, 879.9
deliberately ~, 879.1(3)
~ person, 879.4(5,6)
slyly ~, 879.1(2)
spitting,n., 289.2
causing ~, 289.6,12
~ of blood, 289.2(1)
sounds of ~, 460.1(11)
vessel for ~ into, 289.13
splash,n., 459.1; 917.7; 1036.10, 14
splash,v., 459.2; 1034.30; 1036.7, 9,15
~ around in muddy or dirty water, 1000.6
~ around in watery snow, 1039.2
~ mud upon, 1000.7
~ watery snow over or on, 1039.3
spleen,n., 388.1(3)
inflammation of the ~, 347.12(8)
pert. to the ~, 388.2(11)
splendid,adj., 847.1
excellent, 831.1
ostentatiously ~, 847.3
splendor,n., 847 2
split,adj.
cut, 332.7
separated, 325 8
able to be ~, 332.19
~-off part, 326 10(24,32)
split,n.
break, 802.3,8
cut, 332.3
separation, 325 3,7; see separation,n

~ in a group, party, etc., 325.3(6)
split,v.
break, 802.1,2; see break,v.
cut, 332.1(8,9,18,44,52) ; see cut,v.
separate, 325.1,2; see separate,v.
~ into thin layers, 315.3
~ with a pointed piece of wood, 997.9
splitting,n.
breakage, 802.3
cutting, 332.2; 332.2(3)
separating, 325.3
~ into parts, 332.2(2)
~ of the atom, 332.2(2)
spoil,v., 805.1
decay, 806.1,2; see decay,v.
destroy, 801.1; see destroy,v.
harm, 803.1; see harm,v.
indulge, 1108.1
act of ~ing, 801.2; 803.2; 805.1,7; 806.3
~ by impure mixture, 805.1(1)
something ~ed, 805.8
~ the appearance of, 805.2,4
~ the shape of, 805.4
spoilage, 801.2; 803.2; 805.1; 806.3
spoiled,adj.
decayed, 806.4; see decayed, adj.
indulged, 1108.2
spoke,n.
like the ~s of a wheel, 195.6(4)
spoken,adj., 666.17(5,7) ; 674.4–6; see also say, speak, talk,v.
~ frankly, 671.4(5)
~ without preparation, 48.10
spokesman,n., 671.3(1)
sponge (marine),n., 422.3
like the ~, 422.2
of ~s, 422.1(31,32)
spontaneity,n., 46.12; 810.1; 1092.67
without ~ of feelings, 1097.32
spontaneous,adj.
natural, 810.1
openly emotional, 1092.67
unplanned, 46.12
not happening ~ly, 811.5
talk ~ly, 671.1(1,34,35)
spoon,n.
~-shaped, 507.17(74)
sport,n., 199.9
biological ~, 537.1
sports,n.
a meeting for ~s, 322.1(37)
land for public ~, 1003.2(23)
outdoor ~, participator in, 199.9
water ~, 114.7; 1026.28
spot,n., 501.3
arrangement of ~s on an animal, 501.6
brownish-yellow ~ on the skin, 384.26
eye ~, 501.3(1)
~ on a playing card, 501.3(5)
skin ~s, 501.3(3,6) ; 501.4
white ~ on animal's face, 501.3(2)
spot,v., 501.2
spotless,adj., 899.23,29
spotted,adj., 501.1
~ appearance, 501.5
~ by skin disease, 501.1(12)
spray,n., 1036.10
change into a ~, 1036.14
spray,v., 1034.30; 1036.7,9,15

~ water around medically, 1036.22
spread,adj., 195.6
separated, 325.8
be, become, or lie ~, 195.1
~ open, 195.6(3)
spread,v., 194.1; 195.1–3
separate, 325.1,2; see separate,v.
~ like a bush, 985.24
~ (something), 195.2
tending to ~, 195.5
~ with, 195.3
spreading,adj., 195.5
~ from person to person, 195.5(1)
spreading,n., 195.4
separation, 325.3
descr. of ~, 195.5
device for ~, 195.7
spring,n., 89.2; 110.2; see also jump,n.
spring,v., 89.1; 110.1; see also jump,v.
~ back into shape, able to, 110.5–7
~ up in large amounts, 916.18
spring (season),n., 770.1
beginning of ~, 1055.13
like ~, 770.4
pert. to ~, 770.3
spring (water),n., 1029.36
~ of hot water, 1029.37,38
~ of mineral water, 1029.39
steaming ~, 1029.37
sprinkle,v., 1036.7,9,15
~ with dust, 1001.11
~ with holy water, 845.17
~ with powder, 1001.11
sprite,n., 662.7; see fairy,n.
spun,adj.
woven, 307.2; see woven,adj.
spy,n., 484.3
secret ~ in wartime, 801.5
~ system, 484.7
spying,n., 484.6
squander,v., 224.1(3,6,7,11) ; 225.1
square,adj., 507.17(63)
square,n., 945.8
figure in the shape of a ~, 945.9
~-shaped, 507.17(63)
squeeze,n., 198.2
squeeze,v., 198.1(1,5,10,13,16,20, 23,25,29,34,35)
one who ~s, 198.4
~ out, 198.1(13)
that which ~s, 198.5
~ the throat of, 198.1(3,26,27, 29)
squeezer,n., 198.4,5
squeezing,adj., 198.3
squid,n., 422.3
of ~s, 422.1(9)
squirrel,n., 421.8
group of ~s, 403.5(18)
like the ~, 421.10
pert. to ~s, 421.4,5
stab,n., 332.23
stab,v., 332.22; see pierce,v.
~ with figurative pain, 1137.13
stability,n., 88.2; 526.6
stabilize,v., 88.3
~ by a weight, 947.16
stabilizing,adj.
~ weight, 947.15(1)
stable,adj., 88.1; 526.6
staff,n.
stick, 437.7; see stick,n.
~ of a school, etc., 621.8
stag,n., 413.1
mythical ~, half goat, 412.6

stage,n., 969.27
　period, 769.1
　platform, 1025.23
　~ for addressing audience,
　　969.28
　front of the ~, 969.29
　pert. to the ~, 969.9(2,4)
　spaces on the sides of the ~,
　　969.30
　the ~, 969.27
stain,n., 904.18
　free of moral ~, 845.15
　ink~, 904.23
　moral ~, 891.23
stain,v., 904.5,8,17
　~ morally, 891.22
　~ the reputation, character,
　　or name of, 891.22
　wet and ~, 1034.28
　~ with blood, 352.4(2,5) ;
　　904.24; 1034.28
　~ with smoke, 1050.20,24
　~ with soot, 1050.20
stainable,adj., 904.21
stained,adj., 904.19
　able to be ~, 904.21
　become ~, 904.20
　~ by blood, 352.3(1) ; 352.4(1–
　　5)
　morally ~, 891.24
　morally ~, become, 891.25
　not becoming ~, 904.22
　smoke-~, 1050.21
　soot-~, 1050.21
stainless,adj., 904.22
　make morally ~, 845.15
　morally ~, 845.10
stair,n., 160.1,6; see also stair-
　　case, step (for rising),n.
　arranged like ~, 160.19
　compartment of ~s, 160.11
　construction of ~s, 160.20
　having ~s, 160.18
　passage of ~s, 160.10
　platform between groups of
　　~s, 160.13
　~s, 160.6,7
　winding ~s, central support
　　for, 160.17
staircase,n., 160.6,7; see also
　　stair, step (for rising),n.
　compartment containing ~,
　　160.11
　first support of ~ railing,
　　160.16
　last support of ~ railing,
　　160.16
　moving ~, 160.9
　railing of ~, 160.14
　support of ~ railing, 160.15
　top of ~, 160.12
stale,adj., 759.28
　become or make ~, 759.29
　phrase, attitude, etc., that is
　　~, 759.30
　statement that is ~, etc.,
　　674.9(3,5,7,8,11,18,28,30)
stalk,n., 991.1; see stem (of a
　　plant),n.
　~-shaped, 507.17(58)
stamina,n., 246.8
stammer,v., 671.1(35,96,97)
stamp,n.
　~ collecting, 678.13
　fondness for postage ~s,
　　700.30(26)
　study of ~s, 678.14
stand,n.
　support, 1022.2
　~ for table platter, vessel,
　　etc., 1022.2(30)
　one-legged ~, 1022.2(32)
　three-legged ~, 1022.2(29)
　two-legged ~, 1022.2(4)
　~ with shelves, 1022.2(33)

stand,v., 61.1
　~ for, 324.2(2,4) ; 954.2
　place where one ~s, 782.1(29,
　　30)
　~ something on its end or
　　top, 61.5
standard,n.
　criterion, 946.19
　flag, 957.1
　model, 317.1
　yardstick, 946.19
　~ of measurement, 946.19
stander,n., 61.3
standing,adj., 61.4
standing,n.
　manner of ~, 61.2
stanza,n., 689.12,13
star,n., 1056.1; see also heav-
　　enly body,n.
　among the ~s, 1056.15
　bright ~, 1056.3
　center of ~s, 137.1(5)
　coming from ~s, 1056.21
　consisting of ~s, 1056.23
　covered with ~s, 1056.23,31,32
　determined by the ~s, 1056.27
　dimming ~, 1056.4
　fate influenced by ~s, 1053.24
　five-pointed ~, 1056.39,40
　full of ~s, 1056.23,31,32
　gas around a ~, 1048.1(3)
　group of ~s, 1056.5,6,8–14,16
　group together like ~s, 1056.7
　guiding ~, 1056.2
　influenced by the ~s, 1056.34
　light from ~s, 1065.1(10)
　light of ~s, instrument to
　　measure, 1065.20
　lighted by ~s, 1056.31; 1065.7
　like ~s, 1056.22,24
　like the light of ~s, 1056.8
　mark with a ~-shaped sym-
　　bol, 1056.36
　measured by movement of the
　　~s, 1056.28
　new ~, 1056.4
　North ~, 1056.3
　ornament with a ~, 1056.30
　ornamented by ~s, 1056.29
　pert. to ~s, 1056.20
　position of ~s, instrument to
　　determine, 1053.34,35
　position of ~s as influence on
　　life, 1053.24
　position of ~s on one's
　　birthday, pert. to, 720.6
　prediction by ~s, 772.20(5,6,
　　22,28) ; 1053.36(2)
　science of ~s, 1053.36
　~-shaped, 507.17(76) ; 1056.24
　~-shaped figure, showing a,
　　1056.25,26
　shiny with, or like, ~s,
　　1056.33
　shooting ~, 1053.1(5)
　six-pointed ~, 1056.38
　something like a ~, 1056.35
　stare at the ~s, 1056.17,18
　symbol like a ~, 1056.35,38–
　　40
　symbol like a ~, mark with
　　a, 1056.36
　without ~s, 1056.19
　worship of the ~s, 656.15(23)
starch,n.
　conversion of sugar into ~,
　　pert. to, 449.7
　like ~, 987.17
　pert. to ~, 987.17
stare,n., 484.2
stare,v., 484.1
　~ about idly or dreamily,
　　1054.34–36
　~ in anger, 878.6(10)
starer,n., 484.3

starfish,n., 422.3
　like a ~, 422.2
　of ~es, 422.1(4,16)
staring,adj., 484.4
staring,n.
　~ at the moon, 1054.39
starling,n.
　group of ~s, 403.5(45)
start,n.
　beginning, 729.8,11; see be-
　　ginning,n.
　fright, 576.4
　sudden movement, 89.2;
　　110.2
start,v.
　begin, 729.1,7; see begin,v.
　move in fear, 576.3
　move suddenly, 89.1; 110.1
startle,n., 89.2; 110.2; 576.2,4
startle,v., 89.1,4; 110.1,10;
　　576.3,6
startling,adj., 576.7
starvation,n., 737.2
　cause of ~, 737.10
　die of ~, 737.6
　kill by ~, 737.7
starve,v., 737.3,4,6,7
starving,adj., 737.1
　~ person, animal, or plant,
　　737.5
state,n.
　condition, 44.1
　country or nation, 784.1; see
　　country (nation),n.
　inhabitant of a U.S. ~,
　　784.15(13)
　inhabitants of a U.S. ~,
　　784.17(2)
　nicknames of U.S. ~s, 694.29
　U.S. ~, 784.20
state,v., 674.8; see say,v.
　~ in writing under oath,
　　1086.6
　~ under oath, 1086.1,2
stated, adj. or v., 674.4; see
　　said, adj. or v.
statement,n., 674.9
　~ about business venture,
　　674.9(21)
　ambiguous ~, 674.9(31)
　authoritative ~, 674.9(9)
　curses, ~ containing, 882.3
　derogatory ~, 674.9(16)
　dull ~, 674.9(3,5,7,8,11,18,28,
　　30)
　formal ~, 674.9(20)
　~ in a play, 674.9(2)
　~ in logic, 674.9(19)
　indirect ~, 674.9(6)
　insincere ~, 674.9(10,32)
　make a ~, 674.8
　mathematical ~, 674.9(26)
　meaningless ~, 607.31;
　　674.9(11,23,30)
　nonsensical ~, 607.31;
　　674.9(11,23,30)
　obviously true ~, 674.9(28)
　~ of approval, 850.13
　~ of causes, 674.9(1)
　~ of political platform,
　　674.9(17)
　~ of reasons, 674.9(1)
　pert. to a ~, 674.10
　positive ~s, inclined to make,
　　674.11,12
　public ~ of policy, 674.9(13)
　sarcastic ~, 674.9(4,12) ;
　　1115.7(9)
　senseless ~, 607.31; 674.9(11,
　　23,30)
　series of ~s, 173.9(2)
　sharp ~, 674.9(4,12,15,25) ;
　　876.23
　~ subject to discussion,
　　674.9(27)

sworn ~s, 1086.3
~ that appears true, 812.11
unadorned in ~s, 959.11
unoriginal ~, 674.9(3,5,7,8,11, 18,28,30)
unproved ~, 674.9(19,24,26, 27)
witty ~, 674.9(14,22)
written ~ under oath, 1086.7, 8
static,adj., 59.1
condition of being ~, 59.2(1)
station,n., 782.1,3; see also **place**,n.
military ~, 782.1(19,21)
railroad ~, 782.1(6)
statue,n., 966.18
collection of ~s, 966.19
conventional, traditional, or fixed in style (of ~s), 966.21
hang or burn the ~ of, 966.22
like a ~, 966.20
naked ~, 965.1(36)
~s collectively, 966.19
sculptor of ~s, 966.18
sexual excitement from ~s, 710.33(20)
stone ~, 1006.1(27)
status,n., 44.1
stay,v., 757.1; see **remain**,v.
steadiness,n., 88.2; 526.6
steady,adj., 88.1; 526.6
become ~, 88.4
make ~, 88.3
~ state or condition, 88.2
steady,v., 88.3,4
steal,v., 250.1
~ cattle, 250.1(22)
compulsion to ~, 250.2(6)
compulsion to ~ books, 687.21
~ literary work, 250.1(15,16)
one who ~s, 250.3; see also **robber**,n.
stealing,n., 250.2
descr. of ~, 250.4
~ of books, 250.2(2)
skillful in ~, 7.2(4)
steel,n., 1017.1
articles of ~, 1017.12
bar of ~, 1017.1(1)
convert (iron) into ~, 1017.13
~ furnace, 1017.11
like ~, 1017.2(7)
of the color, strength, or hardness of ~, 1017.2(7)
place of manufacture of ~, 1017.10
relating to ~, 1017.2
tin-coated ~, 1020.16
worker with ~, 1017.8
steep,adj., 164.1; see **high**,adj.
steer,n., 410.1
steer,v., 177.1(8,13)
~ a plane, 177.1(11,13)
~ a ship, 177.1(3,5,8,11,13)
able to be ~ed, 177.7
lever for ~ing, 177.4(10,12)
one who ~s, 177.3
station for ~ing a ship, 177.6(1)
tower for ~ing a ship, 177.6(2)
steersman,n., 177.3
stem (of a plant),n., 991.1
creeping ~, 991.9–11
creeping ~s, structure for, 991.12,14,15
growing from a ~, 991.3
having a ~, 991.2
leaves and ~s, 993.8
~-shaped, 507.17(58)
tree ~, 991.6,7
underground ~, 991.4

woody ~ used in manufacture, 991.8
woody of ~, 997.20,21
stench,n., 445.9; see **odor**,n.
stench,v., 445.11
stenography,n., 682.12(4–8); see also **shorthand**,n.
something written in ~, 682.13
step (for rising),n., 160.1; see also **stair, staircase**,n.
arranged like ~s, 160.19
arrangement in ~s, 311.1(15)
~ for going over fence or wall, 160.5
group of ~s, 160.6
groups of ~s, 160.7
moving ~s, 160.9
~ of a ladder, 160.2
outside ~s of a house, 160.8
part of a ~ for feet, 160.3
scored like ladder ~s, 160.21
vertical part of a ~, 160.4
step (of the feet),n., 108.4
distance of horse's ~, 788.1(13)
~ in walking, 108.4
light in ~, 949.7(5–7)
moving ~ by step, 108.5
~s in a dance, 109.3
slow in ~, 100.6(29)
step,v., 108.1
~ on, 108.2
~ over, 108.3
stepmother,n.
pert. to, like, or fit for a ~, 722.7(10)
stepping,n.
sound of ~, 469.5,6
sterile,adj., 716.1
make ~, 716.4
sterility,n., 716.1
stern,adj., 890.6; see **strict**,adj.
stethoscope,n., 454.20(2)
stick,n.
club or weapon, 437.5
piece of wood, 997.5
staff or rod, 437.7
close with ~s, 997.6
cover with ~s, 997.6
divining ~, 486.5
flaming ~, 1065.107(7,22)
~ for mountain climbing, 159.11
~ for roasting meat, 437.8
forked ~ for hurling missiles, 565.20
orchestra leader's ~, 437.7(1)
~s for fire, 1064.61(2,6)
shepherd's ~, 437.7(3)
symbol of office, ~ as, 437.7(1)
walking ~, 437.7(2,5)
stick,v.
attach, 302.12,16
pierce, 332.22
able to ~, 302.24; see **sticky**, adj.
able to ~ out, 958.4
cause to ~ out, 958.3,10
cause to ~ together, 302.12
causes to ~, that which, 302.14
causing to ~, 302.15
~ out, 172.1(1,7,10,12); 958.1–3
~ out in rounded projection, 958.12
~ out over, 958.2
part that ~s out, 326.1(28,36, 40); 958.7
tendency to ~, 302.19,25
tending to ~, 302.18,24; see also **sticky**,adj.

thing that ~s out, 958.7; see also **projection**,n.
~ together, 302.12,16
~ up, 958.9
~ with, 754.19
stickiness,n., 302.25; see **sticky**,adj.
sticking,adj., 302.18,24; see also **sticky**,adj.
~ easily, 302.24(1,2)
sticking,n.
attachment by ~, 302.13,17
causes ~ together, that which, 302.14
~ out, 958.1,3
~ together, 302.13,17
~ together of bodily tissues, 302.23
stick-to-itive,adj., 754.20
sticky,adj., 302.24
~ condition, 302.25
damp and ~, 302.24(3,10,12); 1034.15
make ~, 302.27
moist and ~, 302.24(3,10,12); 1034.15
semi-liquid and ~, 302.24(9, 11,12,14,16)
~ substance, 302.26
stiff,adj.
severe, 890.6
steady, 88.1
strict, 890.6
stubborn, 553.1
unbending, 442.1; 553.1
unyielding, 442.1; 553.1
that which holds ~, 442.5
stiffen,v., 88.3,4; 442.3,4
stiffness,n., 88.2; 442.2; 553.2
degree of ~, 442.6
lack of ~, 443.2; 444.2
lacking ~, 443.1(4,6,8,11,13); 444.1
lose ~, 443.3(2,3); 444.3
losing ~, 443.4
still,adj.
calm, 1139.15; see **calm**,adj.
inactive, 58.1; see **inactive**, adj.
not moving, 59.1; see **motionless**,adj.
silent, 475.1; see **silent**,adj.
still,v.
become inactive, 58.6
calm, 1139.1
make inactive, 58.3
silence, 475.5
stillness,n.
calmness, 1139.16
lack of motion, 59.2
silence, 475.2
stimulant,n., 52.12; 1100.4
drink, 1.32–34; 748.5(2,7); 749.3
stimulate,v., 52.9; 1100.1
~ by, or as by, electricity, 1066.10
drink that ~s, 1.32–34; 748.5(2,7); 749.3
one who ~s, 52.13
that which ~s, 52.12
stimulated,adj., 1100.6
~ by heat, 1060.44
stimulating,adj., 52.14; 1100.2
~ drink, 1.32–34; 748.5(2,7); 749.3
stimulation,n., 52.11; 1100.1,7
~ by light, pert. to, 101.2
~ of organisms, 101.1
react to ~, 54.2(3)
reacting to ~, 54.3(2,3,4)
reaction to ~, 54.1(4,7,8,9)
stimulus,n., 52.12; 1100.4
biological reaction to ~, 54.1(9); 101.1

movement to or from a ~, 101.1
sting,n., 333.3
sting,v., 333.1,2
~ into action or reaction, 52.9; 1100.1
stinging,adj., 333.4
~ in language, 333.4(2,4–7); 334.1(1,6–8,12,22); 876.22
~ sensation, 333.3; 434.1(7,8, 13,15)
~ substance, 333.5
stinging,n.
adapted for ~, 333.6
sensation of ~, 333.3; 434.1(7, 8,13,15)
stingy,adj., 227.1
be ~, 227.2
greedy and ~, 265.16(2,11)
~ person, 227.3
stink,n., 445.9; see odor,n.
stink,v., 445.11
stinking,adj., 445.10
stir,n., 1100.7; 1101.1
stir,v.
become aroused (of an emotion), 1099.19
have an emotional effect on, 1099.1,12
mix, 320.11
move, 79.1,5; 83 1
stimulate, 52.9
stirred,adj., 1099.3,15
stirrer,n., 320.12
stirring,adj., 52 14: 1099.2,13; 1100.14
stitch,n., 305.2
stitch,v., 305.1
stock,n.
amount, 914.1(1)
ancestry, 723.1
cattle, 403.4
store, 262.1; 915.13
disturbance of prices in the ~ market, 1101.1(12)
~ exchange, 210.12
falling ~ market, 210.13(1)
floating of ~s, 113.7
~ market, 210.12
rising ~ market, 210.13(2)
~s and bonds, 255.10(8)
stock,v., 262.1
stockade,n., 300.7
stocking,n., 979.16
maker or seller of ~s, 205.5(11)
ornament on a ~, 979.18
~s, 979.17
stocky,adj., 1.6; 510.1; 517.7
stolen,adj.
what is ~, 250.5
stomach,n., 347.1
disorders of the ~, 347.12; 389.1(35)
gas in the ~, 1048.1(13)
~-minded, 1091.2
pain in the ~, 1137.56(2,7,10, 13,15,27,30)
pert. to the ~, 347.2
science of the ~, 401 1(17,22, 23)
tube from mouth to ~, 347.6–8
upon the ~, 347.3
wavelike motion of the ~, 93.2(1)
stone,n., 1006.1; see also rock,n.
birth~, 961.16
~ for furnace, 1064.59
precious ~, 961.10–19,21; see gem,n.
~ used in jewelry, 961.10–21
Stone Age,n., 769.9(3,5,9,10,12)

stony,adj., 1006.33; see also rocky,adj.
stool,n.
feces, 293.6
seat, 63.1(2,6,11,13,19,23)
foot~, 63.3
stop,n., 791.3
bring to a ~, 791.1
come to a ~, 791.2
stop,v., 791.1,2
prevent, 78.1
~ a disease, 791.1(1,3)
cause to ~, 791.1
~ doing, 791.1(6); 791.2(2)
~ from doing, 791.1(10,12,16); see also prevent,v.
never, or not, ~ping, 755.1,2
~ temporarily, 791.1(20,21); 791.2(3)
~ the flow of, 791.6
~ the growth or development of, 731.28; 791.1(1,3,8,15)
~ the motion of, 59.4; 791.1(4, 7,8,17,19,20,22)
~ up, 558.1(2,3,4,14,23,24,37, 38,41,50,55)
~ working, 791.2(4,6)
stoppage,n., 791.3
cause of ~, 791.4
causing ~, 791.5
stopper (plug),n., 297.9
remove the ~ from, 298.1(20, 24,26)
storage,n.
building for ~, 998.17
container for ~, 261.1(5)
make more useful by ~, 279.21
place of ~, 262.3; see also storehouse, storeroom,n.
room for ~, 787.7(15,28,33,42)
tank for ~ of water, 262.3(6); 1033.48
store,n.
shop, 212.7
stock, 262.2
store,v., 262.1
collect and ~, 262.1(4,13)
stored,adj.
what is ~, 262.2
storehouse,n., 262.3; see also storeroom,n.
~ for goods, 262.3(18,33)
~ for grain, 262.3(9,13,14,24)
~ for military supplies, 262.3(12,18)
~ for valuables, 262.3(10,11, 21,30–32)
~ for water, 262.3(6,22,28); 1033.48
~ for weapons, 262.3(1,2,12)
~ of information, 262.3(29, 31)
~ of wealth, 262.3(31)
underground ~, 262.3(32)
storeroom,n., 262.3; 787.7(15, 28,33,42); see also storehouse,n.
~ for ammunition, 262.3(18)
~ for clothing, 787.7(15,42)
~ for food, 262.3(16,19); 787.7(28)
~ for glassware or china, 787.7(28)
~ for liquids, 262.3(28)
~ for liquor, 262.3(5)
~ for pots, dishes, etc., 262.3(19); 787.7(28,33)
~ for provisions, 262.3(19); 787.7(28)
~ for valuables, 262.3(10,11, 21,30–32)
~ for weapons, 262.3(1,2,18)
ship's ~, 262.3(17)
stork,n.

group of ~s, 403.5(47)
storm,n.
commotion, 1101.1; see commotion,n.
violence, 4.3
descr. of violent ~s, 4.9
ice ~, 1040.2
~ of frozen rain, 1040.2
protected against ~s, 1042.23
protection against ~s, 1042.25; see also shelter,n.
shut in by ~s, 1042.20
snow~, 1039.7,8; 1042.27(1)
wind~, 1042.27; 1044.7
~ with thunder and lightning, 1044.6,7
without ~s, 1042.26
stormy,adj., 1042.21
full of commotion, 1101.3
violent, 4.1
~ condition, 4.2; 1042.22
story,n., 685.1; see also book, legend, literature, myth, novel, writing,n.
floor, 1025.1
~ about animals, 685.1(5,9)
~ about books, 687.22
amusing ~, 685.1(3)
~ collection, 682.19; 685.2
continuing ~, 685.1(28,29)
end of a ~, 792.6(2); 792.3(1, 2,7)
exciting ~, 1100.4
fairy ~, 662.13
famous ~, 615.5
fantastic ~, 685.1(12)
foolish ~, 685.1(21)
happy ~, 685.1(6,34)
humorous ~, 685.1(6)
incredible ~, 685.1(35)
love ~, 685.1(25)
~ of giants, 662.16
~ of heroism, 685.1(26)
~ of one's own life, 682.16(4, 40)
~ of remembered experiences, 627.27
~ of someone's life, 682.16(6)
outline of a ~, 685.1(27)
part of a ~, 326.1(17)
place where a ~ occurs, 782.8
~ presented on the stage, 685.1(8); see drama, performance (theatrical),n.
put in the form of a ~, 685.4
sad ~, 685.1(33,34); 1128.20
short ~, 685.1(7,17)
tell a ~, 613.17(5,9); 685.3
tell the ~ of, 613.23(4,9)
teller of a ~, 685.5; see also author,n.
~ told from memory, 685.1(14,23)
~ told for pity, 1127.15
~ with a moral, 685.1(2,4,5,9 22)
write a ~, 685.3
writer of a ~, 685.5; see also author,n.
stout,adj.
brave, 575.1; see brave,adj.
fat, 510.1; see fat,adj.
strong, 1.6; see strong,adj.
stove,n., 1061.9
small ~, 1061.9(1)
St. Peter,n.
pert. to ~, 651.10
St. Vitus's dance,n., 378.11(1)
straight,adj., 180.1
forming a ~ line, 180.3
lying in a ~ line, 180.2
moving in a ~ line, 180.3
not ~, 181.1; 183.1
~ of hair, 369.18(4)
standing up ~, 61.4(1)

~ up, 180.1(2,5,12)
~ up and down, 180.1(5–8,13)
straightness,n., 180.1
  weight to measure ~,
    947.15(4) ; 947.17
strain,v.
  pull, 193.1
  sift, 901.2
  stretch, 194.1
  try, 18.1
strainer,n., 901.1
  use a ~ on, 901.2
strange,adj.
  foreign, 538.1
  inexperienced, 620.1
  odd, 536.1,4
  unaccustomed, 629.25
  uncustomary, 629.3
  unfamiliar, 612.23
  unknown, 612.23
  unusual, 536.1,4
  ~ person, act, etc., 536.2,5
stranger,n., 118.3(1) ; 538.4
  hatred of ~s, 880.17(12)
strangle,v., 376.16,17; 796.11,12
  iron collar that ~s, 796.14
strangler,n., 796.13
strangulation,n., 376.18; 796.11
strap,n., 302.32
  leather ~, 302.32(3)
  leather ~ for a dog,
    302.32(15)
  leather ~s for a horse,
    302.32(10)
  shoe ~, 386.7
stratagem,n., 823.13
strategy,n., 7.1; 46.2
  use superior ~ against, 833.17
straw,n.
  ~-colored, 987.28
  cover with ~, 972.1(50)
  like ~, 987.27
  made of ~, 987.26
  pert. to ~, 987.26
  roof of ~, leaves, etc.,
    973.1(10)
strawberry,n.
  of the ~ family, 985.33(8)
stray,adj., 264.4
stray,n., 264.8
stray,v., 128.1; 264.7
streak,n., 502.1
  dirty ~, 904.4
  ~ on the skin, 502.1(10,12–14)
streak,v., 502.3
streaked,adj., 502.2
stream,n.
  current, 1031.1
  flood, 112.2
  flow, 112.2
  pouring, 1036.3
  river, 1029.18,19; see river,n.
  ~ of excess water, 1026.17
stream,v., 112.1
street,n., 123.1; see also road,n.
  signal to leave the ~s,
    956.1(5)
street cleaner,n., 899.30
street cleaning,n.
  department of ~, 899.31
streetcar,n., 192.10
  ~ driver, 192.11
strength,n., 1.2; see also
  strong,adj., vigor,n.
  act of ~, 52.5(39)
  call upon ~, 1.38
  character, ~ of, 1.22
  causing growth and ~, 731.24
  empty of ~ or energy,
    926.21(2,5,7)
  full of ~, 1.1,5–8,10,12,16,18–
    21; see strong,adj.
  get back ~, 1.37; 240.14
  give ~ to, 1.29
  give new ~ to, 1.35

~ giver, 1.32,34
giving ~, 1.31
~-giving drink, 1.34
~-giving medicine, 1.34
lacking bodily ~, 10.1(4,5) ;
  see also weak,adj.
lacking in ~, 10.1(4,15,19,26,
  37,43,45,46,56,63,66,71,75) ;
  see also weak,adj.
lose ~, 10.8
muscular ~, 1.7
reduce in ~, 10.5
regain ~, 1.37; 240.14
restore ~, 1.35
source of ~, 1.28
test of ~, 19.1(2)
~ to endure, 1.17
strengthen,v., 1.29,30
  ~ again, 1.35,37,38
  ~ by addition, 1.29(13)
  ~ foundation or wall, 1006.8
  ~ in color, 1.29(9,17)
  ~ in feeling, 1.29(5)
  ~ in habit, 1.29(5)
  ~ in quality, 1.29(9)
  ~ in volume, 1.29(17)
  ~-ing, 1.31,36
  ~ mentally, 1.29(7)
  ~ morally, 1.29(1,7)
  ~ physically, 1.29(7)
  ~ with brick, 1006.60
  ~ with stone, 1006.60
strenuous,n., 193.19; 194.2; 195.4
stretch,v., 193.18(4,10,13,16,18,
  21,22) ; 194.1; 195.1,2; see
  also spread,v.
  able to ~, 194.5
  ~ across, 194.1(2,9,12)
  ~ out, 194.1(1–10)
  ~ out beyond, 194.1(4)
  ~ out in length, 193.18(10) ;
    194.1(3,8,10)
  ~ out in time, 193.18(16) ;
    194.1(3,8)
  ~ over, 194.1(2,9,12)
  space that something ~es to,
    787.1(2,7,9,15,16,19–21)
  that which ~es out, 194.3
  ~ (the neck), 193.18(4)
  ~ tight, 193.18(21,22) ;
    194.1(13)
stretched,adj., 195.6
  able to be ~, 193.24
  become ~, 194.1; 195.1
  condition of being ~, 193.22
  ~ tight, 193.25
stretcher,n., 193.20; 194.3
  ~ for the wounded, 190.4(6)
stretching,n., 193.19; 194.2;
  195.4
  capable of ~, 194.5
  descr. of ~, 193.21
  ~ of cord, pert. to, 193.23
strict,adj., 890.6
  excessively ~ in moral
    behavior, 843.21
  ~ in demands or require-
    ments, 890.9
  ~ in judging others, 890.10
  ~ in performing official du-
    ties, 890.11
  less ~, become, 890.13
  less ~, make, 890.14
  not ~, 890.12
  treat ~ly, 890.7
strictness,n., 890.6
  practice of ~, 890.7
strike,n.
  blow, 437.2; see blow,n.
  refusal to work, 206.1(8,15,
    16)
strike,v.
  hit, 437.1; see hit,v.
  not work, 209.5
strikebreaker,n., 206.2(1,2,4)

string,n., 302.32; see cord,n.
strip,n.
  ~ of wood or metal for
    support, 326.15(4)
  ~ of wood or metal in a
    blind, 326.15(4)
strip,v.
  remove, 249.1
  take, 247.23
  uncover, 972.6
  undress, 984.12
stripe,n., 502.1
  arrange in ~s, 311.2(1)
stripe,v., 502.3
striped,adj., 502.2
strip-teaser,n., 984.13
strive,v., 18.1
  what one ~s for, 18.6
striving,n., 18.2(4,5,8)
  sexual ~, 709.10
  ~ toward a goal, 18.2(4)
stroke,n.
  attack (of disease), 560.24
  blow, 437.2
  caress, 701.2
  paralysis, 377.15
  touch, 436.2
  finishing ~, 792.20
stroke,v., 436.1; 701.1
strong,adj., 1.1; see also
  strength,n., vigorous,adj.
  not diluted, 1.25
  ~ and active, 57.4(22,24)
  ~ and big, 1.1(1,2) ; 906.8
  ~ and healthy, 1.5
  ~ and manly, 1.1(4)
  ~ and rough, 865.1(13)
  ~ and slim, 1.1(9)
  ~ as metal, 1012.11(4)
  be ~er, 1.27
  become ~, 1.30; 731.3(3,5,15,
    32)
  becoming ~er, 1.30,37;
    907.4(2)
  ~ giant, 1.39
  ~ in body, 1.1(5) ; 1.6
  ~ like brass, 1016.13
  ~ like iron or steel, 1017.2(4,
    7)
  make ~, 1.29,35
  make ~er, 1.29
  ~ man, 1.39
  ~ (of abstractions), 1.18
  ~ (of arguments), 1.24
  ~ (of colors), 1.20
  ~ (of language), 1.19
  ~ (of qualities), 1.18
  ~ (of style), 1.19
  ~ (of water current), 1.21
  ~ (of wind), 1.21
  ~ person, 1.3,4; 906.18(1,6,9,
    14)
  prove ~er, 1.27
  remaining ~, 1.23
  ~, thin, and pliable, 990.14
  ~ thing, 906.18(1,6,9,14)
structural,adj., 727.5
  ~ skill, 727.8
structure,n., 727.4,12,17; see
  also building,n.
structure,n.
  construction, 726.3; 727.2
  ~ across water, 1033.49,52
  ~ against water, 1033.1,5
  ~ alongside water, 1033.10,11,
    17
  commemorative ~, 727.17(4)
  ~ for passage of water,
    1033.22–24,28,29,31,34,39,
    42,44–46
  high ~, 727.17(1,7)
  ~ in water, 1033.10,11
  netlike ~, 727.17(5)
  pert. to ~, 727.5
  roof ~, 727.17(2,3,6,7)

~ to confine water, 1033.1,5
top ~, 727.17(6,7)
struggle,n., 21.2,3
  anguished ~, 21.2(4)
  final ~ before death,
    1137.10(1)
  rough ~, 865.7
  short, quick ~, 21.2(3)
struggle,v., 21.1; 85.1
  ~ at close quarters, 21.1(10,
    14)
  ~ for advantage, 21.1(15)
  ~ for superiority, 21.1(5,15)
  ~ in competition, 21.1(4,5,8,
    12)
  ~ in confusion, 21.1(9,10,14)
  ~ in opposition, 21.1(8,12)
  ~ on equal terms, 21.1(6)
  ~ successfully, 21.1(6)
  ~ to get, 21.1(5)
  ~ with bodily, 21.1(16)
struggler,n., 21.3
strychnine,n., 800.2
  illness caused by ~, 800.13
stubborn,adj., 553.1
  continuing, 754.20
  continue ~ly, 553.4
  ~ person, 553.3
stubbornness,n., 553.2
stuck,adj.
  become ~ together, 302.16
  ~ together, 302.20
student,n., 622.5; see also
  learner,n.
  ~ accepted by a college,
    623.11
  ~ before graduation,
    622.5(23)
  Cambridge ~, 622.5(6)
  clergy ~, 622.5(20)
  college ~, 622.5(2,10)
  devoted ~, 622.5(24)
  fellow ~, 622.5(8,11,19)
  female ~, 622.5(9)
  first-year ~, 622.6(1,3)
  fourth-year ~, 622.6(4,6)
  ~ graduated from a school,
    622.5(16); 623.12; see also
    graduate,n.
  military-school ~, 622.5(5)
  Oxford ~, 622.5(15)
  research ~, 622.5(21)
  research ~s, class of, 622.8
  ~s, 622.7
  second-year ~, 622.6(3,5)
  third-year ~, 622.6(2,6)
studied,adj.
  what is ~, 622.3
studies,n.
  pert. to ~, 622.4
  pert. to adult ~, 622.4(2,5)
studio,n., 203.11(1)
studious,adj., 622.9
study,n., 622.2,3
  room, 787.7(11,17,38)
  course of ~, 622.3
  outside the course of ~,
    623.4–6
  pert. to ~, 622.4
  sphere of ~, 782.9
study,v., 622.1
  examine, 485.1; 624.8
  ~ again, 622.1(6)
  ~ late at night, 622.1(3)
  room in which to ~, 787.7(11,
    17,38)
  ~ with (a teacher), 622.1(2,
    9)
studying,n., 622.2
  fond of ~, 622.9
  given to ~, 622.9
  pert. to ~, 622.4
stuff,v., 319.7; 928.2
stumble,v.
  fall, 168.1

make a mistake, 829.2
stunt,n., 52.5
stunt,v., 731.28; 909.6(1)
stunted,adj., 731.28
  ~ animal, 909.4(1,5,7)
  become ~, 909.7
  make ~, 909.6(1,4)
  ~ person, 909.3(13)
stupefaction,n., 435.1; 597.22
  surprise, 271.3
  causing ~, 597.23
stupefied,adj., 435.3; 597.21
  ~ by liquor, 597.21(3)
stupefy,v., 435.2; 597.20
  surprise, 271.2
  ~ with liquor, 597.20
stupefying,adj., 435.4; 597.23
  surprising, 271.1
stupid,adj., 100.6(23); 597.1,6,
  10,19
  nonsensical, 608.5
  stupefied, 435.3; 597.21
  ~ act, 597.4
  big and ~, 906.3(1)
  cause to appear ~, 597.24
  clumsy and ~, 14.1(6); 597.14
  clumsy and ~ person, 597.15
  coarse and ~, 597.13
  complacently ~, 597.11
  ~ condition, i.e., stupefac-
    tion, 597.22
  ~ condition, i.e., stupidity,
    597.2,18; see stupidity,n.
  ~ from old age, 597.26
  looking ~, 597.25
  make ~, i.e., stupefy,
    597.20
  ~ person, 597.3,15–17,28;
    1054.37
  ~ person intelligent in one
    area, 597.17(5)
  something ~, 597.4,5
stupidity,n., 597.2,4,18
  nonsensicality, 608.6
  ~ from old age, 597.27
  instance of ~, 597.4
stupor,n., 58.2; 435.1; 597.22
  ~ from narcotics, 399.15(6,7)
stuporous,adj., 58.1; 435.3
sturdy,adj., 1.6; 88.1
stutter,v., 671.1(35,95,96)
style,n.
  fashion, 631.1
  manner, 50.1
  descr. of refined artistic or
    literary ~, 859.2
  in English ~, 784.18
  in French ~, 784.19
  strength of language or ~,
    1.19
stylish,adj., 631.7; see also
  fashionable,adj.
  ~ and neat, 902.1(1,6,9)
  ~ and speedy, 631.9
  make ~ and neat, 902.3(2,3)
subconscious,adj., 584.8
subdue,v.
  overcome, 22.23,29
  put down revolt, etc., 22.39
  reduce in sound, 462.15
  weaken, 10.5
  ~ by withholding food, 22.42
subject,n., 671.26
  dealing with ~s of temporary
    interest, 756.4
  wander from the ~, 128.1(3,4,
    12,17); 682.10
  wandering from the ~,
    128.2(2); 128.4
submarine,n., 115.16(13)
  observation tower on a ~,
    480.13(1)
submission,n., 552.2,4
  gesture of ~, 552.8
submissive,adj., 552.3

submissiveness,n., 552.4
submit,v., 552.1
  forced to ~, 22.38
submitter,n., 552.5
subordinate,adj., 313.17; 848.35
subservient,adj.
  slavish, 310.11
  submissive, 552.3
  make ~, 552.9
subsidiary,adj., 556.4; 908.13,40
subsidiary,n., 556.2; 908.14
substance,n., 808.1,7; see also
  matter,n.
  central meaning, 607.3
  main idea, 586.11
  without ~, 10.1(22,31,33,59,
    67); 513.12; 909.11; 949.1(2,
    4,6,7); 1071.3
substitute,adj., 324.5
  ~ actor, 324.4(16)
substitute,n., 324.4
  ~ falsely entered in a contest
    or race, 324.4(13)
  used as a temporary ~, 756.3
substitute,v., 324.1,2
  able to be ~d, 324.6
  falsely ~d for the genuine,
    324.8
substitution,n., 324.3,4
  capable of ~, 324.6
  pert. to ~, 324.7
subtle,adj.
  clever, 595.1,2
  deceptive, 823.7
  delicate, 11.1
  elusive, 244.8
  hard to understand, 604.1
  insubstantial, 513.12
  mysterious, 604.1
  secret in operation, 971.11,12
  shrewd, 595.1,2
  sly, 595.1,2
  thin, 513.12
  unsubstantial, 513.12
subtract,v., 247.20
subtraction,n., 247.21
  involving ~, 247.22
  less by ~, 910.19
  number in ~, 927.1(16,25,27)
  number resulting from ~,
    927.1(25)
suburbs,n., 783.1; 785.1
  inhabitant of the ~, 785.2
  inhabitants of the ~, 785.4
succeed,v., 23.1
  ~ financially, 23.11
  ~ in completing, 23.10
success,n., 22.12; 23.4
  achiever of commercial ~,
    23.14(1–3)
  activities followed to gain ~,
    57.10
  ~ at excessive cost, 23.7
  brilliant ~, 23.6
  critical rather than commer-
    cial ~, 23.8
  financial ~, 23.11
  important to ~, 848.16
  indicating ~, 23.15; 951.5(2)
  lack of ~, 24.2
  promising ~, 23.15
  quality indicating future ~,
    1122.17,18
successful,adj., 22.11; 23.2,3
  ~ act, 52.5(19)
  be ~ against, 23.12,13
  be ~ finally, 1111.33
  ~ in a contest, 23.5
  ~ in an attempt, 23.5
  ~ in battle, 23.5
  ~ person, 23.14
  to be ~, 23.1
successfulness,n., 23.4
suck,v.
  adapted to ~, 134.6

~ from the breast, 360.13
~ in, 134.1; 193.8(1)
operated by ~ing, 134.7
suckle,v., 360.11–13
sudden,adj., 270.1; see also
unexpected,adj.
acting out of ~ feeling, 270.6
~ in movement, 89.3
~ movement, 89.2
sharp and ~, 270.1(2);
334.1(5)
~ thing, 270.3
violent and ~, 270.1(5)
violent and ~, but temporary,
4.11
suddenly,adv.
acting ~, 52.3(1,2); 270.6
bring on ~, 270.4
heavily and ~, 270.5; 948.5
move ~, 89.1,4
suddenness,n., 270.2
suds,n., 899.44
suds,v., 899.46,47
sue,v., 1082.11,14; see lawsuit,n.
suffer,v., 1130.8; 1137.11
allow, 554.1
endure, tolerate, 246.1
cause to ~ emotionally,
1130.1,5
cause to ~ physically,
1137.1,9
sufferer,n., 1130.10; 1137.58
suffering,adj., 1130.7,9; 1137.12
suffering,n., 1130.6; 1137.10; see
also pain,n.
suffocate,v., 376.16,17; 794.29;
796.11
suffocation,n., 376.18; 794.29;
796.11
cause of ~, 376.20; 796.14
disease causing sensation of
~, 351.6(1)
suffrage,n., 254.1
sugar,n., 449.1
amount of ~, instrument to
measure, 449.6
coated with ~, 449.3
~ coating for cakes, etc.,
1059.21
conversion of ~ into starch,
449.7
convert into ~, 449.5
fill with ~, 449.5
full of ~, 448.1; 449.4
paste of ~, 449.1(7)
place to purify ~, 900.7
preserved with ~, 449.3(1)
substitute for ~, 449.2
water and ~, 449.1(20,21,23)
yielding ~, 449.4
sugared,adj., 448.1
sugary,adj., 448.1
suggest,v., 238.1
~ as good, 238.1(4,12,15)
~ changes, 238.1(5)
~ for discussion, 238.1(3)
~ in derogation, 238.1(8)
suggested,adj., 238.5
suggester,n., 238.3
derogatory ~, 238.3(1)
suggestion,n., 238.2
art of ~ by symbols, 238.6
derogatory ~, 238.2(1,2)
self-~, 238.7; 400.6(10)
suggestive,adj.
obscene, 713.1
remindful, 627.32
tempting, 196.5; 196.5(8,11–
14)
suicide,n., 795.1,7
attempts ~, one who, 795.4,5
commit ~, 795.2
commits ~, one who, 795.3
Hindu ~, 795.1(4)
Japanese ~, 795.1(1,3)

pert. to ~, 795.6
sacrificial ~, 795.1(2)
where Judas committed ~,
796.19(1)
suit,n.
set of clothing, 974.35
law~, 1082.1; see lawsuit,n.
men's ~s, 974.22; see also
clothing, coat, jacket,
trousers,n., etc.
suit,v., 817.5,6; 1107.1
suitable,adj., 817.1; 1107.5
be ~, 817.5
be ~ to, 817.6
~ for inspection, 817.4
~ for presentation, 817.4
~ in language, 817.1
~ in time, 817.3
make ~, 817.7
~ to a person, 817.2
~ to a place, 817.2
~ to a time, 817.2
~ to an occasion, 817.2
~ to one's purpose, 46.17
sulk,v., 878.6
sulky,adj., 475.1(2,17); 878.10(2,
5)
be ~, 475.6(5); 876.16; 878.6
~ fit, 878.13
look ~, 876.17; 878.6(13,15,18,
23)
~ person, 475.3; 878.16
sullen,adj., 475.1(2,16);
878.10(2)
be ~, 475.6(5); 876.16; 878.6
look ~, 876.17; 878.6(13,15,18,
23)
make ~, 876.13
~ person, 475.3; 878.16
sulphur,n.
treat with ~, 989.11
sultan,n.
~ of Turkey, 1073.36(22)
~'s concubine or mistress,
1073.41(7)
~'s daughter, mother, sister,
or wife, 1073.41(8)
sum,n., 328.8; 908.37
sum,v., 908.35
summarization,n., 912.4
final ~ in law court, 912.6
summarize,v., 912.2
summarizer,n., 912.3
summary,n., 912.1
be a ~ of, 912.5
final ~ in law court, 912.6
make or give a ~ of, 912.2
~ of previous ownership,
912.1(1)
summer,n., 770.1
beginning of ~, 1055.16
like ~, 770.6
middle of ~, 770.2
pert. to ~, 770.5
spend the ~, 770.11(1,3)
summit,n., 165.1
summon,v., 693.1; see also
call,v.
gesture to ~, 102.1(1,6)
one who ~s spirits, 693.5
~ to court, 275.1(13)
summons,n., 275.2; 693.2
gesture or signal of ~,
956.1(3,12,14)
sumptuous,adj., 223.14(10);
740.20(4); 847.1
sun,n., 1055.1; see also heavenly body,n.
~ and planets, 1053.17
~ as center, 1055.6
coming from the ~, 1055.3
conjunction of planet and ~,
pert. to, 1053.23
dark patch on the ~, 1055.35
darken (the ~), 1055.20

direction of the ~, in the,
1055.43
eclipse of the ~, 1055.18
farthest point from the ~ in
orbit of planet or comet,
1053.21
gas around the ~, 1048.1(3)
god of the ~, 1055.39
highest point of the ~,
165.1(11)
illustrate ~ and planets,
device to, 1053.18
influenced by the ~, 1055.2
instrument used for the ~,
1055.7
jewel in form of ~'s rays,
959.3(20)
light around the ~, 1065.21–
24
light from the ~, 1065.1(12);
see sunlight,n.
lighted by the ~, 1065.6
like the ~, 1055.5
movement away from the ~,
101.1(1)
myth interpretation by the
~, 1055.41
nearest point to the ~ in
orbit of planet or comet,
1053.22
operating by means of the ~,
1055.2
ornament in form of the ~'s
rays, 959.3(20)
path around the ~, 1053.20
path of the ~, 1055.11
pert. to the ~, 1055.2,3
position of the ~, instrument
to determine, 1053.34,35
produced by the ~, 1055.2
protective device against the
~, 568.23
radiation from the ~, 1055.27
ray of ~light, 1065.28
revolution around the ~,
1053.20
revolution around the ~,
time required for, 1055.38
rising of the ~, 775.2; 1055.32;
see also sunrise,n.
rising of the ~, time of,
775.2; 1055.32; see also sunrise,n.
room admitting the ~,
787.7(34,40); 1055.26
science of the ~, 1055.9,10
setting of the ~, 1055.33
setting of the ~, time of,
777.6; 1055.33
shadow of the ~, 1071.1,2
shining of the ~ through
parted clouds, 1055.44
~spot, center of, 1055.37
spot on halo of the ~, 1065.23
~spot, outer part of, 1055.36
stimulation by ~, 101.1(7)
surface of the ~, 1055.34
time when the ~ crosses the
equator, 1055.12–14
time when the ~ is farthest
from the equator, 1055.15–
17
toward the ~, 1055.42
treatise on the ~, 682.15(4)
under the ~, 1055.4
without a ~, 1055.45
worship of the ~, 656.15(9);
1055.8
sunburn,v., 384.25
sunburned,adj., 384.24
Sunday,n., 776.9
pert. to ~, 776.10
strict observance of ~, 643.8,
9
sundial,n., 774.2(8,10,11)

sung,adj., 476.17; see also
sing,v., song,n.
~ by a choir or chorus, 476.18
~ without preparation, 48.10
sunlight,n., 1065.1(1,2,9,12,14)
affect by ~, 1055.28
attraction to ~, 1065.15
burst of ~, 1055.44
expose to ~, 1055.21–23
exposed to ~, 1055.25
fear of ~, 1065.16
illness caused by ~, 1055.29
ocean waters reached by ~,
referring to, 1065.18
penetrated by ~, 1065.14
ray of ~, 1065.28
room exposed to ~, 787.7(34,
40) ; 1055.26
safe against ~, 1055.30,31
sensitiveness to ~, 1065.17
strength of ~, instrument to
measure, 1065.19
use of ~ by plants, 1065.12,13
sunny,adj., 1065.6
happy, 1103.1; 1104.1
sunrise,n., 775.2; 1055.32
goddess of ~, 1055.40
period before ~, 775.3
sunset,n., 777.6; 1055.33
sunshine,n., 1065.1(12) ; see
sunlight,n.
sunshiny,adj., 1065.6
sunspot,n., 1065.23
center of ~, 1055.37
outer part of ~, 1055.36
superb,adj., 831.1
superficial,adj., 139.2; 170.11;
see also shallow,adj.
superficiality,n., 170.12
superfluous,adj., 273.11; 920.1
superior,adj., 833.1
act ~, 871.3; 871.3(3,5)
be ~ in authority, 833.16
be ~ in influence, 833.16
be ~ in number, 833.16
be ~ in power, 833.16
be ~ to, 833.15
~ circumstance, 833.6
~ condition, 833.6
feeling ~, 871.1; 871.1(1,10,39)
government by ~ people,
1073.42(2)
~ in importance, 833.3
~ in influence, 833.3
~ in number, 833.5
~ in order, 833.4
~ in position, 833.4,6
~ in power, 833.3
~ in rank, 833.4
~ people, 833.9
people who feel ~, 871.6
~ person, 833.8
person who feels ~, 871.5
try to be ~, 18.1(25)
try to be ~ to, 18.1(13) ;
833.12
use ~ strategy against, 833.17
superiority,n., 833.2
German ~, belief in, 833.10
give ~ to, 833.7
~ of circumstance, 833.6
~ of condition, 833.6
~ of position, 833.4,6
show of assumed ~, 871.2(7)
test of ~, 19.1(2)
treat with ~, 871.8
try for ~, 18.1(13,25)
supernatural,adj., 662.1; see
also ghostly,adj.
~ action, 662.4(3)
~ being, 662.7; see fairy,
ghost, spirit,n.
~ being, pert. to, 662.8
~ beings, world of, 662.18
belief in ~ beings, 662.9

belief in the ~, 632.6(15)
believing in the ~, 632.18(9)
explanation of the ~ by reasoning, 589.9
~ force, 662.7(38)
~ happening, 29.6(25) ; 662.3
~ influence, 662.4(8)
~ power, 5.1(20) ; 662.4
~ power, person with, 662.5
~ power, pert. to, 662.6
~ practice, 662.4
~ quality, 662.2
~ state, 662.2
~ thing, 662.3
world of ~ beings, 662.18
supervise,v., 8.14; 484.1(24)
~ an examination, 8.14(9)
supervision,n., 8.15
supervisor,n., 8.16
~ of women, children, girls,
etc., in an institution,
8.16(8)
supervisory,adj., 8.17
~ group, 318.1(13,49)
supper,n., 740.16(8)
eat ~, 734.1(13,32)
time for ~, 740.19
supplement,n., 908.14
supplementary,adj., 908.13,40
supplied,adj.
that which is ~, 233.3
supplier,n., 233.4
supplies,n., 915.16
~ for a journey, 915.17
military ~, 915.18
store up ~, 262.1(4–8,10,11,14)
supply,n., 914.1(1)
adequate ~, 915.15
available ~, 915.14
be in excessive ~, 915.10
concealed food ~, 970.52
excessive ~, 915.8
excessive in ~, 915.9
full ~, 915.1,2
have a large or full ~ of,
915.6
having a large or full ~,
915.7
in full ~, 915.4
in large ~, 915.4
~ kept for future, 915.13
large ~, 915.1,2
limited in ~, 917.27,30
~ of good things, 915.3
science of military ~, 190.12;
233.5
source of ~, 728.4(15,21,22,24)
supply,v., 233.1
~ abundantly, 915.11
~ excessively, 915.11
~ food, 233.1(5)
~ with a dowry, 233.1(6)
~ with a room, 233.1(1)
~ with clothing, 233.1(2,9,13)
~ with food, 233.1(1,10,12,15,
17,21,23,24)
~ with money, 233.1(7)
~ with sleeping quarters,
233.1(1)
supplying,n., 233.2
support,n.
backing, 854.3
defense, 854.16,17
a ~, 1022.2; see also column,n.
~ above a door, 1022.2(14)
~ above a window, 1022.2(14)
artificial ~, 1022.2(9)
balcony ~, 1022.2(7)
bridge ~, 1022.2(7,17) ;
1022.17
ceiling ~, 1022.2(13)
chief ~, figuratively, 1022.23
come to the ~ of, 854.15
depend on for ~, 526.3

door ~, 1022.2(17,25)
figurative ~, 1022.23,26
firm ~, 1022.22
floor ~, 1022.2(2,11,13)
~ for arch, 1022.2(27)
~ for arm, hand, foot, head,
etc., 1022.2(1,26,27)
~ for arms of candlestick,
1022.2(22)
~ for cornice, 1022.2(7) ;
1022.19
~ for cooking vessel,
1022.2(30)
~ for genitals (male),
1022.34
~ for hernia or rupture,
1022.33
~ for lever, 1022.2(10)
~ for movable object,
1022.2(26)
~ for pier, 1022.2(27)
~ for ship deck, 1022.2(2)
~ for staircase railing,
160.15,16
~ for statue, 1022.2(5,16)
~ for table platter, vessel,
etc., 1022.2(16)
~ for vase, 1022.2(16)
~ for walking, 1022.2(9,27)
furnish with a ~, 1022.4
gate ~, 1022.2(17)
get the ~ of, 854.20
giving ~, 1022.35
horizontal ~, 1022.2(8,11,14,
25,28)
lose one's ~, 168.1
loyal and unwavering ~
854.4
machine for driving ~s into
the ground, 1022.1
movement to which ~ is
given, 854.11
oblique ~, 1022.2(24)
~ of a cause, principle, party,
etc., in speech or writing,
854.16
~ of broken stones,
1022.2(21)
~ of crossed strips, 991.12,14,
15
~ of person with food, clothing, shelter, etc., 1022.31
one-legged ~, 1022.2(32)
picture ~, 1022.2(15)
pillow ~, 1022.12
protection, ~, and encouragement, 568.20
raise on ~s, 1022.8
raised on ~s, 1022.9
roof ~, 973.6; 1022.2(2) ;
1022.17
~s of a structure, 1022.16
ship ~, 1022.2(24)
solid ~, figuratively, 1022.26
source of figurative ~,
728.4(15)
speak in ~ of, 854.12,13
strip of wood or metal for ~,
326.15(4)
structural ~, 1022.2(6–8,11,12,
18–20,24,27) ; 1022.16
systematic ~ in argument,
854.17
three-legged ~, 1022.2(29)
triangular ~, 1022.2(5)
two-legged ~, 1022.2(4)
unchanging in ~, 531.5
~ under a wall, 1022.2(31)
vertical ~, 1022.2(17,18,19,20,
27) ; 1023.8
wall ~, 1022.2(25)
wall-projection ~, 1022.2(5–
8,23)
window ~, 1022.2(25)
without figurative ~, 1022.38

wooden ~, 997.5(2,9,13,15,21–23)
support,v.
  defend, 854.15
  endure, tolerate, 246.1
  favor, 854.1,12,13
  hold up, 1022.1,3,4,13,24
  support figuratively, 1022.13, 24,27,28,30
  ~ a bridge, 1022.18
  ~ a person, 1022.30
  ~ a roof, 1022.18
  ~ art, artist, etc., 854.2
  bag to ~ the hair, 983.40
  ~ both sides, 854.10
  capable of ~ing in fluid, 1022.36
  ~ candidacy of, 854.9
  ~ figuratively, 1022.13,24,30
  ~ hair with a bag, 983.41
  ~ solidly (figurative), 1022.24
  ~ with a pillow, 1022.11
  ~ with details, 1022.27
  ~ with food, clothing, shelter, etc., 1022.30
  ~ with proof, 812.15,18; 1022.28; see also **prove**,v.
supported,adj.
  ~ economically or emotionally, one who is, 1022.32
  water-~, 1026.5
supporter,n., 854.5
  ~ for the sake of argument or discussion, 854.19
  insincere ~, 854.19
  loyal ~, 854.8
  ~ of an institution, 854.7
  ~ of the Pope, 854.6
suppose,v., 245.1(7); 632.1(4,5, 7,10–13); 633.1
supposition,n., 245.3; 632.7(9, 11)
suppress,v.
  hold or keep back, 558.1
  keep (information, etc.) hidden or secret, 970.50
  put down (revolt, opposition, etc.), 22.39
suppressible,adj., 22.40
suppression,n., 558.2
suppressive,adj., 558.4
sure,adj., 641.1,6; see **certain**, adj.
sureness,n., 641.2,7
surface,n., 139.1
  ~ area, in metric system, 946.43
  bring to the ~, 139.7
  ~ coating, 972.4(3)
  come to the ~, 139.5; 159.1(8, 25)
  cover the ~, 972.1(56)
  ~ features of land, 1003.7
  flat ~, 139.1(1,4,8,9); 519.2
  front ~, 139.1(4)
  give a ~ to, 139.6
  grassy ~, 986.15,19
  inner ~ of a curve, 155.10
  large ~, 139.1(3,11)
  main ~, 139.1(4,6)
  ~ measurement in square feet, 946.42
  on the ~ only, 139.2; 170.11
  outer ~, 139.1(7)
  outer ~ of a curve, 155.11
  plane ~s, having, 139.3
  plane ~s, instrument to measure, 139.4
  rough ~, 139.1(2,12)
  sink (nail, etc.) below the ~, 167.4(1)
surgeon,n., 402.3,7
surgery,n., 402.1,5
  artificial parts, branch of ~ supplying, 401.1(80)

brain ~, 402.1(14,18); 402.5(23,27,28,41)
  ~ by electricity, 1066.24
  childbirth by ~, 402.5(4,5,13, 15,20,21)
  ~ for medical study, 402.1(3–7,11,12,17)
  limb removed by ~, person with, 402.9
  ~ on live animals, 402.1(22)
  ~ on live animals, opponent of, 402.11
  ~ on live animals, supporter of, 402.12
  perform ~, 402.2,6
  removal of specific parts by ~, 402.5
  specific ~, 402.5
  susceptible to ~, 402.10
  ~ to cure deformities, etc., 401.1(60,61)
  ~ to improve appearance, 402.1(2,13,16); 402.5(6,36, 42)
surgical,adj., 402.4,8
  ~ instrument, knife, etc., 402.13
surplus,n., 920.2; see **excess**,n.
surprise,n., 271.3,10
  by ~, 271.7
  cause of ~, 271.10
  cause to jump with ~, 110.10(4)
  feel ~, 271.8
  gaping in ~, 271.5
  holding one's breath in ~, 271.6
  jump in ~, 110.1(28,29)
  show ~, 271.9
  stare in ~, 484.1(7,13)
  staring in ~, 484.4(2)
  state of ~, 271.3
surprise,v., 271.2
surprised,adj., 271.4
  feel ~, 271.8
surprising,adj., 271.1
surrender,n., 230.2; 236.2; 552.2
  flag of ~, 957.11
  signal of ~, 957.11
surrender,v.
  give, 230.1(20,32)
  give up, 236.1
  submit, 552.1
surround,v., 300.1
  ~ by walls, 300.1(12,31,35)
  ~ed by curved lines, 300.5
  ~ed by ice, 1040.26
  something that ~s, 300.4
  ~ to prevent escape, 300.1(29, 30)
  ~ with a line, 300.1(11)
  ~ with armed forces, 300.1(2, 5,37)
  ~ with bushes, 996.31
  ~ with leaves, 300.1(15)
  ~ with shrubs, 996.31
  ~ with trees, 996.31
  ~ with trenches, 300.1(12,22)
surrounding,adj., 300.3
  ~ influences, 783.1(1,6,8)
  ~ mood or tone, 783.1(1,2)
  ~ parts, 783.1(4,6,13)
  ~ places, region, etc., 783.1
  resemblance to ~s, (of animals), 529.9
  ~ space, 787.1(1)
surrounding,n., 300.2; 783.1; see also **environment**,n.
survey,n., 484.2; 485.2
survey,v., 484.1; 485.1
surveying,n., 484.2; 485.2
  instrument used in ~, 944.20(2,4)

measurement unit in ~, 946.26(4,12)
surveyor,n., 484.3; 485.3
survival,n., 750.2,4; 754.2; 757.4
  ~ of species, theory of, 728.17(5)
survive,v., 750.1(15); 757.1
survivor,n., 750.4; 754.1
suspect,v., 632.1(4,11,13,14); 639.1
suspense,n., 268.5,6; 640.2
  holding one's breath in ~, 268.10
  wait in ~, 272.1(6)
suspicion,n., 639.2,4
  open to ~, 884.33
  put under ~, 639.15
  with ~, 639.9
suspicious,adj., 639.3(3,7–9,11, 12,14,16,19,20,22,23,26)
swallow,v., 736.1
swallow (bird),n.
  group of ~s, 403.5(27)
  like a ~, 405.10
  of ~s, 405.9(7,8)
swallowing,n., 736.2
  difficulty in ~, 736.5
  ~ of air, 1045.23
  ~ stones or gravel, 736.4
swamp,n., 1000.14
  full of ~s, 1000.17
  light over ~s, 1065.1(6)
  living or growing in ~s, 1000.18
swampy,adj., 1000.15–17
swan,n.
  female ~, 405.3(6)
  male ~, 405.2(3)
  place for ~s, 405.11(11)
  young ~, 405.4(4)
sway,n., 147.2
  authority, 5.4
  control, 8.2
sway,v., 147.1
  control, 8.1
  persuade, 638.1
  cause to ~, 147.4
swaying,adj., 147.3
swaying,n., 147.2
swear,v.
  curse, 861.12
  put under oath, 1086.9
  take an oath, 1086.2,6
  ~ to tell the truth, 1086.15
swearer,n., 861.11; 1086.4,10
  ~ to the innocence of another, 897.31
swearing,n.
  cursing, 861.10
  statement under oath, 1086.2,3,7,8
swearword,n., 861.13
sweat,n., 291.3
  bad odor of ~, 291.9
  ~ bath, place for, 899.53
  bubbles of ~, 1028.1
  causing ~, 291.13–15
  caused by ~, 291.12
  ~ cloth, 291.17
  pass through like ~, 291.5,6
  pert. to ~, 291.4
  producing ~, 291.16
  secreting ~, 291.8
sweat,v., 291.1
  ~ from heat, 1060.41,42
sweater,n., 976.6
sweating,n., 291.2
  causing ~, 291.13–15
  characterized by ~, 291.10
  increase in ~, 291.7
  pert. to ~, 291.4
  room for ~, 291.18
Swede,n., 784.15(41,42,56,57)
Sweden,n., 784.4(4)

Swedish,adj., 784.16
sweep,v., 899.1(2,17)
  ～ (dust, crumbs, etc.) from
    a surface, 899.32
sweeper,n., 899.33,34
sweet,adj., 448.1
  excessively ～, 448.1(6,8,9)
  ～ in sound, 467.3; 1105.21
  juicy and ～, 448.1(3,5)
  ～ sounds, 467.1,2
swell,v., 518.1,2
  increase, 907.1,2
  ～ (of the penis), 518.1(10)
swelled,adj., 518.4; see **swollen**,
    adj.
swelling,adj., 518.8
swelling,n., 518.3,6
  causing ～, 518.7
swift,adj., 95.1; see **rapid**,adj.
swim,v.
  ～ toward the bottom, 114.2
swimmer,n., 114.1
swimming,adj., 114.3
swimming,n., 114.4,7
  adapted for ～, 114.5
  art of ～, 114.4
  descr. of ～, 114.5
  pert. to ～, 114.5
  pool for ～, 114.6; 1026.19
  used in ～, 114.5
swimming pool,n., 1026.19
  descr. of a large ～, 1026.20
  indoor ～, 114.6
swindle,n., 823.13; 825.7
swindle,v., 825.1
swindler,n., 825.9
  clever ～, 796.3(4)
swine,n., 419.1,5; see **pig**,n.
swing,n., 147.2
swing,v., 147.1
  cause to ～, 147.4
swinging,adj., 147.3
  ～ body or object, 147.5
  ～ weight, 947.15(3)
Switzerland,n., 784.9(10)
  inhabitant of ～, 784.15(58)
  inhabitants of ～, 784.17(6)
  pert. to ～, 784.16
swollen,adj., 518.4
  able to be ～, 518.9
  become ～, 518.1
  becoming ～, 518.3,8
  make ～, 518.2
  ～ (of veins), 353.4(1,3)
  ～ part, 518.10
  ～ state or condition, 518.5
  ～ with gout, 1137.63
sword,n., 332.17
  belt for a ～, 980.7
  holder for a ～, 261.1(41,42)
  ～-shaped, 507.17(35,94)
  weakest part of ～, 332.18
swordsman,n.
  act the boastful ～, 872.5
  boastful ～, 872.19
sycophancy,n., 852.10
sycophant,n., 178.1(3,9,12,13,18,
    22,23); 852.9
  be a ～ to, 178.2
syllable,n., 668.1
  accented ～, 668.1(4)
  add a ～ to a word, 908.19
  add a ～ to the beginning of a
    word, 908.7
  add as a ～ at the beginning
    of a word, 908.7
  added ～ at the beginning of
    a word, 908.8
  added ～ at the end of a
    word, 908.18
  ～ added to a word, 908.20
  addition of a ～ to the end
    of a word, 668.8
  divide into ～s, 668.2
  emphasis on a ～, 670.4(1)

lengthening of a ～ in poetry,
    911.16
lengthening of a short ～,
    668.6
～ of a word, 666.15(1,4,5,8)
omission of ～s, 666.22;
    911.1(16)
pert. to ～s, 668.3
representation of ～s in pic-
    tures, 953.6
shortening of a ～ in poetry,
    911.15
shortening of a long ～, 668.5
similarity in sound of ～s,
    455.7(2)
slurring of a ～, 670.4(7)
sound that is a ～, 668.4
transpose ～s, 668.7
two vowels as one ～, 670.4(17,
    18)
unaccented ～, 668.1(2)
word of eight ～s, 666.8(4)
word of five ～s, 666.8(5)
word of four ～s, 666.8(6,7)
word of one ～, 666.8(3)
word of ten ～s, 666.8(1)
word of three ～s, 666.8(8)
word of two ～s, 666.8(2)
symbol,n., 954.1
  art of ～s, 954.12
  art of suggestion by ～s, 238.6
  be a ～ of, 954.2
  be a condensed ～ of, 911.4
  belief in ～, 954.19
  condensed ～, 911.5
  display by ～s, 954.9
  excessive use of ～s, 954.17
  group of ～s, 954.10
  identifying ～, 954.1(1,5,8,12)
  Indian ～, 954.1(13)
  interpretation of ～s, 954.12
  language of ～s, pert. to,
    664.2(3)
  magic ～, 1056.40
  Nazi ～, 954.1(11)
  ～ of a god, 954.1(14)
  ～ of class, 954.1(5)
  ～ of fertility, 954.1(2)
  ～ of friendship, 954.1(12)
  ～ of government, 1073.85
  ～ of idea, 954.1(5)
  ～ of Moslem political power,
    1073.85
  ～ of power, authority, or
    rule, 954.1(9); 1073.85
  ～ of productivity, 954.1(2)
  ～ of supernatural being,
    954.1(14)
  ～ of Turkish political power,
    1073.86
  post or column with ～s,
    954.21
  primitive ～, 954.1(13)
  represent beforehand by ～,
    953.3
  represent by ～, 953.1(9,10);
    954.2,7,8
  representation by written ～s,
    679.3
  secret ～, 604.3(4); 954.1(3)
  show by ～, 954.8
  starlike ～, 1056.35,37,38–40
  study of ～s, 954.12
  system of ～s, 954.10
  system of written ～s, 679.4
  use ～s, 954.7
  use of ～s, 954.11,17,19
  worship of ～s, 656.15(25);
    954.17
  written or printed ～, 679.1;
    954.1(8); see **letter, punc-
    tuation**,n.
symbolic,adj., 954.3
  ～ artist, 954.14
  consider as ～, 954.6

～ meaning, 954.13
～ representation, 953.10
spiritually ～, 954.5
treat as ～, 954.6
～ writer, 954.14
～ writing, 954.18
symbolism,n., 954.4,5,7,8,11
  ～ by means of animal forms,
    954.22
symbolize,v., 953.1; 954.2,8
  ～ a god or supernatural be-
    ing as an animal, 954.23
symmetrical,adj., 507.13(6);
    529.1(21,23)
  make ～, 950.3
  not ～, 950.18
symmetry,n., 529.2; 950.2
sympathetic,adj., 1129.1,6
  ～ emotional relationship,
    1092.81
  ～ person, 1129.7
sympathize,v., 1129.2,3
sympathizer,n., 1129.12
  secret ～s with the enemy,
    801.5
sympathy,n., 1129.5
  all-inclusive in ～, 259.5
  ask for ～, 1129.19,20
  be sad in ～ with (a
    mourner), 1129.8
  exciting ～, 1129.13–18
  express or show ～, 1129.2
  expressing or showing ～,
    1129.1,10
  expression of ～ with a
    mourner, 1129.9
  feel ～, 1129.2,3
  feeling ～, 1129.1,11
  lack of ～, 1129.22
  lack of ～, act that shows,
    1129.23
  not giving in to ～, 1129.24
  ～ of emotions, 1092.76,81
  trying to evoke ～, 12.8(2)
  without ～, 1129.22
  without ～, cause to be,
    1129.25
symposium,n., 672.2
  contributor to a ～, 633.11
symptom,n., 955
  be a ～ of, 955.6
  before the appearance of ～s,
    955.7
  combination of ～s in the
    middle ear, 955.3
  combination of medical ～s,
    955.2,4
  description of medical ～s,
    955.5
  increasing and decreasing
    medical ～s, 955.8
  medical ～, 955.1
  medical ～s, collectively,
    955.2,4
  not visible as a ～, 483.12(10)
  observable medical ～s, pert.
    to, 955.11
  period before the appearance
    of ～s, pert. to, 955.7
  pert. to medical ～s, 955.9–11
  predict from ～s, 772.11
  science of medical ～s, 955.12
  visible as a ～, 483.1(3)
  warning medical ～, 955.1
synthesis,n., 320.3,4; 321.3,4;
    726.3
synthesize,v., 320.1; 321.1;
    726.1
synthetic,adj.
  artifical, 811.4
  made, 726.4
  put together, 321.8
synthetic,n., 320.4; 726.3
syphilis,n., 379.9(2,6,12,17)
  germ causing ～, 403.21(18)

person with ~, 379.10
test for ~, 401.10(7)
treatment of ~, 400.6(25)
Syria,n.
science of ancient ~, 759.26, 27
syrup,n., 449.1(20,21)
system,n., 50.1
arrangement into a ~, 311.1(7,16,17,20,21,23,27,31, 36)
~ of living for health improvement, 740.13
~ of management, 8.18
systematic,adj., 50.3
make ~, 50.4

T

T.N.T.,n., 802.12
table,n., 1024.9
done or used at a ~, 1024.10
~ for dressing, 974.17
pert. to a ~, 1024.10
place on a ~, 1024.12
~-shaped, 507.17(77)
tact,n., 7.1(6,29,31,32,61) ; 1097.36
requiring ~, 7.8(2–4)
tactful,adj., 1097.36
be ~, 1097.37
tactless,adj., 14.1(19,41,59,71) ; 1097.35
tadpole,n., 424.2
tail,n., 349.1
animal with a cut ~, 911.11
cut ~, 911.11
end of the ~, 349.8
fleshy part of the ~, 349.6
having a ~, 349.3
part of the ~ left after cutting, 349.7; 911.10
pert. to the ~, 349.2
toward the ~, 349.5
with the ~ cut short, 911.12
without a ~, 349.4
tailor,n., 205.5(13)
pert. to a ~, 205.7
tailoring,n.
pert. to ~, 205.7
take,v., 247.1; see also **plunder,** **steal,**v.
accept, 245.1; see **accept,**v.
seize, 247.6; see **seize,**v.
~ a person away, 247.17
~ advantage of, 836.9,10,11
~ apart, 325.1
~ away, 249.1; see **remove,**v.
~ away a person, 247.17
~ away an abstraction, 247.18
~ away an amount, 247.20
~ away privileges, 247.23
~ away secretly, 971.44
~ back, 251.1
~ back a command, 251.1(1)
~ back a statement, etc., 251.1(2,4)
~ back one's belief, 251.1(2,3)
~ for granted, 632.1(4,9,11,12)
~ from a person, 247.23
~ from a place, 247.23
~ in, 134.1; see **absorb,**v.
~ into armed forces, 247.1(13, 18)
~ off, 984.1,2,5–7,9,10,12
~ off a quality or attitude, 984.12
person who ~s continuously from another, 750.17
taken,adj.
able to be ~ back, 251.2
amount ~ away, 247.21
~ by a sovereign, 247.5
not to be ~ away, 247.19
one who is ~, 247.9

that which is ~, 247.5,9; 248.5
unable to be ~ back, 251.3
taker,n., 247.3,25; 248.3
taking,n., 247.2
descr. of ~, 247.4
right of ~ in wartime, 6.1(1)
tale,n., 685.1; see **story,**n.
talent,n., 7.1; see **skill,**n.
without ~, 14.1(30,72)
talented,adj., 7.2; see **skillful,** adj.
talk,n., 671.2; see also **language, speech, talking,**n.
confused ~, 671.2(19)
disrespectful ~, 861.4
effusive ~, 671.2(38)
explanatory ~, 599.3(8)
feces, ~ about, 293.29
foolish ~, 607.26,28,30; 608.1–4; 671.2(1,6,10,14,17–19,29, , 34) ; see also **nonsense,**n.
~ full of sayings, 671.2(20)
incoherent ~, 671.2(35)
incoherent in ~, 671.24,25
informal ~, 671.2(7)
insincere ~, 671.2(5,8)
jesting ~, 671.2(4,5,27,28,31)
loose ~, 671.2(36)
meaningless ~, 607.26,28,30; 608.1–4; see also **nonsense,**n.
mocking ~, 671.2(5,27,31)
morality ~, 671.2(21)
nonsensical ~, 607.26,28,30; 608.1–4; 671.2(1,6,10,14,17–19,29,34) ; see also **nonsense,**n.
nonsensical ~, given to, 607.32
persuasive ~, 638.4
pert. to ~, 671.4
quaint ~, 671.2(41)
rapid ~, 671.23
refraining from ~, 671.20(1,3–8) ; see also **silent,**adj.
ribald ~, 671.2(34)
small ~, 671.2(28)
strange ~, 671.2(41)
teasing ~, 671.2(4,5,27,31)
vehement ~, 671.2(13)
witty ~, 671.2(4,27,32)
talk,v., 671.1
~ about, 671.5
~ about God or religion, 671.1(71,81)
~ about the appearance of, 671.5(6)
~ against, 671.9
~ ambiguously, 671.1(32,44, 73)
~ angrily, 671.1(4,10,40,41,57, 78,109) ; 878.6(1,12,19–22)
approach and ~ to, 132.1(1)
~ authoritatively, 671.1(68)
bad temper, ~ in a, 876.18
~ boastfully, 671.1(103)
~ boringly, 671.1(30,67,77)
breath, ~ with the, 671.1(94, 98,107)
~ carelessly, 671.1(5)
childlike tones, ~ in, 671.1(52)
~ clumsily, 671.1(95–97)
~ complainingly, 671.1(9,40, 41,53,57) ; see also **complain,**v.
~ conceitedly, 871.9
~ confusedly, 671.1(91,92)
~ continually about, 671.5(9)
~ deceitfully, 671.1(62,101) ; see also **deceive,**v.
delay, ~ for purposes of, 768.1(4,9)
delirium, ~ in, 1136.8

~ disrespectfully, 860.14
~ disrespectfully to or about God, the sacred, etc., 861.11,12
~ ecstatically, 671.1(80)
~ effusively, 671.1(42,83)
~ emotionally, 671.1(80,89) ; 1092.71
~ enthusiastically, 671.1(42, 78,80) ; 1095.17
~ evasively, 671.1(73)
~ excessively, 671.1(5,69)
~ excitedly, 671.1(42,78)
~ extravagantly, 671.1(76, 103)
~ familiarly to, 671.8(9)
favor of, ~ in, 854.12,13
~ favorably of, 854.13
~ flatteringly, 671.1(6,61) ; see also **flatter,**v.
~ foolishly, 607.27; 671.1(2,7–9,31,37,38,53,69,70,77,78,83, 99,102,109)
~ for effect, 671.1(25)
~ formally, 671.1(25–28,60,66)
~ frankly, 671.1(59)
~ frivolously, 609.9,10
~ hesitatingly, 671.1(35,52,95–97)
high-pitched tones, ~ in, 671.1(93)
hypocrite, ~ like a, 826.22
~ idly, 671.1(5,14,16–18,36,39, 49,61,70,99–103,106,108)
~ impolitely, 860.14
~ in support of, 854.12,13; see also **support,**v.
inability to ~, 671.21
inability to ~ or hear, 454.22(1) ; 671.21(5)
~ incoherently, 671.1(91,92) ; 671.25
~ indistinctly, 671.1(11,12,40, 41,47,48,53,55–57,64)
~ informally, 671.1(15,17,21–24,63)
~ insincerely, 671.1(62,84,90)
~ insistently, 671.1(105)
~ intimately, 671.1(15,21–24)
~ jestingly, 671.1(3,13,75,101)
~ lengthily, 671.1(26–28,33,66, 69)
~ liquidly, 671.1(11)
~ loudly, 671.1(7,10,19,43,74, 82,105,109)
~ low, 671.1(53,55–57,94,98, 107)
~ maliciously, 671.1(39,49)
~ maliciously of, 891.17
manner of ~ing, 665.8,9
~ meaninglessly, 607.27; 671.1(2,7–9,31,37,38,53,69, 70,77,78,99,102)
~ mockingly, 671.1(50,101) ; see also **ridicule,**v.
~ monotonously, 671.1(30,46)
~ monotonously about, 671.5(4,9)
~ morality, 671.1(51,54,81,84)
~ nasally, 671.1(58,84) ; 826.22
~ nervously, 671.1(92)
~ noisily, 4.13; 671.1(7,10,19, 43,66,74,109)
~ nonsensically, 607.27; 671.1(2,7–9,31,37,38,53,69, 70,77,78,99,102)
~ over, 671.5(7)
~ persuasively, 671.1(6)
~ piously, 671.1(84)
political platform, ~ from a, 1025.26
~ pompously, 671.1(60,68)
preacher, ~ like a, 647.10
~ proudly, 871.9

public, ~ in, 671.1(25–28,51,
60,66,71,72,79,81,88,89)
~ publicly about, 671.5(11)
~ rapidly, 671.1(11,12,16,18,
36–38,47,64,70,77,92,108)
sayings, ~ in, 676.5
~ secretly, 671.1(20)
~ sentimentally, 1094.4
~ sharply, 876.18
~ singingly, 671.1(46)
sleep, ~ in one's, 671.1(86)
~ slightingly of, 671.5(2)
~ slowly, 671.1(29)
~ smoothly, 671.1(6,64)
~ solemnly, 671.1(68)
~ spontaneously, 671.1(1,34,
45)
~ stammeringly, 671.1(35,95–
97)
support of, ~ in, 854.12,13
thin tones, ~ in, 671.1(65,93)
throwing the voice, ~ by,
671.1(104)
~ to, 671.8
~ to a group vehemently,
671.8(7)
~ to a thing, 671.8(3)
~ to an absent or dead person, 671.8(3)
~ to by name, 694.6(2,5)
~ to familiarly, 671.8(9)
~ to oneself, 671.1(85)
~ tritely, 535.8
unable to ~, 454.23; 475.1(1,
4,7,12,19,21,22); 671.21
unable to ~, one who is,
454.24; 671.22
~ unprepared, 48.9; 671.1(1,
34,45)
~ vaguely, 671.1(32,44,73)
~ vehemently, 671.1(43,66,76,
78)
~ vehemently to a group,
671.8(7)
~ violently, 4.13
~ weakly, 671.1(65)
~ with the breath only,
671.1(94,98,107)
~ without preparation, 48.9;
671.1(1,34,45)
~ wittily, 671.1(3,13,75)
talkative,adj., 671.17
conceited and ~ person,
608.20
not ~, 475.1; 671.20; see also
silent,adj.
~ person, 671.19; 871.5(1)
~ woman, 671.19(4)
talkativeness,n., 671.18
talker,n., 671.3; see also
speaker,n.
pert. to a ~, 671.4
talking,adj., 671.4
~ a lot, 671.17; see talkative,
adj.
~ affectedly, 671.4(4)
~ foolishly, 607.32; 608.8;
671.4(1)
~ frankly, 671.4(5)
~ gently, 671.4(6)
~ insincerely, 671.4(3)
~ little, 671.20; see also silent,adj.
talking,n., 671.2; see also language, speech, talk,n.
art of ~ in public, 671.16
careful in ~, 577.1(8,26)
difficulty in ~, 671.21
difficulty in ~, person who
has, 671.22
effective ~, 671.2(25)
enthusiasm for ~, 1095.19
fine ~, 671.2(25)
given to ~ in one's sleep,
671.10

habit of ~ about morals,
671.11
manner of ~ in public, 671.14,
15
nasality in ~, 671.2(33)
pert. to ~, 671.4
stop ~, 475.6
stop from ~, 475.5
unaccustomed to ~, 671.20(9)
tall,adj., 515.1
~ and slim, 997.11
~ person, 515.2
taller,adj.
be ~ than, 515.4; 164.7; 1071.7
tallness,n., 515.1
degree of ~, 515.3
tamable,adj., 22.40
tame,adj.
gentle, 1144.1
reduced in severity, 1142.5
tame,v.
make gentle, 1144.4
reduce in severity, 1142.1
subdue, 22.39
tamed,adj., 1142.5
able to be ~, 22.40; 1144.5
not ~, 1144.7
unable to be ~, 1144.6
tameness,n., 1142.6; 1144.2
tan,adj., 497.2
sunburned, 384.24
tan,n., 497.1(4,5,7,19,24)
tan,v.
sunburn, 384.25; 1055.23
tangerine,n.
cross between grapefruit and
~, 745.1(9)
Tangier,n.
inhabitant of ~, 784.15(59)
pert. to ~, 784.16
tank,n.
~ for water storage, 1033.48
large ~, 261.7(40)
storage ~, 261.4(15); 262.3(6)
tap,v.
hit, 437.1; see hit,v.
open, 298.1; see open,v.
touch, 436.1; see touch,v.
tapeworm,n., 427.7
~ disease, 396 1(27)
tardy,adj., 767 1; see late,adj.
target,n.
object of contempt, 870.16
object of ridicule, 869.13
center of ~, 137.1(3)
task,n., 203.5
taste,n., 446.8,10; see also flavor,n.
broad or liberal in one's ~s,
1109.5,6
descr. of ~ or flavor, 446.13
fore~, 446.9
have ~ or flavor, 446.11
have the ~ of, 446.12
having similar ~s, 1109.8
like tin in ~, 1020.8
perceivable by ~, 446.5
perverted sense of ~, 446.4
pleasurable in ~, 1105.4(3,7)
pleasure to the ~, 1105.2(1,4)
sense of ~, 446.1
uncivilized or unrefined ~,
1109.10
wealthy person of coarse or
showy ~s, 1109.9
taste,v., 446.6
tasteless,adj., 446.18,19
~ because not fresh, 446.20
make ~, 446.21
tasting,n., 446.7
tasty,adj., 446.13
tattle,n., 616.3
tattle,v., 613.1(4–6,14,18,20,26,
28,30); 613.9,10; 616.5;

671.1(5,14,16–18,36,39,49,
61,70,100,102,106,108)
tattler,n., 613.5,11; 616.10
tattletale,n., 613.5,11; 616.10
taught,adj., 621.11; see also
teach,v.
state of being ~, 621.4
what is ~, 622.3
tavern,n., 741.1; 749.37
owner of a ~, 741.2; 749.40(7)
tax,n., 219.18
~ on capacity of ships, 947.39
one tenth part as ~, 938.14
taxi,n., 192.6(10,11,24)
drive a ~, 192.7
driver of a ~, 192.8
measure distance traveled by
a ~, device to, 788.3(7)
ride in a ~, 192.7
tea,n.
belonging to the ~ family,
747.6
chemical in ~, 747.4
kettle for ~, 261.10(9,13)
weak ~, 747.5
teach,v., 621.1,2
~ again, 621.1(18,19)
~ individually, 621.1(2,21)
serving to ~ a moral lesson,
621.5(1)
serving to ~, 621.5
teacher,n., 621.7
alphabet, ~ of the, 621.7(1)
Cambridge, ~ at, 621.7(4)
children's ~, 621.7(7); 721.23
college ~, 621.7(10)
female ~, 621.7(13,14)
German ~, 621.7(9)
learned ~, 621.7(11);
622.17(7)
like a ~, 621.10
Oxford, ~ at, 621.7(4)
pedantic ~, 621.7(7)
pert. to a ~, 621.10
rank of a ~, 621.9
~s, collectively, 621.8
state of being a ~, 621.9
teaching,n., 621.3
art of ~, 621.18
book for ~, 621.19; 687.1(12,
14,16,18–20,23)
branch of ~, 621.16
~ by specific problems,
621.3(3)
descr. of ~, 621.6
development by ~, 621.4(3)
fees paid by students for ~,
621.20
intended for ~, 621.5(1)
medical ~, 621.3(3)
methods of ~, 621.18
~ of both sexes, 621.3(4)
oral ~ in church doctrines,
621.3(2)
pert. to ~, 621.6
pert. to ~ by sermons,
621.6(4)
pert. to moral ~, 621.6(4)
preliminary ~, 621.3(5)
receive ~ from, 622.1(2,9)
rules of ~, 621.18
science of ~, 621.18
secret ~, 621.3(1)
teal,n.
group of ~s, 403.5(70)
team,n., 318.1(6,8,14,17,44,47,
59,87,88,89)
teapot,n.
cover for ~, 972.4(6)
tear (from eyes),n., 1128.1
accompanied by ~s, 1128.8
causing ~s, 1128.7,15
characterized by ~s, 1128.9
come out (of ~s), 1128.16,17
device that causes ~s, 1128.11

dim with ~s, 1070.15,19
fits of ~s, 1127.4
full of ~s, 1128.6
~ gas, 1128.11
~ glands, 1128.10
habitually shedding ~s, 1128.5
in the shape of a ~, 1128.14
let (~s) flow, 1128.18
like ~s, 1128.13
little ~, 1128.2
pert. to ~s, 1128.12
pour ~s, 1036.8
pretended or insincere ~s, 1128.3
producing ~s, 1128.9
stained with ~s, 1128.21
story, etc., that causes ~s, 1128.20
vase for ~s, 1128.19
with the eyes full of ~s, 1128.4
without ~s, 1128.22
tear (rip),n., 337.4
tear,v., 337.1,2; see also **torn,** adj.
~ apart, 337.1(4,5,11,13,15,17)
~ away, 337.1(18)
~ into parts or pieces, 326.12, 13; 337.1(1,2,14,16)
~ off a part or piece, 326.12
~ off the covering of, 337.1(10)
~ open, 337.1(8)
~ out the intestines of, 337.1(3)
serving to ~, 337.6
~ with figurative pain, 1137.13
tearful,adj., 1128.4,6
tearing,n., 337.2
~ out of one's hair, 371.10
tease,v., 875.1,4; see also **annoy,** v.
~ by offering or promising and disappointing, 875.1(5)
~ by reminding of faults, 875.1(6)
~ good-naturedly, jokingly, etc., 875.1(2)
~ unmercifully, 875.1(3)
teaser,n., 875.2
habitual ~, 875.2(1)
teasing,n.
good-humored, humorous, or light ~, 875.3
object of ~, 875.6
technique,n., 50.1(3,6,8,14,15, 17–20,23,30,33,38,40,41,48)
one skilled in ~, 50.2
superiority of ~, 7.1(54)
technocrat,n.
theory, doctrine, or political movement of ~s, 1073.49
teeth,n., 368.2; see also **tooth,** n.
abnormal number of ~, 368.8
around the ~, 368.4(4)
arrangement of ~, 368.10
between the ~, 368.4(3)
cleanser for the ~, 899.5(3)
contact of the ~, 368.11; 735.11
decay of the ~, 368.20
eruption of ~, 368.12
false ~, 368.17
false ~, addition of, 400.6(36)
grinding of the ~, 735.11
having ~, 368.7
inflammation of the sockets of the ~, 368.21
pert. to ~, 368.4
production of ~, 368.12(2)
projecting ~, 368.2(1)
pulling out of ~, 402.5(22)
replacement of ~, 368.13,16

science of the ~, 401.1(10,20, 54,59,71,72,80,81,90)
tighten the ~, 302.10(2,3)
treatise on ~, 682.15(14)
without ~, 368.9
teething,n., 368.12
teetotaler,n., 749.57,58
teetotalism,n., 749.55
telegraphy,n.
system of signals in ~, 956.11
telepathy,n., 433.12
telescope,n., 480.17(1–3,6)
television,n.
transmission of ~ programs through stratosphere, 1046.16
tell,v., 613.1,17
find out, 624.1; see **discover,** v.
~ (a secret), 971.34
~ a secret to, 971.33
~ a story, 613.17(5,9); 685.3
~ about, 613.23
~ about in detail, 327.4; 613.23(2,6–8)
~ about under oath, 613.23(11,12); 1086.2,6
~ by signs, 613.17(12)
~ in detail, 327.4; 613.17(6–8)
inclined to ~, 613.33
~ main points of, 613.17(13)
~ on, 613.8–10
one who ~s, 613.5,19,26
one who ~s on another, 613.11
serving to ~, 613.21
~ (someone), 613.28
that which one ~s, 613.20,25, 30; see also **information, news, report,** n.
~ the story of, 613.23(4,9)
~ to, 613.28
teller,n.
one who counts money, 213.13(3,8,9)
one who tells, 613.5,19,26
~ of stories, 685.5; see also **author,** n.
telling,n., 613.18,24,29
descr. of ~, 613.21,27
telltale,n., 613.5,11; 616.10
temper,n.
condition, 44.1
mood, 1091.5
temperament, 1091.1; see also **nature,** n.
bad ~, 876.2,10; see also **anger,** n.
display of ~, 876.8
excitable ~, 876.20
fit of ~, 876.6
fit of angry and silent ~, 876.9
fit of violent ~, 876.7
hot ~, 876.2; 1100.23
of bad ~, 876.1
of calm or even ~, 1100.25; 1132.12; 1139.15(2–6,8–12,14–21,25–28,31–33,37–40)
of calm or even ~, person, 1100.26; 1132.13; 1139.19
of hot ~, 876.1,20; 1100.23
of sharp ~, 334.1(1); 874.10; 876.1; 1100.23
of sour ~, 876.1
sharp ~, 874.10; 876.2; 1100.23
sour ~, 876.2
temperament,n., 1091.1; see also **nature,** n.
even or calm in ~, 1100.25; 1132.12; 1139.15(2–6,8–12,14–21,25–28,31–33,37–40)
excitable in ~, 1100.23
person of even or calm ~, 1100.26; 1132.12; 1139.19

temperamental,adj., 539.21(5, 6,9,10,13,16–18,21,34,36); 870.3(1); 876.1(4); 1091.1
~ person, 539.22; 870.3
temperance,n., 923.2
~ in drinking, 749.55
~ laws, 749.67,68
~ leader, 749.66
~ society, 749.65
temperate,adj., 923.1; see **moderate,** adj.
temperature,n.
fever, 1063.1; see **fever,** n.
heat, 1060; see **heat,** n.
equal ~, line connecting points of, 1060.60
equal ~, pert. to, 1060.59
instrument to indicate, measure, or register ~, 1046.18(6,7,11); 1060.61,62
melting ~, 1027.22
regulate ~, device to, 1060.63
regulation of bodily ~, 1060.64
strength to endure extremes of ~, 1.17
temporary,adj., 539.24; 756.1
dealing with topics of ~ interest, 756.4
something ~, 756.2
~ substitute, 756.3
tempt,v., 196.1(1,4,15)
~ to wrong, sin, etc., 196.1(12, 16,18,19,22,23)
temptation,n., 196.2,3
tempter,n., 196.4
tempting,adj., 196.5; 196.5(8, 11–15)
~ qualities, 196.6
temptress,n., 196.4(2–4)
ten, n., adj., 938
based on ~s, 938.13
by ~s, 938.12
consisting of ~ parts, 938.3
containing ~, 938.11
divided into ~ parts, 938.3
group of ~, 938.2
multiply by ~, 938.9
number ~ times as great, 938.8
pert. to the number ~, 938.1
system based on ~s, 938.4
~ times as great, 938.10
ten thousand,n., 940.40
tenacious,adj.
clinging tightly, 302.18
continuing, 754.20
holding on, 257.5(2,4)
stubborn, 553.1
tend,v., 179.2; 630.3
take care of, 570.1
cause to ~, 630.4
tendency,n., 179.1(4,5,7,8,15–17); 630.1
concealed ~, 970.53,54
tender,adj.
loving, 700.2
painful, 1137.12
soft, 443.1
sympathetic, 1129.1
tendon,n.
disease of the ~s, 377.9(24)
inflammation of a ~, 377.9(29)
tenfold,adj., 938.7
increase ~, 906.9(2)
tennis,n.
spectators at a ~ match, 484.5
tense,adj.
nervous, 1133.1
stiff, 442.1
stretched tight, 193.25
tight, 303.2

under emotional pressure, 1133.14
tense,v.
stiffen, 442.3,4
stretch tight, 193.18(18,21)
tighten, 303.1,5
become emotionally ~, 1133.16
make emotionally ~, 1133.15
tension,n.
emotional strain, 1133.13
nervousness, 1133.2
stiffness, 442.2
stretched condition, 193.22
tightness, 303.3,6
cord ~, pert. to, 193.23
tent,n., 753.16
camp temporarily without ~s, 757.1(2)
group of ~s, 753.17
Indian ~, 753.16(4,5)
tenth,n.
one-~ part, 938.14
pert. to ~s, 938.1
pert. to every ~, 938.6
terminate,v.
bring to an end, 792.1
come to an end, 792.2
put an end to, 791.10
stop, 791.1; see stop,v.
terminating,adj., 792.15; see final,adj.
terminology,n., 695.1,4
student of ~, 695.2
termite,n.
of ~s, 428.1(14)
terrible,adj., 576.7; 883.17
terrify,v., 576.6
terrifying,adj., 576.7
territory,n., 1003.2(40); 1003.13
place, 782.1; see place,n.
space, 787.1; see space,n.
add new ~, 1003.16
feudal ~, 1074.24
make a ~ out of, 1003.14
outside the limits of a ~, 138.1(14)
portion of ~, 782.1(7)
reduce to status of ~, 1003.14
~ under a government, 1073.89
~ under a ruler or governor, 1073.18
~ under outside government, 1073.4(3)
terse,adj., 665.10; 911.1(5,7,8,14, 15)
terseness,n., 665.9(8,15,16,39,48, 51); 911.1(5,7,8,14,15)
test,n., 19.1,2; see also testing,n.
group of ~s, 318.1(9)
help prepare for a ~, 621.1(2,21)
medical ~s, 401.10
~ of ability, 19.1(6,10,11)
~ of conduct, 19.1(10)
~ of gold, 1013.32
~ of guilt, 19.1(8)
~ of innocence, 19.1(8)
~ of public reaction, 19.1(15)
~ of quality, 19.1(1,6,13,16)
~ of strength, 19.1(2)
~ of superiority, 19.1(2)
~ of value, 19.1(1,6,13,16)
severe ~, 19.1(1,5,8); 1060.12
test,v., 19.2
serving to ~, 19.5
tested,adj.
one who is ~, 19.6
state of being ~, 19.7
tester,n., 19.4
testicle,n., 379.1(21)
inflammation of the ~s, 379.9(8)

sac containing ~s, 379.1(20)
undescended ~s, 379.9(4)
testifier,n., 1086.4
testify,v., 1086.1,2
testimony,n., 1086.3
testing,adj., 19.5
testing,n., 19.2
art of ~, 19.9
means of ~, 19.1
period of ~, 19.12
place for ~, 19.10
practice of ~, 19.9
science of ~, 19.9
treatise on ~, 19.11
texture,n., 307.5; 311.1
th,n.
symbol for ~, 670.21(4)
thank,v., 1110.4
thankful,adj., 1110.1
be ~ for, 1110.7
thankfulness,n., 1110.2
lack of ~, 1110.12
thanks,n., 1110
a giving of ~, 1110.5
deserving of ~, 1110.8
express ~ for, 1110.4
express ~ to, 1110.3
feeling ~, 1110.1
give ~ for, 1110.4
give ~ to, 1110.3
giver of ~, 1110.6
lack of ~, 1110.12
letter of ~ for hospitality, 1110.9
not getting ~, 1110.13
showing ~, 1110.1
thatch,n.
like ~, 972.29
made of ~, 972.29
thatch,v.
~ with reed, 986.6
theater,n., 969.31; see also drama, performance (theatrical),n.
arrange as in a ~, 311.2(5)
~ district of New York City, 969.49
~ for motion pictures, 968.9
person who goes to the ~, 969.38,39
pert. to a ~, 969.32
pert. to the ~, 969.9(2,4)
seats in a ~, 969.33
theme,n.
composition, 682.16(3,7–10, 14,15,20,21,30,32,35–39,41)
subject, 671.26
theology,n., 642.20
branch of ~ defending Christianity, 854.18
theoretical,adj., 585.5; 632.9
~ but impractical, 888.4
theory,n., 585.3; 632.7(11)
able to apply ~, 611.18
based on ~, 632.13
disposed to new ~s, 761.6
part of science subject to ~, 612.26
therapist,n., 400.7; see also doctor,n.
therapy,n., 400.2,6; 400.6(44); see also doctoring, medical science,n.
~ by ~ 400.6(1)
~ by assisting nature, 400.6(30)
~ by baths, 400.6(4,19,20)
~ by books, 400.6(5)
~ by chemicals, 400.6(6)
~ by cold, 400.6(11)
~ by concept that disease is mental, 400.6(8)
~ by drugs, 400.6(21,27,32)
~ by electricity, 400.6(13,34); 1066.23

~ by fever, 400.6(15,25,40)
~ by gases, 400.6(1)
~ by heat, 400.6(34); 1060.26
~ by hobbies, 400.6(31)
~ by hormones, 400.6(14)
~ by hypnosis, 400.6(21); 584.27
~ by light, 400.6(33,34)
~ by manipulation, 400.6(7)
~ by massage, 400.6(26,34)
~ by metals, 1012.30
~ by muscular movements, 400.6(24)
~ by narcotics, 400.6(29)
~ by radium, 400.6(41,42)
~ by self-suggestion, 400.6(10)
~ by shock, 400.6(13,23,28)
~ by sun baths, 400.6(17)
~ by water, 400.6(19,20)
~ by work, 400.6(31)
~ by X-rays, 400.6(41,43,45); 1069.4,6
not reacting readily to ~, 550.7
~ of cancer, 400.6(41,42,45)
~ of emotional disturbances, 400.2(1); 400.6(3,16,21,29,37–39)
~ of insanity, 400.6(13,23,28, 37)
~ of mind and body, 584.6
~ of syphilis, 400.6(25)
~ of tuberculosis, 400.6(9,35)
pert. to ~, 400.3
place of ~, 400.5
practitioner of ~, 400.7
receive ~, 400.4
unorthodox ~, 400.6(12)
thermometer,n., 1060.61
types of ~s, 1060.62
thick,adj., 517.4,7
stupid, 597.1
become sour and ~, 452.6
~ end, 792.10(1,3,4)
~ in arrangement, 517.7
~ in body, 517.7
~ in consistency, 517.4
make sour and ~, 452.4
thicken,v., 517.1,2,8
~ in consistency, 517.1,2
~ in density, 517.8
~ing agent, 517.5
thickening,n., 517.3
thicket,n., 996.27,29
~s, 996.28
thickness,n.
a ~, 517.11
instrument to measure ~, 517.9,10
thick-skinned,adj., 1093.2
thief,n., 250.3
clever ~, 796.3(4)
thievery,n., 250.2; see stealing,n.
thigh,n.
ailment of the ~s, 1137.56(25)
pain in the ~, 1137.56(25)
pert. to the ~, 345.14
thin,adj., 513.1,6,12
insubstantial, 513.12
narrow, 512.1
not dense, 513.12
not fat, 513.1
not thick, 513.6
~ as a hair, 369.10(3)
become ~, 513.5,18
delicate, ~, and small, 11.1(4); 909.1(6)
graceful and ~, 513.1(9,26,27, 30)
hammered ~, able to be, 513.11
long and ~, 513.1(5,16,24,25); 516.1(1–5)

make ~, 513.4,9,16
~ (of the voice), 474.7
pale and ~, 384.11(6)
~ person, 513.3
strong, ~, and pliable, 990.14
tall and ~, 513.1(7,10,14,21,24,
   25); 515.1(2,5,6,8–10,12);
   997.11
~ thing, 513.8,15
weak and ~, 10.1(75)
thing,n., 808.1
essence of a ~, 808.8–10
essential nature of a ~, 808.8
make into a ~, 808.3,4,6
new ~, 808.1(4)
out-of-date ~, 631.16
treat as a concrete ~, 808.3,4,
   6
useful ~s, 808.2
think,v., 585.1
able to ~, 585.6
able to ~ of only one thing at
   a time, 585.9
able to ~ quickly, 585.8
~ about sadness, misfortune,
   etc., constantly, 1125.28,29
~ about with malicious satisfaction, 1107.25,26
~ back, 585.1(34)
inability to ~, 585.10
unable to ~, 585.7; 597.12
~ up, 726.17
thinker,n.
modern ~, 761.15
thinking,n., 585.2; see also
   thought,n.
~ about death, 585.20
advanced region of ~,
   782.1(8)
area of ~ without judgment,
   585.11
capable of ~, 585.6
characteristic ~ of a time,
   762.8
descr. of ~, 585.5
dreamy ~, 585.15
emotional ~, 585.16
given to ~, 585.4,23
incapable of ~, 585.7
incapable of human ~,
   597.12
incoherent in ~, be, 671.25
lack of ~, 597.9
modern ~, 761.18
pert. to ~, 585.5
process of ~, 585.2
rapid ~, 585.19
~ rather than doing, 585.18
result of ~, 585.3
stop ~ about, 585.30
unexplored region of ~,
   782.1(8)
verbalized ~, 585.17
way of ~, 585.22
thin-skinned,adj., 1093.1
third,adj., 932.18
of ~ order, rank, etc., 932.17
~ power (math.), 932.37
recurring every ~ day, 932.36
thirst,n.
become satisfied (of ~)
   1107.12
excessive ~, 748.10
reduce (~), 1107.13
satisfy (~), 1107.11
satisfy (~) to excess, 1107.15
unable to be satisfied (of ~),
   1107.14
thirsty,adj., 748.10; 1038.7
be ~, 748.11
feel ~, 748.11
make ~, 1038.1(6)
thirteen,n., 940.6
thirty,adj., 940.7
thistle,n.

of the ~ family, 985.33(4)
thorn,n., 335.1(2,12,16)
thorny,adj., 335.2; 335.2(1,4,9)
becoming ~, 335.4
thorough,adj., 328.1; see complete,adj.
thoroughness,n., 328.2
thought,adj.
able to be ~ of, 585.28,29
carefully ~ about, 585.25
commonly ~, 585.27
~ of, but not existing, 585.26
thought,n., 585.2,3; see also
   idea, thinking,n.
absorbed in ~, 585.4
absorption in ~, 585.4,12
added ~ to a letter, 682.3(14)
anxious ~s, 1131.4
arouse ~ in, 585.24
capable of ~, 585.6
done after careful ~, 577.6
dreamy ~, 585.15
emotional ~, 585.3(3)
engaged in ~, 585.4
engrossed with one's own ~s,
   one who is, 579.16
full of ~s, 925.26,27
give ~ and care to, 577.8
give external reality to a ~,
   1092.86
impediment to ~, 1097.47
incapable of ~, 585.7
lacking depth of ~, 597.7,8
later ~, 585.3(1)
lost in ~, 581.1(4,14,20);
   585.4(1–4)
lost in ~, one who is, 581.3
pert. to ~, 585.5
psychological group of ~s,
   1056.9
sphere of ~, 782.9
transference of ~ by psychic
   means, 613.29(3)
uncontrolled association of
   ~s, 585.13
under careful ~, 585.21
thoughtful,adj., 581.1(4,14,20);
   585.4
considerate, 1097.36
careful and ~, 577.1(31)
dreamily ~, 585.4(1,2,4)
sadly ~, 585.4(2); 1125.31
thoughtless,adj.
inattentive, 581.1
inconsiderate, 1097.35
stupid, 597.1
thousand, n., adj., 940.29
by the ~, 940.38
consisting of a ~, 940.33
~ dollars, 940.30
numbers beyond a ~, 940.41
pert. to a ~, 940.32
rate per ~, 99.1(4)
total of a ~, 940.31
thousandth, n., adj., 940.34
~ part, 940.35
~ parts, consisting of, 940.36
~ parts, pert. to, 940.37
pert. to a ~, 940.37
thread,n., 306.1
arrangement of ~s, 311.1(46)
form into ~, 306.6,7
having ~s, 306.4
in the form of ~s, 306.3
involving use of two ~s, 306.8
knot in ~, 302.34
like ~s, 306.3
~like structure, 306.5
pert. to ~, 306.2
structure of woven ~s, 307.5
threat,n., 573.4
~s, 573.4
~ to the white race, 573.5
threaten,v., 573.2
~ bodily attack, 573.2(1)

~ emptily, 573.2(3)
~ to expose, 573.2(2)
threatener,n., 573.3
threatening,adj., 573.1
~ action, 573.4
~ appearance, 573.4
look ~, 573.2
~ look, 573.4
looking ~, 573.1
~ sign, 573.4
sound ~, 573.2
~ sound, 573.4
sounding ~, 573.1
stand or advance ~ly,
   573.2(4)
~ to happen, 29.26
three, n. or adj., 932.1
arranged in ~s, 932.16
based on ~, 932.13
~ branches, thing of, 932.22
by ~s, 932.14
card, dice, or domino of ~
   pips, 932.10,11
chord of ~ tones, 932.9
~ copies of, make, 932.35
~ copies, made into, 932.34
divide into ~ parts, 932.20
divided into ~ lobes, 932.21
divided into ~ parts, 932.19
division of man's nature into
   ~ parts, 932.23
group of ~, 932.1
group of ~ animals, 932.7
group of ~ dogs, hares, etc.,
   932.7
group of ~ in love, 932.2
group of ~ in power or office,
   932.5
group of ~ related units,
   932.8
happening every ~ days,
   932.36
~ in one, 932.26,27
involving ~, 932.15,24
made up of ~, 932.15
multiply by ~, 932.29
~ of a kind, 932.3
one of ~ things, 932.33
participated in by ~, 932.24
recurring every ~ days,
   932.36
state of being ~, 932.25
~ times, 932.28
threefold,adj., 932.12
in a ~ manner, 932.28
increase ~, 907.9(9)
threeness,n., 932.25
three-sided,adj., 186.5(8)
threshold,n., 133.7(17)
psychological ~, 133.7(13)
thrift,n., 226.2
thrifty,adj., 226.1
be ~, 226.3
thrill,n., 111.2; 111.2(5)
feel ~s of excitement,
   1100.5(10)
produce ~s, use of techniques
   to, 1100.9
thrill,v., 111.1(7,15,16,18,19,26,
   29,31); 1100.1,5
thrilled,adj., 1100.6
be ~, 1100.5
thriller,n., 1100.4
thrilling,adj., 111.3; 1100.2
~ quality, 1100.3
thrive,v.
grow, 731.3
succeed, 23.1
throat,n., 364.1
inflammation of the ~, 364.13
loose flesh under the ~,
   385.1(4,5,7)
pert. to the ~, 364.2
science of the ~, 401.1(35,66,
   68,73)

sounds made in the ~,
460.1(1–4,6)
wash the ~, 899.35(3)
throaty,adj., 460.3(1,2) ; 460.4
throb,n., 105.4 ; 111.2 ; 910.16
throb,v., 105.3 ; 111.1(1,3,6–8,14–
19,29,31) ; 910.16
throbbing,adj., 105.5 ; 111.3 ;
910.16
throne,n., 63.1 ; 1073.17
entitled to inherit a ~, 6.5
~ for a bishop, 63.1(3)
roof over a ~, 973.1(2)
support of claim to ~, 1073.35
throng,n., 318.9
throng,v., 79.10 ; 318.10,11,13
thronged,adj., 318.12
throw,n., 187.2
throw,v., 187.1
able to be ~n, 187.6
~ (a coin), 187.1(59)
~ around, 187.1(5,8,43,50–52,
55,57)
~ at, 187.1(2,7,30,33–35,56)
~ away, 286.1; see elimi-
nate,v.
~ back, 187.1(41,42)
~ back and forth, 187.1(1,59,
61)
~ back light, heat, or sound,
1065.35
~ down, 187.1(38)
~ down (a structure), 802.24
~ forward, 187.1(39)
~ in, 187.1(28)
~ into, 187.1(37)
~ (missile), 187.1(31)
~ missiles at, 187.1(2,7,35)
~ mud, 187.1(50–52)
~ off, 187.1(3,21) ; 286.1; see
eliminate,v.
~ oneself, 187.1(37,40,58,59)
~ out, 187.1(3,4,19–22,53,61,
62) ; 286.1; see also eliminate,v.
~ out of the window,
187.1(16)
~ over, 187.1(5,8,43,45,50–52,
54,55)
~ over the water, 187.1(63)
place where things are ~n
down, 187.5
~ snowballs, 1039.14
~ stones at, 187.1(30,
56) ; 1006.12
that which is ~n, 187.4
~ (things) around in dis-
order, 903.5
~ through the air, 187.1(63)
~ upward, 187.1(59)
~ (water), 187.1(50–55)
~ words at, 187.1(2,7,35)
throwback,n., 723.10,11
thrower,n.
discus ~, 187.7
throwing,n., 187.2
pert. to ~, 187.3
thrust,n., 197.4
thrust,v., 197.1,2; see push,v.
thumb,n., 344.3
able to touch each finger (of
the ~), 436.10
base of the ~, 344.4
distance from the ~ to the
little finger, 788.1(11)
thunder,n., 1044 ; 1046.4
flash of lightning with ~,
1044.10
like ~ and lightning, 1044.2
sound of ~, 463.1(26,43) ;
1044.5
sound of ~, producing,
1044.4
storm with ~ and lightning,
1044.6,7

thunder,v., 1044.3
thyroid,n.
disorders of the ~ gland,
394.1
secretion of the ~, 287.8(10)
tick (animal),n., 428.3
like a ~, 428.3
of ~s, 428.1(1,23)
ticket,n., 698.2
stub of ~ in case of rain,
1037.17
tickle,v., 1111.23
amuse, 200.1
excite, 1100.1
itch, 434.3
please, 1106.2
pleasure, 1105.3
that which ~s, 1111.26
tickled,adj., 1111.25
tickling,adj., 434.4; 1111.24
tickling,n.
sensitive to ~, 1111.27
tide,n., 1031.1
caused by ~s, 1031.8
channel of the ~, 1031.9
dependent on ~s, 1031.8
having ~s, 1031.8
kinds of ~s, 1031.6
move (of the ~), 1031.7
rough water caused by ~s,
1029.9
water subject to ~s, 1029.10
tidy,adj., 902.1,7; see also neat,
adj.
~ and clean, 899.24
tidy,v., 902.3
tie,n., 977.1(4)
man's ~, 977.2
man's formal ~, 975.8
men's ~s, 974.22
tie,v., 302.28
~ a ship to anchorage,
302.28(32)
~ into a bundle, 302.28(37)
~ into a bundle for fire,
1064.65
~ the arms of, 302.28(33)
~ the wings and legs of,
302.28(44)
~ together, 302.28
~ up, 302.28
~ up an animal or person to
a place, 302.28(42)
~ with a bandage, 302.28(4,7,
41)
~ with a knot, 302.28(18,20,
26,27)
~ with laces, 302.28(19,21–25,
28,34,38)
~ with twigs, 302 28(45) ;
990.12
tiger,n.
baby ~, 406.5
cross between lion and ~,
406.8
female ~, 406.10
like a ~, 406.12,14
pert. to a ~, 406.11,13
small ~, 406.9
young ~, 406.9
tight,adj., 303.2
~ against air, 303.2(1) ;
1043.28; 1045.14(4)
~ against gas, 1048.28
~ against steam leakage,
1048.38
~ against water, 303.2(3) ;
1038.12
~ against wind, 1043.28
become ~, 303.5
draw ~, 193.18(21,22) ; 303.1
fitting ~, 303.2(2)
make ~, 303.1
make ~ against air, 1045.15
pull ~, 193.18(21,22)

stretch ~, 193.18(21,22) ;
194.1(13)
stretched ~, 193.25
tighten,v., 302.10; 303.1,5
~ the fist, 302.10(3)
~ the teeth, 302.10(2,3)
tightness,n., 303.3
cause of ~, 303.4
sensation of ~, 303.6
tile,n.
arranged like ~s, 311.4(5) ;
1006.62
like ~, 1006.62
pert. to ~, 1006.62
square ~, 1006.1(33)
worker with ~, 1006.61
timber,n., 997.1; see wood,n.
time,n., 762.1
action, ~ allowing, 762.1(5)
appointed ~, 762.1(12)
arrange by ~, 762.11
arrangement in ~, 311.1(6)
at the appointed ~, 925.13
at the proper ~, 925.13
bad ~, at a, 765.4,6,7
~ before man, 762.1(4) ; 763
before recorded ~, 766.6(11)
before the proper ~, 765.7
characteristic spirit, etc., of
a ~, 762.8
close in ~, 766.13–17
death, ~ after, 762.1(2)
decisively important ~,
848.11
dividing ~, system of,
774.7(3) ; see calendar,n.
earlier ~s, 762.1(6)
earliest ~s, pert. or belonging
to, 766.6
endless ~, 762.3
error in ~, 774.12,13
exist at the same ~, 764.2
existing at the same ~, 764.1
exists at the same ~, one
who, 764.3
farthest in ~, 767.5
~ flies, 762.6
flowering ~, of, 762.1(1)
for the ~ being, 762.7
future ~, 771.21,22; see future,n.
future ~, pert. to, 771.25
geologic ~, 763.1–5
go on in ~, 762.12; 913.6
grammatical ~, 762.1(11)
happen at the same ~,
764.6; see also happen,v.
happening at the same ~,
764.4,8; see also happening,
adj.
incongruous with the ~,
774.13,14
incorrect ~ to, give, 774.15
insertion of a unit of ~,
323.9
just in ~, 765.3
later ~, 762.1(3)
later in ~, 767.2
make the ~ of earlier, 766.3
measure ~, device to, 774.2;
see timepiece,n.
measurement of ~, 774.1
musical ~, 762.1(9,10)
on ~, 766.10
order in ~, 762.14
out of ~ with surroundings,
774.14
past ~, 771.4–7; see past,n.
period of ~, 769.1–9; see
period,n.
pert. to ~, 762.2
pert. to heat and ~, 1060.54
poetic ~, 762.1(10)
point of ~, 762.4,5
present ~, 771.1

proper ~, 762.1(8,13)
put off to a later ~, 768.1,8;
see **delay**,v.
reckon ~ of incorrectly,
774.15(5)
record of ~, 774.7
same ~, 764.1–8
space and ~, existing in,
762.9
spend ~ dreamily, 1054.36
spend ~ idly, 762.17,18;
1054.36
spend (~) in play, 199.7
spend ~ in the country,
786.4
spend ~ lazily, 762.17,18
spend ~ on, 762.13
spend ~ on unimportant
things, 762.16
spend ~ pleasantly, 762.15
spend ~ with, 762.14
stall for ~, 768.1; see **delay**,v.
up to that ~, 771.15
up to this ~, 771.14
waste ~, 762.19,20
timeliness,n., 765.2; 817.3
timely,adj., 765.1; 817.3
timepiece,n., 774.2
art of making ~s, 774.3
maker of ~s, 774.5
science of making ~s, 774.4
seller of ~s, 774.6
timid,adj., 576.1; 873.14
tin,n., 1020.1
alloy of ~, 1020.2,4,5
~ and copper alloy, 1016.2(2)
article of ~ alloy, 1020.3
coat with ~, 1020.15
~-coated iron or steel,
1020.16
containing ~, 1020.8,10
like ~ in sound or taste,
1020.8
made of ~, 1020.6
~ mine locality, 1020.13
~ miner, 1020.12
objects of ~, 1020.14
pert. to ~, 1020.9
place for work on ~, 1020.17
work done in ~, 1020.7
worker in ~, 1020.11
tinsmith,n., 1020.11
tiny,adj., 909.1; see **small**,adj.
tip,n.
end, 792.10,11
gratuity or payment, 219.8
hint, 239.2
information, 613.30
top, 165.1
demander of ~s, 219.10
demanding of ~s, 219.9
tire,v., 12.3,6
tired,adj., 12.1
~ and bored, 12.1(22);
583.8(12)
~ and dirty, 12.1(1)
~ and wild-eyed, 12.8(1)
become ~ with disappoint-
ment, 1121.8
~ by hard work, 12.1(17);
12.8(3)
easily ~, 12.9
~ emotionally, 12.8(2)
~ from pleasure, 12.1(17)
~ from traveling, 12.1(15,16,
33,34,39,41)
~ from walking, 12.1(15,16,
37)
~ in the feet, 12.1(16)
look ~ to elicit sympathy,
1129.20
~-looking, 12.8
not becoming ~, 12.10
~ of living, 12.1(21,42)
~ of pleasure, 12.1(2)

~ of traveling, 12.1(37)
~ of war, 12.1(31)
tending to be ~, 12.9
tireless,adj., 12.10
tiresome,adj., 12.4; 583.1; see
also **boring**,adj.
~ person, 583.3; 1117.17
tiring,adj., 12.4
tissue,n., 308.1
insert living ~, 323.1(18,23,24,
74)
remove ~ and regrow else-
where, 249.1(17)
treatise on organic ~,
682.15(8)
title,n., 699.2; see also **nobility**
(class), noble, noble-
man,n.
chapter ~, 699.2(4,6)
entitled to inherit a ~, 6.5
give a ~ to, 699.1(2,5–8)
give a new ~ to, 699.1(4)
give a pretentious ~ to,
699.1(3)
having a ~, 699.5
in ~ only, 699.7
Miss, as a ~, 699.8
Mr., as a ~, 699.10
Mrs., as a ~, 699.9
~ of a law, 699.2(6)
~ of honor, 699.2(5)
~ of honor, descr. of, 857.17
page ~, 699.2(4,6)
pert. to a ~, 699.3
style of ~, 699.2(2,7)
use of a person's ~, 699.4
use the proper ~ to, 699.1(1)
with the ~ of one's office,
1077.14
title,v., 699.1
titled,adj., 699.5
self-~, 699.6
T.N.T.,n., 802.12
toad,n., 424.1
immature ~, 424.2
like the ~, 424.4
of ~s, 403.11(1)
pert. to ~s, 424.3
toadstool,n.
of the ~ family, 985.33(1)
toady,n., 178.1(3,9,12,13,18,21);
852.9
toast,n.
drink a ~ to, 856.11
~ in drinking, 748.21; 856.9(8)
tobacco,n., 988.1,2
blowing out ~ smoke, 1057.19
box for ~ storage, 262.3(15)
chemical in ~, 988.3
dealer in ~ supplies, 988.11
ground ~ for breathing in,
988.4
hater of ~ smoke, 880.18(2)
illness from ~, 399.15(8)
Kentucky ~, 988.2
~ left in bottom of pipe,
988.9
~ pipe, 988.8
~ products, 988.10
~ smoke, 1050.5
~ store, 988.12
twist of ~, 988.5
toe,n., 344.1
child's ~s, 344.2
condition of ~s, 344.7
disease of the big ~,
1137.56(14)
having ~s, 344.6(1,3–8,10,11)
having ~s turned inward,
344.6(7)
pain in the big ~, 1137.56(14)
pert. to the ~s, 344.5(3)
~ reflex, 344.8
toenail,n., 344.12(4,5)
care of the ~s, 346.17

trim and polish the ~s,
346.18
together,adv., 51.3(1,2)
act ~, 51.1
answering aloud and ~,
626.9
attach ~, 302.1,12,14,16,28
be ~ in a group, 318.5
bring ~ in a collection, 319.1
bring ~ into a crowd, 318.11
call ~, 693.1(2,6,7,11,12)
come ~, 321.2; see **connect**,v.
come ~ in a collection, 319.2
come ~ in a combination,
320.2
come ~ in a crowd, 318.10
come ~ in a group, 318.5
do ~, 51.1
done ~, 51.5
draw ~, 193.13
draw ~ toward a point,
322.10,11
go ~ in a group, 318.5
hold things ~, 302.10,11
move ~, 79.10
move ~ in a crowd, 318.10
put ~, 321.1; see **connect**,v.
put ~ in a collection, 319.1
put ~ in a combination, 320.1
put ~ into a group, 318.4
stick ~, 302.12,16
stuck ~, 302.20
tie ~, 302.28,30
weave ~, 307.1
toilet,n., 295.1
~ on a ship, 295.1(6)
token,n., 627.34; 951.4; 1091.11
~ of skill, bravery, victory,
etc., 951.8
told,adj.
that which is ~, 613.20,25; see
also **report**,n., **tell**,v.
tolerable,adj., 246.4
tolerance,n., 246.2,3,8
descr. of ~, 246.3
tolerant,adj., 245.8; 246.3
tolerate,v., 245.1(11,12); 246.1;
see also **bear**,v.
ability to ~, 246.8
able to ~, 246.9
willing to ~, 265.23(8); see
patient,adj.
tomb,n., 797.10
building for ~s, 727.12(11)
Egyptian ~, 1006.1(32)
like a ~, 797.12
marker for a ~, 797.13
prehistoric ~, 797.10(3);
1006.21
saint's ~, 797.10(9)
serve as a ~ for, 797.11
structure for ~s, 797.7;
797.10(7)
underground ~, 797.10(2)
ton,n.
British ~, 947.38
charge per ~, 947.39
payment per ~, 219.3(57)
tax per ~, 947.39
weight in ~s, 947.39
tone,n.
attitude, 1091.5
color, 488.1,2
health, 397.2
physiological activity,
57.1(14)
quality, 1091.7
sound, 455.1,6; 474.3
chord of three ~s, 932.9
tongue,n.
animal with ~ like human's,
403.7(2)
bell ~, 458.9
characteristic of the ~, 367.15
coat the ~, 972.1(13)

cover the ~, 972.1(23)
fleshy process behind the ~, 364.6
pert. to the ~, 367.13
science of the ~, 401.1(25)
~-shaped, 507.17(45)
sound formed by the tip of the ~, 670.14(4)
using the ~, 367.14
tonsil,n., 364.5
 inflammation of the ~s, 364.13(3,4)
tool,n., 280.6(10,11,17)
 worker's ~s, 280.1(11,20)
too many, 920.1; see too much
too much, 920.1,3,4,6,19
 ~ of a good thing, 920.20
 ~ to choose from, 920.21
tooth,n., 368.1,3; see also teeth,n.
 ~ache, 1137.56(29)
 around a ~, 368.4(4)
 bone layer of a ~, 354.1(1)
 broken ~, 368.1(13)
 dog's ~, 368.1(4,8)
 elephant's ~, 368.1(16)
 filling of a ~ with gold, 1013.31
 fork ~, 368.3(2,4)
 gear ~, 368.3(1)
 irregular ~, 368.1(13)
 like a ~, 368.5
 parts of a ~, 368.6
 pert. to a ~, 368.4
 projecting ~, 368.1(2)
 saw ~, 368.3(3)
 ~-shaped, 507.17(32)
 snake's ~, 368.1(8)
 walrus's ~, 368.1(16)
 wheel ~, 368.3(1)
top,n., 165.1
 animal's back, ~ of, 165.1(17)
 be at or on the ~ of, 165.3
 edge at the ~, 793.20(1,2)
 put on ~ of, 323.1(70,72,73)
 reach the ~, 165.2
 remove from the ~, 249.2(6)
 remove the ~ from, 249.2(8)
 stand something on its ~, 61.5
 structure on the ~, 727.17(2, 3,6,7)
topic,n., 671.26
topsy-turvy, adj. or adv., 149.4
torch,n.
 electric ~, 1065.107(18)
 flaming ~, 1065.107(7,22)
torment,n., 1130.3,6; 1137.4
torment,v., 1130.1; 1137.1
 annoy, 874.1
tormentor,n., 1130.2; 1137.2
torn,adj.
 able to be ~ apart, 337.9
 become ~, 337.2
 ~ end, 792.10(5)
 looking ~, 337.8
 ~ part, 326.10(19,25,33)
 part ~ off, 337.5
 ~ piece, 326.10(19,25)
 with ~ edges, 337.7
tornado,n., 1042.27; see also cyclone, hurricane, wind-storm,n.
 underground refuge from a ~, 1042.35
torpedo,n., 565.10,15,17
torpid,adj.
 inactive, 58.1
 stupefied, 435.3; 597.21
torpor,n.
 inactivity, 58.2
 stupefaction, 435.1
 spend the summer in ~, 770.11(1)

spend the winter in ~, 770.11(2)
tortoise,n., 425.15
 like a ~, 425.18
 like a ~ shell, 425.19
 pert. to ~s, 425.17
torture,n., 1130.1,3,6; 1137.4; 1138.2,3
 full of ~, 1138.7
 instrument of ~, 1138.4
 involving ~, 1138.8
 method of ~, 1138.3
 prefers ~ to giving up beliefs, one who, 1138.9
 state of ~, 1138.5
torture,v., 1130.1; 1137.1; 1138.1
torturer,n., 1130.2; 1137.2; 1138.6
total,adj., 914.5
 ~ amount, 914.4
 ~ produced, 726.13
total,n., 328.8; 908.37; 914.4; see also whole,n., 914.5
total,v., 908.35,36
totem,n., 954.1; see also symbol,n.
 adoption of ~s, 954.20
 belief in ~s, 954.19
 column, etc., of ~s, 954.21
 use of ~s, 954.19
touch,n., 436.2
 delicate in ~, 949.11
 descr. of ~, 436.3
 insensitive to ~, 1137.38
 insensitiveness to ~, 1137.39
 light in ~, 949.11
 not perceivable by ~, 436.12
 organ of ~ in animals, 343.22
 perceivable by ~, 436.11
 perception through ~, 433.1(1,2,5)
 pert. to ~, 432.12; 433.3; 436.6(2,3)
 quality perceivable by ~, 436.7
 sensation of ~, 434.1(3,5,12–14)
 sense of ~, 432.7; 436.5
 sensitiveness to ~, 1137.32
 sensitiveness to ~, decreased, 1137.34
 skill of ~, 7.1(29)
 skillful in ~, 949.11
touch,v., 436.1
 able to ~ each finger (of the thumb), 436.10
 ~ to examine medically, 436.1(24,27)
 ~ upon, 436.1(1,2)
 ~ with the tongue, 436.1(21, 32)
touching,adj., 436.3
 emotionally affecting, 1099.2
 lie ~, 790.20,21
 lies ~, that which, 790.18,19
 situated ~, 790.17
 spatially ~, 436.3(2–4)
touching,n., 436.2
 caused by ~, 436.8
 causing sensation of ~, 436.9
touchy,adj., 868.9
tough,adj., 441.1
 difficult, 25.1
toughen,v., 441.3,4
 ~ (the mind), 1098.4
tower,n., 727.18
 bell ~, 458.10; 727.18(2)
 castle ~, 727.18(3)
 church ~, 727.18(4)
 having ~s, 727.19,20
 ornamental ~, 727.18(5)
 ~ roof that tapers to a point, 973.1(8)
 signal ~, 727.18(1)

small ~, 727.18(5)
 steering ~, 177.6(2)
town,n., 785.1; see also city,n.
 inhabitant of a ~, 785.2
 pert. to a ~, 785.3
toy,n., 199.12
trace,n.
 small amount, 917.1,16,17
 something left, 757.4,6
 noticeable ~, 917.18
trace,v., 173.12; 486.1
track,n.
 road, 123.1; see road,n.
 ~ of moving ship, etc., 503.1(19); 757.6(4)
 ~ of passing person, animal, or thing, 757.6
track,v., 173.12; 486.1
trade,n.
 business, 210.1
 exchange, 539.13
 purchase and sale, 211.2; 212.2(1)
 pert. to ~, 210.3
trade,v.
 buy and sell, 211.1; 212.1
 do business, 210.2
 exchange, 539.12
trader,n., 210.4; 211.4; 212.3
tradition,n., 629.1(7)
 conformer to ~, 629.7
 conforming or adhering to ~, 629.5(11)
 conforming to scholastic ~s, 629.5(1)
 conformity to ~, 629.6
 make conform to ~, 629.8
 opposition to ~, 544.2(11)
traffic,n.
 business, 210.1; 211.2
 movement, 79.2
 ~ island, 148.15
traffic,v., 210.2; 211.1; 212.1
tragedy,n.
 drama, 969.1(46,47); 969.2
 misfortune, 37.1
 actor in a ~, 969.3,4
 actors in Greek or Roman ~, 969.15(1)
 pert. to ~, 969.9; 969.9(5)
 put on a ~, 969.7
 shoe as symbol of ~, 979.2(8)
 writer of ~, 969.8
tragic,adj.
 causing death, 796.4
 pert. to tragedy, 969.9; 969.9(5)
 sad, 1125.1,6,16
 unfortunate, 37.2
trail,n.
 road, 123.1; see road,n.
 ~ of passing person, animal, or thing, 757.6
trail,v., 173.1,12; 486.1
train,n.
 series, 173.9
 series of happenings, 29.7
 a room on a ~, 787.7(16)
 dining car of a ~, 741.1(9)
 driver of a ~, 192.26
train,v., 621.1(2–6,8,10,17,20,21)
 ~ a plant to grow flat, 991.19
 ~ again, 621.1(18,19)
 serving to ~, 621.5
 structure for ~ing plants to grow flat, 991.18
trained,adj., 621.11
 state of being ~, 621.4
trainer,n., 621.7
training,n., 621.3,4
 development by ~, 621.4(3)
 experience and ~, 621.4(1)
 ~ in society, 621.4(2)
 ~ of trees or shrubs into odd shapes, 998.1(15)

trait,n., 1091.11; see **charac-**
teristic,n.
origin of a ~, 728.8
traitor,n., 659.4; 659.4(1,2,4)
traitorous,adj., 659.1; see **dis-**
loyal,adj.
tramp,n., 128.3
transform,v., 539.1,2
that which ~s, 539.10
transformation,n., 539.3
pert. to ~, 539.8
transient,adj., 120.3; 756.1; see
also **temporary**,adj.
transient,n., 756.2
transition,n.
change, 539.3,16
passage, 120.2
transitory,adj., 120.3; 756.1; see
also **temporary**,adj.
translate,v., 607.17(1,8–10)
change, 539.1(6,30,31,56,58,61,
63)
~ incorrectly, 607.21(1,2,4–7)
~ secret writing, 683.7
translating,adj., 607.19
translation,n., 607.18
change, 539.4
~ of secret symbols, 683.8,10
~ used in learning a foreign
language, 607.18(1,2)
translator,n., 607.20
changer, 539.4
~ of secret symbols, 683.9
translucent,adj., 1065.90
partially ~, 1065.91
~ when wet, 1034.33
transparency,n., 598.1,9,13
destroy the ~ of, 1009.37
transparent,adj., 483.10
clear, 598.1,8
evident, 598.13
obvious, 598.8,13
plain to see, 483.1
not ~, 483.11; 1065.94
not ~, that which is, 1065.95
partially ~, 1065.90
that which is ~, 1065.93
~ when wet, 1034.33
transport,n., 1092.25
transport,v., 190.1
carry away with emotion,
1092.29
transportable,adj., 190.5
transportation,n., 190.2
~ business, person or company in the, 190.3(1)
payment for ~, 219.3(9,16,22,
23,27)
science of military ~, 190.12
transported,adj., 1092.26
trap,n., 244.3
full of ~s, 244.5(4)
lead into a ~, 176.1(6)
trap,v., 244.1
apt to ~, 244.5(1)
~ (game) by flag, 957.10
one who ~s animals, 244.6
serving to ~, 244.5
trapezium,n.
~-shaped, 507.17(79)
trapped,adj.
situation in which one is ~,
244.7
trapper,n.
skillful ~, 996.45,47
trapping,adj., 244.5
trapping,n., 244.2
skill in ~, 7.1(69)
skill in ~ game, 996.46
trash,n., 284.20; 285.1; 888.7,9
trashy,adj., 284.12; 888.1
travel,n., 124.2; see **traveling**,n.
~ business, 124.12
travel,v., 124.1
~ about to sell, 212.1(3,6,12)

~ as actors, 969.17
desire to ~, 124.11(2)
need to ~, 124.11
place one repeatedly ~s over,
782.12
~ to give a theatrical
performance, 969.17
traveler,n., 124.3
~ by sea or ocean, 1029.74
traveling,adj., 124.4
~ actor, 969.18
~ by or on the seas,
1029.72(16)
~ on business, 107.4(4,7);
124.4(1,2)
~ salesman, 212.3(1,4,6–8,12,
14,15)
traveling,n., 124.2
bag or container for ~,
261.16,17
~ by sea or ocean, 1029.73
capable of ~ on the open sea
(of watercraft), 1029.72(19)
designed for ~ on the open
sea, 1029.72(18)
engaged in ~, 124.4
line of ~, 124.7
pert. to ~, 124.5
place to which one is ~,
782.14
plan of ~, 124.8
stage of ~, 124.6
tired from ~, 12.1(39,41)
tired of ~, 12.1(33,34)
while ~, 124.9
year of ~, 124.10
tray,n., 261.5
treacherous,adj.
dangerous, 572.1
deceptive, 823.7,10
disloyal, 659.1; see **disloyal**,
adj.
untrustworthy, 639.12
treachery,n., 659.2; 572.2; 823.7;
see **disloyalty**,n.
treason,n., 659.2; 659.2(3,5); see
also **disloyalty**,n.
behavior just short of ~,
659.5
neglect to inform of ~,
1087.7(6)
treasonous,adj., 659.1(7,9); see
also **disloyal**,adj.
treasure,n., 216.3; 262.2; 700.6;
839.5
treasure,v., 262.1; 700.4;
839.15
treasurer,n., 213.13
treasury,n., 213.15; 262.3
treat,v., 53.1
~ as a celebrity, 848.25
~ as a father does, 1073.11
~ as important, 848.25
~ as less bad, 883.21
~ as less important, 848.40
~ as less serious, 883.21
~ as of low value, 840.6
~ as unimportant, 840.6;
849.8
~ as valueless, 840.6
~ badly, 53.1(1,2,4,6,7,11,12,
13)
~ contemptuously, 870.1
~ cruelly, 53.1(2,6,7,10,11,12,
13); 889.6
cruelly ~ed, 889.8
~ emotionally, 1092.72
~ harmfully, 53.1(15)
~ harshly, 53.1(12,13); 890.5
~ indulgently, 1108.7
~ kindly, 53.1(3)
~ medically, 400.1; 401.4; see
also **therapy**,n.
~ roughly, 53.1(7,8,9,10,15)
~ savagely, 4.30

~ strictly, 890.7
~ unfairly, 635.3
~ with false remedies, 826.18
~ with flattery, 852.1(3)
~ with pride, 871.7,8
~ with superiority, 871.8
~ with X-rays, 1069.5
~ without seriousness,
53.1(14)
treatise,n., 682.16
~ on a subject, 682.15; see
also under the specific subject
~ on one subject, 682.16(21)
treatment,n., 53.2
~ by dramatic performance,
969.37
descr. of ~, 53.2
humiliating ~, 868.17
medical ~, 400.2,6; see
medical science, ther-
apy,n.
medical ~, pert. to, 398.14;
400.3
medical ~, place of, 400.5
not reacting readily to ~,
550.7
~ of emotional disturbances,
400.2(1); 400.6(3,16,21,29,
37–39)
show as proper for ~,
951.1(25)
treaty,n., 541.13; 541.13(1,3,6,8)
addition to a ~, 908.21
tree,n., 996.4
apple ~, 996.4(13)
bottom part of a cut ~, 996.6
boundary of ~s, 996.30
Brooklyn ~, 996.4(1)
central part of a ~, 326.34
clear of ~s, 996.54
climbing ~s, adapted for,
996.12
cone-bearing ~, 996.4(5,12)
cover with ~s, 996.51
covered with ~, 972.5(6);
996.49,50
covered with small ~s,
996.50
covering of ~, 972.4(2)
cultivation of ~s, 996.60,62
cultivation of forest ~s,
996.62
cut a ~ down, 996.7
cut the branches of a ~,
996.5
~ cutter, 205.9(4,5)
cutting or thinning ~s, 996.55
cutting ~s, privilege of,
996.10
drive up ~s, 996.23
enclose with ~, 996.31
evergreen ~, 996.4(5,6,12)
family of ~s, 996.24,25
fence of ~s, 996.30
fence with ~, 996.31
fondness for ~s, 700.30(5)
~ for shade, 1071.9
forest ~, 996.4(7)
forest ~s of a region, 996.1
formed by ~s, 996.21
fruit ~, 996.4(4,13)
fruit ~s, cultivation of,
996.58
grapefruit ~, 996.4(4)
~ growing in a way caused by
the wind, 1043.23
growing on ~s, 731.5(4);
996.13
growth of ~s, 996.27,28
growth on a ~, 731.21(2)
habits of a forest ~, 996.52
having ~s, 996.49
leaf-dropping ~s, 996.20
lemon ~, 996.4(4)

like a ~, 996.16
lime ~, 996.4(4)
line beyond which ~s do not
  grow, 996.53
lined by ~s, 996.22
living in ~s, 996.11
living on ~s, 996.14
low ~s, 996.2
manner of growing of a
  forest ~, 996.52
mark chipped on ~, 503.1(3)
measurement of a ~, device
  for, 996.66,67
nut ~s, cultivation of, 996.58
~ nymph, 996.42
orange ~, 996.4(4)
orange ~s, tract of, 996.29(5)
outline of ~ in fossil or
  mineral, 996.19
peach ~s, tract of, 996.29(6)
pert. to ~s, 996.15
pine ~, 996.4(5,6,12)
pine ~s, tract of, 996.29(7,8)
place of ~s, 996.29
plant with ~s, 996.34,51
raising of ~s, 998.1(1,8,11,15)
row of ~s, 996.30
science of ~s, 996.64
shape like a ~, 996.17
shape of a ~, 996.19
~-shaped, 996.16
~-shaped, become, 996.18
shelter of ~s, 993.10,11
small ~, 996.4(2,3,11)
student of ~s, 996.65
surround with ~s, 996.31
tract of ~s, 996.29
~ trained to grow flat, 991.18
training of ~s into odd
  shapes, 998.1(15)
treatise on ~s, 682.15(22);
  996.68,69
treatise on pine ~s, 996.70
types of ~s, 996.4
value of wood ~s, 996.10
without ~s, 996.56
wood ~s, 996.4(8,12); 996.10
woody part of a ~, 996.71
worship of ~s, 656.15(4);
  996.63
young ~, 996.4(10,11)
tremble,n., 111.2
~ of the voice, 469.1(13–15,24–
  27,29,30)
tremble,v., 111.1; see shake,v.
cause to ~, 111.5
trembling,adj., 111.3
~ sound, 469.1
~ with fear, 111.3(4)
trembling,n., 111.2
fit of ~, 111.2(5)
~ from fear, 111.2(6)
trembly,adj., 111.4
tremendous,adj., 906.12; see
  big,adj.
trench,n., 299.1(6,7,14–16,18,20–
  22,30,34,38); 568.30(7)
trend,n., 179.1(4,5,7,8,14–17);
  630.1
trend,v., 179.2; 630.3
trespass,n., 130.2
trespass,v., 130.1(1,4–6,15,17)
trespasser,n., 130.3
trial,n.
  attempt, 18.2; see attempt,n.
  legal trial, 1082.1; see trial
    (legal),n.
  test, 19.1; see test,n.
  trouble, mental suffering,
    1130.3,6
trial (legal),n., 1082.1; see also
  lawsuit,n.
  dismissed ~, 1082.34
  famous ~, 1082.6
  military or naval ~, 1081.4,5

~ without verdict, 1082.34
triangle,n., 945.2(10)
  figure or ornament in the
    shape of a ~, 945.4
  mathematics of the ~,
    943.1(9)
  point opposite base of a ~,
    335.1(22)
  ~-shaped, 507.17(31,80)
  ~ with three equal sides,
    945.5
  ~ with two equal sides, 945.3
triangular,adj., 507.17(31,80);
  944.5(9)
tribe,n., 722.4
  group, 318.1(14,23,25,26,28,33,
    35,55,57,70,72,79,81)
  pert. to a ~, 722.5
trick,n., 823.13,16; 824.1; 1115.12
  absurd ~, 824.2
  fantastic ~, 824.2
  mischievous ~, 824.3
  perform ~s, 824.6
  play mischievous ~s, 824.4
  player of mischievous ~s,
    824.5
  ~ to deceive the enemy,
    823.13(4)
trick,v., 823.1; 825.1
tricker,n., 823.20; 825.9
trickery,n., 823.13; 825.7
trickster,n., 823.20; 825.9
tricky,adj., 595.2; 823.7,10
  ~ and dishonest, 822.5
  ~ and dishonest act, 822.7
  ~ and dishonest person, 822.6
  ~ and dishonest practice,
    822.7
tricycle,n., 192.17; see cycle,n.
trifle,n., 849.4; 917.1
trifle,v., 199.10; 609.7,10; 762.17–
  20; 826.26
trim,adj., 631.7,8; 902.1,6
trim,v.
  cheat, 825.1
  cut, 332.1
  defeat, 22.1
  neaten, 902.3
trip,n., 124.2; see traveling,n.
  business of managing ~s,
    124.12
  pert. to a ~, 124.5
  take a ~, 124.1; see travel,v.
trip,v.
  blunder, 829.2
  fall, 168.1,4
  move lightly, 90.1
  step, 108.1
  walk, 107.1
Tripoli,n.
  ruler of ~, 1073.36(8)
trite,adj., 535.5; 759.28
  become or make ~, 759.29
  ~ person, 535.7
  ~ phrase, attitude, etc.,
    535.6; 759.30
  speak ~ly, 535.9
triumph,n., 22.2,12; 23.4,5;
  1102.7
  happy over a ~, 22.17; 1102.6
  rejoice over ~, 22.18; 1102.8,9
  token of ~, 951.8
triumph,v., 23.1; 1102.8
  ~ over, 22.1,23,27,28
triumphant,adj., 22.11,15,16,17;
  23.2,5; 1102.6
trolley car,n., 192.10
  ~ driver, 192.11
tropical,adj., 1060.1
  pert. to the ~ regions, 1004.8
tropics,n., 1004.5(11)
  between the ~, 1004.9
  inhabitants of the ~,
    784.17(1)
  region near the ~, 1004.5(9)

tropism,n., 101.1
trouble,n., 25.2; 28.2; 1130.6;
  1131.3,9; 1132.3,5
  that which, if disturbed, will
    cause ~, 267.21
trouble,v., 28.3; 1130.1;
  1131.1; 1132.1
troubled,adj., 1131.8; 1132.4
troublesome,adj., 25.1; 28.1;
  874.4; 1130.4; 1131.2; 1132.2
  ~ person, 874.5
trousers,n., 980.1
  acrobat's ~, 980.1(23)
  child's ~, 980.1(16,19)
  dancer's ~, 980.1(23)
  diplomat's ~, 980.1(22)
  flap covering opening in ~,
    980.5
  golf ~, 980.1(18)
  Indian ~, 980.1(14)
  ~ of early times, 980.1(15)
  Oriental ~, 980.1(14)
  riding ~, 980.1(10)
  short ~, 980.1(11,20)
  sports ~, 980.1(18,20)
  woman's ~, 980.1(1,9,14,16,
    21)
  work ~, 980.1(6,12,13)
trout,n.
  group of ~, 403.5(37,59)
  young ~, 422.4(1)
troy weight,n.
  unit of ~, 947.32,34
truck,n.
  ~ driver, 190.3(3); 192.8
trucker,n., 190.3(3); 192.8
true,adj., 812.1–4; 820.25,26
  genuine, 807.3; 812.1; see
    genuine,adj.
  in good faith, 812.4
  real, 807.3; see real,adj.
  admit as ~, 675.1; see
    admit,v.
  assumed as ~, 812.14
  claim to be ~, 812.12
  deceptively ~, 820.2
  declare ~, 812.12
  not necessarily ~, 820.11
  obviously ~, 812.2
  obviously ~ statement,
    674.9(28)
  prove ~, 812.15; see prove,v.
  statement that appears ~,
    812.11
truly,adv., 812.24
trumpet,n.
  belt for a ~, 980.7
  player of a ~, 479.9(24)
  sounds of a ~, 461.1(1,3,4,6)
trust,n., 632.6(1,2,4–8,14)
  based on ~, 632.14
  not worthy of ~, 639.12
  worthy of ~, 632.25
trust,v., 632.2
trustful,adj., 632.18(1–4,7,10)
trustworthy, 526.6; 632.25
truth,n., 812.1,3,5,8,9
  absolute ~, 812.8
  admission of the ~, 675.2
  appearance of ~, 812.10,11
  art of distinguishing ~ from
    error, 589.15(2)
  declaration of ~, 1086.14,15
  establish the ~ of, 812.15; see
    prove,v.
  evade the ~, 76.1(17); 821.2
  evasion of the ~, 821.1
  fundamental ~, 812.7
  general ~, 812.7
  lover of ~, 700.30(15)
  obvious ~, 812.6,9
  resemblance to ~, 529.8;
    812.10
  self-evident ~, 812.6

solemn declaration of ~,
  812.13; 1086.3; see oath,n.
swear to tell the ~, 1086.15
unadorned in ~s, 959.11
undeniable ~, 812.8
truthful,adj., 812.1; 813.1
truthfulness,n., 812.1; 813.2
  theory of ~ in art or lit-
    erature, 813.5
try,n., 18.2; see attempt,n.
try,v., 18.1
  annoy, 874.1
  cause suffering to, 1130.1
  ~ to attract, 18.1(3)
  ~ to deal with, 18.1(21)
  ~ to do better than, 833.12
  ~ to enforce, 1082.18
  ~ to equal, 18.1(13)
  ~ to gain, 18.1(7)
  ~ to get, 18.1(2,3,5,7,8,12,14,
    16,23,26); 240.11
  ~ to get business, 18.1(16,23)
  ~ to get customers, 18.1(16,
    23)
  ~ to get by legal action,
    1082.18
  ~ to get the love of, 18.1(26)
  ~ to get votes, 18.1(16,23)
  ~ to hold, 18.1(7)
  ~ to seize, 18.1(15,17)
  ~ to surpass, 18.1(13,25);
    833.12
  ~ to win, 18.1(8,26)
trying,adj., 1130.4
trying,n.
  descr. of ~, 18.4
tube,n.
  ~ for escape of smoke, air,
    gases, etc., 1050.27–29
  ~ for waste water, 1033.34
  ~ for water, 1033.23,28,29,31
tuberculosis,n., 374.8
  germ causing ~, 403.21(21)
  pert. to ~, 374.9
  showing signs of ~, 374.12
  sufferer from ~, 374.11
  suffering from ~, 374.10
  treatment of pulmonary ~,
    400.6(9,35)
tuition,n., 621.3; see teach-
    ing,n.
tumor,n., 390.1; 908.5
  science of ~s, 401.1(55)
tumorous,adj., 390.2
tumult,n.
  commotion, 1101.1
  confusion, 605.13; see con-
    fusion,n.
  noise, 463.1; see noise,n.
tune,n., 467.1; 476.4; 478.1
  write ~s, 478.7; 479.23
  writer of ~s, 476.6; 478.6
tuneful,adj., 467.3; 478.3
Tunis,n.
  ruler of ~, 1073.36(4,8)
tunnel,n., 122.1(32,33); 298.9
  worker in underwater ~,
    1026.38
turban,n., 983.2(56); see also
    hat,n.
  inner part of a ~, 983.2(55)
  Persian ~, 983.2(56)
turbulence,n.
  commotion, 1101.1
  confusion, 605.13; see con-
    fusion,n.
turbulent,adj., 4.1; 605.14;
    1101.3
  ~ woman, 708.14(2,15,19)
turf,n., 986.19; 999.1
  race track, 20.12
  like ~, 986.25
  pert. to ~, 999.2
Turk,n., 784.15(46)
turkey (bird),n.

group of ~s, 403.5(55)
young ~, 405.4(12)
Turkey (country),n.
  fondness for ~, 700.30(27)
  official of ~, 1077.1
  ruler in ~, 1073.36(4,14)
  ruler of ~, 1073.36(22,31)
  symbol of political power of
    ~, 1073.86
Turkish,adj., 784.16
  ~ language, 664.4(13)
turmoil,n.
  commotion, 1101.1
  confusion, 605.13; see con-
    fusion,n.
turn,n., 148.2
  period of work, 203.12
  full of ~s, 148.12,13
  having two ~s, 148.11
  make a ~, 148.1
  pen's ~ in writing, 148.2(6)
  sudden ~, 148.2(6)
turn,v., 148.1,6
  ~ around, 150.1,2; see ro-
    tate,v.
  ~ aside, 148.1; 148.6(7,13)
  ~ away, 148.1
  ~ back, 148.1(18,19); 148.6(9,
    10)
  ~ backward, 148.1(17);
    148.6(11)
  ~ inside out, 148.6(3–5)
  ~ limbs backward, 148.6(12)
  ~ limbs forward, 148.6(8)
  ~ over, 149.1,2
  ~ round, 150.1,2; see ro-
    tate,v.
  tendency to ~ toward Mag-
    netic Pole, 148.16
  tending to ~, 148.5
  that on which something ~s,
    148.14
  ~ to the east, 148.1(14)
  twist and ~, 148.1(30,32);
    156.1(35,36)
  ~ upside-down, 149.1(1–3,5,7–
    10)
turned,adj., 148.10
  ~ outward, 148.10(3)
  ~ over, 149.4
  state of being ~, 148.9
  ~ to one side, 148.10(1,2)
  ~ upside-down, 149.4
turning,adj., 148.3,8
  ~ round, 150.4
turning,n., 148.2,7
  ~ back, 148.2(5)
  ~ back of an organ, 148.2(4)
  center of ~, 137.1(1,25)
  clockwise ~, 148.2(2,3)
  counterclockwise ~, 148.2(7)
  ~ toward the left, 148.2(7)
  ~ toward the right, 148.2(2,3)
turning point,n., 539.16
turnip,n.
  ~-shaped, 507.17(49)
turtle,n., 425.1,15,16
  covering on ~s, 972.4(19,24)
  group of ~s, 403.5(3)
  like a ~, 425.18
  like a ~ shell, 355.11(4,5);
    425.19
  pert. to a ~ shell, 355.11(4)
  pert. to ~s, 425.17
  ~ shell, 355.10(1); 972.4(24)
turtledove,n.
  group of ~s, 403.5(21)
twelfth,n. or adj.
  ~ part, 940.4
  pert. to ~s, 940.2
twelve,n., 940.1; see also
    dozen,n.
  by ~s, 940.3
  consisting of ~s, 940.5
  pert. to ~, 940.2

twelvefold,adj., 940.5
twentieth,adj., 939.5
twenty, n. or adj., 939.1
  consisting of ~, 939.2
  consisting of ~ parts, 939.3
  counting by ~, 939.4
  divided into ~ parts, 939.3
  group of ~, 939.1
  pert. to ~, 939.2
twenty-one,n.
  age over ~, 758.1(2)
  age under ~, 758.1(3)
  between fourteen and ~ years
    old, 760.1(1)
  person under ~, 758.2(2)
twice, adj. or adv.
  ~ as great, 931.14
  become ~ as great, 931.13
  make ~ as great, 931.12
twig,n., 990.4,5; see also
    branch,n.
  article made of woven ~s,
    990.15,16
  broom, ~s tied together as
    a, 899.33
  fallen ~s, 990.18
  food, ~s as, 740.6
  having ~s, 990.22,23
  like a ~, 990.14,19
  made of willow ~s, 990.10
  made of woven ~s, 990.13
  remove the ~s from, 990.24
  tie with ~s, 990.12
  tying ~ for, 990.11
  willow ~, 990.9
  woven ~s, 990.15
  woven from ~s, 307.2(2)
  young ~, 990.6
twilight,adj., 775.3; 777.4;
    1065.1(13)
twilight,n., 775.3; 777.4;
    1065.1(13)
  active, etc., in the ~, 777.5
  lighted by ~, 1065.10
twin,adj., 529.1(2,17,19,24);
    931.7,10,15
twin,n., 529.3; 721.5(1,2,7);
    931.2
  developed as a ~, 721.6,7
  give birth to ~s, 717.4
twin,v., 931.11
twinkle,n., 1065.48,49
twinkle,v., 1065.45(2,4,7,8,11,12,
    15,17–21,31,32,34–36);
    1065.47
twinkling,adj., 1065.50
twirl,n., 150.3
twirl,v., 150.1,2
twirling,adj., 150.4
twist,n., 152.3; 155.2; 156.3
  full of ~s, 156.5
  full of ~s, that which is,
    156.4
  pen's ~ in writing, 156.3(3)
twist,v., 152.1,2; 155.1; 156.1,2
  ~ out of shape, 156.1(7,30);
    156.2(4,7–9,15)
  that which ~s, 156.4
twisted,adj., 152.5; 155.4;
    156.5; 181.1
  ~ out of shape, 156.5; 156.5(3,
    6,12,22)
  state of being ~, 156.6
twisting,adj., 152.4; 155.3; 156.5
two, n. or adj., 931.1
  ~ at a time, 931.6
  card of ~ pips, 931.27
  consisting of ~ parts, 931.7
  die of ~ pips, 931.27
  divide into ~ parts, 931.7,8
  divided into ~ lobes, 931.9
  domino of ~ pips, 931.27
  for ~ people, 931.5
  group of ~, 931.1,11
  growing in ~s, 731.5(5)

~ in one, 931.20
in ~s, 931.10
involving ~, 931.16–18
kind, ~ of a, 931.1
more than ~, 916.11
multiply by ~, 931.12,14
natures, having ~ different, 931.3
of ~ people, 931.5
one, ~ in, 931.20
participated in by ~, 931.16,17
pert. to ~, 931.2
political parties, involving ~, 931.17
shared by ~, 931.18
state of being ~, 931.4
~ times, 931.26
whole composed of ~ parts, 931.20
twofold, adj. or adv., 931.15
become ~, 931.13
increase ~, 907.9(3)
make ~, 931.12
twoness,n., 931.4
tying,n.
material for ~, 302.32; see also **cord, rope,**n.
type,n., 317.1
kind, 312.1
model, 317.1
corresponding ~, 317.1(2,6)
earlier ~, 317.1(1)
having many ~s, 312.14
having only one ~, 312.13
of different ~s, 312.10
of no special ~, 312.6
of several ~s, 312.10
opposite ~, 317.1(2,6)
original ~, 317.1(3)
perfect ~, 317.1(4,9)
pert. to a ~, 317.2
primary ~, 317.1(1,24,25)
represent by ~, 953.1(9,10) ; 953.3
representative ~, 317.1(8,11, 15,19,22)
serve as a ~, 317.3
typesetter,n., 690.2(1)
typesetting,n., 690.1(7)
typewritten,adj.
~ manuscript, 682.16(38)
typhoid fever,n., 396.1(12)
resembling ~, 396.2
typhoon,n., 1042.27
typical,adj., 317.2; 535.1,2
be a ~ part of, 326.41(4)
part ~ of the whole, 326.1(13)
tyrannize,v., 8.8; 635.6; 889.7; 890.4; 1073.61
tyrannous,adj., 8.11; 635.6; 889.7; 890.4; 1073.59
tyranny,n., 8.9; 635.6; 889.7; 890.4; 1073.59
tyrant,n., 8.10; 635.6; 889.7; 890.4; 1073.60

U

ugly,adj., 506.1
~ giant, 662.7(43)
~ man, 506.3
~ mythical being, 662.29(6)
~ old woman, 506.2(2) ; 759.18(3,8,11)
~ spirit or supernatural being, 662.7(2,3,19,20,32,43)
~ woman, 506.2; 759.18(3,8,11)
ulcer,n., 383.2
venereal or syphilitic ~, 379.9(2)
ulcerate,v., 383.4,7
ulcerated,adj., 383.3
umbrella,n., 568.23; 1037.29; 1071.8

become ~-shaped, 985.23
umpire,n., 1083.19; see **arbitrator,**n.
unable,adj., 13.3; 14.1(3,4,17,24, 25,27–33,35,36,53–56,62,64, 67–69,72)
unabundant,adj., 43.2; 917.27, 30
unacceptable,adj.
hateful, 880.4
improper, 828.1
offensive, 1118.1
unliked, 880.10
unpleasant, 1117.1
unsuitable, 828.13
~ person, 880.5(4)
unaccompanied,adj., 330.1
unaccustomed,adj., 620.1; 629.3,25
unadorned,adj., 959.9; see **plain,**adj.
unadulterated,adj., 805.9; 900.10
unaffected,adj.
natural, 810.1
emotionally ~, 1099.10
unafraid,adj., 575.1; see **brave,** adj.
unagitated,adj., 1132.9; 1139.15; see also **calm,**adj.
unanimous,adj., 541.4,7
unanxious,adj., 1131.15; see also **calm,**adj.
unappreciated,adj., 1110.13,14
unappreciation,n., 1110.12
unappreciative,adj., 1110.10
unapproachable,adj., 132.8
unarguable,adj., 542.14
unashamed,adj., 884.15
unatonable,adj., 222.5
unattainable,adj.
desire for ~ thing or ideal, 265.2(19) ; 1092.51
one afflicted with a desire for the ~, 1092.52
unattractive,adj., 196.7; 1117.1
~ in appearance, 506.1
unauthentic,adj., 820.1,5; see **false,**adj.
~ works, 820.6
~ writings, 820.6
unavoidable,adj., 76.8
~ and certain to happen, 76.9
make ~, 76.10
unaware,adj., 581.1; 611.3
unawareness,n., 581.2; 611.3
unbalance,n., 950.16
unbalanced,adj., 950.18
unbearable,adj., 246.5
unbearded,adj., 370.3
unbecoming,adj., 506.1; 828.13
unbelievability,n., 639.11
unbelievable,adj., 639.10
unbeliever,n., 639.5
unbelieving,adj., 639.3; see **disbelieving,**adj.
unbending,adj., 442.1; 553.1; see **stiff, stubborn,**adj.
unbiased,adj., 636.1
unbigoted,adj., 636.1
unblemished,adj., 805.9
unborn,adj.
~ child, 721.8; see **fetus,**n.
unbounded,adj., 309.15; 755.3; 906.17; see also **endless, free,**adj.
unbribable,adj., 845.13
unbridled,adj., 4.1; 309.15; see **free, violent,**adj.
unbroken,adj., 328.1; 754.3; see **complete, continuous,**adj.
unbruised,adj., 804.1
unburden,v., 309.11(11,12,15, 28) ; 926.21,29; 948.19,20

uncalm,adj., 1139.20; see also **excited,**adj.
uncalm,v., 1139.22; see also **excite,**v.
uncalmed,adj., 1139.8
uncalmness,n., 1139.21; see also **excitement,**n.
cause ~ in, 1139.22
uncanny,adj., 662.1
mysterious, 604.1(3,6,12,17,18, 24,35,39,45,48,49,55)
strange, 536.1
unceasing,adj., 755.1,2
uncensored,adj., 899.22
uncertain,adj., 640.1,5
be ~, 640.7
difficult and ~, 25.1(12)
feel ~, 640.7
~ of one's ability, 640.5(1,11, 13,15,16)
~ of oneself, 640.5(1,11,13,15, 16)
~ quality, 640.3
~ thing, 640.3
uncertainty,n., 640.2,6
anxious ~, 640.6(2–4)
condition of ~, 640.10
feel ~, 640.7
feeling of ~, 640.6
region of ~, 1071.13
show ~, 640.7
situation of ~, 640.10
unchangeable,adj., 531.1
~ law, 1079.4
unchanged,adj.
continuing ~, 754.3(10)
unchanging,adj., 531.1
boringly ~, 531.3
cause to set in ~ form, 1098.5
continuous and ~ thing, 754.7
~ in arrangement, 531.7
~ in purpose, 531.5
~ in support, 531.5
~ when heated, 531.6
unchaste,adj., 712.1
unchivalrous,adj., 860.10
~ man, 860.11
uncivilized,adj., 863.1; 866.1; see also **unrefined,**adj.
~ act, 866.4
~ behavior, 866.4
belief that ~ culture is superior, 866.6
~ character, 866.4
~ people, 866.3
~ person, 866.2
study of ~ people, 866.5
uncle,n.
pert. to an ~, 722.7(2)
relationship between ~ and nephew, 722.3(1)
state of being an ~, 722.8
unclean,adj., 904.1; see also **dirty,**adj.
~ books, descr. of, 899.22
ceremonially ~, 886.29
ceremonially ~, incapable of being made, 845.4
make ~, 904.5,11
make ceremonially ~, 886.30
make morally ~, 886.26
morally ~, 886.25
~ writing, descr. of, 899.22
uncleanness,n., 904.2,10
moral ~, cause of, 886.28
moral ~, place of, 886.27
unclear,adj., 603.1; see also **confused, mysterious,**adj.
become ~, 603.3
cause to be ~, 603.4
~ in meaning, 603.1; 604.1
something ~, 603.7
use ~ language, 603.9
~ use of words, 667.1(1,2,5)

unclearness,n., 603.2; see also
  confusion, mystery,n.
~ of meaning, 603.2; 604.2
~ of mind, 603.8
one who causes ~, 603.6
uncombed,adj., 903.1(1,6,17,24,
  25) ; 903.13
uncomfortable,adj., 1132.4;
  1137.12; 1141.10,15
burdensome and ~, 948.13(4,
  6)
make ~, 1132.1; 1141.11
physically ~ from eating or
  drinking, 1137.12(1)
uncomfortableness,n.,
  1132.5; 1137.10(3–6,8) ;
  1141.12,16
cause of ~, 1132.3; 1141.14
causing ~, 1132.2; 1141.13
physical ~ from eating or
  drinking, 1137.10(8)
uncommon,adj., 536.1,4
~ person, act, thing, etc.,
  536.2,5
uncomplicated,adj., 26.1; 960.4
uncompromising,adj., 553.1;
  632.18(6) ; 633.17(3,4)
unconcealed,adj., 970.55
unconcerned,adj., 583.8;
  1097.17; 1131.15
unconditional,adj., 309.15(8,25,
  28,34) ; 328.1(1,6,9,13,23,25,
  43,46) ; 925.15
unconquerable,adj., 22.49,51
unconscious,adj.
in a coma, 435.3
not on purpose, 45.14
subconscious, 584.8
unaware, 581.1; 611.3
become ~, 435.6
knock ~, 435.2
unconscious,n., 584.9
force into the ~, 1097.42,45
impediment from the ~,
  1097.47
impulse forced into the ~,
  1097.43
primitive forces in the ~,
  866.7
unconsciousness,n.
coma, 435.1(2,6,8,11,14,16,20,
  21,23,24–27)
unawareness, 581.2; 611.3
agent causing ~, 435.5
causing ~, 435.4
~ from narcotics, 399.15(7)
near-~, 435.1(22,26,27)
soothe to ~, 435.7
unconsecrated,adj., 650.11
unconsolable,adj., 1125.47
uncontrollable,adj., 550.1
~ and very fast, 550.6
uncontrolled,adj., 309.15;
  309.15(1,4–8,10–16,18,20,24,
  25,29–34,36–38)
unconventional,adj., 536.4;
  629.3; 819.16; 828.12
person who lives an ~ life,
  536.7
uncooked,adj., 1061.21
uncorrectible,adj., 815.12
uncountable,adj., 941.8
uncouth,adj.
clumsy, 14.1; see clumsy,adj.
impolite, 860.1; see impolite,
  adj.
unrefined, 863.1; see unrefined,adj.
~ person, 14.3; 860.4,5; 863.3
uncover,v.
find, 487.1
find out, 624.1
remove covering from, 972.6
remove one's hat, 983.9
show, 951.1

uncovered,adj.
bareheaded, 983.7
without a cover, 972.7
uncustomary,adj., 629.3
undamaged,adj., 804.1
undecided,adj., 640.1,5; see uncertain,adj.
remain ~, 640.4
undecorated,adj., 959.9; see
  plain,adj.
undemonstrative,adj., 77.2;
  1097.30
be ~, 77.4
~ person, 77.3
undemonstrativeness,n.,
  77.1(3,8–12,14–20,26,31,32,
  34) ; 1097.30
undeniable,adj., 542.14; 544.7;
  641.1(7–10,12,21) ; 820.25,26
undependable,adj., 527.6;
  539.21,23; 640.1; see also
  dependable and make negative
under, adv. or prep.
lying ~, 65.3(14,18)
~ the earth, 1004.29
underclothing,n., 981.1–3
underestimate,v., 839.25
undergarment,n., 981.1–3
undergo,v., 32.2; 246.1
cause to ~, 32.3
underground,adj., 1004.29
~ cemetery, 797.7
~ passage, 122.1(32,33,35)
~ room, 787.7(13,39,41)
understand,v., 593.1
able to ~, 593.3
easy to ~, 598.8,16,20; see understandable,adj.
hard to ~, 603.1; 604.1; see
  also mysterious, unclear,
  adj.
impossible to ~, 604.1; see
  also mysterious,adj.
~ in a spiritual sense, 1090.8
~ incorrectly, 593.14,17; 827.6;
  see also misunderstand,v.
one who ~s, 593.5
quick to ~, 593.11; 594.1; see
  also intelligent,adj.
slow to ~, 593.12; 597.1; see
  also stupid,adj.
understandable,adj., 585.28,29;
  598.8,16,17
become ~ to, 598.23
~ by the public, 598.18
~ without further explanation, 598.19
~ without further proof,
  598.14
understanding,adj., 593.3;
  1092.78
understanding,n., 592.2;
  1092.76; see also insight,n.
dull in ~, 597.1,6; see also
  stupid,adj.
go beyond ~, 159.1(33)
lacking in ~, 597.1,6; see
  also stupid,adj.
~ of the emotions of others,
  1092.76
pert. to ~, 593.4
range of ~, 593.9
wide range of ~, 593.10
understood,adj.
able to be ~, 585.28,29; 598.16,
  17; see also understandable,adj.
~ by a few only, 604.7
easily ~, 598.16; see also understandable,adj.
generally ~, 593.13
something ~, 593.6
undertake,v., 49.1
undertaker,n., 49.3; 799.3

undertaking,n., 49.6
undervalue,v., 839.25
underwear,n., 981.1–3
undeserved,adj., 841.10
undeservedly,adv., 841.11
undeserving,adj., 841.12
consider ~ of notice, 841.14
undesirable,adj., 920.19
unpleasant, 1117.1
undetectible,adj., 487.5
undeveloped,adj., 733.1,9–11;
  see also immature,adj.
biologically ~, 733.7
~ organ, 733.8
undignified,adj., 867.6; 868.27
undiluted,adj., 1.25
~ alcoholic drink, 1.26
undiscoverable,adj., 487.5
undisguised,adj., 970.56
undissolvable,adj., 1027.31
~ substance, 1027.32
undisturbed,adj.
calm, 1139.15
peaceful, 1140.11
tidy, 902.1
emotionally ~, 1131.15;
  1132.9
undivided,adj., 328.1
undress,n., 984
state of ~, 984.4
undress,v., 984.1,2,5–7,9,10,20,21
~ing room in ancient Greece
  or Rome, 984.15
undressed,adj., 984.3,11,18
partly ~, 974.9
undressing,n.
house for ~, 753.1(9)
watches ~, one who, 484.3(4)
undulant fever,n., 396.1(6)
undying,adj., 755.7; see also
  immortal,adj.
state of being ~, 755.8
unearthly,adj., 662.1; 1004.19,
  39 ; 1090.11
strange, 536.1
unnatural, 811.11
uneasiness,n., 1131.8; 1132.5;
  1133.2; 1134.2; 1141.16
embarrassment, 868.23
~ of conscience, 885.5
~ over guilt, 884.18
~ over sin, 884.18
uneasy,adj., 1131.8; 1132.4;
  1133.1; 1134.1; 1141.15
ill-at-ease, 868.20; 1132.4
~ of conscience, 885.7
uneatable,adj., 734.18
uneducated,adj., 621.12
~ person, 621.13
unemotional,adj., 1097.3,30
~ person, 1097.4
unemployed,adj., 209.6
be ~, 209.5
make ~, 209.7
~ people, 113.14; 209.11
~ person, 113.13; 209.9
unemployment,n., 209.8,12
unending,adj., 755.1,2
unendurable,adj., 246.5
unenergetic,adj., 10.1(3,5,32,34–
  36,38,39,41,60,61,65)
unenthusiastic,adj., 1095.23;
  1097.32
unequal,adj., 534.16,18
unequaled,adj., 534.13
unequality,n., 534.17
unequivalence,n., 534.17
unequivalent,adj., 534.16,18
unethical,adj., 828.11; 886.1;
  see also immoral, im-
  proper,adj.
~ woman, 708.14(1,7)
uneven,adj.
changeable, 539.21,23
rough, 440.1

unbalanced, 950.18
unexcessive,adj., 921.3; 923.1
unexcitable,adj., 1100.25;
  1132.12
  ~ person, 1100.26; 1132.13
unexcited,adj., 1139.15
unexpected,adj., 269.1; see also
  sudden,adj.
  ~ act, 52.5(19)
  what is ~, 269.3
unexpectedly,adv., 1051.4
  bring on ~, 269.4
  what comes ~, 269.3(1)
unexpectedness,n., 269.2
unexplainable,adj., 599 7
  something ~, 599.8
unexplored,adj.
  still ~ area, 612.25
unexpressible,adj., 665.7
unextreme,adj., 922.28; 923.1
unfair,adj., 635.1
  prejudiced, 634.2; see preju-
    diced,adj.
  ~ action, 635.4
  be ~, 634.5
  be ~ to, 635.3
  ~ in exercise of authority or
    power, 635.6
unfairly,adv.
  competing ~, 635.7
  playing ~, 635.7
  represent ~, 635.5; 953.4
  treat ~, 635.3
unfairness,n., 635.2
  prejudice, 634.1; see preju-
    dice,n.
unfaithful,adj., 659.1; see disloyal,adj.
unfamiliar,adj., 536.1; 612.23
unfashionable,adj., 284.8;
  629.3; 631.12; see also old-
  fashioned,adj.
  become ~, 631.14
  make ~, 631.13
unfasten,v., 302.7
unfavorable,adj., 838.1
  ~ emotion, 838.2
  ~ happening, 29.6(14)
  ~ inclination, 838.3
  ~ judgment, 838.2; 894.1,3
  ~ opinion, 838.2; 894.1,3
  ~ result, 838.4
unfeeling,adj., 889.10; 1093.2;
  1097.3,24; 1098.3; 1129.22
  become ~, 1097.6; 1098.2
  make ~, 1097.5; 1098.1;
    1129.25
  ~ person, 1097.4
unfeminine,adj., 707.3(5–10)
  make ~, 708.9
unfinished,adj.
  immature, 733.1,9–11; see
    immature,adj.
  incomplete, 329.1; see in-
    complete,adj.
unfit,adj., 13.3; 14.1(24,25,28,31–
  33,47,54,68,69)
  become ~ for use, 284.19
  declare ~ for use, 284.17
  make ~ for use, 284.14(1,8);
    284.15,16
unfitting,adj., 828.13
unflavored,adj., 446.18,19
unforeseen,adj., 269.1
unforgivable,adj., 897.10
unforgiving,adj., 897.45
unfortunate,adj., 36.3; 838.1;
  see also unfavorable,adj.
  ~ occurrence, 29.6(1,6–9,14,
    17,26–28,32,42,43)
  ~ occurrences, 29.7(8,9)
  that which is ~, 36.1,2; 37.1
unfreeze,v., 1060.52; see melt,v.
unfriendliness,n., 879.14; see
  also hostility,n.

unfriendly,adj., 544.3; 879.1,13;
  see also hostile, opposed,
  adj.
  a split into ~ groups,
    325.3(6)
  bad-tempered and ~ (of ani-
    mals), 879.13(5)
  impolite and ~, 860.7;
    879.13(3)
  less ~, become, 1096.28
  less ~, cause to be, 1096.31
  make ~, 879.10
unfrightened,adj., 575.1; see
  brave,adj.
unfruitful,adj , 716.1
ungainly,adj , 14.1; see clumsy,
  adj.
  ~ in movement, 86.3
ungenerous,adj., 227.1; 887.1;
  see mean, stingy,adj.
ungentle,adj., 1144.8
ungovernable,adj., 550.1
ungoverned,adj., 309.15;
  309.15(1,4–8,10–16,18,24,25,
  29–34,36–38) ; 1087.26
ungraceful,adj., 14.1; see
  clumsy,adj.
  ~ in movement, 86.3
ungracious,adj., 860.1; 1117.1;
  see impolite, unpleasant,
  adj.
ungrammatical,adj., 667.3
  ~ usage, 667.3,4
  use ~ly, 667.5
ungrateful,adj., 1110.10
  ~ person, 1110.11
ungratefulness,n., 1110.12
ungrown,adj., 733.1,9–11; see
  immature,adj.
unhabitual,adj., 629.3
unhappiness,n., 1123.2; 1124.2;
  1125.2,48; see depression,
  gloom, sadness,n.
  in a state of general ~,
    1123.10,11
unhappy,adj., 1123.1; 1124.1;
  1125.1,48; see depressed,
  gloomy, sad,adj.
unharmed,adj., 804.1
unhat,v., 983.5,6
unhatted,adj., 983.7
unhealthful,adj., 389.18
unhealthy,adj., 389.2; 1125.16;
  see also ill,adj.
unheard-of,adj., 536.1; see unusual,adj.
unhidden,adj., 970.55
unhindered,adj., 309.15(21–23,
  26,35–37)
unholy,adj., 650.11
unhonored,adj., 857.21
unhurt,adj., 804.1
unhygienic,adj., 904.10
  make ~, 904.11
unicorn,n.
  like a ~, 408.14
uniform,adj., 531.1,2
  boringly ~, 531.3
  make ~, 529.5
  occurring ~ly, 531.4
uniform,n.
  clothing instead of ~,
    974.1(8)
  servant's ~, 974.1(7)
uniformity,n., 531.1–4
  without ~, 539.21,23
unimaginative,adj., 535.5
  do, act, go, etc., in an ~
    manner, 535.9
  ~ expression, phrase, action,
    etc., 535.6
  ~ person, 535.7
  say or speak in ~ sentiments,
    535.8

unimportant,adj., 849.1–3;
  887.2
  consider ~, 849.8
  ~ for execution, 849.2
  ~ items, 849.5
  light and ~. 949.1(5)
  make ~ and small, 909.6(2)
  ~ part, 326.1(10)
  ~ person, 849.6,7; 909.3(14,15)
  small and ~ person, 909.3(14,
    15)
  small and ~ thing, 909.5(2,10)
  spend time on ~ things,
    762.16
  ~ thing, 849.4; 909.5(2,10)
  ~ things, 849.5
  ~ to war, 849.2
  treat as ~, 840.6; 849.8
  young and ~ person, 849.7
unimprisoned,adj., 309.8
unindulged,adj., 1108.3
uninhabitable,adj., 750.9
uninhabited,adj., 750.24
  ~ land, 1003.11(1)
  ~ place, 750.25
uninhibited,adj., 1092.67
uninjured,adj., 804.1
uninstructed,adj., 621.12
unintelligent,adj., 597.1; see
  stupid,adj.
unintelligible,adj., 604.1
unintentional,adj., 46.12
uninterested,adj., 583.8
  being ~, 583.9
  done in an ~ manner, 583.12
  person who is ~, 583.10
uninteresting,adj., 583.1; see
  also boring,adj.
  be, or become, ~, 583.7
  make ~, 583.6
  person who is ~, 583.3
  something ~, 583.2
unintoxicated,adj., 749.61
uninvolved,adj., 26.1; 960.4
  emotionally ~, 1097.31
union,n., 302.2,5; 320.3,4;
  321.3,4; see also connection, mixture,n.
  control of government by
    labor ~s, advocate of,
    1076.12(27)
  labor ~, 206.1,2
  labor ~, member, 206.1(7)
unique,adj., 534.13; 536.1;
  930.6
  ~ of its kind. 536.3
  ~ person, 534.15
  something ~, 534.15; 930.7
unit,n., 318.1; 930.1,2
  amount per ~, 914.6
  pert. to a ~, 318.2; 930.2
unite,v., 302.1,4; 320.1,2; 321.1,
  2; see also attach, combine, connect,v.
United States,n., 784.9(1,6) ;
  see also America,n.,
  American,adj.
  exaggerated patriotism to the
    ~, 784.8(5)
  government of the ~,
    1073.5(1,2,7)
  make conform to customs of
    the ~, 784.10(1)
unity,n., 321.4; 541.20; 930.1
  destoy the ~ of, 325.1;
    801.1(3) ; see also sepa-
    rate,v.
  device on flag to indicate ~,
    957.17
universal,adj., 40.1; 41.1
  be ~, 40.3
  ~ in application, 41.1(1)
  ~ in effect, 41.1(2)
  ~ in extent, 41.1(2)
  ~ in influence, 41.1(2)

~ in power, 41.1(2)
universality,n., 40.2
universe,n., 1052.1
   description of the ~, 1052.4
   evolution of the ~, 1052.7
   origin of the ~, 1052.5
   pert. to the ~, 1052.2,3
   philosophy of the ~, 1052.7,8
   science of the ~, 1052.8,9
   theory of the ~, 3.13; 1052.6
university,n., 623.1; see
   college, school,n.
unjust,adj., 635.1; 828.11
unjustifiable,adj., 591.1
unjustified,adj., 600.6
unkind,adj., 889.1; 890.1; see
   also cruel, harsh,adj.; see
   kind,adj., and make negative
   speak ~ly, 860.14
unknot,v., 302.31
unknowable,adj., 612.16,17
   concern with ~ things, 612.20
   doctrine of the ~, 612.22
   ~ fact, possibility, or thing,
      612.19
   ~ from experience, 612.18,20
   ~ person, 604.10
   science of ~ things, 612.21
unknowing,adj., 611.3
unknown,adj., 612.23,24;
   970.49
   ~ land, 1003.2(39)
   still ~ area, 612.25,26
   still ~ scientific area, 612.26
   ~ to the mind, 584.8
unlace,v., 302.31
unlawful,adj., 1087.1; see illegal,adj.
unlighted,adj., 1070.1,11; see
   dark,adj.
   ~ by the moon, 1065.11
   ~ by the sun, 1065.11
unlikable,adj., 880.4(1–3) ;
   1117.1
unlike,adj., 540.1; see different,
   adj.
unliked,adj., 880.10; see disliked,adj.
unlimited,adj., 309.15; 309.15(1,
   4–8,10,12–16,20–23,26,28–
   38) ; 755.3; 906.17
unlit,adj., 1065.11; 1070.1,11;
   see dark,adj.
unlivable,adj., 750.9
unlived,adj.
   ~ in, 750.24
   ~in place, 750.25
unload,v., 309.11(11,12,15,28) ;
   926.21,29; 948.19,20
unlock,v., 298.1(19,21–23)
unloosen,v.
   set free, 309.1; see free,v.
   untie, 302.31
unloved,adj., 880.4,10
   state of being ~, 880.11,13
unlucky,adj., 36.3
   make ~, 36.6
   ~ person, 36.4
unmanageable,adj., 550.1
unmanliness,n., 707.10
unmanly,adj., 707.9
   become ~, 707.13
   ~ boy, 707.11
   development of ~ qualities,
      707.14
   make ~, 707.12
   ~ man, 707.11
   presence of ~ qualities, 707.15
unmarred,adj., 805.9
unmarried,adj., 706.2
   favoring ~ state, 706.6
   favors ~ state, one who, 706.7
   ~ person, 705.4; 706.1,8,9
   ~ state, 706.3

unmeaningful,adj., 607.23;
   608.5; see meaningless,
   nonsensical,adj.
unmeasurable,adj., 946.5
   ~ because so deep, 946.5(1)
   ~ because so large, 946.8
   figuratively ~, 946.6
unmeasured,adj.
   figuratively ~, 946.7
unmentionable,adj., 665.7;
   883.9
unmentioned,adj., 475.8
unmerciful,adj., 889.10; 897.45;
   1129.22
   make ~, 1129.25
unnatural,adj.
   abnormal, 536.4; 811.9
   affected, 811.1
   artificial, 811.4,5
   contrary to nature, 536.4;
      811.9,11
   grotesque, 811.6
   man-made, 811.4
   ~ action, 536.5
   ~ figure, 811.8
   frightening and ~, 576.7(4,17,
      18)
   ~ happening, 536.5
   ~ in manner, conduct, etc.,
      811.1
   ~ in shape, appearance, or
      kind, 811.6; see also gro-
      tesque,adj.
   make ~ in manner or con-
      duct, 811.3
   ~ person, 536.5; 537.1; 811.2;
      see also freak,n.
   ~ thing, 536.5; 537.1; 811.7,8,
      10; see also freak,n.
unnecessary,adj., 273.11
   ~ for war, 273.11(7)
   improper and ~, 828.4
   make ~, 273.12
unneeded,adj., 273.11; see unnecessary,adj.
unnervous,adj., 1109.25;
   1131.15; 1135.8
unneurotic,adj., 1135.8
unoccupied,adj., 926.6
   without inhabitants, 750.24
unopposable,adj., 544.7
unoriginal,adj., 535.5
   act, do, or go in an ~ manner, 535.9
   ~ person, 535.7
   ~ phrase, expression, or ac-
      tion, 535.6
   speak in ~ sentiments, 535.8
unornamental,adj., 959.22
unornamented,adj., 959.9; see
   plain,adj.
unpaid,adj., 218.20
unparalleled,adj., 534.13
unpardonable,adj., 897.10
unpeaceful,adj., 1140.13,14
unpenitent,adj., 884.15
unperceivable,adj., 433.10,11;
   483.12(2,7–9,11,14)
   ~ by touch, 436.12
unpersuasive,adj., 638.15
unplanned,adj., 46.12
unpleasant,adj., 1105.29; 1117.1
   be ~, 1117.4
   be ~ to, 1117.3
   burdensome and ~, 948.13(5)
   cause ~ feelings in, 1117.16
   ~ person, 1117.17
   ~ situation, 25.9(11,13)
   sound, ~ in, 466.3
   ~ sounds, 466.1,2,4
unpleasantness,n., 1117.2
unpleasurable,adj., 1105.29
unplug,v., 298.1(20,24,26)
unpolished,adj., 440.1; 1072.8

unrefined (figuratively),
   863.1
unpopular,adj., 880.4,10
   ~ girl at a dance, 1109.17
   ~ person, 880.5(4) ; 1109.17,21
unpopulated,adj., 750.24
   ~ place, 750.25
unprecedented,adj., 29.4;
   536.1
unprejudiced,adj., 636.1
   ~ person, 636.3
unprepared,adj., 48.10
unpretended,adj., 807.3; 813.6,7
unproductive,adj., 716.1–3; see
   also sterile,adj.
   ineffective, 17.1
   ~ land, 1003.11
unprofitable,adj., 16.1; 24.3;
   see also profitable,adj.,
   and make negative
unpunishable,adj., 896.10
unpunished,adj., 896.9
unpunishing,adj., 842.1(3,6)
unqualified,adj., 14.1(25,27–29,
   31–33,35,36,47,52,54,56,62,
   68) ; 309.15(8,25,34) ; 328.1(1,
   3,4,6,9,13,23,25,36,42,46) ;
   925.15
unquestionable,adj., 542.14;
   544.7; 641.1(7–10,12) ; 812.3;
   820.25,26
unreal,adj., 809.1; see also
   imaginary,adj.
   ~ appearance, 483.8(2,3,8,11,
      14,16)
   ~ double, 529.3(4)
   ~ counterpart, 529.3(4)
   ~ image, 483.8(2,3,8,11,14,16)
   ~, like a shadow, 1071.3
   ~ quality or condition, 809.2
   ~ thing, 809.3
unreality,n., 809.2,3
   belief in ~, 632.6(11)
   region of ~, 1071.13
unreasonable,adj., 591.1; 635.1;
   921.1; 923.3
   seeming ~, 591.2,3
   something ~, 591.4,5
unreasoning,adj., 584.8,15;
   585.7; 597.1,6,8,9,19; 985.30
unrefined,adj., 860.1; 863.1;
   see also impolite, uncivilized,adj.
   ~ act, 863.7
   become ~, 863.5
   cause to be ~, 863.6
   ~ person, 863.3
   ~ phrase, 863.8
unrefinement,n., 860.2; 863.2
unregretful,adj., 1126.11
   ~ person, 1126.12
unrelated,adj., 540.1; see different,adj.
unreliable,adj., 527.6; 539.21,23;
   640.1; see also reliable,adj.,
   and make negative
unrelievable,adj., 1125.47;
   1142.9
unrelieved,adj., 1142.7
unremorseful,adj., 884.15;
   1126.11
unresistant,adj., 552.3; see submissive,adj.
unresponsive,adj., 985.30;
   1097.3,30
unrest,n., 549.2; 1132.5; 1134.2
unrestrained,adj., 309.15;
   309.15(1,4–8,10–16,18,20,22–
   26,29–32,34–38)
unrestricted,adj., 309.15;
   309.15(1,4–8,10–16,18,20,22–
   26,29–33,35–38)
unripe,adj., 733.1; see also immature,adj.
unruly,adj., 549.1; 550.1; see

also **disobedient**,adj.
~ behavior, acts, etc., 550.2
likely to become ~, 550.5
~ person, 550.3
~ public demonstration, 550.4
unsafe,adj., 572.1; see **dangerous**,adj.
unsaid,adj., 475.1(18,20–22) ;
475.8,10; 607.6
unsanitary,adj., 904.10
make ~, 904.11
unsatisfaction,n., 1119.21,23;
see also **dissatisfaction**,n.
unsatisfactory,adj., 1105.29;
1119.24
unsatisfiable,adj., 1119.25
unsatisfied,adj., 1119.21,22; see
also **dissatisfied, frustrated**,adj.
always ~, 1119.25
leave ~, 1119.20
state of being ~, 1119.21,23
unsatisfying,adj., 1105.29;
1119.24; see also **dissatisfying**,adj.
unsavory,adj., 446.18,19;
1105.29; 1117.1; 1118.1
unscared,adj., 575.1; see **brave**,
adj.
unscrupulous,adj., 309.15(27) ;
885.9; 886.1,10
unseasonable,adj., 765.4; 828.14
unseemly,adj., 828.1,13
unselfish,adj., 229.1; see **generous**,adj.
unsentimental,adj., 1097.3,24,
30; 1098.3; see also **sentimental**,adj., and make
negative
~ person, 1094.14
unsettle,v., 1101.5,10,12; 1132.1
unsettled,adj., 1101.11; 1132.4;
1139.20
unpopulated, 750.24
unshaded,adj., 1071.14
unshined,adj., 1072.8
unshod,adj., 979.13
unshown,adj., 970.48
unsinning,adj., 845.9
unskilled,adj., 14.1; see also
clumsy, unskillful,adj.
unskillful,adj., 14.1; see also
clumsy,adj.
be ~, 14.4
~ person, 14.3
unskillfulness,n., 14.2
unsociable,adj., 879.13; see
unfriendly,adj.
unsolvable,adj., 601.6
unsoothable,adj., 1139.10
~ person, 1142.13
unsoothed,adj., 1139.8
unsoothing,adj., 1139.3
unsophisticated,adj.
ignorant, 611.3; see **ignorant**,
adj.
inexperienced, 620.1(2–6,14,
15) ; see **inexperienced**,adj.
natural, 810.1; see **natural**,
adj.
unwise, 596.5
~ person, 810.2
unsordid,adj., 887.9
unspeakable,adj., 665.7, 883.9
unspiritual,adj., 1004.38
make ~, 1004.42
unspoiled,adj., 805.9; 1091.23
unspoken,adj., 475.1(8,21,22) ;
475.8,10; 607.6
unspontaneous,adj., 811.5;
1097.30,32
unsportsmanlike,adj., 635.1
unspotted,adj., 899.29; see also
clean,adj.

unstable,adj., 87.1; 539.21,23;
see also **unsteady**,adj.
unstainable,adj., 904.22
unstained,adj., 899.29
unsteady,adj., 87.1; 1007.14
changeable, 539.21
be or become ~, 87.3
cause to be ~, 87.4
~ condition, 87.2
~ in movement, 86.3
move in ~ manner, 86.1(2,5,
11,14,17,19,20)
~ movement, 86.2
~ state, 87.2
unsterile,adj., 904.10; 905.3
make ~, 904.11; 905.1
unstick,v., 302.21
unstop,v., 298.1(20,24,26)
unstrict,adj., 890.12
unstuck,adj.
become ~, 302.21
unsubstantial,adj., 513.12;
909.11; 949.1(2,4,6,7) ;
1071.3
unsuccessful,adj., 24.3
be ~, 24.1
likely to be ~, 24.6
unsuitable,adj., 828.13; see
also **improper**,adj.
be ~ to, 828.16
~ behavior, 55.3(10) ; 828.12
consider ~, 828.17
~ for inspection, 828.15
~ for presentation, 828.15
~ for view, 828.15
~ in time, 765.4,6,7; 828.14
make ~, 828.18
unsuited,adj., 828.13
unsupported,adj., 1022.38
unsuppressible,adj., 22.41
unsuspected,adj.
exist ~, 971.16
unsuspicious,adj., 632.18(1–4,
7,10)
unsymmetrical,adj., 507.14(1,2,
11) ; 950.18
unsympathetic,adj., 889.10;
1129.22; see also **unfeeling**,
adj.
become ~ to suffering, 889.14
make ~, 889.13; 1129.25
unsystematic,adj., 903.6
untactful,adj., 14.1(19,41,51,53,
59) ; 1097.35
untalented,adj., 14.1(30)
untamable,adj., 22.41
untamed,adj., 309.22; 1144.8
~ state, 309.23
untaught,adj., 621.12
~ person, 621.13
untested,adj., 19.13
unthankful,adj., 1110.10
~ person, 1110.11
unthankfulness,n., 1110.12
unthinking,adj., 581.1; 584.8;
585.7; 597.1,6,8,9,19; 985.30
inconsiderate, 1097.35
untidiness,n., 903.2
~ of clothing, 974.8
untidy,adj., 903.1,7
bad-tempered and ~,
903.1(11)
cause to be ~, 903.3
~ condition, 903.2
dirty and ~ person, 903.4
dirty and ~ woman, 903.4
dirty and ~, 903.1(2,8–10,12,
18,20–23)
fat and ~, 903.1(2)
hanging loose and ~, 903.1(1,
6,17,24,25)
~ in habits, 903.1(18–21) ;
903.6
~ of dress, 903.1(1,2,5,6,8–12,
16–18,20,21,23,25)

~ of hair, 903.1(1,6,17,24,25)
~ person, 903.4
red-faced and ~, 903.1(2)
~ state, 903.2
~ woman, 903.4
untie,v., 302.31
~ a horse's bridle, 302.31(2)
untimeliness,n., 765.5; 828.14
untimely,adj., 765.4,6,7; 828.14
untiring,adj., 2.8,10,13; 12.10
untold,adj., 970.49
untouched,adj., 436.13
untrained,adj., 620.1; 621.12
~ person, 621.13
untroubled,adj., 1131.15;
1132.9
untrue,adj., 820.1; see **false**,
adj.
untrustworthy, 527.6; 539.21,
23; see also **trustworthy**,
adj., and make negative
untruth,n., 821.1
untruthful,adj., 821.5,6
untwist,v., 156.8
unused,adj., 284.3,8
unused to,adj., 629.25
unusual,adj., 536.1,4
~ act, 52.5(27) ; 536.2,5
new and ~, 761.1(9–11,16)
~ happening, 29.4(25,31,35,
36) ; 536.2,5
~ person, 536.2,5
~ thing, 536.2,5
unutterable,adj., 665.7; 883.9
unvisited,adj., 125.6; 331.1
~ place, 331.3
unwanted,adj., 920.1,19
unweakening,adj., 1.23
unwelcome,adj., 1105.29
come where ~, 118.1(10,12,13)
go where ~, 119.1(24,25,29)
unwell,adj., 389.2; see **ill**,adj.
menstruating, 292.4
unwhiskered,adj., 370.3
unwholesome,adj., 389.2,18;
803.3(1,5–7,9) ; 886.13
unwieldy,adj., 190.10(3–5) ;
284.12; 906.5
unwilling,adj., 265.26
be ~, 265.28
be ~ because of conscience,
885.6
~ to accept delay, 265.26(8)
~ to be pleasant, 265.26(5)
~ to do favors, 265.26(5,16)
~ to wait, 265.26(8)
unwillingness,n., 265.27
unwind,v., 156.8
unwisdom,n., 596.6; 597.2; see
also **stupidity**,n.
unwise,adj., 596.5; 597.1; see
also **stupid**,adj.
act ~, 596.7
~ person, 596.8
unworldly,adj., 596.5, 662.1,
1004.19,39; 1090.4,11
unworried,adj., 1131.15; 1132 9
unworthy,adj., 841.12
contemptible, 870.8
consider ~, 841.13
consider ~ of notice, 841.14
unwounded,adj., 804 1
unyielding,adj.
stiff, 442.1
stubborn, 553.1; see **stubborn**,adj.

up,adv.
come ~, 159.1
go ~, 159.1
move ~, 89.1(1,17,19,31) ;
159.1; see also **jump**,v
move ~ and down, 162.1,2
push ~, 197.1(1)
slope ~, 154.1(1)
straight ~, 180 1(2,5,12)

straight ~ and down, 180.1(5–8,13)
upbringing,n., 721.17
  affected by ~, 721.18
  art of ~, 721.21
  science of ~, 721.20
upper,adj., 164.4
upset,adj.
  disturbed, 1101.11; 1130.7; 1131.8; 1132.4
  turned over, 149.4
upset,v.
  disturb, 1101.10; 1130.1; 1131.1; 1132.1
  overthrow, 22.34
  overturn, 149.1
upside-down,adj., 149.4
up-to-date,adj., 761.13; see modern,adj.
upward,adj.
  ~ slope, 154.3(1,6–8,11,12)
upward,adv.
  throw ~, 187.1(59)
urge,v., 52.9; 277.1
  ~ on, 277.1(7–9,14,17,18)
  serving to ~, 277.3
  that which ~s, 277.4
urgent,adj., 274.4(2,4,5); 848.4
urging,adj., 277.3
urging,n., 277.2
  descr. of ~, 277.3
urinate,v., 294.1
  ~ like a dog, 294.2
  place to ~, 295.1
  unsuccessful urge to ~, 294.8(19)
  vessel to ~ in, 261.7(13); 294.14
urination,n., 294.3
  ailments of ~, 294.8
  causing ~, 294.9,10
  control ~, ability to, 294.6
  control ~, inability to, 294.7
  difficulty in ~, 294.8(3,8,14,18)
  frequency of ~, 294.8(12,13,16)
  involuntary ~, 294.7
  organs of ~, pert. to, 294.5(3,7)
  pert. to organs of ~ and reproduction, 379.1(2)
  place for ~, 295.1
  vessel for ~, 261.7(13); 294.14
urine,n., 294.4
  analysis of ~, 294.12
  bodily sac for ~, 350.1(9); see bladder,n.
  chemical in the ~, 294.13
  duct for ~, 294.11
  increase ~, medication to, 398.6(5,6)
  lack of ~, 294.8(3)
  like ~, 294.5(4,6)
  pathological condition of ~, 294.8
  pert. to ~, 294.5
  smelling like ~, 294.5(6)
  sugar in the ~, 294.8(5,6,9)
  vessel for ~, 261.7(13); 294.14
urn,n., 261.7(1,39); 261.10(9)
  ~ for ashes of the dead, 798.7
  ~-shaped, 507.17(86)
U.S.,n., 784.9(1,6); see United States,n.
usability,n., 279.18
usable,adj., 279.17
  be ~, 279.19
use,n., 279.2,18
  adapted for ~, 279.8
  be in ~, 279.12
  be of ~, 279.19
  become unfit for ~, 284.19
  bring back to ~, 279.14
  declare unfit for ~, 284.17
  free for other ~s, 309 11(30)

go out of ~, 284.1
go out of ~, tending to, 284.2
habitual ~, 279.2(1)
in general ~, 279.10
lack of ~, 284.4
make unfit for ~, 284.14
no longer in ~, 284.8; 631.12
no longer in ~, that which is, 284.11; 631.16
not in ~, 284.3
pert. to ~, 279.4
put out of ~, 284.10; 631.14
temporary ~, 281.2
use,v., 279.1
  ~ badly, 283.1
  ~ before, 279.1(2)
  easy to ~, 279.9
  ~ economically, 279.1(20)
  find and ~, 279.1(18)
  ~ for the first time, 279.1(6)
  hold and ~, 279.1(22)
  right to ~, 6.1(1); 279.7; 281.2
  ~ skillfully, 279.1(22)
  stop ~ing, 284.6
  take and ~, 279.1(1)
  ~ temporarily, 281.1
  tending to ~, 279.4
  ~ to one's own advantage, 279.1(10)
  ~ too little of, 279.1(19,20)
  ~ too often, 279.1(15)
  ~ up, 282.1
used,adj.
  not yet ~, 284.7
  person ~ by another, 279.15
  ~ practically, 279.5
  process of being ~, 279.2(1)
  something ~, 279.22
  something ~ for advantage, 279.16
  something ~ temporarily, 279.22(8,13)
  ~ too much, 282.6
used to,adj., 629.24; see accustomed,adj.
useful,adj., 279.17; 831.11; 836.2
  be ~, 279.19
  become more ~, 279.20
  belief that the ~ is good, 279.24; 831.22(1,3)
  ~ in assisting, 279.17(15)
  make less ~, 284.14
  make more ~ by storing, 279.21
  ~ thing, 279.22
usefulness,n., 279.18
  concern with ~, 279.23
  decrease the ~ of, 284.14(3,4)
  destroy the ~ of, 284.14(2,5–9)
  lose ~, 284.18
  restore to ~, 191.1(2)
useless,adj., 284.12
  ineffective, 17.1
  make ~, 284.14
  ~ thing or things, 284.20; 285.1
uselessness,n., 284.13
  ineffectiveness, 17.2
user,n., 279.3
usher,n., 131.3; 131.3(8)
usher,v., 131.1(2)
using,adj., 279.4
using,n., 279.2
  way of ~, 279.6
usual,adj., 535.1
  be ~, 535.4
  descr. of that which one ~ly does, has, wears, says, etc., 535.2
utensil,n., 280.6
uterus,n., 379.1(23)
  carry in the ~, 714.5
  inflammation of the ~, 379.9(7)

membrane of ~, 387.1(5)
pain in the ~, 1137.56(20)
utilitarian,adj., 279.17
utilitarianism,n., 279.18,24; 831.22(1)
utility,n., 279.18,22; 280.6
Utopia,n., 1102.23,24
utter,adj., 328.1
utter,v., 674.1; see say,v.
utterance,n., 674.9; see statement,n.

V

V(the letter),n.
  cut in a ~, 332.1(36)
vacancy,n., 284.4; 750.24; 926.1, 6,10–14
vacant,adj., 284.3; 750.24; 926.1, 6,10–12
vacation,n., 209.12
vagabond,n., 128.3; 888.5
vagina,n., 379.1
  contraction of the ~, 379.9(15)
  discharge from the ~, 287.2(4); 287.3(1,3,4); 292.1
  inflammation of the ~, 379.9(16)
  lips at the ~, 379.1(7,8)
  membrane of the ~, 379.1(6)
  plug for the ~ in menstruation, 297.9(1)
  wash the ~, 899.35(2)
vague,adj., 603.1; see unclear, adj.
  ~ form, 507.1(14)
vagueness,n., 603.2,5
  ~ of mind, 603.8
vain,adj.
  conceited, 871.1; see also proud,adj.
  ineffective, 17.1
  unimportant, 849.1
  ~ person, 871.5(2)
  ~ woman, 871.5(2)
valley,n., 170.10
valuable,adj., 279.17; 839.2
  ~ enough, 839.4
  extremely ~, 839.3
  more ~, 839.6
  something ~, 839.5,8
  stored-up ~ things, 839.8
valuable,n., 839.5
  concealed ~s, 970.52
value,n., 279.18; 839.1
  according to ~, 839.13
  certificate of ~, 850.13
  concern with practical ~, 839.9
  consider as having ~, 839.14(4)
  decrease in ~, 839.17,18; 883.11
  decrease the ~, 839.19,21; 883.16
  decrease the ~ of metal, 839.20
  decrease the ~ of money, 839.23,24
  determine the ~ of, 839.14(3–6,8)
  doctrine of ~ in respect to results, 16.29
  express a low opinion of the ~ of, 840.1
  give a ~ to, 839.14
  greater in ~, 924.6
  increase in ~, 839.11,12
  judge the ~ of, 839.14
  lose ~, 839.17; 883.11
  low in ~, 887.2; 888.3
  low opinion of the ~ of (someone), 840.3
  recognize the ~ of, 839.10

set a ~ on, 839.14,15
set a high ~ on, 839.15
set a low ~ on, 839.25,26;
840.1
set too high a ~ on, 839.16
thing of little ~, 888.11
treat as of little ~, 840.6
without ~, 887.2; 888.1,3,4
value,v., 839.14
valueless,adj., 284.12; 887.2;
888.1,3,4; see also worthless,adj.
~ thing, 888.11
treat as ~, 840.6
vanish,v., 143.1
begin to ~, 143.3
~ gradually, 143.1(5)
tending to ~, 143.2
vanity,n., 871.2; see also proud,
adj.
exhibition of ~, 871.2(1)
feel ~, 871.3(4)
hurt the ~ of, 868.1(4)
show ~, 871.3(4)
vanquish,v., 22.1,3,23,24,27,28,
43; see also defeat,v.
vapor,n., 1041.1; 1048.1(11)
blown-out ~, 1045.2
cause to rise as ~, 1048.44
caused by poisonous ~, 1048.9
convert into ~, 1048.39–43
disagreeable ~, 1048.1(5,7)
frozen ~, 1059.7,8
give off ~, 1048.5
giving off ~, 1026.11; 1048.4
harmful ~, 1048.1(5,8)
invisible ~, 1048.1(5)
like ~, 1048.3
pass off as ~, 1048.44,45
poisonous ~, 1048.1(8)
rise as ~, 1048.45
suffocating ~, 1048.1(7)
treatment with ~, place of,
1048.47
vaporous,adj., 1041.2; 1048.3
variable,adj., 539.9,21; see also
changeable, changing,adj.
variation,n., 539.3; 540.2,4; see
also change, difference,n.
subject to ~, 539.24
varied,adj., 312.10; 540.1,9; see
also different,adj.
variety,n., 312.1; 540.2
various,adj., 312.10; 540.1; see
also different,adj.
~ articles, 540.6
vary,v., 312.12; 539.1,2; 540.3;
see also change,v.
vase,n., 261.7(1,38)
~ for ashes of the dead, 798.7
~-shaped, 507.17(86)
vassal,n., 8.19; 310.5; 1074.11
vast,adj., 906.12,17; see also
big,adj.
vaudeville,n., 969.1(48)
vegetable,n., 745.20
belonging to a family of ~s,
745.22
covering of a ~, 972.4(14)
eater of ~s exclusively,
734.28(1)
eating of ~s exclusively,
734.26(12)
edible ~, 745.19
growing or raising of ~s,
745.25; 994.30
neither ~ nor animal, 1008.7
pert. to certain ~s, 745.22
~s, 745.21
seller of ~s, 745.23
science of growing ~s, 994.30
vegetarian,n., 734.28(1); 749.58
vegetarianism,n., 734.26(8);
749.58
vehicle,n., 192.1,6,10,12,23

cycle ~, 192.17; see cycle,n.
desert ~s, 192.2
enemy territory, ~s going
through, 192.2
~ for babies, 192.16
~ for pulling, 192.6(26)
~ for snow, 192.20; see sled,n.
~ for transporting goods,
192.1(5,11,12); 192.6(27);
192.23
~ for wounded or sick, 192.3
horse-drawn ~, 192.12; see
carriage (horse-drawn),n.
man-drawn ~, 192.9
motor ~, 192.6; see auto-
mobile,n.
pert. to ~s, 192.4
police ~, 1078.13
~ pulled along behind,
193.6(1)
rider in a ~, 192.28
slow ~, 100.9
wagon ~, 192.23
veil,n.
Mexican ~, 983.2(33)
Spanish ~, 983.2(33)
vein,n., 353.1
blood in ~s, descr. of,
352.3(19)
enlarged ~, 353.7(5)
enlarged ~s, 353.7(4)
full of ~s, 353.4(4)
having ~s, 353.4(2)
inflammation of a ~, 353.7(3)
into a ~, 353.5
like ~s, 353.4(2)
~ of a leaf, 353.2,3
~ of insect's wing, 353.2,3
pert. to ~s, 353.4(5)
puncture of a ~, 353.6
swollen ~s, descr. of, 353.4(1,
3)
velvet,n.
like ~, 443.1(20,21);
507.17(88)
venereal,adj., 700.25; 709.4,18
~ diseases, 379 9,10
vengeance,n., 221.2
goddess of ~, 896 32
vengeful,adj 221 3
Venice,n.
chief official of ~, 1077.1(12)
inhabitant of ~, 784.15(61)
pert. to ~, 784 16
ventilate,v 1045.7
~ing pipe, 1045.8
Venus (planet),n., 1053.11
veranda,n, 727 21
verbose,adj., 667.6
verboseness,n , 667 7
verge,n., 793 20
be on the ~ of, 793.25
vermin,n
be infested with ~, 403.20
infestation by ~, 403.19
infested with ~, 403.18
kill ~, 1048 7
multiplication of ~, 717.12(7)
verminous,adj., 403.18
versatile,adj., 7 2(5)
verse,n., 689.1,2,12; see poem,
poetry,n.
vertical,adj., 180.1(5–8)
vessel,n., 261 1,7–10; see also
container,n.
boat, 115 1; see boat,n
ship, 115.1; see ship,n
barrel-shaped ~ for liquids,
261.7(11,37)
drinking ~, 261.8
drinking ~ carried on hike or
journey, 261.7(8)
~ for bathing, 261.7(36)
~ for cooking, 261 10
~ for food, 261 9

~ for heating, 261.10
~ for liquids, 261.7
~ for making butter,
261.7(14)
~ for urine, 261.7(13)
~ for washing, 261.7(36)
vest,n., 974.38(26)
woman's ~, 974.38(26); 982.17
veterinarian,n., 401.2(9)
veterinary medicine,n.,
401.1(102)
veto,n., 548.2
veto,v., 548.1
vibrate,v., 105.3; 111.1,5; see
also shake,v.
~ like a balance, 950.9
vibration,n., 105.4; 111.2
sound of ~, 469.1
voice ~, 469.1(13–15,24–27,
29,30)
vice,n., 14.1; 883.23; 886.2,8
area of ~, 883.36
full of ~, 1087.11
viceroy,n.
Turkish ~ of Egypt,
1073.36(15)
vicious,adj., 830.5; 879.1, 883.7,
22; 886.1
victim,n., 236.5; 794.34(2,4);
823.25; 869.13; 1130.10
victor,n., 22.10; 23.14
victorious,adj., 22.11,15; 23.5
victory,n., 22.12; 23.5
celebrating ~, 22.16
easy ~, 22.14
expression of ~, 22.19
happiness over ~, 1102.7
happy over ~, 1102.6
marked by ~, 22.15
pert. to ~, 22.15
rejoice over ~, 22.18; 1102.8,9
rejoicing over ~, 22.17; 1102.6,
7
result of ~, 22.20
song of ~, 22.19
token of ~, 951.8
~ with excessive losses, 22.13
victuals,n., 740.1; see food,n.
view,n., 480.11; see also seeing,
sight, vision,n.
bring into public ~ from obscurity, 615.6
front ~, 185.6
lost to ~, 483.12(9)
~ of the sea, 1029.62
offering a ~, 480.14
on first ~, 483.7
place for a ~, 480.13
point of ~, 480.12
vigilante,n., 1078.16(6)
committee of ~s, 1078.17
methods, activities, etc. of
~s, 1078.18
vigor,n, 1.9; see also
strength,n.
bodily ~, 1.13
give ~, 1.29
lose ~, 10.8; 883.11(2–7)
plant ~, 1.14
reduced in ~, 10.5
time of ~, 1.15
time of greatest ~, 397.4
without ~, 10.1
vigorous,adj., 1.8,12; see also
strong,adj.
be ~, 1.11
become ~, 1.30
~ (of language), 1.19
make ~, 1.29,35
~ (of style), 1.19
young and ~, 1.10
village,n.
inhabitants of a ~, 785.2,4
~ near a large city, 785.1(9)
small ~, 785 1(5)

villain,n., 202.3; 883.25; 886.5; 1088.2
villainous,adj., 202.1; 883.22; 886.1; 1088.9
villainy,n., 202.2; 883.24; 886.2, 7; 1088.1
vine,n.
  shelter for ~s, 993.10,11
  structure for ~s, 991.12,14
  train ~s, 991.13
vinegar,n., 452.8
  referring to ~, 452.9
  turn into ~, 452.10
violate,v., 650.9; 886.30
  rape, 710.13
  ~ laws, 802.29,30; 1087.4
  ~ promises, 802.29; 1122.53
  ~ rules, 802.29
violation,n., 886.29,30
  rape, 710.14
  ~ of decency, 802.30
  ~ of law, 802.29–31; 1087.3,4
  ~ of peace, 802.32,33; 1140.37
  ~ of promises, 802.29; 1122.55
  ~ of rules, 802.29
violence,n., 4.2; 803.2; 865.2
  act with ~, 4.4,13
  acting with ~, 4.1
  ~ against government, 4.18
  behave with ~, 4.4,13
  decrease the ~ of, 10.5(25); 1142.1
  ~ from lack of government or law, 1073.103
  government by ~, 4.18(3)
  marked by ~, 4.8,17
  move with ~, 4.4; 83.1,4; 91.1
  moving with ~, 4.1; 83.3; 91.3
  noise and ~, 4.14
  ~ of a crowd, 4.16
  ~ of action, 4.2
  ~ of motion, 4.2; 83.2; 91.2
  political ~, 4.18
  talk with ~, 4.13
  use ~, 4.5
  with ~, 4.8,17
violent,adj., 4.1,17; 865.1; see also **rough**,adj.
  ~ act, 52.5(33)
  ~ action, 4.3; 865.4
  be ~, 4.4,5,13
  ~ behavior, 4.3; 55.3(15); 865.4
  emotionally ~, 4.12
  ~ in movement, 4.1; 83.3; 91.3
  move ~ly, 4.4; 83.1,4; 91.1
  ~ movement, 4.3; 83.2; 91.2
  moving ~ly, 4.1; 83.3; 91.3
  noisy and ~, 4.15
  ~ person, 865.3
  rapid and ~, 4.6
  rapidly and ~ly, 95.5(2,3)
  sudden and ~ effort, 4.10
  sudden and ~ energy, 4.10
  sudden and ~ feeling, 4.10
  sudden and ~ force, 4.10
  temporary and ~, 4.11
  ~ with excitement, 1100.6(3, 7,11,13,16)
violin,n., 479.8(1,4,6,11,12,25,34, 38); 479.11(4)
  play a ~, 479.10
  ~ player, 479.9
virgin,n., 710.48
  remain a ~, 710.49
  the ~ Mary, 653.11
  worship of the ~ Mary, 656.2(6); 656.15(14)
virginity,n., 710.47(3,5,6,8)
  rob of ~, 710.16
  symbol of ~, 710.50
virtue,n., 843.18; 845.1
  cardinal ~s, 843.19
  sexual ~, 710.47(2,3,5–7); 845.11

symbol of ~, 845.12
virtuous,adj., 843.17; 845.1
  sexually ~, 710.47(2,3,5–7); 845.11
  sexually ~ person, 710.48
visible,adj., 483.1
  ~ as a symptom, 483.1(3)
  be ~, 483.3–6
  ~ by X-rays, 1069.11
  make ~, 483.2
  scarcely ~, 483.12(12)
  something barely ~, 483.8(22)
vision,n., 480.2,4,5; see also **seeing, sight, view**,n.
  aid ~, device to, 480.16,17
  correction of ~, science of, 401.1(56,57,63)
  defects of ~, 481.1,3
  dim the ~, 1065.78
  double ~, 481.1(4,12)
  having ~, 480.10
  having sharp ~, 480.10(5)
  jeweler's glass to aid ~, 961.7
  measure ~, devices to, 480.18, 19
  one who sees ~s, 480.3(2)
  pert. to ~, 480.6,8
  range of ~, 480.11
  science of ~, 401.1(56,57,63); 480.15; 1065.102(2–4)
  without ~, 481.2; see also **blind**,adj.
  without figurative ~, 481.9
visionary,adj.
  imaginary, 809.1; 1065.3
  impractical, 284.21
  unreal, 809.1; 1065.3
visit,n., 125.2
visit,v., 125.1
  ~ing card, 125.5
  ~ points of interest, 848.29
visited,adj.
  not ~, 125.6; 331.1
  place ~, 125.4
  place frequently ~, 782.11,12
  place not ~, 331.3
visitor,n., 125.3
vitamin,n.
  disorders caused by ~ lack, 395.1
  medication for ~ lack, 398.6(13)
vivacious,adj., 752.1; see **lively**, adj.
vocabulary,n., 666.9(1)
  ~ of a subject, etc., 666.9(7)
vocation,n., 204.1; see **occupation**,n.
vogue,n., 631.1; see **fashion**,n.
voice,n., 474.1; see also **sound**,n.
  change sound of ~, 539.1(27, 32)
  confusion of ~s, 473.1–4; 605.13(2)
  deep ~, 1041.8
  in a loud ~, 463.5
  in a low ~, 462.5,12
  loss of the ~, 671.21(3)
  loud of ~, 463.3
  low ~, 474.1(2)
  monotonous tone of ~, 470.1
  ~ of the people, 474.1(3)
  organ of ~, 364.3,4; 474.9,10
  person with a loud ~, 463.6
  pert. to the ~, 474.2
  pronounced with the ~, 474.6
  said with the ~, 474.6
  singing ~, 474.7
  soft and gentle of ~, 462.4
  sounds of the ~, 474.3
  thin (of the ~), 474.7
  throwing the ~, art of, 474.8
  tremble or vibration of the ~, 469.1(13–15,24–27,29,30)

unchanging ~, 474.1(1)
  use of the ~, 474.5
  use the ~, 474.4
  without using the ~, 475.1,10; see also **silent**,adj.
voiceless,adj., 475.1,10; see also **silent**,adj.
void,adj., 17.1; 926.1,2,7
void,n., 926.3,13,15
void,v., 17.5; 926.21
  ~ urine, 294.1; see **urinate**,v.
volcano,n.
  action of a ~, 166.8
  glass from molten lava of a ~, 1009.52
  opening in a ~, 1048.46
  pert. to a ~, 166.2
  rock from a ~, 1006.1(10,20,39)
  rock from action of a ~, descr. of, 1006.30
  science of ~s, 166.7
volley,n., 187.2,4; 565.4
volley,v., 187.1
volume,n., 946.50
  sound, 455.6(4,13); see also **sound**,n.
  decrease in sound ~, 462.15, 16; 910.1(38,39)
  increase in sound ~, 463.9–12
  measure the ~ of, 946.53
  measurement of ~, 946.51,52
  strengthen in ~, 1.29(17)
  unit of sound ~, 455.10
voluntary,adj., 265.23
voluptuous,adj., 709.4; 1105.4,8
vomit,n., 290.5
  bloody ~, 290.6
vomit,v., 290.1,2
  cause a desire to ~, 290.12
  cause a desire to ~, substance that can, 290.15
  cause to ~, 290.8
  causing a desire to ~, 290.14
  causing to ~, 290.7
  desire to ~, 290.17,18
  try to ~, 290.20
  unsuccessful attempt to ~, 290.21
vomiting,n., 290.3,4
  bloody ~, 290.6
  cause ~, 290.8
  causes ~, that which, 290.10, 11
  causing ~, 290.7,9
  feel like ~, 290.17
voodoo,n., 663.1(7,14)
vote,n., 254.6
  affirmative ~, 254.6(1,5,6)
  ~ against membership, 254.6(3)
  collection of ~s, 254.11
  examiner of ~s, 254.13
  extending the ~, advocate of, 254.14
  give the ~ to, 254.2
  negative ~, 254.6(3,4)
  place for ~s, 254.8–10
  record the ~s of, 254.12
  take away the ~, 254.3
  try to get ~s, 18.1(16,23)
vote,v., 254.4
  ~ against, 254.4(2)
  right to ~, 254.1
  right to ~ on laws, 254.1(4)
voter,n., 254.7
  illegal ~, 254.7(3)
voting,n.
  ~ as to government, 254.5(2)
  ~ as to laws, 254.5(4)
  compartment for ~, 787.7(7)
  name a candidate for ~ on, 694.6(19); see **candidate**,n.
vow,n., 1122.3; see **promise**,n.
vow,v., 1122.1; see **promise**,v.
vowel,n.

change into a ~, 670.16
having ~ sounds, 670.17
lengthened ~s in pronunciation, 670.4(6)
~ of two parts, 670.14(5)
pause between ~s, 670.4(9)
separation of ~s in pronunciation, 670.4(5)
system of ~s, 679.4(6)
three ~ sounds, 670.14(12)
two ~s as one syllable,
670.4(17,18)
unaccented ~, 670.14(9)
use as a ~, 670.16
use of a letter as a ~, 679.8
variation of a ~, 670.18-20
vulgar,adj.
coarse, 864.1
common, 535.1,10
in common use, 279.10(1,3-5)
obscene, 713.1
unrefined, 863.1
~ act or action, 863.7; 864.3
become ~, 863.5; 864.5
~ expression, 713.3; 863.8;
1118.7
humorous and ~, 1114.1(7);
1114.2(1,2); 1115.3(1,2);
1115.4
~ language, 713.3; 1114.11;
1118.7
make ~, 863.6; 864.6; 1118.10
~ person, 863.3; 864.4
~ showiness, 951.42
showy and ~, 951.41
showy and ~ person, 951.43
~ word, 666.3(8,23,31,51);
713.3; 863.8; 1118.7
vulgarity,n., 535.10; 713.2,3;
863.2,7; 864.2; 1118.9

W

waffle,n.
device for making ~s, 1062.5
wag,n.
jokester, 1114.5; 1115.6
waving, 147.2
wag,v., 147.1,4
wages,n., 219.3; see **salary**,n.
wagging,adj., 147.3
wagon,n., 192.23
~ maker, 192.24
~ repairer, 192.24
wail,n., 468.1; 1125.18; 1127.3
wail,v., 468.2; 1125.17,19,27;
1127.1
waist,n., 388.1(1)
band for the ~, 980.6
~ of a dress, 982.9
wait,n., 272.2
wait,v., 272.1
~ for in order to attack,
272.1(12)
~ in concealment, 272.1(9)
~ in line, 272.1(10)
~ in suspense, 272.1(6)
keep someone ~ing, 272.6
one who ~s, 272.4
room in which to ~, 787.7(2)
~ secretly, 272.1(9)
those who ~ in line, 272.5
unwilling to ~, 265.26(8); see
impatient,adj.
willing to ~, 265 23(8); see
patient,adj.
waiter,n.
one who waits, 272.4
restaurant server, 205.11-13
waiting,n., 272.2
state of ~, 272.3
waitress,n.
chief ~, 205.13
wake,v., 72.1-6
descr. of ~ing, 72.12

signal to ~, 956.1(9)
wakefulness,n., 72.7
causing ~, 72.13
descr. of ~, 72.12
Wales,n., 784.9(3)
inhabitant of ~, 784.15(11,63)
inhabitants of ~, 784.17(7)
language of ~, 664.4(6,20)
pert. to ~, 784.16
walk,n., 107.2
a ~, 107.2,9; 123.1(1,2,5,9,11-
14,16,17,24,31,35-38,42,47,50,
52-54); 1006.3
walk,v., 107.1
able to ~, 107.7
~ duck-fashion, 107.1(58)
~ lame, 107.1(10,12); 346.15
~ on and injure, 107.1(51)
place to ~, 107.9; 123.1(1,2,5,9,
11-14,16,17,24,31,35-38,42,47,
50,52-54,58); 1006.3
unable to ~ properly, 107.8
~ up and down, 951.33
walker,n., 107.5
tightrope ~, 107.5(1)
walking,adj., 107.4
~ at night, 778.5(1)
walking,n., 107.3
a step in ~, 108.4
adapted for ~, 107.6
~ by night, 107.3(1,2)
given to ~, 107.4
light in ~, 949.7(4-7)
manner of ~, 107.2
measure ~, instrument to,
107.10; 788.3(3,5)
measurement of ~, 946.26(15)
sleep-~, 107.3(1,2)
sounds of ~, 469.5,6
~ stick, 437.7(2,5)
tired from ~, 12.1(37)
wall,n., 1022.2(21); 1024.1
angle of ~, 944.2
attached to a ~, 1024.5
base of ~, 997.4
build a ~, 1006.8
done on a ~, 1024.5
furnish with protective ~s,
568.32
indented place in a ~,
782.1(25)
inside the ~s of a place,
1024.7
interior ~ lining, 1024.3
line a ~, 1024.4
~ of broken stones, 1022.2(21)
outside the ~s, 138.1(10);
1024.6
part of a ~, 1024.1
parts of a protective ~,
568.33-35
pert. to a ~, 1024.5
protective ~, 568.30(3,10);
1024.1(5)
resembling a ~, 1024.5
separate with a ~, 1024.2
straightness of ~, 947.15(4);
947.17
strengthen a ~, 1006.8
wallet,n., 261.15
wall-eye,n., 481.1(31)
walrus,n., 423.5
wand,n., 437.7; see **stick**,n.
~-shaped, 507.17(90)
wander,n., 128.2
wander,v., 128.1; 1054.34
desire to ~, 128.6
~ from the subject, 128.1(3,4,
12,17); 682.10
tendency to ~, 128.5
wanderer,n., 128.3; 1054.35
beach ~, 128.3(1)
wandering,adj., 128.4
~ at night, 778.5(5)

~ from the subject, 128.4;
128.4(4)
~ mentally, 128.4(2)
wandering,n., 128.2
~ at night, 128.2(3)
~ from the subject, 128.2(2);
682.10
want,n., 265.2; see **desire**,n.
want,v., 265.1; see **desire**,v.
war,n., 563.1
activities of ~, 563.24
advocating ~, 563.6
after the ~, 563.19
agreement to end ~, 1140.30,
31
before the ~, 563.19
cause of ~, 563.14
civilian in time of ~, 562.13
end ~, 1140.34
end of ~, temporary, 1140.32
engage in ~, 563.2
fond of ~, 563.5; 879.12
god of ~, 563.21
goddess of ~, 563.22,23
hating ~, 880.19(2)
important to ~, 848.16
land, sea, and air ~, 563.11,12
materials essential to ~,
descr. of, 563.13
nation at ~, 563.4
necessary to ~, 273.6(24)
one engaged in ~, 563.3;
564.1; see also **warrior**,n.
opposition to ~, 544.2(14);
1140.22
pert. to ~, 563.17,18
preparation for ~, 563.7,8,10
readiness for ~, 563.10
reason for ~, 563.14
refuses to fight in ~, one who,
562.14
soldiers engaged in ~, 564.5
stirring up ~, 563.9
threat of ~, 563.16
threatening ~, 563.15
tired of ~, 12.1(31)
unimportant to ~, 849.2
unnecessary for ~, 273.11(7)
ward off,v., 76.1; 78.1
try to ~ by prayer, 76.6
warfare,n., 563.1; see **war**,n.
warlike,adj., 563.5; 879.12
warm,adj., 1060.13,16; see also
heat,n., **hot**,adj.
~ and comfortable, 1060.40
~ and comfortable room,
place, etc., 1141.5
become ~, 1060.15,18
become ~ enough for ice or
snow to melt, 1060.52
emotionally ~, 1092.53
~ from happiness, excite-
ment, liquor, exercise, etc.,
1060.37
growing ~, 1060.51
make ~, 1060.15,17
make ~ and comfortable,
1141.9
warm,v., 1060.15,17,39; see also
heat,v.
warming,adj., 1060.19
warmth,n., 1060.14; see also
heat,n.
be exposed to the ~ of,
1060.38
bodily ~ from excitement,
happiness, liquor, etc.,
1060.37
emotional ~, 1092.54,56,57
expose to the ~ of, 1060.39
lie in the ~ of, 1060.38
warn,v., 574.1
~ of, 574.1(8)
one who ~s, 574.3
serving to ~, 574.5

that which ~s, 574.4
warning,adj., 574.5
~ light, 1065.49(3)
~ signal, 574.6; 956.1(1,2,6,
13) ; 1041.8
~ sound, 455.1(5) ; 468.1(10) ;
574.6
warning,n., 574.2
device to sound a ~, 574.4(1,
4)
signal of ~, 574.6; 956.1(1,2,
6,13) ; 1041.8
sound of ~, 455.1(5) ;
468.1(10) ; 574.6
warrior,n., 564.1; see also soldier,n.
female ~, 564.1(2)
group of ~s, 564.5
Indian ~, 564.1(8)
warship,n., 115.16,17
group of ~s, 115.18
pert. to ~s, 115.19
wart,n., 390.1(20,22) ; 908.5
wary,adj., 577.1; see careful,
adj.
be ~ of, 577.9
wash,n., 899.36
wash,v., 899.35; see also clean,v.
~ away guilt, 845.19
~ away sins, 845.17,19
~ body opening, 899.35(2)
~ clothes, 899.35(4,9)
~ clothes, place to, 899.38
~ hair, 899.35(7)
person who ~es clothes,
899.39
room in which to ~, 295.1(1,
9,11,16) ; 899.37(2)
~ the throat, 899.35(3)
~ the vagina, 899.35(2)
washbasin,n., 899.37(1,3,4)
washing,n., 899.36
agent for ~, 899.37
basin for ~, 899.37(1,3,4)
device for ~, 899.37
~ for purification, 899.36(1)
~ of bodily organ, 899.36(2)
substance for ~, 899.37
wasp,n., 428.3
group of ~s, 403.5(12,77)
nest for ~s, 403.22(42)
of ~s, 428.1(5,24)
waste,n.
refuse, waste products,
285.1; see also refuse,n.
wastefulness, 225.1–3
amount of ~, 914.1(6)
bodily ~, 287.2,3
~ carried by sewers, 285.1(30,
38) ; 1033.37
film of ~ matter, 285.1(16,29)
~ from metals, 285.1(26,28,
32)
lay ~, 801.11; see destroy,v.
~ parts, 285.1(42)
~ parts of an animal,
285.1(13,14)
pipe for carrying off ~,
1033.34
waste,v., 225.1
~ away, 806.1,2; see decay,v.
~d away, 806.4; see decayed,
adj.
~ time, 762.19,20
wasteful,adj., 225.2
be ~ with, 225.1
~ in producing, 225.3
~ person, 225.4
spend ~ly, 224.1(3,6,7,10,11)
wasteland,n., 1003.1(45) ;
1003.11
restore ~, 832.6
waster,n., 225.4
wastrel,n., 225.4
watch,n.

timepiece, 774.2; see timepiece,n.
watching, 484.2
alert ~, 484.2(4)
close ~, 484.2(3)
watch,v., 484.1; see also look,v.
~ over, 568.1; 570.1; see care
for, protect,v.
watcher,n., 484.3; 568.5(1,15–
19) ; 568.9
watchful,adj., 484.4(3) ; 579.4;
see also attentive,adj.
watching,n., 484.2
watchmaker,n., 774.5
watchman,n., 568.5(1,15–18) ;
568.9
go around as a ~, 568.9
water,n., 1026.1
absorb ~, 1034.34
~ animal, 422.3,4; 423.1,3–5,
7,10
animal living both on land
and in ~, 1026.24
animal living both on land
and in ~, descr. of, 1026.25
animal living on ~'s edge,
1026.26
animal living under ~,
1026.36
body of ~, 1029.1,18,19,21,22,
53,63–65
body of ~, man-made,
1029.1(1)
body of ~, portion of,
1029.40
body of ~ between islands,
1029.1(2)
body of ~ for irrigation,
1029.1(1)
border on ~, 1029.81
carbonated drinking ~,
1026.1(13,15)
carried by ~, 1026.5
channel for carrying ~,
1026.18
chemical reaction with ~,
54.1(2)
combine with ~, 1026.14
consisting of ~, 1026.3
consisting of land and ~,
1026.29
containing ~, 1026.4
control ~, device to, 1026.41
cover with ~, 972.1(26,37,47) ;
972.35; 1026.31; 1036.20
covered with ~, 1026.3
covered with ~, become,
1026.32,33
~ covering land at high tide,
1029.10
dash ~ over, 1034.30; see
wet,v.
depth of ~, device to measure, 1026.40(1,4)
depth of ~, measurement of,
946.26(7) ; 947.15(4) ; 947.17
detect ~, device to, 1026.41
distance on ~, measurement
of, 946.26(14)
drain off ~, 1033.41
drinking ~, structure for,
1033.46
enclose ~, 1033.3
faces the ~, part that,
1029.82
fall (of ~), 1029.49
falling ~, 1029.48; see waterfalls,n., below
~falls, 1029.48; see waterfalls,n., below
fill with ~ and sink, 1026.33
flooded with ~, 1026.30
flooded with salt ~, 1026.23(7)
~ fountain, 1033.46
give ~ to animals, 1026.7

go under ~, 1026.32
growing in or on ~, 1026.23(1,
2,5,7)
hardening under ~, 1026.22
height of ~, device to record,
1026.42
history and description of
bodies of ~, 1029.2
hole for flowing ~, 1033.45
hole to reach ~, 1033.38
~ in form of gas, 1048.1(11)
~ in milk, device to measure, 1026.40(3)
~ in the air, 1034.13,14
inland ~, 1029.1(3,5)
inlet of ~, 1029.63
land at the bottom of ~,
1029.100(3)
land in reference to ~,
1029.100
land jutting out into ~,
1029.98,99
land surrounded by ~,
1029.100(4)
land surrounded on three
sides by ~, 1029.100(8)
lie in ~, 1034.27
like ~, 1026.2
living in or on ~, 1026.23(1,2,
5,6)
living on land and ~,
1026.23(1)
living under ~, 1026.30(1,2,5)
lose ~, 1038.2
machinery, ~ for driving,
1029.50
made of ~, 1026.12
made of ~, a compound that
is, 1026.13
mass of ~, 1026.16
measurement of ~, device
for, 1026.40
mile on ~, 946.26(14)
mineral ~, 1026.1(15)
move ~, 1033.39,40,42
move about in ~, 1026.43,44
move like ~, 1031.2,4
movement of ~, 1031.1
movement of ship through ~,
1029.17
moving like ~, 1031.3
narrow body of ~, 1029.1(1,7)
not using ~, 1038.11
ocean ~s, 1029.65
ocean ~s, pert. to, 1029.72
on border of ~, 1029.59
opening for flowing ~,
1033.45
operated by ~, 1027.34
operated by ~ pressure,
1026.22
operating on land and ~,
1026.23(1)
passage for ~, 1033.22
passage made by ~, 1033.32
performed in or on ~,
1026.23(2)
pert. to fresh ~, 1026.23(5)
pert. to hot ~, 1026.23(4)
pert. to ocean or sea ~,
1029.72
pipe carrying ~, 1033.23,28,
29,31,45,46
plant growing in ~, 1026.27
plant growing under ~,
1026.36
plant living both on land and
in ~, 1026.24
~ power, pert. to, 1029.52
protected portion of ~,
1029.11,12
protection against ~, 1033.1,5
pure ~, 1026.1(2)
raise ~, 1033.40
raise ~, device to, 1033.39,42

reaction with ~, chemical, 54.1(2)
relating to ~, 1026.23
relating to ~ and air, 1026.23(3)
remove ~ from, 1038.1
restrict ~, 1033.3
rising above ~, 159.4(2)
rocks in ~, 1029.100(6,11,12)
rough ~ caused by tides, 1029.9
roughness of ~, 1029.68
running ~, structure for, 1033.46
salt ~s of the earth, 1029.67
salty ~, 1026.1(4)
science of ~, 1026.39; 1027.33
sea ~s, 1029.65
sea ~s, pert. to, 1029.72
search for underground ~, 486.1(8)
searcher for underground ~, 486.4(2)
smelling like dirty ~, 1026.6
soapy ~, 899.45
sounds of ~, 459.1
source of ~, 1026.21
sports performed in ~, 114.7; 1026.28
stick for seeking underground ~, 486.5
stimulation by ~, 101.1(8,9)
storage place for ~, 262.3(6, 22,28); 1033.48
stream of excess ~, 1026.17
strength of ~ current, 1.21
stretch of ~, 1029.6,8,9
stretch of ~ with islands, 1029.7
structure across ~, 1033.49,52
structure against the ~, 1033.1
structure alongside the ~, 1033.10
structures alongside the ~, 1033.11
structure to confine ~, 1033.1
~ subject to tides, 1029.10
supply (land) with ~, 1036.23,28
supported by ~, 1026.5
surround with ~, 1036.20
~ suspended in air, 1041.1(3)
tight against ~, 1038.12
treatise on bodies of ~, 682.15(9)
under~, 1026.30,35
under ~, able to function, 1026.34
under~ compartment, 1026.37
under~ land, 1029.100(1–3,6, 7,12,13–16)
under~ tunnel worker, 1026.38
under the ~ of the sea, 1026.35
underground ~, science of, 1026.39(1)
waste ~ carried off, 1033.37
waste ~, pipe or tube for, 1033.34
without ~, 1038.4
worship of ~, 1026.15
watercraft,n., 115.1; see **boat, ship,**n.
waterfalls,n., 1029.48
~ for driving machinery, 1029.50
river ~, 1029.40(2,8)
series of small ~, 1029.51
watery,adj., 1026.2–4
~ and thin, 1026.2(2)
wave,n.

movement, 146.2; 147.2
ocean wave, 1032.1
~ breaking on rocks or shore, 1032.7
breaking or hitting of ~s, 1032.9
break upon rocks or shore (of ~s), 1032.8
floating on the ~s, 113.8(2)
foam of ~s, 1032.7
full of ~s, 1032.5
hair ~, 369.17(3–5); 369.18(7, 8)
having rough and broken ~s, 1032.12
hit upon rocks or shore (of ~s), 1032.8
hollow between ~s, 1032.10
like ~s, 1032.5
move in ~s, 93.1; 1032.2,3
movement in ~s, 93.2
movement of ~s, 1031.1(1,13)
moving in, or like, ~s, 93.3; 1032.4
progress of a ship through ~s, 1032.11
reverberating like ~s, 471.5(1)
rise and fall in ~s, 161.1(1, 5); 1032.2
~s, 1032.6
shaped like ~s, 507.17(84,93)
sound of ~s, 469.7(28); 1032.9
sound of ~s, having or like the, 459.3
wave,v., 111.5; 146.1; 147.1
wavy,adj., 146.4; 147.3
~ in form or shape, 507.17(84)
marked with ~ lines, 502.2(2)
~ (of hair), 369.18
wax,n., 1068.1
coat, cover, fill with, etc., ~, 1068.2
covered with ~, 1068.6
ear ~, 1068.1(4)
exhibition of ~ figures, 951.28(8); 951.30
like ~, 1068.5
made of ~, 1068.7,9
modeled from ~, 1068.9
~ modeling, art of, 1068.8
ornaments of ~, 959.4(4)
polish, shine, rub, or treat with ~, 1068.3
producing ~, 1068.4
waxy,adj., 1068.5–7
~ substance, 1068.1
way,n.
means, manner, etc., 50.1
road, 123.1
by ~ of, 123.9
in the ~, 920.19
weak,adj., 10.1; 830.5
become ~, 10.8
become ~ with disappointment, 1121.8
becoming ~, 10.10
delicate and ~, 11.1(5,6,11)
~ from disease, 10.1(1,6,36, 69)
~ from indulgence in luxuries, 10.1(16)
~ from mental disturbance, 10.1(36)
~ from mixture with water, 10.1(10)
~ from old age, 10.1(8,11–14, 16,19,29,54)
helpless and ~, 10.1(18,48)
~ in appearance, 10.1(70)
~ in argument, 10.1(22,31,33, 59,67)
~ in color, 10.1(9,17,64)

~ in determination, 10.1(73)
~ in excuses, 10.1(22,31,33,59, 67)
~ in flavor, 10.1(30,42)
~ in health, 10.1(9,24)
~ in sound, 10.1(17,64)
~ in the joints, 10.1(51)
make ~, 10.5
~ person, 10.4
sexually ~, 10.1(27)
small and ~, 909.1(20)
~ spot, 10.11
thin and ~, 10.1(75)
without ~ points, 1.24
weaken,v., 10.5,8
~ by depriving of food, 10.5(36)
~ by hunger, 737.7
~ gradually, 10.5(40)
~ secretly, 10.5(40)
~ the body, 10.5(42)
weakened,adj.
state of being ~, 10.7
weakening,adj., 10.10
weakening,n., 10.6,9
weakness,n., 10.2,3,14; 830.1,5
~ from lack of food, 10.2(2)
~ of character, 10.14
wealth,n., 216.2,3
delusions of ~, 1136.1(25)
demon of desire for ~, 216.12
god of ~, 216.11
interest in ~, 214.2
interested in ~, 214.1
means of ~, 216.9
person interested in ~, 214.3
power of ~, 5.4(16)
science of ~, 216.10
seeks ~ by marriage, one who, 214.3(1)
source of ~, 216.9
storehouse of ~, 262.3(31)
wealthy,adj., 216.1
coarse or showy and ~ person, 1109.9
~ class, 216.9
~ families of Japan, 216.8(3)
government by ~ people, 1073.42(14)
make ~, 216.4
newly ~ person, 216.5(1,12,13, 16)
~ person, 216.5
~ person of low tastes, 216.5(17)
~ persons, 216.8
~ persons, behavior of, 216.7
~ persons, descr. or characteristic of, 216.6
~ persons, characteristics of, 216.7
self-satisfied and ~ group, 1107.9
~ youth, 216.5(15)
weapon,n., 565.1; see also **arrow, dagger, gun, sword,** etc.
bearing ~s, 562.10
manufacture of ~s, place for, 262.3(2)
~s, 562.9; 565.2
storage of ~s, place for, 262.3(1,2,12)
wear,v., 974.3,10,11,40
~ away, 801.25,26
~ away by biting, 735.6
wearer,n.
~ of garment of office or profession, 974.42
wearing,adj., 974.4,41
~ away, 801.28
wearing,n.
a ~ away, 801.27
a ~ down, 801.27(1)
weary,adj., 12.1; 583.8

weary,v., 12.3,6; 583.7,10
weasel,n.
 of ~s, 403.11(10)
weather,n., 1046.2; 1047.1; see
 also **climate**,n.
 adapted to changes of ~,
  770.14
 atmospheric ~, 1046.6
 changed by ~, 1047.9
 changes in ~, instrument to
  record or measure, 1046.18
 delayed by ~, 768.12; 1047.14
 dried by ~, 1047.9
 expose to the ~, 1047.8
 hardened by ~, 1047.9
 map of the ~, 1047.15
 normal in ~, 770.12; 1047.5
 period of ~, 1047.6
 pert. to ~, 1047.2
 pert. to ~ of the past, 1047.4
 predict ~, 1047.16
 prediction of ~, 772.14;
  1047.18,19
 prediction of ~, department
  of, 1047.22
 prediction of ~, instrument
  for, 1046.18
 prediction of ~, skillful in,
  1047.21
 predictor of ~, 772.15; 1047.20
 protect against ~, 1047.11
 protected against ~, 1047.10
 protection against ~, 1047.12
 region of ~, 1047.3
 science of ~, 1046.17(3-5)
 seasoned by ~, 1047.9
 violent ~, 4.9
 withstand the ~, 1047.8
weave,v., 156.1,2; 307.1
weaving,adj., 307.7
weaving,n., 156.3; 307.4
 form by ~, 307.1
 formed by ~, 307.2,10; see
  also **woven**,adj.
 machine for ~, 307.8
 material for ~, 307.13
 palm fiber for ~, 993.29
 pert. to ~, 307.11
web,n., 308.1; see **network**,n.
 able to make a ~ for prey,
  308.6
wed,adj., 702.6; see **married**,
 adj.
wed,v., 702.1,2; see **marry**,v.
wedding,n.
 ceremony or celebration of
  marriage, 702.26
 marriage, 702.8; see **marriage**,n.
wedge,n.
 ~-shaped, 507.17(28,75)
wedlock,n., 702.8; see **marriage**,n.
week,n., 779.1
 consisting of a ~, 779.2
 day in the middle of the ~,
  776.1
 days at the end of the ~,
  776.2
 every ~, 779.4(3,6)
 every three ~s, 779.4(5)
 every two ~s, 779.4(1,2)
 twice a ~, 779.4(4)
 two ~s, 779.3
weep,v., 1127.1
 ~ in dissatisfaction,
  1119.3(5)
 start to ~, 1127.1(4)
 story to make one ~, 1127.15
 unable to ~, 1127.17
 ~ until exhausted, 1127.14
weeper,n., 1127.5
 habitual ~, 1127.9,10
weeping,adj., 1127.6
 habitually ~, 1128.5

 not ~, 1127.17
weeping,n., 1127.2
 alternating ~ and laughter,
  1111.9
 causing ~, 1128.7
 distort the face with ~,
  1127.11,12
 fit of ~, 1127.3
 fit of laughter and ~, 1100.10
 fits of ~, 1127.4
 indicative of ~, 1127.8
 put oneself to sleep by ~,
  1127.13
 say while ~, 1127.7
 sound of ~, 1127.3
 stop ~, 1127.18
 wet the face with ~, 1034.4
weepy,adj., 1128.4
weigh,v., 947.19,20
 device to ~, 947.27,28
 ~ heavily upon (of sadness,
  etc.), 1125.38
 ~ more than, 947.5
weighed,adj.
 able to be ~, 947.21
 unable to be ~, 947.22
weight,n., 947.1
 ancient ~ unit, 947.46
 apothecaries' ~ units, 947.33
 avoirdupois ~ units, 947.35
 balancing ~, 947.12,13
 be a heavy ~ upon, 948.8,12
 be of greater ~, 947.5
 boxer's ~, 947.47
 British ~s, descr. of, 946.55
 British ~ units, 947.36-38
 cargo ~, 947.40
 clock ~, 947.15(3)
 container ~, 947.29
 drug ~ system, 947.31(1)
 drug ~ units, 947.32,33
 equal ~, 947.12
 equal distribution of ~, 947.11
 equal in ~, 947.8,10
 equal in ~, make, 947.9
 equality of ~, 947.7
 excessive ~, 947.3,4
 gem ~ system, 947.31(4)
 gem ~ units, 947.32,34,43,44
 greater ~, 947.3
 hanging ~, 947.15(2,4); 947.17
 have a ~ of, 947.20
 having ~, 947.21
 ~ in tons, 947.39
 jewelry ~ system, 947.31(4)
 jewelry ~ units, 947.32,34,43,
  44
 lead ~, 947.15(4); 947.17
 light in ~, 949.1,4
 measurement of ~, 947.26
 metric ~ units, 947.41,42
 opposing ~, 947.13,14
 pearl ~ unit, 947.45
 person of average ~, 949.5
 person of light ~, 949.3
 person's ~, 947.2
 precious metal ~ system,
  947.31(4)
 precious metal ~ units,
  947.32,34
 put a heavy ~ upon, 947.16;
  948.8,11
 ratio of ~, 947.23
 science, system of ~s used in,
  947.31(3)
 science of ~s, 946.23
 smallest ~ unit, 947.32
 specific ~s, 947.15
 stabilizing ~, 947.15(1)
 swinging ~, 947.15(3)
 system of ~s, 946.22; 947.31
 test the ~ of, 947.18
 treatise on ~s, 946.24
 troy ~ units, 947.34
 upsets balance, ~ that, 947.6

 vehicle ~, 947.29
 vessel ~, 947.29
 wall straightness, ~ for measuring, 947.15(4); 947.17
 water depth, ~ for measuring, 947.15(4); 947.17
 without ~, 947.22; 949.1
 wrestler's ~, 947.47
weight,v., 947.16; 948.8,11,12;
  1018.3
weighty,adj., 948.1; see **heavy**,
 adj.
weird,adj.
 mysterious, 604.1(3,6,12,17,18,
  24,35,39,45,48,49,52)
 strange, 536.1
 supernatural, 662.1
 unnatural, 811.11
welcome,adj., 1105.4; 1106.3
welfare,n., 831.9
 general ~, 831.10
 interest in ~ of country,
  community, etc., 784.8(4)
 public ~, 831.10
well,adj., 397.1
 get ~, 398.21
well,n., 728.4; 1033.38
well-being,n., 831.9
 emotional ~, 1092.100
 physical ~, 397.2
well-bred,adj., 858.1
well-known,adj., 615.1; see
  famous,adj.
well-off,adj., 216.1; see
  wealthy,adj.
well-to-do,adj., 216.1; see
  wealthy,adj.
Welsh,adj., 784.16
Welsh,n., 784.17(7)
Welshman,n., 784.15(11,63)
Welshmen,n., 784.17(7)
werewolf,n., 662.29(5)
west,adj., 179.18
 ~ circle of earth, 1004.14
 ~ distance on earth, 1004.12
West,n., 179.20
 countries of the ~, 784.4(2)
Western,adj., 179.18
 ~ Hemisphere, 179.20
 ~ inhabitant, 179.19;
  784.15(44)
Westernize,v., 784.10(6)
wet,adj., 1034.2,8,20,25,26,31
 be thoroughly ~, 1034.24
 ~ because overflowed,
  1034.20
 become somewhat ~, 1034.7
 become thoroughly ~, 1034.23
 become thoroughly ~ by lying
  in water, 1034.27
 dirty and ~, 904.1(2)
 ~ from splashed water,
  1034.31
 ~ ground, 1000.14; see **marsh**,
  swamp,n.
 heavy and ~, 948.4
 ~ land, 1000.14; see **marsh**,
  swamp,n.
 make somewhat ~, 1034.6
 soft and ~, 443.1(15-17);
  443.3(3); 1034.32
 somewhat ~, 1034.8; see
  damp,adj.
 thoroughly ~, 1034.25,26
 transparent or translucent
  when ~, 1034.33
 ~ with rain, 1037.9
wet,v., 1034.1,5,6,19,21,30;
  1035.15
 ~ a little, 1034.6
 ~ after penetrating, 1034.29
 ~ and stain, 1034.28
 ~ by dashing water over,
  1034.30

~ by dipping in and out, 1035.15
~ by flowing over, 1034.19
~ repeatedly, 1034.5
~s thoroughly, that which, 1034.22
that which ~s, 1034.3,22
~ (the face) with weeping, 1034.4
~ thoroughly, 1034.21
~ with blood, 1034.28
~ with dew, 1026.8
wetted,adj., 1034.2,9,20,25,26,31
whale,n., 423.1,3
baby ~, 423.4
group of ~s, 403.5(31,34,52,59,61)
jump of a ~, 110.2(1)
pert. to ~s, 423.2,3
young ~, 423.4
wharf,n., 1033.10; see also dock,n.
bring (a ship) into a ~, 1033.14
come into a ~, 1033.13
fee for tying up at a ~, 1033.16
furnish (a place) with a ~, 1033.12
put (goods) on a ~, 1033.19
storage of goods on a ~, 1033.18
structure protecting a ~, 1033.17
tie up at a ~, 1033.13,14
use of a ~, 1033.18
wharves,n., 1033.11
wheat,n.
beat ~, 437.1(98)
constituent of ~, 987.16
kernels of ~, 987.23
like ~, 987.21
made from ~, 987.21
stick for beating ~, 437.5(11)
wheel,n.
central part of a ~, 137.1(13); 326.35
like the spokes of a ~, 195.6(4)
measure revolutions of a ~, device to, 788.3(1)
~-shaped, 507.17(66,81)
whim,n., 265.2(6,7,10,11,18,26)
whimper,n., 468.1; 1120.2; 1127.3
whimper,v., 468.2; 1120.1; 1127.1
whine,n., 465.1; 468.1; 1120.2,3
whine,v., 465.2; 468.2; 1120.1(2,9,12,15,17)
~ in dissatisfaction, 1119.3(5)
whiner,n., 1120.4
whiny,adj., 468.3; 1120.5,6
whip,n., 437.5
~ of untanned hide, 386.15
part of a ~ below handle, 437.6
whip,v., 437.1; see also hit,v.
~ as punishment, 896.1(3,5,6,7,9,11,13,22,28)
~ with a branch, 990.26
~ with a strip of hide, 386.17
whipping,n., 437.2
sexual desire from ~, 710.33(14,23,27)
whirl,n., 147.2; 148.2; 150.3
whirl,v., 147.1,4; 148.1; 150.1,2
whirling,adj., 147.3; 148.3; 150.4
whirlpool,n., 1031.1(4,6,18)
like a ~, 1031.5
whirlwind,n., 1042.27; see also windstorm,n.
dust ~, 1042.27(3)

whiskers,n., 370.1; see also beard,n.
animal's ~, 370.1(10)
cat's ~, 370.1(10)
whiskey,n., 749.1,3,6; see liquor, (alcoholic),n.
unit of measurement in ~, 946.46(6)
whisper,n., 462.1,9; 472.1
in a ~, 462.12
whisper,v., 462.2,10; 472.2
whispering,adj., 462.3,11,12; 472.3
whistle,n., 461.4; 465.1
~ in the chest, 376.6(3)
sounds of a ~, 461.1(7,8)
whistle,v., 461.5; 465.2
white,adj., 499.1
~ as snow, 1039.22
become ~, 499.7
becoming ~, 499.4
duty of ~ people to govern, 1073.94
make ~, 499.5,6,8,9
mottled black and ~, 499.1(14)
~ of hair, 369.12(1,12)
~ people, 430.10
~ person, 430.9
smooth and ~, 1008.2
soft and ~, 443.1(5)
threat to the ~ race, 573.5
~ with frost, 1059.8
white,n., 499.2
whiten,v., 499.5,7
able to ~, 499.9
agent that ~s, 499.8
~ by sunlight, 1055.23
~ with chalk, 1006.43
whiteness,n., 499.3
whole,adj., 328.1; see complete, adj.
whole,n., 328.8
essential to the ~, 326.44
part essential to the ~, 326.9,45
wholeness,n., 328.2
wholesome,adj., 397.1; 831.11
whore,n., 711.1; see prostitute,n.
whorehouse,n., 711.9; see brothel,n.
wicked,adj., 883.22; see also evil,adj.
~ act, 883.24
~ action, 883.27
~ acts, 883.26
doer of ~ acts, 883.29
doing of ~ acts, 883.28
mean and ~, 887.4
~ person who pretends to goodness, 826.12(4)
~ thing, 883.32
wickedness,n., 883.23; see also evil,n.
area of ~, 883.36–38
reputation for ~, 883.34
wide,adj., 511.1
~ enough for sailing, 116.13
widen,v., 511.3
~ a hole or opening, 511.4
~ed part or organ, 511.8
~ed state, 511.5
~ing, 511.6,7
widow,n.
king's ~, 1073.21(10,11)
width,n., 511.2
wife,n., 703.1(2,3,5–12,14,15)
British nobleman's ~, 1074.25
czar's ~, 1073.41(3)
czar's son's ~, 1073.41(2)
emperor's ~, 1073.21(3)
Indian ~, 703.1(15)
king's ~, 1073.21(9)

living together as husband and ~, state of, 702.20,22
maharajah's ~, 1073.41(5)
man attentive to another's ~, 700.23(6,7)
man whose ~ has died, 706.9
new ~, 703.1(3,11)
pert. to a ~, 703.5
prince's ~, 1073.21(2,7)
provide a ~ for, 703.7
rajah's ~, 1073.41(6)
relationship between husband and ~, pert. to, 703.6
scolding ~, 874.5; 895.8
state of a ~, 702.21
sultan's ~, 1073.41(8)
take a ~, 702.1(11); see also marry,v.
viceroy's ~, 1073.21(13)
wig,n., 372.1
maker of ~s, 372.5
~s, 372.2
use of ~s, 372.3
wearing a ~, 372.4
wild,adj.
angry, 878.10(3)
excited, 1100.6
free, 309.15
uncivilized, 866.1
untamed, 309.22
growing ~, 731.5(3,7,14,17,18)
tired and ~-eyed, 12.8(1)
wildcat,n.
group of ~s, 403.5(10)
will (human),n., 266.1
based on one's own ~, 266.6
controlled by one's ~, 266.7
doctrines or theories of the ~, 266.11
exercise of one's ~, 266.3
exercise one's ~, 266.4
free ~, 266.2
imperfect exercise of one's ~, 266.8
lack or loss of ~ power, 266.10
not controlled by one's ~, 266.9
one dependent on the ~ of another, 526.5
power to exercise one's ~, 266.3,5
will (legal),n., 242.1,2
a judge on ~s, 1083.2(9)
addition to a ~, 242.3; 908.25
cut out of one's ~, 242.14
file (a ~), 242.12
give by ~, 242.4
giver by ~, 242.6
giving by ~, 242.5
having left a ~, 242.9
leaver of a ~, 242.6
not having left a ~, 242.10
one who is appointed to carry out a ~, 242.13
oral (of a ~), 242.11
receiver by a ~, 242.7
what is left by a ~, 242.8
without a ~, 242.10
willing,adj., 265.23
anxiously ~, 265.23(10)
make ~, 265.25
~ to do favors, 265.23(7)
~ to endure, 265.23(8); see also patient,adj.
~ to help, 265.23(1)
~ to wait, 265.23(8); see also patient,adj.
willingness,n., 265.24
willow,n.
made of ~ twigs, 990.10
~ twig, 990.9
win,v., 23.1; 240.1; see also winner,n.
that which one ~s, 240.3
that which one ~s in a con-

test, war, etc., 22.20
try to ~, 18.1(3,5,8,12,14,16,17,
26) ; 240.11
wind,n., 1042.1; 1046.2
~ bringing rain, 1042.1(12) ;
1042.4
carried by the ~, 1042.37
changeable ~, 1042.1(7)
changeable ~, descr. of,
1042.8
cold ~, 1042.1(6)
cool ~, 1042.1(4,10)
desert ~, 1042.1(11)
expose to the ~, 1042.12
full of ~, 1042.5; 1045.14(6)
~ full of dust, 1001.17;
1042.1(12) ; 1042.27(3)
~ full of gusts, descr. of,
1042.7
~ full of sand, 1042.1(11)
god of the ~, 1042.47,48
hot ~, 1042.1(11,12)
influence of ~ on a missile,
1042.36
instrument used for or on ~,
1042.43
light ~, 1042.1(4,15) ; 1042.4
light and changeable ~s near
equator, 1139.18
machine or mill operated by
~, 1043.24
measurement of ~, 1042.41,
42
measurement of ~, instru-
ment for, 1042.43
move with the ~, 1042.11
north ~, 1042.1(2,6,8,9)
open to ~s, 1042.13,14
pert. to ~s, 1042.2
pert. to the west ~, 1042.3
position facing the ~, 1042.17
protected against the ~,
1043.28
protection against ~, 1047.12
row swept by the ~,
311.11(12)
safe against the ~, 1043.28
science of the ~, 1042.40
sea ~, 1042.1(10,14)
short, quick ~, 1042.4
side facing the ~, 1042.38
side facing the ~, pert. to,
1042.15
side of ship toward the ~,
1042.16
sound of blowing ~, 1043.17
south ~, 1042.1(1,12,13)
~storm, 1042.27; see **windstorm**,n., below
strong ~, 1042.1(3,5,6,11) ;
1042.4
strong (of ~), 1.21
sudden ~, 1042.4
swept by ~s, 1042.13,14
tight against ~, 1043.28
upward ~, descr. of, 1042.9
violent, noisy ~, 1042.1(3)
west ~, 1042.1(15,16)
west ~, pert. to, 1042.3
~ with snow or sleet, 1042.4;
1042.27(1)
without ~, 1042.39
without ~s, region, 1139.18
wind,v., 146.1,3; 155.1; 156.1,2
act of ~ing, 146.2; 155.2; 156.3
full of ~ings, 156.5
full of ~ings, that which is,
156.4
that which ~s, 156.4
winding,adj., 146.4; 155.3; 156.5
window,n., 1009.4
arrangement of ~s, 1009.9
arrangement or display in
store ~s, 1009.20

bar separating ~panes,
1009.14
bottom edge of a ~, 1009.12
cover a ~, 972.1(16,20,42) ;
1009.24
~ covering, 1009.23
crosspiece between ~ and
doorway, 1009.16
~ frame, 1009.10,11
front ~ of an automobile,
1009.17
having ~s, 1009.5,6
horizontal crosspiece of a ~,
1009.16
look at things in a store ~,
1009.22
~ of crossed strips, 991.14,15
opening like a ~, 1009.8
projection with a ~, 1009.7
~ repair, 1009.19
~ repairer, 1009.18
separate (the panes of a ~)
with bars, 1009.15
side of a ~, 1009.13
windpipe,n., 375.1
inflammation of the ~, 375.4,5
subdivisions of the ~, 375.2,3
windstorm,n., 1042.27
center of a ~, 1042.29,30
create a ~, conditions that,
1042.33
having or subject to ~s,
1042.28
~ of dust, 1001.17,18
~ of sand, 1007.7
science of ~s, 1042.34
underground refuge from a
~, 1042.35
~ with thunder, 1044.7
windy,adj., 1042.5
~ condition, 1042.6,22
wine,n., 749.6(10) ; 749.17
addiction to ~, 749.44
caused by ~, 749.19(5)
connoisseur of ~s, 734.13(3,
4,6)
derived from ~, 749.19(4)
descr. of ~, 749.19(1,2)
drinker of ~, 748.14
drunk from ~, 749.50(12)
dry (in ref. to ~), 749.19(1)
god of ~, 749.21; see also
Bacchus,n.
hater of ~, 880.18(6)
knowledge about ~s,
749.20(1)
like ~, 749.19(3,5,6)
make ~, 749.28(1,3)
making ~, 749.18
making ~, chemistry of,
749.36(2)
making ~, device for,
749.27(2)
making ~, place for, 749.26(3)
measurement unit of ~,
946.46(8,9) ; 946.47
of the color of ~, 749.19(3)
pert. to ~, 749.19(3–5)
science of ~ making,
749.20(2)
seller of ~, 749.40(9)
shop where ~ is sold, 749.37(6,
26)
study of ~s, 749.20(1)
tasting like ~, 749.19(6)
wing,n., 340.1
building ~, 727.15
cover chicks with ~s, 972.34
having ~s, 340.4
like a ~, 340.3,5
pert. to the ~, 340.2
shaped like a ~, 507.17(4)
without ~s, 340.6
wink,n., 297.13
wink,v., 297.11

~ the eyes, 297.12
time required to ~ the eyes,
297.16
winking,adj., 297.14
winking,n., 297.13,15
winner,n., 22.10; 240.4
descr. of a ~, 22.11
~ of a horse race, 20.14
winter,n., 770.1
beginning of ~, 1055.17
like ~, 770.10
middle of ~, 770.2
pert. to ~, 770.9
spend the ~, 770.11(2,4)
wipe,v., 438.1(3,13,27,29,30) ; see
also **rub**,v.
~ clean, 899.1(1,2,5,7,8,12–16)
~ dust from, 1001.10
wire,n.
measurement unit of ~,
946.26(13)
Wisconsin,n.
inhabitant or native of ~,
784.15(5)
wisdom,n., 596.3
action from practical ~,
596.9,10
claim to all ~, 596.11
goddess of ~, 596.13
hatred of ~, 880.17(10)
lack of ~, 596.6; see also
stupidity,n.
pert. to ~, 596.12
without ~, 596.5
wise,adj., 596.1,2
~ action, 596.9,10
~ person, 596.4
~ woman, 596.4(1)
worldly-~, 596.1(21,24)
wish,v., 265.1; see **desire**,v.
wishbone,n., 354.15
wit,n., 1114.4; see also **humor,
joke, joking**,n., **witty**,adj.
bit of ~, 1115.7
descr. of quiet ~, 1114.6
engage in ~, 1115.1
of quick ~, 1114.9
season with ~, 1114.12
sparkle with ~, 1114.14
talk with ~, 671.1(3,13,75)
witch,n., 660.7; 662.5; 663.2,13
temptress, 196.4; 709.1(1)
ugly woman, 506.2; 759.18(3,
8)
withdraw,v.
draw out, 193.18
go back, 145.1
leave, 141.1; see **leave**,v.
take back, 251.1
withdrawal,n., 141.2; 145.2;
193.19; 251.1
~ from worldly interests,
141.2(1)
wither,v.
decay, 806.1,2; see **decay**,v.
dry up, 1038.1,2; see **dry**,v.
make ineffective, 17.5
~ing but not falling off (of
leaves), 806.18
withered,adj.
decayed, 806.4; see **decayed**,
adj.
dried up, 1038.4
plant with ~ parts, 806.19
withering,n.
decay, 806.3
insect or organism that
causes ~, 806.20
plant disease that causes ~,
806.20
withstand,v., 246.1; 544.1(35,
36)
ability to ~, 246.8
able to ~, 246.9

successfully ~, 23.12,13;
  544.1(35)
witness,n., 480.3; 484.3; 1086.4
  bear ~ (to), 1086.1,2
  call as or to ~, 1086.13
witty,adj., 1114.1,2; see also
  humorous,adj.
  ~ answer, 1115.7(8)
  be ~, 1115.1
  ~ person, 1114.5; 1115.6,10
  ~ remark, 674.9(14,22);
  1115.7
  ~ remarks, sayings, books,
    writings, etc., 676.1(8,14,19,
    20); 1115.8
  ~ sayings, use of, 676.7
wizard,n., 662.5; 663.2,13
  clever person, 595.4
  skilled person, 7.3
wobble,n., 111.2; 147.2
wobble,v., 87.3,4; 111.1; 147.1
wobbly,adj., 87.1; 111.3,4; 147.3
wolf,n.
  change into a ~, 662.30
  delusions of being a ~,
    1136.1(21)
  ~ group, 403.5(51,58)
  like a ~, 407.16
  person changed into, or able
    to become, a ~, 662.29(5,7)
  pert. to a ~, 407.16
  young ~, 407.17
woman,n., 708.1,14; see also
  female, girl, women,n.
  alluring ~, 708.14(7,12,16,22)
  bad-mannered ~, 708.14(10,
    13)
  bad-tempered ~, 708.14(2,9,
    14,15,18–20,23); 876.4,5
  brazen ~, 708.14(10,13)
  coarse ~, 708.14(5)
  complaining ~, 708.14(9,15,
    23)
  contemptible ~, 708.14(11,21)
  descr. of a ~, 708.5; see also
    feminine,adj.
  hot-tempered ~, 708.14(17);
    876.4,5,21
  kept ~, 710.19–21,23; see also
    prostitute,n.
  like a ~, 708.5,8; see also
    feminine,adj.
  like an old ~, 759.19
  lively ~, 708.14(4,8)
  masculine ~, 708.14(2,3)
  old ~, 759.18
  pert. to a ~, 708.5; see also
    feminine,adj.
  sexually loose ~, 711.1; 712.4;
    see also prostitute,n.
  tall ~, 708.14(2)
  turbulent ~, 708.14(2,15,19)
  ugly ~, 506.2
  ugly old ~, 759.18(3,8,11)
  unethical ~, 708.14(1,7)
  worthless ~, 708.14(4,10,11,13)
  young ~, 760.6; see also
    girl,n.
womanhood,n., 708.6
  early ~, 760.2(1)
womanly,adj., 708.5; see also
  feminine,adj.
  state of possessing full ~
    powers, 708.7
womb,n., 379.1(23); see
  uterus,n.
wombat,n.
  pert. to the ~, 418.3
women,n., 708.2; see also female, girl, woman,n.
  equal rights for ~, belief in,
    708.10
  fondness for ~, 700.30(20)
  government by ~, 1073.42(8,
    13)

group of ~, 318.1(10,43,62);
  708.4
hatred of ~, 880.17(6)
~ in Oriental household,
  708.3
pert. to ~, 708.5; see also
  feminine,adj.
place for ~ in ancient Greece
  or Rome, 708.12
rights of ~, concern with,
  708.11
screen used in India to conceal ~, 708.13
types of ~, 708.14
worship of ~, 656.15(7)
won,adj.
  having ~, 22.11
wonder,n., 271.3,10
  holding one's breath in ~,
    271.6
  imaginary place full of ~s,
    809.4
  place that causes ~, 782.1(36)
wonder,v., 271.8
wonderful,adj.
  excellent, 831.1
  surprising, 271.1
woo,v.
  make love to, 700.7
  try to get, 240.11
wood,n., 997.1
  boring into ~, 997.22
  building ~, 997.1(5)
  built of ~, 997.16–18
  burned piece of ~, 997.5(5,
    6); 1064.42(1,3–6)
  burning piece of ~, 1064.42(1,
    5,6); 1065.107(7,22)
  change into ~, 997.24
  close with ~, 997.6
  containing ~, 997.15
  cover with ~, 997.6
  cutter of ~, 205.9(4,5)
  destroying ~, 997.22
  eating ~, 734.27(16,18,34);
    997.22
  fire~, 1064.61(2,6)
  ~ fittings of a house, 997.19
  flaming stick of ~, 1065.107(7,
    22)
  floating ~, 113.12(2)
  ~ for cremation, 1064.61(5,8)
  ~ for sacrifice to gods,
    1064.61(8)
  heap of ~ for burning to
    death, 1064.61(8)
  inner covering of ~, 997.2
  knot in ~, 997.12
  like ~, 997.13,14
  made of ~, 997.16–18
  maker of ~ articles, 205.9(1–
    3,6,7)
  microscopic examination of
    ~, 997.23
  outer covering of ~, 997.3
  pert. to ~, 997.13
  piece of ~, 997.5
  piece of ~ as a support,
    997.5(2,9,13,15,21,22,23)
  piece of ~ for a fire, 997.5(8)
  piece of ~ for signs, 997.5(3,
    15)
  pointed piece of ~, 997.5(24)
  product made with ~, 205.10
  sawed ~, 997.1(2,3)
  skill with ~, 7.1(69)
  strip of ~, 326.15(4)
  things of ~, 997.19
  trees suitable for ~, 996.10
  worker with ~, 205.9
woodcock,n.
  group of ~s, 403.5(24)
woodcutter,n., 205.9(4,5)
wooden,adj., 997.15–18

woodland,n., 996.27,29; see
  forest,n.
woods,n., 996.27,29; see also
  forest,n.
woodsy,adj., 996.36,37,40
woody,adj., 996.36; 997.14,15
  ~ at the base, 997.20
  becoming partly ~ at its
    base, 997.21
  ~ part of tree or plant, 996.71
wool,n., 373.1
  covered with ~, 369.6(22)
woolly,adj., 373.2
  soft and ~, 443.1(7)
word,n., 666.1,3; see also language,n.
  abstract ~, 666.3(1)
  abusive ~, 561.10; 666.3(20);
    861.13
  acceptance of ~s in literal
    meanings only, 607.16
  addition of ~s as explana-
    tion, 599.2(2)
  affected ~, 666.3(14)
  affectionate ~, 700.19
  analyze ~ relationships,
    666.14
  ~ as a motto, 666.3(43); 666.6
  ~ as to sound, 666.3(50)
  ~ as to syllables, 666.8
  attention to ~s rather than
    to meaning, 666.21
  belittling ~, 666.3(35); 840.4
  blasphemous ~, 861.13
  ~ blindness, 692.13(1)
  ~ book, 666.19
  Cockney ~, 666.7(4)
  commonly used ~, 666.3(48,
    49)
  connective ~, 321.5(1–3)
  consisting of ~s, 666.17
  conversational ~, 666.3(13,49)
  curse ~, 666.3(23); 861.13
  depreciatory ~, 666.3(35);
    840.4
  dirty ~, 713.3
  disparaging ~, 666.3(35);
    840.4
  disrespectful ~, 861.13
  economical in use of ~s,
    671.20(2)
  exact ~, 666.3(28)
  exact ~s in writing, 666.9(8)
  excess ~s, 667.9
  excess ~s, one who uses,
    667.8
  excess ~s, use of, 667.7
  excess ~s, using, 667.6
  exclamatory ~, 666.3(23,25)
  explain the meaning of a ~,
    607.20(2)
  explanation of ~s, 599.3(9)
  explanatory ~, 666.3(33)
  express in ~s, 665.1
  expressing ideas in a single
    ~, 586.4
  expression in ~s, 665.2
  expression in ~s, art of,
    665.5
  expressive in ~s, 665.3
  ~ expressive of emotion,
    666.3(22,23,25)
  ~ expressive of idea or pic-
    ture, 666.3(40)
  fanciful ~, 666.3(14)
  favorite ~, 666.3(10,42,43)
  favorite ~ of a group,
    666.3(11)
  filthy ~, 713.3
  flood of ~s, 916.5
  following ~s, 666.12(3)
  ~ for word, 666.17(2,5,6)
  foreign ~, 538.3
  ~ formed by combination,
    666.3(9,37)

~ formed by rearranging letters, 666.3(4)
~ formed for the occasion, 666.3(29)
~ formed of first letters, 666.3(2)
~ formed of parts of others, 666.3(2)
~ found only once, 666.3(29)
four-letter ~, 666.3(46) ; 713.3
full of ~, 925.26,27
~ games, 666.18
~ in advertising, 666.3(43) ; 666.6
~ in drinking, 666.3(47)
in spoken ~s, 666.17(5,7)
incorrect ~, 667.4
indecent ~, 713.3; 863.8
index of ~s, 687.9(5)
inexact ~, 666.3(17)
insert ~s, 323.1(30,36,37,39,40)
insulting ~, 867.4
linking ~, 666.3(3)
list of ~s, 666.9(9)
list of ~s with explanations, 599.3(9)
local ~, 666.3(26,38,49)
long ~, 666.3(41)
long ~s, use of, 665.9(54,55) ; 667.1(7)
love, ~ showing, 700.19
meaning of a ~, 607.2(4)
meaningless ~s, 607.24,26,29; 608.1; see also **nonsense,**n.
meaningless ~s, use of, 667.1(8)
mistake in ~s, 667.3
misuse ~s, 667.5
misuse of ~s, 667.3
misused ~, 667.4
mystical use of ~s, 667.1(3)
native ~, 666.3(49)
new ~, 666.3(29)
new ~, coiner or user of, 666.4
new use of ~s, 667.1(6)
nonsensical ~s, 607.24,26,29; 608.1; see also **nonsense,**n.
number ~, 927.2
obscene ~, 666.3(23,31) ; 713.3
obsolete ~, 666.3(5)
~ of attribute, 666.3(20)
~ of constant meaning, 666.3(18)
~ of grammatical relationship, 666.3(27)
~ of ignorant speakers, 666.3(51)
~ of several meanings, 607.12
offensive ~, 1118.7
old-fashioned ~, 631.16
omission of ~ parts, 666.22–24
omission of ~ sounds, 666.22–24
omission of ~s, 666.25; 911.1(2,10)
origin of ~s, 664.11(4,7,9)
out-of-date ~, 631.16
~ parts, 666.15
~ peculiar to a language 666.3(24)
~ peculiar to England, 666.7(1,3,4)
~ peculiar to French, 666.7(5)
~ peculiar to Greece or Athens, 666.7(2,6)
~ peculiar to Irish, 666 7(7)
pert. to ~s, 666.10
picture ~s, 953.6
placed after a ~, 666.16
placed at the end of a ~, 666.16
play on ~s, 667.10; see **pun,**n.
preceding ~s, 666 12(3)

profane ~, 666.3(23) ; 861.13
related ~s, 666.12
relationship of ~s in a sentence, 666.13
ridiculing ~s, 869.3
row of ~s, 311.11(4)
rush of ~s, 666.9(6) ; 916.5
~s, collectively, 666.9
~s of a drama, 969.14
~s of a musical comedy, 666.9(2)
~s of a musical comedy or play, writer of, 666.11
~s of a play, 969.14
~s of an opera, 666.9(2)
~s of an opera, writer of, 666.11
~s of common origin, 666.12(2,4,9)
~s of opposite meaning, 666.12(1)
~s of same meaning, 666.12(10)
~s on a page, 666.9(8)
~s sounded the same, 666.12(7,8)
~s spelled the same, 666.12(5,6)
~s to express or describe, 666.9(7)
sarcastic ~, 666.3(7)
science of ~s, 664.11
science of ~ meanings, 607.22(2–6)
secret ~, 666.3(16,34,42,52)
secret ~ for passing, 956.1(4)
sharp ~, 666.3(7) ; 876.23
shortened ~, 666.3(12,15)
similarity in sound of ~s, 455.7(2)
skilled use of ~s, 667.1(8)
special ~s of a subject, 666.9(7)
spiritual meaning of ~s, 607.2(2)
spiritual use of ~s, 667.1(3)
splitting of a ~, 666.26
student of ~s, 664.12
student of name ~s, 695.2
study of ~s, 664.11
study of ~s that describe or name things, 695.1(1,3)
substandard ~, 666.3(8)
system of technical ~s, 695.4(1,3,5,6)
technical ~, 666.3(45)
the number of ~s, 666.9(10)
~ to avoid offense, 666.3(21)
too many ~s, 667.9
too many ~s, use of, 667.7
too many ~s, user of, 667.8
too many ~s, using, 667.6
unaccented ~, 666.3(6,19)
~ unchanged when read backward, 666.3(32) ; 666.5
unclear use of ~s, 667.1(1,2,5)
unnecessary ~, 666.3(36,39)
unnecessary ~s, 667.9
unnecessary ~s, use of, 665.9(41,44,52) ; 667.7
unnecessary ~s, user of, 667.8
unnecessary ~s, using, 667.6
unrefined ~, 863.8
~ usage, 667.1
use of ~s, 667.1
use of ~s with several meanings, 607.13,14
~ user, 667.2
vulgar ~, 713.3; 863.8; 1118.7
war about ~s, 666.27
war of ~s, 666.27
without ~s, 475.1; 951.27; see also **silent,**adj.

wordiness,n., 665.9(32,41,44,52, 54,55,60) ; 667.7
wording,n.
alter the ~ of, 607.21(2)
wordy,adj., 667.6
~ language, 664.1(7) ; 665.9(32,41,44,52,54,55) ; 667.7,9
~ person, 667.8
work,n., 203.4; 204.1; see also **occupation,**n.
artistic creation, 726.21
book, 687.1; see **book,**n.
piece of writing, 682.16
something made, 726.3
accept ~, 205.22
addicted to ~, one who is, 203.19
amount of ~, 203.17
avoid ~ by pretense of illness, 209.5(5,7)
disposition toward ~, 203.18
easy and well-paying ~, 26.4
freedom from ~, 209.12
give ~ to, 205.21
household ~, 205.17
out of ~, 209.6
out-of-~ people, 113.14; 209.11
out-of-~ person, 113.13; 209.9
period of ~, 203.12
piece of ~, 203.5
place of ~, 203.11
put out of ~, 209.7
quality of ~, 203.13
relating to ~, 203.6
requiring ~, 203.21
study of effects of ~ on a person, 203.22
type of ~, 203.4; 204.1
~ with animals, 205.2
~ with or on clothing, 205.6
without ~, person, 113.13; 209.9
without ~, persons, 113.14; 209.11
work,v., 203.1,2
cause to ~, 203.2
deprive of chance to ~, 581.11
easy to ~ with, 203.16
manner in which parts ~ together, 203.14
not ~, 209.5
person for whom one ~s, 203.23
pretend to ~, 209.5(2,7)
refusal to ~, 206.1(8,9)
refuses to ~, one who, 206.2(6) ; 209.3
unwillingness to ~, 209.2
unwilling to ~, 209.1
unwilling to ~, one who is, 209.3
worker,n., 203.7
accept a position as a ~, 205.22
animals, ~ with, 205.1
brick, ~ with, 1002.14; 1006.58
clothing ~, 205.5
copper, ~ with, 1016.3
electricity, ~ with, 1066.17
excess ~, 920.8
farm ~, 998.4(2,3,9)
gas fixtures, ~ on, 1048.27
give a position as a ~ to, 205.19
glass, ~ with, 1009.44,45,49
government by ~s, 1073.42(6)
group of ~s, 318.1(14,33,44, 58,59,70,80,87,93,94)
household ~, 205.14
machines, ~ on, 280.8
metals, ~ with, 1012.18
position as a ~, 205.18

restaurant ~, 205.11–13
sand ~, 1007.13
~s, collectively, 203.9
ship ~, 115.11; see also
　sailor,n.
skill of a ~, 7.1(70)
stone~, 1006.58
without sufficient ~s, 203.10
wood, ~ with, 205.9
working,adj., 203.6
~ class, 203.9(5); 314.2(17,20)
~ girl, 203.7(15,36)
hard-~, 203.20
member of the ~ class,
　203.7(31)
not ~, 209.6
not ~ (of machinery), 209.10
not ~, one who is, 209.9
working,n., 203.3
addicted to ~, one who is,
　203.19
method or means of ~, 203.15
process of ~, 203.3
stop ~, 791.2(4,6)
~ together of drugs, 203.3(2)
workman,n., 203.7; see
　worker,n.
workshop,n., 203.11
~ of worker with animals,
　205.3
world,n., 1004.1; see also
　earth,n.
affairs of the ~, person con-
　cerned with, 1004.40
animal found all over the ~,
　1004.35
belonging to this ~, 1004.38
belonging to whole ~,
　1004.32–35
better ~, belief in, 831.22(2)
citizen of the ~, 1004.33
concerned with pleasures of
　this ~, person who is,
　1004.40
concerned with this ~,
　1004.38,41
concerning this ~, 1004.38,41
creator of real or imaginary
　~, 726.19(3)
exhibition of pictures, scen-
　ery, etc., of the ~, 1004.36
inhabitant of this ~, 1004.31
little ~, 1004.2
made up of parts from all
　over the ~, 326.47(16)
miniature ~, 1004.2
northernmost regions of the
　~, 1004.5(12)
not of this ~, 662.1; 1004.19,
　39; 1090.4,11
opposite end of the ~, at the,
　789.1(1)
orderly arrangement of the
　~, 311.1(11)
origin of the ~, 728.6
origin of the ~, theory of,
　728.17(4)
out of this ~, 662.1; 1004.19,
　39; 1090.4,11
outside the ~, 138.1(9,13)
pert. to the ~, 1004.16
pert. to the whole ~, 1004.28
plant found all over the ~,
　1004.35
pleasures of the ~, person
　concerned with, 1004.40
sadness over state of the ~,
　1125.4
supporter of the ~, 948.15
worship of the natural ~,
　656.15(3)
worldly,adj., 1004.16,38,41
-wise, 596.1(21,24)
make ~, 1004.42

not ~, 662.1; 1004.19,31,39;
　1090.4,11
withdrawal from ~ interests,
　141.2(1)
world-wide,adj., 40.1; 41.1;
　1004.28,32
~ point of view, 636.4(3);
　636.6
worm,n., 427.1,4
bloodsucking ~, 427.8,9
creeping like a ~, 427.16
eaten by ~s, 427.17
eating ~s, 734.27(33)
flat ~, 427.12,13
full of ~s, 403.18(5,7)
infested with intestinal ~s,
　403.18(6)
intestinal ~, 427.7
like a ~, 427.3,6,15,16
marks in ~like design,
　503.1(17)
medication for intestinal ~s,
　398.8(1,11,13–16)
multiplication of ~s,
　717.12(7)
pert. to ~s, 427.2,5,14
raising of bloodsucking ~s,
　403.30(4)
raising of silk ~s, 403.30(6)
round~, 427.11,13
science of ~s, 403.26(28)
science of parasitic ~s,
　403.26(16)
wormy,adj., 427.15
worn,adj.
able to be ~ away, 801.32
~ away, 801.29
looking ~ out, 12.8
~ out, 12.1
~ out from luxury, indulgent
　living, age, etc., 10.1(16)
spot or place that is ~ away,
　801.30
worried,adj., 1130.9; 1131.8;
　1132.4; see also anxious,
　adj.
annoyed, 874.6
worry,n., 1130.3,6; 1131.3,9;
　1132.3,5; see also anxiety,n.
annoyance, 874.3,5
become free of ~, 309.21(3,6)
worry,v., 1130.1,8; 1131.1,6;
　1132.1,6
annoy, 874.1
tending to ~, 1131.12
worse,adj.
become ~, 883.11
becoming ~, 883.13
having become ~, 883.14
make ~, 883.16
making ~, 883.17
state of becoming ~, 883.12
world is becoming ~, belief
　that the, 883.19
worship,n., 656.2,15
a meeting for ~, 322.1(12,35)
a meeting for secret ~,
　322.1(16)
a travel to ~, 124.2(4,8)
blind devotion and ~,
　657.1(13)
ceremonies of ~, compiler of,
　656.11
ceremony in public ~, adher-
　ence to, 656.10
ceremony of ~, 656.9
devotion to method in ~,
　50.5(6)
expression of ~, 656.14
fear and ~, 656.2(1)
glorification into object of ~,
　656.7
image for ~, 965.1(26)
leader of public ~, 656.4(1)
object of ~, 656.8

~ of specific things or people,
　656.15
pert. to ~, 656.5
place of ~, 645.1; see
　church,n.
prescribed form of ~,
　656.2(10–12); 819.12
public ~, 656.2(8,9,12)
rules for ~, 656.2(10,12);
　656.9
science of ~, 656.12,13
singing of songs during ~,
　476.2(4)
song of ~, 476.4(27,38); 477;
　656.14; see also hymn,n.
supreme ~ of God, 656.2(7)
worthy of ~, 656.6
worship,v., 656.1
~ in hymns, 477.9
worshiper,n., 656.4,16
group of ~s, 318.1(38,57)
~ in church, 645.3
pert. to a ~, 656.5
~s in church, 645.4
worshipful,adj., 656.3,17
worst,adj., 883.20
~ part, 326.1(12)
worth,n., 279.18; 839.1; see also
　value,n.
express a low opinion of ~ of,
　840.1
expressing a low opinion of
　~ of, 840.2
low opinion of ~, 840.3
of little ~, 888.3
of no ~, 888.1
of no practical ~, 888.4
person of ~, 839.7
recognize the ~ of, 839.10
something of ~, 839.5
worthiness,n., 279.18; 841.2–6
worthless,adj., 284.12; 883.7;
　888.1,3
bad-tempered and ~ person,
　888.5(3)
idle and ~ person, 888.5(2)
~ people, 888.7
~ person, 888.5
showy and ~, 888.2
showy and ~ thing, 888.10;
　951.36(1,3)
small and ~ thing, 909.5(1,
　13)
~ thing, 888.8,10,11
~ things, 888.9
~ woman, 708.14(4,10,11,13);
　888.6
worthy,adj., 279.17; 839.2;
　841.2
be ~ of, 841.1
~ of admiration, 855.8
~ of approval, 850.19
~ of contempt, 870.8
~ of help, 841.3
~ of honor, 857.18
~ of praise, 851.8
~ of respect, 856.15
wound,adj., 156.5; see also
　wind,v.
state of being ~, 156.6
wound,n., 803.2; see injury,n.
wound,v., 803.1; see injure,v.
woven,adj., 307.2; see also
　weave,v.
able to be ~, 307.9
~ from twigs, 307.2(2)
~ material, 307.3
pert. to ~ material, 307.12
state of being ~, 307.6
~ strips of wood or metal,
　307.3(2)
structure of ~ threads, 307.5
wrap,n.
coat, 976.1

covering, 972.4
wrap,v.
　conceal, 970.1,8
　cover, 972.1
　~ a corpse, 797.5
wraps,n.
　concealment, 970.2
　covering, 972.4
　~ for a corpse, 797.20
wreck,n., 801.2,13,16,38; see also
　destruction,n.
wreck,v., 801.1,12,15,33; see
　destroy,v.
wreckage,n., 801.2,13,16,38; see
　also **destruction**,n.
wrestle,v., 21.1
wrestler,n., 21.3
　weight of a ~, 947.47
wrestling,n., 21.2
　invincible in ~, 1.39
　school of ~, 21.4
wretch,n., 887.6
wretched,adj., 883.1,7; 887.1,2;
　888.1; 1125.6,16,34
　one who looks ~, 1125.8
wrinkle,n., 158.4
　~ at the corner of the eye,
　158.4(1)
wrinkle,v., 158.1,2
　~ (the forehead), 158.1(2)
wrinkled,adj., 158.5
　~ place, 158.6
wrist,n., 343.21
　sleeve over the ~, 978.7,8
write,v., 677.3; 682.1,17
　~ a, or one's, name on a list,
　695.6–9
　~ a piece, 682.17
　~ a story, 685.3
　~ able to ~ and read, 682.22
　~ about, 682.1(4,8)
　~ about morality, 682.1(13)
　~ above, 682.1(19)
　~ an introduction, 730.6
　~ at the end of, 682.16
　~ by hand, 677.3; see **hand-
　writing**,n.
　compulsion to ~, 682.21
　desire to ~, 682.21
　~ enthusiastically, 1095.17,18
　~ in another form, 682.1(20)
　~ in sayings, 676.5,6
　inability to ~, mental dis-
　order characterized by,
　1136.1(30)
　~ incorrectly, 682.11
　~ letters, 678.3
　~ letters to, 678.4; 682.1(3)
　loss of ability to ~, 682.24
　~ melodies, 478.7; 479.23
　~ music, 479.23
　~ one's name, 694.5; 696.1;
　see **sign**,v.
　~ one's name under,
　682.1(18); 694.5; 696.1; see
　also **sign**,v.
　~ on the back of, 682.1(6)
　~ on the outside of, 682.1(11,
　19)
　~ on the top of, 682.1(19)
　~ poetry, 689.3
　~ the name of, 682.1(7,11,17)
　~ to by name, 694.6(2)
　~ tunes, 478.7; 479.23
　unable to ~ and read, 682.23
　~ under, 682.1(18)
　~ with another, 682.1(1)
　~ with chalk, 1006.42
　~ with charcoal, 1064.43
writer,n., 682.5,18; 685.5; 686.1;
　687.2,5; 688.3; see also **au-
　thor, poet**,n.
　book ~, 685.5; 686.1; 687.2,5;
　see also **author**,n.

~ by dictation, 682.5(1,5,6);
　682.12(6–8)
country life, ~ on, 786.9
death notices, ~ of, 794.17
drama ~, 969.8
epilogue ~, 792.24
fatigue of a ~, 12.7
history ~, 771.17
hymn ~, 477.14
Italian ~, 965.33
melody ~, 478.6
motion-picture ~, 968.8
music ~, 479.23
pamphlet ~, 687.2
pert. to ~s, 682.6
poetry ~, 689.5; see **poet**,n.
preface ~, 730.8
~'s cramp, 1137.56(31)
shepherd life, ~ on, 786.9
song ~, 476.6
story ~, 685.5; see also
　author,n.
writing,n., 682.2,3,15,16; see
　also **book, handwriting,
　inscription, literature,
　poem**,n.
　act of ~, 682.2
　ancient ~s, art of decipher-
　ing, 682.14(1,3,5)
　ancient ~s, science of,
　682.14(1–5)
　ancient ~, 682.3(13)
　ancient style of ~, 682.7
　automatic ~ in spiritualism,
　682.3(18)
　awkward piece of ~,
　682.16(19)
　Bible, passage of ~ from the,
　682.20(4)
　ceaseless ~, 682.2(1)
　censor ~, 899.17
　Chinese system of ~,
　682.12(3)
　clear ~, 965.26
　collection of ~s, 682.19
　collection of false Biblical ~s,
　682.19(12)
　collection of humorous ~s,
　682.19(1,6)
　country life, ~s on, 786.8
　critical ~, 682.16(28)
　descr. of ~ in ref. to a spe-
　cific author, 686.8
　dirty ~s, 682.16(24); 713.3,4
　dirty ~s, descr. of, 899.22
　Egyptian ~s, science of,
　682.14(4)
　Egyptian ~s, treatise on,
　682.15(7)
　Egyptian system of ~,
　682.12(1)
　enthusiasm for ~, 682.21;
　1095.20
　enthusiastic ~, 1095.16
　explanatory ~, 599.3(5,8)
　false ~, 682.3 (15,16); 820.6
　falsely sacred ~s, 648.4
　filthy ~s, 682.16(24); 713.3,4
　hand~, 677.1; see **handwrit-
　ing**,n.
　handwritten piece of ~,
　682.16(20); see **manu-
　script**,n.
　historical ~s, 771.16(1,2);
　771.19
　immature ~s, 682.16(18)
　incoherent ~, 682.2(1)
　incorrect ~ of words,
　682.2(2)
　introductory piece of ~,
　682.16(16,26,27); see also
　introduction,n.
　judgment, habit of ~ in,
　682.8

key to Egyptian ~, 601.9
key to secret ~, 601.8
learned piece of ~, 682.16(19)
legal documents, art of ~,
　682.14(6)
list of ~s on a subject, 687.12
literary ~s, 682.16; see also
　book, literature, story,n.
margin, ~ in the, 682.3(12)
materials for ~, seller of,
　677.15
materials or instruments for
　~, 677.14
meaningless ~, 682.3(2,16);
　see also **nonsense**,n.
money, ~ produced only for,
　682.16(25)
nonsense ~, 682.3(2,16); see
　also **nonsense**,n.
obscene ~s, 682.16(24); 713.3,4
one person speaking, ~ that
　indicates, 682.16(22)
one subject, piece of ~ on,
　682.15; 682.16(3,7–10,14,15,
　21,32,34–37)
pain from ~, 1137.56(31)
passage of ~, 682.20
passages of ~, selection of,
　682.20(1)
pert. to ~, 682.6
pictorial system of ~,
　682.12(2)
piece of ~, 682.16; see also
　story,n.
place where ~ is done in
　monasteries, 677.17
prepare ~ for publication,
　682.9
rapid ~, 682.2(3)
rough ~ or draft, 682.3(19)
sacred ~s, 648.1
sacred ~s, history of, 650.5
sacred piece of ~, 682.16(31)
sacred subjects, ~s on, 650.7
saints, ~s about, 651.8
secret ~, 683.1–4
selections from ~, 252.5(2,6,
　7)
shepherd life, ~s on, 786.8(2,
　4)
sky~, 1051.13
solve secret ~, 601.7; 683.7
sordid subjects, ~ on,
　682.16(29)
sound system of ~, 682.12(4–
　8)
spirit ~, 682.3(17)
spurious ~, 682.3(15,16);
　820.6
stone for ~ on, 1006.1(43)
story, ~ that tells a,
　682.16(23,33); see also
　story,n.
style of ~, 665.8(8,10,14);
　665.9,10; see also **lan-
　guage**,n.
support, ~ in, 854.16; see
　support,n.
symbolic ~, 954.18
systems of ~, 682.12
table or desk for ~, 677.16
typed piece of ~, 682.16(20,
　38)
unauthentic ~s, 682.3(15,16);
　820.6
uncensored ~, descr. of,
　899.22
unclean ~, 682.16(24); 713.3,
　4
unclean ~, descr. of, 899.22
unfair selections from ~,
　252.5(8)
wander from the subject in
　~, 682.10

910

youthful ~s, 682.16(18)
written,adj., 682.4
~ in capital letters, 679.19
~ on stone or rock, 1006.47,48
something ~, 682.3; see **writing,n.**
something ~ in one's own hand, 682.3(3)
something ~ in shorthand, 682.13
something ~ later or after, 682.3(1,14)
wrong,adj., 827.1; 828.1,11,13; see also **improper, incorrect, unsuitable,adj.**
act ~, 827.9; 883.30; 884.1; see also **sin,v.**
~ act, 828.3
be ~, 827.3,7
go ~ (of circumstances, etc.), 827.8
~ in judgment, 827.12
~ in opinion, 827.12
~ thing, 827.2
wrong,n., 635.4; 883.27,32; 884.2
civil ~, 1087.12
do ~, 827.9; 883.30; 884.1; see also **sin,v.**
full of ~, 827.11
wrong,v., 635.3; 803.1
wrongdoer,n., 883.29; 884.6; 1087.8; see also **criminal,n.**
wrongdoing,n., 883.28; 1087.7
involve in ~, 522.1(3–5); 1088.17
involvement in ~, 522.3; 1088.17

X

X(the letter),n.
cross like an ~, 121.1(6)
cut in an ~, 332.1(13)
X-ray,n., 1069.1
brain ~, 357.8
disease caused by ~s, 1069.7
effect of ~s, instrument to measure, 1065.19
~ energy, 1069.16
examination by ~s, 1069.12–14
impenetrable by ~s, 1069.10
measurement of ~s, device for, 1069.15
pert. to ~s, 1069.2
~ photograph, 1069.8,9
science of ~s, 401.1(88,90)
therapy by ~s, 400.6(41–43, 45); 1069.6
treat with or subject to ~s, 1069.4,5
~ unit, 1069.3
visible by ~s, 1069.11
xylophone,n., 479.8(13,19,33)
player of a ~, 479.9(26)

Y

yarn,n.
story, 685.1; see **story,n.**
thread, 306.1; see **thread,n.**
yawn,n., 298.3
yawn,v., 298.2(4,6,7)
year,n.
by the ~, 781.7
consisting of a thousand ~s, 781.12(5)
consisting of four ~s, 781.12(7)
consisting of twenty ~s, 781.12(14)
every ~, 781.7,8
every eight ~s, 781.12(6)

every fifty ~s, 781.12(10)
every five ~s, 781.12(9)
every four ~s, 781.12(7)
every four hundred ~s, 781.12(8)
every hundred ~s, 781.12(3)
every seven ~s, 781.12(11)
every six ~s, 781.12(12)
every ten ~s, 781.12(4)
every three ~s, 781.12(13)
every twenty ~s, 781.12(14)
every two ~s, 781.12(2)
every two hundred ~s, 781.12(1)
fifteen ~s, pert. to, 781.4(1)
five ~s, 781.3(6)
four ~s, 781.3(5)
four times a ~, 780.3(7,11,12)
half ~, academic, 780.2(2)
hundred ~s, 781.3(2); 781.4
hundred fifty ~s, pert. to, 781.4(2)
in the ~ of our Lord, 781.5
in the ~ of the world, 781.6
lasting a hundred ~s, 781.12(3)
lasting a whole ~, 781.9
lasting all ~, 781.9
lasting eight ~s, 781.12(6)
lasting five ~s, 781.12(9)
lasting four ~s, 781.12(7)
lasting four hundred ~s, 781.12(8)
lasting seven ~s, 781.12(11)
lasting six ~s, 781.12(12)
lasting three ~s, 781.12(13)
lasting twenty ~s, 781.12(14)
lasting two ~s, 781.12(2)
leap ~, 781.1
leap ~, extra day in, 776.7
leap ~, inserted in, 774.8,9
lunar ~, 1054.12
middle of the ~, 781.2
once a ~, 781.8
period of ~s, 781.3,4
person as to ~s old, 758.2
seven ~s, 781.3(7)
six ~s, 781.3(9)
six hundred ~s, 781.3(8); 781.4
six times a ~, 780.3(1–3)
ten ~s, 781.3(3)
thirty-three ~s, 769.8(8)
thousand ~s, 781.3(4); 781.4
three hundred ~s, pert. to, 781.4(3)
three times a ~, 780.3(6)
twelve times a ~, 780.3(4,5)
twice a ~, 780.3(8); 781.11
two ~s, 781.3(1)
yearly,adj., 781.8
yell,n., 464.1
yell,v., 464.2
yellow, adj., n., 500.1,2; 1013.14
become ~, 500.6
becoming ~, 500.3
~-haired, 369.12(3,4,7,11–13)
~-haired person, 369.15
make ~, 500.6,7; 1013.15
~ (of hair), 369.13
~ of hair, 369.12(3,4,7,11–13)
pert. to ~, 500.4
~ pigment, 500.5
sickly ~ of complexion, 384.15,16
straw ~, 987.28
yellow fever,n., 396.1(4,36)
Yeoman of the Guard,n., 564.1(6)
yes,n., 554.5
gesture ~, 102.1(6)
say ~, 541.1; 554.1; see **agree,v.**
saying ~, 554.2,3

saying ~ to a question, 554.4
saying neither ~ nor no, 554.6
word that means ~, 554.5
yield,n., 235.3; 726.11
yield,v.
give, 230.1; see **give,v.**
give forth, 235.1
give in, 552.1; see **submit,v.**
give up, 236.1
produce, 726.8; see **produce,v.**
surrender, 236.1; 552.1; see **submit,v.**
yielding,adj., 552.3
yoga,n.
practitioner of ~, 579.28
young,adj., 760.1
acting ~, 760.1(11)
become ~, 760.12
becoming ~, 760.11
~ female, 760.6; see also **girl, woman,n.**
immature ~ person, 760.3(1)
like a ~ person, 760.1(2–7,9–11)
make ~, 760.13
~ male, 760.5; see also **boy, man,n.**
~ man, 760.5; see also **boy,n.**
persistence of ~ characteristics in adult, 760.15
~ person, 760.3,5,6; see also **boy, girl,n.**
self-important and ~ person, 848.34(2)
state of being ~, 760.2
state of being too ~, 760.9
too ~, 760.8
unimportant and ~ person, 849.7
vigorous and ~, 1.10
~ woman, 760.6; see also **girl, woman,n.**
younger,adj., 760.7
become ~, 760.12
becoming ~, 760.11
make ~, 760.13
youngster,n., 760.3,5,6; see also **boy, child, girl,n.**
youth,n., 760.2,3,5; see also **boy, girl,n.**
symbol of ~, 760.4
youthful,adj., 760.1; see **young, adj.**

Z

Z(the letter),n., 679.1(11,22)
incorrect pronunciation of ~, 670.7(4)
zeal,n.
ardor, 1092.25
desire, 265.1,4
eagerness, 265.20
enthusiasm, 1095.1
zealot,n.
desirer, 265.5
eager person, 265.21
enthusiast, 1095.3
prejudiced person, 634.3
behavior, actions, or nature of a ~, 1095.22
like a ~, 1095.21
zealous,adj.
ardent, 1092.26
desirous, 265.3
eager, 265.19
enthusiastic, 1095.2
zebra,n.
cross between horse and ~, 408.18
like a ~, 403.12
of ~s, 403.11(6,13,14,18)
zero,n., 928.1,4

zinc,n., 1019
  ~ and copper alloy, 1016.2(1,
    5)
  coat with ~, 1019.3
  ~, copper, and nickel alloy,
    1016.2(4)

etching of ~, 1019.6
etching on ~, 1019.5
like ~, 1019.2
pert. to ~, 1019.1
yielding ~, 1019.3
zone,n., 782.1

~s of the earth, 1004.5
~s of the earth, boundaries
  of, 1004.10
zoo,n., 403.22; 951.28(2,4)
  animal in a ~, 301.5(2)